Bankruptcy Rules and Official Forms

2012 Law School Edition

WEST®

A Thomson Reuters business

Mat #41143037

ISBN: 978–0–314–94973–8

ISSN: 1079-381X

EXPLANATION

This publication contains the current Bankruptcy Code (11 U.S.C.) and related provisions of United States Code Titles 18 and 28, as amended through Pub.L. 112–106, approved April 5, 2012. Court rules are amended as received May 10, 2012.

The current bankruptcy court fee schedule, including changes effective in 2012, appears following 28 U.S.C. § 1930.

Judge William H. Brown, Lawrence R. Ahern, III and Nancy Fraas Maclean prepared the "Bankruptcy Highlights" feature, in which they discuss recent bankruptcy law developments, including 2011 amendments to the Federal Rules of Bankruptcy Procedure, recent Supreme Court and lower court decisions relevant to bankruptcy practitioners, and significant legislation from the 112th Congress.

The Official Forms follow the Federal Rules of Bankruptcy Procedure.

For comprehensive coverage of all aspects of bankruptcy law, see *Epstein, Nickles and White, Hornbook on Bankruptcy*.

For researching bankruptcy cases, see West's Bankruptcy Reporter and West's Bankruptcy Digest. Cross-references to the West Key Number System are provided throughout this 2012 Edition. For bankruptcy research on WestlawNext and Westlaw, see the "WestlawNext Online Research Guide" that follows this Explanation.

For additional information or research assistance call the West reference attorneys at 1–800–REF–ATTY (1–800–733–2889). Contact West's editorial department directly with your questions and suggestions by e-mail at west.editor@thomson.com. Visit West's home page at west.thomson.com.

THE PUBLISHER

June, 2012

*

WestlawNext™

THE NEXT GENERATION OF ONLINE RESEARCH

WestlawNext is the world's most advanced legal research system. By leveraging more than a century of information and legal analysis from Westlaw, this easy-to-use system not only helps you find the information you need quickly, but offers time-saving tools to organize and annotate your research online. As with Westlaw.com, WestlawNext includes the editorial enhancements (e.g., case headnotes, topics, key numbers) that make it a perfect complement to West print resources.

- FIND ANYTHING by entering citations, descriptive terms, or Boolean terms and connectors into the WestSearch™ box at the top of every page.

- USE KEYCITE® to determine whether a case, statute, regulation, or administrative decision is good law.

- BROWSE DATABASES right from the home page.

- SAVE DOCUMENTS to folders and add notes and highlighting online.

SIGN ON: next.westlaw.com
LEARN MORE: West.Thomson.com/WestlawNext
FOR HELP: 1–800–WESTLAW (1–800–937–8529)

*

TABLE OF CONTENTS

	Page
BANKRUPTCY HIGHLIGHTS	IX
BANKRUPTCY CODE	1

Chapter

1. General Provisions	6
3. Case Administration	59
5. Creditors, the Debtor, and the Estate	142
7. Liquidation	265
9. Adjustment of Debts of a Municipality	320
11. Reorganization	335
12. Adjustment of Debts of a Family Farmer or Fisherman With Regular Annual Income	410
13. Adjustment of Debts of an Individual With Regular Income	452
15. Ancillary and Other Cross-Border Cases	479

RELATED PROVISIONS OF U.S. CODE TITLES 18 AND 28	493
Title 18, Crimes and Criminal Procedure	494
Title 28, Judiciary and Judicial Procedure	516
Bankruptcy Fees	587
FEDERAL RULES OF BANKRUPTCY PROCEDURE	597

Part

I. Commencement of Case: Proceedings Relating to Petition and Order for Relief	599
II. Officers and Administration; Notices; Meetings; Examinations; Elections; Attorneys and Accountants	628
III. Claims and Distribution to Creditors and Equity Interest Holders; Plans	668
IV. The Debtor: Duties and Benefits	697
V. Bankruptcy Courts and Clerks	712
VI. Collection and Liquidation of the Estate	723
VII. Adversary Proceedings	733
VIII. Appeals to District Court or Bankruptcy Appellate Panel	755
IX. General Provisions	771
X. United States Trustees [Abrogated]	802

OFFICIAL BANKRUPTCY FORMS	803
RELATED UNIFORM LAWS	1003
Uniform Fraudulent Transfer Act	1003
Uniform Commercial Code	1007
FEDERAL TAX LIEN STATUTES—INTERNAL REVENUE CODE	1019
Index	I–1

*

BANKRUPTCY HIGHLIGHTS

By

William Houston Brown
United States Bankruptcy Judge, 1987–2006
Western District of Tennessee

Lawrence R. Ahern III
Burr & Forman LLP
Nashville, Tennessee

———

    I. Amendments to the Federal Rules of Bankruptcy Procedure and Forms
   II. Proposed Amendments to the Federal Rules of Bankruptcy Procedure and Forms Submitted for Public Comment
  III. Amendments to the Federal Rules of Appellate Procedure
  IV. Recent Supreme Court Decisions of Interest to Bankruptcy Practitioners
   V. Recent Circuit Court Bankruptcy Decisions
  VI. 2010 Technical Amendments to Bankruptcy Code
 VII. Pending Amendments to UCC Article 9 and Commentary

———

I. Amendments to the Federal Rules of Bankruptcy Procedure and Forms

Effective December 1, 2011, Bankruptcy Rules 2003, 2019, 3001, 4004 and 6003 were amended, Rules 1004.2 and 3002.1 were added, and Official Forms 1, 9A - 9I, 10 and 25A were amended. An attachment and two supplements to Official Form 10 were added, and Director's Form 240A/B was amended.

Rule 2003 (Meeting of Creditors or Equity Security Holders) was amended to require the prompt filing by the presiding official of a statement upon the adjournment of a meeting of creditors or equity security holders, specifying the date and time to which the meeting is adjourned.

Rule 2019 (Disclosure Regarding Creditors and Equity Security Holders in Chapter 9 and Chapter 11 Cases) was amended to expand the scope of the rule's disclosure requirements by requiring disclosure in Chapter 9 and Chapter 11 cases by all committees or groups that consist of more than one creditor or equity security holder, as well as entities that represent more than one creditor or equity security holder. It also authorizes the court to require disclosure by an individual party in interest when knowledge of that party's economic stake in the debtor would assist the court in evaluating the party's arguments.

Rule 3001 (Proof of Claim), was amended to prescribe in greater detail the supporting information required to accompany a proof of claim in any case, if the claim, or any interest in property of the debtor securing the claim, is based on a writing. Because of the significance of these new requirements and those contained in new Rule 3002.1, they are summarized in a table below.

Rule 4004 (Grant or Denial of Discharge) was amended to permit a party under limited circumstances to seek an extension of time to object to a debtor's discharge after the time for objecting has expired, where the request involves new facts and is made in a motion filed promptly after discovery of the facts.

BANKRUPTCY HIGHLIGHTS

Rule 6003 (Interim and Final Relief Immediately Following the Commencement of the Case-- Applications for Employment; Motions for Use, Sale, or Lease of Property; and Motions for Assumption or Assignment of Executory Contracts) was amended to clarify that the requirement of a 21-day waiting period before a court can enter certain orders at the beginning of a case, including an order approving employment of counsel, does not prevent the court from specifying an effective date for the order that is *nunc pro tunc*--earlier than the date of its issuance.

New Rule 1004.2 (Petition in Chapter 15 Cases) reflects the republication of a new rule. It requires an entity filing a Chapter 15 petition to state the country of the debtor's main interest and to list each country in which a case involving the debtor is pending. As republished, it also sets a deadline for challenging the statement asserting the country of the debtor's main interest, which was changed from "60 days after the notice of the petition has been given" to no later than seven days before the petition hearing.

Rule 3002.1 (Notice Relating to Claims Secured by Security Interest in the Debtor's Principal Residence) is a new rule that implements § 1322(b)(5) of the Bankruptcy Code, which permits a Chapter 13 debtor to cure a default and maintain payments of a home mortgage. It imposes significant filing and other deadlines, particularly on creditors secured by such mortgages, and imposes significant penalties for violation of those requirements. In several instances, new forms will be required to implement the rule. Because of the significance of these new requirements and those contained in amended Rule 3001, they are summarized in a table below.

Form 1 (Petition), was amended to implement new Rule 1004.2 in Chapter 15 cases.

Forms 9A - 9I (Notice of Commencement of Case Under the Bankruptcy Code, Meeting of Creditors and Deadlines), was amended to conform to the amendment of Rule 2003(e).

Form 10 (Proof of Claim), was amended to clarify that, consistent with Rule 3001(c), original or duplicate writings supporting a claim or an interest in property of a debtor securing a claim--not just summaries--must be attached to the proof of claim.

Form 10 Attachment A (Proof of Claim), is new and would be filed with Form 10, as required by new Rule 3001(c)(2). Attachment A includes a statement of the principal and interest due as of the petition date, as well as a statement of prepetition fees, expenses and other charges, and a statement of the amount required to cure any default as of the petition date.

Form 10 Supplement 1 (Proof of Claim), is new and would be used by a home mortgage claim holder to provide the notice required by new Rule 3002.1(b) of any escrow account payment adjustment, interest payment change, as well as any other mortgage payment change while a Chapter 13 case is pending.

Form 10 Supplement 2 (Proof of Claim), is new and would be used in Chapter 13 cases to provide notice of the date incurred and amount of any postpetition fees, expenses and other charges.

Form 25A (Plan of Reorganization in Small Business Case Under Chapter 11), was amended to change the effective date, in a small business Chapter 11 plan, from 11 to 14 days after entry of the order of confirmation, consistent with the 2009 "days are days" time-computation rules amendments.

Director's Form 240 A/B (Reaffirmation), had a technical amendment, effective December 1, 2011, at its page 5, to conform to the amendment of 11 U.S.C.A. § 524(k)(3)(J) by the Bankruptcy Technical Corrections Act of 2010, Public Law 111-327.

The table on the following pages summarizes the new rules contained in amended Rule 3001 and new Rule 3002.1:

BANKRUPTCY HIGHLIGHTS

Summary of Amended Rule 3001(c) and New Rule 3002.1

Applicable to Claims/Chapters:	Requirements: What?	When?	Citation	Penalties for failure:
All Claims, All Chapters if Claim, or Interest in Property of Debtor Securing Claim, is Based on Writing	Original or duplicate. If writing lost or destroyed, statement of circumstances of loss or destruction	Filed with claim	3001(c)(1)	Court may, after notice and hearing, take either or both of following actions: (i) preclude holder from presenting omitted information, in any form, as evidence in any contested matter or adversary proceeding in case, unless court determines that failure was substantially justified or is harmless (ii) award other appropriate relief, including reasonable expenses and attorney's fees caused by failure: 3001(c)(2)(D)
Individual Cases (Chapter 11 or 13) *and ...*				
... claim includes interest, fees, expenses or other prepetition charges	Itemized statement of interest, fees, expenses, or charges		3001(c)(2)(A)	
... security interest is claimed in debtor's property	Statement of amount necessary to cure any default as of petition date		3001(c)(2)(B)	
... security interest is claimed in debtor's principal residence	Attachment prescribed by Official Form		3001(c)(2)(C)	
... escrow account has been established in connection with claim	Escrow account statement prepared as of petition date and in form consistent with applicable nonbankruptcy law			
Only Chapter 13 and Only Claims: Secured by Principal Residence and Provided for under §1322(b)(5) in Debtor's Plan	Holder of claim shall file and serve on debtor, debtor's counsel, and trustee notice of any change in payment amount, including any change that results from interest rate or escrow account adjustment	Filed no later than 21 days before payment in new amount is due	3002.1(b)	Same penalties: 3002.1(i)
	Holder of claim shall file and serve on debtor, debtor's counsel, and trustee notice itemizing all postpetition fees, expenses, or charges that holder asserts are recoverable against debtor or against debtor's principal residence	Served within 180 days after date on which fees, expenses or charges are incurred	3002.1(c)	

	Notice filed and served under 3002.1(b) or (c) shall be prepared as prescribed by Official Form, and filed as supplement to holder's proof of claim		3002.1(d) Notice is not subject to 3001(f)	No penalty specified
	On motion of debtor or trustee, court shall, after notice and hearing, determine whether payment of any claimed fee, expense, or charge is required by underlying agreement and applicable nonbankruptcy law to cure default or maintain payments in accordance with §1322(b)(5)	Filed within one year after service of notice under 3002.1(c)	3002.1(e)	
	Trustee shall file and serve on holder of claim, debtor, and debtor's counsel: notice stating that debtor has paid in full amount required to cure any default on claim. Notice shall also inform holder of its obligation to file and serve response under 3002.1(g).	Filed and served within 30 days after debtor completes all payments under plan	3002.1(f)	
	If debtor contends that final cure payment has been made and all plan payments have been completed, and trustee does not timely file and serve notice required by 3002.1(f), debtor may file and serve notice	No new deadline after trustee's failure		

Holder shall file and serve statement on debtor, debtor's counsel, and trustee indicating (1) whether it agrees that debtor has paid full amount required to cure default on claim, and (2) whether debtor is otherwise current on all payments consistent with §1322(b)(5). Statement shall itemize required cure or postpetition amounts, if any, that holder contends remain unpaid as of date of statement. Statement shall be filed as supplement to holder's proof of claim	Filed and served within 21 days after service of notice under 3002.1(f)	3002.1(g); Statement is not subject to 3001(f)	Same penalties: 3002.1(i)
On motion of debtor or trustee, court shall, after notice and hearing, determine whether debtor has cured default and paid all required postpetition amounts	Filed within 21 days after service of statement under 3002.1(g)	3002.1(h)	No penalty specified

Effective November 1, 2011, the following Forms were also amended to reflect the $7 increase in the Title 11 Administrative Fee and the $4 increase in the Miscellaneous Fee Schedule for a Record Search:

Form 3B (Application for Waiver of Chapter 7 Filing Fee)

Director's Form 132 (Application for Search of Bankruptcy Records)

Director's Form 200 (Required Lists, Schedules, Statements and Fees)

Director's Form 201A (Notice to Individual Consumer Debtor)

II. Proposed Amendments to the Federal Rules of Bankruptcy Procedure and Forms Submitted for Public Comment

The following Federal Rules of Bankruptcy Procedure and Forms are subject to amendment and were submitted for public comment in August, 2011:

Bankruptcy Rule 1007 - relieves individual debtors of the obligation to file Official Form 23 if the provider of a personal financial management course notifies the court that the debtor has completed the course.

Bankruptcy Rule 3007 - allows the use of a negative-notice procedure for claim objections and clarifies the manner for serving them.

Bankruptcy Rule 5009 - reflects the amendment to Bankruptcy Rule 1007 by providing that the Clerk of Court is not required to send notice to a debtor if a course provider has already provided notice that the debtor completed a personal financial management course.

Bankruptcy Rule 9006 - makes various changes to draw attention to the fact that the rule prescribes default deadlines for serving motions and written responses; and applies deadlines to any written response to a motion.

Bankruptcy Rules 9013 and 9014 - conform to the amendments to Bankruptcy Rule 9006.

Official Form 6C - reflects the Supreme Court's decision in *Schwab v. Reilly* by permitting the debtor to state the value of the claimed exemption as the "full fair market value of the exempted property."

Official Form 7 - makes the definition of "insider" consistent with the definition in the Bankruptcy Code.

Official Forms 22A and 22C - aligns the allowable deduction for telecommunication expenses with the IRS list of Other Necessary Expenses; also amends Form 22C to conform to the Supreme Court's decision in *Hamilton v. Lanning*, by directing an above-median-income Chapter 13 debtor to list any changes in the reported income and expenses that have already occurred or are virtually certain to occur during the 12 months following the filing of the petition.

III. Amendments to the Federal Rules of Appellate Procedure and Forms

Effective December 1, 2011, Appellate Rules 4 and 40 were amended. The highlights of these amendments are set forth below.

Rule 4 was amended to clarify that there is a 60-day appeal deadline in cases in which the United States, a federal agency, or a federal employee is a party.

Rule 40 was amended to clarify that there is a 45-day rehearing deadline in cases in which the United States, a federal agency, or a federal employee is a party.

IV. Recent Supreme Court Decisions of Interest to Bankruptcy Practitioners

A. *A bankruptcy court lacks authority under Article III to enter a final judgment on a a state law counterclaim that is not resolved in the process of ruling on the defendant's proof of claim.* Stern v. Marshall, ___ U.S. ___, 131 S. Ct. 2594, ___ L. Ed. 2d ___ (2011).

In a 4-1-4 opinion, the Court rendered a decision that arose from a Chapter 11 debtor's adversary proceeding against a claimant who had filed a defamation claim. The debtor sought to recover for alleged tortious interference with the debtor's expectancy of inheritance from her deceased husband. The Supreme Court, speaking through Chief Justice Roberts, joined by Justices Kennedy, Thomas and Alito and with Justice Scalia concurring, held that the Bankruptcy Court lacked authority under Article III, U.S. Const. Art. 3, § 1 et seq., to enter a final judgment on the tortious interference counterclaim, even though it was asserted in response to a claim against the estate (so, as a counterclaim, it was defined as a "core proceeding" by 28 U.S.C.A. § 157(b)(2)(C)). The counterclaim arose under state common law; it was between two private parties; it did not flow from a federal statutory scheme; it was not a matter of public right; and it would not necessarily be resolved by the process of ruling on the defamation claim. The defendant's claim was not a consent to the Bankruptcy Court's authority to render a final order on the counterclaim and, to the extent that section 157 suggests otherwise by its 1984 "core" classification, it is unconstitutional.

Justice Scalia concurred, arguing that an Article III judge is required in all federal adjudications, unless there is a firmly established historical practice to the contrary. On that basis, rather than on the plurality's more complex, "intuitive balancing of benefits and harms," 131 S. Ct. at 2621, he agreed that an Article III judge was required to hear the case.

Justice Breyer filed a dissenting opinion in which Justices Ginsburg, Sotomayor, and Kagan joined, arguing that the Bankruptcy Court's entry of a final judgment on the state common law counterclaim was constitutional, despite what the plurality saw as similarities between the bankruptcy courts under the 1978 Bankruptcy Code and those exercising core jurisdiction under the 1984 amendments that followed *Northern Pipeline Constr. Co. v. Marathon Pipe Line Co.*, 458 U.S. 50, 102 S. Ct. 2858, 73 L. Ed. 2d 598 (1982).

What is left of the bankruptcy courts' jurisdictional structure under the 1984 amendments remains to be seen. Justice Roberts declared that his opinion addressed a narrow question, with practical consequences that would not be as significant as the dissent suggested. 131 S. Ct. at 2620. However, lower courts are already struggling with the issue. For example, in *In re Blixseth*, 2011 WL 3274042 (Bankr. D. Mont., Aug. 1, 2011), the court concluded that a bankruptcy court has no statutory authority even to render findings and conclusions in core (in contrast with non-core) proceedings that it may not constitutionally hear. Because the *Blixseth* Court could not constitutionally hear the fraudulent conveyance claim in that case as a core proceeding, it found no statutory authority to hear it at all. The *Blixseth* Court granted the parties 14 days in which to request withdrawal of the reference before it dismissed the fraudulent conveyance claims for lack of subject matter jurisdiction.

B. A Chapter 13 debtor may not deduct vehicle ownership costs in calculating "projected disposable income," when the vehicle is unencumbered. Ransom v. FIA Card Services, N.A., ___ U.S. ___, 131 S. Ct. 716, 178 L. Ed. 2d 603 (2011).

An unsecured creditor objected to confirmation of an above-median-income Chapter 13 debtor's proposed plan, as not satisfying the Bankruptcy Code's "projected disposable income" requirement. The Supreme Court, speaking through Justice Kagan, joined the Ninth Circuit in affirming the Bankruptcy Court's denial of confirmation, holding that a debtor who does not make loan or lease payments may not take the car-ownership deduction in calculating projected disposable income. The car-ownership category of expense in the formula for calculation of "projected disposable income" encompasses the actual costs of a car loan or lease and nothing more. The debtor could not use the IRS Local Standards Transportation Ownership Costs for a car that was owned free of debt or lease obligations.

Justice Scalia dissented, agreeing with the three other Courts of Appeals that had held that a debtor who owns a car free and clear is nevertheless entitled to the car-ownership allowance under BAPCPA's "applicable monthly expense amounts specified under the National Standards and Local Standards" language of 11 U.S.C.A. § 707(b)(2)(A)(ii)(I).

C. Change in a credit card interest rate was not a "change in terms" requiring notice, under pre-2009 Regulation Z. Chase Bank USA, N.A. v. McCoy, ___U.S. ___, 131 S. Ct. 871, 178 L. Ed. 2d 716 (2011).

A credit card holder alleged a violation of Regulation Z under the Truth in Lending Act, based on the credit card company's failure to notify him before increasing his interest rate after default. A unanimous Court, speaking through Justice Sotomayor and applying the version of Regulation Z in effect at the time of the transactions (prior to the credit card reforms instituted in 2009), held for the credit card company. The rate increase was not a qualifying "change in terms" that triggered the notice requirements of Reg. Z. The issuer's initial disclosure had provided the card holder with notice that the company could increase rates up to the specified maximum rate after a default or delinquency, and the company acted within the scope of that disclosure when it increased the rate.

V. Recent Circuit Court Bankruptcy Decisions

The monthly **Norton Bankruptcy Law Adviser**, available from Thomson Reuters in print or on WestlawNext and WestLaw, publishes summaries of circuit court decisions affecting bankruptcy and interpreting the Bankruptcy Code. Selected from the **Adviser**, as prepared by Austin L. McMullen, James B. Bailey and Max Smith, of Bradley Arant Boult Cummings, LLP, Nashville,

BANKRUPTCY HIGHLIGHTS

Tennessee, the following circuit court decisions were issued since publication of the 2011 edition of Bankruptcy Highlights. The March issue of the *Adviser* each year contains a more extensive summary of appellate bankruptcy decisions from each circuit.

FIRST CIRCUIT

City Sanitation, LLC v. Allied Waste Servs. of Mass., LLC (In re American Cartage, Inc.), 656 F.3d 82 (1st Cir. 2011). (1) Chapter 7 trustee has exclusive standing to assert commercial tort claims. The right to pursue a commercial tort claim cannot be passed to secured creditors as proceeds of original collateral. (2) Approval of settlement of commercial tort claims by Chapter 7 trustee against individual who managed day-to-day business operations of debtor while in Chapter 11 was within bankruptcy court's discretion.

Laboy v. Doral Mortg. Corp. (In re Vazquez Laboy), 647 F.3d 367 (1st Cir. 2011). After finding willful violation of automatic stay, bankruptcy court erred by not allowing debtors an opportunity to present evidence of damages under Code section now codified as § 362(k).

Samus Holdings, LLC v. LBM Fin., LLC (In re Shamus Holdings, LLC), 642 F.3d 263 (1st Cir. 2011). Section 108(c) tolls the period under state law within which a mortgagee must enforce a mortgage following maturity of the secured debt.

Thunberg v. Wallick (In re Thunberg), 641 F.3d 559 (1st Cir. 2011). Chapter 7 discharge was properly revoked pursuant to § 727(d)(2) when debtor knowingly and fraudulently failed to report acquisition of estate property and did not surrender that property to the trustee.

SECOND CIRCUIT

Smith v. Silverman (In re Smith), 645 F.3d 186 (2d Cir. 2011). Trustee is immune from suit for personal liability for acts taken as a matter of business judgment when acting in accordance with statutory or other duty or pursuant to court order.

Savage & Assocs., P.C. v. K&L Gates LLP (In re Teligent, Inc.), 640 F.3d 53 (2d Cir. 2011). Party with too remote an interest in a settlement agreement lacks standing to challenge bankruptcy court's approval under Fed. R. Bankr. P. 9019. Party that lacked standing to challenge approval of settlement is not estopped from asserting defense that relates to validity of the settlement agreement.

Lockheed Martin Corp. v. Retail Holdings, N.V., 639 F.3d 63 (2d Cir. 2011). Party is not obligated to file a claim in bankruptcy to obtain an asset that it already owned under the terms of a prepetition corporate spin-off agreement. Failure to file a claim does not preclude the party from obtaining control of the asset.

Dish Network Corp. v. DBSD. N. Am., Inc. (In re DBSD N. Am., Inc.), 634 F.3d 79 (2d Cir. 2011). "Gift" of stock by secured creditor to underwater equity holder violated absolute priorities rule. Debtor's plan proposed a small distribution of stock in the reorganized entity to unsecured creditors and a distribution of stock and warrants to the equity interest holder in the debtor. (1) Unsecured creditor with a valid, impaired claim had standing to appeal. (2) Plan violated absolute priority rule in § 1129(b)(2)(B) when it proposed to distribute stock in reorganized entity to equity interest holder in debtor without paying unsecured creditors in full. The distribution to the equity interest holder was characterized as a gift from the secured creditor. The court rejected the gifting doctrine because the doctrine is not incorporated into § 1129(b)(2)(B) and the assets to be distributed were assets of the estate, not assets of the secured creditor. (3) Bankruptcy court appropriately designated creditor's vote as not in good faith under § 1126(e). Debtor's competitor had purchased claims to further its strategic objective of acquiring the debtor's property, not protecting the claims. This was an improper ulterior motive. (4) Bankruptcy court properly disregarded class of claims for voting purposes under § 1129(a)(8). Debtor's competitor had purchased the entire class of claims and its vote was not in good faith under § 1126(e). (5)

Chapter 11 plan met the feasibility requirement of § 1129(a)(11). The plan dramatically deleveraged the debtor, the debtor had received a credit commitment for the first two years of working capital, and there was little risk of default on the debtor's obligations to secured creditors.

Adelphia Recovery Trust v. HSBC Bank USA, Nat'l Ass'n (In re Adelphia Recovery Trust), 634 F.3d 678 (2d Cir. 2011). Bankruptcy court order confirming an asset sale is a final judgment entitled to preclusive effect; when debtor in possession consented to the valuation of payments made to creditor under a loan for purposes of sale approval, the debtor is precluded from challenging that valuation in a subsequent fraudulent conveyance action. Under the equitable doctrine of judicial estoppel, position taken in support of asset sale precluded inconsistent position necessary to maintain fraudulent conveyance actions against parties that did not participate in sale approval.

THIRD CIRCUIT

In re Taylor, 655 F.3d 274 (3d Cir. 2011). Bankruptcy court appropriately imposed sanctions under Bankruptcy Rule 9011 on mortgage lender and its attorneys based on inaccurate and misleading statements in motion for relief from stay and in response to claim objection. Attorneys failed to adequately investigate accuracy of electronic information received through an automated third party provider on lender's behalf.

In re Marcal Paper Mills, Inc., 650 F.3d 311 (3d Cir. 2011). Pension fund withdrawal liability under ERISA when debtor ceased operations constitutes an administrative expense under § 503(b)(1)(A) to the extent attributable to the postpetition time period.

In re Global Indus. Tech., Inc., 645 F.3d 201 (3d Cir. 2011). Insurers whose policies would fund trusts for personal injury claimants pursuant to channeling injunctions under Chapter 11 plan had standing to object to confirmation. The plan purported to be ''insurance neutral'' in that all the insurers' defenses were preserved, except any defense to the antiassignment provisions of the policies. The insurers demonstrated an injury-in-fact sufficient to confer standing in that the prepetition liability exposure of the insurers increased by a factor of 27 due to the plan's promise of a trust to fund injury claims.

Credit Agricole Corp. & Inv. Bank N.Y. Branch v. American Home Mortg. Holdings, Inc. (In re American Home Mortg. Holdings, Inc.), 637 F.3d 246 (3d Cir. 2011). The discounted cash-flow method is a commercially reasonable determinant of value for repurchase agreements under § 562(a). The market price should be used to determine an asset's value when the market is functioning properly. When the market is dysfunctional, and the market price does not reflect an asset's worth, the bankruptcy court should turn to other determinants of value, which may include the discounted cash-flow method.

FOURTH CIRCUIT

Botkin v. DuPont Cmty. Credit Union (In re Botkin), 650 F.3d 396 (4th Cir. 2011). A debtor can avoid a judicial lien under § 522(f) without having previously claimed an exemption on Schedule C in the property subject to the lien.

Calhoun v. United States Trustee, 650 F.3d 338 (4th Cir. 2011). (1) Bankruptcy court properly dismissed Chapter 7 petition for abuse under § 707(b). Debtors' ability to pay creditors was supported by totality of the circumstances, including (a) the dollar amount of the debtors' prepetition payments to creditors, (b) that the petition was not the result of sudden illness, calamity, disability, or unemployment, and (c) the debtors' extravagant monthly expenses. (2) Means test under § 707(b)(1) provides a formula by which a court can presume abuse by above-median-income debtors and a basis to dismiss an abusive case. Means test is not conclusive, the presumption is rebuttable, and court may find abuse even if there is no presumption.

BANKRUPTCY HIGHLIGHTS

Goldman v. Capital City Mortg. Corp. (In re Nieves), 648 F.3d 232 (4th Cir. 2011). For purposes of § 550(b)(1), "knowledge" is satisfied if the transferee knew facts that would lead a reasonable person to believe that the property transferred was voidable. "Good faith," as used in § 550(b)(1), should be determined under an objective standard. Courts should analyze what the transferee knew or should have known. Hence, transferees do not take in good faith if they remain willfully ignorant in the face of facts which cry out for investigation, taking into consideration the customary practices of the industry in which the transferee operates.

Maryland v. Ciotti (In re Ciotti), 638 F.3d 276 (4th Cir. 2011). State income tax liability was nondischargeable under § 523(a)(1)(B) because debtor failed to file a required report with state authorities after the IRS adjusted federal returns to increase tax liability. (1) Debtor argued the required state report was not a "return" under § 523(a)(1)(B). The court disagreed because the information required in the report was equivalent to that required in a return. Also, although the report was not filed under penalty of perjury, criminal penalties are imposed for filing a false report. (2) Debtor argued that since the IRS had provided the report to state authorities, the debt should be discharged. The court disagreed because state law required the taxpayer to file the report.

FIFTH CIRCUIT

Spencer Ad Hoc Equity Comm. v. Idearc, Inc. (In re Idearc, Inc.), No. 10-10858, 2011 WL 4910019 (5th Cir. Oct. 17, 2011) (per curiam). Whether appeal of plan confirmation should be dismissed on equitable mootness grounds depends on three factors: (1) whether a stay of the reorganization has been obtained; (2) whether the reorganization has been substantially consummated; and (3) whether the relief requested would affect either the rights of parties not before the court or the success of the plan. Granting the requested relief would adversely affect the success of the Chapter 11 plan; therefore, the court affirmed the district court's dismissal of the appeal of the confirmation order.

Smith v. H.D. Smith Wholesale Drug Co. (In re McCombs), No. 08-20171, 2011 WL 4553052 (5th Cir. Oct. 4, 2011). (1) Under Texas law, judgment creditor lacked enforceable lien on debtor's homestead property at the time of debtor's petition. (2) Judgment creditor's unenforceable lien did not become enforceable against the sale proceeds of the homestead property that became non-exempt due to operation of § 522(p).

ASARCO, Inc. v. Elliott Mgmt. (In re ASARCO, LLC.), 650 F.3d 593 (5th Cir. 2011). Bankruptcy court did not err in authorizing the debtor to reimburse qualified bidders for expenses incurred in connection with the sale of a substantial asset of the bankruptcy estate. The business judgment standard, as adopted in § 363(b), applied, and the bankruptcy court found that the reimbursement was designed to maximize the value of the estate, was fair, reasonable, appropriate, and in the best interests of all parties.

Reed v. City of Arlington, 650 F.3d 571 (5th Cir. 2011) (en banc). Judicial estoppel does not bar bankruptcy trustee from pursuing a judgment that was unscheduled by the debtor. Trustee receives causes of action subject to defenses that could have been raised against the debtor, but this has been limited to prepetition defenses that would apply if no bankruptcy case were filed. Prohibiting trustee from pursuing the judgment would thwart a core goal of the bankruptcy system--obtaining a maximum and equitable distribution for creditors--by unnecessarily vaporizing the assets effectively belonging to innocent creditors.

Grossman v. Lothian Oil, Inc. (In re Lothian Oil, Inc.), 650 F.3d 539 (5th Cir. 2011). Under § 502(b), bankruptcy court may recharacterize a claim as equity rather than debt when applicable state law would classify the interest as equity rather than debt.

Wells Fargo Bank, N.A. v. Stewart (In re Stewart), 647 F.3d 553 (5th Cir. 2011). Bankruptcy court lacked jurisdiction to require creditor to audit every proof of claim that it had filed in the district, to provide a loan history on every account, and to amend its proofs of claim. The case only involved the estate of a single debtor, not a class of debtors. There was no demonstrated likelihood the debtor would ever again be subject to an incorrect proof of claim filed by the creditor. The bankruptcy court's injunction ranged beyond the case to police other cases untested by the adversary process.

Spicer v. Laguna Madre Oil & Gas II, L.L.C. (In re Texas Wyoming Drilling, Inc.), 647 F.3d 547 (5th Cir. 2011). Chapter 11 plan preserved debtor's avoidance actions against prepetition shareholders when plan and disclosure statement revealed the existence of the avoidance actions, the potential recovery amount, the basis for the actions and that the reorganized debtor intended to pursue the claims.

Evercore Capital Partners II, L.L.C. v. Nancy Sue Davis Trust (In Re Davis Offshore, L.P.), 644 F.3d 259 (5th Cir. 2011). (1) Plan and confirmation order that were not appealed and that contained releases and exculpation provisions essential to reorganization bar the claims of shareholders who had sophisticated financial and legal assistance. (2) Bankruptcy court's holding that confirmation order always prevails over conflicting terms of plan is erroneous.

Roberts v. McConnell (In re Hoff), 644 F.3d 244 (5th Cir. 2011). When a Chapter 7 debtor is the beneficiary of a trust, the bankruptcy trustee has same withdrawal rights to reach trust assets as the debtor-beneficiary.

FNFS, Ltd. v. Harwood (In re Harwood), 637 F.3d 615 (5th Cir. 2011). Loans debtor obtained from a limited partnership that the debtor managed were nondischargeable under § 523(a)(4). An officer of a corporate general partner who is entrusted with the management of a limited partnership and who exercises control over the limited partnership owes a fiduciary duty to the partnership for purposes of nondischargeability under § 523(a)(4). The debtor's failure to record deeds of trust on the debtor's property securing his obligation to repay loans from the limited partnership constituted defalcation for purposes of nondischargeability under § 523(a)(4).

Burnett v. Stewart Title, Inc. (In re Burnett), 635 F.3d 169 (5th Cir. 2011). Section 525(b) does not prohibit private employers from denying employment to applicants based on their bankruptcy status.

Camp v. Ingalls (In re Camp), 631 F.3d 757 (5th Cir. 2011). Florida resident who moved to Texas less than 730 days prepetition was entitled to federal exemptions under § 522(b). Debtor could not claim Florida exemptions because Florida state law expressly limits its exemptions to Florida residents.

Save Our Springs Alliance, Inc. v. WSI (II)-COS, LLC (Save Our Springs (S.O.S.) Alliance, Inc.), 632 F.3d 168 (5th Cir. 2011). (1) Bankruptcy court did not err in denying confirmation of Chapter 11 plan of nonprofit organization. Plan was not feasible under § 1129(a)(11). Prepetition donations to debtor were not evidence of future fundraising ability. Unenforceable voluntary pledges were inadmissible as evidence of feasibility. (2) Debtor that designated itself as a small business debtor in its petition is judicially stopped to argue that it should not be held to the 300-day deadline for confirmation under § 1121(e)(2). Debtor was aware its designation might be incorrect, yet the debtor continued to enjoy the benefits of the designation. Having taken advantage of these benefits, the debtor cannot opportunistically avoid the costs of the designation.

Tax Ease Funding, L.P. v. Thompson (In re Kizzee-Jordan), 626 F.3d 239 (5th Cir. 2011). Third-party lender that pays debtor's tax debt and receives a transfer of the local taxing authority's tax lien holds a "tax claim" and is entitled to interest pursuant to § 511.

SIXTH CIRCUIT

Dickson v. Countrywide Home Loans (In re Dickson), 655 F.3d 585 (6th Cir. 2011). State court judgment during preference period that deemed manufactured home to be an improvement to real property, resulted in a lien that was not a "voluntary transfer" under § 522(g). Accordingly, the lien was avoidable under § 522(h) and § 547.

Hancock v. McDermott, 646 F.3d 356 (6th Cir. 2011). District court properly entered a summary affirmance of bankruptcy court's order denying compensation to debtor's counsel when record established delay and contumacious conduct by counsel. Counsel failed to timely file a brief that met the requirements of the Federal Rules of Bankruptcy Procedure. Counsel responded to district court's show cause order with disrespectful remarks and unacceptable explanations for delay.

United States v. Storey, 640 F.3d 739 (6th Cir. 2011). Nondischargeability of a tax obligation under § 523(a)(1)(c) requires a voluntary, conscious, and intentional evasion. The government must prove that the debtor: 1) had a duty to pay taxes; 2) knew of the duty to pay taxes; and 3) voluntarily and intentionally violated that duty. Nonpayment of taxes alone is insufficient to bar discharge but is relevant to overall analysis. Bankruptcy court's ruling on dischargeability of student loan obligations does not support government's position that debtor voluntarily avoided paying taxes. The treatment of student loans and tax obligations differs significantly in bankruptcy.

Owner Operator Indep. Drivers Ass'n v. Comerica Bank (In re Arctic Express Inc.), 636 F.3d 781 (6th Cir. 2011). Truth-in-Leasing regulations of the Motor Carrier Act-49 U.S.C.A. §§ 14101-02 & 14704; 49 C.F.R. § 376.12--impressed a statutory trust upon maintenance escrow funds held by the debtor in favor of the debtor's beneficiary-lessees. Lender secured by the debtor's cash collateral account, including the trust funds, is not a bona fide purchaser for value of the trust funds. Accordingly, secured lender does not have superior priority in trust funds over that of beneficiary-lessee.

Baud v. Carroll, 634 F.3d 327 (6th Cir. 2011). (1) Chapter 13 plan cannot be confirmed when trustee or holder of an allowed unsecured claim objects to confirmation, the debtor has positive projected disposable income and the plan does not pay unsecured claims in full, unless the plan provides that all of the debtor's projected disposable income will be applied to make payments over a period of time equal to the applicable commitment period imposed by § 1325(b). (2) The calculation of projected disposable income (a) should not include items, such as benefits received under the Social Security Act, that are excluded from the definition of current monthly income set forth in § 101(10A), and (b) should deduct expenses that above-median income debtors are permitted to deduct pursuant to §§ 1325(b)(3) and 707(b)(2)(A)(iii). (3) There is no exception to the temporal requirement of a minimum commitment period set forth in § 1325(b) for debtors with zero or negative projected disposable income.

SEVENTH CIRCUIT

In re Longview Aluminum, L.L.C., No. 10-2780, 2011 WL 3966152 (7th Cir. Sept. 2, 2011). The definition of an "insider" in § 101(31)(B) is not exhaustive. It is not simply the title of "director" or "officer" that renders an individual an insider; rather, it is the set of legal rights that a typical corporate director or officer holds. A member of a limited liability company may be an insider if the member has voting rights and a formal position on the board, even if full membership rights have been limited in other ways.

In re Golf 255, Inc., 652 F.3d 806 (7th Cir. 2011). (1) Debtor's former shareholder did not commit fraud on the court when he signed an involuntary petition. A creditor who makes false representations or encourages others to do so is different than a lying witness, and a witness's lies are not fraud on the court unless a lawyer in the case is complicit in them. Former shareholder signing involuntary petition is in the position of a witness, and although he is, in this case, a lawyer, he was serving as a party, not a lawyer, when he signed the petition. (2) Fraud is not a basis to rescind a bankruptcy sale when there is no proof that the purchaser was a party to any alleged fraud.

Townsquare Media, Inc. v. Brill, 652 F.3d 767 (7th Cir. 2011). Pursuant to 28 U.S.C.A. § 1447(d), a bankruptcy court's order remanding removed claims to state court based upon lack of subject matter jurisdiction is nonappealable.

Matrix IV, Inc. v. American Nat'l Bank & Trust Co. of Chicago, 649 F.3d 539 (7th Cir. 2011). Creditor was collaterally estopped from bringing RICO and common-law fraud claims in a subsequent proceeding when those claims were actually litigated in a § 363 sale hearing and lien-priority adversary proceeding. A bankruptcy court's ruling in a noncore proceeding could not provide res judicata affect. However, collateral estoppel is a narrower basis to preclude the creditor's new action than res judicata, and unlike res judicata, collateral estoppel does not depend upon the core/noncore distinction.

In re XMH Corp., 647 F.3d 690 (7th Cir. 2011). Trademark license, in the absence of a clause expressly authorizing assignment, is not assignable under § 365(c)(1).

United States v. Buchman, 646 F.3d 409 (7th Cir. 2011). The Seventh Circuit does not apply "equitable mootness" to dispose of appellate proceedings. The possibility of financial adjustments among the parties keeps a proceeding alive even if a property sale cannot be upset and rights under a plan of reorganization cannot be revised.

CDX Liquidating Trust v. Venrock Assocs., 640 F.3d 209 (7th Cir. 2011). A derivative suit is a corporate asset, and if the corporation is in bankruptcy the derivative suit is an asset of the estate.

Reeves v. Davis (In re Davis), 638 F.3d 549 (7th Cir. 2011). A creditor seeking exception from discharge under § 523(a)(2)(A) must prove: 1) that the debtor made a false representation or omission, which it knew was false or made with reckless disregard for the truth; 2) that the debtor possessed an intent to deceive or defraud; and 3) that the creditor justifiably relied on the false representation. State court ruling that debtor committed a "deceptive act," did not make a finding as to the debtor's intent and was not entitled to collateral estoppel effect in dischargeability litigation.

Stamat v. Neary, 635 F.3d 974 (7th Cir. 2011). To prevail on a denial of discharge under § 727(a)(4), it must be proven by a preponderance of the evidence that: (1) the debtor made a statement under oath; (2) the statement was false; (3) the debtor knew the statement was false; (4) the debtor made the statement with fraudulent intent; and (5) the statement related materially to the bankruptcy case. Debtors were properly denied a discharge for: failing to disclose business interests, even though they were merely limited partners or the business no longer existed; failing to disclose money borrowed to settle a lawsuit and a refinancing of their home; and, overstating their income.

Regen Capital I, Inc. v. UAL Corp. (In re UAL Corp.), 635 F.3d 312 (7th Cir. 2011). Claim assignment granted assignor the right to collect a cure amount arising from any assumption of executory contract. However, executory contract was never assumed by debtor under the confirmed plan. Assignor's contract was listed in plan under "Assumed Executory Contracts," but plan also provided right to assume or reject executory contracts postconfirmation. Debtor never cured or provided adequate assurance of prompt cure "at the time of assumption" under § 365(b)(1). Court did not rule whether postconfirmation assumption or rejection violated § 365.

Busson-Sokolik v. Milwaukee School of Eng'g (In re Busson-Sokolik), 635 F.3d 261 (7th Cir. 2011). (1) Court adopted "purpose" test to determine whether a loan is "educational" and potentially nondischargeable under § 523(a)(8)(A). The following facts are relevant to inquiry of loan's purpose: (a) creditor is a school; (b) loan was part of a package that included scholarship and grant money toward completion of debtor's education at school; (c) promissory note was signed while debtor was a student; (d) debtor had to be a student to receive the money from the school; and (e) the loan was deposited into debtor's student account at the school. (2) Sanctions against debtor and counsel under Rule 8020 for pursing a frivolous appeal were reduced because debtor is a student and neither party acted in bad faith. The full sanction awarded by district court was not necessary to serve deterrent purposes of Rule 8020.

Follett Higher Educ. Group, Inc. v. Berman (In re Berman), 629 F.3d 761 (7th Cir. 2011). Debtor served as president of a corporation that had a prepetition contract with the creditor. (1) Although an officer of an insolvent corporation may be deemed a fiduciary for creditors under state law, the officer may not be deemed, on that basis alone, a fiduciary under § 523(a)(4). (2) Creditor also failed to establish that debtor's corporation owed a fiduciary duty. Creditor did not prove the existence of an express trust or an implied fiduciary status arising under a contractual relationship.

EIGHTH CIRCUIT

Sanchez v. Northwest Airlines, Inc., No. 10-2393, 2011 WL 4862654 (8th Cir. Oct. 14, 2011). Employee's claim under the Americans with Disabilities Act ("ADA") was not discharged in airline's confirmed Chapter 11 case for failure to file the claim by the administrative expense claims deadline. The airline's notice of deadline to file administrative expense claims specifically stated that no filing was necessary with regard to claims "incurred in the ordinary course of business." The ADA claim arose out of the regular employment relationship and therefore in the ordinary course of business. Given these circumstances, the employee did not receive notice fairly apprising him of the possibility of the ADA claim being barred if not submitted by the administrative claims bar date.

Danduran v. Kaler (In re Danduran), No. 10-3813, 2011 WL 4104923 (8th Cir. Sept. 16, 2011). (1) Homestead exemption only applies to proceeds from sale of real property, not to personal property included in same transaction. (2) Trustee, as objecting party, has burden of proof to establish invalidity of claimed homestead exemption in saving account containing proceeds from combined sale of real and personal property. (3) Trustee failed to meet this burden. Although portion of sale proceeds attributable to real property was initially identifiable, funds were used to satisfy mortgage after combined proceeds were deposited into account. The trustee could not establish whether remaining balance of account included non-homestead funds.

Lange v. Invoa Capital Funding, LLC (In re Qualia Clinical Serv., Inc.), 652 F.3d 933 (8th Cir. 2011). The statutory "improvement in position" test under § 547(c)(5) presupposes that a creditor holds a perfected security interest as of the date of the first testing point. Creditor that entered test period with unperfected security interest, that was properly deemed to have zero value, improved position as against other creditors. Security interest was avoidable preferential transfer.

Kramer v. Cash Link Sys., 652 F.3d 840 (8th Cir. 2011). Under § 727(a)(1), a corporation is not entitled to discharge its debts in a Chapter 7 case. Accordingly, the final decree in the corporate debtor's Chapter 7 case did not grant a discharge, and the plaintiff was free to pursue his claims against the defendant after the expiration of the automatic stay.

Walker v. Sallie Mae Servicing Corp. (In re Walker), 650 F.3d 1227 (8th Cir. 2011). A debtor seeking to discharge an otherwise nondischargeable student debt pursuant to § 523(a)(8) must show that the totality of the circumstances support a finding of undue hardship. It is not clear error to consider the debtor's postpetition financial condition in determining undue hardship. Moreover, any errors in calculating a debtor's net monthly income must be evaluated in the larger context of the undue hardship totality of the circumstances analysis. Hence, even if the debtor's net monthly income may be greater than concluded by the bankruptcy court, the undue hardship determination will not be overturned if the debtor still could not make student loan payments with the correct net income. Finally, allowing a debtor to maintain a "minimal standard of living" must be based upon the unique facts and circumstances present in a particular undue hardship determination.

Wetzel v. Regions Bank, 649 F.3d 831 (8th Cir. 2011). Pursuant to § 541(c)(2), the debtor's interest in disbursements from spendthrift trust was not part of bankruptcy estate. Spendthrift provision in trust was a "restriction on… transfer" under "applicable nonbankruptcy law.".

Burnett v. Burnett (In re Burnett), 646 F.3d 575 (8th Cir. 2011). Chapter 13 plan provided for payment of child and spousal support arrearages and allowed former spouse to return to state court to determine accrued interest on child support arrearage as of petition date. Pursuant to § 1327(a), the former spouse was bound to the terms of the plan and could only litigate accrued interest on the prepetition child support arrearage, not interest on the prepetition spousal support arrearage. Prepetition interest on the spousal support arrearage was not provided for under the plan. The plan was res judicata even though it violated § 1322(a)(2) by not providing for full payment of all prepetition spousal support obligations.

Advanced Control Solutions, Inc. v. Justice, 639 F.3d 838 (8th Cir. 2011). In a case converted from Chapter 13 to Chapter 7, § 707(b)(1) allows bankruptcy court to re-convert Chapter 7 case to Chapter 13 on debtor's motion. "[Section] 706(a) does not co-opt the clear grant of authority that the plain language of § 707(b)(1) provides to bankruptcy courts."

NINTH CIRCUIT

Sherman v. S.E.C. (In re Sherman), No. 09-55880, 2011 WL 4347025 (9th Cir. Sept. 19, 2011). Exception to discharge under § 523(a)(19)(A)(i) only applies to those who have themselves violated securities laws. Debtor was an attorney representing defendants in an SEC enforcement action and was required by a disgorgement order to return fees he had been paid. This obligation was dischargeable since debtor-attorney did not violate securities laws.

California Franchise Tax Bd. v. Kendall (In re Jones), No. 10-60000, 2011 WL 4061190 (9th Cir. Sept. 14, 2011). (1) Under § 1327(b), property of the estate revests in debtor upon plan confirmation, unless plan or order of confirmation provides otherwise. When revesting occurs before a tax debt becomes due, no stay precludes collection under § 362. (2) The § 507(a)(8) lookback period is suspended only when the creditor was specifically precluded from collection, and equitable tolling under principles of *Young v. United States* only apply when the creditor is precluded from collecting the tax debt.

Palmdale Hills Prop., LLC v. Lehman Commercial Paper, Inc. (Palmdale Hills Prop., LLC), 654 F.3d 868 (9th Cir. 2011). Where one debtor holds a claim against another debtor and the second debtor seeks to equitably subordinate the claim of the first debtor, the second debtor must obtain relief from the automatic stay in the first debtor's bankruptcy case.

Grantham v. Cory (In re Flamingo 55, Inc.), 646 F.3d 1253 (9th Cir. 2011). (1) Joint borrowers with the debtor are not in the position of a surety, guarantor, or accommodation maker and thus are not entitled to subrogation pursuant to § 509(a). Instead, the rights of such joint borrowers are governed by § 509(b)(2), which precludes subrogation. (2) The court disagreed with the bankruptcy court's holding that the joint borrowers did not "pay" the debtor's obligation by means of foreclosure on the jointly titled property. The words "pay" and "payment" in § 509(a) should not be read to mean cash payment alone.

AmeriCredit Fin. Servs. Inc. v. Penrod (In re Penrod), 636 F.3d 1175 (9th Cir. 2011), *cert. denied*, 2011 WL 4530304 (U.S. Oct. 3, 2011). Denial of rehearing en banc. Majority of Ninth Circuit judges voted to deny rehearing en banc, sustaining panel decision that "negative equity" is not part of purchase money debt for purposes of hanging sentence at the end of § 1325(a).

Dissenting judges would include "negative equity" in purchase money debt for purposes of hanging sentence at end of § 1325(a). There is now a clear circuit split on this issue.

Barrientos v. Wells Fargo Bank, N.A., 633 F.3d 1186 (9th Cir. 2011). There is no private cause of action for damages under §§ 105 and 524 for violation of discharge injunction. The remedy for violation of the discharge injunction is an order of contempt sought via motion under Rule 9014.

Battle Ground Plaza, LLC v. Ray (In re Ray), 624 F.3d 1124 (9th Cir. 2011). Bankruptcy court lacks jurisdiction over challenge to § 363 sale order when Chapter 11 plan has been confirmed, the debtor discharged and the case closed. The collateral attack on the sale order was based on a state law breach of contract claim independent of the bankruptcy case, so the claim did not arise under the Bankruptcy Code. The breach of contract claim could exist entirely apart from the bankruptcy proceeding and was not dependent on a resolution of any substantial question of bankruptcy law. Ancillary jurisdiction did not exist because reopening the bankruptcy case to determine a state law issue goes beyond what is necessary to effectuate the bankruptcy court's decrees.

TENTH CIRCUIT

HealthTrio, Inc. v. Centennial River Corp. (In re HealthTrio Inc.), 653 F.3d 1154 (10th Cir. 2011). The Tenth Circuit had jurisdiction over Bankruptcy Appellate Panel's order dismissing an appeal for lack of jurisdiction because the underlying bankruptcy court's order for relief was a final order. Pursuant to 28 U.S.C.A. § 158(a), appeals of bankruptcy court orders "shall be taken only to the district court for the judicial district in which the bankruptcy judge is serving." Accordingly, the Tenth Circuit Bankruptcy Appellate Panel was foreclosed from reviewing a Delaware bankruptcy judge's order for relief because the issuing judge was serving outside the judicial district where the appeal was filed.

Chizzali v. Gindi (In re Gindi), 642 F.3d 865 (10th Cir. 2011). (1) Creditor's appeal of state court denial of civil contempt sanction against debtor is not excepted from automatic stay by § 362(b)(1). (2) "Cause" exists for lifting the automatic stay under § 362(d)(1), enabling continuance of state court litigation, when the movant can show that it is likely to prevail in the action. (3) Under Colorado law, service of writ of garnishment creates lien in amount of judgment sought to be satisfied by garnishment. Accordingly, debtor lacks equity, for purposes of relief from the automatic stay under § 362(d)(2), if garnishment lien on bank account exceeds the value of funds in the account.

C.O.P. Coal Dev. Co. v. C.W. Mining Co. (In re C.W. Mining Co.), 641 F.3d 1235 (10th Cir. 2011). (1) Appeal of order approving sale of debtor's contract with appellant that allowed debtor to mine and remove coal from land owned or controlled by appellant was not moot under § 363(m). Even though the contract was sold to a good faith purchaser and the appellant did not seek to stay the sale order, the appeal was not moot because the appellant might be entitled to alternative relief that would not affect the validity of the sale. (2) Contract had not terminated under state law postpetition, so the contract was property of the estate under § 541(b)(2) and could be assumed and sold.

Standiferd v. United States Trustee (In re Standiferd), 641 F.3d 1209 (10th Cir. 2011). After conversion from Chapter 13 to Chapter 7, debtor may be denied discharge under § 727(a)(6)(A) based on preconversion failure to obey Chapter 13 confirmation order. Under § 727(a)(6)(A), the court may deny discharge if the debtor has refused, in the case, to obey any lawful order of the court other than an order to respond to a material question or to testify. Section 348(a) clearly provides that, upon conversion, the case includes the proceedings both before and after conversion; and, a Chapter 13 confirmation order is a lawful order of the court.

Standard Indus., Inc. v. Aquila, Inc. (In re C.W. Mining Co.), 625 F.3d 1240 (10th Cir. 2011). (1) Bankruptcy court has authority to void actions taken in violation of the automatic stay. The court's power to punish contempt is not limited solely to monetary sanctions. (2) Bankruptcy Rules 9014(a) and 9020 permit a party to seek an order of civil contempt by motion. An adversary proceeding is not required.

ELEVENTH CIRCUIT

Florida Dep't of Rev. v. Diaz (In re Diaz), 647 F.3d 1073 (11th Cir. 2011). (1) State sovereign immunity shielded state agencies seeking to collect child support payments from postdischarge claims for violations of the automatic stay. States waived sovereign immunity to the extent necessary to effectuate the in rem functions of bankruptcy courts. Actions for violation of the automatic stay and violation of the discharge injunction are generally subject to such waiver; but since the debtor initiated the underlying proceeding after completion of his Chapter 13 plan and discharge, the stay violation proceeding was not necessary to effectuate the bankruptcy court's in rem jurisdiction. (2) State agencies did not waive sovereign immunity by filing a proof of claim. Litigation waiver only extends to actions seeking damages for violation of the automatic stay while the stay is in effect, and actions seeking damages for violations of the discharge injunction. Hence, the postdischarge automatic stay claim does not fit within the litigation waiver. (3) State agencies did waive sovereign immunity with respect to discharge injunction but did not violate the discharge injunction because a claim for child support is excepted from discharge regardless whether it is provided for by the Chapter 13 plan or even disallowed. (4) Debtor's objection to the state agencies' child support claims only determined the amount of child support debt that would be paid by the bankruptcy estate, not the total amount of the child support debt. Consequently, res judicata and collateral estoppel did not preclude the state agencies from arguing the extent of the debtor's postbankruptcy personal liability for child support.

Jacks v. Wells Fargo Bank, N.A. (In re Jacks), 642 F.3d 1323 (11th Cir. 2011). With regard to the automatic stay: (1) the mere recordation of fees incurred by a lender in its internal records, without any attempt to collect those fees from the debtor or estate or to modify the mortgage, is not an "act" in violation of § 362(a)(3); (2) the mere potential of future liability for fees incurred by a mortgage lender during a bankruptcy is not the creation of a new and enlarged lien as prohibited by § 362(a)(5); and (3) merely recording fees on internal documents is not an attempt to collect a prepetition debt in violation of § 362(a)(6), when the fees were never charged to a debtor's account, added to the balance due on the mortgage, or communicated to the debtor as an attempt to collect. Similarly, § 506(b) and Rule 2016(a) are not violated when a creditor merely records costs that it has incurred in association with a mortgagor's bankruptcy for internal bookkeeping purposes and makes no attempt to collect or otherwise add them to the debtor's balance. Failure to disclose fees on a proof of claim is not a valid basis for a claim objection under § 502(b)(1).

Myers v. Toojay's Mgmt. Corp., 640 F.3d 1278 (11th Cir. 2011). A private employer may refuse employment based upon an applicant's prior bankruptcy, and a debtor must be an employee to be protected from termination under § 525(b). Section 525(a) prohibits government employers from denying employment to an individual based on bankruptcy status. Pursuant to § 525(b), the private sector is prohibited from discriminating against persons who are already employees based upon bankruptcy status.

IRT Partners, L.P. v. Winn-Dixie Stores, Inc. (In re Winn-Dixie Stores, Inc.), 639 F.3d 1053 (11th Cir. 2011). The res judicata effect of confirmation of a Chapter 11 plan precludes creditors from filing amended claims after plan confirmation absent compelling circumstances.

United States v. Mitchell (In re Mitchell), 633 F.3d 1319 (11th Cir. 2011). Tax liability is nondischargeable under § 523(a)(1)(C) when government shows the debtor engaged in willfully evasive conduct. Nonpayment in conjunction with a failure to file tax returns has been deemed to constitute evasive conduct. The following evidenced the debtor's willfulness in evading taxes:

failing to file tax returns in order to avoid collection activity; purchasing a home in another person's name to avoid levy; forming a company to avoid garnishment; letter threatening bankruptcy; placing title to homes in another person's name; closing bank accounts and depositing checks in another account; debtor's discretionary spending; and lack of evidence that debtor's failure to pay was result of inadvertence or mistake.

Alabama Dep't of Econ. & Cmty. Affairs v. Ball Healthcare-Dallas, LLC (In re Lett), 632 F.3d 1216 (11th Cir. 2011). Confirmation of a cram down Chapter 11 plan sufficiently puts at issue application of the absolute priority rule so as to preserve the issue for appeal notwithstanding the absence of an objection to confirmation from an impaired creditor in a dissenting class. Furthermore, appeal was not equitably moot because plan was not "substantially consummated" and effective relief was still available for appellant notwithstanding the commencement of payments to other classes of creditors.

VI.   2010 Technical Amendments to Bankruptcy Code

In the February, 2011 Norton Bankruptcy Law Adviser, the following summary and analysis of the Bankruptcy Technical Corrections Act of 2010, Public Law 111-327, was authored by Honorable Nancy C. Dreher, United Bankruptcy Judge in the District of Minnesota, and her Career Law Clerk, Michael J. Stepan.

On December 16, 2010, the U.S. House of Representatives passed by voice vote a Senate amendment of HR 6198. The President signed the legislation on December 22, 2010, and it is known as the "Bankruptcy Technical Corrections Act of 2010." Pub. L. 111-327. The Act makes "technical corrections" to amendments to the Bankruptcy Code made by the Bankruptcy Abuse Prevention Consumer Protection Act of 2005 (BAPCPA), makes technical corrections to Title 18 relating to the federal crime of bankruptcy fraud, and makes technical corrections to Title 28 relating to appeals and to bankruptcy statistics. The "technical corrections" appear to be mainly just that -- grammatical, typographical, and stylistic fixes to BAPCPA. There are, however, a few corrected cross-references to other sections of the Code, along with subtle but meaning-changing amendments (identified below), that are arguably substantive.

A. Amendments to the Bankruptcy Code

Definitions. The Act amends § 101(13A)(A) (definition of "debtor's principal residence") by inserting "if used as the principal residence by the debtor" after "structure" the first place that it appears and amends § 101(13A)(B) by inserting "if used as the principal residence by the debtor" before the period at the end. In § 101(35)(B) ("insured depository institution" defined), "(23) and (35)" is stricken and replaced with corrected references to "(21B) and (33)(A)". Presumably with the advent of electronic records, § 101 (40B) (definition of "patient records") is amended by replacing the phrase "written document relating to a patient or a" with "record relating to a patient, including a written document or a". In § 101(42) ("petition" defined), "303, and 304" is stricken and replaced with "303 and 1504" since § 304 was deleted from the Code in 2005 and no longer exists. In § 101(51B) (definition of "single asset real estate"), the word "thereto" is inserted before the period at the end. In § 101(51D)(A) ("small business debtor" defined), the phrase "of the filing" is inserted after "date" the first time that it appears.

Applicability of chapters. To correct an erroneous cross-reference in § 103(a), "362(n)" is replaced with "362(o)".

Power of court. The word "may" is inserted after "Procedure" in § 105(d)(2).

Waiver of sovereign immunity. The Act strikes "728," in § 106(a)(1) since § 728 was deleted from the Code in 2005 and no longer exists.

Public access to papers. In § 107(a), the phrase "subsection (b) of this section" is stricken and replaced with "subsections (b) and (c)".

BANKRUPTCY HIGHLIGHTS

Who may be a debtor. In § 109(b)(3)(B), "1978" is replaced with the stylistic correction of "1978". In § 109(h)(1) the phrase "other than paragraph (4) of this subsection" is inserted after "this section" and "preceding" is replaced with "ending on" to make the phrase more grammatically correct.

Penalty for persons who negligently or fraudulently prepare bankruptcy petitions. Section 110(b)(2)(A) is amended by inserting "or on behalf of" after "from". In § 110(h)(1), "a" is replaced with "the" and "or on behalf of" is inserted after "from". Section 110(h)(3)(A) is amended by striking the phrase "found to be in excess of the value of any services" and in clause (i) of § 110(h)(3)(A), that phrase is inserted at the beginning of clause (i) to read: "(i) found to be in excess of the value of any services rendered by the bankruptcy petition preparer during the 12-month period immediately preceding the date of the filing of the petition; or". In § 110(h)(4), "paragraph (2)" is replaced with "paragraph (3)".

Nonprofit budget and credit counseling agencies; financial management instructional courses. Section 111(d)(1)(E) is amended by replacing the period at the end with "; and" and by indenting the left margin of subparagraph 2 to the right for stylistic consistency.

Involuntary cases. Section 303(*l*) is redesignated as subsection (k), since subsection (k) was deleted in 2005.

Debtor reporting requirements. In the introductory sentence of § 308(b) "small business debtor" is deleted and replaced with "debtor in a small business case" for stylistic effect. In § 308(b)(4), subparagraph (A), "(A)" is stricken, and clauses (i) and (ii) of that subparagraph are redesignated as subparagraphs (A) and (B), respectively. In other words, § 308(b)(4)(A)(i) is now § 308(b)(4)(A), and § 308(b)(4)(A)(ii) is now § 308(b)(4)(B). Section 308(b)(4)(B) is redesignated as § 308(b)(5), and § 308(b)(4)(C) is redesignated as § 308(b)(6). Also, to consistently reflect this redesignation, in § 308(b)(4)(B) (now redesignated as § 308(b)(5)), the references to "subparagraph (A)(i)" and "subparagraph (A)(ii)" are replaced with "paragraph (4)(A)" and "paragraph (4)(B)".

Effect of conversion. Section 348(b) is amended by striking "728(a), 728(b)," and "1146(a), 1146(b)," since those provisions have not existed since 2005. Section 348(f)(1)(C)(i) is amended by inserting "of the filing" after "date" the first time that it appears.

Automatic stay. Section 362(a)(8) is stylistically amended by striking "corporate debtor's" and by inserting "of a debtor that is a corporation" after "liability" the first place that it appears. The introductory sentence of § 362(c)(3) is grammatically corrected by inserting "a" after "against" and in § 362(c)(4)(A)(i) the phrase "under a chapter other than chapter 7 after dismissal" is inserted after "refiled". In § 362(d)(4), "hinder, or" replaces "hinder, and". In § 362(*l*)(2), a spelling error is corrected by replacing "nonbankrupcty" with "nonbankruptcy".

Use, sale, or lease of property. The word "only" is stricken in the introductory sentence of § 363(d). Paragraph (1) of § 363(d) is replaced to read: "(1) in the case of a debtor that is a corporation or trust that is not a moneyed business, commercial corporation, or trust, only in accordance with nonbankruptcy law applicable to the transfer of property by a debtor that is such a corporation or trust; and". The word "only" is inserted after "(2)" to begin § 363(d)(4)(2).

Determination of tax liability. In § 505(a)(2)(C) the phrase "any law (other than a bankruptcy law)" is replaced with the simply clearer one of "applicable nonbankruptcy law".

Priorities. Section 507(a)(8)(A)(ii) is amended by striking the period at the end of that subsection and inserting "; or" in its place for internal consistency.

Debtor's duties. In § 521(a)(2)(A), the phrase "the debtor shall" is stricken, and the word "and" is inserted at the end of that subparagraph. In § 521(a)(2)(B), the phrase "the debtor shall" and "and" are stricken. In § 521(a)(2)(C), the designator "(C)" is stricken so that it is now an unnumbered continuation of paragraph (2), and the phrase "except that" is inserted in its place. The word "is" is inserted after "auditor" in paragraphs (3) and (4) of § 521(a) for grammatical correctness.

Exemptions. In § 522(b)(3)(A), the word "at" is stricken the first place it appears and replaced with "to" and the second occurrence of "at" is replaced with "in" to make the text more grammatically correct. The phrase "section 523(a)(5)" is replaced with "such paragraph" in § 522(c)(1).

Exceptions to discharge. The period at the end of § 523(a)(2)(C)(ii)(II) is stricken and replaced with a semicolon. Section 523(a)(3) is corrected by replacing an erroneous reference to "521(1)" with an accurate reference to "521(a)(1)".

Effect of discharge. In the last undesignated paragraph of the quoted matter in § 524(k)(3)(J)(i) beginning with "What if your creditor", the phrase "security property" (the first place it appears) is replaced with "property securing the lien" and, in the last sentence, the word "must" is inserted after "you" to read "you must make a single payment" and the phrase "current value of the security property" is replaced with "amount of the allowed secured claim". In paragraph (5)(B) of § 524(k), the word "that" is stricken and replaced with "that,".

Restrictions on debt relief agencies. The phrase "untrue and" in § 526(a)(2) is replaced with "untrue or" and "a" is inserted after "preparer" in § 526(a)(4).

Disclosures. In the third sentence of the fourth undesignated paragraph of the quoted matter in § 527(b) (that paragraph begins with "Before filing"), the phrase "Schedules and Statement of Financial Affairs, as well as in some cases a Statement of Intention" is replaced with "Schedules, and Statement of Financial Affairs, and in some cases a Statement of Intention,".

Property of the estate. An obviously incorrect reference in § 541(b)(6)(B) to nonexistent "section 529(b)(7)" is replaced with a correct reference to "section 529(b)(6)".

Abandonment of property of the estate. Not unlike the correction to § 523(a)(3), an incorrect reference to "521(1)" in § 554(c) is replaced with an accurate reference of "521(a)(1)".

Duties of trustee. A reference to nonexistent "521(2)(B)" in § 704(a)(3) is corrected to "521(a)(2)(B)".

Dismissal of a case or conversion to a case under chapter 11 or 13. In § 707(a)(3), "521" is replaced with a more accurate reference to "521(a)". The phrase "of the filing" is inserted after "date" in § 707(b)(2)(A)(iii)(I), and the phrase "subparagraph (A)(i) of such paragraph" is replaced with "paragraph (2)(A)(I)" in § 707(b)(3).

Rights of partnership trustee against general partners. Since § 728 was deleted from the Code in 2005, the reference "Notwithstanding section 728(c) of this title, the" is deleted and replaced with "The" in § 723(c).

Treatment of certain liens. The text of § 724(b)(2) is cleaned up by replacing "507(a)(1)" with a more precise reference to "507(a)(1)(C) or 507(a)(2)"; "under each such section" is inserted after "expenses" the first place it appears; "chapter 7 of this title" is replaced with "this chapter"; and an incorrect reference to "507(a)(2)," is replaced with correct references to "507(a)(1)(A), 507(a)(1)(B),".

Distribution of property of the estate. In § 726(b), the reference to "or (8)" is replaced with a more complete reference to "(8), (9), or (10)".

Applicability of other sections of this title. In § 901(a), "333," is inserted after the reference to "301," and "351," is inserted after "350(b)".

Appointment of trustee or examiner. The word "or" is inserted at the end of § 1104(a)(1) and the "; or" in § 1104(a)(2) is stricken and replaced with a period. Superfluous § 1104(a)(3) is stricken in its entirety. In § 1104(b)(2)(B)(ii) "subsection (d)" is replaced with a more accurate reference to "subsection (a)".

Duties of trustee and examiner. In § 1106(a)(1), a reference to "704" is replaced with a more precise reference to "704(a)" and another erroneous reference to "521(1)" in § 1106(a)(2) is replaced with a correct reference to "521(a)(1)".

Claims and interests. Yet another erroneous reference to "521(1)" in § 1111(a) is replaced with a correct reference to "521(a)(1)".

Conversion or dismissal. Section 1112(b)(1) is nonsubstantively amended to read more easily as follows: "(1) Except as provided in paragraph (2) and subsection (c), on request of a party in interest, and after notice and a hearing, the court shall convert a case under this chapter to a case under chapter 7 or dismiss a case under this chapter, whichever is in the best interests of creditors and the estate, for cause unless the court determines that the appointment under section 1104(a) of a trustee or an examiner is in the best interests of creditors and the estate." Similarly, the introductory clause of § 1112(b)(2) is replaced with the following: "(2) The court may not convert a case under this chapter to a case under chapter 7 or dismiss a case under this chapter if the court finds and specifically identifies unusual circumstances establishing that converting or dismissing the case is not in the best interests of creditors and the estate, and the debtor or any other party in interest establishes that--". The phrase "granting such relief" is replaced with the more precise one of "converting or dismissing the case" in § 1112(b)(2)(B). In § 1112(e), the vague reference to "521" is replaced with a more precise reference to "521(a)".

Modification of plan. In § 1127(f)(1), the reference to "subsection (a)" is replaced with "subsection (e)" to dovetail with the addition of § 1127(e) in 2005.

Confirmation of plan. Section 1129(a)(16) is made more grammatically correct by striking the phrase "of the plan" and inserting "under the plan" in its place.

Effect of confirmation. The hardship discharge provision of § 1141(d)(5)(B) is made more complete (and internally consistent with § 1141(d)(5)(C)) by striking the word "and" at the end of clause (i) and by adding, following clause (ii), the following new clause: "(iii) subparagraph (C) permits the court to grant a discharge; and". In turn, the word "unless" in the introductory clause of § 1141(d)(5)(C) is replaced with "the court may grant a discharge if,"; the period at the end of § 1141(d)(5)(C)(ii) is replaced with a semicolon and the phrase "and if the requirements of subparagraph (A) or (B) are met." is added to the end of that clause.

Exemption from securities laws. In § 1145(b), "2(11)" is replaced with "2(a)(11)" each place it appears in the section.

Trustee. In § 1202(b)(1), inaccurate references to "704(2), 704(3), 704(5), 704(6), 704(7), and 704(9)" are replaced with accurate references to "704(a)(2), 704(a)(3), 704(a)(5), 704(a)(6), 704(a)(7), and 704(a)(9)". Similarly, the reference to "704(8)" is replaced with "704(a)(8)" in § 1202(b)(5).

Trustee. Similar to the corrections in § 1202(b)(1), inaccurate references in § 1302(b)(1) to "704(2), 704(3), 704(4), 704(5), 704(6), 704(7), and 704(9)" are replaced with corrected references to "704(a)(2), 704(a)(3), 704(a)(4), 704(a)(5), 704(a)(6), 704(a)(7), and 704(a)(9)".

Debtor engaged in business. The reference to "704(8)" in § 1304(c) is corrected to "704(a)(8)".

Conversion or dismissal. The reference to "subsection (e)" in the introductory clause of § 1307(c) is replaced with "subsection (f)" to coincide with the 2005 redesignation of that subsection. In § 1307(c)(9) and (10), the vague reference to "521" is more precisely referenced by "521(a)". Similar to the correction made to the introductory clause of § 1307(c), the reference to "subsection (e)" in § 1307(d) is replaced with "subsection (f)".

BANKRUPTCY HIGHLIGHTS

Filing of prepetition tax returns. In § 1308(b)(2), the phrase "this subsection" is replaced with "paragraph (1)" each place it appears. In § 1308(b)(2)(A), the reference to "paragraph (1)" is more precisely replaced with "paragraph (1)(A)" and similarly, the phrase "paragraph (2)" in § 1308(b)(2)(B) is replaced with "paragraph (1)(B)".

Contents of plan. In the introductory clause of § 1322(a), the word "shall" is stricken and in § 1322(a)(1) and (2), the word shall is inserted after "(1)" and "(2)", respectively, to begin each paragraph; and in § 1322(a)(3), "shall" is inserted after "claims,". In § 1322(a)(4), the redundant phrase "a plan" is stricken.

Confirmation of plan. In the last sentence of § 1325(a) beginning with "For purposes of paragraph (5)", the word "period" is inserted after "910-day". Congress passed on the opportunity to tag the "hanging sentence" at the end of § 1325(a) with a proper sub-section designation. In § 1325(b)(2)(A)(ii), "548(d)(3))" is a mere typographical correction, adding a missing parenthesis to what previously read "548(d)(3)".

Commencement of case under section 301 [,302,] or 303. In the heading of § 1511, the ", 302," is inserted after "301" to comport with the subject matter of § 1511.

Relief that may be granted upon filing petition for recognition. To correct an erroneous cross-reference in § 1519(f), "362(n)" is replaced with "362(o)".

Relief that may be granted upon recognition. Similar to the correction to § 1519(f), the incorrect reference to "362(n)" is replaced with "362(o)" in § 1521(f).

Coordination of a case under this title and a foreign proceeding. In § 1529(l), "is" is inserted after "States" to make the introductory clause grammatically correct.

Corrections to table of sections. In the table of sections of Chapter 3, the item "333. Appointment of ombudsman." is replaced with "333. Appointment of patient care ombudsman." to more accurately coincide with the actual heading of § 333. Similarly, in the table of sections of Chapter 5, specifically the item for § 562, the word "or" is replaced with "and" to match the actual heading of § 562, i.e., "562. Timing of damage measure in connection with swap agreements, securities contracts, forward contracts, commodity contracts, repurchase agreements, and master netting agreements."

B. Amendments to Title 18

Bankruptcy fraud. In paragraph (1) of 18 U.S.C.A. § 157, the word "bankruptcy" is stricken as redundant. Similarly, in paragraphs (2) and (3), stricken as redundant is the phrase ", including a fraudulent involuntary bankruptcy petition under section 303 of such title".

C. Amendments to Title 28

Appeals. In 28 U.S.C.A. § 158(d)(2)(D), the phrase "appeal in" is replaced with "appeal is" to correct an obvious typographical error.

Bankruptcy statistics. The word "the" is stylistically inserted after "against" in 28 U.S.C.A. § 159(c)(3)(H).

Duties (of United States trustee); supervision by Attorney General. Paragraph (3)(A)(ii) of 28 U.S.C.A. § 586(a) is amended by striking the period at the end and inserting a semicolon; in paragraph (7)(C) the word "identify" is replaced with "determine"; and in paragraph (8) the phrase "the United States trustee shall" is stricken.

D. Technical Correction to Public Law 109-8 (BAPCPA)

Section 1406(b)(1) of Public Law 109-8, 119 Stat. 23, 215, is amended by striking the incomplete word "cept" and replacing it with "Except".

E. Concluding Thoughts

There may be others, but the changes to § 105(d)(2) (adding "may"), § 348(d)(4) (changing "and" to "or"), § 526(a)(2) (changing "and" to "or"), and § 726(b) (adding § 507(a)(9) and 507(a)(10)) are substantive and not merely "technical."

Unfortunately, the introduction of the word "period" in the so-called "dangling" clause or "hanging sentence" appearing at the end of § 1325(a) after § 1325(a)(9) does not solve the many problems of construction--e.g., the vague reference to § 506--created by the 2005 amendments to § 1325(a). See Bankruptcy Law Manual § 13:39.

VII. Pending Amendments to UCC Article 9 and Commentary

Changes to Article 9 of the UCC were proposed by the American Law Institute and the Uniform Law Commission in 2010. Numerous changes were made both in commentary and in statutory amendments that were sent to the states for adoption. The amendments include a July 1, 2013 effective date and several states started the enactment process promptly, with enactment already accomplished in at least nine states. http://www.nccusl.org/shared/legreports/legrpt_act. pdf (last visited August 2, 2011). It is not too soon to understand the new commentary and to start using some of these changes, even though the statutory changes do not go into effect immediately.

The drafters took the approach that, if there was a change that needed to be made and it could be dealt with by a comment to the existing statute, that was the better approach. Therefore, a number of the changes are in the commentary rather than the statute. There are also amended forms, including National Form Financing Statements (which are part of the statute) that have been developed with the International Association of Corporation Administrators (IACA) to take into account some of these changes, particularly the new rules for individual debtors' names and the reduced volume of extraneous information to be included.

The proposed statute and forms and revised comments can be examined in their entirety on Westlaw in the UCC-TEXT database.

The most significant substantive amendments will deal with two sets of issues. The several other amendments also simplify the documentation and administration of secured lending, by clarifying or correcting errors and addressing problems in the existing text or conforming it to recent amendments to other articles of the UCC. Some of these latter changes may be especially important in light of problems with enforcement of mortgages since the recession that began in late 2007.

A. *Debtor's Name for Purposes of Public Filing*

The first major set of issues addressed in the amendments involve the name of the debtor on a UCC-1 financing statement. The name of the debtor is extremely important, of course, for indexing and searching, and the application of the standards in Article 9 can be very unforgiving. Several amendments were proposed regarding a debtor's name, including amendments to UCC § 9-507 regarding name changes and an amendment to UCC § 9-502 that addresses how to name the debtor when the debtor is a trust. However, the most significant changes are those prompted by the difficulty involved in determining a debtor's name, especially if the debtor is a natural person.

1. Individual's Name

Many courts have held that errors in individuals' names, which may seem minor, nevertheless render the filing misleading and insufficient to give third parties notice. See, e.g., *In re Kinderknecht*, 308 B.R. 71 (B.A.P. 10th Cir. 2004) ("Terry J." instead of "Terrance Joseph" misleading); *In re Borden*, 353 B.R. 886 (Bankr. D. Neb. 2006), judgment aff'd, appeal dismissed, 2007 WL 2407032 (D. Neb. 2007) ("Mike" instead of "Michael R." misleading); but see *Peoples Bank v. Bryan Bros. Cattle Co.*, 504 F.3d 549 (5th Cir. 2007) ("Louie Dickerson" instead of "Brooks L. Dickerson" sufficient, because debtor held himself out to community as Louie Dickerson and frequently used nickname in business affairs and nickname appeared in files of searching bank). To deal with this problem, the Committee proposed giving states two alternatives:

"Only-If" Rule: Alternative A requires filers to use the name on the debtor's driver's license, if (1) the license has not in its face expired and (b) the license is issued by the state in which the debtor is located. If the debtor does not have such a driver's license, the filer must use either the individual name of the debtor (i.e., whatever the debtor's name would have been prior to the new revision) or the debtor's surname and first personal name.

"Safe Harbor" Rule: Alternative B leaves in place a requirement that the financing statement use the debtor's "individual name," but provides that the name on the driver's license will also be sufficient. If the debtor does not have a current driver's license issued by the state in which the debtor is located, then using the debtor's surname and first personal name will be sufficient.

Under either option, the driver's license is one of the alternatives. It simply may be the mandatory means of determining the name in a state that adopts Alternative A.

2. Registered Organization's Name

With respect to registered organizations, the changes are less dramatic than those for individuals, but they are nevertheless important. A registered organization is a corporation, LLC or similar entity that is created with what might be thought of as a "birth certificate," issued by a state. However, it was somewhat unclear, after the 2001 revision of Article 9, whether a registered organization's name was the name that the state has recorded in its indexing system or whether it is the name that actually appears on the face of the document filed at the time of organization. This has lead to two types of confusion. The first relates to what qualifies as this record: is it the document filed by the organizers or is it the Secretary of State's database? The second is: what happens if there is inconsistency in the recorded document itself? Numbers may be numerical or spelled out in various places in the document, for example, and there may be other typographical errors in capitalization, spacing and spelling. Answering these questions in 2010 was relatively easy in concept but somewhat lengthy in drafting. The answers involve a new defined term, effective in 2013, and other alterations.

First, under a revised definition, a registered organization is one organized solely under the law of a single state by the filing of a "public organic record" with the jurisdiction. The phrase "public organic record," to be defined in a new UCC § 9-102(a)(68), is a record that is available to the public for inspection and consists of the record filed with the state to form or organize the debtor and any subsequent filings.

Next, amended UCC § 9-503(a)(1) makes clear which name to use from that public organic record: it is the name that is stated to be that name. It is not the name recorded by the filing office in its database, if that is different from the name that appears in the organic record. Also, the name in the title of the document or in the signature block will not control if those are different from the provision that actually states what the entity's name is to be. Prudent filers and searchers should look for the name that is in the body of the document where the name is declared.

B. *Debtor's Change in Location and New Debtor*

The second major category of revisions to be effective in 2013 deals with the effect on a security interest in after-acquired property, in the event of a change of a debtor's location or a new debtors becoming bound by the security agreement. New UCC § 9-316(h) and (i) will address two situations: collateral acquired by a debtor after the debtor's relocation to another jurisdiction and collateral acquired by a new debtor (e.g., a successor) that is located in a different jurisdiction from the original debtor. The new provisions generally increase the likelihood that a secured party who filed a financing statement in the debtor's "old" location or the original debtor's location will be perfected against the collateral in question, but still require diligence in monitoring the transaction and re-filing upon such a change.

THE CODE OF THE LAWS OF THE UNITED STATES OF AMERICA

TITLE 11

BANKRUPTCY

Chapter		Section
1.	General Provisions	101
3.	Case Administration	301
5.	Creditors, the Debtor, and the Estate	501
7.	Liquidation	701
9.	Adjustment of Debts of a Municipality	901
11.	Reorganization	1101
12.	Adjustments of Debts of a Family Farmer or Family Fisherman with Regular Annual Income[1]	1201
13.	Adjustment of Debts of an Individual With Regular Income	1301
15.	Ancillary and Other Cross-Border Cases	1501

[1] So in original. Does not conform to chapter heading.

HISTORICAL AND STATUTORY NOTES

Enacting Clause

Pub.L. 95–598, Title I, § 101, Nov. 6, 1978, 92 Stat. 2549, provided in part: "The law relating to bankruptcy is codified and enacted as title 11 of the United States Code, entitled 'Bankruptcy', and may be cited as 11 U.S.C. § ___."

Amendments

2005 Amendments. Pub.L. 109–8, Title X, § 1007(d), Apr. 20, 2005, 119 Stat. 188, in the item for chapter 12, struck out "Adjustment of Debts of Family Farmers with Regular Annual Income" and inserted "Adjustments of Debts of a Family Farmer or Family Fisherman with Regular Annual Income", which does not conform to the chapter heading.

Pub.L. 109–8, Title VIII, § 801(b), Apr. 20, 2005, 119 Stat. 145, added item for chapter 15.

1994 Amendments. Pub.L. 103–394, Title V, § 501(d)(39), Oct. 22, 1994, 108 Stat. 4147, struck out item for former chapter 15 which read: "United States Trustees".

1986 Amendments. Pub.L. 99–554, Title II, § 257(a), Oct. 27, 1986, 100 Stat. 3114, added item 12.

Effective and Applicability Provisions

2005 Acts. Amendments by Pub.L. 109–8 effective, except as otherwise provided, 180 days after April 20, 2005, and inapplicable with respect to cases commenced under Title 11 before the effective date, see Pub.L. 109–8, § 1501, set out as a note under 11 U.S.C.A. § 101.

1994 Acts. Amendment by Pub.L. 103–394 effective on Oct. 22, 1994, and not to apply with respect to cases commenced under Title 11 of the United States Code before Oct. 22, 1994, see section 702 of Pub.L. 103–394, set out as a note under section 101 of this title.

1978 Acts. Pub.L. 95–598, Title IV, § 402, Nov. 6, 1978, 92 Stat. 2682, as amended by Pub.L. 98–249, § 1(a), Mar. 31, 1984, 98 Stat. 116; Pub.L. 98–271, § 1(a), Apr. 30, 1984, 98 Stat. 163; Pub.L. 98–299, § 1(a), May 25, 1984, 98 Stat. 214; Pub.L. 98–325, § 1(a), June 20, 1984, 98 Stat. 268; Pub.L. 98–353, Title I, §§ 113, 121(a), July 10, 1984, 98 Stat. 343, 345; Pub.L. 98–454, Title X, § 1001, Oct. 5, 1984, 98 Stat. 1745, provided that:

"(a) Except as otherwise provided in this title [sections 401 to 411 of Pub.L. 95–598, this Act [see Tables for classification] shall take effect on October 1, 1979.

"(b) Except as provided in subsections (c) and (d) of this section, the amendments made by title II of this Act [sections 201 to 252 of Pub.L. 95–598] shall not be effective.

"(c) The amendments made by sections 210, 214, 219, 220, 222, 224, 225, 228, 229, 235, 244, 245, 246, 249, and 251 of this Act shall take effect on October 1, 1979.

"(d) The amendments made by sections 217, 218, 230, 247, 302, 314(j), 317, 327, 328, 338, and 411 of this Act shall take effect on the date of enactment of this Act [Nov. 6, 1978]."

[(e) Repealed. Pub.L. 98–454, Title X, § 1001, Oct. 5, 1984, 98 Stat. 1745.]

[Section 121(a) of Pub.L. 98–353 purported to amend section 402(b) of Pub.L. 95–598 by substituting "the date of enactment of the Bankruptcy Amendments and Federal Judgeship Act of 1984 [i.e. July 10, 1984]" for "June 28, 1984". This amendment was not executed as the probable intent of Congress in view of the prior amendment to section 402(b) of Pub.L. 95–598 by section 113 of Pub.L. 98–353.]

[Amendment of section 402(b) of Pub.L. 95–598 by section 113 of Pub.L. 98–353 effective June 27, 1984, see section 122(c) of Pub.L. 98–353, set out as an Effective Date note under section 151 of Title 28, Judiciary and Judicial Procedure.]

Repeals

Pub.L. 95–598, Title IV, § 401(a), Nov. 6, 1978, 92 Stat. 2682, provided that: "The Bankruptcy Act [Act July 1, 1898, c. 541, 30 Stat. 544, as amended] is repealed."

BANKRUPTCY CODE

Savings Provisions

Pub.L. 95–598, Title IV, § 403, Nov. 6, 1978, 92 Stat. 2683, as amended by Pub.L. 98–353, Title III, § 382, July 10, 1984, 98 Stat. 364, provided that:

"(a) A case commenced under the Bankruptcy Act [Act July 1, 1898, c. 541, 30 Stat. 544, as amended], and all matters and proceedings in or relating to any such case, shall be conducted and determined under such Act as if this Act had not been enacted, and the substantive rights of parties in connection with any such bankruptcy case, matter, or proceeding shall continue to be governed by the law applicable to such case, matter, or proceeding as if the [this] Act had not been enacted.

"(b) Notwithstanding subsection (a) of this section, sections 1165, 1167, 1168, 1169, and 1171 of title 11 of the United States Code, as enacted by section 101 of this Act, apply to cases pending under section 77 of the Bankruptcy Act ([former] 11 U.S.C. 205) on the date of enactment of this Act [Nov. 6, 1978] in which the trustee has not filed a plan of reorganization.

"(c) The repeal made by section 401(a) of this Act [repealing the Bankruptcy Act] does not affect any right of a referee in bankruptcy, United States bankruptcy judge, or survivor of a referee in bankruptcy or United States bankruptcy judge to receive any annuity or other payment under the civil service retirement laws.

"(d) The amendments made by section 314 of this Act [see Tables] do not affect the application of chapter 9, chapter 96, section 2516, section 3057, or section 3284 of title 18 of the United States Code to any act of any person—

"(1) committed before October 1, 1979; or

"(2) committed after October 1, 1979, in connection with a case commenced before such date.

"(e) Notwithstanding subsection (a) of this section—

"(1) a fee may not be charged under section 40c(2)(a) of the Bankruptcy Act [former 11 U.S.C.A. § 68(c)(2)(a)] in a case pending under such Act after September 30, 1979, to the extent that such fee exceeds $200,000;

"(2) a fee may not be charged under section 40c(2)(b) of the Bankruptcy Act in a case in which the plan is confirmed after September 30, 1978, or in which the final determination as to the amount of such fee is made after September 30, 1979, notwithstanding an earlier confirmation date, to the extent that such fee exceeds $100,000;

"(3) after September 30, 1979, all moneys collected for payment into the referees' salary and expense fund in cases filed under the Bankruptcy Act shall be collected and paid into the general fund of the Treasury; and

"(4) any balance in the referees' salary and expense fund in the Treasury on October 1, 1979, shall be transferred to the general fund of the Treasury and the referees' salary and expense fund account shall be closed."

Pub.L. 98–353, Title III, § 381, July 10, 1984, 98 Stat. 364, provided that: "This subtitle [§§ 381, 382 of Pub.L. 98–353], [amending subsec. (e) of this note] may be cited as the 'Referees Salary and Expense Fund Act of 1984'."

Separability of Provisions

If any provision of or amendment made by Pub.L. 103–394 or the application of such provision or amendment to any person or circumstance is held to be unconstitutional, the remaining provisions of and amendments made by Pub.L. 103–394 and the application of such provisions and amend-

ments to any person or circumstance shall not be affected thereby, see section 701 of Pub.L. 103–394, set out as a note under section 101 of this title.

Commission on the Bankruptcy Laws of the United States

Pub.L. 91–354, §§ 1–6, July 24, 1970, 84 Stat. 468, as amended by Pub.L. 92–251, Mar. 17, 1972, 86 Stat. 63; Pub.L. 93–56, § 1, July 1, 1973, 87 Stat. 140, established the Commission on the Bankruptcy Laws of the United States, to study and recommend changes to this title, which ceased to exist 30 days after the date of submission of its final report which was required prior to July 31, 1973.

History of Bankruptcy Acts

The bankruptcy laws were revised generally and enacted as Title 11, Bankruptcy, by Pub.L. 96–598, Nov. 6, 1978, 92 Stat. 2549.

Earlier bankruptcy laws included the following Acts:

Apr. 4, 1800, c. 19, 2 Stat. 19, repealed Dec. 19, 1803, ch. 6, 2 Stat. 248.

Aug. 19, 1841, c. 9, 5 Stat. 440, repealed Mar. 3, 1843, ch. 82, 5 Stat. 614.

Mar. 2, 1867, c. 176, 14 Stat. 517, the provisions of which were incorporated in Rev.Stat.Title LXI, §§ 4972 to 5132, were materially amended June 22, 1874, c. 390, 18 Stat. 178, and were repealed June 7, 1878, c. 160, 20 Stat. 99.

The Bankruptcy Act of July 1, 1898, c. 541, 30 Stat. 544, as amended, sometimes called the Nelson Act, repealed by Pub.L. 95–598.

The Chandler Act of July 22, 1938, c. 575, 52 Stat. 883, which revised the Bankruptcy Act generally and materially amended the provisions covering corporate reorganizations, repealed by Pub.L. 95–598.

National Bankruptcy Review Commission

Pub.L. 103–394, Title VI, Oct. 22, 1994, 108 Stat. 4147, provided that:

"Sec. 601. Short title.

"This title [this note] may be cited as the 'National Bankruptcy Review Commission Act'.

"Sec. 602. Establishment.

"There is established the National Bankruptcy Review Commission (referred to as the 'Commission').

"Sec. 603. Duties of the Commission.

"The duties of the Commission are—

"(1) to investigate and study issues and problems relating to title 11, United States Code (commonly known as the 'Bankruptcy Code');

"(2) to evaluate the advisability of proposals and current arrangements with respect to such issues and problems;

"(3) to prepare and submit to the Congress, the Chief Justice, and the President a report in accordance with section 608; and

"(4) to solicit divergent views of all parties concerned with the operation of the bankruptcy system.

"Sec. 604. Membership.

"(a) Number and appointment.—The Commission shall be composed of 9 members as follows:

"(1) Three members appointed by the President, 1 of whom shall be designated as chairman by the President.

"(2) One member shall be appointed by the President pro tempore of the Senate.

Complete Annotation Materials, see Title 11 U.S.C.A.

2

"(3) One member shall be appointed by the Minority Leader of the Senate.

"(4) One member shall be appointed by the Speaker of the House of Representatives.

"(5) One member shall be appointed by the Minority Leader of the House of Representatives.

"(6) Two members appointed by the Chief Justice.

Members of Congress, and officers and employees of the executive branch, shall be ineligible for appointment to the Commission.

"(b) **Term.**—Members of the Commission shall be appointed for the life of the Commission.

"(c) **Quorum.**—Five members of the Commission shall constitute a quorum, but a lesser number may conduct meetings.

"(d) **Appointment deadline.**—The first appointments made under subsection (a) shall be made within 60 days after the date of enactment of this Act [Oct. 22, 1994].

"(e) **First meeting.**—The first meeting of the Commission shall be called by the chairman and shall be held within 210 days after the date of enactment of this Act [Oct. 22, 1994].

"(f) **Vacancy.**—A vacancy on the Commission resulting from the death or resignation of a member shall not affect its powers and shall be filled in the same manner in which the original appointment was made.

"(g) **Continuation of membership.**—If any member of the Commission who was appointed to the Commission as an officer or employee of a government leaves that office, or if any member of the Commission who was not appointed in such a capacity becomes an officer or employee of a government, the member may continue as a member of the Commission for not longer than the 90-day period beginning on the date the member leaves that office or becomes such an officer or employee, as the case may be.

"(h) **Consultation prior to appointment.**—Prior to the appointment of members of the Commission, the President, the President pro tempore of the Senate, the Speaker of the House of Representatives, and the Chief Justice shall consult with each other to ensure fair and equitable representation of various points of view in the Commission and its staff.

"Sec. 605. **Compensation of the Commission.**

"(a) **Pay.**—

"(1) **Nongovernment employees.**—Each member of the Commission who is not otherwise employed by the United States Government shall be entitled to receive the daily equivalent of the annual rate of basic pay payable for level IV of the Executive Schedule under section 5315 of title 5, United States Code [section 5315 of Title 5, Government Organization and Employees], for each day (including travel time) during which he or she is engaged in the actual performance of duties as a member of the Commission.

"(2) **Government employees.**—A member of the Commission who is an officer or employee of the United States Government shall serve without additional compensation.

"(b) **Travel.**—Members of the Commission shall be reimbursed for travel, subsistence, and other necessary expenses incurred by them in the performance of their duties.

"Sec. 606. **Staff of Commission; experts and consultants.**

"(a) **Staff.**—

"(1) **Appointment.**—The chairman of the Commission may, without regard to the civil service laws and regulations, appoint, and terminate an executive director and such other personnel as are necessary to enable the Commission to perform its duties. The employment of an executive director shall be subject to confirmation by the Commission.

"(2) **Compensation.**—The chairman of the Commission may fix the compensation of the executive director and other personnel without regard to the provisions of chapter 51 and subchapter II of chapter 53 of title 5, United States Code [sections 5101 et seq. and 5311 et seq. of Title 5], relating to classification of positions and General Schedule pay rates, except that the rate of pay for the executive director and other personnel may not exceed the rate payable for level V of the Executive Schedule under section 5316 of that title [section 5316 of Title 5].

"(b) **Experts and consultants.**—The Commission may procure temporary and intermittent services of experts and consultants under section 3109(b) of title 5, United States Code [section 3109(b) of Title 5].

"Sec. 607. **Powers of the Commission.**

"(a) **Hearings and meetings.**—The Commission or, on authorization of the Commission, a member of the Commission, may hold such hearings, sit and act at such time and places, take such testimony, and receive such evidence, as the Commission considers appropriate. The Commission or a member of the Commission may administer oaths or affirmations to witnesses appearing before it.

"(b) **Official data.**—The Commission may secure directly from any Federal department, agency, or court information necessary to enable it to carry out this title [this note]. Upon request of the chairman of the Commission, the head of a Federal department or agency or chief judge of a Federal court shall furnish such information, consistent with law, to the Commission.

"(c) **Facilities and support services.**—The Administrator of General Services shall provide to the Commission on a reimbursable basis such facilities and support services as the Commission may request. Upon request of the Commission, the head of a Federal department or agency may make any of the facilities or services of the agency available to the Commission to assist the Commission in carrying out its duties under this title [this note].

"(d) **Expenditures and contracts.**—The Commission or, on authorization of the Commission, a member of the Commission may make expenditures and enter into contracts for the procurement of such supplies, services, and property as the Commission or member considers appropriate for the purposes of carrying out the duties of the Commission. Such expenditures and contracts may be made only to such extent or in such amounts as are provided in appropriation Acts.

"(e) **Mails.**—The Commission may use the United States mails in the same manner and under the same conditions as other Federal departments and agencies of the United States.

"(f) **Gifts.**—The Commission may accept, use, and dispose of gifts or donations of services or property.

"Sec. 608. **Report.**

"The Commission shall submit to the Congress, the Chief Justice, and the President a report not later than 2 years after the date of its first meeting. The report shall contain a detailed statement of the findings and conclusions of the Commission, together with its recommendations for such legislative or administrative action as it considers appropriate.

"Sec. 609. **Termination.**

"The Commission shall cease to exist on the date that is 30 days after the date on which it submits its report under section 608.

"Sec. 610. Authorization of appropriations.

"There is authorized to be appropriated $1,500,000 to carry out this title [this note]."

CROSS REFERENCES

Additional information on bankruptcy filings required, see 15 USCA § 1681c.

Amount of unfunded vested benefits allocable to employer withdrawn from pension plan as including uncollectible amounts for reasons arising out of cases or proceedings under this title, see 29 USCA § 1391.

Applicability of provisions of Securities Act of 1933 to certain classes of securities exchanged in cases under this title, see 15 USCA § 77c.

Applicability of rules to bankruptcy proceedings—

Federal Rules of Civil Procedure, see Fed.Rules Civ. Proc. Rule 81, 28 USCA.

Federal Rules of Evidence, see Fed.Rules Evid. Rule 1101, 28 USCA.

Applicability of this title to district court of—

Guam, see 48 USCA § 1424–4.

Northern Mariana Islands, see 48 USCA § 1821.

Virgin Islands, see 48 USCA § 1614.

Applicability to case under this title of provisions relating to special pay to selected reserve health care professionals in critically short wartime specialties, see 37 USCA § 302g.

Approval by Federal Trade Commission of fees, expenses, and remuneration paid in connection with case brought under this title involving public utility holding company, see 15 USCA § 79k.

Assertion of claim against guarantor providing evidence of financial responsibility in cases where owner or operator is in bankruptcy under this title for corrective action relating to—

Hazardous waste treatment, storage and disposal facilities, see 42 USCA § 6924.

Release of hazardous substances from facilities, see 42 USCA § 9608.

Underground storage tanks, see 42 USCA §§ 6991b and 6991c.

Authority of Attorney General to investigate official acts, records and accounts of trustees in cases under this title, see 28 USCA § 526.

Automatic protection of lands conveyed pursuant to Alaska Native Claims Settlement Act provided such lands are not sold to third parties from judgments resulting from claims arising under this title, see 43 USCA § 1636.

"Bankruptcy Act" defined as this title for purposes of Trust Indenture Act of 1939, see 15 USCA § 77ccc.

Benefit accrual requirements and prohibition on increases where plan sponsor is in bankruptcy, see 29 USCA § 1054.

"Bridge owner" as including bridge in possession or under control of trustee in case under this title for purposes of alteration of bridges over navigable waters, see 33 USCA § 511.

Change of venue in cases or proceedings under this title, see 28 USCA § 1412.

"Company" defined as including trustee in case under this title for purposes of—

Subchapter I of Investment Advisers Act of 1940, see 15 USCA § 80a–2.

Subchapter II of Investment Advisers Act of 1940, see 15 USCA § 80b–2.

Compromise, adjustment or cancellation of farm loans upon discharge of indebtedness in proceeding under this title, see 12 USCA § 1150.

Concealment of assets, false oaths or claims, and bribery in cases under this title, see 18 USCA § 152.

Congressional finding of railroad insolvency and reorganization under this title for purposes of enacting Regional Rail Reorganization Act of 1973, see 45 USCA § 701.

Congressional power to establish uniform bankruptcy laws throughout United States, see USCA Const. Art. I § 8, cl. 4.

Coordination of Internal Revenue Code provisions with cases under this title, see 26 USCA § 6658.

Court procedures for cases under this title, see 28 USCA § 157.

Credits against unemployment tax, see 26 USCA § 3302.

"Debtor" defined under this title as having same meaning for purposes of crimes in bankruptcy, see 18 USCA § 151.

Disclosure of confidential tax returns and return information to trustee in cases under this title, see 26 USCA § 6103.

Duties of United States trustees and supervision by Attorney General, see 28 USCA § 586.

Effect of discharge in bankruptcy under this title on discharge of debt arising from—

Advanced educational assistance loan, see 10 USCA § 2005.

Aviation service agreement, see 37 USCA § 301b.

Child support obligation assigned to State, see 42 USCA § 656.

Critical acquisition positions service agreement, see 37 USCA § 317.

Engineering and scientific career service agreement, see 37 USCA § 315.

Enlistment in elements of Ready Reserve, see 37 USCA § 308g.

Health professionals educational assistance, see 38 USCA § 7635.

Indian Health Scholarship, see 25 USCA § 1613a.

Indian health service loan, see 25 USCA § 1616a.

Multiyear retention bonus for medical officers of armed forces, see 37 USCA § 301d.

Nurse officer agreement, see 10 USCA § 2130a.

Prior service enlistment bonus, see 37 USCA § 308i.

Reenlistment, enlistment, or voluntary extension of enlistment in elements of Ready Reserve, see 37 USCA § 308h.

Reserve affiliation agreement, see 37 USCA § 308e.

Special pay for dental officers of armed forces, see 37 USCA §§ 302b, 302h.

Special pay for medical officers of armed forces, see 37 USCA § 302.

Special pay for nurse anesthetists, see 37 USCA § 302e.

Special pay for registered nurses, see 37 USCA § 302d.

BANKRUPTCY CODE

Effect of Federal debt collection procedure on this title, see 28 USCA § 3003.

Employee protection benefits available under this title deemed waived upon receipt of assistance by employee under—

Milwaukee Railroad Restructuring Act, see 45 USCA § 912.

Rock Island Railroad Transition and Employee Assistance Act, see 45 USCA § 1007.

Employer Retirement Income new reportable events, see 29 USCA § 1343.

Extension of time for paying tax claims in cases under this title, see 26 USCA § 6161.

Fee agreements in cases under this title, see 18 USCA § 155.

"Filing date" as meaning date on which petition filed under this title for purposes of Securities Investor Protection Act of 1970, see 15 USCA § 78lll.

Fraud and consumer issues under this chapter, see 18 USCA § 157.

Immediate assessment for tax deficiencies with respect to certain cases under this title, see 26 USCA § 6871.

Inapplicability of § 421(a) of Title 26 to transfers of stock acquired pursuant to exercise of incentive stock option by debtor in proceeding under this title, see 26 USCA § 422.

Inapplicability to case under this title of provision relating to—

Limitation on net operating loss carry forwards following ownership change for tax purposes, see 26 USCA § 382.

Limitation on pension plan withdrawal liability to employers undergoing reorganization, see 29 USCA § 1405.

Postponement of certain time periods in determining tax liability by reason of service in combat zone, see 26 USCA § 7508.

Priority of government claims, see 31 USCA § 3713.

Transfers to corporation controlled by transferor, see 26 USCA § 351.

Inappropriate transfers included in determining net worth of employer, see 29 USCA § 1362.

Income tax rules relating to individuals' cases under this title, see 26 USCA § 1398.

Inferiority of rights of trustee and other parties under this title to rights of—

Federal Deposit Insurance Corporation as conservator or liquidating agent in connection with avoidance of fraudulent transfers, see 12 USCA § 1821.

National Credit Union Administration Board as conservator or liquidating agent in connection with avoidance of fraudulent transfers, see 12 USCA § 1787.

Insolvency and liquidation of holding companies by trustee pursuant to provisions of this title, see 12 USCA § 1467a.

Interception of wires or oral communications involving fraud under this title, see 18 USCA § 2516.

Intervention by trustee of debtor's estate in case under this title in proceeding before Tax Court to which debtor is party, see 26 USCA § 7464.

Jurisdiction and power of court over Securities Investor Protection Act decrees same as under this title, see 15 USCA § 78eee.

Jurisdiction of district courts in cases under this title, see 28 USCA § 1334.

Jury trials, see 28 USCA § 1411.

Lien of Black Lung Disability Trust Fund treated in same manner as lien for taxes due United States for purposes of this title, see 30 USCA § 934.

Limitations period for concealment of assets of debtor in case under this title begins to run upon final discharge or denial of discharge, see 18 USCA § 3284.

Liquidation proceedings under Securities Investor Protection Act conducted in accordance with chapters 1, 3, and 5 and subchapters I and II of chapter 7 of this title, see 15 USCA § 78fff.

No separate taxable entity resulting from commencement of case under this title, see 26 USCA § 1399.

Nonenforcement of guarantee of legal custody and financial ability for certain aliens when sponsor adjudicated bankrupt under this title, see 8 USCA § 1154.

Notice to creditors of commencement of liquidation proceeding for purposes of Securities Investor Protection Act of 1970 given in manner prescribed by this title, see 15 USCA § 78fff-2.

Notice to Secretary of Treasury of qualification as trustee in case under this title for purposes of Internal Revenue Code, see 26 USCA § 6036.

Original and exclusive jurisdiction of courts under this title over civil actions for adjudication of direct payment procedure for purposes of Securities Investor Protection Act of 1970, see 15 USCA § 78fff-4.

Ownership of copyright, see 17 USCA § 201.

Partition of multiemployer pension plan if reduction in amount of aggregate contributions will result from case or proceeding under this title, see 29 USCA § 1413.

"Person" defined as including trustees in cases under this title for purposes of—

Equal Employment Opportunity Act of 1972, see 42 USCA § 2000e.

Fair housing, see 42 USCA § 3602.

HIV health care services program, see 42 USCA § 300ff-76.

Labor–Management Reporting and Disclosure Act of 1959, see 29 USCA § 402.

National Labor Relations Act, see 29 USCA § 152.

Walsh–Healey provisions, see 41 USCA § 41.

"Personal holding company" for income tax purposes defined as excluding corporation subject to jurisdiction of court in cases under this title, see 26 USCA § 542.

Powers and duties of trustee same as under this title for purposes of Securities Investor Protection Act of 1970, see 15 USCA § 78fff-1.

Priority of—

Claims of United States arising out of any contract authorized by Boulder Canyon Project Act, see 43 USCA § 617p.

Liens for pension plan contribution of employer in cases under this title, see 29 USCA § 1368.

Procedure on default of housing and small business loans, see 38 USCA § 3732.

Complete Annotation Materials, see Title 11 U.S.C.A.

Prohibition on benefit increases while sponsor is in bankruptcy, see 26 USCA § 401.

Public disclosure of data in connection with bankruptcy proceedings for purposes of Commodity Exchange Act, see 7 USCA § 12.

"Qualifying event" as including proceeding in case under this title for purposes of—

> Determination of excise taxes for failure to satisfy continuation coverage requirements of group health plans, see 26 USCA § 4980B.

> Providing group health plan continuation coverage under Employee Retirement Income Security Act of 1974, see 29 USCA § 1163.

"Racketeering activity" for purposes of RICO as including any offense involving fraud connected with case under this title, see 18 USCA § 1961.

Reduction in basis of property held by taxpayer by portion of discharge of indebtedness under this title, see 26 USCA § 1017.

Regulations respecting commodity broker debtors notwithstanding provisions of this title, see 7 USCA § 24.

Reimbursements to multiemployer pension plans for payments due from employers uncollectible as result of employer involvement in cases under this title, see 29 USCA § 1402.

Relationship of Regional Rail Reorganization Act of 1973 to this title, see 45 USCA § 791.

"Reorganization" defined as certain transfers by corporation of all or part of its assets to another corporation in case under this title for purposes of income tax provisions relating to corporate organizations and reorganizations, see 26 USCA § 368.

Rules of bankruptcy, power of Supreme Court to prescribe, see 28 USCA § 2075.

Settlement common stock of Alaska native regional corporation not treated as asset under this title, see 43 USCA § 1606.

Suspension of limitations period for assessment and collection of tax, see 26 USCA § 6503.

Suspension of period on tax assessment in cases under this title where notice of qualification of fiduciary required to be given Secretary of Treasury, see 26 USCA § 6872.

Time for filing petition with Tax Court for redetermination of deficiency, see 26 USCA § 6213.

Treatment of income from discharge of indebtedness under this title for purposes of Internal Revenue Code, see 26 USCA § 108.

Trustee in case under this title deemed importer of record of merchandise consigned to insolvent for purposes of customs duties declaration, see 19 USCA § 1485.

Utilization by courts of facilities or services which pertain to parties in cases filed under this title, see 28 USCA § 156.

Venue of—

> Cases under this title, see 28 USCA § 1408.

> Proceedings arising in or related to cases under this title, see 28 USCA § 1409.

CHAPTER 1—GENERAL PROVISIONS

Sec.
101. Definitions.
102. Rules of construction.
103. Applicability of chapters.
104. Adjustment of dollar amounts.
105. Power of court.
106. Waiver of sovereign immunity.
107. Public access to papers.
108. Extension of time.
109. Who may be a debtor.
110. Penalty for persons who negligently or fraudulently prepare bankruptcy petitions.
111. Nonprofit budget and credit counseling agencies; financial management instructional courses.
112. Prohibition on disclosure of name of minor children.

HISTORICAL AND STATUTORY NOTES

Amendments

2005 Amendments. Pub.L. 109–8, Title I, § 106(e)(2), Apr. 20, 2005, 119 Stat. 41, added item 111.

Pub.L. 109–8, Title II, § 233(b), Apr. 20, 2005, 119 Stat. 74, added item 112.

1994 Amendments. Pub.L 103–394, Title III, § 308(b), Oct. 22, 1994, 108 Stat. 4137, added item 110.

Effective and Applicability Provisions

2005 Acts. Amendments by Pub.L. 109–8 effective, except as otherwise provided, 180 days after April 20, 2005, and inapplicable with respect to cases commenced under Title 11 before the effective date, see Pub.L. 109–8, § 1501, set out as a note under 11 U.S.C.A. § 101.

§ 101. Definitions

In this title the following definitions shall apply:

(1) The term "accountant" means accountant authorized under applicable law to practice public accounting, and includes professional accounting association, corporation, or partnership, if so authorized.

(2) The term "affiliate" means—

(A) entity that directly or indirectly owns, controls, or holds with power to vote, 20 percent or more of the outstanding voting securities of the debtor, other than an entity that holds such securities—

(i) in a fiduciary or agency capacity without sole discretionary power to vote such securities; or

(ii) solely to secure a debt, if such entity has not in fact exercised such power to vote;

(B) corporation 20 percent or more of whose outstanding voting securities are directly or indirectly owned, controlled, or held with power to vote, by the debtor, or by an entity that directly or indirectly owns, controls, or holds with power to vote, 20 percent or more of the outstanding voting securities of the debtor, other than an entity that holds such securities—

(i) in a fiduciary or agency capacity without sole discretionary power to vote such securities; or

(ii) solely to secure a debt, if such entity has not in fact exercised such power to vote;

(C) person whose business is operated under a lease or operating agreement by a debtor, or person substantially all of whose property is operated under an operating agreement with the debtor; or

(D) entity that operates the business or substantially all of the property of the debtor under a lease or operating agreement.

(3) The term "assisted person" means any person whose debts consist primarily of consumer debts and the value of whose nonexempt property is less than $175,750 [1].

(4) The term "attorney" means attorney, professional law association, corporation, or partnership, authorized under applicable law to practice law.

(4A) The term "bankruptcy assistance" means any goods or services sold or otherwise provided to an assisted person with the express or implied purpose of providing information, advice, counsel, document preparation, or filing, or attendance at a creditors' meeting or appearing in a case or proceeding on behalf of another or providing legal representation with respect to a case or proceeding under this title.

(5) The term "claim" means—

(A) right to payment, whether or not such right is reduced to judgment, liquidated, unliquidated, fixed, contingent, matured, unmatured, disputed, undisputed, legal, equitable, secured, or unsecured; or

(B) right to an equitable remedy for breach of performance if such breach gives rise to a right to payment, whether or not such right to an equitable remedy is reduced to judgment, fixed, contingent, matured, unmatured, disputed, undisputed, secured, or unsecured.

(6) The term "commodity broker" means futures commission merchant, foreign futures commission merchant, clearing organization, leverage transaction merchant, or commodity options dealer, as defined in section 761 of this title, with respect to which there is a customer, as defined in section 761 of this title.

(7) The term "community claim" means claim that arose before the commencement of the case concerning the debtor for which property of the kind specified in section 541(a)(2) of this title is liable, whether or not there is any such property at the time of the commencement of the case.

(7A) The term "commercial fishing operation" means—

(A) the catching or harvesting of fish, shrimp, lobsters, urchins, seaweed, shellfish, or other aquatic species or products of such species; or

(B) for purposes of section 109 and chapter 12, aquaculture activities consisting of raising for market any species or product described in subparagraph (A).

(7B) The term "commercial fishing vessel" means a vessel used by a family fisherman to carry out a commercial fishing operation.

(8) The term "consumer debt" means debt incurred by an individual primarily for a personal, family, or household purpose.

(9) The term "corporation"—

(A) includes—

(i) association having a power or privilege that a private corporation, but not an individual or a partnership, possesses;

(ii) partnership association organized under a law that makes only the capital subscribed responsible for the debts of such association;

(iii) joint-stock company;

(iv) unincorporated company or association; or

(v) business trust; but

(B) does not include limited partnership.

(10) The term "creditor" means—

(A) entity that has a claim against the debtor that arose at the time of or before the order for relief concerning the debtor;

(B) entity that has a claim against the estate of a kind specified in section 348(d), 502(f), 502(g), 502(h) or 502(i) of this title; or

(C) entity that has a community claim.

(10A) The term "current monthly income"—

(A) means the average monthly income from all sources that the debtor receives (or in a joint case the debtor and the debtor's spouse receive) without regard to whether such income is taxable income, derived during the 6–month period ending on—

(i) the last day of the calendar month immediately preceding the date of the commencement of the case if the debtor files the schedule of current income required by section 521(a)(1)(B)(ii); or

(ii) the date on which current income is determined by the court for purposes of this title if the debtor does not file the schedule of current income required by section 521(a)(1)(B)(ii); and

(B) includes any amount paid by any entity other than the debtor (or in a joint case the debtor and the debtor's spouse), on a regular basis for the household expenses of the debtor or the debtor's dependents (and in a joint case the debtor's spouse if not otherwise a dependent), but excludes benefits received under the Social Security Act, payments to victims of war crimes or crimes against humanity on account of their status as victims of such crimes, and payments to victims of international terrorism (as defined in section 2331 of title 18) or domestic terrorism (as defined in section 2331 of title 18) on account of their status as victims of such terrorism.

(11) The term "custodian" means—

(A) receiver or trustee of any of the property of the debtor, appointed in a case or proceeding not under this title;

(B) assignee under a general assignment for the benefit of the debtor's creditors; or

(C) trustee, receiver, or agent under applicable law, or under a contract, that is appointed or authorized to take charge of property of the debtor for the purpose of enforcing a lien against such property, or for the purpose of general administration of such property for the benefit of the debtor's creditors.

(12) The term "debt" means liability on a claim.

(12A) The term "debt relief agency" means any person who provides any bankruptcy assistance to an assisted person in return for the payment of money or other valuable consideration, or who is a bankruptcy petition preparer under section 110, but does not include—

(A) any person who is an officer, director, employee, or agent of a person who provides such assistance or of the bankruptcy petition preparer;

(B) a nonprofit organization that is exempt from taxation under section 501(c)(3) of the Internal Revenue Code of 1986;

(C) a creditor of such assisted person, to the extent that the creditor is assisting such assisted person to restructure any debt owed by such assisted person to the creditor;

(D) a depository institution (as defined in section 3 of the Federal Deposit Insurance Act) or any Federal credit union or State credit union (as those terms are defined in section 101 of the Federal Credit Union Act), or any affiliate or subsidiary of such depository institution or credit union; or

(E) an author, publisher, distributor, or seller of works subject to copyright protection under title 17, when acting in such capacity.

(13) The term "debtor" means person or municipality concerning which a case under this title has been commenced.

(13A) The term "debtor's principal residence"—

(A) means a residential structure if used as the principal residence by the debtor, including incidental property, without regard to whether that structure is attached to real property; and

(B) includes an individual condominium or cooperative unit, a mobile or manufactured home, or trailer if used as the principal residence by the debtor.

(14) The term "disinterested person" means a person that—

(A) is not a creditor, an equity security holder, or an insider;

(B) is not and was not, within 2 years before the date of the filing of the petition, a director, officer, or employee of the debtor; and

(C) does not have an interest materially adverse to the interest of the estate or of any class of creditors or equity security holders, by reason of any direct or indirect relationship to, connection with, or interest in, the debtor, or for any other reason.

(14A) The term "domestic support obligation" means a debt that accrues before, on, or after the date of the order for relief in a case under this title, including interest that accrues on that debt as provided under applicable nonbankruptcy law notwithstanding any other provision of this title, that is—

(A) owed to or recoverable by—

(i) a spouse, former spouse, or child of the debtor or such child's parent, legal guardian, or responsible relative; or

(ii) a governmental unit;

(B) in the nature of alimony, maintenance, or support (including assistance provided by a governmental unit) of such spouse, former spouse, or child of the debtor or such child's parent, without regard to whether such debt is expressly so designated;

(C) established or subject to establishment before, on, or after the date of the order for relief in a case under this title, by reason of applicable provisions of—

(i) a separation agreement, divorce decree, or property settlement agreement;

(ii) an order of a court of record; or

(iii) a determination made in accordance with applicable nonbankruptcy law by a governmental unit; and

(D) not assigned to a nongovernmental entity, unless that obligation is assigned voluntarily by the spouse, former spouse, child of the debtor, or such child's parent, legal guardian, or responsible relative for the purpose of collecting the debt.

(15) The term "entity" includes person, estate, trust, governmental unit, and United States trustee.

(16) The term "equity security" means—

(A) share in a corporation, whether or not transferable or denominated "stock", or similar security;

(B) interest of a limited partner in a limited partnership; or

(C) warrant or right, other than a right to convert, to purchase, sell, or subscribe to a share, security, or interest of a kind specified in subparagraph (A) or (B) of this paragraph.

(17) The term "equity security holder" means holder of an equity security of the debtor.

(18) The term "family farmer" means—

(A) individual or individual and spouse engaged in a farming operation whose aggregate debts do not exceed $3,792,650 [1] and not less than 50 percent of whose aggregate noncontingent, liquidated debts (excluding a debt for the principal residence of such individual or such individual and spouse unless such debt arises out of a farming operation), on the date the case is filed, arise out of a farming operation owned or operated by such individual or such individual and spouse, and such individual or such individual and spouse receive from such farming operation more than 50 percent of such individual's or such individual and spouse's gross income for—

(i) the taxable year preceding; or

(ii) each of the 2d and 3d taxable years preceding;

the taxable year in which the case concerning such individual or such individual and spouse was filed; or

(B) corporation or partnership in which more than 50 percent of the outstanding stock or equity is held by one family, or by one family and the relatives of the members of such family, and such family or such relatives conduct the farming operation, and

(i) more than 80 percent of the value of its assets consists of assets related to the farming operation;

(ii) its aggregate debts do not exceed $3,792,650 [1] and not less than 50 percent of its aggregate noncontingent, liquidated debts (excluding a debt for one dwelling which is owned by such corporation or partnership and which a shareholder or partner maintains as a principal residence, unless such debt arises out of a farming operation), on the date the case is filed, arise out of the farming operation owned or operated by such corporation or such partnership; and

(iii) if such corporation issues stock, such stock is not publicly traded.

(19) The term "family farmer with regular annual income" means family farmer whose annual income is sufficiently stable and regular to enable such family farmer to make payments under a plan under chapter 12 of this title.

(19A) The term "family fisherman" means—

(A) an individual or individual and spouse engaged in a commercial fishing operation—

(i) whose aggregate debts do not exceed $1,757,475 [1] and not less than 80 percent of whose aggregate noncontingent, liquidated debts (excluding a debt for the principal residence of such individual or such individual and spouse, unless such debt arises out of a commercial fishing operation), on the date the case is filed, arise out of a commercial fishing operation owned or operated by such individual or such individual and spouse; and

(ii) who receive from such commercial fishing operation more than 50 percent of such individual's or such individual's and spouse's gross income for the taxable year preceding the taxable year in which the case concerning such individual or such individual and spouse was filed; or

(B) a corporation or partnership—

(i) in which more than 50 percent of the outstanding stock or equity is held by—

(I) 1 family that conducts the commercial fishing operation; or

(II) 1 family and the relatives of the members of such family, and such family or such relatives conduct the commercial fishing operation; and

(ii)(I) more than 80 percent of the value of its assets consists of assets related to the commercial fishing operation;

(II) its aggregate debts do not exceed $1,757,475 [1] and not less than 80 percent of its aggregate noncontingent, liquidated debts (excluding a debt for 1 dwelling which is owned by such corporation or partnership and which a shareholder or partner maintains as a principal residence, unless such debt arises out of a commercial fishing operation), on the date the case is filed, arise out of a commercial fishing operation owned or operated by such corporation or such partnership; and

(III) if such corporation issues stock, such stock is not publicly traded.

(19B) The term "family fisherman with regular annual income" means a family fisherman whose annual income is sufficiently stable and regular to enable such family fisherman to make payments under a plan under chapter 12 of this title.

(20) The term "farmer" means (except when such term appears in the term "family farmer") person that received more than 80 percent of such person's gross income during the taxable year of such person immediately preceding the taxable year of such person during which the case under this title concerning such person was commenced from a farming operation owned or operated by such person.

(21) The term "farming operation" includes farming, tillage of the soil, dairy farming, ranching, production or raising of crops, poultry, or livestock, and production of poultry or livestock products in an unmanufactured state.

(21A) The term "farmout agreement" means a written agreement in which—

 (A) the owner of a right to drill, produce, or operate liquid or gaseous hydrocarbons on property agrees or has agreed to transfer or assign all or a part of such right to another entity; and

 (B) such other entity (either directly or through its agents or its assigns), as consideration, agrees to perform drilling, reworking, recompleting, testing, or similar or related operations, to develop or produce liquid or gaseous hydrocarbons on the property.

(21B) The term "Federal depository institutions regulatory agency" means—

 (A) with respect to an insured depository institution (as defined in section 3(c)(2) of the Federal Deposit Insurance Act) for which no conservator or receiver has been appointed, the appropriate Federal banking agency (as defined in section 3(q) of such Act);

 (B) with respect to an insured credit union (including an insured credit union for which the National Credit Union Administration has been appointed conservator or liquidating agent), the National Credit Union Administration;

 (C) with respect to any insured depository institution for which the Resolution Trust Corporation has been appointed conservator or receiver, the Resolution Trust Corporation; and

 (D) with respect to any insured depository institution for which the Federal Deposit Insurance Corporation has been appointed conservator or receiver, the Federal Deposit Insurance Corporation.

(22) The term "financial institution" means—

 (A) a Federal reserve bank, or an entity that is a commercial or savings bank, industrial savings bank, savings and loan association, trust company, federally-insured credit union, or receiver, liquidating agent, or conservator for such entity and, when any such Federal reserve bank, receiver, liquidating agent, conservator or entity is acting as agent or custodian for a customer (whether or not a "customer", as defined in section 741) in connection with a securities contract (as defined in section 741) such customer; or

 (B) in connection with a securities contract (as defined in section 741) an investment company registered under the Investment Company Act of 1940.

(22A) The term "financial participant" means—

 (A) an entity that, at the time it enters into a securities contract, commodity contract, swap agreement, repurchase agreement, or forward contract, or at the time of the date of the filing of the petition, has one or more agreements or transactions described in paragraph (1), (2), (3), (4), (5), or (6) of section 561(a) with the debtor or any other entity (other than an affiliate) of a total gross dollar value of not less than $1,000,000,000 in notional or actual principal amount outstanding (aggregated across counterparties) at such time or on any day during the 15–month period preceding the date of the filing of the petition, or has gross mark-to-market positions of not less than $100,000,000 (aggregated across counterparties) in one or more such agreements or transactions with the debtor or any other entity (other than an affiliate) at such time or on any day during the 15–month period preceding the date of the filing of the petition; or

 (B) a clearing organization (as defined in section 402 of the Federal Deposit Insurance Corporation Improvement Act of 1991).

(23) The term "foreign proceeding" means a collective judicial or administrative proceeding in a foreign country, including an interim proceeding, under a law relating to insolvency or adjustment of debt in which proceeding the assets and affairs of the debtor are subject to control or supervision by a foreign court, for the purpose of reorganization or liquidation.

(24) The term "foreign representative" means a person or body, including a person or body appointed on an interim basis, authorized in a foreign proceeding to administer the reorganization or the liquidation of the debtor's assets or affairs or to act as a representative of such foreign proceeding.

(25) The term "forward contract" means—

 (A) a contract (other than a commodity contract, as defined in section 761) for the purchase, sale, or transfer of a commodity, as defined in section 761(8) of this title, or any similar good, article, service, right, or interest which is presently or in the future becomes the subject of dealing in the forward contract trade, or product or by-product thereof, with a maturity date more than two days after the date the contract is entered into, including, but not limited to, a repurchase or reverse repurchase transaction (whether or not such repurchase or reverse repurchase transaction is a "repurchase agreement", as defined in this section)² consignment, lease, swap, hedge transaction, deposit, loan, option, allocated transaction, unallocated transaction, or any other similar agreement;

 (B) any combination of agreements or transactions referred to in subparagraphs (A) and (C);

 (C) any option to enter into an agreement or transaction referred to in subparagraph (A) or (B);

 (D) a master agreement that provides for an agreement or transaction referred to in subparagraph (A), (B), or (C), together with all supplements to any such master agreement, without regard to whether such master agreement provides for an agreement or transaction that is not a forward contract under this paragraph, except that such master agreement shall be considered to be a forward contract under this paragraph only with respect to each agreement or transaction under such master agreement that is referred to in subparagraph (A), (B), or (C); or

(E) any security agreement or arrangement, or other credit enhancement related to any agreement or transaction referred to in subparagraph (A), (B), (C), or (D), including any guarantee or reimbursement obligation by or to a forward contract merchant or financial participant in connection with any agreement or transaction referred to in any such subparagraph, but not to exceed the damages in connection with any such agreement or transaction, measured in accordance with section 562.

(26) The term "forward contract merchant" means a Federal reserve bank, or an entity the business of which consists in whole or in part of entering into forward contracts as or with merchants in a commodity (as defined in section 761) or any similar good, article, service, right, or interest which is presently or in the future becomes the subject of dealing in the forward contract trade.

(27) The term "governmental unit" means United States; State; Commonwealth; District; Territory; municipality; foreign state; department, agency, or instrumentality of the United States (but not a United States trustee while serving as a trustee in a case under this title), a State, a Commonwealth, a District, a Territory, a municipality, or a foreign state; or other foreign or domestic government.

(27A) The term "health care business"—

(A) means any public or private entity (without regard to whether that entity is organized for profit or not for profit) that is primarily engaged in offering to the general public facilities and services for—

(i) the diagnosis or treatment of injury, deformity, or disease; and

(ii) surgical, drug treatment, psychiatric, or obstetric care; and

(B) includes—

(i) any—

(I) general or specialized hospital;

(II) ancillary ambulatory, emergency, or surgical treatment facility;

(III) hospice;

(IV) home health agency; and

(V) other health care institution that is similar to an entity referred to in subclause (I), (II), (III), or (IV); and

(ii) any long-term care facility, including any—

(I) skilled nursing facility;

(II) intermediate care facility;

(III) assisted living facility;

(IV) home for the aged;

(V) domiciliary care facility; and

(VI) health care institution that is related to a facility referred to in subclause (I), (II), (III), (IV), or (V), if that institution is primarily engaged in offering room, board, laundry, or personal assistance with activities of daily living and incidentals to activities of daily living.

(27B) The term "incidental property" means, with respect to a debtor's principal residence—

(A) property commonly conveyed with a principal residence in the area where the real property is located;

(B) all easements, rights, appurtenances, fixtures, rents, royalties, mineral rights, oil or gas rights or profits, water rights, escrow funds, or insurance proceeds; and

(C) all replacements or additions.

(28) The term "indenture" means mortgage, deed of trust, or indenture, under which there is outstanding a security, other than a voting-trust certificate, constituting a claim against the debtor, a claim secured by a lien on any of the debtor's property, or an equity security of the debtor.

(29) The term "indenture trustee" means trustee under an indenture.

(30) The term "individual with regular income" means individual whose income is sufficiently stable and regular to enable such individual to make payments under a plan under chapter 13 of this title, other than a stockbroker or a commodity broker.

(31) The term "insider" includes—

(A) if the debtor is an individual—

(i) relative of the debtor or of a general partner of the debtor;

(ii) partnership in which the debtor is a general partner;

(iii) general partner of the debtor; or

(iv) corporation of which the debtor is a director, officer, or person in control;

(B) if the debtor is a corporation—

(i) director of the debtor;

(ii) officer of the debtor;

(iii) person in control of the debtor;

(iv) partnership in which the debtor is a general partner;

(v) general partner of the debtor; or

(vi) relative of a general partner, director, officer, or person in control of the debtor;

(C) if the debtor is a partnership—

(i) general partner in the debtor;

(ii) relative of a general partner in, general partner of, or person in control of the debtor;

(iii) partnership in which the debtor is a general partner;

(iv) general partner of the debtor; or

(v) person in control of the debtor;

(D) if the debtor is a municipality, elected official of the debtor or relative of an elected official of the debtor;

(E) affiliate, or insider of an affiliate as if such affiliate were the debtor; and

(F) managing agent of the debtor.

(32) The term "insolvent" means—

(A) with reference to an entity other than a partnership and a municipality, financial condition such that the sum of such entity's debts is greater than all of such entity's property, at a fair valuation, exclusive of—

(i) property transferred, concealed, or removed with intent to hinder, delay, or defraud such entity's creditors; and

(ii) property that may be exempted from property of the estate under section 522 of this title;

(B) with reference to a partnership, financial condition such that the sum of such partnership's debts is greater than the aggregate of, at a fair valuation—

(i) all of such partnership's property, exclusive of property of the kind specified in subparagraph (A)(i) of this paragraph; and

(ii) the sum of the excess of the value of each general partner's nonpartnership property, exclusive of property of the kind specified in subparagraph (A) of this paragraph, over such partner's nonpartnership debts; and

(C) with reference to a municipality, financial condition such that the municipality is—

(i) generally not paying its debts as they become due unless such debts are the subject of a bona fide dispute; or

(ii) unable to pay its debts as they become due.

(33) The term "institution-affiliated party"—

(A) with respect to an insured depository institution (as defined in section 3(c)(2) of the Federal Deposit Insurance Act), has the meaning given it in section 3(u) of the Federal Deposit Insurance Act; and

(B) with respect to an insured credit union, has the meaning given it in section 206(r) of the Federal Credit Union Act.

(34) The term "insured credit union" has the meaning given it in section 101(7) of the Federal Credit Union Act.

(35) The term "insured depository institution"—

(A) has the meaning given it in section 3(c)(2) of the Federal Deposit Insurance Act; and

(B) includes an insured credit union (except in the case of paragraphs (21B) and (33)(A) of this subsection).

(35A) The term "intellectual property" means—

(A) trade secret;

(B) invention, process, design, or plant protected under title 35;

(C) patent application;

(D) plant variety;

(E) work of authorship protected under title 17; or

(F) mask work protected under chapter 9 of title 17;

to the extent protected by applicable nonbankruptcy law.

(36) The term "judicial lien" means lien obtained by judgment, levy, sequestration, or other legal or equitable process or proceeding.

(37) The term "lien" means charge against or interest in property to secure payment of a debt or performance of an obligation.

(38) The term "margin payment" means, for purposes of the forward contract provisions of this title, payment or deposit of cash, a security or other property, that is commonly known in the forward contract trade as original margin, initial margin, maintenance margin, or variation margin, including mark-to-market payments, or variation payments.

(38A) The term "master netting agreement"—

(A) means an agreement providing for the exercise of rights, including rights of netting, setoff, liquidation, termination, acceleration, or close out, under or in connection with one or more contracts that are described in any one or more of paragraphs (1) through (5) of section 561(a), or any security agreement or arrangement or other credit enhancement related to one or more of the foregoing, including any guarantee or reimbursement obligation related to 1 or more of the foregoing; and

(B) if the agreement contains provisions relating to agreements or transactions that are not contracts described in paragraphs (1) through (5) of section 561(a), shall be deemed to be a master netting agreement only with respect to those agreements or transactions that are described in any one or more of paragraphs (1) through (5) of section 561(a).

(38B) The term "master netting agreement participant" means an entity that, at any time before the date of the filing of the petition, is a party to an outstanding master netting agreement with the debtor.

(39) The term "mask work" has the meaning given it in section 901(a)(2) of title 17.

(39A) The term "median family income" means for any year—

(A) the median family income both calculated and reported by the Bureau of the Census in the then most recent year; and

(B) if not so calculated and reported in the then current year, adjusted annually after such most recent year until the next year in which median family income is both calculated and reported by the Bureau of the Census, to reflect the percentage change in the Consumer Price Index for All Urban Consumers during the period of years occurring after such most recent year and before such current year.

(40) The term "municipality" means political subdivision or public agency or instrumentality of a State.

(40A) The term "patient" means any individual who obtains or receives services from a health care business.

(40B) The term "patient records" means any record relating to a patient, including a written document or a record recorded in a magnetic, optical, or other form of electronic medium.

(41) The term "person" includes individual, partnership, and corporation, but does not include governmental unit, except that a governmental unit that—

  (A) acquires an asset from a person—

    (i) as a result of the operation of a loan guarantee agreement; or

    (ii) as receiver or liquidating agent of a person;

  (B) is a guarantor of a pension benefit payable by or on behalf of the debtor or an affiliate of the debtor; or

  (C) is the legal or beneficial owner of an asset of—

    (i) an employee pension benefit plan that is a governmental plan, as defined in section 414(d) of the Internal Revenue Code of 1986; or

    (ii) an eligible deferred compensation plan, as defined in section 457(b) of the Internal Revenue Code of 1986;

shall be considered, for purposes of section 1102 of this title, to be a person with respect to such asset or such benefit.

(41A) The term "personally identifiable information" means—

  (A) if provided by an individual to the debtor in connection with obtaining a product or a service from the debtor primarily for personal, family, or household purposes—

    (i) the first name (or initial) and last name of such individual, whether given at birth or time of adoption, or resulting from a lawful change of name;

    (ii) the geographical address of a physical place of residence of such individual;

    (iii) an electronic address (including an e-mail address) of such individual;

    (iv) a telephone number dedicated to contacting such individual at such physical place of residence;

    (v) a social security account number issued to such individual; or

    (vi) the account number of a credit card issued to such individual; or

  (B) if identified in connection with 1 or more of the items of information specified in subparagraph (A)—

    (i) a birth date, the number of a certificate of birth or adoption, or a place of birth; or

    (ii) any other information concerning an identified individual that, if disclosed, will result in contacting or identifying such individual physically or electronically.

(42) The term "petition" means petition filed under section 301, 302, 303 and [3] 1504 of this title, as the case may be, commencing a case under this title.

(42A) The term "production payment" means a term overriding royalty satisfiable in cash or in kind—

  (A) contingent on the production of a liquid or gaseous hydrocarbon from particular real property; and

  (B) from a specified volume, or a specified value, from the liquid or gaseous hydrocarbon produced from such property, and determined without regard to production costs.

(43) The term "purchaser" means transferee of a voluntary transfer, and includes immediate or mediate transferee of such a transferee.

(44) The term "railroad" means common carrier by railroad engaged in the transportation of individuals or property or owner of trackage facilities leased by such a common carrier.

(45) The term "relative" means individual related by affinity or consanguinity within the third degree as determined by the common law, or individual in a step or adoptive relationship within such third degree.

(46) The term "repo participant" means an entity that, at any time before the filing of the petition, has an outstanding repurchase agreement with the debtor.

(47) The term "repurchase agreement" (which definition also applies to a reverse repurchase agreement)—

  (A) means—

    (i) an agreement, including related terms, which provides for the transfer of one or more certificates of deposit, mortgage related securities (as defined in section 3 of the Securities Exchange Act of 1934), mortgage loans, interests in mortgage related securities or mortgage loans, eligible bankers' acceptances, qualified foreign government securities (defined as a security that is a direct obligation of, or that is fully guaranteed by, the central government of a member of the Organization for Economic Cooperation and Development), or securities that are direct obligations of, or that are fully guaranteed by, the United States or any agency of the United States against the transfer of funds by the transferee of such certificates of deposit, eligible bankers' acceptances, securities, mortgage loans, or interests, with a simultaneous agreement by such transferee to transfer to the transferor thereof certificates of deposit, eligible bankers' acceptance, securities, mortgage loans, or interests of the kind described in this clause, at a date certain not later than 1 year after such transfer or on demand, against the transfer of funds;

(ii) any combination of agreements or transactions referred to in clauses (i) and (iii);

(iii) an option to enter into an agreement or transaction referred to in clause (i) or (ii);

(iv) a master agreement that provides for an agreement or transaction referred to in clause (i), (ii), or (iii), together with all supplements to any such master agreement, without regard to whether such master agreement provides for an agreement or transaction that is not a repurchase agreement under this paragraph, except that such master agreement shall be considered to be a repurchase agreement under this paragraph only with respect to each agreement or transaction under the master agreement that is referred to in clause (i), (ii), or (iii); or

(v) any security agreement or arrangement or other credit enhancement related to any agreement or transaction referred to in clause (i), (ii), (iii), or (iv), including any guarantee or reimbursement obligation by or to a repo participant or financial participant in connection with any agreement or transaction referred to in any such clause, but not to exceed the damages in connection with any such agreement or transaction, measured in accordance with section 562 of this title; and

(B) does not include a repurchase obligation under a participation in a commercial mortgage loan.

(48) The term "securities clearing agency" means person that is registered as a clearing agency under section 17A of the Securities Exchange Act of 1934, or exempt from such registration under such section pursuant to an order of the Securities and Exchange Commission, or whose business is confined to the performance of functions of a clearing agency with respect to exempted securities, as defined in section 3(a)(12) of such Act for the purposes of such section 17A.

(48A) The term "securities self regulatory organization" means either a securities association registered with the Securities and Exchange Commission under section 15A of the Securities Exchange Act of 1934 or a national securities exchange registered with the Securities and Exchange Commission under section 6 of the Securities Exchange Act of 1934.

(49) The term "security"—

(A) includes—

(i) note;

(ii) stock;

(iii) treasury stock;

(iv) bond;

(v) debenture;

(vi) collateral trust certificate;

(vii) pre-organization certificate or subscription;

(viii) transferable share;

(ix) voting-trust certificate;

(x) certificate of deposit;

(xi) certificate of deposit for security;

(xii) investment contract or certificate of interest or participation in a profit-sharing agreement or in an oil, gas, or mineral royalty or lease, if such contract or interest is required to be the subject of a registration statement filed with the Securities and Exchange Commission under the provisions of the Securities Act of 1933, or is exempt under section 3(b) of such Act from the requirement to file such a statement;

(xiii) interest of a limited partner in a limited partnership;

(xiv) other claim or interest commonly known as "security"; and

(xv) certificate of interest or participation in, temporary or interim certificate for, receipt for, or warrant or right to subscribe to or purchase or sell, a security; but

(B) does not include—

(i) currency, check, draft, bill of exchange, or bank letter of credit;

(ii) leverage transaction, as defined in section 761 of this title;

(iii) commodity futures contract or forward contract;

(iv) option, warrant, or right to subscribe to or purchase or sell a commodity futures contract;

(v) option to purchase or sell a commodity;

(vi) contract or certificate of a kind specified in subparagraph (A)(xii) of this paragraph that is not required to be the subject of a registration statement filed with the Securities and Exchange Commission and is not exempt under section 3(b) of the Securities Act of 1933 from the requirement to file such a statement; or

(vii) debt or evidence of indebtedness for goods sold and delivered or services rendered.

(50) The term "security agreement" means agreement that creates or provides for a security interest.

(51) The term "security interest" means lien created by an agreement.

(51A) The term "settlement payment" means, for purposes of the forward contract provisions of this title, a preliminary settlement payment, a partial settlement payment, an interim settlement payment, a settlement payment on account, a final settlement payment, a net settlement payment, or any other similar payment commonly used in the forward contract trade.

(51B) The term "single asset real estate" means real property constituting a single property or project, other than residential real property with fewer than 4 residential units, which generates substantially all of the gross income of a debtor who is not a family farmer and on which no substantial business is being conducted by a debtor other than the business of operating the real property and activities incidental thereto.

(51C) The term "small business case" means a case filed under chapter 11 of this title in which the debtor is a small business debtor.

(51D) The term "small business debtor"—

(A) subject to subparagraph (B), means a person engaged in commercial or business activities (including any affiliate of such person that is also a debtor under this title and excluding a person whose primary activity is the business of owning or operating real property or activities incidental thereto) that has aggregate noncontingent liquidated secured and unsecured debts as of the date of the filing of the petition or the date of the order for relief in an amount not more than $2,343,300 [1] (excluding debts owed to 1 or more affiliates or insiders) for a case in which the United States trustee has not appointed under section 1102(a)(1) a committee of unsecured creditors or where the court has determined that the committee of unsecured creditors is not sufficiently active and representative to provide effective oversight of the debtor; and

(B) does not include any member of a group of affiliated debtors that has aggregate noncontingent liquidated secured and unsecured debts in an amount greater than $2,343,300 [1] (excluding debt owed to 1 or more affiliates or insiders).

(52) The term "State" includes the District of Columbia and Puerto Rico, except for the purpose of defining who may be a debtor under chapter 9 of this title.

(53) The term "statutory lien" means lien arising solely by force of a statute on specified circumstances or conditions, or lien of distress for rent, whether or not statutory, but does not include security interest or judicial lien, whether or not such interest or lien is provided by or is dependent on a statute and whether or not such interest or lien is made fully effective by statute.

(53A) The term "stockbroker" means person—

(A) with respect to which there is a customer, as defined in section 741 of this title; and

(B) that is engaged in the business of effecting transactions in securities—

(i) for the account of others; or

(ii) with members of the general public, from or for such person's own account.

(53B) The term "swap agreement"—

(A) means—

(i) any agreement, including the terms and conditions incorporated by reference in such agreement, which is—

(I) an interest rate swap, option, future, or forward agreement, including a rate floor, rate cap, rate collar, cross-currency rate swap, and basis swap;

(II) a spot, same day-tomorrow, tomorrow-next, forward, or other foreign exchange, precious metals, or other commodity agreement;

(III) a currency swap, option, future, or forward agreement;

(IV) an equity index or equity swap, option, future, or forward agreement;

(V) a debt index or debt swap, option, future, or forward agreement;

(VI) a total return, credit spread or credit swap, option, future, or forward agreement;

(VII) a commodity index or a commodity swap, option, future, or forward agreement;

(VIII) a weather swap, option, future, or forward agreement;

(IX) an emissions swap, option, future, or forward agreement; or

(X) an inflation swap, option, future, or forward agreement;

(ii) any agreement or transaction that is similar to any other agreement or transaction referred to in this paragraph and that—

(I) is of a type that has been, is presently, or in the future becomes, the subject of recurrent dealings in the swap or other derivatives markets (including terms and conditions incorporated by reference therein); and

(II) is a forward, swap, future, option, or spot transaction on one or more rates, currencies, commodities, equity securities, or other equity instruments, debt securities or other debt instruments, quantitative measures associated with an occurrence, extent of an occurrence, or contingency associated with a financial, commercial, or economic consequence, or economic or financial indices or measures of economic or financial risk or value;

(iii) any combination of agreements or transactions referred to in this subparagraph;

(iv) any option to enter into an agreement or transaction referred to in this subparagraph;

(v) a master agreement that provides for an agreement or transaction referred to in clause (i), (ii), (iii), or (iv), together with all supplements to any such master agreement, and without regard to whether the master agreement contains an agreement or transaction that is not a swap agreement under this paragraph, except that the master agreement shall be considered to be a swap agreement under this paragraph only with respect to each agreement or transaction under the master agreement that is referred to in clause (i), (ii), (iii), or (iv); or

(vi) any security agreement or arrangement or other credit enhancement related to any agreements or transactions referred to in clause (i) through (v), including any guarantee or reimbursement obligation by or to a swap participant or financial participant in connection with any agreement or transaction referred to in any such clause, but not to exceed the damages in connection with any such agreement or transaction, measured in accordance with section 562; and

(B) is applicable for purposes of this title only, and shall not be construed or applied so as to challenge or affect the characterization, definition, or treatment of any swap agreement under any other statute, regulation, or rule, including the Gramm–Leach–Bliley Act, the Legal Certainty for Bank Products Act of 2000, the securities laws (as such term is defined in section 3(a)(47) of the Securities Exchange Act of 1934) and the Commodity Exchange Act.

(53C) The term "swap participant" means an entity that, at any time before the filing of the petition, has an outstanding swap agreement with the debtor.

(56A) [4] The term "term overriding royalty" means an interest in liquid or gaseous hydrocarbons in place or to be produced from particular real property that entitles the owner thereof to a share of production, or the value thereof, for a term limited by time, quantity, or value realized.

(53D) The term "timeshare plan" means and shall include that interest purchased in any arrangement, plan, scheme, or similar device, but not including exchange programs, whether by membership, agreement, tenancy in common, sale, lease, deed, rental agreement, license, right to use agreement, or by any other means, whereby a purchaser, in exchange for consideration, receives a right to use accommodations, facilities, or recreational sites, whether improved or unimproved, for a specific period of time less than a full year during any given year, but not necessarily for consecutive years, and which extends for a period of more than three years. A "timeshare interest" is that interest purchased in a timeshare plan which grants the purchaser the right to use and occupy accommodations, facilities, or recreational sites, whether improved or unimproved, pursuant to a timeshare plan.

(54) The term "transfer" means—

(A) the creation of a lien;

(B) the retention of title as a security interest;

(C) the foreclosure of a debtor's equity of redemption; or

(D) each mode, direct or indirect, absolute or conditional, voluntary or involuntary, of disposing of or parting with—

(i) property; or

(ii) an interest in property.

(54A) The term "uninsured State member bank" means a State member bank (as defined in section 3 of the Federal Deposit Insurance Act) the deposits of which are not insured by the Federal Deposit Insurance Corporation.

(55) The term "United States", when used in a geographical sense, includes all locations where the judicial jurisdiction of the United States extends, including territories and possessions of the United States.

(Pub.L. 95–598, Nov. 6, 1978, 92 Stat. 2549; Pub.L. 97–222, § 1, July 27, 1982, 96 Stat. 235; Pub.L. 98–353, Title III, §§ 391, 401, 421, July 10, 1984, 98 Stat. 364, 366, 367; Pub.L. 99–554, Title II, §§ 201, 251, 283(a), Oct. 27, 1986, 100 Stat. 3097, 3104, 3116; Pub.L. 100–506, § 1(a), Oct. 18, 1988, 102 Stat. 2538; Pub.L. 100–597, § 1, Nov. 3, 1988, 102 Stat. 3028; Pub.L. 101–311, Title I, § 101, Title II, § 201, June 25, 1990, 104 Stat. 267, 268; Pub.L. 101–647, Title XXV, § 2522(e), Nov. 29, 1990, 104 Stat. 4867; Pub.L. 102–486, Title XXX, § 3017(a), Oct. 24, 1992, 106 Stat. 3130; Pub.L. 103–394, Title I, § 106, Title II, §§ 208(a), 215, 217(a), 218(a), Title III, § 304(a), Title V, § 501(a), (b)(1), (d)(1), Oct. 22, 1994, 108 Stat. 4111, 4124, 4126–4128, 4132, 4141–4143; Pub.L. 106–554, § 1(a)(5) [Title I, § 112(c)(3), (4)], Dec. 21, 2000, 114 Stat. 2763, 2763A–393; Pub.L. 109–8, Title I, § 102(b), (k), Title II, §§ 211, 226(a), 231(b), Title III, § 306(c), Title IV, §§ 401(a), 414, 432(a), Title VIII, § 802(b), Title IX, § 907(a)(1), (b), (c), Title X, §§ 1004, 1005, 1007(a), Title XI, § 1101(a), (b), Title XII, § 1201, Apr. 20, 2005, 119 Stat. 32, 35, 50, 66, 73, 80, 104, 107, 110, 145, 170, 175, 186, 187, 189, 192; Pub.L. 109–390, § 5(a)(1), Dec. 12, 2006, 120 Stat. 2695; Pub.L. 111–327, § 2(a)(1), Dec. 22, 2010, 124 Stat. 3557.)

1 Dollar amount as adjusted by the Judicial Conference of the United States. See Adjustment of Dollar Amounts notes set out under this section and 11 U.S.C.A. § 104.

2 So in original. A comma should probably appear.

3 So in original. Probably should be "or". See 2010 Amendments note set out under this section.

4 So in original. Par. (56A) was inserted between pars. (53C) and (53D).

HISTORICAL AND STATUTORY NOTES

Revision Notes and Legislative Reports

1978 Acts. Section 101 of title 11 contains 40 definitions:

Paragraph (1) defines "accountant" as an accountant authorized under applicable law to practice accounting. The term includes a professional accounting association, corporation, or partnership if applicable law authorizes such a unit to practice accounting.

Paragraph (2) defines "affiliate." An affiliate is an entity with a close relationship to the debtor. It includes a 20 percent parent or subsidiary of the debtor, whether a corporate, partnership, individual, or estate parent.

The use of "directly or indirectly" in subparagraphs (A) and (B) is intended to cover situations in which there is an opportunity to control, and where the existence of that opportunity operates as indirect control.

"Affiliate" is defined primarily for use in the definition of insider, infra, and for use in the chapter 11 reorganization cases. The definition of "affiliate" does not include an entity acting in a fiduciary or agency capacity if the entity does not have the sole discretionary power to vote 20 percent of the voting securities but hold them solely as security and have not exercised the power to vote. This restriction applies to a corporate affiliate under subparagraph (B) of paragraph (2).

Subsections (C) and (D) of paragraph (2) define affiliate also as those persons and entities whose business or substantially all of whose property is operated under a lease or operating agreement by a debtor and whose business or property is more than 50 percent under the control of the debtor.

The definition of "attorney" in paragraph (3) is similar to the definition of accountant.

Paragraph (4) defines "claim." The effect of the definition is a significant departure from present law. Under present law, "claim" is not defined in straight bankruptcy. Instead it is simply used, along with the concept of provability in section 63 of the Bankruptcy Act [section 103 of former Title 11], to limit the kinds of obligations that are payable in a bankruptcy case. The term is defined in the debtor rehabilitation chapters of present law far more broadly. The definition in paragraph (4) adopts an even broader definition of claim than is found in the present debtor rehabilitation chapters. The definition is any right to payment, whether or not reduced to judgment, liquidated, unliquidated, fixed, contingent, matured, unmatured, disputed, undisputed, legal, equitable, secured, or unsecured. The definition also includes as a claim an equitable right to performance that does not give rise to a right to payment. By this broadest possible definition and by the use of the term throughout the title 11, especially in subchapter I of chapter 5, the bill contemplates that all legal obligations of the debtor, no matter how remote or contingent, will be able to be dealt with in the bankruptcy case. It permits the broadest possible relief in the bankruptcy court.

Paragraph (5) defines "commodity broker" by reference to various terms used and defined in subchapter IV of chapter 7, Commodity Broker Liquidation. The terms are described in connection with section 761, infra.

Paragraph (6) defines "community claim" for those eight States that have community property laws. The definition is keyed to the liability of the debtor's property for a claim against either the debtor or the debtor's spouse. If the debtor's property is liable for a claim against either, that claim is a community claim.

Paragraph (7) defines "consumer debt". The definition is adapted from the definition used in various consumer protection laws. It encompasses only a debt incurred by an individual primarily for a personal, family, or household purpose.

The definition of "corporation" in paragraph (8) is similar to the definition in current law, section 1(8) [section 1(8) of former Title 11]. The term encompasses any association having the power or privilege that a private corporation, but not an individual or partnership, has; partnership associations organized under a law that makes only the capital subscribed responsible for the debts of the partnership; joint-stock company; unincorporated company or association; and business trust. "Unincorporated association" is intended specifically to include a labor union, as well as other bodies that come under that phrase as used under current law. The exclusion of limited partnerships is explicit, and not left to the case law.

Paragraph (9) defines "court" as the bankruptcy judge in the district in which the case is pending except in municipal adjustment and railroad reorganization cases, where "court" means the Federal district judge.

Paragraph (10) defines "creditor" to include holders of prepetition claims against the debtor. However, it also encompasses certain holders of claims that are deemed to arise before the date of the filing of the petition, such as those injured by the rejection of an executory contract or unexpired lease, certain investment tax credit recapture claim holders, "involuntary gap" creditors, and certain holders of the right of setoff. The term also includes the holder of a prepetition community claim. A guarantor of or surety for a claim against the debtor is also a creditor, because he holds a contingent claim against the debtor that becomes fixed when he pays the creditor whose claim he has guaranteed or insured.

Paragraph (11) defines "custodian." There is no similar definition in current law. It is defined to facilitate drafting, and means a prepetition liquidator of the debtor's property, such as an assignee for the benefit of creditors, a receiver of the debtor's property, or administrator of the debtor's property. The definition of custodian to include a receiver or trustee is descriptive, and not meant to be limited to court officers with those titles. The definition is intended to include other officers of the court if their functions are substantially similar to those of a receiver or trustee.

"Debt" is defined in paragraph (12) as a liability on a claim. The terms "debt" and "claim" are coextensive: a creditor has a "claim" against the debtor; the debtor owes a "debt" to the creditor. This definition of "debt" and the definition of "claim" on which it is based, proposed 11 U.S.C. 101(4), does not include a transaction such as a policy loan on an insurance policy. Under that kind of transaction, the debtor is not liable to the insurance company for repayment; the amount owed is merely available to the company for setoff against any benefits that become payable under the policy. As such, the loan is not a claim (it is not a right to payment) that the company can assert against the estate; nor is the debtor's obligation a debt (a liability on a claim) that will be discharged under proposed 11 U.S.C. 523 or 524.

Paragraph (13) defines "debtor." Debtor means person or municipality concerning which a case under title II [probably means 11] has been commenced. This is a change in terminology from present law, which identifies the person by or against whom a petition is filed in a straight bankruptcy liquidation case as the "bankrupt", and a person or municipality that is proceeding under a debtor rehabilitation chapter (chapters VIII through XIII of the Bankruptcy Act) [chapters 8 through 13 of former Title 11] as a "debtor." The term "debtor" is used for both kinds of cases in this bill, for ease of reference in chapters 1, 3, and 5 (which apply to straight bankruptcy and reorganization cases).

Paragraph (14) defines "disinterested person." The definition is adapted from section 158 of chapter X of current law [section 558 of former Title 11], though it is expanded and modified in some respects. A person is a disinterested person if the person is not a creditor, equity security holder, or insider; is not and was not an investment banker of the debtor for any outstanding security of the debtor (the change from underwriter in current law to investment banker is to make the term more descriptive and to avoid conflict with the definition of underwriter in section 2(11) of the Securities Act of 1933 (15 U.S.C. 77b(11)) [15 U.S.C.A. § 77(b)(11)]; has not been an investment banker for a security of the debtor within 3 years before the date of the filing of the petition (the change from five years to three years here conforms the definition with the statute of limitations in the Securities Act of 1933) [15 U.S.C.A. § 77n], or an attorney for such an investment banker; is not an insider of the debtor or of such an investment banker; and does not have an interest materially adverse to the estate.

"Entity" is defined, for convenience, in paragraph (15), to include person, estate, trust, and governmental unit. It is the most inclusive of the various defined terms relating to bodies or units.

Paragraph (16) defines "equity security." The term includes a share or stock in a corporation, a limited partner's interest in a limited partnership, and a warrant or right to subscribe to an equity security. The term does not include a security, such as a convertible debenture, that is convertible into equity security, but has not been converted.

Paragraph (17) defines "equity security holder" for convenience as the holder of an equity securing of the debtor.

Paragraph (18) defines "farmer". It encompasses only those persons for whom farming operations contribute 75 percent or more of their total income.

Paragraphs (19) and (20) define "foreign proceeding" and "foreign representative". A foreign proceeding is a proceeding in another country in which the debtor has some substantial connection for the purpose of liquidating the estate of the debtor or the purpose of financial rehabilitation of the debtor. A foreign representative is the representative of the estate in a foreign proceeding, such as a trustee or administrator.

Paragraph (21) defines "governmental unit" in the broadest sense. The definition encompasses the United States, a State, Commonwealth, District, Territory, municipality, or foreign state, and a department, agency, or instrumentality of any of those entities. "Department, agency, or instrumentality" does not include an entity that owes its existence to State action, such as the granting of a charter or a license but that has no other connection with a State or local government or the Federal Government. The relationship must be an active one in which the department, agency, or instrumentality is actually carrying out some governmental function.

Paragraph (22) defines "indenture." It is similar to the definition of indenture in the Trust Indenture Act of 1939 [15 U.S.C.A. § 77ccc(7)]. An indenture is the instrument under which securities, either debt or equity, of the debtor are outstanding.

Paragraph (23) defines "indenture trustee" as the trustee under an indenture.

Paragraph (24) defines "individual with regular income." The effect of this definition, and of its use in section 109(e), is to expand substantially the kinds of individuals that are eligible for relief under chapter 13, Adjustment of Debts of an Individual with Regular Income. Chapter XIII [chapter 13 of former Title 11] is now available only for wage earners. The definition encompasses all individuals with incomes that are sufficiently stable and regular to enable them to make payments under a chapter 13 plan. Thus, individuals on welfare, social security, fixed pension incomes, or who live on investment incomes, will be able to work out repayment plans with their creditors rather than being forced into straight bankruptcy. Also, self-employed individuals will be eligible to use chapter 13 if they have regular incomes.

However, the definition excludes certain stockbrokers and commodity brokers, in order to prohibit them from proceeding under chapter 13 and avoiding the customer protection provisions of chapter 7.

"Insider", defined in paragraph (25), is a new term. An insider is one who has a sufficiently close relationship with the debtor that his conduct is made subject to closer scrutiny than those dealing at arms length with the debtor. If the debtor is an individual, then a relative of the debtor, a partnership in which the debtor is a general partner, a general partner of the debtor, and a corporation controlled by the debtor are all insiders. If the debtor is a corporation, then a controlling person, a relative of a controlling person, a partnership in which the debtor is a general partner, and a general partner of the debtor are all insiders. If the debtor is a partnership, then a general partner of or in the debtor, a relative of a general partner in the debtor, and a person in control are all insiders. If the debtor is a municipality, then an elected official of the debtor is an insider. In addition, affiliates of the debtor and managing agents are insiders.

The definition of "insolvent" in paragraph (26) is adopted from section 1(19) of current law [section 1(19) of former Title 11]. An entity is insolvent if its debts are greater than its assets, at a fair valuation, exclusive of property exempted or fraudulently transferred. It is the traditional bankruptcy balance sheet test of insolvency. For a partnership, the definition is modified to account for the liability of a general partner for the partnership's debts. The difference in this definition from that in current law is in the exclusion of exempt property for all purposes in the definition of insolvent.

Paragraph (27) defines "judicial lien." It is one of three kinds of liens defined in this section. A judicial lien is a lien obtained by judgment, levy, sequestration, or other legal or equitable process or proceeding.

Paragraph (28) defines "lien." The definition is new and is very broad. A lien is defined as a charge against or interest in property to secure payment of a debt or performance of an obligation. It includes inchoate liens. In general, the concept of lien is divided into three kinds of liens: judicial liens, security interests, and statutory liens. Those three categories are mutually exclusive and are exhaustive except for certain common law liens.

Paragraph (29) defines "municipality." The definition is adapted from the terms used in the chapter IX (municipal bankruptcy) [chapter 9 of former Title 11] amendment to the

Bankruptcy Act enacted in 1976 (Pub.L. 94–260). That amendment spoke in terms of "political subdivision or public agency or instrumentality of a State". Bankruptcy Act sec. 84 [section 404 of former Title 11]. The term municipality is defined by those three terms for convenience. It does not include the District of Columbia or any territories of the United States.

"Person" is defined in paragraph (30). The definition is a change in wording, but not in substance, from the definition in section 1(23) of the Bankruptcy Act [section 1(23) of former Title 11]. The definition is also similar to the one contained in 1 U.S.C. sec. 1, but is repeated here for convenience and ease of reference. Person includes individual partnership, and corporation. The exclusion of governmental units is made explicit in order to avoid any confusion that may arise if, for example, a municipality is incorporated and thus is legally a corporation as well as governmental unit. The definition does not include an estate or a trust, which are included only in the definition of "entity" in proposed 11 U.S.C. 101(14).

"Petition" is defined for convenience in paragraph (31). Petition is a petition under section 301, 302, 303, or 304 of the bankruptcy code—that is, a petition that commences a case under title 11.

Paragraph (32) defines purchaser as a transferee of a voluntary transfer, such as a sale or gift, and includes an immediate or mediate transferee of a purchaser.

The definition of "railroad" in paragraph (33) is derived from section 77 of the Bankruptcy Act [section 205 of former Title 11]. A railroad is a common carrier by railroad engaged in the transportation of individuals or property, or an owner of trackage facilities leased by such a common carrier. The effect of the definition and the use of the term in section 109(d) is to eliminate the limitation now found in section 77 of the Bankruptcy Act that only railroads engaged in interstate commerce may proceed under the railroad reorganization provisions. The limitation may have been inserted because of a doubt that the commerce power could not reach intrastate railroads. Be that as it may, this bill is enacted under the bankruptcy power.

Paragraph (34) defines "relative" as an individual related by affinity or consanguinity within the third degree as determined by the common law, and includes individuals in a step or adoptive relationship. The definition is similar to current law, but adds the latter phrase. This definition should be applied as of the time when the transaction that it concerns took place. Thus, a former spouse is not a relative, but if, for example, for purposes of the preference section, proposed 11 U.S.C. 547(b)(4)(B), the transferee was a spouse of the debtor at the time of the transfer sought to be avoided, then the transferee would be relative and subject to the insider rules, even if the transferee was no longer married to the debtor at the time of the commencement of the case or at the time of the commencement of the preference recovery proceeding.

Paragraph (35) defines "security." The definition is new and is modeled on the most recent draft of the American Law Institute's proposed securities code, with some exceptions. The interest of a limited partner in a limited partnership is included in order to make sure that everything that is defined as an equity security is also a "security." The definition, as with the definition of "entity", "insider", and "person", is open-ended because the term is not susceptible of precise specification. Thus the courts will be able to use the characterization provided in this definition to treat with new kinds of documents on a flexible basis.

Paragraphs (36) and (37) defined "security agreement" and "security interest." A security interest is one of the kinds of liens. It is a lien created by an agreement. Security agreement is defined as the agreement creating the security interest. Though these terms are similar to the same terms in the Uniform Commercial Code, article IX, they are broader. For example, the U.C.C. does not cover real property mortgages. Under this definition, such a mortgage is included, as are all other liens created by agreement, even though not covered by the U.C.C. All U.C.C. security interests and security agreements are, however, security interests and security agreements under this definition. Whether a consignment or a lease constitutes a security interest under the bankruptcy code will depend on whether it constitutes a security interest under applicable State or local law.

Paragraph (38) defines another kind of lien, "statutory lien." The definition, derived from current law, states that a statutory lien is a lien arising solely by force of statute on specified circumstances or conditions and includes a lien of distress for rent (whether statutory, common law, or otherwise). The definition excludes judicial liens and security interests, whether or not they are provided for or are dependent on a statute, and whether or not they are made fully effective by statute. A statutory lien is only one that arises automatically, and is not based on an agreement to give a lien or on judicial action. Mechanics', materialmen's, and warehousemen's liens are examples. Tax liens are also included in the definition of statutory lien.

"Stockbroker" is defined in paragraph (39) as a person engaged in the business of effecting transactions in securities for the account of others or with members of the general public from or for such person's own account, if the person has a customer, as defined. Thus, the definition, derived from a combination of the definitions of "broker" and "dealer" in the Securities Exchange Act of 1934 [15 U.S.C.A. § 78c], encompasses both brokers and dealers. The definition is used in section 109 and in subchapter III of chapter 7, Stockholder Liquidation. The term does not encompass an employee who acts for a principal that "effects" transaction or deals with the public, because such an employee will not have a "customer".

Paragraph (40) defines "transfer." It is derived and adapted, with stylistic changes, from section 1(30) of the Bankruptcy Act [section 1(30) of former Title 11]. A transfer is a disposition of an interest in property. The definition of transfer is as broad as possible. Many of the potentially limiting words in current law are deleted, and the language is simplified. Under this definition, any transfer of an interest in property is a transfer, including a transfer of possession, custody, or control even if there is no transfer of title, because possession, custody, and control are interests in property. A deposit in a bank account or similar account is a transfer. Senate Report No. 95–989.

1982 Acts. House Report No. 97–420, see 1982 U.S. Code Cong. and Adm. News, p. 583.

1984 Acts. Statements by Legislative Leaders, see 1984 U.S. Code Cong. and Adm. News, p. 576.

1986 Acts. House Report No. 99–764 and House Conference Report No. 99–958, see 1986 U.S. Code Cong. and Adm. News, p. 5227.

1988 Acts. Senate Report No. 100–505, see 1988 U.S. Code Cong. and Adm. News, p. 3200.

House Report No. 100–1011, see 1988 U.S. Code Cong. and Adm. News, p. 4115.

1990 Acts. House Report No. 101–484, see 1990 U.S. Code Cong. and Adm. News, p. 223.

House Report No. 101–681(Part I), see 1990 U.S. Code Cong. and Adm. News, p. 6472.

1994 Acts. House Report No. 103–835, see 1994 U.S. Code Cong. and Adm. News, p. 3340.

2000 Acts. House Report No. 106–645 and Statement by President, see 2000 U.S. Code Cong. and Adm. News, p. 2459.

2005 Acts. House Report No. 109–31(Part I), see 2005 U.S. Code Cong. and Adm. News, p. 88.

2006 Acts. House Report No. 109–648(Part I), see 2006 U.S. Code Cong. and Adm. News, p. 1585.

Legislative Statements

Section 101(2) defines "affiliate." The House amendment contains a provision that is a compromise between the definition in the House-passed version of H.R. 8200 and the Senate amendment in the nature of a substitute to H.R. 8200. Subparagraphs (A) and (B) are derived from the Senate amendment and subparagraph (D) is taken from the House bill, while subparagraph (C) represents a compromise, taking the House position with respect to a person whose business is operated under a lease or an operating agreement by the debtor and with respect to a person substantially all of whose property is operated under an operating agreement by the debtor and with respect to a person substantially all of whose property is operated under an operating agreement by the debtor and the Senate position on leased property. Thus, the definition of "affiliate" excludes persons substantially all of whose property is operated under a lease agreement by a debtor, such as a small company which owns equipment all of which is leased to a larger nonrelated company.

Section 101(4)(B) represents a modification of the House-passed bill to include the definition of "claim" a right to an equitable remedy for breach of performance if such breach gives rise to a right to payment. This is intended to cause the liquidation or estimation of contingent rights of payment for which there may be an alternative equitable remedy with the result that the equitable remedy will be susceptible to being discharged in bankruptcy. For example, in some States, a judgment for specific performance may be satisfied by an alternative right to payment, in the event performance is refused; in that event, the creditor entitled to specific performance would have a "claim" for purposes of a proceeding under title 11.

On the other hand, rights to an equitable remedy for a breach of performance with respect to which such breach does not give rise to a right to payment are not "claims" and would therefore not be susceptible to discharge in bankruptcy.

In a case under chapter 9 to title 11, "claim" does not include a right to payment under an industrial development bond issued by a municipality as a matter of convenience for a third party.

Municipalities are authorized, under section 103(c) of the Internal Revenue Code of 1954, as amended [section 103(c) of Title 26, Internal Revenue Code], to issue tax-exempt industrial development revenue bonds to provide for the financing of certain projects for privately owned companies. The bonds are sold on the basis of the credit of the company on whose behalf they are issued, and the principal, interest, and premium, if any, are payable solely from payments made by the company to the trustee under the bond indenture and do not constitute claims on the tax revenues or other funds of the

issuing municipalities. The municipality merely acts as the vehicle to enable the bonds to be issued on a tax-exempt basis. Claims that arise by virtue of these bonds are not among the claims defined by this paragraph and amounts owed by private companies to the holders of industrial development revenue bonds are not to be included among the assets of the municipality that would be affected by the plan.

Section 101(6) defines "community claim" as provided by the Senate amendment in order to indicate that a community claim exists whether or not there is community property in the estate as of the commencement of the case.

Section 101(7) of the House amendment contains a definition of consumer debt identical to the definition in the House bill and Senate amendment. A consumer debt does not include a debt to any extent the debt is secured by real property.

Section 101(9) of the Senate amendment contained a definition of "court." The House amendment deletes the provision as unnecessary in light of the pervasive jurisdiction of a bankruptcy court under all chapters of title 11 as indicated in title II of the House amendment to H.R. 8200.

Section 101(11) defines "debt" to mean liability on a claim, as was contained in the House-passed version of H.R. 8200. The Senate amendment contained language indicating that "debt" does not include a policy loan made by a life insurance company to the debtor. That language is deleted in the House amendment as unnecessary since a life insurance company clearly has no right to have a policy loan repaid by the debtor, although such company does have a right of offset with respect to such policy loan. Clearly, then, a "debt" does not include a policy loan made by a life insurance company. Inclusion of the language contained in the Senate amendment would have required elaboration of other legal relationships not arising by a liability on a claim. Further the language would have required clarification that interest on a policy loan made by a life insurance company is a debt, and that the insurance company does have right to payment to that interest.

Section 101(14) adopts the definition of "entity" contained in the Senate-passed version of H.R. 8200. Since the Senate amendment to H.R. 8200 deleted the U.S. trustee, a corresponding definitional change is made in chapter 15 of the House amendment for U.S. trustees under the pilot program. Adoption by the House amendment of a pilot program for U.S. trustees under chapter 15 requires insertion of "United States trustee" in many sections. Several provisions in chapter 15 of the House amendment that relate to the U.S. trustee were not contained in the Senate amendment in the nature of a substitute.

Section 101(17) defines "farmer," as in the Senate amendment with an income limitation percentage of 80 percent instead of 75 percent.

Section 101(18) contains a new definition of "farming operation" derived from present law and the definition of "farmer" in the Senate amendment. This definition gives a broad construction to the term "farming operation".

Section 101(20) contains a definition of "foreign representative". It clarifies the House bill and Senate amendment by indicating that a foreign representative must be duly selected in a foreign proceeding.

Section 101(35) defines "security" as contained in the Senate amendment. H.R. 8200 as adopted by the House excluded certain commercial notes from the definition of "security", and that exclusion is deleted.

Section 101(40) defines "transfer" as in the Senate amendment. The definition contained in H.R. 8200 as passed by the House included "setoff" in the definition of "transfer". Inclusion of "setoff" is deleted. The effect is that a "setoff" is not subject to being set aside as a preferential "transfer" but will be subject to special rules.

References in Text

Chapter 12, referred to in pars. (7A)(B) and (19B), is chapter 12 of this title, which is classified to 11 U.S.C.A. § 1201 et seq.

The Social Security Act, referred to in par. (10A)(B), is Act Aug. 14, 1935, c. 531, 49 Stat. 620, as amended, which is classified generally to chapter 7 of Title 42, 42 U.S.C.A. § 301 et seq.

Section 501(c)(3) of the Internal Revenue Code of 1986, referred to in par. (12A)(B), is classified to 26 U.S.C.A. § 501(c)(3).

Section 3 of the Federal Deposit Insurance Act, referred to in pars. (12A)(D), (21B)(A), (33)(A), (35)(A), and (54A) is Act Sept. 21, 1950, c. 967, § 2 [3], 64 Stat. 873, which is classified to 12 U.S.C.A. § 1813.

Section 101 of the Federal Credit Union Act, referred to in pars. (12A)(D), (34), is Act June 26, 1934, c. 750, Title I, § 101, formerly § 2, 48 Stat. 1216, as amended, which is classified to 12 U.S.C.A. § 1752.

The Investment Company Act of 1940, referred to in par. (22)(B), is Act Aug. 22, 1940, c. 686, Title I, 54 Stat. 789, as amended, which is classified principally to subchapter 1 of chapter 2D of title 15, 15 U.S.C.A. § 80a–1 et seq. For complete classification, see Short Title set out as 15 U.S.C.A. § 80a–51 and Tables.

Section 402 of the Federal Deposit Insurance Corporation Improvement Act of 1991, referred to in par. (22A)(B), is Pub.L. 102–242, Title IV, § 402, Dec. 19, 1991, 105 Stat. 2372, which is classified to 12 U.S.C.A. § 4402.

Section 206 of the Federal Credit Union Act, referred to in par. (33)(B), is section 206 of Act June 26, 1934, c. 750, Title II, as added Oct. 19, 1970, Pub.L. 91–468, § 1(3), 84 Stat. 1003, which is classified to section 1786 of Title 12.

Sections 414(d) and 457(b) of the Internal Revenue Code of 1986, referred to in par. (41)(C), are sections 414(d) and 457(b), respectively, of Title 26, Internal Revenue Code.

Section 3 of the Securities and Exchange Act of 1934, referred to in par. (47), is Act June 6, 1934, c. 404, Title I, § 3, 48 Stat. 882, which is classified to 15 U.S.C.A. § 78c.

Section 17A of the Securities and Exchange Act of 1934, referred to in par. (48), is section 17A of Act June 6, 1934, c. 404, Title I, as added June 4, 1975, Pub.L. 94–29, § 15, 89 Stat. 141, which is classified to section 78q–1 of Title 15, Commerce and Trade.

Section 3(a)(12) of such Act, referred to in par. (48), is Section 3 of the Securities and Exchange Act of 1934, Act June 6, 1934, c. 404, Title I, 48 Stat. 882, which is classified to 15 U.S.C.A. § 78c(a)(12).

Section 15A of the Securities Exchange Act of 1934, referred to in par. (48A), is June 6, 1934, c. 404, Title I, § 15A, as added June 25, 1938, c. 677, § 1, 52 Stat. 1070, and amended which is classified to 15 U.S.C.A. § 78o–3.

Section 6 of the Securities Exchange Act of 1934, referred to in par. (48A), is June 6, 1934, c. 404, Title I, § 6, 48 Stat. 885, as amended, which is classified to 15 U.S.C.A. § 78c.

The Securities Act of 1933, referred to in par. (49)(A)(xii), is Act May 27, 1933, c. 38, Title I, 48 Stat. 74, as amended, which is classified generally to subchapter I (section 77a et seq.) of chapter 2A of Title 15, Commerce and Trade. For complete classification of this Act to the Code, see section 77a of Title 15 and Tables.

Section 3 of the Securities Act of 1933, referred to in pars. (49)(A)(xii) and (B)(vi), is section 3 of Act May 27, 1933, c. 38, Title I, 48 Stat. 75, which is classified to section 77c of Title 15.

Chapter 11 of this title, referred to in par. (51C), is 11 U.S.C.A. § 1101 et seq.

The Securities Exchange Act of 1934, referred to in par. (53B)(B), is Act June 6, 1934, c. 404, 48 Stat. 881, as amended, which is classified principally to chapter 2B of Title 15, 15 U.S.C.A. § 78a et seq. Section 3(a)(47) of the Act, as amended, is classified to 15 U.S.C.A. § 78c(a)(47). For complete classification, see Short Title set out as 15 U.S.C.A. § 78a and Tables.

The Commodity Exchange Act, referred to in par. (53B), is Act Sept. 21, 1922, c. 369, 42 Stat. 998, as amended, which is classified principally to chapter 1 of Title 7, 7 U.S.C.A. § 1 et seq. For complete classification, see Short Title set out as 7 U.S.C.A. § 1 and Tables.

The Gramm-Leach-Bliley Act, referred to in par. (53B), is Pub.L. 106–102, Nov. 12, 1999, 113 Stat. 1338, also known as the Financial Services Modernization Act of 1999, which principally enacted chapters 93, 94 and 95 of Title 15, 15 U.S.C.A. § 6701 et seq., 15 U.S.C.A. § 6801 et seq., and 15 U.S.C.A. § 6901 et seq., respectively, and amended chapters 16 and 17 of Title 12, 12 U.S.C.A. § 1811 et seq., and 12 U.S.C.A. § 1841 et seq. For complete classification, see Tables.

The Legal Certainty for Bank Products Act of 2000, referred to in par. (53B), is Pub.L. 106–554, § 1(a)(5) [Title IV, §§ 401 to 408], Dec. 21, 2000, 114 Stat. 2763, 2763A–457, which enacted 7 U.S.C.A. §§ 27 and 27a to 27f. For complete classification, see Short Title set out as a note under 7 U.S.C.A. § 1 and Tables.

Amendments

2010 Amendments. Par. (3). By notice dated Feb. 25, 2010, 75 F.R. 8747, dollar amount adjusted by the Judicial Conference of the United States which adjusted "$164,250" to "$175,750". See 11 U.S.C.A. § 104 and Adjustment of Dollar Amounts notes under this section.

Par. (13A)(A). Pub.L. 111–327, § 2(a)(1)(A)(i), inserted "if used as the principal residence by the debtor" following "residential structure".

Par. (13A)(B). Pub.L. 111–327, § 2(a)(1)(A)(ii), inserted "if used as the principal residence by the debtor" following "or trailer".

Par. (18)(A). By notice published Feb. 25, 2010, 75 F.R. 8747, dollar amount adjusted by the Judicial Conference of the United States which adjusted "$3,544,525" to "$3,792,650" each time it appeared. See 11 U.S.C.A. § 104 and Adjustment of Dollar Amounts notes under this section.

Par. (18)(B)(ii). By notice published Feb. 25, 2010, 75 F.R. 8747, dollar amount adjusted by the Judicial Conference of the United States which adjusted "$3,544,525" to "$3,792,650" each time it appeared. See 11 U.S.C.A. § 104 and Adjustment of Dollar Amounts notes under this section.

Par. (19A)(A)(i). By notice published Feb. 25, 2010, 75 F.R. 8747, dollar amount adjusted by the Judicial Conference of the United States which adjusted "$1,642,500" to "$1,757,475" each time it appeared. See 11 U.S.C.A. § 104 and Adjustment of Dollar Amounts notes under this section.

Par. (19A)(B)(ii)(II). By notice published Feb. 25, 2010, 75 F.R. 8747, dollar amount adjusted by the Judicial Conference of the United States which adjusted "$1,642,500" to "$1,757,475" each time it appeared. See 11 U.S.C.A. § 104 and Adjustment of Dollar Amounts notes under this section.

Par. (35)(B). Pub.L. 111–327, § 2(a)(1)(B), struck out "(23) and (35)" and inserted "(21B) and (33)(A)".

Par. (40B). Pub.L. 111–327, § 2(a)(1)(C), struck out "written document relating to a patient or a" and inserted "record relating to a patient, including a written document or a".

Par. (42). Pub.L. 111–327, § 2(a)(1)(D), which directed the substitution of "303 and 1504" for "303, and 304", was executed by making the substitution for "303, or 304" to reflect the probable intent of Congress.

Par. (51B). Pub.L. 111–327, § 2(a)(1)(E), inserted "thereto" before the period at the end.

Par. (51D). By notice published Feb. 25, 2010, 75 F.R. 8747, dollar amount adjusted by the Judicial Conference of the United States which adjusted "$2,190,000" to "$2,343,300" each time it appeared. See 11 U.S.C.A. § 104 and Adjustment of Dollar Amounts notes under this section.

Par. (51D)(A). Pub.L. 111–327, § 2(a)(1)(F), inserted "of the filing" following "debts as of the date".

2007 Amendments. Par. (3). By notice dated Feb. 14, 2007, 72 F.R. 7082, dollar amount adjusted by the Judicial Conference of the United States which adjusted "$150,000" to "$164,250". See 11 U.S.C.A. § 104 and Adjustment of Dollar Amounts notes under this section.

Par. (18)(A). By notice published Feb. 14, 2007, 72 F.R. 7082, dollar amount adjusted by the Judicial Conference of the United States which adjusted "$3,237,000" to "$3,544,525" each time it appeared. See 11 U.S.C.A. § 104 and Adjustment of Dollar Amounts notes under this section.

Par. (18)(B)(ii). By notice published Feb. 14, 2007, 72 F.R. 7082, dollar amount adjusted by the Judicial Conference of the United States which adjusted "$3,237,000" to "$3,544,525" each time it appeared. See 11 U.S.C.A. § 104 and Adjustment of Dollar Amounts notes under this section.

Par. (19A)(A)(i). By notice published Feb. 14, 2007, 72 F.R. 7082, dollar amount adjusted by the Judicial Conference of the United States which adjusted "$1,500,000" to "$1,642,500" each time it appeared. See 11 U.S.C.A. § 104 and Adjustment of Dollar Amounts notes under this section.

Par. (19A)(B)(ii)(II). By notice published Feb. 14, 2007, 72 F.R. 7082, dollar amount adjusted by the Judicial Conference of the United States which adjusted "$1,500,000" to "$1,642,500" each time it appeared. See 11 U.S.C.A. § 104 and Adjustment of Dollar Amounts notes under this section.

Par. (51D). By notice published Feb. 14, 2007, 72 F.R. 7082, dollar amount adjusted by the Judicial Conference of the United States which adjusted "$2,000,000" to "$2,190,000" each time it appeared. See 11 U.S.C.A. § 104 and Adjustment of Dollar Amounts notes under this section.

2006 Amendments. Par. (22)(A). Pub.L. 109–390, § 5(a)(1)(A)(i), struck out "(domestic or foreign)" after "an entity".

Pub.L. 109–390, § 5(a)(1)(A)(ii), inserted "(whether or not a 'customer', as defined in section 741)" after "custodian for a customer".

Par. (22A)(A). Pub.L. 109–390, § 5(a)(1)(B)(i), struck out "on any day during the previous 15–month period" following "actual principal amount outstanding" and following "(other than an affiliate)" and inserted "at such time or on any day during the 15–month period preceding the date of the filing of the petition".

Pub.L. 109–390, § 5(a)(1)(B)(ii), inserted "(aggregated across counterparties)" after "principal amount outstanding".

Par. (25)(A). Pub.L. 109–390, § 5(a)(1)(C)(i), inserted ", as defined in section 761" after "commodity contract".

Pub.L. 109–390, § 5(a)(1)(C)(ii), struck out "repurchase transaction, reverse repurchase transaction," following "but not limited to, a" and inserted "repurchase or reverse repurchase transaction (whether or not such repurchase or reverse repurchase transaction is a 'repurchase agreement', as defined in this section)".

Par. (53B)(A)(i)(II). Pub.L. 109–390, § 5(a)(1)(D)(i)(I), struck out "or precious metals" following "or other foreign exchange" and inserted ", precious metals, or other commodity".

Par. (53B)(A)(i)(VII). Pub.L. 109–390, § 5(a)(1)(D)(i)(II), struck out "or" at the end.

Par. (53B)(A)(i)(VIII). Pub.L. 109–390, § 5(a)(1)(D)(i)(III), struck out "weather derivative, or weather option" following "weather swap," and inserted "option, future, or forward agreement".

Par. (53B)(A)(i)(IX). Pub.L. 109–390, § 5(a)(1)(D)(i)(IV), added subcl. (IX).

Par. (53B)(A)(i)(X). Pub.L. 109–390, § 5(a)(1)(D)(i)(IV), added subcl. (X).

Par. (53B)(A)(ii)(I). Pub.L. 109–390, § 5(a)(1)(D)(ii)(I), inserted "or other derivatives" after "dealings in the swap".

Par. (53B)(A)(ii)(II). Pub.L. 109–390, § 5(a)(1)(D)(ii)(II), struck out "future, or option" following "is a forward, swap," and inserted "future, option, or spot transaction".

Par. (53B)(B). Pub.L. 109–390, § 5(a)(1)(E), struck out "the Securities Act of 1933, the Securities Exchange Act of 1934, the Public Utility Holding Company Act of 1935, the Trust Indenture Act of 1939, the Investment Company Act of 1940, the Investment Advisers Act of 1940, the Securities Investor Protection Act of 1970, the Commodity Exchange Act, the Gramm–Leach–Bliley Act, and the Legal Certainty for Bank Products Act of 2000" following "or rule, including" and inserted "the Gramm–Leach–Bliley Act, the Legal Certainty for Bank Products Act of 2000, the securities laws (as such term is defined in section 3(a)(47) of the Securities Exchange Act of 1934) and the Commodity Exchange Act".

2005 Amendments. Pub.L. 109–8, § 1201(1), in the matter preceding par. (1), struck out "In this title—" and inserted "In this title the following definitions shall apply:".

Pars. (1), (2). Pub.L. 109–8, § 1201(2), (8), inserted "The term" after the paragraph designations and substituted a period for a semicolon at the end of each paragraph.

Par. (3). Pub.L. 109–8, § 226(a)(1), added par. (3).

Pub.L. 109–8, § 1201(2), (8), inserted "The term" after the paragraph designation and substituted a period for a semicolon at the end.

Par. (4).   Pub.L. 109–8, § 1201(2), (8), inserted "The term" after the paragraph designation and substituted a period for a semicolon at the end.

Par. (4A).   Pub.L. 109–8, § 226(a)(2), added par. (4A).

Pub.L. 109–8, § 1201(2), (8), inserted "The term" after the paragraph designation and substituted a period for a semicolon at the end.

Pars. (5) to (7).   Pub.L. 109–8, § 1201(2), (8), inserted "The term" after the paragraph designations and substituted a period for a semicolon at the end of each paragraph.

Par. (7A).   Pub.L. 109–8, § 1007(a)(1), added par. (7A).

Pub.L. 109–8, § 1201(2), (8), inserted "The term" after the paragraph designation and substituted a period for a semicolon at the end.

Par. (7B).   Pub.L. 109–8, § 1007(a)(1), added par. (7B).

Pub.L. 109–8, § 1201(2), (8), inserted "The term" after the paragraph designation and substituted a period for a semicolon at the end.

Pars. (8) to (10).   Pub.L. 109–8, § 1201(2), (8), inserted "The term" after the paragraph designations and substituted a period for a semicolon at the end of each paragraph.

Par. (10A).   Pub.L. 109–8, § 102(b), added par. (10A).

Pub.L. 109–8, § 1201(2), (8), inserted "The term" after the paragraph designation and substituted a period for a semicolon at the end.

Pars. (11), (12).   Pub.L. 109–8, § 1201(2), (8), inserted "The term" after the paragraph designations and substituted a period for a semicolon at the end of each paragraph.

Par. (12A).   Pub.L. 109–8, § 211(1), struck out par. (12A), which formerly read: " 'debt for child support' means a debt of a kind specified in section 523(a)(5) of this title for maintenance or support of a child of the debtor;".

Pub.L. 109–8, § 1201(2), inserted "The term" after the paragraph designation.

Pub.L. 109–8, § 1201(8), which directed the substitution of a period for a semicolon at the end, could not be executed because par. (12A) ended in a period after amendment by Pub.L. 109–8, § 226(a)(3). See below.

Pub.L. 109–8, § 226(a)(3), added par. (12A) relating to "debt relief agency".

Par. (13).   Pub.L. 109–8, § 1201(2), (8), inserted "The term" after the paragraph designation and substituted a period for a semicolon at the end.

Par. (13A).   Pub.L. 109–8, § 306(c)(1), added par. (13A).

Pub.L. 109–8, § 1201(2), (8), inserted "The term" after the paragraph designation and substituted a period for a semicolon at the end.

Par. (14).   Pub.L. 109–8, § 414, rewrote par. (14), which formerly read:

"(14) "disinterested person" means person that—

"(A) is not a creditor, an equity security holder, or an insider;

"(B) is not and was not an investment banker for any outstanding security of the debtor;

"(C) has not been, within three years before the date of the filing of the petition, an investment banker for a security of the debtor, or an attorney for such an invest-

ment banker in connection with the offer, sale, or issuance of a security of the debtor;

"(D) is not and was not, within two years before the date of the filing of the petition, a director, officer, or employee of the debtor or of an investment banker specified in subparagraph (B) or (C) of this paragraph; and

"(E) does not have an interest materially adverse to the interest of the estate or of any class of creditors or equity security holders, by reason of any direct or indirect relationship to, connection with, or interest in, the debtor or an investment banker specified in subparagraph (B) or (C) of this paragraph, or for any other reason;".

Par. (14).   Pub.L. 109–8, § 1201(2), (8), inserted "The term" after the paragraph designation and substituted a period for a semicolon at the end.

Par. (14A).   Pub.L. 109–8, § 211(2), added par. (14A).

Pub.L. 109–8, § 1201(2), (8), inserted "The term" after the paragraph designation and substituted a period for a semicolon at the end.

Pars. (15) to (17).   Pub.L. 109–8, § 1201(2), (8), inserted "The term" after the paragraph designations and substituted a period for a semicolon at the end of each paragraph.

Par. (18).   Pub.L. 109–8, § 1201(2), (8), inserted "The term" after the paragraph designation and substituted a period for a semicolon at the end.

Par. (18)(A).   Pub.L. 109–8, §§ 1004(1), 1005, struck out "$1,500,000" and inserted "$3,237,000", struck out "80" and inserted "50", and struck out "for the taxable year preceding the taxable year" and inserted the following:

"for—

"(i) the taxable year preceding; or

"(ii) each of the 2d and 3d taxable years preceding; the taxable year".

Par. (18)(B)(ii).   Pub.L. 109–8, § 1004(2), struck out "$1,500,000" and inserted "$3,237,000" and struck out "80" and inserted "50".

Par. (19).   Pub.L. 109–8, § 1201(2), (8), inserted "The term" after the paragraph designation and substituted a period for a semicolon at the end.

Par. (19A).   Pub.L. 109–8, § 1007(a)(2), added par. (19A).

Pub.L. 109–8, § 1201(2), (8), inserted "The term" after the paragraph designation and substituted a period for a semicolon at the end.

Par. (19B).   Pub.L. 109–8, § 1007(a)(2), added par. (19B).

Pub.L. 109–8, § 1201(2), (8), inserted "The term" after the paragraph designation and substituted a period for a semicolon at the end.

Pars. (20) to (21B).   Pub.L. 109–8, § 1201(2), (8), inserted "The term" after the paragraph designations and substituted a period for a semicolon at the end of each paragraph.

Par. (22).   Pub.L. 109–8, § 907(b)(1), rewrote par. (22), which formerly read:

"(22) the term 'financial institution'—

"(A) means—

"(i) a Federal reserve bank or an entity (domestic or foreign) that is a commercial or savings bank, industrial savings bank, savings and loan association, trust company, or receiver or conservator for such entity and, when any such Federal reserve bank, receiver, conservator, or entity is acting as agent or custodian for a customer in

11 § 101 BANKRUPTCY CODE — Title 11

connection with a securities contract, as defined in section 741 of this title, the customer; or

"**(ii)** in connection with a securities contract, as defined in section 741 of this title, an investment company registered under the Investment Company Act of 1940; and

"**(B)** includes any person described in subparagraph (A) which operates, or operates as, a multilateral clearing organization pursuant to section 409 of the Federal Deposit Insurance Corporation Improvement Act of 1991;".

Pub.L. 109–8, § 1201(2), (8), inserted "The term" after the paragraph designation and substituted a period for a semicolon at the end.

Par. (22A). Pub.L. 109–8, § 907(b)(2), added par. (22A).

Pub.L. 109–8, § 1201(2), (8), inserted "The term" after the paragraph designation and substituted a period for a semicolon at the end.

Par. (23). Pub.L. 109–8, § 802(b), rewrote par. (23), which formerly read: " 'foreign proceeding' means proceeding, whether judicial or administrative and whether or not under bankruptcy law, in a foreign country in which the debtor's domicile, residence, principal place of business, or principal assets were located at the commencement of such proceeding, for the purpose of liquidating an estate, adjusting debts by composition, extension, or discharge, or effecting a reorganization;".

Pub.L. 109–8, § 1201(2), (8), inserted "The term" after the paragraph designation and substituted a period for a semicolon at the end.

Par. (24). Pub.L. 109–8, § 802(b), rewrote par. (24), which formerly read: " 'foreign representative' means duly selected trustee, administrator, or other representative of an estate in a foreign proceeding;".

Pub.L. 109–8, § 1201(2), (8), inserted "The term" after the paragraph designation and substituted a period for a semicolon at the end.

Par. (25). Pub.L. 109–8, § 907(a)(1)(A)(i), (ii), struck out "means a contract" and inserted "means—"(A) a contract"; and struck out ", or any combination thereof or option thereon;" and inserted ", or any other similar agreement;".

Pub.L. 109–8, § 1201(2), (8), inserted "The term" after the paragraph designation and substituted a period for a semicolon at the end.

Par. (25)(B). Pub.L. 109–8, § 907(a)(1)(A)(iii), added subpar. (B).

Par. (25)(C). Pub.L. 109–8, § 907(a)(1)(A)(iii), added subpar. (C).

Par. (25)(D). Pub.L. 109–8, § 907(a)(1)(A)(iii), added subpar. (D).

Par. (25)(E). Pub.L. 109–8, § 907(a)(1)(A)(iii), added subpar. (E).

Par. (26). Pub.L. 109–8, § 907(b)(3), rewrote par. (26), which formerly read: " 'forward contract merchant' means a person whose business consists in whole or in part of entering into forward contracts as or with merchants in a commodity, as defined in section 761(8) of this title, or any similar good, article, service, right, or interest which is presently or in the future becomes the subject of dealing in the forward contract trade;".

Pub.L. 109–8, § 1201(2), (8), inserted "The term" after the paragraph designation and substituted a period for a semicolon at the end.

Par. (27). Pub.L. 109–8, § 1201(2), (8), inserted "The term" after the paragraph designation and substituted a period for a semicolon at the end.

Par. (27A). Pub.L. 109–8, § 306(c)(2), added par. (27A) relating to "incidental property".

Pub.L. 109–8, § 1201(2), (8), inserted "The term" after the paragraph designation and substituted a period for a semicolon at the end.

Pub.L. 109–8, § 1101(a), redesignated par. (27A) relating to "incidental property" as par. (27B), and added a new par. (27A) relating to "health care business".

Par. (27B). Pub.L. 109–8, § 1101(a)(1), redesignated par. (27A) relating to "incidental property" as par. (27B).

Pub.L. 109–8, § 1201(2), (8), inserted "The term" after the paragraph designation and substituted a period for a semicolon at the end.

Pars. (28) to (34). Pub.L. 109–8, § 1201(2), (8), inserted "The term" after the paragraph designations and substituted a period for a semicolon at the end of each paragraph.

Par. (35). Pub.L. 109–8, § 1201(2), (8), inserted "The term" after the paragraph designation and substituted a period for a semicolon at the end.

Par. (35)(B). Pub.L. 109–8, § 1201(3), struck out "paragraphs (21B) and (33)(A)" and inserted "paragraphs (23) and (35)".

Par. (35A). Pub.L. 109–8, § 1201(4), struck out "; and" at the end and inserted a period.

Pars. (36), (37). Pub.L. 109–8, § 1201(2), (8), inserted "The term" after the paragraph designations and substituted a period for a semicolon at the end of each paragraph.

Par. (38). Pub.L. 109–8, § 1201(2), (4), inserted "The term" after the paragraph designation and substituted a period for "; and" at the end.

Par. (38A). Pub.L. 109–8, § 907(c), added par. (38A).

Pub.L. 109–8, § 1201(2), (8), inserted "The term" after the paragraph designation and substituted a period for a semicolon at the end.

Par. (38B). Pub.L. 109–8, § 907(c), added par. (38B).

Pub.L. 109–8, § 1201(2), (8), inserted "The term" after the paragraph designation and substituted a period for a semicolon at the end.

Par. (39). Pub.L. 109–8, § 1201(2), inserted "The term" after the paragraph designation.

Par. (39A). Pub.L. 109–8, § 102(k), added par. (39A).

Pub.L. 109–8, § 1201(2), (8), inserted "The term" after the paragraph designation and substituted a period for a semicolon at the end.

Par. (40). Pub.L. 109–8, § 1201(2), (8), inserted "The term" after the paragraph designation and substituted a period for a semicolon at the end.

Par. (40A). Pub.L. 109–8, § 1101(b), added par. (40A).

Pub.L. 109–8, § 1201(2), (8), inserted "The term" after the paragraph designation and substituted a period for a semicolon at the end.

Par. (40B). Pub.L. 109–8, § 1101(b), added par. (40B).

Pub.L. 109–8, § 1201(2), (8), inserted "The term" after the paragraph designation and substituted a period for a semicolon at the end.

Par. (41). Pub.L. 109–8, § 1201(2), (8), inserted "The term" after the paragraph designation and substituted a period for a semicolon at the end.

Par. (41A). Pub.L. 109–8, § 231(b), added par. (41A).

Pub.L. 109–8, § 1201(2), (8), inserted "The term" after the paragraph designation and substituted a period for a semicolon at the end.

Pars. (42) to (45). Pub.L. 109–8, § 1201(2), (8), inserted "The term" after the paragraph designations and substituted a period for a semicolon at the end of each paragraph.

Par. (46). Pub.L. 109–8, § 907(a)(1)(B), struck out "on any day during the period beginning 90 days before the date of" and inserted "at any time before".

Pub.L. 109–8, § 1201(2), (8), inserted "The term" after the paragraph designation and substituted a period for a semicolon at the end.

Par. (47). Pub.L. 109–8, § 907(a)(1)(C), rewrote par. (47), which formerly read: " 'repurchase agreement' (which definition also applies to a reverse repurchase agreement) means an agreement, including related terms, which provides for the transfer of certificates of deposit, eligible bankers' acceptances, or securities that are direct obligations of, or that are fully guaranteed as to principal and interest by, the United States or any agency of the United States against the transfer of funds by the transferee of such certificates of deposit, eligible bankers' acceptances, or securities with a simultaneous agreement by such transferee to transfer to the transferor thereof certificates of deposit, eligible bankers' acceptances, or securities as described above, at a date certain not later than one year after such transfers or on demand, against the transfer of funds;".

Pub.L. 109–8, § 1201(2), (8), inserted "The term" after the paragraph designation and substituted a period for a semicolon at the end.

Par. (48). Pub.L. 109–8, § 907(a)(1)(D), inserted ", or exempt from such registration under such section pursuant to an order of the Securities and Exchange Commission," after "1934".

Pub.L. 109–8, § 1201(2), (8), inserted "The term" after the paragraph designation and substituted a period for a semicolon at the end.

Par. (48A). Pub.L. 109–8, § 401(a), added par. (48A).

Pub.L. 109–8, § 1201(2), (8), inserted "The term" after the paragraph designation and substituted a period for a semicolon at the end.

Pars. (49) to (51A). Pub.L. 109–8, § 1201(2), (8), inserted "The term" after the paragraph designations and substituted a period for a semicolon at the end of each paragraph.

Par. (51B). Pub.L. 109–8, § 1201(2), (5), (8), inserted "The term" after the paragraph designation, inserted "who is not a family farmer" after "debtor" the first place it appeared, and struck out "thereto having aggregate noncontingent, liquidated secured debts in an amount no more than $4,000,000." and inserted a period.

Par. (51C). Pub.L. 109–8, § 432(a), struck out par. (51C), which formerly read: " 'small business' means a person engaged in commercial or business activities (but does not include a person whose primary activity is the business of owning or operating real property and activities incidental thereto) whose aggregate noncontingent liquidated secured and unsecured debts as of the date of the petition do not exceed $2,000,000;"; and added new par. (51C).

Pub.L. 109–8, § 1201(2), (8), inserted "The term" after the paragraph designation and substituted a period for a semicolon at the end.

Par. (51D). Pub.L. 109–8, § 432(a), added par. (51D).

Pub.L. 109–8, § 1201(2), (8), inserted "The term" after the paragraph designation and substituted a period for a semicolon at the end.

Pars. (52) to (53A). Pub.L. 109–8, § 1201(2), (8), inserted "The term" after the paragraph designations and substituted a period for a semicolon at the end of each paragraph.

Par. (53B). Pub.L. 109–8, § 907(a)(1)(E), rewrote par. (53B), which formerly read:

"(53B) 'swap agreement' means—

"(A) an agreement (including terms and conditions incorporated by reference therein) which is a rate swap agreement, basis swap, forward rate agreement, commodity swap, interest rate option, forward foreign exchange agreement, spot foreign exchange agreement, rate cap agreement, rate floor agreement, rate collar agreement, currency swap agreement, cross-currency rate swap agreement, currency option, any other similar agreement (including any option to enter into any of the foregoing);

"(B) any combination of the foregoing; or

"(C) a master agreement for any of the foregoing together with all supplements;".

Pub.L. 109–8, § 1201(2), (8), inserted "The term" after the paragraph designation and substituted a period for a semicolon at the end.

Pars. (53C), (53D). Pub.L. 109–8, § 1201(2), (8), inserted "The term" after the paragraph designations and substituted a period for a semicolon at the end of each paragraph.

Par. (54). Pub.L. 109–8, § 1201(2), inserted "The term" after the paragraph designation.

Pub.L. 109–8, § 1201(6), rewrote par. (54), which formerly read: " 'transfer' means every mode, direct or indirect, absolute or conditional, voluntary or involuntary, of disposing of or parting with property or with an interest in property, including retention of title as a security interest and foreclosure of the debtor's equity of redemption;".

Pub.L. 109–8, § 1201(8), substituted a period for a semicolon at the end.

Par. (54A). Pub.L. 109–8, § 1201(4), (7), struck out "; and" at the end and inserted a period, struck out "the term" and inserted "The term", and indented the left margin 2 ems to the right, requiring no change in text.

Pub.L. 109–8, § 1201(8), which directed the substitution of a period for a semicolon at the end, could not be executed because par. (54A) ended in a period after amendment by Pub.L. 109–8, § 1201(4). § See below.

Par. (55). Pub.L. 109–8, § 1201(2), (8), inserted "The term" after the paragraph designation and substituted a period for a semicolon at the end.

Par. (56A). Pub.L. 109–8, § 1201(2), inserted "The term" after the paragraph designation.

Pub.L. 109–8, § 1201(8), which directed the substitution of a period for a semicolon "in each of paragraphs (40) through (55)" at end, was executed to par. (56A), to reflect the probable intent of Congress, because par. (56A) follows par. (53C) in text.

2000 Amendments. Par. (22). Pub.L. 106–554, § 1(a)(5) [Title I, § 112(c)(3)], rewrote par. (22), which formerly read:

" 'financial institution' means a person that is a commercial or savings bank, industrial savings bank, savings and loan association, or trust company and, when any such person is acting as agent or custodian for a customer in connection with a securities contract, as defined in section 741 of this title, such customer;".

Par. (54A). Pub.L. 106–554, § 1(a)(5) [Title I, § 112(c)(4)], added par. (54A).

1994 Amendments. Par. (3). Pub.L. 103–394, § 501(a)(1), redesignated former par. (3) as (21B).

Par. (6). Pub.L. 103–394, § 501(b)(1)(A), substituted "761" for "761(9)".

Par. (12A). Pub.L. 103–394, § 304(a), added par. (12A).

Par. (21B). Pub.L. 103–394, § 501(a)(1), redesignated former par. (3) as (21B).

Par. (22). Pub.L. 103–394, § 501(b)(1)(B), substituted "741" for "741(7)".

Par. (33)(A). Pub.L. 103–394, § 501(d)(1)(A)(i), struck out "(12 U.S.C. 1813(u))" following "section 3(u) of the Federal Deposit Insurance Act".

Par. (33)(B). Pub.L. 103–394, § 501(d)(1)(A)(ii), struck out "(12 U.S.C. 1786(r))" following "Federal Credit Union Act".

Par. (34). Pub.L. 103–394, § 501(d)(1)(B), struck out "(12 U.S.C. 1752(7))" following "Federal Credit Union Act".

Par. (35)(A). Pub.L. 103–394, § 501(d)(1)(C), struck out "(12 U.S.C. 1813(c)(2))" following "Federal Deposit Insurance Act".

Par. (35)(B). Pub.L. 103–394, § 501(b)(1)(C), substituted "paragraphs (21B)" for " paragraphs (3)".

Par. (35A). Pub.L. 103–394, § 501(a)(4), redesignated former par. (56), defining "intellectual property", as (35A).

Par. (39). Pub.L. 103–394, § 501(a)(2), redesignated former par. (39) as (51A).

Pub.L. 103–394, § 501(a)(5), redesignated former par. (57), defining "mask work", as (39).

Par. (41). Pub.L. 103–394, § 106, added par. (41) and struck out former par. (41) which read as follows: "'person' includes individual, partnership, and corporation, but does not include governmental unit, *Provided, however,* That any governmental unit that acquires an asset from a person as a result of operation of a loan guarantee agreement, or as receiver or liquidating agent of a person, will be considered a person for purposes of section 1102 of this title."

Par. (42A). Pub.L. 103–394, § 208(a)(1), added par. (42A).

Par. (48). Pub.L. 103–394, § 501(d)(1)(D), struck out "(15 U.S.C. 78q–1)" following "Securities Exchange Act of 1934", and "(15 U.S.C. 78c(12))" following "section 3(a)(12) of such Act".

Par. (49)(A)(xii). Pub.L. 103–394, § 501(d)(1)(E)(i), struck out "(15 U.S.C. 77a et seq.)" following "Securities Act of 1933", and "(15 U.S.C. 77c(b))" following "section 3(b) of such Act".

Par. (49)(B)(ii). Pub.L. 103–394, § 501(b)(1)(D), substituted "section 761" for "section 761(13)".

Par. (49)(B)(vi). Pub.L. 103–394, § 501(d)(1)(E)(ii), struck out "(15 U.S.C. 77c(b))" following "Securities Act of 1933".

Par. (51A). Pub.L. 103–394, § 501(a)(2), redesignated former par. (39) as (51A).

Par. (51B). Pub.L. 103–394, § 218(a), added par. (51B).

Par. (51C). Pub.L. 103–394, § 217(a), added par. (51C).

Par. (53A)(A). Pub.L. 103–394, § 501(b)(1)(E), substituted "section 741" for "section 741(2)".

Par. (53A). Pub.L. 103–394, § 501(a)(3), redesignated former par. (54), defining "stockbroker", as (53A).

Par. (53B). Pub.L. 103–394, § 501(a)(3), redesignated former par. (55), defining "swap agreement", as (53B).

Par. (53C). Pub.L. 103–394, § 501(a)(3), redesignated former par. (56), defining "swap participant", as (53C).

Par. (53D). Pub.L. 103–394, § 501(a)(3), redesignated former par. (57), defining "timeshare plan", as (53D).

Pub.L. 103–394, § 501(d)(1)(F), substituted "timeshare plan;" for "timeshare plan.".

Par. (54). Pub.L. 103–394, § 501(a)(3), redesignated former par. (54), defining "stockbroker", as (53A).

Par. (55)(A). Pub.L. 103–394, § 215, in par. (55) relating to swap agreement, included agreement which is a spot foreign exchange agreement within definition.

Par. (55). Pub.L. 103–394, § 501(a)(3), redesignated former par. (55), defining "swap agreement", as (53B).

Par. (56). Pub.L. 103–394, § 501(a)(3), redesignated former par. (56), defining "swap participant", as (53C).

Pub.L. 103–394, § 501(a)(4), redesignated former par. (56), defining "intellectual property", as (35A).

Par. (56A). Pub.L. 103–394, § 208(a)(2), added par. (56A), following par. (56) relating to "swap participant".

Par. (57). Pub.L. 103–394, § 501(a)(3), redesignated former par. (57), defining "timeshare plan", as (53D).

Pub.L. 103–394, § 501(a)(5), redesignated former par. (57), defining "mask work", as (39).

1992 Amendments. Par. (21A). Pub.L. 102–486, § 3017(a), added par. (21A).

1990 Amendments. Par. (3). Pub.L. 101–647, § 2522(e)(4), added par. (3). Former par. (3) redesignated (4).

Pars. (4) to (23). Pub.L. 101–647, § 2522(e)(3), redesignated pars. (3) to (22) as (4) to (23). Former par. (23) redesignated (24).

Par. (24). Pub.L. 101–647, § 2522(e)(3), redesignated par. (23) as (24). Former par. (24) redesignated (25).

Pub.L. 101–311, § 201(1), added provisions relating to section 761(8) of this title and similar goods, articles, etc., which are or will be the subject of dealing in a forward contract trade, and provisions relating to repurchase transactions, reverse repurchase transactions, etc.

Par. (25). Pub.L. 101–647, § 2522(e)(3), redesignated par. (24) as (25). Former par. (25) redesignated (26).

Pub.L. 101–311, § 201(2), substituted "a commodity, as defined in section 761(8) of this title, or any similar good, article, service, right, or interest which is presently or in the future becomes the subject of dealing in the forward contract trade" for "commodities".

Par. (26) to (32). Pub.L. 101–647, § 2522(e)(3), redesignated pars. (25) to (31) as (26) to (32), respectively. Former par. (32) redesignated (36).

Par. (33). Pub.L. 101–647, § 2522(e)(2), added par. (33). Former par. (33) redesignated (37).

Par. (34). Pub.L. 101–647, § 2522(e)(2), added par. (34). Former par. (34) redesignated (38).

Pub.L. 101–311, § 201(4), added par. (34). Former par. (34) redesignated (36).

Par. (35). Pub.L. 101–647, § 2522(e)(2), added par. (35). Former par. (35) redesignated (39).

Pub.L. 101–311, § 201(4), added par. (35). Former par. (35) redesignated (37).

Par. (36). Pub.L. 101–647, § 2522(e)(1), redesignated par. (32) as (36). Former par. (36) redesignated (40).

Pub.L. 101–311, § 201(3), redesignated par. (34) as (36). Former par. (36) redesignated (38).

Pars. (37) to (48). Pub.L. 101–647, § 2522(e)(1), redesignated pars. (33) to (44) as (37) to (48), respectively. Former pars. (37) to (48) redesignated (41) to (52), respectively.

Pub.L. 101–311, § 201(3), redesignated former pars. (35) through (48) as (37) through (50), respectively. Former pars. (37) to (48) redesignated (39) to (50), respectively.

Pars. (49), (50). Pub.L. 101–647, § 2522(e)(1), redesignated former pars. (45) and (46) as (49) and (50), respectively. Former pars. (49) and (50) redesignated (53) and (54), both respectively defining "stockbroker".

Pub.L. 101–311, § 201(3), redesignated pars. (47) and (48) as (49) and (50), respectively. Former pars. (49) and (50) redesignated as (51) and (52), respectively.

Pub.L. 101–311, § 101, added pars. (49) and (50). Former pars. (49) and (50) redesignated as (51) and (52), respectively.

Par. (51). Pub.L. 101–647, § 2522(e)(1), redesignated par. (47) as (51). Former par. (51) redesignated as (55) defining "swap agreement".

Pub.L. 101–311, § 201(3), redesignated par. (49) as (51). Former par. (51) redesignated as (53).

Pub.L. 101–311, § 101(1), redesignated par. (49) as (51). Former par. (51) redesignated as (53).

Par. (52). Pub.L. 101–647, § 2522(e)(1), redesignated par. (48) as (52). Former par. (52) redesignated as (56) defining "swap participant".

Pub.L. 101–311, § 201(3), redesignated par. (50) as (52). Former par. (52) redesignated as (54) defining "transfer".

Pub.L. 101–311, § 101(1), redesignated par. (50) as (52). Former par. (52) redesignated as (54).

Par. (53). Pub.L. 101–647, § 2522(e)(1), redesignated par. (49) as (53). Former par. (53) redesignated as (57) defining "timeshare plan".

Pub.L. 101–311, § 201(3), redesignated par. (51) as (53). Former par. (53) redesignated as (55) defining "United States".

Pub.L. 101–311, § 101(1), redesignated par. (51) as (53). Former par. (53) redesignated as (55).

Par. (54). Pub.L. 101–647, § 2522(e)(1), redesignated par. (50) as (54) defining "stockbroker".

Pub.L. 101–311, § 201(3), redesignated par. (52) as (54) defining "transfer". Former par. (54) redesignated as (56) defining "intellectual property").

Pub.L. 101–311, § 101(1), redesignated par. (52) as (54).

Par. (55). Pub.L. 101–647, § 2522(e)(1), redesignated par. (51) as (55) defining "swap agreement".

Pub.L. 101–311, § 201(3), redesignated par. (53) as (55). Former par. (55) redesignated as (57) defining "mask work".

Pub.L. 101–311, § 101(1), redesignated par. (53) as (55).

Par. (56). Pub.L. 101–647, § 2522(e)(1), redesignated par. (52) as (56) defining "swap participant".

Pub.L. 101–311, § 201(3), redesignated par. (54) as (56) defining "intellectual property".

Par. (57). Pub.L. 101–647, § 2522(e)(1), redesignated par. (53) as (57) defining "timeshare plan".

Pub.L. 101–311, § 201(3), redesignated par. (55) as (57) defining "mask work".

1988 Amendments. Par. (31). Pub.L. 100–597, § 1, inserted in subpar. (A) "and a municipality" after "partnership" and added subpar. (C).

Pars. (52), (53). Pub.L. 100–506, § 1(a), added pars. (52) and (53).

1986 Amendments. Par. (14). Pub.L. 99–554, § 201(1), substituted "trust, governmental unit, and United States trustee" for "trust, and governmental unit".

Par. (17), (18). Pub.L. 99–554, § 251(2), (3), and added pars. (17) and (18) redesignated former pars. (17) and (18) as (19) and (20), respectively.

Par. (19). Pub.L. 99–554, § 251(1), (2), redesignated former par. (17) as (19) and inserted "(except when such term appears in the term 'family farmer')" following "means". Former par. (19) was redesignated (21).

Pars. (20) to (25). Pub.L. 99–554, § 251(2), redesignated former pars. (18) to (23) as (20) to (25), respectively. Former pars. (20) to (25) were redesignated as (22) to (27), respectively.

Par. (26). Pub.L. 99–554, § 201(2), substituted "of the United States (but not a United States trustee while serving as a trustee in a case under this title), a State" for "of the United States, a State".

Pub.L. 99–554, § 251(2), redesignated former par. (24) as (26). Former par. (26) was redesignated (28).

Pars. (27) to (42). Pub.L. 99–554, § 251(2), redesignated former pars. (25) to (40) as (27) to (42), respectively. Former pars. (27) to (42) were redesignated (29) to (44), respectively.

Par. (43). Pub.L. 99–554, § 251(2), redesignated former par. (41) as (43). Former par. (43) was redesignated (45).

Par. (43)(A)(xv). Pub.L. 99–554, § 283(a)(1), substituted "security" for "secuity".

Pars. (44) to (50). Pub.L. 99–554, § 251(2), redesignated former pars. (42) to (48) as (44) to (50), respectively. Former pars. (44) to (49) were redesignated (46) to (51), respectively.

Par. (51). Pub.L. 99–554, § 283(a)(2), substituted "States." for "States;".

Pub.L. 99–554, § 251(2), redesignated former par. (49) as (51).

1984 Amendments. Par. (2)(D). Pub.L. 98–353, § 421(a), struck out "or all" after "business".

Par. (8)(B). Pub.L. 98–353, § 421(b), substituted a semicolon for the colon at the end of subpar. (B).

Par. (9)(B). Pub.L. 98–353, § 421(c), added "348(d)" after "section".

Par. (14). Pub.L. 98–353, § 421(d), added "and" after "trust,".

Par. (19). Pub.L. 98–353, § 421(j)(4), added par. (19). Former par. (19) was redesignated as (20).

Pars. (20), (21). Pub.L. 98–353, § 421(j)(3), redesignated pars. (19) (20) and (21) as (20), (21) and (24) respectively.

Par. (22). Pub.L. 98–353, § 421(j)(5), added par. (22). Former par. (22) was redesignated as (25).

Par. (23). Pub.L. 98–353, § 421(j)(5), added par. (23). Former par. (23) was redesignated as (26).

Par. (24). Pub.L. 98–353, § 421(j)(2), redesignated former par. (21) as (24). Former par. (24) was redesignated as (27).

Par. (25). Pub.L. 98–353, § 421(j)(2), redesignated former par. (22) as (25). Former par. (25) was redesignated as (28).

Par. (26). Pub.L. 98–353, § 421(j)(2), redesignated former par. (23) as (26). Former par. (26) was redesignated as (29).

Par. (27). Pub.L. 98–353, § 421(e), (j)(2), redesignated former par. (24) as (27) and substituted "stockbroker" for "stock broker". Former par. (27) was redesignated as (30).

Par. (28). Pub.L. 98–353, § 421(j)(2), redesignated former par. (25) as (28). Former par. (28) was redesignated as (31).

Par. (29). Pub.L. 98–353, § 421(f), (j)(2), redesignated former par. (26) as (29) and, in subpar. (B)(ii), substituted "nonpartnership" and "(A)" for "separate" and "(A)(ii)", respectively, wherever appearing. Former par. (29) was redesignated as (32).

Par. (30). Pub.L. 98–353, § 421(j)(2), redesignated former par. (27) as (30). Former par. (30) was redesignated as (33).

Par. (31). Pub.L. 98–353, § 421(j)(2), redesignated former par. (28) as (31). Former par. (31) was redesignated as (34).

Par. (32). Pub.L. 98–353, § 421(j)(2), redesignated former par. (29) as (32). Former par. (32) was redesignated as (35).

Par. (33). Pub.L. 98–353, § 421(g), (j)(2), redesignated former par. (30) as (33) and added proviso relating to consideration of certain governmental units as persons for purposes of section 1102 of this title. Former par. (33) was redesignated as (36).

Par. (34). Pub.L. 98–353, § 421(j)(2), redesignated former par. (31) as (34). Former par. (34) redesignated (37).

Pars. (35), (36). Pub.L. 98–353, § 421(j)(2), redesignated former pars. (32) and (33) as (35) and (36), respectively. Former pars. (35) and (36), as added by Pub.L. 98–353, § 391(2), redesignated (38) and (39), respectively.

Pub.L. 98–353, § 391, added pars. (35) and (36), and redesignated former pars. (35) and (36) as (37) and (38) which were again redesignated as (40) and (41), respectively.

Par. (37). Pub.L. 98–353, § 421(j)(2), redesignated former par. (34) as (37). Former par. (37) redesignated successively as (39) and again as (42).

Par. (38). Pub.L. 98–353, §§ 391(2), 421(j)(2), added par. (35) and redesignated such par. (35) as (38). Former par. (38) redesignated successively as (40) and again as (43).

Par. (39). Pub.L. 98–353, §§ 391(2), 421(j)(2), added par. (36) and redesignated such par. (36) as (39). Former par. (39) redesignated successively as (41) and again as (45).

Par. (40). Pub.L. 98–353, §§ 391(1), 421(j)(2), redesignated successively former par. (35) as (37) and again as (40). Former par. (40) redesignated successively as (42) and again as (46).

Par. (41). Pub.L. 98–353, §§ 391(1), 401(1), 421(h), (j)(2), redesignated successively former par. (36) as (38) and again as (41), and, in subpar. (B)(vi), substituted "certificate of a kind specified in subparagraph (A)(xii)" for "certificate specified in clause (xii) of subparagraph (A)" and substituted "required to be the subject of a registration statement" for "the subject of such registration statement". Former par. (41) redesignated successively as (43), again as (44), and again as (48).

Par. (42). Pub.L. 98–353, §§ 391(1), 421(j)(2), redesignated successively former par. (37) as (39) and again as (42).

Par. (43). Pub.L. 98–353, §§ 391(1), 421(j)(2), redesignated successively former par. (38) as (40) and again as (43).

Pub.L. 98–353, § 401, redesignated former par. (43), originally par. (41), as (44), and added another par. (43) which was redesignated (47).

Par. (44). Pub.L. 98–353, § 421(j)(6), added par. (44). Former par. (44) originally was par. (41) and was redesignated successively as (43), again as (44), and again as (48).

Pars. (45), (46). Pub.L. 98–353, §§ 391(1), 421(j)(1), redesignated successively former pars. (39) and (40) as (41) and (42), and again as (45) and (46), respectively.

Par. (47). Pub.L. 98–353, §§ 401(2), 421(j)(1), added par. (43) and redesignated such par. (43) as (47).

Par. (48). Pub.L. 98–353, §§ 391(1), 401(1), 421(i), (j)(1), redesignated successively former par. (41) as (43), again as (44), and again as (48), and substituted "and foreclosure of the debtor's equity of redemption; and" for the period at the end.

Par. (49). Pub.L. 98–353, § 421(j)(7), added par. (49).

1982 Amendments. Par. (35). Pub.L. 97–222, § 1(a)(2), added par. (35). Former par. (35) was redesignated (36).

Par. (36). Pub.L. 97–222, § 1(a)(1), (b), (c), redesignated par. (35) as (36) and in par. (36) as so redesignated, substituted "is required to be the subject of a registration statement" for "is the subject of a registration statement" in subpar. (A)(xii) and substituted "forward contract" for "forward commodity contract" in subpar. (B)(iii). Former par. (36) was redesignated (37).

Pars. (37) to (39). Pub.L. 97–222, § 1(a)(1), redesignated pars. (36) to (38) as (37) to (39), respectively. Former pars. (37) to (39) were redesignated (38) to (40), respectively.

Par. (40). Pub.L. 97–222, § 1(a)(1), (d), redesignated par. (39) as (40) and in par. (40) as so redesignated restructured its provisions by dividing the former introductory provisions into subpars. (A) and (B) and by redesignating former subpars. (A) and (B) as cls. (i) and (ii), respectively, of subpar. (B). Former par. (40) was redesignated (41).

Par. (41). Pub.L. 97–222, § 1(a)(1), redesignated par. (40) as (41).

Effective and Applicability Provisions

2010 Acts. Increase of dollar amounts by Judicial Conference of the United States by notice published Feb. 25, 2010, 75 F.R. 8747 effective April 1, 2010, and increase not applicable to cases commenced before the effective date of the adjustments, i.e., April 1, 2010. See Adjustment of Dollar Amounts notes under 11 U.S.C.A. § 104 and this section.

2007 Acts. Increase of dollar amounts by Judicial Conference of the United States by notice published Feb. 14, 2007, 72 F.R. 7082 effective April 1, 2007, and increase not applicable to cases commenced before the effective date of the adjustments, i.e., April 1, 2007. See Adjustment of Dollar Amounts notes under 11 U.S.C.A. § 104 and this section.

2005 Acts. Pub.L. 109–8, Title XV, § 1501, Apr. 20, 2005, 119 Stat. 216, provided that:

"(a) **Effective date.**—Except as otherwise provided in this Act, this Act and the amendments made by this Act [see Tables for classification] shall take effect 180 days after the date of enactment of this Act [Apr. 20, 2005].

"(b) **Application of amendments.**—

"(1) **In general.**—Except as otherwise provided in this Act and paragraph (2), the amendments made by this Act [see Tables for classification] shall not apply with respect to cases commenced under title 11, United States Code, before the effective date of this Act.

"**(2) Certain limitations applicable to debtors.**—The amendments made by sections 308 [amending 11 § 522], 322 [amending 11 U.S.C.A. §§ 104 and 522], and 330 [amending 11 U.S.C.A. §§ 727, 1141, 1228, and 1328] shall apply with respect to cases commenced under title 11, United States Code, on or after the date of the enactment of this Act [Apr. 20, 2005]."

1994 Acts. Section 702 of Pub.L. 103–394 provided that:

"**(a) Effective date.**—Except as provided in subsection (b), this Act [see Short Title of 1994 Amendments set out under this section] shall take effect on the date of the enactment of this Act [Oct. 22, 1994].

"**(b) Application of amendments.**—(1) Except as provided in paragraph (2), the amendments made by this Act shall not apply with respect to cases commenced under title 11 of the United States Code before the date of the enactment of this Act [Oct. 22, 1994].

"(2)(A) Paragraph (1) shall not apply with respect to the amendment made by section 111 [enacting subsecs. (g) and (h) of section 524 of this title and a provision set out as a note under 11 U.S.C.A. § 524].

"**(B)** The amendments made by sections 113 and 117 [amending 11 U.S.C.A. §§ 106 and 330, respectively] shall apply with respect to cases commenced under title 11 of the United States Code before, on, and after the date of the enactment of this Act [Oct. 22, 1994].

"**(C)** Section 1110 of title 11, United States Code, as amended by section 201 of this Act [11 U.S.C.A. § 1110], shall apply with respect to any lease, as defined in such section 1110(c) as so amended, entered into in connection with a settlement of any proceeding in any case pending under title 11 of the United States Code on the date of the enactment of this Act [Oct. 22, 1994].

"**(D)** The amendments made by section 305 [amending 11 U.S.C.A. §§ 1123, 1222, 1322] shall apply only to agreements entered into after the date of enactment of this Act [Oct. 22, 1994]."

1992 Acts. Section 3017(c) of Pub.L. 102–486 provided that:

"(1) Except as provided in paragraph (2), the amendments made by this section [amending this section and 11 U.S.C.A. § 541] shall take effect on the date of the enactment of this Act [Oct. 24, 1992].

"(2) The amendments made by this section [amending this section and 11 U.S.C.A. § 541] shall not apply with respect to cases commenced under title 11 of the United States Code [this title] before the date of the enactment of this Act [Oct. 24, 1992]."

1988 Acts. Section 12 of Pub.L. 100–597 provided that:

"**(a) Effective date.**—Except as provided in subsection (b), this Act and the amendments made by this Act [enacting 11 U.S.C.A. §§ 927 to 929, amending 11 U.S.C.A. §§ 101, 109, 901, 902, 922, 926, 943, and renumbering former section 927 as 930 of this title] shall take effect on the date of the enactment of this Act [Nov. 3, 1988].

"**(b) Application of amendments.**—The amendments made by this Act shall not apply with respect to cases commenced under title 11 of the United States Code before the date of the enactment of this Act [Nov. 3, 1988]."

Section 2 of Pub.L. 100–506 provided that:

"**(a) Effective date.**—Except as provided in subsection (b), this Act and the amendments made by this Act [amending 11 U.S.C.A. §§ 101 and 365] shall take effect on the date of the enactment of this Act [Oct. 18, 1988].

"**(b) Application of amendments.**—The amendments made by this Act shall not apply with respect to any case commenced under title 11 of the United States Code before the date of the enactment of this Act [Oct. 18, 1988]."

1986 Acts. Amendment by Pub.L. 99–554 effective 30 days after Oct. 27, 1986, except as otherwise provided for, see section 302(a) of Pub.L. 99–554, set out as a note under 28 U.S.C.A. § 581.

Amendment by Pub.L. 99–554, § 201, not to become effective in or with respect to certain specified judicial districts until, or apply to cases while pending in such district before, the expiration of the 270–day period beginning 30 days after Oct. 27, 1986, or of the 30–day period beginning on the date the Attorney General certifies under section 303 of Pub.L. 99–554 the region specified in a paragraph of section 581(a) of Title 28, as amended by section 111(a) of Pub.L. 99–554, that includes such district, whichever occurs first, see section 302(d)(1) of Pub.L. 99–554, set out as a note under 28 U.S.C.A. § 581.

Amendment by Pub.L. 99–554, § 201, not to become effective in or with respect to certain specified judicial districts until, or apply to cases while pending in such district before, the expiration of the 2–year period beginning 30 days after Oct. 27, 1986, or of the 30–day period beginning on the date the Attorney General certifies under section 303 of Pub.L. 99–554 the region specified in a paragraph of section 581(a) of Title 28, as amended by section 111(a) of Pub.L. 99–554, that includes such district, whichever occurs first, see section 302(d)(2) of Pub.L. 99–554, set out as a note under 28 U.S.C.A. § 581.

Amendment by Pub.L. 99–554, § 201, not to become effective in or with respect to judicial districts established for the States of Alabama and North Carolina until, or apply to cases while pending in such district before, such district elects to be included in a bankruptcy region established in section 581(a) of Title 28, as amended by section 111(a) of Pub.L. 99–554, or Oct. 1, 2002, whichever occurs first, and, except as otherwise provided for, with respect to cases under chapters 7, 11, 12, and 13 of Title 11 commenced before 30 days after Oct. 27, 1986, and pending in a judicial district in the States of Alabama or North Carolina before any election made under section 302(d)(3)(A) of Pub.L. 99–554 by such district becomes effective or Oct. 1, 2002, whichever occurs first, amendments, by Pub.L. 99–554 not to apply until Oct. 1, 2003, or the expiration of the 1–year period beginning on the date such election becomes effective, whichever occurs first, and further, in any judicial district in Alabama or North Carolina not making the election described in section 302(d)(3)(A) of Pub.L. 99–554, any person appointed under regulations issued by the Judicial Conference to administer estates in cases under Title 11 authorized to establish, etc., a panel of private trustees, and to supervise cases and trustees in cases under chapters 7, 11, 12, and 13 of Title 11, until amendments by sections 201 to 231 of Pub.L. 99–554 effective in such district, see section 302(d)(3)(A) to (F), (H), (I) of Pub.L. 99–554, set out as a note under 28 U.S.C.A. § 581.

Amendment by Pub.L. 99–554, § 201, except as otherwise provided, with respect to cases under chapters 7, 11, 12, and 13 of Title 11 commenced before 30 days after Oct. 27, 1986, and pending in a judicial district referred to in section 581(a) of Title 28, as amended by section 111(a) of Pub.L. 99–554, for which a United States trustee is not authorized before 30 days after Oct. 27, 1986 to be appointed, not applicable until the expiration of the 3–year period beginning on Oct. 27, 1986, or of the 1–year period beginning on the date the Attorney General certifies section 303 of Pub.L. 99–554 the region specified in a paragraph of such section 581(a) that includes, such district, whichever occurs first, see section 302(e)(1), (2) of Pub.L. 99–554, set out as a note under 28 U.S.C.A. § 581.

Amendments by Pub.L. 99–554, § 251, effective 30 days after Oct. 27, 1986, but not to apply with respect to cases commenced under this title before that date, see section 302(a), (c)(1) of Pub.L. 99–554, set out as a note under 28 U.S.C.A. § 581.

Amendment by Pub.L. 99–554, § 283, effective 30 days after Oct. 27, 1986, see section 302(a) of Pub.L. 99–554, set out as a note under 28 U.S.C.A. § 581.

1984 Acts. Section 552, formerly section 553 of Title III (§§ 301 to 553) of Pub.L. 98–353, as redesignated by Pub.L. 98–531, §§ 1(2), Oct. 19, 1984, 98 Stat. 2704, eff. July 10, 1984, provided that:

"**(a)** Except as otherwise provided in this section the amendments made by this title [see Tables for classification] shall become effective to [sic] cases filed 90 days after the date of enactment of this Act [July 10, 1984].

"**(b)** The amendments made by section 426(b) [amending 11 U.S.C.A. § 303] shall become effective upon the date of enactment of this Act [July 10, 1984].

"**(c)** The amendments made by subtitle J [enacting 11 U.S.C.A. § 1113], shall become effective as provided in section 541(c) [set out as a note under 11 U.S.C.A. § 1113]."

Separability of Provisions

Section 701 of Pub.L. 103–394 provided that: "If any provision of this Act or amendment made by this Act [see Short Title of 1994 Amendments note set out under this section] or the application of such provision or amendment to any person or circumstance is held to be unconstitutional, the remaining provisions of and amendments made by this Act and the application of such other provisions and amendments to any person or circumstance shall not be affected thereby."

Section 551 of Title III (§§ 301 to 553) of Pub.L. 98–353 provided that: "If any provision of this title or any amendment made by this title [see Tables for classification], or the application thereof to any person or circumstance is held invalid, the provisions of every other part, and their application shall not be affected thereby."

Savings Provisions

Pub.L. 109–8, Title IX, § 912, as added by Pub.L. 109–390, § 5(d), Dec. 12, 2006, 120 Stat. 2698, provided that: "The meanings of terms used in this title [Title IX of the Bankruptcy Abuse Prevention and Consumer Protection Act of 2005, Pub.L. 109–8, Title IX (§§ 901 to 912), Apr. 20, 2005, 119 Stat. 146; see Tables for complete classification] are applicable for the purposes of this title only, and shall not be construed or applied so as to challenge or affect the characterization, definition, or treatment of any similar terms under any other statute, regulation, or rule, including the Gramm–Leach–Bliley Act [Pub.L. 106–102, Nov. 12, 1999, 113 Stat. 1338; see Tables for complete classification], the Legal Certainty for Bank Products Act of 2000 [Pub.L. 106–554, § 1(a)(5) (Title IV, §§ 401 to 408), Dec. 21, 2000, 114 Stat. 2763, 2763A–457, which enacted 7 U.S.C.A. §§ 27 and 27a to 27f; for complete

classification, see Short Title note set out under 7 U.S.C.A. § 1 and Tables], the securities laws (as such term is defined in section 3(a)(47) of the Securities Exchange Act of 1934) [15 U.S.C.A. § 78c(a)(47)], and the Commodity Exchange Act [Act Sept. 21, 1922, c. 369, 42 Stat. 998, as amended, which is classified principally to chapter 1 of Title 7, 7 U.S.C.A. § 1 et seq.; for complete classification, see Short Title set out as 7 U.S.C.A. § 1 and Tables]."

Short Title

2011 Amendments. Pub.L. 112–64, § 1, Dec. 13, 2011, 125 Stat. 766, provided that: "This Act [amending provisions set out as a note under 11 U.S.C.A. § 107] may be cited as the 'National Guard and Reservist Debt Relief Extension Act of 2011'."

2010 Amendments. Pub.L. 111–327, § 1, Dec. 22, 2010, 124 Stat. 3557, provided that: "This Act [amending 11 U.S.C.A. §§ 101, 103, 104, 106, 107, 109, 110, 111, 303, 308, 348, 362, 363, 505, 507, 521, 522, 523, 524, 526, 527, 541, 554, 704, 707, 723, 724, 726, 901, 1104, 1106, 1111, 1112, 1127, 1129, 1141, 1145, 1202, 1302, 1304, 1307, 1308, 1322, 1325, 1511, 1519, 1521 and 1529, 18 U.S.C.A. § 157, and 28 U.S.C.A. §§ 158, 159 and 586, and amending provisions set out as a note under 11 U.S.C.A. § 507] may be cited as the 'Bankruptcy Technical Corrections Act of 2010'."

2009 Amendments. Pub.L. 111–16, § 1, May 7, 2009, 123 Stat. 1607, provided that: "This Act [amending section 7 of the Classified Information Procedures Act (18 App. U.S.C.A. § 7), 11 U.S.C.A. §§ 109, 322, 332, 342, 521, 704, 749, and 764, 18 U.S.C.A. §§ 983, 1514, 1963, 2252A, 2339B, 3060, 3432, 3509, and 3771, 21 U.S.C.A. § 853, and 28 U.S.C.A. §§ 636, 1453, and 2107, and enacting provisions set out as a note under 11 U.S.C.A. § 109] may be cited as the 'Statutory Time–Periods Technical Amendments Act of 2009'."

2008 Amendments. Pub.L. 110–438, § 1, Oct. 20, 2008, 122 Stat. 5000, provided that: "This Act [amending 11 U.S.C.A. § 707, and enacting provisions set out as a note under 11 U.S.C.A. § 707] may be cited as the 'National Guard and Reservists Debt Relief Act of 2008'."

2006 Amendments. Pub.L. 109–439, § 1, Dec. 20, 2006, 120 Stat. 3285, provided that: "This Act [amending 11 U.S.C.A. § 1325] may be cited as the 'Religious Liberty and Charitable Donation Clarification Act of 2006'."

Pub.L. 109–390, § 1, Dec. 12, 2006, 120 Stat. 2692, provided that: "This Act [amending this section, 11 U.S.C.A. §§ 362, 546, and 741, 12 U.S.C.A. §§ 1787, 1821, 4403, and 4404, and 15 U.S.C.A. § 78eee, and enacting provisions set out as notes under this section] may be cited as the 'Financial Netting Improvements Act of 2006'."

2005 Amendments. Pub.L. 109–8, § 1(a), Apr. 20, 2005, 119 Stat. 23, provided that: "This Act [see Tables for complete classification] may be cited as the 'Bankruptcy Abuse Prevention and Consumer Protection Act of 2005'." This Act is also commonly known as the BAPCPA.

Pub.L. 109–8, Title III, § 332(a), Apr. 20, 2005, 119 Stat. 103, provided that: "This section [amending 11 U.S.C.A. § 303 and 18 U.S.C.A. § 157] may be cited as the 'Involuntary Bankruptcy Improvement Act of 2005'."

2004 Amendments. Pub.L. 108–369, § 1, Oct. 25, 2004, 118 Stat. 1749, provided that: "This Act [enacting provisions set out as a note under 11 U.S.C.A. § 1201 and amending 11 U.S.C.A. §§ 1201 to 1208, 1221 to 1231, and provisions set out as a note under 11 U.S.C.A. § 1201] may be cited as the 'Family Farmer Bankruptcy Relief Act of 2004'."

2003 Amendments. Pub.L. 108–73, § 1, Aug. 15, 2003, 117 Stat. 891, provided that: "This Act [enacting provisions set out as a note under 11 U.S.C.A. § 1201 and amending 11 U.S.C.A. §§ 1201 to 1208, 1221 to 1231, and provisions set out as a note under 11 U.S.C.A. § 1201] may be cited as the 'Family Farmer Bankruptcy Relief Act of 2003'."

2002 Amendments. Pub.L. 107–377, § 1, Dec. 19, 2002, 116 Stat. 3115, provided that: "This Act [amending 11 U.S.C.A. §§ 1201 to 1208, 1221 to 1231, enacting provisions set out as notes under 11 U.S.C.A. § 1201, and amending provisions set out as notes under 11 U.S.C.A. § 1201] may be cited as the 'Protection of Family Farmers Act of 2002'."

1998 Amendments. Pub.L. 105–183, § 1, June 19, 1998, 112 Stat. 517, provided that: "This Act [amending 11 U.S.C.A. §§ 544, 546, 548, 707, and 1325 and enacting provisions set out as a note under 11 U.S.C.A. § 544] may be cited as the 'Religious Liberty and Charitable Donation Protection Act of 1998'."

1994 Amendments. Section 1(a) of Pub.L. 103–394 provided that: "This Act [enacting 11 U.S.C.A. § 110 and 18 U.S.C.A. §§ 156, 157, amending 11 U.S.C.A. §§ 101, 104, 105, 106, 109, 303, 322, 326, 330, 341, 342, 345, 346, 348, 349, 362, 363, 364, 365, 502, 503, 507, 522, 523, 524, 525, 541, 542, 543, 546, 547, 548, 549, 550, 552, 553, 555, 556, 559, 706, 723, 724, 726, 741, 742, 743, 745, 761, 1102, 1104, 1106, 1110, 1112, 1121, 1123, 1124, 1125, 1129, 1145, 1166, 1167, 1168, 1222, 1226, 1302, 1322, 1326, and 1328, rule 7004 of the Federal Rules of Bankruptcy Procedure, 12 U.S.C.A. §§ 1787, 1821, 18 U.S.C.A. §§ 152, 153, 154, 1961, and 28 U.S.C.A. §§ 157, 158, 586, 1334, 2073, 2075, and enacting provisions section out as notes preceding 11 U.S.C.A. § 101 and 11 U.S.C.A. §§ 101, 341, 501, 524] may be cited as the 'Bankruptcy Reform Act of 1994'."

1990 Amendments. Pub.L. 101–647, Title XXXI, § 3101, Nov. 29, 1990, 104 Stat. 4916, provided that: "This title [amending 11 U.S.C.A. §§ 523, 1328 and enacting provisions set out as a note under 11 U.S.C.A. § 523] may be cited as the 'Criminal Victims Protection Act of 1990'."

Pub.L. 101–581, § 1, Nov. 15, 1990, 104 Stat. 2865, provided that: "This Act [amending 11 U.S.C.A. §§ 523, 1328 and enacting provisions set out as notes under 11 U.S.C.A. § 523] may be cited as the 'Criminal Victims Protection Act of 1990'."

1988 Amendments. Pub.L. 100–334, § 1, June 16, 1988, 102 Stat. 610, provided that: "This Act [enacting 11 U.S.C.A. § 1114, amending 11 U.S.C.A. § 1129, enacting provisions set out as a note under 11 U.S.C.A. § 1114, and amending and repealing provisions set out as notes under 11 U.S.C.A. § 1106] may be cited as the 'Retiree Benefits Bankruptcy Protection Act of 1988'."

1986 Amendments. Pub.L. 99–554, § 1, Oct. 27, 1986, 100 Stat. 3088, provided that said Act [enacting 11 U.S.C.A. §§ 307, 1201 to 1231 and 28 U.S.C.A. § 589a, amending 11 U.S.C.A. §§ 101 to 103, 105, 108, 109, 303, 321, 322, 324, 326, 327, 329, 330, 341, 343, 345 to 348, 362 to 365, 502, 503, 521 to 524, 546 to 549, 554, 557, 701, 703 to 707, 724, 726 to 728, 743, 1102, 1104 to 1106, 1112, 1121, 1129, 1163, 1202, 1302, 1306, 1307, 1324 to 1326, Bankruptcy Form No. 1, set out in the Appendix to Title 11, 28 U.S.C.A. §§ 49, 96, 152, 156, 157, 526, 581, 582, 584 to 587, 604, 1334, 1930, repealing 11 U.S.C.A. §§ 1201 to 1231, 1501 to 151326, enacting provisions set out as notes under 28 U.S.C.A. §§ 581, 589, amending provisions set out as a note under 28 U.S.C.A. § 152, and repealing provi-

sions set out as a note preceding 28 U.S.C.A. § 581] may be cited as the "Bankruptcy Judges, United States Trustees, and Family Farmer Bankruptcy Act of 1986". See note set out under 28 U.S.C.A. § 581.

1984 Amendments. Section 361 of Subtitle C (§§ 361 to 363) of Title III of Pub.L. 98–353 provided that: "This subtitle [amending this section and 11 U.S.C.A. §§ 362, 365, 541] may be cited as the 'Leasehold Management Bankruptcy Amendments Act of 1983'."

Adjustment of Dollar Amounts

For adjustment of dollar amounts specified in pars. (3), (18), (19A), (51D) of this section by the Judicial Conference of the United States, effective Apr. 1, 2010, see note set out under 11 U.S.C.A. § 104 of this title.

By notice dated Feb. 25, 2010, 75 F.R. 8747, the Judicial Conference of the United States adjusted the dollar amounts in provisions specified in pars. (3), (18), (19A), (51D) of this section, effective Apr. 1, 2010, as follows:

In par. (3) adjusted $164,250 to $175,750.

In par. (18)(A) and (B)(ii) adjusted $3,544,525 (each time it appears) to $3,792,650 (each time it appears).

In par. (19A)(A)(i) and (B)(ii)(II) adjusted $1,642,500 (each time it appears) to $1,757,475 (each time it appears).

In par. (51D) adjusted $2,190,000 (each time it appears) to $2,343,300 (each time it appears).

By notice dated Feb. 14, 2007, 72 F.R. 7082, the Judicial Conference of the United States adjusted the dollar amounts in provisions specified in pars. (3), (18), (19A), (51D) of this section, effective Apr. 1, 2007, as follows:

In par. (3) adjusted $150,000 to $164,250.

In par. (18) adjusted $3,237,000 (each time it appears) to $3,544,525 (each time it appears).

In par. (19A) adjusted $1,500,000 (each time it appears) to $1,642,500 (each time it appears).

In par. (51D) adjusted $2,000,000 (each time it appears) to $2,190,000 (each time it appears).

Scope of Application

Pub.L. 109–390, § 7, Dec. 12, 2006, 120 Stat. 2700, provided that: "The amendments made by this Act [amending this section, 11 U.S.C.A. §§ 362, 546, and 741, 12 U.S.C.A. §§ 1787, 1821, 4403, and 4404, and 15 U.S.C.A. § 78eee, and enacting provisions set out as notes under this section] shall not apply to any cases commenced under title 11, United States Code, or appointments made under any Federal or State law, before the date of the enactment of this Act [Dec. 12, 2006]."

Nonlimitation of Information

Pub.L. 109–8, Title I, § 102(e), Apr. 20, 2005, 119 Stat. 33, provided that: "Nothing in this title [see Tables for classification] shall limit the ability of a creditor to provide information to a judge (except for information communicated ex parte, unless otherwise permitted by applicable law), United States trustee (or bankruptcy administrator, if any), or trustee."

[Except as otherwise provided, this note effective 180 days after April 20, 2005, and inapplicable with respect to cases commenced under Title 11 before the effective date, see Pub.L. 109–8, Title XV, § 1501, Apr. 20, 2005, 119 Stat. 216, set out as a note under this section.]

Rule of Construction

Pub.L. 109–8, Title X, § 1007(e), Apr. 20, 2005, 119 Stat. 188, provided that: "**Applicability.**—Nothing in this section [amending this section and 11 U.S.C.A. §§ 109, 1203, 1206, and the chapter heading and table of contents for Chapter 12 of Title 11] shall change, affect, or amend the Fishery Conservation and Management Act of 1976 [officially titled the Magnuson-Stevens Fishery Conservation and Management Act, which is Pub.L. 94–265, Apr. 13, 1976, 90 Stat. 331, as amended, and which is principally classified to chapter 38 of Title 16] (16 U.S.C. § 1801 et seq.)."

Pub.L. 109–8, Title XI, § 1101(c), Apr. 20, 2005, 119 Stat. 189, provided that: "The amendments made by subsection (a) of this section [amending this section by redesignating par. (27A) as par. (27B) and inserting a new par. (27A) and pars. (40A) and (40B)] shall not affect the interpretation of section 109(b) of title 11, United States Code."

[Except as otherwise provided, this note effective 180 days after April 20, 2005, and inapplicable with respect to cases commenced under Title 11 before the effective date, see Pub.L. 109–8, Title XV, § 1501, Apr. 20, 2005, 119 Stat. 216, set out as a note under this section.]

Judicial Education

Pub.L. 109–8, Title XII, § 1226, Apr. 20, 2005, 119 Stat. 199, provided that: "The Director of the Federal Judicial Center, in consultation with the Director of the Executive Office for United States Trustees, shall develop materials and conduct such training as may be useful to courts in implementing this Act [see Short Title 2005 Amendments note set out under this section] and the amendments made by this Act, including the requirements relating to the means test under section 707(b), and reaffirmation agreements under section 524, of title 11 of the United States Code, as amended by this Act."

[Except as otherwise provided, this note effective 180 days after April 20, 2005, and inapplicable with respect to cases commenced under Title 11 before the effective date, see Pub.L. 109–8, Title XV, § 1501, Apr. 20, 2005, 119 Stat. 216, set out as a note under this section.]

CROSS REFERENCES

"Commodity broker", as defined under this section, determining powers and duties of Securities Investor Protection Act trustees, see 15 USCA § 78fff–1.

Crime victims' rights, rights afforded and best efforts to accord rights, procedures to promote compliance, see 18 USCA § 3771.

"Forward contract", "repurchase agreement," and "transfer" defined under this section as having same meaning for purposes of—

　Federal credit union insurance, see 12 USCA § 1787.

　Federal deposit insurance, see 12 USCA § 1821.

"Insolvent" defined under this section as having same meaning for purposes of Securities Investor Protection Act decrees, see 15 USCA § 78eee.

List of creditors, unsecured claims, see Official Bankr. Form 4, 11 USCA.

"Margin payment" and "settlement payment" as defined under this section determining exclusion of certain setoffs from automatic stay, see 11 USCA § 362.

"Railroad," as defined under this section, determining bankruptcy fees, see 28 USCA § 1930.

Statement of financial affairs, see Official Bankr. Form 7, 11 USCA.

LIBRARY REFERENCES

American Digest System

Bankruptcy ⚵2011.

Key Number System Topic No. 51.

Corpus Juris Secundum

CJS Bankruptcy § 7, Bankruptcy Code.

CJS Bankruptcy § 8, Bankruptcy Code--Construction and Interpretation.

CJS Bankruptcy § 18, Debt-Relief Agencies.

CJS Bankruptcy § 56, Eligibility to Serve as Trustee or Examiner--Disinterestedness Requirement.

CJS Bankruptcy § 72, Appointment Required in Railroad Reorganization Cases.

CJS Bankruptcy § 78, Eligibility of Creditors to Vote.

CJS Bankruptcy § 85, Appointment Where Debts Exceed $5 Million.

CJS Bankruptcy § 199, Other Proceedings Affecting Liquidation of Estate Assets or Adjustment of Debtor-Creditor/Equity-Security Holder Relationship.

CJS Bankruptcy § 252, Power to Examine Debtor or Any Entity.

CJS Bankruptcy § 319, Corporations.

CJS Bankruptcy § 323, Chapter 7.

CJS Bankruptcy § 324, Chapter 9.

CJS Bankruptcy § 325, Chapter 11.

CJS Bankruptcy § 326, Chapter 12.

CJS Bankruptcy § 327, Chapter 13.

CJS Bankruptcy § 328, Chapter 13--Regular Income.

CJS Bankruptcy § 329, Chapter 13--Debts.

CJS Bankruptcy § 344, List of Creditors and Others.

CJS Bankruptcy § 345, List of Creditors and Others-- Twenty Largest Unsecured Creditors.

CJS Bankruptcy § 347, List of Equity Security Holders.

CJS Bankruptcy § 352, Statement of Current Monthly Income.

CJS Bankruptcy § 359, Designation of Debtor as Health Care Business.

CJS Bankruptcy § 360, Designation of Debtor as Small Business.

CJS Bankruptcy § 369, Person Against Whom Case May be Commenced.

CJS Bankruptcy § 371, Circumstances Under Which Fewer Than Three Claimholders May File.

CJS Bankruptcy § 386, Foreign Proceedings and Representatives, Generally.

CJS Bankruptcy § 478, Persons Protected by and Subject to Stay--Persons Liable for Debtor's Consumer Debts.

CJS Bankruptcy § 500, Setoffs.

CJS Bankruptcy § 502, Police or Regulatory Power.

CJS Bankruptcy § 539, By Governmental Unit.

CJS Bankruptcy § 573, Individual Debtors.

CJS Bankruptcy § 631, Entities Subject to Turnover Duty.

CJS Bankruptcy § 634, Assertion of Claim Against Governmental Unit; Sovereign Immunity.

CJS Bankruptcy § 641, Who Are Custodians.

CJS Bankruptcy § 669, Statutory Liens; Penalty Liens.

CJS Bankruptcy § 675, Transfer for Benefit of Creditor--Creation of Lien or Security Interest.

CJS Bankruptcy § 677, Debtor's Insolvency.

CJS Bankruptcy § 679, Transfer to Occur Within Preference Period--Who Are Insiders Subject to Longer Period.

CJS Bankruptcy § 684, Consumer Debt Transfers.

CJS Bankruptcy § 685, Transfers to Creditors Who Then Give New Value to Debtor.

CJS Bankruptcy § 693, Transfer of Interest or Obligation to Partner in Partnership Debtor.

CJS Bankruptcy § 715, Prepetition Transfers Under Swap Agreement.

CJS Bankruptcy § 752, Right of Seller of Goods.

CJS Bankruptcy § 786, Disqualification of Judge from Allowing Compensation.

CJS Bankruptcy § 812, Who is Entitled to Make Examination.

CJS Bankruptcy § 824, Examination of Corporations.

CJS Bankruptcy § 851, Prepetition Security Interests in Proceeds, Products, Offspring, or Profits.

CJS Bankruptcy § 853, Use of Aircraft, Aircraft Equipment, Vessels, and Railroad Equipment Subject to Financing Agreements.

CJS Bankruptcy § 930, Effect of Default.

CJS Bankruptcy § 1002, Circumstances Justifying Equitable Subordination.

CJS Bankruptcy § 1003, Persons Whose Claims Are Subject to Subordination.

CJS Bankruptcy § 1004, Recharacterization of Debt.

CJS Bankruptcy § 1005, Claim Arising from Purchase or Sale of Security.

CJS Bankruptcy § 1007, Generally; Who May File.

CJS Bankruptcy § 1041, Improper Conduct in Another Case.

CJS Bankruptcy § 1046, Generally; Objections to Discharge.

CJS Bankruptcy § 1060, What Constitutes Debt or Liability on Claim.

CJS Bankruptcy § 1073, Domestic Support Obligations and Other Debts to Spouses and Children.

CJS Bankruptcy § 1075, Domestic Support Obligations and Other Debts to Spouses and Children--Child Support.

CJS Bankruptcy § 1078, Educational Loans.

CJS Bankruptcy § 1087, Evidence; Presumptions.

CJS Bankruptcy § 1092, Costs and Attorney's Fees.

CJS Bankruptcy § 1103, Community Property.

CJS Bankruptcy § 1129, Appointment of Creditors" and Equity Security Holders" Committees.

CJS Bankruptcy § 1169, Generally; Definitions.

CJS Bankruptcy § 1193, Modification of Claims.

CJS Business Trusts § 67, Receivership and Insolvency.

CJS Interest and Usury; Consumer Credit § 483, Closed End Credit.

CJS Interest and Usury; Consumer Credit § 486, Form and Terminology of Disclosure.

CJS Joint-Stock Companies § 1, Definition, Nature, and Status.

§ 102. Rules of construction

In this title—

(1) "after notice and a hearing", or a similar phrase—

    (A) means after such notice as is appropriate in the particular circumstances, and such opportunity for a hearing as is appropriate in the particular circumstances; but

    (B) authorizes an act without an actual hearing if such notice is given properly and if—

        (i) such a hearing is not requested timely by a party in interest; or

        (ii) there is insufficient time for a hearing to be commenced before such act must be done, and the court authorizes such act;

(2) "claim against the debtor" includes claim against property of the debtor;

(3) "includes" and "including" are not limiting;

(4) "may not" is prohibitive, and not permissive;

(5) "or" is not exclusive;

(6) "order for relief" means entry of an order for relief;

(7) the singular includes the plural;

(8) a definition, contained in a section of this title that refers to another section of this title, does not, for the purpose of such reference, affect the meaning of a term used in such other section; and

(9) "United States trustee" includes a designee of the United States trustee.

(Pub.L. 95–598, Nov. 6, 1978, 92 Stat. 2554; Pub.L. 98–353, Title III, § 422, July 10, 1984, 98 Stat. 369; Pub.L. 99–554, Title II, § 202, Oct. 27, 1986, 100 Stat. 3097.)

HISTORICAL AND STATUTORY NOTES

Revision Notes and Legislative Reports

1978 Acts. Section 102 provides seven rules of construction. Some are derived from current law; others are derived from 1 U.S.C. 1; a few are new. They apply generally throughout proposed title 11. These are terms that are not appropriate for definition, but that require an explanation.

Paragraph (1) defines the concept of "after notice and a hearing." The concept is central to the bill and to the separation of the administrative and judicial functions of bankruptcy judges. The phrase means after such notice as is appropriate in the particular circumstances (to be prescribed by either the Rules of Bankruptcy Procedure or by the court in individual circumstances that the Rules do not cover. In many cases, the Rules will provide for combined notice of several proceedings), and such opportunity for a hearing as is appropriate in the particular circumstances. Thus, a hearing will not be necessary in every instance. If there is no objection to the proposed action, the action may go ahead without court action. This is a significant change from present law, which requires the affirmative approval of the bankruptcy judge for almost every action. The change will permit the bankruptcy judge to stay removed from the administration of the bankruptcy or reorganization case, and to become involved only when there is a dispute about a proposed action, that is, only when there is an objection. The phrase "such opportunity for a hearing as is appropriate in the particular circumstances" is designed to permit the Rules and the courts to expedite or dispense with hearings when speed is essential. The language "or similar phrase" is intended to cover the few instances in the bill where "after notice and a hearing" is interrupted by another phrase, such as "after notice to the debtor and a hearing."

Paragraph (2) specifies that "claim against the debtor" includes claim against property of the debtor. This paragraph is intended to cover nonrecourse loan agreements where the creditor's only rights are against property of the debtor, and not against the debtor personally. Thus, such an agreement would give rise to a claim that would be treated as a claim against the debtor personally, for the purposes of the bankruptcy code.

Paragraph (3) is a codification of *American Surety Co. v. Marotta*, 287 U.S. 513 (1933) [53 S.Ct. 260, 77 L.Ed. 466]. It specifies that "includes" and "including" are not limiting.

Paragraph (4) specifies that "may not" is prohibitive and not permissive (such as in "might not").

Paragraph (5) specifies that "or" is not exclusive. Thus, if a party "may do (a) or (b)", then the party may do either or both. The party is not limited to a mutually exclusive choice between the two alternatives.

Paragraph (6) makes clear that "order for relief" means entry of an order for relief. If the court orally orders relief, but the order is not entered until a later time, then any time measurements in the bill are from entry, not from the oral order. In a voluntary case, the entry of the order for relief is the filing of the petition commencing the voluntary case.

Paragraph (7) specifies that the singular includes the plural. The plural, however, generally does not include the singular. The bill uses only the singular, even when the item in question most often is found in plural quantities, in order to avoid the confusion possible if both rules of construction applied. When an item is specified in the plural, the plural is intended. Senate Report No. 95–989.

1984 Acts. Statements by Legislative Leaders, see 1984 U.S.Code Cong. and Adm.News, p. 576.

1986 Acts. House Report No. 99–764 and House Conference Report No. 99–958, see 1986 U.S.Code Cong. and Adm. News, p. 5227.

Legislative Statements

Section 102 specifies various rules of construction but is not exclusive. Other rules of construction that are not set out in title 11 are nevertheless intended to be followed in construing the bankruptcy code. For example, the phrase "on request of a party in interest" or a similar phrase, is used in connection with an action that the court may take in various sections of the Code. The phrase is intended to restrict the court from acting sua sponte. Rules of bankruptcy procedure or court decisions will determine who is a party in interest for the particular purposes of the provision in question, but the court will not be permitted to act on its own.

Although "property" is not construed in this section, it is used consistently throughout the code in its broadest sense, including cash, all interests in property, such as liens, and every kind of consideration including promises to act or forbear to act as in section 548(d).

Section 102(1) expands on a rule of construction contained in H.R. 8200 as passed by the House and in the Senate amendment. The phrase "after notice and a hearing", or a similar phrase, is intended to be construed according to the particular proceeding to mean after such notice as is appropriate in the particular circumstances, and such opportunity, if any, for a hearing as is appropriate in the particular circumstances. If a provision of title 11 authorizes an act to be taken "after notice and a hearing" this means that if appropriate notice is given and no party to whom such notice is sent timely requests a hearing, then the act sought to be taken may be taken without an actual hearing.

In very limited emergency circumstances, there will be insufficient time for a hearing to be commenced before an action must be taken. The action sought to be taken may be taken if authorized by the court at an ex parte hearing of which a record is made in open court. A full hearing after the fact will be available in such an instance.

In some circumstances, such as under section 1128, the bill requires a hearing and the court may act only after a hearing is held. In those circumstances the judge will receive evidence before ruling. In other circumstances, the court may take action "after notice and a hearing," if no party in interest requests a hearing. In that event a court order authorizing the action to be taken is not necessary as the ultimate action taken by the court implies such an authorization.

Section 102(8) is new. It contains a rule of construction indicating that a definition contained in a section in title 11 that refers to another section of title 11 does not, for the purposes of such reference, take the meaning of a term used in the other section. For example, section 522(a)(2) defines "value" for the purposes of section 522. Section 548(d)(2) defines "value" for purposes of section 548. When section 548 is incorporated by reference in section 522, this rule of construction makes clear that the definition of "value" in section 548 governs its meaning in section 522 notwithstanding a different definition of "value" in section 522(a)(2).

Amendments

1986 Amendments. Par. (9). Pub.L. 99–554, § 202, added par. (9).

1984 Amendments. Par. (8). Pub.L. 98–353 substituted "contained" for "continued".

Effective and Applicability Provisions

1986 Acts. Amendment by Pub.L. 99–554 effective 30 days after Oct. 27, 1986, except as otherwise provided for, see section 302(a) of Pub.L. 99–554, set out as a note under section 581 of Title 28, Judiciary and Judicial Procedure.

Amendment by Pub.L. 99–554, § 202, not to become effective in or with respect to certain specified judicial districts until, or apply to cases while pending in such district before, the expiration of the 270-day period beginning 30 days after Oct. 27, 1986, or of the 30-day period beginning on the date the Attorney General certifies under section 303 of Pub.L. 99–554 the region specified in a paragraph of section 581(a) of Title 28, as amended by section 111(a) of Pub.L. 99–554, that includes such district, whichever occurs first, see section

302(d)(1) of Pub.L. 99–554, set out as a note under section 581 of Title 28.

Amendment by Pub.L. 99–554, § 202, not to become effective in or with respect to certain specified judicial districts until, or apply to cases while pending in such district before, the expiration of the 2-year period beginning 30 days after Oct. 27, 1986, or of the 30-day period beginning on the date the Attorney General certifies under section 303 of Pub.L. 99–554 the region specified in a paragraph of section 581(a) of Title 28, as amended by section 111(a) of Pub.L. 99–554, that includes such district, whichever occurs first, see section 302(d)(2) of Pub.L. 99–554, set out as a note under section 581 of Title 28.

Amendment by Pub.L. 99–554, § 202, not to become effective in or with respect to judicial districts established for the States of Alabama and North Carolina until, or apply to cases while pending in such district before, such district elects to be included in a bankruptcy region established in section 581(a) of Title 28, as amended by section 111(a) of Pub.L. 99–554, or Oct. 1, 2002, whichever occurs first, and, except as otherwise provided, with respect to cases under chapters 7, 11, 12 and 13 of Title 11 commenced before 30 days after Oct. 27, 1986, and pending in a judicial district in the States of Alabama or North Carolina before any election made under section 302(d)(3)(A) of Pub.L. 99–554 by such district becomes effective or Oct. 1, 2002, whichever occurs first, amendments by Pub.L. 99–554 not to apply until Oct. 1, 2003, or the expiration of the 1-year period beginning on the date such election becomes effective, whichever occurs first, and further, in any judicial district in Alabama or North Carolina not making the election described in section 302(d)(3)(A) of Pub.L. 99–554, any person appointed under regulations issued by the Judicial Conference to administer estates in cases under Title 11 authorized to establish, etc., a panel of private trustees, and to supervise cases and trustees in cases under chapters 7, 11, 12, and 13 of Title 11, until amendments by sections 201 to 231 of Pub.L. 99–554 effective in such district, see section 302(d)(3)(A) to (F), (H), (I) of Pub.L. 99–554, set out as a note under section 581 of Title 28.

Amendment by Pub.L. 99–554, § 202, except as otherwise provided, with respect to cases under chapters 7, 11, 12, and 13 of Title 11 commenced before 30 days after Oct. 27, 1986, and pending in a judicial district referred to in section 581(a) of Title 28, as amended by section 111(a) of Pub.L. 99–554, for which a United States trustee is not authorized before 30 days after Oct. 27, 1986 to be appointed, not applicable until the expiration of the 3-year period beginning on Oct. 27, 1986, or of the 1-year period beginning on the date the Attorney General certifies under section 303 of Pub.L. 99–554 the region specified in a paragraph of such section 581(a) that includes such district, whichever occurs first, see section 302(e)(1), (2) of Pub.L. 99–554, set out as a note under section 581 of Title 28.

1984 Acts. Amendment by Pub.L. 98–353 effective with respect to cases filed 90 days after July 10, 1984, see section 552(a), formerly 553(a) of Pub.L. 98–353, set out as a note under section 101 of this title.

LIBRARY REFERENCES

American Digest System

Bankruptcy ⟐2021, 2022.

Key Number System Topic No. 51.

Corpus Juris Secundum

CJS Bankruptcy § 8, Bankruptcy Code--Construction and Interpretation.

CJS Bankruptcy § 68, Notice and Hearing Requirements.

CJS Bankruptcy § 101, Chapter 11.

CJS Bankruptcy § 137, Removal or Reinstatement of Debtor as Debtor in Possession.

CJS Bankruptcy § 141, After Notice and a Hearing.

CJS Bankruptcy § 416, Proceedings.

CJS Bankruptcy § 421, Proceedings.

CJS Bankruptcy § 452, Automatic Dismissal of Case of Individual Debtor.

CJS Bankruptcy § 457, Failure to Provide Copy of Debtor's Federal Income Tax Return to Trustee and Requesting Creditors.

CJS Bankruptcy § 458, Failure to File Prepetition Tax Returns in Chapter 13 Case.

CJS Bankruptcy § 459, Failure to File Postpetition Tax Return.

CJS Bankruptcy § 658, Notice.

CJS Bankruptcy § 782, Notice and Hearing.

CJS Bankruptcy § 790, Convening of Meeting by Trustee or Other Judicial Officer.

CJS Bankruptcy § 793, Duties of Trustee or Other Judicial Officer.

CJS Bankruptcy § 800, United States Trustee or Other Judicial Officer; Bankruptcy Judge.

CJS Bankruptcy § 843, Discontinuance or Modification of Debtor's Business.

CJS Bankruptcy § 900, Motion for Authorization to Obtain Credit; Notice and Hearing.

CJS Bankruptcy § 1007, Generally; Who May File.

CJS Bankruptcy § 1203, Requirements for Confirmation; Notice and Hearing.

§ 103. Applicability of chapters

(a) Except as provided in section 1161 of this title, chapters 1, 3, and 5 of this title apply in a case under chapter 7, 11, 12, or 13 of this title, and this chapter, sections 307, 362(*o*), 555 through 557, and 559 through 562 apply in a case under chapter 15.

(b) Subchapters I and II of chapter 7 of this title apply only in a case under such chapter.

(c) Subchapter III of chapter 7 of this title applies only in a case under such chapter concerning a stockbroker.

(d) Subchapter IV of chapter 7 of this title applies only in a case under such chapter concerning a commodity broker.

(e) Scope of application.—Subchapter V of chapter 7 of this title shall apply only in a case under such chapter concerning the liquidation of an uninsured State member bank, or a corporation organized under section 25A of the Federal Reserve Act, which operates, or operates as, a multilateral clearing organization pursuant to section 409 of the Federal Deposit Insurance Corporation Improvement Act of 1991.

(f) Except as provided in section 901 of this title, only chapters 1 and 9 of this title apply in a case under such chapter 9.

(g) Except as provided in section 901 of this title, subchapters I, II, and III of chapter 11 of this title apply only in a case under such chapter.

(h) Subchapter IV of chapter 11 of this title applies only in a case under such chapter concerning a railroad.

(i) Chapter 13 of this title applies only in a case under such chapter.

(j) Chapter 12 of this title applies only in a case under such chapter.

(k) Chapter 15 applies only in a case under such chapter, except that—

> **(1)** sections 1505, 1513, and 1514 apply in all cases under this title; and

> **(2)** section 1509 applies whether or not a case under this title is pending.

(Pub.L. 95–598, Nov. 6, 1978, 92 Stat. 2555; Pub.L. 97–222, § 2, July 27, 1982, 96 Stat. 235; Pub.L. 98–353, Title III, § 423, July 10, 1984, 98 Stat. 369; Pub.L. 99–554, Title II, § 252, Oct. 27, 1986, 100 Stat. 3104; Pub.L. 106–554, § 1(a)(5) [Title I, § 112(c)(5)(A)], Dec. 21, 2000, 114 Stat. 2763, 2763A–394; Pub.L. 109–8, Title VIII, § 802(a), Apr. 20, 2005, 119 Stat. 145; Pub.L. 111–327, § 2(a)(2), Dec. 22, 2010, 124 Stat. 3557.)

HISTORICAL AND STATUTORY NOTES

Revision Notes and Legislative Reports

1978 Acts. Section 103 prescribes which chapters of the proposed bankruptcy code apply in various cases. All cases, other than cases ancillary to foreign proceedings, are filed under chapter 7, 9, 11, or 13, the operative chapters of the proposed bankruptcy code. The general provisions that apply no matter which chapter a case is filed under are found in chapters 1, 3, and 5. Subsection (a) makes this explicit, with an exception for chapter 9. The other provisions, which are self-explanatory, provide the special rules for Stockbroker Liquidations, Commodity Broker Liquidations, Municipal Debt Adjustments, and Railroad Reorganizations. Senate Report No. 95–989.

1982 Acts. House Report No. 97–420, see 1982 U.S.Code Cong. and Adm.News, p. 583.

1984 Acts. Statements by Legislative Leaders, see 1984 U.S.Code Cong. and Adm.News, p. 576.

1986 Acts. House Report No. 99–764 and House Conference Report No. 99–958, see 1986 U.S.Code Cong. and Adm. News, p. 5227.

2000 Acts. House Report No. 106–645 and Statement by President, see 2000 U.S. Code Cong. and Adm. News, p. 2459.

2005 Acts. House Report No. 109–31(Part I), see 2005 U.S. Code Cong. and Adm. News, p. 88.

References in Text

Chapters 1, 3, and 5 of this title, referred to in subsec. (a), are 11 U.S.C.A. §§ 101 et seq., 301 et seq., and 501 et seq.

Chapter 7, 11, 12, or 13 of this title, referred to in subsec. (a), is 11 U.S.C.A. § 701 et seq., 11 U.S.C.A. § 1101 et seq., 11

U.S.C.A. § 1201 et seq., or 11 U.S.C.A. § 1301 et seq., respectively.

Chapter 15, referred to in subsecs. (a) and (k), is chapter 15 of this title, which is classified to 11 U.S.C.A. § 1501 et seq.

Subchapters I and II of chapter 7 of this title, referred to in subsec. (b), are 11 U.S.C.A. §§ 701 et seq. and 721 et seq., respectively.

Subchapter III of chapter 7 of this title, referred to in subsec. (c), is 11 U.S.C.A. § 741 et seq.

Subchapter IV of chapter 7 of this title, referred to in subsecs. (d) and (h), is 11 U.S.C.A. § 761 et seq.

Subchapter V of chapter 7 of this title, referred to in subsec. (e), is 11 U.S.C.A. § 781 et seq.

Section 25A of the Federal Reserve Act, referred to in subsec. (e), is Dec. 23, 1913, c. 6, § 25A, formerly § 25(a), as added Dec. 24, 1919, c. 18, 41 Stat. 378, as amended, which is classified to subchapter II of chapter 6 of Title 12, 12 U.S.C.A. § 611 et seq.

Section 409 of the Federal Deposit Insurance Corporation Improvement Act of 1991, referred to in subsec. (e), is Pub.L. 102–242, Title IV, § 409, as added by Pub.L. 106–554, § 1(a)(5) [Title I, § 112(a)(3)], Dec. 21, 2000, 114 Stat. 2763, 2763A–394, which is classified as 12 U.S.C.A. § 4422.

Chapter 13 of this title, referred to in subsec. (i), is 11 U.S.C.A. § 1301 et seq.

Chapter 12 of this title, referred to in subsec. (j), is 11 U.S.C.A. § 1201 et seq.

Amendments

2010 Amendments. Subsec. (a). Pub.L. 111–327, § 2(a)(2), struck out "362(n)" and inserted "362(o)".

2005 Amendments. Subsec. (a). Pub.L. 109–8, § 802(a)(1), inserted the following: ", and this chapter, sections 307, 362(n), 555 through 557, and 559 through 562 apply in a case under chapter 15" before the period at the end.

Subsec. (k). Pub.L. 109–8, § 802(a)(2), added subsec. (k).

2000 Amendments. Subsecs. (e) to (j). Pub.L. 106–554, § 1(a)(5) [Title I, § 112(c)(5)(A)], added subsec. (e), and redesignated former subsecs. (e) through (i) as (f) through (j), respectively.

1986 Amendments. Subsec. (a). Pub.L. 99–554, § 252(1), added reference to chapter 12.

Subsec. (i). Pub.L. 99–554, § 252(2), added subsec. (i).

1984 Amendments. Subsec. (c). Pub.L. 98–353 substituted "stockbroker" for "stockholder".

1982 Amendments. Subsec. (d). Pub.L. 97–222 struck out "except with respect to section 746(c) which applies to margin payments made by any debtor to a commodity broker or forward contract merchant" following "concerning a commodity broker".

Effective and Applicability Provisions

2005 Acts. Amendments by Pub.L. 109–8 effective, except as otherwise provided, 180 days after April 20, 2005, and inapplicable with respect to cases commenced under Title 11 before the effective date, see Pub.L. 109–8, § 1501, set out as a note under 11 U.S.C.A. § 101.

1986 Acts. Amendment by Pub.L. 99–554 effective 30 days after Oct. 27, 1986, but not applicable to cases commenced under this title before that date, see section 302(a), (c)(1) of

Pub.L. 99–554, set out as a note under section 581 of Title 28, Judiciary and Judicial Procedure.

1984 Acts. Amendment by Pub.L. 98–353 effective with respect to cases filed 90 days after July 10, 1984, see section 552(a), formerly 553(a), of Pub.L. 98–353, set out as a note under section 101 of this title.

CROSS REFERENCES

Confirmation of Chapter 9 plan complying with provisions of this title made applicable by this section, see 11 USCA § 943.

Terms as defined in this title made applicable to Chapter 9 by this section, see 11 USCA § 901.

Terms "property of the estate" and "trustee" made applicable to Chapter 9 by this section, defined for purposes of such chapter, see 11 USCA § 902.

LIBRARY REFERENCES

American Digest System

Bankruptcy ⟊2021.

Key Number System Topic No. 51.

Corpus Juris Secundum

CJS Bankruptcy § 7, Bankruptcy Code.

CJS Bankruptcy § 73, Chapter 9 Cases.

CJS Bankruptcy § 387, Authorization to Act in Foreign Country.

CJS Bankruptcy § 846, Operation of Affairs of Municipal Debtor in Chapter 9 Cases.

CJS Bankruptcy § 1105, Closing.

CJS Bankruptcy § 1121, Requirements for Confirmation.

CJS Bankruptcy § 1169, Generally; Definitions.

§ 104. Adjustment of dollar amounts

(a) On April 1, 1998, and at each 3–year interval ending on April 1 thereafter, each dollar amount in effect under sections 101(3), 101(18), 101(19A), 101(51D), 109(e), 303(b), 507(a), 522(d), 522(f)(3) and 522(f)(4), 522(n), 522(p), 522(q), 523(a)(2)(C), 541(b), 547(c)(9), 707(b), 1322(d), 1325(b), and 1326(b)(3) of this title and section 1409(b) of title 28 immediately before such April 1 shall be adjusted—

    (1) to reflect the change in the Consumer Price Index for All Urban Consumers, published by the Department of Labor, for the most recent 3–year period ending immediately before January 1 preceding such April 1, and

    (2) to round to the nearest $25 the dollar amount that represents such change.

(b) Not later than March 1, 1998, and at each 3–year interval ending on March 1 thereafter, the Judicial Conference of the United States shall publish in the Federal Register the dollar amounts that will become effective on such April 1 under sections 101(3), 101(18), 101(19A), 101(51D), 109(e), 303(b), 507(a), 522(d), 522(f)(3) and 522(f)(4), 522(n), 522(p), 522(q), 523(a)(2)(C), 541(b), 547(c)(9), 707(b), 1322(d), 1325(b),

and 1326(b)(3) of this title and section 1409(b) of title 28.

(c) Adjustments made in accordance with subsection (a) shall not apply with respect to cases commenced before the date of such adjustments.

(Pub.L. 95–598, Nov. 6, 1978, 92 Stat. 2555; Pub.L. 103–394, Title I, § 108(e), Oct. 22, 1994, 108 Stat. 4112; Pub.L. 109–8, Title I, § 102(j), Title II, §§ 224(e)(2), 226(b), Title III, § 322(b), Title IV, § 432(c), Title X, § 1002, Title XII, § 1202, Apr. 20, 2005, 119 Stat. 35, 65, 67, 97, 110, 186, 193; Pub.L. 110–406, § 7, Oct. 13, 2008, 122 Stat. 4293.)

HISTORICAL AND STATUTORY NOTES

Revision Notes and Legislative Reports

1978 Acts. This section requires that the Director of the Administrative Office of the U. S. Courts report to Congress and the President before Oct. 1, 1985, and before May 1 every 6 years thereafter a recommendation for adjustment in dollar amounts found in this title. The Committee feels that regular adjustment of the dollar amounts by the Director will conserve congressional time and yet assure that the relative dollar amounts used in the bill are maintained. Changes in the cost of living should be a significant, but not necessarily the only, factor considered by the Director. The fact that there has been an increase in the cost of living does not necessarily mean that an adjustment of dollar amounts would be needed or warranted. Senate Report No. 95–989.

This section requires the Judicial Conference to report to the Congress every four years after the effective date of the bankruptcy code any changes that have occurred in the cost of living during the preceding four years, and the appropriate adjustments to the dollar amounts in the bill. The dollar amounts are found primarily in the exemption section (11 U.S.C. 522), the wage priority (11 U.S.C. 507), and the eligibility for chapter 13 (11 U.S.C. 109). This section requires that the Conference recommend uniform percentage changes in these amounts based solely on cost of living changes. The dollar amounts in the bill would not change on that recommendation, absent Congressional veto. Instead, Congress is required to take affirmative action, by passing a law amending the appropriate section, if it wishes to accomplish the change.

If the Judicial Conference has policy recommendations concerning the appropriate dollar amounts in the bankruptcy code based other than on cost of living considerations there are adequate channels through which it may communicate its views. This section is solely for the housekeeping function of maintaining the dollar amounts in the code at fairly constant real dollar levels. House Report No. 95–595.

1994 Acts. House Report No. 103–835, see 1994 U.S. Code Cong. and Adm. News, p. 3340.

2005 Acts. House Report No. 109–31(Part I), see 2005 U.S. Code Cong. and Adm. News, p. 88.

Legislative Statements

Section 104 represents a compromise between the House bill and the Senate amendment with respect to the adjustment of dollar amounts in title 11. The House amendment authorizes the Judicial Conference of the United States to transmit a recommendation for the uniform percentage of adjustment for each dollar amount in title 11 and in 28 U.S.C. 1930 to the Congress and to the President before May 1, 1985, and before May 1 of every sixth year thereafter. The requirement in the

House bill that each such recommendation be based only on any change in the cost-of-living increase during the period immediately preceding the recommendation is deleted.

Amendments

2008 Amendments. Subsec. (a). Pub.L. 110–406, § 7(1), (2) struck out former subsec. (a) and redesignated former subsec. (b)(1) as subsec. (a). Prior to deletion, subsec. (a) read:

"**(a)** The Judicial Conference of the United States shall transmit to the Congress and to the President before May 1, 1985, and before May 1 of every sixth year after May 1, 1985, a recommendation for the uniform percentage adjustment of each dollar amount in this title and in section 1930 of title 28."

Subsec. (b)(1). Pub.L. 110–406, § 7(2), redesignated subsec. (b)(1) as subsec. (a) and subpars. (A) and (B) of that subsection as pars. (1) and (2), respectively.

Subsec. (b)(2). Pub.L. 110–406, § 7(3), redesignated subsec. (b)(2) as subsec. (b).

Subsec. (b)(3). Pub.L. 110–406, § 7(4), redesignated subsec. (b)(3) as subsec. (c).

Subsec. (c). Pub.L. 110–406, § 7(4), (5), redesignated subsec. (b)(3) as subsec. (c); and, in subsec. (c), as so redesignated, struck out "paragraph (1)" and inserted "subsection (a)".

2005 Amendments. Subsec. (b)(1). Pub.L. 109–8, § 1202(1)–(4), in introductory provisions, inserted "101(19A)," after "101(18),", "522(f)(3) and 522(f)(4)," after "522(d),", and "541(b), 547(c)(9)," after "523(a)(2)(C)," and substituted "1322(d), 1325(b), and 1326(b)(3) of this title and section 1409(b) of title 28" for "and 1325(b)(3)".

Pub.L. 109–8, § 1002, inserted "101(18)," after "101(3)," in introductory provisions.

Pub.L. 109–8, § 432(c), inserted "101(51D)," after "101(3)," in introductory provisions.

Pub.L. 109–8, § 322(b), inserted "522(p), 522(q)," after "522(n)," in introductory provisions.

Pub.L. 109–8, § 226(b), inserted "101(3)," after "sections" in introductory provisions.

Pub.L. 109–8, § 224(e)(2), inserted "522(n)," after "522(d)," in introductory provisions.

Pub.L. 109–8, § 102(j), substituted "523(a)(2)(C), 707(b), and 1325(b)(3)" for "and 523(a)(2)(C)" in introductory provisions.

Subsec. (b)(2). Pub.L. 109–8, § 1202(1)–(3), (5), inserted "101(19A)," after "101(18),", "522(f)(3) and 522(f)(4)," after "522(d),", and "541(b), 547(c)(9)," after "523(a)(2)(C)," and substituted "1322(d), 1325(b), and 1326(b)(3) of this title and section 1409(b) of title 28" for "and 1325(b)(3) of this title".

Pub.L. 109–8, § 1002, inserted "101(18)," after "101(3),".

Pub.L. 109–8, § 432(c), inserted "101(51D)," after "101(3),".

Pub. L. 109–8, § 322(b), inserted "522(p), 522(q)," after "522(n),".

Pub.L. 109–8, § 226(b), inserted "101(3)," after "sections".

Pub.L. 109–8, § 224(e)(2), inserted "522(n)," after "522(d),".

Pub.L. 109–8, § 102(j), substituted "523(a)(2)(C), 707(b), and 1325(b)(3)" for "and 523(a)(2)(C)".

1994 Amendments. Subsec. (a). Pub.L. 103–394, § 108(e)(1), designated existing provisions as subsec. (a).

Subsec. (b). Pub.L. 103–394, § 108(e)(2), added subsec. (b).

Effective and Applicability Provisions

2005 Acts. Amendments by Pub.L. 109–8, § 322, effective, except as otherwise provided, 180 days after April 20, 2005, and applicable with respect to cases commenced under Title 11 on or after April 20, 2005, see Pub.L. 109–8, § 1501, set out as a note under 11 U.S.C.A. § 101.

Amendments by Pub.L. 109–8 effective, except as otherwise provided, 180 days after April 20, 2005, and inapplicable with respect to cases commenced under Title 11 before the effective date, see Pub.L. 109–8, § 1501, set out as a note under 11 U.S.C.A. § 101.

1994 Acts. Amendment by Pub.L. 103–394 effective on Oct. 22, 1994, and not to apply with respect to cases commenced under Title 11 of the United States Code before Oct. 22, 1994, see section 702 of Pub.L. 103–394, set out as a note under section 101 of this title.

Termination of Reporting Requirements

For termination, effective May 15, 2000, of provisions of law requiring submittal to Congress of any annual, semiannual, or other regular periodic report listed in House Document No. 103–7 (in which a report required under subsec. (a) of this section is listed in the 15th item on page 12, which references a note but probably means this section), see section 3003 of Pub. L. 104–66, as amended, set out as a note under 31 U.S.C.A. § 1113.

Separability of Provisions

If any provision of or amendment made by Pub.L. 103–394 or the application of such provision or amendment to any person or circumstance is held to be unconstitutional, the remaining provisions of and amendments made by Pub.L. 103–394 and the application of such provisions and amendments to any person or circumstance shall not be affected thereby, see section 701 of Pub.L. 103–394, set out as a note under section 101 of this title.

Adjustment of Dollar Amounts

By notice published Feb. 25, 2010, 75 F.R. 8747, the Judicial Conference of the United States increased the dollar amounts in provisions specified in subsec. (b) of this section, effective Apr. 1, 2010, and provided also that these increases do not apply to cases commenced before the effective date of the adjustments, i.e., April 1, 2010. The dollar amounts are adjusted as set out in the following chart.

	Dollar amount to be adjusted	New (adjusted) dollar amount
28 U.S.C.:		
1409(b)—a trustee may commence a proceeding arising in or related to a case to recover:		
(1)—money judgment of or property worth less than	$1,100	$1,175
(2)—a consumer debt less than	$16,425	$17,575

	Dollar amount to be adjusted	New (adjusted) dollar amount
(3)—a non consumer debt against a non insider less than	$10,950	$11,725
11 U.S.C.:		
101(3)—definition of assisted person	$164,250	$175,750
101(18)(A) & (B)(ii)—definition of family farmer	$3,544,525 (each time it appears)	$3,792,650 (each time it appears).
101(19A)(A)(i) & (B)(ii)(II)—definition of family fisherman	$1,642,500 (each time it appears)	$1,757,475 (each time it appears).
101(51D)(A) & (B)—definition of small business debtor	$2,190,000 (each time it appears)	$2,343,300 (each time it appears).
109(e)—allowable debt limits for individual filing bankruptcy under chapter 13	$336,900 (each time it appears)	$360,475 (each time it appears).
	$1,010,650 (each time it appears)	$1,081,400 (each time it appears).
303(b)—minimum aggregate claims needed for the commencement of involuntary chapter 7 or chapter 11 bankruptcy:		
(1)—in paragraph (1)	$13,475	$14,425
(2)—in paragraph (2)	$13,475	$14,425
507(a)—priority expenses and claims		
(1)—in paragraph (4)	$10,950	$11,725
(2)—in paragraph (5)	$10,950	$11,725
(3)—in paragraph (6)	$5,400	$5,775
(4)—in paragraph (7)	$2,425	$2,600
522(d)—value of property exemptions allowed to the debtor		
(1)—in paragraph (1)	$20,200	$21,625
(2)—in paragraph (2)	$3,225	$3,450
(3)—in paragraph (3)	$525	$550
	$10,775	$11,525
(4)—in paragraph (4)	$1,350	$1,450
(5)—in paragraph (5)	$1,075	$1,150
	$10,125	$10,825
(6)—in paragraph (6)	$2,025	$2,175
(7)—in paragraph (8)	$10,775	$11,525
(8)—in paragraph (11)(D)	$20,200	$21,625
522(f)(3)(B)—exception to lien avoidance under certain state laws	$5,475	$5,850
522(f)(4)(B)—items excluded from definition of household goods for lien avoidance purposes........	$550 (each time it appears)	$600 (each time it appears).
522(n)—maximum aggregate value of assets in individual retirement accounts exempted	$1,095,000.............	$1,171,650
522(p)(1)—qualified homestead exemption	$136,875	$146,450
522(q)(1)—state homestead exemption	$136,875	$146,450

	Dollar amount to be adjusted	New (adjusted) dollar amount
523(a)(2)(C)—exceptions to discharge:		
in subclause (i)(I)—consumer debts, incurred ≤ 90 days before filing owed to a single creditor in the aggregate ...	$550	$600
in subclause (i)(II)—cash advances incurred ≤ 70 days before filing in the aggregate	$825	$875
541(b)—property of the estate exclusions:		
(1)—in paragraph (5)(C)—education IRA funds in the aggregate	$5,475	$5,850
(2)—in paragraph (6)(C)—prepurchased tuition credits in the aggregate	$5,475	$5,850
547(c)(9)—preferences, trustee may not avoid a transfer if, in a case filed by a debtor whose debts are not primarily consumer debts, the aggregate value of property is less than	$5,475	$5,850
707(b)—dismissal of a case or conversion to a case under chapter 11 or 13 (means test):		
(1)—in paragraph (2)(A)(i)(I) ..	$6,575	$7,025
(2)—in paragraph (2)(A)(i)(II)	$10,950	$11,725
(3)—in paragraph (2)(A)(ii)(IV)	$1,650	$1,775
(4)—in paragraph (2)(B)(iv)(I)	$6,575	$7,025
(5)—in paragraph (2)(B)(iv)(II)	$10,950	$11,725
(6)—in paragraph (5)(B)	$1,100	$1,175
(7)—in paragraph (6)(C)	$575	$625
(8)—in paragraph (7)(A)(iii) ...	$575	$625
1322(d)(1)(C) & (2)(C)—contents of chapter 13 plan, monthly income	$575 (each time it appears)	$625 (each time it appears).
1325(b)(3) & (b)(4))—chapter 13 confirmation of plan, disposable income	$575 (each time it appears)	$625 (each time it appears).
1326(b)(3)(B)—payments to former chapter 7 trustee	$25	$25

Previous adjustments of the dollar amounts in provisions specified in subsec. (b) of this section were contained in the following:

Notice published Feb. 14, 2007, 72 F.R. 7082, modified Mar. 30, 2007, 72 F.R. 15162, effective Apr. 1, 2007.

Notice published Feb. 18, 2004, 69 F.R. 8482, effective Apr. 1, 2004.

Notice published Feb. 20, 2001, 66 F.R. 10910, effective Apr. 1, 2001.

Notice published Feb. 3, 1998, 63 F.R. 7179, effective Apr. 1, 1998.

LIBRARY REFERENCES

American Digest System

Bankruptcy ⚷2233(3), 2285.1, 2951, 2771.1, 3420(11).

Key Number System Topic No. 51.

Corpus Juris Secundum

CJS Bankruptcy § 7, Bankruptcy Code.

CJS Bankruptcy § 327, Chapter 13.

CJS Bankruptcy § 569, Bankruptcy Code Exemption List.

CJS Bankruptcy § 1087, Evidence; Presumptions.

§ 105.   Power of court

(a) The court may issue any order, process, or judgment that is necessary or appropriate to carry out the provisions of this title. No provision of this title providing for the raising of an issue by a party in interest shall be construed to preclude the court from, sua sponte, taking any action or making any determination necessary or appropriate to enforce or implement court orders or rules, or to prevent an abuse of process.

(b) Notwithstanding subsection (a) of this section, a court may not appoint a receiver in a case under this title.

(c) The ability of any district judge or other officer or employee of a district court to exercise any of the authority or responsibilities conferred upon the court under this title shall be determined by reference to the provisions relating to such judge, officer, or employee set forth in title 28. This subsection shall not be interpreted to exclude bankruptcy judges and other officers or employees appointed pursuant to chapter 6 of title 28 from its operation.

(d) The court, on its own motion or on the request of a party in interest—

(1) shall hold such status conferences as are necessary to further the expeditious and economical resolution of the case; and

(2) unless inconsistent with another provision of this title or with applicable Federal Rules of Bankruptcy Procedure, may issue an order at any such conference prescribing such limitations and conditions as the court deems appropriate to ensure that the case is handled expeditiously and economically, including an order that—

(A) sets the date by which the trustee must assume or reject an executory contract or unexpired lease; or

(B) in a case under chapter 11 of this title—

(i) sets a date by which the debtor, or trustee if one has been appointed, shall file a disclosure statement and plan;

(ii) sets a date by which the debtor, or trustee if one has been appointed, shall solicit acceptances of a plan;

(iii) sets the date by which a party in interest other than a debtor may file a plan;

(iv) sets a date by which a proponent of a plan, other than the debtor, shall solicit acceptances of such plan;

(v) fixes the scope and format of the notice to be provided regarding the hearing on approval of the disclosure statement; or

(vi) provides that the hearing on approval of the disclosure statement may be combined with the hearing on confirmation of the plan.

(Pub.L. 95–598, Nov. 6, 1978, 92 Stat. 2555; Pub.L. 98–353, Title I, § 118, July 10, 1984, 98 Stat. 344; Pub.L. 99–554, Title II, § 203, Oct. 27, 1986, 100 Stat. 3097; Pub.L. 103–394, Title I, § 104(a), Oct. 22, 1994, 108 Stat. 4108; Pub.L. 109–8, Title IV, § 440, Apr. 20, 2005, 119 Stat. 114; Pub.L. 111–327, § 2(a)(3), Dec. 22, 2010, 124 Stat. 3557.)

HISTORICAL AND STATUTORY NOTES

Revision Notes and Legislative Reports

1978 Acts. Section 105 is derived from section 2a(15) of present law [section 11(a)(15) of former Title 11], with two changes. First, the limitation on the power of a bankruptcy judge (the power to enjoin a court being reserved to the district judge) is removed as inconsistent with the increased powers and jurisdiction of the new bankruptcy court. Second, the bankruptcy judge is prohibited from appointing a receiver in a case under title 11 under any circumstances. The bankruptcy code has ample provision for the appointment of a trustee when needed. Appointment of a receiver would simply circumvent the established procedures.

This section is also an authorization, as required under 28 U.S.C. 2283, for a court of the United States to stay the action of a State court. As such, *Toucey v. New York Life Insurance Company*, 314 U.S. 118 (1941) [62 S.Ct. 139, 86 L.Ed. 100, 137 A.L.R. 967], is overruled. Senate Report No. 95–989.

1984 Acts. Statements by Legislative Leaders, see 1984 U.S.Code Cong. and Adm.News, p. 576.

1986 Acts. House Report No. 99–764 and House Conference Report No. 99–958, see 1986 U.S.Code Cong. and Adm. News, p. 5227.

1994 Acts. House Report No. 103–835, see 1994 U.S. Code Cong. and Adm. News, p. 3340.

2005 Acts. House Report No. 109–31(Part I), see 2005 U.S. Code Cong. and Adm. News, p. 88.

References in Text

The Federal Rules of Bankruptcy Procedure, referred to in subsec. (d)(2), are set out in this title.

Amendments

2010 Amendments. Subsec. (d)(2). Pub.L. 111–327, § 2(a)(3), inserted "may" following "Procedure,".

2005 Amendments. Subsec. (d). Pub.L. 109–8, § 440(1), struck ", may" following "party in interest" in the matter preceding par. (1).

Subsec. (d)(1). Pub.L. 109–8, § 440(2), rewrote par. (1), which formerly read:

"(1) hold a status conference regarding any case or proceeding under this title after notice to the parties in interest; and".

1994 Amendments. Subsec. (d). Pub.L. 103–394, § 104(a), added subsec. (d).

1986 Amendments. Subsec. (a). Pub.L. 99–554, § 203, added "No provision of this title providing for the raising of an issue by a party in interest shall be construed to preclude the court from, sua sponte, taking any action or making any determination necessary or appropriate to enforce or implement court orders or rules, or to prevent an abuse of process" following "of this title".

1984 Amendments. Subsec. (a). Pub.L. 98–353, § 118(1), struck out "bankruptcy" preceding "court".

Subsec. (b). Pub.L. 98–353, § 118(1), struck out "bankruptcy" preceding "court".

Subsec. (c). Pub.L. 98–353, § 118(2), added subsec. (c).

Effective and Applicability Provisions

2005 Acts. Amendments by Pub.L. 109–8 effective, except as otherwise provided, 180 days after April 20, 2005, and inapplicable with respect to cases commenced under Title 11 before the effective date, see Pub.L. 109–8, § 1501, set out as a note under 11 U.S.C.A. § 101.

1994 Acts. Amendment by Pub.L. 103–394 effective on Oct. 22, 1994, and not to apply with respect to cases commenced under Title 11 of the United States Code before Oct. 22, 1994, see section 702 of Pub.L. 103–394, set out as a note under section 101 of this title.

1986 Acts. Amendment by Pub.L. 99–554 effective 30 days after Oct. 27, 1986, except as otherwise provided for, see section 302(a) of Pub.L. 99–554, set out as a note under section 581 of Title 28, Judiciary and Judicial Procedure.

Amendment by Pub.L. 99–554, § 203, not to become effective in or with respect to certain specified judicial districts until, or apply to cases while pending in such district before, the expiration of the 270-day period beginning 30 days after Oct. 27, 1986, or of the 30-day period beginning on the date the Attorney General certifies under section 303 of Pub.L. 99–554 the region specified in a paragraph of section 581(a) of Title 28, as amended by section 111(a) of Pub.L. 99–554, that includes such district, whichever occurs first, see section 302(d)(1) of Pub.L. 99–554, set out as a note under section 581 of Title 28.

Amendment by Pub.L. 99–554, § 203, not to become effective in or with respect to certain specified judicial districts until, or apply to cases while pending in such district before, the expiration of the 2-year period beginning 30 days after Oct. 27, 1986, or of the 30-day period beginning on the date the Attorney General certifies under section 303 of Pub.L. 99–554 the region specified in a paragraph of section 581(a) of Title 28, as amended by section 111(a) of Pub.L. 99–554, that includes such district, whichever occurs first, see section 302(d)(2) of Pub.L. 99–554, set out as a note under section 581 of Title 28.

Amendment by Pub.L. 99–554, § 203, not to become effective in or with respect to judicial districts established for the States of Alabama and North Carolina until, or apply to cases while pending in such district before, such district elects to be included in a bankruptcy region established in section 581(a) of Title 28, as amended by section 111(a) of Pub.L. 99–554, or Oct. 1, 2002, whichever occurs first, except that the amendment to subsec. (a) of this section shall become effective as of Dec. 1, 1990, and, except as otherwise provided, with respect to cases under chapters 7, 11, 12, and 13 of Title 11 commenced before 30 days after Oct. 27, 1986, and pending in a judicial district in the States of Alabama or North Carolina before any election made under section 302(d)(3)(A) of Pub.L. 99–554 by such district becomes effective or Oct. 1, 2002, whichever occurs first, amendments by Pub.L. 99–554 not to apply until Oct. 1, 2003, or the expiration of the 1-year period beginning on the date such election becomes effective, whichever occurs first, and, further, in any judicial district in Alabama or North Carolina not making the election described in section 302(d)(3)(A) of Pub.L. 99–554, any person appointed under regulations issued by the Judicial Conference to administer estates in cases under Title 11 authorized to establish, etc., a panel of private trustees, and to supervise cases and trustees in cases under chapters 7, 11, 12, and 13 of Title 11, until amendments by sections 201 to 231 of Pub.L. 99–554 effective in such district, see section 302(d)(3)(A) to (F), (H), and (I) of Pub.L. 99–554, set out as a note under section 581 of Title 28.

Amendment by Pub.L. 99–554, § 203, except as otherwise provided, with respect to cases under chapters 7, 11, 12, and 13 of Title 11 commenced before 30 days after Oct. 27, 1986, and pending in a judicial district referred to in section 581(a) of Title 28, as amended by section 111(a) of Pub.L. 99–554, for which a United States trustee is not authorized before 30 days after Oct. 27, 1986 to be appointed, not applicable until the expiration of the 3-year period beginning on Oct. 27, 1986, or of the 1-year period beginning on the date the Attorney General certifies under section 303 of Pub.L. 99–554 the region specified in a paragraph of such section 581(a) that includes such district, whichever occurs first, see section 302(e)(1), (2) of Pub.L. 99–554, set out as a note under section 581 of Title 28.

1984 Acts. Amendment by Pub.L. 98–353 effective July 10, 1984, see section 122(a) of Pub.L. 98–353, set out as a note under section 151 of Title 28, Judiciary and Judicial Procedure.

Separability of Provisions

If any provision of or amendment made by Pub.L. 103–394 or the application of such provision or amendment to any person or circumstance is held to be unconstitutional, the remaining provisions of and amendments made by Pub.L. 103–394 and the application of such provisions and amendments to any person or circumstance shall not be affected thereby, see section 701 of Pub.L. 103–394, set out as a note under section 101 of this title.

CROSS REFERENCES

Bankruptcy investigations, see 18 USCA § 3057.

LIBRARY REFERENCES

American Digest System

Bankruptcy ⟐2124.1 to 2126.

Key Number System Topic No. 51.

Corpus Juris Secundum

Request for Appointment, CJS Bankruptcy § 67.

Request for Appointment, CJS Bankruptcy § 86.

Contested Matters, CJS Bankruptcy § 140.

Pre-Trial Procedure; Status Conferences and Deadlines for Action, CJS Bankruptcy § 144.

General Statutory Powers, CJS Bankruptcy § 242.

Limitations, CJS Bankruptcy § 244.

Relationship to Automatic Stay, CJS Bankruptcy § 246.

Procedure for Obtaining Injunction, CJS Bankruptcy § 247.

Enjoining Suit or Continuance of Suit, CJS Bankruptcy § 248.

Civil Contempt, CJS Bankruptcy § 253.

Court's Inherent and Statutory Power to Sanction Abuse of Judicial Process, CJS Bankruptcy § 258.

Appointment of Receiver, CJS Bankruptcy § 263.

Parties Defendant; Sovereign Immunity, CJS Bankruptcy § 278.

Amendment, CJS Bankruptcy § 358.

Reinstatement; Modification of Order of Relief, CJS Bankruptcy § 509.

Under Statute, CJS Bankruptcy § 547.

Under Statute--Willful Violation, CJS Bankruptcy § 548.

Exercising Right in Chapter 7 Cases, CJS Bankruptcy § 927.

Revocation or Vacation, CJS Bankruptcy § 1207.

§ 106. Waiver of sovereign immunity

(a) Notwithstanding an assertion of sovereign immunity, sovereign immunity is abrogated as to a governmental unit to the extent set forth in this section with respect to the following:

(1) Sections 105, 106, 107, 108, 303, 346, 362, 363, 364, 365, 366, 502, 503, 505, 506, 510, 522, 523, 524, 525, 542, 543, 544, 545, 546, 547, 548, 549, 550, 551, 552, 553, 722, 724, 726, 744, 749, 764, 901, 922, 926, 928, 929, 944, 1107, 1141, 1142, 1143, 1146, 1201, 1203, 1205, 1206, 1227, 1231, 1301, 1303, 1305, and 1327 of this title.

(2) The court may hear and determine any issue arising with respect to the application of such sections to governmental units.

(3) The court may issue against a governmental unit an order, process, or judgment under such sections or the Federal Rules of Bankruptcy Procedure, including an order or judgment awarding a money recovery, but not including an award of punitive damages. Such order or judgment for costs or fees under this title or the Federal Rules of Bankruptcy Procedure against any governmental unit shall be consistent with the provisions and limitations of section 2412(d)(2)(A) of title 28.

(4) The enforcement of any such order, process, or judgment against any governmental unit shall be consistent with appropriate nonbankruptcy law applicable to such governmental unit and, in the case of a money judgment against the United States, shall be paid as if it is a judgment rendered by a district court of the United States.

(5) Nothing in this section shall create any substantive claim for relief or cause of action not otherwise existing under this title, the Federal Rules of Bankruptcy Procedure, or nonbankruptcy law.

(b) A governmental unit that has filed a proof of claim in the case is deemed to have waived sovereign immunity with respect to a claim against such governmental unit that is property of the estate and that arose out of the same transaction or occurrence out of which the claim of such governmental unit arose.

(c) Notwithstanding any assertion of sovereign immunity by a governmental unit, there shall be offset against a claim or interest of a governmental unit any claim against such governmental unit that is property of the estate.

(Pub.L. 95–598, Nov. 6, 1978, 92 Stat. 2555; Pub.L. 103–394, Title I, § 113, Oct. 22, 1994, 108 Stat. 4117; Pub.L. 111–327, § 2(a)(4), Dec. 22, 2010, 124 Stat. 3557.)

HISTORICAL AND STATUTORY NOTES

Revision Notes and Legislative Reports

1978 Acts. Section 106 provides for a limited waiver of sovereign immunity in bankruptcy cases. Though Congress has the power to waive sovereign immunity for the Federal government completely in bankruptcy cases, the policy followed here is designed to achieve approximately the same result that would prevail outside of bankruptcy. Congress does not, however, have the power to waive sovereign immunity completely with respect to claims of a bankrupt estate against a State, though it may exercise its bankruptcy power through the supremacy clause to prevent or prohibit State action that is contrary to bankruptcy policy.

There is, however, a limited change from the result that would prevail in the absence of bankruptcy; the change is two-fold and is within Congress' power vis-a-vis both the Federal Government and the States. First, the filing of a proof of claim against the estate by a governmental unit is a waiver by that governmental unit of sovereign immunity with respect to compulsory counterclaims, as defined in the Federal Rules of Civil Procedure [set out in Title 28, Judiciary and Judicial Procedure], that is, counterclaims arising out of the same transaction or occurrence. The governmental unit cannot receive a distribution from the estate without subjecting itself to any liability it has to the estate within the confines of a compulsory counterclaim rule. Any other result would be one-sided. The counterclaim by the estate against the governmental unit is without limit.

Second, the estate may offset against the allowed claim of a governmental unit, up to the amount of the governmental unit's claim, any claim that the debtor, and thus the estate, has against the governmental unit, without regard to whether the estate's claim arose out of the same transaction or occurrence as the government's claim. Under this provision, the setoff permitted is only to the extent of the governmental unit's claim. No affirmative recovery is permitted. Subsection (a) governs affirmative recovery.

Though this subsection creates a partial waiver of immunity when the governmental unit files a proof of claim, it does not waive immunity if the debtor or trustee, and not the governmental unit, files proof of a governmental unit's claim under proposed 11 U.S.C. 501(c).

This section does not confer sovereign immunity on any governmental unit that does not already have immunity. It simply recognizes any immunity that exists and prescribes the proper treatment of claims by and against that sovereign. Senate Report No. 92–989.

1994 Acts. House Report No. 103–835, see 1994 U.S. Code Cong. and Adm. News, p. 3340.

Legislative Statements

Section 106(c) relating to sovereign immunity is new. The provision indicates that the use of the term "creditor," "entity," or "governmental unit" in title 11 applies to governmental units notwithstanding any assertion of sovereign immunity and that an order of the court binds governmental units. The provision is included to comply with the requirement in case law that an express waiver of sovereign immunity is required in order to be effective. Section 106(c) codifies *In re Gwilliam*, 519 F.2d 407 (9th Cir., 1975), and *In re Dolard*, 519 F.2d 282 (9th Cir., 1975), permitting the bankruptcy court to determine the amount and dischargeability of tax liabilities owing by the debtor or the estate prior to or during a bankruptcy case whether or not the governmental unit to which such taxes are owed files a proof of claim. Except as provided in sections 106(a) and (b) subsection (c) is not limited to those issues, but permits the bankruptcy court to bind governmental units on other matters as well. For example, section 106(c) permits a trustee or debtor in possession to assert avoiding powers under title 11 against a governmental unit; contrary language in the House report to H.R. 8200 is thereby overruled.

References in Text

The Federal Rules of Bankruptcy Procedure, referred to in subsec. (a)(3) and (5), are set out in this title.

Amendments

2010 Amendments. Subsec. (a)(1). Pub.L. 111–327, § 2(a)(4), struck out "728," following "726,".

1994 Amendments. Subsecs. (a) to (c). Pub.L. 103–394, § 113, amended subsecs. (a) to (c) generally. Prior to amendment, subsecs. (a) to (c) read as follows:

"**(a)** A governmental unit is deemed to have waived sovereign immunity with respect to any claim against such governmental unit that is property of the estate and that arose out of the same transaction or occurrence out of which such governmental unit's claim arose.

"**(b)** There shall be offset against an allowed claim or interest of a governmental unit any claim against such governmental unit that is property of the estate.

"**(c)** Except as provided in subsections (a) and (b) of this section and notwithstanding any assertion of sovereign immunity—

"**(1)** a provision of this title that contains 'creditor', 'entity', or 'governmental unit' applies to governmental units; and

"**(2)** a determination by the court of an issue arising under such a provision binds governmental units."

Effective and Applicability Provisions

1994 Acts. Amendment by section 113 of Pub.L. 103–394 effective on Oct. 22, 1994, and applicable with respect to cases commenced under Title 11 of the United States Code before, on, and after Oct. 22, 1994, see section 702 of Pub.L. 103–394, set out as a note under section 101 of this title.

Separability of Provisions

If any provision of or amendment made by Pub.L. 103–394 or the application of such provision or amendment to any person or circumstance is held to be unconstitutional, the remaining provisions of and amendments made by Pub.L. 103–394 and the application of such provisions and amendments to any person or circumstance shall not be affected thereby, see section 701 of Pub.L. 103–394, set out as a note under section 101 of this title.

LIBRARY REFERENCES

American Digest System

Bankruptcy ⟐2679.

Key Number System Topic No. 51.

Corpus Juris Secundum

Parties Defendant; Sovereign Immunity, CJS Bankruptcy § 278.

Assertion of Claim Against Governmental Unit; Sovereign Immunity, CJS Bankruptcy § 634.

Estate's or Debtor's Right of Setoff, CJS Bankruptcy § 961.

§ 107. Public access to papers

(a) Except as provided in subsections (b) and (c) and subject to section 112, a paper filed in a case under this title and the dockets of a bankruptcy court are public records and open to examination by an entity at reasonable times without charge.

(b) On request of a party in interest, the bankruptcy court shall, and on the bankruptcy court's own motion, the bankruptcy court may—

(1) protect an entity with respect to a trade secret or confidential research, development, or commercial information; or

(2) protect a person with respect to scandalous or defamatory matter contained in a paper filed in a case under this title.

(c)(1) The bankruptcy court, for cause, may protect an individual, with respect to the following types of information to the extent the court finds that disclosure of such information would create undue risk of identity theft or other unlawful injury to the individual or the individual's property:

(A) Any means of identification (as defined in section 1028(d) of title 18) contained in a paper filed, or to be filed, in a case under this title.

(B) Other information contained in a paper described in subparagraph (A).

(2) Upon ex parte application demonstrating cause, the court shall provide access to information protected pursuant to paragraph (1) to an entity acting pursuant to the police or regulatory power of a domestic governmental unit.

(3) The United States trustee, bankruptcy administrator, trustee, and any auditor serving under section 586(f) of title 28—

(A) shall have full access to all information contained in any paper filed or submitted in a case under this title; and

(B) shall not disclose information specifically protected by the court under this title.

(Pub.L. 95–598, Nov. 6, 1978, 92 Stat. 2556; Pub.L. 109–8, Title II, §§ 233(c), 234(a), (c), Apr. 20, 2005, 119 Stat. 74, 75; Pub.L. 111–327, § 2(a)(5), Dec. 22, 2010, 124 Stat. 3557.)

HISTORICAL AND STATUTORY NOTES

Revision Notes and Legislative Reports

1978 Acts. Subsection (a) of this section makes all papers filed in a bankruptcy case and the dockets of the bankruptcy court public and open to examination at reasonable times without charge. "Docket" includes the claims docket, the proceedings docket, and all papers filed in a case.

Subsection (b) permits the court, on its own motion, and requires the court, on the request of a party in interest, to protect trade secrets, confidential research, development, or commercial information, and to protect persons against scandalous or defamatory matter. Senate Report No. 95–989.

2005 Acts. House Report No. 109–31(Part I), see 2005 U.S. Code Cong. and Adm. News, p. 88.

Amendments

2010 Amendments. Subsection (a). Pub.L. 111–327, § 2(a)(5), struck out "subsection (b) of this section" and inserted "subsections (b) and (c)".

2005 Amendments. Subsec. (a). Pub.L. 109–8, § 233(c), inserted "and subject to section 112" after "section".

Pub.L. 109–8, § 234(c), which directed that subsec. (a) is amended by striking "subsection (b)," and inserting "subsections (b) and (c)," was incapable of execution.

Subsec. (c). Pub.L. 109–8, § 234(a), added subsec. (c).

Effective and Applicability Provisions

2005 Acts. Amendments by Pub.L. 109–8 effective, except as otherwise provided, 180 days after April 20, 2005, and inapplicable with respect to cases commenced under Title 11 before the effective date, see Pub.L. 109–8, § 1501, set out as a note under 11 U.S.C.A. § 101.

CROSS REFERENCES

Application for search of records, see Fed.Rules Bankr. Proc. Form B 132, 11 USCA.

Documents relating to adverse interest and conduct of officers of estate, see 18 USCA § 154.

Reporting of obsolete information prohibited, see 15 USCA § 1681c.

LIBRARY REFERENCES

American Digest System

Records ☞32, 31.

Key Number System Topic No. 326.

Corpus Juris Secundum

Protective Orders, CJS Bankruptcy § 147.

Parties Defendant; Sovereign Immunity, CJS Bankruptcy § 278.

Papers Filed as Public Records, CJS Bankruptcy § 286.

Trade Secrets, Confidential Information and Scandalous or Defamatory Matter, CJS Bankruptcy § 831.

Prevention of Identity Theft or Other Unlawful Injury, CJS Bankruptcy § 833.

Discretion of Court in Restricting Public Access, CJS Bankruptcy § 834.

§ 108. Extension of time

(a) If applicable nonbankruptcy law, an order entered in a nonbankruptcy proceeding, or an agreement fixes a period within which the debtor may commence an action, and such period has not expired before the date of the filing of the petition, the trustee may commence such action only before the later of—

    (1) the end of such period, including any suspension of such period occurring on or after the commencement of the case; or

    (2) two years after the order for relief.

(b) Except as provided in subsection (a) of this section, if applicable nonbankruptcy law, an order entered in a nonbankruptcy proceeding, or an agreement fixes a period within which the debtor or an individual protected under section 1201 or 1301 of this title may file any pleading, demand, notice, or proof of claim or loss, cure a default, or perform any other similar act, and such period has not expired before the date of the filing of the petition, the trustee may only file, cure, or perform, as the case may be, before the later of—

    (1) the end of such period, including any suspension of such period occurring on or after the commencement of the case; or

    (2) 60 days after the order for relief.

(c) Except as provided in section 524 of this title, if applicable nonbankruptcy law, an order entered in a nonbankruptcy proceeding, or an agreement fixes a period for commencing or continuing a civil action in a court other than a bankruptcy court on a claim against the debtor, or against an individual with respect to which such individual is protected under section 1201 or 1301 of this title, and such period has not expired before the date of the filing of the petition, then such period does not expire until the later of—

    (1) the end of such period, including any suspension of such period occurring on or after the commencement of the case; or

    (2) 30 days after notice of the termination or expiration of the stay under section 362, 922, 1201, or 1301 of this title, as the case may be, with respect to such claim.

(Pub.L. 95–598, Nov. 6, 1978, 92 Stat. 2556; Pub.L. 98–353, Title III, § 424, July 10, 1984, 98 Stat. 369; Pub.L. 99–554, Title II, § 257(b), Oct. 27, 1986, 100 Stat. 3114; Pub.L. 109–8, Title XII, § 1203, Apr. 20, 2005, 119 Stat. 193.)

HISTORICAL AND STATUTORY NOTES

Revision Notes and Legislative Reports

1978 Acts. Subsections (a) and (b), derived from Bankruptcy Act section 11 [section 29 of former Title 11], permit the trustee, when he steps into the shoes of the debtor, an extension of time for filing an action or doing some other act that is required to preserve the debtor's rights. Subsection (a) extends any statute of limitation for commencing or continuing an action by the debtor for two years after the date of the order for relief, unless it would expire later. Subsection (b) gives the trustee 60 days to take other actions not covered under subsection (a), such as filing a pleading, demand, notice, or proof of claim or loss (such as an insurance claim), unless the period for doing the relevant act expires later than 60 days after the date of the order for relief.

Subsection (c) extends the statute of limitations for creditors. Thus, if a creditor is stayed from commencing or continuing an action against the debtor because of the bankruptcy case, then the creditor is permitted an additional 30 days after notice of the event by which the stay is terminated, whether that event be relief from the automatic stay under proposed 11 U.S.C. 362 or 1301, the closing of the bankruptcy case (which terminates the stay), or the exception from discharge of the debts on which the creditor claims.

In the case of Federal tax liabilities, the Internal Revenue Code [Title 26] suspends the statute of limitations on a tax liability of a taxpayer from running while his assets are in the control or custody of a court and for 6 months thereafter (sec.

6503(b) of the Code) [Title 26]. The amendment applies this rule in a title 11 proceeding. Accordingly, the statute of limitations on collection of a nondischargeable Federal tax liability of a debtor will resume running after 6 months following the end of the period during which the debtor's assets are in the control or custody of the bankruptcy court. This rule will provide the Internal Revenue Service adequate time to collect nondischargeable taxes following the end of the title 11 proceedings. Senate Report No. 95–989.

1984 Acts. Statements by Legislative Leaders, see 1984 U.S.Code Cong. and Adm.News, p. 576.

1986 Acts. House Report No. 99–764 and House Conference Report No. 99–958, see 1986 U.S.Code Cong. and Adm. News, p. 5227.

2005 Acts. House Report No. 109–31(Part I), see 2005 U.S. Code Cong. and Adm. News, p. 88.

Legislative Statements

Extension of time: The House amendment adopts section 108(c)(1) of the Senate amendment which expressly includes any special suspensions of statutes of limitation periods on collection outside bankruptcy when assets are under the authority of a court. For example, section 6503(b) of the Internal Revenue Code [Title 26] suspends collection of tax liabilities while the debtor's assets are in the control or custody of a court, and for 6 months thereafter. By adopting the language of the Senate amendment, the House amendment insures not only that the period for collection of the taxes outside bankruptcy will not expire during the title 11 proceedings, but also that such period will not expire until at least 6 months thereafter, which is the minimum suspension period provided by the Internal Revenue Code [Title 26].

Codifications

Amendment by Pub.L. 99–554, § 257(b)(2)(B), which directed amendment of subsec. (c)(2) by inserting "1201," after "722," was incapable of execution.

Amendments

2005 Amendments. Subsec. (c)(2). Pub.L. 109–8, § 1203, substituted "922, 1201, or" for "922, or".

1986 Amendments. Subsec. (b). Pub.L. 99–554, § 257(b)(1), inserted "1201 or" preceding "1301".

Subsec. (c). Pub.L. 99–554, § 257(b)(2)(A), in the matter preceding par. (1) struck out "section 1301" and inserted "section 1201 or 1301".

Subsec. (c)(2). Pub.L. 99–554, § 257(b)(2)(B), which directed the amendment of subsec. (c) by inserting "1201," after "722," could not be executed because "722," did not appear in text.

1984 Amendments. Subsec. (a). Pub.L. 98–353, § 424(b), added "nonbankruptcy" after "applicable" and "entered in a" in provisions preceding par. (1).

Subsec. (a)(1). Pub.L. 98–353, § 424(a), substituted "or" for "and" after the semicolon.

Subsec. (b). Pub.L. 98–353, § 424(b), added "nonbankruptcy" after "applicable" and "entered in a" in provisions preceding par. (1).

Subsec. (b)(1). Pub.L. 98–353, § 424(a), substituted "or" for "and" after the semicolon.

Subsec. (c). Pub.L. 98–353, § 424(b), added "nonbankruptcy" after "applicable" and "entered in a" in provisions preceding par. (1).

Subsec. (c)(1). Pub.L. 98–353, § 424(a), substituted "or" for "and" after the semicolon.

Effective and Applicability Provisions

2005 Acts. Amendments by Pub.L. 109–8 effective, except as otherwise provided, 180 days after April 20, 2005, and inapplicable with respect to cases commenced under Title 11 before the effective date, see Pub.L. 109–8, § 1501, set out as a note under 11 U.S.C.A. § 101.

1986 Acts. Amendment by Pub.L. 99–554 effective 30 days after Oct. 27, 1986, but not applicable to cases commenced under this title before that date, see section 302(a), (c)(1) of Pub.L. 99–554, set out as a note under section 581 of Title 28, Judiciary and Judicial Procedure.

1984 Acts. Amendment by Pub.L. 98–353 effective with respect to cases filed 90 days after July 10, 1984, see section 552(a), formerly 553(a) of Pub.L. 98–353, set out as a note under section 101 of this title.

LIBRARY REFERENCES

American Digest System

Bankruptcy ⚲2157.

Key Number System Topic No. 51.

Corpus Juris Secundum

Suits by Trustee, CJS Bankruptcy § 105.

Relationship to Automatic Stay, CJS Bankruptcy § 246.

Parties Defendant; Sovereign Immunity, CJS Bankruptcy § 278.

Enlargement, CJS Bankruptcy § 308.

Property Subject to Liens or Mortgages, CJS Bankruptcy § 606.

Prepetition Termination of Contract or Lease--Right to Relief from Forfeiture as Assumable Interest, CJS Bankruptcy § 910.

Postpetition Expiration of Agreement, CJS Bankruptcy § 911.

Modification of Claims; Cram Down of Secured Claims, CJS Bankruptcy § 1174.

Pendency of Other Legal Proceedings--Proceedings in Insolvency, Bankruptcy, or Receivership, CJS Limitations of Actions § 178.

§ 109.   Who may be a debtor

(a) Notwithstanding any other provision of this section, only a person that resides or has a domicile, a place of business, or property in the United States, or a municipality, may be a debtor under this title.

(b) A person may be a debtor under chapter 7 of this title only if such person is not—

(1) a railroad;

(2) a domestic insurance company, bank, savings bank, cooperative bank, savings and loan association, building and loan association, homestead association, a New Markets Venture Capital company as defined in section 351 of the Small Business Investment Act of 1958, a small business investment company licensed by the Small Business Administration under section 301 of the Small Business Investment Act of

1958, credit union, or industrial bank or similar institution which is an insured bank as defined in section 3(h) of the Federal Deposit Insurance Act, except that an uninsured State member bank, or a corporation organized under section 25A of the Federal Reserve Act, which operates, or operates as, a multilateral clearing organization pursuant to section 409 of the Federal Deposit Insurance Corporation Improvement Act of 1991 may be a debtor if a petition is filed at the direction of the Board of Governors of the Federal Reserve System; or

(3)(A) a foreign insurance company, engaged in such business in the United States; or

(B) a foreign bank, savings bank, cooperative bank, savings and loan association, building and loan association, or credit union, that has a branch or agency (as defined in section 1(b) of the International Banking Act of 1978) in the United States.

(c) An entity may be a debtor under chapter 9 of this title if and only if such entity—

(1) is a municipality;

(2) is specifically authorized, in its capacity as a municipality or by name, to be a debtor under such chapter by State law, or by a governmental officer or organization empowered by State law to authorize such entity to be a debtor under such chapter;

(3) is insolvent;

(4) desires to effect a plan to adjust such debts; and

(5)(A) has obtained the agreement of creditors holding at least a majority in amount of the claims of each class that such entity intends to impair under a plan in a case under such chapter;

(B) has negotiated in good faith with creditors and has failed to obtain the agreement of creditors holding at least a majority in amount of the claims of each class that such entity intends to impair under a plan in a case under such chapter;

(C) is unable to negotiate with creditors because such negotiation is impracticable; or

(D) reasonably believes that a creditor may attempt to obtain a transfer that is avoidable under section 547 of this title.

(d) Only a railroad, a person that may be a debtor under chapter 7 of this title (except a stockbroker or a commodity broker), and an uninsured State member bank, or a corporation organized under section 25A of the Federal Reserve Act, which operates, or operates as, a multilateral clearing organization pursuant to section 409 of the Federal Deposit Insurance Corporation Improvement Act of 1991 may be a debtor under chapter 11 of this title.

(e) Only an individual with regular income that owes, on the date of the filing of the petition, noncontingent, liquidated, unsecured debts of less than

$360,475 [1] and noncontingent, liquidated, secured debts of less than $1,081,400 [1], or an individual with regular income and such individual's spouse, except a stockbroker or a commodity broker, that owe, on the date of the filing of the petition, noncontingent, liquidated, unsecured debts that aggregate less than $360,475 [1] and noncontingent, liquidated, secured debts of less than $1,081,400 [1] may be a debtor under chapter 13 of this title.

(f) Only a family farmer or family fisherman with regular annual income may be a debtor under chapter 12 of this title.

(g) Notwithstanding any other provision of this section, no individual or family farmer may be a debtor under this title who has been a debtor in a case pending under this title at any time in the preceding 180 days if—

(1) the case was dismissed by the court for willful failure of the debtor to abide by orders of the court, or to appear before the court in proper prosecution of the case; or

(2) the debtor requested and obtained the voluntary dismissal of the case following the filing of a request for relief from the automatic stay provided by section 362 of this title.

(h)(1) Subject to paragraphs (2) and (3), and notwithstanding any other provision of this section other than paragraph (4) of this subsection, an individual may not be a debtor under this title unless such individual has, during the 180–day period ending on the date of filing of the petition by such individual, received from an approved nonprofit budget and credit counseling agency described in section 111(a) an individual or group briefing (including a briefing conducted by telephone or on the Internet) that outlined the opportunities for available credit counseling and assisted such individual in performing a related budget analysis.

(2)(A) Paragraph (1) shall not apply with respect to a debtor who resides in a district for which the United States trustee (or the bankruptcy administrator, if any) determines that the approved nonprofit budget and credit counseling agencies for such district are not reasonably able to provide adequate services to the additional individuals who would otherwise seek credit counseling from such agencies by reason of the requirements of paragraph (1).

(B) The United States trustee (or the bankruptcy administrator, if any) who makes a determination described in subparagraph (A) shall review such determination not later than 1 year after the date of such determination, and not less frequently than annually thereafter. Notwithstanding the preceding sentence, a nonprofit budget and credit counseling agency may be disapproved by the United States trustee (or the bankruptcy administrator, if any) at any time.

(3)(A) Subject to subparagraph (B), the requirements of paragraph (1) shall not apply with respect to a debtor who submits to the court a certification that—

(i) describes exigent circumstances that merit a waiver of the requirements of paragraph (1);

(ii) states that the debtor requested credit counseling services from an approved nonprofit budget and credit counseling agency, but was unable to obtain the services referred to in paragraph (1) during the 7–day period beginning on the date on which the debtor made that request; and

(iii) is satisfactory to the court.

(B) With respect to a debtor, an exemption under subparagraph (A) shall cease to apply to that debtor on the date on which the debtor meets the requirements of paragraph (1), but in no case may the exemption apply to that debtor after the date that is 30 days after the debtor files a petition, except that the court, for cause, may order an additional 15 days.

(4) The requirements of paragraph (1) shall not apply with respect to a debtor whom the court determines, after notice and hearing, is unable to complete those requirements because of incapacity, disability, or active military duty in a military combat zone. For the purposes of this paragraph, incapacity means that the debtor is impaired by reason of mental illness or mental deficiency so that he is incapable of realizing and making rational decisions with respect to his financial responsibilities; and "disability" means that the debtor is so physically impaired as to be unable, after reasonable effort, to participate in an in person, telephone, or Internet briefing required under paragraph (1).

(Pub.L. 95–598, Nov. 6, 1978, 92 Stat. 2557; Pub.L. 97–320, Title VII, § 703(d), Oct. 15, 1982, 96 Stat. 1539; Pub.L. 98–353, Title III, §§ 301, 425, July 10, 1984, 98 Stat. 352, 369; Pub.L. 99–554, Title II, § 253, Oct. 27, 1986, 100 Stat. 3105; Pub.L. 100–597, § 2, Nov. 3, 1988, 102 Stat. 3028; Pub.L. 103–394, Title I, § 108(a), Title II, § 220, Title IV, § 402, Title V, § 501(d)(2), Oct. 22, 1994, 108 Stat. 4111, 4129, 4141, 4143; Pub.L. 106–554, § 1(a)(5) [Title I, § 112(c)(1), (2)], (8) [§ 1(e)], Dec. 21, 2000, 114 Stat. 2763, 2763A–393, 2763A–665; Pub.L. 109–8, Title I, § 106(a), Title VIII, § 802(d)(1), Title X, § 1007(b), Title XII, § 1204(1), Apr. 20, 2005, 119 Stat. 37, 146, 188, 193; Pub.L. 111–16, § 2(1), May 7, 2009, 123 Stat. 1607; Pub.L. 111–327, § 2(a)(6), Dec. 22, 2010, 124 Stat. 3557.)

1 Dollar amount as adjusted by the Judicial Conference of the United States. See Adjustment of Dollar Amounts notes set out under this section and 11 U.S.C.A. § 104.

HISTORICAL AND STATUTORY NOTES

Revision Notes and Legislative Reports

1978 Acts. This section specifies eligibility to be a debtor under the bankruptcy laws. The first criterion, found in the current Bankruptcy Act section 2a(1) [section 11(a)(1) of former Title 11] requires that the debtor reside or have a domicile, a place of business, or property in the United States.

Subsection (b) defines eligibility for liquidation under chapter 7. All persons are eligible except insurance companies, and certain banking institutions. These exclusions are contained in current law. However, the banking institution exception is expanded in light of changes in various banking laws since the current law was last amended on this point. A change is also made to clarify that the bankruptcy laws cover foreign banks and insurance companies not engaged in the banking or insurance business in the United States but having assets in the United States. Banking institutions and insurance companies engaged in business in this country are excluded from liquidation under the bankruptcy laws because they are bodies for which alternate provision is made for their liquidation under various State or Federal regulatory laws. Conversely, when a foreign bank or insurance company is not engaged in the banking or insurance business in the United States, then those regulatory laws do not apply, and the bankruptcy laws are the only ones available for administration of any assets found in United States.

The first clause of subsection (b) provides that a railroad is not a debtor except where the requirements of section 1174 are met.

Subsection (c) provides that only a person who may be a debtor under chapter 7 and a railroad may also be a debtor under chapter 11, but a stockbroker or commodity broker is eligible for relief only under chapter 7. Subsection (d) establishes dollar limitations on the amount of indebtedness that an individual with regular income can incur and yet file under chapter 13. Senate Report No. 95–989.

Subsection (c) defines eligibility for chapter 9. Only a municipality that is unable to pay its debts as they mature, and that is not prohibited by State law from proceeding under chapter 9, is permitted to be a chapter 9 debtor. The subsection is derived from Bankruptcy Act section 84 [section 404 of former Title 11], with two changes. First, section 84 requires that the municipality be "generally authorized to file a petition under this chapter by the legislature, or by a governmental officer or organization empowered by State law to authorize the filing of a petition." The "generally authorized" language is unclear, and has generated a problem for a Colorado Metropolitan District that attempted to use chapter IX [chapter 9 of former Title 11] in 1976. The "not prohibited" language provides flexibility for both the States and the municipalities involved, while protecting State sovereignty as required by *Ashton v. Cameron County Water District No. 1,* 298 U.S. 513 (1936) [56 S.Ct. 892, 80 L.Ed. 1309, 31 Am. Bankr.Rep.N.S. 96, rehearing denied 57 S.Ct. 5, 299 U.S. 619, 81 L.Ed. 457] and *Bekins v. United States,* 304 U.S. 27 (1938) [58 S.Ct. 811, 82 L.Ed. 1137, 36 Am.Bankr.Rep.N.S. 187, rehearing denied 58 S.Ct. 1043, 1044, 304 U.S. 589, 82 L.Ed. 1549].

The second change deletes the four prerequisites to filing found in section 84 [section 404 of former Title 11]. The prerequisites require the municipality to have worked out a plan in advance, to have attempted to work out a plan without success, to fear that a creditor will attempt to obtain a preference, or to allege that prior negotiation is impracticable. The loopholes in those prerequisites are larger than the requirement itself. It was a compromise from pre-1976 chapter IX [chapter 9 of former Title 11] under which a municipality could file only if it had worked out an adjustment plan in advance. In the meantime, chapter IX protection was unavailable. There was some controversy at the time of the enactment of current chapter IX concerning deletion of the pre-negotiation requirement. It was argued that deletion would lead to a rash of municipal bankruptcies. The prerequisites now contained in section 84 were inserted to assuage that fear. They are largely cosmetic and precatory, however, and do not offer any significant deterrent to use of chapter IX. Instead, other factors, such as a general reluctance on the part of any debtor, especially a municipality, to use the bankruptcy laws, operates as a much more effective deterrent against capricious use.

Subsection (d) permits a person that may proceed under chapter 7 to be a debtor under chapter 11, Reorganization, with two exceptions. Railroads, which are excluded from chapter 7, are permitted to proceed under chapter 11. Stockbrokers and commodity brokers, which are permitted to be debtors under chapter 7, are excluded from chapter 11. The special rules for treatment of customer accounts that are the essence of stockbroker and commodity broker liquidations are available only in chapter 7. Customers would be unprotected under chapter 11. The special protective rules are unavailable in chapter 11 because their complexity would make reorganization very difficult at best, and unintelligible at worst. The variety of options available in reorganization cases make it extremely difficult to reorganize and continue to provide the special customer protection necessary in these cases.

Subsection (e) specifies eligibility for chapter 13, Adjustment of Debts of an Individual with Regular Income. An individual with regular income, or an individual with regular income and the individual's spouse, may proceed under chapter 13. As noted in connection with the definition of the term "individual with regular income", this represents a significant departure from current law. The change might have been too great, however, without some limitation. Thus, the debtor (or the debtor and spouse) must have unsecured debts that aggregate less than $100,000, and secured debts that aggregate less than $500,000. These figures will permit the small sole proprietor, for whom a chapter 11 reorganization is too cumbersome a procedure, to proceed under chapter 13. It does not create a presumption that any sole proprietor within that range is better off in chapter 13 than chapter 11. The conversion rules found in section 1307 will govern the appropriateness of the two chapters for any particular individual. The figures merely set maximum limits.

Whether a small business operated by a husband and wife, the so-called "mom and pop grocery store," will be a partnership and thus excluded from chapter 13, or a business owned by an individual, will have to be determined on the facts of each case. Even if partnership papers have not been filed, for example, the issue will be whether the assets of the grocery store are for the benefit of all creditors of the debtor or only for business creditors, and whether such assets may be the subject of a chapter 13 proceeding. The intent of the section is to follow current law that a partnership by estoppel may be adjudicated in bankruptcy and therefore would not prevent a chapter 13 debtor from subjecting assets in such a partnership to the reach of all creditors in a chapter 13 case. However, if the partnership is found to be a partnership by agreement, even informal agreement, then a separate entity exists and the assets of that entity would be exempt from a case under chapter 13. House Report No. 95–595.

1982 Acts. Senate Report No. 97–536 and Senate Conference Report No. 97–641, see 1982 U.S. Code Cong. and Adm. News, p. 3054.

1984 Acts. Statements by Legislative Leaders, see 1984 U.S. Code Cong. and Adm. News, p. 576.

1986 Acts. House Report No. 99–764 and House Conference Report No. 99–958, see U.S. Code Cong. and Adm. News, p. 5227.

1988 Acts. House Report No. 100–1011, see 1988 U.S. Code Cong. and Adm. News, p. 4115.

1994 Acts. House Report No. 103–835, see 1994 U.S. Code Cong. and Adm. News, p. 3340.

2000 Acts. House Report No. 106–645 and Statement by President, see 2000 U.S. Code Cong. and Adm. News, p. 2459.

2005 Acts. House Report No. 109–31(Part I), see 2005 U.S. Code Cong. and Adm. News, p. 88.

Legislative Statements

Section 109(b) of the House amendment adopts a provision contained in H.R. 8200 as passed by the House. Railroad liquidations will occur under chapter 11, not chapter 7.

Section 109(c) contains a provision which tracks the Senate amendment as to when a municipality may be a debtor under chapter 11 of title 11. As under the Bankruptcy Act [former Title 11], State law authorization and prepetition negotiation efforts are required.

Section 109(e) represents a compromise between H.R. 8200 as passed by the House and the Senate amendment relating to the dollar amounts restricting eligibility to be a debtor under chapter 13 of title 11. The House amendment adheres to the limit of $100,000 placed on unsecured debts in H.R. 8200 as passed by the House. It adopts a midpoint of $350,000 as a limit on secured claims, a compromise between the level of $500,000 in H.R. 8200 as passed by the House and $200,000 as contained in the Senate amendment.

References in Text

Section 351 of the Small Business Investment Act of 1958, referred to in subsec. (b)(2), is section 351 of Pub.L. 85–699, which is classified to 15 U.S.C.A. § 689.

Subsection (c) or (d) of section 301 of the Small Business Investment Act of 1958, referred to in subsec. (b)(2), is subsection (c) or (d) of section 301 of Pub.L. 85–699, Title III, Aug. 21, 1958, which is classified to 15 U.S.C.A. § 681(c) or (d). Subsection (d) of section 301 was repealed by Pub.L. 104–208, Div. D, Title II, § 208(b)(3)(A), Sept. 30, 1996, 110 Stat. 3009–742.

Section 3 of the Federal Deposit Insurance Act, referred to in subsec. (b)(2), is section 2[3] of Act Sept. 21, 1950, c. 967, 64 Stat. 873, which is classified to 12 U.S.C.A. § 1813.

Section 25A of the Federal Reserve Act, referred to in subsecs. (b)(2) and (d), is Dec. 23, 1913, c. 6, § 25A, formerly § 25(a), as added Dec. 24, 1919, c. 18, 41 Stat. 378, as amended, which is classified to subchapter II of chapter 6 of Title 12 (12 U.S.C.A. § 611 et seq.).

Section 409 of the Federal Deposit Insurance Corporation Improvement Act of 1991, referred to in subsecs. (b)(2) and (d), is Pub.L. 102–242, Title IV, § 409, as added by Pub.L. 106–554, § 1(a)(5) [Title I, § 112(a)(3)], Dec. 21, 2000, 114 Stat. 2763, 2763A–391, which is classified as 12 U.S.C.A. § 4422.

Section 1(b) of the International Banking Act of 1978, referred to in subsec. (b)(3)(B), is Pub.L. 95–369, § 1(b), Sept. 17, 1978, 92 Stat. 607, as amended, which is classified to 12 U.S.C.A. § 3101.

Chapter 7 of this title, referred to in subsec. (d), is 11 U.S.C.A. § 701 et seq.

Chapter 11 of this title, referred to in subsec. (d), is 11 U.S.C.A. § 1101 et seq.

Amendments

2010 Amendments. Subsec. (b)(3)(B). Pub.L. 111–327, § 2(a)(6)(A), struck out "1978" and inserted "1978)".

Subsec. (h)(1). Pub.L. 111–327, § 2(a)(6)(B), inserted "other than paragraph (4) of this subsection" following "this section", and struck out "preceding" and inserted "ending on".

Subsec. (e). By notice dated Feb. 25, 2010, 75 F.R. 8747, dollar amount adjusted by the Judicial Conference of the United States which adjusted "$336,900" to "$360,475" each time it appeared and "$1,010,650" to "$1,081,400" each time it appeared. See 11 U.S.C.A. § 104 and Adjustment of Dollar Amounts notes under this section.

2009 Amendments. Subsec. (h)(3)(A)(ii). Pub.L. 111–16, § 2(1), struck out "5–day" and inserted "7–day".

2007 Amendments. Subsec. (e). By notice dated Feb. 14, 2007, 72 F.R. 7082, dollar amount adjusted by the Judicial Conference of the United States which adjusted "$307,675" to "$336,900" each time it appeared and "$922,975" to "$1,010,650" each time it appeared. See 11 U.S.C.A. § 104 and Adjustment of Dollar Amounts notes under this section.

2005 Amendments. Subsec. (b)(2). Pub.L. 109–8, § 1204(1), struck out "subsection (c) or (d) of" preceding "section 301 of the Small Business Investment Act of 1958".

Subsec. (b)(3). Pub.L. 109–8, § 802(d)(1), rewrote par. (3), which formerly read: "**(3)** a foreign insurance company, bank, savings bank, cooperative bank, savings and loan association, building and loan association, homestead association, or credit union, engaged in such business in the United States."

Subsec. (f). Pub.L. 109–8, § 1007(b), inserted "or family fisherman" after "family farmer".

Subsec. (h). Pub.L. 109–8, § 106(a), added subsec. (h).

2004 Amendments. Subsec. (e). By notice dated Feb. 18, 2004, 69 F.R. 8482, dollar amount adjusted by the Judicial Conference of the United States which adjusted "$290,525" to "$307,675" each time it appeared and "$871,550" to "$922,975" each time it appeared. See 11 U.S.C.A. § 104 and Adjustment of Dollar Amounts notes under this section.

2001 Amendments. Subsec. (e). By notice dated Feb. 20, 2001, 66 F.R. 10910, dollar amount adjusted by the Judicial Conference of the United States which adjusted "$269,250" to "$290,525" each time it appeared and "$807,750" to "$871,550" each time it appeared. See 11 U.S.C.A. § 104 and Adjustment of Dollar Amounts notes under this section.

2000 Amendments. Subsec. (b)(2). Pub.L. 106–554, § 1(a)(8)[§ 1(e)], inserted "a New Markets Venture Capital company as defined in section 351 of the Small Business Investment Act of 1958,," after "homestead association".

Pub.L. 106–554, § 1(a)(5) [Title I, § 112(c)(1)], struck "; or" and inserted the following: " , except that an uninsured State member bank, or a corporation organized under section 25A of the Federal Reserve Act, which operates, or operates as, a multilateral clearing organization pursuant to section 409 of the Federal Deposit Insurance Corporation Improvement Act of 1991 may be a debtor if a petition is filed at the direction of the Board of Governors of the Federal Reserve System; or".

Subsec. (d). Pub.L. 106–554, § 1(a)(5) [Title I, § 112(c)(2)], revised subsec. (d). Prior to revision, subsec. (d) read as follows:

"**(d)** Only a person that may be a debtor under chapter 7 of this title, except a stockbroker or a commodity broker, and a railroad may be a debtor under chapter 11 of this title."

1998 Amendments. Subsec. (e). By notice dated Feb. 3, 1998, 63 F.R. 7179, dollar amount adjusted by the Judicial Conference of the United States which adjusted "$250,000" to "$269,250" each time it appeared and "$750,000" to "$807,750" each time it appeared. See 11 U.S.C.A. § 104 and Adjustment of Dollar Amounts notes under this section.

1994 Amendments. Subsec. (b)(2). Pub.L. 103–394, § 220, added a small business investment company licensed by the Small Business Administration under subsection (c) or (d) of section 301 of the Small Business Investment Act of 1958 to the list of institutions which may not be debtors under chapter 7 of this title.

Pub.L. 103–394, § 501(d)(2), struck out "(12 U.S.C. 1813(h))" following "Federal Deposit Insurance Act".

Subsec. (c)(2). Pub.L. 103–394, § 402, substituted "specifically authorized, in its capacity as a municipality or by name," for "generally authorized".

Subsec. (e). Pub.L. 103–394, § 108(a), substituted "$250,000" for "$100,000", wherever appearing, and substituted "$750,000" for "$350,000", wherever appearing.

1988 Amendments. Subsec. (c)(3). Pub.L. 100–597 deleted from definition of debtor an entity "unable to meet such entity's debts as such debts mature".

1986 Amendments. Subsec. (f). Pub.L. 99–554, § 253(1)(B), (2), added subsec. (f). Former subsec. (f) was redesignated (g).

Subsec. (g). Pub.L. 99–554, § 253(1), redesignated former subsec. (f) as (g) and, as so redesignated, added reference to family farmer.

1984 Amendments. Subsec. (a). Pub.L. 98–353, § 425(a), struck out "in the United States," after "only a person that resides".

Subsec. (c)(5)(D). Pub.L. 98–353, § 425(b), substituted "transfer that is avoidable under section 547 of this title" for "preference".

Subsec. (d). Pub.L. 98–353, § 425(c), substituted "stockbroker" for "stockholder".

Subsec. (f). Pub.L. 98–353, § 301, added subsec. (f).

1982 Amendments. Subsec. (b)(2). Pub.L. 97–320 inserted reference to industrial banks or similar institutions which are insured banks as defined in section 3(h) of the Federal Deposit Insurance Act (12 U.S.C. 1813(h)).

Effective and Applicability Provisions

2010 Acts. Increase of dollar amounts by Judicial Conference of the United States by notice published Feb. 25, 2010, 75 F.R. 8747 effective April 1, 2010, and increase not applicable to cases commenced before the effective date of the adjustments, i.e., April 1, 2010. See Adjustment of Dollar Amounts notes under 11 U.S.C.A. § 104 and this section.

2009 Acts. Pub.L. 111–16, § 7, May 7, 2009, 123 Stat. 1609, provided that: "The amendments made by this Act [amending this section, section 7 of the Classified Information Procedures Act (18 App. U.S.C.A. § 7), 11 U.S.C.A. §§ 322, 332, 342, 521, 704, 749, and 764, 18 U.S.C.A. §§ 983, 1514, 1963, 2252A, 2339B, 3060, 3432, 3509, and 3771, 21 U.S.C.A. § 853, and 28 U.S.C.A. §§ 636, 1453, and 2107] shall take effect on December 1, 2009."

2007 Acts. Increase of dollar amounts by Judicial Conference of the United States by notice published Feb. 14, 2007, 72 F.R. 7082 effective April 1, 2007, and increase not applicable to cases commenced before the effective date of the adjustments, i.e., April 1, 2007. See Adjustment of Dollar Amounts notes under 11 U.S.C.A. § 104 and this section.

2005 Acts. Amendments by Pub.L. 109–8 effective, except as otherwise provided, 180 days after April 20, 2005, and inapplicable with respect to cases commenced under Title 11 before the effective date, see Pub.L. 109–8, § 1501, set out as a note under 11 U.S.C.A. § 101.

2004 Acts. Adjustment of dollar amounts by Judicial Conference of the United States by notice dated Feb. 18, 2004, 69 F.R. 8482 effective April 1, 2004, and adjustment not applicable to cases commenced before the effective date of the adjustments, i.e., April 1, 2004. See Adjustment of Dollar Amounts notes under 11 U.S.C.A. § 104 and this section.

2001 Acts. Adjustment of dollar amounts by Judicial Conference of the United States by notice dated Feb. 20, 2001, 66 F.R. 10910 effective April 1, 2001, and adjustment not applicable to cases commenced before the effective date of the adjustments, i.e., April 1, 2001. See Adjustment of Dollar Amounts notes under 11 U.S.C.A. § 104 and this section.

1998 Acts. Adjustment of dollar amounts by Judicial Conference of the United States by notice dated Feb. 3, 1998, 63 F.R. 7179 effective April 1, 1998, and adjustment not applicable to cases commenced before the effective date of the adjustments, i.e., April 1, 1998. See Adjustment of Dollar Amounts notes under 11 U.S.C.A. § 104 and this section.

1994 Acts. Amendments by Pub.L. 103–394 effective on Oct. 22, 1994, and not to apply with respect to cases commenced under Title 11 of the United States Code before Oct. 22, 1994, see section 702 of Pub.L. 103–394, set out as a note under section 101 of this title.

1988 Acts. Amendment by Pub.L. 100–597 effective Nov. 3, 1988, but not applicable to any case commenced under this title before that date, see section 12 of Pub.L. 100–597, set out as a note under section 101 of this title.

1986 Acts. Amendment by Pub.L. 99–554 effective 30 days after Oct. 27, 1986, but not applicable to cases commended under this title before that date, see section 302(a), (c)(1) of Pub.L. 99–554, set out as a note under section 581 of Title 28, Judiciary and Judicial Procedure.

1984 Acts. Amendment by Pub.L. 98–353 effective with respect to cases filed 90 days after July 10, 1984, see section 552(a), formerly 553(a), of Pub.L. 98–353, set out as a note under section 101 of this title.

Separability of Provisions

If any provision of or amendment made by Pub.L. 103–394 or the application of such provision or amendment to any person or circumstance is held to be unconstitutional, the remaining provisions of and amendments made by Pub.L. 103–394 and the application of such provisions and amendments to any person or circumstance shall not be affected thereby, see section 701 of Pub.L. 103–394, set out as a note under section 101 of this title.

Adjustment of Dollar Amounts

For adjustment of dollar amounts specified in subsec. (e) of this section by the Judicial Conference of the United States, effective Apr. 1, 2010, see note set out under 11 U.S.C.A. § 104.

By notice published Feb. 25, 2010, 75 F.R. 8747, the Judicial Conference of the United States adjusted the dollar amounts in provisions specified in subsec. (e) of this section, effective Apr. 1, 2010, as follows:

Adjusted $336,900 (each time it appears) to $360,475 (each time it appears).

Adjusted $1,010,650 (each time it appears) to $1,081,400 (each time it appears).

By notice published Feb. 14, 2007, 72 F.R. 7082, the Judicial Conference of the United States adjusted the dollar amounts in provisions specified in subsec. (e) of this section, effective Apr. 1, 2007, as follows:

Adjusted $307,675 (each time it appears) to $336,900 (each time it appears).

Adjusted $922,975 (each time it appears) to $1,010,650 (each time it appears).

By notice dated Feb. 18, 2004, 69 F.R. 8482, the Judicial Conference of the United States adjusted the dollar amounts in provisions specified in subsec. (e) of this section, effective Apr. 1, 2004, as follows:

Adjusted $290,525 (each time it appears) to $307,675 (each time it appears).

Adjusted $871,550 to $922,975.

By notice dated Feb. 20, 2001, 66 F.R. 10910, the Judicial Conference of the United States adjusted the dollar amounts in provisions specified in subsec. (e) of this section, effective Apr. 1, 2001, as follows:

Adjusted $269,250 (each time it appears) to $290,525 (each time it appears).

Adjusted $807,750 (each time it appears) to $871,550 (each time it appears).

By notice dated Feb. 3, 1998, 63 F.R. 7179, the Judicial Conference of the United States adjusted the dollar amounts in provisions specified in subsec. (e) of this section, effective Apr. 1, 1998, as follows:

Adjusted $250,000 (each time it appears) to $269,250 (each time it appears).

Adjusted $750,000 (each time it appears) to $807,750 (each time it appears).

CROSS REFERENCES

Filing of Chapter 9 petition by certain unincorporated tax or special assessment districts notwithstanding provisions under this section, see 11 USCA § 921.

Nonprejudicial dismissal, except as provided by this section, see 11 USCA § 349.

LIBRARY REFERENCES

American Digest System

Bankruptcy ⟅2222.1 to 2234.

Key Number System Topic No. 51.

Corpus Juris Secundum

Original and Exclusive Jurisdiction of Cases Under Title 11, CJS Bankruptcy § 149.

Sanctions Resulting from Noncompliance With Requirements as to Basis for Filing, CJS Bankruptcy § 256.

Residence or Domicile, Place of Business, or Property in United States, CJS Bankruptcy § 322.

Chapter 7, CJS Bankruptcy § 323.

Chapter 9, CJS Bankruptcy § 324.

Chapter 11, CJS Bankruptcy § 325.

Chapter 12, CJS Bankruptcy § 326.

Chapter 13, CJS Bankruptcy § 327.

Circumstances Requiring 180-Day Wait to Refile, CJS Bankruptcy § 330.

Briefing Required, CJS Bankruptcy § 333.

Temporary Waiver, CJS Bankruptcy § 334.

Commodity-Broker Liquidation Cases, CJS Bankruptcy § 837.

Stockbroker Liquidation Cases, CJS Bankruptcy § 838.

Failure to Complete Financial Management Course, CJS Bankruptcy § 1044.

Generally; Definitions, CJS Bankruptcy § 1169.

Discharge--Grounds for Denial or Revocation of Discharge, CJS Bankruptcy § 1209.

§ 110. Penalty for persons who negligently or fraudulently prepare bankruptcy petitions

(a) In this section—

(1) "bankruptcy petition preparer" means a person, other than an attorney for the debtor or an employee of such attorney under the direct supervision of such attorney, who prepares for compensation a document for filing; and

(2) "document for filing" means a petition or any other document prepared for filing by a debtor in a United States bankruptcy court or a United States district court in connection with a case under this title.

(b)(1) A bankruptcy petition preparer who prepares a document for filing shall sign the document and print on the document the preparer's name and address. If a bankruptcy petition preparer is not an individual, then an officer, principal, responsible person, or partner of the bankruptcy petition preparer shall be required to—

(A) sign the document for filing; and

(B) print on the document the name and address of that officer, principal, responsible person, or partner.

(2)(A) Before preparing any document for filing or accepting any fees from or on behalf of a debtor, the bankruptcy petition preparer shall provide to the debtor a written notice which shall be on an official form prescribed by the Judicial Conference of the United States in accordance with rule 9009 of the Federal Rules of Bankruptcy Procedure.

(B) The notice under subparagraph (A)—

(i) shall inform the debtor in simple language that a bankruptcy petition preparer is not an attorney and may not practice law or give legal advice;

(ii) may contain a description of examples of legal advice that a bankruptcy petition preparer is not authorized to give, in addition to any advice that the

preparer may not give by reason of subsection (e)(2); and

(iii) shall—

(I) be signed by the debtor and, under penalty of perjury, by the bankruptcy petition preparer; and

(II) be filed with any document for filing.

(c)(1) A bankruptcy petition preparer who prepares a document for filing shall place on the document, after the preparer's signature, an identifying number that identifies individuals who prepared the document.

(2)(A) Subject to subparagraph (B), for purposes of this section, the identifying number of a bankruptcy petition preparer shall be the Social Security account number of each individual who prepared the document or assisted in its preparation.

(B) If a bankruptcy petition preparer is not an individual, the identifying number of the bankruptcy petition preparer shall be the Social Security account number of the officer, principal, responsible person, or partner of the bankruptcy petition preparer.

(3) [Repealed. Pub.L. 109–8, Title II, § 221(3)(B), Apr. 20, 2005, 119 Stat. 60]

(d) A bankruptcy petition preparer shall, not later than the time at which a document for filing is presented for the debtor's signature, furnish to the debtor a copy of the document.

(e)(1) A bankruptcy petition preparer shall not execute any document on behalf of a debtor.

(2)(A) A bankruptcy petition preparer may not offer a potential bankruptcy debtor any legal advice, including any legal advice described in subparagraph (B).

(B) The legal advice referred to in subparagraph (A) includes advising the debtor—

(i) whether—

(I) to file a petition under this title; or

(II) commencing a case under chapter 7, 11, 12, or 13 is appropriate;

(ii) whether the debtor's debts will be discharged in a case under this title;

(iii) whether the debtor will be able to retain the debtor's home, car, or other property after commencing a case under this title;

(iv) concerning—

(I) the tax consequences of a case brought under this title; or

(II) the dischargeability of tax claims;

(v) whether the debtor may or should promise to repay debts to a creditor or enter into a reaffirmation agreement with a creditor to reaffirm a debt;

(vi) concerning how to characterize the nature of the debtor's interests in property or the debtor's debts; or

(vii) concerning bankruptcy procedures and rights.

(f) A bankruptcy petition preparer shall not use the word "legal" or any similar term in any advertisements, or advertise under any category that includes the word "legal" or any similar term.

(g) A bankruptcy petition preparer shall not collect or receive any payment from the debtor or on behalf of the debtor for the court fees in connection with filing the petition.

(h)(1) The Supreme Court may promulgate rules under section 2075 of title 28, or the Judicial Conference of the United States may prescribe guidelines, for setting a maximum allowable fee chargeable by a bankruptcy petition preparer. A bankruptcy petition preparer shall notify the debtor of any such maximum amount before preparing any document for filing for the debtor or accepting any fee from or on behalf of the debtor.

(2) A declaration under penalty of perjury by the bankruptcy petition preparer shall be filed together with the petition, disclosing any fee received from or on behalf of the debtor within 12 months immediately prior to the filing of the case, and any unpaid fee charged to the debtor. If rules or guidelines setting a maximum fee for services have been promulgated or prescribed under paragraph (1), the declaration under this paragraph shall include a certification that the bankruptcy petition preparer complied with the notification requirement under paragraph (1).

(3)(A) The court shall disallow and order the immediate turnover to the bankruptcy trustee any fee referred to in paragraph (2)—

(i) found to be in excess of the value of any services rendered by the bankruptcy petition preparer during the 12-month period immediately preceding the date of the filing of the petition; or

(ii) found to be in violation of any rule or guideline promulgated or prescribed under paragraph (1).

(B) All fees charged by a bankruptcy petition preparer may be forfeited in any case in which the bankruptcy petition preparer fails to comply with this subsection or subsection (b), (c), (d), (e), (f), or (g).

(C) An individual may exempt any funds recovered under this paragraph under section 522(b).

(4) The debtor, the trustee, a creditor, the United States trustee (or the bankruptcy administrator, if any) or the court, on the initiative of the court, may file a motion for an order under paragraph (3).

(5) A bankruptcy petition preparer shall be fined not more than $500 for each failure to comply with a court order to turn over funds within 30 days of service of such order.

(i)(1) If a bankruptcy petition preparer violates this section or commits any act that the court finds to be fraudulent, unfair, or deceptive, on the motion of the debtor, trustee, United States trustee (or the bankruptcy administrator, if any), and after notice and a hearing, the court shall order the bankruptcy petition preparer to pay to the debtor—

(A) the debtor's actual damages;

(B) the greater of—

(i) $2,000; or

(ii) twice the amount paid by the debtor to the bankruptcy petition preparer for the preparer's services; and

(C) reasonable attorneys' fees and costs in moving for damages under this subsection.

(2) If the trustee or creditor moves for damages on behalf of the debtor under this subsection, the bankruptcy petition preparer shall be ordered to pay the movant the additional amount of $1,000 plus reasonable attorneys' fees and costs incurred.

(j)(1) A debtor for whom a bankruptcy petition preparer has prepared a document for filing, the trustee, a creditor, or the United States trustee in the district in which the bankruptcy petition preparer resides, has conducted business, or the United States trustee in any other district in which the debtor resides may bring a civil action to enjoin a bankruptcy petition preparer from engaging in any conduct in violation of this section or from further acting as a bankruptcy petition preparer.

(2)(A) In an action under paragraph (1), if the court finds that—

(i) a bankruptcy petition preparer has—

(I) engaged in conduct in violation of this section or of any provision of this title;

(II) misrepresented the preparer's experience or education as a bankruptcy petition preparer; or

(III) engaged in any other fraudulent, unfair, or deceptive conduct; and

(ii) injunctive relief is appropriate to prevent the recurrence of such conduct,

the court may enjoin the bankruptcy petition preparer from engaging in such conduct.

(B) If the court finds that a bankruptcy petition preparer has continually engaged in conduct described in subclause (I), (II), or (III) of clause (i) and that an injunction prohibiting such conduct would not be sufficient to prevent such person's interference with the proper administration of this title, has not paid a penalty imposed under this section, or failed to disgorge all fees ordered by the court the court may enjoin the person from acting as a bankruptcy petition preparer.

(3) The court, as part of its contempt power, may enjoin a bankruptcy petition preparer that has failed to comply with a previous order issued under this section. The injunction under this paragraph may be issued on the motion of the court, the trustee, or the United

States trustee (or the bankruptcy administrator, if any).

(4) The court shall award to a debtor, trustee, or creditor that brings a successful action under this subsection reasonable attorneys' fees and costs of the action, to be paid by the bankruptcy petition preparer.

(k) Nothing in this section shall be construed to permit activities that are otherwise prohibited by law, including rules and laws that prohibit the unauthorized practice of law.

(*l*)(1) A bankruptcy petition preparer who fails to comply with any provision of subsection (b), (c), (d), (e), (f), (g), or (h) may be fined not more than $500 for each such failure.

(2) The court shall triple the amount of a fine assessed under paragraph (1) in any case in which the court finds that a bankruptcy petition preparer—

(A) advised the debtor to exclude assets or income that should have been included on applicable schedules;

(B) advised the debtor to use a false Social Security account number;

(C) failed to inform the debtor that the debtor was filing for relief under this title; or

(D) prepared a document for filing in a manner that failed to disclose the identity of the bankruptcy petition preparer.

(3) A debtor, trustee, creditor, or United States trustee (or the bankruptcy administrator, if any) may file a motion for an order imposing a fine on the bankruptcy petition preparer for any violation of this section.

(4)(A) Fines imposed under this subsection in judicial districts served by United States trustees shall be paid to the United States trustees, who shall deposit an amount equal to such fines in the United States Trustee Fund.

(B) Fines imposed under this subsection in judicial districts served by bankruptcy administrators shall be deposited as offsetting receipts to the fund established under section 1931 of title 28, and shall remain available until expended to reimburse any appropriation for the amount paid out of such appropriation for expenses of the operation and maintenance of the courts of the United States.

(Added Pub.L. 103–394, Title III, § 308(a), Oct. 22, 1994, 108 Stat. 4135; amended Pub.L. 109–8, Title II, § 221, Title XII, § 1205, Apr. 20, 2005, 119 Stat. 59, 194; Pub.L. 110–161, Div. B, Title II, § 212(b), Dec. 26, 2007, 121 Stat. 1914; Pub.L. 111–327, § 2(a)(7), Dec. 22, 2010, 124 Stat. 3558.)

HISTORICAL AND STATUTORY NOTES

Revision Notes and Legislative Reports

1994 Acts. House Report No. 103–835, see 1994 U.S. Code Cong. and Adm. News, p. 3340.

2005 Acts. House Report No. 109–31(Part I), see 2005 U.S. Code Cong. and Adm. News, p. 88.

2007 Acts. House Report No. 110–197, see 2007 U.S. Code Cong. and Adm. News, p. 661.

Statement by President, see 2007 U.S. Code Cong. and Adm. News, p. S34.

References in Text

The Federal Rules of Bankruptcy Procedure, referred to in subsec. (b)(2)(A), are set out in the Appendix to this title.

Chapter 7, 11, 12, or 13, referred to in subsec. (e)(2)(B)(i)(II), is chapter 7, 11, 12, or 13 of this title, 11 U.S.C.A. § 701 et seq., 11 U.S.C.A. § 1101 et seq., 11 U.S.C.A. § 1201 et seq., or 11 U.S.C.A. § 1301 et seq., respectively.

Paragraph (2), referred to in subsec. (h)(4), was redesignated as par. (3) and repealed and a new par. (3) was added by Pub.L. 109–8, Title II, § 221(8)(A), (D), Apr. 20, 2005, 119 Stat. 59. The new par. (3) provides for court orders similar to those provided for in former par. (2).

Amendments

2010 Amendments. Subsec. (b)(2)(A). Pub.L. 111–327, § 2(a)(7)(A), inserted "or on behalf of" following "from".

Subsec. (h)(1). Pub.L. 111–327, § 2(a)(7)(B)(i), struck out "a debtor" and inserted "the debtor", and inserted "or on behalf of" following "from".

Subsec. (h)(3)(A). Pub.L. 111–327, § 2(a)(7)(B)(ii)(I) , struck out "found to be in excess of the value of any services" following "paragraph (2)".

Subsec. (h)(3)(A)(i). Pub.L. 111–327, § 2(a)(7)(B)(ii)(II), inserted "found to be in excess of the value of any services" following "(i)".

Subsec. (h)(4). Pub.L. 111–327, § 2(a)(7)(B)(iii), struck out "paragraph (2)" and inserted " paragraph (3)".

2007 Amendments. Subsec. (*l*)(4)(A). Pub.L. 110–161, Div. B, § 212(b), rewrote subpar. (A), which formerly read: "Fines imposed under this subsection in judicial districts served by United States trustees shall be paid to the United States trustee, who shall deposit an amount equal to such fines in a special account of the United States Trustee System Fund referred to in section 586(e)(2) of title 28. Amounts deposited under this subparagraph shall be available to fund the enforcement of this section on a national basis."

2005 Amendments. Subsec. (a)(1). Pub.L. 109–8, § 221(1), substituted "for the debtor or an employee of such attorney under the direct supervision of such attorney" for "or an employee of an attorney".

Subsec. (b)(1). Pub.L. 109–8, § 221(2)(A), added at the end of par. (1) the following:

"If a bankruptcy petition preparer is not an individual, then an officer, principal, responsible person, or partner of the bankruptcy petition preparer shall be required to—

"**(A)** sign the document for filing; and

"**(B)** print on the document the name and address of that officer, principal, responsible person, or partner."

Subsec. (b)(2). Pub.L. 109–8, § 221(2)(B), rewrote par. (2), which formerly read: "A bankruptcy petition preparer who fails to comply with paragraph (1) may be fined not more than $500 for each such failure unless the failure is due to reasonable cause."

Subsec. (c)(2). Pub.L. 109–8, § 221(3)(A), substituted "(2)(A) Subject to subparagraph (B), for purposes" for "(2) For purposes" and added subpar. (B).

Subsec. (c)(3). Pub.L. 109–8, § 221(3)(B), struck out former par. (3), which read: "A bankruptcy petition preparer who fails to comply with paragraph (1) may be fined not more than $500 for each such failure unless the failure is due to reasonable cause."

Subsec. (d)(1), (2). Pub.L. 109–8, § 221(4), redesignated par. (1) as subsec. (d) and struck out former par. (2), which read: "A bankruptcy petition preparer who fails to comply with paragraph (1) may be fined not more than $500 for each such failure unless the failure is due to reasonable cause."

Subsec. (e)(2). Pub.L. 109–8, § 221(5), rewrote par. (2), which formerly read: "A bankruptcy petition preparer may be fined not more than $500 for each document executed in violation of paragraph (1)."

Subsec. (f)(1), (2). Pub.L. 109–8, § 221(6), redesignated par. (1) as subsec. (f) and struck out par. (2), which formerly read: "A bankruptcy petition preparer shall be fined not more than $500 for each violation of paragraph (1)."

Subsec. (g)(1), (2). Pub.L. 109–8, § 221(7), redesignated par. (1) as subsec. (g) and struck out par. (2), which formerly read: "A bankruptcy petition preparer shall be fined not more than $500 for each violation of paragraph (1)."

Subsec. (h)(1). Pub.L. 109–8, § 221(8)(A),(B), redesignated former par. (1) as par. (2) and inserted a new par. (1).

Subsec. (h)(2). Pub.L. 109–8, § 221(8)(A), (C), redesignated former par. (1) as par. (2). Former par. (2) redesignated par. (3).

Pub.L. 109–8, § 221(8)(C), in redesignated par. (2), substituted "A" for "Within 10 days after the date of the filing of a petition, a bankruptcy petition preparer shall file a", inserted "by the bankruptcy petition preparer shall be filed together with the petition," after "perjury", and added the following at the end: "If rules or guidelines setting a maximum fee for services have been promulgated or prescribed under paragraph (1), the declaration under this paragraph shall include a certification that the bankruptcy petition preparer complied with the notification requirement under paragraph (1)."

Subsec. (h)(3). Pub.L. 109–8, § 221(8)(A), redesignated former par. (2) as par. (3). Former par. (3) redesignated par. (4).

Pub.L. 109–8, § 221(8)(D), inserted a new par. (3) and struck out redesignated par. (3), which read: "The court shall disallow and order the immediate turnover to the bankruptcy trustee of any fee referred to in paragraph (1) found to be in excess of the value of services rendered for the documents prepared. An individual debtor may exempt any funds so recovered under section 522(b)."

Subsec. (h)(4). Pub.L. 109–8, § 221(8)(A), redesignated former par. (3) as par. (4). Former par. (4) redesignated par. (5).

Pub.L. 109–8, § 221(8)(E), in redesignated par. (4), substituted "the United States trustee (or the bankruptcy administrator, if any) or the court, on the initiative of the court," for "or the United States trustee".

Subsec. (h)(5). Pub.L. 109–8, § 221(8)(A), redesignated former par. (4) as par. (5).

Subsec. (i)(1). Pub.L. 109–8, § 221(9), rewrote the matter preceding subpar. (a), which formerly read: "If a bankruptcy case or related proceeding is dismissed because of the failure to file bankruptcy papers, including papers specified in section 521(1) of this title, the negligence or intentional disregard of this title or the Federal Rules of Bankruptcy Procedure by a bankruptcy petition preparer, or if a bankruptcy petition preparer violates this section or commits any fraudulent, unfair, or deceptive act, the bankruptcy court shall certify that fact to the district court, and the district court, on motion of the debtor, the trustee, or a creditor and after a hearing, shall order the bankruptcy petition preparer to pay to the debtor—".

Subsec. (j)(2)(A)(i)(I). Pub.L. 109–8, § 221(10)(A)(i), struck out "a violation of which subjects a person to criminal penalty" after "provision of this title".

Subsec. (j)(2)(B). Pub.L. 109–8, § 221(10)(A)(ii)(I), substituted "has not paid a penalty" for "or has not paid a penalty".

Pub.L. 109–8, § 221(10)(A)(ii)(II), inserted "or failed to disgorge all fees ordered by the court" after "a penalty imposed under this section,".

Subsec. (j)(3). Pub.L. 109–8, § 221(10)(B), (C), inserted a new par. (3) and redesignated former par. (3) as par. (4).

Subsec. (j)(4). Pub.L. 109–8, § 221(10)(B), redesignated former par. (3) as par. (4).

Pub.L. 109–8, § 1205, in redesignated par. (4), struck out "attorney's" and inserted "attorneys' ".

Subsec. (*l*). Pub.L. 109–8, § 221(11), added subsec. (*l*).

Effective and Applicability Provisions

2005 Acts. Amendments by Pub.L. 109–8 effective, except as otherwise provided, 180 days after April 20, 2005, and inapplicable with respect to cases commenced under Title 11 before the effective date, see Pub.L. 109–8, § 1501, set out as a note under 11 U.S.C.A. § 101.

1994 Acts. Section effective on Oct. 22, 1994, and not to apply with respect to cases commenced under Title 11 of the United States Code before Oct. 22, 1994, see section 702 of Pub.L. 103–394, set out as a note under section 101 of this title.

Separability of Provisions

If any provision of or amendment made by Pub.L. 103–394 or the application of such provision or amendment to any person or circumstance is held to be unconstitutional, the remaining provisions of and amendments made by Pub.L. 103–394 and the application of such provisions and amendments to any person or circumstance shall not be affected thereby, see section 701 of Pub.L. 103–394, set out as a note under section 101 of this title.

LIBRARY REFERENCES

American Digest System

Bankruptcy ⬥3030.6 to 3030.12, 3165.5.
Key Number System Topic No. 51.

Corpus Juris Secundum

CJS Bankruptcy § 18, Debt-Relief Agencies.
CJS Bankruptcy § 337, Contents, Signature, and Verification--Certification of Delivery or Receipt of Prefiling Notice.

§ 111. Nonprofit budget and credit counseling agencies; financial management instructional courses

(a) The clerk shall maintain a publicly available list of—

(1) nonprofit budget and credit counseling agencies that provide 1 or more services described in section 109(h) currently approved by the United States trustee (or the bankruptcy administrator, if any); and

(2) instructional courses concerning personal financial management currently approved by the United States trustee (or the bankruptcy administrator, if any), as applicable.

(b) The United States trustee (or bankruptcy administrator, if any) shall only approve a nonprofit budget and credit counseling agency or an instructional course concerning personal financial management as follows:

(1) The United States trustee (or bankruptcy administrator, if any) shall have thoroughly reviewed the qualifications of the nonprofit budget and credit counseling agency or of the provider of the instructional course under the standards set forth in this section, and the services or instructional courses that will be offered by such agency or such provider, and may require such agency or such provider that has sought approval to provide information with respect to such review.

(2) The United States trustee (or bankruptcy administrator, if any) shall have determined that such agency or such instructional course fully satisfies the applicable standards set forth in this section.

(3) If a nonprofit budget and credit counseling agency or instructional course did not appear on the approved list for the district under subsection (a) immediately before approval under this section, approval under this subsection of such agency or such instructional course shall be for a probationary period not to exceed 6 months.

(4) At the conclusion of the applicable probationary period under paragraph (3), the United States trustee (or bankruptcy administrator, if any) may only approve for an additional 1–year period, and for successive 1–year periods thereafter, an agency or instructional course that has demonstrated during the probationary or applicable subsequent period of approval that such agency or instructional course—

(A) has met the standards set forth under this section during such period; and

(B) can satisfy such standards in the future.

(5) Not later than 30 days after any final decision under paragraph (4), an interested person may seek judicial review of such decision in the appropriate district court of the United States.

(c)(1) The United States trustee (or the bankruptcy administrator, if any) shall only approve a nonprofit budget and credit counseling agency that demonstrates that it will provide qualified counselors, maintain adequate provision for safekeeping and payment of client funds, provide adequate counseling with respect to client credit problems, and deal responsibly and effec-

tively with other matters relating to the quality, effectiveness, and financial security of the services it provides.

(2) To be approved by the United States trustee (or the bankruptcy administrator, if any), a nonprofit budget and credit counseling agency shall, at a minimum—

(A) have a board of directors the majority of which—

(i) are not employed by such agency; and

(ii) will not directly or indirectly benefit financially from the outcome of the counseling services provided by such agency;

(B) if a fee is charged for counseling services, charge a reasonable fee, and provide services without regard to ability to pay the fee;

(C) provide for safekeeping and payment of client funds, including an annual audit of the trust accounts and appropriate employee bonding;

(D) provide full disclosures to a client, including funding sources, counselor qualifications, possible impact on credit reports, and any costs of such program that will be paid by such client and how such costs will be paid;

(E) provide adequate counseling with respect to a client's credit problems that includes an analysis of such client's current financial condition, factors that caused such financial condition, and how such client can develop a plan to respond to the problems without incurring negative amortization of debt;

(F) provide trained counselors who receive no commissions or bonuses based on the outcome of the counseling services provided by such agency, and who have adequate experience, and have been adequately trained to provide counseling services to individuals in financial difficulty, including the matters described in subparagraph (E);

(G) demonstrate adequate experience and background in providing credit counseling; and

(H) have adequate financial resources to provide continuing support services for budgeting plans over the life of any repayment plan.

(d) The United States trustee (or the bankruptcy administrator, if any) shall only approve an instructional course concerning personal financial management—

(1) for an initial probationary period under subsection (b)(3) if the course will provide at a minimum—

(A) trained personnel with adequate experience and training in providing effective instruction and services;

(B) learning materials and teaching methodologies designed to assist debtors in understanding personal financial management and that are consistent with stated objectives directly related to the goals of such instructional course;

(C) adequate facilities situated in reasonably convenient locations at which such instructional course is offered, except that such facilities may include the provision of such instructional course by telephone or through the Internet, if such instructional course is effective;

(D) the preparation and retention of reasonable records (which shall include the debtor's bankruptcy case number) to permit evaluation of the effectiveness of such instructional course, including any evaluation of satisfaction of instructional course requirements for each debtor attending such instructional course, which shall be available for inspection and evaluation by the Executive Office for United States Trustees, the United States trustee (or the bankruptcy administrator, if any), or the chief bankruptcy judge for the district in which such instructional course is offered; and

(E) if a fee is charged for the instructional course, charge a reasonable fee, and provide services without regard to ability to pay the fee; and

(2) for any 1–year period if the provider thereof has demonstrated that the course meets the standards of paragraph (1) and, in addition—

(A) has been effective in assisting a substantial number of debtors to understand personal financial management; and

(B) is otherwise likely to increase substantially the debtor's understanding of personal financial management.

(e) The district court may, at any time, investigate the qualifications of a nonprofit budget and credit counseling agency referred to in subsection (a), and request production of documents to ensure the integrity and effectiveness of such agency. The district court may, at any time, remove from the approved list under subsection (a) a nonprofit budget and credit counseling agency upon finding such agency does not meet the qualifications of subsection (b).

(f) The United States trustee (or the bankruptcy administrator, if any) shall notify the clerk that a nonprofit budget and credit counseling agency or an instructional course is no longer approved, in which case the clerk shall remove it from the list maintained under subsection (a).

(g)(1) No nonprofit budget and credit counseling agency may provide to a credit reporting agency information concerning whether a debtor has received or sought instruction concerning personal financial management from such agency.

(2) A nonprofit budget and credit counseling agency that willfully or negligently fails to comply with any requirement under this title with respect to a debtor shall be liable for damages in an amount equal to the sum of—

(A) any actual damages sustained by the debtor as a result of the violation; and

(B) any court costs or reasonable attorneys' fees (as determined by the court) incurred in an action to recover those damages.

(Added Pub.L. 109–8, Title I, § 106(e)(1), Apr. 20, 2005, 119 Stat. 39; amended Pub.L. 111–327, § 2(a)(8), Dec. 22, 2010, 124 Stat. 3558.)

HISTORICAL AND STATUTORY NOTES

Revision Notes and Legislative Reports

2005 Acts. House Report No. 109–31(Part I), see 2005 U.S. Code Cong. and Adm. News, p. 88.

Amendments

2010 Amendments. Subsec. (d)(1)(E). Pub.L. 111–327, § 2(a)(8)(A), struck out the period at the end and inserted "; and".

Pub.L. 111–327, § 2(a)(8)(B), made technical corrections requiring no change in text.

Effective and Applicability Provisions

2005 Acts. Amendments by Pub.L. 109–8 effective, except as otherwise provided, 180 days after April 20, 2005, and inapplicable with respect to cases commenced under Title 11 before the effective date, see Pub.L. 109–8, § 1501, set out as a note under 11 U.S.C.A. § 101.

Debtor Financial Management Training Test Program

Pub.L. 109–8, Title I, § 105, Apr. 20, 2005, 119 Stat. 36, provided that:

"**(a) Development of financial management and training curriculum and materials.**—The Director of the Executive Office for United States Trustees (in this section referred to as the 'Director') shall consult with a wide range of individuals who are experts in the field of debtor education, including trustees who serve in cases under chapter 13 of title 11, United States Code [11 U.S.C.A. § 1301 et seq.], and who operate financial management education programs for debtors, and shall develop a financial management training curriculum and materials that can be used to educate debtors who are individuals on how to better manage their finances.

"**(b) Test.**—

"**(1) Selection of districts.**—The Director shall select 6 judicial districts of the United States in which to test the effectiveness of the financial management training curriculum and materials developed under subsection (a) [of this note].

"**(2) Use.**—For an 18–month period beginning not later than 270 days after the date of the enactment of this Act [April 20, 2005], such curriculum and materials shall be, for the 6 judicial districts selected under paragraph (1), used as the instructional course concerning personal financial management for purposes of section 111 of title 11, United States Code.

"**(c) Evaluation.**—

"**(1) In general.**—During the 18–month period referred to in subsection (b) [of this note], the Director shall evaluate the effectiveness of—

"**(A)** the financial management training curriculum and materials developed under subsection (a) [of this note]; and

"(B) a sample of existing consumer education programs such as those described in the Report of the National Bankruptcy Review Commission (October 20, 1997) that are representative of consumer education programs carried out by the credit industry, by trustees serving under chapter 13 of title 11, United States Code [11 U.S.C.A. § 1301 et seq.], and by consumer counseling groups.

"(2) **Report.**—Not later than 3 months after concluding such evaluation, the Director shall submit a report to the Speaker of the House of Representatives and the President pro tempore of the Senate, for referral to the appropriate committees of the Congress, containing the findings of the Director regarding the effectiveness of such curriculum, such materials, and such programs and their costs."

[Amendments by Pub.L. 109–8 effective, except as otherwise provided, 180 days after April 20, 2005, and inapplicable with respect to cases commenced under Title 11 before the effective date, see Pub.L. 109–8, § 1501, set out as a note under 11 U.S.C.A. § 101.]

LIBRARY REFERENCES

Corpus Juris Secundum

CJS Bankruptcy § 19, Nonprofit Budget and Credit Counseling Agencies; Financial Management Instructional Courses.

CJS Bankruptcy § 1044, Failure to Complete Financial Management Course.

CJS Bankruptcy § 1209, Discharge--Grounds for Denial or Revocation of Discharge.

§ 112.　Prohibition on disclosure of name of minor children

The debtor may be required to provide information regarding a minor child involved in matters under this title but may not be required to disclose in the public records in the case the name of such minor child. The debtor may be required to disclose the name of such minor child in a nonpublic record that is maintained by the court and made available by the court for examination by the United States trustee, the trustee, and the auditor (if any) serving under section 586(f) of title 28, in the case. The court, the United States trustee, the trustee, and such auditor shall not disclose the name of such minor child maintained in such nonpublic record.
(Added Pub.L. 109–8, Title II, § 233(a), Apr. 20, 2005, 119 Stat. 74.)

HISTORICAL AND STATUTORY NOTES

Revision Notes and Legislative Reports

2005 Acts. House Report No. 109–31(Part I), see 2005 U.S. Code Cong. and Adm. News, p. 88.

Effective and Applicability Provisions

2005 Acts. Amendments by Pub.L. 109–8 effective, except as otherwise provided, 180 days after April 20, 2005, and inapplicable with respect to cases commenced under Title 11 before the effective date, see Pub.L. 109–8, § 1501, set out as a note under 11 U.S.C.A. § 101.

LIBRARY REFERENCES

Corpus Juris Secundum

CJS Bankruptcy § 832, Minor Children's Names.

CHAPTER 3—CASE ADMINISTRATION

SUBCHAPTER I—COMMENCEMENT OF A CASE

Sec.
301. Voluntary cases.
302. Joint cases.
303. Involuntary cases.
304. [Repealed.]
305. Abstention.
306. Limited appearance.
307. United States trustee.
308. Debtor reporting requirements.

SUBCHAPTER II—OFFICERS

321. Eligibility to serve as trustee.
322. Qualification of trustee.
323. Role and capacity of trustee.
324. Removal of trustee or examiner.
325. Effect of vacancy.
326. Limitation on compensation of trustee.
327. Employment of professional persons.
328. Limitation on compensation of professional persons.
329. Debtor's transactions with attorneys.
330. Compensation of officers.
331. Interim compensation.
332. Consumer privacy ombudsman.
333. Appointment of patient care ombudsman.

SUBCHAPTER III—ADMINISTRATION

341. Meetings of creditors and equity security holders.
342. Notice.
343. Examination of the debtor.
344. Self-incrimination; immunity.
345. Money of estates.
346. Special provisions related to the treatment of State and local taxes.
347. Unclaimed property.
348. Effect of conversion.
349. Effect of dismissal.
350. Closing and reopening cases.
351. Disposal of patient records.

SUBCHAPTER IV—ADMINISTRATIVE POWERS

361. Adequate protection.
362. Automatic stay.
363. Use, sale, or lease of property.
364. Obtaining credit.
365. Executory contracts and unexpired leases.
366. Utility service.

HISTORICAL AND STATUTORY NOTES

Amendments

2010 Amendments. Pub.L. 111–327, § 2(a)(49), Dec. 22. 2010, 124 Stat. 3562, rewrote item 333 which formerly read: "333. Appointment of ombudsman".

2005 Amendments. Pub.L. 109–8, Title II, § 232(c), Apr. 20, 2005, 119 Stat. 74, added item 332.

Pub.L. 109–8, Title IV, § 434(a)(2), Apr. 20, 2005, 119 Stat. 111, added item 308.

Pub.L. 109–8, Title VII, § 719(a)(2), Apr. 20, 2005, 119 Stat. 133, struck out item 346 and added a new item 346. Prior to striking, former item 346 read: "346. Special Tax Provisions".

Pub.L. 109–8, Title VIII, § 802(d)(4), Apr. 20, 2005, 119 Stat. 146, struck out item 304, which formerly read: "304. Cases ancillary to foreign proceedings."

Pub.L. 109–8, Title XI, § 1102(b), Apr. 20, 2005, 119 Stat. 190, added item 351.

Pub.L. 109–8, Title XI, § 1104(a)(2), Apr. 20, 2005, 119 Stat. 192, added item 333.

1986 Amendments. Pub.L. 99–554, Title II, § 205(b), Oct. 27, 1986, 100 Stat. 3098, added item 307.

Effective and Applicability Provisions

2005 Acts. Amendments by Pub.L. 109–8, § 434, effective, 60 days after the date on which rules are prescribed under 28 U.S.C.A. § 2075, to establish forms to be used to comply with 11 U.S.C.A. § 308, see Pub.L. 109–8, § 434(b), set out as a note under 11 U.S.C.A. § 308.

Amendments by Pub.L. 109–8 effective, except as otherwise provided, 180 days after April 20, 2005, and inapplicable with respect to cases commenced under Title 11 before the effective date, see Pub.L. 109–8, § 1501, set out as a note under 11 U.S.C.A. § 101.

CROSS REFERENCES

Applicability of this chapter to—
Cases under Chapters 7, 11, 12, or 13 of this title, see 11 USCA § 103.
Investor protection liquidation proceedings, see 15 USCA § 78fff.

SUBCHAPTER I—COMMENCEMENT OF A CASE

§ 301. Voluntary cases

(a) A voluntary case under a chapter of this title is commenced by the filing with the bankruptcy court of a petition under such chapter by an entity that may be a debtor under such chapter.

(b) The commencement of a voluntary case under a chapter of this title constitutes an order for relief under such chapter.

(Pub.L. 95–598, Nov. 6, 1978, 92 Stat. 2558; Pub.L. 109–8, Title V, § 501(b), Apr. 20, 2005, 119 Stat. 118.)

HISTORICAL AND STATUTORY NOTES

Revision Notes and Legislative Reports

1978 Acts. Section 301 specifies the manner in which a voluntary bankruptcy case is commenced. The debtor files a petition under this section under the particular operative chapter of the bankruptcy code under which he wishes to proceed. The filing of the petition constitutes an order for relief in the case under that chapter. The section contains no change from current law, except for the use of the phrase "order for relief" instead of "adjudication." The term adjudication is replaced by a less pejorative phrase in light of the clear power of Congress to permit voluntary bankruptcy without the necessity for an adjudication, as under the 1898 act [former Title 11], which was adopted when voluntary bankruptcy was a concept not thoroughly tested. Senate Report No. 95–989.

2005 Acts. House Report No. 109–31(Part I), see 2005 U.S. Code Cong. and Adm. News, p. 88.

Legislative Statements

Sections 301, 302, 303, and 304, are all modified in the House amendment to adopt an idea contained in sections 301 and 303 of the Senate amendment requiring a petition commencing a case to be filed with the bankruptcy court. The exception contained in section 301 of the Senate bill relating to cases filed under chapter 9 is deleted. Chapter 9 cases will be handled by a bankruptcy court as are other title 11 cases.

Amendments

2005 Amendments. Subsec. (a). Pub.L. 109–8, § 501(b)(1), inserted "(a)" before "A voluntary" and struck the last sentence, which read: "The commencement of a voluntary case under a chapter of this title constitutes an order for relief under such chapter."

Subsec. (b). Pub.L. 109–8, § 501(b)(2), inserted subsec. (b).

Effective and Applicability Provisions

2005 Acts. Amendments by Pub.L. 109–8 effective, except as otherwise provided, 180 days after April 20, 2005, and inapplicable with respect to cases commenced under Title 11 before the effective date, see Pub.L. 109–8, § 1501, set out as a note under 11 U.S.C.A. § 101.

CROSS REFERENCES

Applicability of this section in Chapter 9 cases, see 11 USCA § 901.

Automatic stay, see 11 USCA § 362.

Commencement of Chapter 9 cases concerning certain unincorporated tax or special assessment districts, see 11 USCA § 921.

Exemptions elected in estates administered jointly, see 11 USCA § 522.

Fees, see 28 USCA § 1930.

"Petition" defined, see 11 USCA § 101.

Property of estate, see 11 USCA § 541.

LIBRARY REFERENCES

American Digest System

Bankruptcy ⚎2202, 2257.

Key Number System Topic No. 51.

Corpus Juris Secundum

CJS Bankruptcy § 7, Bankruptcy Code.

CJS Bankruptcy § 62, Appointment of Interim Trustee.

CJS Bankruptcy § 264, Cases Under Bankruptcy Code.

CJS Bankruptcy § 365, Commencement and Order for Relief.

§ 302. Joint cases

(a) A joint case under a chapter of this title is commenced by the filing with the bankruptcy court of a single petition under such chapter by an individual that may be a debtor under such chapter and such individual's spouse. The commencement of a joint case under a chapter of this title constitutes an order for relief under such chapter.

(b) After the commencement of a joint case, the court shall determine the extent, if any, to which the debtors' estates shall be consolidated.

(Pub.L. 95–598, Nov. 6, 1978, 92 Stat. 2558.)

HISTORICAL AND STATUTORY NOTES

Revision Notes and Legislative Reports

1978 Acts. A joint case is a voluntary bankruptcy case concerning a wife and husband. Under current law, there is no explicit provision for joint cases. Very often, however, in the consumer debtor context, a husband and wife are jointly liable on their debts, and jointly hold most of their property. A joint case will facilitate consolidation of their estates, to the benefit of both the debtors and their creditors, because the cost of administration will be reduced, and there will be only one filing fee.

Section 302 specifies that a joint case is commenced by the filing of a petition under an appropriate chapter by an individual and that individual's spouse. Thus, one spouse cannot take the other into bankruptcy without the other's knowledge or consent. The filing of the petition constitutes an order for relief under the chapter selected.

Subsection (b) requires the court to determine the extent, if any, to which the estates of the two debtors will be consolidated; that is, assets and liabilities combined in a single pool to pay creditors. Factors that will be relevant in the court's determination include the extent of jointly held property and the amount of jointly-owned debts. The section, of course, is not license to consolidate in order to avoid other provisions of the title to the detriment of either the debtors or their creditors. It is designed mainly for ease of administration. Senate Report No. 95–989.

CROSS REFERENCES

Automatic stay, see 11 USCA § 362.

Exempt property, see 11 USCA § 522.

Fees, see 28 USCA § 1930.

"Petition" defined, see 11 USCA § 101.

Property of estate, see 11 USCA § 541.

LIBRARY REFERENCES

American Digest System

Bankruptcy ⚎2311.

Key Number System Topic No. 51.

Corpus Juris Secundum

CJS Bankruptcy § 7, Bankruptcy Code.

CJS Bankruptcy § 264, Cases Under Bankruptcy Code.

CJS Bankruptcy § 366, Joint Case.

§ 303. Involuntary cases

(a) An involuntary case may be commenced only under chapter 7 or 11 of this title, and only against a person, except a farmer, family farmer, or a corporation that is not a moneyed, business, or commercial corporation, that may be a debtor under the chapter under which such case is commenced.

(b) An involuntary case against a person is commenced by the filing with the bankruptcy court of a petition under chapter 7 or 11 of this title—

(1) by three or more entities, each of which is either a holder of a claim against such person that is not contingent as to liability or the subject of a bona fide dispute as to liability or amount, or an indenture trustee representing such a holder, if such noncontingent, undisputed claims aggregate at least $14,425 ¹ more than the value of any lien on property of the debtor securing such claims held by the holders of such claims;

(2) if there are fewer than 12 such holders, excluding any employee or insider of such person and any transferee of a transfer that is voidable under section 544, 545, 547, 548, 549, or 724(a) of this title, by one or more of such holders that hold in the aggregate at least $14,425 ¹ of such claims;

(3) if such person is a partnership—

(A) by fewer than all of the general partners in such partnership; or

(B) if relief has been ordered under this title with respect to all of the general partners in such partnership, by a general partner in such partnership, the trustee of such a general partner, or a holder of a claim against such partnership; or

(4) by a foreign representative of the estate in a foreign proceeding concerning such person.

(c) After the filing of a petition under this section but before the case is dismissed or relief is ordered, a creditor holding an unsecured claim that is not contingent, other than a creditor filing under subsection (b) of this section, may join in the petition with the same effect as if such joining creditor were a petitioning creditor under subsection (b) of this section.

(d) The debtor, or a general partner in a partnership debtor that did not join in the petition, may file an answer to a petition under this section.

(e) After notice and a hearing, and for cause, the court may require the petitioners under this section to file a bond to indemnify the debtor for such amounts as the court may later allow under subsection (i) of this section.

(f) Notwithstanding section 363 of this title, except to the extent that the court orders otherwise, and until an order for relief in the case, any business of the debtor may continue to operate, and the debtor may continue to use, acquire, or dispose of property as if an involuntary case concerning the debtor had not been commenced.

(g) At any time after the commencement of an involuntary case under chapter 7 of this title but before an order for relief in the case, the court, on request of a party in interest, after notice to the debtor and a hearing, and if necessary to preserve the property of the estate or to prevent loss to the estate, may order the United States trustee to appoint an interim trustee under section 701 of this title to take possession of the property of the estate and to operate any business of the debtor. Before an order for relief, the debtor may regain possession of property in the possession of a trustee ordered appointed under this subsection if the debtor files such bond as the court requires, conditioned on the debtor's accounting for and delivering to the trustee, if there is an order for relief in the case, such property, or the value, as of the date the debtor regains possession, of such property.

(h) If the petition is not timely controverted, the court shall order relief against the debtor in an involuntary case under the chapter under which the petition was filed. Otherwise, after trial, the court shall order relief against the debtor in an involuntary case under the chapter under which the petition was filed, only if—

(1) the debtor is generally not paying such debtor's debts as such debts become due unless such debts are the subject of a bona fide dispute as to liability or amount; or

(2) within 120 days before the date of the filing of the petition, a custodian, other than a trustee, receiver, or agent appointed or authorized to take charge of less than substantially all of the property of the debtor for the purpose of enforcing a lien against such property, was appointed or took possession.

(i) If the court dismisses a petition under this section other than on consent of all petitioners and the debtor, and if the debtor does not waive the right to judgment under this subsection, the court may grant judgment—

(1) against the petitioners and in favor of the debtor for—

(A) costs; or

(B) a reasonable attorney's fee; or

(2) against any petitioner that filed the petition in bad faith, for—

(A) any damages proximately caused by such filing; or

(B) punitive damages.

(j) Only after notice to all creditors and a hearing may the court dismiss a petition filed under this section—

(1) on the motion of a petitioner;

(2) on consent of all petitioners and the debtor; or

(3) for want of prosecution.

(k)(1) If—

(A) the petition under this section is false or contains any materially false, fictitious, or fraudulent statement;

(B) the debtor is an individual; and

(C) the court dismisses such petition,

the court, upon the motion of the debtor, shall seal all the records of the court relating to such petition, and all references to such petition.

(2) If the debtor is an individual and the court dismisses a petition under this section, the court may enter an order prohibiting all consumer reporting agencies (as defined in section 603(f) of the Fair Credit Reporting Act (15 U.S.C. 1681a(f))) from making any consumer report (as defined in section 603(d) of that Act) that contains any information relating to such petition or to the case commenced by the filing of such petition.

(3) Upon the expiration of the statute of limitations described in section 3282 of title 18, for a violation of section 152 or 157 of such title, the court, upon the motion of the debtor and for good cause, may expunge any records relating to a petition filed under this section.

[(l) Redesignated (k)]

(Pub.L. 95–598, Nov. 6, 1978, 92 Stat. 2559; Pub. L. 98–353, Title III, §§ 426, 427, July 10, 1984, 98 Stat. 369; Pub.L. 99–554, Title II, §§ 204, 254, 283(b), Oct. 27, 1986, 100 Stat. 3097, 3105, 3116; Pub.L. 103–394, Title I, § 108(b), Oct. 22, 1994, 108 Stat. 4112; Pub.L. 109–8, Title III, § 332(b), Title VIII, § 802(d)(2), Title XII, § 1234(a), Apr. 20, 2005, 119 Stat. 103, 146, 204; Pub.L. 111–327, § 2(a)(9), Dec. 22, 2010, 124 Stat. 3558.)

¹ Dollar amount as adjusted by the Judicial Conference of the United States. See Adjustment of Dollar Amounts notes set out under this section and 11 U.S.C.A. § 104.

HISTORICAL AND STATUTORY NOTES
Revision Notes and Legislative Reports

1978 Acts. Section 303 governs the commencement of involuntary cases under title 11. An involuntary case may be commenced only under chapter 7, Liquidation, or chapter 11, Reorganization. Involuntary cases are not permitted for municipalities, because to do so may constitute an invasion of State sovereignty contrary to the 10th amendment, and would constitute bad policy, by permitting the fate of a municipality, governed by officials elected by the people of the municipality, to be determined by a small number of creditors of the municipality. Involuntary chapter 13 cases are not permitted either. To do so would constitute bad policy, because chapter 13 only works when there is a willing debtor that wants to repay his creditors. Short of involuntary servitude, it is difficult to keep a debtor working for his creditors when he does not want to pay them back. See chapter 3, supra.

The exceptions contained in current law that prohibit involuntary cases against farmers, ranchers and eleemosynary institutions are continued. Farmers and ranchers are excepted because of the cyclical nature of their business. One drought year or one year of low prices, as a result of which a farmer is temporarily unable to pay his creditors, should not subject him to involuntary bankruptcy. Eleemosynary insti-

tutions, such as churches, schools, and charitable organizations and foundations, likewise are exempt from involuntary bankruptcy.

The provisions for involuntary chapter 11 cases is a slight change from present law, based on the proposed consolidation of the reorganization chapters. Currently, involuntary cases are permitted under chapters X and XII [chapters 10 and 12 of former Title 11] but not under chapter XI [chapter 11 of former Title 11]. The consolidation requires a single rule for all kinds of reorganization proceedings. Because the assets of an insolvent debtor belong equitably to his creditors, the bill permits involuntary cases in order that creditors may realize on their assets through reorganization as well as through liquidation.

Subsection (b) of the section specifies who may file an involuntary petition. As under current law, if the debtor has more than 12 creditors, three creditors must join in the involuntary petition. The dollar amount limitation is changed from current law to $5,000. The new amount applies both to liquidation and reorganization cases in order that there not be an artificial difference between the two chapters that would provide an incentive for one or the other. Subsection (b)(1) makes explicit the right of an indenture trustee to be one of the three petitioning creditors on behalf of the creditors the trustee represents under the indenture. If all of the general partners in a partnership are in bankruptcy, then the trustee of a single general partner may file an involuntary petition against the partnership. Finally, a foreign representative may file an involuntary case concerning the debtor in the foreign proceeding, in order to administer assets in this country. This subsection is not intended to overrule Bankruptcy Rule 104(d), which places certain restrictions on the transfer of claims for the purpose of commencing an involuntary case. That Rule will be continued under section 405(d) of this bill.

Subsection (c) permits creditors other than the original petitioning creditors to join in the petition with the same effect as if the joining creditor had been one of the original petitioning creditors. Thus, if the claim of one of the original petitioning creditors is disallowed, the case will not be dismissed for want of three creditors or want of $5,000 in petitioning claims if the joining creditor suffices to fulfill the statutory requirements.

Subsection (d) permits the debtor to file an answer to an involuntary petition. The subsection also permits a general partner in a partnership debtor to answer an involuntary petition against the partnership if he did not join in the petition. Thus, a partnership petition by less than all of the general partners is treated as an involuntary, not a voluntary, petition.

The court may, under subsection (e), require the petitioners to file a bond to indemnify the debtor for such amounts as the court may later allow under subsection (i). Subsection (i) provides for costs, attorneys fees, and damages in certain circumstances. The bonding requirement will discourage frivolous petitions as well as spiteful petitions based on a desire to embarrass the debtor (who may be a competitor of a petitioning creditor) or to put the debtor out of business without good cause. An involuntary petition may put a debtor out of business even if it is without foundation and is later dismissed.

Subsection (f) is both a clarification and a change from existing law. It permits the debtor to continue to operate any business of the debtor and to dispose of property as if the case had not been commenced. The court is permitted, however, to control the debtor's powers under this subsection by appropriate orders, such as where there is a fear that the debtor may attempt to abscond with assets, dispose of them at less than their fair value, or dismantle his business, all to the detriment of the debtor's creditors.

The court may also, under subsection (g), appoint an interim trustee to take possession of the debtor's property and to operate any business of the debtor, pending trial on the involuntary petition. The court may make such an order only on the request of a party in interest, and after notice to the debtor and a hearing. There must be a showing that a trustee is necessary to preserve the property of the estate or to prevent loss to the estate. The debtor may regain possession by posting a sufficient bond.

Subsection (h) provides the standard for an order for relief on an involuntary petition. If the petition is not timely controverted (the Rules of Bankruptcy Procedure will fix time limits), the court orders relief after a trial, only if the debtor is generally unable to pay its debts as they mature, or if the debtor has failed to pay a major portion of his debts as they become due, or if a custodian was appointed during the 90-day period preceding the filing of the petition. The first two tests are variations of the equity insolvency test. They represent the most significant departure from present law concerning the grounds for involuntary bankruptcy, which requires an act of bankruptcy. Proof of the commission of an act of bankruptcy has frequently required a showing that the debtor was insolvent on a "balance-sheet" test when the act was committed. This bill abolishes the concept of acts of bankruptcy.

The equity insolvency test has been in equity jurisprudence for hundreds of years, and though it is new in the bankruptcy context (except in chapter X [former chapter 10 of former Title 11 (former section 501 et seq. of former Title 11)]), the bankruptcy courts should have no difficulty in applying it. The third test, appointment of a custodian within ninety days before the petition, is provided for simplicity. It is not a partial re-enactment of acts of bankruptcy. If a custodian of all or substantially all of the property of the debtor has been appointed, this paragraph creates an irrebuttable presumption that the debtor is unable to pay its debts as they mature. Moreover, once a proceeding to liquidate assets has been commenced, the debtor's creditors have an absolute right to have the liquidation (or reorganization) proceed in the bankruptcy court and under the bankruptcy laws with all of the appropriate creditor and debtor protections that those laws provide. Ninety days gives creditors ample time in which to seek bankruptcy liquidation after the appointment of a custodian. If they wait beyond the ninety day period, they are not precluded from filing an involuntary petition. They are simply required to prove equity insolvency rather than the more easily provable custodian test.

Subsection (i) permits the court to award costs, reasonable attorney's fees, or damages if an involuntary petition is dismissed other than by consent of all petitioning creditors and the debtor. The damages that the court may award are those that may be caused by the taking of possession of the debtor's property under subsection (g) or section 1104 of the bankruptcy code. In addition, if a petitioning creditor filed the petition in bad faith, the court may award the debtor any damages proximately caused by the filing of the petition. These damages may include such items as loss of business during and after the pendency of the case, and so on. "Or" is not exclusive in this paragraph. The court may grant any or all

of the damages provided for under the provision. Dismissal in the best interests of credits under section 305(a)(1) would not give rise to a damages claim.

Under subsection (j), the court may dismiss the petition by consent only after giving notice to all creditors. The purpose of the subsection is to prevent collusive settlements among the debtor and the petitioning creditors while other creditors, that wish to see relief ordered with respect to the debtor but that did not participate in the case, are left without sufficient protection.

Subsection (k) governs involuntary cases against foreign banks that are not engaged in business in the United States but that have assets located here. The subsection prevents a foreign bank from being placed into bankruptcy in this country unless a foreign proceeding against the bank is pending. The special protection afforded by this section is needed to prevent creditors from effectively closing down a foreign bank by the commencement of an involuntary bankruptcy case in this country unless that bank is involved in a proceeding under foreign law. An involuntary case commenced under this subsection gives the foreign representative and alternative to commencing a case ancillary to a foreign proceeding under section 304. Senate Report No. 95–989.

1984 Acts. Statements by Legislative Leaders, see 1984 U.S. Code Cong. and Adm. News, p. 576.

1986 Acts. House Report No. 99–764 and House Conference Report No. 99–958, see 1986 U.S. Code Cong. and Adm. News, p. 5227.

1994 Acts. House Report No. 103–835, see 1994 U.S. Code Cong. and Adm. News, p. 3340.

2005 Acts. House Report No. 109–31(Part I), see 2005 U.S. Code Cong. and Adm. News, p. 88.

Legislative Statements

Section 303(b)(1) is modified to make clear that unsecured claims against the debtor must be determined by taking into account liens securing property held by third parties.

Section 303(b)(3) adopts a provision contained in the Senate amendment indicating that an involuntary petition may be commenced against a partnership by fewer than all of the general partners in such partnership. Such action may be taken by fewer than all of the general partners notwithstanding a contrary agreement between the partners or State or local law.

Section 303(h)(1) in the House amendment is a compromise of standards found in H.R. 8200 as passed by the House and the Senate amendment pertaining to the standards that must be met in order to obtain an order for relief in an involuntary case under title 11. The language specifies that the court will order such relief only if the debtor is generally not paying debtor's debts as they become due.

Section 303(h)(2) reflects a compromise pertaining to section 543 of title 11 relating to turnover of property by a custodian. It provides an alternative test to support an order for relief in an involuntary case. If a custodian, other than a trustee, receiver, or agent appointed or authorized to take charge of less than substantially all of the property of the debtor for the purpose of enforcing a lien against such property, was appointed or took possession within 120 days before the date of the filing of the petition, then the court may order relief in the involuntary case. The test under section 303(h)(2) differs from section 3a(5) of the Bankruptcy Act [section 21(a)(5) of former Title 11], which requires an involuntary case to be commenced before the earlier of time such custodian was appointed or took possession. The test in section 303(h)(2) authorizes an order for relief to be entered in an involuntary case from the later date on which the custodian was appointed or took possession.

References in Text

Section 603 of the Fair Credit Reporting Act, referred to in subsec. (k)(2), is Pub.L. 90–321, Title VI, § 603, as added Pub.L. 91–508, Title IV, § 601, Oct. 26, 1970, 84 Stat. 1128, and amended, which is classified to 15 U.S.C.A. § 1681a.

Amendments

2010 Amendments. Subsec. (b)(1), (2). By notice dated Feb. 25, 2010, 75 F.R. 8747, dollar amount adjusted by the Judicial Conference of the United States which adjusted "$13,475" to "$14,425". See 11 U.S.C.A. § 104 and Adjustment of Dollar Amounts notes under this section.

Subsec. (k). Pub.L. 111–327, § 2(a)(9), redesignated former subsec. (*l*) as (k).

Subsec. (*l*). Pub.L. 111–327, § 2(a)(9), redesignated former subsec. (*l*) as (k).

2007 Amendments. Subsec. (b)(1), (2). By notice dated Feb. 14, 2007, 72 F.R. 7082, dollar amount adjusted by the Judicial Conference of the United States which adjusted "$12,300" to "$13,475". See 11 U.S.C.A. § 104 and Adjustment of Dollar Amounts notes under this section.

2005 Amendments. Subsec. (b)(1). Pub.L. 109–8, § 1234(a)(1)(A), inserted "as to liability or amount" after "bona fide dispute".

Pub.L. 109–8, § 1234(a)(1)(B), struck "if such claims" and inserted "if such noncontingent, undisputed claims".

Subsec. (h)(1). Pub.L. 109–8, § 1234(a)(2), inserted "as to liability or amount" before the semicolon at the end.

Subsec. (k). Pub.L. 109–8, § 802(d)(2), struck out subsec. (k), which formerly read: "**(k)** Notwithstanding subsection (a) of this section, an involuntary case may be commenced against a foreign bank that is not engaged in such business in the United States only under chapter 7 of this title and only if a foreign proceeding concerning such bank is pending."

Subsec. (*l*). Pub.L. 109–8, § 332(b), added subsec. (*l*).

2004 Amendments. Subsec. (b)(1), (2). By notice dated Feb. 18, 2004, 69 F.R. 8482, dollar amount adjusted by the Judicial Conference of the United States which adjusted "$11,625" to "$12,300". See 11 U.S.C.A. § 104 and Adjustment of Dollar Amounts notes under this section.

2001 Amendments. Subsec. (b)(1), (2). By notice dated Feb. 20, 2001, 66 F.R. 10910, dollar amount adjusted by the Judicial Conference of the United States which adjusted "$10,775" to "$11,625". See 11 U.S.C.A. § 104 and Adjustment of Dollar Amounts notes under this section.

1998 Amendments. Subsec. (b)(1), (2). By notice dated Feb. 3, 1998, 63 F.R. 7179, dollar amount adjusted by the Judicial Conference of the United States which adjusted "$10,000" to "$10,775". See 11 U.S.C.A. § 104 and Adjustment of Dollar Amounts notes under this section.

1994 Amendments. Subsec. (b)(1). Pub.L. 103–394, § 108(b)(1), substituted "if such claims aggregate at least $10,000 more than the value of any lien" for "if such claims aggregate at least $5,000 more than the value of any lien".

Subsec. (b)(2). Pub.L. 103–394, § 108(b)(2), substituted "hold in the aggregate at least $10,000 of such claims" for "hold in the aggregate at least $5,000 of such claims".

1986 Amendments. Subsec. (a). Pub.L. 99–554, § 254, added reference to family farmer.

Subsec. (b). Pub.L. 99–554, § 283(b)(1), substituted "subject of" for "subject on".

Subsec. (g). Pub.L. 99–554, § 204(1), substituted "may order the United States trustee to appoint" for "may appoint".

Subsec. (h)(1). Pub.L. 99–554, § 283(b)(2), substituted "are the" for "that are the".

Subsec. (i)(1)(A). Pub.L. 99–554, § 204(2), substituted "costs; or" for "costs;".

Subsec. (i)(1)(C). Pub.L. 99–554, § 204(2), struck out "(C) any damages proximately caused by the taking of possession of the debtor's property by a trustee appointed under subsection (g) of this section or section 1104 of this title; or".

1984 Amendments. Subsec. (b). Pub.L. 98–353, § 426(a), added "against a person" after "involuntary case".

Subsec. (b)(1). Pub.L. 98–353, § 426(b)(1), added "or the subject of a bona fide dispute," after "liability".

Subsec. (h)(1). Pub.L. 98–353, § 426(b)(2), added "unless such debts that are the subject of a bona fide dispute" after "due".

Subsec. (j)(2). Pub.L. 98–353, § 427, substituted "debtor" for "debtors".

Effective and Applicability Provisions

2010 Acts. Increase of dollar amounts by Judicial Conference of the United States by notice published Feb. 25, 2010, 75 F.R. 8747 effective April 1, 2010, and increase not applicable to cases commenced before the effective date of the adjustments, i.e., April 1, 2010. See Adjustment of Dollar Amounts notes under 11 U.S.C.A. § 104 and this section.

2007 Acts. Increase of dollar amounts by Judicial Conference of the United States by notice published Feb. 14, 2007, 72 F.R. 7082 effective April 1, 2007, and increase not applicable to cases commenced before the effective date of the adjustments, i.e., April 1, 2007. See Adjustment of Dollar Amounts notes under 11 U.S.C.A. § 104 and this section.

2005 Acts. Pub.L. 109–8, Title XII, § 1234(b), Apr. 20, 2005, 119 Stat. 204, provided that: "This section and the amendments made by this section [amending this section] shall take effect on the date of the enactment of this Act [Apr. 20, 2005] and shall apply with respect to cases commenced under title 11 of the United States Code before, on, and after such date."

Amendments by sections 332(b) and 802(d)(2) of Pub.L. 109–8 effective, except as otherwise provided, 180 days after April 20, 2005, and inapplicable with respect to cases commenced under Title 11 before the effective date, see Pub.L. 109–8, § 1501, set out as a note under 11 U.S.C.A. § 101.

2004 Acts. Adjustment of dollar amounts by Judicial Conference of the United States by notice dated Feb. 18, 2004, 69 F.R. 8482 effective April 1, 2004, and adjustment not applicable to cases commenced before the effective date of the adjustments, i.e., April 1, 2004. See Adjustment of Dollar Amounts notes under 11 U.S.C.A. § 104 and this section.

2001 Acts. Adjustment of dollar amounts by Judicial Conference of the United States by notice dated Feb. 20, 2001, 66 F.R. 10910 effective April 1, 2001, and adjustment not applicable to cases commenced before the effective date of the adjustments, i.e., April 1, 2001. See Adjustment of Dollar Amounts notes under 11 U.S.C.A. § 104 and this section.

1998 Acts. Adjustment of dollar amounts by Judicial Conference of the United States by notice dated Feb. 3, 1998, 63 F.R. 7179 effective April 1, 1998, and adjustment not applicable to cases commenced before the effective date of the adjustments, i.e., April 1, 1998. See Adjustment of Dollar Amounts notes under 11 U.S.C.A. § 104 and this section.

1994 Acts. Amendment by Pub.L. 103–394 effective on Oct. 22, 1994, and not to apply with respect to cases commenced under Title 11 of the United States Code before Oct. 22, 1994, see section 702 of Pub.L. 103–394, set out as a note under section 101 of this title.

1986 Acts. Amendment by Pub.L. 99–554 effective 30 days after Oct. 27, 1986, except as otherwise provided for, see section 302(a) of Pub.L. 99–554, set out as a note under section 581 of Title 28, Judiciary and Judicial Procedure.

Amendment by Pub.L. 99–554, § 204, not to become effective in or with respect to certain specified judicial districts until, or apply to cases while pending in such district before, the expiration of the 270-day period beginning 30 days after Oct. 27, 1986, or of the 30-day period beginning on the date the Attorney General certifies under section 303 of Pub.L. 99–554 the region specified in a paragraph of section 581(a) of Title 28, as amended by section 111(a) of Pub.L. 99–554, that includes such district, whichever occurs first, see section 302(d)(1) of Pub.L. 99–554, set out as a note under section 581 of Title 28.

Amendment by Pub.L. 99–554, § 204, not to become effective in or with respect to certain specified judicial districts until, or apply to cases while pending in such districts before, the expiration of the 2-year period beginning 30 days after Oct. 27, 1986, or of the 30-day period beginning on the date the Attorney General certifies under section 303 of Pub.L. 99–554 the region specified in a paragraph of section 581(a) of Title 28, as amended by section 111(a) of Pub.L. 99–554, that includes such district, whichever occurs first, see section 302(d)(2) of Pub.L. 99–554, set out as a note under section 581 of Title 28.

Amendment by Pub.L. 99–554, § 204, not to become effective in or with respect to judicial districts established for the States of Alabama and North Carolina until, or apply to cases while pending in such district before, such district elects to be included in a bankruptcy region established in section 581(a) of Title 28, as amended by section 111(a) of Pub.L. 99–554, or Oct. 1, 2002, whichever occurs first, and, except as otherwise provided, with respect to cases under chapters 7, 11, 12, and 13 of Title 11 commenced before 30 days after Oct. 27, 1986, and pending in a judicial district in the States of Alabama or North Carolina before any election made under section 302(d)(3)(A) of Pub.L. 99–554 by such district becomes effective or Oct. 1, 2002, whichever occurs first, amendments by Pub.L. 99–554 not to apply until Oct. 1, 2003, or the expiration of the 1-year period beginning on the date such election becomes effective, whichever occurs first, and further, in any judicial district in Alabama or North Carolina not making the election described in section 302(d)(3)(A) of Pub.L. 99–554, any person appointed under regulations issued by the Judicial Conference to administer estates in cases under Title 11 authorized to establish, etc., a panel of private trustees, and to supervise cases and trustees in cases under chapters 7, 11, 12, and 13 of Title 11, until amendments by sections 201 to 231 of Pub.L. 99–554 effective in such district, see section 302(d)(3)(A) to (F), (H), and (I) of Pub.L. 99–554, set out as a note under section 581 of Title 28.

Amendment by Pub.L. 99–554, § 204, except as otherwise provided, with respect to cases under chapters 7, 11, 12, and 13 of Title 11 commenced before 30 days after Oct. 27, 1986, and pending in a judicial district referred to in section 581(a) of Title 28, as amended by section 111(a) of Pub.L. 99–554, for which a United States trustee is not authorized before 30 days after Oct. 27, 1986 to be appointed, not applicable until the expiration of the 3-year period beginning on Oct. 27, 1986, or of the 1-year period beginning on the date the Attorney General certifies under section 303 of Pub.L. 99–554 the region specified in a paragraph of such section 581(a) that includes, such district, whichever occurs first, see section 302(e)(1), (2) of Pub.L. 99–554, set out as a note under section 581 of Title 28.

Amendment by Pub.L. 99–554, § 254, effective 30 days after Oct. 27, 1986, but not applicable to cases commenced under this title before that date, see section 302(a), (c)(1) of Pub.L. 99–554, set out as a note under section 581 of Title 28.

Amendment by Pub.L. 99–554, § 283, effective 30 days after Oct. 27, 1986, see section 302(a) of Pub.L. 99–554, set out as a note under section 581 of Title 28.

1984 Acts. Amendment by sections 426(a) and 427 of Pub.L. 98–353 effective with respect to cases filed 90 days after July 10, 1984, and amendment by section 426(b) of Pub.L. 98–353 effective July 10, 1984, see section 552(a), (b) of Pub.L. 98–353, set out as a note under section 101 of this title.

Separability of Provisions

If any provision of or amendment made by Pub.L. 103–394 or the application of such provision or amendment to any person or circumstance is held to be unconstitutional, the remaining provisions of and amendments made by Pub.L. 103–394 and the application of such provisions and amendments to any person or circumstance shall not be affected thereby, see section 701 of Pub.L. 103–394, set out as a note under section 101 of this title.

Adjustment of Dollar Amounts

For adjustment of dollar amounts specified in subsec. (b)(1), (2) of this section by the Judicial Conference of the United States, effective Apr. 1, 2010, see note set out under 11 U.S.C.A. § 104.

By notice published Feb. 25, 2010, 75 F.R. 8747, the Judicial Conference of the United States adjusted the dollar amounts in provisions specified in subsec. (b)(1), (2) of this section, effective Apr. 1, 2010, as follows:

In subsec. (b)(1) adjusted $13,475 to $14,425.

In subsec. (b)(2) adjusted $13,475 to $14,425.

By notice published Feb. 14, 2007, 72 F.R. 7082, the Judicial Conference of the United States adjusted the dollar amounts in provisions specified in subsec. (b)(1), (2) of this section, effective Apr. 1, 2007, as follows:

In subsec. (b)(1) adjusted $12,300 to $13,475.

In subsec. (b)(2) adjusted $12,300 to $13,475.

By notice dated Feb. 18, 2004, 69 F.R. 8482, the Judicial Conference of the United States adjusted the dollar amounts in provisions specified in subsec. (b)(1), (2) of this section, effective Apr. 1, 2004, as follows:

In subsec. (b)(1) adjusted $11,625 to $12,300.

In subsec. (b)(2) adjusted $11,625 to $12,300.

By notice dated Feb. 20, 2001, 66 F.R. 10910, the Judicial Conference of the United States adjusted the dollar amounts in provisions specified in subsec. (b)(1), (2) of this section, effective Apr. 1, 2001, as follows:

> In subsec. (b)(1) adjusted $10,775 to $11,625.

> In subsec. (b)(2) adjusted $10,775 to $11,625.

By notice dated Feb. 3, 1998, 63 F.R. 7179, the Judicial Conference of the United States adjusted the dollar amounts in provisions specified in subsec. (b)(1), (2) of this section, effective Apr. 1, 1998, as follows:

> In subsec. (b)(1) adjusted $10,000 to $10,775.

> In subsec. (b)(2) adjusted $10,000 to $10,775.

CROSS REFERENCES

Allowance of administrative expenses incurred by creditor filing petition, see 11 USCA § 503.

Automatic stay, see 11 USCA § 362.

Exempt property, see 11 USCA § 522.

Fees, see 28 USCA § 1930.

Involuntary case—

> Future adjustments, see 11 USCA § 104.

Jury trials, see 28 USCA § 1411.

Lists, schedules, statements and fees, see Fed.Rules Bankr. Proc. Form B 200, 11 USCA.

"Petition" defined, see 11 USCA § 101.

Postpetition transactions, see 11 USCA § 549.

Property of estate, see 11 USCA § 541.

Sharing of compensation between attorneys, see 11 USCA § 504.

LIBRARY REFERENCES

American Digest System

Bankruptcy ⊕2281 to 2297, 2184, 2187.

Key Number System Topic No. 51.

Corpus Juris Secundum

CJS Bankruptcy § 7, Bankruptcy Code.

CJS Bankruptcy § 50, Chapter 7 Proceedings.

CJS Bankruptcy § 62, Appointment of Interim Trustee.

CJS Bankruptcy § 216, Appearance by Foreign Representative.

CJS Bankruptcy § 264, Cases Under Bankruptcy Code.

CJS Bankruptcy § 278, Parties Defendant; Sovereign Immunity.

CJS Bankruptcy § 311, When Does Right to Trial by Jury Exist.

CJS Bankruptcy § 368, Effect of Case on Debtor's Property and Business.

CJS Bankruptcy § 369, Person Against Whom Case May be Commenced.

CJS Bankruptcy § 371, Circumstances Under Which Fewer Than Three Claimholders May File.

CJS Bankruptcy § 374, Partnership.

CJS Bankruptcy § 376, Joinder of Petitioners.

CJS Bankruptcy § 379, Answer; Defenses and Objections.

CJS Bankruptcy § 381, Default.

CJS Bankruptcy § 384, Protection for Debtor on Dismissal.

CJS Bankruptcy § 839, Involuntary Cases.

[§ 304. Repealed. Pub.L. 109–8, Title VIII, § 802(d)(3), Apr. 20, 2005, 119 Stat. 146]

HISTORICAL AND STATUTORY NOTES

Section, Pub.L. 95–598, Nov. 6, 1978, 92 Stat. 2560, related to cases ancillary to foreign proceedings.

See, now, 11 U.S.C.A. § 1501 et seq. and 28 U.S.C.A. § 1410.

Effective Date of Repeal

Repeal effective, except as otherwise provided, 180 days after April 20, 2005, and inapplicable with respect to cases commenced under Title 11 before the effective date, see Pub.L. 109–8, § 1501, set out as a note under 11 U.S.C.A. § 101.

§ 305. Abstention

(a) The court, after notice and a hearing, may dismiss a case under this title, or may suspend all proceedings in a case under this title, at any time if—

(1) the interests of creditors and the debtor would be better served by such dismissal or suspension; or

(2)(A) a petition under section 1515 for recognition of a foreign proceeding has been granted; and

(B) the purposes of chapter 15 of this title would be best served by such dismissal or suspension.

(b) A foreign representative may seek dismissal or suspension under subsection (a)(2) of this section.

(c) An order under subsection (a) of this section dismissing a case or suspending all proceedings in a case, or a decision not so to dismiss or suspend, is not reviewable by appeal or otherwise by the court of appeals under section 158(d), 1291, or 1292 of title 28 or by the Supreme Court of the United States under section 1254 of title 28.

(Pub.L. 95–598, Nov. 6, 1978, 92 Stat. 2561; Pub.L. 101–650, Title III, § 309(a), Dec. 1, 1990, 104 Stat. 5113; Pub.L. 102–198, § 5, Dec. 9, 1991, 105 Stat. 1623; Pub.L. 109–8, Title VIII, § 802(d)(6), Apr. 20, 2005, 119 Stat. 146.)

HISTORICAL AND STATUTORY NOTES

Revision Notes and Legislative Reports

1978 Acts. A principle of the common law requires a court with jurisdiction over a particular matter to take jurisdiction. This section recognizes that there are cases in which it would be appropriate for the court to decline jurisdiction. Abstention under this section, however, is of jurisdiction over the entire case. Abstention from jurisdiction over a particular proceeding in a case is governed by proposed 28 U.S.C. 1471(c). Thus, the court is permitted, if the interests of creditors and the debtor would be better served by dismissal of the case or suspension of all proceedings in the case, to so order. The court may dismiss or suspend under the first paragraph, for example, if an arrangement is being worked out by creditors and the debtor out of court, there is no prejudice to the results of creditors in that arrangement, and an involuntary case has been commenced by a few recalcitrant creditors to provide a basis for future threats to extract full payment. The less expensive out-of-court workout may better serve the interests in the case. Likewise, if there is pending a foreign proceeding concerning the debtor and the factors specified in proposed 11 U.S.C. 304(c) warrant dismissal or suspension, the court may so act.

Subsection (b) gives a foreign representative authority to appear in the bankruptcy court to request dismissal or suspension. Subsection (c) makes the dismissal or suspension order nonreviewable by appeal or otherwise. The bankruptcy court, based on its experience and discretion is vested with the power of decision. Senate Report No. 95–989.

1990 Acts. Senate Report No. 101–416, see 1990 U.S.Code Cong. and Adm.News, p. 6802.

1991 Acts. House Report No. 102–322, see 1991 U.S.Code Cong. and Adm.News, p. 1303.

2005 Acts. House Report No. 109–31(Part I), see 2005 U.S. Code Cong. and Adm. News, p. 88.

References in Text

Chapter 15 of this title, referred to in subsec. (a)(2)(B), is classified to 11 U.S.C.A. § 1501 et seq.

Amendments

2005 Amendments. Subsec. (a)(2). Pub.L. 109–8, § 802(d)(6), rewrote par. (2), which formerly read:

"(2)(A) there is pending a foreign proceeding; and

"(B) the factors specified in section 304(c) of this title warrant such dismissal or suspension."

1991 Amendments. Subsec. (c). Pub.L. 102–198 substituted "title 28" for "this title", wherever appearing.

1990 Amendments. Subsec. (c). Pub.L. 101–650 declared abstention determinations in bankruptcy cases nonreviewable by the court of appeals or by the Supreme Court.

Effective and Applicability Provisions

2005 Acts. Amendments by Pub.L. 109–8 effective, except as otherwise provided, 180 days after April 20, 2005, and inapplicable with respect to cases commenced under Title 11 before the effective date, see Pub.L. 109–8, § 1501, set out as a note under 11 U.S.C.A. § 101.

LIBRARY REFERENCES

American Digest System

Bankruptcy ⚏2261, 3766.1.

American Digest System

Federal Courts ⚏47.5.

Key Number System Topic Nos. 170B, 51.

Corpus Juris Secundum

CJS Bankruptcy § 174, Motions to Abstain or Remand.

CJS Bankruptcy § 216, Appearance by Foreign Representative.

CJS Bankruptcy § 414, Dismissal or Suspension to Better Serve Interests of Creditors and Debtor.

CJS Bankruptcy § 415, Dismissal or Suspension When Petition for Recognition of Foreign Proceeding Has Been Granted.

CJS Bankruptcy § 416, Proceedings.

CJS Bankruptcy § 1227, Abstention.

§ 306. Limited appearance

An appearance in a bankruptcy court by a foreign representative in connection with a petition or request under section 303 or 305 of this title does not submit such foreign representative to the jurisdiction of any court in the United States for any other purpose, but the bankruptcy court may condition any order under section 303 or 305 of this title on compliance by such foreign representative with the orders of such bankruptcy court.

(Pub.L. 95–598, Nov. 6, 1978, 92 Stat. 2561; Pub.L. 109–8, Title VIII, § 802(d)(5), Apr. 20, 2005, 119 Stat. 146.)

HISTORICAL AND STATUTORY NOTES

Revision Notes and Legislative Reports

1978 Acts. Section 306 permits a foreign representative that is seeking dismissal or suspension under section 305 of an ancillary case or that is appearing in connection with a petition under section 303 or 304 to appear without subjecting himself to the jurisdiction of any other court in the United States, including State courts. The protection is necessary to allow the foreign representative to present his case and the case of the foreign estate, without waiving the normal jurisdictional rules of the foreign country. That is, creditors in this country will still have to seek redress against the foreign estate according to the host country's jurisdictional rules. Any other result would permit local creditors to obtain unfair advantage by filing an involuntary case, thus requiring the foreign representative to appear, and then obtaining local jurisdiction over the representative in connection with his appearance in this country. That kind of bankruptcy law would legalize an ambush technique that has frequently been rejected by the common law in other contexts.

However, the bankruptcy court is permitted under section 306 to condition any relief under section 303, 304, or 305 on the compliance by the foreign representative with the orders of the bankruptcy court. The last provision is not carte blanche to the bankruptcy court to require the foreign representative to submit to jurisdiction in other courts contrary to the general policy of the section. It is designed to enable the bankruptcy court to enforce its own orders that are necessary to the appropriate relief granted under section 303, 304, or 305. Senate Report No. 95–989.

2005 Acts. House Report No. 109–31(Part I), see 2005 U.S. Code Cong. and Adm. News, p. 88.

Amendments

2005 Amendments. Section. Pub.L. 109–8, § 802(d)(5), struck out ", 304," following "under section 303" twice.

Effective and Applicability Provisions

2005 Acts. Amendments by Pub.L. 109–8 effective, except as otherwise provided, 180 days after April 20, 2005, and inapplicable with respect to cases commenced under Title 11 before the effective date, see Pub.L. 109–8, § 1501, set out as a note under 11 U.S.C.A. § 101.

LIBRARY REFERENCES

American Digest System

Appearance ⚏9(1).

American Digest System

Bankruptcy ⚏2058.1.

Key Number System Topic Nos. 31, 51.

Corpus Juris Secundum

CJS Bankruptcy § 216, Appearance by Foreign Representative.

CJS Bankruptcy § 386, Foreign Proceedings and Representatives, Generally.

§ 307. United States trustee

The United States trustee may raise and may appear and be heard on any issue in any case or proceeding under this title but may not file a plan pursuant to section 1121(c) of this title.

(Added Pub.L. 99–554, Title II, § 205(a), Oct. 27, 1986, 100 Stat. 3098.)

HISTORICAL AND STATUTORY NOTES

Revision Notes and Legislative Reports

1986 Acts. House Report No. 99–764 and House Conference Report No. 99–958, see 1986 U.S.Code Cong. and Adm. News, p. 5227.

Effective and Applicability Provisions

1986 Acts. Enactment by Pub.L. 99–554, effective 30 days after Oct. 27, 1986, except as otherwise provided for, see section 302(a) of Pub.L. 99–554, set out as a note under section 581 of Title 28, Judiciary and Judicial Procedure.

Enactment by Pub.L. 99–554, § 205(a), not to become effective in or with respect to certain specified judicial districts until, or apply to cases while pending in such district before, the expiration of the 270-day period beginning 30 days after Oct. 27, 1986, or of the 30-day period beginning on the date the Attorney General certifies under section 303 of Pub.L. 99–554 the region specified in a paragraph of section 581(a) of Title 28, as amended by section 111(a) of Pub.L. 99–554, that includes such district, whichever occurs first, see section 302(d)(1) of Pub.L. 99–554, set out as a note under section 581 of Title 28.

Enactment by Pub.L. 99–554, § 205(a), not to become effective in or with respect to certain specified judicial districts until, or apply to cases while pending in such district before, the expiration of the 2-year period beginning 30 days after Oct. 27, 1986, or of the 30-day period beginning on the date the Attorney General certifies under section 303 of Pub.L. 99–554 the region specified in a paragraph of section 581(a) of Title 28, as amended by section 111(a) of Pub.L. 99–554, that includes such district, whichever occurs first, see section 302(d)(2) of Pub.L. 99–554, set out as a note under section 581 of Title 28.

Enactment by Pub.L. 99–554, § 205(a), not to become effective in or with respect to judicial districts established for the States of Alabama and North Carolina until, or apply to cases while pending in such district before, such district elects to be included in a bankruptcy region established in section 581(a) of Title 28, as amended by section 111(a) of Pub.L. 99–554, or Oct. 1, 2002, whichever occurs first, and, except as otherwise provided for, with respect to cases under chapters 7, 11, 12, and 13 of Title 11 commenced before 30 days after Oct. 27, 1986, and pending in a judicial district in the States of Alabama or North Carolina before an election made under section 302(d)(3)(A) of Pub.L. 99–554 by such district becomes effective or Oct. 1, 2002, whichever occurs first, amendments by Pub.L. 99–554 not to apply until Oct. 1, 2003, or the expiration of the 1-year period beginning on the date such election becomes effective, whichever occurs first, and further, in any judicial district in Alabama or North Carolina not making the election described in section 302(d)(3)(A) of Pub.L. 99–554, any person appointed under regulations issued by the Judicial Conference to administer estates in cases under Title 11 authorized to establish, etc., a panel of private trustees, and to supervise cases and trustees in cases under chapters 7, 11, 12, and 13 of Title 11, until amendments by sections 201 to 231 of Pub.L. 99–554 effective in such district, see section 302(d)(3)(A) to (F), (H), and (I), of Pub.L. 99–554, set out as a note under section 581 of Title 28.

Standing and Authority of Bankruptcy Administrator

Pub.L. 101–650, Title III, § 317(b), Dec. 1, 1990, 104 Stat. 5115, provided that: "A bankruptcy administrator may raise and may appear and be heard on any issue in any case under title 11, United States Code, but may not file a plan pursuant to section 1121(c) of such title."

LIBRARY REFERENCES

American Digest System

Bankruptcy ⟐2204.1, 2205.

Key Number System Topic No. 51.

Corpus Juris Secundum

CJS Bankruptcy § 7, Bankruptcy Code.

CJS Bankruptcy § 44, Authority to Appear and be Heard.

CJS Bankruptcy § 51, Chapter 11 Proceedings.

§ 308. Debtor reporting requirements

(a) For purposes of this section, the term "profitability" means, with respect to a debtor, the amount of money that the debtor has earned or lost during current and recent fiscal periods.

(b) A debtor in a small business case shall file periodic financial and other reports containing information including—

(1) the debtor's profitability;

(2) reasonable approximations of the debtor's projected cash receipts and cash disbursements over a reasonable period;

(3) comparisons of actual cash receipts and disbursements with projections in prior reports;

(4) whether the debtor is—

(A) in compliance in all material respects with postpetition requirements imposed by this title and the Federal Rules of Bankruptcy Procedure; and

(B) timely filing tax returns and other required government filings and paying taxes and other administrative expenses when due;

(5) if the debtor is not in compliance with the requirements referred to in paragraph (4)(A) or filing tax returns and other required government filings and making the payments referred to in paragraph (4)(B), what the failures are and how, at what

cost, and when the debtor intends to remedy such failures; and

(6) such other matters as are in the best interests of the debtor and creditors, and in the public interest in fair and efficient procedures under chapter 11 of this title.

(Added Pub.L. 109–8, Title IV, § 434(a)(1), Apr. 20, 2005, 119 Stat. 111; amended Pub.L. 111–327, § 2(a)(10), Dec. 22, 2010, 124 Stat. 3558.)

HISTORICAL AND STATUTORY NOTES

Revision Notes and Legislative Reports

2005 Acts. House Report No. 109–31(Part I), see 2005 U.S. Code Cong. and Adm. News, p. 88.

References in Text

The Federal Rules of Bankruptcy Procedure, referred to in subsec. (b)(4)(A), are set out in the Appendix to this title.

Chapter 11 of this title, referred to in subsec. (b)(6), is 11 U.S.C.A. § 1101 et seq.

Amendments

2010 Amendments. Subsec. (b). Pub.L. 111–327, § 2(a)(10)(A), struck out "small business debtor" and inserted "debtor in a small business case".

Subsec. (b)(4). Pub.L. 111–327, § 2(a)(10)(B), redesignated former par. (4)(A) as par. (4) and therein redesignated former cls. (i) and (ii) as subpars. (A) and (B), respectively; redesignated former par. (4)(B) as par. (5), and therein struck out "subparagraph (A)(i)" and inserted "paragraph (4)(A)", and struck out "subparagraph (A)(ii)" and inserted "paragraph (4)(B)"; and redesignated former par. (4)(C) as par. (6).

Subsec. (b)(5). Pub.L. 111–327, § 2(a)(10)(B)(ii), redesignated former par. (4)(B) as par. (5), and therein struck out "subparagraph (A)(i)" and inserted "paragraph (4)(A)", and struck out "subparagraph (A)(ii)" and inserted "paragraph (4)(B)".

Subsec. (b)(6). Pub.L. 111–327, § 2(a)(10)(B)(iii), redesignated former par. (4)(C) as par. (6).

Effective and Applicability Provisions

2005 Acts. Pub.L. 109–8, Title IV, § 434(b), Apr. 20, 2005, 119 Stat. 111, provided that: "The amendments made by subsection (a) [enacting this section] shall take effect 60 days after the date on which rules are prescribed under section 2075 of title 28, United States Code, to establish forms to be used to comply with section 308 of title 11, United States Code, as added by subsection (a) [enacting this section]. [See Bankruptcy Form No. 25C, eff. Dec. 1, 2008, set out in the Appendix to this title.]"

Amendments by Pub.L. 109–8 effective, except as otherwise provided, 180 days after April 20, 2005, and inapplicable with respect to cases commenced under Title 11 before the effective date, see Pub.L. 109–8, § 1501, set out as a note under 11 U.S.C.A. § 101.

LIBRARY REFERENCES

Corpus Juris Secundum

CJS Bankruptcy § 758, Debtor's Duties.

SUBCHAPTER II—OFFICERS

§ 321. Eligibility to serve as trustee

(a) A person may serve as trustee in a case under this title only if such person is—

(1) an individual that is competent to perform the duties of trustee and, in a case under chapter 7, 12, or 13 of this title, resides or has an office in the judicial district within which the case is pending, or in any judicial district adjacent to such district; or

(2) a corporation authorized by such corporation's charter or bylaws to act as trustee, and, in a case under chapter 7, 12, or 13 of this title, having an office in at least one of such districts.

(b) A person that has served as an examiner in the case may not serve as trustee in the case.

(c) The United States trustee for the judicial district in which the case is pending is eligible to serve as trustee in the case if necessary.

(Pub.L. 95–598, Nov. 6, 1978, 92 Stat. 2561; Pub. L. 98–353, Title III, § 428, July 10, 1984, 98 Stat. 369; Pub.L. 99–554, Title II, §§ 206, 257(c), Oct. 27, 1986, 100 Stat. 3098, 3114.)

HISTORICAL AND STATUTORY NOTES

Revision Notes and Legislative Reports

1978 Acts. Section 321 is adapted from current Bankruptcy Act section 45 [section 73 of former Title 11] and Bankruptcy Rule 209. Subsection (a) specifies that an individual may serve as trustee in a bankruptcy case only if he is competent to perform the duties of trustee and resides or has an office in the judicial district within which the case is pending, or in an adjacent judicial district. A corporation must be authorized by its charter or bylaws to act as trustee, and, for chapter 7 or 13 cases, must have an office in any of the above mentioned judicial districts. Senate Report No. 95–989.

1984 Acts. Statements by Legislative Leaders, see 1984 U.S.Code Cong. and Adm.News, p. 576.

1986 Acts. House Report No. 99–764 and House Conference Report No. 99–958, see 1986 U.S.Code Cong. and Adm. News, p. 5227.

Legislative Statements

Section 321 indicates that an examiner may not serve as a trustee in the case.

Amendments

1986 Amendments. Subsec. (a). Pub.L. 99–554, § 257(c), added references to chapter 12 in two places.

Subsec. (c). Pub.L. 99–554, § 206, added subsec. (c).

1984 Amendments. Subsec. (b). Pub.L. 98–353 substituted "the case" for "a case" after "an examiner in".

Effective and Applicability Provisions

1986 Acts. Amendment by Pub.L. 99–554 effective 30 days after Oct. 27, 1986, except as otherwise provided for, see section 302(a) of Pub.L. 99–554, set out as a note under section 581 of Title 28, Judiciary and Judicial Procedure.

Amendment by Pub.L. 99–554, § 206, not to become effective in or with respect to certain specified judicial districts until, or apply to cases while pending in such district before, the expiration of the 270-day period beginning 30 days after Oct. 27, 1986, or of the 30-day period beginning on the date the Attorney General certifies under section 303 of Pub.L. 99–554 the region specified in a paragraph of section 581(a) of Title 28, as amended by section 111(a) of Pub.L. 99–554, that includes such district, whichever occurs first, see section 302(d)(1) of Pub.L. 99–554, set out as a note under section 581 of Title 28.

Amendment by Pub.L. 99–554, § 206, not to become effective in or with respect to certain specified judicial districts until, or apply to cases while pending in such district before, the expiration of the 2-year period beginning 30 days after Oct. 27, 1986, or of the 30-day period beginning on the date the Attorney General certifies under section 303 of Pub.L. 99–554 the region specified in a paragraph of section 581(a) of Title 28, as amended by section 111(a) of Pub.L. 99–554, that includes such district, whichever occurs first, see section 302(d)(2) of Pub.L. 99–554, set out as a note under section 581 of Title 28.

Amendment by Pub.L. 99–554, § 206, not to become effective in or with respect to judicial districts established for the States of Alabama and North Carolina until, or apply to cases while pending in such district before, such district elects to be included in a bankruptcy region established in section 581(a) of Title 28, as amended by section 111(a) of Pub.L. 99–554, or Oct. 1, 2002, whichever occurs first, and, except as otherwise provided for, with respect to cases under chapters 7, 11, 12, and 13 of Title 11 commenced before 30 days after Oct. 27, 1986, and pending in a judicial district in the States of Alabama or North Carolina before any election made under section 302(d)(3)(A) of Pub.L. 99–554 by such district becomes effective or Oct. 1, 2002, whichever occurs first, amendments by Pub.L. 99–554 not to apply until Oct. 1, 2003, or the expiration of the 1-year period beginning on the date such election becomes effective whichever occurs first, and further, in any judicial district in Alabama or North Carolina not making the election described in section 302(d)(3)(A) of Pub.L. 99–554, any person appointed under regulations issued by the Judicial Conference to administer estates in cases under Title 11 authorized to establish, etc., a panel of private trustees, and to supervise cases and trustees in cases under chapters 7, 11, 12, and 13 of Title 11, until amendments by sections 201 to 231 of Pub.L. 99–554 effective in such district, see section 302(d)(3)(A) to (F), (H), and (I) of Pub.L. 99–554, set out as a note under section 581 of Title 28.

Amendment by Pub.L. 99–554, § 206, except as otherwise provided, with respect to cases under chapters, 7, 11, 12, and 13 of Title 11 commenced before 30 days after Oct. 27, 1986, and pending in a judicial district referred to in section 581(a) of Title 28, as amended by section 111(a) of Pub.L. 99–554, for which a United States trustee is not authorized before 30 days after Oct. 27, 1986 to be appointed, not applicable until the expiration of the 3-year period beginning on Oct. 27, 1986, or of the 1-year period beginning on the date the Attorney General certifies under section 303 of Pub.L. 99–554 the region specified in a paragraph of such section 581(a) that includes, such district, whichever occurs first, see section 302(e)(1), (2) of Pub.L. 99–554, set out as a note under section 581 of Title 28.

Amendment by Pub.L. 99–554, § 257(c) effective 30 days after Oct. 27, 1986, but not applicable with respect to cases commenced under this title before that date, see section 302(a), (c)(1) of Pub.L. 99–554, set out as a note under section 581 of Title 28.

1984 Acts. Amendment by Pub.L. 98–353 effective with respect to cases filed 90 days after July 10, 1984, see section 552(a), formerly 553(a), of Pub.L. 98–353, set out as a note under section 101 of this title.

LIBRARY REFERENCES

American Digest System

Bankruptcy ⬥3003.

Key Number System Topic No. 51.

Corpus Juris Secundum

CJS Bankruptcy § 46, Service as Bankruptcy Trustee.

CJS Bankruptcy § 55, Eligibility to Serve as Trustee or Examiner.

§ 322.　Qualification of trustee

(a) Except as provided in subsection (b)(1), a person selected under section 701, 702, 703, 1104, 1163, 1202, or 1302 of this title to serve as trustee in a case under this title qualifies if before seven days after such selection, and before beginning official duties, such person has filed with the court a bond in favor of the United States conditioned on the faithful performance of such official duties.

(b)(1) The United States trustee qualifies wherever such trustee serves as trustee in a case under this title.

(2) The United States trustee shall determine—

(A) the amount of a bond required to be filed under subsection (a) of this section; and

(B) the sufficiency of the surety on such bond.

(c) A trustee is not liable personally or on such trustee's bond in favor of the United States for any penalty or forfeiture incurred by the debtor.

(d) A proceeding on a trustee's bond may not be commenced after two years after the date on which such trustee was discharged.

(Pub.L. 95–598, Nov. 6, 1978, 92 Stat. 2562; Pub. L. 98–353, Title III, § 429, July 10, 1984, 98 Stat. 369; Pub.L. 99–554, Title II, §§ 207, 257(d), Oct. 27, 1986, 100 Stat. 3098, 3114; Pub.L. 103–394, Title V, § 501(d)(3), Oct. 22, 1994, 108 Stat. 4143; Pub.L. 111–16, § 2(2), May 7, 2009, 123 Stat. 1607.)

HISTORICAL AND STATUTORY NOTES

Revision Notes and Legislative Reports

1978 Acts. A trustee qualifies in a case by filing, within five days after selection, a bond in favor of the United States, conditioned on the faithful performance of his official duties. This section is derived from the Bankruptcy Act section 50b [section 78(b) of former Title 11]. The court is required to determine the amount of the bond and the sufficiency of the surety on the bond. Subsection (c), derived from Bankruptcy Act section 50i [section 78(i) of former Title 11], relieves the trustee from personal liability and from liability on his bond for any penalty or forfeiture incurred by the debtor. Subsection (d), derived from section 50m [section 78(m) of former Title 11], fixes a two-year statute of limitations on any action on a trustee's bond. Finally, subsection (e) dispenses with the bonding requirement for the United States trustee. Senate Report No. 95–989.

1984 Acts. Statements by Legislative Leaders, see 1984 U.S.Code Cong. and Adm.News, p. 576.

1986 Acts. House Report No. 99–764 and House Conference Report No. 99–958, see 1986 U.S.Code Cong. and Adm. News, p. 5227.

1994 Acts. House Report No. 103–835, see 1994 U.S. Code Cong. and Adm. News, p. 3340.

Legislative Statements

Section 322(a) is modified to include a trustee serving in a railroad reorganization under subchapter IV of chapter 11.

Amendments

2009 Amendments. Subsec. (a). Pub.L. 111–16, § 2(2), struck out "five days" and inserted "seven days".

1994 Amendments. Subsec. (a). Pub.L. 103–394, § 501(d)(3), substituted "1202, or 1302" for "1302, or 1202".

1986 Amendments. Subsec. (a). Pub.L. 99–554, § 207(1), substituted "Except as provided in subsection (b)(1), a person" for "A person".

Pub.L. 99–554, § 257(d), added reference to section 1202 of this title.

Subsec. (b). Pub.L. 99–554, § 207(2), added par. (1), designated existing provisions as par. (2), and, as so designated, substituted "The United States trustee" for "The court", "(A) the amount" for "(1) the amount", and "(B) the sufficiency" for "(2) the sufficiency".

1984 Amendments. Subsec. (b)(1). Pub.L. 98–353 added "required to be" after "bond".

Effective and Applicability Provisions

2009 Acts. Amendments by Pub.L. 111–16 effective Dec. 1, 2009, see Pub.L. 111–16, § 7, set out as a note under 11 U.S.C.A. § 109.

1994 Acts. Amendment by Pub.L. 103–394 effective on Oct. 22, 1994, and not to apply with respect to cases commenced under Title 11 of the United States Code before Oct. 22, 1994, see section 702 of Pub.L. 103–394, set out as a note under section 101 of this title.

1986 Acts. Amendment by Pub.L. 99–554 effective 30 days after Oct. 27, 1986, except as otherwise provided for, see section 302(a) of Pub.L. 99–554, set out as a note under section 581 of Title 28, Judiciary and Judicial Procedure.

Amendment by Pub.L. 99–554, § 207, not to become effective in or with respect to certain specified judicial districts until, or apply to cases while pending in such district before, the expiration of the 270-day period beginning 30 days after Oct. 27, 1986, or of the 30-day period beginning on the date the Attorney General certifies under section 303 of Pub.L. 99–554 the region specified in a paragraph of section 581(a) of Title 28, as amended by section 111(a) of Pub.L. 99–554, that includes such district, whichever occurs first, see section 302(d)(1) of Pub.L. 99–554, set out as a note under section 581 of Title 28.

Amendment by Pub.L. 99–554, § 207, not to become effective in or with respect to certain specified judicial districts until, or apply to cases while pending in such district before, the expiration of the 2-year period beginning 30 days after Oct. 27, 1986, or of the 30-day period beginning on the date the Attorney General certifies under section 303 of Pub.L. 99–554 the region specified in a paragraph of section 581(a) of Title 28, as amended by section 111(a) of Pub.L. 99–554, that includes such district, whichever occurs first, see section

302(d)(2) of Pub.L. 99–554, set out as a note under section 581 of Title 28.

Amendment by Pub.L. 99–554, § 207, not to become effective in or with respect to judicial districts established for the States of Alabama and North Carolina until, or apply to cases while pending in such district before, such district elects to be included in a bankruptcy region established in section 581(a) of Title 28, as amended by section 111(a) of Pub.L. 99–554, or Oct. 1, 2002, whichever occurs first, and, except as otherwise provided for, with respect to cases under chapters 7, 11, 12, and 13 of Title 11 commenced before 30 days after Oct. 27, 1986, and pending in a judicial district in the States of Alabama or North Carolina before any election made under section 302(d)(3)(A) of Pub.L. 99–554 by such district becomes effective or Oct. 1, 2002, whichever occurs first, amendments by Pub.L. 99–554 not to apply until Oct. 1, 2003, or the expiration of the 1-year period beginning on the date such election becomes effective, whichever occurs first, and further, in any judicial district in Alabama or North Carolina not making the election described in section 302(d)(3)(A) of Pub.L. 99–554, any person appointed under regulations issued by the Judicial Conference to administer estates in cases under Title 11 authorized to establish, etc., a panel of private trustees, and to supervise cases and trustees in cases under chapters 7, 11, 12, and 13 of Title 11, until amendments by sections 201 to 231 of Pub.L. 99–554 effective in such district, see section 302(d)(3)(A) to (F), (H), and (I) of Pub.L. 99–554, set out as a note under section 581 of Title 28.

Amendment by Pub.L. 99–554, § 207, except as otherwise provided, with respect to cases under chapters 7, 11, 12, and 13 of Title 11 commenced before 30 days after Oct. 27, 1986, and pending in a judicial district referred to in section 581(a) of Title 28, as amended by section 111(a) of Pub.L. 99–554, for which a United States trustee is not authorized before 30 days after Oct. 27, 1986 to be appointed, not applicable until the expiration of the 3-year period beginning on Oct. 27, 1986, or of the 1-year period beginning on the date the Attorney General certifies under section 303 of Pub.L. 99–554 the region specified in a paragraph of such section 581(a) that includes, such district, whichever occurs first, see section 302(e)(1), (2) of Pub.L. 99–554, set out as a note under section 581 of Title 28.

Amendment by Pub.L. 99–554, § 257(d), effective 30 days after Oct. 27, 1986, but not applicable with respect to cases commenced under this title before that date, see section 302(a), (c)(1) of Pub.L. 99–554, set out as a note under section 581 of Title 28.

1984 Acts. Amendment by Pub.L. 98–353 effective with respect to cases filed 90 days after July 10, 1984, see section 552(a), formerly 553(a), of Pub.L. 98–353, set out as a note under section 101 of this title.

Separability of Provisions

If any provision of or amendment made by Pub.L. 103–394 or the application of such provision or amendment to any person or circumstance is held to be unconstitutional, the remaining provisions of and amendments made by Pub.L. 103–394 and the application of such provisions and amendments to any person or circumstance shall not be affected thereby, see section 701 of Pub.L. 103–394, set out as a note under section 101 of this title.

§ 323. Role and capacity of trustee

(a) The trustee in a case under this title is the representative of the estate.

(b) The trustee in a case under this title has capacity to sue and be sued.

(Pub.L. 95–598, Nov. 6, 1978, 92 Stat. 2562.)

HISTORICAL AND STATUTORY NOTES

Revision Notes and Legislative Reports

1978 Acts. Subsection (a) of this section makes the trustee the representative of the estate. Subsection (b) grants the trustee the capacity to sue and to be sued. If the debtor remains in possession in a chapter 11 case, section 1107 gives the debtor in possession these rights of the trustee: the debtor in possession becomes the representative of the estate, and may sue and be sued. The same applies in a chapter 13 case. Senate Report No. 95–989.

§ 324. Removal of trustee or examiner

(a) The court, after notice and a hearing, may remove a trustee, other than the United States trustee, or an examiner, for cause.

(b) Whenever the court removes a trustee or examiner under subsection (a) in a case under this title, such trustee or examiner shall thereby be removed in all other cases under this title in which such trustee or examiner is then serving unless the court orders otherwise.

(Pub.L. 95–598, Nov. 6, 1978, 92 Stat. 2562; Pub.L. 99–554, Title II, § 208, Oct. 27, 1986, 100 Stat. 3098.)

HISTORICAL AND STATUTORY NOTES

Revision Notes and Legislative Reports

1978 Acts. This section permits the court, after notice and a hearing, to remove a trustee for cause. Senate Report No. 95–989.

1986 Acts. House Report No. 99–764 and House Conference Report No. 99–958, see 1986 U.S.Code Cong. and Adm. News, p. 5227.

Amendments

1986 Amendments. Pub.L. 99–554, § 208, designated existing provisions as subsec. (a), and, as so designated, substituted "a trustee, other than the United States trustee, or an examiner" for "a trustee or an examiner", and added subsec. (b).

Effective and Applicability Provisions

1986 Acts. Amendment by Pub.L. 99–554 effective 30 days after Oct. 27, 1986, except as otherwise provided for, see section 302(a) of Pub.L. 99–554, set out as a note under section 581 of Title 28, Judiciary and Judicial Procedure.

Amendment by Pub.L. 99–554, § 208 not to become effective in or with respect to certain specified judicial districts until, or apply to cases while pending in such district before, the expiration of the 270-day period beginning 30 days after Oct. 27, 1986, or of the 30-day period beginning on the date the Attorney General certifies under section 303 of Pub.L. 99–554 the region specified in a paragraph of section 581(a) of Title 28, as amended by section 111(a) of Pub.L. 99–554, that includes such district, whichever occurs first, see section 302(d)(1) of Pub.L. 99–554, set out as a note under section 581 of Title 28.

Amendment by Pub.L. 99–554, § 208, not to become effective in or with respect to certain specified judicial districts until, or apply to cases while pending in such district before, the expiration of the 2-year period beginning 30 days after Oct. 27, 1986, or of the 30-day period beginning on the date the Attorney General certifies under section 303 of Pub.L. 99–554 the region specified in a paragraph of section 581(a) of Title 28, as amended by section 111(a) of Pub.L. 99–554, that includes such district, whichever occurs first, see section 302(d)(2) of Pub.L. 99–554, set out as a note under section 581 of Title 28.

Amendment by Pub.L. 99–554, § 208, not to become effective in or with respect to judicial districts established for the States of Alabama and North Carolina until, or apply to cases while pending in such district before, such district elects to be included in a bankruptcy region established in section 581(a) of Title 28, as amended by section 111(a) of Pub.L. 99–554, or Oct. 1, 2002, whichever occurs first, and, except as otherwise provided for, with respect to cases under chapters 7, 11, 12, and 13 of Title 11 commenced before 30 days after Oct. 27, 1986, and pending in a judicial district in the States of Alabama or North Carolina before any election made under section 302(d)(3)(A) of Pub.L. 99–554 by such district becomes effective or Oct. 1, 2002, whichever occurs first, amendments by Pub.L. 99–554 not to apply until Oct. 1, 2003, or the expiration of the 1-year period beginning on the date such election becomes effective, whichever occurs first, and further, in any judicial district in Alabama or North Carolina not making the election described in section 302(d)(3)(A) of Pub.L. 99–554, any person appointed under regulations issued by the Judicial Conference to administer estates in cases under Title 11 authorized to establish, etc., a panel of private trustees, and to supervise cases and trustees in cases under chapters 7, 11, 12, and 13 of Title 11, until amendments by sections 201 to 231 of Pub.L. 99–554 effective in such district, see section 302(d)(3)(A) to (F), (H), and (I) of Pub.L. 99–554, set out as a note under section 581 of Title 28.

Amendment by Pub.L. 99–554, § 208, except as otherwise provided, with respect to cases under chapters 7, 11, 12, and 13 of Title 11 commenced before 30 days after Oct. 27, 1986, and pending in a judicial district referred to in section 581(a) of Title 28, as amended by section 111(a) of Pub.L. 99–554, for which a United States trustee is not authorized before 30 days after Oct. 27, 1986 to be appointed, not applicable until the expiration of the 3-year period beginning on Oct. 27, 1986, or of the 1-year period beginning on the date the Attorney General certifies under section 303 of Pub.L. 99–554 the region specified in a paragraph of such section 581(a) that includes, such district, whichever occurs first, see section 302(e)(1), (2) of Pub.L. 99–554, set out as a note under section 581 of Title 28.

CROSS REFERENCES

Adverse interest and conduct of officers of estate, see 18 USCA § 154.

Appointment of trustee or examiner upon removal, see 11 USCA § 1104.

Authority of Attorney General to investigate trustees, see 28 USCA § 526.

Embezzlement by trustee, see 18 USCA § 153.

Successor trustee, see 11 USCA § 703.

LIBRARY REFERENCES

American Digest System

Bankruptcy ⬥3623.1, 3007.

Key Number System Topic No. 51.

Corpus Juris Secundum

CJS Bankruptcy § 41, Appointment, Oath, and Term; Vacancy in and Removal from Office.

CJS Bankruptcy § 110, Removal of Trustee or Examiner for Cause.

CJS Bankruptcy § 111, Removal of Trustee or Examiner for Cause--Grounds for Removal.

CJS Bankruptcy § 127, Breach of Fiduciary Duty or Disqualification of Trustee.

CJS Bankruptcy § 842, Presumption of Reasonableness of Management Decisions.

§ 325. Effect of vacancy

A vacancy in the office of trustee during a case does not abate any pending action or proceeding, and the successor trustee shall be substituted as a party in such action or proceeding.
(Pub.L. 95–598, Nov. 6, 1978, 92 Stat. 2562.)

HISTORICAL AND STATUTORY NOTES

Revision Notes and Legislative Reports

1978 Acts. Section 325, derived from Bankruptcy Act section 46 [section 74 of former Title 11] and Bankruptcy Rule 221(b), specifies that a vacancy in the office of trustee during a case does not abate any pending action or proceeding. The successor trustee, when selected and qualified, is substituted as a party in any pending action or proceeding. Senate Report No. 95–989.

LIBRARY REFERENCES

American Digest System

Bankruptcy ⬥3001, 3008.1.

Key Number System Topic No. 51.

Corpus Juris Secundum

CJS Bankruptcy § 60, Vacancy in Office of Trustee; Substitution of Successor Trustee.

§ 326. Limitation on compensation of trustee

(a) In a case under chapter 7 or 11, the court may allow reasonable compensation under section 330 of this title of the trustee for the trustee's services, payable after the trustee renders such services, not to exceed 25 percent on the first $5,000 or less, 10 percent on any amount in excess of $5,000 but not in excess of $50,000, 5 percent on any amount in excess of $50,000 but not in excess of $1,000,000, and reasonable compensation not to exceed 3 percent of such moneys in excess of $1,000,000, upon all moneys disbursed or turned over in the case by the trustee to parties in interest, excluding the debtor, but including holders of secured claims.

(b) In a case under chapter 12 or 13 of this title, the court may not allow compensation for services or reimbursement of expenses of the United States trustee or of a standing trustee appointed under section 586(b) of title 28, but may allow reasonable compensation under section 330 of this title of a trustee appointed under section 1202(a) or 1302(a) of this title for the trustee's services, payable after the trustee renders such services, not to exceed five percent upon all payments under the plan.

(c) If more than one person serves as trustee in the case, the aggregate compensation of such persons for such service may not exceed the maximum compensation prescribed for a single trustee by subsection (a) or (b) of this section, as the case may be.

(d) The court may deny allowance of compensation for services or reimbursement of expenses of the trustee if the trustee failed to make diligent inquiry into facts that would permit denial of allowance under section 328(c) of this title or, with knowledge of such facts, employed a professional person under section 327 of this title.

(Pub.L. 95–598, Nov. 6, 1978, 92 Stat. 2562; Pub. L. 98–353, Title III, § 430(a), (b), July 10, 1984, 98 Stat. 369; Pub.L. 99–554, Title II, § 209, Oct. 27, 1986, 100 Stat. 3098; Pub.L. 103–394, Title I, § 107, Oct. 22, 1994, 108 Stat. 4111.)

HISTORICAL AND STATUTORY NOTES

Revision Notes and Legislative Reports

1978 Acts. This section is derived in part from section 48c of the Bankruptcy Act [section 76(c) of former Title 11]. It must be emphasized that this section does not authorize compensation of trustees. This section simply fixes the maximum compensation of a trustee. Proposed 11 U.S.C. section 330 authorizes and fixes the standard of compensation. Under section 48c of current law, the maximum limits have tended to become minimums in many cases. This section is not intended to be so interpreted. The limits in this section, together with the limitations found in section 330, are to be applied as outer limits and not as grants or entitlements to the maximum fees specified.

The maximum fee schedule is derived from section 48c(1) of the present act [section 76(c)(1) of former Title 11], but with a change relating to the bases on which the percentage maxima are computed. The maximum fee schedule is based on decreasing percentages of increasing amounts. The amounts are the amounts of money distributed by the trustee to parties in interest, excluding the debtor, but including secured creditors. These amounts were last amended in 1952. Since then, the cost of living has approximately doubled. Thus, the bases were doubled.

It should be noted that the bases on which the maximum fee is computed includes moneys turned over to secured creditors, to cover the situation where the trustee liquidates property subject to a lien and distributes the proceeds. It does not cover cases in which the trustee simply turns over the property to the secured creditor, nor where the trustee abandons the property and the secured creditor is permitted to foreclose. The provision is also subject to the rights of the secured creditor generally under proposed section 506, especially section 506(c). The $150 discretionary fee provision of current law is retained.

Subsection (b) of this section entitles an operating trustee to a reasonable fee, without any limitation based on the maximum provided for a liquidating trustee as in current law, Bankruptcy Act section 48c(2) [section 76(c)(2) of former Title 11].

Subsection (c) permits a maximum fee of five percent on all payments to creditors under a chapter 13 plan to the trustee appointed in the case.

Subsection (d) provides a limitation not found in current law. Even if more than one trustee serves in the case, the maximum fee payable to all trustees does not change. For example, if an interim trustee is appointed and an elected trustee replaces him, the combined total of the fees payable to the interim trustee and the permanent trustee may not exceed the amount specified in this section. Under current law, very often a receiver receives a full fee and a subsequent trustee also receives a full fee. The resultant "double-dipping", especially in cases in which the receiver and the trustee are the same individual, is detrimental to the interests of creditors, by needlessly increasing the cost of administering bankruptcy estates.

Subsection (e) permits the court to deny compensation to a trustee if the trustee has been derelict in his duty by employing counsel, who is not disinterested. Senate Report No. 95–989.

1984 Acts. Statements by Legislative Leaders, see 1984 U.S.Code Cong. and Adm.News, p. 576.

1986 Acts. House Report No. 99–764 and House Conference Report No. 99–958, see 1986 U.S.Code Cong. and Adm. News, p. 5227.

1994 Acts. House Report No. 103–835, see 1994 U.S. Code Cong. and Adm. News, p. 3340.

Legislative Statements

Section 326(a) of the House amendment modifies a provision as contained in H.R. 8200 as passed by the House. The percentage limitation on the fees of a trustee contained in the House bill is retained, but no additional percentage is specified for cases in which a trustee operates the business of the debtor. Section 326(b) of the Senate amendment, is deleted as an unnecessary restatement of the limitation contained in section 326(a) as modified. The provision contained in section 326(a) of the Senate amendment authorizing a trustee to receive a maximum fee of $150 regardless of the availability of assets in the estate is deleted. It will not be necessary in view of the increase in section 326(a) and the doubling of the minimum fee as provided in section 330(b).

Section 326(b) of the House amendment derives from section 326(c) of H.R. 8200 as passed by the House. It is a conforming amendment to indicate a change with respect to the selection of a trustee in a chapter 13 case under section 1302(a) of Title 11.

Amendments

1994 Amendments. Subsec. (a). Pub.L. 103–394, § 107, substituted "25 percent on the first $5,000 or less, 10 percent on any amount in excess of $5,000 but not in excess of $50,000, 5 percent on any amount in excess of $50,000 but not in excess of $1,000,000, and reasonable compensation not to exceed 3 percent of such moneys in excess of $1,000,000" for "fifteen percent of the first $1,000 or less, six percent on any amount in excess of $1,000 but not in excess of $3,000, and three percent on any amount in excess of $3,000".

1986 Amendments. Subsec. (b). Pub.L. 99–554, § 209, substituted "under chapter 12 or 13 of this title" for "under chapter 13 of this title", "expenses of the United States trustee or of a standing trustee appointed under section 586(b) of title 28" for "expenses of a standing trustee appointed under section 1302(d) of this title", and "under section

1202(a) or 1302(a) of this title" for "under section 1302(a) of this title".

1984 Amendments. Subsec. (a). Pub.L. 98–353, § 430(a), substituted "and three percent on any amount in excess of $3000" for "three percent on any amount in excess of $3,000 but not in excess of $20,000, two percent on any amount in excess of $20,000 but not in excess of $50,000, and one percent on any amount in excess of $50,000".

Subsec. (d). Pub.L. 98–353, § 430(b), substituted "(d) The court may deny allowance of compensation for services or reimbursement of expenses of the trustee if the trustee failed to make diligent inquiry into facts that would permit denial of allowance under section 328(c) of this title or, with knowledge of such facts, employed a professional person under section 327 of this title." for "(d) The court may deny allowance of compensation for services and reimbursement of expenses of the trustee if the trustee—

"(1) failed to make diligent inquiry into facts that would permit denial of allowance under section 328(c) of this title; or

"(2) with knowledge of such facts, employed a professional person under section 327 of this title."

Effective and Applicability Provisions

1994 Acts. Amendment by Pub.L. 103–394 effective on Oct. 22, 1994, and not to apply with respect to cases commenced under Title 11 of the United States Code before Oct. 22, 1994, see section 702 of Pub.L. 103–394, set out as a note under section 101 of this title.

1986 Acts. Amendment by Pub.L. 99–554 effective 30 days after Oct. 27, 1986, except as otherwise provided for, see section 302(a) of Pub.L. 99–554, set out as a note under section 581 of Title 28, Judiciary and Judicial Procedure.

Until amendments made by section 209 of Pub.L. 99–554 become effective in a district and apply to a case, for purposes of such case any references in subsec. (b) of this section to chapter 13 of this title, to section 1302(d) of this title, or to section 1302(a) of this title deemed references to other provisions of the Code, see section 302(c)(3)(A)(i) to (iii) of Pub.L. 99–554, set out as a note under section 581 of Title 28.

Amendment by Pub.L. 99–554, § 209, not to become effective in or with respect to certain specified judicial districts until, or apply to cases while pending in such district before, the expiration of the 270-day period beginning 30 days after Oct. 27, 1986, or of the 30-day period beginning on the date the Attorney General certifies under section 303 of Pub.L. 99–554 the region specified in a paragraph of section 581(a) of Title 28, as amended by section 111(a) of Pub.L. 99–554, that includes such district, whichever occurs first, see section 302(d)(1) of Pub.L. 99–554, set out as a note under section 581 of Title 28.

Amendment by Pub.L. 99–554, § 209, not to become effective in or with respect to certain specified judicial districts until, or apply to cases while pending in such district before, the expiration of the 2-year period beginning 30 days after Oct. 27, 1986, or of the 30-day period beginning on the date the Attorney General certifies under section 303 of Pub.L. 99–554 the region specified in a paragraph of section 581(a) of Title 28, as amended by section 111(a) of Pub.L. 99–554, that includes such district, whichever occurs first, see section 302(d)(2) of Pub.L. 99–554, set out as a note under section 581 of Title 28.

Amendment by Pub.L. 99–554, § 209, not to become effective in or with respect to judicial districts established for the States of Alabama and North Carolina until, or apply to cases while pending in such district before, such district elects to be included in a bankruptcy region established in section 581(a) of Title 28, as amended by section 111(a) of Pub.L. 99–554, or Oct. 1, 2002, whichever occurs first, and, except as otherwise provided for, with respect to cases under chapters 7, 11, 12, and 13 of Title 11 commenced before 30 days after Oct. 27, 1986, and pending in a judicial district in the States of Alabama or North Carolina before any election made under section 302(d)(3)(A) of Pub.L. 99–554 by such district becomes effective or Oct. 1, 2002, whichever occurs first, amendments by Pub.L. 99–554 not to apply until Oct. 1, 2003, or the expiration of the 1-year period beginning on the date such election becomes effective, whichever occurs first, and further, in any judicial district in Alabama or North Carolina not making the election described in section 302(d)(3)(A) of Pub.L. 99–554, any person appointed under regulations issued by the Judicial Conference to administer estates in cases under Title 11 authorized to establish, etc., a panel of private trustees, and to supervise cases and trustees in cases under chapters 7, 11, 12, and 13 of Title 11, until amendments by sections 201 to 231 of Pub.L. 99–554 effective in such district, see section 302(d)(3)(A) to (F), (H), and (I) of Pub.L. 99–554, set out as a note under section 581 of Title 28.

Amendment by Pub.L. 99–554, § 209, except as otherwise provided, with respect to cases under chapters 7, 11, 12, and 13 of Title 11 commenced before 30 days after Oct. 27, 1986, and pending in a judicial district referred to in section 581(a) of Title 28, as amended by section 111(a) of Pub.L. 99–554, for which a United States trustee is not authorized before 30 days after Oct. 27, 1986 to be appointed, not applicable until the expiration of the 3-year period beginning on Oct. 27, 1986, or of the 1-year period beginning on the date the Attorney General certifies under section 303 of Pub.L. 99–554 the region specified in a paragraph of such section 581(a) that includes such district, whichever occurs first, see section 302(e)(1), (2) of Pub.L. 99–554, set out as a note under section 581 of Title 28.

1984 Acts. Amendment by Pub.L. 98–353 effective with respect to cases filed 90 days after July 10, 1984, see section 552(a), formerly 553(a), of Pub.L. 98–353, set out as a note under section 101 of this title.

Separability of Provisions

If any provision of or amendment made by Pub.L. 103–394 or the application of such provision or amendment to any person or circumstance is held to be unconstitutional, the remaining provisions of and amendments made by Pub.L. 103–394 and the application of such provisions and amendments to any person or circumstance shall not be affected thereby, see section 701 of Pub.L. 103–394, set out as a note under section 101 of this title.

CROSS REFERENCES

Grain storage facility bankruptcies, expedited determinations, see 11 USCA § 557.

LIBRARY REFERENCES

American Digest System

Bankruptcy ⬤3152.

Key Number System Topic No. 51.

Corpus Juris Secundum

CJS Bankruptcy § 52, Proceedings Under Chapters 12 and 13.

CJS Bankruptcy § 112, General Rule and Limitation.

CJS Bankruptcy § 114, Interim Compensation.

CJS Bankruptcy § 116, Limitation on Compensation Where More Than One Trustee Serves in Case; Effect of Case Conversion.

CJS Bankruptcy § 120, What Constitutes Disbursal of Moneys to Parties in Interest, Excluding Debtor.

CJS Bankruptcy § 121, Effect of Dismissal of Case.

CJS Bankruptcy § 122, Effect of Conversion of Chapter 7 or Chapter 11 Case.

CJS Bankruptcy § 126, Where Trustee Employs Nondisinterested Professional Persons.

CJS Bankruptcy § 647, Payment of Compensation and Expenses of Custodian.

§ 327. Employment of professional persons

(a) Except as otherwise provided in this section, the trustee, with the court's approval, may employ one or more attorneys, accountants, appraisers, auctioneers, or other professional persons, that do not hold or represent an interest adverse to the estate, and that are disinterested persons, to represent or assist the trustee in carrying out the trustee's duties under this title.

(b) If the trustee is authorized to operate the business of the debtor under section 721, 1202, or 1108 of this title, and if the debtor has regularly employed attorneys, accountants, or other professional persons on salary, the trustee may retain or replace such professional persons if necessary in the operation of such business.

(c) In a case under chapter 7, 12, or 11 of this title, a person is not disqualified for employment under this section solely because of such person's employment by or representation of a creditor, unless there is objection by another creditor or the United States trustee, in which case the court shall disapprove such employment if there is an actual conflict of interest.

(d) The court may authorize the trustee to act as attorney or accountant for the estate if such authorization is in the best interest of the estate.

(e) The trustee, with the court's approval, may employ, for a specified special purpose, other than to represent the trustee in conducting the case, an attorney that has represented the debtor, if in the best interest of the estate, and if such attorney does not represent or hold any interest adverse to the debtor or to the estate with respect to the matter on which such attorney is to be employed.

(f) The trustee may not employ a person that has served as an examiner in the case.

(Pub.L. 95–598, Nov. 6, 1978, 92 Stat. 2563; Pub. L. 98–353, Title III, § 430(c), July 10, 1984, 98 Stat. 370; Pub.L. 99–554, Title II, §§ 210, 257(e), Oct. 27, 1986, 100 Stat. 3099, 3114.)

HISTORICAL AND STATUTORY NOTES

Revision Notes and Legislative Reports

1978 Acts. This section authorizes the trustee, subject to the court's approval, to employ professional persons, such as attorneys, accountants, appraisers, and auctioneers, to represent or perform services for the estate. The trustee may employ only disinterested persons that do not hold or represent an interest adverse to the estate.

Subsection (b) is an exception, and authorizes the trustee to retain or replace professional persons that the debtor has employed if necessary in the operation of the debtor's business.

Subsection (c) provides a professional person is not disqualified for employment solely because of the person's prior employment by or representation of a secured or unsecured creditor.

Subsection (d) permits the court to authorize the trustee, if qualified to act as his own counsel or accountant.

Subsection (e) permits the trustee, subject to the court's approval, to employ for a specified special purpose an attorney that has represented the debtor, if such employment is in the best interest of the estate and if the attorney does not hold or represent an interest adverse to the debtor of the estate with respect to the matter on which he is to be employed. This subsection does not authorize the employment of the debtor's attorney to represent the estate generally or to represent the trustee in the conduct of the bankruptcy case. The subsection will most likely be used when the debtor is involved in complex litigation, and changing attorneys in the middle of the case after the bankruptcy case has commenced would be detrimental to the progress of that other litigation. Senate Report No. 95–989.

Subsection (c) is an additional exception. The trustee may employ as his counsel a nondisinterested person if the only reason that the attorney is not disinterested is because of his representation of an unsecured creditor. House Report No. 95–595.

1984 Acts. Statements by Legislative Leaders, see 1984 U.S.Code Cong. and Adm.News, p. 576.

1986 Acts. House Report No. 99–764 and House Conference Report No. 99–958, see 1986 U.S.Code Cong. and Adm. News, p. 5227.

Legislative Statements

Section 327(a) of the House amendment contains a technical amendment indicating that attorneys, and perhaps other officers enumerated therein, represent, rather than assist, the trustee in carrying out the trustee's duties.

Section 327(c) represents a compromise between H.R. 8200 as passed by the House and the Senate amendment. The provision states that former representation of a creditor, whether secured or unsecured, will not automatically disqualify a person from being employed by a trustee, but if such person is employed by the trustee, the person may no longer represent the creditor in connection with the case.

Section 327(f) prevents an examiner from being employed by the trustee.

Codifications

Amendment by Pub.L. 99–554, § 257(e)(1), has been executed to text following "section 721" as the probable intent of

Congress, notwithstanding directory language which required amendment to be executed following "section 721,".

Amendment by Pub.L. 99–554, § 257(e)(2), has been executed to text following "chapter 7" as the probable intent of Congress, notwithstanding directory language which required amendment to be executed following "section 7".

Amendments

1986 Amendments. Subsec. (b). Pub.L. 99–554, § 257(e)(1), added reference to section 1202 of this title. See, also Codifications note under this section.

Subsec. (c). Pub.L. 99–554, § 210, substituted "another creditor or the United States trustee, in which case" for "another creditor, in which case".

Pub.L. 99–554, § 257(e)(2), added reference to chapter 12. See Codifications note under this section.

1984 Amendments. Subsec. (c). Pub.L. 98–353 substituted "In a case under chapter 7 or 11 of this title, a person is not disqualified for employment under this section solely because of such person's employment by or representation of a creditor, unless there is objection by another creditor, in which case the court shall disapprove such employment if there is an actual conflict of interest." for "In a case under chapter 7 or 11 of this title, a person is not disqualified for employment under this section solely because of such person's employment by or representation of a creditor, but may not, while employed by the trustee, represent, in connection with the case, a creditor.".

Effective and Applicability Provisions

1986 Acts. Amendment by Pub.L. 99–554 effective 30 days after Oct. 27, 1986, except as otherwise provided for, see section 302(a) of Pub.L. 99–554, set out as a note under section 581 of Title 28, Judiciary and Judicial Procedure.

Amendment by Pub.L. 99–554, § 210, not to become effective in or with respect to certain specified judicial districts until, or apply to cases while pending in such district before, the expiration of the 270-day period beginning 30 days after Oct. 27, 1986, or of the 30-day period beginning on the date the Attorney General certifies under section 303 of Pub.L. 99–554 the region specified in a paragraph of section 581(a) of Title 28, as amended by section 111(a) of Pub.L. 99–554, that includes such district, whichever occurs first, see section 302(d)(1) of Pub.L. 99–554, set out as a note under section 581 of Title 28.

Amendment by Pub.L. 99–554, § 210, not to become effective in or with respect to certain specified judicial districts until, or apply to cases while pending in such district before, the expiration of the 2-year period beginning 30 days after Oct. 27, 1986, or of the 30-day period beginning on the date the Attorney General certifies under section 303 of Pub.L. 99–554 the region specified in a paragraph of section 581(a) of Title 28, as amended by section 111(a) of Pub.L. 99–554, that includes such district, whichever occurs first, see section 302(d)(2) of Pub.L. 99–554, set out as a note under section 581 of Title 28.

Amendment by Pub.L. 99–554, § 210, not to become effective in or with respect to judicial districts established for the States of Alabama and North Carolina until, or apply to cases while pending in such district before, such district elects to be included in a bankruptcy region established in section 581(a) of Title 28, as amended by section 111(a) of Pub.L. 99–554, or Oct. 1, 2002, whichever occurs first, and, except as otherwise provided for, with respect to cases under chapters 7, 11, 12,

and 13 of Title 11 commenced before 30 days after Oct. 27, 1986, and pending in a judicial district in the States of Alabama or North Carolina before any election made under section 302(d)(3)(A) of Pub.L. 99–554 by such district becomes effective or Oct. 1, 2002, whichever occurs first, amendments by Pub.L. 99–554 not to apply until Oct. 1, 2003, or the expiration of the 1-year period beginning on the date such election becomes effective, whichever occurs first, and further, in any judicial district in Alabama or North Carolina not making the election described in section 302(d)(3)(A) of Pub.L. 99–554, any person appointed under regulations issued by the Judicial Conference to administer estates in cases under Title 11 authorized to establish, etc., a panel of private trustees, and to supervise cases and trustees in cases under chapters 7, 11, 12, and 13 of Title 11, until amendments by sections 201 to 231 of Pub.L. 99–554 effective in such district, see section 302(d)(3)(A) to (F), (H), and (I) of Pub.L. 99–554, set out as a note under section 581 of Title 28.

Amendment by Pub.L. 99–554, § 210, except as otherwise provided, with respect to cases under chapters 7, 11, 12, and 13 of Title 11 commenced before 30 days after Oct. 27, 1986, and pending in a judicial district referred to in section 581(a) of Title 28, as amended by section 111(a) of Pub.L. 99–554, for which a United States trustee is not authorized before 30 days after Oct. 27, 1986 to be appointed, not applicable until the expiration of the 3-year period beginning on Oct. 27, 1986, or of the 1-year period beginning on the date the Attorney General certifies under section 303 of Pub.L. 99–554 the region specified in a paragraph of such section 581(a) that includes, such district, whichever occurs first, see section 302(e)(1), (2) of Pub.L. 99–554, set out as a note under section 581 of Title 28.

Amendment by Pub.L. 99–554, § 257(e), effective 30 days after Oct. 27, 1986, but not applicable to cases commenced under this title before that date, see section 302(a), (c)(1) of Pub.L. 99–554, set out as a note under section 581 of Title 28.

1984 Acts. Amendment by Pub.L. 98–353 effective with respect to cases filed 90 days after July 10, 1984, see section 552(a), formerly 553(a), of Pub.L. 98–353, set out as a note under section 101 of this title.

CROSS REFERENCES

Duty of United States trustee to monitor applications, see 28 USCA § 586.

Qualification for employment by debtor in possession despite prior employment or representation, see 11 USCA § 1107.

LIBRARY REFERENCES

American Digest System

Attorney and Client �köp21.5(6).

American Digest System

Bankruptcy �köp3029.1, 3030.

Key Number System Topic Nos. 45, 51.

Corpus Juris Secundum

CJS Bankruptcy § 45, Supervision of Cases and Bankruptcy Trustees.

CJS Bankruptcy § 91, Right to Employ Professional Persons; Trustee as Attorney or Accountant in Case.

CJS Bankruptcy § 134, Rights, Powers, and Duties of Debtor in Possession--Specific Rights, Powers, and Duties.

CJS Bankruptcy § 149, Original and Exclusive Jurisdiction of Cases Under Title 11.

CJS Bankruptcy § 151, Original But Not Exclusive Jurisdiction of Civil Proceedings.

CJS Bankruptcy § 178, Employment and Compensation of Professional Persons.

CJS Bankruptcy § 760, Disqualification for and Limitations Upon Employment.

CJS Bankruptcy § 761, Relationship Between Employment and Compensation Provisions.

CJS Bankruptcy § 763, Salaried Employees; Employment of Debtor's Attorney.

CJS Bankruptcy § 850, Valuation and Appraisals of Property.

CJS Bankruptcy § 1131, Debtor-In-Possession.

§ 328. Limitation on compensation of professional persons

(a) The trustee, or a committee appointed under section 1102 of this title, with the court's approval, may employ or authorize the employment of a professional person under section 327 or 1103 of this title, as the case may be, on any reasonable terms and conditions of employment, including on a retainer, on an hourly basis, on a fixed or percentage fee basis, or on a contingent fee basis. Notwithstanding such terms and conditions, the court may allow compensation different from the compensation provided under such terms and conditions after the conclusion of such employment, if such terms and conditions prove to have been improvident in light of developments not capable of being anticipated at the time of the fixing of such terms and conditions.

(b) If the court has authorized a trustee to serve as an attorney or accountant for the estate under section 327(d) of this title, the court may allow compensation for the trustee's services as such attorney or accountant only to the extent that the trustee performed services as attorney or accountant for the estate and not for performance of any of the trustee's duties that are generally performed by a trustee without the assistance of an attorney or accountant for the estate.

(c) Except as provided in section 327(c), 327(e), or 1107(b) of this title, the court may deny allowance of compensation for services and reimbursement of expenses of a professional person employed under section 327 or 1103 of this title if, at any time during such professional person's employment under section 327 or 1103 of this title, such professional person is not a disinterested person, or represents or holds an interest adverse to the interest of the estate with respect to the matter on which such professional person is employed. (Pub.L. 95–598, Nov. 6, 1978, 92 Stat. 2563; amended Pub. L. 98–353, Title III, § 431, July 10, 1984, 98 Stat. 370; Pub.L. 109–8, Title XII, § 1206, Apr. 20, 2005, 119 Stat. 194.)

HISTORICAL AND STATUTORY NOTES

Revision Notes and Legislative Reports

1978 Acts. This section, which is parallel to § 326, fixes the maximum compensation allowable to a professional person employed under section 327. It authorizes the trustee, with the court's approval, to employ professional persons on any reasonable terms, including on a retainer, on an hourly or on a contingent fee basis. Subsection (a) further permits the court to allow compensation different from the compensation provided under the trustee's agreement if the prior agreement proves to have been improvident in light of development unanticipatable at the time of the agreement. The court's power includes the power to increase as well as decrease the agreed upon compensation. This provision is permissive, not mandatory, and should not be used by the court if to do so would violate the code of ethics of the professional involved.

Subsection (b) limits a trustee that has been authorized to serve as his own counsel to only one fee for each service. The purpose of permitting the trustee to serve as his own counsel is to reduce costs. It is not included to provide the trustee with a bonus by permitting him to receive two fees for the same service or to avoid the maxima fixed in section 326. Thus, this subsection requires the court to differentiate between the trustee's services as trustee, and his services as trustee's counsel, and to fix compensation accordingly. Services that a trustee normally performs for an estate without assistance of counsel are to be compensated under the limits fixed in section 326. Only services that he performs that are normally performed by trustee's counsel may be compensated under the maxima imposed by this section.

Subsection (c) permits the court to deny compensation for services and reimbursement of expenses if the professional person is not disinterested or if he represents or holds an interest adverse to the estate on the matter on which he is employed. The subsection provides a penalty for conflicts of interest. Senate Report No. 95–989.

1984 Acts. Statements by Legislative Leaders, see 1984 U.S.Code Cong. and Adm.News, p. 576.

2005 Acts. House Report No. 109–31(Part I), see 2005 U.S. Code Cong. and Adm. News, p. 88.

Legislative Statements

Section 328(c) adopts a technical amendment contained in the Senate amendment indicating that an attorney for the debtor in possession is not disqualified for compensation for services and reimbursement of expenses simply because of prior representation of the debtor.

Amendments

2005 Amendments. Subsec. (a). Pub.L. 109–8, § 1206, inserted "on a fixed or percentage fee basis," after "hourly basis,".

1984 Amendments. Subsec. (a). Pub.L. 98–353 substituted "not capable of being anticipated" for "unanticipatable".

Effective and Applicability Provisions

2005 Acts. Amendments by Pub.L. 109–8 effective, except as otherwise provided, 180 days after April 20, 2005, and inapplicable with respect to cases commenced under Title 11 before the effective date, see Pub.L. 109–8, § 1501, set out as a note under 11 U.S.C.A. § 101.

1984 Acts. Amendment by Pub.L. 98–353 effective with respect to cases filed 90 days after July 10, 1984, see section

552(a), formerly 553 of Pub.L. 98–353, set out as a note under section 101 of this title.

LIBRARY REFERENCES

American Digest System

Bankruptcy ⟐3155 to 3205, 3152.

Key Number System Topic No. 51.

Corpus Juris Secundum

CJS Bankruptcy § 112, General Rule and Limitation.

CJS Bankruptcy § 117, Compensation of Trustee Also Serving as Attorney or Accountant for Estate.

CJS Bankruptcy § 126, Where Trustee Employs Nondisinterested Professional Persons.

CJS Bankruptcy § 761, Relationship Between Employment and Compensation Provisions.

§ 329.   Debtor's transactions with attorneys

(a) Any attorney representing a debtor in a case under this title, or in connection with such a case, whether or not such attorney applies for compensation under this title, shall file with the court a statement of the compensation paid or agreed to be paid, if such payment or agreement was made after one year before the date of the filing of the petition, for services rendered or to be rendered in contemplation of or in connection with the case by such attorney, and the source of such compensation.

(b) If such compensation exceeds the reasonable value of any such services, the court may cancel any such agreement, or order the return of any such payment, to the extent excessive, to—

(1) the estate, if the property transferred—

(A) would have been property of the estate; or

(B) was to be paid by or on behalf of the debtor under a plan under chapter 11, 12, or 13 of this title; or

(2) the entity that made such payment.

(Pub.L. 95–598, Nov. 6, 1978, 92 Stat. 2564; Pub. L. 98–353, Title III, § 432, July 10, 1984, 98 Stat. 370; Pub.L. 99–554, Title II, § 257(c), Oct. 27, 1986, 100 Stat. 3114.)

HISTORICAL AND STATUTORY NOTES

Revision Notes and Legislative Reports

1978 Acts. This section, derived in large part from current Bankruptcy Act section 60d [section 96(d) of former Title 11], requires the debtor's attorney to file with the court a statement of the compensation paid or agreed to be paid to the attorney for services in contemplation of and in connection with the case, and the source of the compensation. Payments to a debtor's attorney provide serious potential for evasion of creditor protection provisions of the bankruptcy laws, and serious potential for overreaching by the debtor's attorney, and should be subject to careful scrutiny.

Subsection (b) permits the court to deny compensation to the attorney, to cancel an agreement to pay compensation, or to order the return of compensation paid, if the compensation exceeds the reasonable value of the services provided. The return of payments already made are generally to the trustee

for the benefit of the estate. However, if the property would not have come into the estate in any event, the court will order it returned to the entity that made the payment.

The Bankruptcy Commission recommended a provision similar to this that would have also permitted an examination of the debtor's transactions with insiders. S. 236, 94th Cong., 1st sess., sec. 4–311(b) (1975). Its exclusion here is to permit it to be dealt with by the Rules of Bankruptcy Procedure. It is not intended that the provision be deleted entirely, only that the flexibility of the rules is more appropriate for such evidentiary matters. Senate Report No. 95–989.

1984 Acts. Statements by Legislative Leaders, see 1984 U.S.Code Cong. and Adm.News, p. 576.

1986 Acts. House Report No. 99–764 and House Conference Report No. 99–958, see 1986 U.S.Code Cong. and Adm. News, p. 5227.

Amendments

1986 Amendments. Subsec. (b)(1)(B). Pub.L. 99–554, § 257(c), added reference to chapter 12.

1984 Amendments. Subsec. (a). Pub.L. 98–353, § 432(a), substituted "or" for "and" after "in contemplation of".

Subsec. (b)(1). Pub.L. 98–353, § 432(b), substituted "estate" for "trustee".

Effective and Applicability Provisions

1986 Acts. Amendment by Pub.L. 99–554 effective 30 days after Oct. 27, 1986, but not applicable to cases commenced under this title before that date, see section 302(a), (c)(1) of Pub.L. 99–554, set out as a note under section 581 of Title 28, Judiciary and Judicial Procedure.

1984 Acts. Amendment by Pub.L. 98–353 effective with respect to cases filed 90 days after July 10, 1984, see section 552(a), formerly 553(a), of Pub.L. 98–353, set out as a note under section 101 of this title.

CROSS REFERENCES

Disclosure of compensation, debtor's attorney, see Fed. Rules Bankr.Proc. Form B 203, 11 USCA.

Fee agreements, see 18 USCA § 155.

Lists, schedules, statements and fees, see Fed.Rules Bankr. Proc. Form B 200, 11 USCA.

Property of estate, see 11 USCA § 541.

LIBRARY REFERENCES

American Digest System

Bankruptcy ⟐3170 to 3205.

Key Number System Topic No. 51.

Corpus Juris Secundum

CJS Bankruptcy § 112, General Rule and Limitation.

CJS Bankruptcy § 761, Relationship Between Employment and Compensation Provisions.

§ 330.   Compensation of officers

(a)(1) After notice to the parties in interest and the United States Trustee and a hearing, and subject to sections 326, 328, and 329, the court may award to a trustee, a consumer privacy ombudsman appointed under section 332, an examiner, an ombudsman appointed under section 333, or a professional person employed under section 327 or 1103—

 (A) reasonable compensation for actual, necessary services rendered by the trustee, examiner, ombudsman, professional person, or attorney and by any paraprofessional person employed by any such person; and

 (B) reimbursement for actual, necessary expenses.

(2) The court may, on its own motion or on the motion of the United States Trustee, the United States Trustee for the District or Region, the trustee for the estate, or any other party in interest, award compensation that is less than the amount of compensation that is requested.

(3) In determining the amount of reasonable compensation to be awarded to an examiner, trustee under chapter 11, or professional person, the court shall consider the nature, the extent, and the value of such services, taking into account all relevant factors, including—

 (A) the time spent on such services;

 (B) the rates charged for such services;

 (C) whether the services were necessary to the administration of, or beneficial at the time at which the service was rendered toward the completion of, a case under this title;

 (D) whether the services were performed within a reasonable amount of time commensurate with the complexity, importance, and nature of the problem, issue, or task addressed;

 (E) with respect to a professional person, whether the person is board certified or otherwise has demonstrated skill and experience in the bankruptcy field; and

 (F) whether the compensation is reasonable based on the customary compensation charged by comparably skilled practitioners in cases other than cases under this title.

(4)(A) Except as provided in subparagraph (B), the court shall not allow compensation for—

 (i) unnecessary duplication of services; or

 (ii) services that were not—

  (I) reasonably likely to benefit the debtor's estate; or
  (II) necessary to the administration of the case.

(B) In a chapter 12 or chapter 13 case in which the debtor is an individual, the court may allow reasonable compensation to the debtor's attorney for representing the interests of the debtor in connection with the bankruptcy case based on a consideration of the benefit and necessity of such services to the debtor and the other factors set forth in this section.

(5) The court shall reduce the amount of compensation awarded under this section by the amount of any interim compensation awarded under section 331, and, if the amount of such interim compensation exceeds the amount of compensation awarded under this section, may order the return of the excess to the estate.

(6) Any compensation awarded for the preparation of a fee application shall be based on the level and skill reasonably required to prepare the application.

(7) In determining the amount of reasonable compensation to be awarded to a trustee, the court shall treat such compensation as a commission, based on section 326.

(b)(1) There shall be paid from the filing fee in a case under chapter 7 of this title $45 to the trustee serving in such case, after such trustee's services are rendered.

(2) The Judicial Conference of the United States—

 (A) shall prescribe additional fees of the same kind as prescribed under section 1914(b) of title 28; and

 (B) may prescribe notice of appearance fees and fees charged against distributions in cases under this title;

to pay $15 to trustees serving in cases after such trustees' services are rendered. Beginning 1 year after the date of the enactment of the Bankruptcy Reform Act of 1994, such $15 shall be paid in addition to the amount paid under paragraph (1).

(c) Unless the court orders otherwise, in a case under chapter 12 or 13 of this title the compensation paid to the trustee serving in the case shall not be less than $5 per month from any distribution under the plan during the administration of the plan.

(d) In a case in which the United States trustee serves as trustee, the compensation of the trustee under this section shall be paid to the clerk of the bankruptcy court and deposited by the clerk into the United States Trustee System Fund established by section 589a of title 28.

(Pub.L. 95–598, Nov. 6, 1978, 92 Stat. 2564; Pub.L. 98–353, Title III, §§ 433, 434, July 10, 1984, 98 Stat. 370; Pub.L. 99–554, Title II, §§ 211, 257(f), Oct. 27, 1986, 100 Stat. 3099, 3114; Pub.L. 103–394, Title I, § 117, Title II, § 224(b), Oct. 22, 1994, 108 Stat. 4119, 4130; Pub.L. 109–8, Title II, § 232(b), Title IV, §§ 407, 415, Title XI, 1104(b), Apr. 20, 2005, 119 Stat. 74, 106, 107, 192.)

HISTORICAL AND STATUTORY NOTES

Revision Notes and Legislative Reports

 1978 Acts. Section 330 authorizes the court to award compensation for services and reimbursement of expenses of officers of the estate, and other professionals. The compensation is to be reasonable, for economy in administration is the basic objective. Compensation is to be for actual necessary services, based on the time spent, the nature, the extent and the value of the services rendered, and the cost of comparable services in nonbankruptcy cases. There are the criteria that have been applied by the courts as analytic aids in defining "reasonable" compensation.

The reference to "the cost of comparable services" in a nonbankruptcy case is not intended as a change of existing law. In a bankruptcy cases fees are not a matter for private agreement. There is inherent a "public interest" that "must be considered in awarding fees," *Massachusetts Mutual Life Insurance Co. v. Brock*, 405 F.2d 429, 432 (C.A.5, 1968), cert. denied, 395 U.S. 906 (1969) [89 S.Ct. 1748, 23 L.Ed.2d 220]. An allowance is the result of a balance struck between moderation in the interest of the estate and its security holders and the need to be "generous enough to encourage" lawyers and others to render the necessary and exacting services that bankruptcy cases often require. *In re Yale Express System, Inc.*, 366 F.Supp. 1376, 1381 (S.D.N.Y.1973). The rates for similar kinds of services in private employment is one element, among others, in that balance. Compensation in private employment noted in subsection (a) is a point of reference, not a controlling determinant of what shall be allowed in bankruptcy cases.

One of the major reforms in 1938, especially for reorganization cases, was centralized control over fees in the bankruptcy courts. See *Brown v. Gerdes*, 321 U.S. 178, 182–184 (1944) [64 S.Ct. 487, 88 L.Ed. 659]; *Leiman v. Guttman*, 336 U.S. 1, 4–9, (1949) [69 S.Ct. 371, 93 L.Ed. 453]. It was intended to guard against a recurrence of "the many sordid chapters" in "the history of fees in corporate reorganizations." *Dickinson Industrial Site, Inc. v. Cowan*, 309 U.S. 382, 388 (1940) [60 S.Ct. 595, 84 L.Ed. 819, rehearing denied 60 S.Ct. 806, 309 U.S. 698, 84 L.Ed. 1037]. In the years since then the bankruptcy bar has flourished and prospered, and persons of merit and quality have not eschewed public service in bankruptcy cases merely because bankruptcy courts, in the interest of economy in administration, have not allowed them compensation that may be earned in the private economy of business or the professions. There is no reason to believe that, in generations to come, their successors will be less persuaded by the need to serve in the public interest because of stronger allures of private gain elsewhere.

Subsection (a) provides for compensation of paraprofessional in order to reduce the cost of administering bankruptcy cases. Paraprofessionals can be employed to perform duties which do not require the full range of skills of a qualified professional. Some courts have not hesitated to recognize paraprofessional services as compensable under existing law. An explicit provision to that effect is useful and constructive.

The last sentence of subsection (a) provides that in the case of a public company—defined in section 1101(3)—the court shall refer, after a hearing, all applications to the Securities and Exchange Commission for a report, which shall be advisory only. In Chapter X cases in which the Commission has appeared, it generally filed reports on fee applications. Usually, courts have accorded the SEC's views substantial weight, as representing the opinion of a disinterested agency skilled and experienced in reorganization affairs. The last sentence intends for the advisory assistance of the Commission to be sought only in case of a public company in reorganization under chapter 11.

Subsection (b) reenacts section 249 of Chapter X of the Bankruptcy Act ([former] 11 U.S.C. 649). It is a codification of equitable principles designed to prevent fiduciaries in the case from engaging in the specified transactions since they are in a position to gain inside information or to shape or influence the course of the reorganization. *Wolf v. Weinstein*, 372 U.S. 633 (1963) [83 S.Ct. 969, 10 L.Ed.2d 33, rehearing denied 83 S.Ct. 1522, 373 U.S. 928, 10 L.Ed.2d 427]. The statutory bar of compensation and reimbursement is based on the principle that such transactions involve conflicts of interest. Private gain undoubtedly prompts the purchase or sale of claims or stock interests, while the fiduciary's obligation is to render loyal and disinterested service which his position of trust has imposed upon him. Subsection (b) extends to a trustee, his attorney, committees and their attorneys, or any other persons "acting in the case in a representative or fiduciary capacity." It bars compensation to any of the foregoing, who after assuming to act in such capacity has purchased or sold, directly or indirectly, claims against, or stock in the debtor. The bar is absolute. It makes no difference whether the transaction brought a gain or loss, or neither, and the court is not authorized to approve a purchase or sale, before or after the transaction. The exception is for an acquisition or transfer "otherwise" than by a voluntary purchase or sale, such as an acquisition by bequest. See *Otis & Co. v. Insurance Bldg. Corp.*, 110 F.2d 333, 335 (C.A.1, 1940).

Subsection (c) is intended for no asset liquidation cases where minimal compensation for trustees is needed. The sum of $20 will be allowed in each case, which is double the amount provided under current law. Senate Report No. 95–989.

Section 330 authorizes compensation for services and reimbursement of expenses of officers of the estate. It also prescribes the standards on which the amount of compensation is to be determined. As noted above, the compensation allowable under this section is subject to the maxima set out in sections 326, 328, and 329. The compensation is to be reasonable, for actual necessary services rendered, based on the time, the nature, the extent, and the value of the services rendered, and on the cost of comparable services other than in a case under the bankruptcy code. The effect of the last provision is to overrule *In re Beverly Crest Convalescent Hospital, Inc.*, 548 F.2d 817 (9th Cir.1976, as amended 1977), which set an arbitrary limit on fees payable, based on the amount of a district judge's salary, and other, similar cases that require fees to be determined based on notions of conservation of the estate and economy of administration. If that case were allowed to stand, attorneys that could earn much higher incomes in other fields would leave the bankruptcy arena. Bankruptcy specialists, who enable the system to operate smoothly, efficiently, and expeditiously, would be driven elsewhere, and the bankruptcy field would be occupied by those who could not find other work and those who practice bankruptcy law only occasionally almost as a public service. Bankruptcy fees that are lower than fees in other areas of the legal profession may operate properly when the attorneys appearing in bankruptcy cases do so intermittently, because a low fee in a small segment of a practice can be absorbed by other work. Bankruptcy specialists, however, if required to accept fees in all of their cases that are consistently lower than fees they could receive elsewhere, will not remain in the bankruptcy field.

This subsection provides for reimbursement of actual, necessary expenses. It further provides for compensation of paraprofessionals employed by professional persons employed by the estate of the debtor. The provision is included to reduce the cost of administering bankruptcy cases. In nonbankruptcy areas, attorneys are able to charge for a paraprofessional's time on an hourly basis, and not include it in overhead. If a similar practice does not pertain in bankruptcy cases then the attorney will be less inclined to use paraprofessionals even where the work involved could easily be handled by an attorney's assistant, at much lower cost to the estate. This provision is designed to encourage attorneys to use paraprofessional assistance where possible, and to insure that the estate, not the attorney, will bear the cost, to the benefit of both the estate and the attorneys involved. House Report No. 95–595.

1984 Acts. Statements by Legislative Leaders, see 1984 U.S.Code Cong. and Adm.News, p. 576.

1986 Acts. House Report No. 99–764 and House Conference Report No. 99–958, see 1986 U.S.Code Cong. and Adm. News, p. 5227.

1994 Acts. House Report No. 103–835, see 1994 U.S. Code Cong. and Adm. News, p. 3340.

2005 Acts. House Report No. 109–31(Part I), see 2005 U.S. Code Cong. and Adm. News, p. 88.

Legislative Statements

Section 330(a) contains the standard of compensation adopted in H.R. 8200 as passed by the House rather than the contrary standard contained in the Senate amendment. Attorneys' fees in bankruptcy cases can be quite large and should be closely examined by the court. However bankruptcy legal services are entitled to command the same competency of counsel as other cases. In that light, the policy of this section is to compensate attorneys and other professionals serving in a case under title 11 at the same rate as the attorney or other professional would be compensated for performing comparable services other than in a case under title 11. Contrary language in the Senate report accompanying S. 2266 is rejected, and *Massachusetts Mutual Life Insurance Company v. Brock*, 405 F.2d 429, 432 (5th Cir. 1968) is overruled. Notions of economy of the estate in fixing fees are outdated and have no place in a bankruptcy code.

Section 330(a)(2) of the Senate amendment is deleted although the Securities and Exchange Commission retains a right to file an advisory report under section 1109.

Section 330(b) of the Senate amendment is deleted as unnecessary, as the limitations contained therein are covered by section 328(c) of H.R. 8200 as passed by the House and contained in the House amendment.

Section 330(c) of the Senate amendment providing for a trustee to receive a fee of $20 for each estate from the filing fee paid to the clerk is retained as section 330(b) of the House amendment. The section will encourage private trustees to serve in cases under title 11 and in pilot districts will place less of a burden on the U.S. trustee to serve in no-asset cases.

Section 330(b) of H.R. 8200 as passed by the House is retained by the House amendment as section 330(c) [section 15330].

Amendments

2005 Amendments. Subsec. (a)(1). Pub.L. 109–8, § 232(b), in the matter preceding subparagraph (A), inserted "a consumer privacy ombudsman appointed under section 332," before "an examiner".

Pub.L. 109–8, § 1104(b), inserted "an ombudsman appointed under section 333, or" before "a professional person" in the matter preceding subparagraph (A), and inserted "ombudsman," before "professional person" in subparagraph (A).

Subsec. (a)(3). Pub.L. 109–8, § 407(1), struck "(A) In" and inserted "In" and inserted "to an examiner, trustee under chapter 11, or professional person" after "awarded".

Subsec. (a)(3)(D). Pub.L. 109–8, § 415(1), struck "and" at the end of subpar. (D).

Subsec. (a)(3)(E). Pub.L. 109–8, § 415(2), (3), redesignated subparagraph (E) as subparagraph (F), and added a new subpar. (E).

Subsec. (a)(3)(F). Pub.L. 109–8, § 415(2), redesignated subparagraph (E) as subparagraph (F).

Subsec. (a)(7). Pub.L. 109–8, § 407(2), added par. (7).

1994 Amendments. Subsec. (a). Pub.L. 103–394, § 224(b), completely revised subsec. (a). Prior to revision, subsec. (a) read as follows:

"(a) After notice to any parties in interest and to the United States trustee and a hearing, and subject to sections 326, 328, and 329 of this title, the court may award to a trustee, to an examiner, to a professional person employed under section 327 or 1103 of this title, or to the debtor's attorney—

"(1) reasonable compensation for actual, necessary services rendered by such trustee, examiner, professional person, or attorney, as the case may be, and by any paraprofessional persons employed by such trustee, professional person, or attorney, as the case may be, based on the nature, the extent, and the value of such services, the time spent on such services, and the cost of comparable services other than in a case under this title; and

"(2) reimbursement for actual, necessary expenses."

Subsec. (b)(1). Pub.L. 103–394, § 117(1), designated existing provisions as par. (1).

Subsec. (b)(2). Pub.L. 103–394, § 117(2), added par. (2).

1986 Amendments. Subsec. (a). Pub.L. 99–554, § 211(1), substituted "notice to any parties in interest and to the United States trustee and a hearing" for "notice and a hearing".

Subsec. (c). Pub.L. 99–554, § 257(f), added reference to chapter 12.

Subsec. (d). Pub.L. 99–554, § 211(2), added subsec. (d).

1984 Amendments. Subsec. (a). Pub.L. 98–353, § 433(1), struck out "to any parties in interest and to the United States trustee" after "After notice".

Subsec. (a)(1). Pub.L. 98–353, § 433(2), substituted "nature, the extent, and the value of such services, the time spent on such services" for "time, the nature, the extent, and the value of such services".

Subsec. (b). Pub.L. 98–353, § 434(a), substituted "$45" for "$20".

Subsec. (c). Pub.L. 98–353, § 434(b), added subsec. (c).

Effective and Applicability Provisions

2005 Acts. Amendments by Pub.L. 109–8 effective, except as otherwise provided, 180 days after April 20, 2005, and inapplicable with respect to cases commenced under Title 11 before the effective date, see Pub.L. 109–8, § 1501, set out as a note under 11 U.S.C.A. § 101.

1994 Acts. Amendment by section 117 of Pub.L. 103–394 effective on Oct. 22, 1994, and applicable with respect to cases commenced under Title 11 of the United States Code before, on, and after Oct. 22, 1994, see section 702(a), (b)(2)(B) of Pub.L. 103–394, set out as a note under section 101 of this title.

Amendment by section 224(b) of Pub.L. 103–394 effective Oct. 22, 1994, and shall not apply with respect to cases commenced under this title before Oct. 22, 1994, see section 702(a), (b)(1) of Pub.L. 103–394, set out as a note under section 101 of this title.

1986 Acts. Amendment by Pub.L. 99–554 effective 30 days after Oct. 27, 1986, except as otherwise provided for, see section 302(a) of Pub.L. 99–554, set out as a note under section 581 of Title 28, Judiciary and Judicial Procedure.

Amendment by Pub.L. 99–554, § 211, not to become effective in or with respect to certain specified judicial districts until, or apply to cases while pending in such district before, the expiration of the 270-day period beginning 30 days after Oct. 27, 1986, or of the 30-day period beginning on the date the Attorney General certifies under section 303 of Pub.L. 99–554 the region specified in a paragraph of section 581(a) of Title 28, as amended by section 111(a) of Pub.L. 99–554, that includes such district, whichever occurs first, see section 302(d)(1) of Pub.L. 99–554, set out as a note under section 581 of Title 28.

Amendment by Pub.L. 99–554, § 211, not to become effective in or with respect to certain specified judicial districts until, or apply to cases while pending in such district before, the expiration of the 2-year period beginning 30 days after Oct. 27, 1986, or of the 30-day period beginning on the date the Attorney General certifies under section 303 of Pub.L. 99–554 the region specified in a paragraph of section 581(a) of Title 28, as amended by section 111(a) of Pub.L. 99–554, that includes such district, whichever occurs first, see section 302(d)(2) of Pub.L. 99–554, set out as a note under section 581 of Title 28.

Amendment by Pub.L. 99–554, § 211, not to become effective in or with respect to judicial districts established for the States of Alabama and North Carolina until, or apply to cases while pending in such district before, such district elects to be included in a bankruptcy region established in section 581(a) of Title 28, as amended by section 111(a) of Pub.L. 99–554, or Oct. 1, 2002, whichever occurs first, and, except as otherwise provided for, with respect to cases under chapters 7, 11, 12, and 13 of Title 11 commenced before 30 days after Oct. 27, 1986, and pending in a judicial district in the States of Alabama or North Carolina before any election made under section 302(d)(3)(A) of Pub.L. 99–554 by such district becomes effective or Oct. 1, 2002, whichever occurs first, amendments by Pub.L. 99–554 not to apply until Oct. 1, 2003, or the expiration of the 1-year period beginning on the date such election becomes effective, whichever occurs first, and further, in any judicial district in Alabama or North Carolina not making the election described in section 302(d)(3)(A) of Pub.L. 99–554, any person appointed under regulations issued by the Judicial Conference to administer estates in cases under Title 11 authorized to establish, etc., a panel of private trustees, and to supervise cases and trustees in cases under chapters 7, 11, 12, and 13 of Title 11, until amendments by sections 201 to 231 of Pub.L. 99–554 effective in such district, see section 302(d)(3)(A) to (F), (H), and (I) of Pub.L. 99–554, set out as a note under section 581 of Title 28.

Amendment by Pub.L. 99–554, § 211, except as otherwise provided, with respect to cases under chapters 7, 11, 12, and 13 of Title 11 commenced before 30 days after Oct. 27, 1986, and pending in a judicial district referred to in section 581(a) of Title 28, as amended by section 111(a) of Pub.L. 99–554, for which a United States trustee is not authorized before 30 days after Oct. 27, 1986 to be appointed, not applicable until the expiration of the 3-year period beginning on Oct. 27, 1986, or of the 1-year period beginning on the date the Attorney General certifies under section 303 of Pub.L. 99–554 the region specified in a paragraph of such section 581(a) that includes, such district, whichever occurs first, see section 302(e)(1), (2) of Pub.L. 99–554, set out as a note under section 581 of Title 28.

Amendment by Pub.L. 99–554, § 257(f), effective 30 days after Oct. 27, 1986, but not applicable to cases commenced under this title before that date, see section 302(a), (c)(1) of Pub.L. 99–554, set out as a note under section 581 of Title 28.

1984 Acts. Amendment by Pub.L. 98–353 effective with respect to cases filed 90 days after July 10, 1984, see section 552(a), formerly 553(a), of Pub.L. 98–353, set out as a note under section 101 of this title.

Separability of Provisions

If any provision of or amendment made by Pub.L. 103–394 or the application of such provision or amendment to any person or circumstance is held to be unconstitutional, the remaining provisions of and amendments made by Pub.L. 103–394 and the application of such provisions and amendments to any person or circumstance shall not be affected thereby, see section 701 of Pub.L. 103–394, set out as a note under section 101 of this title.

CROSS REFERENCES

Adverse interest and conduct of officers of estate, see 18 USCA § 154.

Allowances to trustee and trustee's attorney in investor protection liquidation proceedings, see 15 USCA § 78eee.

Approval of Securities and Exchange Commission for payment of fees, expenses and remuneration in cases involving holding companies under this title, see 15 USCA § 79k.

Debtor in possession's right of compensation—

    Chapter 11 cases, see 11 USCA § 1107.

    Chapter 12 cases, see 11 USCA § 1203.

Guidelines for reviewing applications for compensation and reimbursement of expenses, see Fed.Rules Bankr.Proc. Rule 2016, 11 USCA.

Officers' compensation as administrative expense, see 11 USCA § 503.

Supervision by Attorney General, see 28 USCA § 586.

United States Trustee System Fund establishment and purpose, see 28 USCA § 589a.

LIBRARY REFERENCES

American Digest System

    Bankruptcy ⟳3151 to 3205.

    Key Number System Topic No. 51.

Corpus Juris Secundum

    CJS Bankruptcy § 39, United States Trustee System Fund.

    CJS Bankruptcy § 45, Supervision of Cases and Bankruptcy Trustees.

    CJS Bankruptcy § 46, Service as Bankruptcy Trustee.

    CJS Bankruptcy § 112, General Rule and Limitation.

    CJS Bankruptcy § 114, Interim Compensation.

    CJS Bankruptcy § 115, Specific Minimum Compensation of Trustees in Chapters 7, 12, and 13 Cases.

CJS Bankruptcy § 118, Prohibition Against Compensation Sharing.

CJS Bankruptcy § 122, Effect of Conversion of Chapter 7 or Chapter 11 Case.

CJS Bankruptcy § 178, Employment and Compensation of Professional Persons.

CJS Bankruptcy § 761, Relationship Between Employment and Compensation Provisions.

CJS Bankruptcy § 773, Status of Claims for Compensation and Reimbursement.

CJS Bankruptcy § 775, Interim Compensation.

CJS Bankruptcy § 776, Particular Items Compensable and Factors Affecting Amount.

CJS Bankruptcy § 782, Notice and Hearing.

CJS Bankruptcy § 785, Judicial Authority to Deny or Modify Compensation.

§ 331. Interim compensation

A trustee, an examiner, a debtor's attorney, or any professional person employed under section 327 or 1103 of this title may apply to the court not more than once every 120 days after an order for relief in a case under this title, or more often if the court permits, for such compensation for services rendered before the date of such an application or reimbursement for expenses incurred before such date as is provided under section 330 of this title. After notice and a hearing, the court may allow and disburse to such applicant such compensation or reimbursement.

(Pub.L. 95–598, Nov. 6, 1978, 92 Stat. 2564.)

HISTORICAL AND STATUTORY NOTES

Revision Notes and Legislative Reports

1978 Acts. Section 331 permits trustees and professional persons to apply to the court not more than once every 120 days for interim compensation and reimbursement payments. The court may permit more frequent applications if the circumstances warrant, such as in very large cases where the legal work is extensive and merits more frequent payments. The court is authorized to allow and order disbursement to the applicant of compensation and reimbursement that is otherwise allowable under section 330. The only effect of this section is to remove any doubt that officers of the estate may apply for, and the court may approve, compensation and reimbursement during the case, instead of being required to wait until the end of the case, which in some instances, may be years. The practice of interim compensation is followed in some courts today, but has been subject to some question. This section explicitly authorizes it.

This section will apply to professionals such as auctioneers and appraisers only if they are not paid on a per job basis. Senate Report No. 95–989.

LIBRARY REFERENCES

American Digest System

Bankruptcy ⟝3175, 3158.

Key Number System Topic No. 51.

Corpus Juris Secundum

CJS Bankruptcy § 114, Interim Compensation.

CJS Bankruptcy § 761, Relationship Between Employment and Compensation Provisions.

CJS Bankruptcy § 775, Interim Compensation.

CJS Bankruptcy § 782, Notice and Hearing.

§ 332. Consumer privacy ombudsman

(a) If a hearing is required under section 363(b)(1)(B), the court shall order the United States trustee to appoint, not later than 7 days before the commencement of the hearing, 1 disinterested person (other than the United States trustee) to serve as the consumer privacy ombudsman in the case and shall require that notice of such hearing be timely given to such ombudsman.

(b) The consumer privacy ombudsman may appear and be heard at such hearing and shall provide to the court information to assist the court in its consideration of the facts, circumstances, and conditions of the proposed sale or lease of personally identifiable information under section 363(b)(1)(B). Such information may include presentation of—

(1) the debtor's privacy policy;

(2) the potential losses or gains of privacy to consumers if such sale or such lease is approved by the court;

(3) the potential costs or benefits to consumers if such sale or such lease is approved by the court; and

(4) the potential alternatives that would mitigate potential privacy losses or potential costs to consumers.

(c) A consumer privacy ombudsman shall not disclose any personally identifiable information obtained by the ombudsman under this title.

(Added Pub.L. 109–8, Title II, § 232(a), Apr. 20, 2005, 119 Stat. 73; amended Pub.L. 111–16, § 2(3), May 7, 2009, 123 Stat. 1607.)

HISTORICAL AND STATUTORY NOTES

Revision Notes and Legislative Reports

2005 Acts. House Report No. 109–31(Part I), see 2005 U.S. Code Cong. and Adm. News, p. 88.

2009 Amendments. Subsec. (a). Pub.L. 111–16, § 2(3), struck out "5 days" and inserted "7 days".

Effective and Applicability Provisions

2009 Acts. Amendments by Pub.L. 111–16 effective Dec. 1, 2009, see Pub.L. 111–16, § 7, set out as a note under 11 U.S.C.A. § 109.

2005 Acts. Amendments by Pub.L. 109–8 effective, except as otherwise provided, 180 days after April 20, 2005, and inapplicable with respect to cases commenced under Title 11 before the effective date, see Pub.L. 109–8, § 1501, set out as a note under 11 U.S.C.A. § 101.

LIBRARY REFERENCES

Corpus Juris Secundum

CJS Bankruptcy § 764, Consumer Privacy and Patient Care Ombudsmen.

CJS Bankruptcy § 877, Sale or Lease of Personally Identifiable Information.

§ 333. Appointment of patient care ombudsman

(a)(1) If the debtor in a case under chapter 7, 9, or 11 is a health care business, the court shall order, not later than 30 days after the commencement of the case, the appointment of an ombudsman to monitor the quality of patient care and to represent the interests of the patients of the health care business unless the court finds that the appointment of such ombudsman is not necessary for the protection of patients under the specific facts of the case.

(2)(A) If the court orders the appointment of an ombudsman under paragraph (1), the United States trustee shall appoint 1 disinterested person (other than the United States trustee) to serve as such ombudsman.

(B) If the debtor is a health care business that provides long-term care, then the United States trustee may appoint the State Long–Term Care Ombudsman appointed under the Older Americans Act of 1965 for the State in which the case is pending to serve as the ombudsman required by paragraph (1).

(C) If the United States trustee does not appoint a State Long–Term Care Ombudsman under subparagraph (B), the court shall notify the State Long–Term Care Ombudsman appointed under the Older Americans Act of 1965 for the State in which the case is pending, of the name and address of the person who is appointed under subparagraph (A).

(b) An ombudsman appointed under subsection (a) shall—

(1) monitor the quality of patient care provided to patients of the debtor, to the extent necessary under the circumstances, including interviewing patients and physicians;

(2) not later than 60 days after the date of appointment, and not less frequently than at 60–day intervals thereafter, report to the court after notice to the parties in interest, at a hearing or in writing, regarding the quality of patient care provided to patients of the debtor; and

(3) if such ombudsman determines that the quality of patient care provided to patients of the debtor is declining significantly or is otherwise being materially compromised, file with the court a motion or a written report, with notice to the parties in interest immediately upon making such determination.

(c)(1) An ombudsman appointed under subsection (a) shall maintain any information obtained by such ombudsman under this section that relates to patients (including information relating to patient records) as confidential information. Such ombudsman may not review confidential patient records unless the court approves such review in advance and imposes restric-

tions on such ombudsman to protect the confidentiality of such records.

(2) An ombudsman appointed under subsection (a)(2)(B) shall have access to patient records consistent with authority of such ombudsman under the Older Americans Act of 1965 and under non-Federal laws governing the State Long–Term Care Ombudsman program.

(Added Pub.L. 109–8, Title XI, § 1104(a)(1), Apr. 20, 2005, 119 Stat. 191.)

HISTORICAL AND STATUTORY NOTES

Revision Notes and Legislative Reports

2005 Acts. House Report No. 109–31(Part I), see 2005 U.S. Code Cong. and Adm. News, p. 88.

References in Text

Chapter 7, 9, or 11, referred to in subsec. (a)(1), means chapter 7, 9, or 11 of this title, 11 U.S.C.A. § 701 et seq., 11 U.S.C.A. § 901 et seq., or 11 U.S.C.A. § 1101 et seq., respectively.

The Older Americans Act of 1965, referred to in subsecs. (a)(2)(B), (C) and (c)(2), is Pub.L. 89–73, July 14, 1965, 79 Stat. 218, as amended, which is classified principally to chapter 35 of Title 42, 42 U.S.C.A. § 3001 et seq. For complete classification, see Short Title note set out under 42 U.S.C.A. § 3001 and Tables.

Effective and Applicability Provisions

2005 Acts. Enactment of this section by Pub.L. 109–8 effective, except as otherwise provided, 180 days after April 20, 2005, and inapplicable with respect to cases commenced under Title 11 before the effective date, see Pub.L. 109–8, § 1501, set out as a note under 11 U.S.C.A. § 101.

LIBRARY REFERENCES

Corpus Juris Secundum

CJS Bankruptcy § 764, Consumer Privacy and Patient Care Ombudsmen.

SUBCHAPTER III—ADMINISTRATION

§ 341. Meetings of creditors and equity security holders

(a) Within a reasonable time after the order for relief in a case under this title, the United States trustee shall convene and preside at a meeting of creditors.

(b) The United States trustee may convene a meeting of any equity security holders.

(c) The court may not preside at, and may not attend, any meeting under this section including any final meeting of creditors. Notwithstanding any local court rule, provision of a State constitution, any otherwise applicable nonbankruptcy law, or any other requirement that representation at the meeting of creditors under subsection (a) be by an attorney, a creditor holding a consumer debt or any representative of the creditor (which may include an entity or an employee of an entity and may be a representative for more than

1 creditor) shall be permitted to appear at and participate in the meeting of creditors in a case under chapter 7 or 13, either alone or in conjunction with an attorney for the creditor. Nothing in this subsection shall be construed to require any creditor to be represented by an attorney at any meeting of creditors.

(d) Prior to the conclusion of the meeting of creditors or equity security holders, the trustee shall orally examine the debtor to ensure that the debtor in a case under chapter 7 of this title is aware of—

(1) the potential consequences of seeking a discharge in bankruptcy, including the effects on credit history;

(2) the debtor's ability to file a petition under a different chapter of this title;

(3) the effect of receiving a discharge of debts under this title; and

(4) the effect of reaffirming a debt, including the debtor's knowledge of the provisions of section 524(d) of this title.

(e) Notwithstanding subsections (a) and (b), the court, on the request of a party in interest and after notice and a hearing, for cause may order that the United States trustee not convene a meeting of creditors or equity security holders if the debtor has filed a plan as to which the debtor solicited acceptances prior to the commencement of the case.

(Pub.L. 95–598, Nov. 6, 1978, 92 Stat. 2564; Pub.L. 99–554, Title II, § 212, Oct. 27, 1986, 100 Stat. 3099; Pub.L. 103–394, Title I, § 115, Oct. 22, 1994, 108 Stat. 4118; Pub.L. 109–8, Title IV, §§ 402, 413, Apr. 20, 2005, 119 Stat. 104, 107.)

HISTORICAL AND STATUTORY NOTES

Revision Notes and Legislative Reports

1978 Acts. Section [subsection] (a) of this section requires that there be a meeting of creditors within a reasonable time after the order for relief in the case. The Bankruptcy Act [former Title 11] and the current Rules of Bankruptcy Procedure provide for a meeting of creditors, and specify the time and manner of the meeting, and the business to be conducted. This bill leaves those matters to the rules. Under section 405(d) of the bill, the present rules will continue to govern until new rules are promulgated. Thus, pending the adoption of different rules, the present procedure for the meeting will continue.

Subsection (b) authorizes the court to order a meeting of equity security holders in cases where such a meeting would be beneficial or useful, for example, in a chapter 11 reorganization case where it may be necessary for the equity security holders to organize in order to be able to participate in the negotiation of a plan of reorganization.

Subsection (c) makes clear that the bankruptcy judge is to preside at the meeting of creditors. Senate Report No. 95–989.

1986 Acts. House Report No. 99–764 and House Conference Report No. 99–958, see 1986 U.S.Code Cong. and Adm. News, p. 5227.

1994 Acts. House Report No. 103–835, see 1994 U.S. Code Cong. and Adm. News, p. 3340.

2005 Acts. House Report No. 109–31(Part I), see 2005 U.S. Code Cong. and Adm. News, p. 88.

Legislative Statements

Section 341(c) of the Senate amendment is deleted and a contrary provision is added indicating that the bankruptcy judge will not preside at or attend the first meeting of creditors or equity security holders but a discharge hearing for all individuals will be held at which the judge will preside.

References in Text

Chapter 7, referred to in subsecs. (c) and (d), is chapter 7 of this title, 11 U.S.C.A. § 701 et seq.

Chapter 13, referred to in subsec. (c), is chapter 13 of this title, 11 U.S.C.A. § 1301 et seq.

Amendments

2005 Amendments. Subsec. (c). Pub.L. 109–8, § 413, inserted at the end the following: "Notwithstanding any local court rule, provision of a State constitution, any otherwise applicable nonbankruptcy law, or any other requirement that representation at the meeting of creditors under subsection (a) be by an attorney, a creditor holding a consumer debt or any representative of the creditor (which may include an entity or an employee of an entity and may be a representative for more than 1 creditor) shall be permitted to appear at and participate in the meeting of creditors in a case under chapter 7 or 13, either alone or in conjunction with an attorney for the creditor. Nothing in this subsection shall be construed to require any creditor to be represented by an attorney at any meeting of creditors.".

Subsec. (e). Pub.L. 109–8, § 402, added subsec. (e).

1994 Amendments. Subsec. (d). Pub.L. 103–394, § 115, added subsec. (d).

1986 Amendments. Subsec. (a). Pub.L. 99–554, § 212(1), substituted "this title, the United States trustee shall convene and preside at a meeting of creditors" for "this title, there shall be a meeting of creditors".

Subsec. (b). Pub.L. 99–554, § 212(2), substituted "The United States trustee may convene a meeting" for "The court may order a meeting".

Subsec. (c). Pub.L. 99–554, § 212(3), substituted "this section including any final meeting of creditors." for "this section.".

Effective and Applicability Provisions

2005 Acts. Amendments by Pub.L. 109–8 effective, except as otherwise provided, 180 days after April 20, 2005, and inapplicable with respect to cases commenced under Title 11 before the effective date, see Pub.L. 109–8, § 1501, set out as a note under 11 U.S.C.A. § 101.

1994 Acts. Amendment by Pub.L. 103–394 effective on Oct. 22, 1994, and not to apply with respect to cases commenced under Title 11 of the United States Code before Oct. 22, 1994, see section 702 of Pub.L. 103–394, set out as a note under section 101 of this title.

1986 Acts. Amendment by Pub.L. 99–554 effective 30 days after Oct. 27, 1986, except as otherwise provided for, see section 302(a) of Pub.L. 99–554, set out as a note under section 581 of Title 28, Judiciary and Judicial Procedure.

Amendment by Pub.L. 99–554, § 212, not to become effective in or with respect to certain specified judicial districts until, or apply to cases while pending in such district before, the expiration of the 270-day period beginning 30 days after Oct. 27, 1986, or of the 30-day period beginning on the date the Attorney General certifies under section 303 of Pub.L. 99–554 the region specified in a paragraph of section 581(a) of Title 28, as amended by section 111(a) of Pub.L. 99–554, that includes such district, whichever occurs first, see section 302(d)(1) of Pub.L. 99–554, set out as a note under section 581 of Title 28.

Amendment by Pub.L. 99–554, § 212, not to become effective in or with respect to certain specified judicial districts until, or apply to cases while pending in such district before, the expiration of the 2-year period beginning 30 days after Oct. 27, 1986, or of the 30-day period beginning on the date the Attorney General certifies under section 303 of Pub.L. 99–554 the region specified in a paragraph of section 581(a) of Title 28, as amended by section 111(a) of Pub.L. 99–554, that includes such district, whichever occurs first, see section 302(d)(2) of Pub.L. 99–554, set out as a note under section 581 of Title 28.

Amendment by Pub.L. 99–554, § 212, not to become effective in or with respect to judicial districts established for the States of Alabama and North Carolina until, or apply to cases while pending in such district before, such district elects to be included in a bankruptcy region established in section 581(a) of Title 28, as amended by section 111(a) of Pub.L. 99–554, or Oct. 1, 2002, whichever occurs first, and, except as otherwise provided, with respect to cases under chapters 7, 11, 12, and 13 of Title 11 commenced before 30 days after Oct. 27, 1986, and pending in a judicial district in the States of Alabama or North Carolina before any election made under section 302(d)(3)(A) of Pub.L. 99–554 by such district becomes effective or Oct. 1, 2003, whichever occurs first, amendments by Pub.L. 99–554 not to apply until Oct. 1, 1992, or the expiration of the 1-year period beginning on the date such election becomes effective whichever occurs first, and further, in any judicial district in Alabama or North Carolina not making the election described in section 302(d)(3)(A) of Pub.L. 99–554, any person appointed under regulations issued by the Judicial Conference to administer estates in cases under Title 11 authorized to establish, etc., a panel of private trustees, and to supervise cases and trustees in cases under chapters 7, 11, 12, and 13 of Title 11, until amendments by sections 201 to 231 of Pub.L. 99–554 effective in such district, see section 302(d)(3)(A) to (F), (H), and (I) of Pub.L. 99–554, set out as a note under section 581 of Title 28.

Amendment by Pub.L. 99–554, § 212, except as otherwise provided, with respect to cases under chapters 7, 11, 12 and 13 of Title 11 commenced before 30 days after Oct. 27, 1986, and pending in a judicial district referred to in section 581(a) of Title 28, as amended by section 111(a) of Pub.L. 99–554, for which a United States trustee is not authorized before 30 days after Oct. 27, 1986 to be appointed, not applicable until the expiration of the 3-year period beginning on Oct. 27, 1986, or of the 1-year period beginning on the date the Attorney General certifies under section 303 of Pub.L. 99–554 the region specified in a paragraph of such section 581(a) that includes, such district, whichever occurs first, see section 302(e)(1), (2) of Pub.L. 99–554, set out as a note under section 581 of Title 28.

Separability of Provisions

If any provision of or amendment made by Pub.L. 103–394 or the application of such provision or amendment to any person or circumstance is held to be unconstitutional, the remaining provisions of and amendments made by Pub.L.

103–394 and the application of such provisions and amendments to any person or circumstance shall not be affected thereby, see section 701 of Pub.L. 103–394, set out as a note under section 101 of this title.

Participation by Bankruptcy Administrator at Meetings of Creditors and Equity Security Holders

Section 105 of Pub.L. 103–394 provided that:

"**(a) Presiding officer.**—A bankruptcy administrator appointed under section 302(d)(3)(I) of the Bankruptcy Judges, United States Trustees, and Family Farmer Bankruptcy Act of 1986 (28 U.S.C. 581 note; Public Law 99–554; 100 Stat. 3123), as amended by section 317(a) of the Federal Courts Study Committee Implementation Act of 1990 (Public Law 101–650; 104 Stat. 5115), or the bankruptcy administrator's designee may preside at the meeting of creditors convened under section 341(a) of title 11, United States Code [subsec. (a) of this section]. The bankruptcy administrator or the bankruptcy administrator's designee may preside at any meeting of equity security holders convened under section 341(b) of title 11, United States Code [subsec. (b) of this section].

"**(b) Examination of the debtor.**—The bankruptcy administrator or the bankruptcy administrator's designee may examine the debtor at the meeting of creditors and may administer the oath required under section 343 of title 11, United States Code [section 343 of this title]."

CROSS REFERENCES

Election of—

Creditors' committee, see 11 USCA § 705.

Trustee, see 11 USCA § 702.

Inapplicability of this section in railroad reorganization cases, see 11 USCA § 1161.

LIBRARY REFERENCES

American Digest System

Bankruptcy ⬦3024.

Key Number System Topic No. 51.

Corpus Juris Secundum

CJS Bankruptcy § 790, Convening of Meeting by Trustee or Other Judicial Officer.

CJS Bankruptcy § 793, Duties of Trustee or Other Judicial Officer.

CJS Bankruptcy § 794, Time of Initial Meeting.

CJS Bankruptcy § 800, United States Trustee or Other Judicial Officer; Bankruptcy Judge.

CJS Bankruptcy § 801, Creditors.

CJS Bankruptcy § 810, Trustee's Examination of Chapter 7 Debtor Concerning Effects of Bankruptcy.

CJS Bankruptcy § 1105, Closing.

§ 342. Notice

(a) There shall be given such notice as is appropriate, including notice to any holder of a community claim, of an order for relief in a case under this title.

(b) Before the commencement of a case under this title by an individual whose debts are primarily consumer debts, the clerk shall give to such individual written notice containing—

(1) a brief description of—

(A) chapters 7, 11, 12, and 13 and the general purpose, benefits, and costs of proceeding under each of those chapters; and

(B) the types of services available from credit counseling agencies; and

(2) statements specifying that—

(A) a person who knowingly and fraudulently conceals assets or makes a false oath or statement under penalty of perjury in connection with a case under this title shall be subject to fine, imprisonment, or both; and

(B) all information supplied by a debtor in connection with a case under this title is subject to examination by the Attorney General.

(c)(1) If notice is required to be given by the debtor to a creditor under this title, any rule, any applicable law, or any order of the court, such notice shall contain the name, address, and last 4 digits of the taxpayer identification number of the debtor. If the notice concerns an amendment that adds a creditor to the schedules of assets and liabilities, the debtor shall include the full taxpayer identification number in the notice sent to that creditor, but the debtor shall include only the last 4 digits of the taxpayer identification number in the copy of the notice filed with the court.

(2)(A) If, within the 90 days before the commencement of a voluntary case, a creditor supplies the debtor in at least 2 communications sent to the debtor with the current account number of the debtor and the address at which such creditor requests to receive correspondence, then any notice required by this title to be sent by the debtor to such creditor shall be sent to such address and shall include such account number.

(B) If a creditor would be in violation of applicable nonbankruptcy law by sending any such communication within such 90–day period and if such creditor supplies the debtor in the last 2 communications with the current account number of the debtor and the address at which such creditor requests to receive correspondence, then any notice required by this title to be sent by the debtor to such creditor shall be sent to such address and shall include such account number.

(d) In a case under chapter 7 of this title in which the debtor is an individual and in which the presumption of abuse arises under section 707(b), the clerk shall give written notice to all creditors not later than 10 days after the date of the filing of the petition that the presumption of abuse has arisen.

(e)(1) In a case under chapter 7 or 13 of this title of a debtor who is an individual, a creditor at any time may both file with the court and serve on the debtor a notice of address to be used to provide notice in such case to such creditor.

(2) Any notice in such case required to be provided to such creditor by the debtor or the court later than 7 days after the court and the debtor receive such creditor's notice of address, shall be provided to such address.

(f)(1) An entity may file with any bankruptcy court a notice of address to be used by all the bankruptcy courts or by particular bankruptcy courts, as so specified by such entity at the time such notice is filed, to provide notice to such entity in all cases under chapters 7 and 13 pending in the courts with respect to which such notice is filed, in which such entity is a creditor.

(2) In any case filed under chapter 7 or 13, any notice required to be provided by a court with respect to which a notice is filed under paragraph (1), to such entity later than 30 days after the filing of such notice under paragraph (1) shall be provided to such address unless with respect to a particular case a different address is specified in a notice filed and served in accordance with subsection (e).

(3) A notice filed under paragraph (1) may be withdrawn by such entity.

(g)(1) Notice provided to a creditor by the debtor or the court other than in accordance with this section (excluding this subsection) shall not be effective notice until such notice is brought to the attention of such creditor. If such creditor designates a person or an organizational subdivision of such creditor to be responsible for receiving notices under this title and establishes reasonable procedures so that such notices receivable by such creditor are to be delivered to such person or such subdivision, then a notice provided to such creditor other than in accordance with this section (excluding this subsection) shall not be considered to have been brought to the attention of such creditor until such notice is received by such person or such subdivision.

(2) A monetary penalty may not be imposed on a creditor for a violation of a stay in effect under section 362(a) (including a monetary penalty imposed under section 362(k)) or for failure to comply with section 542 or 543 unless the conduct that is the basis of such violation or of such failure occurs after such creditor receives notice effective under this section of the order for relief.

(Pub.L. 95–598, Nov. 6, 1978, 92 Stat. 2565; Pub.L. 98–353, Title III, §§ 302, 435, July 10, 1984, 98 Stat. 352, 370; Pub.L. 103–394, Title II, § 225, Oct. 22, 1994, 108 Stat. 4131; Pub.L. 109–8, Title I, §§ 102(d), 104, Title II, § 234(b), Title III, § 315(a), Apr. 20, 2005, 119 Stat. 33, 35, 75, 88; Pub.L. 111–16, § 2(4), May 7, 2009, 123 Stat. 1607.)

HISTORICAL AND STATUTORY NOTES
Revision Notes and Legislative Reports

1978 Acts. Subsection (a) of section 342 requires the clerk of the bankruptcy court to give notice of the order for relief. The rules will prescribe to whom the notice should be sent and in what manner notice will be given. The rules already prescribe such things, and they will continue to govern unless changed as provided in section 404(a) of the bill. Due process will certainly require notice to all creditors and equity security holders. State and Federal governmental representatives responsible for collecting taxes will also receive notice. In cases where the debtor is subject to regulation, the regulatory agency with jurisdiction will receive notice. In order to insure maximum notice to all parties in interest, the Rules will include notice by publication in appropriate cases and for appropriate issues. Other notices will be given as appropriate.

Subsections (b) and (c) are derived from section 21g of the Bankruptcy Act [section 44(g) of former Title 11]. They specify that the trustee may file notice of the commencement of the case in land recording offices in order to give notice of the pendency of the case to potential transferees of the debtor's real property. Such filing is unnecessary in the county in which the bankruptcy case is commenced. If notice is properly filed, a subsequent purchaser of the property will not be a bona fide purchaser. Otherwise, a purchaser, including a purchaser at a judicial sale, that has no knowledge of the case, is not prevented from obtaining the status of a bona fide purchaser by the mere commencement of the case. "County" is defined in title 1 of the United States Code [1 U.S.C.A. § 2] to include other political subdivisions where counties are not used. Senate Report No. 95–989.

1984 Acts. Statements by Legislative Leaders, see 1984 U.S.Code Cong. and Adm.News, p. 576.

1994 Acts. House Report No. 103–835, see 1994 U.S. Code Cong. and Adm. News, p. 3340.

2005 Acts. House Report No. 109–31(Part I), see 2005 U.S. Code Cong. and Adm. News, p. 88.

Legislative Statements

Section 342(b) and (c) of the Senate amendment are adopted in principle but moved to section 549(c), in lieu of section 342(b) of H.R. 8200 as passed by the House.

Section 342(c) of H.R. 8200 as passed by the House is deleted as a matter to be left to the Rules of Bankruptcy Procedure.

References in Text

Chapters 7, 11, 12, and 13, referred to in subsec. (b)(1), are chapters 7, 11, 12, and 13 of this title, 11 U.S.C.A. § 701 et seq., 11 U.S.C.A. § 1101 et seq., 11 U.S.C.A. § 1201 et seq., and 11 U.S.C.A. § 1301 et seq., respectively.

Chapter 7 of this title, referred to in subsec. (d), is 11 U.S.C.A. § 701 et seq.

Chapter 7 or 13, referred to in subsecs. (e)(1), (f)(1), (2), is chapter 7 or 13 of this title, 11 U.S.C.A. § 701 et seq. or 11 U.S.C.A. § 1301 et seq., respectively.

Amendments

2009 Amendments. Subsec. (e)(2). Pub.L. 111–16, § 2(4), struck out "5 days" and inserted "7 days".

2005 Amendments. Subsec. (b). Pub.L. 109–8, § 104, rewrote subsec. (b), which formerly read:

"**(b)** Prior to the commencement of a case under this title by an individual whose debts are primarily consumer debts, the clerk shall give written notice to such individual that indicates each chapter of this title under which such individual may proceed."

Subsec. (c). Pub.L. 109–8, § 234(b), inserted "last 4 digits of the" before "taxpayer identification number", and added "If the notice concerns an amendment that adds a creditor to the schedules of assets and liabilities, the debtor shall include the full taxpayer identification number in the notice sent to that creditor, but the debtor shall include only the last 4 digits of the taxpayer identification number in the copy of the notice filed with the court." at the end.

Subsec. (c)(1). Pub.L. 109–8, § 315(a)(1)(A), (B), inserted "(1)" after "(c)" and struck out ", but the failure of such notice to contain such information shall not invalidate the legal effect of such notice" following "taxpayer identification number of the debtor".

Subsec. (c)(2). Pub.L. 109–8, § 315(a)(1)(C), added par. (2).

Subsec. (d). Pub.L. 109–8, § 102(d), added subsec. (d).

Subsecs. (e) to (g). Pub.L. 109–8, § 315(a)(2), added subsecs. (e), (f), and (g).

1994 Amendments. Subsec. (c). Pub.L. 103–394, § 225, added subsec. (c).

1984 Amendments. Subsec. (a). Pub.L. 98–353, § 302(1), designated existing provisions as subsec. (a).

Pub.L. 98–353, § 435, added requirement respecting notice to any holder of a community claim.

Subsec. (b). Pub.L. 98–353, § 302(2), added subsec. (b).

Effective and Applicability Provisions

2009 Acts. Amendments by Pub.L. 111–16 effective Dec. 1, 2009, see Pub.L. 111–16, § 7, set out as a note under 11 U.S.C.A. § 109.

2005 Acts. Amendments by Pub.L. 109–8 effective, except as otherwise provided, 180 days after April 20, 2005, and inapplicable with respect to cases commenced under Title 11 before the effective date, see Pub.L. 109–8, § 1501, set out as a note under 11 U.S.C.A. § 101.

1994 Acts. Amendment by Pub.L. 103–394 effective on Oct. 22, 1994, and not to apply with respect to cases commenced under Title 11 of the United States Code before Oct. 22, 1994, see section 702 of Pub.L. 103–394, set out as a note under section 101 of this title.

1984 Acts. Amendment by Pub.L. 98–353 effective with respect to cases filed 90 days after July 10, 1984, see section 552(a), formerly 553(a), of Pub.L. 98–353, set out as a note under section 101 of this title.

Separability of Provisions

If any provision of or amendment made by Pub.L. 103–394 or the application of such provision or amendment to any person or circumstance is held to be unconstitutional, the remaining provisions of and amendments made by Pub.L. 103–394 and the application of such provisions and amendments to any person or circumstance shall not be affected thereby, see section 701 of Pub.L. 103–394, set out as a note under section 101 of this title.

CROSS REFERENCES

Instructions in notice to customers, see 11 USCA § 765.

"Net equity" defined in relation to payments made by customers to trustee within 60 days after notice, see 11 USCA § 741.

Notice in—

    Commodity broker liquidation cases, see 11 USCA § 762.

Investor protection liquidation proceedings, see 15 USCA § 78fff–2.

Stockbroker liquidation cases, see 11 USCA § 743.

LIBRARY REFERENCES

American Digest System

Bankruptcy ⚬2131.

Key Number System Topic No. 51.

Corpus Juris Secundum

CJS Bankruptcy § 285, Captions.

CJS Bankruptcy § 296, Notice by Mail--Proper Mailing Address.

CJS Bankruptcy § 300, Filing and Serving Notice of Address in Case Under Chapter 7 or 13.

CJS Bankruptcy § 301, Notice to Debtor, Creditors, and Indenture Trustees.

CJS Bankruptcy § 337, Contents, Signature, and Verification--Certification of Delivery or Receipt of Prefiling Notice.

CJS Bankruptcy § 365, Commencement and Order for Relief.

CJS Bankruptcy § 432, Presumption of Abuse--Notice.

§ 343.   Examination of the debtor

The debtor shall appear and submit to examination under oath at the meeting of creditors under section 341(a) of this title. Creditors, any indenture trustee, any trustee or examiner in the case, or the United States trustee may examine the debtor. The United States trustee may administer the oath required under this section.

(Pub.L. 95–598, Nov. 6, 1978, 92 Stat. 2565; Pub.L. 98–353, Title III, § 436, July 10, 1984, 98 Stat. 370; Pub.L. 99–554, Title II, § 213, Oct. 27, 1986, 100 Stat. 3099.)

HISTORICAL AND STATUTORY NOTES

Revision Notes and Legislative Reports

1978 Acts. This section, derived from section 21a of the Bankruptcy Act [section 44(a) of former Title 11], requires the debtor to appear at the meeting of creditors and submit to examination under oath. The purpose of the examination is to enable creditors and the trustee to determine if assets have improperly been disposed of or concealed or if there are grounds for objection to discharge. The scope of the examination under this section will be governed by the Rules of Bankruptcy Procedure, as it is today. See rules 205(d), 10–213(c), and 11–26. It is expected that the scope prescribed by these rules for liquidation cases, that is, "only the debtor's acts, conduct, or property, or any matter that may affect the administration of the estate, or the debtor's right to discharge" will remain substantially unchanged. In reorganization cases, the examination would be broader, including inquiry into the liabilities and financial condition of the debtor, the operation of his business, and the desirability of the continuance thereof, and other matters relevant to the case and to the formulation of the plan. Examination of other persons in connection with the bankruptcy case is left completely to the rules, just as examination of witnesses in civil cases is governed by the Federal Rules of Civil Procedure. Senate Report No. 95–989.

1984 Acts. Statements by Legislative Leaders, see 1984 U.S.Code Cong. and Adm.News, p. 576.

1986 Acts. House Report No. 99–764 and House Conference Report No. 99–958, see 1986 U.S.Code Cong. and Adm. News, p. 5227.

Amendments

1986 Amendments. Pub.L. 99–554, § 213, substituted "Creditors, any indenture trustee, any trustee or examiner in the case, or the United States trustee may examine the debtor. The United States trustee may administer the oath required under this section." for "Creditors, any indenture trustee, or any trustee or examiner in the case may examine the debtor.".

1984 Amendments. Pub.L. 98–353 substituted "examine" for "examiner".

Effective and Applicability Provisions

1986 Acts. Amendment by Pub.L. 99–554 effective 30 days after Oct. 27, 1986, except as otherwise provided for, see section 302(a) of Pub.L. 99–554, set out as a note under section 581 of Title 28, Judiciary and Judicial Procedure.

Amendment by Pub.L. 99–554, § 213, not to become effective in or with respect to certain specified judicial districts until, or apply to cases while pending in such district before, the expiration of the 270-day period beginning 30 days after Oct. 27, 1986, or of the 30-day period beginning on the date the Attorney General certifies under section 303 of Pub.L. 99–554 the region specified in a paragraph of section 581(a) of Title 28, as amended by section 111(a) of Pub.L. 99–554, that includes such district, whichever occurs first, see section 302(d)(1) of Pub.L. 99–554, set out as a note under section 581 of Title 28.

Amendment by Pub.L. 99–554, § 213, not to become effective in or with respect to certain specified judicial districts until, or apply to cases while pending in such district before, the expiration of the 2-year period beginning 30 days after Oct. 27, 1986, or of the 30-day period beginning on the date the Attorney General certifies under section 303 of Pub.L. 99–554 the region specified in a paragraph of section 581(a) of Title 28, as amended by section 111(a) of Pub.L. 99–554, that includes such district, whichever occurs first, see section 302(d)(2) of Pub.L. 99–554, set out as a note under section 581 of Title 28.

Amendment by Pub.L. 99–554, § 213, not to become effective in or with respect to judicial districts established for the States of Alabama and North Carolina until, or apply to cases while pending in such district before, such district elects to be included in a bankruptcy region established in section 581(a) of Title 28, as amended by section 111(a) of Pub.L. 99–554, or Oct. 1, 2002, whichever occurs first, and, except as otherwise provided for, with respect to cases under chapters 7, 11, 12, and 13 of Title 11 commenced before 30 days after Oct. 27, 1986, and pending in a judicial district in the States of Alabama or North Carolina before any election made under section 302(d)(3)(A) of Pub.L. 99–554 by such district becomes effective or Oct. 1, 2002, whichever occurs first, amendments by Pub.L. 99–554 not to apply until Oct. 1, 2003, or the expiration of the 1-year period beginning on the date such election becomes effective, whichever occurs first, and further, in any judicial district in Alabama or North Carolina not making the election described in section 302(d)(3)(A) of Pub.L. 99–554, any person appointed under regulations issued by the Judicial Conference to administer estates in cases under Title

11 authorized to establish, etc., a panel of private trustees, and to supervise cases and trustees in cases under chapters 7, 11, 12, and 13 of Title 11, until amendments by sections 201 to 231 of Pub.L. 99–554 effective in such district, see section 302(d)(3)(A) to (F), (H), and (I) of Pub.L. 99–554, set out as a note under section 581 of Title 28.

Amendment by Pub.L. 99–554, § 213, except as otherwise provided, with respect to cases under chapters 7, 11, 12, and 13 of Title 11 commenced before 30 days after Oct. 27, 1986, and pending in a judicial district referred to in section 581(a) of Title 28, as amended by section 111(a) of Pub.L. 99–554, for which a United States trustee is not authorized before 30 days after Oct. 27, 1986 to be appointed, not applicable until the expiration of the 3-year period beginning on Oct. 27, 1986, or of the 1-year period beginning on the date the Attorney General certifies under section 303 of Pub.L. 99–554 the region specified in a paragraph of such section 581(a) that includes, such district, whichever occurs first, see section 302(e)(1), (2) of Pub.L. 99–554, set out as a note under section 581 of Title 28.

1984 Acts. Amendment by Pub.L. 98–353 effective with respect to cases filed 90 days after July 10, 1984, see section 552(a), formerly 553(a), of Pub.L. 98–353, set out as a note under section 101 of this title.

Participation by Bankruptcy Administrator at Meetings of Creditors and Equity Security Holders

The bankruptcy administrator or the bankruptcy's designee may examine the debtor at the meeting of the creditors and may administer the oath required by this section, see section 105 of Pub.L. 103–394, set out as a note under section 341 of this title.

CROSS REFERENCES

Concealment of assets deemed continuing offense, see 18 USCA § 3284.

Concealment of assets; false oaths and claims, see 18 USCA § 152.

Inapplicability of this section in railroad reorganization cases, see 11 USCA § 1161.

LIBRARY REFERENCES

American Digest System

Bankruptcy ☞3040.1 to 3048.

Key Number System Topic No. 51.

Corpus Juris Secundum

CJS Bankruptcy § 797, Debtor's Duty to Attend as Mandatory.

CJS Bankruptcy § 798, Excusing Debtor's Nonattendance.

CJS Bankruptcy § 801, Creditors.

CJS Bankruptcy § 805, Who May Conduct Examination; Debtor's Right to Examine.

CJS Bankruptcy § 807, Scope of Inquiry.

§ 344. Self-incrimination; immunity

Immunity for persons required to submit to examination, to testify, or to provide information in a case under this title may be granted under part V of title 18.

(Pub.L. 95–598, Nov. 6, 1978, 92 Stat. 2565.)

HISTORICAL AND STATUTORY NOTES
Revision Notes and Legislative Reports

1978 Acts. Part V of title 18 of the United States Code [18 U.S.C.A. § 6001 et seq.] governs the granting of immunity to witnesses before Federal tribunals. The immunity provided under part V is only use immunity, not transactional immunity. Part V applies to all proceedings before Federal courts, before Federal grand juries, before administrative agencies, and before Congressional committees. It requires the Attorney General or the U.S. attorney to request or to approve any grant of immunity, whether before a court, grand jury, agency, or congressional committee.

This section carries part V over into bankruptcy cases. Thus, for a witness to be ordered to testify before a bankruptcy court in spite of a claim of privilege, the U.S. attorney for the district in which the court sits would have to request from the district court for that district the immunity order. The rule would apply to both debtors, creditors, and any other witnesses in a bankruptcy case. If the immunity were granted, the witness would be required to testify. If not, he could claim the privilege against self-incrimination.

Part V [section 6001 et seq. of Title 18, Crimes and Criminal Procedure] is a significant departure from current law. Under section 7a(10) of the Bankruptcy Act [section 25(a)(10) of former Title 11] a debtor is required to testify in all circumstances, but any testimony he gives may not be used against him in any criminal proceeding, except testimony given in any hearing on objections to discharge. With that exception, section 7a(10) amounts to a blanket grant of use immunity to all debtors. Immunity for other witnesses in bankruptcy courts today is governed by part V of title 18.

The consequences of a claim of privileges by a debtor under proposed law and under current law differ as well. Under section 14c(6) of current law [section 32(c)(6) of former Title 11], any refusal to answer a material question approved by the court will result in the denial of a discharge, even if the refusal is based on the privilege against self incrimination. Thus, the debtor is confronted with the choice between losing his discharge and opening himself up to possible criminal prosecution.

Under section 727(a)(6) of the proposed title 11, a debtor is only denied a discharge if he refuses to testify after having been granted immunity. If the debtor claims the privilege and the U.S. attorney does not request immunity from the district courts, then the debtor may refuse to testify and still retain his right to a discharge. It removes the Scylla and Charibdis choice for debtors that exists under the Bankruptcy Act [former Title 11]. Senate Report No. 95–989.

CROSS REFERENCES

Applicability of this section in chapter 9 cases, see 11 USCA § 901.

Debtor's duty to surrender records despite grant of immunity under this section, see 11 USCA § 521.

LIBRARY REFERENCES

American Digest System

Bankruptcy ☞3048.

Key Number System Topic No. 51.

Corpus Juris Secundum

CJS Bankruptcy § 10, Other U.S. Code Provisions.

CJS Bankruptcy § 94, Criminal Liability.

CJS Bankruptcy § 624, Surrender of Property of Estate and Recorded Information to Trustee.

CJS Bankruptcy § 808, Scope of Inquiry--Privilege Against Self-Incrimination; Grant of Immunity.

§ 345. Money of estates

(a) A trustee in a case under this title may make such deposit or investment of the money of the estate for which such trustee serves as will yield the maximum reasonable net return on such money, taking into account the safety of such deposit or investment.

(b) Except with respect to a deposit or investment that is insured or guaranteed by the United States or by a department, agency, or instrumentality of the United States or backed by the full faith and credit of the United States, the trustee shall require from an entity with which such money is deposited or invested—

(1) a bond—

(A) in favor of the United States;

(B) secured by the undertaking of a corporate surety approved by the United States trustee for the district in which the case is pending; and

(C) conditioned on—

(i) a proper accounting for all money so deposited or invested and for any return on such money;

(ii) prompt repayment of such money and return; and

(iii) faithful performance of duties as a depository; or

(2) the deposit of securities of the kind specified in section 9303 of title 31;

unless the court for cause orders otherwise.

(c) An entity with which such moneys are deposited or invested is authorized to deposit or invest such moneys as may be required under this section.
(Pub.L. 95–598, Nov. 6, 1978, 92 Stat. 2565; Pub.L. 97–258, § 3(c), Sept. 13, 1982, 96 Stat. 1064; Pub.L. 98–353, Title III, § 437, July 10, 1984, 98 Stat. 370; Pub.L. 99–554, Title II, § 214, Oct. 27, 1986, 100 Stat. 3099; Pub.L. 103–394, Title II, § 210, Oct. 22, 1994, 108 Stat. 4125.)

HISTORICAL AND STATUTORY NOTES

Revision Notes and Legislative Reports

1978 Acts. This section is a significant departure from section 61 of the Bankruptcy Act [section 101 of former Title 11]. It permits a trustee in a bankruptcy case to make such deposit of investment of the money of the estate for which he serves as will yield the maximum reasonable net return on the money, taking into account the safety of such deposit or investment. Under current law, the trustee is permitted to deposit money only with banking institutions. Thus, the trustee is generally unable to secure a high rate of return on money of estates pending distribution, to the detriment of creditors. Under this section, the trustee may make deposits in savings and loans, may purchase government bonds, or make such other deposit or investment as is appropriate.

Under proposed 11 U.S.C. 541(a)(6), and except as provided in subsection (c) of this section, any interest or gain realized on the deposit or investment of funds under this section with become property of the estate, and will thus enhance the recovery of creditors.

In order to protect the creditors, subsection (b) requires certain precautions against loss of the money so deposited or invested. The trustee must require from a person with which he deposits or invests money of an estate a bond in favor of the United States secured by approved corporate surety and conditioned on a proper accounting for all money deposited or invested and for any return on such money. Alternately, the trustee may require the deposit of securities of the kind specified in section 15 of title 6 of the United States Code [31 U.S.C.A. § 9303], which governs the posting of security by banks that receive public moneys on deposit. These bonding requirements do not apply to deposits or investments that are insured or guaranteed the United States or a department, agency, or instrumentality of the United States, or that are backed by the full faith and credit of the United States.

These provisions do not address the question of aggregation of funds by a private chapter 13 trustee and are not to be construed as excluding such possibility. The Rules of Bankruptcy Procedure may provide for aggregation under appropriate circumstances and adequate safeguards in cases where there is a significant need, such as in districts in which there is a standing chapter 13 trustee. In such case, the interest or return on the funds would help defray the cost of administering the cases in which the standing trustee serves. Senate Report No. 95–989.

1982 Acts. House Report No. 97–651, see 1982 U.S.Code Cong. and Adm.News, p. 1895.

1984 Acts. Statements by Legislative Leaders, see 1984 U.S.Code Cong. and Adm.News, p. 576.

1986 Acts. House Report No. 99–764 and House Conference Report No. 99–958, see 1986 U.S.Code Cong. and Adm. News, p. 5227.

1994 Acts. House Report No. 103–835, see 1994 U.S. Code Cong. and Adm. News, p. 3340.

Legislative Statements

The House amendment moves section 345(c) of the House bill to chapter 15 as part of the pilot program for the U.S. trustees. The bond required by section 345(b) may be a blanket bond posted by the financial depository sufficient to cover deposits by trustees in several cases, as is done under current law.

Amendments

1994 Amendments. Subsec. (b). Pub.L. 103–394, § 210(2), added provisions authorizing court for cause to order an alternative to bond or securities requirement.

1986 Amendments. Subsec. (b)(1)(B). Pub.L. 99–554, § 214, substituted "approved by the United States trustee for the district" for "approved by the court for the district".

1984 Amendments. Subsec. (c). Pub.L. 98–353 added subsec. (c).

1982 Amendments. Subsec. (b)(2). Pub.L. 97–258 substituted "9303 of title 31" for "15 of title 6".

Effective and Applicability Provisions

1994 Acts. Amendment by Pub.L. 103–394 effective on Oct. 22, 1994, and not to apply with respect to cases commenced

under Title 11 of the United States Code before Oct. 22, 1994, see section 702 of Pub.L. 103–394, set out as a note under section 101 of this title.

1986 Acts. Amendment by Pub.L. 99–554 effective 30 days after Oct. 27, 1986, except as otherwise provided for, see section 302(a) of Pub.L. 99–554, set out as a note under section 581 of Title 28, Judiciary and Judicial Procedure.

Amendment by Pub.L. 99–554, § 214, not to become effective in or with respect to certain specified judicial districts until, or apply to cases while pending in such district before, the expiration of the 270-day period beginning 30 days after Oct. 27, 1986, or of the 30-day period beginning on the date the Attorney General certifies under section 303 of Pub.L. 99–554 the region specified in a paragraph of section 581(a) of Title 28, as amended by section 111(a) of Pub.L. 99–554, that includes such district, whichever occurs first, see section 302(d)(1) of Pub.L. 99–554, set out as a note under section 581 of Title 28.

Amendment by Pub.L. 99–554, § 214, not to become effective in or with respect to certain specified judicial districts until, or apply to cases while pending in such district before, the expiration of the 2-year period beginning 30 days after Oct. 27, 1986, or of the 30-day period beginning on the date the Attorney General certifies under section 303 of Pub.L. 99–554 the region specified in a paragraph of section 581(a) of Title 28, as amended by section 111(a) of Pub.L. 99–554, that includes such district, whichever occurs first, see section 302(d)(2) of Pub.L. 99–554, set out as a note under section 581 of Title 28.

Amendment by Pub.L. 99–554, § 214, not to become effective in or with respect to judicial districts established for the States of Alabama and North Carolina until, or apply to cases while pending in such district before, such district elects to be included in a bankruptcy region established in section 581(a) of Title 28, as amended by section 111(a) of Pub.L. 99–554, or Oct. 1, 2002, whichever occurs first, and except as otherwise provided, with respect to cases under chapters 7, 11, 12, and 13 of Title 11 commenced before 30 days after Oct. 27, 1986, and pending in a judicial district in the States of Alabama or North Carolina before any election made under section 302(d)(3)(A) of Pub.L. 99–554 by such district becomes effective or Oct. 1, 2002, whichever occurs first, amendments by Pub.L. 99–554 not to apply until Oct. 1, 2003, or the expiration of the 1-year period beginning on the date such election becomes effective, whichever occurs first, and further, in any judicial district in Alabama or North Carolina not making the election described in section 302(d)(3)(A) of Pub.L. 99–554, any person appointed under regulations issued by the Judicial Conference to administer estates in cases under Title 11 authorized to establish, etc., a panel of private trustees, and to supervise cases and trustees in cases under chapters 7, 11, 12, and 13 of Title 11, until amendments by sections 201 to 231 of Pub.L. 99–554 effective in such district, see section 302(d)(3)(A) to (F), (H), and (I) of Pub.L. 99–554, set out as a note under section 581 of Title 28.

Amendment by Pub.L. 99–554, § 214, except as otherwise provided, with respect to cases under chapters 7, 11, 12, and 13 of Title 11 commenced before 30 days after Oct. 27, 1986, and pending in a judicial district referred to in section 581(a) of Title 28, as amended by section 111(a) of Pub.L. 99–554, for which a United States trustee is not authorized before 30 days after Oct. 27, 1986, to be appointed, not applicable until the expiration of the 3-year period beginning on Oct. 27, 1986, or of the 1-year period beginning on the date the Attorney

General certifies under section 303 of Pub.L. 99–554 the region specified in a paragraph of such section 581(a) that includes, such district, whichever occurs first, see section 302(e)(1), (2) of Pub.L. 99–554, set out as a note under section 581 of Title 28.

1984 Acts. Amendment by Pub.L. 98–353 effective with respect to cases filed 90 days after July 10, 1984, see section 552(a), formerly 553(a), of Pub.L. 98–353, set out as a note under section 101 of this title.

Separability of Provisions

If any provision of or amendment made by Pub.L. 103–394 or the application of such provision or amendment to any person or circumstance is held to be unconstitutional, the remaining provisions of and amendments made by Pub.L. 103–394 and the application of such provisions and amendments to any person or circumstance shall not be affected thereby, see section 701 of Pub.L. 103–394, set out as a note under section 101 of this title.

CROSS REFERENCES

Adverse interest and conduct of officers of estate, see 18 USCA § 154.

Duty of United States trustee to deposit or invest money, see 28 USCA § 586.

Embezzlement by trustee, see 18 USCA § 153.

LIBRARY REFERENCES

American Digest System

Bankruptcy ☞3039.

Key Number System Topic No. 51.

Corpus Juris Secundum

CJS Bankruptcy § 48, Approval of Bonding of Estate Moneys.

CJS Bankruptcy § 90, Right to Deposit or Invest Money of Estate.

§ 346. Special provisions related to the treatment of State and local taxes

(a) Whenever the Internal Revenue Code of 1986 provides that a separate taxable estate or entity is created in a case concerning a debtor under this title, and the income, gain, loss, deductions, and credits of such estate shall be taxed to or claimed by the estate, a separate taxable estate is also created for purposes of any State and local law imposing a tax on or measured by income and such income, gain, loss, deductions, and credits shall be taxed to or claimed by the estate and may not be taxed to or claimed by the debtor. The preceding sentence shall not apply if the case is dismissed. The trustee shall make tax returns of income required under any such State or local law.

(b) Whenever the Internal Revenue Code of 1986 provides that no separate taxable estate shall be created in a case concerning a debtor under this title, and the income, gain, loss, deductions, and credits of an estate shall be taxed to or claimed by the debtor, such income, gain, loss, deductions, and credits shall be taxed to or claimed by the debtor under a State or local law imposing a tax on or measured by income and may not be taxed to or claimed by the estate. The trustee shall make such tax returns of income of corporations and of partnerships as are required under any State or local law, but with respect to partnerships, shall make such returns only to the extent such returns are also required to be made under such Code. The estate shall be liable for any tax imposed on such corporation or partnership, but not for any tax imposed on partners or members.

(c) With respect to a partnership or any entity treated as a partnership under a State or local law imposing a tax on or measured by income that is a debtor in a case under this title, any gain or loss resulting from a distribution of property from such partnership, or any distributive share of any income, gain, loss, deduction, or credit of a partner or member that is distributed, or considered distributed, from such partnership, after the commencement of the case, is gain, loss, income, deduction, or credit, as the case may be, of the partner or member, and if such partner or member is a debtor in a case under this title, shall be subject to tax in accordance with subsection (a) or (b).

(d) For purposes of any State or local law imposing a tax on or measured by income, the taxable period of a debtor in a case under this title shall terminate only if and to the extent that the taxable period of such debtor terminates under the Internal Revenue Code of 1986.

(e) The estate in any case described in subsection (a) shall use the same accounting method as the debtor used immediately before the commencement of the case, if such method of accounting complies with applicable nonbankruptcy tax law.

(f) For purposes of any State or local law imposing a tax on or measured by income, a transfer of property from the debtor to the estate or from the estate to the debtor shall not be treated as a disposition for purposes of any provision assigning tax consequences to a disposition, except to the extent that such transfer is treated as a disposition under the Internal Revenue Code of 1986.

(g) Whenever a tax is imposed pursuant to a State or local law imposing a tax on or measured by income pursuant to subsection (a) or (b), such tax shall be imposed at rates generally applicable to the same types of entities under such State or local law.

(h) The trustee shall withhold from any payment of claims for wages, salaries, commissions, dividends, interest, or other payments, or collect, any amount required to be withheld or collected under applicable State or local tax law, and shall pay such withheld or collected amount to the appropriate governmental unit at the time and in the manner required by such tax law, and with the same priority as the claim from which such amount was withheld or collected was paid.

(i)(1) To the extent that any State or local law imposing a tax on or measured by income provides for the carryover of any tax attribute from one taxable period to a subsequent taxable period, the estate shall succeed to such tax attribute in any case in which such estate is subject to tax under subsection (a).

(2) After such a case is closed or dismissed, the debtor shall succeed to any tax attribute to which the estate succeeded under paragraph (1) to the extent consistent with the Internal Revenue Code of 1986.

(3) The estate may carry back any loss or tax attribute to a taxable period of the debtor that ended before the date of the order for relief under this title to the extent that—

    (A) applicable State or local tax law provides for a carryback in the case of the debtor; and

    (B) the same or a similar tax attribute may be carried back by the estate to such a taxable period of the debtor under the Internal Revenue Code of 1986.

(j)(1) For purposes of any State or local law imposing a tax on or measured by income, income is not realized by the estate, the debtor, or a successor to the debtor by reason of discharge of indebtedness in a case under this title, except to the extent, if any, that such income is subject to tax under the Internal Revenue Code of 1986.

(2) Whenever the Internal Revenue Code of 1986 provides that the amount excluded from gross income in respect of the discharge of indebtedness in a case under this title shall be applied to reduce the tax attributes of the debtor or the estate, a similar reduction shall be made under any State or local law imposing a tax on or measured by income to the extent such State or local law recognizes such attributes. Such State or local law may also provide for the reduction of other attributes to the extent that the full amount of income from the discharge of indebtedness has not been applied.

(k)(1) Except as provided in this section and section 505, the time and manner of filing tax returns and the items of income, gain, loss, deduction, and credit of any taxpayer shall be determined under applicable nonbankruptcy law.

(2) For Federal tax purposes, the provisions of this section are subject to the Internal Revenue Code of 1986 and other applicable Federal nonbankruptcy law. (Pub.L. 95–598, Nov. 6, 1978, 92 Stat. 2565; Pub.L. 98–353, Title III, § 438, July 10, 1984, 98 Stat. 370; Pub.L. 99–554, Title II, §§ 257(g), 283(c), Oct. 27, 1986, 100 Stat. 3114, 3116; Pub.L. 103–394, Title V, § 501(d)(4), Oct. 22, 1994, 108 Stat. 4143; Pub.L. 109–8, Title VII, § 719(a)(1), Apr. 20, 2005, 119 Stat. 131.)

HISTORICAL AND STATUTORY NOTES
Revision Notes and Legislative Reports

1978 Acts. Subsection (a) indicates that subsections (b), (c), (d), (e), (g), (h), (i), and (j) apply notwithstanding any State or local tax law, but are subject to Federal tax law.

Subsection (b)(1) provides that in a case concerning an individual under chapter 7 or 11 of title 11, income of the estate is taxable only to the estate and not to the debtor. The second sentence of the paragraph provides that if such individual is a partner, the tax attributes of the partnership are distributable to the partner's estate rather than to the partner, except to the extent that section 728 of title 11 provides otherwise.

Subsection (b)(2) states a general rule that the estate of an individual is to be taxed as an estate. The paragraph is made subject to the remainder of section 346 and section 728 of title 11.

Subsection (b)(3) requires the accounting method, but not necessarily the accounting period, of the estate to be the same as the method used by the individual debtor.

Subsection (c)(1) states a general rule that the estate of a partnership or a corporated debtor is not a separate entity for tax purposes. The income of the debtor is to be taxed as if the case were not commenced, except as provided in the remainder of section 346 and section 728.

Subsection (c)(2) requires the trustee, except as provided in section 728 of title 11, to file all tax returns on behalf of the partnership or corporation during the case.

Subsection (d) indicates that the estate in a chapter 13 case is not a separate taxable entity and that all income of the estate is to be taxed to the debtor.

Subsection (e) establishes a business deduction consisting of allowed expenses of administration except for tax or capital expenses that are not otherwise deductible. The deduction may be used by the estate when it is a separate taxable entity or by the entity to which the income of the estate is taxed when it is not.

Subsection (f) imposes a duty on the trustee to comply with any Federal, State, or local tax law requiring withholding or collection of taxes from any payment of wages, salaries, commissions, dividends, interest, or other payments. Any amount withheld is to be paid to the taxing authority at the same time and with the same priority as the claim from which such amount withheld was paid.

Subsection (g)(1)(A) indicates that neither gain nor loss is recognized on the transfer by law of property from the debtor or a creditor to the estate. Subparagraph (B) provides a similar policy if the property of the estate is returned from the estate to the debtor other than by a sale of property to debtor. Subparagraph (C) also provides for nonrecognition of gain or loss in a case under chapter 11 if a corporate debtor transfers property to a successor corporation or to an affiliate under a joint plan. An exception is made to enable a taxing authority to cause recognition of gain or loss to the extent provided in IRC section 371 (as amended by section 109 of this bill) [section 371 of Title 26, Internal Revenue Code].

Subsection (g)(2) provides that any of the three kinds of transferees specified in paragraph (1) take the property with the same character, holding period, and basis in the hands of the transferor at the time of such transfer. The transferor's basis may be adjusted under section 346(j)(5) even if the discharge of indebtedness occurs after the transfer of property. Of course, no adjustment will occur if the transfer is from the debtor to the estate or if the transfer is from an entity that is not discharged.

Subsection (h) provides that the creation of the estate of an individual under chapter 7 or 11 of title 11 as a separate taxable entity does not affect the number of taxable years for purposes of computing loss carryovers or carrybacks. The section applies with respect to carryovers or carrybacks of the debtor transferred into the estate under section 346(i)(1) of title 11 or back to the debtor under section 346(i)(2) of title 11.

Subsection (i)(1) states a general rule that an estate that is a separate taxable entity nevertheless succeeds to all tax attributes of the debtor. The six enumerated attributes are illustrative and not exhaustive.

Subsection (i)(2) indicates that attributes passing from the debtor into an estate that is a separate taxable entity will return to the debtor if unused by the estate. The debtor is permitted to use any such attribute as though the case had not been commenced.

Subsection (i)(3) permits an estate that is a separate taxable entity to carryback losses of the estate to a taxable period of the debtor that ended before the case was filed. The estate is treated as if it were the debtor with respect to time limitations and other restrictions. The section makes clear that the debtor may not carryback any loss of his own from a tax year during the pendency of the case to such a period until the case is closed. No tolling of any period of limitation is provided with respect to carrybacks by the debtor of postpetition losses.

Subsection (j) sets forth seven special rules treating with the tax effects of forgiveness or discharge of indebtedness. The terms "forgiveness" and "discharge" are redundant, but are used to clarify that "discharge" in the context of a special tax provision in title 11 includes forgiveness of indebtedness whether or not such indebtedness is "discharged" in the bankruptcy sense.

Paragraph (1) states the general rule that forgiveness of indebtedness is not taxable except as otherwise provided in paragraphs (2)–(7). The paragraph is patterned after sections 268, 395, and 520 of the Bankruptcy Act [sections 668, 795 and 920 of former Title 11].

Paragraph (2) disallows deductions for liabilities of a deductible nature in any year during or after the year of cancellation of such liabilities. For the purposes of this paragraph, "a deduction with respect to a liability" includes a capital loss incurred on the disposition of a capital asset with respect to a liability that was incurred in connection with the acquisition of such asset.

Paragraph (3) causes any net operating loss of a debtor that is an individual or corporation to be reduced by any discharge of indebtedness except as provided in paragraphs (2) or (4). If a deduction is disallowed under paragraph (2), then no double counting occurs. Thus, paragraph (3) will reflect the reduction of losses by liabilities that have been forgiven, including deductible liabilities or nondeductible liabilities such as repayment of principal on borrowed funds.

Paragraph (4) specifically excludes two kinds of indebtedness from reduction of net operating losses under paragraph (3) or from reduction of basis under paragraph (5). Subparagraph (A) excludes items of a deductible nature that were not deducted or that could not be deducted such as gambling losses or liabilities for interest owed to a relative of the debtor. Subparagraph (B) excludes indebtedness of a debtor that is an individual or corporation that resulted in deductions which did not offset income and that did not contribute to an unexpired net operating loss or loss carryover. In these situations, the debtor has derived no tax benefit so there is no need to incur an offsetting reduction.

Paragraph (5) provides a two-point test for reduction of basis. The paragraph replaces sections 270, 396, and 522 of the Bankruptcy Act [sections 670, 796, and 922 of former Title 11]. Subparagraph (A) sets out the maximum amount by which basis may be reduced—the total indebtedness forgiven less adjustments made under paragraphs (2) and (3). This avoids double counting. If a deduction is disallowed under paragraph (2) or a carryover is reduced under paragraph (3) then the tax benefit is neutralized, and there is no need to reduce basis. Subparagraph (B) reduces basis to the extent the debtor's total basis of assets before the discharge exceeds total preexisting liabilities still remaining after discharge of indebtedness. This is a "basis solvency" limitation which differs from the usual test of solvency because it measures against the remaining liabilities the benefit aspect of assets, their basis, rather than their value. Paragraph (5) applies so that any transferee of the debtor's property who is required to use the debtor's basis takes the debtor's basis reduced by the lesser of (A) and (B). Thus, basis will be reduced, but never below a level equal to undischarged liabilities.

Paragraph (6) specifies that basis need not be reduced under paragraph (5) to the extent the debtor treats discharged indebtedness as taxable income. This permits the debtor to elect whether to recognize income, which may be advantageous if the debtor anticipates subsequent net operating losses, rather than to reduce basis.

Paragraph (7) establishes two rules excluding from the category of discharged indebtedness certain indebtedness that is exchanged for an equity security issued under a plan or that is forgiven as a contribution to capital by an equity security holder. Subparagraph (A) creates the first exclusion to the extent indebtedness consisting of items not of a deductible nature is exchanged for an equity security, other than the interests of a limited partner in a limited partnership, issued by the debtor or is forgiven as a contribution to capital by an equity security holder. Subparagraph (B) excludes indebtedness consisting of items of a deductible nature, if the exchange of stock for debts has the same effect as a cash payment equal to the value of the equity security, in the amount of the fair market value of the equity security or, if less, the extent to which such exchange has such effect. The two provisions treat the debtor as if it had originally issued stock instead of debt. Subparagraph (B) rectifies the inequity under current law between a cash basis and accrual basis debtor concerning the issuance of stock in exchange for previous services rendered that were of a greater value than the stock. Subparagraph (B) also changes current law by taxing forgiveness of indebtedness to the extent that stock is exchanged for the accrued interest component of a security, because the recipient of such stock would not be regarded as having received money under the *Carman* doctrine. Senate Report No. 95–989.

1984 Acts. Statements by Legislative Leaders, see 1984 U.S.Code Cong. and Adm.News, p. 576.

1986 Acts. House Report No. 99–764 and House Conference Report No. 99–958, see 1986 U.S.Code Cong. and Adm. News, p. 5227.

1994 Acts. House Report No. 103–835, see 1994 U.S. Code Cong. and Adm. News, p. 3340.

2005 Acts. House Report No. 109–31(Part I), see 2005 U.S. Code Cong. and Adm. News, p. 88.

Legislative Statements

Section 346 of the House amendment, together with sections 728 and 1146, represent special tax provisions applicable in bankruptcy. The policy contained in those sections reflects the policy that should he applied in Federal, State, and local taxes in the view of the House Committee on the Judiciary. The House Ways and Means Committee and the Senate Finance Committee did not have time to process a bankruptcy tax bill during the 95th Congress. It is anticipated that early in the 96th Congress, and before the effective date of the bankruptcy code [Oct. 1, 1979], the tax committees of Congress will have an opportunity to consider action with respect to amendments to the Internal Revenue Code [Title 26] and the special tax provisions in title 11. Since the special tax provisions are likely to be amended during the first part of the 96th Congress, it is anticipated that the bench and bar will also study and comment on these special tax provisions prior to their revision.

Special tax provisions: State and local rules. This section provides special tax provisions dealing with the treatment, under State or local, but not Federal, tax law, of the method of taxing bankruptcy estates of individuals, partnerships, and corporations; survival and allocation of tax attributes between the bankrupt and the estate; return filing requirements; and the tax treatment of income from discharge of indebtedness. The Senate bill removed these rules pending adoption of Federal rules on these issues in the next Congress. The House amendment returns the State and local tax rules to section 346 so that they may be studied by the bankruptcy and tax bars who may wish to submit comments to Congress.

Withholding rules: Both the House bill and Senate amendment provide that the trustee is required to comply with the normal withholding rules applicable to the payment of wages and other payments. The House amendment retains this rule for State and local taxes only. The treatment of withholding of Federal taxes will be considered in the next Congress.

Section 726 of the Senate amendment provides that the rule requiring pro rata payment of all expenses within a priority category does not apply to the payment of amounts withheld by a bankruptcy trustee. The purpose of this rule was to insure that the trustee pay the full amount of the withheld taxes to the appropriate governmental tax authority. The House amendment deletes this rule as unnecessary because the existing practice conforms essentially to that rule. If the trustee fails to pay over in full amounts that he withheld, it is a violation of his trustee's duties which would permit the taxing authority to sue the trustee on his bond.

When taxes considered "incurred": The Senate amendment contained rules of general application dealing with when a tax is "incurred" for purposes of the various tax collection rules affecting the debtor and the estate. The House amendment adopts the substance of these rules and transfers them to section 507 of title 11.

Penalty for failure to pay tax: The Senate amendment contains a rule which relieves the debtor and the trustee from certain tax penalties for failure to make timely payment of a tax to the extent that the bankruptcy rules prevent the trustee or the debtor from paying the tax on time. Since most of these penalties relate to Federal taxes, the House amendment deletes these rules pending consideration of Federal tax rules affecting bankruptcy in the next Congress.

References in Text

The Internal Revenue Code of 1986, referred to in text, is classified to Title 26 of the Code.

Amendments

2005 Amendments. Section. Pub.L. 109–8, § 719(a)(1), rewrote this section, which formerly read:

"§ 346. Special tax provisions

"(a) Except to the extent otherwise provided in this section, subsections (b), (c), (d), (e), (g), (h), (i), and (j) of this section apply notwithstanding any State or local law imposing a tax, but subject to the Internal Revenue Code of 1986.

"(b)(1) In a case under chapter 7, 12, or 11 of this title concerning an individual, any income of the estate may be taxed under a State or local law imposing a tax on or measured by income only to the estate, and may not be taxed to such individual. Except as provided in section 728 of this title, if such individual is a partner in a partnership, any gain or loss resulting from a distribution of property from such partnership, or any distributive share of income, gain, loss, deduction, or credit of such individual that is distributed, or considered distributed, from such partnership, after the commencement of the case is gain, loss, income, deduction, or credit, as the case may be, of the estate.

"(2) Except as otherwise provided in this section and in section 728 of this title, any income of the estate in such a case, and any State or local tax on or measured by such income, shall be computed in the same manner as the income and the tax of an estate.

"(3) The estate in such a case shall use the same accounting method as the debtor used immediately before the commencement of the case.

"(c)(1) The commencement of a case under this title concerning a corporation or a partnership does not effect a change in the status of such corporation or partnership for the purposes of any State or local law imposing a tax on or measured by income. Except as otherwise provided in this section and in section 728 of this title, any income of the estate in such case may be taxed only as though such case had not been commenced.

"(2) In such a case, except as provided in section 728 of this title, the trustee shall make any tax return otherwise required by State or local law to be filed by or on behalf of such corporation or partnership in the same manner and form as such corporation or partnership, as the case may be, is required to make such return.

"(d) In a case under chapter 13 of this title, any income of the estate or the debtor may be taxed under a State or local law imposing a tax on or measured by income only to the debtor, and may not be taxed to the estate.

"(e) A claim allowed under section 502(f) or 503 of this title, other than a claim for a tax that is not otherwise deductible or a capital expenditure that is not otherwise deductible, is deductible by the entity to which income of the estate is taxed unless such claim was deducted by another entity, and a deduction for such a claim is deemed to be a deduction attributable to a business.

"(f) The trustee shall withhold from any payment of claims for wages, salaries, commissions, dividends, interest, or other payments, or collect, any amount required to be withheld or collected under applicable State or local tax law, and shall pay such withheld or collected amount to the appropriate governmental unit at the time and in the manner required by such tax law, and with the same priority as the claim from which such amount was withheld was paid.

"(g)(1) Neither gain nor loss shall be recognized on a transfer—

"(A) by operation of law, of property to the estate;

"(B) other than a sale, of property from the estate to the debtor; or

"(C) in a case under chapter 11 or 12 of this title concerning a corporation, of property from the estate to a corporation that is an affiliate participating in a joint plan with the debtor, or that is a successor to the debtor under the plan, except that gain or loss may be recognized to the same extent that such transfer results in the recognition of gain or loss under section 371 of the Internal Revenue Code of 1986.

"(2) The transferee of a transfer of a kind specified in this subsection shall take the property transferred with the same character, and with the transferor's basis, as adjusted under subsection (j)(5) of this section, and holding period.

"(h) Notwithstanding sections 728(a) and 1146(a) of this title, for the purpose of determining the number of taxable periods during which the debtor or the estate may use a loss carryover or a loss carryback, the taxable period of the debtor during which the case is commenced is deemed not to have been terminated by such commencement.

"(i)(1) In a case under chapter 7, 12, or 11 of this title concerning an individual, the estate shall succeed to the debtor's tax attributes, including—

"(A) any investment credit carryover;

"(B) any recovery exclusion;

"(C) any loss carryover;

"(D) any foreign tax credit carryover;

"(E) any capital loss carryover; and

"(F) any claim of right.

"(2) After such a case is closed or dismissed, the debtor shall succeed to any tax attribute to which the estate succeeded under paragraph (1) of this subsection but that was not utilized by the estate. The debtor may utilize such tax attributes as though any applicable time limitations on such utilization by the debtor were suspended during the time during which the case was pending.

"(3) In such a case, the estate may carry back any loss of the estate to a taxable period of the debtor that ended before the order for relief under such chapter the same as the debtor could have carried back such loss had the debtor incurred such loss and the case under this title had not been commenced, but the debtor may not carry back any loss of the debtor from a taxable period that ends after such order to any taxable period of the debtor that ended before such order until after the case is closed.

"(j)(1) Except as otherwise provided in this subsection, income is not realized by the estate, the debtor, or a successor to the debtor by reason of forgiveness or discharge of indebtedness in a case under this title.

"(2) For the purposes of any State or local law imposing a tax on or measured by income, a deduction with respect to a liability may not be allowed for any taxable period during or after which such liability is forgiven or discharged under this title. In this paragraph, 'a deduction with respect to a liability' includes a capital loss incurred on the disposition of a capital asset with respect to a liability that was incurred in connection with the acquisition of such asset.

"(3) Except as provided in paragraph (4) of this subsection, for the purpose of any State or local law imposing a tax on or measured by income, any net operating loss of an individual or corporate debtor, including a net operating loss carryover to such debtor, shall be reduced by the amount of indebtedness forgiven or discharged in a case under this title, except to the extent that such forgiveness or discharge resulted in a disallowance under paragraph (2) of this subsection.

"(4) A reduction of a net operating loss or a net operating loss carryover under paragraph (3) of this subsection or of basis under paragraph (5) of this subsection is not required to the extent that the indebtedness of an individual or corporate debtor forgiven or discharged—

"(A) consisted of items of a deductible nature that were not deducted by such debtor; or

"(B) resulted in an expired net operating loss carryover or other deduction that—

"(i) did not offset income for any taxable period; and

"(ii) did not contribute to a net operating loss in or a net operating loss carryover to the taxable period during or after which such indebtedness was discharged.

"(5) For the purposes of a State or local law imposing a tax on or measured by income, the basis of the debtor's property or of property transferred to an entity required to use the debtor's basis in whole or in part shall be reduced by the lesser of—

"(A)(i) the amount by which the indebtedness of the debtor has been forgiven or discharged in a case under this title; minus

"(ii) the total amount of adjustments made under paragraphs (2) and (3) of this subsection; and

"(B) the amount by which the total basis of the debtor's assets that were property of the estate before such forgiveness or discharge exceeds the debtor's total liabilities that were liabilities both before and after such forgiveness or discharge.

"(6) Notwithstanding paragraph (5) of this subsection, basis is not required to be reduced to the extent that the debtor elects to treat as taxable income, of the taxable period in which indebtedness is forgiven or discharged, the amount of indebtedness forgiven or discharged that otherwise would be applied in reduction of basis under paragraph (5) of this subsection.

"(7) For the purposes of this subsection, indebtedness with respect to which an equity security, other than an interest of a limited partner in a limited partnership, is issued to the creditor to whom such indebtedness was owed, or that is forgiven as a contribution to capital by an equity security holder other than a limited partner in the debtor, is not forgiven or discharged in a case under this title—

"(A) to any extent that such indebtedness did not consist of items of a deductible nature; or

"(B) if the issuance of such equity security has the same consequences under a law imposing a tax on or measured by income to such creditor as a payment in cash to such creditor in an amount equal to the fair market value of such equity security, then to the lesser of—

"(i) the extent that such issuance has the same such consequences; and

"(ii) the extent of such fair market value."

1994 Amendments. Subsec. (a). Pub.L. 103–394, § 501(d)(4)(A), substituted "Internal Revenue Code of 1986" for "Internal Revenue Code of 1954 (26 U.S.C. 1 et seq.)".

Subsec. (g)(1)(C). Pub.L. 103–394, § 501(d)(4)(B), substituted "Internal Revenue Code of 1986" for "Internal Revenue Code of 1954 (26 U.S.C. 371)".

1986 Amendments. Subsec. (a). Pub.L. 99–514, § 2, substituted "Internal Revenue Code of 1986" for "Internal Revenue Code of 1954".

Subsec. (b)(1). Pub.L. 99–554, § 257(g)(1), added reference to chapter 12.

Subsec. (g)(1)(C). Pub.L. 99–554, § 257(g)(2), added reference to chapter 12.

Pub.L. 99–514, § 2, substituted "Internal Revenue Code of 1986" for "Internal Revenue Code of 1954".

Subsec. (i)(1). Pub.L. 99–554, § 257(g)(3), added reference to chapter 12.

Subsec. (j)(7). Pub.L. 99–554, § 283(c), substituted "owed" for "owned".

1984 Amendments. Subsec. (c)(2). Pub.L. 98–353 substituted "corporation" for "operation".

Effective and Applicability Provisions

2005 Acts. Amendments by Pub.L. 109–8 effective, except as otherwise provided, 180 days after April 20, 2005, and inapplicable with respect to cases commenced under Title 11 before the effective date, see Pub.L. 109–8, § 1501, set out as a note under 11 U.S.C.A. § 101.

1994 Acts. Amendment by of Pub.L. 103–394 effective on Oct. 22, 1994, and not to apply with respect to cases commenced under Title 11 of the United States Code before Oct. 22, 1994, see section 702 of Pub.L. 103–394, set out as a note under section 101 of this title.

1986 Acts. Amendment by Pub.L. 99–554, § 257(g), effective 30 days after Oct. 27, 1986, but not applicable with respect to cases commenced under this title before that date, see section 302(a), (c)(1) of Pub.L. 99–554, set out as a note under section 581 of Title 28, Judiciary and Judicial Procedure.

Amendment by Pub.L. 99–554, § 283(c), effective 30 days after Oct. 27, 1986, see section 302(a) of Pub.L. 99–554, set out as a note under section 581 of Title 28.

1984 Acts. Amendment by Pub.L. 98–353 effective with respect to cases filed 90 days after July 10, 1984, see section 552(a), formerly 553(a), of Pub.L. 98–353, set out as a note under section 101 of this title.

Separability of Provisions

If any provision of or amendment made by Pub.L. 103–394 or the application of such provision or amendment to any person or circumstance is held to be unconstitutional, the remaining provisions of and amendments made by Pub.L. 103–394 and the application of such provisions and amendments to any person or circumstance shall not be affected thereby, see section 701 of Pub.L. 103–394, set out as a note under section 101 of this title.

CROSS REFERENCES

Request for determination of tax effects of—

Chapter 12 plan, see 11 USCA § 1231.

Reorganization plan, see 11 USCA § 1146.

American Digest System

Internal Revenue ☞4006.

American Digest System

Taxation ☞1021.1.

Key Number System Topic Nos. 220, 371.

Corpus Juris Secundum

CJS Bankruptcy § 278, Parties Defendant; Sovereign Immunity.

CJS Internal Revenue § 6, Construction and Operation of Revenue Laws.

§ 347. Unclaimed property

(a) Ninety days after the final distribution under section 726, 1226, or 1326 of this title in a case under chapter 7, 12, or 13 of this title, as the case may be, the trustee shall stop payment on any check remaining unpaid, and any remaining property of the estate shall be paid into the court and disposed of under chapter 129 of title 28.

(b) Any security, money, or other property remaining unclaimed at the expiration of the time allowed in a case under chapter 9, 11, or 12 of this title for the presentation of a security or the performance of any other act as a condition to participation in the distribution under any plan confirmed under section 943(b), 1129, 1173, or 1225 of this title, as the case may be, becomes the property of the debtor or of the entity acquiring the assets of the debtor under the plan, as the case may be.

(Pub.L. 95–598, Nov. 6, 1978, 92 Stat. 2568; Pub.L. 99–554, Title II, § 257(h), Oct. 27, 1986, 100 Stat. 3114.)

HISTORICAL AND STATUTORY NOTES

Revision Notes and Legislative Reports

1978 Acts. Section 347 is derived from Bankruptcy Act § 66 [section 106 of former Title 11]. Subsection (a) requires the trustee to stop payment on any distribution check that is unpaid 90 days after the final distribution in a case under chapter 7 or 13. The unclaimed funds, and any other property of the estate are paid into the court and disposed of under chapter 129 of title 28 [section 2041 et seq. of Title 28, Judiciary and Judicial Procedure], which requires the clerk of court to hold the funds for their owner for 5 years, after which they escheat to the Treasury.

Subsection (b) specifies that any property remaining unclaimed at the expiration of the time allowed in a chapter 9 or 11 case for presentation (exchange) of securities or the performance of any other act as a condition to participation in the plan reverts to the debtor or the entity acquiring the assets of the debtor under the plan. Conditions to participation under a plan include such acts as cashing a check, surrendering securities for cancellation, and so on. Similar provisions are found in sections 96(d) and 205 [sections 416(d) and 605 of former Title 11] of current law. Senate Report No. 95–989.

1986 Acts. House Report No. 99–764 and House Conference Report No. 99–958, see 1986 U.S.Code Cong. and Adm. News, p. 5227.

Legislative Statements

Section 347(a) of the House amendment adopts a comparable provision contained in the Senate amendment instructing the trustee to stop payment on any check remaining unpaid more than 90 days after the final distribution in a case under Chapter 7 or 13. Technical changes are made in section 347(b) to cover distributions in a railroad reorganization.

Amendments

1986 Amendments. Subsec. (a). Pub.L. 99–554, § 257(h)(1), added references to section 1226 and chapter 12 of this title.

Subsec. (b). Pub.L. 99–554, § 257(h)(2), added references to chapter 12 and section 1225 of this title.

Effective and Applicability Provisions

1986 Acts. Amendment by Pub.L. 99–554, § 257(h), effective 30 days after Oct. 27, 1986, but not applicable with respect to cases commenced under this title before that date, see section 302(a), (c)(1) of Pub.L. 99–554, set out as a note under section 581 of Title 28, Judiciary and Judicial Procedure.

CROSS REFERENCES

Applicability of subsec. (b) of this section in Chapter 9 cases, see 11 USCA § 901.

Applicability of this section in Chapter 9 cases, see 11 USCA § 901.

"Creditor" defined, see 11 USCA § 101.

American Digest System

Bankruptcy ☞3445, 3652, 3570, 3481, 3683.1, 3715(9.1), 3009.

Key Number System Topic No. 51.

Corpus Juris Secundum

CJS Bankruptcy § 1099, Unclaimed Property.

CJS Bankruptcy § 1162, Implementation of the Plan; Distribution.

CJS Bankruptcy § 1168, Reorganization Plan.

§ 348. Effect of conversion

(a) Conversion of a case from a case under one chapter of this title to a case under another chapter of this title constitutes an order for relief under the chapter to which the case is converted, but, except as provided in subsections (b) and (c) of this section, does not effect a change in the date of the filing of the petition, the commencement of the case, or the order for relief.

(b) Unless the court for cause orders otherwise, in sections 701(a), 727(a)(10), 727(b), 1102(a), 1110(a)(1), 1121(b), 1121(c), 1141(d)(4), 1201(a), 1221, 1228(a), 1301(a), and 1305(a) of this title, "the order for relief under this chapter" in a chapter to which a case has been converted under section 706, 1112, 1208, or 1307 of this title means the conversion of such case to such chapter.

(c) Sections 342 and 365(d) of this title apply in a case that has been converted under section 706, 1112, 1208, or 1307 of this title, as if the conversion order were the order for relief.

(d) A claim against the estate or the debtor that arises after the order for relief but before conversion in a case that is converted under section 1112, 1208, or 1307 of this title, other than a claim specified in section 503(b) of this title, shall be treated for all purposes as if such claim had arisen immediately before the date of the filing of the petition.

(e) Conversion of a case under section 706, 1112, 1208, or 1307 of this title terminates the service of any trustee or examiner that is serving in the case before such conversion.

(f)(1) Except as provided in paragraph (2), when a case under chapter 13 of this title is converted to a case under another chapter under this title—

(A) property of the estate in the converted case shall consist of property of the estate, as of the date of filing of the petition, that remains in the possession of or is under the control of the debtor on the date of conversion;

(B) valuations of property and of allowed secured claims in the chapter 13 case shall apply only in a case converted to a case under chapter 11 or 12, but not in a case converted to a case under chapter 7, with allowed secured claims in cases under chapters 11 and 12 reduced to the extent that they have been paid in accordance with the chapter 13 plan; and

(C) with respect to cases converted from chapter 13—

(i) the claim of any creditor holding security as of the date of the filing of the petition shall continue to be secured by that security unless the full amount of such claim determined under applicable nonbankruptcy law has been paid in full as of the date of conversion, notwithstanding any valuation or determination of the amount of an allowed secured claim made for the purposes of the case under chapter 13; and

(ii) unless a prebankruptcy default has been fully cured under the plan at the time of conversion, in any proceeding under this title or otherwise, the default shall have the effect given under applicable nonbankruptcy law.

(2) If the debtor converts a case under chapter 13 of this title to a case under another chapter under this title in bad faith, the property of the estate in the converted case shall consist of the property of the estate as of the date of conversion.

(Pub.L. 95–598, Nov. 6, 1978, 92 Stat. 2568; Pub.L. 99–554, Title II, § 257(i), Oct. 27, 1986, 100 Stat. 3115; Pub.L. 103–394, Title III, § 311, Title V, § 501(d)(5), Oct. 22, 1994, 108 Stat. 4138, 4144; Pub.L. 109–8, Title III, § 309(a), Title XII, § 1207, Apr. 20, 2005, 119 Stat. 82, 194; Pub.L. 111–327, § 2(a)(11), Dec. 22, 2010, 124 Stat. 3558.)

HISTORICAL AND STATUTORY NOTES

Revision Notes and Legislative Reports

1978 Acts. This section governs the effect of the conversion of a case from one chapter of the bankruptcy code to another chapter. Subsection (a) specifies that the date of the filing of the petition, the commencement of the case, or the order for relief are unaffected by conversion, with some exceptions specified in subsections (b) and (c).

Subsection (b) lists certain sections in the operative chapters of the bankruptcy code in which there is a reference to "the order for relief under this chapter." In those sections, the reference is to be read as a reference to the conversion order if the case has been converted into the particular chapter. Subsection (c) specifies that notice is to be given of the conversion order the same as notice was given of the order for relief, and that the time the trustee (or debtor in possession) has for assuming or rejecting executory contracts recommences, thus giving an opportunity for a newly appointed trustee to familiarize himself with the case.

Subsection (d) provides for special treatment of claims that arise during chapter 11 or 13 cases before the case is converted to a liquidation case. With the exception of claims specified in proposed 11 U.S.C. 503(b) (administrative expenses), preconversion claims are treated the same as prepetition claims.

Subsection (e) provides that conversion of a case terminates the service of any trustee serving in the case prior to conversion. Senate Report No. 95–989.

1986 Acts. House Report No. 99–764 and House Conference Report No. 99–958, see 1986 U.S.Code Cong. and Adm. News, p. 5227.

1994 Acts. House Report No. 103–835, see 1994 U.S. Code Cong. and Adm. News, p. 3340.

2005 Acts. House Report No. 109–31(Part I), see 2005 U.S. Code Cong. and Adm. News, p. 88.

Legislative Statements

The House amendment adopts section 348(b) of the Senate amendment with slight modifications, as more accurately reflecting sections to which this particular effect of conversion should apply.

Section 348(e) of the House amendment is a stylistic revision of similar provisions contained in H.R. 8200 as passed by the House and in the Senate amendment. Termination of services is expanded to cover any examiner serving in the case before conversion, as done in H.R. 8200 as passed by the House.

References in Text

Chapter 7, 11, 12, or 13, referred to in subsec. (f)(1), is chapter 7, 11, 12, or 13 of this title, 11 U.S.C.A. § 701 et seq., 11 U.S.C.A. § 1101 et seq., 11 U.S.C.A. § 1201 et seq., or 11 U.S.C.A. § 1301 et seq., respectively.

Amendments

2010 Amendments. Subsec. (b). Pub.L. 111–327, § 2(a)(11)(A), struck out "728(a), 728(b)," following "727(b),", and struck out "1146(a), 1146(b),"following "1141(d)(4),".

Subsec. (f)(1)(C)(i). Pub.L. 111–327, § 2(a)(11)(B), inserted "of the filing" following "security as of the date".

2005 Amendments. Subsec. (f)(1)(A). Pub.L. 109–8, § 309(a)(1), struck out "and" at the end of subpar. (A).

Subsec. (f)(1)(B). Pub.L. 109–8, § 309(a)(2)(A), struck out "in the converted case, with allowed secured claims" and inserted "only in a case converted to a case under chapter 11 or 12, but not in a case converted to a case under chapter 7, with allowed secured claims in cases under chapters 11 and 12".

Pub.L. 109–8, § 309(a)(2)(B), struck out the period and inserted "; and" at the end of subpar. (B).

Subsec. (f)(1)(C). Pub.L. 109–8, § 309(a)(3), added subpar. (C).

Subsec. (f)(2). Pub.L. 109–8, § 1207, inserted "of the estate" after "bad faith, the property".

1994 Amendments. Subsec. (b). Pub.L. 103–394, § 501(d)(5), substituted "1201(a), 1221, 1228(a), 1301(a), and 1305(a)" for "1301(a), 1305(a), 1201(a), 1221, and 1228(a)", and substituted "1208, or 1307" for "1307, or 1208".

Subsec. (c). Pub.L. 103–394, § 501(d)(5)(B), substituted "1208, or 1307" for "1307, or 1208".

Subsec. (d). Pub.L. 103–394, § 501(d)(5)(B), substituted "1208, or 1307" for "1307, or 1208".

Subsec. (e). Pub.L. 103–394, § 501(d)(5)(B), substituted "1208, or 1307" for "1307, or 1208".

Subsec. (f). Pub.L. 103–394, § 311, added subsec. (f).

1986 Amendments. Subsec. (b). Pub.L. 99–554, § 257(i)(1), substituted references to sections 1201(a), 1221, and 1228(a) of this title for reference to section 1328(a) of this title, and added reference to section 1208 of this title.

Subsec. (c). Pub.L. 99–554, § 257(i)(2), added reference to section 1208 of this title.

Subsec. (d). Pub.L. 99–554, § 257(i)(3), added reference to section 1208 of this title.

Subsec. (e). Pub.L. 99–554, § 257(i)(2), added reference to section 1208 of this title.

Effective and Applicability Provisions

2005 Acts. Amendments by Pub.L. 109–8 effective, except as otherwise provided, 180 days after April 20, 2005, and inapplicable with respect to cases commenced under Title 11 before the effective date, see Pub.L. 109–8, § 1501, set out as a note under 11 U.S.C.A. § 101.

1994 Acts. Amendments by Pub.L. 103–394 effective on Oct. 22, 1994, and not to apply with respect to cases commenced under Title 11 of the United States Code before Oct. 22, 1994, see section 702 of Pub.L. 103–394, set out as a note under section 101 of this title.

1986 Acts. Amendment by Pub.L. 99–554, effective 30 days after Oct. 27, 1986, but not applicable with respect to cases commenced under this title before that date see section 302(a), (c)(1) of Pub.L. 99–554, set out as a note under section 581 of Title 28, Judiciary and Judicial Procedure.

Separability of Provisions

If any provision of or amendment made by Pub.L. 103–394 or the application of such provision or amendment to any person or circumstance is held to be unconstitutional, the remaining provisions of and amendments made by Pub.L. 103–394 and the application of such provisions and amendments to any person or circumstance shall not be affected thereby, see section 701 of Pub.L. 103–394, set out as a note under section 101 of this title.

LIBRARY REFERENCES

American Digest System

Bankruptcy ⬀3673, 3717, 3594, 2332, 2331.

Key Number System Topic No. 51.

Corpus Juris Secundum

CJS Bankruptcy § 109, Termination of Service.

CJS Bankruptcy § 472, Effect of Bad-Faith Conversion on Estate Property.

CJS Bankruptcy § 563, Conversion as Affecting What Property is Included in Estate.

CJS Bankruptcy § 662, Effect of Prepetition or Postpetition Nature of Debts.

CJS Bankruptcy § 836, Chapter 7 Cases.

CJS Bankruptcy § 839, Involuntary Cases.

CJS Bankruptcy § 840, Operation of Debtor's Business.

CJS Bankruptcy § 926, Time for Exercise of Right.

CJS Bankruptcy § 927, Exercising Right in Chapter 7 Cases.

CJS Bankruptcy § 959, Effect of Time of Accrual.

CJS Bankruptcy § 976, Effect of Conversion.

CJS Bankruptcy § 1129, Appointment of Creditors" and Equity Security Holders" Committees.

§ 349. Effect of dismissal

(a) Unless the court, for cause, orders otherwise, the dismissal of a case under this title does not bar the discharge, in a later case under this title, of debts that were dischargeable in the case dismissed; nor does the dismissal of a case under this title prejudice the debtor with regard to the filing of a subsequent petition under this title, except as provided in section 109(g) of this title.

(b) Unless the court, for cause, orders otherwise, a dismissal of a case other than under section 742 of this title—

(1) reinstates—

(A) any proceeding or custodianship superseded under section 543 of this title;

(B) any transfer avoided under section 522, 544, 545, 547, 548, 549, or 724(a) of this title, or preserved under section 510(c)(2), 522(i)(2), or 551 of this title; and

(C) any lien voided under section 506(d) of this title;

(2) vacates any order, judgment, or transfer ordered, under section 522(i)(1), 542, 550, or 553 of this title; and

(3) revests the property of the estate in the entity in which such property was vested immediately before the commencement of the case under this title.

(Pub.L. 95–598, Nov. 6, 1978, 92 Stat. 2569; Pub.L. 98–353, Title III, § 303, July 10, 1984, 98 Stat. 352; Pub.L. 103–394, Title V, § 501(d)(6), Oct. 22, 1994, 108 Stat. 4144.)

HISTORICAL AND STATUTORY NOTES

Revision Notes and Legislative Reports

1978 Acts. Subsection (a) specifies that unless the court for cause orders otherwise, the dismissal of a case is without prejudice. The debtor is not barred from receiving a discharge in a later case of debts that were dischargeable in the case dismissed. Of course, this subsection refers only to pre-discharge dismissals. If the debtor has already received a discharge and it is not revoked, then the debtor would be barred under section 727(a) from receiving a discharge in a subsequent liquidation case for six years. Dismissal of an involuntary [sic] on the merits will generally not give rise to adequate cause so as to bar the debtor from further relief.

Subsection (b) specifies that the dismissal reinstates proceedings or custodianships that were superseded by the bankruptcy case, reinstates avoided transfers, reinstates voided liens, vacates any order, judgment, or transfer ordered as a result of the avoidance of a transfer, and revests the property of the estate in the entity in which the property was vested at the commencement of the case. The court is permitted to order a different result for cause. The basic purpose of the subsection is to undo the bankruptcy case, as far as practicable, and to restore all property rights to the position in which they were found at the commencement of the case. This does not necessarily encompass undoing sales of property from the estate to a good faith purchaser. Where there is a question over the scope of the subsection, the court will make the appropriate orders to protect rights acquired in reliance on the bankruptcy case. Senate Report No. 95–989.

1984 Acts. Statements by Legislative Leaders, see 1984 U.S.Code Cong. and Adm.News, p. 576.

1994 Acts. House Report No. 103–835, see 1994 U.S. Code Cong. and Adm. News, p. 3340.

Legislative Statements

Section 349(b)(2) of the House amendment adds a cross reference to section 553 to reflect the new right of recovery of setoffs created under that section. Corresponding changes are made throughout the House amendment.

Amendments

1994 Amendments. Subsec. (a). Pub.L. 103–394, § 501(d)(6), substituted "109(g)" for "109(f)".

1984 Amendments. Subsec. (a). Pub.L. 98–353 added "; nor does the dismissal of a case under this title prejudice the debtor with regard to the filing of a subsequent petition under this title, except as provided in section 109(f) of this title" before the period.

Effective and Applicability Provisions

1994 Acts. Amendment by Pub.L. 103–394 effective on Oct. 22, 1994, and not to apply with respect to cases commenced under Title 11 of the United States Code before Oct. 22, 1994, see section 702 of Pub.L. 103–394, set out as a note under section 101 of this title.

1984 Acts. Amendment by Pub.L. 98–353 effective with respect to cases filed 90 days after July 10, 1984, see section 552(a), formerly 553(a), of Pub.L. 98–353, set out as a note under section 101 of this title.

Separability of Provisions

If any provision of or amendment made by Pub.L. 103–394 or the application of such provision or amendment to any person or circumstance is held to be unconstitutional, the remaining provisions of and amendments made by Pub.L. 103–394 and the application of such provisions and amendments to any person or circumstance shall not be affected thereby, see section 701 of Pub.L. 103–394, set out as a note under section 101 of this title.

LIBRARY REFERENCES

American Digest System

Bankruptcy ⊕2295, 3594, 3673, 3717.

Key Number System Topic No. 51.

Corpus Juris Secundum

CJS Bankruptcy § 474, Subsequent Case.

CJS Bankruptcy § 836, Chapter 7 Cases.

CJS Bankruptcy § 839, Involuntary Cases.

CJS Bankruptcy § 840, Operation of Debtor's Business.

§ 350. Closing and reopening cases

(a) After an estate is fully administered and the court has discharged the trustee, the court shall close the case.

(b) A case may be reopened in the court in which such case was closed to administer assets, to accord relief to the debtor, or for other cause.

(Pub.L. 95–598, Nov. 6, 1978, 92 Stat. 2569; Pub.L. 98–353, Title III, § 439, July 10, 1984, 98 Stat. 370.)

HISTORICAL AND STATUTORY NOTES

Revision Notes and Legislative Reports

1978 Acts. Subsection (a) requires the court to close a bankruptcy case after the estate is fully administered and the trustee discharged. The Rules of Bankruptcy Procedure will provide the procedure for case closing. Subsection (b) permits reopening of the case to administer assets, to accord relief to the debtor, or for other cause. Though the court may permit reopening of a case so that the trustee may exercise an avoiding power, laches may constitute a bar to an action that has been delayed too long. The case may be reopened in the court in which it was closed. The rules will prescribe the procedure by which a case is reopened and how it will be conducted after reopening. Senate Report No. 95–989.

1984 Acts. Statements by Legislative Leaders, see 1984 U.S.Code Cong. and Adm.News, p. 576.

Amendments

1984 Amendments. Subsec. (b). Pub.L. 98–353 substituted "A" for "a".

Effective and Applicability Provisions

1984 Acts. Amendment by Pub.L. 98–353 effective with respect to cases filed 90 days after July 10, 1984, see section 552(a), formerly 553(a), of Pub.L. 98–353, set out as a note under section 101 of this title.

CROSS REFERENCES

Applicability of subsec. (b) of this section in Chapter 9 cases, see 11 USCA § 901.

Scheduled property deemed abandoned, see 11 USCA § 554.

Successor trustee, see 11 USCA § 703.

§ 351.　Disposal of patient records

If a health care business commences a case under chapter 7, 9, or 11, and the trustee does not have a sufficient amount of funds to pay for the storage of patient records in the manner required under applicable Federal or State law, the following requirements shall apply:

 (1) The trustee shall—

  (A) promptly publish notice, in 1 or more appropriate newspapers, that if patient records are not claimed by the patient or an insurance provider (if applicable law permits the insurance provider to make that claim) by the date that is 365 days after the date of that notification, the trustee will destroy the patient records; and

  (B) during the first 180 days of the 365–day period described in subparagraph (A), promptly attempt to notify directly each patient that is the subject of the patient records and appropriate insurance carrier concerning the patient records by mailing to the most recent known address of that patient, or a family member or contact person for that patient, and to the appropriate insurance carrier an appropriate notice regarding the claiming or disposing of patient records.

 (2) If, after providing the notification under paragraph (1), patient records are not claimed during the 365–day period described under that paragraph, the trustee shall mail, by certified mail, at the end of such 365–day period a written request to each appropriate Federal agency to request permission from that agency to deposit the patient records with that agency, except that no Federal agency is required to accept patient records under this paragraph.

 (3) If, following the 365–day period described in paragraph (2) and after providing the notification under paragraph (1), patient records are not claimed by a patient or insurance provider, or request is not granted by a Federal agency to deposit such records with that agency, the trustee shall destroy those records by—

  (A) if the records are written, shredding or burning the records; or

  (B) if the records are magnetic, optical, or other electronic records, by otherwise destroying those records so that those records cannot be retrieved.

(Added Pub.L. 109–8, Title XI, § 1102(a), Apr. 20, 2005, 119 Stat. 189.)

HISTORICAL AND STATUTORY NOTES

Revision Notes and Legislative Reports

 2005 Acts. House Report No. 109–31(Part I), see 2005 U.S. Code Cong. and Adm. News, p. 88.

References in Text

 Chapter 7, 9, or 11, referred to in the introductory paragraph, means chapter 7, 9, or 11 of this title, 11 U.S.C.A. § 701 et seq., 11 U.S.C.A. § 901 et seq., or 11 U.S.C.A. § 1101 et seq., respectively.

Effective and Applicability Provisions

 2005 Acts. Enactment of this section by Pub.L. 109–8 effective, except as otherwise provided, 180 days after April 20, 2005, and inapplicable with respect to cases commenced under Title 11 before the effective date, see Pub.L. 109–8, § 1501, set out as a note under 11 U.S.C.A. § 101.

SUBCHAPTER IV—ADMINISTRATIVE POWERS

§ 361.　Adequate protection

When adequate protection is required under section 362, 363, or 364 of this title of an interest of an entity in property, such adequate protection may be provided by—

 (1) requiring the trustee to make a cash payment or periodic cash payments to such entity, to the extent that the stay under section 362 of this title, use, sale, or lease under section 363 of this title, or any grant of a lien under section 364 of this title results in a decrease in the value of such entity's interest in such property;

 (2) providing to such entity an additional or replacement lien to the extent that such stay, use, sale, lease, or grant results in a decrease in the value of such entity's interest in such property; or

 (3) granting such other relief, other than entitling such entity to compensation allowable under section 503(b)(1) of this title as an administrative expense, as will result in the realization by such entity of the indubitable equivalent of such entity's interest in such property.

(Pub.L. 95–598, Nov. 6, 1978, 92 Stat. 2569; Pub.L. 98–353, Title III, § 440, July 10, 1984, 98 Stat. 370.)

HISTORICAL AND STATUTORY NOTES

Revision Notes and Legislative Reports

 1978 Acts. Sections 362, 363, and 364 require, in certain circumstances, that the court determine in noticed hearings whether the interest of a secured creditor or co-owner of property with the debtor is adequately protected in connection with the sale or use of property. The interests of which the court may provide protection in the ways described in this section include equitable as well as legal interests. For example, a right to enforce a pledge and a right to recover property delivered to a debtor under a consignment agreement or an agreement of sale or return are interests that may be entitled to protection. This section specifies means by which adequate protection may be provided but, to avoid placing the court in an administrative role, does not require the court to provide it. Instead, the trustee or debtor in possession or the creditor will provide or propose a protection method. If the party that is affected by the proposed action objects, the court will determine whether the protection provided is adequate. The purpose of this section is to illustrate means by which it may be provided and to define the limits of the concept.

The concept of adequate protection is derived from the fifth amendment protection of property interests as enunciated by the Supreme Court. See *Wright v. Union Central Life Ins. Co.*, 311 U.S. 273 (1940) [61 S.Ct. 196, 85 L.Ed. 184, rehearing denied 61 S.Ct. 445, 312 U.S. 711, 85 L.Ed. 1142]; *Louisville Joint Stock Land Bank v. Radford*, 295 U.S. 555 (1935) [55 S.Ct. 854, 79 L.Ed. 1593].

The automatic stay also provides creditor protection. Without it, certain creditors would be able to pursue their own remedies against the debtor's property. Those who acted first would obtain payment of the claims in preference to and to the detriment of other creditors. Bankruptcy is designed to provide an orderly liquidation procedure under which all creditors are treated equally. A race of diligence by creditors for the debtor's assets prevents that.

Subsection (a) defines the scope of the automatic stay, by listing the acts that are stayed by the commencement of the case. The commencement or continuation, including the issuance of process, of a judicial, administrative or other proceeding against the debtor that was or could have been commenced before the commencement of the bankruptcy case is stayed under paragraph (1). The scope of this paragraph is broad. All proceedings are stayed, including arbitration, administrative, and judicial proceedings. Proceeding in this sense encompasses civil actions and all proceedings even if they are not before governmental tribunals.

The stay is not permanent. There is adequate provision for relief from the stay elsewhere in the section. However, it is important that the trustee have an opportunity to inventory the debtor's position before proceeding with the administration of the case. Undoubtedly the court will lift the stay for proceedings before specialized or nongovernmental tribunals to allow those proceedings to come to a conclusion. Any party desiring to enforce an order in such a proceeding would thereafter have to come before the bankruptcy court to collect assets. Nevertheless, it will often be more appropriate to permit proceedings to continue in their place of origin, when no great prejudice to the bankruptcy estate would result, in order to leave the parties to their chosen forum and to relieve the bankruptcy court from many duties that may be handled elsewhere.

Paragraph (2) stays the enforcement, against the debtor or against property of the estate, of a judgment obtained before the commencement of the bankruptcy case. Thus, execution and levy against the debtors' prepetition property are stayed, and attempts to collect a judgment from the debtor personally are stayed.

Paragraph (3) stays any act to obtain possession of property of the estate (that is, property of the debtor as of the date of the filing of the petition) or property from the estate (property over which the estate has control or possession). The purpose of this provision is to prevent dismemberment of the estate. Liquidation must proceed in an orderly fashion. Any distribution of property must be by the trustee after he has had an opportunity to familiarize himself with the various rights and interests involved and with the property available for distribution.

Paragraph (4) stays lien creation against property of the estate. Thus, taking possession to perfect a lien or obtaining court process is prohibited. To permit lien creation after bankruptcy would give certain creditors preferential treatment by making them secured instead of unsecured.

Paragraph (5) stays any act to create or enforce a lien against property of the debtor, that is, most property that is acquired after the date of the filing of the petition, property that is exempted, or property that does not pass to the estate, to the extent that the lien secures a prepetition claim. Again, to permit postbankruptcy lien creation or enforcement would permit certain creditors to receive preferential treatment. It may also circumvent the debtors' discharge.

Paragraph (6) prevents creditors from attempting in any way to collect a prepetition debt. Creditors in consumer cases occasionally telephone debtors to encourage repayment in spite of bankruptcy. Inexperienced, frightened, or ill-counseled debtors may succumb to suggestions to repay notwithstanding their bankruptcy. This provision prevents evasion of the purpose of the bankruptcy laws by sophisticated creditors.

Paragraph (7) stays setoffs of mutual debts and credits between the debtor and creditors. As with all other paragraphs of subsection (a), this paragraph does not affect the right of creditors. It simply stays its enforcement pending an orderly examination of the debtor's and creditors' rights.

Subsection (b) lists seven exceptions to the automatic stay. The effect of an exception is not to make the action immune from injunction.

The court has ample other powers to stay actions not covered by the automatic stay. Section 105, of proposed title 11, derived from Bankruptcy Act, § 2a(15), [section 11(a)(15) of former Title 11], grants the power to issue orders necessary or appropriate to carry out the provisions of title 11. The district court and the bankruptcy court as its adjunct have all the traditional injunctive powers of a court of equity, 28 U.S.C. §§ 151 and 164 as proposed in S. 2266, § 201, and 28 U.S.C. § 1334, as proposed in S. 2266, § 216. Stays or injunctions issued under these other sections will not be automatic upon the commencement of the case, but will be granted or issued under the usual rules for the issuance of injunctions. By excepting an act or action from the automatic stay, the bill simply requires that the trustee move the court into action, rather than requiring the stayed party to request relief from the stay. There are some actions, enumerated in the exceptions, that generally should not be stayed automatically upon the commencement of the case, for reasons of either policy or practicality. Thus, the court will have to determine on a case-by-case basis whether a particular action which may be harming the estate should be stayed.

With respect to stays issued under other powers, or the application of the automatic stay, to governmental actions, this section and the other sections mentioned are intended to be an express waiver of sovereign immunity of the Federal Government, and an assertion of the bankruptcy power over State governments under the supremacy clause notwithstanding a State's sovereign immunity.

The first exception is of criminal proceedings against the debtor. The bankruptcy laws are not a haven for criminal offenders, but are designed to give relief from financial overextension. Thus, criminal actions and proceedings may proceed in spite of bankruptcy.

Paragraph (2) excepts from the stay the collection of alimony, maintenance or support from property that is not property of the estate. This will include property acquired after the commencement of the case, exempted property, and property that does not pass to the estate. The automatic stay is one means of protecting the debtor's discharge. Alimony, maintenance and support obligations are excepted from discharge. Staying collection of them, when not to the detriment of other creditors (because the collection effort is against property that is not property of the estate) does not further that goal. Moreover, it could lead to hardship on the part of the protected spouse or children.

Paragraph (3) excepts any act to perfect an interest in property to the extent that the trustee's rights and powers are limited under section 546(a) of the bankruptcy code. That section permits postpetition perfection of certain liens to be effective against the trustee. If the act of perfection, such as filing, were stayed, the section would be nullified.

Paragraph (4) excepts commencement or continuation of actions and proceedings by governmental units to enforce police or regulatory powers. Thus, where a governmental unit is suing a debtor to prevent or stop violation of fraud, environmental protection, consumer protection, safety, or similar police or regulatory laws, or attempting to fix damages for violation of such a law, the action or proceeding is not stayed under the automatic stay.

Paragraph (5) makes clear that the exception extends to permit an injunction and enforcement of an injunction, and to permit the entry of a money judgment, but does not extend to permit enforcement of a money judgment. Since the assets of the debtor are in the possession and control of the bankruptcy court, and since they constitute a fund out of which all creditors are entitled to share, enforcement by a governmental unit of a money judgment would give it preferential treatment to the detriment of all other creditors.

Paragraph (6) excepts the setoff of any mutual debt and claim for commodity transactions.

Paragraph (7) excepts actions by the Secretary of Housing and Urban Development to foreclose or take possession in a case of a loan insured under the National Housing Act [12 U.S.C.A. § 1701 et seq.]. A general exception for such loans is found in current sections 263 and 517 [sections 663 and 917 of former Title 11], the exception allowed by this paragraph is much more limited.

Subsection (c) of section 362 specifies the duration of the automatic stay. Paragraph (1) terminates a stay of an act against property of the estate when the property ceases to be property of the estate, such as by sale, abandonment, or exemption. It does not terminate the stay against property of the debtor if the property leaves the estate and goes to the debtor. Paragraph (2) terminates the stay of any other act on the earliest of the time the case is closed, the time the case is dismissed, or the time a discharge is granted or denied (unless the debtor is a corporation or partnership in a chapter 7 case).

Subsection (c) governs automatic termination of the stay. Subsections (d) through (g) govern termination of the stay by the court on the request of a party in interest.

Subsection (d) requires the court, upon motion of a party in interest, to grant relief from the stay for cause, such as by terminating, annulling, modifying, or conditioning the stay. The lack of adequate protection of an interest in property is one cause for relief, but is not the only cause. Other causes might include the lack of any connection with or interference with the pending bankruptcy case. Generally, proceedings in which the debtor is a fiduciary or involving postpetition activities of the debtor, need not be stayed because they bear no relationship to the purpose of the automatic stay, which is protection of the debtor and his estate from his creditors.

Upon the court's finding that the debtor has no equity in the property subject to the stay and that the property is not necessary to an effective reorganization of the debtor, the subsection requires the court grant relief from the stay. To aid in this determination, guidelines are established where the property subject to the stay is real property. An exception to "the necessary to an effective reorganization" requirement is made for real property on which no business is being conducted other than operating the real property and activities incident thereto. The intent of this exception is to reach the single-asset apartment type cases which involve primarily tax-shelter investments and for which the bankruptcy laws have provided a too facile method to relay conditions, but not the operating shopping center and hotel cases where attempts at reorganization should be permitted. Property in which the debtor has equity but which is not necessary to an effective reorganization of the debtor should be sold under section 363. Hearings under this subsection are given calendar priority to ensure that court congestion will not unduly prejudice the rights of creditors who may be obviously entitled to relief from the operation of the automatic stay.

Subsection (e) provides protection that is not always available under present law. The subsection sets a time certain within which the bankruptcy court must rule on the adequacy of protection provided for the secured creditor's interest. If the court does not rule within 30 days from a request by motion for relief from the stay, the stay is automatically terminated with respect to the property in question. To accommodate more complex cases, the subsection permits the court to make a preliminary ruling after a preliminary hearing. After a preliminary hearing, the court may continue the stay only if there is a reasonable likelihood that the party opposing relief from the stay will prevail at the final hearing. Because the stay is essentially an injunction, the three stages of the stay may be analogized to the three stages of an injunction. The filing of the petition which gives rise to the automatic stay is similar to a temporary restraining order. The preliminary hearing is similar to the hearing on a preliminary injunction, and the final hearing and order are similar to the hearing and issuance or denial of a permanent injunction. The main difference lies in which party must bring the issue before the court. While in the injunction setting, the party seeking the injunction must prosecute the action, in proceeding for relief from the automatic stay, the enjoined party must move. The difference does not, however, shift the burden of proof. Subsection (g) leaves that burden on the party opposing relief from the stay (that is, on the party seeking continuance of the injunction) on the issue of adequate protection and existence of an equity. It is not, however, intended to be confined strictly to the constitutional requirement. This section and the concept of adequate protection are based as much on policy grounds as on constitutional grounds. Secured creditors should not be deprived of the benefit of their bargain. There may be situations in bankruptcy where giving a secured creditor an absolute right to his bargain may be impossible or seriously detrimental to the policy of the bankruptcy laws. Thus, this section recognizes the availability of alternate means of protecting a secured creditor's interest where such steps are a necessary part of the rehabilitative process. Though the creditor might not be able to retain his lien upon the specific collateral held at the time of filing, the purpose of the section is to insure that the secured creditor receives the value for which he bargained.

The section specifies two exclusive means of providing adequate protection, both of which may require an approximate determination of the value of the protected entity's interest in the property involved. The section does not specify how value is to be determined, nor does it specify when it is to be determined. These matters are left to case-by-case interpretation and development. In light of the restrictive approach of the section to the availability of means of providing adequate protection, this flexibility is important to permit the courts to adapt to varying circumstances and changing modes of financing.

Neither is it expected that the courts will construe the term value to mean, in every case, forced sale liquidation value or full going concern value. There is wide latitude between those two extremes although forced sale liquidation value will be a minimum.

In any particular case, especially a reorganization case, the determination of which entity should be entitled to the difference between the going concern value and the liquidation value must be based on equitable considerations arising from the facts of the case. Finally, the determination of value is binding only for the purposes of the specific hearing and is not to have a res judicata effect.

The first method of adequate protection outlined is the making of cash payments to compensate for the expected decrease in value of the opposing entity's interest. This provision is derived from *In re Bermec Corporation*, 445 F.2d 367 (2d Cir. 1971), though in that case it is not clear whether the payments offered were adequate to compensate the secured creditors for their loss. The use of periodic payments may be appropriate where, for example, the property in question is depreciating at a relatively fixed rate. The periodic payments would be to compensate for the depreciation and might, but need not necessarily, be in the same amount as payments due on the secured obligation.

The second method is the fixing of an additional or replacement lien on other property of the debtor to the extent of the decrease in value or actual consumption of the property involved. The purpose of this method is to provide the protected entity with an alternative means of realizing the value of the original property, if it should decline during the case, by granting an interest in additional property from whose value the entity may realize its loss. This is consistent with the view expressed in *Wright v. Union Central Life Ins. Co.*, 311 U.S. 273 (1940) [61 S.Ct. 196, 85 L.Ed. 184, rehearing denied 61 S.Ct. 445, 312 U.S. 711, 85 L.Ed. 1142], where the Court suggested that it was the value of the secured creditor's collateral, and not necessarily his rights in specific collateral, that was entitled to protection.

The section makes no provision for the granting of an administrative priority as a method of providing adequate protection to an entity as was suggested in *In re Yale Express System, Inc.*, 384 F.2d 990 (2d Cir. 1967), because such protection is too uncertain to be meaningful. Senate Report No. 95–989.

The section specifies four means of providing adequate protection. They are neither exclusive nor exhaustive. They all rely, however, on the value of the protected entity's interest in the property involved. The section does not specify how value is to be determined, nor does it specify when it is to be determined. These matters are left to case-by-case interpretation and development. It is expected that the courts will apply the concept in light of facts of each case and general equitable principles. It is not intended that the courts will develop a hard and fast rule that will apply in every case. The time and method of valuation is not specified precisely, in order to avoid that result. There are an infinite number of variations possible in dealings between debtors and creditors, the law is continually developing, and new ideas are continually being implemented in this field. The flexibility is important to permit the courts to adapt to varying circumstances and changing modes of financing.

Neither is it expected that the courts will construe the term value to mean, in every case, forced sale liquidation value or full going concern value. There is wide latitude between those two extremes. In any particular case, especially a reorganization case, the determination of which entity should be entitled to the difference between the going concern value and the liquidation value must be based on equitable considerations based on the facts of the case. It will frequently be based on negotiation between the parties. Only if they cannot agree will the court become involved.

The first method of adequate protection specified is periodic cash payments by the estate, to the extent of a decrease in value of the opposing entity's interest in the property involved. This provision is derived from *In re Yale Express, Inc.*, 384 F.2d 990 (2d Cir. 1967) (though in that case it is not clear whether the payments required were adequate to compensate the secured creditors for their loss). The use of periodic payments may be appropriate, where for example, the property in question is depreciating at a relatively fixed rate. The periodic payments would be to compensate for the depreciation.

The second method is the provision of an additional or replacement lien on other property to the extent of the decrease in value of the property involved. The purpose of this method is to provide the protected entity with a means of realizing the value of the original property, if it should decline during the case, by granting an interest in additional property from whose value the entity may realize its loss.

The third method is the granting of an administrative expense priority to the protected entity to the extent of his loss. This method, more than the others, requires a prediction as to whether the unencumbered assets that will remain if the case if converted from reorganization to liquidation will be sufficient to pay the protected entity in full. It is clearly the most risky, from the entity's perspective, and should be used only when there is relative certainty that administrative expenses will be able to be paid in full in the event of liquidation.

The fourth method gives the parties and the courts flexibility by allowing such other relief as will result in the realization by the protected entity of the value of its interest in the property involved. Under this provision, the courts will be able to adapt to new methods of financing and to formulate protection that is appropriate to the circumstances of the case if none of the other methods would accomplish the desired result. For example, another form of adequate protection might be the guarantee by a third party outside the judicial process of compensation for any loss incurred in the case. Adequate protection might also, in some circumstances, be provided by permitting a secured creditor to bid in his claim at the sale of the property and to offset the claim against the price bid in.

The paragraph also defines, more clearly than the others, the general concept of adequate protection, by requiring such relief as will result in the realization of value. It is the general category, and as such, is defined by the concept involved rather than any particular method of adequate protection. House Report No. 95–595.

1984 Acts. Statements by Legislative Leaders, see 1984 U.S.Code Cong. and Adm.News, p. 576.

Legislative Statements

Section 361 of the House amendment represents a compromise between H.R. 8200 as passed by the House and the Senate amendment regarding the issue of "adequate protection" of a secured party. The House amendment deletes the provision found in section 361(3) of H.R. 8200 as passed by the House. It would have permitted adequate protection to be provided by giving the secured party an administrative expense regarding any decrease in the value of such party's collateral. In every case there is the uncertainty that the estate will have sufficient property to pay administrative expenses in full.

Section 361(4) of H.R. 8200 as passed by the House is modified in section 361(3) of the House amendment to indicate that the court may grant other forms of adequate protection, other than an administrative expense, which will result in the realization by the secured creditor of the indubitable equivalent of the creditor's interest in property. In the special instance where there is a reserve fund maintained under the security agreement, such as in the typical bondholder case, indubitable equivalent means that the bondholders would be entitled to be protected as to the reserve fund, in addition to the regular payments needed to service the debt. Adequate protection of an interest of an entity in property is intended to protect a creditor's allowed secured claim. To the extent the protection proves to be inadequate after the fact, the creditor is entitled to a first priority administrative expense under section 503(b).

In the special case of a creditor who has elected application of creditor making an election under section 1111(b)(2), that creditor is entitled to adequate protection of the creditor's interest in property to the extent of the value of the collateral not to the extent of the creditor's allowed secured claim, which is inflated to cover a deficiency as a result of such election.

Amendments

1984 Amendments. Par. (1). Pub.L. 98–353 added "a cash payment or" after "make".

Effective and Applicability Provisions

1984 Acts. Amendment by Pub.L. 98–353 effective with respect to cases filed 90 days after July 10, 1984, see section 552(a), formerly 553(a), of Pub.L. 98–353, set out as a note under section 101 of this title.

CROSS REFERENCES

Applicability of this section in Chapter 9 cases, see 11 USCA § 901.

Inapplicability of this section in Chapter 12 cases, see 11 USCA § 1205.

LIBRARY REFERENCES

American Digest System

Bankruptcy ☞3062, 2430.1 to 2434, 3073, 3083.

Key Number System Topic No. 51.

Corpus Juris Secundum

CJS Bankruptcy § 399, Effects of Recognizing Foreign Main Proceeding.

CJS Bankruptcy § 514, Methods of Adequate Protection.

CJS Bankruptcy § 637, Effect of Lien on Recorded Information; Adequate Protection of Lien Holder's Interest.

CJS Bankruptcy § 858, How to Provide Adequate Protection.

CJS Bankruptcy § 898, Credit Secured by Superpriority Lien; Subordination of Existing Liens.

§ 362. Automatic stay

(a) Except as provided in subsection (b) of this section, a petition filed under section 301, 302, or 303 of this title, or an application filed under section 5(a)(3) of the Securities Investor Protection Act of 1970, operates as a stay, applicable to all entities, of—

(1) the commencement or continuation, including the issuance or employment of process, of a judicial, administrative, or other action or proceeding against the debtor that was or could have been commenced before the commencement of the case under this title, or to recover a claim against the debtor that arose before the commencement of the case under this title;

(2) the enforcement, against the debtor or against property of the estate, of a judgment obtained before the commencement of the case under this title;

(3) any act to obtain possession of property of the estate or of property from the estate or to exercise control over property of the estate;

(4) any act to create, perfect, or enforce any lien against property of the estate;

(5) any act to create, perfect, or enforce against property of the debtor any lien to the extent that such lien secures a claim that arose before the commencement of the case under this title;

(6) any act to collect, assess, or recover a claim against the debtor that arose before the commencement of the case under this title;

(7) the setoff of any debt owing to the debtor that arose before the commencement of the case under this title against any claim against the debtor; and

(8) the commencement or continuation of a proceeding before the United States Tax Court concerning a tax liability of a debtor that is a corporation for a taxable period the bankruptcy court may determine or concerning the tax liability of a debtor who is an individual for a taxable period ending before the date of the order for relief under this title.

exceptions

(b) The filing of a petition under section 301, 302, or 303 of this title, or of an application under section 5(a)(3) of the Securities Investor Protection Act of 1970, does not operate as a stay—

(1) under subsection (a) of this section, of the commencement or continuation of a criminal action or proceeding against the debtor;

(2) under subsection (a)—

(A) of the commencement or continuation of a civil action or proceeding—

(i) for the establishment of paternity;

(ii) for the establishment or modification of an order for domestic support obligations;

(iii) concerning child custody or visitation;

(iv) for the dissolution of a marriage, except to the extent that such proceeding seeks to determine the division of property that is property of the estate; or

(v) regarding domestic violence;

(B) of the collection of a domestic support obligation from property that is not property of the estate;

(C) with respect to the withholding of income that is property of the estate or property of the debtor for payment of a domestic support obligation under a judicial or administrative order or a statute;

(D) of the withholding, suspension, or restriction of a driver's license, a professional or occupational license, or a recreational license, under State law, as specified in section 466(a)(16) of the Social Security Act;

(E) of the reporting of overdue support owed by a parent to any consumer reporting agency as specified in section 466(a)(7) of the Social Security Act;

(F) of the interception of a tax refund, as specified in sections 464 and 466(a)(3) of the Social Security Act or under an analogous State law; or

(G) of the enforcement of a medical obligation, as specified under title IV of the Social Security Act;

(3) under subsection (a) of this section, of any act to perfect, or to maintain or continue the perfection of, an interest in property to the extent that the trustee's rights and powers are subject to such perfection under section 546(b) of this title or to the extent that such act is accomplished within the period provided under section 547(e)(2)(A) of this title;

(4) under paragraph (1), (2), (3), or (6) of subsection (a) of this section, of the commencement or continuation of an action or proceeding by a governmental unit or any organization exercising authority under the Convention on the Prohibition of the Development, Production, Stockpiling and Use of Chemical Weapons and on Their Destruction, opened for signature on January 13, 1993, to enforce such governmental unit's or organization's police and regulatory power, including the enforcement of a judgment other than a money judgment, obtained in an action or proceeding by the governmental unit to enforce such governmental unit's or organization's police or regulatory power;

[(5) **Repealed.** Pub.L. 105–277, Div. I, Title VI, § 603(1), Oct. 21, 1998, 112 Stat. 2681–886]

(6) under subsection (a) of this section, of the exercise by a commodity broker, forward contract merchant, stockbroker, financial institution, financial participant, or securities clearing agency of any contractual right (as defined in section 555 or 556) under any security agreement or arrangement or other credit enhancement forming a part of or related to any commodity contract, forward contract or securities contract, or of any contractual right (as defined in section 555 or 556) to offset or net out any termination value, payment amount, or other transfer obligation arising under or in connection with 1 or more such contracts, including any master agreement for such contracts;

(7) under subsection (a) of this section, of the exercise by a repo participant or financial participant of any contractual right (as defined in section 559) under any security agreement or arrangement or other credit enhancement forming a part of or related to any repurchase agreement, or of any contractual right (as defined in section 559) to offset or net out any termination value, payment amount, or other transfer obligation arising under or in connection with 1 or more such agreements, including any master agreement for such agreements;

(8) under subsection (a) of this section, of the commencement of any action by the Secretary of Housing and Urban Development to foreclose a mortgage or deed of trust in any case in which the mortgage or deed of trust held by the Secretary is insured or was formerly insured under the National Housing Act and covers property, or combinations of property, consisting of five or more living units;

(9) under subsection (a), of—

(A) an audit by a governmental unit to determine tax liability;

(B) the issuance to the debtor by a governmental unit of a notice of tax deficiency;

(C) a demand for tax returns; or

(D) the making of an assessment for any tax and issuance of a notice and demand for payment of such an assessment (but any tax lien that would otherwise attach to property of the estate by reason of such an assessment shall not take effect unless such tax is a debt of the debtor that will not be discharged in the case and such property or its proceeds are transferred out of the estate to, or otherwise revested in, the debtor).

(10) under subsection (a) of this section, of any act by a lessor to the debtor under a lease of nonresidential real property that has terminated by the expiration of the stated term of the lease before the commencement of or during a case under this title to obtain possession of such property;

(11) under subsection (a) of this section, of the presentment of a negotiable instrument and the giving of notice of and protesting dishonor of such an instrument;

(12) under subsection (a) of this section, after the date which is 90 days after the filing of such petition, of the commencement or continuation, and conclusion to the entry of final judgment, of an action which involves a debtor subject to reorganization pursuant to chapter 11 of this title and which was brought by the Secretary of Transportation under section 31325 of title 46 (including distribution of any proceeds of sale) to foreclose a preferred ship or fleet mortgage, or a security interest in or relating to a vessel or vessel under construction, held by the Secretary of Transportation under chapter 537 of title 46 or section 109(h) of title 49, or under applicable State law;

(13) under subsection (a) of this section, after the date which is 90 days after the filing of such petition, of the commencement or continuation, and conclusion to the entry of final judgment, of an action which involves a debtor subject to reorganization pursuant to chapter 11 of this title and which was brought by the Secretary of Commerce under section 31325 of title 46 (including distribution of any proceeds of sale) to foreclose a preferred ship or fleet mortgage in a vessel or a mortgage, deed of trust, or other security interest in a fishing facility held by the Secretary of Commerce under chapter 537 of title 46;

(14) under subsection (a) of this section, of any action by an accrediting agency regarding the accreditation status of the debtor as an educational institution;

(15) under subsection (a) of this section, of any action by a State licensing body regarding the licensure of the debtor as an educational institution;

(16) under subsection (a) of this section, of any action by a guaranty agency, as defined in section 435(j) of the Higher Education Act of 1965 or the Secretary of Education regarding the eligibility of the debtor to participate in programs authorized under such Act;

(17) under subsection (a) of this section, of the exercise by a swap participant or financial participant of any contractual right (as defined in section 560) under any security agreement or arrangement or other credit enhancement forming a part of or related to any swap agreement, or of any contractual right (as defined in section 560) to offset or net out any termination value, payment amount, or other transfer obligation arising under or in connection with 1 or more such agreements, including any master agreement for such agreements;

(18) under subsection (a) of the creation or perfection of a statutory lien for an ad valorem property tax, or a special tax or special assessment on real property whether or not ad valorem, imposed by a governmental unit, if such tax or assessment comes due after the date of the filing of the petition;

(19) under subsection (a), of withholding of income from a debtor's wages and collection of amounts withheld, under the debtor's agreement authorizing that withholding and collection for the benefit of a pension, profit-sharing, stock bonus, or other plan established under section 401, 403, 408, 408A, 414, 457, or 501(c) of the Internal Revenue Code of 1986, that is sponsored by the employer of the debtor, or an affiliate, successor, or predecessor of such employer—

   (A) to the extent that the amounts withheld and collected are used solely for payments relating to a loan from a plan under section 408(b)(1) of the Employee Retirement Income Security Act of 1974 or is subject to section 72(p) of the Internal Revenue Code of 1986; or

   (B) a loan from a thrift savings plan permitted under subchapter III of chapter 84 of title 5, that satisfies the requirements of section 8433(g) of such title;

but nothing in this paragraph may be construed to provide that any loan made under a governmental plan under section 414(d), or a contract or account under section 403(b), of the Internal Revenue Code of 1986 constitutes a claim or a debt under this title;

(20) under subsection (a), of any act to enforce any lien against or security interest in real property following entry of the order under subsection (d)(4) as to such real property in any prior case under this title, for a period of 2 years after the date of the entry of such an order, except that the debtor, in a subsequent case under this title, may move for relief from such order based upon changed circumstances or for other good cause shown, after notice and a hearing;

(21) under subsection (a), of any act to enforce any lien against or security interest in real property—

   (A) if the debtor is ineligible under section 109(g) to be a debtor in a case under this title; or

   (B) if the case under this title was filed in violation of a bankruptcy court order in a prior case under this title prohibiting the debtor from being a debtor in another case under this title;

(22) subject to subsection (*l*), under subsection (a)(3), of the continuation of any eviction, unlawful detainer action, or similar proceeding by a lessor against a debtor involving residential property in which the debtor resides as a tenant under a lease or rental agreement and with respect to which the lessor has obtained before the date of the filing of the bankruptcy petition, a judgment for possession of such property against the debtor;

(23) subject to subsection (m), under subsection (a)(3), of an eviction action that seeks possession of the residential property in which the debtor resides as a tenant under a lease or rental agreement based on endangerment of such property or the illegal use of controlled substances on such property, but only if the lessor files with the court, and serves upon the debtor, a certification under penalty of perjury that such an eviction action has been filed, or that the debtor, during the 30–day period preceding the date of the filing of the certification, has endangered property or illegally used or allowed to be used a controlled substance on the property;

(24) under subsection (a), of any transfer that is not avoidable under section 544 and that is not avoidable under section 549;

(25) under subsection (a), of—

(A) the commencement or continuation of an investigation or action by a securities self regulatory organization to enforce such organization's regulatory power;

(B) the enforcement of an order or decision, other than for monetary sanctions, obtained in an action by such securities self regulatory organization to enforce such organization's regulatory power; or

(C) any act taken by such securities self regulatory organization to delist, delete, or refuse to permit quotation of any stock that does not meet applicable regulatory requirements;

(26) under subsection (a), of the setoff under applicable nonbankruptcy law of an income tax refund, by a governmental unit, with respect to a taxable period that ended before the date of the order for relief against an income tax liability for a taxable period that also ended before the date of the order for relief, except that in any case in which the setoff of an income tax refund is not permitted under applicable nonbankruptcy law because of a pending action to determine the amount or legality of a tax liability, the governmental unit may hold the refund pending the resolution of the action, unless the court, on the motion of the trustee and after notice and a hearing, grants the taxing authority adequate protection (within the meaning of section 361) for the secured claim of such authority in the setoff under section 506(a);

(27) under subsection (a) of this section, of the exercise by a master netting agreement participant of any contractual right (as defined in section 555, 556, 559, or 560) under any security agreement or arrangement or other credit enhancement forming a part of or related to any master netting agreement, or of any contractual right (as defined in section 555, 556, 559, or 560) to offset or net out any termination value, payment amount, or other transfer obligation arising under or in connection with 1 or more such master netting agreements to the extent that such participant is eligible to exercise such rights under paragraph (6), (7), or (17) for each individual contract covered by the master netting agreement in issue; and

(28) under subsection (a), of the exclusion by the Secretary of Health and Human Services of the debtor from participation in the medicare program or any other Federal health care program (as defined in section 1128B(f) of the Social Security Act pursuant to title XI or XVIII of such Act).

The provisions of paragraphs (12) and (13) of this subsection shall apply with respect to any such petition filed on or before December 31, 1989.

(c) Except as provided in subsections (d), (e), (f), and (h) of this section—

(1) the stay of an act against property of the estate under subsection (a) of this section continues until such property is no longer property of the estate;

(2) the stay of any other act under subsection (a) of this section continues until the earliest of—

(A) the time the case is closed;

(B) the time the case is dismissed; or

(C) if the case is a case under chapter 7 of this title concerning an individual or a case under chapter 9, 11, 12, or 13 of this title, the time a discharge is granted or denied;

(3) if a single or joint case is filed by or against a debtor who is an individual in a case under chapter 7, 11, or 13, and if a single or joint case of the debtor was pending within the preceding 1–year period but was dismissed, other than a case refiled under a chapter other than chapter 7 after dismissal under section 707(b)—

(A) the stay under subsection (a) with respect to any action taken with respect to a debt or property securing such debt or with respect to any lease shall terminate with respect to the debtor on the 30th day after the filing of the later case;

(B) on the motion of a party in interest for continuation of the automatic stay and upon notice and a hearing, the court may extend the stay in particular cases as to any or all creditors (subject to such conditions or limitations as the court may then impose) after notice and a hearing completed before the expiration of the 30–day period only if the party in interest demonstrates that the filing of the later case is in good faith as to the creditors to be stayed; and

(C) for purposes of subparagraph (B), a case is presumptively filed not in good faith (but such presumption may be rebutted by clear and convincing evidence to the contrary)—

(i) as to all creditors, if—

(I) more than 1 previous case under any of chapters 7, 11, and 13 in which the individual was a debtor was pending within the preceding 1–year period;

(II) a previous case under any of chapters 7, 11, and 13 in which the individual was a debtor was dismissed within such 1–year period, after the debtor failed to—

(aa) file or amend the petition or other documents as required by this title or the court without substantial excuse (but mere inadvertence or negligence shall not be a substantial excuse unless the dismissal was caused by the negligence of the debtor's attorney);

(bb) provide adequate protection as ordered by the court; or

(cc) perform the terms of a plan confirmed by the court; or

(III) there has not been a substantial change in the financial or personal affairs of the debtor since the dismissal of the next most previous case under chapter 7, 11, or 13 or any other reason to conclude that the later case will be concluded—

(aa) if a case under chapter 7, with a discharge; or

(bb) if a case under chapter 11 or 13, with a confirmed plan that will be fully performed; and

(ii) as to any creditor that commenced an action under subsection (d) in a previous case in which the individual was a debtor if, as of the date of dismissal of such case, that action was still pending or had been resolved by terminating, conditioning, or limiting the stay as to actions of such creditor; and

(4)(A)(i) if a single or joint case is filed by or against a debtor who is an individual under this title, and if 2 or more single or joint cases of the debtor were pending within the previous year but were dismissed, other than a case refiled under a chapter other than chapter 7 after dismissal under section 707(b), the stay under subsection (a) shall not go into effect upon the filing of the later case; and

(ii) on request of a party in interest, the court shall promptly enter an order confirming that no stay is in effect;

(B) if, within 30 days after the filing of the later case, a party in interest requests the court may

order the stay to take effect in the case as to any or all creditors (subject to such conditions or limitations as the court may impose), after notice and a hearing, only if the party in interest demonstrates that the filing of the later case is in good faith as to the creditors to be stayed;

(C) a stay imposed under subparagraph (B) shall be effective on the date of the entry of the order allowing the stay to go into effect; and

(D) for purposes of subparagraph (B), a case is presumptively filed not in good faith (but such presumption may be rebutted by clear and convincing evidence to the contrary)—

(i) as to all creditors if—

(I) 2 or more previous cases under this title in which the individual was a debtor were pending within the 1–year period;

(II) a previous case under this title in which the individual was a debtor was dismissed within the time period stated in this paragraph after the debtor failed to file or amend the petition or other documents as required by this title or the court without substantial excuse (but mere inadvertence or negligence shall not be substantial excuse unless the dismissal was caused by the negligence of the debtor's attorney), failed to provide adequate protection as ordered by the court, or failed to perform the terms of a plan confirmed by the court; or

(III) there has not been a substantial change in the financial or personal affairs of the debtor since the dismissal of the next most previous case under this title, or any other reason to conclude that the later case will not be concluded, if a case under chapter 7, with a discharge, and if a case under chapter 11 or 13, with a confirmed plan that will be fully performed; or

(ii) as to any creditor that commenced an action under subsection (d) in a previous case in which the individual was a debtor if, as of the date of dismissal of such case, such action was still pending or had been resolved by terminating, conditioning, or limiting the stay as to such action of such creditor. *Relief from stay*

(d) On request of a party in interest and after notice and a hearing, the court shall grant relief from the stay provided under subsection (a) of this section, such as by terminating, annulling, modifying, or conditioning such stay— *relief from stay for creditor*

(1) for cause, including the lack of adequate protection of an interest in property of such party in interest;

(2) with respect to a stay of an act against property under subsection (a) of this section, if—

(A) the debtor does not have an equity in such property; and

(B) such property is not necessary to an effective reorganization;

(3) with respect to a stay of an act against single asset real estate under subsection (a), by a creditor whose claim is secured by an interest in such real estate, unless, not later than the date that is 90 days after the entry of the order for relief (or such later date as the court may determine for cause by order entered within that 90–day period) or 30 days after the court determines that the debtor is subject to this paragraph, whichever is later—

(A) the debtor has filed a plan of reorganization that has a reasonable possibility of being confirmed within a reasonable time; or

(B) the debtor has commenced monthly payments that—

(i) may, in the debtor's sole discretion, notwithstanding section 363(c)(2), be made from rents or other income generated before, on, or after the date of the commencement of the case by or from the property to each creditor whose claim is secured by such real estate (other than a claim secured by a judgment lien or by an unmatured statutory lien); and

(ii) are in an amount equal to interest at the then applicable nondefault contract rate of interest on the value of the creditor's interest in the real estate; or

(4) with respect to a stay of an act against real property under subsection (a), by a creditor whose claim is secured by an interest in such real property, if the court finds that the filing of the petition was part of a scheme to delay, hinder, or defraud creditors that involved either—

(A) transfer of all or part ownership of, or other interest in, such real property without the consent of the secured creditor or court approval; or

(B) multiple bankruptcy filings affecting such real property.

If recorded in compliance with applicable State laws governing notices of interests or liens in real property, an order entered under paragraph (4) shall be binding in any other case under this title purporting to affect such real property filed not later than 2 years after the date of the entry of such order by the court, except that a debtor in a subsequent case under this title may move for relief from such order based upon changed circumstances or for good cause shown, after notice and a hearing. Any Federal, State, or local governmental unit that accepts notices of interests or liens in real property shall accept any certified copy of an order described in this subsection for indexing and recording.

(e)(1) Thirty days after a request under subsection (d) of this section for relief from the stay of any act against property of the estate under subsection (a) of this section, such stay is terminated with respect to the party in interest making such request, unless the court,

after notice and a hearing, orders such stay continued in effect pending the conclusion of, or as a result of, a final hearing and determination under subsection (d) of this section. A hearing under this subsection may be a preliminary hearing, or may be consolidated with the final hearing under subsection (d) of this section. The court shall order such stay continued in effect pending the conclusion of the final hearing under subsection (d) of this section if there is a reasonable likelihood that the party opposing relief from such stay will prevail at the conclusion of such final hearing. If the hearing under this subsection is a preliminary hearing, then such final hearing shall be concluded not later than thirty days after the conclusion of such preliminary hearing, unless the 30–day period is extended with the consent of the parties in interest or for a specific time which the court finds is required by compelling circumstances.

(2) Notwithstanding paragraph (1), in a case under chapter 7, 11, or 13 in which the debtor is an individual, the stay under subsection (a) shall terminate on the date that is 60 days after a request is made by a party in interest under subsection (d), unless—

(A) a final decision is rendered by the court during the 60–day period beginning on the date of the request; or

(B) such 60–day period is extended—

(i) by agreement of all parties in interest; or

(ii) by the court for such specific period of time as the court finds is required for good cause, as described in findings made by the court.

(f) Upon request of a party in interest, the court, with or without a hearing, shall grant such relief from the stay provided under subsection (a) of this section as is necessary to prevent irreparable damage to the interest of an entity in property, if such interest will suffer such damage before there is an opportunity for notice and a hearing under subsection (d) or (e) of this section.

(g) In any hearing under subsection (d) or (e) of this section concerning relief from the stay of any act under subsection (a) of this section—

(1) the party requesting such relief has the burden of proof on the issue of the debtor's equity in property; and

(2) the party opposing such relief has the burden of proof on all other issues.

(h)(1) In a case in which the debtor is an individual, the stay provided by subsection (a) is terminated with respect to personal property of the estate or of the debtor securing in whole or in part a claim, or subject to an unexpired lease, and such personal property shall no longer be property of the estate if the debtor fails within the applicable time set by section 521(a)(2)—

(A) to file timely any statement of intention required under section 521(a)(2) with respect to such personal property or to indicate in such statement that the debtor will either surrender such personal property or retain it and, if retaining such personal property, either redeem such personal property pursuant to section 722, enter into an agreement of the kind specified in section 524(c) applicable to the debt secured by such personal property, or assume such unexpired lease pursuant to section 365(p) if the trustee does not do so, as applicable; and

(B) to take timely the action specified in such statement, as it may be amended before expiration of the period for taking action, unless such statement specifies the debtor's intention to reaffirm such debt on the original contract terms and the creditor refuses to agree to the reaffirmation on such terms.

(2) Paragraph (1) does not apply if the court determines, on the motion of the trustee filed before the expiration of the applicable time set by section 521(a)(2), after notice and a hearing, that such personal property is of consequential value or benefit to the estate, and orders appropriate adequate protection of the creditor's interest, and orders the debtor to deliver any collateral in the debtor's possession to the trustee. If the court does not so determine, the stay provided by subsection (a) shall terminate upon the conclusion of the hearing on the motion.

(i) If a case commenced under chapter 7, 11, or 13 is dismissed due to the creation of a debt repayment plan, for purposes of subsection (c)(3), any subsequent case commenced by the debtor under any such chapter shall not be presumed to be filed not in good faith.

(j) On request of a party in interest, the court shall issue an order under subsection (c) confirming that the automatic stay has been terminated.

(k)(1) Except as provided in paragraph (2), an individual injured by any willful violation of a stay provided by this section shall recover actual damages, including costs and attorneys' fees, and, in appropriate circumstances, may recover punitive damages.

(2) If such violation is based on an action taken by an entity in the good faith belief that subsection (h) applies to the debtor, the recovery under paragraph (1) of this subsection against such entity shall be limited to actual damages.

(l)(1) Except as otherwise provided in this subsection, subsection (b) (22) shall apply on the date that is 30 days after the date on which the bankruptcy petition is filed, if the debtor files with the petition and serves upon the lessor a certification under penalty of perjury that—

(A) under nonbankruptcy law applicable in the jurisdiction, there are circumstances under which the debtor would be permitted to cure the entire monetary default that gave rise to the judgment for possession, after that judgment for possession was entered; and

(B) the debtor (or an adult dependent of the debtor) has deposited with the clerk of the court, any rent that would become due during the 30–day period after the filing of the bankruptcy petition.

(2) If, within the 30–day period after the filing of the bankruptcy petition, the debtor (or an adult dependent of the debtor) complies with paragraph (1) and files with the court and serves upon the lessor a further certification under penalty of perjury that the debtor (or an adult dependent of the debtor) has cured, under nonbankruptcy law applicable in the jurisdiction, the entire monetary default that gave rise to the judgment under which possession is sought by the lessor, subsection (b)(22) shall not apply, unless ordered to apply by the court under paragraph (3).

(3)(A) If the lessor files an objection to any certification filed by the debtor under paragraph (1) or (2), and serves such objection upon the debtor, the court shall hold a hearing within 10 days after the filing and service of such objection to determine if the certification filed by the debtor under paragraph (1) or (2) is true.

(B) If the court upholds the objection of the lessor filed under subparagraph (A)—

(i) subsection (b)(22) shall apply immediately and relief from the stay provided under subsection (a)(3) shall not be required to enable the lessor to complete the process to recover full possession of the property; and

(ii) the clerk of the court shall immediately serve upon the lessor and the debtor a certified copy of the court's order upholding the lessor's objection.

(4) If a debtor, in accordance with paragraph (5), indicates on the petition that there was a judgment for possession of the residential rental property in which the debtor resides and does not file a certification under paragraph (1) or (2)—

(A) subsection (b)(22) shall apply immediately upon failure to file such certification, and relief from the stay provided under subsection (a)(3) shall not be required to enable the lessor to complete the process to recover full possession of the property; and

(B) the clerk of the court shall immediately serve upon the lessor and the debtor a certified copy of the docket indicating the absence of a filed certification and the applicability of the exception to the stay under subsection (b)(22).

(5)(A) Where a judgment for possession of residential property in which the debtor resides as a tenant under a lease or rental agreement has been obtained by the lessor, the debtor shall so indicate on the bankruptcy petition and shall provide the name and address of the lessor that obtained that pre-petition judgment on the petition and on any certification filed under this subsection.

(B) The form of certification filed with the petition, as specified in this subsection, shall provide for the debtor to certify, and the debtor shall certify—

(i) whether a judgment for possession of residential rental housing in which the debtor resides has been obtained against the debtor before the date of the filing of the petition; and

(ii) whether the debtor is claiming under paragraph (1) that under nonbankruptcy law applicable in the jurisdiction, there are circumstances under which the debtor would be permitted to cure the entire monetary default that gave rise to the judgment for possession, after that judgment of possession was entered, and has made the appropriate deposit with the court.

(C) The standard forms (electronic and otherwise) used in a bankruptcy proceeding shall be amended to reflect the requirements of this subsection.

(D) The clerk of the court shall arrange for the prompt transmittal of the rent deposited in accordance with paragraph (1)(B) to the lessor.

(m)(1) Except as otherwise provided in this subsection, subsection (b) (23) shall apply on the date that is 15 days after the date on which the lessor files and serves a certification described in subsection (b)(23).

(2)(A) If the debtor files with the court an objection to the truth or legal sufficiency of the certification described in subsection (b)(23) and serves such objection upon the lessor, subsection (b)(23) shall not apply, unless ordered to apply by the court under this subsection.

(B) If the debtor files and serves the objection under subparagraph (A), the court shall hold a hearing within 10 days after the filing and service of such objection to determine if the situation giving rise to the lessor's certification under paragraph (1) existed or has been remedied.

(C) If the debtor can demonstrate to the satisfaction of the court that the situation giving rise to the lessor's certification under paragraph (1) did not exist or has been remedied, the stay provided under subsection (a)(3) shall remain in effect until the termination of the stay under this section.

(D) If the debtor cannot demonstrate to the satisfaction of the court that the situation giving rise to the lessor's certification under paragraph (1) did not exist or has been remedied—

(i) relief from the stay provided under subsection (a)(3) shall not be required to enable the lessor to proceed with the eviction; and

(ii) the clerk of the court shall immediately serve upon the lessor and the debtor a certified copy of the court's order upholding the lessor's certification.

(3) If the debtor fails to file, within 15 days, an objection under paragraph (2)(A)—

(A) subsection (b)(23) shall apply immediately upon such failure and relief from the stay provided under subsection (a)(3) shall not be required to enable the lessor to complete the process to recover full possession of the property; and

(B) the clerk of the court shall immediately serve upon the lessor and the debtor a certified copy of the docket indicating such failure.

(n)(1) Except as provided in paragraph (2), subsection (a) does not apply in a case in which the debtor—

(A) is a debtor in a small business case pending at the time the petition is filed;

(B) was a debtor in a small business case that was dismissed for any reason by an order that became final in the 2–year period ending on the date of the order for relief entered with respect to the petition;

(C) was a debtor in a small business case in which a plan was confirmed in the 2–year period ending on the date of the order for relief entered with respect to the petition; or

(D) is an entity that has acquired substantially all of the assets or business of a small business debtor described in subparagraph (A), (B), or (C), unless such entity establishes by a preponderance of the evidence that such entity acquired substantially all of the assets or business of such small business debtor in good faith and not for the purpose of evading this paragraph.

(2) Paragraph (1) does not apply—

(A) to an involuntary case involving no collusion by the debtor with creditors; or

(B) to the filing of a petition if—

(i) the debtor proves by a preponderance of the evidence that the filing of the petition resulted from circumstances beyond the control of the debtor not foreseeable at the time the case then pending was filed; and

(ii) it is more likely than not that the court will confirm a feasible plan, but not a liquidating plan, within a reasonable period of time.

(o) The exercise of rights not subject to the stay arising under subsection (a) pursuant to paragraph (6), (7), (17), or (27) of subsection (b) shall not be stayed by any order of a court or administrative agency in any proceeding under this title.

(Pub.L. 95–598, Nov. 6, 1978, 92 Stat. 2570; Pub.L. 97–222, § 3, July 27, 1982, 96 Stat. 235; Pub.L. 98–353, Title III, §§ 304, 363(b), 392, 441, July 10, 1984, 98 Stat. 352, 363, 365, 371; Pub.L. 99–509, Title V, § 5001(a), Oct. 21, 1986, 100 Stat. 1911; Pub.L. 99–554, Title II, §§ 257(j), 283(d), Oct. 27, 1986, 100 Stat. 3115, 3116; Pub.L. 101–311, Title I, § 102, Title II, § 202, June 25, 1990, 104 Stat. 267, 269; Pub.L. 101–508, Title III, § 3007(a)(1), Nov. 5, 1990, 104 Stat. 1388–28; Pub.L. 103–394, Title I, §§ 101, 116, Title II, §§ 204(a), 218(b), Title III, § 304(b), Title IV, § 401, Title V, § 501(b)(2), (d)(7), Oct. 22, 1994, 108 Stat. 4107, 4119, 4122, 4128, 4132, 4141, 4142,

4144; Pub.L. 105–277, Div. I, Title VI, § 603, Oct. 21, 1998, 112 Stat. 2681–886; Pub.L. 109–8, Title I, § 106(f), Title II, §§ 214, 224(b), Title III, §§ 302, 303, 305(1), 311, 320, Title IV, §§ 401(b), 441, 444, Title VII, §§ 709, 718, Title IX, § 907(d), (o)(1), (2), Title XI, § 1106, Title XII, § 1225, Apr. 20, 2005, 119 Stat. 41, 54, 64, 75, 77, 79, 84, 94, 104, 114, 117, 127, 131, 176, 181, 182, 192, 199; Pub.L. 109–304, § 17(b)(1), Oct. 6, 2006, 120 Stat. 1706; Pub.L. 109–390, § 5(a)(2), Dec. 12, 2006, 120 Stat. 2696; Pub.L. 111–327, § 2(a)(12), Dec. 22, 2010, 124 Stat. 3558.)

HISTORICAL AND STATUTORY NOTES

Revision Notes and Legislative Reports

1978 Acts. The automatic stay is one of the fundamental debtor protections provided by the bankruptcy laws. It gives the debtor a breathing spell from his creditors. It stops all collection efforts, all harassment, and all foreclosure actions. It permits the debtor to attempt a repayment or reorganization plan, or simply to be relieved of the financial pressures that drove him into bankruptcy.

The action commenced by the party seeking relief from the stay is referred to as a motion to make it clear that at the expedited hearing under subsection (e), and at hearings on relief from the stay, the only issue will be the lack of adequate protection, the debtor's equity in the property, and the necessity of the property to an effective reorganization of the debtor, or the existence of other cause for relief from the stay. This hearing will not be the appropriate time at which to bring in other issues, such as counterclaims against the creditor, which, although relevant to the question of the amount of the debt, concern largely collateral or unrelated matters. This approach is consistent with that taken in cases such as *In re Essex Properties, Ltd.*, 430 F.Supp. 1112 (N.D.Cal.1977), that an action seeking relief from the stay is not the assertion of a claim which would give rise to the right or obligation to assert counterclaims. Those counterclaims are not to be handled in the summary fashion that the preliminary hearing under this provision will be. Rather, they will be the subject of more complete proceedings by the trustee to recover property of the estate or to object to the allowance of a claim. However, this would not preclude the party seeking continuance of the stay from presenting evidence on the existence of claims which the court may consider in exercising its discretion. What is precluded is a determination of such collateral claims on the merits at the hearing. Senate Report No. 95–989.

[For additional discussion, see Revision Notes and Legislative Reports, Senate Report No. 95–989, set out under section 361 of this title.]

Paragraph (7) [of subsec. (a)] stays setoffs of mutual debts and credits between the debtor and creditors. As with all other paragraphs of subsection (a), this paragraph does not affect the right of creditors. It simply stays its enforcement pending an orderly examination of the debtor's and creditors' rights.

Subsection (c) governs automatic termination of the stay. Subsections (d) through (g) govern termination of the stay by the court on the request of a party in interest. Subsection (d) requires the court, on request of a party in interest, to grant relief from the stay, such as by terminating, annulling, modifying, or conditioning the stay, for cause. The lack of adequate protection of an interest in property of the party requesting relief from the stay is one cause for relief, but is not the only cause. As noted above, a desire to permit an action to proceed to completion in another tribunal may provide another cause. Other causes might include the lack of any connection with or interference with the pending bankruptcy case. For example, a divorce or child custody proceeding involving the debtor may bear no relation to the bankruptcy case. In that case, it should not be stayed. A probate proceeding in which the debtor is the executor or administrator of another's estate usually will not be related to the bankruptcy case, and should not be stayed. Generally, proceedings in which the debtor is a fiduciary, or involving postpetition activities of the debtor, need not be stayed because they bear no relationship to the purpose of the automatic stay, which is debtor protection from his creditors. The facts of each request will determine whether relief is appropriate under the circumstances.

Subsection (e) provides a protection for secured creditors that is not available under present law. The subsection sets a time certain within which the bankruptcy court must rule on the adequacy of protection provided of the secured creditor's interest. If the court does not rule within 30 days from a request for relief from the stay, the stay is automatically terminated with respect to the property in question. In order to accommodate more complex cases, the subsection permits the court to make a preliminary ruling after a preliminary hearing. After a preliminary hearing, the court may continue the stay only if there is a reasonable likelihood that the party opposing relief from the stay will prevail at the final hearing. Because the stay is essentially an injunction, the three stages of the stay may be analogized to the three stages of an injunction. The filing of the petition which gives rise to the automatic stay is similar to a temporary restraining order. The preliminary hearing is similar to the hearing on a preliminary injunction, and the final hearing and order is similar to a permanent injunction. The main difference lies in which party must bring the issue before the court. While in the injunction setting, the party seeking the injunction must prosecute the action, in proceedings for relief from the automatic stay, the enjoined party must move. The difference does not, however, shift the burden of proof. Subsection (g) leaves that burden on the party opposing relief from the stay (that is, on the party seeking continuance of the injunction) on the issue of adequate protection.

At the expedited hearing under subsection (e), and at all hearings on relief from the stay, the only issue will be the claim of the creditor and the lack of adequate protection or existence of other cause for relief from the stay. This hearing will not be the appropriate time at which to bring in other issues, such as counterclaims against the creditor on largely unrelated matters. Those counterclaims are not to be handled in the summary fashion that the preliminary hearing under this provision will be. Rather, they will be the subject of more complete proceedings by the trustees to recover property of the estate or to object to the allowance of a claim. House Report No. 95–595.

1982 Acts. House Report No. 97–420, see 1982 U.S. Code Cong. and Adm. News, p. 583.

1984 Acts. Statements by Legislative Leaders, see 1984 U.S. Code Cong. and Adm. News, p. 576.

1986 Acts. House Report No. 99–727, House Conference Report No. 99–1012, and Statement by President, see 1986 U.S. Code Cong. and Adm. News, p. 3607.

House Report No. 99–764 and House Conference Report No. 99–958, see 1986 U.S. Code Cong. and Adm. News, p. 5227.

1990 Acts. House Report No. 101–484, see 1990 U.S. Code Cong. and Adm. News, p. 223.

House Report No. 101–881, House Conference Report No. 101–964, and Statement by President, see 1990 U.S. Code Cong. and Adm. News, p. 2017.

1994 Acts. House Report No. 103–835, see 1994 U.S. Code Cong. and Adm. News, p. 3340.

1998 Acts. Statement by President, see 1998 U.S. Code Cong. and Adm. News, p. 576.

2005 Acts. House Report No. 109–31(Part I), see 2005 U.S. Code Cong. and Adm. News, p. 88.

2006 Acts. House Report No. 109–170, see 2006 U.S. Code Cong. and Adm. News, p. 972.

House Report No. 109–648(Part I), see 2006 U.S. Code Cong. and Adm. News, p. 1585.

Legislative Statements

Section 362(a)(1) of the House amendment adopts the provision contained in the Senate amendment enjoining the commencement or continuation of a judicial, administrative, or other proceeding to recover a claim against the debtor that arose before the commencement of the case. The provision is beneficial and interacts with section 362(a)(6), which also covers assessment, to prevent harassment of the debtor with respect to pre-petition claims.

Section 362(a)(7) contains a provision contained in H.R. 8200 as passed by the House. The differing provision in the Senate amendment was rejected. It is not possible that a debt owing to the debtor may be offset against an interest in the debtor.

Section 362(a)(8) is new. The provision stays the commencement or continuation of any proceeding concerning the debtor before the U.S. Tax Court.

Section 362(b)(4) indicates that the stay under section 362(a)(1) does not apply to affect the commencement or continuation of an action or proceeding by a governmental unit to enforce the governmental unit's police or regulatory power. This section is intended to be given a narrow construction in order to permit governmental units to pursue actions to protect the public health and safety and not to apply to actions by a governmental unit to protect a pecuniary interest in property of the debtor or property of the estate.

Section 362(b)(6) of the House amendment adopts a provision contained in the Senate amendment restricting the exception to the automatic stay with respect to setoffs to permit only the setoff of mutual debts and claims. Traditionally, the right of setoff has been limited to mutual debts and claims and the lack of the clarifying term "mutual" in H.R. 8200 as passed by the House created an unintentional ambiguity. Section 362(b)(7) of the House amendment permits the issuance of a notice of tax deficiency. The House amendment rejects section 362(b)(7) in the Senate amendment. It would have permitted a particular governmental unit to obtain a pecuniary advantage without a hearing on the merits contrary to the exceptions contained in sections 362(b)(4) and (5).

Section 362(d) of the House amendment represents a compromise between comparable provisions in the House bill and Senate amendment. Under section 362(d)(1) of the House amendment, the court may terminate, annul, modify, or condition the automatic stay for cause, including lack of adequate protection of an interest in property of a secured party. It is anticipated that the Rules of Bankruptcy Procedure will provide that those hearings will receive priority on the calendar.

Under section 362(d)(2) the court may alternatively terminate, annul, modify, or condition the automatic stay for cause including inadequate protection for the creditor. The court shall grant relief from the stay if there is no equity and it is not necessary to an effective reorganization of the debtor.

The latter requirement is contained in section 362(d)(2). This section is intended to solve the problem of real property mortgage foreclosures of property where the bankruptcy petition is filed on the eve of foreclosure. The section is not intended to apply if the business of the debtor is managing or leasing real property, such as a hotel operation, even though the debtor has no equity if the property is necessary to an effective reorganization of the debtor. Similarly, if the debtor does have an equity in the property, there is no requirement that the property be sold under section 363 of title 11 as would have been required by the Senate amendment.

Section 362(e) of the House amendment represents a modification of provisions in H.R. 8200 as passed by the House and the Senate amendment to make clear that a final hearing must be commenced within 30 days after a preliminary hearing is held to determine whether a creditor will be entitled to relief from the automatic stay. In order to insure that those hearings will in fact occur within such 30–day period, it is anticipated that the rules of bankruptcy procedure provide that such final hearings receive priority on the court calendar.

Section 362(g) places the burden of proof on the issue of the debtor's equity in collateral on the party requesting relief from the automatic stay and the burden on other issues on the debtor.

An amendment has been made to section 362(b) to permit the Secretary of the Department of Housing and Urban Development to commence an action to foreclose a mortgage or deed of trust. The commencement of such an action is necessary for tax purposes. The section is not intended to permit the continuation of such an action after it is commenced nor is the section to be construed to entitle the Secretary to take possession in lieu of foreclosure.

Automatic stay: Sections 362(b)(8) and (9) contained in the Senate amendment are largely deleted in the House amendment. Those provisions add to the list of actions not stayed (a) jeopardy assessments, (b) other assessments, and (c) the issuance of deficiency notices. In the House amendment, jeopardy assessments against property which ceases to be property of the estate is already authorized by section 362(c)(1). Other assessments are specifically stayed under section 362(a)(6), while the issuance of a deficiency notice is specifically permitted. Stay of the assessment and the permission to issue a statutory notice of a tax deficiency will permit the debtor to take his personal tax case to the Tax Court, if the bankruptcy judge authorizes him to do so (as explained more fully in the discussion of section 505.)

References in Text

Chapter 7, 11, or 13, referred to in text, is chapter 7, 11, or 13 of this title, 11 U.S.C.A. § 701 et seq., 11 U.S.C.A. § 1101 et seq., or 11 U.S.C.A. § 1301 et seq., respectively.

Section 5(a)(3) of the Securities Investor Protection Act of 1970, referred to in subsecs. (a) and (b), is section 5(a)(3) of Pub.L. 91–598, Dec. 30, 1970, 84 Stat. 1644, which is classified to section 78eee of Title 15, Commerce and Trade.

Section 466 of the Social Security Act, referred to in subsec. (b)(2)(D) to (F), is Act Aug. 14, 1935, c. 531, Title IV, § 466, as added Aug. 16, 1984, Pub.L. 98–378, § 3(b), 98 Stat. 1306, and amended, which is classified to 42 U.S.C.A. § 666.

Section 464 of the Social Security Act, referred to in subsec. (b)(2)(F), is Act Aug. 14, 1935, c. 531, Title IV, § 464, as added Aug. 13, 1981, Pub.L. 97–35, Title XXIII, § 2331(a), 95 Stat. 860, and amended, which is classified to 42 U.S.C.A. § 664.

Title IV of the Social Security Act, referred to in subsec. (b)(2)(G), is Act Aug. 14, 1935, c. 531, Title IV, § 401 et seq., as added Aug. 22, 1996, Pub.L. 104–193, Title I, § 103(a)(1), 110 Stat. 2113, and amended, which is classified principally to subchapter IV of chapter 7 of Title 42, 42 U.S.C.A. § 601 et seq. For complete classification, see Tables.

The National Housing Act, referred to in subsec. (b)(8), is Act June 27, 1934, c. 847, 48 Stat. 1246, as amended, which is classified principally to chapter 13 (section 1701 et seq.) of Title 12, Banks and Banking. For complete classification of this Act to the Code, see section 1701 of Title 12 and Tables.

Chapter 537 of title 46, referred to in subsecs. (b)(12) and (13), is Loans and Guarantees, 46 U.S.C.A. § 53701 et seq.

The Higher Education Act of 1965, including such Act, referred to in subsec. (b)(16), is Pub.L. 89–329, Nov. 8, 1965, 79 Stat. 1219, as amended, which is classified principally to chapter 28 (§ 1001 et seq.) of Title 20, Education. Section 435(j) of the Act is classified to section 1085(j) of Title 20. For complete classification of this Act to the Code, see Short Title note set out under section 1001 of Title 20 and Tables.

Section 401, 403, 408, 408A, 414, 457, or 501(c) of the Internal Revenue Code of 1986, referred to in subsec. (b)(19), is classified to 26 U.S.C.A. § 401, 403, 408, 408A, 414, 457, or 501(c).

Section 414(d) or section 403(b) of the Internal Revenue Code, referred to in subsec. (b)(19), is classified to 26 U.S.C.A. § 414(d) or 26 U.S.C.A. § 403(b).

Section 408(b)(1) of the Employee Retirement Income Security Act of 1974, referred to in subsec. (b)(19)(A), is Pub.L. 93–406, Title I, § 408(b)(1), Sept. 2, 1974, 88 Stat. 883, as amended, which is classified to 29 U.S.C.A. § 1108(b)(1).

Section 72(p) of the Internal Revenue Code of 1986, referred to in subsec. (b)(19)(A), is classified to 26 U.S.C.A. § 72(p).

Subchapter III of chapter 84 of title 5, referred to in subsec. (b)(19)(B), is 5 U.S.C.A. § 8431 et seq.

Section 1128B(f) of the Social Security Act, referred to in subsec. (b)(28), is Act Aug. 14, 1935, c. 531, Title XI, § 1128B, formerly Title XVIII, § 1877(d), and Title XIX, § 1909, as added and amended Oct. 30, 1972, Pub.L. 92–603, Title II, §§ 242(c), 278(b)(9), 86 Stat. 1419, 1454, which is classified to 42 U.S.C.A. § 1320a–7b(f).

Title XI of such Act, referred to in subsec. (b)(28), means title XI of the Social Security Act, Act Aug. 14, 1935, c. 531, Title XI, § 1101 et seq., 49 Stat. 647, as amended, which is classified principally to subchapter XI of chapter 7 of Title 42, 42 U.S.C.A. § 1301 et seq.

Title XVIII of such Act, referred to in subsec. (b)(28), means title XVIII of the Social Security Act, Act Aug. 14, 1935, c. 531, Title XVIII, § 1801 et seq., as added July 30, 1965, Pub.L. 89–97, Title I, § 102(a), 79 Stat. 291, and amended, which is classified principally to subchapter XVIII of chapter 7 of Title 42, 42 U.S.C.A. § 1395 et seq.

Chapter 7, 9, 11, 12, or 13 of this title, referred to in subsec. (c)(2)(C), is 11 U.S.C.A. § 701 et seq., 11 U.S.C.A. § 901 et seq., 11 U.S.C.A. § 1101 et seq., 11 U.S.C.A. § 1201 et seq., or 11 U.S.C.A. § 1301 et seq., respectively.

Codifications

Renumbering and conforming amendments by Pub.L. 101–508 failed to take into consideration prior renumbering and conforming amendments by Pub.L. 101–311, thereby resulting in two pars. numbered "(14)". To accommodate such duplication, the renumbering reflects changes by Pub.L. 101–311 set out first, and by Pub.L. 101–508 set out second, but does not reflect the minor conforming amendments.

Amendments

2010 Amendments. Subsec. (a)(8). Pub.L. 111–327, § 2(a)(12)(A), struck out "concerning a corporate debtor's tax liability" and inserted "concerning a tax liability of a debtor that is a corporation".

Subsec. (c)(3). Pub.L. 111–327, § 2(a)(12)(B)(i), inserted "a" following "against".

Subsec. (c)(4)(A)(i). Pub.L. 111–327, § 2(a)(12)(B)(ii), inserted "under a chapter other than chapter 7 after dismissal" following "refiled".

Subsec. (d)(4). Pub.L. 111–327, § 2(a)(12)(C), struck out "hinder, and" and inserted "hinder, or".

Subsec. (l)(2). Pub.L. 111–327, § 2(a)(12)(D), struck out "nonbankrupcty" and inserted "nonbankruptcy".

2006 Amendments. Subsec. (b)(6). Pub.L. 109–390, § 5(a)(2)(A), rewrote par. (6), which formerly read: "(6) under subsection (a) of this section, of the setoff by a commodity broker, forward contract merchant, stockbroker, financial institution, financial participant, or securities clearing agency of any mutual debt and claim under or in connection with commodity contracts, as defined in section 761 of this title, forward contracts, or securities contracts, as defined in section 741 of this title, that constitutes the setoff of a claim against the debtor for a margin payment, as defined in section 101, 741, or 761 of this title, or settlement payment, as defined in section 101 or 741 of this title, arising out of commodity contracts, forward contracts, or securities contracts against cash, securities, or other property held by, pledged to, under the control of, or due from such commodity broker, forward contract merchant, stockbroker, financial institution, financial participant, or securities clearing agency to margin, guarantee, secure, or settle commodity contracts, forward contracts, or securities contracts;".

Subsec. (b)(7). Pub.L. 109–390, § 5(a)(2)(A), rewrote par. (7), which formerly read: "(7) under subsection (a) of this section, of the setoff by a repo participant or financial participant, of any mutual debt and claim under or in connection with repurchase agreements that constitutes the setoff of a claim against the debtor for a margin payment, as defined in section 741 or 761 of this title, or settlement payment, as defined in section 741 of this title, arising out of repurchase agreements against cash, securities, or other property held by, pledged to, under the control of, or due from such repo participant or financial participant to margin, guarantee, secure or settle repurchase agreements;".

Subsec. (b)(12). Pub.L. 109–304, § 17(b)(1)(A), struck out "section 207 or title XI of the Merchant Marine Act, 1936" and inserted "chapter 537 of title 46 or section 109(h) of title 49".

Subsec. (b)(13). Pub.L. 109–304, § 17(b)(1)(B), struck out "section 207 or title XI of the Merchant Marine Act, 1936" and inserted "chapter 537 of title 46".

Subsec. (b)(17). Pub.L. 109–390, § 5(a)(2)(B), rewrote par. (17),, which formerly read: "**(17)** under subsection (a), of the setoff by a swap participant or financial participant of a mutual debt and claim under or in connection with one or more swap agreements that constitutes the setoff of a claim against the debtor for any payment or other transfer of property due from the debtor under or in connection with any swap agreement against any payment due to the debtor from the swap participant or financial participant under or in connection with any swap agreement or against cash, securities, or other property held by, pledged to, under the control of, or due from such swap participant or financial participant to margin, guarantee, secure, or settle any swap agreement;".

Subsec. (b)(27). Pub.L. 109–390, § 5(a)(2)(C), rewrote par. (27), which formerly read: "**(27)** under subsection (a), of the setoff by a master netting agreement participant of a mutual debt and claim under or in connection with one or more master netting agreements or any contract or agreement subject to such agreements that constitutes the setoff of a claim against the debtor for any payment or other transfer of property due from the debtor under or in connection with such agreements or any contract or agreement subject to such agreements against any payment due to the debtor from such master netting agreement participant under or in connection with such agreements or any contract or agreement subject to such agreements or against cash, securities, or other property held by, pledged to, under the control of, or due from such master netting agreement participant to margin, guarantee, secure, or settle such agreements or any contract or agreement subject to such agreements, to the extent that such participant is eligible to exercise such offset rights under paragraph (6), (7), or (17) for each individual contract covered by the master netting agreement in issue; and".

2005 Amendments. Subsec. (a)(8). Pub.L. 109–8, § 709, struck out "the debtor" and inserted "a corporate debtor's tax liability for a taxable period the bankruptcy court may determine or concerning the tax liability of a debtor who is an individual for a taxable period ending before the date of the order for relief under this title".

Subsec. (b)(2). Pub.L. 109–8, § 214, rewrote par. (2), which formerly read: "under subsection (a) of this section—

"**(A)** of the commencement or continuation of an action or proceeding for—

"**(i)** the establishment of paternity; or

"**(ii)** the establishment or modification of an order for alimony, maintenance, or support; or

"**(B)** of the collection of alimony, maintenance, or support from property that is not property of the estate;".

Subsec. (b)(6). Pub.L. 109–8, § 907(d)(1)(A), inserted ", pledged to, under the control of," after "held by".

Pub.L. 109–8, § 907(o)(1), substituted "financial institution, financial participant," for "financial institutions," each place such term appeared.

Subsec. (b)(7). Pub.L. 109–8, § 907(d)(1)(B), inserted ", pledged to, under the control of," after "held by".

Pub.L. 109–8, § 907(o)(2), inserted "or financial participant" after "repo participant" each place such term appeared.

Subsec. (b)(17). Pub.L. 109–8, § 224(b)(1), struck out "or" at the end of par. (17).

Pub.L. 109–8, § 907(d)(1)(C), rewrote par. (17), which formerly read: "under subsection (a) of this section, of the setoff by a swap participant, of any mutual debt and claim under or

in connection with any swap agreement that constitutes the setoff of a claim against the debtor for any payment due from the debtor under or in connection with any swap agreement against any payment due to the debtor from the swap participant under or in connection with any swap agreement or against cash, securities, or other property of the debtor held by or due from such swap participant to guarantee, secure or settle any swap agreement;"

Subsec. (b)(18). Pub.L. 109–8, § 224(b)(2), substituted a semicolon for the period at the end of par. (18).

Pub.L.109–8, § 1225, rewrote par. (18), which formerly read: "under subsection (a) of the creation or perfection of a statutory lien for an ad valorem property tax imposed by the District of Columbia, or a political subdivision of a State, if such tax comes due after the filing of the petition;"

Subsec. (b)(19). Pub.L. 109–8, § 224(b)(3), added par. (19).

Subsec. (b)(20), (21). Pub.L. 109–8, § 303(b), added pars. (20) and (21).

Subsec. (b)(22) to (24). Pub.L. 109–8, § 311(a), added pars. (22) to (24).

Subsec. (b)(25). Pub.L. 109–8, § 401(b), added par. (25).

Subsec. (b)(26). Pub.L. 109–8, § 718, added par. (26).

Subsec. (b)(27). Pub.L. 109–8, § 907(d)(1)(D), added par. (27).

Subsec. (b)(28). Pub.L. 109–8, § 1106, added par. (28).

Subsec. (c). Pub.L. 109–8, § 305(1)(A), in the text preceding par. (1), struck out "(e), and (f)" and inserted "(e), (f), and (h)".

Subsec. (c)(1). Pub.L. 109–8, § 302(1), struck out "and" at the end of par. (1).

Subsec. (c)(2). Pub.L. 109–8, § 302(2), struck out the period at the end of par. (2) and inserted a semicolon.

Subsec. (c)(3), (4). Pub.L. 109–8, § 302(3), added pars. (3) and (4).

Subsec. (d)(2). Pub.L. 109–8, § 303(a)(1), struck out "or" at the end of par. (2).

Subsec. (d)(3). Pub.L. 109–8, § 303(a)(2), struck out the period at the end of par. (3) and inserted "; or".

Pub.L. 109–8, § 444(1), inserted "or 30 days after the court determines that the debtor is subject to this paragraph, whichever is later" after "90–day period)".

Subsec. (d)(3)(B). Pub.L. 109–8, § 444(2), rewrote subpar. (B), which formerly read:

"**(B)** the debtor has commenced monthly payments to each creditor whose claim is secured by such real estate (other than a claim secured by a judgment lien or by an unmatured statutory lien), which payments are in an amount equal to interest at a current fair market rate on the value of the creditor's interest in the real estate; or"

Subsec. (d)(4). Pub.L. 109–8, § 303(a)(3), added par. (4) and concluding provisions.

Subsec. (e)(1). Pub.L. 109–8, § 320(1), inserted "(1)" after "(e)".

Subsec. (e)(2). Pub.L. 109–8, § 320(2), added par. (2).

Subsec. (h). Pub.L. 109–8, § 305(1)(B),(C), redesignated former subsec. (h) as subsec. (k), and inserted a new subsec. (h).

Subsec. (i). Pub.L. 109–8, § 106(f), added subsec. (i).

Subsec. (j). Pub.L. 109–8, § 106(f), added subsec. (j).

Subsec. (k). Pub.L. 109–8, § 305(1)(B), redesignated former subsec. (h) as subsec. (k).

Subsec. (k)(1). Pub.L. 109–8, § 441(1)(A), in subsec. (k) as so redesignated, struck out "An" and inserted "**(1)** Except as provided in paragraph (2), an".

Subsec. (k)(2). Pub.L. 109–8, § 441(1)(B), added par. (2).

Subsecs. (*l*) and (m). Pub.L. 109–8, § 311(b), added subsecs. (*l*) and (m).

Subsec. (n). Pub.L. 109–8, § 441(2), added subsec. (n).

Subsec. (*o*). Pub.L. 109–8, § 907(d)(2), inserted subsec. (*o*).

1998 Amendments. Subsec. (b)(4). Pub.L. 105–277, § 603, rewrote par. (4), which formerly read: "under subsection (a)(1) of this section, of the commencement or continuation of an action or proceeding by a governmental unit to enforce such governmental unit's police or regulatory power;".

Subsec. (b)(5). Pub.L. 105–277, § 603(1), struck out par. (5), which formerly read: "under subsection (a)(2) of this section, of the enforcement of a judgment, other than a money judgment, obtained in an action or proceeding by a governmental unit to enforce such governmental unit's police or regulatory power;".

1994 Amendments. Subsec. (a). Pub.L. 103–394, § 501(d)(7)(A), struck out "(15 U.S.C. 78eee(a)(3))" following "Securities Investor Protection Act of 1970".

Subsec. (b)(2). Pub.L. 103–394, § 304(b), completely revised par. (2). Prior to revision, par. (2) read as follows: "under subsection (a) of this section, of the collection of alimony, maintenance, or support from property that is not property of the estate;"

Subsec. (b)(3). Pub.L. 103–394, § 204(a), substituted "of any act to perfect, or to maintain or continue the perfection of, an interest in property" for "of any act to perfect an interest in property".

Subsec. (b)(6). Pub.L. 103–394, § 501(b)(2)(A), substituted "section 761" for "section 761(4)", "section 741" for "section 741(7)", "section 101, 741, or 761" for "section 101(34), 741(5), or 761(15)", and "section 101 or 741" for "section 101(35) or 741(8)".

Subsec. (b)(7). Pub.L. 103–394, § 501(b)(2)(B), substituted "section 741 or 761" for "741(5) or 761(15)", and "section 741" for "section 741(8)".

Subsec. (b)(9). Pub.L. 103–394, § 116, designated a portion of former par. (9) as subpar. (B), and added subpars. (A), (C), and (D).

Subsec. (b)(10). Pub.L. 103–394, § 501(d)(7)(B)(ii), struck out "or" following "possession of such property;".

Subsec. (b)(12). Pub.L. 103–394, § 501(d)(7)(B)(iii), substituted "section 31325 of title 46" for "the Ship Mortgage Act, 1920 (46 App. U.S.C. 911 et seq.)", and struck out "(46 App. U.S.C. 1117 and 1271 et seq., respectively)" following "Merchant Marine Act, 1936".

Subsec. (b)(13). Pub.L. 103–394, § 501(d)(7)(B)(iv), substituted "section 31325 of title 46" for "the Ship Mortgage Act, 1920 (46 App. U.S.C. 911 et seq.)", struck out "(46 App. U.S.C. 1117 and 1271 et seq., respectively)" following "Merchant Marine Act, 1936", and struck out "or" following ";" .

Subsec. (b)(14). Pub.L. 103–394, § 501(d)(7)(B)(vii)(I), substituted "swap agreement; or" for "swap agreement.".

Pub.L. 103–394, § 501(d)(7)(B)(vii)(II), redesignated former par. (14), relating to setoff by a swap participant of any

mutual debt and claim under or in connection with a swap agreement, as par. (17).

Subsec. (b)(15). Pub.L. 103–394, § 501(d)(7)(B)(v), struck out "or" after "educational institution;".

Subsec. (b)(16). Pub.L. 103–394, § 501(d)(7)(B)(vi), substituted "such Act; " for "such Act." and struck out "(20 U.S.C. 1001 et seq.)" following "Higher Education Act of 1965".

Subsec. (b)(17). Pub.L. 103–394, § 501(d)(7)(B)(vii)(II), (III), redesignated former par. (14), relating to setoff by a swap participant of any mutual debt and claim under or in connection with a swap agreement, as par. (17).

Subsec. (b)(18). Pub.L. 103–394, § 401, added par. (18).

Subsec. (b). Pub.L. 103–394, § 501(d)(7)(B)(i), struck out "(15 U.S.C. 78eee(a)(3))" following "Securities Investor Protection Act of 1970".

Subsec. (d)(3). Pub.L. 103–394, § 218(b), added par. (3).

Subsec. (e). Pub.L. 103–394, § 101, substituted "If the hearing under this subsection is a preliminary hearing, then such final hearing shall be concluded not later than thirty days after the conclusion of such preliminary hearing, unless the 30-day period is extended with the consent of the parties in interest or for a specific time which the court finds is required by compelling circumstances.", for "If the hearing under this subsection is a preliminary hearing, then such final hearing shall be commenced not later than thirty days after the conclusion of such preliminary hearing."

1990 Amendments. Subsec. (b)(6). Pub.L. 101–311, § 202, added provisions referring to sections 101(34) and 101(35) of this title.

Subsec. (b)(12). Pub.L. 101—508, §§ 3007(a)(1)(A), 3008, which temporarily directed the striking of "or" after "State law;", could not be executed because of a prior amendment by Pub.L. 101—311. See amendment note for section 102(1) of Pub.L. 101–311, immediately following. See also Effective and Applicability Provisions note under this section.

Pub.L. 101—311, § 102(1), struck out "or" after "State law".

Subsec. (b)(13). Pub.L. 101—508, §§ 3007(a)(1)(B), 3008, which temporarily directed the substitution of a semicolon for a period at end thereof, could not be executed because of a prior amendment by Pub.L. 101—311. See amendment note for section 102(2) of Pub.L. 101—311, immediately following. See also Effective and Applicability Provisions note under this section.

Pub.L. 101—311, § 102(2), substituted "; or" for period at end.

Subsec. (b)(14) to (16). Pub.L. 101—508, §§ 3007(a)(1)(C), 3008, temporarily added pars. (14) to (16). Notwithstanding directory language adding pars. (14) to (16) immediately following par. (13), pars. (14) to (16) were added after par. (14), as added by Pub.L. 101—311, to reflect the probable intent of Congress. See Effective and Applicability Provisions note under this section.

Pub.L. 101—311, § 102(3), added par. (14) relating to the setoff by a swap participant of any mutual debt and claim under or in connection with a swap agreement. Notwithstanding directory language adding par. (14) at end of subsec. (b), par. (14) was added after par.(13) to reflect the probable intent of Congress.

1986 Amendments. Subsec. (b). Pub.L. 99–509, § 5001(a), inserted undesignated provision, following numbered pars., that the provisions of pars. (12) and (13) of this subsection shall apply with respect to any such petition filed on or before December 31, 1989.

Subsec. (b)(6). Pub.L. 99–554, § 283(d)(1), substituted ", financial institutions" for "financial institution," wherever appearing.

Subsec. (b)(9). Pub.L. 99–554, § 283(d)(2), (3), struck out "or" at end of first par. (9) and redesignated as par. (10) the second par. (9) relating to leases of nonresidential property, which was added by section 363(b) of Pub.L. 98–353.

Subsec. (b)(10). Pub.L. 99–554, § 283(d)(3), (4), redesignated par. (9), as added by Pub.L. 98–353, § 363(b), as par. (10), and, in par. (10), as so redesignated, substituted "property; or" for "property.". Former par. (10) was redesignated (11).

Subsec. (b)(11). Pub.L. 99–554, § 283(d)(3), redesignated former par. (10) as (11).

Subsec. (b)(12), (13). Pub.L. 99–509, § 5001(a), added pars. (12) and (13).

Subsec. (c)(2)(C). Pub.L. 99–554, § 257(j), added reference to chapter 12 of this title.

1984 Amendments. Subsec. (a)(1). Pub.L. 98–353, § 441(a)(1), added "action or" after "other".

Subsec. (a)(3). Pub.L. 98–353, § 441(a)(2), added "or to exercise control over property of the estate" after "estate".

Subsec. (b)(3). Pub.L. 98–353, § 441(b)(1), added "or to the extent that such act is accomplished within the period provided under section 547(e)(2)(A) of this title" after "title".

Subsec. (b)(6). Pub.L. 98–353, § 441(b)(2)(A), added "or due from" after "held by".

Pub.L. 98–353, § 441(b)(2)(B), added "Financial institution," after "stockbroker" wherever appearing and substituted "secure, or settle commodity contracts" for "or secure commodity contracts".

Subsec. (b)(7). Pub.L. 98–353, § 392(b), added par. (7). Former par. (7) was redesignated as (8).

Subsec. (b)(8). Pub.L. 98–353, § 392(a), redesignated former par. (7) as (8). Former par. (8) was redesignated as (9).

Pub.L. 98–353, § 441(b)(3)(A), substituted "the" for "said".

Pub.L. 98–353, § 441(b)(3)(B), struck out "or" after "units;".

Subsec. (b)(9). Pub.L. 98–353, § 363(b), added par. (9), relating to leases of nonresidential real property, which resulted in two pars. designated "(9)" in view of renumbering of former par. (8) as (9) by Pub.L. 98–353, § 392(a).

Pub.L. 98–353, § 392(a), redesignated former par. (8) as (9). See note under this section relating to subsec. (b)(8).

Pub.L. 98–353, § 441(b)(4), substituted a semicolon for the period at the end of par. (9).

Subsec. (b)(10). Pub.L. 98–353, § 441(b)(5), added par. (10).

Subsec. (c)(2)(B). Pub.L. 98–353, § 441(c), substituted "or" for "and".

Subsec. (d)(2). Pub.L. 98–353, § 441(d), added "under subsection (a) of this section" after "property".

Subsec. (e). Pub.L. 98–353, § 441(e), added "the conclusion of" after "pending" and substituted "The court shall order such stay continued in effect pending the conclusion of the final hearing under subsection (d) of this section if there is a reasonable likelihood that the party opposing relief from such stay will prevail at the conclusion of such final hearing. If the hearing under this subsection is a preliminary hearing, then such final hearing shall be commenced not later than thirty days after the conclusion of such preliminary hearing." for "If the hearing under this subsection is a preliminary hearing—

"(1) the court shall order such stay so continued if there is a reasonable likelihood that the party opposing relief from such stay will prevail at the final hearing under subsection (d) of this section; and

"(2) such final hearing shall be commenced within thirty days after such preliminary hearing."

Subsec. (f). Pub.L. 98–353, § 441(f), substituted "Upon request of a party in interest, the court, with or" for "The court,".

Subsec. (h). Pub.L. 98–353, § 304, added subsec. (h).

1982 Amendments. Subsec. (a). Pub.L. 97–222, § 3(a), inserted ", or an application filed under section 5(a)(3) of the Securities Investor Protection Act of 1970 (15 U.S.C. 78eee(a)(3))," following "this title" in the provisions preceding par. (1).

Subsec. (b). Pub.L. 97–222, § 3(b), inserted ", or of an application under section 5(a)(3) of the Securities Investor Protection Act of 1970 (15 U.S.C. 78eee(a)(3))," following "this title" in the provisions preceding par. (1).

Subsec. (b)(6). Pub.L. 97–222, § 3(c), substituted provisions that the filing of a bankruptcy petition would not operate as a stay, under subsec. (a) of this section, of the setoff by a commodity broker, forward contract merchant, stockbroker, or securities clearing agency of any mutual debt and claim under or in connection with commodity, forward, or securities contracts that constitutes the setoff of a claim against the debtor for a margin or settlement payment arising out of commodity, forward, or securities contracts against cash, securities, or other property held by any of the above agents to margin, guarantee, or secure commodity, forward, or securities contracts, for provisions that such filing would not operate as a stay under subsection (a)(7) of this section, of the setoff of any mutual debt and claim that are commodity futures contracts, forward commodity contracts, leverage transactions, options, warrants, rights to purchase or sell commodity futures contracts or securities, or options to purchase or sell commodities or securities.

Effective and Applicability Provisions

2005 Acts. Amendments by Pub.L. 109–8 effective, except as otherwise provided, 180 days after April 20, 2005, and inapplicable with respect to cases commenced under Title 11 before the effective date, see Pub.L. 109–8, § 1501, set out as a note under 11 U.S.C.A. § 101.

1994 Acts. Amendments by Pub.L. 103–394 effective on Oct. 22, 1994, and not to apply with respect to cases commenced under this title before Oct. 22, 1994, see section 702 of Pub.L. 103–394, set out as a note under section 101 of this title.

1990 Acts. Section 3007(a)(3) of Pub.L. 101–508 provided that: "The amendments made by this subsection [amending this section and section 541 this title] shall be effective upon date of enactment of this Act [Nov. 5, 1990]."

Section 3008 of Pub.L. 101–508, which provided that the amendments made by this subtitle [subtitle A (§§ 3001–3008) of Title III of Pub.L. 101–508, amending this section, sections 541 and 1328 of this title, and sections 1078, 1078–1, 1078–7, 1085, 1088, and 1091 of Title 20, Education, and provisions set out as a note under section 1078–1 of Title 20, and enacting provisions set out as notes under this section, and section 1328 of this title, and sections 1001, 1078–1, 1078–7, 1085, and 1088 of Title 20] were to cease to be effective on October 1, 1996, was repealed by Pub.L. 102–325, Title XV, § 1558, July 23, 1992, 106 Stat. 841.

1986 Acts. Amendment by Pub.L. 99–554, § 257(j), effective 30 days after Oct. 27, 1986, but not applicable with respect to cases commenced under this title before that date, see section 302(a), (a)(1) of Pub.L. 99–554, set out as a note under section 581 of Title 28, Judiciary and Judicial Procedure.

Amendment by Pub.L. 99–554, § 283(d), effective 30 days after Oct. 27, 1986, see section 302(a) of Pub.L. 99–554, set out as a note under section 581 of Title 28.

Section 5001(b) of Pub.L. 99–509 provided that: "The amendments made by subsection (a) of this section [amending this section and enacting a provision set out as a note under this section] shall apply only to petitions filed under section 362 of title 11, United States Code, which are made after August 1, 1986."

1984 Acts. Amendment by Pub.L. 98–353 effective with respect to cases filed 90 days after July 10, 1984, see section 552(a), formerly 553 of Pub.L. 98–353, set out as a note under section 101 of this title.

Separability of Provisions

If any provision of or amendment made by Pub.L. 103–394 or the application of such provision or amendment to any person or circumstance is held to be unconstitutional, the remaining provisions of and amendments made by Pub.L. 103–394 and the application of such provisions and amendments to any person or circumstance shall not be affected thereby, see section 701 of Pub.L. 103–394, set out as a note under section 101 of this title.

Report to Congressional Committees

Section 5001(a) of Pub.L. 99–509, directed Secretary of Transportation and Secretary of Commerce, before July 1, 1989, to submit reports to Congress on the effects of amendments to 11 U.S.C.A. § 362 by this subsection.

CROSS REFERENCES

Abstention of district court from hearing a proceeding based upon State law as cause of action, provision as not limiting applicability of stay under this section, see 28 USCA § 1334.

Adequate protection in Chapter 12 cases, method of obtaining, see 11 USCA § 1205.

Applicability of this section in Chapter 9 cases, see 11 USCA § 901.

Assessment of taxes against estate, see 11 USCA § 505.

Denial of debtor status to debtor who obtained voluntary dismissal following filing of relief from provisions of this section, see 11 USCA § 109.

Effect of this section on subchapter III of Chapter 7, see 11 USCA § 742.

Enforcement of claims against debtor in Chapter 9 cases, automatic stay of, see 11 USCA § 922.

Extension of time, see 11 USCA § 108.

Grain storage facility bankruptcies, expedited determinations, see 11 USCA § 557.

Priorities, see 11 USCA § 507.

Right of possession of party with security interest in—

    Aircraft equipment and vessel, see 11 USCA § 1110.

    Rolling stock equipment, see 11 USCA § 1168.

Secretary of Commerce or Transportation as mortgagee, see 46 USCA § 31308.

Setoff, see 11 USCA § 553.

Turnover of property to estate, see 11 USCA § 542.

LIBRARY REFERENCES

American Digest System

Bankruptcy ⌖2391 to 2468.

Corpus Juris Secundum

CJS Bankruptcy § 7, Bankruptcy Code.

CJS Bankruptcy § 187, Sanctions for Violating Stay.

CJS Bankruptcy § 202, Procedure; Motion and Stay.

CJS Bankruptcy § 234, Pending Actions.

CJS Bankruptcy § 246, Relationship to Automatic Stay.

CJS Bankruptcy § 256, Sanctions Resulting from Noncompliance With Requirements as to Basis for Filing.

CJS Bankruptcy § 278, Parties Defendant; Sovereign Immunity.

CJS Bankruptcy § 308, Enlargement.

CJS Bankruptcy § 395, Provisional Relief.

CJS Bankruptcy § 399, Effects of Recognizing Foreign Main Proceeding.

CJS Bankruptcy § 400, Relief Available on Recognition.

CJS Bankruptcy § 476, Purpose.

CJS Bankruptcy § 477, Persons Protected by and Subject to Stay.

CJS Bankruptcy § 479, Inception and Duration of Stay.

CJS Bankruptcy § 483, Municipal Bankruptcies.

CJS Bankruptcy § 485, Proceedings Against Debtor.

CJS Bankruptcy § 487, Enforcement of Prepetition Judgment.

CJS Bankruptcy § 488, Tax Court Proceedings.

CJS Bankruptcy § 494, Setoff.

CJS Bankruptcy § 497, Previous or Pending Small Business Bankruptcies.

CJS Bankruptcy § 498, Domestic Relations Claims and Proceedings.

CJS Bankruptcy § 499, Perfection and Enforcement of Liens and Other Property Interests.

CJS Bankruptcy § 500, Setoffs.

CJS Bankruptcy § 501, Criminal Prosecutions.

CJS Bankruptcy § 502, Police or Regulatory Power.

CJS Bankruptcy § 503, Police or Regulatory Power--Labor and Employment Matters.

CJS Bankruptcy § 504, Police or Regulatory Power--Environmental Matters.

CJS Bankruptcy § 505, Taxation.

CJS Bankruptcy § 506, Licenses.

CJS Bankruptcy § 512, Chapter 12 and Chapter 13 Cases.

CJS Bankruptcy § 515, Equity Cushion.

CJS Bankruptcy § 516, Family Farmer Debt Adjustment Cases.

CJS Bankruptcy § 517, Fraud, Bad Faith, or Misconduct.

CJS Bankruptcy § 519, Lack of Equity in Property; Asset Necessary for Reorganization.

CJS Bankruptcy § 520, Single Real Property Asset.

CJS Bankruptcy § 522, Parties; Standing.

CJS Bankruptcy § 525, Evidence.

CJS Bankruptcy § 526, Automatic Relief from Stay.

CJS Bankruptcy § 527, Automatic Relief from Stay--As to Personal Property.

CJS Bankruptcy § 529, Ex Parte Relief from Stay.

CJS Bankruptcy § 530, Determination and Relief.

CJS Bankruptcy § 541, By Private Employer.

CJS Bankruptcy § 547, Under Statute.

CJS Bankruptcy § 548, Under Statute--Willful Violation.

CJS Bankruptcy § 549, Under Statute--Punitive Damages.

CJS Bankruptcy § 608, Time of Redemption.

CJS Bankruptcy § 638, Good-Faith Transfers and Payments Made by Entities Without Notice or Knowledge of Case.

CJS Bankruptcy § 663, Disqualifying or Limiting Factors.

CJS Bankruptcy § 838, Stockbroker Liquidation Cases.

CJS Bankruptcy § 846, Operation of Affairs of Municipal Debtor in Chapter 9 Cases.

CJS Bankruptcy § 853, Use of Aircraft, Aircraft Equipment, Vessels, and Railroad Equipment Subject to Financing Agreements.

CJS Bankruptcy § 868, Remedies for Unauthorized Use of Cash Collateral.

CJS Bankruptcy § 921, Assumption of Leases of Personal Property.

CJS Bankruptcy § 1094, Requirements for Reaffirmation of Debt.

CJS Bankruptcy § 1112, Under Securities Investor Protection Act of 1970.

CJS Bankruptcy § 1166, Interest in Rolling Stock Equipment.

CJS Bankruptcy § 1226, Relief from Automatic Stay.

CJS Bankruptcy § 1261, Particular Matters.

CJS Limitations of Actions § 178, Pendency of Other Legal Proceedings--Proceedings in Insolvency, Bankruptcy, or Receivership.

CJS Securities Reg. & Commodity Futures Trading § 419, Proceedings, Generally.

§ 363. Use, sale, or lease of property

(a) In this section, "cash collateral" means cash, negotiable instruments, documents of title, securities, deposit accounts, or other cash equivalents whenever acquired in which the estate and an entity other than the estate have an interest and includes the proceeds, products, offspring, rents, or profits of property and the fees, charges, accounts or other payments for the use or occupancy of rooms and other public facilities in hotels, motels, or other lodging properties subject to a security interest as provided in section 552(b) of this title, whether existing before or after the commencement of a case under this title.

(b)(1) The trustee, after notice and a hearing, may use, sell, or lease, other than in the ordinary course of business, property of the estate, except that if the debtor in connection with offering a product or a service discloses to an individual a policy prohibiting the transfer of personally identifiable information about individuals to persons that are not affiliated with the debtor and if such policy is in effect on the date of the commencement of the case, then the trustee may not sell or lease personally identifiable information to any person unless—

(A) such sale or such lease is consistent with such policy; or

(B) after appointment of a consumer privacy ombudsman in accordance with section 332, and after notice and a hearing, the court approves such sale or such lease—

(i) giving due consideration to the facts, circumstances, and conditions of such sale or such lease; and

(ii) finding that no showing was made that such sale or such lease would violate applicable nonbankruptcy law.

(2) If notification is required under subsection (a) of section 7A of the Clayton Act in the case of a transaction under this subsection, then—

(A) notwithstanding subsection (a) of such section, the notification required by such subsection to be given by the debtor shall be given by the trustee; and

(B) notwithstanding subsection (b) of such section, the required waiting period shall end on the 15th day after the date of the receipt, by the Federal Trade Commission and the Assistant Attorney General in charge of the Antitrust Division of the Department of Justice, of the notification required under such subsection (a), unless such waiting period is extended—

(i) pursuant to subsection (e)(2) of such section, in the same manner as such subsection (e)(2) applies to a cash tender offer;

(ii) pursuant to subsection (g)(2) of such section; or

(iii) by the court after notice and a hearing.

(c)(1) If the business of the debtor is authorized to be operated under section 721, 1108, 1203, 1204, or 1304 of this title and unless the court orders otherwise, the trustee may enter into transactions, including the sale or lease of property of the estate, in the ordinary course of business, without notice or a hearing, and may use property of the estate in the ordinary course of business without notice or a hearing.

(2) The trustee may not use, sell, or lease cash collateral under paragraph (1) of this subsection unless—

(A) each entity that has an interest in such cash collateral consents; or

(B) the court, after notice and a hearing, authorizes such use, sale, or lease in accordance with the provisions of this section.

(3) Any hearing under paragraph (2)(B) of this subsection may be a preliminary hearing or may be consolidated with a hearing under subsection (e) of this section, but shall be scheduled in accordance with the needs of the debtor. If the hearing under paragraph (2)(B) of this subsection is a preliminary hearing, the court may authorize such use, sale, or lease only if there is a reasonable likelihood that the trustee will prevail at the final hearing under subsection (e) of this section. The court shall act promptly on any request for authorization under paragraph (2)(B) of this subsection.

(4) Except as provided in paragraph (2) of this subsection, the trustee shall segregate and account for any cash collateral in the trustee's possession, custody, or control.

(d) The trustee may use, sell, or lease property under subsection (b) or (c) of this section—

(1) in the case of a debtor that is a corporation or trust that is not a moneyed business, commercial corporation, or trust, only in accordance with nonbankruptcy law applicable to the transfer of property by a debtor that is such a corporation or trust; and

(2) only to the extent not inconsistent with any relief granted under subsection (c), (d), (e), or (f) of section 362.

(e) Notwithstanding any other provision of this section, at any time, on request of an entity that has an interest in property used, sold, or leased, or proposed to be used, sold, or leased, by the trustee, the court, with or without a hearing, shall prohibit or condition such use, sale, or lease as is necessary to provide adequate protection of such interest. This subsection also applies to property that is subject to any unexpired lease of personal property (to the exclusion of such property being subject to an order to grant relief from the stay under section 362).

(f) The trustee may sell property under subsection (b) or (c) of this section free and clear of any interest in such property of an entity other than the estate, only if—

(1) applicable nonbankruptcy law permits sale of such property free and clear of such interest;

(2) such entity consents;

(3) such interest is a lien and the price at which such property is to be sold is greater than the aggregate value of all liens on such property;

(4) such interest is in bona fide dispute; or

(5) such entity could be compelled, in a legal or equitable proceeding, to accept a money satisfaction of such interest.

(g) Notwithstanding subsection (f) of this section, the trustee may sell property under subsection (b) or (c) of this section free and clear of any vested or contingent right in the nature of dower or curtesy.

(h) Notwithstanding subsection (f) of this section, the trustee may sell both the estate's interest, under subsection (b) or (c) of this section, and the interest of any co-owner in property in which the debtor had, at the time of the commencement of the case, an undivided interest as a tenant in common, joint tenant, or tenant by the entirety, only if—

(1) partition in kind of such property among the estate and such co-owners is impracticable;

(2) sale of the estate's undivided interest in such property would realize significantly less for the estate than sale of such property free of the interests of such co-owners;

(3) the benefit to the estate of a sale of such property free of the interests of co-owners outweighs the detriment, if any, to such co-owners; and

(4) such property is not used in the production, transmission, or distribution, for sale, of electric energy or of natural or synthetic gas for heat, light, or power.

(i) Before the consummation of a sale of property to which subsection (g) or (h) of this section applies, or of property of the estate that was community property of the debtor and the debtor's spouse immediately before the commencement of the case, the debtor's spouse, or a co-owner of such property, as the case may be, may purchase such property at the price at which such sale is to be consummated.

(j) After a sale of property to which subsection (g) or (h) of this section applies, the trustee shall distribute to the debtor's spouse or the co-owners of such property, as the case may be, and to the estate, the proceeds of such sale, less the costs and expenses, not including any compensation of the trustee, of such sale, according to the interests of such spouse or co-owners, and of the estate.

(k) At a sale under subsection (b) of this section of property that is subject to a lien that secures an allowed claim, unless the court for cause orders otherwise the holder of such claim may bid at such sale, and, if the holder of such claim purchases such property, such holder may offset such claim against the purchase price of such property.

(l) Subject to the provisions of section 365, the trustee may use, sell, or lease property under subsection (b) or (c) of this section, or a plan under chapter 11, 12, or 13 of this title may provide for the use, sale, or lease of property, notwithstanding any provision in a contract, a lease, or applicable law that is conditioned on the insolvency or financial condition of the debtor, on the commencement of a case under this title concerning the debtor, or on the appointment of or the taking possession by a trustee in a case under this title or a custodian, and that effects, or gives an option to effect, a forfeiture, modification, or termination of the debtor's interest in such property.

(m) The reversal or modification on appeal of an authorization under subsection (b) or (c) of this section of a sale or lease of property does not affect the validity of a sale or lease under such authorization to an entity that purchased or leased such property in good faith, whether or not such entity knew of the pendency of the appeal, unless such authorization and such sale or lease were stayed pending appeal.

(n) The trustee may avoid a sale under this section if the sale price was controlled by an agreement among potential bidders at such sale, or may recover from a party to such agreement any amount by which the value of the property sold exceeds the price at which such sale was consummated, and may recover any costs, attorneys' fees, or expenses incurred in avoiding such sale or recovering such amount. In addition to any recovery under the preceding sentence, the court may grant judgment for punitive damages in favor of the estate and against any such party that entered into such an agreement in willful disregard of this subsection.

(o) Notwithstanding subsection (f), if a person purchases any interest in a consumer credit transaction that is subject to the Truth in Lending Act or any interest in a consumer credit contract (as defined in section 433.1 of title 16 of the Code of Federal Regulations (January 1, 2004), as amended from time to time), and if such interest is purchased through a sale under this section, then such person shall remain subject to all claims and defenses that are related to such consumer credit transaction or such consumer credit contract, to the same extent as such person would be subject to such claims and defenses of the consumer had such interest been purchased at a sale not under this section.

(p) In any hearing under this section—

(1) the trustee has the burden of proof on the issue of adequate protection; and

(2) the entity asserting an interest in property has the burden of proof on the issue of the validity, priority, or extent of such interest.

(Pub.L. 95–598, Nov. 6, 1978, 92 Stat. 2572; Pub.L. 98–353, Title III, § 442, July 10, 1984, 98 Stat. 371; Pub.L. 99–554, Title II, § 257(k), Oct. 27, 1986, 100 Stat. 3115; Pub.L. 103–394, Title I, § 109, Title II, §§ 214(b), 219(c), Title V, § 501(d)(8), Oct. 22, 1994, 108 Stat. 4113, 4126, 4129, 4144; Pub.L. 109–8, Title II, §§ 204, 231(a), Title XII, § 1221(a), Apr. 20, 2005, 119 Stat. 49, 72, 195; Pub.L. 111–327, § 2(a)(13), Dec. 22, 2010, 124 Stat. 3559.)

HISTORICAL AND STATUTORY NOTES

Revision Notes and Legislative Reports

1978 Acts. This section defines the right and powers of the trustee with respect to the use, sale or lease of property and the rights of other parties that have interests in the property involved. It applies in both liquidation and reorganization cases.

Subsection (a) defines "cash collateral" as cash, negotiable instruments, documents of title, securities, deposit accounts, or other cash equivalents in which the estate and an entity other than the estate have an interest, such as a lien or a co-ownership interest. The definition is not restricted to property of the estate that is cash collateral on the date of the filing of the petition. Thus, if "non-cash" collateral is disposed of and the proceeds come within the definition of "cash collateral" as set forth in this subsection, the proceeds would be cash collateral as long as they remain subject to the original lien on the "non-cash" collateral under section 52(b). To illustrate, rents received from real property before or after the commencement of the case would be cash collateral to the extent that they are subject to a lien.

Subsection (b) permits the trustees to use, sell, or lease, other than in the ordinary course of business, property of the estate upon notice and opportunity for objections and hearing thereon.

Subsection (c) governs use, sale, or lease in the ordinary course of business. If the business of the debtor is authorized to be operated under section 721, 1108, or 1304 of the bankruptcy code, then the trustee may use, sell, or lease property in the ordinary course of business or enter into ordinary course transactions without need for notice and hearing. This power is subject to several limitations. First, the court may restrict the trustee's powers in the order authorizing operation of the business. Second, with respect to cash collateral, the trustee may not use, sell, or lease cash collateral except upon court authorization after notice and a hearing, or with the consent of each entity that has an interest in such cash collateral. The same preliminary hearing procedure in the automatic stay section applies to a hearing under this subsection. In addition, the trustee is required to segregate and account for any cash collateral in the trustee's possession, custody, or control.

Under subsections (d) and (e), the use, sale, or lease of property is further limited by the concept of adequate protection. Sale, use, or lease of property in which an entity other than the estate has an interest may be effected only to the extent not inconsistent with any relief from the stay granted to that interest's holder. Moreover, the court may prohibit or condition the use, sale, or lease as is necessary to provide adequate protection of that interest. Again, the trustee has the burden of proof on the issue of adequate protection. Subsection (e) also provides that where a sale of the property is proposed, an entity that has an interest in such property may bid at the sale thereof and set off against the purchase price up to the amount of such entity's claim. No prior valuation under section 506(a) would limit this bidding right, since the bid at the sale would be determinative of value.

Subsection (f) permits sale of property free and clear of any interest in the property of an entity other than the estate. The trustee may sell free and clear if applicable nonbankruptcy law permits it, if the other entity consents, if the interest is a lien and the sale price of the property is greater than the amount secured by the lien, if the interest is in bona fide dispute, or if the other entity could be compelled to accept a money satisfaction of the interest in a legal or equitable proceeding. Sale under this subsection is subject to the adequate protection requirement. Most often, adequate protection in connection with a sale free and clear of other interests will be to have those interests attach to the proceeds of the sale.

At a sale free and clear of other interests, any holder of any interest in the property being sold will be permitted to bid. If that holder is the high bidder, he will be permitted to offset the value of his interest against the purchase price of the property. Thus, in the most common situation, a holder of a lien on property being sold may bid at the sale and, if successful, may offset the amount owed to him that is secured by the lien on the property (but may not offset other amounts owed to him) against the purchase price, and be liable to the trustee for the balance of the sale price, if any.

Subsection (g) permits the trustee to sell free and clear of any vested or contingent right in the nature of dower or curtesy.

Subsection (h) permits sale of a co-owner's interest in property in which the debtor had an undivided ownership interest such as a joint tenancy, a tenancy in common, or a tenancy by the entirety. Such a sale is permissible only if partition is impracticable, if sale of the estate's interest would realize significantly less for the estate than sale of the property free of the interests of the co-owners, and if the benefit to the estate of such a sale outweighs any detriment to the co-owners. This subsection does not apply to a co-owner's interest in a public utility when a disruption of the utilities services could result.

Subsection (i) provides protections for co-owners and spouses with dower, curtesy, or community property rights. It gives a right of first refusal to the co-owner or spouse at the price at which the sale is to be consummated.

Subsection (j) requires the trustee to distribute to the spouse or co-owner the appropriate portion of the proceeds of the sale, less certain administrative expenses.

Subsection (k) permits the trustee to use, sell, or lease property notwithstanding certain bankruptcy or ipso facto clauses that terminate the debtor's interest in the property or that work a forfeiture or modification of that interest. This subsection is not as broad as the anti-ipso facto provision in proposed 11 U.S.C. 541(c)(1).

Subsection (l) protects good faith purchasers of property sold under this section from a reversal on appeal of the sale authorization, unless the authorization for the sale and the sale itself were stayed pending appeal. The purchaser's knowledge of the appeal is irrelevant to the issue of good faith.

Subsection (m) is directed at collusive bidding on property sold under this section. It permits the trustee to void a sale if the price of the sale was controlled by an agreement among potential bidders. The trustees may also recover the excess of the value of the property over the purchase price, and may recover any costs, attorney's fees, or expenses incurred in voiding the sale or recovering the difference. In addition, the court is authorized to grant judgment in favor of the estate and against the collusive bidder if the agreement controlling the sale price was entered into in willful disregard of this subsection. The subsection does not specify the precise measure of damages, but simply provides for punitive damages, to be fixed in light of the circumstances. Senate Report No. 95–989.

1984 Acts. Statements by Legislative Leaders, see 1984 U.S.Code Cong. and Adm.News, p. 576.

1986 Acts. House Report No. 99–764 and House Conference Report No. 99–958, see 1986 U.S.Code Cong. and Adm. News, p. 5227.

1994 Acts. House Report No. 103–835, see 1994 U.S. Code Cong. and Adm. News, p. 3340.

2005 Acts. House Report No. 109–31(Part I), see 2005 U.S. Code Cong. and Adm. News, p. 88.

Legislative Statements

Section 363(a) of the House amendment defines "cash collateral" as defined in the Senate amendment. The broader definition of "soft collateral" contained in H.R. 8200 as passed by the House is deleted to remove limitations that were placed on the use, lease, or sale of inventory, accounts, contract rights, general intangibles, and chattel paper by the trustee or debtor in possession.

Section 363(c)(2) of the House amendment is derived from the Senate amendment. Similarly, sections 363(c)(3) and (4) are derived from comparable provisions in the Senate amendment in lieu of the contrary procedure contained in section 363(c) as passed by the House. The policy of the House amendment will generally require the court to schedule a preliminary hearing in accordance with the needs of the debtor to authorize the trustee or debtor in possession to use, sell, or lease cash collateral. The trustee or debtor in possession may use, sell, or lease cash collateral in the ordinary course of business only "after notice and a hearing."

Section 363(f) of the House amendment adopts an identical provision contained in the House bill, as opposed to an alternative provision contained in the Senate amendment.

Section 363(h) of the House amendment adopts a new paragraph (4) representing a compromise between the House bill and Senate amendment. The provision adds a limitation indicating that a trustee or debtor in possession sell jointly owned property only if the property is not used in the production, transmission, or distribution for sale, of electric energy or of natural or synthetic gas for heat, light, or power. This limitation is intended to protect public utilities from being deprived of power sources because of the bankruptcy of a joint owner.

Section 363(k) of the House amendment is derived from the third sentence of section 363(e) of the Senate amendment. The provision indicates that a secured creditor may bid in the full amount of the creditor's allowed claim, including the secured portion and any unsecured portion thereof in the event the creditor is undersecured, with respect to property that is subject to a lien that secures the allowed claim of the sale of the property.

References in Text

Section 7A of the Clayton Act, referred to in subsec. (b)(2), is section 7A of Act Oct. 15, 1914, c. 323, as added Sept. 30, 1976, Pub.L. 94–435, Title II, § 201, 90 Stat. 1390, which is classified to section 18a of Title 15, Commerce and Trade.

The Truth in Lending Act, referred to in subsec. (o), is Title I of Pub.L. 90–321, May 29, 1968, 82 Stat. 146, as amended, also known as TILA, which is classified principally to subchapter I of chapter 41 of Title 15, 15 U.S.C.A. § 1601 et seq. For complete classification, see Short Title note set out under 15 U.S.C.A. § 1601 and Tables.

Amendments

2010 Amendments. Subsec. (d). Pub.L. 111–327, § 2(a)(13)(A), struck out "only" following "of this section".

Subsec. (d)(1). Pub.L. 111–327, § 2(a)(13)(B), rewrote par. (1), which formerly read: "**(1)** in accordance with applicable nonbankruptcy law that governs the transfer of property by a corporation or trust that is not a moneyed, business, or commercial corporation or trust; and".

Subsec. (d)(2). Pub.L. 111–327, § 2(a)(13)(C), inserted "only" after "(2)".

2005 Amendments. Subsec. (b)(1). Pub.L. 109–8, § 231(a), struck out the period at the end and inserted the following:

", except that if the debtor in connection with offering a product or a service discloses to an individual a policy prohibiting the transfer of personally identifiable information about individuals to persons that are not affiliated with the debtor and if such policy is in effect on the date of the commencement of the case, then the trustee may not sell or lease personally identifiable information to any person unless—

"**(A)** such sale or such lease is consistent with such policy; or

"**(B)** after appointment of a consumer privacy ombudsman in accordance with section 332, and after notice and a hearing, the court approves such sale or such lease—

"**(i)** giving due consideration to the facts, circumstances, and conditions of such sale or such lease; and

"**(ii)** finding that no showing was made that such sale or such lease would violate applicable nonbankruptcy law."

Subsec. (d). Pub.L.109–8, § 1221(a), struck out "only to the extent not inconsistent with any relief granted under section 362(c), 362(d), 362(e), or 362(f) of this title" at the end of the subsection and inserted "only—

"**(1)** in accordance with applicable nonbankruptcy law that governs the transfer of property by a corporation or trust that is not a moneyed, business, or commercial corporation or trust; and

"**(2)** to the extent not inconsistent with any relief granted under subsection (c), (d), (e), or (f) of section 362."

Subsec. (o). Pub.L. 109–8, § 204(1), (2), added a new subsec. (o) and redesignated former subsec. (o) as subsec. (p).

Subsec. (p). Pub.L. 109–8, § 204(1), redesignated former subsec. (o) as subsec. (p).

1994 Amendments. Subsec. (a). Pub.L. 103–394, § 214(b), added provisions stating that "cash collateral" includes the fees, charges, accounts or other payments for the use or occupancy of rooms and other public facilities in hotels, motels, or other lodging properties.

Subsec. (b)(2). Pub.L. 103–394, § 501(d)(8)(A), struck out "(15 U.S.C. 18a)" following "section 7A of the Clayton Act".

Subsec. (b)(2)(A), (B). Pub.L. 103–394, § 109, completely revised subpars. (A) and (B). Prior to revision, subpars. (A) and (B) read as follows:

"**(A)** notwithstanding subsection (a) of such section, such notification shall be given by the trustee; and

"**(B)** notwithstanding subsection (b) of such section, the required waiting period shall end on the tenth day after the date of the receipt of such notification, unless the court, after notice and hearing, orders otherwise."

Subsec. (c)(1). Pub.L. 103–394, § 501(d)(8)(B), substituted "1203, 1204, or 1304" for "1304, 1203, or 1204".

Subsec. (e). Pub.L. 103–394, § 219(c), added sentence directing that subsec. (e) applies to property that is subject to any unexpired lease of personal property.

1986 Amendments. Subsec. (c)(1). Pub.L. 99–554, § 257(k)(1), added reference to sections 1203 and 1204 of this title.

Subsec. (l). Pub.L. 99–554, § 257(k)(2), added reference to chapter 12.

1984 Amendments. Subsec. (a). Pub.L. 98–353, § 442(a), added "whenever acquired" after "equivalents" and added "and includes the proceeds, products, offspring, rents, or profits of property subject to a security interest as provided in section 552(b) of this title, whether existing before or after the commencement of a case under this title" after "interest".

Subsec. (b). Pub.L. 98–353, § 442(b), designated existing provisions as par. (1) and added par. (2).

Subsec. (e). Pub.L. 98–353, § 442(c), added ", with or without a hearing," after "court" and struck out "In any hearing under this section, the trustee has the burden of proof on the issue of adequate protection".

Subsec. (f)(3). Pub.L. 98–353, § 442(d), substituted "all liens on such property" for "such interest".

Subsec. (h). Pub.L. 98–353, § 442(e), substituted "at the time of" for "immediately before".

Subsec. (j). Pub.L. 98–353, § 442(f), substituted "compensation" for "compenation".

Subsec. (k). Pub.L. 98–353, § 442(g), substituted "unless the court for cause orders otherwise the holder of such claim may bid at such sale, and, if the holder" for "if the holder".

Subsec. (l). Pub.L. 98–353, § 442(h), substituted "Subject to the provisions of section 365, the trustee" for "The trustee", "condition" for "conditions", "or the taking" for "a taking", and "interest" for "interests".

Subsec. (n). Pub.L. 98–353, § 442(i), substituted "avoid" for "void", "avoiding" for "voiding", and "In addition to any recovery under the preceding sentence, the court may grant judgment for punitive damages in favor of the estate and against any such party that entered into such an agreement in willful disregard of this subsection." for "The court may grant judgment in favor of the estate and against any such party that entered into such agreement in willful disregard of this subsection for punitive damages in addition to any recovery under the preceding sentence.".

Subsec. (o). Pub.L. 98–353, § 442(j), added subsec. (o).

Effective and Applicability Provisions

2005 Acts. Amendments by Pub.L. 109–8 effective, except as otherwise provided, 180 days after April 20, 2005, and inapplicable with respect to cases commenced under Title 11 before the effective date, see Pub.L. 109–8, § 1501, set out as a note under 11 U.S.C.A. § 101.

Pub.L. 109–8, Title XII, § 1221(d), Apr. 20, 2005, 119 Stat. 196, provided that: "The amendments made by this section [amending this section and 11 U.S.C.A. §§ 541 and 1129, and enacting provisions set out as a note under this section] shall apply to a case pending under title 11, United States Code [11 U.S.C.A. § 101 et seq.], on the date of enactment of this Act [Apr. 20, 2005], or filed under that title on or after that date of enactment, except that the court shall not confirm a plan under chapter 11 of title 11, United States Code [11 U.S.C.A. § 1101 et seq.], without considering whether this section would substantially affect the rights of a party in interest who first acquired rights with respect to the debtor after the date of the filing of the petition. The parties who may appear and be heard in a proceeding under this section include the attorney general of the State in which the debtor is incorporated, was formed, or does business."

1994 Acts. Amendments by Pub.L. 103–394 effective on Oct. 22, 1994, and not to apply with respect to cases commenced under this title before Oct. 22, 1994, see section 702 of Pub.L. 103–394, set out as a note under section 101 of this title.

1986 Acts. Amendment by Pub.L. 99–554 effective 30 days after Oct. 27, 1986, but not applicable with respect to cases commenced under this title before that date, see section 302(a), (c)(1) of Pub.L. 99–554, set out as a note under section 581 of Title 28, Judiciary and Judicial Procedure.

1984 Acts. Amendment by Pub.L. 98–353 effective with respect to cases filed 90 days after July 10, 1984, see section 552(a), formerly 553(a) of Pub.L. 98–353, set out as a note under section 101 of this title.

Separability of Provisions

If any provision of or amendment made by Pub.L. 103–394 or the application of such provision or amendment to any person or circumstance is held to be unconstitutional, the remaining provisions of and amendments made by Pub.L. 103–394 and the application of such provisions and amendments to any person or circumstance shall not be affected thereby, see section 701 of Pub.L. 103–394, set out as a note under section 101 of this title.

Rule of Construction

Pub.L. 109–8, Title XII, § 1221(e), Apr. 20, 2005, 119 Stat. 196, provided that: "Nothing in this section [amending this section and 11 U.S.C.A. §§ 541 and 1129, and enacting provisions set out as a note under this section] shall apply to a case pending under title 11, United States Code [11 U.S.C.A. § 101 et seq.] shall be construed to require the court in which a case under chapter 11 of title 11, United States Code [11 U.S.C.A. § 1101 et seq.], is pending to remand or refer any proceeding, issue, or controversy to any other court or to require the approval of any other court for the transfer of property."

CROSS REFERENCES

Adequate protection in chapter 12 cases, method of obtaining, see 11 USCA § 1205.

Adverse interest and conduct of officers of estate, see 18 USCA § 154.

Confirmation of plan, see 11 USCA § 1129.

Continuity of business operation and use, acquisition or disposition of property by debtor, see 11 USCA § 303.

Grain storage facility bankruptcies, expedited determinations, see 11 USCA § 557.

Identical rights and powers of debtor in Chapter 13 cases, see 11 USCA § 1303.

Postpetition effect of security interest, see 11 USCA § 552.

Priorities, see 11 USCA § 507.

Property of estate, see 11 USCA § 541.

Right of possession of party with security interest in—
    Aircraft equipment and vessels, see 11 USCA § 1110.
    Rolling stock equipment, see 11 USCA § 1168.

Rights and powers of debtor engaged in business, see 11 USCA § 1304.

Sale of property as affecting allowance of claim secured by lien on property of estate, see 11 USCA § 1111.

Sales free of interests, see 11 USCA § 1206.

Setoff, see 11 USCA § 553.

Turnover of property to estate, see 11 USCA § 542.

LIBRARY REFERENCES

American Digest System

Bankruptcy ⟋3061 to 3088, 3776.5(5).

Key Number System Topic No. 51.

Corpus Juris Secundum

CJS Bankruptcy § 104, Chapter 13--Duties If Debtor is Engaged in Business.

CJS Bankruptcy § 139, Adversary Proceedings.

CJS Bankruptcy § 261, Power to Render Declaratory Judgment.

CJS Bankruptcy § 278, Parties Defendant; Sovereign Immunity.

CJS Bankruptcy § 399, Effects of Recognizing Foreign Main Proceeding.

CJS Bankruptcy § 520, Single Real Property Asset.

CJS Bankruptcy § 529, Ex Parte Relief from Stay.

CJS Bankruptcy § 562, Property Acquired Postpetition--Security Interest on Property Acquired Postpetition.

CJS Bankruptcy § 698, Transfers or Obligations Which May be Avoided.

CJS Bankruptcy § 764, Consumer Privacy and Patient Care Ombudsmen.

CJS Bankruptcy § 836, Chapter 7 Cases.

CJS Bankruptcy § 848, Operation of Business or Affairs of Chapter 13 Debtor.

CJS Bankruptcy § 850, Valuation and Appraisals of Property.

CJS Bankruptcy § 851, Prepetition Security Interests in Proceeds, Products, Offspring, or Profits.

CJS Bankruptcy § 852, Prepetition Security Interests Extending to Rents and Similar Charges.

CJS Bankruptcy § 854, Expedited Determination of Disposition of Grain Assets.

CJS Bankruptcy § 856, Motion and Notice.

CJS Bankruptcy § 862, Recovery of Costs of Preserving or Disposing of Property--Sale of Property.

CJS Bankruptcy § 863, Use of Property Subject to Bankruptcy Forfeiture Clause or Other Ipso Facto Clauses.

CJS Bankruptcy § 865, What is Cash Collateral.

CJS Bankruptcy § 866, Use, Sale, or Lease of Property Other Than Cash Collateral.

CJS Bankruptcy § 867, Stay of Order Authorizing Use, Sale, or Lease of Property.

CJS Bankruptcy § 868, Remedies for Unauthorized Use of Cash Collateral.

CJS Bankruptcy § 871, Motion for Authorization.

CJS Bankruptcy § 872, Notice and Hearing; Ex Parte Relief.

CJS Bankruptcy § 874, What Transactions Are Other Than in Ordinary Course of Business.

CJS Bankruptcy § 875, What Transactions Are Other Than in Ordinary Course of Business--Sale of All or Substantially All of Chapter 11 Debtor's Assets.

CJS Bankruptcy § 877, Sale or Lease of Personally Identifiable Information.

CJS Bankruptcy § 879, Service and Content of Notices.

CJS Bankruptcy § 885, Sale of Farmland or Farm Equipment in Chapter 12 Cases.

CJS Bankruptcy § 886, Authorization to Sell Property Free and Clear; Notice.

CJS Bankruptcy § 888, Right of First Refusal of Debtor's Spouse or Co-Owners.

CJS Bankruptcy § 889, Co-Owner or Spouse's Right to Proportionate Share of Proceeds of Sale.

CJS Bankruptcy § 891, Protection of Good-Faith Purchasers and Lessees from Reversal or Modification on Appeal.

CJS Bankruptcy § 892, Setting Aside Confirmed Sale; Remedies for Collusive Bidding.

CJS Bankruptcy § 1148, Protection of Secured Creditors.

CJS Bankruptcy § 1170, Filing and Contents of Plan, Generally.

CJS Bankruptcy § 1179, Use, Sale, or Lease of Property.

CJS Bankruptcy § 1272, Authorization of Sale, Debt, Credit; Priority of Lien.

CJS Estoppel and Waiver § 186, Generally; Rule of Judicial Estoppel.

CJS Mortgages § 363, Agreements or Stipulations--Enforcement and Perfection of Rights Under Agreement.

§ 364. Obtaining credit

(a) If the trustee is authorized to operate the business of the debtor under section 721, 1108, 1203, 1204, or 1304 of this title, unless the court orders otherwise, the trustee may obtain unsecured credit and incur unsecured debt in the ordinary course of business allowable under section 503(b)(1) of this title as an administrative expense.

(b) The court, after notice and a hearing, may authorize the trustee to obtain unsecured credit or to incur unsecured debt other than under subsection (a) of this section, allowable under section 503(b)(1) of this title as an administrative expense.

(c) If the trustee is unable to obtain unsecured credit allowable under section 503(b)(1) of this title as an administrative expense, the court, after notice and a hearing, may authorize the obtaining of credit or the incurring of debt—

(1) with priority over any or all administrative expenses of the kind specified in section 503(b) or 507(b) of this title;

(2) secured by a lien on property of the estate that is not otherwise subject to a lien; or

(3) secured by a junior lien on property of the estate that is subject to a lien.

(d)(1) The court, after notice and a hearing, may authorize the obtaining of credit or the incurring of

debt secured by a senior or equal lien on property of the estate that is subject to a lien only if—

(A) the trustee is unable to obtain such credit otherwise; and

(B) there is adequate protection of the interest of the holder of the lien on the property of the estate on which such senior or equal lien is proposed to be granted.

(2) In any hearing under this subsection, the trustee has the burden of proof on the issue of adequate protection.

(e) The reversal or modification on appeal of an authorization under this section to obtain credit or incur debt, or of a grant under this section of a priority or a lien, does not affect the validity of any debt so incurred, or any priority or lien so granted, to an entity that extended such credit in good faith, whether or not such entity knew of the pendency of the appeal, unless such authorization and the incurring of such debt, or the granting of such priority or lien, were stayed pending appeal.

(f) Except with respect to an entity that is an underwriter as defined in section 1145(b) of this title, section 5 of the Securities Act of 1933, the Trust Indenture Act of 1939, and any State or local law requiring registration for offer or sale of a security or registration or licensing of an issuer of, underwriter of, or broker or dealer in, a security does not apply to the offer or sale under this section of a security that is not an equity security.

(Pub.L. 95–598, Nov. 6, 1978, 92 Stat. 2574; Pub.L. 99–554, Title II, § 257(*l*), Oct. 27, 1986, 100 Stat. 3115; Pub.L. 103–394, Title V, § 501(d)(9), Oct. 22, 1994, 108 Stat. 4144.)

HISTORICAL AND STATUTORY NOTES

Revision Notes and Legislative Reports

1978 Acts. This section is derived from provisions in current law governing certificates of indebtedness, but is much broader. It governs all obtaining of credit and incurring of debt by the estate.

Subsection (a) authorizes the obtaining of unsecured credit and the incurring of unsecured debt in the ordinary course of business if the business of the debtor is authorized to be operated under section 721, 1108, or 1304. The debts so incurred are allowable as administrative expenses under section 503(b)(1). The court may limit the estate's ability to incur debt under this subsection.

Subsection (b) permits the court to authorize the trustee to obtain unsecured credit and incur unsecured debts other than in the ordinary course of business, such as in order to wind up a liquidation case, or to obtain a substantial loan in an operating case. Debt incurred under this subsection is allowable as an administrative expense under section 503(b)(1).

Subsection (c) is closer to the concept of certificates of indebtedness in current law. It authorizes the obtaining of credit and the incurring of debt with some special priority, if the trustee is unable to obtain unsecured credit under subsection (a) or (b). The various priorities are (1) with priority over any or all administrative expenses; (2) secured by a lien on unencumbered property of the estate; or (3) secured by a junior lien on encumbered property. The priorities granted under this subsection do not interfere with existing property rights.

Subsection (d) grants the court the authority to authorize the obtaining of credit and the incurring of debt with a superiority [sic], that is a lien on encumbered property that is senior or equal to the existing lien on the property. The court may authorize such a super-priority [sic] only if the trustee is otherwise unable to obtain credit, and if there is adequate protection of the original lien holder's interest. Again, the trustee has the burden of proof on the issue of adequate protection.

Subsection (e) provides the same protection for credit extenders pending an appeal of an authorization to incur debt as is provided under section 363(l) for purchasers: the credit is not affected on appeal by reversal of the authorization and the incurring of the debt were stayed pending appeal. The protection runs to a good faith lender, whether or not he knew of the pendency of the appeal.

A claim arising as a result of lending or borrowing under this section will be a priority claim, as defined in proposed section 507(a)(1), even if the claim is granted a super-priority over administrative expenses and is to be paid in advance of other first priority claims. Senate Report No. 95–989.

1986 Acts. House Report No. 99–764 and House Conference Report No. 99–958, see 1986 U.S.Code Cong. and Adm. News, p. 5227.

1994 Acts. House Report No. 103–835, see 1994 U.S. Code Cong. and Adm. News, p. 3340.

Legislative Statements

Section 364(f) of the House amendment is new. This provision continues the exemption found in section 3(a)(7) of the Securities Act of 1933 [15 U.S.C.A. § 77c(a)(7)] for certificates of indebtedness issued by a trustee in bankruptcy. The exemption applies to any debt security issued under section 364 of title 11. The section does not intend to change present law which exempts such securities from the Trust Indenture Act, 15 U.S.C. 77aaa, et seq. (1976).

References in Text

Section 5 of the Securities Act of 1933, referred to in subsec. (f), is section 5 of Act May 27, 1933, c. 38, Title I, 48 Stat. 77, which is classified to section 77e of Title 15, Commerce and Trade.

The Trust Indenture Act of 1939, referred to in subsec. (f), is Title III of Act May 27, 1933, c. 38, as added Aug. 3, 1939, c. 411, 53 Stat. 1149, as amended, which is classified generally to subchapter III (§ 77aaa et seq.) of chapter 2A of Title 15, Commerce and Trade. For complete classification of this Act to the Code, see section 77aaa of Title 15 and Tables.

Amendments

1994 Amendments. Subsec. (a). Pub.L. 103–394, § 501(d)(9)(A), substituted "1203, 1204, or 1304" for "1304, 1203, or 1204".

Subsec. (f). Pub.L. 103–394, § 501(d)(9)(B), struck out "(15 U.S.C. 77e)" following "Securities Act of 1933", and struck out "(15 U.S.C. 77aaa et seq.)" following "Trust Indenture Act of 1939".

1986 Amendments. Subsec. (a). Pub.L. 99–554 added reference to sections 1203 and 1204 of this title.

Effective and Applicability Provisions

1994 Acts. Amendment by Pub.L. 103–394 effective on Oct. 22, 1994, and not to apply with respect to cases commenced under this title before Oct. 22, 1994, see section 702 of Pub.L. 103–394, set out as a note under section 101 of this title.

1986 Acts. Amendment by Pub.L. 99–554 effective 30 days after Oct. 27, 1986, but not applicable with respect to cases commenced under this title before that date, see section 302(a), (c)(1) of Pub.L. 99–554, set out as a note under section 581 of Title 28, Judiciary and Judicial Procedure.

Separability of Provisions

If any provision of or amendment made by Pub.L. 103–394 or the application of such provision or amendment to any person or circumstance is held to be unconstitutional, the remaining provisions of and amendments made by Pub.L. 103–394 and the application of such provisions and amendments to any person or circumstance shall not be affected thereby, see section 701 of Pub.L. 103–394, set out as a note under section 101 of this title.

CROSS REFERENCES

Adequate protection in Chapter 12 cases, method of obtaining, see 11 USCA § 1205.

Applicability of subsecs. (c) to (f) of this section in Chapter 9 cases, see 11 USCA § 901.

Enforcement of claims against debtor in Chapter 9 cases, automatic stay of, see 11 USCA § 922.

Priorities, see 11 USCA § 507.

Reversal on appeal of finding of jurisdiction as affecting validity of debt incurred, see 11 USCA § 921.

Rights and powers of debtor engaged in business, see 11 USCA § 1304.

LIBRARY REFERENCES

American Digest System

Bankruptcy ⚭3035.1 to 3038.

Key Number System Topic No. 51.

Corpus Juris Secundum

CJS Bankruptcy § 104, Chapter 13--Duties If Debtor is Engaged in Business.

CJS Bankruptcy § 190, Orders With Respect to Obtaining Credit.

CJS Bankruptcy § 278, Parties Defendant; Sovereign Immunity.

CJS Bankruptcy § 836, Chapter 7 Cases.

CJS Bankruptcy § 848, Operation of Business or Affairs of Chapter 13 Debtor.

CJS Bankruptcy § 895, Unsecured Credit or Debt in Ordinary Course of Business.

CJS Bankruptcy § 896, Unsecured Credit or Debt Other Than in Ordinary Course of Business.

CJS Bankruptcy § 897, Credit With Special Administrative Priority or Secured by First Liens or Junior Liens.

CJS Bankruptcy § 898, Credit Secured by Superpriority Lien; Subordination of Existing Liens.

CJS Bankruptcy § 899, Cross-Collateralization as Inducement to Extend Credit.

CJS Bankruptcy § 900, Motion for Authorization to Obtain Credit; Notice and Hearing.

CJS Bankruptcy § 902, Protection of Lenders from Reversal or Modification of Borrowing Authorization.

CJS Bankruptcy § 903, Securities Registration Inapplicable to Securities Issued to Obtain Credit.

CJS Bankruptcy § 1272, Authorization of Sale, Debt, Credit; Priority of Lien.

§ 365. Executory contracts and unexpired leases

(a) Except as provided in sections 765 and 766 of this title and in subsections (b), (c), and (d) of this section, the trustee, subject to the court's approval, may assume or reject any executory contract or unexpired lease of the debtor.

(b)(1) If there has been a default in an executory contract or unexpired lease of the debtor, the trustee may not assume such contract or lease unless, at the time of assumption of such contract or lease, the trustee—

(A) cures, or provides adequate assurance that the trustee will promptly cure, such default other than a default that is a breach of a provision relating to the satisfaction of any provision (other than a penalty rate or penalty provision) relating to a default arising from any failure to perform nonmonetary obligations under an unexpired lease of real property, if it is impossible for the trustee to cure such default by performing nonmonetary acts at and after the time of assumption, except that if such default arises from a failure to operate in accordance with a nonresidential real property lease, then such default shall be cured by performance at and after the time of assumption in accordance with such lease, and pecuniary losses resulting from such default shall be compensated in accordance with the provisions of this paragraph;

(B) compensates, or provides adequate assurance that the trustee will promptly compensate, a party other than the debtor to such contract or lease, for any actual pecuniary loss to such party resulting from such default; and

(C) provides adequate assurance of future performance under such contract or lease.

(2) Paragraph (1) of this subsection does not apply to a default that is a breach of a provision relating to—

(A) the insolvency or financial condition of the debtor at any time before the closing of the case;

(B) the commencement of a case under this title;

(C) the appointment of or taking possession by a trustee in a case under this title or a custodian before such commencement; or

(D) the satisfaction of any penalty rate or penalty provision relating to a default arising from any failure by the debtor to perform nonmonetary obligations under the executory contract or unexpired lease.

(3) For the purposes of paragraph (1) of this subsection and paragraph (2)(B) of subsection (f), adequate assurance of future performance of a lease of real property in a shopping center includes adequate assurance—

(A) of the source of rent and other consideration due under such lease, and in the case of an assignment, that the financial condition and operating performance of the proposed assignee and its guarantors, if any, shall be similar to the financial condition and operating performance of the debtor and its guarantors, if any, as of the time the debtor became the lessee under the lease;

(B) that any percentage rent due under such lease will not decline substantially;

(C) that assumption or assignment of such lease is subject to all the provisions thereof, including (but not limited to) provisions such as a radius, location, use, or exclusivity provision, and will not breach any such provision contained in any other lease, financing agreement, or master agreement relating to such shopping center; and

(D) that assumption or assignment of such lease will not disrupt any tenant mix or balance in such shopping center.

(4) Notwithstanding any other provision of this section, if there has been a default in an unexpired lease of the debtor, other than a default of a kind specified in paragraph (2) of this subsection, the trustee may not require a lessor to provide services or supplies incidental to such lease before assumption of such lease unless the lessor is compensated under the terms of such lease for any services and supplies provided under such lease before assumption of such lease.

(c) The trustee may not assume or assign any executory contract or unexpired lease of the debtor, whether or not such contract or lease prohibits or restricts assignment of rights or delegation of duties, if—

(1)(A) applicable law excuses a party, other than the debtor, to such contract or lease from accepting performance from or rendering performance to an entity other than the debtor or the debtor in possession, whether or not such contract or lease prohibits or restricts assignment of rights or delegation of duties; and

(B) such party does not consent to such assumption or assignment; or

(2) such contract is a contract to make a loan, or extend other debt financing or financial accommodations, to or for the benefit of the debtor, or to issue a security of the debtor; or

(3) such lease is of nonresidential real property and has been terminated under applicable nonbankruptcy law prior to the order for relief.

[(4) Repealed. Pub.L. 109–8, Title III, § 328(a)(2)(C), Apr. 20, 2005, 119 Stat. 100]

(d)(1) In a case under chapter 7 of this title, if the trustee does not assume or reject an executory contract or unexpired lease of residential real property or of personal property of the debtor within 60 days after the order for relief, or within such additional time as the court, for cause, within such 60-day period, fixes, then such contract or lease is deemed rejected.

(2) In a case under chapter 9, 11, 12, or 13 of this title, the trustee may assume or reject an executory contract or unexpired lease of residential real property or of personal property of the debtor at any time before the confirmation of a plan but the court, on the request of any party to such contract or lease, may order the trustee to determine within a specified period of time whether to assume or reject such contract or lease.

(3) The trustee shall timely perform all the obligations of the debtor, except those specified in section 365(b)(2), arising from and after the order for relief under any unexpired lease of nonresidential real property, until such lease is assumed or rejected, notwithstanding section 503(b)(1) of this title. The court may extend, for cause, the time for performance of any such obligation that arises within 60 days after the date of the order for relief, but the time for performance shall not be extended beyond such 60-day period. This subsection shall not be deemed to affect the trustee's obligations under the provisions of subsection (b) or (f) of this section. Acceptance of any such performance does not constitute waiver or relinquishment of the lessor's rights under such lease or under this title.

(4)(A) Subject to subparagraph (B), an unexpired lease of nonresidential real property under which the debtor is the lessee shall be deemed rejected, and the trustee shall immediately surrender that nonresidential real property to the lessor, if the trustee does not assume or reject the unexpired lease by the earlier of—

(i) the date that is 120 days after the date of the order for relief; or

(ii) the date of the entry of an order confirming a plan.

(B)(i) The court may extend the period determined under subparagraph (A), prior to the expiration of the 120–day period, for 90 days on the motion of the trustee or lessor for cause.

(ii) If the court grants an extension under clause (i), the court may grant a subsequent extension only upon prior written consent of the lessor in each instance.

(5) The trustee shall timely perform all of the obligations of the debtor, except those specified in section 365(b)(2), first arising from or after 60 days after the order for relief in a case under chapter 11 of this title under an unexpired lease of personal property (other than personal property leased to an individual primarily for personal, family, or household purposes), until such lease is assumed or rejected notwithstanding section 503(b)(1) of this title, unless the court, after notice and a hearing and based on the equities of the case, orders otherwise with respect to the obligations or timely performance thereof. This subsection shall not be deemed to affect the trustee's obligations under the provisions of subsection (b) or (f). Acceptance of any such performance does not constitute waiver or relinquishment of the lessor's rights under such lease or under this title.

[(6) to (9) Repealed. Pub.L. 109–8, Title III, § 328(a)(3)(A), Apr. 20, 2005, 119 Stat. 100]

[(10) Redesignated (5)]

(e)(1) Notwithstanding a provision in an executory contract or unexpired lease, or in applicable law, an executory contract or unexpired lease of the debtor may not be terminated or modified, and any right or obligation under such contract or lease may not be terminated or modified, at any time after the commencement of the case solely because of a provision in such contract or lease that is conditioned on—

(A) the insolvency or financial condition of the debtor at any time before the closing of the case;

(B) the commencement of a case under this title; or

(C) the appointment of or taking possession by a trustee in a case under this title or a custodian before such commencement.

(2) Paragraph (1) of this subsection does not apply to an executory contract or unexpired lease of the debtor, whether or not such contract or lease prohibits or restricts assignment of rights or delegation of duties, if—

(A)(i) applicable law excuses a party, other than the debtor, to such contract or lease from accepting performance from or rendering performance to the trustee or to an assignee of such contract or lease, whether or not such contract or lease prohibits or restricts assignment of rights or delegation of duties; and

(ii) such party does not consent to such assumption or assignment; or

(B) such contract is a contract to make a loan, or extend other debt financing or financial accommodations, to or for the benefit of the debtor, or to issue a security of the debtor.

(f)(1) Except as provided in subsections (b) and (c) of this section, notwithstanding a provision in an executory contract or unexpired lease of the debtor, or in applicable law, that prohibits, restricts, or conditions the assignment of such contract or lease, the trustee may assign such contract or lease under paragraph (2) of this subsection.

(2) The trustee may assign an executory contract or unexpired lease of the debtor only if—

(A) the trustee assumes such contract or lease in accordance with the provisions of this section; and

(B) adequate assurance of future performance by the assignee of such contract or lease is provided, whether or not there has been a default in such contract or lease.

(3) Notwithstanding a provision in an executory contract or unexpired lease of the debtor, or in applicable law that terminates or modifies, or permits a party other than the debtor to terminate or modify, such contract or lease or a right or obligation under such contract or lease on account of an assignment of such contract or lease, such contract, lease, right, or obligation may not be terminated or modified under such provision because of the assumption or assignment of such contract or lease by the trustee.

(g) Except as provided in subsections (h)(2) and (i)(2) of this section, the rejection of an executory contract or unexpired lease of the debtor constitutes a breach of such contract or lease—

(1) if such contract or lease has not been assumed under this section or under a plan confirmed under chapter 9, 11, 12, or 13 of this title, immediately before the date of the filing of the petition; or

(2) if such contract or lease has been assumed under this section or under a plan confirmed under chapter 9, 11, 12, or 13 of this title—

(A) if before such rejection the case has not been converted under section 1112, 1208, or 1307 of this title, at the time of such rejection; or

(B) if before such rejection the case has been converted under section 1112, 1208, or 1307 of this title—

(i) immediately before the date of such conversion, if such contract or lease was assumed before such conversion; or

(ii) at the time of such rejection, if such contract or lease was assumed after such conversion.

(h)(1)(A) If the trustee rejects an unexpired lease of real property under which the debtor is the lessor and—

(i) if the rejection by the trustee amounts to such a breach as would entitle the lessee to treat such lease as terminated by virtue of its terms, applicable nonbankruptcy law, or any agreement made by the lessee, then the lessee under such lease may treat such lease as terminated by the rejection; or

(ii) if the term of such lease has commenced, the lessee may retain its rights under such lease (including rights such as those relating to the amount and timing of payment of rent and other amounts payable by the lessee and any right of use, possession, quiet enjoyment, subletting, assignment, or hypothe-

cation) that are in or appurtenant to the real property for the balance of the term of such lease and for any renewal or extension of such rights to the extent that such rights are enforceable under applicable nonbankruptcy law.

(B) If the lessee retains its rights under subparagraph (A)(ii), the lessee may offset against the rent reserved under such lease for the balance of the term after the date of the rejection of such lease and for the term of any renewal or extension of such lease, the value of any damage caused by the nonperformance after the date of such rejection, of any obligation of the debtor under such lease, but the lessee shall not have any other right against the estate or the debtor on account of any damage occurring after such date caused by such nonperformance.

(C) The rejection of a lease of real property in a shopping center with respect to which the lessee elects to retain its rights under subparagraph (A)(ii) does not affect the enforceability under applicable nonbankruptcy law of any provision in the lease pertaining to radius, location, use, exclusivity, or tenant mix or balance.

(D) In this paragraph, "lessee" includes any successor, assign, or mortgagee permitted under the terms of such lease.

(2)(A) If the trustee rejects a timeshare interest under a timeshare plan under which the debtor is the timeshare interest seller and—

(i) if the rejection amounts to such a breach as would entitle the timeshare interest purchaser to treat the timeshare plan as terminated under its terms, applicable nonbankruptcy law, or any agreement made by timeshare interest purchaser, the timeshare interest purchaser under the timeshare plan may treat the timeshare plan as terminated by such rejection; or

(ii) if the term of such timeshare interest has commenced, then the timeshare interest purchaser may retain its rights in such timeshare interest for the balance of such term and for any term of renewal or extension of such timeshare interest to the extent that such rights are enforceable under applicable nonbankruptcy law.

(B) If the timeshare interest purchaser retains its rights under subparagraph (A), such timeshare interest purchaser may offset against the moneys due for such timeshare interest for the balance of the term after the date of the rejection of such timeshare interest, and the term of any renewal or extension of such timeshare interest, the value of any damage caused by the nonperformance after the date of such rejection, of any obligation of the debtor under such timeshare plan, but the timeshare interest purchaser shall not have any right against the estate or the debtor on account of any damage occurring after such date caused by such nonperformance.

(i)(1) If the trustee rejects an executory contract of the debtor for the sale of real property or for the sale of a timeshare interest under a timeshare plan, under which the purchaser is in possession, such purchaser may treat such contract as terminated, or, in the alternative, may remain in possession of such real property or timeshare interest.

(2) If such purchaser remains in possession—

(A) such purchaser shall continue to make all payments due under such contract, but may,[1] offset against such payments any damages occurring after the date of the rejection of such contract caused by the nonperformance of any obligation of the debtor after such date, but such purchaser does not have any rights against the estate on account of any damages arising after such date from such rejection, other than such offset; and

(B) the trustee shall deliver title to such purchaser in accordance with the provisions of such contract, but is relieved of all other obligations to perform under such contract.

(j) A purchaser that treats an executory contract as terminated under subsection (i) of this section, or a party whose executory contract to purchase real property from the debtor is rejected and under which such party is not in possession, has a lien on the interest of the debtor in such property for the recovery of any portion of the purchase price that such purchaser or party has paid.

(k) Assignment by the trustee to an entity of a contract or lease assumed under this section relieves the trustee and the estate from any liability for any breach of such contract or lease occurring after such assignment.

(l) If an unexpired lease under which the debtor is the lessee is assigned pursuant to this section, the lessor of the property may require a deposit or other security for the performance of the debtor's obligations under the lease substantially the same as would have been required by the landlord upon the initial leasing to a similar tenant.

(m) For purposes of this section 365 and sections 541(b)(2) and 362(b)(10), leases of real property shall include any rental agreement to use real property.

(n)(1) If the trustee rejects an executory contract under which the debtor is a licensor of a right to intellectual property, the licensee under such contract may elect—

(A) to treat such contract as terminated by such rejection if such rejection by the trustee amounts to such a breach as would entitle the licensee to treat such contract as terminated by virtue of its own terms, applicable nonbankruptcy law, or an agreement made by the licensee with another entity; or

(B) to retain its rights (including a right to enforce any exclusivity provision of such contract, but excluding any other right under applicable nonbankruptcy law to specific performance of such contract) under such contract and under any agreement supplementary to such contract, to such intellectual property (including any embodiment of such intellectual property to the extent protected by applicable nonbankruptcy law), as such rights existed immediately before the case commenced, for—

(i) the duration of such contract; and

(ii) any period for which such contract may be extended by the licensee as of right under applicable nonbankruptcy law.

(2) If the licensee elects to retain its rights, as described in paragraph (1)(B) of this subsection, under such contract—

(A) the trustee shall allow the licensee to exercise such rights;

(B) the licensee shall make all royalty payments due under such contract for the duration of such contract and for any period described in paragraph (1)(B) of this subsection for which the licensee extends such contract; and

(C) the licensee shall be deemed to waive—

(i) any right of setoff it may have with respect to such contract under this title or applicable nonbankruptcy law; and

(ii) any claim allowable under section 503(b) of this title arising from the performance of such contract.

(3) If the licensee elects to retain its rights, as described in paragraph (1)(B) of this subsection, then on the written request of the licensee the trustee shall—

(A) to the extent provided in such contract, or any agreement supplementary to such contract, provide to the licensee any intellectual property (including such embodiment) held by the trustee; and

(B) not interfere with the rights of the licensee as provided in such contract, or any agreement supplementary to such contract, to such intellectual property (including such embodiment) including any right to obtain such intellectual property (or such embodiment) from another entity.

(4) Unless and until the trustee rejects such contract, on the written request of the licensee the trustee shall—

(A) to the extent provided in such contract or any agreement supplementary to such contract—

(i) perform such contract; or

(ii) provide to the licensee such intellectual property (including any embodiment of such intellectual property to the extent protected by applicable nonbankruptcy law) held by the trustee; and

(B) not interfere with the rights of the licensee as provided in such contract, or any agreement supplementary to such contract, to such intellectual property (including such embodiment), including any right to obtain such intellectual property (or such embodiment) from another entity.

(o) In a case under chapter 11 of this title, the trustee shall be deemed to have assumed (consistent with the debtor's other obligations under section 507), and shall immediately cure any deficit under, any commitment by the debtor to a Federal depository institutions regulatory agency (or predecessor to such agency) to maintain the capital of an insured depository institution, and any claim for a subsequent breach of the obligations thereunder shall be entitled to priority under section 507. This subsection shall not extend any commitment that would otherwise be terminated by any act of such an agency.

(p)(1) If a lease of personal property is rejected or not timely assumed by the trustee under subsection (d), the leased property is no longer property of the estate and the stay under section 362(a) is automatically terminated.

(2)(A) If the debtor in a case under chapter 7 is an individual, the debtor may notify the creditor in writing that the debtor desires to assume the lease. Upon being so notified, the creditor may, at its option, notify the debtor that it is willing to have the lease assumed by the debtor and may condition such assumption on cure of any outstanding default on terms set by the contract.

(B) If, not later than 30 days after notice is provided under subparagraph (A), the debtor notifies the lessor in writing that the lease is assumed, the liability under the lease will be assumed by the debtor and not by the estate.

(C) The stay under section 362 and the injunction under section 524(a) (2) shall not be violated by notification of the debtor and negotiation of cure under this subsection.

(3) In a case under chapter 11 in which the debtor is an individual and in a case under chapter 13, if the debtor is the lessee with respect to personal property and the lease is not assumed in the plan confirmed by the court, the lease is deemed rejected as of the conclusion of the hearing on confirmation. If the lease is rejected, the stay under section 362 and any stay under section 1301 is automatically terminated with respect to the property subject to the lease.

(Pub.L. 95–598, Nov. 6, 1978, 92 Stat. 2574; Pub.L. 98–353, Title III, §§ 362, 402–404, July 10, 1984, 98 Stat. 361, 367; Pub.L. 99–554, Title II, §§ 257(j), (m), 283(e), Oct. 27, 1986, 100 Stat. 3115, 3117; Pub.L. 100–506, § 1(b), Oct. 18, 1988, 102 Stat. 2538; Pub.L. 101–647, Title XXV, § 2522(c), Nov. 29, 1990, 104 Stat. 4866; Pub.L. 102–365, § 19(b)–(e), Sept. 3, 1992, 106 Stat. 982–984; Pub.L. 103–394, Title II, §§ 205(a), 219(a), (b), Title V, § 501(d)(10), Oct. 22, 1994, 108 Stat. 4122, 4128, 4145; Pub.L. 103–429, § 1, Oct. 31, 1994, 108 Stat. 4377;

Pub.L. 109–8, Title III, §§ 309(b), 328(a), Title IV, § 404, Apr. 20, 2005, 119 Stat. 82, 100, 104.)

1 So in original. The comma probably should not appear.

HISTORICAL AND STATUTORY NOTES

Revision Notes and Legislative Reports

1978 Acts. Subsection (a) of this section authorizes the trustee, subject to the court's approval, to assume or reject an executory contract or unexpired lease. Though there is no precise definition of what contracts are executory, it generally includes contracts on which performance remains due to some extent on both sides. A note is not usually an executory contract if the only performance that remains is repayment. Performance on one side of the contract would have been completed and the contract is no longer executory.

Because of the volatile nature of the commodities markets and the special provisions governing commodity broker liquidations in subchapter IV of chapter 7, the provisions governing distribution in section 765(a) will govern if any conflict between those provisions and the provisions of this section arise.

Subsections (b), (c), and (d) provide limitations on the trustee's powers. Subsection (b) requires the trustee to cure any default in the contract or lease and to provide adequate assurance of future performance if there has been a default, before he may assume. This provision does not apply to defaults under ipso facto or bankruptcy clauses, which is a significant departure from present law.

Subsection (b)(3) permits termination of leases entered into prior to the effective date of this title in liquidation cases if certain other conditions are met.

Subsection (b)(4) prohibits the trustee's assumption of an executory contract requiring the other party to make a loan or deliver equipment to or to issue a security of the debtor. The purpose of this subsection is to make it clear that a party to a transaction which is based upon the financial strength of a debtor should not be required to extend new credit to the debtor whether in the form of loans, lease financing, or the purchase or discount of notes.

Subsection (b)(5) provides that in lease situations common to shopping centers, protections must be provided for the lessor if the trustee assumes the lease, including protection against decline in percentage rents, breach of agreements with other tenants, and preservation of the tenant mix. Protection for tenant mix will not be required in the office building situation.

Subsection (c) prohibits the trustee from assuming or assigning a contract or lease if applicable nonbankruptcy law excuses the other party from performance to someone other than the debtor, unless the other party consents. This prohibition applies only in the situation in which applicable law excuses the other party from performance independent of any restrictive language in the contract or lease itself.

Subsection (d) places time limits on assumption and rejection. In a liquidation case, the trustee must assume within 60 days (or within an additional 60 days, if the court, for cause, extends the time). If not assumed, the contract or lease is deemed rejected. In a rehabilitation case, the time limit is not fixed in the bill. However, if the other party to the contract or lease requests the court to fix a time, the court may specify a time within which the trustee must act. This provision will prevent parties in contractual or lease relationships with the debtor from being left in doubt concerning their status vis-a-vis the estate.

Subsection (e) invalidates ipso facto or bankruptcy clauses. These clauses, protected under present law, automatically terminate the contract or lease, or permit the other contracting party to terminate the contract or lease, in the event of bankruptcy. This frequently hampers rehabilitation efforts. If the trustee may assume or assign the contract under the limitations imposed by the remainder of the section, the contract or lease may be utilized to assist in the debtor's rehabilitation or liquidation.

The unenforceability of ipso facto or bankruptcy clauses proposed under this section will require the courts to be sensitive to the rights of the nondebtor party to executory contracts and unexpired leases. If the trustee is to assume a contract or lease, the court will have to insure that the trustee's performance under the contract or lease gives the other contracting party the full benefit of his bargain.

This subsection does not limit the application of an ipso facto or bankruptcy clause if a new insolvency or receivership occurs after the bankruptcy case is closed. That is, the clause is not invalidated in toto, but merely made inapplicable during the case for the purposes of disposition of the executory contract or unexpired lease.

Subsection (f) partially invalidates restrictions on assignment of contracts or leases by the trustee to a third party. The subsection imposes two restrictions on the trustee: he must first assume the contract or lease, subject to all the restrictions on assumption found in the section, and adequate assurance of future performance must be provided to the other contracting party. Paragraph (3) of the subsection invalidates contractual provisions that permit termination or modification in the event of an assignment, as contrary to the policy of this subsection.

Subsection (g) defines the time as of which a rejection of an executory contract or unexpired lease constitutes a breach of the contract or lease. Generally, the breach is as of the date immediately preceding the date of the petition. The purpose is to treat rejection claims as prepetition claims. The remainder of the subsection specifies different times for cases that are converted from one chapter to another. The provisions of this subsection are not a substantive authorization to breach or reject an assumed contract. Rather, they prescribe the rules for the allowance of claims in case an assumed contract is breached, or if a case under chapter 11 in which a contract has been assumed is converted to a case under chapter 7 in which the contract is rejected.

Subsection (h) protects real property lessees of the debtor if the trustee rejects an unexpired lease under which the debtor is the lessor (or sublessor). The subsection permits the lessee to remain in possession of the leased property or to treat the lease as terminated by the rejection. The balance of the term of the lease referred to in paragraph (1) will include any renewal terms that are enforceable by the tenant, but not renewal terms if the landlord had an option to terminate. Thus, the tenant will not be deprived of his estate for the term for which he bargained. If the lessee remains in possession, he may offset the rent reserved under the lease against damages caused by the rejection, but does not have any affirmative rights against the estate for any damages after the rejection that result from the rejection.

Subsection (i) gives a purchaser of real property under a land installment sales contract similar protection. The purchaser, if the contract is rejected, may remain in possession or may treat the contract as terminated. If the purchaser remains in possession, he is required to continue to make the payments due, but may offset damages that occur after rejection. The trustee is required to deliver title, but is relieved of all other obligations to perform.

A purchaser that treats the contract as terminated is granted a lien on the property to the extent of the purchase price paid. A party with a contract to purchase land from the debtor has a lien on the property to secure the price already paid, if the contract is rejected and the purchaser is not yet in possession.

Subsection (k) relieves the trustee and the estate of liability for a breach of an assigned contract or lease that occurs after the assignment. Senate Report No. 95–989.

Subsection (c) prohibits the trustee from assuming or assigning a contract or lease if applicable nonbankruptcy law excuses the other party from performance to someone other than the debtor, unless the other party consents. This prohibition applies only in the situation in which applicable law excuses the other party from performance independent of any restrictive language in the contract or lease itself. The purpose of this subsection, at least in part, is to prevent the trustee from requiring new advances of money or other property. The section permits the trustee to continue to use and pay for property already advanced, but is not designed to permit the trustee to demand new loans or additional transfers of property under lease commitments.

Thus, under this provision, contracts such as loan commitments and letters of credit are nonassignable, and may not be assumed by the trustee.

Subsection (e) invalidates ipso facto or bankruptcy clauses. These clauses, protected under present law, automatically terminate the contract or lease, or permit the other contracting party to terminate the contract or lease, in the event of bankruptcy. This frequently hampers rehabilitation efforts. If the trustee may assume or assign the contract under the limitations imposed by the remainder of the section, then the contract or lease may be utilized to assist in the debtor's rehabilitation or liquidation.

The unenforceability of ipso facto or bankruptcy clauses proposed under this section will require the courts to be sensitive to the rights of the nondebtor party to executory contracts and unexpired leases. If the trustee is to assume a contract or lease, the courts will have to insure that the trustee's performance under the contract or lease gives the other contracting party the full benefit of his bargain. An example of the complexity that may arise in these situations and the need for a determination of all aspects of a particular executory contract or unexpired lease is the shopping center lease under which the debtor is a tenant in a shopping center.

A shopping center is often a carefully planned enterprise, and though it consists of numerous individual tenants, the center is planned as a single unit, often subject to a master lease or financing agreement. Under these agreements, the tenant mix in a shopping center may be as important to the lessor as the actual promised rental payments, because certain mixes will attract higher patronage of the stores in the center, and thus a higher rental for the landlord from those stores that are subject to a percentage of gross receipts rental agreement. Thus, in order to assure a landlord of his bargained for exchange, the court would have to consider such factors as the nature of the business to be conducted by the trustee or his assignee, whether that business complies with the requirements of any master agreement, whether the kind of business proposed will generate gross sales in an amount such that the percentage rent specified in the lease is substantially the same as what would have been provided by the debtor, and whether the business proposed to be conducted would result in a breach of other clauses in master agreements relating, for example, to tenant mix and location.

This subsection does not limit the application of an ipso facto or bankruptcy clause to a new insolvency or receivership after the bankruptcy case is closed. That is, the clause is not invalidated in toto, but merely made inapplicable during the case for the purpose of disposition of the executory contract or unexpired lease. House Report No. 95–595.

1984 Acts. Statements by Legislative Leaders, see 1984 U.S.Code Cong. and Adm.News, p. 576.

1986 Acts. House Report No. 99–764 and House Conference Report No. 99–958, see 1986 U.S.Code Cong. and Adm. News, p. 5227.

1988 Acts. Senate Report No. 100–505, see 1988 U.S.Code Cong. and Adm.News, p. 3200.

1990 Acts. House Report No. 101–681(I), see 1990 U.S.Code Cong. and Adm.News, p. 6472.

1992 Acts. House Report No. 102–205, see U.S.Code Cong. and Adm.News, p. 866.

1994 Acts. House Report No. 103–835, see 1994 U.S. Code Cong. and Adm. News, p. 3340.

House Report No. 103–831, see 1994 U.S. Code Cong. and Adm. News, p. 3579.

2005 Acts. House Report No. 109–31(Part I), see 2005 U.S. Code Cong. and Adm. News, p. 88.

Legislative Statements

Section 365(b)(3) represents a compromise between H.R. 8200 as passed by the House and the Senate amendment. The provision adopts standards contained in section 365(b)(5) of the Senate amendment to define adequate assurance of future performance of a lease of real property in a shopping center.

Section 365(b)(4) of the House amendment indicates that after default the trustee may not require a lessor to supply services or materials without assumption unless the lessor is compensated as provided in the lease.

Section 365(c)(2) and (3) likewise represent a compromise between H.R. 8200 as passed by the House and the Senate amendment. Section 365(c)(2) is derived from section 365(b)(4) of the Senate amendment but does not apply to a contract to deliver equipment as provided in the Senate amendment. As contained in the House amendment, the provision prohibits a trustee or debtor in possession from assuming or assigning an executory contract of the debtor to make a loan, or extend other debt financing or financial accommodations, to or for the benefit of the debtor, or the issuance of a security of the debtor.

Section 365(e) is a refinement of comparable provisions contained in the House bill and Senate amendment. Sections 365(e)(1) and (2)(A) restate section 365(e) of H.R. 8200 as passed by the House. Sections 365(e)(2)(B) expands the section to permit termination of an executory contract or unexpired lease of the debtor if such contract is a contract to make a loan, or extend other debt financing or financial accommodations, to or for the benefit of the debtor, or for the issuance of a security of the debtor.

Characterization of contracts to make a loan, or extend other debt financing or financial accommodations, is limited to the extension of cash or a line of credit and is not intended to embrace ordinary leases or contracts to provide goods or services with payments to be made over time.

Section 365(f) is derived from H.R. 8200 as passed by the House. Deletion of language in section 365(f)(3) of the Senate amendment is done as a matter of style. Restrictions with respect to assignment of an executory contract or unexpired lease are superfluous since the debtor may assign an executory contract or unexpired lease of the debtor only if such contract is first assumed under section 364(f)(2)(A) of the House amendment.

Section 363(h) of the House amendment represents a modification of section 365(h) of the Senate amendment. The House amendment makes clear that in the case of a bankrupt lessor, a lessee may remain in possession for the balance of the term of a lease and any renewal or extension of the term only to the extent that such renewal or extension may be obtained by the lessee without the permission of the landlord or some third party under applicable non-bankruptcy law.

References in Text

Chapter 7, referred to in subsec. (p)(1), is chapter 7 of this title, 11 U.S.C.A. § 701 et seq.

Chapter 11 or 13, referred to in subsec. (p)(3), is chapter 11 or 13 of this title, 11 U.S.C.A. § 1101 et seq. or 11 U.S.C.A. § 1301 et seq., respectively.

Codifications

Amendment to subsec. (c)(1)(A) by Pub.L. 99–554, § 283(e)(1)(1), struck out "or an assignee of such contract or lease" as the probable intent of Congress, notwithstanding directory language requiring "or and assignee of such contract or lease" be struck out.

Amendment by section 501(d)(10)(A) of Pub.L. 103–394, purporting to amend subsec. (d)(6)(C) of this section by substituting "section 40102 of title 49" for "the Federal Aviation Act of 1958 (49 U.S.C. 1301)", could not be executed, as the latter phrase did not appear in text.

Amendment by section 1(2) of Pub.L. 103–429, purporting to amend subsec. (p) of this section by substituting "section 40102(a) of title 49" for "section 101(3) of the Federal Aviation Act of 1958", could not be executed, as subsec. (p) had already been stricken out pursuant to section 510(d)(10)(E) of Pub.L. 103–394.

Amendments

2005 Amendments. Subsec. (b)(1)(A). Pub.L. 109–8, § 328(a)(1)(A), struck out the semicolon at the end of subpar. (A) and inserted the following: "other than a default that is a breach of a provision relating to the satisfaction of any provision (other than a penalty rate or penalty provision) relating to a default arising from any failure to perform nonmonetary obligations under an unexpired lease of real property, if it is impossible for the trustee to cure such default by performing nonmonetary acts at and after the time of assumption, except that if such default arises from a failure to operate in accordance with a nonresidential real property lease, then such default shall be cured by performance at and after the time of assumption in accordance with such lease, and pecuniary losses resulting from such default shall be compensated in accordance with the provisions of this paragraph;".

Subsec. (b)(2)(D). Pub.L. 109–8, § 328(a)(1)(B), struck out "penalty rate or provision" and inserted "penalty rate or penalty provision".

Subsec. (c)(2). Pub.L. 109–8, § 328(a)(2)(A), inserted "or" at the end of par. (2).

Subsec. (c)(3). Pub.L. 109–8, § 328(a)(2)(B), struck out "; or" at the end of par. (3) and inserted a period.

Subsec. (c)(4). Pub.L. 109–8, § 328(a)(2)(C), struck out par. (4), which formerly read:

"(4) such lease is of nonresidential real property under which the debtor is the lessee of an aircraft terminal or aircraft gate at an airport at which the debtor is the lessee under one or more additional nonresidential leases of an aircraft terminal or aircraft gate and the trustee, in connection with such assumption or assignment, does not assume all such leases or does not assume and assign all of such leases to the same person, except that the trustee may assume or assign less than all of such leases with the airport operator's written consent."

Subsec. (d)(4). Pub.L. 109–8, § 404(a), rewrote par. (4), which formerly read:

"(4) Notwithstanding paragraphs (1) and (2), in a case under any chapter of this title, if the trustee does not assume or reject an unexpired lease of nonresidential real property under which the debtor is the lessee within 60 days after the date of the order for relief, or within such additional time as the court, for cause, within such 60–day period, fixes, then such lease is deemed rejected, and the trustee shall immediately surrender such nonresidential real property to the lessor."

Subsec. (d)(5). Pub.L. 109–8, § 328(a)(3), struck out par. (5) and redesignated par. (10) as par. (5). Prior to striking, par. (5) formerly read:

"(5) Notwithstanding paragraphs (1) and (4) of this subsection, in a case under any chapter of this title, if the trustee does not assume or reject an unexpired lease of nonresidential real property under which the debtor is an affected air carrier that is the lessee of an aircraft terminal or aircraft gate before the occurrence of a termination event, then (unless the court orders the trustee to assume such unexpired leases within 5 days after the termination event), at the option of the airport operator, such lease is deemed rejected 5 days after the occurrence of a termination event and the trustee shall immediately surrender possession of the premises to the airport operator; except that the lease shall not be deemed to be rejected unless the airport operator first waives the right to damages related to the rejection. In the event that the lease is deemed to be rejected under this paragraph, the airport operator shall provide the affected air carrier adequate opportunity after the surrender of the premises to remove the fixtures and equipment installed by the affected air carrier."

Subsec. (d)(6). Pub.L. 109–8, § 328(a)(3)(A), struck out par. (6), which formerly read:

"(6) For the purpose of paragraph (5) of this subsection and paragraph (f)(1) of this section, the occurrence of a termination event means, with respect to a debtor which is an affected air carrier that is the lessee of an aircraft terminal or aircraft gate—

"(A) the entry under section 301 or 302 of this title of an order for relief under chapter 7 of this title;

"(B) the conversion of a case under any chapter of this title to a case under chapter 7 of this title; or

"(C) the granting of relief from the stay provided under section 362(a) of this title with respect to aircraft, aircraft engines, propellers, appliances, or spare parts, as defined in section 40102(a) of title 49, except for property of the debtor found by the court not to be necessary to an effective reorganization."

Subsec. (d)(7). Pub.L. 109–8, § 328(a)(3)(A), struck out par. (7), which formerly read:

"(7) Any order entered by the court pursuant to paragraph (4) extending the period within which the trustee of an affected air carrier must assume or reject an unexpired lease of nonresidential real property shall be without prejudice to—

"(A) the right of the trustee to seek further extensions within such additional time period granted by the court pursuant to paragraph (4); and

"(B) the right of any lessor or any other party in interest to request, at any time, a shortening or termination of the period within which the trustee must assume or reject an unexpired lease of nonresidential real property."

Subsec. (d)(8). Pub.L. 109–8, § 328(a)(3)(A), struck out par. (8), which formerly read: "(8) The burden of proof for establishing cause for an extension by an affected air carrier under paragraph (4) or the maintenance of a previously granted extension under paragraph (7)(A) and (B) shall at all times remain with the trustee."

Subsec. (d)(9). Pub.L. 109–8, § 328(a)(3)(A), struck out par. (9), which formerly read: "(9) For purposes of determining cause under paragraph (7) with respect to an unexpired lease of nonresidential real property between the debtor that is an affected air carrier and an airport operator under which such debtor is the lessee of an airport terminal or an airport gate, the court shall consider, among other relevant factors, whether substantial harm will result to the airport operator or airline passengers as a result of the extension or the maintenance of a previously granted extension. In making the determination of substantial harm, the court shall consider, among other relevant factors, the level of actual use of the terminals or gates which are the subject of the lease, the public interest in actual use of such terminals or gates, the existence of competing demands for the use of such terminals or gates, the effect of the court's extension or termination of the period of time to assume or reject the lease on such debtor's ability to successfully reorganize under chapter 11 of this title, and whether the trustee of the affected air carrier is capable of continuing to comply with its obligations under section 365(d)(3) of this title."

Subsec. (d)(10). Pub.L. 109–8, § 328(a)(3)(B), redesignated former par. (10) as par. (5).

Subsec. (f)(1). Pub.L. 109–8, § 328(a)(4), struck out "; except that the trustee may not assign an unexpired lease of nonresidential real property under which the debtor is an affected air carrier that is the lessee of an aircraft terminal or aircraft gate if there has occurred a termination event." and inserted a period at the end.

Pub.L. 109–8, § 404(b), struck out "subsection (c)" following "Except as provided in" and inserted "subsections (b) and (c)".

Subsec. (p). Pub.L. 109–8, § 309(b), added subsec. (p).

1994 Amendments. Subsec. (b)(2)(D). Pub.L. 103–394, § 219(a), added subpar. (D).

Subsec. (d)(6)(C). Pub.L. 103–429, § 1(1), substituted "section 40102(a) of title 49" for "section 101 of the Federal Aviation Act of 1958 (49 App. U.S.C. 1301)".

Pub.L. 103–394, § 501(d)(10)(A), substituted "section 40102 of title 49" for "the Federal Aviation Act of 1958 (49 U.S.C. 1301)", which could not be executed to text. See Codification note under this section.

Subsec. (d)(10). Pub.L. 103–394, § 219(b), added par. (10).

Subsec. (g)(2)(A), (B). Pub.L. 103–394, § 501(d)(10)(B), substituted "1208, or 1307" for "1307, or 1208", wherever appearing.

Subsec. (h). Pub.L. 103–394, § 205(a), reorganized text, retaining par. (1) and (2) designations, in par. (1) as so reorganized added subpar. (A) and (B) and subpar. (A), cl. (i) and (ii) designations, and added subpars. (C) and (D), and in par. (2) as reorganized added subpar. (A) and (B) and subpar. (A), cl. (i) and (ii) designations.

Subsec. (n)(1)(B). Pub.L. 103–394, § 501(d)(10)(C), substituted "a right to enforce" for "a right to to enforce".

Subsec. (o). Pub.L. 103–394, § 501(d)(10)(D), substituted provisions directing that trustee shall be deemed to have assumed any commitment by debtor to a Federal depository institutions regulatory agency (or predecessor to such agency), for provisions directing that trustee shall be deemed to have assumed any commitment by debtor to particular institutions, or to predecessors or successors.

Subsec. (p). Pub.L. 103–429, § 1(2), substituted "section 40102(a) of title 49" for "section 101(3) of the Federal Aviation Act of 1958".

Pub.L. 103–394, § 501(d)(10)(E), struck out subsec. (p), relating to affected air carriers.

1992 Amendments. Subsec. (c)(4). Pub.L. 102–365, § 19(c), added par. (4).

Subsec. (d)(5)–(9). Pub.L. 102–365, § 19(b), added pars. (5) through (9).

Subsec. (f)(1). Pub.L. 102–365, § 19(d), inserted provisions prohibiting the trustee from assigning an unexpired lease of nonresidential real property under which the debtor is an affected air carrier that is the lessee of an aircraft terminal or gate if a termination event has occurred.

Subsec. (p). Pub.L. 102–365, § 19(e), added subsec. (p).

1990 Amendments. Subsec. (o). Pub.L. 101–647 added subsec. (o).

1988 Amendments. Subsec. (n). Pub.L. 100–506, § 1(b), added subsec. (n).

1986 Amendments. Subsec. (c)(1)(A). Pub.L. 99–554, § 283(e)(1)(1), struck out "or an assignee of such contract or lease" following "debtor in possession". See Codifications note set out under this section.

Subsec. (c)(3). Pub.L. 99–554, § 283(e)(1)(2), inserted "is" following "lease" and "and" following "property".

Subsec. (d)(2). Pub.L. 99–554, § 257(j), added reference to chapter 12.

Subsec. (g)(1). Pub.L. 99–554, § 257(m)(1), added reference to chapter 12.

Subsec. (g)(2). Pub.L. 99–554, § 257(m)(2), added references to chapter 12 and section 1208 of this title.

Subsec. (h)(1). Pub.L. 99–554, § 283(e)(2), inserted "or timeshare plan" following "to treat such lease".

Subsec. (m). Pub.L. 99–554, § 283(e)(3), substituted "362(b)(10)" for "362(b)(9)".

1984 Amendments. Subsec. (a). Pub.L. 98–353, § 362(a), substantially reenacted provisions with minor changes in phraseology.

Subsec. (b)(3). Pub.L. 98–353, § 362(a), added reference to par. (2)(B) of subsec. (f) of this section in provisions preceding subpar. (A).

Subsec. (b)(3)(A). Pub.L. 98–353, § 362(a), added provisions relating to financial condition and operating performance in the case of an assignment.

Subsec. (b)(3)(C). Pub.L. 98–353, § 362(a), substituted "that assumption or assignment of such lease is subject to all the provisions thereof, including (but not limited to) provisions such as a radius, location, use, or exclusivity provision, and will not breach any such provision contained in any other lease, financing agreement, or master agreement relating to such shopping center; and" for "that assumption or assignment of such lease will not breach substantially any provision, such as a radius, location, use, or exclusivity provision, in any other lease, financing agreement, or master agreement relating to such shopping center; and".

Subsec. (c)(1)(A). Pub.L. 98–353, § 362(a), substituted "applicable law excuses a party, other than the debtor, to such contract or lease from accepting performance from or rendering performance to an entity other than the debtor or the debtor in possession or an assignee of such contract or lease, whether or not such contract or lease prohibits or restricts assignment of rights or delegation of duties; and" for "applicable law excuses a party, other than the debtor, to such contract or lease from accepting performance from or rendering performance to the trustee or an assignee of such contract or lease, whether or not such contract or lease prohibits or restricts assignment of rights or delegation of duties; and".

Subsec. (c)(3). Pub.L. 98–353, § 362(a), added par. (3).

Subsec. (d)(1). Pub.L. 98–353, § 362(a), added reference to residential real property or personal property of the debtor.

Subsec. (d)(2). Pub.L. 98–353, § 362(a), added reference to residential real property or personal property of the debtor.

Subsec. (d)(3), (4). Pub.L. 98–353, § 362(a), added pars. (3) and (4).

Subsec. (h)(1). Pub.L. 98–353, § 402, substituted "If the trustee rejects an unexpired lease of real property of the debtor under which the debtor is the lessor, or a timeshare interest under a timeshare plan under which the debtor is the timeshare interest seller, the lessee or timeshare interest purchaser under such lease or timeshare plan may treat such lease or timeshare plan as terminated by such rejection, where the disaffirmance by the trustee amounts to such a breach as would entitle the lessee or timeshare interest purchaser to treat such lease as terminated by virtue of its own terms, applicable nonbankruptcy law, or other agreements the lessee or timeshare interest purchaser has made with other parties; or, in the alternative, the lessee or timeshare interest purchaser may remain in possession of the leasehold or timeshare interest under any lease or timeshare plan the term of which has commenced for the balance of such term and for any renewal or extension of such term that is enforceable by such lessee or timeshare interest purchaser under applicable nonbankruptcy law." for "If the trustee rejects an unexpired lease of real property of the debtor under which the debtor is the lessor, the lessee under such lease may treat the lease as terminated by such rejection, or, in the alternative, may remain in possession for the balance of the term of such lease and any renewal or extension of such term that is enforceable by such lessee under applicable nonbankruptcy law.".

Subsec. (h)(2). Pub.L. 98–353, § 403, substituted "If such lessee or timeshare interest purchaser remains in possession as provided in paragraph (1) of this subsection, such lessee or timeshare interest purchaser may offset against the rent reserved under such lease or moneys due for such timeshare interest for the balance of the term after the date of the rejection of such lease or timeshare interest, and any such renewal or extension thereof, any damages occurring after such date caused by the nonperformance of any obligation of the debtor under such lease or timeshare plan after such date, but such lessee or timeshare interest purchaser does not have any rights against the estate on account of any damages arising after such date from such rejection, other than such offset." for "If such lessee remains in possession, such lessee may offset against the rent reserved under such lease for the balance of the term after the date of the rejection of such lease, and any such renewal or extension, any damages occurring after such date caused by the nonperformance of any obligation of the debtor after such date, but such lessee does not have any rights against the estate on account of any damages arising after such date from such rejection, other than such offset.".

Subsec. (i)(1). Pub.L. 98–353, § 404, added provisions relating to timeshare interests under timeshare plans.

Subsecs. (l), (m). Pub.L. 98–353, § 362(b), added subsecs. (l) and (m).

Effective and Applicability Provisions

2005 Acts. Amendments by Pub.L. 109–8 effective, except as otherwise provided, 180 days after April 20, 2005, and inapplicable with respect to cases commenced under Title 11 before the effective date, see Pub.L. 109–8, § 1501, set out as a note under 11 U.S.C.A. § 101.

1994 Acts. Amendments by Pub.L. 103–394 effective on Oct. 22, 1994, and not to apply with respect to cases commenced under this title before Oct. 22, 1994, see section 702 of Pub.L. 103–394, set out as a note under section 101 of this title.

1992 Acts. Section 19(f) of Pub.L. 102–365 provided that:

"The amendments made by this section [amending this section and enacting provisions set out as a note under this section] shall be in effect for the 12–month period that begins on the date of enactment of this Act [Sept. 3, 1992] and shall apply in all proceedings involving an affected air carrier (as defined in section 365(p) of title 11, United States Code, as amended by this section [subsec. (p) of this section]) that are pending during such 12–month period. Not later than 9 months after the date of enactment [Sept. 3, 1992], the Administrator of the Federal Aviation Administration shall report to the Committee on Commerce, Science, and Transportation and Committee on the Judiciary of the Senate and the Committee on the Judiciary and Committee on Public Works and Transportation of the House of Representatives on whether this section shall apply to proceedings that are commenced after such 12–month period."

[Any reference in any provision of law enacted before Jan. 4, 1995, to the Committee on Public Works and Transportation of the House of Representatives treated as referring to the Committee on Transportation and Infrastructure of the House of Representatives, see section 1(a)(9) of Pub.L.

104–14, set out as a note preceding section 21 of Title 2, The Congress.]

1988 Acts. Amendment by Pub.L. 100–506 effective on Oct. 18, 1988, except with respect to any case commenced under this title before such date, see section 2 of Pub.L. 100–506, set out as a note under section 101 of this title.

1986 Acts. Amendment by Pub.L. 99–554, § 257, effective 30 days after Oct. 27, 1986, but not applicable with respect to cases commenced under this title before that date, see section 302(a), (c)(1) of Pub.L. 99–554, set out as a note under section 581 of Title 28, Judiciary and Judicial Procedure.

Amendment by Pub.L. 99–554, § 283, effective 30 days after Oct. 27, 1986, except as otherwise provided for, see section 302(a) of Pub.L. 99–554, set out as a note under section 581 of Title 28.

1984 Acts. Amendment by Pub.L. 98–353 effective with respect to cases filed 90 days after July 10, 1984, see section 552(a), formerly 553(a), of Pub.L. 98–353, set out as a note under section 101 of this title.

Separability of Provisions

If any provision of or amendment made by Pub.L. 103–394 or the application of such provision or amendment to any person or circumstance is held to be unconstitutional, the remaining provisions of and amendments made by Pub.L. 103–394 and the application of such provisions and amendments to any person or circumstance shall not be affected thereby, see section 701 of Pub.L. 103–394, set out as a note under section 101 of this title.

Congressional Findings Concerning Airport Gate Leases

Section 19(a) of Pub.L. 102–365 provided that:

"Congress finds that—

"(1) there are major airports served by an air carrier that has leased a substantial majority of the airport's gates;

"(2) the commerce in the region served by such a major airport can be disrupted if the air carrier that leases most of its gates enters bankruptcy and either discontinues or materially reduces service; and

"(3) it is important that such airports be empowered to continue service in the event of such a disruption."

CROSS REFERENCES

Allowance of claims, see 11 USCA § 502.

Applicability of this section in Chapter 9 cases, see 11 USCA § 901.

Assumption or rejection of certain executory contracts within reasonable time after order for relief, see 11 USCA § 744.

Collective bargaining agreements, see 11 USCA § 1167.

Contents of plan, see 11 USCA § 1222.

Contractual right to liquidate—

Commodities contract or forward contract, see 11 USCA § 556.

Repurchase agreement, see 11 USCA § 559.

Securities contract, see 11 USCA § 555.

Contractual right to terminate a swap agreement, see 11 USCA § 560.

Effect of—

Conversion, see 11 USCA § 348.

Rejection of lease of railroad line, see 11 USCA § 1169.

Grain storage facility bankruptcies, expedited determinations, see 11 USCA § 557.

Impairment of claims or interests by plans which cure certain defaults, see 11 USCA § 1124.

Municipal leases, see 11 USCA § 929.

Provisions in plan for assumption or rejection of certain executory contracts or unexpired leases, see 11 USCA §§ 1123 and 1322.

Right of possession of party with security interest as affected by default—

    Aircraft equipment and vessels, see 11 USCA § 1110.

    Rolling stock equipment, see 11 USCA § 1168.

Setoff, see 11 USCA § 553.

LIBRARY REFERENCES

American Digest System

Bankruptcy ⟜3101 to 3117, 2834.

Key Number System Topic No. 51.

Corpus Juris Secundum

CJS Bankruptcy § 278, Parties Defendant; Sovereign Immunity.

CJS Bankruptcy § 527, Automatic Relief from Stay--As to Personal Property.

CJS Bankruptcy § 540, By Governmental Unit--With Regard to License or Similar Grant.

CJS Bankruptcy § 553, Leases.

CJS Bankruptcy § 663, Disqualifying or Limiting Factors.

CJS Bankruptcy § 838, Stockbroker Liquidation Cases.

CJS Bankruptcy § 905, Substantial Performance Remaining.

CJS Bankruptcy § 913, Rights and Duties Pending Assumption or Rejection.

CJS Bankruptcy § 915, Effect of Rejection.

CJS Bankruptcy § 918, Where Applicable Law Excuses Performance.

CJS Bankruptcy § 919, Effect of Conditional Limitations or Restrictions.

CJS Bankruptcy § 920, Effect of Conditional Limitations or Restrictions--Restrictions on Assignment or Delegation.

CJS Bankruptcy § 921, Assumption of Leases of Personal Property.

CJS Bankruptcy § 922, Necessity of Court Approval; Assumption by Conduct.

CJS Bankruptcy § 926, Time for Exercise of Right.

CJS Bankruptcy § 927, Exercising Right in Chapter 7 Cases.

CJS Bankruptcy § 928, Judicial Forcing of Decision Date on Request of Party to Contract.

CJS Bankruptcy § 930, Effect of Default.

CJS Bankruptcy § 931, Cure of Default or Adequate Assurance of Prompt Cure.

CJS Bankruptcy § 932, Compensation for Losses; Adequate Assurance of Future Performance.

CJS Bankruptcy § 933, Assumption of Shopping Center Leases.

CJS Bankruptcy § 935, Ability to Terminate or Modify Agreement Because of Assignment.

CJS Bankruptcy § 937, Time Limitation on Exercise of Right to Assume or Reject.

CJS Bankruptcy § 939, Relief from Automatic Rejection; Waiver.

CJS Bankruptcy § 941, Surrender of Premises.

CJS Bankruptcy § 943, Exclusion of Collective-Bargaining Agreements Subject to Railway Labor Act.

CJS Bankruptcy § 945, Application for Court Approval of Rejection; Hearing and Notice.

CJS Bankruptcy § 991, Commitment to Maintain Depository Institution Capital.

CJS Bankruptcy § 994, Superpriority Administrative Expense.

CJS Bankruptcy § 1135, Impairment of Claims or Interests--Curing Defaults.

CJS Bankruptcy § 1143, Optional Provisions.

CJS Bankruptcy § 1166, Interest in Rolling Stock Equipment.

CJS Bankruptcy § 1167, Operation of Railroad; Abandonment of Lines.

CJS Bankruptcy § 1179, Use, Sale, or Lease of Property.

CJS Bankruptcy § 1180, Treatment of Executory Contracts and Unexpired Leases.

CJS Bankruptcy § 1189, Contents of Plan, Generally.

CJS Secured Transactions § 27, Other Particular Factors and Tests.

§ 366. Utility service

(a) Except as provided in subsections (b) and (c) of this section, a utility may not alter, refuse, or discontinue service to, or discriminate against, the trustee or the debtor solely on the basis of the commencement of a case under this title or that a debt owed by the debtor to such utility for service rendered before the order for relief was not paid when due.

(b) Such utility may alter, refuse, or discontinue service if neither the trustee nor the debtor, within 20 days after the date of the order for relief, furnishes adequate assurance of payment, in the form of a deposit or other security, for service after such date. On request of a party in interest and after notice and a hearing, the court may order reasonable modification of the amount of the deposit or other security necessary to provide adequate assurance of payment.

(c)(1)(A) For purposes of this subsection, the term "assurance of payment" means—

    (i) a cash deposit;

    (ii) a letter of credit;

    (iii) a certificate of deposit;

    (iv) a surety bond;

    (v) a prepayment of utility consumption; or

    (vi) another form of security that is mutually agreed on between the utility and the debtor or the trustee.

(B) For purposes of this subsection an administrative expense priority shall not constitute an assurance of payment.

(2) Subject to paragraphs (3) and (4), with respect to a case filed under chapter 11, a utility referred to in subsection (a) may alter, refuse, or discontinue utility service, if during the 30–day period beginning on the date of the filing of the petition, the utility does not receive from the debtor or the trustee adequate assurance of payment for utility service that is satisfactory to the utility.

(3)(A) On request of a party in interest and after notice and a hearing, the court may order modification of the amount of an assurance of payment under paragraph (2).

(B) In making a determination under this paragraph whether an assurance of payment is adequate, the court may not consider—

    (i) the absence of security before the date of the filing of the petition;

    (ii) the payment by the debtor of charges for utility service in a timely manner before the date of the filing of the petition; or

    (iii) the availability of an administrative expense priority.

(4) Notwithstanding any other provision of law, with respect to a case subject to this subsection, a utility may recover or set off against a security deposit provided to the utility by the debtor before the date of the filing of the petition without notice or order of the court.

(Pub.L. 95–598, Nov. 6, 1978, 92 Stat. 2578; Pub.L. 98–353, Title III, § 443, July 10, 1984, 98 Stat. 373; Pub.L. 109–8, Title IV, § 417, Apr. 20, 2005, 119 Stat. 108.)

HISTORICAL AND STATUTORY NOTES

Revision Notes and Legislative Reports

1978 Acts. This section gives debtors protection from a cut-off of service by a utility because of the filing of a bankruptcy case. This section is intended to cover utilities that have some special position with respect to the debtor, such as an electric company, gas supplier, or telephone company that is a monopoly in the area so that the debtor cannot easily obtain comparable service from another utility. The utility may not alter, refuse, or discontinue service because of the nonpayment of a bill that would be discharged in the bankruptcy case. Subsection (b) protects the utility company by requiring the trustee or the debtor to provide, within ten days,

adequate assurance of payment for service provided after the date of the petition. Senate Report No. 95–989.

1984 Acts. Statements by Legislative Leaders, see 1984 U.S.Code Cong. and Adm.News, p. 576.

2005 Acts. House Report No. 109–31(Part I), see 2005 U.S. Code Cong. and Adm. News, p. 88.

Legislative Statements

Section 366 of the House amendment represents a compromise between comparable provisions contained in H.R. 8200 as passed by the House and the Senate amendment. Subsection (a) is modified so that the applicable date is the date of the order for relief rather than the date of the filing of the petition. Subsection (b) contains a similar change but is otherwise derived from section 366(b) of the Senate amendment, with the exception that a time period for continued service of 20 days rather than 10 days is adopted.

References in Text

Chapter 11, referred to in subsec. (c)(2), is chapter 11 of this title, 11 U.S.C.A. § 1101 et seq.

Amendments

2005 Amendments. Subsec. (a). Pub.L. 109–8, § 417(1), struck out "subsection (b)" and inserted "subsections (b) and (c)".

Subsec. (c). Pub.L. 109–8, § 417(2), added subsec. (c).

1984 Amendments. Subsec. (a). Pub.L. 98–353 added "of the commencement of a case under this title or" after "basis".

Effective and Applicability Provisions

2005 Acts. Amendments by Pub.L. 109–8 effective, except as otherwise provided, 180 days after April 20, 2005, and inapplicable with respect to cases commenced under Title 11 before the effective date, see Pub.L. 109–8, § 1501, set out as a note under 11 U.S.C.A. § 101.

1984 Acts. Amendment by Pub.L. 98–353 effective with respect to cases filed 90 days after July 10, 1984, see section 552(a), formerly 553(a) of Pub.L. 98–353, set out as a note under section 101 of this title.

CROSS REFERENCES

Applicability of this section in Chapter 9 cases, see 11 USCA § 901.

LIBRARY REFERENCES

American Digest System
    Bankruptcy ⟐2481, 2482.
    Key Number System Topic No. 51.

Corpus Juris Secundum
    CJS Bankruptcy § 278, Parties Defendant; Sovereign Immunity.
    CJS Bankruptcy § 543, Form of Adequate Assurance.

CHAPTER 5—CREDITORS, THE DEBTOR, AND THE ESTATE

SUBCHAPTER I—CREDITORS AND CLAIMS

Sec.
501. Filing of proofs of claims or interests.
502. Allowance of claims or interests.
503. Allowance of administrative expenses.
504. Sharing of compensation.
505. Determination of tax liability.
506. Determination of secured status.
507. Priorities.
508. Effect of distribution other than under this title.
509. Claims of codebtors.
510. Subordination.
511. Rate of interest on tax claims.

SUBCHAPTER II—DEBTOR'S DUTIES AND BENEFITS

521. Debtor's duties.
522. Exemptions.
523. Exceptions to discharge.
524. Effect of discharge.
525. Protection against discriminatory treatment.
526. Restrictions on debt relief agencies.
527. Disclosures.
528. Requirements for debt relief agencies.

SUBCHAPTER III—THE ESTATE

541. Property of the estate.
542. Turnover of property to the estate.
543. Turnover of property by a custodian.
544. Trustee as lien creditor and as successor to certain creditors and purchasers.
545. Statutory liens.
546. Limitations on avoiding powers.
547. Preferences.
548. Fraudulent transfers and obligations.
549. Postpetition transactions.
550. Liability of transferee of avoided transfer.
551. Automatic preservation of avoided transfer.
552. Postpetition effect of security interest.
553. Setoff.
554. Abandonment of property of the estate.
555. Contractual right to liquidate, terminate, or accelerate a securities contract.
556. Contractual right to liquidate, terminate, or accelerate a commodities contract or forward contract.
557. Expedited determination of interests in, and abandonment or other disposition of grain assets.
558. Defenses of the estate.
559. Contractual right to liquidate, terminate, or accelerate a repurchase agreement.
560. Contractual right to liquidate, terminate, or accelerate a swap agreement.
561. Contractual right to terminate, liquidate, accelerate, or offset under a master netting agreement and across contracts; proceedings under chapter 15.
562. Timing of damage measure in connection with swap agreements, securities contracts, forward contracts,

Sec.
SUBCHAPTER III—THE ESTATE—Cont'd
commodity contracts, repurchase agreements, and master netting agreements.

HISTORICAL AND STATUTORY NOTES

Amendments

2010 Amendments. Pub.L. 111–327, § 2(a)(50), Dec. 22, 2010, 124 Stat. 3562, rewrote item 562 which formerly read: "562. Timing of damage measure in connection with swap agreements, securities contracts, forward contracts, commodity contracts, repurchase agreements, or master netting agreements".

2005 Amendments. Pub.L. 109–8, Title VII, § 704(b), Apr. 20, 2005, 119 Stat. 126, added item 511.

Pub.L. 109–8, Title II, § 227(b), April 20, 2005, 119 Stat. 69, added item 526.

Pub.L. 109–8, Title II, § 228(b), April 20, 2005, 119 Stat. 71, added item 527.

Pub.L. 109–8, Title II, § 229(b), April 20, 2005, 119 Stat. 72, added item 528.

Pub.L. 109–8, Title IX, § 907(p)(1), Apr. 20, 2005, 119 Stat. 182, rewrote items 555, 556, 559, and 560, which formerly read:

"555. Contractual right to liquidate a securities contract.

"556. Contractual right to liquidate a commodity contract or forward contract."

"559. Contractual right to liquidate a repurchase agreement.

"560. Contractual right to terminate a swap agreement."

Pub.L. 109–8, Title IX, § 907(k)(2), Apr. 20, 2005, 119 Stat. 181, added item 561.

Pub.L. 109–8, Title IX, § 910(a)(2), Apr. 20, 2005, 119 Stat. 184, added item 562.

1990 Amendments. Pub.L. 101–311, Title I, § 106(b), June 25, 1990, 104 Stat. 268, added item 560.

1986 Amendments. Pub.L. 99–554, Title II, § 283(q), Oct. 27, 1986, 100 Stat. 3118, in item 557, substituted in it "557. Expedited determination of interests in, and abandonment or other disposition of grain assets" for "557. Expedited determination of interests in and disposition of grain", and reenacted items 558 and 559 without change.

1984 Amendments. Pub.L. 98–353, Title III, § 352(b), July 10, 1984, 98 Stat. 361, added item 557.

Pub.L. 98–353, Title III, § 396(b), July 10, 1984, 98 Stat. 366, added item 559.

Pub.L. 98–353, Title III, § 470(b), July 10, 1984, 98 Stat. 380, added item 558.

1982 Amendments. Pub.L. 97–222, § 6(b), July 27, 1982, 96 Stat. 237, added items 555 and 556.

Effective and Applicability Provisions

2005 Acts. Amendments by Pub.L. 109–8 effective, except as otherwise provided, 180 days after April 20, 2005, and inapplicable with respect to cases commenced under Title 11 before the effective date, see Pub.L. 109–8, § 1501, set out as a note under 11 U.S.C.A. § 101.

CROSS REFERENCES

Applicability of this chapter to—

Cases under Chapter 7, 11, 12, or 13 of this title, see 11 USCA § 103.

Investor protection liquidation proceedings, see 15 USCA § 78fff.

SUBCHAPTER I—CREDITORS AND CLAIMS

§ 501.   Filing of proofs of claims or interests

(a) A creditor or an indenture trustee may file a proof of claim. An equity security holder may file a proof of interest.

(b) If a creditor does not timely file a proof of such creditor's claim, an entity that is liable to such creditor with the debtor, or that has secured such creditor, may file a proof of such claim.

(c) If a creditor does not timely file a proof of such creditor's claim, the debtor or the trustee may file a proof of such claim.

(d) A claim of a kind specified in section 502(e)(2), 502(f), 502(g), 502(h) or 502(i) of this title may be filed under subsection (a), (b), or (c) of this section the same as if such claim were a claim against the debtor and had arisen before the date of the filing of the petition.

(e) A claim arising from the liability of a debtor for fuel use tax assessed consistent with the requirements of section 31705 of title 49 may be filed by the base jurisdiction designated pursuant to the International Fuel Tax Agreement (as defined in section 31701 of title 49) and, if so filed, shall be allowed as a single claim.

(Pub.L. 95–598, Nov. 6, 1978, 92 Stat. 2578; Pub.L. 98–353, Title III, § 444, July 10, 1984, 98 Stat. 373; Pub.L. 109–8, Title VII, § 702, Apr. 20, 2005, 119 Stat. 125.)

HISTORICAL AND STATUTORY NOTES

Revision Notes and Legislative Reports

1978 Acts. This section governs the means by which creditors and equity security holders present their claims or interests to the court. Subsection (a) permits a creditor to file a proof of claim or interest. An indenture trustee representing creditors may file a proof of claim on behalf of the creditors he represents.

This subsection is permissive only, and does not require filing of a proof of claim by any creditor. It permits filing where some purpose would be served, such as where a claim that appears on a list filed under proposed 11 U.S.C. 924 or 1111 was incorrectly stated or listed as disputed, contingent, or unliquidated, where a creditor with a lien is undersecured and asserts a claim for the balance of the debt owed him (his unsecured claim, as determined under proposed 11 U.S.C. 506(a)), or in a liquidation case where there will be a distribution of assets to the holders of allowed claims. In other instances, such as in no-asset liquidation cases, in situations where a secured creditor does not assert any claim against the estate and a determination of his claim is not made under proposed 11 U.S.C. 506, or in situations where the claim asserted would be subordinated and the creditor would not recover from the estate in any event, filing of a proof of claim may simply not be necessary. The Rules of Bankruptcy Procedure and practice under the law will guide creditors as to when filing is necessary and when it may be dispensed with. In general, however, unless a claim is listed in a chapter 9 or chapter 11 case and allowed as a result of the list, a proof of claim will be a prerequisite to allowance for unsecured claims, including priority claims and the unsecured portion of a claim asserted by the holder of a lien.

The Rules of Bankruptcy Procedure will set the time limits, the form, and the procedure for filing, which will determine whether claims are timely or tardily filed. The rules governing time limits for filing proofs of claims will continue to apply under section 405(d) of the bill. These provide a 6-month-bar date for the filing of tax claims.

Subsection (b) permits a codebtor, surety, or guarantor to file a proof of claim on behalf of the creditor to which he is liable if the creditor does not timely file a proof of claim.

In liquidation and individual repayment plan cases, the trustee or the debtor may file a proof of claim under subsection (c) if the creditor does not timely file. The purpose of this subsection is mainly to protect the debtor if the creditor's claim is nondischargeable. If the creditor does not file, there would be no distribution on the claim, and the debtor would have a greater debt to repay after the case is closed than if the claim were paid in part or in full in the case or under the plan.

Subsection (d) governs the filing of claims of the kind specified in subsections (f), (g), (h), (i), or (j) of proposed 11 U.S.C. 502. The separation of this provision from the other claim-filing provisions in this section is intended to indicate that claims of the kind specified, which do not become fixed or do not arise until after the commencement of the case, must be treated differently for filing purposes such as the bar date for filing claims. The rules will provide for later filing of claims of these kinds.

Subsection (e) gives governmental units (including tax authorities) at least six months following the date for the first meeting of creditors in a chapter 7 or chapter 13 case within which to file proof of claims. Senate Report No. 95–989.

1984 Acts. Statements by Legislative Leaders, see 1984 U.S.Code Cong. and Adm.News, p. 576.

2005 Acts. House Report No. 109–31(Part I), see 2005 U.S. Code Cong. and Adm. News, p. 88.

Legislative Statements

The House amendment adopts section 501(b) of the Senate amendment leaving the Rules of Bankruptcy Procedure free to determine where a proof of claim must be filed.

Section 501(c) expands language contained in section 501(c) of the House bill and Senate amendment to permit the debtor to file a proof of claim if a creditor does not timely file a proof of the creditor's claim in a case under title 11.

The House amendment deletes section 501(e) of the Senate amendment as a matter to be left to the rules of bankruptcy procedure. It is anticipated that the rules will enable governmental units, like other creditors, to have a reasonable time to file proofs of claim in bankruptcy cases.

For purposes of section 501, a proof of "interest" includes the interest of a general or limited partner in a partnership, the interest of a proprietor in a sole proprietorship, or the interest of a common or preferred stockholder in a corporation.

Amendments

2005 Amendments. Subsec. (e). Pub.L. 109–8, § 702, added subsec. (e).

1984 Amendments. Subsec. (d). Pub.L. 98–353 added "502(e)(2)," preceding "502(f)".

Effective and Applicability Provisions

2005 Acts. Amendments by Pub.L. 109–8 effective, except as otherwise provided, 180 days after April 20, 2005, and inapplicable with respect to cases commenced under Title 11 before the effective date, see Pub.L. 109–8, § 1501, set out as a note under 11 U.S.C.A. § 101.

1984 Acts. Amendment by Pub.L. 98–353 effective with respect to cases filed 90 days after July 10, 1984, see section 552(a), formerly 553 of Pub.L. 98–353, set out as a note under section 101 of this title.

Child Support Creditors or Their Representatives; Appearance Before Court

Pub.L. 103–394, Title IV, § 304(g), Oct. 22, 1994, 108 Stat. 4134, provided that: "Child support creditors or their representatives shall be permitted to appear and intervene without charge, and without meeting any special local court rule requirement for attorney appearances, in any bankruptcy case or proceeding in any bankruptcy court or district court of the United States if such creditors or representatives file a form in such court that contains information detailing the child support debt, its status, and other characteristics."

§ 502. Allowance of claims or interests

(a) A claim or interest, proof of which is filed under section 501 of this title, is deemed allowed, unless a party in interest, including a creditor of a general partner in a partnership that is a debtor in a case under chapter 7 of this title, objects.

(b) Except as provided in subsections (e)(2), (f), (g), (h) and (i) of this section, if such objection to a claim is made, the court, after notice and a hearing, shall determine the amount of such claim in lawful currency of the United States as of the date of the filing of the petition, and shall allow such claim in such amount, except to the extent that—

(1) such claim is unenforceable against the debtor and property of the debtor, under any agreement or applicable law for a reason other than because such claim is contingent or unmatured;

(2) such claim is for unmatured interest;

(3) if such claim is for a tax assessed against property of the estate, such claim exceeds the value of the interest of the estate in such property;

(4) if such claim is for services of an insider or attorney of the debtor, such claim exceeds the reasonable value of such services;

(5) such claim is for a debt that is unmatured on the date of the filing of the petition and that is excepted from discharge under section 523(a)(5) of this title;

(6) if such claim is the claim of a lessor for damages resulting from the termination of a lease of real property, such claim exceeds—

(A) the rent reserved by such lease, without acceleration, for the greater of one year, or 15 percent, not to exceed three years, of the remaining term of such lease, following the earlier of—

(i) the date of the filing of the petition; and

(ii) the date on which such lessor repossessed, or the lessee surrendered, the leased property; plus

(B) any unpaid rent due under such lease, without acceleration, on the earlier of such dates;

(7) if such claim is the claim of an employee for damages resulting from the termination of an employment contract, such claim exceeds—

(A) the compensation provided by such contract, without acceleration, for one year following the earlier of—

(i) the date of the filing of the petition; or

(ii) the date on which the employer directed the employee to terminate, or such employee terminated, performance under such contract; plus

(B) any unpaid compensation due under such contract, without acceleration, on the earlier of such dates;

(8) such claim results from a reduction, due to late payment, in the amount of an otherwise applicable credit available to the debtor in connection with an employment tax on wages, salaries, or commissions earned from the debtor; or

(9) proof of such claim is not timely filed, except to the extent tardily filed as permitted under paragraph (1), (2), or (3) of section 726(a) of this title or under the Federal Rules of Bankruptcy Procedure, except that a claim of a governmental unit shall be timely filed if it is filed before 180 days after the date of the order for relief or such later time as the Federal Rules of Bankruptcy Procedure may provide, and except that in a case under chapter 13, a claim of a governmental unit for a tax with respect to a return filed under section 1308 shall be timely if the claim is filed on or before the date that is 60 days after the date on which such return was filed as required.

(c) There shall be estimated for purpose of allowance under this section—

(1) any contingent or unliquidated claim, the fixing or liquidation of which, as the case may be, would unduly delay the administration of the case; or

(2) any right to payment arising from a right to an equitable remedy for breach of performance.

(d) Notwithstanding subsections (a) and (b) of this section, the court shall disallow any claim of any entity from which property is recoverable under section 542, 543, 550, or 553 of this title or that is a transferee of a transfer avoidable under section 522(f), 522(h), 544, 545, 547, 548, 549, or 724(a) of this title, unless such entity or transferee has paid the amount, or turned over any such property, for which such entity or transferee is liable under section 522(i), 542, 543, 550, or 553 of this title.

(e)(1) Notwithstanding subsections (a), (b), and (c) of this section and paragraph (2) of this subsection, the court shall disallow any claim for reimbursement or contribution of an entity that is liable with the debtor on or has secured the claim of a creditor, to the extent that—

(A) such creditor's claim against the estate is disallowed;

(B) such claim for reimbursement or contribution is contingent as of the time of allowance or disallowance of such claim for reimbursement or contribution; or

(C) such entity asserts a right of subrogation to the rights of such creditor under section 509 of this title.

(2) A claim for reimbursement or contribution of such an entity that becomes fixed after the commencement of the case shall be determined, and shall be allowed under subsection (a), (b), or (c) of this section, or disallowed under subsection (d) of this section, the same as if such claim had become fixed before the date of the filing of the petition.

(f) In an involuntary case, a claim arising in the ordinary course of the debtor's business or financial affairs after the commencement of the case but before the earlier of the appointment of a trustee and the order for relief shall be determined as of the date such claim arises, and shall be allowed under subsection (a), (b), or (c) of this section or disallowed under subsection (d) or (e) of this section, the same as if such claim had arisen before the date of the filing of the petition.

(g)(1) A claim arising from the rejection, under section 365 of this title or under a plan under chapter 9, 11, 12, or 13 of this title, of an executory contract or unexpired lease of the debtor that has not been assumed shall be determined, and shall be allowed under subsection (a), (b), or (c) of this section or disallowed under subsection (d) or (e) of this section, the same as if such claim had arisen before the date of the filing of the petition.

(2) A claim for damages calculated in accordance with section 562 shall be allowed under subsection (a), (b), or (c), or disallowed under subsection (d) or (e), as if such claim had arisen before the date of the filing of the petition.

(h) A claim arising from the recovery of property under section 522, 550, or 553 of this title shall be determined, and shall be allowed under subsection (a), (b), or (c) of this section, or disallowed under subsection (d) or (e) of this section, the same as if such claim had arisen before the date of the filing of the petition.

(i) A claim that does not arise until after the commencement of the case for a tax entitled to priority under section 507(a)(8) of this title shall be determined, and shall be allowed under subsection (a), (b), or (c) of this section, or disallowed under subsection (d) or (e) of this section, the same as if such claim had arisen before the date of the filing of the petition.

(j) A claim that has been allowed or disallowed may be reconsidered for cause. A reconsidered claim may be allowed or disallowed according to the equities of the case. Reconsideration of a claim under this subsection does not affect the validity of any payment or transfer from the estate made to a holder of an allowed claim on account of such allowed claim that is not reconsidered, but if a reconsidered claim is allowed and is of the same class as such holder's claim, such holder may not receive any additional payment or transfer from the estate on account of such holder's allowed claim until the holder of such reconsidered and allowed claim receives payment on account of such claim proportionate in value to that already received by such other holder. This subsection does not alter or modify the trustee's right to recover from a creditor any excess payment or transfer made to such creditor.

(k)(1) The court, on the motion of the debtor and after a hearing, may reduce a claim filed under this section based in whole on an unsecured consumer debt by not more than 20 percent of the claim, if—

(A) the claim was filed by a creditor who unreasonably refused to negotiate a reasonable alternative repayment schedule proposed on behalf of the debtor by an approved nonprofit budget and credit counseling agency described in section 111;

(B) the offer of the debtor under subparagraph (A)—

    (i) was made at least 60 days before the date of the filing of the petition; and

    (ii) provided for payment of at least 60 percent of the amount of the debt over a period not to exceed the repayment period of the loan, or a reasonable extension thereof; and

(C) no part of the debt under the alternative repayment schedule is nondischargeable.

(2) The debtor shall have the burden of proving, by clear and convincing evidence, that—

    (A) the creditor unreasonably refused to consider the debtor's proposal; and

    (B) the proposed alternative repayment schedule was made prior to expiration of the 60–day period specified in paragraph (1)(B)(i).

(Pub.L. 95–598, Nov. 6, 1978, 92 Stat. 2579; Pub.L. 98–353, Title III, § 445, July 10, 1984, 98 Stat. 373; Pub.L. 99–554, Title II, §§ 257(j), 283(f), Oct. 27, 1986, 100 Stat. 3115, 3117; Pub.L. 103–394, Title II, § 213(a), Title III, § 304(h)(1), Oct. 22, 1994, 108 Stat. 4125, 4134; Pub.L. 109–8, Title II, § 201(a), Title VII, § 716(d), Title IX, § 910(b), Apr. 20, 2005, 119 Stat. 42, 130. 184.)

HISTORICAL AND STATUTORY NOTES

Revision Notes and Legislative Reports

1978 Acts. A proof of claim or interest is prima facie evidence of the claim or interest. Thus, it is allowed under subsection (a) unless a party in interest objects. The rules and case law will determine who is a party in interest for purposes of objection to allowance. The case law is well developed on this subject today. As a result of the change in the liability of a general partner's estate for the debts of this partnership, see proposed 11 U.S.C. 723, the category of persons that are parties in interest in the partnership case will be expanded to include a creditor of a partner against whose estate the trustee of the partnership estate may proceed under proposed 11 U.S.C. 723(c).

Subsection (b) prescribes the grounds on which a claim may be disallowed. The court will apply these standards if there is an objection to a proof of claim. The burden of proof on the issue of allowance is left to the Rules of Bankruptcy Procedure. Under the current chapter XIII [section 1001 et seq. of former Title 11] rules, a creditor is required to prove that his claim is free from usury, rule 13–301. It is expected that the rules will make similar provision for both liquidation and individual repayment plan cases. See Bankruptcy Act § 656(b) [section 1056(b) of former Title 11]; H.R. 31, 94th Cong., 1st sess., sec. 6–104(a) (1975).

Paragraph (1) requires disallowance if the claim is unenforceable against the debtor for any reason (such as usury, unconscionability, or failure of consideration) other than because it is contingent or unmatured. All such contingent or unmatured claims are to be liquidated by the bankruptcy court in order to afford the debtor complete bankruptcy relief; these claims are generally not provable under present law.

Paragraph (2) requires disallowance to the extent that the claim is for unmatured interest as of the date of the petition. Whether interest is matured or unmatured on the date of bankruptcy is to be determined without reference to any ipso facto or bankruptcy clause in the agreement creating the claim. Interest disallowed under this paragraph includes postpetition interest that is not yet due and payable, and any portion of prepaid interest that represents an original discounting of the claim, yet that would not have been earned on the date of bankruptcy. For example, a claim on a $1,000 note issued the day before bankruptcy would only be allowed to the extent of the cash actually advanced. If the original discount was 10 percent so that the cash advanced was only $900, then notwithstanding the face amount of note, only $900 would be allowed. If $900 was advanced under the note some time before bankruptcy, the interest component of the note would have to be prorated and disallowed to the extent it was for interest after the commencement of the case.

Section 502(b) thus contains two principles of present law. First, interest stops accruing at the date of the filing of the petition, because any claim for unmatured interest is disallowed under this paragraph. Second, bankruptcy operates as the acceleration of the principal amount of all claims against the debtor. One unarticulated reason for this is that the discounting factor for claims after the commencement of the case is equivalent to contractual interest rate on the claim. Thus, this paragraph does not cause disallowance of claims that have not been discounted to a present value because of the irrebuttable presumption that the discounting rate and the contractual interest rate (even a zero interest rate) are equivalent.

Paragraph (3) requires disallowance of a claim to the extent that the creditor may offset the claim against a debt owing to the debtor. This will prevent double recovery, and permit the claim to be filed only for the balance due. This follows section 68 of the Bankruptcy Act [section 108 of former Title 11].

Paragraph (4) requires disallowance of a property tax claim to the extent that the tax due exceeds the value of the property. This too follows current law to the extent the property tax is ad valorem.

Paragraph (5) prevents overreaching by the debtor's attorneys and concealing of assets by debtors. It permits the court to examine the claim of a debtor's attorney independently of any other provision of this subsection, and to disallow it to the extent that it exceeds the reasonable value of the attorneys' services.

Postpetition alimony, maintenance or support claims are disallowed under paragraph (6). They are to be paid from the debtor's postpetition property, because the claims are nondischargeable.

Paragraph (7), derived from current law, limits the damages allowable to a landlord of the debtor. The history of this provision is set out at length in *Oldden v. Tonto Realty Co.,* 143 F.2d 916 (2d Cir. 1944). It is designed to compensate the landlord for his loss while not permitting a claim so large (based on a long-term lease) as to prevent other general unsecured creditors from recovering a dividend from the estate. The damages a landlord may assert from termination of a lease are limited to the rent reserved for the greater of one year or ten percent of the remaining lease term, not to exceed three years, after the earlier of the date of the filing of the petition and the date of surrender or repossession in a chapter 7 case and 3 years lease payments in a chapter 9, 11, or 13 case. The sliding scale formula for chapter 7 cases is new and designed to protect the long-term lessor. This subsection does not apply to limit administrative expense claims for use of the leased premises to which the landlord is otherwise entitled.

This paragraph will not overrule *Oldden*, or the proposition for which it has been read to stand: To the extent that a landlord has a security deposit in excess of the amount of his claim allowed under this paragraph, the excess comes into the estate. Moreover, his allowed claim is for his total damages, as limited by this paragraph. By virtue of proposed 11 U.S.C. 506(a) and 506(d), the claim will be divided into a secured portion and an unsecured portion in those cases in which the deposit that the landlord holds is less than his damages. As under *Oldden*, he will not be permitted to offset his actual damages against his security deposit and then claim for the balance under this paragraph. Rather, his security deposit will be applied in satisfaction of the claim that is allowed under this paragraph.

As used in section 502(b)(7), the phrase "lease of real property" applies only to a "true" or "bona fide" lease and does not apply to financing leases of real property or interests therein, or to leases of such property which are intended as security.

Historically, the limitation on allowable claims of lessors of real property was based on two considerations. First, the amount of the lessor's damages on breach of a real estate lease was considered contingent and difficult to prove. Partly for this reason, claims of a lessor of real estate were not provable prior to the 1934 amendments to the Bankruptcy Act [former Title 11]. Second, in a true lease of real property, the lessor retains all risk and benefits as to the value of the real estate at the termination of the lease. Historically, it was, therefore, considered equitable to limit the claims of a real estate lessor.

However, these considerations are not present in "lease financing" transactions where, in substance, the "lease" involves a sale of the real estate and the rental payments are in substance the payment of principal and interest on a secured loan or sale. In a financing lease the lessor is essentially a secured or unsecured creditor (depending upon whether his interest is perfected or not) of the debtor, and the lessor's claim should not be subject to the 502(b)(7) limitation. Financing "leases" are in substance installment sales or loans. The "lessors" are essentially sellers or lenders and should be treated as such for purposes of the bankruptcy law.

Whether a "lease" is true or bona fide lease or, in the alternative, a financing "lease" or a lease intended as security, depends upon the circumstances of each case. The distinction between a true lease and a financing transaction is based upon the economic substance of the transaction and not, for example, upon the locus of title, the form of the transaction or the fact that the transaction is denominated as a "lease". The fact that the lessee, upon compliance with the terms of the lease, becomes or has the option to become the owner of the leased property for no additional consideration or for nominal consideration indicates that the transaction is a financing lease or lease intended as security. In such cases, the lessor has no substantial interest in the leased property at the expiration of the lease term. In addition, the fact that the lessee assumes and discharges substantially all the risks and obligations ordinarily attributed to the outright ownership of the property is more indicative of a financing transaction than of a true lease. The rental payments in such cases are in substance payments of principal and interest either on a loan secured by the leased real property or on the purchase of the leased real property. See, e.g., Financial Accounting Standards Board Statement No. 13 and SEC Reg. S–X, 17 C.F.R. sec. 210.3–16(q) (1977); cf. *First National Bank of Chicago v. Irving Trust Co.*, 74 F.2d 263 (2nd Cir. 1934); and Albenda and Lief, "Net Lease Financing Transactions Under the Proposed Bankruptcy Act of 1973," 30 Business Lawyer, 713 (1975).

Paragraph (8) is new. It tracks the landlord limitation on damages provision in paragraph (7) for damages resulting from the breach by the debtor of an employment contract, but limits the recovery to the compensation reserved under an employment contract for the year following the earlier of the date of the petition and the termination of employment.

Subsection (c) requires the estimation of any claim liquidation of which would unduly delay the closing of the estate, such as a contingent claim, or any claim for which applicable law provides only an equitable remedy, such as specific performance. This subsection requires that all claims against the debtor be converted into dollar amounts.

Subsection (d) is derived from present law. It requires disallowance of a claim of a transferee of a voidable transfer in toto if the transferee has not paid the amount or turned over the property received as required under the sections under which the transferee's liability arises.

Subsection (e), also derived from present law, requires disallowance of the claim for reimbursement or contribution of a codebtor, surety or guarantor of an obligation of the debtor, unless the claim of the creditor on such obligation has been paid in full. The provision prevents competition between a creditor and his guarantor for the limited proceeds in the estate.

Subsection (f) specifies that "involuntary gap" creditors receive the same treatment as prepetition creditors. Under the allowance provisions of this subsection, knowledge of the commencement of the case will be irrelevant. The claim is to be allowed "the same as if such claim had arisen before the date of the filing of the petition." Under voluntary petition, proposed 11 U.S.C. 303(f), creditors must be permitted to deal with the debtor and be assured that their claims will be paid. For purposes of this subsection, "creditors" include governmental units holding claims for tax liabilities incurred during the period after the petition is filed and before the earlier of the order for relief or appointment of a trustee.

Subsection (g) gives entities injured by the rejection of an executory contract or unexpired lease, either under section 365 or under a plan or reorganization, a prepetition claim for any resulting damages, and requires that the injured entity be treated as a prepetition creditor with respect to that claim.

Subsection (h) gives a transferee of a setoff that is recovered by one trustee a prepetition claim for the amount recovered.

Subsection (i) answers the nonrecourse loan problem and gives the creditor an unsecured claim for the difference between the value of the collateral and the debt in response to the decision in *Great National Life Ins. Co. v. Pine Gate Associates, Ltd.*, Bankruptcy Case No. B75–4345A (N.D.Ga. Sept. 16, 1977).

The bill, as reported, deletes a provision in the bill as originally introduced (former sec. 502(i)) requiring a tax authority to file a proof of claim for recapture of an investment credit where, during title 11 proceedings, the trustee sells or otherwise disposes of property before the title 11 case began. The tax authority should not be required to submit a formal claim for a taxable event (a sale or other disposition of the asset) of whose occurrence the trustee necessarily knows better than the taxing authority. For procedural purposes, the recapture of investment credit is to be treated as an administrative expense, as to which only a request for payment is required. Senate Report No. 95–989.

Paragraph (9) [of subsec. (b)] requires disallowance of certain employment tax claims. These relate to a Federal tax credit for State unemployment insurance taxes which is disallowed if the State tax is paid late. This paragraph disallows the Federal claim for the tax the same as if the credit had been allowed in full on the Federal return. House Report No. 95–595.

1984 Acts. Statements by Legislative Leaders, see 1984 U.S. Code Cong. and Adm. News, p. 576.

1986 Acts. House Report No. 99–764 and House Conference Report No. 99–958, see 1986 U.S. Code Cong. and Adm. News, p. 5227.

1994 Acts. House Report No. 103–835, see 1994 U.S. Code Cong. and Adm. News, p. 3340.

2005 Acts. House Report No. 109–31(Part I), see 2005 U.S. Code Cong. and Adm. News, p. 88.

Legislative Statements

The House amendment adopts a compromise position in section 502(a) between H.R. 8200, as passed by the House, and the Senate amendment. Section 502(a) has been modified to make clear that a party in interest includes a creditor of a partner in a partnership that is a debtor under chapter 7. Since the trustee of the partnership is given an absolute claim against the estate of each general partner under section 723(c), creditors of the partner must have standing to object to claims against the partnership at the partnership level because no opportunity will be afforded at the partner's level for such objection.

The House amendment contains a provision in section 502(b)(1) that requires disallowance of a claim to the extent that such claim is unenforceable against the debtor and unenforceable against property of the debtor. This is intended to result in the disallowance of any claim for deficiency by an undersecured creditor on a non-recourse loan or under a State antideficiency law, special provision for which is made in section 1111, since neither the debtor personally, nor the property of the debtor is liable for such a deficiency. Similarly claims for usurious interest or which could be barred by an agreement between the creditor and the debtor would be disallowed.

Section 502(b)(7)(A) represents a compromise between the House bill and the Senate amendment. The House amendment takes the provision in H.R. 8200 as passed by the House of Representatives but increases the percentage from 10 to 15 percent.

As used in section 502(b)(7), the phrase "lease of real property" applies only to a "true" or "bona fide" lease and does not apply to financing leases of real property or interests therein, or to leases of such property which are intended as security.

Historically, the limitation on allowable claims of lessors of real property was based on two considerations. First, the

amount of the lessor's damages on breach of a real estate lease was considered contingent and difficult to prove. Partly for this reason, claims of a lessor of real estate were not provable prior to the 1934 amendments, to the Bankruptcy Act. Second, in a true lease of real property, the lessor retains all risks and benefits as to the value of the real estate at the termination of the lease. Historically, it was, therefore, considered equitable to limit the claims of real estate lessor.

However, these considerations are not present in "lease financing" transactions where, in substance, the "lease" involves a sale of the real estate and the rental payments are in substance the payment of principal and interest on a secured loan or sale. In a financing lease the lessor is essentially a secured or unsecured creditor (depending upon whether his interest is perfected or not) of the debtor, and the lessor's claim should not be subject to the 502(b)(7) limitation. Financing "leases" are in substance installment sales or loans. The "lessors" are essentially sellers or lenders and should be treated as such for purposes of the bankruptcy law.

Whether a "lease" is true or bona fide lease or, in the alternative a financing "lease" or a lease intended as security, depends upon the circumstances of each case. The distinction between a true lease and a financing transaction is based upon the economic substance of the transaction and not, for example, upon the locus of title, the form of the transaction or the fact that the transaction is denominated as a "lease." The fact that the lessee, upon compliance with the terms of the lease, becomes or has the option to become the owner of the leased property for no additional consideration or for nominal consideration indicates that the transaction is a financing lease or lease intended as security. In such cases, the lessor has no substantial interest in the leased property at the expiration of the lease term. In addition, the fact that the lessee assumes and discharges substantially all the risks and obligations ordinarily attributed to the outright ownership of the property is more indicative of a financing transaction than of a true lease. The rental payments in such cases are in substance payments of principal and interest either on a loan secured by the leased real property or on the purchase of the leased real property. See, e.g., Financial Accounting Standards Board Statement No. 13 and SEC Reg. S–X, 17 C.F.R. sec. 210.3–16(q) (1977); cf. First National Bank of Chicago v. Irving Trust Co., 74 F.2d 263 (2nd Cir.1934); and Albenda and Lief, "Net Lease Financing Transactions Under the Proposed Bankruptcy Act of 1973," 30 Business Lawyer, 713 (1975).

Section 502(c) of the House amendment presents a compromise between similar provisions contained in the House bill and the Senate amendment. The compromise language is consistent with an amendment to the definition of "claim" in section 104(4)(B) of the House amendment and requires estimation of any right to an equitable remedy for breach of performance if such breach gives rise to a right to payment. To the extent language in the House and Senate reports indicate otherwise, such language is expressly overruled.

Section 502(e) of the House amendment contains language modifying a similar section in the House bill and Senate amendment. Section 502(e)(1) states the general rule requiring the court to disallow any claim for reimbursement or contribution of an entity that is liable with the debtor on, or that has secured, the claim of a creditor to any extent that the creditor's claim against the estate is disallowed. This adopts a policy that a surety's claim for reimbursement or contribution is entitled to no better status than the claim of the creditor assured by such surety. Section 502(e)(1)(B) alternatively disallows any claim for reimbursement or contribution by a surety to the extent such claim is contingent as of the time of allowance. Section 502(e)(2) is clear that to the extent a claim for reimbursement or contribution becomes fixed after the commencement of the case that it is to be considered a prepetition claim for purposes of allowance. The combined effect of sections 502(e)(1)(B) and 502(e)(2) is that a surety or codebtor is generally permitted a claim for reimbursement or contribution to the extent the surety or codebtor has paid the assured party at the time of allowance. Section 502(e)(1)(C) alternatively indicates that a claim for reimbursement or contribution of a surety or codebtor is disallowed to the extent the surety or codebtor requests subrogation under section 509 with respect to the rights of the assured party. Thus, the surety or codebtor has a choice; to the extent a claim for contribution or reimbursement would be advantageous, such as in the case where such a claim is secured, a surety or codebtor may opt for reimbursement or contribution under section 502(e). On the other hand, to the extent the claim for such surety or codebtor by way of subrogation is more advantageous, such as where such claim is secured, the surety may elect subrogation under section 509.

The section changes current law by making the election identical in all other respects. To the extent a creditor's claim is satisfied by a surety or codebtor, other creditors should not benefit by the surety's inability to file a claim against the estate merely because such surety or codebtor has failed to pay such creditor's claim in full. On the other hand, to the extent the creditor's claim against the estate is otherwise disallowed, the surety or codebtor should not be entitled to increased rights by way of reimbursement or contribution, to the detriment of competing claims of other unsecured creditors, than would be realized by way of subrogation.

While the foregoing scheme is equitable with respect to other unsecured creditors of the debtor, it is desirable to preserve present law to the extent that a surety or codebtor is not permitted to compete with the creditor he has assured until the assured party's claim has paid in full [sic]. Accordingly, section 509(c) of the House amendment subordinates both a claim by way of subrogation or a claim for reimbursement or contribution of a surety or codebtor to the claim of the assured party until the assured party's claim is paid in full.

Section 502(h) of the House amendment expands similar provisions contained in the House bill and the Senate amendment to indicate that any claim arising from the recovery of property under section 522(i), 550, or 553 shall be determined as though it were a prepetition claim.

Section 502(i) of the House amendment adopts a provision contained in section 502(j) of H.R. 8200 as passed by the House but that was not contained in the Senate amendment.

Section 502(i) of H.R. 8200 as passed by the House, but was not included in the Senate amendment, is deleted as a matter to be left to the bankruptcy tax bill next year.

The House amendment deletes section 502(i) of the Senate bill but adopts the policy of that section to a limited extent for confirmation of a plan of reorganization in section 1111(b) of the House amendment.

Section 502(j) of the House amendment is new. The provision codifies section 57k of the Bankruptcy Act [section 93(k) of former Title 11].

Allowance of Claims or Interest: The House amendment adopts section 502(b)(9) of the House bill which disallows any

tax claim resulting from a reduction of the Federal Unemployment Tax Act (FUTA) credit (sec. 3302 of the Internal Revenue Code [26 U.S.C.A. § 3302]) on account of a tardy contribution to a State unemployment fund if the contribution is attributable to ways or other compensation paid by the debtor before bankruptcy. The Senate amendment allowed this reduction, but would have subordinated it to other claims in the distribution of the estate's assets by treating it as a punitive (nonpecuniary loss) penalty. The House amendment would also not bar reduction of the FUTA credit on account of a trustee's late payment of a contribution to a State unemployment fund if the contribution was attributable to a trustee's payment of compensation earned from the estate.

Section 511 of the Senate amendment is deleted. Its substance is adopted in section 502(b)(9) of the House amendment which reflects an identical provision contained in H.R. 8200 as passed by the House.

References in Text

Chapter 7 of this title, referred to in subsec. (a), is 11 U.S.C.A. § 701 et seq.

The Federal Rules of Bankruptcy Procedure, referred to in subsec. (b)(9), are set out in this title.

Chapter 13, referred to in subsec. (b)(9), is chapter 13 of this title, 11 U.S.C.A. § 1301.

Chapter 9, 11, 12, or 13 of this title, referred to in subsec. (g), is 11 U.S.C.A. § 901 et seq., 11 U.S.C.A. § 1101 et seq., 11 U.S.C.A. § 1201 et seq., or 11 U.S.C.A. § 1301 et seq., respectively.

Amendments

2005 Amendments. Subsec. (b)(9). Pub.L. 109–8, § 716(d), inserted ", and except that in a case under chapter 13, a claim of a governmental unit for a tax with respect to a return filed under section 1308 shall be timely if the claim is filed on or before the date that is 60 days after the date on which such return was filed as required" before the period at the end of par. (9).

Subsec. (g)(1), (2). Pub.L. 109–8, § 910(b), designated existing text in subsec. (g) as par. (1) and added par. (2).

Subsec. (k). Pub.L. 109–8, § 201(a), added subsec. (k).

1994 Amendments. Subsec. (b)(9). Pub.L. 103–394, § 213(a), added par. (9).

Subsec. (i). Pub.L. 103–394, § 304(h)(1), substituted "section 507(a)(8)" for "section 507(a)(7)".

1986 Amendments. Subsec. (b)(6)(A)(ii). Pub.L. 99–554, § 283(f)(1), substituted "repossessed" for "reposessed".

Subsec. (g). Pub.L. 99–554, § 257(j), added reference to chapter 12.

Subsec. (i). Pub.L. 99–554, § 283(f)(2), substituted "507(a)(7)" for "507(a)(6)".

1984 Amendments. Subsec. (a). Pub.L. 98–353, § 445(a), added "general" before "partner".

Subsec. (b). Pub.L. 98–353, § 445(b)(1)(2), in provisions preceding par. (1), added "(e)(2)," after "subsections" and "in lawful currency of the United States" after "claim" the second place such word appeared.

Subsec. (b)(1). Pub.L. 98–353, § 445(b)(3), substituted "and" for ", and unenforceable against".

Subsec. (b)(3). Pub.L. 98–353, § 445(b)(4), redesignated former par. (4) as (3), and struck out former par. (3), which read "such claim may be offset under section 553 of this title against a debt owing to the debtor;".

Pub.L. 98–353, § 445(b)(5), in par. (3), as so redesignated, added "the" after "exceeds".

Subsec. (b)(4). Pub.L. 98–353, § 445(b)(4), redesignated former par. (5) as (4). Former par. (4) was redesignated as (3).

Subsec. (b)(5). Pub.L. 98–353, § 445(b)(4), redesignated former par. (6) as (5). Former par. (5) was redesignated as (4).

Pub.L. 98–353, § 445(b)(6), in par. (5), as so redesignated, substituted "such claim" for "the claim" and struck out the comma after "petition".

Subsec. (b)(6). Pub.L. 98–353, § 445(b)(4), redesignated former par. (7) as (6). Former par. (6) was redesignated as (5).

Subsec. (b)(7). Pub.L. 98–353, § 445(b)(4), redesignated former par. (8) as (7). Former par. (7) was redesignated as (6).

Pub.L. 98–353, § 445(b)(7)(A), in par. (7), as so redesignated, added "the claim of an employee" before "for damages".

Subsec. (b)(7)(A)(i). Pub.L. 98–353, § 445(b)(7)(B), substituted "or" for "and".

Subsec. (b)(7)(B). Pub.L. 98–353, § 445(b)(7)(C), (D), substituted "any" for "the" and substituted "contract, without" for "contract without".

Subsec. (b)(8). Pub.L. 98–353, § 445(b)(4), redesignated former par. (9) as (8). Former par. (8) was redesignated as (7).

Subsec. (b)(9). Pub.L. 98–353, § 445(b)(4), redesignated former par. (9) as (8).

Subsec. (c)(1). Pub.L. 98–353, § 445(c)(1), added "the" before "fixing" and substituted "administration" for "closing".

Subsec. (c)(2). Pub.L. 98–353, § 445(c)(2), added "right to payment arising from a" after "any" and struck out "if such breach gives rise to a right to payment" after "breach of performance".

Subsec. (e)(1). Pub.L. 98–353, § 445(d)(1), (2), substituted ", (b), and (c)" for "and (b)" and substituted "or has secured" for ", or has secured,".

Subsec. (e)(1)(B). Pub.L. 98–353, § 445(d)(3), added "or disallowance" after "allowance".

Subsec. (e)(1)(C). Pub.L. 98–353, § 445(d)(4), substituted "asserts a right of subrogation to the rights of such creditor" for "requests subrogation" and struck out "to the rights of such creditor" after "of this title".

Subsec. (h). Pub.L. 98–353, § 445(e), substituted "522" for "522(i)".

Subsec. (j). Pub.L. 98–353, § 445(f), added provisions relating to reconsideration of a disallowed claim, and provisions relating to reconsideration of a claim under this subsection.

Effective and Applicability Provisions

2005 Acts. Amendments by Pub.L. 109–8 effective, except as otherwise provided, 180 days after April 20, 2005, and inapplicable with respect to cases commenced under Title 11 before the effective date, see Pub.L. 109–8, § 1501, set out as a note under 11 U.S.C.A. § 101.

1994 Acts. Amendments by Pub.L. 103–394 effective on Oct. 22, 1994, and not to apply with respect to cases commenced under Title 11 of the United States Code before Oct.

22, 1994, see section 702 of Pub.L. 103–394, set out as a note under section 101 of this title.

1986 Acts. Amendments by Pub.L. 99–554, § 257(j) effective 30 days after Oct. 27, 1986, but not to apply with respect to cases commenced under this title before that date, see section 302(a)(c)(1) of Pub.L. 99–554, set out as a note under section 581 of Title 28, Judiciary and Judicial Procedure.

Amendment by Pub.L. 99–554, § 283, effective 30 days after Oct. 27, 1986, except as otherwise provided for, see section 302(a) of Pub.L. 99–554, set out as a note under section 581 of Title 28.

1984 Acts. Amendment by Pub.L. 98–353 effective with respect to cases filed 90 days after July 10, 1984, see section 552(a), formerly 553(a) of Pub.L. 98–353, set out as a note under section 101 of this title.

Separability of Provisions

If any provision of or amendment made by Pub.L. 103–394 or the application of such provision or amendment to any person or circumstance is held to be unconstitutional, the remaining provisions of and amendments made by Pub.L. 103–394 and the application of such provisions and amendments to any person or circumstance shall not be affected thereby, see section 701 of Pub.L. 103–394, set out as a note under section 101 of this title.

CROSS REFERENCES

Acceptance of plan by holders of claims or interests, see 11 USCA § 1126.

Applicability of this section in Chapter 9 cases, see 11 USCA § 901.

Certain claims for which partner and partnership are liable, see 11 USCA § 723.

Claims secured by lien on property of estate, see 11 USCA § 1111.

Creditor as meaning entity having certain claims specified in this section, see 11 USCA § 101.

Deductibility of allowed claim, see 11 USCA § 346.

Discharge of liabilities on claims in—

　　Chapter 7 cases, see 11 USCA § 727.

　　Chapter 13 cases, see 11 USCA § 1328.

　　Chapter 12 cases, see 11 USCA § 1228.

Effect of confirmation in—

　　Chapter 11 cases, see 11 USCA § 1141.

　　Chapter 9 cases, see 11 USCA § 944.

Filing and allowance of postpetition claims, see 11 USCA § 1305.

Liability of exempted property for debtor's debt, see 11 USCA § 522.

Municipal leases, see 11 USCA § 929.

Payment of insurance benefits to retired employees, see 11 USCA § 1114.

Setoff, see 11 USCA § 553.

Trustee as lien creditor and as successor to certain creditors and purchasers, see 11 USCA § 544.

LIBRARY REFERENCES

American Digest System

　　Bankruptcy ☞2921 to 2933, 2821 to 2837.

　　Key Number System Topic No. 51.

Corpus Juris Secundum

CJS Bankruptcy § 278, Parties Defendant; Sovereign Immunity.

CJS Bankruptcy § 662, Effect of Prepetition or Postpetition Nature of Debts.

CJS Bankruptcy § 696, Use of State Law Concerning Fraudulent Transfers or Obligations.

CJS Bankruptcy § 700, Disallowance of Claims of Entities or Transferees Holding Recoverable Property.

CJS Bankruptcy § 952, Claims for Retiree Benefits.

CJS Bankruptcy § 959, Effect of Time of Accrual.

CJS Bankruptcy § 960, Estimation of Value.

CJS Bankruptcy § 963, Co-Debtors, Sureties, and Subrogation.

CJS Bankruptcy § 964, Tax Claims.

CJS Bankruptcy § 965, Termination or Rejection of Lease or Contract.

CJS Bankruptcy § 966, Termination or Rejection of Lease or Contract--Employment Contract.

CJS Bankruptcy § 980, Use and Occupancy Claims; Administrative Rent.

CJS Bankruptcy § 1027, Reconsideration.

CJS Bankruptcy § 1032, Effect of Discharge of Debtor.

CJS Bankruptcy § 1129, Appointment of Creditors" and Equity Security Holders" Committees.

CJS Bankruptcy § 1161, Effect of Confirmation--Discharge.

CJS Bankruptcy § 1209, Discharge--Grounds for Denial or Revocation of Discharge.

§ 503. Allowance of administrative expenses

(a) An entity may timely file a request for payment of an administrative expense, or may tardily file such request if permitted by the court for cause.

(b) After notice and a hearing, there shall be allowed administrative expenses, other than claims allowed under section 502(f) of this title, including—

(1)(A) the actual, necessary costs and expenses of preserving the estate including—

(i) wages, salaries, and commissions for services rendered after the commencement of the case; and

(ii) wages and benefits awarded pursuant to a judicial proceeding or a proceeding of the National Labor Relations Board as back pay attributable to any period of time occurring after commencement of the case under this title, as a result of a violation of Federal or State law by the debtor, without regard to the time of the occurrence of unlawful conduct on which such award is based or to whether any services were rendered, if the court determines that payment of wages and benefits by reason of the operation of this clause will not substantially increase the probability of layoff or termination of current employees, or of nonpayment of domestic support obligations, during the case under this title;

(B) any tax—

(i) incurred by the estate, whether secured or unsecured, including property taxes for which liability is in rem, in personam, or both, except a tax of a kind specified in section 507(a)(8) of this title; or

(ii) attributable to an excessive allowance of a tentative carryback adjustment that the estate received, whether the taxable year to which such adjustment relates ended before or after the commencement of the case;

(C) any fine, penalty, or reduction in credit relating to a tax of a kind specified in subparagraph (B) of this paragraph; and

(D) notwithstanding the requirements of subsection (a), a governmental unit shall not be required to file a request for the payment of an expense described in subparagraph (B) or (C), as a condition of its being an allowed administrative expense;

(2) compensation and reimbursement awarded under section 330(a) of this title;

(3) the actual, necessary expenses, other than compensation and reimbursement specified in paragraph (4) of this subsection, incurred by—

(A) a creditor that files a petition under section 303 of this title;

(B) a creditor that recovers, after the court's approval, for the benefit of the estate any property transferred or concealed by the debtor;

(C) a creditor in connection with the prosecution of a criminal offense relating to the case or to the business or property of the debtor;

(D) a creditor, an indenture trustee, an equity security holder, or a committee representing creditors or equity security holders other than a committee appointed under section 1102 of this title, in making a substantial contribution in a case under chapter 9 or 11 of this title;

(E) a custodian superseded under section 543 of this title, and compensation for the services of such custodian; or

(F) a member of a committee appointed under section 1102 of this title, if such expenses are incurred in the performance of the duties of such committee;

(4) reasonable compensation for professional services rendered by an attorney or an accountant of an entity whose expense is allowable under subparagraph (A), (B), (C), (D), or (E) of paragraph (3) of this subsection, based on the time, the nature, the extent, and the value of such services, and the cost of comparable services other than in a case under this title, and reimbursement for actual, necessary expenses incurred by such attorney or accountant;

(5) reasonable compensation for services rendered by an indenture trustee in making a substantial contribution in a case under chapter 9 or 11 of this title, based on the time, the nature, the extent, and

the value of such services, and the cost of comparable services other than in a case under this title;

(6) the fees and mileage payable under chapter 119 of title 28;

(7) with respect to a nonresidential real property lease previously assumed under section 365, and subsequently rejected, a sum equal to all monetary obligations due, excluding those arising from or relating to a failure to operate or a penalty provision, for the period of 2 years following the later of the rejection date or the date of actual turnover of the premises, without reduction or setoff for any reason whatsoever except for sums actually received or to be received from an entity other than the debtor, and the claim for remaining sums due for the balance of the term of the lease shall be a claim under section 502(b)(6);

(8) the actual, necessary costs and expenses of closing a health care business incurred by a trustee or by a Federal agency (as defined in section 551(1) of title 5) or a department or agency of a State or political subdivision thereof, including any cost or expense incurred—

(A) in disposing of patient records in accordance with section 351; or

(B) in connection with transferring patients from the health care business that is in the process of being closed to another health care business; and

(9) the value of any goods received by the debtor within 20 days before the date of commencement of a case under this title in which the goods have been sold to the debtor in the ordinary course of such debtor's business.

(c) Notwithstanding subsection (b), there shall neither be allowed, nor paid—

(1) a transfer made to, or an obligation incurred for the benefit of, an insider of the debtor for the purpose of inducing such person to remain with the debtor's business, absent a finding by the court based on evidence in the record that—

(A) the transfer or obligation is essential to retention of the person because the individual has a bona fide job offer from another business at the same or greater rate of compensation;

(B) the services provided by the person are essential to the survival of the business; and

(C) either—

(i) the amount of the transfer made to, or obligation incurred for the benefit of, the person is not greater than an amount equal to 10 times the amount of the mean transfer or obligation of a similar kind given to nonmanagement employees for any purpose during the calendar year in which the transfer is made or the obligation is incurred; or

(ii) if no such similar transfers were made to, or obligations were incurred for the benefit of, such nonmanagement employees during such calendar year, the amount of the transfer or obligation is not greater than an amount equal to 25 percent of the amount of any similar transfer or obligation made to or incurred for the benefit of such insider for any purpose during the calendar year before the year in which such transfer is made or obligation is incurred;

(2) a severance payment to an insider of the debtor, unless—

(A) the payment is part of a program that is generally applicable to all full-time employees; and

(B) the amount of the payment is not greater than 10 times the amount of the mean severance pay given to nonmanagement employees during the calendar year in which the payment is made; or

(3) other transfers or obligations that are outside the ordinary course of business and not justified by the facts and circumstances of the case, including transfers made to, or obligations incurred for the benefit of, officers, managers, or consultants hired after the date of the filing of the petition.

(Pub.L. 95–598, Nov. 6, 1978, 92 Stat. 2581; Pub.L. 98–353, Title III, § 446, July 10, 1984, 98 Stat. 374; Pub.L. 99–554, Title II, § 283(g), Oct. 27, 1986, 100 Stat. 3117; Pub.L. 103–394, Title I, § 110, Title II, § 213(c), Title III, § 304(h)(2), Oct. 22, 1994, 108 Stat. 4113, 4126, 4134; Pub.L. 109–8, Title III, §§ 329, 331, Title IV, § 445, Title VII, § 712(b), (c), Title XI, § 1103, Title XII, §§ 1208, 1227(b), Apr. 20, 2005, 119 Stat. 101, 102, 117, 128, 190, 194, 200.)

HISTORICAL AND STATUTORY NOTES

Revision Notes and Legislative Reports

1978 Acts. Subsection (a) of this section permits administrative expense claimants to file with the court a request for payment of an administrative expense. The Rules of Bankruptcy Procedure will specify the time, the form, and the method of such a filing.

Subsection (b) specifies the kinds of administrative expenses that are allowable in a case under the bankruptcy code. The subsection is derived mainly from section 64a(1) of the Bankruptcy Act [section 104(a)(1) of former Title 11], with some changes. The actual, necessary costs and expenses of preserving the estate, including wages, salaries, or commissions for services rendered after the order for relief, and any taxes on, measured by, or withheld from such wages, salaries, or commissions, are allowable as administrative expenses.

In general, administrative expenses include taxes which the trustee incurs in administering the debtor's estate, including taxes on capital gains from sales of property by the trustee and taxes on income earned by the estate during the case. Interest on tax liabilities and certain tax penalties incurred by the trustee are also included in this first priority.

Taxes which the Internal Revenue Service may find due after giving the trustee a so-called "quickie" tax refund and later doing an audit of the refund are also payable as administrative expenses. The tax code [Title 26, Internal Revenue Code] permits the trustee of an estate which suffers a net operating loss to carry back the loss against an earlier profit year of the estate or of the debtor and to obtain a tentative refund for the earlier year, subject, however, to a later full audit of the loss which led to the refund. The bill, in effect, requires the Internal Revenue Service to issue a tentative refund to the trustee (whether the refund was applied for by the debtor or by the trustee), but if the refund later proves to have been erroneous in amount, the Service can request that the tax attributable to the erroneous refund be payable by the estate as an administrative expense.

Postpetition payments to an individual debtor for services rendered to the estate are administrative expenses, and are not property of the estate when received by the debtor. This situation would most likely arise when the individual was a sole proprietor and was employed by the estate to run the business after the commencement of the case. An individual debtor in possession would be so employed, for example. See *Local Loan v. Hunt*, 292 U.S. 234, 243 (1933) [54 S.Ct. 695, 78 L.Ed. 1230].

Compensation and reimbursement awarded officers of the estate under section 330 are allowable as administrative expenses. Actual, necessary expenses, other than compensation of a professional person, incurred by a creditor that files an involuntary petition, by a creditor that recovers property for the benefit of the estate, by a creditor that acts in connection with the prosecution of a criminal offense relating to the case, by a creditor, indenture, trustee, equity security holder, or committee of creditors or equity security holders (other than official committees) that makes a substantial contribution to a reorganization or municipal debt adjustment case, or by a superseded custodian, are all allowable administrative expenses. The phrase "substantial contribution in the case" is derived from Bankruptcy Act §§ 242 and 243 [sections 642 and 643 of former Title 11]. It does not require a contribution that leads to confirmation of a plan, for in many cases, it will be a substantial contribution if the person involved uncovers facts that would lead to a denial of confirmation, such as fraud in connection with the case.

Paragraph (4) permits reasonable compensation for professional services rendered by an attorney or an accountant of an equity whose expense is compensable under the previous paragraph. Paragraph (5) permits reasonable compensation for an indenture trustee in making a substantial contribution in a reorganization or municipal debt adjustment case. Finally, paragraph (6) permits witness fees and mileage as prescribed under chapter 119 of title 28 [section 1821 et seq. of Title 28, Judiciary and Judicial Procedure]. Senate Report No. 95–989.

1984 Acts. Statements by Legislative Leaders, see 1984 U.S. Code Cong. and Adm. News, p. 576.

1986 Acts. House Report No. 99–764 and House Conference Report No. 99–958, see 1986 U.S. Code Cong. and Adm. News, p. 5227.

1994 Acts. House Report No. 103–835, see 1994 U.S. Code Cong. and Adm. News, p. 3340.

2005 Acts. House Report No. 109–31(Part I), see 2005 U.S. Code Cong. and Adm. News, p. 88.

Legislative Statements

Section 503(a) of the House amendment represents a compromise between similar provisions in the House bill and the Senate amendment by leaving to the Rules of Bankruptcy Procedure the determination of the location at which a request for payment of an administrative expense may be filed. The preamble to section 503(b) of the House bill makes a similar change with respect to the allowance of administrative expenses.

Section 503(b)(1) adopts the approach taken in the House bill as modified by some provisions contained in the Senate amendment. The preamble to section 503(b) makes clear that none of the paragraphs of section 503(b) apply to claims or expenses of the kind specified in section 502(f) that arise in the ordinary course of the debtor's business or financial affairs and that arise during the gap between the commencement of an involuntary case and the appointment of a trustee or the order for relief, whichever first occurs. The remainder of section 503(b) represents a compromise between H.R. 8200 as passed by the House and the Senate amendments. Section 503(b)(3)(E) codifies present law in cases such as *Randolph v. Scruggs*, 190 U.S. 533, which accords administrative expense status to services rendered by a prepetition custodian or other party to the extent such services actually benefit the estate. Section 503(b)(4) of the House amendment conforms to the provision contained in H.R. 8200 as passed by the House and deletes language contained in the Senate amendment providing a different standard of compensation under section 330 of that amendment.

Amendments

2005 Amendments. Subsec. (b)(1)(A). Pub.L. 109–8, § 329, rewrote subpar. (A), which formerly read: "**(1)(A)** the actual, necessary costs and expenses of preserving the estate, including wages, salaries, or commissions for services rendered after the commencement of the case;".

Subsec. (b)(1)(B). Pub.L. 109–8, § 712(c)(1), struck out "and" at the end of subpar. (B).

Subsec. (b)(1)(B)(i). Pub.L. 109–8, § 712(b), inserted "whether secured or unsecured, including property taxes for which liability is in rem, in personam, or both," before "except".

Subsec. (b)(1)(C). Pub.L. 109–8, § 712(c)(2), added "and" at the end of subpar. (C).

Subsec. (b)(1)(D). Pub.L. 109–8, § 712(c)(3), added subpar. (D).

Subsec. (b)(4). Pub.L. 109–8, § 1208, inserted "subparagraph (A), (B), (C), (D), or (E) of" before "paragraph (3)".

Subsec. (b)(5). Pub.L. 109–8, § 445(1), struck out "and" at the end of par. (5).

Subsec. (b)(6). Pub.L. 109–8, § 445(2), struck out the period at the end of par. (6) and inserted a semicolon.

Subsec. (b)(7). Pub.L. 109–8, § 445(3), added par. (7).

Subsec. (b)(8). Pub.L. 109–8, § 1103, added par. (8).

Subsec. (b)(9). Pub.L.109–8, § 1227(b), added par. (9).

Subsec. (c). Pub.L. 109–8, § 331, added subsec. (c).

1994 Amendments. Subsec. (a). Pub.L. 103–394, § 213(c), substituted "An entity may timely file a request for payment of an administrative expense, or may tardily file such request if permitted by the court for cause." for "An entity may file a request for payment of an administrative expense."

Subsec. (b)(1)(B)(i). Pub.L. 103–394, § 304(h)(2), substituted "section 507(a)(8)" for "section 507(a)(7)".

Subsec. (b)(3)(F). Pub.L. 103–394, § 110, added subpar. (F).

1986 Amendments. Subsec. (b)(1)(B)(i). Pub.L. 99–554, § 283(g)(1), substituted "507(a)(7)" for "507(a)(6)".

Subsec. (b)(5). Pub.L. 99–554, § 283(g)(2), inserted "and" following "title;".

Subsec. (b)(6). Pub.L. 99–554, § 283(g)(3), substituted "28." for "28; and".

1984 Amendments. Subsec. (b). Pub.L. 98–353, § 446(1), struck out the comma after "be allowed" in provisions preceding par. (1).

Subsec. (b)(1)(C). Pub.L. 98–353, § 446(2), struck out the comma after "credit".

Subsec. (b)(2). Pub.L. 98–353, § 446(3), added "(a)" after "330".

Subsec. (b)(3). Pub.L. 98–353, § 446(4), added a comma after "paragraph (4) of this subsection".

Subsec. (b)(3)(C). Pub.L. 98–353, § 446(5), struck out the comma after "case".

Subsec. (b)(5). Pub.L. 98–353, § 446(6), struck out "and" following "title;".

Subsec. (b)(6). Pub.L. 98–353, § 446(7), substituted "; and" for the period at the end of par. (6).

Effective and Applicability Provisions

2005 Acts. Amendments by Pub.L. 109–8 effective, except as otherwise provided, 180 days after April 20, 2005, and inapplicable with respect to cases commenced under Title 11 before the effective date, see Pub.L. 109–8, § 1501, set out as a note under 11 U.S.C.A. § 101.

1994 Acts. Amendments by Pub.L. 103–394 effective on Oct. 22, 1994, and not to apply with respect to cases commenced under Title 11 of the United States Code before Oct. 22, 1994, see section 702 of Pub.L. 103–394, set out as a note under section 101 of this title.

1986 Acts. Amendment by Pub.L. 99–554 effective 30 days after Oct. 27, 1986, except as otherwise provided for, see section 302(a) of Pub.L. 99–554, set out as a note under section 581 of Title 28, Judiciary and Judicial Procedure.

1984 Acts. Amendment by Pub.L. 98–353 effective with respect to cases filed 90 days after July 10, 1984, see section 552(a), formerly 553(a), of Pub.L. 98–353, set out as a note under section 101 of this title.

Separability of Provisions

If any provision of or amendment made by Pub.L. 103–394 or the application of such provision or amendment to any person or circumstance is held to be unconstitutional, the remaining provisions of and amendments made by Pub.L. 103–394 and the application of such provisions and amendments to any person or circumstance shall not be affected thereby, see section 701 of Pub.L. 103–394, set out as a note under section 101 of this title.

CROSS REFERENCES

Adequate protection, other than granting certain administrative expenses, see 11 USCA § 361.

Applicability of this section in Chapter 9 cases, see 11 USCA § 901.

Claims arising from automatic stay, see 11 USCA § 922.

Discharge of liabilities on claims in Chapter 12 cases, see 11 USCA § 1228.

Deductibility of allowed claim, see 11 USCA § 346.

Deduction of administrative expenses for income tax purposes, see 26 USCA § 1398.

Deduction of administrative expenses from payments received by trustee if plan not confirmed in—

Chapter 13 cases, see 11 USCA § 1326.

Chapter 12 cases, see 11 USCA § 1226.

Distribution of property of estate, see 11 USCA § 726.

Effect of conversion, see 11 USCA § 348.

Grain storage facility bankruptcies, expedited determinations, see 11 USCA § 557.

Method of obtaining adequate protection in Chapter 12 case, see 11 USCA § 1205.

Payment of insurance benefits to retired employees, see 11 USCA § 1114.

Performance of obligations under executory contracts and unexpired leases notwithstanding subsec. (b)(1) of this section, see 11 USCA § 365.

Proof of claim, see Official Bankr. Form 10, 11 USCA.

Unsecured debt as administrative expense or having priority over certain administrative expenses, see 11 USCA § 364.

LIBRARY REFERENCES

American Digest System

Bankruptcy ⬯2871 to 2879, 3151 to 3205.

Key Number System Topic No. 51.

Corpus Juris Secundum

CJS Bankruptcy § 118, Prohibition Against Compensation Sharing.

CJS Bankruptcy § 278, Parties Defendant; Sovereign Immunity.

CJS Bankruptcy § 773, Status of Claims for Compensation and Reimbursement.

CJS Bankruptcy § 774, Necessity of Court Approval.

CJS Bankruptcy § 860, Recovery of Costs of Preserving or Disposing of Property.

CJS Bankruptcy § 895, Unsecured Credit or Debt in Ordinary Course of Business.

CJS Bankruptcy § 896, Unsecured Credit or Debt Other Than in Ordinary Course of Business.

CJS Bankruptcy § 897, Credit With Special Administrative Priority or Secured by First Liens or Junior Liens.

CJS Bankruptcy § 974, Benefit to Estate.

CJS Bankruptcy § 975, Claims Not Allowable.

CJS Bankruptcy § 976, Effect of Conversion.

CJS Bankruptcy § 977, Taxes.

CJS Bankruptcy § 978, Wage and Benefit Claims.

CJS Bankruptcy § 980, Use and Occupancy Claims; Administrative Rent.

CJS Bankruptcy § 981, Use and Occupancy Claims; Administrative Rent--Amount Allowable.

CJS Bankruptcy § 1007, Generally; Who May File.

CJS Bankruptcy § 1021, Court Approval of Administrative Expenses.

CJS Bankruptcy § 1102, Priority of Particular Distribution Classes.

CJS Bankruptcy § 1103, Community Property.

§ 504. Sharing of compensation

(a) Except as provided in subsection (b) of this section, a person receiving compensation or reimbursement under section 503(b)(2) or 503(b)(4) of this title may not share or agree to share—

(1) any such compensation or reimbursement with another person; or

(2) any compensation or reimbursement received by another person under such sections.

(b)(1) A member, partner, or regular associate in a professional association, corporation, or partnership may share compensation or reimbursement received under section 503(b)(2) or 503(b)(4) of this title with another member, partner, or regular associate in such association, corporation, or partnership, and may share in any compensation or reimbursement received under such sections by another member, partner, or regular associate in such association, corporation, or partnership.

(2) An attorney for a creditor that files a petition under section 303 of this title may share compensation and reimbursement received under section 503(b)(4) of this title with any other attorney contributing to the services rendered or expenses incurred by such creditor's attorney.

(c) This section shall not apply with respect to sharing, or agreeing to share, compensation with a bona fide public service attorney referral program that operates in accordance with non-Federal law regulating attorney referral services and with rules of professional responsibility applicable to attorney acceptance of referrals.

(Pub.L. 95–598, Nov. 6, 1978, 92 Stat. 2582; Pub.L. 109–8, Title III, § 326, Apr. 20, 2005, 119 Stat. 99.)

HISTORICAL AND STATUTORY NOTES

Revision Notes and Legislative Reports

1978 Acts. Section 504 prohibits the sharing of compensation, or fee splitting, among attorneys, other professionals, or trustees. The section provides only two exceptions: partners or associates in the same professional association, partnership, or corporation may share compensation inter se; and attorneys for petitioning creditors that join in a petition commencing an involuntary case may share compensation. Senate Report No. 95–989.

2005 Acts. House Report No. 109–31(Part I), see 2005 U.S. Code Cong. and Adm. News, p. 88.

Amendments

2005 Amendments. Subsec. (c). Pub.L. 109–8, § 326, added subsec. (c).

Effective and Applicability Provisions

2005 Acts. Amendments by Pub.L. 109–8 effective, except as otherwise provided, 180 days after April 20, 2005, and inapplicable with respect to cases commenced under Title 11 before the effective date, see Pub.L. 109–8, § 1501, set out as a note under 11 U.S.C.A. § 101.

CROSS REFERENCES

Applicability of restrictions on sharing of compensation to allowances in investor protection liquidation proceedings, see 15 USCA § 78eee.

Applicability of this section in Chapter 9 cases, see 11 USCA § 901.

LIBRARY REFERENCES

American Digest System

Bankruptcy ⟨key⟩3174, 3200, 3155.

Key Number System Topic No. 51.

Corpus Juris Secundum

CJS Bankruptcy § 118, Prohibition Against Compensation Sharing.

CJS Bankruptcy § 761, Relationship Between Employment and Compensation Provisions.

CJS Bankruptcy § 777, Sharing of Compensation.

§ 505. Determination of tax liability

(a)(1) Except as provided in paragraph (2) of this subsection, the court may determine the amount or legality of any tax, any fine or penalty relating to a tax, or any addition to tax, whether or not previously assessed, whether or not paid, and whether or not contested before and adjudicated by a judicial or administrative tribunal of competent jurisdiction.

(2) The court may not so determine—

(A) the amount or legality of a tax, fine, penalty, or addition to tax if such amount or legality was contested before and adjudicated by a judicial or administrative tribunal of competent jurisdiction before the commencement of the case under this title;

(B) any right of the estate to a tax refund, before the earlier of—

(i) 120 days after the trustee properly requests such refund from the governmental unit from which such refund is claimed; or

(ii) a determination by such governmental unit of such request; or

(C) the amount or legality of any amount arising in connection with an ad valorem tax on real or personal property of the estate, if the applicable period for contesting or redetermining that amount under applicable nonbankruptcy law has expired.

(b)(1)(A) The clerk shall maintain a list under which a Federal, State, or local governmental unit responsible for the collection of taxes within the district may—

(i) designate an address for service of requests under this subsection; and

(ii) describe where further information concerning additional requirements for filing such requests may be found.

(B) If such governmental unit does not designate an address and provide such address to the clerk under subparagraph (A), any request made under this subsection may be served at the address for the filing of a tax return or protest with the appropriate taxing authority of such governmental unit.

(2) A trustee may request a determination of any unpaid liability of the estate for any tax incurred during the administration of the case by submitting a tax return for such tax and a request for such a determination to the governmental unit charged with responsibility for collection or determination of such tax at the address and in the manner designated in paragraph (1). Unless such return is fraudulent, or contains a material misrepresentation, the estate, the trustee, the debtor, and any successor to the debtor are discharged from any liability for such tax—

(A) upon payment of the tax shown on such return, if—

(i) such governmental unit does not notify the trustee, within 60 days after such request, that such return has been selected for examination; or

(ii) such governmental unit does not complete such an examination and notify the trustee of any tax due, within 180 days after such request or within such additional time as the court, for cause, permits;

(B) upon payment of the tax determined by the court, after notice and a hearing, after completion by such governmental unit of such examination; or

(C) upon payment of the tax determined by such governmental unit to be due.

(c) Notwithstanding section 362 of this title, after determination by the court of a tax under this section, the governmental unit charged with responsibility for collection of such tax may assess such tax against the estate, the debtor, or a successor to the debtor, as the case may be, subject to any otherwise applicable law. (Pub.L. 95–598, Nov. 6, 1978, 92 Stat. 2582; Pub.L. 98–353, Title III, § 447, July 10, 1984, 98 Stat. 374; Pub.L. 109–8, Title VII, §§ 701(b), 703, 715, Apr. 20, 2005, 119 Stat. 124, 125, 129; Pub.L. 111–327, § 2(a)(14), Dec. 22, 2010, 124 Stat. 3559.)

HISTORICAL AND STATUTORY NOTES

Revision Notes and Legislative Reports

1978 Acts. Subsections (a) and (b) are derived, with only stylistic changes, from section 2a(2A) of the Bankruptcy Act [section 11(a)(2A) of former Title 11]. They permit determination by the bankruptcy court of any unpaid tax liability of the debtor that has not been contested before or adjudicated by a judicial or administrative tribunal of competent jurisdiction before the bankruptcy case, and the prosecution by the trustee of an appeal from an order of such a body if the time for review or appeal has not expired before the commencement of the bankruptcy case. As under current Bankruptcy Act section 2a(2A), *Arkansas Corporation Commissioner v. Thompson*, 313 U.S. 132 (1941) [61 S.Ct. 888, 85 L.Ed. 1244], remains good law to permit abstention where uniformity of assessment is of significant importance.

Section (c) [sic] deals with procedures for obtaining a prompt audit of tax returns filed by the trustee in a liquidation or reorganization case. Under the bill as originally introduced, a trustee who is "in doubt" concerning tax liabilities of the estate incurred during a title 11 proceeding could obtain a discharge from personal liability for himself and the debtor (but not for the debtor or the debtor's successor in a reorganization), provided that certain administrative procedures were followed. The trustee could request a prompt tax audit by the local, State, or Federal governmental unit. The taxing authority would have to notify the trustee and the court within sixty days whether it accepted the return or desired to audit the returns more fully. If an audit were conducted, the tax office would have to notify the trustee of any tax deficiency within 4 months (subject to an extension of time if the court approved). These procedures would apply only to tax years completed on or before the case was closed and for which the trustee had filed a tax return.

The committee bill eliminates the "in doubt" rule and makes mandatory (rather than optional) the trustee's request for a prompt audit of the estate's tax returns. In many cases, the trustee could not be certain that his returns raised no doubt about possible tax issues. In addition, it is desirable not to create a situation where the taxing authority asserts a tax liability against the debtor (as transferee of surplus assets, if any, return to him) after the case is over; in any such situation, the debtor would be called on to defend a tax return which he did not prepare. Under the amendment, all disputes concerning these returns are to be resolved by the bankruptcy court, and both the trustee and the debtor himself do not then face potential post-bankruptcy tax liabilities based on these returns. This result would occur as to the debtor, however, only in a liquidation case.

In a reorganization in which the debtor or a successor to the debtor continues in existence, the trustee could obtain a discharge from personal liability through the prompt audit procedure, but the Treasury could still claim a deficiency against the debtor (or his successor) for additional taxes due on returns filed during the title 11 proceedings. Senate Report No. 95–989.

Subsection (c) is new. It codifies in part the referee's decision in *In re Statmaster Corp.*, 465 F.2d 987 (5th Cir. 1972). Its purpose is to protect the trustee from personal liability for a tax falling on the estate that is not assessed until after the case is closed. If necessary to permit expeditious closing of the case, the court, on request of the trustee, must order the governmental unit charged with the responsibility for collection or determination of the tax to audit the trustee's return or be barred from attempting later collection. The court will be required to permit sufficient time to perform an audit, if the taxing authority requests it. The final order of the court and the payment of the tax determined in that order discharges the trustee, the debtor, and any successor to the debtor from any further liability for the tax. See Plumb, The Tax Recommendations of the Commission on the Bankruptcy Laws: Tax Procedures, 88 Harv.L.Rev. 1360, 1423–42 (1975). House Report No. 95–595.

1984 Acts. Statements by Legislative Leaders, see 1984 U.S.Code Cong. and Adm.News, p. 576.

2005 Acts. House Report No. 109–31(Part I), see 2005 U.S. Code Cong. and Adm. News, p. 88.

Legislative Statements

Section 505 of the House amendment adopts a compromise position with respect to the determination of tax liability from the position taken in H.R. 8200 as passed by the House and in the Senate amendment.

Determinations of tax liability: Authority of bankruptcy court to rule on merits of tax claims.—The House amendment authorizes the bankruptcy court to rule on the merits of any tax claim involving an unpaid tax, fine, or penalty relating to a tax, or any addition to a tax, of the debtor or the estate. This authority applies, in general, whether or not the tax, penalty, fine, or addition to tax had been previously assessed or paid. However, the bankruptcy court will not have jurisdiction to rule on the merits of any tax claim which has been previously adjudicated, in a contested proceeding, before a court of competent jurisdiction. For this purpose, a proceeding in the U.S. Tax Court is to be considered "contested" if the debtor filed a petition in the Tax Court by the commencement of the case and the Internal Revenue Service had filed an answer to the petition. Therefore, if a petition and answer were filed in the Tax Court before the title II petition was filed, and if the debtor later defaults in the Tax Court, then, under res judicata principles, the bankruptcy court could not then rule on the debtor's or the estate's liability for the same taxes.

The House amendment adopts the rule of the Senate bill that the bankruptcy court can, under certain conditions, determine the amount of tax refund claim by the trustee. Under the House amendment, if the refund results from an offset or counterclaim to a claim or request for payment by the Internal Revenue Service, or other tax authority, the trustee would not first have to file an administrative claim for refund with the tax authority.

However, if the trustee requests a refund in other situations, he would first have to submit an administrative claim for the refund. Under the House amendment, if the Internal Revenue Service, or other tax authority does not rule on the refund claim within 120 days, then the bankruptcy court may rule on the merits of the refund claim.

Under the Internal Revenue Code [Title 26, Internal Revenue Code], a suit for refund of Federal taxes cannot be filed until 6 months after a claim for refund is filed with the Internal Revenue Service (sec. 6532(a) [26 U.S.C.A. § 6532(a)]). Because of the bankruptcy aim to close the estate as expeditiously as possible, the House amendment shortens to 120 days the period for the Internal Revenue Service to decide the refund claim.

The House amendment also adopts the substance of the Senate bill rule permitting the bankruptcy court to determine the amount of any penalty, whether punitive or pecuniary in nature, relating to taxes over which it has jurisdiction.

Jurisdiction of the tax court in bankruptcy cases: The Senate amendment provided a detailed series of rules concerning the jurisdiction of the U.S. Tax Court, or similar State or local administrative tribunal to determine personal tax liabilities of an individual debtor. The House amendment deletes these specific rules and relies on procedures to be derived from broad general powers of the bankruptcy court.

Under the House amendment, as under present law, a corporation seeking reorganization under chapter 11 is considered to be personally before the bankruptcy court for purposes of giving that court jurisdiction over the debtor's personal liability for a nondischargeable tax.

The rules are more complex where the debtor is an individual under chapter 7, 11, or 13. An individual debtor or the tax authority can, as under section 17c of the present Bankruptcy Act [section 35(c) of former Title 11], file a request that the bankruptcy court determine the debtor's personal liability for the balance of any nondischargeable tax not satisfied from assets of the estate. The House amendment

intends to retain these procedures and also adds a rule staying commencement or continuation of any proceeding in the Tax Court after the bankruptcy petition is filed, unless and until that stay is lifted by the bankruptcy judge under section 362(a)(8). The House amendment also stays assessment as well as collection of a prepetition claim against the debtor (sec. 362(a)(6)). A tax authority would not, however, be stayed from issuing a deficiency notice during the bankruptcy case (sec. (b)(7)). The Senate amendment repealed the existing authority of the Internal Revenue Service to make an immediate assessment of taxes upon bankruptcy (sec. 6871(a) of the code [26 U.S.C.A. § 6871(a)]). See section of the Senate bill. As indicated, the substance of that provision, also affecting State and local taxes, is contained in section 362(a)(6) of the House amendment. The statute of limitations is tolled under the House amendment while the bankruptcy case is pending.

Where no proceeding in the Tax Court is pending at the commencement of the bankruptcy case, the tax authority can, under the House amendment, file a claim against the estate for a prepetition tax liability and may also file a request that the bankruptcy court hear arguments and decide the merits of an individual debtor's personal liability for the balance of any nondischargeable tax liability not satisfied from assets of the estate. Bankruptcy terminology refers to the latter type of request as a creditor's complaint to determine the dischargeability of a debt. Where such a complaint is filed, the bankruptcy court will have personal jurisdiction over an individual debtor, and the debtor himself would have no access to the Tax Court, or to any other court, to determine his personal liability for nondischargeable taxes.

If a tax authority decides not to file a claim for taxes which would typically occur where there are few, if any, assets in the estate, normally the tax authority would also not request the bankruptcy court to rule on the debtor's personal liability for a nondischargeable tax. Under the House amendment, the tax authority would then have to follow normal procedures in order to collect a nondischargeable tax. For example, in the case of nondischargeable Federal income taxes, the Internal Revenue Service would be required to issue a deficiency notice to an individual debtor, and the debtor could then file a petition in the Tax Court—or a refund suit in a district court—as the forum in which to litigate his personal liability for a nondischargeable tax.

Under the House amendment, as under present law, an individual debtor can also file a complaint to determine dischargeability. Consequently, where the tax authority does not file a claim or a request that the bankruptcy court determine dischargeability of a specific tax liability, the debtor could file such a request on his own behalf, so that the bankruptcy court would then determine both the validity of the claim against assets in the estate and also the personal liability of the debtor for any nondischargeable tax.

Where a proceeding is pending in the Tax Court at the commencement of the bankruptcy case, the commencement of the bankruptcy case automatically stays further action in the Tax Court case unless and until the stay is lifted by the bankruptcy court. The Senate amendment repealed a provision of the Internal Revenue case barring a debtor from filing a petition in the Tax Court after commencement of a bankruptcy case (sec. 6871(b) of the code) [26 U.S.C.A. § 6871(b)]. See section 321 of the Senate bill. As indicated earlier, the equivalent of the code amendment is embodied in section 362(a)(8) of the House amendment, which automatically stays commencement or continuation of any proceeding in the Tax Court until the stay is lifted or the case is terminated. The stay will permit sufficient time for the bankruptcy trustee to determine if he desires to join the Tax Court proceeding on behalf of the estate. Where the trustee chooses to join the Tax Court proceeding, it is expected that he will seek permission to intervene in the Tax Court case and then request that the stay on the Tax Court proceeding be lifted. In such a case, the merits of the tax liability will be determined by the Tax Court, and its decision will bind both the individual debtor as to any taxes which are nondischargeable and the trustee as to the tax claim against the estate.

Where the trustee does not want to intervene in the Tax Court, but an individual debtor wants to have the Tax Court determine the amount of his personal liability for nondischargeable taxes, the debtor can request the bankruptcy court to lift the automatic stay on existing Tax Court proceedings. If the stay is lifted and the Tax Court reaches its decision before the bankruptcy court's decision on the tax claim against the estate, the decision of the Tax Court would bind the bankruptcy court under principles of res judicata because the decision of the Tax Court affected the personal liability of the debtor. If the trustee does not wish to subject the estate to the decision of the Tax Court if the latter court decides the issues before the bankruptcy court rules, the trustee could resist the lifting of the stay on the existing Tax Court proceeding. If the Internal Revenue Service had issued a deficiency notice to the debtor before the bankruptcy case began, but as of the filing of the bankruptcy petition the 90-day period for filing in the Tax Court was still running, the debtor would be automatically stayed from filing a petition in the Tax Court. If either the debtor or the Internal Revenue Service then files a complaint to determine dischargeability in the bankruptcy court, the decision of the bankruptcy court would bind both the debtor and the Internal Revenue Service.

The bankruptcy judge could, however, lift the stay on the debtor to allow him to petition the Tax Court, while reserving the right to rule on the tax authority's claim against assets of the estate. The bankruptcy court could also, upon request by the trustee, authorize the trustee to intervene in the Tax Court for purposes of having the estate also governed by the decision of the Tax Court.

In essence, under the House amendment, the bankruptcy judge will have authority to determine which court will determine the merits of the tax claim both as to claims against the estate and claims against the debtor concerning his personal liability for nondischargeable taxes. Thus, if the Internal Revenue Service, or a State or local tax authority, files a petition to determine dischargeability, the bankruptcy judge can either rule on the merits of the claim and continue the stay on any pending Tax Court proceeding or lift the stay on the Tax Court and hold the dischargeability complaint in abeyance. If he rules on the merits of the complaint before the decision of the Tax Court is reached, the bankruptcy court's decision would bind the debtor as to nondischargeable taxes and the Tax Court would be governed by that decision under principles of res judicata. If the bankruptcy judge does not rule on the merits of the complaint before the decision of the Tax Court is reached, the bankruptcy court will be bound by the decision of the Tax Court as it affects the amount of any claim against the debtor's estate.

If the Internal Revenue Service does not file a complaint to determine dischargeability and the automatic stay on a pending Tax Court proceeding is not lifted, the bankruptcy court could determine the merits of any tax claim against the estate. That decision will not bind the debtor personally because he would not have been personally before the bankruptcy court unless the debtor himself asks the bankruptcy court to rule on his personal liability. In any such situation where no party filed a dischargeability petition, the debtor would have access to the Tax Court to determine his personal liability for a nondischargeable tax debt. While the Tax Court in such a situation could take into account the ruling of the bankruptcy court on claims against the estate in deciding the debtor's personal liability, the bankruptcy court's ruling would not bind the Tax Court under principles of res judicata, because the debtor, in that situation, would not have been personally before the bankruptcy court.

If neither the debtor nor the Internal Revenue Service files a claim against the estate or a request to rule on the debtor's personal liability, any pending tax court proceeding would be stayed until the closing of the bankruptcy case, at which time the stay on the tax court would cease and the tax court case could continue for purposes of deciding the merits of the debtor's personal liability for nondischargeable taxes.

Audit of trustee's returns: Under both bills, the bankruptcy court could determine the amount of any administrative period taxes. The Senate amendment, however, provided for an expedited audit procedure, which was mandatory in some cases. The House amendment (sec. 505(b)), adopts the provision of the House bill allowing the trustee discretion in all cases whether to ask the Internal Revenue Service, or State or local tax authority for a prompt audit of his returns on behalf of the estate. The House amendment, however, adopts the provision of the Senate bill permitting a prompt audit only on the basis of tax returns filed by the trustee for completed taxable periods. Procedures for a prompt audit set forth in the Senate bill are also adopted in modified form.

Under the procedure, before the case can be closed, the trustee may request a tax audit by the local, State or Federal tax authority of all tax returns filed by the trustee. The taxing authority would have to notify the trustee and the bankruptcy court within 60 days whether it accepts returns or desires to audit the returns more fully. If an audit is conducted, the taxing authority would have to notify the trustee of tax deficiency within 180 days after the original request, subject to extensions of time if the bankruptcy court approves. If the trustee does not agree with the results of the audit, the trustee could ask the bankruptcy court to resolve the dispute. Once the trustee's tax liability for administration period taxes has thus been determined, the legal effect in a case under chapter 7 or 11 would be to discharge the trustee and any predecessor of the trustee, and also the debtor, from any further liability for these taxes.

The prompt audit procedure would not be available with respect to any tax liability as to which any return required to be filed on behalf of the estate is not filed with the proper tax authority. The House amendment also specifies that a discharge of the trustee or the debtor which would otherwise occur will not be granted, or will be void if the return filed on behalf of the estate reflects fraud or material misrepresentation of facts.

For purposes of the above prompt audit procedures, it is intended that the tax authority with which the request for audit is to be filed is, as to Federal taxes, the office of the District Director in the district where the bankruptcy case is pending.

Under the House amendment, if the trustee does not request a prompt audit, the debtor would not be discharged from possible transferee liability if any assets are returned to the debtor.

Assessment after decision: As indicated above, the commencement of a bankruptcy case automatically stays assessment of any tax (sec. 362(a)(6)). However, the House amendment provides (sec. 505(c)) that if the bankruptcy court renders a final judgment with regard to any tax (under the rules discussed above), the tax authority may then make an assessment (if permitted to do so under otherwise applicable tax law) without waiting for termination of the case or confirmation of a reorganization plan.

Trustee's authority to appeal tax cases: The equivalent provision in the House bill (sec. 505(b)) and in the Senate bill (sec. 362(h)) authorizing the trustee to prosecute an appeal or review of a tax case are deleted as unnecessary. Section 541(a) of the House amendment provides that property of the estate is to include all legal or equitable interests of the debtor. These interests include the debtor's causes of action, so that the specific provisions of the House and Senate bills are not needed.

Amendments

2010 Amendments. Subsec. (a)(2)(C). Pub.L. 111–327, § 2(a)(14), struck out "any law (other than a bankruptcy law)" and inserted "applicable nonbankruptcy law".

2005 Amendments. Subsec. (a)(2)(A). Pub.L. 109–8, § 701(b)(1), struck out "or" at the end of subpar. (A).

Subsec. (a)(2)(B). Pub.L. 109–8, § 701(b)(2), struck out the period at the end of subpar. (B) and inserted "; or".

Subsec. (a)(2)(C). Pub.L. 109–8, § 701(b)(3), added subpar. (C).

Subsec. (b). Pub.L. 109–8, §§ 703, 715, rewrote subsec. (b), which formerly read:

"**(b)** A trustee may request a determination of any unpaid liability of the estate for any tax incurred during the administration of the case by submitting a tax return for such tax and a request for such a determination to the governmental unit charged with responsibility for collection or determination of such tax. Unless such return is fraudulent, or contains a material misrepresentation, the trustee, the debtor, and any successor to the debtor are discharged from any liability for such tax—

"**(1)** upon payment of the tax shown on such return, if—

"**(A)** such governmental unit does not notify the trustee, within 60 days after such request, that such return has been selected for examination; or

"**(B)** such governmental unit does not complete such an examination and notify the trustee of any tax due, within 180 days after such request or within such additional time as the court, for cause, permits;

"**(2)** upon payment of the tax determined by the court, after notice and a hearing, after completion by such governmental unit of such examination; or

"**(3)** upon payment of the tax determined by such governmental unit to be due."

1984 Amendments. Subsec. (a)(2)(B)(i). Pub.L. 98–353 substituted "or" for "and".

Effective and Applicability Provisions

2005 Acts. Amendments by Pub.L. 109–8 effective, except as otherwise provided, 180 days after April 20, 2005, and inapplicable with respect to cases commenced under Title 11 before the effective date, see Pub.L. 109–8, § 1501, set out as a note under 11 U.S.C.A. § 101.

1984 Acts. Amendment by Pub.L. 98–353 effective with respect to cases filed 90 days after July 10, 1984, see section 552(a), formerly 553(a), of Pub.L. 98–353, set out as a note under section 101 of this title.

CROSS REFERENCES

Declaratory judgments, see 28 USCA § 2201.

LIBRARY REFERENCES

American Digest System

Bankruptcy ⟾2055, 2402(4).

Key Number System Topic No. 51.

Corpus Juris Secundum

CJS Bankruptcy § 261, Power to Render Declaratory Judgment.

CJS Bankruptcy § 278, Parties Defendant; Sovereign Immunity.

CJS Bankruptcy § 1022, Taxes.

§ 506. Determination of secured status

(a)(1) An allowed claim of a creditor secured by a lien on property in which the estate has an interest, or that is subject to setoff under section 553 of this title, is a secured claim to the extent of the value of such creditor's interest in the estate's interest in such property, or to the extent of the amount subject to setoff, as the case may be, and is an unsecured claim to the extent that the value of such creditor's interest or the amount so subject to setoff is less than the amount of such allowed claim. Such value shall be determined in light of the purpose of the valuation and of the proposed disposition or use of such property, and in conjunction with any hearing on such disposition or use or on a plan affecting such creditor's interest.

(2) If the debtor is an individual in a case under chapter 7 or 13, such value with respect to personal property securing an allowed claim shall be determined based on the replacement value of such property as of the date of the filing of the petition without deduction for costs of sale or marketing. With respect to property acquired for personal, family, or household purposes, replacement value shall mean the price a retail merchant would charge for property of that kind considering the age and condition of the property at the time value is determined.

(b) To the extent that an allowed secured claim is secured by property the value of which, after any recovery under subsection (c) of this section, is greater than the amount of such claim, there shall be allowed to the holder of such claim, interest on such claim, and any reasonable fees, costs, or charges provided for under the agreement or State statute under which such claim arose.

(c) The trustee may recover from property securing an allowed secured claim the reasonable, necessary costs and expenses of preserving, or disposing of, such property to the extent of any benefit to the holder of such claim, including the payment of all ad valorem property taxes with respect to the property.

(d) To the extent that a lien secures a claim against the debtor that is not an allowed secured claim, such lien is void, unless—

    (1) such claim was disallowed only under section 502(b)(5) or 502(e) of this title; or

    (2) such claim is not an allowed secured claim due only to the failure of any entity to file a proof of such claim under section 501 of this title.

(Pub.L. 95–598, Nov. 6, 1978, 92 Stat. 2583; Pub.L. 98–353, Title III, § 448, July 10, 1984, 98 Stat. 374; Pub.L. 109–8, Title III, § 327, Title VII, § 712(d), Apr. 20, 2005, 119 Stat. 99, 128.)

HISTORICAL AND STATUTORY NOTES

Revision Notes and Legislative Reports

1978 Acts. Subsection (a) of this section separates an undersecured creditor's claim into two parts: He has a secured claim to the extent of the value of his collateral; and he has an unsecured claim for the balance of his claim. The subsection also provides for the valuation of claims which involve setoffs under section 553. While courts will have to determine value on a case-by-case basis, the subsection makes it clear that valuation is to be determined in light of the purpose of the valuation and the proposed disposition or use of the subject property. This determination shall be made in conjunction with any hearing on such disposition or use of property or on a plan affecting the creditor's interest. To illustrate, a valuation early in the case in a proceeding under sections 361–363 would not be binding upon the debtor or creditor at the time of confirmation of the plan. Throughout the bill, references to secured claims are only to the claim determined to be secured under this subsection, and not to the full amount of the creditor's claim. This provision abolishes the use of the terms "secured creditor" and "unsecured creditor" and substitutes in their places the terms "secured claim" and "unsecured claim."

Subsection (b) codifies current law by entitling a creditor with an oversecured claim to any reasonable fees (including attorney's fees), costs, or charges provided under the agreement under which the claim arose. These fees, costs, and charges are secured claims to the extent that the value of the collateral exceeds the amount of the underlying claim.

Subsection (c) also codifies current law by permitting the trustee to recover from property the value of which is greater than the sum of the claims secured by a lien on that property the reasonable, necessary costs and expenses of preserving, or disposing of, the property. The recovery is limited to the extent of any benefit to the holder of such claim.

Subsection (d) provides that to the extent a secured claim is not allowed, its lien is void unless the holder had neither actual notice nor knowledge of the case, the lien was not listed by the debtor in a chapter 9 or 11 case or such claim was disallowed only under section 502(e). Senate Report No. 95–989.

Subsection (d) permits liens to pass through the bankruptcy case unaffected. However, if a party in interest requests the court to determine and allow or disallow the claim secured by the lien under section 502 and the claim is not allowed, then the lien is void to the extent that the claim is not allowed. The voiding provision does not apply to claims disallowed only under section 502(e), which requires disallowance of certain claims against the debtor by a codebtor, surety, or guarantor for contribution or reimbursement. House Report No. 95–595.

1984 Acts. Statements by Legislative Leaders, see 1984 U.S.Code Cong. and Adm.News, p. 576.

2005 Acts. House Report No. 109–31(Part I), see 2005 U.S. Code Cong. and Adm. News, p. 88.

Legislative Statements

Section 506(a) of the House amendment adopts the provision contained in the Senate amendment and rejects a contrary provision as contained in H.R. 8200 as passed by the House. The provision contained in the Senate amendment and adopted by the House amendment recognizes that an amount subject to set-off is sufficient to recognize a secured status in the holder of such right. Additionally a determination of what portion of an allowed claim is secured and what portion is unsecured is binding only for the purpose for which the determination is made. Thus determinations for purposes of adequate protection is not binding for purposes of "cram down" on confirmation in a case under chapter 11.

Section 506(b) of the House amendment adopts language contained in the Senate amendment and rejects language contained in H.R. 8200 as passed by the House. If the security agreement between the parties provides for attorneys' fees, it will be enforceable under title 11, notwithstanding contrary law, and is recoverable from the collateral after any recovery under section 506(c).

Section 506(c) of the House amendment was contained in H.R. 8200 as passed by the House and adopted, verbatim, in the Senate amendment. Any time the trustee or debtor in possession expends money to provide for the reasonable and necessary cost and expenses of preserving or disposing of a secured creditor's collateral, the trustee or debtor in possession is entitled to recover such expenses from the secured party or from the property securing an allowed secured claim held by such party.

Section 506(d) of the House amendment is derived from H.R. 8200 as passed by the House and is adopted in lieu of the alternative test provided in section 506(d) of the Senate amendment. For purposes of section 506(d) of the House amendment, the debtor is a party in interest.

Determination of Secured Status: The House amendment deletes section 506(d)(3) of the Senate amendment, which insures that a tax lien securing a nondischargeable tax claim is not voided because a tax authority with notice or knowledge of the bankruptcy case fails to file a claim for the liability (as it may elect not to do, if it is clear there are insufficient assets to pay the liability). Since the House amendment retains section 506(d) of the House bill that a lien is not voided unless a party in interest has requested that the court determine and allow or disallow the claim, provision of the Senate amendment is not necessary.

References in Text

Chapter 7 or 13, referred to in subsec. (a)(2), is chapter 7 or 13 of this title, 11 U.S.C.A. § 701 et seq. or 11 U.S.C.A. § 1301 et seq.

Amendments

2005 Amendments. Subsec. (a)(1). Pub.L. 109–8, § 327(1), inserted "(1)" after "(a)".

Subsec. (a)(2). Pub.L. 109–8, § 327(2), added par. (2).

Subsec. (b). Pub.L. 109–8, § 712(d)(1), inserted "or State statute" after "agreement".

Subsec. (c). Pub.L. 109–8, § 712(d)(2), inserted ", including the payment of all ad valorem property taxes with respect to the property" before the period at the end.

1984 Amendments. Subsec. (b). Pub.L. 98–353, § 448(a), added "for" after "provided".

Subsec. (d)(1). Pub.L. 98–353, § 448(b), substituted "such claim was disallowed only under section 502(b)(5) or 502(e) of this title; or" for "a party in interest has not requested that the court determine and allow or disallow such claim under section 502 of this title; or".

Subsec. (d)(2). Pub.L. 98–353, § 448(b), substituted "such claim is not an allowed secured claim due only to the failure of any entity to file a proof of such claim under section 501 of this title." for "such claim was disallowed only under section 502(e) of this title.".

Effective and Applicability Provisions

2005 Acts. Amendments by Pub.L. 109–8 effective, except as otherwise provided, 180 days after April 20, 2005, and inapplicable with respect to cases commenced under Title 11 before the effective date, see Pub.L. 109–8, § 1501, set out as a note under 11 U.S.C.A. § 101.

1984 Acts. Amendment by Pub.L. 98–353 effective with respect to cases filed 90 days after July 10, 1984, see section 552(a), formerly 553(a), of Pub.L. 98–353, set out as a note under section 101 of this title.

CROSS REFERENCES

Applicability of this section in Chapter 9 cases, see 11 USCA § 901.

Automatic preservation of avoided transfer, see 11 USCA § 551.

Claims secured by lien on property of estate, see 11 USCA § 1111.

Contents of plan and interest on interest, see 11 USCA §§ 1123, 1222 and 1322.

Effect of dismissal, see 11 USCA § 349.

Liability of exempted property for debtor's debt, see 11 USCA § 522.

Postpetition effect of security interest, see 11 USCA § 552.

LIBRARY REFERENCES

American Digest System

Bankruptcy ⚖2575.

Key Number System Topic No. 51.

Corpus Juris Secundum

CJS Bankruptcy § 7, Bankruptcy Code.

CJS Bankruptcy § 120, What Constitutes Disbursal of Moneys to Parties in Interest, Excluding Debtor.

CJS Bankruptcy § 278, Parties Defendant; Sovereign Immunity.

CJS Bankruptcy § 505, Taxation.

CJS Bankruptcy § 555, Property Subject to Liens or Mortgages--Liens Securing Unallowed or Undersecured Claims.

CJS Bankruptcy § 562, Property Acquired Postpetition--Security Interest on Property Acquired Postpetition.

CJS Bankruptcy § 619, Recovery from Secured Property of Trustee's Costs and Expenses.

CJS Bankruptcy § 643, Prohibition Against Disbursement from Property.

CJS Bankruptcy § 698, Transfers or Obligations Which May be Avoided.

CJS Bankruptcy § 773, Status of Claims for Compensation and Reimbursement.

CJS Bankruptcy § 851, Prepetition Security Interests in Proceeds, Products, Offspring, or Profits.

CJS Bankruptcy § 852, Prepetition Security Interests Extending to Rents and Similar Charges.

CJS Bankruptcy § 860, Recovery of Costs of Preserving or Disposing of Property.

CJS Bankruptcy § 861, Recovery of Costs of Preserving or Disposing of Property--Preservation of Property; Operating Expenses.

CJS Bankruptcy § 862, Recovery of Costs of Preserving or Disposing of Property--Sale of Property.

CJS Bankruptcy § 967, Generally; Valuation.

CJS Bankruptcy § 969, Interest, Fees, and Costs.

CJS Bankruptcy § 970, Interest, Fees, and Costs--Attorneys" Fees.

CJS Bankruptcy § 971, Liability for Expense of Preservation or Disposition.

CJS Bankruptcy § 1104, Tax Liens and Other Statutory Liens.

CJS Bankruptcy § 1135, Impairment of Claims or Interests--Curing Defaults.

CJS Bankruptcy § 1174, Modification of Claims; Cram Down of Secured Claims.

CJS Bankruptcy § 1176, Curing or Waiving of Defaults.

CJS Bankruptcy § 1193, Modification of Claims.

CJS Bankruptcy § 1194, Treatment of Secured Claims; Cram Down Provisions.

CJS Bankruptcy § 1198, Curing Defaults.

CJS Secured Transactions § 11, Nature of Purchase-Money Security Interest.

CJS Secured Transactions § 12, Loss of Purchase-Money Status.

§ 507. Priorities

(a) The following expenses and claims have priority in the following order:

(1) First:

(A) Allowed unsecured claims for domestic support obligations that, as of the date of the filing of the petition in a case under this title, are owed to or recoverable by a spouse, former spouse, or child of the debtor, or such child's parent, legal guardian, or responsible relative, without regard to whether the claim is filed by such person or is filed by a governmental unit on behalf of such person, on the condition that funds received under this paragraph by a governmental unit under this title after the date of the filing of the petition shall be applied and distributed in accordance with applicable nonbankruptcy law.

(B) Subject to claims under subparagraph (A), allowed unsecured claims for domestic support obligations that, as of the date of the filing of the petition, are assigned by a spouse, former spouse, child of the debtor, or such child's parent, legal guardian, or responsible relative to a governmental unit (unless such obligation is assigned voluntarily by the spouse, former spouse, child, parent, legal guardian, or responsible relative of the child for the purpose of collecting the debt) or are owed directly to or recoverable by a governmental unit under applicable nonbankruptcy law, on the condition that funds received under this paragraph by a governmental unit under this title after the date of the filing of the petition be applied and distributed in accordance with applicable nonbankruptcy law.

(C) If a trustee is appointed or elected under section 701, 702, 703, 1104, 1202, or 1302, the administrative expenses of the trustee allowed under paragraphs (1)(A), (2), and (6) of section 503(b) shall be paid before payment of claims under subparagraphs (A) and (B), to the extent that the trustee administers assets that are otherwise available for the payment of such claims.

(2) Second, administrative expenses allowed under section 503(b) of this title, unsecured claims of any Federal reserve bank related to loans made through programs or facilities authorized under section 13(3) of the Federal Reserve Act (12 U.S.C. 343), and any fees and charges assessed against the estate under chapter 123 of title 28.

(3) Third, unsecured claims allowed under section 502(f) of this title.

(4) Fourth, allowed unsecured claims, but only to the extent of $11,725 [1] for each individual or corporation, as the case may be, earned within 180 days before the date of the filing of the petition or the date of the cessation of the debtor's business, whichever occurs first, for—

(A) wages, salaries, or commissions, including vacation, severance, and sick leave pay earned by an individual; or

(B) sales commissions earned by an individual or by a corporation with only 1 employee, acting as an independent contractor in the sale of goods or services for the debtor in the ordinary course of the debtor's business if, and only if, during the 12 months preceding that date, at least 75 percent of the amount that the individual or corporation earned by acting as an independent contractor in the sale of goods or services was earned from the debtor.

(5) Fifth, allowed unsecured claims for contributions to an employee benefit plan—

(A) arising from services rendered within 180 days before the date of the filing of the petition or the date of the cessation of the debtor's business, whichever occurs first; but only

(B) for each such plan, to the extent of—

(i) the number of employees covered by each such plan multiplied by $11,725 [1]; less

(ii) the aggregate amount paid to such employees under paragraph (4) of this subsection, plus the aggregate amount paid by the estate on behalf of such employees to any other employee benefit plan.

(6) Sixth, allowed unsecured claims of persons—

(A) engaged in the production or raising of grain, as defined in section 557(b) of this title, against a debtor who owns or operates a grain storage facility, as defined in section 557(b) of this title, for grain or the proceeds of grain, or

(B) engaged as a United States fisherman against a debtor who has acquired fish or fish produce from a fisherman through a sale or conversion, and who is engaged in operating a fish produce storage or processing facility—

but only to the extent of $5,775 [1] for each such individual.

(7) Seventh, allowed unsecured claims of individuals, to the extent of $2,600 [1] for each such individual, arising from the deposit, before the commencement of the case, of money in connection with the purchase, lease, or rental of property, or the purchase of services, for the personal, family, or household use of such individuals, that were not delivered or provided.

(8) Eighth, allowed unsecured claims of governmental units, only to the extent that such claims are for—

(A) a tax on or measured by income or gross receipts for a taxable year ending on or before the date of the filing of the petition—

(i) for which a return, if required, is last due, including extensions, after three years before the date of the filing of the petition;

(ii) assessed within 240 days before the date of the filing of the petition, exclusive of—

(I) any time during which an offer in compromise with respect to that tax was pending or in effect during that 240–day period, plus 30 days; and

(II) any time during which a stay of proceedings against collections was in effect in a prior case under this title during that 240–day period, plus 90 days; or

(iii) other than a tax of a kind specified in section 523(a)(1)(B) or 523(a)(1)(C) of this title, not assessed before, but assessable, under applicable law or by agreement, after, the commencement of the case;

(B) a property tax incurred before the commencement of the case and last payable without penalty after one year before the date of the filing of the petition;

(C) a tax required to be collected or withheld and for which the debtor is liable in whatever capacity;

(D) an employment tax on a wage, salary, or commission of a kind specified in paragraph (4) of this subsection earned from the debtor before the date of the filing of the petition, whether or not actually paid before such date, for which a return is last due, under applicable law or under any extension, after three years before the date of the filing of the petition;

(E) an excise tax on—

(i) a transaction occurring before the date of the filing of the petition for which a return, if required, is last due, under applicable law or under any extension, after three years before the date of the filing of the petition; or

(ii) if a return is not required, a transaction occurring during the three years immediately preceding the date of the filing of the petition;

(F) a customs duty arising out of the importation of merchandise—

(i) entered for consumption within one year before the date of the filing of the petition;

(ii) covered by an entry liquidated or reliquidated within one year before the date of the filing of the petition; or

(iii) entered for consumption within four years before the date of the filing of the petition but unliquidated on such date, if the Secretary of the Treasury certifies that failure to liquidate such entry was due to an investigation pending on such date into assessment of antidumping or countervailing duties or fraud, or if information needed for the proper appraisement or classification of such merchandise was not available to the appropriate customs officer before such date; or

(G) a penalty related to a claim of a kind specified in this paragraph and in compensation for actual pecuniary loss.

An otherwise applicable time period specified in this paragraph shall be suspended for any period during which a governmental unit is prohibited under applicable nonbankruptcy law from collecting a tax as a result of a request by the debtor for a hearing and an appeal of any collection action taken or proposed against the debtor, plus 90 days; plus any time during which the stay of proceedings was in effect in a prior case under this title or during which collection was precluded by the existence of 1 or more confirmed plans under this title, plus 90 days.

(9) Ninth, allowed unsecured claims based upon any commitment by the debtor to a Federal depository institutions regulatory agency (or predecessor to such agency) to maintain the capital of an insured depository institution.

(10) Tenth, allowed claims for death or personal injury resulting from the operation of a motor vehicle or vessel if such operation was unlawful because the debtor was intoxicated from using alcohol, a drug, or another substance.

(b) If the trustee, under section 362, 363, or 364 of this title, provides adequate protection of the interest of a holder of a claim secured by a lien on property of the debtor and if, notwithstanding such protection, such creditor has a claim allowable under subsection (a)(2) of this section arising from the stay of action against such property under section 362 of this title, from the use, sale, or lease of such property under section 363 of this title, or from the granting of a lien under section 364(d) of this title, then such creditor's claim under such subsection shall have priority over every other claim allowable under such subsection.

(c) For the purpose of subsection (a) of this section, a claim of a governmental unit arising from an erroneous refund or credit of a tax has the same priority as a claim for the tax to which such refund or credit relates.

(d) An entity that is subrogated to the rights of a holder of a claim of a kind specified in subsection (a)(1), (a)(4), (a)(5), (a)(6), (a)(7), (a)(8), or (a)(9) of this section is not subrogated to the right of the holder of such claim to priority under such subsection.

(Pub.L. 95–598, Nov. 6, 1978, 92 Stat. 2583; Pub.L. 98–353, Title III, §§ 350, 449, July 10, 1984, 98 Stat. 358, 374; Pub.L. 101–647, Title XXV, § 2522(d), Nov. 29, 1990, 104 Stat. 4867; Pub.L. 103–394, Title I, § 108(c), Title II, § 207, Title III, § 304(c), Title V, § 501(b)(3), (d)(11), Oct. 22, 1994, 108 Stat. 4112, 4123, 4132, 4142, 4145; Pub.L. 109–8, Title II, §§ 212, 223, Title VII, §§ 705, 706, Title XIV, § 1401, Title XV, § 1502(a)(1), Apr. 20, 2005, 119 Stat. 51, 62, 126, 214, 216; Pub.L. 111–203, Title XI, § 1101(b), July 21, 2010, 124 Stat. 2115; Pub.L. 111–327, § 2(a)(15), Dec. 22, 2010, 124 Stat. 3559.)

1 Dollar amount as adjusted by the Judicial Conference of the United States. See Adjustment of Dollar Amounts notes set out under this section and 11 U.S.C.A. § 104.

HISTORICAL AND STATUTORY NOTES

Revision Notes and Legislative Reports

1978 Acts. Section 507 specifies the kinds of claims that are entitled to priority in distribution, and the order of their priority. Paragraph (1) grants first priority to allowed administrative expenses and to fees and charges assessed against the estate under chapter 123 of title 28 [section 1911 et seq. of Title 28, Judiciary and Judicial Procedure]. Taxes included as administrative expenses under section 503(b)(1) of the bill generally receive the first priority, but the bill makes certain qualifications: Examples of these specially treated claims are the estate's liability for recapture of an investment tax credit claimed by the debtor before the title 11 case (this liability receives sixth priority) and the estate's employment tax liabilities on wages earned before, but paid after, the petition was filed (this liability generally receives the same priority as the wages).

"Involuntary gap" creditors, granted first priority under current law, are granted second priority by paragraph (2). This priority, covering claims arising in the ordinary course of the debtor's business or financial affairs after a title 11 case has begun but before a trustee is appointed or before the order for relief, includes taxes incurred during the conduct of such activities.

Paragraph (3) expands and increases the wage priority found in current section 64a(2) [section 104(a)(2) of former Title 11]. The amount entitled to priority is raised from $600 to $1800. The former figure was last adjusted in 1926. Inflation has made it nearly meaningless, and the bill brings it more than up to date. The three month limit of current law is retained, but is modified to run from the earlier of the date of the filing of the petition or the date of the cessation of the debtor's business. The priority is expanded to cover vacation, severance, and sick leave pay. The bill adds to the third priority so-called "trust fund" taxes, that is, withheld income taxes and the employees' share of the social security or railroad retirement taxes, but only to the extent that the wages on which taxes are imposed are themselves entitled to third priority.

The employer's share, the employment tax and the employer's share of the social security or railroad retirement tax on third priority compensation, is also included in the third priority category, but only if, and to the extent that the wages and related trust fund taxes have first been paid in full. Because of the claimants urgent need for their wages in the typical cases, the employer's taxes should not be paid before the wage claims entitled to priority, as well as the related trust fund taxes, are fully paid.

Paragraph (4) overrules *United States v. Embassy Restaurant*, 359 U.S. 29 (1958) [79 S.Ct. 554, 3 L.Ed.2d 601], which held that fringe benefits were not entitled to wage priority status. The bill recognizes the realities of labor contract negotiations, where fringe benefits may be substituted for wage demands. The priority granted is limited to claims for contributions to employee benefit plans such as pension plans, health or life insurance plans, and others, arising from services rendered within 120 days before the commencement of the case or the date of cessation of the debtor's business, whichever occurs first. The dollar limit placed on the total of all contributions payable under this paragraph is equal to the difference between the maximum allowable priority under paragraph (3), $1,800, times the number of employees covered by the plan less the actual distributions under paragraph (3) with respect to these employees.

Paragraph (5) is a new priority for consumer creditors— those who have deposited money in connection with the purchase, lease, or rental of property, or the purchase of services, for their personal, family, or household use, that were not delivered or provided. The priority amount is not to exceed $600. In order to reach only those persons most deserving of this special priority, it is limited to individuals whose adjustable gross income from all sources derived does not exceed $20,000. See Senate Hearings, testimony of Prof. Vern Countryman, at pp. 848–849. The income of the husband and wife should be aggregated for the purposes of the $20,000 limit if either or both spouses assert such a priority claim.

The sixth priority is for certain taxes. Priority is given to income taxes for a taxable year that ended on or before the date of the filing of the petition, if the last due date of the return for such year occurred not more than 3 years immediately before the date on which the petition was filed (§ 507(a)(6)(A)(i)). For the purposes of this rule, the last due date of the return is the last date under any extension of time to file the return which the taxing authority may have granted the debtor.

Employment taxes and transfer taxes (including gift, estate, sales, use and other excise taxes) are also given sixth priority if the transaction or event which gave rise to the tax occurred before the petition date, provided that the required return or report of such tax liabilities was last due within 3 years before the petition was filed or was last due after the petition date (§ 507(a)(6)(A)(ii).) The employment taxes covered under this rule are the employer's share of the social security and railroad retirement taxes and required employer payments toward unemployment insurance.

Priority is given to income taxes and other taxes of a kind described in section 507(a)(6)(A)(i) and (ii) which the Federal, State, or local tax authority had assessed within 3 years after the last due date of the return, that is, including any extension of time to file the return, if the debtor filed in title 11 within 240 days after the assessment was made (§ 507(a)(6)(B)(i)). This rule may bring into the sixth priority the debtor's tax liability for some taxable years which would not qualify for priority under the general three-year rule of section 507(a)(6)(A).

The sixth priority category also includes taxes which the tax authority was barred by law from assessing or collecting at any time during the 300 days before the petition under title 11 was filed (§ 507(a)(6)(B)(ii)). In the case of certain Federal taxes, this preserves a priority for tax liabilities for years more than three years before the filing of the petition where the debtor and the Internal Revenue Service were negotiating over an audit of the debtor's returns or were engaged in litigation in the Tax Court. In such situations, the tax law prohibits the service's right to assess a tax deficiency until ninety days after the service sends the taxpayer a deficiency letter or, if the taxpayer files a petition in the Tax Court during that 90-day period, until the outcome of the litigation. A similar priority exists in present law, except that the taxing authority is allowed no time to assess and collect the taxes after the restrictions on assessment (discussed above) are lifted. Some taxpayers have exploited this loophole by filing in bankruptcy immediately after the end of the 90-day period or immediately after the close of Tax Court proceedings. The bill remedies this defect by preserving a priority for taxes the assessment of which was barred by law by giving the tax authority 300 days within which to make the assessment after the lifting of the bar and then to collect or file public notice of its tax lien. Thus, if a taxpayer files a title 11 petition at any time during that 300-day period, the tax deficiency will be entitled to priority. If the petition is filed more than 300 days after the restriction on assessment was lifted, the taxing authority will not have priority for the tax deficiency.

Taxes for which an offer in compromise was withdrawn by the debtor, or rejected by a governmental unit, within 240 days before the petition date (§ 507(a)(6)(B)(iii)) will also receive sixth priority. This rule closes a loophole under present law under which, following an assessment of tax, some taxpayers have submitted a formal offer in compromise, dragged out negotiations with the taxing authority until the tax liability would lose priority under the three-year priority period of present law, and then filed in bankruptcy before the governmental unit could take collection steps.

Also included are certain taxes for which no return or report is required by law (§ 507(a)(6)(C)), if the taxable transaction occurred within three years before the petition was filed.

Taxes (not covered by the third priority) which the debtor was required by law to withhold or collect from others and for which he is liable in any capacity, regardless of the age of the tax claims (§ 507(a)(6)(D)) are included. This category covers the so-called "trust fund" taxes, that is, income taxes which an employer is required to withhold from the pay of his employees, the employees' shares of social security and railroad retirement taxes, and also Federal unemployment insurance. This category also includes excise taxes which a seller of goods or services is required to collect from a buyer and pay over to a taxing authority.

This category also covers the liability of a responsible corporate officer under the Internal Revenue Code [Title 26] for income taxes or for the employees' share of employment taxes which, under the tax law, the employer was required to withhold from the wages of employees. This priority will operate where a person found to be a responsible officer has himself filed a petition under title 11, and the priority covers the debtor's liability as an officer under the Internal Revenue Code [Title 26], regardless of the age of the tax year to which the tax relates.

The priority rules under the bill governing employment taxes can be summarized as follows: In the case of wages earned and actually paid before the petition under title 11 was filed, the liability for the employees' share of the employment taxes, regardless of the prepetition year in which the wages were earned and paid. The employer's share of the employment taxes on all wages earned and paid before the petition receive sixth priority; generally, these taxes will be those for which a return was due within three years before the petition. With respect to wages earned by employees before the petition but actually paid by the trustee after the title 11 case commenced, taxes required to be withheld receives the same priority as the wages themselves. Thus, the employees' share of taxes on third priority wages also receives third priority. Taxes on the balance of such wages receive no priority and are collectible only as general claims because the wages themselves are payable only as general claims and liability for the taxes arises only to the extent the wages are actually paid. The employer's share of employment taxes on third priority wages earned before the petition but paid after the petition was filed receives third priority, but only if the wages in this category have first been paid in full. Assuming there are sufficient funds to pay third priority wages and the related employer taxes in full, the employer's share of taxes on the balance of wage payments becomes a general claim (because the wages themselves are payable as general claims). Both the employees' and the employer's share of employment taxes on wages earned and paid after the petition was filed receive first priority as administrative expenses.

Also covered by this sixth priority are property taxes required to be assessed within 3 years before the filing of the petition (§ 507(a)(6)(E)).

Taxes attributable to a tentative carryback adjustment received by the debtor before the petition was filed, such as a "quickie refund" received under section 6411 of the Internal Revenue Code [section 6411 of Title 26, Internal Revenue Code] (§ 507(a)(6)(F)) are included. However, the tax claim against the debtor will rein a prepetition loss year for which the tax return was last due, including extensions, within 3 years before the petition was filed.

Taxes resulting from a recapture, occasioned by a transfer during bankruptcy, of a tax credit or deduction taken during an earlier tax year (§ 507(a)(6)(G)) are included. A typical example occurs when there is a sale by the trustee of depreciable property during the case and depreciation deductions taken in prepetition years are subject to recapture under section 1250 of the Code [section 1250 of Title 26, Internal Revenue Code].

Taxes owed by the debtor as a transferee of assets from another person who is liable for a tax, if the tax claim against the transferor would have received priority in a chapter 11 case commenced by the transferor within 1 year before the date of the petition filed by the transferee (§ 507(a)(6)(H)), are included.

Also included are certain tax payments required to have been made during the 1 year immediately before the petition was filed, where the debtor had previously entered into a deferred payment agreement (including an offer in compromise) to pay an agreed liability in periodic installments but had become delinquent in one or more installments before the petition was filed (§ 507(a)(6)(I)). This priority covers all types of deferred or part payment agreements. The priority covers only installments which first became due during the 1 year before the petition but which remained unpaid at the date of the petition. The priority does not come into play, however, if before the case began or during the case, the debtor and the taxing authority agree to a further extension of time to pay the delinquent amounts.

Certain tax-related liabilities which are not true taxes or which are not collected by regular assessment procedures (§ 507(a)(6)(J)) are included. One type of liability covered in this category is the liability under section 3505 of the Internal Revenue Code [section 3505 of Title 26, Internal Revenue Code] of a lender who pays wages directly to employees of another employer or who supplies funds to an employer for the payment of wages. Another is the liability under section 6332 of the Internal Revenue Code [section 6332 of Title 26, Internal Revenue Code], of a person who fails to turn over money or property of the taxpayer in response to a levy. Since the taxing authority must collect such a liability from the third party by suit rather than normal assessment procedures, an extra year is added to the normal 3-year priority periods. If a suit was commenced by the taxing authority within the four-year period and before the petition was filed, the priority is also preserved, provided that the suit had not terminated more than 1 year before the date of the filing of the petition.

Also included are certain unpaid customs duties which have not grown unreasonably "stale" (§ 507(a)(6)(K)). These include duties on imports entered for consumption with 3 years before the filing of the petition if the duties are still unliquidated on the petition date. If an import entry has been liquidated (in general, liquidation is in an administrative determination of the value and tariff rate of the item) or reliquidated, within two years of the filing of the petition the customs liability is given priority. If the Secretary of the Treasury certifies that customs duties were not liquidated because of an investigation into possible assessment of antidumping or countervailing duties, or because of fraud penalties, duties not liquidated for this reason during the five years before the importer filed under title 11 also will receive priority.

Subsection (a) of this section also provides specifically that interest on sixth priority tax claims accrued before the filing of the petition is also entitled to sixth priority.

Subsection (b) of this section provides that any fine or penalty which represents compensation for actual pecuniary loss of a governmental unit, and which involves a tax liability entitled to sixth priority, is to receive the same priority.

Subsection (b) also provides that a claim arising from an erroneous refund or credit of tax is to be given the same priority as the tax to which the refund or credit relates. Senate Report No. 95–989.

1984 Acts. Statements by Legislative Leaders, see 1984 U.S. Code Cong. and Adm. News, p. 576.

1990 Acts. House Report No. 101–681(I), see 1990 U.S. Code Cong. and Adm. News, p. 6472.

1994 Acts. House Report No. 103–835, see 1994 U.S. Code Cong. and Adm. News, p. 3340.

2005 Acts. House Report No. 109–31(Part I), see 2005 U.S. Code Cong. and Adm. News, p. 88.

Legislative Statements

Section 507(a)(3) of the House amendment represents a compromise dollar amount and date for the priority between similar provisions contained in H.R. 8200 as passed by the House and the Senate amendments. A similar compromise is contained in section 507(a)(4).

Section 507(a)(5) represents a compromise on amount between the priority as contained in H.R. 8200 as passed by the House and the Senate amendment. The Senate provision for limiting the priority to consumers having less than a fixed gross income is deleted.

Section 507(a)(6) of the House amendment represents a compromise between similar provisions contained in H.R. 8200 as passed by the House and the Senate amendment.

Section 507(b) of the House amendment is new and is derived from the compromise contained in the House amendment with respect to adequate protection under section 361. Subsection (b) provides that to the extent adequate protection of the interest of a holder of a claim proves to be inadequate, then the creditor's claim is given priority over every other allowable claim entitled to distribution under section 507(a). Section 507(b) of the Senate amendment is deleted.

Section 507(c) of the House amendment is new. Section 507(d) of the House amendment prevents subrogation with respect to priority for certain priority claims. Subrogation with respect to priority is intended to be permitted for administrative claims and claims arising during the gap period.

Priorities: Under the House amendment, taxes receive priority as follows:

First. Administration expenses: The amendment generally follows the Senate amendment in providing expressly that taxes incurred during the administration of the estate share the first priority given to administrative expenses generally. Among the taxes which receives first priority, as defined in section 503, are the employees' and the employer's shares of employment taxes on wages earned and paid after the petition is filed. Section 503(b)(1) also includes in administration expenses a tax liability arising from an excessive allowance by a tax authority of a "quickie refund" to the estate. (In the case of Federal taxes, such refunds are allowed under special rules based on net operating loss carrybacks (section 6411 of the Internal Revenue Code) [section 6411 of Title 26, Internal Revenue Code]).

An exception is made to first priority treatment for taxes incurred by the estate with regard to the employer's share of employment taxes on wages earned from the debtor before the petition but paid from the estate after the petition has been filed. In this situation, the employer's tax receives either sixth priority or general claim treatment.

The House amendment also adopts the provisions of the Senate amendment which include in the definition of administrative expenses under section 503 any fine, penalty (including "additions to tax" under applicable tax laws) or reduction in credit imposed on the estate.

Second. "Involuntary gap" claims: "Involuntary gap" creditors are granted second priority by paragraph (2) of section 507(a). This priority includes tax claims arising in the ordinary course of the debtor's business or financial affairs after he has been placed involuntarily in bankruptcy but before a trustee is appointed or before the order for relief.

Third. Certain taxes on prepetition wages: Wage claims entitled to third priority are for compensation which does not exceed $2,000 and was earned during the 90 days before the filing of the bankruptcy petition or the cessation of the debtor's business. Certain employment taxes receive third priority in payment from the estate along with the payment of wages to which the taxes relate. In the case of wages earned before the filing of the petition, but paid by the trustee (rather than by the debtor) after the filing of the petition, claims or the employees' share of the employment taxes (withheld income taxes and the employees' share of the social security or railroad retirement tax) receive third priority to the extent the wage claims themselves are entitled to this priority.

In the case of wages earned from and paid by the debtor before the filing of the petition, the employer's share of the employment taxes on these wages paid by the debtor receives sixth priority or, if not entitled to that priority, are treated only as general claims. Under the House amendment, the employer's share of employment taxes on wages earned by employees of the debtor, but paid by the trustee after the filing of the bankruptcy petition, will also receive sixth priority to the extent that claims for the wages receive third priority. To the extent the claims for wages do not receive third priority, but instead are treated only as general claims, claims for the employer's share of the employment taxes attributable to those wages will also be treated as general claims. In calculating the amounts payable as general wage claims, the trustee must pay the employer's share of employment taxes on such wages.

Sixth priority. The House amendment modifies the provisions of both the House bill and Senate amendment in the case of sixth priority taxes. Under the amendment, the following Federal, State and local taxes are included in the sixth priority:

First. Income and gross receipts taxes incurred before the date of the petition for which the last due date of the return, including all extensions of time granted to file the return, occurred within 3 years before the date on which the petition was filed, or after the petition date. Under this rule, the due date of the return, rather than the date on which the taxes were assessed, determines the priority.

Second. Income and gross receipts taxes assessed at any time within 240 days before the petition date. Under this rule, the date on which the governmental unit assesses the tax, rather than the due date of the return, determines the priority.

If, following assessment of a tax, the debtor submits an offer in compromise to the governmental unit, the House amendment provides that the 240-day period is to be suspended for the duration of the offer and will resume running after the offer is withdrawn or rejected by the governmental unit, but the tax liability will receive priority if the title 11 petition is filed during the balance of the 240-day period or during a minimum of 30 days after the offer is withdrawn or rejected. This rule modifies a provision of the Senate amendment dealing specifically with offers in compromise. Under the modified rule, if, after the assessment, an offer in compromise is submitted by the debtor and is still pending (without having been accepted or rejected) at the date on which a title 11 petition is filed, the underlying liability will receive sixth priority. However, if an assessment of a tax liability is made but the tax is not collected within 240 days, the tax will not receive priority under section 507(a)(6)(A)(i) and the debtor cannot revive a priority for that tax by submitting an offer in compromise.

Third. Income and gross receipts taxes not assessed before the petition date but still permitted, under otherwise applicable tax laws, to be assessed. Thus, for example, a prepetition tax liability is to receive sixth priority under this rule if, under the applicable statute of limitations, the tax liability can still be assessed by the tax authority. This rule also covers situations referred to in section 507(a)(6)(B)(ii) of the Senate amendment where the assessment or collection of a tax was prohibited before the petition pending exhaustion of judicial or administrative remedies, except that the House amendment eliminates the 300-day limitation of the Senate bill. So, for example, if before the petition a debtor was engaged in litigation in the Tax Court, during which the Internal Revenue Code [Title 26] bars the Internal Revenue Service from assessing or collecting the tax, and if the tax court decision is made in favor of the Service before the petition under title 11 is filed, thereby lifting the restrictions on assessment and collection, the tax liability will receive sixth priority even if the tax authority does not make an assessment within 300 days before the petition (provided, of course, that the statute of limitations on assessment has not expired by the petition date).

In light of the above categories of the sixth priority, and tax liability of the debtor (under the Internal Revenue Code [Title 26] or State or local law) as a transferee of property from another person will receive sixth priority without the limitations contained in the Senate amendment so long as the transferee liability had not been assessed by the tax authority by the petition date but could still have been assessed by that date under the applicable tax statute of limitations or, if the transferee liability had been assessed before the petition, the assessment was made no more than 240 days before the petition date.

Also in light of the above categories, the treatment of prepetition tax liabilities arising from an excessive allowance to the debtor of a tentative carryback adjustment, such as a "quickie refund" under section 6411 of the Internal Revenue Code [section 6411 of Title 26, Internal Revenue Code], is revised as follows: If the tax authority has assessed the additional tax before the petition, the tax liability will receive priority if the date of assessment was within 240 days before the petition date. If the tax authority had not assessed the additional tax by the petition, the tax liability will still receive priority so long as, on the petition date, assessment of the liability is not barred by the statute of limitations.

Fourth. Any property tax assessed before the commencement of the case and last payable without penalty within 1 year before the petition, or thereafter.

Fifth. Taxes which the debtor was required by law to withhold or collect from others and for which he is liable in any capacity, regardless of the age of the tax claims. This category covers the so-called "trust fund" taxes, that is, income taxes which an employer is required to withhold from the pay of his employees, and the employees' share of social security taxes.

In addition, this category includes the liability of a responsible officer under the Internal Revenue Code (Sec. 6672 [section 6672 of Title 26, Internal Revenue Code]) for income taxes or for the employees' share of social security taxes which that officer was responsible for withholding from the wages of employees and paying to the Treasury, although he was not himself the employer. This priority will operate when a person found to be a responsible officer has himself filed in title 11, and the priority will cover the debtor's responsible officer liability regardless of the age of the tax year to which the tax relates. The U.S. Supreme Court has interpreted present law to require the same result as will be reached under this rule. *U.S. v. Sotelo*, 436 U.S. 268 (1978) [98 S.Ct. 1795, 56 L.Ed.2d 275, rehearing denied 98 S.Ct. 3126, 438 U.S. 907, 57 L.Ed.2d 1150].

This category also includes the liability under section 3505 of the Internal Revenue Code [section 3505 of Title 26, Internal Revenue Code] of a taxpayer who loans money for the payment of wages or other compensation.

Sixth. The employer's share of employment taxes on wages paid before the petition and on third-priority wages paid postpetition by the estate. The priority rules under the House amendment governing employment taxes can thus be summarized as follows: Claims for the employees' shares of employment taxes attributable to wages both earned and paid before the filing of the petition are to receive sixth priority. In the case of employee wages earned, but not paid, before the filing of the bankruptcy petition, claims for the employees' share of employment taxes receive third priority to the extent the wages themselves receive third priority. Claims which relate to wages earned before the petition, but not paid before the petition (and which are not entitled to the third priority under the rule set out above), will be paid as general claims. Since the related wages will receive no priority, the related employment taxes would also be paid as nonpriority general claims.

The employer's share of the employment taxes on wages earned and paid before the bankruptcy petition will receive sixth priority to the extent the return for these taxes was last due (including extensions of time) within 3 years before the filing of the petition, or was due after the petition was filed. Older tax claims of this nature will be payable as general claims. In the case of wages earned by employees before the petition, but actually paid by the trustee (as claims against the estate) after the title 11 case commenced, the employer's share of the employment taxes on third priority wages will be payable as sixth priority claims and the employer's taxes on prepetition wages which are treated only as general claims will be payable only as general claims. In calculating the amounts payable as general wage claims, the trustee must pay the employer's share of employment taxes on such wages. The House amendment thus deletes the provision of the Senate amendment that certain employer taxes receive third priority and are to be paid immediately after payment of third priority wages and the employees' shares of employment taxes on those wages.

In the case of employment taxes relating to wages earned and paid after the petition, both the employees' shares and the employer's share will receive first priority as administration expenses of the estate.

Seventh. Excise taxes on transactions for which a return, if required, is last due, under otherwise applicable law or under any extension of time to file the return, within 3 years before the petition was filed, or thereafter. If a return is not required with regard to a particular excise tax, priority is given if the transaction or event itself occurred within 3 years before the date on which the title 11 petition was filed. All Federal, State or local taxes generally considered or expressly treated as excises are covered by this category, including sales taxes, estate and gift taxes, gasoline and special fuel taxes, and wagering and truck taxes.

Eighth. Certain unpaid customs duties. The House amendment covers in this category duties on imports entered for consumption within 1 year before the filing of the petition, but which are still unliquidated on the petition date; duties covered by an entry liquidated or reliquidated within 1 year before the petition date; and any duty on merchandise entered for consumption within 4 years before the petition but not liquidated on the petition date, if the Secretary of the Treasury or his delegate certifies that duties were not liquidated because of possible assessment of antidumping or countervailing duties or fraud penalties.

For purposes of the above priority rules, the House amendment adopts the provision of the Senate bill that any tax liability which, under otherwise applicable tax law, is collectible in the form of a "penalty," is to be treated in the same manner as a tax liability. In bankruptcy terminology, such tax liabilities are referred to as pecuniary loss penalties. Thus, any tax liability which under the Internal Revenue Code [Title 26] or State or local tax law is payable as a "penalty," in addition to the liability of a responsible person under section 6672 of the Internal Revenue Code [section 6672 of Title 26, Internal Revenue Code] will be entitled to the priority which the liability would receive if it were expressly labeled as a "tax" under the applicable tax law. However, a tax penalty which is punitive in nature is given subordinated treatment under section 726(a)(4).

The House amendment also adopts the provision of the Senate amendment that a claim arising from an erroneous refund or credit of tax, other than a "quickie refund," is to receive the same priority as the tax to which the refund or credit relates.

The House amendment deletes the express provision of the Senate amendment that a tax liability is to receive sixth priority if it satisfies any one of the subparagraphs of section 507(a)(6) even if the liability fails to satisfy the terms of one or more other subparagraphs. No change of substance is intended by the deletion, however, in light of section 102(5) of the House amendment, providing a rule of construction that the word "or" is not intended to be exclusive.

The House amendment deletes from the express priority categories of the Senate amendment the priority for a debtor's liability as a third party for failing to surrender property

or to pay an obligation in response to a levy for taxes of another, and the priority for amounts provided for under deferred payment agreements between a debtor and the tax authority.

The House amendment also adopts the substance of the definition in section 346(a) the Senate amendment of when taxes are to be considered "incurred" except that the House amendment applies these definitions solely for purposes of determining which category of section 507 tests the priority of a particular tax liability. Thus, for example, the House amendment contains a special rule for the treatment of taxes under the 45-day exception to the preference rules under section 547 and the definitions of when a tax is incurred for priority purposes are not to apply to such preference rules. Under the House amendment, for purposes of the priority rules, a tax on income for a particular period is to be considered "incurred" on the last day of the period. A tax on or measured by some event, such as the payment of wages or a transfer by reason of death or gift, or an excise tax on a sale or other transaction, is to be considered "incurred" on the date of the transaction or event.

References in Text

The Federal Reserve Act, referred to in subsec. (a)(2), is Act Dec. 23, 1913, c. 6, 38 Stat. 251, as amended, which is classified principally to chapter 3 of Title 12, 12 U.S.C.A. § 221 et seq. Section 13(3) of such Act is classified to 12 U.S.C.A. § 343. For complete classification, see References in Text note set out under 12 U.S.C.A. § 226 and Tables.

Codifications

Amendments by Pub.L. 109–8, § 1401, to pars. (4) and (5) of subsec. (a) of this section, as amended by section 212 of Pub.L. 109–8, were made to pars. (3) and (4) of subsec. (a) of this section, as the probable intent of Congress. The redesignation of pars. (3) and (4) as pars. (4) and (5) by section 212 of Pub.L. 109–8 does not take effect until 180 days after April 20, 2005.

Amendments

2010 Amendments. Subsec. (a)(2). Pub.L. 111–203, § 1101(b), inserted "unsecured claims of any Federal reserve bank related to loans made through programs or facilities authorized under section 13(3) of the Federal Reserve Act (12 U.S.C. 343)," after "this title,".

Subsec. (a)(4). By notice published Feb. 25, 2010, 75 F.R. 8747, dollar amount adjusted by the Judicial Conference of the United States which adjusted "$10,950" to "$11,725". See 11 U.S.C.A. § 104 and Adjustment of Dollar Amounts notes under this section.

Subsec. (a)(5)(B)(i). By notice published Feb. 25, 2010, 75 F.R. 8747, dollar amount adjusted by the Judicial Conference of the United States which adjusted "$10,950" to "$11,725". See 11 U.S.C.A. § 104 and Adjustment of Dollar Amounts notes under this section.

Subsec. (a)(6). By notice published Feb. 25, 2010, 75 F.R. 8747, dollar amount adjusted by the Judicial Conference of the United States which adjusted "$5,400" to "$5,775". See 11 U.S.C.A. § 104 and Adjustment of Dollar Amounts notes under this section.

Subsec. (a)(7). By notice published Feb. 25, 2010, 75 F.R. 8747, dollar amount adjusted by the Judicial Conference of the United States which adjusted "$2,425" to "$2,600". See

11 U.S.C.A. § 104 and Adjustment of Dollar Amounts notes under this section.

Subsec. (a)(8)(A)(ii)(II).　Pub.L. 111–327, § 2(a)(15), struck out the period at the end and inserted "; or".

2007 Amendments. Subsec. (a)(4).　By notice published Feb. 14, 2007, 72 F.R. 7082, dollar amount adjusted by the Judicial Conference of the United States which adjusted "$10,000" to "$10,950". See 11 U.S.C.A. § 104 and Adjustment of Dollar Amounts notes under this section.

Subsec. (a)(5)(B)(i).　By notice published Feb. 14, 2007, 72 F.R. 7082, dollar amount adjusted by the Judicial Conference of the United States which adjusted "$10,000" to "$10,950". See 11 U.S.C.A. § 104 and Adjustment of Dollar Amounts notes under this section.

Subsec. (a)(6).　By notice published Feb. 14, 2007, 72 F.R. 7082, dollar amount adjusted by the Judicial Conference of the United States which adjusted "$4,925" to "$5,400". See 11 U.S.C.A. § 104 and Adjustment of Dollar Amounts notes under this section.

Subsec. (a)(7).　By notice published Feb. 14, 2007, 72 F.R. 7082, dollar amount adjusted by the Judicial Conference of the United States which adjusted "$2,225" to "$2,425". See 11 U.S.C.A. § 104 and Adjustment of Dollar Amounts notes under this section.

2005 Amendments. Subsec. (a)(1).　Pub.L. 109–8, § 212(2), (9), redesignated former par. (1) as par. (2) and inserted a new par. (1).

Subsec. (a)(2).　Pub.L. 109–8, § 212(2), (3), redesignated former par. (1) as par. (2) and, in par. (2) as redesignated, substituted "Second" for "First". Former par. (2) redesignated par. (3).

Subsec. (a)(3).　Pub.L. 109–8, § 212(2), (4), redesignated former par. (2) as par. (3) and, in par. (3) as redesignated, substituted "Third" for "Second". Former par. (3) redesignated par. (4).

Subsec. (a)(4).　Pub.L. 109–8, § 212(2), (5), redesignated former par. (3) as par. (4) and, in par. (4) as redesignated, substituted "Fourth" for "Third" and substituted a period for the semicolon at the end. Former par. (4) redesignated par. (5).

Pub.L. 109–8, § 1401, struck out "90" and inserted "180", and struck out "$4,000", which had been adjusted by the Judicial Conference to "$4,925", and inserted "$10,000", in par. (3) before redesignation as par. (4) by Pub.L. 109–8, § 212(2) took effect 180 days after April 20, 2005. See Codifications note set out under this section.

Subsec. (a)(5).　Pub.L. 109–8, § 212(2), (6), redesignated former par. (4) as par. (5) and, in par. (5) as redesignated, substituted "Fifth" for "Fourth". Former par. (5) redesignated par. (6).

Pub.L. 109–8, § 1401(2), struck out "$4,000", which had been adjusted by the Judicial Conference to "$4,925", and inserted "$10,000", in par. (4) before redesignation as par. (5) by Pub.L. 109–8, § 212(2) took effect 180 days after April 20, 2005. See Codifications note set out under this section.

Subsec. (a)(5)(B)(ii).　Pub.L. 109–8, § 1502(a)(1)(A)(i), struck out "paragraph (3)" and inserted "paragraph (4)".

Subsec. (a)(6).　Pub.L. 109–8, § 212(2), (7), redesignated former par. (5) as par. (6) and, in par. (6) as redesignated, substituted "Sixth" for "Fifth". Former par. (6) redesignated par. (7).

Subsec. (a)(7).　Pub.L. 109–8, § 212(1), (2), (8), redesignated former par. (6) as par. (7), substituted "Seventh" for "Sixth" in redesignated par. (7), and struck out former par. (7) which read: "Seventh, allowed claims for debts to a spouse, former spouse, or child of the debtor, for alimony to, maintenance for, or support of such spouse or child, in connection with a separation agreement, divorce decree or other order of a court of record, determination made in accordance with State or territorial law by a governmental unit, or property settlement agreement, but not to the extent that such debt—

"**(A)** is assigned to another entity, voluntarily, by operation of law, or otherwise; or

"**(B)** includes a liability designated as alimony, maintenance, or support, unless such liability is actually in the nature of alimony, maintenance or support."

Subsec. (a)(8).　Pub.L. 109–8, § 705(2), added "An otherwise applicable time period specified in this paragraph shall be suspended for any period during which a governmental unit is prohibited under applicable nonbankruptcy law from collecting a tax as a result of a request by the debtor for a hearing and an appeal of any collection action taken or proposed against the debtor, plus 90 days; plus any time during which the stay of proceedings was in effect in a prior case under this title or during which collection was precluded by the existence of 1 or more confirmed plans under this title, plus 90 days." to the end of par. (8).

Subsec. (a)(8)(A).　Pub.L. 109–8, § 705(1)(A), in the matter preceding cl. (i), inserted "for a taxable year ending on or before the date of the filing of the petition" after "gross receipts".

Subsec. (a)(8)(A)(i).　Pub.L. 109–8, § 705(1)(B), struck out "for a taxable year ending on or before the date of the filing of the petition" before "for which a return, if required, is last due".

Subsec. (a)(8)(A)(ii).　Pub.L. 109–8, § 705(1)(C), rewrote cl. (ii), which formerly read: "**(ii)** assessed within 240 days, plus any time plus 30 days during which an offer in compromise with respect to such tax that was made within 240 days after such assessment was pending, before the date of the filing of the petition; or"

Subsec. (a)(8)(B).　Pub.L. 109–8, § 706, struck out "assessed" and inserted "incurred".

Subsec. (a)(8)(D).　Pub.L. 109–8, § 1502(a)(1)(A)(ii), struck out "paragraph (3)" and inserted "paragraph (4)".

Subsec. (a)(10).　Pub.L. 109–8, § 223, inserted par. (10).

Subsec. (b).　Pub.L. 109–8, § 1502(a)(1)(B), struck out "subsection (a)(1)" and inserted "subsection (a)(2)".

Subsec. (d).　Pub.L. 109–8, § 1502(a)(1)(C), struck out "subsection (a)(3)" and inserted "subsection (a)(1)".

2004 Amendments. Subsec. (a)(3).　By notice dated Feb. 18, 2004, 69 F.R. 8482, dollar amount adjusted by the Judicial Conference of the United States which adjusted "$4,650" to "$4,925". See 11 U.S.C.A. § 104 and Adjustment of Dollar Amounts notes under this section.

Subsec. (a)(4)(B)(i).　By notice dated Feb. 18, 2004, 69 F.R. 8482, dollar amount adjusted by the Judicial Conference of the United States which adjusted "$4,650" to "$4,925". See 11 U.S.C.A. § 104 and Adjustment of Dollar Amounts notes under this section.

Subsec. (a)(5).　By notice dated Feb. 18, 2004, 69 F.R. 8482, dollar amount adjusted by the Judicial Conference of the United States which adjusted "$4,650" to "$4,925". See 11

U.S.C.A. § 104 and Adjustment of Dollar Amounts notes under this section.

Subsec. (a)(6). By notice dated Feb. 18, 2004, 69 F.R. 8482, dollar amount adjusted by the Judicial Conference of the United States which adjusted "$2,100" to "$2,225". See 11 U.S.C.A. § 104 and Adjustment of Dollar Amounts notes under this section.

2001 Amendments. Subsec. (a)(3). By notice dated Feb. 20, 2001, 66 F.R. 10910, dollar amount adjusted by the Judicial Conference of the United States which adjusted "$4,300" to "$4,650". See 11 U.S.C.A. § 104 and Adjustment of Dollar Amounts notes under this section.

Subsec. (a)(4)(B)(i). By notice dated Feb. 20, 2001, 66 F.R. 10910, dollar amount adjusted by the Judicial Conference of the United States which adjusted "$4,300" to "$4,650". See 11 U.S.C.A. § 104 and Adjustment of Dollar Amounts notes under this section.

Subsec. (a)(5). By notice dated Feb. 20, 2001, 66 F.R. 10910, dollar amount adjusted by the Judicial Conference of the United States which adjusted "$4,300" to "$4,650". See 11 U.S.C.A. § 104 and Adjustment of Dollar Amounts notes under this section.

Subsec. (a)(6). By notice dated Feb. 20, 2001, 66 F.R. 10910, dollar amount adjusted by the Judicial Conference of the United States which adjusted "$1,950" to "$2,100". See 11 U.S.C.A. § 104 and Adjustment of Dollar Amounts notes under this section.

1998 Amendments. Subsec. (a)(3). By notice dated Feb. 3, 1998, 63 F.R. 7179, dollar amount adjusted by the Judicial Conference of the United States which adjusted "$4,000" to "$4,300". See 11 U.S.C.A. § 104 and Adjustment of Dollar Amounts notes under this section.

Subsec. (a)(4)(B)(i). By notice dated Feb. 3, 1998, 63 F.R. 7179, dollar amount adjusted by the Judicial Conference of the United States which adjusted "$4,000" to "$4,300". See 11 U.S.C.A. § 104 and Adjustment of Dollar Amounts notes under this section.

Subsec. (a)(5). By notice dated Feb. 3, 1998, 63 F.R. 7179, dollar amount adjusted by the Judicial Conference of the United States which adjusted "$4,000" to "$4,300". See 11 U.S.C.A. § 104 and Adjustment of Dollar Amounts notes under this section.

Subsec. (a)(6). By notice dated Feb. 3, 1998, 63 F.R. 7179, dollar amount adjusted by the Judicial Conference of the United States which adjusted "$1,800" to "$1,950". See 11 U.S.C.A. § 104 and Adjustment of Dollar Amounts notes under this section.

1994 Amendments. Subsec. (a)(3). Pub.L. 103–394, § 207, completely revised par. (3). Prior to revision, par. (3) read as follows:

"(3) Third, allowed unsecured claims for wages, salaries, or commissions, including vacation, severance, and sick leave pay—

"(A) earned by an individual within 90 days before the date of the filing of the petition or the date of the cessation of the debtor's business, whichever occurs first; but only

"(B) to the extent of $2,000 for each such individual."

Subsec. (a)(4)(B)(i). Pub.L. 103–394, § 108(c)(1), substituted "multiplied by $4,000" for "multiplied by $2,000".

Subsec. (a)(5)(A). Pub.L. 103–394, § 501(b)(3), substituted "section 557(b)" for "section 557(b)(1)", and "section 557(b)" for "section 557(b)(2)".

Subsec. (a)(5). Pub.L. 103–394, § 108(c)(2), substituted "but only to the extent of $4,000 for each such individual." for "but only to the extent of $2,000 for each such individual.".

Subsec. (a)(6). Pub.L. 103–394, § 108(c)(3), substituted "allowed unsecured claims of individuals, to the extent of $1,800 for each such individual," for "allowed unsecured claims of individuals, to the extent of $900 for each such individual,".

Subsec. (a)(7). Pub.L. 103–394, § 304(c)(2), (3), added par. (7). Former par. (7) redesignated (8).

Subsec. (a)(8). Pub.L. 103–394, § 304(c)(1), (2), redesignated former par. (7) as (8). Former par. (8) redesignated (9).

Subsec. (a)(9). Pub.L. 103–394, § 304(c)(1), redesignated former par. (8) as (9).

Pub.L. 103–394, § 501(d)(11)(A), substituted "a Federal depository institutions regulatory agency (or predecessor to such agency)" for "the Federal Deposit Insurance Corporation, the Resolution Trust Corporation, the Director of the Office of Thrift Supervision, the Comptroller of the Currency, or the Board of Governors of the Federal Reserve System, or their predecessors or successors,".

Subsec. (d). Pub.L. 103–394, § 501(d)(11)(B), inserted reference to (a)(7), (a)(8), or (a)(9), following reference to (a)(6).

1990 Amendments. Subsec. (a)(8). Pub.L. 101–647 added par. (8).

1984 Amendments. Subsec. (a)(3). Pub.L. 98–353, § 449(a)(1), added a comma following "severance".

Subsec. (a)(4). Pub.L. 98–353, § 449(a)(2), substituted "an employee benefit plan" for "employee benefit plans" in provisions preceding Subpar. (A).

Subsec. (a)(4)(B)(i). Pub.L. 98–353, § 449(a)(3), added "each" following "covered by".

Subsec. (a)(5). Pub.L. 98–353, § 350(3), added par. (5). Former par. (5) was redesignated as (6).

Subsec. (a)(6). Pub.L. 98–353, § 350(1), redesignated former par. (5) as (6) and, as so redesignated, substituted "Sixth" for "Fifth". Former par. (6) was redesignated as (7).

Subsec. (a)(7). Pub.L. 98–353, § 350(2), redesignated former par. (6) as (7) and, as so redesignated, substituted "Seventh" for "Sixth".

Pub.L. 98–353, § 449(a)(4), added "only" following "units,".

Subsec. (c). Pub.L. 98–353, § 449(b), substituted "has the same priority" for "shall be treated the same".

Effective and Applicability Provisions

2010 Acts. Except as otherwise specifically provided, Pub.L. 111–203 and such amendments by Pub.L. 111–203 are effective 1 day after July 21, 2010, see Pub.L. 111–203, § 4, set out as a note under 12 U.S.C.A. § 5301.

Increase of dollar amounts by Judicial Conference of the United States by notice published Feb. 25, 2010, 75 F.R. 8747 effective April 1, 2010, and increase not applicable to cases commenced before the effective date of the adjustments, i.e., April 1, 2010. See Adjustment of Dollar Amounts notes under 11 U.S.C.A. § 104 and this section.

2007 Acts. Increase of dollar amounts by Judicial Conference of the United States by notice published Feb. 14, 2007, 72 F.R. 7082 effective April 1, 2007, and increase not applicable to cases commenced before the effective date of the adjustments, i.e., April 1, 2007. See Adjustment of Dollar Amounts notes under 11 U.S.C.A. § 104 and this section.

2005 Acts. Pub.L. 109–8, Title XIV, § 1406, Apr. 20, 2005, 119 Stat. 215, as amended Pub.L. 111–327, § 3, Dec. 22, 2010, 124 Stat. 3563, provided that:

"(a) **Effective date.**—Except as provided in subsection (b) [of this note], this title and the amendments made by this title [amending this section and 11 U.S.C.A. §§ 523, 548, 1104, 1114, and enacting provisions set out as a note under 11 U.S.C.A. § 523] shall take effect on the date of the enactment of this Act [Apr. 20, 2005].

"(b) **Application of amendments.—**

"(1) **In general.**—Except as provided in paragraph (2), the amendments made by this title [amending this section and 11 U.S.C.A. §§ 523, 548, 1104, 1114, and enacting provisions set out as a note under 11 U.S.C.A. § 523] shall apply only with respect to cases commenced under title 11 of the United States Code [11 U.S.C.A. § 101 et seq.] on or after the date of the enactment of this Act [Apr. 20, 2005].

"(2) **Avoidance period.**—The amendment made by section 1402(1) [amending 11 U.S.C.A. § 548] shall apply only with respect to cases commenced under title 11 of the United States Code more than 1 year after the date of the enactment of this Act [Apr. 20, 2005]."

Amendments by Pub.L. 109–8 effective, except as otherwise provided, 180 days after April 20, 2005, and inapplicable with respect to cases commenced under Title 11 before the effective date, see Pub.L. 109–8, § 1501, set out as a note under 11 U.S.C.A. § 101.

2004 Acts. Adjustment of dollar amounts by Judicial Conference of the United States by notice dated Feb. 18, 2004, 69 F.R. 8482 effective April 1, 2004, and adjustment not applicable to cases commenced before the effective date of the adjustments, i.e., April 1, 2004. See Adjustment of Dollar Amounts notes under 11 U.S.C.A. § 104 and this section.

2001 Acts. Adjustment of dollar amounts by Judicial Conference of the United States by notice dated Feb. 20, 2001, 66 F.R. 10910 effective April 1, 2001, and adjustment not applicable to cases commenced before the effective date of the adjustments, i.e., April 1, 2001. See Adjustment of Dollar Amounts notes under 11 U.S.C.A. § 104 and this section.

1998 Acts. Adjustment of dollar amounts by Judicial Conference of the United States by notice dated Feb. 3, 1998, 63 F.R. 7179 effective April 1, 1998, and adjustment not applicable to cases commenced before the effective date of the adjustments, i.e., April 1, 1998. See Adjustment of Dollar Amounts notes under 11 U.S.C.A. § 104 and this section.

1994 Acts. Amendments by Pub.L. 103–394 effective on Oct. 22, 1994, and not to apply with respect to cases commenced under Title 11 of the United States Code before Oct. 22, 1994, see section 702 of Pub.L. 103–394, set out as a note under section 101 of this title.

1984 Acts. Amendment by Pub.L. 98–353 effective with respect to cases filed 90 days after July 10, 1984, see section 552(a), formerly 553(a) of Pub.L. 98–353, set out as a note under section 101 of this title.

Severability of Provisions

If any provision of Pub.L. 111–203, an amendment made by Pub.L. 111–203, or the application of such provision or amendment to any person or circumstance is held to be unconstitutional, the remainder of Pub.L. 111–203, the amendments made by Pub.L. 111–203, and the application of the provisions of such to any person or circumstance shall not be affected, see 12 U.S.C.A. § 5302.

If any provision of or amendment made by Pub.L. 103–394 or the application of such provision or amendment to any person or circumstance is held to be unconstitutional, the remaining provisions of and amendments made by Pub.L. 103–394 and the application of such provisions and amendments to any person or circumstance shall not be affected thereby, see section 701 of Pub.L. 103–394, set out as a note under section 101 of this title.

Adjustment of Dollar Amounts

For adjustment of dollar amounts specified in subsec. (a)(4), (5), (6), (7) of this section by the Judicial Conference of the United States, effective Apr. 1, 2010, see note set out under 11 U.S.C.A. § 104.

By notice dated Feb. 25, 2010, 75 F.R. 8747, the Judicial Conference of the United States adjusted the dollar amounts in provisions specified in subsec. (a)(4), (5), (6), (7) of this section, effective Apr. 1, 2010, as follows:

In subsec. (a)(4) adjusted $10,950 to $11,725.
In subsec. (a)(5) adjusted $10,950 to $11,725.
In subsec. (a)(6) adjusted $5,400 to $5,775.
In subsec. (a)(7) adjusted $2,425 to $2,600.

By notice dated Feb. 14, 2007, 72 F.R. 7082, the Judicial Conference of the United States adjusted the dollar amounts in provisions specified in subsec. (a)(4), (5), (6), (7) of this section, effective Apr. 1, 2007, as follows:

In subsec. (a)(4) adjusted $10,000 to $10,950.
In subsec. (a)(5) adjusted $10,000 to $10,950.
In subsec. (a)(6) adjusted $4,925 to $5,400.
In subsec. (a)(7) adjusted $2,225 to $2,425.

By notice dated Feb. 18, 2004, 69 F.R. 8482, the Judicial Conference of the United States adjusted the dollar amounts in provisions specified in subsec. (a)(3), (4)(B)(i), (5), (6) of this section, effective Apr. 1, 2004, as follows:

In subsec. (a)(3) adjusted $4,650 to $4,925.
In subsec. (a)(4)(B)(i) adjusted $4,650 to $4,925.
In subsec. (a)(5) adjusted $4,650 to $4,925.
In subsec. (a)(6) adjusted $2,100 to $2,225.

By notice dated Feb. 20, 2001, 66 F.R. 10910, the Judicial Conference of the United States adjusted the dollar amounts in provisions specified in subsec. (a)(3), (4)(B)(i), (5), (6) of this section, effective Apr. 1, 2001, as follows:

In subsec. (a)(3) adjusted $4,300 to $4,650.
In subsec. (a)(4)(B)(i) adjusted $4,300 to $4,650.
In subsec. (a)(5) adjusted $4,300 to $4,650.
In subsec. (a)(6) adjusted $1,950 to $2,100.

By notice dated Feb. 3, 1998, 63 F.R. 7179, the Judicial Conference of the United States adjusted the dollar amounts in provisions specified in subsec. (a)(3), (4)(B)(i), (5), (6) of this section, effective Apr. 1, 1998, as follows:

In subsec. (a)(3) adjusted $4,000 to $4,300.
In subsec. (a)(4)(B)(i) adjusted $4,000 to $4,300.
In subsec. (a)(5) adjusted $4,000 to $4,300.
In subsec. (a)(6) adjusted $1,800 to $1,950.

CROSS REFERENCES

Applicability of subsec. (a)(1) of this section in Chapter 9 cases, see 11 USCA § 901.

Confirmation upon payment of administrative expenses, fees, and charges, see 11 USCA § 943.

Contents of plan in—

Chapter 13 cases, see 11 USCA § 1322.

Chapter 12 cases, see 11 USCA § 1222.

Designation by plan of classes of claims, see 11 USCA § 1123.

Distribution of—

Certain estate property subject to liens, see 11 USCA § 724.

Customer property in commodity broker liquidation cases, see 11 USCA § 766.

Customer property in stockbroker liquidation cases, see 11 USCA § 752.

Property of estate, see 11 USCA § 726.

Executory contracts and unexpired leases, see 11 USCA § 365.

Involuntary cases future adjustments, see 11 USCA § 104.

Proof of claim, see Official Bankr. Form 10, 11 USCA.

Recoupment of funds advanced by Securities Investor Protection Corporation as priority administrative expense, see 15 USCA § 78fff.

Tax or customs duty excepted from discharge, see 11 USCA § 523.

Time of payment of administrative expenses, fees and charges in—

Chapter 13 cases, see 11 USCA § 1326.

Chapter 12 cases, see 11 USCA § 1226.

Treatment of certain claims as affecting confirmation of plan, see 11 USCA § 1129.

Unsecured debt having priority over certain administrative expenses, see 11 USCA § 364.

Unsecured priority claims, see Official Bankr. Form 6, 11 USCA.

LIBRARY REFERENCES

American Digest System

Bankruptcy ☞2951 to 2972, 2823.

Key Number System Topic No. 51.

Corpus Juris Secundum

CJS Bankruptcy § 752, Right of Seller of Goods.

CJS Bankruptcy § 773, Status of Claims for Compensation and Reimbursement.

CJS Bankruptcy § 895, Unsecured Credit or Debt in Ordinary Course of Business.

CJS Bankruptcy § 897, Credit With Special Administrative Priority or Secured by First Liens or Junior Liens.

CJS Bankruptcy § 985, Domestic Relations Claims.

CJS Bankruptcy § 986, Claims Arising in Ordinary Course of Debtor's Business.

CJS Bankruptcy § 987, Wage, Salary, and Commission Claims.

CJS Bankruptcy § 988, Employee Benefit Plan Contributions.

CJS Bankruptcy § 989, Grain and Fish Claims.

CJS Bankruptcy § 990, Consumer Deposits.

CJS Bankruptcy § 991, Commitment to Maintain Depository Institution Capital.

CJS Bankruptcy § 992, Wrongful Death and Personal Injury Claims.

CJS Bankruptcy § 994, Superpriority Administrative Expense.

CJS Bankruptcy § 996, Income and Gross Receipts Taxes.

CJS Bankruptcy § 997, Taxes on Wages, Salaries, and Commissions.

CJS Bankruptcy § 998, Excise Taxes.

CJS Bankruptcy § 999, Customs Duties.

CJS Bankruptcy § 1000, Interest and Penalties.

CJS Bankruptcy § 1064, Debt for Tax or Customs Duty.

CJS Bankruptcy § 1102, Priority of Particular Distribution Classes.

CJS Bankruptcy § 1103, Community Property.

CJS Bankruptcy § 1104, Tax Liens and Other Statutory Liens.

CJS Bankruptcy § 1121, Requirements for Confirmation.

CJS Bankruptcy § 1142, Preservation of Priority.

CJS Bankruptcy § 1170, Filing and Contents of Plan, Generally.

CJS Bankruptcy § 1189, Contents of Plan, Generally.

CJS Bankruptcy § 1195, Amount of Repayment of Unsecured Claims.

CJS Bankruptcy § 1196, Amount of Repayment of Unsecured Claims--Interest.

CJS Bankruptcy § 1208, Discharge.

CJS Receivers § 315, Claims of Political Entities Other Than for Taxes--Debts Due to United States.

§ 508. Effect of distribution other than under this title

If a creditor of a partnership debtor receives, from a general partner that is not a debtor in a case under chapter 7 of this title, payment of, or a transfer of property on account of, a claim that is allowed under this title and that is not secured by a lien on property of such partner, such creditor may not receive any payment under this title on account of such claim until each of the other holders of claims on account of which such holders are entitled to share equally with such creditor under this title has received payment under this title equal in value to the consideration received by such creditor from such general partner.

(Pub.L. 95–598, Nov. 6, 1978, 92 Stat. 2585; Pub.L. 109–8, Title VIII, § 802(d)(7), Apr. 20, 2005, 119 Stat. 146.)

HISTORICAL AND STATUTORY NOTES

Revision Notes and Legislative Reports

1978 Acts. This section prohibits a creditor from receiving any distribution in the bankruptcy case if he has received payment of a portion of his claim in a foreign proceeding, until the other creditors in the bankruptcy case in this country that are entitled to share equally with that creditor have received as much as he has in the foreign proceeding. Senate Report No. 95–989.

2005 Acts. House Report No. 109–31(Part I), see 2005 U.S. Code Cong. and Adm. News, p. 88.

Legislative Statements

Section 508(b) of the House amendment is new and provides an identical rule with respect to a creditor of a partnership who receives payment from a partner, to that of a creditor of a debtor who receives a payment in a foreign proceeding involving the debtor.

Amendments

2005 Amendments. Subsec. (a). Pub.L. 109–8, § 802(d)(7)(A), struck out subsec. (a), which formerly read: "**(a)** If a creditor receives, in a foreign proceeding, payment of, or a transfer of property on account of, a claim that is allowed under this title, such creditor may not receive any payment under this title on account of such claim until each of the other holders of claims on account of which such holders are entitled to share equally with such creditor under this title has received payment under this title equal in value to the consideration received by such creditor in such foreign proceeding."

Subsec. (b). Pub.L. 109–8, § 802(d)(7)(B), struck out "**(b)**".

Effective and Applicability Provisions

2005 Acts. Amendments by Pub.L. 109–8 effective, except as otherwise provided, 180 days after April 20, 2005, and inapplicable with respect to cases commenced under Title 11 before the effective date, see Pub.L. 109–8, § 1501, set out as a note under 11 U.S.C.A. § 101.

LIBRARY REFERENCES

American Digest System

Bankruptcy ☞2964, 2837.

Key Number System Topic No. 51.

Corpus Juris Secundum

CJS Bankruptcy § 984, Effect of Distribution Outside of Bankruptcy.

§ 509. Claims of codebtors

(a) Except as provided in subsection (b) or (c) of this section, an entity that is liable with the debtor on, or that has secured, a claim of a creditor against the debtor, and that pays such claim, is subrogated to the rights of such creditor to the extent of such payment.

(b) Such entity is not subrogated to the rights of such creditor to the extent that—

   (1) a claim of such entity for reimbursement or contribution on account of such payment of such creditor's claim is—

      (A) allowed under section 502 of this title;

      (B) disallowed other than under section 502(e) of this title; or

      (C) subordinated under section 510 of this title; or

   (2) as between the debtor and such entity, such entity received the consideration for the claim held by such creditor.

(c) The court shall subordinate to the claim of a creditor and for the benefit of such creditor an allowed claim, by way of subrogation under this section, or for reimbursement or contribution, of an entity that is liable with the debtor on, or that has secured, such creditor's claim, until such creditor's claim is paid in full, either through payments under this title or otherwise.

(Pub.L. 95–598, Nov. 6, 1978, 92 Stat. 2585; Pub.L. 98–353, Title III, § 450, July 10, 1984, 98 Stat. 375.)

HISTORICAL AND STATUTORY NOTES

Revision Notes and Legislative Reports

1978 Acts. Section 509 deals with codebtors generally, and is in addition to the disallowance provision in section 502(e). This section is based on the notion that the only rights available to a surety, guarantor, or comaker are contribution, reimbursement, and subrogation. The right that applies in a particular situation will depend on the agreement between the debtor and the codebtor, and on whether and how payment was made by the codebtor to the creditor. The claim of a surety or codebtor for contribution or reimbursement is discharged even if the claim is never filed, as is any claim for subrogation even if the surety or codebtor chooses to file a claim for contribution or reimbursement instead.

Subsection (a) subrogates the codebtor (whether as a codebtor, surety, or guarantor) to the rights of the creditor, to the extent of any payment made by the codebtor to the creditor. Whether the creditor's claim was filed under section 501(a) or 501(b) is irrelevant. The right of subrogation will exist even if the primary creditor's claim is allowed by virtue of being listed under proposed 11 U.S.C. 924 or 1111, and not by reason of a proof of claim.

Subsection (b) permits a subrogated codebtor to receive payments in the bankruptcy case only if the creditor has been paid in full, either through payments under the bankruptcy code or otherwise. Senate Report No. 95–989.

1984 Acts. Statements by Legislative Leaders, see 1984 U.S.Code Cong. and Adm.News, p. 576.

Legislative Statements

Section 509 of the House amendment represents a substantial revision of provisions contained in H.R. 8200 as passed by the House and in the Senate amendment. Section 509(a) states a general rule that a surety or co-debtor is subrogated to the rights of a creditor assured by the surety or codebtor to the extent the surety or codebtor pays such creditor. Section 509(b) states a general exception indicating that subrogation is not granted to the extent that a claim of a surety or co-debtor for reimbursement or contribution is allowed under section 502 or disallowed other than under section 502(e). Additionally, section 509(b)(1)(C) provides that such claims for subrogation are subordinated to the extent that a claim of the surety or co-debtor for reimbursement or contribution is subordinated under section 510(a)(1) or 510(b). Section 509(b)(2) reiterates the well-known rule that prevents a debtor that is ultimately liable on the debt from recovering from a surety or a co-debtor. Although the language in section 509(b)(2) focuses in terms of receipt of consideration, legislative history appearing elsewhere indicates that an agreement to share liabilities should prevail over an agreement to share profits throughout title 11. This is particularly important in the context of codebtors who are partners. Section 509(c) subordinates the claim of a surety or co-debtor to the claim of an assured creditor until the creditor's claim is paid in full.

Amendments

1984 Amendments. Subsec. (a). Pub.L. 98–353, § 450(a)(1), substituted "subsection (b) or" for "subsections (b) and".

Pub.L. 98–353, § 450(a)(2), added, "against the debtor" following "a creditor".

Subsec. (b)(1). Pub.L. 98–353, § 450(b), substituted "of such" for "of a" following "account".

Subsec. (c). Pub.L. 98–353, § 450(c) substituted "this section" for "section 509 of this title".

Effective and Applicability Provisions

1984 Acts. Amendment by Pub.L. 98–353 effective with respect to cases filed 90 days after July 10, 1984, see section 552(a), formerly 553(a) of Pub.L. 98–353, set out as a note under section 101 of this title.

CROSS REFERENCES

Applicability of this section in Chapter 9 cases, see 11 USCA § 901.

LIBRARY REFERENCES

American Digest System

Bankruptcy ⬭2823, 2967.1.
Key Number System Topic No. 51.

Corpus Juris Secundum

CJS Bankruptcy § 963, Co-Debtors, Sureties, and Subrogation.

§ 510. Subordination

(a) A subordination agreement is enforceable in a case under this title to the same extent that such agreement is enforceable under applicable nonbankruptcy law.

(b) For the purpose of distribution under this title, a claim arising from rescission of a purchase or sale of a security of the debtor or of an affiliate of the debtor, for damages arising from the purchase or sale of such a security, or for reimbursement or contribution allowed under section 502 on account of such a claim, shall be subordinated to all claims or interests that are senior to or equal the claim or interest represented by such security, except that if such security is common stock, such claim has the same priority as common stock.

(c) Notwithstanding subsections (a) and (b) of this section, after notice and a hearing, the court may—

(1) under principles of equitable subordination, subordinate for purposes of distribution all or part of an allowed claim to all or part of another allowed claim or all or part of an allowed interest to all or part of another allowed interest; or

(2) order that any lien securing such a subordinated claim be transferred to the estate.

(Pub.L. 95–598, Nov. 6, 1978, 92 Stat. 2586; Pub.L. 98–353, Title III, § 451, July 10, 1984, 98 Stat. 375.)

HISTORICAL AND STATUTORY NOTES

Revision Notes and Legislative Reports

1978 Acts. Subsection (a) requires the court to enforce subordination agreements. A subordination agreement will not be enforced, however, in a reorganization case in which the class that is the beneficiary of the agreement has accepted, as specified in proposed 11 U.S.C. 1126, a plan that waives their rights under the agreement. Otherwise, the agreement would prevent just what chapter 11 contemplates: that seniors may give up rights to juniors in the interest of confirmation of a plan and rehabilitation of the debtor. The subsection also requires the court to subordinate in payment any claim for rescission of a purchase or sale of a security of the debtor or of an affiliate, or for damages arising from the purchase or sale of such a security, to all claims and interests that are senior to the claim or interest represented by the security. Thus, the later subordination varies with the claim or interest involved. If the security is a debt instrument, the damages or rescission claim will be granted the status of a general unsecured claim. If the security is an equity security, the damages or rescission claim is subordinated to all creditors and treated the same as the equity security itself.

Subsection (b) authorizes the bankruptcy court, in ordering distribution of assets, to subordinate all or any part of any claim to all or any part of another claim, regardless of the priority ranking of either claim. In addition, any lien securing such a subordinated claim may be transferred to the estate. The bill provides, however, that any subordination ordered under this provision must be based on principles of equitable subordination. These principles are defined by case law, and have generally indicated that a claim may normally be subordinated only if its holder is guilty of misconduct. As originally introduced, the bill provided specifically that a tax claim may not be subordinated on equitable grounds. The bill deletes this express exception, but the effect under the amendment should be much the same in most situations since, under the judicial doctrine of equitable subordination, a tax claim would rarely be subordinated. Senate Report No. 95–989.

1984 Acts. Statements by Legislative Leaders, see 1984 U.S.Code Cong. and Adm.News, p. 576.

Legislative Statements

Section 510(c)(1) of the House amendment represents a compromise between similar provisions in the House bill and Senate amendment. After notice and a hearing, the court may, under principles of equitable subordination, subordinate for purposes of distribution all or part of an allowed claim to all or part of another allowed claim or all or part of an allowed interest to all or part of another allowed interest. As a matter of equity, it is reasonable that a court subordinate claims to claims and interests to interests. It is intended that the term "principles of equitable subordination" follow existing case law and leave to the courts development of this principle. To date, under existing law, a claim is generally subordinated only if holder of such claim is guilty of inequitable conduct, or the claim itself is of a status susceptible to subordination, such as a penalty or a claim for damages arising from the purchase or sale of a security of the debtor. The fact that such a claim may be secured is of no consequence to the issue of subordination. However, it is inconceivable that the status of a claim as a secured claim could ever be grounds for justifying equitable subordination.

Subordination: Since the House amendment authorizes subordination of claims only under principles of equitable subordination, and thus incorporates principles of existing case law, a tax claim would rarely be subordinated under this provision of the bill.

Section 511 of the Senate amendment is deleted. Its substance is adopted in section 502(b)(9) of the House amendment which reflects an identical provision contained in H.R. 8200 as passed by the House.

Amendments

1984 Amendments. Subsec. (b). Pub.L. 98–353 substituted "For the purpose of distribution under this title, a claim arising from rescission of a purchase or sale of a security of the debtor or of an affiliate of the debtor, for damages arising from the purchase or sale of such a security, or for reimbursement or contribution allowed under section 502 on account of such a claim, shall be subordinated to all claims or interests that are senior to or equal the claim or interest represented by such security, except that if such security is common stock, such claim has the same priority as common stock." for "Any claim for recission of a purchase or sale of a security of the debtor or of an affiliate or for damages arising from the purchase or sale of such a security shall be subordinated for purposes of distribution to all claims and interests that are senior or equal to the claim or interest represented by such security.".

Effective and Applicability Provisions

1984 Acts. Amendment by Pub.L. 98–353 effective with respect to cases filed 90 days after July 10, 1984, see section 552(a), formerly 553(a) of Pub.L. 98–353, set out as a note under section 101 of this title.

CROSS REFERENCES

Applicability of this section in Chapter 9 cases, see 11 USCA § 901.

Certain customer claims in stockbroker liquidation proceedings, see 11 USCA § 747.

Confirmation of plan, see 11 USCA § 1129.

Distribution of—

Customer property, see 11 USCA § 752.

Property of estate, see 11 USCA § 726.

Effect of dismissal, see 11 USCA § 349.

Property of estate, see 11 USCA § 541.

Property recoverable by trustee as exempt, see 11 USCA § 522.

Unpaid portion of certain claims as entitled to distribution, see 11 USCA § 766.

LIBRARY REFERENCES

American Digest System

Bankruptcy ⟞2967.1 to 2970, 2972.

Key Number System Topic No. 51.

Corpus Juris Secundum

CJS Bankruptcy § 278, Parties Defendant; Sovereign Immunity.

CJS Bankruptcy § 589, Property Debtor Could Have Exempted Absent Transfer of that Property.

CJS Bankruptcy § 1002, Circumstances Justifying Equitable Subordination.

CJS Bankruptcy § 1004, Recharacterization of Debt.

CJS Bankruptcy § 1005, Claim Arising from Purchase or Sale of Security.

CJS Bankruptcy § 1006, Subordination Agreements.

CJS Bankruptcy § 1102, Priority of Particular Distribution Classes.

CJS Bankruptcy § 1147, Generally; Fairness and Equity.

§ 511.   Rate of interest on tax claims

(a) If any provision of this title requires the payment of interest on a tax claim or on an administrative expense tax, or the payment of interest to enable a creditor to receive the present value of the allowed amount of a tax claim, the rate of interest shall be the rate determined under applicable nonbankruptcy law.

(b) In the case of taxes paid under a confirmed plan under this title, the rate of interest shall be determined as of the calendar month in which the plan is confirmed.

(Added Pub.L. 109–8, Title VII, § 704(a), Apr. 20, 2005, 119 Stat. 125.)

HISTORICAL AND STATUTORY NOTES

Revision Notes and Legislative Reports

2005 Acts. House Report No. 109–31(Part I), see 2005 U.S. Code Cong. and Adm. News, p. 88.

Effective and Applicability Provisions

2005 Acts. Section effective, except as otherwise provided, 180 days after April 20, 2005, and inapplicable with respect to cases commenced under Title 11 before the effective date, see Pub.L. 109–8, § 1501, set out as a note under 11 U.S.C.A. § 101.

SUBCHAPTER II—DEBTOR'S DUTIES AND BENEFITS

§ 521.   Debtor's duties

(a) The debtor shall—

  (1) file—

    (A) a list of creditors; and

    (B) unless the court orders otherwise—

      (i) a schedule of assets and liabilities;

      (ii) a schedule of current income and current expenditures;

      (iii) a statement of the debtor's financial affairs and, if section 342(b) applies, a certificate—

        (I) of an attorney whose name is indicated on the petition as the attorney for the debtor, or a bankruptcy petition preparer signing the petition under section 110(b)(1), indicating that such attorney or the bankruptcy petition preparer delivered to the debtor the notice required by section 342(b); or

        (II) if no attorney is so indicated, and no bankruptcy petition preparer signed the petition, of the debtor that such notice was received and read by the debtor;

(iv) copies of all payment advices or other evidence of payment received within 60 days before the date of the filing of the petition, by the debtor from any employer of the debtor;

(v) a statement of the amount of monthly net income, itemized to show how the amount is calculated; and

(vi) a statement disclosing any reasonably anticipated increase in income or expenditures over the 12–month period following the date of the filing of the petition;

(2) if an individual debtor's schedule of assets and liabilities includes debts which are secured by property of the estate—

(A) within thirty days after the date of the filing of a petition under chapter 7 of this title or on or before the date of the meeting of creditors, whichever is earlier, or within such additional time as the court, for cause, within such period fixes, file with the clerk a statement of his intention with respect to the retention or surrender of such property and, if applicable, specifying that such property is claimed as exempt, that the debtor intends to redeem such property, or that the debtor intends to reaffirm debts secured by such property; and

(B) within 30 days after the first date set for the meeting of creditors under section 341(a), or within such additional time as the court, for cause, within such 30–day period fixes, perform his intention with respect to such property, as specified by subparagraph (A) of this paragraph;

except that nothing in subparagraphs (A) and (B) of this paragraph shall alter the debtor's or the trustee's rights with regard to such property under this title, except as provided in section 362(h);

(3) if a trustee is serving in the case or an auditor is serving under section 586(f) of title 28, cooperate with the trustee as necessary to enable the trustee to perform the trustee's duties under this title;

(4) if a trustee is serving in the case or an auditor is serving under section 586(f) of title 28, surrender to the trustee all property of the estate and any recorded information, including books, documents, records, and papers, relating to property of the estate, whether or not immunity is granted under section 344 of this title;

(5) appear at the hearing required under section 524(d) of this title;

(6) in a case under chapter 7 of this title in which the debtor is an individual, not retain possession of personal property as to which a creditor has an allowed claim for the purchase price secured in whole or in part by an interest in such personal property unless the debtor, not later than 45 days after the first meeting of creditors under section 341(a), either—

(A) enters into an agreement with the creditor pursuant to section 524(c) with respect to the claim secured by such property; or

(B) redeems such property from the security interest pursuant to section 722; and

(7) unless a trustee is serving in the case, continue to perform the obligations required of the administrator (as defined in section 3 of the Employee Retirement Income Security Act of 1974) of an employee benefit plan if at the time of the commencement of the case the debtor (or any entity designated by the debtor) served as such administrator.

If the debtor fails to so act within the 45–day period referred to in paragraph (6), the stay under section 362(a) is terminated with respect to the personal property of the estate or of the debtor which is affected, such property shall no longer be property of the estate, and the creditor may take whatever action as to such property as is permitted by applicable nonbankruptcy law, unless the court determines on the motion of the trustee filed before the expiration of such 45–day period, and after notice and a hearing, that such property is of consequential value or benefit to the estate, orders appropriate adequate protection of the creditor's interest, and orders the debtor to deliver any collateral in the debtor's possession to the trustee.

(b) In addition to the requirements under subsection (a), a debtor who is an individual shall file with the court—

(1) a certificate from the approved nonprofit budget and credit counseling agency that provided the debtor services under section 109(h) describing the services provided to the debtor; and

(2) a copy of the debt repayment plan, if any, developed under section 109(h) through the approved nonprofit budget and credit counseling agency referred to in paragraph (1).

(c) In addition to meeting the requirements under subsection (a), a debtor shall file with the court a record of any interest that a debtor has in an education individual retirement account (as defined in section 530(b)(1) of the Internal Revenue Code of 1986) or under a qualified State tuition program (as defined in section 529(b)(1) of such Code).

(d) If the debtor fails timely to take the action specified in subsection (a)(6) of this section, or in paragraphs (1) and (2) of section 362(h), with respect to property which a lessor or bailor owns and has leased, rented, or bailed to the debtor or as to which a creditor holds a security interest not otherwise voidable under section 522(f), 544, 545, 547, 548, or 549, nothing in this title shall prevent or limit the operation of a provision in the underlying lease or agreement that has the effect of placing the debtor in default under such lease or agreement by reason of the occurrence, pendency, or existence of a proceeding under this title or the insolvency of the debtor. Nothing in this subsection shall be deemed to justify limiting such a provision in any other circumstance.

(e)(1) If the debtor in a case under chapter 7 or 13 is an individual and if a creditor files with the court at any time a request to receive a copy of the petition, schedules, and statement of financial affairs filed by the debtor, then the court shall make such petition, such schedules, and such statement available to such creditor.

(2)(A) The debtor shall provide—

(i) not later than 7 days before the date first set for the first meeting of creditors, to the trustee a copy of the Federal income tax return required under applicable law (or at the election of the debtor, a transcript of such return) for the most recent tax year ending immediately before the commencement of the case and for which a Federal income tax return was filed; and

(ii) at the same time the debtor complies with clause (i), a copy of such return (or if elected under clause (i), such transcript) to any creditor that timely requests such copy.

(B) If the debtor fails to comply with clause (i) or (ii) of subparagraph (A), the court shall dismiss the case unless the debtor demonstrates that the failure to so comply is due to circumstances beyond the control of the debtor.

(C) If a creditor requests a copy of such tax return or such transcript and if the debtor fails to provide a copy of such tax return or such transcript to such creditor at the time the debtor provides such tax return or such transcript to the trustee, then the court shall dismiss the case unless the debtor demonstrates that the failure to provide a copy of such tax return or such transcript is due to circumstances beyond the control of the debtor.

(3) If a creditor in a case under chapter 13 files with the court at any time a request to receive a copy of the plan filed by the debtor, then the court shall make available to such creditor a copy of the plan—

(A) at a reasonable cost; and

(B) not later than 7 days after such request is filed.

(f) At the request of the court, the United States trustee, or any party in interest in a case under chapter 7, 11, or 13, a debtor who is an individual shall file with the court—

(1) at the same time filed with the taxing authority, a copy of each Federal income tax return required under applicable law (or at the election of the debtor, a transcript of such tax return) with respect to each tax year of the debtor ending while the case is pending under such chapter;

(2) at the same time filed with the taxing authority, each Federal income tax return required under applicable law (or at the election of the debtor, a transcript of such tax return) that had not been filed with such authority as of the date of the commencement of the case and that was subsequently filed for any tax year of the debtor ending in the 3–year period ending on the date of the commencement of the case;

(3) a copy of each amendment to any Federal income tax return or transcript filed with the court under paragraph (1) or (2); and

(4) in a case under chapter 13—

(A) on the date that is either 90 days after the end of such tax year or 1 year after the date of the commencement of the case, whichever is later, if a plan is not confirmed before such later date; and

(B) annually after the plan is confirmed and until the case is closed, not later than the date that is 45 days before the anniversary of the confirmation of the plan;

a statement, under penalty of perjury, of the income and expenditures of the debtor during the tax year of the debtor most recently concluded before such statement is filed under this paragraph, and of the monthly income of the debtor, that shows how income, expenditures, and monthly income are calculated.

(g)(1) A statement referred to in subsection (f)(4) shall disclose—

(A) the amount and sources of the income of the debtor;

(B) the identity of any person responsible with the debtor for the support of any dependent of the debtor; and

(C) the identity of any person who contributed, and the amount contributed, to the household in which the debtor resides.

(2) The tax returns, amendments, and statement of income and expenditures described in subsections (e)(2)(A) and (f) shall be available to the United States trustee (or the bankruptcy administrator, if any), the trustee, and any party in interest for inspection and copying, subject to the requirements of section 315(c) of the Bankruptcy Abuse Prevention and Consumer Protection Act of 2005.

(h) If requested by the United States trustee or by the trustee, the debtor shall provide—

(1) a document that establishes the identity of the debtor, including a driver's license, passport, or other document that contains a photograph of the debtor; or

(2) such other personal identifying information relating to the debtor that establishes the identity of the debtor.

(i)(1) Subject to paragraphs (2) and (4) and notwithstanding section 707(a), if an individual debtor in a voluntary case under chapter 7 or 13 fails to file all of the information required under subsection (a)(1) within 45 days after the date of the filing of the petition, the case shall be automatically dismissed effective on the 46th day after the date of the filing of the petition.

(2) Subject to paragraph (4) and with respect to a case described in paragraph (1), any party in interest may request the court to enter an order dismissing the case. If requested, the court shall enter an order of dismissal not later than 7 days after such request.

(3) Subject to paragraph (4) and upon request of the debtor made within 45 days after the date of the filing of the petition described in paragraph (1), the court may allow the debtor an additional period of not to exceed 45 days to file the information required under subsection (a)(1) if the court finds justification for extending the period for the filing.

(4) Notwithstanding any other provision of this subsection, on the motion of the trustee filed before the expiration of the applicable period of time specified in paragraph (1), (2), or (3), and after notice and a hearing, the court may decline to dismiss the case if the court finds that the debtor attempted in good faith to file all the information required by subsection (a)(1)(B)(iv) and that the best interests of creditors would be served by administration of the case.

(j)(1) Notwithstanding any other provision of this title, if the debtor fails to file a tax return that becomes due after the commencement of the case or to properly obtain an extension of the due date for filing such return, the taxing authority may request that the court enter an order converting or dismissing the case.

(2) If the debtor does not file the required return or obtain the extension referred to in paragraph (1) within 90 days after a request is filed by the taxing authority under that paragraph, the court shall convert or dismiss the case, whichever is in the best interests of creditors and the estate.

(Pub.L. 95–598, Nov. 6, 1978, 92 Stat. 2586; Pub.L. 98–353, Title III, §§ 305, 452, July 10, 1984, 98 Stat. 352, 375; Pub.L. 99–554, Title II, § 283(h), Oct. 27, 1986, 100 Stat. 3117; Pub.L. 109–8, Title I, § 106(d), Title II, § 225(b), Title III, §§ 304(1), 305(2), 315(b), 316, Title IV, § 446(a), Title VI, § 603(c), Title VII, § 720, Apr. 20, 2005, 119 Stat. 38, 66, 78, 80, 89, 90, 92, 118, 123, 133; Pub.L. 111–16, § 2(5), (6), May 7, 2009, 123 Stat. 1607; Pub.L. 111–327, § 2(a)(16), Dec. 22, 2010, 124 Stat. 3559.)

HISTORICAL AND STATUTORY NOTES

Revision Notes and Legislative Reports

1978 Acts. This section lists three duties of the debtor in a bankruptcy case. The Rules of Bankruptcy Procedure will specify the means of carrying out these duties. The first duty is to file with the court a list of creditors and, unless the court orders otherwise, a schedule of assets and liabilities and a statement of his financial affairs. Second, the debtor is required to cooperate with the trustee as necessary to enable the trustee to perform the trustee's duties. Finally, the debtor must surrender to the trustee all property of the estate, and any recorded information, including books, documents, records, and papers, relating to property of the estate. This phrase "recorded information, including books, documents, records, and papers," has been used here and throughout the bill as a more general term, and includes such other forms of recorded information as date in computer storage or in other machine readable forms.

The list in this section is not exhaustive of the debtor's duties. Others are listed elsewhere in proposed title 11, such as in section 343, which requires the debtor to submit to examination, or in the Rules of Bankruptcy Procedure, as continued by § 404(a) of S. 2266, such as the duty to attend any hearing on discharge, Rule 402(2). Senate Reports 95–989.

1984 Acts. Statements by Legislative Leaders, see 1984 U.S.Code Cong. and Adm.News, p. 576.

1986 Acts. House Report No. 99–764 and House Conference Report No. 99–958, see 1986 U.S.Code Cong. and Adm. News, p. 5227.

2005 Acts. House Report No. 109–31(Part I), see 2005 U.S. Code Cong. and Adm. News, p. 88.

Legislative Statements

Section 521 of the House amendment modifies a comparable provision contained in the House bill and Senate amendment. The Rules of Bankruptcy Procedure should provide where the list of creditors is to be filed. In addition, the debtor is required to attend the hearing on discharge under section 524(d).

References in Text

Chapter 7, referred to in text, is chapter 7 of this title, 11 U.S.C.A. § 701 et seq.

Chapter 13, referred to in text, is chapter 13 of this title, 11 U.S.C.A. § 1301 et seq.

Section 3 of the Employee Retirement Income Security Act of 1974, referred to in subsec. (a)(7), is Pub.L. 93–406, Title I, § 3, Sept. 2, 1974, 88 Stat. 833, which is classified to 29 U.S.C.A. § 1002.

Section 530(b)(1) of the Internal Revenue Code of 1986, referred to in subsec. (c), is classified to 26 U.S.C.A. § 530(b)(1).

Section 529(b)(1) of such Code, referred to in subsec. (c), is classified to 26 U.S.C.A. § 529(b)(1).

Chapter 11, referred to in subsec. (f), is chapter 11 of this title, 11 U.S.C.A. § 1101 et seq.

Section 315(c) of the Bankruptcy Abuse Prevention and Consumer Protection Act of 2005, referred to in subsec. (g)(2), is Pub.L. 109–8, Title III, § 315(c), Apr. 20, 2005, 119 Stat. 91, which is set out as a note under this section.

Amendments

2010 Amendments. Subsec. (a)(2)(A). Pub.L. 111–327, § 2(a)(16)(A)(i), struck out "the debtor shall" following "such period fixes;", and inserted "and" after the semicolon at the end.

Subsec. (a)(2)(B). Pub.L. 111–327, § 2(a)(16)(A)(ii), struck out "the debtor shall" following "30–day period fixes,", and struck out "and" following the semicolon at the end.

Subsec. (a)(2)(C). Pub.L. 111–327, § 2(a)(16)(A)(iii), struck out the designator "(C)" and inserted except that".

Subsec. (a)(3). Pub.L. 111–327, § 2(a)(16)(B), inserted "is" following "auditor".

Subsec. (a)(4). Pub.L. 111–327, § 2(a)(16)(B), inserted "is" following "auditor".

2009 Amendments. Subsec. (e)(3)(B). Pub.L. 111–16, § 2(5), struck out "5 days" and inserted "7 days".

Subsec. (i)(2). Pub.L. 111–16, § 2(6), struck out "5 days" and inserted "7 days".

2005 Amendments. Subsec. (a). Pub.L. 109–8, § 106(d)(1), inserted "**(a)**" before "The debtor shall—".

Pub.L. 109–8, § 304(1)(C), added concluding provisions.

Subsec. (a)(1). Pub.L. 109–8, § 315(b)(1), rewrote par. (1), which formerly read: "**(1)** file a list of creditors, and unless the court orders otherwise, a schedule of assets and liabilities, a schedule of current income and current expenditures, and a statement of the debtor's financial affairs;"

Subsec. (a)(2). Pub.L. 109–8, § 305(2)(A), struck out "consumer" preceding "debts which are secured by".

Subsec. (a)(2)(B). Pub.L. 109–8, § 305(2)(B)(i), struck out "forty-five days after the filing of a notice of intent under this section" and inserted "30 days after the first date set for the meeting of creditors under section 341(a)".

Pub.L. 109–8, § 305(2)(B)(ii), struck out "forty-five day" and inserted "30–day".

Subsec. (a)(2)(C). Pub.L. 109–8, § 305(2)(C), inserted ", except as provided in section 362(h)" before the semicolon.

Subsec. (a)(3). Pub.L. 109–8, § 603(c), inserted "or an auditor serving under section 586(f) of title 28" after "serving in the case".

Subsec. (a)(4). Pub.L. 109–8, § 304(1)(A), struck out ", and" at the end of par. (4) and inserted a semicolon.

Pub.L. 109–8, § 603(c), inserted "or an auditor serving under section 586(f) of title 28" after "serving in the case".

Subsec. (a)(5). Pub.L. 109–8, § 304(1)(B), struck out the period at the end of par. (5) and inserted "; and".

Pub.L. 109–8, § 446(a)(1), struck "and" at the end of par. (5).

Subsec. (a)(6). Pub.L. 109–8, § 304(1)(C), added par. (6).

Pub.L. 109–8, § 446(a)(2), struck the period at the end of par. (6) and inserted "; and".

Subsec. (a)(7). Pub.L. 109–8, § 446(a)(3), added par. (7).

Subsec. (b). Pub.L. 109–8, § 106(d)(2), added subsec. (b).

Subsec. (c). Pub.L. 109–8, § 225(b), added subsec. (c).

Subsec. (d). Pub.L. 109–8, § 305(2)(D), added subsec. (d).

Subsecs. (e) to (h). Pub.L. 109–8, § 315(b)(2), added subsecs. (e), (f), (g), and (h).

Subsec. (i). Pub.L. 109–8, § 316, added subsec. (i).

Subsec. (j). Pub.L. 109–8, § 720, added subsec. (j).

1986 Amendments. Par. (4). Pub.L. 99–554 added provisions relating to granting of immunity under section 344 of this title.

1984 Amendments. Par. (1). Pub.L. 98–353, § 305(2), added "a schedule of current income and current expenditures," following "liabilities,".

Par. (2). Pub.L. 98–353, § 305(3), added par. (2). Former par. (2) was redesignated as (3).

Par. (3). Pub.L. 98–353, § 305(1), redesignated former par. (2) as (3). Former par. (3) was redesignated as (4).

Pub.L. 98–353, § 452, which directed the insertion of ", whether or not immunity is granted under section 344 of this title" after second reference to "estate" in par. (3) as redesignated above, could not be executed because such reference appeared in par. (4) rather than in par. (3). See 1986 Amendments note under this section relating to par. (4).

Par. (4). Pub.L. 98–353, § 305(1), redesignated former par. (3) as (4). Former par. (4) was redesignated as (5).

Par. (5). Pub.L. 98–353, § 305(1), redesignated former par. (4) as (5).

Effective and Applicability Provisions

2009 Acts. Amendments by Pub.L. 111–16 effective Dec. 1, 2009, see Pub.L. 111–16, § 7, set out as a note under 11 U.S.C.A. 109.

2005 Acts. Pub.L. 109–8, Title VI, § 603(e), Apr. 20, 2005, 119 Stat. 123, provided that: "The amendments made by this section [amending this section and 11 U.S.C.A. § 727, and 28 U.S.C.A. § 586, and enacting provisions set out as a note under 28 U.S.C.A. § 586] shall take effect 18 months after the date of enactment of this Act [Apr. 20, 2005]."

Amendments by Pub.L. 109–8 effective, except as otherwise provided, 180 days after April 20, 2005, and inapplicable with respect to cases commenced under Title 11 before the effective date, see Pub.L. 109–8, § 1501, set out as a note under 11 U.S.C.A. § 101.

1986 Acts. Amendment by Pub.L. 99–554 effective 30 days after Oct. 27, 1986, except as otherwise provided for, see section 302(a) of Pub.L. 99–554, set out as a note under section 581 of Title 28, Judiciary and Judicial Procedure.

1984 Acts. Amendment by Pub.L. 98–353 effective with respect to cases filed 90 days after July 10, 1984, see section 552(a), formerly 553(a), of Pub.L. 98–353, set out as a note under section 101 of this title.

Confidentiality of Tax Information

Pub.L. 109–8, Title III, § 315(c), Apr. 20, 2005, 119 Stat. 91, provided that:

"**(1)** Not later than 180 days after the date of the enactment of this Act [Apr. 20, 2005], the Director of the Administrative Office of the United States Courts shall establish procedures for safeguarding the confidentiality of any tax information required to be provided under this section.

"**(2)** The procedures under paragraph (1) shall include restrictions on creditor access to tax information that is required to be provided under this section.

"**(3)** Not later than 540 days after the date of enactment of this Act [Apr. 20, 2005], the director of the administrative office of the United States courts shall prepare and submit to the President pro tempore of the Senate and the speaker of the House of Representatives a report that—

"**(A)** assesses the effectiveness of the procedures established under paragraph (1); and

"**(B)** If appropriate, includes proposed legislation to—

"**(i)** further protect the confidentiality of tax information; and "(ii) provide penalties for the improper use by any person of the tax information required to be provided under this section."

[Amendments by Pub.L. 109–8 effective, except as otherwise provided, 180 days after April 20, 2005, and inapplicable with respect to cases commenced under Title 11 before the effective date, see Pub.L. 109–8, § 1501, set out as a note under 11 U.S.C.A. § 101.]

Providing Requested Tax Documents to the Court.

Pub.L. 109–8, Title XII, § 1228, Apr. 20, 2005, 119 Stat. 200, provided that:

"(a) **Chapter 7 cases.**—The court shall not grant a discharge in the case of an individual who is a debtor in a case under chapter 7 of title 11, United States Code [11 U.S.C.A. § 701 et seq.], unless requested tax documents have been provided to the court.

"(b) **Chapter 11 and chapter 13 cases.**—The court shall not confirm a plan of reorganization in the case of an individual under chapter 11 or 13 of title 11, United States Code [11 U.S.C.A. § 1101 et seq. or 1301 et seq.], unless requested tax documents have been filed with the court.

"(c) **Document retention.**—The court shall destroy documents submitted in support of a bankruptcy claim not sooner than 3 years after the date of the conclusion of a case filed by an individual under chapter 7, 11, or 13 of title 11, United States Code [11 U.S.C.A. § 701 et seq. or 1101 et seq., or 1301 et seq.]. In the event of a pending audit or enforcement action, the court may extend the time for destruction of such requested tax documents."

[Amendments by Pub.L. 109–8 effective, except as otherwise provided, 180 days after April 20, 2005, and inapplicable with respect to cases commenced under Title 11 before the effective date, see Pub.L. 109–8, § 1501, set out as a note under 11 U.S.C.A. § 101.]

CROSS REFERENCES

Conversion or dismissal of—

Chapter 11 case, see 11 USCA § 1112.

Chapter 13 case, see 11 USCA § 1307.

Debtor's statement of intention, see Official Bankr. Form 8, 11 USCA.

Dismissal of Chapter 7 case, see 11 USCA § 707.

Filing of list, schedule and statement by trustee, see 11 USCA § 1106.

Lists, schedules, statements and fees, see Fed.Rules Bankr. Proc. Form B 200, 11 USCA.

Order converting case, see Fed.Rules Bankr.Proc. Form B 221A et seq., 11 USCA.

Penalty for persons who negligently or fraudulently prepare bankruptcy petitions or failure to file bankruptcy papers, see 11 USCA § 110.

Proof of claim or interest deemed filed if scheduled, see 11 USCA § 1111.

Property scheduled but unadministered before close of case deemed abandoned, see 11 USCA § 554.

Trustee's duty to ensure performance of debtor's intention as specified in subsec. (2)(B) of this section, see 11 USCA § 704.

LIBRARY REFERENCES

American Digest System

Bankruptcy ⚮3022, 3034, 2794.1, 3415.1, 3319, 2321 to 2325.

Key Number System Topic No. 51.

Corpus Juris Secundum

CJS Bankruptcy § 101, Chapter 11.

CJS Bankruptcy § 132, Rights, Powers, and Duties of Debtor in Possession.

CJS Bankruptcy § 337, Contents, Signature, and Verification--Certification of Delivery or Receipt of Prefiling Notice.

CJS Bankruptcy § 344, List of Creditors and Others.

CJS Bankruptcy § 349, Schedules and Statements Regarding Debtor's Assets, Liabilities, Income, Expenditures, and Finances.

CJS Bankruptcy § 350, Statement of Intention With Respect to the Retention or Surrender of Collateral.

CJS Bankruptcy § 351, Evidence of Compliance With Credit Counseling Requirement.

CJS Bankruptcy § 352, Statement of Current Monthly Income.

CJS Bankruptcy § 356, Extension of Time for Filing.

CJS Bankruptcy § 358, Amendment.

CJS Bankruptcy § 451, Dismissal or Conversion on Request of United States Trustee.

CJS Bankruptcy § 452, Automatic Dismissal of Case of Individual Debtor.

CJS Bankruptcy § 457, Failure to Provide Copy of Debtor's Federal Income Tax Return to Trustee and Requesting Creditors.

CJS Bankruptcy § 459, Failure to File Postpetition Tax Return.

CJS Bankruptcy § 527, Automatic Relief from Stay--As to Personal Property.

CJS Bankruptcy § 578, Debtor's Statement of Intention.

CJS Bankruptcy § 608, Time of Redemption.

CJS Bankruptcy § 610, Waiver; Failure to File Timely Statement of Intent.

CJS Bankruptcy § 624, Surrender of Property of Estate and Recorded Information to Trustee.

CJS Bankruptcy § 650, Deemed Abandonment.

CJS Bankruptcy § 758, Debtor's Duties.

CJS Bankruptcy § 1069, Debt Neither Listed Nor Scheduled.

CJS Bankruptcy § 1094, Requirements for Reaffirmation of Debt.

CJS Estoppel and Waiver § 190, Applicability of Judicial Estoppel to Contradictory Positions Taken in Same Proceeding.

CJS Estoppel and Waiver § 191, Applicability of Judicial Estoppel to Inconsistent Statements of Facts or Conclusions of Law.

CJS Estoppel and Waiver § 192, Judicial Estoppel as Restricted to Statements Made Under Oath.

§ 522. Exemptions

(a) In this section—

(1) "dependent" includes spouse, whether or not actually dependent; and

(2) "value" means fair market value as of the date of the filing of the petition or, with respect to property that becomes property of the estate after such date, as of the date such property becomes property of the estate.

(b)(1) Notwithstanding section 541 of this title, an individual debtor may exempt from property of the estate the property listed in either paragraph (2) or, in the alternative, paragraph (3) of this subsection. In joint cases filed under section 302 of this title and individual cases filed under section 301 or 303 of this title by or against debtors who are husband and wife, and whose estates are ordered to be jointly administered under Rule 1015(b) of the Federal Rules of Bankruptcy Procedure, one debtor may not elect to exempt property listed in paragraph (2) and the other debtor elect to exempt property listed in paragraph (3) of this subsection. If the parties cannot agree on the alternative to be elected, they shall be deemed to elect paragraph (2), where such election is permitted under the law of the jurisdiction where the case is filed.

(2) Property listed in this paragraph is property that is specified under subsection (d), unless the State law that is applicable to the debtor under paragraph (3)(A) specifically does not so authorize.

(3) Property listed in this paragraph is—

(A) subject to subsections (o) and (p), any property that is exempt under Federal law, other than subsection (d) of this section, or State or local law that is applicable on the date of the filing of the petition to the place in which the debtor's domicile has been located for the 730 days immediately preceding the date of the filing of the petition or if the debtor's domicile has not been located in a single State for such 730–day period, the place in which the debtor's domicile was located for 180 days immediately preceding the 730–day period or for a longer portion of such 180–day period than in any other place;

(B) any interest in property in which the debtor had, immediately before the commencement of the case, an interest as a tenant by the entirety or joint tenant to the extent that such interest as a tenant by the entirety or joint tenant is exempt from process under applicable nonbankruptcy law; and

(C) retirement funds to the extent that those funds are in a fund or account that is exempt from taxation under section 401, 403, 408, 408A, 414, 457, or 501(a) of the Internal Revenue Code of 1986.

If the effect of the domiciliary requirement under subparagraph (A) is to render the debtor ineligible for any exemption, the debtor may elect to exempt property that is specified under subsection (d).

(4) For purposes of paragraph (3)(C) and subsection (d)(12), the following shall apply:

(A) If the retirement funds are in a retirement fund that has received a favorable determination under section 7805 of the Internal Revenue Code of 1986, and that determination is in effect as of the date of the filing of the petition in a case under this title, those funds shall be presumed to be exempt from the estate.

(B) If the retirement funds are in a retirement fund that has not received a favorable determination under such section 7805, those funds are exempt from the estate if the debtor demonstrates that—

(i) no prior determination to the contrary has been made by a court or the Internal Revenue Service; and

(ii)(I) the retirement fund is in substantial compliance with the applicable requirements of the Internal Revenue Code of 1986; or

(II) the retirement fund fails to be in substantial compliance with the applicable requirements of the Internal Revenue Code of 1986 and the debtor is not materially responsible for that failure.

(C) A direct transfer of retirement funds from 1 fund or account that is exempt from taxation under section 401, 403, 408, 408A, 414, 457, or 501(a) of the Internal Revenue Code of 1986, under section 401(a)(31) of the Internal Revenue Code of 1986, or otherwise, shall not cease to qualify for exemption under paragraph (3)(C) or subsection (d)(12) by reason of such direct transfer.

(D)(i) Any distribution that qualifies as an eligible rollover distribution within the meaning of section 402(c) of the Internal Revenue Code of 1986 or that is described in clause (ii) shall not cease to qualify for exemption under paragraph (3)(C) or subsection (d)(12) by reason of such distribution.

(ii) A distribution described in this clause is an amount that—

(I) has been distributed from a fund or account that is exempt from taxation under section 401, 403, 408, 408A, 414, 457, or 501(a) of the Internal Revenue Code of 1986; and

(II) to the extent allowed by law, is deposited in such a fund or account not later than 60 days after the distribution of such amount.

(c) Unless the case is dismissed, property exempted under this section is not liable during or after the case for any debt of the debtor that arose, or that is determined under section 502 of this title as if such debt had arisen, before the commencement of the case, except—

(1) a debt of a kind specified in paragraph (1) or (5) of section 523(a) (in which case, notwithstanding any provision of applicable nonbankruptcy law to the contrary, such property shall be liable for a debt of a kind specified in such paragraph);

(2) a debt secured by a lien that is—

(A)(i) not avoided under subsection (f) or (g) of this section or under section 544, 545, 547, 548, 549, or 724(a) of this title; and

(ii) not void under section 506(d) of this title; or

(B) a tax lien, notice of which is properly filed;

(3) a debt of a kind specified in section 523(a)(4) or 523(a)(6) of this title owed by an institution-affiliated party of an insured depository institution to a Federal depository institutions regulatory agency acting in its capacity as conservator, receiver, or liquidating agent for such institution; or

(4) a debt in connection with fraud in the obtaining or providing of any scholarship, grant, loan, tuition, discount, award, or other financial assistance for purposes of financing an education at an institution of higher education (as that term is defined in section 101 of the Higher Education Act of 1965 (20 U.S.C. 1001)).

(d) The following property may be exempted under subsection (b)(2) of this section:

(1) The debtor's aggregate interest, not to exceed $21,625 [1] in value, in real property or personal property that the debtor or a dependent of the debtor uses as a residence, in a cooperative that owns property that the debtor or a dependent of the debtor uses as a residence, or in a burial plot for the debtor or a dependent of the debtor.

(2) The debtor's interest, not to exceed $3,450 [1] in value, in one motor vehicle.

(3) The debtor's interest, not to exceed $550 [1] in value in any particular item or $11,525 [1] in aggregate value, in household furnishings, household goods, wearing apparel, appliances, books, animals, crops, or musical instruments, that are held primarily for the personal, family, or household use of the debtor or a dependent of the debtor.

(4) The debtor's aggregate interest, not to exceed $1,450 [1] in value, in jewelry held primarily for the personal, family, or household use of the debtor or a dependent of the debtor.

(5) The debtor's aggregate interest in any property, not to exceed in value $1,150 [1] plus up to $10,825 [1] of any unused amount of the exemption provided under paragraph (1) of this subsection.

(6) The debtor's aggregate interest, not to exceed $2,175 [1] in value, in any implements, professional books, or tools, of the trade of the debtor or the trade of a dependent of the debtor.

(7) Any unmatured life insurance contract owned by the debtor, other than a credit life insurance contract.

(8) The debtor's aggregate interest, not to exceed in value $11,525 [1] less any amount of property of the estate transferred in the manner specified in section 542(d) of this title, in any accrued dividend or interest under, or loan value of, any unmatured life insurance contract owned by the debtor under which the insured is the debtor or an individual of whom the debtor is a dependent.

(9) Professionally prescribed health aids for the debtor or a dependent of the debtor.

(10) The debtor's right to receive—

(A) a social security benefit, unemployment compensation, or a local public assistance benefit;

(B) a veterans' benefit;

(C) a disability, illness, or unemployment benefit;

(D) alimony, support, or separate maintenance, to the extent reasonably necessary for the support of the debtor and any dependent of the debtor;

(E) a payment under a stock bonus, pension, profitsharing, annuity, or similar plan or contract on account of illness, disability, death, age, or length of service, to the extent reasonably necessary for the support of the debtor and any dependent of the debtor, unless—

(i) such plan or contract was established by or under the auspices of an insider that employed the debtor at the time the debtor's rights under such plan or contract arose;

(ii) such payment is on account of age or length of service; and

(iii) such plan or contract does not qualify under section 401(a), 403(a), 403(b), or 408 of the Internal Revenue Code of 1986.

(11) The debtor's right to receive, or property that is traceable to—

(A) an award under a crime victim's reparation law;

(B) a payment on account of the wrongful death of an individual of whom the debtor was a dependent, to the extent reasonably necessary for the support of the debtor and any dependent of the debtor;

(C) a payment under a life insurance contract that insured the life of an individual of whom the debtor was a dependent on the date of such individual's death, to the extent reasonably necessary for the support of the debtor and any dependent of the debtor;

(D) a payment, not to exceed $21,625,[1] on account of personal bodily injury, not including pain and suffering or compensation for actual pecuniary loss, of the debtor or an individual of whom the debtor is a dependent; or

(E) a payment in compensation of loss of future earnings of the debtor or an individual of whom the debtor is or was a dependent, to the extent reasonably necessary for the support of the debtor and any dependent of the debtor.

(12) Retirement funds to the extent that those funds are in a fund or account that is exempt from taxation under section 401, 403, 408, 408A, 414, 457, or 501(a) of the Internal Revenue Code of 1986.

(e) A waiver of an exemption executed in favor of a creditor that holds an unsecured claim against the debtor is unenforceable in a case under this title with respect to such claim against property that the debtor may exempt under subsection (b) of this section. A waiver by the debtor of a power under subsection (f) or (h) of this section to avoid a transfer, under subsection (g) or (i) of this section to exempt property, or under subsection (i) of this section to recover property or to preserve a transfer, is unenforceable in a case under this title.

(f)(1) Notwithstanding any waiver of exemptions but subject to paragraph (3), the debtor may avoid the fixing of a lien on an interest of the debtor in property to the extent that such lien impairs an exemption to which the debtor would have been entitled under subsection (b) of this section, if such lien is—

(A) a judicial lien, other than a judicial lien that secures a debt of a kind that is specified in section 523(a)(5); or

(B) a nonpossessory, nonpurchase-money security interest in any—

   (i) household furnishings, household goods, wearing apparel, appliances, books, animals, crops, musical instruments, or jewelry that are held primarily for the personal, family, or household use of the debtor or a dependent of the debtor;

   (ii) implements, professional books, or tools, of the trade of the debtor or the trade of a dependent of the debtor; or

   (iii) professionally prescribed health aids for the debtor or a dependent of the debtor.

(2)(A) For the purposes of this subsection, a lien shall be considered to impair an exemption to the extent that the sum of—

   (i) the lien;

   (ii) all other liens on the property; and

   (iii) the amount of the exemption that the debtor could claim if there were no liens on the property;

exceeds the value that the debtor's interest in the property would have in the absence of any liens.

(B) In the case of a property subject to more than 1 lien, a lien that has been avoided shall not be considered in making the calculation under subparagraph (A) with respect to other liens.

(C) This paragraph shall not apply with respect to a judgment arising out of a mortgage foreclosure.

(3) In a case in which State law that is applicable to the debtor—

(A) permits a person to voluntarily waive a right to claim exemptions under subsection (d) or prohib-

its a debtor from claiming exemptions under subsection (d); and

(B) either permits the debtor to claim exemptions under State law without limitation in amount, except to the extent that the debtor has permitted the fixing of a consensual lien on any property or prohibits avoidance of a consensual lien on property otherwise eligible to be claimed as exempt property;

the debtor may not avoid the fixing of a lien on an interest of the debtor or a dependent of the debtor in property if the lien is a nonpossessory, nonpurchase-money security interest in implements, professional books, or tools of the trade of the debtor or a dependent of the debtor or farm animals or crops of the debtor or a dependent of the debtor to the extent the value of such implements, professional books, tools of the trade, animals, and crops exceeds $5,850 [1].

(4)(A) Subject to subparagraph (B), for purposes of paragraph (1)(B), the term "household goods" means—

   (i) clothing;

   (ii) furniture;

   (iii) appliances;

   (iv) 1 radio;

   (v) 1 television;

   (vi) 1 VCR;

   (vii) linens;

   (viii) china;

   (ix) crockery;

   (x) kitchenware;

   (xi) educational materials and educational equipment primarily for the use of minor dependent children of the debtor;

   (xii) medical equipment and supplies;

   (xiii) furniture exclusively for the use of minor children, or elderly or disabled dependents of the debtor;

   (xiv) personal effects (including the toys and hobby equipment of minor dependent children and wedding rings) of the debtor and the dependents of the debtor; and

   (xv) 1 personal computer and related equipment.

(B) The term "household goods" does not include—

   (i) works of art (unless by or of the debtor, or any relative of the debtor);

   (ii) electronic entertainment equipment with a fair market value of more than $600 [1] in the aggregate (except 1 television, 1 radio, and 1 VCR);

   (iii) items acquired as antiques with a fair market value of more than $600 [1] in the aggregate;

   (iv) jewelry with a fair market value of more than $600 [1] in the aggregate (except wedding rings); and

(v) a computer (except as otherwise provided for in this section), motor vehicle (including a tractor or lawn tractor), boat, or a motorized recreational device, conveyance, vehicle, watercraft, or aircraft.

(g) Notwithstanding sections 550 and 551 of this title, the debtor may exempt under subsection (b) of this section property that the trustee recovers under section 510(c)(2), 542, 543, 550, 551, or 553 of this title, to the extent that the debtor could have exempted such property under subsection (b) of this section if such property had not been transferred, if—

  (1)(A) such transfer was not a voluntary transfer of such property by the debtor; and

  (B) the debtor did not conceal such property; or

  (2) the debtor could have avoided such transfer under subsection (f)(1)(B) of this section.

(h) The debtor may avoid a transfer of property of the debtor or recover a setoff to the extent that the debtor could have exempted such property under subsection (g)(1) of this section if the trustee had avoided such transfer, if—

  (1) such transfer is avoidable by the trustee under section 544, 545, 547, 548, 549, or 724(a) of this title or recoverable by the trustee under section 553 of this title; and

  (2) the trustee does not attempt to avoid such transfer.

(i)(1) If the debtor avoids a transfer or recovers a setoff under subsection (f) or (h) of this section, the debtor may recover in the manner prescribed by, and subject to the limitations of, section 550 of this title, the same as if the trustee had avoided such transfer, and may exempt any property so recovered under subsection (b) of this section.

(2) Notwithstanding section 551 of this title, a transfer avoided under section 544, 545, 547, 548, 549, or 724(a) of this title, under subsection (f) or (h) of this section, or property recovered under section 553 of this title, may be preserved for the benefit of the debtor to the extent that the debtor may exempt such property under subsection (g) of this section or paragraph (1) of this subsection.

(j) Notwithstanding subsections (g) and (i) of this section, the debtor may exempt a particular kind of property under subsections (g) and (i) of this section only to the extent that the debtor has exempted less property in value of such kind than that to which the debtor is entitled under subsection (b) of this section.

(k) Property that the debtor exempts under this section is not liable for payment of any administrative expense except—

  (1) the aliquot share of the costs and expenses of avoiding a transfer of property that the debtor exempts under subsection (g) of this section, or of recovery of such property, that is attributable to the value of the portion of such property exempted in relation to the value of the property recovered; and

  (2) any costs and expenses of avoiding a transfer under subsection (f) or (h) of this section, or of recovery of property under subsection (i)(1) of this section, that the debtor has not paid.

(l) The debtor shall file a list of property that the debtor claims as exempt under subsection (b) of this section. If the debtor does not file such a list, a dependent of the debtor may file such a list, or may claim property as exempt from property of the estate on behalf of the debtor. Unless a party in interest objects, the property claimed as exempt on such list is exempt.

(m) Subject to the limitation in subsection (b), this section shall apply separately with respect to each debtor in a joint case.

(n) For assets in individual retirement accounts described in section 408 or 408A of the Internal Revenue Code of 1986, other than a simplified employee pension under section 408(k) of such Code or a simple retirement account under section 408(p) of such Code, the aggregate value of such assets exempted under this section, without regard to amounts attributable to rollover contributions under section 402(c), 402(e)(6), 403(a)(4), 403(a) (5), and 403(b)(8) of the Internal Revenue Code of 1986, and earnings thereon, shall not exceed $1,171,650 [1] in a case filed by a debtor who is an individual, except that such amount may be increased if the interests of justice so require.

(o) For purposes of subsection (b)(3)(A), and notwithstanding subsection (a), the value of an interest in—

  (1) real or personal property that the debtor or a dependent of the debtor uses as a residence;

  (2) a cooperative that owns property that the debtor or a dependent of the debtor uses as a residence;

  (3) a burial plot for the debtor or a dependent of the debtor; or

  (4) real or personal property that the debtor or a dependent of the debtor claims as a homestead;

shall be reduced to the extent that such value is attributable to any portion of any property that the debtor disposed of in the 10–year period ending on the date of the filing of the petition with the intent to hinder, delay, or defraud a creditor and that the debtor could not exempt, or that portion that the debtor could not exempt, under subsection (b), if on such date the debtor had held the property so disposed of.

(p)(1) Except as provided in paragraph (2) of this subsection and sections 544 and 548, as a result of electing under subsection (b)(3)(A) to exempt property under State or local law, a debtor may not exempt any amount of interest that was acquired by the debtor during the 1215–day period preceding the date of the filing of the petition that exceeds in the aggregate $146,450 [1] in value in—

(A) real or personal property that the debtor or a dependent of the debtor uses as a residence;

(B) a cooperative that owns property that the debtor or a dependent of the debtor uses as a residence;

(C) a burial plot for the debtor or a dependent of the debtor; or

(D) real or personal property that the debtor or dependent of the debtor claims as a homestead.

(2)(A) The limitation under paragraph (1) shall not apply to an exemption claimed under subsection (b)(3)(A) by a family farmer for the principal residence of such farmer.

(B) For purposes of paragraph (1), any amount of such interest does not include any interest transferred from a debtor's previous principal residence (which was acquired prior to the beginning of such 1215–day period) into the debtor's current principal residence, if the debtor's previous and current residences are located in the same State.

(q)(1) As a result of electing under subsection (b)(3)(A) to exempt property under State or local law, a debtor may not exempt any amount of an interest in property described in subparagraphs (A), (B), (C), and (D) of subsection (p)(1) which exceeds in the aggregate $146,450 [1] if—

(A) the court determines, after notice and a hearing, that the debtor has been convicted of a felony (as defined in section 3156 of title 18), which under the circumstances, demonstrates that the filing of the case was an abuse of the provisions of this title; or

(B) the debtor owes a debt arising from—

(i) any violation of the Federal securities laws (as defined in section 3(a)(47) of the Securities Exchange Act of 1934), any State securities laws, or any regulation or order issued under Federal securities laws or State securities laws;

(ii) fraud, deceit, or manipulation in a fiduciary capacity or in connection with the purchase or sale of any security registered under section 12 or 15(d) of the Securities Exchange Act of 1934 or under section 6 of the Securities Act of 1933;

(iii) any civil remedy under section 1964 of title 18; or

(iv) any criminal act, intentional tort, or willful or reckless misconduct that caused serious physical injury or death to another individual in the preceding 5 years.

(2) Paragraph (1) shall not apply to the extent the amount of an interest in property described in subparagraphs (A), (B), (C), and (D) of subsection (p)(1) is

reasonably necessary for the support of the debtor and any dependent of the debtor.

(Pub.L. 95–598, Nov. 6, 1978, 92 Stat. 2586; Pub.L. 98–353, Title III, §§ 306, 453, July 10, 1984, 98 Stat. 353, 375; Pub.L. 99–554, Title II, § 283(i), Oct. 27, 1986, 100 Stat. 3117; Pub.L. 101–647, Title XXV, § 2522(b), Nov. 29, 1990, 104 Stat. 4866; Pub.L. 103–394, Title I, § 108(d), Title III, §§ 303, 304(d), 310, Title V, § 501(d)(12), Oct. 22, 1994, 108 Stat. 4112, 4132, 4133, 4137, 4145; Pub.L. 106–420, § 4, Nov. 1, 2000, 114 Stat. 1868; Pub.L. 109–8, Title II, §§ 216, 224(a), (e)(1), Title III, §§ 307, 308, 313(a), 322(a), Apr. 20, 2005, 119 Stat. 55, 62, 65, 81, 87, 96; Pub.L. 111–327, § 2(a)(17), Dec. 22, 2010, 124 Stat. 3559.)

[1] Dollar amount as adjusted by the Judicial Conference of the United States. See Adjustment of Dollar Amounts notes set out under this section and 11 U.S.C.A. § 104.

HISTORICAL AND STATUTORY NOTES

Revision Notes and Legislative Reports

1978 Acts. Subsection (a) of this section defines two terms: "dependent" includes the debtor's spouse, whether or not actually dependent; and "value" means fair market value as of the date of the filing of the petition.

Subsection (b) tracks current law. It permits a debtor the exemptions to which he is entitled under other Federal law and the law of the State of his domicile. Some of the items that may be exempted under Federal laws other than title 11 include:

Foreign Service Retirement and Disability payments, 22 U.S.C. 1104 [1] [section 1104 of Title 22, Foreign Relations and Intercourse];

Social security payments, 42 U.S.C. 407 [section 407 of Title 42, The Public Health and Welfare];

Injury or death compensation payments from war risk hazards, 42 U.S.C. 1717 [section 1717 of Title 42];

Wages of fishermen, seamen, and apprentices, 46 U.S.C. 601 [2] [section 601 of Title 46, Shipping];

Civil service retirement benefits, 5 U.S.C. 729, 2265 [3] [sections 729 and 2265 of Title 5, Government Organization and Employees];

Longshoremen's and Harbor Workers' Compensation Act death and disability benefits, 33 U.S.C. 916 [section 916 of Title 33, Navigation and Navigable Waters];

Railroad Retirement Act annuities and pensions, 45 U.S.C. 228(L) [4] [former section 2281 of Title 45, Railroads];

Veterans benefits, 45 U.S.C. 352(E) [5] [section 352(e) of Title 45];

Special pensions paid to winners of the Congressional Medal of Honor, 38 U.S.C. 3101 [6] [section 3101 of Title 38, Veterans' Benefits]; and

Federal homestead lands on debts contracted before issuance of the patent, 43 U.S.C. 175 [section 175 of Title 43, Public Lands].

He may also exempt an interest in property in which the debtor had an interest as a tenant by the entirety or joint tenant to the extent that interest would have been exempt from process under applicable nonbankruptcy law.

Under proposed section 541, all property of the debtor becomes property of the estate, but the debtor is permitted to exempt certain property from property of the estate under this section. Property may be exempted even if it is subject to a lien, but only the unencumbered portion of the property is to be counted in computing the "value" of the property for the purposes of exemption.

As under current law, the debtor will be permitted to convert nonexempt property into exempt property before filing a bankruptcy petition. The practice is not fraudulent as to creditors, and permits the debtor to make full use of the exemptions to which he is entitled under the law. [Ed. Note: cf. Mickelson v. Anderson, Bkrtcy.Minn.1982, 31 B.R. 635.]

Subsection (c) insulates exempt property from prepetition claims other than tax claims (whether or not dischargeable), and other than alimony, maintenance, or support claims that are excepted from discharge. The bankruptcy discharge does not prevent enforcement of valid liens. The rule of *Long v. Bullard*, 117 U.S. 617 (1886) [6 S.Ct. 917, 29 L.Ed. 1004], is accepted with respect to the enforcement of valid liens on nonexempt property as well as on exempt property. Cf. *Louisville Joint Stock Land Bank v. Radford*, 295 U.S. 555, 583 (1935) [55 S.Ct. 854].

Subsection (c)(3) permits the collection of dischargeable taxes from exempt assets. Only assets exempted from levy under section 6334 of the Internal Revenue Code [section 6334 of Title 26, Internal Revenue Code] or under applicable state or local tax law cannot be applied to satisfy these tax claims. This rule applies to prepetition tax claims against the debtor regardless of whether the claims do or do not receive priority and whether they are dischargeable or nondischargeable. Thus, even if a tax is dischargeable vis-a-vis the debtor's after-acquired assets, it may nevertheless be collectible from exempt property held by the estate. (Taxes incurred by the debtor's estate which are collectible as first priority administrative expenses are not collectible from the debtor's estate which are collectible as first priority administrative expenses are not collectible from the debtor's exempt assets.)

Subsection (d) protects the debtor's exemptions, either Federal or State, by making unenforceable in a bankruptcy case a waiver of exemptions or a waiver of the debtor's avoiding powers under the following subsections.

Subsection (e) protects the debtor's exemptions, his discharge, and thus his fresh start by permitting him to avoid certain liens on exempt property. The debtor may avoid a judicial lien on any property to the extent that the property could have been exempted in the absence of the lien, and may similarly avoid a nonpurchase-money security interest in certain household and personal goods. The avoiding power is independent of any waiver of exemptions.

Subsection (f) gives the debtor the ability to exempt property that the trustee recovers under one of the trustee's avoiding powers if the property was involuntarily transferred away from the debtor (such as by the fixing of a judicial lien) and if the debtor did not conceal the property. The debtor is also permitted to exempt property that the trustee recovers as the result of the avoiding of the fixing of certain security interests to the extent that the debtor could otherwise have exempted the property.

Subsection (g) provides that if the trustee does not exercise an avoiding power to recover a transfer of property that would be exempt, the debtor may exercise it and exempt the property, if the transfer was involuntary and the debtor did not conceal the property. If the debtor wishes to preserve his right to pursue any action under this provision, then he must intervene in any action brought by the trustee based on the same cause of action. It is not intended that the debtor be given an additional opportunity to avoid a transfer or that the transferee should have to defend the same action twice.

Rather, the section is primarily designed to give the debtor the rights the trustee could have, but has not, pursued. The debtor is given no greater rights under this provision than the trustee, and thus, the debtor's avoiding powers under proposed sections 544, 545, 547, and 548, are subject to proposed 546, as are the trustee's powers.

These subsections are cumulative. The debtor is not required to choose which he will use to gain an exemption. Instead, he may use more than one in any particular instance, just as the trustee's avoiding powers are cumulative.

Subsection (h) permits recovery by the debtor of property transferred by an avoided transfer from either the initial or subsequent transferees. It also permits preserving a transfer for the benefit of the debtor. In either event, the debtor may exempt the property recovered or preserved.

Subsection (i) makes clear that the debtor may exempt property under the avoiding subsections (f) and (h) only to the extent he has exempted less property than allowed under subsection (b).

Subsection (j) makes clear that the liability of the debtor's exempt property is limited to the debtor's aliquot share of the costs and expenses recovery of property that the trustee recovers and the debtor later exempts, and any costs and expenses of avoiding a transfer by the debtor that the debtor has not already paid.

Subsection (k) requires the debtor to file a list of property that he claims as exempt from property of the estate. Absent an objection to the list, the property is exempted. A dependent of the debtor may file it and thus be protected if the debtor fails to file the list.

Subsection (*l*) provides the rule for a joint case. Senate Report No. 95–989.

[1] Replaced by 22 USCA § 4060(c).

[2] Replaced by 46 USCA §§ 11108, 11109.

[3] Replaced by 5 USCA § 8346.

[4] Replaced by 45 USCA § 231m.

[5] Railroad unemployment benefits are covered by 45 USCA § 352(e).

[6] Veterans benefits generally are covered by 38 USCA § 5301.

Subsection (a) of this section defines two terms: "dependent" includes the debtor's spouse, whether or not actually dependent; and "value" means fair market value as of the date of the filing of the petition.

Subsection (b), the operative subsection of this section, is a significant departure from present law. It permits an individual debtor in a bankruptcy case a choice between exemption systems. The debtor may choose the Federal exemptions prescribed in subsection (d), or he may choose the exemptions to which he is entitled under other Federal law and the law of the State of his domicile. If the debtor chooses the latter, some of the items that may be exempted under other Federal laws include:

—Foreign Service Retirement and Disability payments, 22 U.S.C. 1104 [1] [section 1104 of Title 22, Foreign Relations and Intercourse];

—Social security payments, 42 U.S.C. 407 [section 407 of Title 42, The Public Health and Welfare];

—Injury or death compensation payments from war risk hazards, 42 U.S.C. 1717 [section 1717 of Title 42];

—Wages of fishermen, seamen, and apprentices, 46 U.S.C. 601 [section 601 of Title 46, Shipping];

—Civil service retirement benefits, 5 U.S.C. 729, 2265 [2] [sections 729, 2265 of Title 5, Government Organization and Employees];

—Longshoremen's and Harbor Workers' Compensation Act death and disability benefits, 33 U.S.C. 916 [section 916 of Title 33, Navigation and Navigable Waters];

—Railroad Retirement Act annuities and pensions, 45 U.S.C. 228(*l*) [3]; [former section 228l of Title 45, Railroads];

—Veterans benefits, 45 U.S.C. 352(E) [4] [section 352(e) of Title 45];

—Special pensions paid to winners of the Congressional Medal of Honor, 38 U.S.C. 3101 [section 3101 of Title 38, Veterans' Benefits]; [5] and

—Federal homestead lands on debts contracted before issuance of the patent, 43 U.S.C. 175 [section 175 of Title 43, Public Lands].

He may also exempt an interest in property in which the debtor had an interest as a tenant by the entirety or joint tenant to the extent that interest would have been exempt from process under applicable nonbankruptcy law. The Rules will provide for the situation where the debtor's choice of exemption, Federal or State, was improvident and should be changed, for example, where the court has ruled against the debtor with respect to a major exemption.

Under proposed 11 U.S.C. 541, all property of the debtor becomes property of the estate, but the debtor is permitted to exempt certain property from property of the estate under this section. Property may be exempted even if it is subject to a lien, but only the unencumbered portion of the property is to be counted in computing the "value" of the property for the purposes of exemption. Thus, for example, a residence worth $30,000 with a mortgage of $25,000 will be exemptable to the extent of $5,000. This follows current law. The remaining value of the property will be dealt with in the bankruptcy case as is any interest in property that is subject to a lien.

As under current law, the debtor will be permitted to convert nonexempt property into exempt property before filing a bankruptcy petition. See Hearings, pt. 3, at 1355–58. The practice is not fraudulent as to creditors and permits the debtor to make full use of the exemptions to which he is entitled under the law.

Subsection (c) insulates exempt property from prepetition claims, except tax and alimony, maintenance, or support claims that are excepted from discharge. The bankruptcy discharge will not prevent enforcement of valid liens. The rule of *Long v. Bullard*, 117 U.S. 617 (1886) [6 S.Ct. 917, 29 L.Ed. 1004], is accepted with respect to the enforcement of valid liens on nonexempt property as well as on exempt property. Cf. *Louisville Joint Stock Land Bank v. Radford*, 295 U.S. 555, 583 (1935) [55 S.Ct. 854].

Subsection (d) specifies the Federal exemptions to which the debtor is entitled. They are derived in large part from the Uniform Exemptions Act, promulgated by the Commissioners of Uniform State Laws in August, 1976. Eleven categories of property are exempted. First is a homestead to the extent of $10,000, which may be claimed in real or personal property that the debtor or a dependent of the debtor uses as a residence. Second, the debtor may exempt a motor vehicle to the extent of $1500. Third, the debtor may exempt household goods, furnishings, clothing, and similar household items, held primarily for the personal, family, or household use of the debtor or a dependent of the debtor.

"Animals" includes all animals, such as pets, livestock, poultry, and fish, if they are held primarily for personal, family or household use. The limitation for third category items is $300 on any particular item. The debtor may also exempt up to $750 of personal jewelry.

Paragraph (5) permits the exemption of $500, plus any unused amount of the homestead exemption, in any property, in order not to discriminate against the nonhomeowner. Paragraph (6) grants the debtor up to $1000 in implements, professional books, or tools, of the trade of the debtor a dependent. Paragraph (7) exempts a life insurance contract, other than a credit life insurance contract, owned by the debtor. This paragraph refers to the life insurance contract itself. It does not encompass any other rights under the contract, such as the right to borrow out the loan value. Because of this provision, the trustee may not surrender a life insurance contract, which remains property of the debtor if he chooses the Federal exemptions. Paragraph (8) permits the debtor to exempt up to $5000 in loan value in a life insurance policy owned by the debtor under which the debtor or an individual of whom the debtor is a dependent is the insured. The exemption provided by this paragraph and paragraph (7) will also include the debtor's rights in a group insurance certificate under which the insured is an individual of whom the debtor is a dependent (assuming the debtor has rights in the policy that could be exempted) or the debtor. A trustee is authorized to collect the entire loan value on every life insurance policy owned by the debtor as property of the estate. First, however, the debtor will choose which policy or policies under which the loan value will be exempted. The $5000 figure is reduced by the amount of any automatic premium loan authorized after the date of the filing of the petition under section 542(d). Paragraph (9) exempts professionally prescribed health aids.

Paragraph (10) exempts certain benefits that are akin to future earnings of the debtor. These include social security, unemployment compensation, or public assistance benefits, veteran's benefits, disability, illness, or unemployment benefits, alimony, support, or separate maintenance (but only to the extent reasonably necessary for the support of the debtor and any dependents of the debtor), and benefits under a certain stock bonus, pension, profitsharing, annuity or similar plan based on illness, disability, death, age or length of service. Paragraph (11) allows the debtor to exempt certain compensation for losses. These include crime victim's reparation benefits, wrongful death benefits (with a reasonably necessary for support limitation), life insurance proceeds (same limitation), compensation for bodily injury, not including pain and suffering ($10,000 limitation), and loss of future earnings payments (support limitation). This provision in subparagraph (D)(11) is designed to cover payments in compensation of actual bodily injury, such as the loss of a limb, and is not intended to include the attendant costs that accompany such a loss, such as medical payments, pain and suffering, or loss of earnings. Those items are handled separately by the bill.

Subsection (e) protects the debtor's exemptions, either Federal or State, by making unenforceable in a bankruptcy case a waiver of exemptions or a waiver of the debtor's avoiding powers under the following subsections.

Subsection (f) protects the debtor's exemptions, his discharge, and thus his fresh start by permitting him to avoid certain liens on exempt property. The debtor may avoid a judicial lien on any property to the extent that the property could have been exempted in the absence of the lien, and may similarly avoid a nonpurchase-money security interest in certain household and personal goods. The avoiding power is independent of any waiver of exemptions.

Subsection (g) gives the debtor the ability to exempt property that the trustee recovers under one of the trustee's avoiding powers if the property was involuntarily transferred away from the debtor (such as by the fixing of a judicial lien) and if the debtor did not conceal the property. The debtor is also permitted to exempt property that the trustee recovers as the result of the avoiding of the fixing of certain security interests to the extent that the debtor could otherwise have exempted the property.

If the trustee does not pursue an avoiding power to recover a transfer of property that would be exempt, the debtor may pursue it and exempt the property, if the transfer was involuntary and the debtor did not conceal the property. If the debtor wishes to preserve his right to pursue an action under this provision, then he must intervene in any action brought by the trustee based on the same cause of action. It is not intended that the debtor be given an additional opportunity to avoid a transfer or that the transferee have to defend the same action twice. Rather, the section is primarily designed to give the debtor the rights the trustee could have pursued if the trustee chooses not to pursue them. The debtor is given no greater rights under this provision than the trustee, and thus the debtor's avoiding powers under proposed 11 U.S.C. 544, 545, 547, and 548, are subject to proposed 11 U.S.C. 546, as are the trustee's powers.

These subsections are cumulative. The debtor is not required to choose which he will use to gain an exemption. Instead, he may use more than one in any particular instance, just as the trustee's avoiding powers are cumulative.

Subsection (i) permits recovery by the debtor of property transferred in an avoided transfer from either the initial or subsequent transferees. It also permits preserving a transfer for the benefit of the debtor. Under either case the debtor may exempt the property recovered or preserved.

Subsection (k) makes clear that the debtor's aliquot share of the costs and expenses [for] recovery of property that the trustee recovers and the debtor later exempts, and any costs and expenses of avoiding a transfer by the debtor that the debtor has not already paid.

Subsection (l) requires the debtor to file a list of property that he claims as exempt from property of the estate. Absent an objection to the list, the property is exempted. A dependent of the debtor may file it and thus be protected if the debtor fails to file the list.

Subsection (m) requires the clerk of the bankruptcy court to give notice of any exemptions claimed under subsection (l), in order that parties in interest may have an opportunity to object to the claim.

Subsection (n) provides the rule for a joint case: each debtor is entitled to the Federal exemptions provided under this section or to the State exemptions, whichever the debtor chooses. House Report 95–595.

[1] Replaced by 22 USCA § 4060(c).
[2] Replaced by 5 USCA § 8346.
[3] Replaced by 45 USCA § 231m.
[4] Railroad unemployment benefits are covered by 45 USCA § 352(e).
[5] Veteran benefits generally are covered by 38 USCA § 5301.

1984 Acts. Statements by Legislative Leaders, see 1984 U.S. Code Cong. and Adm. News, p. 576.

1986 Acts. House Report No. 99–764 and House Conference Report No. 99–958, see 1986 U.S. Code Cong. and Adm. News, p. 5227.

House Conference Report No. 99–841 and Statement by President, see 1986 U.S. Code Cong. and Adm. News, p. 4075.

1990 Acts. House Report No. 101–681(I), see 1990 U.S. Code Cong. and Adm. News, p. 6472.

1994 Acts. House Report No. 103–835, see 1994 U.S. Code Cong. and Adm. News, p. 3340.

2005 Acts. House Report No. 109–31(Part I), see 2005 U.S. Code Cong. and Adm. News, p. 88.

Legislative Statements

Section 522 of the House amendment represents a compromise on the issue of exemptions between the position taken in the House bill, and that taken in the Senate amendment. Dollar amounts specified in section 522(d) of the House bill have been reduced from amounts as contained in H.R. 8200 as passed by the House. The States may, by passing a law, determine whether the Federal exemptions will apply as an alternative to State exemptions in bankruptcy cases.

Section 522(c)(1) tracks the House bill and provides that dischargeable tax claims may not be collected out of exempt property.

Section 522(f)(2) is derived from the Senate amendment restricting the debtor to avoidance of nonpossessory, nonpurchase money security interests.

Exemptions: Section 522(c)(1) of the House amendment adopts a provision contained in the House bill that dischargeable taxes cannot be collected from exempt assets. This changes present law, which allows collection of dischargeable taxes from exempt property, a rule followed in the Senate amendment. Nondischargeable taxes, however, will continue to the [be] collectable [sic] out of exempt property. It is anticipated that in the next session Congress will review the exemptions from levy currently contained in the Internal Revenue Code [Title 26] with a view to increasing the exemptions to more realistic levels.

References in Text

The Federal Rules of Bankruptcy Procedure, referred to in subsec. (b), are set out in the Appendix to this title.

Section 401, 403, 408, 408A, 414, 457, or 501(a) of the Internal Revenue Code of 1986, referred to in subsecs. (b)(2)(C), (4)(C), (D)(ii)(I), (d)(12), is classified to 26 U.S.C.A. § 401, 403, 408, 408A, 414, 457, or 501(a).

Section 7805 of the Internal Revenue Code of 1986, referred to in subsec. (b)(4)(A), (B), is 26 U.S.C.A. § 7805.

The Internal Revenue Code of 1986, referred to in subsec. (b)(4)(B)(ii)(I), (II), is classified to Title 26 of the Code.

Section 402(c) of the Internal Revenue Code of 1986, referred to in subsec. (b)(4)(D)(i), is 26 U.S.C.A. § 402(c).

Section 401(a), 403(a), 403(b), or 408, of the Internal Revenue Code of 1986, referred to in subsec. (d)(10)(E)(iii), is classified to 26 U.S.C.A. § 401(a), 403(a), 403(b), or 408.

Section 408 or 408A of the Internal Revenue Code of 1986, referred to in subsec. (n), is classified to 26 U.S.C.A. § 408 or 408A.

Section 402(c), 402(e)(6), 403(a)(4), 403(a)(5), and 403(b)(8) of the Internal Revenue Code of 1986, referred to in subsec.

(n), are classified to 26 U.S.C.A. §§ 402(c), 402(e)(6), 403(a)(4), 403(a)(5), and 403(b)(8).

Section 3(a)(47) of the Securities Exchange Act of 1934, referred to in subsec. (q)(1)(B)(i), is June 6, 1934, c. 404, Title I, § 3(a)(47), 48 Stat. 882, as amended, which is classified to 15 U.S.C.A. § 78c(a)(47).

Section 12 or 15(d) of the Securities Exchange Act of 1934, referred to in subsec. (q)(1)(B)(ii), is June 6, 1934, c. 404, Title I, § 12 or 15, 48 Stat. 892 or 895, as amended, which is classified to 15 U.S.C.A. § 78l or 15 U.S.C.A. § 78o.

Section 6 of the Securities Act of 1933, referred to in subsec. (q)(1)(B)(ii), is Act May 27, 1933, c. 38, Title I, § 6, 48 Stat. 78, which is classified to 15 U.S.C.A. § 77f.

Amendments

2010 Amendments. Subsec. (b)(3)(A). Pub.L. 111–327, § 2(a)(17)(A), struck out "petition at" and inserted "petition to", and struck out "located at" and inserted "located in".

Subsec. (c)(1). Pub.L. 111–327, § 2(a)(17)(B), struck out "section 523(a)(5)" and inserted "such paragraph".

Subsec. (d)(1). By notice dated Feb. 25, 2010, 75 F.R. 8747, dollar amount adjusted by the Judicial Conference of the United States which adjusted "$20,200" to "$21,625". See 11 U.S.C.A. § 104 and Adjustment of Dollar Amounts notes under this section.

Subsec. (d)(2). By notice dated Feb. 25, 2010, 75 F.R. 8747, dollar amount adjusted by the Judicial Conference of the United States which adjusted "$3,225" to "$3,450". See 11 U.S.C.A. § 104 and Adjustment of Dollar Amounts notes under this section.

Subsec. (d)(3). By notice dated Feb. 25, 2010, 75 F.R. 8747, dollar amount adjusted by the Judicial Conference of the United States which adjusted "$525" to "$550" and "$10,775" to "$11,525". See 11 U.S.C.A. § 104 and Adjustment of Dollar Amounts notes under this section.

Subsec. (d)(4). By notice dated Feb. 25, 2010, 75 F.R. 8747, dollar amount adjusted by the Judicial Conference of the United States which adjusted "$1,350" to "$1,450". See 11 U.S.C.A. § 104 and Adjustment of Dollar Amounts notes under this section.

Subsec. (d)(5). By notice dated Feb. 25, 2010, 75 F.R. 8747, dollar amount adjusted by the Judicial Conference of the United States which adjusted "$1,075" to "$1,150" and "$10,125" to "$10,825". See 11 U.S.C.A. § 104 and Adjustment of Dollar Amounts notes under this section.

Subsec. (d)(6). By notice dated Feb. 25, 2010, 75 F.R. 8747, dollar amount adjusted by the Judicial Conference of the United States which adjusted "$2,025" to "$2,175". See 11 U.S.C.A. § 104 and Adjustment of Dollar Amounts notes under this section.

Subsec. (d)(8). By notice dated Feb. 25, 2010, 75 F.R. 8747, dollar amount adjusted by the Judicial Conference of the United States which adjusted "$10,775" to "$11,525". See 11 U.S.C.A. § 104 and Adjustment of Dollar Amounts notes under this section.

Subsec. (d)(11)(D). By notice dated Feb. 25, 2010, 75 F.R. 8747, dollar amount adjusted by the Judicial Conference of the United States which adjusted "$20,200" to "$21,625". See 11 U.S.C.A. § 104 and Adjustment of Dollar Amounts notes under this section.

Subsec. (f)(3). By notice dated Feb. 25, 2010, 75 F.R. 8747, dollar amount adjusted by the Judicial Conference of the United States which adjusted "$5,475" to "$5,850". See 11 U.S.C.A. § 104 and Adjustment of Dollar Amounts notes under this section.

Subsec. (f)(4)(B). By notice dated Feb. 25, 2010, 75 F.R. 8747, dollar amount adjusted by the Judicial Conference of the United States which adjusted "$550" each time it appeared to "$600" each time it appeared. See 11 U.S.C.A. § 104 and Adjustment of Dollar Amounts notes under this section.

Subsec. (n). By notice dated Feb. 25, 2010, 75 F.R. 8747, dollar amount adjusted by the Judicial Conference of the United States which adjusted "$1,095,000" to "$1,171,650". See 11 U.S.C.A. § 104 and Adjustment of Dollar Amounts notes under this section.

Subsec. (p). By notice dated Feb. 25, 2010, 75 F.R. 8747, dollar amount adjusted by the Judicial Conference of the United States which adjusted "$136,875" to "$146,450". See 11 U.S.C.A. § 104 and Adjustment of Dollar Amounts notes under this section.

Subsec. (q). By notice dated Feb. 25, 2010, 75 F.R. 8747, dollar amount adjusted by the Judicial Conference of the United States which adjusted "$136,875" to "$146,450". See 11 U.S.C.A. § 104 and Adjustment of Dollar Amounts notes under this section.

2007 Amendments. Subsec. (d)(1). By notice dated Feb. 14, 2007, 72 F.R. 7082, dollar amount adjusted by the Judicial Conference of the United States which adjusted "$18,450" to "$20,200". See 11 U.S.C.A. § 104 and Adjustment of Dollar Amounts notes under this section.

Subsec. (d)(2). By notice dated Feb. 14, 2007, 72 F.R. 7082, dollar amount adjusted by the Judicial Conference of the United States which adjusted "$2,950" to "$3,225". See 11 U.S.C.A. § 104 and Adjustment of Dollar Amounts notes under this section.

Subsec. (d)(3). By notice dated Feb. 14, 2007, 72 F.R. 7082, dollar amount adjusted by the Judicial Conference of the United States which adjusted "$475" to "$525" and "$9,850" to "$10,775". See 11 U.S.C.A. § 104 and Adjustment of Dollar Amounts notes under this section.

Subsec. (d)(4). By notice dated Feb. 14, 2007, 72 F.R. 7082, dollar amount adjusted by the Judicial Conference of the United States which adjusted "$1,225" to "$1,350". See 11 U.S.C.A. § 104 and Adjustment of Dollar Amounts notes under this section.

Subsec. (d)(5). By notice dated Feb. 14, 2007, 72 F.R. 7082, dollar amount adjusted by the Judicial Conference of the United States which adjusted "$975" to "$1,075" and "$9,250" to "$10,125". See 11 U.S.C.A. § 104 and Adjustment of Dollar Amounts notes under this section.

Subsec. (d)(6). By notice dated Feb. 14, 2007, 72 F.R. 7082, dollar amount adjusted by the Judicial Conference of the United States which adjusted "$1,850" to "$2,025". See 11 U.S.C.A. § 104 and Adjustment of Dollar Amounts notes under this section.

Subsec. (d)(8). By notice dated Feb. 14, 2007, 72 F.R. 7082, dollar amount adjusted by the Judicial Conference of the United States which adjusted "$9,850" to "$10,775". See 11 U.S.C.A. § 104 and Adjustment of Dollar Amounts notes under this section.

Subsec. (d)(11)(D). By notice dated Feb. 14, 2007, 72 F.R. 7082, dollar amount adjusted by the Judicial Conference of the United States which adjusted "$18,450" to "$20,200". See

11 U.S.C.A. § 104 and Adjustment of Dollar Amounts notes under this section.

Subsec. (f)(3). By notice dated Feb. 14, 2007, 72 F.R. 7082, dollar amount adjusted by the Judicial Conference of the United States which adjusted "$5,000" to "$5,475". See 11 U.S.C.A. § 104 and Adjustment of Dollar Amounts notes under this section.

Subsec. (f)(4)(B). By notice dated Feb. 14, 2007, 72 F.R. 7082, dollar amount adjusted by the Judicial Conference of the United States which adjusted "$500" each time it appeared to "$550" each time it appeared. See 11 U.S.C.A. § 104 and Adjustment of Dollar Amounts notes under this section.

Subsec. (n). By notice dated Feb. 14, 2007, 72 F.R. 7082, dollar amount adjusted by the Judicial Conference of the United States which adjusted "$1,000,000" to "$1,095,000". See 11 U.S.C.A. § 104 and Adjustment of Dollar Amounts notes under this section.

Subsec. (p). By notice dated Feb. 14, 2007, 72 F.R. 7082, dollar amount adjusted by the Judicial Conference of the United States which adjusted "$125,000" to "$136,875". See 11 U.S.C.A. § 104 and Adjustment of Dollar Amounts notes under this section.

Subsec. (q). By notice dated Feb. 14, 2007, 72 F.R. 7082, dollar amount adjusted by the Judicial Conference of the United States which adjusted "$125,000" to "$136,875". See 11 U.S.C.A. § 104 and Adjustment of Dollar Amounts notes under this section.

2005 Amendments. Subsec. (b). Pub.L. 109–8, § 224(a)(1), rewrote subsec. (b), which formerly read: "**(b)** Notwithstanding section 541 of this title, an individual debtor may exempt from property of the estate the property listed in either paragraph (1) or, in the alternative, paragraph (2) of this subsection. In joint cases filed under section 302 of this title and individual cases filed under section 301 or 303 of this title by or against debtors who are husband and wife, and whose estates are ordered to be jointly administered under Rule 1015(b) of the Federal Rules of Bankruptcy Procedure, one debtor may not elect to exempt property listed in paragraph (1) and the other debtor elect to exempt property listed in paragraph (2) of this subsection. If the parties cannot agree on the alternative to be elected, they shall be deemed to elect paragraph (1), where such election is permitted under the law of the jurisdiction where the case is filed. Such property is—

"**(1)** property that is specified under subsection (d) of this section, unless the State law that is applicable to the debtor under paragraph (2)(A) of this subsection specifically does not so authorize; or, in the alternative,

"**(2)(A)** any property that is exempt under Federal law, other than subsection (d) of this section, or State or local law that is applicable on the date of the filing of the petition at the place in which the debtor's domicile has been located for the 180 days immediately preceding the date of the filing of the petition, or for a longer portion of such 180–day period than in any other place; and

"**(B)** any interest in property in which the debtor had, immediately before the commencement of the case, an interest as a tenant by the entirety or joint tenant to the extent that such interest as a tenant by the entirety or joint tenant is exempt from process under applicable nonbankruptcy law."

Subsec. (b)(3). Pub.L. 109–8, § 307(2), added "If the effect of the domiciliary requirement under subparagraph (A) is to render the debtor ineligible for any exemption, the debtor may elect to exempt property that is specified under subsection (d)." to the end of par. (3).

Subsec. (b)(3)(A). Pub.L. 109–8, § 307(1)(A), struck out "180 days" and inserted "730 days".

Pub.L. 109–8, § 307(1)(B), struck out ", or for a longer portion of such 180–day period than in any other place" and inserted "or if the debtor's domicile has not been located at a single State for such 730–day period, the place in which the debtor's domicile was located for 180 days immediately preceding the 730–day period or for a longer portion of such 180–day period than in any other place".

Pub.L. 109–8, § 308(1), inserted "subject to subsections (o) and (p)," before "any property".

Subsec. (c)(1). Pub.L. 109–8, § 216(1), rewrote par. (1) which formerly read: "a debt of a kind specified in section 523(a)(1) or 523(a)(5) of this title;"

Subsec. (d). Pub.L. 109–8, § 224(a)(2)(A), in the matter preceding par. (1), substituted "subsection (b)(2)" for "subsection (b)(1)".

Subsec. (d)(12). Pub.L. 109–8, § 224(a)(2)(B), added par. (12).

Subsec. (f)(1)(A). Pub.L. 109–8, § 216(2), substituted "of a kind that is specified in section 523(a)(5); or" for "a debt—

"**(i)** to a spouse, former spouse, or child of the debtor, for alimony to, maintenance for, or support of such spouse or child, in connection with a separation agreement, divorce decree or other order of a court of record, determination made in accordance with State or territorial law by a governmental unit, or property settlement agreement; and

"**(ii)** to the extent that such debt—

"**(I)** is not assigned to another entity, voluntarily, by operation of law, or otherwise; and

"**(II)** includes a liability designated as alimony, maintenance, or support, unless such liability is actually in the nature of alimony, maintenance or support.; or"

Subsec. (f)(4). Pub.L. 109–8, § 313(a), added par. (4).

Subsec. (g)(2). Pub.L. 109–8, § 216(3), substituted "subsection (f)(1)(B)" for "subsection (f)(2)".

Subsec. (n). Pub.L. 109–8, § 224(e)(1), added subsec. (n).

Subsec. (o). Pub.L. 109–8, § 308(2), added subsec. (o).

Subsec. (p). Pub.L. 109–8, § 322(a), added subsec. (p).

Subsec. (q). Pub.L. 109–8, § 322(a), added subsec. (q).

2004 Amendments. Subsec. (d)(1). By notice dated Feb. 18, 2004, 69 F.R. 8482, dollar amount adjusted by the Judicial Conference of the United States which adjusted "$17,425" to "$18,450". See 11 U.S.C.A. § 104 and Adjustment of Dollar Amounts notes under this section.

Subsec. (d)(2). By notice dated Feb. 18, 2004, 69 F.R. 8482, dollar amount adjusted by the Judicial Conference of the United States which adjusted "$2,775" to "$2,950". See 11 U.S.C.A. § 104 and Adjustment of Dollar Amounts notes under this section.

Subsec. (d)(3). By notice dated Feb. 18, 2004, 69 F.R. 8482, dollar amount adjusted by the Judicial Conference of the United States which adjusted "$450" to "$475" and "$9,300" to "$9,850". See 11 U.S.C.A. § 104 and Adjustment of Dollar Amounts notes under this section.

Subsec. (d)(4). By notice dated Feb. 18, 2004, 69 F.R. 8482, dollar amount adjusted by the Judicial Conference of the United States which adjusted "$1,150" to "$1,225". See 11

U.S.C.A. § 104 and Adjustment of Dollar Amounts notes under this section.

Subsec. (d)(5). By notice dated Feb. 18, 2004, 69 F.R. 8482, dollar amount adjusted by the Judicial Conference of the United States which adjusted "$925" to "$975" and "$8,725" to "$9,250". See 11 U.S.C.A. § 104 and Adjustment of Dollar Amounts notes under this section.

Subsec. (d)(6). By notice dated Feb. 18, 2004, 69 F.R. 8482, dollar amount adjusted by the Judicial Conference of the United States which adjusted "$1,750" to "$1,850". See 11 U.S.C.A. § 104 and Adjustment of Dollar Amounts notes under this section.

Subsec. (d)(8). By notice dated Feb. 18, 2004, 69 F.R. 8482, dollar amount adjusted by the Judicial Conference of the United States which adjusted "$9,300" to "$9,850". See 11 U.S.C.A. § 104 and Adjustment of Dollar Amounts notes under this section.

Subsec. (d)(11)(D). By notice dated Feb. 18, 2004, 69 F.R. 8482, dollar amount adjusted by the Judicial Conference of the United States which adjusted "$17,425" to "$18,450". See 11 U.S.C.A. § 104 and Adjustment of Dollar Amounts notes under this section.

2001 Amendments. Subsec. (d)(1). By notice dated Feb. 20, 2001, 66 F.R. 10910, dollar amount adjusted by the Judicial Conference of the United States which adjusted "$16,150" to "$17,425". See 11 U.S.C.A. § 104 and Adjustment of Dollar Amounts notes under this section.

Subsec. (d)(2). By notice dated Feb. 20, 2001, 66 F.R. 10910, dollar amount adjusted by the Judicial Conference of the United States which adjusted "$2,575" to "$2,775". See 11 U.S.C.A. § 104 and Adjustment of Dollar Amounts notes under this section.

Subsec. (d)(3). By notice dated Feb. 20, 2001, 66 F.R. 10910, dollar amount adjusted by the Judicial Conference of the United States which adjusted "$425" to "$450" and "$8,625" to "$9,300". See 11 U.S.C.A. § 104 and Adjustment of Dollar Amounts notes under this section.

Subsec. (d)(4). By notice dated Feb. 20, 2001, 66 F.R. 10910, dollar amount adjusted by the Judicial Conference of the United States which adjusted "$1,075" to "$1,150". See 11 U.S.C.A. § 104 and Adjustment of Dollar Amounts notes under this section.

Subsec. (d)(5). By notice dated Feb. 20, 2001, 66 F.R. 10910, dollar amount adjusted by the Judicial Conference of the United States which adjusted "$850" to "$925" and "$8,075" to "$8,725". See 11 U.S.C.A. § 104 and Adjustment of Dollar Amounts notes under this section.

Subsec. (d)(6). By notice dated Feb. 20, 2001, 66 F.R. 10910, dollar amount adjusted by the Judicial Conference of the United States which adjusted "$1,625" to "$1,750". See 11 U.S.C.A. § 104 and Adjustment of Dollar Amounts notes under this section.

Subsec. (d)(8). By notice dated Feb. 20, 2001, 66 F.R. 10910, dollar amount adjusted by the Judicial Conference of the United States which adjusted "$8,625" to "$9,300". See 11 U.S.C.A. § 104 and Adjustment of Dollar Amounts notes under this section.

Subsec. (d)(11)(D). By notice dated Feb. 20, 2001, 66 F.R. 10910, dollar amount adjusted by the Judicial Conference of the United States which adjusted "$16,150" to "$17,425". See 11 U.S.C.A. § 104 and Adjustment of Dollar Amounts notes under this section.

2000 Amendments. Subsec. (c). Pub.L. 106–420, § 4, struck out "or" at the end of par. (2), substituted "; or" for the period at the end of par. (3), and added par. (4).

1998 Amendments. Subsec. (d)(1). By notice dated Feb. 3, 1998, 63 F.R. 7179, dollar amount adjusted by the Judicial Conference of the United States which adjusted "$15,000" to "$16,150". See 11 U.S.C.A. § 104 and Adjustment of Dollar Amounts notes under this section.

Subsec. (d)(2). By notice dated Feb. 3, 1998, 63 F.R. 7179, dollar amount adjusted by the Judicial Conference of the United States which adjusted "$2,400" to "$2,575". See 11 U.S.C.A. § 104 and Adjustment of Dollar Amounts notes under this section.

Subsec. (d)(3). By notice dated Feb. 3, 1998, 63 F.R. 7179, dollar amount adjusted by the Judicial Conference of the United States which adjusted "$400" to "$425" and "$8,000" to "$8,625". See 11 U.S.C.A. § 104 and Adjustment of Dollar Amounts notes under this section.

Subsec. (d)(4). By notice dated Feb. 3, 1998, 63 F.R. 7179, dollar amount adjusted by the Judicial Conference of the United States which adjusted "$1,000" to "$1,075". See 11 U.S.C.A. § 104 and Adjustment of Dollar Amounts notes under this section.

Subsec. (d)(5). By notice dated Feb. 3, 1998, 63 F.R. 7179, dollar amount adjusted by the Judicial Conference of the United States which adjusted "$800" to "$850" and "$7,500" to "$8,075". See 11 U.S.C.A. § 104 and Adjustment of Dollar Amounts notes under this section.

Subsec. (d)(6). By notice dated Feb. 3, 1998, 63 F.R. 7179, dollar amount adjusted by the Judicial Conference of the United States which adjusted "$1,500" to "$1,625". See 11 U.S.C.A. § 104 and Adjustment of Dollar Amounts notes under this section.

Subsec. (d)(8). By notice dated Feb. 3, 1998, 63 F.R. 7179, dollar amount adjusted by the Judicial Conference of the United States which adjusted "$8,000" to "$8,625". See 11 U.S.C.A. § 104 and Adjustment of Dollar Amounts notes under this section.

Subsec. (d)(11)(D). By notice dated Feb. 3, 1998, 63 F.R. 7179, dollar amount adjusted by the Judicial Conference of the United States which adjusted "$15,000" to "$16,150". See 11 U.S.C.A. § 104 and Adjustment of Dollar Amounts notes under this section.

1994 Amendments. Subsec. (b). Pub.L. 103–394, § 501(d)(12)(A), substituted "Federal Rules of Bankruptcy Procedure" for "Bankruptcy Rules".

Subsec. (d)(1). Pub.L. 103–394, § 108(d)(1), increased the debtor's aggregate interest exemption from $7,500 to $15,000.

Subsec. (d)(2). Pub.L. 103–394, § 108(d)(2), increased the exemption for the debtor's interest in one motor vehicle from $1,200 to $2,400.

Subsec. (d)(3). Pub.L. 103–394, § 108(d)(3), substituted "The debtor's interest, not to exceed $400 in value in any particular item or $8,000 in aggregate value," for "The debtor's interest, not to exceed $200 in value in any particular item or $4,000 in aggregate value,".

Subsec. (d)(4). Pub.L. 103–394, § 108(d)(4), increased the exemption for the debtor's aggregate interest in jewelry from $500 to $1,000.

Subsec. (d)(5). Pub.L. 103–394, § 108(d)(5), substituted "aggregate interest in any property, not to exceed in value

$800 plus up to $7,500" for "aggregate interest in any property, not to exceed in value $400 plus up to $3,750".

Subsec. (d)(6). Pub.L. 103–394, § 108(d)(6), increased the exemption for the debtor's aggregate interest in any implements, professional books or tools, of the trade from $750 to $1,500.

Subsec. (d)(8). Pub.L. 103–394, § 108 (d)(7), increased the debtor's aggregate interest exemption from $4,000 to $8,000.

Subsec. (d)(10)(E)(iii). Pub.L. 103–394, § 501(d)(12)(B)(i), substituted "Internal Revenue Code of 1986" for "Internal Revenue Code of 1954 (26 U.S.C. 401(a), 403(a), 403(b), 408, or 409)"..

Subsec. (d)(11)(D). Pub.L. 103–394, § 108(d)(8), increased the exemption for the debtor's right to receive, or property that is traceable to, a payment on account of personal bodily injury from $7,500 to $15,000.

Subsec. (f)(1)(A). Pub.L. 103–394, § 304(d), added provisions excluding a judicial lien that secures to a specified extent a debt in connection with a separation agreement, divorce decree, or property settlement agreement.

Subsec. (f)(1). Pub.L. 103–394, § 303(1)–(3), designated existing text in entirety as par. (1), redesignated former pars. (1) and (2) as par. (1), subpars. (A) and (B) and former par. (2), subpars. (A) to (C) as par. (1), subpar. (B), cls. (i) to (iii).

Pub.L. 103–394, § 310(1), inserted "but subject to paragraph (3)" after "waiver of exemptions".

Subsec. (f)(2). Pub.L. 103–394, § 303(1)(B), (4), added par. (2) and redesignated former par. (2) as par. (1), subpar. (B).

Subsec. (f)(3). Pub.L. 103–394, § 310(2), added par. (3).

1990 Amendments. Subsec. (c)(3). Pub.L. 101–647 added par. (3).

1986 Amendments. Subsec. (h)(1). Pub.L. 99–554, § 283(i)(1), substituted "553 of this title" for "553 of this tittle".

Subsec. (i)(2). Pub.L. 99–554, § 283(i)(2), substituted "(g) of this section" for "(g) of his section".

1984 Amendments. Subsec. (a)(2). Pub.L. 98–353, § 453(a), added "or, with respect to property that becomes property of an estate after such date, as of the date such property becomes property of the estate" following "petition".

Subsec. (b). Pub.L. 98–353, § 306(a), added provision that in joint cases filed under section 302 of this title and individual cases filed under section 301 or 303 of this title by or against debtors who are husband and wife, and whose estates are ordered to be jointly administered under Rule 1015(b) of the Bankruptcy Rules, one debtor may not elect to exempt property listed in paragraph (1) and the other debtor elect to exempt property listed in paragraph (2) of this subsection, but that if the parties cannot agree on the alternative to be elected, they shall be deemed to elect paragraph (1), where such election is permitted under the law of the jurisdiction where the case is filed.

Subsec. (c). Pub.L. 98–353, § 453(b), substituted "Unless the case is dismissed, property exempted under this section is not liable during or after the case for any debt of the debtor that arose, or that is determined under section 502 of this title as if such debt had arisen, before the commencement of the case, except—

"(1) a debt of a kind specified in section 523(a)(1) or 523(a)(5) of this title; or

"(2) a debt secured by a lien that is—

"(A)(i) not avoided under subsection (f) or (g) of this section or under section 544, 545, 547, 548, 549, or 724(a) of this title; and

"(ii) not void under section 506(d) of this title; or

"(B) a tax lien, notice of which is properly filed." for "Unless the case is dismissed, property exempted under this section is not liable during or after the case for any debt of the debtor that arose, or that is determined under section 502 of this title as if such claim had arisen before the commencement of the case, except—

"(1) a debt of a kind specified in section 523(a)(1) or section 523(a)(5) of this title; or

"(2) a lien that is—

"(A) not avoided under section 544, 545, 547, 548, 549, or 724(a) of this title;

"(B) not voided under section 506(d) of this title; or

"(C)(i) a tax lien, notice of which is properly filed; and

"(ii) avoided under section 545(2) of this title.".

Subsec. (d)(3). Pub.L. 98–353, § 306(b), added "or $4,000 in aggregate value" following "item".

Subsec. (d)(5). Pub.L. 98–353, § 306(c), substituted "The debtor's aggregate interest in any property, not to exceed in value $400 plus up to $3,750 of any unused amount of the exemption provided under paragraph (1) of this subsection" for "The debtor's aggregate interest, not to exceed in value $400 plus any unused amount of the exemption provided under paragraph (1) of this subsection, in any property".

Subsec. (e). Pub.L. 98–353, § 453(c), substituted "an exemption" for "exemptions".

Subsec. (m). Pub.L. 98–353, § 306(d), substituted "Subject to the limitation in subsection (b), this section shall apply separately with respect to each debtor in a joint case" for "This section shall apply separately with respect to each debtor in a joint case".

Effective and Applicability Provisions

2010 Acts. Increase of dollar amounts by Judicial Conference of the United States by notice published Feb. 25, 2010, 75 F.R. 8747 effective April 1, 2010, and increase not applicable to cases commenced before the effective date of the adjustments, i.e., April 1, 2010. See Adjustment of Dollar Amounts notes under 11 U.S.C.A. § 104 and this section.

2007 Acts. Increase of dollar amounts by Judicial Conference of the United States by notice published Feb. 14, 2007, 72 F.R. 7082 effective April 1, 2007, and increase not applicable to cases commenced before the effective date of the adjustments, i.e., April 1, 2007. See Adjustment of Dollar Amounts notes under 11 U.S.C.A. § 104 and this section.

2005 Acts. Amendments by Pub.L. 109–8 effective 180 days after Apr. 20, 2005, with amendments by sections 216, 224(a), (e)(1), 307, and 313(a) of Pub.L. 109–8 not applicable with respect to cases commenced under this title before such effective date, except as otherwise provided, and amendments by sections 308 and 322(a) of Pub.L. 109–8 applicable with respect to cases commenced under this title on or after Apr. 20, 2005, see Pub.L. 109–8, § 1501, set out as a note under 11 U.S.C.A. § 101.

2004 Acts. Adjustment of dollar amounts by Judicial Conference of the United States by notice dated Feb. 18, 2004, 69 F.R. 8482 effective April 1, 2004, and adjustment not applicable to cases commenced before the effective date of the adjustments, i.e., April 1, 2004. See Adjustment of Dollar Amounts notes under 11 U.S.C.A. § 104 and this section.

2001 Acts. Adjustment of dollar amounts by Judicial Conference of the United States by notice dated Feb. 20, 2001, 66 F.R. 10910 effective April 1, 2001, and adjustment not applicable to cases commenced before the effective date of the adjustments, i.e., April 1, 2001. See Adjustment of Dollar Amounts notes under 11 U.S.C.A. § 104 and this section.

1998 Acts. Adjustment of dollar amounts by Judicial Conference of the United States by notice dated Feb. 3, 1998, 63 F.R. 7179 effective April 1, 1998, and adjustment not applicable to cases commenced before the effective date of the adjustments, i.e., April 1, 1998. See Adjustment of Dollar Amounts notes under 11 U.S.C.A. § 104 and this section.

1994 Acts. Amendments by Pub.L. 103–394 effective on Oct. 22, 1994, and not to apply with respect to cases commenced under Title 11 of the United States Code before Oct. 22, 1994, see section 702 of Pub.L. 103–394, set out as a note under section 101 of this title.

1986 Acts. Amendment by Pub.L. 99–554 effective 30 days after Oct. 27, 1986, except as otherwise provided for, see section 302(a) of Pub.L. 99–554, set out as a note under section 581 of Title 28, Judiciary and Judicial Procedure.

1984 Acts. Amendment by Pub.L. 98–353 effective with respect to cases filed 90 days after July 10, 1984, see section 552(a), formerly 553(a) of Pub.L. 98–353, set out as a note under section 101 of this title.

Separability of Provisions

If any provision of or amendment made by Pub.L. 103–394 or the application of such provision or amendment to any person or circumstance is held to be unconstitutional, the remaining provisions of and amendments made by Pub.L. 103–394 and the application of such provisions and amendments to any person or circumstance shall not be affected thereby, see section 701 of Pub.L. 103–394, set out as a note under section 101 of this title.

Adjustment of Dollar Amounts

For adjustment of dollar amounts specified in subsecs. (d)(1) to (6), (8), (11)(D), (f)(3), (4)(B), (n), (p)(1), (q)(1) of this section by the Judicial Conference of the United States, effective Apr. 1, 2010, see note set out under 11 U.S.C.A. § 104 of this title.

By notice dated Feb. 25, 2010, 75 F.R. 8747, the Judicial Conference of the United States adjusted the dollar amounts in provisions specified in subsecs. (d)(1) to (6), (8), (11)(D), (f)(3), (4)(B), (n), (p)(1), (q)(1) of this section, effective Apr. 1, 2010, as follows:

In subsec. (d)(1) adjusted $20,200 to $21,625.

In subsec. (d)(2) adjusted $3,225 to $3,450.

In subsec. (d)(3) adjusted $525 to $550 and $10,775 to $11,525.

In subsec. (d)(4) adjusted $1,350 to $1,450.

In subsec. (d)(5) adjusted $1,075 to $1,150, and $10,125 to $10,825.

In subsec. (d)(6) adjusted $2,025 to $2,175.

In subsec. (d)(8) adjusted $10,775 to $11,525.

In subsec. (d)(11)(D) adjusted $20,200 to $21,625.

In subsec. (f)(3) adjusted $5,475 to $5,850.

In subsec. (f)(4)(B) adjusted $550 (each time it appears) to $600 (each time it appears).

In subsec. (n) adjusted $1,095,000 to $1,171,650.

In subsec. (p)(1) adjusted $136,875 to $146,450.

In subsec. (q)(1) adjusted $136,875 to $146,450.

By notice dated Feb. 14, 2007, 72 F.R. 7082, the Judicial Conference of the United States adjusted the dollar amounts in provisions specified in subsecs. (d)(1) to (6), (8), (11)(D), (f)(3), (4), (n), (p), (q) of this section, effective Apr. 1, 2007, as follows:

In subsec. (d)(1) adjusted $18,450 to $20,200.

In subsec. (d)(2) adjusted $2,950 to $3,225.

In subsec. (d)(3) adjusted $475 to $525 and $9,850 to $10,775.

In subsec. (d)(4) adjusted $1,225 to $1,350.

In subsec. (d)(5) adjusted $975 to $1,075, and $9,250 to $10,125.

In subsec. (d)(6) adjusted $1,850 to $2,025.

In subsec. (d)(8) adjusted $9,850 to $10,775.

In subsec. (d)(11)(D) adjusted $18,450 to $20,200.

In subsec. (f)(3) adjusted $5,000 to $5,475.

In subsec. (f)(4) adjusted $500 (each time it appears) to $550 (each time it appears).

In subsec. (n) adjusted $1,000,000 to $1,095,000.

In subsec. (p) adjusted $125,000 to $136,875.

In subsec. (q) adjusted $125,000 to $136,875.

By notice dated Feb. 18, 2004, 69 F.R. 8482, the Judicial Conference of the United States adjusted the dollar amounts in provisions specified in subsec. (d)(1) to (6), (8), (11)(D) of this section, effective Apr. 1, 2004, as follows:

In subsec. (d)(1) adjusted $17,425 to $18,450.

In subsec. (d)(2) adjusted $2,775 to $2,950.

In subsec. (d)(3) adjusted $450 to $475 and $9,300 to $9,850.

In subsec. (d)(4) adjusted $1,150 to $1,225.

In subsec. (d)(5) adjusted $925 to $975, and $8,725 to $9,250.

In subsec. (d)(6) adjusted $1,750 to $1,850.

In subsec. (d)(8) adjusted $9,300 to $9,850.

In subsec. (d)(11)(D) adjusted $17,425 to $18,450.

By notice dated Feb. 20, 2001, 66 F.R. 10910, the Judicial Conference of the United States adjusted the dollar amounts in provisions specified in subsec. (d)(1) to (6), (8), (11)(D) of this section, effective Apr. 1, 2001, as follows:

In subsec. (d)(1) adjusted $16,150 to $17,425.

In subsec. (d)(2) adjusted $2,575 to $2,775.

In subsec. (d)(3) adjusted $425 to $450 and $8,625 to $9,300.

In subsec. (d)(4) adjusted $1,075 to $1,150.

In subsec. (d)(5) adjusted $850 to $925, and $8,075 to $8,725.

In subsec. (d)(6) adjusted $1,625 to $1,750.

In subsec. (d)(8) adjusted $8,625 to $9,300.

In subsec. (d)(11)(D) adjusted $16,150 to $17,425.

By notice dated Feb. 3, 1998, 63 F.R. 7179, the Judicial Conference of the United States adjusted the dollar amounts in provisions specified in subsec. (d)(1) to (6), (8), (11)(D) of this section, effective Apr. 1, 1998, as follows:

In subsec. (d)(1) adjusted $15,000 to $16,150.

In subsec. (d)(2) adjusted $2,400 to $2,575.

In subsec. (d)(3) adjusted $400 to $425 and $8,000 to $8,625.

In subsec. (d)(4) adjusted $1,000 to $1,075.

In subsec. (d)(5) adjusted $800 to $850 and $7,500 to $8,075.

In subsec. (d)(6) adjusted $1,500 to $1,625.

In subsec. (d)(8) adjusted $8,000 to $8,625.

In subsec. (d)(11)(D) adjusted $15,000 to $16,150.

CROSS REFERENCES

Allowance of claims or interests, see 11 USCA § 502.

Automatic preservation of avoided transfer, see 11 USCA § 551.

Effect of dismissal, see 11 USCA § 349.

Election to terminate debtor's taxable year for purposes of Internal Revenue Code not available to debtor with no assets other than property treated as exempt under this section, see 26 USCA § 1398.

Exempt property as including property treated as exempt under this section for purposes of Federal Debt Collection Act, see 28 USCA § 3014.

Insolvent as meaning financial condition wherein entity's debts are greater than entity's property exclusive of property that may be exempted under this section, see 11 USCA § 101.

Involuntary cases and future adjustments, see 11 USCA § 104.

Penalty for persons who negligently or fraudulently prepare bankruptcy petitions and exempt funds, see 11 USCA § 110.

Postpetition effect of security interest, see 11 USCA § 552.

Property claimed as exempt, see Official Bankr. Form 6, 11 USCA.

Property exempt under this section not subject to enforcement of withdrawal liability for purposes of Employee Retirement Income Security Act Program, see 29 USCA § 1405.

Provisions in plan for use, sale or lease of exempt property, see 11 USCA § 1123.

Redemption, see 11 USCA § 722.

Reduction in basis not allowed for property exempt under this section for purposes of Internal Revenue Code, see 26 USCA § 1017.

Turnover of property to estate, see 11 USCA § 542.

LIBRARY REFERENCES

American Digest System

Bankruptcy ⟐2761 to 2802.

Key Number System Topic No. 51.

Corpus Juris Secundum

CJS Bankruptcy § 278, Parties Defendant; Sovereign Immunity.

CJS Bankruptcy § 400, Relief Available on Recognition.

CJS Bankruptcy § 403, Powers of Foreign Representative on Recognition--Commencement of or Participation in Other Bankruptcy Case.

CJS Bankruptcy § 407, Joint Administration of Estates.

CJS Bankruptcy § 562, Property Acquired Postpetition--Security Interest on Property Acquired Postpetition.

CJS Bankruptcy § 565, Joint Debtors.

CJS Bankruptcy § 566, Property Exempt Under Federal or State Law But Not on the Exemption List, Interests as Tenant by the Entirety or Joint Tenant, and Retirement Funds.

CJS Bankruptcy § 567, Property Exempt Under Federal or State Law But Not on the Exemption List, Interests as Tenant by the Entirety or Joint Tenant, and Retirement Funds--Tenancy by the Entirety or Joint Tenancy.

CJS Bankruptcy § 568, Property Exempt Under Federal or State Law But Not on the Exemption List, Interests as Tenant by the Entirety or Joint Tenant, and Retirement Funds--Retirement Funds.

CJS Bankruptcy § 569, Bankruptcy Code Exemption List.

CJS Bankruptcy § 571, Waiver or Loss of Exemption Power.

CJS Bankruptcy § 572, Operation and Effect of Exemption.

CJS Bankruptcy § 573, Individual Debtors.

CJS Bankruptcy § 574, Dependents or Spouse of Debtor.

CJS Bankruptcy § 575, Restriction of Exemption to Individual With Equity in Property.

CJS Bankruptcy § 576, Filing List of Property Claimed as Exempt.

CJS Bankruptcy § 585, Extension of Time; Effect of Absence of Timely Objection.

CJS Bankruptcy § 589, Property Debtor Could Have Exempted Absent Transfer of that Property.

CJS Bankruptcy § 590, Recovery and Exemption of Property After Transfer Avoided.

CJS Bankruptcy § 592, Requirement that Transfer Debtor Seeks to Set Aside be Involuntary.

CJS Bankruptcy § 594, Requirement that Property be Exempt and be Claimed as Exempt.

CJS Bankruptcy § 595, Requirement that Lien Impair Exemption.

CJS Bankruptcy § 596, Federal or State Law as Governing.

CJS Bankruptcy § 600, Implements, Professional Books, or Tools of Debtor's or Debtor's Dependent's Trade.

CJS Bankruptcy § 601, Nonpossession Component of Security Interest.

CJS Bankruptcy § 602, Purchase-Money Component of Security Interest.

CJS Bankruptcy § 603, Limitation to Property on Bankruptcy Code List of Exemptions.

CJS Bankruptcy § 605, Reopening Case to Avoid Lien.

CJS Bankruptcy § 700, Disallowance of Claims of Entities or Transferees Holding Recoverable Property.

CJS Bankruptcy § 743, Chapter 11 Debtors in Possession.

CJS Bankruptcy § 744, Chapters 7 and 13 Individual Debtors.

CJS Bankruptcy § 1045, Abuse of Bankruptcy Code Provisions; Liability for Certain Debts.

CJS Bankruptcy § 1137, Means of Implementation.

CJS Bankruptcy § 1138, Protection of Exempted Property.

CJS Bankruptcy § 1209, Discharge--Grounds for Denial or Revocation of Discharge.

CJS Estoppel and Waiver § 187, Court's Discretion; Determinative Factors in Applying Judicial Estoppel.

CJS Exemptions § 171, Forfeiture of Exemption--Conversion of Nonexempt Into Exempt Property.

CJS Internal Revenue § 319, Individual Retirement Accounts and Individual Retirement Annuities.

CJS Internal Revenue § 724, Priority.

§ 523. Exceptions to discharge

(a) A discharge under section 727, 1141, 1228(a), 1228(b), or 1328(b) of this title does not discharge an individual debtor from any debt—

(1) for a tax or a customs duty—

(A) of the kind and for the periods specified in section 507(a)(3) or 507(a)(8) of this title, whether or not a claim for such tax was filed or allowed;

(B) with respect to which a return, or equivalent report or notice, if required—

(i) was not filed or given; or

(ii) was filed or given after the date on which such return, report, or notice was last due, under applicable law or under any extension, and after two years before the date of the filing of the petition; or

(C) with respect to which the debtor made a fraudulent return or willfully attempted in any manner to evade or defeat such tax;

(2) for money, property, services, or an extension, renewal, or refinancing of credit, to the extent obtained by—

(A) false pretenses, a false representation, or actual fraud, other than a statement respecting the debtor's or an insider's financial condition;

(B) use of a statement in writing—

(i) that is materially false;

(ii) respecting the debtor's or an insider's financial condition;

(iii) on which the creditor to whom the debtor is liable for such money, property, services, or credit reasonably relied; and

(iv) that the debtor caused to be made or published with intent to deceive; or

(C)(i) for purposes of subparagraph (A)—

(I) consumer debts owed to a single creditor and aggregating more than $600 [1] for luxury goods or services incurred by an individual debtor on or within 90 days before the order for relief under this title are presumed to be nondischargeable; and

(II) cash advances aggregating more than $875 [1] that are extensions of consumer credit under an open end credit plan obtained by an individual debtor on or within 70 days before the order for relief under this title, are presumed to be nondischargeable; and

(ii) for purposes of this subparagraph—

(I) the terms "consumer", "credit", and "open end credit plan" have the same meanings as in section 103 of the Truth in Lending Act; and

(II) the term "luxury goods or services" does not include goods or services reasonably necessary for the support or maintenance of the debtor or a dependent of the debtor;

(3) neither listed nor scheduled under section 521(a)(1) of this title, with the name, if known to the debtor, of the creditor to whom such debt is owed, in time to permit—

(A) if such debt is not of a kind specified in paragraph (2), (4), or (6) of this subsection, timely filing of a proof of claim, unless such creditor had notice or actual knowledge of the case in time for such timely filing; or

(B) if such debt is of a kind specified in paragraph (2), (4), or (6) of this subsection, timely filing of a proof of claim and timely request for a determination of dischargeability of such debt under one of such paragraphs, unless such creditor had notice or actual knowledge of the case in time for such timely filing and request;

(4) for fraud or defalcation while acting in a fiduciary capacity, embezzlement, or larceny;

(5) for a domestic support obligation;

(6) for willful and malicious injury by the debtor to another entity or to the property of another entity;

(7) to the extent such debt is for a fine, penalty, or forfeiture payable to and for the benefit of a governmental unit, and is not compensation for actual pecuniary loss, other than a tax penalty—

(A) relating to a tax of a kind not specified in paragraph (1) of this subsection; or

(B) imposed with respect to a transaction or event that occurred before three years before the date of the filing of the petition;

(8) unless excepting such debt from discharge under this paragraph would impose an undue hardship on the debtor and the debtor's dependents, for—

(A)(i) an educational benefit overpayment or loan made, insured, or guaranteed by a governmental unit, or made under any program funded in whole or in part by a governmental unit or nonprofit institution; or

(ii) an obligation to repay funds received as an educational benefit, scholarship, or stipend; or

(B) any other educational loan that is a qualified education loan, as defined in section 221(d)(1) of the Internal Revenue Code of 1986, incurred by a debtor who is an individual;

(9) for death or personal injury caused by the debtor's operation of a motor vehicle, vessel, or aircraft if such operation was unlawful because the debtor was intoxicated from using alcohol, a drug, or another substance;

(10) that was or could have been listed or scheduled by the debtor in a prior case concerning the debtor under this title or under the Bankruptcy Act in which the debtor waived discharge, or was denied a discharge under section 727(a)(2), (3), (4), (5), (6),

or (7) of this title, or under section 14c(1), (2), (3), (4), (6), or (7) of such Act;

(11) provided in any final judgment, unreviewable order, or consent order or decree entered in any court of the United States or of any State, issued by a Federal depository institutions regulatory agency, or contained in any settlement agreement entered into by the debtor, arising from any act of fraud or defalcation while acting in a fiduciary capacity committed with respect to any depository institution or insured credit union;

(12) for malicious or reckless failure to fulfill any commitment by the debtor to a Federal depository institutions regulatory agency to maintain the capital of an insured depository institution, except that this paragraph shall not extend any such commitment which would otherwise be terminated due to any act of such agency;

(13) for any payment of an order of restitution issued under title 18, United States Code;

(14) incurred to pay a tax to the United States that would be nondischargeable pursuant to paragraph (1);

(14A) incurred to pay a tax to a governmental unit, other than the United States, that would be nondischargeable under paragraph (1);

(14B) incurred to pay fines or penalties imposed under Federal election law;

(15) to a spouse, former spouse, or child of the debtor and not of the kind described in paragraph (5) that is incurred by the debtor in the course of a divorce or separation or in connection with a separation agreement, divorce decree or other order of a court of record, or a determination made in accordance with State or territorial law by a governmental unit;

(16) for a fee or assessment that becomes due and payable after the order for relief to a membership association with respect to the debtor's interest in a unit that has condominium ownership, in a share of a cooperative corporation, or a lot in a homeowners association, for as long as the debtor or the trustee has a legal, equitable, or possessory ownership interest in such unit, such corporation, or such lot, but nothing in this paragraph shall except from discharge the debt of a debtor for a membership association fee or assessment for a period arising before entry of the order for relief in a pending or subsequent bankruptcy case;

(17) for a fee imposed on a prisoner by any court for the filing of a case, motion, complaint, or appeal, or for other costs and expenses assessed with respect to such filing, regardless of an assertion of poverty by the debtor under subsection (b) or (f)(2) of section 1915 of title 28 (or a similar non–Federal law), or the debtor's status as a prisoner, as defined in section 1915(h) of title 28 (or a similar non–Federal law);

(18) owed to a pension, profit-sharing, stock bonus, or other plan established under section 401, 403, 408, 408A, 414, 457, or 501(c) of the Internal Revenue Code of 1986, under—

(A) a loan permitted under section 408(b)(1) of the Employee Retirement Income Security Act of 1974, or subject to section 72(p) of the Internal Revenue Code of 1986; or

(B) a loan from a thrift savings plan permitted under subchapter III of chapter 84 of title 5, that satisfies the requirements of section 8433(g) of such title;

but nothing in this paragraph may be construed to provide that any loan made under a governmental plan under section 414(d), or a contract or account under section 403(b), of the Internal Revenue Code of 1986 constitutes a claim or a debt under this title; or

(19) that—

(A) is for—

(i) the violation of any of the Federal securities laws (as that term is defined in section 3(a)(47) of the Securities Exchange Act of 1934), any of the State securities laws, or any regulation or order issued under such Federal or State securities laws; or

(ii) common law fraud, deceit, or manipulation in connection with the purchase or sale of any security; and

(B) results, before, on, or after the date on which the petition was filed, from—

(i) any judgment, order, consent order, or decree entered in any Federal or State judicial or administrative proceeding;

(ii) any settlement agreement entered into by the debtor; or

(iii) any court or administrative order for any damages, fine, penalty, citation, restitutionary payment, disgorgement payment, attorney fee, cost, or other payment owed by the debtor.

For purposes of this subsection, the term "return" means a return that satisfies the requirements of applicable nonbankruptcy law (including applicable filing requirements). Such term includes a return prepared pursuant to section 6020(a) of the Internal Revenue Code of 1986, or similar State or local law, or a written stipulation to a judgment or a final order entered by a nonbankruptcy tribunal, but does not include a return made pursuant to section 6020(b) of the Internal Revenue Code of 1986, or a similar State or local law.

(b) Notwithstanding subsection (a) of this section, a debt that was excepted from discharge under subsection (a)(1), (a)(3), or (a)(8) of this section, under section 17a(1), 17a(3), or 17a(5) of the Bankruptcy Act, under section 439A of the Higher Education Act of 1965, or under section 733(g) of the Public Health Service Act in a prior case concerning the debtor under this title, or under the Bankruptcy Act, is dischargeable in a case under this title unless, by the terms of subsection (a) of this section, such debt is not dischargeable in the case under this title.

(c)(1) Except as provided in subsection (a)(3)(B) of this section, the debtor shall be discharged from a debt of a kind specified in paragraph (2), (4), or (6) of subsection (a) of this section, unless, on request of the creditor to whom such debt is owed, and after notice and a hearing, the court determines such debt to be excepted from discharge under paragraph (2), (4), or (6), as the case may be, of subsection (a) of this section.

(2) Paragraph (1) shall not apply in the case of a Federal depository institutions regulatory agency seeking, in its capacity as conservator, receiver, or liquidating agent for an insured depository institution, to recover a debt described in subsection (a)(2), (a)(4), (a)(6), or (a)(11) owed to such institution by an institution-affiliated party unless the receiver, conservator, or liquidating agent was appointed in time to reasonably comply, or for a Federal depository institutions regulatory agency acting in its corporate capacity as a successor to such receiver, conservator, or liquidating agent to reasonably comply, with subsection (a)(3)(B) as a creditor of such institution-affiliated party with respect to such debt.

(d) If a creditor requests a determination of dischargeability of a consumer debt under subsection (a)(2) of this section, and such debt is discharged, the court shall grant judgment in favor of the debtor for the costs of, and a reasonable attorney's fee for, the proceeding if the court finds that the position of the creditor was not substantially justified, except that the court shall not award such costs and fees if special circumstances would make the award unjust.

(e) Any institution-affiliated party of an insured depository institution shall be considered to be acting in a fiduciary capacity with respect to the purposes of subsection (a)(4) or (11).

(Pub.L. 95–598, Nov. 6, 1978, 92 Stat. 2590; Pub.L. 96–56, § 3, Aug. 14, 1979, 93 Stat. 387; Pub.L. 97–35, Title XXIII, § 2334(b), Aug. 13, 1981, 95 Stat. 863; Pub.L. 98–353, Title III, §§ 307, 371, 454, July 10, 1984, 98 Stat. 353, 364, 375; Pub.L. 99–554, Title II, §§ 257(n), 281, 283(j), Oct. 27, 1986, 100 Stat. 3115 to 3117; Pub.L. 101–581, § 2(a), Nov. 15, 1990, 104 Stat. 2865; Pub.L. 101–647, Title XXV, § 2522(a), Title XXXI, § 3102(a), Title XXXVI, § 3621, Nov. 29, 1990, 104 Stat. 4865, 4916, 4964; Pub.L. 103–322, Title XXXII, § 320934, Sept. 13, 1994, 108 Stat. 2135; Pub.L. 103–394, Title II, § 221, Title III, §§ 304(e), (h)(3), 306, 309, Title V, § 501(d)(13), Oct. 22, 1994, 108 Stat. 4129, 4133 to 4135, 4137, 4145; Pub.L. 104–134, Title I, § 101[(a)][Title VIII, § 804(b)], Apr. 26, 1996, 110 Stat. 1321–74; renumbered Title I Pub.L. 104–140, § 1(a), May 2, 1996, 110 Stat. 1327; amended Pub.L. 104–193, Title III, § 374(a), Aug. 22, 1996, 110 Stat. 2255; Pub.L. 105–244, Title IX, § 971(a), Oct. 7, 1998, 112 Stat.

1837; Pub.L. 107–204, Title VIII, § 803, July 30, 2002, 116 Stat. 801; Pub.L. 109–8, Title II, §§ 215, 220, 224(c), Title III, §§ 301, 310, 314(a), Title IV, § 412, Title VII, § 714, Title XII, §§ 1209, 1235, Title XIV, § 1404(a), Title XV, § 1502(a)(2), Apr. 20, 2005, 119 Stat. 54, 59, 64, 75, 84, 88, 107, 128, 194, 204, 215, 216; Pub.L. 111–327, § 2(a)(18), Dec. 22, 2010, 124 Stat. 3559.)

1 Dollar amount as adjusted by the Judicial Conference of the United States. See Adjustment of Dollar Amounts notes set out under this section and 11 U.S.C.A. § 104.

HISTORICAL AND STATUTORY NOTES
Revision Notes and Legislative Reports

1978 Acts. This section specifies which of the debtor's debts are not discharged in a bankruptcy case, and certain procedures for effectuating the section. The provision in Bankruptcy Act § 17c [section § 35(c) of former Title 11] granting the bankruptcy courts jurisdiction to determine dischargeability is deleted as unnecessary, in view of the comprehensive grant of jurisdiction prescribed in proposed 28 U.S.C. 1334(b), which is adequate to cover the full jurisdiction that the bankruptcy courts have today over dischargeability and related issues under Bankruptcy Act § 17c [section 35(c) of former Title 11]. The Rules of Bankruptcy Procedure will specify, as they do today, who may request determinations of dischargeability, subject, of course, to proposed 11 U.S.C. 523(c), and when such a request may be made. Proposed 11 U.S.C. 350, providing for reopening of cases, provides one possible procedure for a determination of dischargeability and related issues after a case is closed.

Subsection (a) lists nine kinds of debts excepted from discharge. Taxes that are excepted from discharge are set forth in paragraph (1). These include claims against the debtor which receive priority in the second, third and sixth categories (§ 507(a)(3)(B) and (C) and (6)). These categories include taxes for which the tax authority failed to file a claim against the estate or filed its claim late. Whether or not the taxing authority's claim is secured will also not affect the claim's nondischargeability if the tax liability in question is otherwise entitled to priority.

Also included in the nondischargeable debts are taxes for which the debtor had not filed a required return as of the petition date, or for which a return had been filed beyond its last permitted due date (§ 523(a)(1)(B)). For this purpose, the date of the tax year to which the return relates is immaterial. The late return rule applies, however, only to the late returns filed within three years before the petition was filed, and to late returns filed after the petition in title 11 was filed. For this purpose, the taxable year in question need not be one or more of the three years immediately preceding the filing of the petition.

Tax claims with respect to which the debtor filed a fraudulent return, entry or invoice, or fraudulently attempted to evade or defeat any tax (§ 523(a)(1)(C)) are included. The date of the taxable year with regard to which the fraud occurred is immaterial.

Also included are tax payments due under an agreement for deferred payment of taxes, which a debtor had entered into with the Internal Revenue Service (or State or local tax authority) before the filing of the petition and which relate to a prepetition tax liability (§ 523(a)(1)(D)) are also nondischargeable. This classification applies only to tax claims which would have received priority under section 507(a) if the taxpayer had filed a title 11 petition on the date on which the deferred payment agreement was entered into. This rule also applies only to installment payments which become due during and after the commencement of the title 11 case. Payments which had become due within one year before the filing of the petition receive sixth priority, and will be nondischargeable under the general rule of section 523(a)(1)(A).

The above categories of nondischargeability apply to customs duties as well as to taxes.

Paragraph (2) provides that as under Bankruptcy Act § 17a(2) [section 35(a)(2) of former Title 11], a debt for obtaining money, property, services, or a refinancing extension or renewal of credit by false pretenses, a false representation, or actual fraud, or by use of a statement in writing respecting the debtor's financial condition that is materially false, on which the creditor reasonably relied, and which the debtor made or published with intent to deceive, is excepted from discharge. This provision is modified only slightly from current section 17a(2) [section 35(a)(2) of former Title 11]. First, "actual fraud" is added as a ground for exception from discharge. Second, the creditor must not only have relied on a false statement in writing, but the reliance must have been reasonable. This codifies case law construing present section 17a(2) [section 35(a)(2) of former Title 11]. Third, the phrase "in any manner whatsoever" that appears in current law after "made or published" is deleted as unnecessary, the word "published" is used in the same sense that it is used in defamation cases.

Unscheduled debts are excepted from discharge under paragraph (3). The provision, derived from section 17a(3) [section 35(a)(3) of former Title 11], follows current law, but clarifies some uncertainties generated by the case law construing 17a(3) [section 35(a)(3) of former Title 11]. The debt is excepted from discharge if it was not scheduled in time to permit timely action by the creditor to protect his rights, unless the creditor had notice or actual knowledge of the case.

Paragraph (4) excepts debts for fraud incurred by the debtor while acting in a fiduciary capacity or for defalcation, embezzlement, or misappropriation.

Paragraph (5) provides that debts for willful and malicious conversion or injury by the debtor to another entity or the property of another entity are nondischargeable. Under this paragraph "willful" means deliberate or intentional. To the extent that *Tinker v. Colwell*, 139 U.S. 473 (1902) [24 S.Ct. 505, 48 L.Ed. 754, 11 Am.Bankr.Rep. 568], held that a less strict standard is intended, and to the extent that other cases have relied on *Tinker* to apply a "reckless disregard" standard, they are overruled.

Paragraph (6) excepts from discharge debts to a spouse, former spouse, or child of the debtor for alimony to, maintenance for, or support of the spouse or child. This language, in combination with the repeal of section 456(b) of the Social Security Act (42 U.S.C. 656(b)) [section 656(b) of Title 42, The Public Health and Welfare] by section 326 of the bill, will apply to make nondischargeable only alimony, maintenance, or support owed directly to a spouse or dependent. What constitutes alimony, maintenance, or support, will be determined under the bankruptcy law, not State law. Thus, cases such as *In re Waller*, 494 F.2d 447 (6th Cir. 1974), are overruled, and the result in cases such as *Fife v. Fife*, 1 Utah 2d 281, 265 P.2d 642 (1952) is followed. The proviso, however, makes nondischargeable any debts resulting from an agreement by the debtor to hold the debtor's spouse harmless on joint debts, to the extent that the agreement is in payment of alimony, maintenance, or support of the spouse, as deter-

mined under bankruptcy law considerations as to whether a particular agreement to pay money to a spouse is actually alimony or a property settlement.

Paragraph (7) makes nondischargeable certain liabilities for penalties including tax penalties if the underlying tax with respect to which the penalty was imposed is also nondischargeable (sec. 523(a)(7)). These latter liabilities cover those which, but are penal in nature, as distinct from so-called "pecuniary loss" penalties which, in the case of taxes, involve basically the collection of a tax under the label of a "penalty." This provision differs from the bill as introduced, which did not link the nondischarge of a tax penalty with the treatment of the underlying tax. The amended provision reflects the existing position of the Internal Revenue Service as to tax penalties imposed by the Internal Revenue Code [Title 26] (Rev.Rul. 68–574, 1968–2 C.B. 595).

Paragraph (8) follows generally current law and excerpts [sic] from discharge student loans until such loans have been due and owing for five years. Such loans include direct student loans as well as insured and guaranteed loans. This provision is intended to be self-executing and the lender or institution is not required to file a complaint to determine the nondischargeability of any student loan.

Paragraph (9) excepts from discharge debts that the debtor owed before a previous bankruptcy case concerning the debtor in which the debtor was denied a discharge other than on the basis of the six-year bar.

Subsection (b) of this section permits discharge in a bankruptcy case of an unscheduled debt from a prior case. This provision is carried over from Bankruptcy Act § 17b [section 35(b) of former Title 11]. The result dictated by the subsection would probably not be different if the subsection were not included. It is included nevertheless for clarity.

Subsection (c) requires a creditor who is owed a debt that may be excepted from discharge under paragraph (2), (4), or (5), (false statements, defalcation or larceny misappropriation, or willful and malicious injury) to initiate proceedings in the bankruptcy court for an exception to discharge. If the creditor does not act, the debt is discharged. This provision does not change current law.

Subsection (d) is new. It provides protection to a consumer debtor that dealt honestly with a creditor who sought to have a debt excepted from discharge on the ground of falsity in the incurring of the debt. The debtor may be awarded costs and a reasonable attorney's fee for the proceeding to determine the dischargeability of a debt under subsection (a)(2), if the court finds that the proceeding was frivolous or not brought by its creditor in good faith.

The purpose of the provision is to discourage creditors from initiating proceedings to obtaining a false financial statement exception to discharge in the hope of obtaining a settlement from an honest debtor anxious to save attorney's fees. Such practices impair the debtor's fresh start and are contrary to the spirit of the bankruptcy laws. Senate Report 95–989.

Subsection (a) lists eight kinds of debts excepted from discharge. Taxes that are entitled to priority are excepted from discharge under paragraph (1). In addition, taxes with respect to which the debtor made a fraudulent return or willfully attempted to evade or defeat, or with respect to which a return (if required) was not filed or was not filed after the due date and after one year before the bankruptcy case are excepted from discharge. If the taxing authority's claim has been disallowed, then it would be barred by the more modern rules of collateral estoppel from reasserting that claim against the debtor after the case was closed. See Plumb, The Tax Recommendations of the Commission on the Bankruptcy Laws: Tax Procedures, 88 Harv.L.Rev. 1360, 1388 (1975).

As under Bankruptcy Act § 17a(2) [section 35(a)(2) of former Title 11], a debt for obtaining money, property, services, or an extension or renewal of credit by false pretenses, a false representation, or actual fraud, or by use of a statement in writing respecting the debtor's financial condition that is materially false, on which the creditor reasonably relied, and that the debtor made or published with intent to deceive, is excepted from discharge. This provision is modified only slightly from current section 17a(2). First, "actual fraud" is added as a grounds for exception from discharge. Second, the creditor must not only have relied on a false statement in writing, the reliance must have been reasonable. This codifies case law construing this provision. Third, the phrase "in any manner whatsoever" that appears in current law after "made or published" is deleted as unnecessary. The word "published" is used in the same sense that it is used in slander actions.

Unscheduled debts are excepted from discharge under paragraph (3). The provision, derived from section 17a(3) [section 35(a)(3) of former Title 11], follows current law, but clarifies some uncertainties generated by the case law construing 17a(3). The debt is excepted from discharge if it was not scheduled in time to permit timely action by the creditor to protect his rights, unless the creditor had notice or actual knowledge of the case.

Paragraph (4) excepts debts for embezzlement or larceny. The deletion of willful and malicious conversion from § 17a(2) [section 35(a)(2) of former Title 11] of the Bankruptcy Act is not intended to effect a substantive change. The intent is to include in the category of non-dischargeable debts a conversion under which the debtor willfully and maliciously intends to borrow property for a short period of time with no intent to inflict injury but on which injury is in fact inflicted.

Paragraph (5) excepts from discharge debts to a spouse, former spouse, or child of the debtor for alimony to, maintenance for, or support of, the spouse or child. This language, in combination with the repeal of section 456(b) of the Social Security Act (42 U.S.C. 656(b)) [former section 656(b) of Title 42, The Public Health and Welfare] by section 327 of the bill, will apply to make nondischargeable only alimony, maintenance, or support owed directly to a spouse or dependent. See Hearings, pt. 2, at 942. What constitutes alimony, maintenance, or support, will be determined under the bankruptcy laws, not State law. Thus, cases such as *In re Waller*, 494 F.2d 447 (6th Cir. 1974); Hearings, pt. 3, at 1308–10, are overruled, and the result in cases such as *Fife v. Fife*, 1 Utah 2d 281, 265 P.2d 642 (1952) is followed. This provision will, however, make nondischargeable any debts resulting from an agreement by the debtor to hold the debtor's spouse harmless on joint debts, to the extent that the agreement is in payment of alimony, maintenance, or support of the spouse, as determined under bankruptcy law considerations that are similar to considerations of whether a particular agreement to pay money to a spouse is actually alimony or a property settlement. See Hearings, pt. 3, at 1287–1290.

Paragraph (6) excepts debts for willful and malicious injury by the debtor to another person or to the property of another person. Under this paragraph, "willful" means deliberate or intentional. To the extent that *Tinker v. Colwell*, 193 U.S.

473 (1902) [24 S.Ct. 505, 48 L.Ed. 754, 11 Am.Bankr.Rep. 568], held that a looser standard is intended, and to the extent that other cases have relied on *Tinker* to apply a "reckless disregard" standard, they are overruled.

Paragraph (7) excepts from discharge a debt for a fine, penalty, or forfeiture payable to and for the benefit of a governmental unit, that is not compensation for actual pecuniary loss.

Paragraph (8) [now (9)] excepts from discharge debts that the debtor owed before a previous bankruptcy case concerning the debtor in which the debtor was denied a discharge other than on the basis of the six-year bar.

Subsection (b) of this section permits discharge in a bankruptcy case of an unscheduled debt from a prior case. This provision is carried over from Bankruptcy Act § 17b [section 35(b) of former Title 11]. The result dictated by the subsection would probably not be different if the subsection were not included. It is included nevertheless for clarity.

Subsection (c) requires a creditor who is owed a debt that may be expected from discharge under paragraph (2), (4), or (6) (false statements, embezzlement or larceny, or willful and malicious injury) to initiate proceedings in the bankruptcy court for an exception to discharge. If the creditor does not act, the debt is discharged. This provision does not change current law.

Subsection (d) is new. It provides protection to a consumer debtor that dealt honestly with a creditor who sought to have a debt excepted from discharge on grounds of falsity in the incurring of the debt. The debtor is entitled to costs of and a reasonable attorney's fee for the proceeding to determine the dischargeability of a debt under subsection (a)(2), if the creditor initiated the proceeding and the debt was determined to be dischargeable. The court is permitted to award any actual pecuniary loss that the debtor may have suffered as a result of the proceeding (such as loss of a day's pay). The purpose of the provision is to discourage creditors from initiating false financial statement exception to discharge actions in the hopes of obtaining a settlement from an honest debtor anxious to save attorney's fees. Such practices impair the debtor's fresh start. House Report No. 95–595.

1979 Acts. Senate Report No. 96–230, see 1979 U.S. Code Cong. and Adm. News, p. 936.

1981 Acts. Senate Report No. 97–139 and House Conference Report No. 97–208, see 1981 U.S. Code Cong. and Adm. News, p. 396.

1984 Acts. Statements by Legislative Leaders, see 1984 U.S. Code Cong. and Adm. News, p. 576.

1986 Acts. House Report No. 99–764 and House Conference Report No. 99–958, see 1986 U.S. Code Cong. and Adm. News, p. 5227.

1990 Acts. House Report No. 101–681(Part I), see 1990 U.S. Code Cong. and Adm. News, p. 6472.

Senate Report No. 101–434, see 1990 U.S. Code Cong. and Adm. News, p. 4065.

1994 Acts. House Report Nos. 103–324 and 103–489, and House Conference Report No. 103–711, see 1994 U.S. Code Cong. and Adm. News, p. 1801.

House Report No. 103–835, see 1994 U.S. Code Cong. and Adm. News, p. 3340.

1996 Acts. House Report No. 104–651 and House Conference Report No. 104–725, see 1996 U.S. Code Cong. and Adm. News, p. 2183.

1998 Acts. House Conference Report No. 105–750, see 1998 U.S. Code Cong. and Adm. News, p. 417.

2002 Acts. House Conference Report No. 107–610 and Statement by President, see 2002 U.S. Code Cong. and Adm. News, p. 542.

2005 Acts. House Report No. 109–31(Part I), see 2005 U.S. Code Cong. and Adm. News, p. 88.

Legislative Statements

Section 523(a)(1) represents a compromise between the position taken in the House bill and the Senate amendment. Section 523(a)(2) likewise represents a compromise between the position taken in the House bill and the Senate amendment with respect to the false financial statement exception to discharge. In order to clarify that a "renewal of credit" includes a "refinancing of credit", explicit reference to a refinancing of credit is made in the preamble to section 523(a)(2). A renewal of credit or refinancing of credit that was obtained by a false financial statement within the terms of section 523(a)(2) is nondischargeable. However, each of the provisions of section 523(a)(2) must be proved. Thus, under section 523(a)(2)(A) a creditor must prove that the debt was obtained by false pretenses, a false representation, or actual fraud, other than a statement respecting the debtor's or an insider's financial condition. Subparagraph (A) is intended to codify current case law e.g., *Neal v. Clark*, 95 U.S. 704 (1887) [24 L.Ed. 586], which interprets "fraud" to mean actual or positive fraud rather than fraud implied in law. Subparagraph (A) is mutually exclusive from subparagraph (B). Subparagraph (B) pertains to the so-called false financial statement. In order for the debt to be nondischargeable, the creditor must prove that the debt was obtained by the use of a statement in writing (i) that is materially false; (ii) respecting the debtor's or an insider's financial condition; (iii) on which the creditor to whom the debtor is liable for obtaining money, property, services, or credit reasonably relied; (iv) that the debtor caused to be made or published with intent to deceive. Section 523(a)(2)(B)(iv) is not intended to change from present law since the statement that the debtor causes to be made or published with the intent to deceive automatically includes a statement that the debtor actually makes or publishes with an intent to deceive. Section 523(a)(2)(B) is explained in the House report. Under section 523(a)(2)(B)(i) a discharge is barred only as to that portion of a loan with respect to which a false financial statement is materially false.

In many cases, a creditor is required by state law to refinance existing credit on which there has been no default. If the creditor does not forfeit remedies or otherwise rely to his detriment on a false financial statement with respect to existing credit, then an extension, renewal, or refinancing of such credit is nondischargeable only to the extent of the new money advanced; on the other hand, if an existing loan is in default or the creditor otherwise reasonably relies to his detriment on a false financial statement with regard to an existing loan, then the entire debt is nondischargeable under section 523(a)(2)(B). This codifies the reasoning expressed by the second circuit in *In re Danns*, 558 F.2d 114 (2d Cir. 1977).

Section 523(a)(3) of the House amendment is derived from the Senate amendment. The provision is intended to overrule *Birkett v. Columbia Bank*, 195 U.S. 345 (1904) [25 S.Ct. 38, 49 L.Ed. 231, 12 Am.Bankr.Rep. 691].

Section 523(a)(4) of the House amendment represents a compromise between the House bill and the Senate amendment.

Section 523(a)(5) is a compromise between the House bill and the Senate amendment. The provision excepts from discharge a debt owed to a spouse, former spouse or child of the debtor, in connection with a separation agreement, divorce decree, or property settlement agreement, for alimony to, maintenance for, or support of such spouse or child but not to the extent that the debt is assigned to another entity. If the debtor has assumed an obligation of the debtor's spouse to a third party in connection with a separation agreement, property settlement agreement, or divorce proceeding, such debt is dischargeable to the extent that payment of the debt by the debtor is not actually in the nature of alimony, maintenance, or support of debtor's spouse, former spouse, or child.

Section 523(a)(6) adopts the position taken in the House bill and rejects the alternative suggested in the Senate amendment. The phrase "willful and malicious injury" covers a willful and malicious conversion.

Section 523(a)(7) of the House amendment adopts the position taken in the Senate amendment and rejects the position taken in the House bill. A penalty relating to a tax cannot be nondischargeable unless the tax itself is nondischargeable.

Section 523(a)(8) represents a compromise between the House bill and the Senate amendment regarding educational loans. This provision is broader than current law which is limited to federally insured loans. Only educational loans owing to a governmental unit or a nonprofit institution of higher education are made nondischargeable under this paragraph.

Section 523(b) is new. The section represents a modification of similar provisions contained in the House bill and the Senate amendment.

Section 523(c) of the House amendment adopts the position taken in the Senate amendment.

Section 523(d) represents a compromise between the position taken in the House bill and the Senate amendment on the issue of attorneys' fees in false financial statement complaints to determine dischargeability. The provision contained in the House bill permitting the court to award damages is eliminated. The court must grant the debtor judgment or a reasonable attorneys' fee unless the granting of judgment would be clearly inequitable.

Nondischargeable debts: The House amendment retains the basic categories of nondischargeable tax liabilities contained in both bills, but restricts the time limits on certain nondischargeable taxes. Under the amendment, nondischargeable taxes cover taxes entitled to priority under section 507(a)(6) of title 11 and, in the case of individual debtors under chapters 7, 11, or 13, tax liabilities with respect to which no required return had been filed or as to which a late return had been filed if the return became last due, including extensions, within 2 years before the date of the petition or became due after the petition or as to which the debtor made a fraudulent return, entry or invoice or fraudulently attempted to evade or defeat the tax.

In the case of individuals in liquidation under chapter 7 or in reorganization under chapter 11 of title 11, section 1141(d)(2) incorporates by reference the exceptions to discharge continued in section 523. Different rules concerning the discharge of taxes where a partnership or corporation reorganizes under chapter 11, apply under section 1141.

The House amendment also deletes the reduction rule contained in section 523(e) of the Senate amendment. Under that rule, the amount of an otherwise nondischargeable tax liability would be reduced by the amount which a governmental tax authority could have collected from the debtor's estate if it had filed a timely claim against the estate but which it did not collect because no such claim was filed. This provision is deleted in order not to effectively compel a tax authority to file claim against the estate in "no asset" cases, along with a dischargeability petition. In no-asset cases, therefore, if the tax authority is not potentially penalized by failing to file a claim, the debtor in such cases will have a better opportunity to choose the prepayment forum, bankruptcy court or the Tax Court, in which to litigate his personal liability for a nondischargeable tax.

The House amendment also adopts the Senate amendment provision limiting the nondischargeability of punitive tax penalties, that is, penalties other than those which represent collection of a principal amount of tax liability through the form of a "penalty." Under the House amendment, tax penalties which are basically punitive in nature are to be nondischargeable only if the penalty is computed by reference to a related tax liability which is nondischargeable or, if the amount of the penalty is not computed by reference to a tax liability, the transaction or event giving rise to the penalty occurred during the 3-year period ending on the date of the petition.

References in Text

Section 6020(a) of the Internal Revenue Code of 1986, referred to in subsec. (a), is classified to 26 U.S.C.A. § 6020(a).

Section 6020(b) of the Internal Revenue Code of 1986, referred to in subsec. (a), is classified to 26 U.S.C.A. § 6020(b).

The Consumer Credit Protection Act, referred to in subsec. (a)(2)(C), is Pub.L. 90–321, May 29, 1968, 82 Stat. 146, as amended, which is classified principally to chapter 41 (section 1601 et seq.) of Title 15, Commerce and Trade. For complete classification of this Act to the Code, see Short Title note set out under section 1601 of Title 15 and Tables.

Section 103 of the Truth in Lending Act, referred to in subsec. (a)(2)(C)(ii)(I), is Pub.L. 90–321, Title I, § 103, May 29, 1968, 82 Stat. 147, as amended, which is classified to 15 U.S.C.A. § 1602.

The Social Security Act, referred to in subsec. (a)(5)(A), (18)(B), is Act Aug. 14, 1935, c. 531, 49 Stat. 620, as amended. Section 408(a)(3) of that Act is classified to section 608(a)(3) of Title 42, The Public Health and Welfare. Part D of Title IV of such Act is classified generally to part D (section 651 et seq.) of subchapter IV of chapter 7 of Title 42. For complete classification of this Act to the Code, see section 1305 of Title 42 and Tables.

Section 221(d)(1) of the Internal Revenue Code of 1986, referred to in subsec. (a)(8)(B), is classified to 26 U.S.C.A. § 221(d)(1).

The Bankruptcy Act, referred to in subsecs. (a)(10) and (b), is Act July 1, 1898, c. 541, 30 Stat. 544, as amended, which was classified generally to former Title 11. Sections 14c and 17a of the Bankruptcy Act were classified to sections 32(c) and 35(a) of former Title 11.

Section 401, 403, 408, 408A, 414, 457, or 501(c) of the Internal Revenue Code of 1986, referred to in subsec. (a)(18), is classified to 26 U.S.C.A. § 401, 403, 408, 408A, 414, 457, or 501(c).

Section 408(b)(1) of the Employee Retirement Income Security Act of 1974, referred to in subsec. (a)(18)(A), is Pub.L. 93–406, Title I, § 408(b)(1), Sept. 2, 1974, 88 Stat. 883, as amended, which is classified to 29 U.S.C.A. § 1108(b)(1).

Section 72(p) of the Internal Revenue Code of 1986, referred to in subsec. (a)(18)(A), is classified to 26 U.S.C.A. § 72(p).

Subchapter III of chapter 84 of title 5, referred to in subsec. (a)(18)(B), is 5 U.S.C.A. § 8431 et seq.

Section 414(d) or section 403(b) of the Internal Revenue Code, referred to in the undesignated paragraph following subsec. (a)(18), is classified to 26 U.S.C.A. § 414(d) or 26 U.S.C.A. § 403(b).

Section 3(a)(47) of the Securities Exchange Act of 1934, referred to in subsec. (a)(19)(A)(i), is section 3(a)(47) of Act June 6, 1934, c. 404, Title I, 48 Stat. 882, as amended, which is classified to 15 U.S.C.A. § 78c(a)(47).

Section 439A of the Higher Education Act of 1965, referred to in subsec. (b), is section 439A of Pub.L. 89–329, Title IV, as added Pub.L. 94–482, Title I, § 127(a), Oct. 12, 1976, 90 Stat. 2141, which was classified to section 1087–3 of Title 20, Education, and was repealed by Pub.L. 95–598, Title III, § 317, Nov. 6, 1978, 92 Stat. 2678.

Section 733 of the Public Health Service Act, referred to in subsec. (b), is section 733 of Act July 1, 1944, c. 373, Title VII as added Oct. 12, 1976, Pub.L. 94–484, Title IV, § 401(b)(3), 90 Stat. 2262, which was classified to section 294f of Title 42, The Public Health and Welfare, and which was repealed by Pub.L. 95–598, Title III, § 327, Nov. 6, 1978, 92 Stat. 2679. A subsec. (g), containing similar provisions, was added to section 733 by Pub.L. 97–35, Title XXVII, § 2730, Aug. 13, 1981, 95 Stat. 919. Section 733 was subsequently omitted in the general revision of subchapter V of chapter 6A of Title 42 by Pub.L. 102–408, Title I, § 102, Oct. 13, 1992, 106 Stat. 1992.

Codifications

Amendment by section 215(3) of Pub.L. 109–8, directing the amendment of par. (15) as added by Public Law 103–394, was executed by amending par. (15) of subsec. (a), as the probable intent of Congress.

Amendment by section 304(e) of Pub.L. 103–394, directing the addition of par. (15), was executed by adding par. (15) to subsec. (a), as the probable intent of Congress.

Pub.L. 101–581 and Pub.L. 101–647, § 3102(a), made identical amendments to subsec. (a)(9) of this section. See 1990 Amendments note set out under this section.

Amendment by section 283(j)(1) of Pub.L. 99–554, which redesignated the second par. (9) of subsec. (a) as (10), has been executed by redesignating as (10), par. (9) as enacted by Pub.L. 95–598 as the probable intent of Congress in view of amendment by section 371(2) of Pub.L. 98–353, which directed the addition of par. (9), as presently set out, to follow par. (8).

Amendments

2010 Amendments. Subsec. (a)(2)(C)(i)(I). By notice dated Feb. 25, 2010, 75 F.R. 8747, dollar amount adjusted by the Judicial Conference of the United States which adjusted "$550" to "$600". See 11 U.S.C.A. § 104 and Adjustment of Dollar Amounts notes under this section.

Subsec. (a)(2)(C)(i)(II). By notice dated Feb. 25, 2010, 75 F.R. 8747, dollar amount adjusted by the Judicial Conference of the United States which adjusted "$825" to "$875". See 11

U.S.C.A. § 104 and Adjustment of Dollar Amounts notes under this section.

Subsec. (a)(2)(C)(ii)(II). Pub.L. 111–327, § 2(a)(18)(A), struck out the period at the end and inserted a semicolon.

Subsec. (a)(3). Pub.L. 111–327, § 2(a)(18)(B), struck out "521(1)" and inserted "521(a)(1)".

2007 Amendments. Subsec. (a)(2)(C)(i)(I). By notice dated Feb. 14, 2007, 72 F.R. 7082, dollar amount adjusted by the Judicial Conference of the United States which adjusted "$500" to "$550". See 11 U.S.C.A. § 104 and Adjustment of Dollar Amounts notes under this section.

Subsec. (a)(2)(C)(i)(II). By notice dated Feb. 14, 2007, 72 F.R. 7082, dollar amount adjusted by the Judicial Conference of the United States which adjusted "$750" to "$825". See 11 U.S.C.A. § 104 and Adjustment of Dollar Amounts notes under this section.

2005 Amendments. Subsec. (a). Pub.L. 109–8, § 714(2), added "For purposes of this subsection, the term 'return' means a return that satisfies the requirements of applicable nonbankruptcy law (including applicable filing requirements). Such term includes a return prepared pursuant to section 6020(a) of the Internal Revenue Code of 1986, or similar State or local law, or a written stipulation to a judgment or a final order entered by a nonbankruptcy tribunal, but does not include a return made pursuant to section 6020(b) of the Internal Revenue Code of 1986, or a similar State or local law." at the end of subsec. (a).

Subsec. (a)(1)(A). Pub.L. 109–8, § 1502(a)(2), struck out "507(a)(2)" and inserted "507(a)(3)".

Subsec. (a)(1)(B). Pub.L. 109–8, § 714(1)(A), in the matter preceding cl. (i), inserted "or equivalent report or notice," after "a return,".

Subsec. (a)(1)(B)(i). Pub.L. 109–8, § 714(1)(B), inserted "or given" after "filed".

Subsec. (a)(1)(B)(ii). Pub.L. 109–8, § 714(1)(C)(i), inserted "or given" after "filed".

Pub.L. 109–8, § 714(1)(C)(ii), inserted ", report, or notice" after "return".

Subsec. (a)(2)(C). Pub.L. 109–8, § 310, rewrote subpar. (C), which formerly read: "for purposes of subparagraph (A) of this paragraph, consumer debts owed to a single creditor and aggregating more than $1,225 for 'luxury goods or services' incurred by an individual debtor on or within 60 days before the order for relief under this title, or cash advances aggregating more than $1,225 that are extensions of consumer credit under an open end credit plan obtained by an individual debtor on or within 60 days before the order for relief under this title, are presumed to be nondischargeable; 'luxury goods or services' do not include goods or services reasonably acquired for the support or maintenance of the debtor or a dependent of the debtor; an extension of consumer credit under an open end credit plan is to be defined for purposes of this subparagraph as it is defined in the Consumer Credit Protection Act;".

Subsec. (a)(5). Pub.L. 109–8, § 215(1)(A), rewrote par. (5), which formerly read:

"(5) to a spouse, former spouse, or child of the debtor, for alimony to, maintenance for, or support of such spouse or child, in connection with a separation agreement, divorce decree or other order of a court of record, determination made in accordance with State or territorial law by a govern-

mental unit, or property settlement agreement, but not to the extent that—

"(A) such debt is assigned to another entity, voluntarily, by operation of law, or otherwise (other than debts assigned pursuant to section 408(a)(3) of the Social Security Act, or any such debt which has been assigned to the Federal Government or to a State or any political subdivision of such State); or

"(B) such debt includes a liability designated as alimony, maintenance, or support, unless such liability is actually in the nature of alimony, maintenance, or support;"

Subsec. (a)(8). Pub.L. 109–8, § 220, rewrote par. (8), which formerly read: "for an educational benefit overpayment or loan made, insured or guaranteed by a governmental unit, or made under any program funded in whole or in part by a governmental unit or nonprofit institution, or for an obligation to repay funds received as an educational benefit, scholarship or stipend, unless excepting such debt from discharge under this paragraph will impose an undue hardship on the debtor and the debtor's dependents;"

Subsec. (a)(9). Pub.L. 109–8, § 1209(2), struck out "motor vehicle" and inserted "motor vehicle, vessel, or aircraft".

Subsec. (a)(14A). Pub.L. 109–8, § 314(a), added par. (14A).

Subsec. (a)(14B). Pub.L. 109–8, § 1235, added par. (14B).

Subsec. (a)(15). Pub.L. 109–8, § 215(3), inserted "to a spouse, former spouse, or child of the debtor and" before "not of the kind", inserted "or" after "court of record,", and substituted a semicolon for "unless—

"(A) the debtor does not have the ability to pay such debt from income or property of the debtor not reasonably necessary to be expended for the maintenance or support of the debtor or a dependent of the debtor and, if the debtor is engaged in a business, for the payment of expenditures necessary for the continuation, preservation, and operation of such business; or

"(B) discharging such debt would result in a benefit to the debtor that outweighs the detrimental consequences to a spouse, former spouse, or child of the debtor;"

Pub.L. 109–8, § 1209(1), transferred paragraph (15), as added by Pub.L. 103–394, § 304(e), so as to insert such paragraph after subsection (a)(14A), as added by Pub.L. 109–8, § 314(a).

Subsec. (a)(16). Pub.L. 109–8, § 412, rewrote par. (16), which formerly read:

"(16) for a fee or assessment that becomes due and payable after the order for relief to a membership association with respect to the debtor's interest in a dwelling unit that has condominium ownership or in a housing corporation, but only if such fee or assessment is payable for a period during which—

"(A) the debtor physically occupied a dwelling unit in the condominium or cooperative project; or

"(B) the debtor rented the dwelling unit to a tenant and received payments from the tenant for such period,

"but nothing in this paragraph shall except from discharge the debt of a debtor for a membership association fee or assessment for a period arising before entry of the order for relief in a pending or subsequent bankruptcy case;"

Subsec. (a)(17). Pub.L. 109–8, § 301(1), struck out "by a court" and inserted "on a prisoner by any court".

Pub.L. 109–8, § 301(2), struck out "section 1915(b) or (f)" and inserted "subsection (b) or (f)(2) of section 1915".

Pub.L. 109–8, § 301(3), inserted "(or a similar non–Federal law)" after "title 28" each place it appears.

Subsec. (a)(18). Pub.L. 109–8, § 215(1)(B), struck out par. (18), which formerly read:

"**(18)** owed under State law to a State or municipality that is—

"**(A)** in the nature of support, and

"**(B)** enforceable under part D of title IV of the Social Security Act (42 U.S.C. 601 et seq.); or"

Pub.L. 109–8, § 224(c), inserted par. (18).

Subsec. (a)(19)(B). Pub.L. 109–8, § 1404(a), inserted ", before, on, or after the date on which the petition was filed," after "results".

Subsec. (c)(1). Pub.L. 109–8, § 215(2), substituted "or (6)" for "(6), or (15)" in two places.

Subsec. (e). Pub.L. 109–8, § 1209(3), struck out "a insured" and inserted "an insured".

2004 Amendments. Subsec. (a)(2)(C). By notice dated Feb. 18, 2004, 69 F.R. 8482, dollar amount adjusted by the Judicial Conference of the United States which adjusted "$1,150" to "$1,225" each time it appeared. See 11 U.S.C.A. § 104 and Adjustment of Dollar Amounts notes under this section.

2002 Amendments. Subsec. (a)(17). Pub.L. 107–204, § 803(1), struck out "or" at the end.

Subsec. (a)(18). Pub.L. 107–204, § 803(2), substituted "; or" for the period at the end.

Subsec. (a)(19). Pub.L. 107–204, § 803(3), added par. (19).

2001 Amendments. Subsec. (a)(2)(C). By notice dated Feb. 20, 2001, 66 F.R. 10910, dollar amount adjusted by the Judicial Conference of the United States which adjusted "$1,075" to "$1,150" each time it appeared. See 11 U.S.C.A. § 104 and Adjustment of Dollar Amounts notes under this section.

1998 Amendments. Subsec. (a)(2)(C). By notice dated Feb. 3, 1998, 63 F.R. 7179, dollar amount adjusted by the Judicial Conference of the United States which adjusted "$1,000" to "$1,075" each time it appeared. See 11 U.S.C.A. § 104 and Adjustment of Dollar Amounts notes under this section.

Subsec. (a)(8). Pub.L. 105–244, § 971(a), rewrote par. (8), which formerly read:

"**(8)** for an educational benefit overpayment or loan made, insured or guaranteed by a governmental unit, or made under any program funded in whole or in part by a governmental unit or nonprofit institution, or for an obligation to repay funds received as an educational benefit, scholarship or stipend, unless—

"**(A)** such loan, benefit, scholarship, or stipend overpayment first became due more than 7 years (exclusive of any applicable suspension of the repayment period) before the date of the filing of the petition; or

"**(B)** excepting such debt from discharge under this paragraph will impose an undue hardship on the debtor and the debtor's dependents;".

1996 Amendments. Subsec. (a)(5). Pub.L. 104–193, § 374(a)(4), substituted "section 408(a)(3)" for "section 402(a)(26)".

Subsec. (a)(17). Pub.L. 104–134, § 101[(a)][§ 804(b)], added par. (17).

Subsec. (a)(18). Pub.L. 104–193, § 374(a)(1) to (3), added par. (18).

1994 Amendments. Subsec. (a)(1)(A). Pub.L. 103–394, § 304(h)(3), substituted "507(a)(8)" for "507(a)(7)".

Subsec. (a)(2)(C). Pub.L. 103–394, § 306, substituted "$1,000 for 'luxury goods or services'" for "$500 for 'luxury goods or services'", "incurred by an individual debtor on or within 60 days" for "incurred by an individual debtor on or within forty days", and "obtained by an individual debtor on or within 60 days" for "obtained by an individual debtor on or within twenty days".

Pub.L. 103–394, § 501(d)(13)(A)(ii), struck out "(15 U.S.C. 1601 et seq.)" after "Consumer Credit Protection Act".

Subsec. (a)(13). Pub.L. 103–322, § 320934, added par. (13).

Subsec. (a)(14). Pub.L. 103–394, § 221, added par. (14).

Subsec. (a)(15). Pub.L. 103–394, § 304(e), added par. (15). See Codifications note under this section.

Subsec. (a)(16). Pub.L. 103–394, § 309, added par. (16).

Subsec. (a). Pub.L. 103–394, § 501(d)(13)(A)(i), struck out second comma following "1141".

Subsec. (b). Pub.L. 103–394, § 501(d)(13)(B), struck out "(20 U.S.C. 1087–3)" following "the Higher Education Act of 1965", and "(42 U.S.C. 294f)" following "the Public Health Service Act".

Subsec. (c)(1). Pub.L. 103–394, § 304(e)(2), substituted "(6), or (15)" for "or (6)" wherever appearing.

Subsec. (e). Pub.L. 103–394, § 501(d)(13)(C), substituted "insured depository institution" for "depository institution or insured credit union".

1990 Amendments. Subsec. (a)(8). Pub.L. 101–647, § 3621(1), in introductory provisions substituted "for an educational benefit overpayment or loan made" for "for an educational loan made" and inserted preceding "unless" the phrase "or for an obligation to repay funds received as an educational benefit, scholarship or stipend,".

Subsec. (a)(8)(A). Pub.L. 101–647, § 3621(2), substituted "such loan, benefit, scholarship, or stipend overpayment first became due more than 7 years" for "such loan first became due before five years".

Subsec. (a)(9). Pub.L. 101–581 and Pub.L. 101–647, § 3102(a), made identical amendments, substituting "for death or personal injury caused by the debtor's operation of a motor vehicle if such operation was unlawful because the debtor was intoxicated from using alcohol, a drug, or another substance; 01" for "to any entity, to the extent that such debt arises from a judgment or consent decree entered in a court of record against the debtor wherein liability was incurred by such debtor as a result of the debtor's operation of a motor vehicle while legally intoxicated under the laws or regulations of any jurisdiction within the United States or its territories wherein such motor vehicle was operated and within which such liability was incurred; 01".

Subsec. (a)(11), (12). Pub.L. 101–647, § 2522(a)(1), added pars. (11) and (12).

Subsec. (c)(1). Pub.L. 101–647, § 2522(a)(3)(A), designated existing provision as par. (1).

Subsec. (c)(2). Pub.L. 101–647, § 2522(a)(3)(B), added par. (2).

Subsec. (e). Pub.L. 101–647, § 2522(a)(2), added subsec. (e).

1986 Amendments. Subsec. (a). Pub.L. 99–554, § 257(n), added reference to section 1228(a) and (b) of this title.

Subsec. (a)(1)(A). Pub.L. 99–554, § 283(j)(1)(A), substituted "(7)" for "(6)".

Subsec. (a)(5). Pub.L. 99–554, § 281, inserted ", determination made in accordance with State or territorial law by a governmental unit," following "record", and substituted "decree" for "decree,".

Subsec. (a)(10). Pub.L. 99–554, § 283(j)(1)(B), redesignated par. (9), as added by Pub.L. 95–598, as par. (10). See Codifications note set out under this section.

Subsec. (b). Pub.L. 99–554, § 283(j)(2), substituted "Service" for "Services".

1984 Amendments. Subsec. (a)(2). Pub.L. 98–353, § 454(a)(1)(A), in provisions preceding subpar. (A), struck out "obtaining" following "for".

Pub.L. 98–353, § 454(a)(1)(B), in provisions preceding subpar. (A), substituted "refinancing of credit, to the extent obtained" for "refinance of credit,".

Subsec. (a)(2)(A). Pub.L. 98–353, § 307(a)(1), struck out "or" at the end of subpar. (A).

Subsec. (a)(2)(B). Pub.L. 98–353, § 307(a)(2), added "or" at the end of subpar. (B).

Subsec. (a)(2)(B)(iii). Pub.L. 98–353, § 454(a)(1)(A), struck out "obtaining" preceding "such".

Subsec. (a)(2)(C). Pub.L. 98–353, § 307(a)(3), added subpar. (C).

Subsec. (a)(5). Pub.L. 98–353, § 454(b)(1), added "or other order of a court of record" following "divorce decree," in provisions preceding subpar. (A).

Subsec. (a)(5)(A). Pub.L. 98–353, § 454(b)(2), added ", or any such debt which has been assigned to the Federal Government or to a State or any political subdivision of such State" following "Social Security Act".

Subsec. (a)(8). Pub.L. 98–353, § 454(a)(2), struck out "of higher education" following "a nonprofit institution of".

Pub.L. 98–353, § 371(1), struck out "or" at the end of par. (8).

Subsec. (a)(9). Pub.L. 98–353, § 371(2), added par. (9), relating to debts incurred by persons driving while intoxicated.

Subsec. (c). Pub.L. 98–353, § 454(c), added "of a kind" following "debt".

Subsec. (d). Pub.L. 98–353, § 307(b), substituted "the court shall grant judgment in favor of the debtor for the costs of, and a reasonable attorney's fee for, the proceeding if the court finds that the position of the creditor was not substantially justified, except that the court shall not award such costs and fees if special circumstances would make the award unjust" for "the court shall grant judgment against such creditor and in favor of the debtor for the costs of, and a reasonable attorney's fee for, the proceeding to determine dischargeability, unless such granting of judgment would be clearly inequitable.".

1981 Amendments. Subsec. (a)(5)(A). Pub.L. 97–35 substituted "law, or otherwise (other than debts assigned pursuant to section 402(a)(26) of the Social Security Act);" for "law, or otherwise;".

1979 Amendments. Subsec. (a)(8). Pub.L. 96–56, § 3(1), in the introductory provisions, substituted "for an educational loan made, insured, or guaranteed by a governmental unit, or

made under any program funded in whole or in part by a governmental unit or a nonprofit institution of higher education" for "to a governmental unit, or a nonprofit institution of higher education, for an educational loan".

Subsec. (a)(8)(A). Pub.L. 96–56, § 3(2), inserted "(exclusive of any applicable suspension of the repayment period)" following "before five years".

Effective and Applicability Provisions

2010 Acts. Increase of dollar amounts by Judicial Conference of the United States by notice published Feb. 14, 2007, 75 F.R. 8747 effective April 1, 2010, and increase not applicable to cases commenced before the effective date of the adjustments, i.e., April 1, 2010. See Adjustment of Dollar Amounts notes under 11 U.S.C.A. § 104 and this section.

2007 Acts. Increase of dollar amounts by Judicial Conference of the United States by notice published Feb. 14, 2007, 72 F.R. 7082 effective April 1, 2007, and increase not applicable to cases commenced before the effective date of the adjustments, i.e., April 1, 2007. See Adjustment of Dollar Amounts notes under 11 U.S.C.A. § 104 and this section.

2005 Acts. Pub.L. 109–8, Title XIV, § 1404(b), Apr. 20, 2005, 119 Stat. 215, provided that: **"Effective date upon enactment of Sarbanes–Oxley Act.**—The amendment made by subsection (a) [amending subsec. (a)(19)(B) of this section] is effective beginning July 30, 2002."

Amendments by Pub.L. 109–8, Title XIV, effective, except as otherwise provided, on Apr. 20, 2005, and applicable only with respect to cases commenced under Title 11 on or after Apr. 20, 2005, see Pub.L. 109–8, § 1406, set out as a note under 11 U.S.C.A. § 507.

Amendments by Pub.L. 109–8 effective, except as otherwise provided, 180 days after April 20, 2005, and inapplicable with respect to cases commenced under Title 11 before the effective date, see Pub.L. 109–8, § 1501, set out as a note under 11 U.S.C.A. § 101.

2004 Acts. Adjustment of dollar amounts by Judicial Conference of the United States by notice dated Feb. 18, 2004, 69 F.R. 8482 effective April 1, 2004, and adjustment not applicable to cases commenced before the effective date of the adjustments, i.e., April 1, 2004. See Adjustment of Dollar Amounts notes under 11 U.S.C.A. § 104 and this section.

2001 Acts. Adjustment of dollar amounts by Judicial Conference of the United States by notice dated Feb. 20, 2001, 66 F.R. 10910 effective April 1, 2001, and adjustment not applicable to cases commenced before the effective date of the adjustments, i.e., April 1, 2001. See Adjustment of Dollar Amounts notes under 11 U.S.C.A. § 104 and this section.

1998 Acts. Amendment by Pub.L. 105–244 effective Oct. 1, 1998, except as otherwise provided, see section 3 of Pub.L. 105–244, set out as a note under section 1001 of Title 20.

Pub.L. 105–244, Title IX, § 971(b), Oct. 7, 1998, 112 Stat. 1837, provided that: "The amendment made by subsection (a) [amending subsec. (a)(8) of this section] shall apply only with respect to cases commenced under title 11, United States Code, after the date of enactment of this Act [Oct. 7, 1998]."

Adjustment of dollar amounts by Judicial Conference of the United States by notice dated Feb. 3, 1998, 63 F.R. 7179 effective April 1, 1998, and adjustment not applicable to cases commenced before the effective date of the adjustments, i.e., April 1, 1998. See Adjustment of Dollar Amounts notes under 11 U.S.C.A. § 104 and this section.

1996 Acts. For effective date of Title III of Pub.L. 104–193, see section 395(a) to (c) of Pub.L. 104–193, set out as a note under section 654 of Title 42, The Public Health and Welfare.

Section 374(c) of Pub.L. 104–193 provided that: "The amendments made by this section [amending this section and section 656 of Title 42, The Public Health and Welfare] shall apply only with respect to cases commenced under title 11 of the United States Code [this title] after the date of the enactment of this Act [Aug. 22, 1996]."

1994 Acts. Amendments by Pub.L. 103–394 effective on Oct. 22, 1994, and not to apply with respect to cases commenced under Title 11 of the United States Code before Oct. 22, 1994, see section 702 of Pub.L. 103–394, set out as a note under section 101 of this title.

1990 Acts. Section 3104 of Title XXXI of Pub.L. 101–647 provided that:

"(a) Effective date.—This title and the amendments made by this title [amending this section and section 1328 of this title and enacting provisions set out as a note under section 101 of this title] shall take effect on the date of the enactment of this Act [Nov. 29, 1990].

"(b) Application of amendments.—The amendments made by this title [amending this section and section 1328 of this title] shall not apply with respect to cases commenced under title 11 of the United States Code before the date of the enactment of this Act."

Amendment by section 3621 of Pub.L. 101–647 effective 180 days after Nov. 29, 1990, see section 3631 of Pub.L. 101–647, set out as a note under section 3001 of Title 28, Judiciary and Judicial Procedure.

Section 4 of Pub.L. 101–581 provided that:

"(a) Effective date.—This Act and the amendments made by this Act [amending this section and section 1328 of this title and enacting provisions set out as a note under section 101 of this title] shall take effect on the date of the enactment of this Act [Nov. 15, 1990.]"

"(b) Application of amendments.—The amendments made by this Act [amending this section and section 1328 of this title] shall not apply with respect to cases commenced under title 11 of the United States Code [this title] before the date of the enactment of this Act [Nov. 5, 1990.]"

1986 Acts. Amendment by sections 281 and 283 of Pub.L. 99–554 effective 30 days after Oct. 27, 1986, except as otherwise provided for, see section 302(a) of Pub.L. 99–554, set out as a note under section 581 of Title 28, Judiciary and Judicial Procedure.

Amendment by section 257 of Pub.L. 99–554 effective 30 days after Oct. 27, 1986, but not applicable to cases commenced under this title before that date, see section 302(a), (c)(1) of Pub.L. 99–554, set out as a note under section 581 of Title 28.

1984 Acts. Amendment by Pub.L. 98–353 effective with respect to cases filed 90 days after July 10, 1984, see section 552(a), formerly 553 of Pub.L. 98–353, set out as a note under section 101 of this title.

1981 Acts. Amendment by Pub.L. 97–35 effective on Aug. 13, 1981, see section 2334(c) of Pub.L. 97–35, set out as a note under section 656 of Title 42, The Public Health and Welfare.

Separability of Provisions

If any provision of section 101[a] [Title VIII] of Pub.L. 104–134, an amendment made by such Title, or the application of such provision or amendment to any person or circum-stance is held to be unconstitutional, the remainder of such Title, the amendments made by such Title, and the application of the provisions of such Title to any person or circumstance not affected thereby, see section 101[a] [Title VIII, § 810] of Pub.L. 104–134, set out as a note under section 3626 of Title 18, Crimes and Criminal Procedure.

If any provision of or amendment made by Pub.L. 103–394 or the application of such provision or amendment to any person or circumstance is held to be unconstitutional, the remaining provisions of and amendments made by Pub.L. 103–394 and the application of such provisions and amendments to any person or circumstance shall not be affected thereby, see section 701 of Pub.L. 103–394, set out as a note under section 101 of this title.

Adjustment of Dollar Amounts

For adjustment of dollar amounts specified in subsec. (a)(2)(C)(i)(I), (II) of this section by the Judicial Conference of the United States, effective Apr. 1, 2010, see note set out under 11 U.S.C.A. § 104.

By notice published Feb. 25, 2010, 75 F.R. 8747, the Judicial Conference of the United States adjusted the dollar amounts in provisions specified in subsec. (a)(2)(C)(i)(I), (II) of this section, effective Apr. 1, 2010, as follows:

In subsec. (a)(2)(C)(i)(I) adjusted $550 to $600.

In subsec. (a)(2)(C)(i)(II) adjusted $825 to $875.

By notice published Feb. 14, 2007, 72 F.R. 7082, the Judicial Conference of the United States adjusted the dollar amounts in provisions specified in subsec. (a)(2)(C)(i)(I), (II) of this section, effective Apr. 1, 2007, as follows:

In subsec. (a)(2)(C)(i)(I) adjusted $500 to $550.

In subsec. (a)(2)(C)(i)(II) adjusted $750 to $825.

By notice dated Feb. 18, 2004, 69 F.R. 8482, the Judicial Conference of the United States adjusted the dollar amounts in provisions specified in subsec. (a)(2)(C) of this section, effective Apr. 1, 2004, as follows:

Adjusted $1,150 (each time it appears) to $1,225 (each time it appears).

By notice dated Feb. 20, 2001, 66 F.R. 10910, the Judicial Conference of the United States adjusted the dollar amounts in provisions specified in subsec. (a)(2)(C) of this section, effective Apr. 1, 2001, as follows:

Adjusted $1,075 (each time it appears) to $1,150 (each time it appears).

By notice dated Feb. 3, 1998, 63 F.R. 7179, the Judicial Conference of the United States adjusted the dollar amounts in provisions specified in subsec. (a)(2)(C) of this section, effective Apr. 1, 1998, as follows:

Adjusted $1,000 (each time it appears) to $1,075 (each time it appears).

CROSS REFERENCES

Disallowance of claim to extent claim is for unmatured debt and excepted from discharge as debt for alimony, maintenance or support, see 11 USCA § 502.

Discharge of debtor—

Generally, see Official Bankr. Form 18, 11 USCA.

Chapter 7 cases, see 11 USCA § 727.

Chapter 12 cases, see 11 USCA § 1228.

Chapter 13 cases, see 11 USCA § 1328.

Effect of confirmation, see 11 USCA § 1141.

Extent of priorities for unsecured claims of governmental units, see 11 USCA § 507.

Involuntary cases and future adjustments, see 11 USCA § 104.

Notice of filing, creditors and dates, see Official Bankr. Form 9, 11 USCA.

LIBRARY REFERENCES

American Digest System

Bankruptcy ⚼3341 to 3388, 2185.
Key Number System Topic No. 51.

Corpus Juris Secundum

CJS Bankruptcy § 1032, Effect of Discharge of Debtor.

CJS Bankruptcy § 1040, Failure to Obey Any Lawful Order of Court; Refusal to Testify or Respond.

CJS Bankruptcy § 1060, What Constitutes Debt or Liability on Claim.

CJS Bankruptcy § 1062, Effect of Discharge of Debts.

CJS Bankruptcy § 1064, Debt for Tax or Customs Duty.

CJS Bankruptcy § 1065, False Pretenses, False Representation, or Fraud.

CJS Bankruptcy § 1066, False Pretenses, False Representation, or Actual Fraud--Reliance.

CJS Bankruptcy § 1067, Statement Respecting Debtor's or Insider's Financial Condition.

CJS Bankruptcy § 1068, Statement Respecting Debtor's or Insider's Financial Condition--Reliance.

CJS Bankruptcy § 1069, Debt Neither Listed Nor Scheduled.

CJS Bankruptcy § 1070, Fraud or Defalcation While Acting in Fiduciary Capacity.

CJS Bankruptcy § 1071, Fraud or Defalcation While Acting in Fiduciary Capacity--Determination of Existence of Fiduciary Relationship.

CJS Bankruptcy § 1072, Embezzlement or Larceny.

CJS Bankruptcy § 1073, Domestic Support Obligations and Other Debts to Spouses and Children.

CJS Bankruptcy § 1075, Domestic Support Obligations and Other Debts to Spouses and Children--Child Support.

CJS Bankruptcy § 1076, Debt for Willful and Malicious Injury.

CJS Bankruptcy § 1077, Debt for Fine, Penalty, or Forfeiture.

CJS Bankruptcy § 1078, Educational Loans.

CJS Bankruptcy § 1079, Debt Resulting from Operation of Vehicle, Vessel, or Aircraft While Intoxicated.

CJS Bankruptcy § 1080, Debt Not Discharged in Previous Bankruptcy.

CJS Bankruptcy § 1082, Time for Proceedings.

CJS Bankruptcy § 1087, Evidence; Presumptions.

CJS Bankruptcy § 1088, Burden of Proof.

CJS Bankruptcy § 1090, Weight and Sufficiency of Evidence.

CJS Bankruptcy § 1091, Hearing, Determination, and Judgment.

CJS Bankruptcy § 1092, Costs and Attorney's Fees.

CJS Bankruptcy § 1105, Closing.

CJS Bankruptcy § 1161, Effect of Confirmation--Discharge.

CJS Bankruptcy § 1185, Discharge.

CJS Bankruptcy § 1208, Discharge.

CJS Bankruptcy § 1214, Costs and Fees.

CJS Bankruptcy § 139, Adversary Proceedings.

CJS Bankruptcy § 153, Jurisdiction to Determine Dischargeability of a Debt.

CJS Bankruptcy § 18, Debt-Relief Agencies.

CJS Bankruptcy § 139, Adversary Proceedings.

CJS Bankruptcy § 153, Jurisdiction to Determine Dischargeability of a Debt.

CJS Bankruptcy § 18, Debt-Relief Agencies.

CJS Bankruptcy § 192, Determinations as to Dischargeability of Particular Debts.

CJS Bankruptcy § 192, Determinations as to Dischargeability of Particular Debts.

CJS Bankruptcy § 278, Parties Defendant; Sovereign Immunity.

CJS Bankruptcy § 278, Parties Defendant; Sovereign Immunity.

CJS Bankruptcy § 301, Notice to Debtor, Creditors, and Indenture Trustees.

CJS Bankruptcy § 301, Notice to Debtor, Creditors, and Indenture Trustees.

CJS Bankruptcy § 308, Enlargement.

CJS Bankruptcy § 308, Enlargement.

CJS Bankruptcy § 309, Reduction.

CJS Bankruptcy § 309, Reduction.

CJS Bankruptcy § 985, Domestic Relations Claims.

CJS Bankruptcy § 985, Domestic Relations Claims.

CJS Bankruptcy § 996, Income and Gross Receipts Taxes.

CJS Bankruptcy § 1032, Effect of Discharge of Debtor.

CJS Bankruptcy § 1040, Failure to Obey Any Lawful Order of Court; Refusal to Testify or Respond.

CJS Bankruptcy § 1060, What Constitutes Debt or Liability on Claim.

CJS Bankruptcy § 1062, Effect of Discharge of Debts.

CJS Bankruptcy § 1064, Debt for Tax or Customs Duty.

CJS Bankruptcy § 1065, False Pretenses, False Representation, or Fraud.

CJS Bankruptcy § 1066, False Pretenses, False Representation, or Actual Fraud--Reliance.

CJS Bankruptcy § 1067, Statement Respecting Debtor's or Insider's Financial Condition.

CJS Bankruptcy § 1068, Statement Respecting Debtor's or Insider's Financial Condition--Reliance.

CJS Bankruptcy § 1069, Debt Neither Listed Nor Scheduled.

CJS Bankruptcy § 1070, Fraud or Defalcation While Acting in Fiduciary Capacity.

CJS Bankruptcy § 1071, Fraud or Defalcation While Acting in Fiduciary Capacity--Determination of Existence of Fiduciary Relationship.

CJS Bankruptcy § 1072, Embezzlement or Larceny.

CJS Bankruptcy § 1073, Domestic Support Obligations and Other Debts to Spouses and Children.

CJS Bankruptcy § 1075, Domestic Support Obligations and Other Debts to Spouses and Children--Child Support.

CJS Bankruptcy § 1076, Debt for Willful and Malicious Injury.

CJS Bankruptcy § 1077, Debt for Fine, Penalty, or Forfeiture.

CJS Bankruptcy § 1078, Educational Loans.

CJS Bankruptcy § 1079, Debt Resulting from Operation of Vehicle, Vessel, or Aircraft While Intoxicated.

CJS Bankruptcy § 1080, Debt Not Discharged in Previous Bankruptcy.

CJS Bankruptcy § 1082, Time for Proceedings.

CJS Bankruptcy § 1087, Evidence; Presumptions.

CJS Bankruptcy § 1088, Burden of Proof.

CJS Bankruptcy § 1090, Weight and Sufficiency of Evidence.

CJS Bankruptcy § 1091, Hearing, Determination, and Judgment.

CJS Bankruptcy § 1092, Costs and Attorney's Fees.

CJS Bankruptcy § 1105, Closing.

CJS Bankruptcy § 1161, Effect of Confirmation--Discharge.

CJS Bankruptcy § 1185, Discharge.

CJS Bankruptcy § 1208, Discharge.

CJS Bankruptcy § 1214, Costs and Fees.

CJS Bankruptcy § 996, Income and Gross Receipts Taxes.

CJS Internal Revenue § 636, General Considerations.

CJS Internal Revenue § 636, General Considerations.

CJS Internal Revenue § 852, Attempt to Evade or Defeat Tax.

CJS Internal Revenue § 852, Attempt to Evade or Defeat Tax.

CJS Judgments § 1337, Dischargeability.

CJS Judgments § 1337, Dischargeability.

§ 524.   Effect of discharge *In whatever chapter*

(a) A discharge in a case under this title—

(1) voids any judgment at any time obtained, to the extent that such judgment is a determination of the personal liability of the debtor with respect to any debt discharged under section 727, 944, 1141, 1228, or 1328 of this title, whether or not discharge of such debt is waived;

(2) operates as an injunction against the commencement or continuation of an action, the employment of process, or an act, to collect, recover or offset any such debt as a personal liability of the debtor, whether or not discharge of such debt is waived; and

(3) operates as an injunction against the commencement or continuation of an action, the employment of process, or an act, to collect or recover from, or offset against, property of the debtor of the kind specified in section 541(a)(2) of this title that is acquired after the commencement of the case, on account of any allowable community claim, except a community claim that is excepted from discharge under section 523, 1228(a)(1), or 1328(a)(1), or that would be so excepted, determined in accordance with the provisions of sections 523(c) and 523(d) of this title, in a case concerning the debtor's spouse commenced on the date of the filing of the petition in the case concerning the debtor, whether or not discharge of the debt based on such community claim is waived.

(b) Subsection (a)(3) of this section does not apply if—

(1)(A) the debtor's spouse is a debtor in a case under this title, or a bankrupt or a debtor in a case under the Bankruptcy Act, commenced within six years of the date of the filing of the petition in the case concerning the debtor; and

(B) the court does not grant the debtor's spouse a discharge in such case concerning the debtor's spouse; or

(2)(A) the court would not grant the debtor's spouse a discharge in a case under chapter 7 of this title concerning such spouse commenced on the date of the filing of the petition in the case concerning the debtor; and

(B) a determination that the court would not so grant such discharge is made by the bankruptcy court within the time and in the manner provided for a determination under section 727 of this title of whether a debtor is granted a discharge.

(c) An agreement between a holder of a claim and the debtor, the consideration for which, in whole or in part, is based on a debt that is dischargeable in a case under this title is enforceable only to any extent enforceable under applicable nonbankruptcy law, whether or not discharge of such debt is waived, only if—

(1) such agreement was made before the granting of the discharge under section 727, 1141, 1228, or 1328 of this title;

(2) the debtor received the disclosures described in subsection (k) at or before the time at which the debtor signed the agreement;

(3) such agreement has been filed with the court and, if applicable, accompanied by a declaration or an affidavit of the attorney that represented the debtor during the course of negotiating an agreement under this subsection, which states that—

(A) such agreement represents a fully informed and voluntary agreement by the debtor;

(B) such agreement does not impose an undue hardship on the debtor or a dependent of the debtor; and

(C) the attorney fully advised the debtor of the legal effect and consequences of—

(i) an agreement of the kind specified in this subsection; and

(ii) any default under such an agreement;

(4) the debtor has not rescinded such agreement at any time prior to discharge or within sixty days after such agreement is filed with the court, whichever occurs later, by giving notice of rescission to the holder of such claim;

(5) the provisions of subsection (d) of this section have been complied with; and

(6)(A) in a case concerning an individual who was not represented by an attorney during the course of negotiating an agreement under this subsection, the court approves such agreement as—

(i) not imposing an undue hardship on the debtor or a dependent of the debtor; and

(ii) in the best interest of the debtor.

(B) Subparagraph (A) shall not apply to the extent that such debt is a consumer debt secured by real property.

(d) In a case concerning an individual, when the court has determined whether to grant or not to grant a discharge under section 727, 1141, 1228, or 1328 of this title, the court may hold a hearing at which the debtor shall appear in person. At any such hearing, the court shall inform the debtor that a discharge has been granted or the reason why a discharge has not been granted. If a discharge has been granted and if the debtor desires to make an agreement of the kind specified in subsection (c) of this section and was not represented by an attorney during the course of negotiating such agreement, then the court shall hold a hearing at which the debtor shall appear in person and at such hearing the court shall—

(1) inform the debtor—

(A) that such an agreement is not required under this title, under nonbankruptcy law, or under any agreement not made in accordance with the provisions of subsection (c) of this section; and

(B) of the legal effect and consequences of—

(i) an agreement of the kind specified in subsection (c) of this section; and

(ii) a default under such an agreement; and

(2) determine whether the agreement that the debtor desires to make complies with the requirements of subsection (c)(6) of this section, if the consideration for such agreement is based in whole or in part on a consumer debt that is not secured by real property of the debtor.

(e) Except as provided in subsection (a)(3) of this section, discharge of a debt of the debtor does not affect the liability of any other entity on, or the property of any other entity for, such debt.

(f) Nothing contained in subsection (c) or (d) of this section prevents a debtor from voluntarily repaying any debt.

(g)(1)(A) After notice and hearing, a court that enters an order confirming a plan of reorganization under chapter 11 may issue, in connection with such order, an injunction in accordance with this subsection to supplement the injunctive effect of a discharge under this section.

(B) An injunction may be issued under subparagraph (A) to enjoin entities from taking legal action for the purpose of directly or indirectly collecting, recovering, or receiving payment or recovery with respect to any claim or demand that, under a plan of reorganization, is to be paid in whole or in part by a trust described in paragraph (2)(B)(i), except such legal actions as are expressly allowed by the injunction, the confirmation order, or the plan of reorganization.

(2)(A) Subject to subsection (h), if the requirements of subparagraph (B) are met at the time an injunction described in paragraph (1) is entered, then after entry of such injunction, any proceeding that involves the validity, application, construction, or modification of such injunction, or of this subsection with respect to such injunction, may be commenced only in the district court in which such injunction was entered, and such court shall have exclusive jurisdiction over any such proceeding without regard to the amount in controversy.

(B) The requirements of this subparagraph are that—

(i) the injunction is to be implemented in connection with a trust that, pursuant to the plan of reorganization—

(I) is to assume the liabilities of a debtor which at the time of entry of the order for relief has been named as a defendant in personal injury, wrongful death, or property-damage actions seeking recovery for damages allegedly caused by the presence of, or exposure to, asbestos or asbestos-containing products;

(II) is to be funded in whole or in part by the securities of 1 or more debtors involved in such plan and by the obligation of such debtor or debtors to make future payments, including dividends;

(III) is to own, or by the exercise of rights granted under such plan would be entitled to own if specified contingencies occur, a majority of the voting shares of—

(aa) each such debtor;

(bb) the parent corporation of each such debtor; or

(cc) a subsidiary of each such debtor that is also a debtor; and

(IV) is to use its assets or income to pay claims and demands; and

(ii) subject to subsection (h), the court determines that—

(I) the debtor is likely to be subject to substantial future demands for payment arising out of the same or similar conduct or events that gave rise to the claims that are addressed by the injunction;

(II) the actual amounts, numbers, and timing of such future demands cannot be determined;

(III) pursuit of such demands outside the procedures prescribed by such plan is likely to threaten the plan's purpose to deal equitably with claims and future demands;

(IV) as part of the process of seeking confirmation of such plan—

(aa) the terms of the injunction proposed to be issued under paragraph (1)(A), including any provisions barring actions against third parties pursuant to paragraph (4)(A), are set out in such plan and in any disclosure statement supporting the plan; and

(bb) a separate class or classes of the claimants whose claims are to be addressed by a trust described in clause (i) is established and votes, by at least 75 percent of those voting, in favor of the plan; and

(V) subject to subsection (h), pursuant to court orders or otherwise, the trust will operate through mechanisms such as structured, periodic, or supplemental payments, pro rata distributions, matrices, or periodic review of estimates of the numbers and values of present claims and future demands, or other comparable mechanisms, that provide reasonable assurance that the trust will value, and be in a financial position to pay, present claims and future demands that involve similar claims in substantially the same manner.

(3)(A) If the requirements of paragraph (2)(B) are met and the order confirming the plan of reorganization was issued or affirmed by the district court that has jurisdiction over the reorganization case, then after the time for appeal of the order that issues or affirms the plan—

(i) the injunction shall be valid and enforceable and may not be revoked or modified by any court except through appeal in accordance with paragraph (6);

(ii) no entity that pursuant to such plan or thereafter becomes a direct or indirect transferee of, or successor to any assets of, a debtor or trust that is the subject of the injunction shall be liable with respect to any claim or demand made against such entity by reason of its becoming such a transferee or successor; and

(iii) no entity that pursuant to such plan or thereafter makes a loan to such a debtor or trust or to such a successor or transferee shall, by reason of making the loan, be liable with respect to any claim or demand made against such entity, nor shall any pledge of assets made in connection with such a loan be upset or impaired for that reason;

(B) Subparagraph (A) shall not be construed to—

(i) imply that an entity described in subparagraph (A)(ii) or (iii) would, if this paragraph were not applicable, necessarily be liable to any entity by reason of any of the acts described in subparagraph (A);

(ii) relieve any such entity of the duty to comply with, or of liability under, any Federal or State law regarding the making of a fraudulent conveyance in a transaction described in subparagraph (A)(ii) or (iii); or

(iii) relieve a debtor of the debtor's obligation to comply with the terms of the plan of reorganization, or affect the power of the court to exercise its authority under sections 1141 and 1142 to compel the debtor to do so.

(4)(A)(i) Subject to subparagraph (B), an injunction described in paragraph (1) shall be valid and enforceable against all entities that it addresses.

(ii) Notwithstanding the provisions of section 524(e), such an injunction may bar any action directed against a third party who is identifiable from the terms of such injunction (by name or as part of an identifiable group) and is alleged to be directly or indirectly liable for the conduct of, claims against, or demands on the debtor to the extent such alleged liability of such third party arises by reason of—

(I) the third party's ownership of a financial interest in the debtor, a past or present affiliate of the debtor, or a predecessor in interest of the debtor;

(II) the third party's involvement in the management of the debtor or a predecessor in interest of the debtor, or service as an officer, director or employee of the debtor or a related party;

(III) the third party's provision of insurance to the debtor or a related party; or

(IV) the third party's involvement in a transaction changing the corporate structure, or in a loan or other financial transaction affecting the financial condition, of the debtor or a related party, including but not limited to—

(aa) involvement in providing financing (debt or equity), or advice to an entity involved in such a transaction; or

(bb) acquiring or selling a financial interest in an entity as part of such a transaction.

(iii) As used in this subparagraph, the term "related party" means—

(I) a past or present affiliate of the debtor;

(II) a predecessor in interest of the debtor; or

(III) any entity that owned a financial interest in—

(aa) the debtor;

(bb) a past or present affiliate of the debtor; or

(cc) a predecessor in interest of the debtor.

(B) Subject to subsection (h), if, under a plan of reorganization, a kind of demand described in such plan is to be paid in whole or in part by a trust described in paragraph (2)(B)(i) in connection with which an injunction described in paragraph (1) is to be implemented, then such injunction shall be valid and enforceable with respect to a demand of such kind made, after such plan is confirmed, against the debtor or debtors involved, or against a third party described in subparagraph (A)(ii), if—

(i) as part of the proceedings leading to issuance of such injunction, the court appoints a legal representative for the purpose of protecting the rights of persons that might subsequently assert demands of such kind, and

(ii) the court determines, before entering the order confirming such plan, that identifying such debtor or debtors, or such third party (by name or as part of an identifiable group), in such injunction with respect to such demands for purposes of this subparagraph is fair and equitable with respect to the persons that might subsequently assert such demands, in light of the benefits provided, or to be provided, to such trust on behalf of such debtor or debtors or such third party.

(5) In this subsection, the term "demand" means a demand for payment, present or future, that—

(A) was not a claim during the proceedings leading to the confirmation of a plan of reorganization;

(B) arises out of the same or similar conduct or events that gave rise to the claims addressed by the injunction issued under paragraph (1); and

(C) pursuant to the plan, is to be paid by a trust described in paragraph (2)(B)(i).

(6) Paragraph (3)(A)(i) does not bar an action taken by or at the direction of an appellate court on appeal of an injunction issued under paragraph (1) or of the order of confirmation that relates to the injunction.

(7) This subsection does not affect the operation of section 1144 or the power of the district court to refer a proceeding under section 157 of title 28 or any reference of a proceeding made prior to the date of the enactment of this subsection.

(h) **Application to existing injunctions.**—For purposes of subsection (g)—

(1) subject to paragraph (2), if an injunction of the kind described in subsection (g)(1)(B) was issued before the date of the enactment of this Act, as part of a plan of reorganization confirmed by an order entered before such date, then the injunction shall be considered to meet the requirements of subsection (g)(2)(B) for purposes of subsection (g)(2)(A), and to satisfy subsection (g)(4)(A)(ii), if—

(A) the court determined at the time the plan was confirmed that the plan was fair and equitable in accordance with the requirements of section 1129(b);

(B) as part of the proceedings leading to issuance of such injunction and confirmation of such plan, the court had appointed a legal representative for the purpose of protecting the rights of persons that might subsequently assert demands described in subsection (g)(4)(B) with respect to such plan; and

(C) such legal representative did not object to confirmation of such plan or issuance of such injunction; and

(2) for purposes of paragraph (1), if a trust described in subsection (g)(2)(B)(i) is subject to a court order on the date of the enactment of this Act staying such trust from settling or paying further claims—

(A) the requirements of subsection (g)(2)(B)(ii)(V) shall not apply with respect to such trust until such stay is lifted or dissolved; and

(B) if such trust meets such requirements on the date such stay is lifted or dissolved, such trust shall be considered to have met such requirements continuously from the date of the enactment of this Act.

(i) The willful failure of a creditor to credit payments received under a plan confirmed under this title, unless the order confirming the plan is revoked, the plan is in default, or the creditor has not received payments required to be made under the plan in the manner required by the plan (including crediting the amounts required under the plan), shall constitute a violation of an injunction under subsection (a)(2) if the act of the creditor to collect and failure to credit payments in the manner required by the plan caused material injury to the debtor.

(j) Subsection (a)(2) does not operate as an injunction against an act by a creditor that is the holder of a secured claim, if—

(1) such creditor retains a security interest in real property that is the principal residence of the debtor;

(2) such act is in the ordinary course of business between the creditor and the debtor; and

(3) such act is limited to seeking or obtaining periodic payments associated with a valid security interest in lieu of pursuit of in rem relief to enforce the lien.

(k)(1) The disclosures required under subsection (c)(2) shall consist of the disclosure statement described in paragraph (3), completed as required in that paragraph, together with the agreement specified in subsection (c), statement, declaration, motion and order described, respectively, in paragraphs (4) through (8), and shall be the only disclosures required in connection with entering into such agreement.

(2) Disclosures made under paragraph (1) shall be made clearly and conspicuously and in writing. The terms "Amount Reaffirmed" and "Annual Percentage

Rate" shall be disclosed more conspicuously than other terms, data or information provided in connection with this disclosure, except that the phrases "Before agreeing to reaffirm a debt, review these important disclosures" and "Summary of Reaffirmation Agreement" may be equally conspicuous. Disclosures may be made in a different order and may use terminology different from that set forth in paragraphs (2) through (8), except that the terms "Amount Reaffirmed" and "Annual Percentage Rate" must be used where indicated.

(3) The disclosure statement required under this paragraph shall consist of the following:

(A) The statement: "Part A: Before agreeing to reaffirm a debt, review these important disclosures:";

(B) Under the heading "Summary of Reaffirmation Agreement", the statement: "This Summary is made pursuant to the requirements of the Bankruptcy Code";

(C) The "Amount Reaffirmed", using that term, which shall be—

(i) the total amount of debt that the debtor agrees to reaffirm by entering into an agreement of the kind specified in subsection (c), and

(ii) the total of any fees and costs accrued as of the date of the disclosure statement, related to such total amount.

(D) In conjunction with the disclosure of the "Amount Reaffirmed", the statements—

(i) "The amount of debt you have agreed to reaffirm"; and

(ii) "Your credit agreement may obligate you to pay additional amounts which may come due after the date of this disclosure. Consult your "'credit agreement.".

(E) The "Annual Percentage Rate", using that term, which shall be disclosed as—

(i) if, at the time the petition is filed, the debt is an extension of credit under an open end credit plan, as the terms "credit" and "open end credit plan" are defined in section 103 of the Truth in Lending Act, then—

(I) the annual percentage rate determined under paragraphs (5) and (6) of section 127(b) of the Truth in Lending Act, as applicable, as disclosed to the debtor in the most recent periodic statement prior to entering into an agreement of the kind specified in subsection (c) or, if no such periodic statement has been given to the debtor during the prior 6 months, the annual percentage rate as it would have been so disclosed at the time the disclosure statement is given to the debtor, or to the extent this annual percentage rate is not readily available or not applicable, then

(II) the simple interest rate applicable to the amount reaffirmed as of the date the disclosure

statement is given to the debtor, or if different simple interest rates apply to different balances, the simple interest rate applicable to each such balance, identifying the amount of each such balance included in the amount reaffirmed, or

(III) if the entity making the disclosure elects, to disclose the annual percentage rate under subclause (I) and the simple interest rate under subclause (II); or

(ii) if, at the time the petition is filed, the debt is an extension of credit other than under an open end credit plan, as the terms "credit" and "open end credit plan" are defined in section 103 of the Truth in Lending Act, then—

(I) the annual percentage rate under section 128(a)(4) of the Truth in Lending Act, as disclosed to the debtor in the most recent disclosure statement given to the debtor prior to the entering into an agreement of the kind specified in subsection (c) with respect to the debt, or, if no such disclosure statement was given to the debtor, the annual percentage rate as it would have been so disclosed at the time the disclosure statement is given to the debtor, or to the extent this annual percentage rate is not readily available or not applicable, then

(II) the simple interest rate applicable to the amount reaffirmed as of the date the disclosure statement is given to the debtor, or if different simple interest rates apply to different balances, the simple interest rate applicable to each such balance, identifying the amount of such balance included in the amount reaffirmed, or

(III) if the entity making the disclosure elects, to disclose the annual percentage rate under (I) and the simple interest rate under (II).

(F) If the underlying debt transaction was disclosed as a variable rate transaction on the most recent disclosure given under the Truth in Lending Act, by stating "The interest rate on your loan may be a variable interest rate which changes from time to time, so that the annual percentage rate disclosed here may be higher or lower."

(G) If the debt is secured by a security interest which has not been waived in whole or in part or determined to be void by a final order of the court at the time of the disclosure, by disclosing that a security interest or lien in goods or property is asserted over some or all of the debts the debtor is reaffirming and listing the items and their original purchase price that are subject to the asserted security interest, or if not a purchase-money security interest then listing by items or types and the original amount of the loan.

(H) At the election of the creditor, a statement of the repayment schedule using 1 or a combination of the following—

(i) by making the statement: "Your first payment in the amount of $___ is due on ___ but the future payment amount may be different. Consult your reaffirmation agreement or credit agreement, as applicable.", and stating the amount of the first payment and the due date of that payment in the places provided;

(ii) by making the statement: "Your payment schedule will be:", and describing the repayment schedule with the number, amount, and due dates or period of payments scheduled to repay the debts reaffirmed to the extent then known by the disclosing party; or

(iii) by describing the debtor's repayment obligations with reasonable specificity to the extent then known by the disclosing party.

(I) The following statement: "Note: When this disclosure refers to what a creditor 'may' do, it does not use the word 'may' to give the creditor specific permission. The word 'may' is used to tell you what might occur if the law permits the creditor to take the action. If you have questions about your reaffirming a debt or what the law requires, consult with the attorney who helped you negotiate this agreement reaffirming a debt. If you don't have an attorney helping you, the judge will explain the effect of your reaffirming a debt when the hearing on the reaffirmation agreement is held.".

(J)(i) The following additional statements:

"Reaffirming a debt is a serious financial decision. The law requires you to take certain steps to make sure the decision is in your best interest. If these steps are not completed, the reaffirmation agreement is not effective, even though you have signed it.

"1. Read the disclosures in this Part A carefully. Consider the decision to reaffirm carefully. Then, if you want to reaffirm, sign the reaffirmation agreement in Part B (or you may use a separate agreement you and your creditor agree on).

"2. Complete and sign Part D and be sure you can afford to make the payments you are agreeing to make and have received a copy of the disclosure statement and a completed and signed reaffirmation agreement.

"3. If you were represented by an attorney during the negotiation of your reaffirmation agreement, the attorney must have signed the certification in Part C.

"4. If you were not represented by an attorney during the negotiation of your reaffirmation agreement, you must have completed and signed Part E.

"5. The original of this disclosure must be filed with the court by you or your creditor. If a separate reaffirmation agreement (other than the one in Part B) has been signed, it must be attached.

"6. If you were represented by an attorney during the negotiation of your reaffirmation agreement, your reaffirmation agreement becomes effective upon filing with the court unless the reaffirmation is presumed to be an undue hardship as explained in Part D.

"7. If you were not represented by an attorney during the negotiation of your reaffirmation agreement, it will not be effective unless the court approves it. The court will notify you of the hearing on your reaffirmation agreement. You must attend this hearing in bankruptcy court where the judge will review your reaffirmation agreement. The bankruptcy court must approve your reaffirmation agreement as consistent with your best interests, except that no court approval is required if your reaffirmation agreement is for a consumer debt secured by a mortgage, deed of trust, security deed, or other lien on your real property, like your home.

"Your right to rescind (cancel) your reaffirmation agreement. You may rescind (cancel) your reaffirmation agreement at any time before the bankruptcy court enters a discharge order, or before the expiration of the 60-day period that begins on the date your reaffirmation agreement is filed with the court, whichever occurs later. To rescind (cancel) your reaffirmation agreement, you must notify the creditor that your reaffirmation agreement is rescinded (or canceled).

"What are your obligations if you reaffirm the debt? A reaffirmed debt remains your personal legal obligation. It is not discharged in your bankruptcy case. That means that if you default on your reaffirmed debt after your bankruptcy case is over, your creditor may be able to take your property or your wages. Otherwise, your obligations will be determined by the reaffirmation agreement which may have changed the terms of the original agreement. For example, if you are reaffirming an open end credit agreement, the creditor may be permitted by that agreement or applicable law to change the terms of that agreement in the future under certain conditions.

"Are you required to enter into a reaffirmation agreement by any law? No, you are not required to reaffirm a debt by any law. Only agree to reaffirm a debt if it is in your best interest. Be sure you can afford the payments you agree to make.

"What if your creditor has a security interest or lien? Your bankruptcy discharge does not eliminate any lien on your property. A 'lien' is often referred to as a security interest, deed of trust, mortgage or security deed. Even if you do not reaffirm and your personal liability on the debt is discharged, because of the lien your creditor may still have the right to take the property securing the lien if you do not pay the debt or default on it. If the lien is on an item of personal property that is exempt under your State's law or that the trustee has abandoned, you may be able to redeem the item rather than reaffirm the debt. To redeem, you must make a single payment to the creditor equal to the amount of the allowed secured claim, as agreed by the parties or determined by the court.".

(ii) In the case of a reaffirmation under subsection (m)(2), numbered paragraph 6 in the disclosures required by clause (i) of this subparagraph shall read as follows:

"6. If you were represented by an attorney during the negotiation of your reaffirmation agreement, your reaffirmation agreement becomes effective upon filing with the court.".

(4) The form of such agreement required under this paragraph shall consist of the following:

"Part B: Reaffirmation Agreement. I (we) agree to reaffirm the debts arising under the credit agreement described below.

"Brief description of credit agreement:

"Description of any changes to the credit agreement made as part of this reaffirmation agreement:

"Signature: Date:

"Borrower:

"Co-borrower, if also reaffirming these debts:

"Accepted by creditor:

"Date of creditor acceptance:".

(5) The declaration shall consist of the following:

(A) The following certification:

"Part C: Certification by Debtor's Attorney (If Any).

"I hereby certify that (1) this agreement represents a fully informed and voluntary agreement by the debtor; (2) this agreement does not impose an undue hardship on the debtor or any dependent of the debtor; and (3) I have fully advised the debtor of the legal effect and consequences of this agreement and any default under this agreement.

"Signature of Debtor's Attorney: Date:".

(B) If a presumption of undue hardship has been established with respect to such agreement, such certification shall state that, in the opinion of the attorney, the debtor is able to make the payment.

(C) In the case of a reaffirmation agreement under subsection (m)(2), subparagraph (B) is not applicable.

(6)(A) The statement in support of such agreement, which the debtor shall sign and date prior to filing with the court, shall consist of the following:

"Part D: Debtor's Statement in Support of Reaffirmation Agreement.

"1. I believe this reaffirmation agreement will not impose an undue hardship on my dependents or me. I can afford to make the payments on the reaffirmed debt because my monthly income (take home pay plus any other income received) is $___, and my actual current monthly expenses including monthly payments on post-bankruptcy debt and other reaffirmation agreements total $___, leaving $___ to make the required payments on this reaffirmed debt. I understand that if my income less my monthly expenses does not leave enough to make the payments, this reaffirmation agreement is presumed to be an undue hardship on me and must be reviewed by the court. However, this presumption may be overcome if I explain to the satisfaction of the court how I can afford to make the payments here: ___.

"2. I received a copy of the Reaffirmation Disclosure Statement in Part A and a completed and signed reaffirmation agreement.".

(B) Where the debtor is represented by an attorney and is reaffirming a debt owed to a creditor defined in section 19(b)(1)(A)(iv) of the Federal Reserve Act, the statement of support of the reaffirmation agreement, which the debtor shall sign and date prior to filing with the court, shall consist of the following:

"I believe this reaffirmation agreement is in my financial interest. I can afford to make the payments on the reaffirmed debt. I received a copy of the Reaffirmation Disclosure Statement in Part A and a completed and signed reaffirmation agreement.".

(7) The motion that may be used if approval of such agreement by the court is required in order for it to be effective, shall be signed and dated by the movant and shall consist of the following:

"Part E: Motion for Court Approval (To be completed only if the debtor is not represented by an attorney.). I (we), the debtor(s), affirm the following to be true and correct:

"I am not represented by an attorney in connection with this reaffirmation agreement.

"I believe this reaffirmation agreement is in my best interest based on the income and expenses I have disclosed in my Statement in Support of this reaffirmation agreement, and because (provide any additional relevant reasons the court should consider):

"Therefore, I ask the court for an order approving this reaffirmation agreement."

(8) The court order, which may be used to approve such agreement, shall consist of the following:

"Court Order: The court grants the debtor's motion and approves the reaffirmation agreement described above.".

(*l*) Notwithstanding any other provision of this title the following shall apply:

(1) A creditor may accept payments from a debtor before and after the filing of an agreement of the kind specified in subsection (c) with the court.

(2) A creditor may accept payments from a debtor under such agreement that the creditor believes in good faith to be effective.

(3) The requirements of subsections (c)(2) and (k) shall be satisfied if disclosures required under those subsections are given in good faith.

(m)(1) Until 60 days after an agreement of the kind specified in subsection (c) is filed with the court (or such additional period as the court, after notice and a hearing and for cause, orders before the expiration of such period), it shall be presumed that such agreement is an undue hardship on the debtor if the debtor's monthly income less the debtor's monthly expenses as shown on the debtor's completed and signed statement in support of such agreement required under subsection (k)(6)(A) is less than the scheduled payments on the reaffirmed debt. This presumption shall be reviewed by the court. The presumption may be rebutted in writing by the debtor if the statement includes an explanation that identifies additional sources of funds to make the payments as agreed upon under the terms of such agreement. If the presumption is not rebutted to the satisfaction of the court, the court may disapprove such agreement. No agreement shall be disapproved without notice and a hearing to the debtor and creditor, and such hearing shall be concluded before the entry of the debtor's discharge.

(2) This subsection does not apply to reaffirmation agreements where the creditor is a credit union, as defined in section 19(b)(1)(A)(iv) of the Federal Reserve Act.

(Pub.L. 95–598, Nov. 6, 1978, 92 Stat. 2592; Pub.L. 98–353, Title III, §§ 308, 455, July 10, 1984, 98 Stat. 354, 376; Pub.L. 99–554, Title II, §§ 257(*o*), 282, 283(k), Oct. 27, 1986, 100 Stat. 3115–3117; Pub.L. 103–394, Title I, §§ 103, 111(a), Title V, § 501(d)(14), Oct. 22, 1994, 108 Stat. 4108, 4113, 4145; Pub.L. 109–8, Title II, §§ 202, 203(a), Title XII, § 1210, Apr. 20, 2005, 119 Stat. 43, 194; Pub.L. 111–327, § 2(a)(19), Dec. 22, 2010, 124 Stat. 3559.)

HISTORICAL AND STATUTORY NOTES

Revision Notes and Legislative Reports

1978 Acts. Subsection (a) specifies that a discharge in a bankruptcy case voids any judgment to the extent that it is a determination of the personal liability of the debtor with respect to a prepetition debt, and operates as an injunction against the commencement or continuation of an action, the employment of process, or any act, including telephone calls, letters, and personal contacts, to collect, recover, or offset any discharged debt as a personal liability of the debtor, or from property of the debtor, whether or not the debtor has waived discharge of the debt involved. The injunction is to give complete effect to the discharge and to eliminate any doubt concerning the effect of the discharge as a total prohibition on debt collection efforts. This paragraph has been expanded over a comparable provision in Bankruptcy Act § 14f [section 32(f) of former Title 11] to cover any act to collect, such as dunning by telephone or letter, or indirectly through friends, relatives, or employers, harassment, threats of repossession, and the like. The change is consonant with the new policy

forbidding binding reaffirmation agreements under proposed 11 U.S.C. 524(b), and is intended to insure that once a debt is discharged, the debtor will not be pressured in any way to repay it. In effect, the discharge extinguishes the debt, and creditors may not attempt to avoid that. The language "whether or not discharge of such debt is waived" is intended to prevent waiver of discharge of a particular debt from defeating the purposes of this section. It is directed at waiver of discharge of a particular debt, not waiver of discharge in toto as permitted under section 727(a)(9).

Subsection (a) also codifies the split discharge for debtors in community property states. If community property was in the estate and community claims were discharged, the discharge is effective against community creditors of the non-debtor spouse as well as of the debtor spouse.

Subsection (b) gives further effect to the discharge. It prohibits reaffirmation agreements after the commencement of the case with respect to any dischargeable debt. The prohibition extends to agreements the consideration for which in whole or in part is based on a dischargeable debt, and it applies whether or not discharge of the debt involved in the agreement has been waived. Thus, the prohibition on reaffirmation agreements extends to debts that are based on discharged debts. Thus, "second generation" debts, which included all or a part of a discharged debt could not be included in any new agreement for new money. This subsection will not have any effect on reaffirmations of debts discharged under the Bankruptcy Act [former Title 11]. It will only apply to discharges granted if commenced under the new title 11 bankruptcy code.

Subsection (c) grants an exception to the anti-reaffirmation provision. It permits reaffirmation in connection with the settlement of a proceeding to determine the dischargeability of the debt being reaffirmed, or in connection with a redemption agreement permitted under section 722. In either case, the reaffirmation agreement must be entered into in good faith and must be approved by the court.

Subsection (d) provides the discharge of the debtor does not affect co-debtors or guarantors. Senate Report No. 95–989.

1984 Acts. Statements by Legislative Leaders, see 1984 U.S. Code Cong. and Adm. News, p. 576.

1986 Acts. House Report No. 99–764 and House Conference Report No. 99–958, see 1986 U.S. Code Cong. and Adm. News, p. 5227.

1994 Acts. House Report No. 103–835, see 1994 U.S. Code Cong. and Adm. News, p. 3340.

2005 Acts. House Report No. 109–31(Part I), see 2005 U.S. Code Cong. and Adm. News, p. 88.

Legislative Statements

Section 524(a) of the House amendment represents a compromise between the House bill and the Senate amendment. Section 524(b) of the House amendment is new, and represents standards clarifying the operation of section 524(a)(3) with respect to community property.

Sections 524(c) and (d) represent a compromise between the House bill and Senate amendment on the issue of reaffirmation of a debt discharged in bankruptcy. Every reaffirmation to be enforceable must be approved by the court, and any debtor may rescind a reaffirmation for 30 days from the time the reaffirmation becomes enforceable. If the debtor is an individual the court must advise the debtor of various effects of reaffirmation at a hearing. In addition, to any extent the debt is a consumer debt that is not secured by real property of the debtor reaffirmation is permitted only if the court approves the reaffirmation agreement, before granting a discharge under section 727, 1141, or 1328, as not imposing a hardship on the debtor or a dependent of the debtor and in the best interest of the debtor; alternatively, the court may approve an agreement entered into in good faith that is in settlement of litigation of a complaint to determine dischargeability or that is entered into in connection with redemption under section 722. The hearing on discharge under section 524(d) will be held whether or not the debtor desires to reaffirm any debts.

References in Text

The Bankruptcy Act, referred to in subsec. (b)(1), is Act July 1, 1898, c. 541, 30 Stat. 544, as amended, which was classified generally to former Title 11.

The date of enactment of this subsection, referred to in subsec. (g), is the date of enactment of section 111(a) of Pub.L. 103–394, which enacted subsec. (g) of this section and which was approved Oct. 22, 1994.

The date of enactment of this Act, referred to in subsec. (h), probably means the date of enactment of Pub.L. 103–394, known as the Bankruptcy Reform Act of 1994, which was approved Oct. 22, 1994.

Section 103 of the Truth in Lending Act, referred to in subsec. (k)(3)(E)(i), (ii), is Pub.L. 90–321, Title I, § 103, May 29, 1968, 82 Stat. 147, as amended, which is classified to 15 U.S.C.A. § 1602.

Section 127(b) of the Truth in Lending Act, referred to in subsec. (k)(3)(E)(i)(I), is Pub.L. 90–321, Title I, § 127(b), May 29, 1968, 82 Stat. 153, as amended, which is classified to 15 U.S.C.A. § 1637(b).

Section 128(a)(4) of the Truth in Lending Act, referred to in subsec. (k)(3)(E)(ii)(I), is Pub.L. 90–321, Title I, § 128(a)(4), May 29, 1968, 82 Stat. 155, as amended, which is classified to 15 U.S.C.A. § 1638(a)(4).

The Truth in Lending Act, referred to in subsec. (k)(3)(F), is Title I of Pub.L. 90–321, May 29, 1968, 82 Stat. 146, as amended, also known as TILA, which is classified principally to subchapter I of chapter 41 of Title 15, 15 U.S.C.A. § 1601 et seq. For complete classification, see Short Title note set out under 15 U.S.C.A. § 1601 and Tables.

Section 19(b)(1)(A)(iv) of the Federal Reserve Act, referred to in subsecs. (k)(6)(B), (m)(2), is Act Dec. 23, 1913, c. 6, § 19(b)(1)(A)(iv), 38 Stat. 270, as amended, which is classified to 12 U.S.C.A. § 461(b)(1)(A)(iv).

Amendments

2010 Amendments. Subsec. (k)(3)(J)(i). Pub.L. 111–327, § 2(a)(19)(A), in the undesignated last paragraph, struck out "security property if" and inserted "property securing the lien if", struck out "current value of the security property" and inserted "amount of the allowed secured claim", and inserted "must" following "redeem, you".

Subsec. (k)(5)(B). Pub.L. 111–327, § 2(a)(19)(B), struck "that" and inserted "that,".

2005 Amendments. Subsec. (a)(3). Pub.L. 109–8, § 1210, struck out "section 523, 1228(a)(1), or 1328(a)(1) of this title, or that" and inserted "section 523, 1228(a)(1), or 1328(a)(1), or that". See 1994 and 1986 Amendments notes under this section.

Subsec. (c)(2). Pub.L. 109–8, § 203(a)(1), rewrote par. (2), which formerly read: "(A) such agreement contains a clear and conspicuous statement which advises the debtor that the agreement may be rescinded at any time prior to discharge or within sixty days after such agreement is filed with the court, whichever occurs later, by giving notice of rescission to the holder of such claim; and

"(B) such agreement contains a clear and conspicuous statement which advises the debtor that such agreement is not required under this title, under nonbankruptcy law, or under any agreement not in accordance with the provisions of this subsection;"

Subsec. (i). Pub.L. 109–8, § 202, added subsec. (i).

Subsec. (j). Pub.L. 109–8, § 202, added subsec. (j).

Subsec. (k). Pub.L. 109–8, § 203(a)(2), added subsec. (k).

Subsec. (l). Pub.L. 109–8, § 203(a)(2), added subsec. (k).

Subsec. (m). Pub.L. 109–8, § 203(a)(2), added subsec. (m).

1994 Amendments. Subsec. (a)(3). Pub.L. 103–394, § 501(d)(14)(A), substituted "1328(a)(1)" for "1328(c)(1)". See 1986 and 2005 Amendments notes under this section.

Subsec. (c)(2). Pub.L. 103–394, § 103(a)(1), designated existing provisions as subpar. (A) and added subpar. (B).

Subsec. (c)(3). Pub.L. 103–394, § 103(a)(2), added subpar. (C) and made conforming technical changes to subpars. (A) and (B).

Subsec. (c)(4). Pub.L. 103–394, § 501(d)(14)(B), substituted "rescission" for "recission".

Subsec. (d)(1)(B)(ii). Pub.L. 103–394, § 501(d)(14)(C), inserted "and" following the semicolon.

Subsec. (d). Pub.L. 103–465, § 103(b), in opening par. inserted "and was not represented by an attorney during the course of negotiating such agreement" after "this section".

Subsecs. (g), (h). Pub.L. 103–394, § 111(a), added subsecs. (g) and (h).

1986 Amendments. Subsec. (a)(1). Pub.L. 99–554, § 257(o)(1), added reference to section 1228 of this title.

Subsec. (a)(3). Pub.L. 99–554, § 257(o)(2), which directed the substitution of ", 1228(a)(1), or 1328(a)(1)" for "or 1328(a)(1)" was executed by substituting ", 1228(a)(1), or 1328(c)(1)" for "or 1328(c)(1)" as the probable intent of Congress. See 1994 and 2005 Amendments notes under this section.

Subsec. (c)(1). Pub.L. 99–554, § 257(o)(1), added reference to section 1228 of this title.

Subsec. (d). Pub.L. 99–554, § 257(o)(1), added reference to section 1228 of this title.

Pub.L. 99–554, § 282, substituted "may hold" for "shall hold" and "At any" for "At", and added provisions relating to required appearance by the debtor in person at required hearing held by the court.

Subsec. (d)(2). Pub.L. 99–554, § 283(k), substituted "section" for "subsection" following "subsection (c)(6) of this".

1984 Amendments. Subsec. (a)(2). Pub.L. 98–353, § 308(a), struck out "or from property of the debtor," before "whether or not discharge of such debt is waived".

Pub.L. 98–353, § 455, substituted "an act" for "any act".

Subsec. (a)(3). Pub.L. 98–353, § 455, substituted "an act" for "any act".

Subsec. (c)(2). Pub.L. 98–353, § 308(b)(1), (3), added par. (2). Former par. (2), which had related to situations where the debtor had not rescinded the agreement within 30 days after the agreement became enforceable, was struck out.

Subsec. (c)(3). Pub.L. 98–353, § 308(b)(3), added par. (3). Former par. (3) was redesignated as (5).

Subsec. (c)(4). Pub.L. 98–353, § 308(b)(3), added par. (4). Former par. (4) was redesignated as (6).

Subsec. (c)(5). Pub.L. 98–353, § 308(b)(2), redesignated par. (3) as (5).

Subsec. (c)(6). Pub.L. 98–353, § 308(b)(2), redesignated former par. (4) as (6).

Pub.L. 98–353, § 308(b)(4), struck out provisions relating to court approval of such agreements as are entered into in good faith and are in settlement of litigation under section 523 of this title or provide for redemption under section 722 of this title.

Subsec. (d)(2). Pub.L. 98–353, § 308(c), substituted "subsection (c)(6)" for "subsection (c)(4)".

Subsec. (f). Pub.L. 98–353, § 308(d), added subsec. (f).

Effective and Applicability Provisions

2005 Acts. Amendments by Pub.L. 109–8 effective, except as otherwise provided, 180 days after April 20, 2005, and inapplicable with respect to cases commenced under Title 11 before the effective date, see Pub.L. 109–8, § 1501, set out as a note under 11 U.S.C.A. § 101.

1994 Acts. Amendments by sections 103 and 501(d)(14) of Pub.L. 103–394 effective on Oct. 22, 1994, and not to apply with respect to cases commenced under Title 11 of the United States Code before Oct. 22, 1994, see section 702 of Pub.L. 103–394, set out as a note under section 101 of this title.

Amendment by section 111 of Pub.L. 103–394 [enacting subsecs. (g) and (h) of this section and a provision set out as a note under this section] effective Oct. 22, 1994, see section 702 of Pub.L. 103–394, set out as a note under section 101 of this title.

1986 Acts. Amendment by sections 282 and 283 of Pub.L. 99–554 effective 30 days after Oct. 27, 1986, see section 302(a) of Pub.L. 99–554, set out as a note under section 581 of Title 28, Judiciary and Judicial Procedure.

Amendment by section 257 of Pub.L. 99–554 effective 30 days after Oct. 27, 1986, but not applicable to cases commenced under this title before that date, see section 302(a), (c)(1) of Pub.L. 99–554, set out as a note under Section 581 of Title 28.

1984 Acts. Amendment by Pub.L. 98–353 effective with respect to cases filed 90 days after July 10, 1984, see section 552(a), formerly 553(a) of Pub.L. 98–353, set out as a note under section 101 of this title.

Separability of Provisions

If any provision of or amendment made by Pub.L. 103–394 or the application of such provision or amendment to any person or circumstance is held to be unconstitutional, the remaining provisions of and amendments made by Pub.L. 103–394 and the application of such provisions and amendments to any person or circumstance shall not be affected thereby, see section 701 of Pub.L. 103–394, set out as a note under section 101 of this title.

Rule of Construction

Section 111(b) of Pub.L. 103–394 provided that: "Nothing in subsection (a), or in the amendments made by subsection (a) [enacting subsecs. (g) and (h) of this section], shall be construed to modify, impair, or supersede any other authority the court has to issue injunctions in connection with an order confirming a plan of reorganization."

CROSS REFERENCES

Applicability of subsec. (a)(1), (2) of this section in Chapter 9 cases, see 11 USCA § 901.

Cancellation of indebtedness from discharged farm loans, see 12 USCA § 1150.

Extension of time generally, see 11 USCA § 108.

Meetings of creditors and equity security holders reaffirming a debt, see 11 USCA § 341.

LIBRARY REFERENCES

American Digest System

Bankruptcy ⟺3319, 3411 to 3417, 2363.1 to 2374.

Key Number System Topic No. 51.

Corpus Juris Secundum

CJS Bankruptcy § 140, Contested Matters.

CJS Bankruptcy § 278, Parties Defendant; Sovereign Immunity.

CJS Bankruptcy § 527, Automatic Relief from Stay--As to Personal Property.

CJS Bankruptcy § 533, Discharge as Injunction.

CJS Bankruptcy § 544, Violations of Discharge Injunction.

CJS Bankruptcy § 547, Under Statute.

CJS Bankruptcy § 548, Under Statute--Willful Violation.

CJS Bankruptcy § 810, Trustee's Examination of Chapter 7 Debtor Concerning Effects of Bankruptcy.

CJS Bankruptcy § 921, Assumption of Leases of Personal Property.

CJS Bankruptcy § 1032, Effect of Discharge of Debtor.

CJS Bankruptcy § 1043, Waiver of Discharge.

CJS Bankruptcy § 1055, Hearing to Inform Debtor After Determination.

CJS Bankruptcy § 1062, Effect of Discharge of Debts.

CJS Bankruptcy § 1094, Requirements for Reaffirmation of Debt.

CJS Bankruptcy § 1095, Hearing; Determination of Validity of Reaffirmation.

CJS Bankruptcy § 1161, Effect of Confirmation--Discharge.

§ 525. Protection against discriminatory treatment

(a) Except as provided in the Perishable Agricultural Commodities Act, 1930, the Packers and Stockyards Act, 1921, and section 1 of the Act entitled "An Act making appropriations for the Department of Agriculture for the fiscal year ending June 30, 1944, and for other purposes," approved July 12, 1943, a governmental unit may not deny, revoke, suspend, or refuse to renew a license, permit, charter, franchise, or other similar grant to, condition such a grant to, discriminate with respect to such a grant against, deny employment to, terminate the employment of, or discriminate with respect to employment against, a person that is or has been a debtor under this title or a bankrupt or a debtor under the Bankruptcy Act, or another person with whom such bankrupt or debtor has been associated, solely because such bankrupt or debtor is or has been a debtor under this title or a bankrupt or debtor under the Bankruptcy Act, has been insolvent before the commencement of the case under this title, or during the case but before the debtor is granted or denied a discharge, or has not paid a debt that is dischargeable in the case under this title or that was discharged under the Bankruptcy Act.

(b) No private employer may terminate the employment of, or discriminate with respect to employment against, an individual who is or has been a debtor under this title, a debtor or bankrupt under the Bankruptcy Act, or an individual associated with such debtor or bankrupt, solely because such debtor or bankrupt—

    (1) is or has been a debtor under this title or a debtor or bankrupt under the Bankruptcy Act;

    (2) has been insolvent before the commencement of a case under this title or during the case but before the grant or denial of a discharge; or

    (3) has not paid a debt that is dischargeable in a case under this title or that was discharged under the Bankruptcy Act.

(c)(1) A governmental unit that operates a student grant or loan program and a person engaged in a business that includes the making of loans guaranteed or insured under a student loan program may not deny a student grant, loan, loan guarantee, or loan insurance to a person that is or has been a debtor under this title or a bankrupt or debtor under the Bankruptcy Act, or another person with whom the debtor or bankrupt has been associated, because the debtor or bankrupt is or has been a debtor under this title or a bankrupt or debtor under the Bankruptcy Act, has been insolvent before the commencement of a case under this title or during the pendency of the case but before the debtor is granted or denied a discharge, or has not paid a debt that is dischargeable in the case under this title or that was discharged under the Bankruptcy Act.

(2) In this section, "student loan program" means any program operated under title IV of the Higher Education Act of 1965 or a similar program operated under State or local law.

(Pub.L. 95–598, Nov. 6, 1978, 92 Stat. 2593; Pub.L. 98–353, Title III, § 309, July 10, 1984, 98 Stat. 354; Pub.L. 103–394, Title III, § 313, Title V, § 501(d)(15), Oct. 22, 1994, 108 Stat. 4140, 4145; Pub.L. 109–8, Title XII, § 1211, Apr. 20, 2005, 119 Stat. 194.)

HISTORICAL AND STATUTORY NOTES
Revision Notes and Legislative Reports

1978 Acts. This section is additional debtor protection. It codifies the result of *Perez v. Campbell,* 402 U.S. 637 (1971) [91 S.Ct. 1704, 29 L.Ed.2d 233], which held that a State would frustrate the Congressional policy of a fresh start for a debtor if it were permitted to refuse to renew a drivers license because a tort judgment resulting from an automobile accident had been unpaid as a result of a discharge in bankruptcy.

Notwithstanding any other laws, section 525 prohibits a governmental unit from denying, revoking, suspending, or refusing to renew a license, permit, charter, franchise, or other similar grant to, from conditioning such a grant to, from discrimination with respect to such a grant against, deny employment to, terminate the employment of, or discriminate with respect to employment against, a person that is or has been a debtor or that is or has been associated with a debtor. The prohibition extends only to discrimination or other action based solely on the basis of the bankruptcy, on the basis of insolvency before or during bankruptcy prior to a determination of discharge, or on the basis of nonpayment of a debt discharged in the bankruptcy case (the *Perez* situation). It does not prohibit consideration of other factors, such as future financial responsibility or ability, and does not prohibit imposition of requirements such as net capital rules, if applied nondiscriminatorily.

In addition, the section is not exhaustive. The enumeration of various forms of discrimination against former bankrupts is not intended to permit other forms of discrimination. The courts have been developing the *Perez* rule. This section permits further development to prohibit actions by governmental or quasi-governmental organizations that perform licensing functions, such as a State bar association or a medical society, or by other organizations that can seriously affect the debtors' livelihood or fresh start, such as exclusion from a union on the basis of discharge of a debt to the union's credit union.

The effect of the section, and of further interpretations of the *Perez* rule, is to strengthen the anti-reaffirmation policy found in section 524(b). Discrimination based solely on nonpayment could encourage reaffirmations, contrary to the expressed policy.

The section is not so broad as a comparable section proposed by the Bankruptcy Commission, S. 236, 94th Cong., 1st Sess. § 4–508 (1975), which would have extended the prohibition to any discrimination, even by private parties. Nevertheless, it is not limiting either, as noted. The courts will continue to mark the contours of the anti-discrimination provision in pursuit of sound bankruptcy policy. Senate Report No. 95–989.

1984 Acts. Statements by Legislative Leaders, see 1984 U.S. Code Cong. and Adm. News, p. 576.

1994 Acts. House Report No. 103–835, see 1994 U.S. Code Cong. and Adm. News, p. 3340.

2005 Acts. House Report No. 109–31(Part I), see 2005 U.S. Code Cong. and Adm. News, p. 88.

References in Text

The Perishable Agricultural Commodities Act, 1930, referred to in subsec. (a), is Act June 10, 1930, c. 436, 46 Stat. 531, as amended, which is classified principally to chapter 20A (section 499a et seq.) of Title 7, Agriculture. For complete classification of this Act to the Code, see section 499a of Title 7 and Tables.

The Packers and Stockyards Act, 1921, referred to in subsec. (a), is Act Aug. 15, 1921, c. 64, 42 Stat. 159, which is classified principally to chapter 9 (section 181 et seq.) of Title 7, Agriculture. For complete classification of this Act to the Code, see section 181 of Title 7 and Tables.

Section 1 of an Act entitled "An Act making appropriations for the Department of Agriculture for the fiscal year ending June 30, 1944, and for other purposes," approved July 12, 1943, referred to in subsec. (a), is section 1 of Act July 12, 1943, c. 215, 57 Stat. 422, which is classified to section 204 of Title 7, Agriculture.

The Bankruptcy Act, referred to in subsecs. (a), (b), and (c)(1), is Act July 1, 1898, c. 541, 30 Stat. 544, as amended, which was classified generally to former Title 11.

The Higher Education Act of 1965, referred to in subsec. (c)(2), is Pub.L. 89–329, Nov. 8, 1965, 79 Stat. 1219, as amended. Title IV of the Act is classified generally to subchapter IV of chapter 28 of Title 20, 20 U.S.C.A. § 1070 et seq., and part C of subchapter I of chapter 34 of Title 42, 42 U.S.C.A. § 2751 et seq. For complete classification, see Short Title note set out under 20 U.S.C.A. § 1001 and Tables.

Amendments

2005 Amendments. Subsec. (c)(1). Pub.L. 109–8, § 1211(1), inserted "student" before "grant, loan".

Subsec. (c)(2). Pub.L. 109–8, § 1211(2), struck out "the program operated under part B, D, or E of" and inserted "any program operated under".

1994 Amendments. Subsec. (a). Pub.L. 103–394, § 501(d)(15), struck out "(7 U.S.C. 499a-499s)" following "the Perishable Agricultural Commodities Act, 1930", "(7 U.S.C. 181-229)" following "the Packers and Stockyards Act, 1921", and "(57 Stat. 422; 7 U.S.C. 204)" following "approved July 12, 1943".

Subsec. (c). Pub.L. 103–394, § 313, added subsec. (c).

1984 Amendments. Subsec. (a). Pub.L. 98–353, § 309(1), designated existing provisions as subsec. (a).

Pub.L. 98–353, § 309(2), added "the" before "Perishable".

Subsec. (b). Pub.L. 98–353, § 309(3), added subsec. (b).

Effective and Applicability Provisions

2005 Acts. Amendments by Pub.L. 109–8 effective, except as otherwise provided, 180 days after April 20, 2005, and inapplicable with respect to cases commenced under Title 11 before the effective date, see Pub.L. 109–8, § 1501, set out as a note under 11 U.S.C.A. § 101.

1994 Acts. Amendments by Pub.L. 103–394 effective on Oct. 22, 1994, and not to apply with respect to cases commenced under Title 11 of the United States Code before Oct. 22, 1994, see section 702 of Pub.L. 103–394, set out as a note under section 101 of this title.

1984 Acts. Amendment by Pub.L. 98–353 effective with respect to cases filed 90 days after July 10, 1984, see section 552(a), formerly 553(a) of Pub.L. 98–353, set out as a note under section 101 of this title.

Separability of Provisions

If any provision of or amendment made by Pub.L. 103–394 or the application of such provision or amendment to any person or circumstance is held to be unconstitutional, the remaining provisions of and amendments made by Pub.L. 103–394 and the application of such provisions and amendments to any person or circumstance shall not be affected thereby, see section 701 of Pub.L. 103–394, set out as a note under section 101 of this title.

CROSS REFERENCES

Reporting of obsolete information prohibited, see 15 USCA § 1681c.

LIBRARY REFERENCES

American Digest System

Bankruptcy ⟐2363.1, 2371(1) to 2373.
Key Number System Topic No. 51.

Corpus Juris Secundum

CJS Bankruptcy § 278, Parties Defendant; Sovereign Immunity.

CJS Bankruptcy § 539, By Governmental Unit.

CJS Bankruptcy § 540, By Governmental Unit--With Regard to License or Similar Grant.

CJS Bankruptcy § 541, By Private Employer.

§ 526. Restrictions on debt relief agencies

(a) A debt relief agency shall not—

(1) fail to perform any service that such agency informed an assisted person or prospective assisted person it would provide in connection with a case or proceeding under this title;

(2) make any statement, or counsel or advise any assisted person or prospective assisted person to make a statement in a document filed in a case or proceeding under this title, that is untrue or misleading, or that upon the exercise of reasonable care, should have been known by such agency to be untrue or misleading;

(3) misrepresent to any assisted person or prospective assisted person, directly or indirectly, affirmatively or by material omission, with respect to—

(A) the services that such agency will provide to such person; or

(B) the benefits and risks that may result if such person becomes a debtor in a case under this title; or

(4) advise an assisted person or prospective assisted person to incur more debt in contemplation of such person filing a case under this title or to pay an attorney or bankruptcy petition preparer a fee or charge for services performed as part of preparing for or representing a debtor in a case under this title.

(b) Any waiver by any assisted person of any protection or right provided under this section shall not be enforceable against the debtor by any Federal or State court or any other person, but may be enforced against a debt relief agency.

(c)(1) Any contract for bankruptcy assistance between a debt relief agency and an assisted person that does not comply with the material requirements of this section, section 527, or section 528 shall be void and may not be enforced by any Federal or State court or by any other person, other than such assisted person.

(2) Any debt relief agency shall be liable to an assisted person in the amount of any fees or charges in connection with providing bankruptcy assistance to such person that such debt relief agency has received, for actual damages, and for reasonable attorneys' fees and costs if such agency is found, after notice and a hearing, to have—

(A) intentionally or negligently failed to comply with any provision of this section, section 527, or section 528 with respect to a case or proceeding under this title for such assisted person;

(B) provided bankruptcy assistance to an assisted person in a case or proceeding under this title that is dismissed or converted to a case under another chapter of this title because of such agency's intentional or negligent failure to file any required document including those specified in section 521; or

(C) intentionally or negligently disregarded the material requirements of this title or the Federal Rules of Bankruptcy Procedure applicable to such agency.

(3) In addition to such other remedies as are provided under State law, whenever the chief law enforcement officer of a State, or an official or agency designated by a State, has reason to believe that any person has violated or is violating this section, the State—

(A) may bring an action to enjoin such violation;

(B) may bring an action on behalf of its residents to recover the actual damages of assisted persons arising from such violation, including any liability under paragraph (2); and

(C) in the case of any successful action under subparagraph (A) or (B), shall be awarded the costs of the action and reasonable attorneys' fees as determined by the court.

(4) The district courts of the United States for districts located in the State shall have concurrent jurisdiction of any action under subparagraph (A) or (B) of paragraph (3).

(5) Notwithstanding any other provision of Federal law and in addition to any other remedy provided under Federal or State law, if the court, on its own motion or on the motion of the United States trustee or the debtor, finds that a person intentionally violated this section, or engaged in a clear and consistent pattern or practice of violating this section, the court may—

(A) enjoin the violation of such section; or

(B) impose an appropriate civil penalty against such person.

(d) No provision of this section, section 527, or section 528 shall—

(1) annul, alter, affect, or exempt any person subject to such sections from complying with any law of any State except to the extent that such law is inconsistent with those sections, and then only to the extent of the inconsistency; or

(2) be deemed to limit or curtail the authority or ability—

(A) of a State or subdivision or instrumentality thereof, to determine and enforce qualifications for the practice of law under the laws of that State; or

(B) of a Federal court to determine and enforce the qualifications for the practice of law before that court.

(Added Pub.L. 109–8, Title II, § 227(a), Apr. 20, 2005, 119 Stat. 67; amended Pub.L. 111–327, § 2(a)(20), Dec. 22, 2010, 124 Stat. 3560.)

HISTORICAL AND STATUTORY NOTES

Revision Notes and Legislative Reports

2005 Acts. House Report No. 109–31(Part I), see 2005 U.S. Code Cong. and Adm. News, p. 88.

References in Text

The Federal Rules of Bankruptcy Procedure, referred to in subsec. (c)(2)(C), are set out in the Appendix to this title.

Amendments

2010 Amendments. Subsec. (a)(2). Pub.L. 111–327, § 2(a)(20)(A), struck out "untrue and" and inserted "untrue or".

Subsec. (a)(4). Pub.L. 111–327, § 2(a)(20)(B), inserted "a" following "preparer".

Effective and Applicability Provisions

2005 Acts. Amendments by Pub.L. 109–8 effective, except as otherwise provided, 180 days after April 20, 2005, and inapplicable with respect to cases commenced under Title 11 before the effective date, see Pub.L. 109–8, § 1501, set out as a note under 11 U.S.C.A. § 101.

LIBRARY REFERENCES

Corpus Juris Secundum

CJS Bankruptcy § 18, Debt-Relief Agencies.

§ 527. Disclosures

(a) A debt relief agency providing bankruptcy assistance to an assisted person shall provide—

(1) the written notice required under section 342(b)(1); and

(2) to the extent not covered in the written notice described in paragraph (1), and not later than 3 business days after the first date on which a debt relief agency first offers to provide any bankruptcy assistance services to an assisted person, a clear and conspicuous written notice advising assisted persons that—

(A) all information that the assisted person is required to provide with a petition and thereafter during a case under this title is required to be complete, accurate, and truthful;

(B) all assets and all liabilities are required to be completely and accurately disclosed in the documents filed to commence the case, and the replacement value of each asset as defined in section 506 must be stated in those documents where requested after reasonable inquiry to establish such value;

(C) current monthly income, the amounts specified in section 707(b)(2), and, in a case under chapter 13 of this title, disposable income (determined in accordance with section 707(b)(2)), are required to be stated after reasonable inquiry; and

(D) information that an assisted person provides during their case may be audited pursuant to this title, and that failure to provide such information may result in dismissal of the case under this title or other sanction, including a criminal sanction.

(b) A debt relief agency providing bankruptcy assistance to an assisted person shall provide each assisted person at the same time as the notices required under subsection (a)(1) the following statement, to the extent applicable, or one substantially similar. The statement shall be clear and conspicuous and shall be in a single document separate from other documents or notices provided to the assisted person:

"IMPORTANT INFORMATION ABOUT BANKRUPTCY ASSISTANCE SERVICES FROM AN ATTORNEY OR BANKRUPTCY PETITION PREPARER.

"If you decide to seek bankruptcy relief, you can represent yourself, you can hire an attorney to represent you, or you can get help in some localities from a bankruptcy petition preparer who is not an attorney. THE LAW REQUIRES AN ATTORNEY OR BANKRUPTCY PETITION PREPARER TO GIVE YOU A WRITTEN CONTRACT SPECIFYING WHAT THE ATTORNEY OR BANKRUPTCY PETITION PREPARER WILL DO FOR YOU AND HOW MUCH IT WILL COST. Ask to see the contract before you hire anyone.

"The following information helps you understand what must be done in a routine bankruptcy case to help you evaluate how much service you need. Although bankruptcy can be complex, many cases are routine.

"Before filing a bankruptcy case, either you or your attorney should analyze your eligibility for different forms of debt relief available under the Bankruptcy Code and which form of relief is most likely to be beneficial for you. Be sure you understand the relief you can obtain and its limitations. To file a bankruptcy case, documents called a Petition, Schedules, and Statement of Financial Affairs, and in some cases a Statement of Intention, need to be prepared correctly and filed with the bankruptcy court. You will have to pay a filing fee to the bankruptcy court. Once your case starts, you will have to attend the required first meeting of creditors where you may be questioned by a court official called a 'trustee' and by creditors.

"If you choose to file a chapter 7 case, you may be asked by a creditor to reaffirm a debt. You may want help deciding whether to do so. A creditor is not permitted to coerce you into reaffirming your debts.

"If you choose to file a chapter 13 case in which you repay your creditors what you can afford over 3 to 5 years, you may also want help with preparing your chapter 13 plan and with the confirmation hearing on your plan which will be before a bankruptcy judge.

"If you select another type of relief under the Bankruptcy Code other than chapter 7 or chapter 13, you will want to find out what should be done from someone familiar with that type of relief.

"Your bankruptcy case may also involve litigation. You are generally permitted to represent yourself in litigation in bankruptcy court, but only attorneys, not bankruptcy petition preparers, can give you legal advice.".

(c) Except to the extent the debt relief agency provides the required information itself after reasonably diligent inquiry of the assisted person or others so as to obtain such information reasonably accurately for inclusion on the petition, schedules or statement of financial affairs, a debt relief agency providing bankruptcy assistance to an assisted person, to the extent permitted by nonbankruptcy law, shall provide each assisted person at the time required for the notice required under subsection (a)(1) reasonably sufficient information (which shall be provided in a clear and conspicuous writing) to the assisted person on how to provide all the information the assisted person is required to provide under this title pursuant to section 521, including—

(1) how to value assets at replacement value, determine current monthly income, the amounts specified in section 707(b)(2) and, in a chapter 13 case, how to determine disposable income in accordance with section 707(b)(2) and related calculations;

(2) how to complete the list of creditors, including how to determine what amount is owed and what address for the creditor should be shown; and

(3) how to determine what property is exempt and how to value exempt property at replacement value as defined in section 506.

(d) A debt relief agency shall maintain a copy of the notices required under subsection (a) of this section for 2 years after the date on which the notice is given the assisted person.

(Added Pub.L. 109–8, Title II, § 228(a), Apr. 20, 2005, 119 Stat. 69; amended Pub.L. 111–327, § 2(a)(21), Dec. 22, 2010, 124 Stat. 3560.)

HISTORICAL AND STATUTORY NOTES

Revision Notes and Legislative Reports

2005 Acts. House Report No. 109–31(Part I), see 2005 U.S. Code Cong. and Adm. News, p. 88.

References in Text

Chapter 13, referred to in text, is chapter 13 of this title, 11 U.S.C.A. § 1301 et seq.

Chapter 7, referred to in text, is chapter 7 of this title, 11 U.S.C.A. § 701 et seq.

Amendments

2010 Amendments. Subsec. (b). Pub.L. 111–327, § 2(a)(21), in the fourth paragraph of undesignated matter, struck out "Schedules and Statement of Financial Affairs, as well as in some cases a Statement of Intention" and inserted "Schedules, and Statement of Financial Affairs, and in some cases a Statement of Intention,".

Effective and Applicability Provisions

2005 Acts. Amendments by Pub.L. 109–8 effective, except as otherwise provided, 180 days after April 20, 2005, and inapplicable with respect to cases commenced under Title 11 before the effective date, see Pub.L. 109–8, § 1501, set out as a note under 11 U.S.C.A. § 101.

LIBRARY REFERENCES

Corpus Juris Secundum

CJS Bankruptcy § 18, Debt-Relief Agencies.

§ 528. Requirements for debt relief agencies

(a) A debt relief agency shall—

(1) not later than 5 business days after the first date on which such agency provides any bankruptcy assistance services to an assisted person, but prior to such assisted person's petition under this title being filed, execute a written contract with such assisted person that explains clearly and conspicuously—

(A) the services such agency will provide to such assisted person; and

(B) the fees or charges for such services, and the terms of payment;

(2) provide the assisted person with a copy of the fully executed and completed contract;

(3) clearly and conspicuously disclose in any advertisement of bankruptcy assistance services or of the benefits of bankruptcy directed to the general public (whether in general media, seminars or specific mailings, telephonic or electronic messages, or otherwise) that the services or benefits are with respect to bankruptcy relief under this title; and

(4) clearly and conspicuously use the following statement in such advertisement: "We are a debt relief agency. We help people file for bankruptcy relief under the Bankruptcy Code." or a substantially similar statement.

(b)(1) An advertisement of bankruptcy assistance services or of the benefits of bankruptcy directed to the general public includes—

(A) descriptions of bankruptcy assistance in connection with a chapter 13 plan whether or not chapter 13 is specifically mentioned in such advertisement; and

(B) statements such as "federally supervised repayment plan" or "Federal debt restructuring help" or other similar statements that could lead a reasonable consumer to believe that debt counseling was being offered when in fact the services were directed to providing bankruptcy assistance with a chapter 13 plan or other form of bankruptcy relief under this title.

(2) An advertisement, directed to the general public, indicating that the debt relief agency provides assistance with respect to credit defaults, mortgage foreclosures, eviction proceedings, excessive debt, debt collection pressure, or inability to pay any consumer debt shall—

(A) disclose clearly and conspicuously in such advertisement that the assistance may involve bankruptcy relief under this title; and

(B) include the following statement: "We are a debt relief agency. We help people file for bankruptcy relief under the Bankruptcy Code." or a substantially similar statement.

(Added Pub.L. 109–8, Title II, § 229(a), Apr. 20, 2005, 119 Stat. 71.)

HISTORICAL AND STATUTORY NOTES

Revision Notes and Legislative Reports

2005 Acts. House Report No. 109–31(Part I), see 2005 U.S. Code Cong. and Adm. News, p. 88.

References in Text

Chapter 13, referred to in subsec. (b)(1)(A), (B), is chapter 13 of this title, 11 U.S.C.A. § 1301 et seq.

Effective and Applicability Provisions

2005 Acts. Amendments by Pub.L. 109–8 effective, except as otherwise provided, 180 days after April 20, 2005, and inapplicable with respect to cases commenced under Title 11 before the effective date, see Pub.L. 109–8, § 1501, set out as a note under 11 U.S.C.A. § 101.

LIBRARY REFERENCES

Corpus Juris Secundum

CJS Bankruptcy § 18, Debt-Relief Agencies.

SUBCHAPTER III—THE ESTATE

§ 541. Property of the estate

(a) The commencement of a case under section 301, 302, or 303 of this title creates an estate. Such estate is comprised of all the following property, wherever located and by whomever held:

(1) Except as provided in subsections (b) and (c)(2) of this section, all legal or equitable interests of

the debtor in property as of the commencement of the case.

(2) All interests of the debtor and the debtor's spouse in community property as of the commencement of the case that is—

(A) under the sole, equal, or joint management and control of the debtor; or

(B) liable for an allowable claim against the debtor, or for both an allowable claim against the debtor and an allowable claim against the debtor's spouse, to the extent that such interest is so liable.

(3) Any interest in property that the trustee recovers under section 329(b), 363(n), 543, 550, 553, or 723 of this title.

(4) Any interest in property preserved for the benefit of or ordered transferred to the estate under section 510(c) or 551 of this title.

(5) Any interest in property that would have been property of the estate if such interest had been an interest of the debtor on the date of the filing of the petition, and that the debtor acquires or becomes entitled to acquire within 180 days after such date—

(A) by bequest, devise, or inheritance;

(B) as a result of a property settlement agreement with the debtor's spouse, or of an interlocutory or final divorce decree; or

(C) as a beneficiary of a life insurance policy or of a death benefit plan.

(6) Proceeds, product, offspring, rents, or profits of or from property of the estate, except such as are earnings from services performed by an individual debtor after the commencement of the case.

(7) Any interest in property that the estate acquires after the commencement of the case.

(b) Property of the estate does not include—

(1) any power that the debtor may exercise solely for the benefit of an entity other than the debtor;

(2) any interest of the debtor as a lessee under a lease of nonresidential real property that has terminated at the expiration of the stated term of such lease before the commencement of the case under this title, and ceases to include any interest of the debtor as a lessee under a lease of nonresidential real property that has terminated at the expiration of the stated term of such lease during the case;

(3) any eligibility of the debtor to participate in programs authorized under the Higher Education Act of 1965 (20 U.S.C. 1001 et seq.; 42 U.S.C. 2751 et seq.), or any accreditation status or State licensure of the debtor as an educational institution;

(4) any interest of the debtor in liquid or gaseous hydrocarbons to the extent that—

(A)(i) the debtor has transferred or has agreed to transfer such interest pursuant to a farmout agreement or any written agreement directly related to a farmout agreement; and

(ii) but for the operation of this paragraph, the estate could include the interest referred to in clause (i) only by virtue of section 365 or 544(a)(3) of this title; or

(B)(i) the debtor has transferred such interest pursuant to a written conveyance of a production payment to an entity that does not participate in the operation of the property from which such production payment is transferred; and

(ii) but for the operation of this paragraph, the estate could include the interest referred to in clause (i) only by virtue of section 365 or 542 of this title;

(5) funds placed in an education individual retirement account (as defined in section 530(b)(1) of the Internal Revenue Code of 1986) not later than 365 days before the date of the filing of the petition in a case under this title, but—

(A) only if the designated beneficiary of such account was a child, stepchild, grandchild, or stepgrandchild of the debtor for the taxable year for which funds were placed in such account;

(B) only to the extent that such funds—

(i) are not pledged or promised to any entity in connection with any extension of credit; and

(ii) are not excess contributions (as described in section 4973(e) of the Internal Revenue Code of 1986); and

(C) in the case of funds placed in all such accounts having the same designated beneficiary not earlier than 720 days nor later than 365 days before such date, only so much of such funds as does not exceed $5,850 [1];

(6) funds used to purchase a tuition credit or certificate or contributed to an account in accordance with section 529(b)(1)(A) of the Internal Revenue Code of 1986 under a qualified State tuition program (as defined in section 529(b)(1) of such Code) not later than 365 days before the date of the filing of the petition in a case under this title, but—

(A) only if the designated beneficiary of the amounts paid or contributed to such tuition program was a child, stepchild, grandchild, or stepgrandchild of the debtor for the taxable year for which funds were paid or contributed;

(B) with respect to the aggregate amount paid or contributed to such program having the same designated beneficiary, only so much of such amount as does not exceed the total contributions permitted under section 529(b)(6) of such Code with respect to such beneficiary, as adjusted beginning on the date of the filing of the petition in a case under this title by the annual increase or decrease (rounded to the nearest tenth of 1 percent) in the education expenditure category of the Consumer Price Index prepared by the Department of Labor; and

(C) in the case of funds paid or contributed to such program having the same designated beneficiary not earlier than 720 days nor later than 365 days before such date, only so much of such funds as does not exceed $5,850 [1];

(7) any amount—

(A) withheld by an employer from the wages of employees for payment as contributions—

   (i) to—

      (I) an employee benefit plan that is subject to title I of the Employee Retirement Income Security Act of 1974 or under an employee benefit plan which is a governmental plan under section 414(d) of the Internal Revenue Code of 1986;

      (II) a deferred compensation plan under section 457 of the Internal Revenue Code of 1986; or

      (III) a tax-deferred annuity under section 403(b) of the Internal Revenue Code of 1986;

except that such amount under this subparagraph shall not constitute disposable income as defined in section 1325(b)(2); or

   (ii) to a health insurance plan regulated by State law whether or not subject to such title; or

(B) received by an employer from employees for payment as contributions—

   (i) to—

      (I) an employee benefit plan that is subject to title I of the Employee Retirement Income Security Act of 1974 or under an employee benefit plan which is a governmental plan under section 414(d) of the Internal Revenue Code of 1986;

      (II) a deferred compensation plan under section 457 of the Internal Revenue Code of 1986; or

      (III) a tax-deferred annuity under section 403(b) of the Internal Revenue Code of 1986;

except that such amount under this subparagraph shall not constitute disposable income, as defined in section 1325(b)(2); or

   (ii) to a health insurance plan regulated by State law whether or not subject to such title;

(8) subject to subchapter III of chapter 5, any interest of the debtor in property where the debtor pledged or sold tangible personal property (other than securities or written or printed evidences of indebtedness or title) as collateral for a loan or advance of money given by a person licensed under law to make such loans or advances, where—

(A) the tangible personal property is in the possession of the pledgee or transferee;

(B) the debtor has no obligation to repay the money, redeem the collateral, or buy back the property at a stipulated price; and

(C) neither the debtor nor the trustee have exercised any right to redeem provided under the contract or State law, in a timely manner as provided under State law and section 108(b); or

(9) any interest in cash or cash equivalents that constitute proceeds of a sale by the debtor of a money order that is made—

(A) on or after the date that is 14 days prior to the date on which the petition is filed; and

(B) under an agreement with a money order issuer that prohibits the commingling of such proceeds with property of the debtor (notwithstanding that, contrary to the agreement, the proceeds may have been commingled with property of the debtor),

unless the money order issuer had not taken action, prior to the filing of the petition, to require compliance with the prohibition.

Paragraph (4) shall not be construed to exclude from the estate any consideration the debtor retains, receives, or is entitled to receive for transferring an interest in liquid or gaseous hydrocarbons pursuant to a farmout agreement.

→ **(c)(1)** Except as provided in paragraph (2) of this subsection, an interest of the debtor in property becomes property of the estate under subsection (a)(1), (a)(2), or (a)(5) of this section notwithstanding any provision in an agreement, transfer instrument, or applicable nonbankruptcy law—

(A) that restricts or conditions transfer of such interest by the debtor; or

(B) that is conditioned on the insolvency or financial condition of the debtor, on the commencement of a case under this title, or on the appointment of or taking possession by a trustee in a case under this title or a custodian before such commencement, and that effects or gives an option to effect a forfeiture, modification, or termination of the debtor's interest in property.

(2) A restriction on the transfer of a beneficial interest of the debtor in a trust that is enforceable under applicable nonbankruptcy law is enforceable in a case under this title.

(d) Property in which the debtor holds, as of the commencement of the case, only legal title and not an equitable interest, such as a mortgage secured by real property, or an interest in such a mortgage, sold by the debtor but as to which the debtor retains legal title to service or supervise the servicing of such mortgage or interest, becomes property of the estate under subsection (a)(1) or (2) of this section only to the extent of the debtor's legal title to such property, but not to the extent of any equitable interest in such property that the debtor does not hold.

(e) In determining whether any of the relationships specified in paragraph (5)(A) or (6)(A) of subsection (b) exists, a legally adopted child of an individual (and a child who is a member of an individual's household, if placed with such individual by an authorized placement agency for legal adoption by such individual), or a foster child of an individual (if such child has as the child's principal place of abode the home of the debtor and is a member of the debtor's household) shall be treated as a child of such individual by blood.

(f) Notwithstanding any other provision of this title, property that is held by a debtor that is a corporation described in section 501(c)(3) of the Internal Revenue Code of 1986 and exempt from tax under section 501(a) of such Code may be transferred to an entity that is not such a corporation, but only under the same conditions as would apply if the debtor had not filed a case under this title.

(Pub.L. 95–598, Nov. 6, 1978, 92 Stat. 2594; Pub.L. 98–353, Title III, §§ 363(a), 456, July 10, 1984, 98 Stat. 363, 376; Pub.L. 101–508, Title III, § 3007(a)(2), Nov. 5, 1990, 104 Stat. 1388–28; Pub.L. 102–486, Title XXX, § 3017(b), Oct. 24, 1992, 106 Stat. 3130; Pub.L. 103–394, Title II, §§ 208(b), 223, Oct. 22, 1994, 108 Stat. 4124, 4129; Pub.L. 109–8, Title II, § 225(a), Title III, § 323, Title XII, §§ 1212, 1221(c), 1230, Apr. 20, 2005, 119 Stat. 65, 97, 194, 196, 201; Pub.L. 111–327, § 2(a)(22), Dec. 22, 2010, 124 Stat. 3560.)

1 Dollar amount as adjusted by the Judicial Conference of the United States. See Adjustment of Dollar Amounts notes set out under this section and 11 U.S.C.A. § 104.

HISTORICAL AND STATUTORY NOTES
Revision Notes and Legislative Reports

1978 Acts. This section defines property of the estate, and specifies what property becomes property of the estate. The commencement of a bankruptcy case creates an estate. Under paragraph (1) of subsection (a), the estate is comprised of all legal or equitable interest of the debtor in property, wherever located, as of the commencement of the case. The scope of this paragraph is broad. It includes all kinds of property, including tangible or intangible property, causes of action (see Bankruptcy Act § 70a(6) [section 110(a)(6) of former Title 11]), and all other forms of property currently specified in section 70a of the Bankruptcy Act § 70a [sic] [section 110(a) of former Title 11], as well as property recovered by the trustee under section 542 of proposed title 11, if the property recovered was merely out of the possession of the debtor, yet remained "property of the debtor." The debtor's interest in property also includes "title" to property, which is an interest, just as are a possessory interest, or leasehold interest, for example. The result of *Segal v. Rochelle*, 382 U.S. 375 (1966) [86 S.Ct. 511, 15 L.Ed.2d 428], is followed, and the right to a refund is property of the estate.

Though this paragraph will include choses in action and claims by the debtor against others, it is not intended to expand the debtor's rights against others more than they exist at the commencement of the case. For example, if the debtor has a claim that is barred at the time of the commencement of the case by the statute of limitations, then the trustee would not be able to pursue that claim, because he too would be barred. He could take no greater rights than the debtor himself had. But see proposed 11 U.S.C. 108, which

would permit the trustee a tolling of the statute of limitations if it had not run before the date of the filing of the petition.

Paragraph (1) has the effect of overruling *Lockwood v. Exchange Bank*, 190 U.S. 294 (1903) [23 S.Ct. 751, 47 L.Ed. 1061, 10 Am.Bankr.Rep. 107], because it includes as property of the estate all property of the debtor, even that needed for a fresh start. After the property comes into the estate, then the debtor is permitted to exempt it under proposed 11 U.S.C. 522, and the court will have jurisdiction to determine what property may be exempted and what remains as property of the estate. The broad jurisdictional grant in proposed 28 U.S.C. 1334 would have the effect of overruling *Lockwood* independently of the change made by this provision.

Paragraph (1) also has the effect of overruling *Lines v. Frederick*, 400 U.S. 18 (1970) [91 S.Ct. 113, 27 L.Ed.2d 124].

Situations occasionally arise where property ostensibly belonging to the debtor will actually not be property of the debtor, but will be held in trust for another. For example, if the debtor has incurred medical bills that were covered by insurance, and the insurance company had sent the payment of the bills to the debtor before the debtor had paid the bill for which the payment was reimbursement, the payment would actually be held in a constructive trust for the person to whom the bill was owed. This section and proposed 11 U.S.C. 545 also will not affect various statutory provisions that give a creditor of the debtor a lien that is valid outside as well as inside bankruptcy, or that creates a trust fund for the benefit of a creditor of the debtor. See Packers and Stockyards Act § 206, 7 U.S.C. 196 [7 U.S.C.A. § 196].

Bankruptcy Act § 8 [section 26 of former Title 11] has been deleted as unnecessary. Once the estate is created, no interests in property of the estate remain in the debtor. Consequently, if the debtor dies during the case, only property exempted from property of the estate or acquired by the debtor after the commencement of the case and not included as property of the estate will be available to the representative of the debtor's probate estate. The bankruptcy proceeding will continue in rem with respect to property of the state [sic], and the discharge will apply in personam to relieve the debtor, and thus his probate representative, of liability for dischargeable debts.

The estate also includes the interests of the debtor and the debtor's spouse in community property, subject to certain limitations; property that the trustee recovers under the avoiding powers; property that the debtor acquires by bequest, devise, inheritance, a property settlement agreement with the debtor's spouse, or as the beneficiary of a life insurance policy within 180 days after the petition; and proceeds, product, offspring, rents, and profits of or from property of the estate, except such as are earning from services performed by an individual debtor after the commencement of the case. Proceeds here is not used in a confining sense, as defined in the Uniform Commercial Code, but is intended to be a broad term to encompass all proceeds of property of the estate. The conversion in form of property of the estate does not change its character as property of the estate.

Subsection (b) excludes from property of the estate any power, such as a power of appointment, that the debtor may exercise solely for the benefit of an entity other than the debtor. This changes present law which excludes powers solely benefiting other persons but not other entities.

Subsection (c) invalidates restrictions on the transfer of property of the debtor, in order that all of the interests of the debtor in property will become property of the estate. The provisions invalidated are those that restrict or condition transfer of the debtor's interest, and those that are conditioned on the insolvency or financial condition of the debtor, on the commencement of a bankruptcy case, or on the appointment of a custodian of the debtor's property. Paragraph (2) of subsection (c), however, preserves restrictions on a transfer of a spendthrift trust that the restriction is enforceable nonbankruptcy law to the extent of the income reasonably necessary for the support of a debtor and his dependents.

Subsection (d), derived from section 70c of the Bankruptcy Act [section 110(c) of former Title 11], gives the estate the benefit of all defenses available to the debtor as against an entity other than the estate, including such defenses as statutes of limitations, statutes of frauds, usury, and other personal defenses, and makes waiver by the debtor after the commencement of the case ineffective to bind the estate.

Section 541(e) confirms the current status under the Bankruptcy Act [former Title 11] of bona fide secondary mortgage market transactions as the purchase and sale of assets. Mortgages or interests in mortgages sold in the secondary market should not be considered as part of the debtor's estate. To permit the efficient servicing of mortgages or interests in mortgages the seller often retains the original mortgage notes and related documents, and the purchaser records under State recording statutes the purchaser's ownership of the mortgages or interests in mortgages purchased. Section 541(e) makes clear that the seller's retention of the mortgage documents and the purchaser's decision not to record do not impair the asset sale character of secondary mortgage market transactions. The committee notes that in secondary mortgage market transactions the parties may characterize their relationship as one of trust, agency, or independent contractor. The characterization adopted by the parties should not affect the statutes in bankruptcy on bona fide secondary mortgage market purchases and sales. Senate Report No. 95–989.

1984 Acts. Statements by Legislative Leaders, see 1984 U.S. Code Cong. and Adm. News, p. 576.

1990 Acts. House Report No. 101–881, House Conference Report No. 101–964, and President's Signing Statement, see 1990 U.S. Code Cong. and Adm. News, p. 2017.

1994 Acts. House Report No. 103–835, see 1994 U.S. Code Cong. and Adm. News, p. 3340.

2005 Acts. House Report No. 109–31(Part I), see 2005 U.S. Code Cong. and Adm. News, p. 88.

Legislative Statements

Section 541(a)(7) is new. The provision clarifies that any interest in property that the estate acquires after the commencement of the case is property of the estate; for example, if the estate enters into a contract, after the commencement of the case, such a contract would be property of the estate. The addition of this provision by the House amendment merely clarifies that section 541(a) is an all-embracing definition which includes charges on property, such as liens held by the debtor on property of a third party, or beneficial rights and interests that the debtor may have in property of another. However, only the debtor's interest in such property becomes property of the estate. If the debtor holds bare legal title or holds property in trust for another, only those rights which the debtor would have otherwise had emanating from such interest pass to the estate under section 541. Neither this

section nor section 545 will affect various statutory provisions that give a creditor a lien that is valid both inside and outside bankruptcy against a bona fide purchaser of property from the debtor, or that creates a trust fund for the benefit of creditors meeting similar criteria. See Packers and Stockyards Act § 206, 7 U.S.C. 196 (1976) [7 U.S.C.A. § 196].

Section 541(c)(2) follows the position taken in the House bill and rejects the position taken in the Senate amendment with respect to income limitations on a spend-thrift trust.

Section 541(d) of the House amendment is derived from section 541(e) of the Senate amendment and reiterates the general principle that where the debtor holds bare legal title without any equitable interest, that the estate acquires bare legal title without any equitable interest in the property. The purpose of section 541(d) as applied to the secondary mortgage market is identical to the purpose of section 541(e) of the Senate amendment and section 541(d) will accomplish the same result as would have been accomplished by section 541(e). Even if a mortgage seller retains for purposes of servicing legal title to mortgages or interests in mortgages sold in the secondary mortgage market, the trustee would be required by section 541(d) to turn over the mortgages or interests in mortgages to the purchaser of those mortgages.

The seller of mortgages in the secondary mortgage market will often retain the original mortgage notes and related documents and the seller will not endorse the notes to reflect the sale to the purchaser. Similarly, the purchaser will often not record the purchaser's ownership of the mortgages or interests in mortgages under State recording statutes. These facts are irrelevant and the seller's retention of the mortgage documents and the purchaser's decision not to record do not change the trustee's obligation to turn the mortgages or interests in mortgages over to the purchaser. The application of section 541(d) to secondary mortgage market transactions will not be affected by the terms of the servicing agreement between the mortgage servicer and the purchaser of the mortgages. Under section 541(d), the trustee is required to recognize the purchaser's title to the mortgages or interests in mortgages and to turn this property over to the purchaser. It makes no difference whether the servicer and the purchaser characterize their relationship as one of trust, agency, or independent contractor.

The purpose of section 541(d) as applied to the secondary mortgage market is therefore to make certain that secondary mortgage market sales as they are currently structured are not subject to challenge by bankruptcy trustees and that purchasers of mortgages will be able to obtain the mortgages or interests in mortgages which they have purchased from trustees without the trustees asserting that a sale of mortgages is a loan from the purchaser to the seller.

Thus, as section 541(a)(1) clearly states, the estate is comprised of all legal or equitable interests of the debtor in property as of the commencement of the case. To the extent such an interest is limited in the hands of the debtor, it is equally limited in the hands of the estate except to the extent that defenses which are personal against the debtor are not effective against the estate.

Property of the estate: The Senate amendment provided that property of the estate does not include amounts held by the debtor as trustee and any taxes withheld or collected from others before the commencement of the case. The House amendment removes these two provisions. As to property held by the debtor as a trustee, the House amendment provides that property of the estate will include whatever interest the debtor held in the property at the commencement of the case. Thus, where the debtor held only legal title to the property and the beneficial interest in that property belongs to another, such as exists in the case of property held in trust, the property of the estate includes the legal title, but not the beneficial interest in the property.

As to withheld taxes, the House amendment deletes the rule in the Senate bill as unnecessary since property of the estate does not include the beneficial interest in property held by the debtor as a trustee. Under the Internal Revenue Code of 1954 (section 7501 [26 U.S.C.A. § 7501]), the amounts of withheld taxes are held to be a special fund in trust for the United States. Where the Internal Revenue Service can demonstrate that the amounts of taxes withheld are still in the possession of the debtor at the commencement of the case, then if a trust is created, those amounts are not property of the estate. Compare *In re Shakesteers Coffee Shops*, 546 F.2d 821 (9th Cir. 1976) with *In re Glynn Wholesale Building Materials, Inc.* (S.D.Ga.1978) and *In re Progress Tech Colleges, Inc.*, 42 Aftr 2d 78–5573 (S.D.Ohio 1977).

Where it is not possible for the Internal Revenue Service to demonstrate that the amounts of taxes withheld are still in the possession of the debtor at the commencement of the case, present law generally includes amounts of withheld taxes as property of the estate. See, e.g., *United States v. Randall*, 401 U.S. 513 (1973) [91 S.Ct. 991, 28 L.Ed.2d 273] and *In re Tamasha Town and Country Club*, 483 F.2d 1377 (9th Cir. 1973). Nonetheless, a serious problem exists where "trust fund taxes" withheld from others are held to be property of the estate where the withheld amounts are commingled with other assets of the debtor. The courts should permit the use of reasonable assumptions under which the Internal Revenue Service, and other tax authorities, can demonstrate that amounts of withheld taxes are still in the possession of the debtor at the commencement of the case. For example, where the debtor had commingled that amount of withheld taxes in his general checking account, it might be reasonable to assume that any remaining amounts in that account on the commencement of the case are the withheld taxes. In addition, Congress may consider future amendments to the Internal Revenue Code making clear that amounts of withheld taxes are held by the debtor in a trust relationship and, consequently, that such amounts are not property of the estate.

References in Text

The Higher Education Act of 1965, referred to in subsec. (b)(3), is Pub.L. 89–329, Nov. 8, 1965, 79 Stat. 1219, as amended, which is classified principally to chapter 28 (§ 1001 et seq.) of Title 20, Education. For complete classification of this Act to the Code, see Short Title note set out under section 1001 of Title 20 and Tables.

Section 530(b)(1) of the Internal Revenue Code of 1986, referred to in subsec. (b)(5), is classified to 26 U.S.C.A. § 530(b)(1).

Section 4973(e) of the Internal Revenue Code of 1986, referred to in subsec. (b)(5)(B)(ii), is classified to 26 U.S.C.A. § 4973(e).

"Section 529(b)(1) of such Code" and "section 529(b)(6) of such Code", referred to in subsec. (b)(6), are classified to 26 U.S.C.A. § 529(b)(1) and to 26 U.S.C.A. § 529(b)(6), respectively.

Title I of the Employee Retirement Income Security Act of 1974, referred to in subsec. (b)(7)(A)(i)(I), (B)(i)(I), means Pub.L. 93–406, Title I, Sept. 2, 1974, 88 Stat. 829, which principally enacted subchapter I of chapter 18 of Title 29, 29 U.S.C.A. § 1001 et seq.; see Tables for complete classification.

Section 414(d) of the Internal Revenue Code of 1986, referred to in subsec. (b)(7)(A)(i)(I), (B)(i)(I), is 26 U.S.C.A. § 414(d).

Section 457 of the Internal Revenue Code of 1986, referred to in subsec. (b)(7)(A)(i)(II), (B)(i)(II), is 26 U.S.C.A. § 457.

Section 403(b) of the Internal Revenue Code of 1986, referred to in subsec. (b)(7)(A)(i)(III), (B)(i)(III), is 26 U.S.C.A. § 403(b).

Codifications

Section 223(2) of Pub.L. 103–394, directing that subsec. (b)(4) of this section be amended by striking out the period at the end and inserting "; or", was executed by inserting "or" following the semicolon at the end of subsec. (b)(4)(B)(ii) of this section, as added by section 208(b)(3) of Pub.L. 103–394, as the probable intent of Congress.

Amendments

2010 Amendments. Subsec. (b)(5)(C). By notice dated Feb. 25, 2010, 75 F.R. 8747, dollar amount adjusted by the Judicial Conference of the United States which adjusted "$5,475" to "$5,850". See 11 U.S.C.A. § 104 and Adjustment of Dollar Amounts notes under this section.

Subsec. (b)(6)(B). Pub.L. 111–327, § 2(a)(22), struck out "section 529(b)(7)" and inserted "section 529(b)(6)".

Subsec. (b)(6)(C). By notice dated Feb. 25, 2010, 75 F.R. 8747, dollar amount adjusted by the Judicial Conference of the United States which adjusted "$5,475" to "$5,850". See 11 U.S.C.A. § 104 and Adjustment of Dollar Amounts notes under this section.

2007 Amendments. Subsec. (b)(5)(C). By notice dated Feb. 14, 2007, 72 F.R. 7082, dollar amount adjusted by the Judicial Conference of the United States which adjusted "$5,000" to "$5,475". See 11 U.S.C.A. § 104 and Adjustment of Dollar Amounts notes under this section.

Subsec. (b)(6)(C). By notice dated Feb. 14, 2007, 72 F.R. 7082, dollar amount adjusted by the Judicial Conference of the United States which adjusted "$5,000" to "$5,475". See 11 U.S.C.A. § 104 and Adjustment of Dollar Amounts notes under this section.

2005 Amendments. Subsec. (b)(4). Pub.L. 109–8, § 225(a)(1)(A), struck out "or" at the end of par. (4).

Subsec. (b)(4)(B)(ii). Pub.L.109–8, § 1212, inserted "365 or" before "542".

Subsec. (b)(5). Pub.L. 109–8, § 225(a)(1)(B), (C), inserted new par. (5) and redesignated former par. (5) as par. (9).

Subsec. (b)(6). Pub.L. 109–8, § 225(a)(1)(C), inserted new par. (6)

Subsec. (b)(7). Pub.L. 109–8, § 323, added par. (7).

Subsec. (b)(8). Pub.L.109–8, § 1230, added par. (8).

Subsec. (b)(9). Pub.L. 109–8, § 225(a)(1)(B), redesignated former par. (5) as par. (9).

Subsec. (e). Pub.L. 109–8, § 225(a)(2), added subsec. (e).

Subsec. (f). Pub.L.109–8, § 1221(c), added subsec. (f).

1994 Amendments. Subsec. (b)(4). Pub.L. 103–394, § 208(b), added subpar. (B) and redesignated former subpar. (A) as subpar. (A), cl. (i) and former subpar. (B) as subpar.

(A), cl. (ii) and as so redesignated substituted "the interest referred to in clause (i)" for "such interest".

Subsec. (b)(4)(B). Pub.L. 103–394, § 208(b)(3), added subpar. (B).

Subsec. (b)(5). Pub.L. 103–394, § 223, added par. (5).

1992 Amendments. Subsec. (b). Pub.L. 102–486, § 3017(b), added par. (4) and closing sentence.

1990 Amendments. Subsec. (b)(3). Pub.L. 101–508, § 3007(a)(2), added par. (3).

1984 Amendments. Subsec. (a). Pub.L. 98–353, § 456(a)(1), (2), struck out "under" following "under" and added "and by whomever held" after "located".

Subsec. (a)(3). Pub.L. 98–353, § 456(a)(3), added "329(b), 363(n)," after "section".

Subsec. (a)(5). Pub.L. 98–353, § 456(a)(4), substituted "Any" for "An".

Subsec. (a)(6). Pub.L. 98–353, § 456(a)(5), substituted "or profits" for "and profits".

Subsec. (b). Pub.L. 98–353, § 363(a), substituted "Property of the estate does not include—

"**(1)** any power that the debtor may exercise solely for the benefit of an entity other than the debtor; or

"**(2)** any interest of the debtor as a lessee under a lease of nonresidential real property that has terminated at the expiration of the stated term of such lease before the commencement of the case under this title, and ceases to include any interest of the debtor as a lessee under a lease of nonresidential real property that has terminated at the expiration of the stated term of such lease during the case."

for

"Property of the estate does not include any power that the debtor may only exercise solely for the benefit of an entity other than the debtor.".

Subsec. (c)(1). Pub.L. 98–353, § 456(b)(1), added "in an agreement, transfer instrument, or applicable nonbankruptcy law" after "provision" in matter preceding subpar. (A).

Subsec. (c)(1)(B). Pub.L. 98–353, § 456(b)(2), substituted "taking" for "the taking" and added "before such commencement" after "custodian".

Subsec. (d). Pub.L. 98–353, § 456(c), added "(1) or (2)" after "(a)".

Subsec. (e). Pub.L. 98–353, § 456(d), struck out subsec. (e), which read "The estate shall have the benefit of any defense available to the debtor as against an entity other than the estate, including statutes of limitation, statutes of frauds, usury, and other personal defenses. A waiver of any such defense by the debtor after the commencement of the case does not bind the estate."

Effective and Applicability Provisions

2010 Acts. Increase of dollar amounts by Judicial Conference of the United States by notice published Feb. 25, 2010, 75 F.R. 8747 effective April 1, 2010, and increase not applicable to cases commenced before the effective date of the adjustments, i.e., April 1, 2010. See Adjustment of Dollar Amounts notes under 11 U.S.C.A. § 104 and this section.

2007 Acts. Increase of dollar amounts by Judicial Conference of the United States by notice published Feb. 14, 2007, 72 F.R. 7082 effective April 1, 2007, and increase not applicable to cases commenced before the effective date of the

adjustments, i.e., April 1, 2007. See Adjustment of Dollar Amounts notes under 11 U.S.C.A. § 104 and this section.

2005 Acts. Amendments to this section by Pub.L. 109–8, § 1221, applicable to case pending under this title on April 20, 2005, or filed under this title on or after that date, except that the court shall not confirm a plan under chapter 11 of this title without considering whether this section would substantially affect the rights of a party in interest who first acquired rights with respect to the debtor after the date of the filing of the petition, see Pub.L. 109–8, § 1221(d), set out as a note under 11 U.S.C.A. § 363.

Amendments by Pub.L. 109–8 effective, except as otherwise provided, 180 days after April 20, 2005, and inapplicable with respect to cases commenced under Title 11 before the effective date, see Pub.L. 109–8, § 1501, set out as a note under 11 U.S.C.A. § 101.

1994 Acts. Amendment by Pub.L. 103–394 effective on Oct. 22, 1994, and not to apply with respect to cases commenced under Title 11 of the United States Code before Oct. 22, 1994, see section 702 of Pub.L. 103–394, set out as a note under section 101 of this title.

1992 Acts. Enactment of subsec. (b)(4) by Pub.L. 102–486 effective Oct. 24, 1992, see section 3017(c) of Pub.L. 102–486, set out as a note under section 101 of this title.

1990 Acts. Section 3008 of Pub.L. 101–508, which had provided that the amendment to this section by Pub.L. 101–508 was to cease to be effective on Oct. 1, 1996, was repealed by Pub.L. 102–325, Title XV, § 1558, July 23, 1992, 106 Stat. 841.

1984 Acts. Amendment by Pub.L. 98–353 effective with respect to cases filed 90 days after July 10, 1984, see section 552(a), formerly 553(a) of Pub.L. 98–353, set out as a note under section 101 of this title.

Separability of Provisions

If any provision of or amendment made by Pub.L. 103–394 or the application of such provision or amendment to any person or circumstance is held to be unconstitutional, the remaining provisions of and amendments made by Pub.L. 103–394 and the application of such provisions and amendments to any person or circumstance shall not be affected thereby, see section 701 of Pub.L. 103–394, set out as a note under section 101 of this title.

Adjustment of Dollar Amounts

For adjustment of dollar amounts specified in subsec. (b)(5)(C), (6)(C) of this section by the Judicial Conference of the United States, effective Apr. 1, 2010, see note set out under 11 U.S.C.A. § 104.

By notice published Feb. 25, 2010, 75 F.R. 8747, the Judicial Conference of the United States adjusted the dollar amounts in provisions specified in subsec. (b)(5)(C), (6)(C) of this section, effective Apr. 1, 2010, as follows:

In subsec. (b)(5)(C) adjusted $5,475 to $5,850.

In subsec. (b)(6)(C) adjusted $5,475 to $5,850.

By notice published Feb. 14, 2007, 72 F.R. 7082, the Judicial Conference of the United States adjusted the dollar amounts in provisions specified in subsec. (b)(5)(C), (6)(C) of this section, effective Apr. 1, 2007, as follows:

In subsec. (b)(5)(C) adjusted $5,000 to $5,475.

In subsec. (b)(6)(C) adjusted $5,000 to $5,475.

Community claim defined, see 11 USCA § 101.

Distribution of property of estate, see 11 USCA § 726.

Effect of discharge, see 11 USCA § 524.

Executory contracts and unexpired leases, see 11 USCA § 365.

Exemptions, see 11 USCA § 522.

Ownership of copyright, see 17 USCA § 201.

Property of estate in—

Chapter 13 cases, see 11 USCA § 1306.

Chapter 12 cases, see 11 USCA § 1207.

Special tax provisions concerning estates of partners and partnerships, see 11 USCA § 728.

Trustee considered consignee of merchandise consigned to deceased or insolvent persons, see 19 USCA § 1485.

Venue of action brought under this title by trustee as statutory successor under this section to debtor, see 28 USCA § 1409.

LIBRARY REFERENCES

American Digest System

Bankruptcy ⬩2531 to 2559, 2492.

Key Number System Topic No. 51.

Corpus Juris Secundum

CJS Bailments § 121, Termination of Bailment--Effect of Termination.

CJS Bankruptcy § 152, Exclusive Jurisdiction of Property of Debtor and Estate.

CJS Bankruptcy § 266, Proceedings Arising Under Bankruptcy Code or Arising in or Related to Cases Under Code.

CJS Bankruptcy § 355, Supplemental Schedule to Account for Certain Interests Acquired or Arising After Petition.

CJS Bankruptcy § 358, Amendment.

CJS Bankruptcy § 552, Items and Interests Included.

CJS Bankruptcy § 553, Leases.

CJS Bankruptcy § 556, Spousal and Other Joint Interests.

CJS Bankruptcy § 557, Deposits and Other Property Held in Trust or Custody for Debtor.

CJS Bankruptcy § 559, Rights of Action and Contract Rights.

CJS Bankruptcy § 560, Property of Partners and Partnerships.

CJS Bankruptcy § 561, Property Acquired Postpetition.

CJS Bankruptcy § 572, Operation and Effect of Exemption.

CJS Bankruptcy § 581, Interests Acquired or Arising After Filing of Bankruptcy Petition.

CJS Bankruptcy § 624, Surrender of Property of Estate and Recorded Information to Trustee.

CJS Bankruptcy § 888, Right of First Refusal of Debtor's Spouse or Co-Owners.

CJS Bankruptcy § 1062, Effect of Discharge of Debts.

CJS Bankruptcy § 1103, Community Property.

CJS Estoppel and Waiver § 190, Applicability of Judicial Estoppel to Contradictory Positions Taken in Same Proceeding.

CJS Estoppel and Waiver § 191, Applicability of Judicial Estoppel to Inconsistent Statements of Facts or Conclusions of Law.

CJS Estoppel and Waiver § 192, Judicial Estoppel as Restricted to Statements Made Under Oath.

CJS Gifts § 74, Relation of Parties.

CJS Internal Revenue § 319, Individual Retirement Accounts and Individual Retirement Annuities.

§ 542. Turnover of property to the estate

(a) Except as provided in subsection (c) or (d) of this section, an entity, other than a custodian, in possession, custody, or control, during the case, of property that the trustee may use, sell, or lease under section 363 of this title, or that the debtor may exempt under section 522 of this title, shall deliver to the trustee, and account for, such property or the value of such property, unless such property is of inconsequential value or benefit to the estate.

(b) Except as provided in subsection (c) or (d) of this section, an entity that owes a debt that is property of the estate and that is matured, payable on demand, or payable on order, shall pay such debt to, or on the order of, the trustee, except to the extent that such debt may be offset under section 553 of this title against a claim against the debtor.

(c) Except as provided in section 362(a)(7) of this title, an entity that has neither actual notice nor actual knowledge of the commencement of the case concerning the debtor may transfer property of the estate, or pay a debt owing to the debtor, in good faith and other than in the manner specified in subsection (d) of this section, to an entity other than the trustee, with the same effect as to the entity making such transfer or payment as if the case under this title concerning the debtor had not been commenced.

(d) A life insurance company may transfer property of the estate or property of the debtor to such company in good faith, with the same effect with respect to such company as if the case under this title concerning the debtor had not been commenced, if such transfer is to pay a premium or to carry out a nonforfeiture insurance option, and is required to be made automatically, under a life insurance contract with such company that was entered into before the date of the filing of the petition and that is property of the estate.

(e) Subject to any applicable privilege, after notice and a hearing, the court may order an attorney, accountant, or other person that holds recorded information, including books, documents, records, and papers, relating to the debtor's property or financial affairs, to turn over or disclose such recorded information to the trustee.

(Pub.L. 95–598, Nov. 6, 1978, 92 Stat. 2595; Pub.L. 98–353, Title III, § 457, July 10, 1984, 98 Stat. 376; Pub.L. 103–394, Title V, § 501(d)(16), Oct. 22, 1994, 108 Stat. 4146.)

HISTORICAL AND STATUTORY NOTES
Revision Notes and Legislative Reports

1978 Acts. Subsection (a) of this section requires anyone holding property of the estate on the date of the filing of the petition, or property that the trustee may use, sell, or lease under section 363, to deliver it to the trustee. The subsection also requires an accounting. The holder of property of the estate is excused from the turnover requirement of this subsection if the property held is of inconsequential value to the estate. However, this provision must be read in conjunction with the remainder of the subsection, so that if the property is of inconsequential monetary value, yet has a significant use value for the estate, the holder of the property would not be excused from turnover.

Subsection (b) requires an entity that owes money to the debtor as of the date of the petition, or that holds money payable on demand or payable on order, to pay the money to the order of the trustee. An exception is made to the extent that the entity has a valid right of setoff, as recognized by section 553.

Subsection (c) provides an exception to subsections (a) and (b). It protects an entity that has neither actual notice nor actual knowledge of the case and that transfers, in good faith, property that is deliverable or payable to the trustee to someone other than to the estate or on order of the estate. This subsection codifies the result of *Bank of Marin v. England*, 385 U.S. 99 (1966) [87 S.Ct. 274, 17 L.Ed.2d 197], but does not go so far as to permit bank setoff in violation of the automatic stay, proposed 11 U.S.C. 362(a)(7), even if the bank offsetting the debtor's balance has no knowledge of the case.

Subsection (d) protects life insurance companies that are required by contract to make automatic premium loans from property that might otherwise be property of the estate.

Subsection (e) requires an attorney, accountant, or other professional that holds recorded information relating to the debtor's property or financial affairs, to surrender it to the trustee. This duty is subject to any applicable claim of privilege, such as attorney-client privilege. It is a new provision that deprives accountants and attorneys of the leverage that they have today, under State law lien provisions, to receive payment in full ahead of other creditors when the information they hold is necessary to the administration of the estate. Senate Report No. 95–989.

1984 Acts. Statements by Legislative Leaders, see 1984 U.S. Code Cong. and Adm. News, p. 576.

1994 Acts. House Report No. 103–835, see 1994 U.S. Code Cong. and Adm. News, p. 3340.

Legislative Statements

Section 542(a) of the House amendment modifies similar provisions contained in the House bill and the Senate amendment treating with turnover of property to the estate. The section makes clear that any entity, other than a custodian, is required to deliver property of the estate to the trustee or debtor in possession whenever such property is acquired by the entity during the case, if the trustee or debtor in possession may use, sell, or lease the property under section 363, or if the debtor may exempt the property under section 522, unless the property is of inconsequential value or benefit to the estate. This section is not intended to require an entity to deliver property to the trustee if such entity has obtained an order of the court authorizing the entity to retain possession, custody or control of the property.

The House amendment adopts section 542(c) of the House bill in preference to a similar provision contained in section 542(c) of the Senate amendment. Protection afforded by section 542(c) applies only to the transferor or payor and not to a transferee or payee receiving a transfer or payment, as the case may be. Such transferee or payee is treated under section 549 and section 550 of title 11.

The extent to which the attorney client privilege is valid against the trustee is unclear under current law and is left to be determined by the courts on a case by case basis.

Amendments

1994 Amendments. Subsec. (e). Pub.L. 103–394, § 501(d)(16), substituted "to turn over" for "to to turn over".

1984 Amendments. Subsec. (e). Pub.L. 98–353 added "to turn over or" before "disclose".

Effective and Applicability Provisions

1994 Acts. Amendment by Pub.L. 103–394 effective on Oct. 22, 1994, and not to apply with respect to cases commenced under Title 11 of the United States Code before Oct. 22, 1994, see section 702 of Pub.L. 103–394, set out as a note under section 101 of this title.

1984 Acts. Amendment by Pub.L. 98–353 effective with respect to cases filed 90 days after July 10, 1984, see section 552(a), formerly 553 of Pub.L. 98–353, set out as a note under section 101 of this title.

Separability of Provisions

If any provision of or amendment made by Pub.L. 103–394 or the application of such provision or amendment to any person or circumstance is held to be unconstitutional, the remaining provisions of and amendments made by Pub.L. 103–394 and the application of such provisions and amendments to any person or circumstance shall not be affected thereby, see section 701 of Pub.L. 103–394, set out as a note under section 101 of this title.

CROSS REFERENCES

Assignability or accrual to third persons of farm loan agreements respecting credits or principal and interest, see 42 USCA § 1473.

Concealment of assets, see 18 USCA § 152.

Disallowance of claims of entity from which property is recoverable, see 11 USCA § 502.

Effect of dismissal, see 11 USCA § 349.

Exemptions, see 11 USCA § 522.

LIBRARY REFERENCES
American Digest System

Bankruptcy ⊕3063.1 to 3066(6).
Key Number System Topic No. 51.

Corpus Juris Secundum

CJS Bankruptcy § 278, Parties Defendant; Sovereign Immunity.

CJS Bankruptcy § 589, Property Debtor Could Have Exempted Absent Transfer of that Property.

CJS Bankruptcy § 617, Burden and Standard of Proof.

CJS Bankruptcy § 631, Entities Subject to Turnover Duty.

CJS Bankruptcy § 634, Assertion of Claim Against Governmental Unit; Sovereign Immunity.

CJS Bankruptcy § 636, Applicability of Attorney-Client or Accountant-Client Privilege.

CJS Bankruptcy § 637, Effect of Lien on Recorded Information; Adequate Protection of Lien Holder's Interest.

CJS Bankruptcy § 638, Good-Faith Transfers and Payments Made by Entities Without Notice or Knowledge of Case.

CJS Bankruptcy § 639, Automatic Transfers of Life-Insurance Premiums.

CJS Bankruptcy § 700, Disallowance of Claims of Entities or Transferees Holding Recoverable Property.

§ 543. Turnover of property by a custodian

(a) A custodian with knowledge of the commencement of a case under this title concerning the debtor may not make any disbursement from, or take any action in the administration of, property of the debtor, proceeds, product, offspring, rents, or profits of such property, or property of the estate, in the possession, custody, or control of such custodian, except such action as is necessary to preserve such property.

(b) A custodian shall—

(1) deliver to the trustee any property of the debtor held by or transferred to such custodian, or proceeds, product, offspring, rents, or profits of such property, that is in such custodian's possession, custody, or control on the date that such custodian acquires knowledge of the commencement of the case; and

(2) file an accounting of any property of the debtor, or proceeds, product, offspring, rents, or profits of such property, that, at any time, came into the possession, custody, or control of such custodian.

(c) The court, after notice and a hearing, shall—

(1) protect all entities to which a custodian has become obligated with respect to such property or proceeds, product, offspring, rents, or profits of such property;

(2) provide for the payment of reasonable compensation for services rendered and costs and expenses incurred by such custodian; and

(3) surcharge such custodian, other than an assignee for the benefit of the debtor's creditors that was appointed or took possession more than 120 days before the date of the filing of the petition, for any improper or excessive disbursement, other than a disbursement that has been made in accordance with applicable law or that has been approved, after notice and a hearing, by a court of competent jurisdiction before the commencement of the case under this title.

(d) After notice and hearing, the bankruptcy court—

(1) may excuse compliance with subsection (a), (b), or (c) of this section if the interests of creditors and, if the debtor is not insolvent, of equity security holders would be better served by permitting a custodian to continue in possession, custody, or control of such property, and

(2) shall excuse compliance with subsections (a) and (b)(1) of this section if the custodian is an assignee for the benefit of the debtor's creditors that was appointed or took possession more than 120 days before the date of the filing of the petition, unless compliance with such subsections is necessary to prevent fraud or injustice.

(Pub.L. 95–598, Nov. 6, 1978, 92 Stat. 2595; Pub.L. 98–353, Title III, § 458, July 10, 1984, 98 Stat. 376; Pub.L. 103–394, Title V, § 501(d)(17), Oct. 22, 1994, 108 Stat. 4146.)

HISTORICAL AND STATUTORY NOTES

Revision Notes and Legislative Reports

1978 Acts. This section requires a custodian appointed before the bankruptcy case to deliver to the trustee and to account for property that has come into his possession, custody, or control as a custodian. "Property of the debtor" in section (a) [sic] includes property that was property of the debtor at the time the custodian took the property, but the title to which passed to the custodian. The section requires the court to protect any obligations incurred by the custodian, provide for the payment of reasonable compensation for services rendered and costs and expenses incurred by the custodian, and to surcharge the custodian for any improper or excessive disbursement, unless it has been approved by a court of competent jurisdiction. Subsection (d) reinforces the general abstention policy in § 305 by permitting the bankruptcy court to authorize the custodianship to proceed notwithstanding this section. Senate Report No. 95–989.

1984 Acts. Statements by Legislative Leaders, see 1984 U.S. Code Cong. and Adm. News, p. 576.

1994 Acts. House Report No. 103–835, see 1994 U.S. Code Cong. and Adm. News, p. 3340.

Legislative Statements

Section 543(a) is a modification of similar provisions contained in the House bill and the Senate amendment. The provision clarifies that a custodian may always act as is necessary to preserve property of the debtor. Section 543(c)(3) excepts from surcharge a custodian that is an assignee for the benefit of creditors, who was appointed or took possession before 120 days before the date of the filing of the petition, whichever is later. The provision also prevents a custodian from being surcharged in connection with payments made in accordance with applicable law.

Amendments

1994 Amendments. Subsec. (d)(1). Pub.L. 103–394, § 501(d)(17), struck out comma following "section".

1984 Amendments. Subsec. (a). Pub.L. 98–353, § 458(a), added ", product, offspring, rents, or profits" after "proceeds".

Subsec. (b)(1). Pub.L. 98–353, § 458(b)(1), added "held by" after "debtor", and ", product, offspring, rents, or profits" after "proceeds".

Subsec. (b)(2). Pub.L. 98–353, § 458(b)(2), added ", product, offspring, rents, or profits" after "proceeds".

Subsec. (c)(1). Pub.L. 98–353, § 458(c)(1), added "or proceeds, product, offspring, rents, or profits of such property" after "property".

Subsec. (c)(3). Pub.L. 98–353, § 458(c)(2), added "that has been" before "approved".

Subsec. (d)(1). Pub.L. 98–353, § 458(d), designated existing provisions as par. (1).

Subsec. (d)(2). Pub.L. 98–353, § 458(d), added par. (2).

Effective and Applicability Provisions

1994 Acts. Amendment by Pub.L. 103–394 effective on Oct. 22, 1994, and not to apply with respect to cases commenced under Title 11 of the United States Code before Oct. 22, 1994, see section 702 of Pub.L. 103–394, set out as a note under section 101 of this title.

1984 Acts. Amendment by Pub.L. 98–353 effective with respect to cases filed 90 days after July 10, 1984, see section 552(a)(7), formerly 553 of Pub.L. 98–353, set out as a note under section 101 of this title.

Separability of Provisions

If any provision of or amendment made by Pub.L. 103–394 or the application of such provision or amendment to any person or circumstance is held to be unconstitutional, the remaining provisions of and amendments made by Pub.L. 103–394 and the application of such provisions and amendments to any person or circumstance shall not be affected thereby, see section 701 of Pub.L. 103–394, set out as a note under section 101 of this title.

CROSS REFERENCES

Administrative expenses of superseded custodians, see 11 USCA § 503.

Concealment of assets, see 18 USCA § 152.

Disallowance of claim of entity from which property is recoverable, see 11 USCA § 502.

Effect of dismissal, see 11 USCA § 349.

Order of payment on claims for expenses of superseded custodians, see 11 USCA § 726.

Property recoverable by trustee as exempt, see 11 USCA § 522.

LIBRARY REFERENCES

American Digest System

Bankruptcy ⊗3064, 3066(1) to 3066(6).

Key Number System Topic No. 51.

Corpus Juris Secundum

CJS Bankruptcy § 200, Other Proceedings Affecting Liquidation of Estate Assets or Adjustment of Debtor-Creditor/Equity-Security Holder Relationship--Actions Involving State Law.

CJS Bankruptcy § 278, Parties Defendant; Sovereign Immunity.

CJS Bankruptcy § 589, Property Debtor Could Have Exempted Absent Transfer of that Property.

CJS Bankruptcy § 643, Prohibition Against Disbursement from Property.

CJS Bankruptcy § 644, Delivery of Property to Estate.

CJS Bankruptcy § 645, Report and Account.

CJS Bankruptcy § 646, Protection of Entities to Which Custodian is Obligated.

CJS Bankruptcy § 647, Payment of Compensation and Expenses of Custodian.

CJS Bankruptcy § 648, Court Authorization to Excuse Compliance With Turnover Requirements.

CJS Bankruptcy § 700, Disallowance of Claims of Entities or Transferees Holding Recoverable Property.

CJS Bankruptcy § 1102, Priority of Particular Distribution Classes.

CJS Internal Revenue § 636, General Considerations.

§ 544. Trustee as lien creditor and as successor to certain creditors and purchasers

(a) The trustee shall have, as of the commencement of the case, and without regard to any knowledge of the trustee or of any creditor, the rights and powers of, or may avoid any transfer of property of the debtor or any obligation incurred by the debtor that is voidable by—

(1) a creditor that extends credit to the debtor at the time of the commencement of the case, and that obtains, at such time and with respect to such credit, a judicial lien on all property on which a creditor on a simple contract could have obtained such a judicial lien, whether or not such a creditor exists;

(2) a creditor that extends credit to the debtor at the time of the commencement of the case, and obtains, at such time and with respect to such credit, an execution against the debtor that is returned unsatisfied at such time, whether or not such a creditor exists; or

(3) a bona fide purchaser of real property, other than fixtures, from the debtor, against whom applicable law permits such transfer to be perfected, that obtains the status of a bona fide purchaser and has perfected such transfer at the time of the commencement of the case, whether or not such a purchaser exists.

(b)(1) Except as provided in paragraph (2), the trustee may avoid any transfer of an interest of the debtor in property or any obligation incurred by the debtor that is voidable under applicable law by a creditor holding an unsecured claim that is allowable under section 502 of this title or that is not allowable only under section 502(e) of this title.

(2) Paragraph (1) shall not apply to a transfer of a charitable contribution (as that term is defined in section 548(d)(3)) that is not covered under section 548(a)(1)(B), by reason of section 548(a)(2). Any claim by any person to recover a transferred contribution described in the preceding sentence under Federal or State law in a Federal or State court shall be preempted by the commencement of the case.

(Pub.L. 95–598, Nov. 6, 1978, 92 Stat. 2596; Pub.L. 98–353, Title III, § 459, July 10, 1984, 98 Stat. 377; Pub.L. 105–183, § 3(b), June 19, 1998, 112 Stat. 518.)

HISTORICAL AND STATUTORY NOTES

Revision Notes and Legislative Reports

1978 Acts. Subsection (a) is the "strong arm clause" of current law, now found in Bankruptcy Act § 70c [section 110(c) of former Title 11]. It gives the trustee the rights of a creditor on a simple contract with a judicial lien on the property of the debtor as of the date of the petition; of a creditor with a writ of execution against the property of the debtor unsatisfied as of the date of the petition; and a bona fide purchaser of the real property of the debtor as of the date of the petition. "Simple contract" as used here is derived from Bankruptcy Act § 60a(4) [section 96(a)(4) of former title 11]. The third status, that of a bona fide purchaser of real property, is new.

Subsection (b) is derived from current section 70e [former § 110(e) of former Title 11]. It gives the trustee the rights of actual unsecured creditors under applicable law to void transfers. It follows *Moore v. Bay*, 284 U.S. 4 (1931) [52 S.Ct. 3, 76 L.Ed. 133, 18 Am.Bankr.Rep.N.S. 675.], and overrules those cases that hold section 70e [section 110(e) of former Title 11] gives the trustee the rights of secured creditors. Senate Report No. 95–989.

1984 Acts. Statements by Legislative Leaders, see 1984 U.S.Code Cong. and Adm.News, p. 576.

1998 Acts. Statement by President, see 1998 U.S. Code Cong. and Adm. News, p. 230.

Legislative Statements

Section 544(a)(3) modifies similar provisions contained in the House bill and Senate amendment so as not to require a creditor to perform the impossible in order to perfect his interest. Both the lien creditor test in section 544(a)(1), and the bona fide purchaser test in section 544(a)(3) should not require a transferee to perfect a transfer against an entity with respect to which applicable law does not permit perfection. The avoiding powers under section 544(a)(1), (2), and (3) are new. In particular, section 544(a)(1) overrules *Pacific Finance Corp. v. Edwards*, 309 F.2d 224 (9th Cir. 1962), and *In re Federals, Inc.*, 553 F.2d 509 (6th Cir. 1977), insofar as those cases held that the trustee did not have the status of a creditor who extended credit immediately prior to the commencement of the case.

The House amendment deletes section 544(c) of the House bill.

Amendments

1998 Amendments. Subsec. (b)(1). Pub.L. 105–183, § 3(b)(1), struck out "(b) The trustee" and inserted "(b)(1) Except as provided in paragraph (2), the trustee".

Subsec. (b)(2). Pub.L. 105–183, § 3(b)(2), added par. (2).

1984 Amendments. Subsec. (a)(1). Pub.L. 98–353, § 459(1), added "such" after "obtained".

Subsec. (a)(2). Pub.L. 98–353, § 459(2), substituted "; or" for "; and".

Subsec. (a)(3). Pub.L. 98–353, § 459(3), added ", other than fixtures," after "property"; and "and has perfected such transfer" after "purchaser" the second place it appeared.

Effective and Applicability Provisions

1984 Acts. Amendment by Pub.L. 98–353 effective with respect to cases filed 90 days after July 10, 1984, see section 552(a), formerly 553 of Pub.L. 98–353, set out as a note under section 101 of this title.

Applicability

Pub.L. 105–183, § 5, June 19, 1998, 112 Stat. 518, provided that: "This Act and the amendments made by this Act [amending this section and sections 546, 548, 707, and 1325 of this title and enacting this note and provisions set out as notes under this section and section 101 of this title] shall apply to any case brought under an applicable provision of title 11, United States Code, [this title] that is pending or commenced on or after the date of enactment of this Act [June 19, 1998]."

Rule of Construction

Pub.L. 105–183, § 6, June 19, 1998, 112 Stat. 519, provided that: "Nothing in the amendments made by this Act [amending this section and sections 546, 548, 707, and 1325 of this title and enacting this note and provisions set out as notes under this section and section 101 of this title] is intended to limit the applicability of the Religious Freedom Restoration Act of 1993 (42 U.S.C. 2002bb et seq.)."

CROSS REFERENCES

Applicability of this section in Chapter nine cases, see 11 USCA § 901.

Appointment of trustee upon debtor's refusal to pursue cause of action under this section, see 11 USCA § 926.

Commencement of involuntary cases by transferees of voidable transfer, see 11 USCA § 303.

Disallowance of claims of entity that is transferee of avoidable transfer, see 11 USCA § 502.

Effect of dismissal, see 11 USCA § 349.

Exemptions, see 11 USCA § 522.

Recovery of voidable transfers in investor protection liquidation proceedings, see 15 USCA § 78fff–2.

Venue of action brought under this title by trustee as statutory successor under this section to creditors, see 28 USCA § 1409.

Voidable transfers in—

Commodity broker liquidation cases, see 11 USCA § 764.

Stockbroker liquidation proceedings, see 11 USCA § 749.

LIBRARY REFERENCES

American Digest System

Bankruptcy ⚭2511 to 2516, 2701 to 2706.

Key Number System Topic No. 51.

Corpus Juris Secundum

CJS Bankruptcy § 103, Chapter 13.

CJS Bankruptcy § 130, Debtor in Possession as Same Entity as or Separate Entity from Debtor.

CJS Bankruptcy § 189, Actions Based on State Law.

CJS Bankruptcy § 266, Proceedings Arising Under Bankruptcy Code or Arising in or Related to Cases Under Code.

CJS Bankruptcy § 278, Parties Defendant; Sovereign Immunity.

CJS Bankruptcy § 400, Relief Available on Recognition.

CJS Bankruptcy § 403, Powers of Foreign Representative on Recognition--Commencement of or Participation in Other Bankruptcy Case.

CJS Bankruptcy § 499, Perfection and Enforcement of Liens and Other Property Interests.

CJS Bankruptcy § 562, Property Acquired Postpetition-- Security Interest on Property Acquired Postpetition.

CJS Bankruptcy § 590, Recovery and Exemption of Property After Transfer Avoided.

CJS Bankruptcy § 696, Use of State Law Concerning Fraudulent Transfers or Obligations.

CJS Bankruptcy § 698, Transfers or Obligations Which May be Avoided.

CJS Bankruptcy § 699, Who May Exercise Avoidance and Recovery Powers.

CJS Bankruptcy § 700, Disallowance of Claims of Entities or Transferees Holding Recoverable Property.

CJS Bankruptcy § 702, Venue.

CJS Bankruptcy § 705, Strong-Arm Power.

CJS Bankruptcy § 706, Avoidance of Transfer Avoidable by Bona Fide Purchaser of Real Property.

CJS Bankruptcy § 707, Governing Law.

CJS Bankruptcy § 708, Time When Trustee Acquires Status.

CJS Bankruptcy § 709, Knowledge of or Notice to Trustee or Creditor.

CJS Bankruptcy § 710, Knowledge of or Notice to Debtor.

CJS Bankruptcy § 713, Establishing Trustee's Right to Sue.

CJS Bankruptcy § 715, Prepetition Transfers Under Swap Agreement.

CJS Bankruptcy § 725, Repurchase Agreements.

CJS Bankruptcy § 733, Nature of Proceedings; Right to Jury Trial.

CJS Bankruptcy § 752, Right of Seller of Goods.

CJS Bankruptcy § 755, Commencement of Adversary Proceeding; Venue.

CJS Bankruptcy § 851, Prepetition Security Interests in Proceeds, Products, Offspring, or Profits.

CJS Bankruptcy § 852, Prepetition Security Interests Extending to Rents and Similar Charges.

CJS Bankruptcy § 1109, Voidable Transfers.

CJS Estoppel and Waiver § 186, Generally; Rule of Judicial Estoppel.

§ 545. Statutory liens

The trustee may avoid the fixing of a statutory lien on property of the debtor to the extent that such lien—

(1) first becomes effective against the debtor—

(A) when a case under this title concerning the debtor is commenced;

(B) when an insolvency proceeding other than under this title concerning the debtor is commenced;

(C) when a custodian is appointed or authorized to take or takes possession;

(D) when the debtor becomes insolvent;

(E) when the debtor's financial condition fails to meet a specified standard; or

(F) at the time of an execution against property of the debtor levied at the instance of an entity other than the holder of such statutory lien;

(2) is not perfected or enforceable at the time of the commencement of the case against a bona fide purchaser that purchases such property at the time of the commencement of the case, whether or not such a purchaser exists, except in any case in which a purchaser is a purchaser described in section 6323 of the Internal Revenue Code of 1986, or in any other similar provision of State or local law;

(3) is for rent; or

(4) is a lien of distress for rent.

(Pub.L. 95–598, Nov. 6, 1978, 92 Stat. 2597; Pub.L. 98–353, Title III, § 460, July 10, 1984, 98 Stat. 377; Pub.L. 109–8, Title VII, § 711, Apr. 20, 2005, 119 Stat. 127.)

HISTORICAL AND STATUTORY NOTES

Revision Notes and Legislative Reports

1978 Acts. This section permits the trustee to avoid the fixing of certain statutory liens. It is derived from subsections 67b and 67c of present law [sections 107(b) and (c) former Title 11]. Liens that first become effective on the bankruptcy or insolvency of the debtor are voidable by the trustee. Liens that are not perfected or enforceable on the date of the petition against a bona fide purchaser are voidable. If a transferee is able to perfect under section 546(a) and that perfection relates back to an earlier date, then in spite of the filing of the bankruptcy petition, the trustee would not be able to defeat the lien, because the lien would be perfected and enforceable against a bona fide purchaser that purchased the property on the date of the filing of the petition. Finally, a lien for rent or of distress for rent is voidable, whether the lien is a statutory lien or a common law lien of distress for rent. See proposed 11 U.S.C. 101(37); Bankruptcy Act § 67(c)(1)(C) [section 107(c)(1)(C) of former Title 11]. The trustee may avoid a lien under this section even if the lien has been enforced by sale before the commencement of the case. To that extent, Bankruptcy Act section 67c(5) [section 107(c)(5) of former Title 11] is not followed.

Subsection (b) limits the trustee's power to avoid tax liens under Federal, state, or local law. For example, under section 6323 of the Internal Revenue Code [Title 26]. Once public notice of a tax lien has been filed, the Government is generally entitled to priority over subsequent lienholders. However, certain purchasers who acquire an interest in certain specific kinds of personal property will take free of an existing filed tax lien attaching to such property. Among the specific kinds of personal property which a purchaser can acquire free of an existing tax lien (unless the buyer knows of the existence of the lien) are stocks and securities, motor vehicles, inventory, and certain household goods. Under the present Bankruptcy Act (section 67(c)(1) [section 107(c)(1) of former Title 11]), the trustee may be viewed as a bona fide purchaser, so that he can take over any such designated items free of tax liens even if the tax authority has perfected its lien. However, the reasons for enabling a bona fide purchaser to take these kinds of assets free of an unfiled tax lien, that is, to encourage free movement of these assets in general commerce, do not apply to a trustee in a title 11 case, who is not in the same position as an ordinary bona fide purchaser as to such property. The bill accordingly adds a new subsection (b) to sec. 545 providing, in effect, that a trustee in bankruptcy does not have the right under this section to take otherwise specially treated items of personal property free of a tax lien filed before the filing of the petition. Senate Report No. 95–989.

1984 Acts. Statements by Legislative Leaders, see 1984 U.S.Code Cong. and Adm.News, p. 576.

2005 Acts. House Report No. 109–31(Part I), see 2005 U.S. Code Cong. and Adm. News, p. 88.

Legislative Statements

Section 545 of the House amendment modifies similar provisions contained in the House bill and Senate amendment to make clear that a statutory lien may be avoided under section 545 only to the extent the lien violates the perfection standards of section 545. Thus a Federal tax lien is invalid under section 545(2) with respect to property specified in sections 6323(b) and (c) of the Internal Revenue Code of 1954 [sections 6323(b) and (c) of Title 26, Internal Revenue Code]. As a result of this modification, section 545(b) of the Senate amendment is deleted as unnecessary.

Statutory liens: The House amendment retains the provision of section 545(2) of the House bill giving the trustee in a bankruptcy case the same power which a bona fide purchaser has to take over certain kinds of personal property despite the existence of a tax lien covering that property. The amendment thus retains present law, and deletes section 545(b) of the Senate amendment which would have no longer allowed the trustee to step into the shoes of a bona fide purchaser for this purpose.

References in Text

Section 6323 of the Internal Revenue Code of 1986, referred to in par. (2), is classified to 26 U.S.C.A. § 6323.

Amendments

2005 Amendments. Par. (2). Pub.L. 109–8, § 711, inserted ", except in any case in which a purchaser is a purchaser described in section 6323 of the Internal Revenue Code of 1986, or in any other similar provision of State or local law" before the semicolon at the end.

1984 Amendments. Par. (1)(A). Pub.L. 98–353, § 460(1), struck out "is" following "is".

Par. (1)(C). Pub.L. 98–353, § 460(2), substituted "appointed or authorized to take" for "apponted".

Par. (2). Pub.L. 98–353, § 460(3), substituted "at the time of the commencement of the case" for "on the date of the filing of the petition" wherever appearing.

Effective and Applicability Provisions

2005 Acts. Amendments by Pub.L. 109–8 effective, except as otherwise provided, 180 days after April 20, 2005, and inapplicable with respect to cases commenced under Title 11 before the effective date, see Pub.L. 109–8, § 1501, set out as a note under 11 U.S.C.A. § 101.

1984 Acts. Amendment by Pub.L. 98–353 effective with respect to cases filed 90 days after July 10, 1984, see section 552(a), formerly 553(a) of Pub.L. 98–353, set out as a note under section 101 of this title.

CROSS REFERENCES

Applicability of this section in Chapter nine cases, see 11 USCA § 901.

Appointment of trustee upon debtor's refusal to pursue cause of action under this section, see 11 USCA § 926.

Commencement of involuntary cases by transferees of voidable transfers, see 11 USCA § 303.

Disallowance of claims of entity that is a transferee of an avoidable transfer, see 11 USCA § 502.

Effect of dismissal, see 11 USCA § 349.

Exemptions, see 11 USCA § 522.

Recovery of voidable transfers in investor protection liquidation proceedings, see 15 USCA § 78fff–2.

Voidable transfers in—

    Commodity broker liquidation cases, see 11 USCA § 764.

    Stockbroker liquidation cases, see 11 USCA § 749.

LIBRARY REFERENCES

American Digest System

Bankruptcy ⟺2580.1 to 2585.

Key Number System Topic No. 51.

Corpus Juris Secundum

CJS Bankruptcy § 278, Parties Defendant; Sovereign Immunity.

CJS Bankruptcy § 400, Relief Available on Recognition.

CJS Bankruptcy § 403, Powers of Foreign Representative on Recognition--Commencement of or Participation in Other Bankruptcy Case.

CJS Bankruptcy § 562, Property Acquired Postpetition--Security Interest on Property Acquired Postpetition.

CJS Bankruptcy § 590, Recovery and Exemption of Property After Transfer Avoided.

CJS Bankruptcy § 669, Statutory Liens; Penalty Liens.

CJS Bankruptcy § 698, Transfers or Obligations Which May be Avoided.

CJS Bankruptcy § 699, Who May Exercise Avoidance and Recovery Powers.

CJS Bankruptcy § 700, Disallowance of Claims of Entities or Transferees Holding Recoverable Property.

CJS Bankruptcy § 715, Prepetition Transfers Under Swap Agreement.

CJS Bankruptcy § 725, Repurchase Agreements.

CJS Bankruptcy § 752, Right of Seller of Goods.

CJS Bankruptcy § 851, Prepetition Security Interests in Proceeds, Products, Offspring, or Profits.

CJS Bankruptcy § 852, Prepetition Security Interests Extending to Rents and Similar Charges.

CJS Bankruptcy § 1109, Voidable Transfers.

§ 546. Limitations on avoiding powers

(a) An action or proceeding under section 544, 545, 547, 548, or 553 of this title may not be commenced after the earlier of—

  (1) the later of—

    (A) 2 years after the entry of the order for relief; or

    (B) 1 year after the appointment or election of the first trustee under section 702, 1104, 1163, 1202, or 1302 of this title if such appointment or such election occurs before the expiration of the period specified in subparagraph (A); or

  (2) the time the case is closed or dismissed.

(b)(1) The rights and powers of a trustee under sections 544, 545, and 549 of this title are subject to any generally applicable law that—

    (A) permits perfection of an interest in property to be effective against an entity that acquires rights in such property before the date of perfection; or

    (B) provides for the maintenance or continuation of perfection of an interest in property to be effective against an entity that acquires rights in such property before the date on which action is taken to effect such maintenance or continuation.

    (2) If—

    (A) a law described in paragraph (1) requires seizure of such property or commencement of an action to accomplish such perfection, or maintenance or continuation of perfection of an interest in property; and

    (B) such property has not been seized or such an action has not been commenced before the date of the filing of the petition;

such interest in such property shall be perfected, or perfection of such interest shall be maintained or continued, by giving notice within the time fixed by such law for such seizure or such commencement.

(c)(1) Except as provided in subsection (d) of this section and in section 507(c), and subject to the prior rights of a holder of a security interest in such goods or the proceeds thereof, the rights and powers of the trustee under sections 544(a), 545, 547, and 549 are subject to the right of a seller of goods that has sold goods to the debtor, in the ordinary course of such seller's business, to reclaim such goods if the debtor has received such goods while insolvent, within 45 days before the date of the commencement of a case under this title, but such seller may not reclaim such goods unless such seller demands in writing reclamation of such goods—

    (A) not later than 45 days after the date of receipt of such goods by the debtor; or

    (B) not later than 20 days after the date of commencement of the case, if the 45–day period expires after the commencement of the case.

(2) If a seller of goods fails to provide notice in the manner described in paragraph (1), the seller still may assert the rights contained in section 503(b)(9).

(d) In the case of a seller who is a producer of grain sold to a grain storage facility, owned or operated by the debtor, in the ordinary course of such seller's business (as such terms are defined in section 557 of this title) or in the case of a United States fisherman who has caught fish sold to a fish processing facility owned or operated by the debtor in the ordinary course of such fisherman's business, the rights and powers of the trustee under sections 544(a), 545, 547, and 549 of this title are subject to any statutory or common law right of such producer or fisherman to

reclaim such grain or fish if the debtor has received such grain or fish while insolvent, but—

    (1) such producer or fisherman may not reclaim any grain or fish unless such producer or fisherman demands, in writing, reclamation of such grain or fish before ten days after receipt thereof by the debtor; and

    (2) the court may deny reclamation to such a producer or fisherman with a right of reclamation that has made such a demand only if the court secures such claim by a lien.

(e) Notwithstanding sections 544, 545, 547, 548(a)(1)(B), and 548(b) of this title, the trustee may not avoid a transfer that is a margin payment, as defined in section 101, 741, or 761 of this title, or settlement payment, as defined in section 101 or 741 of this title, made by or to (or for the benefit of) a commodity broker, forward contract merchant, stockbroker, financial institution, financial participant, or securities clearing agency, or that is a transfer made by or to (or for the benefit of) a commodity broker, forward contract merchant, stockbroker, financial institution, financial participant, or securities clearing agency, in connection with a securities contract, as defined in section 741(7), commodity contract, as defined in section 761(4), or forward contract, that is made before the commencement of the case, except under section 548(a)(1)(A) of this title.

(f) Notwithstanding sections 544, 545, 547, 548(a)(1)(B), and 548(b) of this title, the trustee may not avoid a transfer made by or to (or for the benefit of) a repo participant or financial participant, in connection with a repurchase agreement and that is made before the commencement of the case, except under section 548(a)(1)(A) of this title.

(g) Notwithstanding sections 544, 545, 547, 548(a)(1)(B) and 548(b) of this title, the trustee may not avoid a transfer, made by or to (or for the benefit of) a swap participant or financial participant, under or in connection with any swap agreement and that is made before the commencement of the case, except under section 548(a)(1)(A) of this title.

(h) Notwithstanding the rights and powers of a trustee under sections 544(a), 545, 547, 549, and 553, if the court determines on a motion by the trustee made not later than 120 days after the date of the order for relief in a case under chapter 11 of this title and after notice and a hearing, that a return is in the best interests of the estate, the debtor, with the consent of a creditor and subject to the prior rights of holders of security interests in such goods or the proceeds of such goods, may return goods shipped to the debtor by the creditor before the commencement of the case, and the creditor may offset the purchase price of such goods against any claim of the creditor against the debtor that arose before the commencement of the case.

(i)(1) Notwithstanding paragraphs (2) and (3) of section 545, the trustee may not avoid a warehouseman's lien for storage, transportation, or other costs incidental to the storage and handling of goods.

(2) The prohibition under paragraph (1) shall be applied in a manner consistent with any State statute applicable to such lien that is similar to section 7–209 of the Uniform Commercial Code, as in effect on the date of enactment of the Bankruptcy Abuse Prevention and Consumer Protection Act of 2005, or any successor to such section 7–209.

(j) Notwithstanding sections 544, 545, 547, 548(a)(1)(B), and 548(b) the trustee may not avoid a transfer made by or to (or for the benefit of) a master netting agreement participant under or in connection with any master netting agreement or any individual contract covered thereby that is made before the commencement of the case, except under section 548(a)(1)(A) and except to the extent that the trustee could otherwise avoid such a transfer made under an individual contract covered by such master netting agreement.

(Pub.L. 95–598, Nov. 6, 1978, 92 Stat. 2597; Pub.L. 97–222, § 4, July 27, 1982, 96 Stat. 236; Pub.L. 98–353, Title III, §§ 351, 393, 461, July 10, 1984, 98 Stat. 358, 365, 377; Pub.L. 99–554, Title II, §§ 257(d), 283(l), Oct. 27, 1986, 100 Stat. 3114, 3117; Pub.L. 101–311, Title I, § 103, Title II, § 203, June 25, 1990, 104 Stat. 268, 269; Pub.L. 103–394, Title II, §§ 204(b), 209, 216, 222(a), Title V, § 501(b)(4), Oct. 22, 1994, 108 Stat. 4122, 4125, 4126, 4129, 4142; Pub.L. 105–183, § 3(c), June 19, 1998, 112 Stat. 518; Pub.L. 109–8, Title IV, § 406, Title IX, §§ 907(e), (o)(2), (3), Title XII, § 1227(a), Apr. 20, 2005, 119 Stat. 105, 177, 182, 199; Pub.L. 109–390, § 5(b), Dec. 12, 2006, 120 Stat. 2697.)

HISTORICAL AND STATUTORY NOTES

Revision Notes and Legislative Reports

1978 Acts. The trustee's rights and powers under certain of the avoiding powers are limited by section 546. First, if an interest holder against whom the trustee would have rights still has, under applicable nonbankruptcy law, and as of the date of the petition, the opportunity to perfect his lien against an intervening interest holder, then he may perfect his interest against the trustee. If applicable law requires seizure for perfection, then perfection is by notice to the trustee instead. The rights granted to a creditor under this subsection prevail over the trustee only if the transferee has perfected the transfer in accordance with applicable law, and that perfection relates back to a date that is before the commencement of the case.

The phrase "generally applicable law" relates to those provisions of applicable law that apply both in bankruptcy cases and outside of bankruptcy cases. For example, many State laws, under the Uniform Commercial Code, permit perfection of a purchase-money security interest to relate back to defeat an earlier levy by another creditor if the former was perfected within ten days of delivery of the property. U.C.C. § 9–301(2). Such perfection would then be able to defeat an intervening hypothetical judicial lien creditor on the date of the filing of the petition. The purpose of the subsection is to protect, in spite of the surprise intervention of

a bankruptcy petition, those whom State law protects by allowing them to perfect their liens or interests as of an effective date that is earlier than the date of perfection. It is not designed to give the States an opportunity to enact disguised priorities in the form of liens that apply only in bankruptcy cases.

Subsection (b) specifies that the trustee's rights and powers under the strong arm clause, the successor to creditors provision, the preference section, and the postpetition transaction section are all subject to any statutory or common-law right of a seller, in the ordinary course of business, of goods to the debtor to reclaim the goods if the debtor received the goods on credit while insolvent. The seller must demand reclamation within ten days after receipt of the goods by the debtor. As under nonbankruptcy law, the right is subject to any superior rights of secured creditors. The purpose of the provision is to recognize, in part, the validity of section 2–702 of the Uniform Commercial Code, which has generated much litigation, confusion, and divergent decisions in different circuits. The right is subject, however, to the power of the court to deny reclamation and protect the seller by granting him a priority as an administrative expense for his claim arising out of the sale of the goods.

Subsection (c) adds a statute of limitations to the use by the trustee of the avoiding powers. The limitation is two years after his appointment, or the time the case is closed or dismissed, whichever occurs later. Senate Report No. 95–989.

1982 Acts. House Report No. 97–420, see 1982 U.S. Code Cong. and Adm. News, p. 583.

1984 Acts. Statements by Legislative Leaders, see 1984 U.S. Code Cong. and Adm. News, p. 576.

1986 Acts. House Report No. 99–764 and House Conference Report No. 99–958, see 1986 U.S. Code Cong. and Adm. News, p. 5227.

1990 Acts. House Report No. 101–484, see 1990 U.S. Code Cong. and Adm. News, p. 223.

1994 Acts. House Report No. 103–835, see 1994 U.S. Code Cong. and Adm. News, p. 3340.

1998 Acts. Statement by President, see 1998 U.S. Code Cong. and Adm. News, p. 230.

2005 Acts. House Report No. 109–31(Part I), see 2005 U.S. Code Cong. and Adm. News, p. 88.

2006 Acts. House Report No. 109–648(Part I), see 2006 U.S. Code Cong. and Adm. News, p. 1585.

Legislative Statements

Section 546(a) of the House amendment is derived from section 546(c) of the Senate amendment. Section 546(c) of the House amendment is derived from section 546(b) of the Senate amendment. It applies to receipt of goods on credit as well as by cash sales. The section clarifies that a demand for reclamation must be made in writing anytime before 10 days after receipt of the goods by the debtor. The section also permits the court to grant the reclaiming creditor a lien or an administrative expense in lieu of turning over the property.

References in Text

The date of enactment of the Bankruptcy Abuse Prevention and Consumer Protection Act of 2005, referred to in subsec. (i)(2), is April 20, 2005, the approval date of Pub.L. 109–8, 119 Stat. 23.

Codifications

The amendment by Pub.L. 105–183, § 3(c)(3), to subsec. (g) of this section was executed to the first subsec. (g) of this section as the probable intent of Congress since the phrases being amended, "section 548(a)(1)" and "548(a)(2)", appeared only in the first subsec. (g).

Amendments

2006 Amendments. Subsec. (e). Pub.L. 109–390, § 5(b)(1)(A), inserted "(or for the benefit of)" before "a commodity broker".

Pub.L. 109–390, § 5(b)(1)(B), inserted "or that is a transfer made by or to (or for the benefit of) a commodity broker, forward contract merchant, stockbroker, financial institution, financial participant, or securities clearing agency, in connection with a securities contract, as defined in section 741(7), commodity contract, as defined in section 761(4), or forward contract," after "securities clearing agency,".

Subsec. (f). Pub.L. 109–390, § 5(b)(2)(A), struck out "that is a margin payment, as defined in section 741 or 761 of this title, or settlement payment, as defined in section 741 of this title," following "may not avoid a transfer".

Pub.L. 109–390, § 5(b)(2)(B), inserted "(or for the benefit of)" before "a repo participant".

Subsec. (g). Pub.L. 109–390, § 5(b)(3), inserted "(or for the benefit of)" before "a swap participant".

Subsec. (j). Pub.L. 109–390, § 5(b)(4), inserted "(or for the benefit of)" after "made by or to".

2005 Amendments. Subsec. (c). Pub.L. 109–8, § 1227(a), rewrote subsec. (c), which formerly read:

"**(c)** Except as provided in subsection (d) of this section, the rights and powers of a trustee under sections 544(a), 545, 547, and 549 of this title are subject to any statutory or common-law right of a seller of goods that has sold goods to the debtor, in the ordinary course of such seller's business, to reclaim such goods if the debtor has received such goods while insolvent, but—

"**(1)** such a seller may not reclaim any such goods unless such seller demands in writing reclamation of such goods—

"**(A)** before 10 days after receipt of such goods by the debtor; or

"**(B)** if such 10–day period expires after the commencement of the case, before 20 days after receipt of such goods by the debtor; and

"**(2)** the court may deny reclamation to a seller with such a right of reclamation that has made such a demand only if the court—

"**(A)** grants the claim of such a seller priority as a claim of a kind specified in section 503(b) of this title; or

"**(B)** secures such claim by a lien."

Subsec. (e). Pub.L. 109–8, § 907(o)(3), inserted "financial participant," after "financial institution,".

Subsec. (f). Pub.L. 109–8, § 907(o)(2), inserted "or financial participant" after "repo participant" each place such term appeared.

Subsec. (g). Pub.L. 109–8, § 406(1), redesignated the second subsec. (g), as added by Pub.L. 103–394, § 222(a), relating to returns of goods, as subsec. (h).

Pub.L. 109–8, § 907(e)(1), in subsec. (g) as added by Pub.L. 101–311, § 103, struck out "under a swap agreement" after "may not avoid a transfer", struck out "in connection with a swap agreement" and inserted "under or in connection with

any swap agreement", and inserted "or financial participant" after "swap participant".

Subsec. (h). Pub.L. 109–8, § 406(1), (2), redesignated the second subsec. (g), as added by Pub.L. 103–394, § 222(a), as subsec. (h), and as so redesignated, inserted "and subject to the prior rights of holders of security interests in such goods or the proceeds of such goods" after "consent of a creditor".

Subsec. (i). Pub.L. 109–8, § 406(3), added subsec. (i).

Subsec. (j). Pub.L. 109–8, § 907(e)(2), added subsec. (j).

1998 Amendments. Subsec. (e). Pub.L. 105–183, § 3(c)(1), struck out "548(a)(2)" and inserted "548(a)(1)(B)" and struck out "548(a)(1)" and inserted "548(a)(1)(A)".

Subsec. (f). Pub.L. 105–183, § 3(c)(2), struck out "548(a)(2)" and inserted "548(a)(1)(B)" and struck out "548(a)(1)" and inserted "548(a)(1)(A)".

Subsec. (g). Pub.L. 105–183, § 3(c)(3), struck out "section 548(a)(1)" each place it appeared and inserted "section 548(a)(1)(A)" and struck out "548(a)(2)" and inserted "548(a)(1)(B)".

1994 Amendments. Subsec. (a)(1). Pub.L. 103–394, § 216, completely revised par. (1). Prior to revision, par. (1) read as follows:

"two years after the appointment of a trustee under section 702, 1104, 1163, 1302, or 1202 of this title; or".

Subsec. (b). Pub.L. 103–394, § 204(b), completely revised subsec. (b). Prior to revision, subsec. (b) read as follows:

"The rights and powers of a trustee under sections 544, 545, and 549 of this title are subject to any generally applicable law that permits perfection of an interest in property to be effective against an entity that acquires rights in such property before the date of such perfection. If such law requires seizure of such property or commencement of an action to accomplish such perfection, and such property has not been seized or such action has not been commenced before the date of the filing of the petition, such interest in such property shall be perfected by notice within the time fixed by such law for such seizure or commencement."

Subsec. (c)(1). Pub.L. 103–394, § 209, redesignated existing text as opening cl. and subpar. (A) and added subpar. (B).

Subsec. (e). Pub.L. 103–394, § 501(b)(4)(A), substituted "section 101, 741, or 761" for "section 101(34), 741(5), or 761(15)", and "section 101 or 741" for "section 101(35) or 741(8)".

Subsec. (f). Pub.L. 103–394, § 501(b)(4)(B), substituted "section 741 or 761" for "section 741(5) or 761(15)", and "section 741" for "section 741(8)".

Subsec. (g). Pub.L. 103–394, § 222(a), added subsec. (g), relating to return of goods.

1990 Amendments. Subsec. (e). Pub.L. 101–311, § 203, added provisions referring to sections 101(34) and 101(35) of this title.

Subsec. (g). Pub.L. 101–311, § 103, added subsec. (g), relating to swap agreements.

1986 Amendments. Subsec. (a)(1). Pub.L. 99–554, § 257(d), added reference to section 1202 of this title.

Subsec. (e). Pub.L. 99–554, § 283(1), substituted "stockbroker," for "stockbroker".

1984 Amendments. Subsec. (a)(1). Pub.L. 98–353, § 461(a), substituted "or" for "and" following the semicolon at the end.

Subsec. (b). Pub.L. 98–353, § 461(b), substituted "a trustee under sections 544, 545, and" for "the trustee under sections 544, 545, or".

Subsec. (c). Pub.L. 98–353, § 351(1), substituted "Except as provided in subsection (d) of this section, the" for "The".

Pub.L. 98–353, § 461(c)(1)–(4), substituted "a trustee" for "the trustee", struck out "right" before "or common-law", added "of goods that has sold goods to the debtor" after "seller", and struck out "of goods to the debtor" after "business,".

Subsec. (c)(2). Pub.L. 98–353, § 461(c)(5)(A), added "the" after "if".

Subsec. (c)(2)(A). Pub.L. 98–353, § 461(c)(5)(B), substituted "a claim of a kind specified in section 503(b) of this title" for "an administrative expense".

Subsec. (d). Pub.L. 98–353, § 351(3), added subsec. (d). Former subsec. (d) was redesignated as (e).

Subsec. (e). Pub.L. 98–353, § 351(2), redesignated former subsec. (d) as (e).

Pub.L. 98–353, § 461(d), added "financial institution" after "stockbroker".

Subsec. (f). Pub.L. 98–353, § 393, added subsec. (f).

1982 Amendments. Subsec. (d). Pub.L. 97–222 added subsec. (d).

Effective and Applicability Provisions

2005 Acts. Amendments by Pub.L. 109–8 effective, except as otherwise provided, 180 days after April 20, 2005, and inapplicable with respect to cases commenced under Title 11 before the effective date, see Pub.L. 109–8, § 1501, set out as a note under 11 U.S.C.A. § 101.

1994 Acts. Amendments by Pub.L. 103–394 effective on Oct. 22, 1994, and not to apply with respect to cases commenced under Title 11 of the United States Code before Oct. 22, 1994, see section 702 of Pub.L. 103–394, set out as a note under section 101 of this title.

1986 Acts. Amendments by Pub.L. 99–554, § 257(d), effective 30 days after Oct. 27, 1986, but not to apply with respect to cases commenced under this title before that date, see section 302(a), (c)(1) of Pub.L. 99–554, set out as a note under section 581 of Title 28, Judiciary and Judicial Procedure.

Amendment by Pub.L. 99–554, § 283, effective 30 days after Oct. 27, 1986, except as otherwise provided for, see section 302(a) of Pub.L. 99–554, set out as a note under section 581 of Title 28.

1984 Acts. Amendment by Pub.L. 98–353 effective with respect to cases filed 90 days after July 10, 1984, see section 552(a), formerly 553 of Pub.L. 98–353, set out as a note under section 101 of this title.

Separability of Provisions

If any provision of or amendment made by Pub.L. 103–394 or the application of such provision or amendment to any person or circumstance is held to be unconstitutional, the remaining provisions of and amendments made by Pub.L. 103–394 and the application of such provisions and amendments to any person or circumstance shall not be affected thereby, see section 701 of Pub.L. 103–394, set out as a note under section 101 of this title.

Applicability

Applicability of amendments made by Pub.L. 105–183 to any case brought under an applicable provision of this title that is pending or commenced on or after June 19, 1998, see Pub.L. 105–183, § 5, June 19, 1998, 112 Stat. 518, set out as a note under section 544 of this title.

Rule of Construction

Amendments made by Pub.L. 105–183 not intended to limit the applicability of the Religious Freedom Restoration Act of 1993 (42 U.S.C. 2002bb et seq.), see Pub.L. 105–183, § 6, June 19, 1998, 112 Stat. 519, set out as a note under section 544 of this title.

CROSS REFERENCES

Applicability of this section in Chapter nine cases, see 11 USCA § 901.

Automatic stay, see 11 USCA § 362.

Concealment of debtor's assets deemed continuing offense, see 18 USCA § 3284.

LIBRARY REFERENCES

American Digest System

Bankruptcy ⇒2722, 2701 to 2706, 2741 to 2745.

Key Number System Topic No. 51.

Corpus Juris Secundum

CJS Bankruptcy § 278, Parties Defendant; Sovereign Immunity.

CJS Bankruptcy § 499, Perfection and Enforcement of Liens and Other Property Interests.

CJS Bankruptcy § 562, Property Acquired Postpetition--Security Interest on Property Acquired Postpetition.

CJS Bankruptcy § 663, Disqualifying or Limiting Factors.

CJS Bankruptcy § 668, Postpetition Transfers and Postpetition Perfection.

CJS Bankruptcy § 705, Strong-Arm Power.

CJS Bankruptcy § 715, Prepetition Transfers Under Swap Agreement.

CJS Bankruptcy § 716, Return of Goods Shipped to Debtor by Creditor Before Commencement of Case.

CJS Bankruptcy § 718, Commencement of Limitations Period.

CJS Bankruptcy § 719, Tolling of Limitations Period.

CJS Bankruptcy § 723, Particular Applications.

CJS Bankruptcy § 725, Repurchase Agreements.

CJS Bankruptcy § 726, Statute of Limitations.

CJS Bankruptcy § 752, Right of Seller of Goods.

CJS Bankruptcy § 753, Demand for Reclamation.

§ 547. Preferences

(a) In this section—

(1) "inventory" means personal property leased or furnished, held for sale or lease, or to be furnished under a contract for service, raw materials, work in process, or materials used or consumed in a business, including farm products such as crops or livestock, held for sale or lease;

(2) "new value" means money or money's worth in goods, services, or new credit, or release by a transferee of property previously transferred to such

transferee in a transaction that is neither void nor voidable by the debtor or the trustee under any applicable law, including proceeds of such property, but does not include an obligation substituted for an existing obligation;

(3) "receivable" means right to payment, whether or not such right has been earned by performance; and

(4) a debt for a tax is incurred on the day when such tax is last payable without penalty, including any extension.

(b) Except as provided in subsections (c) and (i) of this section, the trustee may avoid any transfer of an interest of the debtor in property—

(1) to or for the benefit of a creditor;

(2) for or on account of an antecedent debt owed by the debtor before such transfer was made;

(3) made while the debtor was insolvent;

(4) made—

(A) on or within 90 days before the date of the filing of the petition; or

(B) between ninety days and one year before the date of the filing of the petition, if such creditor at the time of such transfer was an insider; and

(5) that enables such creditor to receive more than such creditor would receive if—

(A) the case were a case under chapter 7 of this title;

(B) the transfer had not been made; and

(C) such creditor received payment of such debt to the extent provided by the provisions of this title. *defenses to preferences*

(c) The trustee may not avoid under this section a transfer—

(1) to the extent that such transfer was—

(A) intended by the debtor and the creditor to or for whose benefit such transfer was made to be a contemporaneous exchange for new value given to the debtor; and

(B) in fact a substantially contemporaneous exchange;

(2) to the extent that such transfer was in payment of a debt incurred by the debtor in the ordinary course of business or financial affairs of the debtor and the transferee, and such transfer was—

(A) made in the ordinary course of business or financial affairs of the debtor and the transferee; or *not 'and'*

(B) made according to ordinary business terms;

(3) that creates a security interest in property acquired by the debtor— *enabling loan*

(A) to the extent such security interest secures new value that was—

(i) given at or after the signing of a security agreement that contains a description of such property as collateral;

(ii) given by or on behalf of the secured party under such agreement;

(iii) given to enable the debtor to acquire such property; and

(iv) in fact used by the debtor to acquire such property; and

(B) that is perfected on or before 30 days after the debtor receives possession of such property;

(4) to or for the benefit of a creditor, to the extent that, after such transfer, such creditor gave new value to or for the benefit of the debtor—

(A) not secured by an otherwise unavoidable security interest; and

(B) on account of which new value the debtor did not make an otherwise unavoidable transfer to or for the benefit of such creditor;

(5) that creates a perfected security interest in inventory or a receivable or the proceeds of either, except to the extent that the aggregate of all such transfers to the transferee caused a reduction, as of the date of the filing of the petition and to the prejudice of other creditors holding unsecured claims, of any amount by which the debt secured by such security interest exceeded the value of all security interests for such debt on the later of—

(A)(i) with respect to a transfer to which subsection (b)(4)(A) of this section applies, 90 days before the date of the filing of the petition; or

(ii) with respect to a transfer to which subsection (b)(4)(B) of this section applies, one year before the date of the filing of the petition; or

(B) the date on which new value was first given under the security agreement creating such security interest;

(6) that is the fixing of a statutory lien that is not avoidable under section 545 of this title;

(7) to the extent such transfer was a bona fide payment of a debt for a domestic support obligation;

(8) if, in a case filed by an individual debtor whose debts are primarily consumer debts, the aggregate value of all property that constitutes or is affected by such transfer is less than $600; or

(9) if, in a case filed by a debtor whose debts are not primarily consumer debts, the aggregate value of all property that constitutes or is affected by such transfer is less than $5,850 [1] *different on slides*

(d) The trustee may avoid a transfer of an interest in property of the debtor transferred to or for the benefit of a surety to secure reimbursement of such a surety that furnished a bond or other obligation to dissolve a judicial lien that would have been avoidable by the trustee under subsection (b) of this section. The liability of such surety under such bond or obligation shall be discharged to the extent of the value of such property recovered by the trustee or the amount paid to the trustee.

(e)(1) For the purposes of this section—

(A) a transfer of real property other than fixtures, but including the interest of a seller or purchaser under a contract for the sale of real property, is perfected when a bona fide purchaser of such property from the debtor against whom applicable law permits such transfer to be perfected cannot acquire an interest that is superior to the interest of the transferee; and

(B) a transfer of a fixture or property other than real property is perfected when a creditor on a simple contract cannot acquire a judicial lien that is superior to the interest of the transferee.

(2) For the purposes of this section, except as provided in paragraph (3) of this subsection, a transfer is made—

(A) at the time such transfer takes effect between the transferor and the transferee, if such transfer is perfected at, or within 30 days after, such time, except as provided in subsection (c)(3)(B);

(B) at the time such transfer is perfected, if such transfer is perfected after such 30 days; or

(C) immediately before the date of the filing of the petition, if such transfer is not perfected at the later of—

(i) the commencement of the case; or
(ii) 30 days after such transfer takes effect between the transferor and the transferee.

(3) For the purposes of this section, a transfer is not made until the debtor has acquired rights in the property transferred.

(f) For the purposes of this section, the debtor is presumed to have been insolvent on and during the 90 days immediately preceding the date of the filing of the petition.

(g) For the purposes of this section, the trustee has the burden of proving the avoidability of a transfer under subsection (b) of this section, and the creditor or party in interest against whom recovery or avoidance is sought has the burden of proving the nonavoidability of a transfer under subsection (c) of this section.

(h) The trustee may not avoid a transfer if such transfer was made as a part of an alternative repayment schedule between the debtor and any creditor of the debtor created by an approved nonprofit budget and credit counseling agency.

(i) If the trustee avoids under subsection (b) a transfer made between 90 days and 1 year before the date of the filing of the petition, by the debtor to an entity that is not an insider for the benefit of a creditor that is an insider, such transfer shall be considered to be avoided under this section only with respect to the creditor that is an insider.

(Pub.L. 95–598, Nov. 6, 1978, 92 Stat. 2597; Pub.L. 98–353, Title III, §§ 310, 462, July 10, 1984, 98 Stat. 355, 377; Pub.L. 99–554, Title II, § 283(m), Oct. 27, 1986, 100 Stat. 3117; Pub.L. 103–394, Title II, § 203, Title III, § 304(f), Oct. 22, 1994, 108 Stat. 4121, 4133; Pub.L. 109–8, Title II, §§ 201(b), 217, Title IV, §§ 403, 409, Title XII, § 1213(a), 1222, Apr. 20, 2005, 119 Stat. 42, 55, 104, 106, 194, 196.)

¹ Dollar amount as adjusted by the Judicial Conference of the United States. See Adjustment of Dollar Amounts notes set out under this section and 11 U.S.C.A. § 104.

HISTORICAL AND STATUTORY NOTES

Revision Notes and Legislative Reports

1978 Acts. This section is a substantial modification of present law. It modernizes the preference provisions and brings them more into conformity with commercial practice and the Uniform Commercial Code.

Subsection (a) contains three definitions. Inventory, new value, and receivable are defined in their ordinary senses, but are defined to avoid any confusion or uncertainty surrounding the terms.

Subsection (b) is the operative provision of the section. It authorizes the trustee to avoid a transfer if five conditions are met. These are the five elements of a preference action. First, the transfer must be to or for the benefit of a creditor. Second, the transfer must be for or on account of an antecedent debt owed by the debtor before the transfer was made. Third, the transfer must have been made when the debtor was insolvent. Fourth, the transfer must have been made during the 90 days immediately preceding the commencement of the case. If the transfer was to an insider, the trustee may avoid the transfer if it was made during the period that begins one year before the filing of the petition and ends 90 days before the filing, if the insider to whom the transfer was made had reasonable cause to believe the debtor was insolvent at the time the transfer was made.

Finally, the transfer must enable the creditor to whom or for whose benefit it was made to receive a greater percentage of his claim than he would receive under the distributive provisions of the bankruptcy code. Specifically, the creditor must receive more than he would if the case were a liquidation case, if the transfer had not been made, and if the creditor received payment of the debt to the extent provided by the provisions of the code.

The phrasing of the final element changes the application of the greater percentage test from that employed under current law. Under this language, the court must focus on the relative distribution between classes as well as the amount that will be received by the members of the class of which the creditor is a member. The language also requires the court to focus on the allowability of the claim for which the preference was made. If the claim would have been entirely disallowed, for example, then the test of paragraph (5) will be met, because the creditor would have received nothing under the distributive provisions of the bankruptcy code.

The trustee may avoid a transfer of a lien under this section even if the lien has been enforced by sale before the commencement of the case.

Subsection (b)(2) of this section in effect exempts from the preference rules payments by the debtor of tax liabilities, regardless of their priority status.

Subsection (c) contains exceptions to the trustee's avoiding power. If a creditor can qualify under any one of the exceptions, then he is protected to that extent. If he can qualify under several, he is protected by each to the extent that he can qualify under each.

The first exception is for a transfer that was intended by all parties to be a contemporaneous exchange for new value, and was in fact substantially contemporaneous. Normally, a check is a credit transaction. However, for the purposes of this paragraph, a transfer involving a check is considered to be "intended to be contemporaneous", and if the check is presented for payment in the normal course of affairs, which the Uniform Commercial Code specifies as 30 days, U.C.C. § 3–503(2)(a), that will amount to a transfer that is "in fact substantially contemporaneous."

The second exception protects transfers in the ordinary course of business (or of financial affairs, where a business is not involved) transfers. For the case of a consumer, the paragraph uses the phrase "financial affairs" to include such nonbusiness activities as payment of monthly utility bills. If the debt on account of which the transfer was made was incurred in the ordinary course of both the debtor and the transferee, if the transfer was made not later than 45 days after the debt was incurred, if the transfer itself was made in the ordinary course of both the debtor and the transferee, and if the transfer was made according to ordinary business terms, then the transfer is protected. The purpose of this exception is to leave undisturbed normal financial relations, because it does not detract from the general policy of the preference section to discourage unusual action by either the debtor or his creditors during the debtor's slide into bankruptcy.

The third exception is for enabling loans in connection with which the debtor acquires the property that the loan enabled him to purchase after the loan is actually made.

The fourth exception codifies the net result rule in section 60c of current law [section 96(c) of former Title 11]. If the creditor and the debtor have more than one exchange during the 90-day period, the exchanges are netted out according to the formula in paragraph (4). Any new value that the creditor advances must be unsecured in order for it to qualify under this exception.

Paragraph (5) codifies the improvement in position test, and thereby overrules such cases as *DuBay v. Williams*, 417 F.2d 1277 (C.A.9, 1966), and *Grain Merchants of Indiana, Inc. v. Union Bank and Savings Co.*, 408 F.2d 209 (C.A.7, 1969). A creditor with a security interest in a floating mass, such as inventory or accounts receivable, is subject to preference attack to the extent he improves his position during the 90-day period before bankruptcy. The test is a two-point test, and requires determination of the secured creditor's position 90 days before the petition and on the date of the petition. If new value was first given after 90 days before the case, the date on which it was first given substitutes for the 90-day point.

Paragraph (6) excepts statutory liens validated under section 545 from preference attack. It also protects transfers in satisfaction of such liens, and the fixing of a lien under section 365(j), which protects a vendee whose contract to purchase real property from the debtor is rejected.

Subsection (d), derived from section 67a of the Bankruptcy Act [section 107(a) of former Title 11], permits the trustee to avoid a transfer to reimburse a surety that posts a bond to dissolve a judicial lien that would have been avoidable under this section. The second sentence protects the surety from double liability.

Subsection (e) determines when a transfer is made for the purposes of the preference section. Paragraph (1) defines when a transfer is perfected. For real property, a transfer is perfected when it is valid against a bona fide purchaser. For personal property and fixtures, a transfer is perfected when it is valid against a creditor on a simple contract that obtains a judicial lien after the transfer is perfected. "Simple contract" as used here is derived from Bankruptcy Act § 60a(4) [section 96(a)(4) of former Title 11]. Paragraph (2) specifies that a transfer is made when it takes effect between the transferor and the transferee if it is perfected at or within 10 days after that time. Otherwise, it is made when the transfer is perfected. If it is not perfected before the commencement of the case, it is made immediately before the commencement of the case. Paragraph (3) specifies that a transfer is not made until the debtor has acquired rights in the property transferred. This provision, more than any other in the section, overrules *DuBay and Grain Merchants*, and in combination with subsection (b)(2), overrules *In re King-Porter Co.*, 446 F.2d 722 (5th Cir. 1971).

Subsection (e) is designed to reach the different results under the 1962 version of Article 9 of the U.C.C. and under the 1972 version because different actions are required under each version in order to make a security agreement affective between the parties.

Subsection (f) creates a presumption of insolvency for the 90 days preceding the bankruptcy case. The presumption is as defined in Rule 301 of the Federal Rules of Evidence [Title 28, Judiciary and Judicial Procedure], made applicable in bankruptcy cases by sections 224 and 225 of the bill. The presumption requires the party against whom the presumption exists to come forward with some evidence to rebut the presumption, but the burden of proof remains on the party in whose favor the presumption exists. Senate Report No. 95–989.

1984 Acts. Statements by Legislative Leaders, see 1984 U.S. Code Cong. and Adm. News, p. 576.

1986 Acts. House Report No. 99–764 and House Conference Report No. 99–958, see 1986 U.S. Code Cong. and Adm. News, p. 5227.

1994 Acts. House Report No. 103–835, see 1994 U.S. Code Cong. and Adm. News, p. 3340.

2005 Acts. House Report No. 109–31(Part I), see 2005 U.S. Code Cong. and Adm. News, p. 88.

Legislative Statements

No limitation is provided for payments to commodity brokers as in section 766 of the Senate amendment other than the amendment to section 548 of title 11. Section 547(c)(2) protects most payments.

Section 547(b)(2) of the House amendment adopts a provision contained in the House bill and rejects an alternative contained in the Senate amendment relating to the avoidance of a preferential transfer that is payment of a tax claim owing to a governmental unit. As provided, section 106(c) of the House amendment overrules contrary language in the House report with the result that the Government is subject to avoidance of preferential transfers.

Contrary to language contained in the House report, payment of a debt by means of a check is equivalent to a cash payment, unless the check is dishonored. Payment is considered to be made when the check is delivered for purposes of sections 547(c)(1) and (2).

Section 547(c)(6) of the House bill is deleted and is treated in a different fashion in section 553 of the House amendment.

Section 547(c)(6) represents a modification of a similar provision contained in the House bill and Senate amendment. The exception relating to satisfaction of a statutory lien is deleted. The exception for a lien created under title 11 is deleted since such a lien is a statutory lien that will not be avoidable in a subsequent bankruptcy.

Section 547(e)(1)(B) is adopted from the House bill and Senate amendment without change. It is intended that the simple contract test used in this section will be applied as under section 544(a)(1) not to require a creditor to perfect against a creditor on a simple contract in the event applicable law makes such perfection impossible. For example, a purchaser from a debtor at an improperly noticed bulk sale may take subject to the rights of a creditor on a simple contract of the debtor for 1 year after the bulk sale. Since the purchaser cannot perfect against such a creditor on a simple contract, he should not be held responsible for failing to do the impossible. In the event the debtor goes into bankruptcy within a short time after the bulk sale, the trustee should not be able to use the avoiding powers under section 544(a)(1) or 547 merely because State law has made some transfers of personal property subject to the rights of a creditor on a simple contract to acquire a judicial lien with no opportunity to perfect against such a creditor.

Preferences: The House amendment deletes from the category of transfers on account of antecedent debts which may be avoided under the preference rules, section 547(b)(2), the exception in the Senate amendment for taxes owed to governmental authorities. However, for purposes of the "ordinary course" exception to the preference rules contained in section 547(c)(2), the House amendment specifies that the 45-day period referred to in section 547(c)(2)(B) is to begin running, in the case of taxes from the last due date, including extensions, of the return with respect to which the tax payment was made.

Amendments

2010 Amendments. Subsec. (c)(9). By notice dated Feb. 25, 2010, 75 F.R. 8747, dollar amount adjusted by the Judicial Conference of the United States which adjusted "$5,475" to "$5,850". See 11 U.S.C.A. § 104 and Adjustment of Dollar Amounts notes under this section.

2007 Amendments. Subsec. (c)(9). By notice dated Feb. 14, 2007, 72 F.R. 7082, dollar amount adjusted by the Judicial Conference of the United States which adjusted "$5,000" to "$5,475". See 11 U.S.C.A. § 104 and Adjustment of Dollar Amounts notes under this section.

2005 Amendments. Subsec. (b). Pub.L.109–8, § 1213(a)(1), struck out "subsection (c)" and inserted "subsections (c) and (i)" in introductory provisions.

Subsec. (c)(2). Pub.L. 109–8, § 409(1), rewrote par. (2), which formerly read:

"**(2)** to the extent that such transfer was—

"**(A)** in payment of a debt incurred by the debtor in the ordinary course of business or financial affairs of the debtor and the transferee;

"**(B)** made in the ordinary course of business or financial affairs of the debtor and the transferee; and

"**(C)** made according to ordinary business terms;"

Subsec. (c)(3)(B). Pub.L.109–8, § 1222, struck out "20" and inserted "30".

Subsec. (c)(7). Pub.L. 109–8, § 217, rewrote par. (7) which formerly read:

"**(7)** to the extent such transfer was a bona fide payment of a debt to a spouse, former spouse, or child of the debtor, for alimony to, maintenance for, or support of such spouse or child, in connection with a separation agreement, divorce decree or other order of a court of record, determination made in accordance with State or territorial law by a governmental unit, or property settlement agreement, but not to the extent that such debt—

"**(A)** is assigned to another entity, voluntarily, by operation of law, or otherwise; or

"**(B)** includes a liability designated as alimony, maintenance, or support, unless such liability is actually in the nature of alimony, maintenance or support; or"

Subsec. (c)(8). Pub.L. 109–8, § 409(2), struck the period at the end and inserted "; or".

Subsec. (c)(9). Pub.L. 109–8, § 409(3), added par. (9).

Subsec. (e)(2)(A). Pub.L. 109–8, § 403, struck "10" prior to "days" and inserted "30".

Subsec. (e)(2)(B). Pub.L. 109–8, § 403, struck "10" prior to "days" and inserted "30".

Subsec. (e)(2)(C)(ii). Pub.L. 109–8, § 403, struck "10" prior to "days" and inserted "30".

Subsec. (h). Pub.L. 109–8, § 201(b), added subsec. (h).

Subsec. (i). Pub.L.109–8, § 1213(a)(2), added subsec. (i).

1994 Amendments. Subsec. (c)(3)(B). Pub.L. 103–394, § 203(1), substituted "20 days" for "10 days".

Subsec. (c)(7), (8). Pub.L. 103–394, § 304(f), added par. (7). Former par. (7) redesignated (8).

Subsec. (e)(2)(A). Pub.L. 103–394, § 203(2), inserted reference to subsec. (c)(3)(B).

1986 Amendments. Subsec. (b)(4)(B). Pub.L. 99–554 inserted "and" following the semicolon.

1984 Amendments. Subsec. (a)(2). Pub.L. 98–353, § 462(a)(1), added "including proceeds of such property," after "law,".

Subsec. (a)(4). Pub.L. 98–353, § 462(a)(2), struck out ", without penalty" after "any extension" and added "without penalty" after "payable".

Subsec. (b). Pub.L. 98–353, § 462(b)(1), substituted "of an interest of the debtor in property" for "of property of the debtor" in provisions preceding par. (1).

Subsec. (b)(4)(B). Pub.L. 98–353, § 462(b)(2), substituted "between ninety days and one year before the date of the filing of the petition, if such creditor at the time of such transfer was an insider;" for "between 90 days and one year before the date of the filing of the petition, if such creditor, at the time of such transfer—

"**(i)** was an insider; and

"**(ii)** had reasonable cause to believe the debtor was insolvent at the time of such transfer; and".

Subsec. (c)(2)(A). Pub.L. 98–353, § 462(d)(1), added "by the debtor" after "incurred".

Subsec. (c)(2)(B). Pub.L. 98–353, § 462(c), struck out subpar. (B), which read "made not later than 45 days after such debt was incurred;". Former subpar. (C) was redesignated as (B).

Subsec. (c)(2)(C). Pub.L. 98–353, § 462(c), redesignated former subpar. (D) as (C). Former subpar. (C) was redesignated as (B).

Subsec. (c)(2)(D). Pub.L. 98–353, § 462(c), redesignated former subpar. (D) as (C).

Subsec. (c)(3). Pub.L. 98–353, § 462(d)(2), substituted "that creates" for "of".

Subsec. (c)(3)(B). Pub.L. 98–353, § 462(d)(3), added "on or" after "perfected" and substituted "the debtor receives possession of such property" for "such security interest attaches".

Subsec. (c)(5). Pub.L. 98–353, § 462(d)(4), substituted "that creates" for "of" at the beginning of par. (5), and "all security interests" for "all security interest".

Subsec. (c)(5)(A)(ii). Pub.L. 98–353, § 462(d)(5), substituted "or" for "and".

Subsec. (c)(5)(B). Pub.L. 98–353, § 310(1), struck out "or" following "interest;".

Subsec. (c)(6). Pub.L. 98–353, § 310(2), substituted "; or" for the period at the end of par. (6).

Subsec. (c)(7). Pub.L. 98–353, § 310(3), added par. (7).

Subsec. (d). Pub.L. 98–353, § 462(e), substituted "The" for "A" before "trustee may avoid", added "an interest in" after "transfer of", added "to or for the benefit of a surety" after "transferred", and added "such" after "reimbursement of".

Subsec. (e)(2)(C)(i). Pub.L. 98–353, § 462(f), substituted "or" for "and".

Subsec. (g). Pub.L. 98–353, § 462(g), added subsec. (g).

Effective and Applicability Provisions

2010 Acts. Increase of dollar amounts by Judicial Conference of the United States by notice published Feb. 25, 2010, 75 F.R. 8747 effective April 1, 2010, and increase not applicable to cases commenced before the effective date of the adjustments, i.e., April 1, 2010. See Adjustment of Dollar Amounts notes under 11 U.S.C.A. § 104 and this section.

2007 Acts. Increase of dollar amounts by Judicial Conference of the United States by notice published Feb. 14, 2007, 72 F.R. 7082 effective April 1, 2007, and increase not applicable to cases commenced before the effective date of the adjustments, i.e., April 1, 2007. See Adjustment of Dollar Amounts notes under 11 U.S.C.A. § 104 and this section.

2005 Acts. Pub.L. 109–8, Title XII, § 1213(b), Apr. 20, 2005, 119 Stat. 195, provided that: "The amendments made by this section [amending this section] shall apply to any case that is pending or commenced on or after the date of enactment of this Act [Apr. 20, 2005]."

Amendments by Pub.L. 109–8 effective, except as otherwise provided, 180 days after April 20, 2005, and inapplicable with respect to cases commenced under Title 11 before the effective date, see Pub.L. 109–8, § 1501, set out as a note under 11 U.S.C.A. § 101.

1994 Acts. Amendments by Pub.L. 103–394 effective on Oct. 22, 1994, and not to apply with respect to cases commenced under Title 11 of the United States Code before Oct. 22, 1994, see section 702 of Pub.L. 103–394, set out as a note under section 101 of this title.

1986 Acts. Amendment by Pub.L. 99–554 effective 30 days after Oct. 27, 1986, except as otherwise provided for, see section 302(a) of Pub.L. 99–554, set out as a note under section 581 of Title 28, Judiciary and Judicial Procedure.

1984 Acts. Amendment by Pub.L. 98–353 effective with respect to cases filed 90 days after July 10, 1984, see section 552(a), formerly 553(a), of Pub.L. 98–353, set out as a note under section 101 of this title.

Separability of Provisions

If any provision of or amendment made by Pub.L. 103–394 or the application of such provision or amendment to any person or circumstance is held to be unconstitutional, the remaining provisions of and amendments made by Pub.L. 103–394 and the application of such provisions and amendments to any person or circumstance shall not be affected thereby, see section 701 of Pub.L. 103–394, set out as a note under section 101 of this title.

Adjustment of Dollar Amounts

For adjustment of dollar amounts specified in subsec. (c)(9) of this section by the Judicial Conference of the United States, effective Apr. 1, 2010, see note set out under 11 U.S.C.A. § 104.

By notice published Feb. 25, 2010, 75 F.R. 8747, the Judicial Conference of the United States adjusted the dollar amounts in provisions specified in subsec. (c)(9) of this section, effective Apr. 1, 2010, as follows:

    Adjusted $5,475 to $5,850.

By notice published Feb. 14, 2007, 72 F.R. 7082, the Judicial Conference of the United States adjusted the dollar amounts in provisions specified in subsec. (c)(9) of this section, effective Apr. 1, 2007, as follows:

    Adjusted $5,000 to $5,475.

CROSS REFERENCES

Applicability of this section in Chapter nine cases, see 11 USCA § 901.

Appointment of trustee upon debtor's refusal to pursue cause of action under this section, see 11 USCA § 926.

Automatic stay, see 11 USCA § 362.

Commencement of involuntary cases by transferees of voidable transfers, see 11 USCA § 303.

Disallowance of claims of entity that is transferee of avoidable transfer, see 11 USCA § 502.

Effect of dismissal, see 11 USCA § 349.

Exemptions, see 11 USCA § 522.

Persons who may be debtors in Chapter nine case, see 11 USCA § 109.

Recovery of voidable transfers in investor protection liquidation proceedings, see 15 USCA § 78fff–2.

Transfers to defeat cases under this title, see 18 USCA § 152.

Voidable transfers in—

    Commodity broker liquidation cases, see 11 USCA § 764.

    Stockbroker liquidation cases, see 11 USCA § 749.

LIBRARY REFERENCES

American Digest System

Bankruptcy ⇔2601 to 2623, 2726(3), 2726.1(2).

Key Number System Topic No. 51.

Corpus Juris Secundum

CJS Bankruptcy § 103, Chapter 13.

CJS Bankruptcy § 191, Proceedings to Determine, Avoid, or Recover Preferences.

CJS Bankruptcy § 200, Other Proceedings Affecting Liquidation of Estate Assets or Adjustment of Debtor-Creditor/Equity-Security Holder Relationship--Actions Involving State Law.

CJS Bankruptcy § 278, Parties Defendant; Sovereign Immunity.

CJS Bankruptcy § 400, Relief Available on Recognition.

CJS Bankruptcy § 403, Powers of Foreign Representative on Recognition--Commencement of or Participation in Other Bankruptcy Case.

CJS Bankruptcy § 499, Perfection and Enforcement of Liens and Other Property Interests.

CJS Bankruptcy § 562, Property Acquired Postpetition--Security Interest on Property Acquired Postpetition.

CJS Bankruptcy § 590, Recovery and Exemption of Property After Transfer Avoided.

CJS Bankruptcy § 668, Postpetition Transfers and Postpetition Perfection.

CJS Bankruptcy § 674, Transfer for Benefit of Creditor.

CJS Bankruptcy § 675, Transfer for Benefit of Creditor--Creation of Lien or Security Interest.

CJS Bankruptcy § 676, Antecedent Debt.

CJS Bankruptcy § 677, Debtor's Insolvency.

CJS Bankruptcy § 678, Transfer to Occur Within Preference Period.

CJS Bankruptcy § 679, Transfer to Occur Within Preference Period--Who Are Insiders Subject to Longer Period.

CJS Bankruptcy § 680, Effect of Giving Creditor More Than Under Bankruptcy Distribution.

CJS Bankruptcy § 682, Payments of Debts Incurred by Debtor in Ordinary Course of Business.

CJS Bankruptcy § 683, Security Interest in Inventory, Receivables, or Proceeds Thereof.

CJS Bankruptcy § 684, Consumer Debt Transfers.

CJS Bankruptcy § 685, Transfers to Creditors Who Then Give New Value to Debtor.

CJS Bankruptcy § 686, Transfers Creating Purchase Money Security Interests Securing New Value.

CJS Bankruptcy § 687, What Constitutes New Value.

CJS Bankruptcy § 688, Contemporaneous Exchanges for New Value.

CJS Bankruptcy § 690, Fraudulent and Preferential Transfers Distinguished.

CJS Bankruptcy § 698, Transfers or Obligations Which May be Avoided.

CJS Bankruptcy § 699, Who May Exercise Avoidance and Recovery Powers.

CJS Bankruptcy § 700, Disallowance of Claims of Entities or Transferees Holding Recoverable Property.

CJS Bankruptcy § 715, Prepetition Transfers Under Swap Agreement.

CJS Bankruptcy § 725, Repurchase Agreements.

CJS Bankruptcy § 727, Who May Commence.

CJS Bankruptcy § 729, Burden of Proof, Generally.

CJS Bankruptcy § 730, Burden of Proof as to Nonavoidability of Transfer.

CJS Bankruptcy § 731, Presumption of Insolvency.

CJS Bankruptcy § 752, Right of Seller of Goods.

CJS Bankruptcy § 841, Fiduciary Duties of Trustees and Debtors in Possession.

CJS Bankruptcy § 851, Prepetition Security Interests in Proceeds, Products, Offspring, or Profits.

CJS Bankruptcy § 852, Prepetition Security Interests Extending to Rents and Similar Charges.

CJS Bankruptcy § 1109, Voidable Transfers.

§ 548. Fraudulent transfers and obligations

(a)(1) The trustee may avoid any transfer (including any transfer to or for the benefit of an insider under an employment contract) of an interest of the debtor in property, or any obligation (including any obligation to or for the benefit of an insider under an employment contract) incurred by the debtor, that was made or incurred on or within 2 years before the date of the filing of the petition, if the debtor voluntarily or involuntarily—

(A) made such transfer or incurred such obligation with actual intent to hinder, delay, or defraud any entity to which the debtor was or became, on or after the date that such transfer was made or such obligation was incurred, indebted; or

(B)(i) received less than a reasonably equivalent value in exchange for such transfer or obligation; and

(ii)(I) was insolvent on the date that such transfer was made or such obligation was incurred, or became insolvent as a result of such transfer or obligation;

(II) was engaged in business or a transaction, or was about to engage in business or a transaction, for which any property remaining with the debtor was an unreasonably small capital;

(III) intended to incur, or believed that the debtor would incur, debts that would be beyond the debtor's ability to pay as such debts matured; or

(IV) made such transfer to or for the benefit of an insider, or incurred such obligation to or for the benefit of an insider, under an employment contract and not in the ordinary course of business.

(2) A transfer of a charitable contribution to a qualified religious or charitable entity or organization shall not be considered to be a transfer covered under paragraph (1)(B) in any case in which—

(A) the amount of that contribution does not exceed 15 percent of the gross annual income of the debtor for the year in which the transfer of the contribution is made; or

(B) the contribution made by a debtor exceeded the percentage amount of gross annual income specified in subparagraph (A), if the transfer was consistent with the practices of the debtor in making charitable contributions.

(b) The trustee of a partnership debtor may avoid any transfer of an interest of the debtor in property, or any obligation incurred by the debtor, that was made or incurred on or within 2 years before the date of the filing of the petition, to a general partner in the debtor, if the debtor was insolvent on the date such transfer was made or such obligation was incurred, or became insolvent as a result of such transfer or obligation.

(c) Except to the extent that a transfer or obligation voidable under this section is voidable under section 544, 545, or 547 of this title, a transferee or obligee of such a transfer or obligation that takes for value and in good faith has a lien on or may retain any interest transferred or may enforce any obligation incurred, as the case may be, to the extent that such transferee or obligee gave value to the debtor in exchange for such transfer or obligation.

(d)(1) For the purposes of this section, a transfer is made when such transfer is so perfected that a bona fide purchaser from the debtor against whom applicable law permits such transfer to be perfected cannot acquire an interest in the property transferred that is superior to the interest in such property of the transferee, but if such transfer is not so perfected before the commencement of the case, such transfer is made immediately before the date of the filing of the petition.

(2) In this section—

(A) "value" means property, or satisfaction or securing of a present or antecedent debt of the debtor, but does not include an unperformed promise to furnish support to the debtor or to a relative of the debtor;

(B) a commodity broker, forward contract merchant, stockbroker, financial institution, financial participant, or securities clearing agency that receives a margin payment, as defined in section 101, 741, or 761 of this title, or settlement payment, as defined in section 101 or 741 of this title, takes for value to the extent of such payment;

(C) a repo participant or financial participant that receives a margin payment, as defined in section 741 or 761 of this title, or settlement payment, as defined in section 741 of this title, in connection with a repurchase agreement, takes for value to the extent of such payment;

(D) a swap participant or financial participant that receives a transfer in connection with a swap agreement takes for value to the extent of such transfer; and

(E) a master netting agreement participant that receives a transfer in connection with a master netting agreement or any individual contract covered thereby takes for value to the extent of such trans-

fer, except that, with respect to a transfer under any individual contract covered thereby, to the extent that such master netting agreement participant otherwise did not take (or is otherwise not deemed to have taken) such transfer for value.

(3) In this section, the term "charitable contribution" means a charitable contribution, as that term is defined in section 170(c) of the Internal Revenue Code of 1986, if that contribution—

(A) is made by a natural person; and

(B) consists of—

(i) a financial instrument (as that term is defined in section 731(c)(2)(C) of the Internal Revenue Code of 1986); or

(ii) cash.

(4) In this section, the term "qualified religious or charitable entity or organization" means—

(A) an entity described in section 170(c)(1) of the Internal Revenue Code of 1986; or

(B) an entity or organization described in section 170(c)(2) of the Internal Revenue Code of 1986.

(e)(1) In addition to any transfer that the trustee may otherwise avoid, the trustee may avoid any transfer of an interest of the debtor in property that was made on or within 10 years before the date of the filing of the petition, if—

(A) such transfer was made to a self-settled trust or similar device;

(B) such transfer was by the debtor;

(C) the debtor is a beneficiary of such trust or similar device; and

(D) the debtor made such transfer with actual intent to hinder, delay, or defraud any entity to which the debtor was or became, on or after the date that such transfer was made, indebted.

(2) For the purposes of this subsection, a transfer includes a transfer made in anticipation of any money judgment, settlement, civil penalty, equitable order, or criminal fine incurred by, or which the debtor believed would be incurred by—

(A) any violation of the securities laws (as defined in section 3(a)(47) of the Securities Exchange Act of 1934 (15 U.S.C. 78c(a)(47))), any State securities laws, or any regulation or order issued under Federal securities laws or State securities laws; or

(B) fraud, deceit, or manipulation in a fiduciary capacity or in connection with the purchase or sale of any security registered under section 12 or 15(d) of the Securities Exchange Act of 1934 (15 U.S.C. 78l and 78o(d)) or under section 6 of the Securities Act of 1933 (15 U.S.C. 77f).

(Pub.L. 95–598, Nov. 6, 1978, 92 Stat. 2600; Pub.L. 97–222, § 5, July 27, 1982, 96 Stat. 236; Pub.L. 98–353, Title III, §§ 394, 463, July 10, 1984, 98 Stat. 365, 378; Pub.L. 99–554,

Title II, § 283(n), Oct. 27, 1986, 100 Stat. 3117; Pub.L. 101–311, Title I, § 104, Title II, § 204, June 25, 1990, 104 Stat. 268, 269; Pub.L. 103–394, Title V, § 501(b)(5), Oct. 22, 1994, 108 Stat. 4142; Pub.L. 105–183, §§ 2, 3(a), June 19, 1998, 112 Stat. 517; Pub.L. 109–8, Title IX, § 907(f), (o)(4) to (6), Title XIV, § 1402, Apr. 20, 2005, 119 Stat. 177, 182, 214.)

HISTORICAL AND STATUTORY NOTES

Revision Notes and Legislative Reports

1978 Acts. This section is derived in large part from section 67d of the Bankruptcy Act [section 107(d) of former Title 11]. It permits the trustee to avoid transfers by the debtor in fraud of his creditors. Its history dates from the statute of 13 Eliz. c. 5 (1570).

The trustee may avoid fraudulent transfers or obligations if made with actual intent to hinder, delay, or defraud a past or future creditor. Transfers made for less than a reasonably equivalent consideration are also vulnerable if the debtor was or thereby becomes insolvent, was engaged in business with an unreasonably small capital, or intended to incur debts that would be beyond his ability to repay.

The trustee of a partnership debtor may avoid any transfer of partnership property to a partner in the debtor if the debtor was or thereby became insolvent.

If a transferee's only liability to the trustee is under this section, and if he takes for value and in good faith, then subsection (c) grants him a lien on the property transferred, or other similar protection.

Subsection (d) specifies that for the purposes of fraudulent transfer section, a transfer is made when it is valid against a subsequent bona fide purchaser. If not made before the commencement of the case, it is considered made immediately before then. Subsection (d) also defines "value" to mean property, or the satisfaction or securing of a present or antecedent debt, but does not include an unperformed promise to furnish support to the debtor or a relative of the debtor. Senate Report No. 95–989.

1982 Acts. House Report No. 97–420, see 1982 U.S. Code Cong. and Adm. News, p. 583.

1984 Acts. Statements by Legislative Leaders, see 1984 U.S. Code Cong. and Adm. News, p. 576.

1986 Acts. House Report No. 99–764 and House Conference Report No. 99–958, see 1986 U.S. Code Cong. and Adm. News, p. 5227.

1990 Acts. House Report No. 101–484, see 1990 U.S. Code Cong. and Adm. News, p. 223.

1994 Acts. House Report No. 103–835, see 1994 U.S. Code Cong. and Adm. News, p. 3340.

1998 Acts. Statement by President, see 1998 U.S. Code Cong. and Adm. News, p. 230.

2005 Acts. House Report No. 109–31(Part I), see 2005 U.S. Code Cong. and Adm. News, p. 88.

Legislative Statements

Section 548(d)(2) is modified to reflect general application of a provision contained in section 766 of the Senate amendment with respect to commodity brokers. In particular, section 548(d)(2)(B) of the House amendment makes clear that a commodity broker who receives a margin payment is considered to receive the margin payment in return for "value" for purposes of section 548.

References in Text

The Internal Revenue Code of 1986, referred to in subsec. (d)(3) and (4), is classified generally to Title 26.

Section 3(a)(47) of the Securities Exchange Act of 1934, referred to in subsec. (e)(2)(A), is June 6, 1934, c. 404, Title I, § 3(a)(47), 48 Stat. 882, as amended, which is classified to 15 U.S.C.A. § 78c(a)(47).

Section 12 of the Securities Exchange Act of 1934, referred to in subsec. (e)(2)(B), is June 6, 1934, c. 404, Title I, § 12, 48 Stat. 892, as amended, which is classified to 15 U.S.C.A. § 78l.

Section 15(d) of the Securities Exchange Act of 1934, referred to in subsec. (e)(2)(B), is June 6, 1934, c. 404, Title I, § 15(d), 48 Stat. 895, as amended, which is classified to 15 U.S.C.A. § 78o.

Section 6 of the Securities Act of 1933, referred to in subsec. (e)(2)(B), is Act May 27, 1933, c. 38, Title I, § 6, 48 Stat. 78, as amended, which is classified to 15 U.S.C.A. § 77f.

Amendments

2005 Amendments. Subsec. (a). Pub.L. 109–8, § 1402(1), (2), struck out "one year" and inserted "2 years", and inserted "(including any transfer to or for the benefit of an insider under an employment contract)" after "avoid any transfer", and "(including any obligation to or for the benefit of an insider under an employment contract)" after "or any obligation".

Subsec. (a)(1)(B)(ii)(II) to (IV). Pub.L. 109–8, § 1402(3), struck out "or" at the end of subcl. (II), struck out the period at the end of subcl. (III) and inserted "; or", and added subcl. (IV).

Subsec. (b). Pub.L. 109–8, § 1402(1), struck out "one year" and inserted "2 years",

Subsec. (d)(2)(B). Pub.L. 109–8, § 907(o)(4), inserted "financial participant," after "financial institution,".

Subsec. (d)(2)(C). Pub.L. 109–8, § 907(f)(1), struck out "and" at the end of subpar. (C).

Pub.L. 109–8, § 907(o)(5), inserted "or financial participant" after "repo participant".

Subsec. (d)(2)(D). Pub.L. 109–8, § 907(f)(2), substituted "; and" for the period at the end of subpar. (D).

Pub.L. 109–8, § 907(o)(6), inserted "or financial participant" after "swap participant".

Subsec. (d)(2)(E). Pub.L. 109–8, § 907(f)(3), added subpar. (E).

Subsec. (e). Pub.L. 109–8, § 1402(4), added subsec. (e).

1998 Amendments. Subsec. (a)(1). Pub.L. 105–183, § 3(a)(1), inserted "(1)" after "(a)".

Subsec. (a)(1)(A). Pub.L. 105–183, § 3(a)(2), struck out "(1) made" and inserted "(A) made".

Subsec. (a)(1)(B)(i). Pub.L. 105–183, § 3(a)(3), struck out "(2)(A)" and inserted "(B)(i)".

Subsec. (a)(1)(B)(ii)(I). Pub.L. 105–183, § 3(a)(4), struck out "(B)(i)" and inserted "(ii)(I)".

Subsec. (a)(1)(B)(ii)(II). Pub.L. 105–183, § 3(a)(5), struck out "(ii) was" and inserted "(II) was".

Subsec. (a)(1)(B)(ii)(III). Pub.L. 105–183, § 3(a)(6), struck out "(iii)" and inserted "(III)".

Subsec. (a)(2). Pub.L. 105–183, § 3(a)(7), added par. (2).

Subsec. (d). Pub.L. 105–183, § 2, added pars. (3) and (4).

1994 Amendments. Subsec. (d)(2)(B). Pub.L. 103–394, § 501(b)(5)(A), substituted "section 101, 741, or 761" for "section 101(34), 741(5), or 761(15)", and "section 101 or 741" for "section 101(35) or 741(8)".

Subsec. (d)(2)(C). Pub.L. 103–394, § 501(b)(5)(B), substituted "section 741 or 761" for "section 741(5) or 761(15)", and "section 741" for "section 741(8)".

1990 Amendments. Subsec. (d)(2)(B). Pub.L. 101–311, § 204, added provisions referring to sections 101(34) and 101(35) of this title.

Subsec. (d)(2)(D). Pub.L. 101–311, § 104, added subpar. (D).

1986 Amendments. Subsec. (d)(2)(B). Pub.L. 99–554 substituted ", financial institution" for "financial institution,".

1984 Amendments. Subsec. (a). Pub.L. 98–353, § 463(a)(1), substituted "if the debtor voluntarily or involuntarily" for "if the debtor" in provisions preceding par. (1).

Subsec. (a)(1). Pub.L. 98–353, § 463(a)(2), substituted "was made" for "occurred".

Subsec. (a)(2)(B)(ii). Pub.L. 98–353, § 463(a)(3), added "or a transaction" after "engaged in business".

Subsec. (c). Pub.L. 98–353, § 463(b)(1), added "or may retain" after "lien on" and struck out ", may retain any lien transferred," before "or may enforce any obligation incurred".

Subsec. (d)(1). Pub.L. 98–353, § 463(c)(1), substituted "is so" for "becomes so far", "applicable law permits such transfer to be" for "such transfer could have been", and "is made" for "occurs".

Subsec. (d)(2)(B). Pub.L. 98–353, § 463(c)(2), added "financial institution," after "stockbroker".

Subsec. (d)(2)(C). Pub.L. 98–353, § 394; added subpar. (C).

1982 Amendments. Subsec. (d)(2)(B). Pub.L. 97–222 substituted "a commodity broker, forward contract merchant, stockbroker, or securities clearing agency that receives a margin payment, as defined in section 741(5) or 761(15) of this title, or settlement payment, as defined in section 741(8) of this title, takes for value to the extent of such payment" for "a commodity broker or forward contract merchant that receives a margin payment, as defined in section 761(15) of this title, takes for value".

Effective and Applicability Provisions

2005 Acts. Amendments by Pub.L. 109–8, Title XIV, effective, except as otherwise provided, on Apr. 20, 2005, and applicable only with respect to cases commenced under Title 11 on or after Apr. 20, 2005. Amendments by Pub.L. 109–8, § 1402(1), to subsecs. (a) and (b) of this section applicable only with respect to cases commenced under Title 11 more than 1 year after April 20, 2005; see Pub.L. 109–8, § 1406, set out as a note under 11 U.S.C.A. § 507.

Amendments by Pub.L. 109–8 effective, except as otherwise provided, 180 days after April 20, 2005, and inapplicable with respect to cases commenced under Title 11 before the effective date, see Pub.L. 109–8, § 1501, set out as a note under 11 U.S.C.A. § 101.

1994 Acts. Amendment by Pub.L. 103–394 effective on Oct. 22, 1994, and not to apply with respect to cases commenced under Title 11 of the United States Code before Oct. 22, 1994, see section 702 of Pub.L. 103–394, set out as a note under section 101 of this title.

1986 Acts. Amendment by Pub.L. 99–554, effective 30 days after Oct. 27, 1986, except as otherwise provided for, see section 302(a) of Pub.L. 99–554, set out as a note under section 581 of Title 28, Judiciary and Judicial Procedure.

1984 Acts. Amendment by Pub.L. 98–353 effective with respect to cases filed 90 days after July 10, 1984, see section 552(a), formerly 553(a), of Pub.L. 98–353, set out as a note under section 101 of this title.

Separability of Provisions

If any provision of or amendment made by Pub.L. 103–394 or the application of such provision or amendment to any person or circumstance is held to be unconstitutional, the remaining provisions of and amendments made by Pub.L. 103–394 and the application of such provisions and amendments to any person or circumstance shall not be affected thereby, see section 701 of Pub.L. 103–394, set out as a note under section 101 of this title.

Applicability

Applicability of amendments made by Pub.L. 105–183 to any case brought under an applicable provision of this title that is pending or commenced on or after June 19, 1998, see Pub.L. 105–183, § 5, June 19, 1998, 112 Stat. 518, set out as a note under section 544 of this title.

Rule of Construction

Amendments made by Pub.L. 105–183 not intended to limit the applicability of the Religious Freedom Restoration Act of 1993 (42 U.S.C. 2002bb et seq.), see Pub.L. 105–183, § 6, June 19, 1998, 112 Stat. 519, set out as a note under section 544 of this title.

CROSS REFERENCES

Applicability of this section in Chapter nine cases, see 11 USCA § 901.

Appointment of trustee upon debtor's refusal to pursue cause of action under this section, see 11 USCA § 926.

Commencement of involuntary cases by transferees of voidable transfers, see 11 USCA § 303.

Disallowance of claims of entity that is transferee of avoidable transfer, see 11 USCA § 502.

Effect of dismissal, see 11 USCA § 349.

Exemptions, see 11 USCA § 522.

Inappropriate transfers included in determining net worth of employer, see 29 USCA § 1362.

Recovery of voidable transfers in investor protection liquidation proceedings, see 15 USCA § 78fff–2.

Transfers to defeat cases under this title, see 18 USCA § 152.

Voidable transfers in—

    Commodity broker liquidation cases, see 11 USCA § 764.

    Stockbroker liquidation cases, see 11 USCA § 749.

LIBRARY REFERENCES

American Digest System

Bankruptcy ⊕2641 to 2651.

Key Number System Topic No. 51.

Corpus Juris Secundum

CJS Bankruptcy § 103, Chapter 13.

CJS Bankruptcy § 189, Actions Based on State Law.

CJS Bankruptcy § 200, Other Proceedings Affecting Liquidation of Estate Assets or Adjustment of Debtor-Creditor/Equity-Security Holder Relationship--Actions Involving State Law.

CJS Bankruptcy § 278, Parties Defendant; Sovereign Immunity.

CJS Bankruptcy § 400, Relief Available on Recognition.

CJS Bankruptcy § 403, Powers of Foreign Representative on Recognition--Commencement of or Participation in Other Bankruptcy Case.

CJS Bankruptcy § 562, Property Acquired Postpetition--Security Interest on Property Acquired Postpetition.

CJS Bankruptcy § 590, Recovery and Exemption of Property After Transfer Avoided.

CJS Bankruptcy § 662, Effect of Prepetition or Postpetition Nature of Debts.

CJS Bankruptcy § 668, Postpetition Transfers and Postpetition Perfection.

CJS Bankruptcy § 690, Fraudulent and Preferential Transfers Distinguished.

CJS Bankruptcy § 691, Actual and Constructive Fraud.

CJS Bankruptcy § 692, Less Than Reasonably Equivalent Value.

CJS Bankruptcy § 693, Transfer of Interest or Obligation to Partner in Partnership Debtor.

CJS Bankruptcy § 694, When Transfer is Deemed Made.

CJS Bankruptcy § 695, Bona Fide Purchasers from Debtor.

CJS Bankruptcy § 696, Use of State Law Concerning Fraudulent Transfers or Obligations.

CJS Bankruptcy § 698, Transfers or Obligations Which May be Avoided.

CJS Bankruptcy § 700, Disallowance of Claims of Entities or Transferees Holding Recoverable Property.

CJS Bankruptcy § 715, Prepetition Transfers Under Swap Agreement.

CJS Bankruptcy § 725, Repurchase Agreements.

CJS Bankruptcy § 733, Nature of Proceedings; Right to Jury Trial.

CJS Bankruptcy § 734, Burden of Proof.

CJS Bankruptcy § 739, Trustee.

CJS Bankruptcy § 746, Sufficiency of Pleadings.

CJS Bankruptcy § 851, Prepetition Security Interests in Proceeds, Products, Offspring, or Profits.

CJS Bankruptcy § 852, Prepetition Security Interests Extending to Rents and Similar Charges.

CJS Bankruptcy § 1109, Voidable Transfers.

CJS Bankruptcy § 1197, Disposable Income.

CJS Fraudulent Conveyances § 96, Fair or Valuable Consideration.

§ 549. Postpetition transactions

(a) Except as provided in subsection (b) or (c) of this section, the trustee may avoid a transfer of property of the estate—

    (1) that occurs after the commencement of the case; and

    (2)(A) that is authorized only under section 303(f) or 542(c) of this title; or

    (B) that is not authorized under this title or by the court.

(b) In an involuntary case, the trustee may not avoid under subsection (a) of this section a transfer made after the commencement of such case but before the order for relief to the extent any value, including services, but not including satisfaction or securing of a debt that arose before the commencement of the case, is given after the commencement of the case in exchange for such transfer, notwithstanding any notice or knowledge of the case that the transferee has.

(c) The trustee may not avoid under subsection (a) of this section a transfer of an interest in real property to a good faith purchaser without knowledge of the commencement of the case and for present fair equivalent value unless a copy or notice of the petition was filed, where a transfer of an interest in such real property may be recorded to perfect such transfer, before such transfer is so perfected that a bona fide purchaser of such real property, against whom applicable law permits such transfer to be perfected, could not acquire an interest that is superior to such interest of such good faith purchaser. A good faith purchaser without knowledge of the commencement of the case and for less than present fair equivalent value has a lien on the property transferred to the extent of any present value given, unless a copy or notice of the petition was so filed before such transfer was so perfected.

(d) An action or proceeding under this section may not be commenced after the earlier of—

    (1) two years after the date of the transfer sought to be avoided; or

    (2) the time the case is closed or dismissed.

(Pub.L. 95–598, Nov. 6, 1978, 92 Stat. 2601; Pub.L. 98–353, Title III, § 464, July 10, 1984, 98 Stat. 379; Pub.L. 99–554, Title II, § 283(o), Oct. 27, 1986, 100 Stat. 3117; Pub.L. 103–394, Title V, § 501(d)(18), Oct. 22, 1994, 108 Stat. 4146; Pub.L. 109–8, Title XII, § 1214, Apr. 20, 2005, 119 Stat. 195.)

HISTORICAL AND STATUTORY NOTES

Revision Notes and Legislative Reports

1978 Acts. This section modifies section 70d of current law [section 110(d) of former Title 11]. It permits the trustee to avoid transfers of property that occur after the commencement of the case. The transfer must either have been unauthorized, or authorized under a section that protects only the transferor. Subsection (b) protects "involuntary gap" transferees to the extent of any value (including services, but not including satisfaction of a debt that arose before the commencement of the case), given after commencement in exchange for the transfer. Notice or knowledge of the transferee is irrelevant in determining whether he is protected under this provision. Senate Report No. 95–989.

1984 Acts. Statements by Legislative Leaders, see 1984 U.S. Code Cong. and Adm. News, p. 576.

1986 Acts. House Report No. 99–764 and House Conference Report No. 99–958, see 1986 U.S. Code Cong. and Adm. News, p. 5227.

1994 Acts. House Report No. 103–835, see 1994 U.S. Code Cong. and Adm. News, p. 3340.

2005 Acts. House Report No. 109–31(Part I), see 2005 U.S. Code Cong. and Adm. News, p. 88.

Legislative Statements

Section 549 of the House amendment has been redrafted in order to incorporate section 342(b) and (c) of the Senate amendment. Those sections have been consolidated and redrafted in section 549(c) of the House amendment. Section 549(d) of the House amendment adopts a provision contained in section 549(c) of the Senate amendment.

Amendments

2005 Amendments. Subsec. (c). Pub.L.109–8, § 1214, inserted "an interest in" after "transfer of" each place it appeared, struck out "such property" and inserted "such real property" following "a bona fide purchaser of", and struck out "the interest" and inserted "such interest".

1994 Amendments. Subsec. (b). Pub.L. 103–394, § 501(d)(18), inserted "the trustee may not avoid under subsection (a) of this section" following "In an involuntary case,".

1986 Amendments. Subsec. (b). Pub.L. 99–554 substituted "made" for "that occurs", and "to the extent" for "is valid against the trustee to the extent of", and inserted "is" preceding "given".

1984 Amendments. Subsec. (a). Pub.L. 98–353, § 464(a)(1), (2), substituted "(b) or (c)" for "(b) and (c)" in provisions preceding par. (1) and inserted "only" between "authorized" and "under" in par. (2)(A). In the original of Pub.L. 98–353, subsec. (a)(2) of section 464 thereof ended with a period but was followed by pars. (3), (4), and (5). Such pars. (3), (4), and (5) purported to amend subsec. (a) of this section in ways not susceptible of execution. In a predecessor bill [S. 445], these pars. (3), (4), and (5) formed a part of a subsec. (b) of section 361 thereof which amended subsec. (b) of this section. Such subsec. (b) of section 361 of S. 445 was not carried into Pub.L. 98–353, § 464.

Subsec. (c). Pub.L. 98–353, § 464(c), substituted "The trustee may not avoid under subsection (a) of this section a transfer of real property to a good faith purchaser without knowledge of the commencement of the case and for present fair equivalent value unless a copy or notice of the petition was filed, where a transfer of such real property may be recorded to perfect such transfer, before such transfer is so perfected that a bona fide purchaser of such property, against whom applicable law permits such transfer to be perfected, could not acquire an interest that is superior to the interest of such good faith purchaser. A good faith purchaser without knowledge of the commencement of the case and for less than present fair equivalent value has a lien on the property transferred to the extent of any present value given, unless a copy or notice of the petition was so filed before such transfer was so perfected." for "The trustee may not avoid under subsection (a) of this section a transfer, to a good faith purchaser without knowledge of the commencement of the case and for present fair equivalent value or to a purchaser at a judicial sale, of real property located other than in the county in which the case is commenced, unless a copy of the petition was filed in the office where conveyances of real property in such county are recorded before such transfer

was so far perfected that a bona fide purchaser of such property against whom applicable law permits such transfer to be perfected cannot acquire an interest that is superior to the interest of such good faith or judicial sale purchaser. A good faith purchaser, without knowledge of the commencement of the case and for less than present fair equivalent value, of real property located other than in the county in which the case is commenced, under a transfer that the trustee may avoid under this section, has a lien on the property transferred to the extent of any present value given, unless a copy of the petition was so filed before such transfer was so perfected.".

Subsec. (d)(1). Pub.L. 98–353, § 464(d), substituted "or" for "and".

Effective and Applicability Provisions

2005 Acts. Amendments by Pub.L. 109–8 effective, except as otherwise provided, 180 days after April 20, 2005, and inapplicable with respect to cases commenced under Title 11 before the effective date, see Pub.L. 109–8, § 1501, set out as a note under 11 U.S.C.A. § 101.

1994 Acts. Amendment by Pub.L. 103–394 effective on Oct. 22, 1994, and not to apply with respect to cases commenced under Title 11 of the United States Code before Oct. 22, 1994, see section 702 of Pub.L. 103–394, set out as a note under section 101 of this title.

1986 Acts. Amendment by Pub.L. 99–554 effective 30 days after Oct. 27, 1986, except as otherwise provided for, see section 302(a) of Pub.L. 99–554, set out as a note under section 581 of Title 28, Judiciary and Judicial Procedure.

1984 Acts. Amendment by Pub.L. 98–353 effective with respect to cases filed 90 days after July 10, 1984, see section 552(a), formerly 553(a), of Pub.L. 98–353, set out as a note under section 101 of this title.

Separability of Provisions

If any provision of or amendment made by Pub.L. 103–394 or the application of such provision or amendment to any person or circumstance is held to be unconstitutional, the remaining provisions of and amendments made by Pub.L. 103–394 and the application of such provisions and amendments to any person or circumstance shall not be affected thereby, see section 701 of Pub.L. 103–394, set out as a note under section 101 of this title.

CROSS REFERENCES

Applicability of subsecs. (a), (c) and (d) of this section in Chapter 9 cases, see 11 USCA § 901.

Appointment of trustee upon debtor's refusal to pursue cause of action under this section, see 11 USCA § 926.

Commencement of involuntary cases by transferees of voidable transfers, see 11 USCA § 303.

Disallowance of claims of entity that is transferee of avoidable transfer, see 11 USCA § 502.

Effect of dismissal, see 11 USCA § 349.

Exemptions, see 11 USCA § 522.

Inappropriate transfers included in determining net worth of employer, see 29 USCA § 1362.

Recovery of voidable transfers in investor liquidation proceedings, see 15 USCA § 78fff–2.

Voidable transfers in—
  Commodity broker liquidation cases, see 11 USCA § 764.
  Stockbroker liquidation cases, see 11 USCA § 749.

LIBRARY REFERENCES

American Digest System
  Bankruptcy ⟜2722, 2588.
  Key Number System Topic No. 51.

Corpus Juris Secundum
  CJS Bankruptcy § 278, Parties Defendant; Sovereign Immunity.
  CJS Bankruptcy § 399, Effects of Recognizing Foreign Main Proceeding.
  CJS Bankruptcy § 590, Recovery and Exemption of Property After Transfer Avoided.
  CJS Bankruptcy § 638, Good-Faith Transfers and Payments Made by Entities Without Notice or Knowledge of Case.
  CJS Bankruptcy § 668, Postpetition Transfers and Postpetition Perfection.
  CJS Bankruptcy § 698, Transfers or Obligations Which May be Avoided.
  CJS Bankruptcy § 699, Who May Exercise Avoidance and Recovery Powers.
  CJS Bankruptcy § 700, Disallowance of Claims of Entities or Transferees Holding Recoverable Property.
  CJS Bankruptcy § 703, Burden of Proof.
  CJS Bankruptcy § 726, Statute of Limitations.
  CJS Bankruptcy § 752, Right of Seller of Goods.
  CJS Bankruptcy § 1109, Voidable Transfers.

§ 550. Liability of transferee of avoided transfer

  (a) Except as otherwise provided in this section, to the extent that a transfer is avoided under section 544, 545, 547, 548, 549, 553(b), or 724(a) of this title, the trustee may recover, for the benefit of the estate, the property transferred, or, if the court so orders, the value of such property, from—

  (1) the initial transferee of such transfer or the entity for whose benefit such transfer was made; or

  (2) any immediate or mediate transferee of such initial transferee.

  (b) The trustee may not recover under section[1] (a)(2) of this section from—

  (1) a transferee that takes for value, including satisfaction or securing of a present or antecedent debt, in good faith, and without knowledge of the voidability of the transfer avoided; or

  (2) any immediate or mediate good faith transferee of such transferee.

  (c) If a transfer made between 90 days and one year before the filing of the petition—

  (1) is avoided under section 547(b) of this title; and

  (2) was made for the benefit of a creditor that at the time of such transfer was an insider;

the trustee may not recover under subsection (a) from a transferee that is not an insider.

  (d) The trustee is entitled to only a single satisfaction under subsection (a) of this section.

  (e)(1) A good faith transferee from whom the trustee may recover under subsection (a) of this section has a lien on the property recovered to secure the lesser of—

  (A) the cost, to such transferee, of any improvement made after the transfer, less the amount of any profit realized by or accruing to such transferee from such property; and

  (B) any increase in the value of such property as a result of such improvement, of the property transferred.

  (2) In this subsection, "improvement" includes—

  (A) physical additions or changes to the property transferred;

  (B) repairs to such property;

  (C) payment of any tax on such property;

  (D) payment of any debt secured by a lien on such property that is superior or equal to the rights of the trustee; and

  (E) preservation of such property.

  (f) An action or proceeding under this section may not be commenced after the earlier of—

  (1) one year after the avoidance of the transfer on account of which recovery under this section is sought; or

  (2) the time the case is closed or dismissed.

(Pub.L. 95–598, Nov. 6, 1978, 92 Stat. 2601; Pub.L. 98–353, Title III, § 465, July 10, 1984, 98 Stat. 379; Pub.L. 103–394, Title II, § 202, Oct. 22, 1994, 108 Stat. 4121.)

1 So in original. Probably should be "subsection".

HISTORICAL AND STATUTORY NOTES

Revision Notes and Legislative Reports

  1978 Acts. Section 550 prescribes the liability of a transferee of an avoided transfer, and enunciates the separation between the concepts of avoiding a transfer and recovering from the transferee. Subsection (a) permits the trustee to recover from the initial transferee of an avoided transfer or from any immediate or mediate transferee of the initial transferee. The words "to the extent that" in the lead in to this subsection are designed to incorporate the protection of transferees found in proposed 11 U.S.C. 549(b) and 548(c). Subsection (b) limits the liability of an immediate or mediate transferee of the initial transferee if such secondary transferee takes for value, in good faith and without knowledge of the voidability of the transfer. An immediate or mediate good faith transferee of a protected secondary transferee is also shielded from liability. This subsection is limited to the trustee's right to recover from subsequent transferees under subsection (a)(2). It does not limit the trustee's rights against the initial transferee under subsection (a)(1). The phrase "good faith" in this paragraph is intended to prevent a transferee from whom the trustee could recover from transferring the recoverable property to an innocent transferee, and receiving a retransfer from him, that is, "washing" the transaction through an innocent third party. In order for the transferee to be excepted from liability under this paragraph, he himself must be a good faith transferee. Subsection (c) is a further limitation on recovery. It specifies that the trustee is entitled to only one satisfactory, under subsection (a), even if more than one transferee is liable.

Subsection (d) protects good faith transferees, either initial or subsequent, to the extent of the lesser of the cost of any improvement the transferee makes in the transferred property and the increase in value of the property as a result of the improvement. Paragraph (2) of the subsection defines improvement to include physical additions or changes to the property, repairs, payment of taxes on the property, payment of a debt secured by a lien on the property, discharge of a lien on the property, and preservation of the property.

Subsection (e) establishes a statute of limitations on avoidance by the Trustee. The limitation is one year after the avoidance of the transfer or the time the case is closed or dismissed, whichever is earlier. Senate Report No. 95–989.

1984 Acts. Statements by Legislative Leaders, see 1984 U.S. Code Cong. and Adm. News, p. 576.

1994 Acts. House Report No. 103–835, see 1994 U.S. Code Cong. and Adm. News, p. 3340.

Legislative Statements

Section 550(a)(1) of the House amendment has been modified in order to permit recovery from an entity for whose benefit an avoided transfer is made in addition to a recovery from the initial transferee of the transfer. Section 550(c) would still apply, and the trustee is entitled only to a single satisfaction. The liability of a transferee under section 550(a) applies only "to the extent that a transfer is avoided". This means that liability is not imposed on a transferee to the extent that a transferee is protected under a provision such as section 548(c) which grants a good faith transferee for value of a transfer that is avoided only as a fraudulent transfer, a lien on the property transferred to the extent of value given.

Section 550(b) of the House amendment is modified to indicate that value includes satisfaction or securing of a present antecedent debt. This means that the trustee may not recover under subsection (a)(2) from a subsequent transferee that takes for "value", provided the subsequent transferee also takes in good faith and without knowledge of the transfer avoided.

Section 550(e) of the House amendment is derived from section 550(e) of the Senate amendment.

Amendments

1994 Amendments. Subsecs. (c) to (f). Pub.L. 103–394, § 202, added subsec. (c) and redesignated former subsecs. (c) through (e) as (d) through (f), respectively.

1984 Amendments. Subsec. (a). Pub.L. 98–353, § 465(a), substituted "549, 553(b), or 724(a) of this title" for "549, or 724(a) of this title".

Subsec. (d)(1)(A). Pub.L. 98–353, § 465(b)(1), added "or accruing to" after "by".

Subsec. (d)(1)(B). Pub.L. 98–353, § 465(b)(2), substituted "the value of such property" for "value".

Subsec. (d)(2)(D). Pub.L. 98–353, § 465(b)(3), substituted "payment of any debt secured by a lien on such property that is superior or equal to the rights of the trustee; and" for "payment of any debt secured by a lien on such property."

Subsec. (d)(2)(E). Pub.L. 98–353, § 465(b)(3), (4), struck out subpar. (E) which read "discharge of any lien against such property that is superior or equal to the rights of the trustee; and" and redesignated former subpar. (F) as (E).

Subsec. (d)(2)(F). Pub.L. 98–353, § 465(b)(4), redesignated former subpar. (F) as (E).

Subsec. (e)(1). Pub.L. 98–353, § 465(c), substituted "or" for "and".

Effective and Applicability Provisions

1994 Acts. Amendment by Pub.L. 103–394 effective on Oct. 22, 1994, and not to apply with respect to cases commenced under Title 11 of the United States Code before Oct. 22, 1994, see section 702 of Pub.L. 103–394, set out as a note under section 101 of this title.

1984 Acts. Amendment by Pub.L. 98–353 effective with respect to cases filed 90 days after July 10, 1984, see section 552(a), formerly 553(a), of Pub.L. 98–353, set out as a note under section 101 of this title.

Separability of Provisions

If any provision of or amendment made by Pub.L. 103–394 or the application of such provision or amendment to any person or circumstance is held to be unconstitutional, the remaining provisions of and amendments made by Pub.L. 103–394 and the application of such provisions and amendments to any person or circumstance shall not be affected thereby, see section 701 of Pub.L. 103–394, set out as a note under section 101 of this title.

CROSS REFERENCES

Allowance of claims or interests, see 11 USCA § 502.

Applicability of this section in Chapter 9 cases, see 11 USCA § 901.

Appointment of trustee upon debtor's refusal to pursue cause of action under this section, see 11 USCA § 926.

Effect of dismissal, see 11 USCA § 349.

Exemptions, see 11 USCA § 522.

LIBRARY REFERENCES

American Digest System

Bankruptcy ⊂⇒2701.

Key Number System Topic No. 51.

Corpus Juris Secundum

CJS Bankruptcy § 278, Parties Defendant; Sovereign Immunity.

CJS Bankruptcy § 400, Relief Available on Recognition.

CJS Bankruptcy § 403, Powers of Foreign Representative on Recognition--Commencement of or Participation in Other Bankruptcy Case.

CJS Bankruptcy § 589, Property Debtor Could Have Exempted Absent Transfer of that Property.

CJS Bankruptcy § 590, Recovery and Exemption of Property After Transfer Avoided.

CJS Bankruptcy § 638, Good-Faith Transfers and Payments Made by Entities Without Notice or Knowledge of Case.

CJS Bankruptcy § 663, Disqualifying or Limiting Factors.

CJS Bankruptcy § 700, Disallowance of Claims of Entities or Transferees Holding Recoverable Property.

CJS Bankruptcy § 726, Statute of Limitations.

§ 551. Automatic preservation of avoided transfer

Any transfer avoided under section 522, 544, 545, 547, 548, 549, or 724(a) of this title, or any lien void under section 506(d) of this title, is preserved for the benefit of the estate but only with respect to property of the estate.

(Pub.L. 95–598, Nov. 6, 1978, 92 Stat. 2602.)

HISTORICAL AND STATUTORY NOTES

Revision Notes and Legislative Reports

1978 Acts. This section is a change from present law. It specifies that any avoided transfer is automatically preserved for the benefit of the estate. Under current law, the court must determine whether or not the transfer should be preserved. The operation of the section is automatic, unlike current law, even though preservation may not benefit the estate in every instance. A preserved lien may be abandoned by the trustee under proposed 11 U.S.C. 554 if the preservation does not benefit the estate. The section as a whole prevents junior lienors from improving their position at the expense of the estate when a senior lien is avoided. Senate Report No. 95–989.

1984 Acts. Statements by Legislative Leaders, see 1984 U.S.Code Cong. and Adm.News, p. 576.

Legislative Statements

Section 551 is adopted from the House bill and the alternative in the Senate amendment is rejected. The section is clarified to indicate that a transfer avoided or a lien that is void is preserved for the benefit of the estate, but only with respect to property of the estate. This prevents the trustee from asserting an avoided tax lien against after acquired property of the debtor.

CROSS REFERENCES

Applicability of this section in Chapter 9 cases, see 11 USCA § 901.

Effect of dismissal, see 11 USCA § 349.

Exemptions, see 11 USCA § 522.

LIBRARY REFERENCES

American Digest System

Bankruptcy ⊂⇒2706.

Key Number System Topic No. 51.

Corpus Juris Secundum

CJS Bankruptcy § 278, Parties Defendant; Sovereign Immunity.

CJS Bankruptcy § 589, Property Debtor Could Have Exempted Absent Transfer of that Property.

CJS Bankruptcy § 590, Recovery and Exemption of Property After Transfer Avoided.

CJS Bankruptcy § 622, Effect on Junior and Senior Lien Holders.

§ 552. Postpetition effect of security interest

(a) Except as provided in subsection (b) of this section, property acquired by the estate or by the debtor after the commencement of the case is not subject to any lien resulting from any security agreement entered into by the debtor before the commencement of the case.

(b)(1) Except as provided in sections 363, 506(c), 522, 544, 545, 547, and 548 of this title, if the debtor and an entity entered into a security agreement before the commencement of the case and if the security interest created by such security agreement extends to property of the debtor acquired before the commencement of the case and to proceeds, products, offspring, or profits of such property, then such security interest extends to such proceeds, products, offspring, or profits acquired by the estate after the commencement of the case to the extent provided by such security agreement and by applicable nonbankruptcy law, except to any extent that the court, after notice and a hearing and based on the equities of the case, orders otherwise.

(2) Except as provided in sections 363, 506(c), 522, 544, 545, 547, and 548 of this title, and notwithstanding section 546(b) of this title, if the debtor and an entity entered into a security agreement before the commencement of the case and if the security interest created by such security agreement extends to property of the debtor acquired before the commencement of the case and to amounts paid as rents of such property or the fees, charges, accounts, or other payments for the use or occupancy of rooms and other public facilities in hotels, motels, or other lodging properties, then such security interest extends to such rents and such fees, charges, accounts, or other payments acquired by the estate after the commencement of the case to the extent provided in such security agreement, except to any extent that the court, after notice and a hearing and based on the equities of the case, orders otherwise.

(Pub.L. 95–598, Nov. 6, 1978, 92 Stat. 2602; Pub.L. 98–353, Title III, § 466, July 10, 1984, 98 Stat. 380; Pub.L. 103–394, Title II, § 214(a), Oct. 22, 1994, 108 Stat. 4126; Pub.L. 109–8, Title XII, § 1204(2), Apr. 20, 2005, 119 Stat. 194.)

HISTORICAL AND STATUTORY NOTES

Revision Notes and Legislative Reports

1978 Acts. Under the Uniform Commercial Code, article 9, creditors may take security interests in after-acquired property. Section 552 governs the effect of such a prepetition security interest in postpetition property. It applies to all security interests as defined in section 101(37) of the bankruptcy code, not only to U.C.C. security interests.

As a general rule, if a security agreement is entered into before the commencement of the case, then property that the estate acquires is not subject to the security interest created by a provision in the security agreement extending the security interest to after-acquired property. Subsection (b) provides an important exception consistent with the Uniform Commercial Code. If the security agreement extends to proceeds, product, offspring, rents, or profits of the property in question, then the proceeds would continue to be subject to the security interest pursuant to the terms of the security agreement and provisions of applicable law, except to the extent that where the estate acquires the proceeds at the expense of other creditors holding unsecured claims, the expenditure resulted in an improvement in the position of the secured party.

The exception covers the situation where raw materials, for example, are converted into inventory, or inventory into accounts, at some expense to the estate, thus depleting the fund available for general unsecured creditors, but is limited to the benefit inuring to the secured party thereby. Situations in which the estate incurs expense in simply protecting collateral are governed by 11 U.S.C. 506(c). In ordinary circumstances, the risk of loss in continued operations will remain with the estate. Senate Report No. 95–989.

Under the Uniform Commercial Code, Article 9, creditors may take security interests in after-acquired property. This section governs the effect of such a prepetition security interest in postpetition property. It applies to all security interests as defined in section 101 of the bankruptcy code, not only to U.C.C. security interests.

As a general rule, if a security agreement is entered into before the case, then property that the estate acquires is not subject to the security interest created by the security agreement. Subsection (b) provides the only exception. If the security agreement extends to proceeds, product, offspring, rents, or profits of property that the debtor had before the commencement of the case, then the proceeds, etc., continue to be subject to the security interest, except to the extent that the estate acquired the proceeds to the prejudice of other creditors holding unsecured claims. "Extends to" as used here would include an automatically arising security interest in proceeds, as permitted under the 1972 version of the Uniform Commercial Code, as well as an interest in proceeds specifically designated, as required under the 1962 Code or similar statutes covering property not covered by the Code. "Prejudice" is not intended to be a broad term here, but is designed to cover the situation where the estate expends funds that result in an increase in the value of collateral. The exception is to cover the situation where raw materials, for example, are converted into inventory, or inventory into accounts, at some expense to the estate, thus depleting the fund available for general unsecured creditors. The term "proceeds" is not limited to the technical definition of that term in the U.C.C., but covers any property into which property subject to the security interest is converted. House Report No. 95–595.

1984 Acts. Statements by Legislative Leaders, see 1984 U.S. Code Cong. and Adm. News, p. 576.

1994 Acts. House Report No, 103–835, see 1994 U.S. Code Cong. and Adm. News, p. 3340.

2005 Acts. House Report No. 109–31(Part I), see 2005 U.S. Code Cong. and Adm. News, p. 88.

Legislative Statements

Section 552(a) is derived from the House bill and the alternative provision in the Senate amendment is rejected. Section 552(b) represents a compromise between the House bill and the Senate amendment. Proceeds coverage, but not after acquired property clauses, are valid under title 11. The provision allows the court to consider the equities in each case. In the course of such consideration the court may evaluate any expenditures by the estate relating to proceeds

and any related improvement in position of the secured party. Although this section grants a secured party a security interest in proceeds, product, offspring, rents, or profits, the section is explicitly subject to other sections of title 11. For example, the trustee or debtor in possession may use, sell, or lease proceeds, product, offspring, rents or profits under section 363.

Amendments

2005 Amendments. Subsec. (b)(1). Pub.L. 109–8, § 1204(2), struck out "product" each place it appeared and inserted "products".

1994 Amendments. Subsec. (b). Pub.L. 103–394, § 214(a), designated existing provisions as par. (1) and as so designated, struck out "rents" before ", or profits" wherever appearing, and added par. (2).

1984 Amendments. Subsec. (b). Pub.L. 98–353, § 466, added "522," after "506(c),", substituted "an entity entered" for "a secured party enter", and substituted "except to any extent" for "except to the extent".

Effective and Applicability Provisions

2005 Acts. Amendments by Pub.L. 109–8 effective, except as otherwise provided, 180 days after April 20, 2005, and inapplicable with respect to cases commenced under Title 11 before the effective date, see Pub.L. 109–8, § 1501, set out as a note under 11 U.S.C.A. § 101.

1994 Acts. Amendment by Pub.L. 103–394 effective on Oct. 22, 1994, and not to apply with respect to cases commenced under Title 11 of the United States Code before Oct. 22, 1994, see section 702 of Pub.L. 103–394, set out as a note under section 101 of this title.

1984 Acts. Amendment by Pub.L. 98–353 effective with respect to cases filed 90 days after July 10, 1984, see section 552, formerly 553, of Pub.L. 98–353, set out as a note under section 101 of this title.

Separability of Provisions

If any provision of or amendment made by Pub.L. 103–394 or the application of such provision or amendment to any person or circumstance is held to be unconstitutional, the remaining provisions of and amendments made by Pub.L. 103–394 and the application of such provisions and amendments to any person or circumstance shall not be affected thereby, see section 701 of Pub.L. 103–394, set out as a note under section 101 of this title.

CROSS REFERENCES

Applicability of this section in Chapter 9 cases, see 11 USCA § 901.

"Cash collateral" as including proceeds, products, offspring, rents or profits of property subject to security interest as provided in this section, see 11 USCA § 363.

Special revenues acquired by debtor after commencement of Chapter 9 case subject to security interest, see 11 USCA § 928.

LIBRARY REFERENCES

American Digest System

Bankruptcy ⟳2573, 2558.

Key Number System Topic No. 51.

Corpus Juris Secundum

CJS Bankruptcy § 278, Parties Defendant; Sovereign Immunity.

CJS Bankruptcy § 399, Effects of Recognizing Foreign Main Proceeding.

CJS Bankruptcy § 562, Property Acquired Postpetition--Security Interest on Property Acquired Postpetition.

CJS Bankruptcy § 668, Postpetition Transfers and Postpetition Perfection.

CJS Bankruptcy § 851, Prepetition Security Interests in Proceeds, Products, Offspring, or Profits.

CJS Bankruptcy § 852, Prepetition Security Interests Extending to Rents and Similar Charges.

§ 553.   Setoff

(a) Except as otherwise provided in this section and in sections 362 and 363 of this title, this title does not affect any right of a creditor to offset a mutual debt owing by such creditor to the debtor that arose before the commencement of the case under this title against a claim of such creditor against the debtor that arose before the commencement of the case, except to the extent that—

(1) the claim of such creditor against the debtor is disallowed;

(2) such claim was transferred, by an entity other than the debtor, to such creditor—

(A) after the commencement of the case; or

(B)(i) after 90 days before the date of the filing of the petition; and

(ii) while the debtor was insolvent (except for a setoff of a kind described in section 362(b)(6), 362(b)(7), 362(b)(17), 362(b)(27), 555, 556, 559, 560, or 561); or

(3) the debt owed to the debtor by such creditor was incurred by such creditor—

(A) after 90 days before the date of the filing of the petition;

(B) while the debtor was insolvent; and

(C) for the purpose of obtaining a right of setoff against the debtor (except for a setoff of a kind described in section 362(b)(6), 362(b)(7), 362(b)(17), 362(b)(27), 555, 556, 559, 560, or 561).

(b)(1) Except with respect to a setoff of a kind described in section 362(b)(6), 362(b)(7), 362(b)(17), 362(b)(27), 555, 556, 559, 560, 561, 365(h), 546(h), or 365(i)(2) of this title, if a creditor offsets a mutual debt owing to the debtor against a claim against the debtor on or within 90 days before the date of the filing of the petition, then the trustee may recover from such creditor the amount so offset to the extent that any insufficiency on the date of such setoff is less than the insufficiency on the later of—

(A) 90 days before the date of the filing of the petition; and

(B) the first date during the 90 days immediately preceding the date of the filing of the petition on which there is an insufficiency.

(2) In this subsection, "insufficiency" means amount, if any, by which a claim against the debtor exceeds a mutual debt owing to the debtor by the holder of such claim.

(c) For the purposes of this section, the debtor is presumed to have been insolvent on and during the 90 days immediately preceding the date of the filing of the petition.

(Pub.L. 95–598, Nov. 6, 1978, 92 Stat. 2602; Pub.L. 98–353, Title III, §§ 395, 467, July 10, 1984, 98 Stat. 365, 380; Pub.L. 101–311, Title I, § 105, June 25, 1990, 104 Stat. 268; Pub.L. 103–394, Title II, §§ 205(b), 222(b), Title V, § 501(d)(19), Oct. 22, 1994, 108 Stat. 4123, 4129, 4146; Pub.L. 109–8, Title IX, § 907(n), Apr. 20, 2005, 119 Stat. 181.)

HISTORICAL AND STATUTORY NOTES

Revision Notes and Legislative Reports

1978 Acts. This section preserves, with some changes, the right of setoff in bankruptcy cases now found in section 68 of the Bankruptcy Act [section 108 of former Title 11]. One exception to the right is the automatic stay, discussed in connection with proposed 11 U.S.C. 362. Another is the right of the trustee to use property under section 363 that is subject to a right of setoff.

The section states that the right of setoff is unaffected by the bankruptcy code except to the extent that the creditor's claim is disallowed, the creditor acquired (other than from the debtor) the claim during the 90 days preceding the case while the debtor was insolvent, the debt being offset was incurred for the purpose of obtaining a right of setoff, while the debtor was insolvent and during the 90-day prebankruptcy period, or the creditor improved his position in the 90-day period (similar to the improvement in position test found in the preference section 547(c)(5)). Only the last exception is an addition to current law.

As under section 547(f), the debtor is presumed to have been insolvent during the 90 days before the case. Senate Report No. 95–989.

1984 Acts. Statements by Legislative Leaders, see 1984 U.S. Code Cong. and Adm. News, p. 576.

1990 Acts. House Report No. 101–484, see 1990 U.S. Code Cong. and Adm. News, p. 223.

1994 Acts. House Report No. 103–835, see 1994 U.S. Code Cong. and Adm. News, p. 3340.

2005 Acts. House Report No. 109–31(Part I), see 2005 U.S. Code Cong. and Adm. News, p. 88.

Legislative Statements

Section 553 of the House amendment is derived from a similar provision contained in the Senate amendment, but is modified to clarify application of a two-point test with respect to setoffs.

Amendments

2005 Amendments. Subsec. (a)(2)(B)(ii). Pub.L. 109–8, § 907(n)(1), inserted before the semicolon the following: "(except for a setoff of a kind described in section 362(b)(6), 362(b)(7), 362(b)(17), 362(b)(27), 555, 556, 559, 560, or 561)".

Subsec. (a)(3)(C). Pub.L. 109–8, § 907(n)(2), inserted before the period the following: "(except for a setoff of a kind described in section 362(b)(6), 362(b)(7), 362(b)(17), 362(b)(27), 555, 556, 559, 560, or 561)".

Subsec. (b)(1). Pub.L. 109–8, § 907(n)(3), substituted "362(b)(17), 362(b)(27), 555, 556, 559, 560, 561," for "362(b)(14)," in introductory provisions.

1994 Amendments. Subsec. (a)(1). Pub.L. 103–394, § 501(d)(19)(A), struck out "other than under section 502(b)(3) of this title" after "is disallowed".

Subsec. (b)(1). Pub.L. 103–394, § 205(b), substituted "365(h)" for "365(h)(2)".

Pub.L. 103–394, § 222(b), inserted "546(h)," after "365(h),".

Pub.L. 103–394, § 501(d)(19)(B), substituted "362(b)(14)," for "362(b)(14),,".

1990 Amendments. Subsec. (b)(1). Pub.L. 101–311 added reference to section 362(b)(14) of this title.

1984 Amendments. Subsec. (b)(1). Pub.L. 98–353, § 395, added ", 362(b)(7)" after "362(b)(6)".

Pub.L. 98–353, § 467, substituted ", 365(h)(2), or 365(i)(2)" for "or 365(h)(1)".

Effective and Applicability Provisions

2005 Acts. Amendments by Pub.L. 109–8 effective, except as otherwise provided, 180 days after April 20, 2005, and inapplicable with respect to cases commenced under Title 11 before the effective date, see Pub.L. 109–8, § 1501, set out as a note under 11 U.S.C.A. § 101.

1994 Acts. Amendments by Pub.L. 103–394 effective on Oct. 22, 1994, and not to apply with respect to cases commenced under Title 11 of the United States Code before Oct. 22, 1994, see section 702 of Pub.L. 103–394, set out as a note under section 101 of this title.

1984 Acts. Amendment by Pub.L. 98–353 effective with respect to cases filed 90 days after July 10, 1984, see section 552(a), formerly 553(a), of Pub.L. 98–353, set out as a note under section 101 of this title.

Separability of Provisions

If any provision of or amendment made by Pub.L. 103–394 or the application of such provision or amendment to any person or circumstance is held to be unconstitutional, the remaining provisions of and amendments made by Pub.L. 103–394 and the application of such provisions and amendments to any person or circumstance shall not be affected thereby, see section 701 of Pub.L. 103–394, set out as a note under section 101 of this title.

CROSS REFERENCES

Allowance of claims or interests, see 11 USCA § 502.

Applicability of this section in Chapter 9 cases, see 11 USCA § 901.

Determination of secured status, see 11 USCA § 506.

Effect of dismissal, see 11 USCA § 349.

Recovered property as exempt, see 11 USCA § 522.

Stay of pending actions in investor protection liquidation proceedings, see 15 USCA § 78eee.

LIBRARY REFERENCES

American Digest System

Bankruptcy ⟨key⟩2622, 2671 to 2680.

Key Number System Topic No. 51.

Corpus Juris Secundum

CJS Bankruptcy § 278, Parties Defendant; Sovereign Immunity.

CJS Bankruptcy § 534, Discharge as Injunction--Setoff.

CJS Bankruptcy § 589, Property Debtor Could Have Exempted Absent Transfer of that Property.

CJS Bankruptcy § 590, Recovery and Exemption of Property After Transfer Avoided.

CJS Bankruptcy § 617, Burden and Standard of Proof.

CJS Bankruptcy § 662, Effect of Prepetition or Postpetition Nature of Debts.

CJS Bankruptcy § 663, Disqualifying or Limiting Factors.

CJS Bankruptcy § 664, Procedure.

CJS Bankruptcy § 671, Preference Distinguished from Fraudulent Transfer and Setoff.

CJS Bankruptcy § 698, Transfers or Obligations Which May be Avoided.

CJS Bankruptcy § 700, Disallowance of Claims of Entities or Transferees Holding Recoverable Property.

CJS Bankruptcy § 961, Estate's or Debtor's Right of Setoff.

CJS Internal Revenue § 790, Mitigation of Effect of Limitations and Other Provisions Precluding Correction of Error.

§ 554. Abandonment of property of the estate

(a) After notice and a hearing, the trustee may abandon any property of the estate that is burdensome to the estate or that is of inconsequential value and benefit to the estate.

(b) On request of a party in interest and after notice and a hearing, the court may order the trustee to abandon any property of the estate that is burdensome to the estate or that is of inconsequential value and benefit to the estate.

(c) Unless the court orders otherwise, any property scheduled under section 521(a)(1) of this title not otherwise administered at the time of the closing of a case is abandoned to the debtor and administered for purposes of section 350 of this title.

(d) Unless the court orders otherwise, property of the estate that is not abandoned under this section and that is not administered in the case remains property of the estate.

(Pub.L. 95–598, Nov. 6, 1978, 92 Stat. 2603; Pub.L. 98–353, Title III, § 468, July 10, 1984, 98 Stat. 380; Pub.L. 99–554, Title II, § 283(p), Oct. 27, 1986, 100 Stat. 3118; Pub.L. 111–327, § 2(a)(23), Dec. 22, 2010, 124 Stat. 3560.)

HISTORICAL AND STATUTORY NOTES

Revision Notes and Legislative Reports

1978 Acts. Under this section the court may authorize the trustee to abandon any property of the estate that is burdensome to the estate or that is of inconsequential value to the estate. Abandonment may be to any party with a possessory interest in the property abandoned. In order to aid administration of the case, subsection (b) deems the court to have authorized abandonment of any property that is scheduled under section 521(1) and that is not administered before the case is closed. That property is deemed abandoned to the debtor. Subsection (c) specifies that if property is neither abandoned nor administered it remains property of the estate. Senate Report No. 95–989.

1984 Acts. Statements by Legislative Leaders, see 1984 U.S.Code Cong. and Adm.News, p. 576.

1986 Acts. House Report No. 99–764 and House Conference Report No. 99–958, see 1986 U.S.Code Cong. and Adm. News, p. 5227.

Legislative Statements

Section 554(b) is new and permits a party in interest to request the court to order the trustee to abandon property of the estate that is burdensome to the estate or that is of inconsequential value to the estate.

Amendments

2010 Amendments. Subsec. (c). Pub.L. 111–327, § 2(a)(23), struck out "521(1)" and inserted "521(a)(1)".

1986 Amendments. Subsec. (c). Pub.L. 99–554 substituted "521(1)" for "521(a)(1)".

1984 Amendments. Subsec. (a). Pub.L. 98–353, § 468(a), added "and benefit" after "value".

Subsec. (b). Pub.L. 98–353, § 468(a), added "and benefit" after "value".

Subsec. (c). Pub.L. 98–353, § 468(b), substituted "Unless the court orders otherwise, any property scheduled under section 521(a)(1) of this title not otherwise administered at the time of the closing of a case is abandoned to the debtor and administered for purposes of section 350 of this title." for "Unless the court orders otherwise, any property that is scheduled under section 521(1) of this title and that is not administered before a case is closed under section 350 of this title is deemed abandoned.".

Subsec. (d). Pub.L. 98–353, § 468(c), struck out "section (a) or (b) of" after "not abandoned under".

Effective and Applicability Provisions

1986 Acts. Amendment by Pub.L. 99–554 effective 30 days after Oct. 27, 1986, except as otherwise provided, see section 302(a) of Pub.L. 99–554, set out as a note under section 581 of Title 28, Judiciary and Judicial Procedure.

1984 Acts. Amendment by Pub.L. 98–353 effective with respect to cases filed 90 days after July 10, 1984, see section 552(a), formerly 553(a) of Pub.L. 98–353, set out as a note under section 101 of this title.

CROSS REFERENCES

Grain storage facility bankruptcies, expedited determinations, see 11 USCA § 557.

Redemption, see 11 USCA § 722.

LIBRARY REFERENCES

American Digest System

Bankruptcy ⊃3131 to 3137.

Key Number System Topic No. 51.

Corpus Juris Secundum

CJS Bankruptcy § 139, Adversary Proceedings.

CJS Bankruptcy § 261, Power to Render Declaratory Judgment.

CJS Bankruptcy § 530, Determination and Relief.

CJS Bankruptcy § 650, Deemed Abandonment.

CJS Bankruptcy § 651, Effect of Abandonment.

CJS Bankruptcy § 654, Compelled Abandonment.

CJS Bankruptcy § 658, Notice.

CJS Bankruptcy § 1106, Reopening.

§ 555. Contractual right to liquidate, terminate, or accelerate a securities contract

The exercise of a contractual right of a stockbroker, financial institution, financial participant, or securities clearing agency to cause the liquidation, termination, or acceleration of a securities contract, as defined in section 741 of this title, because of a condition of the kind specified in section 365(e)(1) of this title shall not be stayed, avoided, or otherwise limited by operation of any provision of this title or by order of a court or administrative agency in any proceeding under this title unless such order is authorized under the provisions of the Securities Investor Protection Act of 1970 or any statute administered by the Securities and Exchange Commission. As used in this section, the term "contractual right" includes a right set forth in a rule or bylaw of a derivatives clearing organization (as defined in the Commodity Exchange Act), a multilateral clearing organization (as defined in the Federal Deposit Insurance Corporation Improvement Act of 1991), a national securities exchange, a national securities association, a securities clearing agency, a contract market designated under the Commodity Exchange Act, a derivatives transaction execution facility registered under the Commodity Exchange Act, or a board of trade (as defined in the Commodity Exchange Act), or in a resolution of the governing board thereof, and a right, whether or not in writing, arising under common law, under law merchant, or by reason of normal business practice.

(Added Pub.L. 97–222, § 6(a), July 27, 1982, 96 Stat. 236; amended Pub.L. 98–353, Title III, § 469, July 10, 1984, 98 Stat. 380; Pub.L. 103–394, Title V, § 501(b)(6), (d)(20), Oct. 22, 1994, 108 Stat. 4143, 4146; Pub.L. 109–8, Title IX, § 907(g), (o)(7), Apr. 20, 2005, 119 Stat. 177, 182.)

HISTORICAL AND STATUTORY NOTES

Revision Notes and Legislative Reports

1982 Acts. House Report No. 97–420, see 1982 U.S. Code Cong. and Adm. News, p. 583.

1984 Acts. Statements by Legislative Leaders, see 1984 U.S. Code Cong. and Adm. News, p. 576.

1994 Acts. House Report No. 103–835, see 1994 U.S. Code Cong. and Adm. News, p. 3340.

2005 Acts. House Report No. 109–31(Part I), see 2005 U.S. Code Cong. and Adm. News, p. 88.

References in Text

The Securities Investor Protection Act of 1970, referred to in text, is Pub.L. 91–598, Dec. 30, 1970, 84 Stat. 1636, as amended, which is classified generally to chapter 2B–1 (section 78aaa et seq.) of Title 15, Commerce and Trade. For complete classification of this Act to the Code, see section 78aaa of Title 15 and Tables.

The Commodity Exchange Act, referred to in text, is Act Sept. 21, 1922, c. 369, 42 Stat. 998, as amended, which is classified principally to chapter 1 of Title 7, 7 U.S.C.A. § 1 et seq. For complete classification, see Short Title set out as 7 U.S.C.A. § 1 and Tables.

The Federal Deposit Insurance Corporation Improvement Act of 1991, referred to in text, is Pub.L. 102–242, Dec. 19, 1991, 105 Stat. 2236. See Tables for classification.

Amendments

2005 Amendments. Heading. Pub.L. 109–8, § 907(g)(1), rewrote the section heading, which formerly read: "**Contractual right to liquidate a securities contract**".

Pub.L. 109–8, § 907(g)(2), substituted "liquidation, termination, or acceleration" for "liquidation" in the first sentence.

Pub.L. 109–8, § 907(o)(7)(A), inserted "financial participant," after "financial institution,".

Pub.L. 109–8, § 907(o)(7)(B), rewrote the second sentence, substituting "As used in this section, the term 'contractual right' includes a right set forth in a rule or bylaw of a derivatives clearing organization (as defined in the Commodity Exchange Act), a multilateral clearing organization (as defined in the Federal Deposit Insurance Corporation Improvement Act of 1991), a national securities exchange, a national securities association, a securities clearing agency, a contract market designated under the Commodity Exchange Act, a derivatives transaction execution facility registered under the Commodity Exchange Act, or a board of trade (as defined in the Commodity Exchange Act), or in a resolution of the governing board thereof, and a right, whether or not in writing, arising under common law, under law merchant, or by reason of normal business practice." for "As used in this section, the term 'contractual right' includes a right set forth in a rule or bylaw of a national securities exchange, a national securities association, or a securities clearing agency."

1994 Amendments. Pub.L. 103–394, § 501(b)(6), substituted "section 741 of this title" for "section 741(7)".

Pub.L. 103–394, § 501(d)(20), struck out "(15 U.S.C. 78aaa et seq.)" after "Securities Investor Protection Act of 1970".

1984 Amendments. Pub.L. 98–353 added ", financial institution," after "stockbroker".

Effective and Applicability Provisions

2005 Acts. Amendments by Pub.L. 109–8 effective, except as otherwise provided, 180 days after April 20, 2005, and inapplicable with respect to cases commenced under Title 11 before the effective date, see Pub.L. 109–8, § 1501, set out as a note under 11 U.S.C.A. § 101.

1994 Acts. Amendments by Pub.L. 103–394 effective on Oct. 22, 1994, and not to apply with respect to cases commenced under Title 11 of the United States Code before Oct. 22, 1994, see section 702 of Pub.L. 103–394, set out as a note under section 101 of this title.

1984 Acts. Amendment by Pub.L. 98–353 effective with respect to cases filed 90 days after July 10, 1984, see section 552(a), formerly 553(a) of Pub.L. 98–353, set out as a note under section 101 of this title.

Separability of Provisions

If any provision of or amendment made by Pub.L. 103–394 or the application of such provision or amendment to any person or circumstance is held to be unconstitutional, the remaining provisions of and amendments made by Pub.L. 103–394 and the application of such provisions and amendments to any person or circumstance shall not be affected thereby, see section 701 of Pub.L. 103–394, set out as a note under section 101 of this title.

LIBRARY REFERENCES

American Digest System

Bankruptcy ⟷2367, 2701.

Key Number System Topic No. 51.

Corpus Juris Secundum

CJS Bankruptcy § 7, Bankruptcy Code.

CJS Bankruptcy § 663, Disqualifying or Limiting Factors.

§ 556. Contractual right to liquidate, terminate, or accelerate a commodities contract or forward contract

The contractual right of a commodity broker, financial participant, or forward contract merchant to cause the liquidation, termination, or acceleration of a commodity contract, as defined in section 761 of this title, or forward contract because of a condition of the kind specified in section 365(e)(1) of this title, and the right to a variation or maintenance margin payment received from a trustee with respect to open commodity contracts or forward contracts, shall not be stayed, avoided, or otherwise limited by operation of any provision of this title or by the order of a court in any proceeding under this title. As used in this section, the term "contractual right" includes a right set forth in a rule or bylaw of a derivatives clearing organization (as defined in the Commodity Exchange Act), a multilateral clearing organization (as defined in the Federal Deposit Insurance Corporation Improvement Act of 1991), a national securities exchange, a national securities association, a securities clearing agency, a contract market designated under the Commodity Exchange Act, a derivatives transaction execution facility registered under the Commodity Exchange Act, or a board of trade (as defined in the Commodity Exchange Act) or in a resolution of the governing board thereof and a right, whether or not evidenced in writing, arising under common law, under law merchant or by reason of normal business practice.

(Added Pub.L. 97–222, § 6(a), July 27, 1982, 96 Stat. 236; amended Pub.L. 101–311, Title II, § 205, June 25, 1990, 104 Stat. 270; Pub.L. 103–394, Title V, § 501(b)(7), Oct. 22, 1994, 108 Stat. 4143; Pub.L. 109–8, Title IX, § 907(h), (o)(8), Apr. 20, 2005, 119 Stat. 178, 182.)

HISTORICAL AND STATUTORY NOTES

Revision Notes and Legislative Reports

1982 Acts. House Report No. 97–420, see 1982 U.S. Code Cong. and Adm. News, p. 583.

1990 Acts. House Report No. 101–484, see 1990 U.S. Code Cong. and Adm. News, p. 223.

1994 Acts. House Report No. 103–835, see 1994 U.S. Code Cong. and Adm. News, p. 3340.

2005 Acts. House Report No. 109–31(Part I), see 2005 U.S. Code Cong. and Adm. News, p. 88.

References in Text

The Commodity Exchange Act, referred to in text, is Act Sept. 21, 1922, c. 369, 42 Stat. 998, as amended, which is classified principally to chapter 1 of Title 7, 7 U.S.C.A. § 1. For complete classification, see Short Title set out as 7 U.S.C.A. § 1 and Tables.

The Federal Deposit Insurance Corporation Improvement Act of 1991, referred to in text, is Pub.L. 102–242, Dec. 19, 1991, 105 Stat. 2236. See Tables for classification.

Amendments

2005 Amendments. Pub.L. 109–8, (h)(1), rewrote the section heading, which formerly read: "Contractual right to liquidate a commodities contract or forward contract".

Pub.L. 109–8, § 907(h)(2), in the first sentence, substituted "liquidation, termination, or acceleration" for "liquidation".

Pub.L. 109–8, § 907(o)(8), in the first sentence, inserted ", financial participant," after "commodity broker".

Pub.L. 109–8, § 907(h)(3), in the second sentence, substituted "As used in this section, the term 'contractual right' includes a right set forth in a rule or bylaw of a derivatives clearing organization (as defined in the Commodity Exchange Act), a multilateral clearing organization (as defined in the Federal Deposit Insurance Corporation Improvement Act of 1991), a national securities exchange, a national securities association, a securities clearing agency, a contract market designated under the Commodity Exchange Act, a derivatives transaction execution facility registered under the Commodity Exchange Act, or a board of trade (as defined in the Commodity Exchange Act) or in a resolution of the governing board thereof and a right," for "As used in this section, the term 'contractual right' includes a right set forth in a rule or bylaw of a clearing organization or contract market or in a resolution of the governing board thereof and a right,".

1994 Amendments. Pub.L. 103–394, § 501(b)(7), substituted "section 761 of this title" for "section 761(4)".

1990 Amendments. Pub.L. 101–311 added provisions relating to rights arising under common law, law merchant, or normal business practice.

Effective and Applicability Provisions

2005 Acts. Amendments by Pub.L. 109–8 effective, except as otherwise provided, 180 days after April 20, 2005, and inapplicable with respect to cases commenced under Title 11 before the effective date, see Pub.L. 109–8, § 1501, set out as a note under 11 U.S.C.A. § 101.

1994 Acts. Amendment by Pub.L. 103–394 effective on Oct. 22, 1994, and not to apply with respect to cases commenced under Title 11 of the United States Code before Oct. 22, 1994, see section 702 of Pub.L. 103–394, set out as a note under section 101 of this title.

Separability of Provisions

If any provision of or amendment made by Pub.L. 103–394 or the application of such provision or amendment to any person or circumstance is held to be unconstitutional, the remaining provisions of and amendments made by Pub.L.

103–394 and the application of such provisions and amendments to any person or circumstance shall not be affected thereby, see section 701 of Pub.L. 103–394, set out as a note under section 101 of this title.

LIBRARY REFERENCES

American Digest System

Bankruptcy ⟐2367, 2701.

Key Number System Topic No. 51.

Corpus Juris Secundum

CJS Bankruptcy § 663, Disqualifying or Limiting Factors.

§ 557. Expedited determination of interests in, and abandonment or other disposition of grain assets

(a) This section applies only in a case concerning a debtor that owns or operates a grain storage facility and only with respect to grain and the proceeds of grain. This section does not affect the application of any other section of this title to property other than grain and proceeds of grain.

(b) In this section—

(1) "grain" means wheat, corn, flaxseed, grain sorghum, barley, oats, rye, soybeans, other dry edible beans, or rice;

(2) "grain storage facility" means a site or physical structure regularly used to store grain for producers, or to store grain acquired from producers for resale; and

(3) "producer" means an entity which engages in the growing of grain.

(c)(1) Notwithstanding sections 362, 363, 365, and 554 of this title, on the court's own motion the court may, and on the request of the trustee or an entity that claims an interest in grain or the proceeds of grain the court shall, expedite the procedures for the determination of interests in and the disposition of grain and the proceeds of grain, by shortening to the greatest extent feasible such time periods as are otherwise applicable for such procedures and by establishing, by order, a timetable having a duration of not to exceed 120 days for the completion of the applicable procedure specified in subsection (d) of this section. Such time periods and such timetable may be modified by the court, for cause, in accordance with subsection (f) of this section.

(2) The court shall determine the extent to which such time periods shall be shortened, based upon—

(A) any need of an entity claiming an interest in such grain or the proceeds of grain for a prompt determination of such interest;

(B) any need of such entity for a prompt disposition of such grain;

(C) the market for such grain;

(D) the conditions under which such grain is stored;

(E) the costs of continued storage or disposition of such grain;

(F) the orderly administration of the estate;

(G) the appropriate opportunity for an entity to assert an interest in such grain; and

(H) such other considerations as are relevant to the need to expedite such procedures in the case.

(d) The procedures that may be expedited under subsection (c) of this section include—

(1) the filing of and response to—

    (A) a claim of ownership;

    (B) a proof of claim;

    (C) a request for abandonment;

    (D) a request for relief from the stay of action against property under section 362(a) of this title;

    (E) a request for determination of secured status;

    (F) a request for determination of whether such grain or the proceeds of grain—

        (i) is property of the estate;

        (ii) must be turned over to the estate; or

        (iii) may be used, sold, or leased; and

    (G) any other request for determination of an interest in such grain or the proceeds of grain;

(2) the disposition of such grain or the proceeds of grain, before or after determination of interests in such grain or the proceeds of grain, by way of—

    (A) sale of such grain;

    (B) abandonment;

    (C) distribution; or

    (D) such other method as is equitable in the case;

(3) subject to sections 701, 702, 703, 1104, 1202, and 1302 of this title, the appointment of a trustee or examiner and the retention and compensation of any professional person required to assist with respect to matters relevant to the determination of interests in or disposition of such grain or the proceeds of grain; and

(4) the determination of any dispute concerning a matter specified in paragraph (1), (2), or (3) of this subsection.

(e)(1) Any governmental unit that has regulatory jurisdiction over the operation or liquidation of the debtor or the debtor's business shall be given notice of any request made or order entered under subsection (c) of this section.

(2) Any such governmental unit may raise, and may appear and be heard on, any issue relating to grain or the proceeds of grain in a case in which a request is made, or an order is entered, under subsection (c) of this section.

(3) The trustee shall consult with such governmental unit before taking any action relating to the disposition of grain in the possession, custody, or control of the debtor or the estate.

(f) The court may extend the period for final disposition of grain or the proceeds of grain under this section beyond 120 days if the court finds that—

(1) the interests of justice so require in light of the complexity of the case; and

(2) the interests of those claimants entitled to distribution of grain or the proceeds of grain will not be materially injured by such additional delay.

(g) Unless an order establishing an expedited procedure under subsection (c) of this section, or determining any interest in or approving any disposition of grain or the proceeds of grain, is stayed pending appeal—

(1) the reversal or modification of such order on appeal does not affect the validity of any procedure, determination, or disposition that occurs before such reversal or modification, whether or not any entity knew of the pendency of the appeal; and

(2) neither the court nor the trustee may delay, due to the appeal of such order, any proceeding in the case in which such order is issued.

(h)(1) The trustee may recover from grain and the proceeds of grain the reasonable and necessary costs and expenses allowable under section 503(b) of this title attributable to preserving or disposing of grain or the proceeds of grain, but may not recover from such grain or the proceeds of grain any other costs or expenses.

(2) Notwithstanding section 326(a) of this title, the dollar amounts of money specified in such section include the value, as of the date of disposition, of any grain that the trustee distributes in kind.

(i) In all cases where the quantity of a specific type of grain held by a debtor operating a grain storage facility exceeds ten thousand bushels, such grain shall be sold by the trustee and the assets thereof distributed in accordance with the provisions of this section.

(Added Pub.L. 98–353, Title III, § 352(a), July 10, 1984, 98 Stat. 359; amended Pub.L. 99–554, Title II, § 257(p), Oct. 27, 1986, 100 Stat. 3115.)

HISTORICAL AND STATUTORY NOTES

Revision Notes and Legislative Reports

1984 Acts. Statements by Legislative Leaders, see 1984 U.S. Code Cong. and Adm.News, p. 576.

1986 Acts. House Report No. 99–764 and House Conference Report No. 99–958, see 1986 U.S.Code Cong. and Adm. News, p. 5227.

Amendments

1986 Amendments. Subsec. (d)(3). Pub.L. 99–554 added reference to section 1202 of this title.

Effective and Applicability Provisions

1986 Acts. Amendment by Pub.L. 99–554 effective 30 days after Oct. 27, 1986, but not applicable to cases commenced under this title before that date, see section 302(a)(c)(1) of

Pub.L. 99–554, set out as a note under section 581 of Title 28, Judiciary and Judicial Procedure.

1984 Acts. Section effective with respect to cases filed 90 days after July 10, 1984, see section 552(a), formerly 553(a), of Pub.L. 98–353, set out as a note under section 101 of this title.

CROSS REFERENCES

Applicability of this section in Chapter nine cases, see 11 USCA § 901.

Priorities, see 11 USCA § 507.

Rights and powers of trustee subject to right of seller who is "producer" of "grain" sold to "grain storage facility" owned or operated by debtor, as such terms are defined under this section, see 11 USCA § 546.

LIBRARY REFERENCES

American Digest System

Bankruptcy ⟅2127.1, 2204.1, 3066(1), 3137, 2437, 2897.1.

Key Number System Topic No. 51.

Corpus Juris Secundum

CJS Bankruptcy § 7, Bankruptcy Code.

CJS Bankruptcy § 307, Computation.

CJS Bankruptcy § 616, Prosecution and Defense of Proceedings; Expedited Procedures.

CJS Bankruptcy § 854, Expedited Determination of Disposition of Grain Assets.

CJS Bankruptcy § 989, Grain and Fish Claims.

§ 558. Defenses of the estate

The estate shall have the benefit of any defense available to the debtor as against any entity other than the estate, including statutes of limitation, statutes of frauds, usury, and other personal defenses. A waiver of any such defense by the debtor after the commencement of the case does not bind the estate.

(Added Pub.L. 98–353, Title III, § 470(a), July 10, 1984, 98 Stat. 380.)

HISTORICAL AND STATUTORY NOTES

Revision Notes and Legislative Reports

1984 Acts. Statements by Legislative Leaders, see 1984 U.S.Code Cong. and Adm.News, p. 576.

Effective and Applicability Provisions

1984 Acts. Section effective with respect to cases filed 90 days after July 10, 1984, see section 552(a), formerly 553(a), of Pub.L. 98–353, set out as a note under section 101 of this title.

LIBRARY REFERENCES

American Digest System

Bankruptcy ⟅2151, 2157.

Key Number System Topic No. 51.

Corpus Juris Secundum

CJS Bankruptcy § 106, Suits Against Trustee.

§ 559. Contractual right to liquidate, terminate, or accelerate a repurchase agreement

The exercise of a contractual right of a repo participant or financial participant to cause the liquidation, termination, or acceleration of a repurchase agreement because of a condition of the kind specified in section 365(e)(1) of this title shall not be stayed, avoided, or otherwise limited by operation of any provision of this title or by order of a court or administrative agency in any proceeding under this title, unless, where the debtor is a stockbroker or securities clearing agency, such order is authorized under the provisions of the Securities Investor Protection Act of 1970 or any statute administered by the Securities and Exchange Commission. In the event that a repo participant or financial participant liquidates one or more repurchase agreements with a debtor and under the terms of one or more such agreements has agreed to deliver assets subject to repurchase agreements to the debtor, any excess of the market prices received on liquidation of such assets (or if any such assets are not disposed of on the date of liquidation of such repurchase agreements, at the prices available at the time of liquidation of such repurchase agreements from a generally recognized source or the most recent closing bid quotation from such a source) over the sum of the stated repurchase prices and all expenses in connection with the liquidation of such repurchase agreements shall be deemed property of the estate, subject to the available rights of setoff. As used in this section, the term "contractual right" includes a right set forth in a rule or bylaw of a derivatives clearing organization (as defined in the Commodity Exchange Act), a multilateral clearing organization (as defined in the Federal Deposit Insurance Corporation Improvement Act of 1991), a national securities exchange, a national securities association, a securities clearing agency, a contract market designated under the Commodity Exchange Act, a derivatives transaction execution facility registered under the Commodity Exchange Act, or a board of trade (as defined in the Commodity Exchange Act) or in a resolution of the governing board thereof and a right, whether or not evidenced in writing, arising under common law, under law merchant or by reason of normal business practice.

(Added Pub.L. 98–353, Title III, § 396(a), July 10, 1984, 98 Stat. 366; amended Pub.L. 103–394, Title V, § 501(d)(21), Oct. 22, 1994, 108 Stat. 4146; Pub.L. 109–8, Title IX, § 907(i), (o)(9), Apr. 20, 2005, 119 Stat. 178, 182.)

HISTORICAL AND STATUTORY NOTES

Revision Notes and Legislative Reports

1984 Acts. Statements by Legislative Leaders, see 1984 U.S. Code Cong. and Adm. News, p. 576.

1994 Acts. House Report No. 103–835, see 1994 U.S. Code Cong. and Adm. News, p. 3340.

2005 Acts. House Report No. 109–31(Part I), see 2005 U.S. Code Cong. and Adm. News, p. 88.

References in Text

The Securities Investor Protection Act of 1970, referred to in text, is Pub. L. 91–598, Dec. 30, 1970, 84 Stat. 1636, as amended, which is classified generally to chapter 2B–1 (section 78aaa et seq.) of Title 15, Commerce and Trade. For complete classification of this Act to the Code, see section 78aaa of Title 15 and Tables.

The Commodity Exchange Act, referred to in text, is Act Sept. 21, 1922, c. 369, 42 Stat. 998, as amended, which is classified principally to chapter 1 of Title 7, 7 U.S.C.A. § 1. For complete classification, see Short Title set out as 7 U.S.C.A. § 1 and Tables.

The Federal Deposit Insurance Corporation Improvement Act of 1991, referred to in text, is Pub.L. 102–242, Dec. 19, 1991, 105 Stat. 2236. See Tables for classification.

Amendments

2005 Amendments. Pub.L. 109–8, § 907(i)(1), rewrote the section heading, which formerly read: "Contractual right to liquidate a repurchase agreement".

Pub.L. 109–8, § 907(i)(2), in the first sentence, substituted "liquidation, termination, or acceleration" for "liquidation".

Pub.L. 109–8, § 907(i)(3), in the third sentence, substituted "As used in this section, the term 'contractual right' includes a right set forth in a rule or bylaw of a derivatives clearing organization (as defined in the Commodity Exchange Act), a multilateral clearing organization (as defined in the Federal Deposit Insurance Corporation Improvement Act of 1991), a national securities exchange, a national securities association, a securities clearing agency, a contract market designated under the Commodity Exchange Act, a derivatives transaction execution facility registered under the Commodity Exchange Act, or a board of trade (as defined in the Commodity Exchange Act) or in a resolution of the governing board thereof and a right," for "As used in this section, the term 'contractual right' includes a right set forth in a rule or bylaw, applicable to each party to the repurchase agreement, of a national securities exchange, a national securities association, or a securities clearing agency, and a right,".

Pub.L. 109–8, § 907(o)(9), inserted "or financial participant" after "repo participant" each place such term appeared.

1994 Amendments. Pub.L. 103–394, § 501(d)(21), struck out "(15 U.S.C. 78aaa et seq.)" following "the Securities Investor Protection Act of 1970".

Effective and Applicability Provisions

2005 Acts. Amendments by Pub.L. 109–8 effective, except as otherwise provided, 180 days after April 20, 2005, and inapplicable with respect to cases commenced under Title 11 before the effective date, see Pub.L. 109–8, § 1501, set out as a note under 11 U.S.C.A. § 101.

1994 Acts. Amendment by Pub.L. 103–394 effective on Oct. 22, 1994, and not to apply with respect to cases commenced under Title 11 of the United States Code before Oct. 22, 1994, see section 702 of Pub.L. 103–394, set out as a note under section 101 of this title.

1984 Acts. Section effective with respect to cases filed 90 days after July 10, 1984, see section 552(a), formerly 553(a), of Pub.L. 98–353, set out as a note under section 101 of this title.

Separability of Provisions

If any provision of or amendment made by Pub.L. 103–394 or the application of such provision or amendment to any person or circumstance is held to be unconstitutional, the remaining provisions of and amendments made by Pub.L. 103–394 and the application of such provisions and amendments to any person or circumstance shall not be affected thereby, see section 701 of Pub.L. 103–394, set out as a note under section 101 of this title.

LIBRARY REFERENCES

American Digest System

Bankruptcy ⟐2367, 2701.

Key Number System Topic No. 51.

Corpus Juris Secundum

CJS Bankruptcy § 7, Bankruptcy Code.

CJS Bankruptcy § 663, Disqualifying or Limiting Factors.

§ 560. Contractual right to liquidate, terminate, or accelerate a swap agreement

The exercise of any contractual right of any swap participant or financial participant to cause the liquidation, termination, or acceleration of one or more swap agreements because of a condition of the kind specified in section 365(e)(1) of this title or to offset or net out any termination values or payment amounts arising under or in connection with the termination, liquidation, or acceleration of one or more swap agreements shall not be stayed, avoided, or otherwise limited by operation of any provision of this title or by order of a court or administrative agency in any proceeding under this title. As used in this section, the term "contractual right" includes a right set forth in a rule or bylaw of a derivatives clearing organization (as defined in the Commodity Exchange Act), a multilateral clearing organization (as defined in the Federal Deposit Insurance Corporation Improvement Act of 1991), a national securities exchange, a national securities association, a securities clearing agency, a contract market designated under the Commodity Exchange Act, a derivatives transaction execution facility registered under the Commodity Exchange Act, or a board of trade (as defined in the Commodity Exchange Act) or in a resolution of the governing board thereof and a right, whether or not evidenced in writing, arising under common law, under law merchant, or by reason of normal business practice.

(Added Pub.L. 101–311, Title I, § 106(a), June 25, 1990, 104 Stat. 268; amended Pub.L. 109–8, Title IX, § 907(j), (o)(10), Apr. 20, 2005, 119 Stat. 178, 182.)

HISTORICAL AND STATUTORY NOTES

Revision Notes and Legislative Reports

1990 Acts. House Report No. 101–484, see 1990 U.S.Code Cong. and Adm.News, p. 223.

2005 Acts. House Report No. 109–31(Part I), see 2005 U.S. Code Cong. and Adm. News, p. 88.

References in Text

The Commodity Exchange Act, referred to in text, is Act Sept. 21, 1922, c. 369, 42 Stat. 998, as amended, which is classified principally to chapter 1 of Title 7, 7 U.S.C.A. § 1.

For complete classification, see Short Title set out as 7 U.S.C.A. § 1 and Tables.

The Federal Deposit Insurance Corporation Improvement Act of 1991, referred to in text, is Pub.L. 102–242, Dec. 19, 1991, 105 Stat. 2236. See Tables for classification.

Amendments

2005 Amendments. Pub.L. 109–8, § 907(j)(1), rewrote the section heading, which formerly read: "Contractual right to terminate a swap agreement".

Pub.L. 109–8, § 907(j)(2), (3), in the first sentence, substituted "liquidation, termination, or acceleration of one or more swap agreements" for "termination of a swap agreement", and substituted "in connection with the termination, liquidation, or acceleration of one or more swap agreements" for "in connection with any swap agreement".

Pub.L. 109–8, § 907(o)(10), in the first sentence, inserted "or financial participant" after "swap participant".

Pub.L. 109–8, (j)(4), in the second sentence, substituted "As used in this section, the term 'contractual right' includes a right set forth in a rule or bylaw of a derivatives clearing organization (as defined in the Commodity Exchange Act), a multilateral clearing organization (as defined in the Federal Deposit Insurance Corporation Improvement Act of 1991), a national securities exchange, a national securities association, a securities clearing agency, a contract market designated under the Commodity Exchange Act, a derivatives transaction execution facility registered under the Commodity Exchange Act, or a board of trade (as defined in the Commodity Exchange Act) or in a resolution of the governing board thereof and a right," for "As used in this section, the term 'contractual right' includes a right, ".

Effective and Applicability Provisions

2005 Acts. Amendments by Pub.L. 109–8 effective, except as otherwise provided, 180 days after April 20, 2005, and inapplicable with respect to cases commenced under Title 11 before the effective date, see Pub.L. 109–8, § 1501, set out as a note under 11 U.S.C.A. § 101.

LIBRARY REFERENCES

American Digest System

Bankruptcy �961 2367, 2701.

Key Number System Topic No. 51.

Corpus Juris Secundum

CJS Bankruptcy § 663, Disqualifying or Limiting Factors.

§ 561. Contractual right to terminate, liquidate, accelerate, or offset under a master netting agreement and across contracts; proceedings under chapter 15

(a) Subject to subsection (b), the exercise of any contractual right, because of a condition of the kind specified in section 365(e)(1), to cause the termination, liquidation, or acceleration of or to offset or net termination values, payment amounts, or other transfer obligations arising under or in connection with one or more (or the termination, liquidation, or acceleration of one or more)—

(1) securities contracts, as defined in section 741(7);

(2) commodity contracts, as defined in section 761(4);

(3) forward contracts;

(4) repurchase agreements;

(5) swap agreements; or

(6) master netting agreements,

shall not be stayed, avoided, or otherwise limited by operation of any provision of this title or by any order of a court or administrative agency in any proceeding under this title.

(b)(1) A party may exercise a contractual right described in subsection (a) to terminate, liquidate, or accelerate only to the extent that such party could exercise such a right under section 555, 556, 559, or 560 for each individual contract covered by the master netting agreement in issue.

(2) If a debtor is a commodity broker subject to subchapter IV of chapter 7—

(A) a party may not net or offset an obligation to the debtor arising under, or in connection with, a commodity contract traded on or subject to the rules of a contract market designated under the Commodity Exchange Act or a derivatives transaction execution facility registered under the Commodity Exchange Act against any claim arising under, or in connection with, other instruments, contracts, or agreements listed in subsection (a) except to the extent that the party has positive net equity in the commodity accounts at the debtor, as calculated under such subchapter; and

(B) another commodity broker may not net or offset an obligation to the debtor arising under, or in connection with, a commodity contract entered into or held on behalf of a customer of the debtor and traded on or subject to the rules of a contract market designated under the Commodity Exchange Act or a derivatives transaction execution facility registered under the Commodity Exchange Act against any claim arising under, or in connection with, other instruments, contracts, or agreements listed in subsection (a).

(3) No provision of subparagraph (A) or (B) of paragraph (2) shall prohibit the offset of claims and obligations that arise under—

(A) a cross-margining agreement or similar arrangement that has been approved by the Commodity Futures Trading Commission or submitted to the Commodity Futures Trading Commission under paragraph (1) or (2) of section 5c(c) of the Commodity Exchange Act and has not been abrogated or rendered ineffective by the Commodity Futures Trading Commission; or

(B) any other netting agreement between a clearing organization (as defined in section 761) and another entity that has been approved by the Commodity Futures Trading Commission.

(c) As used in this section, the term "contractual right" includes a right set forth in a rule or bylaw of a derivatives clearing organization (as defined in the Commodity Exchange Act), a multilateral clearing organization (as defined in the Federal Deposit Insurance Corporation Improvement Act of 1991), a national securities exchange, a national securities association, a securities clearing agency, a contract market designated under the Commodity Exchange Act, a derivatives transaction execution facility registered under the Commodity Exchange Act, or a board of trade (as defined in the Commodity Exchange Act) or in a resolution of the governing board thereof, and a right, whether or not evidenced in writing, arising under common law, under law merchant, or by reason of normal business practice.

(d) Any provisions of this title relating to securities contracts, commodity contracts, forward contracts, repurchase agreements, swap agreements, or master netting agreements shall apply in a case under chapter 15, so that enforcement of contractual provisions of such contracts and agreements in accordance with their terms will not be stayed or otherwise limited by operation of any provision of this title or by order of a court in any case under this title, and to limit avoidance powers to the same extent as in a proceeding under chapter 7 or 11 of this title (such enforcement not to be limited based on the presence or absence of assets of the debtor in the United States).

(Added Pub.L. 109–8, Title IX, § 907(k)(1), Apr. 20, 2005, 119 Stat. 179.)

HISTORICAL AND STATUTORY NOTES

Revision Notes and Legislative Reports

2005 Acts. House Report No. 109–31(Part I), see 2005 U.S. Code Cong. and Adm. News, p. 88.

References in Text

Subchapter IV of chapter 7, referred to in subsec. (b)(2), is subchapter IV of chapter 7 of this title, 11 U.S.C.A. § 761 et seq.

The Commodity Exchange Act, referred to in subsecs. (b)(2)(A) and (c), is Act Sept. 21, 1922, c. 369, 42 Stat. 998, as amended, which is classified principally to chapter 1 of Title 7, 7 U.S.C.A. § 1 et seq. For complete classification, see Short Title set out as 7 U.S.C.A. § 1 and Tables.

Section 5c(c) of the Commodity Exchange Act, referred to in subsec. (b)(2)(A), is Act Sept. 21, 1922, c. 369, § 5c, as added and amended Dec. 21, 2000, Pub.L. 106–554, § 1(a)(5) [Title I, § 113, Title II, § 251(h)], 114 Stat. 2763, 2763A–399, 2763a–444, which is classified to 7 U.S.C.A. § 7a–2.

The Federal Deposit Insurance Corporation Improvement Act of 1991, referred to in subsec. (c), is Pub.L. 102–242, Dec. 19, 1991, 105 Stat. 2236. See Tables for classification.

Chapter 15, referred to in subsec. (d), is chapter 15 of this title, 11 U.S.C.A. § 1501 et seq.

Chapter 7 or 11 of this title, referred to in subsec. (d), is 11 U.S.C.A. § 701 et seq., or 11 U.S.C.A. 1101 et seq., respectively.

Effective and Applicability Provisions

2005 Acts. Amendments by Pub.L. 109–8 effective, except as otherwise provided, 180 days after April 20, 2005, and inapplicable with respect to cases commenced under Title 11 before the effective date, see Pub.L. 109–8, § 1501, set out as a note under 11 U.S.C.A. § 101.

LIBRARY REFERENCES

Corpus Juris Secundum

CJS Bankruptcy § 663, Disqualifying or Limiting Factors.

§ 562. Timing of damage measurement in connection with swap agreements, securities contracts, forward contracts, commodity contracts, repurchase agreements, and master netting agreements

(a) If the trustee rejects a swap agreement, securities contract (as defined in section 741), forward contract, commodity contract (as defined in section 761), repurchase agreement, or master netting agreement pursuant to section 365(a), or if a forward contract merchant, stockbroker, financial institution, securities clearing agency, repo participant, financial participant, master netting agreement participant, or swap participant liquidates, terminates, or accelerates such contract or agreement, damages shall be measured as of the earlier of—

(1) the date of such rejection; or

(2) the date or dates of such liquidation, termination, or acceleration.

(b) If there are not any commercially reasonable determinants of value as of any date referred to in paragraph (1) or (2) of subsection (a), damages shall be measured as of the earliest subsequent date or dates on which there are commercially reasonable determinants of value.

(c) For the purposes of subsection (b), if damages are not measured as of the date or dates of rejection, liquidation, termination, or acceleration, and the forward contract merchant, stockbroker, financial institution, securities clearing agency, repo participant, financial participant, master netting agreement participant, or swap participant or the trustee objects to the timing of the measurement of damages—

(1) the trustee, in the case of an objection by a forward contract merchant, stockbroker, financial institution, securities clearing agency, repo participant, financial participant, master netting agreement participant, or swap participant; or

(2) the forward contract merchant, stockbroker, financial institution, securities clearing agency, repo participant, financial participant, master netting

agreement participant, or swap participant, in the case of an objection by the trustee,

has the burden of proving that there were no commercially reasonable determinants of value as of such date or dates.

(Added Pub.L. 109–8, Title IX, § 910(a)(1), Apr. 20, 2005, 119 Stat. 184.)

HISTORICAL AND STATUTORY NOTES

Revision Notes and Legislative Reports

2005 Acts. House Report No. 109–31(Part I), see 2005 U.S. Code Cong. and Adm. News, p. 88.

Effective and Applicability Provisions

2005 Acts. Amendments by Pub.L. 109–8 effective, except as otherwise provided, 180 days after April 20, 2005, and inapplicable with respect to cases commenced under Title 11 before the effective date, see Pub.L. 109–8, § 1501, set out as a note under 11 U.S.C.A. § 101.

LIBRARY REFERENCES

Corpus Juris Secundum

CJS Bankruptcy § 7, Bankruptcy Code.

CJS Bankruptcy § 965, Termination or Rejection of Lease or Contract.

CHAPTER 7—LIQUIDATION

SUBCHAPTER I—OFFICERS AND ADMINISTRATION

Sec.
701. Interim trustee.
702. Election of trustee.
703. Successor trustee.
704. Duties of trustee.
705. Creditors' committee.
706. Conversion.
707. Dismissal of a case or conversion to a case under chapter 11 or 13.

SUBCHAPTER II—COLLECTION, LIQUIDATION, AND DISTRIBUTION OF THE ESTATE

721. Authorization to operate business.
722. Redemption.
723. Rights of partnership trustee against general partners.
724. Treatment of certain liens.
725. Disposition of certain property.
726. Distribution of property of the estate.
727. Discharge.
[728. Repealed.]

SUBCHAPTER III—STOCKBROKER LIQUIDATION

741. Definitions for this subchapter.
742. Effect of section 362 of this title in this subchapter.
743. Notice.
744. Executory contracts.
745. Treatment of accounts.
746. Extent of customer claims.
747. Subordination of certain customer claims.
748. Reduction of securities to money.
749. Voidable transfers.
750. Distribution of securities.
751. Customer name securities.
752. Customer property.
753. Stockbroker liquidation and forward contract merchants, commodity brokers, stockbrokers, financial institutions, financial participants, securities clearing agencies, swap participants, repo participants, and master netting agreement participants.

SUBCHAPTER IV—COMMODITY BROKER LIQUIDATION

761. Definitions for this subchapter.
762. Notice to the Commission and right to be heard.
763. Treatment of accounts.
764. Voidable transfers.
765. Customer instructions.
766. Treatment of customer property.
767. Commodity broker liquidation and forward contract merchants, commodity brokers, stockbrokers, financial institutions, financial participants, securities clearing agencies, swap participants, repo participants, and master netting agreement participants.

Sec.
SUBCHAPTER V—CLEARING BANK LIQUIDATION

781. Definitions.
782. Selection of trustee.
783. Additional powers of trustee.
784. Right to be heard.

HISTORICAL AND STATUTORY NOTES

Amendments

2005 Amendments. Pub.L. 109–8, Title I, § 102(k), Apr. 20, 2005, 119 Stat. 35, rewrote item 707, which formerly read: "Sec. 707. Dismissal.".

Pub.L. 109–8, Title VII, § 719(b)(2), Apr. 20, 2005, 119 Stat. 133, struck out item 728, which formerly read: "728. Special tax provisions.".

Pub.L. 109–8, Title IX, § 907(p)(2), Apr. 20, 2005, 119 Stat. 182, added items 753 and 767.

2000 Amendments. Pub.L. 106–554, § 1(a)(5) [Title I, § 112(d)], Dec. 21, 2000, 114 Stat. 2763, 2763A–396, added items relating to subchapter V and sections 781 to 784 of this title.

1984 Amendments. Pub.L. 98–353, Title III, § 471, July 10, 1984, 98 Stat. 380, substituted "Successor" for "Succesor" in item 703.

Effective and Applicability Provisions

2005 Acts. Amendments by Pub.L. 109–8 effective, except as otherwise provided, 180 days after April 20, 2005, and inapplicable with respect to cases commenced under Title 11 before the effective date, see Pub.L. 109–8, § 1501, set out as a note under 11 U.S.C.A. § 101.

CROSS REFERENCES

Amount received for claim through liquidation under this chapter as standard for confirmation requirement in—

Chapter eleven cases, see 11 USCA § 1129.

Chapter thirteen cases, see 11 USCA § 1325.

Chapter twelve cases, see 11 USCA § 1225.

Amount received for claim through liquidation under this chapter as standard for discharge requirement in—

Chapter thirteen cases, see 11 USCA § 1328.

Chapter twelve cases, see 11 USCA § 1228.

Applicability of income tax provisions to cases under this chapter, see 26 USCA § 1398.

Certain provisions respecting commodity brokers under this chapter, see 7 USCA § 24.

Chapters 1, 3 and 5 of this title applicable in case under this chapter, see 11 USCA § 103.

Commencement of involuntary cases, see 11 USCA § 303.

Conversion to this chapter from—

Chapter eleven, see 11 USCA § 1112.

Chapter thirteen, see 11 USCA § 1307.

Chapter twelve, see 11 USCA § 1208.

Debtor's duty under this chapter to file statement of intentions with respect to schedule of assets and liabilities, see 11 USCA § 521.

Denial of discharge under this chapter as affecting operation of injunction, see 11 USCA § 524.

Determination of net worth of person subject to liability for termination of single-employer plans includes improper transfers of assets in cases under this chapter, see 29 USCA § 1362.

Distribution of certain proceeds and property under this chapter as requirement for confirmation of plan, see 11 USCA § 1173.

Duration of automatic stay in case concerning an individual under this chapter, see 11 USCA § 362.

Duties of trustee in investor protection liquidation proceedings same as under this chapter, see 15 USCA § 78fff–1.

Duties of United States trustees, see 28 USCA § 586.

Effect of confirmation, see 11 USCA § 1141.

Effect of distribution other than under this title, see 11 USCA § 508.

Eligibility to serve as trustee, see 11 USCA § 321.

Employment of professional persons, see 11 USCA § 327.

Executory contracts and unexpired leases, see 11 USCA § 365.

Filing fees, see 28 USCA § 1930.

Limitation on compensation of trustee, see 11 USCA § 326.

Liquidation in railroad reorganization case as if under this chapter, see 11 USCA § 1174.

Meetings of creditors and equity security holders and oral examination of debtor, see 11 USCA § 341.

Objection to allowance of claims by creditor of partner in partnership that is debtor under this chapter, see 11 USCA § 502.

Payment of trustee from filing fee, see 11 USCA § 330.

Persons required to make returns of income under this chapter, see 26 USCA § 6012.

Persons who may be debtors under this chapter, see 11 USCA § 109.

Property of estate in cases converted to this chapter from—

Chapter thirteen, see 11 USCA § 1306.

Chapter twelve, see 11 USCA § 1207.

Recommendation by trustee of conversion from chapter 11 to this chapter, see 11 USCA § 1106.

Special tax provisions, see 11 USCA § 346.

Stay of action against codebtor in cases converted to this chapter from—

Chapter thirteen, see 11 USCA § 1301.

Chapter twelve, see 11 USCA § 1201.

Transfers enabling creditor to receive more than under this chapter, see 11 USCA § 547.

Treatment of debtor's estate in cases under this chapter as taxpayer for certain income tax purposes, see 26 USCA § 108.

Unclaimed property, see 11 USCA § 347.

SUBCHAPTER I—OFFICERS AND ADMINISTRATION

CROSS REFERENCES

Applicability of this subchapter in investor protection liquidation proceedings, see 15 USCA § 78fff.

Subchapter applicable only in case under this chapter, see 11 USCA § 103.

§ 701. Interim trustee

(a)(1) Promptly after the order for relief under this chapter, the United States trustee shall appoint one disinterested person that is a member of the panel of private trustees established under section 586(a)(1) of title 28 or that is serving as trustee in the case immediately before the order for relief under this chapter to serve as interim trustee in the case.

(2) If none of the members of such panel is willing to serve as interim trustee in the case, then the United States trustee may serve as interim trustee in the case.

(b) The service of an interim trustee under this section terminates when a trustee elected or designated under section 702 of this title to serve as trustee in the case qualifies under section 322 of this title.

(c) An interim trustee serving under this section is a trustee in a case under this title.

(Pub.L. 95–598, Nov. 6, 1978, 92 Stat. 2604; Pub.L. 99–554, Title II, § 215, Oct. 27, 1986, 100 Stat. 3100.)

HISTORICAL AND STATUTORY NOTES

Revision Notes and Legislative Reports

1978 Acts. This section requires the court to appoint an interim trustee. The appointment must be made from the panel of private trustees established and maintained by the Director of the Administrative Office under proposed 28 U.S.C. 604(e).

Subsection (a) requires the appointment of an interim trustee to be made promptly after the order for relief, unless a trustee is already serving in the case, such as before a conversion from a reorganization to a liquidation case.

Subsection (b) specifies that the appointment of an interim trustee expires when the permanent trustee is elected or designated under section 702.

Subsection (c) makes clear that an interim trustee is a trustee in a case under the bankruptcy code.

Subsection (d) provides that in a commodity broker case where speed is essential the interim trustee must be appointed by noon of the business day immediately following the order for relief. Senate Report No. 95–989.

1986 Acts. House Report No. 99–764 and House Conference Report No. 99–958, see 1986 U.S.Code Cong. and Adm. News, p. 5227.

Legislative Statements

The House amendment deletes section 701(d) of the Senate amendment. It is anticipated that the Rules of Bankruptcy Procedure will require the appointment of an interim trustee at the earliest practical moment in commodity broker bankruptcies, but no later than noon of the day after the date of the filing of the petition, due to the volatility of such cases.

Amendments

1986 Amendments. Subsec. (a). Pub.L. 99–554, § 215, designated existing provisions as par. (1), and, in par. (1) as so designated, substituted "the United States trustee shall appoint" for "the court shall appoint", "586(a)(1)" for "604(f)", and "that is serving" for "that was serving", and added par. (2).

Effective and Applicability Provisions

1986 Acts. Amendment by Pub.L. 99–554 effective 30 days after Oct. 27, 1986, except as otherwise provided for, see section 302(a) of Pub.L. 99–554, set out as a note under section 581 of Title 28, Judiciary and Judicial Procedure.

Amendment by Pub.L. 99–554, § 215, not to become effective in or with respect to certain specified judicial districts until, or apply to cases while pending in such district before, the expiration of the 270-day period beginning 30 days after Oct. 27, 1986, or of the 30-day period beginning on the date the Attorney General certifies under section 303 of Pub.L. 99–554 the region specified in a paragraph of section 581(a) of Title 28, as amended by section 111(a) of Pub.L. 99–554, that includes such district, whichever occurs first, see section 302(d)(1) of Pub.L. 99–554, set out as a note under section 581 of Title 28.

Amendment by Pub.L. 99–554, § 215, not to become effective in or with respect to certain specified judicial districts until, or apply to cases while pending in such district before, the expiration of the 2-year period beginning 30 days after Oct. 27, 1986, or of the 30-day period beginning on the date the Attorney General certifies under section 303 of Pub.L. 99–554 the region specified in a paragraph of section 581(a) of Title 28, as amended by section 111(a) of Pub.L. 99–554, that includes such district, whichever occurs first, see section 302(d)(2) of Pub.L. 99–554, set out as a note under section 581 of Title 28.

Amendment by Pub.L. 99–554, § 215, not to become effective in or with respect to judicial districts established for the States of Alabama and North Carolina until, or apply to cases while pending in such district before, such district elects to be included in a bankruptcy region established in section 581(a) of Title 28, as amended by section 111(a) of Pub.L. 99–554, or Oct. 1, 2002, whichever occurs first, and, except as otherwise provided, with respect to cases under chapters 7, 11, 12, and 13 of Title 11 commenced before 30 days after Oct. 27, 1986, and pending in a judicial district in the States of Alabama or North Carolina before any election made under section 302(d)(3)(A) of Pub.L. 99–554 by such district becomes effective or Oct. 1, 2002, whichever occurs first, amendments by Pub.L. 99–554 not to apply until Oct. 1, 2003, or the expiration of the 1-year period beginning on the date such election becomes effective, whichever occurs first, and further, in any judicial district in Alabama or North Carolina not making the election described in section 302(d)(3)(A) of Pub.L. 99–554, any person appointed under regulations issued by the Judicial Conference to administer estates in cases under Title 11 authorized to establish, etc., a panel of private trustees, and to supervise cases and trustees in cases under chapters 7, 11, 12 and 13 of Title 11, until amendments by sections 201 to 231 of Pub.L. 99–554 effective in such district, see section 302(d)(3)(A) to (F), (H), and (I) of Pub.L. 99–554, set out as a note under section 581 of Title 28.

Amendment by Pub.L. 99–554, § 215, except as otherwise provided, with respect to cases under chapters 7, 11, 12, and 13 of Title 11 commenced before 30 days after Oct. 27, 1986, and pending in a judicial district referred to in section 581(a) of Title 28, as amended by section 111(a) of Pub.L. 99–554, for which a United States trustee is not authorized before 30 days after Oct. 27, 1986 to be appointed, not applicable until the expiration of the 3-year period beginning on Oct. 27, 1986 or of the 1-year period beginning on the date the Attorney

General certifies under section 303 of Pub.L. 99–554 the region specified in a paragraph of such section 581(a) that includes, such district, whichever occurs first, see section 302(e)(1)(2) of Pub.L. 99–554, set out as a note under section 581 of Title 28.

CROSS REFERENCES

Appointment of interim trustee after commencement of involuntary case, see 11 USCA § 303.

Effect of conversion, see 11 USCA § 348.

Grain storage facility bankruptcies, expedited appointment of trustee, see 11 USCA § 557.

Qualification of trustee, see 11 USCA § 322.

LIBRARY REFERENCES

American Digest System

Bankruptcy ⊕3002.

Key Number System Topic No. 51.

Corpus Juris Secundum

CJS Bankruptcy § 7, Bankruptcy Code.

CJS Bankruptcy § 46, Service as Bankruptcy Trustee.

CJS Bankruptcy § 50, Chapter 7 Proceedings.

CJS Bankruptcy § 55, Eligibility to Serve as Trustee or Examiner.

CJS Bankruptcy § 56, Eligibility to Serve as Trustee or Examiner--Disinterestedness Requirement.

CJS Bankruptcy § 62, Appointment of Interim Trustee.

CJS Bankruptcy § 81, Election of Successor Trustee.

CJS Bankruptcy § 109, Termination of Service.

§ 702. Election of trustee

(a) A creditor may vote for a candidate for trustee only if such creditor—

(1) holds an allowable, undisputed, fixed, liquidated, unsecured claim of a kind entitled to distribution under section 726(a)(2), 726(a)(3), 726(a)(4), 752(a), 766(h), or 766(i) of this title;

(2) does not have an interest materially adverse, other than an equity interest that is not substantial in relation to such creditor's interest as a creditor, to the interest of creditors entitled to such distribution; and

(3) is not an insider.

(b) At the meeting of creditors held under section 341 of this title, creditors may elect one person to serve as trustee in the case if election of a trustee is requested by creditors that may vote under subsection (a) of this section, and that hold at least 20 percent in amount of the claims specified in subsection (a)(1) of this section that are held by creditors that may vote under subsection (a) of this section.

(c) A candidate for trustee is elected trustee if—

(1) creditors holding at least 20 percent in amount of the claims of a kind specified in subsection (a)(1)

of this section that are held by creditors that may vote under subsection (a) of this section vote; and

(2) such candidate receives the votes of creditors holding a majority in amount of claims specified in subsection (a)(1) of this section that are held by creditors that vote for a trustee.

(d) If a trustee is not elected under this section, then the interim trustee shall serve as trustee in the case.

(Pub.L. 95–598, Nov. 6, 1978, 92 Stat. 2604; Pub.L. 97–222, § 7, July 27, 1982, 96 Stat. 237; Pub.L. 98–353, Title III, § 472, July 10, 1984, 98 Stat. 380.)

HISTORICAL AND STATUTORY NOTES

Revision Notes and Legislative Reports

1978 Acts. Subsection (a) of this section specifies which creditors may vote for a trustee. Only a creditor that holds an allowable, undisputed, fixed, liquidated, unsecured claim that is not entitled to priority, that does not have an interest materially adverse to the interest of general unsecured creditors, and that is not an insider may vote for a trustee. The phrase "materially adverse" is currently used in the Rules of Bankruptcy Procedure, rule 207(d). The application of the standard requires a balancing of various factors, such as the nature of the adversity. A creditor with a very small equity position would not be excluded from voting solely because he holds a small equity in the debtor. The Rules of Bankruptcy Procedure also currently provide for temporary allowance of claims, and will continue to do so for the purposes of determining who is eligible to vote under this provision.

Subsection (b) permits creditors at the meeting of creditors to elect one person to serve as trustee in the case. Creditors holding at least 20 percent in amount of the claims specified in the preceding paragraph must request election before creditors may elect a trustee. Subsection (c) specifies that a candidate for trustee is elected trustee if creditors holding at least 20 percent in amount of those claims actually vote, and if the candidate receives a majority in amount of votes actually cast.

Subsection (d) specifies that if a trustee is not elected, then the interim trustee becomes the permanent trustee and serves in the case permanently. Senate Report No. 95–989.

1982 Acts. House Report No. 97–420, see 1982 U.S.Code Cong. and Adm.News, p. 583.

1984 Acts. Statements by Legislative Leaders, see 1984 U.S.Code Cong. and Adm.News, p. 576.

Legislative Statements

The House amendment adopts section 702(a)(2) of the Senate amendment. An insubstantial equity interest does not disqualify a creditor from voting for a candidate for trustee.

Amendments

1984 Amendments. Subsec. (b). Pub.L. 98–353, § 472(a), inserted "held" after "meeting of creditors".

Subsec. (c)(1). Pub.L. 98–353, § 472(b)(1), inserted "of a kind" after "claims".

Subsec. (c)(2). Pub.L. 98–353, § 472(b)(2), substituted "for a trustee" for "for trustee".

Subsec. (d). Pub.L. 98–353, § 472(c), substituted "this section" for "subsection (c) of this section".

1982 Amendments. Subsec. (a)(1). Pub.L. 97–222 substituted "726(a)(4), 752(a), 766(h), or 766(i)" for "or 726(a)(4)".

Effective and Applicability Provisions

1984 Acts. Amendment by Pub.L. 98–353 effective with respect to cases filed 90 days after July 10, 1984, see section 552(a), formerly 553(a), of Pub.L. 98–353, set out as a note under section 101 of this title.

CROSS REFERENCES

Grain storage facility bankruptcies, expedited appointment of trustee, see 11 USCA § 557.

Qualification of trustee, see 11 USCA § 322.

Time for bringing action, see 11 USCA § 546.

LIBRARY REFERENCES

American Digest System

Bankruptcy ⚘3004.1, 3005.

Key Number System Topic No. 51.

Corpus Juris Secundum

CJS Bankruptcy § 56, Eligibility to Serve as Trustee or Examiner--Disinterestedness Requirement.

CJS Bankruptcy § 62, Appointment of Interim Trustee.

CJS Bankruptcy § 78, Eligibility of Creditors to Vote.

CJS Bankruptcy § 79, Solicitation and Voting of Proxies.

CJS Bankruptcy § 80, Report to Court; Disputed Election.

CJS Bankruptcy § 82, Meeting of Creditors and Election Procedures.

CJS Bankruptcy § 109, Termination of Service.

CJS Bankruptcy § 809, Voting and Elections.

CJS Bankruptcy § 1129, Appointment of Creditors" and Equity Security Holders" Committees.

§ 703. Successor trustee

(a) If a trustee dies or resigns during a case, fails to qualify under section 322 of this title, or is removed under section 324 of this title, creditors may elect, in the manner specified in section 702 of this title, a person to fill the vacancy in the office of trustee.

(b) Pending election of a trustee under subsection (a) of this section, if necessary to preserve or prevent loss to the estate, the United States trustee may appoint an interim trustee in the manner specified in section 701(a).

(c) If creditors do not elect a successor trustee under subsection (a) of this section or if a trustee is needed in a case reopened under section 350 of this title, then the United States trustee—

(1) shall appoint one disinterested person that is a member of the panel of private trustees established under section 586(a)(1) of title 28 to serve as trustee in the case; or

(2) may, if none of the disinterested members of such panel is willing to serve as trustee, serve as trustee in the case.

(Pub.L. 95–598, Nov. 6, 1978, 92 Stat. 2605; Pub.L. 98–353, Title III, § 473, July 10, 1984, 98 Stat. 381; Pub.L. 99–554, Title II, § 216, Oct. 27, 1986, 100 Stat. 3100.)

HISTORICAL AND STATUTORY NOTES

Revision Notes and Legislative Reports

1978 Acts. If the office of trustee becomes vacant during the case, this section makes provision for the selection of a successor trustee. The office might become vacant through death, resignation, removal, failure to qualify under section 322 by posting bond, or the reopening of a case. If it does, creditors may elect a successor in the same manner as they may elect a trustee under the previous section. Pending the election of a successor, the court may appoint an interim trustee in the usual manner if necessary to preserve or prevent loss to the estate. If creditors do not elect a successor, or if a trustee is needed in a reopened case, then the court appoints a disinterested member of the panel of private trustees to serve. Senate Report No. 95–989.

1984 Acts. Statements by Legislative Leaders, see 1984 U.S.Code Cong. and Adm.News, p. 576.

1986 Acts. House Report No. 99–764 and House Conference Report No. 99–958, see 1986 U.S.Code Cong. and Adm. News, p. 5227.

Amendments

1986 Amendments. Subsec. (b). Pub.L. 99–554, § 216, substituted "the United States trustee may appoint" for "the court may appoint" and "manner specified in section 701(a)" for "manner and subject to the provisions of section 701 of this title".

Subsec. (c). Pub.L. 99–554, § 216, substituted "this section or" for "this section, or", "then the United States trustee" for "then the court", designated part of existing provisions as par. (1), and, in par. (1) as so designated, substituted "586(a)(1)" for "604(f)", "in the case; or" for "in the case.", and added par. (2).

1984 Amendments. Subsec. (b). Pub.L. 98–353 substituted "and subject to the provisions of section 701 of this title" for "specified in section 701(a) of this title. Sections 701(b) and 701(c) of this title apply to such interim trustee".

Effective and Applicability Provisions

1986 Acts. Amendment by Pub.L. 99–554 effective 30 days after Oct. 27, 1986, except as otherwise provided for, see section 302(a) of Pub.L. 99–554, set out as a note under section 581 of Title 28, Judiciary and Judicial Procedure.

Amendment by Pub.L. 99–554, § 216, not to become effective in or with respect to certain specified judicial districts until, or apply to cases while pending in such district before, the expiration of the 270-day period beginning 30 days after Oct. 27, 1986, or of the 30-day period beginning on the date the Attorney General certifies under section 303 of Pub.L. 99–554 the region specified in a paragraph of section 581(a) of Title 28, as amended by section 111(a) of Pub.L. 99–554, that includes such district, whichever occurs first, see section 302(d)(1) of Pub.L. 99–554, set out as a note under section 581 of Title 28.

Amendment by Pub.L. 99–554, § 216, not to become effective in or with respect to certain specified judicial districts until, or apply to cases while pending in such district before, the expiration of the 2-year period beginning 30 days after Oct. 27, 1986, or of the 30-day period beginning on the date the Attorney General certifies under section 303 of Pub.L.

99–554 the region specified in a paragraph of section 581(a) of Title 28, as amended by section 111(a) of Pub.L. 99–554, that includes such district, whichever occurs first, see section 302(d)(2) of Pub.L. 99–554, set out as a note under section 581 of Title 28.

Amendment by Pub.L. 99–554, § 216, not to become effective in or with respect to judicial districts established for the States of Alabama and North Carolina until, or apply to cases while pending in such district before, such district elects to be included in a bankruptcy region established in section 581(a) of Title 28, as amended by section 111(a) of Pub.L. 99–554, or Oct. 1, 2002, whichever occurs first, and, except as otherwise provided, with respect to cases under chapters 7, 11, 12, and 13 of Title 11 commenced before 30 days after Oct. 27, 1986, and pending in a judicial district in the States of Alabama or North Carolina before any election made under section 302(d)(3)(A) of Pub.L. 99–554 by such district becomes effective or Oct. 1, 2002, whichever occurs first, amendments by Pub.L. 99–554 not to apply until Oct. 1, 2003, or the expiration of the 1-year period beginning on the date such election becomes effective, whichever occurs first, and further, in any judicial district in Alabama or North Carolina not making the election described in section 302(d)(3)(A) of Pub.L. 99–554, any person appointed under regulations issued by the Judicial Conference to administer estates in cases under Title 11 authorized to establish, etc., a panel of private trustees, and to supervise cases and trustees in cases under chapters 7, 11, 12, and 13 of Title 11, until amendments by sections 201 to 231 of Pub.L. 99–554 effective in such district, see section 302(d)(3)(A) to (F), (H), and (I) of Pub.L. 99–554, set out as a note under section 581 of Title 28.

Amendment by Pub.L. 99–554, § 216, except as otherwise provided, with respect to cases under chapters 7, 11, 12, and 13 of Title 11 commenced before 30 days after Oct. 27, 1986, and pending in a judicial district referred to in section 581(a) of Title 28, as amended by section 111(a) of Pub.L. 99–554, for which a United States trustee is not authorized before 30 days after Oct. 27, 1986 to be appointed, not applicable until the expiration of the 3-year period beginning on Oct. 27, 1986, or of the 1-year period beginning on the date the Attorney General certifies under section 303 of Pub.L. 99–554 the region specified in a paragraph of such section 581(a) that includes, such district, whichever occurs first, see section 302(e)(1), (2) of Pub.L. 99–554, set out as a note under section 581 of Title 28.

1984 Acts. Amendment by Pub.L. 98–353 effective with respect to cases filed 90 days after July 10, 1984, see section 552(a), formerly 553(a), of Pub.L. 98–353, set out as a note under section 101 of this title.

CROSS REFERENCES

Effect of vacancy in office of trustee, see 11 USCA § 325.

Grain storage facility bankruptcies, expedited appointment of trustee, see 11 USCA § 557.

Qualification of trustee, see 11 USCA § 322.

LIBRARY REFERENCES

American Digest System

Bankruptcy ⊕3001, 3002, 3004.1, 3007.

Key Number System Topic No. 51.

Corpus Juris Secundum

CJS Bankruptcy § 46, Service as Bankruptcy Trustee.

CJS Bankruptcy § 50, Chapter 7 Proceedings.

CJS Bankruptcy § 56, Eligibility to Serve as Trustee or Examiner--Disinterestedness Requirement.

CJS Bankruptcy § 62, Appointment of Interim Trustee.

CJS Bankruptcy § 63, Appointment of Trustee in Re-opened Case.

CJS Bankruptcy § 81, Election of Successor Trustee.

§ 704. Duties of trustee

(a) The trustee shall—

(1) collect and reduce to money the property of the estate for which such trustee serves, and close such estate as expeditiously as is compatible with the best interests of parties in interest;

(2) be accountable for all property received;

(3) ensure that the debtor shall perform his intention as specified in section 521(a)(2)(B) of this title;

(4) investigate the financial affairs of the debtor;

(5) if a purpose would be served, examine proofs of claims and object to the allowance of any claim that is improper;

(6) if advisable, oppose the discharge of the debtor;

(7) unless the court orders otherwise, furnish such information concerning the estate and the estate's administration as is requested by a party in interest;

(8) if the business of the debtor is authorized to be operated, file with the court, with the United States trustee, and with any governmental unit charged with responsibility for collection or determination of any tax arising out of such operation, periodic reports and summaries of the operation of such business, including a statement of receipts and disbursements, and such other information as the United States trustee or the court requires;

(9) make a final report and file a final account of the administration of the estate with the court and with the United States trustee;

(10) if with respect to the debtor there is a claim for a domestic support obligation, provide the applicable notice specified in subsection (c);

(11) if, at the time of the commencement of the case, the debtor (or any entity designated by the debtor) served as the administrator (as defined in section 3 of the Employee Retirement Income Security Act of 1974) of an employee benefit plan, continue to perform the obligations required of the administrator; and

(12) use all reasonable and best efforts to transfer patients from a health care business that is in the process of being closed to an appropriate health care business that—

(A) is in the vicinity of the health care business that is closing;

(B) provides the patient with services that are substantially similar to those provided by the health care business that is in the process of being closed; and

(C) maintains a reasonable quality of care.

(b)(1) With respect to a debtor who is an individual in a case under this chapter—

(A) the United States trustee (or the bankruptcy administrator, if any) shall review all materials filed by the debtor and, not later than 10 days after the date of the first meeting of creditors, file with the court a statement as to whether the debtor's case would be presumed to be an abuse under section 707(b); and

(B) not later than 7 days after receiving a statement under subparagraph (A), the court shall provide a copy of the statement to all creditors.

(2) The United States trustee (or bankruptcy administrator, if any) shall, not later than 30 days after the date of filing a statement under paragraph (1), either file a motion to dismiss or convert under section 707(b) or file a statement setting forth the reasons the United States trustee (or the bankruptcy administrator, if any) does not consider such a motion to be appropriate, if the United States trustee (or the bankruptcy administrator, if any) determines that the debtor's case should be presumed to be an abuse under section 707(b) and the product of the debtor's current monthly income, multiplied by 12 is not less than—

(A) in the case of a debtor in a household of 1 person, the median family income of the applicable State for 1 earner; or

(B) in the case of a debtor in a household of 2 or more individuals, the highest median family income of the applicable State for a family of the same number or fewer individuals.

(c)(1) In a case described in subsection (a)(10) to which subsection (a)(10) applies, the trustee shall—

(A)(i) provide written notice to the holder of the claim described in subsection (a)(10) of such claim and of the right of such holder to use the services of the State child support enforcement agency established under sections 464 and 466 of the Social Security Act for the State in which such holder resides, for assistance in collecting child support during and after the case under this title;

(ii) include in the notice provided under clause (i) the address and telephone number of such State child support enforcement agency; and

(iii) include in the notice provided under clause (i) an explanation of the rights of such holder to payment of such claim under this chapter;

(B)(i) provide written notice to such State child support enforcement agency of such claim; and

(ii) include in the notice provided under clause (i) the name, address, and telephone number of such holder; and

(C) at such time as the debtor is granted a discharge under section 727, provide written notice to such holder and to such State child support enforcement agency of—

(i) the granting of the discharge;

(ii) the last recent known address of the debtor;

(iii) the last recent known name and address of the debtor's employer; and

(iv) the name of each creditor that holds a claim that—

(I) is not discharged under paragraph (2), (4), or (14A) of section 523(a); or

(II) was reaffirmed by the debtor under section 524(c).

(2)(A) The holder of a claim described in subsection (a)(10) or the State child support enforcement agency of the State in which such holder resides may request from a creditor described in paragraph (1)(C)(iv) the last known address of the debtor.

(B) Notwithstanding any other provision of law, a creditor that makes a disclosure of a last known address of a debtor in connection with a request made under subparagraph (A) shall not be liable by reason of making such disclosure.

(Pub.L. 95–598, Nov. 6, 1978, 92 Stat. 2605; Pub.L. 98–353, Title III, §§ 311(a), 474, July 10, 1984, 98 Stat. 355, 381; Pub.L. 99–554, Title II, § 217, Oct. 27, 1986, 100 Stat. 3100; Pub.L. 109–8, Title I, § 102(c), Title II, § 219(a), Title IV, § 446(b), Title XI, § 1105(a), Apr. 20, 2005, 119 Stat. 32, 55, 118, 192; Pub.L. 111–16, § 2(7), May 7, 2009, 123 Stat. 1607; Pub.L. 111–327, § 2(a)(24), Dec. 22, 2010, 124 Stat. 3560.)

HISTORICAL AND STATUTORY NOTES
Revision Notes and Legislative Reports

1978 Acts. The essential duties of the trustee are enumerated in this section. Others, or elaborations on these, may be prescribed by the Rules of Bankruptcy Procedure to the extent not inconsistent with those prescribed by this section. The duties are derived from section 47a of the Bankruptcy Act [section 75(a) of former Title 11].

The trustee's principal duty is to collect and reduce to money the property of the estate for which he serves, and to close up the estate as expeditiously as is compatible with the best interests of parties in interest. He must be accountable for all property received, and must investigate the financial affairs of the debtor. If a purpose would be served (such as if there are assets that will be distributed), the trustee is required to examine proofs of claims and object to the allowance of any claim that is improper. If advisable, the trustee must oppose the discharge of the debtor, which is for the benefit of general unsecured creditors whom the trustee represents.

The trustee is responsible to furnish such information concerning the estate and its administration as is requested by a party in interest. If the business of the debtor is authorized to be operated, then the trustee is required to file with

governmental units charged with the responsibility for collection or determination of any tax arising out of the operation of the business periodic reports and summaries of the operation, including a statement of receipts and disbursements, and such other information as the court requires. He is required to give constructive notice of the commencement of the case in the manner specified under section 342(b). Senate Report No. 95–989.

1984 Acts. Statements by Legislative Leaders, see 1984 U.S.Code Cong. and Adm.News, p. 576.

1986 Acts. House Report No. 99–764 and House Conference Report No. 99–958, see 1986 U.S.Code Cong. and Adm. News, p. 5227.

2005 Acts. House Report No. 109–31(Part I), see 2005 U.S. Code Cong. and Adm. News, p. 88.

Legislative Statements

Section 704(8) of the Senate amendment is deleted in the House amendment. Trustees should give constructive notice of the commencement of the case in the manner specified under section 549(c) of title 11.

References in Text

Section 3 of the Employee Retirement Income Security Act of 1974, referred to in subsec. (a)(11), is Pub.L. 93–406, Title I, § 3, Sept. 2, 1974, 88 Stat. 833, which is classified to 29 U.S.C.A. § 1002.

Section 464 of the Social Security Act, referred to in subsec. (c)(1)(A)(i), is Act Aug. 14, 1935, c. 531, Title IV, § 464, as added Aug. 13, 1981, Pub.L. 97–35, Title XXIII, § 2331(a), 95 Stat. 860, and amended, which is classified to 42 U.S.C.A. § 664.

Section 466 of the Social Security Act, referred to in subsec. (c)(1)(A)(i), is Act Aug. 14, 1935, c. 531, Title IV, § 466, as added Aug. 16, 1984, Pub.L. 98–378, § 3(b), 98 Stat. 1306, and amended, which is classified to 42 U.S.C.A. § 666.

Amendments

2010 Amendments. Subsec. (a)(3). Pub.L. 111–327, § 2(a)(24), struck out "521(2)(B)" and inserted "521(a)(2)(B)".

2009 Amendments. Subsec. (b)(1)(B). Pub.L. 111–16, § 2(7), struck out "5 days" and inserted "7 days".

2005 Amendments. Subsec. (a). Pub.L. 109–8, § 102(c)(1), inserted "(a)" before "The trustee shall—".

Subsec. (a)(8). Pub.L. 109–8, § 219(a)(1)(A), struck out 'and' at the end of par. (8).

Subsec. (a)(9). Pub.L. 109–8, § 219(a)(1)(B), substituted a semicolon for the period at the end of par. (9).

Subsec. (a)(10). Pub.L. 109–8, § 219(a)(1)(C), added par. (10).

Pub.L. 109–8, § 446(b)(1), struck "and" at the end of par. (10).

Subsec. (a)(11). Pub.L. 109–8, § 446(b)(2), added par. (11).

Subsec. (a)(12). Pub.L. 109–8, § 1105(a), added par. (12).

Subsec. (b). Pub.L. 109–8, § 102(c)(2), inserted subsec. (b).

Subsec. (c). Pub.L. 109–8, § 219(a)(2), added subsec. (c).

1986 Amendments. Par. (8). Pub.L. 99–554, § 217(1), substituted "with the court, with the United States trustee, and with" for "with the court and with" and "information as the United States trustee or the court" for "information as the court".

Par. (9). Pub.L. 99–554, § 217(2), substituted "with the court and with the United States trustee." for "with the court.".

1984 Amendments. Par. (1). Pub.L. 98–353, § 474, substituted "close such estate" for "close up such estate".

Par. (3). Pub.L. 98–353, § 311(a)(2), added par. (3). Former par. (3) was redesignated as (4).

Pars. (4) to (9). Pub.L. 98–353, § 311(a)(1), redesignated pars. (3) to (8) as (4) to (9), respectively.

Effective and Applicability Provisions

2009 Acts. Amendments by Pub.L. 111–16 effective Dec. 1, 2009, see Pub.L. 111–16, § 7, set out as a note under 11 U.S.C.A. § 109.

2005 Acts. Amendments by Pub.L. 109–8 effective, except as otherwise provided, 180 days after April 20, 2005, and inapplicable with respect to cases commenced under Title 11 before the effective date, see Pub.L. 109–8, § 1501, set out as a note under 11 U.S.C.A. § 101.

1986 Acts. Amendment by Pub.L. 99–554 effective 30 days after Oct. 27, 1986, except as otherwise provided for, see section 302(a) of Pub.L. 99–554, set out as a note under section 581 of Title 28, Judiciary and Judicial Procedure.

Amendment by Pub.L. 99–554, § 217, not to become effective in or with respect to certain specified judicial districts until, or apply to cases while pending in such district before, the expiration of the 270-day period beginning 30 days after Oct. 27, 1986, or of the 30-day period beginning on the date the Attorney General certifies under section 303 of Pub.L. 99–554 the region specified in a paragraph of section 581(a) of Title 28, as amended by section 111(a) of Pub.L. 99–554, that includes such district, whichever occurs first, see section 302(d)(1) of Pub.L. 99–554, set out as a note under section 581 of Title 28.

Amendment by Pub.L. 99–554, § 217, not to become effective in or with respect to certain specified judicial districts until, or apply to cases while pending in such district before, the expiration of the 2-year period beginning 30 days after Oct. 27, 1986, or of the 30-day period beginning on the date the Attorney General certifies under section 303 of Pub.L. 99–554 the region specified in a paragraph of section 581(a) of Title 28, as amended by section 111(a) of Pub.L. 99–554, that includes such district, whichever occurs first, see section 302(d)(2) of Pub.L. 99–554, set out as a note under section 581 of Title 28.

Amendment by Pub.L. 99–554, § 217, not to become effective in or with respect to judicial districts established for the States of Alabama and North Carolina until, or apply to cases while pending in such district before, such district elects to be included in a bankruptcy region established in section 581(a) of Title 28, as amended by section 111(a) of Pub.L. 99–554, or Oct. 1, 2002, whichever occurs first, and, except as otherwise provided for, with respect to cases under chapters 7, 11, 12 and 13 of Title 11 commenced before 30 days after Oct. 27, 1986, and pending in a judicial district in the States of Alabama or North Carolina before any election made under section 302(d)(3)(A) of Pub.L. 99–554 by such district becomes effective or Oct. 1, 2002, whichever occurs first, amendments by Pub.L. 99–554 not to apply until Oct. 1, 2003, or the expiration of the 1-year period beginning on the date such election becomes effective, whichever occurs first, and further, in any judicial district in Alabama or North Carolina not making the election described in section 302(d)(3)(A) of Pub.L. 99–554, any person appointed under regulations issued by the Judicial Conference to administer estates in cases under Title 11 authorized to establish, etc., a panel of private trustees, and to supervise cases and trustees in cases under chapters 7, 11, 12 and 13 of Title 11, until amendments by sections 201 to 231 of Pub.L. 99–554 effective in such district, see section 302(d)(3)(A) to (F), (H), and (I) of Pub.L. 99–554, set out as a note under section 581 of Title 28.

Amendment by Pub.L. 99–554, § 217, except as otherwise provided, with respect to cases under chapters 7, 11, 12, and 13 of Title 11 commenced before 30 days after Oct. 27, 1986, and pending in a judicial district referred to in section 581(a) of Title 28, as amended by section 111(a) of Pub.L. 99–554, for which a United States trustee is not authorized before 30 days after Oct. 27, 1986 to be appointed, not applicable until the expiration of the 3-year period beginning on Oct. 27, 1986, or of the 1-year period beginning on the date the Attorney General certifies under section 303 of Pub.L. 99–554 the region specified in a paragraph of such section 581(a) that includes, such district, whichever occurs first, see section 302(e)(1), (2) of Pub.L. 99–554, set out as a note under section 581 of Title 28.

1984 Acts. Amendment by Pub.L. 98–353 effective with respect to cases filed 90 days after July 10, 1984, see section 552(a), formerly 553(a), of Pub.L. 98–353, set out as a note under section 101 of this title.

CROSS REFERENCES

Duties of trustee in—

Chapter eleven cases, see 11 USCA § 1106.

Chapter thirteen cases, see 11 USCA § 1302.

Chapter twelve cases, see 11 USCA § 1202.

Multiemployer plan termination proceedings, see 29 USCA § 1342.

Filing of reports and summaries by debtor engaged in business, see 11 USCA § 1304.

Powers and duties of trustee in investor protection liquidation proceedings, see 15 USCA § 78fff–1.

LIBRARY REFERENCES

American Digest System

Bankruptcy ⟨key⟩3008.1, 3009, 3011.

Key Number System Topic No. 51.

Corpus Juris Secundum

CJS Bankruptcy § 96, Duty to File Inventory and Collect and Reduce to Money Property of Estate.

CJS Bankruptcy § 97, Duty to Investigate Debtor and to Examine Proofs of Claims.

CJS Bankruptcy § 101, Chapter 11.

CJS Bankruptcy § 102, Chapter 12.

CJS Bankruptcy § 103, Chapter 13.

CJS Bankruptcy § 104, Chapter 13--Duties If Debtor is Engaged in Business.

CJS Bankruptcy § 177, Governmental Regulations.

CJS Bankruptcy § 301, Notice to Debtor, Creditors, and Indenture Trustees.

CJS Bankruptcy § 431, Presumption of Abuse.

CJS Bankruptcy § 578, Debtor's Statement of Intention.

CJS Bankruptcy § 626, Collection and Reduction to Money of Property of Estate in Chapter 7 Cases.

CJS Bankruptcy § 632, Absolute Nature of Turnover Duty.

CJS Bankruptcy § 764, Consumer Privacy and Patient Care Ombudsmen.

CJS Bankruptcy § 805, Who May Conduct Examination; Debtor's Right to Examine.

CJS Bankruptcy § 836, Chapter 7 Cases.

CJS Bankruptcy § 841, Fiduciary Duties of Trustees and Debtors in Possession.

CJS Bankruptcy § 848, Operation of Business or Affairs of Chapter 13 Debtor.

CJS Bankruptcy § 1097, Trustee's Duties and Liabilities.

CJS Bankruptcy § 1105, Closing.

CJS Bankruptcy § 1115, Generally; Definitions.

CJS Bankruptcy § 1130, Powers and Duties of Committee.

§ 705.   Creditors' committee

(a) At the meeting under section 341(a) of this title, creditors that may vote for a trustee under section 702(a) of this title may elect a committee of not fewer than three, and not more than eleven, creditors, each of whom holds an allowable unsecured claim of a kind entitled to distribution under section 726(a)(2) of this title.

(b) A committee elected under subsection (a) of this section may consult with the trustee or the United States trustee in connection with the administration of the estate, make recommendations to the trustee or the United States trustee respecting the performance of the trustee's duties, and submit to the court or the United States trustee any question affecting the administration of the estate.

(Pub.L. 95–598, Nov. 6, 1978, 92 Stat. 2605; Pub.L. 99–554, Title II, § 218, Oct. 27, 1986, 100 Stat. 3100.)

HISTORICAL AND STATUTORY NOTES

Revision Notes and Legislative Reports

1978 Acts. This section is derived from section 44b of the Bankruptcy Act [section 72(b) of former Title 11] without substantial change. It permits election by general unsecured creditors of a committee of not fewer than 3 members and not more than 11 members to consult with the trustee in connection with the administration of the estate, to make recommendations to the trustee respecting the performance of his duties, and to submit to the court any question affecting the administration of the estate. There is no provision for compensation or reimbursement of its counsel. Senate Report No. 95–989.

1986 Acts. House Report No. 99–764 and House Conference Report No. 99–958, see 1986 U.S.Code Cong. and Adm. News, p. 5227.

Legislative Statements

Section 705(a) of the House amendment adopts a provision contained in the Senate amendment that limits a committee of creditors to not more than 11; the House bill contained no maximum limitation.

Amendments

1986 Amendments. Subsec. (b). Pub.L. 99–554, § 218, substituted "with the trustee or the United States trustee in

connection" for "with the trustee in connection", "to the trustee or the United States trustee respecting" for "to the trustee respecting", and "to the court or the United States trustee any question" for "to the court any question".

Effective and Applicability Provisions

1986 Acts. Amendment by Pub.L. 99–554 effective 30 days after Oct. 27, 1986, except as otherwise provided for, see section 302(a) of Pub.L. 99–554, set out as a note under section 581 of Title 28, Judiciary and Judicial Procedure.

Amendment by Pub.L. 99–554, § 218, not to become effective in or with respect to certain specified judicial districts until, or apply to cases while pending in such district before, the expiration of the 270-day period beginning 30 days after Oct. 27, 1986, or of the 30-day period beginning on the date the Attorney General certifies under section 303 of Pub.L. 99–554 the region specified in a paragraph of section 581(a) of Title 28, as amended by section 111(a) of Pub.L. 99–554, that includes such district, whichever occurs first, see section 302(d)(1) of Pub.L. 99–554, set out as a note under section 581 of Title 28.

Amendment by Pub.L. 99–554, § 218, not to become effective in or with respect to certain specified judicial districts until, or apply to cases while pending in such district before, the expiration of the 2-year period beginning 30 days after Oct. 27, 1986, or of the 30-day period beginning on the date the Attorney General certifies under section 303 of Pub.L. 99–554 the region specified in a paragraph of section 581(a) of Title 28, as amended by section 111(a) of Pub.L. 99–554, that includes such district, whichever occurs first, see section 302(d)(2) of Pub.L. 99–554, set out as a note under section 581 of Title 28.

Amendment by Pub.L. 99–554, § 218, not to become effective in or with respect to judicial districts established for the States of Alabama and North Carolina until, or apply to cases while pending in such district before, such district elects to be included in a bankruptcy region established in section 581(a) of Title 28, as amended by section 111(a) of Pub.L. 99–554, or Oct. 1, 2002, whichever occurs first, and, except as otherwise provided, with respect to cases under chapters 7, 11, 12, and 13 of Title 11 commenced before 30 days after Oct. 27, 1986, and pending in a judicial district in the States of Alabama or North Carolina before any election made under section 302(d)(3)(A) of Pub.L. 99–554 by such district becomes effective or Oct. 1, 2002, whichever occurs first, amendments by Pub.L. 99–554 not to apply until Oct. 1, 2003, or the expiration of the 1-year period beginning on the date such election becomes effective, whichever occurs first, and further, in any judicial district in Alabama or North Carolina not making the election described in section 302(d)(3)(A) of Pub.L. 99–554, any person appointed under regulations issued by the Judicial Conference to administer estates in cases under Title 11 authorized to establish, etc., a panel of private trustees, and to supervise cases and trustees in cases under chapters 7, 11, 12, and 13 of Title 11, until amendments by sections 201 to 231 of Pub.L. 99–554 effective in such district, see section 302(d)(3)(A) to (F), (H), and (I) of Pub.L. 9–554, set out as a note under section 581 of Title 28.

Amendment by Pub.L. 99–554, § 218, except as otherwise provided, with respect to cases under chapters 7, 11, 12, and 13 of Title 11 commenced before 30 days after Oct. 27, 1986, and pending in a judicial district referred to in section 581(a) of Title 28, as amended by section 111(a) of Pub.L. 99–554, for which a United States trustee is not authorized before 30 days after Oct. 27, 1986 to be appointed, not applicable until the expiration of the 3-year period beginning on Oct. 27, 1986, or of the 1-year period beginning on the date the Attorney General certifies under section 303 of Pub.L. 99–554 the region specified in a paragraph of such section 581(a) that includes, such district, whichever occurs first, see section 302(e)(1), (2) of Pub.L. 99–554, set out as a note under section 581 of Title 28.

CROSS REFERENCES

Appointment of creditors' and equity security holders' committees in chapter 11 cases, see 11 USCA § 1102.

Powers and duties of committees in chapter 11 cases, see 11 USCA § 1103.

LIBRARY REFERENCES

American Digest System

Bankruptcy ⊜3024.

Key Number System Topic No. 51.

Corpus Juris Secundum

CJS Bankruptcy § 79, Solicitation and Voting of Proxies.

CJS Bankruptcy § 522, Parties; Standing.

CJS Bankruptcy § 764, Consumer Privacy and Patient Care Ombudsmen.

CJS Bankruptcy § 809, Voting and Elections.

CJS Bankruptcy § 856, Motion and Notice.

CJS Bankruptcy § 857, Approval of Agreement.

CJS Bankruptcy § 870, Agreement or Stipulation for Use of Cash Collateral.

CJS Bankruptcy § 901, Motion for Authorization to Obtain Credit; Approval of Agreement.

CJS Bankruptcy § 1100, Solicitation and Voting of Proxies in Chapter 7 Liquidations.

CJS Bankruptcy § 1115, Generally; Definitions.

§ 706. Conversion

(a) The debtor may convert a case under this chapter to a case under chapter 11, 12, or 13 of this title at any time, if the case has not been converted under section 1112, 1208, or 1307 of this title. Any waiver of the right to convert a case under this subsection is unenforceable.

(b) On request of a party in interest and after notice and a hearing, the court may convert a case under this chapter to a case under chapter 11 of this title at any time.

(c) The court may not convert a case under this chapter to a case under chapter 12 or 13 of this title unless the debtor requests or consents to such conversion.

(d) Notwithstanding any other provision of this section, a case may not be converted to a case under another chapter of this title unless the debtor may be a debtor under such chapter.

(Pub.L. 95–598, Nov. 6, 1978, 92 Stat. 2606; Pub.L. 99–554, Title II, § 257(q), Oct. 27, 1986, 100 Stat. 3115; Pub.L. 103–394, Title V, § 501(d)(22), Oct. 22, 1994, 108 Stat. 4146; Pub.L. 109–8, Title I, § 101, Apr. 20, 2005, 119 Stat. 27.)

HISTORICAL AND STATUTORY NOTES

Revision Notes and Legislative Reports

1978 Acts. Subsection (a) of this section gives the debtor the one-time absolute right of conversion of a liquidation case to a reorganization or individual repayment plan case. If the case has already once been converted from chapter 11 or 13 to chapter 7, then the debtor does not have that right. The policy of the provision is that the debtor should always be given the opportunity to repay his debts, and a waiver of the right to convert a case is unenforceable.

Subsection (b) permits the court, on request of a party in interest and after notice and a hearing, to convert the case to chapter 11 at any time. The decision whether to convert is left in the sound discretion of the court, based on what will most inure to the benefit of all parties in interest.

Subsection (c) is part of the prohibition against involuntary chapter 13 cases, and prohibits the court from converting a case to chapter 13 without the debtor's consent.

Subsection (d) reinforces section 109 by prohibiting conversion to a chapter unless the debtor is eligible to be a debtor under that chapter. Senate Report No. 95–989.

1986 Acts. House Report No. 99–764 and House Conference Report No. 99–958, see 1986 U.S.Code Cong. and Adm. News, p. 5227.

1994 Acts. House Report No. 103–835, see 1994 U.S. Code Cong. and Adm. News, p. 3340.

2005 Acts. House Report No. 109–31(Part I), see 2005 U.S. Code Cong. and Adm. News, p. 88.

Legislative Statements

Section 706(a) of the House amendment adopts a provision contained in the Senate amendment indicating that a waiver of the right to convert a case under section 706(a) is unenforceable. The explicit reference in title 11 forbidding the waiver of certain rights is not intended to imply that other rights, such as the right to file a voluntary bankruptcy case under section 301, may be waived.

Section 706 of the House amendment adopts a similar provision contained in H.R. 8200 as passed by the House. Competing proposals contained in section 706(c) and section 706(d) of the Senate amendment are rejected.

Amendments

2005 Amendments. Subsec. (c). Pub.L. 109–8, § 101, inserted "or consents to" after "requests".

1994 Amendments. Subsec. (a). Pub.L. 103–394, § 501(d)(22), substituted "1208, or 1307" for "1307, or 1208".

1986 Amendments. Subsec. (a). Pub.L. 99–554, § 257(q)(1), added references to chapter 12 and section 1208 of this title.

Subsec. (c). Pub.L. 99–554, § 257(q)(2), added reference to chapter 12.

Effective and Applicability Provisions

2005 Acts. Amendments by Pub.L. 109–8 effective, except as otherwise provided, 180 days after April 20, 2005, and inapplicable with respect to cases commenced under Title 11 before the effective date, see Pub.L. 109–8, § 1501, set out as a note under 11 U.S.C.A. § 101.

1994 Acts. Amendment by Pub.L. 103–394 effective on Oct. 22, 1994, and not to apply with respect to cases commenced

under Title 11 of the United States Code before Oct. 22, 1994, see section 702 of Pub.L. 103–394, set out as a note under section 101 of this title.

1986 Acts. Amendment by Pub.L. 99–554 effective 30 days after Oct. 27, 1986, but not applicable to cases commenced under this title before that date, see section 302(a), (c)(1) of Pub.L. 99–554, set out as a note under section 581 of Title 28, Judiciary and Judicial Procedure.

Separability of Provisions

If any provision of or amendment made by Pub.L. 103–394 or the application of such provision or amendment to any person or circumstance is held to be unconstitutional, the remaining provisions of and amendments made by Pub.L. 103–394 and the application of such provisions and amendments to any person or circumstance shall not be affected thereby, see section 701 of Pub.L. 103–394, set out as a note under section 101 of this title.

CROSS REFERENCES

Conversion or dismissal of—
> Chapter eleven cases, see 11 USCA § 1112.
> Chapter thirteen cases, see 11 USCA § 1307.
> Chapter twelve cases, see 11 USCA § 1208.

Effect of conversion, see 11 USCA § 348.

Termination of debtor's taxable period in—
> Chapter eleven cases, see 11 USCA § 1146.
> Chapter twelve cases, see 11 USCA § 1231.

LIBRARY REFERENCES

American Digest System

Bankruptcy ☞2331, 2332.

Key Number System Topic No. 51.

Corpus Juris Secundum

CJS Bankruptcy § 109, Termination of Service.

CJS Bankruptcy § 244, Limitations.

CJS Bankruptcy § 420, Conversion of Previously Converted Case.

CJS Bankruptcy § 421, Proceedings.

CJS Bankruptcy § 927, Exercising Right in Chapter 7 Cases.

§ 707.   Dismissal of a case or conversion to a case under chapter 11 or 13

(a) The court may dismiss a case under this chapter only after notice and a hearing and only for cause, including—

> **(1)** unreasonable delay by the debtor that is prejudicial to creditors;

> **(2)** nonpayment of any fees or charges required under chapter 123 of title 28; and

> **(3)** failure of the debtor in a voluntary case to file, within fifteen days or such additional time as the court may allow after the filing of the petition commencing such case, the information required by paragraph (1) of section 521(a), but only on a motion by the United States trustee.

(b)(1) After notice and a hearing, the court, on its own motion or on a motion by the United States trustee, trustee (or bankruptcy administrator, if any), or any party in interest, may dismiss a case filed by an individual debtor under this chapter whose debts are primarily consumer debts, or, with the debtor's consent, convert such a case to a case under chapter 11 or 13 of this title, if it finds that the granting of relief would be an abuse of the provisions of this chapter. In making a determination whether to dismiss a case under this section, the court may not take into consideration whether a debtor has made, or continues to make, charitable contributions (that meet the definition of "charitable contribution" under section 548(d)(3)) to any qualified religious or charitable entity or organization (as that term is defined in section 548(d)(4)).

(2)(A)(i) In considering under paragraph (1) whether the granting of relief would be an abuse of the provisions of this chapter, the court shall presume abuse exists if the debtor's current monthly income reduced by the amounts determined under clauses (ii), (iii), and (iv), and multiplied by 60 is not less than the lesser of—

> **(I)** 25 percent of the debtor's nonpriority unsecured claims in the case, or $7,025 [1], whichever is greater; or

> **(II)** $11,725 [1].

(ii)(I) The debtor's monthly expenses shall be the debtor's applicable monthly expense amounts specified under the National Standards and Local Standards, and the debtor's actual monthly expenses for the categories specified as Other Necessary Expenses issued by the Internal Revenue Service for the area in which the debtor resides, as in effect on the date of the order for relief, for the debtor, the dependents of the debtor, and the spouse of the debtor in a joint case, if the spouse is not otherwise a dependent. Such expenses shall include reasonably necessary health insurance, disability insurance, and health savings account expenses for the debtor, the spouse of the debtor, or the dependents of the debtor. Notwithstanding any other provision of this clause, the monthly expenses of the debtor shall not include any payments for debts. In addition, the debtor's monthly expenses shall include the debtor's reasonably necessary expenses incurred to maintain the safety of the debtor and the family of the debtor from family violence as identified under section 302 of the Family Violence Prevention and Services Act, or other applicable Federal law. The expenses included in the debtor's monthly expenses described in the preceding sentence shall be kept confidential by the court. In addition, if it is demonstrated that it is reasonable and necessary, the debtor's monthly expenses may also include an additional allowance for food and clothing of up to 5 percent of the food and clothing categories as specified by the National Standards issued by the Internal Revenue Service.

(II) In addition, the debtor's monthly expenses may include, if applicable, the continuation of actual expenses paid by the debtor that are reasonable and necessary for care and support of an elderly, chronically ill, or disabled household member or member of the debtor's immediate family (including parents, grandparents, siblings, children, and grandchildren of the debtor, the dependents of the debtor, and the spouse of the debtor in a joint case who is not a dependent) and who is unable to pay for such reasonable and necessary expenses.

(III) In addition, for a debtor eligible for chapter 13, the debtor's monthly expenses may include the actual administrative expenses of administering a chapter 13 plan for the district in which the debtor resides, up to an amount of 10 percent of the projected plan payments, as determined under schedules issued by the Executive Office for United States Trustees.

(IV) In addition, the debtor's monthly expenses may include the actual expenses for each dependent child less than 18 years of age, not to exceed $1,775 [1] per year per child, to attend a private or public elementary or secondary school if the debtor provides documentation of such expenses and a detailed explanation of why such expenses are reasonable and necessary, and why such expenses are not already accounted for in the National Standards, Local Standards, or Other Necessary Expenses referred to in subclause (I).

(V) In addition, the debtor's monthly expenses may include an allowance for housing and utilities, in excess of the allowance specified by the Local Standards for housing and utilities issued by the Internal Revenue Service, based on the actual expenses for home energy costs if the debtor provides documentation of such actual expenses and demonstrates that such actual expenses are reasonable and necessary.

(iii) The debtor's average monthly payments on account of secured debts shall be calculated as the sum of—

(I) the total of all amounts scheduled as contractually due to secured creditors in each month of the 60 months following the date of the filing of the petition; and

(II) any additional payments to secured creditors necessary for the debtor, in filing a plan under chapter 13 of this title, to maintain possession of the debtor's primary residence, motor vehicle, or other property necessary for the support of the debtor and the debtor's dependents, that serves as collateral for secured debts;

divided by 60.

(iv) The debtor's expenses for payment of all priority claims (including priority child support and alimony claims) shall be calculated as the total amount of debts entitled to priority, divided by 60.

(B)(i) In any proceeding brought under this subsection, the presumption of abuse may only be rebutted by demonstrating special circumstances, such as a serious medical condition or a call or order to active duty in the Armed Forces, to the extent such special circumstances that justify additional expenses or adjustments of current monthly income for which there is no reasonable alternative.

(ii) In order to establish special circumstances, the debtor shall be required to itemize each additional expense or adjustment of income and to provide—

(I) documentation for such expense or adjustment to income; and

(II) a detailed explanation of the special circumstances that make such expenses or adjustment to income necessary and reasonable.

(iii) The debtor shall attest under oath to the accuracy of any information provided to demonstrate that additional expenses or adjustments to income are required.

(iv) The presumption of abuse may only be rebutted if the additional expenses or adjustments to income referred to in clause (i) cause the product of the debtor's current monthly income reduced by the amounts determined under clauses (ii), (iii), and (iv) of subparagraph (A) when multiplied by 60 to be less than the lesser of—

(I) 25 percent of the debtor's nonpriority unsecured claims, or $7,025 [1], whichever is greater; or

(II) $11,725 [1].

(C) As part of the schedule of current income and expenditures required under section 521, the debtor shall include a statement of the debtor's current monthly income, and the calculations that determine whether a presumption arises under subparagraph (A)(i), that show how each such amount is calculated.

(D) Subparagraphs (A) through (C) shall not apply, and the court may not dismiss or convert a case based on any form of means testing—

(i) if the debtor is a disabled veteran (as defined in section 3741(1) of title 38), and the indebtedness occurred primarily during a period during which he or she was—

(I) on active duty (as defined in section 101(d)(1) of title 10); or

(II) performing a homeland defense activity (as defined in section 901(1) of title 32); or

(ii) with respect to the debtor, while the debtor is—

(I) on, and during the 540–day period beginning immediately after the debtor is released from, a period of active duty (as defined in section 101(d)(1) of title 10) of not less than 90 days; or

(II) performing, and during the 540–day period beginning immediately after the debtor is no longer performing, a homeland defense activity (as defined in section 901(1) of title 32) performed for a period of not less than 90 days;

if after September 11, 2001, the debtor while a member of a reserve component of the Armed Forces or a member of the National Guard, was called to such active duty or performed such homeland defense activity.

(3) In considering under paragraph (1) whether the granting of relief would be an abuse of the provisions of this chapter in a case in which the presumption in paragraph (2)(A)(i) does not arise or is rebutted, the court shall consider—

(A) whether the debtor filed the petition in bad faith; or

(B) the totality of the circumstances (including whether the debtor seeks to reject a personal services contract and the financial need for such rejection as sought by the debtor) of the debtor's financial situation demonstrates abuse.

(4)(A) The court, on its own initiative or on the motion of a party in interest, in accordance with the procedures described in rule 9011 of the Federal Rules of Bankruptcy Procedure, may order the attorney for the debtor to reimburse the trustee for all reasonable costs in prosecuting a motion filed under section 707(b), including reasonable attorneys' fees, if—

(i) a trustee files a motion for dismissal or conversion under this subsection; and

(ii) the court—

(I) grants such motion; and

(II) finds that the action of the attorney for the debtor in filing a case under this chapter violated rule 9011 of the Federal Rules of Bankruptcy Procedure.

(B) If the court finds that the attorney for the debtor violated rule 9011 of the Federal Rules of Bankruptcy Procedure, the court, on its own initiative or on the motion of a party in interest, in accordance with such procedures, may order—

(i) the assessment of an appropriate civil penalty against the attorney for the debtor; and

(ii) the payment of such civil penalty to the trustee, the United States trustee (or the bankruptcy administrator, if any).

(C) The signature of an attorney on a petition, pleading, or written motion shall constitute a certification that the attorney has—

(i) performed a reasonable investigation into the circumstances that gave rise to the petition, pleading, or written motion; and

(ii) determined that the petition, pleading, or written motion—

(I) is well grounded in fact; and

(II) is warranted by existing law or a good faith argument for the extension, modification, or reversal of existing law and does not constitute an abuse under paragraph (1).

(D) The signature of an attorney on the petition shall constitute a certification that the attorney has no knowledge after an inquiry that the information in the schedules filed with such petition is incorrect.

(5)(A) Except as provided in subparagraph (B) and subject to paragraph (6), the court, on its own initiative or on the motion of a party in interest, in accordance with the procedures described in rule 9011 of the Federal Rules of Bankruptcy Procedure, may award a debtor all reasonable costs (including reasonable attorneys' fees) in contesting a motion filed by a party in interest (other than a trustee or United States trustee (or bankruptcy administrator, if any)) under this subsection if—

(i) the court does not grant the motion; and

(ii) the court finds that—

(I) the position of the party that filed the motion violated rule 9011 of the Federal Rules of Bankruptcy Procedure; or

(II) the attorney (if any) who filed the motion did not comply with the requirements of clauses (i) and (ii) of paragraph (4)(C), and the motion was made solely for the purpose of coercing a debtor into waiving a right guaranteed to the debtor under this title.

(B) A small business that has a claim of an aggregate amount less than $1,175 [1] shall not be subject to subparagraph (A)(ii)(I).

(C) For purposes of this paragraph—

(i) the term "small business" means an unincorporated business, partnership, corporation, association, or organization that—

(I) has fewer than 25 full-time employees as determined on the date on which the motion is filed; and

(II) is engaged in commercial or business activity; and

(ii) the number of employees of a wholly owned subsidiary of a corporation includes the employees of—

(I) a parent corporation; and

(II) any other subsidiary corporation of the parent corporation.

(6) Only the judge or United States trustee (or bankruptcy administrator, if any) may file a motion under section 707(b), if the current monthly income of the debtor, or in a joint case, the debtor and the debtor's spouse, as of the date of the order for relief, when multiplied by 12, is equal to or less than—

(A) in the case of a debtor in a household of 1 person, the median family income of the applicable State for 1 earner;

(B) in the case of a debtor in a household of 2, 3, or 4 individuals, the highest median family income of the applicable State for a family of the same number or fewer individuals; or

(C) in the case of a debtor in a household exceeding 4 individuals, the highest median family income of the applicable State for a family of 4 or fewer individuals, plus $625 [1] per month for each individual in excess of 4.

(7)(A) No judge, United States trustee (or bankruptcy administrator, if any), trustee, or other party in interest may file a motion under paragraph (2) if the current monthly income of the debtor, including a veteran (as that term is defined in section 101 of title 38), and the debtor's spouse combined, as of the date of the order for relief when multiplied by 12, is equal to or less than—

(i) in the case of a debtor in a household of 1 person, the median family income of the applicable State for 1 earner;

(ii) in the case of a debtor in a household of 2, 3, or 4 individuals, the highest median family income of the applicable State for a family of the same number or fewer individuals; or

(iii) in the case of a debtor in a household exceeding 4 individuals, the highest median family income of the applicable State for a family of 4 or fewer individuals, plus $625 [1] per month for each individual in excess of 4.

(B) In a case that is not a joint case, current monthly income of the debtor's spouse shall not be considered for purposes of subparagraph (A) if—

(i)(I) the debtor and the debtor's spouse are separated under applicable nonbankruptcy law; or

(II) the debtor and the debtor's spouse are living separate and apart, other than for the purpose of evading subparagraph (A); and

(ii) the debtor files a statement under penalty of perjury—

(I) specifying that the debtor meets the requirement of subclause (I) or (II) of clause (i); and

(II) disclosing the aggregate, or best estimate of the aggregate, amount of any cash or money payments received from the debtor's spouse attributed to the debtor's current monthly income.

(c)(1) In this subsection—

(A) the term "crime of violence" has the meaning given such term in section 16 of title 18; and

(B) the term "drug trafficking crime" has the meaning given such term in section 924(c)(2) of title 18.

(2) Except as provided in paragraph (3), after notice and a hearing, the court, on a motion by the victim of a crime of violence or a drug trafficking crime, may when it is in the best interest of the victim dismiss a voluntary case filed under this chapter by a debtor who is an individual if such individual was convicted of such crime.

(3) The court may not dismiss a case under paragraph (2) if the debtor establishes by a preponderance of the evidence that the filing of a case under this chapter is necessary to satisfy a claim for a domestic support obligation.

(Pub.L. 95–598, Nov. 6, 1978, 92 Stat. 2606; Pub.L. 98–353, Title III, §§ 312, 475, July 10, 1984, 98 Stat. 355, 381; Pub.L. 99–554, Title II, § 219, Oct. 27, 1986, 100 Stat. 3100; Pub.L. 105–183, § 4(b), June 19, 1998, 112 Stat. 518; Pub.L. 109–8, Title I, § 102(a), (f), Apr. 20, 2005, 119 Stat. 27, 33; Pub.L. 110–438, § 2, Oct. 20, 2008, 122 Stat. 5000; Pub.L. 111–320, Title II, § 202(a), Dec. 20, 2010, 124 Stat. 3509; Pub.L. 111–327, § 2(a)(25), Dec. 22, 2010, 124 Stat. 3560.)

[1] Dollar amount as adjusted by the Judicial Conference of the United States. See Adjustment of Dollar Amounts notes set out under this section and 11 U.S.C.A. § 104.

HISTORICAL AND STATUTORY NOTES

Revision Notes and Legislative Reports

1978 Acts. This section authorizes the court to dismiss a liquidation case only for cause, such as unreasonable delay by the debtor that is prejudicial to creditors or nonpayment of any fees and charges required under chapter 123 of title 28 [section 1911 et seq. of Title 28, Judiciary and Judicial Procedure]. These causes are not exhaustive, but merely illustrative. The section does not contemplate, however, that the ability of the debtor to repay his debts in whole or in part constitutes adequate cause for dismissal. To permit dismissal on that ground would be to enact a non-uniform mandatory chapter 13, in lieu of the remedy of bankruptcy. Senate Report No. 95–989.

1984 Acts. Statements by Legislative Leaders, see 1984 U.S.Code Cong. and Adm.News, p. 576.

1986 Acts. House Report No. 99–764 and House Conference Report No. 99–958, see 1986 U.S.Code Cong. and Adm. News, p. 5227.

1998 Acts. Statement by President, see 1998 U.S. Code Cong. and Adm. News, p. 230.

2005 Acts. House Report No. 109–31(Part I), see 2005 U.S. Code Cong. and Adm. News, p. 88.

Legislative Statements

Section 707 of the House amendment indicates that the court may dismiss a case only after notice and a hearing.

References in Text

Chapter 11 of this title, referred to in subsec. (b)(1), is 11 U.S.C.A. § 1101 et seq.

Chapter 13 of this title, referred to in subsec. (b)(1), (2)(A)(ii)(III), (iii)(II), is 11 U.S.C.A. § 1301 et seq.

The Family Violence Prevention and Services Act, referred to in subsec. (b)(2)(A)(ii)(I), is Pub.L. 98–457, Title III, § 301 et seq., as revised by Pub.L. 111–320, § 201, Dec. 20, 2010, 124 Stat. 3484, which is classified principally to chapter 110 of Title 42, 42 U.S.C.A. § 10401 et seq. Section 302 of the Act is classified to 42 U.S.C.A. § 10402.

The Federal Rules of Bankruptcy Procedure, referred to in subsec. (b)(4)(A), (B), (5)(A), are set out in the Appendix to this title.

Amendments

2010 Amendments. Subsec. (a)(3). Pub.L. 111–327, § 2(a)(25)(A), struck out "521" and inserted "521(a)".

Subsec. (b)(2)(A)(i)(I). By notice published Feb. 25, 2010, 75 F.R. 8747, dollar amount adjusted by the Judicial Conference of the United States which adjusted "$6,575" to "$7,025". See 11 U.S.C.A. § 104 and Adjustment of Dollar Amounts notes under this section.

Subsec. (b)(2)(A)(i)(II). By notice published Feb. 25, 2010, 75 F.R. 8747, dollar amount adjusted by the Judicial Conference of the United States which adjusted "$10,950" to "$11,725". See 11 U.S.C.A. § 104 and Adjustment of Dollar Amounts notes under this section.

Subsec. (b)(2)(A)(ii)(I). Pub.L. 111–320, § 202(a), struck out "section 309 of the Family Violence Prevention and Services Act" and inserted "section 302 of the Family Violence Prevention and Services Act".

Subsec. (b)(2)(A)(ii)(IV). By notice published Feb. 25, 2010, 75 F.R. 8747, dollar amount adjusted by the Judicial Conference of the United States which adjusted "$1,650" to "$1,775". See 11 U.S.C.A. § 104 and Adjustment of Dollar Amounts notes under this section.

Subsec. (b)(2)(A)(iii)(I). Pub.L. 111–327, § 2(a)(25)(B)(i), inserted "of the filing" following " date".

Subsec. (b)(2)(B)(iv)(I). By notice published Feb. 25, 2010, 75 F.R. 8747, dollar amount adjusted by the Judicial Conference of the United States which adjusted "$6,575" to "$7,025". See 11 U.S.C.A. § 104 and Adjustment of Dollar Amounts notes under this section.

Subsec. (b)(2)(B)(iv)(II). By notice published Feb. 25, 2010, 75 F.R. 8747, dollar amount adjusted by the Judicial Conference of the United States which adjusted "$10,950" to "$11,725". See 11 U.S.C.A. § 104 and Adjustment of Dollar Amounts notes under this section.

Subsec. (b)(3). Pub.L. 111–327, § 2(a)(25)(B)(ii), struck out "subparagraph (A)(i) of such paragraph" and inserted "paragraph (2)(A)(i)".

Subsec. (b)(5)(B). By notice published Feb. 25, 2010, 75 F.R. 8747, dollar amount adjusted by the Judicial Conference of the United States which adjusted "$1,100" to "$1,175". See 11 U.S.C.A. § 104 and Adjustment of Dollar Amounts notes under this section.

Subsec. (b)(6)(C). By notice published Feb. 25, 2010, 75 F.R. 8747, dollar amount adjusted by the Judicial Conference of the United States which adjusted "$575" to "$625". See 11 U.S.C.A. § 104 and Adjustment of Dollar Amounts notes under this section.

Subsec. (b)(7)(A)(iii). By notice published Feb. 25, 2010, 75 F.R. 8747, dollar amount adjusted by the Judicial Conference of the United States which adjusted "$575" to "$625". See 11 U.S.C.A. § 104 and Adjustment of Dollar Amounts notes under this section.

2008 Amendments. Subsec. (b)(2)(D). Pub.L. 110–438, § 2, rewrote subpar. (D), which formerly read:

"**(D)** Subparagraphs (A) through (C) shall not apply, and the court may not dismiss or convert a case based on any form of means testing, if the debtor is a disabled veteran (as defined in section 3741(1) of title 38), and the indebtedness occurred primarily during a period during which he or she was—

"**(i)** on active duty (as defined in section 101(d)(1) of title 10); or

"**(ii)** performing a homeland defense activity (as defined in section 901(1) of title 32)."

2007 Amendments. Subsec. (b)(2)(A)(i)(I). By notice published Feb. 14, 2007, 72 F.R. 7082, dollar amount adjusted by the Judicial Conference of the United States which adjusted "$6,000" to "$6,575". See 11 U.S.C.A. § 104 and Adjustment of Dollar Amounts notes under this section.

Subsec. (b)(2)(A)(i)(II). By notice published Feb. 14, 2007, 72 F.R. 7082, dollar amount adjusted by the Judicial Conference of the United States which adjusted "$10,000" to "$10,950". See 11 U.S.C.A. § 104 and Adjustment of Dollar Amounts notes under this section.

Subsec. (b)(2)(A)(ii)(IV). By notice published Feb. 14, 2007, 72 F.R. 7082, dollar amount adjusted by the Judicial Conference of the United States which adjusted "$1,500" to "$1,650". See 11 U.S.C.A. § 104 and Adjustment of Dollar Amounts notes under this section.

Subsec. (b)(2)(B)(iv)(I). By notice published Feb. 14, 2007, 72 F.R. 7082, modified Mar. 30, 2007, 72 F.R. 15162, dollar amount adjusted by the Judicial Conference of the United States which adjusted "$6,000" to "$6,575". See 11 U.S.C.A. § 104 and Adjustment of Dollar Amounts notes under this section.

Subsec. (b)(2)(B)(iv)(II). By notice published Feb. 14, 2007, 72 F.R. 7082, modified Mar. 30, 2007, 72 F.R. 15162, dollar amount adjusted by the Judicial Conference of the United States which adjusted "$10,000" to "$10,950". See 11 U.S.C.A. § 104 and Adjustment of Dollar Amounts notes under this section.

Subsec. (b)(5)(B). By notice published Feb. 14, 2007, 72 F.R. 7082, dollar amount adjusted by the Judicial Conference of the United States which adjusted "$1,000" to "$1,100". See 11 U.S.C.A. § 104 and Adjustment of Dollar Amounts notes under this section.

Subsec. (b)(6)(C). By notice published Feb. 14, 2007, 72 F.R. 7082, dollar amount adjusted by the Judicial Conference of the United States which adjusted "$525" to "$575". See 11 U.S.C.A. § 104 and Adjustment of Dollar Amounts notes under this section.

Subsec. (b)(7)(A)(iii). By notice published Feb. 14, 2007, 72 F.R. 7082, dollar amount adjusted by the Judicial Conference of the United States which adjusted "$525" to "$575". See 11 U.S.C.A. § 104 and Adjustment of Dollar Amounts notes under this section.

2005 Amendments. Heading. Pub.L. 109–8, § 102(a)(1), struck the existing section heading, which formerly read, "**§ 707. Dismissal**", and inserted "**§ 707. Dismissal of a case or conversion to a case under chapter 11 or 13**".

Subsec. (b). Pub.L. 109–8, § 102(a)(2), rewrote subsec. (b), which formerly read:

"**(b)** After notice and a hearing, the court, on its own motion or on a motion by the United States trustee, but not at the request or suggestion of any party in interest, may dismiss a case filed by an individual debtor under this chapter whose debts are primarily consumer debts if it finds that the granting of relief would be a substantial abuse of the provisions of this chapter. There shall be a presumption in favor of granting the relief requested by the debtor. In making a determination whether to dismiss a case under this section, the court may not take into consideration whether a debtor has made, or continues to make, charitable contributions (that meet the definition of 'charitable contribution"under section

548(d)(3)) to any qualified religious or charitable entity or organization (as that term is defined in section 548(d)(4)).”

Subsec. (c). Pub.L. 109–8, § 102(f), added subsec. (c).

1998 Amendments. Subsec. (b). Pub.L. 105–183, § 4(b), added at the end “In making a determination whether to dismiss a case under this section, the court may not take into consideration whether a debtor has made, or continues to make, charitable contributions (that meet the definition of ‘charitable contribution’ under section 548(d)(3)) to any qualified religious or charitable entity or organization (as that term is defined in section 548(d)(4)).”.

1986 Amendments. Subsec. (a)(3). Pub.L. 99–554, § 219(a), added par. (3).

Subsec. (b). Pub.L. 99–554, § 219(b), substituted “motion or on a motion by the United States trustee, but not” for “motion and not”.

1984 Amendments. Subsec. (a). Pub.L. 98–353, § 312(1), designated existing provisions as subsec. (a).

Subsec. (a)(1). Pub.L. 98–353, § 475, substituted “or” for “and”.

Subsec. (a)(2). Pub.L. 98–353, § 475, substituted “or” for “and”.

Subsec. (b). Pub.L. 98–353, § 312(2), added subsec. (b).

Effective and Applicability Provisions

2010 Acts. Increase of dollar amounts by Judicial Conference of the United States by notice published Feb. 25, 2010, 75 F.R. 8747 effective April 1, 2010, and increase not applicable to cases commenced before the effective date of the adjustments, i.e., April 1, 2010. See Adjustment of Dollar Amounts notes under 11 U.S.C.A. § 104 and this section.

2008 Acts. Pub.L. 110–438, § 4, Oct. 20, 2008, 122 Stat. 5002, as amended Pub.L. 112–64, § 2, Dec. 13, 2011, 125 Stat. 766, provided that:

“**(a) Effective date.**—Except as provided in subsection (b), this Act and the amendments made by this Act [amending this section and enacting provisions set out as a note under 11 U.S.C.A. § 101] shall take effect 60 days after the date of enactment of this Act [Oct. 20, 2008].

“**(b) Application of amendments.**—The amendments made by this Act [amending this section] shall apply only with respect to cases commenced under title 11 of the United States Code [11 U.S.C.A. § 101 et seq.] in the 7–year period beginning on the effective date of this Act [set out in this note].”

2007 Acts. Increase of dollar amounts by Judicial Conference of the United States by notice published Feb. 14, 2007, 72 F.R. 7082, modified Mar. 30, 2007, 72 F.R. 15162, effective April 1, 2007, and increase not applicable to cases commenced before the effective date of the adjustments, i.e., April 1, 2007. See Adjustment of Dollar Amounts notes under 11 U.S.C.A. § 104 and this section.

2005 Acts. Amendments by Pub.L. 109–8 effective, except as otherwise provided, 180 days after April 20, 2005, and inapplicable with respect to cases commenced under Title 11 before the effective date, see Pub.L. 109–8, § 1501, set out as a note under 11 U.S.C.A. § 101.

1986 Acts. Amendment by Pub.L. 99–554 effective 30 days after Oct. 27, 1986, except as otherwise provided for, see section 302(a) of Pub.L. 99–554, set out as a note under section 581 of Title 28, Judiciary and Judicial Procedure.

Amendment by Pub.L. 99–554, § 219, not to become effective in or with respect to certain specified judicial districts until, or apply to cases while pending in such district before, the expiration of the 270-day period beginning 30 days after Oct. 27, 1986, or of the 30-day period beginning on the date the Attorney General certifies under section 303 of Pub.L. 99–554 the region specified in a paragraph of section 581(a) of Title 28, as amended by section 111(a) of Pub.L. 99–554, that includes such district, whichever occurs first, see section 302(d)(1) of Pub.L. 99–554, set out as a note under section 581 of Title 28.

Amendment by Pub.L. 99–554, § 219, not to become effective in or with respect to certain specified judicial districts until, or apply to cases while pending in such district before, the expiration of the 2-year period beginning 30 days after Oct. 27, 1986, or of the 30-day period beginning on the date the Attorney General certifies under section 303 of Pub.L. 99–554 the region specified in a paragraph of section 581(a) of Title 28, as amended by section 111(a) of Pub.L. 99–554, that includes such district, whichever occurs first, see section 302(d)(2) of Pub.L. 99–554, set out as a note under section 581 of Title 28.

Amendment by Pub.L. 99–554, § 219, not to become effective in or with respect to judicial districts established for the States of Alabama and North Carolina until, or apply to cases while pending in such district before, such district elects to be included in a bankruptcy region established in section 581(a) of Title 28, as amended by section 111(a) of Pub.L. 99–554, or Oct. 1, 2002, whichever occurs first, and, except as otherwise provided, with respect to cases under chapters 7, 11, 12, and 13 of Title 11 commenced before 30 days after Oct. 27, 1986, and pending in a judicial district in the States of Alabama or North Carolina before any election made under section 302(d)(3)(A) of Pub.L. 99–554 by such district becomes effective or Oct. 1, 2002, whichever occurs first, amendments by Pub.L. 99–554 not to apply until Oct. 1, 2003, or the expiration of the 1-year period beginning on the date such election becomes effective, whichever occurs first, and further, in any judicial district in Alabama or North Carolina not making the election described in section 302(d)(3)(A) of Pub.L. 99–554, any person appointed under regulations issued by the Judicial Conference to administer estates in cases under Title 11 authorized to establish, etc., a panel of private trustees, and to supervise cases and trustees in cases under chapters 7, 11, 12, and 13 of Title 11, until amendments by sections 201 to 231 of Pub.L. 99–554 effective in such district, see section 302(d)(3)(A) to (F), (H), and (I) of Pub.L. 99–554, set out as a note under section 581 of Title 28.

Amendment by Pub.L. 99–554, § 219, except as otherwise provided, with respect to cases under chapters 7, 11, 12, and 13 of Title 11 commenced before 30 days after Oct. 27, 1986, and pending in a judicial district referred to in section 581(a) of Title 28, as amended by section 111(a) of Pub.L. 99–554, for which a United States trustee is not authorized before 30 days after Oct. 27, 1986 to be appointed, not applicable until the expiration of the 3-year period beginning on Oct. 27, 1986, or of the 1-year period beginning on the date the Attorney General certifies under section 303 of Pub.L. 99–554 the region specified in a paragraph of such section 581(a) that includes, such district, whichever occurs first, see section 302(e)(1), (2) of Pub.L. 99–554, set out as a note under section 581 of Title 28.

1984 Acts. Amendment by Pub.L. 98–353 effective with respect to cases filed 90 days after July 10, 1984, see section

552(a), formerly 553(a), of Pub.L. 98–353, set out as a note under section 101 of this title.

Applicability

Applicability of amendments made by Pub.L. 105–183 to any case brought under an applicable provision of this title that is pending or commenced on or after June 19, 1998, see Pub.L. 105–153, § 5, June 19, 1998, 112 Stat. 518, set out as a note under section 544 of this title.

Adjustment of Dollar Amounts

For adjustment of dollar amounts specified in subsec. (b)(2)(A)(i)(I), (II), (ii)(IV), (B)(iv)(I), (II), (5)(B), (6)(C), (7)(A)(iii) of this section by the Judicial Conference of the United States, effective Apr. 1, 2010, see note set out under 11 U.S.C.A. § 104 of this title.

By notice dated Feb. 25, 2010, 75 F.R. 8747, the Judicial Conference of the United States adjusted the dollar amounts in provisions specified in subsec. (b)(2)(A)(i)(I), (II), (ii)(IV), (B)(iv)(I), (II), (5)(B), (6)(C), (7)(A)(iii) of this section, effective Apr. 1, 2010, as follows:

In subsec. (b)(2)(A)(i)(I) adjusted $6,575 to $7,025.
In subsec. (b)(2)(A)(i)(II) adjusted $10,950 to $11,725.
In subsec. (b)(2)(A)(ii)(IV) adjusted $1,650 to $1,775.
In subsec. (b)(2)(B)(iv)(I) adjusted $6,575 to $7,025.
In subsec. (b)(2)(B)(iv)(II) adjusted $10,950 to $11,725.
In subsec. (b)(5)(B) adjusted $1,100 to $1,175.
In subsec. (b)(6)(C) adjusted $575 to $625.
In subsec. (b)(7)(A)(iii) adjusted $575 to $625.

By notice dated Feb. 14, 2007, 72 F.R. 7082, modified Mar. 30, 2007, 72 F.R. 15162, the Judicial Conference of the United States adjusted the dollar amounts in provisions specified in subsec. (b)(2)(A)(i)(I), (II), (ii)(IV), (B)(iv)(I), (II), (5)(B), (6)(C), (7)(A)(iii) of this section, effective Apr. 1, 2007, as follows:

In subsec. (b)(2)(A)(i)(I) adjusted $6,000 to $6,575.
In subsec. (b)(2)(A)(i)(II) adjusted $10,000 to $10,950.
In subsec. (b)(2)(A)(ii)(IV) adjusted $1,500 to $1,650.
In subsec. (b)(2)(B)(iv)(I) adjusted $6,000 to $6,575.
In subsec. (b)(2)(B)(iv)(II) adjusted $10,000 to $10,950.
In subsec. (b)(5)(B) adjusted $1,000 to $1,100.
In subsec. (b)(6)(C) adjusted $525 to $575.
In subsec. (b)(7)(A)(iii) adjusted $525 to $575.

Schedules of Reasonable and Necessary Expenses

Pub.L. 109–8, Title I, § 107, Apr. 20, 2005, 119 Stat. 42, provided that: "For purposes of section 707(b) of title 11, United States Code [subsec. (b) of this section], as amended by this Act [Bankruptcy Abuse Prevention and Consumer Protection Act of 2005, Pub.L. 109–8, April 20, 2005, 119 Stat. 23, see Tables for classification], the Director of the Executive Office for United States Trustees shall, not later than 180 days after the date of enactment of this Act [April 20, 2005], issue schedules of reasonable and necessary administrative expenses of administering a chapter 13 plan [chapter 13 of this title is 11 U.S.C.A. § 1301 et seq.] for each judicial district of the United States."

Rule of Construction

Amendments made by Pub.L. 105–183 not intended to limit the applicability of the Religious Freedom Restoration Act of 1993 (42 U.S.C. 2002bb et seq.), see Pub.L. 105–183, § 6, June 19, 1998, 112 Stat. 519, set out as a note under section 544 of this title.

Rules Promulgated by Supreme Court

United States Supreme Court to prescribe general rules implementing the practice and procedure to be followed under subsec. (b) of this section, with section 2075 of Title 28, Judiciary and Judicial Procedure, to apply with respect to such general rules, see section 320 of Pub.L. 98–353, set out as a note under section 2075 of Title 28.

CROSS REFERENCES

Conversion or dismissal of—
Chapter eleven cases, see 11 USCA § 1112.
Chapter thirteen cases, see 11 USCA § 1307.
Crime victims' rights, rights afforded and best efforts to accord rights, procedures to promote compliance, see 18 USCA § 3771.
Dismissal of Chapter nine cases, see 11 USCA § 930.
Effect of dismissal, see 11 USCA § 349.

LIBRARY REFERENCES

American Digest System

Bankruptcy ⟶2259.1 to 2264(3).
Key Number System Topic No. 51.

Corpus Juris Secundum

CJS Bankruptcy § 50, Chapter 7 Proceedings.
CJS Bankruptcy § 301, Notice to Debtor, Creditors, and Indenture Trustees.
CJS Bankruptcy § 336, Contents, Signature, and Verification.
CJS Bankruptcy § 352, Statement of Current Monthly Income.
CJS Bankruptcy § 431, Presumption of Abuse.
CJS Bankruptcy § 433, Presumption of Abuse--Rebuttal by Showing of Special Circumstances.
CJS Bankruptcy § 434, Considerations Absent Presumption.
CJS Bankruptcy § 435, Sanctions Against Debtor's Attorney.
CJS Bankruptcy § 436, Sanctions Against Party Filing Motion to Dismiss or Convert.
CJS Bankruptcy § 438, What Constitutes Cause.
CJS Bankruptcy § 451, Dismissal or Conversion on Request of United States Trustee.
CJS Bankruptcy § 453, Chapter 7.
CJS Bankruptcy § 1197, Disposable Income.
CJS Interest and Usury; Consumer Credit § 524, Liability of Cardholder.
CJS PEONAGE § 2, Constitutional and Statutory Provisions, Generally.

SUBCHAPTER II—COLLECTION, LIQUIDATION, AND DISTRIBUTION OF THE ESTATE

CROSS REFERENCES

Applicability of this subchapter in investor protection liquidation proceedings, see 15 USCA § 78fff.

Subchapter applicable only in case under this chapter, see 11 USCA § 103.

§ 721. Authorization to operate business

The court may authorize the trustee to operate the business of the debtor for a limited period, if such operation is in the best interest of the estate and consistent with the orderly liquidation of the estate. (Pub.L. 95–598, Nov. 6, 1978, 92 Stat. 2606.)

HISTORICAL AND STATUTORY NOTES

Revision Notes and Legislative Reports

1978 Acts. This section is derived from section 2a(5) of the Bankruptcy Act [section 11(a)(5) of former Title 11]. It permits the court to authorize the operation of any business of the debtor for a limited period, if the operation is in the best interest of the estate and consistent with orderly liquidation of the estate. An example is the operation of a watch company to convert watch movements and cases into completed watches which will bring much higher prices than the component parts would have brought. Senate Report No. 95–989.

CROSS REFERENCES

Authorization to operate business in Chapter eleven cases, see 11 USCA § 1108.

Debtor engaged in business in Chapter thirteen cases, see 11 USCA § 1304.

Executory contracts and unexpired leases, see 11 USCA § 365.

Executory contracts in stockbroker liquidation cases, see 11 USCA § 744.

Obtaining credit, see 11 USCA § 364.

Retention or replacement of professional persons, see 11 USCA § 327.

Treatment of accounts in—

    Commodity broker liquidation cases, see 11 USCA § 763.

    Stockbroker liquidation cases, see 11 USCA § 745.

Use, sale or lease of property, see 11 USCA § 363.

Utility service, see 11 USCA § 366.

LIBRARY REFERENCES

American Digest System

Bankruptcy �köm3025.1.

Key Number System Topic No. 51.

Corpus Juris Secundum

CJS Bankruptcy § 836, Chapter 7 Cases.

CJS Bankruptcy § 895, Unsecured Credit or Debt in Ordinary Course of Business.

§ 722. Redemption → personal use

An individual debtor may, whether or not the debtor has waived the right to redeem under this section, redeem tangible personal property intended primarily for personal, family, or household use, from a lien securing a dischargeable consumer debt, if such property is exempted under section 522 of this title or has been abandoned under section 554 of this title, by

paying the holder of such lien the amount of the allowed secured claim of such holder that is secured by such lien in full at the time of redemption.

(Pub.L. 95–598, Nov. 6, 1978, 92 Stat. 2606; Pub.L. 109–8, Title III, § 304(2), Apr. 20, 2005, 119 Stat. 79.)

HISTORICAL AND STATUTORY NOTES

Revision Notes and Legislative Reports

1978 Acts. This section is new and is broader than rights of redemption under the Uniform Commercial Code. It authorizes an individual debtor to redeem tangible personal property intended primarily for personal, family, or household use, from a lien securing a nonpurchase money dischargeable consumer debt. It applies only if the debtor's interest in the property is exempt or has been abandoned.

This right to redeem is a very substantial change from current law. To prevent abuses such as may occur when the debtor deliberately allows the property to depreciate in value, the debtor will be required to pay the fair market value of the goods or the amount of the claim if the claim is less. The right is personal to the debtor and not assignable. Senate Report No. 95–989.

This section is new and is broader than rights of redemption under the Uniform Commercial Code. It authorizes an individual debtor to redeem tangible personal property intended primarily for personal, family, or household use, from a lien securing a dischargeable consumer debt. It applies only if the debtor's interest in the property is exempt or has been abandoned.

The right to redeem extends to the whole of the property, not just the debtor's exempt interest in it. Thus, for example, if a debtor owned a $2,000 car, subject to a $1,200 lien, the debtor could exempt his $800 interest in the car. The debtor is permitted a $1,500 exemption in a car, proposed 11 U.S.C. 522(d)(2). This section permits him to pay the holder of the lien $1,200 and redeem the entire car, not just the remaining $700 of his exemption. The redemption is accomplished by paying the holder of the lien the amount of the allowed claim secured by the lien. The provision amounts to a right of first refusal for the debtor in consumer goods that might otherwise be repossessed. The right of redemption under this section is not waivable. House Report No. 95–595.

2005 Acts. House Report No. 109–31(Part I), see 2005 U.S. Code Cong. and Adm. News, p. 88.

Legislative Statements

Section 722 of the House amendment adopts the position taken in H.R. 8200 as passed by the House and rejects the alternative contained in section 722 of the Senate amendment.

Amendments

2005 Amendments. Pub.L. 109–8, § 304(2), inserted "in full at the time of redemption" before the period at the end of the section.

Effective and Applicability Provisions

2005 Acts. Amendments by Pub.L. 109–8 effective, except as otherwise provided, 180 days after April 20, 2005, and inapplicable with respect to cases commenced under Title 11 before the effective date, see Pub.L. 109–8, § 1501, set out as a note under 11 U.S.C.A. § 101.

American Digest System

Bankruptcy ☞3034.

Key Number System Topic No. 51.

Corpus Juris Secundum

CJS Bankruptcy § 278, Parties Defendant; Sovereign Immunity.

CJS Bankruptcy § 527, Automatic Relief from Stay--As to Personal Property.

CJS Bankruptcy § 609, Filing of Motion; Notice.

CJS Bankruptcy § 610, Waiver; Failure to File Timely Statement of Intent.

§ 723. Rights of partnership trustee against general partners

(a) If there is a deficiency of property of the estate to pay in full all claims which are allowed in a case under this chapter concerning a partnership and with respect to which a general partner of the partnership is personally liable, the trustee shall have a claim against such general partner to the extent that under applicable nonbankruptcy law such general partner is personally liable for such deficiency.

(b) To the extent practicable, the trustee shall first seek recovery of such deficiency from any general partner in such partnership that is not a debtor in a case under this title. Pending determination of such deficiency, the court may order any such partner to provide the estate with indemnity for, or assurance of payment of, any deficiency recoverable from such partner, or not to dispose of property.

(c) The trustee has a claim against the estate of each general partner in such partnership that is a debtor in a case under this title for the full amount of all claims of creditors allowed in the case concerning such partnership. Notwithstanding section 502 of this title, there shall not be allowed in such partner's case a claim against such partner on which both such partner and such partnership are liable, except to any extent that such claim is secured only by property of such partner and not by property of such partnership. The claim of the trustee under this subsection is entitled to distribution in such partner's case under section 726(a) of this title the same as any other claim of a kind specified in such section.

(d) If the aggregate that the trustee recovers from the estates of general partners under subsection (c) of this section is greater than any deficiency not recovered under subsection (b) of this section, the court, after notice and a hearing, shall determine an equitable distribution of the surplus so recovered, and the trustee shall distribute such surplus to the estates of the general partners in such partnership according to such determination.

(Pub.L. 95–598, Nov. 6, 1978, 92 Stat. 2606; Pub.L. 98–353, Title III, § 476, July 10, 1984, 98 Stat. 381; Pub.L. 103–394,

Title II, § 212, Oct. 22, 1994, 108 Stat. 4125; Pub.L. 111–327, § 2(a)(26), Dec. 22, 2010, 124 Stat. 3560.)

HISTORICAL AND STATUTORY NOTES

Revision Notes and Legislative Reports

1978 Acts. This section is a significant departure from present law. It repeals the jingle rule, which, for ease of administration, denied partnership creditors their rights against general partners by permitting general partners' individual creditors to share in their estates first to the exclusion of partnership creditors. The result under this section more closely tracks generally applicable partnership law, without a significant administrative burden.

Subsection (a) specifies that each general partner in a partnership debtor is liable to the partnership's trustee for any deficiency of partnership property to pay in full all administrative expenses and all claims against the partnership.

Subsection (b) requires the trustee to seek recovery of the deficiency from any general partner that is not a debtor in a bankruptcy case. The court is empowered to order that partner to indemnify the estate or not to dispose of property pending a determination of the deficiency. The language of the subsection is directed to cases under the bankruptcy code. However, if, during the early stages of the transition period, a partner in a partnership is proceeding under the Bankruptcy Act [former Title 11] while the partnership is proceeding under the bankruptcy code, the trustee should not first seek recovery against the Bankruptcy Act partner. Rather, the Bankruptcy Act partner should be deemed for the purposes of this section and the rights of the trustee to be proceeding under title 11.

Subsection (c) requires the partnership trustee to seek recovery of the full amount of the deficiency from the estate of each general partner that is a debtor in a bankruptcy case. The trustee will share equally with the partners' individual creditors in the assets of the partners' estates. Claims of partnership creditors who may have filed against the partner will be disallowed to avoid double counting.

Subsection (d) provides for the case where the total recovery from all of the bankrupt general partners is greater than the deficiency of which the trustee sought recovery. This case would most likely occur for a partnership with a large number of general partners. If the situation arises, the court is required to determine an equitable redistribution of the surplus to the estate of the general partners. The determination will be based on factors such as the relative liability of each of the general partners under the partnership agreement and the relative rights of each of the general partners in the profits of the enterprise under the partnership agreement. Senate Report No. 95–989.

1984 Acts. Statements by Legislative Leaders, see 1984 U.S.Code Cong. and Adm.News, p. 576.

1994 Acts. House Report No. 103–835, see 1994 U.S. Code Cong. and Adm. News, p. 3340.

Legislative Statements

Section 723(c) of the House amendment is a compromise between similar provisions contained in the House bill and Senate amendment. The section makes clear that the trustee of a partnership has a claim against each general partner for the full amount of all claims of creditors allowed in the case concerning the partnership. By restricting the trustee's rights to claims of "creditors," the trustee of the partnership will not have a claim against the general partners for administrative expenses or claims allowed in the case concerning the partnership. As under present law, sections of the Bankruptcy Act [former title 11] applying to codebtors and sureties apply to the relationship of a partner with respect to a partnership debtor. See sections 501(b), 502(e), 506(d)(2), 509, 524(d), and 1301 of title 11.

References in Text

Section 728(a), (b) of this title, referred to in subsec. (b), is subsecs. (a) and (b) of 11 U.S.C.A. § 728, which was repealed by Pub.L. 109–8, Title VII, § 719(b)(1), Apr. 20, 2005, 119 Stat. 133.

Amendments

2010 Amendments. Subsec. (c). Pub.L. 111–327, § 2(a)(26), struck out "Notwithstanding section 728(c) of this title, the" and inserted "The" preceding "trustee has a claim"–.

1994 Amendments. Subsec. (a). Pub.L. 103–394, § 212, substituted provisions directing that trustee shall have a claim against general partner to the extent that under applicable nonbankruptcy law general partner is personally liable for deficiency, for provisions directing that trustee shall have a claim for full amount of deficiency.

1984 Amendments. Subsec. (a). Pub.L. 98–353, § 476, substituted provisions that the trustee shall have a claim for the full amount of the deficiency against a general partner who is personally liable with respect to claims concerning partnerships which are allowed in a case under this chapter, for provisions that each general partner in the partnership would be liable to the trustee for the full amount of such deficiency.

Subsec. (c). Pub.L. 98–353, § 476(b), substituted "such partner's case" for "such case" wherever appearing, "by property of such partnership" for "be property of such partnership", and "a kind specified in such section" for "the kind specified in such section".

Effective and Applicability Provisions

1994 Acts. Amendment by Pub.L. 103–394 effective on Oct. 22, 1994, and not to apply with respect to cases commenced under Title 11 of the United States Code before Oct. 22, 1994, see section 702 of Pub.L. 103–394, set out as a note under section 101 of this title.

1984 Acts. Amendment by Pub.L. 98–353 effective with respect to cases filed 90 days after July 10, 1984, see section 552(a), formerly 553(a), of Pub.L. 98–353, set out as a note under section 101 of this title.

Separability of Provisions

If any provision of or amendment made by Pub.L. 103–394 or the application of such provision or amendment to any person or circumstance is held to be unconstitutional, the remaining provisions of and amendments made by Pub.L. 103–394 and the application of such provisions and amendments to any person or circumstance shall not be affected thereby, see section 701 of Pub.L. 103–394, set out as a note under section 101 of this title.

CROSS REFERENCES

Property of estate, see 11 USCA § 541.

LIBRARY REFERENCES

American Digest System

Bankruptcy ⟐2559.
Key Number System Topic No. 51.

Corpus Juris Secundum

CJS Bankruptcy § 560, Property of Partners and Partnerships.

CJS Bankruptcy § 613, Rights of Partnership Trustee Against General Partners in Chapter 7 Cases.

CJS Bankruptcy § 1097, Trustee's Duties and Liabilities.

§ 724. Treatment of certain liens

(a) The trustee may avoid a lien that secures a claim of a kind specified in section 726(a)(4) of this title.

(b) Property in which the estate has an interest and that is subject to a lien that is not avoidable under this title (other than to the extent that there is a properly perfected unavoidable tax lien arising in connection with an ad valorem tax on real or personal property of the estate) and that secures an allowed claim for a tax, or proceeds of such property, shall be distributed—

(1) first, to any holder of an allowed claim secured by a lien on such property that is not avoidable under this title and that is senior to such tax lien;

(2) second, to any holder of a claim of a kind specified in section 507(a)(1)(C) or 507(a)(2) (except that such expenses under each such section, other than claims for wages, salaries, or commissions that arise after the date of the filing of the petition, shall be limited to expenses incurred under this chapter and shall not include expenses incurred under chapter 11 of this title), 507(a)(1)(A), 507(a)(1)(B), 507(a)(3), 507(a)(4), 507(a)(5), 507(a)(6), or 507(a)(7) of this title, to the extent of the amount of such allowed tax claim that is secured by such tax lien;

(3) third, to the holder of such tax lien, to any extent that such holder's allowed tax claim that is secured by such tax lien exceeds any amount distributed under paragraph (2) of this subsection;

(4) fourth, to any holder of an allowed claim secured by a lien on such property that is not avoidable under this title and that is junior to such tax lien;

(5) fifth, to the holder of such tax lien, to the extent that such holder's allowed claim secured by such tax lien is not paid under paragraph (3) of this subsection; and

(6) sixth, to the estate.

(c) If more than one holder of a claim is entitled to distribution under a particular paragraph of subsection (b) of this section, distribution to such holders under such paragraph shall be in the same order as distribution to such holders would have been other than under this section.

(d) A statutory lien the priority of which is determined in the same manner as the priority of a tax lien under section 6323 of the Internal Revenue Code of 1986 shall be treated under subsection (b) of this section the same as if such lien were a tax lien.

(e) Before subordinating a tax lien on real or personal property of the estate, the trustee shall—

(1) exhaust the unencumbered assets of the estate; and

(2) in a manner consistent with section 506(c), recover from property securing an allowed secured claim the reasonable, necessary costs and expenses of preserving or disposing of such property.

(f) Notwithstanding the exclusion of ad valorem tax liens under this section and subject to the requirements of subsection (e), the following may be paid from property of the estate which secures a tax lien, or the proceeds of such property:

(1) Claims for wages, salaries, and commissions that are entitled to priority under section 507(a)(4).

(2) Claims for contributions to an employee benefit plan entitled to priority under section 507(a)(5).

(Pub.L. 95–598, Nov. 6, 1978, 92 Stat. 2607; Pub.L. 98–353, Title III, § 477, July 10, 1984, 98 Stat. 381; Pub.L. 99–554, Title II, § 283(r), Oct. 27, 1986, 100 Stat. 3118; Pub.L. 103–394, Title III, § 304(h)(4), Title V, § 501(d)(23), Oct. 22, 1994, 108 Stat. 4134, 4146; Pub.L. 109–8, Title VII, § 701(a), Apr. 20, 2005, 119 Stat. 124; Pub.L. 111–327, § 2(a)(27), Dec. 22, 2010, 124 Stat. 3560.)

HISTORICAL AND STATUTORY NOTES

Revision Notes and Legislative Reports

1978 Acts. Subsection (a) of section 724 permits the trustee to avoid a lien that secures a fine, penalty, forfeiture, or multiple, punitive, or exemplary damages claim to the extent that the claim is not compensation for actual pecuniary loss. The subsection follows the policy found in section 57j of the Bankruptcy Act [section 93(j) of former Title 11] of protecting unsecured creditors from the debtor's wrongdoing, but expands the protection afforded. The lien is made voidable rather than void in chapter 7, in order to permit the lien to be revived if the case is converted to chapter 11 under which penalty liens are not voidable. To make the lien void would be to permit the filing of a chapter 7, the voiding of the lien, and the conversion to a chapter 11, simply to avoid a penalty lien, which should be valid in a reorganization case.

Subsection (b) governs tax liens. This provision retains the rule of present bankruptcy law (section 67(C)(3) of the Bankruptcy Act [section 107(c)(3) of former Title 11]) that a tax lien on personal property, if not avoidable by the trustee, is subordinated in payment to unsecured claims having a higher priority than unsecured tax claims. Those other claims may be satisfied from the amount that would otherwise have been applied to the tax lien, and any excess of the amount of the lien is then applied to the tax. Any personal property (or sale proceeds) remaining is to be used to satisfy claims secured by liens which are junior to the tax lien. Any proceeds remaining are next applied to pay any unpaid balance of the tax lien.

Subsection (d) specifies that any statutory lien whose priority is determined in the same manner as a tax lien is to be treated as a tax lien under this section, even if the lien does not secure a claim for taxes. An example is the ERISA [29 U.S.C.A. § 1001 et seq.] lien. Senate Report No. 95–989.

Subsection (b) governs tax liens. It is derived from section 67c(3) of the Bankruptcy Act [section 107(c)(3) of former Title 11], without substantial modification in result. It subordinates tax liens to administrative expense and wage claims, and solves certain circuity of liens problems that arise in connection with the subordination. The order of distribution of property subject to a tax lien is as follows: First, to holders of liens senior to the tax lien; second, to administrative expenses, wage claims, and consumer creditors that are granted priority, but only to the extent of the amount of the allowed tax claim secured by the lien. In other words, the priority claimants step into the shoes of the tax collector. Third, to the tax claimant, to the extent that priority claimants did not use up his entire claim. Fourth, to junior lien holders. Fifth, to the tax collector to the extent that he was not paid under paragraph (3). Finally, any remaining property goes to the estate. The result of these provisions are to leave senior and junior lienors and holders of unsecured claims undisturbed. If there are any liens that are equal in status to the tax lien, they share pari passu with the tax lien under the distribution provisions of this subsection. House Report No. 95–595.

1984 Acts. Statements by Legislative Leaders, see 1984 U.S.Code Cong. and Adm.News, p. 576.

1986 Acts. House Report No. 99–764 and House Conference Report No. 99–958, see 1986 U.S.Code Cong. and Adm. News, p. 5227.

House Conference Report No. 99–841 and Statement by President, see 1986 U.S.Code Cong. and Adm.News, p. 4075.

1994 Acts. House Report No. 103–835, see 1994 U.S. Code Cong. and Adm. News, p. 3340.

2005 Acts. House Report No. 109–31(Part I), see 2005 U.S. Code Cong. and Adm. News, p. 88.

Legislative Statements

Section 724 of the House amendment adopts the provision taken in the House bill and rejects the provision taken in the Senate amendment. In effect, a tax claim secured by a lien is treated as a claim between the fifth and sixth priority in a case under chapter 7 rather than as a secured claim.

Treatment of certain liens: The House amendment modifies present law by requiring the subordination of tax liens on both real and personal property to the payment of claims having a priority. This means that assets are to be distributed from the debtor's estate to pay higher priority claims before the tax claims are paid, even though the tax claims are properly secured. Under present law and the Senate amendment only tax liens on personal property, but not on real property, are subordinated to the payment of claims having a priority above the priority for tax claims.

References in Text

Chapter 11 of this title, referred to in subsec. (b)(2), is 11 U.S.C.A. § 1101 et seq.

Section 6323 of the Internal Revenue Code of 1986, referred to in subsec. (d), is classified to section 6323 of Title 26, Internal Revenue Code.

Amendments

2010 Amendments. Subsec. (b)(2). Pub.L. 111–327, § 2(a)(27), struck out "507(a)(1)" and inserted "507(a)(1)(C) or 507(a)(2)", inserted "under each such section" following "such expenses", struck out "chapter 7 of this title" and inserted "this chapter", and struck out "507(a)(2)," and inserted "507(a)(1)(A), 507(a)(1)(B),".

2005 Amendments. Subsec. (b). Pub.L. 109–8, § 701(a)(1), in the matter preceding par. (1), inserted "(other than to the extent that there is a properly perfected unavoidable tax lien arising in connection with an ad valorem tax on real or personal property of the estate)" after "under this title".

Subsec. (b)(2). Pub.L. 109–8, § 701(a)(2), inserted "(except that such expenses, other than claims for wages, salaries, or commissions that arise after the date of the filing of the petition, shall be limited to expenses incurred under chapter 7 of this title and shall not include expenses incurred under chapter 11 of this title)" after "507(a)(1)".

Subsec. (e). Pub.L. 109–8, § 701(a)(3), added subsec. (e).

Subsec. (f). Pub.L. 109–8, § 701(a)(3), added subsec. (f).

1994 Amendments. Subsec. (b)(2). Pub.L. 103–394, § 304(h)(4), substituted "507(a)(6), or 507(a)(7)" for "or 507(a)(6)".

Subsec. (d). Pub.L. 103–394, § 501(d)(23), substituted "Internal Revenue Code of 1986" for "Internal Revenue Code of 1954 (26 U.S.C. 6323)".

1986 Amendments. Subsec. (b)(2). Pub.L. 99–554 added reference to section 507(a)(6) of this title.

1984 Amendments. Subsec. (b). Pub.L. 98–353, § 477(a)(1), substituted "a tax" for "taxes" in provisions preceding par. (1).

Subsec. (b)(2). Pub.L. 98–353, § 477(a)(2), substituted "any holder of a claim of a kind specified" for "claims specified", "section 507(a)(1)" for "sections 507(a)(1)", and "or 507(a)(5) of this title" for "and 507(a)(5) of this title".

Subsec. (b)(3). Pub.L. 98–353, § 477(a)(3), substituted "allowed tax claim" for "allowed claim".

Subsec. (c). Pub.L. 98–353, § 477(b), substituted "holder of a claim is entitled" for "creditor is entitled" and "holders" for "creditors" wherever appearing.

Subsec. (d). Pub.L. 98–353, § 477(c), substituted "the priority of which" for "whose priority" and "the same as if such lien were a tax lien" for "the same as a tax lien".

Effective and Applicability Provisions

2005 Acts. Amendments by Pub.L. 109–8 effective, except as otherwise provided, 180 days after April 20, 2005, and inapplicable with respect to cases commenced under Title 11 before the effective date, see Pub.L. 109–8, § 1501, set out as a note under 11 U.S.C.A. § 101.

1994 Acts. Amendments by Pub.L. 103–394 effective on Oct. 22, 1994, and not to apply with respect to cases commenced under Title 11 of the United States Code before Oct. 22, 1994, see section 702 of Pub.L. 103–394, set out as a note under section 101 of this title.

1986 Acts. Amendment by Pub.L. 99–554 effective 30 days after Oct. 27, 1986, except as otherwise provided, see section 302(a) of Pub.L. 99–554, set out as a note under section 581 of Title 28, Judiciary and Judicial Procedure.

1984 Acts. Amendment by Pub.L. 98–353 effective with respect to cases filed 90 days after July 10, 1984, see section

552(a), formerly 553(a), of Pub.L. 98–353, set out as a note under section 101 of this title.

Separability of Provisions

If any provision of or amendment made by Pub.L. 103–394 or the application of such provision or amendment to any person or circumstance is held to be unconstitutional, the remaining provisions of and amendments made by Pub.L. 103–394 and the application of such provisions and amendments to any person or circumstance shall not be affected thereby, see section 701 of Pub.L. 103–394, set out as a note under section 101 of this title.

CROSS REFERENCES

Automatic preservation of avoided transfer, see 11 USCA § 551.

Commencement of involuntary cases by transferees of voidable transfers, see 11 USCA § 303.

Disallowance of claims of entity that is transferee of avoidable transfer, see 11 USCA § 502.

Effect of dismissal, see 11 USCA § 349.

Exemptions, see 11 USCA § 522.

Liability of transferee of avoided transfer, see 11 USCA § 550.

Recovery of voidable transfers in investor protection liquidation proceedings, see 15 USCA § 78fff–2.

Voidable transfers in commodity broker liquidation cases, see 11 USCA § 764.

LIBRARY REFERENCES

American Digest System

Bankruptcy ⊂⊃2951 to 2972, 3442.1, 3443.

Key Number System Topic No. 51.

Corpus Juris Secundum

CJS Bankruptcy § 278, Parties Defendant; Sovereign Immunity.

CJS Bankruptcy § 400, Relief Available on Recognition.

CJS Bankruptcy § 403, Powers of Foreign Representative on Recognition--Commencement of or Participation in Other Bankruptcy Case.

CJS Bankruptcy § 590, Recovery and Exemption of Property After Transfer Avoided.

CJS Bankruptcy § 669, Statutory Liens; Penalty Liens.

CJS Bankruptcy § 698, Transfers or Obligations Which May be Avoided.

CJS Bankruptcy § 700, Disallowance of Claims of Entities or Transferees Holding Recoverable Property.

CJS Bankruptcy § 1104, Tax Liens and Other Statutory Liens.

§ 725. Disposition of certain property

After the commencement of a case under this chapter, but before final distribution of property of the estate under section 726 of this title, the trustee, after notice and a hearing, shall dispose of any property in which an entity other than the estate has an interest, such as a lien, and that has not been disposed of under another section of this title.

(Pub.L. 95–598, Nov. 6, 1978, 92 Stat. 2607; Pub.L. 98–353, Title III, § 478, July 10, 1984, 98 Stat. 381.)

HISTORICAL AND STATUTORY NOTES
Revision Notes and Legislative Reports

1978 Acts. This section requires the court to determine the appropriate disposition of property in which the estate and an entity other than the estate have an interest. It would apply, for example, to property subject to a lien or property co-owned by the estate and another entity. The court must make the determination with respect to property that is not disposed of under another section of the bankruptcy code, such as by abandonment under section 554, by sale or distribution under 363, or by allowing foreclosure by a secured creditor by lifting the stay under section 362. The purpose of the section is to give the court appropriate authority to ensure that collateral or its proceeds is returned to the proper secured creditor, that consigned or bailed goods are returned to the consignor or bailor and so on. Current law is curiously silent on this point, though case law has grown to fill the void. The section is in lieu of a section that would direct a certain distribution to secured creditors. It gives the court greater flexibility to meet the circumstances, and it is broader, permitting disposition of property subject to a co-ownership interest. Senate Report No. 95–989.

1984 Acts. Statements by Legislative Leaders, see 1984 U.S.Code Cong. and Adm.News, p. 576.

Legislative Statements

Section 725 of the House amendment adopts the substance contained in both the House bill and Senate amendment but transfers an administrative function to the trustee in accordance with the general thrust of this legislation to separate the administrative and the judicial functions where appropriate.

Amendments

1984 Amendments. Pub.L. 98–353 substituted "distribution of property of the estate" for "distribution".

Effective and Applicability Provisions

1984 Acts. Amendment by Pub.L. 98–353 effective with respect to cases filed 90 days after July 10, 1984, see section 552(a), formerly 553(a), of Pub.L. 98–353, set out as a note under section 101 of this title.

LIBRARY REFERENCES
American Digest System

Bankruptcy ⟝3442.1.
Key Number System Topic No. 51.

Corpus Juris Secundum

CJS Bankruptcy § 139, Adversary Proceedings.
CJS Bankruptcy § 261, Power to Render Declaratory Judgment.
CJS Bankruptcy § 1097, Trustee's Duties and Liabilities.

§ 726. Distribution of property of the estate

(a) Except as provided in section 510 of this title, property of the estate shall be distributed—

(1) first, in payment of claims of the kind specified in, and in the order specified in, section 507 of this title, proof of which is timely filed under section 501

of this title or tardily filed on or before the earlier of—

  (A) the date that is 10 days after the mailing to creditors of the summary of the trustee's final report; or

  (B) the date on which the trustee commences final distribution under this section;

(2) second, in payment of any allowed unsecured claim, other than a claim of a kind specified in paragraph (1), (3), or (4) of this subsection, proof of which is—

  (A) timely filed under section 501(a) of this title;

  (B) timely filed under section 501(b) or 501(c) of this title; or

  (C) tardily filed under section 501(a) of this title, if—

    (i) the creditor that holds such claim did not have notice or actual knowledge of the case in time for timely filing of a proof of such claim under section 501(a) of this title; and

    (ii) proof of such claim is filed in time to permit payment of such claim;

(3) third, in payment of any allowed unsecured claim proof of which is tardily filed under section 501(a) of this title, other than a claim of the kind specified in paragraph (2)(C) of this subsection;

(4) fourth, in payment of any allowed claim, whether secured or unsecured, for any fine, penalty, or forfeiture, or for multiple, exemplary, or punitive damages, arising before the earlier of the order for relief or the appointment of a trustee, to the extent that such fine, penalty, forfeiture, or damages are not compensation for actual pecuniary loss suffered by the holder of such claim;

(5) fifth, in payment of interest at the legal rate from the date of the filing of the petition, on any claim paid under paragraph (1), (2), (3), or (4) of this subsection; and

(6) sixth, to the debtor.

(b) Payment on claims of a kind specified in paragraph (1), (2), (3), (4), (5), (6), (7), (8), (9), or (10) of section 507(a) of this title, or in paragraph (2), (3), (4), or (5) of subsection (a) of this section, shall be made pro rata among claims of the kind specified in each such particular paragraph, except that in a case that has been converted to this chapter under section 1112, 1208, or 1307 of this title, a claim allowed under section 503(b) of this title incurred under this chapter after such conversion has priority over a claim allowed under section 503(b) of this title incurred under any other chapter of this title or under this chapter before such conversion and over any expenses of a custodian superseded under section 543 of this title.

(c) Notwithstanding subsections (a) and (b) of this section, if there is property of the kind specified in section 541(a)(2) of this title, or proceeds of such property, in the estate, such property or proceeds shall be segregated from other property of the estate, and such property or proceeds and other property of the estate shall be distributed as follows:

(1) Claims allowed under section 503 of this title shall be paid either from property of the kind specified in section 541(a)(2) of this title, or from other property of the estate, as the interest of justice requires.

(2) Allowed claims, other than claims allowed under section 503 of this title, shall be paid in the order specified in subsection (a) of this section, and, with respect to claims of a kind specified in a particular paragraph of section 507 of this title or subsection (a) of this section, in the following order and manner:

(A) First, community claims against the debtor or the debtor's spouse shall be paid from property of the kind specified in section 541(a)(2) of this title, except to the extent that such property is solely liable for debts of the debtor.

(B) Second, to the extent that community claims against the debtor are not paid under subparagraph (A) of this paragraph, such community claims shall be paid from property of the kind specified in section 541(a)(2) of this title that is solely liable for debts of the debtor.

(C) Third, to the extent that all claims against the debtor including community claims against the debtor are not paid under subparagraph (A) or (B) of this paragraph such claims shall be paid from property of the estate other than property of the kind specified in section 541(a)(2) of this title.

(D) Fourth, to the extent that community claims against the debtor or the debtor's spouse are not paid under subparagraph (A), (B), or (C) of this paragraph, such claims shall be paid from all remaining property of the estate.

(Pub.L. 95–598, Nov. 6, 1978, 92 Stat. 2608; Pub.L. 98–353, Title III, § 479, July 10, 1984, 98 Stat. 381; Pub.L. 99–554, Title II, §§ 257(r), 283(s), Oct. 27, 1986, 100 Stat. 3115, 3118; Pub.L. 103–394, Title II, § 213(b), Title III, § 304(h)(5), Title V, § 501(d)(24), Oct. 22, 1994, 108 Stat. 4126, 4134, 4146; Pub.L. 109–8, Title VII, § 713, Title XII, § 1215, Apr. 20, 2005, 119 Stat. 128, 195; Pub.L. 111–327, § 2(a)(28), Dec. 22, 2010, 124 Stat. 3560.)

HISTORICAL AND STATUTORY NOTES

Revision Notes and Legislative Reports

1978 Acts. This section is the general distribution section for liquidation cases. It dictates the order in which distribution of property of the estate, which has usually been reduced to money by the trustee under the requirements of section 704(1).

First, property is distributed among priority claimants, as determined by section 507, and in the order prescribed by section 507. Second, distribution is to general unsecured creditors. This class excludes priority creditors and the two classes of subordinated creditors specified below. The provi-

sion is written to permit distribution to creditors that tardily file claims if their tardiness was due to lack of notice or knowledge of the case. Though it is in the interest of the estate to encourage timely filing, when tardy filing is not the result of a failure to act by the creditor, the normal subordination penalty should not apply. Third distribution is to general unsecured creditors who tardily file. Fourth distribution is to holders of fine, penalty, forfeiture, or multiple, punitive, or exemplary damage claims. More of these claims are disallowed entirely under present law. They are simply subordinated here.

Paragraph (4) provides that punitive penalties, including prepetition tax penalties, are subordinated to the payment of all other classes of claims, except claims for interest accruing during the case. In effect, these penalties are payable out of the estate's assets only if and to the extent that a surplus of assets would otherwise remain at the close of the case for distribution back to the debtor.

Paragraph (5) provides that postpetition interest on prepetition claims is also to be paid to the creditor in a subordinated position. Like prepetition penalties, such interest will be paid from the estate only if and to the extent that a surplus of assets would otherwise remain for return to the debtor at the close of the case.

This section also specifies that interest accrued on all claims (including priority and nonpriority tax claims) which accrued before the date of the filing of the title 11 petition is to be paid in the same order of distribution of the estate's assets as the principal amount of the related claims.

Any surplus is paid to the debtor under paragraph (6).

Subsection (b) follows current law. It specifies that claims within a particular class are to be paid pro rata. This provision will apply, of course, only when there are inadequate funds to pay the holders of claims of a particular class in full. The exception found in the section, which also follows current law, specifies that liquidation administrative expenses are to be paid ahead of reorganization administrative expenses if the case has been converted from a reorganization case to a liquidation case, or from an individual repayment plan case to a liquidation case.

Subsection (c) governs distributions in cases in which there is community property and other property of the estate. The section requires the two kinds of property to be segregated. The distribution is as follows: First, administrative expenses are to be paid, as the court determines on any reasonable equitable basis, from both kinds of property. The court will divide administrative expenses according to such factors as the amount of each kind of property in the estate, the cost of preservation and liquidation of each kind of property, and whether any particular administrative expenses are attributable to one kind of property or the other. Second, claims are to be paid as provided under subsection (a) (the normal liquidation case distribution rules) in the following order and manner: First, community claims against the debtor or the debtor's spouse are paid from community property, except such as is liable solely for the debts of the debtor.

Second, community claims against the debtor, to the extent not paid under the first provision, are paid from community property that is solely liable for the debts of the debtor. Third, community claims, to the extent they remain unpaid, and all other claims against the debtor, are paid from noncommunity property. Fourth, if any community claims against the debtor or the debtor's spouse remain unpaid, they are paid from whatever property remains in the estate. This would occur if community claims against the debtor's spouse are large in amount and most of the estate's property is property solely liable, under nonbankruptcy law, for debts of the debtor.

The marshalling rules in this section apply only to property of the estate. However, they will provide a guide to the courts in the interpretation of proposed 11 U.S.C. 725, relating to distribution of collateral, in cases in which there is community property. If a secured creditor has a lien on both community and non-community property, the marshalling rules here—by analogy would dictate that the creditor be satisfied first out of community property, and then out of separate property. Senate Report No. 95–989.

1984 Acts. Statements by Legislative Leaders, see 1984 U.S.Code Cong. and Adm.News, p. 576.

1986 Acts. House Report No. 99–764 and House Conference Report No. 99–958, see 1986 U.S.Code Cong. and Adm. News, p. 5227.

1994 Acts. House Report No. 103–835, see 1994 U.S. Code Cong. and Adm. News, p. 3340.

2005 Acts. House Report No. 109–31(Part I), see 2005 U.S. Code Cong. and Adm. News, p. 88.

Legislative Statements

Section 726(a)(4) adopts a provision contained in the Senate amendment subordinating prepetition penalties and penalties arising in the involuntary gap period to the extent the penalties are not compensation for actual pecuniary laws.

The House amendment deletes a provision following section 726(a)(6) of the Senate amendment providing that the term "claim" includes interest due owed before the date of the filing of the petition as unnecessary since a right to payment for interest due is a right to payment which is within the definition of "claim" in section 101(4) of the House amendment.

Amendments

2010 Amendments. Subsec. (b). Pub.L. 111–327, § 2(a)(28), struck out "or (8)" and inserted "(8), (9), or (10)".

2005 Amendments. Subsec. (a)(1). Pub.L. 109–8, § 713, struck out "before the date on which the trustee commences distribution under this section;" and inserted "on or before the earlier of—".

Subsec. (a)(1)(A). Pub.L. 109–8, § 713, added subpar. (A).

Subsec. (a)(1)(B). Pub.L. 109–8, § 713, added subpar. (B).

Subsec. (b). Pub.L. 109–8, § 1215, struck out "1009," preceding "1112, 1208, or 1307 of this title".

1994 Amendments. Subsec. (a)(1). Pub.L. 103–394, § 213(b), added provisions relating to proof timely filed or tardily filed.

Subsec. (b). Pub.L. 103–394, § 304(h)(5), substituted ", (7), or (8)" for "or (7)".

Pub.L. 103–394, § 501(d)(24), substituted "chapter under section 1009, 1112," for "chapter under section 1112".

1986 Amendments. Subsec. (b). Pub.L. 99–554, § 257(r), added reference to section 1208 of this title.

Pub.L. 99–554, § 283(s), added reference to par. (7) of section 507(a) of this title.

1984 Amendments. Subsec. (b). Pub.L. 98–353, § 479(a), substituted "each such particular paragraph" for "a particular paragraph", "a claim allowed under section 503(b) of this title"

for "administrative expenses" wherever appearing, and "has priority over" for "have priority over".

Subsec. (c)(1). Pub.L. 98–353, § 479(b)(1), substituted "Claims allowed under section 503 of this title" for "Administrative expenses".

Subsec. (c)(2). Pub.L. 98–353, § 479(b)(2), substituted "Allowed claims, other than claims allowed under section 503 of this title," for "Claims other than for administrative expenses".

Effective and Applicability Provisions

2005 Acts. Amendments by Pub.L. 109–8 effective, except as otherwise provided, 180 days after April 20, 2005, and inapplicable with respect to cases commenced under Title 11 before the effective date, see Pub.L. 109–8, § 1501, set out as a note under 11 U.S.C.A. § 101.

1994 Acts. Amendments by Pub.L. 103–394 effective on Oct. 22, 1994, and not to apply with respect to cases commenced under Title 11 of the United States Code before Oct. 22, 1994, see section 702 of Pub.L. 103–394, set out as a note under section 101 of this title.

1986 Acts. Amendments by Pub.L. 99–554, § 257(r), effective 30 days after Oct. 27, 1986, but not to apply with respect to cases commenced under this title before that date, see section 302(a), (c)(1) of Pub.L. 99–554, set out as a note under section 581 of Title 28, Judiciary and Judicial Procedure.

Amendment by Pub.L. 99–554, § 283, effective 30 days after Oct. 27, 1986, see section 302(a) of Pub.L. 99–554, set out as a note under section 581 of Title 28.

1984 Acts. Amendment by Pub.L. 98–353 effective with respect to cases filed 90 days after July 10, 1984, see section 552(a), formerly 553(a), of Pub.L. 98–353, set out as a note under section 101 of this title.

Separability of Provisions

If any provision of or amendment made by Pub.L. 103–394 or the application of such provision or amendment to any person or circumstance is held to be unconstitutional, the remaining provisions of and amendments made by Pub.L. 103–394 and the application of such provisions and amendments to any person or circumstance shall not be affected thereby, see section 701 of Pub.L. 103–394, set out as a note under section 101 of this title.

CROSS REFERENCES

Customer property, distribution in—

    Commodity broker liquidation cases, see 11 USCA § 766.

    Stockbroker liquidation cases, see 11 USCA § 752.

Distribution in Chapter eleven cases, see 11 USCA § 1143.

Distribution of securities in stockbroker liquidation cases, see 11 USCA § 750.

Election of creditors holding certain claims entitled to distribution to creditors' committee, see 11 USCA § 705.

Election of trustee by creditors holding claims entitled to distribution, see 11 USCA § 702.

Impairment of claims and interests and objection to claims filed untimely, see 11 USCA § 502.

Ownership of copyright, see 17 USCA § 201.

Payment stopped on checks remaining unpaid 90 days after final distribution, see 11 USCA § 347.

Priorities of distribution in investor liquidation proceedings, see 15 USCA § 78fff.

Student Loan Marketing Association of the Robert T. Stafford Student Loan Program deemed person within meaning of this title for purposes of distribution of its property pursuant to this section, see 20 USCA § 1087–2.

LIBRARY REFERENCES

American Digest System

Bankruptcy ⇔3442.1, 3443.

Key Number System Topic No. 51.

Corpus Juris Secundum

CJS Bankruptcy § 278, Parties Defendant; Sovereign Immunity.

CJS Bankruptcy § 669, Statutory Liens; Penalty Liens.

CJS Bankruptcy § 1097, Trustee's Duties and Liabilities.

CJS Bankruptcy § 1099, Unclaimed Property.

CJS Bankruptcy § 1102, Priority of Particular Distribution Classes.

CJS Bankruptcy § 1103, Community Property.

CJS Bankruptcy § 1111, Customer Property.

CJS Bankruptcy § 1114, Treatment of Customer Property.

§ 727. Discharge

(a) The court shall grant the debtor a discharge, unless—

(1) the debtor is not an individual;

(2) the debtor, with intent to hinder, delay, or defraud a creditor or an officer of the estate charged with custody of property under this title, has transferred, removed, destroyed, mutilated, or concealed, or has permitted to be transferred, removed, destroyed, mutilated, or concealed—

(A) property of the debtor, within one year before the date of the filing of the petition; or

(B) property of the estate, after the date of the filing of the petition;

(3) the debtor has concealed, destroyed, mutilated, falsified, or failed to keep or preserve any recorded information, including books, documents, records, and papers, from which the debtor's financial condition or business transactions might be ascertained, unless such act or failure to act was justified under all of the circumstances of the case;

(4) the debtor knowingly and fraudulently, in or in connection with the case—

(A) made a false oath or account;

(B) presented or used a false claim;

(C) gave, offered, received, or attempted to obtain money, property, or advantage, or a promise of money, property, or advantage, for acting or forbearing to act; or

(D) withheld from an officer of the estate entitled to possession under this title, any recorded information, including books, documents, records, and papers, relating to the debtor's property or financial affairs;

(5) the debtor has failed to explain satisfactorily, before determination of denial of discharge under this paragraph, any loss of assets or deficiency of assets to meet the debtor's liabilities;

(6) the debtor has refused, in the case—

(A) to obey any lawful order of the court, other than an order to respond to a material question or to testify;

(B) on the ground of privilege against self-incrimination, to respond to a material question approved by the court or to testify, after the debtor has been granted immunity with respect to the matter concerning which such privilege was invoked; or

(C) on a ground other than the properly invoked privilege against self-incrimination, to respond to a material question approved by the court or to testify;

(7) the debtor has committed any act specified in paragraph (2), (3), (4), (5), or (6) of this subsection, on or within one year before the date of the filing of the petition, or during the case, in connection with another case, under this title or under the Bankruptcy Act, concerning an insider;

(8) the debtor has been granted a discharge under this section, under section 1141 of this title, or under section 14, 371, or 476 of the Bankruptcy Act, in a case commenced within 8 years before the date of the filing of the petition;

(9) the debtor has been granted a discharge under section 1228 or 1328 of this title, or under section 660 or 661 of the Bankruptcy Act, in a case commenced within six years before the date of the filing of the petition, unless payments under the plan in such case totaled at least—

(A) 100 percent of the allowed unsecured claims in such case; or

(B)(i) 70 percent of such claims; and

(ii) the plan was proposed by the debtor in good faith, and was the debtor's best effort;

(10) the court approves a written waiver of discharge executed by the debtor after the order for relief under this chapter;

(11) after filing the petition, the debtor failed to complete an instructional course concerning personal financial management described in section 111, except that this paragraph shall not apply with respect to a debtor who is a person described in section 109(h)(4) or who resides in a district for which the United States trustee (or the bankruptcy administrator, if any) determines that the approved instructional courses are not adequate to service the additional individuals who would otherwise be required to complete such instructional courses under this section (The United States trustee (or the bankruptcy administrator, if any) who makes a determination described in this paragraph shall review such determi-

nation not later than 1 year after the date of such determination, and not less frequently than annually thereafter.); or

(12) the court after notice and a hearing held not more than 10 days before the date of the entry of the order granting the discharge finds that there is reasonable cause to believe that—

    (A) section 522(q)(1) may be applicable to the debtor; and

    (B) there is pending any proceeding in which the debtor may be found guilty of a felony of the kind described in section 522(q)(1)(A) or liable for a debt of the kind described in section 522(q)(1)(B).

(b) Except as provided in section 523 of this title, a discharge under subsection (a) of this section discharges the debtor from all debts that arose before the date of the order for relief under this chapter, and any liability on a claim that is determined under section 502 of this title as if such claim had arisen before the commencement of the case, whether or not a proof of claim based on any such debt or liability is filed under section 501 of this title, and whether or not a claim based on any such debt or liability is allowed under section 502 of this title.

(c)(1) The trustee, a creditor, or the United States trustee may object to the granting of a discharge under subsection (a) of this section.

(2) On request of a party in interest, the court may order the trustee to examine the acts and conduct of the debtor to determine whether a ground exists for denial of discharge.

(d) On request of the trustee, a creditor, or the United States trustee, and after notice and a hearing, the court shall revoke a discharge granted under subsection (a) of this section if—

(1) such discharge was obtained through the fraud of the debtor, and the requesting party did not know of such fraud until after the granting of such discharge;

(2) the debtor acquired property that is property of the estate, or became entitled to acquire property that would be property of the estate, and knowingly and fraudulently failed to report the acquisition of or entitlement to such property, or to deliver or surrender such property to the trustee;

(3) the debtor committed an act specified in subsection (a)(6) of this section; or

(4) the debtor has failed to explain satisfactorily—

    (A) a material misstatement in an audit referred to in section 586(f) of title 28; or

    (B) a failure to make available for inspection all necessary accounts, papers, documents, financial records, files, and all other papers, things, or property belonging to the debtor that are request-

ed for an audit referred to in section 586(f) of title 28.

(e) The trustee, a creditor, or the United States trustee may request a revocation of a discharge—

(1) under subsection (d)(1) of this section within one year after such discharge is granted; or

(2) under subsection (d)(2) or (d)(3) of this section before the later of—

    (A) one year after the granting of such discharge; and

    (B) the date the case is closed.

(Pub.L. 95–598, Nov. 6, 1978, 92 Stat. 2609; Pub.L. 98–353, Title III, § 480, July 10, 1984, 98 Stat. 382; Pub.L. 99–554, Title II, §§ 220, 257(s), Oct. 27, 1986, 100 Stat. 3101, 3116; Pub.L. 109–8, Title I, § 106(b), Title III, §§ 312(1), 330(a), Title VI, § 603(d), Apr. 20, 2005, 119 Stat. 38, 86, 101, 123.)

HISTORICAL AND STATUTORY NOTES

Revision Notes and Legislative Reports

1978 Acts. This section is the heart of the fresh start provisions of the bankruptcy law. Subsection (a) requires the court to grant a debtor a discharge unless one of nine conditions is met. The first condition is that the debtor is not an individual. This is a change from present law, under which corporations and partnerships may be discharged in liquidation cases, though they rarely are. The change in policy will avoid trafficking in corporate shells and in bankrupt partnerships. "Individual" includes a deceased individual, so that if the debtor dies during the bankruptcy case, he will nevertheless be released from his debts, and his estate will not be liable for them. Creditors will be entitled to only one satisfaction—from the bankruptcy estate and not from the probate estate.

The next three grounds for denial of discharge center on the debtor's wrongdoing in or in connection with the bankruptcy case. They are derived from Bankruptcy Act § 14c [section 32(c) of former Title 11]. If the debtor, with intent to hinder, delay, or defraud his creditors or an officer of the estate, has transferred, removed, destroyed, mutilated, or concealed, or has permitted any such action with respect to, property of the debtor within the year preceding the case, or property of the estate after the commencement of the case, then the debtor is denied discharge. The debtor is also denied discharge if he has concealed, destroyed, mutilated, falsified, or failed to keep or preserve any books and records from which his financial condition might be ascertained, unless the act or failure to act was justified under all the circumstances of the case. The fourth ground for denial of discharge is the commission of a bankruptcy crime, although the standard of proof is preponderance of the evidence rather than proof beyond a reasonable doubt. These crimes include the making of a false oath or account, the use or presentation of a false claim, the giving or receiving of money for acting or forbearing to act, and the withholding from an officer of the estate entitled to possession of books and records relating to the debtor's financial affairs.

The fifth ground for denial of discharge is the failure of the debtor to explain satisfactorily any loss of assets or deficiency of assets to meet the debtor's liabilities. The sixth ground concerns refusal to testify. It is a change from present law, under which the debtor may be denied discharge for legitimately exercising his right against self-incrimination. Under this provision, the debtor may be denied discharge if he refuses to obey any lawful order of the court, or if he refuses to testify after having been granted immunity or after improperly invoking the constitutional privilege against self-incrimination.

The seventh ground for denial of discharge is the commission of an act specified in grounds two through six during the year before the debtor's case in connection with another bankruptcy case concerning an insider.

The eighth ground for denial of discharge is derived from § 14c(5) of the Bankruptcy Act [section 32(c)(5) of former Title 11]. If the debtor has been granted a discharge in a case commenced within 6 years preceding the present bankruptcy case, he is denied discharge. This provision, which is no change from current law with respect to straight bankruptcy, is the 6-year bar to discharge. Discharge under chapter 11 will bar a discharge for 6 years. As under current law, confirmation of a composition wage earner plan under chapter 13 is a basis for invoking the 6-year bar.

The ninth ground is approval by the court of a waiver of discharge.

Subsection (b) specifies that the discharge granted under this section discharges the debtor from all debts that arose before the date of the order for relief. It is irrelevant whether or not a proof of claim was filed with respect to the debt, and whether or not the claim based on the debt was allowed.

Subsection (c) permits the trustee, or a creditor, to object to discharge. It also permits the court, on request of a party in interest, to order the trustee to examine the acts and conduct of the debtor to determine whether a ground for denial of discharge exists.

Subsection (d) requires the court to revoke a discharge already granted in certain circumstances. If the debtor obtained the discharge through fraud, if he acquired and concealed property of the estate, or if he refused to obey a court order or to testify, the discharge is to be revoked.

Subsection (e) permits the trustee or a creditor to request revocation of a discharge within 1 year after the discharge is granted, on the grounds of fraud, and within one year of discharge or the date of the closing of the case, whichever is later, on other grounds. Senate Report No. 95–989.

1984 Acts. Statements by Legislative Leaders, see 1984 U.S.Code Cong. and Adm.News, p. 576.

1986 Acts. House Report No. 99–764 and House Conference Report No. 99–958, see 1986 U.S.Code Cong. and Adm. News, p. 5227.

2005 Acts. House Report No. 109–31(Part I), see 2005 U.S. Code Cong. and Adm. News, p. 88.

Legislative Statements

Sections 727(a)(8) and (9) of the House amendment represent a compromise between provisions contained in section 727(a)(8) of the House bill and Senate amendment. Section 727(a)(8) of the House amendment adopts section 727(a)(8) of the House bill. However, section 727(a)(9) of the House amendment contains a compromise based on section 727(a)(8) of the Senate amendment with respect to the circumstances under which a plan by way of composition under Chapter XIII of the Bankruptcy Act [chapter 13 of former Title 11 (section 1001 et seq.)] should be a bar to discharge in a subsequent proceeding under Title 11. The paragraph provides that a discharge under section 660 or 661 of the

Bankruptcy Act [sections 1060 or 1061 of former Title 11] or section 1328 of Title 11 in a case commenced within 6 years before the date of the filing of the petition in a subsequent case, operates as a bar to discharge unless, first, payments under the plan totaled at least 100 percent of the allowed unsecured claims in the case; or second, payments under the plan totaled at least 70 percent of the allowed unsecured claims in the case and the plan was proposed by the debtor in good faith and was the debtor's best effort.

It is expected that the Rules of Bankruptcy Procedure will contain a provision permitting the debtor to request a determination of whether a plan is the debtor's "best effort" prior to confirmation of a plan in a case under chapter 13 of title 11. In determining whether a plan is the debtor's "best effort" the court will evaluate several factors. Different facts and circumstances in cases under chapter 13 operate to make any rule of thumb of limited usefulness. The court should balance the debtor's assets, including family income, health insurance, retirement benefits, and other wealth, a sum which is generally determinable, against the foreseeable necessary living expenses of the debtor and the debtor's dependents, which unfortunately is rarely quantifiable. In determining the expenses of the debtor and the debtor's dependents, the court should consider the stability of the debtor's employment, if any, the age of the debtor, the number of the debtor's dependents and their ages, the condition of equipment and tools necessary to the debtor's employment or to the operation of his business, and other foreseeable expenses that the debtor will be required to pay during the period of the plan, other than payments to be made to creditors under the plan.

Section 727(a)(10) of the House amendment clarifies a provision contained in section 727(a)(9) of the House bill and Senate amendment indicating that a discharge may be barred if the court approves a waiver of discharge executed in writing by the debtor after the order for relief under chapter 7.

Section 727(b) of the House amendment adopts a similar provision contained in the Senate amendment modifying the effect of discharge. The provision makes clear that the debtor is discharged from all debts that arose before the date of the order for relief under chapter 7 in addition to any debt which is determined under section 502 as if it were a prepetition claim. Thus, if a case is converted from chapter 11 or chapter 13 to a case under chapter 7, all debts prior to the time of conversion are discharged, in addition to debts determined after the date of conversion of a kind specified in section 502, that are to be determined as prepetition claims. This modification is particularly important with respect to an individual debtor who files a petition under chapter 11 or chapter 13 of title 11 if the case is converted to chapter 7. The logical result of the House amendment is to equate the result that obtains whether the case is converted from another chapter to chapter 7, or whether the other chapter proceeding is dismissed and a new case is commenced by filing a petition under chapter 7.

References in Text

The Bankruptcy Act, referred to in subsec. (a)(7), is Act July 1, 1898, c. 541, 30 Stat. 544, as amended, which was classified generally to former Title 11, prior to repeal of such Act by Pub.L. 95–598, Title IV, § 401(a), Nov. 6, 1978, 92 Stat. 2692.

Sections 14, 371, and 476 of the Bankruptcy Act, referred to in subsec. (a)(8), are section 14 of Act July 1, 1898, c. 541, 30

Stat. 550, and sections 371 and 476 of Act July 1, 1898, c. 541, as added June 22, 1938, c. 575, § 1, 52 Stat. 912, 924, which were classified to sections 32, 771, and 876 of former Title 11, respectively.

Sections 660 and 661 of the Bankruptcy Act, referred to in subsec. (a)(9), are sections 660 and 661 of Act July 1, 1898, c. 541, as added June 22, 1938, c. 575, § 1, 52 Stat. 935, 936, which were classified, respectively, to sections 1060 and 1061 of former Title 11.

Amendments

2005 Amendments. Subsec. (a)(8). Pub.L. 109–8, § 312(1), struck out "six" and inserted "8".

Subsec. (a)(9). Pub.L. 109–8, § 106(b)(1), struck "or" at the end of the paragraph.

Subsec. (a)(10). Pub.L. 109–8, § 106(b)(2), struck the period and inserted "; or" at the end of the paragraph.

Pub.L. 109–8, § 330(a)(1), struck out "or" at the end of par. (10).

Subsec. (a)(11). Pub.L. 109–8, § 106(b)(3), added par. (11).

Pub.L. 109–8, § 330(a)(2), struck out the period at the end of par. (11) and inserted "; or".

Subsec. (a)(12). Pub.L. 109–8, § 330(a)(3), added par. (12).

Subsec. (d)(2). Pub.L. 109–8, § 603(d)(1), struck "or" at the end of the paragraph.

Subsec. (d)(3). Pub.L. 109–8, § 603(d)(2), struck the period at the end of paragraph (3) and inserted "; or"

Subsec. (d)(4). Pub.L. 109–8, § 603(d)(3), added par. (4).

1986 Amendments. Subsec. (a)(9). Pub.L. 99–554, § 257(s), added reference to section 1228 of this title.

Subsec. (c)(1). Pub.L. 99–554, § 220, substituted "The trustee, a creditor, or the United States trustee may object" for "The trustee or a creditor may object".

Subsec. (d). Pub.L. 99–554, § 220, substituted ", a creditor, or the United States trustee," for "or a creditor," in provisions preceding par. (1).

Subsec. (d)(2). Pub.L. 99–554, § 220, substituted "acquisition of or entitlement to such property" for "acquisition of, or entitlement to, such property".

Subsec. (e). Pub.L. 99–554, § 220, substituted "The trustee, a creditor, or the United States trustee may" for "The trustee or a creditor may" in provisions preceding par. (1).

Subsec. (e)(1). Pub.L. 99–554, § 220, substituted "section within" for "section, within" and "discharge is granted" for "discharge was granted".

Subsec. (e)(2). Pub.L. 99–554, § 220, substituted "section before" for "section, before" in provisions preceding subpar. (A).

Subsec. (e)(2)(A). Pub.L. 99–554, § 220, substituted "discharge; and" for "discharge; or".

1984 Amendments. Subsec. (a)(6)(C). Pub.L. 98–353, § 480(a)(1), substituted "properly" for "property".

Subsec. (a)(7). Pub.L. 98–353, § 480(a)(2), inserted ", under this title or under the Bankruptcy Act," after "another case".

Subsec. (a)(8). Pub.L. 98–353, § 480(a)(3), substituted "371," for "371".

Subsec. (c)(1). Pub.L. 98–353, § 480(b), substituted "to the granting of a discharge" for "to discharge".

Subsec. (e)(2)(A). Pub.L. 98–353, § 480(c), substituted "or" for "and".

Effective and Applicability Provisions

2005 Acts. Amendments by sections 106(b), 312(1), and 330(a) of Pub.L. 109–8 effective 180 days after Apr. 20, 2005, with amendments by sections 106(b) and 312(1) of Pub.L. 109–8 not applicable with respect to cases commenced under this title before such effective date, except as otherwise provided, and amendment by section 330(a) of Pub.L. 109–8 applicable with respect to cases commenced under this title on or after Apr. 20, 2005, see Pub.L. 109–8, § 1501, set out as a note under 11 U.S.C.A. § 101.

Amendments by Pub.L. 109–8, § 603, effective 18 months after Apr. 20, 2005, see Pub.L. 109–8, § 603(e), set out as a note under 11 U.S.C.A. § 521.

1986 Acts. Amendment by section 257 Pub.L. 99–554 effective 30 days after Oct. 27, 1986, except as otherwise provided for, see section 302(a) of Pub.L. 99–554, set out as a note under section 581 of Title 28, Judiciary and Judicial Procedure.

Amendment by Pub.L. 99–554, § 220 not to become effective in or with respect to certain specified judicial districts until, or apply to cases while pending in such district before, the expiration of the 270-day period beginning 30 days after Oct. 27, 1986, or of the 30-day period beginning on the date the Attorney General certifies under section 303 of Pub.L. 99–554 the region specified in a paragraph of section 581(a) of Title 28, as amended by section 111(a) of Pub.L. 99–554, that includes such district, whichever occurs first, see section 302(d)(1) of Pub.L. 99–554, set out as a note under section 581 of Title 28.

Amendment by Pub.L. 99–554, § 220, not to become effective in or with respect to certain specified judicial districts until, or apply to cases while pending in such district before, the expiration of the 2-year period beginning 30 days after Oct. 27, 1986, or of the 30-day period beginning on the date the Attorney General certifies under section 303 of Pub.L. 99–554 the region specified in a paragraph of section 581(a) of Title 28, as amended by section 111(a) of Pub.L. 99–554, that includes such district, whichever occurs first, see section 302(d)(2) of Pub.L. 99–554, set out as a note under section 581 of Title 28.

Amendment by Pub.L. 99–554, § 220, not to become effective in or with respect to judicial districts established for the States of Alabama and North Carolina until, or apply to cases while pending in such district before, such district elects to be included in a bankruptcy region established in section 581(a) of Title 28, as amended by section 111(a) of Pub.L. 99–554, or Oct. 1, 2002, whichever occurs first, and, except as otherwise provided, with respect to cases under chapters 7, 11, 12, and 13 of Title 11 commenced before 30 days after Oct. 27, 1986, and pending in a judicial district in the States of Alabama or North Carolina before any election made under section 302(d)(3)(A) of Pub.L. 99–554 by such district becomes effective or Oct. 1, 2002, whichever occurs first, amendments by Pub.L. 99–554 not to apply until Oct. 1, 2003, or the expiration of the 1-year period beginning on the date such election becomes effective, whichever occurs first, and further, in the case, in any judicial district in Alabama or North Carolina not making the election described in section 302(d)(3)(A) of Pub.L. 99–554, any person appointed under regulations issued by the Judicial Conference to administer estates in cases under Title 11 authorized to establish, etc., a panel of private trustees, and to supervise cases and trustees in cases under chapters 7, 11, 12, and 13 of Title 11, until amendments by sections 201 to 231 of Pub.L. 99–554 effective in such district, see section 302(d)(3)(A) to (F), (H), and (I) of Pub.L. 99–554, set out as a note under section 581 of Title 28.

Amendment by Pub.L. 99–554, § 220, except as otherwise provided, with respect to cases under chapters 7, 11, 12, and 13 of Title 11 commenced before 30 days after Oct. 27, 1986, and pending in a judicial district referred to in section 581(a) of Title 28, as amended by section 111(a) of Pub.L. 99–554, for which a United States trustee is not authorized before 30 days after Oct. 27, 1986 to be appointed, not applicable until the expiration of the 3-year period beginning on Oct. 27, 1986, or of the 1-year period beginning on the date the Attorney General certifies under section 303 of Pub.L. 99–554 the region specified in a paragraph of such section 581(a) that includes, such district, whichever occurs first, see section 302(e)(1), (2) of Pub.L. 99–554, as amended, set out as a note under section 581 of Title 28.

Amendment by Pub.L. 99–554, § 257(s), effective 30 days after Oct. 27, 1986, but not applicable to cases commenced under this title before that date, see section 302(a), (c)(1) of Pub.L. 99–554, set out as a note under section 581 of Title 28.

1984 Acts. Amendment by Pub.L. 98–353 effective with respect to cases filed 90 days after July 10, 1984, see section 552(a), formerly 553(a), of Pub.L. 98–353, set out as a note under section 101 of this title.

CROSS REFERENCES

Cancellation of indebtedness from discharged farm loans, see 12 USCA § 1150.

Concealment of assets; false oaths and claims, see 18 USCA § 152.

Confirmation of plan as affecting discharge in—

Chapter eleven cases, see 11 USCA § 1141.

Chapter nine cases, see 11 USCA § 944.

Discharge in Chapter thirteen cases, see 11 USCA § 1328.

Duty of trustee to oppose discharge, see 11 USCA § 704.

Effect of—

Conversion, see 11 USCA § 348.

Discharge, see 11 USCA § 524.

Exceptions to discharge, see 11 USCA § 523.

Nondischargeability of capital improvement loans for multi-family housing projects in proceedings under this section, see 12 USCA § 1715z–1a.

LIBRARY REFERENCES

American Digest System

Bankruptcy ⟳3251 to 3322, 3411.

Key Number System Topic No. 51.

Corpus Juris Secundum

CJS Bankruptcy § 50, Chapter 7 Proceedings.

CJS Bankruptcy § 139, Adversary Proceedings.

CJS Bankruptcy § 287, Complaints.

CJS Bankruptcy § 301, Notice to Debtor, Creditors, and Indenture Trustees.

CJS Bankruptcy § 308, Enlargement.

CJS Bankruptcy § 309, Reduction.

CJS Bankruptcy § 315, Judgments--Relief from Judgment or Order; Collateral Attack.

CJS Bankruptcy § 808, Scope of Inquiry--Privilege Against Self-Incrimination; Grant of Immunity.

CJS Bankruptcy § 1030, Nature of and Right to Discharge.

CJS Bankruptcy § 1032, Effect of Discharge of Debtor.

CJS Bankruptcy § 1034, Debtor Not Individual.

CJS Bankruptcy § 1035, Transfers With Intent to Hinder, Delay, or Defraud.

CJS Bankruptcy § 1036, Transfers With Intent to Hinder, Delay, or Defraud--Showing of Actual Intent.

CJS Bankruptcy § 1037, Failure to Keep or Preserve Financial Records.

CJS Bankruptcy § 1038, False Oath or Account.

CJS Bankruptcy § 1039, Failure to Explain Loss or Deficiency of Assets.

CJS Bankruptcy § 1040, Failure to Obey Any Lawful Order of Court; Refusal to Testify or Respond.

CJS Bankruptcy § 1041, Improper Conduct in Another Case.

CJS Bankruptcy § 1042, Prior Discharges.

CJS Bankruptcy § 1043, Waiver of Discharge.

CJS Bankruptcy § 1044, Failure to Complete Financial Management Course.

CJS Bankruptcy § 1045, Abuse of Bankruptcy Code Provisions; Liability for Certain Debts.

CJS Bankruptcy § 1046, Generally; Objections to Discharge.

CJS Bankruptcy § 1049, Pleading of Grounds of Objection; Amendments.

CJS Bankruptcy § 1050, Evidence; Presumptions and Burden of Proof.

CJS Bankruptcy § 1052, Weight and Sufficiency of Evidence.

CJS Bankruptcy § 1053, Weight and Sufficiency of Evidence--Standard of Proof.

CJS Bankruptcy § 1054, Hearing, Determination, and Order.

CJS Bankruptcy § 1056, Revocation or Vacation of Discharge.

CJS Bankruptcy § 1057, Revocation or Vacation of Discharge--Time When Revocation May be Sought.

CJS Bankruptcy § 1062, Effect of Discharge of Debts.

CJS Bankruptcy § 1094, Requirements for Reaffirmation of Debt.

CJS Bankruptcy § 1106, Reopening.

CJS Bankruptcy § 1190, Requirement of Good Faith in Proposal of Plan.

CJS Bankruptcy § 1209, Discharge--Grounds for Denial or Revocation of Discharge.

[§ 728. Repealed. Pub.L. 109–8, Title VII, § 719(b)(1), Apr. 20, 2005, 119 Stat. 133]

HISTORICAL AND STATUTORY NOTES

Section, Pub.L. 95–598, Nov. 6, 1978, 92 Stat. 2611; Pub.L. 98–353, Title III, § 481, July 10, 1984, 98 Stat. 382; Pub.L.

99–554, Title II, § 257(t), Oct. 27, 1986, 100 Stat. 3116, related to special tax provisions applying to state and local taxation.

See, now, 11 U.S.C.A. § 346.

Effective Date of Repeal

Amendments by Pub.L. 109–8 effective, except as otherwise provided, 180 days after April 20, 2005, and inapplicable with respect to cases commenced under Title 11 before the effective date, see Pub.L. 109–8, § 1501, set out as a note under 11 U.S.C.A. § 101.

SUBCHAPTER III—STOCKBROKER LIQUIDATION

CROSS REFERENCES

Subchapter applicable only in case under chapter concerning stockholder, see 11 USCA § 103.

§ 741. Definitions for this subchapter

In this subchapter—

(1) "Commission" means Securities and Exchange Commission;

(2) "customer" includes—

(A) entity with whom a person deals as principal or agent and that has a claim against such person on account of a security received, acquired, or held by such person in the ordinary course of such person's business as a stockbroker, from or for the securities account or accounts of such entity—

(i) for safekeeping;

(ii) with a view to sale;

(iii) to cover a consummated sale;

(iv) pursuant to a purchase;

(v) as collateral under a security agreement; or

(vi) for the purpose of effecting registration of transfer; and

(B) entity that has a claim against a person arising out of—

(i) a sale or conversion of a security received, acquired, or held as specified in subparagraph (A) of this paragraph; or

(ii) a deposit of cash, a security, or other property with such person for the purpose of purchasing or selling a security;

(3) "customer name security" means security—

(A) held for the account of a customer on the date of the filing of the petition by or on behalf of the debtor;

(B) registered in such customer's name on such date or in the process of being so registered under instructions from the debtor; and

(C) not in a form transferable by delivery on such date;

(4) "customer property" means cash, security, or other property, and proceeds of such cash, security, or property, received, acquired, or held by or for the account of the debtor, from or for the securities account of a customer—

(A) including—

(i) property that was unlawfully converted from and that is the lawful property of the estate;

(ii) a security held as property of the debtor to the extent such security is necessary to meet a net equity claim of a customer based on a security of the same class and series of an issuer;

(iii) resources provided through the use or realization of a customer's debit cash balance or a debit item includible in the Formula for Determination of Reserve Requirement for Brokers and Dealers as promulgated by the Commission under the Securities Exchange Act of 1934; and

(iv) other property of the debtor that any applicable law, rule, or regulation requires to be set aside or held for the benefit of a customer, unless including such property as customer property would not significantly increase customer property; but

(B) not including—

(i) a customer name security delivered to or reclaimed by a customer under section 751 of this title; or

(ii) property to the extent that a customer does not have a claim against the debtor based on such property;

(5) "margin payment" means payment or deposit of cash, a security, or other property, that is commonly known to the securities trade as original margin, initial margin, maintenance margin, or variation margin, or as a mark-to-market payment, or that secures an obligation of a participant in a securities clearing agency;

(6) "net equity" means, with respect to all accounts of a customer that such customer has in the same capacity—

(A)(i) aggregate dollar balance that would remain in such accounts after the liquidation, by sale or purchase, at the time of the filing of the petition, of all securities positions in all such accounts, except any customer name securities of such customer; minus

(ii) any claim of the debtor against such customer in such capacity that would have been owing immediately after such liquidation; plus

(B) any payment by such customer to the trustee, within 60 days after notice under section 342 of this title, of any business related claim of the debtor against such customer in such capacity;

(7) "securities contract"—

(A) means—

(i) a contract for the purchase, sale, or loan of a security, a certificate of deposit, a mortgage loan, any interest in a mortgage loan, a group or index of securities, certificates of deposit, or mortgage loans or interests therein (including an interest therein or based on the value thereof), or option on any of the foregoing, including an option to purchase or sell any such security, certificate of deposit, mortgage loan, interest, group or index, or option, and including any repurchase or reverse repurchase transaction on any such security, certificate of deposit, mortgage loan, interest, group or index, or option (whether or not such repurchase or reverse repurchase transaction is a "repurchase agreement", as defined in section 101);

(ii) any option entered into on a national securities exchange relating to foreign currencies;

(iii) the guarantee (including by novation) by or to any securities clearing agency of a settlement of cash, securities, certificates of deposit, mortgage loans or interests therein, group or index of securities, or mortgage loans or interests therein (including any interest therein or based on the value thereof), or option on any of the foregoing, including an option to purchase or sell any such security, certificate of deposit, mortgage loan, interest, group or index, or option (whether or not such settlement is in connection with any agreement or transaction referred to in clauses (i) through (xi));

(iv) any margin loan;

(v) any extension of credit for the clearance or settlement of securities transactions;

(vi) any loan transaction coupled with a securities collar transaction, any prepaid forward securities transaction, or any total return swap transaction coupled with a securities sale transaction;

(vii) any other agreement or transaction that is similar to an agreement or transaction referred to in this subparagraph;

(viii) any combination of the agreements or transactions referred to in this subparagraph;

(ix) any option to enter into any agreement or transaction referred to in this subparagraph;

(x) a master agreement that provides for an agreement or transaction referred to in clause (i), (ii), (iii), (iv), (v), (vi), (vii), (viii), or (ix), together with all supplements to any such master agreement, without regard to whether the master agreement provides for an agreement or transaction that is not a securities contract under this subparagraph, except that such master agreement shall be considered to be a securities contract under this subparagraph only with respect to each agreement or transaction under such master agreement that is referred to in clause (i), (ii), (iii), (iv), (v), (vi), (vii), (viii), or (ix); or

(xi) any security agreement or arrangement or other credit enhancement related to any agreement or transaction referred to in this subparagraph, including any guarantee or reimbursement obligation by or to a stockbroker, securities clearing agency, financial institution, or financial participant in connection with any agreement or transaction referred to in this subparagraph, but not to exceed the damages in connection with any such agreement or transaction, measured in accordance with section 562; and

(B) does not include any purchase, sale, or repurchase obligation under a participation in a commercial mortgage loan;

(8) "settlement payment" means a preliminary settlement payment, a partial settlement payment, an interim settlement payment, a settlement payment on account, a final settlement payment, or any other similar payment commonly used in the securities trade; and

(9) "SIPC" means Securities Investor Protection Corporation.

(Pub.L. 95–598, Nov. 6, 1978, 92 Stat. 2611; Pub.L. 97–222, § 8, July 27, 1982, 96 Stat. 237; Pub.L. 98–353, Title III, § 482, July 10, 1984, 98 Stat. 382; Pub.L. 103–394, Title V, § 501(d)(25), Oct. 22, 1994, 108 Stat. 4146; Pub.L. 109–8, Title IX, § 907(a)(2), Apr. 20, 2005, 119 Stat. 173; Pub.L. 109–390, § 5(a)(3), Dec. 12, 2006, 120 Stat. 2697)

HISTORICAL AND STATUTORY NOTES
Revision Notes and Legislative Reports

1978 Acts. Section 741 sets forth definitions for subchapter III of chapter 7.

Paragraph (1) defines "Commission" to mean the Securities and Exchange Commission.

Paragraph (2) defines "customer" to include anybody that interacts with the debtor in a capacity that concerns securities transactions. The term embraces cash or margin customers of a broker or dealer in the broadest sense.

Paragraph (3) defines "customer name security" in a restrictive fashion to include only non-transferrable securities that are registered, or in the process of being registered in a customer's own name. The securities must not be endorsed by the customer and the stockbroker must not be able to legally transfer the securities by delivery, by a power of attorney, or otherwise.

Paragraph (4) defines "customer property" to include all property of the debtor that has been segregated for customers or property that should have been segregated but was unlawfully converted. Clause (i) refers to customer property not properly segregated by the debtor or customer property converted and then recovered so as to become property of the estate. Unlawfully converted property that has been transferred to a third party is excluded until it is recovered as property of the estate by virtue of the avoiding powers. The concept excludes customer name securities that have been delivered to or reclaimed by a customer and any property properly belonging to the stockholder, such as money deposited by a customer to pay for securities that the stockholder has distributed to such customer.

Paragraph (5) defines "net equity" to establish the extent to which a customer will be entitled to share in the single and separate fund. Accounts of a customer are aggregated and offset only to the extent the accounts are held by the customer in the same capacity. Thus, a personal account is separate from an account held as trustee. In a community property state an account held for the community is distinct from an account held as separate property.

The net equity is computed by liquidating all securities positions in the accounts and crediting the account with any amount due to the customer. Regardless of the actual dates, if any, of liquidation, the customer is only entitled to the liquidation value at the time of the filing of the petition. To avoid double counting, the liquidation value of customer name securities belonging to a customer is excluded from net equity. Thus, clause (ii) includes claims against a customer resulting from the liquidation of a security under clause (i). The value of a security on which trading has been suspended at the time of the filing of the petition will be estimated. Once the net liquidation value is computed, any amount that the customer owes to the stockbroker is subtracted including any amount that would be owing after the hypothetical liquidation, such as brokerage fees. Debts owed by the customer to the debtor, other than in a securities related transaction, will not reduce the net equity of the customer. Finally, net equity is increased by any payment by the customer to the debtor actually paid within 60 days after notice. The principal reason a customer would make such a payment is to reclaim customer name securities under § 751.

Paragraph (6) defines "1934 Act" to mean the Securities Exchange Act of 1934 [15 U.S.C.A. § 78a et seq.].

Paragraph (7) defines "SIPC" to mean the Securities Investor Protection Corporation. Senate Report No. 95–989.

1982 Acts. House Report No. 97–420, see 1982 U.S.Code Cong. and Adm.News, p. 583.

1984 Acts. Statements by Legislative Leaders, see 1984 U.S.Code Cong. and Adm.News, p. 576.

1994 Acts. House Report No. 103–835, see 1994 U.S. Code Cong. and Adm. News, p. 3340.

2005 Acts. House Report No. 109–31(Part I), see 2005 U.S. Code Cong. and Adm. News, p. 88.

2006 Acts. House Report No. 109–648(Part I), see 2006 U.S. Code Cong. and Adm. News, p. 1585.

Legislative Statements

Section 741(6) of the House bill and Senate amendment is deleted by the House amendment since the defined term is used only in section 741(4)(A)(iii). A corresponding change is made in that section.

References in Text

The Securities Exchange Act of 1934, referred to in par. (4)(A)(iii), is Act June 6, 1934, c. 404, 48 Stat. 881, as amended, which is classified principally to chapter 2B (section 78a et seq.) of Title 15, Commerce and Trade. For complete classification of this Act to the Code, see section 78l of Title 15 and Tables.

Amendments

2006 Amendments. Par. (7)(A)(i). Pub.L. 109–390, § 5(a)(3)(A)(i), struck out "mortgage loan, or" following "a certificate of deposit, a" and inserted "mortgage loan,".

Pub.L. 109–390, § 5(a)(3)(A)(ii), inserted before the semicolon "(whether or not such repurchase or reverse repurchase transaction is a 'repurchase agreement', as defined in section 101)".

Par. (7)(A)(iii). Pub.L. 109–390, § 5(a)(3)(B)(i), inserted "(including by novation)" after "the guarantee".

Pub.L. 109–390, § 2(a)(3)(B)(ii), inserted before the semicolon "(whether or not such settlement is in connection with any agreement or transaction referred to in clauses (i) through (xi))".

Par. (7)(A)(v). Pub.L. 109–390, § 5(a)(3)(D), (E), redesignated former cl. (v) as (vii) and added a new cl. (v).

Par. (7)(A)(vi). Pub.L. 109–390, § 5(a)(3)(D), (E), redesignated former cl. (vi) as (viii) and added a new cl. (vi).

Par. (7)(A)(vii). Pub.L. 109–390, § 5(a)(3)(D), redesignated former cl. (v) as (vii). Former cl. (vii) redesignated (ix).

Par. (7)(A)(viii). Pub.L. 109–390, § 5(a)(3)(C), struck out "or (vii)" each place it appeared and inserted "(vii), (viii), or (ix)" in cl. (viii) before redesignation as cl. (x).

Pub.L. 109–390, § 5(a)(3)(D), redesignated former cl. (vi) as (viii). Former cl. (viii) redesignated (x).

Par. (7)(A)(ix). Pub.L. 109–390, § 5(a)(3)(D), redesignated former cl. (vii) as (ix). Former cl. (ix) redesignated (xi).

Par. (7)(A)(x). Pub.L. 109–390, § 5(a)(3)(D), redesignated former cl. (viii) as (x).

Par. (7)(A)(xi). Pub.L. 109–390, § 5(a)(3)(D), redesignated former cl. (ix) as (xi).

2005 Amendments. Par. (7). Pub.L. 109–8, § 907(a)(2), rewrote par. (7), which formerly read: "'securities contract' means contract for the purchase, sale, or loan of a security, including an option for the purchase or sale of a security, certificate of deposit, or group or index of securities (including any interest therein or based on the value thereof), or any option entered into on a national securities exchange relating to foreign currencies, or the guarantee of any settlement of cash or securities by or to a securities clearing agency;"

1994 Amendments. Par. (4)(A)(iii). Pub.L. 103–394, § 501(d)(25), struck out "(15 U.S.C. 78a et seq.)" following "the Securities Exchange Act of 1934".

1984 Amendments. Par. (2)(A). Pub.L. 98–353, § 482(1), substituted "with whom a person deals" for "with whom the debtor deals", "that has a claim" for "that holds a claim", "against such person" for "against the debtor", "held by such person" for "held by the debtor", and "such person's business as a stockbroker," for "business as a stockbroker".

Par. (2)(B). Pub.L. 98–353, § 482(2)(A), (B), substituted "has a claim" for "holds a claim" and "against a person" for "against the debtor" in provisions preceding cl. (i).

Par. (2)(B)(ii). Pub.L. 98–353, § 482(2)(C), substituted "such person" for "the debtor".

Par. (4)(A)(i). Pub.L. 98–353, § 482(3), substituted "from and that is the lawful" for "and that is".

Par. (6)(A)(i). Pub.L. 98–353, § 482(4), substituted "petition," for "petition" and "except any customer name" for "except customer name".

Par. (7). Pub.L. 98–353, § 482(5), added provisions relating to options for the purchase or sale of certificates of deposit, or a group or index of securities (including any interest therein or based on the value thereof), or any option entered into on a national securities exchange relating to foreign currencies.

Par. (8). Pub.L. 98–353, § 482(6), substituted "settlement payment on account, a final settlement payment," for "settlement payment on account,".

1982 Amendments. Par. (4). Pub.L. 97–222, § 8(1), struck out "at any time" following "security, or property," in the provisions preceding subpar. (A), and inserted "of a customer" after "claim" in subpar. (A)(ii).

Par. (5). Pub.L. 97–222, § 8(3), added par. (5). Former par. (5) was redesignated (6).

Par. (6). Pub.L. 97–222, § 8(2), (4), redesignated former par. (5) as (6) and as so redesignated, in the provisions preceding subpar. (A), substituted "all accounts of a customer that such customer has" for "the aggregate of all of a customer's accounts that such customer holds", in subpar. (A)(2) inserted "in such capacity", and in subpar. (B) inserted "in such capacity". Former par. (6) was redesignated (9).

Pars. (7), (8). Pub.L. 97–222, § 8(5), added pars. (7) and (8).

Par. (9). Pub.L. 97–222, § 8(2), (6), redesignated former par. (6) as (9) and in par. (9), as so redesignated substituted "Securities" for "Security".

Effective and Applicability Provisions

2005 Acts. Amendments by Pub.L. 109–8 effective, except as otherwise provided, 180 days after April 20, 2005, and inapplicable with respect to cases commenced under Title 11 before the effective date, see Pub.L. 109–8, § 1501, set out as a note under 11 U.S.C.A. § 101.

1994 Acts. Amendment by Pub.L. 103–394 effective on Oct. 22, 1994, and not to apply with respect to cases commenced under Title 11 of the United States Code before Oct. 22, 1994, see section 702 of Pub.L. 103–394, set out as a note under section 101 of this title.

1984 Acts. Amendment by Pub.L. 98–353 effective with respect to cases filed 90 days after July 10, 1984, see section 552(a), formerly 553(a), of Pub.L. 98–353, set out as a note under section 101 of this title.

Separability of Provisions

If any provision of or amendment made by Pub.L. 103–394 or the application of such provision or amendment to any person or circumstance is held to be unconstitutional, the remaining provisions of and amendments made by Pub.L. 103–394 and the application of such provisions and amendments to any person or circumstance shall not be affected thereby, see section 701 of Pub.L. 103–394, set out as a note under section 101 of this title.

CROSS REFERENCES

Certain persons acting as agent or custodian for customer in connection with "securities contract" as defined under this section considered a financial institution for purposes of this title, see 11 USCA § 101.

Contractual right to liquidate "securities contract" as defined under this section not stayed, avoided or limited by operation of any provision of this title, see 11 USCA § 555.

"Customer" defined under this section as determining who is a stockbroker for purposes of this title, see 11 USCA § 101.

Definitions applicable in—

Chapter eleven cases, see 11 USCA § 1101.

Chapter nine cases, see 11 USCA § 902.

Commodity broker liquidation cases, see 11 USCA § 761.

Railroad reorganization cases, see 11 USCA § 1162.

Limitation on power of trustee to avoid transfer of "margin payment" and "settlement payment" as defined under this section, see 11 USCA § 546.

Receipt of "margin payment" or "settlement payment" as defined under this section is taking for value for purposes of avoidance of fraudulent transfers and obligations, see 11 USCA § 548.

"Securities contract" as defined under this section as having same meaning for purposes of—

Federal credit union insurance, see 12 USCA § 1787.

Federal deposit insurance corporation, see 12 USCA § 1821.

Setoff of mutual debt in connection with "securities contract", "margin payment" or "settlement payment", not stayed by filing of petitions for voluntary cases, joint cases or involuntary cases or protective decrees in investor protection liquidation proceedings, see 11 USCA § 362.

LIBRARY REFERENCES

American Digest System

Bankruptcy ☞3461.

Key Number System Topic No. 51.

Corpus Juris Secundum

CJS Bankruptcy § 7, Bankruptcy Code.

CJS Bankruptcy § 385, Governing Statutes, Generally.

CJS Bankruptcy § 500, Setoffs.

CJS Bankruptcy § 838, Stockbroker Liquidation Cases.

CJS Bankruptcy § 1110, Customer Name Securities.

CJS Bankruptcy § 1111, Customer Property.

§ 742. Effect of section 362 of this title in this subchapter

Notwithstanding section 362 of this title, SIPC may file an application for a protective decree under the Securities Investor Protection Act of 1970. The filing of such application stays all proceedings in the case under this title unless and until such application is dismissed. If SIPC completes the liquidation of the debtor, then the court shall dismiss the case.

(Pub.L. 95–598, Nov. 6, 1978, 92 Stat. 2613; Pub.L. 97–222, § 9, July 27, 1982, 96 Stat. 237; Pub.L. 103–394, Title V, § 501(d)(26), Oct. 22, 1994, 108 Stat. 4146.)

HISTORICAL AND STATUTORY NOTES

Revision Notes and Legislative Reports

1978 Acts. Section 742 indicates that the automatic stay does not prevent SIPC from filing an application for a protective decree under SIPA. If SIPA does file such an application, then all bankruptcy proceedings are suspended until the SIPC action is completed. If SIPC completes liquidation of the stockbroker then the bankruptcy case is dismissed. Senate Report No. 95–989.

1982 Acts. House Report No. 97–420, see 1982 U.S.Code Cong. and Adm.News, p. 583.

1994 Acts. House Report No. 103–835, see 1994 U.S. Code Cong. and Adm. News, p. 3340.

Legislative Statements

Section 742 of the House amendment deletes a sentence contained in the Senate amendment requiring the trustee in an interstate stock-brokerage liquidation to comply with the provisions of subchapter IV of chapter 7 if the debtor is also a commodity broker. The House amendment expands the requirement to require the SIPC trustee to perform such duties, if the debtor is a commodity broker, under section 7(b) of the Securities Investor Protection Act [15 U.S.C. 78ggg(b)]. The requirement is deleted from section 742 since the trustee of an intrastate stockbroker will be bound by the provisions of subchapter IV of chapter 7 if the debtor is also a commodity broker by reason of section 103 of title 11.

References in Text

The Securities Investor Protection Act of 1970, referred to in text, is Pub.L. 91–598, Dec. 30, 1970, 84 Stat. 1636, as amended, which is classified generally to chapter 2B–1 (section 78aaa et seq.) of Title 15, Commerce and Trade. For complete classification of this Act to the Code, see section 78aaa of Title 15 and Tables.

Amendments

1994 Amendments. Pub.L. 103–394, § 501(d)(26), struck out "(15 U.S.C. 78aaa et seq.)" following "the Securities Investor Protection Act of 1970".

1982 Amendments. Pub.L. 97–222 substituted "title" for "chapter" following "all proceedings in the case under this".

Effective and Applicability Provisions

1994 Acts. Amendment by Pub.L. 103–394 effective on Oct. 22, 1994, and not to apply with respect to cases commenced under Title 11 of the United States Code before Oct. 22, 1994, see section 702 of Pub.L. 103–394, set out as a note under section 101 of this title.

Separability of Provisions

If any provision of or amendment made by Pub.L. 103–394 or the application of such provision or amendment to any person or circumstance is held to be unconstitutional, the remaining provisions of and amendments made by Pub.L. 103–394 and the application of such provisions and amendments to any person or circumstance shall not be affected thereby, see section 701 of Pub.L. 103–394, set out as a note under section 101 of this title.

CROSS REFERENCES

Automatic stay of enforcement of claims against debtor in Chapter 9 cases, see 11 USCA § 922.

Effect of dismissal, see 11 USCA § 349.

Stay of action against codebtor in Chapter 13 cases, see 11 USCA § 1301.

LIBRARY REFERENCES

American Digest System

Bankruptcy ☞3461.
Key Number System Topic No. 51.

Corpus Juris Secundum

CJS Bankruptcy § 838, Stockbroker Liquidation Cases.

CJS Bankruptcy § 1112, Under Securities Investor Protection Act of 1970.

§ 743. Notice

The clerk shall give the notice required by section 342 of this title to SIPC and to the Commission. (Pub.L. 95–598, Nov. 6, 1978, 92 Stat. 2613; Pub.L. 99–554, Title II, § 283(t), Oct. 27, 1986, 100 Stat. 3118); Pub.L. 103–394, Title V, § 501(d)(27), Oct. 22, 1994, 108 Stat. 4146.)

HISTORICAL AND STATUTORY NOTES
Revision Notes and Legislative Reports

1978 Acts. Section 743 requires that notice of the order for relief be given to SIPC and to the SEC in every stockbroker case. Senate Report No. 95–989.

1986 Acts. House Report No. 99–764 and House Conference Report No. 99–958, see 1986 U.S.Code Cong. and Adm. News, p. 5227.

1994 Acts. House Report No. 103–835, see 1994 U.S. Code Cong. and Adm. News, p. 3340.

Codifications

Pub.L. 99–554, Title II, § 283(t), Oct. 27, 1986, 100 Stat. 3118, provided that this section be amended by striking out "(d)", which amendment was incapable of execution in view of present language of text.

Amendments

1994 Amendments. Pub.L. 103–394, § 501(d)(27), substituted "section 342" for "section 342(a)".

Effective and Applicability Provisions

1994 Acts. Amendment by Pub.L. 103–394 effective on Oct. 22, 1994, and not to apply with respect to cases commenced under Title 11 of the United States Code before Oct. 22, 1994, see section 702 of Pub.L. 103–394, set out as a note under section 101 of this title.

Separability of Provisions

If any provision of or amendment made by Pub.L. 103–394 or the application of such provision or amendment to any person or circumstance is held to be unconstitutional, the remaining provisions of and amendments made by Pub.L. 103–394 and the application of such provisions and amendments to any person or circumstance shall not be affected thereby, see section 701 of Pub.L. 103–394, set out as a note under section 101 of this title.

CROSS REFERENCES

Notice in Chapter nine cases, see 11 USCA § 923.

Notice to the Commodity Futures Trading Commission, see 11 USCA § 762.

LIBRARY REFERENCES
American Digest System

Bankruptcy ☞3461.
Key Number System Topic No. 51.

§ 744. Executory contracts

Notwithstanding section 365(d)(1) of this title, the trustee shall assume or reject, under section 365 of this title, any executory contract of the debtor for the purchase or sale of a security in the ordinary course of the debtor's business, within a reasonable time after the date of the order for relief, but not to exceed 30 days. If the trustee does not assume such a contract within such time, such contract is rejected.

(Pub.L. 95–598, Nov. 6, 1978, 92 Stat. 2613; Pub.L. 97–222, § 10, July 27, 1982, 96 Stat. 238.)

HISTORICAL AND STATUTORY NOTES

Revision Notes and Legislative Reports

1978 Acts. Section 744 instructs the court to give the trustee a reasonable time, not to exceed 30 days, to assume or reject any executory contract of the stockbroker to buy or sell securities. Any contract not assumed within the time fixed by the court is considered to be rejected. Senate Report No. 95–989.

1982 Acts. House Report No. 97–420, see 1982 U.S.Code Cong. and Adm.News, p. 583.

Amendments

1982 Amendments. Pub.L. 97–222 inserted "but" following "relief,".

CROSS REFERENCES

Effect of rejection of lease of railroad line, see 11 USCA § 1169.

LIBRARY REFERENCES

American Digest System

Bankruptcy ⟜3461.

Key Number System Topic No. 51.

Corpus Juris Secundum

CJS Bankruptcy § 99, Powers and Duties in Stockholder or Commodity Broker Liquidation Cases.

CJS Bankruptcy § 278, Parties Defendant; Sovereign Immunity.

CJS Bankruptcy § 838, Stockbroker Liquidation Cases.

CJS Bankruptcy § 927, Exercising Right in Chapter 7 Cases.

§ 745. Treatment of accounts

(a) Accounts held by the debtor for a particular customer in separate capacities shall be treated as accounts of separate customers.

(b) If a stockbroker or a bank holds a customer net equity claim against the debtor that arose out of a transaction for a customer of such stockbroker or bank, each such customer of such stockbroker or bank shall be treated as a separate customer of the debtor.

(c) Each trustee's account specified as such on the debtor's books, and supported by a trust deed filed with, and qualified as such by, the Internal Revenue Service, and under the Internal Revenue Code of 1986, shall be treated as a separate customer account for each beneficiary under such trustee account.

(Pub.L. 95–598, Nov. 6, 1978, 92 Stat. 2613; Pub.L. 97–222, § 11, July 27, 1982, 96 Stat. 238; Pub.L. 98–353, Title III, § 483, July 10, 1984, 98 Stat. 383; Pub.L. 103–394, Title V, § 501(d)(28), Oct. 22, 1994, 108 Stat. 4146.)

HISTORICAL AND STATUTORY NOTES

Revision Notes and Legislative Reports

1978 Acts. Section 745(a) indicates that each account held by a customer in a separate capacity is to be considered a separate account. This prevents the offset of accounts held in different capacities.

Subsection (b) indicates that a bank or another stockbroker that is a customer of a debtor is considered to hold its customers accounts in separate capacities. Thus a bank or other stockbroker is not treated as a mutual fund for purposes of bulk investment. This protects unrelated customers of a bank or other stockholder [sic] from having their accounts offset.

Subsection (c) effects the same result with respect to a trust so that each beneficiary is treated as the customer of the debtor rather than the trust itself. This eliminates any doubt whether a trustee holds a personal account in a separate capacity from his trustee's account. Senate Report No. 95–989.

1982 Acts. House Report No. 97–420, see 1982 U.S.Code Cong. and Adm.News, p. 583.

1986 Acts. House Conference Report No. 99–841 and Statement by President, see 1986 U.S.Code Cong. and Adm. News, p. 4075.

1994 Acts. House Report No. 103–835, see 1994 U.S. Code Cong. and Adm. News, p. 3340.

References in Text

The Internal Revenue Code of 1986, referred to in subsec. (c), is classified to Title 26, Internal Revenue Code.

Amendments

1994 Amendments. Subsec. (d). Pub.L. 103–394, § 501(d)(28), substituted "Internal Revenue Code of 1986" for "Internal Revenue Code of 1954 (26 U.S.C. 1 et seq.)".

1984 Amendments. Subsec. (a). Pub.L. 98–353 inserted "the debtor for" after "by".

1982 Amendments. Subsec. (c). Pub.L. 97–222 substituted "Each" for "A".

Effective and Applicability Provisions

1994 Acts. Amendment by Pub.L. 103–394 effective on Oct. 22, 1994, and not to apply with respect to cases commenced under Title 11 of the United States Code before Oct. 22, 1994, see section 702 of Pub.L. 103–394, set out as a note under section 101 of this title.

1984 Acts. Amendment by Pub.L. 98–353 effective with respect to cases filed 90 days after July 10, 1984, see section 552(a), formerly 553(a), of Pub.L. 98–353, set out as a note under section 101 of this title.

Separability of Provisions

If any provision of or amendment made by Pub.L. 103–394 or the application of such provision or amendment to any person or circumstance is held to be unconstitutional, the remaining provisions of and amendments made by Pub.L. 103–394 and the application of such provisions and amendments to any person or circumstance shall not be affected thereby, see section 701 of Pub.L. 103–394, set out as a note under section 101 of this title.

CROSS REFERENCES

Stockbroker defined, see 11 USCA § 101.

Treatment of accounts in commodity broker liquidation cases, see 11 USCA § 763.

LIBRARY REFERENCES

American Digest System

Bankruptcy ☞3461.

Key Number System Topic No. 51.

Corpus Juris Secundum

CJS Bankruptcy § 1108, Treatment of Accounts.

§ 746. Extent of customer claims

(a) If, after the date of the filing of the petition, an entity enters into a transaction with the debtor, in a manner that would have made such entity a customer had such transaction occurred before the date of the filing of the petition, and such transaction was entered into by such entity in good faith and before the qualification under section 322 of this title of a trustee, such entity shall be deemed a customer, and the date of such transaction shall be deemed to be the date of the filing of the petition for the purpose of determining such entity's net equity.

(b) An entity does not have a claim as a customer to the extent that such entity transferred to the debtor cash or a security that, by contract, agreement, understanding, or operation of law, is—

(1) part of the capital of the debtor; or

(2) subordinated to the claims of any or all creditors.

(Pub.L. 95–598, Nov. 6, 1978, 92 Stat. 2613; Pub.L. 97–222, § 12, July 27, 1982, 96 Stat. 238.)

HISTORICAL AND STATUTORY NOTES

Revision Notes and Legislative Reports

1978 Acts. Section 746(a) protects entities who deal in good faith with the debtor after the filing of the petition and before a trustee is appointed by deeming such entities to be customers. The principal application of this section will be in an involuntary case before the order for relief, because § 701(b) requires prompt appointment of an interim trustee after the order for relief.

Subsection (b) indicates that an entity who holds securities that are either part of the capital of the debtor or that are subordinated to the claims of any creditor of the debtor is not a customer with respect to those securities. This subsection will apply when the stockbroker has sold securities in itself to the customer or when the customer has otherwise placed such securities in an account with the stockbroker. Senate Report No. 95–989.

1982 Acts. House Report No. 97–420, see 1982 U.S.Code Cong. and Adm.News, p. 583.

Amendments

1982 Amendments. Pub.L. 97–222, § 12(c), substituted "claims" for "claim" in section catchline.

Subsec. (a). Pub.L. 97–222, § 12(a), substituted "enters into" for "effects, with respect to cash or a security,", struck out "with respect to such cash or security" wherever appear-

ing, and substituted "the date of the filing of the petition" for "such date", and "entered into" for "effected".

Subsec. (b). Pub.L. 97–222, § 12(b), substituted "transferred to the debtor" for "has a claim for" in the provisions preceding par. (1), and struck out "is" in par. (2).

CROSS REFERENCES

Allowance of claims or interests, see 11 USCA § 502.

LIBRARY REFERENCES

American Digest System

Bankruptcy ☞3461.

Key Number System Topic No. 51.

§ 747. Subordination of certain customer claims

Except as provided in section 510 of this title, unless all other customer net equity claims have been paid in full, the trustee may not pay in full or pay in part, directly or indirectly, any net equity claim of a customer that was, on the date the transaction giving rise to such claim occurred—

(1) an insider;

(2) a beneficial owner of at least five percent of any class of equity securities of the debtor, other than—

(A) nonconvertible stock having fixed preferential dividend and liquidation rights; or

(B) interests of limited partners in a limited partnership;

(3) a limited partner with a participation of at least five percent in the net assets or net profits of the debtor; or

(4) an entity that, directly or indirectly, through agreement or otherwise, exercised or had the power to exercise control over the management or policies of the debtor.

(Pub.L. 95–598, Nov. 6, 1978, 92 Stat. 2613; Pub.L. 97–222, § 13, July 27, 1982, 96 Stat. 238.)

HISTORICAL AND STATUTORY NOTES

Revision Notes and Legislative Reports

1978 Acts. Section 747 subordinates to other customer claims, all claims of a customer who is an insider, a five percent owner of the debtor, or otherwise in control of the debtor. Senate Report No. 95–989.

1982 Acts. House Report No. 97–420, see 1982 U.S.Code Cong. and Adm.News, p. 583.

Amendments

1982 Amendments. Pub.L. 97–222 substituted "the transaction giving rise to such claim occurred" for "such claim arose" in provisions preceding par. (1).

CROSS REFERENCES

Insider defined, see 11 USCA § 101.

LIBRARY REFERENCES

American Digest System

Bankruptcy ☞3461.

Key Number System Topic No. 51.

§ 748. Reduction of securities to money

As soon as practicable after the date of the order for relief, the trustee shall reduce to money, consistent with good market practice, all securities held as property of the estate, except for customer name securities delivered or reclaimed under section 751 of this title.
(Pub.L. 95–598, Nov. 6, 1978, 92 Stat. 2614.)

HISTORICAL AND STATUTORY NOTES

Revision Notes and Legislative Reports

1978 Acts. Section 748 requires the trustee to liquidate all securities, except for customer name securities, of the estate in a manner consistent with good market practice. The trustee should refrain from flooding a thin market with a large percentage of shares in any one issue. If the trustee holds restricted securities or securities in which trading has been suspended, then the trustee must arrange to liquidate such securities in accordance with the securities laws. A private placement may be the only exemption available with the customer of the debtor the best prospect for such a placement. The subsection does not permit such a customer to bid in his net equity as part of the purchase price; a contrary result would permit a customer to receive a greater percentage on his net equity claim than other customers. Senate Report No. 95–989.

CROSS REFERENCES

Reduction of certain securities and property to money in commodity broker liquidation cases, see 11 USCA § 766.

LIBRARY REFERENCES

American Digest System

Bankruptcy ⊙3461.
Key Number System Topic No. 51.

Corpus Juris Secundum

CJS Bankruptcy § 99, Powers and Duties in Stockholder or Commodity Broker Liquidation Cases.

CJS Bankruptcy § 626, Collection and Reduction to Money of Property of Estate in Chapter 7 Cases.

CJS Bankruptcy § 838, Stockbroker Liquidation Cases.

§ 749. Voidable transfers

(a) Except as otherwise provided in this section, any transfer of property that, but for such transfer, would have been customer property, may be avoided by the trustee, and such property shall be treated as customer property, if and to the extent that the trustee avoids such transfer under section 544, 545, 547, 548, or 549 of this title. For the purpose of such sections, the property so transferred shall be deemed to have been property of the debtor and, if such transfer was made to a customer or for a customer's benefit, such customer shall be deemed, for the purposes of this section, to have been a creditor.

(b) Notwithstanding sections 544, 545, 547, 548, and 549 of this title, the trustee may not avoid a transfer made before seven days after the order for relief if

such transfer is approved by the Commission by rule or order, either before or after such transfer, and if such transfer is—

(1) a transfer of a securities contract entered into or carried by or through the debtor on behalf of a customer, and of any cash, security, or other property margining or securing such securities contract; or

(2) the liquidation of a securities contract entered into or carried by or through the debtor on behalf of a customer.

(Pub.L. 95–598, Nov. 6, 1978, 92 Stat. 2614; Pub.L. 97–222, § 14, July 27, 1982, 96 Stat. 238; Pub.L. 111–16, § 2(8), May 7, 2009, 123 Stat. 1607.)

HISTORICAL AND STATUTORY NOTES

Revision Notes and Legislative Reports

1978 Acts. Section 749 indicates that if the trustee avoids a transfer, property recovered is customer property to any extent it would have been customer property but for the transfer. The section clarifies that a customer who receives a transfer of property of the debtor is a creditor and that property in a customer's account is property of a creditor for purposes of the avoiding powers. Senate Report No. 95–989.

1982 Acts. House Report No. 97–420, see 1982 U.S.Code Cong. and Adm.News, p. 583.

Amendments

2009 Amendments. Subsec. (b). Pub.L. 111–16, § 2(8), struck out "five days" and inserted "seven days".

1982 Amendments. Pub.L. 97–222 substituted "(a) Except as otherwise provided in this section, any" for "Any", and "but" for "except", inserted "such property", substituted "or 549" for "549, or 724(a)", and added subsec. (b).

Effective and Applicability Provisions

2009 Acts. Amendments by Pub.L. 111–16 effective Dec. 1, 2009, see Pub.L. 111–16, § 7, set out as a note under 11 U.S.C.A. § 109.

CROSS REFERENCES

Voidable transfers in commodity broker liquidation cases, see 11 USCA § 764.

LIBRARY REFERENCES

American Digest System

Bankruptcy ⊙3461.
Key Number System Topic No. 51.

Corpus Juris Secundum

CJS Bankruptcy § 278, Parties Defendant; Sovereign Immunity.

CJS Bankruptcy § 1109, Voidable Transfers.

§ 750. Distribution of securities

The trustee may not distribute a security except under section 751 of this title.
(Pub.L. 95–598, Nov. 6, 1978, 92 Stat. 2614.)

HISTORICAL AND STATUTORY NOTES

Revision Notes and Legislative Reports

1978 Acts. Section 750 forbids the trustee from distributing a security other than a customer name security. The term "distribution" refers to a distribution to customers in satisfaction of net equity claims and is not intended to preclude the trustee from liquidating securities under proposed 11 U.S.C. 748. Senate Report No. 95–989.

CROSS REFERENCES

Distribution in Chapter eleven cases, see 11 USCA § 1143.

Distribution of property of estate, see 11 USCA § 726.

LIBRARY REFERENCES

American Digest System

Bankruptcy ☞3461.

Key Number System Topic No. 51.

Corpus Juris Secundum

CJS Bankruptcy § 1110, Customer Name Securities.

§ 751. Customer name securities

The trustee shall deliver any customer name security to or on behalf of the customer entitled to such security, unless such customer has a negative net equity. With the approval of the trustee, a customer may reclaim a customer name security after payment to the trustee, within such period as the trustee allows, of any claim of the debtor against such customer to the extent that such customer will not have a negative net equity after such payment.
(Pub.L. 95–598, Nov. 6, 1978, 92 Stat. 2614.)

HISTORICAL AND STATUTORY NOTES

Revision Notes and Legislative Reports

1978 Acts. Section 751 requires the trustee to deliver a customer name security to the customer entitled to such security unless the customer has a negative net equity. The customer's net equity will be negative when the amount owed by the customer to the stockbroker exceeds the liquidation value of the non-customer name securities in the customer's account. If the customer is a net debtor of the stockbroker, then the trustee may permit the customer to repay debts to the stockbroker so that the customer will no longer be in debt to the stockbroker. If the customer refuses to pay such amount, then the court may order the customer to endorse the security in order that the trustee may liquidate such property. Senate Report No. 95–989.

LIBRARY REFERENCES

American Digest System

Bankruptcy ☞3461.

Key Number System Topic No. 51.

Corpus Juris Secundum

CJS Bankruptcy § 626, Collection and Reduction to Money of Property of Estate in Chapter 7 Cases.

CJS Bankruptcy § 838, Stockbroker Liquidation Cases.

CJS Bankruptcy § 1110, Customer Name Securities.

§ 752. Customer property

(a) The trustee shall distribute customer property ratably to customers on the basis and to the extent of such customers' allowed net equity claims and in priority to all other claims, except claims of the kind specified in section 507(a)(2) of this title that are attributable to the administration of such customer property.

(b)(1) The trustee shall distribute customer property in excess of that distributed under subsection (a) of this section in accordance with section 726 of this title.

(2) Except as provided in section 510 of this title, if a customer is not paid the full amount of such customer's allowed net equity claim from customer property, the unpaid portion of such claim is a claim entitled to distribution under section 726 of this title.

(c) Any cash or security remaining after the liquidation of a security interest created under a security agreement made by the debtor, excluding property excluded under section 741(4)(B) of this title, shall be apportioned between the general estate and customer property in the same proportion as the general estate of the debtor and customer property were subject to such security interest.
(Pub.L. 95–598, Nov. 6, 1978, 92 Stat. 2614; Pub.L. 97–222, § 15, July 27, 1982, 96 Stat. 238; Pub.L. 98–353, Title III, § 484, July 10, 1984, 98 Stat. 383; Pub.L. 109–8, Title XV, § 1502(a)(3), Apr. 20, 2005, 119 Stat. 216.)

HISTORICAL AND STATUTORY NOTES

Revision Notes and Legislative Reports

1978 Acts. Section 752(a) requires the trustee to distribute customer property to customers based on the amount of their net equity claims. Customer property is to be distributed in priority to all claims except expenses of administration entitled to priority under § 507(1). It is anticipated that the court will apportion such administrative claims on an equitable basis between the general estate and the customer property of the debtor.

Subsection (b)(1) indicates that in the event customer property exceeds customers net equity claims and administrative expenses, the excess pours over into the general estate. This event would occur if the value of securities increased dramatically after the order for relief but before liquidation by the trustee. Subsection (b)(2) indicates that the unpaid portion of a customer's net equity claim is entitled to share in the general estate as an unsecured claim unless subordinated by the court under proposed 11 U.S.C. 501. A net equity claim of a customer that is subordinated under section 747 is entitled to share in distribution under section 726(a)(2) unless subordinated under section 510 independently of the subordination under section 747.

Subsection (c) provides for apportionment between customer property and the general estate of any equity of the debtor in property remaining after a secured creditor liquidates a security interest. This might occur if a stockbroker hypothecates securities of his own and of his customers if the value of the hypothecated securities exceeds the debt owed to the secured party. The apportionment is to be made according to the ratio of customer property and general property of the debtor that comprised the collateral. The subsection refers to cash and securities of customers to include any customer property unlawfully converted by the stockbroker in the course of such a transaction. The apportionment is made subject to section 741(4)(B) to insure that property in a customer's account that is owed to the stockbroker will not be considered customer property. This recognizes the right of the stockbroker to withdraw money that has been erroneously placed in a customer's account or that is otherwise owing to the stockbroker. Senate Report No. 95–989.

1982 Acts. House Report No. 97–420, see 1982 U.S.Code Cong. and Adm.News, p. 583.

1984 Acts. Statements by Legislative Leaders, see 1984 U.S.Code Cong. and Adm.News, p. 576.

2005 Acts. House Report No. 109–31(Part I), see 2005 U.S. Code Cong. and Adm. News, p. 88.

Codifications

Amendment by section 484(a)(3) of Pub.L. 98–353, directing that subsec. (a) of this section be amended by inserting "such" before "customer property", has been executed by inserting "such" before "customer property" following "the administration of" as the probable intent of Congress.

Amendments

2005 Amendments. Subsec. (a). Pub.L. 109–8, § 1502(a)(3), struck out "507(a)(1)" and inserted "507(a)(2)".

1984 Amendments. Subsec. (a). Pub.L. 98–353, § 484(a), substituted "customers' allowed" for "customers allowed", "except claims of the kind" for "except claims", and "the administration of such customer property" for "the administration of customer property". See Codifications note set out under this section.

Subsec. (b)(2). Pub.L. 98–353, § 484(b), substituted "section 726 of this title" for "section 726(a) of this title".

1982 Amendments. Subsec. (c). Pub.L. 97–222 substituted "Any cash or security remaining after the liquidation of a security interest created under a security agreement made by the debtor, excluding property excluded under section 741(4)(B) of this title, shall be apportioned between the general estate and customer property in the same proportion as the general estate of the debtor and customer property were subject to such security interest" for "Subject to section 741(4)(B) of this title, any cash or security remaining after the liquidation of a security interest created under a security agreement made by the debtor shall be apportioned between the general estate and customer property in the proportion that the general property of the debtor and the cash or securities of customers were subject to such security interest".

Effective and Applicability Provisions

2005 Acts. Amendments by Pub.L. 109–8 effective, except as otherwise provided, 180 days after April 20, 2005, and inapplicable with respect to cases commenced under Title 11 before the effective date, see Pub.L. 109–8, § 1501, set out as a note under 11 U.S.C.A. § 101.

1984 Acts. Amendment by Pub.L. 98–353 effective with respect to cases filed 90 days after July 10, 1984, see section 552(a), formerly 553(a), of Pub.L. 98–353, set out as a note under section 101 of this title.

CROSS REFERENCES

Distribution in Chapter eleven cases, see 11 USCA § 1143.

Distribution of—

Customer property in commodity broker liquidation cases, see 11 USCA § 766.

Property of the estate, see 11 USCA § 726.

Election of trustee by creditors holding claims entitled to distribution, see 11 USCA § 702.

Priorities, see 11 USCA § 507.

LIBRARY REFERENCES

American Digest System

Bankruptcy ⚮3461.

Key Number System Topic No. 51.

Corpus Juris Secundum

CJS Bankruptcy § 99, Powers and Duties in Stockholder or Commodity Broker Liquidation Cases.

CJS Bankruptcy § 838, Stockbroker Liquidation Cases.

CJS Bankruptcy § 1111, Customer Property.

§ 753. Stockbroker liquidation and forward contract merchants, commodity brokers, stockbrokers, financial institutions, financial participants, securities clearing agencies, swap participants, repo participants, and master netting agreement participants

Notwithstanding any other provision of this title, the exercise of rights by a forward contract merchant, commodity broker, stockbroker, financial institution, financial participant, securities clearing agency, swap participant, repo participant, or master netting agreement participant under this title shall not affect the priority of any unsecured claim it may have after the exercise of such rights.

(Added Pub.L. 109–8, Title IX, § 907(m), Apr. 20, 2005, 119 Stat. 181.)

HISTORICAL AND STATUTORY NOTES

Revision Notes and Legislative Reports

2005 Acts. House Report No. 109–31(Part I), see 2005 U.S. Code Cong. and Adm. News, p. 88.

Effective and Applicability Provisions

2005 Acts. Amendments by Pub.L. 109–8 effective, except as otherwise provided, 180 days after April 20, 2005, and inapplicable with respect to cases commenced under Title 11 before the effective date, see Pub.L. 109–8, § 1501, set out as a note under 11 U.S.C.A. § 101.

LIBRARY REFERENCES

Corpus Juris Secundum

CJS Bankruptcy § 7, Bankruptcy Code.

CJS Bankruptcy § 385, Governing Statutes, Generally.

SUBCHAPTER IV—COMMODITY BROKER LIQUIDATION

CROSS REFERENCES

Certain terms defined under this section as having same meaning for purposes of Commodity Exchange Act, see 7 USCA § 24.

Powers and duties of trustee in investor liquidation proceedings, see 15 USCA § 78fff–1.

Subchapter generally applicable only in case under chapter concerning commodity broker, see 11 USCA § 103.

§ 761.   Definitions for this subchapter

In this subchapter—

   (1) "Act" means Commodity Exchange Act;

   (2) "clearing organization" means a derivatives clearing organization registered under the Act;

   (3) "Commission" means Commodity Futures Trading Commission;

   (4) "commodity contract" means—

     (A) with respect to a futures commission merchant, contract for the purchase or sale of a commodity for future delivery on, or subject to the rules of, a contract market or board of trade;

     (B) with respect to a foreign futures commission merchant, foreign future;

     (C) with respect to a leverage transaction merchant, leverage transaction;

     (D) with respect to a clearing organization, contract for the purchase or sale of a commodity for future delivery on, or subject to the rules of, a contract market or board of trade that is cleared by such clearing organization, or commodity option traded on, or subject to the rules of, a contract market or board of trade that is cleared by such clearing organization;

     (E) with respect to a commodity options dealer, commodity option;

     (F) any other agreement or transaction that is similar to an agreement or transaction referred to in this paragraph;

     (G) any combination of the agreements or transactions referred to in this paragraph;

     (H) any option to enter into an agreement or transaction referred to in this paragraph;

     (I) a master agreement that provides for an agreement or transaction referred to in subparagraph (A), (B), (C), (D), (E), (F), (G), or (H), together with all supplements to such master agreement, without regard to whether the master agreement provides for an agreement or transaction that is not a commodity contract under this paragraph, except that the master agreement shall be considered to be a commodity contract under this paragraph only with respect to each agreement or transaction under the master agreement that is referred to in subparagraph (A), (B), (C), (D), (E), (F), (G), or (H); or

     (J) any security agreement or arrangement or other credit enhancement related to any agreement or transaction referred to in this paragraph, including any guarantee or reimbursement obligation by or to a commodity broker or financial participant in connection with any agreement or

transaction referred to in this paragraph, but not to exceed the damages in connection with any such agreement or transaction, measured in accordance with section 562;

   (5) "commodity option" means agreement or transaction subject to regulation under section 4c(b) of the Act;

   (6) "commodity options dealer" means person that extends credit to, or that accepts cash, a security, or other property from, a customer of such person for the purchase or sale of an interest in a commodity option;

   (7) "contract market" means a registered entity;

   (8) "contract of sale", "commodity", "derivatives clearing organization", "future delivery", "board of trade", "registered entity", and "futures commission merchant" have the meanings assigned to those terms in the Act;

   (9) "customer" means—

     (A) with respect to a futures commission merchant—

       (i) entity for or with whom such futures commission merchant deals and that holds a claim against such futures commission merchant on account of a commodity contract made, received, acquired, or held by or through such futures commission merchant in the ordinary course of such futures commission merchant's business as a futures commission merchant from or for the commodity futures account of such entity; or

       (ii) entity that holds a claim against such futures commission merchant arising out of—

         (I) the making, liquidation, or change in the value of a commodity contract of a kind specified in clause (i) of this subparagraph;

         (II) a deposit or payment of cash, a security, or other property with such futures commission merchant for the purpose of making or margining such a commodity contract; or

         (III) the making or taking of delivery on such a commodity contract;

     (B) with respect to a foreign futures commission merchant—

       (i) entity for or with whom such foreign futures commission merchant deals and that holds a claim against such foreign futures commission merchant on account of a commodity contract made, received, acquired, or held by or through such foreign futures commission merchant in the ordinary course of such foreign futures commission merchant's business as a foreign futures commission merchant from or for the foreign futures account of such entity; or

       (ii) entity that holds a claim against such foreign futures commission merchant arising out of—

(I) the making, liquidation, or change in value of a commodity contract of a kind specified in clause (i) of this subparagraph;

(II) a deposit or payment of cash, a security, or other property with such foreign futures commission merchant for the purpose of making or margining such a commodity contract; or

(III) the making or taking of delivery on such a commodity contract;

(C) with respect to a leverage transaction merchant—

(i) entity for or with whom such leverage transaction merchant deals and that holds a claim against such leverage transaction merchant on account of a commodity contract engaged in by or with such leverage transaction merchant in the ordinary course of such leverage transaction merchant's business as a leverage transaction merchant from or for the leverage account of such entity; or

(ii) entity that holds a claim against such leverage transaction merchant arising out of—

(I) the making, liquidation, or change in value of a commodity contract of a kind specified in clause (i) of this subparagraph;

(II) a deposit or payment of cash, a security, or other property with such leverage transaction merchant for the purpose of entering into or margining such a commodity contract; or

(III) the making or taking of delivery on such a commodity contract;

(D) with respect to a clearing organization, clearing member of such clearing organization with whom such clearing organization deals and that holds a claim against such clearing organization on account of cash, a security, or other property received by such clearing organization to margin, guarantee, or secure a commodity contract in such clearing member's proprietary account or customers' account; or

(E) with respect to a commodity options dealer—

(i) entity for or with whom such commodity options dealer deals and that holds a claim on account of a commodity contract made, received, acquired, or held by or through such commodity options dealer in the ordinary course of such commodity options dealer's business as a commodity options dealer from or for the commodity options account of such entity; or

(ii) entity that holds a claim against such commodity options dealer arising out of—

(I) the making of, liquidation of, exercise of, or a change in value of, a commodity

contract of a kind specified in clause (i) of this subparagraph; or

(II) a deposit or payment of cash, a security, or other property with such commodity options dealer for the purpose of making, exercising, or margining such a commodity contract;

(10) "customer property" means cash, a security, or other property, or proceeds of such cash, security, or property, received, acquired, or held by or for the account of the debtor, from or for the account of a customer—

(A) including—

(i) property received, acquired, or held to margin, guarantee, secure, purchase, or sell a commodity contract;

(ii) profits or contractual or other rights accruing to a customer as a result of a commodity contract;

(iii) an open commodity contract;

(iv) specifically identifiable customer property;

(v) warehouse receipt or other document held by the debtor evidencing ownership of or title to property to be delivered to fulfill a commodity contract from or for the account of a customer;

(vi) cash, a security, or other property received by the debtor as payment for a commodity to be delivered to fulfill a commodity contract from or for the account of a customer;

(vii) a security held as property of the debtor to the extent such security is necessary to meet a net equity claim based on a security of the same class and series of an issuer;

(viii) property that was unlawfully converted from and that is the lawful property of the estate; and

(ix) other property of the debtor that any applicable law, rule, or regulation requires to be set aside or held for the benefit of a customer, unless including such property as customer property would not significantly increase customer property; but

(B) not including property to the extent that a customer does not have a claim against the debtor based on such property;

(11) "foreign future" means contract for the purchase or sale of a commodity for future delivery on, or subject to the rules of, a board of trade outside the United States;

(12) "foreign futures commission merchant" means entity engaged in soliciting or accepting orders for the purchase or sale of a foreign future or that, in connection with such a solicitation or acceptance, accepts cash, a security, or other property, or extends credit to margin, guarantee, or secure any trade or contract that results from such a solicitation or acceptance;

(13) "leverage transaction" means agreement that is subject to regulation under section 19 of the Commodity Exchange Act, and that is commonly known to the commodities trade as a margin account, margin contract, leverage account, or leverage contract;

(14) "leverage transaction merchant" means person in the business of engaging in leverage transactions;

(15) "margin payment" means payment or deposit of cash, a security, or other property, that is commonly known to the commodities trade as original margin, initial margin, maintenance margin, or variation margin, including mark-to-market payments, settlement payments, variation payments, daily settlement payments, and final settlement payments made as adjustments to settlement prices;

(16) "member property" means customer property received, acquired, or held by or for the account of a debtor that is a clearing organization, from or for the proprietary account of a customer that is a clearing member of the debtor; and

(17) "net equity" means, subject to such rules and regulations as the Commission promulgates under the Act, with respect to the aggregate of all of a customer's accounts that such customer has in the same capacity—

    (A) the balance remaining in such customer's accounts immediately after—

        (i) all commodity contracts of such customer have been transferred, liquidated, or become identified for delivery; and

        (ii) all obligations of such customer in such capacity to the debtor have been offset; plus

    (B) the value, as of the date of return under section 766 of this title, of any specifically identifiable customer property actually returned to such customer before the date specified in subparagraph (A) of this paragraph; plus

    (C) the value, as of the date of transfer, of—

        (i) any commodity contract to which such customer is entitled that is transferred to another person under section 766 of this title; and

        (ii) any cash, security, or other property of such customer transferred to such other person under section 766 of this title to margin or secure such transferred commodity contract.

(Pub.L. 95–598, Nov. 6, 1978, 92 Stat. 2615; Pub.L. 97–222, § 16, July 27, 1982, 96 Stat. 238; Pub.L. 98–353, Title III, § 485, July 10, 1984, 98 Stat. 383; Pub.L. 103–394, Title V, § 501(d)(29), Oct. 22, 1994, 108 Stat. 4146; Pub.L. 106–554, § 1(a)(5) [Title I, § 112(c)(6)], Dec. 21, 2000, 114 Stat. 2763, 2763A–395; Pub.L. 109–8, Title IX, § 907(a)(3), Apr. 20, 2005, 119 Stat. 174.)

Amendment of Par. (4)(F)

Pub.L. 111–203, Title VII, §§ 724(b)(1), 754, July 21, 2010, 124 Stat. 1684, 1754, provided that, except as otherwise provided, effective on the later of 360 days after July 21, 2010, or, to the extent a provision requires a rulemaking, not less than 60 days after publication of the final rule or regulation, par. (4)(F) is amended by striking subpar. (F) and inserting a new subpar. (F) to read:

(F)(i) any other contract, option, agreement, or transaction that is similar to a contract, option, agreement, or transaction referred to in this paragraph; and

(ii) with respect to a futures commission merchant or a clearing organization, any other contract, option, agreement, or transaction, in each case, that is cleared by a clearing organization;

Amendment of Par. (9)(A)(i)

Pub.L. 111–203, Title VII, §§ 724(b)(2), 754, July 21, 2010, 124 Stat. 1684, 1754, provided that, except as otherwise provided, effective on the later of 360 days after July 21, 2010, or, to the extent a provision requires a rulemaking, not less than 60 days after publication of the final rule or regulation, par. (9)(A)(i) is amended by striking "the commodity futures account" and inserting "a commodity contract account".

HISTORICAL AND STATUTORY NOTES

Revision Notes and Legislative Reports

1978 Acts. Paragraph (1) defines "Act" to mean the Commodity Exchange Act [7 U.S.C.A. § 1 et seq.].

Paragraph (2) defines "clearing organization" to mean an organization that clears (i.e., matches purchases and sales) commodity futures contracts made on or subject to the rules of a contract market or commodity options transactions made on or subject to the rules of a commodity option exchange. Although commodity option trading on exchanges is currently prohibited, it is anticipated that CFTC may permit such trading in the future.

Paragraphs (3) and (4) define terms "Commission" and "commodity futures contract".

Paragraph (5) defines "commodity contract" to mean a commodity futures contract (§ 761(4)), a commodity option (§ 761(6)), or a leverage contract (§ 761(15)).

Paragraph (b) [probably should be "(6)" defines "commodity option" by reference to section 4c(b) of the Commodity Exchange Act [7 U.S.C.A. § 6c(b)].

Paragraphs (7), (8), and (9), define "commodity options dealer," "contract market," "contract of sale," "commodity," "future delivery," "board of trade," and "futures commission merchant."

Paragraph (10) defines the term "customer" to mean with respect to a futures commission merchant or a foreign futures commission merchant, the entity for whom the debtor carries a commodity futures contract or foreign future, or with whom such a contract is carried (such as another commodity broker), or from whom the debtor has received, acquired, or holds cash, securities, or other property arising out of or connected with specified transactions involving commodity futures contracts or foreign futures. This section also defines "customer" in the context of leverage transaction merchants, clearing organizations, and commodity options dealers. Persons associated with a commodity broker, such as its employees, officers, or partners, may be customers under this definition.

The definition of "customer" serves to isolate that class of persons entitled to the protection subchapter IV provides to customers. In addition, section 101(5) defines "commodity broker" to mean a futures commission merchant, foreign futures commission merchant, clearing organization, leverage transaction merchant, or commodity options dealer, with respect to which there is a customer. Accordingly, the definition of customer also serves to designate those entities which must utilize chapter 7 and are precluded from reorganizing under chapter 11.

Paragraph (11) defines "customer property" to mean virtually all property or proceeds thereof, received, acquired, or held by or for the account of the debtor for a customer arising out of or in connection with a transaction involving a commodity contract.

Paragraph (12) defines "distribution share" to mean the amount to which a customer is entitled under section 765(a).

Paragraphs (13), (14), (15), and (16), define "foreign future," "foreign futures commission merchant," "leverage transaction," and "leverage transaction merchant."

Paragraph (17) defines "margin payment" to mean a payment or deposit commonly known to the commodities trade as original margin, initial margin, or variation margin.

Paragraph (18) defines "member property."

Paragraph (19) defines "net equity" to be the sum of (A) the value of all customer property remaining in a customer's account immediately after all commodity contracts of such customer have been transferred, liquidated, or become identified for delivery and all obligations of such customer to the debtor have been offset (such as margin payments, whether or not called, and brokerage commissions) plus (B) the value of specifically identifiable customer property previously returned to the customer by the trustee, plus (C) if the trustee has transferred any commodity contract to which the customer is entitled or any margin or security for such contract, the value of such contract and margin or security. Net equity, therefore, will be the total amount of customer property to which a customer is entitled as of the date of the filing of the bankruptcy petition, although valued at subsequent dates. The Commission is given authority to promulgate rules and regulations to further refine this definition. Senate Report No. 95–989.

Paragraph (8) is a dynamic definition of "contractual commitment". The definition will vary depending on the character of the debtor in each case. If the debtor is a futures commission merchant or a clearing organization, then subparagraphs (A) and (D) indicate that the definition means a contract of sale of a commodity for future delivery on a contract market. If the debtor is a foreign futures commission merchant, a leverage transaction merchant, or a commodity options dealer, then subparagraphs (B), (C), and (E) indicate that the definition means foreign future, leverage transaction, or commodity option, respectively.

Paragraph (9) defines "customer" in a similar style. It is anticipated that a debtor with multifaceted characteristics will have separate estates for each different kind of customer. Thus, a debtor that is a leverage transaction merchant and a commodity options dealer would have separate estates for the leverage transaction customers and for the options customers,

and a general estate for other creditors. Customers for each kind of commodity broker, except the clearing organization, arise from either of two relationships. In subparagraphs (A), (B), (C), and (E), clause (i) treats with customers to the extent of contractual commitments with the debtor in either a broker or a dealer relationship. Clause (ii) treats with customers to the extent of proceeds from contractual commitments or deposits for the purpose of making contractual commitments. The customer of the clearing organization is a member with a proprietary or customers' account.

Paragraph (10) defines "customer property" to include all property in customer accounts and property that should have been in those accounts but was diverted through conversion or mistake. Clause (i) refers to customer property not properly segregated by the debtor or customer property converted and then recovered so as to become property of the estate. Clause (vii) is intended to exclude property that would cost more to recover from a third party than the value of the property itself. Subparagraph (B) excludes property in a customer's account that belongs to the commodity broker, such as a contract placed in the account by error, or cash due the broker for a margin payment that the broker has made.

Paragraph (15) defines "net equity" to include the value of all contractual commitments at the time of liquidation or transfer less any obligations owed by the customer to the debtor, such as brokerage fees. In addition, the term includes the value of any specifically identifiable property as of the date of return to the customer and the value of any customer property transferred to another commodity broker as of the date of transfer. This definition places the risk of market fluctuations on the customer until commitments leave the estate. House Report No. 95–595.

1982 Acts. House Report No. 97–420, see 1982 U.S.Code Cong. and Adm.News, p. 583.

1984 Acts. Statements by Legislative Leaders, see 1984 U.S.Code Cong. and Adm.News, p. 576.

1994 Acts. House Report No. 103–835, see 1994 U.S. Code Cong. and Adm. News, p. 3340.

2000 Acts. House Report No. 106–645 and Statement by President, see 2000 U.S. Code Cong. and Adm. News, p. 2459.

2005 Acts. House Report No. 109–31(Part I), see 2005 U.S. Code Cong. and Adm. News, p. 88.

Legislative Statements

Subchapter IV of chapter 7 represents a compromise between similar chapters in the House bill and Senate amendment. Section 761(2) of the House amendment defines "clearing organization" to cover an organization that clears commodity contracts on a contract market or a board of trade; the expansion of the definition is intended to include clearing organizations that clear commodity options. Section 761(4) of the House amendment adopts the term "commodity contract" as used in section 761(5) of the Senate amendment but with the more precise substantive definitions contained in section 761(8) of the House bill. The definition is modified to insert "board of trade" to cover commodity options. Section 761(5) of the House amendment adopts the definition contained in section 761(6) of the Senate amendment in preference to the definition contained in section 761(4) of the House bill which erroneously included onions. Section 761(9) of the House amendment represents a compromise between similar provisions contained in section 761(10) of the Senate amendment and section 761(9) of the House bill. The compromise adopts the substance contained in the House bill and adopts the terminology of "commodity contract" in lieu of "contractual commitment" as suggested in the Senate amendment. Section 761(10) of the House amendment represents a compromise between similar sections in the House bill and Senate amendment regarding the definition of "customer property." The definition of "distribution share" contained in section 761(12) of the Senate amendment is deleted as unnecessary. Section 761(12) of the House amendment adopts a definition of "foreign futures commission merchant" similar to the definition contained in section 761(14) of the Senate amendment. The definition is modified to cover either an entity engaged in soliciting orders or the purchase or sale of a foreign future, or an entity that accepts cash, a security, or other property for credit in connection with such a solicitation or acceptance. Section 761(13) of the House amendment adopts a definition of "leverage transaction" identical to the definition contained in section 761(15) of the Senate amendment. Section 761(15) of the House amendment adopts the definition of "margin payment" contained in section 761(17) of the Senate amendment. Section 761(17) of the House amendment adopts a definition of "net equity" derived from section 761(15) of the House bill.

References in Text

The Commodity Exchange Act or the Act, referred to in pars. (1), (8), and (17), is Act Sept. 21, 1922, c. 369, 42 Stat. 998, as amended, which is classified generally to chapter 1 (section 1 et seq.) of Title 7, Agriculture. For complete classification of this Act to the Code, see section 1 of Title 7 and Tables.

Section 4c of the Commodity Exchange Act, referred to in par. (5), is section 4c of Act Sept. 21, 1922, c. 369, as added June 15, 1936, c. 545, § 5, 49 Stat. 1494, which is classified to section 6c of Title 7, Agriculture.

Section 19 of the Commodity Exchange Act, referred to in par. (13), is section 19 of Act Sept. 21, 1922, c. 369, as added Sept. 30, 1978, Pub.L. 95–405, § 23, 92 Stat. 876, which is classified to section 23 of Title 7.

Amendments

2010 Amendments. Par. (4)(F). Pub.L. 111–203, § 724(b)(1), rewrote subpar. (F), which formerly read: **"(F)** any other agreement or transaction that is similar to an agreement or transaction referred to in this paragraph;".

Par. (9)(A)(i). Pub.L. 111–203, § 724(b)(2), struck out "the commodity futures account" and inserting "a commodity contract account".

2005 Amendments. Par. (4)(D). Pub.L. 109–8, § 907(a)(3)(A), struck out "or" at the end of subpar. (D).

Par. (4)(F) to (J). Pub.L. 109–8, § 907(a)(3)(B), added subpars. (F) to (J).

2000 Amendments. Par. (2). Pub.L. 106–554, § 1(a)(5) [Title I, § 112(c)(6)(A)], revised par. (2). Prior to amendment, par. (2) read as follows:

"(2) 'clearing organization' means organization that clears commodity contracts made on, or subject to the rules of, a contract market or board of trade;".

Par. (7). Pub.L. 106–554, § 1(a)(5) [Title I, § 112(c)(6)(B)], revised par. (7). Prior to amendment, par. (7) read as follows:

"(7) 'contract market' means board of trade designated as a contract market by the Commission under the Act;".

Par. (8). Pub.L. 106–554, § 1(a)(5) [Title I, § 112(c)(6)(C)], revised par. (8). Prior to amendment, par. (8) read as follows:

"(8) 'contract of sale', 'commodity', 'future delivery', 'board of trade', and 'futures commission merchant' have the meanings assigned to those terms in the Act;".

1994 Amendments. Par. (1). Pub.L. 103–394, § 501(d)(29)(A), struck out "(7 U.S.C. 1 et seq.)" following "Commodity Exchange Act".

Par. (5). Pub.L. 103–394, § 501(d)(29)(B), struck out "(7 U.S.C. 6c(b))" following "section 4c(b) of the Act".

Par. (13). Pub.L. 103–394, § 501(d)(29)(C), struck out "(7 U.S.C. 23)" following "the Commodity Exchange Act".

1984 Amendments. Par. (10)(A)(viii). Pub.L. 98–353 substituted "from and that is the lawful property of the estate" for "and that is property of the estate".

1982 Amendments. Par. (2). Pub.L. 97–222, § 16(1), inserted "made" following "commodity contracts".

Par. (4). Pub.L. 97–222, § 16(2), substituted "with respect to" for "if the debtor is" wherever appearing, and substituted "cleared by such clearing organization, or commodity option traded on, or subject to the rules of, a contract market or board of trade that is cleared by such clearing organization" for "cleared by the debtor" in subpar. (D).

Par. (9). Pub.L. 97–222, § 16(3), substituted "with respect to" for "if the debtor is" wherever appearing, in subpar. (A) substituted "such futures commission merchant" for "the debtor" wherever appearing and "such futures commission merchant's" for "the debtor's", in subpar. (B) substituted "such foreign futures commission merchant" for "the debtor" wherever appearing and "such foreign futures commission merchant's" for "the debtor's", in subpar. (C) substituted "such leverage transaction merchant" for "the debtor" wherever appearing and "such leverage transaction merchant's" for "the debtor's", inserted "or" after the semicolon in cl. (i), and substituted "holds" for "hold" in cl. (ii), in subpar. (D) substituted "such clearing organization" for "the debtor" wherever appearing, and in subpar. (E) substituted "such commodity options dealer" for "the debtor" wherever appearing and "such commodity options dealer's" for "the debtor's".

Par. (10). Pub.L. 97–222, § 16(4), struck out "at any time" following "security, or property," in the provisions preceding subpar. (A).

Par. (12). Pub.L. 97–222, § 16(5), inserted a comma after "property" and struck out the comma after "credit".

Par. (13). Pub.L. 97–222, § 16(6), substituted "section 19 of the Commodity Exchange Act (7 U.S.C. 23)" for "section 217 of the Commodity Futures Trading Commission Act of 1974 (7 U.S.C. 15a)".

Par. (14). Pub.L. 97–222, § 16(7), struck out "that is engaged" following "means person".

Par. (15). Pub.L. 97–222, § 16(8), substituted "mark-to-market payments, settlement payments, variation payments, daily settlement payments, and final settlement payments made as adjustments to settlement prices" for "a daily variation settlement payment".

Par. (16). Pub.L. 97–222, § 16(9), struck out "at any time" following "customer property".

Par. (17). Pub.L. 97–222, § 16(10), in the provisions preceding subpar. (A) substituted "has" for "holds", in subpar. (A) inserted "the" after "(A)" in provisions preceding cl. (i), and "in such capacity" after "customer" in cl. (ii).

Effective and Applicability Provisions

2010 Acts. Unless as otherwise provided, Pub.L. 111–203, Title VII, subtitle A, § 711 et seq., shall take effect on the later of 360 days after July 21, 2010, or, to the extent a provision requires a rulemaking, not less than 60 days after publication of the final rule or regulation, see Pub.L. 111–203, § 754, set out as a note under 7 U.S.C.A. § 1a.

2005 Acts. Amendments by Pub.L. 109–8 effective, except as otherwise provided, 180 days after April 20, 2005, and inapplicable with respect to cases commenced under Title 11 before the effective date, see Pub.L. 109–8, § 1501, set out as a note under 11 U.S.C.A. § 101.

1994 Acts. Amendment by Pub.L. 103–394 effective on Oct. 22, 1994, and not to apply with respect to cases commenced under Title 11 of the United States Code before Oct. 22, 1994, see section 702 of Pub.L. 103–394, set out as a note under section 101 of this title.

1984 Acts. Amendment by Pub.L. 98–353 effective with respect to cases filed 90 days after July 10, 1984, see section 552(a), formerly 553(a), of Pub.L. 98–353, set out as a note under section 101 of this title.

Savings Provisions

Notwithstanding any other provision of Title VII of Pub.L. 111–203, § 701 et seq., nothing in subtitle A of such title, § 701 et seq., shall be construed as divesting any appropriate Federal banking agency of any authority it may have to establish or enforce, with respect to a person for which such agency is the appropriate Federal banking agency, prudential or other standards pursuant to authority by Federal law other than Title VII of Pub.L. 111–203, see 15 U.S.C.A. § 8324.

Unless otherwise provided by the amendments made by Title VII of Pub.L. 111–203, § 711 et seq., the amendments made by that subtitle do not divest any appropriate Federal banking agency, the Commodity Futures Trading Commission, the Securities and Exchange Commission, or other Federal or State agency of any authority derived from any other applicable law, see Pub.L. 111–203, § 743, set out as a note under 7 U.S.C.A. § 1a.

Severability of Provisions

If any provision of Pub.L. 111–203, an amendment made by Pub.L. 111–203, or the application of such provision or amendment to any person or circumstance is held to be unconstitutional, the remainder of Pub.L. 111–203, the amendments made by Pub.L. 111–203, and the application of the provisions of such to any person or circumstance shall not be affected, see 12 U.S.C.A. § 5302.

Separability of Provisions

If any provision of or amendment made by Pub.L. 103–394 or the application of such provision or amendment to any person or circumstance is held to be unconstitutional, the remaining provisions of and amendments made by Pub.L. 103–394 and the application of such provisions and amendments to any person or circumstance shall not be affected thereby, see section 701 of Pub.L. 103–394, set out as a note under section 101 of this title.

CROSS REFERENCES

Certain terms having same meanings as under this section, see 7 USCA § 24.

Commodity broker defined, see 11 USCA § 101.

"Commodity contract" defined under this section as having same meaning for purposes of Federal deposit insurance corporation, see 12 USCA § 1821.

Contractual right to liquidate "commodity contract" as defined under this section not stayed, avoided or limited by operation of any provision of this title, see 11 USCA § 556.

Definitions applicable in—

Chapter eleven cases, see 11 USCA § 1101.

Chapter nine cases, see 11 USCA § 902.

Railroad reorganization cases, see 11 USCA § 1162.

Stockbroker liquidation cases, see 11 USCA § 741.

Limitation on power of trustee to avoid transfer of "margin payment" as defined in this section, see 11 USCA § 546.

Reception of margin payments by commodity brokers or forward contract merchants as taking for value, see 11 USCA § 548.

Setoff of mutual debt in connection with "commodity contracts" or "margin payment" not stayed by filing of petitions for voluntary cases, joint cases or involuntary cases or protective decrees in investor protection liquidation proceedings, see 11 USCA § 362.

LIBRARY REFERENCES

American Digest System

Bankruptcy ⟜3461.

Key Number System Topic No. 51.

Corpus Juris Secundum

CJS Bankruptcy § 7, Bankruptcy Code.

CJS Bankruptcy § 385, Governing Statutes, Generally.

CJS Bankruptcy § 500, Setoffs.

CJS Bankruptcy § 837, Commodity-Broker Liquidation Cases.

CJS Bankruptcy § 1114, Treatment of Customer Property.

§ 762. Notice to the Commission and right to be heard

(a) The clerk shall give the notice required by section 342 of this title to the Commission.

(b) The Commission may raise and may appear and be heard on any issue in a case under this chapter.
(Pub.L. 95–598, Nov. 6, 1978, 92 Stat. 2618.)

HISTORICAL AND STATUTORY NOTES

Revision Notes and Legislative Reports

1978 Acts. Section 762 provides that the Commission shall be given such notice as is appropriate of an order for relief in a bankruptcy case and that the Commission may raise and may appear and may be heard on any issue in case involving a commodity broker liquidation. Senate Report No. 95–989.

CROSS REFERENCES

Notice in—

Chapter nine cases, see 11 USCA § 923.

Stockbroker liquidation proceedings, see 11 USCA § 743.

LIBRARY REFERENCES

American Digest System

Bankruptcy ⟜3461.

Key Number System Topic No. 51.

§ 763.   Treatment of accounts

(a) Accounts held by the debtor for a particular customer in separate capacities shall be treated as accounts of separate customers.

(b) A member of a clearing organization shall be deemed to hold such member's proprietary account in a separate capacity from such member's customers' account.

(c) The net equity in a customer's account may not be offset against the net equity in the account of any other customer.

(Pub.L. 95–598, Nov. 6, 1978, 92 Stat. 2618; Pub.L. 98–353, Title III, § 486, July 10, 1984, 98 Stat. 383.)

HISTORICAL AND STATUTORY NOTES

Revision Notes and Legislative Reports

1978 Acts. Section 763 provides for separate treatment of accounts held in separate capacities. A deficit in one account held for a customer may not be offset against the net equity in another account held by the same customer in a separate capacity or held by another customer. Senate Report No. 95–989.

1984 Acts. Statements by Legislative Leaders, see 1984 U.S.Code Cong. and Adm.News, p. 576.

Amendments

1984 Amendments. Subsec. (a). Pub.L. 98–353 substituted "by the debtor for" for "by" and "treated as" for "deemed to be".

Effective and Applicability Provisions

1984 Acts. Amendment by Pub.L. 98–353 effective with respect to cases filed 90 days after July 10, 1984, see section 552(a), formerly 553(a), of Pub.L. 98–353, set out as a note under section 101 of this title.

CROSS REFERENCES

Treatment of accounts in stockbroker liquidation cases, see 11 USCA § 745.

LIBRARY REFERENCES

American Digest System

Bankruptcy ⟜3461.

Key Number System Topic No. 51.

§ 764.   Voidable transfers

(a) Except as otherwise provided in this section, any transfer by the debtor of property that, but for such transfer, would have been customer property, may be avoided by the trustee, and such property shall be treated as customer property, if and to the extent that the trustee avoids such transfer under section 544, 545, 547, 548, 549, or 724(a) of this title. For the purpose of such sections, the property so transferred shall be deemed to have been property of the debtor, and, if such transfer was made to a customer or for a customer's benefit, such customer shall be deemed, for the purposes of this section, to have been a creditor.

(b) Notwithstanding sections 544, 545, 547, 548, 549, and 724(a) of this title, the trustee may not avoid a transfer made before seven days after the order for relief, if such transfer is approved by the Commission by rule or order, either before or after such transfer, and if such transfer is—

(1) a transfer of a commodity contract entered into or carried by or through the debtor on behalf of a customer, and of any cash, securities, or other property margining or securing such commodity contract; or

(2) the liquidation of a commodity contract entered into or carried by or through the debtor on behalf of a customer.

(Pub.L. 95–598, Nov. 6, 1978, 92 Stat. 2618; Pub.L. 97–222, § 17, July 27, 1982, 96 Stat. 240; Pub.L. 98–353, Title III, § 487, July 10, 1984, 98 Stat. 383; Pub.L. 111–16, § 2(9), May 7, 2009, 123 Stat. 1607.)

HISTORICAL AND STATUTORY NOTES

Revision Notes and Legislative Reports

1978 Acts. Section 764 permits the trustee to void any transfer of property that, except for such transfer, would have been customer property, to the extent permitted under section 544, 545, 547, 548, 549, or 724(a). Senate Report No. 95–989.

Section 764 indicates the extent to which the avoiding powers may be used by the trustee under subchapter IV of chapter 7. If property recovered would have been customer property if never transferred, then subsection (a) indicates that it will be so treated when recovered.

Subsection (b) prohibits avoiding any transaction that occurs before or within five days after the petition if the transaction is approved by the Commission and concerns an open contractual commitment. This enables the Commission to exercise its discretion to protect the integrity of the market by insuring that transactions cleared with other brokers will not be undone on a preference or a fraudulent transfer theory.

Subsection (c) insulates variation margin payments and other deposits from the avoiding powers except to the extent of actual fraud under section 548(a)(1). This facilitates prepetition transfers and protects the ordinary course of business in the market. House Report No. 95–595.

1982 Acts. House Report No. 97–420, see 1982 U.S.Code Cong. and Adm.News, p. 583.

1984 Acts. Statements by Legislative Leaders, see 1984 U.S.Code Cong. and Adm.News, p. 576.

Legislative Statements

Section 764 of the House amendment is derived from the House bill.

Amendments

2009 Amendments. Subsec. (b). Pub.L. 111–16, § 2(9), struck out "five days" and inserted "seven days".

1984 Amendments. Subsec. (a). Pub.L. 98–353 substituted "any transfer by the debtor" for "any transfer".

1982 Amendments. Subsec. (a). Pub.L. 97–222, § 17(a), substituted "but" for "except", inserted "such property" after "trustee, and", and substituted "shall be" for "is" wherever appearing.

Subsec. (b). Pub.L. 97–222, § 17(b), substituted "order for relief" for "date of the filing of the petition".

Subsec. (c). Pub.L. 97–222, § 17(c), struck out subsec. (c) which had provided that the trustee could not avoid a transfer that was a margin payment to or deposit with a commodity broker or forward contract merchant or was a settlement payment made by a clearing organization and that occurred before the commencement of the case.

Effective and Applicability Provisions

2009 Acts. Amendments by Pub.L. 111–16 effective Dec. 1, 2009, see Pub.L. 111–16, § 7, set out as a note under 11 U.S.C.A. § 109.

1984 Acts. Amendment by Pub.L. 98–353 effective with respect to cases filed 90 days after July 10, 1984, see section 552(a), formerly 553(a), of Pub.L. 98–353, set out as a note under section 101 of this title.

CROSS REFERENCES

Voidable transfers in stockbroker liquidation cases, see 11 USCA § 749.

LIBRARY REFERENCES

American Digest System

Bankruptcy ☞3461.

Key Number System Topic No. 51.

Corpus Juris Secundum

CJS Bankruptcy § 99, Powers and Duties in Stockholder or Commodity Broker Liquidation Cases.

CJS Bankruptcy § 278, Parties Defendant; Sovereign Immunity.

§ 765.   Customer instructions

(a) The notice required by section 342 of this title to customers shall instruct each customer—

(1) to file a proof of such customer's claim promptly, and to specify in such claim any specifically identifiable security, property, or commodity contract; and

(2) to instruct the trustee of such customer's desired disposition, including transfer under section 766 of this title or liquidation, of any commodity contract specifically identified to such customer.

(b) The trustee shall comply, to the extent practicable, with any instruction received from a customer regarding such customer's desired disposition of any commodity contract specifically identified to such customer. If the trustee has transferred, under section 766 of this title, such a commodity contract, the trustee shall transmit any such instruction to the commodity broker to whom such commodity contract was so transferred.

(Pub.L. 95–598, Nov. 6, 1978, 92 Stat. 2619; Pub.L. 97–222, § 18, July 27, 1982, 96 Stat. 240; Pub.L. 98–353, Title III, § 488, July 10, 1984, 98 Stat. 383.)

HISTORICAL AND STATUTORY NOTES

Revision Notes and Legislative Reports

1978 Acts. For Revision Notes and Legislative Reports for this section, see Revision Notes and Legislative Reports set out under section 766 of this title.

1982 Acts. House Report No. 97–420, see 1982 U.S.Code Cong. and Adm.News, p. 583.

1984 Acts. Statements by Legislative Leaders, see 1984 U.S.Code Cong. and Adm.News, p. 576.

Amendments

1984 Amendments. Subsec. (a). Pub.L. 98–353 substituted "notice required by" for "notice under".

1982 Amendments. Subsec. (b). Pub.L. 97–222 substituted "commodity contract" for "commitment".

Effective and Applicability Provisions

1984 Acts. Amendment by Pub.L. 98–353 effective with respect to cases filed 90 days after July 10, 1984, see section 552(a), formerly 553(a), of Pub.L. 98–353, set out as a note under section 101 of this title.

CROSS REFERENCES

Executory contracts and unexpired leases, see 11 USCA § 365.

LIBRARY REFERENCES

American Digest System

Bankruptcy ☞3461.

Key Number System Topic No. 51.

Corpus Juris Secundum

CJS Bankruptcy § 99, Powers and Duties in Stockholder or Commodity Broker Liquidation Cases.

CJS Bankruptcy § 837, Commodity-Broker Liquidation Cases.

§ 766.   Treatment of customer property

(a) The trustee shall answer all margin calls with respect to a specifically identifiable commodity contract of a customer until such time as the trustee returns or transfers such commodity contract, but the trustee may not make a margin payment that has the effect of a distribution to such customer of more than that to which such customer is entitled under subsection (h) or (i) of this section.

(b) The trustee shall prevent any open commodity contract from remaining open after the last day of trading in such commodity contract, or into the first day on which notice of intent to deliver on such commodity contract may be tendered, whichever occurs first. With respect to any commodity contract that has remained open after the last day of trading in such commodity contract or with respect to which delivery must be made or accepted under the rules of the contract market on which such commodity contract was made, the trustee may operate the business of the debtor for the purpose of—

(1) accepting or making tender of notice of intent to deliver the physical commodity underlying such commodity contract;

(2) facilitating delivery of such commodity; or

(3) disposing of such commodity if a party to such commodity contract defaults.

(c) The trustee shall return promptly to a customer any specifically identifiable security, property, or commodity contract to which such customer is entitled, or shall transfer, on such customer's behalf, such security, property, or commodity contract to a commodity broker that is not a debtor under this title, subject to such rules or regulations as the Commission may prescribe, to the extent that the value of such security, property, or commodity contract does not exceed the amount to which such customer would be entitled under subsection (h) or (i) of this section if such security, property, or commodity contract were not returned or transferred under this subsection.

(d) If the value of a specifically identifiable security, property, or commodity contract exceeds the amount to which the customer of the debtor is entitled under subsection (h) or (i) of this section, then such customer to whom such security, property, or commodity contract is specifically identified may deposit cash with the trustee equal to the difference between the value of such security, property, or commodity contract and such amount, and the trustee then shall—

(1) return promptly such security, property, or commodity contract to such customer; or

(2) transfer, on such customer's behalf, such security, property, or commodity contract to a commodity broker that is not a debtor under this title, subject to such rules or regulations as the Commission may prescribe.

(e) Subject to subsection (b) of this section, the trustee shall liquidate any commodity contract that—

(1) is identified to a particular customer and with respect to which such customer has not timely instructed the trustee as to the desired disposition of such commodity contract;

(2) cannot be transferred under subsection (c) of this section; or

(3) cannot be identified to a particular customer.

(f) As soon as practicable after the commencement of the case, the trustee shall reduce to money, consistent with good market practice, all securities and other property, other than commodity contracts, held as property of the estate, except for specifically identifiable securities or property distributable under subsection (h) or (i) of this section.

(g) The trustee may not distribute a security or other property except under subsection (h) or (i) of this section.

(h) Except as provided in subsection (b) of this section, the trustee shall distribute customer property ratably to customers on the basis and to the extent of such customers' allowed net equity claims, and in priority to all other claims, except claims of a kind specified in section 507(a)(2) of this title that are attributable to the administration of customer property. Such distribution shall be in the form of—

(1) cash;

(2) the return or transfer, under subsection (c) or (d) of this section, of specifically identifiable customer securities, property, or commodity contracts; or

(3) payment of margin calls under subsection (a) of this section.

Notwithstanding any other provision of this subsection, a customer net equity claim based on a proprietary account, as defined by Commission rule, regulation, or order, may not be paid either in whole or in part, directly or indirectly, out of customer property unless all other customer net equity claims have been paid in full.

(i) If the debtor is a clearing organization, the trustee shall distribute—

(1) customer property, other than member property, ratably to customers on the basis and to the extent of such customers' allowed net equity claims based on such customers' accounts other than proprietary accounts, and in priority to all other claims, except claims of a kind specified in section 507(a)(2) of this title that are attributable to the administration of such customer property; and

(2) member property ratably to customers on the basis and to the extent of such customers' allowed net equity claims based on such customers' proprietary accounts, and in priority to all other claims, except claims of a kind specified in section 507(a)(2) of this title that are attributable to the administration of member property or customer property.

(j)(1) The trustee shall distribute customer property in excess of that distributed under subsection (h) or (i) of this section in accordance with section 726 of this title.

(2) Except as provided in section 510 of this title, if a customer is not paid the full amount of such customer's allowed net equity claim from customer property, the unpaid portion of such claim is a claim entitled to distribution under section 726 of this title.

(Pub.L. 95–598, Nov. 6, 1978, 92 Stat. 2619; Pub.L. 97–222, § 19, July 27, 1982, 96 Stat. 240; Pub.L. 98–353, Title III, § 489, July 10, 1984, 98 Stat. 383; Pub.L. 109–8, Title XV, § 1502(a)(4), Apr. 20, 2005, 119 Stat. 216.)

HISTORICAL AND STATUTORY NOTES

Revision Notes and Legislative Reports

1978 Acts. [Section 765] Subsection (a) of this section [now section 766(h)] provides that with respect to liquidation of commodity brokers which are not clearing organizations, the trustee shall distribute customer property to customers on the basis and to the extent of such customers' allowed net equity claims, and in priority to all other claims. This section grants customers' claims first priority in the distribution of the estate. Subsection (b) [now section 766(i)] grants the same priority to member property and other customer property in the liquidation of a clearing organization. A fundamental purpose of these provisions is to ensure that the property entrusted by customers to their brokers will not be subject to the risks of the broker's business and will be available for disbursement to customers if the broker becomes bankrupt.

As a result of section 765, a customer need not trace any funds in order to avoid treatment as a general creditor as was required by the Seventh Circuit in *In re Rosenbaum Grain Corporation.*

Section 766 lists certain transfers which are not voidable by the trustee of a commodity broker. Subsection (a) exempts transfers approved by the Commission by rule or order, either before or after the transfer. It is expected that the Commission will use this power sparingly and only when necessary to effectuate the remedial purposes of this legislation, bearing in mind that the immediate transfer of customer accounts from bankrupt commodity brokers to solvent commodity brokers is one of the primary goals of this subchapter. The committee considered and rejected a provision in subsection (b) that would have exempted payments made to a commodity broker. The Commission may not by rule exempt such transfers. The Commission's prompt attention to the promulgation of such rules and regulations is expected.

Subsection (b) [now section 764(c)] provides for the nonavoidability of margin payments made by a commodity broker, other than a clearing organization. If such payments are made by or to a clearing organization, they are nonavoidable pursuant to subsection (c). All other margin payments made by a commodity broker, other than a clearing organization, are nonavoidable if they meet the conditions set forth in subsection (b). Subsections (b)(1) and (b)(2) parallel the requirements for avoidance of fraudulent transfers and obligations under section 548. Subsection (b)(3) adds a requirement that there be collusion between the transferee and transferor in order for such payments to be voidable. It would be unfair to permit recovery from an innocent commodity broker since such brokers are, for the most part, simply conduits for margin payments and do not retain margin for use in their operations. Subsection (b)(4) would permit recovery of a subsequent transferee only if it had actual knowledge at the time of that subsequent transfer of the scheme to defraud. Again it should be noted that if the transfer is a margin payment and the subsequent transferee is a clearing organization, the transfer is nonavoidable under section 766(c).

Subsection (c) [now section 548(d)(2)] overrules *Seligson v. New York Produce Exchange,* and provides as a matter of law that margin payments made by or to a clearing organization are not voidable.

Section 767 sets forth the procedures to be followed by the trustee. It should be emphasized that many of the duties imposed on the trustee are required to be discharged by the trustee immediately upon his appointment. The earlier these duties are discharged the less potential market disruption can result.

The initial duty of the trustee is to endeavor to transfer to another commodity broker or brokers all identified customer accounts together with the customer property margining such

accounts, to the extent the trustee deems appropriate. Although it is preferable for all such accounts to be transferred, exigencies may dictate a partial transfer. The requirement that the value of the accounts and property transferred not exceed the customer's distribution share may necessitate a slight delay until the trustee can submit to the court, for its disapproval, an estimate of each customer's distribution share pursuant to section 768.

Subsection (c) [now section 766(e)] provides that contemporaneously with the estimate of the distribution share and the transfer of identified customer accounts and property, subsection (c) provides that the trustee should make arrangements for the liquidation of all commodity contracts maintained by the debtor that are not identifiable to specific customers. These contracts would, of course, include all such contracts held in the debtor's proprietary account.

At approximately the same time, the trustee should notify each customer of the debtor's bankruptcy and instruct each customer immediately to submit a claim including any claim to a specifically identifiable security or other property, and advise the trustee as to the desired disposition of commodity contracts carried by the debtor for the customer.

This requirement is placed upon the trustee to insure that producers who have hedged their production in the commodities market are allowed the opportunity to preserve their positions. The theory of the commodity market is that it exists for producers and buyers of commodities and not for the benefit of the speculators whose transactions now comprise the overwhelming majority of trades. Maintenance of positions by hedges may require them to put up additional margin payments in the hours and days following the commodity broker bankruptcy, which they may be unable or unwilling to do. In such cases, their positions will be quickly liquidated by the trustee, but they must have the opportunity to make those margin payments before they are summarily liquidated out of the market to the detriment of their growing crop. The failure of the customer to advise the trustee as to disposition of the customer's commodity contract will not delay a transfer of a contract pursuant to subsection (b) so long as the contract can otherwise be identified to the customer. Nor will the failure of the customer to submit a claim prevent the customer from recovering the net equity in that customer's account, absent a claim the customer cannot participate in the determination of the net equity in the account.

If the customer submits instructions pursuant to subsection (a) after the customer's commodity contracts are transferred to another commodity broker, the trustee must transmit the instruction to the transferee. If the customer's commodity contracts are not transferred before the customer's instructions are received, the trustee must attempt to comply with the instruction, subject to the provisions of section 767(d).

Under subsection (d) [now section 766(e)], the trustee has discretion to liquidate any commodity contract carried by the debtor at any time. This discretion must be exercised with restraint in such cases, consistent with the purposes of this subchapter and good business practices. The committee intends that hedged accounts will be given special consideration before liquidation as discussed in connection with subsection (c).

Subsection (e) [now section 766(c)] instructs the trustee as to the disposition of any security or other property, not disposed of pursuant to subsection (b) or (d), that is specifically identifiable to a customer and to which the customer is entitled. Such security or other property must be returned to the customer or promptly transferred to another commodity broker for the benefit of the customer. If the value of the security or other property retained or transferred, together with any other distribution made by the trustee to or on behalf of the customer, exceeds the customer's distribution share the customer must deposit cash with the trustee equal to that difference before the return or transfer of the security or other property.

Subsection (f) [now section 766(a)] requires the trustee to answer margin calls on specifically identifiable customer commodity contracts, but only to the extent that the margin payment, together with any other distribution made by the trustee to or on behalf of the customer, does not exceed the customer's distribution share.

Subsection (g) [now section 766(b)] requires the trustee to liquidate all commodity futures contracts prior to the close of trading in that contract, or the first day on which notice of intent to deliver on that contract may be tendered, whichever occurs first. If the customer desires that the contract be kept open for delivery, the contract should be transferred to another commodity broker pursuant to subsection (b).

If for some reason the trustee is unable to transfer a contract on which delivery must be made or accepted and is unable to close out such contract, the trustee is authorized to operate the business of the debtor for the purpose of accepting or making tender of notice of intent to deliver the physical commodity underlying the contract, facilitating delivery of the physical commodity or disposing of the physical commodity in the event of a default. Any property received, not previously held, by the trustee in connection with its operation of the business of the debtor for these purposes, is not by the terms of this subchapter specifically included in the definition of customer property.

Finally, subsection (h) [now section 766(f)] requires the trustee to liquidate the debtor's estate as soon as practicable and consistent with good market practice, except for specifically identifiable securities or other property distributable under subsection (e).

Section 768 is an integral part of the commodity broker liquidation procedures outlined in section 767. Prompt action by the trustee to transfer or liquidate customer commodity contracts is necessary to protect customers, the debtor's estate, and the marketplace generally. However, transfers of customer accounts and property valued in excess of the customer's distribution share are prohibited. Since a determination of the customer's distribution share requires a determination of the customer's net equity and the total dollar value of customer property held by or for the account of the debtor, it is possible that the customer's distribution share will not be determined, and thus the customer's contracts and property will not be transferred, on a timely basis. To avoid this problem, and to expedite transfers of customer property, section 768 permits the trustee to make distributions to customers in accordance with a preliminary estimate of the debtor's customer property and each customer's distribution share.

It is acknowledged that the necessity for prompt action may not allow the trustee to assemble all relevant facts before such an estimate is made. However, the trustee is expected to develop as accurate an estimate as possible based on the available facts. Further, in order to permit expeditious action, section 768 does not require that notice be given to customers or other creditors before the court approves or disapproves the estimate. Nor does section 768 require that

customer claims be received pursuant to section 767(a) before the trustee may act upon and in accordance with the estimate. If the estimate is inaccurate, the trustee is absolved of liability for a distribution share so long as the distribution did not exceed the customer's estimated distribution share. However, a trustee may have a claim back against a customer who received more than its actual distribution share. Senate Report No. 95–989.

Section 765(a) indicates that a customer must file a proof of claim, including any claim to specifically identifiable property, within such time as the court fixes.

Subsection (c) [subsec. (c) of section 765 of H. Bill] sets forth the general rule requiring the trustee to liquidate contractual commitments that are either not specifically identifiable or with respect to which a customer has not instructed the trustee during the time fixed by the court. Subsection (d) [subsec. (d) of section 765 of H. Bill] indicates an exception to the time limits in the rule by requiring the trustee to liquidate any open contractual commitment before the last day of trading or the first day during which delivery may be demanded, whichever first occurs, if transfer cannot be effectuated.

Section 766(a) indicates that the trustee may distribute securities or other property only under section 768. This does not preclude a distribution of cash under section 767(a) or distribution of any excess customer property under section 767(c) to the general estate.

Subsection (b) indicates that the trustee shall liquidate all securities and other property that is not specifically identifiable property as soon as practicable after the commencement of the case and in accordance with good market practice. If securities are restricted or trading has been suspended, the trustee will have to make an exempt sale or file a registration statement. In the event of a private placement, a customer is not entitled to "bid in" his net equity claim. To do so would enable him to receive a greater percentage recovery than other customers.

Section 767(a) provides for the trustee to distribute customer property pro rata according to customers' net equity claims. The court will determine an equitable portion of customer property to pay administrative expenses. Paragraphs (2) and (3) indicate that the return of specifically identifiable property constitutes a distribution of net equity.

Subsection (b) indicates that if the debtor is a clearing organization, customer property is to be segregated into customers' accounts and proprietary accounts and distributed accordingly without offset. This protects a member's customers from having their claims offset against the member's proprietary account. Subsection (c)(1) indicates that any excess customer property will pour over into the general estate. This unlikely event would occur only if customers fail to file proofs of claim. Subsection (c)(2) indicates that to the extent customers are not paid in full, they are entitled to share in the general estate as unsecured creditors, unless subordinated by the court under proposed 11 U.S.C. 510.

Section 768(a) requires the trustee to return specifically identifiable property to the extent that such distribution will not exceed a customer's net equity claim. Thus, if the customer owes money to a commodity broker, this will be offset under section 761(15)(A)(ii). If the value of the specifically identifiable property exceeds the net equity claim, then the customer may deposit cash with the trustee to make up the difference after which the trustee may return or transfer the customer's property.

Subsection (c) permits the trustee to answer all margin calls, to the extent of the customer's net equity claim, with respect to any specifically identifiable open contractual commitment. It should be noted that any payment under subsections (a) or (c) will be considered a reduction of the net equity claim under section 767(a). Thus the customer's net equity claim is a dynamic amount that varies with distributions of specifically identifiable property or margin payments on such property. This approach differs from the priority given to specifically identifiable property under subchapter III of chapter 7 by limiting the priority effect to a right to receive specific property as part of, rather than in addition to, a ratable share of customer property. This policy is designed to protect the small customer who is unlikely to have property in specifically identifiable form as compared with the professional trader. The CFTC is authorized to make rules defining specifically identifiable property under section 302 of the bill, in title III. House Report No. 95–595.

1982 Acts. House Report No. 97–420, see 1982 U.S.Code Cong. and Adm.News, p. 583.

1984 Acts. Statements by Legislative Leaders, see 1984 U.S.Code Cong. and Adm.News, p. 576.

2005 Acts. House Report No. 109–31(Part I), see 2005 U.S. Code Cong. and Adm. News, p. 88.

Legislative Statements

Sections 765 and 766 of the House amendment represent a consolidation and redraft of sections 765, 766, 767, and 768 of the House bill and sections 765, 766, 767, and 768 of the Senate amendment. In particular, section 765(a) of the House amendment is derived from section 765(a) of the House bill and section 767(a) of the Senate amendment. Under section 765(a) of the House amendment customers are notified of the opportunity to immediately file proofs of claim and to identify specifically identifiable securities, property, or commodity contracts. The customer is also afforded an opportunity to instruct the trustee regarding the customer's desires concerning disposition of the customer's commodity contracts. Section 767(b) [probably should be 765(b)] makes clear that the trustee must comply with instructions received to the extent practicable, but in the event the trustee has transferred commodity contracts to a commodity broker, such instructions shall be forwarded to the broker.

Section 766(a) of the House amendment is derived from section 768(c) of the House bill and section 767(f) of the Senate amendment. Section 766(b) of the House amendment is derived from section 765(d) of the House bill, and section 767(g) of the Senate amendment. Section 766(c) of the House amendment is derived from section 768(a) of the House bill and section 767(e) of the Senate amendment. Section 766(d) of the House amendment is derived from section 768(b) of the House bill and the second sentence of section 767(e) of the Senate amendment.

Section 766(e) of the House amendment is derived from section 765(c) of the House bill and sections 767(c) and (d) of the Senate amendment. The provision clarifies that the trustee may liquidate a commodity contract only if the commodity contract cannot be transferred to a commodity broker under section 766(c), cannot be identified to a particular customer, or has been identified with respect to a particular customer, but with respect to which the customer's instructions have not been received.

Section 766(f) of the House amendment is derived from section 766(b) of the House bill and section 767(h) of the Senate amendment. The term "all securities and other property" is not intended to include a commodity contract. Section 766(g) of the House amendment is derived from section 766(a) of the House bill. Section 766(h) of the House amendment is derived from section 767(a) of the House bill and section 765(a) of the Senate amendment. In order to induce private trustees to undertake the difficult and risky job of liquidating a commodity broker, the House amendment contains a provision insuring that a pro rata share of administrative claims will be paid. The provision represents a compromise between the position taken in the House bill, subordinating customer property to all expenses of administration, and the position taken in the Senate amendment requiring the distribution of customer property in advance of any expenses of administration. The position in the Senate amendment is rejected since customers, in any event, would have to pay a brokerage commission or fee in the ordinary course of business. The compromise provision requires customers to pay only those administrative expenses that are attributable to the administration of customer property.

Section 766(i) of the House amendment is derived from section 767(b) of the House bill and contains a similar compromise with respect to expenses of administration as the compromise detailed in connection with section 766(h) of the House amendment. Section 766(j) of the House amendment is derived from section 767(c) of the House bill. No counterpart is contained in the Senate amendment. The provision takes account of the rare case where the estate has customer property in excess of customer claims and administrative expenses attributable to those claims. The section also specifies that to the extent a customer is not paid in full out of customer property, that the unpaid claim will be treated the same as any other general unsecured creditor.

Section 768 of the Senate amendment was deleted from the House amendment as unwise. The provision in the Senate amendment would have permitted the trustee to distribute customer property based upon an estimate of value of the customer's account, with no provision for recapture of excessive disbursements. Moreover, the section would have exonerated the trustee from any liability for such an excessive disbursement. Furthermore, the section is unclear with respect to the customer's rights in the event the trustee makes a distribution less than the share to which the customer is entitled. The provision is deleted in the House amendment so that this difficult problem may be handled on a case-by-case basis by the courts as the facts and circumstances of each case require.

Section 769 of the Senate amendment is deleted in the House amendment as unnecessary. The provision was intended to codify *Board of Trade v. Johnson,* 264 U.S. 1 (1924) [Ill.1924, 44 S.Ct. 232]. *Board of Trade against Johnson* is codified in section 363(f) of the House amendment which indicates the only five circumstances in which property may be sold free and clear of an interest in such property of an entity other than the estate.

Section 770 of the Senate amendment is deleted in the House amendment as unnecessary. That section would have permitted commodity brokers to liquidate commodity contracts, notwithstanding any contrary order of the court. It would require an extraordinary circumstance, such as a threat to the national security, to enjoin a commodity broker from liquidating a commodity contract. However, in those circumstances, an injunction must prevail. Failure of the House amendment to incorporate section 770 of the Senate amendment does not imply that the automatic stay prevents liquidation of commodity contracts by commodity brokers. To the contrary, whenever by contract, or otherwise, a commodity broker is entitled to liquidate a position as a result of a condition specified in a contract, other than a condition or default of the kind specified in section 365(b)(2) of title 11, the commodity broker may engage in such liquidation. To this extent, the commodity broker's contract with his customer is treated no differently than any other contract under section 365 of Title 11.

Amendments

2005 Amendments. Subsec. (h). Pub.L. 109–8, § 1502(a)(4)(A), struck out "507(a)(1)" and inserted "507(a)(2)".

Subsec. (i). Pub.L. 109–8, § 1502(a)(4)(B), struck out "507(a)(1)" each place it appeared and inserted "507(a)(2)".

1984 Amendments. Subsec. (j)(2). Pub.L. 98–353 substituted "section 726 of this title" for "section 726(a) of this title".

1982 Amendments. Subsec. (a). Pub.L. 97–222, § 19(a), inserted "to such customer" after "distribution".

Subsec. (b). Pub.L. 97–222, § 19(b), struck out "that is being actively traded as of the date of the filing of the petition" after "any open commodity contract" and inserted "the" after "rules of".

Subsec. (d). Pub.L. 97–222, § 19(c), substituted "the amount to which the customer of the debtor is entitled under subsection (h) or (i) of this section, then such" for "such amount, then the" and "the trustee then shall" for "the trustee shall".

Subsec. (h). Pub.L. 97–222, § 19(d), added provision that notwithstanding any other provision of this subsection, a customer net equity claim based on a proprietary account, as defined by Commission rule, regulation, or order, may not be paid either in whole or in part, directly or indirectly, out of customer property unless all other customer net equity claims have been paid in full.

Effective and Applicability Provisions

2005 Acts. Amendments by Pub.L. 109–8 effective, except as otherwise provided, 180 days after April 20, 2005, and inapplicable with respect to cases commenced under Title 11 before the effective date, see Pub.L. 109–8, § 1501, set out as a note under 11 U.S.C.A. § 101.

1984 Acts. Amendment by Pub.L. 98–353 effective with respect to cases filed 90 days after July 10, 1984, see section 552(a), formerly 553(a), of Pub.L. 98–353, set out as a note under section 101 of this title.

CROSS REFERENCES

Distribution in Chapter eleven cases, see 11 USCA § 1143.

Distribution of—

    Customer property in stockbroker liquidation cases, see 11 USCA § 752.

    Property of estate, see 11 USCA § 726.

Election of trustee by creditors holding claims entitled to distribution, see 11 USCA § 702.

Executory contracts and unexpired leases, see 11 USCA § 365.

Provisions relating to transferability of customer property and commodity contracts, see 7 USCA § 24.

LIBRARY REFERENCES

American Digest System

    Bankruptcy ⟜3461.

    Key Number System Topic No. 51.

Corpus Juris Secundum

    CJS Bankruptcy § 99, Powers and Duties in Stockholder or Commodity Broker Liquidation Cases.

    CJS Bankruptcy § 837, Commodity-Broker Liquidation Cases.

    CJS Bankruptcy § 1114, Treatment of Customer Property.

§ 767. Commodity broker liquidation and forward contract merchants, commodity brokers, stockbrokers, financial institutions, financial participants, securities clearing agencies, swap participants, repo participants, and master netting agreement participants

Notwithstanding any other provision of this title, the exercise of rights by a forward contract merchant, commodity broker, stockbroker, financial institution, financial participant, securities clearing agency, swap participant, repo participant, or master netting agreement participant under this title shall not affect the priority of any unsecured claim it may have after the exercise of such rights.

(Added Pub.L. 109–8, Title IX, § 907(*l*), Apr. 20, 2005, 119 Stat. 181.)

HISTORICAL AND STATUTORY NOTES

Revision Notes and Legislative Reports

2005 Acts. House Report No. 109–31(Part I), see 2005 U.S. Code Cong. and Adm. News, p. 88.

Effective and Applicability Provisions

2005 Acts. Amendments by Pub.L. 109–8 effective, except as otherwise provided, 180 days after April 20, 2005, and inapplicable with respect to cases commenced under Title 11 before the effective date, see Pub.L. 109–8, § 1501, set out as a note under 11 U.S.C.A. § 101.

LIBRARY REFERENCES

Corpus Juris Secundum

    CJS Bankruptcy § 7, Bankruptcy Code.

    CJS Bankruptcy § 385, Governing Statutes, Generally.

SUBCHAPTER V—CLEARING BANK LIQUIDATION

HISTORICAL AND STATUTORY NOTES

Amendments

2000 Amendments. Pub.L. 106–554, § 1(a)(5) [Title I, § 112(c)(5)(B)], Dec. 21, 2000, 114 Stat. 2763, 2763A–394, added subchapter heading.

§ 781. Definitions

For purposes of this subchapter, the following definitions shall apply:

(1) **Board.**—The term "Board" means the Board of Governors of the Federal Reserve System.

(2) **Depository institution.**—The term "depository institution" has the same meaning as in section 3 of the Federal Deposit Insurance Act.

(3) **Clearing bank.**—The term "clearing bank" means an uninsured State member bank, or a corporation organized under section 25A of the Federal Reserve Act, which operates, or operates as, a multilateral clearing organization pursuant to section 409 of the Federal Deposit Insurance Corporation Improvement Act of 1991.

(Added Pub.L. 106–554, § 1(a)(5) [Title I, § 112(c)(5)(B)], Dec. 21, 2000, 114 Stat. 2763, 2763A–394.)

HISTORICAL AND STATUTORY NOTES
Revision Notes and Legislative Reports

2000 Acts. House Report No. 106–645 and Statement by President, see 2000 U.S. Code Cong. and Adm. News, p. 2459.

References in Text

Section 3 of the Federal Deposit Insurance Act, referred to in par. (2), is Act Sept. 21, 1950, c. 967, § 2[3], 64 Stat. 873, which is classified to 12 U.S.C.A. § 1813.

Section 25A of the Federal Reserve Act, referred to in par. (3), is Dec. 23, 1913, c. 6, § 25A, formerly § 25(a), as added Dec. 24, 1919, c. 18, 41 Stat. 378, as amended, which is classified to subchapter II of chapter 6 of Title 12, 12 U.S.C.A. § 611 et seq.

Section 409 of the Federal Deposit Insurance Corporation Improvement Act of 1991, referred to in par. (3), is Pub.L. 102–242, Title IV, § 409, as added by Pub.L. 106–554, § 1(a)(5) [Title I, § 112(a)(3)], Dec. 21, 2000, 114 Stat. 2763, 2763A–392, which is classified as 12 U.S.C.A. § 4422.

LIBRARY REFERENCES
American Digest System

Bankruptcy ⬯3471.

Key Number System Topic No. 51.

Corpus Juris Secundum

CJS Bankruptcy § 1115, Generally; Definitions.

CJS Bankruptcy § 1116, Distribution of Property.

§ 782. Selection of trustee

(a) **In general.**—

(1) **Appointment.**—Notwithstanding any other provision of this title, the conservator or receiver who files the petition shall be the trustee under this chapter, unless the Board designates an alternative trustee.

(2) **Successor.**—The Board may designate a successor trustee if required.

(b) **Authority of trustee.**—Whenever the Board appoints or designates a trustee, chapter 3 and sections 704 and 705 of this title shall apply to the Board in the same way and to the same extent that they apply to a United States trustee.

(Added Pub.L. 106–554, § 1(a)(5) [Title I, § 112(c)(5)(B)], Dec. 21, 2000, 114 Stat. 2763, 2763A–394.)

HISTORICAL AND STATUTORY NOTES
Revision Notes and Legislative Reports

2000 Acts. House Report No. 106–645 and Statement by President, see 2000 U.S. Code Cong. and Adm. News, p. 2459.

References in Text

Chapter 3, referred to in subsec. (b), is classified to 11 U.S.C.A. § 301 et seq.

LIBRARY REFERENCES
American Digest System

Bankruptcy ⬯3471.

Key Number System Topic No. 51.

Corpus Juris Secundum

CJS Bankruptcy § 809, Voting and Elections.

CJS Bankruptcy § 1115, Generally; Definitions.

§ 783. Additional powers of trustee

(a) **Distribution of property not of the estate.**—The trustee under this subchapter has power to distribute property not of the estate, including distributions to customers that are mandated by subchapters III and IV of this chapter.

(b) **Disposition of institution.**—The trustee under this subchapter may, after notice and a hearing—

(1) sell the clearing bank to a depository institution or consortium of depository institutions (which consortium may agree on the allocation of the clearing bank among the consortium);

(2) merge the clearing bank with a depository institution;

(3) transfer contracts to the same extent as could a receiver for a depository institution under paragraphs (9) and (10) of section 11(e) of the Federal Deposit Insurance Act;

(4) transfer assets or liabilities to a depository institution; and

(5) transfer assets and liabilities to a bridge depository institution as provided in paragraphs (1), (3)(A), (5), and (6) of section 11(n) of the Federal Deposit Insurance Act, paragraphs (9) through (13) of such section, and subparagraphs (A) through (H) and subparagraph (K) of paragraph (4) of such section 11(n), except that—

(A) the bridge depository institution to which such assets or liabilities are transferred shall be treated as a clearing bank for the purpose of this subsection; and

(B) any references in any such provision of law to the Federal Deposit Insurance Corporation shall be construed to be references to the appointing agency and that references to deposit insurance shall be omitted.

(c) Certain transfers included.—Any reference in this section to transfers of liabilities includes a ratable transfer of liabilities within a priority class.

(Added Pub.L. 106–554, § 1(a)(5) [Title I, § 112(c)(5)(B)], Dec. 21, 2000, 114 Stat. 2763, 2763A–395; amended Pub.L. 110–289, Div. A, Title VI, § 1604(b)(3), July 30, 2008, 122 Stat. 2829.)

HISTORICAL AND STATUTORY NOTES

Revision Notes and Legislative Reports

2000 Acts. House Report No. 106–645 and Statement by President, see 2000 U.S. Code Cong. and Adm. News, p. 2459.

References in Text

Subchapters III and IV of this chapter, referred to in subsec. (a), are 11 U.S.C.A. §§ 741 et seq. and 761 et seq.

Paragraphs (9) and (10) of section 11(e) of the Federal Deposit Insurance Act, referred to in subsec. (b)(3), are classified to 12 U.S.C.A. § 1821(e)(9), (10).

Paragraphs (1), (3)(A), (5), and (6) of section 11(n) of the Federal Deposit Insurance Act, paragraphs (9) through (13) of such section, and subparagraphs (A) through (H) and subparagraph (K) of paragraph (4) of such section 11(n), referred to in subsec. (b)(5), are classified to 12 U.S.C.A. § 1821(n)(1), (3)(A), (5), (6), and (4)(A) to (K).

Codifications

Amendment by Pub.L. 110–289, § 1604(b)(3), which directed striking out "bridge bank" and inserting "bridge depository institution", was executed to both locations where the term appeared in subsec. (b)(5), as the probable intent of Congress. See 2008 Amendments note set out under this section.

Amendments

2008 Amendments. Subsec. (b)(5). Pub.L. 110–289, Div. A, Title VI, § 1604(b)(3), struck out "bridge bank" and inserted "bridge depository institution" in two locations. See Codifications note set out under this section.

LIBRARY REFERENCES

American Digest System

Bankruptcy ⟘3471.
Key Number System Topic No. 51.

Corpus Juris Secundum

CJS Bankruptcy § 1116, Distribution of Property.

§ 784.   Right to be heard

The Board or a Federal reserve bank (in the case of a clearing bank that is a member of that bank) may raise and may appear and be heard on any issue in a case under this subchapter.

(Added Pub.L. 106–554, § 1(a)(5) [Title I, § 112(c)(5)(B)], Dec. 21, 2000, 114 Stat. 2763, 2763A–395.)

HISTORICAL AND STATUTORY NOTES

Revision Notes and Legislative Reports

2000 Acts. House Report No. 106–645 and Statement by President, see 2000 U.S. Code Cong. and Adm. News, p. 2459.

LIBRARY REFERENCES

American Digest System

Bankruptcy ⟘3471.
Key Number System Topic No. 51.

Corpus Juris Secundum

CJS Bankruptcy § 1115, Generally; Definitions.
CJS Bankruptcy § 1116, Distribution of Property.

CHAPTER 9—ADJUSTMENT OF DEBTS OF A MUNICIPALITY

SUBCHAPTER I—GENERAL PROVISIONS

Sec.
901. Applicability of other sections of this title.
902. Definitions for this chapter.
903. Reservation of State power to control municipalities.
904. Limitation on jurisdiction and powers of court.

SUBCHAPTER II—ADMINISTRATION

921. Petition and proceedings relating to petition.
922. Automatic stay of enforcement of claims against the debtor.
923. Notice.
924. List of creditors.
925. Effect of list of claims.
926. Avoiding powers.
927. Limitation on recourse.
928. Post petition effect of security interest.
929. Municipal leases.
930. Dismissal.

SUBCHAPTER III—THE PLAN

941. Filing of plan.
942. Modification of plan.
943. Confirmation.
944. Effect of confirmation.
945. Continuing jurisdiction and closing of the case.
946. Effect of exchange of securities before the date of the filing of the petition.

HISTORICAL AND STATUTORY NOTES

Amendments

1988 Amendments. Pub.L. 100–597, § 11, Nov. 3, 1988, 102 Stat. 3030, added items 927 to 929 and redesignated as 930 former item 927.

SUBCHAPTER I—GENERAL PROVISIONS

CROSS REFERENCES

Allowance of administrative expenses of substantial contributors in cases under this chapter, see 11 USCA § 503.

Chapter one of this title and this chapter solely applicable in cases under this chapter except as provided in § 901 of this title, see 11 USCA § 103.

Claims arising from rejection of executory contracts or unexpired leases under this chapter's plans, see 11 USCA § 502.

Definitions applicable in this title, see 11 USCA § 101.

Duration of automatic stay, see 11 USCA § 362.

Entities which may be debtors under this chapter, see 11 USCA § 109.

Executory contracts and unexpired leases under this chapter, see 11 USCA § 365.

Filing fees, see 28 USCA § 1930.

Unclaimed property, see 11 USCA § 347.

§ 901. Applicability of other sections of this title

(a) Sections 301, 333, 344, 347(b), 349, 350(b) 351,,[1] 361, 362, 364(c), 364(d), 364(e), 364(f), 365, 366, 501, 502, 503, 504, 506, 507(a)(2), 509, 510, 524(a)(1), 524(a)(2), 544, 545, 546, 547, 548, 549(a), 549(c), 549(d), 550, 551, 552, 553, 555, 556, 557, 559, 560, 561, 562, 1102, 1103, 1109, 1111(b), 1122, 1123(a)(1), 1123(a)(2), 1123(a)(3), 1123(a)(4), 1123(a)(5), 1123(b), 1123(d), 1124, 1125, 1126(a), 1126(b), 1126(c), 1126(e), 1126(f), 1126(g), 1127(d), 1128, 1129(a)(2), 1129(a)(3), 1129(a)(6), 1129(a)(8), 1129(a)(10), 1129(b)(1), 1129(b)(2)(A), 1129(b)(2)(B), 1142(b), 1143, 1144, and 1145 of this title apply in a case under this chapter.

(b) A term used in a section of this title made applicable in a case under this chapter by subsection (a) of this section or section 103(e) of this title has the meaning defined for such term for the purpose of such applicable section, unless such term is otherwise defined in section 902 of this title.

(c) A section made applicable in a case under this chapter by subsection (a) of this section that is operative if the business of the debtor is authorized to be operated is operative in a case under this chapter. (Pub.L. 95–598, Nov. 6, 1978, 92 Stat. 2621; Pub.L. 98–353, Title III, §§ 353, 490, July 10, 1984, 98 Stat. 361, 383; Pub.L. 100–597, § 3, Nov. 3, 1988, 102 Stat. 3028; Pub.L. 109–8, Title V, § 502, Title XII, § 1216, Title XV, § 1502(a)(5), Apr. 20, 2005, 119 Stat. 118, 195, 216; Pub.L. 111–327, § 2(a)(29), Dec. 22, 2010, 124 Stat. 3560.)

[1] So in original. The second comma probably should follow "350(b)".

HISTORICAL AND STATUTORY NOTES

Revision Notes and Legislative Reports

1978 Acts. Section 901 makes applicable appropriate provisions of other chapters of proposed title 11. The general rule set out in section 103(e) is that only the provisions of chapters 1 and 9 apply in a chapter 9 case. Section 901 is the exception, and specifies other provisions that do apply. They are as follows:

§ 301. Voluntary cases. Application of this section makes clear, as under current chapter IX [former chapter 9 (section 401 et seq.) of former Title 11], that a municipal case can be commenced only by the municipality itself. There are no involuntary chapter 9 cases.

§ 344. Self-incrimination; immunity. Application of this section is of no substantive effect for the administration of the case, but merely provides that the general rules in part V of title 18 [section 6001 et seq. of Title 18, Crimes and Criminal Procedure] govern immunity.

§ 347(b). Unclaimed property. This provision currently appears in section 96(d) of chapter IX [section 416(d) of this former Title 11].

§ 349. Effect of dismissal. This section governs the effect of a dismissal of a chapter 9 case. It provides in substance that rights that existed before the case that were disturbed by the commencement of the case are reinstated. This section does not concern grounds for dismissal, which are found in § 926.

§ 361. **Adequate protection.** Section 361 provides the general standard for the protection of secured creditors whose property is used in a case under title 11. Its importance lies in its application to sections 362 and 364.

§ 362. **Automatic stay.** The automatic stay provisions of the general portions of the title are incorporated into chapter 9. There is an automatic stay provided in current Bankruptcy Act section 85(e) [section 405(e) of former title 11]. The thrust of section 362 is the same as that of section 85(e), but, of course, its application in chapter 9 is modernized and drafted to conform with the stay generally applicable under the bankruptcy code. An additional part of the automatic stay applicable only to municipal cases is included in section 922.

§§ 364(c), 364(d), 364(e). **Obtaining credit.** This section governs the borrowing of money by a municipality in reorganization. It is narrower than a comparable provision in current law, section 82(b)(2) [section 402(b)(2) of former title 11]. The difference lies mainly in the removal under the bill of the authority of the court to supervise borrowing by the municipality in instances in which none of the special bankruptcy powers are involved. That is, if a municipality could borrow money outside of the bankruptcy court, then it should have the same authority in bankruptcy court, under the doctrine of *Ashton v. Cameron Water District No. 1*, 298 U.S. 513 (1936) [Tex.1936, 56 S.Ct. 892, 80 L.Ed. 1309, 31 Am. Bankr.Rep.N.S. 96, rehearing denied 57 S.Ct. 5, 299 U.S. 619, 81 L.Ed. 457] and *National League of Cities v. Usery*, 426 U.S. 833 (1976) [Dist.Col.1976, 96 S.Ct. 2465, 49 L.Ed.2d 245, on remand 429 F.Supp. 703]. Only when the municipality needs special authority, such as subordination of existing liens, or special priority for the borrowed funds, will the court become involved in the authorization.

§ 365. **Executory contracts and unexpired leases.** The applicability of section 365 incorporates the general power of a bankruptcy court to authorize the assumption or rejection of executory contracts or unexpired leases found in other chapters of the title. This section is comparable to section 82(b)(1) [section 402(b)(1) of former Title 11] of current law.

§ 366. **Utility service.** This section gives a municipality the same authority as any other debtor with respect to continuation of utility service during the proceeding, provided adequate assurance of future payment is provided. No comparable explicit provision is found in current law, although the case law seems to support the same result.

§ 501. **Filing of proofs of claims.** This section permits filing of proofs of claims in a chapter 9 case. Note, however, that section 924 permits listing of creditors' claims, as under chapter 11 and under section 85(b) of chapter IX [section 405(b) of former Title 11].

§ 502. **Allowance of claims.** This section applies the general allowance rules to chapter 9 cases. This is no change from current law.

§ 503. **Administrative expenses.** Administrative expenses as defined in section 503 will be paid in a chapter 9 case, as provided under section 89(1) of current law [section 409(1) of former Title 11].

§ 504. **Sharing of compensation.** There is no comparable provision in current law. However, this provision applies

generally throughout the proposed law, and will not affect the progress of the case, only the interrelations between attorneys and other professionals that participate in the case.

§ 506. **Determination of secured status.** Section 506 specifies that claims secured by a lien should be separated, to the extent provided, into secured and unsecured claims. It applies generally. Current law follows this result, though there is no explicit provision.

§ 507(1). **Priorities.** Paragraph (1) of section 507 requires that administrative expenses be paid first. This rule will apply in chapter 9 cases. It is presently found in section 89(1) [section 409(1) of former Title 11]. The two other priorities presently found in section 89 have been deleted. The second, for claims arising within 3 months before the case is commenced, is deleted from the statute, but may be within the court's equitable power to award, under the case of *Fosdick v. Schall*, 99 U.S. 235 (1878). Leaving the provision to the courts permits greater flexibility, as under railroad cases, than an absolute three-month rule. The third priority under current law, for claims which are entitled to priority under the laws of the United States, is deleted because of the proposed amendment to section 3466 of the Revised Statutes [former 31 U.S.C.A. § 191, see 31 U.S.C.A. § 3713(a)] contained in section 321(a) of title III of the bill, which previously has given the United States an absolute first priority in Chapter X [former Chapter 10 (section 501 et seq.) of former Title 11] and section 77 [section 205 of former Title 1] cases. Because the priority rules are regularized and brought together in the bankruptcy laws by this bill, the need for incorporation of priorities elsewhere specified is eliminated.

§ 509. **Claims of codebtors.** This section provides for the treatment of sureties, guarantors, and codebtors. The general rule of postponement found in the other chapters will apply in chapter 9. This section adopts current law.

§ 510. **Subordination of claims.** This section permits the court to subordinate, on equitable grounds, any claim, and requires enforcement of contractual subordination agreements, and subordination of securities rescission claims. The section recognizes the inherent equitable power of the court under current law, and the practice followed with respect to contractual provisions.

§ 547. **Preferences.** Incorporation of section 547 will permit the debtor to recover preferences. This power will be used primarily when those who gave the preferences have been replaced by new municipal officers or when creditors coerced preferential payments. Unlike Bankruptcy Act § 85(h) [section 405(h) of former Title 11], the section does not permit the appointment of a trustee for the purpose of pursuing preferences. Moreover, this bill does not incorporate the other avoiding powers of a trustee for chapter 9, found in current section 85(h).

§ 550. **Liability of transfers.** Incorporation of this section is made necessary by the incorporation of the preference section, and permits recovery by the debtor from a transferee of an avoided preference.

§ 551. **Automatic preservation of avoided transfer.** Application of section 551 requires preservation of any avoided preference for the benefit of the estate.

§ 552. **Postpetition effect of security interest.** This section will govern the applicability after the commencement of the case of security interests granted by the debtor before the commencement of the case.

§ 553. **Setoff.** Under current law, certain setoff is stayed. Application of this section preserves that result, though the setoffs that are permitted under section 553 are better defined than under present law. Application of this section is necessary to stay the setoff and to provide the offsetting creditor with the protection to which he is entitled under present law.

§ 1122. **Classification of claims.** This section is derived from current section 88(b) [section 408(b) of former Title 11], and is substantially similar.

§ 1123(a)(1)–(4), (b). **Contents of plan.** The general provisions governing contents of a chapter 11 plan are made applicable here, with two exceptions relating to the rights of stockholders, which are not applicable in chapter 9 cases. This section expands current law by specifying the contents of a plan in some detail. Section 91 of current law [section 411 of former Title 11] speaks only in general terms. The substance of the two sections is substantially the same, however.

§ 1124. **Impairment of claims.** The confirmation standards adopted in chapter 9 are the same as those of chapter 11. This changes current chapter IX [former chapter 9 (section 401 et seq.) of former Title 11], which requires compliance with the fair and equitable rule. The greater flexibility of proposed chapter 11 is carried over into chapter 9, for there appears to be no reason why the confirmation standards for the two chapters should be different, or why the elimination of the fair and equitable rule from corporate reorganizations should not be followed in municipal debt adjustments. The current chapter IX rule is based on the confirmation rules of current chapter X [chapter 10 of former Title 11]. The change in the latter suggests a corresponding change in the former. Section 1124 is one part of the new confirmation standard. It defines impairment, for use in section 1129.

§ 1125. **Postpetition disclosure and solicitation.** The change in the confirmation standard necessitates a corresponding change in the disclosure requirements for solicitation of acceptances of a plan. Under current chapter IX [former chapter 9 (section 401 et seq.) of former Title 11] there is no disclosure requirement. Incorporation of section 1125 will insure that creditors receive adequate information before they are required to vote on a plan.

§ 1126(a), (b), (c), (e), (f), (g). **Acceptance of plan.** Section 1126 incorporates the current chapter IX [former chapter 9 (section 401 et seq.) of former Title 11] acceptance requirement: two-thirds in amount and a majority in number, Bankruptcy Act § 92 [section 412 of former Title 11]. Section 1125 permits exclusion of certain acceptances from the computation if the acceptances were obtained in bad faith or, unlike current law, if there is a conflict of interest motivating the acceptance.

§ 1127(d). **Modification of plan.** This section governs the change of a creditor's vote on the plan after a modification is proposed. It is derived from current section 92(e) [section 412(e) of former Title 11].

§ 1128. **Hearing on confirmation.** This section requires a hearing on the confirmation of the plan, and permits parties in interest to object. It is the same as Bankruptcy Act §§ 93 and 94(a) [section 413 and section 414(a) of former Title 11], though the provision, comparable to section 206 of current chapter X [section 606 of former Title 11], permitting a labor organization to appear and be heard on the economic soundness of the plan, has been deleted as more appropriate for the Rules.

§ 1129(a)(2), (3), (8), (b)(1), (2). **Confirmation of plan.** This section provides the boiler-plate language that the plan be proposed in good faith and that it comply with the provisions of the chapter, and also provides the financial standard for confirmation, which replaces the fair and equitable rule. See § 1124, supra.

§ 1142(b). **Execution of plan.** Derived from Bankruptcy Act § 96(b) [section 416(b) of former Title 11], this section permits the court to order execution and delivery of instruments in order to execute the plan.

§ 1143. **Distribution.** This section is the same in substance as section 96(d) [section 416(d) of former Title 11], which requires presentment or delivery of securities within five years, and bars creditors that do not act within that time.

§ 1144. **Revocation of order of confirmation.** This section permits the court to revoke the order of confirmation and the discharge if the confirmation of the plan was procured by fraud. There is no comparable provision in current chapter IX [former chapter 9 (section 401 et seq.) of former Title 11]. House Report No. 95–595.

1984 Acts. Statements by Legislative Leaders, see 1984 U.S.Code Cong. and Adm.News, p. 576.

1988 Acts. House Report No. 100–1011, see 1988 U.S.Code Cong. and Adm.News, p. 4115.

2005 Acts. House Report No. 109–31(Part I), see 2005 U.S. Code Cong. and Adm. News, p. 88.

Legislative Statements

Chapter 9 of the House amendment represents a compromise between chapter 9 of the House bill and 9 of the Senate amendment. In most respects this chapter follows current law with respect to the adjustment of debts of a municipality. Stylistic changes and minor substantive revisions have been made in order to conform this chapter with other new chapters of the bankruptcy code [this title]. There are few major differences between the House bill and the Senate amendment on this issue. Section 901 indicates the applicability of other sections of title 11 in cases under chapter 9. Included are sections providing for creditors' committees under sections 1102 and 1103.

References in Text

Section 103(e) of this title, referred to in subsec. (b), was redesignated subsec. (f) and a new subsec. (e) was added by Pub.L. 106–554, § 1(a)(5) [Title I, § 112(c)(5)(A)], Dec. 21, 2000, 114 Stat. 2763, 2763A–394.

Amendments

2010 Amendments. Subsec. (a). Pub.L. 111–327, § 2(a)(29), inserted "333," following "301,", and inserted "351," following "350(b)".

2005 Amendments. Subsec. (a). Pub.L. 109–8, § 502, inserted "555, 556," after "553," and inserted "559, 560, 561, 562," after "557,".

Pub.L.109–8, § 1216, inserted "1123(d)," after "1123(b),".

Pub.L. 109–8, § 1502(a)(5), struck out "507(a)(1)" and inserted "507(a)(2)".

1988 Amendments. Subsec. (a). Pub.L. 100–597 inserted reference to section "1129(a)(6)," after "1129(a)(3),".

1984 Amendments. Subsec. (a). Pub.L. 98–353, § 353, added "557," after "553".

Pub.L. 98–353, § 490, substituted "1111(b)," for "1111(b)" preceding "1122".

Effective and Applicability Provisions

2005 Acts. Amendments by Pub.L. 109–8 effective, except as otherwise provided, 180 days after April 20, 2005, and inapplicable with respect to cases commenced under Title 11 before the effective date, see Pub.L. 109–8, § 1501, set out as a note under 11 U.S.C.A. § 101.

1988 Acts. Amendment by Pub.L. 100–597 effective Nov. 3, 1988, but not applicable to any case commenced under this title before that date, see section 12 of Pub.L. 100–597, set out as a note under section 101 of this title.

1984 Acts. Amendment by Pub.L. 98–353 effective with respect to cases filed 90 days after July 10, 1984, see section 552(a), formerly 553(a), of Pub.L. 98–353, set out as a note under section 101 of this title.

CROSS REFERENCES

Chapters one and nine of this title solely applicable in cases under Chapter nine except as provided in this section, see 11 USCA § 103.

Confirmation in Chapter nine cases upon compliance with provisions of this title made applicable by this section, see 11 USCA § 943.

LIBRARY REFERENCES

American Digest System

Bankruptcy ⟲3481.

Key Number System Topic No. 51.

Corpus Juris Secundum

CJS Bankruptcy § 7, Bankruptcy Code.

CJS Bankruptcy § 51, Chapter 11 Proceedings.

CJS Bankruptcy § 73, Chapter 9 Cases.

CJS Bankruptcy § 278, Parties Defendant; Sovereign Immunity.

CJS Bankruptcy § 279, Intervention.

CJS Bankruptcy § 483, Municipal Bankruptcies.

CJS Bankruptcy § 773, Status of Claims for Compensation and Reimbursement.

CJS Bankruptcy § 846, Operation of Affairs of Municipal Debtor in Chapter 9 Cases.

CJS Bankruptcy § 851, Prepetition Security Interests in Proceeds, Products, Offspring, or Profits.

CJS Bankruptcy § 898, Credit Secured by Superpriority Lien; Subordination of Existing Liens.

CJS Bankruptcy § 902, Protection of Lenders from Reversal or Modification of Borrowing Authorization.

CJS Bankruptcy § 923, Application for Approval.

CJS Bankruptcy § 1105, Closing.

CJS Bankruptcy § 1118, Filing of Plan and Disclosure Statement; Hearing on Objections.

CJS Bankruptcy § 1119, Acceptance of Rejection of Plan by Claim Holders.

CJS Bankruptcy § 1120, Modification of Plan Before Confirmation.

CJS Bankruptcy § 1121, Requirements for Confirmation.

CJS Bankruptcy § 1122, Objections to Confirmation.

CJS Bankruptcy § 1123, Hearing and Order.

CJS Bankruptcy § 1125, Continuing Jurisdiction; Closing of Case.

§ 902. Definitions for this chapter

In this chapter—

(1) "property of the estate", when used in a section that is made applicable in a case under this chapter by section 103(e) or 901 of this title, means property of the debtor;

(2) "special revenues" means—

(A) receipts derived from the ownership, operation, or disposition of projects or systems of the debtor that are primarily used or intended to be used primarily to provide transportation, utility, or other services, including the proceeds of borrowings to finance the projects or systems;

(B) special excise taxes imposed on particular activities or transactions;

(C) incremental tax receipts from the benefited area in the case of tax-increment financing;

(D) other revenues or receipts derived from particular functions of the debtor, whether or not the debtor has other functions; or

(E) taxes specifically levied to finance one or more projects or systems, excluding receipts from general property, sales, or income taxes (other than tax-increment financing) levied to finance the general purposes of the debtor;

(3) "special tax payer" means record owner or holder of legal or equitable title to real property against which a special assessment or special tax has been levied the proceeds of which are the sole source of payment of an obligation issued by the debtor to defray the cost of an improvement relating to such real property;

(4) "special tax payer affected by the plan" means special tax payer with respect to whose real property the plan proposes to increase the proportion of special assessments or special taxes referred to in paragraph (2) of this section assessed against such real property; and

(5) "trustee", when used in a section that is made applicable in a case under this chapter by section 103(e) or 901 of this title, means debtor, except as provided in section 926 of this title.

(Pub.L. 95–598, Nov. 6, 1978, 92 Stat. 2622; Pub.L. 98–353, Title III, § 491, July 10, 1984, 98 Stat. 383; Pub.L. 100–597, § 4, Nov. 3, 1988, 102 Stat. 3028.)

HISTORICAL AND STATUTORY NOTES

Revision Notes and Legislative Reports

1978 Acts. There are six definitions for use in chapter 9. Paragraph (1) defines what claims are included in a chapter 9 case and adopts the definition now found in section 81(1) [section 401(1) of former Title 11]. All claims against the petitioner generally will be included, with one significant exception. Municipalities are authorized, under section 103(c) of the Internal Revenue Code of 1954 [section 103(c) of Title 26, Internal Revenue Code], as amended, to issue tax-exempt industrial development revenue bonds to provide for the financing of certain projects for privately owned companies. The bonds are sold on the basis of the credit of the company on whose behalf they are issued, and the principal, interest, and premium, if any, are payable solely from payments made by the company to the trustee under the bond indenture and do not constitute claims on the tax revenues or other funds of the issuing municipalities. The municipality merely acts as the vehicle to enable the bonds to be issued on a tax-exempt basis. Claims that arise by virtue of these bonds are not among the claims defined by this paragraph and amounts owed by private companies to the holders of industrial development revenue bonds are not to be included among the assets of the municipality that would be affected by the plan. See Cong. Record, 94th Cong., 1st Sess. H.R. 12073 (statement by Mr. Don Edwards, floor manager of the bill in the House). Paragraph (2) defines the court which means the federal district court or federal district judge before which the case is pending. Paragraph (3) specifies that when the term "property of the estate" is used in a section in another chapter made applicable in chapter 9 cases, the term means "property of the debtor". Paragraphs (4) and (5) adopt the definition of "special taxpayer affected by the plan" that appears in current sections 81(10) and 81(11) [section 401(10) and (11) of former Title 11] of the Bankruptcy Act. Paragraph (6) provides that "trustee" means "debtor" when used in conjunction with chapter 9. Senate Report No. 95–989.

There are only four definitions for use only in chapter 9. The first specifies that when the term "property of the estate" is used in a section in another chapter made applicable in chapter 9 cases, the term will mean "property of the debtor". Paragraphs (2) and (3) adopt the definition of "special taxpayer affected by the plan" that appears in current section 81(10) and 81(11) [section 401(10) and (11) of former Title 11]. Paragraphs [sic] (4) provides for "trustee" the same treatment as provided for "property of the estate", specifying that it means "debtor" when used in conjunction with chapter 9. House Report No. 95–595.

1984 Acts. Statements by Legislative Leaders, see 1984 U.S.Code Cong. and Adm.News, p. 576.

1988 Acts. House Report No. 100–1011, see 1988 U.S.Code Cong. and Adm.News, p. 4115.

Legislative Statements

Section 902(2) of the Senate amendment is deleted since the bankruptcy court will have jurisdiction over all cases under chapter 9. The concept of a claim being materially and adversely affected reflected in section 902(1) of the Senate amendment has been deleted and replaced with the new concept of "impairment" set forth in section 1124 of the House amendment and incorporated by reference into chapter 9.

References in Text

Section 103(e) of this title, referred to in pars. (1) and (5), was redesignated section 103(f) and a new section 103(e) was added by Pub.L. 106–554, § 1(a)(5) [Title I, § 112(c)(5)(A)], Dec. 21, 2000, 114 Stat. 2763, 2763A–394.

Amendments

1988 Amendments. Par. (2). Pub.L. 100–597, § 4(1), (2), redesignated former par. (2) as (3) and added par. (2).

Pars. (3) to (5). Pub.L. 100–597, § 4(1), redesignated former pars. (2) to (4) as (3) to (5), respectively.

1984 Amendments. Par. (2). Pub.L. 98–353 substituted "legal or equitable title to real property against which a special assessment or special tax has been levied" for "title, legal or equitable, to real property against which has been levied a special assessment or special tax".

Effective and Applicability Provisions

1988 Acts. Amendment by Pub.L. 100–597 effective Nov. 3, 1988, but not applicable to any case commenced under this title before that date, see section 12 of Pub.L. 100–597, set out as a note under section 101 of this title.

1984 Acts. Amendment by Pub.L. 98–353 effective with respect to cases filed 90 days after July 10, 1984, see section 552(a), formerly 553(a), of Pub.L. 98–353, set out as a note under section 101 of this title.

CROSS REFERENCES

Definitions applicable in—

　Cases under this title, see 11 USCA § 101.

　Chapter eleven cases, see 11 USCA § 1101.

　Commodity broker liquidation cases, see 11 USCA § 761.

　Railroad reorganization cases, see 11 USCA § 1162.

　Stockbroker liquidation cases, see 11 USCA § 741.

LIBRARY REFERENCES

American Digest System

Bankruptcy ☞3481.

Key Number System Topic No. 51.

Corpus Juris Secundum

CJS Bankruptcy § 73, Chapter 9 Cases.

CJS Bankruptcy § 846, Operation of Affairs of Municipal Debtor in Chapter 9 Cases.

CJS Bankruptcy § 1122, Objections to Confirmation.

§ 903.　Reservation of State power to control municipalities

This chapter does not limit or impair the power of a State to control, by legislation or otherwise, a municipality of or in such State in the exercise of the political or governmental powers of such municipality, including expenditures for such exercise, but—

　(1) a State law prescribing a method of composition of indebtedness of such municipality may not bind any creditor that does not consent to such composition; and

　(2) a judgment entered under such a law may not bind a creditor that does not consent to such composition.

(Pub.L. 95–598, Nov. 6, 1978, 92 Stat. 2622; Pub.L. 98–353, Title III, § 492, July 10, 1984, 98 Stat. 383.)

HISTORICAL AND STATUTORY NOTES

Revision Notes and Legislative Reports

1978 Acts. Section 903 is derived, with stylistic changes, from section 83 of current Chapter IX [section 403 of former Title 11]. It sets forth the primary authority of a State, through its constitution, laws, and other powers, over its municipalities. The proviso in section 83, prohibiting State composition procedures for municipalities, is retained. Deletion of the provision would "permit all States to enact their own versions of Chapter IX [former chapter 9 (section 401 et seq.) of former Title 11]", Municipal Insolvency, 50 Am.Bankr. L.J. 55, 65, which would frustrate the constitutional mandate of uniform bankruptcy laws. Constitution of the United States, Art. I, Sec. 8.

This section provides that the municipality can consent to the court's orders in regard to use of its income or property. It is contemplated that such consent will be required by the court for the issuance of certificates of indebtedness under section 364(c). Such consent could extend to enforcement of the conditions attached to the certificates or the municipal services to be provided during the proceedings. Senate Report No. 95–989.

1984 Acts. Statements by Legislative Leaders, see 1984 U.S.Code Cong. and Adm.News, p. 576.

Legislative Statements

Section 903 of the House amendment represents a stylistic revision of section 903 of the Senate amendment. To the extent section 903 of the House bill would have changed present law, such section is rejected.

Amendments

1984 Amendments. Par. (2). Pub.L. 98–353 struck out "to" preceding "that does not consent".

Effective and Applicability Provisions

1984 Acts. Amendment by Pub.L. 98–353 effective with respect to cases filed 90 days after July 10, 1984, see section 552(a), formerly 553(a), of Pub.L. 98–353, set out as a note under section 101 of this title.

CROSS REFERENCES

Authorization by state to be debtor under this chapter, see 11 USCA § 109.

LIBRARY REFERENCES

American Digest System

Bankruptcy ☞3481.

Key Number System Topic No. 51.

Corpus Juris Secundum

CJS Bankruptcy § 846, Operation of Affairs of Municipal Debtor in Chapter 9 Cases.

§ 904. Limitation on jurisdiction and powers of court

Notwithstanding any power of the court, unless the debtor consents or the plan so provides, the court may not, by any stay, order, or decree, in the case or otherwise, interfere with—

(1) any of the political or governmental powers of the debtor;

(2) any of the property or revenues of the debtor; or

(3) the debtor's use or enjoyment of any income-producing property.

(Pub.L. 95–598, Nov. 6, 1978, 92 Stat. 2622.)

HISTORICAL AND STATUTORY NOTES

Revision Notes and Legislative Reports

1978 Acts. This section adopts the policy of section 82(c) of current law [section 402(c) of former Title 11]. The only change in this section from section 82(c) is to conform the section to the style and cross-references of S. 2266. Senate Report No. 95–989.

This section adopts the policy of section 82(c) of current law [section 402(c) of former Title 11]. The *Usery* case underlines the need for this limitation on the court's powers. The only change in this section from section 82(c) is to conform the section to the style and cross-references of H.R. 8200. This section makes clear that the court may not interfere with the choices a municipality makes as to what services and benefits it will provide to its inhabitants. House Report No. 95–595.

CROSS REFERENCES

Power of court, see 11 USCA § 105.

LIBRARY REFERENCES

American Digest System

Bankruptcy ☞3481.

Key Number System Topic No. 51.

Corpus Juris Secundum

CJS Bankruptcy § 214, Power of Bankruptcy Judges to Hear Cases and Proceedings.

CJS Bankruptcy § 846, Operation of Affairs of Municipal Debtor in Chapter 9 Cases.

SUBCHAPTER II—ADMINISTRATION

HISTORICAL AND STATUTORY NOTES

Amendments

1984 Amendments. Pub.L. 98–353, Title III, § 493, July 10, 1984, 98 Stat. 383, corrected a typographical error in the original by substituting "SUBCHAPTER" for "SUBCHAPER" in the subchapter heading.

§ 921. Petition and proceedings relating to petition

(a) Notwithstanding sections 109(d) and 301 of this title, a case under this chapter concerning an unincorporated tax or special assessment district that does not have such district's own officials is commenced by the filing under section 301 of this title of a petition under this chapter by such district's governing authority or the board or body having authority to levy taxes or assessments to meet the obligations of such district.

(b) The chief judge of the court of appeals for the circuit embracing the district in which the case is commenced shall designate the bankruptcy judge to conduct the case.

(c) After any objection to the petition, the court, after notice and a hearing, may dismiss the petition if the debtor did not file the petition in good faith or if the petition does not meet the requirements of this title.

(d) If the petition is not dismissed under subsection (c) of this section, the court shall order relief under this chapter notwithstanding section 301(b).

(e) The court may not, on account of an appeal from an order for relief, delay any proceeding under this chapter in the case in which the appeal is being taken; nor shall any court order a stay of such proceeding pending such appeal. The reversal on appeal of a finding of jurisdiction does not affect the validity of any debt incurred that is authorized by the court under section 364(c) or 364(d) of this title.

(Pub.L. 95–598, Nov. 6, 1978, 92 Stat. 2622; Pub.L. 98–353, Title III, § 494, July 10, 1984, 98 Stat. 383; Pub.L. 109–8, Title V, § 501(a), Apr. 20, 2005, 119 Stat. 118.)

HISTORICAL AND STATUTORY NOTES

Revision Notes and Legislative Reports

1978 Acts. Section 905 adopts the procedures for selection of the judge for the chapter 9 case as found in current section 82(d) [section 402(d) of former Title 11]. It is expected that the large chapter 9 case might take up almost all the judicial time of the presiding judge and involve very complex legal questions. Selection should not be left to chance or the luck of the draw. This provision will insure that calendar demands and levels of experience can be considered in the selection of the judge in a chapter 9 case. Senate Report No. 95–989.

Subsection (a) is derived from section 85(a) [section 405(a) of former Title 11], second sentence, of current law. There is no substantive change in the law. The subsection permits a municipality that does not have its own officers to be moved into chapter 9 by the action of the body or board that has authority to levy taxes for the municipality.

Subsection (b) permits a party in interest to object to the filing of the petition not later than 15 days after notice. This provision tracks the third sentence of section 85(a) [section 405(a) of former Title 11], except that the provision for publication in section 85(a) is left to the Rules (See Rule 9–14 [Rules of Bankruptcy Procedure, this title]), and therefore the determinative date is left less definite.

Subsection (c) permits the court to dismiss a petition not filed in good faith or not filed in compliance with the requirements of the chapter. This provision is the fourth sentence of section 85(a) [section 405(a) of former Title 11].

Subsection (d) directs the court to order relief on the petition if it does not dismiss the case under subsection (c).

Subsection (e) contains the fifth and sixth sentences of section 85(a) [section 405(a) of former Title 11]. House Report No. 95–595.

1984 Acts. Statements by Legislative Leaders, see 1984 U.S.Code Cong. and Adm.News, p. 576.

2005 Acts. House Report No. 109–31(Part I), see 2005 U.S. Code Cong. and Adm. News, p. 88.

Legislative Statements

Section 905 of the Senate amendment is incorporated as section 921(b) of the House amendment with the difference that the chief judge of the circuit embracing the district in which the case is commenced designates a bankruptcy judge to conduct the case in lieu of a district judge as under present law. It is intended that a municipality may commence a case in any district in which the municipality is located, as under present law. Section 906 of the Senate amendment has been

adopted in substance in section 109(c) of the House amendment.

Amendments

2005 Amendments. Subsec. (d). Pub.L. 109–8, § 501(a), inserted "notwithstanding section 301(b)" before the period at the end.

1984 Amendments. Subsec. (a). Pub.L. 98–353, § 494(c), substituted "109(d)" for "109(c)".

Subsec. (c). Pub.L. 98–353, § 494(a)(1), substituted "any" for "an".

Pub.L. 98–353, § 494(a)(2), substituted "petition if the debtor did not file the petition in good faith" for "petition, if the debtor did not file the petition in good faith,".

Subsec. (d). Pub.L. 98–353, § 494(b), (d), redesignated former subsec. (e) as (d), and in subsec. (d), as so redesignated, substituted a reference to "subsection (c)" for a reference to "subsection (d)". Prior to such redesignation and amendment, no former subsec. (d) had been enacted.

Subsec. (e). Pub.L. 98–353, § 494(b), redesignated former subsec. (f) as (e). Former subsec. (e) was redesignated as (d).

Subsec. (f). Pub.L. 98–353, § 494(b), redesignated former subsec. (f) as (e).

Effective and Applicability Provisions

2005 Acts. Amendments by Pub.L. 109–8 effective, except as otherwise provided, 180 days after April 20, 2005, and inapplicable with respect to cases commenced under Title 11 before the effective date, see Pub.L. 109–8, § 1501, set out as a note under 11 U.S.C.A. § 101.

1984 Acts. Amendment by Pub.L. 98–353 effective with respect to cases filed 90 days after July 10, 1984, see section 552(a), formerly 553(a), of Pub.L. 98–353, set out as a note under section 101 of this title.

LIBRARY REFERENCES

American Digest System

Bankruptcy ⟜3481.

Key Number System Topic No. 51.

Corpus Juris Secundum

CJS Bankruptcy § 339, Who May File on Behalf of Debtor Who is Not an Individual.

CJS Bankruptcy § 365, Commencement and Order for Relief.

§ 922.   Automatic stay of enforcement of claims against the debtor

(a) A petition filed under this chapter operates as a stay, in addition to the stay provided by section 362 of this title, applicable to all entities, of—

(1) the commencement or continuation, including the issuance or employment of process, of a judicial, administrative, or other action or proceeding against an officer or inhabitant of the debtor that seeks to enforce a claim against the debtor; and

(2) the enforcement of a lien on or arising out of taxes or assessments owed to the debtor.

(b) Subsections (c), (d), (e), (f), and (g) of section 362 of this title apply to a stay under subsection (a) of this section the same as such subsections apply to a stay under section 362(a) of this title.

(c) If the debtor provides, under section 362, 364, or 922 of this title, adequate protection of the interest of the holder of a claim secured by a lien on property of the debtor and if, notwithstanding such protection such creditor has a claim arising from the stay of action against such property under section 362 or 922 of this title or from the granting of a lien under section 364(d) of this title, then such claim shall be allowable as an administrative expense under section 503(b) of this title.

(d) Notwithstanding section 362 of this title and subsection (a) of this section, a petition filed under this chapter does not operate as a stay of application of pledged special revenues in a manner consistent with section 927 of this title to payment of indebtedness secured by such revenues.

(Pub.L. 95–598, Nov. 6, 1978, 92 Stat. 2623; Pub.L. 98–353, Title III, § 495, July 10, 1984, 98 Stat. 384; Pub.L. 100–597, § 5, Nov. 3, 1988, 102 Stat. 3029.)

HISTORICAL AND STATUTORY NOTES

Revision Notes and Legislative Reports

1978 Acts. The automatic stay provided under section 362 of title 11 is incomplete for a municipality, because there is the possibility of action by a creditor against an officer or inhabitant of the municipality to collect taxes due the municipality. Section 85(e)(1) of current chapter IX [section 405(e)(1) of former Title 11] stays such actions. Section 922 carries over that protection into the proposed chapter 9. Subsection (b) applies the provisions for relief from the stay that apply generally in section 362 to the stay under section 922. House Report No. 95–595.

1984 Acts. Statements by Legislative Leaders, see 1984 U.S.Code Cong. and Adm.News, p. 576.

1988 Acts. House Report No. 100–1011, see 1988 U.S.Code Cong. and Adm.News, p. 4115.

Amendments

1988 Amendments. Subsecs. (c), (d). Pub.L. 100–597 added subsecs. (c) and (d).

1984 Amendments. Subsec. (a)(1). Pub.L. 98–353, § 495(1), substituted "a judicial" for "judicial".

Pub.L. 98–353, § 495(2), substituted "action or proceeding" for "proceeding".

Effective and Applicability Provisions

1988 Acts. Amendment by Pub.L. 100–597 effective Nov. 3, 1988, but not applicable to any case commenced under this title before that date, see section 12 of Pub.L. 100–597, set out as a note under section 101 of this title.

1984 Acts. Amendment by Pub.L. 98–353 effective with respect to cases filed 90 days after July 10, 1984, see section 552(a), formerly 553(a), of Pub.L. 98–353, set out as a note under section 101 of this title.

CROSS REFERENCES

Effect of § 362 of this title in stockbroker liquidation cases, see 11 USCA § 742.

Extension of time generally, see 11 USCA § 108.

Stay of action against codebtor in—

    Chapter thirteen cases, see 11 USCA § 1301.

    Chapter twelve cases, see 11 USCA § 1201.

LIBRARY REFERENCES

American Digest System

Bankruptcy ⟊3481.

Key Number System Topic No. 51.

Corpus Juris Secundum

CJS Bankruptcy § 278, Parties Defendant; Sovereign Immunity.

CJS Bankruptcy § 483, Municipal Bankruptcies.

CJS Bankruptcy § 846, Operation of Affairs of Municipal Debtor in Chapter 9 Cases.

§ 923.   Notice

There shall be given notice of the commencement of a case under this chapter, notice of an order for relief under this chapter, and notice of the dismissal of a case under this chapter. Such notice shall also be published at least once a week for three successive weeks in at least one newspaper of general circulation published within the district in which the case is commenced, and in such other newspaper having a general circulation among bond dealers and bondholders as the court designates.

(Pub.L. 95–598, Nov. 6, 1978, 92 Stat. 2623.)

HISTORICAL AND STATUTORY NOTES

Revision Notes and Legislative Reports

1978 Acts. The notice provisions in section 923 are significantly more sparse than those provided under section 85(d) of chapter IX [section § 405(d) of former Title 11]. The exact contours of the notice to be given under chapter 9 are left to the Rules [Rules of Bankruptcy Procedure, this title]. Because the Rules deal with notice in a municipal case (Rule 9–14), and because section 405(d) of title IV of the bill continues those Rules in effect to the extent not inconsistent with the bill, the notice provisions of current law and Rules would continue to apply. House Report No. 95–595.

Legislative Statements

Section 923 of the House amendment represents a compromise with respect to the notice provisions contained in comparable provisions of the House bill and Senate amendment. As a general matter, title 11 leaves most procedural issues to be determined by the Rules of Bankruptcy Procedure. Section 923 of the House amendment contains certain important aspects of procedure that have been retained from present law. It is anticipated that the Rules of Bankruptcy Procedure will adopt rules similar to the present rules for chapter IX of the Bankruptcy Act [former chapter 9 (section 401 et seq.) of former Title 11].

CROSS REFERENCES

Notice in—

    Commodity broker liquidation cases, see 11 USCA § 762.

    Stockbroker liquidation cases, see 11 USCA § 743.

Notice of order for relief, see 11 USCA § 342.

LIBRARY REFERENCES

American Digest System

Bankruptcy ⊕3481.

Key Number System Topic No. 51.

Corpus Juris Secundum

CJS Bankruptcy § 305, Notice to Bond Dealers and Bondholders in Chapter 9 Municipal-Debt-Adjustment Cases.

CJS Bankruptcy § 365, Commencement and Order for Relief.

§ 924. List of creditors

The debtor shall file a list of creditors.

(Pub.L. 95–598, Nov. 6, 1978, 92 Stat. 2623.)

HISTORICAL AND STATUTORY NOTES

Revision Notes and Legislative Reports

1978 Acts. This section adopts the provision presently contained in section 85(b) of Chapter IX [section 405(b) of former Title 11]. A list of creditors, as complete and accurate as practicable, must be filed with the court. Senate Report No. 95–989.

This section directs the debtor to file a list of creditors with the court. A comparable provision is presently contained in section 85(b) of chapter IX [section 405(b) of former Title 11]. The Rules, [Rules of Bankruptcy Procedure, this title], in Rule 9–7, copy the provisions of section 85(b), with additional matter. As noted above, section 405(d) of title IV will continue those Rules in effect. Because the form, time of filing, and nature of the list, are procedural matters that may call for some flexibility, those details have been left to the Rules. House Report No. 95–595.

Legislative Statements

Section 924 of the House amendment is derived from section 924 of the House bill with the location of the filing of the list of creditors to be determined by the rules of bankruptcy procedure. The detailed requirements of section 724 [924] of the Senate bill are anticipated to be incorporated in the rules of bankruptcy procedure.

CROSS REFERENCES

Duty of—

    Debtor to file list of creditors, see 11 USCA § 521.

    Trustee to file list of creditors in Chapter 11 cases, see 11 USCA § 1106.

LIBRARY REFERENCES

American Digest System

Bankruptcy ⊕3481.

Key Number System Topic No. 51.

Corpus Juris Secundum

CJS Bankruptcy § 344, List of Creditors and Others.

§ 925. Effect of list of claims

A proof of claim is deemed filed under section 501 of this title for any claim that appears in the list filed under section 924 of this title, except a claim that is listed as disputed, contingent, or unliquidated.

(Pub.L. 95–598, Nov. 6, 1978, 92 Stat. 2623.)

HISTORICAL AND STATUTORY NOTES

Revision Notes and Legislative Reports

1978 Acts. Section 926 [now section 925] follows the policy contained in section 88(a) of the present Act [section 408(a) of former Title 11], though certain details are left to the Rules. The language of section 926 is the same as that of proposed 11 U.S.C. 1111, which applies in chapter 11 cases. The list of creditors filed under section 924 is given weight as prima facie evidence of the claims listed (except claims that are listed as disputed, contingent, or unliquidated), which are deemed filed under section 501, obviating the need for listed creditors to file proofs of claim. Senate Report No. 95–989.

Legislative Statements

Section 925 of the Senate amendment regarding venue and fees has been deleted.

LIBRARY REFERENCES

American Digest System

Bankruptcy ⊕3481.

Key Number System Topic No. 51.

§ 926. Avoiding powers

(a) If the debtor refuses to pursue a cause of action under section 544, 545, 547, 548, 549(a), or 550 of this title, then on request of a creditor, the court may appoint a trustee to pursue such cause of action.

(b) A transfer of property of the debtor to or for the benefit of any holder of a bond or note, on account of such bond or note, may not be avoided under section 547 of this title.

(Pub.L. 95–598, Nov. 6, 1978, 92 Stat. 2623; Pub.L. 100–597, § 6, Nov. 3, 1988, 102 Stat. 3029.)

HISTORICAL AND STATUTORY NOTES

Revision Notes and Legislative Reports

1978 Acts. This section [928 (now section 926)] adopts current section 85(h) [section 405(h) of former Title 11] which provides for a trustee to be appointed for the purpose of pursuing an action under an avoiding power, if the debtor refuses to do so. This section is necessary because a municipality might, by reason of political pressure or desire for future good relations with a particular creditor or class of creditors, make payments to such creditors in the days preceding the petition to the detriment of all other creditors. No change in the elected officials of such a city would automatically occur upon filing of the petition, and it might be very awkward for those same officials to turn around and demand the return of the payments following the filing of the petition. Hence, the need for a trustee for such purpose.

The general avoiding powers are incorporated by reference in section 901 and are broader than under current law. Preferences, fraudulent conveyances, and other kinds of transfers will thus be voidable.

Incorporated by reference also is the power to accept or reject executory contracts and leases (section 365). Within the definition of executory contracts are collective bargaining agreements between the city and its employees. Such contracts may be rejected despite contrary State laws. Courts should readily allow the rejection of such contracts where they are burdensome, the rejection will aid in the municipality's reorganization and in consideration of the equities of each case. On the last point, "[e]quities in favor of the city in chapter 9 will be far more compelling than the equities in favor of the employer in chapter 11. Onerous employment obligations may prevent a city from balancing its budget for some time. The prospect of an unbalanced budget may preclude judicial confirmation of the plan. Unless a city can reject its labor contracts, lack of funds may force cutbacks in police, fire, sanitation, and welfare services, imposing hardships on many citizens. In addition, because cities in the past have often seemed immune to the constraint of "profitability" faced by private businesses, their wage contracts may be relatively more onerous than those in the private sector." Executory Contracts and Municipal Bankruptcy, 85 Yale L.J. 957, 965 (1976) (footnote omitted). Rejection of the contracts may require the municipalities to renegotiate such contracts by state collective bargaining laws. It is intended that the power to reject collective bargaining agreements will pre-empt state termination provisions, but not state collective bargaining laws. Thus, a city would not be required to maintain existing employment terms during the renegotiation period. Senate Report No. 95–989.

1988 Acts. House Report No. 100–1011, see 1988 U.S.Code Cong. and Adm.News, p. 4115.

Legislative Statements

Section 926 of the House amendment is derived from section 928 of the Senate bill. The provision enables creditors to request the court to appoint a trustee to pursue avoiding powers if the debtor refuses to exercise those powers. Section 901 of the House amendment makes a corresponding change to incorporate avoiding powers included in the Senate amendment, but excluded from the House bill.

Amendments

1988 Amendments. Subsec. (a). Pub.L. 100–597, § 6(1), designated existing provision as subsec. (a).

Subsec. (b). Pub.L. 100–597, § 6(2), added subsec. (b).

Effective and Applicability Provisions

1988 Acts. Amendment by Pub.L. 100–597 effective Nov. 3, 1988, but not applicable to any case commenced under this title before that date, see section 12 of Pub.L. 100–597, set out as a note under section 101 of this title.

CROSS REFERENCES

Appointment of trustee in—

    Chapter eleven cases, see 11 USCA § 1104.

    Chapter thirteen cases, see 11 USCA § 1302.

    Railroad reorganization cases, see 11 USCA § 1163.

Trustee defined when used in sections made applicable to cases under this chapter, see 11 USCA § 902.

LIBRARY REFERENCES

American Digest System

Bankruptcy ⏄3481.

Key Number System Topic No. 51.

Corpus Juris Secundum

CJS Bankruptcy § 56, Eligibility to Serve as Trustee or Examiner--Disinterestedness Requirement.

CJS Bankruptcy § 73, Chapter 9 Cases.

CJS Bankruptcy § 100, Chapter 9.

CJS Bankruptcy § 278, Parties Defendant; Sovereign Immunity.

CJS Bankruptcy § 846, Operation of Affairs of Municipal Debtor in Chapter 9 Cases.

§ 927. Limitation on recourse

The holder of a claim payable solely from special revenues of the debtor under applicable nonbankruptcy law shall not be treated as having recourse against the debtor on account of such claim pursuant to section 1111(b) of this title.

(Added Pub.L. 100–597, § 7(2), Nov. 3, 1988, 102 Stat. 3029.)

HISTORICAL AND STATUTORY NOTES

Revision Notes and Legislative Reports

1988 Acts. House Report No. 100–1011, see 1988 U.S.Code Cong. and Adm.News, p. 4115.

Effective and Applicability Provisions

1988 Acts. Section effective Nov. 3, 1988, but not applicable to any case commenced under this title before that date, see section 12 of Pub.L. 100–597, set out as an Effective Date of 1988 Amendment note under section 101 of this title.

Prior Provisions

A prior section 927, Pub.L. 95–598, Nov. 6, 1978, 92 Stat. 2623, as amended, relating to dismissal of cases under this chapter, was renumbered 930 by Pub.L. 100–597.

LIBRARY REFERENCES

American Digest System

Bankruptcy ⏄3481.

Key Number System Topic No. 51.

§ 928. Post petition effect of security interest

(a) Notwithstanding section 552(a) of this title and subject to subsection (b) of this section, special revenues acquired by the debtor after the commencement of the case shall remain subject to any lien resulting from any security agreement entered into by the debtor before the commencement of the case.

(b) Any such lien on special revenues, other than municipal betterment assessments, derived from a project or system shall be subject to the necessary operating expenses of such project or system, as the case may be.

(Added Pub.L. 100–597, § 8, Nov. 3, 1988, 102 Stat. 3029.)

HISTORICAL AND STATUTORY NOTES

Revision Notes and Legislative Reports

1988 Acts. House Report No. 100–1011, see 1988 U.S.Code Cong. and Adm.News, p. 4115.

Effective and Applicability Provisions

1988 Acts. Section effective Nov. 3. 1988, but not applicable to any case commenced under this title before that date, see section 12 of Pub.L. 100–597, set out as an Effective Date of 1988 Amendment note under section 101 of this title.

LIBRARY REFERENCES

American Digest System

Bankruptcy ⊆3481.

Key Number System Topic No. 51.

Corpus Juris Secundum

CJS Bankruptcy § 278, Parties Defendant; Sovereign Immunity.

§ 929. Municipal leases

A lease to a municipality shall not be treated as an executory contract or unexpired lease for the purposes of section 365 or 502(b)(6) of this title solely by reason of its being subject to termination in the event the debtor fails to appropriate rent.

(Added Pub.L. 100–597, § 9, Nov. 3, 1988, 102 Stat. 3030.)

HISTORICAL AND STATUTORY NOTES

Revision Notes and Legislative Reports

1988 Acts. House Report No. 100–1011, see 1988 U.S.Code Cong. and Adm.News, p. 4115.

Effective and Applicability Provisions

1988 Acts. Section effective Nov. 3, 1988, but not applicable to any case commenced under this title before that date, see section 12 of Pub.L. 100–597, set out as an Effective Date of 1988 Amendment note under section 101 of this title.

LIBRARY REFERENCES

American Digest System

Bankruptcy ⊆3481.

Key Number System Topic No. 51.

Corpus Juris Secundum

CJS Bankruptcy § 278, Parties Defendant; Sovereign Immunity.

§ 930. Dismissal

(a) After notice and a hearing, the court may dismiss a case under this chapter for cause, including—

  (1) want of prosecution;

  (2) unreasonable delay by the debtor that is prejudicial to creditors;

  (3) failure to propose a plan within the time fixed under section 941 of this title;

  (4) if a plan is not accepted within any time fixed by the court;

  (5) denial of confirmation of a plan under section 943(b) of this title and denial of additional time for filing another plan or a modification of a plan; or

  (6) if the court has retained jurisdiction after confirmation of a plan—

    (A) material default by the debtor with respect to a term of such plan; or

    (B) termination of such plan by reason of the occurrence of a condition specified in such plan.

(b) The court shall dismiss a case under this chapter if confirmation of a plan under this chapter is refused.

(Pub.L. 95–598, Nov. 6, 1978, 92 Stat. 2623, § 927; Pub.L. 98–353, Title III, § 496, July 10, 1984, 98 Stat. 384; renumbered § 930, Pub.L. 100–597, § 7(1), Nov. 3, 1988, 102 Stat. 3029.)

HISTORICAL AND STATUTORY NOTES

Revision Notes and Legislative Reports

1978 Acts. Section 927 conforms to section 98 [section 418 of former Title 11] of current law. The Section [sic] permits dismissal by the court for unreasonable delay by the debtor, failure to propose a plan, failure of acceptance of a plan, or default by the debtor under a conformed plan. Mandatory dismissal is required if confirmation is refused. Senate Report No. 95–989.

Section 926 [now 927] generally conforms to section 98(a) [section 418(a) of former title 11] of current law. Stylistic changes have been made to conform the language with that used in chapter 11, section 1112. The section permits dismissal by the court for unreasonable delay by the debtor that is prejudicial to creditors, failure to propose a plan, failure of confirmation of a plan, or material default by the debtor under a confirmed plan. The only significant change from current law lies in the second ground. Currently, section 98(a)(2) provides for dismissal if a proposed plan is not accepted, and section 98(b) *requires* dismissal if an accepted plan is not confirmed. In order to provide greater flexibility to the court, the debtor, and creditors, the bill allows the court to permit the debtor to propose another plan if the first plan is not confirmed. In that event the debtor need not, as under current law, commence the case all over again. This could provide savings in time and administrative expenses if a plan is denied confirmation. House Report No. 95–595.

1984 Acts. Statements by Legislative Leaders, see 1984 U.S.Code Cong. and Adm.News, p. 576.

1988 Acts. House Report No. 100–1011, see 1988 U.S.Code Cong. and Adm.News, p. 4115.

Legislative Statements

Section 927(b) of the House amendment is derived from section 927(b) of the Senate bill. The provision requires mandatory dismissal if confirmation of a plan is refused.

The House amendment deletes section 929 of the Senate amendment as unnecessary since the bankruptcy court has original exclusive jurisdiction of all cases under chapter 9.

The House amendment deletes section 930 of the Senate amendment and incorporates section 507(a)(1) by reference.

Amendments

1984 Amendments. Subsec. (b). Pub.L. 98–353 substituted "confirmation of a plan under this chapter" for "confirmation".

Effective and Applicability Provisions

1984 Acts. Amendment by Pub.L. 98–353 effective with respect to cases filed 90 days after July 10, 1984, see section 552(a), formerly 553(a), of Pub.L. 98–353, set out as a note under section 101 of this title.

CROSS REFERENCES

Conversion or dismissal of—

  Chapter eleven cases, see 11 USCA § 1112.

  Chapter thirteen cases, see 11 USCA § 1307.

Dismissal of Chapter seven cases, see 11 USCA § 707.

Effect of dismissal, see 11 USCA § 349.

LIBRARY REFERENCES

American Digest System

Bankruptcy �köm3481.

Key Number System Topic No. 51.

Corpus Juris Secundum

CJS Bankruptcy § 1123, Hearing and Order.

CJS Bankruptcy § 1125, Continuing Jurisdiction; Closing of Case.

SUBCHAPTER III—THE PLAN

§ 941. Filing of plan

The debtor shall file a plan for the adjustment of the debtor's debts. If such a plan is not filed with the petition, the debtor shall file such a plan at such later time as the court fixes.

(Pub.L. 95–598, Nov. 6, 1978, 92 Stat. 2624.)

HISTORICAL AND STATUTORY NOTES

Revision Notes and Legislative Reports

1978 Acts. Section 941 gives the debtor the exclusive right to propose a plan, and directs that the debtor propose one either with the petition or within such time as the court directs. The section follows section 90(a) of current law [section 410(a) of former Title 11]. Senate Report No. 95–989.

1984 Acts. Statements by Legislative Leaders, see 1984 U.S.Code Cong. and Adm.News, p. 576.

CROSS REFERENCES

Dismissal for failure to timely propose plan, see 11 USCA § 930.

Filing of plan in Chapter thirteen cases, see 11 USCA § 1321.

Who may file a plan in Chapter eleven cases, see 11 USCA § 1121.

LIBRARY REFERENCES

American Digest System

Bankruptcy ⊫3481.

Key Number System Topic No. 51.

Corpus Juris Secundum

CJS Bankruptcy § 1118, Filing of Plan and Disclosure Statement; Hearing on Objections.

§ 942. Modification of plan

The debtor may modify the plan at any time before confirmation, but may not modify the plan so that the plan as modified fails to meet the requirements of this chapter. After the debtor files a modification, the plan as modified becomes the plan.

(Pub.L. 95–598, Nov. 6, 1978, 92 Stat. 2624.)

HISTORICAL AND STATUTORY NOTES

Revision Notes and Legislative Reports

1978 Acts. Section 942 permits the debtor to modify the plan at any time before confirmation, as does section 90(a) of current law [section 410(a) of former Title 11]. Senate Report No.95–989.

Legislative Statements

The House amendment deletes section 942 of the Senate amendment in favor of incorporating section 1125 by cross-reference. Similarly, the House amendment does not incorporate section 944 or 945 of the Senate amendment since incorporation of several sections in chapter 11 in section 901 is sufficient.

CROSS REFERENCES

Modification of plan after confirmation in—

Chapter thirteen cases, see 11 USCA § 1329.

Chapter twelve cases, see 11 USCA § 1229.

Modification of plan before confirmation in—

Chapter thirteen cases, see 11 USCA § 1323.

Chapter twelve cases, see 11 USCA § 1223.

Modification of plan in Chapter eleven cases, see 11 USCA § 1127.

LIBRARY REFERENCES

American Digest System

Bankruptcy ⊫3481.

Key Number System Topic No. 51.

Corpus Juris Secundum

CJS Bankruptcy § 1120, Modification of Plan Before Confirmation.

§ 943. Confirmation

(a) A special tax payer may object to confirmation of a plan.

(b) The court shall confirm the plan if—

    (1) the plan complies with the provisions of this title made applicable by sections 103(e) and 901 of this title;

    (2) the plan complies with the provisions of this chapter;

    (3) all amounts to be paid by the debtor or by any person for services or expenses in the case or incident to the plan have been fully disclosed and are reasonable;

    (4) the debtor is not prohibited by law from taking any action necessary to carry out the plan;

    (5) except to the extent that the holder of a particular claim has agreed to a different treatment of such claim, the plan provides that on the effective date of the plan each holder of a claim of a kind specified in section 507(a)(2) of this title will receive on account of such claim cash equal to the allowed amount of such claim;

    (6) any regulatory or electoral approval necessary under applicable nonbankruptcy law in order to carry out any provision of the plan has been obtained, or such provision is expressly conditioned on such approval; and

(7) the plan is in the best interests of creditors and is feasible.

(Pub.L. 95–598, Nov. 6, 1978, 92 Stat. 2624; Pub.L. 98–353, Title III, § 497, July 10, 1984, 98 Stat. 384; Pub.L. 100–597, § 10, Nov. 3, 1988, 102 Stat. 3030; Pub.L. 109–8, Title XV, § 1502(a)(6), Apr. 20, 2005, 119 Stat. 216.)

HISTORICAL AND STATUTORY NOTES

Revision Notes and Legislative Reports

1978 Acts. Section 946 [now this section] is adopted from current section 94 [section 414 of former Title 11]. The test for confirmation is whether or not the plan is fair and equitable and feasible. The fair and equitable test tracts current chapter X [former chapter 10 (section 501 et seq.) of this title] and is known as the strict priority rule. Creditors must be provided, under the plan, the going concern value of their claims. The going concern value contemplates a "comparison of revenues and expenditures taking into account the taxing power and the extent to which tax increases are both necessary and feasible" Municipal Insolvency, supra, at p. 64, and is intended to provide more of a return to creditors than the liquidation value if the city's assets could be liquidated like those of a private corporation. Senate Report No. 95–989.

In addition to the confirmation requirements incorporated from section 1129 by section 901, this section specifies additional requirements. Paragraph (1) requires compliance with the provisions of the title made applicable in chapter 9 cases. This provision follows section 94(b)(2) [section 414(b)(2) of former Title 11]. Paragraph (2) requires compliance with the provisions of chapter 9, as does section 94(b)(2) [section 414(b)(2) of former Title 11]. Paragraph (3) adopts section 94(b)(4) [section 414(b)(4) of former Title 11], requiring disclosure and reasonableness of all payments to be made in connection with the plan or the case. Paragraph (4), copied from section 92(b)(6) [probably should be "94(b)(6)", which was section 414(b)(6) of former Title 11], requires that the debtor not be prohibited by law from taking any action necessary to carry out the plan. Paragraph (5) departs from current law by requiring that administrative expenses be paid in full, but not necessarily in cash. Finally, paragraph (6) requires that the plan be in the best interest of creditors and feasible. The best interest test was deleted in section 94(b)(1) of current chapter IX [section 414(b)(1) of former Title 11] from previous chapter IX [former chapter 9 (section 401 et seq.) of former Title 11], because it was redundant with the fair and equitable rule. However, this bill proposes a new confirmation standard generally for reorganization, one element of which is the best interest of creditors test; see section 1129(a)(7). In that section, the test is phrased in terms of liquidation of the debtor. Because that is not possible in a municipal case, the test here is phrased in its more traditional form, using the words of art "best interest of creditors." The best interest of creditors test here is in addition to the financial standards imposed on the plan by section 1129(a)(8) and 1129(b), just as those provisions are in addition to the comparable best interest test in chapter 11, 11 U.S.C. 1129(a)(7). The feasibility requirement, added in the revision of chapter IX [former chapter 9 (section 401 et seq.) of former Title 11] last year, is retained. House Report No. 95–595.

1984 Acts. Statements by Legislative Leaders, see 1984 U.S.Code Cong. and Adm.News, p. 576.

1988 Acts. House Report No. 100–1011, see 1988 U.S.Code Cong. and Adm.News, p. 4115.

2005 Acts. House Report No. 109–31(Part I), see 2005 U.S. Code Cong. and Adm. News, p. 88.

Legislative Statements

Section 943(a) of the House amendment makes clear that a special taxpayer may object to confirmation of a plan. Section 943(b) of the House amendment is derived from section 943 of the House bill respecting confirmation of a plan under chapter 9. It must be emphasized that these standards of confirmation are in addition to standards in section 1129 that are made applicable to chapter 9 by section 901 of the House amendment. In particular, if the requirements of section 1129(a)(8) are not complied with, then the proponent may request application of section 1129(b). The court will then be required to confirm the plan if it complies with the "fair and equitable" test and is in the best interests of creditors. The best interests of creditors test does not mean liquidation value as under chapter XI of the Bankruptcy Act [former chapter 11 (section 701 et seq.) of former Title 11]. In making such a determination, it is expected that the court will be guided by standards set forth in *Kelley v. Everglades Drainage District*, 319 U.S. 415 (1943) [Fla.1943, 63 S.Ct. 1141, 87 L.Ed. 1485, rehearing denied 63 S.Ct. 1444, 320 U.S. 214, 87 L.Ed. 1851, motion denied 64 S.Ct. 783, 321 U.S. 754, 88 L.Ed. 1054] and *Fano v. Newport Heights Irrigation Dist.*, 114 F.2d 563 (9th Cir. 1940), as under present law, the bankruptcy court should make findings as detailed as possible to support a conclusion that this test has been met. However, it must be emphasized that unlike current law, the fair and equitable test under section 1129(b) will not apply if section 1129(a)(8) has been satisfied in addition to the other confirmation standards specified in section 943 and incorporated by reference in section 901 of the House amendment. To the extent that *American United Mutual Life Insurance Co. v. City of Avon Park*, 311 U.S. 138 (1940) [Fla.1940, 61 S.Ct. 157, 85 L.Ed. 91, 136 A.L.R. 860, rehearing denied 61 S.Ct. 395, 311 U.S. 730, 85 L.Ed. 475] and other cases are to the contrary, such cases are overruled to that extent.

References in Text

Section 103(e) of this title, referred to in subsec. (b), was redesignated subsec. (f) and a new subsec. (e) was added by Pub.L. 106–554, § 1(a)(5) [Title I, § 112(c)(5)(A)], Dec. 21, 2000, 114 Stat. 2763, 2763A–394.

Amendments

2005 Amendments. Subsec. (b)(5). Pub.L. 109–8, § 1502(a)(6), struck out "507(a)(1)" and inserted "507(a)(2)".

1988 Amendments. Subsec. (b)(5)–(7). Pub.L. 100–597, § 10(1)–(3), struck out "and" at the end of par. (5); added par. (6); and redesignated former par. (6) as (7).

1984 Amendments. Subsec. (b)(4). Pub.L. 98–353, § 497(1), struck out "to be taken" following "necessary".

Subsec. (b)(5). Pub.L. 98–353, § 497(2), substituted provisions requiring the plan to provide payment of cash in an amount equal to the allowed amount of a claim except to the extent that the holder of a particular claim has agreed to different treatment of such claim, for provisions which required the plan to provide for payment of property of a value equal to the allowed amount of such claim except to the extent that the holder of a particular claim has waived such payment on such claim.

Effective and Applicability Provisions

2005 Acts. Amendments by Pub.L. 109–8 effective, except as otherwise provided, 180 days after April 20, 2005, and inapplicable with respect to cases commenced under Title 11 before the effective date, see Pub.L. 109–8, § 1501, set out as a note under 11 U.S.C.A. § 101.

1988 Acts. Amendment by Pub.L. 100–597 effective Nov. 3, 1988, but not applicable to any case commenced under this title before that date, see section 12 of Pub.L. 100–597, set out as a note under section 101 of this title.

1984 Acts. Amendment by Pub.L. 98–353 effective with respect to cases filed 90 days after July 10, 1984, see section 552(a), formerly 553(a), of Pub.L. 98–353, set out as a note under section 101 of this title.

CROSS REFERENCES

Confirmation hearing in—
>   Chapter eleven cases, see 11 USCA § 1128.
>   Chapter thirteen cases, see 11 USCA § 1324.
>   Chapter twelve cases, see 11 USCA § 1224.

Confirmation of plan in—
>   Chapter eleven cases, see 11 USCA § 1129.
>   Chapter thirteen cases, see 11 USCA § 1325.
>   Chapter twelve cases, see 11 USCA § 1225.
>   Railroad reorganization cases, see 11 USCA § 1173.

Dismissal for denial of confirmation of plan, see 11 USCA § 930.

Unclaimed property, see 11 USCA § 347.

LIBRARY REFERENCES

American Digest System

Bankruptcy ☞3481.

Key Number System Topic No. 51.

Corpus Juris Secundum

CJS Bankruptcy § 1099, Unclaimed Property.

CJS Bankruptcy § 1121, Requirements for Confirmation.

CJS Bankruptcy § 1122, Objections to Confirmation.

§ 944.   Effect of confirmation

(a) The provisions of a confirmed plan bind the debtor and any creditor, whether or not—

(1) a proof of such creditor's claim is filed or deemed filed under section 501 of this title;

(2) such claim is allowed under section 502 of this title; or

(3) such creditor has accepted the plan.

(b) Except as provided in subsection (c) of this section, the debtor is discharged from all debts as of the time when—

(1) the plan is confirmed;

(2) the debtor deposits any consideration to be distributed under the plan with a disbursing agent appointed by the court; and

(3) the court has determined—

>   **(A)** that any security so deposited will constitute, after distribution, a valid legal obligation of the debtor; and

>   **(B)** that any provision made to pay or secure payment of such obligation is valid.

(c) The debtor is not discharged under subsection (b) of this section from any debt—

(1) excepted from discharge by the plan or order confirming the plan; or

(2) owed to an entity that, before confirmation of the plan, had neither notice nor actual knowledge of the case.

(Pub.L. 95–598, Nov. 6, 1978, 92 Stat. 2624.)

HISTORICAL AND STATUTORY NOTES

Revision Notes and Legislative Reports

1978 Acts. [Section 947] Subsection (a) [now section 944(a)] makes the provisions of a confirmed plan binding on the debtor and creditors. It is derived from section 95(a) of chapter 9 [section 415(a) of former Title 11].

Subsections (b) and (c) [now section 944(b) and (c)] provide for the discharge of a municipality. The discharge is essentially the same as that granted under section 95(b) of the Bankruptcy Act [section 415(b) of former Title 11]. Senate Report No. 95–989.

CROSS REFERENCES

Discharge in—
>   Chapter seven cases, see 11 USCA § 727.
>   Chapter thirteen cases, see 11 USCA § 1328.
>   Chapter twelve cases, see 11 USCA § 1228.

Effect of confirmation in—
>   Chapter eleven cases, see 11 USCA § 1141.
>   Chapter thirteen cases, see 11 USCA § 1327.
>   Chapter twelve cases, see 11 USCA § 1227.

Effect of discharge, see 11 USCA § 524.

Exceptions to discharge, see 11 USCA § 523.

LIBRARY REFERENCES

American Digest System

Bankruptcy ☞3481.

Key Number System Topic No. 51.

Corpus Juris Secundum

CJS Bankruptcy § 278, Parties Defendant; Sovereign Immunity.

CJS Bankruptcy § 1062, Effect of Discharge of Debts.

CJS Bankruptcy § 1124, Effect of Confirmation.

§ 945.   Continuing jurisdiction and closing of the case

(a) The court may retain jurisdiction over the case for such period of time as is necessary for the successful implementation of the plan.

(b) Except as provided in subsection (a) of this section, the court shall close the case when administration of the case has been completed.

(Pub.L. 95–598, Nov. 6, 1978, 92 Stat. 2625; Pub.L. 98–353, Title III, § 498, July 10, 1984, 98 Stat. 384.)

HISTORICAL AND STATUTORY NOTES

Revision Notes and Legislative Reports

1978 Acts. Section 948 [now this section] permits the court to retain jurisdiction over the case to ensure successful execution of the plan. The provision is the same as that found in section 96(e) of Chapter 9 of the present Act [former section 416(e) of former Title 11]. Senate Report No. 95–989.

1984 Acts. Statements by Legislative Leaders, see 1984 U.S.Code Cong. and Adm.News, p. 576.

Amendments

1984 Amendments. Subsec. (a). Pub.L. 98–353 substituted "implementation" for "execution".

Effective and Applicability Provisions

1984 Acts. Amendment by Pub.L. 98–353 effective with respect to cases filed 90 days after July 10, 1984, see section 552(a), formerly 553(a), of Pub.L. 98–353, set out as a note under section 101 of this title.

CROSS REFERENCES

Closing and reopening cases, see 11 USCA § 350.

LIBRARY REFERENCES

American Digest System

Bankruptcy ⟝3481.

Key Number System Topic No. 51.

Corpus Juris Secundum

CJS Bankruptcy § 1105, Closing.

CJS Bankruptcy § 1125, Continuing Jurisdiction; Closing of Case.

§ 946.   Effect of exchange of securities before the date of the filing of the petition

The exchange of a new security under the plan for a claim covered by the plan, whether such exchange occurred before or after the date of the filing of the petition, does not limit or impair the effectiveness of the plan or of any provision of this chapter. The amount and number specified in section 1126(c) of this title include the amount and number of claims formerly held by a creditor that has participated in any such exchange.

(Pub.L. 95–598, Nov. 6, 1978, 92 Stat. 2625.)

HISTORICAL AND STATUTORY NOTES

Revision Notes and Legislative Reports

1978 Acts. [Section 949] This section [now section 946], which follows section 97 of current law [section 417 of former Title 11], permits an exchange of a security before the case is filed to constitute an acceptance of the plan if the exchange was under a proposal that later becomes the plan. Section Report No. 95–989.

Legislative Statements

The House amendment deletes section 950 of the Senate amendment as unnecessary. The constitutionality of chapter 9 of the House amendment is beyond doubt.

LIBRARY REFERENCES

American Digest System

Bankruptcy ⟝3481.

Key Number System Topic No. 51.

Corpus Juris Secundum

CJS Bankruptcy § 1119, Acceptance of Rejection of Plan by Claim Holders.

CHAPTER 11—REORGANIZATION

SUBCHAPTER I—OFFICERS AND ADMINISTRATION

Sec.
1101. Definitions for this chapter.
1102. Creditors' and equity security holders' committees.
1103. Powers and duties of committees.
1104. Appointment of trustee or examiner.
1105. Termination of trustee's appointment.
1106. Duties of trustee and examiner.
1107. Rights, powers, and duties of debtor in possession.
1108. Authorization to operate business.
1109. Right to be heard.
1110. Aircraft equipment and vessels.
1111. Claims and interests.
1112. Conversion or dismissal.
1113. Rejection of collective bargaining agreements.
1114. Payment of insurance benefits to retired employees.
1115. Property of the estate.
1116. Duties of trustee or debtor in possession in small business cases.

SUBCHAPTER II—THE PLAN

1121. Who may file a plan.
1122. Classification of claims or interests.
1123. Contents of plan.
1124. Impairment of claims or interests.
1125. Postpetition disclosure and solicitation.
1126. Acceptance of plan.
1127. Modification of plan.
1128. Confirmation hearing.
1129. Confirmation of plan.

SUBCHAPTER III—POSTCONFIRMATION MATTERS

1141. Effect of confirmation.
1142. Implementation of plan.
1143. Distribution.
1144. Revocation of an order of confirmation.
1145. Exemption from securities laws.
1146. Special tax provisions.

SUBCHAPTER IV—RAILROAD REORGANIZATION

1161. Inapplicability of other sections.
1162. Definition.
1163. Appointment of trustee.
1164. Right to be heard.
1165. Protection of the public interest.
1166. Effect of subtitle IV of title 49 and of Federal, State, or local regulations.
1167. Collective bargaining agreements.
1168. Rolling stock equipment.
1169. Effect of rejection of lease of railroad line.
1170. Abandonment of railroad line.
1171. Priority claims.
1172. Contents of plan.
1173. Confirmation of plan.
1174. Liquidation.

HISTORICAL AND STATUTORY NOTES

Amendments

2005 Amendments. Pub.L. 109–8, Title III, § 321(a)(2), Apr. 20, 2005, 119 Stat. 95, added item 1115.

Pub.L. 109–8, Title IV, § 436(b), Apr. 20, 2005, 119 Stat. 113, added item 1116.

1988 Amendments. Pub.L. 100–334, § 2(c), June 16, 1988, 102 Stat. 613, added item 1114.

1984 Amendments. Pub.L. 98–353, Title III, § 514(b), July 10, 1984, 98 Stat. 387 substituted "Implementation" for "Execution" in item 1142.

Pub.L. 98–353, Title III, § 541(b), July 10, 1984, 98 Stat. 391 added item 1113.

1983 Amendments. Pub.L. 97–449, § 5(a)(1), Jan. 12, 1983, 96 Stat. 2442, substituted "subtitle IV of title 49" for "Interstate Commerce Act" in item 1166.

CROSS REFERENCES

Allowance of administrative expenses of substantial contributors to cases under this chapter, see 11 USCA § 503.

Applicability of income tax provisions to cases under this chapter, see 26 USCA § 1398.

Chapters one, three, and five of this title applicable in cases under this chapter except as provided in § 1161 of this title, see 11 USCA § 103.

Claims arising from rejection under chapter plans of executory contracts or unexpired leases, see 11 USCA § 502.

Commencement of involuntary cases, see 11 USCA § 303.

Conversion to this chapter from—

Chapter seven, see 11 USCA § 706.

Chapter thirteen, see 11 USCA § 1307.

Core proceedings, see 28 USCA § 157.

Distress termination of single-employer plans in cases under this chapter, see 29 USCA § 1341.

Duration of automatic stay, see 11 USCA § 362.

Duties of United States trustees, see 28 USCA § 586.

Employment of professional persons, see 11 USCA § 327.

Establishment, operation and termination of Bankruptcy Appellate Panel Service and undue delay or increased costs, see 28 USCA § 158.

Executory contracts and unexpired leases, see 11 USCA § 365.

Filing fees, see 28 USCA § 1930.

Jurisdiction of courts in termination proceedings of employer plans brought by Pension Benefit Guaranty Corporation same as jurisdiction of courts in cases under this chapter, see 29 USCA § 1342.

Limitation on compensation of trustee, see 11 USCA § 326.

Persons required to make returns of income under this chapter, see 26 USCA § 6012.

Persons who may be debtors under this chapter, see 11 USCA § 109.

Powers of Courts to set date to file disclosure, see 11 USCA § 105.

Property of estate in cases converted from Chapter 13, see 11 USCA § 1306.

Provisions concerning reorganization plan of investment companies not to affect or derogate from powers of courts with reference to reorganizations under this title, see 15 USCA § 80a–25.

Return of excessive attorney compensation if transferred property was to be paid by debtor under plan under this chapter, see 11 USCA § 329.

Rights and powers of debtor in Chapter twelve case not encompassing certain duties of trustee serving in case under this chapter, see 11 USCA § 1203.

Special tax provisions, see 11 USCA § 346.

Stay of action against Chapter thirteen codebtor in cases converted to this chapter, see 11 USCA § 1301.

Supplemental injunctions and notice and hearings, see 11 USCA § 524.

Treatment of debtor's estate in cases under this chapter as taxpayer for certain income tax purposes, see 26 USCA § 108.

Unclaimed property, see 11 USCA § 347.

Use, sale or lease of property under plan under this chapter, see 11 USCA § 363.

SUBCHAPTER I—OFFICERS AND ADMINISTRATION

CROSS REFERENCES

Subchapter applicable only in case under this chapter except as provided in § 901 of this title, see 11 USCA § 103.

§ 1101. Definitions for this chapter

In this chapter—

(1) "debtor in possession" means debtor except when a person that has qualified under section 322 of this title is serving as trustee in the case;

(2) "substantial consummation" means—

(A) transfer of all or substantially all of the property proposed by the plan to be transferred;

(B) assumption by the debtor or by the successor to the debtor under the plan of the business or of the management of all or substantially all of the property dealt with by the plan; and

(C) commencement of distribution under the plan.

(Pub.L. 95–598, Nov. 6, 1978, 92 Stat. 2626.)

HISTORICAL AND STATUTORY NOTES

Revision Notes and Legislative Reports

1978 Acts. This section contains definitions of three terms that are used in chapter 11. Paragraph (1) defines debtor in possession to mean the debtor, except when a trustee who has qualified is serving in the case.

Paragraph (2), derived from section 229a of current law [section 629(a) of former Title 11], defines substantial consummation. Substantial consummation of a plan occurs when transfer of all or substantially all of the property proposed by the plan to be transferred is actually transferred; when the debtor (or its successor) has assumed the business of the debtor or the management of all or substantially all of the

property dealt with by the plan; and when distribution under the plan has commenced.

Paragraph (3) defines for purposes of Chapter 11 a public company to mean "a debtor who, within 12 months prior to the filing of a petition for relief under this chapter, had outstanding liabilities of $5 million or more, exclusive of liabilities for goods, services, or taxes and not less than 1,000 security holders." There are, as noted, special safeguards for public investors related to the reorganization of a public company, as so defined.

Both requirements must be met: liabilities, excluding tax obligations and trade liabilities, must be $5 million or more; and (2) the number of holders of securities, debt or equity, or both, must be not less than 1,000. The amount and number are to be determined as of any time within 12 months prior to the filing of the petition for reorganization. Senate Report No. 95–989.

CROSS REFERENCES

Definitions applicable in—

Cases under this title, see 11 USCA § 101.

Chapter nine cases, see 11 USCA § 902.

Commodity broker liquidation cases, see 11 USCA § 761.

Railroad reorganization cases, see 11 USCA § 1162.

Stockbroker liquidation cases, see 11 USCA § 741.

LIBRARY REFERENCES

American Digest System

Bankruptcy ⟨⊃3501, 3569.

Key Number System Topic No. 51.

Corpus Juris Secundum

CJS Bankruptcy § 7, Bankruptcy Code.

CJS Bankruptcy § 130, Debtor in Possession as Same Entity as or Separate Entity from Debtor.

CJS Bankruptcy § 131, Debtor as Debtor in Possession.

CJS Bankruptcy § 135, Replacement of Debtor in Possession by Trustee; Restoration of Debtor to Possession.

CJS Bankruptcy § 624, Surrender of Property of Estate and Recorded Information to Trustee.

CJS Bankruptcy § 1131, Debtor-In-Possession.

CJS Bankruptcy § 1163, Modification of the Plan.

CJS Bankruptcy § 1271, Equitable Mootness.

§ 1102. Creditors' and equity security holders' committees

(a)(1) Except as provided in paragraph (3), as soon as practicable after the order for relief under chapter 11 of this title, the United States trustee shall appoint a committee of creditors holding unsecured claims and may appoint additional committees of creditors or of equity security holders as the United States trustee deems appropriate.

(2) On request of a party in interest, the court may order the appointment of additional committees of creditors or of equity security holders if necessary to assure adequate representation of creditors or of equity security holders. The United States trustee shall appoint any such committee.

(3) On request of a party in interest in a case in which the debtor is a small business debtor and for cause, the court may order that a committee of creditors not be appointed.

(4) On request of a party in interest and after notice and a hearing, the court may order the United States trustee to change the membership of a committee appointed under this subsection, if the court determines that the change is necessary to ensure adequate representation of creditors or equity security holders. The court may order the United States trustee to increase the number of members of a committee to include a creditor that is a small business concern (as described in section 3(a)(1) of the Small Business Act), if the court determines that the creditor holds claims (of the kind represented by the committee) the aggregate amount of which, in comparison to the annual gross revenue of that creditor, is disproportionately large.

(b)(1) A committee of creditors appointed under subsection (a) of this section shall ordinarily consist of the persons, willing to serve, that hold the seven largest claims against the debtor of the kinds represented on such committee, or of the members of a committee organized by creditors before the commencement of the case under this chapter, if such committee was fairly chosen and is representative of the different kinds of claims to be represented.

(2) A committee of equity security holders appointed under subsection (a)(2) of this section shall ordinarily consist of the persons, willing to serve, that hold the seven largest amounts of equity securities of the debtor of the kinds represented on such committee.

(3) A committee appointed under subsection (a) shall—

    (A) provide access to information for creditors who—

        (i) hold claims of the kind represented by that committee; and

        (ii) are not appointed to the committee;

    (B) solicit and receive comments from the creditors described in subparagraph (A); and

    (C) be subject to a court order that compels any additional report or disclosure to be made to the creditors described in subparagraph (A).

(Pub.L. 95–598, Nov. 6, 1978, 92 Stat. 2626; Pub.L. 98–353, Title III, § 499, July 10, 1984, 98 Stat. 384; Pub.L. 99–554, Title II, § 221, Oct. 27, 1986, 100 Stat. 3101; Pub.L. 103–394, Title II, § 217(b), Oct. 22, 1994, 108 Stat. 4127; Pub.L. 109–8, Title IV, §§ 405, 432(b), Apr. 20, 2005, 119 Stat. 105, 110.)

HISTORICAL AND STATUTORY NOTES

Revision Notes and Legislative Reports

1978 Acts. This section provides for the election and appointment of committees. Subsection (c) provides that this section does not apply in case of a public company, as to which a trustee, appointed under section 1104(a) will have

responsibility to administer the estate and to formulate a plan as provided in section 1106(a).

There is no need for the election or appointment of committees for which the appointment of a trustee is mandatory. In the case of a public company there are likely to be several committees, each representing a different class of security holders and seeking authority to retain accountants, lawyers, and other experts, who will expect to be paid. If in the case of a public company creditors or stockholders wish to organize committees, they may do so, as authorized under section 1109(a). Compensation and reimbursement will be allowed for contributions to the reorganization pursuant to section 503(b)(3) and (4). Senate Report No. 95–989.

This section provides for the appointment of creditors' and equity security holders' committees, which will be the primary negotiating bodies for the formulation of the plan of reorganization. They will represent the various classes of creditors and equity security holders from which they are selected. They will also provide supervision of the debtor in possession and of the trustee, and will protect their constituents' interests.

Subsection (a) requires the court to appoint at least one committee. That committee is to be composed of creditors holding unsecured claims. The court is authorized to appoint such additional committees as are necessary to assure adequate representation of creditors and equity security holders. The provision will be relied upon in cases in which the debtor proposes to affect several classes of debt or equity holders under the plan, and in which they need representation.

Subsection (b) contains precatory language directing the court to appoint the persons holding the seven largest claims against the debtor of the kinds represented on a creditors' committee, or the members of a prepetition committee organized by creditors before the order for relief under chapter 11. The court may continue prepetition committee members only if the committee was fairly chosen and is representative of the different kinds of claims to be represented. The court is restricted to the appointment of persons in order to exclude governmental holders of claims or interests.

Paragraph (2) of subsection (b) requires similar treatment for equity security holders' committees. The seven largest holders are normally to be appointed, but the language is only precatory.

Subsection (c) authorizes the court, on request of a party in interest, to change the size or the membership of a creditors' or equity security holders' committee if the membership of the committee is not representative of the different kinds of claims or interests to be represented. This subsection is intended, along with the nonbinding nature of subsection (b), to afford the court latitude in appointing a committee that is manageable and representative in light of the circumstances of the case. House Report No. 95–595.

1984 Acts. Statements by Legislative Leaders, see 1984 U.S.Code Cong. and Adm.News, p. 576.

1986 Acts. House Report No. 99–764 and House Conference Report No. 99–958, see 1986 U.S.Code Cong. and Adm. News, p. 5227.

1994 Acts. House Report No. 103–835, see 1994 U.S. Code Cong. and Adm. News, p. 3340.

2005 Acts. House Report No. 109–31(Part I), see 2005 U.S. Code Cong. and Adm. News, p. 88.

Legislative Statements

Section 1102(a) of the House amendment adopts a compromise between the House bill and Senate amendment requiring appointment of a committee of creditors holding unsecured claims by the court; the alternative of creditor committee election is rejected.

Section 1102(b) of the House amendment represents a compromise between the House bill and the Senate amendment by preventing the appointment of creditors who are unwilling to serve on a creditors committee.

References in Text

Section 3(a)(1) of the Small Business Act, referred to in subsec. (a)(4), is section 3(a)(1) of Pub.L. 85–536 § 2[3], July 18, 1958, 72 Stat. 384, as amended, which is classified to 15 U.S.C.A. § 632(a)(1). For complete classification, see Short Title note under 15 U.S.C.A. § 631 and Tables.

Amendments

2005 Amendments. Subsec. (a)(3). Pub.L. 109–8, § 432(b), inserted "debtor" after "small business".

Subsec. (a)(4). Pub.L. 109–8, § 405(a), added par. (4).

Subsec. (b)(3). Pub.L. 109–8, § 405(b), added par. (3).

1994 Amendments. Subsec. (a)(1). Pub.L. 103–394, § 217(b)(1), inserted reference to par. (3).

Subsec. (a)(3). Pub.L. 103–394, § 217(b)(2), added par. (3).

1986 Amendments. Subsec. (a)(1). Pub.L. 99–554, § 221(1), substituted "under chapter 11 of this title, the United States trustee shall appoint" for "under this chapter, the court shall appoint" and added "and may appoint additional committees of creditors or of equity security holders as the United States trustee deems appropriate" following "unsecured claims".

Subsec. (a)(2). Pub.L. 99–554, § 221(1), substituted "The United States trustee shall appoint" for "The court shall appoint".

Subsec. (c). Pub.L. 99–554, § 221(2), struck out subsec. (c) which read as follows: "On request of a party in interest and after notice and a hearing, the court may change the membership or the size of a committee appointed under subsection (a) of this section if the membership of such committee is not representative of the different kinds of claims or interests to be represented.".

1984 Amendments. Subsec. (b)(1). Pub.L. 98–353 substituted "commencement of the case" for "order for relief".

Effective and Applicability Provisions

2005 Acts. Amendments by Pub.L. 109–8 effective, except as otherwise provided, 180 days after April 20, 2005, and inapplicable with respect to cases commenced under Title 11 before the effective date, see Pub.L. 109–8, § 1501, set out as a note under 11 U.S.C.A. § 101.

1994 Acts. Amendment by Pub.L. 103–394 effective on Oct. 22, 1994, and not to apply with respect to cases commenced under Title 11 of the United States Code before Oct. 22, 1994, see section 702 of Pub.L. 103–394, set out as a note under section 101 of this title.

1986 Acts. Amendment by Pub.L. 99–554 effective 30 days after Oct. 27, 1986, except as otherwise provided for, see section 302(a) of Pub.L. 99–554, set out as a note under section 581 of Title 28, Judiciary and Judicial Procedure.

Amendment by Pub.L. 99–554, § 221, not to become effective in or with respect to certain specified judicial districts until, or apply to cases while pending in such district before, the expiration of the 270–day period beginning 30 days after Oct. 27, 1986, or of the 30–day period beginning on the date the Attorney General certifies under section 303 of Pub.L. 99–554 the region specified in a paragraph of section 581(a) of Title 28, as amended by section 111(a) of Pub.L. 99–554, that includes such district, whichever occurs first, see section 302(d)(1) of Pub.L. 99–554, set out as a note under section 581 of Title 28.

Amendment by Pub.L. 99–554, § 221, not to become effective in or with respect to certain specified judicial districts until, or apply to cases while pending in such district before, the expiration of the 2–year period beginning 30 days after Oct. 27, 1986, or of the 30–day period beginning on the date the Attorney General certifies under section 303 of Pub.L. 99–554 the region specified in a paragraph of section 581(a) of Title 28, as amended by section 111(a) of Pub.L. 99–554, that includes such district, whichever occurs first, see section 302(d)(2) of Pub.L. 99–554, set out as a note under section 581 of Title 28.

Amendment by Pub.L. 99–554, § 221, not to become effective in or with respect to judicial districts established for the States of Alabama and North Carolina until, or apply to cases while pending in such district before, such district elects to be included in a bankruptcy region established in section 581(a) of Title 28, as amended by section 111(a) of Pub.L. 99–554, or Oct. 1, 2002, whichever occurs first, and, except as otherwise provided for, with respect to cases under chapters 7, 11, 12, and 13 of Title 11 commenced before 30 days after Oct. 27, 1986, and pending in a judicial district in the States of Alabama or North Carolina before any election made under section 302(d)(3)(A) of Pub.L. 99–554 by such district becomes effective or Oct. 1, 2002, whichever occurs first, amendments by Pub.L. 99–554 not to apply until Oct. 1, 2003, or the expiration of the 1–year period beginning on the date such election becomes effective, whichever occurs first, and further, in any judicial district in Alabama or North Carolina not making the election described in section 302(d)(3)(A) of Pub.L. 99–554, any person appointed under regulations issued by the Judicial Conference to administer estates in cases under Title 11 authorized to establish, etc., a panel of private trustees, and to supervise cases and trustees in cases under chapters 7, 11, 12 and 13 of Title 11, until amendments by sections 201 to 231 of Pub.L. 99–554 effective in such district, see section 302(d)(3)(A) to (F), (H), (I), of Pub.L. 99–554, set out as a note under section 581 of Title 28.

Amendment by Pub.L. 99–554, § 221, except as otherwise provided, with respect to cases under chapters 7, 11, 12 and 13 of Title 11 commenced before 30 days after Oct. 27, 1986, and pending in a judicial district referred to in section 581(a) of Title 28, as amended by section 111(a) of Pub.L. 99–554, for which a United States trustee is not authorized before 30 days after Oct. 27, 1986 to be appointed, not applicable until the expiration of the 3–year period beginning on Oct. 27, 1986, or of the 1–year period beginning on the date the Attorney General certifies under section 303 of Pub.L. 99–554 the region specified in a paragraph of such section 581(a) that includes, such district, whichever occurs first, see section 302(e)(1), (2) of Pub.L. 99–554, set out as a note under section 581 of Title 28.

1984 Acts. Amendment by Pub.L. 98–353 effective with respect to cases filed 90 days after July 10, 1984, see section 552(a), formerly 553(a), of Pub.L. 98–353, set out as a note under section 101 of this title.

If any provision of or amendment made by Pub.L. 103–394 or the application of such provision or amendment to any person or circumstance is held to be unconstitutional, the remaining provisions of and amendments made by Pub.L. 103–394 and the application of such provisions and amendments to any person or circumstance shall not be affected thereby, see section 701 of Pub.L. 103–394, set out as a note under section 101 of this title.

CROSS REFERENCES

Allowance of creditor committee expenses, see 11 USCA § 503.

Applicability of this section in Chapter nine cases, see 11 USCA § 901.

Creditors' committees in Chapter seven cases, see 11 USCA § 705.

Disallowance of administrative expenses for creditors' and equity security holders' committees, see 11 USCA § 503.

Effect of conversion, see 11 USCA § 348.

Inapplicability of subsec. (a)(1) of this section to railroad reorganization cases, see 11 USCA § 1161.

Limitation on compensation of professional persons, see 11 USCA § 328.

"Person" defined for purposes of this section, see 11 USCA § 101.

LIBRARY REFERENCES

American Digest System

Bankruptcy ⚬3024.

Key Number System Topic No. 51.

Corpus Juris Secundum

CJS Bankruptcy § 51, Chapter 11 Proceedings.

CJS Bankruptcy § 82, Meeting of Creditors and Election Procedures.

CJS Bankruptcy § 522, Parties; Standing.

CJS Bankruptcy § 764, Consumer Privacy and Patient Care Ombudsmen.

CJS Bankruptcy § 809, Voting and Elections.

CJS Bankruptcy § 840, Operation of Debtor's Business.

CJS Bankruptcy § 856, Motion and Notice.

CJS Bankruptcy § 857, Approval of Agreement.

CJS Bankruptcy § 870, Agreement or Stipulation for Use of Cash Collateral.

CJS Bankruptcy § 901, Motion for Authorization to Obtain Credit; Approval of Agreement.

CJS Bankruptcy § 1129, Appointment of Creditors'' and Equity Security Holders'' Committees.

CJS Bankruptcy § 1130, Powers and Duties of Committee.

§ 1103. Powers and duties of committees

(a) At a scheduled meeting of a committee appointed under section 1102 of this title, at which a majority of the members of such committee are present, and with the court's approval, such committee may select and authorize the employment by such committee of one or more attorneys, accountants, or other agents, to represent or perform services for such committee.

(b) An attorney or accountant employed to represent a committee appointed under section 1102 of this title may not, while employed by such committee, represent any other entity having an adverse interest in connection with the case. Representation of one or more creditors of the same class as represented by the committee shall not per se constitute the representation of an adverse interest.

(c) A committee appointed under section 1102 of this title may—

(1) consult with the trustee or debtor in possession concerning the administration of the case;

(2) investigate the acts, conduct, assets, liabilities, and financial condition of the debtor, the operation of the debtor's business and the desirability of the continuance of such business, and any other matter relevant to the case or to the formulation of a plan;

(3) participate in the formulation of a plan, advise those represented by such committee of such committee's determinations as to any plan formulated, and collect and file with the court acceptances or rejections of a plan;

(4) request the appointment of a trustee or examiner under section 1104 of this title; and

(5) perform such other services as are in the interest of those represented.

(d) As soon as practicable after the appointment of a committee under section 1102 of this title, the trustee shall meet with such committee to transact such business as may be necessary and proper.
(Pub.L. 95–598, Nov. 6, 1978, 92 Stat. 2627; Pub.L. 98–353, Title III, §§ 324, 500, July 10, 1984, 98 Stat. 358, 384.)

HISTORICAL AND STATUTORY NOTES

Revision Notes and Legislative Reports

1978 Acts. This section defines the powers and duties of a committee elected or appointed under section 1102.

Under subsection (a) the committee may, if authorized by the court, employ one or more attorneys, accountants, or other agents to represent or perform services for the committee. Normally one attorney should suffice; more than one may be authorized for good cause. The same considerations apply to the services of others, if the need for any at all is demonstrated.

Under subsections (c) and (d) the committee, like any party in interest, may confer with the trustee or debtor regarding the administration of the estate; may advise the court on the need for a trustee under section 1104(b). The committee may investigate matters specified in paragraph (2) of subsection (c), but only if authorized by the court and if no trustee or examiner is appointed. Senate Report No. 95–989.

Subsection (a) of this section authorizes a committee appointed under section 1102 to select and authorize the employment of counsel, accountants, or other agents, to represent or perform services for the committee. The committee's selection and authorization is subject to the court's approval, and may only be done at a meeting of the committee at which a majority of its members are present. The subsection provides for the employment of more than one attorney. However, this will be the exception, and not the rule; cause must be shown to depart from the normal standard.

Subsection (b) requires a committee's counsel to cease representation of any other entity in connection with the case after he begins to represent the committee. This will prevent the potential of severe conflicts of interest.

Subsection (c) lists a committee's functions in a chapter 11 case. The committee may consult with the trustee or debtor in possession concerning the administration of the case, may investigate the acts, conduct, assets, liabilities and financial condition of the debtor, the operation of the debtor's business, and the desirability of the continuance of the business, and any other matter relevant to the case or to the formulation of a plan. The committee may participate in the formulation of a plan, advise those it represents of the committee's recommendation with respect to any plan formulated, and collect and file acceptances. These will be its most important functions. The committee may also determine the need for the appointment of a trustee, if one has not previously been appointed, and perform such other services as are in the interest of those represented.

Subsection (d) requires the trustee and each committee to meet as soon as practicable after their appointments to transact such business as may be necessary and proper. House Report No. 95–595.

1984 Acts. Statements by Legislative Leaders, see 1984 U.S.Code Cong. and Adm.News, p. 576.

Amendments

1984 Amendments. Subsec. (b). Pub.L. 98–353, § 324, substituted "An attorney or accountant" for "A person".

Pub.L. 98–353, § 500(a)(1), substituted "entity having an adverse interest" for "entity".

Pub.L. 98–353, § 500(a)(2), added provision that representation of one or more creditors of the same class as represented by the committee shall not per se constitute the representation of an adverse interest.

Subsec. (c)(3). Pub.L. 98–353, § 500(b)(1)(A), substituted "determinations" for "recommendations".

Pub.L. 98–353, § 500(b)(1)(B), substituted "acceptances or rejections" for "acceptances".

Subsec. (c)(4). Pub.L. 98–353, § 500(b)(2), struck out ", if a trustee or examiner, as the case may be, has not previously been appointed under this chapter in the case" following "section 1104 of this title".

Effective and Applicability Provisions

1984 Acts. Amendment by Pub.L. 98–353 effective with respect to cases filed 90 days after July 10, 1984, see section 552(a), formerly 553(a), of Pub.L. 98–353, set out as a note under section 101 of this title.

CROSS REFERENCES

Applicability of this section in Chapter nine cases, see 11 USCA § 901.

Compensation of officers, see 11 USCA § 330.

Creditors' committees in Chapter seven cases, see 11 USCA § 705.

Interim compensation for professional persons, see 11 USCA § 331.

Limitation on compensation of professional persons, see 11 USCA § 328.

LIBRARY REFERENCES

American Digest System

Attorney and Client ⟐21.5(6).

Bankruptcy ⟐3024.

Key Number System Topic Nos. 45, 51.

Corpus Juris Secundum

CJS Bankruptcy § 101, Chapter 11.

CJS Bankruptcy § 761, Relationship Between Employment and Compensation Provisions.

CJS Bankruptcy § 773, Status of Claims for Compensation and Reimbursement.

CJS Bankruptcy § 840, Operation of Debtor's Business.

CJS Bankruptcy § 1130, Powers and Duties of Committee.

§ 1104. Appointment of trustee or examiner

(a) At any time after the commencement of the case but before confirmation of a plan, on request of a party in interest or the United States trustee, and after notice and a hearing, the court shall order the appointment of a trustee—

(1) for cause, including fraud, dishonesty, incompetence, or gross mismanagement of the affairs of the debtor by current management, either before or after the commencement of the case, or similar cause, but not including the number of holders of securities of the debtor or the amount of assets or liabilities of the debtor; or

(2) if such appointment is in the interests of creditors, any equity security holders, and other interests of the estate, without regard to the number of holders of securities of the debtor or the amount of assets or liabilities of the debtor.

[**(3)** Repealed. Pub.L. 111–327, § 2(a)(30)(A)(iii), Dec. 22, 2010, 124 Stat. 3560]

(b)(1) Except as provided in section 1163 of this title, on the request of a party in interest made not later than 30 days after the court orders the appointment of a trustee under subsection (a), the United States trustee shall convene a meeting of creditors for the purpose of electing one disinterested person to serve as trustee in the case. The election of a trustee shall be conducted in the manner provided in subsections (a), (b), and (c) of section 702 of this title.

(2)(A) If an eligible, disinterested trustee is elected at a meeting of creditors under paragraph (1), the United States trustee shall file a report certifying that election.

(B) Upon the filing of a report under subparagraph (A)—

(i) the trustee elected under paragraph (1) shall be considered to have been selected and appointed for purposes of this section; and

(ii) the service of any trustee appointed under subsection (a) shall terminate.

(C) The court shall resolve any dispute arising out of an election described in subparagraph (A).

(c) If the court does not order the appointment of a trustee under this section, then at any time before the confirmation of a plan, on request of a party in interest or the United States trustee, and after notice and a hearing, the court shall order the appointment of an examiner to conduct such an investigation of the debtor as is appropriate, including an investigation of any allegations of fraud, dishonesty, incompetence, misconduct, mismanagement, or irregularity in the management of the affairs of the debtor of or by current or former management of the debtor, if—

(1) such appointment is in the interests of creditors, any equity security holders, and other interests of the estate; or

(2) the debtor's fixed, liquidated, unsecured debts, other than debts for goods, services, or taxes, or owing to an insider, exceed $5,000,000.

(d) If the court orders the appointment of a trustee or an examiner, if a trustee or an examiner dies or resigns during the case or is removed under section 324 of this title, or if a trustee fails to qualify under section 322 of this title, then the United States trustee, after consultation with parties in interest, shall appoint, subject to the court's approval, one disinterested person other than the United States trustee to serve as trustee or examiner, as the case may be, in the case.

(e) The United States trustee shall move for the appointment of a trustee under subsection (a) if there are reasonable grounds to suspect that current members of the governing body of the debtor, the debtor's chief executive or chief financial officer, or members of the governing body who selected the debtor's chief executive or chief financial officer, participated in actual fraud, dishonesty, or criminal conduct in the management of the debtor or the debtor's public financial reporting.

(Pub.L. 95–598, Nov. 6, 1978, 92 Stat. 2627; Pub.L. 99–554, Title II, § 222, Oct. 27, 1986, 100 Stat. 3102; Pub.L. 103–394, Title II, § 211(a), Title V, § 501(d)(30), Oct. 22, 1994, 108 Stat. 4125, 4146; Pub.L. 109–8, Title IV, §§ 416, 442(b), Title XIV, § 1405, Apr. 20, 2005, 119 Stat. 107, 116, 215; Pub.L. 111–327, § 2(a)(30), Dec. 22, 2010, 124 Stat. 3560.)

HISTORICAL AND STATUTORY NOTES

Revision Notes and Legislative Reports

1978 Acts. Subsection (a) provides for the mandatory appointment of a disinterested trustee in the case of a public company, as defined in section 1101(3), within 10 days of the order for relief, or of a successor, in the event of a vacancy, as soon as practicable.

Section 156 of chapter X [section 516 (556) of former Title 11] requires the appointment of a disinterested trustee if the debtor's liabilities are $250,000 or over. Section 1104(a) marks a substantial change. The appointment of a trustee is

mandatory only for a public company, which under section 1101(3), has $5 million in liabilities, excluding tax and trade obligations, and 1,000 security holders. In view of past experience, cases involving public companies will under normal circumstances probably be relatively few in number but of vast importance in terms of public investor interest.

In case of a nonpublic company, the appointment or election of a trustee is discretionary if the interests of the estate and its security holders would be served thereby. A test based on probable costs and benefits of a trusteeship is not practical. The appointment may be made at any time prior to confirmation of the plan.

In case of a nonpublic company, if no trustee is appointed, the court may under subsection (c) appoint an examiner, if the appointment would serve the interests of the estate and security holders. The purpose of his appointment is specified in section 1106(b). Senate Report No. 95–989.

Subsection (a) of this section governs the appointment of trustees in reorganization cases. The court is permitted to order the appointment of one trustee at any time after the commencement of the case if a party in interest so requests. The court may order appointment only if the protection afforded by a trustee is needed and the costs and expenses of a trustee would not be disproportionately higher than the value of the protection afforded.

The protection afforded by a trustee would be needed, for example, in cases where the current management of the debtor has been fraudulent or dishonest, or has grossly mismanaged the company, or where the debtor's management has abandoned the business. A trustee would not necessarily be needed to investigate misconduct of former management of the debtor, because an examiner appointed under this section might well be able to serve that function adequately without displacing the current management. Generally, a trustee would not be needed in any case where the protection afforded by a trustee could equally be afforded by an examiner. Though the device of examiner appears in current chapter X [chapter 10 (section 501 et seq.) of former Title 11], it is rarely used because of the nearly absolute presumption in favor of the appointment of a trustee. Its use here will give the courts, debtors, creditors, and equity security holders greater flexibility in handling the affairs of an insolvent debtor, permitting the court to tailor the remedy to the case.

The second test, relating to the costs and expenses of a trustee, is not intended to be a strict cost/benefit analysis. It is included to require the court to have due regard for any additional costs or expenses that the appointment of a trustee would impose on the estate.

Subsection (b) permits the court, at any time after the commencement of the case and on request of a party in interest, to order the appointment of an examiner, if the court has not ordered the appointment of a trustee. The examiner would be appointed to conduct such an investigation of the debtor as is appropriate under the particular circumstances of the case, including an investigation of any allegations of fraud, dishonesty, or gross mismanagement of the debtor of or by current or former management of the debtor. The standards for the appointment of an examiner are the same as those for the appointment of a trustee: the protection must be needed, and the costs and expenses must not be disproportionately high.

By virtue of proposed 11 U.S.C. 1109, an indenture trustee and the Securities and Exchange Commission will be parties in interest for the purpose of requesting the appointment of a trustee or examiner.

Subsection (c) directs that the United States trustee actually select and appoint the trustee or examiner ordered appointed under this section. The United States trustee is required to consult with various parties in interest before selecting and appointing a trustee. He is not bound to select one of the members of the panel of private trustees established under proposed 28 U.S.C. 586(a)(1) which exists only for the purpose of providing trustees for chapter 7 cases. Neither is he precluded from selecting a panel member if the member is qualified to serve as chapter 11 trustee. Appointment by the United States trustee will remove the court from the often criticized practice of appointing an officer that will appear in litigation before the court against an adverse party. House Report No. 95–595.

1986 Acts. House Report No. 99–764 and House Conference Report No. 99–958, see 1986 U.S.Code Cong. and Adm. News, p. 5227.

1994 Acts. House Report No. 103–835, see 1994 U.S. Code Cong. and Adm. News, p. 3340.

2005 Acts. House Report No. 109–31(Part I), see 2005 U.S. Code Cong. and Adm. News, p. 88.

Legislative Statements

Section 1104 of the House amendment represents a compromise between the House bill and the Senate amendment concerning the appointment of a trustee or examiner. The method of appointment rather than election, is derived from the House bill; the two alternative standards of appointment are derived with modifications from the Senate amendment, instead of the standard stated in the House bill. For example, if the current management of the debtor gambled away rental income before the filing of the petition, a trustee should be appointed after the petition, whether or not postpetition mismanagement can be shown. However, under no circumstances will cause include the number of security holders of the debtor or the amount of assets or liabilities of the debtor. The standard also applies to the appointment of an examiner in those circumstances in which mandatory appointment, as previously detailed, is not required.

Amendments

2010 Amendments. Subsec. (a)(1). Pub.L. 111–327, § 2(a)(30)(A)(i), inserted "or" following the semicolon at the end.

Subsec. (a)(2). Pub.L. 111–327, § 2(a)(30)(A)(ii), struck out "; or" at the end and inserted a period.

Subsec. (a)(3). Pub.L. 111–327, § 2(a)(30)(A)(iii), struck out par. (3), which formerly read: "**(3)** if grounds exist to convert or dismiss the case under section 1112, but the court determines that the appointment of a trustee or an examiner is in the best interests of creditors and the estate."

Subsec. (b)(2)(B)(ii). Pub.L. 111–327, § 2(a)(30)(B), struck out "subsection (d)" and inserted "subsection (a)".

2005 Amendments. Subsec. (a)(1). Pub.L. 109–8, § 442(b)(1), struck "or" at the end of par. (1).

Subsec. (a)(2). Pub.L. 109–8, § 442(b)(2), struck the period at the end of par. (2) and inserted "; "or".

Subsec. (a)(3). Pub.L. 109–8, § 442(b)(3), added par. (3).

Subsec. (b), (b)(1). Pub.L. 109–8, § 416(1), inserted "**(1)**" after "**(b)**".

Subsec. (b)(2). Pub.L. 109–8, § 416(2), added par. (2).

Subsec. (e). Pub.L. 109–8, § 1405, added subsec. (e).

1994 Amendments. Subsec. (b). Pub.L. 103–394, § 211(a), added subsec. (b) and redesignated former subsec. (b) as (c).

Subsec. (c). Pub.L. 103–394, § 211(a)(1), redesignated former subsec. (b) as (c) and former subsec. (c) as (d).

Subsec. (d). Pub.L. 103–394, § 211(a)(1), redesignated former subsec. (c) as (d).

Pub.L. 103–394, § 501(d)(30), substituted "parties in interest," for "parties in interest".

1986 Amendments. Subsec. (a). Pub.L. 99–554, § 222(1), added "or the United States trustee" following "party in interest".

Subsec. (b). Pub.L. 99–554, § 222(2), added "or the United States trustee" following "party in interest".

Subsec. (c). Pub.L. 99–554, § 222(3), substituted "the United States trustee after consultation with parties in interest shall appoint, subject to the court's approval, one disinterested person other than the United States trustee to serve" for "the court shall appoint one disinterested person to serve".

Effective and Applicability Provisions

2005 Acts. Amendments by Pub.L. 109–8, Title XIV, effective, except as otherwise provided, on Apr. 20, 2005, and applicable only with respect to cases commenced under Title 11 on or after Apr. 20, 2005, see Pub.L. 109–8, § 1406, set out as a note under 11 U.S.C.A. § 507.

Amendments by Pub.L. 109–8 effective, except as otherwise provided, 180 days after April 20, 2005, and inapplicable with respect to cases commenced under Title 11 before the effective date, see Pub.L. 109–8, § 1501, set out as a note under 11 U.S.C.A. § 101.

1994 Acts. Amendments by Pub.L. 103–394 effective on Oct. 22, 1994, and not to apply with respect to cases commenced under Title 11 of the United States Code before Oct. 22, 1994, see section 702 of Pub.L. 103–394, set out as a note under section 101 of this title.

1986 Acts. Amendment by Pub.L. 99–554 effective 30 days after Oct. 27, 1986, except as otherwise provided for, see section 302(a) of Pub.L. 99–554, set out as a note under section 581 of Title 28, Judiciary and Judicial Procedure.

Amendment by Pub.L. 99–554, § 222, not to become effective in or with respect to certain specified judicial districts until, or apply to cases while pending in such district before, the expiration of the 270–day period beginning 30 days after Oct. 27, 1986, or of the 30–day period beginning on the date the Attorney General certifies under section 303 of Pub.L. 99–554 the region specified in a paragraph of section 581(a) of Title 28, as amended by section 111(a) of Pub.L. 99–554, that includes such district, whichever occurs first, see section 302(d)(1) of Pub.L. 99–554, set out as a note under section 581 of Title 28.

Amendment by Pub.L. 99–554, § 222, not to become effective in or with respect to certain specified judicial districts until, or apply to cases while pending in such district before, the expiration of the 2–year period beginning 30 days after Oct. 27, 1986, or of the 30–day period beginning on the date the Attorney General certifies under section 303 of Pub.L. 99–554 the region specified in a paragraph of section 581(a) of Title 28, as amended by section 111(a) of Pub.L. 99–554, that includes such district, whichever occurs first, see section 302(d)(2) of Pub.L. 99–554, set out as a note under section 581 of Title 28.

Amendment by Pub.L. 99–554, § 222, not to become effective in or with respect to judicial districts established for the States of Alabama and North Carolina until, or apply to cases while pending in such district before, such district elects to be included in a bankruptcy region established in section 581(a) of Title 28, as amended by section 111(a) of Pub.L. 99–554, or Oct. 1, 2002, whichever occurs first, and, except as otherwise provided for, with respect to cases under chapters 7, 11, 12, and 13 of Title 11 commenced before 30 days after Oct. 27, 1986, and pending in a judicial district in the States of Alabama or North Carolina before any election made under section 302(d)(3)(A) of Pub.L. 99–554 by such district becomes effective or Oct. 1, 2992, whichever occurs first, amendments by Pub.L. 99–554 not to apply until Oct. 1, 2003, or the expiration of the 1–year period beginning on the date such election becomes effective, whichever occurs first, and further, in any judicial district in Alabama or North Carolina not making the election described in section 302(d)(3)(A) of Pub.L. 99–554, any person appointed under regulations issued by the Judicial Conference to administer estates in cases under Title 11 authorized to establish, etc., a panel of private trustees, and to supervise cases and trustees in cases under chapters 7, 11, 12, and 13 of Title 11, until amendments by sections 201 to 231 of Pub.L. 99–554 effective in such district, see section 302(d)(3)(A) to (F), (H), (I), of Pub.L. 99–554, set out as a note under section 581 of Title 28.

Amendment by Pub.L. 99–554, § 222, except as otherwise provided, with respect to cases under chapters 7, 11, 12, and 13 of Title 11 commenced before 30 days after Oct. 27, 1986, and pending in a judicial district referred to in section 581(a) of Title 28, as amended by section 111(a) of Pub.L. 99–554, for which a United States trustee is not authorized before 30 days after Oct. 27, 1986 to be appointed, not applicable until the expiration of the 3–year period beginning on Oct. 27, 1986, or of the 1–year period beginning on the date the Attorney General certifies under section 303 of Pub.L. 99–554 the region specified in a paragraph of such section 581(a) that includes, such district, whichever occurs first, see section 302(e)(1), (2) of Pub.L. 99–554 set out as a note under section 581 of Title 28.

Separability of Provisions

If any provision of or amendment made by Pub.L. 103–394 or the application of such provision or amendment to any person or circumstance is held to be unconstitutional, the remaining provisions of and amendments made by Pub.L. 103–394 and the application of such provisions and amendments to any person or circumstance shall not be affected thereby, see section 701 of Pub.L. 103–394, set out as a note under section 101 of this title.

CROSS REFERENCES

Appointment of Secretary of Transportation as sole trustee, see 46 USCA § 50305.

Appointment of trustee in—

     Chapter thirteen cases, see 11 USCA § 1302.

     Chapter twelve cases, see 11 USCA § 1202.

     Railroad reorganization cases, see 11 USCA § 1163.

Election of trustee in Chapter seven cases, see 11 USCA § 702.

Grain storage facility bankruptcies, expedited appointment of trustee or examiner, see 11 USCA § 557.

Inapplicability of this section to railroad reorganization cases, see 11 USCA § 1161.

Qualification of trustee, see 11 USCA § 322.

Time for bringing action, see 11 USCA § 546.

LIBRARY REFERENCES

American Digest System

Bankruptcy ⟶3623.1 to 3626.

Key Number System Topic No. 51.

Corpus Juris Secundum

CJS Bankruptcy § 51, Chapter 11 Proceedings.

CJS Bankruptcy § 56, Eligibility to Serve as Trustee or Examiner--Disinterestedness Requirement.

CJS Bankruptcy § 64, Bases for Appointment.

CJS Bankruptcy § 65, Bases for Appointment--Appointment for Cause.

CJS Bankruptcy § 66, Bases for Appointment--Appointment in Interests of Creditors, Equity Security Holders, or Estate.

CJS Bankruptcy § 67, Request for Appointment.

CJS Bankruptcy § 68, Notice and Hearing Requirements.

CJS Bankruptcy § 70, General Factors Considered in Appointment.

CJS Bankruptcy § 71, Appointment by U.S. Trustee; Judicial Approval.

CJS Bankruptcy § 72, Appointment Required in Railroad Reorganization Cases.

CJS Bankruptcy § 82, Meeting of Creditors and Election Procedures.

CJS Bankruptcy § 84, Appointment in Interests of Creditors, Equity Security Holders, or Estate.

CJS Bankruptcy § 85, Appointment Where Debts Exceed $5 Million.

CJS Bankruptcy § 86, Request for Appointment.

CJS Bankruptcy § 135, Replacement of Debtor in Possession by Trustee; Restoration of Debtor to Possession.

CJS Bankruptcy § 396, Examiner.

CJS Bankruptcy § 809, Voting and Elections.

CJS Bankruptcy § 842, Presumption of Reasonableness of Management Decisions.

CJS Bankruptcy § 868, Remedies for Unauthorized Use of Cash Collateral.

CJS Bankruptcy § 1130, Powers and Duties of Committee.

§ 1105.   Termination of trustee's appointment

At any time before confirmation of a plan, on request of a party in interest or the United States trustee, and after notice and a hearing, the court may terminate the trustee's appointment and restore the debtor to possession and management of the property of the estate and of the operation of the debtor's business.

(Pub.L. 95–598, Nov. 6, 1978, 92 Stat. 2628; Pub.L. 98–353, Title III, § 501, July 10, 1984, 98 Stat. 384; Pub.L. 99–554, Title II, § 223, Oct. 27, 1986, 100 Stat. 3102.)

HISTORICAL AND STATUTORY NOTES

Revision Notes and Legislative Reports

1978 Acts. This section authorizes the court to terminate the trustee's appointment and to restore the debtor to possession and management of the property of the estate and to operation of the debtor's business. Section 1104(a) provides that this section does not apply in the case of a public company, for which the appointment of a trustee is mandatory. Senate Report No. 95–989.

This section authorizes the court to terminate the trustee's appointment and to restore the debtor to possession and management of the property of the estate, and to operation of the debtor's business. This section would permit the court to reverse its decision to order the appointment of a trustee in light of new evidence. House Report No. 95–595.

1984 Acts. Statements by Legislative Leaders, see 1984 U.S.Code Cong. and Adm.News, p. 576.

1986 Acts. House Report No. 99–764 and House Conference Report No. 99–958, see 1986 U.S.Code Cong. and Adm. News, p. 5227.

Amendments

1986 Amendments. Pub.L. 99–554, § 223, added "or the United States trustee" following "party in interest".

1984 Amendments. Pub.L. 98–353 substituted "estate and of the" for "estate, and".

Effective and Applicability Provisions

1986 Acts. Amendment by Pub.L. 99–554 effective 30 days after Oct. 27, 1986, except as otherwise provided for, see section 302(a) of Pub.L. 99–554, set out as a note under section 581 of Title 28, Judiciary and Judicial Procedure.

Amendment by Pub.L. 99–554, § 223, not to become effective in or with respect to certain specified judicial districts until, or apply to cases while pending in such district before, the expiration of the 270–day period beginning 30 days after Oct. 27, 1986, or of the 30–day period beginning on the date the Attorney General certifies under section 303 of Pub.L. 99–554 the region specified in a paragraph of section 581(a) of Title 28, as amended by section 111(a) of Pub.L. 99–554, that includes such district, whichever occurs first, see section 302(d)(1) of Pub.L. 99–554, set out as a note under section 581 of Title 28.

Amendment by Pub.L. 99–554, § 223, not to become effective in or with respect to certain specified judicial districts until, or apply to cases while pending in such district before, the expiration of the 2–year period beginning 30 days after Oct. 27, 1986, or of the 30–day period beginning on the date the Attorney General certifies under section 303 of Pub.L. 99–554 the region specified in a paragraph of section 581(a) of Title 28, as amended by section 111(a) of Pub.L. 99–554, that includes such district, whichever occurs first, see section 302(d)(2) of Title 28.

Amendment by Pub.L. 99–554, § 223, not to become effective in or with respect to judicial districts established for the States of Alabama and North Carolina until, or apply to cases while pending in such district before, such district elects to be included in a bankruptcy region established in section 581(a) of Title 28, as amended by section 111(a) of Pub.L. 99–554, or Oct. 1, 2002, whichever occurs first, and, except as otherwise provided for, with respect to cases under chapters 7, 11, 12, and 13 of Title 11 commenced before 30 days after Oct. 27,

1986, and pending in a judicial district in the States of Alabama or North Carolina before any election made under section 302(d)(3)(A) of Pub.L. 99–554 by such district becomes effective or Oct. 1, 2002, whichever occurs first, amendments by Pub.L. 99–554 not to apply until Oct. 1, 2003, or the expiration of the 1–year period beginning on the date such election becomes effective, whichever occurs first, and further, in any judicial district in Alabama or North Carolina not making the election described in section 302(d)(3)(A) of Pub.L. 99–554, any person appointed under regulations issued by the Judicial Conference to administer estates in cases under Title 11 authorized to establish, etc., a panel of private trustees, and to supervise cases and trustees in cases under chapters 7, 11, 12, and 13 of Title 11, until amendments by sections 201 to 231 of Pub.L. 99–554 effective in such district, see section 302(d)(3)(A) to (F), (H), (I) of Pub.L. 99–554, set out as a note under section 581 of Title 28.

Amendment by Pub.L. 99–554, § 223, except as otherwise provided, with respect to cases under chapters 7, 11, 12, and 13 of Title 11 commenced before 30 days after Oct. 27, 1986, and pending in a judicial district referred to in section 581(a) of Title 28, as amended by section 111(a) of Pub.L. 99–554, for which a United States trustee is not authorized before 30 days after Oct. 27, 1986 to be appointed, not applicable until the expiration of the 3–year period beginning on Oct. 27, 1986, or of the 1–year period beginning on the date the Attorney General certifies under section 303 of Pub.L. 99–554, the region specified in a paragraph of such section 581(a) that includes, such district, whichever occurs first, see section 302(e)(1), (2) of Pub.L. 99–554, set out as a note under section 581 of Title 28.

1984 Acts. Amendment by Pub.L. 98–353 effective with respect to cases filed 90 days after July 10, 1984, see section 552(a), formerly 553(a), of Pub.L. 98–353, set out as a note under section 101 of this title.

CROSS REFERENCES

Effect of vacancy in office of trustee, see 11 USCA § 325.

Inapplicability of this section to railroad reorganization cases, see 11 USCA § 1161.

Removal of trustee, see 11 USCA § 324.

LIBRARY REFERENCES

American Digest System

Bankruptcy ⟳3623.1 to 3626.

Key Number System Topic No. 51.

Corpus Juris Secundum

CJS Bankruptcy § 51, Chapter 11 Proceedings.

CJS Bankruptcy § 72, Appointment Required in Railroad Reorganization Cases.

CJS Bankruptcy § 109, Termination of Service.

CJS Bankruptcy § 135, Replacement of Debtor in Possession by Trustee; Restoration of Debtor to Possession.

CJS Bankruptcy § 842, Presumption of Reasonableness of Management Decisions.

§ 1106.   Duties of trustee and examiner

(a) A trustee shall—

(1) perform the duties of the trustee, as specified in paragraphs (2), (5), (7), (8), (9), (10), (11), and (12) of section 704(a);

(2) if the debtor has not done so, file the list, schedule, and statement required under section 521(a)(1) of this title;

(3) except to the extent that the court orders otherwise, investigate the acts, conduct, assets, liabilities, and financial condition of the debtor, the operation of the debtor's business and the desirability of the continuance of such business, and any other matter relevant to the case or to the formulation of a plan;

(4) as soon as practicable—

  (A) file a statement of any investigation conducted under paragraph (3) of this subsection, including any fact ascertained pertaining to fraud, dishonesty, incompetence, misconduct, mismanagement, or irregularity in the management of the affairs of the debtor, or to a cause of action available to the estate; and

  (B) transmit a copy or a summary of any such statement to any creditors' committee or equity security holders' committee, to any indenture trustee, and to such other entity as the court designates;

(5) as soon as practicable, file a plan under section 1121 of this title, file a report of why the trustee will not file a plan, or recommend conversion of the case to a case under chapter 7, 12, or 13 of this title or dismissal of the case;

(6) for any year for which the debtor has not filed a tax return required by law, furnish, without personal liability, such information as may be required by the governmental unit with which such tax return was to be filed, in light of the condition of the debtor's books and records and the availability of such information;

(7) after confirmation of a plan, file such reports as are necessary or as the court orders; and

(8) if with respect to the debtor there is a claim for a domestic support obligation, provide the applicable notice specified in subsection (c).

(b) An examiner appointed under section 1104(d) of this title shall perform the duties specified in paragraphs (3) and (4) of subsection (a) of this section, and, except to the extent that the court orders otherwise, any other duties of the trustee that the court orders the debtor in possession not to perform.

(c)(1) In a case described in subsection (a)(8) to which subsection (a)(8) applies, the trustee shall—

  (A)(i) provide written notice to the holder of the claim described in subsection (a)(8) of such claim and of the right of such holder to use the services of the State child support enforcement agency established under sections 464 and 466 of the Social Security Act for the State in which such holder resides, for assistance in collecting child support during and after the case under this title; and

  (ii) include in the notice required by clause (i) the address and telephone number of such State child support enforcement agency;

  (B)(i) provide written notice to such State child support enforcement agency of such claim; and

  (ii) include in the notice required by clause (i) the name, address, and telephone number of such holder; and

  (C) at such time as the debtor is granted a discharge under section 1141, provide written notice to such holder and to such State child support enforcement agency of—

    (i) the granting of the discharge;

    (ii) the last recent known address of the debtor;

    (iii) the last recent known name and address of the debtor's employer; and

    (iv) the name of each creditor that holds a claim that—

      (I) is not discharged under paragraph (2), (4), or (14A) of section 523(a); or

      (II) was reaffirmed by the debtor under section 524(c).

(2)(A) The holder of a claim described in subsection (a)(8) or the State child enforcement support agency of the State in which such holder resides may request from a creditor described in paragraph (1)(C)(iv) the last known address of the debtor.

(B) Notwithstanding any other provision of law, a creditor that makes a disclosure of a last known address of a debtor in connection with a request made under subparagraph (A) shall not be liable by reason of making such disclosure.

(Pub.L. 95–598, Nov. 6, 1978, 92 Stat. 2628; Pub.L. 98–353, Title III, §§ 311(b)(1), 502, July 10, 1984, 98 Stat. 355, 384; Pub.L. 99–554, Title II, § 257(c), Oct. 27, 1986, 100 Stat. 3114; Pub.L. 103–394, Title II, § 211(b), Oct. 22, 1994, 108 Stat. 4125; Pub.L. 109–8, Title II, § 219(b), Title IV, § 446(c), Title XI, § 1105(b), Apr. 20, 2005, 119 Stat. 56, 118, 192; Pub.L. 111–327, § 2(a)(31), Dec. 22, 2010, 124 Stat. 3560.)

HISTORICAL AND STATUTORY NOTES
Revision Notes and Legislative Reports

1978 Acts. Subsection (a) of this section prescribes the trustee's duties. He is required to perform the duties of a trustee in a liquidation case specified in section 704(2), (4), (6), (7), (8), and (9). These include reporting and informational duties, and accountability for all property received. Paragraph (2) of this subsection requires the trustee to file with the court, if the debtor has not done so, the list of creditors, schedule of assets and liabilities, and statement of affairs required under section 521(1).

Paragraph (3) of S. 1106 requires the trustee to investigate the acts, conduct, assets, liabilities, and financial condition of the debtor, the operation of the debtor's business, and the desirability of the continuance of the business, and any other matter relevant to the case or to the formulation of a plan. Paragraph (4) requires the trustee to report the results of his investigation to the court and to creditors' committees, equity security holders' committees, indenture trustees and any other entity the court designates.

Paragraph (5) requires the trustee to file a plan or to report why a plan cannot be formulated, or to recommend conversion to liquidation or to an individual repayment plan case, or dismissal. It is anticipated that the trustee will consult with creditors and other parties in interest in the formulation of a plan, just as the debtor in possession would.

Paragraph (6) [now (7)] requires final reports by the trustee, as the court orders.

Subsection (b) gives the trustee's investigative duties to an examiner, if one is appointed. The court is authorized to give the examiner additional duties as the circumstances warrant.

Paragraphs (3), (4), and (5) of subsection (a) are derived from sections 165 and 169 of chapter X (11 U.S.C. 565, 569) [former sections 565 and 569 of former Title 11, respectively]. Senate Report No. 95–989.

1984 Acts. Statements by Legislative Leaders, see 1984 U.S.Code Cong. and Adm.News, p. 576.

1986 Acts. House Report No. 99–764 and House Conference Report No. 99–958, see 1986 U.S.Code Cong. and Adm. News, p. 5227.

1994 Acts. House Report No. 103–835, see 1994 U.S. Code Cong. and Adm. News, p. 3340.

2005 Acts. House Report No. 109–31(Part I), see 2005 U.S. Code Cong. and Adm. News, p. 88.

References in Text

Section 464 of the Social Security Act, referred to in subsec. (c)(1)(A)(i), is Act Aug. 14, 1935, c. 531, Title IV, § 464, as added Aug. 13, 1981, Pub.L. 97–35, Title XXIII, § 2331(a), 95 Stat. 860, and amended, which is classified to 42 U.S.C.A. § 664.

Section 466 of the Social Security Act, referred to in subsec. (c)(1)(A)(i), is Act Aug. 14, 1935, c. 531, Title IV, § 466, as added Aug. 16, 1984, Pub.L. 98–378, § 3(b), 98 Stat. 1306, and amended, which is classified to 42 U.S.C.A. § 666.

Amendments

2010 Amendments. Subsec. (a)(1). Pub.L. 111–327, § 2(a)(31)(A), struck out "704" and inserted "704(a)".

Subsec. (a)(2). Pub.L. 111–327, § 2(a)(31)(B), struck out "521(1)" and inserted "521(a)(1)".

2005 Amendments. Subsec. (a)(1). Pub.L. 109–8, § 446(c), rewrote par. (1), which formerly read:

"**(1)** perform the duties of a trustee specified in sections 704(2), 704(5), 704(7), 704(8), and 704(9) of this title;"

Pub.L. 109–8, § 1105(b), struck out "and (11)" and inserted "(11), and (12)".

Subsec. (a)(6). Pub.L. 109–8, § 219(b)(1)(A), struck out "and" at the end of par. (6).

Subsec. (a)(7). Pub.L. 109–8, § 219(b)(1)(B), substituted "; and" for the period at the end of par. (7).

Subsec. (a)(8). Pub.L. 109–8, § 219(b)(1)(C), added par. (8).

Subsec. (c). Pub.L. 109–8, § 219(b)(2), added subsec. (c).

1994 Amendments. Subsec. (b). Pub.L. 103–394, § 211(b), substituted "An examiner appointed under section 1104(d)" for "An examiner appointed under section 1104(c)".

1986 Amendments. Subsec. (a)(5). Pub.L. 99–554, § 257(c), added reference to chapter 12.

1984 Amendments. Subsec. (a)(1). Pub.L. 98–353, § 311(b)(1), substituted "704(5), 704(7), 704(8), and 704(9)" for "704(4), 704(6), 704(7) and 704(8)".

Subsec. (b). Pub.L. 98–353, § 502, inserted ", except to the extent that the court orders otherwise," before "any other".

Effective and Applicability Provisions

2005 Acts. Amendments by Pub.L. 109–8 effective, except as otherwise provided, 180 days after April 20, 2005, and inapplicable with respect to cases commenced under Title 11 before the effective date, see Pub.L. 109–8, § 1501, set out as a note under 11 U.S.C.A. § 101.

1994 Acts. Amendment by Pub.L. 103–394 effective on Oct. 22, 1994, and not to apply with respect to cases commenced under Title 11 of the United States Code before Oct. 22, 1994, see section 702 of Pub.L. 103–394, set out as a note under section 101 of this title.

1986 Acts. Amendment by Pub.L. 99–554 effective 30 days after Oct. 27, 1986, but not applicable to cases commenced under this title before that date, see section 302(a), (c)(1), of Pub.L. 99–554, set out as a note under section 581 of Title 28, Judiciary and Judicial Procedure.

1984 Acts. Amendment by Pub.L. 98–353 effective with respect to cases filed 90 days after July 10, 1984, see section 552(a), formerly 553(a), of Pub.L. 98–353, set out as a note under section 101 of this title.

Separability of Provisions

If any provision of or amendment made by Pub.L. 103–394 or the application of such provision or amendment to any person or circumstance is held to be unconstitutional, the remaining provisions of and amendments made by Pub.L. 103–394 and the application of such provisions and amendments to any person or circumstance shall not be affected thereby, see section 701 of Pub.L. 103–394, set out as a note under section 101 of this title.

Payment of Certain Benefits to Retired Former Employees

Pub.L. 99–500, § 101(b) [Title VI, § 608], Oct. 18, 1986, 100 Stat. 1783–39, 1783–74, and Pub.L. 99–591, § 101(b) [Title VI, § 608], Oct. 30, 1986, 100 Stat. 3341–74, as amended by Pub.L. 100–41, May 15, 1987, 101 Stat. 309; Pub.L. 100–99, Aug. 18, 1987, 101 Stat. 716; Pub.L. 100–334, § 3(a), June 16, 1988, 102 Stat. 613, provided that:

"**(a)(1)** Subject to paragraphs (2), (3), (4), and (5), and notwithstanding title 11 of the United States Code [this title], the trustee shall pay benefits to retired former employees under a plan, fund, or program maintained or established by the debtor prior to filing a petition (through the purchase of insurance or otherwise) for the purpose of providing medical, surgical, or hospital care benefits, or benefits in the event of sickness, accident, disability, or death.

"**(2)** The level of benefits required to be paid by this subsection may be modified prior to confirmation of a plan under section 1129 of such title [section 1129 of this title] if—

"**(A)** the trustee and an authorized representative of the former employees with respect to whom such benefits are payable agree to the modification of such benefit payments; or

"**(B)** the court finds that a modification proposed by the trustee meets the standards of section 1113(b)(1)(A) of such title [section 1113(b)(1)(A) of this title] and the balance of the equities clearly favors the modification.

If such benefits are covered by a collective bargaining agreement, the authorized representative shall be the labor organization that is signatory to such collective bargaining agreement unless there is a conflict of interest.

"**(3)** The trustee shall pay benefits in accordance with this subsection until—

"**(A)** the dismissal of the case involved; or

"**(B)** the effective date of a plan confirmed under section 1129 of such title which provides for the continued payment after confirmation of the plan of all such benefits at the level established under paragraph (2) of this subsection, at any time prior to the confirmation of the plan, for the duration of the period the debtor (as defined in such title) has obligated itself to provide such benefits.

"**(4)** No such benefits paid between the filing of a petition in a case covered by this section and the time a plan confirmed under section 1129 of such title with respect to such case becomes effective shall be deducted or offset from the amount allowed as claims for any benefits which remain unpaid, or from the amount to be paid under the plan with respect to such claims for unpaid benefits, whether such claims for unpaid benefits are based upon or arise from a right to future benefits or from any benefit not paid as a result of modifications allowed pursuant to this section.

"**(5)** No claim for benefits covered by this section shall be limited by section 502(b)(7) of such title [section 502(b)(7) of this title].

"**(b)(1)** Notwithstanding any provision of title 11 of the United States Code [this title], the trustee shall pay an allowable claim of any person for a benefit paid—

"**(A)** before the filing of the petition under title 11 of the United States Code; and

"**(B)** directly or indirectly to a retired former employee under a plan, fund, or program described in subsection (a)(1);

if, as determined by the court, such person is entitled to recover from such employee, or any provider of health care to such employee, directly or indirectly, the amount of such benefit for which such person receives no payment from the debtor.

"**(2)** For purposes of paragraph (1), the term 'provider of health care' means a person who—

"**(A)** is the direct provider of health care (including a physician, dentist, nurse, podiatrist, optometrist, physician assistant, or ancillary personnel employed under the supervision of a physician); or

"**(B)** administers a facility or institution (including a hospital, alcohol and drug abuse treatment facility, outpatient facility, or health maintenance organization) in which health care is provided.

"**(c)** This section is effective with respect to cases commenced under chapter 11, of title 11, United States Code [this chapter], in which a plan for reorganization has not been confirmed by the court and in which any such benefit is still being paid on October 2, 1986, and in cases that become subject to chapter 11, title 11, United States Code, after October 2, 1986 and before the date of the enactment of the Retiree Benefits Bankruptcy Protection Act of 1988 [June 16, 1988].

"**(d)** This section shall not apply during any period in which a case is subject to chapter 7, title 11, United States Code [11 U.S.C.A. § 701 et seq.]."

Similar provisions were contained in Pub.L. 99–656, § 2, Nov. 14, 1986, 100 Stat. 3668, as amended by Pub.L. 100–41, May 15, 1987, 101 Stat. 309; Pub.L. 100–99, Aug. 18, 1987, 101 Stat. 716, and were repealed by Pub.L. 100–334, § 3(b), June 16, 1988, 102 Stat. 614.

CROSS REFERENCES

Duties of trustees in—

    Chapter thirteen cases, see 11 USCA § 1302.

    Chapter twelve cases, see 11 USCA § 1202.

Powers and duties of trustee in investor protection liquidation proceedings, see 15 USCA § 78fff–1.

Rights and powers of debtor in Chapter twelve case not encompassing duties specified in subsec. (a)(3) and (4) of this section, see 11 USCA § 1203.

LIBRARY REFERENCES

American Digest System

    Bankruptcy ⬥3627, 3008.1, 3009.

    Key Number System Topic No. 51.

Corpus Juris Secundum

    CJS Bankruptcy § 101, Chapter 11.

    CJS Bankruptcy § 102, Chapter 12.

    CJS Bankruptcy § 104, Chapter 13--Duties If Debtor is Engaged in Business.

    CJS Bankruptcy § 132, Rights, Powers, and Duties of Debtor in Possession.

    CJS Bankruptcy § 136, Rights, Powers, and Duties of Debtor in Possession.

    CJS Bankruptcy § 805, Who May Conduct Examination; Debtor's Right to Examine.

    CJS Bankruptcy § 841, Fiduciary Duties of Trustees and Debtors in Possession.

    CJS Bankruptcy § 847, Operation of Family Farm in Chapter 12 Cases.

    CJS Bankruptcy § 1131, Debtor-In-Possession.

§ 1107. Rights, powers, and duties of debtor in possession

(a) Subject to any limitations on a trustee serving in a case under this chapter, and to such limitations or conditions as the court prescribes, a debtor in possession shall have all the rights, other than the right to compensation under section 330 of this title, and powers, and shall perform all the functions and duties, except the duties specified in sections 1106(a)(2), (3), and (4) of this title, of a trustee serving in a case under this chapter.

(b) Notwithstanding section 327(a) of this title, a person is not disqualified for employment under section 327 of this title by a debtor in possession solely because of such person's employment by or representation of the debtor before the commencement of the case.

(Pub.L. 95–598, Nov. 6, 1978, 92 Stat. 2628; Pub.L. 98–353, Title III, § 503, July 10, 1984, 98 Stat. 384.)

HISTORICAL AND STATUTORY NOTES

Revision Notes and Legislative Reports

1978 Acts. This section places a debtor in possession in the shoes of a trustee in every way. The debtor is given the rights and powers of a chapter 11 trustee. He is required to perform the functions and duties of a chapter 11 trustee (except the investigative duties). He is also subject to any limitations on a chapter 11 trustee, and to such other limitations and conditions as the court prescribes cf. *Wolf v. Weinstein*, 372 U.S. 633, 649–650 (1963). Senate Report No. 95–989.

1984 Acts. Statements by Legislative Leaders, see 1984 U.S.Code Cong. and Adm.News, p. 576.

Legislative Statements

The House amendment adopts section 1107(b) of the Senate amendment which clarifies a point not covered by the House bill.

Amendments

1984 Amendments. Subsec. (a). Pub.L. 98–353 substituted "on a trustee serving in a case" for "on a trustee" preceding "under this chapter".

Effective and Applicability Provisions

1984 Acts. Amendment by Pub.L. 98–353 effective with respect to cases filed 90 days after July 10, 1984, see section 552(a), formerly 553(a), of Pub.L. 98–353, set out as a note under section 101 of this title.

CROSS REFERENCES

Debtor engaged in business in Chapter thirteen cases, see 11 USCA § 1304.

Debtor's duties, see 11 USCA § 521.

Inapplicability of this section in railroad reorganization cases, see 11 USCA § 1161.

Limitation on compensation of professional persons, see 11 USCA § 328.

Rights and powers of debtor in—

    Chapter thirteen cases, see 11 USCA § 1303.

    Chapter twelve cases, see 11 USCA § 1203.

LIBRARY REFERENCES

American Digest System

Attorney and Client ⬤⇒21.5(6).

American Digest System

Bankruptcy ⬤⇒3029.1, 3622.

Key Number System Topic Nos. 45, 51.

Corpus Juris Secundum

CJS Bankruptcy § 131, Debtor as Debtor in Possession.

CJS Bankruptcy § 132, Rights, Powers, and Duties of Debtor in Possession.

CJS Bankruptcy § 134, Rights, Powers, and Duties of Debtor in Possession--Specific Rights, Powers, and Duties.

CJS Bankruptcy § 135, Replacement of Debtor in Possession by Trustee; Restoration of Debtor to Possession.

CJS Bankruptcy § 190, Orders With Respect to Obtaining Credit.

CJS Bankruptcy § 276, Standing.

CJS Bankruptcy § 278, Parties Defendant; Sovereign Immunity.

CJS Bankruptcy § 657, Standing; Motion.

CJS Bankruptcy § 760, Disqualification for and Limitations Upon Employment.

CJS Bankruptcy § 761, Relationship Between Employment and Compensation Provisions.

CJS Bankruptcy § 763, Salaried Employees; Employment of Debtor's Attorney.

CJS Bankruptcy § 840, Operation of Debtor's Business.

CJS Bankruptcy § 841, Fiduciary Duties of Trustees and Debtors in Possession.

CJS Bankruptcy § 843, Discontinuance or Modification of Debtor's Business.

CJS Bankruptcy § 844, Railroad Reorganizations.

CJS Bankruptcy § 851, Prepetition Security Interests in Proceeds, Products, Offspring, or Profits.

CJS Bankruptcy § 852, Prepetition Security Interests Extending to Rents and Similar Charges.

CJS Bankruptcy § 854, Expedited Determination of Disposition of Grain Assets.

CJS Bankruptcy § 860, Recovery of Costs of Preserving or Disposing of Property.

CJS Bankruptcy § 871, Motion for Authorization.

CJS Bankruptcy § 874, What Transactions Are Other Than in Ordinary Course of Business.

CJS Bankruptcy § 876, Requirement of Business Justification.

CJS Bankruptcy § 889, Co-Owner or Spouse's Right to Proportionate Share of Proceeds of Sale.

CJS Bankruptcy § 891, Protection of Good-Faith Purchasers and Lessees from Reversal or Modification on Appeal.

CJS Bankruptcy § 892, Setting Aside Confirmed Sale; Remedies for Collusive Bidding.

CJS Bankruptcy § 895, Unsecured Credit or Debt in Ordinary Course of Business.

CJS Bankruptcy § 896, Unsecured Credit or Debt Other Than in Ordinary Course of Business.

CJS Bankruptcy § 897, Credit With Special Administrative Priority or Secured by First Liens or Junior Liens.

CJS Bankruptcy § 898, Credit Secured by Superpriority Lien; Subordination of Existing Liens.

CJS Bankruptcy § 900, Motion for Authorization to Obtain Credit; Notice and Hearing.

CJS Bankruptcy § 1131, Debtor-In-Possession.

§ 1108.   Authorization to operate business

Unless the court, on request of a party in interest and after notice and a hearing, orders otherwise, the trustee may operate the debtor's business.

(Pub.L. 95–598, Nov. 6, 1978, 92 Stat. 2629; Pub.L. 98–353, Title III, § 504, July 10, 1984, 98 Stat. 384.)

HISTORICAL AND STATUTORY NOTES

Revision Notes and Legislative Reports

1978 Acts. This section permits the debtor's business to continue to be operated, unless the court orders otherwise. Thus, in a reorganization case, operation of the business will be the rule, and it will not be necessary to go to the court to obtain an order authorizing operation. Senate Report No. 95–989.

This section does not presume that a trustee will be appointed to operate the business of the debtor. Rather, the power granted to trustee under this section is one of the powers that a debtor in possession acquires by virtue of proposed 11 U.S.C. 1107. House Report No. 95–595.

1984 Acts. Statements by Legislative Leaders, see 1984 U.S.Code Cong. and Adm.News, p. 576.

Legislative Statements

The House amendment adopts section 1108 of the House bill in preference to the style of an identical substantive provision contained in the Senate amendment. Throughout title 11 references [sic] to a "trustee" is read to include other parties under various sections of the bill. For example, section 1107 applies to give the debtor in possession all the rights and powers of a trustee in a case under chapter 11; this includes the power of the trustee to operate the debtor's business under section 1108.

Amendments

1984 Amendments. Pub.L. 98–353 inserted ", on request of a party in interest and after notice and a hearing," after "court".

Effective and Applicability Provisions

1984 Acts. Amendment by Pub.L. 98–353 effective with respect to cases filed 90 days after July 10, 1984, see section 552(a), formerly 553(a), of Pub.L. 98–353, set out as a note under section 101 of this title.

CROSS REFERENCES

Authorization to operate business in Chapter seven cases, see 11 USCA § 721.

Executory contracts and unexpired leases, see 11 USCA § 365.

Executory contracts in stockbroker liquidation cases, see 11 USCA § 744.

Obtaining credit, see 11 USCA § 364.

Retention or replacement of professional persons, see 11 USCA § 327.

Treatment of accounts in—

Commodity broker liquidation cases, see 11 USCA § 763.

Stockbroker liquidation cases, see 11 USCA § 745.

Use, sale or lease of property, see 11 USCA § 363.

Utility service, see 11 USCA § 366.

LIBRARY REFERENCES

American Digest System

Bankruptcy ⟂3621, 3009.

Key Number System Topic No. 51.

Corpus Juris Secundum

CJS Bankruptcy § 101, Chapter 11.

CJS Bankruptcy § 840, Operation of Debtor's Business.

CJS Bankruptcy § 842, Presumption of Reasonableness of Management Decisions.

CJS Bankruptcy § 895, Unsecured Credit or Debt in Ordinary Course of Business.

§ 1109. Right to be heard

(a) The Securities and Exchange Commission may raise and may appear and be heard on any issue in a case under this chapter, but the Securities and Exchange Commission may not appeal from any judgment, order, or decree entered in the case.

(b) A party in interest, including the debtor, the trustee, a creditors' committee, an equity security holders' committee, a creditor, an equity security holder, or any indenture trustee, may raise and may appear and be heard on any issue in a case under this chapter. (Pub.L. 95–598, Nov. 6, 1978, 92 Stat. 2629.)

HISTORICAL AND STATUTORY NOTES

Revision Notes and Legislative Reports

1978 Acts. Subsection (a) provides, in unqualified terms, that any creditor, equity security holder, or an indenture trustee shall have the right to be heard as a party in interest under this chapter in person, by an attorney, or by a committee. It is derived from section 206 of chapter X (11 U.S.C. 606) [section 606 of former Title 11].

Subsection (b) provides that the Securities and Exchange Commission may appear by filing an appearance in a case of a public company and may appear in other cases if authorized or requested by the court. As a party in interest in either case, the Commission may raise and be heard on any issue. The Commission may not appeal from a judgment, order, or decree in a case, but may participate in any appeal by any other party in interest. This is the present law under section 208 of chapter X (11 U.S.C. 608) [section 608 of former Title 11]. Senate Report No. 95–989.

Section 1109 authorizes the Securities and Exchange Commission and any indenture trustee to intervene in the case at any time on any issue. They may raise an issue or may appear and be heard on an issue that is raised by someone else. The section, following current law, denies the right of appeal to the Securities and Exchange Commission. It does not, however, prevent the Commission from joining or participating in an appeal taken by a true party in interest. The Commission is merely prevented from initiating the appeal in any capacity. House Report No. 95–595.

Legislative Statements

Section 1109 of the House amendment represents a compromise between comparable provisions in the House bill and Senate amendment. As previously discussed the section gives the Securities and Exchange Commission the right to appear and be heard and to raise any issue in a case under chapter 11; however, the Securities and Exchange Commission is not a party in interest and the Commission may not appeal from any judgment, order, or decree entered in the case. Under section 1109(b) a party in interest, including the debtor, the trustee, creditors committee, equity securities holders committee, a creditor, an equity security holder, or an indentured trustee, may raise and may appear and be heard on any issue in a case under chapter 11. Section 1109(c) of the Senate amendment has been moved to subchapter IV pertaining to Railroad Reorganizations.

CROSS REFERENCES

Applicability of this section in Chapter 9 cases, see 11 USCA § 901.

Right of Commodity Futures Trading Commission to be heard in commodity broker liquidation cases, see 11 USCA § 762.

Right of Interstate Commerce Commission, Department of Transportation, and State or local regulatory commission to be heard in railroad reorganization, see 11 USCA § 1164.

LIBRARY REFERENCES

American Digest System

Bankruptcy ☞3771, 2205, 2206.

Key Number System Topic No. 51.

Corpus Juris Secundum

CJS Bankruptcy § 67, Request for Appointment.

CJS Bankruptcy § 86, Request for Appointment.

CJS Bankruptcy § 101, Chapter 11.

CJS Bankruptcy § 120, What Constitutes Disbursal of Moneys to Parties in Interest, Excluding Debtor.

CJS Bankruptcy § 277, Real Party in Interest; Capacity.

CJS Bankruptcy § 279, Intervention.

CJS Bankruptcy § 1122, Objections to Confirmation.

CJS Bankruptcy § 1240, Parties.

§ 1110. Aircraft equipment and vessels

(a)(1) Except as provided in paragraph (2) and subject to subsection (b), the right of a secured party with a security interest in equipment described in paragraph (3), or of a lessor or conditional vendor of such equipment, to take possession of such equipment in compliance with a security agreement, lease, or conditional sale contract, and to enforce any of its other rights or remedies, under such security agreement, lease, or conditional sale contract, to sell, lease, or otherwise retain or dispose of such equipment, is not limited or otherwise affected by any other provision of this title or by any power of the court.

(2) The right to take possession and to enforce the other rights and remedies described in paragraph (1) shall be subject to section 362 if—

(A) before the date that is 60 days after the date of the order for relief under this chapter, the trustee, subject to the approval of the court, agrees to perform all obligations of the debtor under such security agreement, lease, or conditional sale contract; and

(B) any default, other than a default of a kind specified in section 365(b)(2), under such security agreement, lease, or conditional sale contract—

(i) that occurs before the date of the order is cured before the expiration of such 60–day period;

(ii) that occurs after the date of the order and before the expiration of such 60–day period is cured before the later of—

(I) the date that is 30 days after the date of the default; or

(II) the expiration of such 60–day period; and

(iii) that occurs on or after the expiration of such 60–day period is cured in compliance with the terms of such security agreement, lease, or conditional sale contract, if a cure is permitted under that agreement, lease, or contract.

(3) The equipment described in this paragraph—

(A) is—

(i) an aircraft, aircraft engine, propeller, appliance, or spare part (as defined in section 40102 of title 49) that is subject to a security interest granted by, leased to, or conditionally sold to a debtor that, at the time such transaction is entered into, holds an air carrier operating certificate issued pursuant to chapter 447 of title 49 for aircraft capable of carrying 10 or more individuals or 6,000 pounds or more of cargo; or

(ii) a vessel documented under chapter 121 of title 46 that is subject to a security interest granted by, leased to, or conditionally sold to a debtor that is a water carrier that, at the time such transaction is entered into, holds a certificate of public convenience and necessity or permit issued by the Department of Transportation; and

(B) includes all records and documents relating to such equipment that are required, under the terms of the security agreement, lease, or conditional sale contract, to be surrendered or returned by the debtor in connection with the surrender or return of such equipment.

(4) Paragraph (1) applies to a secured party, lessor, or conditional vendor acting in its own behalf or acting as trustee or otherwise in behalf of another party.

(b) The trustee and the secured party, lessor, or conditional vendor whose right to take possession is protected under subsection (a) may agree, subject to the approval of the court, to extend the 60–day period specified in subsection (a)(1).

(c)(1) In any case under this chapter, the trustee shall immediately surrender and return to a secured party, lessor, or conditional vendor, described in subsection (a)(1), equipment described in subsection (a)(3), if at any time after the date of the order for relief under this chapter such secured party, lessor, or conditional vendor is entitled pursuant to subsection (a)(1) to take possession of such equipment and makes a written demand for such possession to the trustee.

(2) At such time as the trustee is required under paragraph (1) to surrender and return equipment described in subsection (a)(3), any lease of such equipment, and any security agreement or conditional sale contract relating to such equipment, if such security agreement or conditional sale contract is an executory contract, shall be deemed rejected.

(d) With respect to equipment first placed in service on or before October 22, 1994, for purposes of this section—

(1) the term 'lease' includes any written agreement with respect to which the lessor and the debtor, as lessee, have expressed in the agreement or in a substantially contemporaneous writing that the agreement is to be treated as a lease for Federal income tax purposes; and

(2) the term "security interest" means a purchase- money equipment security interest.

(Pub.L. 95–598, Nov. 6, 1978, 92 Stat. 2629; Pub.L. 103–272, § 5(c), July 5, 1994, 108 Stat. 1373; Pub.L. 103–394, Title II, § 201(a), Oct. 22, 1994, 108 Stat. 4119; Pub.L. 106–181, Title VII, § 744(b), Apr. 5, 2000, 114 Stat. 177; Pub.L. 109–304, § 17(b)(2), Oct. 6, 2006, 120 Stat. 1707.)

HISTORICAL AND STATUTORY NOTES
Revision Notes and Legislative Reports

1978 Acts. This section, to a large degree, preserves the protection given lessors and conditional vendors of aircraft to a certificated air carrier or of vessels to a certificated water carrier under sections 116(5) and 116(6) of present Chapter X [sections 516(5) and 516(6) of former Title 11]. It is modified to conform with the consolidation of Chapters X [former chapter 10, section 501 et seq.] and XI [former chapter 11 (section 701 et seq.) of former Title 11] and with the new chapter 11 generally. It is also modified to give the trustee in a reorganization case an opportunity to continue in possession of the equipment in question by curing defaults and by making the required lease or purchase payments. This removes the absolute veto power over a reorganization that lessors and conditional vendors have under present law, while entitling them to protection of their investment.

The section overrides the automatic stay or any power of the court to enjoin taking of possession of certain leased, conditionally sold, or liened equipment, unless, [sic] the trustee agrees to perform the debtor's obligations and cures all prior defaults (other than defaults under ipso facto or bankruptcy clauses) within 60 days after the order for relief. The trustee and the equipment financer are permitted to extend the 60-day period by agreement. During the first 60 days, the automatic stay will apply to prevent foreclosure unless the creditor gets relief from the stay.

The effect of this section will be the same if the debtor has granted the security interest to the financer or if the debtor is leasing equipment from a financer that has leveraged the lease and leased the equipment subject to a security interest of a third party. Senate Report No. 95–989.

1994 Acts. House Report No. 103–180, see 1994 U.S. Code Cong. and Adm. News, p. 818.

House Report No. 103–835, see 1994 U.S. Code Cong. and Adm. News, p. 3340.

2000 Acts. House Conference Report No. 106–513 and Statement by President, see 2000 U.S. Code Cong. and Adm. News, p. 80.

2006 Acts. House Report No. 109–170, see 2006 U.S. Code Cong. and Adm. News, p. 972.

Legislative Statements

Section 1110 of the House amendment adopts an identical provision contained in the House bill without modifications contained in the Senate amendment. This section protects a limited class of financiers of aircraft and vessels and is intended to be narrowly construed to prevent secured parties or lessors from gaining the protection of the section unless the interest of such lessor or secured party is explicitly enumerated therein. It should be emphasized that under section 1110(a) a debtor in possession or trustee is given 60 days after the order for relief in a case under chapter 11, to have an opportunity to comply with the provisions of section 1110(a).

During this time the automatic stay will apply and may not be lifted prior to the expiration of the 60-day period. Under section 1110(b), the debtor and secured party or lessor are given an opportunity to extend the 60-day period, but no right to reduce the period is intended. It should additionally be noted that under section 1110(a) the trustee or debtor in possession is not required to assume the executory contract or unexpired lease under section 1110; rather, if the trustee or debtor in possession complies with the requirements of section 1110(a), the trustee or debtor in possession is entitled to retain the aircraft or vessels subject to the normal requirements of section 365. The discussion regarding aircraft and vessels likewise applies with respect to railroad rolling stock in a railroad reorganization under section 1168.

References in Text

Chapter 447 of Title 49, referred to in subsec. (a)(3)(A)(i), is classified to 49 U.S.C.A. § 44701 et seq.

Chapter 121 of this title, referred to in subsec. (a)(3)(A)(ii), is Documentation of Vessels, 46 U.S.C.A. § 12101 et seq.

Amendments

2006 Amendments. Subsec. (a)(3)(A)(ii). Pub.L. 109–304, § 17(b)(2), struck out "documented vessel (as defined in section 30101(1) of title 46)" and inserted "vessel documented under chapter 121 of title 46".

2000 Amendments. Pub.L. 106–181, Title VII, § 744(b), rewrote the section, which read:

"**(a)(1)** The right of a secured party with a security interest in equipment described in paragraph (2) or of a lessor or conditional vendor of such equipment to take possession of such equipment in compliance with a security agreement, lease, or conditional sale contract is not affected by section 362, 363, or 1129 or by any power of the court to enjoin the taking of possession unless—

"**(A)** before the date that is 60 days after the date of the order for relief under this chapter, the trustee, subject to the court's approval, agrees to perform all obligations of the debtor that become due on or after the date of the order under such security agreement, lease, or conditional sale contract; and

"**(B)** any default, other than a default of a kind specified in section 365(b)(2), under such security agreement, lease, or conditional sale contract—

"**(i)** that occurs before the date of the order is cured before the expiration of such 60–day period; and

"**(ii)** that occurs after the date of the order is cured before the later of—

"**(I)** the date that is 30 days after the date of the default; or

"**(II)** the expiration of such 60–day period.

"**(2)** Equipment is described in this paragraph if it is—

"**(A)** an aircraft, aircraft engine, propeller, appliance, or spare part (as defined in section 40102 of title 49) that is subject to a security interest granted by, leased to, or conditionally sold to a debtor that is a citizen of the United States (as defined in section 40102 of title 49) holding an air carrier operating certificate issued by the Secretary of Transportation pursuant to chapter 447 of title 49 for aircraft capable of carrying 10 or more individuals or 6,000 pounds or more of cargo; or

"**(B)** a documented vessel (as defined in section 30101(1) of title 46) that is subject to a security interest granted by, leased to, or conditionally sold to a debtor that is a water carrier that holds a certificate of public convenience and necessity or permit issued by the Interstate Commerce Commission.

"**(3)** Paragraph (1) applies to a secured party, lessor, or conditional vendor acting in its own behalf or acting as trustee or otherwise in behalf of another party.

"**(b)** The trustee and the secured party, lessor, or conditional vendor whose right to take possession is protected under subsection (a) may agree, subject to the court's approval, to extend the 60–day period specified in subsection (a)(1).

"**(c)** With respect to equipment first placed in service on or prior to the date of enactment of this subsection, for purposes of this section—

"**(1)** the term 'lease' includes any written agreement with respect to which the lessor and the debtor, as lessee, have expressed in the agreement or in a substantially contemporaneous writing that the agreement is to be treated as a lease for Federal income tax purposes; and

"**(2)** the term 'security interest' means a purchase-money equipment security interest."

1994 Amendments. Subsec. (a). Pub.L. 103–272, § 5(c), substituted "section 40102(a) of title 49" for "section 101 of the Federal Aviation Act of 1958 (49 U.S.C. 1301)", "section 30101 of title 46" for "subsection B(4) of the Ship Mortgage Act, 1920 (46 U.S.C. 911(4))", and "Secretary of Transportation" for "Civil Aeronautics Board".

Pub.L. 103–394, § 201(a), in subsec. (a) designated existing text as par. (1), as so designated, substituted provisions directing that the right to take possession of certain equipment is not affected by section 362, 363, or 1129, for provisions directing that the right to take possession of certain equipment is not affected by section 362 or 363 of this title, redesignated former pars. (1) and (2) as par. (1), subpars. (A) and (B), respectively, and added pars. (2) and (3) and subsecs. (c) and (d).

Effective and Applicability Provisions

2000 Acts. Amendment by Pub.L. 106–181 applicable only to fiscal years beginning after September 30, 1999, see section 3 of Pub.L. 106–181, set out as a note under section 106 of this title.

1994 Acts. Amendment by Pub.L. 103–394 effective on Oct. 22, 1994, with this section as amended by section 201 of Pub.L. 103–394 applicable with respect to any lease, as defined by subsec. (c) of this section as so amended, entered into in connection with a settlement of any proceeding in any case pending under Title 11 of the United States Code on Oct. 22,

1994, see section 702 of Pub.L. 103–394, set out as a note under section 101 of this title.

Separability of Provisions

If any provision of or amendment made by Pub.L. 103–394 or the application of such provision or amendment to any person or circumstance is held to be unconstitutional, the remaining provisions of and amendments made by Pub.L. 103–394 and the application of such provisions and amendments to any person or circumstance shall not be affected thereby, see section 701 of Pub.L. 103–394, set out as a note under section 101 of this title.

Abolition of Interstate Commerce Commission and Transfer of Functions

Interstate Commerce Commission abolished and functions of Commission transferred, except as otherwise provided in Pub.L. 104–88, to Surface Transportation Board effective Jan. 1, 1996, by section 702 of Title 49, Transportation, and section 101 of Pub.L. 104–88, set out as a note under section 701 of Title 49. References to Interstate Commerce Commission deemed to refer to Surface Transportation Board, a member or employee of the Board, or Secretary of Transportation, as appropriate, see section 205 of Pub.L. 104–88, set out as a note under section 701 of Title 49.

Aircraft Equipment Settlement Leases Act of 1993

Pub.L. 103–7, Mar. 17, 1993, 107 Stat. 36, provided:

"**Section 1. Short Title.**

"This Act [this note] may be cited as the 'Aircraft Equipment Settlement Leases Act of 1993'.

"**Sec. 2. Treatment of Aircraft Equipment Settlement Leases with the Pension Benefit Guaranty Corporation.**

"In the case of any settlement of liability under title IV of the Employee Retirement Income Security Act of 1974 [29 U.S.C.A. § 1301 et seq.], entered into by the Pension Benefit Guaranty Corporation and one or more other parties, if—

"**(1)** such settlement was entered into before, on, or after the date of the enactment of this Act [Mar. 17, 1993],

"**(2)** at least one party to such settlement was a debtor under title 11 of the United States Code [this title], and

"**(3)** an agreement that is entered into as part of such settlement provides that such agreement is to be treated as a lease,

then such agreement shall be treated as a lease for purposes of section 1110 of such title 11 [this section]."

Termination of Civil Aeronautics Board and Transfer of Certain Functions

All functions, powers, and duties of the Civil Aeronautics Board were terminated or transferred by section 1551 of Title 49, Appendix, Transportation, effective in part on Dec. 31, 1981, in part on Jan. 1, 1983, and in part on Jan. 1, 1985.

CROSS REFERENCES

Effect of conversion, see 11 USCA § 348.

Rights of certain secured parties in rolling stock equipment, see 11 USCA § 1168.

LIBRARY REFERENCES

American Digest System

Bankruptcy ⚵3504.

Key Number System Topic No. 51.

CJS Bankruptcy § 477, Persons Protected by and Subject to Stay.

CJS Bankruptcy § 853, Use of Aircraft, Aircraft Equipment, Vessels, and Railroad Equipment Subject to Financing Agreements.

§ 1111.　Claims and interests

(a) A proof of claim or interest is deemed filed under section 501 of this title for any claim or interest that appears in the schedules filed under section 521(a)(1) or 1106(a)(2) of this title, except a claim or interest that is scheduled as disputed, contingent, or unliquidated.

(b)(1)(A) A claim secured by a lien on property of the estate shall be allowed or disallowed under section 502 of this title the same as if the holder of such claim had recourse against the debtor on account of such claim, whether or not such holder has such recourse, unless—

(i) the class of which such claim is a part elects, by at least two-thirds in amount and more than half in number of allowed claims of such class, application of paragraph (2) of this subsection; or

(ii) such holder does not have such recourse and such property is sold under section 363 of this title or is to be sold under the plan.

(B) A class of claims may not elect application of paragraph (2) of this subsection if—

(i) the interest on account of such claims of the holders of such claims in such property is of inconsequential value; or

(ii) the holder of a claim of such class has recourse against the debtor on account of such claim and such property is sold under section 363 of this title or is to be sold under the plan.

(2) If such an election is made, then notwithstanding section 506(a) of this title, such claim is a secured claim to the extent that such claim is allowed.

(Pub.L. 95–598, Nov. 6, 1978, 92 Stat. 2630; Pub.L. 111–327, § 2(a)(32), Dec. 22, 2010, 124 Stat. 3561.)

HISTORICAL AND STATUTORY NOTES

Revision Notes and Legislative Reports

1978 Acts. Senate Report No. 95–989 and House Report No. 95–595, see 1978 U.S.Code Cong. and Adm.News, p. 5787.

This section dispenses with the need for every creditor and equity security holder to file a proof of claim or interest in a reorganization case. Usually the debtor's schedules are accurate enough that they will suffice to determine the claims or interests allowable in the case. Thus, the section specifies that any claim or interest included on the debtor's schedules is deemed filed under section 501. This does not apply to claims or interests that are scheduled as disputed, contingent, or unliquidated. Senate Report No. 95–989.

Legislative Statements

A discussion of section 1111(b) of the House amendment is best considered in the context of confirmation and will therefore, [sic] be discussed in connection with section 1129.

Amendments

2010　Amendments. Subsec.　(a).　Pub.L.　111–327, § 2(a)(32), struck out "521(1)" and inserted "521(a)(1)".

CROSS REFERENCES

Applicability of subsec. (b) of this section in Chapter nine cases, see 11 USCA § 901.

Effect of list of claims in Chapter nine cases, see 11 USCA § 925.

Election as affecting confirmation of plan, see 11 USCA § 1129.

Filing and allowance of postpetition claims in Chapter thirteen cases, see 11 USCA § 1305.

Limitation on recourse of claim payable solely from special revenues of debtor, see 11 USCA § 927.

LIBRARY REFERENCES

American Digest System

Bankruptcy ⚮2892.1, 2894, 2852.

Key Number System Topic No. 51.

CJS Bankruptcy § 968, Nonrecourse Claims Secured by Liens; Election.

CJS Bankruptcy § 1014, Scheduling as Filing.

CJS Bankruptcy § 1141, Provisions for Satisfaction of Claims; Relation to Recovery in Liquidation.

§ 1112.　Conversion or dismissal

(a) The debtor may convert a case under this chapter to a case under chapter 7 of this title unless—

(1) the debtor is not a debtor in possession;

(2) the case originally was commenced as an involuntary case under this chapter; or

(3) the case was converted to a case under this chapter other than on the debtor's request.

(b)(1) Except as provided in paragraph (2) and subsection (c), on request of a party in interest, and after notice and a hearing, the court shall convert a case under this chapter to a case under chapter 7 or dismiss a case under this chapter, whichever is in the best interests of creditors and the estate, for cause unless the court determines that the appointment under section 1104(a) of a trustee or an examiner is in the best interests of creditors and the estate.

(2) The court may not convert a case under this chapter to a case under chapter 7 or dismiss a case under this chapter if the court finds and specifically identifies unusual circumstances establishing that converting or dismissing the case is not in the best interests of creditors and the estate, and the debtor or any other party in interest establishes that—

(A) there is a reasonable likelihood that a plan will be confirmed within the timeframes established in sections 1121(e) and 1129(e) of this title, or if such sections do not apply, within a reasonable period of time; and

(B) the grounds for converting or dismissing the case include an act or omission of the debtor other than under paragraph (4)(A)—

    (i) for which there exists a reasonable justification for the act or omission; and

    (ii) that will be cured within a reasonable period of time fixed by the court.

(3) The court shall commence the hearing on a motion under this subsection not later than 30 days after filing of the motion, and shall decide the motion not later than 15 days after commencement of such hearing, unless the movant expressly consents to a continuance for a specific period of time or compelling circumstances prevent the court from meeting the time limits established by this paragraph.

(4) For purposes of this subsection, the term 'cause' includes—

(A) substantial or continuing loss to or diminution of the estate and the absence of a reasonable likelihood of rehabilitation;

(B) gross mismanagement of the estate;

(C) failure to maintain appropriate insurance that poses a risk to the estate or to the public;

(D) unauthorized use of cash collateral substantially harmful to 1 or more creditors;

(E) failure to comply with an order of the court;

(F) unexcused failure to satisfy timely any filing or reporting requirement established by this title or by any rule applicable to a case under this chapter;

(G) failure to attend the meeting of creditors convened under section 341(a) or an examination ordered under rule 2004 of the Federal Rules of Bankruptcy Procedure without good cause shown by the debtor;

(H) failure timely to provide information or attend meetings reasonably requested by the United States trustee (or the bankruptcy administrator, if any);

(I) failure timely to pay taxes owed after the date of the order for relief or to file tax returns due after the date of the order for relief;

(J) failure to file a disclosure statement, or to file or confirm a plan, within the time fixed by this title or by order of the court;

(K) failure to pay any fees or charges required under chapter 123 of title 28;

(L) revocation of an order of confirmation under section 1144;

(M) inability to effectuate substantial consummation of a confirmed plan;

(N) material default by the debtor with respect to a confirmed plan;

(O) termination of a confirmed plan by reason of the occurrence of a condition specified in the plan; and

(P) failure of the debtor to pay any domestic support obligation that first becomes payable after the date of the filing of the petition.

(c) The court may not convert a case under this chapter to a case under chapter 7 of this title if the debtor is a farmer or a corporation that is not a moneyed, business, or commercial corporation, unless the debtor requests such conversion.

(d) The court may convert a case under this chapter to a case under chapter 12 or 13 of this title only if—

(1) the debtor requests such conversion;

(2) the debtor has not been discharged under section 1141(d) of this title; and

(3) if the debtor requests conversion to chapter 12 of this title, such conversion is equitable.

(e) Except as provided in subsections (c) and (f), the court, on request of the United States trustee, may convert a case under this chapter to a case under chapter 7 of this title or may dismiss a case under this chapter, whichever is in the best interest of creditors and the estate if the debtor in a voluntary case fails to file, within fifteen days after the filing of the petition commencing such case or such additional time as the court may allow, the information required by paragraph (1) of section 521(a), including a list containing the names and addresses of the holders of the twenty largest unsecured claims (or of all unsecured claims if there are fewer than twenty unsecured claims), and the approximate dollar amounts of each of such claims.

(f) Notwithstanding any other provision of this section, a case may not be converted to a case under another chapter of this title unless the debtor may be a debtor under such chapter.

(Pub.L. 95–598, Nov. 6, 1978, 92 Stat. 2630; Pub.L. 98–353, Title III, § 505, July 10, 1984, 98 Stat. 384; Pub.L. 99–554, Title II, §§ 224, 256, Oct. 27, 1986, 100 Stat. 3102, 3114; Pub.L. 103–394, Title II, § 217(c), Oct. 22, 1994, 108 Stat. 4127; Pub.L. 109–8, Title IV, § 442(a), Apr. 20, 2005, 119 Stat. 115; Pub.L. 111–327, § 2(a)(33), Dec. 22, 2010, 124 Stat. 3561.)

HISTORICAL AND STATUTORY NOTES

Revision Notes and Legislative Reports

1978 Acts. This section brings together all of the conversion and dismissal rules for chapter 11 cases. Subsection (a) gives the debtor an absolute right to convert a voluntarily commenced chapter 11 case in which the debtor remains in possession to a liquidation case.

Subsection (b) gives wide discretion to the court to make an appropriate disposition of the case sua sponte or upon motion of a party in interest, or the court is permitted to convert a reorganization case to a liquidation case or to dismiss the case, whichever is in the best interest of creditors and the estate, but only for cause. Cause may include the continuing loss to or diminution of the estate of an insolvent debtor, the absence of a reasonable likelihood of rehabilitation, the inability to effectuate a plan, unreasonable delay by the debtor that is prejudicial to creditors, failure to file a plan within the appropriate time limits, denial of confirmation and any opportunity to modify or propose a new plan, revocation of confirmation and denial of confirmation of a modified plan, inability to effectuate substantial consummation of a confirmed plan, material default by the debtor under the plan, and termination of the plan by reason of the occurrence of a condition specified in the plan. This list is not exhaustive. The court will be able to consider other factors as they arise, and to use its equitable powers to reach an appropriate result in individual cases. The power of the court to act sua sponte should be used sparingly and only in emergency situations.

Subsection (c) prohibits the court from converting a case concerning a farmer or an eleemosynary institution to a liquidation case unless the debtor consents.

Subsection (d) prohibits conversion of a reorganization case to a chapter 13 case unless the debtor requests conversion and his discharge had not been granted or has been revoked.

Subsection (e) reinforces section 109 by prohibiting conversion of a chapter 11 case to a case under another chapter proceedings under which the debtor is not permitted to proceed. Senate Report No. 95–989.

1984 Acts. Statements by Legislative Leaders, see 1984 U.S.Code Cong. and Adm.News, p. 576.

1986 Acts.. House Report No. 99–764 and House Conference Report No. 99–958, see 1986 U.S.Code Cong. and Adm. News, p. 5227.

1994 Acts. House Report No. 103–835, see 1994 U.S. Code Cong. and Adm. News, p. 3340.

2005 Acts. House Report No. 109–31(Part I), see 2005 U.S. Code Cong. and Adm. News, p. 88.

Legislative Statements

Section 1112 of the House amendment represents a compromise between the House bill and Senate amendment with respect to the factors constituting cause for conversion of a case to chapter 7 or dismissal. The House amendment combines two separate factors contained in section 1112(b)(1) and section 1112(b)(2) of the Senate amendment. Section 1112(b)(1) of the House amendment permits the court to convert a case to a case under chapter 7 or to dismiss the case if there is both a continuing loss to or diminution of the estate and the absence of a reasonable likelihood of rehabilitation; requiring both factors to be present simultaneously represents a compromise from the House bill which eliminated both factors from the list of causes enumerated.

Sections 1112(c) and 1112(d) of the House amendment is derived from the House bill which differs from the Senate amendment only as a matter of style.

References in Text

Chapter 7 of this title, referred to in text, is 11 U.S.C.A. § 701 et seq.

The Federal Rules of Bankruptcy Procedure, referred to in subsec. (b)(4)(G), are set out in the Appendix to this title.

Chapter 123 of title 28, referred to in subsec. (b)(4)(K), is 28 U.S.C.A. § 1911 et seq.

Chapter 12 or 13 of this title, referred to in subsec. (d), is 11 U.S.C.A. § 1201 et seq. or 11 U.S.C.A. § 1301 et seq., respectively.

Amendments

2010 Amendments. Subsec. (b)(1). Pub.L. 111–327, § 2(a)(33)(A)(i), rewrote par. (1), which formerly read: "**(1)** Except as provided in paragraph (2) of this subsection, subsection (c) of this section, and section 1104(a)(3), on request of a party in interest, and after notice and a hearing, absent unusual circumstances specifically identified by the court that establish that the requested conversion or dismissal is not in the best interests of creditors and the estate, the court shall convert a case under this chapter to a case under chapter 7 or dismiss a case under this chapter, whichever is in the best interests of creditors and the estate, if the movant establishes cause."

Subsec. (b)(2). Pub.L. 111–327, § 2(a)(33)(A)(ii)(I), rewrote the matter preceding subpar. (A), which formerly read: "**(2)** The relief provided in paragraph (1) shall not be granted absent unusual circumstances specifically identified by the court that establish that such relief is not in the best interests of creditors and the estate, if the debtor or another party in interest objects and establishes that—".

Subsec. (b)(2)(B). Pub.L. 111–327, § 2(a)(33)(A)(ii)(II), struck out "granting such relief" and inserted "converting or dismissing the case".

Subsec. (e). Pub.L. 111–327, § 2(a)(33)(B), struck out "521" and inserted "521(a)".

2005 Amendments. Subsec. (b). Pub.L. 109–8, § 442(a), rewrote subsec. (b), which formerly read:

"**(b)** Except as provided in subsection (c) of this section, on request of a party in interest or the United States trustee or bankruptcy administrator, and after notice and a hearing, the court may convert a case under this chapter to a case under chapter 7 of this title or may dismiss a case under this chapter, whichever is in the best interest of creditors and the estate, for cause, including-

"**(1)** continuing loss to or diminution of the estate and absence of a reasonable likelihood of rehabilitation;

"**(2)** inability to effectuate a plan;

"**(3)** unreasonable delay by the debtor that is prejudicial to creditors;

"**(4)** failure to propose a plan under section 1121 of this title within any time fixed by the court;

"**(5)** denial of confirmation of every proposed plan and denial of a request made for additional time for filing another plan or a modification of a plan;

"**(6)** revocation of an order of confirmation under section 1144 of this title, and denial of confirmation of another plan or a modified plan under section 1129 of this title;

"**(7)** inability to effectuate substantial consummation of a confirmed plan;

"**(8)** material default by the debtor with respect to a confirmed plan;

"**(9)** termination of a plan by reason of the occurrence of a condition specified in the plan;

"**(10)** nonpayment of any fees or charges required under chapter 123 of title 28."

1994 Amendments. Subsec. (b). Pub.L. 103–394, § 217(c), added provisions authorizing the court to convert or dismiss a case on request of bankruptcy administrator.

1986 Amendments. Subsec. (b). Pub.L. 99–554, § 224(1)(A), added "or the United States trustee" following "party in interest".

Subsec. (b)(10). Pub.L. 99–554, § 224(1)(B)–(D), added par. (10).

Subsec. (d). Pub.L. 99–554, § 256(1), added reference to chapter 12.

Subsec. (d)(3). Pub.L. 99–554, § 256(2)–(4), added par. (3).

Subsec. (e). Pub.L. 99–554, § 224(3), added subsec. (e). Former subsec. (e) was redesignated (f).

Subsec. (f). Pub.L. 99–554, § 224(2), redesignated former subsec. (e) as (f).

1984 Amendments. Subsec. (a)(2). Pub.L. 98–353, § 505(a)(1), substituted "originally was commenced as an involuntary case under this chapter" for "is an involuntary case originally commenced under this chapter".

Subsec. (a)(3). Pub.L. 98–353, § 505(a)(2), substituted "other than on" for "on other than".

Subsec. (b)(5). Pub.L. 98–353, § 505(b)(1), added "a request made for" before "additional".

Subsec. (b)(8). Pub.L. 98–353, § 505(b)(2), substituted "or" for "and".

Effective and Applicability Provisions

2005 Acts. Amendments by Pub.L. 109–8 effective, except as otherwise provided, 180 days after April 20, 2005, and inapplicable with respect to cases commenced under Title 11 before the effective date, see Pub.L. 109–8, § 1501, set out as a note under 11 U.S.C.A. § 101.

1994 Acts. Amendment by Pub.L. 103–394 effective on Oct. 22, 1994, and not to apply with respect to cases commenced under Title 11 of the United States Code before Oct. 22, 1994, see section 702 of Pub.L. 103–394, set out as a note under section 101 of this title.

1986 Acts. Amendment by Pub.L. 99–554 effective 30 days after Oct. 27, 1986, except as otherwise provided for, see section 302(a) of Pub.L. 99–554, set out as a note under section 581 of Title 28, Judiciary and Judicial Procedure.

Amendment by Pub.L. 99–554, § 224, not to become effective in or with respect to certain specified judicial districts until, or apply to cases while pending in such district before, the expiration of the 270–day period beginning 30 days after Oct. 27, 1986, or of the 30–day period beginning on the date the Attorney General certifies under section 303 of Pub.L. 99–554 the region specified in a paragraph of section 581(a) of Title 28, as amended by section 111(a) of Pub.L. 99–554, that includes such district, whichever occurs first, see section 302(d)(1) of Pub.L. 99–554, set out as a note under section 581 of Title 28.

Amendment by Pub.L. 99–554, § 224, not to become effective in or with respect to certain specified judicial districts until, or apply to cases while pending in such district before, the expiration of the 2–year period beginning 30 days after Oct. 27, 1986, or of the 30–day period beginning on the date the Attorney General certifies under section 303 of Pub.L. 99–554 the region specified in a paragraph of section 581(a) of Title 28, as amended by section 111(a) of Pub.L. 99–554, that includes such district, whichever occurs first, see section 302(d)(2) of Pub.L. 99–554, set out as a note under section 581 of Title 28.

Amendment by Pub.L. 99–554, § 224, not to become effective in or with respect to judicial districts established for the States of Alabama and North Carolina until, or apply to cases while pending in such district before, such district elects to be included in a bankruptcy region established in section 581(a) of Title 28, as amended by section 111(a) of Pub.L. 99–554, or Oct. 1, 2002, whichever occurs first, and, except as otherwise provided for, with respect to cases under chapters 7, 11, 12, and 13 of Title 11 commenced before 30 days after Oct. 27, 1986, and pending in a judicial district in the States of Alabama or North Carolina before any election made under section 302(d)(3)(A) of Pub.L. 99–554 by such district becomes effective or Oct. 1, 2002, whichever occurs first, amendments by Pub.L. 99–554 not to apply until Oct. 1, 2003, or the expiration of the 1–year period beginning on the date such election becomes effective, whichever occurs first, and further, in any judicial district in Alabama or North Carolina not making the election described in section 302(d)(3)(A) of Pub.L. 99–554, any person appointed under regulations issued by the Judicial Conference to administer estates in cases under Title 11 authorized to establish, etc., a panel of private trustees, and to supervise cases and trustees in cases under chapters 7, 11, 12, and 13 of Title 11, until amendments by sections 201 to 231 of Pub.L. 99–554 effective in such district, see section 302(d)(3)(A) to (F), (H), (I) of Pub.L. 99–554, set out as a note under section 581 of Title 28.

Amendment by Pub.L. 99–554, § 224, except as otherwise provided, with respect to cases under chapters 7, 11, 12, and 13 of Title 11 commenced before 30 days after Oct. 27, 1986, and pending in a judicial district referred to in section 581(a) of Title 28, as amended by section 111(a) of Pub.L. 99–554, for which a United States trustee is not authorized before 30 days after Oct. 27, 1986 to be appointed, not applicable until the expiration of the 3–year period beginning on Oct. 27, 1986, or of the 1–year period beginning on the date the Attorney General certifies under section 303 of Pub.L. 99–554 the region specified in a paragraph of such section 581(a) that includes, such district, whichever occurs first, see section 302(e)(1), (2) of Pub.L. 99–554, set out as a note under section 581 of Title 28.

Amendments by Pub.L. 99–554, § 256, not to apply with respect to cases commenced under Title 11, Bankruptcy, before 30 days after Oct. 27, 1986, see section 302(c)(1) of Pub.L. 99–554, set out as a note under section 581 of Title 28.

1984 Acts. Amendment by Pub.L. 98–353 effective with respect to cases filed 90 days after July 10, 1984, see section 552(a), formerly 553(a), of Pub.L. 98–353, set out as a note under section 101 of this title.

Separability of Provisions

If any provision of or amendment made by Pub.L. 103–394 or the application of such provision or amendment to any person or circumstance is held to be unconstitutional, the remaining provisions of and amendments made by Pub.L. 103–394 and the application of such provisions and amendments to any person or circumstance shall not be affected thereby, see section 701 of Pub.L. 103–394, set out as a note under section 101 of this title.

CROSS REFERENCES

Conversion of—

Chapter seven cases, see 11 USCA § 706.

Chapter thirteen cases, see 11 USCA § 1307.

Chapter twelve cases, see 11 USCA § 1208.

Dismissal of—

    Chapter nine cases, see 11 USCA § 930.

    Chapter seven cases, see 11 USCA § 707.

Distribution of property of estate converted to Chapter seven, see 11 USCA § 726.

Effect of conversion, see 11 USCA § 348.

Effect of dismissal, see 11 USCA § 349.

Executory contracts and unexpired leases, see 11 USCA § 365.

Liquidation of estate in railroad reorganization cases, see 11 USCA § 1174.

Termination of debtor's taxable period for cases converted to Chapter seven, see 11 USCA § 728.

LIBRARY REFERENCES

American Digest System

Bankruptcy ⟜3591(1) to 3594.

Key Number System Topic No. 51.

Corpus Juris Secundum

CJS Bankruptcy § 64, Bases for Appointment.

CJS Bankruptcy § 109, Termination of Service.

CJS Bankruptcy § 442, What Constitutes Cause.

CJS Bankruptcy § 451, Dismissal or Conversion on Request of United States Trustee.

CJS Bankruptcy § 797, Debtor's Duty to Attend as Mandatory.

CJS Bankruptcy § 927, Exercising Right in Chapter 7 Cases.

CJS Bankruptcy § 1102, Priority of Particular Distribution Classes.

CJS Bankruptcy § 1157, Acceptance of the Plan--Eligibility to Vote; Impairment.

§ 1113. Rejection of collective bargaining agreements

(a) The debtor in possession, or the trustee if one has been appointed under the provisions of this chapter, other than a trustee in a case covered by subchapter IV of this chapter and by title I of the Railway Labor Act, may assume or reject a collective bargaining agreement only in accordance with the provisions of this section.

(b)(1) Subsequent to filing a petition and prior to filing an application seeking rejection of a collective bargaining agreement, the debtor in possession or trustee (hereinafter in this section "trustee" shall include a debtor in possession), shall—

(A) make a proposal to the authorized representative of the employees covered by such agreement, based on the most complete and reliable information available at the time of such proposal, which provides for those necessary modifications in the employees benefits and protections that are necessary to permit the reorganization of the debtor and assures that all creditors, the debtor and all of the affected parties are treated fairly and equitably; and

(B) provide, subject to subsection (d)(3), the representative of the employees with such relevant information as is necessary to evaluate the proposal.

(2) During the period beginning on the date of the making of a proposal provided for in paragraph (1) and ending on the date of the hearing provided for in subsection (d)(1), the trustee shall meet, at reasonable times, with the authorized representative to confer in good faith in attempting to reach mutually satisfactory modifications of such agreement.

(c) The court shall approve an application for rejection of a collective bargaining agreement only if the court finds that—

(1) the trustee has, prior to the hearing, made a proposal that fulfills the requirements of subsection (b)(1);

(2) the authorized representative of the employees has refused to accept such proposal without good cause; and

(3) the balance of the equities clearly favors rejection of such agreement.

(d)(1) Upon the filing of an application for rejection the court shall schedule a hearing to be held not later than fourteen days after the date of the filing of such application. All interested parties may appear and be heard at such hearing. Adequate notice shall be provided to such parties at least ten days before the date of such hearing. The court may extend the time for the commencement of such hearing for a period not exceeding seven days where the circumstances of the case, and the interests of justice require such extension, or for additional periods of time to which the trustee and representative agree.

(2) The court shall rule on such application for rejection within thirty days after the date of the commencement of the hearing. In the interests of justice, the court may extend such time for ruling for such additional period as the trustee and the employees' representative may agree to. If the court does not rule on such application within thirty days after the date of the commencement of the hearing, or within such additional time as the trustee and the employees' representative may agree to, the trustee may terminate or alter any provisions of the collective bargaining agreement pending the ruling of the court on such application.

(3) The court may enter such protective orders, consistent with the need of the authorized representative of the employee to evaluate the trustee's proposal and the application for rejection, as may be necessary to prevent disclosure of information provided to such representative where such disclosure could compromise the position of the debtor with respect to its competitors in the industry in which it is engaged.

(e) If during a period when the collective bargaining agreement continues in effect, and if essential to the continuation of the debtor's business, or in order to avoid irreparable damage to the estate, the court, after notice and a hearing, may authorize the trustee to implement interim changes in the terms, conditions, wages, benefits, or work rules provided by a collective bargaining agreement. Any hearing under this paragraph shall be scheduled in accordance with the needs of the trustee. The implementation of such interim changes shall not render the application for rejection moot.

(f) No provision of this title shall be construed to permit a trustee to unilaterally terminate or alter any provisions of a collective bargaining agreement prior to compliance with the provisions of this section.

(Added Pub.L. 98–353, Title III, § 541(a), July 10, 1984, 98 Stat. 390.)

HISTORICAL AND STATUTORY NOTES

Revision Notes and Legislative Reports

1984 Acts. Statements by Legislative Leaders, see 1984 U.S.Code Cong. and Adm.News, p. 576.

References in Text

The Railway Labor Act, referred to in subsec. (a), is Act May 20, 1926, c. 347, 44 Stat. 577, as amended. Title I of the Railway Labor Act is classified principally to subchapter I (section 151 et seq.) of chapter 8 of Title 45, Railroads. For complete classification of this Act to the Code, see section 151 of Title 45 and Tables.

Effective and Applicability Provisions

1984 Acts. Section 541(c) of Pub.L. 98–353 provided that: "The amendments made by this section [enacting this section] shall become effective upon the date of enactment of this Act [July 10, 1984]; provided that this section shall not apply to cases filed under title 11 of the United States Code [this title] which were commenced prior to the date of enactment of this section [July 10, 1984]."

LIBRARY REFERENCES

American Digest System

Bankruptcy ⟜3113, 3117.
Key Number System Topic No. 51.

Corpus Juris Secundum

CJS Bankruptcy § 101, Chapter 11.

CJS Bankruptcy § 134, Rights, Powers, and Duties of Debtor in Possession--Specific Rights, Powers, and Duties.

CJS Bankruptcy § 943, Exclusion of Collective-Bargaining Agreements Subject to Railway Labor Act.

CJS Bankruptcy § 944, Status of Agreement Pending Rejection.

CJS Bankruptcy § 945, Application for Court Approval of Rejection; Hearing and Notice.

CJS Bankruptcy § 946, Burden and Degree of Proof.

CJS Bankruptcy § 947, Entry of Judgment; Protective Orders and Interim Relief.

CJS Bankruptcy § 949, Nine-Element Test.

CJS Bankruptcy § 950, Bildisco Case.

CJS Bankruptcy § 978, Wage and Benefit Claims.

§ 1114. Payment of insurance benefits to retired employees

(a) For purposes of this section, the term "retiree benefits" means payments to any entity or person for the purpose of providing or reimbursing payments for retired employees and their spouses and dependents, for medical, surgical, or hospital care benefits, or benefits in the event of sickness, accident, disability, or death under any plan, fund, or program (through the purchase of insurance or otherwise) maintained or established in whole or in part by the debtor prior to filing a petition commencing a case under this title.

(b)(1) For purposes of this section, the term "authorized representative" means the authorized representative designated pursuant to subsection (c) for persons receiving any retiree benefits covered by a collective bargaining agreement or subsection (d) in the case of persons receiving retiree benefits not covered by such an agreement.

(2) Committees of retired employees appointed by the court pursuant to this section shall have the same rights, powers, and duties as committees appointed under sections 1102 and 1103 of this title for the purpose of carrying out the purposes of sections 1114 and 1129(a)(13) and, as permitted by the court, shall have the power to enforce the rights of persons under this title as they relate to retiree benefits.

(c)(1) A labor organization shall be, for purposes of this section, the authorized representative of those persons receiving any retiree benefits covered by any collective bargaining agreement to which that labor organization is signatory, unless (A) such labor organization elects not to serve as the authorized representative of such persons, or (B) the court, upon a motion by any party in interest, after notice and hearing, determines that different representation of such persons is appropriate.

(2) In cases where the labor organization referred to in paragraph (1) elects not to serve as the authorized representative of those persons receiving any retiree benefits covered by any collective bargaining agreement to which that labor organization is signatory, or in cases where the court, pursuant to paragraph (1) finds different representation of such persons appropriate, the court, upon a motion by any party in interest, and after notice and a hearing, shall appoint a committee of retired employees if the debtor seeks to modify or not pay the retiree benefits or if the court otherwise determines that it is appropriate, from among such persons, to serve as the authorized representative of such persons under this section.

(d) The court, upon a motion by any party in interest, and after notice and a hearing, shall order the appointment of a committee of retired employees if the debtor seeks to modify or not pay the retiree benefits or if the court otherwise determines that it is appropriate, to serve as the authorized representative, under this section, of those persons receiving any retiree benefits not covered by a collective bargaining agreement. The United States trustee shall appoint any such committee.

(e)(1) Notwithstanding any other provision of this title, the debtor in possession, or the trustee if one has been appointed under the provisions of this chapter (hereinafter in this section "trustee" shall include a debtor in possession), shall timely pay and shall not modify any retiree benefits, except that—

　(A) the court, on motion of the trustee or authorized representative, and after notice and a hearing, may order modification of such payments, pursuant to the provisions of subsections (g) and (h) of this section, or

　(B) the trustee and the authorized representative of the recipients of those benefits may agree to modification of such payments,

after which such benefits as modified shall continue to be paid by the trustee.

(2) Any payment for retiree benefits required to be made before a plan confirmed under section 1129 of this title is effective has the status of an allowed administrative expense as provided in section 503 of this title.

(f)(1) Subsequent to filing a petition and prior to filing an application seeking modification of the retiree benefits, the trustee shall—

　(A) make a proposal to the authorized representative of the retirees, based on the most complete and reliable information available at the time of such proposal, which provides for those necessary modifications in the retiree benefits that are necessary to permit the reorganization of the debtor and assures that all creditors, the debtor and all of the affected parties are treated fairly and equitably; and

　(B) provide, subject to subsection (k)(3), the representative of the retirees with such relevant information as is necessary to evaluate the proposal.

(2) During the period beginning on the date of the making of a proposal provided for in paragraph (1), and ending on the date of the hearing provided for in subsection (k)(1), the trustee shall meet, at reasonable times, with the authorized representative to confer in good faith in attempting to reach mutually satisfactory modifications of such retiree benefits.

(g) The court shall enter an order providing for modification in the payment of retiree benefits if the court finds that—

　(1) the trustee has, prior to the hearing, made a proposal that fulfills the requirements of subsection (f);

　(2) the authorized representative of the retirees has refused to accept such proposal without good cause; and

　(3) such modification is necessary to permit the reorganization of the debtor and assures that all creditors, the debtor, and all of the affected parties are treated fairly and equitably, and is clearly favored by the balance of the equities;

except that in no case shall the court enter an order providing for such modification which provides for a modification to a level lower than that proposed by the trustee in the proposal found by the court to have complied with the requirements of this subsection and subsection (f): *Provided, however,* That at any time after an order is entered providing for modification in the payment of retiree benefits, or at any time after an agreement modifying such benefits is made between the trustee and the authorized representative of the recipients of such benefits, the authorized representative may apply to the court for an order increasing those benefits which order shall be granted if the increase in retiree benefits sought is consistent with the standard set forth in paragraph (3): *Provided further,* That neither the trustee nor the authorized representative is precluded from making more than one motion for a modification order governed by this subsection.

(h)(1) Prior to a court issuing a final order under subsection (g) of this section, if essential to the continuation of the debtor's business, or in order to avoid irreparable damage to the estate, the court, after notice and a hearing, may authorize the trustee to implement interim modifications in retiree benefits.

(2) Any hearing under this subsection shall be scheduled in accordance with the needs of the trustee.

(3) The implementation of such interim changes does not render the motion for modification moot.

(i) No retiree benefits paid between the filing of the petition and the time a plan confirmed under section 1129 of this title becomes effective shall be deducted or offset from the amounts allowed as claims for any benefits which remain unpaid, or from the amounts to be paid under the plan with respect to such claims for unpaid benefits, whether such claims for unpaid benefits are based upon or arise from a right to future unpaid benefits or from any benefits not paid as a result of modifications allowed pursuant to this section.

(j) No claim for retiree benefits shall be limited by section 502(b)(7) of this title.

(k)(1) Upon the filing of an application for modifying retiree benefits, the court shall schedule a hearing to be held not later than fourteen days after the date of the filing of such application. All interested parties may appear and be heard at such hearing. Adequate notice shall be provided to such parties at least ten days before the date of such hearing. The court may extend the time for the commencement of such hearing for a period not exceeding seven days where the circumstances of the case, and the interests of justice require such extension, or for additional periods of time to which the trustee and the authorized representative agree.

(2) The court shall rule on such application for modification within ninety days after the date of the commencement of the hearing. In the interests of justice, the court may extend such time for ruling for such additional period as the trustee and the authorized representative may agree to. If the court does not rule on such application within ninety days after the date of the commencement of the hearing, or within such additional time as the trustee and the authorized representative may agree to, the trustee may implement the proposed modifications pending the ruling of the court on such application.

(3) The court may enter such protective orders, consistent with the need of the authorized representative of the retirees to evaluate the trustee's proposal and the application for modification, as may be necessary to prevent disclosure of information provided to such representative where such disclosure could compromise the position of the debtor with respect to its competitors in the industry in which it is engaged.

(*l*) If the debtor, during the 180–day period ending on the date of the filing of the petition—

(1) modified retiree benefits; and

(2) was insolvent on the date such benefits were modified;

the court, on motion of a party in interest, and after notice and a hearing, shall issue an order reinstating as of the date the modification was made, such benefits as in effect immediately before such date unless the court finds that the balance of the equities clearly favors such modification.

(m) This section shall not apply to any retiree, or the spouse or dependents of such retiree, if such retiree's gross income for the twelve months preceding the filing of the bankruptcy petition equals or exceeds $250,000, unless such retiree can demonstrate to the satisfaction of the court that he is unable to obtain health, medical, life, and disability coverage for himself, his spouse, and his dependents who would otherwise be covered by the employer's insurance plan, comparable to the coverage provided by the employer on the day before the filing of a petition under this title.

(Added Pub.L. 100–334, § 2(a), June 16, 1988, 102 Stat. 610; amended Pub.L. 109–8, Title IV, § 447, Title XIV, § 1403, Apr. 20, 2005, 119 Stat. 118, 215.)

HISTORICAL AND STATUTORY NOTES

Revision Notes and Legislative Reports

1988 Acts. Senate Report No. 100–119, see 1988 U.S.Code Cong. and Adm.News, p. 683.

2005 Acts. House Report No. 109–31(Part I), see 2005 U.S. Code Cong. and Adm. News, p. 88.

Amendments

2005 Amendments. Subsec. (d). Pub.L. 109–8, § 447, struck "appoint" and inserted "order the appointment of", and added at the end: "The United States trustee shall appoint any such committee.".

Subsec. (*l*). Pub.L. 109–8, § 1403, redesignated former subsec. (*l*) as subsec. (m), and added a new subsec. (*l*).

Subsec. (m). Pub.L. 109–8, § 1403(1), redesignated former subsec. (*l*) as subsec. (m).

Effective and Applicability Provisions

2005 Acts. Amendments by Pub.L. 109–8 effective, except as otherwise provided, 180 days after April 20, 2005, and inapplicable with respect to cases commenced under Title 11 before the effective date, see Pub.L. 109–8, § 1501, set out as a note under 11 U.S.C.A. § 101.

Amendments by Pub.L. 109–8, Title XIV, effective, except as otherwise provided, on Apr. 20, 2005, and applicable only with respect to cases commenced under Title 11 on or after Apr. 20, 2005, see Pub.L. 109–8, § 1406, set out as a note under 11 U.S.C.A. § 507.

1988 Acts. Section 4 of Pub.L. 100–334 provided that:

"**(a) General Effective Date.**—Except as provided in subsection (b), this Act and the amendments made by this Act [enacting this section, amending section 1129 of this title, enacting provisions set out as a note under section 101 of this title, and amending and repealing provisions set out as notes under section 1106 of this title] shall take effect on the date of the enactment of this Act [June 16, 1988].

"**(b) Application of Amendments.**—The amendments made by section 2 [enacting this section and amending section 1129 of this title] shall not apply with respect to cases commenced under title 11 of the United States Code [this title] before the date of the enactment of this Act [June 16, 1988]."

Payment of Certain Benefits to Retired Former Employees

For payment of benefits by bankruptcy trustee to retired employees in enumerated circumstances with respect to cases commenced under this chapter in which a plan for reorganization had not been confirmed by the court and in which any such benefit was still being paid on October 2, 1986, and in cases that became subject to this chapter after October 2, 1986, and before June 16, 1988, see section 101(b) [title VI, § 608] of Pub.L. 99–500, and Pub.L. 99–591, as amended, set out as a note under section 1106 of this title.

CROSS REFERENCES

Confirmation of plan if plan provides for continuation of "retiree benefits" as defined under this section, see 11 USCA § 1129.

LIBRARY REFERENCES

American Digest System

Bankruptcy ⚖3113.

Key Number System Topic No. 51.

Corpus Juris Secundum

CJS Bankruptcy § 101, Chapter 11.

CJS Bankruptcy § 134, Rights, Powers, and Duties of Debtor in Possession--Specific Rights, Powers, and Duties.

CJS Bankruptcy § 947, Entry of Judgment; Protective Orders and Interim Relief.

CJS Bankruptcy § 952, Claims for Retiree Benefits.

CJS Bankruptcy § 954, Preliminary Proposal for Modification; Duty to Supply Relevant Information and Negotiate.

CJS Bankruptcy § 955, Hearing on Application for Modification; Entry of Judgment.

CJS Bankruptcy § 956, Requests to Increase Benefits.

CJS Bankruptcy § 957, Emergency Modifications.

CJS Bankruptcy § 979, Pension Claims and Retiree Benefits.

CJS Bankruptcy § 1141, Provisions for Satisfaction of Claims; Relation to Recovery in Liquidation.

§ 1115.   Property of the estate

(a) In a case in which the debtor is an individual, property of the estate includes, in addition to the property specified in section 541—

(1) all property of the kind specified in section 541 that the debtor acquires after the commencement of the case but before the case is closed, dismissed, or converted to a case under chapter 7, 12, or 13, whichever occurs first; and

(2) earnings from services performed by the debtor after the commencement of the case but before the case is closed, dismissed, or converted to a case under chapter 7, 12, or 13, whichever occurs first.

(b) Except as provided in section 1104 or a confirmed plan or order confirming a plan, the debtor shall remain in possession of all property of the estate.
(Added Pub.L. 109–8, Title III, § 321(a)(1), Apr. 20, 2005, 119 Stat. 94.)

HISTORICAL AND STATUTORY NOTES

Revision Notes and Legislative Reports

2005 Acts. House Report No. 109–31(Part I), see 2005 U.S. Code Cong. and Adm. News, p. 88.

References in Text

Chapter 7, 12, or 13, referred to in subsec. (a)(1), (2), is chapter 7, 12, or 13 of this title, 11 U.S.C.A. § 701 et seq., 11 U.S.C.A. § 1201 et seq., or 11 U.S.C.A. § 1301 et seq., respectively.

Effective and Applicability Provisions

2005 Acts. Amendments by Pub.L. 109–8 effective, except as otherwise provided, 180 days after April 20, 2005, and inapplicable with respect to cases commenced under Title 11 before the effective date, see Pub.L. 109–8, § 1501, set out as a note under 11 U.S.C.A. § 101.

LIBRARY REFERENCES

Corpus Juris Secundum

CJS Bankruptcy § 561, Property Acquired Postpetition.

CJS Bankruptcy § 624, Surrender of Property of Estate and Recorded Information to Trustee.

CJS Bankruptcy § 1149, Protection of Unsecured Creditors and Equityholders.

§ 1116.   Duties of trustee or debtor in possession in small business cases

In a small business case, a trustee or the debtor in possession, in addition to the duties provided in this title and as otherwise required by law, shall—

(1) append to the voluntary petition or, in an involuntary case, file not later than 7 days after the date of the order for relief—

(A) its most recent balance sheet, statement of operations, cash-flow statement, and Federal income tax return; or

(B) a statement made under penalty of perjury that no balance sheet, statement of operations, or cash-flow statement has been prepared and no Federal tax return has been filed;

(2) attend, through its senior management personnel and counsel, meetings scheduled by the court or the United States trustee, including initial debtor interviews, scheduling conferences, and meetings of creditors convened under section 341 unless the court, after notice and a hearing, waives that requirement upon a finding of extraordinary and compelling circumstances;

(3) timely file all schedules and statements of financial affairs, unless the court, after notice and a hearing, grants an extension, which shall not extend such time period to a date later than 30 days after the date of the order for relief, absent extraordinary and compelling circumstances;

(4) file all postpetition financial and other reports required by the Federal Rules of Bankruptcy Procedure or by local rule of the district court;

(5) subject to section 363(c)(2), maintain insurance customary and appropriate to the industry;

(6)(A) timely file tax returns and other required government filings; and

(B) subject to section 363(c)(2), timely pay all taxes entitled to administrative expense priority except those being contested by appropriate proceedings being diligently prosecuted; and

(7) allow the United States trustee, or a designated representative of the United States trustee, to inspect the debtor's business premises, books, and records at reasonable times, after reasonable prior written notice, unless notice is waived by the debtor.
(Added Pub.L. 109–8, Title IV, § 436(a), Apr. 20, 2005, 119 Stat. 112.)

HISTORICAL AND STATUTORY NOTES

Revision Notes and Legislative Reports

2005 Acts. House Report No. 109–31(Part I), see 2005 U.S. Code Cong. and Adm. News, p. 88.

References in Text
The Federal Rules of Bankruptcy Procedure, referred to in par. (4), are set out in the Appendix to this title.

Effective and Applicability Provisions

2005 Acts. Amendments by Pub.L. 109–8 effective, except as otherwise provided, 180 days after April 20, 2005, and inapplicable with respect to cases commenced under Title 11 before the effective date, see Pub.L. 109–8, § 1501, set out as a note under 11 U.S.C.A. § 101.

LIBRARY REFERENCES

Corpus Juris Secundum

CJS Bankruptcy § 356, Extension of Time for Filing.

CJS Bankruptcy § 799, Corporate Debtors and Debtors in Small Business Cases.

SUBCHAPTER II—THE PLAN

CROSS REFERENCES

Subchapter applicable only in case under this chapter except as provided in § 901 of this title, see 11 USCA § 103.

§ 1121. Who may file a plan

(a) The debtor may file a plan with a petition commencing a voluntary case, or at any time in a voluntary case or an involuntary case.

(b) Except as otherwise provided in this section, only the debtor may file a plan until after 120 days after the date of the order for relief under this chapter.

(c) Any party in interest, including the debtor, the trustee, a creditors' committee, an equity security holders' committee, a creditor, an equity security holder, or any indenture trustee, may file a plan if and only if—

(1) a trustee has been appointed under this chapter;

(2) the debtor has not filed a plan before 120 days after the date of the order for relief under this chapter; or

(3) the debtor has not filed a plan that has been accepted, before 180 days after the date of the order for relief under this chapter, by each class of claims or interests that is impaired under the plan.

(d)(1) Subject to paragraph (2), on request of a party in interest made within the respective periods specified in subsections (b) and (c) of this section and after notice and a hearing, the court may for cause reduce or increase the 120-day period or the 180-day period referred to in this section.

(2)(A) The 120–day period specified in paragraph (1) may not be extended beyond a date that is 18 months after the date of the order for relief under this chapter.

(B) The 180–day period specified in paragraph (1) may not be extended beyond a date that is 20 months after the date of the order for relief under this chapter.

(e) In a small business case—

(1) only the debtor may file a plan until after 180 days after the date of the order for relief, unless that period is—

(A) extended as provided by this subsection, after notice and a hearing; or

(B) the court, for cause, orders otherwise;

(2) the plan and a disclosure statement (if any) shall be filed not later than 300 days after the date of the order for relief; and

(3) the time periods specified in paragraphs (1) and (2), and the time fixed in section 1129(e) within which the plan shall be confirmed, may be extended only if—

(A) the debtor, after providing notice to parties in interest (including the United States trustee), demonstrates by a preponderance of the evidence that it is more likely than not that the court will confirm a plan within a reasonable period of time;

(B) a new deadline is imposed at the time the extension is granted; and

(C) the order extending time is signed before the existing deadline has expired.

(Pub.L. 95–598, Nov. 6, 1978, 92 Stat. 2631; Pub.L. 98–353, Title III, § 506, July 10, 1984, 98 Stat. 385; Pub.L. 99–554, Title II, § 283(u), Oct. 27, 1986, 100 Stat. 3118; Pub.L. 103–394, Title II, § 217(d), Oct. 22, 1994, 108 Stat. 4127; Pub.L. 109–8, Title IV, §§ 411, 437, Apr. 20, 2005, 119 Stat. 106, 113.)

HISTORICAL AND STATUTORY NOTES

Revision Notes and Legislative Reports

1978 Acts. Subsection (a) permits the debtor to file a reorganization plan with a petition commencing a voluntary case or at any time during a voluntary or involuntary case.

Subsection (b) gives the debtor the exclusive right to file a plan during the first 120 days of the case. There are exceptions, however, enumerated in subsection (c). If a trustee has been appointed, if the debtor does not meet the 120-day deadline, or if the debtor fails to obtain the required consent within 180 days after the filing of the petition, any party in interest may propose a plan. This includes the debtor, the trustee, a creditors' committee, an equity security holders' committee, a creditor, an equity security holder, and an indenture trustee. The list is not exhaustive. In the case of a public company, a trustee is appointed within 10 days of the petition. In such a case, for all practical purposes, any party in interest may file a plan.

Subsection (d) permits the court, for cause, to increase or reduce the 120-day and 180-day periods specified. Since, [sic] the debtor has an exclusive privilege for 6 months during which others may not file a plan, the granted extension should be based on a showing of some promise of probable success. An extension should not be employed as a tactical device to put pressure on parties in interest to yield to a plan they consider unsatisfactory. Senate Report No. 95–989.

1984 Acts. Statements by Legislative Leaders, see 1984 U.S.Code Cong. and Adm.News, p. 576.

1986 Acts. House Report No. 99–764 and House Conference Report No. 99–958, see 1986 U.S.Code Cong. and Adm. News, p. 5227.

1994 Acts. House Report No. 103–835, see 1994 U.S. Code Cong. and Adm. News, p. 3340.

2005 Acts. House Report No. 109–31(Part I), see 2005 U.S. Code Cong. and Adm. News, p. 88.

Legislative Statements

Section 1121 of the House amendment is derived from section 1121 of the House bill; section 1121(c)(1) will be satisfied automatically in a case under subchapter IV of title 11.

Amendments

2005 Amendments. Subsec. (d), (d)(1). Pub.L. 109–8, § 411(1), struck "On" at the beginning of the subsection and inserted "**(1)** Subject to paragraph (2), on".

Subsec. (d)(2). Pub.L. 109–8, § 411(2), added par. (2).

Subsec. (e). Pub.L. 109–8, § 437, rewrote subsec. (e), which formerly read:

"**(e)** In a case in which the debtor is a small business and elects to be considered a small business—

"**(1)** only the debtor may file a plan until after 100 days after the date of the order for relief under this chapter;

"**(2)** all plans shall be filed within 160 days after the date of the order for relief; and

"**(3)** on request of a party in interest made within the respective periods specified in paragraphs (1) and (2) and after notice and a hearing, the court may—

"**(A)** reduce the 100–day period or the 160–day period specified in paragraph (1) or (2) for cause; and

"**(B)** increase the 100–day period specified in paragraph (1) if the debtor shows that the need for an increase is caused by circumstances for which the debtor should not be held accountable."

1994 Amendments. Subsec. (e). Pub.L. 103–394, § 217(d), added subsec. (e).

1986 Amendments. Subsec. (d). Pub.L. 99–554 added reference to subsection (b) of this section.

1984 Amendments. Subsec. (c)(3). Pub.L. 98–353, § 506(a), substituted "of claims or interests that is" for "the claims or interests of which are".

Subsec. (d). Pub.L. 98–353, § 506(b), added "made within the respective periods specified in subsection (c) of this section" following "interest".

Effective and Applicability Provisions

2005 Acts. Amendments by Pub.L. 109–8 effective, except as otherwise provided, 180 days after April 20, 2005, and inapplicable with respect to cases commenced under Title 11 before the effective date, see Pub.L. 109–8, § 1501, set out as a note under 11 U.S.C.A. § 101.

1994 Acts. Amendment by Pub.L. 103–394 effective on Oct. 22, 1994, and not to apply with respect to cases commenced under Title 11 of the United States Code before Oct. 22, 1994, see section 702 of Pub.L. 103–394, set out as a note under section 101 of this title.

1986 Acts. Amendment by Pub.L. 99–554 effective 30 days after Oct. 27, 1986, except as otherwise provided for, see section 302(a) of Pub.L. 99–554, set out as a note under section 581 of Title 28, Judiciary and Judicial Procedure.

1984 Acts. Amendment by Pub.L. 98–353 effective with respect to cases filed 90 days after July 10, 1984, see section

552(a), formerly 553(a), of Pub.L. 98–353, set out as a note under section 101 of this title.

Separability of Provisions

If any provision of or amendment made by Pub.L. 103–394 or the application of such provision or amendment to any person or circumstance is held to be unconstitutional, the remaining provisions of and amendments made by Pub.L. 103–394 and the application of such provisions and amendments to any person or circumstance shall not be affected thereby, see section 701 of Pub.L. 103–394, set out as a note under section 101 of this title.

CROSS REFERENCES

Effect of conversion, see 11 USCA § 348.

Failure to propose plan as cause for conversion or dismissal, see 11 USCA § 1112.

Filing of plan by trustee, see 11 USCA § 1106.

Filing of plan in—

    Chapter nine cases, see 11 USCA § 941.

    Chapter thirteen cases, see 11 USCA § 1321.

    Chapter twelve cases, see 11 USCA § 1221.

United States trustee not permitted to file plan, see 11 USCA § 307.

LIBRARY REFERENCES

American Digest System

Bankruptcy ☞3533.1 to 3535.

Key Number System Topic No. 51.

Corpus Juris Secundum

CJS Bankruptcy § 1133, Who May File; Time for Filing.

§ 1122. Classification of claims or interests

(a) Except as provided in subsection (b) of this section, a plan may place a claim or an interest in a particular class only if such claim or interest is substantially similar to the other claims or interests of such class.

(b) A plan may designate a separate class of claims consisting only of every unsecured claim that is less than or reduced to an amount that the court approves as reasonable and necessary for administrative convenience.

(Pub.L. 95–598, Nov. 6, 1978, 92 Stat. 2631.)

HISTORICAL AND STATUTORY NOTES

Revision Notes and Legislative Reports

1978 Acts. This section codifies current case law surrounding the classification of claims and equity securities. It requires classification based on the nature of the claims or interests classified, and permits inclusion of claims or interests in a particular class only if the claim or interest being included is substantially similar to the other claims or interests of the class.

Subsection (b), also a codification of existing practice, contains an exception. The plan may designate a separate class of claims consisting only of every unsecured claim that is less than or reduced to an amount that the court approves as reasonable and necessary for administrative convenience. Senate Report No. 95–989.

Applicability of this section in Chapter 9 cases, see 11 USCA § 901.

Contents of plan filed in—

Chapter thirteen cases, see 11 USCA § 1322.

Chapter twelve cases, see 11 USCA § 1222.

Filing and allowance of postpetition claims in Chapter 13 cases, see 11 USCA § 1305.

Filing of proofs of claims or interests, see 11 USCA § 501.

LIBRARY REFERENCES

American Digest System

Bankruptcy ⚖3550.

Key Number System Topic No. 51.

Corpus Juris Secundum

CJS Bankruptcy § 1121, Requirements for Confirmation.

CJS Bankruptcy § 1163, Modification of the Plan.

CJS Bankruptcy § 1173, Classification and Discrimination.

CJS Bankruptcy § 1178, Payments--Time for Completion.

CJS Bankruptcy § 1189, Contents of Plan, Generally.

CJS Bankruptcy § 1192, Classification and Discrimination.

§ 1123. Contents of plan

(a) Notwithstanding any otherwise applicable non-bankruptcy law, a plan shall—

(1) designate, subject to section 1122 of this title, classes of claims, other than claims of a kind specified in section 507(a)(2), 507(a)(3), or 507(a)(8) of this title, and classes of interests;

(2) specify any class of claims or interests that is not impaired under the plan;

(3) specify the treatment of any class of claims or interests that is impaired under the plan;

(4) provide the same treatment for each claim or interest of a particular class, unless the holder of a particular claim or interest agrees to a less favorable treatment of such particular claim or interest;

(5) provide adequate means for the plan's implementation, such as—

(A) retention by the debtor of all or any part of the property of the estate;

(B) transfer of all or any part of the property of the estate to one or more entities, whether organized before or after the confirmation of such plan;

(C) merger or consolidation of the debtor with one or more persons;

(D) sale of all or any part of the property of the estate, either subject to or free of any lien, or the distribution of all or any part of the property of the estate among those having an interest in such property of the estate;

(E) satisfaction or modification of any lien;

(F) cancellation or modification of any indenture or similar instrument;

(G) curing or waiving of any default;

(H) extension of a maturity date or a change in an interest rate or other term of outstanding securities;

(I) amendment of the debtor's charter; or

(J) issuance of securities of the debtor, or of any entity referred to in subparagraph (B) or (C) of this paragraph, for cash, for property, for existing securities, or in exchange for claims or interests, or for any other appropriate purpose;

(6) provide for the inclusion in the charter of the debtor, if the debtor is a corporation, or of any corporation referred to in paragraph (5)(B) or (5)(C) of this subsection, of a provision prohibiting the issuance of nonvoting equity securities, and providing, as to the several classes of securities possessing voting power, an appropriate distribution of such power among such classes, including, in the case of any class of equity securities having a preference over another class of equity securities with respect to dividends, adequate provisions for the election of directors representing such preferred class in the event of default in the payment of such dividends;

(7) contain only provisions that are consistent with the interests of creditors and equity security holders and with public policy with respect to the manner of selection of any officer, director, or trustee under the plan and any successor to such officer, director, or trustee; and

(8) in a case in which the debtor is an individual, provide for the payment to creditors under the plan of all or such portion of earnings from personal services performed by the debtor after the commencement of the case or other future income of the debtor as is necessary for the execution of the plan.

(b) Subject to subsection (a) of this section, a plan may—

(1) impair or leave unimpaired any class of claims, secured or unsecured, or of interests;

(2) subject to section 365 of this title, provide for the assumption, rejection, or assignment of any executory contract or unexpired lease of the debtor not previously rejected under such section;

(3) provide for—

(A) the settlement or adjustment of any claim or interest belonging to the debtor or to the estate; or

(B) the retention and enforcement by the debtor, by the trustee, or by a representative of the estate appointed for such purpose, of any such claim or interest;

(4) provide for the sale of all or substantially all of the property of the estate, and the distribution of the

proceeds of such sale among holders of claims or interests;

(5) modify the rights of holders of secured claims, other than a claim secured only by a security interest in real property that is the debtor's principal residence, or of holders of unsecured claims, or leave unaffected the rights of holders of any class of claims; and

(6) include any other appropriate provision not inconsistent with the applicable provisions of this title.

(c) In a case concerning an individual, a plan proposed by an entity other than the debtor may not provide for the use, sale, or lease of property exempted under section 522 of this title, unless the debtor consents to such use, sale, or lease.

(d) Notwithstanding subsection (a) of this section and sections 506(b), 1129(a)(7), and 1129(b) of this title, if it is proposed in a plan to cure a default the amount necessary to cure the default shall be determined in accordance with the underlying agreement and applicable nonbankruptcy law.

(Pub.L. 95–598, Nov. 6, 1978, 92 Stat. 2631; Pub.L. 98–353, Title III, § 507, July 10, 1984, 98 Stat. 385; Pub.L. 103–394, Title II, § 206, Title III, §§ 304(h)(6), 305(a), Title V, § 501(d)(31), Oct. 22, 1994, 108 Stat. 4123, 4134, 4146; Pub.L. 109–8, Title III, § 321(b), Title XV, § 1502(a)(7), Apr. 20, 2005, 119 Stat. 95, 216.)

HISTORICAL AND STATUTORY NOTES

Revision Notes and Legislative Reports

1978 Acts. Subsection (a) specifies what a plan of reorganization must contain. The plan must designate classes of claims and interests, and specify, by class, the claims or interests that are unimpaired under the plan. Priority claims are not required to be classified because they may not have arisen when the plan is filed. The plan must provide the same treatment for each claim or interest of a particular class, unless the holder of a particular claim or interest agrees to a different, but not better, treatment of his claim or interest.

Paragraph (3) applies to claims, not creditors. Thus, if a creditor is undersecured, and thus has a secured claim and an unsecured claim, this paragraph will be applied independently to each of his claims.

Paragraph (4) of subsection (a) is derived from section 216 of chapter X [section 616 of former Title 11] with some modifications. It requires the plan to provide adequate means for the plans [sic] execution. These means may include retention by the debtor of all or any part of the property of the estate, transfer of all or any part of the property of the estate to one or more entities, whether organized pre- or postconfirmation, merger or consolidation of the debtor with one or more persons, sale and distribution of all or any part of the property of the estate, satisfaction or modification of any lien, cancellation or modification of any indenture or similar instrument, curing or waiving of any default, extension of maturity dates or change in interest rates of securities, amendment of the debtor's charter, and issuance of securities.

Subparagraph (C), as it applies in railroad cases, has the effect of overruling *St. Joe Paper Co. v. Atlantic Coast Line R.R.*, 347 U.S. 298 (1954). [Fla.1954, 74 S.Ct. 574, 98 L.Ed. 710, rehearing denied 74 S.Ct. 734, 347 U.S. 980, 98 L.Ed. 1118]. It will allow the trustee or creditors to propose a plan of merger with another railroad without the consent of the debtor, and the debtor will be bound under proposed 11 U.S.C. 1141(a). See Hearings, pt. 3, at 1616. "Similar instrument" referred to in subparagraph (F) might include a deposit with an agent for distribution, other than an indenture trustee, such as an agent under an agreement in a railroad conditional sale or lease financing agreement.

Paragraphs (5) and (6) and subsection (b) are derived substantially from section 216 of Chapter X (11 U.S.C. 616) [section 616 of former Title 11]. Paragraph (5) requires the plan to prohibit the issuance of nonvoting equity securities, and to provide for an appropriate distribution of voting power among the various classes of equity securities. Paragraph (6) requires that the plan contain only provisions that are consistent with the interests of creditors and equity security holders, and with public policy with respect to the selection of officers, directors, and trustees, and their successors.

Subsection (b) specifies the matters that the plan may propose. The plan may impair or leave unimpaired any claim or interest. The plan may provide for the assumption or rejection of executory contracts or unexpired leases not previously rejected under section 365. The plan may also provide for the treatment of claims by the debtor against other entities that are not settled before the confirmation of the plan. The plan may propose settlement or adjustment of any claim or equity security belonging to the estate, or may propose retention and enforcement of such claim or interest by the debtor or by an agent appointed for that purpose.

The plan may also propose the sale of all or substantially all of the property of the estate, and the distribution of the proceeds of the sale among creditors and equity security holders. This would be a liquidating plan. The subsection permits the plan to include any other appropriate provision not inconsistent with the applicable provisions of the bankruptcy code.

Subsection (c) protects an individual debtor's exempt property by prohibiting its use, sale, or lease under a plan proposed by someone other than the debtor, unless the debtor consents. Senate Report No. 95–989.

1984 Acts. Statements by Legislative Leaders, see 1984 U.S.Code Cong. and Adm.News, p. 576.

1994 Acts. House Report No. 103–835, see 1994 U.S. Code Cong. and Adm. News, p. 3340.

2005 Acts. House Report No. 109–31(Part I), see 2005 U.S. Code Cong. and Adm. News, p. 88.

Legislative Statements

Section 1123 of the House amendment represents a compromise between similar provisions in the House bill and Senate amendment. The section has been clarified to clearly indicate that both secured and unsecured claims, or either of them, may be impaired in a case under title 11. In addition assumption or rejection of an executory contract under a plan must comply with section 365 of title 11. Moreover, section 1123(a)(1) has been substantively modified to permit classification of certain kinds of priority claims. This is important for purposes of confirmation under section 1129(a)(9).

Section 1123(a)(5) of the House amendment is derived from a similar provision in the House bill and Senate amendment but deletes the language pertaining to "fair upset price" as an unnecessary restriction. Section 1123 is also intended to indicate that a plan may provide for any action specified in section 1123 in the case of a corporation without a resolution of the board of directors. If the plan is confirmed, then any action proposed in the plan may be taken notwithstanding any otherwise applicable nonbankruptcy law in accordance with section 1142(a) of title 11.

Amendments

2005 Amendments. Subsec. (a)(1). Pub.L. 109–8, § 1502(a)(7), struck out "507(a)(1), 507(a)(2)" and inserted "507(a)(2), 507(a)(3)".

Subsec. (a)(6). Pub.L. 109–8, § 321(b)(1), struck out "and" at the end of par. (6).

Subsec. (a)(7). Pub.L. 109–8, § 321(b)(2), struck out the period at the end of par. (7) and inserted "; and".

Subsec. (a)(8). Pub.L. 109–8, § 321(b)(3), added par. (8).

1994 Amendments. Subsec. (a)(1). Pub.L. 103–394, § 304(h)(6), substituted "507(a)(8)" for "507(a)(7)".

Pub.L. 103–394, § 501(d)(31), which directed that a comma be inserted after "title" the last place it appears, required no change to text due to earlier amendment by section 507(a)(2)(B) of Pub.L. 98–353, which among other changes added a comma after "title" the last place it appears.

Subsec. (b)(5), (6). Pub.L. 103–394, § 206, added par. (5) and redesignated former par. (5) as (6).

Subsec. (d). Pub.L. 103–394, § 305(a), added subsec. (d).

1984 Amendments. Subsec. (a). Pub.L. 98–353, § 507(a)(1), in provisions preceding par. (1), substituted "Notwithstanding any otherwise applicable nonbankruptcy law, a" for "A".

Subsec. (a)(1). Pub.L. 98–353, § 507(a)(2)(A), added a comma after "classes of claims".

Pub.L. 98–353, § 507(a)(2)(B), substituted "507(a)(7) of this title," for "507(a)(6) of this title".

Subsec. (a)(3). Pub.L. 98–353, § 507(a)(3), struck out "shall" before "specify the treatment".

Subsec. (a)(5). Pub.L. 98–353, § 507(a)(4), substituted "implementation" for "execution".

Subsec. (a)(5)(G). Pub.L. 98–353, § 507(a)(5), added "of" after "waiving".

Subsec. (b)(2). Pub.L. 98–353, § 507(b)(1), substituted "rejection, or assignment" for "or rejection".

Pub.L. 98–353, § 507(b)(2) substituted "under such section" for "under section 365 of this title".

Effective and Applicability Provisions

2005 Acts. Amendments by Pub.L. 109–8 effective, except as otherwise provided, 180 days after April 20, 2005, and inapplicable with respect to cases commenced under Title 11 before the effective date, see Pub.L. 109–8, § 1501, set out as a note under 11 U.S.C.A. § 101.

1994 Acts. Amendments by sections 206, 304(h)(6), and 501(d)(31) of Pub.L. 103–394 effective on Oct. 22, 1994, and not to apply with respect to cases commenced under Title 11 of the United States Code before Oct. 22, 1994, see section 702 of Pub.L. 103–394, set out as a note under section 101 of this title.

Amendment by section 305(a) of Pub.L. 103–394 effective Oct. 22, 1994, and applicable only to agreements entered into

after Oct. 22, 1994, see section 702 of Pub.L.103–394, set out as a note under section 101 of this title.

1984 Acts. Amendment by Pub.L. 98–353 effective with respect to cases filed 90 days after July 10, 1984, see section 552(a), formerly 553(a), of Pub.L. 98–353, set out as a note under section 101 of this title.

Separability of Provisions

If any provision of or amendment made by Pub.L. 103–394 or the application of such provision or amendment to any person or circumstance is held to be unconstitutional, the remaining provisions of and amendments made by Pub.L. 103–394 and the application of such provisions and amendments to any person or circumstance shall not be affected thereby, see section 701 of Pub.L. 103–394, set out as a note under section 101 of this title.

CROSS REFERENCES

Applicability of subsecs. (a)(1) to (5) and (b) of this section in Chapter 9 cases, see 11 USCA § 901.

Contents of plan filed in—

    Chapter thirteen cases, see 11 USCA § 1322.

    Chapter twelve cases, see 11 USCA § 1222.

    Railroad reorganization cases, see 11 USCA § 1172.

LIBRARY REFERENCES

American Digest System

Bankruptcy ⟐3548.1 to 3565.

Key Number System Topic No. 51.

Corpus Juris Secundum

CJS Bankruptcy § 923, Application for Approval.

CJS Bankruptcy § 1134, Impairment of Claims or Interests.

CJS Bankruptcy § 1135, Impairment of Claims or Interests--Curing Defaults.

CJS Bankruptcy § 1137, Means of Implementation.

CJS Bankruptcy § 1138, Protection of Exempted Property.

CJS Bankruptcy § 1143, Optional Provisions.

CJS Bankruptcy § 1145, Specification of Unimpaired Classes of Claims.

CJS Bankruptcy § 1146, Treatment of Impaired Classes; Equality Within Class.

CJS Bankruptcy § 1163, Modification of the Plan.

CJS Bankruptcy § 1168, Reorganization Plan.

§ 1124. Impairment of claims or interests

Except as provided in section 1123(a)(4) of this title, a class of claims or interests is impaired under a plan unless, with respect to each claim or interest of such class, the plan—

    (1) leaves unaltered the legal, equitable, and contractual rights to which such claim or interest entitles the holder of such claim or interest; or

    (2) notwithstanding any contractual provision or applicable law that entitles the holder of such claim or interest to demand or receive accelerated payment of such claim or interest after the occurrence of a default—

(A) cures any such default that occurred before or after the commencement of the case under this title, other than a default of a kind specified in section 365(b)(2) of this title or of a kind that section 365(b)(2) expressly does not require to be cured;

(B) reinstates the maturity of such claim or interest as such maturity existed before such default;

(C) compensates the holder of such claim or interest for any damages incurred as a result of any reasonable reliance by such holder on such contractual provision or such applicable law;

(D) if such claim or such interest arises from any failure to perform a nonmonetary obligation, other than a default arising from failure to operate a nonresidential real property lease subject to section 365(b)(1)(A), compensates the holder of such claim or such interest (other than the debtor or an insider) for any actual pecuniary loss incurred by such holder as a result of such failure; and

(E) does not otherwise alter the legal, equitable, or contractual rights to which such claim or interest entitles the holder of such claim or interest.

(Pub.L. 95–598, Nov. 6, 1978, 92 Stat. 2633; Pub.L. 98–353, Title III, § 508, July 10, 1984, 98 Stat. 385; Pub.L. 103–394, Title II, § 213(d), Oct. 22, 1994, 108 Stat. 4126; Pub.L. 109–8, Title III, § 328(b), Apr. 20, 2005, 119 Stat. 100.)

HISTORICAL AND STATUTORY NOTES

Revision Notes and Legislative Reports

1978 Acts. The basic concept underlying this section is not new. It rests essentially on Section [sic] 107 of Chapter X (11 U.S.C. 507) [section 507 of former Title 11], which states that creditors or stockholders or any class thereof "shall be deemed to be 'affected' by a plan only if their or its interest shall be materially and adversely affected thereby."

This section is designed to indicate when contractual rights of creditors or interest holders are not materially affected. It specifies three ways in which the plan may leave a claim or interest unimpaired.

First, the plan may propose not to alter the legal, equitable, or contractual rights to which the claim or interest entitled its holder.

Second, a claim or interest is unimpaired by curing the effect of a default and reinstating the original terms of an obligation when maturity was brought on or accelerated by the default. The intervention of bankruptcy and the defaults represent a temporary crisis which the plan of reorganization is intended to clear away. The holder of a claim or interest who under the plan is restored to his original position, when others receive less or get nothing at all, is fortunate indeed and has no cause to complain. Curing of the default and the assumption of the debt in accordance with its terms is an important reorganization technique for dealing with a particular class of claims, especially secured claims.

Third, a claim or interest is unimpaired if the plan provides for their payment in cash. In the case of a debt liability, the cash payment is for the allowed amount of the claim, which does not include a redemption premium. If it is an equity security with a fixed liquidation preference, such as a preferred stock, the allowed amount is such liquidation preference, with no redemption premium. With respect to any other equity security, such as a common stock, cash payment must be equal to the "value of such holder's interest in the debtor."

Section 1124 does not include payment "in property" other than cash. Except for a rare case, claims or interests are not by their terms payable in property, but a plan may so provide and those affected thereby may accept or reject the proposed plan. They may not be forced to accept a plan declaring the holders' claims or interests to be "unimpaired." Senate Report No. 95–989.

This section is new. It is designed to indicate when contractual rights of creditors or interest holders are not materially affected. The section specifies three ways in which the plan may leave a claim or interest unimpaired.

First, the plan may propose not to alter the legal, equitable, or contractual rights to which the claim or interest entitled its holder.

Second, the plan is permitted to reinstate a claim or interest and thus leave it unimpaired. Reinstatement consists of curing any default (other than a default under an ipso facto or bankruptcy clause) and reinstatement of the maturity of the claim or interest. Further, the plan may not otherwise alter any legal, equitable, or contractual right to which the claim or interest entitles its holder.

Third, the plan may leave a claim or interest unimpaired by paying its amount in full other than in securities of the debtor, an affiliate of the debtor participating in a joint plan, or a successor to the debtor. These securities are excluded because determination of their value would require a valuation of the business being reorganized. Use of them to pay a creditor or equity security holder without his consent may be done only under section 1129(b) and only after a valuation of the debtor. Under this paragraph, the plan must pay the allowed amount of the claim in full, in cash or other property, or, in the case of an equity security, must pay the greatest of any fixed liquidation preference to which the terms of the equity security entitle its holder, any fixed price at which the debtor, under the terms of the equity security may redeem such equity security, and the value, as of the effective date of the plan, of the holder's interest in the debtor. The value of the holder's interest need not be determined precisely by valuing the debtor's business if such value of clearly below redemption or liquidation preference values. If such value would require a full-scale valuation of the business, then such interest should be treated as impaired. But, if the debtor corporation is clearly insolvent, then the value of the common stock holder's interest in the debtor is zero, and offering them nothing under the plan of reorganization will not impair their rights.

"Value, as of the effective date of the plan," as used in paragraph (3) and in proposed 11 U.S.C. 1179(a)(7)(B), 1129(a)(9), 1129(b), 1172(2), 1325(a)(4), 1325(a)(5)(B), and 1328(b), indicates that the promised payment under the plan must be discounted to present value as of the effective date of the plan. The discounting should be based only on the unpaid balance of the amount due under the plan, until that amount, including interest, is paid in full. House Report No. 95–595.

1984 Acts. Statements by Legislative Leaders, see 1984 U.S.Code Cong. and Adm.News, p. 576.

1994 Acts. House Report No. 103–835, see 1994 U.S. Code Cong. and Adm. News, p. 3340.

2005 Acts. House Report No. 109–31(Part I), see 2005 U.S. Code Cong. and Adm. News, p. 88.

Legislative Statements

Section 1124 of the House amendment is derived from a similar provision in the House bill and Senate amendment. The section defines the new concept of "impairment" of claims or interests; the concept differs significantly from the concept of "materially and adversely affected" under the Bankruptcy Act [former Title 11]. Section 1124(3) of the House amendment provides that a holder of a claim or interest is not impaired, if the plan provides that the holder will receive the allowed amount of the holder's claim, or in the case of an interest with a fixed liquidation preference or redemption price, the greater of such price. This adopts the position contained in the House bill and rejects the contrary standard contained in the Senate amendment.

Section 1124(3) of the House amendment rejects a provision contained in section 1124(3)(B)(iii) of the House bill which would have considered a class of interest not to be impaired by virtue of the fact that the plan provided cash or property for the value of the holder's interest in the debtor.

The effect of the House amendment is to permit an interest not to be impaired only if the interest has a fixed liquidation preference or redemption price. Therefore, a class of interests such as common stock, must either accept a plan under section 1129(a)(8), or the plan must satisfy the requirements of section 1129(b)(2)(C) in order for a plan to be confirmed.

A compromise reflected in section 1124(2)(C) of the House amendment indicates that a class of claims is not impaired under the circumstances of section 1124(2) if damages are paid to rectify reasonable reliance engaged in by the holder of a claim or interest arising from the prepetition breach of a contractual provision, such as an ipso facto or bankruptcy clause, or law. Where the rights of third parties are concerned, such as in the case of lease premises which have been rerented to a third party, it is not intended that there will be adequate damages to compensate the third party.

Amendments

2005 Amendments. Par. (2)(A). Pub.L. 109–8, § 328(b)(1), inserted "or of a kind that section 365(b)(2) expressly does not require to be cured" before the semicolon at the end.

Par. (2)(C). Pub.L. 109–8, § 328(b)(2), struck out "and" at the end of subpar. (C).

Par. (2)(D). Pub.L. 109–8, § 328(b)(3), (4), redesignated former subpar. (D) as subpar. (E), and inserted a new subpar. (D), respectively.

Par. (2)(E). Pub.L. 109–8, § 328(b)(3), redesignated former subpar. (D) as subpar. (E).

1994 Amendments. Par. (3). Pub.L. 103–394, § 213(d), struck out par. (3), which stated that a class of claims or interests is impaired under a plan unless the plan provides that on the plan's effective date, the holder of such claim or interest receives cash equal to certain amounts.

1984 Amendments. Par. (2)(A). Pub.L. 98–353, § 508(1), substituted "cures any such default that occurred before or after the commencement of the case under this title," for "cures any such default, other than a default of a kind specified in section 365(b)(2) of this title, that occurred

before or after the commencement of the case under this title;".

Par. (3)(B)(i). Pub.L. 98–353, § 508(2), substituted "or" for "and".

Effective and Applicability Provisions

2005 Acts. Amendments by Pub.L. 109–8 effective, except as otherwise provided, 180 days after April 20, 2005, and inapplicable with respect to cases commenced under Title 11 before the effective date, see Pub.L. 109–8, § 1501, set out as a note under 11 U.S.C.A. § 101.

1994 Acts. Amendment by Pub.L. 103–394 effective on Oct. 22, 1994, and not to apply with respect to cases commenced under Title 11 of the United States Code before Oct. 22, 1994, see section 702 of Pub.L. 103–394, set out as a note under section 101 of this title.

1984 Acts. Amendment by Pub.L. 98–353 effective with respect to cases filed 90 days after July 10, 1984, see section 552(a), formerly 553(a), of Pub.L. 98–353, set out as a note under section 101 of this title.

Separability of Provisions

If any provision of or amendment made by Pub.L. 103–394 or the application of such provision or amendment to any person or circumstance is held to be unconstitutional, the remaining provisions of and amendments made by Pub.L. 103–394 and the application of such provisions and amendments to any person or circumstance shall not be affected thereby, see section 701 of Pub.L. 103–394, set out as a note under section 101 of this title.

CROSS REFERENCES

Allowance of claims or interests, see 11 USCA § 502.

Applicability of this section in Chapter nine cases, see 11 USCA § 901.

Claims and interests generally, see 11 USCA § 1111.

Filing of proofs of claims or interests, see 11 USCA § 501.

LIBRARY REFERENCES

American Digest System

Bankruptcy ⚎3536.1, 3537.

Key Number System Topic No. 51.

Corpus Juris Secundum

CJS Bankruptcy § 1134, Impairment of Claims or Interests.

CJS Bankruptcy § 1135, Impairment of Claims or Interests--Curing Defaults.

CJS Bankruptcy § 1156, Deemed Acceptance or Rejection; Unimpaired Classes.

CJS Bankruptcy § 1157, Acceptance of the Plan--Eligibility to Vote; Impairment.

§ 1125. Postpetition disclosure and solicitation

(a) In this section—

(1) "adequate information" means information of a kind, and in sufficient detail, as far as is reasonably practicable in light of the nature and history of the debtor and the condition of the debtor's books and records, including a discussion of the potential material Federal tax consequences of the plan to

the debtor, any successor to the debtor, and a hypothetical investor typical of the holders of claims or interests in the case, that would enable such a hypothetical investor of the relevant class to make an informed judgment about the plan, but adequate information need not include such information about any other possible or proposed plan and in determining whether a disclosure statement provides adequate information, the court shall consider the complexity of the case, the benefit of additional information to creditors and other parties in interest, and the cost of providing additional information; and

(2) "investor typical of holders of claims or interests of the relevant class" means investor having—

(A) a claim or interest of the relevant class;

(B) such a relationship with the debtor as the holders of other claims or interests of such class generally have; and

(C) such ability to obtain such information from sources other than the disclosure required by this section as holders of claims or interests in such class generally have.

(b) An acceptance or rejection of a plan may not be solicited after the commencement of the case under this title from a holder of a claim or interest with respect to such claim or interest, unless, at the time of or before such solicitation, there is transmitted to such holder the plan or a summary of the plan, and a written disclosure statement approved, after notice and a hearing, by the court as containing adequate information. The court may approve a disclosure statement without a valuation of the debtor or an appraisal of the debtor's assets.

(c) The same disclosure statement shall be transmitted to each holder of a claim or interest of a particular class, but there may be transmitted different disclosure statements, differing in amount, detail, or kind of information, as between classes.

(d) Whether a disclosure statement required under subsection (b) of this section contains adequate information is not governed by any otherwise applicable nonbankruptcy law, rule, or regulation, but an agency or official whose duty is to administer or enforce such a law, rule, or regulation may be heard on the issue of whether a disclosure statement contains adequate information. Such an agency or official may not appeal from, or otherwise seek review of, an order approving a disclosure statement.

(e) A person that solicits acceptance or rejection of a plan, in good faith and in compliance with the applicable provisions of this title, or that participates, in good faith and in compliance with the applicable provisions of this title, in the offer, issuance, sale, or purchase of a security, offered or sold under the plan, of the debtor, of an affiliate participating in a joint plan with the debtor, or of a newly organized successor to the debtor under the plan, is not liable, on account of such solicitation or participation, for violation of any applicable law, rule, or regulation governing solicitation of acceptance or rejection of a plan or the offer, issuance, sale, or purchase of securities.

(f) Notwithstanding subsection (b), in a small business case—

(1) the court may determine that the plan itself provides adequate information and that a separate disclosure statement is not necessary;

(2) the court may approve a disclosure statement submitted on standard forms approved by the court or adopted under section 2075 of title 28; and

(3)(A) the court may conditionally approve a disclosure statement subject to final approval after notice and a hearing;

(B) acceptances and rejections of a plan may be solicited based on a conditionally approved disclosure statement if the debtor provides adequate information to each holder of a claim or interest that is solicited, but a conditionally approved disclosure statement shall be mailed not later than 25 days before the date of the hearing on confirmation of the plan; and

(C) the hearing on the disclosure statement may be combined with the hearing on confirmation of a plan.

(g) Notwithstanding subsection (b), an acceptance or rejection of the plan may be solicited from a holder of a claim or interest if such solicitation complies with applicable nonbankruptcy law and if such holder was solicited before the commencement of the case in a manner complying with applicable nonbankruptcy law.

(Pub.L. 95–598, Nov. 6, 1978, 92 Stat. 2633; Pub.L. 98–353, Title III, § 509, July 10, 1984, 98 Stat. 385; Pub.L. 103–394, Title II, § 217(e), Oct. 22, 1994, 108 Stat. 4127; Pub.L. 109–8, Title IV, §§ 408, 431, Title VII, § 717, Apr. 20, 2005, 119 Stat. 106, 109, 131.)

HISTORICAL AND STATUTORY NOTES

Revision Notes and Legislative Reports

1978 Acts. This section extends disclosure requirements in connection with solicitations to all cases under chapter 11. Heretofore this subject was dealt with by the Bankruptcy Act [former Title 11] mainly in the special contexts of railroad reorganizations and chapter X [former Chapter 10 (section 501 et seq.) of former Title 11 cases.

Subsection (a) defines (1) the subject matter of disclosure as "adequate information" and relates the standard of adequacy to an (2) "investor typical of holders or claims or interests of the relevant class." "Investor" is used broadly here, for it will almost always include a trade creditor or other creditors who originally had no investment intent or interest. It refers to the investment-type decision by those called upon to accept a plan to modify their claims or interests, which typically will involve acceptance of new securities or of a cash payment in lieu thereof.

Both the kind and form of information are left essentially to the judicial discretion of the court, guided by the specification in subparagraph (a)(1) that it be of a kind and in sufficient detail that a reasonable and typical investor can make an informed judgment about the plan. The information required will necessarily be governed by the circumstances of the case.

Reporting and audit standards devised for solvent and continuing businesses do not necessarily fit a debtor in reorganization. Subsection (a)(1) expressly incorporates consideration of the nature and history of the debtor and the condition of its books and records into the determination of what is reasonably practicable to supply. These factors are particularly pertinent to historical data and to discontinued operations of no future relevance.

A plan is necessarily predicated on knowledge of the assets and liabilities being dealt with and on factually supported expectations as to the future course of the business sufficient to meet the feasibility standard in section 1130(a)(11) [now section 1129(a)(11)] of this title. It may thus be necessary to provide estimates or judgments for that purpose. Yet it remains practicable to describe, in such detail as may be relevant and needed, the basis for the plan and the data on which supporters of the plan rely.

Subsection (b) establishes the jurisdiction of the court over this subject by prohibiting solicitation of acceptance or rejection of a plan after the commencement of the case, unless the person solicited receives, before or at the time of the solicitation, a written disclosure statement approved by the court, after notice and hearing, as containing adequate information. As under present law, determinations of value, by appraisal or otherwise, are not required if not needed to accomplish the purpose specified in subsection (a)(1).

Subsection (c) requires that the same disclosure statement be transmitted to each member of a class. It recognizes that the information needed for an informed judgment about the plan may differ among classes. A class whose rights under the plan center on a particular fund or asset would have no use for an extensive description of other matters that could not affect them.

Subsection (d) relieves the court of the need to follow any otherwise applicable Federal or state law in determining the adequacy of the information contained in the disclosure statement submitted for its approval. It authorizes an agency or official, Federal or state, charged with administering cognate laws so preempted to advise the court on the adequacy of proposed disclosure statement. But they are not authorized to appeal the court's decision.

Solicitations with respect to a plan do not involve just mere requests for opinions. Acceptance of the plan vitally affects creditors and shareholders, and most frequently the solicitation involves an offering of securities in exchange for claims or interests. The present bankruptcy statute [former Title 11] has exempted such offerings under each of its chapters from the registration and disclosure requirements of the Securities Act of 1933 [section 77a et seq. of Title 15, Commerce and Trade], an exemption also continued by section 1145(a)(2) of this title. The extension of the disclosure requirements to all chapter 11 cases justifies the coordinate extension of these exemptions. By the same token, no valid purpose is served not to exempt from the requirements of similar state laws in a matter under the exclusive jurisdiction of the Federal bankruptcy laws.

Subsection (e) exonerates any person who, in good faith and in compliance with this title, solicits or participates in the offer, issuance, sale or purchase, under the plan, of a security from any liability, on account of such solicitation or participation, for violation of any law, rule, or regulation governing the offer, issuance, sale, or purchase of securities. This exoneration is coordinate with the exemption from Federal or State registration or licensing requirements provided by section 1145 of this title.

In the nonpublic case, the court, when approving the disclosure statement, has before it the texts of the plan, a proposed disclosure document, and such other information the plan proponents and other interested parties may present at the hearing. In the final analysis the exoneration which subsection (e) grants must depend on the good faith of the plan proponents and of those who participate in the preparation of the disclosure statement and in the solicitation. Subsection (e) does not affect civil or criminal liability for defects and inadequacies that are beyond the limits of the exoneration that good faith provides.

Section 1125 applies to public companies as well, subject to the qualifications of subsection (f). In case of a public company no solicitations of acceptance is permitted unless authorized by the court upon or after approval of the plan pursuant to section 1128(c). In addition to the documents specified in subsection (b), subsection (f) requires transmission of the opinion and order of the court approving the plan and, if filed, the advisory report of the Securities and Exchange Commission or a summary thereof prepared by the Commission. Senate Report No. 95–989.

This section is new. It is the heart of the consolidation of the various reorganization chapters found in current law. It requires disclosure before solicitation of acceptances of a plan or reorganization.

Subsection (a) contains two definitions. First, "adequate information" is defined to mean information of a kind, and insufficient [sic] detail, as far as is reasonably practical in light of the nature and history of the debtor and the condition of the debtor's books and records, that would enable a hypothetical reasonable investor typical of holders of claims or interests of the relevant class to make an informed judgment about the plan. Second, "investor typical of holders of claims or interests of the relevant class" is defined to mean an investor having a claim or interest of the relevant class, having such a relationship with the debtor as the holders of other claims or interests of the relevant class have, and having such ability to obtain information from sources other than the disclosure statement as holders of claims or interests of the relevant class have, and having such ability to obtain information from sources other than the disclosure statement as holders of claims or interests of the relevant class have. That is, the hypothetical investor against which the disclosure is measured must not be an insider if other members of the class are not insiders, and so on. In other words, the adequacy of disclosure is measured against the typical investor, not an extraordinary one.

The Supreme Court's rulemaking power will not extend to rulemaking that will prescribe what constitutes adequate information. That standard is a substantive standard. Precisely what constitutes adequate information in any particular instance will develop on a case-by-case basis. Courts will take a practical approach as to what is necessary under the circumstances of each case, such as the cost of preparation of the statements, the need for relative speed in solicitation and confirmation, and, of course, the need for investor protection. There will be a balancing of interests in each case. In reorganization cases, there is frequently great uncertainty. Therefore the need for flexibility is greatest.

Subsection (b) is the operative subsection. It prohibits solicitation of acceptances or rejections of a plan after the commencement of the case unless, at the time of the solicitation or before, there is transmitted to the solicitee the plan or a summary of the plan, and a written disclosure statement approved by the court as containing adequate information. The subsection permits approval of the statement without the necessity of a valuation of the debtor or an appraisal of the debtor's assets. However, in some cases, a valuation or appraisal will be necessary to develop adequate information. The court will be able to determine what is necessary in light of the facts and circumstances of each particular case.

Subsection (c) requires that the same disclosure statement go to all members of a particular class, but permits different disclosure to different classes.

Subsection (d) excepts the disclosure statements from the requirements of the securities laws (such as section 14 of the 1934 Act [section 78n of Title 15, Commerce and Trade] and section 5 of the 1933 Act [section 77e of Title 15]), and from similar State securities laws (blue sky laws, for example). The subsection permits an agency or official whose duty is to administer or enforce such laws (such as the Securities and Exchange Commission or State Corporation Commissioners) to appear and be heard on the issue of whether a disclosure statement contains adequate information, but the agencies and officials are not granted the right of appeal from an adverse determination in any capacity. They may join in an appeal by a true party in interest, however.

Subsection (e) is a safe harbor provision, and is necessary to make the exemption provided by subsection (d) effective. Without it, a creditor that solicited an acceptance or rejection in reliance on the court's approval of a disclosure statement would be potentially liable under antifraud sections designed to enforce the very sections of the securities laws from which subsection (d) excuses compliance. The subsection protects only persons that solicit in good faith and in compliance with the applicable provisions of the reorganization chapter. It provides protection from legal liability as well as from equitable liability based on an injunctive action by the SEC [Securities and Exchange Commission] or other agency or official. House Report No. 95–595.

1984 Acts. Statements by Legislative Leaders, see 1984 U.S.Code Cong. and Adm.News, p. 576.

1994 Acts. House Report No. 103–835, see 1994 U.S. Code Cong. and Adm. News, p. 3340.

2005 Acts. House Report No. 109–31(Part I), see 2005 U.S. Code Cong. and Adm. News, p. 88.

Legislative Statements

Section 1125 of the House amendment is derived from section 1125 of the House bill and Senate amendment except with respect to section 1125(f) of the Senate amendment. It will not be necessary for the court to consider the report of the examiner prior to approval of a disclosure statement. The investigation of the examiner is to proceed on an independent basis from the procedure of the reorganization under chapter 11. In order to ensure that the examiner's report will be expeditious and fair, the examiner is precluded from serving as a trustee in the case or from representing a trustee if a trustee is appointed, whether the case remains in chapter 11 or is converted to chapter 7 or 13.

Amendments

2005 Amendments. Subsec. (a)(1). Pub.L. 109–8, § 431(1), inserted "and in determining whether a disclosure statement provides adequate information, the court shall consider the complexity of the case, the benefit of additional information to creditors and other parties in interest, and the cost of providing additional information" following "possible or proposed plan".

Pub.L. 109–8, § 717(1), inserted "including a discussion of the potential material Federal tax consequences of the plan to the debtor, any successor to the debtor, and a hypothetical investor typical of the holders of claims or interests in the case," after "records,".

Pub.L. 109–8, § 717(2), struck out "a hypothetical reasonable investor typical of holders of claims or interests" and inserted "such a hypothetical investor".

Subsec. (f). Pub.L. 109–8, § 431(2), rewrote subsec. (f), which formerly read:

"**(f)** Notwithstanding subsection (b), in a case in which the debtor has elected under section 1121(e) to be considered a small business—

"**(1)** the court may conditionally approve a disclosure statement subject to final approval after notice and a hearing;

"**(2)** acceptances and rejections of a plan may be solicited based on a conditionally approved disclosure statement as long as the debtor provides adequate information to each holder of a claim or interest that is solicited, but a conditionally approved disclosure statement shall be mailed at least 10 days prior to the date of the hearing on confirmation of the plan; and

"**(3)** a hearing on the disclosure statement may be combined with a hearing on confirmation of a plan.

Subsec. (g). Pub.L. 109–8, § 408, added subsec. (g).

1994 Amendments. Subsec. (f). Pub.L. 103–394, § 217(e), added subsec. (f).

1984 Amendments. Subsec. (a)(1). Pub.L. 98–353, § 509(a)(1), added ", but adequate information need not include such information about any other possible or proposed plan" after "plan".

Subsec. (a)(2)(B). Pub.L. 98–353, § 509(a)(2), added "the" after "with".

Subsec. (a)(2)(C). Pub.L. 98–353, § 509(a)(3), added "of" after "holders".

Subsec. (d). Pub.L. 98–353, § 509(b)(1), added "required under subsection (b) of this section" after "Whether a disclosure statement" the first place phase appears.

Pub.L. 98–353, § 509(b)(2), added ", or otherwise seek review of," after "appeal from".

Subsec. (e). Pub.L. 98–353, § 509(c)(1), added "acceptance or rejection of a plan" after "solicits".

Pub.L. 98–353, § 509(c)(2), added "solicitation of acceptance or rejection of a plan or" following "governing".

Effective and Applicability Provisions

2005 Acts. Amendments by Pub.L. 109–8 effective, except as otherwise provided, 180 days after April 20, 2005, and inapplicable with respect to cases commenced under Title 11 before the effective date, see Pub.L. 109–8, § 1501, set out as a note under 11 U.S.C.A. § 101.

1994 Acts. Amendment by Pub.L. 103–394 effective on Oct. 22, 1994, and not to apply with respect to cases commenced

under Title 11 of the United States Code before Oct. 22, 1994, see section 702 of Pub.L. 103–394, set out as a note under section 101 of this title.

1984 Acts. Amendment by Pub.L. 98–353 effective with respect to cases filed 90 days after July 10, 1984, see section 552(a), formerly 553(a), of Pub.L. 98–353, set out as a note under section 101 of this title.

Separability of Provisions

If any provision of or amendment made by Pub.L. 103–394 or the application of such provision or amendment to any person or circumstance is held to be unconstitutional, the remaining provisions of and amendments made by Pub.L. 103–394 and the application of such provisions and amendments to any person or circumstance shall not be affected thereby, see section 701 of Pub.L. 103–394, set out as a note under section 101 of this title.

CROSS REFERENCES

Applicability of this section in Chapter nine cases, see 11 USCA § 901.

Duty of United States trustee to file comments with respect to plans and disclosure statements filed in connection with hearings under this section, see 28 USCA § 586.

Exemption from securities laws of certain transactions in which disclosure statements are provided, see 11 USCA § 1145.

LIBRARY REFERENCES

American Digest System

Bankruptcy ⬤3539.1, 3540.

Key Number System Topic No. 51.

Corpus Juris Secundum

CJS Bankruptcy § 299, Notice of Not Less Than 25 Days.

CJS Bankruptcy § 1118, Filing of Plan and Disclosure Statement; Hearing on Objections.

CJS Bankruptcy § 1119, Acceptance of Rejection of Plan by Claim Holders.

CJS Bankruptcy § 1151, Filing and Contents of Disclosure Statement.

CJS Bankruptcy § 1153, In Small Business Cases.

CJS Bankruptcy § 1156, Deemed Acceptance or Rejection; Unimpaired Classes.

CJS Bankruptcy § 1163, Modification of the Plan.

CJS Bankruptcy § 1175, Amount of Repayment of Unsecured Claims.

CJS Bankruptcy § 1240, Parties.

§ 1126. Acceptance of plan

(a) The holder of a claim or interest allowed under section 502 of this title may accept or reject a plan. If the United States is a creditor or equity security holder, the Secretary of the Treasury may accept or reject the plan on behalf of the United States.

(b) For the purposes of subsections (c) and (d) of this section, a holder of a claim or interest that has accepted or rejected the plan before the commencement of the case under this title is deemed to have accepted or rejected such plan, as the case may be, if—

(1) the solicitation of such acceptance or rejection was in compliance with any applicable nonbankruptcy law, rule, or regulation governing the adequacy of disclosure in connection with such solicitation; or

(2) if there is not any such law, rule, or regulation, such acceptance or rejection was solicited after disclosure to such holder of adequate information, as defined in section 1125(a) of this title.

(c) A class of claims has accepted a plan if such plan has been accepted by creditors, other than any entity designated under subsection (e) of this section, that hold at least two-thirds in amount and more than one-half in number of the allowed claims of such class held by creditors, other than any entity designated under subsection (e) of this section, that have accepted or rejected such plan.

(d) A class of interests has accepted a plan if such plan has been accepted by holders of such interests, other than any entity designated under subsection (e) of this section, that hold at least two-thirds in amount of the allowed interests of such class held by holders of such interests, other than any entity designated under subsection (e) of this section, that have accepted or rejected such plan.

(e) On request of a party in interest, and after notice and a hearing, the court may designate any entity whose acceptance or rejection of such plan was not in good faith, or was not solicited or procured in good faith or in accordance with the provisions of this title.

(f) Notwithstanding any other provision of this section, a class that is not impaired under a plan, and each holder of a claim or interest of such class, are conclusively presumed to have accepted the plan, and solicitation of acceptances with respect to such class from the holders of claims or interests of such class is not required.

(g) Notwithstanding any other provision of this section, a class is deemed not to have accepted a plan if such plan provides that the claims or interests of such class do not entitle the holders of such claims or interests to receive or retain any property under the plan on account of such claims or interests.

(Pub.L. 95–598, Nov. 6, 1978, 92 Stat. 2634; Pub.L. 98–353, Title III, § 510, July 10, 1984, 98 Stat. 386.)

HISTORICAL AND STATUTORY NOTES

Revision Notes and Legislative Reports

1978 Acts. Subsection (a) of this section permits the holder of a claim or interest allowed under section 502 to accept or reject a proposed plan of reorganization. The subsection also incorporates a provision now found in section 199 of chapter X [section 599 of former Title 11] that authorizes the Secretary of the Treasury to accept or reject a plan on behalf of the United States when the United States is a creditor or equity security holder.

Subsection (b) governs acceptances and rejections of plans obtained before commencement of a reorganization for a nonpublic company. Paragraph (3) expressly states that subsection (b) does not apply to a public company.

Prepetition solicitation is a common practice under chapter XI [former chapter 11 (section 701 et seq.) of former Title 11] today, and chapter IX [former chapter 9 (section 401 et seq.) of former Title 11] current makes explicit provision for it. Section 1126(b) counts a prepetition acceptance or rejection toward the required amounts and number of acceptances only if the solicitation of the acceptance or rejection was in compliance with any applicable nonbankruptcy law, rule, or regulation governing the adequacy of disclosure in connection with such solicitation. If there is not any such applicable law, rule, or regulation, then the acceptance or rejection is counted only if it was solicited after disclosure of adequate information, to the holder, as defined in section 1125(a)(1). This permits the court to ensure that the requirements of section 1125 are not avoided by prepetition solicitation.

Subsection (c) specifies the required amount and number of acceptances for a class of creditors. A class of creditors has accepted a plan if at least two-thirds in amount and more than one-half in number of the allowed claims of the class that are voted are cast in favor of the plan. The amount and number are computed on the basis of claims actually voted for or against the plan, not as under chapter X [former chapter 10 (section 501 et seq.) of former Title 11] on the basis of the allowed claims in the class. Subsection (f) excludes from all these calculations claims not voted in good faith, and claims procured or solicited not in good faith or not in accordance with the provisions of this title.

Subsection (c) requires that the same disclosure statement be transmitted to each member of a class. It recognizes that the information needed for an informed judgment about the plan may differ among classes. A class whose rights under the plan center on a particular fund or asset would have no use for an extensive description of other matters that could not affect them.

Subsection (d) relieves the court of the need to follow any otherwise applicable Federal or state law in determining the adequacy of the information contained in the disclosure statement submitted for its approval. It authorizes an agency or official, Federal or state, charged with administering cognate laws so pre-empted to advise the court on the adequacy of proposed disclosure statement. But they are not authorized to appeal the court's decision.

Solicitations with respect to a plan do not involve just mere requests for opinions. Acceptance of the plan vitally affects creditors and shareholders, and most frequently the solicitation involves an offering of securities in exchange for claims or interests. The present Bankruptcy Act [former Title 11] has exempted such offerings under each of its chapters from the registration and disclosure requirements of the Securities Act of 1933 [section 77a of Title 15, Commerce and Trade], et seq., an exemption also continued by section 1145 of this title. The extension of the disclosure requirements to all chapter 11 cases is justified by the integration of the separate chapters into the single chapter 11. By the same token, no valid purpose is served by failing to provide exemption from the requirements of similar state laws in a matter under the exclusive jurisdiction of the Federal bankruptcy laws.

Under subsection (d), with respect to a class of equity securities, it is sufficient for acceptance of the plan if the amount of securities voting for the plan is at least two-thirds of the total actually voted.

Subsection (e) provides that no acceptances are required from any class whose claims or interests are unimpaired under the plan or in the order confirming the plan.

Subsection (g) provides that any class denied participation under the plan is conclusively deemed to have rejected the plan. There is obviously no need to submit a plan for a vote by a class that is to receive nothing. But under subsection (g) the excluded class is like a class that has not accepted, and is a dissenting class for purposes of confirmation under section 1130. Senate Report No. 95–989.

1984 Acts. Statements by Legislative Leaders, see 1984 U.S.Code Cong. and Adm.News, p. 576.

Legislative Statements

Section 1126 of the House amendment deletes section 1126(e) as contained in the House bill. Section 105 of the bill constitutes sufficient power in the court to designate exclusion of a creditor's claim on the basis of a conflict of interest. Section 1126(f) of the House amendment adopts a provision contained in section 1127(f) of the Senate bill indicating that a class that is not impaired under a plan is deemed to have accepted a plan and solicitation of acceptances from such class is not required.

Amendments

1984 Amendments. Subsec. (b)(2). Pub.L. 98–353, § 510(a), substituted "1125(a)" for "1125(a)(1)".

Subsec. (d). Pub.L. 98–353, § 510(b), added a comma after "such interests".

Subsec. (f). Pub.L. 98–353, § 510(c)(1), substituted ", and each holder of a claim or interest of such class, are conclusively presumed" for "is deemed".

Pub.L. 98–353, § 510(c)(2), substituted "solicitation" for "solicititation".

Pub.L. 98–353, § 510(c)(3), substituted "interests" for "interest".

Subsec. (g). Pub.L. 98–353, § 510(d), substituted "receive or retain any property" for "any payment or compensation".

Effective and Applicability Provisions

1984 Acts. Amendment by Pub.L. 98–353 effective with respect to cases filed 90 days after July 10, 1984, see section 552(a), formerly 553(a), of Pub.L. 98–353, set out as a note under section 101 of this title.

CROSS REFERENCES

Amount and number of claims within class as including claims formerly held by certain creditors, see 11 USCA § 946.

Applicability of subsecs. (a) to (c) and (e) to (g) of this section in Chapter nine cases, see 11 USCA § 901.

LIBRARY REFERENCES

American Digest System

Bankruptcy ☞3541.1 to 3547.

Key Number System Topic No. 51.

Corpus Juris Secundum

CJS Bankruptcy § 1118, Filing of Plan and Disclosure Statement; Hearing on Objections.

CJS Bankruptcy § 1119, Acceptance of Rejection of Plan by Claim Holders.

CJS Bankruptcy § 1134, Impairment of Claims or Interests.

CJS Bankruptcy § 1151, Filing and Contents of Disclosure Statement.

CJS Bankruptcy § 1156, Deemed Acceptance or Rejection; Unimpaired Classes.

CJS Bankruptcy § 1157, Acceptance of the Plan--Eligibility to Vote; Impairment.

CJS Bankruptcy § 1158, Number of Creditors and Amount of Claims Concurring; Withdrawal.

§ 1127. Modification of plan

(a) The proponent of a plan may modify such plan at any time before confirmation, but may not modify such plan so that such plan as modified fails to meet the requirements of sections 1122 and 1123 of this title. After the proponent of a plan files a modification of such plan with the court, the plan as modified becomes the plan.

(b) The proponent of a plan or the reorganized debtor may modify such plan at any time after confirmation of such plan and before substantial consummation of such plan, but may not modify such plan so that such plan as modified fails to meet the requirements of sections 1122 and 1123 of this title. Such plan as modified under this subsection becomes the plan only if circumstances warrant such modification and the court, after notice and a hearing, confirms such plan as modified, under section 1129 of this title.

(c) The proponent of a modification shall comply with section 1125 of this title with respect to the plan as modified.

(d) Any holder of a claim or interest that has accepted or rejected a plan is deemed to have accepted or rejected, as the case may be, such plan as modified, unless, within the time fixed by the court, such holder changes such holder's previous acceptance or rejection.

(e) If the debtor is an individual, the plan may be modified at any time after confirmation of the plan but before the completion of payments under the plan, whether or not the plan has been substantially consummated, upon request of the debtor, the trustee, the United States trustee, or the holder of an allowed unsecured claim, to—

(1) increase or reduce the amount of payments on claims of a particular class provided for by the plan;

(2) extend or reduce the time period for such payments; or

(3) alter the amount of the distribution to a creditor whose claim is provided for by the plan to the extent necessary to take account of any payment of such claim made other than under the plan.

(f)(1) Sections 1121 through 1128 and the requirements of section 1129 apply to any modification under subsection (e).

(2) The plan, as modified, shall become the plan only after there has been disclosure under section 1125 as the court may direct, notice and a hearing, and such modification is approved.

(Pub.L. 95–598, Nov. 6, 1978, 92 Stat. 2635; Pub.L. 98–353, Title III, § 511, July 10, 1984, 98 Stat. 386; Pub.L. 109–8, Title III, § 321(e), Apr. 20, 2005, 119 Stat. 96; Pub.L. 111–327, § 2(a)(34), Dec. 22, 2010, 124 Stat. 3561.)

HISTORICAL AND STATUTORY NOTES
Revision Notes and Legislative Reports

1978 Acts. Under subsection (a) the proponent may file a proposal to modify a plan prior to confirmation. In the case of a public company the modifying proposal may be filed prior to approval.

Subsection (b) provides that a party in interest eligible to file a plan may file instead of a plan a proposal to modify a plan filed by another. Under subsection (c) a party in interest objecting to some feature of a plan may submit a proposal to modify the plan to meet the objection.

After a plan has been confirmed, but before its substantial consummation, a plan may be modified by leave of court, which subsection (d) provides shall be granted for good cause. Subsection (e) provides that a proposal to modify a plan is subject to the disclosure requirements of section 1125 and as provided in subsection (f). It provides that a creditor or stockholder who voted for or against a plan is deemed to have accepted or rejected the modifying proposal. But if the modification materially and adversely affects any of their interests, they must be afforded an opportunity to change their vote in accordance with the disclosure and solicitation requirements of section 1125.

Under subsection (g) a plan, if modified prior to confirmation, shall be confirmed if it meets the requirements of section 1130. Senate Report No. 95–989.

Subsection (a) permits the proponent of a plan to modify it at any time before confirmation, subject, of course, to the requirements of sections 1122 and 1123, governing classification and contents of a plan. After the proponent of a plan files a modification with the court, the plan as modified becomes the plan, and is to be treated the same as an original plan.

Subsection (b) permits modification of a plan after confirmation under certain circumstances. The modification must be proposed before substantial consummation of the plan. The requirements of sections 1122 and 1123 continue to apply. The plan as modified under this subsection becomes the plan only if the court confirms the plan as modified under section 1129 and the circumstances warrant the modification.

Subsection (c) requires the proponent of a modification to comply with the disclosure provisions of section 1125. Of course, if the modification were sufficiently minor, the court might determine that additional disclosure was not required under the circumstances.

Subsection (d) simplifies modification procedure by deeming any creditor or equity security holder that has already accepted or rejected the plan to have accepted or rejected the modification, unless, within the time fixed by the court, the creditor or equity security holder changes this previous acceptance or rejection. House Report No. 95–595.

1984 Acts. Statements by Legislative Leaders, see 1984 U.S. Code Cong. and Adm. News, p. 576.

2005 Acts. House Report No. 109–31(Part I), see 2005 U.S. Code Cong. and Adm. News, p. 88.

Legislative Statements

Section 1127(a) of the House amendment adopts a provision contained in the House bill permitting only the proponent of a plan to modify the plan and rejection the alternative of open modification contained in the Senate amendment.

Amendments

2010 Amendments. Subsec. (f)(1). Pub.L. 111–327, § 2(a)(34), struck out "subsection (a)" and inserted "subsection (e)".

2005 Amendments. Subsec. (e). Pub.L. 109–8, § 321(e), added subsec. (e).

Subsec. (f). Pub.L. 109–8, § 321(e), added subsec. (f).

1984 Amendments. Subsec. (a). Pub.L. 98–353, § 511(a)(1), added "of a plan" after "After the proponent".

Pub.L. 98–353, § 511(a)(2), added "of such plan" after "modification".

Subsec. (b). Pub.L. 98–353, § 511(b), substituted "circumstances warrant such modification and the court, after notice and a hearing, confirms such plan as modified, under section 1129 of this title" for "the court, after notice and a hearing, confirms such plan, as modified, under section 1129 of this title, and circumstances warrant such modification".

Effective and Applicability Provisions

2005 Acts. Amendments by Pub.L. 109–8 effective, except as otherwise provided, 180 days after April 20, 2005, and inapplicable with respect to cases commenced under Title 11 before the effective date, see Pub.L. 109–8, § 1501, set out as a note under 11 U.S.C.A. § 101.

1984 Acts. Amendment by Pub.L. 98–353 effective with respect to cases filed 90 days after July 10, 1984, see section 552(a), formerly 553(a), of Pub.L. 98–353, set out as a note under section 101 of this title.

CROSS REFERENCES

Applicability of subsec. (d) of this section in Chapter nine cases, see 11 USCA § 901.

Modification of plan after confirmation in—

Chapter thirteen cases, see 11 USCA § 1329.

Chapter twelve cases, see 11 USCA § 1229.

Modification of plan before confirmation in—

Chapter thirteen cases, see 11 USCA § 1323.

Chapter twelve cases, see 11 USCA § 1223.

Modification of plan in Chapter nine cases, see 11 USCA § 942.

LIBRARY REFERENCES

American Digest System

Bankruptcy ⟷3569.

Key Number System Topic No. 51.

Corpus Juris Secundum

CJS Bankruptcy § 1120, Modification of Plan Before Confirmation.

CJS Bankruptcy § 1163, Modification of the Plan.

CJS Bankruptcy § 1261, Particular Matters.

§ 1128. Confirmation hearing

(a) After notice, the court shall hold a hearing on confirmation of a plan.

(b) A party in interest may object to confirmation of a plan.

(Pub.L. 95–598, Nov. 6, 1978, 92 Stat. 2635.)

HISTORICAL AND STATUTORY NOTES

Revision Notes and Legislative Reports

1978 Acts. [Section 1129 (now section 1128)] Subsection (a) requires that there be a hearing in every case on the confirmation of the plan. Notice is required.

Subsection (b) permits any party in interest to object to the confirmation of the plan. The Securities and Exchange Commission and indenture trustees, as parties in interest under section 1109, may object to confirmation of the plan. Senate Report No. 95–989.

CROSS REFERENCES

Applicability of this section in Chapter nine cases, see 11 USCA § 901.

Confirmation hearing in—

Chapter thirteen cases, see 11 USCA § 1324.

Chapter twelve cases, see 11 USCA § 1224.

Duty of United States trustee to file comments with respect to plans and disclosure statements filed in connection with hearings under this section, see 28 USCA § 586.

Right to be heard in cases under this chapter, see 11 USCA § 1109.

LIBRARY REFERENCES

American Digest System

Bankruptcy ⟷3566.1, 3567.

Key Number System Topic No. 51.

Corpus Juris Secundum

CJS Bankruptcy § 1122, Objections to Confirmation.

CJS Bankruptcy § 1123, Hearing and Order.

§ 1129. Confirmation of plan

(a) The court shall confirm a plan only if all of the following requirements are met:

(1) The plan complies with the applicable provisions of this title.

(2) The proponent of the plan complies with the applicable provisions of this title.

(3) The plan has been proposed in good faith and not by any means forbidden by law.

(4) Any payment made or to be made by the proponent, by the debtor, or by a person issuing securities or acquiring property under the plan, for services or for costs and expenses in or in connection with the case, or in connection with the plan and incident to the case, has been approved by, or is subject to the approval of, the court as reasonable.

(5)(A)(i) The proponent of the plan has disclosed the identity and affiliations of any individual proposed to serve, after confirmation of the plan, as a director, officer, or voting trustee of the debtor, an affiliate of the debtor participating in a joint plan with the debtor, or a successor to the debtor under the plan; and

(ii) the appointment to, or continuance in, such office of such individual, is consistent with the interests of creditors and equity security holders and with public policy; and

(B) the proponent of the plan has disclosed the identity of any insider that will be employed or retained by the reorganized debtor, and the nature of any compensation for such insider.

(6) Any governmental regulatory commission with jurisdiction, after confirmation of the plan, over the rates of the debtor has approved any rate change provided for in the plan, or such rate change is expressly conditioned on such approval.

(7) With respect to each impaired class of claims or interests—

(A) each holder of a claim or interest of such class—

(i) has accepted the plan; or

(ii) will receive or retain under the plan on account of such claim or interest property of a value, as of the effective date of the plan, that is not less than the amount that such holder would so receive or retain if the debtor were liquidated under chapter 7 of this title on such date; or

(B) if section 1111(b)(2) of this title applies to the claims of such class, each holder of a claim of such class will receive or retain under the plan on account of such claim property of a value, as of the effective date of the plan, that is not less than the value of such holder's interest in the estate's interest in the property that secures such claims.

(8) With respect to each class of claims or interests—

(A) such class has accepted the plan; or

(B) such class is not impaired under the plan.

(9) Except to the extent that the holder of a particular claim has agreed to a different treatment of such claim, the plan provides that—

(A) with respect to a claim of a kind specified in section 507(a)(2) or 507(a)(3) of this title, on the effective date of the plan, the holder of such claim will receive on account of such claim cash equal to the allowed amount of such claim;

(B) with respect to a class of claims of a kind specified in section 507(a)(1), 507(a)(4), 507(a)(5), 507(a)(6), or 507(a)(7) of this title, each holder of a claim of such class will receive—

(i) if such class has accepted the plan, deferred cash payments of a value, as of the effective date of the plan, equal to the allowed amount of such claim; or

(ii) if such class has not accepted the plan, cash on the effective date of the plan equal to the allowed amount of such claim;

(C) with respect to a claim of a kind specified in section 507(a)(8) of this title, the holder of such claim will receive on account of such claim regular installment payments in cash—

(i) of a total value, as of the effective date of the plan, equal to the allowed amount of such claim;

(ii) over a period ending not later than 5 years after the date of the order for relief under section 301, 302, or 303; and

(iii) in a manner not less favorable than the most favored nonpriority unsecured claim provided for by the plan (other than cash payments made to a class of creditors under section 1122(b)); and

(D) with respect to a secured claim which would otherwise meet the description of an unsecured claim of a governmental unit under section 507(a)(8), but for the secured status of that claim, the holder of that claim will receive on account of that claim, cash payments, in the same manner and over the same period, as prescribed in subparagraph (C).

(10) If a class of claims is impaired under the plan, at least one class of claims that is impaired under the plan has accepted the plan, determined without including any acceptance of the plan by any insider.

(11) Confirmation of the plan is not likely to be followed by the liquidation, or the need for further financial reorganization, of the debtor or any successor to the debtor under the plan, unless such liquidation or reorganization is proposed in the plan.

(12) All fees payable under section 1930 of title 28, as determined by the court at the hearing on confirmation of the plan, have been paid or the plan provides for the payment of all such fees on the effective date of the plan.

(13) The plan provides for the continuation after its effective date of payment of all retiree benefits, as that term is defined in section 1114 of this title, at the level established pursuant to subsection (e)(1)(B) or (g) of section 1114 of this title, at any time prior to confirmation of the plan, for the duration of the period the debtor has obligated itself to provide such benefits.

(14) If the debtor is required by a judicial or administrative order, or by statute, to pay a domestic support obligation, the debtor has paid all amounts payable under such order or such statute for such obligation that first become payable after the date of the filing of the petition.

(15) In a case in which the debtor is an individual and in which the holder of an allowed unsecured claim objects to the confirmation of the plan—

  (A) the value, as of the effective date of the plan, of the property to be distributed under the plan on account of such claim is not less than the amount of such claim; or

  (B) the value of the property to be distributed under the plan is not less than the projected disposable income of the debtor (as defined in section 1325(b)(2)) to be received during the 5–year period beginning on the date that the first payment is due under the plan, or during the period for which the plan provides payments, whichever is longer.

(16) All transfers of property under the plan shall be made in accordance with any applicable provisions of nonbankruptcy law that govern the transfer of property by a corporation or trust that is not a moneyed, business, or commercial corporation or trust.

(b)(1) Notwithstanding section 510(a) of this title, if all of the applicable requirements of subsection (a) of this section other than paragraph (8) are met with respect to a plan, the court, on request of the proponent of the plan, shall confirm the plan notwithstanding the requirements of such paragraph if the plan does not discriminate unfairly, and is fair and equitable, with respect to each class of claims or interests that is impaired under, and has not accepted, the plan.

(2) For the purpose of this subsection, the condition that a plan be fair and equitable with respect to a class includes the following requirements:

  (A) With respect to a class of secured claims, the plan provides—

    (i)(I) that the holders of such claims retain the liens securing such claims, whether the property subject to such liens is retained by the debtor or transferred to another entity, to the extent of the allowed amount of such claims; and

    (II) that each holder of a claim of such class receive on account of such claim deferred cash payments totaling at least the allowed amount of such claim, of a value, as of the effective date of the plan, of at least the value of such holder's interest in the estate's interest in such property;

    (ii) for the sale, subject to section 363(k) of this title, of any property that is subject to the liens securing such claims, free and clear of such liens, with such liens to attach to the proceeds of such sale, and the treatment of such liens on proceeds under clause (i) or (iii) of this subparagraph; or

    (iii) for the realization by such holders of the indubitable equivalent of such claims.

  (B) With respect to a class of unsecured claims—

    (i) the plan provides that each holder of a claim of such class receive or retain on account of such claim property of a value, as of the effective date of the plan, equal to the allowed amount of such claim; or

    (ii) the holder of any claim or interest that is junior to the claims of such class will not receive or retain under the plan on account of such junior claim or interest any property, except that in a case in which the debtor is an individual, the debtor may retain property included in the estate under section 1115, subject to the requirements of subsection (a)(14) of this section.

  (C) With respect to a class of interests—

    (i) the plan provides that each holder of an interest of such class receive or retain on account of such interest property of a value, as of the effective date of the plan, equal to the greatest of the allowed amount of any fixed liquidation preference to which such holder is entitled, any fixed redemption price to which such holder is entitled, or the value of such interest; or

    (ii) the holder of any interest that is junior to the interests of such class will not receive or retain under the plan on account of such junior interest any property.

(c) Notwithstanding subsections (a) and (b) of this section and except as provided in section 1127(b) of this title, the court may confirm only one plan, unless the order of confirmation in the case has been revoked under section 1144 of this title. If the requirements of subsections (a) and (b) of this section are met with respect to more than one plan, the court shall consider the preferences of creditors and equity security holders in determining which plan to confirm.

(d) Notwithstanding any other provision of this section, on request of a party in interest that is a governmental unit, the court may not confirm a plan if the principal purpose of the plan is the avoidance of taxes or the avoidance of the application of section 5 of the Securities Act of 1933. In any hearing under this subsection, the governmental unit has the burden of proof on the issue of avoidance.

(e) In a small business case, the court shall confirm a plan that complies with the applicable provisions of this title and that is filed in accordance with section 1121(e) not later than 45 days after the plan is filed unless the time for confirmation is extended in accordance with section 1121(e)(3).

(Pub.L. 95–598, Nov. 6, 1978, 92 Stat. 2635; Pub.L. 98–353, Title III, § 512, July 10, 1984, 98 Stat. 386; Pub.L. 99–554, Title II, §§ 225, 283(v), Oct. 27, 1986, 100 Stat. 3102, 3118; Pub.L. 100–334, § 2(b), June 16, 1988, 102 Stat. 613; Pub.L. 103–394, Title III, § 304(h)(7), Title V, § 501(d)(32), Oct. 22, 1994, 108 Stat. 4134, 4146; Pub.L. 109–8, Title II, § 213(1), Title III, § 321(c), Title IV, § 438, Title VII, § 710, Title XII, § 1221(b), Title XV, § 1502(a)(8), Apr. 20, 2005, 119 Stat. 52, 95, 113, 127, 196, 216; Pub.L. 111–327, § 2(a)(35), Dec. 22, 2010, 124 Stat. 3561.)

HISTORICAL AND STATUTORY NOTES

Revision Notes and Legislative Reports

1978 Acts. [Section 1130 (now section 1129)] Subsection (a) enumerates the requirement governing confirmation of a plan. The court is required to confirm a plan if and only if all of the requirements are met.

Paragraph (1) requires that the plan comply with the applicable provisions of chapter 11, such as sections 1122 and 1123, governing classification and contents of plan.

Paragraph (2) requires that the proponent of the plan comply with the applicable provisions of chapter 11, such as section 1125 regarding disclosure.

Paragraph (3) requires that the plan have been proposed in good faith, and not by any means forbidden by law.

Paragraph (4) is derived from section 221 of chapter X [section 621 of former Title 11]. It requires that any payment made or promised by the proponent, the debtor, or person issuing securities or acquiring property under the plan, for services or for costs and expenses in, or in connection with the case, or in connection with the plan and incident to the case, be disclosed to the court. In addition, any payment made before confirmation must have been reasonable, and any payment to be fixed after confirmation must be subject to the approval of the court as reasonable.

Paragraph (5) is also derived from section 221 of chapter X [section 621 of former Title 11]. It requires the plan to disclose the identity and affiliations of any individual proposed to serve, after confirmation, as a director, officer, or voting trustee of the reorganized debtor. The appointment to or continuance in one of these offices by the individual must be consistent with the interests of creditors and equity security holders and with public policy. The plan must also disclose the identity of any insider that will be employed or retained by the reorganized debtor, and the nature of any compensation to be paid to the insider.

Paragraph (6) permits confirmation only if any regulatory commission that will have jurisdiction over the debtor after confirmation of the plan has approved any rate change provided for in the plan. As an alternative, the rate change may be conditioned on such approval.

Paragraph (7) provides that in the case of a public company the court shall confirm the plan if it finds the plan to be fair and equitable and the plan either (1) has been accepted by classes of claims or interests as provided in section 1126, or (2), if not so accepted, satisfies the requirements of subsection (b) of this section.

Paragraphs (8) and (9) apply only in nonpublic cases. Paragraph (8) does not apply the fair and equitable standards in two situations. The first occurs if there is unanimous consent of all affected holders of claims and interests. It is also sufficient for purposes of confirmation if each holder of a claim or interest receives or retains consideration of a value, as of the effective date of the plan, that is not less than each would have or receive if the debtor were liquidated under chapter 7 of this title. This standard adapts the test of "best interest of creditors" as interpreted by the courts under chapter XI [former chapter 11 (section 701 et seq.) of former Title 11]. It is given broader application in chapter 11 of this title since a plan under chapter 11 may affect not only unsecured claims but secured claims and stock as well.

Under paragraph (9)(A), if a class of claims or interests has not accepted the plan, the court will confirm the plan if, for the dissenting class and any class of equal rank, the negotiat-

ed plan provides in value no less than under a plan that is fair and equitable. Such review and determination are not required for any other classes that accepted the plan.

Paragraph 9(A) would permit a senior creditor to adjust his participation for the benefit of stockholders. In such a case, junior creditors, who have not been satisfied in full, may not object if, absent the "give-up", they are receiving all that a fair and equitable plan would give them. To illustrate, suppose the estate is valued at $1.5 million and claims and stock are:

		Claims and stock (millions)	Equity (millions)
(1)	Senior debt...............	$1.2	$1.2
(2)	Junior debt...............	.5	.3
(3)	Stock....................	(1)	—
	Total..................	1.7	1.5

Under the plan, the senior creditor gives up $100,000 in value for the benefit of stockholders as follows:

		Millions
(1)	Senior debt..........................	$1.1
(2)	Junior debt..........................	.3
(3)	Stock...............................	.1
	Total................................	1.5

1 No value.

If the junior creditors dissent, the court may nevertheless confirm the plan since under the fair and equitable standard they had an equity of only $300,000 and the allocation to equity security holders did not affect them.

Paragraph 9(A)[(9)(A)] provides a special alternative with respect to secured claims. A plan may be confirmed against a dissenting class of secured claims if the plan or order of confirmation provides for the realization of their security (1) by the retention of the property subject to such security; (2) by a sale of the property and transfer of the claim to the proceeds of sale if the secured creditors were permitted to bid at the sale and set off against the purchase price up to the allowed amount of their claims; or (3) by such other method that will assure them the realization of the indubitable equivalent of the allowed amount of their secured claims. The indubitable equivalent language is intended to follow the strict approach taken by Judge Learned Hand in *In Re Murel Holding Corp.*, 7 5 [75] F.2d 941 (2nd Cir. 1935).

Paragraph (9)(B) provides that, if a class of claims or interests is excluded from participation under the plan, the court may nevertheless confirm the plan if it determines that no class on a parity with or junior to such participates under the plan. In the previous illustration, no confirmation would be permitted if the negotiated plan would grant a participation to stockholders but nothing for junior creditors. As noted elsewhere, by reason of section 1126(g), an excluded class is a dissenting class under section 1130.

Paragraph (10) states that, to be confirmed, the plan must provide that each holder of a claim under section 507 will receive property, as therein noted, of a value equal to the allowed amount of the claim. There are two exceptions: (A) The holder thereof may agree to a different settlement in part or in whole; (B) where a debtor's business is reorganized under chapter 11, this provision requires that taxes entitled to priority (including administrative claims or taxes) must be paid in cash not later than 120 days after the plan is confirmed, unless the Secretary of the Treasury agrees to other terms or kinds of payment. The bill, as introduced, required full payment in cash within 60 days after the plan is confirmed.

Paragraph (11) requires a determination regarding feasibility of the plan. It is a slight elaboration of the law that has developed in the application of the word "feasible" in Chapter X of the present Act [former chapter 10 (section 501 et seq.) of former Title 11].

Paragraph (12) requires that at least one class must accept the plan, but any claims or interests held by insiders are not to be included for purposes of determining the number and amount of acceptances.

Subsection (b) provides that if, in the case of a public company, the plan meets the requirements of subsection (a) (except paragraphs (8) and (9) which do not apply to such a company), the court is to confirm the plan if the plan or the order of confirmation provides adequate protection for the realization of the value of the claims or interests of each class not accepting the plan. The intent is to incorporate inclusively, as a guide to the meaning of subsection (a) the provisions of section 216(7) (11 U.S.C. 616(7)) [section 616(7) of former Title 11] with respect to claims and section 216(8) (11 U.S.C. 616(8)) [section 616(8) of former Title 11] with respect to equity security interests.

Under subsection (c) the court may confirm only one plan, unless the order of confirmation has been revoked under section 1144. If the requirements for confirmation are met with respect to more than one plan, the court shall consider the preferences of creditors and stockholders in deciding which plan to confirm.

Subsection (d) provides that the bankruptcy court may not confirm a plan of reorganization if its principal purpose is the avoidance of taxes or the avoidance of section 5 of the Securities Act of 1933 (15 U.S.C. 77e) [section 77e of Title 15, Commerce and Trade]. This rule modifies a similar provision of present law (section 269 of the Bankruptcy Act) [section 669 of former title 11]. Senate Report No. 95–989.

Paragraph (7) [of subsec. (a)] incorporates the former "best interest of creditors" test found in chapter 11, but spells out precisely what is intended. With respect to each class, the holders of the claims or interests of that class must receive or retain under the plan on account of those claims or interest property of a value, as of the effective date of the plan, that is not less than the amount that they would so receive or retain if the debtor were liquidated under chapter 7 on the effective date of the plan.

In order to determine the hypothetical distribution in a liquidation, the court will have to consider the various subordination provisions of proposed 11 U.S.C. 510, 726(a)(3), 726(a)(4), and the postponement provisions of proposed 11 U.S.C. 724. Also applicable in appropriate cases will be the rules governing partnership distributions under proposed 11 U.S.C. 723, and distributions of community property under proposed 11 U.S.C. 726(c). Under subparagraph (A), a particular holder is permitted to accept less than liquidation value, but his acceptance does not bind the class.

Property under subparagraph (B) may include securities of the debtor. Thus, the provision will apply in cases in which the plan in confirmed under proposed 11 U.S.C. 1129(b).

Paragraph (8) is central to the confirmation standards. It requires that each class either have accepted the plan or be unimpaired.

Paragraph (9) augments the requirements of paragraph (8) by requiring payment of each priority claim in full. It permits payments over time and payment other than in cash, but payment in securities is not intended to be permitted without consent of the priority claimant even if the class has consented. It also permits a particular claimant to accept less than full payment.

Subsection (b) permits the court to confirm a plan notwithstanding failure of compliance with paragraph (8) of subsection (a). The plan must comply with all other paragraphs of subsection (a), including paragraph (9). This subsection contains the so-called cramdown. It requires simply that the plan meet certain standards of fairness to dissenting creditors or equity security holders. The general principle of the subsection permits confirmation notwithstanding nonacceptance by an impaired class if that class and all below it in priority are treated according to the absolute priority rule. The dissenting class must be paid in full before any junior class may share under the plan. If it is paid in full, then junior classes may share. Treatment of classes of secured creditors is slightly different because they do not fall in the priority ladder, but the principle is the same.

Specifically, the court may confirm a plan over the objection of a class of secured claims if the members of that class are unimpaired or if they are to receive under the plan property of a value equal to the allowed amount of their secured claims, as determined under proposed 11 U.S.C. 506(a). The property is to be valued as of the effective date of the plan, thus recognizing the time-value of money. As used throughout this subsection, "property" includes both tangible and intangible property, such as a security of the debtor or a successor to the debtor under a reorganization plan.

The court may confirm over the dissent of a class of unsecured claims, including priority claims, only if the members of the class are unimpaired, if they will receive under the plan property of a value equal to the allowed amount of their unsecured claims, or if no class junior will share under the plan. That is, if the class is impaired, then they must be paid in full or, if paid less than in full, then no class junior may receive anything under the plan. This codifies the absolute priority rule from the dissenting class on down.

With respect to classes of equity, the court may confirm over a dissent if the members of the class are unimpaired, if they receive their liquidation preference or redemption rights, if any, or if no class junior shares under the plan. This, too, is a codification of the absolute priority rule with respect to equity. If a partnership agreement subordinates limited partners to general partners to any degree, then the general principles of paragraph (3) of this subsection would apply to prevent the general partners from being squeezed out.

One requirement applies generally to all classes before the court may confirm under this subsection. No class may be paid more than in full.

The partial codification of the absolute priority rule here is not intended to deprive senior creditor [sic] of compensation for being required to take securities in the reorganized debtor that are of an equal priority with the securities offered to a junior class. Under current law, seniors are entitled to compensation for their loss of priority, and the increased risk put upon them by being required to give up their priority will be reflected in a lower value of the securities given to them than the value of comparable securities given to juniors that have not lost a priority position.

Finally, the proponent must request use of this subsection. The court may not confirm notwithstanding nonacceptance unless the proponent requests and the court may then confirm only if subsection (b) is complied with. The court may not rewrite the plan.

A more detailed explanation follows:

The test to be applied by the court is set forth in the various paragraphs of section 1129(b). The elements of the test are new [,] departing from both the absolute priority rule and the best interests of creditors tests found under the Bankruptcy Act [former Title 11]. The court is not permitted to alter the terms of the plan. It must merely decide whether the plan complies with the requirements of section 1129(b). If so, the plan is confirmed, if not the plan is denied confirmation.

The procedure followed is simple. The court examines each class of claims or interests designated under section 1123(a)(1) to see if the requirements of section 1129(b) are met. If the class is a class of secured claims, then paragraph (1) contains two tests that must be complied with in order for confirmation to occur. First, under subparagraph (A), the court must be able to find that the consideration given under the plan on account of the secured claim does not exceed the allowed amount of the claim. This condition is not prescribed as a matter of law under section 1129(a), because if the secured claim is compensated in securities of the debtor, a valuation of the business would be necessary to determine the value of the consideration. While section 1129(a) does not contemplate a valuation of the debtor's business, such a valuation will almost always be required under section 1129(b) in order to determine the value of the consideration to be distributed under the plan. Once the valuation is performed, it becomes a simple matter to impose the criterion that no claim will be paid more than in full.

Application of the test under subparagraph (A) also requires a valuation of the consideration "as of the effective date of the plan". This contemplates a present value analysis that will discount value to be received in the future; of course, if the interest rate paid is equivalent to the discount rate used, the present value and face future value will be identical. On the other hand, if no interest is proposed to be paid, the present value will be less than the face future value. For example, consider an allowed secured claim of $1,000 in a class by itself. One plan could propose to pay $1,000 on account of this claim as of the effective date of the plan. Another plan could propose to give a note with a $1,000 face amount due five years after the effective date of the plan on account of this claim. A third plan could propose to give a note in a face amount of $1,000 due five years from the effective date of the plan plus six percent annual interest commencing on the effective date of the plan on account of this claim. The first plan clearly meets the requirements of subparagraph (A) because the amount received on account of the second claim has an equivalent present value as of the effective date of the plan equal to the allowed amount of such claim.

The second plan also meets the requirements of subparagraph (A) because the present value of the five years note as of the effective date of the plan will never exceed the allowed amount of the secured claim; the higher the discount rate, the less present value the note will have. Whether the third plan complies with subparagraph (A) depends on whether the

discount rate is less than six percent. Normally, the interest rate used in the plan will be prima facie evidence of the discount rate because the interest rate will reflect an arms length determination of the risk of the security involved and feasibility considerations will tend to understate interest payments. If the court found the discount rate to be greater than or equal to the interest rate used in the plan, then subparagraph (A) would be complied with because the value of the note as of the effective date of the plan would not exceed the allowed amount of the second claim. If, however, the court found the discount rate to be less than the interest rate proposed under the plan, then the present value of the note would exceed $1,000 and the plan would fail of confirmation. On the other hand, it is important to recognize that the future principal amount of a note in excess of the allowed amount of a secured claim may have a present value less than such allowed amount, if the interest rate under the plan is correspondingly less than the discount rate.

Even if the requirements of subparagraph (A) are complied with, the class of secured claims must satisfy one of the three clauses in paragraph (B) in order to pass muster. It is sufficient for confirmation if the class has accepted the plan, or if the claims of the class are unimpaired, or if each holder of a secured claim in the class will receive property of a value as of the effective date of the plan equal to the allowed amount of such claim (unless he has agreed to accept less). It is important to note that under section 506(a), the allowed amount of the secured claim will not include any extent to which the amount of such claim exceeds the value of the property securing such claim. Thus, instead of focusing on secured creditors or unsecured creditors, the statute focuses on secured claims and unsecured claims.

After the court has applied paragraph (1) to each class of secured claims, it then applies paragraph (2) to each class of unsecured claims. Again two separate components must be tested. Subparagraph (A) is identical with the test under section 1129(b)(1)(A) insofar as the holder of an unsecured claim is not permitted to receive property of a value as of the effective date of the plan on account of such claim that is greater than the allowed amount of such claim. In addition, subparagraph (B) requires compliance with one of four conditions. The conditions in clauses (i)–(iii) mirror the conditions of acceptance unimpairment, or full value found in connection with secured claims in section 1129(b)(1)(B).

The condition contained in section 1129(b)(2)(B)(iv) provides another basis for confirming the plan with respect to a class of unsecured claims. It will be of greatest use when an impaired class that has not accepted the plan is to receive less than full value under the plan. The plan may be confirmed under clause (iv) in those circumstances if the class is not unfairly discriminated against with respect to equal classes and if junior classes will receive nothing under the plan. The second criterion is the easier to understand. It is designed to prevent a senior class from giving up consideration to a junior class unless every intermediate class consents, is paid in full, or is unimpaired. This gives intermediate creditors a great deal of leverage in negotiating with senior or secured creditors who wish to have a plan that gives value to equity. One aspect of this test that is not obvious is that whether one class is senior, equal, or junior to another class is relative and not absolute. Thus from the perspective of trade creditors holding unsecured claims, claims of senior and subordinated debentures may be entitled to share on an equal basis with the trade claims. However, from the perspective of the senior unsecured debt, the subordinated debentures are junior.

This point illustrates the lack of precision in the first criterion which demands that a class not be unfairly discriminated against with respect to equal classes. From the perspective of unsecured trade claims, there is no unfair discrimination as long as the total consideration given all other classes of equal rank does not exceed the amount that would result from an exact aliquot distribution. Thus if trade creditors, senior debt, and subordinate debt are each owed $100 and the plan proposes to pay the trade debt $15, the senior debt $30, and the junior debt $0, the plan would not unfairly discriminate against the trade debt nor would any other allocation of consideration under the plan between the senior and junior debt be unfair as to the trade debt as long as the aggregate consideration is less than $30. The senior debt could take $25 and give up $5 to the junior debt and the trade debt would have no cause to complain because as far as it is concerned the junior debt is an equal class.

However, in this latter case the senior debt would have been unfairly discriminated against because the trade debt was being unfairly over-compensated; of course the plan would also fail unless the senior debt was unimpaired, received full value, or accepted the plan, because from its perspective a junior class received property under the plan. Application of the test from the perspective of senior debt is best illustrated by the plan that proposes to pay trade debt $15, senior debt $25, and junior debt $0. Here the senior debt is being unfairly discriminated against with respect to the equal trade debt even though the trade debt receives less than the senior debt. The discrimination arises from the fact that the senior debt is entitled to the rights of the junior debt which in this example entitle the senior debt to share on a 2:1 basis with the trade debt.

Finally, it is necessary to interpret the first criterion from the perspective of subordinated debt. The junior debt is subrogated to the rights of senior debt once the senior debt is paid in full. Thus, while the plan that pays trade debt $15, senior debt $25, and junior debt $0 is not unfairly discriminatory against the junior debt, a plan that proposes to pay trade debt $55, senior debt $100, and junior debt $1, would be unfairly discriminatory. In order to avoid discriminatory treatment against the junior debt, at least $10 would have to be received by such debt under those facts.

The criterion of unfair discrimination is not derived from the fair and equitable rule or from the best interests of creditors test. Rather it preserves just treatment of a dissenting class from the class's own perspective.

If each class of secured claims satisfies the requirements of section 1129(b)(1) and each class of unsecured claims satisfies the requirements of section 1129(b)(2), then the court must still see if each class of interests satisfies section 1129(b)(3) before the plan may be confirmed. Again, two separate criteria must be met. Under subparagraph (A) if the interest entitles the holder thereof to a fixed liquidation preference or if such interest may be redeemed at a fixed price, then the holder of such interest must not receive under the plan on account of such interest property of a value as of the effective date of the plan greater than the greater of these two values of the interest. Preferred stock would be an example of an interest likely to have liquidation preference or redemption price.

If an interest such as most common stock or the interest of a general partnership has neither a fixed liquidation prefer-

ence nor a fixed redemption price, then the criterion in subparagraph (A) is automatically fulfilled. In addition subparagraph (B) contains five clauses that impose alternative conditions of which at least one must be satisfied in order to warrant confirmation. The first two clauses contain requirements of acceptance or unimpairment similar to the first two clauses in paragraphs (1)(B) and (2)(B). Clause (iii) is similar to the unimpairment test contained in section 1124(3)(B), except that it will apply to cover the issuance securities of the debtor of a value as of the effective date of the plan equal to the greater of any fixed liquidation preference or redemption price. The fourth clause allows confirmation if junior interests are not compensated under the plan and the fifth clause allows confirmation if there are no junior interests. These clauses recognized that as long as senior classes receive no more than full payment, the objection of a junior class will not defeat confirmation unless a class junior to it is receiving value under the plan and the objecting class is impaired. While a determination of impairment may be made under section 1124(3)(B)(iii) without a precise valuation of the business when common stock is clearly under water, once section 1129(b) is used, a more detailed valuation is a necessary byproduct. Thus, if no property is given to a holder of an interest under the plan, the interest should be clearly worthless in order to find unimpairment under section 1124(3)(B)(iii) and section 1129(a)(8); otherwise, since a class of interests receiving no property is deemed to object under section 1126(g), the more precise valuation of section 1129(b) should be used.

If all of the requirements of section 1129(b) are complied with, then the court may confirm the plan subject to other limitations such as those found in section 1129(a) and (d).

Subsection (c) of section 1129 governs confirmation when more than one plan meets the requirements of the section. The court must consider the preferences of creditors and equity security holders in determining which plan to confirm.

Subsection (d) requires the court to deny confirmation if the principal purpose of the plan is the avoidance of taxes (through use of sections 346 and 1146, and applicable provisions of State law or the Internal Revenue Code [Title 26] governing bankruptcy reorganizations) or the avoidance of section 5 of the Securities Act of 1933 [section 77e of Title 15, Commerce and Trade] (through use of section 1145). House Report No. 95–595.

1984 Acts. Statements by Legislative Leaders, see 1984 U.S.Code Cong. and Adm.News, p. 576.

1986 Acts. House Report No. 99–764 and House Conference Report No. 99–958, see 1986 U.S.Code Cong. and Adm. News, p. 5227.

1988 Acts. Senate Report No. 100–119, see 1988 U.S.Code Cong. and Adm.News, p. 683.

1994 Acts. House Report No. 103–835, see 1994 U.S. Code Cong. and Adm. News, p. 3340.

2005 Acts. House Report No. 109–31(Part I), see 2005 U.S. Code Cong. and Adm. News, p. 88.

Legislative Statements

Section 1129 of the House amendment relates to confirmation of a plan in a case under chapter 11. Section 1129(a)(3) of the House amendment adopts the position taken in the Senate amendment and section 1129(a)(5) takes the position adopted in the House bill. Section 1129(a)(7) adopts the position taken in the House bill in order to insure that the dissenting members of an accepting class will receive at least what they would otherwise receive under the best interest of creditors test; it also requires that even the members of a class that has rejected the plan be protected by the best interest of creditors test for those rare cramdown cases where a class of creditors would receive more on liquidation than under reorganization of the debtor. Section 1129(a)(7)(C) is discussed in connection with section 1129(b) and section 1111(b). Section 1129(a)(8) of the House amendment adopts the provision taken in the House bill which permits confirmation of a plan as to a particular class without resort to the fair and equitable test if the class has accepted a plan or is unimpaired under the plan.

Section 1129(a)(9) represents a compromise between a similar provision contained in the House bill and the Senate amendment. Under subparagraph (A) claims entitled to priority under section 507(a)(1) or (2) are entitled to receive cash on the effective date of the plan equal to the amount of the claim. Under subparagraph (B) claims entitled to priority under section 507(a)(3), (4), or (5), are entitled to receive deferred cash payments of a present value as of the effective date of the plan equal to the amount of the claims if the class has accepted the plan or cash payments on the effective date of the plan otherwise. Tax claims entitled to priority under section 507(a)(6) of different governmental units may not be contained in one class although all claims of one such unit may be combined and such unit may be required to take deferred cash payments over a period not to exceed 6 years after the date of assessment of the tax with the present value equal to the amount of the claim.

Section 1129(a)(10) is derived from section 1130(a)(12) of the Senate amendment.

Section 1129(b) is new. Together with section 1111(b) and section 1129(a)(7)(C), this section provides when a plan may be confirmed, notwithstanding the failure of an impaired class to accept the plan under section 1129(a)(8). Before discussing section 1129(b) an understanding of section 1111(b) is necessary. Section 1111(b)(1), the general rule that a secured claim is to be treated as a recourse claim in chapter 11 whether or not the claim is nonrecourse by agreement or applicable law. This preferred status for a nonrecourse loan terminates if the property securing the loan is sold under section 363 or is to be sold under the plan.

The preferred status also terminates if the class of which the secured claim is a part elects application of section 1111(b)(2). Section 1111(b)(2) provides that an allowed claim is a secured claim to the full extent the claim is allowed rather than to the extent of the collateral as under section 506(a). A class may elect application of paragraph (2) only if the security is not of inconsequential value and, if the creditor is a recourse creditor, the collateral is not sold under section 363 or to be sold under the plan. Sale of property under section 363 or under the plan is excluded from treatment under section 1111(b) because of the secured party's right to bid in the full amount of his allowed claim at any sale of collateral under section 363(k) of the House amendment.

As previously noted, section 1129(b) sets forth a standard by which a plan may be confirmed notwithstanding the failure of an impaired class to accept the plan.

Paragraph (1) makes clear that this alternative confirmation standard, referred to as "cram down," will be called into play only on the request of the proponent of the plan. Under this cramdown test, the court must confirm the plan if the plan does not discriminate unfairly, and is "fair and equita-

ble," with respect to each class of claims or interests that is impaired under, and has not accepted, the plan. The requirement of the House bill that a plan not "discriminate unfairly" with respect to a class is included for clarity; the language in the House report interpreting that requirement, in the context of subordinated debentures, applies equally under the requirements of section 1129(b)(1) of the House amendment.

Although many of the factors interpreting "fair and equitable" are specified in paragraph (2), others, which were explicated in the description of section 1129(b) in the House report, were omitted from the House amendment to avoid statutory complexity and because they would undoubtedly be found by a court to be fundamental to "fair and equitable" treatment of a dissenting class. For example, a dissenting class should be assured that no senior class receives more than 100 percent of the amount of its claims. While that requirement was explicitly included in the House bill, the deletion is intended to be one of style and not one of substance.

Paragraph (2) provides guidelines for a court to determine whether a plan is fair and equitable with respect to a dissenting class. It must be emphasized that the fair and equitable requirement applies only with respect to dissenting classes. Therefore, unlike the fair and equitable rule contained in chapter X [former chapter 10 (section 501 et seq.) of former Title 11] and section 77 of the Bankruptcy Act [section 205 of former Title 11] under section 1129(b)(2), senior accepting classes are permitted to give up value to junior classes as long as no dissenting intervening class receives less than the amount of its claims in full. If there is no dissenting intervening class and the only dissent is from a class junior to the class to which value have [sic] been given up, then the plan may still be fair and equitable with respect to the dissenting class, as long as no class senior to the dissenting class has received more than 100 percent of the amount of its claims.

Paragraph (2) contains three subparagraphs, each of which applies to a particular kind of class of claims or interests that is impaired and has not accepted the plan. Subparagraph (A) applies when a class of secured claims is impaired and has not accepted the plan. The provision applies whether or not section 1111(b) applies. The plan may be crammed down notwithstanding the dissent of a secured class only if the plan complies with clause (i), (ii), or (iii).

Clause (i) permits cramdown if the dissenting class of secured claims will retain its lien on the property whether the property is retained by the debtor or transferred. It should be noted that the lien secures the allowed secured claim held by such holder. The meaning of "allowed secured claim" will vary depending on whether section 1111(b)(2) applies to such class.

If section 1111(b)(2) applies then the "electing" class is entitled to have the entire allowed amount of the debt related to such property secured by a lien even if the value of the collateral is less than the amount of the debt. In addition, the plan must provide for the holder to receive, on account of the allowed secured claims, payments, either present or deferred, of a principal face amount equal to the amount of the debt and of a present value equal to the value of the collateral.

For example, if a creditor loaned $15,000,000 to a debtor secured by real property worth $18,000,000 and the value of the real property had dropped to $12,000,000 by the date when the debtor commenced a proceeding under chapter 11, the plan could be confirmed notwithstanding the dissent of the creditor as long as the lien remains on the collateral to secure a $15,000,000 debt, the face amount of present or extended payments to be made to the creditor under the plan is at least $15,000,000, and the present value of the present or deferred payments is not less than $12,000,000. The House report accompanying the House bill described what is meant by "present value".

Clause (ii) is self explanatory. Clause (iii) requires the court to confirm the plan notwithstanding the dissent of the electing secured class if the plan provides for the realization by the secured class of the indubitable equivalents of the secured claims. The standard of "indubitable equivalents" is taken from *In re Murel Holding Corp.*, 75 F.2d 941 (2d Cir. 1935) (Learned Hand, Jr.).

Abandonment of the collateral to the creditor would clearly satisfy indubitable equivalence, as would a lien on similar collateral. However, present cash payments less than the secured claim would not satisfy the standard because the creditor is deprived of an opportunity to gain from a future increase in value of the collateral. Unsecured notes as to the secured claim or equity securities of the debtor would not be the indubitable equivalent. With respect to an oversecured creditor, the secured claim will never exceed the allowed claim.

Although the same language applies, a different result pertains with respect to a class of secured claims to which section 1111(b)(2) does not apply. This will apply to all claims secured by a right of setoff. The court must confirm the plan notwithstanding the dissent of such a class of secured claims if any of three alternative requirements is met. Under clause (i) the plan may be confirmed if the class retains a right of setoff or a lien securing the allowed secured claims of the class and the holders will receive payments of a present value equal to the allowed amount of their secured claims. Contrary to electing classes of secured creditors who retain a lien under subparagraph (A)(i)(I) to the extent of the entire claims secured by such lien, nonelecting creditors retain a lien on collateral only to the extent of their allowed secured claims and not to the extent of any deficiency, and such secured creditors must receive present or deferred payments with a present value equal to the allowed secured claim, which in turn is only the equivalent of the value of the collateral under section 506(a).

Any deficiency claim of a nonelecting class of secured claims is treated as an unsecured claim and is not provided for under subparagraph (A). The plan may be confirmed under clause (ii) if the plan proposes to sell the property free and clear of the secured party's lien as long as the lien will attach to the proceeds and will receive treatment under clause (i) or (iii). Clause (iii) permits confirmation if the plan provides for the realization by the dissenting nonelecting class of secured claims of the indubitable equivalent of the secured claims of such class.

Contrary to an "electing" class to which section 1111(b)(2) applies, the nonelecting class need not be protected with respect to any future appreciation in value of the collateral since the secured claim of such a class is never undersecured by reason of section 506(a). Thus the lien secures only the value of interest of such creditor in the collateral. To the extent deferred payments exceed that amount, they represent interest. In the event of a subsequent default, the portion of the face amount of deferred payments representing unaccrued interest will not be secured by the lien.

Subparagraph (B) applies to a dissenting class of unsecured claims. The court must confirm the plan notwithstanding the dissent of a class of impaired unsecured claims if the plan provides for such claims to receive property with a present value equal to the allowed amount of the claims. Unsecured claims may receive any kind of "property," which is used in its broadest sense, as long as the present value of the property given to the holders of unsecured claims is equal to the allowed amount of the claims. Some kinds of property, such as securities, may require difficult valuations by the court; in such circumstances the court need only determine that there is a reasonable likelihood that the property given the dissenting class of impaired unsecured claims equals the present value of such allowed claims.

Alternatively, under clause (ii), the court must confirm the plan if the plan provides that holders of any claims or interests junior to the interests of the dissenting class of impaired unsecured claims will not receive any property under the plan on account of such junior claims or interests. As long as senior creditors have not been paid more than in full, and classes of equal claims are being treated so that the dissenting class of impaired unsecured claims is not being discriminated against unfairly, the plan may be confirmed if the impaired class of unsecured claims receives less than 100 cents on the dollar (or nothing at all) as long as no class junior to the dissenting class receives anything at all. Such an impaired dissenting class may not prevent confirmation of a plan by objection merely because a senior class has elected to give up value to a junior class that is higher in priority than the impaired dissenting class of unsecured claims as long as the above safeguards are met.

Subparagraph (C) applies to a dissenting class of impaired interests. Such interests may include the interests of general or limited partners in a partnership, the interests of a sole proprietor in a proprietorship, or the interest of common or preferred stockholders in a corporation. If the holders of such interests are entitled to a fixed liquidation preference or fixed redemption price on account of such interests then the plan may be confirmed notwithstanding the dissent of such class of interests as long as it provides the holders property of a present value equal to the greatest of the fixed redemption price, or the value of such interests. In the event there is no fixed liquidation preference or redemption price, then the plan may be confirmed as long as it provides the holders of such interests property of a present value equal to the value of such interests. If the interests are "under water" then they will be valueless and the plan may be confirmed notwithstanding the dissent of that class of interests even if the plan provides that the holders of such interests will not receive any property on account of such interests.

Alternatively, under clause (ii), the court must confirm the plan notwithstanding the dissent of a class of interests if the plan provides that holders of any interests junior to the dissenting class of interests will not receive or retain any property on account of such junior interests. Clearly, if there are no junior interests junior to the class of dissenting interests, then the condition of clause (ii) is satisfied. The safeguards that no claim or interest receive more than 100 percent of the allowed amount of such claim or interest and that no class be discriminated against unfairly will insure that the plan is fair and equitable with respect to the dissenting class of interests.

Except to the extent of the treatment of secured claims under subparagraph (A) of this statement, the House report remains an accurate description of confirmation of section 1129(b). Contrary to the example contained in the Senate report, a senior class will not be able to give up value to a junior class over the dissent of an intervening class unless the intervening class receives the full amount, as opposed to value, of its claims or interests.

One last point deserves explanation with respect to the admittedly complex subject of confirmation. Section 1129(a)(7)(C) in effect exempts secured creditors making an election under section 1111(b)(2) from application of the best interest of creditors test. In the absence of an election the amount such creditors receive in a plan of liquidation would be the value of their collateral plus any amount recovered on the deficiency in the case of a recourse loan. However, under section 1111(b)(2), the creditors are given an allowed secured claim to the full extent the claim is allowed and have no unsecured deficiency. Since section 1129(b)(2)(A) makes clear that an electing class need receive payments of a present value only equal to the value of the collateral, it is conceivable that under such a "cram down" the electing creditors would receive nothing with respect to their deficiency. The advantage to the electing creditors is that they have a lien securing the full amount of the allowed claim so that if the value of the collateral increases after the case is closed, the deferred payments will be secured claims. Thus it is both reasonable and necessary to exempt such electing class from application of section 1129(a)(7) as a logical consequence of permitting election under section 1111(b)(2).

Section 1131 of the Senate amendment is deleted as unnecessary in light of the protection given a secured creditor under section 1129(b) of the House amendment.

Payment of taxes in reorganizations: Under the provisions of section 1141 as revised by the House amendment, an individual in reorganization under chapter 11 will not be discharged from any debt, including prepetition tax liabilities, which are nondischargeable under section 523. Thus, an individual debtor whose plan of reorganization is confirmed under chapter 11 will remain liable for prepetition priority taxes, as defined in section 507, and for tax liabilities which receive no priority but are nondischargeable under section 523, including no return, late return, and fraud liabilities.

In the case of a partnership or a corporation in reorganization under chapter 11 of title 11, section 1141(d)(1) of the House amendment adopts a provision limiting the taxes that must be provided for in a plan before a plan can be confirmed to taxes which receive priority under section 507. In addition, the House amendment makes dischargeable, in effect, tax liabilities attributable to no return, late return, or fraud situations. The amendment thus does not adopt a shareholder continuity test such as was contained in section 1141(d)(2)(A)(iii) of the Senate amendment. However, the House amendment amends section 1106, relating to duties of the trustee, to require the trustee to furnish, on request of a tax authority and without personal liability, information available to the trustee concerning potential prepetition tax liabilities for unfiled returns of the debtor. Depending on the condition of the debtor's books and records, this information may include schedules and files available to the business. The House amendment also does not prohibit a tax authority from disallowing any tax benefit claimed after the reorganization if the item originated in a deduction, credit, or other item improperly reported before the reorganization occurred. It may also be appropriate for the Congress to consider in the future imposing civil or criminal liability on corporate officers for preparing a false or fraudulent tax return. The House amendment also contemplates that the Internal Revenue Service will monitor the relief from liabilities under this provision

and advise the Congress if, and to the extent, any significant tax abuse may be resulting from the provision.

Medium of payment of taxes: Federal, State, and local taxes incurred during the administration period of the estate, and during the "gap" period in an involuntary case, are to be paid solely in cash. Taxes relating to third priority wages are to be paid, under the general rules, in cash on the effective date of the plan, if the class has not accepted the plan, in an amount equal to the allowed amount of the claim. If the class has accepted the plan, the taxes must be paid in cash but the payments must be made at the time the wages are paid which may be paid in deferred periodic installments having a value, on the effective date of the plan, equal to the allowed amount of the tax claims. Prepetition taxes entitled to sixth priority under section 507(a)(6) also must be paid in cash, but the plan may also permit the debtor whether a corporation, partnership, or an individual, to pay the allowed taxes in installments over a period not to exceed 6 years following the date on which the tax authority assesses the tax liability, provided the value of the deferred payments representing principal and interest, as of the effective date of the plan, equals the allowed amount of the tax claim.

The House amendment also modifies the provisions of both bills dealing with the time when tax liabilities of a debtor in reorganization may be assessed by the tax authority. The House amendment follows the Senate amendment in deleting the limitation in present law under which a priority tax assessed after a reorganization plan is confirmed must be assessed within 1 year after the date of the filing of the petition. The House amendment specifies broadly that after the bankruptcy court determines the liability of the estate for a prepetition tax or for an administration period tax, the governmental unit may thereafter assess the tax against the estate, debtor, or successor to the debtor. The party to be assessed will, of course, depend on whether the case is under chapter 7, 11, or 13, whether the debtor is an individual, partnership, or a corporation, and whether the court is determining an individual debtor's personal liability for a nondischargeable tax. Assessment of the tax may only be made, however, within the limits of otherwise applicable law, such as the statute of limitations under the tax law.

Tax avoidance purpose: The House bill provided that no reorganization plan may be approved if the principal purpose of the plan is the avoidance of taxes. The Senate amendment modified the rule so that the bankruptcy court need make a determination of tax avoidance purpose only if it is asked to do so by the appropriate tax authority. Under the Senate amendment, if the tax authority does not request the bankruptcy court to rule on the purpose of the plan, the tax authority would not be barred from later asserting a tax avoidance motive with respect to allowance of a deduction or other tax benefit claimed after the reorganization. The House amendment adopts the substance of the Senate amendment, but does not provide a basis by which a tax authority may collaterally attack confirmation of a plan of reorganization other than under section 1144.

References in Text

Section 5 of the Securities Act of 1933, referred to in subsec. (d), is section 5 of Act May 27, 1933, c. 38, Title I, 48 Stat. 77, which is classified to section 77e of Title 15, Commerce and Trade.

Amendments

2010 Amendments. Subsec. (a)(16). Pub.L. 111–327, § 2(a)(35), struck out "of the plan" and inserted "under the plan".

2005 Amendments. Subsec. (a)(9). Pub.L. 109–8, § 1502(a)(8), struck out "507(a)(1) or 507(a)(2)" and inserted "507(a)(2) or 507(a)(3)" in subparagraph (A), and struck out "507(a)(3)" and inserted "507(a)(1)" in subparagraph (B).

Subsec. (a)(9)(B). Pub.L. 109–8, § 710(1), struck out "and" at the end of subpar. (B).

Subsec. (a)(9)(C). Pub.L. 109–8, § 710(2), struck out "deferred cash payments, over a period not exceeding six years after the date of assessment of such claim, of a value, as of the effective date of the plan, equal to the allowed amount of such claim." and inserted "regular installment payments in cash–"

Subsec. (a)(9)(C)(i). Pub.L. 109–8, § 710(2), added cl. (i).

Subsec. (a)(9)(C)(ii). Pub.L. 109–8, § 710(2), added cl. (ii).

Subsec. (a)(9)(C)(iii). Pub.L. 109–8, § 710(2), added cl. (iii).

Subsec. (a)(9)(D). Pub.L. 109–8, § 710(3), added subpar. (D).

Subsec. (a)(14). Pub.L. 109–8, § 213(1), added par. (14).

Subsec. (a)(15). Pub.L. 109–8, § 321(c)(1), added par. (15).

Subsec. (a)(16). Pub.L.109–8, § 1221(b), added subsec. (a)(16).

Subsec. (b)(2)(B)(ii). Pub.L. 109–8, § 321(c)(2), inserted ", except that in a case in which the debtor is an individual, the debtor may retain property included in the estate under section 1115, subject to the requirements of subsection (a)(14) of this section" before the period at the end of cl. (ii).

Subsec. (e). Pub.L. 109–8, § 438, added subsec. (e).

1994 Amendments. Subsec. (a)(4). Pub.L. 103–394, § 501(d)(32)(A)(i), substituted a period for a semicolon.

Subsec. (a)(9)(B). Pub.L. 103–394, § 304(h)(7)(i), inserted reference to section 507(a)(7) of this title.

Subsec. (a)(9)(C). Pub.L. 103–394, § 304(h)(7)(ii), substituted "507(a)(8)" for "507(a)(7)".

Subsec. (a)(12). Pub.L. 103–394, § 501(d)(32)(A)(ii), inserted "of title 28" following "section 1930".

Subsec. (d). Pub.L. 103–394, § 501(d)(32)(B), struck out "(15 U.S.C. 77e)" following "section 5 of the Securities Act of 1933".

1988 Amendments. Subsec. (a)(13). Pub.L. 100–334 added par. (13).

1986 Amendments. Subsec. (a)(7). Pub.L. 99–554, § 283(v)(1), substituted "to each" for "to of each".

Subsec. (a)(9)(B). Pub.L. 99–554, § 283(v)(2), added reference to section 507(a)(6) of this title. .

Subsec. (a)(9)(C). Pub.L. 99–554, § 283(v)(3), substituted "507(a)(7)" for "507(a)(6)".

Subsec. (a)(12). Pub.L. 99–554, § 225, added par. (12).

1984 Amendments. Subsec. (a)(1). Pub.L. 98–353, § 512(a)(1), substituted "title" for "chapter".

Subsec. (a)(2). Pub.L. 98–353, § 512(a)(2), substituted "title" for "chapter".

Subsec. (a)(4). Pub.L. 98–353, § 512(a)(3), substituted "Any payment made or to be made by the proponent, by the debtor, or by a person issuing securities or acquiring property under the plan, for services or for costs and expenses in or in connection with the case, or in connection with the plan and incident to the case, has been approved by, or is subject to the approval of, the court as reasonable;" for "Any payment made or promised by the proponent, by the debtor, or by a person issuing securities or acquiring property under the plan, for services or for costs and expenses in, or in connection with, the case, or in connection with the plan and incident to the case, has been disclosed to the court; and (B)(i) any such payment made before confirmation of the plan is reasonable; or (ii) if such payment is to be fixed after confirmation of the plan, such payment is subject to the approval of the court as reasonable.".

Subsec. (a)(5)(A)(ii). Pub.L. 98–353, § 512(a)(4), substituted "; and" for the period at the end thereof.

Subsec. (a)(5)(B). Pub.L. 98–353, § 512(a)(5), substituted "the" for "The".

Subsec. (a)(6). Pub.L. 98–353, § 512(a)(6), added "governmental" after "Any".

Subsec. (a)(7). Pub.L. 98–353, § 512(a)(7)(A), substituted "of each impaired class of claims or interests" for "each class".

Subsec. (a)(7)(B). Pub.L. 98–353, § 512(a)(7)(B), substituted "holder's" for "creditor's".

Subsec. (a)(8). Pub.L. 98–353, § 512(a)(8), added "of claims or interests" after "each class".

Subsec. (a)(10). Pub.L. 98–353, § 512(a)(9), substituted "If a class of claims is impaired under the plan, at least one class of claims that is impaired under the plan has accepted the plan, determined without including any acceptance of the plan by any insider." for "At least one class of claims has accepted the plan, determined without including any acceptance of the plan by any insider holding a claim of such class.".

Subsec. (b)(2)(A)(i)(I). Pub.L. 98–353, § 512(b)(1), substituted "liens" for "lien" wherever appearing.

Subsec. (b)(2)(A)(ii). Pub.L. 98–353, § 512(b)(1), substituted "liens" for "lien" wherever appearing.

Subsec. (b)(2)(B)(ii). Pub.L. 98–353, § 512(b)(2), added "under the plan" after "retain".

Subsec. (b)(2)(C)(i). Pub.L. 98–353, § 512(b)(3)(A), substituted "interest" for "claim".

Pub.L. 98–353, § 512(b)(3)(B), substituted "or the value" for "and the value".

Subsec. (d). Pub.L. 98–353, § 512(c)(1), added "the application of" after "avoidance".

Pub.L. 98–353, § 512(c)(2), added provisions requiring that in any hearing under this subsection, the governmental unit has the burden of proof on the issue of avoidance.

Effective and Applicability Provisions

2005 Acts. Amendments to this section by Pub.L. 109–8, § 1221, applicable to case pending under this title on Apr. 20, 2005, or filed under this title on or after that date, except that the court shall not confirm a plan under chapter 11 of this title without considering whether this section would substantially affect the rights of a party in interest who first acquired rights with respect to the debtor after the date of the filing of the petition, see Pub.L. 109–8, § 1221(d), set out as a note under 11 U.S.C.A. § 363.

Amendments by Pub.L. 109–8 effective, except as otherwise provided, 180 days after April 20, 2005, and inapplicable with respect to cases commenced under Title 11 before the effective date, see Pub.L. 109–8, § 1501, set out as a note under 11 U.S.C.A. § 101.

1994 Acts. Amendments by Pub.L. 103–394 effective on Oct. 22, 1994, and not to apply with respect to cases commenced under Title 11 of the United States Code before Oct. 22, 1994, see section 702 of Pub.L. 103–394, set out as a note under section 101 of this title.

1988 Acts. Amendment by Pub.L. 100–334 effective on June 16, 1988, but not applicable to cases commenced under this title before that date, see section 4 of Pub.L. 100–334, set out as an Effective Date note under section 1114 of this title.

1986 Acts. Amendment by Pub.L. 99–554 effective 30 days after Oct. 27, 1986, except as otherwise provided for, see section 302(a) of Pub.L. 99–554, set out as a note under section 581 of Title 28, Judiciary and Judicial Procedure.

Amendment by Pub.L. 99–554, § 225, not to become effective in or with respect to certain specified judicial districts until, or apply to cases while pending in such district before, the expiration of the 270–day period beginning 30 days after Oct. 27, 1986, or of the 30–day period beginning on the date the Attorney General certifies under section 303 of Pub.L. 99–554 the region specified in a paragraph of section 581(a) of Title 28, as amended by section 111(a) of Pub.L. 99–554, that includes such district, whichever occurs first, see section 302(d)(1) of Pub.L. 99–554, set out as a note under section 581 of Title 28.

Amendment by Pub.L. 99–554, § 225, not to become effective in or with respect to certain specified judicial districts until, or apply to cases while pending in such district before, the expiration of the 2–year period beginning 30 days after Oct. 27, 1986, or of the 30–day period beginning on the date the Attorney General certifies under section 303 of Pub.L. 99 554 the region specified in a paragraph of section 581(a) of Title 28, as amended by section 111(a) of Pub.L. 99–554, that includes such district, whichever occurs first, see section 302(d)(2) of Pub.L. 99–554, set out as a note under section 581 of Title 28.

Amendment by Pub.L. 99–554, § 225, not to become effective in or with respect to judicial districts established for the States of Alabama and North Carolina until, or apply to cases while pending in such district before, such district elects to be included in a bankruptcy region established in section 581(a) of Title 28, as amended by section 111(a) of Pub.L. 99–554, or Oct. 1, 2002, whichever occurs first, and, except as otherwise provided for, with respect to cases under chapters 7, 11, 12, and 13 of Title 11 commenced before 30 days after Oct. 27, 1986, and pending in a judicial district in the States of Alabama or North Carolina before any election made under section 302(d)(3)(A) of Pub.L. 99–554 by such district becomes effective or Oct. 1, 2002, whichever occurs first, amendments by Pub.L. 99–554 not to apply until Oct. 1, 2003, or the expiration of the 1–year period beginning on the date such election becomes effective, whichever occurs first, and further, in any judicial district in Alabama or North Carolina not making the election described in section 302(d)(3)(A) of Pub.L. 99–554, any person appointed under regulations issued by the Judicial Conference to administer estates in cases under Title 11 authorized to establish, etc., a panel of private trustees, and to supervise cases and trustees in cases under chapters 7, 11, 12, and 13 of Title 11, until amendments by sections 201 to 231 of Pub.L. 99–554 effective in such district, see section 302(d)(3)(A) to (F), (H), (I) of Pub.L. 99–554, set out as a note under section 581 of Title 28.

Amendment by Pub.L. 99–554, § 225, except as otherwise provided, with respect to cases under chapters 7, 11, 12, and 13 of Title 11 commenced before 30 days after Oct. 27, 1986,

and pending in a judicial district referred to in section 581(a) of Title 28, as amended by section 111(a) of Pub.L. 99–554, for which a United States trustee is not authorized before 30 days after Oct. 27, 1986 to be appointed, not applicable until the expiration of the 3–year period beginning on Oct. 27, 1986, or of the 1–year period beginning on the date the Attorney General certifies under section 303 of Pub.L. 99–554 the region specified in a paragraph of such section 581(a) that includes, such district, whichever occurs first, see section 302(e)(1), (2) of Pub.L. 99–554, set out as a note under section 581 of Title 28.

1984 Acts. Amendment by Pub.L. 98–353 effective with respect to cases filed 90 days after July 10, 1984, see section 552(a), formerly 553(a), of Pub.L. 98–353, set out as a note under section 101 of this title.

Separability of Provisions

If any provision of or amendment made by Pub.L. 103–394 or the application of such provision or amendment to any person or circumstance is held to be unconstitutional, the remaining provisions of and amendments made by Pub.L. 103–394 and the application of such provisions and amendments to any person or circumstance shall not be affected thereby, see section 701 of Pub.L. 103–394, set out as a note under section 101 of this title.

CROSS REFERENCES

Applicability of subsecs. (a)(2), (3), (6), (8), (10) and (b)(1), (2)(A), (2)(B) of this section in Chapter nine cases, see 11 USCA § 901.

Confirmation of plan in—

    Chapter nine cases, see 11 USCA § 943.

    Chapter thirteen cases, see 11 USCA § 1325.

    Chapter twelve cases, see 11 USCA § 1225.

    Railroad reorganization cases, see 11 USCA § 1173.

Denial of confirmation of plan as cause for conversion or dismissal, see 11 USCA § 1112.

Effect of confirmation in cases under this chapter, see 11 USCA § 1141.

Inapplicability of subsecs. (a)(7) and (c) of this section in railroad reorganization cases, see 11 USCA § 1161.

Payment of insurance benefits to retired employees, see 11 USCA § 1114.

Revocation of order of confirmation in cases under this chapter, see 11 USCA § 1144.

Special tax provisions for certain dispositions of securities or instruments under confirmed plan, see 11 USCA § 1146.

Supplemental injunctions and plan fair and equitable, see 11 USCA § 524.

Unclaimed property, see 11 USCA § 347.

LIBRARY REFERENCES

American Digest System

    Bankruptcy ⬤➾3548.1 to 3565.

    Key Number System Topic No. 51.

Corpus Juris Secundum

    CJS Bankruptcy § 952, Claims for Retiree Benefits.

    CJS Bankruptcy § 1099, Unclaimed Property.

    CJS Bankruptcy § 1121, Requirements for Confirmation.

    CJS Bankruptcy § 1133, Who May File; Time for Filing.

CJS Bankruptcy § 1135, Impairment of Claims or Interests--Curing Defaults.

CJS Bankruptcy § 1139, Good Faith and Legality.

CJS Bankruptcy § 1140, Feasibility.

CJS Bankruptcy § 1141, Provisions for Satisfaction of Claims; Relation to Recovery in Liquidation.

CJS Bankruptcy § 1142, Preservation of Priority.

CJS Bankruptcy § 1147, Generally; Fairness and Equity.

CJS Bankruptcy § 1148, Protection of Secured Creditors.

CJS Bankruptcy § 1149, Protection of Unsecured Creditors and Equityholders.

CJS Bankruptcy § 1155, By One Class.

CJS Bankruptcy § 1157, Acceptance of the Plan--Eligibility to Vote; Impairment.

CJS Bankruptcy § 1163, Modification of the Plan.

CJS Bankruptcy § 1168, Reorganization Plan.

CJS Bankruptcy § 1261, Particular Matters.

CJS Secured Transactions § 27, Other Particular Factors and Tests.

SUBCHAPTER III—POSTCONFIRMATION MATTERS

CROSS REFERENCES

Subchapter applicable only in case under this chapter except as provided in § 901 of this title, see 11 USCA § 103.

§ 1141. Effect of confirmation

(a) Except as provided in subsections (d)(2) and (d)(3) of this section, the provisions of a confirmed plan bind the debtor, any entity issuing securities under the plan, any entity acquiring property under the plan, and any creditor, equity security holder, or general partner in the debtor, whether or not the claim or interest of such creditor, equity security holder, or general partner is impaired under the plan and whether or not such creditor, equity security holder, or general partner has accepted the plan.

(b) Except as otherwise provided in the plan or the order confirming the plan, the confirmation of a plan vests all of the property of the estate in the debtor.

(c) Except as provided in subsections (d)(2) and (d)(3) of this section and except as otherwise provided in the plan or in the order confirming the plan, after confirmation of a plan, the property dealt with by the plan is free and clear of all claims and interests of creditors, equity security holders, and of general partners in the debtor.

(d)(1) Except as otherwise provided in this subsection, in the plan, or in the order confirming the plan, the confirmation of a plan—

(A) discharges the debtor from any debt that arose before the date of such confirmation, and any debt of a kind specified in section 502(g), 502(h), or 502(i) of this title, whether or not—

(i) a proof of the claim based on such debt is filed or deemed filed under section 501 of this title;

(ii) such claim is allowed under section 502 of this title; or

(iii) the holder of such claim has accepted the plan; and

(B) terminates all rights and interests of equity security holders and general partners provided for by the plan.

(2) A discharge under this chapter does not discharge a debtor who is an individual from any debt excepted from discharge under section 523 of this title.

(3) The confirmation of a plan does not discharge a debtor if—

(A) the plan provides for the liquidation of all or substantially all of the property of the estate;

(B) the debtor does not engage in business after consummation of the plan; and

(C) the debtor would be denied a discharge under section 727(a) of this title if the case were a case under chapter 7 of this title.

(4) The court may approve a written waiver of discharge executed by the debtor after the order for relief under this chapter.

(5) In a case in which the debtor is an individual—

(A) unless after notice and a hearing the court orders otherwise for cause, confirmation of the plan does not discharge any debt provided for in the plan until the court grants a discharge on completion of all payments under the plan;

(B) at any time after the confirmation of the plan, and after notice and a hearing, the court may grant a discharge to the debtor who has not completed payments under the plan if—

(i) the value, as of the effective date of the plan, of property actually distributed under the plan on account of each allowed unsecured claim is not less than the amount that would have been paid on such claim if the estate of the debtor had been liquidated under chapter 7 on such date;

(ii) modification of the plan under section 1127 is not practicable; and

(iii) subparagraph (C) permits the court to grant a discharge; and

(C) the court may grant a discharge if, after notice and a hearing held not more than 10 days before the date of the entry of the order granting the discharge, the court finds that there is no reasonable cause to believe that—

(i) section 522(q)(1) may be applicable to the debtor; and

(ii) there is pending any proceeding in which the debtor may be found guilty of a felony of the kind described in section 522(q)(1)(A) or liable for a debt of the kind described in section 522(q)(1)(B);

and if the requirements of subparagraph (A) or (B) are met.

(6) Notwithstanding paragraph (1), the confirmation of a plan does not discharge a debtor that is a corporation from any debt—

(A) of a kind specified in paragraph (2)(A) or (2)(B) of section 523(a) that is owed to a domestic governmental unit, or owed to a person as the result of an action filed under subchapter III of chapter 37 of title 31 or any similar State statute; or

(B) for a tax or customs duty with respect to which the debtor—

(i) made a fraudulent return; or

(ii) willfully attempted in any manner to evade or to defeat such tax or such customs duty.

(Pub.L. 95–598, Nov. 6, 1978, 92 Stat. 2638; Pub.L. 98–353, Title III, § 513, July 10, 1984, 98 Stat. 387; Pub.L. 109–8, Title III, §§ 321(d), 330(b), Title VII, § 708, Apr. 20, 2005, 119 Stat. 95, 101, 126; Pub.L. 111–327, § 2(a)(36), Dec. 22, 2010, 124 Stat. 3561.)

HISTORICAL AND STATUTORY NOTES

Revision Notes and Legislative Reports

1978 Acts. Subsection (a) of this section makes the provisions of a confirmed plan binding on the debtor, any entity issuing securities under the plan, any entity acquiring property under the plan, and any creditor, equity security holder, or general partner in the debtor, whether or not the claim or interest of the creditor, equity security holder, or partner is impaired under the plan and whether or not he has accepted the plan. There are two exceptions, enumerated in paragraph (2) and (3) of subsection (d).

Unless the plan or the order confirming the plan provides otherwise, the confirmation of a plan vests all of the property of the estate in the debtor and releases it from all claims and interests of creditors, equity security holders and general partners.

Subsection (d) contains the discharge for a reorganized debtor. Paragraph (1) specifies that the confirmation of a plan discharges the debtor from any debt that arose before the date of the order for relief unless the plan or the order confirming the plan provides otherwise. The discharge is effective against those claims whether or not proof of the claim is filed (or deemed filed), and whether or not the claim is allowed. The discharge also terminates all rights and interests of equity security holders and general partners provided for by the plan. The paragraph permits the plan or the order confirming the plan to provide otherwise, and excepts certain debts from the discharge as provided in paragraphs (2) and (3).

Paragraph (2) of subsection (d) makes clear what taxes remain nondischargeable in the case of a corporate debtor emerging from a reorganization under chapter 11. Nondischargeable taxes in such a reorganization are the priority taxes (under section 507) and tax payments which come due during and after the proceeding under a deferred or part-payment agreement which the debtor had entered into with the tax authority before the bankruptcy proceedings began. On the other hand, a corporation which is taken over by its creditors through a plan of reorganization will not continue to be liable for nonpriority taxes arising from the corporation's

prepetition fraud, failure to file a return, or failure to file a timely return, since the creditors who take over the reorganized company should not bear the burden of acts for which the creditors were not at fault.

Paragraph (3) specifies that the debtor is not discharged by the confirmation of a plan if the plan is a liquidating plan and if the debtor would be denied discharge in a liquidation case under section 727. Specifically, if all or substantially all of the distribution under the plan is of all or substantially all of the property of the estate or the proceeds of it, if the business, if any, of the debtor does not continue, and if the debtor would be denied a discharge under section 727 (such as if the debtor were not an individual or if he had committed an act that would lead to a denial of discharge), the chapter 11 discharge is not granted.

Paragraph (4) authorizes the court to approve a waiver of discharge by the debtor. Senate Report No. 95–989.

Paragraph (2) [of subsec. (d)] makes applicable to an individual debtor the general exceptions to discharge that are enumerated in section 523(a) of the bankruptcy code [this title]. House Report No. 95–595.

1984 Acts. Statements by Legislative Leaders, see 1984 U.S.Code Cong. and Adm.News, p. 576.

2005 Acts. House Report No. 109–31(Part I), see 2005 U.S. Code Cong. and Adm. News, p. 88.

Legislative Statements

Section 1141(d) of the House amendment is derived from a comparable provision contained in the Senate amendment. However, section 1141(d)(2) of the House amendment is derived from the House bill as preferable to the Senate amendment. It is necessary for a corporation or partnership undergoing reorganization to be able to present its creditors with a fixed list of liabilities upon which the creditors or third parties can make intelligent decisions. Retaining an exception for discharge with respect to nondischargeable taxes would leave an undesirable uncertainty surrounding reorganizations that is unacceptable. Section 1141(d)(3) is derived from the Senate amendment. Section 1141(d)(4) is likewise derived from the Senate amendment.

References in Text

Chapter 7, referred to in subsec. (d)(5)(B)(i), is chapter 7 of this title, 11 U.S.C.A. § 701 et seq.

Subchapter III of chapter 37 of title 31, referred to in subsec. (d)(6)(A), is 31 U.S.C.A. § 3721 et seq.

Codifications

Amendment by Pub.L. 109–8, § 330(b), adding a new subparagraph (C) "at the end" of subsection (d) "as amended by section 321 [of Pub.L. 109–8, which added a new paragraph (5) to subsection (d) of this section]" was executed by adding the new subparagraph to the end of paragraph (5) of subsection (d), as the probable intent of Congress.

Amendments

2010 Amendments. Subsec. (d)(5)(B)(i). Pub.L. 111–327, § 2(a)(36)(A)(i), struck out "and" at the end following the semicolon.

Subsec. (d)(5)(B)(iii). Pub.L. 111–327, § 2(a)(36)(A)(ii), added cl. (iii).

Subsec. (d)(5)(C). Pub.L. 111–327, § 2(a)(36)(B)(i), struck out "unless" and inserted "the court may grant a discharge if,".

Pub.L. 111–327, § 2(a)(36)(B)(iii), added the undesignated matter at the end following cl. (ii) reading, "and if the requirements of subparagraph (A) or (B) are met.".

Subsec. (d)(5)(C)(ii). Pub.L. 111–327, § 2(a)(36)(B)(ii), struck out the period at the end and inserted a semicolon.

2005 Amendments. Subsec. (d)(2). Pub.L. 109–8, § 321(d)(1), struck out "The confirmation of a plan does not discharge an individual debtor" and inserted "A discharge under this chapter does not discharge a debtor who is an individual".

Subsec. (d)(5). Pub.L. 109–8, § 321(d)(2), added par. (5).

Subsec. (d)(5)(C). Pub.L. 109–8, § 330(b), added subpar. (C). See Codifications note under this section.

Subsec. (d)(6). Pub.L. 109–8, § 708, added par. (6).

1984 Amendments. Subsec. (a). Pub.L. 98–353, § 513(a), substituted "any creditor, equity security holder, or general partner in" for "any creditor or equity security holder of, or general partner in,".

Subsec. (c). Pub.L. 98–353, § 513(b), substituted "Except as provided in subsections (d)(2) and (d)(3) of this section and except as otherwise provided in the plan or in the order confirming the plan, after confirmation of a plan, the property dealt with by the plan is free and clear of all claims and interests of creditors, equity security holders, and of general partners in the debtor." for "After confirmation of a plan, the property dealt with by the plan is free and clear of all claims and interests of creditors, of equity security holders, and of general partners in the debtor, except as otherwise provided in the plan or in the order confirming the plan.".

Effective and Applicability Provisions

2005 Acts. Amendments by Pub.L. 109–8 effective 180 days after Apr. 20, 2005, with amendments by sections 321(d) and 708 of Pub.L. 109–8 not applicable with respect to cases commenced under this title before such effective date, except as otherwise provided, and amendment by section 330(b) of Pub.L. 109–8 applicable with respect to cases commenced under this title on or after Apr. 20, 2005, see Pub.L. 109–8, § 1501, set out as a note under 11 U.S.C.A. § 101.

1984 Acts. Amendment by Pub.L. 98–353 effective with respect to cases filed 90 days after July 10, 1984, see section 552(a), formerly 553(a), of Pub.L. 98–353, set out as a note under section 101 of this title.

CROSS REFERENCES

Confirmation of plan filed under this chapter, see 11 USCA § 1129.

Discharge under Chapter seven, see 11 USCA § 727.

Effect of confirmation of plans filed in—

    Chapter nine cases, see 11 USCA § 944.

    Chapter thirteen cases, see 11 USCA § 1327.

    Chapter twelve cases, see 11 USCA § 1227.

Effect of conversion, see 11 USCA § 348.

Effect of discharge, see 11 USCA § 524.

Exceptions to discharge, see 11 USCA § 523.

Failure of discharge as cause for conversion, see 11 USCA § 1112.

Nondischargeability of capital improvement loans for multi-family housing projects in proceedings under this section, see 12 USCA § 1715z–1a.

Supplemental injunctions, debtor and plan of reorganization, see 11 USCA § 524.

LIBRARY REFERENCES

American Digest System

Bankruptcy ⟳3568(1) to 3568(3).

Key Number System Topic No. 51.

Corpus Juris Secundum

CJS Bankruptcy § 158, What Are Proceedings Arising in Cases Under Title 11.

CJS Bankruptcy § 278, Parties Defendant; Sovereign Immunity.

CJS Bankruptcy § 301, Notice to Debtor, Creditors, and Indenture Trustees.

CJS Bankruptcy § 840, Operation of Debtor's Business.

CJS Bankruptcy § 1047, Time for Proceedings; Extension of Time.

CJS Bankruptcy § 1094, Requirements for Reaffirmation of Debt.

CJS Bankruptcy § 1160, Effect of Confirmation.

CJS Bankruptcy § 1161, Effect of Confirmation--Discharge.

§ 1142.   Implementation of plan

(a) Notwithstanding any otherwise applicable non-bankruptcy law, rule, or regulation relating to financial condition, the debtor and any entity organized or to be organized for the purpose of carrying out the plan shall carry out the plan and shall comply with any orders of the court.

(b) The court may direct the debtor and any other necessary party to execute or deliver or to join in the execution or delivery of any instrument required to effect a transfer of property dealt with by a confirmed plan, and to perform any other act, including the satisfaction of any lien, that is necessary for the consummation of the plan.

(Pub.L. 95–598, Nov. 6, 1978, 92 Stat. 2639; Pub.L. 98–353, Title III, § 514(a), (c), (d), July 10, 1984, 98 Stat. 387.)

HISTORICAL AND STATUTORY NOTES

Revision Notes and Legislative Reports

1978 Acts. Senate Report No. 95–989 and House Report No. 95–595, see 1978 U.S.Code Cong. and Adm.News, p. 5787.

1984 Acts. Statements by Legislative Leaders, see 1984 U.S.Code Cong. and Adm.News, p. 576.

Amendments

1984 Amendments. Pub.L. 98–353, § 514(a), substituted "Implementation" for "Execution" in the section catchline.

Subsec. (a). Pub.L. 98–353, § 514(c), struck out the comma after "shall carry out the plan".

Subsec. (b). Pub.L. 98–353, § 514(d), added "a" following "by".

Effective and Applicability Provisions

1984 Acts. Amendment by Pub.L. 98–353 effective with respect to cases filed 90 days after July 10, 1984, see section 552(a), formerly 553 of Pub.L. 98–353, set out as a note under section 101 of this title.

Applicability of subsec. (b) of this section in Chapter nine cases, see 11 USCA § 901.

Supplemental injunctions, debtor and plan of reorganization, see 11 USCA § 524.

LIBRARY REFERENCES

American Digest System

Bankruptcy ⟳3570.

Key Number System Topic No. 51.

Corpus Juris Secundum

CJS Bankruptcy § 278, Parties Defendant; Sovereign Immunity.

CJS Bankruptcy § 1125, Continuing Jurisdiction; Closing of Case.

CJS Bankruptcy § 1137, Means of Implementation.

CJS Bankruptcy § 1162, Implementation of the Plan; Distribution.

§ 1143.   Distribution

If a plan requires presentment or surrender of a security or the performance of any other act as a condition to participation in distribution under the plan, such action shall be taken not later than five years after the date of the entry of the order of confirmation. Any entity that has not within such time presented or surrendered such entity's security or taken any such other action that the plan requires may not participate in distribution under the plan.
(Pub.L. 95–598, Nov. 6, 1978, 92 Stat. 2639.)

HISTORICAL AND STATUTORY NOTES

Revision Notes and Legislative Reports

1978 Acts. Section 1143 fixes a 5-year limitation on presentment or surrender of securities or the performance of any other act that is a condition to participation in distribution under the plan. The 5 years runs from the date of the entry of the order of confirmation. Any entity that does not take the appropriate action with the 5-year period is barred from participation in the distribution under the plan. Senate Report No. 95–989.

CROSS REFERENCES

Applicability of this section in Chapter nine cases, see 11 USCA § 901.

Distribution of property of estate in Chapter seven cases, see 11 USCA § 726.

Distribution of securities in stockbroker liquidation cases, see 11 USCA § 750.

Ownership of copyright, see 17 USCA § 201.

LIBRARY REFERENCES

American Digest System

Bankruptcy ⟳3570.

Key Number System Topic No. 51.

Corpus Juris Secundum

CJS Bankruptcy § 278, Parties Defendant; Sovereign Immunity.

CJS Bankruptcy § 1162, Implementation of the Plan; Distribution.

§ 1144.   Revocation of an order of confirmation

On request of a party in interest at any time before 180 days after the date of the entry of the order of confirmation, and after notice and a hearing, the court may revoke such order if and only if such order was procured by fraud. An order under this section revoking an order of confirmation shall—

(1) contain such provisions as are necessary to protect any entity acquiring rights in good faith reliance on the order of confirmation; and

(2) revoke the discharge of the debtor.

(Pub.L. 95–598, Nov. 6, 1978, 92 Stat. 2639; Pub.L. 98–353, Title III, § 515, July 10, 1984, 98 Stat. 387.)

HISTORICAL AND STATUTORY NOTES

Revision Notes and Legislative Reports

1978 Acts. If an order of confirmation was procured by fraud, then the court may revoke the order on request of a party in interest if the request is made before 180 days after the date of the entry of the order of confirmation. The order revoking the order of confirmation must revoke the discharge of the debtor, and contain such provisions as are necessary to protect any entity acquiring rights in good faith reliance on the order of confirmation. Senate Report No. 95–989.

1984 Acts. Statements by Legislative Leaders, see 1984 U.S.Code Cong. and Adm.News, p. 576.

Amendments

1984 Amendments. Pub.L. 98–353 added "if and only" following "revoke such order".

Effective and Applicability Provisions

1984 Acts. Amendment by Pub.L. 98–353 effective with respect to cases filed 90 days after July 10, 1984, see section 552(a), formerly 553(a), of Pub.L. 98–353, set out as a note under section 101 of this title.

CROSS REFERENCES

Applicability of this section in Chapter nine cases, see 11 USCA § 901.

Confirmation of one plan as affected by revocation, see 11 USCA § 1129.

Revocation of confirmation order as cause for conversion or dismissal, see 11 USCA § 1112.

Revocation of order of confirmation in—

Chapter thirteen cases, see 11 USCA § 1330.

Chapter twelve cases, see 11 USCA § 1230.

Supplemental injunctions, see 11 USCA § 524.

LIBRARY REFERENCES

American Digest System

Bankruptcy ⟳3569.

Key Number System Topic No. 51.

Corpus Juris Secundum

CJS Bankruptcy § 315, Judgments--Relief from Judgment or Order; Collateral Attack.

CJS Bankruptcy § 1123, Hearing and Order.

CJS Bankruptcy § 1164, Revocation of Order of Confirmation.

§ 1145. Exemption from securities laws

(a) Except with respect to an entity that is an underwriter as defined in subsection (b) of this section, section 5 of the Securities Act of 1933 and any State or local law requiring registration for offer or sale of a security or registration or licensing of an issuer of, underwriter of, or broker or dealer in, a security do not apply to—

(1) the offer or sale under a plan of a security of the debtor, of an affiliate participating in a joint plan with the debtor, or of a successor to the debtor under the plan—

(A) in exchange for a claim against, an interest in, or a claim for an administrative expense in the case concerning, the debtor or such affiliate; or

(B) principally in such exchange and partly for cash or property;

(2) the offer of a security through any warrant, option, right to subscribe, or conversion privilege that was sold in the manner specified in paragraph (1) of this subsection, or the sale of a security upon the exercise of such a warrant, option, right, or privilege;

(3) the offer or sale, other than under a plan, of a security of an issuer other than the debtor or an affiliate, if—

(A) such security was owned by the debtor on the date of the filing of the petition;

(B) the issuer of such security is—

(i) required to file reports under section 13 or 15(d) of the Securities Exchange Act of 1934; and

(ii) in compliance with the disclosure and reporting provision of such applicable section; and

(C) such offer or sale is of securities that do not exceed—

(i) during the two-year period immediately following the date of the filing of the petition, four percent of the securities of such class outstanding on such date; and

(ii) during any 180-day period following such two-year period, one percent of the securities outstanding at the beginning of such 180-day period; or

(4) a transaction by a stockbroker in a security that is executed after a transaction of a kind specified in paragraph (1) or (2) of this subsection in such security and before the expiration of 40 days after the first date on which such security was bona fide offered to the public by the issuer or by or through an underwriter, if such stockbroker provides, at the time of or before such transaction by such stockbroker, a disclosure statement approved under section 1125 of this title, and, if the court orders, information supplementing such disclosure statement.

(b)(1) Except as provided in paragraph (2) of this subsection and except with respect to ordinary trading transactions of an entity that is not an issuer, an entity is an underwriter under section 2(a)(11) of the Securities Act of 1933, if such entity—

(A) purchases a claim against, interest in, or claim for an administrative expense in the case concerning, the debtor, if such purchase is with a view to distribution of any security received or to be received in exchange for such a claim or interest;

(B) offers to sell securities offered or sold under the plan for the holders of such securities;

(C) offers to buy securities offered or sold under the plan from the holders of such securities, if such offer to buy is—

(i) with a view to distribution of such securities; and

(ii) under an agreement made in connection with the plan, with the consummation of the plan, or with the offer or sale of securities under the plan; or

(D) is an issuer, as used in such section 2(a)(11), with respect to such securities.

(2) An entity is not an underwriter under section 2(a)(11) of the Securities Act of 1933 or under paragraph (1) of this subsection with respect to an agreement that provides only for—

(A)(i) the matching or combining of fractional interests in securities offered or sold under the plan into whole interests; or

(ii) the purchase or sale of such fractional interests from or to entities receiving such fractional interests under the plan; or

(B) the purchase or sale for such entities of such fractional or whole interests as are necessary to adjust for any remaining fractional interests after such matching.

(3) An entity other than an entity of the kind specified in paragraph (1) of this subsection is not an underwriter under section 2(a)(11) of the Securities Act of 1933 with respect to any securities offered or sold to such entity in the manner specified in subsection (a)(1) of this section.

(c) An offer or sale of securities of the kind and in the manner specified under subsection (a)(1) of this section is deemed to be a public offering.

(d) The Trust Indenture Act of 1939 does not apply to a note issued under the plan that matures not later than one year after the effective date of the plan.

(Pub.L. 95–598, Nov. 6, 1978, 92 Stat. 2639; Pub.L. 98–353, Title III, § 516, July 10, 1984, 98 Stat. 387; Pub.L. 103–394, Title V, § 501(d)(33), Oct. 22, 1994, 108 Stat. 4146; Pub.L. 111–327, § 2(a)(37), Dec. 22, 2010, 124 Stat. 3561.)

HISTORICAL AND STATUTORY NOTES

Revision Notes and Legislative Reports

1978 Acts. This section, derived from similar provisions found in sections 264, 393, and 518 of the Bankruptcy Act [sections 664, 793, and 918 of former title 11], provides a limited exemption from the securities laws for securities issued under a plan of reorganization and for certain other securities. Subsection (a) exempts from the requirements of section 5 of the Securities Act of 1933 [section 77e of Title 15, Commerce and Trade] and from any State or local law requiring registration or licensing of an issuer of, underwriter of, or broker or dealer in, a security, the offer or sale of certain securities.

Paragraph (1) of subsection (a) exempts the offer or sale under section 364 of any security that is not an equity security or convertible into an equity security. This paragraph is designed to facilitate the issuance of certificates of indebtedness, and should be read in light of the amendment made in section 306 of title III to section 3(a)(7) of the 1933 act [section 77c(a)(7) of Title 15, Commerce and Trade].

Paragraph (2) of subsection (a) exempts the offer or sale of any security of the debtor, a successor to the debtor, or an affiliate in a joint plan, distributed under a plan if such security is exchanged in principal part for securities of the debtor or for allowed claims or administrative expenses. This exemption is carried over from present law, except as to administrative claims, but is limited to prevent distribution of securities to other than claim holders or equity security holders of the debtor or the estate.

Paragraph (3) of subsection (a) exempts the offer or sale of any security that arises from the exercise of a subscription right or from the exercise of a conversion privilege when such subscription right or conversion privilege was issued under a plan. This exemption is necessary in order to enhance the marketability of subscription rights or conversion privileges, including warrants, offered or sold under a plan. This is present law.

Paragraph (4) of subsection (a) exempts sales of portfolio securities, excluding securities of the debtor or its affiliate, owned by the debtor on the date of the filing of the petition. The purpose of this exemption is to allow the debtor or trustee to sell or distribute, without allowing manipulation schemes, restricted portfolio securities held or acquired by the debtor. Subparagraph (B) of section 1145(a)(4) limits the exemption to securities of a company that is required to file reports under section 13 of the Securities Act [section 78m of Title 15, Commerce and Trade] and that is in compliance with all requirements for the continuance of trading those securities. This limitation effectively prevents selling into the market "cats and dogs" of a nonreporting company. Subparagraph (C) places a limitation on the amount of restricted securities that may be distributed. During the case, the trustee may sell up to 4 percent of each class of restricted securities at any time during the first 2 years and 1 percent during any 180-day period thereafter. This relaxation of the resale rules for debtors in holding restricted securities is similar to but less extensive than the relaxation in SEC [Securities and Exchange Commission] Rule 114(c)(3)(v) for the estates of deceased holders of securities.

Paragraph (5) contains an exemption for brokers and dealers (stockbrokers, as defined in title 11) akin to the exemption provided by section 4(3)(A) of the Securities Act of 1933 [section 77d(3)(A) of Title 15, Commerce and Trade]. Instead of being required to supply a prospectus, however, the stockbroker is required to supply the approved disclosure statement, and if the court orders, information supplementing the disclosure statement. Under present law, the stockholders is not required to supply anything.

Subsection (b) is new. The subsection should be read in light of the amendment in section 306 of Title III to the 1933 act [section 77c(a)(7), (9), (10) of Title 15, Commerce and Trade]. It specifies the standards under which a creditor, equity security holder, or other entity acquiring securities under the plan may resell them. The Securities Act places limitations on sales by underwriters. This subsection defines who is an underwriter, and thus restricted, and who is free to resell. Paragraph (1) enumerates real underwriters that participate in a classical underwriting. A person is an underwriter if he purchases a claim against, interest in, or claim for an administrative expense in the case concerning, the debtor, with a view to distribution or interest. This provision covers the purchase of a certificate of indebtedness issued under proposed 11 U.S.C. 364 and purchased from the debtor, if the purchase of the certificate was with a view to distribution.

A person is also an underwriter if he offers to sell securities offered or sold under the plan for the holders of such securities, or offers to buy securities offered or sold under the plan from the holders of such securities, if the offer to buy is with a view to distribution of the securities and under an agreement made in connection with the plan, with the consummation of the plan or with the offer or sale of securities under the plan. Finally, a person is an underwriter if he is an issuer, as used in section 2(11) of the Securities Act of 1933 [section 77b(11) of Title 15, Commerce and Trade].

Paragraph (2) of subsection (b) exempts from the definition of underwriter any entity to the extent that any agreement that would bring the entity under the definition in paragraph (1) provides only for the matching combination of fractional interests in the covered securities or the purchase or sale of fractional interests. This paragraph and paragraph (1) are modeled after former rule 133 of the Securities and Exchange Commission.

Paragraph (3) specifies that if an entity is not an underwriter under the provisions of paragraph (1), as limited by paragraph (2), then the entity is not an underwriter for the purposes of the Securities Act of 1933 [section 77a et seq. of Title 15, Commerce and Trade] with respect to the covered securities, that is, those offered or sold in an exempt transaction specified in subsection (a)(2). This makes clear that the current definition of underwriter in section 2(11) of the Securities Act of 1933 [section 77b(11) of Title 15] does not apply to such a creditor. The definition in that section technically applies to any person that purchases securities with "a view to distribution." If literally applied, it would prevent any creditor in a bankruptcy case from selling securities received without filing a registration statement or finding another exemption.

Subsection (b) is a first run transaction exemption and does not exempt a creditor that, for example, some years later becomes an underwriter by reacquiring securities originally issued under a plan.

Subsection (c) makes an offer or sale of securities under the plan in an exempt transaction (as specified in subsection (a)(2)) a public offering, in order to prevent characterization of the distribution as a "private placement" which would result in restrictions, under rule 144 of the SEC [Securities and Exchange Commission] on the resale of the securities. Senate Report No. 95–989.

1984 Acts. Statements by Legislative Leaders, see 1984 U.S. Code Cong. and Adm. News, p. 576.

1994 Acts. House Report No. 103–835, see 1994 U.S. Code Cong. and Adm. News, p. 3340.

Legislative Statements

Section 1145 of the House amendment deletes a provision contained in section 1145(a)(1) of the House bill in favor of a more adequate provision contained in section 364(f) of the House amendment. In addition, section 1145(d) has been added to indicate that the Trust Indenture Act [section 77aaa et seq. of Title 15, Commerce and Trade] does not apply to a commercial note issued under a plan, if the note matures not later than 1 year after the effective date of the plan. Some commercial notes receive such an exemption under 304(a)(4) of the Trust Indenture Act of 1939 (15 U.S.C. § 77ddd(a)(4)) [section 77ddd(a)(4) of Title 15] and others may receive protection by incorporation by reference into the Trust indenture Act of securities exempt under section 3a(3), (7), (9), or (10) of the Securities Act of 1933 [section 77c(a)(3), (7), (9) and (10) of Title 15, respectively].

In light of the amendments made to the Securities Act of 1933 [section 77a et seq. of Title 15, Commerce and Trade] in title III of the House amendment to H.R. 8200, a specific exemption from the Trust Indenture Act [section 77aaa et seq. of Title 15, Commerce and Trade] is required in order to create certainty regarding plans of reorganization. Section 1145(d) is not intended to imply that commercial notes issued under a plan that matures more than 1 year after the effective date of the plan are automatically covered by the Trust Indenture Act of 1939 since such notes may fall within another exemption thereto.

One other point with respect to Section [sic] 1145 deserves comment. Section 1145(a)(3) grants a debtor in possession or trustee in chapter 11 an extremely narrow portfolio security exemption from section 5 of the Securities Act of 1933 [section 77e of Title 15, Commerce and Trade] or any comparable State law. The provision was considered by Congress and adopted after much study. The exemption is reasonable and is more restrictive than comparable provisions under the Securities Act [section 77a et seq. of Title 15, Commerce and Trade] relating to the estates of decedents. Subsequent to passage of H.R. 8200 by the House of Representatives, the Securities and Exchange Commission promulgated Rule 148 to treat with this problem under existing law. Members of Congress received opinions from attorneys indicating dissatisfaction with the Commission's rule although the rule has been amended, the ultimate limitation of 1 percent promulgated by the Commission is wholly unacceptable.

The Commission rule would permit a trustee or debtor in possession to distribute securities at the rate of 1 percent every 6 months. Section 1145(a)(3) permits the trustee to distribute 4 percent of the securities during the 2-year period immediately following the date of the filing of the petition. In addition, the security must be of a reporting company under section 13 of the Securities and Exchange Act of 1934 [section 78m of Title 15, Commerce and Trade], and must be in compliance with all applicable requirements for the continuing of trading in the security on the date that the trustee offers or sells the security.

With these safeguards the trustee or debtor in possession should be able to distribute 4 percent of the securities of a class at any time during the 2-year period immediately following the date of the filing of the petition in the interests of expediting bankruptcy administration. The same rationale that applies in expeditiously terminating decedents' estates applies no less to an estate under title 11.

References in Text

Section 5 of the Securities Act of 1933, referred to in subsec. (a), is section 5 of Act May 27, 1933, c. 38, Title I, 48 Stat. 77, which is classified to section 77e of Title 15, Commerce and Trade.

Section 13 or 15 of the Securities Exchange Act of 1934, referred to in subsec. (a)(3)(B)(i), are section 13 and 15 of Act June 6, 1934, c. 404, Title I, 48 Stat. 894, 895, which are classified to sections 78m and 78o, respectively, of Title 15.

Section 2(a)(11) of the Securities Act of 1933, referred to in subsec. (b), is subsec. (a)(11) of section 2 of Act May 27, 1933, c. 38, Title I, 48 Stat. 74, as amended, which is classified to 15 U.S.C.A. § 77b(a)(11).

The Trust Indenture Act of 1939, referred to in subsec. (d), is Title III of Act May 27, 1933, ch. 38, as added Aug. 3, 1939, ch. 411, 53 Stat. 1149, as amended, which is classified generally to subchapter III (section 77aaa et seq.) of chapter 2A of Title 15. For complete classification of this Act to the Code, see section 77aaa of Title 15 and Tables.

Amendments

2010 Amendments. Subsec. (b)(1). Pub.L. 111–327, § 2(a)(37), in the prefatory material preceding subpar. (A), struck out "2(11)" and inserted "2(a)(11)".

Subsec. (b)(1)(D). Pub.L. 111–327, § 2(a)(37), struck out "2(11)" and inserted "2(a)(11)".

Subsec. (b)(2). Pub.L. 111–327, § 2(a)(37), in the prefatory material preceding subpar. (A)(i), struck out "2(11)" and inserted "2(a)(11)".

Subsec. (b)(3). Pub.L. 111–327, § 2(a)(37), struck out "2(11)" and inserted "2(a)(11)".

1994 Amendments. Subsec. (a). Pub.L. 103–394, § 501(d)(33)(A)(i), (ii), substituted "do not apply to" for "does not apply to" and struck out "(15 U.S.C. 77e)" after "Securities Act of 1933".

Subsec. (a)(3)(B). Pub.L. 103–394, § 501(d)(33)(A)(iii), in cl. (i) struck out "(15 U.S.C. 78m or 78o(d))" after "Securities Exchange Act of 1934".

Subsec. (b)(1). Pub.L. 103–394, § 501(d)(33)(B), struck out "(15 U.S.C. 77b(11))" after "Securities Act of 1933".

Subsec. (d). Pub.L. 103–394, § 501(d)(33)(C), struck out "(15 U.S.C. 77aaa et seq.)" after "Trust Indenture Act of 1939".

1984 Amendments. Subsec. (a)(3)(B)(i). Pub.L. 98–353, § 516(a)(1), added "or 15(d)" following "13".

Pub.L. 98–353, § 516(a)(1), added "or 78o(d)" following "78m".

Subsec. (a)(3)(B)(ii). Pub.L. 98–353, § 516(a)(2), substituted "in compliance with the disclosure and reporting provision of such applicable section; and" for "in compliance with all applicable requirements for the continuance of trading in such security on the date of such offer or sale; and".

Subsec. (a)(4). Pub.L. 98–353, § 516(a)(3), substituted "by a stockbroker" for "by a stockholder" and "by such stockbroker" for "by such stockholder", respectively.

Subsec. (b)(1). Pub.L. 98–353, § 516(b)(1), added "and except with respect to ordinary trading transactions of an entity that is not an issuer" following "subsection".

Subsec. (b)(1)(C). Pub.L. 98–353, § 516(b)(2), substituted "from" for "for".

Subsec. (b)(2)(A)(i). Pub.L. 98–353, § 516(b)(3), substituted "or combining" for "combination".

Subsec. (b)(2)(A)(ii). Pub.L. 98–353, § 516(b)(4), substituted "from or to" for "among".

Subsec. (d). Pub.L. 98–353, § 516(c), struck out "commercial" preceding "note issued under the plan".

Effective and Applicability Provisions

1994 Acts. Amendment by Pub.L. 103–394 effective on Oct. 22, 1994, and not to apply with respect to cases commenced under Title 11 of the United States Code before Oct. 22, 1994, see section 702 of Pub.L. 103–394, set out as a note under section 101 of this title.

1984 Acts. Amendment by Pub.L. 98–353 effective with respect to cases filed 90 days after July 10, 1984, see section 552(a), formerly 553(a), of Pub.L. 98–353, set out as a note under section 101 of this title.

Separability of Provisions

If any provision of or amendment made by Pub.L. 103–394 or the application of such provision or amendment to any person or circumstance is held to be unconstitutional, the remaining provisions of and amendments made by Pub.L. 103–394 and the application of such provisions and amendments to any person or circumstance shall not be affected thereby, see section 701 of Pub.L. 103–394, set out as a note under section 101 of this title.

CROSS REFERENCES

Applicability of term "security" to offers or sales under § 364 of this title to underwriters, see 11 USCA § 364.

Applicability of this section in Chapter nine cases, see 11 USCA § 901.

Protection of securities customers, see 15 USCA § 78eee.

Racketeering activity defined as offense involving fraud in sale of securities in case under this title, see 18 USCA § 1961.

Securities exempted from Securities Act of 1933, see 15 USCA § 77c.

LIBRARY REFERENCES

American Digest System

Securities Regulation ⚎11.15 to 11.21, 14.17, 247, 248, 262.1.

Key Number System Topic No. 349B.

Corpus Juris Secundum

CJS Bankruptcy § 903, Securities Registration Inapplicable to Securities Issued to Obtain Credit.

CJS Securities Reg. & Commodity Futures Trading § 62, Other Exemptions.

§ 1146. Special tax provisions

(a) The issuance, transfer, or exchange of a security, or the making or delivery of an instrument of transfer under a plan confirmed under section 1129 of this title, may not be taxed under any law imposing a stamp tax or similar tax.

(b) The court may authorize the proponent of a plan to request a determination, limited to questions of law, by a State or local governmental unit charged with responsibility for collection or determination of a tax on or measured by income, of the tax effects, under section 346 of this title and under the law imposing such tax, of the plan. In the event of an actual controversy, the court may declare such effects after the earlier of—

(1) the date on which such governmental unit responds to the request under this subsection; or

(2) 270 days after such request.

[(c) Redesignated (a)]

[(d) Redesignated (b)]

(Pub.L. 95–598, Nov. 6, 1978, 92 Stat. 2641; Pub.L. 98–353, Title III, § 517, July 10, 1984, 98 Stat. 388; Pub.L. 109–8, Title VII, § 719(b)(3), Apr. 20, 2005, 119 Stat. 133.)

HISTORICAL AND STATUTORY NOTES

Revision Notes and Legislative Reports

1978 Acts. Section 1146 provides special tax rules applicable to Title 11 reorganizations. Subsection (a) provides that the taxable period of an individual debtor terminates on the date of the order for relief, unless the case has been converted into a reorganization from a liquidation proceeding.

Subsection (b) requires the trustee of the estate of an individual debtor in a reorganization to file a tax return for each taxable period while the case is pending after the order for relief. For corporations in chapter 11, the trustee is required to file the tax returns due while the case is pending (section 346(c)(2)).

Subsection (c) exempts from Federal, State, or local stamp taxes the issuance, transfer, or exchange of a security, or the making or delivery of an instrument of transfer under a plan. This subsection is derived from section 267 of the present Bankruptcy Act [section 667 of former Title 11].

Subsection (d) permits the court to authorize the proponent of a reorganization plan to request from the Internal Revenue Service (or State or local tax authority) an advance ruling on the tax effects of the proposed plan. If a ruling is not obtained within 270 days after the request was made, or if a ruling is obtained but the proponent of the plan disagrees with the ruling, the bankruptcy court may resolve the dispute and determine the tax effects of the proposed plan.

Subsection (e) provides that prepetition taxes which are nondischargeable in a reorganization, and all taxes arising during the administration period of the case, may be assessed and collected from the debtor or the debtor's successor in a reorganization (see sec. 505(c) of the bill). Senate Report No. 95–989.

Section 1146 of title 11 specifies five subsections which embody special tax provisions that apply in a case under chapter 11 of title 11. Subsection (a) indicates that the tax year of an individual debtor terminates on the date of the order for relief under chapter 11. Termination of the taxable year of the debtor commences the tax period of the estate. If the case was converted from chapter 7 of title 11 then the estate is created as a separate taxable entity dating from the order for relief under chapter 7. If multiple conversion of the case occurs, then the estate is treated as a separate taxable entity on the date of the order for relief under the first chapter under which the estate is a separate taxable entity.

Subsection (d) permits the court to authorize the proponent of a plan to request a taxing authority to declare the tax effects of such plan. In the event of an actual controversy, the court may declare the tax effects of the plan of reorganization at any time after the earlier of action by such taxing authority or 270 days after the request. Such a declaration, unless appealed, becomes a final judgment and binds any tax authority that was requested by the proponent to determine the tax effects of the plan. House Report No. 95–595.

1984 Acts. Statements by Legislative Leaders, see 1984 U.S.Code Cong. and Adm.News, p. 576.

2005 Acts. House Report No. 109–31(Part I), see 2005 U.S. Code Cong. and Adm. News, p. 88.

Legislative Statements

Section 1146 of the House amendment represents a compromise between the House bill and Senate amendment.

Special tax provisions: reorganization: The House bill provided rules on the effect of bankruptcy on the taxable year of the debtor and on tax return filing requirements for State and local taxes only. The House bill also exempted from State or local stamp taxes the issuance, transfer, or exchange of a security, or the making or delivery of an instrument of transfer under a plan. The House bill also authorized the bankruptcy court to declare the tax effects of a reorganization plan after the proponent of the plan had requested a ruling from State or local tax authority and either had received an unfavorable ruling or the tax authority had not issued a ruling within 270 days.

The Senate amendment deleted the rules concerning the taxable years of the debtor and tax return filing requirements since the Federal rules were to be considered in the next Congress. It broadened the rule exempting transfers of securities to include Federal stamp or similar taxes, if any. In addition, the Senate amendment deleted the provision which permitted the bankruptcy court to determine the tax effects of a plan.

The House amendment retains the State and local rules in the House bill with one modification. Under the House amendment, the power of the bankruptcy court to declare the tax effects of the plan is limited to issues of law and not to questions of fact such as the allowance of specific deductions. Thus, the bankruptcy court could declare whether the reorganization qualified for taxfree status under State or local tax rules, but it could not declare the dollar amount of any tax attributes that survive the reorganization.

Amendments

2005 Amendments. Subsec. (a). Pub.L. 109–8, § 719(b)(3), struck out former subsec. (a) and redesignated subsec. (c) as subsec. (a). Prior to striking, subsec. (a) read: "**(a)** For the purposes of any State or local law imposing a tax on or measured by income, the taxable period of a debtor that is an individual shall terminate on the date of the order for relief under this chapter, unless the case was converted under section 706 of this title."

Subsec. (b). Pub.L. 109–8, § 719(b)(3), struck out former subsec. (b) and redesignated subsec. (d) as subsec. (b). Prior to striking, subsec. (b) read: "**(b)** The trustee shall make a State or local tax return of income for the estate of an individual debtor in a case under this chapter for each taxable period after the order for relief under this chapter during which the case is pending."

Subsec. (c). Pub.L. 109–8, § 719(b)(3)(B), redesignated former subsec. (c) as subsec. (a).

Subsec. (d). Pub.L. 109–8, § 719(b)(3)(B), redesignated former subsec. (d) as subsec. (b).

1984 Amendments. Subsec. (c). Pub.L. 98–353, § 517(a), struck out "State or local" preceding "law imposing a stamp tax".

Subsec. (d)(1). Pub.L. 98–353, § 517(b), substituted "or" for "and".

Effective and Applicability Provisions

2005 Acts. Amendments by Pub.L. 109–8 effective, except as otherwise provided, 180 days after April 20, 2005, and inapplicable with respect to cases commenced under Title 11 before the effective date, see Pub.L. 109–8, § 1501, set out as a note under 11 U.S.C.A. § 101.

1984 Acts. Amendment by Pub.L. 98–353 effective with respect to cases filed 90 days after July 10, 1984, see section 552(a), formerly 553(a), of Pub.L. 98–353, set out as a note under section 101 of this title.

CROSS REFERENCES

Declaratory judgments, see 28 USCA § 2201.

Determination of—

    Number of taxable periods during which debtor may use loss carryover or carryback, see 11 USCA § 346.

    Tax liability, see 11 USCA § 505.

Effect of conversion, see 11 USCA § 348.

Special tax provisions in Chapter 7 cases, see 11 USCA § 728.

LIBRARY REFERENCES

American Digest System

    Taxation ☞1079.1, 982, 1021.1, 105.5.

    Key Number System Topic No. 371.

Corpus Juris Secundum

    CJS Bankruptcy § 261, Power to Render Declaratory Judgment.

    CJS Bankruptcy § 278, Parties Defendant; Sovereign Immunity.

SUBCHAPTER IV—RAILROAD REORGANIZATION

CROSS REFERENCES

"Carrier subject to liquidation" as meaning carrier subject to proceeding under this subchapter, see 45 USCA § 915.

Collective bargaining agreement, manner of assumption or rejection by trustee other than a trustee in a case covered by this subchapter, see 11 USCA § 1113.

Subchapter applicable only in cases under this chapter concerning railroad, see 11 USCA § 103.

Temporary operating approval granted to carrier subject to this subchapter as of January 14, 1983, see 45 USCA § 1017.

§ 1161.　Inapplicability of other sections

Sections 341, 343, 1102(a)(1), 1104, 1105, 1107, 1129(a)(7), and 1129(c) of this title do not apply in a case concerning a railroad.

(Pub.L. 95–598, Nov. 6, 1978, 92 Stat. 2641.)

HISTORICAL AND STATUTORY NOTES

Revision Notes and Legislative Reports

1978 Acts. This section makes inapplicable sections of the bill which are either inappropriate in railroad reorganizations, or relate to matters which are otherwise dealt with in subchapter IV. Senate Report No. 95–989.

CROSS REFERENCES

Applicability of Chapters 1, 3, and 5 of this title to cases under Chapters 7, 11, or 13 of this title except as provided in this section, see 11 USCA § 103.

LIBRARY REFERENCES

American Digest System

Bankruptcy ⟜3651.

Key Number System Topic No. 51.

Corpus Juris Secundum

CJS Bankruptcy § 7, Bankruptcy Code.

CJS Bankruptcy § 72, Appointment Required in Railroad Reorganization Cases.

CJS Bankruptcy § 84, Appointment in Interests of Creditors, Equity Security Holders, or Estate.

CJS Bankruptcy § 85, Appointment Where Debts Exceed $5 Million.

CJS Bankruptcy § 109, Termination of Service.

CJS Bankruptcy § 132, Rights, Powers, and Duties of Debtor in Possession.

CJS Bankruptcy § 844, Railroad Reorganizations.

CJS Bankruptcy § 943, Exclusion of Collective-Bargaining Agreements Subject to Railway Labor Act.

§ 1162.　Definition

In this subchapter, "Board" means the "Surface Transportation Board".

(Added Pub.L. 104–88, Title III, § 302(1), Dec. 29, 1995, 109 Stat. 943.)

HISTORICAL AND STATUTORY NOTES

Revision Notes and Legislative Reports

1995 Acts. House Report No. 104–311 and House Conference Report No. 104–422, see 1995 U.S. Code Cong. and Adm. News, p. 793.

Effective and Applicability Provisions

1995 Acts. Section effective Jan. 1, 1996, see section 2 of Pub.L. 104–88, set out as a note under section 701 of Title 49, Transportation.

Prior Provisions

A prior section 1162, Pub.L. 95–598, Nov. 6, 1978, 92 Stat. 2641, defined the term "Commission" to mean the "Interstate Commerce Commission" for purposes of this subchapter and was repealed by Pub.L. 104–88, Title III, § 302(1), Dec. 29, 1995, 109 Stat. 943.

LIBRARY REFERENCES

American Digest System

Bankruptcy ⟜3651.

Key Number System Topic No. 51.

§ 1163.　Appointment of trustee

As soon as practicable after the order for relief the Secretary of Transportation shall submit a list of five disinterested persons that are qualified and willing to serve as trustees in the case. The United States trustee shall appoint one of such persons to serve as trustee in the case.

(Pub.L. 95–598, Nov. 6, 1978, 92 Stat. 2641; Pub.L. 99–554, Title II, § 226, Oct. 27, 1986, 100 Stat. 3102.)

HISTORICAL AND STATUTORY NOTES

Revision Notes and Legislative Reports

1978 Acts. [Section 1166 (now section 1163)] Requires the court to appoint a trustee in every case. Since the trustee may employ whatever help he needs, multiple trusteeships are unnecessary and add to the cost of administration. The present requirement of section 77(c)(1) [section 205(c)(1) of former Title 11] that the trustee be approved by the Interstate Commerce Commission is unnecessary, since the trustee will be selected either from the panel established under section 606(f) of title 28 [section 606(f) of Title 28, Judiciary and Judicial Procedure], or someone certified by the Director of the Administrative Office of the United States Courts as qualified to become a member of that panel. Senate Report No. 95–989.

[Section 1162] This section [now section 1163] requires the appointment of an independent trustee in a railroad reorganization case. The court may appoint one or more disinterested persons to serve as trustee in the case. House Report No. 95–595.

1986 Acts. House Report No. 99–764 and House Conference Report No. 99–958, see 1986 U.S.Code Cong. and Adm. News, p. 5227.

Legislative Statements

Section 1163 of the House amendment represents a compromise between the House bill and Senate amendment with respect to the appointment of a trustee in a railroad reorganization. As soon as practicable after the order for relief, the Secretary of Transportation is required to submit a list of five disinterested persons who are qualified to serve as trustee and the court will then appoint one trustee from the list to serve as trustee in the case.

The House amendment deletes section 1163 of the Senate amendment in order to cover intrastate railroads in a case under subchapter IV of chapter 11. The bill does not confer jurisdiction on the Interstate Commerce Commission with respect to intrastate railroads.

Amendments

1986 Amendments. Pub.L. 99–554, § 226, substituted "relief the Secretary" for "relief, the Secretary" and "The United States trustee shall appoint" for "The court shall appoint".

Effective and Applicability Provisions

1986 Acts. Amendment by Pub.L. 99–554 effective 30 days after Oct. 27, 1986, except as otherwise provided for, see section 302(a) of Pub.L. 99–554, set out as a note under section 581 of Title 28, Judiciary and Judicial Procedure.

Amendment by Pub.L. 99–554, § 226, not to become effective in or with respect to certain specified judicial districts until, or apply to cases while pending in such district before, the expiration of the 270–day period beginning 30 days after Oct. 27, 1986, or of the 30–day period beginning on the date the Attorney General certifies under section 303 of Pub.L. 99–554 the region specified in a paragraph of section 581(a) of Title 28, as amended by section 111(a) of Pub.L. 99–554, that includes such district, whichever occurs first, see section 302(d)(1) of Pub.L. 99–554, set out as a note under section 581 of Title 28.

Amendment by Pub.L. 99–554, § 226, not to become effective in or with respect to certain specified judicial districts until, or apply to cases while pending in such district before, the expiration of the 2–year period beginning 30 days after Oct. 27, 1986, or of the 30–day period beginning on the date the Attorney General certifies under section 303 of Pub.L. 99–554 the region specified in a paragraph of section 581(a) of Title 28, as amended by section 111(a) of Pub.L. 99–554, that includes such district, whichever occurs first, see section 302(d)(2) of Pub.L. 99–554, set out as a note under section 581 of Title 28.

Amendment by Pub.L. 99–554, § 226, not to become effective in or with respect to judicial districts established for the States of Alabama and North Carolina until, or apply to cases while pending in such district before, such district elects to be included in a bankruptcy region established in section 581(a) of Title 28, as amended by section 111(a) of Pub.L. 99–554, or Oct. 1, 2002, whichever occurs first, and, except as otherwise provided for, with respect to cases under chapters 7, 11, 12, and 13 of Title 11 commenced before 30 days after Oct. 27, 1986, and pending in a judicial district in the States of Alabama or North Carolina before any election made under section 302(d)(3)(A) of Pub.L. 99–554 by such district becomes effective or Oct. 1, 2002, whichever occurs first, amendments by Pub.L. 99–554 not to apply until Oct. 1, 2003, or the expiration of the 1–year period beginning on the date such election becomes effective, whichever occurs first, and further, in any judicial district in Alabama or North Carolina not making the election described in section 302(d)(3)(A) of Pub.L. 99–554, any person appointed under regulations issued by the Judicial Conference to administer estates in cases under Title 11 authorized to establish, etc., a panel of private trustees, and to supervise cases and trustees in cases under chapters 7, 11, 12, and 13 of Title 11, until amendments by sections 201 to 231 of Pub.L. 99–554 effective in such district, see section 302(d)(3)(A) to (F), (H), (I) of Pub.L. 99–554, set out as a note under section 581 of Title 28.

Amendment by Pub.L. 99–554, § 226, except as otherwise provided, with respect to cases under chapters 7, 11, 12, and 13 of Title 11 commenced before 30 days after Oct. 27, 1986, and pending in a judicial district referred to in section 581(a) of Title 28, as amended by section 111(a) of Pub.L. 99–554, for which a United States trustee is not authorized before 30 days after Oct. 27, 1986 to be appointed, not applicable until the expiration of the 3–year period beginning on Oct. 27, 1986, or of the 1–year period beginning on the date the Attorney General certifies under section 303 of Pub.L. 99–554 the region specified in a paragraph of such section 581(a) that includes, such district, whichever occurs first, see section 302(e)(1), (2) of Pub.L. 99–554, set out as a note under section 581 of Title 28.

CROSS REFERENCES

Appointment of trustee in—

    Cases under this chapter, see 11 USCA § 1104.

    Chapter thirteen cases, see 11 USCA § 1302.

    Chapter twelve cases, see 11 USCA § 1202.

Collective bargaining agreement, manner of assumption or rejection by trustee other than a trustee in a case covered by this subchapter, see 11 USCA § 1113.

Election of trustee in Chapter seven cases, see 11 USCA § 702.

Guarantees of certificates, see 45 USCA § 662.

Qualification of trustee, see 11 USCA § 322.

Time for bringing action, see 11 USCA § 546.

LIBRARY REFERENCES

American Digest System

Bankruptcy ⚷3651.

Key Number System Topic No. 51.

Corpus Juris Secundum

CJS Bankruptcy § 51, Chapter 11 Proceedings.

CJS Bankruptcy § 56, Eligibility to Serve as Trustee or Examiner--Disinterestedness Requirement.

CJS Bankruptcy § 72, Appointment Required in Railroad Reorganization Cases.

CJS Bankruptcy § 82, Meeting of Creditors and Election Procedures.

CJS Bankruptcy § 132, Rights, Powers, and Duties of Debtor in Possession.

CJS Bankruptcy § 844, Railroad Reorganizations.

§ 1164.   Right to be heard

The Board, the Department of Transportation, and any State or local commission having regulatory jurisdiction over the debtor may raise and may appear and be heard on any issue in a case under this chapter, but may not appeal from any judgment, order, or decree entered in the case.

(Pub.L. 95–598, Nov. 6, 1978, 92 Stat. 2641; Pub.L. 104–88, Title III, § 302(2), Dec. 29, 1995, 109 Stat. 943.)

HISTORICAL AND STATUTORY NOTES

Revision Notes and Legislative Reports

1978 Acts. [Section 1163] This section [now section 1164] gives the same right to raise, and appear and be heard on, any issue in a railroad reorganization case to the Interstate Commerce Commission, the Department of Transportation, and any State or local commission having regulatory jurisdiction over the debtor as is given to the SEC [Securities and Exchange Commission] and indenture trustees under section 1109 in ordinary reorganization cases. The right of appeal is denied the ICC [Interstate Commerce Commission], the Department of Transportation, and State and local regulatory agencies, the same as it is denied the SEC. House Report No. 95–595.

1995 Acts. House Report No. 104–311 and House Conference Report No. 104–422, see 1995 U.S. Code Cong. and Adm. News, p. 793.

Legislative Statements

Section 1164 of the Senate amendment is deleted as a matter to be left to the Rules of Bankruptcy Procedure. It is anticipated that the rules will require a petition in a railroad reorganization to be filed with the Interstate Commerce Commission and the Secretary of Transportation in a case concerning an interstate railroad.

Section 1164 of the House amendment is derived from section 1163 of the House bill. The section makes clear that the Interstate Commerce Commission, the Department of Transportation, and any State or local commission having regulatory jurisdiction over the debtor may raise and appear and be heard on any issue in a case under subchapter IV of chapter 11, but may not appeal from any judgment, order, or decree in the case. As under section 1109 of title 11, such intervening parties are not parties in interest.

Amendments

1995 Amendments. Pub.L. 104–88, § 302(2), substituted "Board" for "Commission".

Effective and Applicability Provisions

1995 Acts. Amendment by Pub.L. 104–88 effective Jan. 1, 1996, see section 2 of Pub.L. 104–88, set out as a note under section 701 of Title 49, Transportation.

CROSS REFERENCES

Right of Commodity Futures Trading Commission to be heard, see 11 USCA § 762.

Right of Securities and Exchange Commission and party in interest to be heard in case under this chapter, see 11 USCA § 1109.

LIBRARY REFERENCES

American Digest System

Bankruptcy ⊜3651.

Key Number System Topic No. 51.

Corpus Juris Secundum

CJS Bankruptcy § 279, Intervention.

CJS Bankruptcy § 1240, Parties.

§ 1165.   Protection of the public interest

In applying sections 1166, 1167, 1169, 1170, 1171, 1172, 1173, and 1174 of this title, the court and the trustee shall consider the public interest in addition to the interests of the debtor, creditors, and equity security holders.

(Pub.L. 95–598, Nov. 6, 1978, 92 Stat. 2641.)

HISTORICAL AND STATUTORY NOTES

Revision Notes and Legislative Reports

1978 Acts. Section 1165 requires the court, in consideration of the relief to be granted upon the filing of an involuntary

petition, to take into account the "public interest" in the preservation of the debtor's rail service. This is an important factor in railroad reorganization, which distinguishes them from other business reorganizations. Hence, this section modifies the provisions in sections 303 and 305 that govern generally when the business of a debtor may continue to operate, when relief under the Act sought should be granted, and when the petition should be dismissed.

Section 1167 [now section 1165] imposes on the trustee the obligations, in addition to his other duties and responsibilities, to take into account the "public interest" in the preservation of the debtor's rail service. Senate Report No. 95–989.

Legislative Statements

Section 1165 of the House amendment represents a modification of sections 1165 and 1167 of the Senate amendment requiring the court and the trustee to consider the broad, general public interest in addition to the interests of the debtor, creditors, and equity security holders in applying specific sections of the subchapter.

Savings Provisions

Section to apply to cases pending under section 77 of the Bankruptcy Act [section 205 of former Title 11] on Nov. 6, 1978, in which the trustee had not filed a plan of reorganization, see section 403(b) of Pub. L. 95–598, set out as a note preceding section 101 of this title.

LIBRARY REFERENCES

American Digest System

Bankruptcy ⊜3651.

Key Number System Topic No. 51.

Corpus Juris Secundum

CJS Bankruptcy § 844, Railroad Reorganizations.

CJS Bankruptcy § 943, Exclusion of Collective-Bargaining Agreements Subject to Railway Labor Act.

§ 1166.   Effect of subtitle IV of title 49 and of Federal, State, or local regulations

Except with respect to abandonment under section 1170 of this title, or merger, modification of the financial structure of the debtor, or issuance or sale of securities under a plan, the trustee and the debtor are subject to the provisions of subtitle IV of title 49 that are applicable to railroads, and the trustee is subject to orders of any Federal, State, or local regulatory body to the same extent as the debtor would be if a petition commencing the case under this chapter had not been filed, but—

(1) any such order that would require the expenditure, or the incurring of an obligation for the expenditure, of money from the estate is not effective unless approved by the court; and

(2) the provisions of this chapter are subject to section 601(b) of the Regional Rail Reorganization Act of 1973.

(Pub.L. 95–598, Nov. 6, 1978, 92 Stat. 2642; Pub.L. 97–449, § 5(a)(2), Jan. 12, 1983, 96 Stat. 2442; Pub.L. 98–353, Title III, § 518, July 10, 1984, 98 Stat. 388; Pub.L. 103–394, Title V, § 501(d)(34), Oct. 22, 1994, 108 Stat. 4146.)

HISTORICAL AND STATUTORY NOTES

Revision Notes and Legislative Reports

1978 Acts. Section 1168 [now this section] makes the trustee subject to the Interstate Commerce Act [section 10101 et seq. of Title 49, Transportation] and to lawful orders of the Interstate Commerce Commission, the U.S. Department of Transportation, and State and regulatory bodies. The approval of the court is required, however, if the order requires the expenditure of money or the incurring of an expenditure other than the payment of certain interline accounts. The limitation of "lawful orders" of State commissions to those involving "safety, location of tracks, and terminal facilities," which is contained in present section 77(c)(2) [section 205(c)(2) of former Title 11], is eliminated.

Subsection (1) further provides that the debtor must pay in cash all amounts owed other carriers for current balances owed for interline freight, passenger and per diem, including incentive per diem, for periods both prior and subsequent to the filing of the petition, without the necessity of court approval.

Subsection (2) makes the provisions of the chapter subject to section 601(b) of the Regional Rail Reorganization Act [section 791(b) of Title 45, Railroads], which excludes the Interstate Commerce Commission from any participation in the reorganization of certain northeast railroads that have transferred their rail properties to Consolidated Rail Corporation (Conrail). Senate Report No. 95–989.

Section 1164 [now 1166] makes the debtor railroad subject to the provisions of the Interstate Commerce Act [section 10101 et seq. of Title 49, Transportation] that are applicable to railroads, and the trustee subject to the orders of the Interstate Commerce Commission to the same extent as the debtor would have been if the case had not been commenced. There are several exceptions. The section does not apply with respect to abandonment of rail lines, which is provided for under section 1169, or with respect to merger under a plan, modification of the financial structure of the debtor by reason of the plan, or the issuance or sale of securities under a plan. Further, the orders of the ICC [Interstate Commerce Commission] are not effective if the order would require the expenditure or the incurring of an obligation for the expenditure of money from the estate, unless approved by the court, and the provisions of this chapter are subject to section 601(b) of the Regional Rail Reorganization Act of 1973 [section 791(b) of Title 45, Railroads].

[Section 1165 (now section 1166)] The same rules apply with respect to Federal, State, or local regulations. The trustee is subject to the orders of a Federal, State, or local regulatory body to the same extent as the debtor would be if the case had not been commenced. However, any order that would require the expenditure, or the incurring of an obligation for the expenditure, of money is not effective under [until] approved by the court. House Report No. 95–595.

1983 Acts. Detailed Explanation prepared by the Office of the Law Revision Counsel, see 1982 U.S.Code Cong. and Adm.News, p. 4220.

1984 Acts. Statements by Legislative Leaders, see 1984 U.S.Code Cong. and Adm.News, p. 576.

1994 Acts. House Report No. 103–835, see 1994 U.S. Code Cong. and Adm. News, p. 3340.

Legislative Statements

Section 1166 of the House amendment is derived from sections 1164 and 1165 of the House bill. An alternative proposal contained in section 1168(1) of the Senate bill is rejected as violative of the principle or [sic] equal treatment of all creditors under title 11.

References in Text

Section 601(b) of Regional Rail Reorganization Act of 1973, referred to in par. (2), is section 601(b) of Pub.L. 93–236, Title VI, Jan. 2, 1974, 87 Stat. 1021, which is classified to section 791(b) of Title 45, Railroads.

Codifications

Pub.L. 98–353, Title III, § 518, July 10, 1984, 98 Stat. 388, substituted "subtitle IV of title 49" for "the Interstate Commerce Act (49 U.S.C. 1 et seq.)", which amendment was previously made by Pub.L. 97–449, thereby requiring no further change in text.

Amendments

1994 Amendments. Par. (2). Pub.L. 103–394, § 501(d)(34), struck out "(45 U.S.C. 791(b))" after "Regional Rail Reorganization Act of 1973".

1984 Amendments. Pub.L. 98–353, § 518, substituted "subtitle IV of title 49" for "the Interstate Commerce Act (49 U.S.C. 1 et seq.)". See Codifications note set out under this section.

1983 Amendments. Heading. Pub.L. 97–449, § 5(a)(2)(A), substituted "subtitle IV of title 49" for "Interstate Commerce Act".

Pub.L. 97–449, § 5(a)(2)(B), substituted "subtitle IV of title 49" for "the Interstate Commerce Act (49 U.S.C. § 1 et seq.)" following "subject to the provisions of" in text.

Effective and Applicability Provisions

1994 Acts. Amendment by Pub.L. 103–394 effective on Oct. 22, 1994, and not to apply with respect to cases commenced under Title 11 of the United States Code before Oct. 22, 1994, see section 702 of Pub.L. 103–394, set out as a note under section 101 of this title.

1984 Acts. Amendment by Pub.L. 98–353 effective with respect to cases filed 90 days after July 10, 1984, see section 552(a), formerly 553(a), of Pub.L. 98–353, set out as a note under section 101 of this title.

Separability of Provisions

If any provision of or amendment made by Pub.L. 103–394 or the application of such provision or amendment to any person or circumstance is held to be unconstitutional, the remaining provisions of and amendments made by Pub.L. 103–394 and the application of such provisions and amendments to any person or circumstance shall not be affected thereby, see section 701 of Pub.L. 103–394, set out as a note under section 101 of this title.

CROSS REFERENCES

Management and operation of property according to state law, see 28 USCA § 959.

LIBRARY REFERENCES

American Digest System

Bankruptcy ⟲3653.
Key Number System Topic No. 51.

Corpus Juris Secundum

CJS Bankruptcy § 9, Title 28 of the U.S. Code.

CJS Bankruptcy § 845, Railroad Reorganizations--Effect of Federal, State, or Local Regulations.

CJS Bankruptcy § 1167, Operation of Railroad; Abandonment of Lines.

§ 1167. Collective bargaining agreements

Notwithstanding section 365 of this title, neither the court nor the trustee may change the wages or working conditions of employees of the debtor established by a collective bargaining agreement that is subject to the Railway Labor Act except in accordance with section 6 of such Act.

(Pub.L. 95–598, Nov. 6, 1978, 92 Stat. 2642; Pub.L. 103–394, Title V, § 501(d)(35), Oct. 22, 1994, 108 Stat. 4146.)

HISTORICAL AND STATUTORY NOTES

Revision Notes and Legislative Reports

1978 Acts. Section 1176 [now this section] is derived from present section 77(n) [section 205(n) of former Title 11]. It provides that notwithstanding the general section governing the rejection of executory contracts (section 365), neither the court nor the trustee may change the wages or working conditions of employees of the debtor established by a collective bargaining agreement that is subject to the Railway Labor Act [section 151 et seq. of Title 45, Railroads], except in accordance with section 6 of that Act [section 156 of Title 45]. As reported by the subcommittee this section provided that wages and salaries of rail employees could not be affected by the trustee, but that work rules could be rejected by the trustee. The reorganization court was given the authority to review the trustee's decisions and to settle any disputes arising from the rejection. This provision was withdrawn by the full committee, and hearings will be conducted next year by the Human Resources Committee in the area of rail labor contracts and the trustee's ability to reject them in a bankruptcy situation. Senate Report No. 95–989.

Section 1167 is derived from present section 77(n) [section 205(n) of former title 11]. It provides that notwithstanding the general section governing the rejection of executory contracts (section 365), neither the court nor the trustee may change the wages or working conditions of employees of the debtor established by a collective bargaining agreement that is subject to the Railway Labor Act [section 151 et seq. of Title 45, Railroads], except in accordance with section 6 of that Act [section 156 of Title 45]. The subject of railway labor is too delicate and has too long a history for this code to upset established relationships. The balance has been struck over the years. This provision continues that balance unchanged. House Report No. 95–595.

1994 Acts. House Report No. 103–835, see 1994 U.S. Code Cong. and Adm. News, p. 3340.

References in Text

The Railway Labor Act, referred to in text, is Act May 20, 1926, c. 347, 44 Stat. 577, as amended, which is classified principally to chapter 8 (section 151 et seq.) of Title 45, Railroads. Section 6 of such Act is classified to section 156 of Title 15. For complete classification of this Act to the Code, see section 151 of Title 45 and Tables.

Amendments

1994 Amendments. Pub.L. 103–394, § 501(d)(35), struck out "(45 U.S.C. 151 et seq.)" after "Railway Labor Act" and "(45 U.S.C. 156)" after "section 6 of such Act".

Effective and Applicability Provisions

1994 Acts. Amendment by Pub.L. 103–394 effective on Oct. 22, 1994, and not to apply with respect to cases commenced under Title 11 of the United States Code before Oct. 22, 1994, see section 702 of Pub.L. 103–394, set out as a note under section 101 of this title.

Savings Provisions

Section to apply to cases pending under section 77 of the Bankruptcy Act [section 205 of former Title 11] on Nov. 6, 1978, in which the trustee had not filed a plan of reorganization, see section 403(b) of Pub. L. 95–598, set out as a note preceding section 101 of this title.

Separability of Provisions

If any provision of or amendment made by Pub.L. 103–394 or the application of such provision or amendment to any person or circumstance is held to be unconstitutional, the remaining provisions of and amendments made by Pub.L. 103–394 and the application of such provisions and amendments to any person or circumstance shall not be affected thereby, see section 701 of Pub.L. 103–394, set out as a note under section 101 of this title.

CROSS REFERENCES

Authorization of trustee to operate business, see 11 USCA § 1108.

LIBRARY REFERENCES

American Digest System

Bankruptcy ⟶3653.
Key Number System Topic No. 51.

Corpus Juris Secundum

CJS Bankruptcy § 943, Exclusion of Collective-Bargaining Agreements Subject to Railway Labor Act.

CJS Bankruptcy § 1167, Operation of Railroad; Abandonment of Lines.

§ 1168. Rolling stock equipment

(a)(1) The right of a secured party with a security interest in or of a lessor or conditional vendor of equipment described in paragraph (2) to take possession of such equipment in compliance with an equipment security agreement, lease, or conditional sale contract, and to enforce any of its other rights or remedies under such security agreement, lease, or conditional sale contract, to sell, lease, or otherwise retain or dispose of such equipment, is not limited or otherwise affected by any other provision of this title or by any power of the court, except that right to take possession and enforce those other rights and remedies shall be subject to section 362, if—

(A) before the date that is 60 days after the date of commencement of a case under this chapter, the trustee, subject to the court's approval, agrees to perform all obligations of the debtor under such security agreement, lease, or conditional sale contract; and

(B) any default, other than a default of a kind described in section 365(b)(2), under such security agreement, lease, or conditional sale contract—

(i) that occurs before the date of commencement of the case and is an event of default therewith is cured before the expiration of such 60–day period;

(ii) that occurs or becomes an event of default after the date of commencement of the case and before the expiration of such 60–day period is cured before the later of—

(I) the date that is 30 days after the date of the default or event of the default; or

(II) the expiration of such 60–day period; and

(iii) that occurs on or after the expiration of such 60–day period is cured in accordance with the terms of such security agreement, lease, or conditional sale contract, if cure is permitted under that agreement, lease, or conditional sale contract.

(2) The equipment described in this paragraph—

(A) is rolling stock equipment or accessories used on rolling stock equipment, including superstructures or racks, that is subject to a security interest granted by, leased to, or conditionally sold to a debtor; and

(B) includes all records and documents relating to such equipment that are required, under the terms of the security agreement, lease, or conditional sale contract, that is to be surrendered or returned by the debtor in connection with the surrender or return of such equipment.

(3) Paragraph (1) applies to a secured party, lessor, or conditional vendor acting in its own behalf or acting as trustee or otherwise in behalf of another party.

(b) The trustee and the secured party, lessor, or conditional vendor whose right to take possession is protected under subsection (a) may agree, subject to the court's approval, to extend the 60–day period specified in subsection (a)(1).

(c)(1) In any case under this chapter, the trustee shall immediately surrender and return to a secured party, lessor, or conditional vendor, described in subsection (a)(1), equipment described in subsection (a)(2), if at any time after the date of commencement of the case under this chapter such secured party, lessor, or conditional vendor is entitled pursuant to subsection (a)(1) to take possession of such equipment and makes a written demand for such possession of the trustee.

(2) At such time as the trustee is required under paragraph (1) to surrender and return equipment described in subsection (a)(2), any lease of such equipment, and any security agreement or conditional sale contract relating to such equipment, if such security

agreement or conditional sale contract is an executory contract, shall be deemed rejected.

(d) With respect to equipment first placed in service on or prior to October 22, 1994, for purposes of this section—

(1) the term "lease" includes any written agreement with respect to which the lessor and the debtor, as lessee, have expressed in the agreement or in a substantially contemporaneous writing that the agreement is to be treated as a lease for Federal income tax purposes; and

(2) the term "security interest" means a purchase- money equipment security interest.

(e) With respect to equipment first placed in service after October 22, 1994, for purposes of this section, the term "rolling stock equipment" includes rolling stock equipment that is substantially rebuilt and accessories used on such equipment.

(Pub.L. 95–598, Nov. 6, 1978, 92 Stat. 2642; Pub.L. 98–353, Title III, § 519, July 10, 1984, 98 Stat. 388; Pub.L. 103–394, Title II, § 201(b), Oct. 22, 1994, 108 Stat. 4120; Pub.L. 106–181, Title VII, § 744(a), Apr. 5, 2000, 114 Stat. 175.)

HISTORICAL AND STATUTORY NOTES

Revision Notes and Legislative Reports

1978 Acts. Section 1175 [now this section] continues the protection accorded in present section 77(j) [section 205(j) of former Title 11] to the rights of holders of purchase-money equipment security, and of lessors or conditional vendors of railroad rolling stock, but accords to the trustee a limited period within which to assume the debtor's obligation and to cure any defaults. The rights of such lenders are not affected by the automatic stay and related provisions of sections 362 and 363, or by any power of the court, unless (1) within 60 days after the commencement of the case (or such longer period as may be agreed to by the secured party, lessor or conditional vendor) the trustees, with the approval of the court, agrees [sic] to perform all of the debtor's obligations under the security agreement, lease or conditional sale contract, and (2) all defaults are cured within the 60-day period. Defaults described in section 365(b)(2)—defaults which are breaches of provisions relating to the insolvency or financial condition of the debtor, or the commencement of a case under this title, or the appointment of a trustee—are for obvious reasons, excepted. Senate Report No. 95–989.

[Section 1166] This section, [now section 1168] derived with changes from the last sentence of present section 77(j) [section 205(j) of former Title 11], protects the interests of rolling stock equipment financers, while providing the trustee with some opportunity to cure defaults, agree to make payments, and retain and use the equipment. The provision is parallel to section 1110, concerning aircraft equipment and vessels. House Report No. 95–595.

1984 Acts. Statements by Legislative Leaders, see 1984 U.S.Code Cong. and Adm.News, p. 576.

1994 Acts. House Report No. 103–835, see 1994 U.S. Code Cong. and Adm. News, p. 3340.

2000 Acts. House Conference Report No. 106–513 and Statement by President, see 2000 U.S. Code Cong. and Adm. News, p. 80.

11 § 1168

BANKRUPTCY CODE

Title 11

Legislative Statements

Section 1168 of the House amendment incorporates a provision contained in section 1166 of the House bill instead of the provision contained in section 1175 of the Senate amendment for the reasons stated in connection with the discussion of section 1110 of the House amendment.

Amendments

2000 Amendments. Pub.L. 106–181, Title VII, § 744(a), rewrote the section, which read:

"(a)(1) The right of a secured party with a security interest in or of a lessor or conditional vendor of equipment described in paragraph (2) to take possession of such equipment in compliance with an equipment security agreement, lease, or conditional sale contract is not affected by section 362, 363, or 1129 or by any power of the court to enjoin the taking of possession, unless—

"(A) before the date that is 60 days after the date of commencement of a case under this chapter, the trustee, subject to the court's approval, agrees to perform all obligations of the debtor that become due on or after the date of commencement of the case under such security agreement, lease, or conditional sale contract; and

"(B) any default, other than a default of a kind described in section 365(b)(2), under such security agreement, lease, or conditional sale contract—

"(i) that occurs before the date of commencement of the case and is an event of default therewith is cured before the expiration of such 60–day period; and

"(ii) that occurs or becomes an event of default after the date of commencement of the case is cured before the later of—

"(I) the date that is 30 days after the date of the default or event of default; or

"(II) the expiration of such 60-day period.

"(2) Equipment is described in this paragraph if it is rolling stock equipment or accessories used on such equipment, including superstructures and racks, that is subject to a security interest granted by, leased to, or conditionally sold to the debtor.

"(3) Paragraph (1) applies to a secured party, lessor, or conditional vendor acting in its own behalf or acting as trustee or otherwise in behalf of another party.

"(b) The trustee and the secured party, lessor, or conditional vendor whose right to take possession is protected under subsection (a) may agree, subject to the court's approval, to extend the 60-day period specified in subsection (a)(1).

"(c) With respect to equipment first placed in service on or prior to the date of enactment of this subsection, for purposes of this section—

"(1) the term 'lease' includes any written agreement with respect to which the lessor and the debtor, as lessee, have expressed in the agreement or in a substantially contemporaneous writing that the agreement is to be treated as a lease for Federal income tax purposes; and

"(2) the term 'security interest' means a purchase-money equipment security interest.

"(d) With respect to equipment first placed in service after the date of enactment of this subsection, for purposes of this section, the term 'rolling stock equipment' includes rolling stock equipment that is substantially rebuilt and accessories used on such equipment."

1994 Amendments. Pub.L. 103–394, § 201(b), completely revised section, substituting provisions directing that the right to take possession of certain equipment is not affected by section 362, 363, or 1129, for provisions directing that the right to take possession of certain equipment is not affected by section 362 or 363 of this title.

1984 Amendments. Subsec. (b). Pub.L. 98–353 added a comma following "approval".

Effective and Applicability Provisions

2000 Acts. Amendment by Pub.L. 106–181 applicable only to fiscal years beginning after September 30, 1999, see section 3 of Pub.L. 106–181, set out as a note under section 106 of this title.

1994 Acts. Amendment by Pub.L. 103–394 effective on Oct. 22, 1994, and not to apply with respect to cases commenced under Title 11 of the United States Code before Oct. 22, 1994, see section 702 of Pub.L. 103–394, set out as a note under section 101 of this title.

1984 Acts. Amendment by Pub.L. 98–353 effective with respect to cases filed 90 days after July 10, 1984, see section 552(a), formerly 553(a), of Pub.L. 98–353, set out as a note under section 101 of this title.

Savings Provisions

Section to apply to cases pending under section 77 of the Bankruptcy Act [section 205 of former Title 11] on Nov. 6, 1978, in which the trustee had not filed a plan of reorganization, see section 403(b) of Pub. L. 95–598, set out as a note preceding section 101 of this title.

Separability of Provisions

If any provision of or amendment made by Pub.L. 103–394 or the application of such provision or amendment to any person or circumstance is held to be unconstitutional, the remaining provisions of and amendments made by Pub.L. 103–394 and the application of such provisions and amendments to any person or circumstance shall not be affected thereby, see section 701 of Pub.L. 103–394, set out as a note under section 101 of this title.

CROSS REFERENCES

Rights of certain secured parties in aircraft equipment and vessels, see 11 USCA § 1110.

LIBRARY REFERENCES

American Digest System

Bankruptcy �441 3654.

Key Number System Topic No. 51.

Corpus Juris Secundum

CJS Bankruptcy § 853, Use of Aircraft, Aircraft Equipment, Vessels, and Railroad Equipment Subject to Financing Agreements.

CJS Bankruptcy § 1166, Interest in Rolling Stock Equipment.

§ 1169. Effect of rejection of lease of railroad line

(a) Except as provided in subsection (b) of this section, if a lease of a line of railroad under which the debtor is the lessee is rejected under section 365 of this title, and if the trustee, within such time as the court fixes, and with the court's approval, elects not to operate the leased line, the lessor under such lease, after such approval, shall operate the line.

(b) If operation of such line by such lessor is impracticable or contrary to the public interest, the court, on request of such lessor, and after notice and a hearing, shall order the trustee to continue operation of such line for the account of such lessor until abandonment is ordered under section 1170 of this title, or until such operation is otherwise lawfully terminated, whichever occurs first.

(c) During any such operation, such lessor is deemed a carrier subject to the provisions of subtitle IV of title 49 that are applicable to railroads.

(Pub.L. 95–598, Nov. 6, 1978, 92 Stat. 2643; Pub.L. 97–449, § 5(a)(3), Jan. 12, 1983, 96 Stat. 2442; Pub.L. 98–353, Title III, § 520, July 10, 1984, 98 Stat. 388.)

HISTORICAL AND STATUTORY NOTES

Revision Notes and Legislative Reports

1978 Acts. Section 1177 [now this section] continues, essentially without change, the provisions relating to the rejection by the trustee of a lease of a line of railroad now contained in section 77(c)(6) [section 205(c)(6) of former Title 11]. Subsection (a) requires the lessor of a line of railroad to operate it if the lease is rejected by the trustee and the trustee, with the approval of the court, elects not to operate the leased line. Subsection (b), however, further provides that if operation by the lessor is impractical or contrary to the public interest, the court shall require the trustee to operate the line for the account of the lessor until the operation is lawfully terminated. Subsection (c) provides that during such operation, the lessor is a carrier subject to the Interstate Commerce Act [section 10101 et seq. of Title 49, Transportation]. Senate Report No. 95–989.

[Section 1168] This section [now section 1169] governs the effect of the rejection by the trustee of an unexpired lease of railroad line under which the debtor is the lessee. If the trustee rejects such a lease, and if the trustee, within such time as the court allows, and with the approval of the court, elects not to operate the leased line, then the lessor under the lease must operate the line.

Subsection (b) excuses the lessor from the requirement to operate the line under certain circumstances. If operation of the line by the lessor is impracticable or contrary to the public interest, the court, on request of the lessor, must order the trustee to continue operation of the line for the account of the lessor until abandonment is ordered under section 1169, governing abandonments generally, or until the operation is otherwise lawfully terminated, such as by an order of the ICC.

Subsection (c) deems the lessor a carrier subject to the provisions of the Interstate Commerce Act [section 10101 et seq. of Title 49, Transportation] during the operation of the line before abandonment. House Report No. 95–595.

1983 Acts. Detailed Explanation prepared by the Office of the Law Revision Counsel, see 1982 U.S.Code Cong. and Adm.News, p. 4220.

1984 Acts. Statements by Legislative Leaders, see 1984 U.S.Code Cong. and Adm.News, p. 576.

Legislative Statements

Section 1169 of the Senate amendment is deleted from the House amendment as unnecessary since 28 U.S.C. 1407 [section 1407 of Title 28, Judiciary and Judicial Procedure] treating with the judicial panel on multi-district litigation will apply by its terms to cases under title 11.

Codifications

Pub.L. 98–353, Title III, § 520, July 10, 1984, 98 Stat. 388, substituted "subtitle IV of title 49" for "the Interstate Commerce Act (49 U.S.C. 1 et seq.)", which amendment was previously made by Pub.L. 97–449, thereby requiring no further change in text.

Amendments

1984 Amendments. Pub.L. 98–353, § 520, substituted "subtitle IV of title 49" for "the Interstate Commerce Act (49 U.S.C. 1 et seq.)". See codifications note set out under this section.

1983 Amendments. Subsec. (c). Pub.L. 97–449 substituted "subtitle IV of title 49" for "the Interstate Commerce Act (49 U.S.C. 1 et seq.)" after "subject to the provisions of".

Effective and Applicability Provisions

1984 Acts. Amendment by Pub.L. 98–353 effective with respect to cases filed 90 days after July 10, 1984, see section 552(a), formerly 553(a), of Pub.L. 98–353, set out as a note under section 101 of this title.

Savings Provisions

Section to apply to cases pending under section 77 of the Bankruptcy Act [section 205 of former Title 11] on Nov. 6, 1978, in which the trustee had not filed a plan of reorganization, see section 403(b) of Pub. L. 95–598, set out as a note preceding section 101 of this title.

CROSS REFERENCES

Executory contracts in stockbroker liquidation cases, see 11 USCA § 744.

LIBRARY REFERENCES

American Digest System

Bankruptcy ⟐3653.

Key Number System Topic No. 51.

Corpus Juris Secundum

CJS Bankruptcy § 1167, Operation of Railroad; Abandonment of Lines.

§ 1170.   Abandonment of railroad line

(a) The court, after notice and a hearing, may authorize the abandonment of all or a portion of a railroad line if such abandonment is—

    (1)(A) in the best interest of the estate; or

    (B) essential to the formulation of a plan; and

    (2) consistent with the public interest.

(b) If, except for the pendency of the case under this chapter, such abandonment would require approval by the Board under a law of the United States, the trustee shall initiate an appropriate application for such abandonment with the Board. The court may fix a time within which the Board shall report to the court on such application.

(c) After the court receives the report of the Board, or the expiration of the time fixed under subsection (b) of this section, whichever occurs first, the court may authorize such abandonment, after notice to the Board, the Secretary of Transportation, the trustee, any party in interest that has requested notice, any affected shipper or community, and any other entity prescribed by the court, and a hearing.

(d)(1) Enforcement of an order authorizing such abandonment shall be stayed until the time for taking an appeal has expired, or, if an appeal is timely taken, until such order has become final.

(2) If an order authorizing such abandonment is appealed, the court, on request of a party in interest, may authorize suspension of service on a line or a portion of a line pending the determination of such appeal, after notice to the Board, the Secretary of Transportation, the trustee, any party in interest that has requested notice, any affected shipper or community, and any other entity prescribed by the court, and a hearing. An appellant may not obtain a stay of the enforcement of an order authorizing such suspension by the giving of a supersedeas bond or otherwise, during the pendency of such appeal.

(e)(1) In authorizing any abandonment of a railroad line under this section, the court shall require the rail carrier to provide a fair arrangement at least as protective of the interests of employees as that established under section 11326(a) of title 49.

(2) Nothing in this subsection shall be deemed to affect the priorities or timing of payment of employee protection which might have existed in the absence of this subsection.

(Pub.L. 95–598, Nov. 6, 1978, 92 Stat. 2643; Pub.L. 96–448, Title II, § 227(a), Oct. 14, 1980, 94 Stat. 1931; Pub.L. 98–353, Title III, § 521, July 10, 1984, 98 Stat. 388; Pub.L. 104–88, Title III, § 302(2), Dec. 29, 1995, 109 Stat. 943; Pub.L. 109–8, Title XII, § 1217, Apr. 20, 2005, 119 Stat. 195.)

HISTORICAL AND STATUTORY NOTES

Revision Notes and Legislative Reports

1978 Acts. Subsection (a) of section 1178 [now this section] permits the court to authorize the abandonment of a railroad line if the abandonment is consistent with the public interest and either in the best interest of the estate or essential to the formulation of a plan. This avoids the normal abandonment requirements of generally applicable railroad regulatory law.

Subsection (b) permits some participation by the Interstate Commerce Commission in the abandonment process. The Commission's role, however, is only advisory. The Commission will represent the public interest, while the trustee and various creditors and equity security holders will represent the interests of those who have invested money in the enterprise. The court will balance the various interests and make an appropriate decision. The subsection specifies that if, except for the pendency of the railroad reorganization case, the proposed abandonment would require Commission ap-

proval, then the trustee, with the approval of the court, must initiate an application for the abandonment with the Commission. The court may then fix a time within which the Commission must report to the court on the application.

Subsection (c) permits the court to act after it has received the report of the Commission or the time fixed under subsection (b) has expired, whichever occurs first. The court may then authorize the abandonment after notice and a hearing. The notice must go to the Commission, the Secretary of Transportation, the trustee, and party in interest that has requested notice, any affected shipper or community, and any other entity that the court specifies.

Subsection (d) stays the enforcement of an abandonment until the time for taking an appeal has expired, or if an appeal has been taken, until the order has become final. However, the court may, and after notice and a hearing, on request of a party in interest authorize termination of service on the line or a portion of the line pending the determination of the appeal. The notice required is the same as that required under subsection (c). If the court authorizes termination of service pending determination of the appeal, an appellant may not obtain a stay of the enforcement of the order authorizing termination, either by the giving of a supersedeas bond or otherwise, during the pendency of the appeal. Senate Report No. 95–989.

1980 Acts. House Report No. 96–1035 and House Conference Report No. 96–1430, see 1980 U.S.Code Cong. and Adm.News, p. 3978.

1984 Acts. Statements by Legislative Leaders, see 1984 U.S.Code Cong. and Adm.News, p. 576.

1995 Acts. House Report No. 104–311 and House Conference Report No. 104–422, see 1995 U.S. Code Cong. and Adm. News, p. 793.

2005 Acts. House Report No. 109–31(Part I), see 2005 U.S. Code Cong. and Adm. News, p. 88.

Amendments

2005 Amendments. Subsec. (e)(1). Pub.L.109–8, § 1217, struck out "section 11347" and inserted "section 11326(a)".

1995 Amendments. Subsec. (b). Pub.L. 104–88, § 302(2), substituted "Board" for "Commission".

Subsec. (c). Pub.L. 104–88, § 302(2), substituted "Board" for "Commission".

Subsec. (d)(2). Pub.L. 104–88, § 302(2), substituted "Board" for "Commission".

1984 Amendments. Subsec. (a). Pub.L. 98–353, § 521(a), added "of all or a portion" following "the abandonment".

Subsec. (c). Pub.L. 98–353, § 521(b), added a comma following "abandonment".

Subsec. (d)(2). Pub.L. 98–353, § 521(c)(1), substituted "such abandonment" for "the abandonment of a railroad line".

Pub.L. 98–353, § 521(c)(2), substituted "suspension" for "termination".

1980 Amendments. Subsec. (e). Pub.L. 96–448 added subsec. (e).

Effective and Applicability Provisions

2005 Acts. Amendments by Pub.L. 109–8 effective, except as otherwise provided, 180 days after April 20, 2005, and inapplicable with respect to cases commenced under Title 11 before the effective date, see Pub.L. 109–8, § 1501, set out as a note under 11 U.S.C.A. § 101.

1995 Acts. Amendment by Pub.L. 104–88 effective Jan. 1, 1996, see section 2 of Pub.L. 104–88, set out as a note under section 701 of Title 49, Transportation.

1984 Acts. Amendment by Pub.L. 98–353 effective with respect to cases filed 90 days after July 10, 1984, see section 552(a), formerly 553(a), of Pub.L. 98–353, set out as a note under section 101 of this title.

1980 Acts. Section 710 of Pub.L. 96–448 provided that:

"**(a)** Except as provided in subsections (b), (c), and (d) of this section, the provisions of this Act and the amendments made by this Act shall take effect on October 1, 1980.

"**(b)** Section 206 of this Act [enacting former section 10712 of Title 49, Transportation], shall take effect on January 1, 1981.

"**(c)** Section 218(b) of this Act [amending former section 10705 of Title 49] shall take effect on October 1, 1983.

"**(d)** Section 701 of this Act [enacting section 1018 of Title 45, Railroads and amending sections 231, 825, 906, 913, 914, 1002, 1005, 1007, and 1008 of Title 45] shall take effect on the date of enactment of this Act [Oct. 14, 1980]."

CROSS REFERENCES

Abandonment of lines of Milwaukee Railroad in cases pending under § 77 of Bankruptcy Act on November 4, 1979, see 45 USCA § 915.

Abandonment of lines of Milwaukee Railroad under this section, see 45 USCA § 904.

Abandonment of property of estate, see 11 USCA § 554.

LIBRARY REFERENCES

American Digest System

Bankruptcy ☞3653.

Key Number System Topic No. 51.

Corpus Juris Secundum

CJS Bankruptcy § 1167, Operation of Railroad; Abandonment of Lines.

CJS Bankruptcy § 1168, Reorganization Plan.

§ 1171. Priority claims

(a) There shall be paid as an administrative expense any claim of an individual or of the personal representative of a deceased individual against the debtor or the estate, for personal injury to or death of such individual arising out of the operation of the debtor or the estate, whether such claim arose before or after the commencement of the case.

(b) Any unsecured claim against the debtor that would have been entitled to priority if a receiver in equity of the property of the debtor had been appointed by a Federal court on the date of the order for relief under this title shall be entitled to the same priority in the case under this chapter.

(Pub.L. 95–598, Nov. 6, 1978, 92 Stat. 2643; Pub.L. 98–353, Title III, § 522, July 10, 1984, 98 Stat. 388.)

HISTORICAL AND STATUTORY NOTES

Revision Notes and Legislative Reports

1978 Acts. [Section 1170] This section [now section 1171] is derived from current law. Subsection (a) grants an adminis-

trative expense priority to the claim of any individual (or of the personal representative of a deceased individual) against the debtor or the estate for personal injury to or death of the individual arising out of the operation of the debtor railroad or the estate, whether the claim arose before or after commencement of the case. The priority under current law, found in section 77(n) [section 205(n) of former Title 11], applies only to employees of the debtor. This subsection expands the protection provided.

Subsection (b) follows present section 77(b) of the Bankruptcy Act [section 205(b) of former Title] by giving priority to any unsecured claims that would be entitled to priority if a receiver in equity of the property of the debtor had been appointed by a Federal court on the date of the order for relief under the bankruptcy laws. As under current law, the courts will determine the precise contours of the priority recognized by this subsection in each case. House Report No. 95–595.

1984 Acts. Statements by Legislative Leaders, see 1984 U.S.Code Cong. and Adm.News, p. 576.

Legislative Statements

Section 1171 of the House amendment is derived from section 1170 of the House bill in lieu of section 1173(a)(9) of the Senate amendment.

Amendments

1984 Amendments. Subsec. (b). Pub.L. 98–353 substituted "the same" for "such".

Effective and Applicability Provisions

1984 Acts. Amendment by Pub.L. 98–353 effective with respect to cases filed 90 days after July 10, 1984, see section 552(a), formerly 553(a), of Pub.L. 98–353, set out as a note under section 101 of this title.

Savings Provisions

Section to apply to cases pending under section 77 of the Bankruptcy Act [section 205 of former Title 11] on Nov. 6, 1978, in which the trustee had not filed a plan of reorganization, see section 403(b) of Pub. L. 95–598, set out as a note preceding section 101 of this title.

CROSS REFERENCES

Allowance of administrative expenses, see 11 USCA § 503.

Priorities, see 11 USCA § 507.

LIBRARY REFERENCES

American Digest System

Bankruptcy ☞3651.

Key Number System Topic No. 51.

§ 1172. Contents of plan

(a) In addition to the provisions required or permitted under section 1123 of this title, a plan—

(1) shall specify the extent to and the means by which the debtor's rail service is proposed to be continued, and the extent to which any of the debtor's rail service is proposed to be terminated; and

(2) may include a provision for—

(A) the transfer of any or all of the operating railroad lines of the debtor to another operating railroad; or

(B) abandonment of any railroad line in accordance with section 1170 of this title.

(b) If, except for the pendency of the case under this chapter, transfer of, or operation of or over, any of the debtor's rail lines by an entity other than the debtor or a successor to the debtor under the plan would require approval by the Board under a law of the United States, then a plan may not propose such a transfer or such operation unless the proponent of the plan initiates an appropriate application for such a transfer or such operation with the Board and, within such time as the court may fix, not exceeding 180 days, the Board, with or without a hearing, as the Board may determine, and with or without modification or condition, approves such application, or does not act on such application. Any action or order of the Board approving, modifying, conditioning, or disapproving such application is subject to review by the court only under sections 706(2)(A), 706(2)(B), 706(2)(C), and 706(2)(D) of title 5.

(c)(1) In approving an application under subsection (b) of this section, the Board shall require the rail carrier to provide a fair arrangement at least as protective of the interests of employees as that established under section 11326(a) of title 49.

(2) Nothing in this subsection shall be deemed to affect the priorities or timing of payment of employee protection which might have existed in the absence of this subsection.

(Pub.L. 95–598, Nov. 6, 1978, 92 Stat. 2644; Pub.L. 96–448, Title II, § 227(b), Oct. 14, 1980, 94 Stat. 1931; Pub.L. 104–88, Title III, § 302(2), Dec. 29, 1995, 109 Stat. 943; Pub.L. 109–8, Title XII, § 1218, Apr. 20, 2005, 119 Stat. 195.)

HISTORICAL AND STATUTORY NOTES

Revision Notes and Legislative Reports

1978 Acts. Section 1170 [now this section] adds to the general provisions required or permitted in reorganization plans by section 1123. Subsection (1) requires that a reorganization plan under the railroad subchapter specify the means by which the value of the claims of creditors and the interests of equity holders which are materially and adversely affected by the plan are to be realized. Subsection (2) permits a plan to include provisions for the issuance of warrants. Subsection (3) requires that the plan provide for fixed charges by probable earnings for their payment. Subsection (4) requires that the plan specify the means by which, and the extent to which, the debtor's rail service is to be continued, and shall identify any rail service to be terminated. Subsection (5) permits other appropriate provisions not inconsistent with the chapter. With the exception of subsection (4), the requirements are comparable to those of present section 77(b) [section 205(b) of former Title 11]; subsection (4) emphasizes the public interest in the preservation of rail transportation.

Section 1171 imposes on the court, rather than the Interstate Commerce Commission, as in present section 77 [section 205 of former title 11], the responsibility for the plan of

reorganization. The Commission is empowered to make final decisions subject only to review by the court under the standards of the Administrative Procedure Act [sections 551 et seq. and 701 et seq. of Title 5, Government Organization and Employees] as to any part of the plan which deals with transportation matters, such as the grant of operating rights of or over, or transfer of, the debtor's rail lines to other carriers.

Subsection (a) requires the trustee to file a plan of reorganization within 18 months after the petition is filed, and permits the court, for good cause shown, to extend such time limit. Subsection (b) permits a plan to be proposed by any interested person, and permits the trustee to revise his plan at any time before it is approved by the court.

Subsections (c), (d) and (e) require the court, when a plan is submitted by the trustee or, if the court deems it worthy of consideration, a plan submitted is proposed by any other person proposes the transfer of, or operation of or over, any of the debtor's lines by other carriers, to refer to such provisions of the plan to the Interstate Commerce Commission. The Commission, within 240 days, and after a hearing if the Commission so determines, is to report to the court the effects of such provisions of the plan in the light of national transportation policy and sections 5(3)(f)(A), (B), and (D), (F)–(I) of the Interstate Commerce Act [section 11350(b)(1), (2), (4), (6)–(9) of Title 49, Transportation]. The report of the Commission is conclusive in all further hearings on the plan by the court, subject only to review pursuant to 5 U.S.C. 706(2)(A)–(D). Senate Report no. 95–989.

[Section 1171 (now section 1172)] A plan in a railroad reorganization case may include provisions in addition to those required and permitted under an ordinary reorganization plan. It may provide for the transfer of any or all of the operating railroad lines of the debtor to another operating railroad.

Paragraph (1) contemplates a liquidating plan for the debtor's rail lines, much as occurred in the Penn Central case by transfer of operating lines to ConRail. Such a liquidating plan is not per se contrary to the public interest, and the court will have to determine on a case-by-case basis, with the guidance of the Interstate Commerce Commission and of other parties in interest, whether the particular plan proposed is in the public interest, as required under proposed 11 U.S.C. 1172(3).

The plan may also provide for abandonment in accordance with section 1169, governing abandonment generally. Neither of these provisions in a plan, transfer or abandonment of lines, requires ICC approval. Confirmation of the plan by the court authorizes the debtor to comply with the plan in accordance with section 1142(a) notwithstanding any bankruptcy law to the contrary. House Report No. 95–595.

1980 Acts. House Report No. 96–1035 and House Conference Report No. 96–1430, see 1980 U.S.Code Cong. and Adm.News, p. 3978.

1995 Acts. House Report No. 104–311 and House Conference Report No. 104–422, see 1995 U.S. Code Cong. and Adm. News, p. 793.

2005 Acts. House Report No. 109–31(Part I), see 2005 U.S. Code Cong. and Adm. News, p. 88.

Legislative Statements

Section 1172 of the House amendment is derived from section 1171 of the House bill in preference to section 1170 of the Senate amendment with the exception that section 1170(4) of the Senate amendment is incorporated into section 1172(a)(1) of the House amendment.

Section 1172(b) of the House amendment is derived from section 1171(c) of the Senate amendment. The section gives the Interstate Commerce Commission the exclusive power to approve or disapprove the transfer of, or operation of or over, any of the debtor's rail lines over which the Commission has jurisdiction, subject to review under the Administrative Procedures Act [sections 551 et seq. and 701 et seq. of Title 5, Government Organization and Employees]. The section does not apply to a transfer of railroad lines to a successor of the debtor under a plan of reorganization by merger or otherwise.

The House amendment deletes section 1171(a) of the Senate amendment as a matter to be determined by the Rules of Bankruptcy Procedure. It is anticipated that the rules will specify the period of time, such as 18 months, within which a trustee must file with the court a proposed plan of reorganization for the debtor or a report why a plan cannot be formulated. Incorporation by reference of section 1121 in section 1161 of title 11 means that a party in interest will also have a right to file a plan of reorganization. This differs from the position taken in the Senate amendment which would have permitted the Interstate Commerce Commission to file a plan of reorganization.

Amendments

2005 Amendments. Subsec. (c)(1). Pub.L.109–8, § 1218, struck out "section 11347" and inserted "section 11326(a)".

1995 Amendments. Subsec. (b). Pub.L. 104–88, § 302(2), substituted "Board" for "Commission".

Subsec. (c)(1). Pub.L. 104–88, § 302(2), substituted "Board" for "Commission".

1980 Amendments. Subsec. (c). Pub.L. 96–448 added subsec. (c).

Effective and Applicability Provisions

2005 Acts. Amendments by Pub.L. 109–8 effective, except as otherwise provided, 180 days after April 20, 2005, and inapplicable with respect to cases commenced under Title 11 before the effective date, see Pub.L. 109–8, § 1501, set out as a note under 11 U.S.C.A. § 101.

1995 Acts. Amendment by Pub.L. 104–88 effective Jan. 1, 1996, see section 2 of Pub.L. 104–88, set out as a note under section 701 of Title 49, Transportation.

1980 Acts. Amendment by Pub.L. 96–448 effective Oct. 1, 1980, see section 710(a) of Pub.L. 96–448, set out as a note under section 1170 of Title 11, Bankruptcy.

CROSS REFERENCES

Contents of plan filed in—

    Chapter thirteen cases, see 11 USCA § 1322.

    Chapter twelve cases, see 11 USCA § 1222.

LIBRARY REFERENCES

American Digest System

Bankruptcy ⇌3652.

Key Number System Topic No. 51.

Corpus Juris Secundum

CJS Bankruptcy § 1168, Reorganization Plan.

§ 1173. Confirmation of plan

(a) The court shall confirm a plan if—

(1) the applicable requirements of section 1129 of this title have been met;

(2) each creditor or equity security holder will receive or retain under the plan property of a value, as of the effective date of the plan, that is not less than the value of property that each such creditor or equity security holder would so receive or retain if all of the operating railroad lines of the debtor were sold, and the proceeds of such sale, and the other property of the estate, were distributed under chapter 7 of this title on such date;

(3) in light of the debtor's past earnings and the probable prospective earnings of the reorganized debtor, there will be adequate coverage by such prospective earnings of any fixed charges, such as interest on debt, amortization of funded debt, and rent for leased railroads, provided for by the plan; and

(4) the plan is consistent with the public interest.

(b) If the requirements of subsection (a) of this section are met with respect to more than one plan, the court shall confirm the plan that is most likely to maintain adequate rail service in the public interest. (Pub.L. 95–598, Nov. 6, 1978, 92 Stat. 2644; Pub.L. 98–353, Title III, § 523, July 10, 1984, 98 Stat. 388.)

HISTORICAL AND STATUTORY NOTES

Revision Notes and Legislative Reports

1978 Acts. Section 1173 adapts the provisions dealing with reorganization plans generally contained in section 1130 to the particular requirements of railroad reorganization plans, as set out in present section 77(e) [section 205(e) of former Title 11]. Subsection (a) specifies the findings which the court must make before approving a plan: (1) The plan complies with the applicable provisions of the chapter; (2) the proponent of the plan complies with the applicable provisions of the chapter; (3) the plan has been proposed in good faith; (4) any payments for services or for costs or expenses in connection with the case or the plan are disclosed to the court and are reasonable, or, if to be paid later, are subject to the approval of the court as reasonable; (5) the proponent of the plan has disclosed the identity and affiliations of the individuals who will serve as directors, officers, or voting trustees, such appointments or continuations in office are consistent with the interests of creditors, equity security holders, and the proponent the public, and has disclosed the identity and compensation of any insider who will be employed or retained under the plan; (6) that rate changes proposed in the plan have been approved by the appropriate regulatory commission, or that the plan is contingent on such approval; (7) that confirmation of the plan is not likely to be followed by further reorganization or liquidation, unless it is contemplated by the plan; (8) that the plan, if there is more than one, is the one most likely to maintain adequate rail service and (9) that the plan provides the priority traditionally accorded by section 77(b) [section 205(b) of former Title 11] to claims by rail creditors for necessary services rendered during the 6 months preceding the filing of the petition in bankruptcy.

Subsection (b) continues the present power of the court in section 77(e) [section 205(e) of former Title 11] to confirm a plan over the objections of creditors or equity security holders who are materially and adversely affected. The subsection also confirms the authority of the court to approve a transfer of all or part of a debtor's property or its merger over the objections of equity security holders if it finds (1) that the "public interest" in continued rail transportation outweighs any adverse effect on creditors and equity security holders, and (2) that the plan is fair and equitable, affords due recognition to the rights of each class, and does not discriminate unfairly against any class.

Subsection (c) permits modification of a plan confirmed by a final order only for fraud. Senate Report No. 95–989.

[Section 1172] This section [now section 1173] requires the court to confirm a plan if the applicable requirements of section 1129 (relating to confirmation of reorganization plans generally) are met, if the best interest test is met, and if the plan is compatible with the public interest.

The test in this paragraph is similar to the test prescribed for ordinary corporate reorganizations. However, since a railroad cannot liquidate its assets and sell them for scrap to satisfy its creditors, the test focuses on the value of the railroad as a going concern. That is, the test is based on what the assets, sold as operating rail lines, would bring.

The public interest requirement, found in current law, will now be decided by the court, with the ICC [Interstate Commerce Commission] representing the public interest before the court, rather than in the first instance by the ICC. Liquidation of the debtor is not, per se, contrary to the public interest. House Report No. 95–595.

1984 Acts. Statements by Legislative Leaders, see 1984 U.S.Code Cong. and Adm.News, p. 576.

Legislative Statements

Section 1173 of the House amendment concerns confirmation of a plan of railroad reorganization and is derived from section 1172 of the House bill as modified. In particular, section 1173(a)(3) of the House amendment is derived from section 1170(3) of the Senate amendment. Section 1173(b) is derived from section 1173(a)(8) of the Senate amendment.

Amendments

1984 Amendments. Subsec. (a)(4). Pub.L. 98–353 substituted "consistent" for "compatible".

Effective and Applicability Provisions

1984 Acts. Amendment by Pub.L. 98–353 effective with respect to cases filed 90 days after July 10, 1984, see section 552(a), formerly 553(a), of Pub.L. 98–353, set out as a note under section 101 of this title.

CROSS REFERENCES

Confirmation of plan in—

　Chapter nine cases, see 11 USCA § 943.

　Chapter thirteen cases, see 11 USCA § 1325.

　Chapter twelve cases, see 11 USCA § 1225.

Effect of confirmation in cases under this chapter, see 11 USCA § 1141.

Nonrecognition of gain or loss for income tax purposes of exchanges of stock and securities in reorganizations confirmed under this section, see 26 USCA § 354.

Revocation of order of confirmation in cases under this chapter, see 11 USCA § 1144.

Unclaimed property, see 11 USCA § 347.

LIBRARY REFERENCES

American Digest System

　Bankruptcy ⚖3652.

　Key Number System Topic No. 51.

Corpus Juris Secundum

　CJS Bankruptcy § 1099, Unclaimed Property.

　CJS Bankruptcy § 1168, Reorganization Plan.

§ 1174.　Liquidation

On request of a party in interest and after notice and a hearing, the court may, or, if a plan has not been confirmed under section 1173 of this title before five years after the date of the order for relief, the court shall, order the trustee to cease the debtor's operation and to collect and reduce to money all of the property of the estate in the same manner as if the case were a case under chapter 7 of this title.

(Pub.L. 95–598, Nov. 6, 1978, 92 Stat. 2644.)

HISTORICAL AND STATUTORY NOTES

Revision Notes and Legislative Reports

1978 Acts. Section 1174 permits the court to convert the case to a liquidation under chapter 7 if the court finds that the debtor cannot be reorganized, or if various time limits specified in the subchapter are not met. Section 77 [section 205 of former Title 11] does not authorize a liquidation of a railroad under the Bankruptcy Act [former Title 11]. If the railroad is not reorganizable, the only action open to the court is to dismiss the petition, which would in all likelihood be followed by a State court receivership, with all of its attendant disadvantages. If reorganization is impossible, the debtor should be liquidated under the Bankruptcy Act. Senate Report No. 95–989.

Legislative Statements

Section 1174 of the House amendment represents a compromise between the House bill and Senate amendment on the issue of liquidation of a railroad. The provision permits a party in interest at any time to request liquidation. In addition, if a plan has not been confirmed under section 1173 of the House amendment before 5 years after the date of order for relief, the court must order the trustee to cease the debtor's operation and to collect and reduce to money all of the property of the estate in the same manner as if the case were a case under chapter 7 of title 11. The approach differs from the conversion to chapter 7 under section 1174 of the Senate bill in order to make special provisions contained in subchapter IV of chapter 11 applicable to liquidation. However, maintaining liquidation in the context of chapter 11 is not intended to delay liquidation of the railroad to a different extent than if the case were converted to chapter 7.

Although the House amendment does not adopt provisions contained in section 1170(1), (2), (3), or (5), of the Senate amendment such provisions are contained explicitly or implicitly in section 1123 of the House amendment.

CROSS REFERENCES

Conversion of—

    Chapter eleven cases, see 11 USCA § 1112.

    Chapter seven cases, see 11 USCA § 706.

    Chapter thirteen cases, see 11 USCA § 1307.

    Chapter twelve cases, see 11 USCA § 1208.

Dismissal of—

    Chapter nine cases, see 11 USCA § 930.

    Chapter seven cases, see 11 USCA § 707.

LIBRARY REFERENCES

American Digest System

    Bankruptcy ⟲3651.

    Key Number System Topic No. 51.

Corpus Juris Secundum

    CJS Bankruptcy § 7, Bankruptcy Code.

    CJS Bankruptcy § 843, Discontinuance or Modification of Debtor's Business.

    CJS Bankruptcy § 844, Railroad Reorganizations.

CHAPTER 12—ADJUSTMENT OF DEBTS OF A FAMILY FARMER OR FISHERMAN WITH REGULAR ANNUAL INCOME

SUBCHAPTER I—OFFICERS, ADMINISTRATION, AND THE ESTATE

Sec.
1201. Stay of action against codebtor.
1202. Trustee.
1203. Rights and powers of debtor.
1204. Removal of debtor as debtor in possession.
1205. Adequate protection.
1206. Sales free of interests.
1207. Property of the estate.
1208. Conversion or dismissal.

SUBCHAPTER II—THE PLAN

1221. Filing of plan.
1222. Contents of plan.
1223. Modification of plan before confirmation.
1224. Confirmation hearing.
1225. Confirmation of plan.
1226. Payments.
1227. Effect of confirmation.
1228. Discharge.
1229. Modification of plan after confirmation.
1230. Revocation of an order of confirmation.
1231. Special tax provisions.

HISTORICAL AND STATUTORY NOTES

Amendments

2005 Amendments. Chapter Heading. Pub.L. 109–8, Title X, § 1007(c)(1), Apr. 20, 2005, 119 Stat. 188, inserted **"OR FISHERMAN"** after **"FAMILY FARMER"**.

Effective and Applicability Provisions

2005 Acts. Amendments by Pub.L. 109–8 effective, except as otherwise provided, 180 days after April 20, 2005, and inapplicable with respect to cases commenced under Title 11 before the effective date, see Pub.L. 109–8, § 1501, set out as a note under 11 U.S.C.A. § 101.

Reenactment of Chapter

This chapter as in effect on June 30, 2005, reenacted effective July 1, 2005, see Pub.L. 109–8, § 1001(a), set out as a note under 11 U.S.C.A. § 1201.

Repeal of chapter; extension of provisions

Pub.L. 99–554, Title III, § 302(f), Oct. 27, 1986, 100 Stat. 3124, as amended Pub.L. 103–65, § 1, Aug. 6, 1993, 107 Stat. 311, which provided that, effective Oct. 1, 1998, this chapter is repealed, but that all cases commenced or pending under this chapter, and all matters and proceedings in or relating to such cases, shall be conducted and determined under this chapter as if such chapter had not been repealed, and that the substantive rights of parties in connection with such cases, matters, and proceedings shall continue to be governed under the laws applicable to such cases, matters, and proceedings as if such chapter had not been repealed, was superceded by the reenactment of this chapter by Pub.L. 109–8, Title X,

§ 1001(a), Apr. 20, 2005, 119 Stat. 185, set out as a note under 11 U.S.C.A. § 1201.

Pub.L. 105–277, Div. C, Title I, § 149, Oct. 21, 1998, 112 Stat. 2681–610, as amended Pub.L. 106–5, §§ 1, 2, Mar. 30, 1999, 113 Stat. 9; Pub.L. 106–70, §§ 1, 2, Oct. 9, 1999, 113 Stat. 1031; Pub.L. 107–8, §§ 1, 2, May 11, 2001, 115 Stat. 10; Pub.L. 107–17, §§ 1, 2, June 26, 2001, 115 Stat. 151; Pub.L. 107–170, §§ 1, 2, May 7, 2002, 116 Stat. 133; Pub.L. 107–171, Title X, § 10814, May 13, 2002, 116 St. 532; Pub.L. 107–377, § 2, Dec. 19, 2002, 116 Stat. 3115; Pub.L. 108–73, § 2(a), Aug. 15, 2003, 117 Stat. 891; Pub.L. 108–369, § 2(a), Oct. 25, 2004, 118 Stat. 1749, provided that, to take effect on January 1, 2004, chapter 12 of Title 11 [this chapter; 11 U.S.C.A. § 1201 et seq.], as in effect on December 31, 2003, is reenacted for the period beginning on January 1, 2004, and ending on July 1, 2005, but that all cases commenced or pending under this chapter 12, as reenacted under section 149(a) of Pub.L. 105–277, and all matters and proceedings in or relating to such cases, shall be conducted and determined under such chapter as if such chapter were continued in effect after July 1, 2005, and that the substantive rights of parties in connection with such cases, matters, and proceedings shall continue to be governed under the law applicable to such cases, matters, and proceedings as if such chapter were continued in effect after July 1, 2005, was superceded by the reenactment of this chapter by Pub.L. 109–8, Title X, § 1001(a), Apr. 20, 2005, 119 Stat. 185, set out as a note under 11 U.S.C.A. § 1201.

SUBCHAPTER I—OFFICERS, ADMINISTRATION, AND THE ESTATE

§ 1201. Stay of action against codebtor

(a) Except as provided in subsections (b) and (c) of this section, after the order for relief under this chapter, a creditor may not act, or commence or continue any civil action, to collect all or any part of a consumer debt of the debtor from any individual that is liable on such debt with the debtor, or that secured such debt, unless—

(1) such individual became liable on or secured such debt in the ordinary course of such individual's business; or

(2) the case is closed, dismissed, or converted to a case under chapter 7 of this title.

(b) A creditor may present a negotiable instrument, and may give notice of dishonor of such an instrument.

(c) On request of a party in interest and after notice and a hearing, the court shall grant relief from the stay provided by subsection (a) of this section with respect to a creditor, to the extent that—

(1) as between the debtor and the individual protected under subsection (a) of this section, such individual received the consideration for the claim held by such creditor;

    (2) the plan filed by the debtor proposes not to pay such claim; or

    (3) such creditor's interest would be irreparably harmed by continuation of such stay.

(d) Twenty days after the filing of a request under subsection (c)(2) of this section for relief from the stay provided by subsection (a) of this section, such stay is terminated with respect to the party in interest making such request, unless the debtor or any individual that is liable on such debt with the debtor files and serves upon such party in interest a written objection to the taking of the proposed action.

(Added and amended Pub.L. 99–554, Title II, § 255, Title III, § 302(f), Oct. 27, 1986, 100 Stat. 3105, 3124; Pub.L. 103–65, § 1, Aug. 6, 1993, 107 Stat. 311; Pub.L. 105–277, Div. C, Title I, § 149(a), Oct. 21, 1998, 112 Stat. 2681–610; Pub.L. 106–5, § 1(1),(2), Mar. 30, 1999, 113 Stat. 9; Pub.L. 106–70, § 1, Oct. 9, 1999, 113 Stat. 1031; Pub.L. 107–8, § 1, May 11, 2001, 115 Stat. 10; Pub.L. 107–17, § 1, June 26, 2001, 115 Stat. 151; Pub.L. 107–170, § 1, May 7, 2002, 116 Stat. 133; Pub.L. 107–171, Title X, § 10814(a), May 13, 2002, 116 Stat. 532; Pub.L. 107–377, § 2(a), Dec. 19, 2002, 116 Stat. 3115; Pub.L. 108–73, § 2(a), Aug. 15, 2003, 117 Stat. 891; Pub.L. 108–369, § 2(a), Oct. 25, 2004, 118 Stat. 1749; Pub.L. 109–8, Title X, § 1001(a)(1), Apr. 20, 2005, 119 Stat. 185.)

HISTORICAL AND STATUTORY NOTES

Revision Notes and Legislative Reports

1986 Acts. House Report No. 99–764 and House Conference Report No. 99–958, see 1986 U.S. Code Cong. and Adm. News, p. 5227.

1993 Acts. House Report No. 103–32, see 1993 U.S. Code Cong. and Adm. News, p. 373.

1998 Acts. Statement by President, see 1998 U.S. Code Cong. and Adm. News, p. 582.

1999 Acts. Statement by President, see 1999 U.S. Code Cong. and Adm. News, p. 4.

Statement by President, see 1999 U.S. Code Cong. and Adm. News, p. 102.

2001 Acts. House Report No. 107–2, see 2001 U.S. Code Cong. and Adm. News, p. 6.

2005 Acts. House Report No. 109–31(Part I), see 2005 U.S. Code Cong. and Adm. News, p. 88.

Amendments

2005 Amendments. Pub.L. 109–8, § 1001(a)(1), reenacted this section as in effect on June 30, 2005, requiring no change in text; see Pub.L. 109–8, § 1001, set out as a note under this section.

2004 Amendments. Pub.L. 108–369, § 2(a), extended effective date of repeal of this section to July 1, 2005, and so required no change in text.

2003 Amendments. Pub.L. 108–73, § 2(a), extended effective date of repeal of this section to Jan. 1, 2004, and so required no change in text.

2002 Amendments. Pub.L. 107–377, § 2(a), extended effective date of repeal of this section to July 1, 2003, and so required no change in text.

Pub.L. 107–171, § 10814(a), extended effective date of repeal of this section to Jan. 1, 2003, and so required no change in text.

Pub.L. 107–170, § 1, extended effective date of repeal of this section to June 1, 2002, and so required no change in text.

2001 Amendments. Pub.L. 107–17, § 1, extended effective date of repeal of this section to Oct. 1, 2001, and so required no change in text.

Pub.L. 107–8, § 1, extended effective date of repeal of this section to June 1, 2001, and so required no change in text.

1999 Amendments. Pub.L. 106–70, § 1, extended effective date of repeal of this section to July 1, 2000, and so required no change in text.

Pub.L. 106–5, § 1(1), (2), extended effective date of repeal of this section to Oct. 1, 1999, and so required no change in text.

1998 Amendments. Pub.L. 105–277, § 149(a), temporarily reenacted this section, which had been repealed effective Oct. 1, 1998 by Pub.L. 99–554, § 302(f).

1993 Amendments. Pub.L. 103–65, § 1, extended effective date of repeal of this section to Oct. 1, 1998, and so required no change in text.

1986 Amendments. Pub.L. 99–554, § 302(f), as amended by Pub.L. 103–65, § 1, repealed section effective Oct. 1, 1998. Prior to amendment by Pub.L. 103–65, repeal of section was to have taken effect on Oct. 1, 1993.

Effective and Applicability Provisions

2005 Acts. Amendments by Pub.L. 109–8 effective, except as otherwise provided, 180 days after April 20, 2005, and inapplicable with respect to cases commenced under Title 11 before the effective date, see Pub.L. 109–8, § 1501, set out as a note under 11 U.S.C.A. § 101.

2004 Acts. Pub.L. 108–369, § 2(b), Oct. 25, 2004, 118 Stat. 1749, provided that: "The amendments made by subsection (a) [amending this section, 11 U.S.C.A. §§ 1202 to 1208, 1221 to 1231, and provisions set out as a note under this section] are deemed to have taken effect on January 1, 2004."

2003 Acts. Pub.L. 108–73, § 2(b), Aug. 15, 2003, 117 Stat. 891, provided that: "The amendments made by subsection (a) [amending this section, 11 U.S.C.A. §§ 1202 to 1208, 1221 to 1231, and provisions set out as a note under this section] take effect on July 1, 2003."

2002 Acts. Pub.L. 107–377, § 2(b), Dec. 19, 2002, 116 Stat. 3115, provided that: "The amendments made by subsection (a) [amending this section and 11 U.S.C.A. §§ 1202 to 1208, 1221 to 1231] shall take effect on January 1, 2003."

Pub.L. 107–171, Title X, § 10814(b), May 13, 2002, 116 Stat. 532, provided that: "The amendments made by subsection (a) [amending this section, 11 U.S.C.A. §§ 1202 to 1208, 1221 to 1231, and provisions set out as a note under this section] shall take effect on June 1, 2002."

Pub.L. 107–170, § 2, May 7, 2002, 116 Stat. 133, provided that: "The amendments made by section 1 [amending this section, 11 U.S.C.A. §§ 1202 to 1208, 1221 to 1231, and provisions set out as a note under this section] shall take effect on October 1, 2001."

2001 Acts. Pub.L. 107–17, § 2, June 26, 2001, 115 Stat. 151, provided that: "The amendments made by section 1 [amending this section, 11 U.S.C.A. §§ 1202 to 1208, 1221 to 1231, and provisions set out as a note under this section] shall take effect on June 1, 2001."

Pub.L. 107–8, § 2, May 11, 2001, 115 Stat. 10, provided that: "The amendments made by section 1 [amending this section, 11 U.S.C.A. §§ 1202 to 1208, 1221 to 1231, and provisions set out as a note under this section] shall take effect on July 1, 2000."

1999 Acts. Section 2 of Pub.L. 106–70 provided that: "The amendments made by section 1 [amending this section, 11 U.S.C.A. §§ 1202 to 1208, 1221 to 1231, and provisions set out as a note under this section] shall take effect on October 1, 1999."

Section 2 of Pub.L. 106–5 provided that: "The amendments made by section 1 [amending this section and 11 U.S.C.A. §§ 1202 to 1208, 1221 to 1231, and provisions set out as a note under this section] shall take effect on April 1, 1999."

1998 Acts. Section 149 of Pub.L. 105–277, as amended Pub.L. 106–5, § 1, Mar. 30, 1999, 113 Stat. 9; Pub.L. 106–70, § 1, Oct. 9, 1999, 113 Stat. 1031; Pub.L. 107–8, § 1, May 11, 2001, 115 Stat. 10; Pub.L. 107–17, § 1, June 26, 2001, 115 Stat. 151; Pub.L. 107–170, § 1, May 7, 2002, 116 Stat. 133; Pub.L.107–171, Title X, § 10814(a), May 13, 2002, 116 Stat. 532; Pub.L. 107–377, § 2(a), Dec. 19, 2002, 116 Stat. 3115; Pub.L. 108–73, § 2(a), Aug. 15, 2003, 117 Stat. 891; Pub.L. 108–369, § 2(a), Oct. 25, 2004, 118 Stat. 1749, provided that:

"**(a)** Chapter 12 of title 11 of the United States Code [this chapter; 11 U.S.C.A. § 1201 et seq.], as in effect on December 31, 2003, is hereby reenacted for the period beginning on January 1, 2004, and ending on July 1, 2005.

"**(b)** All cases commenced or pending under chapter 12 of title 11, United States Code [this chapter; 11 U.S.C.A. § 1201 et seq.], as reenacted under subsection (a) [of this note], and all matters and proceedings in or relating to such cases, shall be conducted and determined under such chapter as if such chapter were continued in effect after July 1, 2004. The substantive rights of parties in connection with such cases, matters, and proceedings shall continue to be governed under the law applicable to such cases, matters, and proceedings as if such chapter were continued in effect after July 1, 2005.

"**(c)** [Repealed. Pub.L. 106–5, § 1(3), March 30, 1999, 113 Stat. 9.]"

1993 Acts. Amendment by Pub.L. 103–65, extending to Oct. 1, 1998 the date of repeal of this chapter, to take effect Aug. 6, 1993, see section 3 of Pub.L. 103–65, set out as a note under 11 U.S.C.A. § 1221.

1986 Acts. Section repealed effective Oct. 1, 1998, see section 302(f) of Pub.L. 99–554, as amended, set out in a note under section 581 of Title 28. However, for extension of provisions, see section 149 of Pub.L. 105–277, set out as a note under this section.

Section effective 30 days after Oct. 27, 1986, but not applicable to cases commenced under this title before that date, see section 302(a), (c)(1) of Pub.L. 99–554, set out as a note under 28 U.S.C.A. § 581.

Reenactment of Chapter 12

Pub.L. 109–8, Title X, § 1001(a), (b), Apr. 20, 2005, 119 Stat. 185, 186, provided that:

"**(a) Reenactment.—**

"**(1) In general.**—Chapter 12 of title 11, United States Code [this chapter], as reenacted by section 149 of division C of the Omnibus Consolidated and Emergency Supplemental Appropriations Act, 1999 (Public Law 105–277) [Pub.L. 105–277, Div. C, Title I, § 149, Oct. 21, 1998, 112 Stat.

2681–610, as amended, set out as a note under this section], and as in effect on June 30, 2005, is hereby reenacted.

"**(2) Effective date of reenactment.**—Paragraph (1) shall take effect on July 1, 2005.

"**(b) Amendments.**—Chapter 12 of title 11, United States Code, as reenacted by subsection (a) [of this note], is amended by this Act [Pub.L. 109–8, Apr. 20, 2005, 119 Stat. 23; see Tables for classifications]."

Repeal of Chapter; Extension of Provisions

Pub.L. 99–554, Title III, § 302(f), Oct. 27, 1986, 100 Stat. 3124, as amended Pub.L. 103–65, § 1, Aug. 6, 1993, 107 Stat. 311, which provided that, effective Oct. 1, 1998, this chapter is repealed, but that all cases commenced or pending under this chapter, and all matters and proceedings in or relating to such cases, shall be conducted and determined under this chapter as if such chapter had not been repealed, and that the substantive rights of parties in connection with such cases, matters, and proceedings shall continue to be governed under the laws applicable to such cases, matters, and proceedings as if such chapter had not been repealed, was superceded by the reenactment of this chapter by Pub.L. 109–8, Title X, § 1001(a), Apr. 20, 2005, 119 Stat. 185, set out as a note under this section.

Pub.L. 105–277, Div. C, Title I, § 149, Oct. 21, 1998, 112 Stat. 2681–610, as amended Pub.L. 106–5, §§ 1, 2, Mar. 30, 1999, 113 Stat. 9; Pub.L. 106–70, §§ 1, 2, Oct. 9, 1999, 113 Stat. 1031; Pub.L. 107–8, §§ 1, 2, May 11, 2001, 115 Stat. 10; Pub.L. 107–17, §§ 1, 2, June 26, 2001, 115 Stat. 151; Pub.L. 107–170, §§ 1, 2, May 7, 2002, 116 Stat. 133; Pub.L. 107–171, Title X, § 10814, May 13, 2002, 116 St. 532; Pub.L. 107–377, § 2, Dec. 19, 2002, 116 Stat. 3115; Pub.L. 108–73, § 2(a), Aug. 15, 2003, 117 Stat. 891; Pub.L. 108–369, § 2(a), Oct. 25, 2004, 118 Stat. 1749, which provided that, to take effect on January 1, 2004, chapter 12 of Title 11 [this chapter; 11 U.S.C.A. § 1201 et seq.], as in effect on December 31, 2003, is reenacted for the period beginning on January 1, 2004, and ending on July 1, 2005, but that all cases commenced or pending under this chapter 12, as reenacted under section 149(a) of Pub.L. 105–277, and all matters and proceedings in or relating to such cases, shall be conducted and determined under such chapter as if such chapter were continued in effect after July 1, 2005, and that the substantive rights of parties in connection with such cases, matters, and proceedings shall continue to be governed under the law applicable to such cases, matters, and proceedings as if such chapter were continued in effect after July 1, 2005, was superceded by the reenactment of this chapter by Pub.L. 109–8, Title X, § 1001(a), Apr. 20, 2005, 119 Stat. 185, set out as a note under this section.

CROSS REFERENCES

Automatic stay, see 11 USCA § 362.

Automatic stay of enforcement of claims against debtor in Chapter nine cases, see 11 USCA § 922.

Claims of codebtors, see 11 USCA § 509.

Effect of conversion, see 11 USCA § 348.

Effect of § 362 of this title in stockbroker liquidation cases, see 11 USCA § 742.

Extension of time generally, see 11 USCA § 108.

LIBRARY REFERENCES

American Digest System

Bankruptcy ⇔2396, 2422.5(1), 2440, 2404.

Key Number System Topic No. 51.

Corpus Juris Secundum

CJS Bankruptcy § 7, Bankruptcy Code.

CJS Bankruptcy § 278, Parties Defendant; Sovereign Immunity.

CJS Bankruptcy § 478, Persons Protected by and Subject to Stay--Persons Liable for Debtor's Consumer Debts.

CJS Bankruptcy § 508, Against Codebtor or Surety.

CJS Bankruptcy § 526, Automatic Relief from Stay.

CJS Bankruptcy § 1169, Generally; Definitions.

§ 1202. Trustee

(a) If the United States trustee has appointed an individual under section 586(b) of title 28 to serve as standing trustee in cases under this chapter and if such individual qualifies as a trustee under section 322 of this title, then such individual shall serve as trustee in any case filed under this chapter. Otherwise, the United States trustee shall appoint one disinterested person to serve as trustee in the case or the United States trustee may serve as trustee in the case if necessary.

(b) The trustee shall—

(1) perform the duties specified in sections 704(a)(2), 704(a)(3), 704(a)(5), 704(a)(6), 704(a)(7), and 704(a)(9) of this title;

(2) perform the duties specified in section 1106(a)(3) and 1106(a)(4) of this title if the court, for cause and on request of a party in interest, the trustee, or the United States trustee, so orders;

(3) appear and be heard at any hearing that concerns—

    (A) the value of property subject to a lien;

    (B) confirmation of a plan;

    (C) modification of the plan after confirmation; or

    (D) the sale of property of the estate;

(4) ensure that the debtor commences making timely payments required by a confirmed plan;

(5) if the debtor ceases to be a debtor in possession, perform the duties specified in sections 704(a)(8), 1106(a)(1), 1106(a)(2), 1106(a)(6), 1106(a)(7), and 1203; and

(6) if with respect to the debtor there is a claim for a domestic support obligation, provide the applicable notice specified in subsection (c).

(c)(1) In a case described in subsection (b)(6) to which subsection (b)(6) applies, the trustee shall—

    (A)(i) provide written notice to the holder of the claim described in subsection (b)(6) of such claim and of the right of such holder to use the services of the State child support enforcement agency established under sections 464 and 466 of the Social Security Act for the State in which such holder resides, for assis-

tance in collecting child support during and after the case under this title; and

    (ii) include in the notice provided under clause (i) the address and telephone number of such State child support enforcement agency;

    (B)(i) provide written notice to such State child support enforcement agency of such claim; and

    (ii) include in the notice provided under clause (i) the name, address, and telephone number of such holder; and

    (C) at such time as the debtor is granted a discharge under section 1228, provide written notice to such holder and to such State child support enforcement agency of—

        (i) the granting of the discharge;

        (ii) the last recent known address of the debtor;

        (iii) the last recent known name and address of the debtor's employer; and

        (iv) the name of each creditor that holds a claim that—

            (I) is not discharged under paragraph (2), (4), or (14A) of section 523(a); or

            (II) was reaffirmed by the debtor under section 524(c).

(2)(A) The holder of a claim described in subsection (b)(6) or the State child support enforcement agency of the State in which such holder resides may request from a creditor described in paragraph (1)(C)(iv) the last known address of the debtor.

(B) Notwithstanding any other provision of law, a creditor that makes a disclosure of a last known address of a debtor in connection with a request made under subparagraph (A) shall not be liable by reason of making that disclosure.

(Added and amended Pub.L. 99–554, Title II, §§ 227, 255, Title III, § 302(f), Oct. 27, 1986, 100 Stat. 3103, 3106, 3124; Pub.L. 103–65, § 1, Aug. 6, 1993, 107 Stat. 311; Pub.L. 105–277, Div. C, Title I, § 149(a), Oct. 21, 1998, 112 Stat. 2681–610; Pub.L. 106–5, §§ 1(1), (2), Mar. 30, 1999, 113 Stat. 9; Pub.L. 106–70, § 1, Oct. 9, 1999, 113 Stat. 1031; Pub.L. 107–8, § 1, May 11, 2001, 115 Stat. 10; Pub.L. 107–17, § 1, June 26, 2001, 115 Stat. 151; Pub.L. 107–170, § 1, May 7, 2002, 116 Stat. 133; Pub.L. 107–171, Title X, § 10814(a), May 13, 2002, 116 Stat. 532; Pub.L. 107–377, § 2(a), Dec. 19, 2002, 116 Stat. 3115; Pub.L. 108–73, § 2(a), Aug. 15, 2003, 117 Stat. 891; Pub.L. 108–369, § 2(a), Oct. 25, 2004, 118 Stat. 1749; Pub.L. 109–8, Title II, § 219(c), Title X, § 1001(a)(1), Apr. 20, 2005, 119 Stat. 57, 185; Pub.L. 111–327, § 2(a)(38), Dec. 22, 2010, 124 Stat. 3561.)

HISTORICAL AND STATUTORY NOTES

Revision Notes and Legislative Reports

  1986 Acts. House Report No. 99–764 and House Conference Report No. 99–958, see 1986 U.S. Code Cong. and Adm. News, p. 5227.

  1993 Acts. House Report No. 103–32, see 1993 U.S. Code Cong. and Adm. News, p. 373.

1998 Acts. Statement by President, see 1998 U.S. Code Cong. and Adm. News, p. 582.

1999 Acts. Statement by President, see 1999 U.S. Code Cong. and Adm. News, p. 4.

Statement by President, see 1999 U.S. Code Cong. and Adm. News, p. 102.

2001 Acts. House Report No. 107–2, see 2001 U.S. Code Cong. and Adm. News, p. 6.

2005 Acts. House Report No. 109–31(Part I), see 2005 U.S. Code Cong. and Adm. News, p. 88.

References in Text

Section 464 of the Social Security Act, referred to in subsec. (c)(1)(A)(i), is Act Aug. 14, 1935, c. 531, Title IV, § 464, as added Aug. 13, 1981, Pub.L. 97–35, Title XXIII, § 2331(a), 95 Stat. 860, and amended, which is classified to 42 U.S.C.A. § 664.

Section 466 of the Social Security Act, referred to in subsec. (c)(1)(A)(i), is Act Aug. 14, 1935, c. 531, Title IV, § 466, as added Aug. 16, 1984, Pub.L. 98–378, § 3(b), 98 Stat. 1306, and amended, which is classified to 42 U.S.C.A. § 666.

Amendments

2010 Amendments. Subsec. (b)(1). Pub.L. 111–327, § 2(a)(38)(A), struck out "704(2), 704(3), 704(5), 704(6), 704(7), and 704(9)" and inserted "704(a)(2), 704(a)(3), 704(a)(5), 704(a)(6), 704(a)(7), and 704(a)(9)".

Subsec. (b)(5). Pub.L. 111–327, § 2(a)(38)(B), struck out "704(8)" and inserted "704(a)(8)".

2005 Amendments. Pub.L. 109 8, § 1001(a)(1), reenacted this section as in effect on June 30, 2005, requiring no change in text; see Pub.L. 109–8, § 1001, set out as a note under 11 U.S.C.A. § 1201.

Subsec. (b)(4). Pub.L. 109–8, § 219(c)(1)(A), struck out "and" at the end of par. (4).

Subsec. (b)(5). Pub.L. 109–8, § 219(c)(1)(B), substituted "; and" for the period at the end of par. (5).

Subsec. (b)(6). Pub.L. 109–8, § 219(c)(1)(C), added par. (6).

Subsec. (c). Pub.L. 109–8, § 219(c)(2), added subsec. (c).

2004 Amendments. Pub.L. 108–369, § 2(a), extended effective date of repeal of this section to July 1, 2005, and so required no change in text.

2003 Amendments. Pub.L. 108–73, § 2(a), extended effective date of repeal of this section to Jan. 1, 2004, and so required no change in text.

2002 Amendments. Pub.L. 107–377, § 2(a), extended effective date of repeal of this section to July 1, 2003, and so required no change in text.

Pub.L. 107–171, § 10814(a), extended effective date of repeal of this section to Jan. 1, 2003, and so required no change in text.

Pub.L. 107–170, § 1, extended effective date of repeal of this section to June 1, 2002, and so required no change in text.

2001 Amendments. Pub.L. 107–17, § 1, extended effective date of repeal of this section to October 1, 2001, and so required no change in text.

Pub.L. 107–8, § 1, extended effective date of repeal of this section to June 1, 2001, and so required no change in text.

1999 Amendments. Pub.L. 106–70, § 1, extended effective date of repeal of this section to July 1, 2000, and so required no change in text.

Pub.L. 106–5, § 1(1), (2), extended effective date of repeal of this section to Oct. 1, 1999, and so required no change in text.

1998 Amendments. Pub.L. 105–277, § 149(a), temporarily reenacted this section, which had been repealed effective Oct. 1, 1998 by Pub.L. 99–554, § 302(f).

1993 Amendments. Pub.L. 103–65, § 1, extended effective date of repeal of this section to Oct. 1, 1998, and so required no change in text.

1986 Amendments. Pub.L. 99–554, § 302(f), as amended by Pub.L. 103–65, § 1, repealed section effective Oct. 1, 1998. Prior to amendment by Pub.L. 103–65, repeal of section was to have taken effect on Oct. 1, 1993.

Subsecs. (c) and (d). Pub.L. 99–554, § 227, struck out subsecs. (c) and (d) which read as follows:

"(c) If the number of cases under this chapter commenced in a particular judicial district so warrants, the court may appoint one or more individuals to serve as standing trustee for such district in cases under this chapter.

"(d)(1) A court that has appointed an individual under subsection (a) of this section to serve as standing trustee in cases under this chapter shall set for such individual—

"(A) a maximum annual compensation not to exceed the lowest annual rate of basic pay in effect for grade GS–16 of the General Schedule prescribed under section 5332 of title 5; and

"(B) a percentage fee not to exceed the sum of—

"(i) not to exceed ten percent of the payments made under the plan of such debtor, with respect to payments in an aggregate amount not to exceed $450,000; and

"(ii) three percent of payments made under the plan of such debtor, with respect to payments made after the aggregate amount of payments made under the plan exceeds $450,000;

based on such maximum annual compensation and the actual, necessary expenses incurred by such individual as standing trustee.

"(2) Such individual shall collect such percentage fee from all payments under plans in the cases under this chapter for which such individual serves as standing trustee. Such individual shall pay annually to the Treasury—

"(A) any amount by which the actual compensation received by such individual exceeds five percent of all such payments made under plans in cases under this chapter for which such individual serves as standing trustee; and

"(B) any amount by which the percentage fee fixed under paragraph (1)(B) of this subsection for all such cases exceeds—

"(i) such individual's actual compensation for such cases, as adjusted under subparagraph (A) of this paragraph; plus

"(ii) the actual, necessary expenses incurred by such individual as standing trustee in such cases.".

Effective and Applicability Provisions

2005 Acts. Amendments by Pub.L. 109–8 effective, except as otherwise provided, 180 days after April 20, 2005, and inapplicable with respect to cases commenced under Title 11 before the effective date, see Pub.L. 109–8, § 1501, set out as a note under 11 U.S.C.A. § 101.

2004 Acts. Amendment by Pub.L. 108–369, § 2(a), extending to July 1, 2005, the date of repeal of this chapter, to take effect Jan. 1, 2004, see Pub.L. 108–369, § 2(b), set out as a note under 11 U.S.C.A. § 1201.

2003 Acts. Amendment by Pub.L. 108–73, § 2(a), extending to Jan. 1, 2004, the date of repeal of this chapter, to take effect July 1, 2003, see Pub.L. 108–73, § 2(b), set out as a note under 11 U.S.C.A. § 1201.

2002 Acts. Amendment by Pub.L. 107–377, § 2(a), extending to July 1, 2003, the date of repeal of this chapter, to take effect Jan. 1, 2003, see Pub.L. 107–377, § 2(b), set out as a note under 11 U.S.C.A. § 1201.

Amendment by Pub.L. 107–171, extending to Jan. 1, 2003, the date of repeal of this chapter, to take effect June 1, 2002, see section 10814(b) of Pub.L. 107–171, set out as a note under 11 U.S.C.A. § 1201.

Amendment by Pub.L. 107–170, extending to June 1, 2002, the date of repeal of this chapter, to take effect October 1, 2001, see section 2 of Pub.L. 107–170, set out as a note under 11 U.S.C.A. § 1201.

2001 Acts. Amendment by Pub.L. 107–17, extending to October 1, 2001, the date of repeal of this chapter, to take effect June 1, 2001, see section 2 of Pub.L. 107–17, set out as a note under 11 U.S.C.A. § 1201.

Amendment by Pub.L. 107–8, extending to June 1, 2001, the date of repeal of this chapter, to take effect July 1, 2000, see section 2 of Pub.L. 107–8, set out as a note under 11 U.S.C.A. § 1201.

1999 Acts. Amendment by Pub.L. 106–70, extending to July 1, 2000, the date of repeal of this chapter, to take effect Oct. 1, 1999, see section 2 of Pub.L. 106–70, set out as a note under section 1201 of this title.

Amendment by Pub.L. 106–5, extending to Oct. 1, 1999 the date of repeal of this chapter, to take effect Apr. 1, 1999, see section 2 of Pub.L. 106–5, set out as a note under section 1201 of this title.

1998 Acts. Section reenacted, eff. Oct. 1, 1998, for the period beginning on Oct. 1, 1998, and ending on Apr. 1, 1999, but all cases commenced or pending under this chapter 12, as reenacted under section 149(a) of Pub.L. 105–277, and all matters and proceedings in or relating to such cases, to be conducted and determined under such chapter as if such chapter were continued in effect after Apr. 1, 1999, and the substantive rights of parties in connection with such cases, matters, and proceedings to continue to be governed under the law applicable to such cases, matters, and proceedings as if such chapter were continued in effect after Apr. 1, 1999, see section 149 of Pub.L. 105–277, set out as a note under section 1201 of this title.

1993 Acts. Amendment by Pub.L. 103–65, extending to Oct. 1, 1998 the date of repeal of this chapter, to take effect Aug. 6, 1993, see section 3 of Pub.L. 103–65, set out as a note under section 1221 of this title.

1986 Acts. Section repealed effective Oct. 1, 1998, see section 302(f) of Pub.L. 99–554, as amended, set out in a note under section 581 of Title 28. However, for extension of provisions, see section 149 of Pub.L. 105–277, set out as a note under section 1201 of this title.

Enactment by Pub.L. 99–554 effective 30 days after Oct. 27, 1986, except as otherwise provided for, see section 302(a) of Pub.L. 99–554, set out as a note under section 581 of Title 28, Judiciary and Judicial Procedure.

Enactment by Pub.L. 99–554, § 255, not to apply with respect to cases commenced under Title 11, Bankruptcy,

before 30 days after Oct. 27, 1986, see section 302(c)(1) of Pub.L. 99–554, set out as a note under section 581 of Title 28.

Enactment by section 255 of Pub.L. 99–554 to take effect 30 days after Oct. 27, 1986, and before amendment made by section 227 of Pub.L. 99–554, striking out subsecs. (c) and (d) of this section, see section 302(c)(2) of Pub.L. 99–554, set out as a note under section 581 of Title 28.

Amendment by Pub.L. 99–554, § 227, not to become effective in or with respect to certain specified judicial districts until, or apply to cases while pending in such district before, the expiration of the 270–day period beginning 30 days after Oct. 27, 1986, or of the 30–day period beginning on the date the Attorney General certifies under section 303 of Pub.L. 99–554 the region specified in a paragraph of section 581(a) of Title 28, as amended by section 111(a) of Pub.L. 99–554, that includes such district, whichever occurs first, see section 302(d)(1) of Pub.L. 99–554, set out as a note under section 581 of Title 28.

Amendment by Pub.L. 99–554, § 227, not to become effective in or with respect to certain specified judicial districts until, or apply to cases while pending in such district before, the expiration of the 2–year period beginning 30 days after Oct. 27, 1986, or of the 30–day period beginning on the date the Attorney General certifies under section 303 of Pub.L. 99–554 the region specified in a paragraph of section 581(a) of Title 28, as amended by section 111(a) of Pub.L. 99–554, that includes such district, whichever occurs first, see section 302(d)(2) of Pub.L. 99–554, set out as a note under section 581 of Title 28.

Amendment by Pub.L. 99–554, § 227, not to become effective in or with respect to judicial districts established for the States of Alabama and North Carolina until, or apply to cases while pending in such district before, such district elects to be included in a bankruptcy region established in section 581(a) of Title 28, as amended by section 111(a) of Pub.L. 99–554, or Oct. 1, 2002, whichever occurs first, and except as otherwise provided for, with respect to cases under chapters 7, 11, 12, and 13 of Title 11 commenced before 30 days after Oct. 27, 1986, and pending in a judicial district in the States of Alabama or North Carolina before any election made under section 302(d)(3)(A) of Pub.L. 99–554 by such district becomes effective or Oct. 1, 2002, whichever occurs first, amendments by Pub.L. 99–554 not to apply until Oct. 1, 2003, or the expiration of the 1–year period beginning on the date such election becomes effective, whichever occurs first, and further, in any judicial district in Alabama or North Carolina not making the election described in section 302(d)(3)(A) of Pub.L. 99–554, any person appointed under regulations issued by the Judicial Conference to administer estates in cases under Title 11 authorized to establish, etc., a panel of private trustees, and to supervise cases and trustees in cases under chapters 7, 11, 12, and 13 of Title 11, until amendments by section 201 to 231 of Pub.L. 99–554 becomes effective in such district, see section 302(d)(3)(A) to (F), (H), (I) of Pub.L. 99–554, set out as a note under section 581 of Title 28.

Amendment by Pub.L. 99–554, § 227, except as otherwise provided, with respect to cases under chapters 7, 11, 12, and 13 of Title 11 commenced before 30 days after Oct. 27, 1986, and pending in a judicial district referred to in section 581(a) of Title 28, as amended by section 111(a) of Pub.L. 99–554, for which a United States trustee is not authorized before 30 days after Oct. 27, 1986 to be appointed, not applicable until the expiration of the 3–year period beginning on Oct. 27, 1986, or of the 1–year period beginning on the date the Attorney

General certifies under section 303 of Pub.L. 99–554 the region specified in a paragraph of such section 581(a) that includes, such district, whichever occurs first, see section 302(e)(1), (2) of Pub.L. 99–554, set out as a note under section 581 of Title 28.

Reenactment of Chapter

This section as in effect on June 30, 2005, reenacted effective July 1, 2005, see Pub.L. 109–8, § 1001(a), set out as a note under 11 U.S.C.A. § 1201.

Repeal of Chapter; Extension of Provisions

Pub.L. 99–554, Title III, § 302(f), Oct. 27, 1986, 100 Stat. 3124, as amended Pub.L. 103–65, § 1, Aug. 6, 1993, 107 Stat. 311, which provided that, effective Oct. 1, 1998, this chapter is repealed, but that all cases commenced or pending under this chapter, and all matters and proceedings in or relating to such cases, shall be conducted and determined under this chapter as if such chapter had not been repealed, and that the substantive rights of parties in connection with such cases, matters, and proceedings shall continue to be governed under the laws applicable to such cases, matters, and proceedings as if such chapter had not been repealed, was superceded by the reenactment of this chapter by Pub.L. 109–8, Title X, § 1001(a), Apr. 20, 2005, 119 Stat. 185, set out as a note under 11 U.S.C.A. § 1201.

Pub.L. 105–277, Div. C, Title I, § 149, Oct. 21, 1998, 112 Stat. 2681–610, as amended Pub.L. 106–5, §§ 1, 2, Mar. 30, 1999, 113 Stat. 9; Pub.L. 106–70, §§ 1, 2, Oct. 9, 1999, 113 Stat. 1031; Pub.L. 107–8, §§ 1, 2, May 11, 2001, 115 Stat. 10; Pub.L. 107–17, §§ 1, 2, June 26, 2001, 115 Stat. 151; Pub.L. 107–170, §§ 1, 2, May 7, 2002, 116 Stat. 133; Pub.L. 107–171, Title X, § 10814, May 13, 2002, 116 St. 532; Pub.L. 107–377, § 2, Dec. 19, 2002, 116 Stat. 3115; Pub.L. 108–73, § 2(a), Aug. 15, 2003, 117 Stat. 891; Pub.L. 108–369, § 2(a), Oct. 25, 2004, 118 Stat. 1749, provided that, to take effect on January 1, 2004, chapter 12 of Title 11 [this chapter; 11 U.S.C.A. § 1201 et seq.], as in effect on December 31, 2003, is reenacted for the period beginning on January 1, 2004, and ending on July 1, 2005, but that all cases commenced or pending under this chapter 12, as reenacted under section 149(a) of Pub.L. 105–277, and all matters and proceedings in or relating to such cases, shall be conducted and determined under such chapter as if such chapter were continued in effect after July 1, 2005, and that the substantive rights of parties in connection with such cases, matters, and proceedings shall continue to be governed under the law applicable to such cases, matters, and proceedings as if such chapter were continued in effect after July 1, 2005, was superceded by the reenactment of this chapter by Pub.L. 109–8, Title X, § 1001(a), Apr. 20, 2005, 119 Stat. 185, set out as a note under 11 U.S.C.A. § 1201.

References in Subsection (a) Temporarily Deemed to be References to Other Provisions

Until the amendments made by subtitle A (sections 201 to 231) of Title II of Pub.L. 99–554 become effective in a district and apply to a case, in subsec. (a) of this section—

(1) the first two references to the United States trustee are deemed to be references to the court, and

(2) any reference to section 586(b) of Title 28, Judiciary and Judicial Procedure, is deemed to be a reference to subsec. (c) of this section,

see section 302(c)(3)(B), (d), (e) of Pub.L. 99–554, set out as an Effective Date note under section 581 of Title 28.

CROSS REFERENCES

Appointment of trustee in—

Chapter eleven cases, see 11 USCA § 1104.

Chapter thirteen cases, see 11 USCA § 1302.

Railroad reorganization cases, see 11 USCA § 1163.

Compensation of officers, see 11 USCA § 330.

Election of trustee in Chapter seven case, see 11 USCA § 702.

Eligibility to serve as trustee, see 11 USCA § 321.

Grain storage facility bankruptcies, expedited appointment of trustee or examiner, see 11 USCA § 557.

Limitation on compensation of trustee, see 11 USCA § 326.

Qualification of trustee, see 11 USCA § 322.

Removal of trustee, see 11 USCA § 324.

Retention or replacement of professional persons, see 11 USCA § 327.

Role and capacity of trustee, see 11 USCA § 323.

Time of bringing action, see 11 USCA § 546.

Time of payment of percentage fee fixed for standing trustee, see 11 USCA § 1226.

LIBRARY REFERENCES

American Digest System

Bankruptcy ☞3672, 3009, 3008.1.

Key Number System Topic No. 51.

Corpus Juris Secundum

CJS Bankruptcy § 46, Service as Bankruptcy Trustee.

CJS Bankruptcy § 52, Proceedings Under Chapters 12 and 13.

CJS Bankruptcy § 56, Eligibility to Serve as Trustee or Examiner--Disinterestedness Requirement.

CJS Bankruptcy § 74, Chapter 12 Cases.

CJS Bankruptcy § 102, Chapter 12.

CJS Bankruptcy § 137, Removal or Reinstatement of Debtor as Debtor in Possession.

CJS Bankruptcy § 578, Debtor's Statement of Intention.

CJS Bankruptcy § 805, Who May Conduct Examination; Debtor's Right to Examine.

CJS Bankruptcy § 847, Operation of Family Farm in Chapter 12 Cases.

§ 1203. Rights and powers of debtor

Subject to such limitations as the court may prescribe, a debtor in possession shall have all the rights, other than the right to compensation under section 330, and powers, and shall perform all the functions and duties, except the duties specified in paragraphs (3) and (4) of section 1106(a), of a trustee serving in a case under chapter 11, including operating the debtor's farm or commercial fishing operation.

(Added and amended Pub.L. 99–554, Title II, § 255, Title III, § 302(f), Oct. 27, 1986, 100 Stat. 3107, 3124; Pub.L. 103–65, § 1, Aug. 6, 1993, 107 Stat. 311; Pub.L. 105–277, Div. C, Title I, § 149(a), Oct. 21, 1998, 112 Stat. 2681–610; Pub.L. 106–5, § 1(1), (2), Mar. 30, 1999, 113 Stat. 9; Pub.L. 106–70, § 1, Oct.

9, 1999, 113 Stat. 1031; Pub.L. 107–8, § 1, May 11, 2001, 115 Stat. 10; Pub.L. 107–17, § 1, June 26, 2001, 115 Stat. 151; Pub.L. 107–170, § 1, May 7, 2002, 116 Stat. 133; Pub.L. 107–171, Title X, § 10814(a), May 13, 2002, 116 Stat. 532; Pub.L. 107–377, § 2(a), Dec. 19, 2002, 116 Stat. 3115; Pub.L. 108–73, § 2(a), Aug. 15, 2003, 117 Stat. 891; Pub.L. 108–369, § 2(a), Oct. 25, 2004, 118 Stat. 1749; Pub.L. 109–8, Title X, §§ 1001(a)(1), 1007(c)(2), Apr. 20, 2005, 119 Stat. 185, 188.)

HISTORICAL AND STATUTORY NOTES

Revision Notes and Legislative Reports

1986 Acts. House Report No. 99–764 and House Conference Report No. 99–958, see 1986 U.S. Code Cong. and Adm. News, p. 5227.

1993 Acts. House Report No. 103–32, see 1993 U.S. Code Cong. and Adm. News, p. 373.

1998 Acts. Statement by President, see 1998 U.S. Code Cong. and Adm. News, p. 582.

1999 Acts. Statement by President, see 1999 U.S. Code Cong. and Adm. News, p. 4.

Statement by President, see 1999 U.S. Code Cong. and Adm. News, p. 102.

2001 Acts. House Report No. 107–2, see 2001 U.S. Code Cong. and Adm. News, p. 6.

2005 Acts. House Report No. 109–31(Part I), see 2005 U.S. Code Cong. and Adm. News, p. 88.

Amendments

2005 Amendments. Pub.L. 109–8, § 1001(a)(1), reenacted this section as in effect on June 30, 2005, requiring no change in text; see Pub.L. 109–8, § 1001, set out as a note under 11 U.S.C.A. § 1201.

Pub.L. 109–8, § 1007(c)(2), inserted "or commercial fishing operation" after "farm".

2004 Amendments. Pub.L. 108–369, § 2(a), extended effective date of repeal of this section to July 1, 2005, and so required no change in text.

2003 Amendments. Pub.L. 108–73, § 2(a), extended effective date of repeal of this section to Jan. 1, 2004, and so required no change in text.

2002 Amendments. Pub.L. 107–377, § 2(a), extended effective date of repeal of this section to July 1, 2003, and so required no change in text.

Pub.L. 107–171, § 10814(a), extended effective date of repeal of this section to Jan. 1, 2003, and so required no change in text.

Pub.L. 107–170, § 1, extended effective date of repeal of this section to June 1, 2002, and so required no change in text.

2001 Amendments. Pub.L. 107–17, § 1, extended effective date of repeal of this section to Oct. 1, 2001, and so required no change in text.

Pub.L. 107–8, § 1, extended effective date of repeal of this section to June 1, 2001, and so required no change in text.

1999 Amendments. Pub.L. 106–70, § 1, extended effective date of repeal of this section to July 1, 2000, and so required no change in text.

Pub.L. 106–5, § 1(1), (2), extended effective date of repeal of this section to Oct. 1, 1999, and so required no change in text.

1998 Amendments. Pub.L. 105–277, § 149(a), temporarily reenacted this section, which had been repealed effective Oct. 1, 1998 by Pub.L. 99–554, § 302(f).

1993 Amendments. Pub.L. 103–65, § 1, extended effective date of repeal of this section to Oct. 1, 1998.

1986 Amendments. Pub.L. 99–554, § 302(f), as amended by Pub.L. 103–65, § 1, repealed section effective Oct. 1, 1998. Prior to amendment by Pub.L. 103–65, repeal of section was to have taken effect on Oct. 1, 1993.

Effective and Applicability Provisions

2005 Acts. Amendments by Pub.L. 109–8 effective, except as otherwise provided, 180 days after April 20, 2005, and inapplicable with respect to cases commenced under Title 11 before the effective date, see Pub.L. 109–8, § 1501, set out as a note under 11 U.S.C.A. § 101.

2004 Acts. Amendment by Pub.L. 108–369, § 2(a), extending to July 1, 2005, the date of repeal of this chapter, to take effect Jan. 1, 2004, see Pub.L. 108–369, § 2(b), set out as a note under 11 U.S.C.A. § 1201.

2003 Acts. Amendment by Pub.L. 108–73, § 2(a), extending to Jan. 1, 2004, the date of repeal of this chapter, to take effect July 1, 2003, see Pub.L. 108–73, § 2(b), set out as a note under 11 U.S.C.A. § 1201.

2002 Acts. Amendment by Pub.L. 107–377, § 2(a), extending to July 1, 2003, the date of repeal of this chapter, to take effect Jan. 1, 2003, see Pub.L. 107–377, § 2(b), set out as a note under 11 U.S.C.A. § 1201.

Amendment by Pub.L. 107–171, extending to Jan. 1, 2003, the date of repeal of this chapter, to take effect June 1, 2002, see section 10814(b) of Pub.L. 107–171, set out as a note under 11 U.S.C.A. § 1201.

Amendment by Pub.L. 107–170, extending to June 1, 2002, the date of repeal of this chapter, to take effect October 1, 2001, see section 2 of Pub.L. 107–170, set out as a note under 11 U.S.C.A. § 1201.

2001 Acts. Amendment by Pub.L. 107–17, extending to October 1, 2001, the date of repeal of this chapter, to take effect June 1, 2001, see section 2 of Pub.L. 107–17, set out as a note under 11 U.S.C.A. § 1201.

Amendment by Pub.L. 107–8, extending to June 1, 2001, the date of repeal of this chapter, to take effect July 1, 2000, see section 2 of Pub.L. 107–8, set out as a note under 11 U.S.C.A. § 1201.

1999 Acts. Amendment by Pub.L. 106–70, extending to July 1, 2000, the date of repeal of this chapter, to take effect Oct. 1, 1999, see section 2 of Pub.L. 106–70, set out as a note under section 1201 of this title.

Amendment by Pub.L. 106–5, extending to Oct. 1, 1999 the date of repeal of this chapter, to take effect Apr. 1, 1999, see section 2 of Pub.L. 106–5, set out as a note under section 1201 of this title.

1998 Acts. Section reenacted, eff. Oct. 1, 1998, for the period beginning on Oct. 1, 1998, and ending on Apr. 1, 1999, but all cases commenced or pending under this chapter 12, as reenacted under section 149(a) of Pub.L. 105–277, and all matters and proceedings in or relating to such cases, to be conducted and determined under such chapter as if such chapter were continued in effect after Apr. 1, 1999, and the substantive rights of parties in connection with such cases, matters, and proceedings to continue to be governed under the law applicable to such cases, matters, and proceedings as if such chapter were continued in effect after Apr. 1, 1999, see section 149 of Pub.L. 105–277, set out as a note under section 1201 of this title.

1993 Acts. Amendment by Pub.L. 103–65, extending to Oct. 1, 1998 the date of repeal of this chapter, to take effect Aug. 6, 1993, see section 3 of Pub.L. 103–65, set out as a note under section 1221 of this title.

1986 Acts. Section repealed effective Oct. 1, 1998, see section 302(f) of Pub.L. 99–554, as amended, set out in a note under section 581 of Title 28. However, for extension of provisions, see section 149 of Pub.L. 105–277, set out as a note under section 1201 of this title.

Section effective 30 days after Oct. 27, 1986, but not applicable to cases commenced under this title before that date, see section 302(a), (c)(1) of Pub.L. 99–554, set out as a note under section 581 of Title 28, Judiciary and Judicial Procedure.

Reenactment of Chapter

This section as in effect on June 30, 2005, reenacted effective July 1, 2005, see Pub.L. 109–8, § 1001(a), set out as a note under 11 U.S.C.A. § 1201.

Repeal of Chapter; Extension of Provisions

Pub.L. 99–554, Title III, § 302(f), Oct. 27, 1986, 100 Stat. 3124, as amended Pub.L. 103–65, § 1, Aug. 6, 1993, 107 Stat. 311, which provided that, effective Oct. 1, 1998, this chapter is repealed, but that all cases commenced or pending under this chapter, and all matters and proceedings in or relating to such cases, shall be conducted and determined under this chapter as if such chapter had not been repealed, and that the substantive rights of parties in connection with such cases, matters, and proceedings shall continue to be governed under the laws applicable to such cases, matters, and proceedings as if such chapter had not been repealed, was superceded by the reenactment of this chapter by Pub.L. 109–8, Title X, § 1001(a), Apr. 20, 2005, 119 Stat. 185, set out as a note under 11 U.S.C.A. § 1201.

Pub.L. 105–277, Div. C, Title I, § 149, Oct. 21, 1998, 112 Stat. 2681–610, as amended Pub.L. 106–5, §§ 1, 2, Mar. 30, 1999, 113 Stat. 9; Pub.L. 106–70, §§ 1, 2, Oct. 9, 1999, 113 Stat. 1031; Pub.L. 107–8, §§ 1, 2, May 11, 2001, 115 Stat. 10; Pub.L. 107–17, §§ 1, 2, June 26, 2001, 115 Stat. 151; Pub.L. 107–170, §§ 1, 2, May 7, 2002, 116 Stat. 133; Pub.L. 107–171, Title X, § 10814, May 13, 2002, 116 St. 532; Pub.L. 107–377, § 2, Dec. 19, 2002, 116 Stat. 3115; Pub.L. 108–73, § 2(a), Aug. 15, 2003, 117 Stat. 891; Pub.L. 108–369, § 2(a), Oct. 25, 2004, 118 Stat. 1749, provided that, to take effect on January 1, 2004, chapter 12 of Title 11 [this chapter; 11 U.S.C.A. § 1201 et seq.], as in effect on December 31, 2003, is reenacted for the period beginning on January 1, 2004, and ending on July 1, 2005, but that all cases commenced or pending under this chapter 12, as reenacted under section 149(a) of Pub.L. 105–277, and all matters and proceedings in or relating to such cases, shall be conducted and determined under such chapter as if such chapter were continued in effect after July 1, 2005, and that the substantive rights of parties in connection with such cases, matters, and proceedings shall continue to be governed under the law applicable to such cases, matters, and proceedings as if such chapter were continued in effect after July 1, 2005, was superceded by the reenactment of this chapter by Pub.L. 109–8, Title X, § 1001(a), Apr. 20, 2005, 119 Stat. 185, set out as a note under 11 U.S.C.A. § 1201.

CROSS REFERENCES

Obtaining credit, see 11 USCA § 364.

Rights and powers of debtor in—

Chapter eleven cases, see 11 USCA § 1107.

Chapter thirteen cases, see 11 USCA § 1303.

Use, sale or lease of property, see 11 USCA § 363.

LIBRARY REFERENCES

American Digest System

Bankruptcy ⟝3672.

Key Number System Topic No. 51.

Corpus Juris Secundum

CJS Bankruptcy § 102, Chapter 12.

CJS Bankruptcy § 136, Rights, Powers, and Duties of Debtor in Possession.

CJS Bankruptcy § 190, Orders With Respect to Obtaining Credit.

CJS Bankruptcy § 276, Standing.

CJS Bankruptcy § 278, Parties Defendant; Sovereign Immunity.

CJS Bankruptcy § 761, Relationship Between Employment and Compensation Provisions.

CJS Bankruptcy § 763, Salaried Employees; Employment of Debtor's Attorney.

CJS Bankruptcy § 847, Operation of Family Farm in Chapter 12 Cases.

CJS Bankruptcy § 851, Prepetition Security Interests in Proceeds, Products, Offspring, or Profits.

CJS Bankruptcy § 852, Prepetition Security Interests Extending to Rents and Similar Charges.

CJS Bankruptcy § 854, Expedited Determination of Disposition of Grain Assets.

CJS Bankruptcy § 871, Motion for Authorization.

CJS Bankruptcy § 874, What Transactions Are Other Than in Ordinary Course of Business.

CJS Bankruptcy § 876, Requirement of Business Justification.

CJS Bankruptcy § 885, Sale of Farmland or Farm Equipment in Chapter 12 Cases.

CJS Bankruptcy § 889, Co-Owner or Spouse's Right to Proportionate Share of Proceeds of Sale.

CJS Bankruptcy § 891, Protection of Good-Faith Purchasers and Lessees from Reversal or Modification on Appeal.

CJS Bankruptcy § 892, Setting Aside Confirmed Sale; Remedies for Collusive Bidding.

CJS Bankruptcy § 895, Unsecured Credit or Debt in Ordinary Course of Business.

CJS Bankruptcy § 896, Unsecured Credit or Debt Other Than in Ordinary Course of Business.

CJS Bankruptcy § 897, Credit With Special Administrative Priority or Secured by First Liens or Junior Liens.

CJS Bankruptcy § 898, Credit Secured by Superpriority Lien; Subordination of Existing Liens.

CJS Bankruptcy § 900, Motion for Authorization to Obtain Credit; Notice and Hearing.

§ 1204. Removal of debtor as debtor in possession

(a) On request of a party in interest, and after notice and a hearing, the court shall order that the debtor shall not be a debtor in possession for cause, including fraud, dishonesty, incompetence, or gross mismanagement of the affairs of the debtor, either before or after the commencement of the case.

(b) On request of a party in interest, and after notice and a hearing, the court may reinstate the debtor in possession.

(Added and amended Pub.L. 99–554, Title II, § 255, Title III, § 302(f), Oct. 27, 1986, 100 Stat. 3107, 3124; Pub.L. 103–65, § 1, Aug. 6, 1993, 107 Stat. 311; Pub.L. 105–277, Div. C, Title I, § 149(a), Oct. 21, 1998, 112 Stat. 2681–610; Pub.L. 106–5, § 1(1), (2), Mar. 30, 1999, 113 Stat. 9; Pub.L. 106–70, § 1, Oct. 9, 1999, 113 Stat. 1031; Pub.L. 107–8, § 1, May 11, 2001, 115 Stat. 10; Pub.L. 107–17, § 1, June 26, 2001, 115 Stat. 151; Pub.L. 107–170, § 1, May 7, 2002, 116 Stat. 133; Pub.L. 107–171, Title X, § 10814(a), May 13, 2002, 116 Stat. 532; Pub.L. 107–377, § 2(a), Dec. 19, 2002, 116 Stat. 3115; Pub.L. 108–73, § 2(a), Aug. 15, 2003, 117 Stat. 891; Pub.L. 108–369, § 2(a), Oct. 25, 2004, 118 Stat. 1749; Pub.L. 109–8, Title X, § 1001(a)(1), Apr. 20, 2005, 119 Stat. 185.)

HISTORICAL AND STATUTORY NOTES

Revision Notes and Legislative Reports

1986 Acts. House Report No. 99–764 and House Conference Report No. 99–958, see 1986 U.S. Code Cong. and Adm. News, p. 5227.

1993 Acts. House Report No. 103–32, see 1993 U.S. Code Cong. and Adm. News, p. 373.

1998 Acts. Statement by President, see 1998 U.S. Code Cong. and Adm. News, p. 582.

1999 Acts. Statement by President, see 1999 U.S. Code Cong. and Adm. News, p. 4.

Statement by President, see 1999 U.S. Code Cong. and Adm. News, p. 102.

2001 Acts. House Report No. 107–2, see 2001 U.S. Code Cong. and Adm. News, p. 6.

2005 Acts. House Report No. 109–31(Part I), see 2005 U.S. Code Cong. and Adm. News, p. 88.

Amendments

2005 Amendments. Pub.L. 109–8, § 1001(a)(1), reenacted this section as in effect on June 30, 2005, requiring no change in text; see Pub.L. 109–8, § 1001, set out as a note under 11 U.S.C.A. § 1201.

2004 Amendments. Pub.L. 108–369, § 2(a), extended effective date of repeal of this section to July 1, 2005, and so required no change in text.

2003 Amendments. Pub.L. 108–73, § 2(a), extended effective date of repeal of this section to Jan. 1, 2004, and so required no change in text.

2002 Amendments. Pub.L. 107–377, § 2(a), extended effective date of repeal of this section to July 1, 2003, and so required no change in text.

Pub.L. 107–171, § 10814(a), extended effective date of repeal of this section to Jan. 1, 2003, and so required no change in text.

Pub.L. 107–170, § 1, extended effective date of repeal of this section to June 1, 2002, and so required no change in text.

2001 Amendments. Pub.L. 107–17, § 1, extended effective date of repeal of this section to Oct. 1, 2001, and so required no change in text.

Pub.L. 107–8, § 1, extended effective date of repeal of this section to June 1, 2001, and so required no change in text.

1999 Amendments. Pub.L. 106–70, § 1, extended effective date of repeal of this section to July 1, 2000, and so required no change in text.

Pub.L. 106–5, § 1(1), (2), extended effective date of repeal of this section to Oct. 1, 1999, and so required no change in text.

1998 Amendments. Pub.L. 105–277, § 149(a), temporarily reenacted this section, which had been repealed effective Oct. 1, 1998 by Pub.L. 99–554, § 302(f).

1993 Amendments. Pub.L. 103–65, § 1, extended effective date of repeal of this section to Oct. 1, 1998.

1986 Amendments. Pub.L. 99–554, § 302(f), as amended by Pub.L. 103–65, § 1, repealed section effective Oct. 1, 1998. Prior to amendment by Pub.L. 103–65, repeal of section was to have taken effect on Oct. 1, 1993.

Effective and Applicability Provisions

2005 Acts. Amendments by Pub.L. 109–8 effective, except as otherwise provided, 180 days after April 20, 2005, and inapplicable with respect to cases commenced under Title 11 before the effective date, see Pub.L. 109–8, § 1501, set out as a note under 11 U.S.C.A. § 101.

2004 Acts. Amendment by Pub.L. 108–369, § 2(a), extending to July 1, 2005, the date of repeal of this chapter, to take effect Jan. 1, 2004, see Pub.L. 108–369, § 2(b), set out as a note under 11 U.S.C.A. § 1201.

2003 Acts. Amendment by Pub.L. 108–73, § 2(a), extending to Jan. 1, 2004, the date of repeal of this chapter, to take effect July 1, 2003, see Pub.L. 108–73, § 2(b), set out as a note under 11 U.S.C.A. § 1201.

2002 Acts. Amendment by Pub.L. 107–377, § 2(a), extending to July 1, 2003, the date of repeal of this chapter, to take effect Jan. 1, 2003, see Pub.L. 107–377, § 2(b), set out as a note under 11 U.S.C.A. § 1201.

Amendment by Pub.L. 107–171, extending to Jan. 1, 2003, the date of repeal of this chapter, to take effect June 1, 2002, see section 10814(b) of Pub.L. 107–171, set out as a note under 11 U.S.C.A. § 1201.

Amendment by Pub.L. 107–170, extending to June 1, 2002, the date of repeal of this chapter, to take effect October 1, 2001, see section 2 of Pub.L. 107–170, set out as a note under 11 U.S.C.A. § 1201.

2001 Acts. Amendment by Pub.L. 107–17, extending to October 1, 2001, the date of repeal of this chapter, to take effect June 1, 2001, see section 2 of Pub.L. 107–17, set out as a note under 11 U.S.C.A. § 1201.

Amendment by Pub.L. 107–8, extending to June 1, 2001, the date of repeal of this chapter, to take effect July 1, 2000, see section 2 of Pub.L. 107–8, set out as a note under 11 U.S.C.A. § 1201.

1999 Acts. Amendment by Pub.L. 106–70, extending to July 1, 2000, the date of repeal of this chapter, to take effect Oct. 1, 1999, see section 2 of Pub.L. 106–70, set out as a note under section 1201 of this title.

Amendment by Pub.L. 106–5, extending to Oct. 1, 1999 the date of repeal of this chapter, to take effect Apr. 1, 1999, see section 2 of Pub.L. 106–5, set out as a note under section 1201 of this title.

1998 Acts. Section reenacted, eff. Oct. 1, 1998, for the period beginning on Oct. 1, 1998, and ending on Apr. 1, 1999, but all cases commenced or pending under this chapter 12, as reenacted under section 149(a) of Pub.L. 105–277, and all matters and proceedings in or relating to such cases, to be conducted and determined under such chapter as if such chapter were continued in effect after Apr. 1, 1999, and the substantive rights of parties in connection with such cases, matters, and proceedings to continue to be governed under the law applicable to such cases, matters, and proceedings as if such chapter were continued in effect after Apr. 1, 1999, see section 149 of Pub.L. 105–277, set out as a note under section 1201 of this title.

1993 Acts. Amendment by Pub.L. 103–65, extending to Oct. 1, 1998 the date of repeal of this chapter, to take effect Aug. 6, 1993, see section 3 of Pub.L. 103–65, set out as a note under section 1221 of this title.

1986 Acts. Section repealed effective Oct. 1, 1998, see section 302(f) of Pub.L. 99–554, as amended, set out in a note under section 581 of Title 28. However, for extension of provisions, see section 149 of Pub.L. 105–277, set out as a note under section 1201 of this title.

Section effective 30 days after Oct. 27, 1986, but not applicable to cases commenced under this title before that date, see section 302(a), (c)(1) of Pub.L. 99–554, set out as a note under section 581 of Title 28, Judiciary and Judicial Procedure.

Reenactment of Chapter

This section as in effect on June 30, 2005, reenacted effective July 1, 2005, see Pub.L. 109–8, § 1001(a), set out as a note under 11 U.S.C.A. § 1201.

Repeal of Chapter; Extension of Provisions

Pub.L. 99–554, Title III, § 302(f), Oct. 27, 1986, 100 Stat. 3124, as amended Pub.L. 103–65, § 1, Aug. 6, 1993, 107 Stat. 311, which provided that, effective Oct. 1, 1998, this chapter is repealed, but that all cases commenced or pending under this chapter, and all matters and proceedings in or relating to such cases, shall be conducted and determined under this chapter as if such chapter had not been repealed, and that the substantive rights of parties in connection with such cases, matters, and proceedings shall continue to be governed under the laws applicable to such cases, matters, and proceedings as if such chapter had not been repealed, was superceded by the reenactment of this chapter by Pub.L. 109–8, Title X, § 1001(a), Apr. 20, 2005, 119 Stat. 185, set out as a note under 11 U.S.C.A. § 1201.

Pub.L. 105–277, Div. C, Title I, § 149, Oct. 21, 1998, 112 Stat. 2681–610, as amended Pub.L. 106–5, §§ 1, 2, Mar. 30, 1999, 113 Stat. 9; Pub.L. 106–70, §§ 1, 2, Oct. 9, 1999, 113 Stat. 1031; Pub.L. 107–8, §§ 1, 2, May 11, 2001, 115 Stat. 10; Pub.L. 107–17, §§ 1, 2, June 26, 2001, 115 Stat. 151; Pub.L. 107–170, §§ 1, 2, May 7, 2002, 116 Stat. 133; Pub.L. 107–171, Title X, § 10814, May 13, 2002, 116 St. 532; Pub.L. 107–377, § 2, Dec. 19, 2002, 116 Stat. 3115; Pub.L. 108–73, § 2(a), Aug. 15, 2003, 117 Stat. 891; Pub.L. 108–369, § 2(a), Oct. 25, 2004, 118 Stat. 1749, provided that, to take effect on January 1, 2004, chapter 12 of Title 11 [this chapter; 11 U.S.C.A. § 1201 et seq.], as in effect on December 31, 2003, is reenacted for the period beginning on January 1, 2004, and ending on July 1, 2005, but that all cases commenced or pending under this chapter 12, as reenacted under section 149(a) of Pub.L. 105–277, and all matters and proceedings in or relating to such cases, shall be conducted and determined under such chapter as if such chapter were continued in effect after July 1, 2005, and that the substantive rights of parties in connection with such cases, matters, and proceedings shall continue to be governed under the law applicable to such cases, matters, and proceedings as if such chapter were continued in effect after July 1, 2005, was superceded by the reenactment of this chapter by Pub.L. 109–8, Title X, § 1001(a), Apr. 20, 2005, 119 Stat. 185, set out as a note under 11 U.S.C.A. § 1201.

CROSS REFERENCES

Obtaining credit, see 11 USCA § 364.

Revocation of an order of confirmation, see 11 USCA § 1230.

Use, sale or lease of property, see 11 USCA § 363.

LIBRARY REFERENCES

American Digest System

Bankruptcy ⟶3672.

Key Number System Topic No. 51.

Corpus Juris Secundum

CJS Bankruptcy § 130, Debtor in Possession as Same Entity as or Separate Entity from Debtor.

CJS Bankruptcy § 136, Rights, Powers, and Duties of Debtor in Possession.

CJS Bankruptcy § 137, Removal or Reinstatement of Debtor as Debtor in Possession.

CJS Bankruptcy § 624, Surrender of Property of Estate and Recorded Information to Trustee.

CJS Bankruptcy § 847, Operation of Family Farm in Chapter 12 Cases.

§ 1205. Adequate protection

(a) Section 361 does not apply in a case under this chapter.

(b) In a case under this chapter, when adequate protection is required under section 362, 363, or 364 of this title of an interest of an entity in property, such adequate protection may be provided by—

(1) requiring the trustee to make a cash payment or periodic cash payments to such entity, to the extent that the stay under section 362 of this title, use, sale, or lease under section 363 of this title, or any grant of a lien under section 364 of this title results in a decrease in the value of property securing a claim or of an entity's ownership interest in property;

(2) providing to such entity an additional or replacement lien to the extent that such stay, use, sale, lease, or grant results in a decrease in the value of property securing a claim or of an entity's ownership interest in property;

(3) paying to such entity for the use of farmland the reasonable rent customary in the community where the property is located, based upon the rental value, net income, and earning capacity of the property; or

(4) granting such other relief, other than entitling such entity to compensation allowable under section 503(b)(1) of this title as an administrative expense, as will adequately protect the value of property securing a claim or of such entity's ownership interest in property.

(Added and amended Pub.L. 99–554, Title II, § 255, Title III, § 302(f), Oct. 27, 1986, 100 Stat. 3107, 3124; Pub.L. 103–65, § 1, Aug. 6, 1993, 107 Stat. 311; Pub.L. 105–277, Div. C, Title I, § 149(a), Oct. 21, 1998, 112 Stat. 2681–610; Pub.L. 106–5, § 1(1), (2), Mar. 30, 1999, 113 Stat. 9; Pub.L. 106–70, § 1, Oct. 9, 1999, 113 Stat. 1031; Pub.L. 107–8, § 1, May 11, 2001, 115 Stat. 10; Pub.L. 107–17, § 1, June 26, 2001, 115 Stat. 151; Pub.L. 107–170, § 1, May 7, 2002, 116 Stat. 133; Pub.L. 107–171, Title X, § 10814(a), May 13, 2002, 116 Stat. 532; Pub.L. 107–377, § 2(a), Dec. 19, 2002, 116 Stat. 3115; Pub.L. 108–73, § 2(a), Aug. 15, 2003, 117 Stat. 891; Pub.L. 108–369, § 2(a), Oct. 25, 2004, 118 Stat. 1749; Pub.L. 109–8, Title X, § 1001(a)(1), Apr. 20, 2005, 119 Stat. 185.)

HISTORICAL AND STATUTORY NOTES

Revision Notes and Legislative Reports

1986 Acts. House Report No. 99–764 and House Conference Report No. 99–958, see 1986 U.S. Code Cong. and Adm. News, p. 5227.

1993 Acts. House Report No. 103–32, see 1993 U.S. Code Cong. and Adm. News, p. 373.

1998 Acts. Statement by President, see 1998 U.S. Code Cong. and Adm. News, p. 582.

1999 Acts. Statement by President, see 1999 U.S. Code Cong. and Adm. News, p. 4.

Statement by President, see 1999 U.S. Code Cong. and Adm. News, p. 102.

2001 Acts. House Report No. 107–2, see 2001 U.S. Code Cong. and Adm. News, p. 6.

2005 Acts. House Report No. 109–31(Part I), see 2005 U.S. Code Cong. and Adm. News, p. 88.

Amendments

2005 Amendments. Pub.L. 109–8, § 1001(a)(1), reenacted this section as in effect on June 30, 2005, requiring no change in text; see Pub.L. 109–8, § 1001, set out as a note under 11 U.S.C.A. § 1201.

2004 Amendments. Pub.L. 108–369, § 2(a), extended effective date of repeal of this section to July 1, 2005, and so required no change in text.

2003 Amendments. Pub.L. 108–73, § 2(a), extended effective date of repeal of this section to Jan. 1, 2004, and so required no change in text.

2002 Amendments. Pub.L. 107–377, § 2(a), extended effective date of repeal of this section to July 1, 2003, and so required no change in text.

Pub.L. 107–171, § 10814(a), extended effective date of repeal of this section to Jan. 1, 2003, and so required no change in text.

Pub.L. 107–170, § 1, extended effective date of repeal of this section to June 1, 2002, and so required no change in text.

2001 Amendments. Pub.L. 107–17, § 1, extended effective date of repeal of this section to Oct. 1, 2001, and so required no change in text.

Pub.L. 107–8, § 1, extended effective date of repeal of this section to June 1, 2001, and so required no change in text.

1999 Amendments. Pub.L. 106–70, § 1, extended effective date of repeal of this section to July 1, 2000, and so required no change in text.

Pub.L. 106–5, § 1(1), (2), extended effective date of repeal of this section to Oct. 1, 1999, and so required no change in text.

1998 Amendments. Pub.L. 105–277, § 149(a), temporarily reenacted this section, which had been repealed effective Oct. 1, 1998 by Pub.L. 99–554, § 302(f).

1993 Amendments. Pub.L. 103–65, § 1, extended effective date of repeal of this section to Oct. 1, 1998.

1986 Amendments. Pub.L. 99–554, § 302(f), as amended by Pub.L. 103–65, § 1, repealed section effective Oct. 1, 1998. Prior to amendment by Pub.L. 103–65, repeal of section was to have taken effect on Oct. 1, 1993.

Effective and Applicability Provisions

2005 Acts. Amendments by Pub.L. 109–8 effective, except as otherwise provided, 180 days after April 20, 2005, and inapplicable with respect to cases commenced under Title 11 before the effective date, see Pub.L. 109–8, § 1501, set out as a note under 11 U.S.C.A. § 101.

2004 Acts. Amendment by Pub.L. 108–369, § 2(a), extending to July 1, 2005, the date of repeal of this chapter, to take effect Jan. 1, 2004, see Pub.L. 108–369, § 2(b), set out as a note under 11 U.S.C.A. § 1201.

2003 Acts. Amendment by Pub.L. 108–73, § 2(a), extending to Jan. 1, 2004, the date of repeal of this chapter, to take effect July 1, 2003, see Pub.L. 108–73, § 2(b), set out as a note under 11 U.S.C.A. § 1201.

2002 Acts. Amendment by Pub.L. 107–377, § 2(a), extending to July 1, 2003, the date of repeal of this chapter, to take effect Jan. 1, 2003, see Pub.L. 107–377, § 2(b), set out as a note under 11 U.S.C.A. § 1201.

Amendment by Pub.L. 107–171, extending to Jan. 1, 2003, the date of repeal of this chapter, to take effect June 1, 2002, see section 10814(b) of Pub.L. 107–171, set out as a note under 11 U.S.C.A. § 1201.

Amendment by Pub.L. 107–170, extending to June 1, 2002, the date of repeal of this chapter, to take effect October 1, 2001, see section 2 of Pub.L. 107–170, set out as a note under 11 U.S.C.A. § 1201.

2001 Acts. Amendment by Pub.L. 107–17, extending to October 1, 2001, the date of repeal of this chapter, to take effect June 1, 2001, see section 2 of Pub.L. 107–17, set out as a note under 11 U.S.C.A. § 1201.

Amendment by Pub.L. 107–8, extending to June 1, 2001, the date of repeal of this chapter, to take effect July 1, 2000, see section 2 of Pub.L. 107–8, set out as a note under 11 U.S.C.A. § 1201.

1999 Acts. Amendment by Pub.L. 106–70, extending to July 1, 2000, the date of repeal of this chapter, to take effect Oct. 1, 1999, see section 2 of Pub.L. 106–70, set out as a note under section 1201 of this title.

Amendment by Pub.L. 106–5, extending to Oct. 1, 1999 the date of repeal of this chapter, to take effect Apr. 1, 1999, see section 2 of Pub.L. 106–5, set out as a note under section 1201 of this title.

1998 Acts. Section reenacted, eff. Oct. 1, 1998, for the period beginning on Oct. 1, 1998, and ending on Apr. 1, 1999, but all cases commenced or pending under this chapter 12, as reenacted under section 149(a) of Pub.L. 105–277, and all matters and proceedings in or relating to such cases, to be conducted and determined under such chapter as if such chapter were continued in effect after Apr. 1, 1999, and the substantive rights of parties in connection with such cases, matters, and proceedings to continue to be governed under the law applicable to such cases, matters, and proceedings as if such chapter were continued in effect after Apr. 1, 1999, see section 149 of Pub.L. 105–277, set out as a note under section 1201 of this title.

1993 Acts. Amendment by Pub.L. 103–65, extending to Oct. 1, 1998 the date of repeal of this chapter, to take effect Aug. 6, 1993, see section 3 of Pub.L. 103–65, set out as a note under section 1221 of this title.

1986 Acts. Section repealed effective Oct. 1, 1998, see section 302(f) of Pub.L. 99–554, as amended, set out in a note under section 581 of Title 28. However, for extension of provisions, see section 149 of Pub.L. 105–277, set out as a note under section 1201 of this title.

Section effective 30 days after Oct. 27, 1986, but not applicable to cases commenced under this title before that date, see section 302(a), (c)(1) of Pub.L. 99–554, set out as a note under section 581 of Title 28, Judiciary and Judicial Procedure.

Reenactment of Chapter

This section as in effect on June 30, 2005, reenacted effective July 1, 2005, see Pub.L. 109–8, § 1001(a), set out as a note under 11 U.S.C.A. § 1201.

Repeal of Chapter; Extension of Provisions

Pub.L. 99–554, Title III, § 302(f), Oct. 27, 1986, 100 Stat. 3124, as amended Pub.L. 103–65, § 1, Aug. 6, 1993, 107 Stat. 311, which provided that, effective Oct. 1, 1998, this chapter is repealed, but that all cases commenced or pending under this chapter, and all matters and proceedings in or relating to such cases, shall be conducted and determined under this chapter as if such chapter had not been repealed, and that the substantive rights of parties in connection with such cases, matters, and proceedings shall continue to be governed under the laws applicable to such cases, matters, and proceedings as if such chapter had not been repealed, was superceded by the reenactment of this chapter by Pub.L. 109–8, Title X, § 1001(a), Apr. 20, 2005, 119 Stat. 185, set out as a note under 11 U.S.C.A. § 1201.

Pub.L. 105–277, Div. C, Title I, § 149, Oct. 21, 1998, 112 Stat. 2681–610, as amended Pub.L. 106–5, §§ 1, 2, Mar. 30, 1999, 113 Stat. 9; Pub.L. 106–70, §§ 1, 2, Oct. 9, 1999, 113 Stat. 1031; Pub.L. 107–8, §§ 1, 2, May 11, 2001, 115 Stat. 10; Pub.L. 107–17, §§ 1, 2, June 26, 2001, 115 Stat. 151; Pub.L. 107–170, §§ 1, 2, May 7, 2002, 116 Stat. 133; Pub.L. 107–171, Title X, § 10814, May 13, 2002, 116 St. 532; Pub.L. 107–377, § 2, Dec. 19, 2002, 116 Stat. 3115; Pub.L. 108–73, § 2(a), Aug. 15, 2003, 117 Stat. 891; Pub.L. 108–369, § 2(a), Oct. 25, 2004, 118 Stat. 1749, provided that, to take effect on January 1, 2004, chapter 12 of Title 11 [this chapter; 11 U.S.C.A. § 1201 et seq.], as in effect on December 31, 2003, is reenacted for the period beginning on January 1, 2004, and ending on July 1, 2005, but that all cases commenced or pending under this chapter 12, as reenacted under section 149(a) of Pub.L. 105–277, and all matters and proceedings in or relating to such cases, shall be conducted and determined under such chapter as if such chapter were continued in effect after July 1, 2005, and that the substantive rights of parties in connection with such cases, matters, and proceedings shall continue to be governed under the law applicable to such cases, matters, and proceedings as if such chapter were continued in effect after July 1, 2005, was superceded by the reenactment of this chapter by Pub.L. 109–8, Title X, § 1001(a), Apr. 20, 2005, 119 Stat. 185, set out as a note under 11 U.S.C.A. § 1201.

LIBRARY REFERENCES

American Digest System

Bankruptcy ⬤�067330;2430.1 to 2434, 3035.1 to 3038, 3062.

Key Number System Topic No. 51.

Corpus Juris Secundum

CJS Bankruptcy § 278, Parties Defendant; Sovereign Immunity.

CJS Bankruptcy § 516, Family Farmer Debt Adjustment Cases.

CJS Bankruptcy § 858, How to Provide Adequate Protection.

§ 1206. Sales free of interests

After notice and a hearing, in addition to the authorization contained in section 363(f), the trustee in a case under this chapter may sell property under section 363(b) and (c) free and clear of any interest in such property of an entity other than the estate if the property is farmland, farm equipment, or property used to carry out a commercial fishing operation (including a commercial fishing vessel), except that the proceeds of such sale shall be subject to such interest.
(Added and amended Pub.L. 99–554, Title II, § 255, Title III, § 302(f), Oct. 27, 1986, 100 Stat. 3108, 3124; Pub.L. 103–65, § 1, Aug. 6, 1993, 107 Stat. 311; Pub.L. 105–277, Div. C, Title I, § 149(a), Oct. 21, 1998, 112 Stat. 2681–610; Pub.L. 106–5, § 1(1), (2), Mar. 30, 1999, 113 Stat. 9; Pub.L. 106–70, § 1, Oct. 9, 1999, 113 Stat. 1031; Pub.L. 107–8, § 1, May 11, 2001, 115 Stat. 10; Pub.L. 107–17, § 1, June 26, 2001, 115 Stat. 151; Pub.L. 107–170, § 1, May 7, 2002, 116 Stat. 133; Pub.L. 107–171, Title X, § 10814(a), May 13, 2002, 116 Stat. 532; Pub.L. 107–377, § 2(a), Dec. 19, 2002, 116 Stat. 3115; Pub.L. 108–73, § 2(a), Aug. 15, 2003, 117 Stat. 891; Pub.L. 108–369, § 2(a), Oct. 25, 2004, 118 Stat. 1749; Pub.L. 109–8, Title X, §§ 1001(a)(1), 1007(c)(3), Apr. 20, 2005, 119 Stat. 185, 188.)

HISTORICAL AND STATUTORY NOTES

Revision Notes and Legislative Reports

1986 Acts. House Report No. 99–764 and House Conference Report No. 99–958, see 1986 U.S. Code Cong. and Adm. News, p. 5227.

1993 Acts. House Report No. 103–32, see 1993 U.S. Code Cong. and Adm. News, p. 373.

1998 Acts. Statement by President, see 1998 U.S. Code Cong. and Adm. News, p. 582.

1999 Acts. Statement by President, see 1999 U.S. Code Cong. and Adm. News, p. 4.

Statement by President, see 1999 U.S. Code Cong. and Adm. News, p. 102.

2001 Acts. House Report No. 107-2, see 2001 U.S. Code Cong. and Adm. News, p. 6.

2005 Acts. House Report No. 109-31(Part I), see 2005 U.S. Code Cong. and Adm. News, p. 88.

Amendments

2005 Amendments. Pub.L. 109-8, § 1001(a)(1), reenacted this section as in effect on June 30, 2005, requiring no change in text; see Pub.L. 109-8, § 1001, set out as a note under 11 U.S.C.A. 1201.

Pub.L. 109-8, § 1007(c)(3), struck out "if the property is farmland or farm equipment" and inserted "if the property is farmland, farm equipment, or property used to carry out a commercial fishing operation (including a commercial fishing vessel)".

2004 Amendments. Pub.L. 108-369, § 2(a), extended effective date of repeal of this section to July 1, 2005, and so required no change in text.

2003 Amendments. Pub.L. 108-73, § 2(a), extended effective date of repeal of this section to Jan. 1, 2004, and so required no change in text.

2002 Amendments. Pub.L. 107-377, § 2(a), extended effective date of repeal of this section to July 1, 2003, and so required no change in text.

Pub.L. 107-171, § 10814(a), extended effective date of repeal of this section to Jan. 1, 2003, and so required no change in text.

Pub.L. 107-170, § 1, extended effective date of repeal of this section to June 1, 2002, and so required no change in text.

2001 Amendments. Pub.L. 107-17, § 1, extended effective date of repeal of this section to Oct. 1, 2001, and so required no change in text.

Pub.L. 107-8, § 1, extended effective date of repeal of this section to June 1, 2001, and so required no change in text.

1999 Amendments. Pub.L. 106-70, § 1, extended effective date of repeal of this section to July 1, 2000, and so required no change in text.

Pub.L. 106-5, § 1(1), (2), extended effective date of repeal of this section to Oct. 1, 1999, and so required no change in text.

1998 Amendments. Pub.L. 105-277, § 149(a), temporarily reenacted this section, which had been repealed effective Oct. 1, 1998 by Pub.L. 99-554, § 302(f).

1993 Amendments. Pub.L. 103-65, § 1, extended effective date of repeal of this section to Oct. 1, 1998.

1986 Amendments. Pub.L. 99-554, § 302(f), as amended by Pub.L. 103-65, § 1, repealed section effective Oct. 1, 1998. Prior to amendment by Pub.L. 103-65, repeal of section was to have taken effect on Oct. 1, 1993.

Effective and Applicability Provisions

2005 Acts. Amendments by Pub.L. 109-8 effective, except as otherwise provided, 180 days after April 20, 2005, and inapplicable with respect to cases commenced under Title 11 before the effective date, see Pub.L. 109-8, § 1501, set out as a note under 11 U.S.C.A. § 101.

2004 Acts. Amendment by Pub.L. 108-369, § 2(a), extending to July 1, 2005, the date of repeal of this chapter, to take

effect Jan. 1, 2004, see Pub.L. 108-369, § 2(b), set out as a note under 11 U.S.C.A. § 1201.

2003 Acts. Amendment by Pub.L. 108-73, § 2(a), extending to Jan. 1, 2004, the date of repeal of this chapter, to take effect July 1, 2003, see Pub.L. 108-73, § 2(b), set out as a note under 11 U.S.C.A. § 1201.

2002 Acts. Amendment by Pub.L. 107-377, § 2(a), extending to July 1, 2003, the date of repeal of this chapter, to take effect Jan. 1, 2003, see Pub.L. 107-377, § 2(b), set out as a note under 11 U.S.C.A. § 1201.

Amendment by Pub.L. 107-171, extending to Jan. 1, 2003, the date of repeal of this chapter, to take effect June 1, 2002, see section 10814(b) of Pub.L. 107-171, set out as a note under 11 U.S.C.A. § 1201.

Amendment by Pub.L. 107-170, extending to June 1, 2002, the date of repeal of this chapter, to take effect October 1, 2001, see section 2 of Pub.L. 107-170, set out as a note under 11 U.S.C.A. § 1201.

2001 Acts. Amendment by Pub.L. 107-17, extending to October 1, 2001, the date of repeal of this chapter, to take effect June 1, 2001, see section 2 of Pub.L. 107-17, set out as a note under 11 U.S.C.A. § 1201.

Amendment by Pub.L. 107-8, extending to June 1, 2001, the date of repeal of this chapter, to take effect July 1, 2000, see section 2 of Pub.L. 107-8, set out as a note under 11 U.S.C.A. § 1201.

1999 Acts. Amendment by Pub.L. 106-70, extending to July 1, 2000, the date of repeal of this chapter, to take effect Oct. 1, 1999, see section 2 of Pub.L. 106-70, set out as a note under section 1201 of this title.

Amendment by Pub.L. 106-5, extending to Oct. 1, 1999 the date of repeal of this chapter, to take effect Apr. 1, 1999, see section 2 of Pub.L. 106-5, set out as a note under section 1201 of this title.

1998 Acts. Section reenacted, eff. Oct. 1, 1998, for the period beginning on Oct. 1, 1998, and ending on Apr. 1, 1999, but all cases commenced or pending under this chapter 12, as reenacted under section 149(a) of Pub.L. 105-277, and all matters and proceedings in or relating to such cases, to be conducted and determined under such chapter as if such chapter were continued in effect after Apr. 1, 1999, and the substantive rights of parties in connection with such cases, matters, and proceedings to continue to be governed under the law applicable to such cases, matters, and proceedings as if such chapter were continued in effect after Apr. 1, 1999, see section 149 of Pub.L. 105-277, set out as a note under section 1201 of this title.

1993 Acts. Amendment by Pub.L. 103-65, extending to Oct. 1, 1998 the date of repeal of this chapter, to take effect Aug. 6, 1993, see section 3 of Pub.L. 103-65, set out as a note under section 1221 of this title.

1986 Acts. Section repealed effective Oct. 1, 1998, see section 302(f) of Pub.L. 99-554, as amended, set out in a note under section 581 of Title 28. However, for extension of provisions, see section 149 of Pub.L. 105-277, set out as a note under section 1201 of this title.

Section effective 30 days after Oct. 27, 1986, but not applicable to cases commenced under this title before that date, see section 302(a), (c)(1) of Pub.L. 99-554, set out as a note under section 581 of Title 28, Judiciary and Judicial Procedure.

Reenactment of Chapter

This section as in effect on June 30, 2005, reenacted effective July 1, 2005, see Pub.L. 109–8, § 1001(a), set out as a note under 11 U.S.C.A. § 1201.

Repeal of Chapter; Extension of Provisions

Pub.L. 99–554, Title III, § 302(f), Oct. 27, 1986, 100 Stat. 3124, as amended Pub.L. 103–65, § 1, Aug. 6, 1993, 107 Stat. 311, which provided that, effective Oct. 1, 1998, this chapter is repealed, but that all cases commenced or pending under this chapter, and all matters and proceedings in or relating to such cases, shall be conducted and determined under this chapter as if such chapter had not been repealed, and that the substantive rights of parties in connection with such cases, matters, and proceedings shall continue to be governed under the laws applicable to such cases, matters, and proceedings as if such chapter had not been repealed, was superceded by the reenactment of this chapter by Pub.L. 109–8, Title X, § 1001(a), Apr. 20, 2005, 119 Stat. 185, set out as a note under 11 U.S.C.A. § 1201.

Pub.L. 105–277, Div. C, Title I, § 149, Oct. 21, 1998, 112 Stat. 2681–610, as amended Pub.L. 106–5, §§ 1, 2, Mar. 30, 1999, 113 Stat. 9; Pub.L. 106–70, §§ 1, 2, Oct. 9, 1999, 113 Stat. 1031; Pub.L. 107–8, §§ 1, 2, May 11, 2001, 115 Stat. 10; Pub.L. 107–17, §§ 1, 2, June 26, 2001, 115 Stat. 151; Pub.L. 107–170, §§ 1, 2, May 7, 2002, 116 Stat. 133; Pub.L. 107–171, Title X, § 10814, May 13, 2002, 116 St. 532; Pub.L. 107–377, § 2, Dec. 19, 2002, 116 Stat. 3115; Pub.L. 108–73, § 2(a), Aug. 15, 2003, 117 Stat. 891; Pub.L. 108–369, § 2(a), Oct. 25, 2004, 118 Stat. 1749, provided that, to take effect on January 1, 2004, chapter 12 of Title 11 [this chapter; 11 U.S.C.A. § 1201 et seq.], as in effect on December 31, 2003, is reenacted for the period beginning on January 1, 2004, and ending on July 1, 2005, but that all cases commenced or pending under this chapter 12, as reenacted under section 149(a) of Pub.L. 105–277, and all matters and proceedings in or relating to such cases, shall be conducted and determined under such chapter as if such chapter were continued in effect after July 1, 2005, and that the substantive rights of parties in connection with such cases, matters, and proceedings shall continue to be governed under the law applicable to such cases, matters, and proceedings as if such chapter were continued in effect after July 1, 2005, was superceded by the reenactment of this chapter by Pub.L. 109–8, Title X, § 1001(a), Apr. 20, 2005, 119 Stat. 185, set out as a note under 11 U.S.C.A. § 1201.

LIBRARY REFERENCES

American Digest System

Bankruptcy ⊙⇒3078(1) to 3078(3), 3073.
Key Number System Topic No. 51.

Corpus Juris Secundum

CJS Bankruptcy § 278, Parties Defendant; Sovereign Immunity.

CJS Bankruptcy § 885, Sale of Farmland or Farm Equipment in Chapter 12 Cases.

§ 1207. Property of the estate

(a) Property of the estate includes, in addition to the property specified in section 541 of this title—

(1) all property of the kind specified in such section that the debtor acquires after the commence-ment of the case but before the case is closed, dismissed, or converted to a case under chapter 7 of this title, whichever occurs first; and

(2) earnings from services performed by the debtor after the commencement of the case but before the case is closed, dismissed, or converted to a case under chapter 7 of this title, whichever occurs first.

(b) Except as provided in section 1204, a confirmed plan, or an order confirming a plan, the debtor shall remain in possession of all property of the estate.

(Added and amended Pub.L. 99–554, Title II, § 255, Title III, § 302(f), Oct. 27, 1986, 100 Stat. 3108, 3124; Pub.L. 103–65, § 1, Aug. 6, 1993, 107 Stat. 311; Pub.L. 105–277, Div. C, Title I, § 149(a), Oct. 21, 1998, 112 Stat. 2681–610; Pub.L. 106–5, § 1(1), (2), Mar. 30, 1999, 113 Stat. 9; Pub.L. 106–70, § 1, Oct. 9, 1999, 113 Stat. 1031; Pub.L. 107–8, § 1, May 11, 2001, 115 Stat. 10; Pub.L. 107–17, § 1, June 26, 2001, 115 Stat. 151; Pub.L. 107–170, § 1, May 7, 2002, 116 Stat. 133; Pub.L. 107–171, Title X, § 10814(a), May 13, 2002, 116 Stat. 532; Pub.L. 107–377, § 2(a), Dec. 19, 2002, 116 Stat. 3115; Pub.L. 108–73, § 2(a), Aug. 15, 2003, 117 Stat. 891; Pub.L. 108–369, § 2(a), Oct. 25, 2004, 118 Stat. 1749; Pub.L. 109–8, Title X, § 1001(a)(1), Apr. 20, 2005, 119 Stat. 185.)

HISTORICAL AND STATUTORY NOTES

Revision Notes and Legislative Reports

1986 Acts. House Report No. 99–764 and House Conference Report No. 99–958, see 1986 U.S. Code Cong. and Adm. News, p. 5227.

1993 Acts. House Report No. 103–32, see 1993 U.S. Code Cong. and Adm. News, p. 373.

1998 Acts. Statement by President, see 1998 U.S. Code Cong. and Adm. News, p. 582.

1999 Acts. Statement by President, see 1999 U.S. Code Cong. and Adm. News, p. 4.

Statement by President, see 1999 U.S. Code Cong. and Adm. News, p. 102.

2001 Acts. House Report No. 107–2, see 2001 U.S. Code Cong. and Adm. News, p. 6.

2005 Acts. House Report No. 109–31(Part I), see 2005 U.S. Code Cong. and Adm. News, p. 88.

Amendments

2005 Amendments. Pub.L. 109–8, § 1001(a)(1), reenacted this section as in effect on June 30, 2005, requiring no change in text; see Pub.L. 109–8, § 1001, set out as a note under 11 U.S.C.A. § 1201.

2004 Amendments. Pub.L. 108–369, § 2(a), extended effective date of repeal of this section to July 1, 2005, and so required no change in text.

2003 Amendments. Pub.L. 108–73, § 2(a), extended effective date of repeal of this section to Jan. 1, 2004, and so required no change in text.

2002 Amendments. Pub.L. 107–377, § 2(a), extended effective date of repeal of this section to July 1, 2003, and so required no change in text.

Pub.L. 107–171, § 10814(a), extended effective date of repeal of this section to Jan. 1, 2003, and so required no change in text.

Pub.L. 107–170, § 1, extended effective date of repeal of this section to June 1, 2002, and so required no change in text.

2001 Amendments. Pub.L. 107–17, § 1, extended effective date of repeal of this section to Oct. 1, 2001, and so required no change in text.

Pub.L. 107–8, § 1, extended effective date of repeal of this section to June 1, 2001, and so required no change in text.

1999 Amendments. Pub.L. 106–70, § 1, extended effective date of repeal of this section to July 1, 2000, and so required no change in text.

Pub.L. 106–5, § 1(1), (2), extended effective date of repeal of this section to Oct. 1, 1999, and so required no change in text.

1998 Amendments. Pub.L. 105–277, § 149(a), temporarily reenacted this section, which had been repealed effective Oct. 1, 1998 by Pub.L. 99–554, § 302(f).

1993 Amendments. Pub.L. 103–65, § 1, extended effective date of repeal of this section to Oct. 1, 1998.

1986 Amendments. Pub.L. 99–554, § 302(f), as amended by Pub.L. 103–65, § 1, repealed section effective Oct. 1, 1998. Prior to amendment by Pub.L. 103–65, repeal of section was to have taken effect on Oct. 1, 1993.

Effective and Applicability Provisions

2005 Acts. Amendments by Pub.L. 109–8 effective, except as otherwise provided, 180 days after April 20, 2005, and inapplicable with respect to cases commenced under Title 11 before the effective date, see Pub.L. 109–8, § 1501, set out as a note under 11 U.S.C.A. § 101.

2004 Acts. Amendment by Pub.L. 108–369, § 2(a), extending to July 1, 2005, the date of repeal of this chapter, to take effect Jan. 1, 2004, see Pub.L. 108–369, § 2(b), set out as a note under 11 U.S.C.A. § 1201.

2003 Acts. Amendment by Pub.L. 108–73, § 2(a), extending to Jan. 1, 2004, the date of repeal of this chapter, to take effect July 1, 2003, see Pub.L. 108–73, § 2(b), set out as a note under 11 U.S.C.A. § 1201.

2002 Acts. Amendment by Pub.L. 107–377, § 2(a), extending to July 1, 2003, the date of repeal of this chapter, to take effect Jan. 1, 2003, see Pub.L. 107–377, § 2(b), set out as a note under 11 U.S.C.A. § 1201.

Amendment by Pub.L. 107–171, extending to Jan. 1, 2003, the date of repeal of this chapter, to take effect June 1, 2002, see section 10814(b) of Pub.L. 107–171, set out as a note under 11 U.S.C.A. § 1201.

Amendment by Pub.L. 107–170, extending to June 1, 2002, the date of repeal of this chapter, to take effect October 1, 2001, see section 2 of Pub.L. 107–170, set out as a note under 11 U.S.C.A. § 1201.

2001 Acts. Amendment by Pub.L. 107–17, extending to October 1, 2001, the date of repeal of this chapter, to take effect June 1, 2001, see section 2 of Pub.L. 107–17, set out as a note under 11 U.S.C.A. § 1201.

Amendment by Pub.L. 107–8, extending to June 1, 2001, the date of repeal of this chapter, to take effect July 1, 2000, see section 2 of Pub.L. 107–8, set out as a note under 11 U.S.C.A. § 1201.

1999 Acts. Amendment by Pub.L. 106–70, extending to July 1, 2000, the date of repeal of this chapter, to take effect Oct. 1, 1999, see section 2 of Pub.L. 106–70, set out as a note under section 1201 of this title.

Amendment by Pub.L. 106–5, extending to Oct. 1, 1999 the date of repeal of this chapter, to take effect Apr. 1, 1999, see section 2 of Pub.L. 106–5, set out as a note under section 1201 of this title.

1998 Acts. Section reenacted, eff. Oct. 1, 1998, for the period beginning on Oct. 1, 1998, and ending on Apr. 1, 1999, but all cases commenced or pending under this chapter 12, as reenacted under section 149(a) of Pub.L. 105–277, and all matters and proceedings in or relating to such cases, to be conducted and determined under such chapter as if such chapter were continued in effect after Apr. 1, 1999, and the substantive rights of parties in connection with such cases, matters, and proceedings to continue to be governed under the law applicable to such cases, matters, and proceedings as if such chapter were continued in effect after Apr. 1, 1999, see section 149 of Pub.L. 105–277, set out as a note under section 1201 of this title.

1993 Acts. Amendment by Pub.L. 103–65, extending to Oct. 1, 1998 the date of repeal of this chapter, to take effect Aug. 6, 1993, see section 3 of Pub.L. 103–65, set out as a note under section 1221 of this title.

1986 Acts. Section repealed effective Oct. 1, 1998, see section 302(f) of Pub.L. 99–554, as amended, set out in a note under section 581 of Title 28. However, for extension of provisions, see section 149 of Pub.L. 105–277, set out as a note under section 1201 of this title.

Section effective 30 days after Oct. 27, 1986, but not applicable to cases commenced under this title before that date, see section 302(a), (c)(1) of Pub.L. 99–554, set out as a note under section 581 of Title 28, Judiciary and Judicial Procedure.

Reenactment of Chapter

This section as in effect on June 30, 2005, reenacted effective July 1, 2005, see Pub.L. 109–8, § 1001(a), set out as a note under 11 U.S.C.A. § 1201.

Repeal of Chapter; Extension of Provisions

Pub.L. 99–554, Title III, § 302(f), Oct. 27, 1986, 100 Stat. 3124, as amended Pub.L. 103–65, § 1, Aug. 6, 1993, 107 Stat. 311, which provided that, effective Oct. 1, 1998, this chapter is repealed, but that all cases commenced or pending under this chapter, and all matters and proceedings in or relating to such cases, shall be conducted and determined under this chapter as if such chapter had not been repealed, and that the substantive rights of parties in connection with such cases, matters, and proceedings shall continue to be governed under the laws applicable to such cases, matters, and proceedings as if such chapter had not been repealed, was superceded by the reenactment of this chapter by Pub.L. 109–8, Title X, § 1001(a), Apr. 20, 2005, 119 Stat. 185, set out as a note under 11 U.S.C.A. § 1201.

Pub.L. 105–277, Div. C, Title I, § 149, Oct. 21, 1998, 112 Stat. 2681–610, as amended Pub.L. 106–5, §§ 1, 2, Mar. 30, 1999, 113 Stat. 9; Pub.L. 106–70, §§ 1, 2, Oct. 9, 1999, 113 Stat. 1031; Pub.L. 107–8, §§ 1, 2, May 11, 2001, 115 Stat. 10; Pub.L. 107–17, §§ 1, 2, June 26, 2001, 115 Stat. 151; Pub.L. 107–170, §§ 1, 2, May 7, 2002, 116 Stat. 133; Pub.L. 107–171, Title X, § 10814, May 13, 2002, 116 St. 532; Pub.L. 107–377, § 2, Dec. 19, 2002, 116 Stat. 3115; Pub.L. 108–73, § 2(a), Aug. 15, 2003, 117 Stat. 891; Pub.L. 108–369, § 2(a), Oct. 25, 2004, 118 Stat. 1749, provided that, to take effect on January 1, 2004, chapter 12 of Title 11 [this chapter; 11 U.S.C.A. § 1201 et seq.], as in effect on December 31, 2003, is reenacted for the period beginning on January 1, 2004, and ending on July 1, 2005, but that all cases commenced or pending under this chapter 12, as reenacted under section 149(a) of Pub.L. 105–277, and all matters and proceedings in or relating to such cases, shall be conducted and determined under such chapter as if such chapter were continued in effect after July 1, 2005, and that the substantive rights of parties in connection with such cases, matters, and proceedings shall continue to be governed under the law applicable to such cases, matters, and proceedings as if such chapter were continued in effect after July 1, 2005, was superceded by the reenactment of this chapter by Pub.L. 109–8, Title X, § 1001(a), Apr. 20, 2005, 119 Stat. 185, set out as a note under 11 U.S.C.A. § 1201.

LIBRARY REFERENCES

American Digest System

Bankruptcy ⊕2558.

Key Number System Topic No. 51.

Corpus Juris Secundum

CJS Bankruptcy § 136, Rights, Powers, and Duties of Debtor in Possession.

CJS Bankruptcy § 561, Property Acquired Postpetition.

CJS Bankruptcy § 624, Surrender of Property of Estate and Recorded Information to Trustee.

§ 1208.   Conversion or dismissal

(a) The debtor may convert a case under this chapter to a case under chapter 7 of this title at any time. Any waiver of the right to convert under this subsection is unenforceable.

(b) On request of the debtor at any time, if the case has not been converted under section 706 or 1112 of this title, the court shall dismiss a case under this chapter. Any waiver of the right to dismiss under this subsection is unenforceable.

(c) On request of a party in interest, and after notice and a hearing, the court may dismiss a case under this chapter for cause, including—

(1) unreasonable delay, or gross mismanagement, by the debtor that is prejudicial to creditors;

(2) nonpayment of any fees and charges required under chapter 123 of title 28;

(3) failure to file a plan timely under section 1221 of this title;

(4) failure to commence making timely payments required by a confirmed plan;

(5) denial of confirmation of a plan under section 1225 of this title and denial of a request made for additional time for filing another plan or a modification of a plan;

(6) material default by the debtor with respect to a term of a confirmed plan;

(7) revocation of the order of confirmation under section 1230 of this title, and denial of confirmation of a modified plan under section 1229 of this title;

(8) termination of a confirmed plan by reason of the occurrence of a condition specified in the plan;

(9) continuing loss to or diminution of the estate and absence of a reasonable likelihood of rehabilitation; and

(10) failure of the debtor to pay any domestic support obligation that first becomes payable after the date of the filing of the petition.

(d) On request of a party in interest, and after notice and a hearing, the court may dismiss a case under this chapter or convert a case under this chapter to a case under chapter 7 of this title upon a showing that the debtor has committed fraud in connection with the case.

(e) Notwithstanding any other provision of this section, a case may not be converted to a case under another chapter of this title unless the debtor may be a debtor under such chapter.

(Added and amended Pub.L. 99–554, Title II, § 255, Title III, § 302(f), Oct. 27, 1986, 100 Stat. 3108, 3124; Pub.L. 103–65, § 1, Aug. 6, 1993, 107 Stat. 311; Pub.L. 105–277, Div. C, Title I, § 149(a), Oct. 21, 1998, 112 Stat. 2681–610; Pub.L. 106–5, § 1(1), (2), Mar. 30, 1999, 113 Stat. 9; Pub.L. 106–70, § 1, Oct. 9, 1999, 113 Stat. 1031; Pub.L. 107–8, § 1, May 11, 2001, 115 Stat. 10; Pub.L. 107–17, § 1, June 26, 2001, 115 Stat. 151; Pub.L. 107–170, § 1, May 7, 2002, 116 Stat. 133; Pub.L. 107–171, Title X, § 10814(a), May 13, 2002, 116 Stat. 532; Pub.L. 107–377, § 2(a), Dec. 19, 2002, 116 Stat. 3115; Pub.L. 108–73, § 2(a), Aug. 15, 2003, 117 Stat. 891; Pub.L. 108–369, § 2(a), Oct. 25, 2004, 118 Stat. 1749; Pub.L. 109–8, Title II, § 213(2), Title X, § 1001(a)(1), Apr. 20, 2005, 119 Stat. 52, 185.)

HISTORICAL AND STATUTORY NOTES

Revision Notes and Legislative Reports

1986 Acts. House Report No. 99–764 and House Conference Report No. 99–958, see 1986 U.S. Code Cong. and Adm. News, p. 5227.

1993 Acts. House Report No. 103–32, see 1993 U.S. Code Cong. and Adm. News, p. 373.

1998 Acts. Statement by President, see 1998 U.S. Code Cong. and Adm. News, p. 582.

1999 Acts. Statement by President, see 1999 U.S. Code Cong. and Adm. News, p. 4.

Statement by President, see 1999 U.S. Code Cong. and Adm. News, p. 102.

2001 Acts. House Report No. 107–2, see 2001 U.S. Code Cong. and Adm. News, p. 6.

2005 Acts. House Report No. 109–31(Part I), see 2005 U.S. Code Cong. and Adm. News, p. 88.

Amendments

2005 Amendments. Pub.L. 109–8, § 1001(a)(1), reenacted this section as in effect on June 30, 2005, requiring no change in text; see Pub.L. 109–8, § 1001, set out as a note under 11 U.S.C.A. § 1201.

Subsec. (c)(8). Pub.L. 109–8, § 213(2)(A), struck out "or" at the end of par. (8).

Subsec. (c)(9). Pub.L. 109–8, § 213(2)(B), substituted "; and" for the period at the end of par. (9).

Subsec. (c)(10). Pub.L. 109–8, § 213(2)(C), added par. (10).

2004 Amendments. Pub.L. 108–369, § 2(a), extended effective date of repeal of this section to July 1, 2005, and so required no change in text.

2003 Amendments. Pub.L. 108–73, § 2(a), extended effective date of repeal of this section to Jan. 1, 2004, and so required no change in text.

2002 Amendments. Pub.L. 107–377, § 2(a), extended effective date of repeal of this section to July 1, 2003, and so required no change in text.

Pub.L. 107–171, § 10814(a), extended effective date of repeal of this section to Jan. 1, 2003, and so required no change in text.

Pub.L. 107–170, § 1, extended effective date of repeal of this section to June 1, 2002, and so required no change in text.

2001 Amendments. Pub.L. 107–17, § 1, extended effective date of repeal of this section to Oct. 1, 2001, and so required no change in text.

Pub.L. 107–8, § 1, extended effective date of repeal of this section to June 1, 2001, and so required no change in text.

1999 Amendments. Pub.L. 106–70, § 1, extended effective date of repeal of this section to July 1, 2000, and so required no change in text.

Pub.L. 106–5, § 1(1), (2), extended effective date of repeal of this section to Oct. 1, 1999, and so required no change in text.

1998 Amendments. Pub.L. 105–277, § 149(a), temporarily reenacted this section, which had been repealed effective Oct. 1, 1998 by Pub.L. 99–554, § 302(f).

1993 Amendments. Pub.L. 103–65, § 1, extended effective date of repeal of this section to Oct. 1, 1998.

1986 Amendments. Pub.L. 99–554, § 302(f), as amended by Pub.L. 103–65, § 1, repealed section effective Oct. 1, 1998. Prior to amendment by Pub.L. 103–65, repeal of section was to have taken effect on Oct. 1, 1993.

Effective and Applicability Provisions

2005 Acts. Amendments by Pub.L. 109–8 effective, except as otherwise provided, 180 days after April 20, 2005, and inapplicable with respect to cases commenced under Title 11 before the effective date, see Pub.L. 109–8, § 1501, set out as a note under 11 U.S.C.A. § 101.

2004 Acts. Amendment by Pub.L. 108–369, § 2(a), extending to July 1, 2005, the date of repeal of this chapter, to take effect Jan. 1, 2004, see Pub.L. 108–369, § 2(b), set out as a note under 11 U.S.C.A. § 1201.

2003 Acts. Amendment by Pub.L. 108–73, § 2(a), extending to Jan. 1, 2004, the date of repeal of this chapter, to take effect July 1, 2003, see Pub.L. 108–73, § 2(b), set out as a note under 11 U.S.C.A. § 1201.

2002 Acts. Amendment by Pub.L. 107–377, § 2(a), extending to July 1, 2003, the date of repeal of this chapter, to take effect Jan. 1, 2003, see Pub.L. 107–377, § 2(b), set out as a note under 11 U.S.C.A. § 1201.

Amendment by Pub.L. 107–171, extending to Jan. 1, 2003, the date of repeal of this chapter, to take effect June 1, 2002, see section 10814(b) of Pub.L. 107–171, set out as a note under 11 U.S.C.A. § 1201.

Amendment by Pub.L. 107–170, extending to June 1, 2002, the date of repeal of this chapter, to take effect Oct. 1, 2001, see section 2 of Pub.L. 107–170, set out as a note under 11 U.S.C.A. § 1201.

2001 Acts. Amendment by Pub.L. 107–17, extending to Oct. 1, 2001, the date of repeal of this chapter, to take effect June 1, 2001, see section 2 of Pub.L. 107–17, set out as a note under 11 U.S.C.A. § 1201.

Amendment by Pub.L. 107–8, extending to June 1, 2001, the date of repeal of this chapter, to take effect July 1, 2000, see section 2 of Pub.L. 107–8, set out as a note under 11 U.S.C.A. § 1201.

1999 Acts. Amendment by Pub.L. 106–70, extending to July 1, 2000, the date of repeal of this chapter, to take effect Oct. 1, 1999, see section 2 of Pub.L. 106–70, set out as a note under section 1201 of this title.

Amendment by Pub.L. 106–5, extending to Oct. 1, 1999, the date of repeal of this chapter, to take effect Apr. 1, 1999, see section 2 of Pub.L. 106–5, set out as a note under section 1201 of this title.

1998 Acts. Section reenacted, eff. Oct. 1, 1998, for the period beginning on Oct. 1, 1998, and ending on Apr. 1, 1999, but all cases commenced or pending under this chapter 12, as reenacted under section 149(a) of Pub.L. 105–277, and all matters and proceedings in or relating to such cases, to be conducted and determined under such chapter as if such chapter were continued in effect after Apr. 1, 1999, and the substantive rights of parties in connection with such cases, matters, and proceedings to continue to be governed under the law applicable to such cases, matters, and proceedings as if such chapter were continued in effect after Apr. 1, 1999, see section 149 of Pub.L. 105–277, set out as a note under section 1201 of this title.

1993 Acts. Amendment by Pub.L. 103–65, extending to Oct. 1, 1998 the date of repeal of this chapter, to take effect Aug. 6, 1993, see section 3 of Pub.L. 103–65, set out as a note under section 1221 of this title.

1986 Acts. Section repealed effective Oct. 1, 1998, see section 302(f) of Pub.L. 99–554, as amended, set out in a note under section 581 of Title 28. However, for extension of provisions, see section 149 of Pub.L. 105–277, set out as a note under section 1201 of this title.

Section effective 30 days after Oct. 27, 1986, but not applicable to cases commenced under this title before that date, see section 302(a), (c)(1) of Pub.L. 99–554, set out as a note under section 581 of Title 28, Judiciary and Judicial Procedure.

Reenactment of Chapter

This section as in effect on June 30, 2005, reenacted effective July 1, 2005, see Pub.L. 109–8, § 1001(a), set out as a note under 11 U.S.C.A. § 1201.

Repeal of Chapter; Extension of Provisions

Pub.L. 99–554, Title III, § 302(f), Oct. 27, 1986, 100 Stat. 3124, as amended Pub.L. 103–65, § 1, Aug. 6, 1993, 107 Stat. 311, which provided that, effective Oct. 1, 1998, this chapter is repealed, but that all cases commenced or pending under this chapter, and all matters and proceedings in or relating to such cases, shall be conducted and determined under this chapter as if such chapter had not been repealed, and that the substantive rights of parties in connection with such cases, matters, and proceedings shall continue to be governed under the laws applicable to such cases, matters, and proceedings as if such chapter had not been repealed, was superceded by the reenactment of this chapter by Pub.L. 109–8, Title X, § 1001(a), Apr. 20, 2005, 119 Stat. 185, set out as a note under 11 U.S.C.A. § 1201.

Pub.L. 105–277, Div. C, Title I, § 149, Oct. 21, 1998, 112 Stat. 2681–610, as amended Pub.L. 106–5, §§ 1, 2, Mar. 30, 1999, 113 Stat. 9; Pub.L. 106–70, §§ 1, 2, Oct. 9, 1999, 113 Stat. 1031; Pub.L. 107–8, §§ 1, 2, May 11, 2001, 115 Stat. 10; Pub.L. 107–17, §§ 1, 2, June 26, 2001, 115 Stat. 151; Pub.L. 107–170, §§ 1, 2, May 7, 2002, 116 Stat. 133; Pub.L. 107–171, Title X, § 10814, May 13, 2002, 116 St. 532; Pub.L. 107–377, § 2, Dec. 19, 2002, 116 Stat. 3115; Pub.L. 108–73, § 2(a), Aug. 15, 2003, 117 Stat. 891; Pub.L. 108–369, § 2(a), Oct. 25, 2004, 118 Stat. 1749, provided that, to take effect on January 1, 2004, chapter 12 of Title 11 [this chapter; 11 U.S.C.A. § 1201 et seq.], as in effect on December 31, 2003, is reenacted for the period beginning on January 1, 2004, and ending on July 1, 2005, but that all cases commenced or pending under this chapter 12, as reenacted under section 149(a) of Pub.L. 105–277, and all matters and proceedings in or relating to such cases, shall be conducted and determined under such chapter as if such chapter were continued in effect after July 1, 2005, and that the substantive rights of parties in connection with such cases, matters, and proceedings shall continue to be governed under the law applicable to such cases, matters, and proceedings as if such chapter were continued in effect after July 1, 2005, was superceded by the reenactment of this chapter by Pub.L. 109–8, Title X, § 1001(a), Apr. 20, 2005, 119 Stat. 185, set out as a note under 11 U.S.C.A. § 1201.

CROSS REFERENCES

Conversion from Chapter seven, see 11 USCA § 706.

Dismissal of Chapter thirteen cases where not converted under this section, see 11 USCA § 1307.

Distribution of property of estate converted to Chapter seven, see 11 USCA § 726.

Effect of—

Conversion, see 11 USCA § 348.

Dismissal, see 11 USCA § 349.

Executory contracts and unexpired leases, see 11 USCA § 365.

Liquidation of estate in railroad reorganization cases, see 11 USCA § 1174.

Termination of debtor's taxable period for cases converted to Chapter 7, see 11 USCA § 728.

LIBRARY REFERENCES

American Digest System

Bankruptcy ⬤3673.

Key Number System Topic No. 51.

Corpus Juris Secundum

CJS Bankruptcy § 109, Termination of Service.

CJS Bankruptcy § 455, Chapter 12.

CJS Bankruptcy § 927, Exercising Right in Chapter 7 Cases.

CJS Bankruptcy § 1102, Priority of Particular Distribution Classes.

SUBCHAPTER II—THE PLAN

§ 1221.   Filing of plan

The debtor shall file a plan not later than 90 days after the order for relief under this chapter, except that the court may extend such period if the need for an extension is attributable to circumstances for which the debtor should not justly be held accountable.

(Added and amended Pub.L. 99–554, Title II, § 255, Title III, § 302(f), Oct. 27, 1986, 100 Stat. 3109, 3124; Pub.L. 103–65, §§ 1, 2, Aug. 6, 1993, 107 Stat. 311; Pub.L. 105–277, Div. C, Title I, § 149(a), Oct. 21, 1998, 112 Stat. 2681–610; Pub.L. 106–5, § 1(1), (2), Mar. 30, 1999, 113 Stat. 9; Pub.L. 106–70, § 1, Oct. 9, 1999, 113 Stat. 1031; Pub.L. 107–8, § 1, May 11, 2001, 115 Stat. 10; Pub.L. 107–17, § 1, June 26, 2001, 115 Stat. 151; Pub.L. 107–170, § 1, May 7, 2002, 116 Stat. 133; Pub.L. 107–171, Title X, § 10814(a), May 13, 2002, 116 Stat. 532; Pub.L. 107–377, § 2(a), Dec. 19, 2002, 116 Stat. 3115; Pub.L. 108–73, § 2(a), Aug. 15, 2003, 117 Stat. 891; Pub.L. 108–369, § 2(a), Oct. 25, 2004, 118 Stat. 1749; Pub.L. 109–8, Title X, § 1001(a)(1), Apr. 20, 2005, 119 Stat. 185.)

HISTORICAL AND STATUTORY NOTES

Revision Notes and Legislative Reports

1986 Acts. House Report No. 99–764 and House Conference Report No. 99–958, see 1986 U.S. Code Cong. and Adm. News, p. 5227.

1993 Acts. House Report No. 103–32, see 1993 U.S. Code Cong. and Adm. News, p. 373.

1998 Acts. Statement by President, see 1998 U.S. Code Cong. and Adm. News, p. 582.

1999 Acts. Statement by President, see 1999 U.S. Code Cong. and Adm. News, p. 4.

Statement by President, see 1999 U.S. Code Cong. and Adm. News, p. 102.

2001 Acts. House Report No. 107–2, see 2001 U.S. Code Cong. and Adm. News, p. 6.

2005 Acts. House Report No. 109–31(Part I), see 2005 U.S. Code Cong. and Adm. News, p. 88.

Amendments

2005 Amendments. Pub.L. 109–8, § 1001(a)(1), reenacted this section as in effect on June 30, 2005, requiring no change in text; see Pub.L. 109–8, § 1001, set out as a note under 11 U.S.C.A. § 1201.

2004 Amendments. Pub.L. 108–369, § 2(a), extended effective date of repeal of this section to July 1, 2005, and so required no change in text.

2003 Amendments. Pub.L. 108–73, § 2(a), extended effective date of repeal of this section to Jan. 1, 2004, and so required no change in text.

2002 Amendments. Pub.L. 107–377, § 2(a), extended effective date of repeal of this section to July 1, 2003, and so required no change in text.

Pub.L. 107–171, § 10814(a), extended effective date of repeal of this section to Jan. 1, 2003, and so required no change in text.

Pub.L. 107–170, § 1, extended effective date of repeal of this section to June 1, 2002, and so required no change in text.

2001 Amendments. Pub.L. 107–17, § 1, extended effective date of repeal of this section to Oct. 1, 2001, and so required no change in text.

Pub.L. 107–8, § 1, extended effective date of repeal of this section to June 1, 2001, and so required no change in text.

1999 Amendments. Pub.L. 106–70, § 1, extended effective date of repeal of this section to July 1, 2000, and so required no change in text.

Pub.L. 106–5, § 1(1), (2), extended effective date of repeal of this section to Oct. 1, 1999, and so required no change in text.

1998 Amendments. Pub.L. 105–277, § 149(a), temporarily reenacted this section, which had been repealed effective Oct. 1, 1998 by Pub.L. 99–554, § 302(f).

1993 Amendments. Pub.L. 103–65, § 1, extended effective date of repeal of this section to Oct. 1, 1998.

Pub.L. 103–65, § 2, substituted "the need for an extension is attributable to circumstances for which the debtor should not justly be held accountable" for "an extension is substantially justified".

1986 Amendments. Pub.L. 99–554, § 302(f), as amended by Pub.L. 103–65, § 1, repealed section effective Oct. 1, 1998. Prior to amendment by Pub.L. 103–65, repeal of section was to have taken effect on Oct. 1, 1993.

Effective and Applicability Provisions

2005 Acts. Amendments by Pub.L. 109–8 effective, except as otherwise provided, 180 days after April 20, 2005, and inapplicable with respect to cases commenced under Title 11 before the effective date, see Pub.L. 109–8, § 1501, set out as a note under 11 U.S.C.A. § 101.

2004 Acts. Amendment by Pub.L. 108–369, § 2(a), extending to July 1, 2005, the date of repeal of this chapter, to take effect Jan. 1, 2004, see Pub.L. 108–369, § 2(b), set out as a note under 11 U.S.C.A. § 1201.

2003 Acts. Amendment by Pub.L. 108–73, § 2(a), extending to Jan. 1, 2004, the date of repeal of this chapter, to take effect July 1, 2003, see Pub.L. 108–73, § 2(b), set out as a note under 11 U.S.C.A. § 1201.

2002 Acts. Amendment by Pub.L. 107–377, § 2(a), extending to July 1, 2003, the date of repeal of this chapter, to take effect Jan. 1, 2003, see Pub.L. 107–377, § 2(b), set out as a note under 11 U.S.C.A. § 1201.

Amendment by Pub.L. 107–171, extending to Jan. 1, 2003, the date of repeal of this chapter, to take effect June 1, 2002, see section 10814(b) of Pub.L. 107–171, set out as a note under 11 U.S.C.A. § 1201.

Amendment by Pub.L. 107–170, extending to June 1, 2002, the date of repeal of this chapter, to take effect October 1, 2001, see section 2 of Pub.L. 107–170, set out as a note under 11 U.S.C.A. § 1201.

2001 Acts. Amendment by Pub.L. 107–17, extending to October 1, 2001, the date of repeal of this chapter, to take effect June 1, 2001, see section 2 of Pub.L. 107–17, set out as a note under 11 U.S.C.A. § 1201.

Amendment by Pub.L. 107–8, extending to June 1, 2001, the date of repeal of this chapter, to take effect July 1, 2000, see section 2 of Pub.L. 107–8, set out as a note under 11 U.S.C.A. § 1201.

1999 Acts. Amendment by Pub.L. 106–70, extending to July 1, 2000, the date of repeal of this chapter, to take effect Oct. 1, 1999, see section 2 of Pub.L. 106–70, set out as a note under section 1201 of this title.

Amendment by Pub.L. 106–5, extending to Oct. 1, 1999 the date of repeal of this chapter, to take effect Apr. 1, 1999, see section 2 of Pub.L. 106–5, set out as a note under section 1201 of this title.

1998 Acts. Section reenacted, eff. Oct. 1, 1998, for the period beginning on Oct. 1, 1998, and ending on Apr. 1, 1999, but all cases commenced or pending under this chapter 12, as reenacted under section 149(a) of Pub.L. 105–277, and all matters and proceedings in or relating to such cases, to be conducted and determined under such chapter as if such chapter were continued in effect after Apr. 1, 1999, and the substantive rights of parties in connection with such cases, matters, and proceedings to continue to be governed under the law applicable to such cases, matters, and proceedings as if such chapter were continued in effect after Apr. 1, 1999, see section 149 of Pub.L. 105–277, set out as a note under 11 U.S.C.A. § 1201.

1993 Acts. Section 3 of Pub.L. 103–65 provided that:

"**(a) Effective date.**—Except as provided in subsection (b), this Act and the amendments made by this Act [amending this section and provisions set out as a note under 28 U.S.C.A. § 581, and extending the date of repeal of this chapter to Oct. 1, 1998] shall take effect on the date of the enactment of this Act [Aug. 6, 1993].

"**(b) Application of amendment made by section 2.**—The amendment made by section 2 [amending this section] shall not apply with respect to cases commenced under title 11 of the United States Code [this title] before the date of the enactment of this Act [Aug. 6, 1993]."

1986 Acts. Section repealed effective Oct. 1, 1998, see section 302(f) of Pub.L. 99–554, as amended, set out as a note under 28 U.S.C.A. § 581. However, for extension of provisions, see section 149 of Pub.L. 105–277, set out as a note under 11 U.S.C.A. § 1201.

Section effective 30 days after Oct. 27, 1986, but not applicable to cases commenced under this title before that date, see section 302(a), (c)(1) of Pub.L. 99–554, set out as a note under 28 U.S.C.A. § 581.

Reenactment of Chapter

This section as in effect on June 30, 2005, reenacted effective July 1, 2005, see Pub.L. 109–8, § 1001(a), set out as a note under 11 U.S.C.A. § 1201.

Repeal of Chapter; Extension of Provisions

Pub.L. 99–554, Title III, § 302(f), Oct. 27, 1986, 100 Stat. 3124, as amended Pub.L. 103–65, § 1, Aug. 6, 1993, 107 Stat. 311, which provided that, effective Oct. 1, 1998, this chapter is repealed, but that all cases commenced or pending under this chapter, and all matters and proceedings in or relating to such cases, shall be conducted and determined under this chapter as if such chapter had not been repealed, and that the substantive rights of parties in connection with such cases, matters, and proceedings shall continue to be governed under the laws applicable to such cases, matters, and proceedings as if such chapter had not been repealed, was superceded by the reenactment of this chapter by Pub.L. 109–8, Title X, § 1001(a), Apr. 20, 2005, 119 Stat. 185, set out as a note under 11 U.S.C.A. § 1201.

Pub.L. 105–277, Div. C, Title I, § 149, Oct. 21, 1998, 112 Stat. 2681–610, as amended Pub.L. 106–5, §§ 1, 2, Mar. 30, 1999, 113 Stat. 9; Pub.L. 106–70, §§ 1, 2, Oct. 9, 1999, 113

Stat. 1031; Pub.L. 107–8, §§ 1, 2, May 11, 2001, 115 Stat. 10; Pub.L. 107–17, §§ 1, 2, June 26, 2001, 115 Stat. 151; Pub.L. 107–170, §§ 1, 2, May 7, 2002, 116 Stat. 133; Pub.L. 107–171, Title X, § 10814, May 13, 2002, 116 St. 532; Pub.L. 107–377, § 2, Dec. 19, 2002, 116 Stat. 3115; Pub.L. 108–73, § 2(a), Aug. 15, 2003, 117 Stat. 891; Pub.L. 108–369, § 2(a), Oct. 25, 2004, 118 Stat. 1749, provided that, to take effect on January 1, 2004, chapter 12 of Title 11 [this chapter; 11 U.S.C.A. § 1201 et seq.], as in effect on December 31, 2003, is reenacted for the period beginning on January 1, 2004, and ending on July 1, 2005, but that all cases commenced or pending under this chapter 12, as reenacted under section 149(a) of Pub.L. 105–277, and all matters and proceedings in or relating to such cases, shall be conducted and determined under such chapter as if such chapter were continued in effect after July 1, 2005, and that the substantive rights of parties in connection with such cases, matters, and proceedings shall continue to be governed under the law applicable to such cases, matters, and proceedings as if such chapter were continued in effect after July 1, 2005, was superceded by the reenactment of this chapter by Pub.L. 109–8, Title X, § 1001(a), Apr. 20, 2005, 119 Stat. 185, set out as a note under 11 U.S.C.A. § 1201.

CROSS REFERENCES

Conversion or dismissal for failure to timely file plan, see 11 USCA § 1208.

Effect of conversion, see 11 USCA § 348.

Filing of plan in—

Chapter nine cases, see 11 USCA § 941.

Chapter thirteen cases, see 11 USCA § 1321.

Who may file plan in Chapter eleven cases, see 11 USCA § 1121.

LIBRARY REFERENCES

American Digest System

Bankruptcy ☞3681.

Key Number System Topic No. 51.

Corpus Juris Secundum

CJS Bankruptcy § 1170, Filing and Contents of Plan, Generally.

§ 1222. Contents of plan

(a) The plan shall—

(1) provide for the submission of all or such portion of future earnings or other future income of the debtor to the supervision and control of the trustee as is necessary for the execution of the plan;

(2) provide for the full payment, in deferred cash payments, of all claims entitled to priority under section 507, unless—

(A) the claim is a claim owed to a governmental unit that arises as a result of the sale, transfer, exchange, or other disposition of any farm asset used in the debtor's farming operation, in which case the claim shall be treated as an unsecured claim that is not entitled to priority under section 507, but the debt shall be treated in such manner only if the debtor receives a discharge; or

(B) the holder of a particular claim agrees to a different treatment of that claim;

(3) if the plan classifies claims and interests, provide the same treatment for each claim or interest within a particular class unless the holder of a particular claim or interest agrees to less favorable treatment; and

(4) notwithstanding any other provision of this section, a plan may provide for less than full payment of all amounts owed for a claim entitled to priority under section 507(a)(1)(B) only if the plan provides that all of the debtor's projected disposable income for a 5–year period beginning on the date that the first payment is due under the plan will be applied to make payments under the plan.

(b) Subject to subsections (a) and (c) of this section, the plan may—

(1) designate a class or classes of unsecured claims, as provided in section 1122 of this title, but may not discriminate unfairly against any class so designated; however, such plan may treat claims for a consumer debt of the debtor if an individual is liable on such consumer debt with the debtor differently than other unsecured claims;

(2) modify the rights of holders of secured claims, or of holders of unsecured claims, or leave unaffected the rights of holders of any class of claims;

(3) provide for the curing or waiving of any default;

(4) provide for payments on any unsecured claim to be made concurrently with payments on any secured claim or any other unsecured claim;

(5) provide for the curing of any default within a reasonable time and maintenance of payments while the case is pending on any unsecured claim or secured claim on which the last payment is due after the date on which the final payment under the plan is due;

(6) subject to section 365 of this title, provide for the assumption, rejection, or assignment of any executory contract or unexpired lease of the debtor not previously rejected under such section;

(7) provide for the payment of all or part of a claim against the debtor from property of the estate or property of the debtor;

(8) provide for the sale of all or any part of the property of the estate or the distribution of all or any part of the property of the estate among those having an interest in such property;

(9) provide for payment of allowed secured claims consistent with section 1225(a)(5) of this title, over a period exceeding the period permitted under section 1222(c);

(10) provide for the vesting of property of the estate, on confirmation of the plan or at a later time, in the debtor or in any other entity;

(11) provide for the payment of interest accruing after the date of the filing of the petition on unsecured claims that are nondischargeable under section 1228(a), except that such interest may be paid only to the extent that the debtor has disposable income available to pay such interest after making provision for full payment of all allowed claims; and

(12) include any other appropriate provision not inconsistent with this title.

(c) Except as provided in subsections (b)(5) and (b)(9), the plan may not provide for payments over a period that is longer than three years unless the court for cause approves a longer period, but the court may not approve a period that is longer than five years.

(d) Notwithstanding subsection (b)(2) of this section and sections 506(b) and 1225(a)(5) of this title, if it is proposed in a plan to cure a default, the amount necessary to cure the default, shall be determined in accordance with the underlying agreement and applicable nonbankruptcy law.

(Added and amended Pub.L. 99–554, Title II, § 255, Title III, § 302(f), Oct. 27, 1986, 100 Stat. 3109, 3124; Pub.L. 103–65, § 1, Aug. 6, 1993, 107 Stat. 311; Pub.L. 103–394, Title III, § 305(b), Oct. 22, 1994, 108 Stat. 4134; Pub.L. 105–277, Div. C, Title I, § 149(a), Oct. 21, 1998, 112 Stat. 2681–610; Pub.L. 106–5, § 1(1), (2), Mar. 30, 1999, 113 Stat. 9; Pub.L. 106–70, § 1, Oct. 9, 1999, 113 Stat. 1031; Pub.L. 107–8, § 1, May 11, 2001, 115 Stat. 10; Pub.L. 107–17, § 1, June 26, 2001, 115 Stat. 151; Pub.L. 107–170, § 1, May 7, 2002, 116 Stat. 133; Pub.L. 107–171, Title X, § 10814(a), May 13, 2002 116 Stat. 532; Pub.L. 107–377, § 2(a), Dec. 19, 2002, 116 Stat. 3115; Pub.L. 108–73, § 2(a), Aug. 15, 2003, 117 Stat. 891; Pub.L. 108–369, § 2(a), Oct. 25, 2004, 118 Stat. 1749; Pub.L. 109–8, Title II, § 213(3), (4) Title X, §§ 1001(a)(1), 1003(a), Apr. 20, 2005, 119 Stat. 52, 185, 186.)

HISTORICAL AND STATUTORY NOTES

Revision Notes and Legislative Reports

1986 Acts. House Report No. 99–764 and House Conference Report No. 99–958, see 1986 U.S. Code Cong. and Adm. News, p. 5227.

1993 Acts. House Report No. 103–32, see 1993 U.S. Code Cong. and Adm. News, p. 373.

1994 Acts. House Report No. 103–835, see 1994 U.S. Code Cong. and Adm. News, p. 3340.

1998 Acts. Statement by President, see 1998 U.S. Code Cong. and Adm. News, p. 582.

1999 Acts. Statement by President, see 1999 U.S. Code Cong. and Adm. News, p. 4.

Statement by President, see 1999 U.S. Code Cong. and Adm. News, p. 102.

2001 Acts. House Report No. 107–2, see 2001 U.S. Code Cong. and Adm. News, p. 6.

2005 Acts. House Report No. 109–31(Part I), see 2005 U.S. Code Cong. and Adm. News, p. 88.

Amendments

2005 Amendments. Pub.L. 109–8, § 1001(a)(1), reenacted this section as in effect on June 30, 2005, requiring no change in text; see Pub.L. 109–8, § 1001, set out as a note under 11 U.S.C.A. § 1201.

Subsec. (a)(2). Pub.L. 109–8, § 213(3)(A), struck out "and" at the end of par. (2).

Pub.L. 109–8, § 1003(a), rewrote par. (2) which formerly read: "(2) provide for the full payment, in deferred cash payments, of all claims entitled to priority under section 507 of this title, unless the holder of a particular claim agrees to a different treatment of such claim; and".

Subsec. (a)(3). Pub.L. 109–8, § 213(3)(B), substituted "; and" for the period at the end of par. (3).

Subsec. (a)(4). Pub.L. 109–8, § 213(3)(C), added par. (4).

Subsec. (b)(10). Pub.L. 109–8, § 213(4)(A), struck out "and" at the end of par. (10).

Subsec. (b)(11), (12). Pub.L. 109–8, § 213(4)(B), (C), added a new par. (11) and renumbered former par. (11) as par. (12).

2004 Amendments. Pub.L. 108–369, § 2(a), extended effective date of repeal of this section to July 1, 2005, and so required no change in text.

2003 Amendments. Pub.L. 108–73, § 2(a), extended effective date of repeal of this section to Jan. 1, 2004, and so required no change in text.

2002 Amendments. Pub.L. 107–377, § 2(a), extended effective date of repeal of this section to July 1, 2003, and so required no change in text.

Pub.L. 107–171, § 10814(a), extended effective date of repeal of this section to Jan. 1, 2003, and so required no change in text.

Pub.L. 107–170, § 1, extended effective date of repeal of this section to June 1, 2002, and so required no change in text.

2001 Amendments. Pub.L. 107–17, § 1, extended effective date of repeal of this section to Oct. 1, 2001, and so required no change in text.

Pub.L. 107–8, § 1, extended effective date of repeal of this section to June 1, 2001, and so required no change in text.

1999 Amendments. Pub.L. 106–70, § 1, extended effective date of repeal of this section to July 1, 2000, and so required no change in text.

Pub.L. 106–5, § 1(1), (2), extended effective date of repeal of this section to Oct. 1, 1999, and so required no change in text.

1998 Amendments. Pub.L. 105–277, § 149(a), temporarily reenacted this section, which had been repealed effective Oct. 1, 1998 by Pub.L. 99–554, § 302(f).

1994 Amendments. Subsec. (d). Pub.L. 103–394, § 305(b), added subsec. (d).

1993 Amendments. Pub.L. 103–65, § 1, extended effective date of repeal of this section to Oct. 1, 1998.

1986 Amendments. Pub.L. 99–554, § 302(f), as amended by Pub.L. 103–65, § 1, repealed section effective Oct. 1, 1998. Prior to amendment by Pub.L. 103–65, repeal of section was to have taken effect on Oct. 1, 1993.

Effective and Applicability Provisions

2005 Acts. Pub.L. 109–8, Title X, § 1003(c), Apr. 20, 2005, 119 Stat. 186, provided that: "This section and the amendments made by this section [amending subsec. (a)(2) of this section and 11 U.S.C.A. § 1231(b)] shall take effect on the date of the enactment of this Act [Apr. 20, 2005] and shall not apply with respect to cases commenced under title 11 of the United States Code before such date."

Amendment by section 213(3), (4), Pub.L. 109–8 effective, except as otherwise provided, 180 days after April 20, 2005, and inapplicable with respect to cases commenced under Title 11 before the effective date, see Pub.L. 109–8, § 1501, set out as a note under 11 U.S.C.A. § 101.

2004 Acts. Amendment by Pub.L. 108–369, § 2(a), extending to July 1, 2005, the date of repeal of this chapter, to take effect Jan. 1, 2004, see Pub.L. 108–369, § 2(b), set out as a note under 11 U.S.C.A. § 1201.

2003 Acts. Amendment by Pub.L. 108–73, § 2(a), extending to Jan. 1, 2004, the date of repeal of this chapter, to take effect July 1, 2003, see Pub.L. 108–73, § 2(b), set out as a note under 11 U.S.C.A. § 1201.

2002 Acts. Amendment by Pub.L. 107–377, § 2(a), extending to July 1, 2003, the date of repeal of this chapter, to take effect Jan. 1, 2003, see Pub.L. 107–377, § 2(b), set out as a note under 11 U.S.C.A. § 1201.

Amendment by Pub.L. 107–171, extending to Jan. 1, 2003, the date of repeal of this chapter, to take effect June 1, 2002, see section 10814(b) of Pub.L. 107–171, set out as a note under 11 U.S.C.A. § 1201.

Amendment by Pub.L. 107–170, extending to June 1, 2002, the date of repeal of this chapter, to take effect October 1, 2001, see section 2 of Pub.L. 107–170, set out as a note under 11 U.S.C.A. § 1201.

2001 Acts. Amendment by Pub.L. 107–17, extending to October 1, 2001, the date of repeal of this chapter, to take effect June 1, 2001, see section 2 of Pub.L. 107–17, set out as a note under 11 U.S.C.A. § 1201.

Amendment by Pub.L. 107–8, extending to June 1, 2001, the date of repeal of this chapter, to take effect July 1, 2000, see section 2 of Pub.L. 107–8, set out as a note under 11 U.S.C.A. § 1201.

1999 Acts. Amendment by Pub.L. 106–70, extending to July 1, 2000, the date of repeal of this chapter, to take effect Oct. 1, 1999, see section 2 of Pub.L. 106–70, set out as a note under section 1201 of this title.

Amendment by Pub.L. 106–5, extending to Oct. 1, 1999 the date of repeal of this chapter, to take effect Apr. 1, 1999, see section 2 of Pub.L. 106–5, set out as a note under section 1201 of this title.

1998 Acts. Section reenacted, eff. Oct. 1, 1998, for the period beginning on Oct. 1, 1998, and ending on Apr. 1, 1999, but all cases commenced or pending under this chapter 12, as reenacted under section 149(a) of Pub.L. 105–277, and all matters and proceedings in or relating to such cases, to be conducted and determined under such chapter as if such chapter were continued in effect after Apr. 1, 1999, and the substantive rights of parties in connection with such cases, matters, and proceedings to continue to be governed under the law applicable to such cases, matters, and proceedings as if such chapter were continued in effect after Apr. 1, 1999, see section 149 of Pub.L. 105–277, set out as a note under 11 U.S.C.A. § 1201.

1994 Acts. Amendment by Pub.L. 103–394 effective on Oct. 22, 1994, and applicable only to agreements entered into after Oct. 22, 1994, see section 702 of Pub.L. 103–394, set out as a note under 11 U.S.C.A. § 101.

1993 Acts. Amendment by Pub.L. 103–65, extending to Oct. 1, 1998 the date of repeal of this chapter, to take effect Aug. 6, 1993, see section 3 of Pub.L. 103–65, set out as a note under 11 U.S.C.A. § 1221.

1986 Acts. Section repealed effective Oct. 1, 1998, see section 302(f) of Pub.L. 99–554, as amended, set out in a note under 28 U.S.C.A. § 581. However, for extension of provisions, see section 149 of Pub.L. 105–277, set out as a note under 11 U.S.C.A. § 1201.

Section effective 30 days after Oct. 27, 1986, but not applicable to cases commenced under this title before that date, see section 302(a), (c)(1) of Pub.L. 99–554, set out as a note under section 581 of Title 28, Judiciary and Judicial Procedure.

Separability of Provisions

If any provision of or amendment made by Pub.L. 103–394 or the application of such provision or amendment to any person or circumstance is held to be unconstitutional, the remaining provisions of and amendments made by Pub.L. 103–394 and the application of such provisions and amendments to any person or circumstance shall not be affected thereby, see section 701 of Pub.L. 103–394, set out as a note under section 101 of this title.

Reenactment of Chapter

This section as in effect on June 30, 2005, reenacted effective July 1, 2005, see Pub.L. 109–8, § 1001(a), set out as a note under 11 U.S.C.A. § 1201.

Repeal of Chapter; Extension of Provisions

Pub.L. 99–554, Title III, § 302(f), Oct. 27, 1986, 100 Stat. 3124, as amended Pub.L. 103–65, § 1, Aug. 6, 1993, 107 Stat. 311, which provided that, effective Oct. 1, 1998, this chapter is repealed, but that all cases commenced or pending under this chapter, and all matters and proceedings in or relating to such cases, shall be conducted and determined under this chapter as if such chapter had not been repealed, and that the substantive rights of parties in connection with such cases, matters, and proceedings shall continue to be governed under the laws applicable to such cases, matters, and proceedings as if such chapter had not been repealed, was superceded by the reenactment of this chapter by Pub.L. 109–8, Title X, § 1001(a), Apr. 20, 2005, 119 Stat. 185, set out as a note under 11 U.S.C.A. § 1201.

Pub.L. 105–277, Div. C, Title I, § 149, Oct. 21, 1998, 112 Stat. 2681–610, as amended Pub.L. 106–5, §§ 1, 2, Mar. 30, 1999, 113 Stat. 9; Pub.L. 106–70, §§ 1, 2, Oct. 9, 1999, 113 Stat. 1031; Pub.L. 107–8, §§ 1, 2, May 11, 2001, 115 Stat. 10; Pub.L. 107–17, §§ 1, 2, June 26, 2001, 115 Stat. 151; Pub.L. 107–170, §§ 1, 2, May 7, 2002, 116 Stat. 133; Pub.L. 107–171, Title X, § 10814, May 13, 2002, 116 St. 532; Pub.L. 107–377, § 2, Dec. 19, 2002, 116 Stat. 3115; Pub.L. 108–73, § 2(a), Aug. 15, 2003, 117 Stat. 891; Pub.L. 108–369, § 2(a), Oct. 25, 2004, 118 Stat. 1749, provided that, to take effect on January 1, 2004, chapter 12 of Title 11 [this chapter; 11 U.S.C.A. § 1201 et seq.], as in effect on December 31, 2003, is reenacted for the period beginning on January 1, 2004, and ending on July 1, 2005, but that all cases commenced or pending under this chapter 12, as reenacted under section 149(a) of Pub.L. 105–277, and all matters and proceedings in or relating to such cases, shall be conducted and determined under such chapter as if such chapter were continued in effect after July 1, 2005, and that the substantive rights of parties in connection with such cases, matters, and proceedings shall continue to be governed under the law applicable to such cases, matters, and proceedings as if such chapter were continued in effect after July 1, 2005, was superceded by the reenactment of this chapter by Pub.L. 109–8, Title X, § 1001(a), Apr. 20, 2005, 119 Stat. 185, set out as a note under 11 U.S.C.A. § 1201.

CROSS REFERENCES

Contents of plan filed in—
     Chapter eleven cases, see 11 USCA § 1123.
     Chapter thirteen cases, see 11 USCA § 1322.
     Railroad reorganization cases, see 11 USCA § 1172.

LIBRARY REFERENCES

American Digest System
     Bankruptcy ⟐3682.
     Key Number System Topic No. 51.

Corpus Juris Secundum
     CJS Bankruptcy § 923, Application for Approval.
     CJS Bankruptcy § 1170, Filing and Contents of Plan, Generally.
     CJS Bankruptcy § 1171, Modification of Plan.
     CJS Bankruptcy § 1173, Classification and Discrimination.
     CJS Bankruptcy § 1174, Modification of Claims; Cram Down of Secured Claims.
     CJS Bankruptcy § 1175, Amount of Repayment of Unsecured Claims.
     CJS Bankruptcy § 1176, Curing or Waiving of Defaults.
     CJS Bankruptcy § 1177, Payments.
     CJS Bankruptcy § 1178, Payments--Time for Completion.
     CJS Bankruptcy § 1179, Use, Sale, or Lease of Property.
     CJS Bankruptcy § 1180, Treatment of Executory Contracts and Unexpired Leases.
     CJS Bankruptcy § 1182, Effect of Confirmation.
     CJS Bankruptcy § 1185, Discharge.

§ 1223. Modification of plan before confirmation

(a) The debtor may modify the plan at any time before confirmation, but may not modify the plan so that the plan as modified fails to meet the requirements of section 1222 of this title.

(b) After the debtor files a modification under this section, the plan as modified becomes the plan.

(c) Any holder of a secured claim that has accepted or rejected the plan is deemed to have accepted or rejected, as the case may be, the plan as modified, unless the modification provides for a change in the rights of such holder from what such rights were under the plan before modification, and such holder changes such holder's previous acceptance or rejection.

(Added and amended Pub.L. 99–554, Title II, § 255, Title III, § 302(f), Oct. 27, 1986, 100 Stat. 3110, 3124; Pub.L. 103–65, § 1, Aug. 6, 1993, 107 Stat. 311; Pub.L. 105–277, Div. C, Title I, § 149(a), Oct. 21, 1998, 112 Stat. 2681–610; Pub.L. 106–5, § 1(1), (2), Mar. 30, 1999, 113 Stat. 9; Pub.L. 106–70, § 1, Oct. 9, 1999, 113 Stat. 1031; Pub.L. 107–8, § 1, May 11, 2001, 115

Stat. 10; Pub.L. 107–17, § 1, June 26, 2001, 115 Stat. 151; Pub.L. 107–170, § 1, May 7, 2002, 116 Stat. 133; Pub.L. 107–171, Title X, § 10814(a), May 13, 2002, 116 Stat. 532; Pub.L. 107–377, § 2(a), Dec. 19, 2002, 116 Stat. 3115; Pub.L. 108–73, § 2(a), Aug. 15, 2003, 117 Stat. 891; Pub.L. 108–369, § 2(a), Oct. 25, 2004, 118 Stat. 1749; Pub.L. 109–8, Title X, § 1001(a)(1), Apr. 20, 2005, 119 Stat. 185.)

HISTORICAL AND STATUTORY NOTES

Revision Notes and Legislative Reports

1986 Acts. House Report No. 99–764 and House Conference Report No. 99–958, see 1986 U.S. Code Cong. and Adm. News, p. 5227.

1993 Acts. House Report No. 103–32, see 1993 U.S. Code Cong. and Adm. News, p. 373.

1998 Acts. Statement by President, see 1998 U.S. Code Cong. and Adm. News, p. 582.

1999 Acts. Statement by President, see 1999 U.S. Code Cong. and Adm. News, p. 4.

Statement by President, see 1999 U.S. Code Cong. and Adm. News, p. 102.

2001 Acts. House Report No. 107–2, see 2001 U.S. Code Cong. and Adm. News, p. 6.

2005 Acts. House Report No. 109–31(Part I), see 2005 U.S. Code Cong. and Adm. News, p. 88.

Amendments

2005 Amendments. Pub.L. 109–8, § 1001(a)(1), reenacted this section as in effect on June 30, 2005, requiring no change in text; see Pub.L. 109–8, § 1001, set out as a note under 11 U.S.C.A. § 1201.

2004 Amendments. Pub.L. 108–369, § 2(a), extended effective date of repeal of this section to July 1, 2005, and so required no change in text.

2003 Amendments. Pub.L. 108–73, § 2(a), extended effective date of repeal of this section to Jan. 1, 2004, and so required no change in text.

2002 Amendments. Pub.L. 107–377, § 2(a), extended effective date of repeal of this section to July 1, 2003, and so required no change in text.

Pub.L. 107–171, § 10814(a), extended effective date of repeal of this section to Jan. 1, 2003, and so required no change in text.

Pub.L. 107–170, § 1, extended effective date of repeal of this section to June 1, 2002, and so required no change in text.

2001 Amendments. Pub.L. 107–17, § 1, extended effective date of repeal of this section to Oct. 1, 2001, and so required no change in text.

Pub.L. 107–8, § 1, extended effective date of repeal of this section to June 1, 2001, and so required no change in text.

1999 Amendments. Pub.L. 106–70, § 1, extended effective date of repeal of this section to July 1, 2000, and so required no change in text.

Pub.L. 106–5, § 1(1), (2), extended effective date of repeal of this section to Oct. 1, 1999, and so required no change in text.

1998 Amendments. Pub.L. 105–277, § 149(a), temporarily reenacted this section, which had been repealed effective Oct. 1, 1998 by Pub.L. 99–554, § 302(f).

1993 Amendments. Pub.L. 103–65, § 1, extended effective date of repeal of this section to Oct. 1, 1998.

1986 Amendments. Pub.L. 99–554, § 302(f), as amended by Pub.L. 103–65, § 1, repealed section effective Oct. 1, 1998. Prior to amendment by Pub.L. 103–65, repeal of section was to have taken effect on Oct. 1, 1993.

Effective and Applicability Provisions

2005 Acts. Amendments by Pub.L. 109–8 effective, except as otherwise provided, 180 days after April 20, 2005, and inapplicable with respect to cases commenced under Title 11 before the effective date, see Pub.L. 109–8, § 1501, set out as a note under 11 U.S.C.A. § 101.

2004 Acts. Amendment by Pub.L. 108–369, § 2(a), extending to July 1, 2005, the date of repeal of this chapter, to take effect Jan. 1, 2004, see Pub.L. 108–369, § 2(b), set out as a note under 11 U.S.C.A. § 1201.

2003 Acts. Amendment by Pub.L. 108–73, § 2(a), extending to Jan. 1, 2004, the date of repeal of this chapter, to take effect July 1, 2003, see Pub.L. 108–73, § 2(b), set out as a note under 11 U.S.C.A. § 1201.

2002 Acts. Amendment by Pub.L. 107–377, § 2(a), extending to July 1, 2003, the date of repeal of this chapter, to take effect Jan. 1, 2003, see Pub.L. 107–377, § 2(b), set out as a note under 11 U.S.C.A. § 1201.

Amendment by Pub.L. 107–171, extending to Jan. 1, 2003, the date of repeal of this chapter, to take effect June 1, 2002, see section 10814(b) of Pub.L. 107–171, set out as a note under 11 U.S.C.A. § 1201.

Amendment by Pub.L. 107–170, extending to June 1, 2002, the date of repeal of this chapter, to take effect October 1, 2001, see section 2 of Pub.L. 107–170, set out as a note under 11 U.S.C.A. § 1201.

2001 Acts. Amendment by Pub.L. 107–17, extending to October 1, 2001, the date of repeal of this chapter, to take effect June 1, 2001, see section 2 of Pub.L. 107–17, set out as a note under 11 U.S.C.A. § 1201.

Amendment by Pub.L. 107–8, extending to June 1, 2001, the date of repeal of this chapter, to take effect July 1, 2000, see section 2 of Pub.L. 107–8, set out as a note under 11 U.S.C.A. § 1201.

1999 Acts. Amendment by Pub.L. 106–70, extending to July 1, 2000, the date of repeal of this chapter, to take effect Oct. 1, 1999, see section 2 of Pub.L. 106–70, set out as a note under 11 U.S.C.A. § 1201.

Amendment by Pub.L. 106–5, extending to Oct. 1, 1999 the date of repeal of this chapter, to take effect Apr. 1, 1999, see section 2 of Pub.L. 106–5, set out as a note under 11 U.S.C.A. § 1201.

1998 Acts. Section reenacted, eff. Oct. 1, 1998, for the period beginning on Oct. 1, 1998, and ending on Apr. 1, 1999, but all cases commenced or pending under this chapter 12, as reenacted under section 149(a) of Pub.L. 105–277, and all matters and proceedings in or relating to such cases, to be conducted and determined under such chapter as if such chapter were continued in effect after Apr. 1, 1999, and the substantive rights of parties in connection with such cases, matters, and proceedings to continue to be governed under the law applicable to such cases, matters, and proceedings as if such chapter were continued in effect after Apr. 1, 1999, see section 149 of Pub.L. 105–277, set out as a note under 11 U.S.C.A. § 1201.

1993 Acts. Amendment by Pub.L. 103–65, extending to Oct. 1, 1998 the date of repeal of this chapter, to take effect Aug. 6, 1993, see section 3 of Pub.L. 103–65, set out as a note under 11 U.S.C.A. § 1221.

1986 Acts. Section repealed effective Oct. 1, 1998, see section 302(f) of Pub.L. 99–554, as amended, set out in a note under 28 U.S.C.A. § 581. However, for extension of provisions, see section 149 of Pub.L. 105–277, set out as a note under 11 U.S.C.A. § 1201.

Section effective 30 days after Oct. 27, 1986, but not applicable to cases commenced under this title before that date, see section 302(a), (c)(1) of Pub.L. 99–554, set out as a note under 28 U.S.C.A. § 581.

Reenactment of Chapter

This section as in effect on June 30, 2005, reenacted effective July 1, 2005, see Pub.L. 109–8, § 1001(a), set out as a note under 11 U.S.C.A. § 1201.

Repeal of Chapter; Extension of Provisions

Pub.L. 99–554, Title III, § 302(f), Oct. 27, 1986, 100 Stat. 3124, as amended Pub.L. 103–65, § 1, Aug. 6, 1993, 107 Stat. 311, which provided that, effective Oct. 1, 1998, this chapter is repealed, but that all cases commenced or pending under this chapter, and all matters and proceedings in or relating to such cases, shall be conducted and determined under this chapter as if such chapter had not been repealed, and that the substantive rights of parties in connection with such cases, matters, and proceedings shall continue to be governed under the laws applicable to such cases, matters, and proceedings as if such chapter had not been repealed, was superceded by the reenactment of this chapter by Pub.L. 109–8, Title X, § 1001(a), Apr. 20, 2005, 119 Stat. 185, set out as a note under 11 U.S.C.A. § 1201.

Pub.L. 105–277, Div. C, Title I, § 149, Oct. 21, 1998, 112 Stat. 2681–610, as amended Pub.L. 106–5, §§ 1, 2, Mar. 30, 1999, 113 Stat. 9; Pub.L. 106–70, §§ 1, 2, Oct. 9, 1999, 113 Stat. 1031; Pub.L. 107–8, §§ 1, 2, May 11, 2001, 115 Stat. 10; Pub.L. 107–17, §§ 1, 2, June 26, 2001, 115 Stat. 151; Pub.L. 107–170, §§ 1, 2, May 7, 2002, 116 Stat. 133; Pub.L. 107–171, Title X, § 10814, May 13, 2002, 116 St. 532; Pub.L. 107–377, § 2, Dec. 19, 2002, 116 Stat. 3115; Pub.L. 108–73, § 2(a), Aug. 15, 2003, 117 Stat. 891; Pub.L. 108–369, § 2(a), Oct. 25, 2004, 118 Stat. 1749, provided that, to take effect on January 1, 2004, chapter 12 of Title 11 [this chapter; 11 U.S.C.A. § 1201 et seq.], as in effect on December 31, 2003, is reenacted for the period beginning on January 1, 2004, and ending on July 1, 2005, but that all cases commenced or pending under this chapter 12, as reenacted under section 149(a) of Pub.L. 105–277, and all matters and proceedings in or relating to such cases, shall be conducted and determined under such chapter as if such chapter were continued in effect after July 1, 2005, and that the substantive rights of parties in connection with such cases, matters, and proceedings shall continue to be governed under the law applicable to such cases, matters, and proceedings as if such chapter were continued in effect after July 1, 2005, was superceded by the reenactment of this chapter by Pub.L. 109–8, Title X, § 1001(a), Apr. 20, 2005, 119 Stat. 185, set out as a note under 11 U.S.C.A. § 1201.

CROSS REFERENCES

Modification of plan filed in—

Chapter eleven cases, see 11 USCA § 1127.

Chapter nine cases, see 11 USCA § 942.

Chapter thirteen cases, see 11 USCA § 1323.

American Digest System

    Bankruptcy ☞3684, 3682.

    Key Number System Topic No. 51.

Corpus Juris Secundum

    CJS Bankruptcy § 1171, Modification of Plan.

§ 1224. Confirmation hearing

After expedited notice, the court shall hold a hearing on confirmation of the plan. A party in interest, the trustee, or the United States trustee may object to the confirmation of the plan. Except for cause, the hearing shall be concluded not later than 45 days after the filing of the plan.

(Added and amended Pub.L. 99–554, Title II, § 255, Title III, § 302(f), Oct. 27, 1986, 100 Stat. 3110, 3124; Pub.L. 103–65, § 1, Aug. 6, 1993, 107 Stat. 311; Pub.L. 105–277, Div. C, Title I, § 149(a), Oct. 21, 1998, 112 Stat. 2681–610; Pub.L. 106–5, § 1(1), (2), Mar. 30, 1999, 113 Stat. 9; Pub.L. 106–70, § 1, Oct. 9, 1999, 113 Stat. 1031; Pub.L. 107–8, § 1, May 11, 2001, 115 Stat. 10; Pub.L. 107–17, § 1, June 26, 2001, 115 Stat. 151; Pub.L. 107–170, § 1, May 7, 2002, 116 Stat. 133; Pub.L. 107–171, Title X, § 10814(a), May 13, 2002, 116 Stat. 532; Pub.L. 107–377, § 2(a), Dec. 19, 2002, 16 Stat. 3115; Pub.L. 108–73, § 2(a), Aug. 15, 2003, 117 Stat. 891; Pub.L. 108–369, § 2(a), Oct. 25, 2004, 118 Stat. 1749; Pub.L. 109–8, Title X, § 1001(a)(1), Apr. 20, 2005, 119 Stat. 185.)

HISTORICAL AND STATUTORY NOTES

Revision Notes and Legislative Reports

    1986 Acts. House Report No. 99–764 and House Conference Report No. 99–958, see 1986 U.S. Code Cong. and Adm. News, p. 5227.

    1993 Acts. House Report No. 103–32, see 1993 U.S. Code Cong. and Adm. News, p. 373.

    1998 Acts. Statement by President, see 1998 U.S. Code Cong. and Adm. News, p. 582.

    1999 Acts. Statement by President, see 1999 U.S. Code Cong. and Adm. News, p. 4.

    Statement by President, see 1999 U.S. Code Cong. and Adm. News, p. 102.

    2001 Acts. House Report No. 107–2, see 2001 U.S. Code Cong. and Adm. News, p. 6.

    2005 Acts. House Report No. 109–31(Part I), see 2005 U.S. Code Cong. and Adm. News, p. 88.

Amendments

    2005 Amendments. Pub.L. 109–8, § 1001(a)(1), reenacted this section as in effect on June 30, 2005, requiring no change in text; see Pub.L. 109–8, § 1001, set out as a note under 11 U.S.C.A. § 1201.

    2004 Amendments. Pub.L. 108–369, § 2(a), extended effective date of repeal of this section to July 1, 2005, and so required no change in text.

    2003 Amendments. Pub.L. 108–73, § 2(a), extended effective date of repeal of this section to Jan. 1, 2004, and so required no change in text.

    2002 Amendments. Pub.L. 107–377, § 2(a), extended effective date of repeal of this section to July 1, 2003, and so required no change in text.

    Pub.L. 107–171, § 10814(a), extended effective date of repeal of this section to Jan. 1, 2003, and so required no change in text.

    Pub.L. 107–170, § 1, extended effective date of repeal of this section to June 1, 2002, and so required no change in text.

    2001 Amendments. Pub.L. 107–17, § 1, extended effective date of repeal of this section to Oct. 1, 2001, and so required no change in text.

    Pub.L. 107–8, § 1, extended effective date of repeal of this section to June 1, 2001, and so required no change in text.

    1999 Amendments. Pub.L. 106–70, § 1, extended effective date of repeal of this section to July 1, 2000, and so required no change in text.

    Pub.L. 106–5, § 1(1), (2), extended effective date of repeal of this section to Oct. 1, 1999, and so required no change in text.

    1998 Amendments. Pub.L. 105–277, § 149(a), temporarily reenacted this section, which had been repealed effective Oct. 1, 1998 by Pub.L. 99–554, § 302(f).

    1993 Amendments. Pub.L. 103–65, § 1, extended effective date of repeal of this section to Oct. 1, 1998.

    1986 Amendments. Pub.L. 99–554, § 302(f), as amended by Pub.L. 103–65, § 1, repealed section effective Oct. 1, 1998. Prior to amendment by Pub.L. 103–65, repeal of section was to have taken effect on Oct. 1, 1993.

Effective and Applicability Provisions

    2005 Acts. Amendments by Pub.L. 109–8 effective, except as otherwise provided, 180 days after April 20, 2005, and inapplicable with respect to cases commenced under Title 11 before the effective date, see Pub.L. 109–8, § 1501, set out as a note under 11 U.S.C.A. § 101.

    2004 Acts. Amendment by Pub.L. 108–369, § 2(a), extending to July 1, 2005, the date of repeal of this chapter, to take effect Jan. 1, 2004, see Pub.L. 108–369, § 2(b), set out as a note under 11 U.S.C.A. § 1201.

    2003 Acts. Amendment by Pub.L. 108–73, § 2(a), extending to Jan. 1, 2004, the date of repeal of this chapter, to take effect July 1, 2003, see Pub.L. 108–73, § 2(b), set out as a note under 11 U.S.C.A. § 1201.

    2002 Acts. Amendment by Pub.L. 107–377, § 2(a), extending to July 1, 2003, the date of repeal of this chapter, to take effect Jan. 1, 2003, see Pub.L. 107–377, § 2(b), set out as a note under 11 U.S.C.A. § 1201.

    Amendment by Pub.L. 107–171, extending to Jan. 1, 2003, the date of repeal of this chapter, to take effect June 1, 2002, see section 10814(b) of Pub.L. 107–171, set out as a note under 11 U.S.C.A. § 1201.

    Amendment by Pub.L. 107–170, extending to June 1, 2002, the date of repeal of this chapter, to take effect October 1, 2001, see section 2 of Pub.L. 107–170, set out as a note under 11 U.S.C.A. § 1201.

    2001 Acts. Amendment by Pub.L. 107–17, extending to October 1, 2001, the date of repeal of this chapter, to take effect June 1, 2001, see section 2 of Pub.L. 107–17, set out as a note under 11 U.S.C.A. § 1201.

    Amendment by Pub.L. 107–8, extending to June 1, 2001, the date of repeal of this chapter, to take effect July 1, 2000, see section 2 of Pub.L. 107–8, set out as a note under 11 U.S.C.A. § 1201.

1999 Acts. Amendment by Pub.L. 106–70, extending to July 1, 2000, the date of repeal of this chapter, to take effect Oct. 1, 1999, see section 2 of Pub.L. 106–70, set out as a note under 11 U.S.C.A. § 1201.

Amendment by Pub.L. 106–5, extending to Oct. 1, 1999 the date of repeal of this chapter, to take effect Apr. 1, 1999, see section 2 of Pub.L. 106–5, set out as a note under 11 U.S.C.A. § 1201.

1998 Acts. Section reenacted, eff. Oct. 1, 1998, for the period beginning on Oct. 1, 1998, and ending on Apr. 1, 1999, but all cases commenced or pending under this chapter 12, as reenacted under section 149(a) of Pub.L. 105–277, and all matters and proceedings in or relating to such cases, to be conducted and determined under such chapter as if such chapter were continued in effect after Apr. 1, 1999, and the substantive rights of parties in connection with such cases, matters, and proceedings to continue to be governed under the law applicable to such cases, matters, and proceedings as if such chapter were continued in effect after Apr. 1, 1999, see section 149 of Pub.L. 105–277, set out as a note under 11 U.S.C.A. § 1201.

1993 Acts. Amendment by Pub.L. 103–65, extending to Oct. 1, 1998 the date of repeal of this chapter, to take effect Aug. 6, 1993, see section 3 of Pub.L. 103–65, set out as a note under 11 U.S.C.A. § 1221.

1986 Acts. Section repealed effective Oct. 1, 1998, see section 302(f) of Pub.L. 99–554, as amended, set out in a note under 28 U.S.C.A. § 581. However, for extension of provisions, see section 149 of Pub.L. 105–277, set out as a note under 11 U.S.C.A. § 1201.

Section effective 30 days after Oct. 27, 1986, but not applicable to cases commenced under this title before that date, see section 302(a), (c)(1) of Pub.L. 99–554, set out as a note under 28 U.S.C.A. § 581.

Reenactment of Chapter

This section as in effect on June 30, 2005, reenacted effective July 1, 2005, see Pub.L. 109–8, § 1001(a), set out as a note under 11 U.S.C.A. § 1201.

Repeal of Chapter; Extension of Provisions

Pub.L. 99–554, Title III, § 302(f), Oct. 27, 1986, 100 Stat. 3124, as amended Pub.L. 103–65, § 1, Aug. 6, 1993, 107 Stat. 311, which provided that, effective Oct. 1, 1998, this chapter is repealed, but that all cases commenced or pending under this chapter, and all matters and proceedings in or relating to such cases, shall be conducted and determined under this chapter as if such chapter had not been repealed, and that the substantive rights of parties in connection with such cases, matters, and proceedings shall continue to be governed under the laws applicable to such cases, matters, and proceedings as if such chapter had not been repealed, was superceded by the reenactment of this chapter by Pub.L. 109–8, Title X, § 1001(a), Apr. 20, 2005, 119 Stat. 185, set out as a note under 11 U.S.C.A. § 1201.

Pub.L. 105–277, Div. C, Title I, § 149, Oct. 21, 1998, 112 Stat. 2681–610, as amended Pub.L. 106–5, §§ 1, 2, Mar. 30, 1999, 113 Stat. 9; Pub.L. 106–70, §§ 1, 2, Oct. 9, 1999, 113 Stat. 1031; Pub.L. 107–8, §§ 1, 2, May 11, 2001, 115 Stat. 10; Pub.L. 107–17, §§ 1, 2, June 26, 2001, 115 Stat. 151; Pub.L. 107–170, §§ 1, 2, May 7, 2002, 116 Stat. 133; Pub.L. 107–171, Title X, § 10814, May 13, 2002, 116 St. 532; Pub.L. 107–377, § 2, Dec. 19, 2002, 116 Stat. 3115; Pub.L. 108–73, § 2(a), Aug. 15, 2003, 117 Stat. 891; Pub.L. 108–369, § 2(a), Oct. 25, 2004,

118 Stat. 1749, provided that, to take effect on January 1, 2004, chapter 12 of Title 11 [this chapter; 11 U.S.C.A. § 1201 et seq.], as in effect on December 31, 2003, is reenacted for the period beginning on January 1, 2004, and ending on July 1, 2005, but that all cases commenced or pending under this chapter 12, as reenacted under section 149(a) of Pub.L. 105–277, and all matters and proceedings in or relating to such cases, shall be conducted and determined under such chapter as if such chapter were continued in effect after July 1, 2005, and that the substantive rights of parties in connection with such cases, matters, and proceedings shall continue to be governed under the law applicable to such cases, matters, and proceedings as if such chapter were continued in effect after July 1, 2005, was superceded by the reenactment of this chapter by Pub.L. 109–8, Title X, § 1001(a), Apr. 20, 2005, 119 Stat. 185, set out as a note under 11 U.S.C.A. § 1201.

CROSS REFERENCES

Confirmation hearing in—

 Chapter eleven cases, see 11 USCA § 1128.

 Chapter thirteen cases, see 11 USCA § 1324.

Duties of United States trustee, see 28 USCA § 586.

LIBRARY REFERENCES

American Digest System

Bankruptcy ⟪3683.1.

Key Number System Topic No. 51.

§ 1225. Confirmation of plan

(a) Except as provided in subsection (b), the court shall confirm a plan if—

 (1) the plan complies with the provisions of this chapter and with the other applicable provisions of this title;

 (2) any fee, charge, or amount required under chapter 123 of title 28, or by the plan, to be paid before confirmation, has been paid;

 (3) the plan has been proposed in good faith and not by any means forbidden by law;

 (4) the value, as of the effective date of the plan, of property to be distributed under the plan on account of each allowed unsecured claim is not less than the amount that would be paid on such claim if the estate of the debtor were liquidated under chapter 7 of this title on such date;

 (5) with respect to each allowed secured claim provided for by the plan—

  (A) the holder of such claim has accepted the plan;

  (B)(i) the plan provides that the holder of such claim retain the lien securing such claim; and

  (ii) the value, as of the effective date of the plan, of property to be distributed by the trustee or the debtor under the plan on account of such claim is not less than the allowed amount of such claim; or

(C) the debtor surrenders the property securing such claim to such holder;

(6) the debtor will be able to make all payments under the plan and to comply with the plan; and

(7) the debtor has paid all amounts that are required to be paid under a domestic support obligation and that first become payable after the date of the filing of the petition if the debtor is required by a judicial or administrative order, or by statute, to pay such domestic support obligation.

(b)(1) If the trustee or the holder of an allowed unsecured claim objects to the confirmation of the plan, then the court may not approve the plan unless, as of the effective date of the plan—

(A) the value of the property to be distributed under the plan on account of such claim is not less than the amount of such claim;

(B) the plan provides that all of the debtor's projected disposable income to be received in the three-year period, or such longer period as the court may approve under section 1222(c), beginning on the date that the first payment is due under the plan will be applied to make payments under the plan; or

(C) the value of the property to be distributed under the plan in the 3–year period, or such longer period as the court may approve under section 1222(c), beginning on the date that the first distribution is due under the plan is not less than the debtor's projected disposable income for such period.

(2) For purposes of this subsection, "disposable income" means income which is received by the debtor and which is not reasonably necessary to be expended—

(A) for the maintenance or support of the debtor or a dependent of the debtor or for a domestic support obligation that first becomes payable after the date of the filing of the petition; or

(B) for the payment of expenditures necessary for the continuation, preservation, and operation of the debtor's business.

(c) After confirmation of a plan, the court may order any entity from whom the debtor receives income to pay all or any part of such income to the trustee.

(Added and amended Pub.L. 99–554, Title II, § 255, Title III, § 302(f), Oct. 27, 1986, 100 Stat. 3110, 3124; Pub.L. 103–65, § 1, Aug. 6, 1993, 107 Stat. 311; Pub.L. 105–277, Div. C, Title I, § 149(a), Oct. 21, 1998, 112 Stat. 2681–610; Pub.L. 106–5, § 1(1), (2), Mar. 30, 1999, 113 Stat. 9; Pub.L. 106–70, § 1, Oct. 9, 1999, 113 Stat. 1031; Pub.L. 107–8, § 1, May 11, 2001, 115 Stat. 10; Pub.L. 107–17, § 1, June 26, 2001, 115 Stat. 151; Pub.L. 107–170, § 1, May 7, 2002, 116 Stat. 133; Pub.L. 107–171, Title X, § 10814(a), May 13, 2002, 116 Stat. 532; Pub.L. 107–377, § 2(a), Dec. 19, 2002, 116 Stat. 3115; Pub.L. 108–73, § 2(a), Aug. 15, 2003, 117 Stat. 891; Pub.L. 108–369, § 2(a), Oct. 25, 2004, 118 Stat. 1749; Pub.L. 109–8, Title II, §§ 213(5), 218, Title X, §§ 1001(a)(1), 1006(a), Apr. 20, 2005, 119 Stat. 52, 55, 185, 187.)

HISTORICAL AND STATUTORY NOTES

Revision Notes and Legislative Reports

1986 Acts. House Report No. 99–764 and House Conference Report No. 99–958, see 1986 U.S. Code Cong. and Adm. News, p. 5227.

1993 Acts. House Report No. 103–32, see 1993 U.S. Code Cong. and Adm. News, p. 373.

1998 Acts. Statement by President, see 1998 U.S. Code Cong. and Adm. News, p. 582.

1999 Acts. Statement by President, see 1999 U.S. Code Cong. and Adm. News, p. 4.

Statement by President, see 1999 U.S. Code Cong. and Adm. News, p. 102.

2001 Acts. House Report No. 107–2, see 2001 U.S. Code Cong. and Adm. News, p. 6.

2005 Acts. House Report No. 109–31(Part I), see 2005 U.S. Code Cong. and Adm. News, p. 88.

Amendments

2005 Amendments. Pub.L. 109–8, § 1001(a)(1), reenacted this section as in effect on June 30, 2005, requiring no change in text; see Pub.L. 109–8, § 1001, set out as a note under 11 U.S.C.A. § 1201.

Subsec. (a)(5). Pub.L. 109–8, § 213(5)(A), struck out "and" at the end of par. (5).

Subsec. (a)(6). Pub.L. 109–8, § 213(5)(B), substituted "; and" for the period at the end of par. (6).

Subsec. (a)(7). Pub.L. 109–8, § 213(5)(C), added par. (7).

Subsec. (b)(1)(A). Pub.L. 109–8, § 1006(a)(1), struck out "or" at the end of subpar. (A).

Subsec. (b)(1)(B). Pub.L. 109–8, § 1006(a)(2), struck out the period at the end of subpar. (B) and inserted "; or".

Subsec. (b)(1)(C). Pub.L. 109–8, § 1006(a)(3), added subpar. (C).

Subsec. (b)(2)(A). Pub.L. 109–8, § 218, inserted "or for a domestic support obligation that first becomes payable after the date of the filing of the petition" after "dependent of the debtor".

2004 Amendments. Pub.L. 108–369, § 2(a), extended effective date of repeal of this section to July 1, 2005, and so required no change in text.

2003 Amendments. Pub.L. 108–73, § 2(a), extended effective date of repeal of this section to Jan. 1, 2004, and so required no change in text.

2002 Amendments. Pub.L. 107–377, § 2(a), extended effective date of repeal of this section to July 1, 2003, and so required no change in text.

Pub.L. 107–171, § 10814(a), extended effective date of repeal of this section to Jan. 1, 2003, and so required no change in text.

Pub.L. 107–170, § 1, extended effective date of repeal of this section to June 1, 2002, and so required no change in text.

2001 Amendments. Pub.L. 107–17, § 1, extended effective date of repeal of this section to October 1, 2001, and so required no change in text.

Pub.L. 107–8, § 1, extended effective date of repeal of this section to June 1, 2001, and so required no change in text.

1999 Amendments. Pub.L. 106–70, § 1, extended effective date of repeal of this section to July 1, 2000, and so required no change in text.

Pub.L. 106–5, § 1(1), (2), extended effective date of repeal of this section to Oct. 1, 1999, and so required no change in text.

1998 Amendments. Pub.L. 105–277, § 149(a), temporarily reenacted this section, which had been repealed effective Oct. 1, 1998 by Pub.L. 99–554, § 302(f).

1993 Amendments. Pub.L. 103–65, § 1, extended effective date of repeal of this section to Oct. 1, 1998.

1986 Amendments. Pub.L. 99–554, § 302(f), as amended by Pub.L. 103–65, § 1, repealed section effective Oct. 1, 1998. Prior to amendment by Pub.L. 103–65, repeal of section was to have taken effect on Oct. 1, 1993.

Effective and Applicability Provisions

2005 Acts. Amendments by Pub.L. 109–8 effective, except as otherwise provided, 180 days after April 20, 2005, and inapplicable with respect to cases commenced under Title 11 before the effective date, see Pub.L. 109–8, § 1501, set out as a note under 11 U.S.C.A. § 101.

2004 Acts. Amendment by Pub.L. 108–369, § 2(a), extending to July 1, 2005, the date of repeal of this chapter, to take effect Jan. 1, 2004, see Pub.L. 108–369, § 2(b), set out as a note under 11 U.S.C.A. § 1201.

2003 Acts. Amendment by Pub.L. 108–73, § 2(a), extending to Jan. 1, 2004, the date of repeal of this chapter, to take effect July 1, 2003, see Pub.L. 108–73, § 2(b), set out as a note under 11 U.S.C.A. § 1201.

2002 Acts. Amendment by Pub.L. 107–377, § 2(a), extending to July 1, 2003, the date of repeal of this chapter, to take effect Jan. 1, 2003, see Pub.L. 107–377, § 2(b), set out as a note under 11 U.S.C.A. § 1201.

Amendment by Pub.L. 107–171, extending to Jan. 1, 2003, the date of repeal of this chapter, to take effect June 1, 2002, see section 10814(b) of Pub.L. 107–171, set out as a note under 11 U.S.C.A. § 1201.

Amendment by Pub.L. 107–170, extending to June 1, 2002, the date of repeal of this chapter, to take effect October 1, 2001, see section 2 of Pub.L. 107–170, set out as a note under 11 U.S.C.A. § 1201.

2001 Acts. Amendment by Pub.L. 107–17, extending to October 1, 2001, the date of repeal of this chapter, to take effect June 1, 2001, see section 2 of Pub.L. 107–17, set out as a note under 11 U.S.C.A. § 1201.

Amendment by Pub.L. 107–8, extending to June 1, 2001, the date of repeal of this chapter, to take effect July 1, 2000, see section 2 of Pub.L. 107–8, set out as a note under 11 U.S.C.A. § 1201.

1999 Acts. Amendment by Pub.L. 106–70, extending to July 1, 2000, the date of repeal of this chapter, to take effect Oct. 1, 1999, see section 2 of Pub.L. 106–70, set out as a note under 11 U.S.C.A. § 1201.

Amendment by Pub.L. 106–5, extending to Oct. 1, 1999 the date of repeal of this chapter, to take effect Apr. 1, 1999, see section 2 of Pub.L. 106–5, set out as a note under 11 U.S.C.A. § 1201.

1998 Acts. Section reenacted, eff. Oct. 1, 1998, for the period beginning on Oct. 1, 1998, and ending on Apr. 1, 1999, but all cases commenced or pending under this chapter 12, as reenacted under section 149(a) of Pub.L. 105–277, and all matters and proceedings in or relating to such cases, to be conducted and determined under such chapter as if such chapter were continued in effect after Apr. 1, 1999, and the substantive rights of parties in connection with such cases, matters, and proceedings to continue to be governed under the law applicable to such cases, matters, and proceedings as if such chapter were continued in effect after Apr. 1, 1999, see section 149 of Pub.L. 105–277, set out as a note under 11 U.S.C.A. § 1201.

1993 Acts. Amendment by Pub.L. 103–65, extending to Oct. 1, 1998 the date of repeal of this chapter, to take effect Aug. 6, 1993, see section 3 of Pub.L. 103–65, set out as a note under 11 U.S.C.A. § 1221.

1986 Acts. Section repealed effective Oct. 1, 1998, see section 302(f) of Pub.L. 99–554, as amended, set out in a note under 28 U.S.C.A. § 581. However, for extension of provisions, see section 149 of Pub.L. 105–277, set out as a note under 28 U.S.C.A. § 1201.

Section effective 30 days after Oct. 27, 1986, but not applicable to cases commenced under this title before that date, see section 302(a), (c)(1) of Pub.L. 99–554, set out as a note under 28 U.S.C.A. § 581.

Reenactment of Chapter

This section as in effect on June 30, 2005, reenacted effective July 1, 2005, see Pub.L. 109–8, § 1001(a), set out as a note under 11 U.S.C.A. § 1201.

Repeal of Chapter; Extension of Provisions

Pub.L. 99–554, Title III, § 302(f), Oct. 27, 1986, 100 Stat. 3124, as amended Pub.L. 103–65, § 1, Aug. 6, 1993, 107 Stat. 311, which provided that, effective Oct. 1, 1998, this chapter is repealed, but that all cases commenced or pending under this chapter, and all matters and proceedings in or relating to such cases, shall be conducted and determined under this chapter as if such chapter had not been repealed, and that the substantive rights of parties in connection with such cases, matters, and proceedings shall continue to be governed under the laws applicable to such cases, matters, and proceedings as if such chapter had not been repealed, was superceded by the reenactment of this chapter by Pub.L. 109–8, Title X, § 1001(a), Apr. 20, 2005, 119 Stat. 185, set out as a note under 11 U.S.C.A. § 1201.

Pub.L. 105–277, Div. C, Title I, § 149, Oct. 21, 1998, 112 Stat. 2681–610, as amended Pub.L. 106–5, §§ 1, 2, Mar. 30, 1999, 113 Stat. 9; Pub.L. 106–70, §§ 1, 2, Oct. 9, 1999, 113 Stat. 1031; Pub.L. 107–8, §§ 1, 2, May 11, 2001, 115 Stat. 10; Pub.L. 107–17, §§ 1, 2, June 26, 2001, 115 Stat. 151; Pub.L. 107–170, §§ 1, 2, May 7, 2002, 116 Stat. 133; Pub.L. 107–171, Title X, § 10814, May 13, 2002, 116 St. 532; Pub.L. 107–377, § 2, Dec. 19, 2002, 116 Stat. 3115; Pub.L. 108–73, § 2(a), Aug. 15, 2003, 117 Stat. 891; Pub.L. 108–369, § 2(a), Oct. 25, 2004, 118 Stat. 1749, provided that, to take effect on January 1, 2004, chapter 12 of Title 11 [this chapter; 11 U.S.C.A. § 1201 et seq.], as in effect on December 31, 2003, is reenacted for the period beginning on January 1, 2004, and ending on July 1, 2005, but that all cases commenced or pending under this chapter 12, as reenacted under section 149(a) of Pub.L. 105–277, and all matters and proceedings in or relating to such cases, shall be conducted and determined under such chapter as if such chapter were continued in effect after July 1, 2005, and that the substantive rights of parties in connection with such cases, matters, and proceedings shall continue to be governed under the law applicable to such cases, matters, and proceedings as if such chapter were continued in effect after July 1, 2005, was superceded by the reenactment of this chapter by Pub.L. 109–8, Title X, § 1001(a), Apr. 20, 2005, 119 Stat. 185, set out as a note under 11 U.S.C.A. § 1201.

CROSS REFERENCES

Confirmation of plan in—

    Chapter eleven cases, see 11 USCA § 1129.

    Chapter nine cases, see 11 USCA § 943.

    Chapter thirteen cases, see 11 USCA § 1325.

    Railroad reorganization cases, see 11 USCA § 1173.

Conversion or dismissal, see 11 USCA § 1208.

Unclaimed property, see 11 USCA § 347.

LIBRARY REFERENCES

American Digest System

Bankruptcy ⚲3683.1, 3682, 3685.

Key Number System Topic No. 51.

Corpus Juris Secundum

CJS Bankruptcy § 1099, Unclaimed Property.

CJS Bankruptcy § 1172, Need for Good Faith.

CJS Bankruptcy § 1174, Modification of Claims; Cram Down of Secured Claims.

CJS Bankruptcy § 1175, Amount of Repayment of Unsecured Claims.

CJS Bankruptcy § 1176, Curing or Waiving of Defaults.

CJS Bankruptcy § 1182, Effect of Confirmation.

§ 1226.   Payments

(a) Payments and funds received by the trustee shall be retained by the trustee until confirmation or denial of confirmation of a plan. If a plan is confirmed, the trustee shall distribute any such payment in accordance with the plan. If a plan is not confirmed, the trustee shall return any such payments to the debtor, after deducting—

    (1) any unpaid claim allowed under section 503(b) of this title; and

    (2) if a standing trustee is serving in the case, the percentage fee fixed for such standing trustee.

(b) Before or at the time of each payment to creditors under the plan, there shall be paid—

    (1) any unpaid claim of the kind specified in section 507(a)(2) of this title; and

    (2) if a standing trustee appointed under section 1202(c) of this title is serving in the case, the percentage fee fixed for such standing trustee under section 1202(d) of this title.

(c) Except as otherwise provided in the plan or in the order confirming the plan, the trustee shall make payments to creditors under the plan.

(Added and amended Pub.L. 99–554, Title II, § 255, Title III, § 302(f), Oct. 27, 1986, 100 Stat. 3111, 3124; Pub.L. 103–65, § 1, Aug. 6, 1993, 107 Stat. 311; Pub.L. 103–394, Title V, § 501(d)(36), Oct. 22, 1994, 108 Stat. 4147; Pub.L. 105–277, Div. C, Title I, § 149(a), Oct. 21, 1998, 112 Stat. 2681–610;

Pub.L. 106–5, § 1(1), (2), Mar. 30, 1999, 113 Stat. 9; Pub.L. 106–70, § 1, Oct. 9, 1999, 113 Stat. 1031; Pub.L. 107–8, § 1, May 11, 2001, 115 Stat. 10; Pub.L. 107–17, § 1, June 26, 2001, 115 Stat. 151; Pub.L. 107–170, § 1, May 7, 2002, 116 Stat. 133; Pub.L. 107–171, Title X, § 10814(a), May 13, 2002, 116 Stat. 532; Pub.L. 107–377, § 2(a), Dec. 19, 2002, 116 Stat. 3115; Pub.L. 108–73, § 2(a), Aug. 15, 2003, 117 Stat. 891; Pub.L. 108–369, § 2(a), Oct. 25, 2004, 118 Stat. 1749; Pub.L. 109–8, Title X, § 1001(a)(1), Title XV, § 1502(a)(9), Apr. 20, 2005, 119 Stat. 185, 217.)

HISTORICAL AND STATUTORY NOTES

Revision Notes and Legislative Reports

1986 Acts. House Report No. 99–764 and House Conference Report No. 99–958, see 1986 U.S. Code Cong. and Adm. News, p. 5227.

1993 Acts. House Report No. 103–32, see 1993 U.S. Code Cong. and Adm. News, p. 373.

1994 Acts. House Report No. 103–835, see 1994 U.S. Code Cong. and Adm. News, p. 3340.

1998 Acts. Statement by President, see 1998 U.S. Code Cong. and Adm. News, p. 582.

1999 Acts. Statement by President, see 1999 U.S. Code Cong. and Adm. News, p. 4.

Statement by President, see 1999 U.S. Code Cong. and Adm. News, p. 102.

2001 Acts. House Report No. 107–2, see 2001 U.S. Code Cong. and Adm. News, p. 6.

2005 Acts. House Report No. 109–31(Part I), see 2005 U.S. Code Cong. and Adm. News, p. 88.

References in Text

Section 1202(c) and (d) of this title, referred to in subsec. (b)(2), were repealed by section 227 of Pub.L. 99–554, and provisions relating to appointment of and fixing percentage fees for standing trustees are contained in section 586(b) and (e) of Title 28, Judiciary and Judicial Procedure, as amended by section 113(b) and (c) of Pub.L. 99–554.

Amendments

2005 Amendments. Pub.L. 109–8, § 1001(a)(1), reenacted this section as in effect on June 30, 2005, requiring no change in text; see Pub.L. 109–8, § 1001, set out as a note under 11 U.S.C.A. § 1201.

Subsec. (b)(1). Pub.L. 109–8, § 1502(a)(9), struck out "507(a)(1)" and inserted "507(a)(2)".

2004 Amendments. Pub.L. 108–369, § 2(a), extended effective date of repeal of this section to July 1, 2005, and so required no change in text.

2003 Amendments. Pub.L. 108–73, § 2(a), extended effective date of repeal of this section to Jan. 1, 2004, and so required no change in text.

2002 Amendments. Pub.L. 107–377, § 2(a), extended effective date of repeal of this section to July 1, 2003, and so required no change in text.

Pub.L. 107–171, § 10814(a), extended effective date of repeal of this section to Jan. 1, 2003, and so required no change in text.

Pub.L. 107–170, § 1, extended effective date of repeal of this section to June 1, 2002, and so required no change in text.

2001 Amendments. Pub.L. 107–17, § 1, extended effective date of repeal of this section to Oct. 1, 2001, and so required no change in text.

Pub.L. 107–8, § 1, extended effective date of repeal of this section to June 1, 2001, and so required no change in text.

1999 Amendments. Pub.L. 106–70, § 1, extended effective date of repeal of this section to July 1, 2000, and so required no change in text.

Pub.L. 106–5, § 1(1), (2), extended effective date of repeal of this section to Oct. 1, 1999, and so required no change in text.

1998 Amendments. Pub.L. 105–277, § 149(a), temporarily reenacted this section, which had been repealed effective Oct. 1, 1998 by Pub.L. 99–554, § 302(f).

1994 Amendments. Subsec. (b)(2). Pub.L. 103–394, § 501(d)(36), substituted "1202(c)" for "1202(d)" and "1202(d)" for "1202(e)".

1993 Amendments. Pub.L. 103–65, § 1, extended effective date of repeal of this section to Oct. 1, 1998.

1986 Amendments. Pub.L. 99–554, § 302(f), as amended by Pub.L. 103–65, § 1, repealed section effective Oct. 1, 1998. Prior to amendment by Pub.L. 103–65, repeal of section was to have taken effect on Oct. 1, 1993.

Effective and Applicability Provisions

2005 Acts. Amendments by Pub.L. 109–8 effective, except as otherwise provided, 180 days after April 20, 2005, and inapplicable with respect to cases commenced under Title 11 before the effective date, see Pub.L. 109–8, § 1501, set out as a note under 11 U.S.C.A. § 101.

2004 Acts. Amendment by Pub.L. 108–369, § 2(a), extending to July 1, 2005, the date of repeal of this chapter, to take effect Jan. 1, 2004, see Pub.L. 108–369, § 2(b), set out as a note under 11 U.S.C.A. § 1201.

2003 Acts. Amendment by Pub.L. 108–73, § 2(a), extending to Jan. 1, 2004, the date of repeal of this chapter, to take effect July 1, 2003, see Pub.L. 108–73, § 2(b), set out as a note under 11 U.S.C.A. § 1201.

2002 Acts. Amendment by Pub.L. 107–377, § 2(a), extending to July 1, 2003, the date of repeal of this chapter, to take effect Jan. 1, 2003, see Pub.L. 107–377, § 2(b), set out as a note under 11 U.S.C.A. § 1201.

Amendment by Pub.L. 107–171, extending to Jan. 1, 2003, the date of repeal of this chapter, to take effect June 1, 2002, see section 10814(b) of Pub.L. 107–171, set out as a note under 11 U.S.C.A. § 1201.

Amendment by Pub.L. 107–170, extending to June 1, 2002, the date of repeal of this chapter, to take effect October 1, 2001, see section 2 of Pub.L. 107–170, set out as a note under 11 U.S.C.A. § 1201.

2001 Acts. Amendment by Pub.L. 107–17, extending to October 1, 2001, the date of repeal of this chapter, to take effect June 1, 2001, see section 2 of Pub.L. 107–17, set out as a note under 11 U.S.C.A. § 1201.

Amendment by Pub.L. 107–8, extending to June 1, 2001, the date of repeal of this chapter, to take effect July 1, 2000, see section 2 of Pub.L. 107–8, set out as a note under 11 U.S.C.A. § 1201.

1999 Acts. Amendment by Pub.L. 106–70, extending to July 1, 2000, the date of repeal of this chapter, to take effect Oct. 1, 1999, see section 2 of Pub.L. 106–70, set out as a note under 11 U.S.C.A. § 1201.

Amendment by Pub.L. 106–5, extending to Oct. 1, 1999 the date of repeal of this chapter, to take effect Apr. 1, 1999, see section 2 of Pub.L. 106–5, set out as a note under 11 U.S.C.A. § 1201.

1998 Acts. Section reenacted, eff. Oct. 1, 1998, for the period beginning on Oct. 1, 1998, and ending on Apr. 1, 1999, but all cases commenced or pending under this chapter 12, as reenacted under section 149(a) of Pub.L. 105–277, and all matters and proceedings in or relating to such cases, to be conducted and determined under such chapter as if such chapter were continued in effect after Apr. 1, 1999, and the substantive rights of parties in connection with such cases, matters, and proceedings to continue to be governed under the law applicable to such cases, matters, and proceedings as if such chapter were continued in effect after Apr. 1, 1999, see section 149 of Pub.L. 105–277, set out as a note under 11 U.S.C.A. § 1201.

1994 Acts. Amendment by Pub.L. 103–394 effective on Oct. 22, 1994, and not to apply with respect to cases commenced under Title 11 of the United States Code before Oct. 22, 1994, see section 702 of Pub.L. 103–394, set out as a note under 11 U.S.C.A. § 101.

1993 Acts. Amendment by Pub.L. 103–65, extending to Oct. 1, 1998 the date of repeal of this chapter, to take effect Aug. 6, 1993, see section 3 of Pub.L. 103–65, set out as a note under 11 U.S.C.A. § 1221.

1986 Acts. Section repealed effective Oct. 1, 1998, see section 302(f) of Pub.L. 99–554, as amended, set out in a note under 28 U.S.C.A. § 581. However, for extension of provisions, see section 149 of Pub.L. 105–277, set out as a note under 11 U.S.C.A. § 1201.

Section effective 30 days after Oct. 27, 1986, but not applicable to cases commenced under this title before that date, see section 302(a), (c)(1) of Pub.L. 99–554, set out as a note under 28 U.S.C.A. § 581.

Separability of Provisions

If any provision of or amendment made by Pub.L. 103–394 or the application of such provision or amendment to any person or circumstance is held to be unconstitutional, the remaining provisions of and amendments made by Pub.L. 103–394 and the application of such provisions and amendments to any person or circumstance shall not be affected thereby, see section 701 of Pub.L. 103–394, set out as a note under 11 U.S.C.A. § 101.

Reenactment of Chapter

This section as in effect on June 30, 2005, reenacted effective July 1, 2005, see Pub.L. 109–8, § 1001(a), set out as a note under 11 U.S.C.A. § 1201.

Repeal of Chapter; Extension of Provisions

Pub.L. 99–554, Title III, § 302(f), Oct. 27, 1986, 100 Stat. 3124, as amended Pub.L. 103–65, § 1, Aug. 6, 1993, 107 Stat. 311, which provided that, effective Oct. 1, 1998, this chapter is repealed, but that all cases commenced or pending under this chapter, and all matters and proceedings in or relating to such cases, shall be conducted and determined under this chapter as if such chapter had not been repealed, and that the substantive rights of parties in connection with such cases, matters, and proceedings shall continue to be governed under the laws applicable to such cases, matters, and proceedings as if such chapter had not been repealed, was superceded by the reenactment of this chapter by Pub.L. 109–8, Title X,

§ 1001(a), Apr. 20, 2005, 119 Stat. 185, set out as a note under 11 U.S.C.A. § 1201.

Pub.L. 105–277, Div. C, Title I, § 149, Oct. 21, 1998, 112 Stat. 2681–610, as amended Pub.L. 106–5, §§ 1, 2, Mar. 30, 1999, 113 Stat. 9; Pub.L. 106–70, §§ 1, 2, Oct. 9, 1999, 113 Stat. 1031; Pub.L. 107–8, §§ 1, 2, May 11, 2001, 115 Stat. 10; Pub.L. 107–17, §§ 1, 2, June 26, 2001, 115 Stat. 151; Pub.L. 107–170, §§ 1, 2, May 7, 2002, 116 Stat. 133; Pub.L. 107–171, Title X, § 10814, May 13, 2002, 116 St. 532; Pub.L. 107–377, § 2, Dec. 19, 2002, 116 Stat. 3115; Pub.L. 108–73, § 2(a), Aug. 15, 2003, 117 Stat. 891; Pub.L. 108–369, § 2(a), Oct. 25, 2004, 118 Stat. 1749, provided that, to take effect on January 1, 2004, chapter 12 of Title 11 [this chapter; 11 U.S.C.A. § 1201 et seq.], as in effect on December 31, 2003, is reenacted for the period beginning on January 1, 2004, and ending on July 1, 2005, but that all cases commenced or pending under this chapter 12, as reenacted under section 149(a) of Pub.L. 105–277, and all matters and proceedings in or relating to such cases, shall be conducted and determined under such chapter as if such chapter were continued in effect after July 1, 2005, and that the substantive rights of parties in connection with such cases, matters, and proceedings shall continue to be governed under the law applicable to such cases, matters, and proceedings as if such chapter were continued in effect after July 1, 2005, was superceded by the reenactment of this chapter by Pub.L. 109–8, Title X, § 1001(a), Apr. 20, 2005, 119 Stat. 185, set out as a note under 11 U.S.C.A. § 1201.

CROSS REFERENCES

Payment stopped on checks remaining unpaid 90 days after final distribution, see 11 USCA § 347.

Payments in Chapter thirteen cases, see 11 USCA § 1326.

LIBRARY REFERENCES

American Digest System

Bankruptcy ⟳3685.

Key Number System Topic No. 51.

Corpus Juris Secundum

CJS Bankruptcy § 1099, Unclaimed Property.

CJS Bankruptcy § 1177, Payments.

§ 1227.   Effect of confirmation

(a) Except as provided in section 1228(a) of this title, the provisions of a confirmed plan bind the debtor, each creditor, each equity security holder, and each general partner in the debtor, whether or not the claim of such creditor, such equity security holder, or such general partner in the debtor is provided for by the plan, and whether or not such creditor, such equity security holder, or such general partner in the debtor has objected to, has accepted, or has rejected the plan.

(b) Except as otherwise provided in the plan or the order confirming the plan, the confirmation of a plan vests all of the property of the estate in the debtor.

(c) Except as provided in section 1228(a) of this title and except as otherwise provided in the plan or in the order confirming the plan, the property vesting in the debtor under subsection (b) of this section is free and clear of any claim or interest of any creditor provided for by the plan.

(Added and amended Pub.L. 99–554, Title II, § 255, Title III, § 302(f), Oct. 27, 1986, 100 Stat. 3112, 3124; Pub.L. 103–65, § 1, Aug. 6, 1993, 107 Stat. 311; Pub.L. 105–277, Div. C, Title I, § 149(a), Oct. 21, 1998, 112 Stat. 2681–610; Pub.L. 106–5, § 1(1), (2), Mar. 30, 1999, 113 Stat. 9; Pub.L. 106–70, § 1, Oct. 9, 1999, 113 Stat. 1031; Pub.L. 107–8, § 1, May 11, 2001, 115 Stat. 10; Pub.L. 107–17, § 1, June 26, 2001, 115 Stat. 151; Pub.L. 107–170, § 1, May 7, 2002, 116 Stat. 133; Pub.L. 107–171, Title X, § 10814(a), May 13, 2002, 116 Stat. 532; Pub.L. 107–377, § 2(a), Dec. 19, 2002, 116 Stat. 3115; Pub.L. 108–73, § 2(a), Aug. 15, 2003, 117 Stat. 891; Pub.L. 108–369, § 2(a), Oct. 25, 2004, 118 Stat. 1749; Pub.L. 109–8, Title X, § 1001(a)(1), Apr. 20, 2005, 119 Stat. 185.)

HISTORICAL AND STATUTORY NOTES

Revision Notes and Legislative Reports

1986 Acts. House Report No. 99–764 and House Conference Report No. 99–958, see 1986 U.S. Code Cong. and Adm. News, p. 5227.

1993 Acts. House Report No. 103–32, see 1993 U.S. Code Cong. and Adm. News, p. 373.

1998 Acts. Statement by President, see 1998 U.S. Code Cong. and Adm. News, p. 582.

1999 Acts. Statement by President, see 1999 U.S. Code Cong. and Adm. News, p. 4.

Statement by President, see 1999 U.S. Code Cong. and Adm. News, p. 102.

2001 Acts. House Report No. 107–2, see 2001 U.S. Code Cong. and Adm. News, p. 6.

2005 Acts. House Report No. 109–31(Part I), see 2005 U.S. Code Cong. and Adm. News, p. 88.

Amendments

2005 Amendments. Pub.L. 109–8, § 1001(a)(1), reenacted this section as in effect on June 30, 2005, requiring no change in text; see Pub.L. 109–8, § 1001, set out as a note under 11 U.S.C.A. § 1201.

2004 Amendments. Pub.L. 108–369, § 2(a), extended effective date of repeal of this section to July 1, 2005, and so required no change in text.

2003 Amendments. Pub.L. 108–73, § 2(a), extended effective date of repeal of this section to Jan. 1, 2004, and so required no change in text.

2002 Amendments. Pub.L. 107–377, § 2(a), extended effective date of repeal of this section to July 1, 2003, and so required no change in text.

Pub.L. 107–171, § 10814(a), extended effective date of repeal of this section to Jan. 1, 2003, and so required no change in text.

Pub.L. 107–170, § 1, extended effective date of repeal of this section to June 1, 2002, and so required no change in text.

2001 Amendments. Pub.L. 107–17, § 1, extended effective date of repeal of this section to October 1, 2001, and so required no change in text.

Pub.L. 107–8, § 1, extended effective date of repeal of this section to June 1, 2001, and so required no change in text.

1999 Amendments. Pub.L. 106–70, § 1, extended effective date of repeal of this section to July 1, 2000, and so required no change in text.

Pub.L. 106–5, § 1(1), (2), extended effective date of repeal of this section to Oct. 1, 1999, and so required no change in text.

1998 Amendments. Pub.L. 105–277, § 149(a), temporarily reenacted this section, which had been repealed effective Oct. 1, 1998 by Pub.L. 99–554, § 302(f).

1993 Amendments. Pub.L. 103–65, § 1, extended effective date of repeal of this section to Oct. 1, 1998.

1986 Amendments. Pub.L. 99–554, § 302(f), as amended by Pub.L. 103–65, § 1, repealed section effective Oct. 1, 1998. Prior to amendment by Pub.L. 103–65, repeal of section was to have taken effect on Oct. 1, 1993.

Effective and Applicability Provisions

2005 Acts. Amendments by Pub.L. 109–8 effective, except as otherwise provided, 180 days after April 20, 2005, and inapplicable with respect to cases commenced under Title 11 before the effective date, see Pub.L. 109–8, § 1501, set out as a note under 11 U.S.C.A. § 101.

2004 Acts. Amendment by Pub.L. 108–369, § 2(a), extending to July 1, 2005, the date of repeal of this chapter, to take effect Jan. 1, 2004, see Pub.L. 108–369, § 2(b), set out as a note under 11 U.S.C.A. § 1201.

2003 Acts. Amendment by Pub.L. 108–73, § 2(a), extending to Jan. 1, 2004, the date of repeal of this chapter, to take effect July 1, 2003, see Pub.L. 108–73, § 2(b), set out as a note under 11 U.S.C.A. § 1201.

2002 Acts. Amendment by Pub.L. 107–377, § 2(a), extending to July 1, 2003, the date of repeal of this chapter, to take effect Jan. 1, 2003, see Pub.L. 107–377, § 2(b), set out as a note under 11 U.S.C.A. § 1201.

Amendment by Pub.L. 107–171, extending to Jan. 1, 2003, the date of repeal of this chapter, to take effect June 1, 2002, see section 10814(b) of Pub.L. 107–171, set out as a note under 11 U.S.C.A. § 1201.

Amendment by Pub.L. 107–170, extending to June 1, 2002, the date of repeal of this chapter, to take effect October 1, 2001, see section 2 of Pub.L. 107–170, set out as a note under 11 U.S.C.A. § 1201.

2001 Acts. Amendment by Pub.L. 107–17, extending to October 1, 2001, the date of repeal of this chapter, to take effect June 1, 2001, see section 2 of Pub.L. 107–17, set out as a note under 11 U.S.C.A. § 1201.

Amendment by Pub.L. 107–8, extending to June 1, 2001, the date of repeal of this chapter, to take effect July 1, 2000, see section 2 of Pub.L. 107–8, set out as a note under 11 U.S.C.A. § 1201.

1999 Acts. Amendment by Pub.L. 106–70, extending to July 1, 2000, the date of repeal of this chapter, to take effect Oct. 1, 1999, see section 2 of Pub.L. 106–70, set out as a note under 11 U.S.C.A. § 1201.

Amendment by Pub.L. 106–5, extending to Oct. 1, 1999 the date of repeal of this chapter, to take effect Apr. 1, 1999, see section 2 of Pub.L. 106–5, set out as a note under 11 U.S.C.A. § 1201.

1998 Acts. Section reenacted, eff. Oct. 1, 1998, for the period beginning on Oct. 1, 1998, and ending on Apr. 1, 1999, but all cases commenced or pending under this chapter 12, as reenacted under section 149(a) of Pub.L. 105–277, and all matters and proceedings in or relating to such cases, to be conducted and determined under such chapter as if such chapter were continued in effect after Apr. 1, 1999, and the substantive rights of parties in connection with such cases,

matters, and proceedings to continue to be governed under the law applicable to such cases, matters, and proceedings as if such chapter were continued in effect after Apr. 1, 1999, see section 149 of Pub.L. 105–277, set out as a note under 11 U.S.C.A. § 1201.

1993 Acts. Amendment by Pub.L. 103–65, extending to Oct. 1, 1998 the date of repeal of this chapter, to take effect Aug. 6, 1993, see section 3 of Pub.L. 103–65, set out as a note under 11 U.S.C.A. § 1221.

1986 Acts. Section repealed effective Oct. 1, 1998, see section 302(f) of Pub.L. 99–554, as amended, set out in a note under 28 U.S.C.A. § 581. However, for extension of provisions, see section 149 of Pub.L. 105–277, set out as a note under 11 U.S.C.A. § 1201.

Section effective 30 days after Oct. 27, 1986, but not applicable to cases commenced under this title before that date, see section 302(a), (c)(1) of Pub.L. 99–554, set out as a note under 28 U.S.C.A. § 581.

Reenactment of Chapter

This section as in effect on June 30, 2005, reenacted effective July 1, 2005, see Pub.L. 109–8, § 1001(a), set out as a note under 11 U.S.C.A. § 1201.

Repeal of Chapter; Extension of Provisions

Pub.L. 99–554, Title III, § 302(f), Oct. 27, 1986, 100 Stat. 3124, as amended Pub.L. 103–65, § 1, Aug. 6, 1993, 107 Stat. 311, which provided that, effective Oct. 1, 1998, this chapter is repealed, but that all cases commenced or pending under this chapter, and all matters and proceedings in or relating to such cases, shall be conducted and determined under this chapter as if such chapter had not been repealed, and that the substantive rights of parties in connection with such cases, matters, and proceedings shall continue to be governed under the laws applicable to such cases, matters, and proceedings as if such chapter had not been repealed, was superceded by the reenactment of this chapter by Pub.L. 109–8, Title X, § 1001(a), Apr. 20, 2005, 119 Stat. 185, set out as a note under 11 U.S.C.A. § 1201.

Pub.L. 105–277, Div. C, Title I, § 149, Oct. 21, 1998, 112 Stat. 2681–610, as amended Pub.L. 106–5, §§ 1, 2, Mar. 30, 1999, 113 Stat. 9; Pub.L. 106–70, §§ 1, 2, Oct. 9, 1999, 113 Stat. 1031; Pub.L. 107–8, §§ 1, 2, May 11, 2001, 115 Stat. 10; Pub.L. 107–17, §§ 1, 2, June 26, 2001, 115 Stat. 151; Pub.L. 107–170, §§ 1, 2, May 7, 2002, 116 Stat. 133; Pub.L. 107–171, Title X, § 10814, May 13, 2002, 116 St. 532; Pub.L. 107–377, § 2, Dec. 19, 2002, 116 Stat. 3115; Pub.L. 108–73, § 2(a), Aug. 15, 2003, 117 Stat. 891; Pub.L. 108–369, § 2(a), Oct. 25, 2004, 118 Stat. 1749, provided that, to take effect on January 1, 2004, chapter 12 of Title 11 [this chapter; 11 U.S.C.A. § 1201 et seq.], as in effect on December 31, 2003, is reenacted for the period beginning on January 1, 2004, and ending on July 1, 2005, but that all cases commenced or pending under this chapter 12, as reenacted under section 149(a) of Pub.L. 105–277, and all matters and proceedings in or relating to such cases, shall be conducted and determined under such chapter as if such chapter were continued in effect after July 1, 2005, and that the substantive rights of parties in connection with such cases, matters, and proceedings shall continue to be governed under the law applicable to such cases, matters, and proceedings as if such chapter were continued in effect after July 1, 2005, was superceded by the reenactment of this chapter by Pub.L. 109–8, Title X, § 1001(a), Apr. 20,

2005, 119 Stat. 185, set out as a note under 11 U.S.C.A. § 1201.

CROSS REFERENCES

Effect of confirmation in—
Chapter eleven cases, see 11 USCA § 1141.
Chapter nine cases, see 11 USCA § 944.
Chapter thirteen cases, see 11 USCA § 1327.

LIBRARY REFERENCES

American Digest System
Bankruptcy ⬭3683.1.
Key Number System Topic No. 51.

Corpus Juris Secundum
CJS Bankruptcy § 278, Parties Defendant; Sovereign Immunity.
CJS Bankruptcy § 1182, Effect of Confirmation.

§ 1228. Discharge

(a) Subject to subsection (d), as soon as practicable after completion by the debtor of all payments under the plan, and in the case of a debtor who is required by a judicial or administrative order, or by statute, to pay a domestic support obligation, after such debtor certifies that all amounts payable under such order or such statute that are due on or before the date of the certification (including amounts due before the petition was filed, but only to the extent provided for by the plan) have been paid, other than payments to holders of allowed claims provided for under section 1222(b)(5) or 1222(b)(9) of this title, unless the court approves a written waiver of discharge executed by the debtor after the order for relief under this chapter, the court shall grant the debtor a discharge of all debts provided for by the plan allowed under section 503 of this title or disallowed under section 502 of this title, except any debt—

(1) provided for under section 1222(b)(5) or 1222(b)(9) of this title; or

(2) of the kind specified in section 523(a) of this title.

(b) Subject to subsection (d), at any time after the confirmation of the plan and after notice and a hearing, the court may grant a discharge to a debtor that has not completed payments under the plan only if—

(1) the debtor's failure to complete such payments is due to circumstances for which the debtor should not justly be held accountable;

(2) the value, as of the effective date of the plan, of property actually distributed under the plan on account of each allowed unsecured claim is not less than the amount that would have been paid on such claim if the estate of the debtor had been liquidated under chapter 7 of this title on such date; and

(3) modification of the plan under section 1229 of this title is not practicable.

(c) A discharge granted under subsection (b) of this section discharges the debtor from all unsecured debts provided for by the plan or disallowed under section 502 of this title, except any debt—

(1) provided for under section 1222(b)(5) or 1222(b)(9) of this title; or

(2) of a kind specified in section 523(a) of this title.

(d) On request of a party in interest before one year after a discharge under this section is granted, and after notice and a hearing, the court may revoke such discharge only if—

(1) such discharge was obtained by the debtor through fraud; and

(2) the requesting party did not know of such fraud until after such discharge was granted.

(e) After the debtor is granted a discharge, the court shall terminate the services of any trustee serving in the case.

(f) The court may not grant a discharge under this chapter unless the court after notice and a hearing held not more than 10 days before the date of the entry of the order granting the discharge finds that there is no reasonable cause to believe that—

(1) section 522(q)(1) may be applicable to the debtor; and

(2) there is pending any proceeding in which the debtor may be found guilty of a felony of the kind described in section 522(q)(1)(A) or liable for a debt of the kind described in section 522(q)(1)(B).

(Added and amended Pub.L. 99–554, Title II, § 255, Title III, § 302(f), Oct. 27, 1986, 100 Stat. 3112, 3124; Pub.L. 103–65, § 1, Aug. 6, 1993, 107 Stat. 311; Pub.L. 105–277, Div. C, Title I, § 149(a), Oct. 21, 1998, 112 Stat. 2681–610; Pub.L. 106–5, § 1(1), (2), Mar. 30, 1999, 113 Stat. 9; Pub.L. 106–70, § 1, Oct. 9, 1999, 113 Stat. 1031; Pub.L. 106–518, Title II, § 208, Nov. 13, 2000, 114 Stat. 2415; Pub.L. 107–8, § 1, May 11, 2001, 115 Stat. 10; Pub.L. 107–17, § 1, June 26, 2001, 115 Stat. 151; Pub.L. 107–170, § 1, May 7, 2002, 116 Stat. 133; Pub.L. 107–171, Title X, § 10814(a), May 13, 2002, 116 Stat. 532; Pub.L. 107–377, § 2(a), Dec. 19, 2002, 116 Stat. 3115; Pub.L. 108–73, § 2(a), Aug. 15, 2003, 117 Stat. 891; Pub.L. 108–369, § 2(a), Oct. 25, 2004, 118 Stat. 1749; Pub.L. 109–8, Title II, § 213(6), Title III, § 330(c), Title X, § 1001(a)(1), Apr. 20, 2005, 119 Stat. 53, 101, 102, 185.)

HISTORICAL AND STATUTORY NOTES

Revision Notes and Legislative Reports

1986 Acts. House Report No. 99–764 and House Conference Report No. 99–958, see 1986 U.S. Code Cong. and Adm. News, p. 5227.

1993 Acts. House Report No. 103–32, see 1993 U.S. Code Cong. and Adm. News, p. 373.

1998 Acts. Statement by President, see 1998 U.S. Code Cong. and Adm. News, p. 582.

1999 Acts. Statement by President, see 1999 U.S. Code Cong. and Adm. News, p. 4.

Statement by President, see 1999 U.S. Code Cong. and Adm. News, p. 102.

2001 Acts. House Report No. 107–2, see 2001 U.S. Code Cong. and Adm. News, p. 6.

2005 Acts. House Report No. 109–31(Part I), see 2005 U.S. Code Cong. and Adm. News, p. 88.

Amendments

2005 Amendments. Pub.L. 109–8, § 1001(a)(1), reenacted this section as in effect on June 30, 2005, requiring no change in text; see Pub.L. 109–8, § 1001, set out as a note under 11 U.S.C.A. § 1201.

Subsec. (a). Pub.L. 109–8, § 213(6), in the matter preceding par. (1), inserted ", and in the case of a debtor who is required by a judicial or administrative order, or by statute, to pay a domestic support obligation, after such debtor certifies that all amounts payable under such order or such statute that are due on or before the date of the certification (including amounts due before the petition was filed, but only to the extent provided for by the plan) have been paid" after "completion by the debtor of all payments under the plan".

Pub.L. 109–8, § 330(c)(1), struck out "As" and inserted "Subject to subsection (d), as".

Subsec. (b). Pub.L. 109–8, § 330(c)(2), struck out "At" and inserted "Subject to subsection (d), at".

Subsec. (f). Pub.L. 109–8, § 330(c)(3), added subsec. (f).

2004 Amendments. Pub.L. 108–369, § 2(a), extended effective date of repeal of this section to July 1, 2005, and so required no change in text.

2003 Amendments. Pub.L. 108–73, § 2(a), extended effective date of repeal of this section to Jan. 1, 2004, and so required no change in text.

2002 Amendments. Pub.L. 107–377, § 2(a), extended effective date of repeal of this section to July 1, 2003, and so required no change in text.

Pub.L. 107–171, § 10814(a), extended effective date of repeal of this section to Jan. 1, 2003, and so required no change in text.

Pub.L. 107–170, § 1, extended effective date of repeal of this section to June 1, 2002, and so required no change in text.

2001 Amendments. Pub.L. 107–17, § 1, extended effective date of repeal of this section to October 1, 2001, and so required no change in text.

Pub.L. 107–8, § 1, extended effective date of repeal of this section to June 1, 2001, and so required no change in text.

2000 Amendments. Pub.L. 106–518, § 208, struck out "1222(b)(10)" each place it appeared and inserted "1222(b)(9)".

1999 Amendments. Pub.L. 106–70, § 1, extended effective date of repeal of this section to July 1, 2000, and so required no change in text.

Pub.L. 106–5, § 1(1), (2), extended effective date of repeal of this section to Oct. 1, 1999, and so required no change in text.

1998 Amendments. Pub.L. 105–277, § 149(a), temporarily reenacted this section, which had been repealed effective Oct. 1, 1998 by Pub.L. 99–554, § 302(f).

1993 Amendments. Pub.L. 103–65, § 1, extended effective date of repeal of this section to Oct. 1, 1998.

1986 Amendments. Pub.L. 99–554, § 302(f), as amended by Pub.L. 103–65, § 1, repealed section effective Oct. 1, 1998.

Prior to amendment by Pub.L. 103–65, repeal of section was to have taken effect on Oct. 1, 1993.

Effective and Applicability Provisions

2005 Acts. Amendments by sections 213(6) and 330(c) of Pub.L. 109–8 effective 180 days after Apr. 20, 2005, with amendments by section 213(6) of Pub.L. 109–8 not applicable with respect to cases commenced under this title before such effective date, except as otherwise provided, and amendment by section 330(c) of Pub.L. 109–8 applicable with respect to cases commenced under this title on or after Apr. 20, 2005, see Pub.L. 109–8, § 1501, set out as a note under 11 U.S.C.A. § 101.

2004 Acts. Amendment by Pub.L. 108–369, § 2(a), extending to July 1, 2005, the date of repeal of this chapter, to take effect Jan. 1, 2004, see Pub.L. 108–369, § 2(b), set out as a note under 11 U.S.C.A. § 1201.

2003 Acts. Amendment by Pub.L. 108–73, § 2(a), extending to Jan. 1, 2004, the date of repeal of this chapter, to take effect July 1, 2003, see Pub.L. 108–73, § 2(b), set out as a note under 11 U.S.C.A. § 1201.

2002 Acts. Amendment by Pub.L. 107–377, § 2(a), extending to July 1, 2003, the date of repeal of this chapter, to take effect Jan. 1, 2003, see Pub.L. 107–377, § 2(b), set out as a note under 11 U.S.C.A. § 1201.

Amendment by Pub.L. 107–171, extending to Jan. 1, 2003, the date of repeal of this chapter, to take effect June 1, 2002, see section 10814(b) of Pub.L. 107–171, set out as a note under 11 U.S.C.A. § 1201.

Amendment by Pub.L. 107–170, extending to June 1, 2002, the date of repeal of this chapter, to take effect October 1, 2001, see section 2 of Pub.L. 107–170, set out as a note under 11 U.S.C.A. § 1201.

2001 Acts. Amendment by Pub.L. 107–17, extending to October 1, 2001, the date of repeal of this chapter, to take effect June 1, 2001, see section 2 of Pub.L. 107–17, set out as a note under 11 U.S.C.A. § 1201.

Amendment by Pub.L. 107–8, extending to June 1, 2001, the date of repeal of this chapter, to take effect July 1, 2000, see section 2 of Pub.L. 107–8, set out as a note under 11 U.S.C.A. § 1201.

1999 Acts. Amendment by Pub.L. 106–70, extending to July 1, 2000, the date of repeal of this chapter, to take effect Oct. 1, 1999, see section 2 of Pub.L. 106–70, set out as a note under 11 U.S.C.A. § 1201.

Amendment by Pub.L. 106–5, extending to Oct. 1, 1999 the date of repeal of this chapter, to take effect Apr. 1, 1999, see section 2 of Pub.L. 106–5, set out as a note under 11 U.S.C.A. § 1201.

1998 Acts. Section reenacted, eff. Oct. 1, 1998, for the period beginning on Oct. 1, 1998, and ending on Apr. 1, 1999, but all cases commenced or pending under this chapter 12, as reenacted under section 149(a) of Pub.L. 105–277, and all matters and proceedings in or relating to such cases, to be conducted and determined under such chapter as if such chapter were continued in effect after Apr. 1, 1999, and the substantive rights of parties in connection with such cases, matters, and proceedings to continue to be governed under the law applicable to such cases, matters, and proceedings as if such chapter were continued in effect after Apr. 1, 1999, see section 149 of Pub.L. 105–277, set out as a note under 11 U.S.C.A. § 1201.

1993 Acts. Amendment by Pub.L. 103–65, extending to Oct. 1, 1998 the date of repeal of this chapter, to take effect Aug. 6, 1993, see section 3 of Pub.L. 103–65, set out as a note under 11 U.S.C.A. § 1221.

1986 Acts. Section repealed effective Oct. 1, 1998, see section 302(f) of Pub.L. 99–554, as amended, set out in a note under 28 U.S.C.A. § 581. However, for extension of provisions, see section 149 of Pub.L. 105–277, set out as a note under 11 U.S.C.A. § 1201.

Section effective 30 days after Oct. 27, 1986, but not applicable to cases commenced under this title before that date, see section 302(a), (c)(1) of Pub.L. 99–554, set out as a note under 28 U.S.C.A. § 581.

Reenactment of Chapter

This section as in effect on June 30, 2005, reenacted effective July 1, 2005, see Pub.L. 109–8, § 1001(a), set out as a note under 11 U.S.C.A. § 1201.

Repeal of Chapter; Extension of Provisions

Pub.L. 99–554, Title III, § 302(f), Oct. 27, 1986, 100 Stat. 3124, as amended Pub.L. 103–65, § 1, Aug. 6, 1993, 107 Stat. 311, which provided that, effective Oct. 1, 1998, this chapter is repealed, but that all cases commenced or pending under this chapter, and all matters and proceedings in or relating to such cases, shall be conducted and determined under this chapter as if such chapter had not been repealed, and that the substantive rights of parties in connection with such cases, matters, and proceedings shall continue to be governed under the laws applicable to such cases, matters, and proceedings as if such chapter had not been repealed, was superceded by the reenactment of this chapter by Pub.L. 109–8, Title X, § 1001(a), Apr. 20, 2005, 119 Stat. 185, set out as a note under 11 U.S.C.A. § 1201.

Pub.L. 105–277, Div. C, Title I, § 149, Oct. 21, 1998, 112 Stat. 2681–610, as amended Pub.L. 106–5, §§ 1, 2, Mar. 30, 1999, 113 Stat. 9; Pub.L. 106–70, §§ 1, 2, Oct. 9, 1999, 113 Stat. 1031; Pub.L. 107–8, §§ 1, 2, May 11, 2001, 115 Stat. 10; Pub.L. 107–17, §§ 1, 2, June 26, 2001, 115 Stat. 151; Pub.L. 107–170, §§ 1, 2, May 7, 2002, 116 Stat. 133; Pub.L. 107–171, Title X, § 10814, May 13, 2002, 116 St. 532; Pub.L. 107–377, § 2, Dec. 19, 2002, 116 Stat. 3115; Pub.L. 108–73, § 2(a), Aug. 15, 2003, 117 Stat. 891; Pub.L. 108–369, § 2(a), Oct. 25, 2004, 118 Stat. 1749, provided that, to take effect on January 1, 2004, chapter 12 of Title 11 [this chapter; 11 U.S.C.A. § 1201 et seq.], as in effect on December 31, 2003, is reenacted for the period beginning on January 1, 2004, and ending on July 1, 2005, but that all cases commenced or pending under this chapter 12, as reenacted under section 149(a) of Pub.L. 105–277, and all matters and proceedings in or relating to such cases, shall be conducted and determined under such chapter as if such chapter were continued in effect after July 1, 2005, and that the substantive rights of parties in connection with such cases, matters, and proceedings shall continue to be governed under the law applicable to such cases, matters, and proceedings as if such chapter were continued in effect after July 1, 2005, was superceded by the reenactment of this chapter by Pub.L. 109–8, Title X, § 1001(a), Apr. 20, 2005, 119 Stat. 185, set out as a note under 11 U.S.C.A. § 1201.

CROSS REFERENCES

Cancellation of indebtedness from discharged farm loans, see 12 USCA § 1150.

Discharge in—

Chapter seven cases, see 11 USCA § 727.

Chapter thirteen cases, see 11 USCA § 1328.

Effect of—

Conversion, see 11 USCA § 348.

Discharge, see 11 USCA § 524.

Exceptions to discharge, see 11 USCA § 523.

LIBRARY REFERENCES

American Digest System

Bankruptcy ⟝3674.

Key Number System Topic No. 51.

Corpus Juris Secundum

CJS Bankruptcy § 109, Termination of Service.

CJS Bankruptcy § 301, Notice to Debtor, Creditors, and Indenture Trustees.

CJS Bankruptcy § 1062, Effect of Discharge of Debts.

CJS Bankruptcy § 1094, Requirements for Reaffirmation of Debt.

CJS Bankruptcy § 1182, Effect of Confirmation.

CJS Bankruptcy § 1185, Discharge.

§ 1229. Modification of plan after confirmation

(a) At any time after confirmation of the plan but before the completion of payments under such plan, the plan may be modified, on request of the debtor, the trustee, or the holder of an allowed unsecured claim, to—

(1) increase or reduce the amount of payments on claims of a particular class provided for by the plan;

(2) extend or reduce the time for such payments; or

(3) alter the amount of the distribution to a creditor whose claim is provided for by the plan to the extent necessary to take account of any payment of such claim other than under the plan.

(b)(1) Sections 1222(a), 1222(b), and 1223(c) of this title and the requirements of section 1225(a) of this title apply to any modification under subsection (a) of this section.

(2) The plan as modified becomes the plan unless, after notice and a hearing, such modification is disapproved.

(c) A plan modified under this section may not provide for payments over a period that expires after three years after the time that the first payment under the original confirmed plan was due, unless the court, for cause, approves a longer period, but the court may not approve a period that expires after five years after such time.

(d) A plan may not be modified under this section—

(1) to increase the amount of any payment due before the plan as modified becomes the plan;

(2) by anyone except the debtor, based on an increase in the debtor's disposable income, to increase the amount of payments to unsecured creditors required for a particular month so that the aggregate of such payments exceeds the debtor's disposable income for such month; or

(3) in the last year of the plan by anyone except the debtor, to require payments that would leave the debtor with insufficient funds to carry on the farming operation after the plan is completed.

(Added and amended Pub.L. 99–554, Title II, § 255, Title III, § 302(f), Oct. 27, 1986, 100 Stat. 3113, 3124; Pub.L. 103–65, § 1, Aug. 6, 1993, 107 Stat. 311; Pub.L. 105–277, Div. C, Title I, § 149(a), Oct. 21, 1998, 112 Stat. 2681–610; Pub.L. 106–5, § 1(1), (2), Mar. 30, 1999, 113 Stat. 9; Pub.L. 106–70, § 1, Oct. 9, 1999, 113 Stat. 1031; Pub.L. 107–8, § 1, May 11, 2001, 115 Stat. 10; Pub.L. 107–17, § 1, June 26, 2001, 115 Stat. 151; Pub.L. 107–170, § 1, May 7, 2002, 116 Stat. 133; Pub.L. 107–171, Title X, § 10814(a), May 13, 2002, 116 Stat. 532; Pub.L. 107–377, § 2(a), Dec. 19, 2002, 116 Stat. 3115; Pub.L. 108–73, § 2(a), Aug. 15, 2003, 117 Stat. 891; Pub.L. 108–369, § 2(a), Oct. 25, 2004, 118 Stat. 1749; Pub.L. 109–8, Title X, §§ 1001(a)(1), 1006(b), Apr. 20, 2005, 199 Stat. 185, 187.)

HISTORICAL AND STATUTORY NOTES

Revision Notes and Legislative Reports

1986 Acts. House Report No. 99–764 and House Conference Report No. 99–958, see 1986 U.S. Code Cong. and Adm. News, p. 5227.

1993 Acts. House Report No. 103–32, see 1993 U.S. Code Cong. and Adm. News, p. 373.

1998 Acts. Statement by President, see 1998 U.S. Code Cong. and Adm. News, p. 582.

1999 Acts. Statement by President, see 1999 U.S. Code Cong. and Adm. News, p. 4.

Statement by President, see 1999 U.S. Code Cong. and Adm. News, p. 102.

2001 Acts. House Report No. 107–2, see 2001 U.S. Code Cong. and Adm. News, p. 6.

2005 Acts. House Report No. 109–31(Part I), see 2005 U.S. Code Cong. and Adm. News, p. 88.

Amendments

2005 Amendments. Pub.L. 109–8, § 1001(a)(1), reenacted this section as in effect on June 30, 2005, requiring no change in text; see Pub.L. 109–8, § 1001, set out as a note under 11 U.S.C.A. § 1201.

Subsec. (d). Pub.L. 109–8, § 1006(b), added subsec. (d).

2004 Amendments. Pub.L. 108–369, § 2(a), extended effective date of repeal of this section to July 1, 2005, and so required no change in text.

2003 Amendments. Pub.L. 108–73, § 2(a), extended effective date of repeal of this section to Jan. 1, 2004, and so required no change in text.

2002 Amendments. Pub.L. 107–377, § 2(a), extended effective date of repeal of this section to July 1, 2003, and so required no change in text.

Pub.L. 107–171, § 10814(a), extended effective date of repeal of this section to Jan. 1, 2003, and so required no change in text.

Pub.L. 107–170, § 1, extended effective date of repeal of this section to June 1, 2002, and so required no change in text.

2001 Amendments. Pub.L. 107–17, § 1, extended effective date of repeal of this section to October 1, 2001, and so required no change in text.

Pub.L. 107–8, § 1, extended effective date of repeal of this section to June 1, 2001, and so required no change in text.

1999 Amendments. Pub.L. 106–70, § 1, extended effective date of repeal of this section to July 1, 2000, and so required no change in text.

Pub.L. 106–5, § 1(1), (2), extended effective date of repeal of this section to Oct. 1, 1999, and so required no change in text.

1998 Amendments. Pub.L. 105–277, § 149(a), temporarily reenacted this section, which had been repealed effective Oct. 1, 1998 by Pub.L. 99–554, § 302(f).

1993 Amendments. Pub.L. 103–65, § 1, extended effective date of repeal of this section to Oct. 1, 1998.

1986 Amendments. Pub.L. 99–554, § 302(f), as amended by Pub.L. 103–65, § 1, repealed section effective Oct. 1, 1998. Prior to amendment by Pub.L. 103–65, repeal of section was to have taken effect on Oct. 1, 1993.

Effective and Applicability Provisions

2005 Acts. Amendments by Pub.L. 109–8 effective, except as otherwise provided, 180 days after April 20, 2005, and inapplicable with respect to cases commenced under Title 11 before the effective date, see Pub.L. 109–8, § 1501, set out as a note under 11 U.S.C.A. § 101.

2004 Acts. Amendment by Pub.L. 108–369, § 2(a), extending to July 1, 2005, the date of repeal of this chapter, to take effect Jan. 1, 2004, see Pub.L. 108–369, § 2(b), set out as a note under 11 U.S.C.A. § 1201.

2003 Acts. Amendment by Pub.L. 108–73, § 2(a), extending to Jan. 1, 2004, the date of repeal of this chapter, to take effect July 1, 2003, see Pub.L. 108–73, § 2(b), set out as a note under 11 U.S.C.A. § 1201.

2002 Acts. Amendment by Pub.L. 107–377, § 2(a), extending to July 1, 2003, the date of repeal of this chapter, to take effect Jan. 1, 2003, see Pub.L. 107–377, § 2(b), set out as a note under 11 U.S.C.A. § 1201.

Amendment by Pub.L. 107–171, extending to Jan. 1, 2003, the date of repeal of this chapter, to take effect June 1, 2002, see section 10814(b) of Pub.L. 107–171, set out as a note under 11 U.S.C.A. § 1201.

Amendment by Pub.L. 107–170, extending to June 1, 2002, the date of repeal of this chapter, to take effect October 1, 2001, see section 2 of Pub.L. 107–170, set out as a note under 11 U.S.C.A. § 1201.

2001 Acts. Amendment by Pub.L. 107–17, extending to October 1, 2001, the date of repeal of this chapter, to take effect June 1, 2001, see section 2 of Pub.L. 107–17, set out as a note under 11 U.S.C.A. § 1201.

Amendment by Pub.L. 107–8, extending to June 1, 2001, the date of repeal of this chapter, to take effect July 1, 2000, see section 2 of Pub.L. 107–8, set out as a note under 11 U.S.C.A. § 1201.

1999 Acts. Amendment by Pub.L. 106–70, extending to July 1, 2000, the date of repeal of this chapter, to take effect Oct. 1, 1999, see section 2 of Pub.L. 106–70, set out as a note under 11 U.S.C.A. § 1201.

Amendment by Pub.L. 106–5, extending to Oct. 1, 1999, the date of repeal of this chapter, to take effect Apr. 1, 1999, see section 2 of Pub.L. 106–5, set out as a note under 11 U.S.C.A. § 1201.

1998 Acts. Section reenacted, eff. Oct. 1, 1998, for the period beginning on Oct. 1, 1998, and ending on Apr. 1, 1999, but all cases commenced or pending under this chapter 12, as reenacted under section 149(a) of Pub.L. 105–277, and all matters and proceedings in or relating to such cases, to be conducted and determined under such chapter as if such chapter were continued in effect after Apr. 1, 1999, and the substantive rights of parties in connection with such cases, matters, and proceedings to continue to be governed under the law applicable to such cases, matters, and proceedings as if such chapter were continued in effect after Apr. 1, 1999, see section 149 of Pub.L. 105–277, set out as a note under 11 U.S.C.A. § 1201.

1993 Acts. Amendment by Pub.L. 103–65, extending to Oct. 1, 1998, the date of repeal of this chapter, to take effect Aug. 6, 1993, see section 3 of Pub.L. 103–65, set out as a note under 11 U.S.C.A. § 1221.

1986 Acts. Section repealed effective Oct. 1, 1998, see section 302(f) of Pub.L. 99–554, as amended, set out in a note under 28 U.S.C.A. § 581. However, for extension of provisions, see section 149 of Pub.L. 105–277, set out as a note under 11 U.S.C.A. § 1201.

Section effective 30 days after Oct. 27, 1986, but not applicable to cases commenced under this title before that date, see section 302(a), (c)(1) of Pub.L. 99–554, set out as a note under 28 U.S.C.A. § 581.

Reenactment of Chapter

This section as in effect on June 30, 2005, reenacted effective July 1, 2005, see Pub.L. 109–8, § 1001(a), set out as a note under 11 U.S.C.A. § 1201.

Repeal of Chapter; Extension of Provisions

Pub.L. 99–554, Title III, § 302(f), Oct. 27, 1986, 100 Stat. 3124, as amended Pub.L. 103–65, § 1, Aug. 6, 1993, 107 Stat. 311, which provided that, effective Oct. 1, 1998, this chapter is repealed, but that all cases commenced or pending under this chapter, and all matters and proceedings in or relating to such cases, shall be conducted and determined under this chapter as if such chapter had not been repealed, and that the substantive rights of parties in connection with such cases, matters, and proceedings shall continue to be governed under the laws applicable to such cases, matters, and proceedings as if such chapter had not been repealed, was superceded by the reenactment of this chapter by Pub.L. 109–8, Title X, § 1001(a), Apr. 20, 2005, 119 Stat. 185, set out as a note under 11 U.S.C.A. § 1201.

Pub.L. 105–277, Div. C, Title I, § 149, Oct. 21, 1998, 112 Stat. 2681–610, as amended Pub.L. 106–5, §§ 1, 2, Mar. 30, 1999, 113 Stat. 9; Pub.L. 106–70, §§ 1, 2, Oct. 9, 1999, 113 Stat. 1031; Pub.L. 107–8, §§ 1, 2, May 11, 2001, 115 Stat. 10; Pub.L. 107–17, §§ 1, 2, June 26, 2001, 115 Stat. 151; Pub.L. 107–170, §§ 1, 2, May 7, 2002, 116 Stat. 133; Pub.L. 107–171, Title X, § 10814, May 13, 2002, 116 St. 532; Pub.L. 107–377, § 2, Dec. 19, 2002, 116 Stat. 3115; Pub.L. 108–73, § 2(a), Aug. 15, 2003, 117 Stat. 891; Pub.L. 108–369, § 2(a), Oct. 25, 2004, 118 Stat. 1749, provided that, to take effect on January 1, 2004, chapter 12 of Title 11 [this chapter; 11 U.S.C.A. § 1201 et seq.], as in effect on December 31, 2003, is reenacted for the period beginning on January 1, 2004, and ending on July 1, 2005, but that all cases commenced or pending under this chapter 12, as reenacted under section 149(a) of Pub.L. 105–277, and all matters and proceedings in or relating to such cases, shall be conducted and determined under such chapter as if such chapter were continued in effect after July 1, 2005, and that the substantive rights of parties in connection with such cases, matters, and proceedings shall continue to be governed under the law applicable to such cases, matters, and proceedings as if such chapter were continued in effect after July 1, 2005, was superceded by the reenactment of this chapter by Pub.L. 109–8, Title X, § 1001(a), Apr. 20, 2005, 119 Stat. 185, set out as a note under 11 U.S.C.A. § 1201.

CROSS REFERENCES

Conversion or dismissal upon denial of confirmation of modified plan, see 11 USCA § 1208.

Duties of United States trustee, see 28 USCA § 586.

Modification of plan in—

    Chapter eleven cases, see 11 USCA § 1127.

    Chapter nine cases, see 11 USCA § 942.

    Chapter thirteen cases, see 11 USCA § 1329.

LIBRARY REFERENCES

American Digest System

Bankruptcy ☜3684.

Key Number System Topic No. 51.

Corpus Juris Secundum

CJS Bankruptcy § 1178, Payments--Time for Completion.

CJS Bankruptcy § 1183, Modification of Plan After Confirmation.

CJS Bankruptcy § 1185, Discharge.

§ 1230.   Revocation of an order of confirmation

(a) On request of a party in interest at any time within 180 days after the date of the entry of an order of confirmation under section 1225 of this title, and after notice and a hearing, the court may revoke such order if such order was procured by fraud.

(b) If the court revokes an order of confirmation under subsection (a) of this section, the court shall dispose of the case under section 1207 of this title, unless, within the time fixed by the court, the debtor proposes and the court confirms a modification of the plan under section 1229 of this title.

(Added and amended Pub.L. 99–554, Title II, § 255, Title III, § 302(f), Oct. 27, 1986, 100 Stat. 3113, 3124; Pub.L. 103–65, § 1, Aug. 6, 1993, 107 Stat. 311; Pub.L. 105–277, Div. C, Title I, § 149(a), Oct. 21, 1998, 112 Stat. 2681–610; Pub.L. 106–5, § 1(1), (2), Mar. 30, 1999, 113 Stat. 9; Pub.L. 106–70, § 1, Oct. 9, 1999, 113 Stat. 1031; Pub.L. 107–8, § 1, May 11, 2001, 115 Stat. 10; Pub.L. 107–17, § 1, June 26, 2001, 115 Stat. 151; Pub.L. 107–170, § 1, May 7, 2002, 116 Stat. 133; Pub.L. 107–171, Title X, § 10814(a), May 13, 2002, 116 Stat. 532; Pub.L. 107–377, § 2(a), Dec. 19, 2002, 116 Stat. 3115; Pub.L. 108–73, § 2(a), Aug. 15, 2003, 117 Stat. 891; Pub.L. 108–369, § 2(a), Oct. 25, 2004, 118 Stat. 1749; Pub.L. 109–8, Title X, § 1001(a)(1), Apr. 20, 2005, 119 Stat. 185.)

HISTORICAL AND STATUTORY NOTES

Revision Notes and Legislative Reports

1986 Acts. House Report No. 99–764 and House Conference Report No. 99–958, see 1986 U.S. Code Cong. and Adm. News, p. 5227.

1993 Acts. House Report No. 103–32, see 1993 U.S. Code Cong. and Adm. News, p. 373.

1998 Acts. Statement by President, see 1998 U.S. Code Cong. and Adm. News, p. 582.

1999 Acts. Statement by President, see 1999 U.S. Code Cong. and Adm. News, p. 4.

Statement by President, see 1999 U.S. Code Cong. and Adm. News, p. 102.

2001 Acts. House Report No. 107–2, see 2001 U.S. Code Cong. and Adm. News, p. 6.

2005 Acts. House Report No. 109–31(Part I), see 2005 U.S. Code Cong. and Adm. News, p. 88.

Amendments

2005 Amendments. Pub.L. 109–8, § 1001(a)(1), reenacted this section as in effect on June 30, 2005, requiring no change in text; see Pub.L. 109–8, § 1001, set out as a note under 11 U.S.C.A. § 1201.

2004 Amendments. Pub.L. 108–369, § 2(a), extended effective date of repeal of this section to July 1, 2005, and so required no change in text.

2003 Amendments. Pub.L. 108–73, § 2(a), extended effective date of repeal of this section to Jan. 1, 2004, and so required no change in text.

2002 Amendments. Pub.L. 107–377, § 2(a), extended effective date of repeal of this section to July 1, 2003, and so required no change in text.

Pub.L. 107–171, § 10814(a), extended effective date of repeal of this section to Jan. 1, 2003, and so required no change in text.

Pub.L. 107–170, § 1, extended effective date of repeal of this section to June 1, 2002, and so required no change in text.

2001 Amendments. Pub.L. 107–17, § 1, extended effective date of repeal of this section to Oct. 1, 2001, and so required no change in text.

Pub.L. 107–8, § 1, extended effective date of repeal of this section to June 1, 2001, and so required no change in text.

1999 Amendments. Pub.L. 106–70, § 1, extended effective date of repeal of this section to July 1, 2000, and so required no change in text.

Pub.L. 106–5, § 1(1), (2), extended effective date of repeal of this section to Oct. 1, 1999, and so required no change in text.

1998 Amendments. Pub.L. 105–277, § 149(a), temporarily reenacted this section, which had been repealed effective Oct. 1, 1998 by Pub.L. 99–554, § 302(f).

1993 Amendments. Pub.L. 103–65, § 1, extended effective date of repeal of this section to Oct. 1, 1998.

1986 Amendments. Pub.L. 99–554, § 302(f), as amended by Pub.L. 103–65, § 1, repealed section effective Oct. 1, 1998. Prior to amendment by Pub.L. 103–65, repeal of section was to have taken effect on Oct. 1, 1993.

Effective and Applicability Provisions

2005 Acts. Amendments by Pub.L. 109–8 effective, except as otherwise provided, 180 days after April 20, 2005, and

inapplicable with respect to cases commenced under Title 11 before the effective date, see Pub.L. 109–8, § 1501, set out as a note under 11 U.S.C.A. § 101.

2004 Acts. Amendment by Pub.L. 108–369, § 2(a), extending to July 1, 2005, the date of repeal of this chapter, to take effect Jan. 1, 2004, see Pub.L. 108–369, § 2(b), set out as a note under 11 U.S.C.A. § 1201.

2003 Acts. Amendment by Pub.L. 108–73, § 2(a), extending to Jan. 1, 2004, the date of repeal of this chapter, to take effect July 1, 2003, see Pub.L. 108–73, § 2(b), set out as a note under 11 U.S.C.A. § 1201.

2002 Acts. Amendment by Pub.L. 107–377, § 2(a), extending to July 1, 2003, the date of repeal of this chapter, to take effect Jan. 1, 2003, see Pub.L. 107–377, § 2(b), set out as a note under 11 U.S.C.A. § 1201.

Amendment by Pub.L. 107–171, extending to Jan. 1, 2003, the date of repeal of this chapter, to take effect June 1, 2002, see section 10814(b) of Pub.L. 107–171, set out as a note under 11 U.S.C.A. § 1201.

Amendment by Pub.L. 107–170, extending to June 1, 2002, the date of repeal of this chapter, to take effect October 1, 2001, see section 2 of Pub.L. 107–170, set out as a note under 11 U.S.C.A. § 1201.

2001 Acts. Amendment by Pub.L. 107–17, extending to October 1, 2001, the date of repeal of this chapter, to take effect June 1, 2001, see section 2 of Pub.L. 107–17, set out as a note under 11 U.S.C.A. § 1201.

Amendment by Pub.L. 107–8, extending to June 1, 2001, the date of repeal of this chapter, to take effect July 1, 2000, see section 2 of Pub.L. 107–8, set out as a note under 11 U.S.C.A. § 1201.

1999 Acts. Amendment by Pub.L. 106–70, extending to July 1, 2000, the date of repeal of this chapter, to take effect Oct. 1, 1999, see section 2 of Pub.L. 106–70, set out as a note under 11 U.S.C.A. § 1201.

Amendment by Pub.L. 106–5, extending to Oct. 1, 1999, the date of repeal of this chapter, to take effect Apr. 1, 1999, see section 2 of Pub.L. 106–5, set out as a note under 11 U.S.C.A. § 1201.

1998 Acts. Section reenacted, eff. Oct. 1, 1998, for the period beginning on Oct. 1, 1998, and ending on Apr. 1, 1999, but all cases commenced or pending under this chapter 12, as reenacted under section 149(a) of Pub.L. 105–277, and all matters and proceedings in or relating to such cases, to be conducted and determined under such chapter as if such chapter were continued in effect after Apr. 1, 1999, and the substantive rights of parties in connection with such cases, matters, and proceedings to continue to be governed under the law applicable to such cases, matters, and proceedings as if such chapter were continued in effect after Apr. 1, 1999, see section 149 of Pub.L. 105–277, set out as a note under 11 U.S.C.A. § 1201.

1993 Acts. Amendment by Pub.L. 103–65, extending to Oct. 1, 1998, the date of repeal of this chapter, to take effect Aug. 6, 1993, see section 3 of Pub.L. 103–65, set out as a note under 11 U.S.C.A. § 1221.

1986 Acts. Section repealed effective Oct. 1, 1998, see section 302(f) of Pub.L. 99–554, as amended, set out in a note under 28 U.S.C.A. § 581. However, for extension of provisions, see section 149 of Pub.L. 105–277, set out as a note under 11 U.S.C.A. § 1201.

Section effective 30 days after Oct. 27, 1986, but not applicable to cases commenced under this title before that date, see section 302(a), (c)(1) of Pub.L. 99–554, set out as a note under 28 U.S.C.A. § 581.

Reenactment of Chapter

This section as in effect on June 30, 2005, reenacted effective July 1, 2005, see Pub.L. 109–8, § 1001(a), set out as a note under 11 U.S.C.A. § 1201.

Repeal of Chapter; Extension of Provisions

Pub.L. 99–554, Title III, § 302(f), Oct. 27, 1986, 100 Stat. 3124, as amended Pub.L. 103–65, § 1, Aug. 6, 1993, 107 Stat. 311, which provided that, effective Oct. 1, 1998, this chapter is repealed, but that all cases commenced or pending under this chapter, and all matters and proceedings in or relating to such cases, shall be conducted and determined under this chapter as if such chapter had not been repealed, and that the substantive rights of parties in connection with such cases, matters, and proceedings shall continue to be governed under the laws applicable to such cases, matters, and proceedings as if such chapter had not been repealed, was superceded by the reenactment of this chapter by Pub.L. 109–8, Title X, § 1001(a), Apr. 20, 2005, 119 Stat. 185, set out as a note under 11 U.S.C.A. § 1201.

Pub.L. 105–277, Div. C, Title I, § 149, Oct. 21, 1998, 112 Stat. 2681–610, as amended Pub.L. 106–5, §§ 1, 2, Mar. 30, 1999, 113 Stat. 9; Pub.L. 106–70, §§ 1, 2, Oct. 9, 1999, 113 Stat. 1031; Pub.L. 107–8, §§ 1, 2, May 11, 2001, 115 Stat. 10; Pub.L. 107–17, §§ 1, 2, June 26, 2001, 115 Stat. 151; Pub.L. 107–170, §§ 1, 2, May 7, 2002, 116 Stat. 133; Pub.L. 107–171, Title X, § 10814, May 13, 2002, 116 St. 532; Pub.L. 107–377, § 2, Dec. 19, 2002, 116 Stat. 3115; Pub.L. 108–73, § 2(a), Aug. 15, 2003, 117 Stat. 891; Pub.L. 108–369, § 2(a), Oct. 25, 2004, 118 Stat. 1749, provided that, to take effect on January 1, 2004, chapter 12 of Title 11 [this chapter; 11 U.S.C.A. § 1201 et seq.], as in effect on December 31, 2003, is reenacted for the period beginning on January 1, 2004, and ending on July 1, 2005, but that all cases commenced or pending under this chapter 12, as reenacted under section 149(a) of Pub.L. 105–277, and all matters and proceedings in or relating to such cases, shall be conducted and determined under such chapter as if such chapter were continued in effect after July 1, 2005, and that the substantive rights of parties in connection with such cases, matters, and proceedings shall continue to be governed under the law applicable to such cases, matters, and proceedings as if such chapter were continued in effect after July 1, 2005, was superceded by the reenactment of this chapter by Pub.L. 109–8, Title X, § 1001(a), Apr. 20, 2005, 119 Stat. 185, set out as a note under 11 U.S.C.A. § 1201.

CROSS REFERENCES

Conversion or dismissal upon denial of confirmation of modified plan, see 11 USCA § 1208.

Revocation of order of confirmation in—

    Chapter eleven cases, see 11 USCA § 1144.

    Chapter thirteen cases, see 11 USCA § 1330.

LIBRARY REFERENCES

American Digest System

Bankruptcy ⟺3684.

Key Number System Topic No. 51.

Corpus Juris Secundum

CJS Bankruptcy § 315, Judgments--Relief from Judgment or Order; Collateral Attack.

CJS Bankruptcy § 1184, Revocation or Vacation.

§ 1231.   Special tax provisions

(a) The issuance, transfer, or exchange of a security, or the making or delivery of an instrument of transfer under a plan confirmed under section 1225 of this title, may not be taxed under any law imposing a stamp tax or similar tax.

(b) The court may authorize the proponent of a plan to request a determination, limited to questions of law, by any governmental unit charged with responsibility for collection or determination of a tax on or measured by income, of the tax effects, under section 346 of this title and under the law imposing such tax, of the plan. In the event of an actual controversy, the court may declare such effects after the earlier of—

    (1) the date on which such governmental unit responds to the request under this subsection; or

    (2) 270 days after such request.

(c), (d) Redesignated (a), (b)

(Added and amended Pub.L. 99–554, Title II, § 255, Title III, § 302(f), Oct. 27, 1986, 100 Stat. 3113, 3124; Pub.L. 103–65, § 1, Aug. 6, 1993, 107 Stat. 311; Pub.L. 105–277, Div. C, Title I, § 149(a), Oct. 21, 1998, 112 Stat. 2681–610; Pub.L. 106–5, § 1(1), (2), Mar. 30, 1999, 113 Stat. 9; Pub.L. 106–70, § 1, Oct. 9, 1999, 113 Stat. 1031; Pub.L. 107–8, § 1, May 11, 2001, 115 Stat. 10; Pub.L. 107–17, § 1, June 26, 2001, 115 Stat. 151; Pub.L. 107–170, § 1, May 7, 2002, 116 Stat. 133; Pub.L. 107–171, Title X, § 10814(a), May 13, 2002, 116 Stat. 532; Pub.L. 107–377, § 2(a), Dec. 19, 2002, 116 Stat. 3115; Pub.L. 108–73, § 2(a), Aug. 15, 2003, 117 Stat. 891; Pub.L. 108–369, § 2(a), Oct. 25, 2004, 118 Stat. 1749; Pub.L. 109–8, Title VII, § 719(b)(4), Title X, §§ 1001(a)(1), 1003(b), Apr. 20, 2005, 119 Stat. 133, 185, 186.)

HISTORICAL AND STATUTORY NOTES

Revision Notes and Legislative Reports

1986 Acts. House Report No. 99–764 and House Conference Report No. 99–958, see 1986 U.S. Code Cong. and Adm. News, p. 5227.

1993 Acts. House Report No. 103–32, see 1993 U.S. Code Cong. and Adm. News, p. 373.

1998 Acts. Statement by President, see 1998 U.S. Code Cong. and Adm. News, p. 582.

1999 Acts. Statement by President, see 1999 U.S. Code Cong. and Adm. News, p. 4.

Statement by President, see 1999 U.S. Code Cong. and Adm. News, p. 102.

2001 Acts. House Report No. 107–2, see 2001 U.S. Code Cong. and Adm. News, p. 6.

2005 Acts. House Report No. 109–31(Part I), see 2005 U.S. Code Cong. and Adm. News, p. 88.

Amendments

2005 Amendments. Pub.L. 109–8, § 1001(a)(1), reenacted this section as in effect on June 30, 2005, requiring no change in text; see Pub.L. 109–8, § 1001, set out as a note under 11 U.S.C.A. § 1201.

Subsec. (a). Pub.L. 109–8, § 719(b)(4), struck out former subsec. (a) and redesignated subsec. (c) as subsec. (a). Prior to striking, subsec. (a) read: "**(a)** For the purpose of any State or local law imposing a tax on or measured by income, the taxable period of a debtor that is an individual shall terminate on the date of the order for relief under this chapter, unless the case was converted under section 706 of this title."

Subsec. (b). Pub.L. 109–8, § 719(b)(4), struck out former subsec. (b) and redesignated subsec. (d) as subsec. (b). Prior to striking, subsec. (b) read: "**(b)** The trustee shall make a State or local tax return of income for the estate of an individual debtor in a case under this chapter for each taxable period after the order for relief under this chapter during which the case is pending."

Pub.L. 109–8, § 1003(b), struck out "a State or local governmental unit" and inserted "any governmental unit" in subsec. (d) before redesignation as subsec. (b) by Pub.L. 109–8, § 719(b)(4)(B), such redesignation being effective 180 days after April 20, 2005.

Subsec. (c). Pub.L. 109–8, § 719(b)(4)(B), redesignated former subsec. (c) as subsec. (a).

Subsec. (d). Pub.L. 109–8, § 719(b)(4)(B), redesignated former subsec. (d) as subsec. (b).

2004 Amendments. Pub.L. 108–369, § 2(a), extended effective date of repeal of this section to July 1, 2005, and so required no change in text.

2003 Amendments. Pub.L. 108–73, § 2(a), extended effective date of repeal of this section to Jan. 1, 2004, and so required no change in text.

2002 Amendments. Pub.L. 107–377, § 2(a), extended effective date of repeal of this section to July 1, 2003, and so required no change in text.

Pub.L. 107–171, § 10814(a), extended effective date of repeal of this section to Jan. 1, 2003, and so required no change in text.

Pub.L. 107–170, § 1, extended effective date of repeal of this section to June 1, 2002, and so required no change in text.

2001 Amendments. Pub.L. 107–17, § 1, extended effective date of repeal of this section to Oct. 1, 2001, and so required no change in text.

Pub.L. 107–8, § 1, extended effective date of repeal of this section to June 1, 2001, and so required no change in text.

1999 Amendments. Pub.L. 106–70, § 1, extended effective date of repeal of this section to July 1, 2000, and so required no change in text.

Pub.L. 106–5, § 1(1), (2), extended effective date of repeal of this section to Oct. 1, 1999, and so required no change in text.

1998 Amendments. Pub.L. 105–277, § 149(a), temporarily reenacted this section, which had been repealed effective Oct. 1, 1998 by Pub.L. 99–554, § 302(f).

1993 Amendments. Pub.L. 103–65, § 1, extended effective date of repeal of this section to Oct. 1, 1998.

1986 Amendments. Pub.L. 99–554, § 302(f), as amended by Pub.L. 103–65, § 1, repealed section effective Oct. 1, 1998. Prior to amendment by Pub.L. 103–65, repeal of section was to have taken effect on Oct. 1, 1993.

Effective and Applicability Provisions

2005 Acts. Amendment to subsec. (b) of this section, which was formerly designated as subsec. (d) of this section, effective Apr. 20, 2005, and not applicable with respect to cases commenced under this title before that date, see Pub.L. 109–8, § 1003(c), set out as a note under 11 U.S.C.A. § 1222.

Amendments by Pub.L. 109–8 effective, except as otherwise provided, 180 days after April 20, 2005, and inapplicable with respect to cases commenced under Title 11 before the effective date, see Pub.L. 109–8, § 1501, set out as a note under 11 U.S.C.A. § 101.

2004 Acts. Amendment by Pub.L. 108–369, § 2(a), extending to July 1, 2005, the date of repeal of this chapter, to take effect Jan. 1, 2004, see Pub.L. 108–369, § 2(b), set out as a note under 11 U.S.C.A. § 1201.

2003 Acts. Amendment by Pub.L. 108–73, § 2(a), extending to Jan. 1, 2004, the date of repeal of this chapter, to take effect July 1, 2003, see Pub.L. 108–73, § 2(b), set out as a note under 11 U.S.C.A. § 1201.

2002 Acts. Amendment by Pub.L. 107–377, § 2(a), extending to July 1, 2003, the date of repeal of this chapter, to take effect Jan. 1, 2003, see Pub.L. 107–377, § 2(b), set out as a note under 11 U.S.C.A. § 1201.

Amendment by Pub.L. 107–171, extending to Jan. 1, 2003, the date of repeal of this chapter, to take effect June 1, 2002, see section 10814(b) of Pub.L. 107–171, set out as a note under 11 U.S.C.A. § 1201.

Amendment by Pub.L. 107–170, extending to June 1, 2002, the date of repeal of this chapter, to take effect October 1, 2001, see section 2 of Pub.L. 107–170, set out as a note under 11 U.S.C.A. § 1201.

2001 Acts. Amendment by Pub.L. 107–17, extending to October 1, 2001, the date of repeal of this chapter, to take effect June 1, 2001, see section 2 of Pub.L. 107–17, set out as a note under 11 U.S.C.A. § 1201.

Amendment by Pub.L. 107–8, extending to June 1, 2001, the date of repeal of this chapter, to take effect July 1, 2000, see section 2 of Pub.L. 107–8, set out as a note under 11 U.S.C.A. § 1201.

1999 Acts. Amendment by Pub.L. 106–70, extending to July 1, 2000, the date of repeal of this chapter, to take effect Oct. 1, 1999, see section 2 of Pub.L. 106–70, set out as a note under 11 U.S.C.A. § 1201.

Amendment by Pub.L. 106–5, extending to Oct. 1, 1999, the date of repeal of this chapter, to take effect Apr. 1, 1999, see section 2 of Pub.L. 106–5, set out as a note under 11 U.S.C.A. § 1201.

1998 Acts. Section reenacted, eff. Oct. 1, 1998, for the period beginning on Oct. 1, 1998, and ending on Apr. 1, 1999, but all cases commenced or pending under this chapter 12, as reenacted under section 149(a) of Pub.L. 105–277, and all matters and proceedings in or relating to such cases, to be conducted and determined under such chapter as if such chapter were continued in effect after Apr. 1, 1999, and the substantive rights of parties in connection with such cases, matters, and proceedings to continue to be governed under the law applicable to such cases, matters, and proceedings as if such chapter were continued in effect after Apr. 1, 1999, see section 149 of Pub.L. 105–277, set out as a note under 11 U.S.C.A. § 1201.

1993 Acts. Amendment by Pub.L. 103–65, extending to Oct. 1, 1998, the date of repeal of this chapter, to take effect Aug.

6, 1993, see section 3 of Pub.L. 103–65, set out as a note under 11 U.S.C.A. § 1221.

1986 Acts. Section repealed effective Oct. 1, 1998, see section 302(f) of Pub.L. 99–554, as amended, set out in a note under 28 U.S.C.A. § 581. However, for extension of provisions, see section 149 of Pub.L. 105–277, set out as a note under 11 U.S.C.A. § 1201.

Section effective 30 days after Oct. 27, 1986, but not applicable to cases commenced under this title before that date, see section 302(a), (c)(1) of Pub.L. 99–554, set out as a note under 28 U.S.C.A. § 581.

Reenactment of Chapter

This section as in effect on June 30, 2005, reenacted effective July 1, 2005, see Pub.L. 109–8, § 1001(a), set out as a note under 11 U.S.C.A. § 1201.

Repeal of Chapter; Extension of Provisions

Pub.L. 99–554, Title III, § 302(f), Oct. 27, 1986, 100 Stat. 3124, as amended Pub.L. 103–65, § 1, Aug. 6, 1993, 107 Stat. 311, which provided that, effective Oct. 1, 1998, this chapter is repealed, but that all cases commenced or pending under this chapter, and all matters and proceedings in or relating to such cases, shall be conducted and determined under this chapter as if such chapter had not been repealed, and that the substantive rights of parties in connection with such cases, matters, and proceedings shall continue to be governed under the laws applicable to such cases, matters, and proceedings as if such chapter had not been repealed, was superceded by the reenactment of this chapter by Pub.L. 109–8, Title X, § 1001(a), Apr. 20, 2005, 119 Stat. 185, set out as a note under 11 U.S.C.A. § 1201.

Pub.L. 105–277, Div. C, Title I, § 149, Oct. 21, 1998, 112 Stat. 2681–610, as amended Pub.L. 106–5, §§ 1, 2, Mar. 30, 1999, 113 Stat. 9; Pub.L. 106–70, §§ 1, 2, Oct. 9, 1999, 113

Stat. 1031; Pub.L. 107–8, §§ 1, 2, May 11, 2001, 115 Stat. 10; Pub.L. 107–17, §§ 1, 2, June 26, 2001, 115 Stat. 151; Pub.L. 107–170, §§ 1, 2, May 7, 2002, 116 Stat. 133; Pub.L. 107–171, Title X, § 10814, May 13, 2002, 116 St. 532; Pub.L. 107–377, § 2, Dec. 19, 2002, 116 Stat. 3115; Pub.L. 108–73, § 2(a), Aug. 15, 2003, 117 Stat. 891; Pub.L. 108–369, § 2(a), Oct. 25, 2004, 118 Stat. 1749, provided that, to take effect on January 1, 2004, chapter 12 of Title 11 [this chapter; 11 U.S.C.A. § 1201 et seq.], as in effect on December 31, 2003, is reenacted for the period beginning on January 1, 2004, and ending on July 1, 2005, but that all cases commenced or pending under this chapter 12, as reenacted under section 149(a) of Pub.L. 105–277, and all matters and proceedings in or relating to such cases, shall be conducted and determined under such chapter as if such chapter were continued in effect after July 1, 2005, and that the substantive rights of parties in connection with such cases, matters, and proceedings shall continue to be governed under the law applicable to such cases, matters, and proceedings as if such chapter were continued in effect after July 1, 2005, was superceded by the reenactment of this chapter by Pub.L. 109–8, Title X, § 1001(a), Apr. 20, 2005, 119 Stat. 185, set out as a note under 11 U.S.C.A. § 1201.

LIBRARY REFERENCES

American Digest System

Taxation ⬅982, 1021.1, 1079.1.

Key Number System Topic No. 371.

Corpus Juris Secundum

CJS Bankruptcy § 278, Parties Defendant; Sovereign Immunity.

CJS Bankruptcy § 1169, Generally; Definitions.

CHAPTER 13—ADJUSTMENT OF DEBTS OF AN INDIVIDUAL WITH REGULAR INCOME

SUBCHAPTER I—OFFICERS, ADMINISTRATION, AND THE ESTATE

Sec.
1301. Stay of action against codebtor.
1302. Trustee.
1303. Rights and powers of debtor.
1304. Debtor engaged in business.
1305. Filing and allowance of postpetition claims.
1306. Property of the estate.
1307. Conversion or dismissal.
1308. Filing of prepetition tax returns.

SUBCHAPTER II—THE PLAN

1321. Filing of plan.
1322. Contents of plan.
1323. Modification of plan before confirmation.
1324. Confirmation hearing.
1325. Confirmation of plan.
1326. Payments.
1327. Effect of confirmation.
1328. Discharge.
1329. Modification of plan after confirmation.
1330. Revocation of an order of confirmation.

HISTORICAL AND STATUTORY NOTES

Amendments

2005 Amendments. Pub.L. 109–8, Title VII, § 716(b)(2), Apr. 20, 2005, 119 Stat. 130, added item 1308.

Effective and Applicability Provisions

2005 Acts. Amendments by Pub.L. 109–8 effective, except as otherwise provided, 180 days after April 20, 2005, and inapplicable with respect to cases commenced under Title 11 before the effective date, see Pub.L. 109–8, § 1501, set out as a note under 11 U.S.C.A. § 101.

CROSS REFERENCES

Chapters 1, 3 and 5 of this title applicable in cases under this chapter, see 11 USCA § 103.

Claims arising from rejection of executory contracts or unexpired leases by plans under this chapter, see 11 USCA § 502.

Compensation of trustee, see 11 USCA § 330.

Conversion from—

    Chapter eleven, see 11 USCA § 1112.

    Chapter seven, see 11 USCA § 706.

    Chapter thirteen, see 11 USCA § 348.

Core proceedings, see 28 USCA § 157.

Duration of automatic stay, see 11 USCA § 362.

Eligibility to serve as trustee, see 11 USCA § 321.

Executory contracts and unexpired leases, see 11 USCA § 365.

Filing fees, see 28 USCA § 1930.

Inapplicability of restrictions on garnishment to orders of bankruptcy courts under this chapter, see 15 USCA § 1673.

"Individual with regular income" defined, see 11 USCA § 101.

Individuals who may be debtors under this chapter, see 11 USCA § 109.

Limitation on compensation of trustee, see 11 USCA § 326.

Recommendation by trustee of conversion from Chapter eleven to this chapter, see 11 USCA § 1106.

Return of excessive attorney compensation if transferred property was to be paid by debtor under plan under this chapter, see 11 USCA § 329.

Special tax provisions, see 11 USCA § 346.

Supervision of United States trustees' duties by Attorney General, see 28 USCA § 586.

Unclaimed property, see 11 USCA § 347.

Use, sale or lease of property under plan under this chapter, see 11 USCA § 363.

SUBCHAPTER I—OFFICERS, ADMINISTRATION, AND THE ESTATE

§ 1301. Stay of action against codebtor

(a) Except as provided in subsections (b) and (c) of this section, after the order for relief under this chapter, a creditor may not act, or commence or continue any civil action, to collect all or any part of a consumer debt of the debtor from any individual that is liable on such debt with the debtor, or that secured such debt, unless—

(1) such individual became liable on or secured such debt in the ordinary course of such individual's business; or

(2) the case is closed, dismissed, or converted to a case under chapter 7 or 11 of this title.

(b) A creditor may present a negotiable instrument, and may give notice of dishonor of such an instrument.

(c) On request of a party in interest and after notice and a hearing, the court shall grant relief from the stay provided by subsection (a) of this section with respect to a creditor, to the extent that—

(1) as between the debtor and the individual protected under subsection (a) of this section, such individual received the consideration for the claim held by such creditor;

(2) the plan filed by the debtor proposes not to pay such claim; or

(3) such creditor's interest would be irreparably harmed by continuation of such stay.

(d) Twenty days after the filing of a request under subsection (c)(2) of this section for relief from the stay provided by subsection (a) of this section, such stay is terminated with respect to the party in interest making such request, unless the debtor or any individual that is liable on such debt with the debtor files and serves upon such party in interest a written objection to the taking of the proposed action.

(Pub.L. 95–598, Nov. 6, 1978, 92 Stat. 2645; Pub.L. 98–353, Title III, §§ 313, 524, July 10, 1984, 98 Stat. 355, 388.)

HISTORICAL AND STATUTORY NOTES

Revision Notes and Legislative Reports

1978 Acts. Subsection (a) automatically stays the holder of a claim based on a consumer debt of the chapter 13 debtor from acting or proceeding in any way, except as authorized pursuant to subsections (b) and (c), against an individual or the property of an individual liable with the chapter 13 debtor, unless such codebtor became liable in the ordinary course of his business, or unless the case is closed, dismissed, or converted to another chapter.

Under the terms of the agreement with the codebtor who is not in bankruptcy, the creditor has a right to collect all payments to the extent they are not made by the debtor at the time they are due. To the extent to which a chapter 13 plan does not propose to pay a creditor his claims, the creditor may obtain relief from the court from the automatic stay and collect such claims from the codebtor. Conversely, a codebtor obtains the benefit of any payments made to the creditor under the plan. If a debtor defaults on scheduled payments under the plan, then the codebtor would be liable for the remaining deficiency; otherwise, payments not made under the plan may never be made by the codebtor. The obligation of the codebtor to make the creditor whole at the time payments are due remains.

The automatic stay under this section pertains only to the collection of a consumer debt, defined by section 101(7) of this title to mean a debt incurred by an individual primarily for a personal, family, or household purpose. Therefore, not all debts owed by a chapter 13 debtor will be subject to the stay of the codebtor, particularly those business debts incurred by an individual with regular income, as defined by section 101(24) of this title, engaged in business, that is permitted by virtue of section 109(b) and section 1304 to obtain chapter 13 relief.

Subsection (b) excepts the giving of notice of dishonor of a negotiable instrument from the reach of the codebtor stay.

Under subsection (c), if the codebtor has property out of which the creditor's claim can be satisfied, the court can grant relief from the stay absent the transfer of a security interest in that property by the codebtor to the creditor. Correspondingly, if there is reasonable cause to believe that property is about to be disposed of by the codebtor which could be used to satisfy his obligation to the creditor, the court should lift the stay to allow the creditor to perfect his rights against such property. Likewise, if property is subject to rapid depreciation or decrease in value the stay should be lifted to allow the creditor to protect his rights to reach such property. Otherwise, the creditor's interest would be irreparably harmed by such stay. Property which could be used to satisfy the claim could be disposed of or encumbered and placed beyond the reach of the creditor. The creditor should be allowed to protect his rights to reach property which could satisfy his claim and prevent its erosion in value, disposal, or encumbrance. Senate Report No. 95–989.

This section is new. It is designed to protect a debtor operating under a chapter 13 individual repayment plan case by insulating him from indirect pressures from his creditors exerted through friends or relatives that may have cosigned an obligation of the debtor. The protection is limited, however, to ensure that the creditor involved does not lose the benefit of the bargain he made for a cosigner. He is entitled to full compensation, including any interest, fees, and costs provided for by the agreement under which the debtor obtained his loan. The creditor is simply required to share with other creditors to the extent that the debtor will repay him under the chapter 13 plan. The creditor is delayed, but his substantive rights are not affected.

Subsection (a) is the operative subsection. It stays action by a creditor after an order for relief under chapter 13. The creditor may not act, or commence or continue any civil action, to collect all or any part of a consumer debt of the debtor from any individual that is liable on such debt with the debtor, or that has secured the debt, unless the individual became liable or secured the debt in the ordinary course of his business, or the case is closed, dismissed, or converted to chapter 7 or 11.

Subsection (b) permits the creditor, notwithstanding the stay, to present a negotiable instrument and to give notice of dishonor of the instrument, in order to preserve his substantive rights against the codebtor as required by applicable nonbankruptcy law.

Subsection (c) requires the court to grant relief from the stay in certain circumstances. The court must grant relief to the extent that the debtor does not propose to pay, under the plan, the amount owed to the creditor. The court must also grant relief to the extent that the debtor was really the codebtor in the transaction, that is, to the extent that the nondebtor party actually received the consideration for the claim held by the creditor. Finally, the court must grant relief to the extent that the creditor's interest would be irreparably harmed by the stay, for example, where the codebtor filed bankruptcy himself, or threatened to leave the locale, or lost his job. House Report No. 95–595.

1984 Acts. Statements by Legislative Leaders, see 1984 U.S.Code Cong. and Adm.News, p. 576.

Legislative Statements

Section 1301 of the House amendment is identical with the provision contained in section 1301 of the House bill and adopted by the Senate amendment. Section 1301(c)(1) indicates that a basis for lifting the stay is that the debtor did not receive consideration for the claim by the creditor, or in other words, the debtor is really the "codebtor." As with other sections in title 11, the standard of receiving consideration is a general rule, but where two co-debtors have agreed to share liabilities in a different manner than profits it is the individual who does not ultimately bear the liability that is protected by the stay under section 1301.

Amendments

1984 Amendments. Subsec. (c)(3). Pub.L. 98–353, § 524, added "continuation of" after "by".

Subsec. (d). Pub.L. 98–353, § 313, added subsec. (d).

Effective and Applicability Provisions

1984 Acts. Amendment by Pub.L. 98–353 effective with respect to cases filed 90 days after July 10, 1984, see section

552(a), formerly 553(a), of Pub.L. 98–353, set out as a note under 11 U.S.C.A. § 101.

CROSS REFERENCES

Automatic stay, see 11 USCA § 362.

Automatic stay of enforcement of claims against debtor in Chapter nine cases, see 11 USCA § 922.

Claims of codebtors, see 11 USCA § 509.

Effect of conversion, see 11 USCA § 348.

Effect of § 362 of this title in stockbroker liquidation cases, see 11 USCA § 742.

Extension of time generally, see 11 USCA § 108.

LIBRARY REFERENCES

American Digest System

Bankruptcy ⟳2396, 2404, 2425, 2437, 2440.

Key Number System Topic No. 51.

Corpus Juris Secundum

CJS Bankruptcy § 7, Bankruptcy Code.

CJS Bankruptcy § 278, Parties Defendant; Sovereign Immunity.

CJS Bankruptcy § 478, Persons Protected by and Subject to Stay--Persons Liable for Debtor's Consumer Debts.

CJS Bankruptcy § 508, Against Codebtor or Surety.

CJS Bankruptcy § 526, Automatic Relief from Stay.

CJS Bankruptcy § 921, Assumption of Leases of Personal Property.

§ 1302. Trustee

(a) If the United States trustee appoints an individual under section 586(b) of title 28 to serve as standing trustee in cases under this chapter and if such individual qualifies under section 322 of this title, then such individual shall serve as trustee in the case. Otherwise, the United States trustee shall appoint one disinterested person to serve as trustee in the case or the United States trustee may serve as a trustee in the case.

(b) The trustee shall—

(1) perform the duties specified in sections 704(a)(2), 704(a)(3), 704(a)(4), 704(a)(5), 704(a)(6), 704(a)(7), and 704(a)(9) of this title;

(2) appear and be heard at any hearing that concerns—

(A) the value of property subject to a lien;

(B) confirmation of a plan; or

(C) modification of the plan after confirmation;

(3) dispose of, under regulations issued by the Director of the Administrative Office of the United States Courts, moneys received or to be received in a case under chapter XIII of the Bankruptcy Act;

(4) advise, other than on legal matters, and assist the debtor in performance under the plan;

(5) ensure that the debtor commences making timely payments under section 1326 of this title; and

(6) if with respect to the debtor there is a claim for a domestic support obligation, provide the applicable notice specified in subsection (d).

(c) If the debtor is engaged in business, then in addition to the duties specified in subsection (b) of this section, the trustee shall perform the duties specified in sections 1106(a)(3) and 1106(a)(4) of this title.

(d)(1) In a case described in subsection (b)(6) to which subsection (b)(6) applies, the trustee shall—

(A)(i) provide written notice to the holder of the claim described in subsection (b)(6) of such claim and of the right of such holder to use the services of the State child support enforcement agency established under sections 464 and 466 of the Social Security Act for the State in which such holder resides, for assistance in collecting child support during and after the case under this title; and

(ii) include in the notice provided under clause (i) the address and telephone number of such State child support enforcement agency;

(B)(i) provide written notice to such State child support enforcement agency of such claim; and

(ii) include in the notice provided under clause (i) the name, address, and telephone number of such holder; and

(C) at such time as the debtor is granted a discharge under section 1328, provide written notice to such holder and to such State child support enforcement agency of—

(i) the granting of the discharge;

(ii) the last recent known address of the debtor;

(iii) the last recent known name and address of the debtor's employer; and

(iv) the name of each creditor that holds a claim that—

(I) is not discharged under paragraph (2) or (4) of section 523(a); or

(II) was reaffirmed by the debtor under section 524(c).

(2)(A) The holder of a claim described in subsection (b)(6) or the State child support enforcement agency of the State in which such holder resides may request from a creditor described in paragraph (1)(C)(iv) the last known address of the debtor.

(B) Notwithstanding any other provision of law, a creditor that makes a disclosure of a last known address of a debtor in connection with a request made under subparagraph (A) shall not be liable by reason of making that disclosure.

(Pub.L. 95–598, Nov. 6, 1978, 92 Stat. 2645; Pub.L. 98–353, Title III, §§ 314, 525, July 10, 1984, 98 Stat. 356, 388; Pub.L. 99–554, Title II, §§ 228, 283(w), Oct. 27, 1986, 100 Stat. 3103, 3118; Pub.L. 103–394, Title V, § 501(d)(37), Oct. 22, 1994, 108 Stat. 4147; Pub.L. 109–8, Title II, § 219(d), Apr. 20, 2005, 119 Stat. 58; Pub.L. 111–327, § 2(a)(39), Dec. 22, 2010, 124 Stat. 3561.)

HISTORICAL AND STATUTORY NOTES

Revision Notes and Legislative Reports

1978 Acts. The principal administrator in a chapter 13 case is the chapter 13 trustee. Experience under chapter XIII of the Bankruptcy Act [former chapter 13 (section 1001 et seq.) of former Title 11] has shown that the more efficient and effective wage earner programs have been conducted by standing chapter XIII trustees who exercise a broad range of responsibilities in both the design and the effectuation of debtor plans.

Subsection (a) provides administrative flexibility by permitting the bankruptcy judge to appoint an individual from the panel of trustees established pursuant to 28 U.S.C. § 604(f) and qualified under section 322 of title 11, either to serve as a standing trustee in all chapter 13 cases filed in the district or a portion thereof, or to serve in a single case.

Subsection (b)(1) makes it clear that the chapter 13 trustee is no mere disbursing agent of the monies paid to him by the debtor under the plan [section 1322(a)(1)], by imposing upon him certain relevant duties of a liquidation trustee prescribed by section 704 of this title.

Subsection (b)(2) requires the chapter 13 trustee to appear before and be heard by the bankruptcy court whenever the value of property secured by a lien or the confirmation or modification of a plan after confirmation as provided by sections 1323–1325 is considered by the court.

Subsection (b)(3) requires the chapter 13 trustee to advise and counsel the debtor while under chapter 13, except on matters more appropriately left to the attorney for the debtor. The chapter 13 trustee must also assist the debtor in performance under the plan by attempting to tailor the requirements of the plan to the changing needs and circumstances of the debtor during the extension period.

Subsection (c) imposes on the trustee in a chapter 13 case filed by a debtor engaged in business the investigative and reporting duties normally required of a chapter 11 debtor or trustee as prescribed by section 1106(a)(3) and (4). Notes of Committee on the Judiciary, Senate Report No. 95–989.

Subsection (d) gives the trustee an additional duty if the debtor is engaged in business, as defined in section 1304. The trustee must perform the duties specified in sections 1106(a)(3) and 1106(a)(4), relating to investigation of the debtor. House Report No. 95–595.

1984 Acts. Statements by Legislative Leaders, see 1984 U.S.Code Cong. and Adm.News, p. 576.

1986 Acts. House Report No. 99–764 and House Conference Report No. 99–958, see 1986 U.S.Code Cong. and Adm. News, p. 5227.

1994 Acts. House Report No. 103–835, see 1994 U.S. Code Cong. and Adm. News, p. 3340.

2005 Acts. House Report No. 109–31(Part I), see 2005 U.S. Code Cong. and Adm. News, p. 88.

Legislative Statements

Section 1302 of the House amendment adopts a provision contained in the Senate amendment instead of the position taken in the House bill. Sections 1302(d) and (e) are modeled on the standing trustee system contained in the House bill with the court assuming supervisory functions in districts not under the pilot program.

References in Text

Chapter XIII of the Bankruptcy Act, referred to in subsec. (b)(3), is chapter XIII of Act July 1, 1898, c. 541, as added June 22, 1938, c. 575, § 1, 52 Stat. 930, which was classified to chapter 13 (section 1001 et seq.) of former Title 11.

Section 464 of the Social Security Act, referred to in subsec. (d)(1)(A)(i), is Act Aug. 14, 1935, c. 531, Title IV, § 464, as added Aug. 13, 1981, Pub.L. 97–35, Title XXIII, § 2331(a), 95 Stat. 860, and amended, which is classified to 42 U.S.C.A. § 664.

Section 466 of the Social Security Act, referred to in subsec. (d)(1)(A)(i), is Act Aug. 14, 1935, c. 531, Title IV, § 466, as added Aug. 16, 1984, Pub.L. 98–378, § 3(b), 98 Stat. 1306, and amended, which is classified to 42 U.S.C.A. § 666.

Amendments

2010 Amendments. Subsec. (b)(1). Pub.L. 111–327, § 2(a)(39), struck out "704(2), 704(3), 704(4), 704(5), 704(6), 704(7), and 704(9)" and inserted "704(a)(2), 704(a)(3), 704(a)(4), 704(a)(5), 704(a)(6), 704(a)(7), and 704(a)(9)".

2005 Amendments. Subsec. (b)(4). Pub.L. 109–8, § 219(d)(1)(A), struck out "and" at the end of par. (4).

Subsec. (b)(5). Pub.L. 109–8, § 219(d)(1)(B), substituted "; and" for the period at the end of par. (5).

Subsec. (b)(6). Pub.L. 109–8, § 219(d)(1)(C), added par. (6).

Subsec. (d). Pub.L. 109–8, § 219(d)(2), added subsec. (d).

1994 Amendments. Subsec. (b)(3). Pub.L. 103–394, § 501(d)(37), struck out "and" after "Bankruptcy Act;".

1986 Amendments. Subsec. (a). Pub.L. 99–554, § 228(1), substituted "If the United States trustee appoints" for "If the court has appointed", "section 586(b) of title 28" for "subsection (d) of this section", and "the United States trustee shall appoint one disinterested person to serve as trustee in the case or the United States trustee may serve as a trustee in the case" for "the court shall appoint a person to serve as trustee in the case".

Subsecs. (d) and (e). Pub.L. 99–554, § 228(2), struck out subsecs. (d) and (e) which read as follows:

"**(d)** If the number of cases under this chapter commenced in a particular judicial district so warrant, the court may appoint one or more individuals to serve as standing trustee for such district in cases under this chapter.

"**(e)(1)** A court that has appointed an individual under subsection (d) of this section to serve as standing trustee in cases under this chapter shall set for such individual—

"**(A)** a maximum annual compensation, not to exceed the lowest annual rate of basic pay in effect for grade GS–16 of the General Schedule prescribed under section 5332 of title 5; and

"**(B)** a percentage fee, not to exceed ten percent, based on such maximum annual compensation and the actual, necessary expenses incurred by such individual as standing trustee.

"**(2)** Such individual shall collect such percentage fee from all payments under plans in the cases under this chapter for which such individual serves as standing trustee. Such individual shall pay annually to the Treasury—

"**(A)** any amount by which the actual compensation received by such individual exceeds five percent of all such payments made under plans in cases under this chapter for which such individual serves as standing trustee; and

"**(B)** any amount by which the percentage fee fixed under paragraph (1)(B) of this subsection for all such cases exceeds—

"**(i)** such individual's actual compensation for such cases, as adjusted under subparagraph (A) of this paragraph; plus

"**(ii)** the actual, necessary expenses incurred by such individual as standing trustee in such cases.".

Pub.L. 99–554, § 283(w), which directed the amendment of subsec. (e)(1) by substituting "set for such individual" for "fix" could not be executed in view of the repeal of subsec. (e) by section 228(2) of Pub.L. 99–554.

1984 Amendments. Subsec. (b)(1). Pub.L. 98–353, § 314(1), substituted "perform the duties specified in sections 704(2), 704(3), 704(4), 704(5), 704(6), 704(7), and 704(9) of this title;" for "perform the duties specified in sections 704(2), 704(3), 704(4), 704(5), 704(6), and 704(8) of this title;".

Subsec. (b)(2). Pub.L. 98–353, § 314(2), struck out "and" at the end thereof.

Subsec. (b)(3). Pub.L. 98–353, § 525(a), added par. (3). Former par. (3) was redesignated as (4).

Pub.L. 98–353, § 314(3), substituted "; and" for the period at the end thereof.

Subsec. (b)(4). Pub.L. 98–353, § 525(a), redesignated former par. (3) as (4). Another par. (4), as added by Pub.L. 98–353, § 314(4), was redesignated par. (5).

Subsec. (b)(5). Pub.L. 98–353, § 314(4), added par. (5), originally enacted as par. (4) and subsequently redesignated.

Pub.L. 98–353, § 525(a), redesignated former par. (4) as (5).

Subsec. (e)(1). Pub.L. 98–353, § 525(b)(1), which directed the amendment of par. (4) by substituting "set for such individual" for "fix", was executed to par. (1) as the probable intent of Congress.

Subsec. (e)(1)(A). Pub.L. 98–353, § 525(b)(2), struck out "for such individual" after "a maximum annual compensation".

Subsec. (e)(2)(A). Pub.L. 98–353, § 525(b)(3)(A), substituted "received by" for "of".

Pub.L. 98–353, § 525(b)(3)(B), substituted "of all such payments made" for "upon all payments".

Effective and Applicability Provisions

2005 Acts. Amendments by Pub.L. 109–8 effective, except as otherwise provided, 180 days after April 20, 2005, and inapplicable with respect to cases commenced under Title 11 before the effective date, see Pub.L. 109–8, § 1501, set out as a note under 11 U.S.C.A. § 101.

1994 Acts. Amendment by Pub.L. 103–394 effective on Oct. 22, 1994, and not to apply with respect to cases commenced under Title 11 of the United States Code before Oct. 22, 1994, see section 702 of Pub.L. 103–394, set out as a note under section 101 of this title.

1986 Acts. Amendment by section 283 of Pub.L. 99–554 effective 30 days after Oct. 27, 1986, except as otherwise provided for, see section 302(a) of Pub.L. 99–554, set out as a note under section 581 of Title 28, Judiciary and Judicial Procedure.

Amendment by Pub.L. 99–554, § 228, not to become effective in or with respect to certain specified judicial districts until, or apply to cases while pending in such district before, the expiration of the 270–day period beginning 30 days after Oct. 27, 1986, or of the 30–day period beginning on the date the Attorney General certifies under section 303 of Pub.L.

99–554 the region specified in a paragraph of section 581(a) of Title 28, as amended by section 111(a) of Pub.L. 99–554, that includes such district, whichever occurs first, see section 302(d)(1) of Pub.L. 99–554, set out as a note under section 581 of Title 28.

Amendment by Pub.L. 99–554, § 228, not to become effective in or with respect to certain specified judicial districts until, or apply to cases while pending in such district before, the expiration of the 2–year period beginning 30 days after Oct. 27, 1986, or of the 30–day period beginning on the date the Attorney General certifies under section 303 of Pub.L. 99–554 the region specified in a paragraph of section 581(a) of Title 28, as amended by section 111(a) of Pub.L. 99–554, that includes such district, whichever occurs first, see section 302(d)(2) of Pub.L. 99–554, set out as a note under section 581 of Title 28.

Amendment by Pub.L. 99–554, § 228, not to become effective in or with respect to judicial districts established for the States of Alabama and North Carolina until, or apply to cases while pending in such district before, such district elects to be included in a bankruptcy region established in section 581(a) of Title 28, as amended by section 111(a) of Pub.L. 99–554, or Oct. 1, 2002, whichever occurs first, and, except as otherwise provided for, with respect to cases under chapters 7, 11, 12, and 13 of Title 11 commenced before 30 days after Oct. 27, 1986, and pending in a judicial district in the States of Alabama or North Carolina before any election made under section 302(d)(3)(A) of Pub.L. 99–554 by such district becomes effective or Oct. 1, 2002, whichever occurs first, amendments by Pub.L. 99–554 not to apply until Oct. 1, 2003, or the expiration of the 1–year period beginning on the date such election becomes effective, whichever occurs first, and further, in any judicial district in Alabama or North Carolina not making the election described in section 302(d)(3)(A) of Pub.L. 99–554, any person appointed under regulations issued by the Judicial Conference to administer estates in cases under Title 11 authorized to establish, etc., a panel of private trustees, and to supervise cases and trustees in cases under chapters 7, 11, 12, and 13 of Title 11, until amendments by sections 201 to 231 of Pub.L. 99–554 effective in such district, see section 302(d)(3)(A) to (F), (H), (I) of Pub.L. 99–554, set out as a note under section 581 of Title 28.

Amendment by Pub.L. 99–554, § 228, except as otherwise provided, with respect to cases under chapters 7, 11, 12, and 13 of Title 11 commenced before 30 days after Oct. 27, 1986, and pending in a judicial district referred to in section 581(a) of Title 28, as amended by section 111(a) of Pub.L. 99–554, for which a United States trustee is not authorized before 30 days after Oct. 27, 1986 to be appointed, not applicable until the expiration of the 3–year period beginning on Oct. 27, 1986, or of the 1–year period beginning on the date the Attorney General certifies under section 303 of Pub.L. 99–554 the region specified in a paragraph of such section 581(a) that includes, such district, whichever occurs first, see section 302(e)(1), (2) of Pub.L. 99–554, set out as a note under section 581 of Title 28.

1984 Acts. Amendment by Pub.L. 98–353 effective with respect to cases filed 90 days after July 10, 1984, see section 552(a), formerly 553(a), of Pub.L. 98–353, set out as a note under section 101 of this title.

Separability of Provisions

If any provision of or amendment made by Pub.L. 103–394 or the application of such provision or amendment to any person or circumstance is held to be unconstitutional, the remaining provisions of and amendments made by Pub.L. 103–394 and the application of such provisions and amendments to any person or circumstance shall not be affected thereby, see section 701 of Pub.L. 103–394, set out as a note under section 101 of this title.

CROSS REFERENCES

Appointment of trustee in—

    Chapter eleven cases, see 11 USCA § 1104.

    Chapter twelve cases, see 11 USCA § 1202.

    Railroad reorganization cases, see 11 USCA § 1163.

Compensation of officers, see 11 USCA § 330.

Election of trustee, see 11 USCA § 702.

Eligibility to serve as trustee, see 11 USCA § 321.

Grain storage facility bankruptcies, expedited appointment of trustee or examiner, see 11 USCA § 557.

    Limitation on compensation of trustee, see 11 USCA § 326.

    Qualification of trustee, see 11 USCA § 322.

    Removal of trustee, see 11 USCA § 324.

    Role and capacity of trustee, see 11 USCA § 323.

    Time of bringing action, see 11 USCA § 546.

LIBRARY REFERENCES

American Digest System

Bankruptcy ☞3703, 3008.1, 3009.

Key Number System Topic No. 51.

Corpus Juris Secundum

CJS Bankruptcy § 46, Service as Bankruptcy Trustee.

CJS Bankruptcy § 52, Proceedings Under Chapters 12 and 13.

CJS Bankruptcy § 56, Eligibility to Serve as Trustee or Examiner--Disinterestedness Requirement.

CJS Bankruptcy § 75, Chapter 13 Cases.

CJS Bankruptcy § 103, Chapter 13.

CJS Bankruptcy § 104, Chapter 13--Duties If Debtor is Engaged in Business.

CJS Bankruptcy § 578, Debtor's Statement of Intention.

CJS Bankruptcy § 805, Who May Conduct Examination; Debtor's Right to Examine.

CJS Bankruptcy § 848, Operation of Business or Affairs of Chapter 13 Debtor.

§ 1303. Rights and powers of debtor

Subject to any limitations on a trustee under this chapter, the debtor shall have, exclusive of the trustee, the rights and powers of a trustee under sections 363(b), 363(d), 363(e), 363(f), and 363(*l*), of this title. (Pub.L. 95–598, Nov. 6, 1978, 92 Stat. 2646.)

HISTORICAL AND STATUTORY NOTES

Revision Notes and Legislative Reports

1978 Acts. A chapter 13 debtor is vested with the identical rights and powers, and is subject to the same limitations in regard to their exercise, as those given a liquidation trustee by virtue of section 363(b), (d), (e), (f), and (h) of title 11,

relating to the sale, use or lease of property. Notes of Committee on the Judiciary, Senate Report No. 95–989.

Legislative Statements

Section 1303 of the House amendment specifies rights and powers that the debtor has exclusive of the trustees. The section does not imply that the debtor does not also possess other powers concurrently with the trustee. For example, although section 1323 is not specified in section 1303, certainly it is intended that the debtor has the power to sue and be sued.

CROSS REFERENCES

Rights and powers of debtor in—

    Chapter eleven cases, see 11 USCA § 1107.

    Chapter twelve cases, see 11 USCA § 1203.

LIBRARY REFERENCES

American Digest System

Bankruptcy ☞3703.

Key Number System Topic No. 51.

Corpus Juris Secundum

CJS Bankruptcy § 104, Chapter 13--Duties If Debtor is Engaged in Business.

CJS Bankruptcy § 278, Parties Defendant; Sovereign Immunity.

CJS Bankruptcy § 699, Who May Exercise Avoidance and Recovery Powers.

CJS Bankruptcy § 848, Operation of Business or Affairs of Chapter 13 Debtor.

CJS Bankruptcy § 851, Prepetition Security Interests in Proceeds, Products, Offspring, or Profits.

CJS Bankruptcy § 852, Prepetition Security Interests Extending to Rents and Similar Charges.

CJS Bankruptcy § 874, What Transactions Are Other Than in Ordinary Course of Business.

CJS Bankruptcy § 876, Requirement of Business Justification.

CJS Bankruptcy § 891, Protection of Good-Faith Purchasers and Lessees from Reversal or Modification on Appeal.

CJS Estoppel and Waiver § 192, Judicial Estoppel as Restricted to Statements Made Under Oath.

§ 1304. Debtor engaged in business

(a) A debtor that is self-employed and incurs trade credit in the production of income from such employment is engaged in business.

(b) Unless the court orders otherwise, a debtor engaged in business may operate the business of the debtor and, subject to any limitations on a trustee under sections 363(c) and 364 of this title and to such limitations or conditions as the court prescribes, shall have, exclusive of the trustee, the rights and powers of the trustee under such sections.

(c) A debtor engaged in business shall perform the duties of the trustee specified in section 704(a)(8) of this title.

(Pub.L. 95–598, Nov. 6, 1978, 92 Stat. 2646; Pub.L. 98–353, Title III, §§ 311(b)(2), 526, July 10, 1984, 98 Stat. 355, 389; Pub.L. 111–327, § 2(a)(40), Dec. 22, 2010, 124 Stat. 3562.)

HISTORICAL AND STATUTORY NOTES

Revision Notes and Legislative Reports

1978 Acts. Increased access to the simpler, speedier, and less expensive debtor relief provisions of chapter 13 is accomplished by permitting debtors engaged in business to proceed under chapter 13, provided their income is sufficiently stable and regular to permit compliance with a chapter 13 plan [section 101(24)] and that the debtor (or the debtor and spouse) do not owe liquidated, noncontingent unsecured debts of $50,000, or liquidated, noncontingent secured debts of $200,000 (§ 109(d)).

Section 1304(a) states that a self-employed individual who incurs trade credit in the production of income is a debtor engaged in business.

Subsection (b) empowers a chapter 13 debtor engaged in business to operate his business, subject to the rights, powers and limitations that pertain to a trustee under sections 363(c) and 364 of title 11, and subject to such further limitations and conditions as the court may prescribe.

Subsection (c) requires a chapter 13 debtor engaged in business to file with the court certain financial statements relating to the operation of the business. Notes of Committee on the Judiciary, Senate Report No. 95–989.

1984 Acts. Statements by Legislative Leaders, see 1984 U.S.Code Cong. and Adm.News, p. 576.

Legislative Statements

Section 1304(b) of the House amendment adopts the approach taken in the comparable section of the Senate amendment as preferable to the position taken in the House bill.

Amendments

2010 Amendments. Subsec. (c). Pub.L. 111–327, § 2(a)(40), struck out "704(8)" and inserted "704(a)(8)".

1984 Amendments. Subsec. (b). Pub.L. 98–353, § 526, struck out the comma after "of the debtor".

Subsec. (c). Pub.L. 98–353, § 311(b)(2), substituted "section 704(8)" for "section 704(7)".

Effective and Applicability Provisions

1984 Acts. Amendment by Pub.L. 98–353 effective with respect to cases filed 90 days after July 10, 1984, see section 552(a), formerly 553(a), of Pub.L. 98–353, set out as a note under section 101 of this title.

CROSS REFERENCES

Authorization of trustee to operate business in—

 Chapter eleven cases, see 11 USCA § 1108.

 Chapter seven cases, see 11 USCA § 721.

Obtaining credit, see 11 USCA § 364.

Rights, powers and duties of debtor in possession in Chapter 11 cases, see 11 USCA § 1107.

Use, sale or lease of property, see 11 USCA § 363.

LIBRARY REFERENCES

American Digest System

Bankruptcy ⚮3703.

Key Number System Topic No. 51.

Corpus Juris Secundum

CJS Bankruptcy § 104, Chapter 13--Duties If Debtor is Engaged in Business.

CJS Bankruptcy § 699, Who May Exercise Avoidance and Recovery Powers.

CJS Bankruptcy § 848, Operation of Business or Affairs of Chapter 13 Debtor.

CJS Bankruptcy § 851, Prepetition Security Interests in Proceeds, Products, Offspring, or Profits.

CJS Bankruptcy § 852, Prepetition Security Interests Extending to Rents and Similar Charges.

CJS Bankruptcy § 871, Motion for Authorization.

CJS Bankruptcy § 874, What Transactions Are Other Than in Ordinary Course of Business.

CJS Bankruptcy § 891, Protection of Good-Faith Purchasers and Lessees from Reversal or Modification on Appeal.

CJS Bankruptcy § 895, Unsecured Credit or Debt in Ordinary Course of Business.

CJS Bankruptcy § 896, Unsecured Credit or Debt Other Than in Ordinary Course of Business.

CJS Bankruptcy § 897, Credit With Special Administrative Priority or Secured by First Liens or Junior Liens.

CJS Bankruptcy § 898, Credit Secured by Superpriority Lien; Subordination of Existing Liens.

CJS Bankruptcy § 900, Motion for Authorization to Obtain Credit; Notice and Hearing.

§ 1305. Filing and allowance of postpetition claims

(a) A proof of claim may be filed by any entity that holds a claim against the debtor—

 (1) for taxes that become payable to a governmental unit while the case is pending; or

 (2) that is a consumer debt, that arises after the date of the order for relief under this chapter, and that is for property or services necessary for the debtor's performance under the plan.

(b) Except as provided in subsection (c) of this section, a claim filed under subsection (a) of this section shall be allowed or disallowed under section 502 of this title, but shall be determined as of the date such claim arises, and shall be allowed under section 502(a), 502(b), or 502(c) of this title, or disallowed under section 502(d) or 502(e) of this title, the same as if such claim had arisen before the date of the filing of the petition.

(c) A claim filed under subsection (a)(2) of this section shall be disallowed if the holder of such claim knew or should have known that prior approval by the trustee of the debtor's incurring the obligation was practicable and was not obtained.

(Pub.L. 95–598, Nov. 6, 1978, 92 Stat. 2647.)

HISTORICAL AND STATUTORY NOTES

Revision Notes and Legislative Reports

1978 Acts. Section 1305, exclusively applicable in chapter 13 cases, supplements the provisions of sections 501–511 of title 11, dealing with the filing and allowance of claims. Sections 501–511 apply in chapter 13 cases by virtue of section 103(a) of this title. Section 1305(a) provides for the filing of a proof of claim for taxes and other obligations incurred after the filing of the chapter 13 case. Subsection (b) prescribes that section 502 of title 11 governs the allowance of section 1305(a) claims, except that its standards shall be applied as of the date of allowance of the claim, rather than the date of filing of the petition. Subsection (c) requires the disallowance of a postpetition claim for property or services necessary for the debtor's performance under the plan, if the holder of the claim knew or should have known that prior approval by the trustee of the debtor's incurring of the obligation was practicable and was not obtained. Senate Report No. 95–989.

Subsection (a) permits the filing of a proof of a claim against the debtor that is for taxes that become payable to a governmental unit while the case is pending, or that arises after the date of the filing of the petition for property or services that are necessary for the debtor's performance under the plan, such as auto repairs in order that the debtor will be able to get to work, or medical bills. The effect of the latter provision, in paragraph (2), is to treat postpetition credit extended to a chapter 13 debtor the same as a prepetition claim for purposes of allowance, distribution, and so on. House Report No. 95–595.

Legislative Statements

Section 1305(a)(2) of the House amendment modifies similar provisions contained in the House and Senate bills by restricting application of the paragraph to a consumer debt. Debts of the debtor that are not consumer debts should not be subjected to section 1305(c) or section 1328(d) of the House amendment.

Section 1305(b) of the House amendment represents a technical modification of similar provisions contained in the House bill and Senate amendment.

The House amendment deletes section 1305(d) of the Senate amendment as unnecessary. Section 502(b)(1) is sufficient to disallow any claim to the extent the claim represents the usurious interest or any other charge forbidden by applicable law. It is anticipated that the Rules of Bankruptcy Procedure may require a creditor filing a proof of claim in a case under chapter 13 to include an affirmative statement as contemplated by section 1305(d) of the Senate amendment.

CROSS REFERENCES

Allowance and filing of claims and interests in Chapter 11 cases, see 11 USCA § 1111.

Discharge of certain consumer debts, see 11 USCA § 1328.

Effect of conversion, see 11 USCA § 348.

Filing of proofs of claims or interests, see 11 USCA § 501.

Provisions in plans for payment of claims, see 11 USCA § 1322.

LIBRARY REFERENCES

American Digest System

Bankruptcy ⬅2830, 2895.1, 2832.1, 2921.

Key Number System Topic No. 51.

Corpus Juris Secundum

CJS Bankruptcy § 278, Parties Defendant; Sovereign Immunity.

CJS Bankruptcy § 959, Effect of Time of Accrual.

CJS Bankruptcy § 964, Tax Claims.

CJS Bankruptcy § 1007, Generally; Who May File.

CJS Bankruptcy § 1189, Contents of Plan, Generally.

CJS Bankruptcy § 1208, Discharge.

§ 1306. Property of the estate

(a) Property of the estate includes, in addition to the property specified in section 541 of this title—

(1) all property of the kind specified in such section that the debtor acquires after the commencement of the case but before the case is closed, dismissed, or converted to a case under chapter 7, 11, or 12 of this title, whichever occurs first; and

(2) earnings from services performed by the debtor after the commencement of the case but before the case is closed, dismissed, or converted to a case under chapter 7, 11, or 12 of this title, whichever occurs first.

(b) Except as provided in a confirmed plan or order confirming a plan, the debtor shall remain in possession of all property of the estate.

(Pub.L. 95–598, Nov. 6, 1978, 92 Stat. 2647; Pub.L. 99–554, Title II, § 257(u), Oct. 27, 1986, 100 Stat. 3116.)

HISTORICAL AND STATUTORY NOTES

Revision Notes and Legislative Reports

1978 Acts. Section 541 is expressly made applicable to chapter 13 cases by section 103(a). Section 1306 broadens the definition of property of the estate for chapter 13 purposes to include all property acquired and all earnings from services performed by the debtor after the commencement of the case.

Subsection (b) nullifies the effect of section 521(3), otherwise applicable, by providing that a chapter 13 debtor need not surrender possession of property of the estate, unless required by the plan or order of confirmation. Notes of Committee on the Judiciary, Senate Report No. 95–989.

1986 Acts. House Report No. 99–764 and House Conference Report No. 99–958, see 1986 U.S.Code Cong. and Adm. News, p. 5227.

Legislative Statements

Section 1306(a)(2) adopts a provision contained in the Senate amendment in preference to a similar provision contained in the House bill.

Amendments

1986 Amendments. Subsec. (a)(1). Pub.L. 99–554, § 257(u)(1), added reference to chapter 12.

Subsec. (a)(2). Pub.L. 99–554, § 257(u)(2), added reference to chapter 12.

Effective and Applicability Provisions

1986 Acts. Amendment by Pub.L. 99–554 effective 30 days after Oct. 27, 1986, but not applicable to cases commenced under this title before that date, see section 302(a), (c)(1) of Pub.L. 99–554, set out as a note under section 581 of Title 28, Judiciary and Judicial Procedure.

CROSS REFERENCES

Ownership of copyright, see 17 USCA § 201.

LIBRARY REFERENCES

American Digest System

Bankruptcy ⇨2558, 3715(11).

Key Number System Topic No. 51.

Corpus Juris Secundum

CJS Bankruptcy § 75, Chapter 13 Cases.

CJS Bankruptcy § 561, Property Acquired Postpetition.

CJS Bankruptcy § 624, Surrender of Property of Estate and Recorded Information to Trustee.

§ 1307. Conversion or dismissal

(a) The debtor may convert a case under this chapter to a case under chapter 7 of this title at any time. Any waiver of the right to convert under this subsection is unenforceable.

(b) On request of the debtor at any time, if the case has not been converted under section 706, 1112, or 1208 of this title, the court shall dismiss a case under this chapter. Any waiver of the right to dismiss under this subsection is unenforceable.

(c) Except as provided in subsection (f) of this section, on request of a party in interest or the United States trustee and after notice and a hearing, the court may convert a case under this chapter to a case under chapter 7 of this title, or may dismiss a case under this chapter, whichever is in the best interests of creditors and the estate, for cause, including—

(1) unreasonable delay by the debtor that is prejudicial to creditors;

(2) nonpayment of any fees and charges required under chapter 123 of title 28;

(3) failure to file a plan timely under section 1321 of this title;

(4) failure to commence making timely payments under section 1326 of this title;

(5) denial of confirmation of a plan under section 1325 of this title and denial of a request made for additional time for filing another plan or a modification of a plan;

(6) material default by the debtor with respect to a term of a confirmed plan;

(7) revocation of the order of confirmation under section 1330 of this title, and denial of confirmation of a modified plan under section 1329 of this title;

(8) termination of a confirmed plan by reason of the occurrence of a condition specified in the plan other than completion of payments under the plan;

(9) only on request of the United States trustee, failure of the debtor to file, within fifteen days, or such additional time as the court may allow, after the filing of the petition commencing such case, the information required by paragraph (1) of section 521(a);

(10) only on request of the United States trustee, failure to timely file the information required by paragraph (2) of section 521(a); or

(11) failure of the debtor to pay any domestic support obligation that first becomes payable after the date of the filing of the petition.

(d) Except as provided in subsection (f) of this section, at any time before the confirmation of a plan under section 1325 of this title, on request of a party in interest or the United States trustee and after notice and a hearing, the court may convert a case under this chapter to a case under chapter 11 or 12 of this title.

(e) Upon the failure of the debtor to file a tax return under section 1308, on request of a party in interest or the United States trustee and after notice and a hearing, the court shall dismiss a case or convert a case under this chapter to a case under chapter 7 of this title, whichever is in the best interest of the creditors and the estate.

(f) The court may not convert a case under this chapter to a case under chapter 7, 11, or 12 of this title if the debtor is a farmer, unless the debtor requests such conversion.

(g) Notwithstanding any other provision of this section, a case may not be converted to a case under another chapter of this title unless the debtor may be a debtor under such chapter.

(Pub.L. 95–598, Nov. 6, 1978, 92 Stat. 2647; Pub.L. 98–353, Title III, §§ 315, 527, July 10, 1984, 98 Stat. 356, 389; Pub.L. 99–554, Title II, §§ 229, 257(v), Oct. 27, 1986, 100 Stat. 3103, 3116; Pub.L. 109–8, Title II, § 213(7), Title VII, § 716(c), Apr. 20, 2005, 119 Stat. 53, 130; Pub.L. 111–327, § 2(a)(41), Dec. 22, 2010, 124 Stat. 3562.)

HISTORICAL AND STATUTORY NOTES

Revision Notes and Legislative Reports

1978 Acts. Subsections (a) and (b) confirm, without qualification, the rights of a chapter 13 debtor to convert the case to a liquidating bankruptcy case under chapter 7 of title 11, at any time, or to have the chapter 13 case dismissed. Waiver of any such right is unenforceable. Subsection (c) specifies various conditions for the exercise of the power of the court to convert a chapter 13 case to one under chapter 7 or to dismiss the case. Subsection (d) deals with the conversion of a chapter 13 case to one under chapter 11. Subsection (e) prohibits conversion of the chapter 13 case filed by a farmer to chapter 7 or 11 except at the request of the debtor. No case is to be converted from chapter 13 to any other chapter, unless the debtor is an eligible debtor under the new chapter. Senate Report No. 95–989.

Subsection (f) reinforces section 109 by prohibiting conversion to a chapter under which the debtor is not eligible to proceed. House Report No. 95–595.

1984 Acts. Statements by Legislative Leaders, see 1984 U.S.Code Cong. and Adm.News, p. 576.

1986 Acts. House Report No. 99–764 and House Conference Report No. 99–958, see 1986 U.S.Code Cong. and Adm. News, p. 5227.

2005 Acts. House Report No. 109–31(Part I), see 2005 U.S. Code Cong. and Adm. News, p. 88.

Legislative Statements

Section 1307(a) is derived from the Senate amendment in preference to a comparable provision contained in the House bill.

References in Text

Chapter 7 of this title, referred to in text, is 11 U.S.C.A. § 701 et seq.

Amendments

2010 Amendments. Subsec. (c). Pub.L. 111–327, § 2(a)(41)(A)(i), struck out "subsection (e)" and inserted "subsection (f)".

Subsec. (c)(9). Pub.L. 111–327, § 2(a)(41)(A)(ii), struck out "521" and inserted "521(a)".

Subsec. (c)(10). Pub.L. 111–327, § 2(a)(41)(A)(iii), struck out "521" and inserted "521(a)".

Subsec. (d). Pub.L. 111–327, § 2(a)(41)(B), struck out "subsection (e)" and inserted "subsection (f)".

2005 Amendments. Subsec. (c)(9). Pub.L. 109–8, § 213(7)(A), struck out "or" at the end of par. (9).

Subsec. (c)(10). Pub.L. 109–8, § 213(7)(B), substituted "; or" for the period at the end of par. (10).

Subsec. (c)(11). Pub.L. 109–8, § 213(7)(C), added par. (11).

Subsec. (e). Pub.L. 109–8, § 716(c), redesignated subsec. (e) as subsec. (f) and inserted a new subsec. (e).

Subsec. (f). Pub.L. 109–8, § 716(c)(1), redesignated subsec. (e) as subsec. (f). Former subsec. (f) was redesignated subsec. (g).

Subsec. (g). Pub.L. 109–8, § 716(c)(1), redesignated subsec. (f) as subsec. (g).

1986 Amendments. Subsec. (b). Pub.L. 99–554, § 257(v)(1), added reference to section 1208 of this title.

Subsec. (c). Pub.L. 99–554, § 229(1)(A), added "or the United States trustee" following "party in interest" in provisions preceding par. (1).

Subsec. (c)(9), (10). Pub.L. 99–554, § 229(1)(B)–(D), added pars. (9) and (10).

Subsec. (d). Pub.L. 99–554, § 229(2), added "or the United States trustee" following "party in interest".

Pub.L. 99–554, § 257(v)(2), added reference to chapter 12.

Subsec. (e). Pub.L. 99–554, § 257(v)(3), added reference to chapter 12.

1984 Amendments. Subsec. (b). Pub.L. 98–353, § 527(a), added a comma after "time".

Subsec. (c)(4). Pub.L. 98–353, § 315(2), added par. (4). Former par. (4) was redesignated as (5).

Subsec. (c)(5). Pub.L. 98–353, § 315(1), redesignated former par. (4) as (5). Former par. (5) was redesignated as (6).

Pub.L. 98–353, § 527(b)(1), added "a request made for" before "additional".

Subsec. (c)(6). Pub.L. 98–353, § 315(1), redesignated former par. (5) as (6). Former par. (6) was redesignated as (7).

Subsec. (c)(7). Pub.L. 98–353, § 315(1), redesignated former par. (6) as (7). Former par. (7) was redesignated as (8).

Pub.L. 98–353, § 527(b)(2), substituted "; or" for "; and".

Subsec. (c)(8). Pub.L. 98–353, § 315(1), redesignated former par. (7) as (8).

Pub.L. 98–353, § 527(b)(3), added "other than completion of payments under the plan" after "in the plan".

Effective and Applicability Provisions

2005 Acts. Amendments by Pub.L. 109–8 effective, except as otherwise provided, 180 days after April 20, 2005, and inapplicable with respect to cases commenced under Title 11 before the effective date, see Pub.L. 109–8, § 1501, set out as a note under 11 U.S.C.A. § 101.

1986 Acts. Amendment by Pub.L. 99–554 effective 30 days after Oct. 27, 1986, except as otherwise provided for, see section 302(a) of Pub.L. 99–554, set out as a note under section 581 of Title 28, Judiciary and Judicial Procedure.

Amendment by Pub.L. 99–554, § 229, not to become effective in or with respect to certain specified judicial districts until, or apply to cases while pending in such district before, the expiration of the 270–day period beginning 30 days after Oct. 27, 1986, or of the 30–day period beginning on the date the Attorney General certifies under section 303 of Pub.L. 99–554 the region specified in a paragraph of section 581(a) of Title 28, as amended by section 111(a) of Pub.L. 99–554, that includes such district, whichever occurs first, see section 302(d)(1) of Pub.L. 99–554, set out as a note under section 581 of Title 28.

Amendment by Pub.L. 99–554, § 229, not to become effective in or with respect to certain specified judicial districts until, or apply to cases while pending in such district before, the expiration of the 2–year period beginning 30 days after Oct. 27, 1986, or of the 30–day period beginning on the date the Attorney General certifies under section 303 of Pub.L. 99–554 the region specified in a paragraph of section 581(a) of Title 28, as amended by section 111(a) of Pub.L. 99–554, that includes such district, whichever occurs first, see section 302(d)(2) of Pub.L. 99–554, set out as a note under section 581 of Title 28.

Amendment by Pub.L. 99–554, § 229, not to become effective in or with respect to judicial districts established for the States of Alabama and North Carolina until, or apply to cases while pending in such district before, such district elects to be included in a bankruptcy region established in section 581(a) of Title 28, as amended by section 111(a) of Pub.L. 99–554, or Oct. 1, 2002, whichever occurs first, and, except as otherwise provided for, with respect to cases under chapters 7, 11, 12, and 13 of Title 11 commenced before 30 days after Oct. 27, 1986, and pending in a judicial district in the States of Alabama or North Carolina before any election made under section 302(d)(3)(A) of Pub.L. 99–554 by such district becomes effective or Oct. 1, 2002, whichever occurs first, amendments by Pub.L. 99–554 not to apply, until Oct. 1, 2003, or the expiration of the 1–year period beginning on the date such election becomes effective, whichever occurs first, and further, in any judicial district in Alabama or North Carolina not making the election described in section 302(d)(3)(A) of Pub.L. 99–554, any person appointed under regulations issued by the Judicial Conference to administer estates in cases under Title 11 authorized to establish, etc., a panel of private trustees, and to supervise cases and trustees in cases under chapters 7, 11, 12, and 13 of Title 11, until amendments by sections 201 to 231 of Pub.L. 99–554 effective in such district, see section 302(d)(3)(A) to (F), (H), (I) of Pub.L. 99–554, set out as a note under section 581 of Title 28.

Amendments by Pub.L. 99–554, § 257(v), not to apply with respect to cases commenced under Title 11, Bankruptcy, before 30 days after Oct. 27 1986, see section 302(c)(1) of Pub.L. 99–554, set out as a note under section 581 of Title 28.

Amendment by Pub.L. 99–554, § 229 except as otherwise provided, with respect to cases under chapters 7, 11, 12, and 13 of Title 11 commenced before 30 days after Oct. 27, 1986, and pending in a judicial district referred to in section 581(a) of Title 28, as amended by section 111(a) of Pub.L. 99–554, for which a United States trustee is not authorized before 30 days after Oct. 27, 1986 to be appointed, not applicable until the expiration of the 3–year period beginning on Oct. 27, 1986, or of the 1–year period beginning on the date the Attorney General certifies under section 303 of Pub.L. 99–554 the region specified in a paragraph of such section 581(a) that includes, such district, whichever occurs first, see section 302(e)(1), (2) of Pub.L. 99–554, set out as a note under section 581 of Title 28.

1984 Acts. Amendment by Pub.L. 98–353 effective as to cases filed 90 days after July 10, 1984, see section 552(a), formerly 553(a), of Pub.L. 98–353, set out as a note under section 101 of this title.

CROSS REFERENCES

Conversion from Chapter seven, see 11 USCA § 706.

Conversion or dismissal upon revocation of order of confirmation, see 11 USCA § 1330.

Dismissal of—

Chapter nine cases, see 11 USCA § 930.

Chapter seven case, see 11 USCA § 707.

Distribution of property of estate converted to Chapter seven, see 11 USCA § 726.

Effect of—

Conversion, see 11 USCA § 348.

Dismissal, see 11 USCA § 349.

Executory contracts and unexpired leases, see 11 USCA § 365.

Liquidation of estate in railroad reorganization case, see 11 USCA § 1174.

LIBRARY REFERENCES

American Digest System

Bankruptcy ⇒3716.10 to 3717.

Key Number System Topic No. 51.

Corpus Juris Secundum

CJS Bankruptcy § 52, Proceedings Under Chapters 12 and 13.

CJS Bankruptcy § 109, Termination of Service.

CJS Bankruptcy § 448, What Constitutes Cause.

CJS Bankruptcy § 451, Dismissal or Conversion on Request of United States Trustee.

CJS Bankruptcy § 456, Chapter 13.

CJS Bankruptcy § 458, Failure to File Prepetition Tax Returns in Chapter 13 Case.

CJS Bankruptcy § 927, Exercising Right in Chapter 7 Cases.

CJS Bankruptcy § 1102, Priority of Particular Distribution Classes.

§ 1308.   Filing of prepetition tax returns

(a) Not later than the day before the date on which the meeting of the creditors is first scheduled to be held under section 341(a), if the debtor was required to file a tax return under applicable nonbankruptcy law, the debtor shall file with appropriate tax authorities all tax returns for all taxable periods ending during the 4–year period ending on the date of the filing of the petition.

(b)(1) Subject to paragraph (2), if the tax returns required by subsection (a) have not been filed by the date on which the meeting of creditors is first scheduled to be held under section 341(a), the trustee may hold open that meeting for a reasonable period of time to allow the debtor an additional period of time to file any unfiled returns, but such additional period of time shall not extend beyond—

(A) for any return that is past due as of the date of the filing of the petition, the date that is 120 days after the date of that meeting; or

(B) for any return that is not past due as of the date of the filing of the petition, the later of—

(i) the date that is 120 days after the date of that meeting; or

(ii) the date on which the return is due under the last automatic extension of time for filing that return to which the debtor is entitled, and for which request is timely made, in accordance with applicable nonbankruptcy law.

(2) After notice and a hearing, and order entered before the tolling of any applicable filing period determined under paragraph (1), if the debtor demonstrates by a preponderance of the evidence that the failure to file a return as required under paragraph (1) is attributable to circumstances beyond the control of the debtor, the court may extend the filing period established by the trustee under paragraph (1) for—

(A) a period of not more than 30 days for returns described in paragraph (1)(A); and

(B) a period not to extend after the applicable extended due date for a return described in paragraph (1)(B).

(c) For purposes of this section, the term "return" includes a return prepared pursuant to subsection (a) or (b) of section 6020 of the Internal Revenue Code of 1986, or a similar State or local law, or a written stipulation to a judgment or a final order entered by a nonbankruptcy tribunal.

(Added Pub.L. 109–8, Title VII, § 716(b)(1), Apr. 20, 2005, 119 Stat. 129; amended Pub.L. 111–327, § 2(a)(42), Dec. 22, 2010, 124 Stat. 3562.)

HISTORICAL AND STATUTORY NOTES

Revision Notes and Legislative Reports

2005 Acts. House Report No. 109–31(Part I), see 2005 U.S. Code Cong. and Adm. News, p. 88.

Subsection (a) or (b) of section 6020 of the Internal Revenue Code of 1986, referred to in subsec. (c), is classified to 26 U.S.C.A. § 6020(a) or (b).

Amendments

2010 Amendments. Subsec. (b)(2). Pub.L. 111–327, § 2(a)(42)(C), in the matter preceding subpar. (A), struck out "this subsection" and inserted "paragraph (1)" in three places.

Subsec. (b)(2)(A). Pub.L. 111–327, § 2(a)(42)(A), struck out "paragraph (1)" and inserted "paragraph (1)(A)".

Subsec. (b)(2)(B). Pub.L. 111–327, § 2(a)(42)(B), struck out "paragraph (2)" and inserted "paragraph (1)(B)".

Effective and Applicability Provisions

2005 Acts. Amendments by Pub.L. 109–8 effective, except as otherwise provided, 180 days after April 20, 2005, and inapplicable with respect to cases commenced under Title 11 before the effective date, see Pub.L. 109–8, § 1501, set out as a note under 11 U.S.C.A. § 101.

LIBRARY REFERENCES

Corpus Juris Secundum

CJS Bankruptcy § 1018, Extension of Time; Excuse for Delay.

SUBCHAPTER II—THE PLAN

§ 1321.   Filing of plan

The debtor shall file a plan.

(Pub.L. 95–598, Nov. 6, 1978, 92 Stat. 2648.)

HISTORICAL AND STATUTORY NOTES

Revision Notes and Legislative Reports

1978 Acts. Chapter 13 contemplates the filing of a plan only by the debtor. Senate Report No. 95–989.

CROSS REFERENCES

Conversion or dismissal for failure to timely file plan, see 11 USCA § 1307.

Filing of plan in—

Chapter nine cases, see 11 USCA § 941.

Chapter twelve cases, see 11 USCA § 1221.

Who may file plan in Chapter eleven cases, see 11 USCA § 1121.

LIBRARY REFERENCES

American Digest System

Bankruptcy ⊕3704.1.

Key Number System Topic No. 51.

§ 1322.   Contents of plan

(a) The plan—

(1) shall provide for the submission of all or such portion of future earnings or other future income of the debtor to the supervision and control of the trustee as is necessary for the execution of the plan;

(2) shall provide for the full payment, in deferred cash payments, of all claims entitled to priority under section 507 of this title, unless the holder of a particular claim agrees to a different treatment of such claim;

(3) if the plan classifies claims, shall provide the same treatment for each claim within a particular class; and

(4) notwithstanding any other provision of this section, may provide for less than full payment of all amounts owed for a claim entitled to priority under section 507(a)(1)(B) only if the plan provides that all of the debtor's projected disposable income for a 5–year period beginning on the date that the first payment is due under the plan will be applied to make payments under the plan.

(b) Subject to subsections (a) and (c) of this section, the plan may—

(1) designate a class or classes of unsecured claims, as provided in section 1122 of this title, but may not discriminate unfairly against any class so designated; however, such plan may treat claims for a consumer debt of the debtor if an individual is liable on such consumer debt with the debtor differently than other unsecured claims;

(2) modify the rights of holders of secured claims, other than a claim secured only by a security interest in real property that is the debtor's principal residence, or of holders of unsecured claims, or leave unaffected the rights of holders of any class of claims;

(3) provide for the curing or waiving of any default;

(4) provide for payments on any unsecured claim to be made concurrently with payments on any secured claim or any other unsecured claim;

(5) notwithstanding paragraph (2) of this subsection, provide for the curing of any default within a reasonable time and maintenance of payments while the case is pending on any unsecured claim or secured claim on which the last payment is due after the date on which the final payment under the plan is due;

(6) provide for the payment of all or any part of any claim allowed under section 1305 of this title;

(7) subject to section 365 of this title, provide for the assumption, rejection, or assignment of any executory contract or unexpired lease of the debtor not previously rejected under such section;

(8) provide for the payment of all or part of a claim against the debtor from property of the estate or property of the debtor;

(9) provide for the vesting of property of the estate, on confirmation of the plan or at a later time, in the debtor or in any other entity;

(10) provide for the payment of interest accruing after the date of the filing of the petition on unse-

cured claims that are nondischargeable under section 1328(a), except that such interest may be paid only to the extent that the debtor has disposable income available to pay such interest after making provision for full payment of all allowed claims; and

(11) include any other appropriate provision not inconsistent with this title.

(c) Notwithstanding subsection (b)(2) and applicable nonbankruptcy law—

(1) a default with respect to, or that gave rise to, a lien on the debtor's principal residence may be cured under paragraph (3) or (5) of subsection (b) until such residence is sold at a foreclosure sale that is conducted in accordance with applicable nonbankruptcy law; and

(2) in a case in which the last payment on the original payment schedule for a claim secured only by a security interest in real property that is the debtor's principal residence is due before the date on which the final payment under the plan is due, the plan may provide for the payment of the claim as modified pursuant to section 1325(a)(5) of this title.

(d)(1) If the current monthly income of the debtor and the debtor's spouse combined, when multiplied by 12, is not less than—

(A) in the case of a debtor in a household of 1 person, the median family income of the applicable State for 1 earner;

(B) in the case of a debtor in a household of 2, 3, or 4 individuals, the highest median family income of the applicable State for a family of the same number or fewer individuals; or

(C) in the case of a debtor in a household exceeding 4 individuals, the highest median family income of the applicable State for a family of 4 or fewer individuals, plus $625 [1] per month for each individual in excess of 4,

the plan may not provide for payments over a period that is longer than 5 years.

(2) If the current monthly income of the debtor and the debtor's spouse combined, when multiplied by 12, is less than—

(A) in the case of a debtor in a household of 1 person, the median family income of the applicable State for 1 earner;

(B) in the case of a debtor in a household of 2, 3, or 4 individuals, the highest median family income of the applicable State for a family of the same number or fewer individuals; or

(C) in the case of a debtor in a household exceeding 4 individuals, the highest median family income of the applicable State for a family of 4 or fewer individuals, plus $625 [1] per month for each individual in excess of 4,

the plan may not provide for payments over a period that is longer than 3 years, unless the court, for cause, approves a longer period, but the court may not approve a period that is longer than 5 years.

(e) Notwithstanding subsection (b)(2) of this section and sections 506(b) and 1325(a)(5) of this title, if it is proposed in a plan to cure a default, the amount necessary to cure the default, shall be determined in accordance with the underlying agreement and applicable nonbankruptcy law.

(f) A plan may not materially alter the terms of a loan described in section 362(b)(19) and any amounts required to repay such loan shall not constitute "disposable income" under section 1325.

(Pub.L. 95–598, Nov. 6, 1978, 92 Stat. 2648; Pub.L. 98–353, Title III, §§ 316, 528, July 10, 1984, 98 Stat. 356, 389; Pub.L. 103–394, Title III, §§ 301, 305(c), Oct. 22, 1994, 108 Stat. 4131, 4134; Pub.L. 109–8, Title II, §§ 213(8), (9), 224(d), Title III, § 318(1), Apr. 20, 2005, 119 Stat. 53, 65, 93; Pub.L. 111–327, § 2(a)(43), Dec. 22, 2010, 124 Stat. 3562.)

[1] Dollar amount as adjusted by the Judicial Conference of the United States. See Adjustment of Dollar Amounts notes set out under this section and 11 U.S.C.A. § 104.

HISTORICAL AND STATUTORY NOTES

Revision Notes and Legislative Reports

1978 Acts. Chapter 13 is designed to serve as a flexible vehicle for the repayment of part or all of the allowed claims of the debtor. Section 1322 emphasizes that purpose by fixing a minimum of mandatory plan provisions.

Subsection (a) requires that the plan submit whatever portion of the future income of the debtor is necessary to implement the plan to the control of the trustee, mandates payment in full of all section 507 priority claims, and requires identical treatment for all claims of a particular class.

Subsection (b) permits a chapter 13 plan to (1) divide unsecured claims not entitled to priority under section 507 into classes in the manner authorized for chapter 11 claims; (2) modify the rights of holders of secured and unsecured claims, except claims wholly secured by real estate mortgages; (3) cure or waive any default; (4) propose payments on unsecured claims concurrently with payments on any secured claim or any other class of unsecured claims; (5) provide for curing any default on any secured or unsecured claim on which the final payment is due after the proposed final payment under the plan; (6) provide for payment of any allowed postpetition claim; (7) assume or reject any previously unrejected executory contract or unexpired lease of the debtor; (8) propose the payment of all or any part of any claim from property of the estate or of the debtor; (9) provide for the vesting of property of the estate; and (10) include any other provision not inconsistent with other provisions of title 11.

Subsection (c) limits the payment period under the plan to 3 years, except that a 4-year payment period may be permitted by the court. Senate Report No. 95–989.

1984 Acts. Statements by Legislative Leaders, see 1984 U.S.Code Cong. and Adm.News, p. 576.

1994 Acts. House Report No. 103–835, see 1994 U.S. Code Cong. and Adm. News, p. 3340.

2005 Acts. House Report No. 109–31(Part I), see 2005 U.S. Code Cong. and Adm. News, p. 88.

Legislative Statements

Section 1322(b)(2) of the House amendment represents a compromise agreement between similar provisions in the House bill and Senate amendment. Under the House amendment, the plan may modify the rights of holders of secured claims other than a claim secured by a security interest in real property that is the debtor's principal residence. It is intended that a claim secured by the debtor's principal residence may be treated with under section 1322(b)(5) of the House amendment.

Section 1322(c) adopts a 5-year period derived from the House bill in preference to a 4-year period contained in the Senate amendment. A conforming change is made in section 1329(c) adopting the provision in the House bill in preference to a comparable provision in the Senate amendment.

Tax payments in wage earner plans: The House bill provided that a wage earner plan had to provide that all priority claims would be paid in full. The Senate amendment contained a special rule in section 1325(c) requiring that Federal tax claims must be paid in cash, but that such tax claims can be paid in deferred cash installments under the general rules applicable to the payment of debts in a wage earner plan, unless the Internal Revenue Service negotiates with the debtor for some different medium or time for payment of the tax liability.

The House bill adopts the substance of the Senate amendment rule under section 1322(a)(2) of the House amendment. A wage earner plan must provide for full payment in deferred cash payments, of all priority claims, unless the holder of a particular claim agrees with a different treatment of such claim.

Amendments

2010 Amendments. Subsec. (a). Pub.L. 111–327, § 2(a)(43)(A), in the matter preceding par. (1), struck out "shall" following "The plan".

Subsec. (a)(1). Pub.L. 111–327, § 2(a)(43)(B), inserted "shall" following "(1)".

Subsec. (a)(2). Pub.L. 111–327, § 2(a)(43)(C), inserted "shall" following "(2)".

Subsec. (a)(3). Pub.L. 111–327, § 2(a)(43)(D), inserted "shall" following "claims,".

Subsec. (a)(4). Pub.L. 111–327, § 2(a)(43)(E), struck out "a plan" following "this section,".

Subsec. (d)(1)(C). By notice dated Feb. 25, 2010, 75 F.R. 8747, dollar amount adjusted by the Judicial Conference of the United States which adjusted "$575" to "$625". See 11 U.S.C.A. § 104 and Adjustment of Dollar Amounts notes under this section.

Subsec. (d)(2)(C). By notice dated Feb. 25, 2010, 75 F.R. 8747, dollar amount adjusted by the Judicial Conference of the United States which adjusted "$575" to "$625". See 11 U.S.C.A. § 104 and Adjustment of Dollar Amounts notes under this section.

2007 Amendments. Subsec. (d)(1)(C). By notice dated Feb. 14, 2007, 72 F.R. 7082, dollar amount adjusted by the Judicial Conference of the United States which adjusted "$525" to "$575". See 11 U.S.C.A. § 104 and Adjustment of Dollar Amounts notes under this section.

Subsec. (d)(2)(C). By notice dated Feb. 14, 2007, 72 F.R. 7082, dollar amount adjusted by the Judicial Conference of the United States which adjusted "$525" to "$575". See 11 U.S.C.A. § 104 and Adjustment of Dollar Amounts notes under this section.

2005 Amendments. Subsec. (a)(2). Pub.L. 109–8, § 213(8)(A), struck out "and" at the end of par. (2).

Subsec. (a)(3). Pub.L. 109–8, § 213(8)(B), substituted "; and" for the period at the end of par. (3).

Subsec. (a)(4). Pub.L. 109–8, § 213(8)(C), added par. (4).

Subsec. (b)(9). Pub.L. 109–8, § 213(9)(A), substituted a semicolon for "; and" at the end of par. (9).

Subsec. (b)(10), (11). Pub.L. 109–8, § 213(9)(B), (C), redesignated former par. (10) as par. (11) and added a new par. (10).

Subsec. (d). Pub.L. 109–8, § 318(1), rewrote subsec. (d), which formerly read: "**(d)** The plan may not provide for payments over a period that is longer than three years, unless the court, for cause, approves a longer period, but the court may not approve a period that is longer than five years."

Subsec. (f). Pub.L. 109–8, § 224(d), added subsec. (f).

1994 Amendments. Subsec. (c). Pub.L. 103–394, § 301, added subsec. (c). Former subsec. (c) redesignated (d).

Subsec. (d). Pub.L. 103–394, § 301(1), redesignated former subsec. (c) as (d).

Subsec. (e). Pub.L. 103–394, § 305(c), added subsec. (e).

1984 Amendments. Subsec. (a)(2). Pub.L. 98–353, § 528(a) added a comma after "payments".

Subsec. (b)(1). Pub.L. 98–353, § 316(1), substituted "designate a class or classes of unsecured claims, as provided in section 1122 of this title, but may not discriminate unfairly against any class so designated; however, such plan may treat claims for a consumer debt of the debtor if an individual is liable on such consumer debt with the debtor differently than other unsecured claims;" for "designate a class or classes of unsecured claims, as provided in section 1122 of this title, but may not discriminate unfairly against any class so designated;".

Subsec. (b)(2). Pub.L. 98–353, § 528(b)(1), added ", or leave unaffected the rights of the holders of any class of claims" following "unsecured claims".

Subsec. (b)(4). Pub.L. 98–353, § 528(b)(2), added "other" after "claim or any".

Subsec. (b)(7). Pub.L. 98–353, § 528(b)(3)(A), added "subject to section 365 of this title," before "provide".

Pub.L. 98–353, § 528(b)(3)(B), substituted ", rejection, or assignment" for "or rejection".

Pub.L. 98–353, § 528(b)(3)(C), substituted "under such section" for "under section 365 of this title".

Subsec. (b)(8). Pub.L. 98–353, § 528(b)(4), struck out "any" preceding "part of a claim".

Effective and Applicability Provisions

2010 Acts. Increase of dollar amounts by Judicial Conference of the United States by notice published Feb. 25, 2010, 75 F.R. 8747 effective April 1, 2010, and increase not applicable to cases commenced before the effective date of the adjustments, i.e., April 1, 2010. See Adjustment of Dollar Amounts notes under 11 U.S.C.A. § 104 and this section.

2007 Acts. Increase of dollar amounts by Judicial Conference of the United States by notice published Feb. 14, 2007,

72 F.R. 7082 effective April 1, 2007, and increase not applicable to cases commenced before the effective date of the adjustments, i.e., April 1, 2007. See Adjustment of Dollar Amounts notes under 11 U.S.C.A. § 104 and this section.

2005 Acts. Amendments by Pub.L. 109–8 effective, except as otherwise provided, 180 days after April 20, 2005, and inapplicable with respect to cases commenced under Title 11 before the effective date, see Pub.L. 109–8, § 1501, set out as a note under 11 U.S.C.A. § 101.

1994 Acts. Amendment by section 301 of Pub.L. 103–394 [enacting subsec. (c) of this section and redesignating former subsec. (c) as (d)] effective on Oct. 22, 1994, and not to apply with respect to cases commenced under Title 11 of the United States Code before Oct. 22, 1994, see section 702 of Pub.L. 103–394, set out as a note under section 101 of this title.

Amendment by section 305(c) of Pub.L. 103–394 [enacting subsec. (e) of this section] effective Oct. 22, 1994, and applicable only to agreements entered into after Oct. 22, 1994, see section 702 of Pub.L. 103–394, set out as a note under section 101 of this title.

1984 Acts. Amendment by Pub. L. 98–353 effective as to cases filed 90 days after July 10, 1984, see section 552(a), formerly 553(a), of Pub. L. 98–353, set out as a note under section 101 of this title.

Separability of Provisions

If any provision of or amendment made by Pub.L. 103–394 or the application of such provision or amendment to any person or circumstance is held to be unconstitutional, the remaining provisions of and amendments made by Pub.L. 103–394 and the application of such provisions and amendments to any person or circumstance shall not be affected thereby, see section 701 of Pub.L. 103–394, set out as a note under section 101 of this title.

Adjustment of Dollar Amounts

For adjustment of dollar amounts specified in subsec. (d)(1)(C), (2)(C) of this section by the Judicial Conference of the United States, effective Apr. 1, 2010, see note set out under 11 U.S.C.A. § 104.

By notice published Feb. 25, 2010, 75 F.R. 8747, the Judicial Conference of the United States adjusted the dollar amounts in provisions specified in subsec. (d)(1)(C) and (2)(C) of this section, effective Apr. 1, 2010, as follows:

Adjusted $575 (each time it appears) to $625 (each time it appears).

By notice published Feb. 14, 2007, 72 F.R. 7082, the Judicial Conference of the United States adjusted the dollar amounts in provisions specified in subsec. (d) of this section, effective Apr. 1, 2007, as follows:

Adjusted $525 (each time it appears) to $575 (each time it appears).

CROSS REFERENCES

Contents of plan filed in—
    Chapter eleven cases, see 11 USCA § 1123.
    Chapter twelve cases, see 11 USCA § 1222.
    Railroad reorganization cases, see 11 USCA § 1172.

LIBRARY REFERENCES

American Digest System
    Bankruptcy ☞3704.1 to 3714.

Key Number System Topic No. 51.

§ 1323. Modification of plan before confirmation

(a) The debtor may modify the plan at any time before confirmation, but may not modify the plan so that the plan as modified fails to meet the requirements of section 1322 of this title.

(b) After the debtor files a modification under this section, the plan as modified becomes the plan.

(c) Any holder of a secured claim that has accepted or rejected the plan is deemed to have accepted or rejected, as the case may be, the plan as modified, unless the modification provides for a change in the rights of such holder from what such rights were under the plan before modification, and such holder changes such holder's previous acceptance or rejection.
(Pub.L. 95–598, Nov. 6, 1978, 92 Stat. 2649.)

HISTORICAL AND STATUTORY NOTES
Revision Notes and Legislative Reports

1978 Acts. The debtor is permitted to modify the plan before confirmation without court approval so long as the modified plan, which becomes the plan on filing, complies with the requirements of section 1322.

The original acceptance or rejection of a plan by the holder of a secured claim remains binding unless the modified plan changes the rights of the holder and the holder withdraws or alters its earlier acceptance or rejection. Senate Report No. 95–989.

CROSS REFERENCES

Modification of plan filed in—
    Chapter eleven cases, see 11 USCA § 1127.
    Chapter nine cases, see 11 USCA § 942.
    Chapter twelve cases, see 11 USCA § 1223.

LIBRARY REFERENCES
American Digest System
    Bankruptcy ☞3713.
Key Number System Topic No. 51.

§ 1324. Confirmation hearing

(a) Except as provided in subsection (b) and after notice, the court shall hold a hearing on confirmation of the plan. A party in interest may object to confirmation of the plan.

(b) The hearing on confirmation of the plan may be held not earlier than 20 days and not later than 45 days after the date of the meeting of creditors under section 341(a), unless the court determines that it would be in the best interests of the creditors and the estate to hold such hearing at an earlier date and there is no objection to such earlier date.
(Pub.L. 95–598, Nov. 6, 1978, 92 Stat. 2649; Pub.L. 98–353, Title III, § 529, July 10, 1984, 98 Stat. 389; Pub.L. 99–554, Title II, § 283(x), Oct. 27, 1986, 100 Stat. 3118; Pub.L. 109–8, Title III, § 317, Apr. 20, 2005, 119 Stat. 92.)

HISTORICAL AND STATUTORY NOTES

Revision Notes and Legislative Reports

1978 Acts. Any party in interest may object to the confirmation of a plan, as distinguished from merely rejecting a plan. An objection to confirmation is predicated on failure of the plan or the procedures employed prior to confirmation to conform with the requirements of chapter 13. The bankruptcy judge is required to provide notice and an opportunity for hearing any such objection to confirmation. Senate Report No. 95–989.

1984 Acts. Statements by Legislative Leaders, see 1984 U.S.Code Cong. and Adm.News, p. 576.

1986 Acts. House Report No. 99–764 and House Conference Report No. 99–958, see 1986 U.S.Code Cong. and Adm. News, p. 5227.

2005 Acts. House Report No. 109–31(Part I), see 2005 U.S. Code Cong. and Adm. News, p. 88.

Amendments

2005 Amendments. Section. Pub.L. 109–8, § 317(1), struck out "After" and inserted "(a) Except as provided in subsection (b) and after".

Subsec. (b). Pub.L. 109–8, § 317(2), added subsec. (b).

1986 Amendments. Pub.L. 99–554 struck out "the" following "object to".

1984 Amendments. Pub.L. 98–353 struck out "the" preceding "confirmation of the plan".

Effective and Applicability Provisions

2005 Acts. Amendments by Pub.L. 109–8 effective, except as otherwise provided, 180 days after April 20, 2005, and inapplicable with respect to cases commenced under Title 11 before the effective date, see Pub.L. 109–8, § 1501, set out as a note under 11 U.S.C.A. § 101.

1986 Acts. Amendment by Pub.L. 99–554 effective 30 days after Oct. 27, 1986, see section 302(a) of Pub.L. 99–554, set out as a note under section 581 of Title 28, Judiciary and Judicial Procedure.

1984 Acts. Amendment by Pub.L. 98–353 effective with respect to cases filed 90 days after July 10, 1984, see section 552(a), formerly 553(a), of Pub.L. 98–353, set out as a note under section 101 of this title.

CROSS REFERENCES

Confirmation hearing in—

    Chapter eleven cases, see 11 USCA § 1128.

    Chapter twelve cases, see 11 USCA § 1224.

Duties of United States trustee, see 28 USCA § 586.

LIBRARY REFERENCES

American Digest System

Bankruptcy ⚲3715(1) to 3715(8).

Key Number System Topic No. 51.

§ 1325. Confirmation of plan

(a) Except as provided in subsection (b), the court shall confirm a plan if—

    (1) the plan complies with the provisions of this chapter and with the other applicable provisions of this title;

    (2) any fee, charge, or amount required under chapter 123 of title 28, or by the plan, to be paid before confirmation, has been paid;

    (3) the plan has been proposed in good faith and not by any means forbidden by law;

    (4) the value, as of the effective date of the plan, of property to be distributed under the plan on account of each allowed unsecured claim is not less than the amount that would be paid on such claim if the estate of the debtor were liquidated under chapter 7 of this title on such date;

    (5) with respect to each allowed secured claim provided for by the plan—

      (A) the holder of such claim has accepted the plan;

      (B)(i) the plan provides that—

        (I) the holder of such claim retain the lien securing such claim until the earlier of—

          (aa) the payment of the underlying debt determined under nonbankruptcy law; or

          (bb) discharge under section 1328; and

        (II) if the case under this chapter is dismissed or converted without completion of the plan, such lien shall also be retained by such holder to the extent recognized by applicable nonbankruptcy law;

      (ii) the value, as of the effective date of the plan, of property to be distributed under the plan on account of such claim is not less than the allowed amount of such claim; and

      (iii) if—

        (I) property to be distributed pursuant to this subsection is in the form of periodic payments, such payments shall be in equal monthly amounts; and

        (II) the holder of the claim is secured by personal property, the amount of such payments shall not be less than an amount sufficient to provide to the holder of such claim adequate protection during the period of the plan; or

      (C) the debtor surrenders the property securing such claim to such holder;

    (6) the debtor will be able to make all payments under the plan and to comply with the plan;

    (7) the action of the debtor in filing the petition was in good faith;

    (8) the debtor has paid all amounts that are required to be paid under a domestic support obligation and that first become payable after the date of the filing of the petition if the debtor is required by a judicial or administrative order, or by statute, to pay such domestic support obligation; and

    (9) the debtor has filed all applicable Federal, State, and local tax returns as required by section 1308.

For purposes of paragraph (5), section 506 shall not apply to a claim described in that paragraph if the creditor has a purchase money security interest securing the debt that is the subject of the claim, the debt was incurred within the 910–day period preceding the date of the filing of the petition, and the collateral for that debt consists of a motor vehicle (as defined in section 30102 of title 49) acquired for the personal use of the debtor, or if collateral for that debt consists of any other thing of value, if the debt was incurred during the 1–year period preceding that filing.

(b)(1) If the trustee or the holder of an allowed unsecured claim objects to the confirmation of the plan, then the court may not approve the plan unless, as of the effective date of the plan—

(A) the value of the property to be distributed under the plan on account of such claim is not less than the amount of such claim; or

(B) the plan provides that all of the debtor's projected disposable income to be received in the applicable commitment period beginning on the date that the first payment is due under the plan will be applied to make payments to unsecured creditors under the plan.

(2) For purposes of this subsection, the term "disposable income" means current monthly income received by the debtor (other than child support payments, foster care payments, or disability payments for a dependent child made in accordance with applicable nonbankruptcy law to the extent reasonably necessary to be expended for such child) less amounts reasonably necessary to be expended—

(A)(i) for the maintenance or support of the debtor or a dependent of the debtor, or for a domestic support obligation, that first becomes payable after the date the petition is filed; and

(ii) for charitable contributions (that meet the definition of "charitable contribution" under section 548(d)(3)) to a qualified religious or charitable entity or organization (as defined in section 548(d)(4)) in an amount not to exceed 15 percent of gross income of the debtor for the year in which the contributions are made; and

(B) if the debtor is engaged in business, for the payment of expenditures necessary for the continuation, preservation, and operation of such business.

(3) Amounts reasonably necessary to be expended under paragraph (2), other than subparagraph (A)(ii) of paragraph (2), shall be determined in accordance with subparagraphs (A) and (B) of section 707(b)(2), if the debtor has current monthly income, when multiplied by 12, greater than—

(A) in the case of a debtor in a household of 1 person, the median family income of the applicable State for 1 earner;

(B) in the case of a debtor in a household of 2, 3, or 4 individuals, the highest median family income of the applicable State for a family of the same number or fewer individuals; or

(C) in the case of a debtor in a household exceeding 4 individuals, the highest median family income of the applicable State for a family of 4 or fewer individuals, plus $625 [1] per month for each individual in excess of 4.

(4) For purposes of this subsection, the "applicable commitment period"—

(A) subject to subparagraph (B), shall be—

(i) 3 years; or

(ii) not less than 5 years, if the current monthly income of the debtor and the debtor's spouse combined, when multiplied by 12, is not less than—

(I) in the case of a debtor in a household of 1 person, the median family income of the applicable State for 1 earner;

(II) in the case of a debtor in a household of 2, 3, or 4 individuals, the highest median family income of the applicable State for a family of the same number or fewer individuals; or

(III) in the case of a debtor in a household exceeding 4 individuals, the highest median family income of the applicable State for a family of 4 or fewer individuals, plus $625 [1] per month for each individual in excess of 4; and

(B) may be less than 3 or 5 years, whichever is applicable under subparagraph (A), but only if the plan provides for payment in full of all allowed unsecured claims over a shorter period.

(c) After confirmation of a plan, the court may order any entity from whom the debtor receives income to pay all or any part of such income to the trustee. (Pub.L. 95–598, Nov. 6, 1978, 92 Stat. 2649; Pub.L. 98–353, Title III, §§ 317, 530, July 10, 1984, 98 Stat. 356, 389; Pub.L. 99–554, Title II, § 283(y), Oct. 27, 1986, 100 Stat. 3118; Pub.L. 105–183, § 4(a), June 19, 1998, 112 Stat. 518; Pub.L. 109–8, Title I, § 102(g), (h), Title II, § 213(10), Title III, §§ 306(a), (b), 309(c)(1), 318(2), (3), Title VII, § 716(a), Apr. 20, 2005, 119 Stat. 33, 53, 80, 83, 93 129; Pub.L. 109–439, § 2, Dec. 20, 2006, 120 Stat. 3285; Pub.L. 111–327, § 2(a)(44), Dec. 22, 2010, 124 Stat. 3562.)

[1] Dollar amount as adjusted by the Judicial Conference of the United States. See Adjustment of Dollar Amounts notes set out under this section and 11 U.S.C.A. § 104.

HISTORICAL AND STATUTORY NOTES

Revision Notes and Legislative Reports

1978 Acts. The bankruptcy court must confirm a plan if (1) the plan satisfies the provisions of chapter 13 and other applicable provisions of title 11; (2) it is proposed in good faith; (3) it is in the best interests of creditors, and defined by subsection (a)(4) of Section 1325; (4) it has been accepted by the holder of each allowed secured claim provided for the plan or where the holder of any such secured claim is to receive value under the plan not less than the amount of the allowed secured claim, or where the debtor surrenders to the holder the collateral securing any such allowed secured claim; (5) the plan is feasible; and (6) the requisite fees and charges have been paid.

Subsection (b) authorizes the court to order an entity, as defined by section 101(15), to pay any income of the debtor to the trustee. Any governmental unit is an entity subject to such an order. Senate Report No. 95–989.

1984 Acts. Statements by Legislative Leaders, see 1984 U.S.Code Cong. and Adm.News, p. 576.

1986 Acts. House Report No. 99–764 and House Conference Report No. 99–958, see 1986 U.S.Code Cong. and Adm. News, p. 5227.

1998 Acts. Statement by President, see 1998 U.S. Code Cong. and Adm. News, p. 230.

2005 Acts. House Report No. 109–31(Part I), see 2005 U.S. Code Cong. and Adm. News, p. 88.

Legislative Statements

Section 1325(a)(5)(B) of the House amendment modifies the House bill and Senate amendment to significantly protect secured creditors in chapter 13. Unless the secured creditor accepts the plan, the plan must provide that the secured creditor retain the lien securing the creditor's allowed secured claim in addition to receiving value, as of the effective date of the plan of property to be distributed under the plan on account of the claim not less than the allowed amount of the claim. To this extent, a secured creditor in a case under chapter 13 is treated identically with a recourse creditor under section 1111(b)(1) of the House amendment except that the secured creditor in a case under chapter 13 may receive any property of a value as of the effective date of the plan equal to the allowed amount of the creditor's secured claim rather than being restricted to receiving deferred cash payments. Of course, the secured creditors' lien only secures the value of the collateral and to the extent property is distributed of a present value equal to the allowed amount of the creditor's secured claim the creditor's lien will have been satisfied in full. Thus the lien created under section 1325(a)(5)(B)(i) is effective only to secure deferred payments to the extent of the amount of the allowed secured claim. To the extent the deferred payments exceed the value of the allowed amount of the secured claim and the debtor subsequently defaults, the lien will not secure unaccrued interest represented in such deferred payments.

Amendments

2010 Amendments. Subsec. (a). Pub.L. 111–327, § 2(a)(44)(A), in the undesignated matter at the end, inserted "period" after "910–day".

Subsec. (b)(2)(A)(ii). Pub.L. 111–327, § 2(a)(44)(B), struck out "548(d)(3)" and inserted "548(d)(3))".

Subsec. (b)(3)(C). By notice dated Feb. 25, 2010, 75 F.R. 8747, dollar amount adjusted by the Judicial Conference of the United States which adjusted "$575" to "$625". See 11 U.S.C.A. § 104 and Adjustment of Dollar Amounts notes under this section.

Subsec. (b)(4)(A)(ii)(III). By notice dated Feb. 25, 2010, 75 F.R. 8747, dollar amount adjusted by the Judicial Conference of the United States which adjusted "$575" to "$625". See 11 U.S.C.A. § 104 and Adjustment of Dollar Amounts notes under this section.

2007 Amendments. Subsec. (b)(3)(C). By notice dated Feb. 14, 2007, 72 F.R. 7082, dollar amount adjusted by the

Judicial Conference of the United States which adjusted "$525" to "$575". See 11 U.S.C.A. § 104 and Adjustment of Dollar Amounts notes under this section.

Subsec. (b)(4)(A)(ii)(III). By notice dated Feb. 14, 2007, 72 F.R. 7082, dollar amount adjusted by the Judicial Conference of the United States which adjusted "$525" to "$575". See 11 U.S.C.A. § 104 and Adjustment of Dollar Amounts notes under this section.

2006 Amendments. Subsec. (b)(3). Pub.L. 109–439, § 2, inserted ", other than subparagraph (A)(ii) of paragraph (2)," after "paragraph (2)".

2005 Amendments. Subsec. (a). Pub.L. 109–8, § 306(b), added "For purposes of paragraph (5), section 506 shall not apply to a claim described in that paragraph if the creditor has a purchase money security interest securing the debt that is the subject of the claim, the debt was incurred within the 910–day preceding the date of the filing of the petition, and the collateral for that debt consists of a motor vehicle (as defined in section 30102 of title 49) acquired for the personal use of the debtor, or if collateral for that debt consists of any other thing of value, if the debt was incurred during the 1–year period preceding that filing." to the end of subsec. (a).

Subsec. (a)(5). Pub.L. 109–8, § 102(g)(1), struck "and" at the end of par. (5).

Subsec. (a)(5)(B)(i). Pub.L. 109–8, § 306(a), rewrote cl. (i), which formerly read: "the plan provides that the holder of such claim retain the lien securing such claim; and".

Pub.L. 109–8, § 309(c)(1)(A), struck out "and" at the end of cl. (i).

Subsec. (a)(5)(B)(ii). Pub.L. 109–8, § 309(c)(1)(B), struck out "or" at the end of cl. (ii) and inserted "and".

Subsec. (a)(5)(B)(iii). Pub.L. 109–8, § 309(c)(1)(C), added cl. (iii).

Subsec. (a)(6). Pub.L. 109–8, § 102(g)(2), struck the period at the end of par. (6) and inserted a semicolon.

Subsec. (a)(7). Pub.L. 109–8, § 102(g)(3), added par. (7).

Subsec. (a)(8). Pub.L. 109–8, § 213(10), added par. (8).

Subsec. (a)(9). Pub.L. 109–8, § 716(a), added par. (9).

Subsec. (b)(1)(B). Pub.L. 109–8, § 102(h)(1), inserted "to unsecured creditors" after "to make payments".

Pub.L. 109–8, § 318(2), struck out "three-year period" and inserted "applicable commitment period".

Subsec. (b)(2). Pub.L. 109–8, § 102(h)(2), rewrote par. (2), which formerly read:

"(2) For purposes of this subsection, 'disposable income' means income which is received by the debtor and which is not reasonably necessary to be expended—

"(A) for the maintenance or support of the debtor or a dependent of the debtor, including charitable contributions (that meet the definition of 'charitable contribution' under section 548(d)(3)) to a qualified religious or charitable entity or organization (as that term is defined in section 548(d)(4)) in an amount not to exceed 15 percent of the gross income of the debtor for the year in which the contributions are made; and

"(B) if the debtor is engaged in business, for the payment of expenditures necessary for the continuation, preservation, and operation of such business."

Subsec. (b)(3). Pub.L. 109–8, § 102(h)(2), added par. (3).

Subsec. (b)(4). Pub.L. 109–8, § 318(3), added par. (4).

1998 Amendments. Subsec. (b)(2)(A). Pub.L. 105–183, § 4(a), inserted before the semicolon ", including charitable contributions (that meet the definition of 'charitable contribution' under section 548(d)(3)) to a qualified religious or charitable entity or organization (as that term is defined in section 548(d)(4)) in an amount not to exceed 15 percent of the gross income of the debtor for the year in which the contributions are made".

1986 Amendments. Subsec. (b)(2)(A). Pub.L. 99–554 substituted "; and" for "; or".

1984 Amendments. Subsec. (a). Pub.L. 98–353, § 317(1), substituted "Except as provided in subsection (b), the" for "The".

Subsec. (a)(1). Pub.L. 98–353, § 530, added "the" before "other".

Subsec. (b). Pub.L. 98–353, § 317(3), added subsec. (b). Former subsec. (b) was redesignated as (c).

Subsec. (c). Pub.L. 98–353, § 317(2), redesignated former subsec. (b) as (c).

Effective and Applicability Provisions

2010 Acts. Increase of dollar amounts by Judicial Conference of the United States by notice published Feb. 25, 2010, 75 F.R. 8747 effective April 1, 2010, and increase not applicable to cases commenced before the effective date of the adjustments, i.e., April 1, 2010. See Adjustment of Dollar Amounts notes under 11 U.S.C.A. § 104 and this section.

2007 Acts. Increase of dollar amounts by Judicial Conference of the United States by notice published Feb. 14, 2007, 72 F.R. 7082 effective April 1, 2007, and increase not applicable to cases commenced before the effective date of the adjustments, i.e., April 1, 2007. See Adjustment of Dollar Amounts notes under 11 U.S.C.A. § 104 and this section.

2005 Acts. Amendments by Pub.L. 109–8 effective, except as otherwise provided, 180 days after April 20, 2005, and inapplicable with respect to cases commenced under Title 11 before the effective date, see Pub.L. 109–8, § 1501, set out as a note under 11 U.S.C.A. § 101.

1986 Acts. Amendment by Pub.L. 99–554 effective 30 days after Oct. 27, 1986, see section 302(a) of Pub.L. 99–554, set out as a note under section 581 of Title 28, Judiciary and Judicial Procedure.

1984 Acts. Amendment by Pub.L. 98–353 effective with respect to cases filed 90 days after July 10, 1984, see section 552(a), formerly 553(a), of Pub.L. 98–353, set out as a note under section 101 of this title.

Adjustment of Dollar Amounts

For adjustment of dollar amounts specified in subsec. (b)(3) and (4) of this section by the Judicial Conference of the United States, effective Apr. 1, 2010, see note set out under 11 U.S.C.A. § 104.

By notice published Feb. 25, 2010, 75 F.R. 8747, the Judicial Conference of the United States adjusted the dollar amounts in provisions specified in subsec. (b)(3) and (4) of this section, effective Apr. 1, 2010, as follows:

Adjusted $575 (each time it appears) to $625 (each time it appears).

By notice published Feb. 14, 2007, 72 F.R. 7082, the Judicial Conference of the United States adjusted the dollar amounts in provisions specified in subsec. (b) of this section, effective Apr. 1, 2007, as follows:

Adjusted $525 (each time it appears) to $575 (each time it appears).

Applicability

Applicability of amendments made by Pub.L. 105–183 to any case brought under an applicable provision of this title that is pending or commenced on or after June 19, 1998, see Pub.L. 105–183, § 5, June 19, 1998, 112 Stat. 518, set out as a note under section 544 of this title.

Rule of Construction

Amendments made by Pub.L. 105–183 not intended to limit the applicability of the Religious Freedom Restoration Act of 1993 (42 U.S.C. 2002bb et seq.), see Pub.L. 105–183, § 6, June 19, 1998, 112 Stat. 519, set out as a note under section 544 of this title.

CROSS REFERENCES

Confirmation of plan in—

    Chapter eleven cases, see 11 USCA § 1129.

    Chapter nine cases, see 11 USCA § 943.

    Chapter twelve cases, see 11 USCA § 1225.

    Railroad reorganization cases, see 11 USCA § 1173.

Conversion or dismissal, see 11 USCA § 1307.

LIBRARY REFERENCES

American Digest System

Bankruptcy ⊂⇒3704.1 to 3714, 3715(9.1).

Key Number System Topic No. 51.

Corpus Juris Secundum

CJS Bankruptcy § 352, Statement of Current Monthly Income.

CJS Bankruptcy § 431, Presumption of Abuse.

CJS Bankruptcy § 1187, Requirement of Good Faith in Filing Petition.

CJS Bankruptcy § 1188, Filing and Requisites of Plan, Generally.

CJS Bankruptcy § 1189, Contents of Plan, Generally.

CJS Bankruptcy § 1190, Requirement of Good Faith in Proposal of Plan.

CJS Bankruptcy § 1194, Treatment of Secured Claims; Cram Down Provisions.

CJS Bankruptcy § 1195, Amount of Repayment of Unsecured Claims.

CJS Bankruptcy § 1197, Disposable Income.

CJS Bankruptcy § 1198, Curing Defaults.

CJS Bankruptcy § 1201, Time for Completion.

CJS Bankruptcy § 1202, Generally; Objections to Confirmation.

CJS Bankruptcy § 1203, Requirements for Confirmation; Notice and Hearing.

CJS Bankruptcy § 1204, Effect of Confirmation.

CJS Bankruptcy § 1205, Postconfirmation Modification.

CJS Secured Transactions § 11, Nature of Purchase-Money Security Interest.

CJS Secured Transactions § 12, Loss of Purchase-Money Status.

§ 1326. Payments

(a)(1) Unless the court orders otherwise, the debtor shall commence making payments not later than 30 days after the date of the filing of the plan or the order for relief, whichever is earlier, in the amount—

(A) proposed by the plan to the trustee;

(B) scheduled in a lease of personal property directly to the lessor for that portion of the obligation that becomes due after the order for relief, reducing the payments under subparagraph (A) by the amount so paid and providing the trustee with evidence of such payment, including the amount and date of payment; and

(C) that provides adequate protection directly to a creditor holding an allowed claim secured by personal property to the extent the claim is attributable to the purchase of such property by the debtor for that portion of the obligation that becomes due after the order for relief, reducing the payments under subparagraph (A) by the amount so paid and providing the trustee with evidence of such payment, including the amount and date of payment.

(2) A payment made under paragraph (1)(A) shall be retained by the trustee until confirmation or denial of confirmation. If a plan is confirmed, the trustee shall distribute any such payment in accordance with the plan as soon as is practicable. If a plan is not confirmed, the trustee shall return any such payments not previously paid and not yet due and owing to creditors pursuant to paragraph (3) to the debtor, after deducting any unpaid claim allowed under section 503(b).

(3) Subject to section 363, the court may, upon notice and a hearing, modify, increase, or reduce the payments required under this subsection pending confirmation of a plan.

(4) Not later than 60 days after the date of filing of a case under this chapter, a debtor retaining possession of personal property subject to a lease or securing a claim attributable in whole or in part to the purchase price of such property shall provide the lessor or secured creditor reasonable evidence of the maintenance of any required insurance coverage with respect to the use or ownership of such property and continue to do so for so long as the debtor retains possession of such property.

(b) Before or at the time of each payment to creditors under the plan, there shall be paid—

(1) any unpaid claim of the kind specified in section 507(a)(2) of this title;

(2) if a standing trustee appointed under section 586(b) of title 28 is serving in the case, the percentage fee fixed for such standing trustee under section 586(e)(1)(B) of title 28; and

(3) if a chapter 7 trustee has been allowed compensation due to the conversion or dismissal of the debtor's prior case pursuant to section 707(b), and some portion of that compensation remains unpaid in a case converted to this chapter or in the case dismissed under section 707(b) and refiled under this chapter, the amount of any such unpaid compensation, which shall be paid monthly—

(A) by prorating such amount over the remaining duration of the plan; and

(B) by monthly payments not to exceed the greater of—

(i) $25 [1]; or

(ii) the amount payable to unsecured nonpriority creditors, as provided by the plan, multiplied by 5 percent, and the result divided by the number of months in the plan.

(c) Except as otherwise provided in the plan or in the order confirming the plan, the trustee shall make payments to creditors under the plan.

(d) Notwithstanding any other provision of this title—

(1) compensation referred to in subsection (b)(3) is payable and may be collected by the trustee under that paragraph, even if such amount has been discharged in a prior case under this title; and

(2) such compensation is payable in a case under this chapter only to the extent permitted by subsection (b)(3).

(Pub.L. 95–598, Nov. 6, 1978, 92 Stat. 2650; Pub.L. 98–353, Title III, §§ 318(a), 531, July 10, 1984, 98 Stat. 357, 389; Pub.L. 99–554, Title II, §§ 230, 283(z), Oct. 27, 1986, 100 Stat. 3103, 3118; Pub.L. 103–394, Title III, § 307, Oct. 22, 1994, 108 Stat. 4135; Pub.L. 109–8, Title III, § 309(c)(2), Title XII, § 1224, Title XV, § 1502(a)(10), Apr. 20, 2005, 119 Stat. 83, 199, 217.)

[1] Dollar amount as adjusted by the Judicial Conference of the United States. See Adjustment of Dollar Amounts notes set out under this section and 11 U.S.C.A. § 104.

HISTORICAL AND STATUTORY NOTES

Revision Notes and Legislative Reports

1978 Acts. Section 1326 supplements the priorities provisions of section 507. Subsection (a) requires accrued costs of administration and filing fees, as well as fees due the chapter 13 trustee, to be disbursed before payments to creditors under the plan. Subsection (b) makes it clear that the chapter 13 trustee is normally to make distribution to creditors of the payments made under the plan by the debtor. Senate Report No. 95–989.

Subsection (a) requires that before or at the time of each payment any outstanding administrative expenses [and] any percentage fee due for a private standing chapter 13 trustee be paid in full. House Report No. 95–595.

1984 Acts. Statements by Legislative Leaders, see 1984 U.S.Code Cong. and Adm.News, p. 576.

1986 Acts. House Report No. 99–764 and House Conference Report No. 99–958, see 1986 U.S.Code Cong. and Adm. News, p. 5227.

1994 Acts. House Report No. 103–835, see 1994 U.S. Code Cong. and Adm. News, p. 3340.

2005 Acts. House Report No. 109–31(Part I), see 2005 U.S. Code Cong. and Adm. News, p. 88.

Legislative Statements

Section 1326(a)(2) of the House amendment adopts a comparable provision contained in the House bill providing for standing trustees.

Amendments

2010 Amendments. Subsec. (b)(3)(B)(i). By notice dated Feb. 25, 2010, 75 F.R. 8747, dollar amount adjusted by the Judicial Conference of the United States which retained original amount of "$25" as "$25", resulting in no change in text. See 11 U.S.C.A. § 104 and Adjustment of Dollar Amounts notes under this section.

2007 Amendments. Subsec. (b)(3)(B)(i). By notice dated Feb. 14, 2007, 72 F.R. 7082, dollar amount adjusted by the Judicial Conference of the United States which retained original amount of "$25" as "$25", resulting in no change in text. See 11 U.S.C.A. § 104 and Adjustment of Dollar Amounts notes under this section.

2005 Amendments. Subsec. (a). Pub.L. 109–8, § 309(c)(2), rewrote subsec. (a), which formerly read:

"(a)(1) Unless the court orders otherwise, the debtor shall commence making the payments proposed by a plan within 30 days after the plan is filed.

"(2) A payment made under this subsection shall be retained by the trustee until confirmation or denial of confirmation of a plan. If a plan is confirmed, the trustee shall distribute any such payment in accordance with the plan as soon as practicable. If a plan is not confirmed, the trustee shall return any such payment to the debtor, after deducting any unpaid claim allowed under section 503(b) of this title."

Subsec. (b). Pub.L.109–8, § 1224(1), struck out "and" at the end of par. (1), struck out the period at the end of par. (2) and inserted "; and", and added par. (3).

Subsec. (b)(1). Pub.L. 109–8, § 1502(a)(10), struck out "507(a)(1)" and inserted "507(a)(2)".

Subsec. (d). Pub.L.109–8, § 1224(2), added subsec. (d).

1994 Amendments. Subsec. (a)(2). Pub.L. 103–394, § 307, added provisions directing trustee to distribute payment as soon as practicable.

1986 Amendments. Subsec. (a)(2). Pub.L. 99–554, 283(z), substituted "payment" for "payments" in last sentence.

Subsec. (b)(2). Pub.L. 99–554, § 230, substituted "586(b) of title 28" for "1302(d) of this title" and "586(e)(1)(B) of title 28" for "1302(e) of this title".

1984 Amendments. Subsec. (a). Pub.L. 98–353, § 318(a)(2), added subsec. (a). Former subsec. (a) was redesignated as (b).

Subsec. (b). Pub.L. 98–353, § 318(a)(1), redesignated former subsec. (a) as (b). Former subsec. (b) was redesignated as (c).

Subsec. (b)(2). Pub.L. 98–353, § 531, added "of this title" after "1302(d)".

Subsec. (c). Pub.L. 98–353, § 318(a)(1), redesignated former subsec. (b) as (c).

Effective and Applicability Provisions

2010 Acts. Increase of dollar amounts by Judicial Conference of the United States by notice published Feb. 25, 2010, 75 F.R. 8747 effective April 1, 2010, and increase not applicable to cases commenced before the effective date of the adjustments, i.e., April 1, 2010. See Adjustment of Dollar Amounts notes under 11 U.S.C.A. § 104 and this section.

2007 Acts. Increase of dollar amounts by Judicial Conference of the United States by notice published Feb. 14, 2007, 72 F.R. 7082 effective April 1, 2007, and increase not applicable to cases commenced before the effective date of the adjustments, i.e., April 1, 2007. See Adjustment of Dollar Amounts notes under 11 U.S.C.A. § 104 and this section.

2005 Acts. Amendments by Pub.L. 109–8 effective, except as otherwise provided, 180 days after April 20, 2005, and inapplicable with respect to cases commenced under Title 11 before the effective date, see Pub.L. 109–8, § 1501, set out as a note under 11 U.S.C.A. § 101.

1994 Acts. Amendment by Pub.L. 103–394 effective on Oct. 22, 1994, and not to apply with respect to cases commenced under Title 11 of the United States Code before Oct. 22, 1994, see section 702 of Pub.L. 103–394, set out as a note under section 101 of this title.

1986 Acts. Amendment by section 283 of Pub.L. 99–554 effective 30 days after Oct. 27, 1986, except as otherwise provided for, see section 302(a) of Pub.L. 99–554, set out as a note under section 581 of Title 28, Judiciary and Judicial Procedure.

Amendment by Pub.L. 99–554, § 230, not to become effective in or with respect to certain specified judicial districts until, or apply to cases while pending in such district before, the expiration of the 270–day period beginning 30 days after Oct. 27, 1986, or of the 30–day period beginning on the date the Attorney General certifies under section 303 of Pub.L. 99–554 the region specified in a paragraph of section 581(a) of Title 28, as amended by section 111(a) of Pub.L. 99–554, that includes such district, whichever occurs first, see section 302(d)(1) of Pub.L. 99–554, set out as a note under section 581 of Title 28.

Amendment by Pub.L. 99–554, § 230, not to become effective in or with respect to certain specified judicial districts until, or apply to cases while pending in such district before, the expiration of the 2–year period beginning 30 days after Oct. 27, 1986, or of the 30–day period beginning on the date the Attorney General certifies under section 303 of Pub.L. 99–554 the region specified in a paragraph of section 581(a) of Title 28, as amended by section 111(a) of Pub.L. 99–554, that includes such district, whichever occurs first, see section 302(d)(2) of Pub.L. 99–554, set out as a note under section 581 of Title 28.

Amendment by Pub.L. 99–554, § 230, not to become effective in or with respect to judicial districts established for the States of Alabama and North Carolina until, or apply to cases while pending in such district before, such district elects to be included in a bankruptcy region established in section 581(a) of Title 28, as amended by section 111(a) of Pub.L. 99–554, or Oct. 1, 2002, whichever occurs first, and, except as otherwise provided for, with respect to cases under chapters 7, 11, 12, and 13 of Title 11 commenced before 30 days after Oct. 27, 1986, and pending in a judicial district in the States of Alabama or North Carolina before any election made under section 302(d)(3)(A) of Pub.L. 99–554 by such district becomes effective or Oct. 1, 2002, whichever occurs first, amendments by Pub.L. 99–554 not to apply until Oct. 1, 2003, or the expiration of the 1–year period beginning on the date such election becomes effective, whichever occurs first, and further, in any judicial district in Alabama or North Carolina not making the election described in section 302(d)(3)(A) of Pub.L.

99–554, any person appointed under regulations issued by the Judicial Conference to administer estates in cases under Title 11 authorized to establish, etc., a panel of private trustees, and to supervise cases and trustees in cases under chapters 7, 11, 12, and 13 of Title 11, until amendments by sections 201 to 231 of Pub.L. 99–554 effective in such district, see section 302(d)(3)(A) to (F), (H), (I) of Pub.L. 99–554, set out as a note under section 581 of Title 28.

Amendment by Pub.L. 99–554, § 230, except as otherwise provided, with respect to cases under chapters 7, 11, 12, and 13 of Title 11 commenced before 30 days after Oct. 27, 1986, and pending in a judicial district referred to in section 581(a) of Title 28, as amended by section 111(a) of Pub.L. 99–554, for which a United States trustee is not authorized before 30 days after Oct. 27, 1986 to be appointed, not applicable until the expiration of the 3–year period beginning on Oct. 27, 1986, or of the 1–year period beginning on the date the Attorney General certifies under section 303 of Pub.L. 99–554 the region specified in a paragraph of such section 581(a) that includes, such district, whichever occurs first, see section 302(e)(1), (2) of Pub.L. 99–554, set out as a note under section 581 of Title 28.

1984 Acts. Amendment by Pub.L. 98–353 effective with respect to cases filed 90 days after July 10, 1984, see section 552(a), formerly 553(a), of Pub.L. 98–353, set out as a note under section 101 of this title.

Separability of Provisions

If any provision of or amendment made by Pub.L. 103–394 or the application of such provision or amendment to any person or circumstance is held to be unconstitutional, the remaining provisions of and amendments made by Pub.L. 103–394 and the application of such provisions and amendments to any person or circumstance shall not be affected thereby, see section 701 of Pub.L. 103–394, set out as a note under section 101 of this title.

Adjustment of Dollar Amounts

For adjustment of dollar amounts specified in subsec. (b)(3)(B) of this section by the Judicial Conference of the United States, effective Apr. 1, 2010, see note set out under 11 U.S.C.A. § 104.

By notice published Feb. 25, 2010, 75 F.R. 8747, the Judicial Conference of the United States purported to adjust the dollar amounts in provisions specified in subsec. (b)(3)(B) of this section, effective Apr. 1, 2010, as follows:

Adjusted $25 to $25 [resulting in no change in text].

By notice published Feb. 14, 2007, 72 F.R. 7082, the Judicial Conference of the United States purported to adjust the dollar amounts in provisions specified in subsec. (b)(3) of this section, effective Apr. 1, 2007, as follows:

Adjusted $25 to $25 [resulting in no change in text].

CROSS REFERENCES

Conversion or dismissal for failure to commence making timely payments under this section, see 11 USCA § 1307.

Duty of trustee to ensure that debtor commences making timely payments under this section, see 11 USCA § 1302.

Payment stopped on checks remaining unpaid 90 days after final distribution, see 11 USCA § 347.

LIBRARY REFERENCES

American Digest System

Bankruptcy ☞3712.

Bankruptcy ☞3714.

Key Number System Topic No. 51.

Corpus Juris Secundum

CJS Bankruptcy § 103, Chapter 13.

CJS Bankruptcy § 1099, Unclaimed Property.

§ 1327. Effect of confirmation

(a) The provisions of a confirmed plan bind the debtor and each creditor, whether or not the claim of such creditor is provided for by the plan, and whether or not such creditor has objected to, has accepted, or has rejected the plan.

(b) Except as otherwise provided in the plan or the order confirming the plan, the confirmation of a plan vests all of the property of the estate in the debtor.

(c) Except as otherwise provided in the plan or in the order confirming the plan, the property vesting in the debtor under subsection (b) of this section is free and clear of any claim or interest of any creditor provided for by the plan.

(Pub.L. 95–598, Nov. 6, 1978, 92 Stat. 2650.)

HISTORICAL AND STATUTORY NOTES

Revision Notes and Legislative Reports

1978 Acts. Subsection (a) binds the debtor and each creditor to the provisions of a confirmed plan, whether or not the claim of the creditor is provided for by the plan and whether or not the creditor has accepted, rejected, or objected to the plan. Unless the plan itself or the order confirming the plan otherwise provides, confirmation is deemed to vest all property of the estate in the debtor, free and clear of any claim or interest of any creditor provided for by the plan. Senate Report No. 95–989.

CROSS REFERENCES

Effect of confirmation in—

Chapter eleven cases, see 11 USCA § 1141.

Chapter nine cases, see 11 USCA § 944.

Chapter twelve cases, see 11 USCA § 1227.

LIBRARY REFERENCES

American Digest System

Bankruptcy ☞3715(9.1) to 3715(13).

Key Number System Topic No. 51.

Corpus Juris Secundum

CJS Bankruptcy § 278, Parties Defendant; Sovereign Immunity.

CJS Bankruptcy § 1204, Effect of Confirmation.

§ 1328. Discharge

(a) Subject to subsection (d), as soon as practicable after completion by the debtor of all payments under the plan, and in the case of a debtor who is required by a judicial or administrative order, or by statute, to pay a domestic support obligation, after such debtor certifies that all amounts payable under such order or such statute that are due on or before the date of the certification (including amounts due before the petition was filed, but only to the extent provided for by the plan) have been paid, unless the court approves a written waiver of discharge executed by the debtor after the order for relief under this chapter, the court shall grant the debtor a discharge of all debts provided for by the plan or disallowed under section 502 of this title, except any debt—

(1) provided for under section 1322(b)(5);

(2) of the kind specified in section 507(a)(8)(C) or in paragraph (1)(B), (1)(C), (2), (3), (4), (5), (8), or (9) of section 523(a);

(3) for restitution, or a criminal fine, included in a sentence on the debtor's conviction of a crime; or

(4) for restitution, or damages, awarded in a civil action against the debtor as a result of willful or malicious injury by the debtor that caused personal injury to an individual or the death of an individual.

(b) Subject to subsection (d), at any time after the confirmation of the plan and after notice and a hearing, the court may grant a discharge to a debtor that has not completed payments under the plan only if—

(1) the debtor's failure to complete such payments is due to circumstances for which the debtor should not justly be held accountable;

(2) the value, as of the effective date of the plan, of property actually distributed under the plan on account of each allowed unsecured claim is not less than the amount that would have been paid on such claim if the estate of the debtor had been liquidated under chapter 7 of this title on such date; and

(3) modification of the plan under section 1329 of this title is not practicable.

(c) A discharge granted under subsection (b) of this section discharges the debtor from all unsecured debts provided for by the plan or disallowed under section 502 of this title, except any debt—

(1) provided for under section 1322(b)(5) of this title; or

(2) of a kind specified in section 523(a) of this title.

(d) Notwithstanding any other provision of this section, a discharge granted under this section does not discharge the debtor from any debt based on an allowed claim filed under section 1305(a)(2) of this title if prior approval by the trustee of the debtor's incurring such debt was practicable and was not obtained.

(e) On request of a party in interest before one year after a discharge under this section is granted, and after notice and a hearing, the court may revoke such discharge only if—

(1) such discharge was obtained by the debtor through fraud; and

(2) the requesting party did not know of such fraud until after such discharge was granted.

(f) Notwithstanding subsections (a) and (b), the court shall not grant a discharge of all debts provided for in the plan or disallowed under section 502, if the debtor has received a discharge—

(1) in a case filed under chapter 7, 11, or 12 of this title during the 4–year period preceding the date of the order for relief under this chapter, or

(2) in a case filed under chapter 13 of this title during the 2–year period preceding the date of such order.

(g)(1) The court shall not grant a discharge under this section to a debtor unless after filing a petition the debtor has completed an instructional course concerning personal financial management described in section 111.

(2) Paragraph (1) shall not apply with respect to a debtor who is a person described in section 109(h)(4) or who resides in a district for which the United States trustee (or the bankruptcy administrator, if any) determines that the approved instructional courses are not adequate to service the additional individuals who would otherwise be required to complete such instructional course by reason of the requirements of paragraph (1).

(3) The United States trustee (or the bankruptcy administrator, if any) who makes a determination described in paragraph (2) shall review such determination not later than 1 year after the date of such determination, and not less frequently than annually thereafter.

(h) The court may not grant a discharge under this chapter unless the court after notice and a hearing held not more than 10 days before the date of the entry of the order granting the discharge finds that there is no reasonable cause to believe that—

(1) section 522(q)(1) may be applicable to the debtor; and

(2) there is pending any proceeding in which the debtor may be found guilty of a felony of the kind described in section 522(q)(1)(A) or liable for a debt of the kind described in section 522(q)(1)(B).

(Pub.L. 95–598, Nov. 6, 1978, 92 Stat. 2650; Pub.L. 98–353, Title III, § 532, July 10, 1984, 98 Stat. 389; Pub.L. 101–508, Title III, § 3007(b)(1), Nov. 5, 1990, 104 Stat. 1388–28; Pub.L. 101–581, §§ 2(b), 3, Nov. 15, 1990, 104 Stat. 2865; Pub.L. 101–647, Title XXXI, §§ 3102(b), 3103, Nov. 29, 1990, 104 Stat. 4916; Pub.L. 103–394, Title III, § 302, Title V, § 501(d)(38), Oct. 22, 1994, 108 Stat. 4132, 4147; Pub.L. 109–8, Title I, § 106(c), Title II, § 213(11), Title III, §§ 312(2), 314(b), 330(d), Title VII, § 707, Apr. 20, 2005, 119 Stat. 38, 53, 87, 88, 102, 126.)

HISTORICAL AND STATUTORY NOTES

Revision Notes and Legislative Reports

1978 Acts. The court is to enter a discharge, unless waived, as soon as practicable after completion of payments under the plan. The debtor is to be discharged of all debts provided for by the plan or disallowed under section 502, except a debt provided for under the plan the last payment on which was not due until after the completion of the plan, or a debt incurred for willful and malicious conversion of or injury to the property or person of another.

Subsection (b) is the successor to Bankruptcy Act Section [sic] 661 [Section 1061 of former title 11]. This subsection permits the bankruptcy judge to grant the debtor a discharge at any time after confirmation of a plan, if the court determines, after notice and hearing, that the failure to complete payments under the plan is due to circumstances for which the debtor should not justly be held accountable, the distributions made to each creditor under the plan equal in value the amount that would have been paid to the creditor had the estate been liquidated under chapter 7 of title 11 at the date of the hearing under this subsection, and that modification of the plan is impracticable. The discharge granted under subsection (b) relieves the debtor from all unsecured debts provided for by the plan or disallowed under section 502, except nondischargeable debts described in section 523(a) of title 11 or debts of the type covered by section 1322(b)(5).

Subsection (d) excepts from any chapter 13 discharge a debt based on an allowed section 1305(a)(2) postpetition claim, if prior trustee approval of the incurring of the debt was practicable but was not obtained.

A chapter 13 discharge obtained through fraud and before the moving party gained knowledge of the fraud may be revoked by the court under subsection (e), after notice and hearing, at the request of any party in interest made within 1 year after the discharge was granted. Senate Report No. 95–989.

1984 Acts. Statements by Legislative Leaders, see 1984 U.S.Code Cong. and Adm.News, p. 576.

1990 Acts. House Report No. 101–681(I), see 1990 U.S.Code Cong. and Adm.News, p. 6472.

Senate Report No. 101–434, see 1990 U.S.Code Cong. and Adm.News, p. 4065.

House Report No. 101–881, House Conference Report No. 101–964, and President's Signing Statement, see 1990 U.S.Code Cong. and Adm.News, p. 2017.

1994 Acts. House Report No. 103–835, see 1994 U.S. Code Cong. and Adm. News, p. 3340.

2005 Acts. House Report No. 109–31(Part I), see 2005 U.S. Code Cong. and Adm. News, p. 88.

Legislative Statements

Section 1328(a) adopts a provision contained in the Senate amendment permitting the court to approve a waiver of discharge by the debtor. It is anticipated that such a waiver must be in writing executed after the order for relief in a case under chapter 13.

References in Text

Chapter 7, 11, or 12 of this title, referred to in subsec. (f)(1), is 11 U.S.C.A. § 701 et seq., 11 U.S.C.A. § 1101 et seq., or 11 U.S.C.A. § 1201 et seq., respectively.

Chapter 13 of this title, referred to in subsec. (f)(2), is 11 U.S.C.A. § 1301 et seq.

Codifications

Pub.L. 101–581, §§ 2(b), 3(1) to (3) and Pub.L. 101–647, §§ 3102(b), 3103(1)–(3), contained identical amendments to subsec. (a)(2) and (a)(1)–(3) of this section.

Amendments by Pub.L. 101–581, § 2(b), and Pub.L. 101–647, § 3102(b), which both inserted "or 523(a)(9)" following "523(a)(5)", were incapable of literal execution in view of prior amendment by Pub.L. 101–508, which substituted "paragraph (5) or (8) of section 523(a)" for "section 523(a)(5)", thereby deleting language subsequently amended. See also 1990 Amendments note set out under this section.

Amendments

2005 Amendments. Subsec. (a). Pub.L. 109–8, § 213(11), inserted ", and in the case of a debtor who is required by a judicial or administrative order, or by statute, to pay a domestic support obligation, after such debtor certifies that all amounts payable under such order or such statute that are due on or before the date of the certification (including amounts due before the petition was filed, but only to the extent provided for by the plan) have been paid" after "completion by the debtor of all payments under the plan".

Pub.L. 109–8, § 330(d)(1), struck out "As" and inserted "Subject to subsection (d), as".

Pub.L. 109–8, § 314(b), struck out former pars. (1) through (3) of subsec. (a) and inserted new pars. (1) to (4). Prior to deletion, pars. (1) to (3) read:

"**(1)** provided for under section 1322(b)(5) of this title;

"**(2)** of the kind specified in paragraph (5), (8), or (9) of section 523(a) of this title; or

"**(3)** for restitution, or a criminal fine, included in a sentence on the debtor's conviction of a crime."

Subsec. (a)(2). Pub.L. 109–8, § 707, struck out "paragraph" and inserted "section 507(a)(8)(C) or in paragraph (1)(B), (1)(C),".

Subsec. (b). Pub.L. 109–8, § 330(d)(2), struck out "At" and inserted "Subject to subsection (d), at".

Subsec. (f). Pub.L. 109–8, § 312(2), added subsec. (f).

Subsec. (g). Pub.L. 109–8, § 106(c), added subsec. (g).

Subsec. (h). Pub.L. 109–8, § 330(d)(3), added subsec. (h).

1994 Amendments. Subsec. (a)(2). Pub.L. 103–394, § 501(d)(38)(A), substituted "(5), (8), or (9)" for "(5) or (8)".

Subsec. (a)(3). Pub.L. 103–394, § 302, added provisions excluding any debt for a criminal fine from the debts the court shall grant discharge of.

Pub.L. 103–394, § 501(d)(38)(B), struck out par. (3) as added by Pub.L. 101–647, § 3103(3), requiring no change in text. See 1990 Amendment notes set out under this section.

1990 Amendments. Subsec. (a)(1). Pub.L. 101–581, § 3(1), and Pub.L. 101–647, § 3103(1), made identical amendments striking "or" at end.

Subsec. (a)(2). Pub.L. 101–581, § 3(2), and Pub.L. 101–647, § 3103(2), made identical amendments substituting "; or" for period at end.

Pub.L. 101–581, § 2(b), and Pub.L. 101–647, § 3102(b), which directed identical insertions of "or 523(a)(9)" after "523(a)(5)", could not be executed because of a prior amendment by Pub.L. 101–508. See amendment note set out under this section.

Pub.L. 101–508, §§ 3007(b)(1), 3008, temporarily substituted "paragraph (5) or (8) of section 523(a)" for "section 523(a)(5)". See Effective and Applicability Provisions of 1990 Amendments note under this section.

Subsec. (a)(3). Pub.L. 101–581, § 3(3), and Pub.L. 101–647, § 3103(3), made identical amendments adding par. (3).

1984 Amendments. Subsec. (e)(1). Pub.L. 98–353, § 532(1), added "by the debtor" after "obtained".

Subsec. (e)(2). Pub.L. 98–353, § 532(2), substituted "the requesting party did not know of such fraud until" for "knowledge of such fraud came to the requesting party".

Effective and Applicability Provisions

2005 Acts. Amendments Pub.L. 109–8 effective 180 days after Apr. 20, 2005, with amendments by sections 106(c), 213(11), 312(2), 314(b), and 707 of Pub.L. 109–8 not applicable with respect to cases commenced under this title before such effective date, except as otherwise provided, and amendment by section 330(d) of Pub.L. 109–8 applicable with respect to cases commenced under this title on or after Apr. 20, 2005, see Pub.L. 109–8, § 1501, set out as a note under 11 U.S.C.A. § 101.

1994 Acts. Amendments by Pub.L. 103–394 effective on Oct. 22, 1994, and not to apply with respect to cases commenced under Title 11 of the United States Code before Oct. 22, 1994, see section 702 of Pub.L. 103–394, set out as a note under section 101 of this title.

1990 Acts. Amendment by Pub.L. 101–647 effective Nov. 29, 1990, but not applicable with respect to cases commenced under this title before Nov. 29, 1990, see section 3104 of Pub.L. 101–647, set out as an Effective Date of 1990 Amendments note under section 523 of this title.

Amendment by Pub.L. 101–581 effective Nov. 15, 1990, but not applicable with respect to cases commenced under this title before Nov. 15, 1990, see section 4 of Pub.L. 101–581, set out as an Effective Date of 1990 Amendment note under section 523 of this title.

Section 3007(b)(2) of Pub.L. 101–508 provided that: "The amendment made by paragraph (1) [amending this section] shall not apply to any case under the provisions of title 11, United States Code, commenced before the date of the enactment of this Act [Nov. 5, 1990]."

Section 3008 of Pub.L. 101–508, which had provided that the amendment to this section by Pub.L. 101–508 was to cease to be effective on Oct. 1, 1996, was repealed by Pub.L. 102–325, Title XV, § 1558, July 23, 1992, 106 Stat. 841.

1984 Acts. Amendment by Pub.L. 98–353 effective with respect to cases filed 90 days after July 10, 1984, see section 552(a), formerly 553(a), of Pub.L. 98–353, set out as a note under section 101 of this title.

Separability of Provisions

If any provision of or amendment made by Pub.L. 103–394 or the application of such provision or amendment to any person or circumstance is held to be unconstitutional, the remaining provisions of and amendments made by Pub.L. 103–394 and the application of such provisions and amendments to any person or circumstance shall not be affected thereby, see section 701 of Pub.L. 103–394, set out as a note under section 101 of this title.

CROSS REFERENCES

Cancellation of indebtedness from discharged farm loans, see 12 USCA § 1150.

Discharge in—

Chapter seven cases, see 11 USCA § 727.

Chapter twelve cases, see 11 USCA § 1228.

Effect of, discharge, see 11 USCA § 524.

Exceptions to discharge, see 11 USCA § 523.

Nondischargeability of capital improvement loans for multifamily housing projects in proceedings under this section, see 12 USCA § 1715z–1a.

LIBRARY REFERENCES

American Digest System

Bankruptcy ⚖3718(1) to 3718(10).

Key Number System Topic No. 51.

Corpus Juris Secundum

CJS Bankruptcy § 139, Adversary Proceedings.

CJS Bankruptcy § 301, Notice to Debtor, Creditors, and Indenture Trustees.

CJS Bankruptcy § 1046, Generally; Objections to Discharge.

CJS Bankruptcy § 1056, Revocation or Vacation of Discharge.

CJS Bankruptcy § 1062, Effect of Discharge of Debts.

CJS Bankruptcy § 1078, Educational Loans.

CJS Bankruptcy § 1094, Requirements for Reaffirmation of Debt.

CJS Bankruptcy § 1189, Contents of Plan, Generally.

CJS Bankruptcy § 1190, Requirement of Good Faith in Proposal of Plan.

CJS Bankruptcy § 1208, Discharge.

CJS Bankruptcy § 1209, Discharge--Grounds for Denial or Revocation of Discharge.

§ 1329. Modification of plan after confirmation

(a) At any time after confirmation of the plan but before the completion of payments under such plan, the plan may be modified, upon request of the debtor, the trustee, or the holder of an allowed unsecured claim, to—

(1) increase or reduce the amount of payments on claims of a particular class provided for by the plan;

(2) extend or reduce the time for such payments;

(3) alter the amount of the distribution to a creditor whose claim is provided for by the plan to the extent necessary to take account of any payment of such claim other than under the plan; or

(4) reduce amounts to be paid under the plan by the actual amount expended by the debtor to purchase health insurance for the debtor (and for any dependent of the debtor if such dependent does not otherwise have health insurance coverage) if the debtor documents the cost of such insurance and demonstrates that—

(A) such expenses are reasonable and necessary;

(B)(i) if the debtor previously paid for health insurance, the amount is not materially larger than the cost the debtor previously paid or the cost necessary to maintain the lapsed policy; or

(ii) if the debtor did not have health insurance, the amount is not materially larger than the reasonable cost that would be incurred by a debtor who purchases health insurance, who has similar income, expenses, age, and health status, and who lives in the same geographical location with the same number of dependents who do not otherwise have health insurance coverage; and

(C) the amount is not otherwise allowed for purposes of determining disposable income under section 1325(b) of this title;

and upon request of any party in interest, files proof that a health insurance policy was purchased.

(b)(1) Sections 1322(a), 1322(b), and 1323(c) of this title and the requirements of section 1325(a) of this title apply to any modification under subsection (a) of this section.

(2) The plan as modified becomes the plan unless, after notice and a hearing, such modification is disapproved.

(c) A plan modified under this section may not provide for payments over a period that expires after the applicable commitment period under section 1325(b)(1)(B) after the time that the first payment under the original confirmed plan was due, unless the court, for cause, approves a longer period, but the court may not approve a period that expires after five years after such time.

(Pub.L. 95–598, Nov. 6, 1978, 92 Stat. 2651; Pub.L. 98–353, Title III, §§ 319, 533, July 10, 1984, 98 Stat. 357, 389; Pub.L. 109–8, Title I, § 102(i), Title III, § 318(4), Apr. 20, 2005, 119 Stat. 34, 94.)

HISTORICAL AND STATUTORY NOTES

Revision Notes and Legislative Reports

1978 Acts. At any time prior to the completion of payments under a confirmed plan, the plan may be modified, after notice and hearing, to change the amount of payments to creditors or a particular class of creditors and to extend or reduce the payment period. A modified plan may not contain any provision which could not be included in an original plan as prescribed by section 1322. A modified plan may not call for payments to be made beyond four years as measured from the date of the commencement of payments under the original plan. Senate Report No. 95–989.

1984 Acts. Statements by Legislative Leaders, see 1984 U.S.Code Cong. and Adm.News, p. 576.

2005 Acts. House Report No. 109–31(Part I), see 2005 U.S. Code Cong. and Adm. News, p. 88.

Amendments

2005 Amendments. Subsec. (a)(2). Pub.L. 109–8, § 102(i)(1), struck out "or" at the end.

Subsec. (a)(3). Pub.L. 109–8, § 102(i)(2), struck out the period and inserted "; or".

Subsec. (a)(4). Pub.L. 109–8, § 102(i)(3), added par. (4).

Subsec. (c). Pub.L. 109–8, § 318(4), struck out "three years" and inserted "the applicable commitment period under section 1325(b)(1)(B)".

1984 Amendments. Subsec. (a). Pub.L. 98–353, § 319, added provisions respecting requests by the debtor, the trustee, or the holder of an allowed unsecured claim for modification.

Pub.L. 98–353, § 533(1), added "of the plan" after "confirmation".

Pub.L. 98–353, § 533(2), substituted "such plan" for "a plan".

Subsec. (a)(3). Pub.L. 98–353, § 533(3), substituted "plan to" for "plan, to".

Effective and Applicability Provisions

2005 Acts. Amendments by Pub.L. 109–8 effective, except as otherwise provided, 180 days after April 20, 2005, and inapplicable with respect to cases commenced under Title 11 before the effective date, see Pub.L. 109–8, § 1501, set out as a note under 11 U.S.C.A. § 101.

1984 Acts. Amendment by Pub.L. 98–353 effective with respect to cases filed 90 days after July 10, 1984, see section 552(a), formerly 553(a), of Pub.L. 98–353, set out as a note under section 101 of this title.

CROSS REFERENCES

Conversion or dismissal upon denial of confirmation of modified plan, see 11 USCA § 1307.

Duties of United States trustee, see 28 USCA § 586.

Modification of plan in—

    Chapter eleven cases, see 11 USCA § 1127.

    Chapter nine cases, see 11 USCA § 942.

    Chapter twelve cases, see 11 USCA § 1229.

LIBRARY REFERENCES

American Digest System

Bankruptcy ⇒3713.

Key Number System Topic No. 51.

Corpus Juris Secundum

CJS Bankruptcy § 1191, Modification Prior to Confirmation.

CJS Bankruptcy § 1205, Postconfirmation Modification.

CJS Bankruptcy § 1206, Postconfirmation Modification-- Procedure and Burden of Proof.

§ 1330. Revocation of an order of confirmation

(a) On request of a party in interest at any time within 180 days after the date of the entry of an order of confirmation under section 1325 of this title, and after notice and a hearing, the court may revoke such order if such order was procured by fraud.

(b) If the court revokes an order of confirmation under subsection (a) of this section, the court shall dispose of the case under section 1307 of this title, unless, within the time fixed by the court, the debtor proposes and the court confirms a modification of the plan under section 1329 of this title.

(Pub.L. 95–598, Nov. 6, 1978, 92 Stat. 2651.)

HISTORICAL AND STATUTORY NOTES

Revision Notes and Legislative Reports

1978 Acts. The court may revoke an order of confirmation procured by fraud, after notice and hearing, on application of a party in interest filed within 180 days after the entry of the order. Thereafter, unless a modified plan is confirmed, the court is to convert or dismiss the chapter 13 case as provided in section 1307. Senate Report No. 95–989.

Legislative Statements

Section 1331 of the House bill and Senate amendment is deleted in the House amendment.

Special tax provision: Section 1331 of title 11 of the House bill and the comparable provisions in sections 1322 and 1327(d) of the Senate amendment, pertaining to assessment and collection of taxes in wage earner plans, are deleted, and the governing rule is placed in section 505(c) of the House amendment. The provisions of both bills allowing assessment and collection of taxes after confirmation of the wage-earner plan are modified to allow assessment and collection after the court fixes the fact and amount of a tax liability, including administrative period taxes, regardless of whether this occurs before or after confirmation of the plan. The provision of the House bill limiting the collection of taxes to those assessed before one year after the filing of the petition is eliminated, thereby leaving the period of limitations on assessment of these nondischargeable tax liabilities the usual period provided by the Internal Revenue Code [Title 26].

CROSS REFERENCES

Conversion or dismissal upon revocation of order of confirmation, see 11 USCA § 1307.

Revocation of order of confirmation in—

Chapter eleven cases, see 11 USCA § 1144.

Chapter twelve cases, see 11 USCA § 1230.

LIBRARY REFERENCES

American Digest System

Bankruptcy ⚯3715(14).

Key Number System Topic No. 51.

Corpus Juris Secundum

CJS Bankruptcy § 315, Judgments--Relief from Judgment or Order; Collateral Attack.

CJS Bankruptcy § 1207, Revocation or Vacation.

CHAPTER 15—ANCILLARY AND OTHER CROSS–BORDER CASES

Sec.
1501. Purpose and scope of application.

SUBCHAPTER I—GENERAL PROVISIONS

1502. Definitions.
1503. International obligations of the United States.
1504. Commencement of ancillary case.
1505. Authorization to act in a foreign country.
1506. Public policy exception.
1507. Additional assistance.
1508. Interpretation.

SUBCHAPTER II—ACCESS OF FOREIGN REPRESENTATIVES AND CREDITORS TO THE COURT

1509. Right of direct access.
1510. Limited jurisdiction.
1511. Commencement of case under section 301 or 303 [1].
1512. Participation of a foreign representative in a case under this title.
1513. Access of foreign creditors to a case under this title.
1514. Notification to foreign creditors concerning a case under this title.

SUBCHAPTER III—RECOGNITION OF A FOREIGN PROCEEDING AND RELIEF

1515. Application for recognition.
1516. Presumptions concerning recognition.
1517. Order granting recognition.
1518. Subsequent information.
1519. Relief that may be granted upon filing petition for recognition.
1520. Effects of recognition of a foreign main proceeding.
1521. Relief that may be granted upon recognition.
1522. Protection of creditors and other interested persons.
1523. Actions to avoid acts detrimental to creditors.
1524. Intervention by a foreign representative.

SUBCHAPTER IV—COOPERATION WITH FOREIGN COURTS AND FOREIGN REPRESENTATIVES

1525. Cooperation and direct communication between the court and foreign courts or foreign representatives.
1526. Cooperation and direct communication between the trustee and foreign courts or foreign representatives.
1527. Forms of cooperation.

SUBCHAPTER V—CONCURRENT PROCEEDINGS

1528. Commencement of a case under this title after recognition of a foreign main proceeding.
1529. Coordination of a case under this title and a foreign proceeding.
1530. Coordination of more than 1 foreign proceeding.
1531. Presumption of insolvency based on recognition of a foreign main proceeding.

Sec.
SUBCHAPTER V—CONCURRENT PROCEEDINGS—Cont'd

1532. Rule of payment in concurrent proceedings.
[1] So in original. Item does not conform to section catchline.

HISTORICAL AND STATUTORY NOTES

Prior Provisions

A prior chapter 15, consisting of sections 1501 to 151326, related to a pilot program for a United States trustee system, prior to repeal by Pub.L. 99–554, Title II, § 231, Oct. 27, 1986, 100 Stat. 3103.

§ 1501. Purpose and scope of application

(a) The purpose of this chapter is to incorporate the Model Law on Cross-Border Insolvency so as to provide effective mechanisms for dealing with cases of cross-border insolvency with the objectives of—

(1) cooperation between—

(A) courts of the United States, United States trustees, trustees, examiners, debtors, and debtors in possession; and

(B) the courts and other competent authorities of foreign countries involved in cross-border insolvency cases;

(2) greater legal certainty for trade and investment;

(3) fair and efficient administration of cross-border insolvencies that protects the interests of all creditors, and other interested entities, including the debtor;

(4) protection and maximization of the value of the debtor's assets; and

(5) facilitation of the rescue of financially troubled businesses, thereby protecting investment and preserving employment.

(b) This chapter applies where—

(1) assistance is sought in the United States by a foreign court or a foreign representative in connection with a foreign proceeding;

(2) assistance is sought in a foreign country in connection with a case under this title;

(3) a foreign proceeding and a case under this title with respect to the same debtor are pending concurrently; or

(4) creditors or other interested persons in a foreign country have an interest in requesting the commencement of, or participating in, a case or proceeding under this title.

(c) This chapter does not apply to—

(1) a proceeding concerning an entity, other than a foreign insurance company, identified by exclusion in section 109(b);

(2) an individual, or to an individual and such individual's spouse, who have debts within the limits

specified in section 109(e) and who are citizens of the United States or aliens lawfully admitted for permanent residence in the United States; or

(3) an entity subject to a proceeding under the Securities Investor Protection Act of 1970, a stockbroker subject to subchapter III of chapter 7 of this title, or a commodity broker subject to subchapter IV of chapter 7 of this title.

(d) The court may not grant relief under this chapter with respect to any deposit, escrow, trust fund, or other security required or permitted under any applicable State insurance law or regulation for the benefit of claim holders in the United States.

(Added Pub.L. 109–8, Title VIII, § 801(a), Apr. 20, 2005, 119 Stat. 135.)

HISTORICAL AND STATUTORY NOTES

Revision Notes and Legislative Reports

2005 Acts. House Report No. 109–31(Part I), see 2005 U.S. Code Cong. and Adm. News, p. 88.

References in Text

The Securities Investor Protection Act of 1970, referred to in subsec. (c)(3), is Pub.L. 91–598, Dec. 30, 1970, 84 Stat. 1636, also known as SIPA, which is classified principally to chapter 2B–1 of Title 15, 15 U.S.C.A. § 78aaa et seq.

Subchapter III of chapter 7 of this title, referred to in subsec. (c)(3), is 11 U.S.C.A. § 741 et seq.

Subchapter IV of chapter 7 of this title, referred to in subsec. (c)(3), is 11 U.S.C.A. § 761 et seq.

Effective and Applicability Provisions

2005 Acts. Amendments by Pub.L. 109–8 effective, except as otherwise provided, 180 days after April 20, 2005, and inapplicable with respect to cases commenced under Title 11 before the effective date, see Pub.L. 109–8, § 1501, set out as a note under 11 U.S.C.A. § 101.

Prior Provisions

Prior section 1501, Pub.L. 95–598, Title I, § 101, Nov. 6, 1978, 92 Stat. 2652, set forth applicability of chapter, which provided a pilot program for a United States trustee system, and was repealed by Pub.L. 99–554, Title II, § 231, Oct. 27, 1986, 100 Stat. 3103, effective 30 days after Oct. 27, 1986, except as otherwise provided for, see Pub.L. 99–554, § 302, set out as a note under 28 U.S.C.A. § 581.

LIBRARY REFERENCES

Corpus Juris Secundum

CJS Bankruptcy § 7, Bankruptcy Code.

CJS Bankruptcy § 385, Governing Statutes, Generally.

CJS Bankruptcy § 400, Relief Available on Recognition.

SUBCHAPTER I—GENERAL PROVISIONS

§ 1502. Definitions

For the purposes of this chapter, the term—

(1) "debtor" means an entity that is the subject of a foreign proceeding;

(2) "establishment" means any place of operations where the debtor carries out a nontransitory economic activity;

(3) "foreign court" means a judicial or other authority competent to control or supervise a foreign proceeding;

(4) "foreign main proceeding" means a foreign proceeding pending in the country where the debtor has the center of its main interests;

(5) "foreign nonmain proceeding" means a foreign proceeding, other than a foreign main proceeding, pending in a country where the debtor has an establishment;

(6) "trustee" includes a trustee, a debtor in possession in a case under any chapter of this title, or a debtor under chapter 9 of this title;

(7) "recognition" means the entry of an order granting recognition of a foreign main proceeding or foreign nonmain proceeding under this chapter; and

(8) "within the territorial jurisdiction of the United States", when used with reference to property of a debtor, refers to tangible property located within the territory of the United States and intangible property deemed under applicable nonbankruptcy law to be located within that territory, including any property subject to attachment or garnishment that may properly be seized or garnished by an action in a Federal or State court in the United States.

(Added Pub.L. 109–8, Title VIII, § 801(a), Apr. 20, 2005, 119 Stat. 135.)

HISTORICAL AND STATUTORY NOTES

Revision Notes and Legislative Reports

2005 Acts. House Report No. 109–31(Part I), see 2005 U.S. Code Cong. and Adm. News, p. 88.

References in Text

Chapter 9 of this title, referred to in par. (6), is 11 U.S.C.A. § 901 et seq.

Effective and Applicability Provisions

2005 Acts. Amendments by Pub.L. 109–8 effective, except as otherwise provided, 180 days after April 20, 2005, and inapplicable with respect to cases commenced under Title 11 before the effective date, see Pub.L. 109–8, § 1501, set out as a note under 11 U.S.C.A. § 101.

LIBRARY REFERENCES

Corpus Juris Secundum

CJS Bankruptcy § 386, Foreign Proceedings and Representatives, Generally.

CJS Bankruptcy § 398, Order Recognizing Foreign Proceeding.

CJS Bankruptcy § 399, Effects of Recognizing Foreign Main Proceeding.

§ 1503. International obligations of the United States

To the extent that this chapter conflicts with an obligation of the United States arising out of any treaty or other form of agreement to which it is a party with one or more other countries, the requirements of the treaty or agreement prevail.

(Added Pub.L. 109–8, Title VIII, § 801(a), Apr. 20, 2005, 119 Stat. 136.)

HISTORICAL AND STATUTORY NOTES

Revision Notes and Legislative Reports

   2005 Acts. House Report No. 109–31(Part I), see 2005 U.S. Code Cong. and Adm. News, p. 88.

Effective and Applicability Provisions

   2005 Acts. Amendments by Pub.L. 109–8 effective, except as otherwise provided, 180 days after April 20, 2005, and inapplicable with respect to cases commenced under Title 11 before the effective date, see Pub.L. 109–8, § 1501, set out as a note under 11 U.S.C.A. § 101.

LIBRARY REFERENCES

Corpus Juris Secundum

   CJS Bankruptcy § 385, Governing Statutes, Generally.

§ 1504. Commencement of ancillary case

A case under this chapter is commenced by the filing of a petition for recognition of a foreign proceeding under section 1515.

(Added Pub.L. 109–8, Title VIII, § 801(a), Apr. 20, 2005, 119 Stat. 136.)

HISTORICAL AND STATUTORY NOTES

Revision Notes and Legislative Reports

   2005 Acts. House Report No. 109–31(Part I), see 2005 U.S. Code Cong. and Adm. News, p. 88.

Effective and Applicability Provisions

   2005 Acts. Amendments by Pub.L. 109–8 effective, except as otherwise provided, 180 days after April 20, 2005, and inapplicable with respect to cases commenced under Title 11 before the effective date, see Pub.L. 109–8, § 1501, set out as a note under 11 U.S.C.A. § 101.

LIBRARY REFERENCES

Corpus Juris Secundum

   CJS Bankruptcy § 7, Bankruptcy Code.

   CJS Bankruptcy § 390, Petition for Recognition of Foreign Proceeding.

§ 1505. Authorization to act in a foreign country

A trustee or another entity (including an examiner) may be authorized by the court to act in a foreign country on behalf of an estate created under section 541. An entity authorized to act under this section may act in any way permitted by the applicable foreign law.

(Added Pub.L. 109–8, Title VIII, § 801(a), Apr. 20, 2005, 119 Stat. 136.)

HISTORICAL AND STATUTORY NOTES

Revision Notes and Legislative Reports

   2005 Acts. House Report No. 109–31(Part I), see 2005 U.S. Code Cong. and Adm. News, p. 88.

Effective and Applicability Provisions

   2005 Acts. Amendments by Pub.L. 109–8 effective, except as otherwise provided, 180 days after April 20, 2005, and inapplicable with respect to cases commenced under Title 11 before the effective date, see Pub.L. 109–8, § 1501, set out as a note under 11 U.S.C.A. § 101.

LIBRARY REFERENCES

Corpus Juris Secundum

   CJS Bankruptcy § 7, Bankruptcy Code.

   CJS Bankruptcy § 387, Authorization to Act in Foreign Country.

§ 1506. Public policy exception

Nothing in this chapter prevents the court from refusing to take an action governed by this chapter if the action would be manifestly contrary to the public policy of the United States.

(Added Pub.L. 109–8, Title VIII, § 801(a), Apr. 20, 2005, 119 Stat. 136.)

HISTORICAL AND STATUTORY NOTES

Revision Notes and Legislative Reports

   2005 Acts. House Report No. 109–31(Part I), see 2005 U.S. Code Cong. and Adm. News, p. 88.

Effective and Applicability Provisions

   2005 Acts. Amendments by Pub.L. 109–8 effective, except as otherwise provided, 180 days after April 20, 2005, and inapplicable with respect to cases commenced under Title 11 before the effective date, see Pub.L. 109–8, § 1501, set out as a note under 11 U.S.C.A. § 101.

LIBRARY REFERENCES

Corpus Juris Secundum

   CJS Bankruptcy § 385, Governing Statutes, Generally.

§ 1507. Additional assistance

(a) Subject to the specific limitations stated elsewhere in this chapter the court, if recognition is granted, may provide additional assistance to a foreign representative under this title or under other laws of the United States.

(b) In determining whether to provide additional assistance under this title or under other laws of the United States, the court shall consider whether such additional assistance, consistent with the principles of comity, will reasonably assure—

   (1) just treatment of all holders of claims against or interests in the debtor's property;

(2) protection of claim holders in the United States against prejudice and inconvenience in the processing of claims in such foreign proceeding;

(3) prevention of preferential or fraudulent dispositions of property of the debtor;

(4) distribution of proceeds of the debtor's property substantially in accordance with the order prescribed by this title; and

(5) if appropriate, the provision of an opportunity for a fresh start for the individual that such foreign proceeding concerns.

(Added Pub.L. 109–8, Title VIII, § 801(a), Apr. 20, 2005, 119 Stat. 136.)

HISTORICAL AND STATUTORY NOTES

Revision Notes and Legislative Reports

2005 Acts. House Report No. 109–31(Part I), see 2005 U.S. Code Cong. and Adm. News, p. 88.

Effective and Applicability Provisions

2005 Acts. Amendments by Pub.L. 109–8 effective, except as otherwise provided, 180 days after April 20, 2005, and inapplicable with respect to cases commenced under Title 11 before the effective date, see Pub.L. 109–8, § 1501, set out as a note under 11 U.S.C.A. § 101.

LIBRARY REFERENCES

Corpus Juris Secundum

CJS Bankruptcy § 401, Additional Assistance.

§ 1508. Interpretation

In interpreting this chapter, the court shall consider its international origin, and the need to promote an application of this chapter that is consistent with the application of similar statutes adopted by foreign jurisdictions.

(Added Pub.L. 109–8, Title VIII, § 801(a), Apr. 20, 2005, 119 Stat. 137.)

HISTORICAL AND STATUTORY NOTES

Revision Notes and Legislative Reports

2005 Acts. House Report No. 109–31(Part I), see 2005 U.S. Code Cong. and Adm. News, p. 88.

Effective and Applicability Provisions

2005 Acts. Amendments by Pub.L. 109–8 effective, except as otherwise provided, 180 days after April 20, 2005, and inapplicable with respect to cases commenced under Title 11 before the effective date, see Pub.L. 109–8, § 1501, set out as a note under 11 U.S.C.A. § 101.

LIBRARY REFERENCES

Corpus Juris Secundum

CJS Bankruptcy § 385, Governing Statutes, Generally.

SUBCHAPTER II—ACCESS OF FOREIGN REPRESENTATIVES AND CREDITORS TO THE COURT

§ 1509. Right of direct access

(a) A foreign representative may commence a case under section 1504 by filing directly with the court a petition for recognition of a foreign proceeding under section 1515.

(b) If the court grants recognition under section 1517, and subject to any limitations that the court may impose consistent with the policy of this chapter—

(1) the foreign representative has the capacity to sue and be sued in a court in the United States;

(2) the foreign representative may apply directly to a court in the United States for appropriate relief in that court; and

(3) a court in the United States shall grant comity or cooperation to the foreign representative.

(c) A request for comity or cooperation by a foreign representative in a court in the United States other than the court which granted recognition shall be accompanied by a certified copy of an order granting recognition under section 1517.

(d) If the court denies recognition under this chapter, the court may issue any appropriate order necessary to prevent the foreign representative from obtaining comity or cooperation from courts in the United States.

(e) Whether or not the court grants recognition, and subject to sections 306 and 1510, a foreign representative is subject to applicable nonbankruptcy law.

(f) Notwithstanding any other provision of this section, the failure of a foreign representative to commence a case or to obtain recognition under this chapter does not affect any right the foreign representative may have to sue in a court in the United States to collect or recover a claim which is the property of the debtor.

(Added Pub.L. 109–8, Title VIII, § 801(a), Apr. 20, 2005, 119 Stat. 137.)

HISTORICAL AND STATUTORY NOTES

Revision Notes and Legislative Reports

2005 Acts. House Report No. 109–31(Part 1), see 2005 U.S. Code Cong. and Adm. News, p. 88.

Effective and Applicability Provisions

2005 Acts. Amendments by Pub.L. 109–8 effective, except as otherwise provided, 180 days after April 20, 2005, and inapplicable with respect to cases commenced under Title 11 before the effective date, see Pub.L. 109–8, § 1501, set out as a note under 11 U.S.C.A. § 101.

LIBRARY REFERENCES

Corpus Juris Secundum

CJS Bankruptcy § 7, Bankruptcy Code.

CJS Bankruptcy § 386, Foreign Proceedings and Representatives, Generally.

CJS Bankruptcy § 390, Petition for Recognition of Foreign Proceeding.

CJS Bankruptcy § 402, Powers of Foreign Representative on Recognition.

§ 1510. Limited jurisdiction

The sole fact that a foreign representative files a petition under section 1515 does not subject the foreign representative to the jurisdiction of any court in the United States for any other purpose.
(Added Pub.L. 109–8, Title VIII, § 801(a), Apr. 20, 2005, 119 Stat. 138.)

HISTORICAL AND STATUTORY NOTES
Revision Notes and Legislative Reports
2005 Acts. House Report No. 109–31(Part I), see 2005 U.S. Code Cong. and Adm. News, p. 88.

Effective and Applicability Provisions
2005 Acts. Amendments by Pub.L. 109–8 effective, except as otherwise provided, 180 days after April 20, 2005, and inapplicable with respect to cases commenced under Title 11 before the effective date, see Pub.L. 109–8, § 1501, set out as a note under 11 U.S.C.A. § 101.

LIBRARY REFERENCES
Corpus Juris Secundum
CJS Bankruptcy § 386, Foreign Proceedings and Representatives, Generally.

§ 1511. Commencement of case under section 301, 302, or 303

(a) Upon recognition, a foreign representative may commence—

(1) an involuntary case under section 303; or

(2) a voluntary case under section 301 or 302, if the foreign proceeding is a foreign main proceeding.

(b) The petition commencing a case under subsection (a) must be accompanied by a certified copy of an order granting recognition. The court where the petition for recognition has been filed must be advised of the foreign representative's intent to commence a case under subsection (a) prior to such commencement.
(Added Pub.L. 109–8, Title VIII, § 801(a), Apr. 20, 2005, 119 Stat. 138; amended Pub.L. 111–327, § 2(a)(45), Dec. 22, 2010, 124 Stat. 3562.)

HISTORICAL AND STATUTORY NOTES
Revision Notes and Legislative Reports
2005 Acts. House Report No. 109–31(Part I), see 2005 U.S. Code Cong. and Adm. News, p. 88.

Amendments
2010 Amendments. Section heading. Pub.L. 111–327, § 2(a)(45), inserted ", 302," following "301".

Effective and Applicability Provisions
2005 Acts. Amendments by Pub.L. 109–8 effective, except as otherwise provided, 180 days after April 20, 2005, and inapplicable with respect to cases commenced under Title 11 before the effective date, see Pub.L. 109–8, § 1501, set out as a note under 11 U.S.C.A. § 101.

LIBRARY REFERENCES
Corpus Juris Secundum
CJS Bankruptcy § 403, Powers of Foreign Representative on Recognition--Commencement of or Participation in Other Bankruptcy Case.

§ 1512. Participation of a foreign representative in a case under this title

Upon recognition of a foreign proceeding, the foreign representative in the recognized proceeding is entitled to participate as a party in interest in a case regarding the debtor under this title.
(Added Pub.L. 109–8, Title VIII, § 801(a), Apr. 20, 2005, 119 Stat. 138.)

HISTORICAL AND STATUTORY NOTES
Revision Notes and Legislative Reports
2005 Acts. House Report No. 109–31(Part I), see 2005 U.S. Code Cong. and Adm. News, p. 88.

Effective and Applicability Provisions
2005 Acts. Amendments by Pub.L. 109–8 effective, except as otherwise provided, 180 days after April 20, 2005, and inapplicable with respect to cases commenced under Title 11 before the effective date, see Pub.L. 109–8, § 1501, set out as a note under 11 U.S.C.A. § 101.

LIBRARY REFERENCES
Corpus Juris Secundum
CJS Bankruptcy § 403, Powers of Foreign Representative on Recognition--Commencement of or Participation in Other Bankruptcy Case.

§ 1513. Access of foreign creditors to a case under this title

(a) Foreign creditors have the same rights regarding the commencement of, and participation in, a case under this title as domestic creditors.

(b)(1) Subsection (a) does not change or codify present law as to the priority of claims under section 507 or 726, except that the claim of a foreign creditor under those sections shall not be given a lower priority than that of general unsecured claims without priority solely because the holder of such claim is a foreign creditor.

(2)(A) Subsection (a) and paragraph (1) do not change or codify present law as to the allowability of foreign revenue claims or other foreign public law claims in a proceeding under this title.

(B) Allowance and priority as to a foreign tax claim or other foreign public law claim shall be governed by any applicable tax treaty of the United States, under the conditions and circumstances specified therein.
(Added Pub.L. 109–8, Title VIII, § 801(a), Apr. 20, 2005, 119 Stat. 138.)

HISTORICAL AND STATUTORY NOTES

Revision Notes and Legislative Reports

2005 Acts. House Report No. 109–31(Part I), see 2005 U.S. Code Cong. and Adm. News, p. 88.

Effective and Applicability Provisions

2005 Acts. Amendments by Pub.L. 109–8 effective, except as otherwise provided, 180 days after April 20, 2005, and inapplicable with respect to cases commenced under Title 11 before the effective date, see Pub.L. 109–8, § 1501, set out as a note under 11 U.S.C.A. § 101.

LIBRARY REFERENCES

Corpus Juris Secundum

CJS Bankruptcy § 7, Bankruptcy Code.

CJS Bankruptcy § 388, Rights of Foreign Creditors in Bankruptcy Cases.

§ 1514. Notification to foreign creditors concerning a case under this title

(a) Whenever in a case under this title notice is to be given to creditors generally or to any class or category of creditors, such notice shall also be given to the known creditors generally, or to creditors in the notified class or category, that do not have addresses in the United States. The court may order that appropriate steps be taken with a view to notifying any creditor whose address is not yet known.

(b) Such notification to creditors with foreign addresses described in subsection (a) shall be given individually, unless the court considers that, under the circumstances, some other form of notification would be more appropriate. No letter or other formality is required.

(c) When a notification of commencement of a case is to be given to foreign creditors, such notification shall—

    (1) indicate the time period for filing proofs of claim and specify the place for filing such proofs of claim;

    (2) indicate whether secured creditors need to file proofs of claim; and

    (3) contain any other information required to be included in such notification to creditors under this title and the orders of the court.

(d) Any rule of procedure or order of the court as to notice or the filing of a proof of claim shall provide such additional time to creditors with foreign addresses as is reasonable under the circumstances.

(Added Pub.L. 109–8, Title VIII, § 801(a), Apr. 20, 2005, 119 Stat. 138.)

HISTORICAL AND STATUTORY NOTES

Revision Notes and Legislative Reports

2005 Acts. House Report No. 109–31(Part I), see 2005 U.S. Code Cong. and Adm. News, p. 88.

Effective and Applicability Provisions

2005 Acts. Amendments by Pub.L. 109–8 effective, except as otherwise provided, 180 days after April 20, 2005, and inapplicable with respect to cases commenced under Title 11 before the effective date, see Pub.L. 109–8, § 1501, set out as a note under 11 U.S.C.A. § 101.

LIBRARY REFERENCES

Corpus Juris Secundum

CJS Bankruptcy § 7, Bankruptcy Code.

CJS Bankruptcy § 388, Rights of Foreign Creditors in Bankruptcy Cases.

SUBCHAPTER III—RECOGNITION OF A FOREIGN PROCEEDING AND RELIEF

§ 1515. Application for recognition

(a) A foreign representative applies to the court for recognition of a foreign proceeding in which the foreign representative has been appointed by filing a petition for recognition.

(b) A petition for recognition shall be accompanied by—

    (1) a certified copy of the decision commencing such foreign proceeding and appointing the foreign representative;

    (2) a certificate from the foreign court affirming the existence of such foreign proceeding and of the appointment of the foreign representative; or

    (3) in the absence of evidence referred to in paragraphs (1) and (2), any other evidence acceptable to the court of the existence of such foreign proceeding and of the appointment of the foreign representative.

(c) A petition for recognition shall also be accompanied by a statement identifying all foreign proceedings with respect to the debtor that are known to the foreign representative.

(d) The documents referred to in paragraphs (1) and (2) of subsection (b) shall be translated into English. The court may require a translation into English of additional documents.

(Added Pub.L. 109–8, Title VIII, § 801(a), Apr. 20, 2005, 119 Stat. 139.)

HISTORICAL AND STATUTORY NOTES

Revision Notes and Legislative Reports

2005 Acts. House Report No. 109–31(Part I), see 2005 U.S. Code Cong. and Adm. News, p. 88.

Effective and Applicability Provisions

2005 Acts. Amendments by Pub.L. 109–8 effective, except as otherwise provided, 180 days after April 20, 2005, and inapplicable with respect to cases commenced under Title 11 before the effective date, see Pub.L. 109–8, § 1501, set out as a note under 11 U.S.C.A. § 101.

Corpus Juris Secundum

CJS Bankruptcy § 390, Petition for Recognition of Foreign Proceeding.

§ 1516.　Presumptions concerning recognition

(a) If the decision or certificate referred to in section 1515(b) indicates that the foreign proceeding is a foreign proceeding and that the person or body is a foreign representative, the court is entitled to so presume.

(b) The court is entitled to presume that documents submitted in support of the petition for recognition are authentic, whether or not they have been legalized.

(c) In the absence of evidence to the contrary, the debtor's registered office, or habitual residence in the case of an individual, is presumed to be the center of the debtor's main interests.

(Added Pub.L. 109–8, Title VIII, § 801(a), Apr. 20, 2005, 119 Stat. 139.)

HISTORICAL AND STATUTORY NOTES

Revision Notes and Legislative Reports

2005 Acts. House Report No. 109–31(Part I), see 2005 U.S. Code Cong. and Adm. News, p. 88.

Effective and Applicability Provisions

2005 Acts. Amendments by Pub.L. 109–8 effective, except as otherwise provided, 180 days after April 20, 2005, and inapplicable with respect to cases commenced under Title 11 before the effective date, see Pub.L. 109–8, § 1501, set out as a note under 11 U.S.C.A. § 101.

Corpus Juris Secundum

CJS Bankruptcy § 386, Foreign Proceedings and Representatives, Generally.

CJS Bankruptcy § 390, Petition for Recognition of Foreign Proceeding.

§ 1517.　Order granting recognition

(a) Subject to section 1506, after notice and a hearing, an order recognizing a foreign proceeding shall be entered if—

(1) such foreign proceeding for which recognition is sought is a foreign main proceeding or foreign nonmain proceeding within the meaning of section 1502;

(2) the foreign representative applying for recognition is a person or body; and

(3) the petition meets the requirements of section 1515.

(b) Such foreign proceeding shall be recognized—

(1) as a foreign main proceeding if it is pending in the country where the debtor has the center of its main interests; or

(2) as a foreign nonmain proceeding if the debtor has an establishment within the meaning of section 1502 in the foreign country where the proceeding is pending.

(c) A petition for recognition of a foreign proceeding shall be decided upon at the earliest possible time. Entry of an order recognizing a foreign proceeding constitutes recognition under this chapter.

(d) The provisions of this subchapter do not prevent modification or termination of recognition if it is shown that the grounds for granting it were fully or partially lacking or have ceased to exist, but in considering such action the court shall give due weight to possible prejudice to parties that have relied upon the order granting recognition. A case under this chapter may be closed in the manner prescribed under section 350.

(Added Pub.L. 109–8, Title VIII, § 801(a), Apr. 20, 2005, 119 Stat. 139.)

HISTORICAL AND STATUTORY NOTES

Revision Notes and Legislative Reports

2005 Acts. House Report No. 109–31(Part I), see 2005 U.S. Code Cong. and Adm. News, p. 88.

Effective and Applicability Provisions

2005 Acts. Amendments by Pub.L. 109–8 effective, except as otherwise provided, 180 days after April 20, 2005, and inapplicable with respect to cases commenced under Title 11 before the effective date, see Pub.L. 109–8, § 1501, set out as a note under 11 U.S.C.A. § 101.

Corpus Juris Secundum

CJS Bankruptcy § 397, Hearing and Notice of Hearing.

CJS Bankruptcy § 398, Order Recognizing Foreign Proceeding.

CJS Bankruptcy § 1105, Closing.

§ 1518.　Subsequent information

From the time of filing the petition for recognition of a foreign proceeding, the foreign representative shall file with the court promptly a notice of change of status concerning—

(1) any substantial change in the status of such foreign proceeding or the status of the foreign representative's appointment; and

(2) any other foreign proceeding regarding the debtor that becomes known to the foreign representative.

(Added Pub.L. 109–8, Title VIII, § 801(a), Apr. 20, 2005, 119 Stat. 140.)

HISTORICAL AND STATUTORY NOTES

Revision Notes and Legislative Reports

2005 Acts. House Report No. 109–31(Part I), see 2005 U.S. Code Cong. and Adm. News, p. 88.

Effective and Applicability Provisions

2005 Acts. Amendments by Pub.L. 109–8 effective, except as otherwise provided, 180 days after April 20, 2005, and inapplicable with respect to cases commenced under Title 11 before the effective date, see Pub.L. 109–8, § 1501, set out as a note under 11 U.S.C.A. § 101.

LIBRARY REFERENCES

Corpus Juris Secundum

CJS Bankruptcy § 394, Notice of Changes in Status.

§ 1519. Relief that may be granted upon filing petition for recognition

(a) From the time of filing a petition for recognition until the court rules on the petition, the court may, at the request of the foreign representative, where relief is urgently needed to protect the assets of the debtor or the interests of the creditors, grant relief of a provisional nature, including—

(1) staying execution against the debtor's assets;

(2) entrusting the administration or realization of all or part of the debtor's assets located in the United States to the foreign representative or another person authorized by the court, including an examiner, in order to protect and preserve the value of assets that, by their nature or because of other circumstances, are perishable, susceptible to devaluation or otherwise in jeopardy; and

(3) any relief referred to in paragraph (3), (4), or (7) of section 1521(a).

(b) Unless extended under section 1521(a)(6), the relief granted under this section terminates when the petition for recognition is granted.

(c) It is a ground for denial of relief under this section that such relief would interfere with the administration of a foreign main proceeding.

(d) The court may not enjoin a police or regulatory act of a governmental unit, including a criminal action or proceeding, under this section.

(e) The standards, procedures, and limitations applicable to an injunction shall apply to relief under this section.

(f) The exercise of rights not subject to the stay arising under section 362(a) pursuant to paragraph (6), (7), (17), or (27) of section 362(b) or pursuant to section 362(o) shall not be stayed by any order of a court or administrative agency in any proceeding under this chapter.

(Added Pub.L. 109–8, Title VIII, § 801(a), Apr. 20, 2005, 119 Stat. 140; amended Pub.L. 111–327, § 2(a)(46), Dec. 22, 2010, 124 Stat. 3562.)

HISTORICAL AND STATUTORY NOTES

Revision Notes and Legislative Reports

2005 Acts. House Report No. 109–31(Part I), see 2005 U.S. Code Cong. and Adm. News, p. 88.

Amendments

2010 Amendments. Subsec. (f). Pub.L. 111–327, § 2(a)(46), struck out "362(n)" and inserted "362(o)".

Effective and Applicability Provisions

2005 Acts. Amendments by Pub.L. 109–8 effective, except as otherwise provided, 180 days after April 20, 2005, and inapplicable with respect to cases commenced under Title 11 before the effective date, see Pub.L. 109–8, § 1501, set out as a note under 11 U.S.C.A. § 101.

LIBRARY REFERENCES

Corpus Juris Secundum

CJS Bankruptcy § 389, Cooperation and Communication With Foreign Courts and Foreign Representatives.

CJS Bankruptcy § 395, Provisional Relief.

§ 1520. Effects of recognition of a foreign main proceeding

(a) Upon recognition of a foreign proceeding that is a foreign main proceeding—

(1) sections 361 and 362 apply with respect to the debtor and the property of the debtor that is within the territorial jurisdiction of the United States;

(2) sections 363, 549, and 552 apply to a transfer of an interest of the debtor in property that is within the territorial jurisdiction of the United States to the same extent that the sections would apply to property of an estate;

(3) unless the court orders otherwise, the foreign representative may operate the debtor's business and may exercise the rights and powers of a trustee under and to the extent provided by sections 363 and 552; and

(4) section 552 applies to property of the debtor that is within the territorial jurisdiction of the United States.

(b) Subsection (a) does not affect the right to commence an individual action or proceeding in a foreign country to the extent necessary to preserve a claim against the debtor.

(c) Subsection (a) does not affect the right of a foreign representative or an entity to file a petition commencing a case under this title or the right of any party to file claims or take other proper actions in such a case.

(Added Pub.L. 109–8, Title VIII, § 801(a), Apr. 20, 2005, 119 Stat. 141.)

HISTORICAL AND STATUTORY NOTES

Revision Notes and Legislative Reports

2005 Acts. House Report No. 109–31(Part I), see 2005 U.S. Code Cong. and Adm. News, p. 88.

Effective and Applicability Provisions

2005 Acts. Amendments by Pub.L. 109–8 effective, except as otherwise provided, 180 days after April 20, 2005, and inapplicable with respect to cases commenced under Title 11 before the effective date, see Pub.L. 109–8, § 1501, set out as a note under 11 U.S.C.A. § 101.

§ 1521. Relief that may be granted upon recognition

(a) Upon recognition of a foreign proceeding, whether main or nonmain, where necessary to effectuate the purpose of this chapter and to protect the assets of the debtor or the interests of the creditors, the court may, at the request of the foreign representative, grant any appropriate relief, including—

(1) staying the commencement or continuation of an individual action or proceeding concerning the debtor's assets, rights, obligations or liabilities to the extent they have not been stayed under section 1520(a);

(2) staying execution against the debtor's assets to the extent it has not been stayed under section 1520(a);

(3) suspending the right to transfer, encumber or otherwise dispose of any assets of the debtor to the extent this right has not been suspended under section 1520(a);

(4) providing for the examination of witnesses, the taking of evidence or the delivery of information concerning the debtor's assets, affairs, rights, obligations or liabilities;

(5) entrusting the administration or realization of all or part of the debtor's assets within the territorial jurisdiction of the United States to the foreign representative or another person, including an examiner, authorized by the court;

(6) extending relief granted under section 1519(a); and

(7) granting any additional relief that may be available to a trustee, except for relief available under sections 522, 544, 545, 547, 548, 550, and 724(a).

(b) Upon recognition of a foreign proceeding, whether main or nonmain, the court may, at the request of the foreign representative, entrust the distribution of all or part of the debtor's assets located in the United States to the foreign representative or another person, including an examiner, authorized by the court, provided that the court is satisfied that the interests of creditors in the United States are sufficiently protected.

(c) In granting relief under this section to a representative of a foreign nonmain proceeding, the court must be satisfied that the relief relates to assets that, under the law of the United States, should be administered in the foreign nonmain proceeding or concerns information required in that proceeding.

(d) The court may not enjoin a police or regulatory act of a governmental unit, including a criminal action or proceeding, under this section.

(e) The standards, procedures, and limitations applicable to an injunction shall apply to relief under paragraphs (1), (2), (3), and (6) of subsection (a).

(f) The exercise of rights not subject to the stay arising under section 362(a) pursuant to paragraph (6), (7), (17), or (27) of section 362(b) or pursuant to section 362(o) shall not be stayed by any order of a court or administrative agency in any proceeding under this chapter.

(Added Pub.L. 109–8, Title VIII, § 801(a), Apr. 20, 2005, 119 Stat. 141; amended Pub.L. 111–327, § 2(a)(47), Dec. 22, 2010, 124 Stat. 3562.)

HISTORICAL AND STATUTORY NOTES

Revision Notes and Legislative Reports

2005 Acts. House Report No. 109–31(Part I), see 2005 U.S. Code Cong. and Adm. News, p. 88.

Amendments

2010 Amendments. Subsec. (f). Pub.L. 111–327, § 2(a)(47), struck out "362(n)" and inserted "362(o)".

Effective and Applicability Provisions

2005 Acts. Amendments by Pub.L. 109–8 effective, except as otherwise provided, 180 days after April 20, 2005, and inapplicable with respect to cases commenced under Title 11 before the effective date, see Pub.L. 109–8, § 1501, set out as a note under 11 U.S.C.A. § 101.

§ 1522. Protection of creditors and other interested persons

(a) The court may grant relief under section 1519 or 1521, or may modify or terminate relief under subsection (c), only if the interests of the creditors and other interested entities, including the debtor, are sufficiently protected.

(b) The court may subject relief granted under section 1519 or 1521, or the operation of the debtor's business under section 1520(a)(3), to conditions it considers appropriate, including the giving of security or the filing of a bond.

(c) The court may, at the request of the foreign representative or an entity affected by relief granted under section 1519 or 1521, or at its own motion, modify or terminate such relief.

(d) Section 1104(d) shall apply to the appointment of an examiner under this chapter. Any examiner shall comply with the qualification requirements imposed on a trustee by section 322.

(Added Pub.L. 109–8, Title VIII, § 801(a), Apr. 20, 2005, 119 Stat. 142.)

HISTORICAL AND STATUTORY NOTES

Revision Notes and Legislative Reports

2005 Acts. House Report No. 109–31(Part I), see 2005 U.S. Code Cong. and Adm. News, p. 88.

Effective and Applicability Provisions

2005 Acts. Amendments by Pub.L. 109–8 effective, except as otherwise provided, 180 days after April 20, 2005, and inapplicable with respect to cases commenced under Title 11 before the effective date, see Pub.L. 109–8, § 1501, set out as a note under 11 U.S.C.A. § 101.

LIBRARY REFERENCES

Corpus Juris Secundum

CJS Bankruptcy § 395, Provisional Relief.

CJS Bankruptcy § 396, Examiner.

CJS Bankruptcy § 399, Effects of Recognizing Foreign Main Proceeding.

CJS Bankruptcy § 400, Relief Available on Recognition.

§ 1523. Actions to avoid acts detrimental to creditors

(a) Upon recognition of a foreign proceeding, the foreign representative has standing in a case concerning the debtor pending under another chapter of this title to initiate actions under sections 522, 544, 545, 547, 548, 550, 553, and 724(a).

(b) When a foreign proceeding is a foreign nonmain proceeding, the court must be satisfied that an action under subsection (a) relates to assets that, under United States law, should be administered in the foreign nonmain proceeding.

(Added Pub.L. 109–8, Title VIII, § 801(a), Apr. 20, 2005, 119 Stat. 142.)

HISTORICAL AND STATUTORY NOTES

Revision Notes and Legislative Reports

2005 Acts. House Report No. 109–31(Part I), see 2005 U.S. Code Cong. and Adm. News, p. 88.

Effective and Applicability Provisions

2005 Acts. Amendments by Pub.L. 109–8 effective, except as otherwise provided, 180 days after April 20, 2005, and inapplicable with respect to cases commenced under Title 11 before the effective date, see Pub.L. 109–8, § 1501, set out as a note under 11 U.S.C.A. § 101.

LIBRARY REFERENCES

Corpus Juris Secundum

CJS Bankruptcy § 403, Powers of Foreign Representative on Recognition--Commencement of or Participation in Other Bankruptcy Case.

§ 1524. Intervention by a foreign representative

Upon recognition of a foreign proceeding, the foreign representative may intervene in any proceedings in a State or Federal court in the United States in which the debtor is a party.

(Added Pub.L. 109–8, Title VIII, § 801(a), Apr. 20, 2005, 119 Stat. 142.)

HISTORICAL AND STATUTORY NOTES

Revision Notes and Legislative Reports

2005 Acts. House Report No. 109–31(Part I), see 2005 U.S. Code Cong. and Adm. News, p. 88.

Effective and Applicability Provisions

2005 Acts. Amendments by Pub.L. 109–8 effective, except as otherwise provided, 180 days after April 20, 2005, and inapplicable with respect to cases commenced under Title 11 before the effective date, see Pub.L. 109–8, § 1501, set out as a note under 11 U.S.C.A. § 101.

LIBRARY REFERENCES

Corpus Juris Secundum

CJS Bankruptcy § 403, Powers of Foreign Representative on Recognition--Commencement of or Participation in Other Bankruptcy Case.

SUBCHAPTER IV—COOPERATION WITH FOREIGN COURTS AND FOREIGN REPRESENTATIVES

§ 1525. Cooperation and direct communication between the court and foreign courts or foreign representatives

(a) Consistent with section 1501, the court shall cooperate to the maximum extent possible with a foreign court or a foreign representative, either directly or through the trustee.

(b) The court is entitled to communicate directly with, or to request information or assistance directly from, a foreign court or a foreign representative, subject to the rights of a party in interest to notice and participation.

(Added Pub.L. 109–8, Title VIII, § 801(a), Apr. 20, 2005, 119 Stat. 143.)

HISTORICAL AND STATUTORY NOTES

Revision Notes and Legislative Reports

2005 Acts. House Report No. 109–31(Part I), see 2005 U.S. Code Cong. and Adm. News, p. 88.

Effective and Applicability Provisions

2005 Acts. Amendments by Pub.L. 109–8 effective, except as otherwise provided, 180 days after April 20, 2005, and inapplicable with respect to cases commenced under Title 11 before the effective date, see Pub.L. 109–8, § 1501, set out as a note under 11 U.S.C.A. § 101.

LIBRARY REFERENCES

Corpus Juris Secundum

CJS Bankruptcy § 389, Cooperation and Communication With Foreign Courts and Foreign Representatives.

§ 1526. Cooperation and direct communication between the trustee and foreign courts or foreign representatives

(a) Consistent with section 1501, the trustee or other person, including an examiner, authorized by the court, shall, subject to the supervision of the court, cooperate to the maximum extent possible with a foreign court or a foreign representative.

(b) The trustee or other person, including an examiner, authorized by the court is entitled, subject to the supervision of the court, to communicate directly with a foreign court or a foreign representative.

(Added Pub.L. 109–8, Title VIII, § 801(a), Apr. 20, 2005, 119 Stat. 143.)

HISTORICAL AND STATUTORY NOTES

Revision Notes and Legislative Reports

2005 Acts. House Report No. 109–31(Part I), see 2005 U.S. Code Cong. and Adm. News, p. 88.

Effective and Applicability Provisions

2005 Acts. Amendments by Pub.L. 109–8 effective, except as otherwise provided, 180 days after April 20, 2005, and inapplicable with respect to cases commenced under Title 11 before the effective date, see Pub.L. 109–8, § 1501, set out as a note under 11 U.S.C.A. § 101.

LIBRARY REFERENCES

Corpus Juris Secundum

CJS Bankruptcy § 389, Cooperation and Communication With Foreign Courts and Foreign Representatives.

CJS Bankruptcy § 396, Examiner.

§ 1527. Forms of cooperation

Cooperation referred to in sections 1525 and 1526 may be implemented by any appropriate means, including—

(1) appointment of a person or body, including an examiner, to act at the direction of the court;

(2) communication of information by any means considered appropriate by the court;

(3) coordination of the administration and supervision of the debtor's assets and affairs;

(4) approval or implementation of agreements concerning the coordination of proceedings; and

(5) coordination of concurrent proceedings regarding the same debtor.

(Added Pub.L. 109–8, Title VIII, § 801(a), Apr. 20, 2005, 119 Stat. 143.)

HISTORICAL AND STATUTORY NOTES

Revision Notes and Legislative Reports

2005 Acts. House Report No. 109–31(Part I), see 2005 U.S. Code Cong. and Adm. News, p. 88.

Effective and Applicability Provisions

2005 Acts. Amendments by Pub.L. 109–8 effective, except as otherwise provided, 180 days after April 20, 2005, and inapplicable with respect to cases commenced under Title 11 before the effective date, see Pub.L. 109–8, § 1501, set out as a note under 11 U.S.C.A. § 101.

LIBRARY REFERENCES

Corpus Juris Secundum

CJS Bankruptcy § 389, Cooperation and Communication With Foreign Courts and Foreign Representatives.

CJS Bankruptcy § 396, Examiner.

SUBCHAPTER V—CONCURRENT PROCEEDINGS

§ 1528. Commencement of a case under this title after recognition of a foreign main proceeding

After recognition of a foreign main proceeding, a case under another chapter of this title may be commenced only if the debtor has assets in the United States. The effects of such case shall be restricted to the assets of the debtor that are within the territorial jurisdiction of the United States and, to the extent necessary to implement cooperation and coordination under sections 1525, 1526, and 1527, to other assets of the debtor that are within the jurisdiction of the court under sections 541(a) of this title, and 1334(e) of title 28, to the extent that such other assets are not subject to the jurisdiction and control of a foreign proceeding that has been recognized under this chapter.

(Added Pub.L. 109–8, Title VIII, § 801(a), Apr. 20, 2005, 119 Stat. 143.)

HISTORICAL AND STATUTORY NOTES

Revision Notes and Legislative Reports

2005 Acts. House Report No. 109–31(Part I), see 2005 U.S. Code Cong. and Adm. News, p. 88.

Effective and Applicability Provisions

2005 Acts. Amendments by Pub.L. 109–8 effective, except as otherwise provided, 180 days after April 20, 2005, and inapplicable with respect to cases commenced under Title 11 before the effective date, see Pub.L. 109–8, § 1501, set out as a note under 11 U.S.C.A. § 101.

§ 1529. Coordination of a case under this title and a foreign proceeding

If a foreign proceeding and a case under another chapter of this title are pending concurrently regarding the same debtor, the court shall seek cooperation and coordination under sections 1525, 1526, and 1527, and the following shall apply:

(1) If the case in the United States is pending at the time the petition for recognition of such foreign proceeding is filed—

(A) any relief granted under section 1519 or 1521 must be consistent with the relief granted in the case in the United States; and

(B) section 1520 does not apply even if such foreign proceeding is recognized as a foreign main proceeding.

(2) If a case in the United States under this title commences after recognition, or after the date of the filing of the petition for recognition, of such foreign proceeding—

(A) any relief in effect under section 1519 or 1521 shall be reviewed by the court and shall be modified or terminated if inconsistent with the case in the United States; and

(B) if such foreign proceeding is a foreign main proceeding, the stay and suspension referred to in section 1520(a) shall be modified or terminated if inconsistent with the relief granted in the case in the United States.

(3) In granting, extending, or modifying relief granted to a representative of a foreign nonmain proceeding, the court must be satisfied that the relief relates to assets that, under the laws of the United States, should be administered in the foreign nonmain proceeding or concerns information required in that proceeding.

(4) In achieving cooperation and coordination under sections 1528 and 1529, the court may grant any of the relief authorized under section 305.

(Added Pub.L. 109–8, Title VIII, § 801(a), Apr. 20, 2005, 119 Stat. 144; amended Pub.L. 111–327, § 2(a)(48), Dec. 22, 2010, 124 Stat. 3562.)

HISTORICAL AND STATUTORY NOTES

Revision Notes and Legislative Reports

2005 Acts. House Report No. 109–31(Part I), see 2005 U.S. Code Cong. and Adm. News, p. 88.

Amendments

2010 Amendments. Par. (1). Pub.L. 111–327, § 2(a)(48), which directed amendment of par. (1) by inserting "is" after "States", was executed by making the insertion only in introductory provisions to reflect the probable intent of Congress.

Effective and Applicability Provisions

2005 Acts. Amendments by Pub.L. 109–8 effective, except as otherwise provided, 180 days after April 20, 2005, and inapplicable with respect to cases commenced under Title 11 before the effective date, see Pub.L. 109–8, § 1501, set out as a note under 11 U.S.C.A. § 101.

LIBRARY REFERENCES

Corpus Juris Secundum

CJS Bankruptcy § 405, Coordination of Foreign Proceeding With Domestic Bankruptcy Case.

§ 1530. Coordination of more than 1 foreign proceeding

In matters referred to in section 1501, with respect to more than 1 foreign proceeding regarding the debtor, the court shall seek cooperation and coordination under sections 1525, 1526, and 1527, and the following shall apply:

(1) Any relief granted under section 1519 or 1521 to a representative of a foreign nonmain proceeding after recognition of a foreign main proceeding must be consistent with the foreign main proceeding.

(2) If a foreign main proceeding is recognized after recognition, or after the filing of a petition for recognition, of a foreign nonmain proceeding, any relief in effect under section 1519 or 1521 shall be reviewed by the court and shall be modified or terminated if inconsistent with the foreign main proceeding.

(3) If, after recognition of a foreign nonmain proceeding, another foreign nonmain proceeding is recognized, the court shall grant, modify, or terminate relief for the purpose of facilitating coordination of the proceedings.

(Added Pub.L. 109–8, Title VIII, § 801(a), Apr. 20, 2005, 119 Stat. 144.)

HISTORICAL AND STATUTORY NOTES

Revision Notes and Legislative Reports

2005 Acts. House Report No. 109–31(Part I), see 2005 U.S. Code Cong. and Adm. News, p. 88.

Effective and Applicability Provisions

2005 Acts. Amendments by Pub.L. 109–8 effective, except as otherwise provided, 180 days after April 20, 2005, and inapplicable with respect to cases commenced under Title 11 before the effective date, see Pub.L. 109–8, § 1501, set out as a note under 11 U.S.C.A. § 101.

LIBRARY REFERENCES

Corpus Juris Secundum

CJS Bankruptcy § 406, Coordination of Multiple Foreign Proceedings.

§ 1531. Presumption of insolvency based on recognition of a foreign main proceeding

In the absence of evidence to the contrary, recognition of a foreign main proceeding is, for the purpose of commencing a proceeding under section 303, proof that the debtor is generally not paying its debts as such debts become due.

(Added Pub.L. 109–8, Title VIII, § 801(a), Apr. 20, 2005, 119 Stat. 144.)

HISTORICAL AND STATUTORY NOTES

Revision Notes and Legislative Reports

2005 Acts. House Report No. 109–31(Part I), see 2005 U.S. Code Cong. and Adm. News, p. 88.

Effective and Applicability Provisions

2005 Acts. Amendments by Pub.L. 109–8 effective, except as otherwise provided, 180 days after April 20, 2005, and inapplicable with respect to cases commenced under Title 11 before the effective date, see Pub.L. 109–8, § 1501, set out as a note under 11 U.S.C.A. § 101.

§ 1532. Rule of payment in concurrent proceedings

Without prejudice to secured claims or rights in rem, a creditor who has received payment with respect to its claim in a foreign proceeding pursuant to a law relating to insolvency may not receive a payment for the same claim in a case under any other chapter of this title regarding the debtor, so long as the payment to other creditors of the same class is proportionately less than the payment the creditor has already received. (Added Pub.L. 109–8, Title VIII, § 801(a), Apr. 20, 2005, 119 Stat. 145.)

HISTORICAL AND STATUTORY NOTES

Revision Notes and Legislative Reports

2005 Acts. House Report No. 109–31(Part I), see 2005 U.S. Code Cong. and Adm. News, p. 88.

Effective and Applicability Provisions

2005 Acts. Amendments by Pub.L. 109–8 effective, except as otherwise provided, 180 days after April 20, 2005, and inapplicable with respect to cases commenced under Title 11 before the effective date, see Pub.L. 109–8, § 1501, set out as a note under 11 U.S.C.A. § 101.

LIBRARY REFERENCES

Corpus Juris Secundum

CJS Bankruptcy § 385, Governing Statutes, Generally.

[§§ 15101 to 151326. Repealed. Pub.L. 99–554, Title II, § 231, Oct. 27, 1986, 100 Stat. 3103]

HISTORICAL AND STATUTORY NOTES

Section 15101, Pub.L. 95–598, Nov. 6, 1978, 92 Stat. 2652, defined terms "entity" and "governmental unit".

Section 15102, Pub.L. 95–598, Nov. 6, 1978, 92 Stat. 2652, set forth rule of construction.

Section 15103, Pub.L. 95–598, Nov. 6, 1978, 92 Stat. 2652; Pub.L. 98–353, Title III, §§ 311(b)(3), 318(b), July 10, 1984, 98 Stat. 355, 357, set forth applicability of subchapters and sections.

Section 15303, Pub.L. 95–598, Nov. 6, 1978, 92 Stat. 2653, set forth provisions relating to involuntary cases.

Section 15321, Pub.L. 95–598, Nov. 6, 1978, 92 Stat. 2653, related to eligibility to serve as trustee.

Section 15322, Pub.L. 95–598, Nov. 6, 1978, 92 Stat. 2653, related to qualifications of trustees.

Section 15324, Pub.L. 95–598, Nov. 6, 1978, 92 Stat. 2653, related to removal of trustee or examiner.

Section 15326, Pub.L. 95–598, Nov. 6, 1978, 92 Stat. 2653, related to limitation on compensation of trustees.

Section 15330, Pub.L. 95–598, Nov. 6, 1978, 92 Stat. 2653, set forth compensation of officers.

Section 15343, Pub.L. 95–598, Nov. 6, 1978, 92 Stat. 2653, related to examination of the debtor.

Section 15345, Pub.L. 95–598, Nov. 6, 1978, 92 Stat. 2654; Pub.L. 97–258, § 3(c), Sept. 13, 1982, 96 Stat. 1064, related to money of estates.

Section 15701, Pub.L. 95–598, Nov. 6, 1978, 92 Stat. 2654, related to appointment, etc., of interim trustee.

Section 15703, Pub.L. 95–598, Nov. 6, 1978, 92 Stat. 2654, related to successor trustee.

Section 15704, Pub.L. 95–598, Nov. 6, 1978, 92 Stat. 2655, related to duties of trustees.

Section 15727, Pub.L. 95–598, Nov. 6, 1978, 92 Stat. 2655, set forth provisions relating to discharge under section 727(a) of this title.

Section 151102, Pub.L. 95–598, Nov. 6, 1978, 92 Stat. 2655, set forth provisions relating to creditors' and equity security holders' committees.

Section 151104, Pub.L. 95–598, Nov. 6, 1978, 92 Stat. 2655, related to appointment of trustee or examiner in reorganization matters.

Section 151105, Pub.L. 95–598, Nov. 6, 1978, 92 Stat. 2656, related to termination of trustee's appointment.

Section 151163, Pub.L. 95–598, Nov. 6, 1978, 92 Stat. 2656, related to appointment of trustee.

Section 151302, Pub.L. 95–598, Nov. 6, 1978, 92 Stat. 2656; Pub.L. 98–353, Title III, §§ 311(b)(4), 534, July 10, 1984, 98 Stat. 355, 390, related to functions of trustee with respect to adjustment of debts of an individual with regular income.

Section 151326, Pub.L. 95–598, Nov. 6, 1978, 92 Stat. 2657, set forth provisions relating to payments.

Effective and Applicability Provisions of Repeal

Repeal of sections by Pub.L. 99–554 effective 30 days after Oct. 27, 1986, except as otherwise provided for, see section 302 of Pub.L. 99–554, set out as a note under section 581 of Title 28, Judiciary and Judicial Procedure.

Repeal of sections not applicable in or with respect to Northern District of Alabama until March 1, 1987, or the effective date of any election made under section 302(d)(3)(A) of Pub.L. 99–554, whichever occurs first, see section 302(d)(3)(H) of Pub.L. 99–554, set out as a note under section 581 of Title 28.

Pub.L. 95–598, Title IV, § 408(c), Nov. 6, 1978, 92 Stat. 2687, as amended Pub.L. 98–166, Title II, § 200, Nov. 28, 1983, 97 Stat. 1081; Pub.L. 98–353, Title III, § 323, July 10, 1984, 98 Stat. 358; Pub.L. 99–429, Sept. 30, 1986, 100 Stat. 985; Pub.L. 99–500, § 101(b) [Title II, § 200], Oct. 18, 1986, 100 Stat. 1783–39, 1783–45, and Pub.L. 99–591, § 101(b) [Title II, § 200], Oct. 30, 1986, 100 Stat. 3341–39, 3341–45; Pub.L. 99–554, Title III, § 307(a), Oct. 27, 1986, 100 Stat. 3125, which provided for the repeal of this chapter at a prospective date, was repealed by Pub.L. 99–554, Title III, § 307(b), Oct. 27, 1986, 100 Stat. 3125.

RELATED PROVISIONS

OF

U.S. CODE TITLES 18 AND 28

TITLE 18—CRIMES AND CRIMINAL PROCEDURE

CHAPTER 9—BANKRUPTCY

Sec.
151. Definition.
152. Concealment of assets; false oaths and claims; bribery.
153. Embezzlement against estate.
154. Adverse interest and conduct of officers.
155. Fee agreements in cases under title 11 and receiverships.
156. Knowing disregard of bankruptcy law or rule.
157. Bankruptcy fraud.
158. Designation of United States attorneys and agents of the Federal Bureau of Investigation to address abusive reaffirmations of debt and materially fraudulent statements in bankruptcy schedules.

CHAPTER 96—RACKETEER INFLUENCED AND CORRUPT ORGANIZATIONS

1961. Definitions.

CHAPTER 119—WIRE AND ELECTRONIC COMMUNICATIONS INTERCEPTION AND INTERCEPTION OF ORAL COMMUNICATIONS

2516. Authorization for interception of wire, oral, or electronic communications.

CHAPTER 203—ARREST AND COMMITMENT

3057. Bankruptcy investigations.

CHAPTER 213—LIMITATIONS

3284. Concealment of bankrupt's assets.

CHAPTER 601—IMMUNITY OF WITNESSES

6001. Definitions.

TITLE 28—JUDICIARY AND JUDICIAL PROCEDURE

PART I—ORGANIZATION OF COURTS

CHAPTER 6—BANKRUPTCY JUDGES

Sec.
151. Designation of bankruptcy courts.
152. Appointment of bankruptcy judges.
153. Salaries; character of service.
154. Division of business; chief judge.[1]
155. Temporary transfer of bankruptcy judges.
156. Staff; expenses.
157. Procedures.
158. Appeals.
159. Bankruptcy statistics.

[1] So in original. Does not conform to section catchline.

CHAPTER 17—RESIGNATION AND RETIREMENT OF JUSTICES AND JUDGES

372. Retirement for disability; substitute judge on failure to retire.

CHAPTER 21—GENERAL PROVISIONS APPLICABLE TO COURTS AND JUDGES

455. Disqualification of justice, judge, or magistrate judge.

PART II—DEPARTMENT OF JUSTICE

CHAPTER 39—UNITED STATES TRUSTEES

581. United States trustees.
582. Assistant United States trustees.
583. Oath of office.
584. Official stations.
585. Vacancies.
586. Duties; supervision by Attorney General.
587. Salaries.
588. Expenses.
589. Staff and other employees.
589a. United States Trustee System Fund.
589b. Bankruptcy data.

PART III—COURT OFFICERS AND EMPLOYEES

CHAPTER 41—ADMINISTRATIVE OFFICE OF UNITED STATES COURTS

604. Duties of Director generally.

CHAPTER 44—ALTERNATIVE DISPUTE RESOLUTION

651. Authorization of alternative dispute resolution.
652. Jurisdiction.
653. Neutrals.
654. Arbitration.

Complete Annotation Materials, see Title 18 U.S.C.A.

CHAPTER 44—ALTERNATIVE DISPUTE
RESOLUTION—Cont'd

655. Arbitrators.
656. Subpoenas.
657. Arbitration award and judgment.
658. Compensation of arbitrators and neutrals.

CHAPTER 57—GENERAL PROVISIONS APPLICABLE
TO COURT OFFICERS AND EMPLOYEES

959. Trustees and receivers suable; management; State
laws.

PART IV—JURISDICTION AND VENUE

CHAPTER 85—DISTRICT COURTS; JURISDICTION

1334. Bankruptcy cases and proceedings.

CHAPTER 87—DISTRICT COURTS; VENUE

1408. Venue of cases under title 11.

CHAPTER 87—DISTRICT COURTS; VENUE—Cont'd

1409. Venue of proceedings arising under title 11 or arising
in or related to cases under title 11.
1410. Venue of cases ancillary to foreign proceedings.
1411. Jury trials.
1412. Change of venue.
1413. Venue of cases under chapter 5 of title 3.

CHAPTER 89—DISTRICT COURTS; REMOVAL OF
CASES FROM
STATE COURTS

1452. Removal of claims related to bankruptcy cases.

PART V—PROCEDURE

CHAPTER 123—FEES AND COSTS

1930. Bankruptcy fees.

[Miscellaneous Fee Schedule]

CHAPTER 131—RULES OF COURTS

2075. Bankruptcy rules.

TITLE 18

CRIMES AND CRIMINAL PROCEDURE

CHAPTER 9—BANKRUPTCY

HISTORICAL AND STATUTORY NOTES

Amendments

2005 Amendments. Pub.L. 109–8, Title II, § 203(b)(2), Apr. 20, 2005, 119 Stat. 49, added item 158 "Designation of United States attorneys and agents of the Federal Bureau of Investigation to address abusive reaffirmations of debt and materially fraudulent statements in bankruptcy schedules.".

1994 Amendments. Section Analysis. Pub.L. 103–394, Title III, § 312(a)(2), Oct. 22, 1994, 108 Stat. 4140, substituted in item 153 "against estate" for "by trustee or officer", and added items 156 and 157.

1978 Amendments. Pub.L. 95–598, Title III, § 314(b)(2), (d)(3), (e)(3), (f)(3), Nov. 6, 1978, 92 Stat. 2677, substituted in item 151 "Definition" for "Definitions"; struck from item 153 ", receiver" following "trustee" and from item 154 "referees and other" preceding "officers"; and substituted in item 155 "cases under title 11 and receiverships" for "bankruptcy proceedings".

§ 151. Definition

As used in this chapter, the term "debtor" means a debtor concerning whom a petition has been filed under Title 11.

(June 25, 1948, c. 645, 62 Stat. 689; Nov. 6, 1978, Pub.L. 95–598, Title III, § 314(b)(1), 92 Stat. 2676; Sept. 13, 1994, Pub.L. 103–322, Title XXXIII, § 330008(5), 108 Stat. 2143.)

HISTORICAL AND STATUTORY NOTES

Revision Notes and Legislative Reports

1948 Acts. Based on § 52(f) of Title 11, U.S.C., 1940, ed., Bankruptcy (July 1, 1898, c. 541, § 29f as added June 22, 1938, c. 575, § 1, 52 Stat. 857).

Definition of "bankruptcy" was added to avoid repetitious references to said Title 11.

Minor changes in phraseology were made. 80th Congress House Report No. 304.

1994 Acts. House Report Nos. 103–324 and 103–489, and House Conference Report No. 103–711, see 1994 U.S. Code Cong. and Adm. News, p. 1801.

Amendments

1994 Amendments. Pub.L. 103–322, § 330008(5), substituted "means" for "mean".

1978 Amendments. Pub.L. 95–598 substituted "Definition" for "Definitions" in section catchline and definition of "debtor" as a debtor concerning whom a petition has been filed under title 11 for definition of "bankrupt" as a debtor by or against whom a petition has been filed under Title 11 and struck out definition of "bankruptcy" as including any proceeding arrangement, or plan pursuant to Title 11.

Effective and Applicability Provisions

1978 Acts. Amendment by Pub.L. 95–598 effective Oct. 1, 1979, see section 402(a) of Pub.L. 95–598, set out as a note preceding section 101 of Title 11, Bankruptcy.

Savings Provisions

Amendment by section 314 of Pub. L. 95–598 not to affect the application of this chapter to any act of any person (1) committed before Oct. 1, 1979, or (2) committed after Oct. 1, 1979, in connection with a case commenced before such date, see section 403(d) of Pub. L. 95–598, set out preceding section 101 of Title 11, Bankruptcy.

CROSS REFERENCES

Meaning of words and phrases in bankruptcy proceedings, see 11 USCA § 101.

LIBRARY REFERENCES

American Digest System

Bankruptcy ⚌2221.

Corpus Juris Secundum

CJS Bankruptcy § 10, Other U.S. Code Provisions.

§ 152. Concealment of assets; false oaths and claims; bribery

A person who—

(1) knowingly and fraudulently conceals from a custodian, trustee, marshal, or other officer of the court charged with the control or custody of property, or, in connection with a case under title 11, from creditors or the United States Trustee, any property belonging to the estate of a debtor;

(2) knowingly and fraudulently makes a false oath or account in or in relation to any case under title 11;

(3) knowingly and fraudulently makes a false declaration, certificate, verification, or statement under penalty of perjury as permitted under section 1746 of title 28, in or in relation to any case under title 11;

(4) knowingly and fraudulently presents any false claim for proof against the estate of a debtor, or uses any such claim in any case under title 11, in a personal capacity or as or through an agent, proxy, or attorney;

(5) knowingly and fraudulently receives any material amount of property from a debtor after the filing of a case under title 11, with intent to defeat the provisions of title 11;

(6) knowingly and fraudulently gives, offers, receives, or attempts to obtain any money or property, remuneration, compensation, reward, advantage, or promise thereof for acting or forbearing to act in any case under title 11;

(7) in a personal capacity or as an agent or officer of any person or corporation, in contemplation of a case under title 11 by or against the person or any other person or corporation, or with intent to defeat the provisions of title 11, knowingly and fraudulently transfers or conceals any of his property or the property of such other person or corporation;

(8) after the filing of a case under title 11 or in contemplation thereof, knowingly and fraudulently conceals, destroys, mutilates, falsifies, or makes a false entry in any recorded information (including books, documents, records, and papers) relating to the property or financial affairs of a debtor; or

(9) after the filing of a case under title 11, knowingly and fraudulently withholds from a custodian, trustee, marshal, or other officer of the court or a United States Trustee entitled to its possession, any recorded information (including books, documents, records, and papers) relating to the property or financial affairs of a debtor,

shall be fined under this title, imprisoned not more than 5 years, or both.

(June 25, 1948, c. 645, 62 Stat. 689; June 12, 1960, Pub.L. 86–519, § 2, 74 Stat. 217; Sept. 2, 1960, Pub.L. 86–701, 74 Stat. 753; Oct. 18, 1976, Pub.L. 94–550, § 4, 90 Stat. 2535; Nov. 6, 1978, Pub.L. 95–598, Title III, § 314(a), (c), 92 Stat. 2676, 2677; Nov. 18, 1988, Pub.L. 100–690, Title VII, § 7017, 102 Stat. 4395; Sept. 13, 1994, Pub.L. 103–322, Title XXXIII, § 330016(1)(K), 108 Stat. 2147; Oct. 22, 1994, Pub.L. 103–394, Title III, § 312(a)(1)(A), 108 Stat. 4138; Oct. 11, 1996, Pub.L. 104–294, Title VI, § 601(a)(1), 110 Stat. 3498.)

HISTORICAL AND STATUTORY NOTES

Revision Notes and Legislative Reports

1948 Acts. Based on § 52(b) of Title 11, U.S.C., 1940 ed., Bankruptcy (July 1, 1898, c. 541, § 29b, 30 Stat. 554; May 27, 1926, c. 406, § 11 (part), 44 Stat. 665; June 22, 1938, c. 575, § 1 (part), 52 Stat. 855).

Section was broadened to apply to one who gives or offers a bribe.

Minor changes were made in phraseology. 80th Congress House Report No. 304.

1960 Acts. Senate Report No. 1477, see 1960 U.S. Code Cong. and Adm. News, p. 2396.

Senate Report No. 974, see 1960 U.S. Code Cong. and Adm. News, p. 3307.

1976 Acts. House Report No. 94–1616, see 1976 U.S. Code Cong. and Adm. News, p. 5644.

1988 Acts. For Related Reports, see 1988 U.S. Code Cong. and Adm. News, p. 5937.

1994 Acts. House Report Nos. 103–324 and 103–489, and House Conference Report No. 103–711, see 1994 U.S. Code Cong. and Adm. News, p. 1801.

House Report No. 103–835, see 1994 U.S. Code Cong. and Adm. News, p. 3340.

1996 Acts. House Report No. 104–788, see 1996 U.S. Code Cong. and Adm. News, p. 4021.

Amendments

1996 Amendments. Pub.L. 104–294, § 601(a)(1), substituted "fined under this title" for "fined not more than $5,000".

1994 Amendments. Pub.L. 103–394, § 312(a)(1)(A), designated existing provisions as opening cl., pars. (1) to (9), and closing cl., and in pars. (1) and (9) as so designated added reference to United States Trustee.

Pub.L. 103–322, § 330016(1)(K), substituted "under this title" for "not more than $5,000" in tenth undesignated paragraph.

1988 Amendments. Pub.L. 100–690 substituted "penalty of perjury" for "penalty or perjury".

1978 Amendments. Pub.L. 95–598 substituted, wherever appearing, "debtor" for "bankrupt", "case under title 11" for "bankruptcy proceeding", and "provisions of title 11" for "bankruptcy law"; and substituted "a custodian" for "the receiver, custodian", wherever appearing, and "recorded information, including books, documents, records, and papers, relating to the property or financial affairs" for "document affecting or relating to the property or affairs".

1976 Amendments. Pub.L. 94–550 added paragraph covering the knowing and fraudulent making of a false declaration, certificate, verification, or statement under penalty of perjury as permitted under section 1746 of Title 28 or in relation to any bankruptcy proceeding.

1960 Amendments. Pub.L. 86–701 included fraudulent transfers and concealment of property by persons in their individual capacity, within sixth paragraph.

Pub.L. 86–519 deleted words "under oath" which followed "knowingly and fraudulently presents" in third paragraph.

Effective and Applicability Provisions

1994 Acts. Amendment by Pub.L. 103–394 effective on Oct. 22, 1994, and not to apply with respect to cases commenced under Title 11 of the United States Code before Oct. 22, 1994, see section 702 of Pub.L. 103–394, set out as a note under section 101 of Title 11, Bankruptcy.

1978 Acts. Amendment by Pub.L. 95–598 effective Oct. 1, 1979, see section 402(a) of Pub.L. 95–598, set out as a note preceding section 101 of Title 11, Bankruptcy.

Separability of Provisions

If any provision of or amendment made by Pub.L. 103–394 or the application of such provision or amendment to any person or circumstance is held to be unconstitutional, the remaining provisions of and amendments made by Pub.L. 103–394 and the application of such provisions and amendments to any person or circumstance shall not be affected thereby, see section 701 of Pub.L. 103–394, set out as a note under section 101 of Title 11, Bankruptcy.

Savings Provisions

Amendment by section 314 of Pub. L. 95–598 not to affect the application of this chapter to any act of any person (1) committed before Oct. 1, 1979, or (2) committed after Oct. 1, 1979, in connection with a case commenced before such date, see section 403(d) of Pub. L. 95–598, set out preceding section 101 of Title 11, Bankruptcy.

CROSS REFERENCES

Bankruptcy investigations; duties of United States attorney, see 18 USCA § 3057.

Discharges, refusal to grant when offense committed under this section, see 11 USCA § 727.

Examination of bankrupt, evidence as inadmissible in criminal proceedings, see 11 USCA § 521.

Limitation of prosecutions, see 18 USCA §§ 3282 and 3284.

LIBRARY REFERENCES

American Digest System

Bankruptcy ⬥3861.

Corpus Juris Secundum

CJS Bankruptcy § 94, Criminal Liability.

CJS Bankruptcy § 384, Protection for Debtor on Dismissal.

§ 153.   Embezzlement against estate

(a) Offense.—A person described in subsection (b) who knowingly and fraudulently appropriates to the person's own use, embezzles, spends, or transfers any property or secretes or destroys any document belonging to the estate of a debtor shall be fined under this title, imprisoned not more than 5 years, or both.

(b) Person to whom section applies.—A person described in this subsection is one who has access to property or documents belonging to an estate by virtue of the person's participation in the administration of the estate as a trustee, custodian, marshal, attorney, or other officer of the court or as an agent, employee, or other person engaged by such an officer to perform a service with respect to the estate.

(June 25, 1948, c. 645, 62 Stat. 690; Nov. 6, 1978, Pub.L. 95–598, Title III, § 314(a)(1), (d)(1), (2), 92 Stat. 2676, 2677; Sept. 13, 1994, Pub.L. 103–322, Title XXXIII, § 330016(1)(K), 108 Stat. 2147; Oct. 22, 1994, Pub.L. 103–394, Title III, § 312(a)(1)(A), 108 Stat. 4139; Oct. 11, 1996, Pub.L. 104–294, Title VI, § 601(a)(1), 110 Stat. 3498.)

HISTORICAL AND STATUTORY NOTES

Revision Notes and Legislative Reports

1948 Acts. Based on § 52(a) of Title 11, U.S.C., 1940 ed., Bankruptcy (July 1, 1898, c. 541, § 29a, 30 Stat. 554; May 27, 1926, c. 406, § 11 (part), 44 Stat. 665; June 22, 1938, c. 575, § 1 (part), 52 Stat. 855).

Minor changes were made in phraseology. 80th Congress House Report No. 304.

1960 Acts. Senate Report No. 1477, see 1960 U.S. Code Cong. and Adm. News, p. 2396.

Senate Report No. 974, see 1960 U.S. Code Cong. and Adm. News, p. 3307.

1994 Acts. House Report Nos. 103–324 and 103–489, and House Conference Report No. 103–711, see 1994 U.S. Code Cong. and Adm. News, p. 1801.

House Report No. 103–835, see 1994 U.S. Code Cong. and Adm. News, p. 3340.

1996 Acts. House Report No. 104–788, see 1996 U.S. Code Cong. and Adm. News, p. 4021.

Amendments

1996 Amendments. Subsec. (a). Pub.L. 104–294, § 601(a)(1), substituted "fined under this title" for "fined not more than $5,000".

1994 Amendments. Pub.L. 103–394, § 312(a)(1)(A), completely revised section. Prior to revision, section read as follows:

"**§ 153. Embezzlement by trustee or officer**

"Whoever knowingly and fraudulently appropriates to his own use, embezzles, spends, or transfers any property or secretes or destroys any document belonging to the estate of a debtor which came into his charge as trustee, custodian, marshal, or other officer of the court, shall be fined under this title or imprisoned not more than five years, or both."

Pub.L. 103–322, § 330016(1)(K), substituted "under this title" for "not more than $5,000" wherever appearing.

1978 Amendments. Pub.L. 95–598 deleted from heading ", receiver" following "trustee" and in text "receiver," preceding "custodian" and substituted "debtor" for "bankrupt".

Effective and Applicability Provisions

1994 Acts. Amendment by Pub.L. 103–394 effective on Oct. 22, 1994, and not to apply with respect to cases commenced under Title 11 of the United States Code before Oct. 22, 1994, see section 702 of Pub.L. 103–394, set out as a note under section 101 of Title 11, Bankruptcy.

1978 Acts. Amendment by Pub.L. 95–598 effective Oct. 1, 1979, see section 402(a) of Pub.L. 95–598, set out as a note preceding section 101 of Title 11, Bankruptcy.

Savings Provisions

Amendment by section 314 of Pub. L. 95–598 not to affect the application of this chapter to any act of any person (1) committed before Oct. 1, 1979, or (2) committed after Oct. 1, 1979, in connection with a case commenced before such date, see section 403(d) of Pub. L. 95–598, set out preceding section 101 of Title 11, Bankruptcy.

Separability of Provisions

If any provision of or amendment made by Pub.L. 103–394 or the application of such provision or amendment to any person or circumstance is held to be unconstitutional, the remaining provisions of and amendments made by Pub.L. 103–394 and the application of such provisions and amendments to any person or circumstance shall not be affected thereby, see section 701 of Pub.L. 103–394, set out as a note under section 101 of Title 11, Bankruptcy.

CROSS REFERENCES

Debts of bankrupt created by fraud, embezzlement, misappropriation or defalcation while acting as an officer or in any fiduciary capacity as not affected by a discharge, see 11 USCA § 523.

Embezzlement by court officers, generally, see 18 USCA § 645.

LIBRARY REFERENCES

American Digest System

Bankruptcy ☞3861.

Corpus Juris Secundum

CJS Bankruptcy § 94, Criminal Liability.

CJS United States Marshals § 21, Criminal Responsibility.

§ 154. Adverse interest and conduct of officers

A person who, being a custodian, trustee, marshal, or other officer of the court—

(1) knowingly purchases, directly or indirectly, any property of the estate of which the person is such an officer in a case under title 11;

(2) knowingly refuses to permit a reasonable opportunity for the inspection by parties in interest of the documents and accounts relating to the affairs of estates in the person's charge by parties when directed by the court to do so; or

(3) knowingly refuses to permit a reasonable opportunity for the inspection by the United States Trustee of the documents and accounts relating to the affairs of an estate in the person's charge,

shall be fined under this title and shall forfeit the person's office, which shall thereupon become vacant.

(June 25, 1948, c. 645, 62 Stat. 690; Nov. 6, 1978, Pub.L. 95–598, Title III, § 314(a)(2), (e)(1), (2), 92 Stat. 2676, 2677; Sept. 13, 1994, Pub.L. 103–322, Title XXXIII, § 330016(1)(G), 108 Stat. 2147; Oct. 22, 1994, Pub.L. 103–394, Title III, § 312(a)(1)(A), 108 Stat. 4139; Oct. 11, 1996, Pub.L. 104–294, Title VI, § 601(a)(1), 110 Stat. 3498.)

HISTORICAL AND STATUTORY NOTES

Revision Notes and Legislative Reports

1948 Acts. Based on § 52(c) of Title 11, U.S.C., 1940 ed., Bankruptcy (July 1, 1898, c. 541, § 29c, 30 Stat. 554; June 22, 1938, c. 575, § 1, (part), 52 Stat. 856).

Minor changes were made in phraseology. 80th Congress House Report No. 304.

1994 Acts. House Report Nos. 103–324 and 103–489, and House Conference Report No. 103–711, see 1994 U.S. Code Cong. and Adm. News, p. 1801.

House Report No. 103–835, see 1994 U.S. Code Cong. and Adm. News, p. 3340.

1996 Acts. House Report No. 104–788, see 1996 U.S. Code Cong. and Adm. News, p. 4021.

Amendments

1996 Amendments. Pub.L. 104–294, § 601(a)(1), substituted "fined under this title" for "fined not more than $5,000".

1994 Amendments. Pub.L. 103–394, § 312(a)(1)(A), designated portion of existing text as pars. (1) and (2), added par. (3), and increased maximum fine from $500 to $5,000.

Pub.L. 103–322, § 330016(1)(G), substituted "under this title" for "not more than $500".

1978 Amendments. Pub.L. 95–598 struck out from section heading "referees and other" preceding "officers", initial par. "Whoever knowingly acts as a referee in a case in which he is directly or indirectly interested; or", and "referee, receiver," preceding "custodian" and substituted "case under title 11" for "bankruptcy proceeding".

Effective and Applicability Provisions

1994 Acts. Amendment by Pub.L. 103–394 effective on Oct. 22, 1994, and not to apply with respect to cases commenced under Title 11 of the United States Code before Oct. 22, 1994, see section 702 of Pub.L. 103–394, set out as a note under section 101 of Title 11, Bankruptcy.

1978 Acts. Amendment by Pub.L. 95–598 effective Oct. 1, 1979, see section 402(a) of Pub.L. 95–598, set out as a note preceding section 101 of Title 11, Bankruptcy.

Savings Provisions

Amendment by section 314 of Pub. L. 95–598 not to affect the application of this chapter to any act of any person (1) committed before Oct. 1, 1979, or (2) committed after Oct. 1, 1979, in connection with a case commenced before such date, see section 403(d) of Pub. L. 95–598, set out preceding section 101 of Title 11, Bankruptcy.

Separability of Provisions

If any provision of or amendment made by Pub.L. 103–394 or the application of such provision or amendment to any person or circumstance is held to be unconstitutional, the remaining provisions of and amendments made by Pub.L. 103–394 and the application of such provisions and amendments to any person or circumstance shall not be affected thereby, see section 701 of Pub.L. 103–394, set out as a note under section 101 of Title 11, Bankruptcy.

LIBRARY REFERENCES

American Digest System

Officer ☞121.

United States ☞52.

Corpus Juris Secundum

CJS Bankruptcy § 94, Criminal Liability.

CJS United States Marshals § 21, Criminal Responsibility.

§ 155. Fee agreements in cases under title 11 and receiverships

Whoever, being a party in interest, whether as a debtor, creditor, receiver, trustee or representative of any of them, or attorney for any such party in interest, in any receivership or case under title 11 in any United States court or under its supervision, knowingly and fraudulently enters into any agreement, express or implied, with another such party in interest or attorney for another such party in interest, for the purpose of fixing the fees or other compensation to be paid to any party in interest or to any attorney for any party in interest for services rendered in connection therewith, from the assets of the estate, shall be fined under this title or imprisoned not more than one year, or both.

(June 25, 1948, c. 645, 62 Stat. 690; May 24, 1949, c. 139, § 4, 63 Stat. 90; Nov. 6, 1978, Pub.L. 95–598, Title III, § 314(f)(1), (2) 92 Stat. 2677; Sept. 13, 1994, Pub.L. 103–322, Title XXXII, § 330016(1)(K), 108 Stat. 2147.)

HISTORICAL AND STATUTORY NOTES

Revision Notes and Legislative Reports

1948 Acts. Based on § 572a of Title 28, U.S.C., 1940 ed., Judicial Code and Judiciary (Aug. 25, 1937, c. 777, 50 Stat. 810.

Words "upon conviction" were deleted as surplusage since punishment can be imposed only after a conviction.

A fine of "$5,000" was substituted for "$10,000" and "one year" for "five years", to reduce the offense to the grade of a misdemeanor and the punishment to an amount and term proportionate to the gravity of the offense.

Minor changes were made in phraseology. 80th Congress House Report No. 304.

1949 Acts. This amendment [see section 4] clarifies section 155 of Title 18, U.S.C., by restating the first paragraph thereof in closer conformity with the original law, as it existed at the time of the enactment of the revision of Title 18.

Senate Report No. 303 and House Report No. 352, see 1949 U.S. Code Cong. Service, p. 1248.

1994 Acts. House Report Nos. 103–324 and 103–489, and House Conference Report No. 103–711, see 1994 U.S. Code Cong. and Adm. News, p. 1801.

Amendments

1994 Amendments. Pub.L. 103–322, § 330016(1)(K), substituted "under this title" for "not more than $5,000" wherever appearing.

1978 Amendments. Pub.L. 95–598 substituted in the heading "cases under title 11 and receiverships" for "bankruptcy proceedings" and in the text "or cases under title 11" for ", bankruptcy or reorganization proceeding", inserted "knowingly and fraudulently" following "supervision,", and deleted penalty provision for a judge of a United States court to knowingly approve the payment of any fees or compensation that were fixed.

1949 Amendments. Act May 24, 1949, amended section to clarify it by inserting "or attorney for any such party in interest" in two places, and by inserting "in any United States court or under its supervision" in lieu of "in or under the supervision of any court of the United States."

Effective and Applicability Provisions

1978 Acts. Amendment by Pub.L. 95–598 effective Oct. 1, 1979, see section 402(a) of Pub.L. 95–598, set out as a note preceding section 101 of Title 11, Bankruptcy.

Savings Provisions

Amendment by section 314 of Pub. L. 95–598 not to affect the application of this chapter to any act of any person (1) committed before Oct. 1, 1979, or (2) committed after Oct. 1, 1979, in connection with a case commenced before such date, see section 403(d) of Pub. L. 95–598, set out preceding section 101 of Title 11, Bankruptcy.

LIBRARY REFERENCES

American Digest System

Bankruptcy ☞3191, 3861.

Corpus Juris Secundum

CJS Bankruptcy § 94, Criminal Liability.

CJS Receivers § 474, Right To, and Propriety Of, Allowance--Forfeiture by Negligence, Misconduct, or Unsuccessful Administration.

§ 156. Knowing disregard of bankruptcy law or rule

(a) Definitions.—In this section—

(1) the term "bankruptcy petition preparer" means a person, other than the debtor's attorney or an employee of such an attorney, who prepares for compensation a document for filing; and

(2) the term "document for filing" means a petition or any other document prepared for filing by a debtor in a United States bankruptcy court or a United States district court in connection with a case under title 11.

(b) Offense.—If a bankruptcy case or related proceeding is dismissed because of a knowing attempt by a bankruptcy petition preparer in any manner to disregard the requirements of title 11, United States Code, or the Federal Rules of Bankruptcy Procedure, the bankruptcy petition preparer shall be fined under this title, imprisoned not more than 1 year, or both.

(Added Pub.L. 103–394, Title III, § 312(a)(1)(B), Oct. 22, 1994, 108 Stat. 4140; amended Pub.L. 109–8, Title XII, § 1220, Apr. 20, 2005, 119 Stat. 195.)

HISTORICAL AND STATUTORY NOTES

Revision Notes and Legislative Reports

1994 Acts. House Report No. 103–835, see 1994 U.S. Code Cong. and Adm. News, p. 3340.

2005 Acts. House Report No. 109–31(Part I), see 2005 U.S. Code Cong. and Adm. News, p. 88.

References in Text

The Federal Rules of Bankruptcy Procedure, referred to in subsec. (b), are set out in Title 11, Bankruptcy.

Amendments

2005 Amendments. Subsec. (a). Pub.L.109–8, § 1220, in the first undesignated paragraph, inserted "**(1)** the term" before "bankruptcy", and struck out the period at the end and inserted "; and"; and in the second undesignated paragraph, inserted "**(2)** the term" before "document", and struck out "this title" and inserted "title 11".

Effective and Applicability Provisions

2005 Acts. Except as otherwise provided, amendments by Pub.L. 109–8 effective 180 days after April 20, 2005, and inapplicable with respect to cases commenced under Title 11 before the effective date, see Pub.L. 109–8, § 1501, set out as a note under 11 U.S.C.A. § 101.

1994 Acts. Section effective on Oct. 22, 1994, and not to apply with respect to cases commenced under Title 11 of the United States Code before Oct. 22, 1994, see section 702 of Pub.L. 103–394, set out as a note under section 101 of Title 11, Bankruptcy.

Separability of Provisions

If any provision of or amendment made by Pub.L. 103–394 or the application of such provision or amendment to any person or circumstance is held to be unconstitutional, the remaining provisions of and amendments made by Pub.L. 103–394 and the application of such provisions and amendments to any person or circumstance shall not be affected thereby, see section 701 of Pub.L. 103–394, set out as a note under section 101 of Title 11, Bankruptcy.

LIBRARY REFERENCES

American Digest System

Bankruptcy ⟲3861.

Corpus Juris Secundum

CJS Bankruptcy § 94, Criminal Liability.

§ 157. Bankruptcy fraud

A person who, having devised or intending to devise a scheme or artifice to defraud and for the purpose of executing or concealing such a scheme or artifice or attempting to do so—

(1) files a petition under title 11, including a fraudulent involuntary petition under section 303 of such title;

(2) files a document in a proceeding under title 11; or

(3) makes a false or fraudulent representation, claim, or promise concerning or in relation to a proceeding under title 11, at any time before or after the filing of the petition, or in relation to a proceeding falsely asserted to be pending under such title,

shall be fined under this title, imprisoned not more than 5 years, or both.

(Added Pub.L. 103–394, Title III, § 312(a)(1)(B), Oct. 22, 1994, 108 Stat. 4140; amended Pub.L. 109–8, Title III, § 332(c), Apr. 20, 2005, 119 Stat. 103; Pub.L. 111–327, § 2(b), Dec. 22, 2010, 124 Stat. 3562.)

HISTORICAL AND STATUTORY NOTES

Revision Notes and Legislative Reports

1994 Acts. House Report No. 103–835, see 1994 U.S. Code Cong. and Adm. News, p. 3340.

2005 Acts. House Report No. 109–31(Part I), see 2005 U.S. Code Cong. and Adm. News, p. 88.

Amendments

2010 Amendments. Par. (1). Pub.L. 111–327, § 2(b)(1), struck out "bankruptcy" following "involuntary".

Par. (2). Pub.L. 111–327, § 2(b)(2), struck out ", including a fraudulent involuntary bankruptcy petition under section 303 of such title" following "title 11".

Par. (3). Pub.L. 111–327, § 2(b)(2), struck out ", including a fraudulent involuntary bankruptcy petition under section 303 of such title" following "title 11".

2005 Amendments. Pars. (1) to (3). Pub.L. 109–8, § 332(c), inserted ", including a fraudulent involuntary bankruptcy petition under section 303 of such title" after "title 11" wherever appearing, to reflect the probable intent of Congress.

Effective and Applicability Provisions

2005 Acts. Except as otherwise provided, amendments by Pub.L. 109–8 effective 180 days after April 20, 2005, and inapplicable with respect to cases commenced under Title 11 before the effective date, see Pub.L. 109–8, § 1501, set out as a note under 11 U.S.C.A. § 101.

1994 Acts. Section effective on Oct. 22, 1994, and not to apply with respect to cases commenced under Title 11 of the United States Code before Oct. 22, 1994, see section 702 of Pub.L. 103–394, set out as a note under section 101 of Title 11, Bankruptcy.

Separability of Provisions

If any provision of or amendment made by Pub.L. 103–394 or the application of such provision or amendment to any person or circumstance is held to be unconstitutional, the remaining provisions of and amendments made by Pub.L. 103–394 and the application of such provisions and amendments to any person or circumstance shall not be affected thereby, see section 701 of Pub.L. 103–394, set out as a note under section 101 of Title 11, Bankruptcy.

American Digest System

Bankruptcy ⊕3861, 3862.

Corpus Juris Secundum

CJS Bankruptcy § 94, Criminal Liability.

CJS Bankruptcy § 384, Protection for Debtor on Dismissal.

§ 158. Designation of United States attorneys and agents of the Federal Bureau of Investigation to address abusive reaffirmations of debt and materially fraudulent statements in bankruptcy schedules

(a) In general.—The Attorney General of the United States shall designate the individuals described in subsection (b) to have primary responsibility in carrying out enforcement activities in addressing violations of section 152 or 157 relating to abusive reaffirmations of debt. In addition to addressing the violations referred to in the preceding sentence, the individuals described under subsection (b) shall address violations of section 152 or 157 relating to materially fraudulent statements in bankruptcy schedules that are intentionally false or intentionally misleading.

(b) United States attorneys and agents of the Federal Bureau of Investigation.—The individuals referred to in subsection (a) are—

(1) the United States attorney for each judicial district of the United States; and

(2) an agent of the Federal Bureau of Investigation for each field office of the Federal Bureau of Investigation.

(c) Bankruptcy investigations.—Each United States attorney designated under this section shall, in addition to any other responsibilities, have primary responsibility for carrying out the duties of a United States attorney under section 3057.

(d) Bankruptcy procedures.—The bankruptcy courts shall establish procedures for referring any case that may contain a materially fraudulent statement in a bankruptcy schedule to the individuals designated under this section.

(Added Pub.L. 109–8, Title II, § 203(b)(1), Apr. 20, 2005, 119 Stat. 49.)

HISTORICAL AND STATUTORY NOTES

Revision Notes and Legislative Reports

2005 Acts. House Report No. 109–31(Part I), see 2005 U.S. Code Cong. and Adm. News, p. 88.

Effective and Applicability Provisions

2005 Acts. Except as otherwise provided, amendments by Pub.L. 109–8 effective 180 days after April 20, 2005, and inapplicable with respect to cases commenced under Title 11 before the effective date, see Pub.L. 109–8, § 1501, set out as a note under 11 U.S.C.A. § 101.

LIBRARY REFERENCES

Corpus Juris Secundum

CJS Bankruptcy § 10, Other U.S. Code Provisions.

CHAPTER 96—RACKETEER INFLUENCED AND CORRUPT ORGANIZATIONS

§ 1961. Definitions

As used in this chapter—

(1) "racketeering activity" means (A) any act or threat involving murder, kidnapping, gambling, arson, robbery, bribery, extortion, dealing in obscene matter, or dealing in a controlled substance or listed chemical (as defined in section 102 of the Controlled Substances Act), which is chargeable under State law and punishable by imprisonment for more than one year; (B) any act which is indictable under any of the following provisions of title 18, United States Code: Section 201 (relating to bribery), section 224 (relating to sports bribery), sections 471, 472, and 473 (relating to counterfeiting), section 659 (relating to theft from interstate shipment) if the act indictable under section 659 is felonious, section 664 (relating to embezzlement from pension and welfare funds), sections 891–894 (relating to extortionate credit transactions), section 1028 (relating to fraud and related activity in connection with identification documents), section 1029 (relating to fraud and related activity in connection with access devices), section 1084 (relating to the transmission of gam-

bling information), section 1341 (relating to mail fraud), section 1343 (relating to wire fraud), section 1344 (relating to financial institution fraud), section 1425 (relating to the procurement of citizenship or nationalization unlawfully), section 1426 (relating to the reproduction of naturalization or citizenship papers), section 1427 (relating to the sale of naturalization or citizenship papers), sections 1461–1465 (relating to obscene matter), section 1503 (relating to obstruction of justice), section 1510 (relating to obstruction of criminal investigations), section 1511 (relating to the obstruction of State or local law enforcement), section 1512 (relating to tampering with a witness, victim, or an informant), section 1513 (relating to retaliating against a witness, victim, or an informant), section 1542 (relating to false statement in application and use of passport), section 1543 (relating to forgery or false use of passport), section 1544 (relating to misuse of passport), section 1546 (relating to fraud and misuse of visas, permits, and other documents), sections 1581–1592 (relating to peonage, slavery, and trafficking in persons).,[1] section 1951 (relating to interference with commerce, robbery, or extortion), section 1952 (relating to racketeering), section 1953 (relating to interstate transportation of wagering paraphernalia), section 1954 (relating to unlawful welfare fund payments), section 1955 (relating to the prohibition of illegal gambling businesses), section 1956 (relating to the laundering of monetary instruments), section 1957 (relating to engaging in monetary transactions in property derived from specified unlawful activity), section 1958 (relating to use of interstate commerce facilities in the commission of murder-for-hire), section 1960 (relating to illegal money transmitters), sections 2251, 2251A, 2252, and 2260 (relating to sexual exploitation of children), sections 2312 and 2313 (relating to interstate transportation of stolen motor vehicles), sections 2314 and 2315 (relating to interstate transportation of stolen property), section 2318 (relating to trafficking in counterfeit labels for phonorecords, computer programs or computer program documentation or packaging and copies of motion pictures or other audiovisual works), section 2319 (relating to criminal infringement of a copyright), section 2319A (relating to unauthorized fixation of and trafficking in sound recordings and music videos of live musical performances), section 2320 (relating to trafficking in goods or services bearing counterfeit marks), section 2321 (relating to trafficking in certain motor vehicles or motor vehicle parts), sections 2341–2346 (relating to trafficking in contraband cigarettes), sections 2421–24 (relating to white slave traffic), sections 175–178 (relating to biological weapons), sections 229–229F (relating to chemical weapons), section 831 (relating to nuclear materials), (C) any act which is indictable under title 29, United States Code, section 186 (dealing with restrictions on payments and loans to labor organizations) or section 501(c) (relating to embezzlement from union funds), (D) any offense involving fraud connected with a case under title 11 (except a case under section 157 of this title), fraud in the sale of securities, or the felonious manufacture, importation, receiving, concealment, buying, selling, or otherwise dealing in a controlled substance or listed chemical (as defined in section 102 of the Controlled Substances Act), punishable under any law of the United States, (E) any act which is indictable under the Currency and Foreign Transactions Reporting Act, (F) any act which is indictable under the Immigration and Nationality Act, section 274 (relating to bringing in and harboring certain aliens), section 277 (relating to aiding or assisting certain aliens to enter the United States), or section 278 (relating to importation of alien for immoral purpose) if the act indictable under such section of such Act was committed for the purpose of financial gain, or (G) any act that is indictable under any provision listed in section 2332b(g)(5)(B);

(2) "State" means any State of the United States, the District of Columbia, the Commonwealth of Puerto Rico, any territory or possession of the United States, any political subdivision, or any department, agency, or instrumentality thereof;

(3) "person" includes any individual or entity capable of holding a legal or beneficial interest in property;

(4) "enterprise" includes any individual, partnership, corporation, association, or other legal entity, and any union or group of individuals associated in fact although not a legal entity;

(5) "pattern of racketeering activity" requires at least two acts of racketeering activity, one of which occurred after the effective date of this chapter and the last of which occurred within ten years (excluding any period of imprisonment) after the commission of a prior act of racketeering activity;

(6) "unlawful debt" means a debt (A) incurred or contracted in gambling activity which was in violation of the law of the United States, a State or political subdivision thereof, or which is unenforceable under State or Federal law in whole or in part as to principal or interest because of the laws relating to usury, and (B) which was incurred in connection with the business of gambling in violation of the law of the United States, a State or political subdivision thereof, or the business of lending money or a thing of value at a rate usurious under State or Federal law, where the usurious rate is at least twice the enforceable rate;

(7) "racketeering investigator" means any attorney or investigator so designated by the Attorney General and charged with the duty of enforcing or carrying into effect this chapter;

(8) "racketeering investigation" means any inquiry conducted by any racketeering investigator for the purpose of ascertaining whether any person has been involved in any violation of this chapter or of any final order, judgment, or decree of any court of the United States, duly entered in any case or proceeding arising under this chapter;

(9) "documentary material" includes any book, paper, document, record, recording, or other material; and

(10) "Attorney General" includes the Attorney General of the United States, the Deputy Attorney General of the United States, the Associate Attorney General of the United States, any Assistant Attorney General of the United States, or any employee of the Department of Justice or any employee of any department or agency of the United States so designated by the Attorney General to carry out the powers conferred on the Attorney General by this chapter. Any department or agency so designated may use in investigations authorized by this chapter either the investigative provisions of this chapter or the investi-

gative power of such department or agency otherwise conferred by law.

(Added Pub.L. 91–452, Title IX, § 901(a), Oct. 15, 1970, 84 Stat. 941; amended Pub.L. 95–575, § 3(c), Nov. 2, 1978, 92 Stat. 2465; Pub.L. 95–598, Title III, § 314(g), Nov. 6, 1978, 92 Stat. 2677; Pub.L. 98–473, Title II, §§ 901(g), 1020, Oct. 12, 1984, 98 Stat. 2136, 2143; Pub.L. 98–547, Title II, § 205, Oct. 25, 1984, 98 Stat. 2770; Pub.L. 99–570, Title XIII, § 1365(b), Oct. 27, 1986, 100 Stat. 3207–35; Pub.L. 99–646, § 50(a), Nov. 10, 1986, 100 Stat. 3605; Pub.L. 100–690, Title VII, §§ 7013, 7020(c), 7032, 7054, 7514, Nov. 18, 1988, 102 Stat. 4395, 4396, 4398, 4402, 4489; Pub.L. 101–73, Title IX, § 968, Aug. 9, 1989, 103 Stat. 506; Pub.L. 101–647, Title XXXV, § 3560, Nov. 29, 1990, 104 Stat. 4927; Pub.L. 103–322, Title IX, § 90104, Title XVI, § 160001(f), Title XXXIII, § 330021(1), Sept. 13, 1994, 108 Stat. 1987, 2037, 2150; Pub.L. 103–394, Title III, § 312(b), Oct. 22, 1994, 108 Stat. 4140; Pub.L. 104–132, Title IV, § 433, Apr. 24, 1996, 110 Stat. 1274; Pub.L. 104–153, § 3, July 2, 1996, 110 Stat. 1386; Pub.L. 104–208, Div. C, Title II, § 202, Sept. 30, 1996, 110 Stat. 3009–565; Pub.L. 104–294, Title VI, §§ 601(b)(3), (i)(3), 604(b)(6), Oct. 11, 1996, 110 Stat. 3499, 3501, 3506; Pub.L. 107–56, Title VIII, § 813, Oct. 26, 2001, 115 Stat. 382; Pub.L. 107–273, Div. B, Title IV, § 4005(f)(1), Nov. 2, 2002, 116 Stat. 1813; Pub.L. 108–193, § 5(b), Dec. 19, 2003, 117 Stat. 2879; Pub.L. 108–458, Title VI, § 6802(e), Dec. 17, 2004, 118 Stat. 3767; Pub.L. 109–164, Title I, § 103(c), Jan. 10, 2006, 119 Stat. 3563; Pub.L. 109–177, Title IV, § 403(a), Mar. 9, 2006, 120 Stat. 243.)

1 So in original.

HISTORICAL AND STATUTORY NOTES
Revision Notes and Legislative Reports

1970 Acts. House Report No. 91–1549, see 1970 U.S. Code Cong. and Adm. News, p. 4007.

1978 Acts. Senate Report No. 95–962 and House Conference Report No. 95–1778, see 1978 U.S. Code Cong. and Adm. News, p. 5518.

1984 Acts. House Report No. 98–1030 and House Conference Report No. 98–1159, see 1984 U.S. Code Cong. and Adm. News, p. 3182.

House Report No. 98–1087, see 1984 U.S. Code Cong. and Adm. News, p. 4628.

1986 Acts. Statement by President, see 1986 U.S. Code Cong. and Adm. News, p. 5393.

House Report No. 99–797, see 1986 U.S. Code Cong. and Adm. News, p. 6138.

1988 Acts. For Related Reports, see 1988 U.S. Code Cong. and Adm. News, p. 5937.

1989 Acts. House Report No. 101–54(Parts I–VII) and House Conference Report No. 101–222, see 1989 Code Cong. and Adm. News, p. 86.

1990 Acts. House Report Nos. 101–681(Parts I and II), 101–736, Senate Report No. 101–460, and Statement by President, see 1990 U.S. Code Cong. and Adm. News, p. 6472.

1994 Acts. House Report Nos. 103–324, 103–489, and House Conference Report No. 103–711, see 1994 U.S. Code Cong. and Adm. News, p. 1801.

House Report No. 103–835, see 1994 U.S. Code Cong. and Adm. News, p. 3340.

1996 Acts. Senate Report No. 104–179 and House Conference Report No. 104–518, see 1996 U.S. Code Cong. and Adm. News, p. 924.

House Report No. 104–556, see 1996 U.S. Code Cong. and Adm. News, p. 1074.

House Report No. 104–788, see 1996 U.S. Code Cong. and Adm. News, p. 4021.

2002 Acts. House Conference Report No. 107–685 and Statement by President, see 2002 U.S. Code Cong. and Adm. News, p. 1120.

2003 Acts. House Report No. 108–264(Parts I and II), see 2003 U.S. Code Cong. and Adm. News, p. 2408.

2004 Acts. House Conference Report No. 108–796, see 2004 U.S. Code Cong. and Adm. News, p. 3178.

Statement by President, see 2004 U.S. Code Cong. and Adm. News, p. S51.

2006 Acts. House Report No. 109–317(Parts I and II), see 2005 U.S. Code Cong. and Adm. News, p. 1888.

Statement by President, see 2005 U.S. Code Cong. and Adm. News, p. S56.

House Conference Report No. 109–333, see 2006 U.S. Code Cong. and Adm. News, p. 184.

Statement by President, see 2006 U.S. Code Cong. and Adm. News, p. S7.

References in Text

Section 102 of the Controlled Substances Act, referred to in par. (1), is section 102 of Pub.L. 91–513, Title II, Oct. 27, 1970, 84 Stat. 1242, as amended, which is classified to section 802 of Title 21, Food and Drugs.

Sections 201, 224, 471, 472, 473, 659, 664, 891 to 894, 1028, 1029, 1084, 1341, 1343, 1344, 1461 to 1465, 1503, 1510, 1511, 1512, 1513, 1542, 1543, 1544, 1546, 1581 to 1591, 1951, 1952, 1953, 1954, 1955, 1956, 1957, 1958, 2251, 2252, 2312, 2313, 2314, 2315, 2321, 2341 to 2346, and 2421 to 2424 of title 18, United States Code, referred to in par. (1)(B), are sections 201, 224, 471, 472, 473, 659, 664, 891 to 894, 1028, 1029, 1084, 1341, 1343, 1344, 1461 to 1465, 1503, 1510, 1511, 1512, 1513, 1452, 1543, 1544, 1546, 1581 to 1591, 1951, 1952, 1953, 1954, 1955, 1956, 1957, 1958, 2251, 2252, 2312, 2313, 2314, 2315, 2321, 2341 to 2346, and 2421 to 2424 of this title, respectively.

The Currency and Foreign Transaction Reporting Act, as amended, referred to in par. (1)(E), was Pub.L. 91–508, Title II, Oct. 26, 1970, 84 Stat. 1118, which was classified generally to chapter 21 (section 1051 et seq.) of Title 31, Money and Finance prior to the revision of this title by Pub.L. 97–258, Sept. 12, 1982, 96 Stat. 995. For complete classification of this Act to the Code see section 5311 et seq. of revised Title 31 and Tables.

The Immigration and Nationality Act and such Act, referred to in par. (1)(F), is Act June 27, 1952, c. 477, 66 Stat. 163, as amended, which is classified principally to chapter 12 (section 1101 et seq.) of Title 8, Aliens and Nationality. Sections 274, 277 and 278 of such Act are classified to sections 1324, 1327 and 1328 of Title 8, respectively. For complete classification of this Act to the Code, see Tables.

The effective date of this chapter, referred to in par. (5), is Oct. 15, 1970.

Codifications

Section 5(b) of Pub.L. 108–193, which directed that paragraph (1)(A) of this section be amended by striking "sections 1581–1588 (relating to peonage and slavery)" and inserting "sections 1581–1591 (relating to peonage, slavery, and trafficking in persons)", was executed to paragraph (1)(B) of this section as the probable intent of Congress.

Amendments

2006 Amendments. Par. (1)(B). Pub.L. 109–177, § 403(a), inserted "section 1960 (relating to illegal money transmitters)," before "sections 2251".

Pub.L. 109–164, § 103(c), in par. (1)(B), struck out "1581–1591" and inserted "1581–1592".

2004 Amendments. Par. (1)(B). Pub.L. 108–458, § 6802(e), inserted "sections 175–178 (relating to biological weapons) , sections 229–229F (relating to chemical weapons), section 831 (relating to nuclear materials)," before "(C) any act which is indictable under title 29".

2003 Amendments. Par. (1)(B). Pub.L. 108–193, § 5(b), struck out "sections 1581–1588 (relating to peonage and slavery)" and inserted "sections 1581–1591 (relating to peonage, slavery, and trafficking in persons)".

2002 Amendments. Par. (1). Pub.L. 107–273, § 4005(f)(1), amended the directory language of section 813(2) of Pub.L. 107–56, and thus required no change in text.

2001 Amendments. Par. (1). Pub.L. 107–56, § 813, substituted "(F)" for "or (F)" and inserted ", or (G) any act that is indictable under any provision listed in section 2332b(g)(5)(B)" after "committed for the purpose of financial gain".

1996 Amendments. Par. (1). Pub.L. 104–294, § 604(b)(6), amending Pub.L. 103–322, § 160001(f), substituted "sections 2251, 2251A, 2252, and 2258" for "sections 2251–2252".

Par. (1)(B). Pub.L. 104–294, § 601(i)(3), substituted "2252, and 2260" for "2252, and 2258".

Pub.L. 104–208, § 202, added provisions relating to sections 1425, 1426 and 1427 of this title, and struck out provisions relating to violations of sections 1028, 1542, 1543, 1544 and 1546 of this title committed for financial gain.

Pub.L. 104–153, § 3, inserted ", section 2318 (relating to trafficking in counterfeit labels for phonorecords, computer programs or computer program documentation or packaging and copies of motion pictures or other audiovisual works), section 2319 (relating to criminal infringement of a copyright), section 2319A (relating to unauthorized fixation of and trafficking in sound recordings and music videos of live musical performances), section 2320 (relating to trafficking in goods or services bearing counterfeit marks)" after "sections 2314 and 2315 (relating to interstate transportation of stolen property)".

Pub.L. 104–132, § 433, established certain alien smuggling-related crimes as Rico-predicate offenses.

Par. (1)(D). Pub.L. 104–294, § 601(b)(3), substituted "section 157 of this title" for "section 157 of that title".

1994 Amendments. Par. (1). Pub.L. 103–322, § 330021(1), substituted "kidnapping" for "kidnaping".

Pub.L. 103–322, § 90104, substituted "a controlled substance or listed chemical (as defined in section 102 of the Controlled Substances Act)" for "narcotic or other dangerous drugs" wherever appearing.

Pub.L. 103–322, § 160001(f), as amended Pub.L. 104–294, § 604(b)(6), substituted "sections 2251, 2251A, 2252, and 2258" for "sections 2251–2252".

Pub.L. 103–394, § 312(b), inserted "(except in cases under section 157 of that title)" after "offense involving fraud connected with a case under title 11".

1990 Amendments. Par. (1)(B). Pub.L. 101–647, § 3560(1), (2), substituted "relating to" for "relative to" in the parenthetical provision following "section 1029" and struck out "sections 2251 through 2252 (relating to sexual exploitation of children)," before ", section 1958".

1989 Amendments. Par. (1). Pub.L. 101–73 inserted "section 1344 (relating to financial institution fraud)," after "section 1343 (relating to wire fraud),".

1988 Amendments. Par. (1)(B). Pub.L. 100–690, § 7514, inserted "sections 2251 through 2252 (relating to sexual exploitation of children),".

Par. (1). Pub.L. 100–690, § 7032, substituted "section 2321" for "section 2320".

Pub.L. 100–690, § 7054, inserted ", section 1029 (relative to fraud and related activity in connection with access devices)" and ", section 1958 (relating to use of interstate commerce facilities in the commission of murder-for-hire), sections 2251-2252 (relating to sexual exploitation of children)".

Pub.L. 100–690, § 7013, made technical amendment to directory language of Pub.L. 99–646.

Par. (10). Pub.L. 100–690, § 7020(c), added "the Associate Attorney General of the United States," following "Deputy Attorney General of the United States,".

1986 Amendments. Par. (1). Pub.L. 99–646, as amended by Pub.L. 100–690, § 7013, inserted "section 1512 (relating to tampering with a witness, victim, or an informant), section 1513 (relating to retaliating against a witness, victim, or an informant)," after "obstruction of State of local law enforcement),".

Par. (1)(B). Pub.L. 99–570, § 1365(b), inserted "section 1956 (relating to the laundering of monetary instruments), section 1957 (relating to engaging in monetary transactions in property derived from specified unlawful activity)," after "section 1955 (relating to the prohibition of illegal gambling businesses),".

1984 Amendments. Par. (1). Pub.L. 98–473, § 901(g)(2), added ", or (E) any act which is indictable under the Currency and Foreign Transactions Reporting Act".

Par. (1)(A). Pub.L. 98–473, § 1020(1), added "dealing in obscene matter," after "extortion,".

Par. (1)(B). Pub.L. 98–473, § 1020(2), added "sections 1461–1465 (relating to obscene matter)," after "section 1343 (relating to wire fraud),".

Pub.L. 98–547, § 205(2), inserted reference to section 2320 (relating to trafficking in certain motor vehicles or motor vehicle parts).

Pub.L. 98–547, § 205(1), inserted reference to sections 2312 and 2313 (relating to interstate transportation of stolen motor vehicles).

1978 Amendments. Par. (1)(B). Pub.L. 95–575 inserted "sections 2341–2346 (relating to trafficking in contraband cigarettes)," following "sections 2314 and 2315 (relating to interstate transportation of stolen property),".

Par. (1) (D). Pub.L. 95–598 substituted "fraud connected with a case under title 11" for "bankruptcy fraud".

Effective and Applicability Provisions

2002 Acts. Amendment by section 4005(f)(1) of Pub.L. 107–273, as therein provided, effective Oct. 26, 2001, which is the date of enactment of Pub.L. 107–56, to which such amendment relates.

1996 Acts. Amendment by section 604 of Pub.L. 104–294 effective Sept. 13, 1994, see section 604(d) of Pub.L. 104–294, set out as a note under section 13 of this title.

1994 Acts. Amendment by Pub.L. 103–394 effective on Oct. 22, 1994, and not to apply with respect to cases commenced under Title 11 of the United States Code before Oct. 22, 1994, see section 702 of Pub.L. 103–394, set out as a note under section 101 of Title 11, Bankruptcy.

1978 Acts. Amendment by Pub.L. 95–598 effective Oct. 1, 1979, see section 402(a) of Pub.L. 95–598, set out as an Effective Date note preceding section 101 of Title 11, Bankruptcy.

Amendment by Pub.L. 95–575 effective Nov. 2, 1978, see section 4 of Pub.L. 95–575, set out as an Effective Date note under section 2341 of this title.

Severability of Provisions

If any provision of Division C of Pub.L. 104–208 or the application of such provision to any person or circumstances is held to be unconstitutional, the remainder of Division C of Pub.L. 104–208 and the application of the provisions of Division C of Pub.L. 104–208 to any person or circumstance not to be affected thereby, see section 1(e) of Pub.L. 104–208, set out as a note under section 1101 of Title 8, Aliens and Nationality.

Amendment by section 314 of Pub.L. 95–598 not to affect the application of chapter 9 [section 151 et seq.], chapter 96 [section 1961 et seq.], or section 2516, 3057, or 3284 of this title to any act of any person (1) committed before Oct. 1, 1979, or (2) committed after Oct. 1, 1979, in connection with a case commenced before such date, see section 403(d) of Pub.L. 95–598, set out preceding section 151 of this title.

If any provision of or amendment made by Pub.L. 103–394 or the application of such provision or amendment to any person or circumstance is held to be unconstitutional, the remaining provisions of and amendments made by Pub.L. 103–394 and the application of such provisions and amendments to any person or circumstance shall not be affected thereby, see section 701 of Pub.L. 103–394, set out as a note under section 101 of Title 11, Bankruptcy.

If any provision of Pub.L. 101–73 or the application thereof to any person or circumstance is held invalid, the remainder of Pub.L. 101–73 and the application of the provision to other persons not similarly situated or to other circumstances not to be affected thereby, see section 1221 of Pub.L. 101–73, set out as a note under section 1811 of Title 12, Banks and Banking.

Section 1301 of Pub.L. 91–452 provided that: "If the provisions of any part of this Act [see Short Title note set out above] or the application thereof to any person or circumstances be held invalid, the provisions of the other parts and their application to other persons or circumstances shall not be affected thereby."

Short Title

1984 Amendments. Pub.L. 98–473, Title II, § 301, Oct. 12, 1984, 98 Stat. 2040, provided that: "This title [probably means chapter III of title II of Pub.L. 98–473 which enacted sections 853, 854, and 970 of Title 21, Food and Drugs, and sections 1589, 1600, 1613a, and 1616 of Title 19, Customs Duties, amended section 1963 of this title and sections 1602, 1605, 1606, 1607, 1608, 1609, 1610, 1611, 1612, 1613, 1614, 1615, 1618, 1619, and 1644 of Title 19, sections 824, 848, and 881 of Title 21, and section 524 of Title 28, Judiciary and Judicial Procedure, and repealed section 7607 of Title 26, Internal

Revenue Code] may be cited as the 'Comprehensive Forfeiture Act of 1984'."

1970 Acts. Section 1 of Pub.L. 91–452 provided in part that: "This Act [enacting sections 841 to 848, 1511, 1623, 1955, 1961 to 1968, 3331 to 3334, 3503, 3504, 3575 to 3578, and 6001 to 6005 of this title, and section 1826 of Title 28, Judiciary and Judicial Procedure, amending sections 835, 1073, 1505, 1954, 2424, 2516, 2517, 3148, 3486, and 3500 of this title, sections 15, 87f, 135c, 499m, and 2115 of Title 7, Agriculture, section 25 of Title 11, Bankruptcy, section 1820 of Title 12, Banks and Banking, sections 49, 77v, 78u, 79r, 80a–41, 80b–9, 155, 717m, 1271, and 1714 of Title 15, Commerce and Trade, section 825f of Title 16, Conservation, section 1333 of Title 19, Customs Duties, section 373 of Title 21, Food and Drugs, section 161 of Title 29, Labor, section 506 of Title 33, Navigation and Navigable Waters, sections 405 and 2201 of Title 42, The Public Health and Welfare, sections 157 and 362 of Title 45, Railroads, section 1124 of Title 46, Shipping, section 409 of Title 47, Telegraphs, Telephones, and Radio telegraphs, sections 9, 43, 46, 916, 1017, and 1484 of former Title 49, Transportation, section 792 of Title 50, War and National Defense, and sections 643a, 1152, 2026, and former section 2155 of Title 50, Appendix, repealing sections 837, 895, 1406, and 2514 of this title, sections 32 and 33 of Title 15; sections 4874 and 7493 of Title 26, Internal Revenue Code, section 827 of Title 46, sections 47 and 48 of former Title 49, and sections 121 to 144 of Title 50, enacting provisions set out as notes under this section and sections 841, 1511, 1955, preceding 3331, preceding 3481, 3504, and 6001 of this title, and repealing provisions set out as a note under section 2510 of this title] may be cited as the 'Organized Crime Control Act of 1970'."

This chapter is commonly known as the Racketeer Influenced and Corrupt Organizations Act or RICO.

References to Coupons, Authorization Cards, or Access Devices under Food and Nutrition Act of 2008

References in any Federal, State, tribal, or local law to a "coupon", "authorization card", or other access device provided under the Food and Nutrition Act of 2008, 7 U.S.C.A. § 2011 et seq., considered to be a reference to a "benefit" provided under that Act, see Pub.L. 110–234, § 4115(d), and Pub.L. 110–246, § 4115(d), set out as a note under 7 U.S.C.A. § 2012.

President's Commission on Organized Crime; Taking of Testimony and Receipt of Evidence

Pub.L. 98–368, July 17, 1984, 98 Stat. 490, provided for the Commission established by Ex. Ord. No. 12435, formerly set out below, authority relating to taking of testimony, receipt of evidence, subpoena power, testimony of persons in custody, immunity, service of process, witness fees, access to other records and information, Federal protection for members and staff, closure of meetings, rules, and procedures, for the period of July 17, 1984, until the earlier of 2 years or the expiration of the Commission.

Congressional Statement of Findings and Purpose

Section 1 of Pub.L. 91–452 provided in part that: "The Congress finds that (1) organized crime in the United States is a highly sophisticated, diversified, and widespread activity that annually drains billions of dollars from America's economy by unlawful conduct and the illegal use of force, fraud, and corruption; (2) organized crime derives a major portion of its power through money obtained from such illegal endeavors as syndicated gambling, loan sharking, the theft and fencing of property, the importation and distribution of narcotics and other dangerous drugs, and other forms of social exploitation; (3) this money and power are increasingly used to infiltrate and corrupt legitimate business and labor unions and to subvert and corrupt our democratic processes; (4) organized crime activities in the United States weaken the stability of the Nation's economic system, harm innocent investors and competing organizations, interfere with free competition, seriously burden interstate and foreign commerce, threaten the domestic security, and undermine the general welfare of the Nation and its citizens; and (5) organized crime continues to grow because of defects in the evidence-gathering process of the law inhibiting the development of the legally admissible evidence necessary to bring criminal and other sanctions or remedies to bear the unlawful activities of those engaged in organized crime and because the sanctions and remedies available to the Government are unnecessarily limited in scope and impact.

"It is the purpose of this Act [see Short Title note above] to seek the eradication of organized crime in the United States by strengthening the legal tools in the evidence-gathering process, by establishing new penal prohibitions, and by providing enhanced sanctions and new remedies to deal with the unlawful activities of those engaged in organized crime."

Liberal Construction of Provisions; Supersedure of Federal or State Laws; Authority of Attorneys Representing United States

Section 904 of Pub.L. 91–452 provided that:

"(a) The provisions of this title [enacting this chapter and amending sections 1505, 2516, and 2517 of this title] shall be liberally construed to effectuate its remedial purposes.

"(b) Nothing in this title shall supersede any provision of Federal, State, or other law imposing criminal penalties or affording civil remedies in addition to those provided for in this title.

"(c) Nothing contained in this title shall impair the authority of any attorney representing the United States to—

"(1) lay before any grand jury impaneled by any district court of the United States any evidence concerning any alleged racketeering violation of law;

"(2) invoke the power of any such court to compel the production of any evidence before any such grand jury; or

"(3) institute any proceeding to enforce any order or process issued in execution of such power or to punish disobedience of any such order or process by any person."

LIBRARY REFERENCES

American Digest System

RICO ⟐1–98.

Key Number System Topic No. 319H.

Corpus Juris Secundum

CJS Abatement and Revival § 172, Federal Statutes.

CJS Aliens § 1677, Prohibited Acts.

CJS Arbitration § 16, Nonsignatories.

CJS Bankruptcy § 10, Other U.S. Code Provisions.

CJS Bankruptcy § 94, Criminal Liability.

CJS Contribution § 26, Other Wrongs and Wrongdoers.

CJS Courts § 280, State Courts; Cases Arising Under Federal Law--Particular Federal Statutes.

CJS Federal Courts § 16, Discretion to Decline Exercise.

CJS Federal Courts § 114, Actions Under Banking Laws.

CJS Federal Courts § 637, Subsequent Appeals; Law-Of-The-Case Doctrine.

CJS Limitations of Actions § 132, Continuing Wrongs.

CJS Limitations of Actions § 286, Rico Claims.

CJS Products Liability § 120, Elevators, Silos and Other Agriculture Structures.

CJS Release § 72, General Release--Release Encompassing Federally Guaranteed Constitutional Right.

CJS RICO (Racketeer Influenced & Corrupt Orgs.) § 12, State Law Felonies.

CJS RICO (Racketeer Influenced & Corrupt Orgs.) § 13, Federal Offenses.

CJS RICO (Racketeer Influenced & Corrupt Orgs.) § 17, Relation and Continuity.

CJS RICO (Racketeer Influenced & Corrupt Orgs.) § 32, "But-For" and Proximate Causation; Direct Injury.

CJS RICO (Racketeer Influenced & Corrupt Orgs.) § 35, Pleading.

CHAPTER 119—WIRE AND ELECTRONIC COMMUNICATIONS INTERCEPTION AND INTERCEPTION OF ORAL COMMUNICATIONS

§ 2516.　Authorization for interception of wire, oral, or electronic communications

(1) The Attorney General, Deputy Attorney General, Associate Attorney General[1], or any Assistant Attorney General, any acting Assistant Attorney General, or any Deputy Assistant Attorney General or acting Deputy Assistant Attorney General in the Criminal Division or National Security Division specially designated by the Attorney General, may authorize an application to a Federal judge of competent jurisdiction for, and such judge may grant in conformity with section 2518 of this chapter an order authorizing or approving the interception of wire or oral communications by the Federal Bureau of Investigation, or a Federal agency having responsibility for the investigation of the offense as to which the application is made, when such interception may provide or has provided evidence of—

(a) any offense punishable by death or by imprisonment for more than one year under sections 2122 and 2274 through 2277 of title 42 of the United States Code (relating to the enforcement of the Atomic Energy Act of 1954), section 2284 of title 42 of the United States Code (relating to sabotage of nuclear facilities or fuel), or under the following chapters of this title: chapter 10 (relating to biological weapons)[2] chapter 37 (relating to espionage), chapter 55 (relating to kidnapping), chapter 90 (relating to protection of trade secrets), chapter 105 (relating to sabotage), chapter 115 (relating to treason), chapter 102 (relating to riots), chapter 65 (relating to malicious mischief), chapter 111 (relating to destruction of vessels), or chapter 81 (relating to piracy);

(b) a violation of section 186 or section 501(c) of title 29, United States Code (dealing with restrictions on payments and loans to labor organizations), or any offense which involves murder, kidnapping, robbery, or extortion, and which is punishable under this title;

(c) any offense which is punishable under the following sections of this title: section 37 (relating to violence at international airports), section 43 (relating to animal enterprise terrorism), section 81 (arson within special maritime and territorial jurisdiction), section 201 (bribery of public officials and witnesses), section 215 (relating to bribery of bank officials), section 224 (bribery in sporting contests), subsection (d), (e), (f), (g), (h), or (i) of section 844 (unlawful use of explosives), section 1032 (relating to concealment of assets), section 1084 (transmission of wagering information), section 751 (relating to escape), section 832 (relating to nuclear and weapons of mass destruction threats), section 842 (relating to explosive materials), section 930 (relating to possession of weapons in Federal facilities), section 1014 (relating to loans and credit applications generally; renewals and discounts), section 1114 (relating to officers and employees of the United States), section 1116 (relating to protection of foreign officials), sections 1503, 1512, and 1513 (influencing or injuring an officer, juror, or witness generally), section 1510 (obstruction of criminal investigations), section 1511 (obstruction of State or local law enforcement), section 1591 (sex trafficking of children by force, fraud, or coercion), section 1751 (Presidential and Presidential staff assassination, kidnapping, and assault), section 1951 (interference with commerce by threats or violence), section 1952 (interstate and foreign travel or transportation in aid of racketeering enterprises), section 1958 (relating to use of interstate commerce facilities in the commission of murder for hire), section 1959 (relating to violent crimes in aid of racketeering activity), section 1954 (offer, acceptance, or solicitation to influence operations of employee benefit plan), section 1955 (prohibition of business enterprises of gambling), section 1956 (laundering of monetary instruments), section 1957 (relating to engaging in monetary transactions in property derived from specified unlawful activity), section 659 (theft from interstate shipment), section 664 (embezzlement from pension and welfare funds), section 1343 (fraud by wire, radio, or television), section 1344 (relating to bank fraud), section 1992 (relating to terrorist attacks against mass transportation), sections 2251 and 2252 (sexual exploitation of children), section 2251A (selling or buying of children), section 2252A (relating to material constituting or containing child pornography), section 1466A (relating to child obscenity), section 2260 (production of sexually explicit depictions of a minor for importation into the United States), sections 2421, 2422, 2423, and 2425 (relating to transportation for illegal sexual activity and related crimes), sections 2312, 2313, 2314, and 2315 (interstate transportation of stolen property), section 2321 (relating to trafficking in certain motor vehicles or motor vehicle parts), section 2340A (relating to torture), section 1203 (relating to hostage taking), section 1029 (relating to fraud and related activity in connection with access devices), section 3146 (relating to penalty for failure to appear), section 3521(b)(3) (relating to witness relocation and assistance), section 32 (relating to destruction of aircraft or aircraft facilities), section 38 (relating to aircraft parts fraud), section 1963 (violations with respect to racketeer influenced and corrupt organizations), section 115 (relating to threatening or retaliating against a Federal official), section 1341 (relating to mail fraud), a felony violation of section 1030 (relating to computer fraud and abuse), section 351 (violations with respect to congressional, Cabinet, or Supreme Court assassinations, kidnapping, and assault), section 831 (relating to prohibited transactions involving nuclear materials), section 33 (relating to destruction of motor vehicles or motor vehicle facilities), section 175 (relating to biological weapons), section 175c (relating to variola virus), section 956 (conspiracy to harm persons or property overseas), section[3] a felony violation of section 1028 (relating to production of false identification documentation), section 1425 (relating to the procurement of citizenship or nationalization unlawfully), section 1426 (relating to the reproduction of naturalization or citizenship papers), section 1427 (relating to the sale of naturalization or citizenship papers), section 1541 (relating to passport issuance without authority), section 1542 (relating to false statements in passport applications), section 1543 (relating to forgery or false use of passports), section 1544 (relating to misuse of passports), or section 1546 (relating to fraud and misuse of visas, permits, and other documents);

(d) any offense involving counterfeiting punishable under section 471, 472, or 473 of this title;

(e) any offense involving fraud connected with a case under title 11 or the manufacture, importation, receiving, concealment, buying, selling, or otherwise dealing in narcotic drugs, marihuana, or other dangerous drugs, punishable under any law of the United States;

(f) any offense including extortionate credit transactions under sections 892, 893, or 894 of this title;

(**g**) a violation of section 5322 of title 31, United States Code (dealing with the reporting of currency transactions), or section 5324 of title 31, United States Code (relating to structuring transactions to evade reporting requirement prohibited);

(**h**) any felony violation of sections 2511 and 2512 (relating to interception and disclosure of certain communications and to certain intercepting devices) of this title;

(**i**) any felony violation of chapter 71 (relating to obscenity) of this title;

(**j**) any violation of section 60123(b) (relating to destruction of a natural gas pipeline), section 46502 (relating to aircraft piracy), the second sentence of section 46504 (relating to assault on a flight crew with dangerous weapon), or section 46505(b)(3) or (c) (relating to explosive or incendiary devices, or endangerment of human life, by means of weapons on aircraft) of title 49;

(**k**) any criminal violation of section 2778 of title 22 (relating to the Arms Export Control Act);

(*l*) the location of any fugitive from justice from an offense described in this section;

(**m**) a violation of section 274, 277, or 278 of the Immigration and Nationality Act (8 U.S.C. 1324, 1327, or 1328) (relating to the smuggling of aliens);

(**n**) any felony violation of sections 922 and 924 of title 18, United States Code (relating to firearms);

(**o**) any violation of section 5861 of the Internal Revenue Code of 1986 (relating to firearms);

(**p**) a felony violation of section 1028 (relating to production of false identification documents), section 1542 (relating to false statements in passport applications), section 1546 (relating to fraud and misuse of visas, permits, and other documents, [4] section 1028A (relating to aggravated identity theft)) [5] of this title or a violation of section 274, 277, or 278 of the Immigration and Nationality Act (relating to the smuggling of aliens); or [6]

(**q**) any criminal violation of section 229 (relating to chemical weapons): or sections [7] 2332, 2332a, 2332b, 2332d, 2332f, 2332g, 2332h [8] 2339, 2339A, 2339B, 2339C, or 2339D of this title (relating to terrorism);

(**r**) any criminal violation of section 1 (relating to illegal restraints of trade or commerce), 2 (relating to illegal monopolizing of trade or commerce), or 3 (relating to illegal restraints of trade or commerce in territories or the District of Columbia) of the Sherman Act (15 U.S.C. 1, 2, 3); or

(**s**) any conspiracy to commit any offense described in any subparagraph of this paragraph.

(2) The principal prosecuting attorney of any State, or the principal prosecuting attorney of any political subdivision thereof, if such attorney is authorized by a statute of that State to make application to a State court judge of competent jurisdiction for an order authorizing or approving the interception of wire, oral, or electronic communications, may apply to such judge for, and such judge may grant in conformity with section 2518 of this chapter and with the applicable State statute an order authorizing, or approving the interception of wire, oral, or electronic communications by investigative or law enforcement officers having responsibility for the investigation of the offense as to which the application is made, when such interception may provide or has provided evidence of the commission of the offense of murder, kidnapping, gambling, robbery, bribery, extortion, or dealing in narcotic drugs, marihuana or other dangerous drugs, or other crime dangerous to life, limb, or property, and punishable by imprisonment for more than one year, designated in any applicable State statute authorizing such interception, or any conspiracy to commit any of the foregoing offenses.

(3) Any attorney for the Government (as such term is defined for the purposes of the Federal Rules of Criminal Procedure) may authorize an application to a Federal judge of competent jurisdiction for, and such judge may grant, in conformity with section 2518 of this title, an order authorizing or approving the interception of electronic communications by an investigative or law enforcement officer having responsibility for the investigation of the offense as to which the application is made, when such interception may provide or has provided evidence of any Federal felony. (Added Pub.L. 90–351, Title III, § 802, June 19, 1968, 82 Stat. 216; amended Pub.L. 91–452, Title VIII, § 810, Title IX, § 902(a), Title XI, § 1103, Oct. 15, 1970, 84 Stat. 940, 947, 959; Pub.L. 91–644, Title IV, § 16, Jan. 2, 1971, 84 Stat. 1891; Pub.L. 95–598, Title III, § 314(h), Nov. 6, 1978, 92 Stat. 2677; Pub.L. 97–285, §§ 2(e), 4(e), Oct. 6, 1982, 96 Stat. 1220, 1221; Pub.L. 98–292, § 8, May 21, 1984, 98 Stat. 206; Pub.L. 98–473, Title II, § 1203(c), Oct. 12, 1984, 98 Stat. 2152; Pub.L. 99–508, Title I, §§ 101(c)(1)(A), 104, 105, Oct. 21, 1986, 100 Stat. 1851, 1855; Pub.L. 99–570, Title I, § 1365(c), Oct. 27, 1986, 100 Stat. 3207–35; Pub.L. 100–690, Title VI, § 6461, Title VII, §§ 7036, 7053(d), 7525, Nov. 18, 1988, 102 Stat. 4374, 4399, 4402, 4502; Pub.L. 101–298, § 3(b), May 22, 1990, 104 Stat. 203; Pub.L. 101–647, Title XXV, § 2531, Title XXXV, § 3568, Nov. 29, 1990, 104 Stat. 4879, 4928; Pub.L. 103–272, § 5(e)(11), July 5, 1994, 108 Stat. 1374; Pub.L. 103–322, Title XXXIII, §§ 330011(c)(1), (q)(1), (r), 330021(1), Sept. 13, 1994, 108 Stat. 2144, 2145, 2150; Pub.L. 103–414, Title II, § 208, Oct. 25, 1994, 108 Stat. 4292; Pub.L. 103–429, § 7(a)(4)(A), Oct. 31, 1994, 108 Stat. 4389; Pub.L. 104–132, Title IV, § 434, Apr. 24, 1996, 110 Stat. 1274; Pub.L. 104–208, Div. C, Title II, § 201, Sept. 30, 1996, 110 Stat. 3009–564; Pub.L. 104–287, § 6(a)(2), Oct. 11, 1996, 110 Stat. 3398; Pub.L. 104–294, Title I, § 102, Title VI, § 601(d), Oct. 11, 1996, 110 Stat. 3491, 3499; Pub.L. 105–318, § 6(b), Oct. 30, 1998, 112 Stat. 3011; Pub.L. 106–181, Title V, § 506(c)(2)(B), Apr. 5, 2000, 114 Stat. 139; Pub.L. 107–56, Title II, §§ 201, 202, Oct. 26, 2001, 115 Stat. 278; Pub.L. 107–197, Title III, § 301(a), June 25, 2002, 116 Stat. 728; Pub.L. 107–273, Div. B, Title IV, §§ 4002(c)(1), 4005(a)(1), Nov. 2, 2002, 116 Stat. 1808,

1812; Pub.L. 108–21, Title II, § 201, Apr. 30, 2003, 117 Stat. 659; Pub.L. 108–458, Title VI, § 6907, Dec. 17, 2004, 118 Stat. 3774; Pub.L. 109–162, Title XI, § 1171(b), Jan. 5, 2006, 119 Stat. 3123; Pub.L. 109–177, Title I, §§ 110(b)(3)(C), 113, Title V, § 506(a)(6), Mar. 9, 2006, 120 Stat. 208, 209, 248.)

1 See Codifications note set out under this section.

2 So in original. A comma probably should appear.

3 So in original. The word "section" probably should not appear.

4 So in original. Probably should read "other documents),".

5 So in original. The second closing parenthesis probably should not appear.

6 So in original. The word "or" probably should not appear.

7 So in original. Probably should be "weapons) or section".

8 So in original. A comma probably should appear.

HISTORICAL AND STATUTORY NOTES

Revision Notes and Legislative Reports

1968 Acts. Senate Report No. 90–1097, see 1968 U.S. Code Cong. and Adm. News, p. 2112.

1970 Acts. House Report No. 91–1549, see 1970 U.S. Code Cong. and Adm. News, p. 4007.

1971 Acts. Senate Report No. 91–1253 and Conference Report No. 91–1768, see 1970 U.S. Code Cong. and Adm. News, p. 5804.

1982 Acts. House Report No. 97–803, see 1982 U.S. Code Cong. and Adm. News, p. 2428.

1984 Acts. House Report No. 98–536, see 1984 U.S. Code Cong. and Adm. News, p. 492.

House Report No. 98–1030 and House Conference Report No. 98–1159, see 1984 U.S. Code Cong. and Adm. News, p. 3182.

1986 Acts. Senate Report No. 99–541, see 1986 U.S. Code Cong. and Adm. News, p. 3555.

Statement by President, see 1986 U.S. Code Cong. and Adm. News, p. 5393.

1988 Acts. For Related Reports, see 1988 U.S. Code Cong. and Adm. News, p. 5937.

1990 Acts. Senate Report No. 101–210, and Statement by President, see 1990 U.S. Code Cong. and Adm. News, p. 186.

1994 Acts. House Report No. 103–180, see 1994 U.S. Code Cong. and Adm. News, p. 818.

House Report Nos. 103–324, 103–489, and House Conference Report No. 103–711, see 1994 U.S. Code Cong. and Adm. News, p. 1801.

House Report No. 103–827, see 1994 U.S. Code Cong. and Adm. News, p. 3489.

House Report No. 103–831, see 1994 U.S. Code Cong. and Adm. News, p. 3579.

1996 Acts. Senate Report No. 104–179 and House Conference Report No. 104–518, see 1996 U.S. Code Cong. and Adm. News, p. 924.

House Report No. 104–573, see 1996 U.S. Code Cong. and Adm. News, p. 3831.

House Report No. 104–788, see 1996 U.S. Code Cong. and Adm. News, p. 4021.

1998 Acts. Statement by President, see 1998 U.S. Code Cong. and Adm. News, p. 709.

2000 Acts. House Conference Report No. 106–513 and Statement by President, see 2000 U.S. Code Cong. and Adm. News, p. 80.

2002 Acts. House Report No. 107–307 and Statement by President, see 2002 U.S. Code Cong. and Adm. News, p. 521.

House Conference Report No. 107–685 and Statement by President, see 2002 U.S. Code Cong. and Adm. News, p. 1120.

2003 Acts. House Conference Report No. 108–66 and Statement by President, see 2003 U.S. Code Cong. and Adm. News, p. 683.

2004 Acts. House Conference Report No. 108–796, see 2004 U.S. Code Cong. and Adm. News, p. 3178.

Statement by President, see 2004 U.S. Code Cong. and Adm. News, p. S51.

2006 Acts. House Report No. 109–233, see 2005 U.S. Code Cong. and Adm. News, p. 1636.

House Conference Report No. 109–333, see 2006 U.S. Code Cong. and Adm. News, p. 184.

Statement by President, see 2006 U.S. Code Cong. and Adm. News, p. S7.

References in Text

The Atomic Energy Act of 1954, referred to in par. (1)(a), is classified generally to 42 U.S.C.A. § 2011 et seq.

Chapters 10, 37, 55, 90, 105, 115, 102, 65, 111, and 81, referred to in par. (1)(a), are 18 U.S.C.A. §§ 175 et seq., 791 et seq., 1201 et seq., 1831 et seq., 2151 et seq., 2381 et seq., 2101 et seq., 1361 et seq., 2271 et seq., and 1651 et seq., respectively.

The Arms Export Control Act, referred to in par. (1)(k), is Pub.L. 90–629, Oct. 22, 1968, 82 Stat. 1320, as amended, which is classified generally to chapter 39 of Title 22, Foreign Relations and Intercourse (22 U.S.C.A. § 2751 et seq.). For complete classification of this Act to the Code, see Short Title note set out under 22 U.S.C.A. § 2751 and Tables.

Sections 274, 277, and 278 of the Immigration and Nationality Act, referred to in par. (1)(m) and (p), are sections 274, 277, and 278 of Act June 27, 1952, c. 477, 66 Stat. 163, as amended, which are classified to 8 U.S.C.A. §§ 1324, 1327, and 1328.

Sections 1, 2, or 3 of the Sherman Act, referred to in par. (1)(r), are sections 1, 2, or 3, of Act July 2, 1890, c. 647, 26 Stat. 209, also known as the Sherman Anti-Trust Act, which are classified to 15 U.S.C.A. § 1, 2, or 3.

Codifications

Pub.L. 98–473, § 1203(c)(4), which directed the amendment of the first par. of par. (1) by inserting "Deputy Attorney General, Associate Attorney General," after "Attorney General." was executed by making the insertion after the first reference to "Attorney General," to reflect the probable intent of Congress.

Section 102 of Pub.L. 104–294, which directed that par. (1)(c) of this section be amended by inserting "chapter 90 (relating to protection of trade secrets)," following "chapter 37 (relating to espionage),", could not be executed to text, as par. (1)(c) does not contain phrase "chapter 37 (relating to espionage),".

Amendment to par. (1)(c) by section 1365(c) of Pub.L. 99–570 was executed by inserting "section 1956 (laundering of monetary instruments), section 1957 (relating to engaging in monetary transactions in property derived from specified unlawful activity)," after "section 1955 (prohibition of business enterprises of gambling)," as the probable intent of Congress.

Amendment by section 601(d)(1) of Pub.L. 104–294, which directed that "or" be struck out after the semicolon in par. (1)(*l*), could not be executed in view of prior identical amendment by section 201(2) of Pub.L. 104–208.

Amendment by section 601(d)(2) of Pub.L. 104–294, which directed that "or" be substituted for "and" following the semicolon in par. (1)(n), could not be executed as the word "and" does not appear at the end of par. (1)(n). See also 2002 Amendments notes set out under this section.

Amendments

2006 Amendments. Par. (1). Pub.L. 109–177, § 506(a)(6), inserted "or National Security Division" after "the Criminal Division".

Par. (1)(a). Pub.L. 109–177, § 113(a), inserted "chapter 10 (relating to biological weapons)" after "under the following chapters of this title:".

Par. (1)(c). Pub.L. 109–177, § 110(b)(3)(C), struck out "1992 (relating to wrecking trains),".

Pub.L. 109–177, § 113(b)(1), inserted "section 37 (relating to violence at international airports), section 43 (relating to animal enterprise terrorism)," after "the following sections of this title:".

Pub.L. 109–177, § 113(b)(2), inserted "section 832 (relating to nuclear and weapons of mass destruction threats), section 842 (relating to explosive materials), section 930 (relating to possession of weapons in Federal facilities)," after "section 751 (relating to escape),".

Pub.L. 109–177, § 113(b)(3), inserted "section 1114 (relating to officers and employees of the United States), section 1116 (relating to protection of foreign officials)," after "section 1014 (relating to loans and credit applications generally; renewals and discounts),".

Pub.L. 109–177, § 113(b)(4), inserted "section 1992 (relating to terrorist attacks against mass transportation)," after "section 1344 (relating to bank fraud),".

Pub.L. 109–177, § 113(b)(5), inserted "section 2340A (relating to torture)," after "section 2321 (relating to trafficking in certain motor vehicles or motor vehicle parts),".

Pub.L. 109–177, § 113(b)(6), inserted "section 81 (arson within special maritime and territorial jurisdiction)," before "section 201 (bribery of public officials and witnesses)".

Pub.L. 109–177, § 113(b)(7), inserted "section 956 (conspiracy to harm persons or property overseas)," after "section 175c (relating to variola virus)".

Par. (1)(g). Pub.L. 109–177, § 113(c), before the semicolon at the end, inserted ", or section 5324 of title 31, United States Code (relating to structuring transactions to evade reporting requirement prohibited)".

Par. (1)(j). Pub.L. 109–177, § 113(d), struck out "or" before "section 46502 (relating to aircraft piracy)" and inserted a comma after "section 60123(b) (relating to the destruction of a natural gas pipeline)"; and inserted ", the second sentence of section 46504 (relating to assault on a flight crew with dangerous weapon), or section 46505(b)(3) or (c) (relating to explosive or incendiary devices, or endangerment of human life, by means of weapons on aircraft)" before "of title 49".

Par. (1)(p). Pub.L. 109–177, § 113(e), inserted ", section 1028A (relating to aggravated identity theft)" after "other documents".

Par. (1)(q). Pub.L. 109–162, § 1171(b), struck out the semicolon after "(relating to chemical weapons)" and substituted "section 2332" for "sections 2332".

Pub.L. 109–177, § 113(f), inserted "2339" after "2232h"; struck out "or" before "2339C"; and inserted ", or 2339D" after "2339C".

Pub.L. 109–177, § 113(g)(1), struck out "or" after the semicolon at the end.

Par. (1)(r). Pub.L. 109–177, § 113(g)(2), (3), redesignated former subpar. (r) as (s) and inserted a new subpar. (r).

Par. (1)(s). Pub.L. 109–177, § 113(g)(2), redesignated former subpar. (r) as subpar. (s).

2004 Amendments. Par. (1)(a). Pub.L. 108–458, § 6907(1), inserted "2122 and" following "sections".

Par. (1)(c). Pub.L. 108–458, § 6907(2), inserted "section 175c (relating to variola virus)," following "section 175 (relating to biological weapons),".

Par. (1)(q). Pub.L. 108–458, § 6907(3), inserted "2332g, 2332h," following "2332f,".

2003 Amendments. Par. (1)(a). Pub.L. 108–21, § 201(1), inserted "chapter 55 (relating to kidnapping)," after "chapter 37 (relating to espionage),".

Par. (1)(c). Pub.L. 108–21, § 201(2)(A), inserted "section 1591 (sex trafficking of children by force, fraud, or coercion)," after "section 1511 (obstruction of State or local law enforcement),".

Pub.L. 108–21, § 201(2)(B), inserted "section 2251A (selling or buying of children), section 2252A (relating to material constituting or containing child pornography), section 1466A (relating to child obscenity), section 2260 (production of sexually explicit depictions of a minor for importation into the United States), sections 2421, 2422, 2423, and 2425 (relating to transportation for illegal sexual activity and related crimes)," after "sections 2251 and 2252 (sexual exploitation of children),".

2002 Amendments. Par. (1)(n). Pub.L. 107–273, § 4002(c)(1), repealed section 601(d)(2) of Pub.L. 104–294, and thus required no change in text. See Codifications and 1996 Amendments notes set out under this section.

Par. (1)(q). Pub.L. 107–197, § 301(a), inserted "2332f," after "2332d," and substituted "2339B, or 2339C" for "or 2339B".

Pub.L. 107–273, § 4005(a)(1), adjusted the margins and thus required no change in text.

2001 Amendments. Par. (1)(c). Pub.L. 107–56, § 202, struck out "and section 1341 (relating to mail fraud)," and inserted "section 1341 (relating to mail fraud), a felony violation of section 1030 (relating to computer fraud and abuse),".

Par. (1)(p). Pub.L. 107–56, § 201(1), redesignated par. (1)(p) set out second as par. (1)(r).

Par. (1)(q). Pub.L. 107–56, § 201(2), added subpar. (q).

Par. (1)(r). Pub.L. 107–56, § 201(1), temporarily redesignated par. (1)(p) set out second as par. (1)(r). See Sunset Provisions note set out below.

2000 Amendments. Par. (1)(c). Pub.L. 106–181, § 506(c)(2)(B), inserted "section 38 (relating to aircraft parts fraud)," after "section 32 (relating to destruction of aircraft or aircraft facilities),".

1998 Amendments. Par. (1)(a). Pub.L. 105–318, § 6(b) inserted "chapter 90 (relating to protection of trade secrets)," following "to espionage),".

1996 Amendments. Par. (1)(c). Pub.L. 104–294, § 102, directed the insertion of "chapter 90 (relating to protection of trade secrets)," following "chapter 37 (relating to espionage),", which could not be executed to text. See Codification note set out under this section.

Pub.L. 104–208, § 201(1), added provisions relating to felony violation of section 1028, 1425, 1426, 1427, 1541, 1542, 1543, 1544 or 1546 of this title.

Par. (1)(j). Pub.L. 104–287, § 6(a)(2), amending Pub.L. 103–272, § 5(e)(11); Pub.L. 103–429, § 7(a)(4)(A), substituted "section 46502" for "46502".

Par. (1)(*l*). Pub.L. 104–294, § 601(d)(1), directed that "or" be struck out after the semicolon, which could not be executed to text. See Codifications note set out under this section.

Pub.L. 104–208, § 201(2), struck out "or" after the semicolon.

Par. (1)(m). Pub.L. 104–208, § 201(4), added par. (m). Former par. (m) redesignated (n).

Par. (1)(n). Pub.L. 104–294, § 601(d)(2), directed "or" be substituted for "and" following the semicolon, which could not be executed to text. See Codifications note set out under this section.

Pub.L. 104–208, § 201(3), redesignated former par. (m) as (n).

Par. (1)(*o*), (p). Pub.L. 104–208, § 201(3), redesignated former pars. (n) and (o) as (o) and (p) [set first], respectively.

Pub.L. 104–132, § 434, added par. (*o*) and redesignated former par. (*o*) as (p) [set second].

1994 Amendments. Par. (1). Pub.L. 103–414, § 208, inserted "or acting Deputy Assistant Attorney General" following "Deputy Assistant Attorney General".

Par. (1)(c). Pub.L. 103–322, § 330021(1), substituted "kidnapping" for "kidnaping" wherever appearing.

Par. (1)(j). Pub.L. 103–272, § 5(e)(11), as amended Pub.L. 103–429, § 7(a)(4)(A); Pub.L. 104–287, § 6(a)(2), substituted "section 60123(b) (relating to destruction of a natural gas pipeline) or section 46502 (relating to aircraft piracy) of title 49;" for "section 11(c)(2) of the Natural Gas Pipeline Safety Act of 1968 (relating to destruction of a natural gas pipeline) or subsection 902(i) or (n) of the Federal Aviation Act of 1958 (relating to aircraft piracy);".

1990 Amendments. Par. (1)(c). Pub.L. 101–647, § 2531(1)(A) to (E), inserted before the provisions as indicated: "section 215 (relating to bribery of bank officials)," before "section 224"; "section 1014 (relating to loans and credit applications generally; renewals and discounts)," before "sections 1503,"; "section 1032 (relating to concealment of assets)," before "section 1084"; "section 1344 (relating to bank fraud)," before "sections 2251 and 2252"; and struck "the section in chapter 65 relating to destruction of an energy facility," preceding "and section 1341 (relating to mail fraud)".

Pub.L. 101–298, § 3(b), as amended Pub.L. 103–322, § 330011(c)(1), inserted "section 175 (relating to biological weapons)," following "section 33 (relating to destruction of motor vehicles or motor vehicle facilities),".

Par. (1)(j). Pub.L. 101–647, § 2531(3), as amended Pub.L. 103–322, § 330011(r), substituted "any violation of section 11(c)(2) of the Natural Gas Pipeline Safety Act of 1968 (relating to destruction of a natural gas pipeline) or subsection (i) or (n) of section 902 of the Federal Aviation Act of 1958 (relating to aircraft piracy)" for "any violation of section 1679a(c)(2) (relating to destruction of a natural gas pipeline)

or subsection (i) or (n) of section 1472 (relating to aircraft piracy) of title 49, of the United States Code". See Repeals note set out under this section.

Pub.L. 101–647, § 3568, which substituted "any violation of section 11(c)(2) of the Natural Gas Pipeline Safety Act of 1968 (relating to destruction of a natural gas pipeline) or section 902(i) or (n) of the Federal Aviation Act of 1958 (relating to aircraft piracy)" for "any violation of section 1679(c)(2) (relating to destruction of a natural gas pipeline) or subsection (i) or (n) of section 1472 (relating to aircraft piracy) of title 49, of the United States Code", was repealed by section 330011(q)(1) of Pub.L. 103–322. See Repeals note set out under this section.

Par. (1)(m), (n). Pub.L. 101–647, § 2531(2)(A)–(C), struck subpar. "(m) any conspiracy to commit any of the foregoing offenses."; struck from subpar. (m) relating to firearms) the word "and"; and substituted at the end of subpar. (n) "; and" for the period.

Par. (1)(*o*). Pub.L. 101–647, § 2531(2)(D), added subpar. (*o*).

1988 Amendments. Pub.L. 100–690, § 7036(a)(1), substituted "Associate Attorney General, or any" for "Associate Attorney General, any".

Par. (1)(a). Pub.L. 100–690, § 7036(c)(1), substituted "(relating to riots)," for "(relating to riots);".

Par. (1)(c). Pub.L. 100–690, § 7036(a)(2), struck out comma following "to mail fraud),", requiring no change in text.

Pub.L. 100–690, § 7036(b), substituted "section 2321" for "the second section 2320", and struck out "section 2252 or 2253 (sexual exploitation of children)," following "exploitation of children),".

Pub.L. 100–690, § 7053(d), substituted "1958" for "1952A", and "1959" for "1952B".

Par. (1)(i). Pub.L. 100–690, § 7525, added subpar. (i). Former subpar. (i) was redesignated (j).

Par. (1)(j). Pub.L. 100–690, § 7525, redesignated former subpar. (i) as (j). Former subpar. (j) was redesignated (k).

Pub.L. 100–690, § 7036(c)(2), struck out "or;" following "Export Control Act);".

Par. (1)(k). Pub.L. 100–690, § 7525, redesignated former subpar. (j) as (k). Former subpar. (k) was redesignated (*l*).

Pub.L. 100–690, § 7036(c)(3), substituted "section; or" for "section;".

Par. (1)(*l*). Pub.L. 100–690, § 7525, redesignated former subpar. (k) as (*l*). Former subpar. (*l*) was redesignated (m).

Par. (1)(m). Pub.L. 100–690, § 7525, redesignated former subpar. (*l*) as (m).

Par. (1)(m), (n). Pub.L. 100–690, § 6461, added subpars. (m) and (n).

1986 Amendments. Catchline. Pub.L. 99–508, § 101(c)(1)(A), substituted "wire, oral, or electronic communications" for "wire or oral communications".

Par. (1). Pub.L. 99–508, § 104, substituted "any Assistant Attorney General, any acting Assistant Attorney General, or any Deputy Assistant Attorney General in the Criminal Division specially designated for "or any Assistant Attorney General specially designated".

Par. (1)(a). Pub.L. 99–508, § 105(a)(5), added "section 2284 of title 42 of the United States Code (relating to sabotage of nuclear facilities or fuel)," following "Atomic Energy Act of 1954,", "chapter 65 (relating to malicious mischief), chapter

111 (relating to destruction of vessels), or chapter 81 (relating to piracy)" following "relating to riots)", and struck out "or" following "(relating to treason),".

Par. (1)(c). Pub.L. 99–570, § 1356(c), added references to section 1956 (laundering of monetary instruments) and section 1957 (relating to engaging in monetary transactions in property derived from specified unlawful activity). See Codification note set out under this section.

Pub.L. 99–508, § 105(a)(1), added "section 751 (relating to escape)," following "wagering information),", "the second section 2320 (relating to trafficking in certain motor vehicles or motor vehicle parts), section 1203 (relating to hostage taking), section 1029 (relating to fraud and related activity in connection with access devices), section 3146 (relating to penalty for failure to appear), section 3521(b)(3) (relating to witness relocation and assistance), section 32 (relating to destruction of aircraft or aircraft facilities)," following "stolen property),", "section 1952A (relating to use of interstate commerce facilities in the commission of murder for hire), section 1952B (relating to violent crimes in aid of racketeering activity)," following "racketeering enterprises),", ", section 115 (relating to threatening or retaliating against a Federal official), the section in chapter 65 relating to destruction of an energy facility, and section 1341 (relating to mail fraud)," following "corrupt organizations)", ", section 831 (relating to prohibited transactions involving nuclear materials), section 33 (relating to destruction of motor vehicles or motor vehicle facilities), or section 1992 (relating to wrecking trains)" following "Court assassinations, kidnaping, and assault)", and substituted "2312, 2313, 2314," for "2314" and "section 351" for "or section 351".

Par. (1)(h). Pub.L. 99–508, § 105(a)(3), added par. (h). Former par. (h) was redesignated (l).

Pars. (1)(i) to (k). Pub.L. 99–508, § 105(a)(3), added pars. (i) to (k).

Par. (1)(l). Pub.L. 99–508, § 105(a)(4), redesignated former par. (h) as (l).

Par. (2). Pub.L. 99–508, § 101(c)(1)(A), substituted "wire, oral, or electronic communications" for "wire or oral communications" wherever appearing in text.

Par. (3). Pub.L. 99–508, § 105(b), added par. (3).

1984 Amendments. Par. (1). Pub.L. 98–473, § 1203(c)(4), added "Deputy Attorney General, Associate Attorney General," after "Attorney General".

Par. (1)(c). Pub.L. 98–473, § 1203(c)(1), added "section 1343 (fraud by wire, radio, or television), section 2252 or 2253 (sexual exploitation of children)," after "section 664 (embezzlement from pension and welfare funds),".

Pub.L. 98–292 added "sections 2251 and 2252 (sexual exploitation of children)," after "section 664 (embezzlement from pension and welfare funds),".

Pub.L. 98–473, § 1203(c)(2), added references to sections 1512 and 1513 after "1503".

Par. (1)(g). Pub.L. 98–473, § 1203(c)(3), added par. (g). Former par. (g) was redesignated par. (h).

Par. (1)(h). Pub.L. 98–473, § 1203(c)(3), redesignated par. (g) as par. (h).

1982 Amendments. Par. (1)(c). Pub.L. 97–285, §§ 2(e), 4(e), substituted "(Presidential and Presidential staff assassination, kidnaping, and assault)" for "(Presidential assassinations, kidnaping, and assault)" following "section 1751" and substituted "(violations with respect to congressional, Cabinet,

or Supreme Court assassinations, kidnaping, and assault)" for "(violations with respect to congressional assassination, kidnaping, and assault)" following "section 351".

1978 Amendments. Par. (1)(e). Pub.L. 95–598 substituted "fraud connected with a case under title 11" for "bankruptcy fraud".

1971 Amendments. Par. (1)(c). Pub.L. 91–644 added provision authorizing interception of communications with respect to section 351 offense (violations with respect to congressional assassination, kidnaping, and assault).

1970 Amendments. Par. (1)(c). Pub.L. 91–452 added provisions authorizing applicability to sections 844(d), (e), (f), (g), (h), or (i), 1511, 1955, and 1963 of this title.

Effective and Applicability Provisions

2002 Acts. Amendment made by section 4002(c)(1) of Pub.L. 107–273, as therein provided, effective Oct. 11, 1996, which is the date of enactment of Pub.L. 104–294, to which such amendment relates.

2000 Acts. Amendment by Pub.L. 106–181 applicable only to fiscal years beginning after September 30, 1999, see section 3 of Pub.L. 106–181, set out as a note under section 106 of Title 49.

1996 Acts. Section 6(a) of Pub.L. 104–287 provided in part that amendment by such section 6(a), amending this section and section 6101 of Title 31, Money and Finance, was effective July 5, 1994.

1994 Acts. Section 7(a) of Pub.L. 103–429 provided in part that amendment of this section by section 7(a) of Pub.L. 103–429 is effective July 5, 1994.

Section 330011(c)(1) of Pub.L. 103–322 provided in part that the amendment made by such section, amending section 3(b) of Pub.L. 101–298, was to take effect on the date on which section 3(b) of Pub.L. 101–298 took effect [section 3(b) of Pub.L. 101–298 took effect on the date of enactment of Pub.L. 101–298, which was approved May 22, 1990].

Section 330011(q)(1) of Pub.L. 103–322 provided in part that the amendment made by such section, repealing section 3568 of Pub.L. 101–647, was to take effect on the date section 3568 of Pub.L. 101–647 took effect [section 3568 of Pub.L. 101–647 took effect on the date of enactment of Pub.L. 101–647, which was approved Nov. 29, 1990].

Section 330011(r) of Pub.L. 103–322 provided in part that the amendment made by such section, amending language of section 2531(3) of Pub.L. 101–647, was to take effect on the date section 2531(3) of Pub.L. 101–647 took effect [section 2531(3) of Pub.L. 101–647 took effect on the date of enactment of Pub.L. 101–647, which was approved Nov. 29, 1990].

1986 Acts. Except as otherwise provided in section 111 of Pub.L. 99–508, amendment by Pub.L. 99–508 effective 90 days after Oct. 21, 1986, see section 111 of Pub.L. 99–508 set out as a note under section 2510 of this title.

1978 Acts. Amendment by Pub.L. 95–598 effective Oct. 1, 1979, see section 402(a) of Pub.L. 95–598, set out as a note preceding section 101 of Title 11, Bankruptcy.

Sunset Provisions

Provision that amendments by Pub.L. 107–56, Title II, Oct. 26, 2001, 115 Stat. 278, with certain exclusions, shall cease to have effect on March 10, 2006, except with respect to any particular foreign intelligence investigation that began before that date, or with respect to any particular offense or potential offense that began or occurred before that, such provisions to continue in effect, was repealed by Pub.L. 109–177, § 102(a), see Pub.L. 107–56, § 224, as amended, set out as a note under 18 U.S.C.A. § 2510.

Repeals

Section 3568 of Pub.L. 101–647, which made an identical amendment to par. (1)(j) of this section as did section 2531(3) of Pub.L. 101–647, was repealed by section 330011(q)(1) of Pub.L. 103–322.

Paragraph (2) of section 601(d) of Pub.L. 104–294, cited in the credit of this section, was repealed by section 4002(c)(1) of Pub.L. 107–273, effective Oct. 11, 1996.

Severability of Provisions

If any provision of Division C of Pub.L. 104–208 or the application of such provision to any person or circumstances is held to be unconstitutional, the remainder of Division C of Pub.L. 104–208 and the application of the provisions of Division C of Pub.L. 104–208 to any person or circumstance not to be affected thereby, see section 1(e) of Pub.L. 104–208, set out as a note under section 1101 of Title 8, Aliens and Nationality.

Amendment by section 314 of Pub.L. 95–598 not to affect the application of this section to any act of any person (1) committed before Oct. 1, 1979, or (2) committed after Oct. 1, 1979, in connection with a case commenced before such date, see section 403(d) of Pub.L. 95–598, set out preceding section 101 of Title 11, Bankruptcy.

References to Coupons, Authorization Cards, or Access Devices under Food and Nutrition Act of 2008

References in any Federal, State, tribal, or local law to a "coupon", "authorization card", or other access device provided under the Food and Nutrition Act of 2008, 7 U.S.C.A. § 2011 et seq., considered to be a reference to a "benefit" provided under that Act, see Pub.L. 110–234, § 4115(d), and Pub.L. 110–246, § 4115(d), set out as a note under 7 U.S.C.A. § 2012.

LIBRARY REFERENCES

American Digest System

Telecommunications ⊕510–530.

Key Number System Topic No. 372.

Corpus Juris Secundum

CJS Attorney General § 73, Independent Counsel.

CJS Bankruptcy § 10, Other U.S. Code Provisions.

CJS Military Justice § 343, Interception of Wire and Oral Communications.

CJS Telecommunications § 257, Executive Authorization of Application.

CJS Telecommunications § 258, Judicial Action on Application.

CHAPTER 203—ARREST AND COMMITMENT

§ 3057. Bankruptcy investigations

(a) Any judge, receiver, or trustee having reasonable grounds for believing that any violation under chapter 9 of this title or other laws of the United States relating to insolvent debtors, receiverships or reorganization plans has been committed, or that an investigation should be had in connection therewith, shall report to the appropriate United States attorney all the facts and circumstances of the case, the names of the witnesses and the offense or offenses believed to have been committed. Where one of such officers has made such report, the others need not do so.

(b) The United States attorney thereupon shall inquire into the facts and report thereon to the judge, and if it appears probable that any such offense has been committed, shall without delay, present the matter to the grand jury, unless upon inquiry and examination he decides that the ends of public justice do not require investigation or prosecution, in which case he shall report the facts to the Attorney General for his direction.

(June 25, 1948, c. 645, 62 Stat. 818; May 24, 1949, c. 139, § 48, 63 Stat. 96; Nov. 6, 1978, Pub.L. 95–598, Title III, § 314(i), 92 Stat. 2677.)

HISTORICAL AND STATUTORY NOTES

Revision Notes and Legislative Reports

1948 Acts. Based on section 52(e)(1), (2) of Title 11, U.S.C., 1940 ed., Bankruptcy (July 1, 1898, c. 541, § 29e(1), (2), as

added by May 27, 1926, c. 406, § 11, 44 Stat. 665, 666; June 22, 1938, c. 575, § 1, 52 Stat. 840, 856).

Remaining provisions of section 52 of Title 11, U.S.C., 1940 ed., Bankruptcy, constitute sections 151 to 154, and 3284 of this title.

The words "or laws relating to insolvent debtors, receiverships, or reorganization plans" were inserted to avoid reference to "Title 11".

Minor changes were made in phraseology.

1949 Acts. This section [section 48] clarifies the meaning of section 3057 of Title 18, U.S.C., by expressly limiting to laws "of the United States", violations of laws which are to be reported to the United States attorney.

Senate Report No. 303 and House Report No. 352, see 1949 U.S. Code Cong. Service, p. 1248.

1978 Acts. Senate Report No. 95–989 and House Report No. 95–595, see 1978 U.S. Code Cong. and Adm. News, p. 5787.

Amendments

1978 Amendments. Subsec. (a). Pub.L. 95–598, § 314(i), substituted "judge" for "referee" and "violation under chapter 9 of this title" for "violations of the bankruptcy laws".

Subsec. (b). Pub.L. 95–598, § 314(i)(1), substituted "judge" for "referee".

1949 Amendments. Subsec. (a). Act May 24, 1949, substituted "or other laws of the United States" for "or laws".

Effective and Applicability Provisions

1978 Acts. Amendment by Pub.L. 95–598 effective Oct. 1, 1979, see section 402(a) of Pub.L. 95–598, set out as an Effective Dates note preceding section 101 of Title 11, Bankruptcy.

Savings Provisions of Pub.L. 95–598

Amendment by section 314 of Pub.L. 95–598 not to affect the application of chapter 9 [§ 151 et seq.], chapter 96 [§ 1961 et seq.], or section 2516, 3057, or 3284 of this title to any act of any person (1) committed before Oct. 1, 1979, or (2) committed after Oct. 1, 1979, in connection with a case commenced before such date, see section 403(d) of Pub.L. 95–598, set out preceding section 151 of this title.

Transfer of Functions

All functions of all other officers of the Department of Justice and all functions of all agencies and employees of such Department were, with a few exceptions, transferred to the Attorney General, with power vested in him to authorize their performance or the performance of any of his functions by any of such officers, agencies, and employees, by Reorg. Plan No. 2, of 1950, §§ 1, 2, eff. May 24, 1950, 15 F.R. 3173, 64

Stat. 1261, set out in Appendix 1 to Title 5, Government Organization and Employees.

LIBRARY REFERENCES

American Digest System

Bankruptcy ⊜3861.

Key Number System Topic No. 51.

Indictments and informations ⊜3.

Key Number System Topic No. 210.

Corpus Juris Secundum

CJS Bankruptcy § 10, Other U.S. Code Provisions.

CJS Bankruptcy § 94, Criminal Liability.

CJS Bankruptcy § 1275, Prosecutions.

CHAPTER 213—LIMITATIONS

§ 3284. Concealment of bankrupt's assets

The concealment of assets of a debtor in a case under title 11 shall be deemed to be a continuing offense until the debtor shall have been finally discharged or a discharge denied, and the period of limitations shall not begin to run until such final discharge or denial of discharge.

(June 25, 1948, c. 645, 62 Stat. 828; Nov. 6, 1978, Pub.L. 95–598, Title III, § 314(k), 92 Stat. 2678.)

HISTORICAL AND STATUTORY NOTES
Revision Notes and Legislative Reports

1948 Acts. Based on section 52(d) of Title 11, U.S.C., 1940 ed., Bankruptcy (May 27, 1926, c. 406, § 11(d), 44 Stat. 665; June 22, 1938, c. 575, § 1, 52 Stat. 856).

The 3-year-limitation provision was omitted as unnecessary in view of the general statute, section 3282 of this title.

The words "or a discharge denied" and "or denial of discharge" were added on the recommendation of the Department of Justice to supply an omission in existing law.

Other subsections of said section 52 of Title 11, U.S.C., 1940 ed., are incorporated in sections 151–154 and 3057 of this title.

Other minor changes of phraseology were made.

1978 Acts. Senate Report No. 95–989 and House Report No. 95–595, see 1978 U.S. Code Cong. and Adm. News, p. 5787.

Amendments

1978 Amendments. Pub.L. 95–598 substituted "debtor in a case under title 11" for "bankrupt or other debtor".

Effective and Applicability Provisions

1978 Acts. Amendment by Pub.L. 95–598 effective Oct. 1, 1979, see section 402(a) of Pub.L. 95–598, set out as an Effective Date note preceding section 101 of Title 11, Bankruptcy.

Savings Provisions

Amendment by section 314 of Pub.L. 95–598 not to affect the application of this section to any act of any person (1) committed before Oct. 1, 1979, or (2) committed after Oct. 1, 1979, in connection with a case commenced before such date, see section 403(d) of Pub.L. 95–598, set out preceding section 101 of Title 11, Bankruptcy.

CROSS REFERENCES

Bankruptcy investigations, see 18 USCA § 3057.

Five year limitation on offenses relating to bankruptcy, see 18 USCA § 3282.

Offenses relating to bankruptcy, see 18 USCA § 151 et seq.

LIBRARY REFERENCES
American Digest System

Criminal Law ⊜150, 154.

Key Number System Topic No. 110.

Corpus Juris Secundum

CJS Bankruptcy § 10, Other U.S. Code Provisions.

CJS Bankruptcy § 94, Criminal Liability.

PART V—IMMUNITY OF WITNESSES

CHAPTER 601—IMMUNITY OF WITNESSES

§ 6001. Definitions

As used in this chapter—

(1) "agency of the United States" means any executive department as defined in section 101 of title

5, United States Code, a military department as defined in section 102 of title 5, United States Code, the Nuclear Regulatory Commission, the Board of Governors of the Federal Reserve System, the China

Trade Act registrar appointed under 53 Stat. 1432 (15 U.S.C. sec. 143), the Commodity Futures Trading Commission, the Federal Communications Commission, the Federal Deposit Insurance Corporation, the Federal Maritime Commission, the Federal Power Commission, the Federal Trade Commission, the Surface Transportation Board, the National Labor Relations Board, the National Transportation Safety Board, the Railroad Retirement Board, an arbitration board established under 48 Stat. 1193 (45 U.S.C. sec. 157), the Securities and Exchange Commission, or a board established under 49 Stat. 31 (15 U.S.C. sec. 715d);

(2) "other information" includes any book, paper, document, record, recording, or other material;

(3) "proceeding before an agency of the United States" means any proceeding before such an agency with respect to which it is authorized to issue subpenas and to take testimony or receive other information from witnesses under oath; and

(4) "court of the United States" means any of the following courts: the Supreme Court of the United States, a United States court of appeals, a United States district court established under chapter 5, title 28, United States Code, a United States bankruptcy court established under chapter 6, title 28, United States Code, the District of Columbia Court of Appeals, the Superior Court of the District of Columbia, the District Court of Guam, the District Court of the Virgin Islands, the United States Court of Federal Claims, the Tax Court of the United States, the Court of International Trade, and the Court of Appeals for the Armed Forces.

(Added Pub.L. 91–452, Title II, § 201(a), Oct. 15, 1970, 84 Stat. 926; amended Pub.L. 95–405, § 25, Sept. 30, 1978, 92 Stat. 877; Pub.L. 95–598, Title III, § 314(l), Nov. 6, 1978, 92 Stat. 2678; Pub.L. 96–417, Title VI, § 601(1), Oct. 10, 1980, 94 Stat. 1744; Pub.L. 97–164, Title I, § 164(1), Apr. 2, 1982, 96 Stat. 50; Pub.L. 102–550, Title XV, § 1543, Oct. 28, 1992, 106 Stat. 4069; Pub.L. 102–572, Title IX, § 902(b)(1), Oct. 29, 1992, 106 Stat. 4519; Pub.L. 103–272, § 4(d), July 5, 1994, 108 Stat. 1361; Pub.L. 103–322, Title XXXIII, § 330013(2), (3), Sept. 13, 1994, 108 Stat. 2146; Pub.L. 103–337, Div. A, Title IX, § 924(d)(1)(B), Oct. 5, 1994, 108 Stat. 2832; Pub.L. 104–88, Title III, § 303(2), Dec. 29, 1995, 109 Stat. 943.)

HISTORICAL AND STATUTORY NOTES
Revision Notes and Legislative Reports
1970 Acts. House Report No. 91–1549, see 1970 U.S. Code Cong. and Adm. News, p. 4007.

1978 Acts. Senate Report No. 95–850 and Hose Conference Report No. 95–1628, see 1978 U.S. Code Cong. and Adm. News, p. 2087.

Senate Report No. 95–989 and House Report No. 95–595, see 1978 U.S. Code Cong. and Adm. News, p. 5787.

1980 Acts. House Report No. 96–1235, see 1980 U.S. Code Cong. and Adm. News, p. 3729.

1982 Acts. Senate Report No. 97–275, see 1982 U.S. Code Cong. and Adm. News, p. 11.

1992 Acts. House Report No. 102–760, House Conference Report No. 102–1017, and Statement by President, see 1992 U.S. Code Cong. and Adm. News, p. 3281.

1994 Acts. House Report No. 103–180, see 1994 U.S. Code Cong. and Adm. News, p. 818.

House Report Nos. 103–324 and 103–489, and House Conference Report No. 103–711, see 1994 U.S. Code Cong. and Adm. News, p. 1801.

House Report No. 103–499 and House Conference Report No. 103–701, see 1994 U.S. Code Cong. and Adm. News, p. 2091.

1995 Acts. House Report No. 104–311 and House Conference Report No. 104–422, see 1995 U.S. Code Cong. and Adm. News, p. 793.

Amendments
1995 Amendments. Par. (1). Pub.L. 104–88, § 303(2), substituted "Surface Transportation Board" for "Interstate Commerce Commission".

1994 Amendments. Pub.L. 103–322, § 330013(3), substituted "chapter" for "part" in the introductory text.

Par. (1). Pub.L. 103–272, § 4(d), deleted "the Civil Aeronautics Board" from list of U.S. agencies.

Pub.L. 103–322, § 330013(2), substituted "Nuclear Regulatory Commission" for "Atomic Energy Commission" and deleted "the Subversive Activities Control Board,".

Par. (4). Pub.L. 103–337, § 924(d)(1)(B), substituted "Court of Appeals for the Armed Forces" for "Court of Military Appeals".

1992 Amendments. Par. (1). Pub.L. 102–550, § 1543, added reference to the Board of Governors of the Federal Reserve System.

Par. (4). Pub.L. 102–572, § 902(b)(1), substituted "United States Court of Federal Claims" for "United States Claims Court".

1982 Amendments. Par. (4). Pub.L. 97–164 substituted "the United States Claims Court" for "the United States Court of Claims, the United States Court of Customs and Patent Appeals".

1980 Amendments. Par. (4). Pub.L. 96–417 redesignated the Customs Court as the Court of International Trade.

1978 Amendments. Par. (1). Pub.L. 95–405 inserted "the Commodity Futures Trading Commission," following "Civil Aeronautics Board,".

Par. (4). Pub.L. 95–598 inserted "a United States bankruptcy court established under chapter 6, title 28, United States Code," following "title 28, United States Code,".

Effective and Applicability Provisions
1995 Acts. Amendment by Pub.L. 104–88 effective Jan. 1, 1996, see section 2 of Pub.L. 104–88, set out as a note under section 701 of Title 49, Transportation.

1992 Acts. Except as otherwise provided, amendment by Pub.L. 102–550 effective Oct. 28, 1992, see section 2 of Pub.L. 102–550, set out as a note under section 5301 of Title 42, The Public Health and Welfare.

1982 Acts. Amendment by Pub.L. 97–164 effective Oct. 1, 1982, see section 402 of Pub.L. 97–164, set out as an Effective Date of 1982 Amendment note under section 171 of Title 28, Judiciary and Judicial Procedure.

1980 Acts. Amendment by Pub.L. 96–417 effective Nov. 1, 1980, and applicable with respect to civil actions pending on or commenced on or after such date, see section 701(a) of Pub.L. 96–417, set out as an Effective Date of 1980 Amendment note under section 251 of Title 28, Judiciary and Judicial Procedure.

1978 Acts. Amendment by Pub.L. 95–598 effective Oct. 1, 1979, see section 402(a) of Pub.L. 95–598, set out as an Effective Dates note preceding section 101 of Title 11, Bankruptcy.

Amendment by Pub.L. 95–405 effective Oct. 1, 1978, see section 28 of Pub.L. 95–405, set out as an Effective Date of 1978 Amendment note under section 2 of Title 7, Agriculture.

1970 Acts. Section 260 of Pub.L. 91–452 provided that: "The provisions of part V of title 18, United States Code, added by title II of this Act [this part], and the amendments and repeals made by title II of this Act [sections 835, 895, 1406, 1954, 2424, 2514 and 3486 of this title, sections 15, 87(f), 135c, 499m(f), and 2115 of Title 7, Agriculture, section 25 of former Title 11, Bankruptcy, section 1820 of Title 12, Banks and Banking, sections 32, 33, 49, 77v, 78u(d), 79r(e), 80a–41, 80b–9, 155, 717m, 1271, and 1714 of Title 15, Commerce and Trade, section 825f of Title 16, Conservation, section 1333 of Title 19, Customs Duties, section 373 of Title 21, Food and Drugs, sections 4874 and 7493 of Title 26, Internal Revenue Code, section 161(3) of Title 29, Labor, section 506 of Title 33, Navigation and Navigable Waters, sections 405(f) and 2201 of Title 42, The Public Health and Welfare, sections 157 and 362 of Title 45, Railroads, sections 827 and 1124 of Title 46, Shipping, section 409(l) of Title 47, Telegraphs, Telephones, and Radiotelegraphs, sections 9, 43, 46, 47, 48, 916, and 1017 of former Title 49, Transportation, and section 1484 of Title 49, Appendix, section 792 of Title 50, War and National Defense, and sections 643a, 1152, 2026, and 2155(b) of Title 50, Appendix], shall take effect on the sixtieth day following the date of the enactment of this Act [Oct. 15, 1970]. No amendment to or repeal of any provision of law under title II of this Act shall affect any immunity to which any individual is entitled under such provision by reason of any testimony or other information given before such day."

Change of Name

References to United States Claims Court deemed to refer to United States Court of Federal Claims and references to Claims Court deemed to refer to Court of Federal Claims, see section 902(b) of Pub.L. 102–572, set out as a note under section 171 of Title 28, Judiciary and Judicial Procedure.

Savings Provisions

Amendment by section 314 of Pub.L. 95–598 not to affect the application of chapter 9 [§ 151 et seq.], chapter 96 [§ 1961 et seq.], or section 2516, 3057, or 3284 of this title to any act of any person (1) committed before Oct. 1, 1979, or (2) committed after Oct. 1, 1979, in connection with a case commenced before such date, see section 403(d) of Pub.L. 95–598, set out preceding section 101 of Title 11, Bankruptcy.

Amendment or Repeal of Inconsistent Provisions

Section 259 of Pub.L. 91–452 provided that: "In addition to the provisions of law specifically amended or specifically repealed by this title [see Effective Date note set out under this section], any other provision of law inconsistent with the provisions of part V of title 18, United States Code (added by title II of this Act) [this part], is to that extent amended or repealed."

Abolition of the Atomic Energy Commission

The Atomic Energy Commission was abolished and all functions were transferred to the Administrator of the Energy Research and Development Administration (unless otherwise specifically provided) by section 5814 of Title 42, The Public Health and Welfare. The Energy Research and Development Administration was terminated and functions vested by law in the Administrator thereof were transferred to the Secretary of Energy (unless otherwise specifically provided) by sections 7151(a) and 7293 of Title 42.

Termination of Civil Aeronautics Board and Transfer of Certain Functions

All functions, powers, and duties of the Civil Aeronautics Board were terminated or transferred by former section 1551 of Title 49, Transportation, effective in part on Dec. 31, 1981, in part on Jan. 1, 1983, and in part on Jan. 1, 1985.

Termination of Federal Power Commission

The Federal Power Commission, referred to in par. (1) was terminated and the functions, personnel, property, funds, etc., thereof were transferred to the Secretary of Energy (except for certain functions which were transferred to the Federal Energy Regulatory Commission) by sections 7151(b), 7171(a), 7172(a), 7291, and 7293 of Title 42, The Public Health and Welfare.

Subversive Activities Control Board

The Subversive Activities Control Board was established by Act Sept. 23, 1950, c. 1024, § 12, 64 Stat. 997, and ceased to operate June 30, 1973.

LIBRARY REFERENCES

American Digest System

Criminal Law ⟲42.

Key Number System Topic No. 110.

Witnesses ⟲297, 304.

Key Number System Topic No. 410.

Corpus Juris Secundum

CJS Bankruptcy § 10, Other U.S. Code Provisions.

CJS Bankruptcy § 94, Criminal Liability.

CJS Criminal Law § 98, Use and Derivative Use Immunity.

CJS Criminal Law § 656, Privilege Against Self-Incrimination--Immunity of Witness.

TITLE 28
JUDICIARY AND JUDICIAL PROCEDURE

PART I—ORGANIZATION OF COURTS
CHAPTER 6—BANKRUPTCY JUDGES

HISTORICAL AND STATUTORY NOTES

Codifications

Chapter heading and section analysis of chapter 6, as added by Pub.L. 95–598, Title II, § 201(a), Nov. 6, 1978, 92 Stat. 2657, and amended Pub.L. 97–164, Title I, § 110(d), Apr. 2, 1982, 96 Stat. 29, effective June 28, 1984, pursuant to Pub.L. 95–598, Title IV, § 402(b), Nov. 6, 1978, 92 Stat. 2682, as amended by Pub.L. 98–249, § 1(a), Mar. 31, 1984, 98 Stat. 116; Pub.L. 98–271, § 1(a), Apr. 30, 1984, 98 Stat. 163; Pub.L. 98–299, § 1(a), May 25, 1984, 98 Stat. 214; Pub.L. 98–325, § 1(a), June 20, 1984, 98 Stat. 268, set out as a note preceding section 101 of Title 11, Bankruptcy, read as follows:

CHAPTER 6—BANKRUPTCY COURTS

Sec.
151. Creation and composition of bankruptcy courts.
152. Appointment of bankruptcy judges.
153. Tenure and residence of bankruptcy judges.
154. Salaries of bankruptcy judges.
155. Chief judge; precedence of bankruptcy judges.
156. Division of business among bankruptcy judges.
157. Times of holding court.
158. Accommodations at places for holding court.
159. Vacant judgeship as affecting proceedings.
160. Appellate panels.

Section 402(b) of Pub.L. 95–598 was amended by section 113 of Pub.L. 98–353 by substituting "shall not be effective" for "shall take effect on June 28, 1984", thereby eliminating the addition of the chapter heading and section analysis of chapter 6 by section 201(a) of Pub.L. 95–598, effective June 27, 1984, pursuant to section 122(c) of Pub.L. 98–353, set out as an Effective and Applicability Provisions note under section 151 of this title.

Section 121(a) of Pub.L. 98–353 directed that section 402(b) of Pub.L. 95–598 be amended by substituting "the date of enactment of the Bankruptcy Amendments and Federal Judgeship Act of 1984 [i.e. July 10, 1984]" for "June 28, 1984". This amendment was not executed in view of the prior amendment to section 402(b) of Pub.L. 95–598 by section 113 of Pub.L. 98–353.

Amendments

2005 Amendments. Pub.L. 109–8, Title VI, § 601(b), April 20, 2005, 119 Stat. 120, added item 159.

Effective and Applicability Provisions

2005 Acts. Amendments by Pub.L. 109–8, Title VI, § 601, effective 18 months after Apr. 20, 2005, see Pub.L. 109–8, § 601(c), set out as a note under 28 U.S.C.A. § 159.

Except as otherwise provided, amendments by Pub.L. 109–8 effective 180 days after April 20, 2005, and inapplicable with respect to cases commenced under Title 11 before the effective date, see Pub.L. 109–8, § 1501, set out as a note under 11 U.S.C.A. § 101.

Courts During Transition

Pub.L. 95–598, Title IV, § 404, Nov. 6, 1978, 92 Stat. 2683, as amended by Pub.L. 98–249, § 1(b), Mar. 31, 1984, 98 Stat. 116; Pub.L. 98–271, § 1(b), Apr. 30, 1984, 98 Stat. 163; Pub.L. 98–299, § 1(b), May 25, 1984, 98 Stat. 214; Pub.L. 98–325, § 1(b), June 20, 1984, 98 Stat. 268; Pub.L. 98–353, Title I, § 121(b), July 10, 1984, 98 Stat. 345, which provided that, for purposes of Pub.L. 95–598, which enacted Title 11, Bankruptcy, and the amendments made by Pub.L. 95–598, the courts of bankruptcy as defined under section 1(10) of former Title 11, created by section 11(a) of former Title 11, and existing on Sept. 30, 1979, continue to be courts of bankruptcy during the transition period beginning Oct. 1, 1979, and ending June 27, 1984, made provision for extension of the term of office of referees in bankruptcy serving on Nov. 6, 1978, and for such a referee to have the title of United States bankruptcy judge, established for each State a merit screening committee to pass on qualifications of such a referee and determine if the term of such referee should be extended, and set forth the rules and provisions applicable to United States bankruptcy judges during the transition period, was repealed by Pub.L. 98–353, Title I, § 114, 122(a), July 10, 1984, 98 Stat. 343, 346, eff. July 10, 1984.

[Section 121(b) of Pub.L. 98–353 purported to amend section 404 of Pub.L. 95–598 by substituting "the day before the date of enactment of the Bankruptcy Amendments and Federal Judgeship Act of 1984 [i.e. July 9, 1984]" for "June 27, 1984" each place it appeared. This amendment was not executed as the probable intent of Congress in view of the repeal of section 404 of Pub.L. 95–598 by section 114 of Pub.L. 98–353.]

Extension and Termination of Term of Office of Bankruptcy Judge Serving on June 27, 1984

Section 121(e) of Pub.L. 98–353 provided that: "The term of office of any bankruptcy judge who was serving on June 27, 1984, is extended to and shall expire at the end of the day of enactment of this Act [July 10, 1984]."

[Section 121(e) of Pub.L. 98–353 effective June 27, 1984, see section 122(c) of Pub.L. 98–353, set out as an Effective and Applicability Provisions note under section 151 of this title.]

For prior extensions of the term of office of bankruptcy judges see:

Pub.L. 98–325, § 2, June 20, 1984, 98 Stat. 268.

Pub.L. 98–299, § 2, May 25, 1984, 98 Stat. 214.

Pub.L. 98–271, § 2, Apr. 30, 1984, 98 Stat. 163.

Pub.L. 98–249, § 2, Mar. 31, 1984, 98 Stat. 116.

Judicial Administration During Transition

Pub.L. 95–598, Title IV, § 407, Nov. 6, 1978, 92 Stat. 2686, which provided that the Director of the Administrative Office of the United States Courts appoint a committee of not fewer than seven United States bankruptcy judges to advise the Director with respect to matters arising during the transition period, or that are relevant to the purposes of the transition period, and directed that during the transition period, the chief judge of each circuit summon at least one bankruptcy judge from each judicial district within the circuit to the judicial conference of such circuit called and held under section 332 of this title, was repealed by Pub.L. 98–353, Title I, §§ 114, 122(a), July 10, 1984, 98 Stat. 343, 346, eff. July 10, 1984.

Transition Study

Pub.L. 95–598, Title IV, § 406, Nov. 6, 1978, 92 Stat. 2686, as amended by Pub.L. 98–249, § 1(c), Mar. 31, 1984, 98 Stat. 116; Pub.L. 98–271, § 1(c), Apr. 30, 1984, 98 Stat. 163; Pub.L. 98–299, § 1(c), May 25, 1984, 98 Stat. 214; Pub.L. 98–325, § 1(c), June 20, 1984, 98 Stat. 268; Pub.L. 98–353, Title I, § 121(c), July 10, 1984, 98 Stat. 346, which provided that during the transition period, Oct. 1, 1979 to June 27, 1984, the Director of the Administrative Office of the United States Courts make continuing studies and surveys in the judicial districts to determine the number of bankruptcy judges needed after June 27, 1984, to provide for the expeditious and effective administration of justice, their regular places of offices, and the places where the court will be held, and that the Director report to the judicial councils of the circuits and the Judicial Conference of the United States his recommendations, the judicial councils advise the Conference stating their recommendations, and the Conference advise the Congress and the President, before Jan. 3, 1983, the number of bankruptcy judges needed after June 27, 1984, and the locations at which they were to serve, was repealed by Pub.L. 98–353, Title I, §§ 114, 122(a), July 10, 1984, 98 Stat. 343, 346 eff. July 10, 1984.

[Section 121(c) of Pub.L. 98–353 purported to amend section 406 of Pub.L. 95–598 by substituting "the day before the date of enactment of the Bankruptcy Amendments and Federal Judgeship Act of 1984 [i.e. July 9, 1984]" for "June 27, 1984" each place it appeared. This amendment was not executed as the probable intent of Congress in view of the repeal of section 406 of Pub.L. 95–598 by section 114 of Pub.L. 98–353.]

CROSS REFERENCES

Court of the United States defined as including bankruptcy court established under this chapter for purposes of immunity of witnesses, see 18 USCA § 6001.

Power of Bankruptcy Court, see 11 USCA § 105.

Recall of judges and magistrates, see 28 USCA § 375.

§ 151. Designation of bankruptcy courts

In each judicial district, the bankruptcy judges in regular active service shall constitute a unit of the district court to be known as the bankruptcy court for that district. Each bankruptcy judge, as a judicial officer of the district court, may exercise the authority conferred under this chapter with respect to any action, suit, or proceeding and may preside alone and hold a regular or special session of the court, except as otherwise provided by law or by rule or order of the district court.

(Added Pub.L. 98–353, Title I, § 104(a), July 10, 1984, 98 Stat. 336.)

HISTORICAL AND STATUTORY NOTES

Revision Notes and Legislative Reports

1984 Acts. Statements by Legislative Leaders, see 1984 U.S.Code Cong. and Adm.News, p. 576.

Codifications

This section as added by Pub.L. 95–598, Title II, § 201(a), Nov. 6, 1978, 92 Stat. 2657, effective June 28, 1984, pursuant to Pub.L. 95–598, Title IV, § 402(b), Nov. 6, 1978, 92 Stat. 2682, as amended by Pub.L. 98–249, § 1(a), Mar. 31, 1984, 98 Stat. 116; Pub.L. 98–271, § 1(a), Apr. 30, 1984, 98 Stat. 163; Pub.L. 98–299, § 1(a), May 25, 1984, 98 Stat. 214; Pub.L. 98–325, § 1(a), June 20, 1984, 98 Stat. 268, set out as a note preceding section 101 of Title 11, Bankruptcy, read as follows:

§ 151. Creation and composition of bankruptcy courts

(a) There shall be in each judicial district, as an adjunct to the district court for such district, a bankruptcy court which shall be a court of record known as the United States Bankruptcy Court for the district.

(b) Each bankruptcy court shall consist of the bankruptcy judge or judges for the district in regular active service. Justices or judges designated and assigned shall be competent to sit as judges of the bankruptcy court.

(c) Except as otherwise provided by law, or rule or order of court, the judicial power of a bankruptcy court with respect to any action, suit or proceeding may be exercised by a single bankruptcy judge, who may preside alone and hold a regular or special session of court at the same time other sessions are held by other bankruptcy judges.

Section 402(b) of Pub.L. 95–598 was amended by section 113 of Pub.L. 98–353 by substituting "shall not be effective" for "shall take effect on June 28, 1984", thereby eliminating the addition of section 151 by section 201(a) of Pub.L. 95–598, effective June 27, 1984, pursuant to section 122(c) of Pub.L. 98–353, set out as an Effective and Applicability Provisions note under this section.

Section 121(a) of Pub.L. 98–353 directed that section 402(b) of Pub.L. 95–598 be amended by substituting "the date of enactment of the Bankruptcy Amendments and Federal Judgeship Act of 1984 [i.e. July 10, 1984]" for "June 28, 1984". This amendment was not executed in view of the prior amendment to section 402(b) of Pub.L. 95–598 by section 113 of Pub.L. 98–353.

Effective and Applicability Provisions

1984 Acts. Section 122 of Title I of Pub.L. 98–353 provided that:

"(a) Except as otherwise provided in this section, this title and the amendments made by this title [Title I of Pub.L. 98–353, enacting this chapter, and sections 1408 to 1412 and 1452 of this title, amending sections 372, 634, 957, 1334, 1360, and 1930 of this title, sections 8331, 8334, 8336, 8339, 8341, and 8344 of Title 5, Government Organization and Employees, and section 105 of Title 11, Bankruptcy, enacting provisions set out as notes preceding section 151 of this title and under sections 151, 152, 153, 634, and 1334 of this title and section 8331 of Title 5, amending provisions set out as notes preceding sections 151 and 1471 of this title and section 101 of Title 11, and repealing provisions set out as notes preceding this section and section 1471 of this title] shall take effect on the date of the enactment of this Act [July 10, 1984].

"**(b)** Section 1334(c)(2) of title 28, United States Code [section 1334(c)(2) of this title], and section 1411(a) of title 28, United States Code, as added by this Act [section 1411(a) of this title], shall not apply with respect to cases under title 11 of the United States Code [Title 11] that are pending on the date of enactment of this Act [July 10, 1984], or to proceedings arising in or related to such cases.

"**(c)** Sections 108(b) [enacting provisions set out as a note under section 634 of this title], 113 [amending section 402(b) of Pub.L. 95–598, set out as a note preceding section 101 of Title 11], and 121(e) [enacting provisions set out as a note preceding section 151 of this title] shall take effect on June 27, 1984."

Separability of Provisions

Section 119 of Pub.L. 98–353 provided that: "If any provision of this Act [see Short Title of 1984 Amendments note set out under this section] or the application thereof to any person or circumstance is held invalid, the remainder of this Act, or the application of that provision to persons or circumstances other than those as to which it is held invalid, is not affected thereby."

Short Title

1984 Amendments. Section 1 of Pub.L. 98–353 provided: That this Act [enacting this chapter and sections 1408 to 1412 and 1452 of this title and sections 557, 558, 559, and 1113 of Title 11, Bankruptcy, amending sections 44, 98, 131, 133, 371, 372, 634, 957, 1334, 1360, and 1930 of this title, sections 8331, 8334, 8336, 8339, 8341, 8344, 8701, 8706, 8714a, and 8714b of Title 5, Government Organization and Employees, and sections 101, 102, 103, 105, 108, 109, 303, 321, 322, 326, 327, 328, 329, 330, 342, 343, 345, 346, 349, 350, 361, 362, 363, 365, 366, 501, 502, 503, 505, 506, 507, 509, 510, 521, 522, 523, 524, 525, 541, 542, 543, 544, 545, 546, 547, 548, 549, 550, 552, 553, 554, 555, 702, 703, 704, 707, 723, 724, 725, 726, 727, 728, 741, 745, 752, 761, 763, 764, 765, 766, 901, 902, 903, 921, 922, 927, 943, 945, 1102, 1103, 1105, 1106, 1107, 1108, 1112, 1121, 1123, 1124, 1125, 1126, 1127, 1129, 1141, 1142, 1144, 1145, 1146, 1166, 1168, 1169, 1170, 1171, 1173, 1301, 1302, 1304, 1307, 1322, 1324, 1325, 1326, 1328, 1329, 15103, and 151302 of Title 11, Bankruptcy Rules 2002 and 3001, Title 11, and Bankruptcy Form No. 1, Title 11, enacting provisions set out as notes preceding section 151 of this title and under sections 44, 133, 151, 152, 153, 371, 634, 1334, and 2075 of this title, sections 8331 and 8706 of Title 5, and preceding section 101 and sections 101, 365, and 1113 of Title 11, amending provisions set out as notes preceding sections 151, 581 and 1471 of this title and section 101 of Title 11, and repealing provisions set out as notes preceding this section and section 1471 of this title] may be cited as the 'Bankruptcy Amendments and Federal Judgeship Act of 1984'."

LIBRARY REFERENCES

American Digest System

Bankruptcy ⟐2122.
Key Number System Topic No. 51.

Corpus Juris Secundum

CJS Bankruptcy § 9, Title 28 of the U.S. Code.
CJS Bankruptcy § 20, Bankruptcy Court as Unit of District Court.
CJS Bankruptcy § 23, Sessions and Hearings; Court Always Open.

§ 152. Appointment of bankruptcy judges

(a)(1) Each bankruptcy judge to be appointed for a judicial district, as provided in paragraph (2), shall be appointed by the court of appeals of the United States for the circuit in which such district is located. Such appointments shall be made after considering the recommendations of the Judicial Conference submitted pursuant to subsection (b). Each bankruptcy judge shall be appointed for a term of fourteen years, subject to the provisions of subsection (e). However, upon the expiration of the term, a bankruptcy judge may, with the approval of the judicial council of the circuit, continue to perform the duties of the office until the earlier of the date which is 180 days after the expiration of the term or the date of the appointment of a successor. Bankruptcy judges shall serve as judicial officers of the United States district court established under Article III of the Constitution.

(2) The bankruptcy judges appointed pursuant to this section shall be appointed for the several judicial districts as follows:

Districts	Judges
Alabama:	
Northern	5
Middle	2
Southern	2
Alaska	2
Arizona	7
Arkansas:	
Eastern and Western	3
California:	
Northern	9
Eastern	6
Central	21
Southern	4
Colorado	5
Connecticut	3
Delaware	1
District of Columbia	1
Florida:	
Northern	1
Middle	8
Southern	5
Georgia:	
Northern	8
Middle	3
Southern	2
Hawaii	1
Idaho	2
Illinois:	

Districts	Judges
Northern	10
Central	3
Southern	1
Indiana:	
Northern	3
Southern	4
Iowa:	
Northern	2
Southern	2
Kansas	4
Kentucky:	
Eastern	2
Western	3
Louisiana:	
Eastern	2
Middle	1
Western	3
Maine	2
Maryland	4
Massachusetts	5
Michigan:	
Eastern	4
Western	3
Minnesota	4
Mississippi:	
Northern	1
Southern	2
Missouri:	
Eastern	3
Western	3
Montana	1
Nebraska	2
Nevada	3
New Hampshire	1
New Jersey	8
New Mexico	2
New York:	
Northern	2
Southern	9
Eastern	6
Western	3
North Carolina:	
Eastern	2
Middle	2
Western	2
North Dakota	1
Ohio:	
Northern	8
Southern	7
Oklahoma:	
Northern	2
Eastern	1
Western	3
Oregon	5
Pennsylvania:	
Eastern	5
Middle	2
Western	4

Districts	Judges
Puerto Rico	2
Rhode Island	1
South Carolina	2
South Dakota	2
Tennessee:	
Eastern	3
Middle	3
Western	4
Texas:	
Northern	6
Eastern	2
Southern	6
Western	4
Utah	3
Vermont	1
Virginia:	
Eastern	5
Western	3
Washington:	
Eastern	2
Western	5
West Virginia:	
Northern	1
Southern	1
Wisconsin:	
Eastern	4
Western	2
Wyoming	1

(3) Whenever a majority of the judges of any court of appeals cannot agree upon the appointment of a bankruptcy judge, the chief judge of such court shall make such appointment.

(4) The judges of the district courts for the territories shall serve as the bankruptcy judges for such courts. The United States court of appeals for the circuit within which such a territorial district court is located may appoint bankruptcy judges under this chapter for such district if authorized to do so by the Congress of the United States under this section.

(b)(1) The Judicial Conference of the United States shall, from time to time, and after considering the recommendations submitted by the Director of the Administrative Office of the United States Courts after such Director has consulted with the judicial council of the circuit involved, determine the official duty stations of bankruptcy judges and places of holding court.

(2) The Judicial Conference shall, from time to time, submit recommendations to the Congress regarding the number of bankruptcy judges needed and the districts in which such judges are needed.

(3) Not later than December 31, 1994, and not later than the end of each 2–year period thereafter, the Judicial Conference of the United States shall conduct a comprehensive review of all judicial districts to assess the continuing need for the bankruptcy judges authorized by this section, and shall report to the Congress its findings and any recommendations for the

elimination of any authorized position which can be eliminated when a vacancy exists by reason of resignation, retirement, removal, or death.

(c)(1) Each bankruptcy judge may hold court at such places within the judicial district, in addition to the official duty station of such judge, as the business of the court may require.

(2)(A) Bankruptcy judges may hold court at such places within the United States outside the judicial district as the nature of the business of the court may require, and upon such notice as the court orders, upon a finding by either the chief judge of the bankruptcy court (or, if the chief judge is unavailable, the most senior available bankruptcy judge) or by the judicial council of the circuit that, because of emergency conditions, no location within the district is reasonably available where the bankruptcy judges could hold court.

(B) Bankruptcy judges may transact any business at special sessions of court held outside the district pursuant to this paragraph that might be transacted at a regular session.

(C) If a bankruptcy court issues an order exercising its authority under subparagraph (A), the court—

(i) through the Administrative Office of the United States Courts, shall—

(I) send notice of such order, including the reasons for the issuance of such order, to the Committee on the Judiciary of the Senate and the Committee on the Judiciary of the House of Representatives; and

(II) not later than 180 days after the expiration of such court order submit a brief report to the Committee on the Judiciary of the Senate and the Committee on the Judiciary of the House of Representatives describing the impact of such order, including—

(aa) the reasons for the issuance of such order;

(bb) the duration of such order;

(cc) the impact of such order on litigants; and

(dd) the costs to the judiciary resulting from such order; and

(ii) shall provide reasonable notice to the United States Marshals Service before the commencement of any special session held pursuant to such order.

(d) With the approval of the Judicial Conference and of each of the judicial councils involved, a bankruptcy judge may be designated to serve in any district adjacent to or near the district for which such bankruptcy judge was appointed.

(e) A bankruptcy judge may be removed during the term for which such bankruptcy judge is appointed, only for incompetence, misconduct, neglect of duty, or physical or mental disability and only by the judicial council of the circuit in which the judge's official duty station is located. Removal may not occur unless a

majority of all of the judges of such council concur in the order of removal. Before any order of removal may be entered, a full specification of charges shall be furnished to such bankruptcy judge who shall be accorded an opportunity to be heard on such charges.

(Added Pub.L. 98–353, Title I, § 104(a), July 10, 1984, 98 Stat. 336; amended Pub.L. 99–554, Title I, § 101, Oct. 27, 1986, 100 Stat. 3088; Pub.L. 100–587, Nov. 3, 1988, 102 Stat. 2982; Pub.L. 101–650, Title III, § 304, Dec. 1, 1990, 104 Stat. 5105; Pub.L. 102–361, §§ 2, 4, Aug. 26, 1992, 106 Stat. 965, 966; Pub.L. 109–8, Title XII, § 1223(d), Apr. 20, 2005, 119 Stat. 198; Pub.L. 109–63, § 2(c), Sept. 9, 2005, 119 Stat. 1994.)

HISTORICAL AND STATUTORY NOTES

Revision Notes and Legislative Reports

1984 Acts. Statements by Legislative Leaders, see 1984 U.S. Code Cong. and Adm. News, p. 576.

1986 Acts. House Report No. 99–764 and House Conference Report No. 99–958, see 1986 U.S. Code Cong. and Adm. News, p. 5227.

1988 Acts. House Report No. 100–756, see 1988 U.S. Code Cong. and Adm. News, p. 3979.

1990 Acts. Senate Report No. 101–416, Related House Reports, and Statement by President, see 1990 U.S. Code Cong. and Adm. News, p. 6802.

1992 Acts. House Report No. 102–825, see 1992 U.S. Code Cong. and Adm. News, p. 855.

2005 Acts. House Report No. 109–31(Part I), see 2005 U.S. Code Cong. and Adm. News, p. 88.

Codifications

This section as added by Pub.L. 95–598, Title II, § 201(a), Nov. 6, 1978, 92 Stat. 2657, effective June 28, 1984, pursuant to Pub.L. 95–598, Title IV, § 402(b), Nov. 6, 1978, 92 Stat. 2682, as amended by Pub.L. 98–249, § 1(a), Mar. 31, 1984, 98 Stat. 116; Pub.L. 98–271, § 1(a), Apr. 30, 1984, 98 Stat. 163; Pub.L. 98–299, § 1(a), May 25, 1984, 98 Stat. 214; Pub.L. 98–325, § 1(a), June 20, 1984, 98 Stat. 268, set out as a note preceding section 101 of Title 11, Bankruptcy, read as follows:

"**§ 152. Appointment of bankruptcy judges**

"The President shall appoint, by and with the advice and consent of the Senate, bankruptcy judges for the several judicial districts. In each instance, the President shall give due consideration to the recommended nominee or nominees of the Judicial Council of the Circuit within which an appointment is to be made."

Section 402(b) of Pub.L. 95–598 was amended by section 113 of Pub.L. 98–353 by substituting "shall not be effective" for "shall take effect on June 28, 1984", thereby eliminating the addition of section 152 by section 201(a) of Pub.L. 95–598, effective June 27, 1984, pursuant to section 122(c) of Pub.L. 98–353, set out as an Effective and Applicability Provisions note under 28 U.S.C.A. § 151.

Section 121(a) of Pub.L. 98–353 directed that section 402(b) of Pub.L. 95–598 be amended by substituting "the date of enactment of the Bankruptcy Amendments and Federal Judgeship Act of 1984 [i.e. July 10, 1984]" for "June 28, 1984". This amendment was not executed in view of the prior amendment to section 402(b) of Pub.L. 95–598 by section 113 of Pub.L. 98–353.

Amendments

2005 Amendments. Subsec. (a)(1). Pub.L. 109–8, § 1223(d)(1), rewrote the first sentence, substituting "Each bankruptcy judge to be appointed for a judicial district, as provided in paragraph (2), shall be appointed by the court of appeals of the United States for the circuit in which such district is located." for "The United States court of appeals for the circuit shall appoint bankruptcy judges for the judicial districts established in paragraph (2) in such numbers as are established in such paragraph."

Subsec. (a)(2). Pub.L. 109–8, § 1223(d)(2), in the item relating to the middle district of Georgia, substituted "3" for "2" and struck out the collective item relating to the number of judges for the middle and southern districts of Georgia, which had read: "Middle and Southern .... 1".

Subsec. (c)(1). Pub.L. 109–63, § 2(c)(1), redesignated the undesignated par. as par. (1).

Subsec. (c)(2). Pub.L. 109–63, § 2(c)(2), added par. (2).

1992 Amendments. Subsec. (a)(2). Pub.L. 102–361, § 2, amended par. (2) as follows:

(1) in the item relating to the district of Arizona by striking "5" and inserting "7";

(2) in the item relating to the central district of California by striking "19" and inserting "21";

(3) in the item relating to the district of Connecticut by striking "2" and inserting "3";

(4) in the item relating to the middle district of Florida by striking "4" and inserting "8";

(5) in the item relating to the southern district of Florida by striking "3" and inserting "5";

(6) in the item relating to the northern district of Georgia by striking "6" and inserting "8";

(7) in the item relating to Georgia by adding at the end the following:

"Middle and Southern .... 1";

(8) in the item relating to the district of Maryland by striking "3" and inserting "4";

(9) in the item relating to the district of Massachusetts by striking "4" and inserting "5";

(10) in the item relating to the district of New Jersey by striking "7" and inserting "8";

(11) in the item relating to the southern district of New York by striking "7" and inserting "9";

(12) in the item relating to the eastern district of Pennsylvania by striking "3" and inserting "5";

(13) in the item relating to the middle district of Tennessee by striking "2" and inserting "3";

(14) in the item relating to the western district of Tennessee by striking "3" and inserting "4";

(15) in the item relating to the northern district of Texas by striking "5" and inserting "6"; and

(16) in the item relating to the eastern district of Virginia by striking "4" and inserting "5".

Subsec. (b)(3). Pub.L. 102–361, § 4, added par. (3).

1990 Amendments. Subsec. (a)(1). Pub.L. 101–650 provided for extension of terms of office of bankruptcy judges until the earlier of 180 days after expiration of the term or appointment of a successor.

1988 Amendments. Subsec. (a)(2). Pub.L. 100–587 amended par. (2) as follows:

(1) in the item relating to the district of Alaska by striking "1" and inserting "2",

(2) in the item relating to the district of Colorado by striking "4" and inserting "5",

(3) in the item relating to the district of Kansas by striking "3" and inserting "4",

(4) in the item relating to the eastern district of Kentucky by striking "1" and inserting "2",

(5) in the item relating to the eastern district of Texas by striking "1" and inserting "2",

(6) in the item relating to the western district of Texas, by striking "3" and inserting "4", and

(7) in the item relating to the district of Arizona, by striking "4" and inserting "5".

1986 Amendments. Subsec. (a)(2). Pub.L. 99–554 amended subsec. (a)(2) as follows:

(1) in the item relating to the eastern district and the western district of Arkansas by striking out "2" and inserting in lieu thereof "3",

(2) in the item relating to the northern district of California by striking out "7" and inserting in lieu thereof "9",

(3) in the item relating to the eastern district of California by striking out "4" and inserting in lieu thereof "6",

(4) in the item relating to the central district of California by striking out "12" and inserting in lieu thereof "19",

(5) in the item relating to the southern district of California by striking out "3" and inserting in lieu thereof "4",

(6) in the item relating to the middle district of Florida by striking out "2" and inserting in lieu thereof "4",

(7) in the item relating to the northern district of Georgia by striking out "4" and inserting in lieu thereof "6",

(8) in the item relating to the southern district of Georgia by striking out "1" and inserting in lieu thereof "2",

(9) in the item relating to the district of Idaho by striking out "1" and inserting in lieu thereof "2",

(10) in the item relating to the northern district of Illinois by striking out "8" and inserting in lieu thereof "10",

(11) in the item relating to the central district of Illinois by striking out "2" and inserting in lieu thereof "3",

(12) in the item relating to the northern district of Indiana by striking out "2" and inserting in lieu thereof "3",

(13) in the item relating to the northern district of Iowa by striking out "1" and inserting in lieu thereof "2",

(14) in the item relating to the southern district of Iowa by striking out "1" and inserting in lieu thereof "2",

(15) in the item relating to the western district of Kentucky by striking out "2" and inserting in lieu thereof "3",

(16) in the item relating to the western district of Louisiana by striking out "2" and inserting in lieu thereof "3",

(17) in the item relating to the district of Maryland by striking out "2" and inserting in lieu thereof "3",

(18) in the item relating to the western district of Michigan by striking out "2" and inserting in lieu thereof "3",

(19) in the item relating to the district of Nebraska by striking out "1" and inserting in lieu thereof "2",

(20) in the item relating to the district of Nevada by striking out "2" and inserting in lieu thereof "3",

(21) in the item relating to the district of New Jersey by striking out "5" and inserting in lieu thereof "7",

(22) in the item relating to the western district of North Carolina by striking out "1" and inserting in lieu thereof "2",

(23) in the item relating to the northern district of Oklahoma by striking out "1" and inserting in lieu thereof "2",

(24) in the item relating to the western district of Oklahoma by striking out "2" and inserting in lieu thereof "3",

(25) in the item relating to the district of Oregon by striking out "4" and inserting in lieu thereof "5",

(26) in the item relating to the western district of Pennsylvania by striking out "3" and inserting in lieu thereof "4",

(27) in the item relating to the district of South Carolina by striking out "1" and inserting in lieu thereof "2",

(28) in the item relating to the district of South Dakota by striking out "1" and inserting in lieu thereof "2",

(29) in the item relating to the eastern district of Tennessee by striking out "2" and inserting in lieu thereof "3",

(30) in the item relating to the western district of Tennessee by striking out "2" and inserting in lieu thereof "3",

(31) in the item relating to the northern district of Texas by striking out "4" and inserting in lieu thereof "5",

(32) in the item relating to the southern district of Texas by striking out "3" and inserting in lieu thereof "6",

(33) in the item relating to the western district of Texas by striking out "2" and inserting in lieu thereof "3",

(34) in the item relating to the district of Utah by striking out "2" and inserting in lieu thereof "3",

(35) in the item relating to the eastern district of Virginia by striking out "3" and inserting in lieu thereof "4",

(36) in the item relating to the eastern district of Washington by striking out "1" and inserting in lieu thereof "2",

(37) in the item relating to the western district of Washington by striking out "4" and inserting in lieu thereof "5", and

(38) in the item relating to the eastern district of Wisconsin by striking out "3" and inserting in lieu thereof "4".

Effective and Applicability Provisions

2005 Acts. Pub.L. 109–8, Title XII, § 1223(e), Apr. 20, 2005, 119 Stat. 198, provided that: "The amendments made by this section [amending this section and enacting provisions set out as notes under this section and 28 U.S.C.A. § 1] shall take effect on the date of the enactment of this Act [Apr. 20, 2005]."

Except as otherwise provided, amendments by Pub.L. 109–8 effective 180 days after April 20, 2005, and inapplicable with respect to cases commenced under Title 11 before the effective date, see Pub.L. 109–8, § 1501, set out as a note under 11 U.S.C.A. § 101.

1986 Acts. Amendment by Pub.L. 99–554 effective on Oct. 27, 1986, see section 302(b) of Pub.L. 99–554, set out as a note under section 581 of this title.

1984 Acts. Section effective July 10, 1984, see section 122(a) of Pub.L. 98–353, set out as a note under section 151 of this title.

Termination of Reporting Requirements

For termination of reporting provisions of subsec. (b)(2) of this section, effective May 15, 2000, see Pub.L. 104–66, § 3003, as amended, set out as a note under 31 U.S.C.A.

§ 1113, and the 16th item on page 12 of House Document No. 103–7.

Temporary Judgeships: Appointments, Vacancies, and Extensions

Pub.L. 109–8, Title XII, § 1223(b), (c), Apr. 20, 2005, 119 Stat. 196, 198, provided that:

"**(b) Temporary Judgeships.—**

"**(1) Appointments.**—The following bankruptcy judges shall be appointed in the manner prescribed in section 152(a)(1) of title 28, United States Code, for the appointment of bankruptcy judges provided for in section 152(a)(2) of such title:

"**(A)** One additional bankruptcy judge for the eastern district of California.

"**(B)** Three additional bankruptcy judges for the central district of California.

"**(C)** Four additional bankruptcy judges for the district of Delaware.

"**(D)** Two additional bankruptcy judges for the southern district of Florida.

"**(E)** One additional bankruptcy judge for the southern district of Georgia.

"**(F)** Three additional bankruptcy judges for the district of Maryland.

"**(G)** One additional bankruptcy judge for the eastern district of Michigan.

"**(H)** One additional bankruptcy judge for the southern district of Mississippi.

"**(I)** One additional bankruptcy judge for the district of New Jersey.

"**(J)** One additional bankruptcy judge for the eastern district of New York.

"**(K)** One additional bankruptcy judge for the northern district of New York.

"**(L)** One additional bankruptcy judge for the southern district of New York.

"**(M)** One additional bankruptcy judge for the eastern district of North Carolina.

"**(N)** One additional bankruptcy judge for the eastern district of Pennsylvania.

"**(O)** One additional bankruptcy judge for the middle district of Pennsylvania.

"**(P)** One additional bankruptcy judge for the district of Puerto Rico.

"**(Q)** One additional bankruptcy judge for the western district of Tennessee.

"**(R)** One additional bankruptcy judge for the eastern district of Virginia.

"**(S)** One additional bankruptcy judge for the district of South Carolina.

"**(T)** One additional bankruptcy judge for the district of Nevada.

"**(2) Vacancies.—**

"**(A) Districts with single appointments.**—Except as provided in subparagraphs (B), (C), (D), and (E), the first vacancy occurring in the office of bankruptcy judge in each of the judicial districts set forth in paragraph (1)—

"**(i)** occurring 5 years or more after the appointment date of the bankruptcy judge appointed under paragraph (1) to such office; and "(ii) resulting from the death, retirement, resignation, or removal of a bankruptcy judge;

shall not be filled.

"(B) **Central district of California.**—The 1st, 2d, and 3d vacancies in the office of bankruptcy judge in the central district of California—

"(i) occurring 5 years or more after the respective 1st, 2d, and 3d appointment dates of the bankruptcy judges appointed under paragraph (1)(B); and

"(ii) resulting from the death, retirement, resignation, or removal of a bankruptcy judge;

shall not be filled.

"(C) **District of Delaware.**—The 1st, 2d, 3d, and 4th vacancies in the office of bankruptcy judge in the district of Delaware—

"(i) occurring 5 years or more after the respective 1st, 2d, 3d, and 4th appointment dates of the bankruptcy judges appointed under paragraph (1)(F); and

"(ii) resulting from the death, retirement, resignation, or removal of a bankruptcy judge;

shall not be filled.

"(D) **Southern district of Florida.**—The 1st and 2d vacancies in the office of bankruptcy judge in the southern district of Florida—

"(i) occurring 5 years or more after the respective 1st and 2d appointment dates of the bankruptcy judges appointed under paragraph (1)(D); and

"(ii) resulting from the death, retirement, resignation, or removal of a bankruptcy judge;

shall not be filled.

"(E) **District of Maryland.**—The 1st, 2d, and 3d vacancies in the office of bankruptcy judge in the district of Maryland—

"(i) occurring 5 years or more after the respective 1st, 2d, and 3d appointment dates of the bankruptcy judges appointed under paragraph (1)(F); and

"(ii) resulting from the death, retirement, resignation, or removal of a bankruptcy judge;

shall not be filled.

"(c) **Extensions.**—

"(1) **In general.**—The temporary office of bankruptcy judges authorized for the northern district of Alabama, the district of Delaware, the district of Puerto Rico, and the eastern district of Tennessee under paragraphs (1), (3), (7), and (9) of section 3(a) of the Bankruptcy Judgeship Act of 1992 (28 U.S.C. 152 note) are extended until the first vacancy occurring in the office of a bankruptcy judge in the applicable district resulting from the death, retirement, resignation, or removal of a bankruptcy judge and occurring 5 years after the date of the enactment of this Act [April 20, 2005].

"(2) **Applicability of other provisions.**—All other provisions of section 3 of the Bankruptcy Judgeship Act of 1992 (28 U.S.C. 152 note) remain applicable to the temporary office of bankruptcy judges referred to in this subsection."

[Amendments by Pub.L. 109–8, § 1223, effective Apr. 20, 2005, see Pub.L. 109–8, § 1223(e), set out as a note under this section.]

Temporary Appointment of Additional Judges

Section 3 of Pub.L. 102–361, as amended Pub.L. 104–317, Title III, § 307, Oct. 19, 1996, 110 Stat. 3852, provided that:

"(a) **Appointments.**—The following bankruptcy judges shall be appointed in the manner prescribed in section 152(a)(1) of title 28, United States Code [subsec. (a)(1) of this section]:

"(1) 1 additional bankruptcy judge for the northern district of Alabama.

"(2) 1 additional bankruptcy judge for the district of Colorado.

"(3) 1 additional bankruptcy judge for the district of Delaware.

"(4) 1 additional bankruptcy judge for the southern district of Illinois.

"(5) 1 additional bankruptcy judge for the district of New Hampshire.

"(6) 1 additional bankruptcy judge for the middle district of North Carolina.

"(7) 1 additional bankruptcy judge for the district of Puerto Rico.

"(8) 1 additional bankruptcy judge for the district of South Carolina.

"(9) 1 additional bankruptcy judge for the eastern district of Tennessee.

"(10) 1 additional bankruptcy judge for the western district of Texas.

"(b) **Vacancies.**—The first vacancy in the office of bankruptcy judge in each of the judicial districts set forth in subsection (a), resulting from the death, retirement, resignation, or removal of a bankruptcy judge, and occurring 5 years or more after the appointment date of the judge named to fill the temporary judgeship position shall not be filled. In the case of a vacancy resulting from the expiration of the term of a bankruptcy judge not described in the preceding sentence, that judge shall be eligible for reappointment as a bankruptcy judge in that district."

Appointment to Fill Vacancies; Nominations; Qualifications

Section 120 of Pub.L. 98–353, as amended Pub.L. 99–554, Title I, § 102, Oct. 22, 1986, 100 Stat. 3089; Pub.L. 104–317, Title III, § 303, Oct. 19, 1996, 110 Stat. 3852, provided that:

"(a)(1) Whenever a court of appeals is authorized to fill a vacancy that occurs on a bankruptcy court of the United States, such court of appeals shall appoint to fill that vacancy a person whose character, experience, ability, and impartiality qualify such person to serve in the Federal judiciary.

"(2) It is the sense of the Congress that the courts of appeals should consider for appointment under section 152 of title 28, United States Code [this section], to the first vacancy which arises after the date of the enactment of this Act [July 10, 1984] in the office of each bankruptcy judge, the bankruptcy judge who holds such office immediately before such vacancy arises, if such bankruptcy judge requests to be considered for such appointment.

"(3) When filling vacancies, the court of appeals may consider reappointing incumbent bankruptcy judges under procedures prescribed by regulations issued by the Judicial Conference of the United States.

"(b) The judicial council of the circuit involved shall assist the court of appeals by evaluating potential nominees and by recommending to such court for consideration for appointment to each vacancy on the bankruptcy court persons who are qualified to be bankruptcy judges under regulations prescribed by the Judicial Conference of the United States. In the case of the first vacancy which arises after the date of the enactment of this Act [July 10, 1984] in the office of each bankruptcy judge, such potential nominees shall include the bankruptcy judge who holds such office immediately before such vacancy arises, if such bankruptcy judge requests to be considered for such appointment and the judicial council determines that such judge is qualified under subsection (c) of this section to continue to serve. Such potential nominees shall receive consideration equal to that given all other potential nominees for such position. All incumbent nominees seeking reappointment thereafter may be considered for such a reappointment, pursuant to a majority vote of the judges of the appointing court of appeals, under procedures authorized under subsection (a)(3).

"(c) Before transmitting to the court of appeals the names of the persons the judicial council for the circuit deems best qualified to fill any existing vacancy, the judicial council shall have determined that—

"(1) public notice of such vacancy has been given and an effort has been made, in the case of each such vacancy, to identify qualified candidates, without regard to race, color, sex, religion, or national origin,

"(2) such persons are members in good standing of at least one State bar, the District of Columbia bar, or the bar of the Commonwealth of Puerto Rico, and members in good standing of every other bar of which they are members,

"(3) such persons possess, and have a reputation for, integrity and good character,

"(4) such persons are of sound physical and mental health,

"(5) such persons possess and have demonstrated commitment to equal justice under law,

"(6) such persons possess and have demonstrated outstanding legal ability and competence, as evidenced by substantial legal experience, ability to deal with complex legal problems, aptitude for legal scholarship and writing, and familiarity with courts and court processes, and

"(7) such persons [sic] demeanor, character, and personality indicate that they would exhibit judicial temperament if appointed to the position of United States bankruptcy judge."

Extension and Termination of Term of Office of Bankruptcy Judge and Part-Time Bankruptcy Judge Serving on July 10, 1984; Practice of Law by Part-Time Bankruptcy Judge

Section 106 of Pub.L. 98–353 provided that:

"(a) Notwithstanding section 152 of title 28, United States Code, as added by this Act [this section], the term of office of a bankruptcy judge who is serving on the date of enactment of this Act [July 10, 1984] is extended to and expires four years after the date such bankruptcy judge was last appointed to such office or on October 1, 1986, whichever is later.

"(b)(1) Notwithstanding section 153(a) of title 28, United States Code, as added by this Act [section 153(a) of this title], and notwithstanding subsection (a) of this section, a bankruptcy judge serving on a part-time basis on the date of enactment of this Act [July 10, 1984] may continue to serve on such basis for a period not to exceed two years from the date of enactment of this Act [July 10, 1984].

"(2) Notwithstanding the provisions of section 153(b) of title 28, United States Code [section 153(b) of this title], a bankruptcy judge serving on a part-time basis may engage in the practice of law but may not engage in any other practice,

business, occupation, or employment inconsistent with the expeditious, proper, and impartial performance of such bankruptcy judge's duties as a judicial officer. The Judicial Conference of the United States may promulgate appropriate rules and regulations to implement this paragraph."

Extension and Termination of Term of Office of Part-Time Bankruptcy Judge Serving on July 2, 1986, In District of Oregon, Western District of Michigan, and Eastern District of Oklahoma

Pub.L. 99–349, Title I, July 2, 1986, 100 Stat. 718, provided that: "Notwithstanding the provisions of section 106(b)(1) of the Bankruptcy Amendments and Federal Judgeship Act of 1984 [section 106(b)(1) of Pub.L. 98–353, set out as a note under this section], a bankruptcy judge serving on a part-time basis on the date of enactment of this Act [July 2, 1986] may continue to serve as a part-time judge for such district until December 31, 1986, or until such time as a full-time bankruptcy judge for such district is appointed, whichever is earlier: *Provided,* That these provisions shall apply only to part-time bankruptcy judges serving in the district of Oregon, the western district of Michigan, and the eastern district of Oklahoma."

CROSS REFERENCES

Appeals, hearing of, see 28 USCA § 158.

Definition of Bankruptcy judge as including a judge appointed under this section for purposes of civil service retirement, see 5 USCA § 8331.

Removal of judges for disability to be in accordance with provisions of this section, see 28 USCA § 372.

Retirement of bankruptcy judges and magistrates, see 28 USCA § 377.

LIBRARY REFERENCES

American Digest System

Bankruptcy ⊸2123, 2124.1.

Key Number System Topic No. 51.

Corpus Juris Secundum

CJS Bankruptcy § 23, Sessions and Hearings; Court Always Open.

CJS Bankruptcy § 27, Qualifications for Appointment.

CJS Bankruptcy § 32, Removal of Judge; Substitution for Disabled Judge.

§ 153. Salaries; character of service

(a) Each bankruptcy judge shall serve on a full-time basis and shall receive as full compensation for his services, a salary at an annual rate that is equal to 92 percent of the salary of a judge of the district court of the United States as determined pursuant to section 135, to be paid at such times as the Judicial Conference of the United States determines.

(b) A bankruptcy judge may not engage in the practice of law and may not engage in any other practice, business, occupation, or employment inconsistent with the expeditious, proper, and impartial performance of such bankruptcy judge's duties as a judicial officer. The Conference may promulgate appropriate rules and regulations to implement this subsection.

(c) Each individual appointed under this chapter shall take the oath or affirmation prescribed by section 453 of this title before performing the duties of the office of bankruptcy judge.

(d) A bankruptcy judge appointed under this chapter shall be exempt from the provisions of subchapter I of chapter 63 of title 5.

(Added Pub.L. 98–353, Title I, § 104(a), July 10, 1984, 98 Stat. 338; amended Pub.L. 100–202, § 101(a) [Title IV, § 408(a)], Dec. 22, 1987, 101 Stat. 1329–26; Pub.L. 100–702, Title X, § 1003(a)(1), Nov. 19, 1988, 102 Stat. 4665.)

HISTORICAL AND STATUTORY NOTES

Revision Notes and Legislative Reports

1984 Acts. Statements by Legislative Leaders, see 1984 U.S.Code Cong. and Adm.News, p. 576.

1988 Acts. House Report No. 100–889, see 1988 U.S.Code Cong. and Adm.News, p. 5982.

Codifications

This section as added by Pub.L. 95–598, Title II, § 201(a), Nov. 6, 1978, 92 Stat. 2657, effective June 28, 1984, pursuant to Pub.L. 95–598, Title IV, § 402(b), Nov. 6, 1978, 92 Stat. 2682, as amended by Pub.L. 98–249, § 1(a), Mar. 31, 1984, 98 Stat. 116; Pub.L. 98–271, § 1(a), Apr. 30, 1984, 98 Stat. 163; Pub.L. 98–299, § 1(a), May 25, 1984, 98 Stat. 214; Pub.L. 98–325, § 1(a), June 20, 1984, 98 Stat. 268, set out as a note preceding section 101 of Title 11, Bankruptcy, read as follows:

§ 153. Tenure and residence of bankruptcy judges

(a) Each bankruptcy judge shall hold office for a term of 14 years, but may continue to perform the duties of his office until his successor takes office, unless such office has been eliminated.

(b) Removal of a bankruptcy judge during the term for which he is appointed shall be only for incompetency, misconduct, neglect of duty, or physical or mental disability. Removal shall be by the judicial council of the circuit or circuits in which the bankruptcy judge serves, but removal may not occur unless a majority of all the judges of such circuit council or councils concur in the order of removal. Before any order of removal may be entered, a full specification of the charges shall be furnished to the bankruptcy judge, and he shall be accorded an opportunity to be heard on the charges. Any cause for removal of any bankruptcy judge coming to the knowledge of the Director of the Administrative Office of the United States Courts shall be reported by him to the chief judge of the circuit or circuits in which he serves, and a copy of the report shall at the same time be transmitted to the circuit council or councils and to the bankruptcy judge.

(c) Each bankruptcy judge shall reside in the district or one of the districts for which he is appointed, or within 20 miles of his official station.

(d) If the public interest and the nature of the business of a bankruptcy court require that a bankruptcy judge should maintain his abode at or near a particular part of the district the judicial council of the circuit may so declare and may make an appropriate order. If the bankruptcy judges of such a district are unable to agree as to which of them shall maintain his abode at or near the place or within the area

specified in such an order the judicial council of the circuit may decide which of them shall do so.

Section 402(b) of Pub.L. 95–598 was amended by section 113 of Pub.L. 98–353 by substituting "shall not be effective" for "shall take effect on June 28, 1984", thereby eliminating the addition of section 153 by section 201(a) of Pub.L. 95–598, effective June 27, 1984, pursuant to section 122(c) of Pub.L. 98–353, set out as an Effective Date note under section 151 of this title.

Section 121(a) of Pub.L. 98–353 directed that section 402(b) of Pub.L. 95–598 be amended by substituting "the date of enactment of the Bankruptcy Amendments and Federal Judgeship Act of 1984 [i.e. July 10, 1984]" for "June 28, 1984". This amendment was not executed in view of the prior amendment to section 402(b) of Pub.L. 95–598 by section 113 of Pub.L. 98–353.

Amendments

1988 Amendments. Subsec. (d). Pub.L. 100–702 added subsec. (d).

1987 Amendments. Subsec. (a). Pub.L. 100–202 substituted salary at a rate equal to 92 percent of the salary of a district court judge as determined pursuant to section 135 of this title, for salary at a rate determined under section 225 of the Federal Salary Act of 1967 [2 U.S.C.A. § 351 et seq.] as adjusted by section 461 of this title.

Effective and Applicability Provisions

1987 Acts. Section 101(a) [Title IV, § 408(d)] of Pub.L. 100–202 provided that: "This section [amending this section, section 634 of this title, and section 356 of Title 2, The Congress] shall become effective October 1, 1988, and any salary affected by the provisions of this section shall be adjusted at the beginning of the first applicable pay period commencing on or after such date of enactment [probably should read "such date", meaning Oct. 1, 1988]."

1984 Acts. Section effective July 10, 1984, see section 122(a) of Pub.L. 98–353, set out as a note under section 151 of this title.

Continuation of Salaries of Bankruptcy Judges in Effect on June 27, 1984

Section 105(a) of Pub.L. 98–353 provided that: "The salary of a bankruptcy judge in effect on June 27, 1984, shall remain in effect until changed as a result of a determination or adjustment made pursuant to section 153(a) of title 28, United States Code, as added by this Act [subsec. (a) of this section]."

Increase in Salaries

1988—Salaries of bankruptcy judges continued at $72,500 per annum by Ex. Ord. No. 12622, Dec. 31, 1987, 53 F.R. 222, formerly set out as a note under section 5332 of Title 5, Government Organization and Employees.

1987—Salaries of bankruptcy judges increased to $72,500 per annum, on recommendation of the President of the United States, see note set out under section 358 of Title 2, The Congress.

Salaries of bankruptcy judges increased to $70,500 effective on the first day of the first pay period beginning on or after January 1, 1987, by Ex. Ord. No. 12578, Dec. 31, 1986, 52 F.R. 505, formerly set out as a note under section 5332 of Title 5.

1985—Salaries of bankruptcy judges increased to $68,400 effective on the first day of the first pay period beginning on or after Jan. 1, 1985, by Ex. Ord. No. 12496, Dec. 28, 1984, 50

F.R. 211, as amended by Ex. Ord. No. 12540, Dec. 30, 1985, 51 F.R. 577, formerly set out as a note under section 5332 of Title 5.

1984—Salaries of bankruptcy judges (full-time) and bankruptcy judges (part-time) (maximum rate) increased to $66,100 and $33,100, respectively, effective on the first day of the first pay period beginning on or after Jan. 1, 1984, by Ex. Ord. No. 12456, Dec. 30, 1983, 49 F.R. 347, as amended Ex. Ord. No. 12477, May 23, 1984, 49 F.R. 22041; Ex. Ord. No. 12487, Sept. 14, 1984, 49 F.R. 36493, formerly set out as a note under section 5332 of Title 5.

1982—Salaries of bankruptcy judges and referees in bankruptcy (full-time), or referees in bankruptcy (part-time) (maximum rate) increased to $63,600 and $31,800, respectively, effective on the first day of the first pay period beginning on or after Oct. 1, 1982, by Ex. Ord. No. 12387, Oct. 8, 1982, 47 F.R. 44981, formerly set out as a note under section 5332 of Title 5, Government Organization and Employees. Ex. Ord. No. 12387 further provided that pursuant to section 101(e) of Pub.L. 97–276 funds are not available to pay a salary at a rate which exceeds the rate in effect on Sept. 30, 1982, which was $58,500 for bankruptcy judges and referees in bankruptcy (full-time), and $30,600 for referees in bankruptcy (part-time) (maximum rate).

Maximum rate payable to bankruptcy judges after Dec. 17, 1982, increased from $58,500 to $63,600, see Pub.L. 97–377, Title I, § 129(b)–(d), Dec. 21, 1982, 96 Stat. 1914, set out as a note under section 5318 of Title 5.

1981—Salaries of bankruptcy judges and referees in bankruptcy (full-time), or referees in bankruptcy (part-time) (maximum rate) increased to $61,200 and $30,600, respectively, effective on the first day of the first pay period beginning on or after Oct. 1, 1981, by Ex. Ord. No. 12330, Oct. 15, 1981, 46 F.R. 50921, formerly set out as a note under section 5332 of Title 5. Ex. Ord. No. 12330 further provided that pursuant to section 101(c) of Pub.L. 97–51 funds are not available to pay a salary at a rate which exceeds the rate in effect on Sept. 30, 1981, which was $51,167.50 for bankruptcy judges and referees in bankruptcy (full-time), and $25,583.75 for referees in bankruptcy (part-time) (maximum rate).

1980—Salaries of bankruptcy judges and referees in bankruptcy (full-time), or referees in bankruptcy (part-time) (maximum rate) increased to $58,400 and $29,200, respectively, effective on the first day of the first pay period beginning on or after Oct. 1, 1980, by Ex. Ord. No. 12248, Oct. 16, 1980, 45 F.R. 69199, formerly set out as a note under section 5332 of Title 5. Ex. Ord. No. 12248 further provided that pursuant to section 101(c) of Pub.L. 96–369 funds are not available to pay a salary which exceeds the rate in effect on Sept. 30, 1980, which was $51,167.50 for bankruptcy judges and referees in bankruptcy (full-time), and $25,583.75 for referees in bankruptcy (part-time) (maximum rate).

For limitations on use of funds for period Oct. 1, 1980 through June 5, 1981, appropriated by any Act to pay the salary or pay of any individual in legislative, executive, or judicial branch in position equal to or above level V of the Executive Schedule, see section 101(c) of Pub.L. 96–369 and section 101(c) of Pub.L. 96–536, set out as notes under section 5318 of Title 5.

1979—Salaries of bankruptcy judges increased to $53,500 effective on the first day of the first applicable pay period beginning on or after Oct. 1, 1979, by Ex. Ord. No. 12165, Oct. 9, 1979, 44 F.R. 58671, as amended by Ex. Ord. No. 12200, Mar. 12, 1980, 45 F.R. 16443, formerly set out as a note under

section 5332 of Title 5. Ex. Ord. No. 12165 further provided that pursuant to Pub.L. 96–86 funds appropriated for fiscal year 1980 may not be used to pay a salary at a rate which exceeds an increase of 5.5 percent over the applicable rate payable for such position or office in effect on Sept. 30, 1978, which was $51,167.50 for bankruptcy judges.

Part–Time Bankruptcy Judges

For provision that notwithstanding subsecs. (a) and (b) of this section, a bankruptcy judge serving on a part-time basis on July 10, 1984, may continue to serve on such basis for two years from such date, and may engage in the practice of law, see section 106 of Pub.L. 98–353, set out as a note under section 152 of this title.

Transition Provisions

Section 1003(b) of Pub.L. 100–702 provided that:

"(1) If an individual who is exempted from the Leave Act by operation of amendments under this section [amending this section and sections 156, 631, 634, 712, 752, and 794 of this title] and who was previously subject to the provisions of subchapter I of chapter 63 of title 5, United States Code [section 6301 et seq. of Title 5, Government Organization and Employees], without a break in service, again becomes subject to this subchapter on completion of his service as an exempted officer, the unused annual leave and sick leave standing to his credit when he was exempted from this subchapter is deemed to have remained to his credit.

"(2) In computing an annuity under section 8339 of title 5, United States Code [section 8339 of Title 5], the total service of a person specified in paragraph (1) of this subsection who retired on an immediate annuity or dies leaving a survivor or survivors entitled to an annuity includes, without regard to the limitations imposed by subsection (f) of section 8339 of title 5, United States Code [section 8339(f) of Title 5], the days of unused sick leave standing to his credit when he was exempted from subchapter I of chapter 63 of title 5, United States Code [section 6301 et seq. of Title 5], except that these days will not be counted in determining average pay or annuity eligibility."

LIBRARY REFERENCES

American Digest System

Bankruptcy ⬅2123.

Key Number System Topic No. 51.

Corpus Juris Secundum

CJS Bankruptcy § 31, Restrictions and Limitations on Activities and Practices of Judges.

§ 154. Division of businesses; chief judge

(a) Each bankruptcy court for a district having more than one bankruptcy judge shall by majority vote promulgate rules for the division of business among the bankruptcy judges to the extent that the division of business is not otherwise provided for by the rules of the district court.

(b) In each district court having more than one bankruptcy judge the district court shall designate one judge to serve as chief judge of such bankruptcy court. Whenever a majority of the judges of such district court cannot agree upon the designation as chief judge, the chief judge of such district court shall make such designation. The chief judge of the bankruptcy court shall ensure that the rules of the bankruptcy court and of the district court are observed and that the business of the bankruptcy court is handled effectively and expeditiously.

(Added Pub.L. 98–353, Title I, § 104(a), July 10, 1984, 98 Stat. 339.)

HISTORICAL AND STATUTORY NOTES

Revision Notes and Legislative Reports

1984 Acts. Statements by Legislative Leaders, see 1984 U.S.Code Cong. and Adm.News, p. 576.

Codifications

This section as added by Pub.L. 95–598, Title II, § 201(a), Nov. 6, 1978, 92 Stat. 2657, effective June 28, 1984, pursuant to Pub.L. 95–598, Title IV, § 402(b), Nov. 6, 1978, 92 Stat. 2682, as amended by Pub.L. 98–249, § 1(a), Mar. 31, 1984, 98 Stat. 116; Pub.L. 98–271, § 1(a), Apr. 30, 1984, 98 Stat. 163; Pub.L. 98–299, § 1(a), May 25, 1984, 98 Stat. 214; Pub.L. 98–325, § 1(a), June 20, 1984, 98 Stat. 268, set out as a note preceding section 101 of Title 11, Bankruptcy, read as follows:

§ 154. Salaries of bankruptcy judges

Each judge of a bankruptcy court shall receive a salary at an annual rate of $50,000, subject to adjustment under section 225 of the Federal Salary Act of 1967 (2 U.S.C. 351–361), and section 461 of this title.

Section 402(b) of Pub.L. 95–598 was amended by section 113 of Pub.L. 98–353 by substituting "shall not be effective" for "shall take effect on June 28, 1984", thereby eliminating the addition of section 154 by section 201(a) of Pub.L. 95–598, effective June 27, 1984, pursuant to section 122(c) of Pub.L. 98–353, set out as an Effective Date note under section 151 of this title.

Section 121(a) of Pub.L. 98–353 directed that section 402(b) of Pub.L. 95–598 be amended by substituting "the date of enactment of the Bankruptcy Amendments and Federal Judgeship Act of 1984 [i.e. July 10, 1984]" for "June 28, 1984". This amendment was not executed in view of the prior amendment to section 402(b) of Pub.L. 95–598 by section 113 of Pub.L. 98–353.

Effective and Applicability Provisions

1984 Acts. Section effective July 10, 1984, see section 122(a) of Pub.L. 98–353, set out as a note under section 151 of this title.

LIBRARY REFERENCES

American Digest System

Bankruptcy ⟐2127.1, 2129.
Key Number System Topic No. 51.

Corpus Juris Secundum

CJS Bankruptcy § 29, Chief Judge; Division of Business.

§ 155.   Temporary transfer of bankruptcy judges

(a) A bankruptcy judge may be transferred to serve temporarily as a bankruptcy judge in any judicial district other than the judicial district for which such bankruptcy judge was appointed upon the approval of the judicial council of each of the circuits involved.

(b) A bankruptcy judge who has retired may, upon consent, be recalled to serve as a bankruptcy judge in any judicial district by the judicial council of the circuit within which such district is located. Upon recall, a bankruptcy judge may receive a salary for such service in accordance with regulations promulgated by the Judicial Conference of the United States, subject to the restrictions on the payment of an annuity in section 377 of this title or in subchapter III of chapter 83, and chapter 84, of title 5 which are applicable to such judge.

(Added Pub.L. 98–353, Title I, § 104(a), July 10, 1984, 98 Stat. 339; amended Pub.L. 99–651, Title II, § 202(a), Nov. 14, 1986, 100 Stat. 3648; Pub.L. 100–659, § 4(a), Nov. 15, 1988, 102 Stat. 3918.)

HISTORICAL AND STATUTORY NOTES

Revision Notes and Legislative Reports

1984 Acts. Statements by Legislative Leaders, see 1984 U.S.Code Cong. and Adm.News, p. 576.

1986 Acts. House Report No. 99–417, see 1986 U.S.Code Cong. and Adm.News, p. 6165.

1988 Acts. Senate Report No. 100–293, and House Conference Report No. 100–1072, see 1988 U.S.Code Cong. and Adm.News, p. 5564.

Codifications

This section as added by Pub.L. 95–598, Title II, § 201(a), Nov. 6, 1978, 92 Stat. 2658, effective June 28, 1984, pursuant to Pub.L. 95–598, Title IV, § 402(b), Nov. 6, 1978, 92 Stat. 2682, as amended by Pub.L. 98–249, § 1(a), Mar. 31, 1984, 98 Stat. 116; Pub.L. 98–271, § 1(a), Apr. 30, 1984, 98 Stat. 163; Pub.L. 98–299, § 1(a), May 25, 1984, 98 Stat. 214; Pub.L. 98–325, § 1(a), June 20, 1984, 98 Stat. 268, set out as a note preceding section 101 of Title 11, Bankruptcy, read as follows:

§ 155. Chief judge; precedence of bankruptcy judges

(a) In each district having more than one judge the bankruptcy judge in regular active service who is senior in commission and under seventy years of age shall be the chief judge of the bankruptcy court. If all the bankruptcy judges in regular active service are 70 years of age or older the youngest shall act as chief judge until a judge has been appointed and qualified who is under 70 years of age, but a judge may not act as chief judge until he has served as a bankruptcy judge for one year.

(b) The chief judge shall have precedence and preside at any session which he attends.

Other bankruptcy judges shall have precedence and preside according to the seniority of their commissions. Judges whose commissions bear the same date shall have precedence according to seniority in age.

(c) A judge whose commission extends over more than one district shall be junior to all bankruptcy judges except in the district in which he resided at the time he entered upon the duties of his office.

(d) If a chief judge desires to be relieved of his duties as chief judge while retaining his active status as a bankruptcy judge, he may so certify to the chief judge of the court of appeals for the circuit in which the bankruptcy judge serves, and thereafter the bankruptcy judge in active service next in precedence and willing to serve shall be designated by the chief judge of the court of appeals as the chief judge of the bankruptcy court.

(e) If a chief judge is temporarily unable to perform his duties as such, they shall be performed by the bankruptcy judge in active service, present in the district and able and qualified to act, who is next in precedence.

(f) Service as a referee in bankruptcy or as a bankruptcy judge under the Bankruptcy Act shall be taken into account in the determination of seniority of commission under this section.

Section 402(b) of Pub.L. 95–598 was amended by section 113 of Pub.L. 98–353 by substituting "shall not be effective" for "shall take effect on June 28, 1984", thereby eliminating the addition of section 155 by section 201(a) of Pub.L. 95–598, effective June 27, 1984, pursuant to section 122(c) of Pub.L. 98–353, set out as an Effective Date note under section 151 of this title.

Section 121(a) of Pub.L. 98–353 directed that section 402(b) of Pub.L. 95–598 be amended by substituting "the date of enactment of the Bankruptcy Amendments and Federal Judgeship Act of 1984 [i.e. July 10, 1984]" for "June 28, 1984". This amendment was not executed in view of the prior amendment to section 402(b) of Pub.L. 95–598 by section 113 of Pub.L. 98–353.

Amendments

1988 Amendments. Subsec. (b). Pub.L. 100–659, § 4(a), inserted "section 377 of this title or in" after "annuity in" and "which are applicable to such judge" after "title 5", respectively.

1986 Amendments. Subsec. (b). Pub.L. 99–651, § 202(a), added reference to chapter 84 of Title 5.

Effective and Applicability Provisions

1988 Acts. Amendment to this section by Pub.L. 100–659 to take effect on Nov. 15, 1988, and shall apply to bankruptcy judges and magistrates who retire on or after Nov. 15, 1988, with special election provisions for bankruptcy judges, etc., who left office on or after July 31, 1987, and before Nov. 15, 1988, see section 9 of Pub.L. 100–659, set out as a note under section 377 of this title.

1986 Acts. Section 203 of Title II of Pub.L. 99–651 provided that: "This title and the amendments made by this title [enacting section 375 of this title, and amending sections 155, 374, 631, 633, 636, and 797 of this title] take effect on January 1, 1987."

1984 Acts. Section effective July 10, 1984, see section 122(a) of Pub.L. 98–353, set out as a note under section 151 of this title.

CROSS REFERENCES

Recall of retired judges—

Generally, see 28 USCA § 375.

Actual abode deemed official station for purposes of residency, see 28 USCA § 374.

Practicing attorney not eligible for recall, see 28 USCA § 377.

LIBRARY REFERENCES

American Digest System

Bankruptcy ⊕2123.

Key Number System Topic No. 51.

§ 156.   Staff; expenses

(a) Each bankruptcy judge may appoint a secretary, a law clerk, and such additional assistants as the Director of the Administrative Office of the United States Courts determines to be necessary. A law clerk appointed under this section shall be exempt from the provisions of subchapter I of chapter 63 of title 5, unless specifically included by the appointing judge or by local rule of court.

(b) Upon certification to the judicial council of the circuit involved and to the Director of the Administrative Office of the United States Courts that the number of cases and proceedings pending within the jurisdiction under section 1334 of this title within a judicial district so warrants, the bankruptcy judges for such district may appoint an individual to serve as clerk of such bankruptcy court. The clerk may appoint, with the approval of such bankruptcy judges, and in such number as may be approved by the Director, necessary deputies, and may remove such deputies with the approval of such bankruptcy judges.

(c) Any court may utilize facilities or services, either on or off the court's premises, which pertain to the provision of notices, dockets, calendars, and other administrative information to parties in cases filed under the provisions of title 11, United States Code, where the costs of such facilities or services are paid for out of the assets of the estate and are not charged to the United States. The utilization of such facilities or services shall be subject to such conditions and limitations as the pertinent circuit council may prescribe.

(d) No office of the bankruptcy clerk of court may be consolidated with the district clerk of court office without the prior approval of the Judicial Conference and the Congress.

(e) In a judicial district where a bankruptcy clerk has been appointed pursuant to subsection (b), the bankruptcy clerk shall be the official custodian of the records and dockets of the bankruptcy court.

(f) For purposes of financial accountability in a district where a bankruptcy clerk has been certified, such clerk shall be accountable for and pay into the Treasury all fees, costs, and other monies collected by such clerk except uncollected fees not required by an Act of Congress to be prepaid. Such clerk shall make returns thereof to the Director of the Administrative Office of the United States Courts and the Director of the Executive Office For United States Trustees, under regulations prescribed by such Directors.

(Added Pub.L. 98–353, Title I, § 104(a), July 10, 1984, 98 Stat. 339; amended Pub.L. 99–554, Title I, §§ 103, 142, 144(a), Oct. 27, 1986, 100 Stat. 3090, 3096; Pub.L. 100–702, Title X, § 1003(a)(3), Nov. 19, 1988, 102 Stat. 4665.)

HISTORICAL AND STATUTORY NOTES

Revision Notes and Legislative Reports

1984 Acts. Statements by Legislative Leaders, see 1984 U.S. Code Cong. and Adm. News, p. 576.

1986 Acts. House Report No. 99–764 and House Conference Report No. 99–958, see 1986 U.S. Code Cong. and Adm. News, p. 5227.

1988 Acts. House Report No. 100–889, see 1988 U.S. Code Cong. and Adm. News, p. 5982.

Codifications

This section as added by Pub.L. 95–598, Title II, § 201(a), Nov. 6, 1978, 92 Stat. 2659, effective June 28, 1984, pursuant to Pub.L. 95–598, Title IV, § 402(b), Nov. 6, 1978, 92 Stat. 2682, as amended by Pub.L. 98–249, § 1(a), Mar. 31, 1984, 98 Stat. 116; Pub.L. 98–271, § 1(a), Apr. 30, 1984, 98 Stat. 163; Pub.L. 98–299, § 1(a), May 25, 1984, 98 Stat. 214; Pub.L. 98–325, § 1(a), June 20, 1984, 98 Stat. 268, set out as a note preceding section 101 of Title 11, Bankruptcy, read as follows:

§ 156. Division of business among bankruptcy judges

The business of a bankruptcy court having more than one judge shall be divided among the judges as provided by the rules and orders of the court.

The chief judge of the bankruptcy court shall be responsible for the observance of such rules and orders, and shall divide the business and assign the cases so far as such rules and orders do not otherwise prescribe.

If the bankruptcy judges in any district are unable to agree upon the adoption of rules or orders for that purpose the judicial council of the circuit shall make the necessary orders.

Section 402(b) of Pub.L. 95–598 was amended by section 113 of Pub.L. 98–353 by substituting "shall not be effective" for "shall take effect on June 28, 1984", thereby eliminating the addition of section 156 by section 201(a) of Pub.L. 95–598, effective June 27, 1984, pursuant to section 122(c) of Pub.L. 98–353, set out as an Effective Date note under section 151 of this title.

Section 121(a) of Pub.L. 98–353 directed that section 402(b) of Pub.L. 95–598 be amended by substituting "the date of enactment of the Bankruptcy Amendments and Federal Judgeship Act of 1984 [i.e. July 10, 1984]" for "June 28, 1984". This amendment was not executed in view of the prior amendment to section 402(b) of Pub.L. 95–598 by section 113 of Pub.L. 98–353.

Amendments

1988 Amendments. Subsec. (a). Pub.L. 100–702 added provision that a law clerk appointed under this section be exempt from the provisions of subchapter I of chapter 63 of title 5, unless specifically included by the appointing judge or by local rule of court.

1986 Amendments. Subsec. (d). Pub.L. 99–554, § 103, added subsec. (d).

Subsec. (e). Pub.L. 99–554, § 142, added subsec. (e).

Subsec. (f). Pub.L. 99–554, § 144(a), added subsec. (f).

Effective and Applicability Provisions

1986 Acts. Amendment of subsec. (d) by section 103 of Pub.L. 99–554 effective on Oct. 27, 1986, see section 302(b) of Pub.L. 99–554, set out as a note under section 581 of this title.

Enactment of subsecs. (e) and (f) by sections 142 and 144(a) of Pub.L. 99–554 effective 30 days after Oct. 27, 1986, except as otherwise provided for, see section 302(a) of Pub.L. 99–554, set out as a note under section 581 of this title.

1984 Acts. Section effective July 10, 1984, see section 122(a) of Pub.L. 98–353, set out as a note under section 151 of this title.

§ 157. Procedures

(a) Each district court may provide that any or all cases under title 11 and any or all proceedings arising under title 11 or arising in or related to a case under title 11 shall be referred to the bankruptcy judges for the district.

(b)(1) Bankruptcy judges may hear and determine all cases under title 11 and all core proceedings arising under title 11, or arising in a case under title 11, referred under subsection (a) of this section, and may enter appropriate orders and judgments, subject to review under section 158 of this title.

(2) Core proceedings include, but are not limited to—

(A) matters concerning the administration of the estate;

(B) allowance or disallowance of claims against the estate or exemptions from property of the estate, and estimation of claims or interests for the purposes of confirming a plan under chapter 11, 12, or 13 of title 11 but not the liquidation or estimation of contingent or unliquidated personal injury tort or wrongful death claims against the estate for purposes of distribution in a case under title 11;

(C) counterclaims by the estate against persons filing claims against the estate;

(D) orders in respect to obtaining credit;

(E) orders to turn over property of the estate;

(F) proceedings to determine, avoid, or recover preferences;

(G) motions to terminate, annul, or modify the automatic stay;

(H) proceedings to determine, avoid, or recover fraudulent conveyances;

(I) determinations as to the dischargeability of particular debts;

(J) objections to discharges;

(K) determinations of the validity, extent, or priority of liens;

(L) confirmations of plans;

(M) orders approving the use or lease of property, including the use of cash collateral;

(N) orders approving the sale of property other than property resulting from claims brought by the estate against persons who have not filed claims against the estate;

(O) other proceedings affecting the liquidation of the assets of the estate or the adjustment of the debtor-creditor or the equity security holder relationship, except personal injury tort or wrongful death claims; and

(P) recognition of foreign proceedings and other matters under chapter 15 of title 11.

(3) The bankruptcy judge shall determine, on the judge's own motion or on timely motion of a party, whether a proceeding is a core proceeding under this subsection or is a proceeding that is otherwise related to a case under title 11. A determination that a proceeding is not a core proceeding shall not be made solely on the basis that its resolution may be affected by State law.

(4) Non-core proceedings under section 157(b)(2)(B) of title 28, United States Code, shall not be subject to the mandatory abstention provisions of section 1334(c)(2).

(5) The district court shall order that personal injury tort and wrongful death claims shall be tried in the district court in which the bankruptcy case is pending, or in the district court in the district in which the claim arose, as determined by the district court in which the bankruptcy case is pending.

(c)(1) A bankruptcy judge may hear a proceeding that is not a core proceeding but that is otherwise related to a case under title 11. In such proceeding, the bankruptcy judge shall submit proposed findings of fact and conclusions of law to the district court, and any final order or judgment shall be entered by the district judge after considering the bankruptcy judge's proposed findings and conclusions and after reviewing de novo those matters to which any party has timely and specifically objected.

(2) Notwithstanding the provisions of paragraph (1) of this subsection, the district court, with the consent of all the parties to the proceeding, may refer a proceeding related to a case under title 11 to a bankruptcy judge to hear and determine and to enter appropriate orders and judgments, subject to review under section 158 of this title.

(d) The district court may withdraw, in whole or in part, any case or proceeding referred under this section, on its own motion or on timely motion of any party, for cause shown. The district court shall, on timely motion of a party, so withdraw a proceeding if the court determines that resolution of the proceeding requires consideration of both title 11 and other laws of the United States regulating organizations or activities affecting interstate commerce.

(e) If the right to a jury trial applies in a proceeding that may be heard under this section by a bankruptcy judge, the bankruptcy judge may conduct the jury trial if specially designated to exercise such jurisdiction by the district court and with the express consent of all the parties.

(Added Pub.L. 98–353, Title I, § 104(a), July 10, 1984, 98 Stat. 340; amended Pub.L. 99–554, Title I, §§ 143, 144(b), Oct. 27, 1986, 100 Stat. 3096; Pub.L. 103–394, Title I, § 112, Oct. 22, 1994, 108 Stat. 4117; Pub.L. 109–8, Title VIII, § 802(c)(1), Apr. 20, 2005, 119 Stat. 145.)

HISTORICAL AND STATUTORY NOTES

Revision Notes and Legislative Reports

1984 Acts. Statements by Legislative Leaders, see 1984 U.S. Code Cong. and Adm. News, p. 576.

1986 Acts. House Report No. 99–764 and House Conference Report No. 99–958, see 1986 U.S. Code Cong. and Adm. News, p. 5227.

1994 Acts. House Report No. 103–835, see 1994 U.S. Code Cong. and Adm. News, p. 3340.

2005 Acts. House Report No. 109–31(Part I), see 2005 U.S. Code Cong. and Adm. News, p. 88.

References in Text

Chapter 11, 12, or 13 of title 11, referred to in subsec. (b)(2)(B), is 11 U.S.C.A. § 1101 et seq., 11 U.S.C.A. § 1201 et seq., or 11 U.S.C.A. § 1301 et seq., respectively.

Chapter 15 of title 11, referred to in subsec. (b)(2)(P), is 11 U.S.C.A. § 1501 et seq.

Codifications

This section as added by Pub.L. 95–598, Title II, § 201(a), Nov. 6, 1978, 92 Stat. 2659, effective June 28, 1984, pursuant to Pub.L. 95–598, Title IV, § 402(b), Nov. 6, 1978, 92 Stat. 2682, as amended by Pub.L. 98–249, § 1(a), Mar. 31, 1984, 98 Stat. 116; Pub.L. 98–271, § 1(a), Apr. 30, 1984, 98 Stat. 163; Pub.L. 98–299, § 1(a), May 25, 1984, 98 Stat. 214; Pub.L. 98–325, § 1(a), June 20, 1984, 98 Stat. 268, set out as a note preceding section 101 of Title 11, Bankruptcy, read as follows:

"**§ 157. Times of holding court**

"**(a)** The bankruptcy court at each designated location shall be deemed to be in continuous session on all business days throughout the year.

"**(b)** Each bankruptcy court may establish by local rule or order schedules of court sessions at designated places of holding court other than the headquarters office of the court. Such schedules may be pretermitted by order of the court.

"**(c)** Bankruptcy court may be held at any place within the territory served, in any case, on order of the bankruptcy court, for the convenience of the parties, on such notice as the bankruptcy court orders."

Section 402(b) of Pub.L. 95–598 was amended by section 113 of Pub.L. 98–353 by substituting "shall not be effective" for "shall take effect on June 28, 1984", thereby eliminating the addition of section 157 by section 201(a) of Pub.L. 95–598, effective June 27, 1984, pursuant to section 122(c) of Pub.L. 98–353, set out as an Effective Date note under section 151 of this title.

Section 121(a) of Pub.L. 98–353 directed that section 402(b) of Pub.L. 95–598 be amended by substituting "the date of enactment of the Bankruptcy Amendments and Federal

Judgeship Act of 1984 [i.e. July 10, 1984]" for "June 28, 1984". This amendment was not executed in view of the prior amendment to section 402(b) of Pub.L. 95–598 by section 113 of Pub.L. 98–353.

Amendments

2005 Amendments. Subsec. (b)(2)(N). Pub.L. 109–8, § 802(c)(1)(A), struck out "and" at the end of subpar. (N).

Subsec. (b)(2)(O). Pub.L. 109–8, § 802(c)(1)(B), struck out the period at the end and inserted "; and".

Subsec. (b)(2)(P). Pub.L. 109–8, § 802(c)(1)(C), added subpar. (P).

1994 Amendments. Subsec. (e). Pub.L. 103–394, § 112, added subsec. (e).

1986 Amendments. Subsec. (b)(2)(B). Pub.L. 99–554, § 143, added reference to chapter 12.

Pub.L. 99–554, § 144(b)(1), substituted "interests" for "interest".

Subsec. (b)(2)(G). Pub.L. 99–554, § 144(b)(2), substituted "annul," for "annul".

Effective and Applicability Provisions

2005 Acts. Except as otherwise provided, amendments by Pub.L. 109–8 effective 180 days after April 20, 2005, and inapplicable with respect to cases commenced under Title 11 before the effective date, see Pub.L. 109–8, § 1501, set out as a note under 11 U.S.C.A. § 101.

1994 Acts. Amendment by Pub.L. 103–394 effective on Oct. 22, 1994, and not to apply with respect to cases commenced under Title 11 of the United States Code before Oct. 22, 1994, see section 702 of Pub.L. 103–394, set out as a note under section 101 of Title 11, Bankruptcy.

1986 Acts. Amendment by Pub.L. 99–554 effective 30 days after Oct. 27, 1986, except as otherwise provided for, see section 302(a) of Pub.L. 99–554, set out as a note under section 581 of this title.

1984 Acts. Section effective July 10, 1984, see section 122(a) of Pub.L. 98–353, set out as a note under section 151 of this title.

Separability of Provisions

If any provision of or amendment made by Pub.L. 103–394 or the application of such provision or amendment to any person or circumstance is held to be unconstitutional, the remaining provisions of and amendments made by Pub.L. 103–394 and the application of such provisions and amendments to any person or circumstance shall not be affected thereby, see section 701 of Pub.L. 103–394, set out as a note under section 101 of Title 11, Bankruptcy.

CROSS REFERENCES

Supplemental injunctions and power of district court to refer proceedings, see 11 USCA § 524.

LIBRARY REFERENCES

American Digest System

Bankruptcy ⚬2041.1 to 2063, 2101 to 2105, 2130.
Key Number System Topic No. 51.

Corpus Juris Secundum

CJS Bankruptcy § 9, Title 28 of the U.S. Code.
CJS Bankruptcy § 21, Powers of District Court in Relation to Bankruptcy Judges.

CJS Bankruptcy § 158, What Are Proceedings Arising in Cases Under Title 11.

CJS Bankruptcy § 163, Constitutional Underpinnings; the Northern Pipeline Case.

CJS Bankruptcy § 164, Judicial Determination Whether Proceeding is Core.

CJS Bankruptcy § 166, Relationship to Bankruptcy Code.

CJS Bankruptcy § 167, Relationship to State Law.

CJS Bankruptcy § 169, Broad or Narrow Construction.

CJS Bankruptcy § 170, Catchall Provisions.

CJS Bankruptcy § 171, Proceeding Falling Within Enumerated Category May be Noncore.

CJS Bankruptcy § 173, Automatic Stay; Injunctive Relief.

CJS Bankruptcy § 174, Motions to Abstain or Remand.

CJS Bankruptcy § 175, Equitable Subordination and Reclamation.

CJS Bankruptcy § 176, Contracts and Leases.

CJS Bankruptcy § 177, Governmental Regulations.

CJS Bankruptcy § 178, Employment and Compensation of Professional Persons.

CJS Bankruptcy § 180, Breach of Warranty.

CJS Bankruptcy § 183, State Law Basis for Counterclaims.

CJS Bankruptcy § 185, Effect of Disputed Liability or Unmatured Claim.

CJS Bankruptcy § 187, Sanctions for Violating Stay.

CJS Bankruptcy § 189, Actions Based on State Law.

CJS Bankruptcy § 190, Orders With Respect to Obtaining Credit.

CJS Bankruptcy § 191, Proceedings to Determine, Avoid, or Recover Preferences.

CJS Bankruptcy § 192, Determinations as to Dischargeability of Particular Debts.

CJS Bankruptcy § 193, Objections to Discharge.

CJS Bankruptcy § 194, Determination of Validity, Extent, or Priority of Liens.

CJS Bankruptcy § 195, Confirmations of Plans.

CJS Bankruptcy § 196, Orders Approving Use or Lease of Property, Including Use of Cash Collateral.

CJS Bankruptcy § 197, Orders Approving Certain Sales of Property.

CJS Bankruptcy § 198, Recognition of Foreign Proceedings and Other Matters Under Chapter 15.

CJS Bankruptcy § 199, Other Proceedings Affecting Liquidation of Estate Assets or Adjustment of Debtor-Creditor/Equity-Security Holder Relationship.

CJS Bankruptcy § 200, Other Proceedings Affecting Liquidation of Estate Assets or Adjustment of Debtor-Creditor/Equity-Security Holder Relationship--Actions Involving State Law.

CJS Bankruptcy § 208, Exclusion of Personal-Injury-Tort and Wrongful-Death Claims.

CJS Bankruptcy § 214, Power of Bankruptcy Judges to Hear Cases and Proceedings.

CJS Bankruptcy § 215, Core Proceedings.

CJS Bankruptcy § 218, District Court's De Novo Review.

CJS Bankruptcy § 219, Consent to Final Determination by Bankruptcy Judge.

CJS Bankruptcy § 221, Consent to Final Determination by Bankruptcy Judge--Waiver of Objection.

CJS Bankruptcy § 222, Personal-Injury-Tort and Wrongful-Death Claims.

CJS Bankruptcy § 224, Discretionary Withdrawal.

CJS Bankruptcy § 225, Mandatory Withdrawal.

CJS Bankruptcy § 226, Mandatory Withdrawal--What Are Other Federal Laws Regulating Organizations or Activities Affecting Interstate Commerce.

CJS Bankruptcy § 227, Impact on Withdrawal of Core or Noncore Nature of Proceeding.

CJS Bankruptcy § 228, Timeliness of Court's Withdrawal Sua Sponte or Withdrawal Motion.

CJS Bankruptcy § 235, Referral of Removed Claim to Bankruptcy Judge.

CJS Bankruptcy § 274, Personal-Injury-Tort and Wrongful-Death Claims.

CJS Bankruptcy § 310, General Procedures.

CJS Bankruptcy § 311, When Does Right to Trial by Jury Exist.

CJS Bankruptcy § 615, Core Nature of Turnover Proceedings.

CJS Bankruptcy § 733, Nature of Proceedings; Right to Jury Trial.

CJS Bankruptcy § 900, Motion for Authorization to Obtain Credit; Notice and Hearing.

CJS Bankruptcy § 1046, Generally; Objections to Discharge.

CJS Bankruptcy § 1162, Implementation of the Plan; Distribution.

CJS Bankruptcy § 1216, Review of Bankruptcy Court's Proposed Findings and Conclusions.

CJS Juries § 96, Insolvency; Bankruptcy Proceedings.

§ 158. Appeals

(a) The district courts of the United States shall have jurisdiction to hear appeals [1]

(1) from final judgments, orders, and decrees;

(2) from interlocutory orders and decrees issued under section 1121(d) of title 11 increasing or reducing the time periods referred to in section 1121 of such title; and

(3) with leave of the court, from other interlocutory orders and decrees;

and, with leave of the court, from interlocutory orders and decrees, of bankruptcy judges entered in cases and proceedings referred to the bankruptcy judges under section 157 of this title. An appeal under this subsection shall be taken only to the district court for the judicial district in which the bankruptcy judge is serving.

(b)(1) The judicial council of a circuit shall establish a bankruptcy appellate panel service composed of bankruptcy judges of the districts in the circuit who are appointed by the judicial council in accordance with paragraph (3), to hear and determine, with the consent of all the parties, appeals under subsection (a) unless the judicial council finds that—

(A) there are insufficient judicial resources available in the circuit; or

(B) establishment of such service would result in undue delay or increased cost to parties in cases under title 11.

Not later than 90 days after making the finding, the judicial council shall submit to the Judicial Conference of the United States a report containing the factual basis of such finding.

(2)(A) A judicial council may reconsider, at any time, the finding described in paragraph (1).

(B) On the request of a majority of the district judges in a circuit for which a bankruptcy appellate panel service is established under paragraph (1), made after the expiration of the 1–year period beginning on the date such service is established, the judicial council of the circuit shall determine whether a circumstance specified in subparagraph (A) or (B) of such paragraph exists.

(C) On its own motion, after the expiration of the 3–year period beginning on the date a bankruptcy appellate panel service is established under paragraph (1), the judicial council of the circuit may determine whether a circumstance specified in subparagraph (A) or (B) of such paragraph exists.

(D) If the judicial council finds that either of such circumstances exists, the judicial council may provide for the completion of the appeals then pending before such service and the orderly termination of such service.

(3) Bankruptcy judges appointed under paragraph (1) shall be appointed and may be reappointed under such paragraph.

(4) If authorized by the Judicial Conference of the United States, the judicial councils of 2 or more circuits may establish a joint bankruptcy appellate panel comprised of bankruptcy judges from the districts within the circuits for which such panel is established, to hear and determine, upon the consent of all the parties, appeals under subsection (a) of this section.

(5) An appeal to be heard under this subsection shall be heard by a panel of 3 members of the bankruptcy appellate panel service, except that a member of such service may not hear an appeal originating in the district for which such member is appointed or designated under section 152 of this title.

(6) Appeals may not be heard under this subsection by a panel of the bankruptcy appellate panel service unless the district judges for the district in which the appeals occur, by majority vote, have authorized such service to hear and determine appeals originating in such district.

(c)(1) Subject to subsections (b) and (d)(2), each appeal under subsection (a) shall be heard by a 3–judge panel of the bankruptcy appellate panel service established under subsection (b)(1) unless—

(A) the appellant elects at the time of filing the appeal; or

(B) any other party elects, not later than 30 days after service of notice of the appeal;

to have such appeal heard by the district court.

(2) An appeal under subsections (a) and (b) of this section shall be taken in the same manner as appeals in civil proceedings generally are taken to the courts of appeals from the district courts and in the time provided by Rule 8002 of the Bankruptcy Rules.

(d)(1) The courts of appeals shall have jurisdiction of appeals from all final decisions, judgments, orders, and decrees entered under subsections (a) and (b) of this section.

(2)(A) The appropriate court of appeals shall have jurisdiction of appeals described in the first sentence of subsection (a) if the bankruptcy court, the district court, or the bankruptcy appellate panel involved, acting on its own motion or on the request of a party to the judgment, order, or decree described in such first sentence, or all the appellants and appellees (if any) acting jointly, certify that—

(i) the judgment, order, or decree involves a question of law as to which there is no controlling decision of the court of appeals for the circuit or of the Supreme Court of the United States, or involves a matter of public importance;

(ii) the judgment, order, or decree involves a question of law requiring resolution of conflicting decisions; or

(iii) an immediate appeal from the judgment, order, or decree may materially advance the progress of the case or proceeding in which the appeal is taken;

and if the court of appeals authorizes the direct appeal of the judgment, order, or decree.

(B) If the bankruptcy court, the district court, or the bankruptcy appellate panel—

(i) on its own motion or on the request of a party, determines that a circumstance specified in clause (i), (ii), or (iii) of subparagraph (A) exists; or

(ii) receives a request made by a majority of the appellants and a majority of appellees (if any) to make the certification described in subparagraph (A);

then the bankruptcy court, the district court, or the bankruptcy appellate panel shall make the certification described in subparagraph (A).

(C) The parties may supplement the certification with a short statement of the basis for the certification.

(D) An appeal under this paragraph does not stay any proceeding of the bankruptcy court, the district court, or the bankruptcy appellate panel from which the appeal is taken, unless the respective bankruptcy court, district court, or bankruptcy appellate panel, or the court of appeals in which the appeal is pending, issues a stay of such proceeding pending the appeal.

(E) Any request under subparagraph (B) for certification shall be made not later than 60 days after the entry of the judgment, order, or decree.

(Added Pub.L. 98–353, Title I, § 104(a), July 10, 1984, 98 Stat. 341; amended Pub.L. 101–650, Title III, § 305, Dec. 1, 1990, 104 Stat. 5105; Pub.L. 103–394, Title I, §§ 102, 104(c), (d), Oct. 22, 1994, 108 Stat. 4108–4110; Pub.L. 109–8, Title XII, § 1233(a), Apr. 20, 2005, 119 Stat. 202; Pub.L. 111–327, § 2(c)(1), Dec. 22, 2010, 124 Stat. 3563.)

1 So in original.

HISTORICAL AND STATUTORY NOTES

Revision Notes and Legislative Reports

1984 Acts. Statements by Legislative Leaders, see 1984 U.S. Code Cong. and Adm. News, p. 576.

1990 Acts. Senate Report No. 101–416, Related House Reports, and Statement by President, see 1990 U.S. Code Cong. and Adm. News, p. 6802.

1994 Acts. House Report No. 103–835, see 1994 U.S. Code Cong. and Adm. News, p. 3340.

2005 Acts. House Report No. 109–31(Part I), see 2005 U.S. Code Cong. and Adm. News, p. 88.

Codifications

Amendment by section 102 of Pub.L. 103–394, which directed amendment of subsec. (a) by striking "from" the first place it appeared and all that followed through "decrees," and making a substitution for such language, was executed by striking through "decrees," the first place it appeared, as the probable intent of Congress.

This section (section 158) and section 159 as added by Pub.L. 95–598, Title II, § 201(a), Nov. 6, 1978, 92 Stat. 2659, and section 160, as added by Pub.L. 95–598, Title II, § 201(a), Nov. 6, 1978, 92 Stat. 2659, and amended Pub.L. 97–164, Title I, § 110(d), Apr. 2, 1982, 96 Stat. 29, effective June 28, 1984, pursuant to Pub.L. 95–598, Title IV, § 402(b), Nov. 6, 1978, 92 Stat. 2682, as amended by Pub.L. 98–249, § 1(a), Mar. 31, 1984, 98 Stat. 116; Pub.L. 98–271, § 1(a), Apr. 30, 1984, 98 Stat. 163; Pub.L. 98–299, § 1(a), May 25, 1984, 98 Stat. 214; Pub.L. 98–325, § 1(a), June 20, 1984, 98 Stat. 268, set out as a note preceding section 101 of Title II, Bankruptcy, read as follows:

"§ 158. **Accommodations at places for holding court**

"Court shall be held only at places where Federal quarters and accommodations are available, or suitable quarters and accommodations are furnished without cost to the United States. The foregoing restrictions shall not, however, preclude the Administrator of General Services, at the request of the Director of the Administrative Office of the United States Courts, from providing such court quarters and accommodations as the Administrator determines can appropriately be made available at places where court is authorized by law to be held, but only if such court quarters and accommodations have been approved as necessary by the judicial council of the appropriate circuit.

"**§ 159. Vacant judgeship as affecting proceedings**

"When the office of a bankruptcy judge becomes vacant, all pending process, pleadings and proceedings shall, when necessary, be continued by the clerk until a judge is appointed or designated to hold such court.

"**§ 160. Appellate panels**

"**(a)** If the circuit council of a circuit orders application of this section to a district within such circuit, the chief judge of each circuit shall designate panels of three bankruptcy judges to hear appeals from judgments, orders, and decrees of the bankruptcy court of the United States for such district. Except as provided in section 293(b) of this title, a panel shall be composed only of bankruptcy judges for districts located in the circuit in which the appeal arises. The chief judge shall designate a sufficient number of such panels so that appeals may be heard and disposed of expeditiously.

"**(b)** A panel designated under subsection (a) of this section may not hear an appeal from a judgment, order, or decree entered by a member of the panel.

"**(c)** When hearing an appeal, a panel designated under subsection (a) of this section shall sit at a place convenient to the parties to the appeal."

Section 402(b) of Pub.L. 95–598 was amended by section 113 of Pub.L. 98–353 by substituting "shall not be effective" for "shall take effect on June 28, 1984", thereby eliminating the additions of sections 158 to 160 by section 201(a) of Pub.L. 95–598, effective June 27, 1984, pursuant to section 122(c) of Pub.L. 98–353, set out as an Effective Date note under section 151 of this title.

Section 121(a) of Pub.L. 98–353 directed that section 402(b) of Pub.L. 95–598 be amended by substituting "the date of enactment of the Bankruptcy Amendments and Federal Judgeship Act of 1984 [i.e. July 10, 1984]" for "June 28, 1984". This amendment was not executed in view of the prior amendment to section 402(b) of Pub.L. 95–598 by section 113 of Pub.L. 98–353.

Amendments

2010 Amendments. Subsec. (d)(2)(D). Pub.L. 111–327, § 2(c)(1), struck out "appeal in" and inserted "appeal is".

2005 Amendments. Subsec. (c)(1). Pub.L.109–8, § 1233(a)(1), struck out "Subject to subsection (b)," and inserted "Subject to subsections (b) and (d)(2),".

Subsec. (d). Pub.L.109–8, § 1233(a)(2), inserted "(1)" after "(d)", and added paragraph (2).

1994 Amendments. Subsec. (a). Pub.L. 103–394, § 102, designated existing provision "from final judgments, orders, and decrees," following "jurisdiction to hear appeals" as par. (1), and added pars. (2) and (3).

Subsec. (b). Pub.L. 103–465, § 104(c), added pars. (1), (2), (3), (5), and (6), redesignated former par. (2) as (4), and struck out former pars. (1), (3), and (4), which authorized establishment of bankruptcy appellate panel without conditions, prohibited referral of appeal to panel unless authorized by majority vote of district judges, and provided that panel shall consist of 3 bankruptcy judges.

Subsec. (c). Pub.L. 103–465, § 104(d), designated existing text as par. (2) and added par. (1).

1990 Amendments. Subsec. (b)(2). Pub.L. 101–650, § 305(2), added par. (2). Former par. (2) redesignated (3).

Subsec. (b)(3), (4). Pub.L. 101–650, § 305(1), redesignated former pars. (2) and (3) as (3) and (4), respectively.

Effective and Applicability Provisions

2005 Acts. Except as otherwise provided, amendments by Pub.L. 109–8 effective 180 days after April 20, 2005, and inapplicable with respect to cases commenced under Title 11 before the effective date, see Pub.L. 109–8, § 1501, set out as a note under 11 U.S.C.A. § 101.

1994 Acts. Amendments by Pub.L. 103–394 effective on Oct. 22, 1994, and not to apply with respect to cases commenced under Title 11 of the United States Code before Oct. 22, 1994, see section 702 of Pub.L. 103–394, set out as a note under 11 U.S.C.A. § 101.

1984 Acts. Section effective July 10, 1984, see section 122(a) of Pub.L. 98–353, set out as a note under 28 U.S.C.A. § 151.

Separability of Provisions

If any provision of or amendment made by Pub.L. 103–394 or the application of such provision or amendment to any person or circumstance is held to be unconstitutional, the remaining provisions of and amendments made by Pub.L. 103–394 and the application of such provisions and amendments to any person or circumstance shall not be affected thereby, see section 701 of Pub.L. 103–394, set out as a note under 11 U.S.C.A. § 101.

Procedural Rules

Pub.L. 109–8, Title XII, § 1233(b), Apr. 20, 2005, 119 Stat. 203, provided that:

"**(1) Temporary application.**—A provision of this subsection shall apply to appeals under section 158(d)(2) of title 28, United States Code, until a rule of practice and procedure relating to such provision and such appeals is promulgated or amended under chapter 131 of such title [28 U.S.C.A. § 2071 et seq.].

"**(2) Certification.**—A district court, a bankruptcy court, or a bankruptcy appellate panel may make a certification under section 158(d)(2) of title 28, United States Code, only with respect to matters pending in the respective bankruptcy court, district court, or bankruptcy appellate panel.

"**(3) Procedure.**—Subject to any other provision of this subsection, an appeal authorized by the court of appeals under section 158(d)(2)(A) of title 28, United States Code, shall be taken in the manner prescribed in subdivisions (a)(1), (b), (c), and (d) of rule 5 of the Federal Rules of Appellate Procedure. For purposes of subdivision (a)(1) of rule 5—

"**(A)** a reference in such subdivision to a district court shall be deemed to include a reference to a bankruptcy court and a bankruptcy appellate panel, as appropriate; and

"**(B)** a reference in such subdivision to the parties requesting permission to appeal to be served with the petition shall be deemed to include a reference to the parties to the judgment, order, or decree from which the appeal is taken.

"**(4) Filing of petition with attachment.**—A petition requesting permission to appeal, that is based on a certification made under subparagraph (A) or (B) of section 158(d)(2) shall—

"**(A)** be filed with the circuit clerk not later than 10 days after the certification is entered on the docket of the bankruptcy court, the district court, or the bankruptcy appellate panel from which the appeal is taken; and

"**(B)** have attached a copy of such certification.

"(5) **References in rule 5.**—For purposes of rule 5 of the Federal Rules of Appellate Procedure—

"(A) a reference in such rule to a district court shall be deemed to include a reference to a bankruptcy court and to a bankruptcy appellate panel; and

"(B) a reference in such rule to a district clerk shall be deemed to include a reference to a clerk of a bankruptcy court and to a clerk of a bankruptcy appellate panel.

"(6) **Application of rules.**—The Federal Rules of Appellate Procedure [set out in Title 28, Judiciary and Judicial Procedure] shall apply in the courts of appeals with respect to appeals authorized under section 158(d)(2)(A), to the extent relevant and as if such appeals were taken from final judgments, orders, or decrees of the district courts or bankruptcy appellate panels exercising appellate jurisdiction under subsection (a) or (b) of section 158 of title 28, United States Code."

[Except as otherwise provided, amendments by Pub.L. 109–8 effective 180 days after April 20, 2005, and inapplicable with respect to cases commenced under Title 11 before the effective date, see Pub.L. 109–8, § 1501, set out as a note under 11 U.S.C.A. § 101.]

CROSS REFERENCES

Orders and decisions not reviewable under this section—

Abstention from exercising jurisdiction generally, see 28 USCA § 1334.

Dismissal or suspension of bankruptcy case on abstention grounds, see 11 USCA § 305.

Remand orders, see 28 USCA § 1452.

LIBRARY REFERENCES

American Digest System

Bankruptcy ⊕3761 to 3775.

Key Number System Topic No. 51.

Corpus Juris Secundum

CJS Bankruptcy § 9, Title 28 of the U.S. Code.

CJS Bankruptcy § 21, Powers of District Court in Relation to Bankruptcy Judges.

CJS Bankruptcy § 22, Bankruptcy Appellate Panels.

CJS Bankruptcy § 174, Motions to Abstain or Remand.

CJS Bankruptcy § 219, Consent to Final Determination by Bankruptcy Judge.

CJS Bankruptcy § 241, Review of Remand Orders.

CJS Bankruptcy § 1213, Certification to Court of Appeals from Bankruptcy Court.

CJS Bankruptcy § 1218, Bankruptcy Appellate Panel.

CJS Bankruptcy § 1219, District Court.

CJS Bankruptcy § 1220, District Court--Election.

CJS Bankruptcy § 1221, Court of Appeals.

CJS Bankruptcy § 1226, Relief from Automatic Stay.

CJS Bankruptcy § 1231, Confirmation of Plan.

CJS Bankruptcy § 1232, Particular Orders.

CJS Federal Courts § 428, Appeal Advancing Termination of Litigation.

CJS Labor Relations § 517, Interference, Coercion, or Restraint--Work Rules.

§ 159.   Bankruptcy statistics

(a) The clerk of the district court, or the clerk of the bankruptcy court if one is certified pursuant to section 156(b) of this title, shall collect statistics regarding debtors who are individuals with primarily consumer debts seeking relief under chapters 7, 11, and 13 of title 11. Those statistics shall be in a standardized format prescribed by the Director of the Administrative Office of the United States Courts (referred to in this section as the "Director").

(b) The Director shall—

(1) compile the statistics referred to in subsection (a);

(2) make the statistics available to the public; and

(3) not later than July 1, 2008, and annually thereafter, prepare, and submit to Congress a report concerning the information collected under subsection (a) that contains an analysis of the information.

(c) The compilation required under subsection (b) shall—

(1) be itemized, by chapter, with respect to title 11;

(2) be presented in the aggregate and for each district; and

(3) include information concerning—

(A) the total assets and total liabilities of the debtors described in subsection (a), and in each category of assets and liabilities, as reported in the schedules prescribed pursuant to section 2075 of this title and filed by debtors;

(B) the current monthly income, average income, and average expenses of debtors as reported on the schedules and statements that each such debtor files under sections 521 and 1322 of title 11;

(C) the aggregate amount of debt discharged in cases filed during the reporting period, determined as the difference between the total amount of debt and obligations of a debtor reported on the schedules and the amount of such debt reported in categories which are predominantly nondischargeable;

(D) the average period of time between the date of the filing of the petition and the closing of the case for cases closed during the reporting period;

(E) for cases closed during the reporting period—

(i) the number of cases in which a reaffirmation agreement was filed; and

(ii)(I) the total number of reaffirmation agreements filed;

(II) of those cases in which a reaffirmation agreement was filed, the number of cases in which the debtor was not represented by an attorney; and

(III) of those cases in which a reaffirmation agreement was filed, the number of cases in which the reaffirmation agreement was approved by the court;

(F) with respect to cases filed under chapter 13 of title 11, for the reporting period—

(i)(I) the number of cases in which a final order was entered determining the value of property securing a claim in an amount less than the amount of the claim; and

(II) the number of final orders entered determining the value of property securing a claim;

(ii) the number of cases dismissed, the number of cases dismissed for failure to make payments under the plan, the number of cases refiled after dismissal, and the number of cases in which the plan was completed, separately itemized with respect to the number of modifications made before completion of the plan, if any; and

(iii) the number of cases in which the debtor filed another case during the 6–year period preceding the filing;

(G) the number of cases in which creditors were fined for misconduct and any amount of punitive damages awarded by the court for creditor misconduct; and

(H) the number of cases in which sanctions under rule 9011 of the Federal Rules of Bankruptcy Procedure were imposed against the debtor's attorney or damages awarded under such Rule.

(Added Pub.L. 109–8, Title VI, § 601(a), Apr. 20, 2005, 119 Stat. 119; amended Pub.L. 111–327, § 2(c)(2), Dec. 22, 2010, 124 Stat. 3563.)

HISTORICAL AND STATUTORY NOTES

Revision Notes and Legislative Reports

2005 Acts. House Report No. 109–31(Part I), see 2005 U.S. Code Cong. and Adm. News, p. 88.

References in Text

Chapters 7 and 11 of title 11, referred to in subsec. (a), are 11 U.S.C.A. § 701 et seq. and 11 U.S.C.A. § 1101 et seq., respectively.

Chapter 13 of title 11, referred to in subsecs. (a) and (c)(3)(F), is 11 U.S.C.A. § 1301 et seq.

The Federal Rules of Bankruptcy Procedure, referred to in subsec. (c)(3)(H), are set out in Title 11.

Amendments

2010 Amendments. Subsec. (c)(3)(H). Pub.L. 111–327, § 2(c)(2), inserted "the" following "against".

Effective and Applicability Provisions

2005 Acts. Pub.L. 109–8, Title VI, § 601(c), Apr. 20, 2005, 119 Stat. 120, provided that: "The amendments made by this section [enacting this section] shall take effect 18 months after the date of enactment of this Act [April 20, 2005]."

Except as otherwise provided, amendments by Pub.L. 109–8 effective 180 days after April 20, 2005, and inapplicable with respect to cases commenced under Title 11 before the effective date, see Pub.L. 109–8, § 1501, set out as a note under 11 U.S.C.A. § 101.

LIBRARY REFERENCES

American Digest System

Clerks of Courts ⚲64.1.

Key Number System Topic No. 79.

§§ 160 to 170.   Reserved for future legislation

CHAPTER 17—RESIGNATION AND RETIREMENT OF JUSTICES AND JUDGES

§ 372.   Retirement for disability; substitute judge on failure to retire

(a) Any justice or judge of the United States appointed to hold office during good behavior who becomes permanently disabled from performing his duties may retire from regular active service, and the President shall, by and with the advice and consent of the Senate, appoint a successor.

Any justice or judge of the United States desiring to retire under this section shall certify to the President his disability in writing.

Whenever an associate justice of the Supreme Court, a chief judge of a circuit or the chief judge of the Court of International Trade, desires to retire under this section, he shall furnish to the President a certificate of disability signed by the Chief Justice of the United States.

A circuit or district judge, desiring to retire under this section, shall furnish to the President a certificate of disability signed by the chief judge of his circuit.

A judge of the Court of International Trade desiring to retire under this section, shall furnish to the President a certificate of disability signed by the chief judge of his court.

Each justice or judge retiring under this section after serving ten years continuously or otherwise shall, during the remainder of his lifetime, receive the salary of the office. A justice or judge retiring under this section who has served less than ten years in all shall, during the remainder of his lifetime, receive one-half the salary of the office.

(b) Whenever any judge of the United States appointed to hold office during good behavior who is eligible to retire under this section does not do so and a certificate of his disability signed by a majority of the members of the Judicial Council of his circuit in the case of a circuit or district judge, or by the Chief Justice of the United States in the case of the Chief Judge of the Court of International Trade, or by the chief judge of his court in the case of a judge of the Court of International Trade, is presented to the President and the President finds that such judge is unable to discharge efficiently all the duties of his office by reason of permanent mental or physical disability and that the appointment of an additional judge is necessary for the efficient dispatch of business, the President may make such appointment by and with the advice and consent of the Senate. Whenever any such additional judge is appointed, the vacancy subsequently caused by the death, resignation, or retirement of the disabled judge shall not be filled. Any judge whose disability causes the appointment of an additional judge shall, for purpose of precedence, service as chief judge, or temporary performance of the duties of that office, be treated as junior in commission to the other judges of the circuit, district, or court.

[(c) Repealed. Pub.L. 107–273, Div. C, Title I, § 11043(a)(1)(B), Nov. 2, 2002, 116 Stat. 1855]

(June 25, 1948, c. 646, 62 Stat. 903; May 24, 1949, c. 139, § 67, 63 Stat. 99; Feb. 10, 1954, c. 6, § 4(a), 68 Stat. 12; Sept. 2, 1957, Pub.L. 85–261, 71 Stat. 586; Oct. 10, 1980, Pub.L. 96–417, Title V, § 501(9), 94 Stat. 1742; Oct. 15, 1980, Pub.L. 96–458, § 3(a), (b), 94 Stat. 2036, 2040; Apr. 2, 1982, Pub.L. 97–164, Title I, § 112, 96 Stat. 29; July 10, 1984, Pub.L. 98–353, Title I, § 107, 98 Stat. 342; Nov. 19, 1988, Pub.L. 100–702, Title IV, § 403(c), 102 Stat. 4651; Dec. 1, 1990, Pub.L. 101–650, Title III, § 321, Title IV, § 402, 104 Stat. 5117, 5122; Oct. 29, 1992, Pub.L. 102–572, Title IX, § 902(b)(1), 106 Stat. 4516; Nov. 2, 2002, Pub.L. 107–273, Div. C, Title I, § 11043(a)(1), 116 Stat. 1855.)

HISTORICAL AND STATUTORY NOTES

Revision Notes and Legislative Reports

1948 Acts. Based on Title 28, U.S.C., 1940 ed., §§ 375b, 375c, and 375d (Aug. 5, 1939, c. 433, §§ 1 to 3, 53 Stat. 1204, 1205).

This section consolidates sections 375b, 375c, and 375d of Title 28, U.S.C., 1940 ed.

Said section 375e of Title 28, U.S.C., 1940 ed. providing that term "senior circuit judge" includes the Chief Justice of the United States Court of Appeals for the District of Columbia, and the term "judicial circuit" includes the District of Columbia, was omitted from this revision as unnecessary. Such district is included as a judicial circuit by section 41 of this title.

Words "justice or judge of the United States" were used to describe members of all courts who hold office during good behavior. (See reviser's note [now Revision Notes and Legislative Reports] under section 371 of this title.)

Term "chief judge" was substituted for "Chief Justice" of the Court of Claims, "presiding judge" of the Court of Customs and Patent Appeals and "senior circuit judge." (See reviser's note [now Revision Notes and Legislative Reports] under section 136 of this title.)

For clarity and convenience the requirement that certificates of disability be submitted "to the President," was made explicit.

The revised section requires a judge of the Customs Court to furnish a certificate of disability signed by the chief judge of his court, instead of by the chief judge of the Court of Customs and Patent Appeals as in said section 375c of Title 28, U.S.C., 1940 ed. This change insures signing of the certificate of disability by the chief judge possessing knowledge of the facts.

Changes were made in phraseology and arrangement. 80th Congress House Report No. 308.

1949 Acts. Subsection (a) of this section amends section 372 of Title 28, U.S.C., to express the requirement that appointment of successors to justices or judges must be made with confirmation by the Senate. Subsection (b) of this section clarifies the intent of section 372 of Title 28, U.S.C., and conforms with the language of section 371 of such title.

1954 Acts. House Report No. 1005 and Conference Report No. 1133, see 1954 U.S. Code Cong. and Adm. News p. 2006.

1957 Acts. Senate Report No. 1094, see 1957 U.S. Code Cong. and Adm. News, p. 1833.

1980 Acts. House Report No. 96–1235, see 1980 U.S. Code Cong. and Adm. News, p. 3729.

Senate Report No. 96–362, see 1980 U.S. Code Cong. and Adm. News, p. 4315.

1982 Acts. Senate Report No. 97–275, see 1982 U.S. Code Cong. and Adm. News, p. 11.

1984 Acts. Statements by Legislative Leaders, see 1984 U.S. Code Cong. and Adm. News, p. 576.

1988 Acts. House Report No. 100–889, see 1988 U.S. Code Cong. and Adm. News, p. 5982.

1990 Acts. Senate Report No. 101–416, related House Reports, and President's Signing Statement, see 1990 U.S. Code Cong. and Adm. News, p. 6802.

2002 Acts. House Conference Report No. 107–685 and Statement by President, see 2002 U.S. Code Cong. and Adm. News, p. 1120.

Amendments

2002 Amendments. Pub.L. 107–273, § 11043(a)(1)(A), struck out "; judicial discipline" following "failure to retire" in section heading.

Subsec. (c). Pub.L. 107–273, § 11043(a)(1)(B), struck out subsec. (c), which prior thereto read:

"(1) Any person alleging that a circuit, district, or bankruptcy judge, or a magistrate judge, has engaged in conduct prejudicial to the effective and expeditious administration of the business of the courts, or alleging that such a judge or magistrate judge is unable to discharge all the duties of office by reason of mental or physical disability, may file with the clerk of the court of appeals for the circuit a written complaint containing a brief statement of the facts constituting such conduct. In the interests of the effective and expeditious administration of the business of the courts and on the basis of information available to the chief judge of the circuit, the chief judge may, by written order stating reasons therefor, identify a complaint for purposes of this subsection and thereby dispense with filing of a written complaint.

"(2) Upon receipt of a complaint filed under paragraph (1) of this subsection, the clerk shall promptly transmit such complaint to the chief judge of the circuit, or, if the conduct complained of is that of the chief judge, to that circuit judge in regular active service next senior in date of commission (hereafter, for purposes of this subsection only, included in the term "chief judge"). The clerk shall simultaneously transmit a copy of the complaint to the judge or magistrate judge whose conduct is the subject of the complaint.

"(3) After expeditiously reviewing a complaint, the chief judge, by written order stating his reasons, may—

"(A) dismiss the complaint, if he finds it to be (i) not in conformity with paragraph (1) of this subsection, (ii) directly related to the merits of a decision or procedural ruling, or (iii) frivolous; or

"(B) conclude the proceeding if he finds that appropriate corrective action has been taken or that action on the complaint is no longer necessary because of intervening events.

The chief judge shall transmit copies of his written order to the complainant and to the judge or magistrate judge whose conduct is the subject of the complaint.

"(4) If the chief judge does not enter an order under paragraph (3) of this subsection, such judge shall promptly—

"(A) appoint himself and equal numbers of circuit and district judges of the circuit to a special committee to investigate the facts and allegations contained in the complaint;

"(B) certify the complaint and any other documents pertaining thereto to each member of such committee; and

"(C) provide written notice to the complainant and the judge or magistrate judge whose conduct is the subject of the complaint of the action taken under this paragraph.

A judge appointed to a special committee under this paragraph may continue to serve on that committee after becoming a senior judge or, in the case of the chief judge of the circuit, after his or her term as chief judge terminates under subsection (a)(3) or (c) of section 45 of this title. If a judge appointed to a committee under this paragraph dies, or retires from office under section 371(a) of this title, while serving on the committee, the chief judge of the circuit may appoint another circuit or district judge, as the case may be, to the committee.

"(5) Each committee appointed under paragraph (4) of this subsection shall conduct an investigation as extensive as it considers necessary, and shall expeditiously file a comprehensive written report thereon with the judicial council of the circuit. Such report shall present both the findings of the investigation and the committee's recommendations for necessary and appropriate action by the judicial council of the circuit.

"(6) Upon receipt of a report filed under paragraph (5) of this subsection, the judicial council—

"(A) may conduct any additional investigation which it considers to be necessary;

"(B) shall take such action as is appropriate to assure the effective and expeditious administration of the business of the courts within the circuit, including, but not limited to, any of the following actions:

"(i) directing the chief judge of the district of the magistrate judge whose conduct is the subject of the complaint to take such action as the judicial council considers appropriate;

"(ii) certifying disability of a judge appointed to hold office during good behavior whose conduct is the subject of the complaint, pursuant to the procedures and standards provided under subsection (b) of this section;

"(iii) requesting that any such judge appointed to hold office during good behavior voluntarily retire, with the provision that the length of service requirements under section 371 of this title shall not apply;

"(iv) ordering that, on a temporary basis for a time certain, no further cases be assigned to any judge or magistrate judge whose conduct is the subject of a complaint;

"(v) censuring or reprimanding such judge or magistrate judge by means of private communication;

"(vi) censuring or reprimanding such judge or magistrate judge by means of public announcement; or

"(vii) ordering such other action as it considers appropriate under the circumstances, except that (I) in no circumstances may the council order removal from office of any judge appointed to hold office during good behavior, and (II) any removal of a magistrate judge shall be in accordance with section 631 of this title and any removal of a bankruptcy judge shall be in accordance with section 152 of this title;

"(C) may dismiss the complaint; and

"(D) shall immediately provide written notice to the complainant and to such judge or magistrate judge of the action taken under this paragraph.

"(7)(A) In addition to the authority granted under paragraph (6) of this subsection, the judicial council may, in its discretion, refer any complaint under this subsection, together with the record of any associated proceedings and its recommendations for appropriate action, to the Judicial Conference of the United States.

"(B) In any case in which the judicial council determines, on the basis of a complaint and an investigation under this subsection, or on the basis of information otherwise available to the council, that a judge appointed to hold office during good behavior may have engaged in conduct—

"(i) which might constitute one or more grounds for impeachment under article II of the Constitution; or

"(ii) which, in the interest of justice, is not amenable to resolution by the judicial council,

the judicial council shall promptly certify such determination, together with any complaint and a record of any associated proceedings, to the Judicial Conference of the United States.

"(C) A judicial council acting under authority of this paragraph shall, unless contrary to the interests of justice, immediately submit written notice to the complainant and to the judge or magistrate judge whose conduct is the subject of the action taken under this paragraph.

"(8)(A) Upon referral or certification of any matter under paragraph (7) of this subsection, the Judicial Conference, after consideration of the prior proceedings and such additional investigation as it considers appropriate, shall by majority vote take such action, as described in paragraph (6)(B) of this subsection, as it considers appropriate. If the Judicial Conference concurs in the determination of the council, or makes its own determination, that consideration of impeachment may be warranted, it shall so certify and transmit the determination and the record of proceedings to the House of Representatives for whatever action the House of Representatives considers to be necessary. Upon receipt of the determination and record of proceedings in the House of Representatives, the Clerk of the House of Representatives shall make available to the public the determination and any reasons for the determination.

"(B) If a judge or magistrate judge has been convicted of a felony and has exhausted all means of obtaining direct review of the conviction, or the time for seeking further direct review of the conviction has passed and no such review has been sought, the Judicial Conference may, by majority vote and without referral or certification under paragraph (7), transmit to the House of Representatives a determination that consideration of impeachment may be warranted, together with appropriate court records, for whatever action the House of Representatives considers to be necessary.

"(9)(A) In conducting any investigation under this subsection, the judicial council, or a special committee appointed under paragraph (4) of this subsection, shall have full subpoena powers as provided in section 332(d) of this title.

"(B) In conducting any investigation under this subsection, the Judicial Conference, or a standing committee appointed by the Chief Justice under section 331 of this title, shall have full subpoena powers as provided in that section.

"(10) A complainant, judge, or magistrate judge aggrieved by a final order of the chief judge under paragraph (3) of this subsection may petition the judicial council for review thereof. A complainant, judge, or magistrate judge aggrieved by an action of the judicial council under paragraph (6) of this subsection may petition the Judicial Conference of the United States for review thereof. The Judicial Conference, or the standing committee established under section 331 of this title, may grant a petition filed by a complainant, judge, or magistrate judge under this paragraph. Except as expressly provided in this paragraph, all orders and determinations, including denials of petitions for review, shall be final and conclusive and shall not be judicially reviewable on appeal or otherwise.

"(11) Each judicial council and the Judicial Conference may prescribe such rules for the conduct of proceedings under this subsection, including the processing of petitions for review, as each considers to be appropriate. Such rules shall contain provisions requiring that—

"(A) adequate prior notice of any investigation be given in writing to the judge or magistrate judge whose conduct is the subject of the complaint;

"(B) the judge or magistrate judge whose conduct is the subject of the complaint be afforded an opportunity to appear (in person or by counsel) at proceedings conducted by the investigating panel, to present oral and documentary evidence, to compel the attendance of witnesses or the production of documents, to cross-examine witnesses, and to present argument orally or in writing; and

"(C) the complainant be afforded an opportunity to appear at proceedings conducted by the investigating panel, if the panel concludes that the complainant could offer substantial information.

Any such rule shall be made or amended only after giving appropriate public notice and an opportunity for comment. Any rule promulgated under this subsection shall be a matter of public record, and any such rule promulgated by a judicial council may be modified by the Judicial Conference. No rule promulgated under this subsection may limit the period of time within which a person may file a complaint under this subsection.

"(12) No judge or magistrate judge whose conduct is the subject of an investigation under this subsection shall serve upon a special committee appointed under paragraph (4) of this subsection, upon a judicial council, upon the Judicial Conference, or upon the standing committee established under section 331 of this title, until all related proceedings under this subsection have been finally terminated.

"(13) No person shall be granted the right to intervene or to appear as amicus curiae in any proceeding before a judicial council or the Judicial Conference under this subsection.

"(14) Except as provided in paragraph (8), all papers, documents, and records of proceedings related to investigations conducted under this subsection shall be confidential and shall not be disclosed by any person in any proceeding except to the extent that—

"(A) the judicial council of the circuit in its discretion releases a copy of a report of a special investigative committee under paragraph (5) to the complainant whose complaint initiated the investigation by that special committee and to the judge or magistrate judge whose conduct is the subject of the complaint;

"(B) the judicial council of the circuit, the Judicial Conference of the United States, or the Senate or the House of Representatives by resolution, releases any such material which is believed necessary to an impeachment investigation or trial of a judge under article I of the Constitution; or

"(C) such disclosure is authorized in writing by the judge or magistrate judge who is the subject of the complaint and by the chief judge of the circuit, the Chief Justice, or the chairman of the standing committee established under section 331 of this title.

"(15) Each written order to implement any action under paragraph (6)(B) of this subsection, which is issued by a judicial council, the Judicial Conference, or the standing committee established under section 331 of this title, shall be made available to the public through the appropriate clerk's office of the court of appeals for the circuit. Unless contrary to the interests of justice, each such order issued under this paragraph shall be accompanied by written reasons therefor.

"(16) Upon the request of a judge or magistrate judge whose conduct is the subject of a complaint under this subsection, the judicial council may, if the complaint has been finally dismissed under paragraph (6)(C), recommend that the Director of the Administrative Office of the United States Courts award reimbursement, from funds appropriated to the Federal judiciary, for those reasonable expenses, including attorneys' fees, incurred by that judge or magistrate judge during the investigation which would not have been incurred but for the requirements of this subsection.

"(17) Except as expressly provided in this subsection, nothing in this subsection shall be construed to affect any other provision of this title, the Federal Rules of Civil Procedure, the Federal Rules of Criminal Procedure, the Federal Rules of Appellate Procedure, or the Federal Rules of Evidence.

"(18) The United States Court of Federal Claims, the Court of International Trade, and the Court of Appeals for the Federal Circuit shall each prescribe rules, consistent with the foregoing provisions of this subsection, establishing procedures for the filing of complaints with respect to the conduct of any judge of such court and for the investigation and resolution of such complaints. In investigating and taking action with respect to any such complaint, each such court shall have the powers granted to a judicial council under this subsection."

1992 Amendments. Subsec. (c)(18). Pub.L. 102–572 substituted "United States Court of Federal Claims" for "United States Claims Court."

1990 Amendments. Subsec. (c)(1). Pub.L. 101–650, § 402(a), authorized the chief judge, in the interests of administration of the business of the courts and on basis of information available to the chief judge of the circuit, by written order stating reasons therefor to identify a complaint for purposes of this subsection and dispense with filing of a written complaint.

Subsec. (c)(3)(B). Pub.L. 101–650, § 402(f), authorized the chief judge to conclude the proceeding if action on the complaint is no longer necessary because of intervening events.

Subsec. (c)(4). Pub.L. 101–650, § 402(b), authorized a judge appointed to a special committee to continue service on the committee upon becoming a senior judge or upon termination of a term as a chief judge and authorized the chief judge of the circuit to appoint another circuit or district judge to the committee upon the death or retirement of a serving judge.

Subsec. (c)(6). Pub.L. 101–650, § 402(g), added subpar. (C) and redesignated former subpar. (C) as (D).

Subsec. (c)(7)(B). Pub.L. 101–650, § 402(i)(1)(A), (B), substituted: in introductory text, "may have engaged in conduct" for "has engaged in conduct"; and, in cl. (i), "article II" for "article I".

Subsec. (c)(8). Pub.L. 101–650, § 402(d), designated existing provisions as subpar. (A) and added subpar. (B).

Pub.L. 101–650, § 402(c)(1), inserted at end "Upon receipt of the determination and record of proceedings in the House of Representatives, the Clerk of the House of Representatives shall make available to the public the determination and any reasons for the determination."

Subsec. (c)(11). Pub.L. 101–650, § 402(e), prohibited any judicial council or Judicial Conference rule from limiting the period of time within which a person may file a complaint under this subsection.

Subsec. (c)(14). Pub.L. 101–650, § 402(c)(2)(A), (B), substituted in introductory text "Except as provided in paragraph (8), all" for "All" and "except to the extent that" for "unless".

Subsec. (c)(14)(A). Pub.L. 101–650, § 402(c)(2)(E), added subpar. (A). Former subpar. (A) redesignated (B).

Subsec. (c)(14)(B). Pub.L. 101–650, § 402(c)(2)(D), redesignated subpar. (A) as (B). Former subpar. (B) redesignated (C).

Pub.L. 101–650, § 402(c)(2)(C), substituted "disclosure is authorized" for "authorized" in former subpar. (B) immediately prior to redesignation thereof as subpar. (C) by section 402(c)(2)(D) of Pub.C. 101–650. See 1990 Amendments note for subsec. (c)(14)(C) under this section.

Subsec. (c)(14)(C). Pub.L. 101–650, § 402(c)(2)(D), (i)(2), redesignated subpar. (B), as amended by section 402(c)(2)(C) of Pub.L. 101–650, as subpar. (C); and, in subpar. (C), as so redesignated, substituted "subject of the complaint" for "subject to the complaint".

Subsec. (c)(16). Pub.L. 101–650, § 402(h)(2), added par. (16). Former par. (16) redesignated (17).

Subsec. (c)(17), (18). Pub.L. 101–650, § 402(h)(1), redesignated pars. (16) and (17) as (17) and (18), respectively.

1988 Amendments. Subsec. (c)(11). Pub.L. 100–702 inserted requirement that judicial council or Judicial Conference rule be made or amended only after the public be given appropriate notice and opportunity for comment.

1984 Amendments. Subsec. (c)(6)(B)(vii). Pub.L. 98–353 substituted "section 152" for "section 153".

1982 Amendments. Subsec. (a). Pub.L. 97–164, § 112(a), struck out references to the chief judge of the Court of Claims and the chief judge of the Court of Customs and Patent Appeals in the paragraph requiring that, in the case of the retirement for disability of either of those chief judges, the

certificate of disability be signed by the Chief Justice of the United States and struck out references to judges of the Court of Claims and of the Court of Customs and Patent Appeals in the paragraph requiring that, in the case of the retirement for disability of a judge of either of those courts, the certificate of disability be signed by the chief judge of the appropriate court.

Subsec. (b). Pub.L. 97–164, § 112(b), struck out references to the Chief Judge of the Court of Claims, to the Chief Judge of the Court of Customs and Patent Appeals, and to the judges of those courts.

Subsec. (c)(17). Pub.L. 97–164, § 112(c), substituted "United States Claims Court, the Court of International Trade, and the Court of Appeals for the Federal Circuit" for "Court of Claims, the Court of Customs and Patent Appeals, and the Customs Court".

1980 Amendments. Pub.L. 96–458, § 3(b), added "judicial discipline" in section catchline.

Subsecs. (a), (b). Pub.L. 96–417 redesignated the Customs Court as the Court of International Trade.

Subsec. (c). Pub.L. 96–458, § 3(a), added subsec. (c).

1957 Amendments. Subsec. (b). Pub.L. 85–261 added subsec. (b).

1954 Amendments. Act Feb. 10, 1954, amended section by adding to catchline "; substitute judge on failure to retire" (but without adding any provisions on such subject to the text of the section, see 1957 Amendments note under this section), and by adding, after "retire" in third, fourth, and fifth paragraphs, the words "under this section".

1949 Amendments. Act May 24, 1949, added the provision that appointment of successors to justices or judges must be made by and with the consent of the Senate, and inserted the words "continuously or otherwise" following "Each justice or judge" in the last paragraph.

Effective and Applicability Provisions

1992 Acts. Amendment by Pub.L. 102–572 effective Oct. 29, 1992, see section 911 of Pub.L. 102–572, set out as a note under section 171 of this title.

1990 Acts. Amendment by section 402 of Pub.L. 101–650 effective 90 days after Dec. 1, 1990, see section 407 of Pub.L. 101–650, set out as a note under section 332 of this title.

1988 Acts. Amendment by Pub.L. 100–702 effective Dec. 1, 1988, see section 407 of Pub.L. 100–702, set out as a note under section 2071 of this title.

1984 Acts. Amendment by Pub.L. 98–353 effective July 10, 1984, see section 122(a) of Pub.L. 98–353, set out as a note under section 151 of this title.

1982 Acts. Amendment by Pub.L. 97–164 effective Oct. 1, 1982, see section 402 of Pub.L. 97–164, set out as a note under section 171 of this title.

1980 Acts. Amendment by Pub.L. 96–458 effective Oct. 1, 1981, see section 7 of Pub.L. 96–458, set out as a note under section 331 of this title.

Amendment by Pub.L. 96–417 effective on Nov. 1, 1980, and applicable with respect to civil actions pending on or commenced on or after such date, see section 701(a) of Pub.L. 96–417, as amended, set out as a note under section 251 of this title.

Change of Name

References to United States Claims Court deemed to refer to United States Court of Federal Claims and references to Claims Court deemed to refer to Court of Federal Claims, see section 902(b) of Pub.L. 102–572, set out as a note under section 171 of Title 28, Judiciary and Judicial Procedure.

"United States magistrate judge" substituted for "United States magistrate" in text pursuant to section 321 of Pub.L. 101–650, set out as a note under 28 U.S.C.A. § 631.

Transfer of Functions

Any reference in any provision of law enacted before Jan. 4, 1995, to a function, duty, or authority of the Clerk of the House of Representatives treated as referring, with respect to that function, duty, or authority, to the officer of the House of Representatives exercising that function, duty, or authority, as determined by the Committee on House Oversight of the House of Representatives, see section 2(1) of Pub.L. 104–14, set out as a note preceding section 21 of Title 2, The Congress.

Computation of Judicial Service, District of Alaska

Inclusion of service as judge of the District Court for the Territory of Alaska in the computation of years of judicial service for judges of the United States District Court for the District of Alaska, see Pub.L. 89–70, July 8, 1965, 79 Stat. 213, set out as a note under section 371 of this title.

Extension of Time For Report by National Commission on Judicial Discipline and Removal

Pub.L. 102–368, Title I, Sept. 23, 1992, 106 Stat. 1118, provided in part that: "Notwithstanding the requirement of section 415 of Public Law 101–650 [set out as a note under this section] to submit the report mandated by said section not later than one year after the date of the Commission's first meeting, the National Commission on Judicial Discipline and Removal shall submit to each House of Congress, the Chief Justice of the United States, and the President, the report mandated in said section no later than August 1, 1993."

Judicial Service in Hawaii

Certain judicial service in Hawaii as included within computation of aggregate years of judicial service, see section 14(d) of Pub.L. 86–3, Mar. 18, 1959, 73 Stat. 10, set out as a note under section 371 of this title.

National Commission on Judicial Discipline and Removal

Subtitle II (sections 408 to 418) of Title IV of Pub.L. 101–650, as amended Pub.L. 102–198, § 8(a),(b)(2), Dec. 9, 1991, 105 Stat. 1625, 1626, provided that:

"Sec. 408. Short Title.

"This subtitle [subtitle II of Title IV of Pub.L. 101–650] may be cited as the 'National Commission on Judicial Discipline and Removal Act'.

"Sec. 409. Establishment.

"There is hereby established a commission to be known as the 'National Commission on Judicial Discipline and Removal' (hereinafter in this subtitle referred to as the 'Commission').

"Sec. 410. Duties of Commission.

"The duties of the Commission are—

"(1) to investigate and study the problems and issues involved in the tenure (including discipline and removal) of an article III judge;

"(2) to evaluate the advisability of proposing alternatives to current arrangements with respect to such problems and

issues, including alternatives for discipline or removal of judges that would require amendment to the Constitution; and

"(3) to prepare and submit to the Congress, the Chief Justice of the United States, and the President a report in accordance with section 415.

"Sec. 411. Membership.

"(a) Number and appointment.—The Commission shall be composed of 13 members as follows:

"(1) Three appointed by the President pro tempore of the Senate.

"(2) Three appointed by the Speaker of the House of Representatives.

"(3) Three appointed by the Chief Justice of the United States.

"(4) Three appointed by the President.

"(5) One appointed by the Conference of Chief Justices of the States of the United States.

"(b) Term.—Members of the Commission shall be appointed for the life of the Commission.

"(c) Quorum.—Six members of the Commission shall constitute a quorum, but a lesser number may conduct meetings.

"(d) Chairman.—The members of the Commission shall select one of the members to be the Chairman.

"(e) Vacancy.—A vacancy on the Commission resulting from the death or resignation of a member shall not affect its powers and shall be filled in the same manner in which the original appointment was made.

"(f) Continuation of membership.—If any member of the Commission who was appointed to the Commission as a Member of Congress or as an officer or employee of a government leaves that office, or if any member of the Commission who was appointed from persons who are not officers or employees of a government becomes an officer or employee of a government, the member may continue as a member of the Commission for not longer than the 90–day period beginning on the date the member leaves that office or becomes such an officer or employee, as the case may be.

"Sec. 412. Compensation of the Commission.

"(a) Pay.—(1) Except as provided in paragraph (2), each member of the Commission who is not otherwise employed by the United States Government shall be entitled to receive the daily equivalent of the annual rate of basic pay payable for GS–18 of the General Schedule under section 5332 of title 5, United States Code [section 5332 of Title 5, Government Organization and Employees], for each day (including travel time) during which he or she is engaged in the actual performance of duties as a member of the Commission.

"(2) A member of the Commission who is an officer or employee of the United States Government shall serve without additional compensation.

"(b) Travel.—All members of the Commission shall be reimbursed for travel, subsistence, and other necessary expenses incurred by them in the performance of their duties.

"Sec. 413. Director and staff of Commission; experts and consultants.

"(a) Director.—The Commission shall, without regard to section 5311(b) of title 5, United States Code [section 5311(b) of Title 5], have a Director who shall be appointed by the Chairman and who shall be paid at a rate not to exceed the rate of basic pay payable for level V of the Executive Schedule under section 5316 of such title [section 5316 of Title 5].

"**(b) Staff.**—The Chairman of the Commission may appoint and fix the pay of such additional personnel as the Chairman finds necessary to enable the Commission to carry out its duties. Such personnel may be appointed without regard to the provisions of title 5, United States Code [Title 5], governing appointments in the competitive service, and may be paid without regard to the provisions of chapter 51 and subchapter III of chapter 53 of such title [section 5101 et seq. and section 5331 et seq. of Title 5] relating to classification and General Schedule pay rates, except that the annual rate of pay for any individual so appointed may not exceed a rate equal to the annual rate of basic pay payable for GS–18 of the General Schedule under section 5332 of such title [section 5332 of Title 5].

"**(c) Experts and consultants.**—The Commission may procure temporary and intermittent services of experts and consultants under section 3109(b) of title 5, United States Code [section 3109(b) of Title 5].

"**Sec. 414. Powers of Commission.**

"**(a) Hearings and sessions.**—The Commission or, on authorization of the Commission, a member of the Commission may, for the purpose of carrying out this subtitle, hold such hearings, sit and act at such times and places, take such testimony, and receive such evidence, as the Commission considers appropriate. The Commission may administer oaths or affirmations to witnesses appearing before it.

"**(b) Obtaining official data.**—The Commission may secure directly from any department, agency, or entity within the executive or judicial branch of the Federal Government information necessary to enable it to carry out this subtitle. Upon request of the Chairman of the Commission, the head of such department or agency shall furnish such information to the Commission.

"**(c) Facilities and support services.**—The Administrator of General Services shall provide to the Commission on a reimbursable basis such facilities and support services as the Commission may request. Upon request of the Commission, the head of any Federal agency is authorized to make any of the facilities and services of such agency available to the Commission to assist the Commission in carrying out its duties under this subtitle.

"**(d) Expenditures and contracts.**—The Commission or, on authorization of the Commission, a member of the Commission may make expenditures and enter into contracts for the procurement of such supplies, services, and property as the Commission or member considers appropriate for the purposes of carrying out the duties of the Commission. Such expenditures and contracts may be made only to such extent or in such amounts as are provided in appropriation Acts.

"**(e) Mails.**—The Commission may use the United States mails in the same manner and under the same conditions as other departments and agencies of the United States.

"**(f) Gifts.**—The Commission may accept, use, and dispose of gifts or donations of services or property.

"**Sec. 415. Report.**

"The Commission shall submit to each House of Congress, the Chief Justice of the United States, and the President a report not later than one year after the date of its first meeting. The report shall contain a detailed statement of the findings and conclusions of the Commission, together with its recommendations for such legislative or administrative action as it considers appropriate.

"**Sec. 416. Termination.**

"The Commission shall cease to exist on the date 30 days after the date it submits its report to the President and the Congress under section 415.

"**Sec. 417. Authorization of appropriations.**

"There is authorized to be appropriated the sum of $750,000 to carry out the provisions of this subtitle.

"**Sec. 418. Effective date.**

"This subtitle shall take effect on the date of the enactment of this Act [Dec. 1, 1990]."

[References in laws to the rates of pay for GS–16, 17, or 18, or to maximum rates of pay under the General Schedule, to be considered references to rates payable under specified sections of Title 5, Government Organization and Employees, see section 529 [Title I, § 101(c)(1)] of Pub.L. 101–509, set out in a note under section 5376 of Title 5.]

[For provisions extending the time for submission by the National Commission on Judicial Discipline and Removal of the report required by section 415 of Pub.L. 101–650, see Pub.L. 102–368, Title 1, Sept. 23, 1992, 106 Stat. 1118, set out as a note under this section.]

[For termination, effective May 15, 2000, of reporting provisions pertaining to the findings and conclusions of the Commission of Pub.L. 101–650, § 415 set out above, see Pub.L. 104–66, § 3003, as amended, set out as a note under 31 U.S.C.A. § 1113, and the 4th item on page 181 of House Document No. 103–7.]

CROSS REFERENCES

Assignment of retired justices or judges to active duty, see 28 USCA § 294.

Court of Federal Claims judges election of annuity payments upon retirement not entitled to receive annuity or salary in senior status under this section, see 28 USCA § 178.

Court of Veterans Appeals, applicability of this section in prescribing rules and establishing procedures for filing of complaints against any judge, see 38 USCA § 7253.

Duties of Director of Administrative Office of United States Courts, see 28 USCA § 604.

Employee defined as including retired judge under this section for purposes of life insurance for federal employees, see 5 USCA § 8701.

Judicial Conference of the United States, see 28 USCA § 331.

Justices and judges appointed to hold office during good behavior—

Court of Appeals, see USCA Const. Art. III § 1.

Court of International Trade, see 28 USCA § 252.

District Courts, see USCA Const. Art. III § 1.

Supreme Court, see USCA Const. Art. III § 1.

Thrift Savings Fund, see 5 USCA § 8440a.

LIBRARY REFERENCES

American Digest System

Judges ⚫11(1), 15(1), 22(11).

Key Number System Topic No. 227.

CHAPTER 21—GENERAL PROVISIONS APPLICABLE TO COURTS AND JUDGES

§ 455. Disqualification of justice, judge, or magistrate judge

(a) Any justice, judge, or magistrate judge of the United States shall disqualify himself in any proceeding in which his impartiality might reasonably be questioned.

(b) He shall also disqualify himself in the following circumstances:

(1) Where he has a personal bias or prejudice concerning a party, or personal knowledge of disputed evidentiary facts concerning the proceeding;

(2) Where in private practice he served as lawyer in the matter in controversy, or a lawyer with whom he previously practiced law served during such association as a lawyer concerning the matter, or the judge or such lawyer has been a material witness concerning it;

(3) Where he has served in governmental employment and in such capacity participated as counsel, adviser or material witness concerning the proceeding or expressed an opinion concerning the merits of the particular case in controversy;

(4) He knows that he, individually or as a fiduciary, or his spouse or minor child residing in his household, has a financial interest in the subject matter in controversy or in a party to the proceeding, or any other interest that could be substantially affected by the outcome of the proceeding;

(5) He or his spouse, or a person within the third degree of relationship to either of them, or the spouse of such a person:

(i) Is a party to the proceeding, or an officer, director, or trustee of a party;

(ii) Is acting as a lawyer in the proceeding;

(iii) Is known by the judge to have an interest that could be substantially affected by the outcome of the proceeding;

(iv) Is to the judge's knowledge likely to be a material witness in the proceeding.

(c) A judge should inform himself about his personal and fiduciary financial interests, and make a reasonable effort to inform himself about the personal financial interests of his spouse and minor children residing in his household.

(d) For the purposes of this section the following words or phrases shall have the meaning indicated:

(1) "proceeding" includes pretrial, trial, appellate review, or other stages of litigation;

(2) the degree of relationship is calculated according to the civil law system;

(3) "fiduciary" includes such relationships as executor, administrator, trustee, and guardian;

(4) "financial interest" means ownership of a legal or equitable interest, however small, or a relationship as director, adviser, or other active participant in the affairs of a party, except that:

(i) Ownership in a mutual or common investment fund that holds securities is not a "financial interest" in such securities unless the judge participates in the management of the fund;

(ii) An office in an educational, religious, charitable, fraternal, or civic organization is not a "financial interest" in securities held by the organization;

(iii) The proprietary interest of a policyholder in a mutual insurance company, of a depositor in a mutual savings association, or a similar proprietary interest, is a "financial interest" in the organization only if the outcome of the proceeding could substantially affect the value of the interest;

(iv) Ownership of government securities is a "financial interest" in the issuer only if the outcome of the proceeding could substantially affect the value of the securities.

(e) No justice, judge, or magistrate judge shall accept from the parties to the proceeding a waiver of any ground for disqualification enumerated in subsection (b). Where the ground for disqualification arises only under subsection (a), waiver may be accepted provided it is preceded by a full disclosure on the record of the basis for disqualification.

(f) Notwithstanding the preceding provisions of this section, if any justice, judge, magistrate judge, or bankruptcy judge to whom a matter has been assigned would be disqualified, after substantial judicial time has been devoted to the matter, because of the appearance or discovery, after the matter was assigned to him or her, that he or she individually or as a fiduciary, or his or her spouse or minor child residing in his or her household, has a financial interest in a party (other than an interest that could be substantially affected by the outcome), disqualification is not required if the justice, judge, magistrate judge, bankruptcy judge, spouse or minor child, as the case may be, divests himself or herself of the interest that provides the grounds for the disqualification.

(June 25, 1948, c. 646, 62 Stat. 908; Dec. 5, 1974, Pub.L. 93–512, § 1, 88 Stat. 1609; Nov. 6, 1978, Pub.L. 95–598, Title II, § 214(a), (b), 92 Stat. 2661; Nov. 19, 1988, Pub.L. 100–702, Title X, § 1007, 102 Stat. 4667; Dec. 1, 1990, Pub.L. 101–650, Title III, § 321, 104 Stat. 5117.)

HISTORICAL AND STATUTORY NOTES

Revision Notes and Legislative Reports

1948 Acts. Based on Title 28, U.S.C., 1940 ed., § 24 (Mar. 3, 1911, c. 231, § 20, 36 Stat. 1090 [Derived from R.S. § 601]).

Section 24 of Title 28, U.S.C., 1940 ed., applied only to district judges. The revised section is made applicable to all justices and judges of the United States.

The phrase "in which he has a substantial interest" was substituted for "concerned in interest in any suit."

The provision of section 24 of Title 28, U.S.C., 1940 ed., as to giving notice of disqualification to the "senior circuit judge," and words "and thereupon such proceedings shall be had as are provided in sections 17 and 18 of this title," were omitted as unnecessary and covered by section 291 et seq. of this title relating to designation and assignment of judges. Such provision is not made by statute in case of disqualification or incapacity, for other cause. See sections 140, 143, and 144 of this title. If a judge or clerk of court is remiss in failing to notify the chief judge of the district or circuit, the judicial council of the circuit has ample power under section 332 of this title to apply a remedy.

Relationship to a party's attorney is included in the revised section as a basis of disqualification in conformity with the views of judges cognizant of the grave possibility of undesirable consequences resulting from a less inclusive rule.

Changes were made in phraseology. 80th Congress House Report No. 308.

1974 Acts. House Report No. 93–1453, see 1974 U.S.Code Cong. and Adm.News, p. 6351.

1978 Acts. Senate Report No. 95–989 and House Report No. 95–595, see 1978 U.S. Code Cong. and Adm. News, p. 5787.

1988 Acts. House Report No. 100–889, see 1988 U.S.Code Cong. and Adm.News, p. 5982.

Amendments

1988 Amendments. Subsec. (f). Pub.L. 100–702 added subsec. (f).

1978 Amendments. Pub.L. 95–598 struck out references to referees in bankruptcy in the section catchline and in subsecs. (a) and (e).

1974 Amendments. Pub.L. 93–512 substituted "Disqualification of justice, judge, magistrate, or referee in bankruptcy" for "Interest of justice or judge" in section catchline, reorganized structure of provisions, and expanded applicability to include magistrates and referees in bankruptcy and grounds for which disqualification may be based, and added provisions relating to waiver of disqualification.

Change of Name

"United States magistrate judge" substituted for "United States magistrate" in text pursuant to section 321 of Pub.L. 101–650, set out as a note under 28 U.S.C.A. § 631.

Effective and Applicability Provisions

1978 Acts. Amendment by Pub.L. 95–598 effective Oct. 1, 1979, see section 402(c) of Pub.L. 95–598, set out as a note preceding section 101 of Title 11, Bankruptcy. For procedures relating to bankruptcy matters during transition period, see note preceding section 151 of this title.

1974 Acts. Section 3 of Pub.L. 93–512 provided that: "This Act [amending this section] shall not apply to the trial of any proceeding commenced prior to the date of this Act [Dec. 5, 1974], nor to appellate review of any proceeding which was fully submitted to the reviewing court prior to the date of this Act."

CROSS REFERENCES

Application to other courts, see 28 USCA § 460.

Arbitrators subject to disqualification rules under this section, see 28 USCA § 656.

Bias or prejudice of judge, see 28 USCA § 144.

Disqualification of trial judge to hear appeal, see 28 USCA § 47.

United States Court of Veterans affairs, judges and proceedings of subject to this section, see 38 USCA § 7264.

LIBRARY REFERENCES

American Digest System

Judges ⟜39 to 56.

Key Number System Topic No. 227.

Corpus Juris Secundum

CJS Bankruptcy § 34, Bias or Knowledge.

CJS Bankruptcy § 35, Personal or Family Involvement.

CJS Bankruptcy § 36, Involvement of Former Law Associate.

CJS Bankruptcy § 37, Financial or Other Interest.

CJS Constitutional Law § 1624, Right to Qualified and Competent Judge--Disqualification of Judge or Magistrate.

CJS Federal Civil Procedure § 888, Disqualification.

CJS Federal Courts § 525, Effect of Transfer of Cause or Proceedings Therefor.

CJS Federal Courts § 630, Application of Rules to Particular Errors.

CJS Judges § 235, Consent.

CJS Judges § 243, Federal Statutes.

CJS Judges § 248, Business, Political, and Social Relations.

CJS Judges § 257, Judge as Witness.

CJS Judges § 266, Particular Statements or Expressions--Public Comment.

CJS Judges § 319, Review.

CJS Justices of the Peace § 50, Disqualification to Act.

CJS Mandamus § 83, Judges--Recusal.

PART II—DEPARTMENT OF JUSTICE

CHAPTER 39—UNITED STATES TRUSTEES

HISTORICAL AND STATUTORY NOTES

Amendments

2005 Amendments. Pub.L. 109–8, Title VI, § 602(b), Apr. 20, 2005, 119 Stat. 122, added item 589b "Bankruptcy data.".

1986 Amendments. Pub.L. 99–554, Title I, § 115(b), Oct. 27, 1986, 100 Stat. 3095, added item 589a.

Effective and Applicability Provisions

2005 Acts. Except as otherwise provided, amendments by Pub.L. 109–8 effective 180 days after April 20, 2005, and inapplicable with respect to cases commenced under Title 11 before the effective date, see Pub.L. 109–8, § 1501, set out as a note under 11 U.S.C.A. § 101.

United States Trustee Pilot; Repeal of Bankruptcy Provisions Relating to United States Trustees

Pub.L. 95–598, Title IV, § 408, Nov. 6, 1978, 92 Stat. 2686, as amended Pub.L. 98–166, Title II, § 200, Nov. 28, 1983, 97 Stat. 1081; Pub.L. 98–353, Title III, § 323, July 10, 1984, 98 Stat. 358; Pub.L. 99–429, Sept. 30, 1986, 100 Stat. 985; Pub.L. 99–500, Title I, § 101(b) [Title II, § 200], Oct. 18, 1986, 100 Stat. 1783–39, 1783–45, and Pub.L. 99–591, Title I, § 101(b), [Title II, § 2001, Oct. 30, 1986, 100 Stat. 3341–45; Pub.L. 99–554, Title III, § 307(a), Oct. 27, 1986, 100 Stat. 3125, which provided that the Attorney General conduct such studies and surveys as necessary to evaluate the needs, feasibility, and effectiveness of the United States trustee system, and report the result of such studies and surveys to the Congress, the President, and the Judicial Conference of the United States, beginning on or before January 3, 1980, and annually thereafter during the transition period; that not later than January 3, 1984, the Attorney General report to the Congress, the President, and the Judicial Conference of the United States, as to the feasibility, projected annual cost and effectiveness of the United States trustee system, as determined on the basis of the studies and surveys respecting the operation of the United States trustee system in the districts, together with recommendations as to the desirability and method of proceeding with implementation of the United States trustee system in all judicial districts of the United States; and that chapter 15 of title 11 of the United States Code [section 1501 et seq. of Title 11, Bankruptcy] and chapter 39 of title 28 of the United States Code [this chapter] are repealed, and all references to the United States trustee contained in title 28 of the United States Code [this title] are deleted, as of 30 days after the effective date of the Bankruptcy Judges, United States Trustees, and Family Farmer Bankruptcy Act of 1986 [see section 302 of Pub.L. 99–554, set out as a note under 28 U.S.C.A. § 581], with service of any United States trustee, of any assistant United States trustee, and of any employee employed or appointed under the authority of such chapter 39 is terminated on such date, was repealed by Pub.L. 99–554, Title III, § 307(b), Oct. 27, 1986, 100 Stat. 3125 [set out as a note under 28 U.S.C.A. § 581].

§ 581. United States trustees

(a) The Attorney General shall appoint one United States trustee for each of the following regions composed of Federal judicial districts (without regard to section 451):

(1) The judicial districts established for the States of Maine, Massachusetts, New Hampshire, and Rhode Island.

(2) The judicial districts established for the States of Connecticut, New York, and Vermont.

(3) The judicial districts established for the States of Delaware, New Jersey, and Pennsylvania.

(4) The judicial districts established for the States of Maryland, North Carolina, South Carolina, Virginia, and West Virginia and for the District of Columbia.

(5) The judicial districts established for the States of Louisiana and Mississippi.

(6) The Northern District of Texas and the Eastern District of Texas.

(7) The Southern District of Texas and the Western District of Texas.

(8) The judicial districts established for the States of Kentucky and Tennessee.

(9) The judicial districts established for the States of Michigan and Ohio.

(10) The Central District of Illinois and the Southern District of Illinois; and the judicial districts established for the State of Indiana.

(11) The Northern District of Illinois; and the judicial districts established for the State of Wisconsin.

(12) The judicial districts established for the States of Minnesota, Iowa, North Dakota, and South Dakota.

(13) The judicial districts established for the States of Arkansas, Nebraska, and Missouri.

(14) The District of Arizona.

(15) The Southern District of California; and the judicial districts established for the State of Hawaii, and for Guam and the Commonwealth of the Northern Mariana Islands.

(16) The Central District of California.

(17) The Eastern District of California and the Northern District of California; and the judicial district established for the State of Nevada.

(18) The judicial districts established for the States of Alaska, Idaho (exclusive of Yellowstone National Park), Montana (exclusive of Yellowstone National Park), Oregon, and Washington.

(19) The judicial districts established for the States of Colorado, Utah, and Wyoming (including those portions of Yellowstone National Park situated in the States of Montana and Idaho).

(20) The judicial districts established for the States of Kansas, New Mexico, and Oklahoma.

(21) The judicial districts established for the States of Alabama, Florida, and Georgia and for the Commonwealth of Puerto Rico and the Virgin Islands of the United States.

(b) Each United States trustee shall be appointed for a term of five years. On the expiration of his term, a United States trustee shall continue to perform the duties of his office until his successor is appointed and qualifies.

(c) Each United States trustee is subject to removal by the Attorney General.

(Added Pub.L. 95–598, Title II, § 224(a), Nov. 6, 1978, 92 Stat. 2662; amended Pub.L. 99–554, Title I, § 111(a) to (c), Oct. 27, 1986, 100 Stat. 3090, 3091.)

HISTORICAL AND STATUTORY NOTES

Revision Notes and Legislative Reports

1978 Acts. Senate Report No. 95–989 and House Report No. 95–595, see 1978 U.S. Code Cong. and Adm. News, p. 5787.

1986 Acts. House Report No. 99–764 and House Conference Report No. 99–958, see 1986 U.S. Code Cong. and Adm. News, p. 5227.

Codifications

Section 408(c) of Pub.L. 95–598, as amended, which provided for the repeal of this section and the deletion of any references to United States Trustees in this title at a prospective date, was repealed by section 307(b) of Pub.L. 99–554. See note set out preceding this section.

Amendments

1986 Amendments. Subsec. (a). Pub.L. 99–554, § 111(a), substituted in provision preceding par. (1) "regions composed of Federal judicial districts (without regard to section 451)" for "districts or groups of districts".

Subsec. (a)(1). Pub.L. 99–554, § 111(a), substituted "The judicial districts established for the States of Maine, Massachusetts, New Hampshire, and Rhode Island" for "District of Maine, District of New Hampshire, District of Massachusetts, and District of Rhode Island".

Subsec. (a)(2). Pub.L. 99–554, § 111(a), substituted "The judicial districts established for the States of Connecticut, New York, and Vermont" for "Southern District of New York".

Subsec. (a)(3). Pub.L. 99–554, § 111(a), substituted "The judicial districts established for the States of Delaware, New Jersey, and Pennsylvania" for "District of Delaware and District of New Jersey".

Subsec. (a)(4). Pub.L. 99–554, § 111(a), substituted "The judicial districts established for the States of Maryland, North Carolina, South Carolina, Virginia, and West Virginia and for the District of Columbia" for "Eastern District of Virginia and District of District of Columbia".

Subsec. (a)(5). Pub.L. 99–554, § 111(a), substituted "The judicial districts established for the States of Louisiana and Mississippi" for "Northern District of Alabama".

Subsec. (a)(6). Pub.L. 99–554, § 111(a), substituted "The Northern District of Texas and the Eastern District of Texas" for "Northern District of Texas".

Subsec. (a)(7). Pub.L. 99–554, § 111(a), substituted "The Southern District of Texas and the Western District of Texas" for "Northern District of Illinois".

Subsec. (a)(8). Pub.L. 99–554, § 111(a), substituted "The judicial districts established for the States of Kentucky and Tennessee" for "District of Minnesota, District of North Dakota, District of South Dakota".

Subsec. (a)(9). Pub.L. 99–554, § 111(a), substituted "The judicial districts established for the States of Michigan and Ohio" for "Central District of California".

Subsec. (a)(10). Pub.L. 99–554, § 111(a), substituted "The Central District of Illinois and the Southern District of Illinois; and the judicial districts established for the State of Indiana" for "District of Colorado and District of Kansas".

Subsec. (a)(11) to (21). Pub.L. 99–554, § 111(a), added pars. (11) to (21).

Subsec. (b). Pub.L. 99–554, § 111(b), substituted "five years" for "seven years" and "office" for "Office".

Subsec. (c). Pub.L. 99–554, § 111(c), struck out "for cause" after "removal".

Effective and Applicability Provisions

1978 Acts. Section effective Oct. 1, 1979, see section 402(c) of Pub.L. 95–598, as amended, set out as a note preceding 11 U.S.C.A. § 101.

Effective and Applicability Provisions of 1986 Amendments; Transition and Administrative Provisions

Pub.L. 99–554, Title III, Oct. 27, 1986, 100 Stat. 3118, as amended Pub.L. 101–650, Title III, § 317(a), (c), Dec. 1, 1990, 104 Stat. 5115, 5116; Pub.L. 103–65, § 1, Aug. 6, 1993, 107 Stat. 311; Pub.L. 106–518, Title V, § 501, Nov. 13, 2000, 114 Stat. 2421; Pub.L. 109–8, Title X, § 1001(c), Apr. 20, 2005, 119 Stat. 186, provided that:

"**Sec. 301. Incumbent United States Trustees.**

"**(a) Area for which appointed.** Notwithstanding any paragraph of section 581(a) of title 28, United States Code, as in effect before the effective date of this Act, a United States trustee serving in such office on the effective date of this Act shall serve the remaining term of such office as United States trustee for the region specified in a paragraph of such section, as amended by this Act, that includes the site at which the primary official station of the United States trustee is located immediately before the effective date of this Act.

"**(b) Term of office.** Notwithstanding section 581(b) of title 28, United States Code [28 U.S.C.A. § 581(b)], as in effect before the effective date of this Act, the term of office of any United States trustee serving in such office on the date of the enactment of this Act [Oct. 27, 1986] shall expire—

"(1) 2 years after the expiration date of such term of office under such section, as so in effect, or

"(2) 4 years after the date of the enactment of this Act [Oct. 27, 1986],

whichever occurs first.

"**Sec. 302. Effective dates; Application of Amendments.**

"**(a) General effective date.** Except as provided in subsections (b), (c), (d), (e), and (f), this Act and the amendments made by this Act [see Short Title of 1986 Amendment note set out under this section] shall take effect 30 days after the date of the enactment of this Act [Oct. 27, 1986].

"**(b) Amendments relating to bankruptcy judges and incumbent United States trustees.** Subtitle A of title I [amending 28 U.S.C.A. §§ 152 and 156 and provisions set out as a note under 28 U.S.C.A. § 152], and sections 301 [set out as a note under 28 U.S.C.A. § 581] and 307(a) [amending provisions formerly set out as a note preceding 28 U.S.C.A. § 581], shall take effect on the date of the enactment of this Act [Oct. 27, 1986].

"**(c) Amendments relating to family farmers. (1)** The amendments made by subtitle B of title II [enacting 11 U.S.C.A. §§ 1201 to 1231, and amending 11 U.S.C.A. §§ 101, 103, 108, 109, 303, 321, 322, 327, 329, 330, 346, 347, 348, 362, 363, 364, 365, 502, 523, 524, 546, 557, 706, 726, 727, 728, 1106, 1112, 1306, and 1307] shall not apply with respect to cases commenced under title 11 of the United States Code before the effective date of this Act.

"(2) Section 1202 of title 11 of the United States Code [11 U.S.C.A. § 1202] (as added by the amendment made by section 255 of this Act) shall take effect on the effective date of this Act and before the amendment made by section 227 of this Act [amending 11 U.S.C.A. § 1202].

"(3) Until the amendments made by subtitle A of title II of this Act [enacting 11 U.S.C.A. § 307, amending 11 U.S.C.A. §§ 101, 102, 105, 303, 321, 322, 324, 326, 327, 330, 341, 343, 345, 701, 703, 704, 705, 707, 727, 1102, 1104, 1105, 1112, 1129, 1163, 1202, 1302, 1307, and 1326, and repealing 11 U.S.C.A. §§ 1501 to 151326] become effective in a district and apply to a case, for purposes of such case—

"(A)(i) any reference in section 326(b) of title 11 of the United States Code [11 U.S.C.A. § 326(b)] to chapter 13 of title 11 of the United States Code [11 U.S.C.A. § 1301 et seq.] shall be deemed to be a reference to chapter 12 or chapter 13 of title 11 of the United States Code [11 U.S.C.A. § 1201 et seq. or 1301 et seq.],

"(ii) any reference in such section 326(b) to section 1302(d) of title 11 of the United States Code [11 U.S.C.A. §§ 326(b) to 1302(d)] shall be deemed to be a reference to section 1302(d) of title 11 of the United States Code [11 U.S.C.A. § 1302(d)] or section 586(b) of title 28 of the United States Code [28 U.S.C.A. § 586(b)], and

"(iii) any reference in such section 326(b) to section 1302(a) of title 11 of the United States Code [11 U.S.C.A. §§ 326(b) to 1302(a)] shall be deemed to be a reference to section 1202(a) or section 1302(a) of title 11 of the United States Code [11 U.S.C.A. § 1202(a) or 1302(a)], and

"(B)(i) the first two references in section 1202(a) of title 11 of the United States Code [11 U.S.C.A. § 1202(a)] (as added by the amendment made by section 255 of this Act) to the United States trustee shall be deemed to be a reference to the court, and

"(ii) any reference in such section 1202(a) [11 U.S.C.A. § 1202(a)] to section 586(b) of title 28 of the United States Code [28 U.S.C.A. § 586(b)] shall be deemed to be a reference to section 1202(c) of title 11 of the United States Code [11 U.S.C.A. § 1202(c)] (as so added).

"(d) **Application of amendments to judicial districts.**

"(1) **Certain regions not currently served by United States trustees.** (A) The amendments made by subtitle A of title II of this Act [enacting 11 U.S.C.A. § 307, amending 11 U.S.C.A. §§ 101, 102, 105, 303, 321, 322, 324, 326, 327, 330, 341, 343, 345, 701, 703, 704, 705, 707, 727, 1102, 1104, 1105, 1112, 1129, 1163, 1202, 1302, 1307, and 1326, and repealing 11 U.S.C.A. §§ 1501 to 151326], and section 1930(a)(6) of title 28 of the United States Code [28 U.S.C.A. § 1930(a)(6)] (as added by section 117(4) of this Act), shall not—

"(i) become effective in or with respect to a judicial district specified in subparagraph (B) until, or

"(ii) apply to cases while pending in such district before, the expiration of the 270–day period beginning on the effective date of this Act or of the 30–day period beginning on the date the Attorney General certifies under section 303 of this Act the region specified in a paragraph of section 581(a) of Title 28, United States Code [subsec. (a) of this section], as amended by section 111(a) of this Act, that includes such district, whichever occurs first.

"(B) Subparagraph (A) applies to the following:

"(i) The judicial district established for the Commonwealth of Puerto Rico.

"(ii) The District of Connecticut.

"(iii) The judicial districts established for the State of New York (other than the Southern District of New York).

"(iv) The District of Vermont.

"(v) The judicial districts established for the State of Pennsylvania.

"(vi) The judicial district established for the Virgin Islands of the United States.

"(vii) The District of Maryland.

"(viii) The judicial districts established for the State of North Carolina.

"(ix) The District of South Carolina.

"(x) The judicial districts established for the State of West Virginia.

"(xi) The Western District of Virginia.

"(xii) The Eastern District of Texas.

"(xiii) The judicial districts established for the State of Wisconsin.

"(xiv) The judicial districts established for the State of Iowa.

"(xv) The judicial districts established for the State of New Mexico.

"(xvi) The judicial districts established for the State of Oklahoma.

"(xvii) The District of Utah.

"(xviii) The District of Wyoming (including those portions of Yellowstone National Park situated in the States of Montana and Idaho).

"(xix) The judicial districts established for the State of Alabama.

"(xx) The judicial districts established for the State of Florida.

"(xxi) The judicial districts established for the State of Georgia.

"(2) **Certain remaining judicial districts not currently served by United States trustees.** (A) The amendments made by subtitle A of title II of this Act [enacting 11 U.S.C.A. § 307, amending 11 U.S.C.A. §§ 101, 102, 105, 303, 321, 322, 324, 326, 327, 330, 341, 343, 345, 701, 703, 704, 705, 707, 727, 1102, 1104, 1105, 1112, 1129, 1163, 1202, 1302, 1307, and 1326, and repealing 11 U.S.C.A. §§ 1501 to 151326], and section 1930(a)(6) of title 28 of the United States Code [28 U.S.C.A. § 1930(a)(6)] (as added by section 117(4) of this Act), shall not—

"(i) become effective in or with respect to a judicial district specified in subparagraph (B) until, or

"(ii) apply to cases while pending in such district before, the expiration of the 2–year period beginning on the effective date of this Act or of the 30–day period beginning on the date the Attorney General certifies under section 303 of this Act the region specified in a paragraph of section 581(a) of title 28, United States Code [subsec. (a) of this section], as amended by section 111(a) of this Act, that includes such district, whichever occurs first.

"(B) Subparagraph (A) applies to the following:

"(i) The judicial districts established for the State of Louisiana.

"(ii) The judicial districts established for the State of Mississippi.

"(iii) The Southern District of Texas and the Western District of Texas.

"(iv) The judicial districts established for the State of Kentucky.

"(v) The judicial districts established for the State of Tennessee.

"(vi) The judicial districts established for the State of Michigan.

"(vii) The judicial districts established for the State of Ohio.

"(viii) The judicial districts established for the State of Illinois (other than the Northern District of Illinois).

"(ix) The judicial districts established for the State of Indiana.

"(x) The judicial districts established for the State of Arkansas.

"(xi) The judicial districts established for the State of Nebraska.

"(xii) The judicial districts established for the State of Missouri.

"(xiii) The District of Arizona.

"(xiv) The District of Hawaii.

"(xv) The judicial district established for Guam.

"(xvi) The judicial district established for the Commonwealth of the Northern Mariana Islands.

"(xvii) The judicial districts established for the State of California (other than the Central District of California).

"(xviii) The District of Nevada.

"(xix) The District of Alaska.

"(xx) The District of Idaho.

"(xxi) The District of Montana.

"(xxii) The District of Oregon.

"(xxiii) The judicial districts established for the State of Washington.

"(3) **Judicial districts for the States of Alabama and North Carolina.** (A) Notwithstanding paragraphs (1) and (2), and any other provision of law, the amendments made by subtitle A of title II of this Act [enacting 11 U.S.C.A. § 307, amending 11 U.S.C.A. §§ 101, 102, 105, 303, 321, 322, 324, 326, 327, 330, 341, 343, 345, 701, 703, 704, 705, 707, 727, 1102, 1104, 1105, 1112, 1129, 1163, 1202, 1302, 1307, and 1326, and repealing 11 U.S.C.A. §§ 1501 to 151326], and section 1930(a)(6) of title 28 of the United States Code [28 U.S.C.A. § 1930(a)(6)] (as added by section 117(4) of this Act), shall not—

"(i) become effective in or with respect to a judicial district specified in subparagraph (E) until, or

"(ii) apply to cases while pending in such district before, such district elects to be included in a bankruptcy region established in section 581(a) of Title 28, United States Code [subsec. (a) of this section], as amended by section 111(a) of this Act, except that the amendment to section 105(a) of title 11, United States Code [11 U.S.C.A. § 105(a)], shall become effective as of the date of the enactment of the Federal Courts Study Committee Implementation Act of 1990 [Dec. 1, 1990].

"(B) Any election under subparagraph (A) shall be made upon a majority vote of the chief judge of such district and each bankruptcy judge in such judicial district in favor of such election.

"(C) Notice that an election has been made under subparagraph (A) shall be given, not later than 10 days after such election, to the Attorney General and the appropriate Federal Circuit Court of Appeals for such district.

"(D) Any election made under subparagraph (A) shall become effective on the date the amendments made by subtitle A of title II of this Act become effective in the region that includes such district or 30 days after the Attorney General

receives the notice required under subparagraph (C), whichever occurs later.

"(E) Subparagraph (A) applies to the following:

"(i) The judicial districts established for the State of Alabama.

"(ii) The judicial districts established for the State of North Carolina.

"(F)(i) Subject to clause (ii), with respect to cases under chapters 7, 11, 12, and 13 of title 11, United States Code [11 U.S.C.A. §§ 701 et seq., 1101 et seq., 1201 et seq., and 1301 et seq., respectively]—

"(I) commenced before the effective date of this Act, and

"(II) pending in a judicial district in the State of Alabama or the State of North Carolina before any election made under subparagraph (A) by such district becomes effective,

the amendments made by section 113 [amending 28 U.S.C.A. § 586] and subtitle A of title II of this Act, and section 1930(a)(6) of title 28 of the United States Code [28 U.S.C.A. § 1930(a)(6)] (as added by section 117(4) of this Act), shall not apply until the expiration of the 1–year period beginning on the date such election becomes effective.

"(ii) For purposes of clause (i), the amendments made by section 113 [amending 28 U.S.C.A. § 586] and subtitle A of title II of this Act, and section 1930(a)(6) of title 28 of the United States Code [28 U.S.C.A. § 1930(a)(6)] (as added by section 117(4) of this Act), shall not apply with respect to a case under chapter 7, 11, 12, or 13 of title 11, United States Code [11 U.S.C.A. § 701 et seq., 1101 et seq., 1201 et seq., or 1301 et seq., respectively], if—

"(I) the trustee in the case files the final report and account of administration of the estate, required under section 704 of such title [11 U.S.C.A. § 704], or

"(II) a plan is confirmed under section 1129, 1225, or 1325 of such title [11 U.S.C.A. § 1129, 1225, or 1325, respectively],

before the expiration of the 1–year period beginning on the date such election becomes effective.

"(G) Notwithstanding section 589a of title 28, United States Code [28 U.S.C.A. § 589a], as added by section 115 of this Act, funds collected as a result of the amendments made by section 117 of this Act [amending 28 U.S.C.A. § 1930] in a judicial district in the State of Alabama or the State of North Carolina under section 1930(a) of title 28, United States Code [28 U.S.C.A. § 1930(a)], before the date the amendments made by subtitle A of title II of this Act take effect in such district shall be deposited in the general receipts of the Treasury.

"(H) The repeal made by section 231 of this Act [repealing chapter 15 of Title 11] shall not apply in or with respect to the Northern District of Alabama until March 1, 1987, or the effective date of any election made under subparagraph (A) by such district, whichever occurs first.

"(I) In any judicial district in the State of Alabama or the State of North Carolina that has not made the election described in subparagraph (A), any person who is appointed under regulations issued by the Judicial Conference of the United States to administer estates in cases under title 11 of the United States Code [11 U.S.C.A. § 101 et seq.] may—

"(i) establish, maintain, and supervise a panel of private trustees that are eligible and available to serve as trustees in cases under title 11, United States Code, and "(ii) supervise the administration of cases and trustees in cases under chapters 7, 11, 12, and 13 of title 11, United States Code [11 U.S.C.A. §§ 701 et seq., 1101 et seq., 1201 et seq., and 1301 et seq., respectively],

until the amendments made by subtitle A of title II take effect in such district.

"(e) **Application of United States Trustee System and quarterly fees to certain cases.**

"(1) **In general.** Subject to paragraph (2), with respect to cases under chapters 7, 11, 12, and 13 of title 11, United States Code [11 U.S.C.A. §§ 701 et seq., 1101 et seq., 1201 et seq., and 1301 et seq., respectively]—

"(A) commenced before the effective date of this Act, and

"(B) pending in a judicial district referred to in section 581(a)of title 28, United States Code [subsec. (a) of this section], as amended by section 111(a) of this Act, for which a United States trustee is not authorized before the effective date of this Act to be appointed,

the amendments made by section 113 [amending 28 U.S.C.A. § 586] and subtitle A of title II of this Act [enacting 11 U.S.C.A. § 307, amending 11 U.S.C.A. §§ 101, 102, 105, 303, 321, 322, 324, 326, 327, 330, 341, 343, 345, 701, 703, 704, 705, 707, 727, 1102, 1104, 1105, 1112, 1129, 1163, 1202, 1302, 1307, and 1326, and repealing 11 U.S.C.A. § 1501 to 151326], and section 1930(a)(6) of title 28 of the United States Code [28 U.S.C.A. § 1930(a)(6)] (as added by section 117(4) of this Act), shall not apply until the expiration of the 3–year period beginning on the effective date of this Act, or of the 1–year period beginning on the date the Attorney General certifies under section 303 of this Act the region specified in a paragraph of such section 581(a) [subsec. (a) of this section], as so amended, that includes such district, whichever occurs first.

"(2) **Amendments inapplicable.** For purposes of paragraph (1), the amendments made by section 113 [amending 28 U.S.C.A. § 586] and subtitle A of title II of this Act, and section 1930(a)(6) of title 28 of the United States Code [28 U.S.C.A. § 1930(a)(6)] (as added by section 117(4) of this Act), shall not apply with respect to a case under chapter 7, 11, 12, or 13 of title 11, United States Code [11 U.S.C.A. § 701 et seq., 1101 et seq., 1201 et seq., or 1301 et seq., respectively], if—

"(A) the trustee in the case files the final report and account of administration of the estate, required under section 704 of such title [11 U.S.C.A. § 704], or

"(B) a plan is confirmed under section 1129, 1225, or 1325 of such title [11 U.S.C.A. § 1129, 1225, or 1325, respectively],

before the expiration of the 3–year period, or the expiration of the 1–year period, specified in paragraph (1), whichever occurs first.

"(3) **Rule of construction regarding fees for cases.** This Act [see Short Title of 1986 Amendments note set out under this section] and the amendments made by section 117(4) of this Act [amending 28 U.S.C.A. § 1930] shall not be construed to require the payment of a fee under paragraph (6) of section 1930(a) of Title 28, United States Code [28 U.S.C.A. § 1930(a)], in a case under Title 11 of the United States Code for any conduct or period occurring before such paragraph becomes effective in the district in which such case is pending.

"(f) [Repealed. **Pub.L. 109–8, Title X, § 1001(c), Apr. 20, 2005, 119 Stat. 186.**]

"**Sec. 303.**—Certification of judicial districts; notice and publication of certification.

"(a) **Certification by Attorney General.** The Attorney General may certify in writing a region specified in a paragraph of section 581(a) of title 28, United States Code [subsec. (a) of this section] (other than paragraph (16)), as amended by section 111(a) of this Act, to the appropriate court of appeals of the United States, for the purpose of informing such court that certain amendments made by this Act will become effective in accordance with section 302 of this Act [section 302 of this note].

"(b) **Notice and publication of certification.** Whenever the Attorney General transmits a certification under subsection (a), the Attorney General shall simultaneously—

"(1) transmit a copy of such certification to the Speaker of the House of Representatives and to the President pro tempore of the Senate, and

"(2) publish such certification in the Federal Register.

"**Sec. 304. Administrative provisions.**

"(a) **Cooperative arrangements.** The Attorney General and the Director of the Administrative Office of the United States Courts may enter into agreements under which United States trustees may—

"(1) use—

"(A) the services, equipment, personnel, records, reports, and data compilations, in any form, of the courts of the United States, and

"(B) the facilities of such courts, and

"(2) cooperate in the use by the courts of the United States of—

"(A) the services, equipment, personnel, records, reports, and data compilations, in any form, of United States trustees, and

"(B) the facilities of such trustees,

to prevent duplication during the 2–year period beginning on the effective date of this Act.

"(b) **Information and documents relating to bankruptcy cases and United States trustees.** The Director of the Administrative Office of the United States Courts shall make available to United States trustees, at the request of the Attorney General and on a continuing basis, all records, reports, and data compilations relating to—

"(1) cases and proceedings under title 11 of the United States Code [11 U.S.C.A. § 101 et seq.], and

"(2) the duties of United States trustees under titles 11 and 28 of the United States Code.

"**Sec. 305. Application of certain Bankruptcy Rules.**

"(a) **Rules relating to the United States Trustee System.** If a United States trustee is not authorized, before the effective date of this Act to be appointed for a judicial district referred to in section 581(a) of title 28, United States Code [subsec. (a) of this section], as amended by section 111(a) of this Act, then part X of the Bankruptcy Rules [set out in Title 11, Bankruptcy] shall not apply to cases in such district until the amendments made by subtitle A of title II of this Act [Pub.L. 99–554, Title II, §§ 201 to 231; see Tables for classification] become effective under section 302 of this Act [section 302 of this note] in such district.

"(b) **Rules relating to Chapter 12 of Title 11.** The rules prescribed under section 2075 of title 28, United States Code [28 U.S.C.A. § 2075], and in effect on the date of the enactment of this Act [Oct. 27, 1986] shall apply to cases filed under chapter 12 of title 11, United States Code [11 U.S.C.A.

§ 1201 et seq.], to the extent practicable and not inconsistent with the amendments made by title II of this Act [Pub.L. 99–554, Title II, §§ 201 to 283; see Tables for classification].

"Sec. 306.　Salary of incumbent United States trustees.

"For service as a United States trustee in the period beginning on the effective date of this Act and ending on the expiration under section 301 of this Act of their respective terms of office, the salary payable to United States trustees serving in such offices on the effective date of this Act shall be fixed in accordance with section 587 of title 28, United States Code [28 U.S.C.A. § 587], as amended by section 114(a) of this Act.

"Sec. 307.　Preservation of United States Trustee System during pendency of legislation; repealer.

"(a) Temporary delay of Repeal of United States Trustee System. Effective immediately before November 10, 1986, section 408(c) of the Act of November 6, 1978 (Pub.L. 95–598; 92 Stat. 2687) [formerly set out as a note preceding this section], is amended by striking out 'November 10, 1986' and inserting in lieu thereof '30 days after the effective date of the Bankruptcy Judges, United States Trustees, and Family Farmer Bankruptcy Act of 1986 [Pub.L. 99–554]'.

"(b) Conforming amendment. Section 408 of the Act of November 6, 1978 (Pub.L. 95–598; 92 Stat. 2687) [formerly set out as a note preceding this section], is repealed.

[Section 302(b) of Pub.L. 99–554 provided in part that the amendment by subsec. (a) is effective Oct. 27, 1986.]

"Sec. 308.　Consideration of current private trustees for appointment by United States trustees.

"(a) Trustees in bankruptcy cases under Chapter 7. It is the sense of the Congress that individuals who are serving before the effective date of this Act, as trustees in cases under chapter 7 of title 11, United States Code [11 U.S.C.A. § 701 et seq.], should be considered by United States trustees for appointment under section 586(a)(1) of title 28, United States Code [28 U.S.C.A. § 586(a)(1)], to the panels of private trustees that are established as a result of the amendments made by this Act [see Short Title of 1986 Amendments note under this section].

"(b) Standing trustees in bankruptcy cases under Chapter 13. It is the sense of the Congress that individuals who are serving before the effective date of this Act, as standing trustees in cases under chapter 13 of title 11, United States Code [11 U.S.C.A. § 1301 et seq.], should be considered by the United States trustees for appointment under section 586(b) of title 28, United States Code [28 U.S.C.A. § 586(b)], as standing trustees who are appointed as a result of the amendments made by this Act [see Short Title of 1986 Amendments note set out under this section].

"Sec. 309.　Appointment of United States trustees by the Attorney General.

"It is the sense of the Congress that individuals otherwise qualified who are serving, before the effective date of this Act, as estate administrators under title 11 of the United States Code [11 U.S.C.A. § 101 et seq.] should be considered by the Attorney General for appointment under sections 581 and 582 of title 28, United States Code [this section and 28 U.S.C.A. § 582], to new positions of United States trustee and assistant United States trustee resulting from the amendments made by this Act [see Short Title of 1986 Amendments note set out under this section].

"Sec. 310.　Electronic case management demonstration project.

"(a) Establishment of project. Not later than 1 year after the effective date of this Act, the Director of the Executive Office for United States Trustees, in consultation with the Director of the Administrative Office of the United States Courts, shall establish an electronic case management demonstration project to be carried out in 3 Federal judicial districts that have a sufficiently large and varied bankruptcy caseload so as to provide a meaningful evaluation of the cost and effectiveness of such system. A contract for such project shall be awarded—

"(1) on the basis of competitive bids submitted by qualified nongovernmental entities that are able to design an automated joint information system for use by the United States courts and by United States trustees, and

"(2) in accordance with the Federal Property and Administrative Services Act of 1949 [see chapters 1 to 11 of Title 40, Public Buildings, Property, and Works, and division C (except sections 3302, 3307(e), 3501(b), 3509, 3906, 4710, and 4711) of subtitle I of Title 41, Public Contracts], the Office of Federal Procurement Policy Act [see division B (except sections 1123, 2303, 2304, and 2313) of subtitle I of Title 41], and title 31 of the United States Code.

"(b) Study by General Accounting Office [now Government Accountability Office]. Not later than 1 year after the electronic case management system begins to operate in all of the judicial districts participating in the demonstration project carried out under subsection (a), the General Accounting Office [now Government Accountability Office] shall conduct a study to compare the cost and effectiveness of such system with the cost and effectiveness of case management systems used in Federal judicial districts that are not participating in such project.

"(c) Term of project. The demonstration project required by subsection (a) shall be carried out until—

"(1) the expiration of the 2–year period beginning on the date the electronic case management system begins to operate in all of the judicial districts participating in such project, or

"(2) legislation is enacted to extend, expand, modify, or terminate the operation of such project,

whichever occurs first.

"(d) Use by clerks of the courts. The electronic case management system demonstrated under the project required by subsection (a) shall provide the clerk of court in each district in which such system is operated, with a means of—

"(1) maintaining a complete electronic case file of all relevant information contained in petitions and schedules (and any amendments thereto) relating to debtors in cases under title 11 of the United States Code [11 U.S.C.A. § 101 et seq.], including—

"(A) a complete list of creditors in each such case, as listed by the debtor,

"(B) a complete list of assets scheduled by the debtor, the value of such asset, and any action taken by the trustee or debtor in possession with regard to such asset during the pendency of such case,

"(C) a complete list of debts and, with respect to each debt—

"(i) any priority of such debt under title 11 of the United States Code [11 U.S.C.A. § 101 et seq.],

"(ii) whether such debt is secured or unsecured, and

"(iii) whether such debt is contingent or noncontingent, and

"(D) the debtor's statements of current expenses and income, and

"(2) maintaining all calendars and dockets and producing all notices required to be sent in cases under title 11 of the United States Code [11 U.S.C.A. § 101 et seq.].

"(e) Use by United States trustees. The electronic case management system demonstrated under the project required by subsection (a) shall provide, at a minimum, the United States trustee in each district in which such system is operated with—

"(1) complete electronic case files which contain, in addition to the information listed in subsection (d), records of case openings, case closings, hearings, and the filing of all motions, trustee appointments, pleadings, and responses, as well as a record of the responses by the United States trustee to those motions, trustee appointments, and pleadings,

"(2) a means to generate standardized forms for motions, appointments, pleadings, and responses,

"(3) a means to generate standard management reports and letters on an exception basis,

"(4) a means to maintain accounting records, reports, and information required to be maintained by debtors in possession and trustees in cases under title 11 of the United States Code [11 U.S.C.A. § 101 et seq.],

"(5) a means to calculate and record distribution to creditors, final applications and orders for distribution, and final case closing reports, and

"(6) a means to monitor the payment of filing and other required fees.

"(f) Availability to certain governmental entities. Unlimited access to information maintained in the electronic case management system demonstrated under the project required by subsection (a) shall be provided at no charge to the following:

"(1) The Congress.

"(2) The Executive Office for the United States Trustees.

"(3) The Administrative Office of the United States Courts.

"(4) The clerks of the courts in judicial districts in which such system is operated and persons who review case information, in accordance with section 107(a) of title 11, United States Code [11 U.S.C.A. § 107(a)], in the offices of the clerks.

"(5) The judges on the bankruptcy and district courts in districts in which such system is operated.

"(6) Trustees in cases pending in districts in which such system is operated.

"(g) Fees for other users. (1) The entity which is awarded a contract to provide the electronic case management system demonstrated under this project may, under guidelines established by the Director of the Executive Office for the United States Trustees in the provisions of such contract, collect reasonable fees from assets of the estate of the debtor in bankruptcy for providing notices and services to the court and trustees under the demonstration project.

"(2) Access to information maintained in electronic case files pursuant to the demonstration project may be provided to persons other than those specified in subsection (f), but such access shall be limited to viewing such information only.

A reasonable charge for such access may be collected by the entity which is awarded a contract under this section, in accordance with the guidelines established by the Director of the Executive Office for the United States Trustees in such contract. A reasonable portion of any charge so collected may be required by the Director to be remitted to the Executive Office for United States Trustees and deposited in the United States Trustee System Fund established in section 589a of title 28, United States Code [28 U.S.C.A. § 589a].

"(h) Security. Access provided under subsection (f) to an entity or an individual shall be subject to such security limitations as may be imposed by the Congress or the head of the affected entity.

"Sec. 311. Cases pending under the Bankruptcy Act.

"At the end of one calendar year following the date the amendments made by subtitle A of title II of this Act [amendments by Pub.L. 99–554, Title II, §§ 201 to 231, which were approved Oct. 27, 1986; see Tables for classification] take effect in a district in which any case is still pending under the Bankruptcy Act [section 1 et seq. of former Title 11, Bankruptcy, see notes set out preceding 11 U.S.C.A. § 101], the district court shall withdraw the reference of any such case and, after notice and a hearing, determine the status of the case. Such case shall be remanded to the bankruptcy judge with such instructions as are necessary for the prompt closing of the case and with a requirement that a progress report on the case be provided by the bankruptcy judge after such interval as the district court deems appropriate."

[For termination of reporting provisions pertaining to certification of judicial districts, effective May 15, 2000, see Pub.L. 104–66, § 3003, as amended, set out as a note under 31 U.S.C.A. § 1113, and the 13th item on page 117 of House Document No. 103–7.]

[Amendments by Pub.L. 109–8 effective, except as otherwise provided, 180 days after April 20, 2005, and inapplicable with respect to cases commenced under Title 11 before the effective date, see Pub.L. 109–8, § 1501, set out as a note under 11 U.S.C.A. § 101.]

Short Title

1986 Amendments. Section 1 of Pub.L. 99–554 provided: "That this Act [enacting section 589a of this title and sections 307, and 1201 to 1231 of Title 11, Bankruptcy, amending sections 49, 96, 152, 156, 157, 528, 581, 582, 584 to 587, 604, 1334, and 1930 of this title and sections 101 to 103, 105, 108, 109, 303, 321, 322, 324, 326, 327, 329, 330, 341, 343, 345 to 348, 362 to 365, 502, 503, 521 to 524, 546 to 549, 554, 557, 701, 703 to 707, 724, 726 to 728, 743, 1102, 1104 to 1106, 1112, 1121, 1129, 1163, 1202, 1302, 1306, 1307, and 1324 to 1326 of Title 11, Bankruptcy Form No. 1, set out in the Appendix to Title 11, repealing sections 1201 to 1231 and 1501 to 151326 of Title 11, enacting provisions set out as notes under sections 581 and 589 of this title, amending provisions set out as a note under section 152 of this title and preceding section 581 of this title, and repealing provisions set out as notes under preceding section 581 of this title] may be cited as the 'Bankruptcy Judges, United States Trustees, and Family Farmer Bankruptcy Act of 1986'."

Bankruptcy Crimes

Pub.L. 109–162, Title XI, § 1175, Jan. 5, 2006, 119 Stat. 3125, provided that:

"The Director of the Executive Office for United States Trustees shall prepare an annual report to the Congress detailing—

"(1) the number and types of criminal referrals made by the United States Trustee Program;

"(2) the outcomes of each criminal referral;

"(3) for any year in which the number of criminal referrals is less than for the prior year, an explanation of the decrease; and

"(4) the United States Trustee Program's efforts to prevent bankruptcy fraud and abuse, particularly with respect to the establishment of uniform internal controls to detect common, higher risk frauds, such as a debtor's failure to disclose all assets."

CROSS REFERENCES

Appointment of acting United States trustee by Attorney General to serve until vacancy is filled by appointment under this section, see 28 USCA § 585.

LIBRARY REFERENCES

American Digest System

Bankruptcy ⊕3004.1, 3007.

Key Number System Topic No. 51.

Corpus Juris Secundum

CJS Bankruptcy § 9, Title 28 of the U.S. Code.

CJS Bankruptcy § 38, Nationwide System; Not in Effect in North Carolina and Alabama.

CJS Bankruptcy § 41, Appointment, Oath, and Term; Vacancy in and Removal from Office.

§ 582. Assistant United States trustees

(a) The Attorney General may appoint one or more assistant United States trustees in any region when the public interest so requires.

(b) Each assistant United States trustee is subject to removal by the Attorney General.

(Added Pub.L. 95–598, Title II, § 224(a), Nov. 6, 1978, 92 Stat. 2663; amended Pub.L. 99–554, Title I, § 111(d), Oct. 27, 1986, 100 Stat. 3091.)

HISTORICAL AND STATUTORY NOTES

Revision Notes and Legislative Reports

1978 Acts. Senate Report No. 95–989 and House Report No. 95–595, see 1978 U.S.Code Cong. and Adm.News, p. 5787.

1986 Acts. House Report No. 99–764 and House Conference Report No. 99–958, see 1986 U.S.Code Cong. and Adm. News, p. 5227.

Codifications

Section 408(c) of Pub.L. 95–598, as amended, which provided for the repeal of this section and the deletion of any references to United States Trustees in this title at a prospective date, was repealed by section 307(b) of Pub.L. 99–554. See note set out preceding section 581 of this title.

Amendments

1986 Amendments. Subsec. (a). Pub.L. 99–554, § 111(d)(1), substituted "region" for "district".

Subsec. (b). Pub.L. 99–554, § 111(d)(2), struck out "for cause" after "removal".

Effective and Applicability Provisions

1986 Acts. Amendment by Pub.L. 99–554 effective 30 days after Oct. 27, 1986, except as otherwise provided, see section 302(a) of Pub.L. 99–554, as amended, set out as a note under section 581 of this title.

1978 Acts. Section effective Oct. 1, 1979, see section 402(c) of Pub.L. 95–598, as amended, set out as a note preceding section 101 of Title 11, Bankruptcy.

Appointment of United States Trustees by Attorney General

Appointment of United States Trustees by the Attorney General of individuals otherwise qualified, serving as estate administrators under Title 11, Bankruptcy, before effective date of Pub.L. 99–554, see section 309 of Pub.L. 99–554, as amended; set out as a note under section 581 of this title.

LIBRARY REFERENCES

American Digest System

Bankruptcy ⊕3004.1, 3007.

Key Number System Topic No. 51.

Corpus Juris Secundum

CJS Bankruptcy § 41, Appointment, Oath, and Term; Vacancy in and Removal from Office.

§ 583. Oath of office

Each United States trustee and assistant United States trustee, before taking office, shall take an oath to execute faithfully his duties.

(Added Pub.L. 95–598, Title II, § 224(a), Nov. 6, 1978, 92 Stat. 2663.)

HISTORICAL AND STATUTORY NOTES

Revision Notes and Legislative Reports

1978 Acts. Senate Report No. 95–989 and House Report No. 95–595, see 1978 U.S.Code Cong. and Adm.News, p. 5787.

Codifications

Section 408(c) of Pub.L. 95–598, as amended, which provided for the repeal of this section and the deletion of any references to United States Trustees in this title at a prospective date, was repealed by section 307(b) of Pub.L. 99–554. See note set out preceding section 581 of this title.

Effective and Applicability Provisions

1978 Acts. Section effective Oct. 1, 1979, see section 402(c) of Pub.L. 95–598, as amended, set out as a note preceding section 101 of Title 11, Bankruptcy.

LIBRARY REFERENCES

American Digest System

Bankruptcy ⊕3003.

Key Number System Topic No. 51.

Corpus Juris Secundum

CJS Bankruptcy § 41, Appointment, Oath, and Term; Vacancy in and Removal from Office.

§ 584. Official stations

The Attorney General may determine the official stations of the United States trustees and assistant United States trustees within the regions for which they were appointed.

(Added Pub.L. 95–598, Title II, § 224(a), Nov. 6, 1978, 92 Stat. 2663; amended Pub.L. 99–554, Title I, § 144(d), Oct. 27, 1986, 100 Stat. 3096.)

HISTORICAL AND STATUTORY NOTES
Revision Notes and Legislative Reports

1978 Acts. Senate Report No. 95–989 and House Report No. 95–595, see 1978 U.S.Code Cong. and Adm.News, p. 5787.

1986 Acts. House Report No. 99–764 and House Conference Report No. 99–958, see 1986 U.S.Code Cong. and Adm. News, p. 5227.

Codifications

Section 408(c) of Pub.L. 95–598, as amended, which provided for the repeal of this section and the deletion of any references to United States Trustees in this title at a prospective date, was repealed by section 307(b) of Pub.L. 99–554. See note set out preceding section 581 of this title.

Amendments

1986 Amendments. Pub.L. 99–554 substituted "regions" for "districts".

Effective and Applicability Provisions

1986 Acts. Amendment by Pub.L. 99–554 effective 30 days after Oct. 27, 1986, except as otherwise provided, see section 302(a) of Pub.L. 99–554, as amended, set out as a note under section 581 of this title.

1978 Acts. Section effective Oct. 1, 1979, see section 402(c) of Pub.L. 95–598, as amended, set out as a note preceding section 101 of Title 11, Bankruptcy.

LIBRARY REFERENCES
American Digest System
Bankruptcy ⟜3001.
Key Number System Topic No. 51.

§ 585. Vacancies

(a) The Attorney General may appoint an acting United States trustee for a region in which the office of the United States trustee is vacant. The individual so appointed may serve until the date on which the vacancy is filled by appointment under section 581 of this title or by designation under subsection (b) of this section.

(b) The Attorney General may designate a United States trustee to serve in not more than two regions for such time as the public interest requires.

(Added Pub.L. 95–598, Title II, § 224(a), Nov. 6, 1978, 92 Stat. 2663; amended Pub.L. 99–554, Title I, § 112, Oct. 27, 1986, 100 Stat. 3091.)

HISTORICAL AND STATUTORY NOTES
Revision Notes and Legislative Reports

1978 Acts. Senate Report No. 95–989 and House Report No. 95–595, see 1978 U.S. Code Cong. and Adm. News, p. 5787.

1986 Acts. House Report No. 99–764 and House Conference Report No. 99–958, see 1986 U.S. Code Cong. and Adm. News, p. 5227.

Codifications

Section 408(c) of Pub.L. 95–598, as amended, which provided for the repeal of this section and the deletion of any references to United States Trustees in this title at a prospective date, was repealed by section 307(b) of Pub.L. 99–554. See note set out preceding section 581 of this title.

Amendments

1986 Amendments. Subsec. (a). Pub.L. 99–554, § 112, designated existing provision as subsec. (a), and in subsec. (a) as so designated, substituted "for a region" for "for a district", struck out ", or may designate a United States trustee for another judicial district for another judicial district to serve as trustee for the district in which such vacancy exists" after "is vacant", "or designated" after "so appointed", and "the earlier of 90 days after such appointment or designation, as the case may be, or" after "serve until" and inserted "or by designation under subsection (b) of this section" after "581 of this title".

Subsec. (b). Pub.L. 99–554, § 112, added subsec. (b).

Effective and Applicability Provisions

1986 Acts. Amendment by Pub.L. 99–554 effective 30 days after Oct. 27, 1986, except as otherwise provided, see section 302(a) of Pub.L. 99–554, as amended, set out as a note under section 581 of this title.

1978 Acts. Section effective Oct. 1, 1979, see section 402(c) of Pub.L. 95–598, as amended, set out as a note preceding section 101 of Title 11, Bankruptcy.

LIBRARY REFERENCES
American Digest System
Bankruptcy ⟜3004.1, 3007.
Key Number System Topic No. 51.

Corpus Juris Secundum
CJS Bankruptcy § 41, Appointment, Oath, and Term; Vacancy in and Removal from Office.

§ 586. Duties; supervision by Attorney General

(a) Each United States trustee, within the region for which such United States trustee is appointed, shall—

(1) establish, maintain, and supervise a panel of private trustees that are eligible and available to serve as trustees in cases under chapter 7 of title 11;

(2) serve as and perform the duties of a trustee in a case under title 11 when required under title 11 to serve as trustee in such a case;

(3) supervise the administration of cases and trustees in cases under chapter 7, 11, 12, 13, or 15 of title

11 by, whenever the United States trustee considers it to be appropriate—

(A)(i) reviewing, in accordance with procedural guidelines adopted by the Executive Office of the United States Trustee (which guidelines shall be applied uniformly by the United States trustee except when circumstances warrant different treatment), applications filed for compensation and reimbursement under section 330 of title 11; and

(ii) filing with the court comments with respect to such application and, if the United States Trustee considers it to be appropriate, objections to such application;

(B) monitoring plans and disclosure statements filed in cases under chapter 11 of title 11 and filing with the court, in connection with hearings under sections 1125 and 1128 of such title, comments with respect to such plans and disclosure statements;

(C) monitoring plans filed under chapters 12 and 13 of title 11 and filing with the court, in connection with hearings under sections 1224, 1229, 1324, and 1329 of such title, comments with respect to such plans;

(D) taking such action as the United States trustee deems to be appropriate to ensure that all reports, schedules, and fees required to be filed under title 11 and this title by the debtor are properly and timely filed;

(E) monitoring creditors' committees appointed under title 11;

(F) notifying the appropriate United States attorney of matters which relate to the occurrence of any action which may constitute a crime under the laws of the United States and, on the request of the United States attorney, assisting the United States attorney in carrying out prosecutions based on such action;

(G) monitoring the progress of cases under title 11 and taking such actions as the United States trustee deems to be appropriate to prevent undue delay in such progress;

(H) in small business cases (as defined in section 101 of title 11), performing the additional duties specified in title 11 pertaining to such cases; and

(I) monitoring applications filed under section 327 of title 11 and, whenever the United States trustee deems it to be appropriate, filing with the court comments with respect to the approval of such applications;

(4) deposit or invest under section 345 of title 11 money received as trustee in cases under title 11;

(5) perform the duties prescribed for the United States trustee under title 11 and this title, and such duties consistent with title 11 and this title as the Attorney General may prescribe;

(6) make such reports as the Attorney General directs, including the results of audits performed under section 603(a) of the Bankruptcy Abuse Prevention and Consumer Protection Act of 2005;

(7) in each of such small business cases—

(A) conduct an initial debtor interview as soon as practicable after the date of the order for relief but before the first meeting scheduled under section 341(a) of title 11, at which time the United States trustee shall—

(i) begin to investigate the debtor's viability;

(ii) inquire about the debtor's business plan;

(iii) explain the debtor's obligations to file monthly operating reports and other required reports;

(iv) attempt to develop an agreed scheduling order; and

(v) inform the debtor of other obligations;

(B) if determined to be appropriate and advisable, visit the appropriate business premises of the debtor, ascertain the state of the debtor's books and records, and verify that the debtor has filed its tax returns; and

(C) review and monitor diligently the debtor's activities, to determine as promptly as possible whether the debtor will be unable to confirm a plan; and

(8) in any case in which the United States trustee finds material grounds for any relief under section 1112 of title 11, apply promptly after making that finding to the court for relief.

(b) If the number of cases under chapter 12 or 13 of title 11 commenced in a particular region so warrants, the United States trustee for such region may, subject to the approval of the Attorney General, appoint one or more individuals to serve as standing trustee, or designate one or more assistant United States trustees to serve in cases under such chapter. The United States trustee for such region shall supervise any such individual appointed as standing trustee in the performance of the duties of standing trustee.

(c) Each United States trustee shall be under the general supervision of the Attorney General, who shall provide general coordination and assistance to the United States trustees.

(d)(1) The Attorney General shall prescribe by rule qualifications for membership on the panels established by United States trustees under paragraph (a)(1) of this section, and qualifications for appointment under subsection (b) of this section to serve as standing trustee in cases under chapter 12 or 13 of title 11. The Attorney General may not require that an individual be an attorney in order to qualify for appointment under subsection (b) of this section to serve as standing trustee in cases under chapter 12 or 13 of title 11.

(2) A trustee whose appointment under subsection (a)(1) or under subsection (b) is terminated or who

ceases to be assigned to cases filed under title 11, United States Code, may obtain judicial review of the final agency decision by commencing an action in the district court of the United States for the district for which the panel to which the trustee is appointed under subsection (a)(1), or in the district court of the United States for the district in which the trustee is appointed under subsection (b) resides, after first exhausting all available administrative remedies, which if the trustee so elects, shall also include an administrative hearing on the record. Unless the trustee elects to have an administrative hearing on the record, the trustee shall be deemed to have exhausted all administrative remedies for purposes of this paragraph if the agency fails to make a final agency decision within 90 days after the trustee requests administrative remedies. The Attorney General shall prescribe procedures to implement this paragraph. The decision of the agency shall be affirmed by the district court unless it is unreasonable and without cause based on the administrative record before the agency.

(e)(1) The Attorney General, after consultation with a United States trustee that has appointed an individual under subsection (b) of this section to serve as standing trustee in cases under chapter 12 or 13 of title 11, shall fix—

(A) a maximum annual compensation for such individual consisting of—

(i) an amount not to exceed the highest annual rate of basic pay in effect for level V of the Executive Schedule; and

(ii) the cash value of employment benefits comparable to the employment benefits provided by the United States to individuals who are employed by the United States at the same rate of basic pay to perform similar services during the same period of time; and

(B) a percentage fee not to exceed—

(i) in the case of a debtor who is not a family farmer, ten percent; or

(ii) in the case of a debtor who is a family farmer, the sum of—

(I) not to exceed ten percent of the payments made under the plan of such debtor, with respect to payments in an aggregate amount not to exceed $450,000; and

(II) three percent of payments made under the plan of such debtor, with respect to payments made after the aggregate amount of payments made under the plan exceeds $450,000;

based on such maximum annual compensation and the actual, necessary expenses incurred by such individual as standing trustee.

(2) Such individual shall collect such percentage fee from all payments received by such individual under plans in the cases under chapter 12 or 13 of title 11 for which such individual serves as standing trustee. Such individual shall pay to the United States trustee, and the United States trustee shall deposit in the United States Trustee System Fund—

(A) any amount by which the actual compensation of such individual exceeds 5 per centum upon all payments received under plans in cases under chapter 12 or 13 of title 11 for which such individual serves as standing trustee; and

(B) any amount by which the percentage for all such cases exceeds—

(i) such individual's actual compensation for such cases, as adjusted under subparagraph (A) of paragraph (1); plus

(ii) the actual, necessary expenses incurred by such individual as standing trustee in such cases. Subject to the approval of the Attorney General, any or all of the interest earned from the deposit of payments under plans by such individual may be utilized to pay actual, necessary expenses without regard to the percentage limitation contained in subparagraph (d)(1)(B) of this section.

(3) After first exhausting all available administrative remedies, an individual appointed under subsection (b) may obtain judicial review of final agency action to deny a claim of actual, necessary expenses under this subsection by commencing an action in the district court of the United States for the district where the individual resides. The decision of the agency shall be affirmed by the district court unless it is unreasonable and without cause based upon the administrative record before the agency.

(4) The Attorney General shall prescribe procedures to implement this subsection.

(f)(1) The United States trustee for each district is authorized to contract with auditors to perform audits in cases designated by the United States trustee, in accordance with the procedures established under section 603(a) of the Bankruptcy Abuse Prevention and Consumer Protection Act of 2005.

(2)(A) The report of each audit referred to in paragraph (1) shall be filed with the court and transmitted to the United States trustee. Each report shall clearly and conspicuously specify any material misstatement of income or expenditures or of assets identified by the person performing the audit. In any case in which a material misstatement of income or expenditures or of assets has been reported, the clerk of the district court (or the clerk of the bankruptcy court if one is certified under section 156(b) of this title) shall give notice of the misstatement to the creditors in the case.

(B) If a material misstatement of income or expenditures or of assets is reported, the United States trustee shall—

(i) report the material misstatement, if appropriate, to the United States Attorney pursuant to section 3057 of title 18; and

(ii) if advisable, take appropriate action, including but not limited to commencing an adversary proceeding to revoke the debtor's discharge pursuant to section 727(d) of title 11.

(Added Pub.L. 95–598, Title II, § 224(a), Nov. 6, 1978, 92 Stat. 2663; amended Pub.L. 99–554, Title I, § 113, Oct. 27, 1986, 100 Stat. 3091; Pub.L. 101–509, Title V, § 529 [Title I, § 110(a)], Nov. 5, 1990, 104 Stat. 1427, 1452; Pub.L. 103–394, Title II, § 224(a), Title V, § 502, Oct. 22, 1994, 108 Stat. 4130, 4147; Pub.L. 109–8, Title IV, § 439, Title VI, § 603(b), Title VIII, § 802(c)(3), Title XII, § 1231, Apr. 20, 2005, 119 Stat. 113, 122, 146, 201; Pub.L. 111–327, § 2(c)(3), Dec. 22, 2010, 124 Stat. 3563.)

HISTORICAL AND STATUTORY NOTES

Revision Notes and Legislative Reports

1978 Acts. Senate Report No. 95–989 and House Report No. 95–595, see 1978 U.S. Code Cong. and Adm. News, p. 5787.

1986 Acts. House Report No. 99–764 and House Conference Report No. 99–958, see 1986 U.S. Code Cong. and Adm. News, p. 5227.

1994 Acts. House Report No. 103–835, see 1994 U.S. Code Cong. and Adm. News, p. 3340.

2005 Acts. House Report No. 109–31(Part I), see 2005 U.S. Code Cong. and Adm. News, p. 88.

References in Text

Chapter 12 or 13 of title 11, referred to in text, is 11 U.S.C.A. § 1201 et seq. or 11 U.S.C.A. § 1301 et seq., respectively.

Chapter 7, 11, 12, 13, or 15 of title 11, referred to in subsec. (a)(3), is 11 U.S.C.A. § 701 et seq., 11 U.S.C.A. § 1101 et seq., 11 U.S.C.A. § 1201 et seq., 11 U.S.C.A. § 1301 et seq., or 11 U.S.C.A. § 1501 et seq., respectively.

Level V of the Executive Schedule, referred to in subsec. (e)(1)(A)(i), is set out in section 5316 of Title 5, Government Organization and Employees.

Section 603(a) of the Bankruptcy Abuse Prevention and Consumer Protection Act of 2005, referred to in subsecs. (a)(6) and (f)(1), is Pub.L. 109–8, Title VII, § 603(a), Apr. 20, 2005, 119 Stat. 122, which is set out as a note under this section.

Codifications

Section 408(c) of Pub.L. 95–598, as amended, which provided for the repeal of this section and the deletion of any references to United States Trustees in this title at a prospective date, was repealed by section 307(b) of Pub.L. 99–554. See note set out preceding section 581 of this title.

Amendments

2010 Amendments. Subsec. (a)(3)(A)(ii). Pub.L. 111–327, § 2(c)(3)(A), struck out the period at the end and inserted a semicolon.

Subsec. (a)(7)(C). Pub.L. 111–327, § 2(c)(3)(B), struck out "identify" and inserted "determine".

Subsec. (a)(8). Pub.L. 111–327, § 2(c)(3)(C), struck out "the United States trustee shall" following "title 11,".

2005 Amendments. Subsec. (a)(3). Pub.L. 109–8, § 802(c)(3), in the matter preceding subpar. (A), struck out "or 13" and inserted "13, or 15".

Subsec. (a)(3)(G). Pub.L. 109–8, § 439(1)(A), struck out "and" at the end of subpar. (G).

Subsec. (a)(3)(H). Pub.L. 109–8, § 439(1)(B), (C), redesignated former subpar. (H) as (I), and inserted a new subpar. (H).

Subsec. (a)(3)(I). Pub.L. 109–8, § 439(1)(B), redesignated former subpar. (H) as (I).

Subsec. (a)(5). Pub.L. 109–8, § 439(2), struck out "and" at the end of par. (5).

Subsec. (a)(6). Pub.L. 109–8, § 439(3), struck out the period at the end of par. (6) and inserted a semicolon.

Pub.L. 109–8, § 603(b)(1), rewrote par. (6), which formerly read: "make such reports as the Attorney General directs;".

Subsec. (a)(7). Pub.L. 109–8, § 439(4), added par. (7).

Subsec. (a)(8). Pub.L. 109–8, § 439(4), added par. (8).

Subsec. (d). Pub.L.109–8, § 1231(a), inserted "(1)" after "(d)" and added paragraph (2).

Subsec. (e)(3), (4). Pub.L.109–8, § 1231(b), added pars. (3) and (4).

Subsec. (f). Pub.L. 109–8, § 603(b)(2), added subsec. (f).

1994 Amendments. Subsec. (a)(3)(A). Pub.L. 103–394, § 224(a), completely revised subpar. (A). Prior to revision, subpar. (A) read as follows:

"monitoring applications for compensation and reimbursement filed under section 330 of title 11 and, whenever the United States trustee deems it to be appropriate, filing with the court comments with respect to any of such applications;"

Subsec. (a)(3). Pub.L. 103–394, § 502, inserted "12," after "11,".

1990 Amendments. Subsec. (e)(1)(A). Pub.L. 101–509 substituted designated provisions setting maximum amount as amount not to exceed highest level V annual rate and cash value of employment benefits, for undesignated provisions setting such amount as annual rate for step 1 of grade GS–16 of the General Schedule.

1986 Amendments. Subsec. (a). Pub.L. 99–554, § 113(a)(1), substituted in provision preceding par. (1) "the region for which such United States trustee is appointed" for "his district".

Subsec. (a)(3). Pub.L. 99–554, § 113(a)(2), substituted "title 11 by, whenever the United States trustee considers it to be appropriate—" for "title 11;" and added subpars. (A) to (H).

Subsec. (a)(5). Pub.L. 99–554, § 113(a)(3), inserted "and this title, and such duties consistent with title 11 and this title as the Attorney General may prescribe" after "title 11".

Subsec. (b). Pub.L. 99–554, § 113(b), substituted "under chapter 12 or 13 of title 11 commenced in a particular region so warrants, the United States trustee for such region" for "under chapter 13 of title 11 commenced in a particular judicial district so warrant, the United States trustee for such district", "trustees to serve in cases" for "trustee, in cases" and "for such region shall" for "for such district shall".

Subsec. (d). Pub.L. 99–554, § 113(c), substituted "paragraph (a)(1) of this section" for "subsection (a)(1) of this section" and substituted "chapter 12 or 13" for "chapter 13" in two places.

Subsec. (e)(1). Pub.L. 99–554, § 113(c), substituted in provision preceding subpar. (A) "chapter 12 or 13" for "chapter 13", in subpar. (A) "annual rate of basic pay in effect for step 1 of grade" for "lowest annual rate of basic pay in effect for grade" and in subpar. (B) provision specifying the percentage fee in the case of a debtor who is not a family farmer and in the case of a debtor who is a family farmer for provision specifying the percentage fee without such a distinction.

Subsec. (e)(2). Pub.L. 99–554, § 113(c), substituted in provision preceding subpar. (A) "from all payments received by such individual under plans" for "from all payments under plans", "chapter 12 or 13" for "chapter 13" and "deposit in the United States Trustee System Fund" for "pay to the Treasury", in subpar. (A) substituted "5 per centum" for "five percent" and "received under plans in cases under chapter 12 or 13" for "under plans in cases under chapter 13", and in subpar. (B) substituted "individual's" for "individual" and "subparagraph (A) of paragraph (i)" for "subparagraph (A) of this paragraph", in cl. (i) and, in cl. (ii), inserted provision that, subject to the approval of the Attorney General, any and all of the interest earned from the deposit of payments under plans by such individual be utilized to pay actual, necessary expenses without regard to the percentage limitation contained in subpar. (d)(1)(B) of this section.

Effective and Applicability Provisions

2005 Acts. Amendments by Pub.L. 109–8, § 603, effective 18 months after Apr. 20, 2005, see Pub.L. 109–8, § 603(e), set out as a note under 11 U.S.C.A. 521.

Except as otherwise provided, amendments by Pub.L. 109–8 effective 180 days after April 20, 2005, and inapplicable with respect to cases commenced under Title 11 before the effective date, see Pub.L. 109–8, § 1501, set out as a note under 11 U.S.C.A. § 101.

1994 Acts. Amendments by Pub.L. 103–394 effective on Oct. 22, 1994, and not to apply with respect to cases commenced under Title 11 of the United States Code before Oct. 22, 1994, see section 702 of Pub.L. 103–394, set out as a note under section 101 of Title 11, Bankruptcy.

1990 Acts. Amendment by Pub.L. 101–509 effective on such date as the President shall determine, but not earlier than 90 days, and not later than 180 days, after Nov. 5, 1990, see section 529 [Title III, § 305] of Pub.L. 101–509, set out as a note under section 5301 of Title 5, Government Organization and Employees. [See also related provisions in Ex. Ord. No. 12748, Feb. 1, 1991, 56 F.R. 4521, set out under that section.]

1986 Acts. Effective date and applicability of amendment by Pub.L. 99–554 dependent upon the judicial district involved, see section 302(d), (e) of Pub.L. 99–554, set out as a note under section 581 of this title.

1978 Acts. Section effective Oct. 1, 1979, see section 402(c) of Pub.L. 95–598, as amended, set out as a note preceding section 101 of Title 11, Bankruptcy.

Separability of Provisions

If any provision of or amendment made by Pub.L. 103–394 or the application of such provision or amendment to any person or circumstance is held to be unconstitutional, the remaining provisions of and amendments made by Pub.L. 103–394 and the application of such provisions and amendments to any person or circumstance shall not be affected thereby, see section 701 of Pub.L. 103–394, set out as a note under section 101 of Title 11, Bankruptcy.

Audit Procedures

Pub.L. 109–8, Title VI, § 603(a), Apr. 20, 2005, 119 Stat. 122, provided that:

"**(a) In general.—**

"**(1) Establishment of procedures.**—The Attorney General (in judicial districts served by United States trustees) and the Judicial Conference of the United States (in judicial districts served by bankruptcy administrators) shall establish procedures to determine the accuracy, veracity, and completeness of petitions, schedules, and other information that the debtor is required to provide under sections 521 and 1322 of title 11, United States Code, and, if applicable, section 111 of such title [11 U.S.C.A. § 111], in cases filed under chapter 7 or 13 of such title [11 U.S.C.A. § 701 or 1301 et seq.] in which the debtor is an individual. Such audits shall be in accordance with generally accepted auditing standards and performed by independent certified public accountants or independent licensed public accountants, provided that the Attorney General and the Judicial Conference, as appropriate, may develop alternative auditing standards not later than 2 years after the date of enactment of this Act [April 20, 2005].

"**(2) Procedures.**—Those procedures required by paragraph (1) shall—

"**(A)** establish a method of selecting appropriate qualified persons to contract to perform those audits;

"**(B)** establish a method of randomly selecting cases to be audited, except that not less than 1 out of every 250 cases in each Federal judicial district shall be selected for audit;

"**(C)** require audits of schedules of income and expenses that reflect greater than average variances from the statistical norm of the district in which the schedules were filed if those variances occur by reason of higher income or higher expenses than the statistical norm of the district in which the schedules were filed; and

"**(D)** establish procedures for providing, not less frequently than annually, public information concerning the aggregate results of such audits including the percentage of cases, by district, in which a material misstatement of income or expenditures is reported."

[Enactment of this note by Pub.L. 109–8, § 603, effective 18 months after Apr. 20, 2005, see Pub.L. 109–8, § 603(e), set out as a note under 11 U.S.C.A. § 521.]

[Except as otherwise provided, amendments by Pub.L. 109–8 effective 180 days after April 20, 2005, and inapplicable with respect to cases commenced under Title 11 before the effective date, see Pub.L. 109–8, § 1501, set out as a note under 11 U.S.C.A. § 101.]

Application to All Standing Trustees

Section 529 [Title I, § 110(b)] of Pub.L. 101–509 provided that: "The amendment made by subsection (a) [amending this section] shall apply to any trustee to whom the provisions of section 302(d)(3) of the Bankruptcy Judges, United States Trustees, and Family Farmer Bankruptcy Act of 1986 (Public Law 99–54 [Pub.L. 99–554]; 100 Stat. 3121) [set out in a note under section 581 of this title] apply."

CROSS REFERENCES

Appointment of disinterested person from panel of private trustees established under this section to serve as—

Interim trustee, see 11 USCA § 701.

Successor trustee, see 11 USCA § 703.

Appointment of standing trustee to serve in cases under—

Chapter thirteen of Bankruptcy, see 11 USCA § 1302.

Chapter twelve of Bankruptcy, see 11 USCA § 1202.

Compensation for services or reimbursement of expenses not allowable for standing trustee appointed under this section, see 11 USCA § 326.

Payments to standing trustee; percentage fee fixed under this section, see 11 USCA § 1326.

LIBRARY REFERENCES

American Digest System

Bankruptcy ⊜3008.1, 3011.

Key Number System Topic No. 51.

Corpus Juris Secundum

CJS Bankruptcy § 38, Nationwide System; Not in Effect in North Carolina and Alabama.

CJS Bankruptcy § 39, United States Trustee System Fund.

CJS Bankruptcy § 45, Supervision of Cases and Bankruptcy Trustees.

CJS Bankruptcy § 46, Service as Bankruptcy Trustee.

CJS Bankruptcy § 49, Small Business Cases.

CJS Bankruptcy § 50, Chapter 7 Proceedings.

CJS Bankruptcy § 51, Chapter 11 Proceedings.

CJS Bankruptcy § 52, Proceedings Under Chapters 12 and 13.

CJS Bankruptcy § 61, Appointment to Panels of Trustees.

CJS Bankruptcy § 74, Chapter 12 Cases.

CJS Bankruptcy § 75, Chapter 13 Cases.

CJS Bankruptcy § 76, Judicial Review.

CJS Bankruptcy § 125, Court Review of Standing Trustee Fee.

CJS Bankruptcy § 128, Judicial Review of Denial of Standing Trustee's Expense Claim.

CJS Bankruptcy § 147, Protective Orders.

§ 587. Salaries

Subject to sections 5315 through 5317 of title 5, the Attorney General shall fix the annual salaries of United States trustees and assistant United States trustees at rates of compensation not in excess of the rate of basic compensation provided for Executive Level IV of the Executive Schedule set forth in section 5315 of title 5, United States Code.

(Added Pub.L. 95–598, Title II, § 224(a), Nov. 6, 1978, 92 Stat. 2664; amended Pub.L. 99–554, Title I, § 114(a), Oct. 27, 1986, 100 Stat. 3093.)

HISTORICAL AND STATUTORY NOTES

Revision Notes and Legislative Reports

1978 Acts. Senate Report No. 95–989 and House Report No. 95–595, see 1978 U.S.Code Cong. and Adm.News, p. 5787.

1986 Acts. House Report No. 99–764 and House Conference Report No. 99–958, see 1986 U.S.Code Cong. and Adm. News, p. 5227.

Codifications

Section 408(c) of Pub.L. 95–598, as amended, which provided for the repeal of this section and the deletion of any references to United States Trustees in this title at a prospective date, was repealed by section 307(b) of Pub.L. 99–554. See note set out preceding section 581 of this title.

Amendments

1986 Amendments. Pub.L. 99–554 substituted "Subject to sections 5315 through 5317 of title 5, the" for "The" and "in excess of the rate of basic compensation provided for Executive Level IV of the Executive Schedule set forth in section 5315 of title 5, United States Code" for "to exceed the lowest annual rate of basic pay in effect for grade GS–16 of the General Schedule prescribed under section 5332 of title 5".

Effective and Applicability Provisions

1986 Acts. Amendment by Pub.L. 99–554 effective 30 days after Oct. 27, 1986, except as otherwise provided, see section 302(a) of Pub.L. 99–554, as amended, set out as a note under section 581 of this title.

1978 Acts. Section effective Oct. 1, 1979, see section 402(c) of Pub.L. 95–598, as amended, set out as a note preceding section 101 of Title 11, Bankruptcy.

LIBRARY REFERENCES

American Digest System

Bankruptcy ⊜3001.

Key Number System Topic No. 51.

Corpus Juris Secundum

CJS Bankruptcy § 41, Appointment, Oath, and Term; Vacancy in and Removal from Office.

§ 588. Expenses

Necessary office expenses of the United States trustee shall be allowed when authorized by the Attorney General.

(Added Pub.L. 95–598, Title II, § 224(a), Nov. 6, 1978, 92 Stat. 2664.)

HISTORICAL AND STATUTORY NOTES

Revision Notes and Legislative Reports

1978 Acts. Senate Report No. 95–989 and House Report No. 95–595, see 1978 U.S.Code Cong. and Adm.News, p. 5787.

Codifications

Section 408(c) of Pub.L. 95–598, as amended, which provided for the repeal of this section and the deletion of any references to United States Trustees in this title at a prospective date, was repealed by section 307(b) of Pub.L. 99–554. See note set out preceding section 581 of this title.

Effective and Applicability Provisions

1978 Acts. Section effective Oct. 1, 1979, see section 402(c) of Pub.L. 95–598, as amended, set out as a note preceding section 101 of Title 11, Bankruptcy.

LIBRARY REFERENCES

American Digest System

Bankruptcy ⊜3001.

Key Number System Topic No. 51.

§ 589. Staff and other employees

The United States trustee may employ staff and other employees on approval of the Attorney General.

(Added Pub.L. 95–598, Title II, § 224(a), Nov. 6, 1978, 92 Stat. 2664.)

HISTORICAL AND STATUTORY NOTES

Revision Notes and Legislative Reports

1978 Acts. Senate Report No. 95–989 and House Report No. 95–595, see 1978 U.S.Code Cong. and Adm.News, p. 5787.

Codifications

Section 408(c) of Pub.L. 95–598, as amended, which provided for the repeal of this section and the deletion of any references to United States Trustees in this title at a prospective date, was repealed by section 307(b) of Pub.L. 99–554. See note set out preceding section 581 of this title.

Effective and Applicability Provisions

1978 Acts. Section effective Oct. 1, 1979, see section 402(c) of Pub.L. 95–598, as amended, set out as a note preceding section 101 of Title 11, Bankruptcy.

Temporary Suspension of Limitation on Appointments

Pub.L. 99–554, Title I, § 114(b), Oct. 27, 1986, 100 Stat. 3093, provided that: "During the period beginning on the effective date of this Act [see section 302 of Pub.L. 99–554, as amended, set out as a note under section 581 of this title], and ending on October 1, 1989, the provisions of title 5 of the United States Code [Title 5, Government Organization and Employees] governing appointments in the competitive service shall not apply with respect to appointments under section 589 of title 28, United States Code [this section]."

LIBRARY REFERENCES

American Digest System

Bankruptcy ⇒3008.
Key Number System Topic No. 51.

Corpus Juris Secundum

CJS Bankruptcy § 41, Appointment, Oath, and Term; Vacancy in and Removal from Office.

§ 589a.   United States Trustee System Fund

(a) There is hereby established in the Treasury of the United States a special fund to be known as the "United States Trustee System Fund" (hereinafter in this section referred to as the "Fund"). Monies in the Fund shall be available to the Attorney General without fiscal year limitation in such amounts as may be specified in appropriations Acts for the following purposes in connection with the operations of United States trustees—

(1) salaries and related employee benefits;

(2) travel and transportation;

(3) rental of space;

(4) communication, utilities, and miscellaneous computer charges;

(5) security investigations and audits;

(6) supplies, books, and other materials for legal research;

(7) furniture and equipment;

(8) miscellaneous services, including those obtained by contract; and

(9) printing.

(b) For the purpose of recovering the cost of services of the United States Trustee System, there shall be deposited as offsetting collections to the appropriation "United States Trustee System Fund", to remain available until expended, the following—

(1)(A) 40.46 percent of the fees collected under section 1930(a)(1)(A); and

(B) 28.33 percent of the fees collected under section 1930(a)(1)(B);

(2) 55 percent of the fees collected under section 1930(a)(3) of this title;

(3) one-half of the fees collected under section 1930(a)(4) of this title;

(4) one-half of the fees collected under section 1930(a)(5) of this title;

(5) 100 percent of the fees collected under section 1930(a)(6) of this title;

(6) three-fourths of the fees collected under the last sentence of section 1930(a) of this title;

(7) the compensation of trustees received under section 330(d) of title 11 by the clerks of the bankruptcy courts;

(8) excess fees collected under section 586(e)(2) of this title;

(9) interest earned on Fund investment; and

(10) fines imposed under section 110(l) of title 11, United States Code.

(c) Amounts in the Fund which are not currently needed for the purposes specified in subsection (a) shall be kept on deposit or invested in obligations of, or guaranteed by, the United States.

(d) The Attorney General shall transmit to the Congress, not later than 120 days after the end of each fiscal year, a detailed report on the amounts deposited in the Fund and a description of expenditures made under this section.

(e) There are authorized to be appropriated to the Fund for any fiscal year such sums as may be necessary to supplement amounts deposited under subsection (b) for the purposes specified in subsection (a).

(Added Pub.L. 99–554, Title I, § 115(a), Oct. 27, 1986, 100 Stat. 3094; amended Pub.L. 101–162, Title IV, § 406(c), Nov. 21, 1989, 103 Stat. 1016; Pub.L. 102–140, Title I, § 111(b), (c), Oct. 28, 1991, 105 Stat. 795; Pub.L. 103–121, Title I, § 111(a)(2), (b)(2), (3), Oct. 27, 1993, 107 Stat. 1164; Pub.L. 104–91, Title I, § 101(a), Jan. 6, 1996, 110 Stat. 11, as amended Pub.L. 104–99, Title II, § 211, Jan. 26, 1996, 110 Stat. 37; Pub.L. 104–208, Div. A, Title I, § 101(a) [Title I, § 109(b)], Sept. 30, 1996, 110 Stat. 3009–18; Pub.L. 106–113, Div. B, § 1000(a)(1) [Title I, § 113], Nov. 29, 1999, 113 Stat. 1535, 1501A–6, 1501A–20; Pub.L. 109–8, Title III, § 325(b), Apr. 20, 2005, 119 Stat. 99; Pub.L. 109–13, Div. A, Title VI, § 6058(a), May 11, 2005, 119 Stat. 297; Pub.L. 110–161, Div. B, Title II, § 212(a), Dec. 26, 2007, 121 Stat. 1914.)

HISTORICAL AND STATUTORY NOTES

Revision Notes and Legislative Reports

1986 Acts. House Report No. 99–764 and House Conference Report No. 99–958, see 1986 U.S. Code Cong. and Adm. News, p. 5227.

1989 Acts. Statement by President, see 1989 U.S. Code Cong. and Adm. News, p. 733–3.

1999 Acts. Statement by President, see 1999 U.S. Code Cong. and Adm. News, p. 290.

2005 Acts. House Report No. 109–31(Part I), see 2005 U.S. Code Cong. and Adm. News, p. 88.

House Conference Report No. 109–72, see 2005 U.S. Code Cong. and Adm. News, p. 240.

2007 Acts. House Report No. 110–197, see 2007 U.S. Code Cong. and Adm. News, p. 661.

Statement by President, see 2007 U.S. Code Cong. and Adm. News, p. S34.

Codifications

Section 101(a) of Pub.L. 104–91, as amended by section 211 of Pub.L. 104–99, provided in part that section 111(b) and (c) of the General Provisions for the Department of Justice in Title I of the Departments of Commerce, Justice, and State, the Judiciary, and Related Agencies Appropriations Act, 1996 (H.R. 2076) as passed by the House of Representatives on Dec. 6, 1995, was enacted into permanent law. Such section 111(b) and (c) of H.R. 2076 amended subsecs. (b) and (f) of this section. See 1996 Amendments notes set out under this section.

Amendments

2007 Amendments. Subsec. (b)(8). Pub.L. 110–161, Div. B, § 212(a)(1), struck out "and".

Subsec. (b)(9). Pub.L. 110–161, Div. B, § 212(a)(2), struck out the period and inserted "; and".

Subsec. (b)(10). Pub.L. 110–161, Div. B, § 212(a)(3), added par. (10).

2005 Amendments. Subsec. (b)(1). Pub.L. 109–8, § 325(b)(1), as amended by Pub.L. 109–13, § 6058(a), added par. (1) and struck out former par. (1), which read as follows: "27.42 percent of the fees collected under section 1930(a)(1) of this title;".

Subsec. (b)(2). Pub.L. 109–8, § 325(b)(2), as amended by Pub.L. 109–13, § 6058(a), substituted "55 percent" for "one-half".

Subsec. (b)(4). Amendment by Pub.L. 109–8, § 325(b)(3), which struck out "one-half" and inserted "100 percent", was omitted in the amendment of Pub.L. 109–8, § 325 by Pub.L. 109–13, § 6058(a); thus, the language of subsec. (b)(4) reverted to "100 percent" after that amendment.

1999 Amendments. Subsec. (b)(1). Pub.L. 106–113 [§ 113] substituted "27.42 percent" for "23.08 percent".

Subsec. (b)(9). Pub.L. 106–113 [Title I] added par. (9).

1996 Amendments. Subsec. (b). Pub.L. 104–208, § 101(a) [§ 109(b)], substituted provisions requiring amounts to be deposited as offsetting collections to the appropriation "United States Trustee System Fund" for the purpose of recovering the cost of services of the United States Trustee System for provisions requiring amounts to be deposited in the Fund.

Subsec. (b)(2). Pub.L. 104–208, § 101(a) [§ 109(b)], increased the percentage of fees to be deposited under § 1930(a)(3) from 37.5% to 50%.

Subsec. (b)(5). Pub.L. 104–208, § 101(a) [§ 109(b)], increased the fees collected under § 1930(a)(6) from 60% until a reorganization plan is confirmed to 100%.

Pub.L. 104–91, § 101(a), as amended by Pub.L. 104–99, § 211, inserted provisions relating to confirmation of reorganization plan. See Codifications note set out under this section.

Subsec. (b)(8). Pub.L. 104–208, § 101(a) [§ 109(b)], added par. (8).

Subsec. (c). Pub.L. 104–208, § 101(a) [§ 109(b)], struck out par. (1) designation, struck out reference to the exception provided in par. (2), and struck out par. (2), which required the Secretary of the Treasury on each Nov. 1, to transfer certain Fund amounts exceeding 110% into the general fund of the Treasury.

Subsec. (d). Pub.L. 104–208, § 101(a) [§ 109(b)], struck out par. (1) designation, and struck out par. (2), which required the Secretary in certain instances to include in the report a recommendation regarding the manner in which fees payable under § 1930(a) of title 28 may be modified to cause the annual amount deposited to more closely approximate the annual amount expended.

Subsec. (f). Pub.L. 104–208, § 101(a) [§ 109(b)], struck out subsec. (f), which required 12.5% of fees collected under § 1930(a)(3), 40% of fees collected under § 1930(a)(6) until a reorganization plan is confirmed, and 100% of the fees collected under § 1930(a)(6) after the reorganization plan is confirmed, to be deposited to the Fund as offsetting collections.

Subsec. (f)(2). Pub.L. 104–91, § 101(a), as amended Pub.L. 104–99, § 211, inserted provisions relating to confirmation of reorganization plan. See Codifications note set out under this section.

Subsec. (f)(3). Pub.L. 104–91, § 101(a), as amended Pub.L. 104–99, § 211, added par. (3). See Codifications note set out under this section.

1993 Amendments. Subsec. (b)(1). Pub.L. 103–121, § 111(a)(2), substituted "23.08 per centum" for "one-fourth".

Subsec. (b)(2). Pub.L. 103–121, § 111(b)(2), substituted "37.5 per centum" for "50 per centum".

Subsec. (f)(1). Pub.L. 103–121, § 111(b)(3), substituted "12.5 per centum" for "16.7 per centum".

1991 Amendments. Subsec. (b)(2). Pub.L. 102–140, § 111(b)(1), substituted "50 per centum" for "three-fifths".

Subsec. (b)(5). Pub.L. 102–140, § 111(b)(2), substituted "60 per centum" for "all".

Subsec. (f). Pub.L. 102–140, § 111(c), added subsec. (f).

1989 Amendments. Subsec. (b)(1). Pub.L. 101–162, § 406(c), substituted "one-fourth" for "one-third".

Effective and Applicability Provisions

2005 Acts. Pub.L. 109–13, Div. A, Title VI, § 6058(b), May 11, 2005, 119 Stat. 297, provided that: "This section [amending this section and 28 U.S.C.A. § 1930, enacting provisions set out as a note under this section, and amending provisions set out as notes under this section and 28 U.S.C.A. §§ 1930 and 1931] and the amendment made by this section shall take effect immediately after the enactment of the Bankruptcy Abuse Prevention and Consumer Protection Act of 2005 [Pub.L. 109–8, approved Apr. 20, 2005]."

Except as otherwise provided, amendments by Pub.L. 109–8 effective 180 days after April 20, 2005, and inapplicable with respect to cases commenced under Title 11 before the effective date, see Pub.L. 109–8, § 1501, set out as a note under 11 U.S.C.A. § 101.

1999 Acts. Pub.L. 106–113, Div. B, § 1000(a)(1), [Title I, § 113], Nov. 29, 1999, 113 Stat. 1535, 1501A–20, provided in part that section 113 (amending this section and section 1930 of this title and provisions set out as a note under section 1931 of this title) is "[e]ffective 30 days after the enactment of this Act [Department of Commerce, Justice, and State, the Judiciary and Related Agencies Appropriations Act, 2000, Pub.L. 106–113, Div. B, § 1000(a)(1), Nov. 29, 1999, 113 Stat. 1535, 1501A–3; see Tables for complete classification]".

1996 Acts. Pub.L. 104–208, Div. A, Title I, § 101(a) [Title I, § 109(c)], Sept. 30, 1996, 110 Stat. 3009–19, provided that: "Notwithstanding any other provision of law or of this Act [Pub.L. 104–208, Sept. 30, 1996, 110 Stat. 3009, see Tables for classification] the amendments to 28 U.S.C. 589a [this section] made by subsection (b) of this section shall take effect upon enactment of this Act [probably means the date of enactment of Pub.L. 104–208, 110 Stat. 3009, which was approved Sept. 30, 1996]."

1993 Acts. Section 111(a) of Pub.L. 103–121 provided in part that amendment by section 111(a)(2) of Pub.L. 103–121, amending subsec. (b)(1) of this section, is effective 30 days after Oct. 27, 1993.

Section 111(b) of Pub.L. 103–121 provided in part that amendment by section 111(b)(2) and (3) of Pub.L. 103–121, amending subsecs. (b)(2) and (f)(1) of this section, is effective 30 days after Oct. 27, 1993.

1991 Acts. Section 111 of Pub.L. 102–140 provided that the amendment made by that section is effective 60 days after Oct. 28, 1991.

1986 Acts. Enactment by Pub.L. 99–554 effective 30 days after Oct. 27, 1986, except as otherwise provided, see section 302(a) of Pub.L. 99–554, as amended, set out as a note under section 581 of this title.

Sunset Provisions

Pub.L. 109–8, Title III, § 325(d), Apr. 20, 2005, 119 Stat. 99, as amended Pub.L. 109–13, Div. A, Title VI, § 6058(b), May 11, 2005, 119 Stat. 297, which set forth a two-year effective period for the original amendments by Pub.L. 109–8 to this section, has been omitted. The amendment by Pub.L. 109–13, § 6058(a), to Pub.L. 109–8, § 325, omitted this note in the reenactment of the section, to take effect immediately after the enactment of the Bankruptcy Abuse Prevention and Consumer Protection Act of 2005 [Pub.L. 109–8, Apr. 20, 2005, 119 Stat. 23], see Pub.L. 109–13, § 6058(b), set out as an Effective and Applicability Provisions note under this section.

Termination of Reporting Requirements

For termination of reporting provisions of this section, effective May 15, 2000, see Pub.L. 104–66, § 3003, as amended, set out as a note under 31 U.S.C.A. § 1113, and the 9th item on page 119 of House Document No. 103–7.

Reporting requirement of subsec. (d) of this section excepted from termination under Pub.L. 104–66, § 3003(a)(1), as amended, set out in a note under 31 U.S.C.A. § 1113, see Pub.L. 106–197, § 1, set out as a note under 31 U.S.C.A. § 1113.

Compensation of Bankruptcy trustee to be deposited by clerk of bankruptcy court into Fund established by this section, see 11 USCA § 330.

LIBRARY REFERENCES

American Digest System

Attorney General ☞6.

Bankruptcy ☞3001.

United States ☞81.

Key Number System Topic Nos. 393, 46, 51.

Corpus Juris Secundum

CJS Bankruptcy § 9, Title 28 of the U.S. Code.

CJS Bankruptcy § 39, United States Trustee System Fund.

CJS Bankruptcy § 40, United States Trustee System Fund--Quarterly Fees.

§ 589b.   Bankruptcy data

(a) Rules.—The Attorney General shall, within a reasonable time after the effective date of this section, issue rules requiring uniform forms for (and from time to time thereafter to appropriately modify and approve)—

(1) final reports by trustees in cases under chapters 7, 12, and 13 of title 11; and

(2) periodic reports by debtors in possession or trustees in cases under chapter 11 of title 11.

(b) Reports.—Each report referred to in subsection (a) shall be designed (and the requirements as to place and manner of filing shall be established) so as to facilitate compilation of data and maximum possible access of the public, both by physical inspection at one or more central filing locations, and by electronic access through the Internet or other appropriate media.

(c) Required information.—The information required to be filed in the reports referred to in subsection (b) shall be that which is in the best interests of debtors and creditors, and in the public interest in reasonable and adequate information to evaluate the efficiency and practicality of the Federal bankruptcy system. In issuing rules proposing the forms referred to in subsection (a), the Attorney General shall strike the best achievable practical balance between—

(1) the reasonable needs of the public for information about the operational results of the Federal bankruptcy system;

(2) economy, simplicity, and lack of undue burden on persons with a duty to file reports; and

(3) appropriate privacy concerns and safeguards.

(d) Final reports.—The uniform forms for final reports required under subsection (a) for use by trustees under chapters 7, 12, and 13 of title 11 shall, in addition to such other matters as are required by law or as the Attorney General in the discretion of the Attorney

General shall propose, include with respect to a case under such title—

(1) information about the length of time the case was pending;

(2) assets abandoned;

(3) assets exempted;

(4) receipts and disbursements of the estate;

(5) expenses of administration, including for use under section 707(b), actual costs of administering cases under chapter 13 of title 11;

(6) claims asserted;

(7) claims allowed; and

(8) distributions to claimants and claims discharged without payment,

in each case by appropriate category and, in cases under chapters 12 and 13 of title 11, date of confirmation of the plan, each modification thereto, and defaults by the debtor in performance under the plan.

(e) **Periodic reports.**—The uniform forms for periodic reports required under subsection (a) for use by trustees or debtors in possession under chapter 11 of title 11 shall, in addition to such other matters as are required by law or as the Attorney General in the discretion of the Attorney General shall propose, include—

(1) information about the industry classification, published by the Department of Commerce, for the businesses conducted by the debtor;

(2) length of time the case has been pending;

(3) number of full-time employees as of the date of the order for relief and at the end of each reporting period since the case was filed;

(4) cash receipts, cash disbursements and profitability of the debtor for the most recent period and cumulatively since the date of the order for relief;

(5) compliance with title 11, whether or not tax returns and tax payments since the date of the order for relief have been timely filed and made;

(6) all professional fees approved by the court in the case for the most recent period and cumulatively since the date of the order for relief (separately reported, for the professional fees incurred by or on behalf of the debtor, between those that would have been incurred absent a bankruptcy case and those not); and

(7) plans of reorganization filed and confirmed and, with respect thereto, by class, the recoveries of the holders, expressed in aggregate dollar values and, in the case of claims, as a percentage of total claims of the class allowed.

(Added Pub.L. 109–8, Title VI, § 602(a), Apr. 20, 2005, 119 Stat. 120.)

HISTORICAL AND STATUTORY NOTES

Revision Notes and Legislative Reports

2005 Acts. House Report No. 109–31(Part I), see 2005 U.S. Code Cong. and Adm. News, p. 88.

References in Text

The effective date of this section, referred to in subsec. (a), means 180 days after April 20, 2005. See Pub.L. 109–8, § 1501, set out as an Effective and Applicability Provisions note for 2005 Acts under 11 U.S.C.A. § 101.

Chapters 7, 12, and 13 of title 11, referred to in subsecs. (a)(1) and (d), are 11 U.S.C.A. § 701 et seq., 11 U.S.C.A. § 1201 et seq., and 11 U.S.C.A. § 1301 et seq., respectively.

Chapter 11 of title 11, referred to in subsecs. (a)(2) and (e), is 11 U.S.C.A. § 1101 et seq.

Effective and Applicability Provisions

2005 Acts. Except as otherwise provided, amendments by Pub.L. 109–8 effective 180 days after April 20, 2005, and inapplicable with respect to cases commenced under Title 11 before the effective date, see Pub.L. 109–8, § 1501, set out as a note under 11 U.S.C.A. § 101.

PART III—COURT OFFICERS AND EMPLOYEES

CHAPTER 41—ADMINISTRATIVE OFFICE OF UNITED STATES COURTS

§ 604. Duties of Director generally

(a) The Director shall be the administrative officer of the courts, and under the supervision and direction of the Judicial Conference of the United States, shall:

(1) Supervise all administrative matters relating to the offices of clerks and other clerical and administrative personnel of the courts;

(2) Examine the state of the dockets of the courts; secure information as to the courts' need of assistance; prepare and transmit semiannually to the chief judges of the circuits, statistical data and reports as to the business of the courts;

(3) Submit to the annual meeting of the Judicial Conference of the United States, at least two weeks prior thereto, a report of the activities of the Administrative Office and the state of the business of the courts, together with the statistical data submitted to the chief judges of the circuits under paragraph (a)(2) of this section, and the Director's recommendations, which report, data and recommendations shall be public documents.

(4) Submit to Congress and the Attorney General copies of the report, data and recommendations required by paragraph (a)(3) of this section;

(5) Fix the compensation of clerks of court, deputies, librarians, criers, messengers, law clerks, secretaries, stenographers, clerical assistants, and other employees of the courts whose compensation is not otherwise fixed by law, and, notwithstanding any other provision of law, pay on behalf of Justices and judges of the United States appointed to hold office during good behavior, United States magistrate judges, bankruptcy judges appointed under chapter 6 of this title, judges of the District Court of Guam, judges of the District Court for the Northern Mariana Islands, judges of the District Court of the Virgin Islands, bankruptcy judges and magistrate judges retired under section 377 of this title, and judges retired under section 373 of this title, who are,[1] aged 65 or over, any increases in the cost of Federal Employees' Group Life Insurance imposed after April 24, 1999, including any expenses generated by such payments, as authorized by the Judicial Conference of the United States;

(6) Determine and pay necessary office expenses of courts, judges, and those court officials whose expenses are by law allowable, and the lawful fees of United States magistrate judges;

(7) Regulate and pay annuities to widows and surviving dependent children of justices and judges of the United States, judges of the United States Court of Federal Claims, bankruptcy judges, United States magistrate judges, Directors of the Federal Judicial Center, and Directors of the Administrative Office, and necessary travel and subsistence expenses incurred by judges, court officers and employees, and officers and employees of the Administrative Office, and the Federal Judicial Center, while absent from their official stations on official business, without regard to the per diem allowances and amounts for reimbursement of actual and necessary expenses established by the Administrator of General Services under section 5702 of title 5, except that the reimbursement of subsistence expenses may not exceed that authorized by the Director for judges of the United States under section 456 of this title;

(8) Disburse appropriations and other funds for the maintenance and operation of the courts;

(9) Establish pretrial services pursuant to section 3152 of title 18, United States Code;

(10) (A) Purchase, exchange, transfer, distribute, and assign the custody of lawbooks, equipment, supplies, and other personal property for the judicial branch of Government (except the Supreme Court unless otherwise provided pursuant to paragraph (17)); (B) provide or make available readily to each court appropriate equipment for the interpretation of proceedings in accordance with section 1828 of this title; and (C) enter into and perform contracts and other transactions upon such terms as the Director may deem appropriate as may be necessary to

the conduct of the work of the judicial branch of Government (except the Supreme Court unless otherwise provided pursuant to paragraph (17)), and contracts for nonpersonal services providing pretrial services, agencies for the interpretation of proceedings, and for the provision of special interpretation services pursuant to section 1828 of this title may be awarded without regard to section 6101(b) to (d) of title 41;

(11) Audit vouchers and accounts of the courts, the Federal Judicial Center, the offices providing pretrial services, and their clerical and administrative personnel;

(12) Provide accommodations for the courts, the Federal Judicial Center, the offices providing pretrial services and their clerical and administrative personnel;

(13) Lay before Congress, annually, statistical tables that will accurately reflect the business transacted by the several bankruptcy courts, and all other pertinent data relating to such courts;

(14) Pursuant to section 1827 of this title, establish a program for the certification and utilization of interpreters in courts of the United States;

(15) Pursuant to section 1828 of this title, establish a program for the provision of special interpretation services in courts of the United States;

(16) (A) In those districts where the Director considers it advisable based on the need for interpreters, authorize the full-time or part-time employment by the court of certified interpreters; (B) where the Director considers it advisable based on the need for interpreters, appoint certified interpreters on a full-time or part-time basis, for services in various courts when he determines that such appointments will result in the economical provision of interpretation services; and (C) pay out of moneys appropriated for the judiciary interpreters' salaries, fees, and expenses, and other costs which may accrue in accordance with the provisions of sections 1827 and 1828 of this title;

(17) In the Director's discretion, (A) accept and utilize voluntary and uncompensated (gratuitous) services, including services as authorized by section 3102(b) of title 5, United States Code; and (B) accept, hold, administer, and utilize gifts and bequests of personal property for the purpose of aiding or facilitating the work of the judicial branch of Government, but gifts or bequests of money shall be covered into the Treasury;

(18) Establish procedures and mechanisms within the judicial branch for processing fines, restitution, forfeitures of bail bonds or collateral, and assessments;

(19) Regulate and pay annuities to bankruptcy judges and United States magistrate judges in ac-

cordance with section 377 of this title and paragraphs (1)(B) and (2) of section 2(c) of the Retirement and Survivors' Annuities for Bankruptcy Judges and Magistrates Act of 1988;

(20) Periodically compile—

(A) the rules which are prescribed under section 2071 of this title by courts other than the Supreme Court;

(B) the rules which are prescribed under section 358 of this title; and

(C) the orders which are required to be publicly available under section 360(b) of this title;

so as to provide a current record of such rules and orders;

(21) Establish a program of incentive awards for employees of the judicial branch of the United States Government, other than any judge who is entitled to hold office during good behavior;

(22) Receive and expend, either directly or by transfer to the United States Marshals Service or other Government agency, funds appropriated for the procurement, installation, and maintenance of security equipment and protective services for the United States Courts in courtrooms and adjacent areas, including building ingress/egress control, inspection of packages, directed security patrols, and other similar activities;

(23) Regulate and pay annuities to judges of the United States Court of Federal Claims in accordance with section 178 of this title; and

(24) Perform such other duties as may be assigned to him by the Supreme Court or the Judicial Conference of the United States.

(b) The clerical and administrative personnel of the courts shall comply with all requests by the Director for information or statistical data as to the state of court dockets.

(c) Inspection of court dockets outside the continental United States may be made through United States officials residing within the jurisdiction where the inspection is made.

(d) The Director, under the supervision and direction of the conference, shall:

(1) supervise all administrative matters relating to the offices of the United States magistrate judges;

(2) gather, compile, and evaluate all statistical and other information required for the performance of his duties and the duties of the conference with respect to such officers;

(3) lay before Congress annually statistical tables and other information which will accurately reflect the business which has come before the various United States magistrate judges, including (A) the number of matters in which the parties consented to the exercise of jurisdiction by a magistrate judge, (B) the number of appeals taken pursuant to the decisions of magistrate judges and the disposition of such appeals, and (C) the professional background and qualifications of individuals appointed under section 631 of this title to serve as magistrate judges;

(4) prepare and distribute a manual, with annual supplements and periodic revisions, for the use of such officers, which shall set forth their powers and duties, describe all categories of proceedings that may arise before them, and contain such other information as may be required to enable them to discharge their powers and duties promptly, effectively, and impartially.

(e) The Director may promulgate appropriate rules and regulations approved by the conference and not inconsistent with any provision of law, to assist him in the performance of the duties conferred upon him by subsection (d) of this section. Magistrate judges shall keep such records and make such reports as are specified in such rules and regulations.

(f) The Director may make, promulgate, issue, rescind, and amend rules and regulations (including regulations prescribing standards of conduct for Administrative Office employees) as may be necessary to carry out the Director's functions, powers, duties, and authority. The Director may publish in the Federal Register such rules, regulations, and notices for the judicial branch of Government as the Director determines to be of public interest; and the Director of the Federal Register hereby is authorized to accept and shall publish such materials.

(g)(1) When authorized to exchange personal property, the Director may exchange or sell similar items and may apply the exchange allowance or proceeds of sale in such cases in whole or in part payment for the property acquired, but any transaction carried out under the authority of this subsection shall be evidenced in writing.

(2) The Director hereby is authorized to enter into contracts for public utility services and related terminal equipment for periods not exceeding ten years.

(3)(A) In order to promote the recycling and reuse of recyclable materials, the Director may provide for the sale or disposal of recyclable scrap materials from paper products and other consumable office supplies held by an entity within the judicial branch.

(B) The sale or disposal of recyclable materials under subparagraph (A) shall be consistent with the procedures provided in sections 541–555 of title 40 for the sale of surplus property.

(C) Proceeds from the sale of recyclable materials under subparagraph (A) shall be deposited as offsetting collections to the fund established under section 1931 of this title and shall remain available until expended to reimburse any appropriations for the operation and maintenance of the judicial branch.

(4) The Director is hereby authorized:

(A) to enter into contracts for the acquisition of severable services for a period that begins in one fiscal year and ends in the next fiscal year to the same extent as the head of an executive agency under the authority of section 3902 of Title 41, United States Code;

(B) to enter into contracts for multiple years for the acquisition of property and services to the same extent as executive agencies under the authority of section 3903 of Title 41, United States Code; and

(C) to make advance, partial, progress or other payments under contracts for property or services to the same extent as executive agencies under the authority of section 255 of title 41, United States Code.

(h)(1) The Director shall, out of funds appropriated for the operation and maintenance of the courts, provide facilities and pay necessary expenses incurred by the judicial councils of the circuits and the Judicial Conference under chapter 16 of this title, including mileage allowance and witness fees, at the same rate as provided in section 1821 of this title. Administrative and professional assistance from the Administrative Office of the United States Courts may be requested by each judicial council and the Judicial Conference for purposes of discharging their duties under chapter 16 of this title.

(2) The Director of the Administrative Office of the United States Courts shall include in his annual report filed with the Congress under this section a summary of the number of complaints filed with each judicial council under chapter 16 of this title, indicating the general nature of such complaints and the disposition of those complaints in which action has been taken. (June 25, 1948, c. 646, 62 Stat. 914; Aug. 3, 1956, c. 944, § 3, 70 Stat. 1026; Dec. 20, 1967, Pub.L. 90–219, Title II, § 203, 81 Stat. 669; Oct. 17, 1968, Pub.L. 90–578, Title II, § 201, Title IV, § 402(b)(2), 82 Stat. 1114, 1118; Aug. 22, 1972, Pub.L. 92–397, § 4, 86 Stat. 580; Jan. 3, 1975, Pub.L. 93–619, Title II, § 204, 88 Stat. 2089; Oct. 28, 1978, Pub.L. 95–539, §§ 3, 4, 92 Stat. 2043; Nov. 6, 1978, Pub.L. 95–598, Title II, § 225, 92 Stat. 2664; Oct. 10, 1979, Pub.L. 96–82, § 5, 93 Stat. 645; Oct. 15, 1980, Pub.L. 96–458, § 5, 94 Stat. 2040; Dec. 12, 1980, Pub.L. 96–523, § 1(c)(1), 94 Stat. 3040; Sept. 27, 1982, Pub.L. 97–267, § 7, 96 Stat. 1139; Oct. 27, 1986, Pub.L. 99–554, Title I, § 116, 100 Stat. 3095; Dec. 11, 1987, Pub.L. 100–185, § 2, 101 Stat. 1279; Nov. 15, 1988, Pub.L. 100–659, § 6(a), 102 Stat. 3918; Nov. 19, 1988, Pub.L. 100–702, Title IV, § 402(a), Title X, §§ 1008, 1010, 1011, 1020(a)(2), 102 Stat. 4650, 4667, 4668, 4671; Oct. 30, 1990, Pub.L. 101–474, § 5(r), 104 Stat. 1101; Nov. 29, 1990, Pub.L. 101–647, Title XXV, § 2548, 104 Stat. 4888; Dec. 1, 1990, Pub.L. 101–650, Title III, §§ 306(e)(1), 321, 325(c)(1), 104 Stat. 5111, 5117, 5121; Oct. 29, 1992, Pub.L. 102–572, Title V, § 503, Title IX, § 902(b)(1), 106 Stat. 4513, 4516; Nov. 29, 1999, Pub.L. 106–113, § 1000(a)(1) [Title III, § 305], 113 Stat. 1535, 1501A–37; Nov. 13, 2000, Pub.L. 106–518, Title II, § 204, Title III, § 304(d), 114 Stat. 2414, 2418; Aug. 21, 2002, Pub.L. 107–217, § 3(g)(1), 116 Stat. 1299; Nov. 2, 2002, Pub.L. 107–273, Div. C, Title I, § 11043(e), 116 Stat. 1855; Nov. 30, 2005, Pub.L. 109–115,

Div. A, Title IV, § 407(a), 119 Stat. 2470; Jan. 7, 2008, Pub.L. 110–177, Title V, § 502(a), 121 Stat. 2542; Mar. 11, 2009, Pub.L. 111–8, Div. D, Title III, § 307(a), 123 Stat. 648; Jan. 4, 2011, Pub.L. 111–350, § 5(g)(2), 124 Stat. 3848.)

1 So in original. The comma probably should not appear.

HISTORICAL AND STATUTORY NOTES

Revision Notes and Legislative Reports

1948 Acts. Based on sections 726–1 and 726a of Title 18, U.S.C., 1940 ed., Criminal Code and Criminal Procedure, and sections 1130(a), (b), and 1131 of Title 26, U.S.C., 1940 ed., Internal Revenue Code, Title 28, U.S.C., 1940 ed., §§ 9, 128, 222a, 245, 268a, 278a, 302–306, 374b, 446, 447, 450, 544, 545, 547, 557, 558, 560, 561, 561a, 562, 563, 565, 566, 595, and 596 and sections 11–204 and 11–403, District of Columbia Code, 1940 ed. (R.S. §§ 1075, 1085; Mar. 3, 1891, c. 517, §§ 2, 9, 26 Stat. 826, 829; Feb. 9, 1893, c. 74, § 4, 27 Stat. 435; July 30, 1894, c. 172, § 1, 28 Stat. 160; Mar. 3, 1901, c. 854, § 224, 31 Stat. 1224; June 30, 1902, c. 1329, 32 Stat. 528; Mar. 3, 1905, c. 1487, 33 Stat. 1259; Mar. 3, 1911, c. 231, § 5, 36 Stat. 1088; Mar. 3, 1911, c. 231, § 118a, as added June 17, 1930, c. 509, 46 Stat. 774; Mar. 3, 1911, c. 231, § 118b, as added Feb. 17, 1936, c. 75, 49 Stat. 1140; Mar. 3, 1911, c. 231, §§ 140, 163, 171, 189–193, 291, 36 Stat. 1136, 1140, 1141, 1143, 1167; Mar. 3, 1911, c. 231, §§ 304, 305, 308, as added Aug. 7, 1939, c. 501, § 1, 53 Stat. 1223; Aug. 23, 1912, c. 350, 37 Stat. 412; Feb. 26, 1919, c. 49, §§ 1, 2, 3, 4, 5, 7, 8, 40 Stat. 1182; July 19, 1919, c. 24, § 1, 41 Stat. 210; Nov. 4, 1919, c. 93, § 1, 41 Stat. 338; Feb. 11, 1921, c. 46, 41 Stat. 1099; Feb. 22, 1921, c. 70, § 7, 41 Stat. 1144; Mar. 4, 1921, c. 161, 41 Stat. 1412; June 1, 1922, c. 204, Title II, 42 Stat. 616; Jan. 3, 1923, c. 21, Title II, 42 Stat. 1084; Mar. 4, 1923, c. 265, 42 Stat. 1488; May 28, 1924, c. 204, Title II, 43 Stat. 221; Feb. 27, 1925, c. 364, Title II, 43 Stat. 1030; Apr. 29, 1926, c. 195, Title II, 44 Stat. 346, 347; May 21, 1928, c. 659, 45 Stat. 645; Mar. 2, 1929, c. 488, § 1, 45 Stat. 1475; June 16, 1930, c. 494, 46 Stat. 589; May 17, 1932, c. 190, 47 Stat. 158; June 25, 1936, c. 804, 49 Stat. 1921; Apr. 27, 1938, c. 180, Title II, § 1, 52 Stat. 264; Feb. 10, 1939, c. 2, §§ 1130(a), (b), 1131, 53 Stat. 162, 163; June 29, 1939, c. 248, Title II, 53 Stat. 902; May 14, 1940, c. 189, Titles III, IV, 54 Stat. 204, 209, 210; June 28, 1941, c. 258, Title IV, 55 Stat. 300–302; July 2, 1942, c. 472, Title IV, 56 Stat. 503, 504; June 28, 1943, c. 173, Title II, § 201, 57 Stat. 242, 243; June 26, 1944, c. 277, Title II, § 201, 58 Stat. 357; Dec. 7, 1944, c. 522, § 1, 58 Stat. 796; May 21, 1945, c. 129, Titles II, IV, 59 Stat. 184, 199; July 5, 1946, c. 541, Title IV, 60 Stat. 478, 479).

For purposes of uniformity, all provisions of law governing the regulation and allowance of office, travel, and subsistence expenses of all officers and employees of the courts, except those provisions relating to Supreme Court officers and employees, are incorporated in subsection (a)(6)(7) of this section. Likewise the provisions respecting the compensation of court officers and employees, except those of the Supreme Court, are incorporated in subsection (a)(5). In each instance the power to fix and determine such salaries and expenses is transferred to the Director of the Administrative Office of the United States Courts. This change is in conformity with the Administrative Office Act 1939 included in this chapter.

Compensation of bailiffs however is provided by sections 713 and 755 of this title and that of court reporters by section 753 of this title.

Salaries and travel expenses of Court of Claims Commissioners are covered by section 792 of this title.

The language "and the lawful fees of United States Commissioners" in subsection (a)(6) and "the offices of the United States Commissioners" in subsection (a)(9) is new. It conforms with sections 633, 636 and 639 of this title.

Subsection (a)(5)(7) covers the provisions of section 726–1 and 726a of Title 18, U.S.C., 1940 ed., which provided that probation officers' salaries, should not be less than $1,800 nor more than $3,600 per annum and their traveling expenses should not exceed more than 4 cents per mile.

Words, "and officers and employees of the Administrative Office" were added in subsection (a)(7) to expressly authorize travel and subsistence expenses of such officers and employees.

The power to fix such pay and allowances is transferred to the Director as above indicated, and conforms with the Administrative Office Act of 1939. For further explanation of the general supervision of probation officers, see reviser's note [now Revision Notes and Legislative Reports] under section 3654, H.Rept. to accompany H.R. 3190 for revision of Title 18, U.S.C.

Subsection (a)(8) covers the provisions of section 1131 of Title 26, U.S.C., 1940 ed. Such section 1131 authorized the Tax Court, successor to the Board of Tax Appeals, to make expenditures for personal services, rent, law books, reference books, periodicals, and provided that all expenditures should be paid out of appropriations for the Tax Court, on itemized vouchers approved by the court.

Two reference to "officials and employees covered by this chapter" were changed to "clerical and administrative personnel," following the language of paragraph (a)(1), conferring general power to supervise such personnel as respects administrative matters.

Similar language was used in paragraph (b) instead of "The clerks of the district courts, their deputies and assistants, and all other employees of said courts."

The provisions of section 374b of Title 28, U.S.C., 1940 ed., based on successive Acts relating to classification and compensation of secretaries and law clerks were omitted as temporary and unnecessary in revision, in view of subsection (a)(5) of this section under which the salaries of all personnel are necessarily limited by current appropriation Acts.

For increases in basic rates of compensation for other judicial officers and employees see, also, section 521 of Act June 30, 1945, c. 212.

The designation "senior circuit judges" was changed to "chief judges of the circuits" in conformity with section 45 of this title.

Provisions of section 11–204 of District of Columbia Code, 1940 ed., relating to appointment of clerk of the United States Court of Appeals for the District of Columbia, and deputy clerk, crier, and messenger thereof, and the provisions relating to accounting for fees, are incorporated in sections 711 and 713 of this title. Provisions of said section, requiring the clerk of such court to give bond, were omitted as covered by section 952 of this title. Provisions of said section, relating to regulation of clerk's fees by such court were omitted so as to render uniform the method of such regulation as prescribed by section 1913 of this title, and the provisions of said section, placing a maximum of five hundred dollars per year on the office expenditures of the clerk of such court, were omitted as inconsistent with this consolidated section.

For distribution of other provisions of sections on which this section is based, see Distribution Table.

Changes were made in phraseology and arrangement. 80th Congress House Report No. 308.

By Senate amendment, all provisions relating to the Tax Court were eliminated, therefore, as finally enacted, sections 1130(a)(b) and 1131 of Title 26 U.S.C., Internal Revenue Code [1940 ed.], did not constitute part of the source of this section. However, no change in the text of the section was necessary. See 80th Congress Senate Report No. 1559.

As finally enacted, part of Act July 9, 1947, c. 211, Title IV, 61 Stat. 304, 305, which was classified to Title 28 U.S.C., 1946 ed., § 374b, became one of the sources of this section and was accordingly included in the schedule of repeals by Senate amendment. See 80th Congress Senate Report No. 1559.

1956 Acts. House Report No. 2170 and Conference Report No. 2934, see 1956 U.S. Code Cong. and Adm. News, p. 4354.

1967 Acts. Senate Report No. 781 and Conference Report No. 996, see 1967 U.S. Code Cong. and Adm. News, p. 2402.

1968 Acts. House Report No. 1629, see 1968 U.S. Code Cong. and Adm. News, p. 4252.

1972 Acts. House Report No. 92–1148, see 1972 U.S. Code Cong. and Adm. News, p. 3007.

1975 Acts. House Report No. 93–1508, see 1974 U.S. Code Cong. and Adm. News, p. 7401.

1978 Acts. House Report No. 95–1687, see 1978 U.S. Code Cong. and Adm. News, p. 4652.

Senate Report No. 95–989 and House Report No. 95–595, see 1978 U.S. Code Cong. and Adm. News, p. 5787.

1979 Acts. Senate Report No. 96–74 and House Conference Report No. 96–444, see 1979 U.S. Code Cong. and Adm. News, p. 1469.

1980 Acts. Senate Report No. 96–362, see 1980 U.S. Code Cong. and Adm. News, p. 4315.

House Report No. 96–1279, see 1980 U.S. Code Cong. and Adm. News, p. 6530.

1982 Acts. Senate Report No. 97–77 and House Conference Report No. 97–792, see 1982 U.S. Code Cong. and Adm. News, p. 2377.

1986 Acts. House Report No. 99–764 and House Conference Report No. 99–958, see 1986 U.S. Code Cong. and Adm. News, p. 5227.

1987 Acts. House Report No. 100–390, see 1987 U.S. Code Cong. and Adm. News, p. 2137.

1988 Acts. Senate Report No. 100–293 and House Conference Report No. 100–1072, see 1988 U.S. Code Cong. and Adm. News, p. 5564.

House Report No. 100–889, see 1988 U.S. Code Cong. and Adm. News, p. 5982.

1990 Acts. House Report No. 101–770, see 1990 U.S. Code Cong. and Adm. News, p. 1709.

House Report No. 101–681(Part I), see 1990 U.S. Code Cong. and Adm. News, p. 6472.

Senate Report No. 101–416, Related House Reports, and President's Signing Statement, see 1990 U.S. Code Cong. and Adm. News, p. 6802.

1992 Acts. House Report No. 102–1006, see 1992 U.S. Code Cong. and Adm. News, p. 3921.

1999 Acts. Statement by President, see 1999 U.S. Code Cong. and Adm. News, p. 290.

2002 Acts. House Report No. 107–479, see 2002 U.S. Code Cong. and Adm. News, p. 827.

House Conference Report No. 107–685 and Statement by President, see 2002 U.S. Code Cong. and Adm. News, p. 1120.

2005 Acts. House Conference Report No. 109–307, see 2005 U.S. Code Cong. and Adm. News, p. 1260.

Statement by President, see 2005 U.S. Code Cong. and Adm. News, p. S42.

2008 Acts. House Report No. 110–218(Part I), see 2007 U.S. Code Cong. and Adm. News, p. 827.

2009 Acts. Statement by President, see 2009 U.S. Code Cong. and Adm. News, p. S11.

References in Text

Chapter 6 of this title, referred to in subsec. (a)(5), is chapter 6 of part I of this title, which is classified to 28 U.S.C.A. § 151 et seq.

Section 2(c) of the Retirement and Survivors' Annuities for Bankruptcy Judges and Magistrates Act of 1988, referred to in subsec. (a)(19), is section 2(c) of Pub.L. 100–659, Nov. 15, 1988, 102 Stat. 3916, which is set out as a note under section 377 of this title.

Section 255 of Title 41, referred to in subsec. (g)(4)(C), was repealed by Pub.L. 111–350, § 7(b), Jan. 4, 2011, 124 Stat. 3855. See Table preceding Title 41, Public Contracts, for disposition of former Title 41 sections to new Title 41 positive law section.

Codifications

Pub.L. 101–650, § 306(e)(1)(A), directing amendment of Pub.L. 100–702, § 402(1), probably intended amendment of section 402(a)(1) of pub.L. 100–702, which provided for redesignation of subsec. (a)(19) to be subsec. (a)(23) of this section, redesignated as subsec. (a)(24) by Pub.L. 101–650, § 306(e)(1)(B)(ii).

Amendment by Pub.L. 109–115, Div. A, § 407(a), which directed that this section is amended by adding "section (4) at the end of section '(g)' " was executed by adding par. (4) to the end of subsec. (g), as the probable intent of Congress.

In subsec. (g)(4)(A), "section 3902 of Title 41" substituted for section 253l of title 41" on authority of Pub.L. 111–350, § 6(c), Jan. 4, 2011, 124 Stat. 3854, which Act enacted Title 41, Public Contracts.

In subsec. (g)(4)(B), "section 3903 of Title 41" substituted for section 254c of title 41" on authority of Pub.L. 111–350, § 6(c), Jan. 4, 2011, 124 Stat. 3854, which Act enacted Title 41, Public Contracts.

Amendments

2011 Amendments. Subsec. (a)(10)(C). Pub.L. 111–350, § 5(g)(2), struck out "section 3709 of the Revised Statutes of the United States (41 U.S.C. 5)" and inserted "section 6101(b) to (d) of title 41".

2009 Amendments. Subsec. (a)(5). Pub.L. 111–8, Div. D, § 307(a), following "hold office during good behavior", struck out "magistrate judges appointed under section 631 of this title," and inserted ", United States magistrate judges, bankruptcy judges appointed under chapter 6 of this title, judges of the District Court of Guam, judges of the District Court for the Northern Mariana Islands, judges of the District Court of the Virgin Islands, bankruptcy judges and magistrate judges retired under section 377 of this title, and judges retired under section 373 of this title, who are".

2008 Amendments. Subsec. (a)(5). Pub.L. 110–177, § 502(a), inserted "magistrate judges appointed under section 631 of this title," following "hold office during good behavior".

2005 Amendments. Subsec. (g)(4). Pub.L. 109–115, § 407(a), added par. (4).

2002 Amendments. Subsec. (a)(20)(B). Pub.L. 107–273, § 11043(e)(1)(A), substituted "section 358 of this title" for "section 372(c)(11) of this title".

Subsec. (a)(20)(C). Pub.L. 107–273, § 11043(e)(1)(B), substituted "section 360(b) of this title" for "section 372(c)(15) of this title".

Subsec. (g)(3)(B). Pub.L. 107–217, § 3(g)(1), struck out "section 203 of the Federal Property and Administrative Services Act of 1949 (40 U.S.C. 484)" and substituted "sections 541–555 of title 40".

Subsec. (h)(1). Pub.L. 107–273, § 11043(e)(2)(A), substituted "chapter 16 of this title" for "section 372 of this title" wherever appearing.

Subsec. (h)(2). Pub.L. 107–273, § 11043(e)(2)(B), substituted "chapter 16 of this title" for "section 372(c) of this title".

2000 Amendments. Subsec. (a)(8). Pub.L. 106–518, § 304(d), rewrote par. (8), which formerly read: "Disburse, directly or through the several United States marshals, moneys appropriated for the maintenance and operation of the courts;".

Subsec. (a)(24). Pub.L. 106–518, § 204, struck out the second par. (24), which formerly read: "Lay before Congress, annually, statistical tables that will accurately reflect the business imposed on the Federal courts by the savings and loan crisis."

1999 Amendments. Subsec. (a)(5). Pub.L. 106–113 [§ 305] inserted provisions regarding payment on behalf of Justices and judges of the United States appointed to hold office during good behavior, aged 65 or over, any increases in the cost of Federal Employees' Group Life Insurance imposed after April 24, 1999, including expenses.

1992 Amendments. Subsec. (a)(7), (23), Pub.L. 102–572, § 902(b)(1), substituted "United States Court of Federal Claims" for "United States Claims Court".

Subsec. (g)(3). Pub.L. 102–572, § 503, added par. (3).

1990 Amendments. Subsec. (a)(7). Pub.L. 101–650, § 325(c)(1), amended Pub.L. 100–702, § 1011, resulting in the substitution of ", except that" for ": Provided, That" in par. (7), and deleted directory language which would have required substitution of a comma for a semicolon at the end of par. (7) as it existed prior to amendment by Pub.L. 100–702. See 1988 Amendments note under this section.

Pub.L. 101–650, § 306(e)(1)(B)(i), inserted "judges of the United States Claims Court," preceding "bankruptcy judges".

Subsec. (a)(19). Pub.L. 101–474, § 5(r), and Pub.L. 101–650, § 306(e)(1)(A), identically amended Pub.L. 100–702, § 402(a)(1), redesignating par. (19) as (23). See 1988 Amendments note under this section.

Subsec. (a)(23). Pub.L. 101–650, § 306(e)(1)(B)(iii), added par. (23). Former par. (23) redesignated (24).

Pub.L. 101–474, § 5(r), and Pub.L. 101–650, § 306(e)(1)(A), identically amended Pub.L. 100–702, § 402(a)(1), redesignating par. (19) as (23). See 1988 Amendments note under this section.

Subsec. (a)(24). Pub.L. 101–650, § 306(e)(1)(B)(ii), redesignated par. (23), relating to performance of other duties, as (24).

Pub.L. 101–647 added par. (24) relating to statistical tables.

1988 Amendments. Subsec. (a)(2). Pub.L. 100–702, § 1020(a)(2), substituted "semiannually" for "quarterly".

Subsec. (a)(7). Pub.L. 100–702, § 1011, which directed substitution of a comma for a semicolon at the end of par. (7) and added thereafter "without regard to the per diem allowances and amounts for reimbursement of actual and necessary expenses established by the Administrator of General Services under section 5702 of title 5: *Provided*, That the reimbursement of subsistence expenses may not exceed that authorized by the Director for judges of the United States under section 456 of this title;", was executed by inserting said provisions following the comma at the end of par. (7), as the probable intent of Congress.

Pub.L. 100–659, § 6(a)(1), inserted after "United States," the words "bankruptcy judges, United States magistrates,".

Subsec. (a)(14) to (17). Pub.L. 100–702, § 1008(1), redesignated second par. (14) relating to the provision of special interpretation services in courts of the United States, through par. (17) as pars. (15) through (18), respectively.

Subsec. (a)(18). Pub.L. 100–702, § 1008(1), redesignated par. (17) as (18). Former par. (18), as added by Pub.L. 100–659, redesignated (19).

Pub.L. 100–659, § 6(a)(3), added par. (18). Former par. (18) redesignated (19).

Subsec. (a)(19). Pub.L. 100–702, § 1008(1), redesignated par. (19), as added by Pub.L. 100–702, § 402(a)(2), as (20).

Pub.L. 100–702, § 402(a), which directed the redesignation of par. (18) as (23) and the addition of par. (19) was executed by redesignating par. (19), relating to performance of other duties, as (23) and adding par. (19), relating to compilation of rules and orders, to reflect the probable intent of Congress.

Pub.L. 100–659, § 6(a)(2), redesignated par. (18), relating to performance of other duties, as (19).

Subsec. (a)(20). Pub.L. 100–702, § 1008(1), redesignated par. (19), as added by Pub.L. 100–702, § 402(a)(2), as par. (20).

Subsec. (a)(21). Pub.L. 100–702, § 1008(2), added par. (21).

Subsec. (a)(22). Pub.L. 100–702, § 1010, added par. (22).

Subsec. (a)(23). Pub.L. 100–702, § 402(a)(1), redesignated par. (19), relating to performance of other duties, as (23).

1987 Amendments. Subsec. (a)(17), (18). Pub.L. 100–185, § 2, added par. (17) and redesignated former par. (17) as (18).

1986 Amendments. Subsec. (f). Pub.L. 99–554 struck out subsec. (f) as added by section 225(b) of Pub.L. 95–598, which related to the Director naming qualified persons to membership on the panel of trustees, their number, qualifications, removal, etc.

1982 Amendments. Subsec. (a)(9). Pub.L. Pub.L. 97–267, § 7(1), struck out "agencies" following "pretrial services".

Subsec. (a)(10). Pub.L. 97–267, § 7(2), substituted "providing pretrial services" for "for pretrial services agencies".

Subsec. (a)(11), (12). Pub.L. 97–267, § 7(3), (4), substituted "offices providing pretrial services" for "pretrial service agencies" in par. (11), and "offices providing pretrial services" for "pretrial services agencies" in par. (12), respectively.

1980 Amendments. Subsec. (a)(16)(A). Pub.L. 96–523 added "(b)" following "3102".

Subsec. (h). Pub.L. 96–458 added subsec. (h).

1979 Amendments. Subsec. (d)(3). Pub.L. 96–82 added cls. (A), (B), and (C).

1978 Amendments. Subsec. (a)(10). Pub.L. 95–539, § 3(a), expanded the duties of the Director to include providing or making available equipment for interpretation of proceedings in accordance with section 1828 of this title and to include entering into and performing contracts necessary to the conduct of the work of the judicial branch and exempted from the provisions of section 5 of Title 41 contracts for nonpersonal services for pretrial agencies, for interpretation of proceedings, and for special interpretation services pursuant to section 1828 of this title.

Subsec. (a)(13), (14). Pub.L. 95–598, § 225(a), added par. (13), relating to annual statistical tables reflecting the business of the several bankruptcy courts and redesignated former par. (13), relating to provision of special interpretation services in courts of the United States, as (14).

Subsec. (a)(13) to (16). Pub.L. 95–539, § 3(b), (c), added pars. (13) to (16). Former par. (13) redesignated (17).

Subsec. (a)(17). Pub.L. 95–539, § 3(b), redesignated former par. (13) as (17).

Subsec. (f). Pub.L. 95–598, § 225(b), added subsec. (f), relating to the naming of qualified persons to membership on the panel of trustees.

Subsecs. (f), (g). Pub.L. 95–539, § 4, added subsecs. (f) and (g).

1975 Amendments. Subsec. (a)(9). Pub.L. 93–619 added par. (9). Former par. (9) redesignated (10).

Subsec. (a)(10). Pub.L. 93–619 redesignated former par. (9) as (10), and in par. (10) as so redesignated, substituted "the offices of the United States magistrates and commissioners, and the offices of pretrial services agencies" for "and the Administrative Office and the offices of the United States magistrates". Former par. (10) redesignated (11).

Subsec. (a)(11). Pub.L. 93–619 redesignated former par. (10) as par. (11), and in par. (11), as so redesignated, added reference to pretrial service agencies. Former par. (11) redesignated (12).

Subsec. (a)(12). Pub.L. 93–619 redesignated former par. (11) as (12), and in par. (12) as so redesignated, added reference to pretrial service agencies. Former par. (12) redesignated (13).

Subsec. (a)(13). Pub.L. 93–619 redesignated former par. (12) as (13).

1972 Amendments. Subsec. (a)(7). Pub.L. Pub.L. 92–397 substituted "children of justices and judges of the United States" for "children of judges".

1968 Amendments. Subsec. (a)(9). Pub.L. 90–578, § 201(a), substituted "United States magistrates" for "United States Commissioners".

Subsecs. (d), (e). Pub.L. 90–578, § 201(b), added subsecs. (d) and (e).

1967 Amendments. Subsec. (a)(7). Pub.L. 90–219, § 203(a), inserted ", Directors of the Federal Judicial Center, and Directors of the Administrative Office," following "judges" and "and the Federal Judicial Center," following "Administrative Office".

Subsec. (a)(9). Pub.L. 90–219, § 203(b), inserted ", the Federal Judicial Center," following "courts."

Subsec. (a)(10). Pub.L. 90–219, § 203(c), inserted ", the Federal Judicial Center," following "courts."

Subsec. (a)(11). Pub.L. 90–219, § 203(c), inserted ", the Federal Judicial Center," following "courts".

1956 Amendments. Subsec. (a)(7). Act Aug. 3, 1956, inserted "annuities to widows and surviving dependent children of judges and" following "Regulate and pay".

Effective and Applicability Provisions

2009 Acts. Pub.L. 111–8, Div. D, Title III, § 307(c), Mar. 11, 2009, 123 Stat. 649, provided that: "Subsection (b) [enacting provisions set out as a note under 5 U.S.C.A. § 8701] and the amendment made by subsection (a) [amending this section] shall apply with respect to any payment made on or after the first day of the first applicable pay period beginning on or after the date of the enactment of Public Law 110–177 [Jan. 7, 2008]."

2008 Acts. Pub.L. 110–177, Title V, § 502(c), Jan. 7, 2008, 121 Stat. 2542, provided that: "Subsection (b) [enacting provisions set out as a note under 5 U.S.C.A. § 8701] and the amendment made by subsection (a) [amending this section] shall apply with respect to any payment made on or after the first day of the first applicable pay period beginning on or after the date of enactment of this Act [Jan. 7, 2008]."

1992 Acts. Amendment by section 902(b)(1) of Pub.L. 102–572 effective Oct. 29, 1992, see section 911 of Pub.L. 102–572, set out as a note under section 171 of this title.

Amendment by Pub.L. 102–572 effective Jan. 1, 1993, see section 1101(a) of Pub.L. 102–572, set out as a note under section 905 of Title 2, The Congress.

1990 Acts. Amendment by section 306(e)(1) of Pub.L. 101–650 applicable to judges of, and senior judges in active service with, the United States Court of Federal Claims on or after Dec. 1, 1990, see section 306(f) of Pub.L. 101–650, set out as a note under section 8331 of Title 5, Government Organization and Employees.

1988 Acts. Amendment by section 402(a) of Pub.L. 100–702 effective Dec. 1, 1988, see section 407 of Pub.L. 100–702, set out as a note under section 2071 of this title.

Amendment of this section by Pub.L. 100–659 to take effect on Nov. 15, 1988, and shall apply to bankruptcy judges and magistrates who retire on or after Nov. 15, 1988, with special election provisions for bankruptcy judges, etc., who left office on or after July 31, 1987, and before Nov. 15, 1988, see section 9 of Pub.L. 100–659, set out as a note under section 377 of this title.

1986 Acts. Amendment by Pub.L. 99–554 effective 30 days after Oct. 27, 1986, except as otherwise provided, see section 302(a) of Pub.L. 99–554, as amended, set out as a note under section 581 of this title.

1980 Acts. Amendment by Pub.L. 96–523 effective sixty days after Dec. 12, 1980, see section 3 of Pub.L. 96–523, set out as a note under section 3102 of Title 5, Government Organization and Employees.

Amendment by Pub.L. 96–458 effective Oct. 1, 1981, see section 7 of Pub.L. 96–458, set out as a note under section 331 of this title.

1978 Acts. Amendment by Pub.L. 95–598 effective Oct. 1, 1979, see section 402(c) of Pub.L. 95–598, as amended, set out as a note preceding section 101 of Title 11, Bankruptcy.

Amendment by Pub.L. 95–539 effective Oct. 28, 1978, see section 10(a) of Pub.L. 95–539, set out as a note under section 602 of this title.

1968 Acts. Amendment by Pub.L. 90–578 effective Oct. 17, 1968, except when a later effective date is applicable, which is the earlier of date when implementation of amendment by appointment of magistrates and assumption of office takes place or third anniversary of enactment of Pub.L. 90–578 on Oct. 17, 1968, see section 403 of Pub.L. 90–578, set out as a note under section 631 of this title.

Termination of Reporting Requirements

For termination, effective May 15, 2000, of provisions in subsecs. (a)(4), (d)(3), and (h)(2) of this section relating to reporting certain information annually to Congress, see Pub.L. 104–66, § 3003, as amended, set out as a note under 31 U.S.C.A. § 1113 and page 12 of House Document No. 103–7.

Change of Name

References to United States Claims Court deemed to refer to United States Court of Federal Claims and references to Claims Court deemed to refer to Court of Federal Claims, see section 902(b) of Pub.L. 102–572, set out as a note under section 171 of Title 28, Judiciary and Judicial Procedure.

"United States magistrate judge" substituted for "United States magistrate" in text pursuant to section 321 of Pub.L. 101–650, set out as a note under 28 U.S.C.A. § 631. Previously, United States commissioners, referred to in text, were replaced by United States magistrates pursuant to Pub.L. 90–578, Oct. 17, 1968, 82 Stat. 1118. See chapter 43 of Title 28, 28 U.S.C.A. § 631 et seq.

Authority; Termination

Pub.L. 109–115, Div. A, Title IV, § 407(c), Nov. 30, 2005, 119 Stat. 2471, which provided that the authorities granted in this section [Pub.L. 109–115, Div. A, Title IV, § 407, 119 Stat. 2470, which amended subsec. (g)(4) of this section and 28 U.S.C.A. § 612] shall expire on September 30, 2010, was repealed by Pub.L. 111–8, Div. D, Title III, § 308, Mar. 11, 2009, 123 Stat. 649.

Compensation and Appointment of Secretaries and Law Clerks

Provisions authorizing the appointment and compensation of secretaries and law clerks to circuit and district judges in such number and at such rates of compensation as may be determined by the Judicial Conference of the United States were contained in the following appropriation Acts:

Dec. 12, 1985, Pub.L. 99–180, Title IV, § 400, 99 Stat. 1154.

Aug. 30, 1984, Pub.L. 98–411, Title IV, § 400, 98 Stat. 1571.

Nov. 28, 1983, Pub.L. 98–166, Title IV, § 400, 97 Stat. 1099.

Dec. 21, 1982, Pub.L. 97–377, § 101(d) [S. 2956, Title IV, § 400], 96 Stat. 1866.

Dec. 15, 1981, Pub.L. 97–92, § 101(h) [incorporating Pub.L. 96–536, § 101(o); H.R. 7584, Title IV, § 400], 95 Stat. 1190.

Dec. 16, 1980, Pub.L. 96–536, § 101(o) [H.R. 7584, Title IV, § 400], 94 Stat. 3169.

Sept. 24, 1979, Pub.L. 96–68, Title IV, § 400, 93 Stat. 428.

Oct. 10, 1978, Pub.L. 95–431, Title IV, § 401, 92 Stat. 1037.

Aug. 2, 1977, Pub.L. 95–86, Title IV, § 401, 91 Stat. 435.

July 14, 1976, Pub.L. 94–362, Title IV, § 401, 90 Stat. 953.

Oct. 21, 1975, Pub.L. 94–121, Title IV, § 401, 89 Stat. 630.

Oct. 5, 1974, Pub.L. 93–433, Title IV, § 401, 88 Stat. 1202.

Nov. 27, 1973, Pub.L. 93–162, Title IV, § 401, 87 Stat. 651.

Oct. 25, 1972, Pub.L. 92–544, Title IV, § 401, 86 Stat. 1126.

Aug. 10, 1971, Pub.L. 92–77, Title IV, § 401, 85 Stat. 262.

Oct. 21, 1970, Pub.L. 91–472, Title IV, § 401, 84 Stat. 1056.

Dec. 24, 1969, Pub.L. 91–153, Title IV, § 401, 83 Stat. 419.

Aug. 9, 1968, Pub.L. 90–470, Title IV, § 401, 82 Stat. 685.

Nov. 8, 1967, Pub.L. 90–133, Title IV, § 401, 81 Stat. 427.

Nov. 8, 1966, Pub.L. 89–797, Title IV, § 401, 80 Stat. 1499.

Sept. 2, 1965, Pub.L. 89–164, Title IV, § 401, 79 Stat. 638.

Aug. 31, 1964, Pub.L. 88–527, Title IV, § 401, 78 Stat. 729.

Dec. 30, 1963, Pub.L. 88–245, Title IV, § 401, 77 Stat. 795.

Oct. 18, 1962, Pub.L. 87–843, Title IV, § 401, 76 Stat. 1099.

Sept. 21, 1961, Pub.L. 87–264, Title III, § 301, 75 Stat. 555.

Aug. 31, 1960, Pub.L. 86–678, Title III, § 301, 74 Stat. 566.

July 13, 1959, Pub.L. 86–84, Title III, § 301, 73 Stat. 192.

June 30, 1958, Pub.L. 85–474, Title III, § 301, 72 Stat. 254.

June 11, 1957, Pub.L. 85–40, Title III, § 301, 70 Stat. 65.

June 20, 1956, c. 414, Title III, § 301, 70 Stat. 310.

July 7, 1955, c. 279, Title III, § 301, 69 Stat. 276.

July 2, 1954, c. 455, Title II, § 201, 68 Stat. 410.

Aug. 1, 1953, c. 304, Title II, § 201, 67 Stat. 334.

July 10, 1952, c. 651, Title IV, § 401, 66 Stat. 569.

Oct. 22, 1951, c. 533, Title IV, § 401, 65 Stat. 596.

Sept. 6, 1950, c. 896, ch. III, Title IV, § 401, 64 Stat. 631.

Increases in Compensation Rates

Increases in rates of basic compensation fixed pursuant to subsec. (a)(5) of this section, see notes under section 603 of this title.

Limitation on Aggregate Salaries of Secretaries and Law Clerks

1967—Pub.L. 90–206, Title II, § 213(b), Dec. 16, 1967, 81 Stat. 635, provided that: "The limitations provided by applicable law on the effective date of this section [see Effective and Applicability Provisions of 1967 amendments note set out under section 5332 of Title 5, Government Organization and Employees] with respect to the aggregate salaries payable to secretaries and law clerks of circuit and district judges are hereby increased by amounts which reflect the respective applicable increases provided by section 202(a) of this title [amending section 5332(a) of Title 5] in corresponding rates of compensation for officers and employees subject to section 5332 of title 5, United States Code [section 5332 of Title 5]."

Section 213(b) of Pub.L. 90–206 effective as of the beginning of the first pay period which begins on or after Oct. 1, 1967, see section 220(a)(2) of Pub.L. 90–206, set out as a note

under section 5332 of Title 5, Government Organization and Employees.

1966—Pub.L. 89–504, Title II, § 202(b), July 18, 1966, 80 Stat. 294, provided that: "The limitations provided by applicable law on the effective date of this section with respect to the aggregate salaries payable to secretaries and law clerks of circuit and district judges are hereby increased by amounts which reflect the respective applicable increases provided by section 102(a) of title I of this Act [amending section 1113(b) of former Title 5, Executive Departments and Government Officers and Employees] in corresponding rates of compensation for officers and employees subject to the Classification Act of 1949, as amended [chapter 51 and subchapter III of chapter 53 of Title 5, Government Organization and Employees]."

Provision effective the first day of the first pay period which begins on or after July 1, 1966, see section 203 of Pub.L. 89–504, set out as a note under section 603 of this title.

1965—Pub.L. 89–301, § 12(b), Oct. 29, 1965, 79 Stat. 1122, provided that: "The limitations provided by applicable law on the effective date of this section with respect to the aggregate salaries payable to secretaries and law clerks of circuit and district judges are hereby increased by amounts which reflect the respective applicable increases provided by section 2(a) of this Act [amending section 1113(b) of former Title 5, Executive Departments and Government Officers and Employees] in corresponding rates of compensation for officers and employees subject to the Classification Act of 1949, as amended [chapter 51 and subchapter III of chapter 53 of Title 5, Government Organization and Employees]."

1964—Pub.L. 88–426, Title IV, § 402(b), Aug. 14, 1964, 78 Stat. 433, provided that: "The limitations provided by applicable law on the effective date of this section with respect to the aggregate salaries payable to secretaries and law clerks of circuit and district judges are hereby increased by amounts which reflect the respective applicable increases provided by title I of this Act in corresponding rates of compensation for officers and employees subject to the Classification Act of 1949, as amended [chapter 51 and subchapter III of chapter 53 of Title 5, Government Organization and Employees]."

1962—Pub.L. 87–793, Title VI, § 1004(b), Oct. 11, 1962, 76 Stat. 866, provided that: "The limitations provided by applicable law on the effective date of this section with respect to the aggregate salaries payable to secretaries and law clerks of circuit and district judges are hereby increased by two amounts, the first amount to be effective for the period beginning as of the first day of the first pay period which begins on or after the date of enactment of this Act [Oct. 11, 1962], and ending immediately prior to the first day of the first pay period which begins on or after January 1, 1964, and the second amount to be effective on the first day of the first pay period which begins on or after January 1, 1964, and thereafter, which reflect the respective applicable increases provided by title II of this part in corresponding rates of compensation for officers and employees subject to the Classification Act of 1949, as amended [chapter 51 and subchapter III of chapter 53 of Title 5, Government Organization and Employees]."

1960—Pub.L. 86–568, Title I, § 116(b), July 1, 1960, 74 Stat. 303, provided that: "The limitations provided by applicable law on the effective date of this section with respect to the aggregate salaries payable to secretaries and law clerks of circuit and district judges are hereby increased by the amounts necessary to pay the additional basic compensation provided by this part."

Words "this part", referred to in section 116(b) of Pub.L. 86–568 [this note], means Part B of Pub.L. 86–568, which enacted section 932e of former Title 5, Executive Departments and Government Officers and Employees, amended section 753 of this title, sections 1113, 2091, 2252 and 3002 of former Title 5, sections 867 and 870 of Title 22, Foreign Relations and Intercourse, and sections 4103, 4107 and 4108 of Title 38, Veterans' Benefits and enacted notes set out under sections 603 and 604 of this title, sections 60a and 60f of Title 2, The Congress, sections 1113 and 2252 of former Title 5, section 590h of Title 16, Conservation, and section 867 of Title 22.

1958—Pub.L. 85–462, § 3(b), June 20, 1958, 72 Stat. 207, provided that: "The limitations of $13,485 and $18,010 with respect to the aggregate salaries payable to secretaries and law clerks of circuit and district judges, contained in the paragraph designated "Salaries of supporting personnel" in the Judiciary Appropriation Act, 1958 (71 Stat. 65; Public Law 85–49), or any subsequent appropriation Act, shall be increased by the amounts necessary to pay the additional basic compensation provided by this Act."

1955—Act June 28, 1955, c. 189, § 3(b), 69 Stat. 175, provided that: "The limitations of $10,560 and $14,355 with respect to the aggregate salaries payable to secretaries and law clerks of circuit and district judges, contained in the paragraph under the heading 'SALARIES OF SUPPORTING PERSONNEL' in the Judiciary Appropriation Act, 1955 (Public Law 470, Eighty-third Congress), or in any subsequent appropriation Act, shall be increased by the amounts necessary to pay the additional basic compensation provided by this Act."

1951—Act Oct. 24, 1951, c. 554, § 1(d), 65 Stat. 613, provided that: "The limitations of $9,600 and $13,050 with respect to the aggregate salaries payable to secretaries and law clerks of circuit and district judges, contained in the sixteenth paragraph under the head 'Miscellaneous salaries' in the Judiciary Appropriation Act, 1951 (Public Law 759, Eighty-first Congress), or in any subsequent appropriation Act, shall be increased by the amounts necessary to pay the additional basic compensation provided by this Act."

The particular paragraph of the "Judiciary Appropriation Act, 1951 (Public Law 759, Eighty-first Congress)", referred to in section 1(d) of Act Oct. 24, 1951, c. 554 [this note], is Act Sept. 6, 1950, c. 896, ch. III, Title IV, § 401 (part), 64 Stat. 631. The salary limitations therein, also referred to above, were identical with those in the Judiciary Appropriation Act, 1952 (Act Oct. 22, 1951, c. 533, Title IV, § 401 (part), 65 Stat. 596).

1970 Increase in Pay Rates of Judicial Branch Employees Whose Rates of Pay Are Fixed by Administrative Action

Adjustment of rates of pay of judicial branch employees whose rates of pay are fixed by administrative action by not to exceed the amounts of the adjustment for corresponding rates for employees subject to section 2(a) of Pub.L. 91–231, which raised corresponding rates by 6 percent, effective on the first day of the first pay period which begins on or after Dec. 27, 1969, see Pub.L. 91–231, set out as a note under section 5332 of Title 5, Government Organization and Employees.

Reports by Director of Administrative Office of United States Courts

For requirement that Director of Administrative Office of the United States Courts include statistical information about implementation of chapter 44 of this title in annual report under section 604(a)(3) of this title, see section 903(a) of Pub.L. 100–702, set out as a note under section 651 of this title.

Travel and Subsistence Expenses

Pub.L. 87–139, § 6, Aug. 14, 1961, 75 Stat. 340, provided that: "The Director of the Administrative Office of the United States Courts shall promulgate, in accordance with section 604(a)(7) and section 456 of title 28 of the United States Code [subsec. (a)(7) of this section and section 456 of this title], such regulations as he may deem necessary to effectuate the increases provided by this Act [amending section 553 of this title, section 68b of Title 2, The Congress, sections 73b–2, 836 and 837 of former Title 5, Executive Departments and Government Officers and Employees, and sections 287o, 287q and 1471 of Title 22, Foreign Relations and Intercourse]."

CROSS REFERENCES

Actual abode of recalled judge or magistrate deemed official station for purposes of this section, see 28 USCA § 374.

Annual report to Judicial Conference under this section to include administration and operation pretrial services for previous year, see 18 USCA § 3155.

Classification and general schedule pay rates, see 5 USCA §§ 5101 et seq. and 5331 et seq.

Duties of Supreme Court Marshal, see 28 USCA § 672.

Expenses of judges and United States attorneys, see 28 USCA §§ 456, 460, 549, and 566.

Juror travel allowance not to exceed maximum rate per mile that Director prescribes pursuant to this section, see 28 USCA § 1871.

Notification to Attorney General of receipt of payment of unpaid fines, see 18 USCA § 3612.

Office expenses of clerks of court, see 28 USCA § 961.

Overtime pay, see 5 USCA § 5541 et seq.

Specification by Director in payment of fine as provided under this section, see 18 USCA § 3611.

Supreme Court officers and employees; compensation and disbursement, see 28 USCA § 671 et seq.

LIBRARY REFERENCES

American Digest System

Federal Courts ⇐1.1.

Judges ⇐22(11).

Key Number System Topic Nos. 170B, 227.

CHAPTER 44—ALTERNATIVE DISPUTE RESOLUTION

HISTORICAL AND STATUTORY NOTES

Amendments

1998 Amendments. Chapter heading and analysis. Pub.L. 105–315, § 12(b)(1), Oct. 30, 1998, 112 Stat. 2898, rewrote the chapter heading and analysis, which formerly read:

"**CHAPTER 44—ARBITRATION**

"**Sec.**

"651. Authorization of arbitration.

"652. Jurisdiction.

"653. Powers of arbitrator; arbitration hearing.

"654. Arbitration award and judgment.

"655. Trial de novo.

"656. Certification of arbitrators.

"657. Compensation of arbitrators.

"658. District courts that may authorize arbitration."

§ 651. Authorization of alternative dispute resolution

(a) **Definition.**—For purposes of this chapter, an alternative dispute resolution process includes any process or procedure, other than an adjudication by a presiding judge, in which a neutral third party participates to assist in the resolution of issues in controversy, through processes such as early neutral evaluation, mediation, minitrial, and arbitration as provided in sections 654 through 658.

(b) **Authority.**—Each United States district court shall authorize, by local rule adopted under section 2071(a), the use of alternative dispute resolution processes in all civil actions, including adversary proceedings in bankruptcy, in accordance with this chapter, except that the use of arbitration may be authorized only as provided in section 654. Each United States district court shall devise and implement its own alternative dispute resolution program, by local rule adopted under section 2071(a), to encourage and promote the use of alternative dispute resolution in its district.

(c) **Existing alternative dispute resolution programs.**—In those courts where an alternative dispute resolution program is in place on the date of the enactment of the Alternative Dispute Resolution Act of 1998, the court shall examine the effectiveness of that program and adopt such improvements to the program as are consistent with the provisions and purposes of this chapter [28 U.S.C.A. § 651 et seq.].

(d) **Administration of alternative dispute resolution programs.**—Each United States district court shall designate an employee, or a judicial officer, who is knowledgeable in alternative dispute resolution practices and processes to implement, administer, oversee, and evaluate the court's alternative dispute resolution program. Such person may also be responsible for recruiting, screening, and training attorneys to serve as neutrals and arbitrators in the court's alternative dispute resolution program.

(e) **Title 9 not affected.**—This chapter [28 U.S.C.A. § 651 et seq.] shall not affect title 9, United States Code.

(f) **Program support.**—The Federal Judicial Center and the Administrative Office of the United States Courts are authorized to assist the district courts in the establishment and improvement of alternative dispute resolution programs by identifying particular practices employed in successful programs and providing additional assistance as needed and appropriate.

(Added Pub.L. 100–702, Title IX, § 901(a), Nov. 19, 1988, 102 Stat. 4659; amended Pub.L. 105–315, § 3, Oct. 30, 1998, 112 Stat. 2993.)

HISTORICAL AND STATUTORY NOTES

Revision Notes and Legislative Reports

1988 Acts. House Report No. 100–889, see 1988 U.S. Code Cong. and Adm. News, p. 5982.

References in Text

The enactment of the Alternative Dispute Resolution Act of 1998, referred to in subsec. (c), is the enactment of Pub.L. 105–315, 112 Stat. 2993, which was approved Oct. 30, 1998.

Amendments

1998 Amendments. Pub.L. 105–315, § 3, rewrote the section, which formerly read:

"**§ 651. Authorization of arbitration**

"(a) **Authority of Certain District Courts.**—Each United States district court described in section 658 may authorize by local rule the use of arbitration in any civil action, including an adversary proceeding in bankruptcy. A district court described in section 658(1) may refer any such action to arbitration as set forth in section 652(a). A district court described in section 658(2) may refer only such actions to arbitration as are set forth in section 652(a)(1)(A).

"(b) **Title 9 Not Affected.**—This chapter shall not affect title 9."

Effective and Applicability Provisions

1988 Acts. Section 906 of Title IX of Pub.L. 100–702, as amended Pub.L. 103–192, § 1(a), Dec. 14, 1993, 107 Stat. 2292, which provided that, effective December 31, 1994, this chapter, as added by section 901 of Pub.L. 100–702, and the item relating to this chapter in the table of chapters at the beginning of part III of this title, were repealed, except that the provisions of this chapter were to continue to apply through final disposition of all actions in which referral to arbitration was made before the date of repeal, was itself repealed by Pub.L. 103–420, § 3(b), Oct. 25, 1994, 108 Stat. 4345.

Section 907 of Title IX of Pub.L. 100–702 provided that: "This title and the amendments made by this title [enacting this chapter, provisions set out as notes under this section and section 652 of this title] shall take effect 180 days after the date of enactment of this Act [Nov. 19, 1988]."

Findings and Declaration of Policy

Pub.L. 105–315, § 2, Oct. 30, 1998, 112 Stat. 2993, provided that:

"Congress finds that—

"(1) alternative dispute resolution, when supported by the bench and bar, and utilizing properly trained neutrals in a program adequately administered by the court, has the potential to provide a variety of benefits, including greater satisfaction of the parties, innovative methods of resolving disputes, and greater efficiency in achieving settlements;

"(2) certain forms of alternative dispute resolution, including mediation, early neutral evaluation, minitrials, and voluntary arbitration, may have potential to reduce the large backlog of cases now pending in some Federal courts throughout the United States, thereby allowing the courts to process their remaining cases more efficiently; and

"(3) the continued growth of Federal appellate court-annexed mediation programs suggests that this form of alternative dispute resolution can be equally effective in resolving disputes in the Federal trial courts; therefore, the district courts should consider including mediation in their local alternative dispute resolution programs."

Authorization of Appropriations

Pub.L. 105–315, § 11, Oct. 30, 1998, 112 Stat. 2998, provided that: "There are authorized to be appropriated for each fiscal year such sums as may be necessary to carry out chapter 44 of title 28, United States Code [28 U.S.C.A. § 651 et seq.], as amended by this Act [Alternative Dispute Resolution Act of 1998, Pub.L. 105–315, Oct. 30, 1998, 112 Stat. 2993, amending sections 651 to 658 of this title, amending a provision set out as a note under section 652 of this title, and enacting notes set out under this section]."

Section 905 of Title IX of Pub.L. 100–702, as amended Pub.L. 103–192, § 1(b), Dec. 14, 1993, 107 Stat. 2292; Pub.L. 103–420, § 3(a), Oct. 25, 1994, 108 Stat. 4345; Pub.L. 105–53, § 1, Oct. 6, 1997, 111 Stat. 1173, provided that: "There are authorized to be appropriated for each fiscal year to the judicial branch such sums as may be necessary to carry out the purposes of chapter 44 [this chapter], as added by section 901 of this Act. Funds appropriated under this section shall be allocated by the Administrative Office of the United States Courts to Federal judicial districts and the Federal Judicial Center. The funds so appropriated are authorized to remain available until expended."

Effect on Judicial Rulemaking Powers

Section 904 of Title IX of Pub.L. 100–702 provided that: "Nothing in this title [enacting this chapter and provisions set out as notes under this section and section 652 of this title], or in chapter 44 [this chapter], as added by section 901 of this Act, is intended to abridge, modify, or enlarge the rule making powers of the Federal judiciary."

Model Procedures

Section 902 of Title IX of Pub.L. 100–702 provided that: "The Judicial Conference of the United States may develop model rules relating to procedures for arbitration under chapter 44 [this chapter], as added by section 901 of this Act. No model rule may supersede any provision of such chapter 44, this title [enacting this chapter and provisions set out as notes under this section and section 652 of this title], or any law of the United States."

Reports by Director of Administrative Office of United States Courts and by Federal Judicial Center

Pub.L. 100–702, Title IX, § 903, Nov. 19, 1988, 102 Stat. 4663, provided that:

"(a) **Annual Report by Director of Administrative Office of the United States Courts.**—The Director of the Administrative Office of the United States Courts shall include in the annual report of the activities of the Administrative Office required under section 604(a)(3) [section 604(a)(3) of this title], statistical information about the implementation of chapter 44 [this chapter], as added by section 901 of this Act."

"(b) **Report by Federal Judicial Center.**—Not later than 5 years after the date of enactment of this Act [Nov. 19, 1988], the Federal Judicial Center, in consultation with the Director of the Administrative Office of the United States Courts, shall submit to the Congress a report on the implementation of chapter 44 [this chapter], as added by section 901 of this Act, which shall include the following:

"(1) A description of the arbitration programs authorized by such chapter, as conceived and as implemented in the judicial districts in which such programs are authorized.

"(2) A determination of the level of satisfaction with the arbitration programs in those judicial districts by a sampling of court personnel, attorneys, and litigants whose cases have been referred to arbitration.

"(3) A summary of those program features that can be identified as being related to program acceptance both within and across judicial districts.

"(4) A description of the levels of satisfaction relative to the cost per hearing of each program.

"(5) Recommendations to the Congress on whether to terminate or continue chapter 44, or alternatively, to enact an arbitration provision in title 28, United States Code [this title], authorizing arbitration in all Federal district courts."

[For termination, effective May 15, 2000, of reporting provisions of this note, see Pub.L. 104–66, § 3003, as amended, set out as a note under 31 U.S.C.A. § 1113, and the 11th item on page 12 of House Document No. 103–7.]

Treatment of Expired Provisions

Pub.L. 103–192, § 2, Dec. 14, 1993, 107 Stat. 2292, provided that: "Chapter 44 of title 28, United States Code [this chapter], and the item relating to that chapter in the table of chapters at the beginning of part III of such title [analysis preceding section 601 of this title], shall be effective on or after the date of the enactment of this Act [Dec. 14, 1993] as if such chapter and item had not been repealed by section 906 of the Judicial Improvements and Access to Justice Act [section 906 of Pub.L. 100–702, set out as an Effective Date of Repeal note under this section] as such section was in effect on the day before the date of the enactment of this Act [Dec. 14, 1993]."

LIBRARY REFERENCES

American Digest System

Alternative Dispute Resolution ⟪100.
Key Number System Topic No. 25T.

Corpus Juris Secundum

CJS Arbitration § 5, Statutory Provisions--Federal Provisions.

CJS Bankruptcy § 146, Submission to Arbitration.

---

§ 652. Jurisdiction

(a) **Consideration of alternative dispute resolution in appropriate cases.**—Notwithstanding any provision of law to the contrary and except as provided in subsections (b) and (c), each district court shall, by local rule adopted under section 2071(a), require that litigants in all civil cases consider the use of an alternative dispute resolution process at an appropriate stage in the litigation. Each district court shall provide litigants in all civil cases with at least one alternative dispute resolution process, including, but not limited to, mediation, early neutral evaluation, minitrial, and arbitration as authorized in sections 654 through 658. Any district court that elects to require the use of alternative dispute resolution in certain cases may do so only with respect to mediation, early neutral evaluation, and, if the parties consent, arbitration.

(b) **Actions exempted from consideration of alternative dispute resolution.**—Each district court may exempt from the requirements of this section specific cases or categories of cases in which use of alternative dispute resolution would not be appropriate. In defining these exemptions, each district court shall consult with members of the bar, including the United States Attorney for that district.

(c) **Authority of the Attorney General.**—Nothing in this section shall alter or conflict with the authority of the Attorney General to conduct litigation on behalf of the United States, with the authority of any Federal agency authorized to conduct litigation in the United States courts, or with any delegation of litigation authority by the Attorney General.

(d) **Confidentiality provisions.**—Until such time as rules are adopted under chapter 131 of this title [28 U.S.C.A. § 2071 et seq.] providing for the confidentiality of alternative dispute resolution processes under this chapter [28 U.S.C.A. § 651 et seq.], each district court shall, by local rule adopted under section 2071(a), provide for the confidentiality of the alternative dispute resolution processes and to prohibit disclosure of confidential dispute resolution communications.

(Added Pub.L. 100–702, Title IX, § 901(a), Nov. 19, 1988, 102 Stat. 4659; amended Pub.L. 105–315, § 4, Oct. 30, 1998, 112 Stat. 2994.)

HISTORICAL AND STATUTORY NOTES

Revision Notes and Legislative Reports

1988 Acts. House Report No. 100–889, see 1988 U.S.Code Cong. and Adm.News, p. 5982.

Amendments

1998 Amendments. Pub.L. 105–258, § 4, rewrote the section, which formerly read:

"§ 652. Jurisdiction

"(a) **Actions That May Be Referred to Arbitration.**—(1) Notwithstanding any provision of law to the contrary and except as provided in subsections (b) and (c) of this section, and section 901(c) of the Judicial Improvements and Access to Justice Act, a district court that authorizes arbitration under section 651 may—

"(A) allow the referral to arbitration of any civil action (including any adversary proceeding in bankruptcy) pending before it if the parties consent to arbitration, and

"(B) require the referral to arbitration of any civil action pending before it if the relief sought consists only of money damages not in excess of $100,000 or such lesser amount as the district court may set, exclusive of interest and costs.

"(2) For purposes of paragraph (1)(B), a district court may presume damages are not in excess of $100,000 unless counsel certifies that damages exceed such amount.

"(b) **Actions That May Not Be Referred Without Consent of Parties.**—Referral to arbitration under subsection (a)(1)(B) may not be made—

"(1) of an action based on an alleged violation of a right secured by the Constitution of the United States, or

"(2) if jurisdiction is based in whole or in part on section 1343 of this title.

"(c) **Exceptions From Arbitration.**—Each district court shall establish by local rule procedures for exempting, sua sponte or on motion of a party, any case from arbitration in which the objectives of arbitration would not be realized—

"(1) because the case involves complex or novel legal issues,

"(2) because legal issues predominate over factual issues, or

"(3) for other good cause.

"(d) **Safeguards in Consent Cases.**—In any civil action in which arbitration by consent is allowed under subsection (a)(1)(A), the district court shall by local rule establish procedures to ensure that—

"(1) consent to arbitration is freely and knowingly obtained, and

"(2) no party or attorney is prejudiced for refusing to participate in arbitration."

Effective and Applicability Provisions

1988 Acts. Section 906 of Pub.L. 100–702, as amended, which provided that, effective Dec. 31, 1994, this section was repealed, with certain exceptions, was itself repealed by Pub.L. 103–420, § 3(b), Oct. 25, 1994, 108 Stat. 4345. See section 906 of Pub.L. 100–702, set out as a note under section 651 of this title.

Section effective 180 days after Nov. 19, 1988, see section 907 of Pub.L. 100–702, set out as a note under section 651 of this title.

Treatment of Expired Provisions

This section to continue to be effective on or after Dec. 14, 1993 as if it had not been repealed by section 906 of Pub.L. 100–702, as such section was in effect on the day before such date, see Treatment of Expired Provisions note set out under section 651 of this title.

Exception to Limitation on Money Damages

Section 901(c) of Pub.L. 100–702, which provided that notwithstanding this section a district court listed in section 658 of this title whose local rule on Nov. 19, 1988 provided for a limitation on money damages with respect to cases referred to arbitration of not more than $150,000 may continue to apply the higher limitation, was repealed by Pub.L. 105–315, § 12(a), Oct. 30, 1998, 112 Stat. 2998.

American Digest System

  Alternative Dispute Resolution ⊕125.
  Key Number System Topic No. 25T.

§ 653.   Neutrals

  (a) Panel of neutrals.—Each district court that authorizes the use of alternative dispute resolution processes shall adopt appropriate processes for making neutrals available for use by the parties for each category of process offered. Each district court shall promulgate its own procedures and criteria for the selection of neutrals on its panels.

  (b) Qualifications and training.—Each person serving as a neutral in an alternative dispute resolution process should be qualified and trained to serve as a neutral in the appropriate alternative dispute resolution process. For this purpose, the district court may use, among others, magistrate judges who have been trained to serve as neutrals in alternative dispute resolution processes, professional neutrals from the private sector, and persons who have been trained to serve as neutrals in alternative dispute resolution processes. Until such time as rules are adopted under chapter 131 of this title [28 U.S.C.A. § 2071 et seq.] relating to the disqualification of neutrals, each district court shall issue rules under section 2071(a) relating to the disqualification of neutrals (including, where appropriate, disqualification under section 455 of this title, other applicable law, and professional responsibility standards).

(Added Pub.L. 100–702, Title IX, § 901(a), Nov. 19, 1988, 102 Stat. 4660; amended Pub.L. 105–315, § 5, Oct. 30, 1998, 112 Stat. 2995.)

HISTORICAL AND STATUTORY NOTES

Revision Notes and Legislative Reports

  1988 Acts. House Report No. 100–889, see 1988 U.S.Code Cong. and Adm. News, p. 5982.

Amendments

  1998 Amendments. Pub.L. 105–315, § 5, rewrote the section, which formerly read:

  "**§ 653. Powers of arbitrator; arbitration hearing**

  "**(a) Powers.**—An arbitrator to whom an action is referred under section 652 shall have, within the judicial district of the district court which referred the action to arbitration, the power—

    "(1) to conduct arbitration hearings,

    "(2) to administer oaths and affirmations, and

    "(3) to make awards.

  "**(b) Time for Beginning Arbitration Hearing.**—An arbitration hearing under this chapter shall begin within a time period specified by the district court, but in no event later than 180 days after the filing of an answer, except that the arbitration proceeding shall not, in the absence of the consent of the parties, commence until 30 days after the disposition by the district court of any motion to dismiss the complaint, motion for judgment on the pleadings, motion to join necessary parties, or motion for summary judgment, if the motion

was filed during a time period specified by the district court. The 180–day and 30–day periods specified in the preceding sentence may be modified by the court for good cause shown.

  "**(c) Subpoenas.**—Rule 45 of the Federal Rules of Civil Procedure (relating to subpoenas) applies to subpoenas for the attendance of witnesses and the production of documentary evidence at an arbitration hearing under this chapter."

Effective and Applicability Provisions

  1988 Acts. Section 906 of Pub.L. 100–702, as amended, which provided that, effective Dec. 31, 1994, this section was repealed, with certain exceptions, was itself repealed by Pub.L. 103–420, § 3(b), Oct. 25, 1994, 108 Stat. 4345. See section 906 of Pub.L. 100–702, set out as a note under section 651 of this title.

  Section effective 180 days after Nov. 19, 1988, see section 907 of Pub.L. 100–702, set out as a note under section 651 of this title.

Treatment of Expired Provisions

  This section to continue to be effective on or after Dec. 14, 1993 as if it had not been repealed by section 906 of Pub.L. 100–702 as such section was in effect on the day before such date, see Treatment of Expired Provisions note set out under section 651 of this title.

American Digest System

  Alternative Dispute Resolution ⊕221, 314, 472.
  Key Number System Topic No. 25T.

§ 654.   Arbitration

  (a) Referral of actions to arbitration.—Notwithstanding any provision of law to the contrary and except as provided in subsections (a), (b), and (c) of section 652 and subsection (d) of this section, a district court may allow the referral to arbitration of any civil action (including any adversary proceeding in bankruptcy) pending before it when the parties consent, except that referral to arbitration may not be made where—

    (1) the action is based on an alleged violation of a right secured by the Constitution of the United States;

    (2) jurisdiction is based in whole or in part on section 1343 of this title; or

    (3) the relief sought consists of money damages in an amount greater than $150,000.

  (b) Safeguards in consent cases.—Until such time as rules are adopted under chapter 131 of this title relating to procedures described in this subsection, the district court shall, by local rule adopted under section 2071(a), establish procedures to ensure that any civil action in which arbitration by consent is allowed under subsection (a)—

    (1) consent to arbitration is freely and knowingly obtained; and

(2) no party or attorney is prejudiced for refusing to participate in arbitration.

(c) Presumptions.—For purposes of subsection (a)(3), a district court may presume damages are not in excess of $150,000 unless counsel certifies that damages exceed such amount.

(d) Existing programs.—Nothing in this chapter is deemed to affect any program in which arbitration is conducted pursuant to section [1] title IX of the Judicial Improvements and Access to Justice Act (Public Law 100–702), as amended by section 1 of Public Law 105–53.

(Added Pub.L. 100–702, Title IX, § 901(a), Nov. 19, 1988, 102 Stat. 4660; amended Pub.L. 105–315, § 6, Oct. 30, 1998, 112 Stat. 2995.)

[1] So in original. The word "section" probably should not appear.

HISTORICAL AND STATUTORY NOTES

Revision Notes and Legislative Reports

1988 Acts. House Report No. 100–889, see 1988 U.S. Code Cong. and Adm. News, p. 5982.

References in Text

Title IX of the Judicial Improvements and Access to Justice Act, referred to in subsec. (d), is Pub.L. 100–702, Title IX, Nov. 19, 1988, 102 Stat. 4663. See Codifications note under this section.

Codifications

Section title IX of the Judicial Improvements and Access to Justice Act, referred to in subsec. (d), probably should read section 905 of title IX of the Judicial Improvements and Access to Justice Act, which is Pub.L. 100–702, Title IX, § 905, Nov. 19, 1988, 102 Stat. 4663, set out as a note under section 651 of this title.

Amendments

1998 Amendments. Pub.L. 105–315, § 6, rewrote the section, which formerly read:

"**§ 654. Arbitration award and judgment**

"**(a) Filing and Effect of Arbitration Award.**—An arbitration award made by an arbitrator under this chapter, along with proof of service of such award on the other party by the prevailing party or by the plaintiff, shall, promptly after the arbitration hearing is concluded, be filed with the clerk of the district court that referred the case to arbitration. Such award shall be entered as the judgment of the court after the time has expired for requesting a trial de novo under section 655. The judgment so entered shall be subject to the same provisions of law and shall have the same force and effect as a judgment of the court in a civil action, except that the judgment shall not be subject to review in any other court by appeal or otherwise.

"**(b) Sealing of Arbitration Award.**—The district court shall provide by local rule that the contents of any arbitration award made under this chapter shall not be made known to any judge who might be assigned to the case—

"**(1)** except as necessary for the court to determine whether to assess costs or attorney fees under section 655,

"**(2)** until the district court has entered final judgment in the action or the action has been otherwise terminated, or

"**(3)** except for purposes of preparing the report required by section 903(b) of the Judicial Improvements and Access to Justice Act.

"**(c) Taxation of Costs.**—The district court may by rule allow for the inclusion of costs as provided in section 1920 of this title as a part of the arbitration award."

Effective and Applicability Provisions

1988 Acts. Section 906 of Pub.L. 100–702, as amended, which provided that, effective Dec. 31, 1994, this section was repealed, with certain exceptions, was itself repealed by Pub.L. 103–420, § 3(b), Oct. 25, 1994, 108 Stat. 4345. See section 906 of Pub.L. 100–702, set out as a note under section 651 of this title.

Section effective 180 days after Nov. 19, 1988, see section 907 of Pub.L. 100–702, set out as a note under section 651 of this title.

Treatment of Expired Provisions

This section to continue to be effective on or after Dec. 14, 1993 as if it had not been repealed by section 906 of Pub.L. 100–702 as such section was in effect on the day before such date, see Treatment of Expired Provisions note set out under section 651 of this title.

LIBRARY REFERENCES

American Digest System

Alternative Dispute Resolution ⇌112, 118.

Bankruptcy ⇌3031.

Key Number System Topic Nos. 25T, 51.

§ 655. Arbitrators

(a) Powers of arbitrators.—An arbitrator to whom an action is referred under section 654 shall have the power, within the judicial district of the district court which referred the action to arbitration—

(1) to conduct arbitration hearings;

(2) to administer oaths and affirmations; and

(3) to make awards.

(b) Standards for certification.—Each district court that authorizes arbitration shall establish standards for the certification of arbitrators and shall certify arbitrators to perform services in accordance with such standards and this chapter. The standards shall include provisions requiring that any arbitrator—

(1) shall take the oath or affirmation described in section 453; and

(2) shall be subject to the disqualification rules under section 455.

(c) Immunity.—All individuals serving as arbitrators in an alternative dispute resolution program under this chapter are performing quasi-judicial functions and are entitled to the immunities and protections that the law accords to persons serving in such capacity.

(Added Pub.L. 100–702, Title IX, § 901(a), Nov. 19, 1988, 102 Stat. 4661; amended Pub.L. 105–315, § 7, Oct. 30, 1998, 112 Stat. 2996.)

HISTORICAL AND STATUTORY NOTES
Revision Notes and Legislative Reports
1988 Acts. House Report No. 100–889, see 1988 U.S.Code Cong. and Adm.News, p. 5982.

Amendments
1998 Amendments. Pub.L. 105–315, § 7, rewrote the section, which formerly read:

"§ 655. Trial de novo

"(a) Time for Demand.—Within 30 days after the filing of an arbitration award with a district court under section 654, any party may file a written demand for a trial de novo in the district court.

"(b) Restoration to Court Docket.—Upon a demand for a trial de novo, the action shall be restored to the docket of the court and treated for all purposes as if it had not been referred to arbitration. In such a case, any right of trial by jury that a party otherwise would have had, as well as any place on the court calendar which is no later than that which a party otherwise would have had, are preserved.

"(c) Limitation on Admission of Evidence.—The court shall not admit at the trial de novo any evidence that there has been an arbitration proceeding, the nature or amount of any award, or any other matter concerning the conduct of the arbitration proceeding, unless—

"(1) the evidence would otherwise be admissible in the court under the Federal Rules of Evidence, or

"(2) the parties have otherwise stipulated.

"(d) Taxation of Arbitrator Fees as Cost.—(1)(A) A district court may provide by rule that, in any trial de novo under this section, arbitrator fees paid under section 657 may be taxed as costs against the party demanding the trial de novo.

"(B) Such rule may provide that a party demanding a trial de novo under subsection (a), other than the United States or its agencies or officers, shall deposit a sum equal to such arbitrator fees as advanced payment of such costs, unless the party is permitted to proceed in forma pauperis.

"(2) Arbitrator fees shall not be taxed as costs under paragraph (1)(A), and any sum deposited under paragraph (1)(B) shall be returned to the party demanding the trial de novo, if—

"(A) the party demanding the trial de novo obtains a final judgment more favorable than the arbitration award, or

"(B) the court determines that the demand for the trial de novo was made for good cause.

"(3) Any arbitrator fees taxed as costs under paragraph (1)(A), and any sum deposited under paragraph (1)(B) that is not returned to the party demanding the trial de novo, shall be paid to the Treasury of the United States.

"(4) Any rule under this subsection shall provide that no penalty for demanding a trial de novo, other than that provided in this subsection, shall be assessed by the court.

"(e) Assessment of Costs and Attorney Fees.—In any trial de novo demanded under subsection (a) in which arbitration was done by consent of the parties, a district court may assess costs, as provided in section 1920 of this title, and reasonable attorney fees against the party demanding the trial de novo if—

"(1) such party fails to obtain a judgment, exclusive of interest and costs, in the court which is substantially more favorable to such party than the arbitration award, and

"(2) the court determines that the party's conduct in seeking a trial de novo was in bad faith."

Effective and Applicability Provisions
1988 Acts. Section 906 of Pub.L. 100–702, as amended, which provided that, effective Dec. 31, 1994, this section was repealed, with certain exceptions, was itself repealed by Pub.L. 103–420, § 3(b), Oct. 25, 1994, 108 Stat. 4345. See section 906 of Pub.L. 100–702, set out as a note under section 651 of this title.

Section effective 180 days after Nov. 19, 1988, see section 907 of Pub.L. 100–702, set out as a note under section 651 of this title.

Treatment of Expired Provisions
This section to continue to be effective on or after Dec. 14, 1993 as if it had not been repealed by section 906 of Pub.L. 100–702 as such section was in effect on the day before such date, see Treatment of Expired Provisions note set out under section 651 of this title.

LIBRARY REFERENCES
American Digest System
Alternative Dispute Resolution ⟾224, 228, 247, 256.

Key Number System Topic No. 25T.

§ 656. Subpoenas
Rule 45 of the Federal Rules of Civil Procedure (relating to subpoenas) applies to subpoenas for the attendance of witnesses and the production of documentary evidence at an arbitration hearing under this chapter.

(Added Pub.L. 100–702, Title IX, § 901(a), Nov. 19, 1988, 102 Stat. 4662; amended Pub.L. 105–315, § 8, Oct. 30, 1998, 112 Stat. 2996.)

HISTORICAL AND STATUTORY NOTES
Revision Notes and Legislative Reports
1988 Acts. House Report No. 100–889, see 1988 U.S.Code Cong. and Adm.News, p. 5982.

Amendments
1998 Amendments. Pub.L. 105–315, § 8, rewrote the section, which formerly read:

"§ 656. Certification of arbitrators

"(a) Standards for Certification.—Each district court listed in section 658 shall establish standards for the certification of arbitrators and shall certify arbitrators to perform services in accordance with such standards and this chapter. The standards shall include provisions requiring that any arbitrator—

"(1) shall take the oath or affirmation described in section 453, and

"(2) shall be subject to the disqualification rules of section 455.

"(b) Treatment of Arbitrator as Independent Contractor and Special Government Employee.—An arbitrator is an independent contractor and is subject to the provisions of sections 201 through 211 of title 18 to the same extent as such provisions apply to a special Government employee of the executive branch. A person may not be barred from the practice of law because such person is an arbitrator."

Effective and Applicability Provisions

1988 Acts. Section 906 of Pub.L. 100–702, as amended, which provided that, effective Dec. 31, 1994, this section was repealed, with certain exceptions, was itself repealed by Pub.L. 103–420, § 3(b), Oct. 25, 1994, 108 Stat. 4345. See section 906 of Pub.L. 100–702, set out as a note under section 651 of this title.

Section effective 180 days after Nov. 19, 1988, see section 907 of Pub.L. 100–702, set out as a note under section 651 of this title.

Treatment of Expired Provisions

This section to continue to be effective on or after Dec. 14, 1993 as if it had not been repealed by section 906 of Pub.L. 100–702 as such section was in effect on the day before such date, see Treatment of Expired Provisions note set out under section 651 of this title.

LIBRARY REFERENCES

American Digest System

Alternative Dispute Resolution ⚷253.
Key Number System Topic No. 25T.

Corpus Juris Secundum

CJS Banks and Banking § 805, Abstraction, Generally.

§ 657.   Arbitration award and judgment

(a) Filing and effect of arbitration award.—An arbitration award made by an arbitrator under this chapter, along with proof of service of such award on the other party by the prevailing party or by the plaintiff, shall be filed promptly after the arbitration hearing is concluded with the clerk of the district court that referred the case to arbitration. Such award shall be entered as the judgment of the court after the time has expired for requesting a trial de novo. The judgment so entered shall be subject to the same provisions of law and shall have the same force and effect as a judgment of the court in a civil action, except that the judgment shall not be subject to review in any other court by appeal or otherwise.

(b) Sealing of arbitration award.—The district court shall provide, by local rule adopted under section 2071(a), that the contents of any arbitration award made under this chapter shall not be made known to any judge who might be assigned to the case until the district court has entered final judgment in the action or the action has otherwise terminated.

(c) Trial de novo of arbitration awards.—

(1) **Time for filing demand.**—Within 30 days after the filing of an arbitration award with a district court under subsection (a), any party may file a written demand for a trial de novo in the district court.

(2) **Action restored to court docket.**—Upon a demand for a trial de novo, the action shall be restored to the docket of the court and treated for

all purposes as if it had not been referred to arbitration.

(3) **Exclusion of evidence of arbitration.**—The court shall not admit at the trial de novo any evidence that there has been an arbitration proceeding, the nature or amount of any award, or any other matter concerning the conduct of the arbitration proceeding, unless—

(A) the evidence would otherwise be admissible in the court under the Federal Rules of Evidence; or

(B) the parties have otherwise stipulated.

(Added Pub.L. 100–702, Title IX, § 901(a), Nov. 19, 1988, 102 Stat. 4662; amended Pub.L. 105–315, § 9, Oct. 30, 1998, 112 Stat. 2997.)

HISTORICAL AND STATUTORY NOTES

Revision Notes and Legislative Reports

1988 Acts. House Report No. 100–889, see 1988 U.S. Code Cong. and Adm. News, p. 5982.

Amendments

1998 Amendments. Pub.L. 105–315, § 9, rewrote the section, which formerly read:

"**§ 657.   Compensation of arbitrators**

"**(a) Compensation.**—The district court may, subject to limits set by the Judicial Conference of the United States, establish and pay the amount of compensation, if any, that each arbitrator shall receive for services rendered in each case.

"**(b) Transportation Allowances.**—Under regulations prescribed by the Director of the Administrative Office of the United States Courts, a district court may reimburse arbitrators for actual transportation expenses necessarily incurred in the performance of duties under this chapter."

Effective and Applicability Provisions

1988 Acts. Section 906 of Pub.L. 100–702, as amended, which provided that, effective Dec. 31, 1994, this section was repealed, with certain exceptions, was itself repealed by Pub.L. 103–420, § 3(b), Oct. 25, 1994, 108 Stat. 4345. See section 906 of Pub.L. 100–702, set out as a note under section 651 of this title.

Section effective 180 days after Nov. 19, 1988, see section 907 of Pub.L. 100–702, set out as a note under section 651 of this title.

Treatment of Expired Provisions

This section to continue to be effective on or after Dec. 14, 1993 as if it had not been repealed by section 906 of Pub.L. 100–702 as such section was in effect on the day before such date, see Treatment of Expired Provisions note set out under section 651 of this title.

LIBRARY REFERENCES

American Digest System

Alternative Dispute Resolution ⚷302, 319, 353, 363.
Key Number System Topic No. 25T.

§ 658.   Compensation of arbitrators and neutrals

(a) **Compensation.**—The district court shall, subject to regulations approved by the Judicial Conference of the United States, establish the amount of compensation, if any, that each arbitrator or neutral shall receive for services rendered in each case under this chapter.

(b) **Transportation allowances.**—Under regulations prescribed by the Director of the Administrative Office of the United States Courts, a district court may reimburse arbitrators and other neutrals for actual transportation expenses necessarily incurred in the performance of duties under this chapter.

(Added Pub.L. 100–702, Title IX, § 901(a), Nov. 19, 1988, 102 Stat. 4662; amended Pub.L. 105–315, § 10, Oct. 30, 1998, 112 Stat. 2997.)

HISTORICAL AND STATUTORY NOTES

Amendments

1998 Amendments. Pub.L. 105–315, § 10, rewrote the section, which formerly read:

"**§ 658. District courts that may authorize arbitration**

"The district courts for the following judicial districts may authorize the use of arbitration under this chapter:

"(1) Northern District of California, Middle District of Florida, Western District of Michigan, Western District of Missouri, District of New Jersey, Eastern District of New York, Middle District of North Carolina, Western District of Oklahoma, Eastern District of Pennsylvania, and Western District of Texas.

"(2) Ten additional judicial districts, which shall be approved by the Judicial Conference of the United States. The Judicial Conference shall give notice of the 10 districts approved under this paragraph to the Federal Judicial Center and to the public."

Effective and Applicability Provisions

1988 Acts. Section 906 of Pub.L. 100–702, as amended, which provided that, effective Dec. 31, 1994, this section was repealed, with certain exceptions, was itself repealed by Pub.L. 103–420, § 3(b), Oct. 25, 1994, 108 Stat. 4345. See section 906 of Pub.L. 100–702, set out as a note under section 651 of this title.

Section effective 180 days after Nov. 19, 1988, see section 907 of Pub.L. 100–702, set out as a note under section 651 of this title.

Treatment of Expired Provisions

This section to continue to be effective on or after Dec. 14, 1993 as if it had not been repealed by section 906 of Pub.L. 100–702 as such section was in effect on the day before such date, see Treatment of Expired Provisions note set out under section 651 of this title.

LIBRARY REFERENCES

American Digest System

Alternative Dispute Resolution ⬤⟿246.

Key Number System Topic No. 25T.

Corpus Juris Secundum

CJS Bankruptcy § 146, Submission to Arbitration.

CHAPTER 57—GENERAL PROVISIONS APPLICABLE TO COURT OFFICERS AND EMPLOYEES

§ 959.   Trustees and receivers suable; management; State laws

(a) Trustees, receivers or managers of any property, including debtors in possession, may be sued, without leave of the court appointing them, with respect to any of their acts or transactions in carrying on business connected with such property. Such actions shall be subject to the general equity power of such court so far as the same may be necessary to the ends of justice, but this shall not deprive a litigant of his right to trial by jury.

(b) Except as provided in section 1166 of title 11, a trustee, receiver or manager appointed in any cause pending in any court of the United States, including a debtor in possession, shall manage and operate the property in his possession as such trustee, receiver or manager according to the requirements of the valid laws of the State in which such property is situated, in the same manner that the owner or possessor thereof would be bound to do if in possession thereof.

(June 25, 1948, c. 646, 62 Stat. 926; Nov. 6, 1978, Pub.L. 95–598, Title II, § 235, 92 Stat. 2667.)

HISTORICAL AND STATUTORY NOTES

Revision Notes and Legislative Reports

1948 Acts. Based on Title 28, U.S.C., 1940 ed., §§ 124, 125 (Mar. 3, 1911, c. 231, §§ 65, 66, 36 Stat. 1104).

Section consolidates part of section 124 of Title 28, U.S.C., 1940 ed., with section 125 of the same title. The criminal penalty for violation of said section 124 is incorporated in section 1911 of Title 18, Crimes and Criminal Procedure (H.R. 1600, 80th Cong.).

Section was extended and made applicable to trustees and debtors in possession. The provision at the end of subsection (a) for preserving the right to a jury trial was added to clarify the intent of section 125 of Title 28, U.S.C., 1940 ed., as construed in *Vany v. Receiver of Toledo, St. L. and K.C.R.R. Co.*, C.C.1895, 67 F. 379.

Changes in phraseology were made. 80th Congress House Report No. 308.

1978 Acts. Senate Report No. 95–989 and House Report No. 95–595, see 1978 U.S.Code Cong. and Adm.News, p. 5787.

Amendments

1978 Amendments. Subsec. (b). Pub.L. 95–598 substituted "Except as provided in section 1166 of title 11, a trustee" for "A trustee".

Effective and Applicability Provisions

1978 Acts. Amendment by Pub.L. 95–598 effective Oct. 1, 1979, see section 402(c) of Pub.L. 95–598, as amended, set out as a note preceding section 101 of Title 11, Bankruptcy.

CROSS REFERENCES

Capacity to sue or be sued, see Fed.Rules Civ.Proc. Rule 17, 28 USCA.

Mismanagement of property by receiver, criminal penalty, see 18 USCA § 1911.

Process and orders affecting property in different districts, see 28 USCA § 1692.

Receivers of property in different districts; jurisdiction, see 28 USCA § 754.

LIBRARY REFERENCES

American Digest System

Bankruptcy ⚏2153.

Receivers ⚏29, 71, 147, 168, 174(1).

Key Number System Topic Nos. 323, 51.

Corpus Juris Secundum

CJS Bankruptcy § 9, Title 28 of the U.S. Code.

CJS Bankruptcy § 89, Trustee as Representative of Estate and Fiduciary.

CJS Bankruptcy § 106, Suits Against Trustee.

CJS Bankruptcy § 108, Suits Against Trustee--Relating to Trustee's Conduct of Business.

CJS Bankruptcy § 134, Rights, Powers, and Duties of Debtor in Possession--Specific Rights, Powers, and Duties.

CJS Bankruptcy § 136, Rights, Powers, and Duties of Debtor in Possession.

CJS Bankruptcy § 206, Nonbankruptcy Federal-Court Actions.

CJS Bankruptcy § 242, General Statutory Powers.

CJS Bankruptcy § 311, When Does Right to Trial by Jury Exist.

CJS Bankruptcy § 842, Presumption of Reasonableness of Management Decisions.

CJS Federal Civil Procedure § 58, Receivers.

CJS Receivers § 390, Authority of Court or Receiver.

PART IV—JURISDICTION AND VENUE

CHAPTER 85—DISTRICT COURTS; JURISDICTION

§ 1334. Bankruptcy cases and proceedings

(a) Except as provided in subsection (b) of this section, the district courts shall have original and exclusive jurisdiction of all cases under title 11.

(b) Except as provided in subsection (e)(2), and notwithstanding any Act of Congress that confers exclusive jurisdiction on a court or courts other than the district courts, the district courts shall have original but not exclusive jurisdiction of all civil proceedings arising under title 11, or arising in or related to cases under title 11.

(c)(1) Except with respect to a case under chapter 15 of title 11, nothing in this section prevents a district court in the interest of justice, or in the interest of comity with State courts or respect for State law, from abstaining from hearing a particular proceeding arising under title 11 or arising in or related to a case under title 11.

(2) Upon timely motion of a party in a proceeding based upon a State law claim or State law cause of action, related to a case under title 11 but not arising under title 11 or arising in a case under title 11, with respect to which an action could not have been commenced in a court of the United States absent jurisdiction under this section, the district court shall abstain from hearing such proceeding if an action is commenced, and can be timely adjudicated, in a State forum of appropriate jurisdiction.

(d) Any decision to abstain or not to abstain made under subsection (c) (other than a decision not to abstain in a proceeding described in subsection (c)(2))

is not reviewable by appeal or otherwise by the court of appeals under section 158(d), 1291, or 1292 of this title or by the Supreme Court of the United States under section 1254 of this title. Subsection (c) and this subsection shall not be construed to limit the applicability of the stay provided for by section 362 of title 11, United States Code, as such section applies to an action affecting the property of the estate in bankruptcy.

(e) The district court in which a case under title 11 is commenced or is pending shall have exclusive jurisdiction—

(1) of all the property, wherever located, of the debtor as of the commencement of such case, and of property of the estate; and

(2) over all claims or causes of action that involve construction of section 327 of title 11, United States Code, or rules relating to disclosure requirements under section 327.

(June 25, 1948, c. 646, 62 Stat. 931; Nov. 6, 1978, Pub.L. 95–598, Title II, § 238(a), 92 Stat. 2667; July 10, 1984, Pub.L. 98–353, Title I, § 101(a), 98 Stat. 333; Oct. 27, 1986, Pub.L. 99–554, Title I, § 144(e), 100 Stat. 3096; Dec. 1, 1990, Pub.L. 101–650, Title III, § 309(b), 104 Stat. 5113; Oct. 22, 1994, Pub.L. 103–394, Title I, § 104(b), 108 Stat. 4109; Apr. 20, 2005, Pub.L. 109–8, Title III, § 324(a), Title VIII, § 802(c)(2), Title XII, § 1219, 119 Stat. 98, 145, 195.)

HISTORICAL AND STATUTORY NOTES

Revision Notes and Legislative Reports

1948 Acts. Based on Title 28, U.S.C., 1940 ed., §§ 41(19) and 371(6) (Mar. 3, 1911, c. 231, §§ 24, par. 19, 256, par. 6, 36 Stat. 1093, 1160).

Changes in phraseology were made.

1984 Acts. Statements by Legislative Leaders, see 1984 U.S. Code Cong. and Adm. News, p. 576.

1986 Acts. House Report No. 99–764 and House Conference Report No. 99–958, see 1986 U.S. Code Cong. and Adm. News, p. 5227.

1990 Acts. Senate Report No. 101–416, House Report Nos. 101–123, 101–512, 101–514, 101–734, and 101–735, and Statement by President, see 1990 U.S. Code Cong. and Adm. News, p. 6802.

1994 Acts. House Report No. 103–835, see 1994 U.S. Code Cong. and Adm. News, p. 3340.

2005 Acts. House Report No. 109–31(Part I), see 2005 U.S. Code Cong. and Adm. News, p. 88.

References in Text

Chapter 15 of title 11, referred to in subsec. (c), is 11 U.S.C.A. § 1501 et seq.

Codifications

This section was amended by Pub.L. 95–598, Title II, § 238(a), Nov. 6, 1978, 92 Stat. 2668, effective June 28, 1984, pursuant to Pub.L. 95–598, Title IV, § 402(b), Nov. 6, 1978, 92 Stat. 2682, as amended by Pub.L. 98–249, § 1(a), Mar. 31, 1984, 98 Stat. 116; Pub.L. 98–271, § 1(a), Apr. 30, 1984, 98 Stat. 163; Pub.L. 98–299, § 1(a), May 25, 1984, 98 Stat. 214; Pub.L. 98–325, § 1(a), June 20, 1984, 98 Stat. 268, set out as an Effective and Applicability Provisions note preceding section 101 of Title 11, Bankruptcy, to read as follows:

"§ 1334. Bankruptcy appeals

"**(a)** The district courts for districts for which panels have not been ordered appointed under section 160 of this title shall have jurisdiction of appeals from all final judgments, orders, and decrees of bankruptcy courts.

"**(b)** The district courts for such districts shall have jurisdiction of appeals from interlocutory orders and decrees of bankruptcy courts, but only by leave of the district court to which the appeal is taken.

"**(c)** A district court may not refer an appeal under that section to a magistrate or to a special master."

Section 402(b) of Pub.L. 95–598 was amended by section 113 of Pub.L. 98–353 by substituting "shall not be effective" for "shall take effect on June 28, 1984", thereby eliminating the amendment by section 238(a) of Pub.L. 95–598, effective June 27, 1984, pursuant to section 122(c) of Pub.L. 98–353, set out as an Effective and Applicability Provisions note under 28 U.S.C.A. § 151.

Section 121(a) of Pub.L. 98–353 directed that section 402(b) of Pub.L. 95–598 be amended by substituting "the date of enactment of the Bankruptcy Amendments and Federal Judgeship Act of 1984 [i.e. July 10, 1984]" for "June 28, 1984". This amendment was not executed in view of the prior amendment to section 402(b) of Pub.L. 95–598 by section 113 of Pub.L. 98–353.

Amendments

2005 Amendments. Subsec. (b). Pub.L. 109–8, § 324(a)(1), struck out "Notwithstanding" and inserted "Except as provided in subsection (e)(2), and notwithstanding".

Subsec. (c)(1). Pub.L. 109–8, § 802(c)(2), struck out "Nothing in" and inserted "Except with respect to a case under chapter 15 of title 11, nothing in".

Subsec. (d). Pub.L. 109–8, § 1219, struck out "made under this subsection" and inserted "made under subsection (c)", and substituted "Subsection (c) and this subsection" for "This subsection".

Subsec. (e). Pub.L. 109–8, § 324(a)(2), rewrote subsec. (e), which formerly read: "The district court in which a case under title 11 is commenced or is pending shall have exclusive jurisdiction of all of the property, wherever located, of the debtor as of the commencement of such case, and of property of the estate."

1994 Amendments. Subsecs. (c) to (e). Pub.L. 103–465, § 104(b), redesignated portion of existing subsec. (c)(2) as (d) and as so redesignated, inserted "(other than a decision not to abstain in a proceeding described in subsection (c)(2))" after "under this subsection", and redesignated former subsec. (d) as (e).

1990 Amendments. Subsec. (c)(2). Pub.L. 101–650 declared abstention determinations, including determination not to abstain, in bankruptcy cases and proceedings nonreviewable by the court of appeals or by the Supreme Court.

1986 Amendments. Subsec. (d). Pub.L. 99–554 substituted "and of property of the estate" for "and of the estate".

1984 Amendments. Catchline. Pub.L. 98–353 substituted "cases" for "matters".

Subsec. (a). Pub.L. 98–353 designated existing provision as subsec. (a), and in subsec. (a) as so designated, substituted "Except as provided in subsection (b) of this section, the district" for "The district" and "original and exclusive jurisdiction of all cases under title 11" for "original jurisdiction, exclusive of the courts of the States, of all matters and proceedings in bankruptcy".

Subsecs. (b) to (d). Pub.L. 98–353 added subsecs. (b) to (d).

1978 Amendments. Pub.L. 95–598 directed the general amendment of section to relate to bankruptcy appeals, which amendment did not become effective pursuant to section 402(b) of Pub.L. 95–598, as amended, set out as an Effective and Applicability Provisions note preceding section 101 of Title 11, Bankruptcy. Sec. Codifications note set out under this section.

Effective and Applicability Provisions

2005 Acts. Pub.L. 109–8, Title III, § 324(b), Apr. 20, 2005, 119 Stat. 98, provided that: "This section [amending subsecs. (b) and (e) of this section] shall only apply to cases filed after the date of enactment of this Act [Apr. 20, 2005]."

Except as otherwise provided, amendments by Pub.L. 109–8 effective 180 days after April 20, 2005, and inapplicable with respect to cases commenced under Title 11 before the effective date, see Pub.L. 109–8, § 1501, set out as a note under 11 U.S.C.A. § 101.

1994 Acts. Amendment by Pub.L. 103–394 effective on Oct. 22, 1994, and not to apply with respect to cases commenced under Title 11 of the United States Code before Oct. 22, 1994, see section 702 of Pub.L. 103–394, set out as a note under section 101 of Title 11, Bankruptcy.

1986 Acts. Amendment by Pub.L. 99–554 effective 30 days after Oct. 27, 1986, except as otherwise provided for, see section 302(a) of Pub.L. 99–554, as amended, set out as a note under section 581 of this title.

1984 Acts. Amendment by Pub.L. 98–353, except for subsec. (c)(2), effective July 10, 1984, see section 122(a) of Pub.L. 98–353, set out as a note under section 151 of this title.

Subsec. (c)(2) not applicable with respect to cases under Title 11, Bankruptcy, that are pending on July 10, 1984, or to proceedings arising in or related to such cases, see section 122(b) of Pub.L. 98–353, set out as a note under section 151 of this title.

Separability of Provisions

If any provision of or amendment made by Pub.L. 103–394 or the application of such provision or amendment to any person or circumstance is held to be unconstitutional, the remaining provisions of and amendments made by Pub.L. 103–394 and the application of such provisions and amendments to any person or circumstance shall not be affected thereby, see section 701 of Pub.L. 103–394, set out as a note under section 101 of Title 11, Bankruptcy.

Jurisdiction Over and Transfer of Bankruptcy Cases and Proceedings

Section 115 of Pub.L. 98–353 provided that:

"(a) On the date of the enactment of this Act [July 10, 1984] the appropriate district court of the United States shall have jurisdiction of—

"(1) cases, and matters and proceedings in cases, under the Bankruptcy Act [former Title 11, Bankruptcy] that are pending immediately before such date in the bankruptcy courts continued by section 404(a) of the Act of November 6, 1978 (Public Law 95–598; 92 Stat. 2687) [Pub.L. 95–598, Title IV, § 404(a), Nov. 6, 1978, 92 Stat. 2683, formerly set out as a note preceding section 151 of this title], and

"(2) cases under title 11 of the United States Code [Title 11, Bankruptcy], and proceedings arising under title 11 of the United States Code or arising in or related to cases under title 11 of the United States Code, that are pending immediately before such date in the bankruptcy courts continued by section 404(a) of the Act of November 6, 1978 (Public Law 95–598; 92 Stat. 2687).

"(b) On the date of the enactment of this Act [July 10, 1984], there shall be transferred to the appropriate district court of the United States appeals from final judgments, orders, and decrees of the bankruptcy courts pending immediately before such date in the bankruptcy appellate panels appointed under section 405(c) of the Act of November 6, 1978 (Public Law 95–598; 92 Stat. 2685) [formerly set out as a note preceding section 1471 of this title]."

CROSS REFERENCES

Appointment of clerk for bankruptcy court where warranted by number of cases and proceedings pending, see 28 USCA § 156.

Non-core proceedings not subject to mandatory abstention provisions, see 28 USCA § 157.

Removal of claims related to bankruptcy cases, see 28 USCA § 1452.

Venue, see 28 USCA §§ 1408 and 1409.

LIBRARY REFERENCES
American Digest System

Bankruptcy ⚫2041.1 to 2063.

Federal Courts ⚫47.5, 65.

Key Number System Topic Nos. 51, 170B.

Corpus Juris Secundum

CJS Bankruptcy § 9, Title 28 of the U.S. Code.

CJS Bankruptcy § 21, Powers of District Court in Relation to Bankruptcy Judges.

CJS Bankruptcy § 149, Original and Exclusive Jurisdiction of Cases Under Title 11.

CJS Bankruptcy § 151, Original But Not Exclusive Jurisdiction of Civil Proceedings.

CJS Bankruptcy § 152, Exclusive Jurisdiction of Property of Debtor and Estate.

CJS Bankruptcy § 158, What Are Proceedings Arising in Cases Under Title 11.

CJS Bankruptcy § 174, Motions to Abstain or Remand.

CJS Bankruptcy § 202, Procedure; Motion and Stay.

CJS Bankruptcy § 204, Showing Necessary to Obtain Mandatory Abstention.

CJS Bankruptcy § 205, Timely Adjudication in State Court.

CJS Bankruptcy § 206, Nonbankruptcy Federal-Court Actions.

CJS Bankruptcy § 207, Appealability of Ruling on Motion.

CJS Bankruptcy § 208, Exclusion of Personal-Injury-Tort and Wrongful-Death Claims.

CJS Bankruptcy § 210, Effect of Existence of State Law Claims.

CJS Bankruptcy § 211, Judicial Economy.

CJS Bankruptcy § 214, Power of Bankruptcy Judges to Hear Cases and Proceedings.

CJS Bankruptcy § 240, Grounds for Motion; Bases for Exercise of Discretion.

CJS Bankruptcy § 262, Postconfirmation Powers.

CJS Bankruptcy § 317, The Bankruptcy "Case".

CJS Bankruptcy § 1162, Implementation of the Plan; Distribution.

CJS Bankruptcy § 1227, Abstention.

CJS Bankruptcy § 1261, Particular Matters.

CJS Federal Courts § 90, Requirement of Case or Controversy; Ripeness.

CHAPTER 87—DISTRICT COURTS; VENUE

§ 1408. Venue of cases under title 11

Except as provided in section 1410 of this title, a case under title 11 may be commenced in the district court for the district—

(1) in which the domicile, residence, principal place of business in the United States, or principal

assets in the United States, of the person or entity that is the subject of such case have been located for the one hundred and eighty days immediately preceding such commencement, or for a longer portion of such one-hundred-and-eighty-day period than the domicile, residence, or principal place of business, in the United States, or principal assets in the United

States, of such person were located in any other district; or

(2) in which there is pending a case under title 11 concerning such person's affiliate, general partner, or partnership.

(Added Pub.L. 98–353, Title I, § 102(a), July 10, 1984, 98 Stat. 334.)

HISTORICAL AND STATUTORY NOTES

Revision Notes and Legislative Reports

1984 Acts. Statements by Legislative Leaders, see 1984 U.S. Code Cong. and Adm. News, p. 576.

Effective and Applicability Provisions

1984 Acts. Section effective July 10, 1984, see section 122(a) of Pub.L. 98–353, set out as a note under section 151 of this title.

Prior Provisions

A prior section 1408, added by Pub.L. 95–598, Title II, § 240(a), Nov. 6, 1978, 92 Stat. 2668, which related to bankruptcy appeals, did not become effective pursuant to section 402(b) of Pub.L. 95–598, as amended, set out as an Effective and Applicability Provisions note preceding section 101 of Title 11, Bankruptcy.

LIBRARY REFERENCES

American Digest System

Bankruptcy ⟠2081 to 2083.

Key Number System Topic No. 51.

Corpus Juris Secundum

CJS Bankruptcy § 9, Title 28 of the U.S. Code.

CJS Bankruptcy § 264, Cases Under Bankruptcy Code.

CJS Bankruptcy § 317, The Bankruptcy "Case".

§ 1409. Venue of proceedings arising under title 11 or arising in or related to cases under title 11

(a) Except as otherwise provided in subsections (b) and (d), a proceeding arising under title 11 or arising in or related to a case under title 11 may be commenced in the district court in which such case is pending.

(b) Except as provided in subsection (d) of this section, a trustee in a case under title 11 may commence a proceeding arising in or related to such case to recover a money judgment of or property worth less than $1,175 [1] or a consumer debt of less than $17,575 [1], or a debt (excluding a consumer debt) against a noninsider of less than $11,725 [1], only in the district court for the district in which the defendant resides.

(c) Except as provided in subsection (b) of this section, a trustee in a case under title 11 may commence a proceeding arising in or related to such case as statutory successor to the debtor or creditors under section 541 or 544(b) of title 11 in the district court for the district where the State or Federal court sits in which, under applicable nonbankruptcy venue provi-

sions, the debtor or creditors, as the case may be, may have commenced an action on which such proceeding is based if the case under title 11 had not been commenced.

(d) A trustee may commence a proceeding arising under title 11 or arising in or related to a case under title 11 based on a claim arising after the commencement of such case from the operation of the business of the debtor only in the district court for the district where a State or Federal court sits in which, under applicable nonbankruptcy venue provisions, an action on such claim may have been brought.

(e) A proceeding arising under title 11 or arising in or related to a case under title 11, based on a claim arising after the commencement of such case from the operation of the business of the debtor, may be commenced against the representative of the estate in such case in the district court for the district where the State or Federal court sits in which the party commencing such proceeding may, under applicable nonbankruptcy venue provisions, have brought an action on such claim, or in the district court in which such case is pending.

(Added Pub.L. 98–353, Title I, § 102(a), July 10, 1984, 98 Stat. 334; amended Pub.L. 109–8, Title IV, § 410, Apr. 20, 2005, 119 Stat. 106.)

[1] Dollar amount as adjusted by the Judicial Conference of the United States. See Adjustment of Dollar Amounts notes set out under this section and 11 U.S.C.A. § 104.

HISTORICAL AND STATUTORY NOTES

Revision Notes and Legislative Reports

1984 Acts. Statements by Legislative Leaders, see 1984 U.S. Code Cong. and Adm. News, p. 576.

2005 Acts. House Report No. 109–31(Part I), see 2005 U.S. Code Cong. and Adm. News, p. 88.

Amendments

2010 Amendments. Subsec. (b). By notice published Feb. 25, 2010, 75 F.R. 8747, dollar amount adjusted by the Judicial Conference of the United States which adjusted "$1,100" to "$1,175", "$16,425" to "$17,575", and "$10,950" to "$11,725". See 11 U.S.C.A. § 104 and Adjustment of Dollar Amounts notes under this section.

2007 Amendments. Subsec. (b). By notice published Feb. 14, 2007, 72 F.R. 7082, dollar amount adjusted by the Judicial Conference of the United States which adjusted "$1,000" to "$1,100", "$15,000" to "$16,425", and "$10,000" to "$10,950". See 11 U.S.C.A. § 104 and Adjustment of Dollar Amounts notes under this section.

2005 Amendments. Subsec. (b). Pub.L. 109–8, § 410, inserted ", or a debt (excluding a consumer debt) against a noninsider of less than $10,000," after "5,000" and substituted "$15,000" for "$5,000".

Effective and Applicability Provisions

2010 Acts. Increase of dollar amounts by Judicial Conference of the United States by notice published Feb. 25, 2010, 75 F.R. 8747 effective April 1, 2010, and increase not applicable to cases commenced before the effective date of the adjustments, i.e., April 1, 2010. See Adjustment of Dollar Amounts notes under 11 U.S.C.A. § 104 and this section.

2007 Acts. Increase of dollar amounts by Judicial Conference of the United States by notice published Feb. 14, 2007, 72 F.R. 7082 effective April 1, 2007, and increase not applicable to cases commenced before the effective date of the adjustments, i.e., April 1, 2007. See Adjustment of Dollar Amounts notes under 11 U.S.C.A. § 104 and this section.

2005 Acts. Except as otherwise provided, amendments by Pub.L. 109–8 effective 180 days after April 20, 2005, and inapplicable with respect to cases commenced under Title 11 before the effective date, see Pub.L. 109–8, § 1501, set out as a note under 11 U.S.C.A. § 101.

1984 Acts. Section effective July 10, 1984, see section 122(a) of Pub.L. 98–353, set out as a note under section 151 of this title.

Adjustment of Dollar Amounts

For adjustment of dollar amounts specified in subsec. (b) of this section by the Judicial Conference of the United States, effective Apr. 1, 2010, see note set out under 11 U.S.C.A. § 104.

By notice published Feb. 25, 2010, 75 F.R. 8747, the Judicial Conference of the United States adjusted the dollar amounts in provisions specified in subsec. (b) of this section, effective Apr. 1, 2010, as follows:

    Adjusted $1,100 to $1,175.
    Adjusted $16,425 to $17,575.
    Adjusted $10,950 to $11,725.

By notice published Feb. 14, 2007, 72 F.R. 7082, the Judicial Conference of the United States adjusted the dollar amounts in provisions specified in subsec. (b) of this section, effective Apr. 1, 2007, as follows:

    Adjusted $1,000 to $1,100.
    Adjusted $15,000 to $16,425.
    Adjusted $10,000 to $10,950.

LIBRARY REFERENCES

American Digest System

Bankruptcy ⚷2081 to 2083.
Key Number System Topic No. 51.

Corpus Juris Secundum

CJS Bankruptcy § 266, Proceedings Arising Under Bankruptcy Code or Arising in or Related to Cases Under Code.

CJS Bankruptcy § 317, The Bankruptcy "Case".

CJS Bankruptcy § 576, Filing List of Property Claimed as Exempt.

CJS Bankruptcy § 702, Venue.

CJS Bankruptcy § 755, Commencement of Adversary Proceeding; Venue.

§ 1410.   Venue of cases ancillary to foreign proceedings

A case under chapter 15 of title 11 may be commenced in the district court of the United States for the district—

(1) in which the debtor has its principal place of business or principal assets in the United States;

(2) if the debtor does not have a place of business or assets in the United States, in which there is pending against the debtor an action or proceeding in a Federal or State court; or

(3) in a case other than those specified in paragraph (1) or (2), in which venue will be consistent with the interests of justice and the convenience of the parties, having regard to the relief sought by the foreign representative.

(Added Pub.L. 98–353, Title I, § 102(a), July 10, 1984, 98 Stat. 335; amended Pub.L. 109–8, Title VIII, § 802(c)(4), Apr. 20, 2005, 119 Stat. 146.)

HISTORICAL AND STATUTORY NOTES

Revision Notes and Legislative Reports

1984 Acts. Statements by Legislative Leaders, see 1984 U.S. Code Cong. and Adm. News, p. 576.

2005 Acts. House Report No. 109–31(Part I), see 2005 U.S. Code Cong. and Adm. News, p. 88.

References in Text

Chapter 15 of title 11, referred to in text, is 11 U.S.C.A. § 1501 et seq.

Amendments

2005 Amendments. Pub.L. 109–8, § 802(c)(4), rewrote the text of the section, which formerly read:

"**§ 1410. Venue of cases ancillary to foreign proceedings**

"**(a)** A case under section 304 of title 11 to enjoin the commencement or continuation of an action or proceeding in a State or Federal court, or the enforcement of a judgment, may be commenced only in the district court for the district where the State or Federal court sits in which is pending the action or proceeding against which the injunction is sought.

"**(b)** A case under section 304 of title 11 to enjoin the enforcement of a lien against a property, or to require the turnover of property of an estate, may be commenced only in the district court for the district in which such property is found.

"**(c)** A case under section 304 of title 11, other than a case specified in subsection (a) or (b) of this section, may be commenced only in the district court for the district in which is located the principal place of business in the United States, or the principal assets in the United States, of the estate that is the subject of such case."

Effective and Applicability Provisions

2005 Acts. Except as otherwise provided, amendments by Pub.L. 109–8 effective 180 days after April 20, 2005, and inapplicable with respect to cases commenced under Title 11 before the effective date, see Pub.L. 109–8, § 1501, set out as a note under 11 U.S.C.A. § 101.

1984 Acts. Section effective July 10, 1984, see section 122(a) of Pub.L. 98–353, set out as a note under section 151 of this title.

CROSS REFERENCES

Commencement of bankruptcy cases in district courts having venue except as provided by this section, see 28 USCA § 1408.

LIBRARY REFERENCES

American Digest System

Bankruptcy ⬤2081 to 2083.

Key Number System Topic No. 51.

Corpus Juris Secundum

CJS Bankruptcy § 9, Title 28 of the U.S. Code.

CJS Bankruptcy § 264, Cases Under Bankruptcy Code.

§ 1411. Jury trials

(a) Except as provided in subsection (b) of this section, this chapter and title 11 do not affect any right to trial by jury that an individual has under applicable nonbankruptcy law with regard to a personal injury or wrongful death tort claim.

(b) The district court may order the issues arising under section 303 of title 11 to be tried without a jury. (Added Pub.L. 98–353, Title I, § 102(a), July 10, 1984, 98 Stat. 335.)

HISTORICAL AND STATUTORY NOTES

Revision Notes and Legislative Reports

1984 Acts. Statements by Legislative Leaders, see 1984 U.S. Code Cong. and Adm. News, p. 576.

Effective and Applicability Provisions

1984 Acts. Section, except subsec. (a), effective July 10, 1984, see section 122(a) of Pub.L. 98–353, set out as a note under section 151 of this title.

Subsec. (a) not applicable with respect to cases under Title 11, Bankruptcy, that are pending on July 10, 1984, or to proceedings arising in or related to such cases, see section 122(b) of Pub.L. 98–353, set out as a note under section 151 of this title.

LIBRARY REFERENCES

American Digest System

Bankruptcy ⬤2130.

Jury ⬤14.

Key Number System Topic Nos. 51, 230.

Corpus Juris Secundum

CJS Bankruptcy § 9, Title 28 of the U.S. Code.

CJS Bankruptcy § 311, When Does Right to Trial by Jury Exist.

§ 1412. Change of venue

A district court may transfer a case or proceeding under title 11 to a district court for another district, in the interest of justice or for the convenience of the parties. (Added Pub.L. 98–353, Title I, § 102(a), July 10, 1984, 98 Stat. 335.)

HISTORICAL AND STATUTORY NOTES

Revision Notes and Legislative Reports

1984 Acts. Statements by Legislative Leaders, see 1984 U.S. Code Cong. and Adm. News, p. 576.

Effective and Applicability Provisions

1984 Acts. Section effective July 10, 1984, see section 122(a) of Pub.L. 98–353, set out as a note under section 151 of this title.

LIBRARY REFERENCES

American Digest System

Bankruptcy ⬤2083 to 2091.

Key Number System Topic No. 51.

Corpus Juris Secundum

CJS Bankruptcy § 9, Title 28 of the U.S. Code.

CJS Bankruptcy § 271, Interests of Justice or Convenience of Parties; Factors Affecting Grant or Denial.

CJS Bankruptcy § 272, Cases and Proceedings in Improper Venues.

CJS Bankruptcy § 273, Adversary Proceedings.

§ 1413. Venue of cases under chapter 5 of title 3

Notwithstanding the preceding provisions of this chapter, a civil action under section 1346(g) may be brought in the United States district court for the district in which the employee is employed or in the United States District Court for the District of Columbia. (Added Pub.L. 104–331, § 3(b)(2)(A), Oct. 26, 1996, 110 Stat. 4069.)

HISTORICAL AND STATUTORY NOTES

Revision Notes and Legislative Reports

1996 Acts. House Report No. 104–820, see 1996 U.S. Code Cong. and Adm. News, p. 4348.

Codifications

Amendment by Pub.L. 104–331, § 3(b)(2)(A), which directed the addition of this section to the end of chapter 37 of this title, was executed by adding this section to the end of this chapter, as the probable intent of Congress.

Effective and Applicability Provisions

1996 Acts. Amendment by Pub.L. 104–331, § 3(b)(2)(B), effective October 1, 1997, see section 3(d) of Pub.L. 104–331, set out as a note under section 1296 of this title.

LIBRARY REFERENCES

American Digest System

Federal Courts ⬤74.

Key Number System Topic No. 170B.

CHAPTER 89—DISTRICT COURTS; REMOVAL OF CASES FROM STATE COURTS

§ 1452. Removal of claims related to bankruptcy cases

(a) A party may remove any claim or cause of action in a civil action other than a proceeding before the United States Tax Court or a civil action by a governmental unit to enforce such governmental unit's police or regulatory power, to the district court for the district where such civil action is pending, if such district court has jurisdiction of such claim or cause of action under section 1334 of this title.

(b) The court to which such claim or cause of action is removed may remand such claim or cause of action on any equitable ground. An order entered under this subsection remanding a claim or cause of action, or a decision to not remand, is not reviewable by appeal or otherwise by the court of appeals under section 158(d), 1291, or 1292 of this title or by the Supreme Court of the United States under section 1254 of this title. (Added Pub.L. 98–353, Title I, § 103(a), July 10, 1984, 98 Stat. 335; amended Pub.L. 101–650, Title III, § 309(c), Dec. 1, 1990, 104 Stat. 5113.)

HISTORICAL AND STATUTORY NOTES

Revision Notes and Legislative Reports

1984 Acts. Statements by Legislative Leaders, see 1984 U.S. Code Cong. and Adm. News, p. 576.

1990 Acts. Senate Report No. 101–416, House Report Nos. 101–123, 101–512, 101–514, 101–734, and 101–735, and State-

ment by President, see 1990 U.S. Code Cong. and Adm. News, p. 6802.

Amendments

1990 Amendments. Subsec. (b). Pub.L. 101–650 declared remand determinations nonreviewable by the court of appeals or by the Supreme Court.

Effective and Applicability Provisions

1984 Acts. Section effective July 10, 1984, see section 122(a) of Pub.L. 98–353, set out as a note under section 151 of this title.

LIBRARY REFERENCES

American Digest System

Bankruptcy ⟐2086.

Key Number System Topic No. 51.

Corpus Juris Secundum

CJS Bankruptcy § 9, Title 28 of the U.S. Code.

CJS Bankruptcy § 139, Adversary Proceedings.

CJS Bankruptcy § 174, Motions to Abstain or Remand.

CJS Bankruptcy § 235, Referral of Removed Claim to Bankruptcy Judge.

CJS Bankruptcy § 240, Grounds for Motion; Bases for Exercise of Discretion.

CJS Bankruptcy § 241, Review of Remand Orders.

CJS Bankruptcy § 1223, Remand.

PART V—PROCEDURE

CHAPTER 123—FEES AND COSTS

§ 1930. Bankruptcy fees

(a) The parties commencing a case under title 11 shall pay to the clerk of the district court or the clerk of the bankruptcy court, if one has been certified pursuant to section 156(b) of this title, the following filing fees:

   (1) For a case commenced under—

      (A) chapter 7 of title 11, $245, and

      (B) chapter 13 of title 11, $235.

   (2) For a case commenced under chapter 9 of title 11, equal to the fee specified in paragraph (3) for filing a case under chapter 11 of title 11. The amount by which the fee payable under this paragraph exceeds $300 shall be deposited in the fund established under section 1931 of this title.

   (3) For a case commenced under chapter 11 of title 11 that does not concern a railroad, as defined in section 101 of title 11, $1,000.

   (4) For a case commenced under chapter 11 of title 11 concerning a railroad, as so defined, $1,000.

   (5) For a case commenced under chapter 12 of title 11, $200.

   (6) In addition to the filing fee paid to the clerk, a quarterly fee shall be paid to the United States trustee, for deposit in the Treasury, in each case under chapter 11 of title 11 for each quarter (including any fraction thereof) until the case is converted or dismissed, whichever occurs first. The fee shall be $325 for each quarter in which disbursements total less than $15,000; $650 for each quarter in which disbursements total $15,000 or more but less than $75,000; $975 for each quarter in which disbursements total $75,000 or more but less than $150,000; $1,625 for each quarter in which disbursements total $150,000 or more but less than $225,000; $1,950 for each quarter in which disbursements total $225,000 or more but less than $300,000; $4,875 for each quarter in which disbursements total $300,000 or more but less than $1,000,000; $6,500 for each quarter in which disbursements total $1,000,000 or more but less than $2,000,000; $9,750 for each quar-

ter in which disbursements total $2,000,000 or more but less than $3,000,000; $10,400 for each quarter in which disbursements total $3,000,000 or more but less than $5,000,000; $13,000 for each quarter in which disbursements total $5,000,000 or more but less than $15,000,000; $20,000 for each quarter in which disbursements total $15,000,000 or more but less than $30,000,000; $30,000 for each quarter in which disbursements total more than $30,000,000. The fee shall be payable on the last day of the calendar month following the calendar quarter for which the fee is owed.

(7) In districts that are not part of a United States trustee region as defined in section 581 of this title, the Judicial Conference of the United States may require the debtor in a case under chapter 11 of title 11 to pay fees equal to those imposed by paragraph (6) of this subsection. Such fees shall be deposited as offsetting receipts to the fund established under section 1931 of this title and shall remain available until expended.

An individual commencing a voluntary case or a joint case under title 11 may pay such fee in installments. For converting, on request of the debtor, a case under chapter 7, or 13 of title 11, to a case under chapter 11 of title 11, the debtor shall pay to the clerk of the district court or the clerk of the bankruptcy court, if one has been certified pursuant to section 156(b) of this title, a fee of the amount equal to the difference between the fee specified in paragraph (3) and the fee specified in paragraph (1).

(b) The Judicial Conference of the United States may prescribe additional fees in cases under title 11 of the same kind as the Judicial Conference prescribes under section 1914(b) of this title.

(c) Upon the filing of any separate or joint notice of appeal or application for appeal or upon the receipt of any order allowing, or notice of the allowance of, an appeal or a writ of certiorari $5 shall be paid to the clerk of the court, by the appellant or petitioner.

(d) Whenever any case or proceeding is dismissed in any bankruptcy court for want of jurisdiction, such court may order the payment of just costs.

(e) The clerk of the court may collect only the fees prescribed under this section.

(f)(1) Under the procedures prescribed by the Judicial Conference of the United States, the district court or the bankruptcy court may waive the filing fee in a case under chapter 7 of title 11 for an individual if the court determines that such individual has income less than 150 percent of the income official poverty line (as defined by the Office of Management and Budget, and revised annually in accordance with section 673(2) of the Omnibus Budget Reconciliation Act of 1981) applicable to a family of the size involved and is unable to pay that fee in installments. For purposes of this paragraph, the term "filing fee" means the filing fee

required by subsection (a), or any other fee prescribed by the Judicial Conference under subsections (b) and (c) that is payable to the clerk upon the commencement of a case under chapter 7.

(2) The district court or the bankruptcy court may waive for such debtors other fees prescribed under subsections (b) and (c).

(3) This subsection does not restrict the district court or the bankruptcy court from waiving, in accordance with Judicial Conference policy, fees prescribed under this section for other debtors and creditors. (Added Pub.L. 95–598, Title II, § 246(a), Nov. 6, 1978, 92 Stat. 2671; amended Pub.L. 98–353, Title I, § 111(a), (b), July 10, 1984, 98 Stat. 342; Pub.L. 99–500, Title I, § 101(b) [Title IV, § 407(b)], Oct. 18, 1986, 100 Stat. 1783–64; Pub.L. 99–554, Title I, §§ 117, 144(f), Oct. 27, 1986, 100 Stat. 3095, 3097; Pub.L. 99–591, Title I, § 101(b) [Title IV, § 407(b)], Oct. 30, 1986, 100 Stat. 3341–64; Pub.L. 101–162, Title IV, § 406(a), Nov. 21, 1989, 103 Stat. 1016; Pub.L. 102–140, Title I, § 111(a), Oct. 28, 1991, 105 Stat. 795; Pub.L. 103–121, Title I, § 111(a)(1), (b)(1), Oct. 27, 1993, 107 Stat. 1164; Pub.L. 104–91, Title I, § 101(a), Jan. 6, 1996, 110 Stat. 11; Pub.L. 104–99, Title II, § 211, Jan. 26, 1996, 110 Stat. 37; Pub.L. 104–208, Div. A, Title I, § 101(a) [Title I, § 109(a)], Sept. 30, 1996, 110 Stat. 3009–18; Pub.L. 106–113, Div. B, § 1000(a)(1) [Title I, § 113], Nov. 29, 1999, 113 Stat. 1535, 1501A–20; Pub.L. 106–518, Title I, §§ 103 to 105, Nov. 13, 2000, 114 Stat. 2411; Pub.L. 109–8, Title III, § 325(a), Title IV, § 418, Apr. 20, 2005, 119 Stat. 98, 108; Pub.L. 109–13, Div. A, Title VI, § 6058(a), May 11, 2005, 119 Stat. 297; Pub.L. 109–171, Title X, § 10101(a), Feb. 8, 2006, 120 Stat. 184; Pub.L. 110–161, Div. B, Title II, § 213(a), Dec. 26, 2007, 121 Stat. 1914.)

JUDICIAL CONFERENCE SCHEDULE OF FEES

Bankruptcy Court Miscellaneous Fee Schedule (28 U.S.C. § 1930)

(Effective November 1, 2011)

The fees included in the Bankruptcy Court Miscellaneous Fee Schedule are to be charged for services provided by the bankruptcy courts.

• The United States should not be charged fees under this schedule, with the exception of those specifically prescribed in Items 1, 3 and 5 when the information requested is available through remote electronic access.

• Federal agencies or programs that are funded from judiciary appropriations (agencies, organizations, and individuals providing services authorized by the Criminal Justice Act, 18 U.S.C. § 3006A, and bankruptcy administrators) should not be charged any fees under this schedule.

(1) For reproducing any document, $.50 per page. This fee applies to services rendered on behalf of the United States if the document requested is available through electronic access.

(2) For certification of any document, $11.

For exemplification of any document, $21.

(3) For reproduction of an audio recording of a court proceeding, $30. This fee applies to services rendered on behalf of the United States if the recording is available electronically.

(4) For filing an amendment to the debtor's schedules of creditors, lists of creditors, or mailing list, $30, except:

- The bankruptcy judge may, for good cause, waive the charge in any case.
- This fee must not be charged if—
  - the amendment is to change the address of a creditor or an attorney for a creditor listed on the schedules; or
  - the amendment is to add the name and address of an attorney for a creditor listed on the schedules.

(5) For conducting a search of the bankruptcy court records, $30 per name or item searched. This fee applies to services rendered on behalf of the United States if the information requested is available through electronic access.

(6) For filing a complaint, $293, except:

- If the trustee or debtor-in-possession files the complaint, the fee must be paid only by the estate, to the extent there is an estate.
- This fee must not be charged if—
  - the debtor is the plaintiff; or
  - a child support creditor or representative files the complaint and submits the form required by § 304(g) of the Bankruptcy Reform Act of 1994.

(7) For filing any document that is not related to a pending case or proceeding, $46.

(8) Administrative fee for filing a case under Title 11 or when a motion to divide a joint case under Title 11 is filed, $46.

(9) For payment to trustees pursuant to 11 U.S.C. § 330(b)(2), a $15 fee applies in the following circumstances:

- For filing a petition under Chapter 7.
- For filing a motion to reopen a Chapter 7 case.
- For filing a motion to divide a joint Chapter 7 case.
- For filing a motion to convert a case to a Chapter 7 case.
- For filing a notice of conversion to a Chapter 7 case.

(10) In addition to any fees imposed under Item 9, above, the following fees must be collected:

- For filing a motion to convert a Chapter 12 case to a Chapter 7 case or a notice of conversion pursuant to 11 U.S.C. § 1208(a), $45.
- For filing a motion to convert a Chapter 13 case to a Chapter 7 case or a notice of conversion pursuant to 11 U.S.C. § 1307(a), $10.

The fee amounts in this item are derived from the fees prescribed in 28 U.S.C. § 1930(a).

If the trustee files the motion to convert, the fee is payable only from the estate that exists prior to conversion.

If the filing fee for the chapter to which the case is requested to be converted is less than the fee paid at the commencement of the case, no refund may be provided.

(11) For filing a motion to reopen, the following fees apply:

- For filing a motion to reopen a Chapter 7 case, $245.
- For filing a motion to reopen a Chapter 9 case, $1000.
- For filing a motion to reopen a Chapter 11 case, $1000.
- For filing a motion to reopen a Chapter 12 case, $200.
- For filing a motion to reopen a Chapter 13 case, $235.
- For filing a motion to reopen a Chapter 15 case, $1000.

The fee amounts in this item are derived from the fees prescribed in 28 U. S. C. § 1930(a).

The reopening fee must be charged when a case has been closed without a discharge being entered.

The court may waive this fee under appropriate circumstances or may defer payment of the fee from trustees pending discovery of additional assets. If payment is deferred, the fee should be waived if no additional assets are discovered.

The reopening fee must not be charged in the following situations:

- to permit a party to file a complaint to obtain a determination under Rule 4007(b); or
- when a debtor files a motion to reopen a case based upon an alleged violation of the terms of the discharge under 11 U.S.C. § 524; or
- when the reopening is to correct an administrative error.

(12) For retrieval of a record from a Federal Records Center, National Archives, or other storage location removed from the place of business of the court, $53.

(13) For a check paid into the court which is returned for lack of funds, $53.

(14) For filing an appeal or cross appeal from a judgment, order, or decree, $293.

This fee is collected in addition to the statutory fee of $5 that is collected under 28 U.S.C. § 1930 (c) when a notice of appeal is filed.

Parties filing a joint notice of appeal should pay only one fee.

If a trustee or debtor-in-possession is the appellant, the fee must be paid only by the estate, to the extent there is an estate.

Upon notice from the court of appeals that a direct appeal or direct cross-appeal has been authorized, an additional fee of $157* must be collected.

*The approved increase in the notice of appeal fee necessitates that the supplemental direct appeal fee be reduced to ensure that the total fee for filing a direct appeal does not exceed the established appellate filing fee of $450.

(15) For filing a case under Chapter 15 of the Bankruptcy Code, $1000.

This fee is derived from and equal to the fee prescribed in 28 U.S.C. § 1930(a)(3) for filing a case commenced under Chapter 11 of Title 11.

(16) The court may charge and collect fees commensurate with the cost of providing copies of the local rules of court. The court may also distribute copies of the local rules without charge.

(17) The clerk shall assess a charge for the handling of registry funds deposited with the court, to be assessed from interest earnings and in accordance with the detailed fee schedule issued by the Director of the Administrative Office of the United States Courts.

For management of registry funds invested through the Court Registry Investment System, a fee at a rate of 2.5 basis points shall be assessed from interest earnings.

(18) For a motion filed by the debtor to divide a joint case filed under 11 U.S.C. § 302, the following fees apply:

- For filing a motion to divide a joint Chapter 7 case, $245.
- For filing a motion to divide a joint Chapter 11 case, $1000.

- For filing a motion to divide a joint Chapter 12 case, $200.
- For filing a motion to divide a joint Chapter 13 case, $235.

These fees are derived from and equal to the filing fees prescribed in 28 U.S.C. § 1930(a).

(19) For filing the following motions, $176:

- To terminate, annul, modify or condition the automatic stay;
- To compel abandonment of property of the estate pursuant to Rule 6007(b) of the Federal Rules of Bankruptcy Procedure; or
- To withdraw the reference of a case or proceeding under 28 U.S.C. § 157(d).

This fee must not be collected in the following situations:

- For a motion for relief from the co-debtor stay;
- For a stipulation for court approval of an agreement for relief from a stay; or
- For a motion filed by a child support creditor or its representative, if the form required by § 304(g) of the Bankruptcy Reform Act of 1994 is filed.

ELECTRONIC PUBLIC ACCESS FEE SCHEDULE (Eff. 4/1/2012)

(Issued in Accordance with 28 U.S.C. §§ 1913, 1914, 1926, 1930, 1932)

As directed by Congress, the Judicial Conference has determined that the following fees are necessary to reimburse expenses incurred by the judiciary in providing electronic public access to court records. These fees shall apply to the United States unless otherwise stated. No fees under this schedule shall be charged to federal agencies or programs which are funded from judiciary appropriations, including, but not limited to, agencies, organizations, and individuals providing services authorized by the Criminal Justice Act, 18 U.S.C. § 3006A, and bankruptcy administrator programs. Furthermore, the fee increase from eight cents per page to ten cents per page has been suspended for local, state, and federal government entities until 4/1/2015.

I. For electronic access to court data via a federal judiciary Internet site: ten cents per page, with the total for any document, docket sheet, or case-specific report not to exceed the fee for thirty pages- provided however that transcripts of federal court proceedings shall not be subject to the thirty-page fee limit. For electronic access to an audio file of a court hearing via a federal judiciary Internet site: $2.40 per audio file. Attorneys of record and parties in a case (including pro se litigants) receive one free electronic copy of all documents filed electronically, if receipt is required by law or directed by the filer. No fee is owed under this provision until an account holder accrues charges of more than $15 in a quarterly billing cycle. Consistent with Judicial Conference policy, courts may, upon a showing of cause, exempt indigents, bankruptcy case trustees, individual researchers associated with educational institutions, courts, section 501(c)(3) not-for-profit organizations, court appointed pro bono attorneys, and pro bono ADR neutrals from payment of these fees. Courts must find that parties from the classes of persons or entities listed above seeking exemption have demonstrated that an exemption is necessary in order to avoid unreasonable burdens and to promote public access to information. For individual researchers, courts must also find that the defined research project is intended for academic research, and not

for commercial purposes or internet redistribution. Any user granted an exemption agrees not to sell for profit the data obtained as a result. Any transfer of data obtained as the result of a fee exemption is prohibited unless expressly authorized by the court. Exemptions may be granted for a definite period of time and may be revoked at the discretion of the court granting the exemption.

II. For printing copies of any record or document accessed electronically at a public terminal in the courthouse: ten cents per page. This fee shall apply to services rendered on behalf of the United States if the record requested is remotely available through electronic access.

III. For every search of court records conducted by the PACER Service Center, $26 per name or item searched.

IV. For the PACER Service Center to reproduce on paper any record pertaining to a PACER account, if this information is remotely available through electronic access, 50 cents per page.

V. For a check paid to the PACER Service Center which is returned for lack of funds, $45.

JUDICIAL CONFERENCE POLICY NOTES

Courts should not exempt local, state or federal government agencies, members of the media, attorneys or others not members of one of the groups listed above. Exemptions should be granted as the exception, not the rule. A court may not use this exemption language to exempt all users. An exemption applies only to access related to the case or purpose for which it was given. The prohibition on transfer of information received without fee is not intended to bar a quote or reference to information received as a result of a fee exemption in a scholarly or other similar work.

The electronic public access fee applies to electronic court data viewed remotely from the public records of individual cases in the court, including filed documents and the docket sheet. Audio files of court hearings do not include naturalization ceremonies or appellate oral arguments. Electronic court data may be viewed free at public terminals at the courthouse and courts may provide other local court information at no cost. Examples of information that can be provided at no cost include: local rules, court forms, news items, court calendars, opinions, and other information—such as court hours, court location, telephone listings—determined locally to benefit the public and the court.

STATEMENT RESPECTING 1988 AMENDMENTS FROM ADMINISTRATIVE OFFICE OF UNITED STATES COURTS

The Director of the Administrative Office of the United States Courts in a memorandum to the Chief Judges of the United States Courts of Appeals, United States District Courts, and United States Bankruptcy Courts, dated April 19, 1988, provided in part that: "The amendment establishing a fee for filing a petition ancillary to a foreign proceeding under § 304 of the Bankruptcy Code will become effective May 1, 1988. The amendment expanding the exemption for services rendered 'to the United States' to include services rendered to bankruptcy administrators simply expresses a policy which has been in effect since the creation of the bankruptcy administrator program by Congress in the Bankruptcy Judges, United States Trustees and Family Farmer Bankruptcy Act of 1986. [Pub.L. No. 99–554, § 302(d)(3)(I).]"

Statement from 1989 Meeting of Judicial Conference

The Judicial Conference, at the September 20, 1989 meeting, provided in part that Item 21 takes effect on December 21, 1989. The Conference further provided that: "The remaining fees, Items 20 and 22, take effect on January 11, 1990, pending approval of the Appropriations Committees."

Registry Fund Fees—Item 19
(54 FR 20407, May 11, 1989)

Effective June 12, 1989, a fee will be assessed for handling funds deposited in noncriminal proceedings with the court and held in interest bearing accounts or instruments pursuant to 28 U.S.C. § 2041 and Federal Rules of Civil Procedure rule 67. For new accounts, i.e., investments made on or after June 12, 1989, the fee will be equal to the first 45 days income earned on the deposit. Each subsequent deposit of new principal in the same case or proceeding will be subject to the fee. Reinvestment of prior deposits will not be subject to the fee. For existing accounts, i.e., investments held by the court prior to June 12, 1989, a fee will be assessed equal to the first 45 days of income earned beginning 30 days after June 12, 1989. Subsequent deposits of new principal in the same account will be subject to the fee. Subsequent reinvestment of existing deposits will not be subject to the fee.

The fee will apply only once to each sum deposited regardless of the length of time deposits are held and will not exceed income actually earned on the account.

The fee does not apply in the District Courts of Guam, Northern Mariana Islands, the Virgin Islands, the United States Claims Court, or other courts whose fees are not set under 28 U.S.C. § 1930.

Registry Fund Fees—Item 19
(55 F.R. 42867, October 24, 1990)

Effective December 1, 1990, the registry fee assessment provisions were revised and converted from a one-time charge equal to all income earned in the first 45 days of the investment to a charge of 10 percent of the income earned while funds are held in the court registry. Additionally, the fee was extended to any funds placed in the court's registry and

invested regardless of the nature of the action underlying the deposit.

The new method will not be applied on investments in cases from which a fee has been exacted based on the prior method (interest earned in the first 45 days the funds were invested or the first 45 days following July 12, 1989). The new method will also not be applied in cases where the investment instrument has a maturity date greater than one year, but where a fee under the prior method applies but has not been deducted.

The fee does not apply in the District Courts of Guam, the Northern Mariana Islands, the Virgin Islands, the United States Claims Court, or any other federal court whose fees are not set under 28 U.S.C. §§ 1913, 1914, and 1930.

Registry Fund Fees—Item 19
(56 F.R. 56356, November 4, 1991)

Effective February 3, 1992, the registry fee assessment provisions are revised and converted from a charge equal to 10 percent of the income earned while funds are held in the court's registry to a variable rate based on the amount deposited with the court and, in certain cases, the length of time funds are held in the court's registry.

The revised fee will be a fee of 10 percent of the total income received during each income period from investments of less than $100,000,000 of registry funds in income-bearing accounts. On investments exceeding $100,000,000 the 10 percent fee shall be reduced by one percent for each increment of $50,000,000 over the initial $100,000,000. For those deposits where funds are placed in the registry by court order for a time certain, for example, by the terms of an adjudicated trust, the fee will be further reduced. This further reduction will amount to 2.5 percent for each five-year interval or part thereof. The total minimum fee to be charged will be no less than two percent of the income on investments.

The following table sets out the fee schedule promulgated by this notice:

REGISTRY—SCHEDULE OF FEES

[% of income earned]

Amount of deposit *	0–5 yrs.	>5–10 yrs.	>10–15 yrs.	>15 yrs.
less than 100M	10	7.5	5.0	2.5
100M–<150M	9	6.5	4.0	2.0
150M–<200M	8	5.5	3.0	2.0
200M–<250M	7	4.5	2.0	2.0
250M–<300M	6	3.5	2.0	2.0
300M–<350M	5	2.5	2.0	2.0
350M–<400M	4	2.0	2.0	2.0
400M–<450M	3	2.0	2.0	2.0
over 450M	2	2.0	2.0	2.0

* Except where otherwise authorized by the Director, each deposit into any account is treated separately in determining the fee.

The new fee applies to all earnings applied to investments on and after the effective date of this change, except for earnings on investments in cases being administered under the provisions of the May 11, 1989 notice [54 FR 20407], i.e., to which the fee equal to the first 45 days income is applicable.

The fee, as modified herein, will continue to apply to any case where the court has authorized the investment of funds placed in its custody or held by it in trust in its registry regardless of the nature of the underlying action.

The fee does not apply in the District Court of Guam, the Northern Mariana Islands, the Virgin Islands, the United States Claims Court, or any other Federal court whose fees are not set under 28 U.S.C. §§ 1913, 1914, and 1930.

HISTORICAL AND STATUTORY NOTES
Revision Notes and Legislative Reports

1978 Acts. Senate Report No. 95–989 and House Report No. 95–595, see 1978 U.S. Code Cong. and Adm. News, p. 5787.

1984 Acts. Statements by Legislative Leaders, see 1984 U.S. Code Cong. and Adm. News, p. 576.

1986 Acts. House Report No. 99–764 and House Conference Report No. 99–958, see 1986 U.S. Code Cong. and Adm. News, p. 5227.

Statement by President, see 1986 U.S. Code Cong. and Adm. News, p. 5627.

1989 Acts. Statement by President, see 1989 U.S. Code Cong. and Adm. News, p. 733–3.

1991 Acts. Statement by President, see 1991 U.S. Code Cong. and Adm. News, p. 507.

1999 Acts. Statement by President, see 1999 U.S. Code Cong. and Adm. News, p. 290.

2005 Acts. House Report No. 109–31(Part I), see 2005 U.S. Code Cong. and Adm. News, p. 88.

House Conference Report No. 109–72, see 2005 U.S. Code Cong. and Adm. News, p. 240.

2006 Acts. House Conference Report No. 109–362, see 2006 U.S. Code Cong. and Adm. News, p. 3.

Statement by President, see 2006 U.S. Code Cong. and Adm. News, p. S3.

2007 Acts. House Report No. 110–197, see 2007 U.S. Code Cong. and Adm. News, p. 661.

Statement by President, see 2007 U.S. Code Cong. and Adm. News, p. S34.

References in Text

Chapter 7, 11, 12, or 13 of title 11, referred to in text, is 11 U.S.C.A. § 701 et seq., 11 U.S.C.A. § 1101 et seq., 11 U.S.C.A. § 1201 et seq., or 11 U.S.C.A. § 1301 et seq., respectively.

Section 673(2) of the Omnibus Budget Reconciliation Act of 1981, referred to in subsec. (f)(1), is Pub.L. 97–35, Title VI, § 673(2), Aug. 13, 1981, as added Pub.L. 105–285, Title II, § 201, Oct. 27, 1998, 112 Stat. 2729, which is classified to 42 U.S.C.A. § 9902(2).

Codifications

Pub.L. 99–591 is a corrected version of Pub.L. 99–500.

The Chapter 11 filing fee will not change from its current amount of $1,000. It appears that Congress intended to increase chapter 11 filing fees from $1,000 to $2,750. However, there is a drafting error in the language of the Deficit Reduction Act of 2005 which references the incorrect statutory subsection [Pub.L. 109–171, Title X, § 10101(a)(2), Feb. 8, 2006, 120 Stat. 184]. Thus, the chapter 11 fee, at this time, is unaltered. See 2006 Amendments note set out under this section.

Section 101(a) of Pub.L. 104–91, as amended by section 211 of Pub.L. 104–99, provided in part that section 111(a) of the General Provisions for the Department of Justice in Title I of the Departments of Commerce, Justice, and State, the Judiciary, and Related Agencies Appropriations Act, 1996 (H.R. 2076) as passed by the House of Representatives on Dec. 6, 1995, was enacted into permanent law. Such section 111(a) of H.R. 2076 amended subsec. (a)(6) of this section. See 1996 Amendments note set out under this section.

Amendments

2007 Amendments. Subsec. (a)(6). Pub.L. 110–161, Div. B, § 213(a), struck out "The fee shall be $250 for each quarter in which disbursements total less than $15,000; $500 for each quarter in which disbursements total $15,000 or more but less

than $75,000; $750 for each quarter in which disbursements total $75,000 or more but less than $150,000; $1,250 for each quarter in which disbursements total $150,000 or more but less than $225,000; $1,500 for each quarter in which disbursements total $225,000 or more but less than $300,000; $3,750 for each quarter in which disbursements total $300,000 or more but less than $1,000,000; $5,000 for each quarter in which disbursements total $1,000,000 or more but less than $2,000,000; $7,500 for each quarter in which disbursements total $2,000,000 or more but less than $3,000,000; $8,000 for each quarter in which disbursements total $3,000,000 or more but less than $5,000,000; $10,000 for each quarter in which disbursements total $5,000,000 or more. The fee shall be payable on the last day of the calendar month following the calendar quarter for which the fee is owed." and inserted "The fee shall be $325 for each quarter in which disbursements total less than $15,000; $650 for each quarter in which disbursements total $15,000 or more but less than $75,000; $975 for each quarter in which disbursements total $75,000 or more but less than $150,000; $1,625 for each quarter in which disbursements total $150,000 or more but less than $225,000; $1,950 for each quarter in which disbursements total $225,000 or more but less than $300,000; $4,875 for each quarter in which disbursements total $300,000 or more but less than $1,000,000; $6,500 for each quarter in which disbursements total $1,000,000 or more but less than $2,000,000; $9,750 for each quarter in which disbursements total $2,000,000 or more but less than $3,000,000; $10,400 for each quarter in which disbursements total $3,000,000 or more but less than $5,000,000; $13,000 for each quarter in which disbursements total $5,000,000 or more but less than $15,000,000; $20,000 for each quarter in which disbursements total $15,000,000 or more but less than $30,000,000; $30,000 for each quarter in which disbursements total more than $30,000,000. The fee shall be payable on the last day of the calendar month following the calendar quarter for which the fee is owed.".

2006 Amendments. Subsec. (a)(1)(A). Pub.L. 109–171, § 10101(a)(1)(A), struck out "$220" and inserted "$245".

Subsec. (a)(1)(B). Pub.L. 109–171, § 10101(a)(1)(B), struck out "$150" and inserted "$235".

Subsec. (a)(2). Pub.L. 109–171, § 10101(a)(2), which purported to strike out "$1,000" and insert "$2,750", in par. (2), was incapable of execution. See Codifications note set out under this section.

2005 Amendments. Subsec. (a)(1). Pub.L. 109–8, § 325(a)(1), as amended by Pub.L. 109–13, § 6058(a), added par. (1) and struck out former par. (1), which read as follows: "For a case commenced under chapter 7 or 13 of title 11, $155."

Pub.L. 109–8, § 325(a)(2), in subsec. (a)(3), struck out "$800" and inserted "$1000".

Subsec. (a)(3). Pub.L. 109–8, Sec. 325(a)(2), as amended by Pub.L. 109–13, § 6058(a), substituted "$1,000" for "$800".

Subsec. (f). Pub.L. 109–8, § 418(2), added subsec. (f).

2000 Amendments. Subsec. (a). Pub.L. 106–518, § 104, in the undesignated portion at the end, struck out "$400" and inserted "the amount equal to the difference between the fee specified in paragraph (3) and the fee specified in paragraph (1)".

Subsec. (a)(2). Pub.L. 106–518, § 103, struck out "$300" and inserted "equal to the fee specified in paragraph (3) for filing a case under chapter 11 of title 11. The amount by which the fee payable under this paragraph exceeds $300 shall be deposited in the fund established under section 1931 of this title".

Subsec. (a)(7). Pub.L. 106–518, § 105, added par. (7).

1999 Amendments. Subsec. (a)(1). Pub.L. 106–113, § 1000(a)(1) [§ 113] struck out "$130" and inserted "$155".

1996 Amendments. Subsec. (a)(3). Pub.L. 104–208, § 101(a) [§ 109(a)], inserted a dollar sign preceding "800".

Subsec. (a)(6). Pub.L. 104–208, § 101(a) [§ 109(a)], substituted provisions setting quarterly fees at $500 for disbursements between $15,000 and $75,000, $750 for those between $75,000 and $150,000, $1,250 for those between $150,000 and $225,000, $1,500 for those between $225,000 and $300,000, $3,750 for those between $300,000 and $1,000,000, $5,000 for those between $1,000,000 and $2,000,000, $7,500 for those between $2,000,000 and $3,000,000, $8,000 for those between $3,000,000 and $5,000,000, and $10,000 for those over $5,000,000 for provisions setting quarterly fees at $500 for disbursements between $15,000 and $150,000, $1,250 for those between $150,000 and $300,000, $3,750 for those between $300,000 and $3,000,000, and $5,000 for those over $3,000,000.

Pub.L. 104–91, § 101(a), as amended Pub.L. 104–99, § 211, struck out "a plan is confirmed or" preceding "the case is converted". See Codifications note set out under this section.

1993 Amendments. Subsec. (a)(1). Pub.L. 103–121, § 111(a)(1), increased filing fee for chapter 7 or 13 cases from $120 to $130.

Subsec. (a)(3). Pub.L. 103–121, § 111(a)(1), increased filing fee for chapter 11 cases from $600 to $800.

1991 Amendments. Subsec. (a)(3). Pub.L. 102–140, § 111(a)(1), substituted "$600" for "$500".

Subsec. (a)(6). Pub.L. 102–140, § 111(a)(2), substituted "$250" for "$150", "$500" for "$300", "$1,250" for "$750", "$3,750" for "$2,250", and "$5,000" for "$3,000".

1989 Amendments. Subsec. (a)(1). Pub.L. 101–162, § 406(a), substituted "$120" for "$90".

1986 Amendments. Subsec. (a). Pub.L. 99–554, § 117(5), in provision following numbered pars., inserted provision that for conversion, on request of the debtor, of a case under chapter 7 or 13 of title 11 to a case under chapter 11 of title 11, the debtor pay to the clerk of the court a fee of $400.

Pub.L. 99–554, § 144(f), substituted "of the district court or the clerk of the bankruptcy court, if one has been certified pursuant to section 156(b) of this title" for "of the court" wherever appearing.

Subsec. (a)(1). Pub.L. 99–500 and Pub.L. 99–591, and Pub.L. 99–554, § 117(1), amended par. (1) identically, substituting "$90" for "$60".

Subsec. (a)(3). Pub.L. 99–554, § 117(2), substituted "$500" for "$200".

Subsec. (a)(4). Pub.L. 99–554, § 117(3), substituted "$1,000" for "$500".

Subsec. (a)(5), (6). Pub.L. 99–554, § 117(4), added pars. (5) and (6).

1984 Amendments. Catchline. Pub.L. 98–353, § 111(b), substituted "fees" for "courts".

Subsecs. (a), (c), (e). Pub.L. 98–353, § 111(a), substituted "clerk of the court" for "clerk of the bankruptcy court".

Effective and Applicability Provisions

2007 Acts. Pub.L. 110–161, Div. B, Title II, § 213(b), Dec. 26, 2007, 121 Stat. 1914, provided that: "This section and the amendment made by this section [amending this section] shall take effect January 1, 2008, or the date of the enactment of this Act [Dec. 26, 2007], whichever is later."

2006 Acts. Pub.L. 109–171, Title X, § 10101(c), Feb. 8, 2006, 120 Stat. 184, provided that: "This section and the amendments made by this section [amending this section and enacting provisions set out as a note under 28 U.S.C.A. § 1931] shall take effect 60 days after the date of the enactment of this Act [Feb. 8, 2006]."

2005 Acts. Amendment by Pub.L. 109–13, § 6058(a), amending Pub.L. 109–8, § 325, which amended this section, effective immediately after the enactment of the Bankruptcy Abuse Prevention and Consumer Protection Act of 2005 [Pub.L. 109–8, Apr. 20, 2005, 119 Stat. 23], see Pub.L. 109–13, § 6058(b), set out as a note under 28 U.S.C.A. § 589a.

Except as otherwise provided, amendments by Pub.L. 109–8 effective 180 days after April 20, 2005, and inapplicable with respect to cases commenced under Title 11 before the effective date, see Pub.L. 109–8, § 1501, set out as a note under 11 U.S.C.A. § 101.

1999 Acts. Amendment by Pub.L. 106–113, [§ 113], effective 30 days after Nov. 29, 1999, see Pub.L. 106–113, [§ 113], set out as a note under section 589a of this title.

1993 Acts. Section 111(a) of Pub.L. 103–121 provided in part that amendment by section 111(a)(1) of Pub.L. 103–121, amending subsec. (a)(1) of this section, is effective 30 days after Oct. 27, 1993.

Section 111(b) of Pub.L. 103–121 provided in part that amendment by section 111(b)(1) of Pub.L. 103–121, amending subsec. (a)(3) of this section, is effective 30 days after Oct. 27, 1993.

1991 Acts. Amendment by Pub.L. 102–140 effective 60 days after the date of the enactment of Pub.L. 102–140, which was approved Oct. 28, 1991, see section 111(a) of Pub.L. 102–140, set out as a note under section 589a of this title.

1986 Acts. Amendment by Pub.L. 99–554 effective 30 days after Oct. 27, 1986, except as otherwise provided for, see section 302(a) of Pub.L. 99–554, set out as a note under section 581 of this title.

Amendment by Pub.L. 99–554, § 117(4), not to become effective in or with respect to certain specified judicial districts until, or apply to cases while pending in such district before, the expiration of the 270-day period beginning 30 days after Oct. 27, 1986, or of the 30-day period beginning on the date the Attorney General certifies under section 303 of Pub.L. 99–554 the region specified in a paragraph of section 581(a) of Title 28, as amended by section 111(a) of Pub.L. 99–554, that includes such district, whichever occurs first, see section 302(d)(1) of Pub.L. 99–554, set out as a note under section 581 of this title.

Amendment by Pub.L. 99–554, § 117(4), not to become effective in or with respect to certain specified judicial districts until, or apply to cases while pending in such district before, the expiration of the 2-year period beginning 30 days after Oct. 27, 1986, or of the 30-day period beginning on the date the Attorney General certifies under section 303 of Pub.L. 99–554 the region specified in a paragraph of section 581(a) of Title 28, as amended by section 111(a) of Pub.L. 99–554, that includes such district, whichever occurs first, see section 302(d)(2) of Pub.L. 99–554, set out as a note under section 581 of this title.

Amendment by Pub.L. 99–554, § 117(4), not to become effective in or with respect to judicial districts established for the States of Alabama and North Carolina until, or apply to cases while pending in such district before, such district elects to be included in a bankruptcy region established in section 581(a) of Title 28, as amended by section 111(a) of Pub.L. 99–554, or Oct. 1, 2002, whichever occurs first, and, except as otherwise provided for, with respect to cases under chapters 7, 11, 12, and 13 of Title 11 commenced before 30 days after Oct. 27, 1986, and pending in a judicial district in the States of Alabama or North Carolina before any election made under section 302(d)(3)(A) of Pub.L. 99–554 by such district becomes effective or Oct. 1, 2002, whichever occurs first, amendments by Pub.L. 99–554 not to apply until Oct. 1, 2003, or the expiration of the 1-year period beginning on the date such election becomes effective, whichever occurs first, and further, in any judicial district in Alabama or North Carolina not making the election described in section 302(d)(3)(A) of Pub.L. 99–554, any person appointed under regulations issued by the Judicial Conference to administer estates in cases under Title 11 authorized to establish, etc., a panel of private trustees, and to supervise cases and trustees in cases under chapters 7, 11, 12, and 13 of Title 11, until amendments by sections 201 to 231 of Pub.L. 99–554 effective in such district, see section 302(d)(3)(A) to (F), (H), (I) of Pub.L. 99–554, set out as a note under section 581 of this title.

Deposit in the general receipts of the Treasury of funds collected as a result of the amendments made by section 117 of Pub.L. 99–554 in a judicial district in the States of Alabama or North Carolina under section 1930(a) of Title 28 before the date the amendments made by sections 201 to 231 of Pub.L. 99–554 take effect in such districts, and notwithstanding section 589a of Title 28, see section 302(d)(3)(G) of Pub.L. 99–554, set out as a note under section 581 of this title.

Amendment by Pub.L. 99–554, § 117(4), except as otherwise provided, with respect to cases under chapters 7, 11, 12, and 13 of Title 11 commenced before 30 days after Oct. 27, 1986, and pending in a judicial district referred to in section 581(a) of Title 28, as amended by section 111(a) of Pub.L. 99–554, for which a United States trustee is not authorized before 30 days after Oct. 27, 1986 to be appointed, not applicable until the expiration of the 3-year period beginning on Oct. 27, 1986, or of the 1-year period beginning on the date the Attorney General certifies under section 303 of Pub.L. 99–554 the region specified in a paragraph of such section 581(a) that includes, such district, whichever occurs first, see section 302(e)(1), (2) of Pub.L. 99–554, set out as a note under section 581 of this title.

Rule of construction regarding fees for cases under Title 11 for any conduct or period occurring before section 1930(a)(6) of Title 28 becomes effective in the district in which such case is pending, see section 302(e)(3) of Pub.L. 99–554, set out as a note under section 581 of this title.

1984 Acts. Amendment by Pub.L. 98–353 effective July 10, 1984, see section 122(a) of Pub.L. 98–353, set out as a note under section 151 of this title.

1979 Acts. Section effective Oct. 1, 1979, see section 402(c) of Pub.L. 95–598, set out as a note preceding section 101 of Title 11, Bankruptcy.

Use of Increased Receipts

Pub.L. 109–8, Title III, § 325(e), Apr. 20, 2005, 119 Stat. 99, which pertained to the use of increased receipts from fees under subsec. (a) of this section, was omitted in the general amendment of Pub.L. 109–8, § 325, by Pub.L. 109–13, Div. A, Title VI, § 6058(a), May 11, 2005, 119 Stat. 297. Such amendment by Pub.L. 109–13, § 6058(a), effective immediately after the enactment of the Bankruptcy Abuse Prevention and Consumer Protection Act of 2005 [Pub.L. 109–8, Apr. 20, 2005, 119 Stat. 23], see Pub.L. 109–13, § 6058(b), set out as a note under 28 U.S.C.A. § 589a.

[Except as otherwise provided, amendments by Pub.L. 109–8 effective 180 days after April 20, 2005, and inapplicable with respect to cases commenced under Title 11 before the effective date, see Pub.L. 109–8, § 1501, set out as a note under 11 U.S.C.A. § 101.]

Miscellaneous Fees

Section 406(a) of Pub.L. 101–162 provided in part that: "Pursuant to section 1930(b) of title 28 [subsec. (b) of this section] the Judicial Conference of the United States shall prescribe a fee of $60 on motions seeking relief from the automatic stay under 11 U.S.C. section 362(b) [section 362(b) of Title 11, Bankruptcy] and motions to compel abandonment of property of the estate. The fees established pursuant to the preceding two sentences shall take effect 30 days after the enactment of this Act [Nov. 21, 1989]."

Accrual and Payment of Quarterly Fees in Chapter 11 Cases After Jan. 27, 1996; Confirmation Status of Plans

Section 101(a) of Pub.L. 104–91, as amended Pub.L. 104–99, Title II, § 211, Jan. 26, 1996, 110 Stat. 37; Pub.L. 104–208, Div. A, Title I, § 101(a) [Title I, § 109(d)], Sept. 30, 1996, 110 Stat. 3009–19, provided, in part: "That, notwithstanding any other provision of law, the fees under 28 U.S.C. 1930(a)(6) [subsec. (a)(6) of this section] shall accrue and be payable from and after January 27, 1996, in all cases (including, without limitation, any cases pending as of that date), regardless of confirmation status of their plans."

Collection and Disposition of Fees in Bankruptcy Cases

Section 404(a) of Pub. L. 101–162 provided that: "For fiscal year 1990 and hereafter, such fees as shall be collected for the preparation and mailing of notices in bankruptcy cases as prescribed by the Judicial Conference of the United States pursuant to 28 U.S.C. 1930(b) [subsec. (b) of this section] shall be deposited to the 'Courts of Appeals, District Courts, and Other Judicial Services, Salaries and Expenses' appropriation to be used for salaries and other expenses incurred in providing these services."

Court Fees for Electronic Access to Information

Judicial Conference to prescribe reasonable fees for collection by courts under this section for access to information available through automatic data processing equipment and fees to be deposited in Judiciary Automation Fund, see section 303 of Pub.L. 102–140, set out as a note under section 1913 of this title.

Issuance of Notices to Creditors and Other Interested Parties

Section 403 of Pub.L. 101–162 provided that: "Notwithstanding any other provision of law, for fiscal year 1990 and hereafter, (a) The Administrative Office of the United States Courts, or any other agency or instrumentality of the United

States, is prohibited from restricting solely to staff of the Clerks of the United States Bankruptcy Courts the issuance of notices to creditors and other interested parties. (b) The Administrative Office shall permit and encourage the preparation and mailing of such notices to be performed by or at the expense of the debtors, trustees or such other interested parties as the Court may direct and approve. (c) The Director of the Administrative Office of the United States Courts shall make appropriate provisions for the use of and accounting for any postage required pursuant to such directives."

Report on Bankruptcy Fees

Section 111(d) of Pub.L. 103–121 provided that:

"**(1) Report required.**—Not later than March 31, 1998, the Judicial Conference of the United States shall submit to the Committees on the Judiciary of the House of Representatives and the Senate, a report relating to the bankruptcy fee system and the impact of such system on various participants in bankruptcy cases.

"**(2) Contents of report.**—Such report shall include—

"**(A)(i)** an estimate of the costs and benefits that would result from waiving bankruptcy fees payable by debtors who are individuals, and

"**(ii)** recommendations regarding various revenue sources to offset the net cost of waiving such fees; and

"**(B)(i)** an evaluation of the effects that would result in cases under chapters 11 and 13 of title 11, United States Code [sections 1101 et seq. and 1301 et seq., respectively, of Title 11, Bankruptcy], from using a graduated bankruptcy fee system based on assets, liabilities, or both of the debtor, and

"**(ii)** recommendations regarding various methods to implement such a graduated bankruptcy fee system.

"**(3) Waiver of fees in selected districts.**—For purposes of carrying out paragraphs (1) and (2), the Judicial Conference of the United States shall carry out in not more than six judicial districts, throughout the 3–year period beginning on October 1, 1994, a program under which fees payable under section 1930 of title 28, United States Code [this section], may be waived in cases under chapter 7 of title 11, United States Code [section 701 et seq. of Title 11], for debtors who are individuals unable to pay such fees in installments.

"**(4) Study of graduated fee system.**—For purposes of carrying out paragraphs (1) and (2), the Judicial Conference of the United States shall carry out, in not fewer than six judicial districts, a study to estimate the results that would occur in cases under chapters 11 and 13 of title 11, United States Code [sections 1101 et seq. and 1301 et seq., respectively, of Title 11], if filing fees payable under section 1930 of title 28, United States Code [this section], were paid on a graduated scale based on assets, liabilities, or both of the debtor."

CHAPTER 131—RULES OF COURT

§ 2075. Bankruptcy rules

The Supreme Court shall have the power to prescribe by general rules, the forms of process, writs, pleadings, and motions, and the practice and procedure in cases under title 11.

Such rules shall not abridge, enlarge, or modify any substantive right.

The Supreme Court shall transmit to Congress not later than May 1 of the year in which a rule prescribed under this section is to become effective a copy of the proposed rule. The rule shall take effect no earlier than December 1 of the year in which it is transmitted to Congress unless otherwise provided by law.

The bankruptcy rules promulgated under this section shall prescribe a form for the statement required under section 707(b)(2)(C) of title 11 and may provide general rules on the content of such statement.

(Added Pub.L. 88–623, § 1, Oct. 3, 1964, 78 Stat. 1001; amended Pub.L. 95–598, Title II, § 247, Nov. 6, 1978, 92 Stat. 2672; Pub.L. 103–394, Title I, § 104(f), Oct. 22, 1994, 108 Stat. 4110; Pub.L. 109–8, Title XII, § 1232, Apr. 20, 2005, 119 Stat. 202.)

HISTORICAL AND STATUTORY NOTES

Revision Notes and Legislative Reports

1964 Acts. Senate Report No. 1561, see 1964 U.S. Code Cong. and Adm. News, p. 3804.

1978 Acts. Senate Report No. 95–989 and House Report No. 95–595, see 1978 U.S. Code Cong. and Adm. News, p. 5787.

1994 Acts. House Report No. 103–835, see 1994 U.S. Code Cong. and Adm. News, p. 3340.

2005 Acts. House Report No. 109–31(Part I), see 2005 U.S. Code Cong. and Adm. News, p. 88.

Amendments

2005 Amendments. Pub.L.109–8, § 1232, inserted at the end the following new undesignated paragraph: "The bankruptcy rules promulgated under this section shall prescribe a form for the statement required under section 707(b)(2)(C) of title 11 and may provide general rules on the content of such statement."

1994 Amendments. Pub.L. 103–394, § 104(f), added the third undesignated paragraph and struck out the former third undesignated paragraph which read as follows: "Such rules shall not take effect until they have been reported to Congress by the Chief Justice at or after the beginning of a regular session thereof but not later than the first day of May and until the expiration of ninety days after they have been thus reported."

1978 Amendments. Pub.L. 95–598 substituted "in cases under title 11" for "under the Bankruptcy Act" and struck out provisions directing that all laws in conflict with bankruptcy rules be of no further force or effect after such rules have taken effect.

Effective and Applicability Provisions

2005 Acts. Except as otherwise provided, amendments by Pub.L. 109–8 effective 180 days after April 20, 2005, and inapplicable with respect to cases commenced under Title 11 before the effective date, see Pub.L. 109–8, § 1501, set out as a note under 11 U.S.C.A. § 101.

1994 Acts. Amendment by Pub.L. 103–394 effective on Oct. 22, 1994, and not to apply with respect to cases commenced under Title 11 of the United States Code before Oct. 22, 1994, see section 702 of Pub.L. 103–394, set out as a note under section 101 of Title 11, Bankruptcy.

1978 Acts. Amendment by Pub.L. 95–598 effective Nov. 6, 1978, see section 402(d) of Pub.L. 95–598, set out as a note preceding section 101 of Title 11, Bankruptcy.

Separability of Provisions

If any provision of or amendment made by Pub.L. 103–394 or the application of such provision or amendment to any person or circumstance is held to be unconstitutional, the remaining provisions of and amendments made by Pub.L. 103–394 and the application of such provisions and amendments to any person or circumstance shall not be affected thereby, see section 701 of Pub.L. 103–394, set out as a note under section 101 of Title 11, Bankruptcy.

Additional Rulemaking Power

Pub.L. 95–598, Title IV, § 410, Nov. 6, 1978, 92 Stat. 2687, provided that: "The Supreme Court may issue such additional rules of procedure, consistent with Acts of Congress, as may be necessary for the orderly transfer of functions and records and the orderly transition to the new bankruptcy court system created by this Act [see Tables for complete classification of Pub.L. 95–598]."

Applicability of Rules to Cases Under Title 11

Pub.L. 95–598, Title IV, § 405(d), Nov. 6, 1978, 92 Stat. 2685, provided that: "The rules prescribed under section 2075 of title 28 of the United States Code and in effect on September 30, 1979, shall apply to cases under title 11, to the extent not inconsistent with the amendments made by this Act, or with this Act [see Tables for complete classification of Pub.L. 95–598], until such rules are repealed or superseded by rules prescribed and effective under such section, as amended by section 248 of this Act."

Rules Promulgated by Supreme Court

Pub.L. 98–353, Title III, § 320, July 10, 1984, 98 Stat. 357, provided that: "The Supreme Court shall prescribe general rules implementing the practice and procedure to be followed under section 707(b) of title 11, United States Code [section 707(b) of Title 11, Bankruptcy]. Section 2075 of title 28, United States Code [this section], shall apply with respect to the general rules prescribed under this section."

LIBRARY REFERENCES

American Digest System

Bankruptcy ⟿2129.

Key Number System Topic No. 51.

Corpus Juris Secundum

CJS Bankruptcy § 9, Title 28 of the U.S. Code.

CJS Bankruptcy § 11, Federal Rules of Bankruptcy Procedure.

CJS Bankruptcy § 138, Rules of Practice and Procedure.

CJS Bankruptcy § 1153, In Small Business Cases.

BANKRUPTCY RULES

Amendments received to May 10, 2012

Part		Rule
I.	Commencement of Case: Proceedings Relating to Petition and Order for Relief	1002
II.	Officers and Administration; Notices; Meetings; Examinations; Elections; Attorneys and Accountants	2001
III.	Claims and Distribution to Creditors and Equity Interest Holders; Plans	3001
IV.	The Debtor: Duties and Benefits	4001
V.	Bankruptcy Courts and Clerks	5001
VI.	Collection and Liquidation of the Estate	6001
VII.	Adversary Proceedings	7001
VIII.	Appeals to District Court or Bankruptcy Appellate Panel	8001
IX.	General Provisions	9001
X.	United States Trustees [Abrogated]	X–1001

Rule 1001. Scope of Rules and Forms; Short Title

The Bankruptcy Rules and Forms govern procedure in cases under title 11 of the United States Code. The rules shall be cited as the Federal Rules of Bankruptcy Procedure and the forms as the Official Bankruptcy Forms. These rules shall be construed to secure the just, speedy, and inexpensive determination of every case and proceeding.

(As amended Mar. 30, 1987, eff. Aug. 1, 1987; Apr. 30, 1991, eff. Aug. 1, 1991.)

ADVISORY COMMITTEE NOTES

Section 247 of Public Law 95–598, 92 Stat. 2549 amended 28 U.S.C. § 2075 by omitting the last sentence. The effect of the amendment is to require that procedural rules promulgated pursuant to 28 U.S.C. § 2075 be consistent with the bankruptcy statute, both titles 11 and 28 U.S.C. Thus, although Rule 1001 sets forth the scope of the bankruptcy rules and forms, any procedural matters contained in title 11 or 28 U.S.C. with respect to cases filed under 11 U.S.C. would control. See 1 Collier, Bankruptcy ¶3.04[2][c] (15th ed. 1980).

28 U.S.C. § 151 establishes a United States Bankruptcy Court in each district as an adjunct to the district court. This provision does not, however, become effective until April 1, 1984. Public Law 95–598, § 402(b). From October 1, 1979 through March 31, 1984, the courts of bankruptcy as defined in § 1(10) of the Bankruptcy Act [former § 1(10) of this title], and created in § 2a of that Act [former § 11(a) of this title], continue to be the courts of bankruptcy. Public Law 95–598, § 404(a). From their effective date these rules and forms are to be applicable in cases filed under chapters 7, 9, 11 and 13 of title 11 regardless of whether the court is established by the Bankruptcy Act or by 28 U.S.C. § 151. Rule 9001 contains a broad and general definition of "bankruptcy court," "court" and "United States Bankruptcy Court" for this purpose.

"Bankruptcy Code" or "Code" as used in these rules means title 11 of the United States Code, the codification of the bankruptcy law. Public Law 95–598, § 101. See Rule 9001.

"Bankruptcy Act" as used in the notes to these rules means the Bankruptcy Act of 1898 as amended which was repealed by § 401(a) of Public Law 95–598.

These rules apply to all cases filed under the Code except as otherwise specifically stated.

The final sentence of the rule is derived from former Bankruptcy Rule 903. The objective of "expeditious and economical administration" of cases under the Code has frequently been recognized by the courts to be "a chief purpose of the bankruptcy laws." See Katchen v. Landy, 382 U.S. 323, 328 (1966); Bailey v. Glover, 88 U.S. (21 Wall.) 342, 346–47 (1874); Ex parte Christy, 44 U.S. (3 How.) 292, 312–14, 320–22 (1845). The rule also incorporates the wholesome mandate of the last sentence of Rule 1 of the Federal Rules of Civil Procedure. 2 Moore, Federal Practice ¶1.13 (2d ed. 1980); 4 Wright & Miller, Federal Practice and Procedure—Civil § 1029 (1969).

1987 Amendments

Title I of the Bankruptcy Amendments and Federal Judgeship Act of 1984, Pub.L. No. 98–353, 98 Stat. 333 (hereinafter the 1984 amendments), created a new bankruptcy judicial system in which the role of the district court was substantially increased. 28 U.S.C. § 1334 confers on the United States district courts original and exclusive jurisdiction over all cases under title 11 of the United States Code and original but not exclusive jurisdiction over civil proceedings arising under title 11 and civil proceedings arising in or related to a case under title 11.

Pursuant to 28 U.S.C. § 157(a) the district court may but need not refer cases and proceedings within the district court's jurisdiction to the bankruptcy judges for the district. Judgments or orders of the bankruptcy judges entered pursuant to 28 U.S.C. § 157(b)(1) and (c)(2) are subject to appellate review by the district courts or bankruptcy appellate panels under 28 U.S.C. § 158(a).

Rule 81(a)(1) F.R.Civ.P. provides that the civil rules do not apply to proceedings in bankruptcy, except as they may be made applicable by rules promulgated by the Supreme Court, e.g., Part VII of these rules. This amended Bankruptcy Rule 1001 makes the Bankruptcy Rules applicable to cases and proceedings under title 11, whether before the district judges or the bankruptcy judges of the district.

1991 Amendments

The citation to these rules is amended to conform to the citation form of the Federal Rules of Civil Procedure, Federal Rules of Appellate Procedure, and Federal Rules of Criminal Procedure.

CROSS REFERENCES

Promulgation of bankruptcy rules by Supreme Court, see 28 USCA § 2075.

Scope of rules, see Federal Rules of Appellate Procedure Rule 1, 28 USCA.

Applicability of rules, see Fed.Rules Civ.Proc. Rule 81, 28 USCA.

Scope of rules, see Fed.Rules Civ.Proc. Rule 1, 28 USCA.

Applicability of rules, see Fed.Rules Evid. Rule 1101, 28 USCA.

Scope of rules, see Fed.Rules Evid. Rule 101, 28 USCA.

LIBRARY REFERENCES

American Digest System

Bankruptcy ⟸2129.

Key Number System Topic No. 51.

Corpus Juris Secundum

CJS Bankruptcy § 17, Official Forms.

CJS Bankruptcy § 138, Rules of Practice and Procedure.

PART I—COMMENCEMENT OF CASE: PROCEEDINGS RELATING TO PETITION AND ORDER FOR RELIEF

Rule
1002. Commencement of Case.
1003. Involuntary Petition.
1004. Involuntary Petition Against a Partnership.
1004.1. Petition for an Infant or Incompetent Person.
1004.2. Petition in Chapter 15 Cases.
1005. Caption of Petition.
1006. Filing Fee.
1007. Lists, Schedules, Statements, and Other Documents; Time Limits.
1008. Verification of Petitions and Accompanying Papers.
1009. Amendments of Voluntary Petitions, Lists, Schedules and Statements.
1010. Service of Involuntary Petition and Summons; Petition for Recognition of a Foreign Nonmain Proceeding.
1011. Responsive Pleading or Motion in Involuntary and Cross–Border Cases.
1012. [Abrogated Mar. 30, 1987, eff. Aug. 1, 1987].
1013. Hearing and Disposition of Petition in Involuntary Cases.
1014. Dismissal and Change of Venue.
1015. Consolidation or Joint Administration of Cases Pending in Same Court.
1016. Death or Incompetency of Debtor.
1017. Dismissal or Conversion of Case; Suspension.
1018. Contested Involuntary Petitions; Contested Petitions Commencing Chapter 15 Cases; Proceedings to Vacate Order for Relief; Applicability of Rules in Part VII Governing Adversary Proceedings.
1019. Conversion of a Chapter 11 Reorganization Case, Chapter 12 Family Farmer's Debt Adjustment Case, or Chapter 13 Individual's Debt Adjustment Case to a Chapter 7 Liquidation Case.
1020. Small Business Chapter 11 Reorganization Case.
1021. Health Care Business Case.

Rule 1002. Commencement of Case

(a) Petition

A petition commencing a case under the Code shall be filed with the clerk.

(b) Transmission to United States trustee

The clerk shall forthwith transmit to the United States trustee a copy of the petition filed pursuant to subdivision (a) of this rule.

(As amended Mar. 30, 1987, eff. Aug. 1, 1987; Apr. 30, 1991, eff. Aug. 1, 1991.)

ADVISORY COMMITTEE NOTES

Under §§ 301–303 of the Code, a voluntary or involuntary case is commenced by filing a petition with the bankruptcy court. The voluntary petition may request relief under chapter 7, 9, 11, or 13 whereas an involuntary petition may be filed under only chapter 7 or 11. Section 109 of the Code specifies the types of debtors for whom the different forms of relief are available and § 303(a) indicates the persons against whom involuntary petitions may be filed.

The rule in subdivision (a) is in harmony with the Code in that it requires the filing to be with the bankruptcy court.

The number of copies of the petition to be filed is specified in this rule but a local rule may require additional copies. This rule provides for filing sufficient copies for the court's files and for the trustee in a chapter 7 or 13 case.

Official Form No. 1 may be used to seek relief voluntarily under any of the chapters. Only the original need be signed and verified, but the copies must be conformed to the original. See Rules 1008 and 9011(c). As provided in § 362(a) of the Code, the filing of a petition acts as a stay of certain acts and proceedings against the debtor, property of the debtor, and property of the estate.

1987 Amendments

Rules 1002(a), governing a voluntary petition, 1003(a), governing an involuntary petition, and 1003(e), governing a petition in a case ancillary to a foreign proceedings, are combined into this Rule 1002. If a bankruptcy clerk has been appointed for the district, the petition is filed with the bankruptcy clerk. Otherwise, the petition is filed with the clerk of the district court.

The elimination of the reference to the Official Forms of the petition is not intended to change the practice. Rule 9009 provides that the Official Forms "shall be observed and used" in cases and proceedings under the Code.

Subdivision (b) which provided for the distribution of copies of the petition to agencies of the United States has been deleted. Some of these agencies no longer wish to receive copies of the petition, while others not included in subdivision (b) have now requested copies. The Director of the Administrative Office will determine on an ongoing basis which government agencies will be provided a copy of the petition.

The number of copies of a petition that must be filed is a matter for local rule.

1991 Amendments

Subdivision (b) is derived from Rule X–1002(a). The duties of the United States trustee pursuant to the Code and 28 U.S.C. § 586(a) require that the United States trustee be apprised of the commencement of every case under chapters 7, 11, 12 and 13 and this is most easily accomplished by providing that office with a copy of the petition. Although 28 U.S.C. § 586(a) does not give the United States trustee an administrative role in chapter 9 cases, § 1102 of the Code requires the United States trustee to appoint committees and that section is applicable in chapter 9 cases pursuant to § 901(a). It is therefore appropriate that the United States trustee receive a copy of every chapter 9 petition.

Notwithstanding subdivision (b), pursuant to Rule 5005(b)(3), the clerk is not required to transmit a copy of the petition to the United States trustee if the United States trustee requests that it not be transmitted. Many rules require the clerk to transmit a certain document to the United

States trustee, but Rule 5005(b)(3) relieves the clerk of that duty under this or any other rule if the United States trustee requests that such document not be transmitted.

CROSS REFERENCES

Commencement of voluntary cases, see 11 USCA § 301.

Debtors for whom relief available, see 11 USCA § 109.

Joint cases, see 11 USCA § 302.

Number of copies—

　　Involuntary petition, see Fed.Rules Bankr.Proc. Rule 1003, 11 USCA.

　　Schedules, statements, and lists, see Fed.Rules Bankr. Proc. Rule 1007, 11 USCA.

Signing and verification of petitions, see Fed.Rules Bankr. Proc. Rules 1008 and 9011, 11 USCA.

Stay of acts and proceedings against debtor and estate property, see 11 USCA § 362.

LIBRARY REFERENCES

American Digest System

Bankruptcy ⟐2202, 2251, 2257, 2281, 2311, 3030.6 to 3030.12.

Key Number System Topic No. 51.

Rule 1003.　Involuntary Petition

(a) Transferor or transferee of claim

A transferor or transferee of a claim shall annex to the original and each copy of the petition a copy of all documents evidencing the transfer, whether transferred unconditionally, for security, or otherwise, and a signed statement that the claim was not transferred for the purpose of commencing the case and setting forth the consideration for and terms of the transfer. An entity that has transferred or acquired a claim for the purpose of commencing a case for liquidation under chapter 7 or for reorganization under chapter 11 shall not be a qualified petitioner.

(b) Joinder of petitioners after filing

If the answer to an involuntary petition filed by fewer than three creditors avers the existence of 12 or more creditors, the debtor shall file with the answer a list of all creditors with their addresses, a brief statement of the nature of their claims, and the amounts thereof. If it appears that there are 12 or more creditors as provided in § 303(b) of the Code, the court shall afford a reasonable opportunity for other creditors to join in the petition before a hearing is held thereon.

(As amended Mar. 30, 1987, eff. Aug. 1, 1987.)

ADVISORY COMMITTEE NOTES

Subdivision (a). Official Form No. 11 (Involuntary Case: Creditors' Petition), is prescribed for use by petitioning creditors to have a debtor's assets liquidated under chapter 7 of the Code or the business reorganized under chapter 11. It contains the required allegations as specified in § 303(b) of the Code. Official Form 12 is prescribed for use by fewer

than all the general partners to obtain relief for the partnership as governed by § 303(b)(3) of the Code and Rule 1004(b).

Although the number of copies to be filed is specified in Rule 1002, a local rule may require additional copies.

Only the original need be signed and verified, but the copies must be conformed to the original. See Rules 1008 and 9011(c). The petition must be filed with the bankruptcy court. This provision implements § 303(b) which provides that an involuntary case is commenced by filing the petition with the court.

As provided in § 362 of the Code, the filing of the petition acts as a stay of certain acts and proceedings against the debtor, the debtor's property and property of the estate.

Subdivision (c) retains the explicitness of former Bankruptcy Rule 104(d) that a transfer of a claim for the purpose of commencing a case under the Code is a ground for disqualification of a party to the transfer as a petitioner.

Section 303(b) "is not intended to overrule Bankruptcy Rule 104(d), which places certain restrictions on the transfer of claims for the purpose of commencing an involuntary case." House Report No. 95–595, 95th Cong., 1st Sess. (1977) 322; Senate Report No. 95–989, 95th Cong., 2d Sess. (1978) 33.

The subdivision requires disclosure of any transfer of the petitioner's claim as well as a transfer to the petitioner and applies to transfers for security as well as unconditional transfers. Cf. In re 69th & Crandon Bldg. Corp., 97 F.2d 392, 395 (7th Cir.), cert. denied, 305 U.S. 629 (1938), recognizing the right of a creditor to sign a bankruptcy petition notwithstanding a prior assignment of his claim for the purpose of security. This rule does not, however, qualify the requirement of § 303(b)(1) that a petitioning creditor must have a claim not contingent as to liability.

Subdivision (d). Section 303(c) of the Code permits a creditor to join in the petition at any time before the case is dismissed or relief is ordered. While this rule does not require the court to give all creditors notice of the petition, the list of creditors filed by the debtor affords a petitioner the information needed to enable him to give notice for the purpose of obtaining the co-petitioners required to make the petition sufficient. After a reasonable opportunity has been afforded other creditors to join in an involuntary petition, the hearing on the petition should be held without further delay.

Subdivision (e). This subdivision implements § 304. A petition for relief under § 304 may only be filed by a foreign representative who is defined in § 101(20) generally as a representative of an estate in a foreign proceeding. The term "foreign proceeding" is defined in § 101(19).

Section 304(b) permits a petition filed thereunder to be contested by a party in interest. Subdivision (e)(2) therefore requires that the summons and petition be served on any person against whom the relief permitted by § 304(b) is sought as well as on any other party the court may direct.

The rules applicable to the procedure when an involuntary petition is filed are made applicable generally when a case ancillary to a foreign proceeding is commenced. These rules include Rule 1010 with respect to issuance and service of a summons, Rule 1011 concerning responsive pleadings and motions, and Rule 1018 which makes various rules in Part VII applicable in proceedings on contested petitions.

The venue for a case ancillary to a foreign proceeding is provided in 28 U.S.C. § 1474.

1987 Amendments

The subject matter of subdivisions (a), (b), and (e) has been incorporated in Rules 1002, 1010, 1011, and 1018.

CROSS REFERENCES

Case ancillary to foreign proceeding—

Commencement of and contested petitions, see 11 USCA § 304.

Foreign proceeding and foreign representative defined, see 11 USCA § 101.

Debtors for whom relief available, see 11 USCA § 109.

Number of copies—

Voluntary petition, see Fed.Rules Bankr.Proc. Rule 1002, 11 USCA.

Requisite allegations and joinder of parties, see 11 USCA § 303.

Signing and verification of petitions, see Fed.Rules Bankr. Proc. Rules 1008 and 9011, 11 USCA.

Stay of acts and proceedings against debtor and estate property, see 11 USCA § 362.

LIBRARY REFERENCES

American Digest System

Bankruptcy ⬤⇒2202, 2283.1 to 2289.

Key Number System Topic No. 51.

Corpus Juris Secundum

CJS Bankruptcy § 375, Transferee of Claim.

CJS Bankruptcy § 376, Joinder of Petitioners.

Rule 1004. Involuntary Petition Against a Partnership

After filing of an involuntary petition under § 303(b)(3) of the Code, (1) the petitioning partners or other petitioners shall promptly send to or serve on each general partner who is not a petitioner a copy of the petition; and (2) the clerk shall promptly issue a summons for service on each general partner who is not a petitioner. Rule 1010 applies to the form and service of the summons.

(As amended Apr. 29, 2002, eff. Dec. 1, 2002.)

ADVISORY COMMITTEE NOTES

This rule is adapted from former Bankruptcy Rule 105 and complements §§ 301 and 303(b)(3) of the Code.

Subdivision (a) specifies that while all general partners must consent to the filing of a voluntary petition, it is not necessary that they all execute the petition. It may be executed and filed on behalf of the partnership by fewer than all.

Subdivision (b) implements § 303(b)(3) of the Code which provides that an involuntary petition may be filed by fewer than all the general partners or, when all the general partners are debtors, by a general partner, trustee of the partner or creditors of the partnership. Rule 1010, which governs service of a petition and summons in an involuntary case, specifies the time and mode of service on the partnership. When a petition is filed against a partnership under § 303(b)(3), this rule requires an additional service on the nonfiling general partners. It is the purpose of this subdivision to protect the interests of the nonpetitioning partners and the partnership.

2002 Amendments

Section 303(b)(3)(A) of the Code provides that fewer than all of the general partners in a partnership may commence an involuntary case against the partnership. There is no counterpart provision in the Code setting out the manner in which a partnership commences a voluntary case. The Supreme Court has held in the corporate context that applicable nonbankruptcy law determines whether authority exists for a particular debtor to commence a bankruptcy case. *See Price v. Gurney*, 324 U.S. 100 (1945). The lower courts have followed this rule in the partnership context as well. *See, e.g., Jolly v. Pittore*, 170 B.R. 793 (S.D.N.Y. 1994); *Union Planters National Bank v. Hunters Horn Associates*, 158 B.R. 729 (Bankr. M.D. Tenn. 1993); *In re Channel 64 Joint Venture*, 61 B.R. 255 (Bankr. S.D. Oh. 1986). Rule 1004(a) could be construed as requiring the consent of all of the general partners to the filing of a voluntary petition, even if fewer than all of the general partners would have the authority under applicable nonbankruptcy law to commence a bankruptcy case for the partnership. Since this is a matter of substantive law beyond the scope of these rules, Rule 1004(a) is deleted as is the designation of subdivision (b).

The rule is retitled to reflect that it applies only to involuntary petitions filed against partnerships.

Changes Made After Publication and Comments. No changes since publication.

CROSS REFERENCES

Commencement of—

Involuntary cases, see 11 USCA § 303.

Voluntary cases, see 11 USCA § 301.

Contested petition by general partners, see Fed.Rules Bankr.Proc. Rule 1011, 11 USCA.

No change in status for purposes of state or local income tax law, see 11 USCA § 346.

Person defined to include partnership, see 11 USCA § 101.

LIBRARY REFERENCES

American Digest System

Bankruptcy ⬤⇒2227, 2281, 2290.1, 2202.

Key Number System Topic No. 51.

Corpus Juris Secundum

CJS Bankruptcy § 378, Service of Summons and Petition.

Rule 1004.1. Petition for an Infant or Incompetent Person

If an infant or incompetent person has a representative, including a general guardian, committee, conservator, or similar fiduciary, the representative may file a voluntary petition on behalf of the infant or incompetent person. An infant or incompetent person who does not have a duly appointed representative may file a voluntary petition by next friend or guardian ad litem. The court shall appoint a guardian ad litem for an infant or incompetent person who is a debtor and is not otherwise represented or shall make any other order to protect the infant or incompetent debtor.

(Added Apr. 29, 2002, eff. Dec. 1, 2002.)

ADVISORY COMMITTEE NOTES
2002 Adoption

This rule is derived from Rule 17(c) F.R. Civ. P. It does not address the commencement of a case filed on behalf of a missing person. *See, e.g., In re King*, 234 B.R. 515 (Bankr. D.N.M. 1999).

Changes Made After Publication and Comments. No changes were made.

LIBRARY REFERENCES
American Digest System

Bankruptcy ⚏2255.1.

Key Number System Topic No. 51.

Corpus Juris Secundum

CJS Bankruptcy § 338, Who May File on Individual Debtor's Behalf.

Rule 1004.2.   Petition in Chapter 15 Cases

(a) Designating Center of Main Interests

A petition for recognition of a foreign proceeding under chapter 15 of the Code shall state the country where the debtor has its center of main interests. The petition shall also identify each country in which a foreign proceeding by, regarding, or against the debtor is pending.

(b) Challenging Designation

The United States trustee or a party in interest may file a motion for a determination that the debtor's center of main interests is other than as stated in the petition for recognition commencing the chapter 15 case. Unless the court orders otherwise, the motion shall be filed no later than seven days before the date set for the hearing on the petition. The motion shall be transmitted to the United States trustee and served on the debtor, all persons or bodies authorized to administer foreign proceedings of the debtor, all entities against whom provisional relief is being sought under § 1519 of the Code, all parties to litigation pending in the United States in which the debtor was a party as of the time the petition was filed, and such other entities as the court may direct.

(Adopted Apr. 26, 2011, eff. Dec. 1, 2011.)

ADVISORY COMMITTEE NOTES
2011 Adoption

This rule is new. Subdivision (a) directs any entity that files a petition for recognition of a foreign proceeding under chapter 15 of the Code to state in the petition the center of the debtor's main interests. The petition must also list each country in which a foreign proceeding involving the debtor is pending. This information will assist the court and parties in interest in determining whether the foreign proceeding is a foreign main or nonmain proceeding.

Subdivision (b) sets a deadline of seven days before the date set for the hearing on the petition for recognition for filing a motion challenging the statement in the petition as to the country in which the debtor's center of main interests is located.

Rule 1005.   Caption of Petition

The caption of a petition commencing a case under the Code shall contain the name of the court, the title of the case, and the docket number. The title of the case shall include the following information about the debtor: name, employer identification number, last four digits of the social-security number or individual debtor's taxpayer-identification number, any other federal taxpayer-identification number, and all other names used within eight years before filing the petition. If the petition is not filed by the debtor, it shall include all names used by the debtor which are known to the petitioners.

(As amended Mar. 30, 1987, eff. Aug. 1, 1987; Mar. 27, 2003, eff. Dec. 1, 2003; Apr. 23, 2008, eff. Dec. 1, 2008.)

ADVISORY COMMITTEE NOTES

The title of the case should include all names used by the debtor, such as trade names, former married names and maiden name. See also Official Form No. 1 and the Advisory Committee Note to that Form. Additional names of the debtor are also required to appear in the caption of each notice to creditors. See Rule 2002(m).

2003 Amendments

The rule is amended to implement the Judicial Conference policy to limit the disclosure of a party's social security number and similar identifiers. Under the rule, as amended, only the last four digits of the debtor's social security number need be disclosed. Publication of the employer identification number does not present the same identity theft or privacy protection issues. Therefore, the caption must include the full employer identification number.

Debtors must submit with the petition a statement setting out their social security numbers. This enables the clerk to include the full social security number on the notice of the section 341 meeting of creditors, but the statement itself is not submitted in the case or maintained in the case file.

2008 Amendments

The rule is amended to require the disclosure of all names used by the debtor in the past eight years. Section 727(a)(8) was amended in 2005 to extend the time between chapter 7 discharges from six to eight years, and the rule is amended to implement that change. The rule also is amended to require the disclosure of the last four digits of an individual debtor's taxpayer-identification number. This truncation of the number applies only to individual debtors. This is consistent with the requirements of Rule 9037.

CROSS REFERENCES

Conformance of captions of creditor notices with this rule, see Fed.Rules Bankr.Proc. Rule 2002, 11 USCA.

General requirements of form for petition, see Fed.Rules Bankr.Proc. Rule 9004, 11 USCA.

LIBRARY REFERENCES

American Digest System

Bankruptcy ⟝2257, 2290.1, 2311.

Key Number System Topic No. 51.

Corpus Juris Secundum

CJS Bankruptcy § 285, Captions.

CJS Bankruptcy § 336, Contents, Signature, and Verification.

Rule 1006.   Filing Fee

(a) General requirement

Every petition shall be accompanied by the filing fee except as provided in subdivisions (b) and (c) of this rule. For the purpose of this rule, "filing fee" means the filing fee prescribed by 28 U.S.C. § 1930(a)(1)–(a)(5) and any other fee prescribed by the Judicial Conference of the United States under 28 U.S.C. § 1930(b) that is payable to the clerk upon the commencement of a case under the Code.

(b) Payment of filing fee in installments

(1) Application to pay filing fee in installments

A voluntary petition by an individual shall be accepted for filing if accompanied by the debtor's signed application, prepared as prescribed by the appropriate Official Form, stating that the debtor is unable to pay the filing fee except in installments.

(2) Action on application

Prior to the meeting of creditors, the court may order the filing fee paid to the clerk or grant leave to pay in installments and fix the number, amount and dates of payment. The number of installments shall not exceed four, and the final installment shall be payable not later than 120 days after filing the petition. For cause shown, the court may extend the time of any installment, provided the last installment is paid not later than 180 days after filing the petition.

(3) Postponement of attorney's fees

All installments of the filing fee must be paid in full before the debtor or chapter 13 trustee may make further payments to an attorney or any other person who renders services to the debtor in connection with the case.

(c) Waiver of filing fee

A voluntary chapter 7 petition filed by an individual shall be accepted for filing if accompanied by the debtor's application requesting a waiver under 28 U.S.C. § 1930(f), prepared as prescribed by the appropriate Official Form.

(As amended Mar. 30, 1987, eff. Aug. 1, 1987; Apr. 23, 1996, eff. Dec. 1, 1996; Apr. 23, 2008, eff. Dec. 1, 2008.)

ADVISORY COMMITTEE NOTES

1983 Enactments

28 U.S.C. § 1930 specifies the filing fees for petitions under chapters 7, 9, 11 and 13 of the Code. It also permits the payment in installments by individual debtors.

Subdivision (b) is adapted from former Bankruptcy Rule 107. The administrative cost of installments in excess of four is disproportionate to the benefits conferred. Prolonging the period beyond 180 days after the commencement of the case causes undesirable delays in administration. Paragraph (2) accordingly continues the imposition of a maximum of four on the number of installments and retains the maximum period of installment payments allowable on an original application at 120 days. Only in extraordinary cases should it be necessary to give an applicant an extension beyond the four months. The requirement of paragraph (3) that filing fees be paid in full before the debtor may pay an attorney for services in connection with the case codifies the rule declared in In re Latham, 271 Fed. 538 (N.D.N.Y.1921), and In re Darr, 232 Fed. 415 (N.D.Cal.1916).

1987 Amendments

Subdivision (b)(3) is expanded to prohibit payments by the debtor or the chapter 13 trustee not only to attorneys but to any person who renders services to the debtor in connection with the case.

1996 Amendments

The Judicial Conference prescribes miscellaneous fees pursuant to 28 U.S.C. § 1930(b). In 1992, a $30 miscellaneous administrative fee was prescribed for all chapter 7 and chapter 13 cases. The Judicial Conference fee schedule was amended in 1993 to provide that an individual debtor may pay this fee in installments.

Subdivision (a) of this rule is amended to clarify that every petition must be accompanied by any fee prescribed under 28 U.S.C. § 1930(b) that is required to be paid when a petition is filed, as well as the filing fee prescribed by 28 U.S.C. § 1930(a). By defining "filing fee" to include Judicial Conference fees, the procedures set forth in subdivision (b) for paying the filing fee in installments will also apply with respect to any Judicial Conference fee required to be paid at the commencement of the case.

GAP Report on Rule 1006. No changes since publication, except for a stylistic change in subdivision (a).

2008 Amendments

Subdivision (a) is amended to include a reference to new subdivision (c), which deals with fee waivers under 28 U.S.C. § 1930(f), which was added in 2005.

Subdivision (b)(1) is amended to delete the sentence requiring a disclosure that the debtor has not paid an attorney or other person in connection with the case. Inability to pay the filing fee in installments is one of the requirements for a fee waiver under the 2005 revisions to 28 U.S.C. § 1930(f). If the attorney payment prohibition were retained, payment of an attorney's fee would render many debtors ineligible for installment payments and thus enhance their eligibility for the fee waiver. The deletion of this prohibition from the rule, which was not statutorily required, ensures that debtors who have the financial ability to pay the fee in installments will do so rather than request a waiver.

Subdivision (b)(3) is amended in conformance with the changes to subdivision (b)(1) to reflect the 2005 amendments. The change is meant to clarify that subdivision (b)(3) refers to payments made after the debtor has filed the bankruptcy case and after the debtor has received permission to pay the fee in installments. Otherwise, the subdivision may conflict with the intent and effect of the amendments to subdivision (b)(1).

CROSS REFERENCES

District court; filing and miscellaneous fees; rules of court, see 28 USCA § 1914.

Enlargement of time for payment of filing fee installments permitted as limited under this rule, see Fed.Rules Bankr. Proc. Rule 9006, 11 USCA.

Specific amount of fee, see 28 USCA § 1930.

LIBRARY REFERENCES

American Digest System

Bankruptcy ⬚2128, 2190, 2261.
Key Number System Topic No. 51.

Corpus Juris Secundum

CJS Bankruptcy § 288, Applications.
CJS Bankruptcy § 308, Enlargement.
CJS Bankruptcy § 341, Fee for Filing Petition.
CJS Bankruptcy § 342, Fee for Filing Petition--Waiver.

Rule 1007. Lists, Schedules, Statements, and Other Documents; Time Limits

(a) Corporate ownership statement, list of creditors and equity security holders, and other lists

(1) Voluntary case

In a voluntary case, the debtor shall file with the petition a list containing the name and address of each entity included or to be included on Schedules D, E, F, G, and H as prescribed by the Official Forms. If the debtor is a corporation, other than a governmental unit, the debtor shall file with the petition a corporate ownership statement containing the information described in Rule 7007.1. The debtor shall file a supplemental statement promptly upon any change in circumstances that renders the corporate ownership statement inaccurate.

(2) Involuntary case

In an involuntary case, the debtor shall file, within seven days after entry of the order for relief, a list containing the name and address of each entity included or to be included on Schedules D, E, F, G, and H as prescribed by the Official Forms.

(3) Equity security holders

In a chapter 11 reorganization case, unless the court orders otherwise, the debtor shall file within 14 days after entry of the order for relief a list of the debtor's equity security holders of each class showing the number and kind of interests registered in the name of each holder, and the last known address or place of business of each holder.

(4) Chapter 15 case

In addition to the documents required under § 1515 of the Code, a foreign representative filing a petition for recognition under chapter 15 shall file with the petition: (A) a corporate ownership statement containing the information described in Rule 7007.1; and (B) unless the court orders otherwise, a list containing the names and addresses of all persons or bodies authorized to administer foreign proceedings of the debtor, all parties to litigation pending in the United States in which the debtor is a party at the time of the filing of the petition, and all entities against whom provisional relief is being sought under § 1519 of the Code.

(5) Extension of time

Any extension of time for the filing of the lists required by this subdivision may be granted only on motion for cause shown and on notice to the United States trustee and to any trustee, committee elected under § 705 or appointed under § 1102 of the Code, or other party as the court may direct.

(b) Schedules, statements, and other documents required

(1) Except in a chapter 9 municipality case, the debtor, unless the court orders otherwise, shall file the following schedules, statements, and other documents, prepared as prescribed by the appropriate Official Forms, if any:

    (A) schedules of assets and liabilities;

    (B) a schedule of current income and expenditures;

    (C) a schedule of executory contracts and unexpired leases;

    (D) a statement of financial affairs;

    (E) copies of all payment advices or other evidence of payment, if any, received by the debtor from an employer within 60 days before the filing of the petition, with redaction of all but the last four digits of the debtor's social-security number or individual taxpayer-identification number; and

    (F) a record of any interest that the debtor has in an account or program of the type specified in § 521(c) of the Code.

(2) An individual debtor in a chapter 7 case shall file a statement of intention as required by § 521(a) of the Code, prepared as prescribed by the appropriate Official Form. A copy of the statement of intention shall be served on the trustee and the creditors named in the statement on or before the filing of the statement.

(3) Unless the United States trustee has determined that the credit counseling requirement of § 109(h) does not apply in the district, an individual debtor must file a statement of compliance with the credit counseling requirement, prepared as prescribed by the appropriate Official Form which must include one of the following:

(**A**) an attached certificate and debt repayment plan, if any, required by § 521(b);

(**B**) a statement that the debtor has received the credit counseling briefing required by § 109(h)(1) but does not have the certificate required by § 521(b);

(**C**) a certification under § 109(h)(3); or

(**D**) a request for a determination by the court under § 109(h)(4).

(**4**) Unless § 707(b)(2)(D) applies, an individual debtor in a chapter 7 case shall file a statement of current monthly income prepared as prescribed by the appropriate Official Form, and, if the current monthly income exceeds the median family income for the applicable state and household size, the information, including calculations, required by § 707(b), prepared as prescribed by the appropriate Official Form.

(**5**) An individual debtor in a chapter 11 case shall file a statement of current monthly income, prepared as prescribed by the appropriate Official Form.

(**6**) A debtor in a chapter 13 case shall file a statement of current monthly income, prepared as prescribed by the appropriate Official Form, and, if the current monthly income exceeds the median family income for the applicable state and household size, a calculation of disposable income made in accordance with § 1325(b)(3), prepared as prescribed by the appropriate Official Form.

(**7**) An individual debtor in a chapter 7 or chapter 13 case shall file a statement of completion of a course concerning personal financial management, prepared as prescribed by the appropriate Official Form. An individual debtor shall file the statement in a chapter 11 case in which § 1141(d)(3) applies.

(**8**) If an individual debtor in a chapter 11, 12, or 13 case has claimed an exemption under § 522(b)(3)(A) in property of the kind described in § 522(p)(1) with a value in excess of the amount set out in § 522(q)(1), the debtor shall file a statement as to whether there is any proceeding pending in which the debtor may be found guilty of a felony of a kind described in § 522(q)(1)(A) or found liable for a debt of the kind described in § 522(q)(1)(B).

[Text of subdivision (c) effective until December 1, 2012, absent contrary Congressional action.]

(**c**) **Time limits**

In a voluntary case, the schedules, statements, and other documents required by subdivision (b)(1), (4), (5), and (6) shall be filed with the petition or within 14 days thereafter, except as otherwise provided in subdivisions (d), (e), (f), and (h) of this rule. In an involuntary case, the list in subdivision (a)(2), and the schedules,

statements, and other documents required by subdivision (b)(1) shall be filed by the debtor within 14 days of the entry of the order for relief. In a voluntary case, the documents required by paragraphs (A), (C), and (D) of subdivision (b)(3) shall be filed with the petition. Unless the court orders otherwise, a debtor who has filed a statement under subdivision (b)(3)(B), shall file the documents required by subdivision (b)(3)(A) within 14 days of the order for relief. In a chapter 7 case, the debtor shall file the statement required by subdivision (b)(7) within 60 days after the first date set for the meeting of creditors under § 341 of the Code, and in a chapter 11 or 13 case no later than the date when the last payment was made by the debtor as required by the plan or the filing of a motion for a discharge under § 1141(d)(5)(B) or § 1328(b) of the Code. The court may, at any time and in its discretion, enlarge the time to file the statement required by subdivision (b)(7). The debtor shall file the statement required by subdivision (b)(8) no earlier than the date of the last payment made under the plan or the date of the filing of a motion for a discharge under §§ 1141(d)(5)(B),[1] 1228(b), or 1328(b) of the Code. Lists, schedules, statements, and other documents filed prior to the conversion of a case to another chapter shall be deemed filed in the converted case unless the court directs otherwise. Except as provided in § 1116(3), any extension of time to file schedules, statements, and other documents required under this rule may be granted only on motion for cause shown and on notice to the United States trustee, any committee elected under § 705 or appointed under § 1102 of the Code, trustee, examiner, or other party as the court may direct. Notice of an extension shall be given to the United States trustee and to any committee, trustee, or other party as the court may direct.

[Text of subdivision (c) effective December 1, 2012, absent contrary Congressional action.]

(**c**) **Time limits**

In a voluntary case, the schedules, statements, and other documents required by subdivision (b)(1), (4), (5), and (6) shall be filed with the petition or within 14 days thereafter, except as otherwise provided in subdivisions (d), (e), (f), and (h) of this rule. In an involuntary case, the schedules, statements, and other documents required by subdivision (b)(1) shall be filed by the debtor within 14 days after the entry of the order for relief. In a voluntary case, the documents required by paragraphs (A), (C), and (D) of subdivision (b)(3) shall be filed with the petition. Unless the court orders otherwise, a debtor who has filed a statement under subdivision (b)(3)(B), shall file the documents required by subdivision (b)(3)(A) within 14 days of the order for relief. In a chapter 7 case, the debtor shall file the statement required by subdivision (b)(7) within 60 days after the first date set for the meeting of creditors under § 341 of the Code, and in a chapter 11 or 13 case no later than the date when the last payment was

Rule 1007

made by the debtor as required by the plan or the filing of a motion for a discharge under § 1141(d)(5)(B) or § 1328(b) of the Code. The court may, at any time and in its discretion, enlarge the time to file the statement required by subdivision (b)(7). The debtor shall file the statement required by subdivision (b)(8) no earlier than the date of the last payment made under the plan or the date of the filing of a motion for a discharge under §§ 1141(d)(5)(B), [1] 1228(b), or 1328(b) of the Code. Lists, schedules, statements, and other documents filed prior to the conversion of a case to another chapter shall be deemed filed in the converted case unless the court directs otherwise. Except as provided in § 1116(3), any extension of time to file schedules, statements, and other documents required under this rule may be granted only on motion for cause shown and on notice to the United States trustee, any committee elected under § 705 or appointed under § 1102 of the Code, trustee, examiner, or other party as the court may direct. Notice of an extension shall be given to the United States trustee and to any committee, trustee, or other party as the court may direct.

(d) List of 20 largest creditors in chapter 9 municipality case or chapter 11 reorganization case

In addition to the list required by subdivision (a) of this rule, a debtor in a chapter 9 municipality case or a debtor in a voluntary chapter 11 reorganization case shall file with the petition a list containing the name, address and claim of the creditors that hold the 20 largest unsecured claims, excluding insiders, as prescribed by the appropriate Official Form. In an involuntary chapter 11 reorganization case, such list shall be filed by the debtor within 2 days after entry of the order for relief under § 303(h) of the Code.

(e) List in chapter 9 municipality cases

The list required by subdivision (a) of this rule shall be filed by the debtor in a chapter 9 municipality case within such time as the court shall fix. If a proposed plan requires a revision of assessments so that the proportion of special assessments or special taxes to be assessed against some real property will be different from the proportion in effect at the date the petition is filed, the debtor shall also file a list showing the name and address of each known holder of title, legal or equitable, to real property adversely affected. On motion for cause shown, the court may modify the requirements of this subdivision and subdivision (a) of this rule.

(f) Statement of social security number

An individual debtor shall submit a verified statement that sets out the debtor's social security number, or states that the debtor does not have a social security number. In a voluntary case, the debtor shall submit the statement with the petition. In an involuntary case, the debtor shall submit the statement within 14 days after the entry of the order for relief.

(g) Partnership and partners

The general partners of a debtor partnership shall prepare and file the list required under subdivision (a), the schedules of the assets and liabilities, schedule of current income and expenditures, schedule of executory contracts and unexpired leases, and statement of financial affairs of the partnership. The court may order any general partner to file a statement of personal assets and liabilities within such time as the court may fix.

(h) Interests acquired or arising after petition

If, as provided by § 541(a)(5) of the Code, the debtor acquires or becomes entitled to acquire any interest in property, the debtor shall within 14 days after the information comes to the debtor's knowledge or within such further time the court may allow, file a supplemental schedule in the chapter 7 liquidation case, chapter 11 reorganization case, chapter 12 family farmer's debt adjustment case, or chapter 13 individual debt adjustment case. If any of the property required to be reported under this subdivision is claimed by the debtor as exempt, the debtor shall claim the exemptions in the supplemental schedule. The duty to file a supplemental schedule in accordance with this subdivision continues notwithstanding the closing of the case, except that the schedule need not be filed in a chapter 11, chapter 12, or chapter 13 case with respect to property acquired after entry of the order confirming a chapter 11 plan or discharging the debtor in a chapter 12 or chapter 13 case.

(i) Disclosure of list of security holders

After notice and hearing and for cause shown, the court may direct an entity other than the debtor or trustee to disclose any list of security holders of the debtor in its possession or under its control, indicating the name, address and security held by any of them. The entity possessing this list may be required either to produce the list or a true copy thereof, or permit inspection or copying, or otherwise disclose the information contained on the list.

(j) Impounding of lists

On motion of a party in interest and for cause shown the court may direct the impounding of the lists filed under this rule, and may refuse to permit inspection by any entity. The court may permit inspection or use of the lists, however, by any party in interest on terms prescribed by the court.

(k) Preparation of list, schedules, or statements on default of debtor

If a list, schedule, or statement, other than a statement of intention, is not prepared and filed as required by this rule, the court may order the trustee, a petitioning creditor, committee, or other party to prepare and file any of these papers within a time fixed by the court. The court may approve reimbursement of the cost incurred in complying with such an order as an administrative expense.

(*l*) Transmission to United States trustee

The clerk shall forthwith transmit to the United States trustee a copy of every list, schedule, and statement filed pursuant to subdivision (a)(1), (a)(2), (b), (d), or (h) of this rule.

(m) Infants and incompetent persons

If the debtor knows that a person on the list of creditors or schedules is an infant or incompetent person, the debtor also shall include the name, address, and legal relationship of any person upon whom process would be served in an adversary proceeding against the infant or incompetent person in accordance with Rule 7004(b)(2).

(As amended Mar. 30, 1987, eff. Aug. 1, 1987; Apr. 30, 1991, eff. Aug. 1, 1991; Apr. 23, 1996, eff. Dec. 1, 1996; Apr. 23, 2001, eff. Dec. 1, 2001; Mar. 27, 2003, eff. Dec. 1, 2003; Apr. 25, 2005, eff. Dec. 1, 2005; Apr. 23, 2008, eff. Dec. 1, 2008; Mar. 26, 2009, eff. Dec. 1, 2009; Apr. 28, 2010, eff. Dec. 1, 2010; Apr. 23, 2012, eff. Dec. 1, 2012, absent contrary Congressional action.)

1 So in original. Probably should be only one section symbol.

ADVISORY COMMITTEE NOTES

1983 Enactments

This rule is an adaptation of former Rules 108, 8–106, 10–108 and 11–11. As specified in the rule, it is applicable in all types of cases filed under the Code.

Subdivision (a) requires at least a list of creditors with their names and addresses to be filed with the petition. This list is needed for notice of the meeting of creditors (Rule 2002) and notice of the order for relief (§ 342 of the Code). The list will also serve to meet the requirements of § 521(1) of the Code. Subdivision (a) recognizes that it may be impossible to file the schedules required by § 521(1) and subdivision (b) of the rule at the time the petition is filed but in order for the case to proceed expeditiously and efficiently it is necessary that the clerk have the names and addresses of creditors. It should be noted that subdivision (d) of the rule requires a special list of the 20 largest unsecured creditors in chapter 9 and 11 cases. That list is for the purpose of selecting a committee of unsecured creditors.

Subdivision (b) is derived from former Rule 11–11 and conforms with § 521. This subdivision indicates the forms to be used. The court may dispense with the filing of schedules and the statement of affairs pursuant to § 521.

Subdivisions (c) and (f) specify the time periods for filing the papers required by the rule as well as the number of copies. The provisions dealing with an involuntary case are derived from former Bankruptcy Rule 108. Under the Code, a chapter 11 case may be commenced by an involuntary petition (§ 303(a)), whereas under the Act [former Title 11], a Chapter XI [former § 1101 et seq. of this title] case could have been commenced only by a voluntary petition. A motion for an extension of time to file the schedules and statements is

required to be made on notice to parties, as the court may direct, including a creditors' committee if one has been appointed under § 1102 of the Code and a trustee or examiner if one has been appointed pursuant to § 1104 of the Code. Although written notice is preferable, it is not required by the rule; in proper circumstances the notice may be by telephone or otherwise.

Subdivision (d) is new and requires that a list of the 20 largest unsecured creditors, excluding insiders as defined in § 101(25) of the Code, be filed with the petition. The court, pursuant to § 1102 of the Code, is required to appoint a committee of unsecured creditors as soon as practicable after the order for relief. That committee generally is to consist of the seven largest unsecured creditors who are willing to serve. The list should, as indicated on Official Form No. 9, specify the nature and amount of the claim. It is important for the court to be aware of the different types of claims existing in the case and this form should supply such information.

Subdivision (e) applies only in chapter 9 municipality cases. It gives greater discretion to the court to determine the time for filing a list of creditors and any other matter related to the list. A list of creditors must at some point be filed since one is required by § 924 of the Code. When the plan affects special assessments, the definitions in § 902(2) and (3) for "special tax payer" and "special tax payer affected by the plan" become relevant.

Subdivision (g) is derived from former Rules 108(c) and 11–11. Nondebtor general partners are liable to the partnership's trustee for any deficiency in the partnership's estate to pay creditors in full as provided by § 723 of the Code. Subdivision (g) authorizes the court to require a partner to file a statement of personal assets and liabilities to provide the trustee with the relevant information.

Subdivision (h) is derived from former Bankruptcy Rule 108(e) for chapter 7, 11 and 13 purposes. It implements the provisions in and language of § 541(a)(5) of the Code.

Subdivisions (i) and (j) are adapted from §§ 165 and 166 of the Act [former §§ 565 and 566 of this title] and former Rule 10–108(b) and (c) without change in substance. The term "party in interest" is not defined in the Code or the rules, but reference may be made to § 1109(b) of the Code. In the context of this subdivision, the term would include the debtor, the trustee, any indenture trustee, creditor, equity security holder or committee appointed pursuant to § 1102 of the Code.

Subdivision (k) is derived from former Rules 108(d) and 10–108(a).

1987 Amendments

Subdivisions (b), (c), and (g) are amended to provide for the filing of a schedule of current income and current expenditures and the individual debtor's statement of intention. These documents are required by the 1984 amendments to § 521 of the Code. Official Form No. 6A is prescribed for use by an individual debtor for filing a schedule of current income and current expenditures in a chapter 7 or chapter 11 case. Although a partnership or corporation is also required by § 521(1) to file a schedule of current income and current expenditures, no Official Form is prescribed therefor.

The time for filing the statement of intention is governed by § 521(2)(A). A copy of the statement of intention must be served on the trustee and the creditors named in the statement within the same time. The provisions of subdivision (c) governing the time for filing when a chapter 11 or chapter 13 case is converted to a chapter 7 case have been omitted from subdivision (c) as amended. Filing after conversion is now governed exclusively by Rule 1019.

Subdivision (f) has been abrogated. The number of copies of the documents required by this rule will be determined by local rule.

Subdivision (h) is amended to include a direct reference to § 541(a)(5).

Subdivision (k) provides that the court may not order an entity other than the debtor to prepare and file the statement of intention.

1991 Amendments

References to Official Form numbers and to the Chapter 13 Statement are deleted and subdivision (b) is amended in anticipation of future revision and renumbering of the Official Forms. The debtor in a chapter 12 or chapter 13 case shall file the list, schedules and statements required in subdivisions (a)(1), (b)(1), and (h). It is expected that the information currently provided in the Chapter 13 Statement will be included in the schedules and statements as revised not later than the effective date of these rule amendments.

Subdivisions (a)(4) and (c) are amended to provide the United States trustee with notice of any motion to extend the time for the filing of any lists, schedules, or statements. Such notice enables the United States trustee to take appropriate steps to avoid undue delay in the administration of the case. See 28 U.S.C. § 586(a)(3)(G). Subdivisions (a)(4) and (c) are amended further to provide notice to committees elected under § 705 or appointed pursuant to § 1102 of the Code. Committees of retired employees appointed pursuant to § 1114 are not included.

The additions of references to unexpired leases in subdivisions (b)(1) and (g) indicate that the schedule requires the inclusion of unexpired leases as well as other executory contracts.

The words "with the court" in subdivisions (b)(1), (e), and (g) are deleted as unnecessary. See Rules 5005(a) and 9001(3).

Subdivision (l), which is derived from Rule X–1002(a), provides the United States trustee with the information required to perform certain administrative duties such as the appointment of a committee of unsecured creditors. In a chapter 7 case, the United States trustee should be aware of the debtor's intention with respect to collateral that secures a consumer debt so that the United States trustee may monitor the progress of the case. Pursuant to § 307 of the Code, the United States trustee has standing to raise, appear and be heard on issues and the lists, schedules and statements contain information that, when provided to the United States trustee, enable that office to participate effectively in the case. The United States trustee has standing to move to dismiss a chapter 7 or 13 case for failure to file timely the list, schedules or statement required by § 521(l) of the Code. See §§ 707(a)(3) and 1307(c)(9). It is therefore necessary for the United States trustee to receive notice of any extension of time to file such documents. Upon request, the United States trustee also may receive from the trustee or debtor in possession a list of equity security holders.

1996 Amendments

Subdivision (c) is amended to provide that schedules and statements filed prior to the conversion of a case to another chapter shall be deemed filed in the converted case, whether or not the case was a chapter 7 case prior to conversion. This amendment is in recognition of the 1991 amendments to the Official Forms that abrogated the Chapter 13 Statement and made the same forms for schedules and statements applicable in all cases.

This subdivision also contains a technical correction. The phrase "superseded case" creates the erroneous impression that conversion of a case results in a new case that is distinct from the original case. The effect of conversion of a case is governed by § 348 of the Code.

GAP Report on Rule 1007(c). No changes since publication, except for stylistic changes.

2001 Amendments

Subdivision (m) is added to enable the person required to mail notices under Rule 2002 to mail them to the appropriate guardian or other representative when the debtor knows that a creditor or other person listed is an infant or incompetent person.

The proper mailing address of the representative is determined in accordance with Rule 7004(b)(2), which requires mailing to the person's dwelling house or usual place of abode or at the place where the person regularly conducts a business or profession.

CHANGES MADE AFTER PUBLICATION AND COMMENTS

No changes were made.

2003 Amendments

This rule is amended to require the debtor to file a corporate ownership statement setting out the information described in Rule 7007.1. Requiring debtors to file the statement provides the court with an opportunity to make judicial disqualification determinations at the outset of the case. This could reduce problems later in the case by preventing the initial assignment of the case to a judge who holds a financial interest in a parent company of the debtor or some other entity that holds a significant ownership interest in the debtor. Moreover, by including the disclosure statement filing requirement at the commencement of the case, the debtor does not have to make the same disclosure filing each time it is involved in an adversary proceeding throughout the case. The debtor also must file supplemental statements as changes in ownership might arise.

The rule is amended to add a requirement that a debtor submit a statement setting out the debtor's social security number. The addition is necessary because of the corresponding amendment to Rule 1005 which now provides that the caption of the petition includes only the final four digits of the debtor's social security number. The debtor submits the statement, but it is not filed, nor is it included in the case file. The statement provides the information necessary to include on the service copy of the notice required under Rule 2002(a)(1). It will also provide the information to facilitate the ability of creditors to search the court record by a search of a social security number already in the creditor's possession.

2005 Amendments

Notice to creditors and other parties in interest is essential to the operation of the bankruptcy system. Sending notice requires a convenient listing of the names and addresses of the entities to whom notice must be sent, and virtually all of the bankruptcy courts have adopted a local rule requiring the submission of a list of these entities with the petition and in a particular format. These lists are commonly called the "mailing matrix."

Given the universal adoption of these local rules, the need for such lists in all cases is apparent. Consequently, the rule is amended to require the debtor to submit such a list at the commencement of the case. This list may be amended when necessary. See Rule 1009(a).

The content of the list is described by reference to Schedules D through H of the Official Forms rather than by reference to creditors or persons holding claims. The cross reference to the Schedules as the source of the names for inclusion in the list ensures that persons such as codebtors or nondebtor parties to executory contracts and unexpired leases will receive appropriate notices in the case.

While this rule renders unnecessary, in part, local rules on the subject, this rule does not direct any particular format or form for the list to take. Local rules still may govern those particulars of the list.

Subdivision (c) is amended to reflect that subdivision (a)(1) no longer requires the debtor to file a schedule of liabilities with the petition in lieu of a list of creditors. The filing of the list is mandatory, and subdivision (b) of the rule requires the filing of schedules. Thus, subdivision (c) no longer needs to account for the possibility that the debtor can delay filing a schedule of liabilities when the petition is accompanied by a list of creditors. Subdivision (c) simply addresses the situation in which the debtor does not file schedules or statements with the petition, and the procedure for seeking an extension of time for filing.

Other changes are stylistic.

2008 Amendments

The title of this rule is expanded to refer to "documents" in conformity with the 2005 amendments to § 521 and related provisions of the Bankruptcy Code that include a wider range of documentary requirements.

Subdivision (a) is amended to require that any foreign representative filing a petition for recognition to commence a case under chapter 15, which was added to the Code in 2005, file a list of entities with whom the debtor is engaged in litigation in the United States. The foreign representative filing the petition for recognition must also list any entities against whom provisional relief is being sought as well as all persons or bodies authorized to administer foreign proceedings of the debtor. This should ensure that entities most interested in the case, or their representatives, will receive notice of the petition under Rule 2002(q).

Subdivision (a)(4) is amended to require the foreign representative who files a petition for recognition under chapter 15 to file the documents described in § 1515 of the Code as well as a corporate ownership statement. The subdivision is also amended to identify the foreign representative in language that more closely follows the text of the Code. Former subdivision (a)(4) is renumbered as subdivision (a)(5) and stylistic changes were made to the subdivision.

Subdivision (b)(1) addresses schedules, statements, and other documents that the debtor must file unless the court orders otherwise and other than in a case under chapter 9. This subdivision is amended to include documentary requirements added by the 2005 amendments to § 521 that apply to the same group of debtors and have the same time limits as the existing requirements of (b)(1). Consistent with the E–Government Act of 2002, Pub. L. No. 107–347, the payment advices should be redacted before they are filed.

Subdivision (b)(2) is amended to conform to the renumbering of the subsections of § 521.

Subdivisions (b)(3) through (b)(8) are new and implement the 2005 amendments to the Code. Subdivision (b)(3) provides for the filing of a document relating to the credit counseling requirement provided by the 2005 amendments to § 109 in the context of an Official Form that warns the debtor of the consequences of failing to comply with the credit counseling requirement.

Subdivision (b)(4) addresses the filing of information about current monthly income, as defined in § 101, for certain chapter 7 debtors and, if required, additional calculations of expenses required by the 2005 amendments to § 707(b).

Subdivision (b)(5) addresses the filing of information about current monthly income, as defined in § 101, for individual chapter 11 debtors. The 2005 amendments to § 1129(a)(15) condition plan confirmation for individual debtors on the commitment of disposable income, as defined in § 1325(b)(2), which is based on current monthly income.

Subdivision (b)(6) addresses the filing of information about current monthly income, as defined in § 101, for chapter 13 debtors and, if required, additional calculations of expenses. These changes are necessary because the 2005 amendments to § 1325 require that the determination of disposable income begin with current monthly income.

Subdivision (b)(7) reflects the 2005 amendments to §§ 727 and 1328 of the Code that condition the receipt of a discharge on the completion of a personal financial management course, with certain exceptions. Certain individual chapter 11 debtors may also be required to complete a personal financial management course under § 727(a)(11) as incorporated by § 1141(d)(3)(C). To evidence compliance with that requirement, the subdivision requires the debtor to file the appropriate Official Form certifying that the debtor has completed the personal financial management course.

Subdivision (b)(8) requires an individual debtor in a case under chapter 11, 12, or 13 to file a statement that there are no reasonable grounds to believe that the restrictions on a homestead exemption as set out in § 522(q) of the Code are applicable. Sections 1141(d)(5)(C), 1228(f), and 1328(h) each provide that the court shall not enter a discharge order unless it finds that there is no reasonable cause to believe that § 522(q) applies. Requiring the debtor to submit a statement to that effect in cases under chapters 11, 12, and 13 in which an exemption is claimed in excess of the amount allowed under § 522(q)(1) provides the court with a basis to conclude, in the absence of any contrary information, that § 522(q) does not apply. Creditors receive notice under Rule 2002(f)(11) of the time to request postponement of the entry of the discharge to permit an opportunity to challenge the debtor's assertions in the Rule 1007(b)(8) statement in appropriate cases.

Subdivision (c) is amended to include time limits for the filing requirements added to subdivision (b) due to the 2005 amendments to the Code, and to make conforming amendments. Separate time limits are provided for the documentation of credit counseling and for the statement of the completion of the financial management course. While most documents relating to credit counseling must be filed with the voluntary petition, the credit counseling certificate and debt repayment plan can be filed within 15 days of the filing of a voluntary petition if the debtor files a statement under subdivision (b)(3)(B) with the petition. Sections 727(a)(11), 1141(d)(3), and 1328(g) of the Code require individual debtors to complete a personal financial management course prior to the entry of a discharge. The amendment allows the court to enlarge the deadline for the debtor to file the statement of completion. Because no party is harmed by the enlargement, no specific restriction is placed on the court's discretion to enlarge the deadline, even after its expiration.

Subdivision (c) of the rule is also amended to recognize the limitation on the extension of time to file schedules and statements when the debtor is a small business debtor. Section 1116(3), added to the Code in 2005, establishes a specific standard for courts to apply in the event that the debtor in possession or the trustee seeks an extension for filing these forms for a period beyond 30 days after the order for relief.

2009 Amendments

The rule is amended to implement changes in connection with the amendment to Rule 9006(a) and the manner by which time is computed under the rules. Each deadline in the rule of fewer than 30 days is amended to substitute a deadline that is a multiple of seven days. Throughout the rules, deadlines are amended in the following manner:

- 5–day periods become 7–day periods
- 10–day periods become 14–day periods
- 15–day periods become 14–day periods
- 20–day periods become 21–day periods
- 25–day periods become 28–day periods

2010 Amendments

Subdivision (a)(2). Subdivision (a)(2) is amended to shorten the time for a debtor to file a list of the creditors included on the various schedules filed or to be filed in the case. This list provides the information necessary for the clerk to provide notice of the § 341 meeting of creditors in a timely manner.

Subdivision (c). Subdivision (c) is amended to provide additional time for individual debtors in chapter 7 to file the statement of completion of a course in personal financial management. This change is made in conjunction with an amendment to Rule 5009 requiring the clerk to provide notice to debtors of the consequences of not filing the statement in a timely manner.

2012 Amendments

*[Effective December 1, 2012,
absent contrary Congressional action.]*

Subdivision (c). In subdivision (c), the time limit for a debtor in an involuntary case to file the list required by subdivision (a)(2) is deleted as unnecessary. Subdivision (a)(2) provides that the list must be filed within seven days after the entry of the order for relief. The other change to subdivision (c) is stylistic.

Because this amendment is being made to conform to an amendment to Rule 1007(a)(2) that took effect on December 1, 2010, final approval is sought without publication.

CROSS REFERENCES

Committee of seven unsecured creditors appointed in reorganization case, see 11 USCA § 1102.

Compliance with this rule upon conversion to liquidation case, see Fed.Rules Bankr.Proc. Rule 1019, 11 USCA.

Duty of debtor to—

Inform trustee as to property location and name and address of money and property obligors, see Fed.Rules Bankr.Proc. Rule 4002, 11 USCA.

Prepare and file schedule and statement, see 11 USCA § 521.

Enlargement of time for filing list of twenty largest unsecured creditors not permitted, see Fed.Rules Bankr.Proc. Rule 9006, 11 USCA.

Filing of proof of interest by equity security holder obviated by list filed by debtor, see Fed.Rules Bankr.Proc. Rule 3003, 11 USCA.

Immunity from self-incrimination, see 11 USCA § 344.

Insider for purposes of list of 20 unsecured claims defined, see 11 USCA § 101.

List of exempt property to be filed—

By dependent of debtor, see Fed.Rules Bankr.Proc. Rule 4003, 11 USCA.

With schedule of assets, see Fed.Rules Bankr.Proc. Rule 4003, 11 USCA.

Motions; form and service, see Fed.Rules Bankr.Proc. Rule 9013, 11 USCA.

Notice required for—

Creditors' meetings, see Fed.Rules Bankr.Proc. Rule 2002, 11 USCA.

Order for relief, see 11 USCA § 342.

LIBRARY REFERENCES

American Digest System

Bankruptcy ⊜2321 to 2325.

Key Number System Topic No. 51.

Corpus Juris Secundum

CJS Bankruptcy § 296, Notice by Mail--Proper Mailing Address.

CJS Bankruptcy § 308, Enlargement.

CJS Bankruptcy § 344, List of Creditors and Others.

CJS Bankruptcy § 345, List of Creditors and Others--Twenty Largest Unsecured Creditors.

CJS Bankruptcy § 346, List of Property Owners Adversely Affected in Chapter 9 Case.

CJS Bankruptcy § 347, List of Equity Security Holders.

CJS Bankruptcy § 348, List of Administrators and Others in Chapter 15 Case.

CJS Bankruptcy § 349, Schedules and Statements Regarding Debtor's Assets, Liabilities, Income, Expenditures, and Finances.

CJS Bankruptcy § 350, Statement of Intention With Respect to the Retention or Surrender of Collateral.

CJS Bankruptcy § 351, Evidence of Compliance With Credit Counseling Requirement.

CJS Bankruptcy § 352, Statement of Current Monthly Income.

CJS Bankruptcy § 353, Statement of Completion of Course in Personal Financial Management.

CJS Bankruptcy § 354, Statement as to Social Security Number.

CJS Bankruptcy § 355, Supplemental Schedule to Account for Certain Interests Acquired or Arising After Petition.

CJS Bankruptcy § 356, Extension of Time for Filing.

CJS Bankruptcy § 357, Other Considerations.

CJS Bankruptcy § 358, Amendment.

CJS Bankruptcy § 522, Parties; Standing.

CJS Bankruptcy § 576, Filing List of Property Claimed as Exempt.

CJS Bankruptcy § 578, Debtor's Statement of Intention.

CJS Bankruptcy § 581, Interests Acquired or Arising After Filing of Bankruptcy Petition.

CJS Bankruptcy § 764, Consumer Privacy and Patient Care Ombudsmen.

CJS Bankruptcy § 857, Approval of Agreement.

CJS Bankruptcy § 870, Agreement or Stipulation for Use of Cash Collateral.

CJS Bankruptcy § 877, Sale or Lease of Personally Identifiable Information.

CJS Bankruptcy § 901, Motion for Authorization to Obtain Credit; Approval of Agreement.

CJS Bankruptcy § 1054, Hearing, Determination, and Order.

CJS Bankruptcy § 1105, Closing.

Rule 1008. Verification of Petitions and Accompanying Papers

All petitions, lists, schedules, statements and amendments thereto shall be verified or contain an unsworn declaration as provided in 28 U.S.C. § 1746.

(As amended Apr. 30, 1991, eff. Aug. 1, 1991.)

ADVISORY COMMITTEE NOTES

This rule retains the requirement under the Bankruptcy Act [former Title 11] and rules that petitions and accompanying papers must be verified. Only the original need be signed and verified, but the copies must be conformed to the original. See Rule 9011(c).

The verification may be replaced by an unsworn declaration as provided in 28 U.S.C. § 1746. See also, Official Form No. 1 and Advisory Committee Note.

1991 Amendments

The amendments to this rule are stylistic.

CROSS REFERENCES

Signing and verification of papers, see Fed.Rules Bankr. Proc. Rule 9011, 11 USCA.

LIBRARY REFERENCES

American Digest System

Bankruptcy ⊂⇒2257, 2291, 2311, 2322, 2325.
Key Number System Topic No. 51.

Corpus Juris Secundum

CJS Bankruptcy § 284, Signature and Verification of Basis for Filing.

CJS Bankruptcy § 336, Contents, Signature, and Verification.

CJS Bankruptcy § 357, Other Considerations.

CJS Bankruptcy § 390, Petition for Recognition of Foreign Proceeding.

Rule 1009. Amendments of Voluntary Petitions, Lists, Schedules and Statements

(a) General right to amend

A voluntary petition, list, schedule, or statement may be amended by the debtor as a matter of course at any time before the case is closed. The debtor shall give notice of the amendment to the trustee and to any entity affected thereby. On motion of a party in interest, after notice and a hearing, the court may order any voluntary petition, list, schedule, or statement to be amended and the clerk shall give notice of the amendment to entities designated by the court.

(b) Statement of intention

The statement of intention may be amended by the debtor at any time before the expiration of the period provided in § 521(a) of the Code. The debtor shall give notice of the amendment to the trustee and to any entity affected thereby.

(c) Statement of social security number

If a debtor becomes aware that the statement of social security number submitted under Rule 1007(f) is incorrect, the debtor shall promptly submit an amended verified statement setting forth the correct social security number. The debtor shall give notice of the amendment to all of the entities required to be included on the list filed under Rule 1007(a)(1) or (a)(2).

(d) Transmission to United States trustee

The clerk shall promptly transmit to the United States trustee a copy of every amendment filed or submitted under subdivision (a), (b), or (c) of this rule.

(As amended Mar. 30, 1987, eff. Aug. 1, 1987; Apr. 30, 1991, eff. Aug. 1, 1991; Apr. 12, 2006, eff. Dec. 1, 2006; Apr. 23, 2008, eff. Dec. 1, 2008.)

ADVISORY COMMITTEE NOTES

This rule continues the permissive approach adopted by former Bankruptcy Rule 110 to amendments of voluntary petitions and accompanying papers. Notice of any amendment is required to be given to the trustee. This is particularly important with respect to any amendment of the schedule of property affecting the debtor's claim of exemptions.

Notice of any amendment of the schedule of liabilities is to be given to any creditor whose claim is changed or newly listed.

The rule does not continue the provision permitting the court to order an amendment on its own initiative. Absent a request in some form by a party in interest, the court should not be involved in administrative matters affecting the estate.

If a list or schedule is amended to include an additional creditor, the effect on the dischargeability of the creditor's claim is governed by the provisions of § 523(a)(3) of the Code.

1987 Amendments

Subdivision (a) is amended to require notice and a hearing in the event a party in interest other than the debtor seeks to amend. The number of copies of the amendment will be determined by local rule of court.

Subdivision (b) is added to treat amendments of the statement of intention separately from other amendments. The intention of the individual debtor must be performed within 45 days of the filing of the statement, unless the court extends the period. Subdivision (b) limits the time for amendment to the time for performance under § 521(2)(B) of the Code or any extension granted by the court.

1991 Amendments

The amendments to subdivision (a) are stylistic.

Subdivision (c) is derived from Rule X–1002(a) and is designed to provide the United States trustee with current information to enable that office to participate effectively in the case.

2006 Amendments

Subdivision (c). Rule 2002(a)(1) provides that the notice of the § 341 meeting of creditors include the debtor's social security number. It provides creditors with the full number while limiting publication of the social security number otherwise to the final four digits of the number to protect the debtor's identity from others who do not have the same need for that information. If, however, the social security number that the debtor submitted under Rule 1007(f) is incorrect, then the only notice to the entities contained on the list filed under Rule 1007(a)(1) or (a)(2) would be incorrect. This amendment adds a new subdivision (c) that directs the debtor to submit a verified amended statement of social security number and to give notice of the new statement to all entities in the case who received the notice containing the erroneous social security number.

Subdivision (d). Former subdivision (c) becomes subdivision (d) and is amended to include new subdivision (c) amendments in the list of documents that the clerk must transmit to the United States trustee.

Other amendments are stylistic.

2008 Amendments

Subdivision (b) is amended to conform to the 2005 amendments to § 521 of the Code.

CROSS REFERENCES

Dischargeability of debts added to list or schedule, see 11 USCA § 523.

Motions; form and service, see Fed.Rules Bankr.Proc. Rule 9013, 11 USCA.

Amended and supplemental pleadings, see Fed.Rules Civ. Proc. Rule 15, 28 USCA.

LIBRARY REFERENCES

American Digest System

Bankruptcy ⊗2325.

Key Number System Topic No. 51.

Corpus Juris Secundum

CJS Bankruptcy § 343, Amendment.

CJS Bankruptcy § 358, Amendment.

CJS Bankruptcy § 578, Debtor's Statement of Intention.

CJS Bankruptcy § 1094, Requirements for Reaffirmation of Debt.

Rule 1010. Service of Involuntary Petition and Summons; Petition for Recognition of a Foreign Nonmain Proceeding

(a) Service of involuntary petition and summons; service of petition for recognition of foreign nonmain proceeding

On the filing of an involuntary petition or a petition for recognition of a foreign nonmain proceeding, the clerk shall forthwith issue a summons for service. When an involuntary petition is filed, service shall be made on the debtor. When a petition for recognition of a foreign nonmain proceeding is filed, service shall be made on the debtor, any entity against whom provisional relief is sought under § 1519 of the Code, and on any other party as the court may direct. The summons shall be served with a copy of the petition in the manner provided for service of a summons and complaint by Rule 7004(a) or (b). If service cannot be so made, the court may order that the summons and petition be served by mailing copies to the party's last known address, and by at least one publication in a manner and form directed by the court. The summons and petition may be served on the party anywhere. Rule 7004(e) and Rule 4(*l*) F.R.Civ.P. apply when service is made or attempted under this rule.

(b) Corporate ownership statement

Each petitioner that is a corporation shall file with the involuntary petition a corporate ownership statement containing the information described in Rule 7007.1.

(As amended Mar. 30, 1987, eff. Aug. 1, 1987; Apr. 30, 1991, eff. Aug. 1, 1991; Apr. 22, 1993, eff. Aug. 1, 1993; Apr. 11, 1997, eff. Dec. 1, 1997; Apr. 23, 2008, eff. Dec. 1, 2008.)

ADVISORY COMMITTEE NOTES

This rule provides the procedure for service of the involuntary petition and summons. It does not deal with service of a summons and complaint instituting an adversary proceeding pursuant to Part VII.

While this rule is similar to former Bankruptcy Rule 111, it substitutes the clerk of the bankruptcy court for the clerk of the district court as the person who is to issue the summons.

The modes of service prescribed by the rule are personal or by mail, when service can be effected in one of these ways in the United States. Such service is to be made in the manner prescribed in adversary proceedings by Rule 7004(a) and (b). If service must be made in a foreign country, the mode of service is one of that set forth in Rule 4(i) F.R.Civ.P.

When the method set out in Rule 7004(a) and (b) cannot be utilized, service by publication coupled with mailing to the last known address is authorized. Cf. Rule 7004(c). The court determines the form and manner of publication as provided in Rule 9007. The publication need not set out the petition or the order directing service by publication. In order to apprise the debtor fairly, however, the publication should include all the information required to be in the summons by Official Form No. 13 and a notice indicating how service is being effected and how a copy of the petition may be obtained.

There are no territorial limits on the service authorized by this rule, which continues the practice under the former rules and Act. There must, however, be a basis for jurisdiction pursuant to § 109(a) of the Code for the court to order relief. Venue provisions are set forth in 28 U.S.C. § 1472.

Subdivision (f) of Rule 7004 and subdivisions (g) and (h) of Rule 4 F.R.Civ.P. govern time and proof of service and amendment of process or of proof of service.

Rule 1004 provides for transmission to nonpetitioning partners of a petition filed against the partnership by fewer than all the general partners.

1987 Amendments

The rule has been broadened to include service of a petition commencing a case ancillary to a foreign proceeding, previously included in Rule 1003(e)(2).

1991 Amendments

Reference to the Official Form number is deleted in anticipation of future revision and renumbering of the Official Forms.

Rule 4(g) and (h) F.R.Civ.P. made applicable by this rule refers to Rule 4(g) and (h) F.R.Civ.P. in effect on January 1, 1990, notwithstanding any subsequent amendment thereto. See Rule 7004(g).

1993 Amendments

This rule is amended to delete the reference to the Official Form. The Official Form for the summons was abrogated in 1991. Other amendments are stylistic and make no substantive change.

1997 Amendments

The amendments to this rule are technical, are promulgated solely to conform to changes in subdivision designations in Rule 4, F.R.Civ.P., and in Rule 7004, and are not intended to effectuate any material change in substance.

In 1996, the letter designation of subdivision (f) of Rule 7004 (Summons; Time Limit for Service) was changed to subdivision (e). In 1993, the provisions of Rule 4, F.R.Civ.P., relating to proof of service contained in Rule 4(g) (Return) and Rule 4(h) (Amendments), were placed in the new subdivision (l) of Rule 4 (Proof of Service). The technical amendments to Rule 1010 are designed solely to conform to these new subdivision designations.

The 1996 amendments to Rule 7004 and the 1993 amendments to Rule 4, F.R.Civ.P., have not affected the availability of service by first class mail in accordance with Rule 7004(b) for the service of a summons and petition in an involuntary case commenced under § 303 or an ancillary case commenced under § 304 of the Code.

GAP Report on Rule 1010. These amendments, which are technical and conforming, were not published for comment.

2008 Amendments

This rule is amended to implement the 2005 amendments to the Code, which repealed § 304 and replaced it with chapter 15 governing ancillary and other cross-border cases. Under chapter 15, a foreign representative commences a case by filing a petition for recognition of a pending foreign nonmain proceeding. The amendment requires service of the summons and petition on the debtor and any entity against whom the representative is seeking provisional relief. Until the court enters a recognition order under § 1517, no stay is in effect unless the court enters some form of provisional relief under § 1519. Thus, only those entities against whom specific provisional relief is sought need to be served. The court may, however, direct that service be made on additional entities as appropriate.

This rule does not apply to a petition for recognition of a foreign main proceeding.

The rule is also amended by renumbering the prior rule as subdivision (a) and adding a new subdivision (b) requiring any corporate creditor that files or joins an involuntary petition to file a corporate ownership statement.

CROSS REFERENCES

Applicability of this rule to—

Involuntary case ancillary to foreign proceeding, see Fed. Rules Bankr.Proc. Rule 1003, 11 USCA.

Involuntary partnership petitions, see Fed.Rules Bankr. Proc. Rule 1004, 11 USCA.

Form and manner of service by publication, see Fed.Rules Bankr.Proc. Rules 9007 and 9008, 11 USCA.

Jurisdictional basis for service, see 11 USCA § 109.

Process, see Fed.Rules Civ.Proc. Rule 4, 28 USCA.

LIBRARY REFERENCES

American Digest System

Bankruptcy ⟚2158, 2290.1, 2341.

Key Number System Topic No. 51.

Corpus Juris Secundum

CJS Bankruptcy § 378, Service of Summons and Petition.

CJS Bankruptcy § 391, Service of Summons and Petition.

Rule 1011. Responsive Pleading or Motion in Involuntary and Cross–Border Cases

(a) Who may contest petition

The debtor named in an involuntary petition, or a party in interest to a petition for recognition of a foreign proceeding, may contest the petition. In the case of a petition against a partnership under Rule

1004, a nonpetitioning general partner, or a person who is alleged to be a general partner but denies the allegation, may contest the petition.

(b) Defenses and objections; when presented

Defenses and objections to the petition shall be presented in the manner prescribed by Rule 12 F. R. Civ. P. and shall be filed and served within 21 days after service of the summons, except that if service is made by publication on a party or partner not residing or found within the state in which the court sits, the court shall prescribe the time for filing and serving the response.

(c) Effect of motion

Service of a motion under Rule 12(b) F.R.Civ.P. shall extend the time for filing and serving a responsive pleading as permitted by Rule 12(a) F.R.Civ.P.

(d) Claims against petitioners

A claim against a petitioning creditor may not be asserted in the answer except for the purpose of defeating the petition.

(e) Other pleadings

No other pleadings shall be permitted, except that the court may order a reply to an answer and prescribe the time for filing and service.

(f) Corporate ownership statement

If the entity responding to the involuntary petition or the petition for recognition of a foreign proceeding is a corporation, the entity shall file with its first appearance, pleading, motion, response, or other request addressed to the court a corporate ownership statement containing the information described in Rule 7007.1.

(As amended Mar. 30, 1987, eff. Aug. 1, 1987; Apr. 26, 2004, eff. Dec. 1, 2004; Apr. 23, 2008, eff. Dec. 1, 2008; Mar. 26, 2009, eff. Dec. 1, 2009.)

ADVISORY COMMITTEE NOTES

This rule is derived from former Bankruptcy Rule 112. A petition filed by fewer than all the general partners under Rule 1004(b) to have an order for relief entered with respect to the partnership is referred to as a petition against the partnership because of the adversary character of the proceeding it commences. Cf. § 303(b)(3) of the Code; 2 Collier Bankruptcy ¶303.05[5][a] (15th ed.1981); id. ¶¶18.33[2], 18.46 (14th ed.1966). One who denies an allegation of membership in the firm is nevertheless recognized as a party entitled to contest a petition filed against a partnership under subdivision (b) of Rule 1004 in view of the possible consequences to him of an order for relief against the entity alleged to include him as a member. See § 723 of the Code; Francis v. McNeal, 228 U.S. 695 (1913); Manson v. Williams, 213 U.S. 453 (1909); Carter v. Whisler, 275 Fed. 743, 746–747 (8th Cir.1921). The rule preserves the features of the former Act and Rule 112 and the Code permitting no response by creditors to an involuntary petition or petition against a partnership under rule 1004(b).

Subdivision (b): Rule 12 F.R.Civ.P. has been looked to by the courts as prescribing the mode of making a defense or objection to a petition in bankruptcy. See Fada of New York, Inc. v. Organization Service Co., Inc., 125 F.2d 120 (2d Cir.1942); In the Matter of McDougald, 17 F.R.D. 2, 5 (W.D.Ark.1955); In the Matter of Miller, 6 Fed.Rules Serv. 12f.26, Case No. 1 (N.D.Ohio 1942); Tatum v. Acadian Production Corp. of La., 35 F.Supp. 40, 50 (E.D.La.1940); 2 Collier, supra ¶303.07 (15th ed.1981); 2 id. at 134–40 (14th ed.1966). As pointed out in the Note accompanying former Bankruptcy rule 915 an objection that a debtor is neither entitled to the benefits of the Code nor amenable to an involuntary petition goes to jurisdiction of the subject matter and may be made at any time consistent with Rule 12(h)(3) F.R.Civ.P. Nothing in this rule recognizes standing in a creditor or any other person not authorized to contest a petition to raise an objection that a person eligible to file a voluntary petition cannot be the subject of an order for relief on an involuntary petition. See Seligson & King, Jurisdiction and Venue in Bankruptcy, 36 Ref.J. 36, 38–40 (1962).

As Collier has pointed out with respect to the Bankruptcy Act, "the mechanics of the provisions in § 18a and b relating to time for appearance and pleading are unnecessarily confusing. . . . It would seem, though, to be more straightforward to provide, as does Federal Rule 12(a), that the time to respond runs from the date of service rather than the date of issuance of process." 2 Collier, supra at 119. The time normally allowed for the service and filing of an answer or motion under Rule 1011 runs from the date of the issuance of the summons. Compare Rule 7012. Service of the summons and petition will ordinarily be made by mail under Rule 1010 and must be served within 10 days of the issuance of the summons under Rule 7004(e), which governs the time of service. When service is made by publication, the court should fix the time for service and filing of the response in the light of all the circumstances so as to afford a fair opportunity to the debtor to enter a defense or objection without unduly delaying the hearing on the petition. Cf. Rule 12(a) F.R.Civ.P.

Subdivision (c): Under subdivision (c), the timely service of a motion permitted by Rule 12(b), (e), (f), or (h) F.R.Civ.P. alters the time within which an answer must be filed. If the court denies a motion or postpones its disposition until trial on the merits, the answer must be served within 10 days after notice of the court's action. If the court grants a motion for a more definite statement, the answer may be served any time within 10 days after the service of the more definite statement.

Many of the rules governing adversary proceedings apply to proceedings on a contested petition unless the court otherwise directs as provided in Rule 1018. The specific provisions of this Rule 1011 or 7005, however, govern the filing of an answer or motion responsive to a petition. The rules of Part VII are adaptations of the corresponding Federal Rules of Civil Procedure, and the effect of Rule 1018 is thus to make the provisions of Civil Rules 5, 8, 9, 15, and 56, inter alia, generally applicable to the making of defenses and objections to the petition. Rule 1018 follows prior law and practice in this respect. See 2 Collier, Bankruptcy ¶¶18.39–18.41 (14th ed.1966).

Subdivision (d). This subdivision adopts the position taken in many cases that an affirmative judgment against a petitioning creditor cannot be sought by a counterclaim filed in an answer to an involuntary petition. See, e.g., Georgia

Jewelers, Inc., v. Bulova Watch Co., 302 F.2d 362, 369–70 (5th Cir.1962); Associated Electronic Supply Co. of Omaha v. C.B.S. Electronic Sales Corp., 288 F.2d 683, 684–85 (8th Cir. 1961). The subdivision follows Harris v. Capehart-Farnsworth Corp., 225 F.2d 268 (8th Cir.1955), in permitting the debtor to challenge the standing of a petitioner by filing a counterclaim against him. It does not foreclose the court from rejecting a counterclaim that cannot be determined without unduly delaying the decision upon the petition. See In the Matter of Bichel Optical Laboratories, Inc., 299 F.Supp. 545 (D.Minn.1969).

Subdivision (e). This subdivision makes it clear that no reply needs to be made to an answer, including one asserting a counterclaim, unless the court orders otherwise.

1987 Amendments

The rule has been broadened to make applicable in ancillary cases the provisions concerning responsive pleadings to involuntary petitions.

2004 Amendments

The amendment to Rule 1004 that became effective on December 1, 2002, deleted former subdivision (a) of that rule leaving only the provisions relating to involuntary petitions against partnerships. The rule no longer includes subdivisions. Therefore, this technical amendment changes the reference to Rule 1004(b) to Rule 1004.

2008 Amendments

The rule is amended to reflect the 2005 amendments to the Code, which repealed § 304 and added chapter 15. Section 304 covered cases ancillary to foreign proceedings, while chapter 15 governs ancillary and other cross-border cases and introduces the concept of a petition for recognition of a foreign proceeding.

The rule is also amended in tandem with the amendment to Rule 1010 to require the parties responding to an involuntary petition and a petition for recognition of a foreign proceeding to file corporate ownership statements to assist the court in determining whether recusal is necessary.

2009 Amendments

The rule is amended to implement changes in connection with the amendment to Rule 9006(a) and the manner by which time is computed under the rules. The deadline in the rule is amended to substitute a deadline that is a multiple of seven days. Throughout the rules, deadlines are amended in the following manner:

* 5–day periods become 7–day periods
* 10–day periods become 14–day periods
* 15–day periods become 14–day periods
* 20–day periods become 21–day periods
* 25–day periods become 28–day periods

CROSS REFERENCES

Applicability of this rule to involuntary case ancillary to foreign proceeding, see Fed.Rules Bankr.Proc. Rule 1003, 11 USCA.

Entry of default upon failure to plead within time, see Fed.Rules Bankr.Proc. Rule 1013, 11 USCA.

Motions; form and service, see Fed.Rules Bankr.Proc. Rule 9013, 11 USCA.

Responsive pleadings, see 11 USCA § 303.

Pleadings—

Amended and supplemental, see Fed.Rules Civ.Proc. Rule 15, 28 USCA.

Capacity, fraud, and other special matters, see Fed.Rules Civ.Proc. Rule 9, 28 USCA.

General rules, see Fed.Rules Civ.Proc. Rule 8, 28 USCA.

Service and filing, see Fed.Rules Civ.Proc. Rule 5, 28 USCA.

Summary judgment, see Fed.Rules Civ.Proc. Rule 56, 28 USCA.

LIBRARY REFERENCES

American Digest System

Bankruptcy ⚯2294, 2341.

Key Number System Topic No. 51.

Corpus Juris Secundum

CJS Bankruptcy § 379, Answer; Defenses and Objections.

CJS Bankruptcy § 380, Other Pleadings.

CJS Bankruptcy § 392, Answer; Defenses and Objections.

CJS Bankruptcy § 393, Other Pleadings.

Rule 1012. [Abrogated Mar. 30, 1987, eff. Aug. 1, 1987]

ADVISORY COMMITTEE NOTES

This rule is abrogated. The discovery rules apply whenever an involuntary petition is contested. Rule 1018.

Rule 1013. Hearing and Disposition of Petition in Involuntary Cases

(a) Contested petition

The court shall determine the issues of a contested petition at the earliest practicable time and forthwith enter an order for relief, dismiss the petition, or enter any other appropriate order.

(b) Default

If no pleading or other defense to a petition is filed within the time provided by Rule 1011, the court, on the next day, or as soon thereafter as practicable, shall enter an order for the relief requested in the petition.

(c) [Abrogated]

(As amended Apr. 30, 1991, eff. Aug. 1, 1991; Apr. 22, 1993, eff. Aug. 1, 1993.)

ADVISORY COMMITTEE NOTES

This rule is adapted from former Bankruptcy Rule 115(a) and (c) and applies in chapter 7 and 11 cases. The right to trial by jury under § 19a of the Bankruptcy Act [former § 42(a) of this title] has been abrogated and the availability of a trial by jury is within the discretion of the bankruptcy judge pursuant to 28 U.S.C. § 1480(b). Rule 9015 governs the demand for a jury trial.

Subdivision (b) of Rule 1013 is derived from former Bankruptcy Rule 115(c) and § 18(e) of the Bankruptcy Act [former § 41(e) of this title]. If an order for relief is not entered on default, dismissal will ordinarily be appropriate but the court may postpone definitive action. See also Rule 9024 with respect to setting aside an order for relief on default for cause.

Subdivision (e) of former Bankruptcy Rule 115 has not been carried over because its provisions are covered by § 303(i) of the Code.

1991 Amendments

Reference to the Official Form number is deleted in anticipation of future revision and renumbering of the Official Forms.

1993 Amendments

Subdivision (c) is abrogated because the official form for the order for relief was abrogated in 1991. Other amendments are stylistic and make no substantive change.

CROSS REFERENCES

Costs, counsel fees, expenses and damages upon dismissal of petition, see 11 USCA § 303.

Power of court to render judgments, see 11 USCA § 105.

Setting aside default for cause, see Fed.Rules Bankr.Proc. Rule 9024, 11 USCA.

Instructions to jury; objection, see Fed.Rules Civ.Proc. Rule 51, 28 USCA.

Juries of less than twelve; majority verdict, see Fed.Rules Civ.Proc. Rule 48, 28 USCA.

Jurors, see Fed.Rules Civ.Proc. Rule 47, 28 USCA.

Jury trial of right, see Fed.Rules Civ.Proc. Rule 38, 28 USCA.

Motion for directed verdict and for judgment notwithstanding verdict, see Fed.Rules Civ.Proc. Rule 50, 28 USCA.

Special verdicts and interrogatories, see Fed.Rules Civ. Proc. Rule 49, 28 USCA.

Trial by jury or by court, see Fed.Rules Civ.Proc. Rule 39, 28 USCA.

LIBRARY REFERENCES

American Digest System

Bankruptcy ⚯2130, 2295.1 to 2297.

Jury ⚯19(9).

Key Number System Topic Nos. 230, 51.

Corpus Juris Secundum

CJS Bankruptcy § 381, Default.

Rule 1014. Dismissal and Change of Venue

(a) Dismissal and Transfer of Cases

(1) Cases Filed in Proper District

If a petition is filed in the proper district, the court, on the timely motion of a party in interest or on its own motion, and after hearing on notice to the petitioners, the United States trustee, and other entities as directed by the court, may transfer the case to any other district if the court determines that the transfer is in the interest of justice or for the convenience of the parties.

(2) Cases Filed in Improper District

If a petition is filed in an improper district, the court, on the timely motion of a party in interest or on its own motion, and after hearing on notice to the petitioners, the United States trustee, and other entities as directed by the court, may dismiss the case or transfer it to any other district if the court determines that transfer is in the interest of justice or for the convenience of the parties.

(b) Procedure when petitions involving the same debtor or related debtors are filed in different courts

If petitions commencing cases under the Code or seeking recognition under chapter 15 are filed in different districts by, regarding, or against (1) the same debtor, (2) a partnership and one or more of its general partners, (3) two or more general partners, or (4) a debtor and an affiliate, on motion filed in the district in which the petition filed first is pending and after hearing on notice to the petitioners, the United States trustee, and other entities as directed by the court, the court may determine, in the interest of justice or for the convenience of the parties, the district or districts in which the case or cases should proceed. Except as otherwise ordered by the court in the district in which the petition filed first is pending, the proceedings on the other petitions shall be stayed by the courts in which they have been filed until the determination is made.

(As amended Mar. 30, 1987, eff. Aug. 1, 1987; Apr. 30, 1991, eff. Aug. 1, 1991; Apr. 30, 2007, eff. Dec. 1, 2007; Apr. 28, 2010, eff. Dec. 1, 2010.)

ADVISORY COMMITTEE NOTES

This rule is derived from former Bankruptcy Rule 116 which contained venue as well as transfer provisions. Public Law 95–598, however, placed the venue provisions in 28 U.S.C. § 1472, and no purpose is served by repeating them in this rule. Transfer of cases is provided in 28 U.S.C. § 1475 but this rule adds the procedure for obtaining transfer. Pursuant to 28 U.S.C. § 1472, proper venue for cases filed under the Code is either the district of domicile, residence, principal place of business, or location of principal assets for 180 days or the longer portion thereof immediately preceding the petition. 28 U.S.C. § 1475 permits the court to transfer a case in the interest of justice and for the convenience of the parties. If the venue is improper, the court may retain or transfer the case in the interest of justice and for the convenience of the parties pursuant to 28 U.S.C. § 1477.

Subdivision (a) of the rule is derived from former Bankruptcy Rule 116(b). It implements 28 U.S.C. §§ 1475 and 1477 and clarifies the procedure to be followed in requesting and effecting transfer of a case. Subdivision (a) protects the parties against being subjected to a transfer except on a timely motion of a party in interest. If the transfer would result in fragmentation or duplication of administration, increase expense, or delay closing the estate, such a factor would bear on the timeliness of the motion as well as on the propriety of the transfer under the standards prescribed in subdivision (a). Subdivision (a) of the rule requires the interest of justice and the convenience of the parties to be the grounds of any transfer of a case or of the retention of a case filed in an improper district as does 28 U.S.C. § 1477. Cf. 28 U.S.C. § 1404(a) (district court may transfer any civil action "[f]or the convenience of parties and witnesses, in the interest of justice"). It also expressly requires a hearing on notice to the petitioner or petitioners before the transfer of any case may be ordered. Under this rule, a motion by a party in interest is necessary. There is no provision for the court to act on its own initiative.

Subdivision (b) is derived from former Bankruptcy Rule 116(c). It authorizes the court in which the first petition is filed under the Code by or against a debtor to entertain a motion seeking a determination whether the case so commenced should continue or be transferred and consolidated or administered jointly with another case commenced by or against the same or related person in another court under a different chapter of the Code. Subdivision (b) is correlated with 28 U.S.C. § 1472 which authorizes petitioners to file cases involving a partnership and partners or affiliated debtors.

The reference in subdivision (b) to petitions filed "by" a partner or "by" any other of the persons mentioned is to be understood as referring to voluntary petitions. It is not the purpose of this subdivision to permit more than one case to be filed in the same court because a creditor signing an involuntary petition happens to be a partner, a partnership, or an affiliate of a debtor.

Transfers of adversary proceedings in cases under title 11 are governed by Rule 7087 and 28 U.S.C. § 1475.

1987 Amendments

Both paragraphs 1 and 2 of subdivision (a) are amended to conform to the standard for transfer in 28 U.S.C. § 1412. Formerly, 28 U.S.C. § 1477 authorized a court either to transfer or retain a case which had been commenced in a district where venue was improper. However, 28 U.S.C. § 1412, which supersedes 28 U.S.C. § 1477, authorizes only the transfer of a case. The rule is amended to delete the reference to retention of a case commenced in the improper district. Dismissal of a case commenced in the improper district as authorized by 28 U.S.C. § 1406 has been added to the rule. If a timely motion to dismiss for improper venue is not filed, the right to object to venue is waived.

The last sentence of the rule has been deleted as unnecessary.

1991 Amendments

Subdivision (b) is amended to provide that a motion for transfer of venue under this subdivision shall be filed in the district in which the first petition is pending. If the case commenced by the first petition has been transferred to another district prior to the filing of a motion to transfer a related case under this subdivision, the motion must be filed in the district to which the first petition had been transferred.

The other amendments to this rule are consistent with the responsibilities of the United States trustee in the supervision and administration of cases pursuant to 28 U.S.C. § 586(a)(3). The United States trustee may appear and be heard on issues

relating to the transfer of the case or dismissal due to improper venue. See § 307 of the Code.

2007 Amendments

Courts have generally held that they have the authority to dismiss or transfer cases on their own motion. The amendment recognizes this authority and also provides that dismissal or transfer of the case may take place only after notice and a hearing.

Other amendments are stylistic.

2010 Amendments

Subdivision (b). Subdivision (b) of the rule is amended to provide that petitions for recognition of a foreign proceeding are included among those that are governed by the procedure for determining where cases should go forward when multiple petitions involving the same debtor are filed. The amendment adds a specific reference to chapter 15 petitions and also provides that the rule governs proceedings regarding a debtor as well as those that are filed by or against a debtor.

Other changes are stylistic.

CROSS REFERENCES

Change of venue, see 28 USCA § 1404.

Motions; form and service, see Fed.Rules Bankr.Proc. Rule 9013, 11 USCA.

Transfer of adversary proceeding, see Fed.Rules Bankr. Proc. Rule 7087, 11 USCA.

LIBRARY REFERENCES

American Digest System

Bankruptcy ⚎2081 to 2091.

Key Number System Topic No. 51.

Corpus Juris Secundum

CJS Bankruptcy § 269, Filing of Petitions Involving Same or Related Debtors in Different Courts.

CJS Bankruptcy § 272, Cases and Proceedings in Improper Venues.

Rule 1015.   Consolidation or Joint Administration of Cases Pending in Same Court

(a) Cases involving same debtor

If two or more petitions by, regarding, or against the same debtor are pending in the same court, the court may order consolidation of the cases.

(b) Cases Involving Two or More Related Debtors

If a joint petition or two or more petitions are pending in the same court by or against (1) a husband and wife, or (2) a partnership and one or more of its general partners, or (3) two or more general partners, or (4) a debtor and an affiliate, the court may order a joint administration of the estates. Prior to entering an order the court shall give consideration to protecting creditors of different estates against potential conflicts of interest. An order directing joint administration of individual cases of a husband and wife shall, if one spouse has elected the exemptions under § 522(b)(2) of the Code and the other has elected the exemptions under § 522(b)(3), fix a reasonable time within which either may amend the election so that both shall have elected the same exemptions. The order shall notify the debtors that unless they elect the same exemptions within the time fixed by the court, they will be deemed to have elected the exemptions provided by § 522(b)(2).

(c) Expediting and protective orders

When an order for consolidation or joint administration of a joint case or two or more cases is entered pursuant to this rule, while protecting the rights of the parties under the Code, the court may enter orders as may tend to avoid unnecessary costs and delay.

(As amended Mar. 30, 1987, eff. Aug. 1, 1987; Apr. 23, 2008, eff. Dec. 1, 2008; Apr. 28, 2010, eff. Dec. 1, 2010.)

ADVISORY COMMITTEE NOTES

Subdivision (a) of this rule is derived from former Bankruptcy Rule 117(a). It applies to cases when the same debtor is named in both voluntary and involuntary petitions, when husband and wife have filed a joint petition pursuant to § 302 of the Code, and when two or more involuntary petitions are filed against the same debtor. It also applies when cases are pending in the same court by virtue of a transfer of one or more petitions from another court. Subdivision (c) allows the court discretion regarding the order of trial of issues raised by two or more involuntary petitions against the same debtor.

Subdivision (b) recognizes the propriety of joint administration of estates in certain kinds of cases. The election or appointment of one trustee for two or more jointly administered estates is authorized by Rule 2009. The authority of the court to order joint administration under subdivision (b) extends equally to the situation when the petitions are filed under different sections, e.g., when one petition is voluntary and the other involuntary, and when all of the petitions are filed under the same section of the Code.

Consolidation of cases implies a unitary administration of the estate and will ordinarily be indicated under the circumstances to which subdivision (a) applies. This rule does not deal with the consolidation of cases involving two or more separate debtors. Consolidation of the estates of separate debtors may sometimes be appropriate, as when the affairs of an individual and a corporation owned or controlled by that individual are so intermingled that the court cannot separate their assets and liabilities. Consolidation, as distinguished from joint administration, is neither authorized nor prohibited by this rule since the propriety of consolidation depends on substantive considerations and affects the substantive rights of the creditors of the different estates. For illustrations of the substantive consolidation of separate estates, see Sampsell v. Imperial Paper & Color Corp., 313 U.S. 215 [61 S.Ct. 904, 85 L.Ed. 1293] (1941). See also Chemical Bank N.Y. Trust Co. v. Kheel, 369 F.2d 845 (2d Cir. 1966); Seligson & Mandell, Multi-Debtor Petition—Consolidation of Debtors and Due Process of Law, 73 Com.L.J. 341 (1968); Kennedy, Insolvency and the Corporate Veil in the United States in Proceedings of the 8th International Symposium on Comparative Law 232, 248–55 (1971).

Joint administration as distinguished from consolidation may include combining the estates by using a single docket for the matters occurring in the administration, including the listing of filed claims, the combining of notices to creditors of the different estates, and the joint handling of other purely administrative matters that may aid in expediting the cases and rendering the process less costly.

Subdivision (c) is an adaptation of the provisions of Rule 42(a) F.R.Civ.P. for the purposes of administration of estates under this rule. The rule does not deal with filing fees when an order for the consolidation of cases or joint administration of estates is made.

A joint petition of husband and wife, requiring the payment of a single filing fee, is permitted by § 302 of the Code. Consolidation of such a case, however, rests in the discretion of the court; see § 302(b) of the Code.

1987 Amendments

The amendment to subdivision (b) implements the provisions of § 522(b) of the Code, as enacted by the 1984 amendments.

2008 Amendments

The rule is amended to conform to the change in the numbering of § 522(b) of the Code that was made as a part of the 2005 amendments. Former subsections (b)(1) and (b)(2) of § 522 were renumbered as subsections (b)(2) and (b)(3), respectively. The rule is amended to make the parallel change.

2010 Amendments

Subdivision (a). By amending subdivision (a) to include cases regarding the same debtor, the rule explicitly recognizes that the court's authority to consolidate cases when more than one petition is filed includes the authority to consolidate cases when one or more of the petitions is filed under chapter 15. This amendment is made in conjunction with the amendment to Rule 1014(b), which also governs petitions filed under chapter 15 regarding the same debtor as well as those filed by or against the debtor.

CROSS REFERENCES

Election of trustees in liquidation cases when joint administration ordered, see Fed.Rules Bankr.Proc. Rule 2009, 11 USCA.

Joint cases, see 11 USCA § 302.

Consolidation, see Fed.Rules Civ.Proc. Rule 42, 28 USCA.

LIBRARY REFERENCES

American Digest System

Bankruptcy ⟶2084.1 to 2085, 2311, 2769.

Key Number System Topic No. 51.

Corpus Juris Secundum

CJS Bankruptcy § 407, Joint Administration of Estates.

CJS Bankruptcy § 408, Consolidation of Cases Against Single Debtor.

CJS Bankruptcy § 565, Joint Debtors.

Rule 1016. Death or Incompetency of Debtor

Death or incompetency of the debtor shall not abate a liquidation case under chapter 7 of the Code. In such event the estate shall be administered and the case concluded in the same manner, so far as possible, as though the death or incompetency had not occurred. If a reorganization, family farmer's debt adjustment, or individual's debt adjustment case is pending under chapter 11, chapter 12, or chapter 13, the case may be dismissed; or if further administration is possible and in the best interest of the parties, the case may proceed and be concluded in the same manner, so far as possible, as though the death or incompetency had not occurred.

(As amended Apr. 30, 1991, eff. Aug. 1, 1991.)

ADVISORY COMMITTEE NOTES

This rule is derived from former Rules 118 and 11–16. In a chapter 11 reorganization case or chapter 13 individual's debt adjustment case, the likelihood is that the case will be dismissed.

1991 Amendments

This rule is amended to conform to 25 F.R.Civ.P. and to include chapter 12 cases.

CROSS REFERENCES

Exemptions, see 11 USCA § 522.

Property of estate, see 11 USCA § 541.

LIBRARY REFERENCES

American Digest System

Bankruptcy ⊅2201.

Key Number System Topic No. 51.

Corpus Juris Secundum

CJS Bankruptcy § 363, Chapter 7.

CJS Bankruptcy § 364, Chapters 11, 12, or 13.

Rule 1017. Dismissal or Conversion of Case; Suspension

(a) Voluntary dismissal; dismissal for want of prosecution or other cause

Except as provided in §§ 707(a)(3), 707(b), 1208(b), and 1307(b) of the Code, and in Rule 1017(b), (c), and (e), a case shall not be dismissed on motion of the petitioner, for want of prosecution or other cause, or by consent of the parties, before a hearing on notice as provided in Rule 2002. For the purpose of the notice, the debtor shall file a list of creditors with their addresses within the time fixed by the court unless the list was previously filed. If the debtor fails to file the list, the court may order the debtor or another entity to prepare and file it.

(b) Dismissal for failure to pay filing fee

(1) If any installment of the filing fee has not been paid, the court may, after a hearing on notice to the debtor and the trustee, dismiss the case.

(2) If the case is dismissed or closed without full payment of the filing fee, the installments collected

shall be distributed in the same manner and proportions as if the filing fee had been paid in full.

(c) Dismissal of voluntary chapter 7 or chapter 13 case for failure to timely file list of creditors, schedules, and statement of financial affairs

The court may dismiss a voluntary chapter 7 or chapter 13 case under § 707(a)(3) or § 1307(c)(9) after a hearing on notice served by the United States trustee on the debtor, the trustee, and any other entities as the court directs.

(d) Suspension

The court shall not dismiss a case or suspend proceedings under § 305 before a hearing on notice as provided in Rule 2002(a).

(e) Dismissal of an individual debtor's chapter 7 case, or conversion to a case under chapter 11 or 13, for abuse

The court may dismiss or, with the debtor's consent, convert an individual debtor's case for abuse under § 707(b) only on motion and after a hearing on notice to the debtor, the trustee, the United States trustee, and any other entity as the court directs.

(1) Except as otherwise provided in § 704(b)(2), a motion to dismiss a case for abuse under § 707(b) or (c) may be filed only within 60 days after the first date set for the meeting of creditors under § 341(a), unless, on request filed before the time has expired, the court for cause extends the time for filing the motion to dismiss. The party filing the motion shall set forth in the motion all matters to be considered at the hearing. In addition, a motion to dismiss under § 707(b)(1) and (3) shall state with particularity the circumstances alleged to constitute abuse.

(2) If the hearing is set on the court's own motion, notice of the hearing shall be served on the debtor no later than 60 days after the first date set for the meeting of creditors under § 341(a). The notice shall set forth all matters to be considered by the court at the hearing.

(f) Procedure for dismissal, conversion, or suspension

(1) Rule 9014 governs a proceeding to dismiss or suspend a case, or to convert a case to another chapter, except under §§ 706(a), 1112(a), 1208(a) or (b), or 1307(a) or (b).

(2) Conversion or dismissal under §§ 706(a), 1112(a), 1208(b), or 1307(b) shall be on motion filed and served as required by Rule 9013.

(3) A chapter 12 or chapter 13 case shall be converted without court order when the debtor files a notice of conversion under §§ 1208(a) or 1307(a). The filing date of the notice becomes the date of the conversion order for the purposes of applying § 348(c) and Rule 1019. The clerk shall promptly

transmit a copy of the notice to the United States trustee.

(As amended Mar. 30, 1987, eff. Aug. 1, 1987; Apr. 30, 1991, eff. Aug. 1, 1991; Apr. 22, 1993, eff. Aug. 1, 1993; Apr. 29, 1999, eff. Dec. 1, 1999; Apr. 17, 2000, eff. Dec. 1, 2000; Apr. 23, 2008, eff. Dec. 1, 2008.)

ADVISORY COMMITTEE NOTES

Subdivision (a) of this rule is derived from former Bankruptcy Rule 120(a). While the rule applies to voluntary and involuntary cases, the "consent of the parties" referred to is that of petitioning creditors and the debtor in an involuntary case. The last sentence recognizes that the court should not be confined to petitioning creditors in its choice of parties on whom to call for assistance in preparing the list of creditors when the debtor fails to do so. This subdivision implements §§ 303(j), 707, 1112 and 1307 of the Code by specifying the manner of and persons to whom notice shall be given and requiring the court to hold a hearing on the issue of dismissal.

Subdivision (b) is derived from former Bankruptcy Rule 120(b). A dismissal under this subdivision can occur only when the petition has been permitted to be filed pursuant to Rule 1006(b). The provision for notice in paragraph (3) is correlated with the provision in Rule 4006 when there is a waiver, denial, or revocation of a discharge. As pointed out in the Note accompanying Rule 4008, the purpose of notifying creditors of a debtor that no discharge has been granted is to correct their assumption to the contrary so that they can take appropriate steps to protect their claims.

Subdivision (c) is new and specifies the notice required for a hearing on dismissal or suspension pursuant to § 305 of the Code. The suspension to which this subdivision refers is that of the case; it does not concern abstention of the court in hearing an adversary proceeding pursuant to 28 U.S.C. § 1478(b).

Subdivision (d). Any proceeding, whether by a debtor or other party, to dismiss or convert a case under §§ 706, 707, 1112, or 1307 is commenced by a motion pursuant to Rule 9014.

1987 Amendments

Subdivision (d) is amended to provide that dismissal or conversion pursuant to §§ 706(a), 707(b), 1112(a), and 1307(b) is not automatically a contested matter under Rule 9014. Conversion or dismissal under these sections is initiated by the filing and serving of a motion as required by Rule 9013. No hearing is required on these motions unless the court directs.

Conversion of a chapter 13 case to a chapter 7 case as authorized by § 1307(a) is accomplished by the filing of a notice of conversion. The notice of conversion procedure is modeled on the voluntary dismissal provision of Rule 41(a)(1) F.R.Civ.P. Conversion occurs on the filing of the notice. No court order is required.

Subdivision (e) is new and provides the procedure to be followed when a court on its own motion has made a preliminary determination that an individual debtor's chapter 7 case may be dismissed pursuant to § 707(b) of the Code, which was added by the 1984 amendments. A debtor's failure to attend the hearing is not a ground for dismissal pursuant to § 707(b).

1991 Amendments

Subdivision (a) is amended to clarify that all entities required to receive notice under Rule 2002, including but not limited to creditors, are entitled to the 20 day notice of the hearing to dismiss the case. The United States trustee receives the notice pursuant to Rule 2002(k).

The word "petition" is changed to "case" in subdivisions (a), (b), and (c) to conform to §§ 707, 930, 1112, 1208, and 1307.

Subdivision (d) is amended to conform to § 348(c) of the Code which refers to the "conversion order."

Subdivisions (a) and (d) are amended to provide procedures for dismissal or conversion of a chapter 12 case. Procedures for dismissal or conversion under § 1208(a) and (b) are the same as the procedures for dismissal or conversion of a chapter 13 case under § 1307(a) and (b).

Subdivision (e) is amended to conform to the 1986 amendment to § 707(b) of the Code which permits the United States trustee to make a motion to dismiss a case for substantial abuse. The time limit for such a motion is added by this subdivision. In general, the facts that are the basis for a motion to dismiss under § 707(b) exist at the time the case is commenced and usually can be discovered early in the case by reviewing the debtor's schedules and examining the debtor at the meeting of creditors. Since dismissal for substantial abuse has the effect of denying the debtor a discharge in the chapter 7 case based on matters which may be discovered early, a motion to dismiss under § 707(b) is analogous to an objection to discharge pursuant to Rule 4004 and, therefore, should be required to be made within a specified time period. If matters relating to substantial abuse are not discovered within the time period specified in subdivision (e) because of the debtor's false testimony, refusal to obey a court order, fraudulent schedules or other fraud, and the debtor receives a discharge, the debtor's conduct may constitute the basis for revocation of the discharge under § 727(d) and (e) of the Code.

1993 Amendments

Subdivision (d) is amended to clarify that the date of the filing of a notice of conversion in a chapter 12 or chapter 13 case is treated as the date of the conversion order for the purpose of applying Rule 1019. Other amendments are stylistic and make no substantive change.

1999 Amendments

Subdivision (b)(3), which provides that notice of dismissal for failure to pay the filing fee shall be sent to all creditors within 30 days after the dismissal, is deleted as unnecessary. Rule 2002(f) provides for notice to creditors of the dismissal of a case.

Rule 2002(a) and this rule currently require notice to all creditors of a hearing on dismissal of a voluntary chapter 7 case for the debtor's failure to file a list of creditors, schedules, and statement of financial affairs within the time provided in § 707(a)(3) of the Code. A new subdivision (c) is added to provide that the United States trustee, who is the only entity with standing to file a motion to dismiss under § 707(a)(3) or § 1307(c)(9), is required to serve the motion on only the debtor, the trustee, and any other entities as the court directs. This amendment, and the amendment to Rule 2002, will have the effect of avoiding the expense of sending notices of the motion to all creditors in a chapter 7 case.

New subdivision **(f)** is the same as current subdivision (d), except that it provides that a motion to suspend all proceedings in a case or to dismiss a case for substantial abuse of chapter 7 under § 707(b) is governed by Rule 9014.

Other amendments to this rule are stylistic or for clarification.

Gap Report on Rule 1017. No changes since publication, except for stylistic changes in Rule 1017(e) and (f).

2000 Amendments

This rule is amended to permit the court to grant a timely request filed by the United States trustee for an extension of time to file a motion to dismiss a chapter 7 case under § 707(b), whether the court rules on the request before or after the expiration of the 60–day period.

Reporter's Note on Text of Rule 1017(e). The above text of Rule 1017(e) is not based on the text of the rule in effect on this date. The above text embodies amendments that have been promulgated by the Supreme Court in April 1999 and, unless Congress acts with respect to the amendments, will become effective on December 1, 1999.

GAP Report on Rule 1017(e). No changes since publication.

2008 Amendments

Subdivision (e) is amended to implement the 2005 amendments to § 707 of the Code. These statutory amendments permit conversion of a chapter 7 case to a case under chapter 11 or 13, change the basis for dismissal or conversion from "substantial abuse" to "abuse," authorize parties other than the United States trustee to bring motions under § 707(b) under certain circumstances, and add § 707(c) to create an explicit ground for dismissal based on the request of a victim of a crime of violence or drug trafficking. The conforming amendments to subdivision (e) preserve the time limits already in place for § 707(b) motions, except to the extent that § 704(b)(2) sets the deadline for the United States trustee to act. In contrast to the grounds for a motion to dismiss under § 707(b)(2), which are quite specific, the grounds under § 707(b)(1) and (3) are very general. Therefore, to enable the debtor to respond, subdivision (e) requires that motions to dismiss under § 707(b)(1) and (3) state with particularity the circumstances alleged to constitute abuse.

CROSS REFERENCES

Conversion of—

Individual debt adjustment case, see 11 USCA § 1307.

Liquidation case, see 11 USCA § 706.

Reorganization case, see 11 USCA § 1112.

Dismissal of—

Individual debt adjustment case, see 11 USCA § 1307.

Involuntary petition, see 11 USCA § 303.

Liquidation case, see 11 USCA § 707.

Reorganization case, see 11 USCA § 1112.

Enlargement of thirty-day period for notice of dismissal for failure to pay filing fee not permitted, see Fed.Rules Bankr. Proc. Rule 9006, 11 USCA.

Motions; form and service, see Fed.Rules Bankr.Proc. Rule 9013, 11 USCA.

LIBRARY REFERENCES

American Digest System

Bankruptcy ⬦2252.1 to 2254, 2259.1 to 2264(3), 2295.1, 2331, 2332, 3591(1) to 3594, 3673, 3716.10 to 3717.

Key Number System Topic No. 51.

Corpus Juris Secundum

CJS Bankruptcy § 54, Notices.

CJS Bankruptcy § 308, Enlargement.

CJS Bankruptcy § 344, List of Creditors and Others.

CJS Bankruptcy § 416, Proceedings.

CJS Bankruptcy § 421, Proceedings.

CJS Bankruptcy § 427, Proceedings.

CJS Bankruptcy § 429, Proceedings.

CJS Bankruptcy § 451, Dismissal or Conversion on Request of United States Trustee.

CJS Bankruptcy § 457, Failure to Provide Copy of Debtor's Federal Income Tax Return to Trustee and Requesting Creditors.

CJS Bankruptcy § 458, Failure to File Prepetition Tax Returns in Chapter 13 Case.

CJS Bankruptcy § 459, Failure to File Postpetition Tax Return.

CJS Bankruptcy § 466, Filing of Lists, Inventories, Schedules, and Statements.

CJS Bankruptcy § 794, Time of Initial Meeting.

CJS Bankruptcy § 1054, Hearing, Determination, and Order.

Rule 1018. Contested Involuntary Petitions; Contested Petitions Commencing Chapter 15 Cases; Proceedings to Vacate Order for Relief; Applicability of Rules in Part VII Governing Adversary Proceedings

Unless the court otherwise directs and except as otherwise prescribed in Part I of these rules, the following rules in Part VII apply to all proceedings contesting an involuntary petition or a chapter 15 petition for recognition, and to all proceedings to vacate an order for relief: Rules 7005, 7008–7010, 7015, 7016, 7024–7026, 7028–7037, 7052, 7054, 7056, and 7062. The court may direct that other rules in Part VII shall also apply. For the purposes of this rule a reference in the Part VII rules to adversary proceedings shall be read as a reference to proceedings contesting an involuntary petition or a chapter 15 petition for recognition, or proceedings to vacate an order for relief. Reference in the Federal Rules of Civil Procedure to the complaint shall be read as a reference to the petition. (As amended Mar. 30, 1987, eff. Aug. 1, 1987; Apr. 28, 2010, eff. Dec. 1, 2010.)

ADVISORY COMMITTEE NOTES

The rules in Part VII to which this rule refers are adaptations of the Federal Rules of Civil Procedure for the purpose of governing the procedure in adversary proceedings in cases under the Code. See the Note accompanying Rule 7001 infra. Because of the special need for dispatch and expedition in the determination of the issues in an involuntary petition, see Acme Harvester Co. v. Beekman Lumber Co., 222 U.S. 300, 309 (1911), the objective of some of the Federal Rules of Civil Procedure and their adaptations in Part VII to facilitate the settlement of multiple controversies involving many persons in a single lawsuit is not compatible with the exigencies of bankruptcy administration. See United States F. & G. Co. v. Bray, 225 U.S. 205, 218 (1912). For that reason Rules 7013, 7014 and 7018–7023 will rarely be appropriate in a proceeding on a contested petition.

Certain terms used in the Federal Rules of Civil Procedure have altered meanings when they are made applicable in cases under the Code by these rules. See Rule 9002 infra. This Rule 1018 requires that the terms "adversary proceedings" when used in the rules in Part VII and "complaint" when used in the Federal Rules of Civil Procedure be given altered meanings when they are made applicable to proceedings relating to a contested petition or proceedings to vacate any order for relief. A motion to vacate an order for relief, whether or not made on a petition that was or could have been contested, is governed by the rules in Part VII referred to in this Rule 1018.

1987 Amendments

Rule 1018 is amended to include within its terms a petition commencing an ancillary case when it is contested. This provision was formerly included in Rule 1003(e)(4).

Although this rule does not contain an explicit authorization for the entry of an order for relief when a debtor refuses to cooperate in discovery relating to a contested involuntary petition, the court has ample power under Rule 37(b) F.R.Civ. P., as incorporated by Rule 7037, to enter an order for relief under appropriate circumstances. Rule 37(b) authorizes the court to enter judgment by default or an order that "facts shall be taken as established."

2010 Amendments

The rule is amended to reflect the enactment of chapter 15 of the Code in 2005. As to chapter 15 cases, the rule applies to contests over the petition for recognition and not to all matters that arise in the case. Thus, proceedings governed by § 1519(e) and § 1521(e) of the Code must comply with Rules 7001(7) and 7065, which provide that actions for injunctive relief are adversary proceedings governed by Part VII of the rules. The rule is also amended to clarify that it applies to contests over an involuntary petition, and not to matters merely "relating to" a contested involuntary petition. Matters that may arise in a chapter 15 case or an involuntary case, other than contests over the petition itself, are governed by the otherwise applicable rules.

Other changes are stylistic.

CROSS REFERENCES

Applicability of this rule to involuntary case ancillary to foreign proceeding, see Fed.Rules Bankr.Proc. Rule 1003, 11 USCA.

Effect of amendment of Federal Rules of Civil Procedure, see Fed.Rules Bankr.Proc. Rule 9032, 11 USCA.

LIBRARY REFERENCES

American Digest System

Bankruptcy ⊙2294 to 2297, 2341.

Key Number System Topic No. 51.

Corpus Juris Secundum

CJS Bankruptcy § 397, Hearing and Notice of Hearing.

Rule 1019. Conversion of a Chapter 11 Reorganization Case, Chapter 12 Family Farmer's Debt Adjustment Case, or Chapter 13 Individual's Debt Adjustment Case to a Chapter 7 Liquidation Case

When a chapter 11, chapter 12, or chapter 13 case has been converted or reconverted to a chapter 7 case:

(1) Filing of lists, inventories, schedules, statements

(A) Lists, inventories, schedules, and statements of financial affairs theretofore filed shall be deemed to be filed in the chapter 7 case, unless the court directs otherwise. If they have not been previously filed, the debtor shall comply with Rule 1007 as if an order for relief had been entered on an involuntary petition on the date of the entry of the order directing that the case continue under chapter 7.

(B) If a statement of intention is required, it shall be filed within 30 days after entry of the order of conversion or before the first date set for the meeting of creditors, whichever is earlier. The court may grant an extension of time for cause only on written motion filed, or oral request made during a hearing, before the time has expired. Notice of an extension shall be given to the United States trustee and to any committee, trustee, or other party as the court may direct.

(2) New filing periods

(A) A new time period for filing a motion under § 707(b) or (c), a claim, a complaint objecting to discharge, or a complaint to obtain a determination of dischargeability of any debt shall commence under Rules [1] 1017, 3002, 4004, or 4007, but a new time period shall not commence if a chapter 7 case had been converted to a chapter 11, 12, or 13 case and thereafter reconverted to a chapter 7 case and the time for filing a motion under § 707(b) or (c), a claim, a complaint objecting to discharge, or a complaint to obtain a determination of the dischargeability of any debt, or any extension thereof, expired in the original chapter 7 case.

(B) A new time period for filing an objection to a claim of exemptions shall commence under Rule 4003(b) after conversion of a case to chapter 7 unless:

(i) the case was converted to chapter 7 more than one year after the entry of the first order confirming a plan under chapter 11, 12, or 13; or

(ii) the case was previously pending in chapter 7 and the time to object to a claimed exemption had expired in the original chapter 7 case.

(3) Claims filed before conversion

All claims actually filed by a creditor before conversion of the case are deemed filed in the chapter 7 case.

(4) Turnover of records and property

After qualification of, or assumption of duties by the chapter 7 trustee, any debtor in possession or trustee previously acting in the chapter 11, 12, or 13 case shall, forthwith, unless otherwise ordered, turn over to the chapter 7 trustee all records and property of the estate in the possession or control of the debtor in possession or trustee.

(5) Filing final report and schedule of postpetition debts

(A) Conversion of Chapter 11 or Chapter 12 case

Unless the court directs otherwise, if a chapter 11 or chapter 12 case is converted to chapter 7, the debtor in possession or, if the debtor is not a debtor in possession, the trustee serving at the time of conversion, shall:

(i) not later than 14 days after conversion of the case, file a schedule of unpaid debts incurred after the filing of the petition and before conversion of the case, including the name and address of each holder of a claim; and

(ii) not later than 30 days after conversion of the case, file and transmit to the United States trustee a final report and account;

(B) Conversion of Chapter 13 case

Unless the court directs otherwise, if a chapter 13 case is converted to chapter 7,

(i) the debtor, not later than 14 days after conversion of the case, shall file a schedule of unpaid debts incurred after the filing of the petition and before conversion of the case, including the name and address of each holder of a claim; and

(ii) the trustee, not later than 30 days after conversion of the case, shall file and transmit to the United States trustee a final report and account;

(C) Conversion after confirmation of a plan

Unless the court orders otherwise, if a chapter 11, chapter 12, or chapter 13 case is converted to chapter 7 after confirmation of a plan, the debtor shall file:

(i) a schedule of property not listed in the final report and account acquired after the filing of the petition but before conversion, except if the case is converted from chapter 13 to chapter 7 and § 348(f)(2) does not apply;

(ii) a schedule of unpaid debts not listed in the final report and account incurred after confirmation but before the conversion; and

(iii) a schedule of executory contracts and unexpired leases entered into or assumed after the filing of the petition but before conversion.

(D) Transmission to United States trustee

The clerk shall forthwith transmit to the United States trustee a copy of every schedule filed pursuant to Rule 1019(5).

(6) Postpetition claims; preconversion administrative expenses; notice

A request for payment of an administrative expense incurred before conversion of the case is timely filed under § 503(a) of the Code if it is filed before conversion or a time fixed by the court. If the request is filed by a governmental unit, it is timely if it is filed before conversion or within the later of a time fixed by the court or 180 days after the date of the conversion. A claim of a kind specified in § 348(d) may be filed in accordance with Rules 3001(a)-(d) and 3002. Upon the filing of the schedule of unpaid debts incurred after commencement of the case and before conversion, the clerk, or some other person as the court may direct, shall give notice to those entities listed on the schedule of the time for filing a request for payment of an administrative expense and, unless a notice of insufficient assets to pay a dividend is mailed in accordance with Rule 2002(e), the time for filing a claim of a kind specified in § 348(d).

(7) [Abrogated]

(As amended Mar. 30, 1987, eff. Aug. 1, 1987; Apr. 30, 1991, eff. Aug. 1, 1991; Apr. 23, 1996, eff. Dec. 1, 1996; Apr. 11, 1997, eff. Dec. 1, 1997; Apr. 29, 1999, eff. Dec. 1, 1999; Apr. 23, 2008, eff. Dec. 1, 2008; Mar. 26, 2009, eff. Dec. 1, 2009; Apr. 28, 2010, eff. Dec. 1, 2010.)

1 So in original. Probably should be "Rule".

ADVISORY COMMITTEE NOTES

1983 Enactments

This rule is derived from former Bankruptcy Rule 122 and implements § 348 of the Code. The rule applies to proceedings in a chapter 7 case following supersession of a case commenced under chapter 11 or 13, whether the latter was initiated by an original petition or was converted from a pending chapter 7 or another chapter case. The rule is not intended to invalidate any action taken in the superseded case before its conversion to chapter 7.

Paragraph (1). If requirements applicable in the superseded case respecting the filing of schedules of debts and property, or lists of creditors and inventory, and of statements of financial affairs have been complied with before the order directing conversion to liquidation, these documents will ordinarily provide all the information about the debts, property, financial affairs, and contracts of the debtor needed for the administration of the estate. If the information submitted in the superseded case is inadequate for the purposes of administration, however, the court may direct the preparation of further informational material and the manner and time of its submission pursuant to paragraph (1). If no schedules, lists, inventories, or statements were filed in the superseded case, this paragraph imposes the duty on the debtor to file schedules and a statement of affairs pursuant to Rule 1007 as if an involuntary petition had been filed on the date when the court directed the conversion of the case to a liquidation case.

Paragraphs (2) and (3). Paragraph (2) requires notice to be given to all creditors of the order of conversion. The notice is to be included in the notice of the meeting of creditors and Official Form No. 16 may be adapted for use. A meeting of creditors may have been held in the superseded case as required by § 341(a) of the Code but that would not dispense with the need to hold one in the ensuing liquidation case. Section 701(a) of the Code permits the court to appoint the trustee acting in the chapter 11 or 13 case as interim trustee in the chapter 7 case. Section 702(a) of the Code allows creditors to elect a trustee but only at the meeting of creditors held under § 341. The right to elect a trustee is not lost because the chapter 7 case follows a chapter 11 or 13 case. Thus a meeting of creditors is necessary. The date fixed for the meeting of creditors will control at least the time for filing claims pursuant to Rule 3002(c). That time will remain applicable in the ensuing chapter 7 case except as paragraph (3) provides, if that time had expired in an earlier chapter 7 case which was converted to the chapter 11 or 13 case, it is not revived in the subsequent chapter 7 case. The same is true if the time for filing a complaint objecting to discharge or to determine nondischargeability of a debt had expired. Paragraph (3), however, recognizes that such time may be extended by the court under Rule 4004 or 4007 on motion made within the original prescribed time.

Paragraph (4) renders it unnecessary to file anew claims that had been filed in the chapter 11 or 13 case before conversion to chapter 7.

Paragraph (5) contemplates that typically, after the court orders conversion of a chapter case to liquidation, a trustee under chapter 7 will forthwith take charge of the property of the estate and proceed expeditiously to liquidate it. The court may appoint the interim trustee in the chapter 7 case pursuant to § 701(a) of the Code. If creditors do not elect a trustee under § 702, the interim trustee becomes the trustee.

Paragraph (6) requires the trustee or debtor in possession acting in the chapter 11 or 13 case to file a final report and schedule of debts incurred in that case. This schedule will provide the information necessary for giving the notice required by paragraph (7) of the rule.

Paragraph (7) requires that claims that arose in the chapter 11 or 13 case be filed within 60 days after entry of the order converting the case to one under chapter 7. Claims not scheduled pursuant to paragraph (6) of the rule or arising from the rejection of an executory contract entered into during the chapter case may be filed within a time fixed by the court. Pursuant to § 348(c) of the Code, the conversion order is treated as the order for relief to fix the time for the trustee to assume or reject executory contracts under § 365(d).

Paragraph (8) permits the extension of the time for filing claims when claims are not timely filed but only with respect to any surplus that may remain in the estate. See also § 726(a)(2)(C) and (3) of the Code.

1987 Amendments

Paragraph (1) is amended to provide for the filing of a statement of intention in a case converted to chapter 7. Paragraph (1)(B) is added to provide for the filing of the statement of intention when a case is converted to chapter 7. The time for filing the statement of intention and for an extension of that time is governed by § 521(2)(A) of the Code. An extension of time for other required filings is governed by Rule 1007(c), which paragraph (1)(A) incorporates by reference. Because of the amendment to Rule 1007(c), the filing of new lists, schedules, and statements is now governed exclusively by Rule 1019(1).

Paragraph (3) of the rule is expanded to include the effect of conversion of a chapter 11 or 13 case to a chapter 7 case. On conversion of a case from chapter 11 or 13 to a chapter 7 case, parties have a new period within which to file claims or complaints relating to the granting of the discharge or the dischargeability of a debt. This amendment is consistent with the holding and reasoning of the court in *F & M Marquette Nat'l Bank v. Richards*, 780 F.2d 24 (8th Cir.1985).

Paragraph (4) is amended to deal directly with the status of claims which are properly listed on the schedules filed in a chapter 11 case and deemed filed pursuant to § 1111(a) of the Code. Section 1111(a) is only applicable to the chapter 11 case. On conversion of the chapter 11 case to a chapter 7 case, paragraph (4) governs the status of claims filed in the chapter 11 case. The Third Circuit properly construed paragraph (4) as applicable to claims deemed filed in the superseded chapter 11 case. *In re Crouthamel Potato Chip Co.*, 786 F.2d 141 (3d Cir.1986).

The amendment to paragraph (4) changes that result by providing that only claims that are actually filed in the chapter 11 case are treated as filed in the superseding chapter 7 cases. When chapter 11 cases are converted to chapter 7 cases, difficulties in obtaining and verifying the debtors' records are common. It is unfair to the chapter 7 trustee and creditors to require that they be bound by schedules which may not be subject to verification.

Paragraph (6) is amended to place the obligation on the chapter 13 debtor to file a schedule of unpaid debts incurred during the superseded chapter 13 case.

1991 Amendments

This rule is amended to include conversion of a case from chapter 12 to chapter 7 and to implement the United States trustee system.

The amendments to paragraph (1)(A) are stylistic. Reference to the statement of executory contracts is deleted to conform to the amendment to Rule 1007(b)(1) which changes the statement to a schedule of executory contracts and unexpired leases.

Paragraph (1)(B) is amended to enable the United States trustee to monitor the progress of the case and to take appropriate action to enforce the debtor's obligation to perform the statement of intention in a timely manner.

Paragraph (2) is deleted because notice of conversion of the case is required by Rules 1017(d), 2002(f)(2), and 9022. The United States trustee, who supervises trustees pursuant to 28 U.S.C. § 586(a), may give notice of the conversion to the trustee in the superseded case.

Paragraph (6), renumbered as paragraph (5), is amended to reduce to 15 days the time for filing a schedule of postpetition debts and requires inclusion of the name and address of each creditor in connection with the postpetition debt. These changes will enable the clerk to send postpetition creditors a timely notice of the meeting of creditors held pursuant to § 341(a) of the Code. The amendments to this paragraph also provide the United States trustee with the final report and account of the superseded case, and with a copy of every schedule filed after conversion of the case. Conversion to chapter 7 terminates the service of the trustee in the superseded case pursuant to § 348(e) of the Code. Sections 704(a)(9), 1106(a)(1), 1107(a), 1202(b)(1), 1203 and 1302(b)(1) of the Code require the trustee or debtor in possession to file a final report and account with the court and the United States trustee. The words "with the court" are deleted as unnecessary. See Rules 5005(a) and 9001(3).

Paragraph (7), renumbered as paragraph (6), is amended to conform the time for filing postpetition claims to the time for filing prepetition claims pursuant to paragraph (3) (renumbered as paragraph (2)) of this rule and Rule 3002(c). This paragraph is also amended to eliminate the need for a court order to provide notice of the time for filing claims. It is anticipated that this notice will be given together with the notice of the meeting of creditors. It is amended further to avoid the need to fix a time for filing claims arising under § 365(d) if it is a no asset case upon conversion. If assets become available for distribution, the court may fix a time for filing such claims pursuant to Rule 3002(c)(4).

The additions of references to unexpired leases in paragraph (1)(A) and in paragraphs (6) and (7) (renumbered as paragraphs (5) and (6)) are technical amendments to clarify that unexpired leases are included as well as other executory contracts.

1996 Amendments

Subdivision (7) is abrogated to conform to the abrogation of Rule 3002(c)(6).

GAP Report on Rule 1019. No changes were made to the text of the rule. The Committee Note was changed to conform to the proposed changes to Rule 3002 (see GAP Report on Rule 3002 below).

1997 Amendments

The amendments to subdivisions (3) and (5) are technical corrections and stylistic changes. The phrase "superseded case" is deleted because it creates the erroneous impression that conversion of a case results in a new case that is distinct from the original case. Similarly, the phrase "original petition" is deleted because it erroneously implies that there is a second petition with respect to a converted case. See § 348 of the Code.

GAP Report on Rule 1019. No changes to the published draft.

1999 Amendments

Paragraph (1)(B) is amended to clarify that a motion for an extension of time to file a statement of intention must be made by written motion filed before the time expires, or by oral request made at a hearing before the time expires.

Subdivision (6) is amended to provide that a holder of an administrative expense claim incurred after the commencement of the case, but before conversion to chapter 7, is required to file a request for payment under § 503(a) within a time fixed by the court, rather than a proof of claim under § 501 and Rules 3001(a)-(d) and 3002. The 180-day period applicable to governmental units is intended to conform to § 502(b)(9) of the Code and Rule 3002(c)(1). It is unnecessary for the court to fix a time for filing requests for payment if it appears that there are not sufficient assets to pay preconversion administrative expenses. If a time for filing a request for payment of an administrative expense is fixed by the court, it may be enlarged as provided in Rule 9006(b). If an administrative expense claimant fails to timely file the request, it may be tardily filed under § 503(a) if permitted by the court for cause.

The final sentence of Rule 1019(6) is deleted because it is unnecessary in view of the other amendments to this paragraph. If a party has entered into a postpetition contract or lease with the trustee or debtor that constitutes an administrative expense, a timely request for payment must be filed in accordance with this paragraph and § 503(b) of the Code. The time for filing a proof of claim in connection with the rejection of any other executory contract or unexpired lease is governed by Rule 3002(c)(4).

The phrase "including the United States, any state, or any subdivision thereof" is deleted as unnecessary. Other amendments to this rule are stylistic.

Gap Report on Rule 1019. The proposed amendments to Rule 1019(6) were changed to delete the deadline for filing requests for payment of preconversion administrative expenses that would be applicable in all cases, and to provide instead that the court may fix such a deadline. The committee note was revised to clarify that it is not necessary for the court to fix a deadline where there are insufficient assets to pay preconversion administrative expenses.

2008 Amendments

Subdivision (2) is amended to include a new filing period for motions under § 707(b) and (c) of the Code when a case is converted to chapter 7. The establishment of a deadline for filing such motions is not intended to express a position as to whether such motions are permitted under the Code.

2009 Amendments

The rule is amended to implement changes in connection with the amendment to Rule 9006(a) and the manner by which time is computed under the rules. The deadlines in the rule are amended to substitute a deadline that is a multiple of seven days. Throughout the rules, deadlines are amended in the following manner:

- 5–day periods become 7–day periods
- 10–day periods become 14–day periods
- 15–day periods become 14–day periods
- 20–day periods become 21–day periods
- 25–day periods become 28–day periods

2010 Amendments

Subdivision (2). Subdivision (2) is redesignated as subdivision (2)(A), and a new subdivision (2)(B) is added to the rule. Subdivision (2)(B) provides that a new time period to object to a claim of exemption arises when a case is converted to chapter 7 from chapter 11, 12, or 13. The new time period does not arise, however, if the conversion occurs more than one year after the first order confirming a plan, even if the plan was subsequently modified. A new objection period also does not arise if the case was previously pending under chapter 7 and the objection period had expired in the prior chapter 7 case.

CROSS REFERENCES

Appointment of interim trustee, see Fed.Rules Bankr.Proc. Rule 2001, 11 USCA.

Election of trustee, see 11 USCA § 702.

Enlargement of twenty-day period for notice of order of conversion to liquidation case not permitted, see Fed.Rules Bankr.Proc. Rule 9006, 11 USCA.

Failure to effect plan or substantial consummation of confirmed plan, see 11 USCA § 1112.

Meeting of creditors or equity security holders, see Fed. Rules Bankr.Proc. Rule 2003, 11 USCA.

LIBRARY REFERENCES

American Digest System

Bankruptcy ⇒3591(1) to 3594, 3673, 3716.20(1) to 3716.20(12), 3717.

Key Number System Topic No. 51.

Corpus Juris Secundum

CJS Bankruptcy § 358, Amendment.

CJS Bankruptcy § 466, Filing of Lists, Inventories, Schedules, and Statements.

CJS Bankruptcy § 467, Filing Periods.

CJS Bankruptcy § 468, Preconversion Claims.

CJS Bankruptcy § 469, Turnover of Records and Property.

CJS Bankruptcy § 470, Filing Final Report and Schedule of Postpetition Debts.

CJS Bankruptcy § 578, Debtor's Statement of Intention.

CJS Bankruptcy § 586, Effect of Conversion on Time Allowed for Objection.

CJS Bankruptcy § 627, Turnover of Records and Property to Chapter 7 Trustee Upon Conversion of Chapter 11, 12, or 13 Case.

CJS Bankruptcy § 794, Time of Initial Meeting.

Rule 1020. Small Business Chapter 11 Reorganization Case

(a) Small business debtor designation

In a voluntary chapter 11 case, the debtor shall state in the petition whether the debtor is a small business debtor. In an involuntary chapter 11 case, the debtor shall file within 14 days after entry of the order for relief a statement as to whether the debtor is a small business debtor. Except as provided in subdivision (c), the status of the case as a small business case shall be in accordance with the debtor's statement under this subdivision, unless and until the court enters an order finding that the debtor's statement is incorrect.

(b) Objecting to designation

Except as provided in subdivision (c), the United States trustee or a party in interest may file an objection to the debtor's statement under subdivision (a) no later than 30 days after the conclusion of the meeting of creditors held under § 341(a) of the Code, or within 30 days after any amendment to the statement, whichever is later.

(c) Appointment of committee of unsecured creditors

If a committee of unsecured creditors has been appointed under § 1102(a)(1), the case shall proceed as a small business case only if, and from the time when, the court enters an order determining that the committee has not been sufficiently active and representative to provide effective oversight of the debtor and that the debtor satisfies all the other requirements for being a small business. A request for a determination under this subdivision may be filed by the United States trustee or a party in interest only within a reasonable time after the failure of the committee to be sufficiently active and representative. The debtor may file a request for a determination at any time as to whether the committee has been sufficiently active and representative.

(d) Procedure for objection or determination

Any objection or request for a determination under this rule shall be governed by Rule 9014 and served on: the debtor; the debtor's attorney; the United States trustee; the trustee; any committee appointed under § 1102 or its authorized agent, or, if no committee of unsecured creditors has been appointed under § 1102, the creditors included on the list filed under Rule 1007(d); and any other entity as the court directs. (Added Apr. 11, 1997, eff. Dec. 1, 1997; amended Apr. 23, 2008, eff. Dec. 1, 2008; Mar, 26, 2009, eff. Dec. 1, 2009.)

ADVISORY COMMITTEE NOTES

1997 Amendments

This rule is designed to implement §§ 1121(e) and 1125(f), which were added to the Code by the Bankruptcy Reform Act of 1994.

GAP Report on Rule 1020. The phrase "or by a later date as the court, for cause, may fix" at the end of the published draft was deleted. The general provisions on reducing or extending time periods under Rule 9006 will be applicable.

2008 Amendments

Under the Code, as amended in 2005, there are no longer any provisions permitting or requiring a small business debtor to elect to be treated as a small business. Therefore, the election provisions in the rule are eliminated.

The 2005 amendments to the Code include several provisions relating to small business cases under chapter 11.

Section 101 includes definitions of "small business debtor" and "small business case." The purpose of the new language in this rule is to provide a procedure for informing the parties, the United States trustee, and the court of whether the debtor is a small business debtor, and to provide procedures for resolving disputes regarding the proper characterization of the debtor. Because it is important to resolve such disputes early in the case, a time limit for objecting to the debtor's self-designation is imposed. Rule 9006(b)(1), which governs enlargement of time, is applicable to the time limits set forth in this rule.

An important factor in determining whether the debtor is a small business debtor is whether the United States trustee has appointed a committee of unsecured creditors under § 1102, and whether such a committee is sufficiently active and representative. Subdivision (c), relating to the appointment and activity of a committee of unsecured creditors, is designed to be consistent with the Code's definition of "small business debtor."

2009 Amendments

The rule is amended to implement changes in connection with the amendment to Rule 9006(a) and the manner by which time is computed under the rules. The deadline in the rule is amended to substitute a deadline that is a multiple of seven days. Throughout the rules, deadlines are amended in the following manner:

- 5–day periods become 7–day periods
- 10–day periods become 14–day periods
- 15–day periods become 14–day periods
- 20–day periods become 21–day periods
- 25–day periods become 28–day periods

LIBRARY REFERENCES

American Digest System

Bankruptcy ⟷3501.

Key Number System Topic No. 51.

Corpus Juris Secundum

CJS Bankruptcy § 360, Designation of Debtor as Small Business.

CJS Bankruptcy § 361, Status of Case as Small Business Case.

CJS Bankruptcy § 362, Procedure on Objection or Request for Determination.

CJS Bankruptcy § 470, Filing Final Report and Schedule of Postpetition Debts.

Rule 1021. Health Care Business Case

(a) Health care business designation

Unless the court orders otherwise, if a petition in a case under Chapter 7, chapter 9, or chapter 11 states that the debtor is a health care business, the case shall proceed as a case in which the debtor is a health care business.

(b) Motion

The United States trustee or a party in interest may file a motion to determine whether the debtor is a health care business. The motion shall be transmitted to the United States trustee and served on: the debtor; the trustee; any committee elected under § 705 or appointed under § 1102 of the Code or its authorized agent, or, if the case is a chapter 9 municipality case or a chapter 11 reorganization case and no committee of unsecured creditors has been appointed under § 1102, the creditors included on the list filed under Rule 1007(d); and any other entity as the court directs. The motion shall be governed by Rule 9014.

(Added Apr. 23, 2008, eff. Dec. 1, 2008.)

ADVISORY COMMITTEE NOTES

2008 Adoption

Section 101(27A) of the Code, added by the 2005 amendments, defines a health care business. This rule provides procedures for designating the debtor as a health care business. The debtor in a voluntary case, or petitioning creditors in an involuntary case, make that designation by checking the appropriate box on the petition. The rule also provides procedures for resolving disputes regarding the status of the debtor as a health care business.

LIBRARY REFERENCES

Corpus Juris Secundum

CJS Bankruptcy § 359, Designation of Debtor as Health Care Business.

PART II—OFFICERS AND ADMINISTRATION; NOTICES; MEETINGS; EXAMINATIONS; ELECTIONS; ATTORNEYS AND ACCOUNTANTS

Rule

2001. Appointment of Interim Trustee Before Order for Relief in a Chapter 7 Liquidation Case.

2002. Notices to Creditors, Equity Security Holders, Administrators in Foreign Proceedings, Persons Against Whom Provisional Relief is Sought in Ancillary and Other Cross–Border Cases, United States, and United States Trustee.

2003. Meeting of Creditors or Equity Security Holders.

2004. Examination.

2005. Apprehension and Removal of Debtor to Compel Attendance for Examination.

2006. Solicitation and Voting of Proxies in Chapter 7 Liquidation Cases.

2007. Review of Appointment of Creditors' Committee Organized Before Commencement of the Case.

2007.1. Appointment of Trustee or Examiner in a Chapter 11 Reorganization Case.

2007.2. Appointment of Patient Care Ombudsman in a Health Care Business Case.

2008. Notice to Trustee of Selection.

2009. Trustees for Estates When Joint Administration Ordered.

2010. Qualification by Trustee; Proceeding on Bond.

2011. Evidence of Debtor in Possession or Qualification of Trustee.

2012. Substitution of Trustee or Successor Trustee; Accounting.

2013. Public Record of Compensation Awarded to Trustees, Examiners, and Professionals.

2014. Employment of Professional Persons.

2015. Duty to Keep Records, Make Reports, and Give Notice of Case or Change of Status.

2015.1. Patient Care Ombudsman.

2015.2. Transfer of Patient in Health Care Business Case.

2015.3. Reports of Financial Information on Entities in Which a Chapter 11 Estate Holds a Controlling or Substantial Interest.

2016. Compensation for Services Rendered and Reimbursement of Expenses.

2017. Examination of Debtor's Transactions with Debtor's Attorney.

2018. Intervention; Right to Be Heard.

2019. Disclosure Regarding Creditors and Equity Security Holders in Chapter 9 and Chapter 11 Cases.

2020. Review of Acts by United States Trustee.

Rule 2001. Appointment of Interim Trustee Before Order for Relief in a Chapter 7 Liquidation Case

(a) Appointment

At any time following the commencement of an involuntary liquidation case and before an order for relief, the court on written motion of a party in interest may order the appointment of an interim trustee under § 303(g) of the Code. The motion shall set forth the necessity for the appointment and may be granted only after hearing on notice to the debtor, the petitioning creditors, the United States trustee, and other parties in interest as the court may designate.

(b) Bond of movant

An interim trustee may not be appointed under this rule unless the movant furnishes a bond in an amount approved by the court, conditioned to indemnify the debtor for costs, attorney's fee, expenses, and damages allowable under § 303(i) of the Code.

(c) Order of Appointment

The order directing the appointment of an interim trustee shall state the reason the appointment is necessary and shall specify the trustee's duties.

(d) Turnover and report

Following qualification of the trustee selected under § 702 of the Code, the interim trustee, unless otherwise ordered, shall (1) forthwith deliver to the trustee all the records and property of the estate in possession or subject to control of the interim trustee and, (2) within 30 days thereafter file a final report and account.

(As amended Mar. 30, 1987, eff. Aug. 1, 1987; Apr. 30, 1991, eff. Aug. 1, 1991.)

ADVISORY COMMITTEE NOTES

This rule is adapted from former Bankruptcy Rule 201. See also former Chapter X Rule 10–201. In conformity with title 11 of the United States Code, this rule substitutes "interim trustee" for "receiver." Subdivision (a) and (e) of Rule 201 are not included because the provisions contained therein are found in detail in § 303(g) of the Code, or they are inconsistent with § 701 of the Code. Similarly, the provisions in Rule 201(d) relating to a debtor's counterbond are not included because of their presence in § 303(g).

Subdivision (a) makes it clear that the court may not on its own motion order the appointment of an interim trustee before an order for relief is entered. Appointment may be ordered only on motion of a party in interest.

Subdivision (b) requires those seeking the appointment of an interim trustee to furnish a bond. The bond may be the same one required of petitioning creditors under § 303(e) of the Code to indemnify the debtor for damages allowed by the court under § 303(i).

Subdivision (c) requires that the order specify which duties enumerated in § 303(g) shall be performed by the interim trustee. Reference should be made to Rule 2015 for additional duties required of an interim trustee including keeping records and filing periodic reports with the court.

Subdivision (d) requires turnover of records and property to the trustee selected under § 702 of the Code, after qualification. That trustee may be the interim trustee who becomes the trustee because of the failure of creditors to elect one under § 702(d) or the trustee elected by creditors under § 702(b), (c).

1991 Amendments

This rule is amended to conform to § 303(g) of the Code which provides that the United States trustee appoints the interim trustee. See Rule X–1003. This rule does not apply to the exercise by the court of the power to act sua sponte pursuant to § 105(a) of the Code.

CROSS REFERENCES

Duty to keep and file records and reports, see Fed.Rules Bankr.Proc. Rule 2015, 11 USCA.

Interim trustee, see 11 USCA § 701.

Motions; form and service, see Fed.Rules Bankr.Proc. Rule 9013, 11 USCA.

Security; proceedings against sureties, see Fed.Rules Bankr.Proc. Rule 9025, 11 USCA.

LIBRARY REFERENCES

American Digest System

Bankruptcy ⚌3002, 3006, 3011.
Key Number System Topic No. 51.

Corpus Juris Secundum

CJS Bankruptcy § 50, Chapter 7 Proceedings.
CJS Bankruptcy § 62, Appointment of Interim Trustee.
CJS Bankruptcy § 368, Effect of Case on Debtor's Property and Business.

Rule 2002. Notices to Creditors, Equity Security Holders, Administrators in Foreign Proceedings, Persons Against Whom Provisional Relief is Sought in Ancillary and Other Cross–Border Cases, United States, and United States Trustee

(a) Twenty–one–day notices to parties in interest

Except as provided in subdivisions (h), (i), (l), (p), and (q) of this rule, the clerk, or some other person as the court may direct, shall give the debtor, the trustee, all creditors and indenture trustees at least 21 days' notice by mail of:

(1) the meeting of creditors under § 341 or § 1104(b) of the Code, which notice, unless the court orders otherwise, shall include the debtor's employer identification number, social security number, and any other federal taxpayer identification number;

(2) a proposed use, sale, or lease of property of the estate other than in the ordinary course of business, unless the court for cause shown shortens the time or directs another method of giving notice;

(3) the hearing on approval of a compromise or settlement of a controversy other than approval of an agreement pursuant to Rule 4001(d), unless the court for cause shown directs that notice not be sent;

(4) in a chapter 7 liquidation, a chapter 11 reorganization case, or a chapter 12 family farmer debt adjustment case, the hearing on the dismissal of the case or the conversion of the case to another chapter, unless the hearing is under § 707(a)(3) or § 707(b) or is on dismissal of the case for failure to pay the filing fee;

(5) the time fixed to accept or reject a proposed modification of a plan;

(6) a hearing on any entity's request for compensation or reimbursement of expenses if the request exceeds $1,000;

(7) the time fixed for filing proofs of claims pursuant to Rule 3003(c); and

(8) the time fixed for filing objections and the hearing to consider confirmation of a chapter 12 plan.

(b) Twenty–eight–day notices to parties in interest

Except as provided in subdivision (l) of this rule, the clerk, or some other person as the court may direct, shall give the debtor, the trustee, all creditors and indenture trustees not less than 28 days' notice by mail of the time fixed (1) for filing objections and the hearing to consider approval of a disclosure statement or, under § 1125(f), to make a final determination whether the plan provides adequate information so that a separate disclosure statement is not necessary; and (2) for filing objections and the hearing to consider confirmation of a chapter 9, chapter 11, or chapter 13 plan.

(c) Content of notice

(1) Proposed Use, Sale, or Lease of Property

Subject to Rule 6004, the notice of a proposed use, sale, or lease of property required by subdivision (a)(2) of this rule shall include the time and place of any public sale, the terms and conditions of any private sale and the time fixed for filing objections. The notice of a proposed use, sale, or lease of property, including real estate, is sufficient if it generally describes the property. The notice of a proposed sale or lease of personally identifiable information under § 363(b)(1) of the Code shall state whether the sale is consistent with any policy prohibiting the transfer of the information.

(2) Notice of hearing on compensation

The notice of a hearing on an application for compensation or reimbursement of expenses required by subdivision (a)(6) of this rule shall identify the applicant and the amounts requested.

(3) Notice of hearing on confirmation when plan provides for an injunction

If a plan provides for an injunction against conduct not otherwise enjoined under the Code, the notice required under Rule 2002(b)(2) shall:

(**A**) include in conspicuous language (bold, italic, or underlined text) a statement that the plan proposes an injunction;

(**B**) describe briefly the nature of the injunction; and

(**C**) identify the entities that would be subject to the injunction.

(d) Notice to equity security holders

In a chapter 11 reorganization case, unless otherwise ordered by the court, the clerk, or some other person as the court may direct, shall in the manner and form directed by the court give notice to all equity security holders of (1) the order for relief; (2) any meeting of equity security holders held pursuant to § 341 of the Code; (3) the hearing on the proposed sale of all or substantially all of the debtor's assets; (4) the hearing on the dismissal or conversion of a case to another chapter; (5) the time fixed for filing objections to and the hearing to consider approval of a disclosure statement; (6) the time fixed for filing objections to and the hearing to consider confirmation of a plan; and (7) the time fixed to accept or reject a proposed modification of a plan.

(e) Notice of no dividend

In a chapter 7 liquidation case, if it appears from the schedules that there are no assets from which a dividend can be paid, the notice of the meeting of creditors may include a statement to that effect; that it is unnecessary to file claims; and that if sufficient assets become available for the payment of a dividend, further notice will be given for the filing of claims.

(f) Other notices

Except as provided in subdivision (*l*) of this rule, the clerk, or some other person as the court may direct, shall give the debtor, all creditors, and indenture trustees notice by mail of:

(1) the order for relief;

(2) the dismissal or the conversion of the case to another chapter, or the suspension of proceedings under § 305;

(3) the time allowed for filing claims pursuant to Rule 3002;

(4) the time fixed for filing a complaint objecting to the debtor's discharge pursuant to § 727 of the Code as provided in Rule 4004;

(5) the time fixed for filing a complaint to determine the dischargeability of a debt pursuant to § 523 of the Code as provided in Rule 4007;

(6) the waiver, denial, or revocation of a discharge as provided in Rule 4006;

(7) entry of an order confirming a chapter 9, 11, or 12 plan;

(8) a summary of the trustee's final report in a chapter 7 case if the net proceeds realized exceed $1,500;

(9) a notice under Rule 5008 regarding the presumption of abuse;

(10) a statement under § 704(b)(1) as to whether the debtor's case would be presumed to be an abuse under § 707(b); and

(11) the time to request a delay in the entry of the discharge under §§ 1141(d)(5)(C), 1228(f), and 1328(h). Notice of the time fixed for accepting or rejecting a plan pursuant to Rule 3017(c) shall be given in accordance with Rule 3017(d).

(g) Addressing notices

(1) Notices required to be mailed under Rule 2002 to a creditor, indenture trustee, or equity security holder shall be addressed as such entity or an authorized agent has directed in its last request filed in the particular case. For the purposes of this subdivision—

(**A**) a proof of claim filed by a creditor or indenture trustee that designates a mailing address constitutes a filed request to mail notices to that address, unless a notice of no dividend has been given under Rule 2002(e) and a later notice of possible dividend under Rule 3002(c)(5) has not been given; and

(**B**) a proof of interest filed by an equity security holder that designates a mailing address constitutes a filed request to mail notices to that address.

(2) Except as provided in § 342(f) of the Code, if a creditor or indenture trustee has not filed a request designating a mailing address under Rule 2002(g)(1) or Rule 5003(e), the notices shall be mailed to the address shown on the list of creditors or schedule of liabilities, whichever is filed later. If an equity security holder has not filed a request designating a mailing address under Rule 2002(g)(1) or Rule 5003(e), the notices shall be mailed to the address shown on the list of equity security holders.

(3) If a list or schedule filed under Rule 1007 includes the name and address of a legal representative of an infant or incompetent person, and a person other than that representative files a request or proof of claim designating a name and mailing address that differs from the name and address of the representative included in the list or schedule, unless the court orders otherwise, notices under Rule 2002 shall be mailed to the representative included in the list or schedules and to the name and address designated in the request or proof of claim.

(4) Notwithstanding Rule 2002(g)(1)-(3), an entity and a notice provider may agree that when the notice provider is directed by the court to give a notice, the notice provider shall give the notice to the

entity in the manner agreed to and at the address or addresses the entity supplies to the notice provider. That address is conclusively presumed to be a proper address for the notice. The notice provider's failure to use the supplied address does not invalidate any notice that is otherwise effective under applicable law.

(5) A creditor may treat a notice as not having been brought to the creditor's attention under § 342(g)(1) only if, prior to issuance of the notice, the creditor has filed a statement that designates the name and address of the person or organizational subdivision of the creditor responsible for receiving notices under the Code, and that describes the procedures established by the creditor to cause such notices to be delivered to the designated person or subdivision.

(h) Notices to creditors whose claims are filed

In a chapter 7 case, after 90 days following the first date set for the meeting of creditors under § 341 of the Code, the court may direct that all notices required by subdivision (a) of this rule be mailed only to the debtor, the trustee, all indenture trustees, creditors that hold claims for which proofs of claim have been filed, and creditors, if any, that are still permitted to file claims by reason of an extension granted pursuant to Rule 3002(c)(1) or (c)(2). In a case where notice of insufficient assets to pay a dividend has been given to creditors pursuant to subdivision (e) of this rule, after 90 days following the mailing of a notice of the time for filing claims pursuant to Rule 3002(c)(5), the court may direct that notices be mailed only to the entities specified in the preceding sentence.

(i) Notices to committees

Copies of all notices required to be mailed pursuant to this rule shall be mailed to the committees elected under § 705 or appointed under § 1102 of the Code or to their authorized agents. Notwithstanding the foregoing subdivisions, the court may order that notices required by subdivision (a)(2), (3) and (6) of this rule be transmitted to the United States trustee and be mailed only to the committees elected under § 705 or appointed under § 1102 of the Code or to their authorized agents and to the creditors and equity security holders who serve on the trustee or debtor in possession and file a request that all notices be mailed to them. A committee appointed under § 1114 shall receive copies of all notices required by subdivisions (a)(1), (a)(5), (b), (f)(2), and (f)(7), and such other notices as the court may direct.

(j) Notices to the United States

Copies of notices required to be mailed to all creditors under this rule shall be mailed (1) in a chapter 11 reorganization case, to the Securities and Exchange Commission at any place the Commission designates, if the Commission has filed either a notice of appearance in the case or a written request to receive notices; (2) in a commodity broker case, to the Commodity Futures Trading Commission at Washington, D.C.; (3) in a chapter 11 case, to the Internal Revenue Service at its address set out in the register maintained under Rule 5003(e) for the district in which the case is pending; (4) if the papers in the case disclose a debt to the United States other than for taxes, to the United States attorney for the district in which the case is pending and to the department, agency, or instrumentality of the United States through which the debtor became indebted; or (5) if the filed papers disclose a stock interest of the United States, to the Secretary of the Treasury at Washington, D.C.

(k) Notices to United States trustee

Unless the case is a chapter 9 municipality case or unless the United States trustee requests otherwise, the clerk, or some other person as the court may direct, shall transmit to the United States trustee notice of the matters described in subdivisions (a)(2), (a)(3), (a)(4), (a)(8), (b), (f)(1), (f)(2), (f)(4), (f)(6), (f)(7), (f)(8), and (q) of this rule and notice of hearings on all applications for compensation or reimbursement of expenses. Notices to the United States trustee shall be transmitted within the time prescribed in subdivision (a) or (b) of this rule. The United States trustee shall also receive notice of any other matter if such notice is requested by the United States trustee or ordered by the court. Nothing in these rules requires the clerk or any other person to transmit to the United States trustee any notice, schedule, report, application or other document in a case under the Securities Investor Protection Act, 15 U.S.C. § 78aaa et. [1] seq.

(l) Notice by publication

The court may order notice by publication if it finds that notice by mail is impracticable or that it is desirable to supplement the notice.

(m) Orders designating matter of notices

The court may from time to time enter orders designating the matters in respect to which, the entity to whom, and the form and manner in which notices shall be sent except as otherwise provided by these rules.

(n) Caption

The caption of every notice given under this rule shall comply with Rule 1005. The caption of every notice required to be given by the debtor to a creditor shall include the information required to be in the notice by § 342(c) of the Code.

(o) Notice of Order for Relief in Consumer Case.

In a voluntary case commenced by an individual debtor whose debts are primarily consumer debts, the clerk or some other person as the court may direct shall give the trustee and all creditors notice by mail of the order for relief within 21 days from the date thereof.

(p) Notice to a creditor with a foreign address

(1) If, at the request of the United States trustee or a party in interest, or on its own initiative, the court finds that a notice mailed within the time prescribed by these rules would not be sufficient to give a creditor with a foreign address to which notices under these rules are mailed reasonable notice under the circumstances, the court may order that the notice be supplemented with notice by other means or that the time prescribed for the notice by mail be enlarged.

(2) Unless the court for cause orders otherwise, a creditor with a foreign address to which notices under this rule are mailed shall be given at least 30 days' notice of the time fixed for filing a proof of claim under Rule 3002(c) or Rule 3003(c).

(3) Unless the court for cause orders otherwise, the mailing address of a creditor with a foreign address shall be determined under Rule 2002(g).

(q) Notice of petition for recognition of foreign proceeding and of court's intention to communicate with foreign courts and foreign representatives

(1) Notice of Petition for Recognition.

The clerk, or some other person as the court may direct, shall forthwith give the debtor, all persons or bodies authorized to administer foreign proceedings of the debtor, all entities against whom provisional relief is being sought under § 1519 of the Code, all parties to litigation pending in the United States in which the debtor is a party at the time of the filing of the petition, and such other entities as the court may direct, at least 21 days' notice by mail of the hearing on the petition for recognition of a foreign proceeding. The notice shall state whether the petition seeks recognition as a foreign main proceeding or foreign nonmain proceeding.

(2) Notice of Court's Intention to Communicate with Foreign Courts and Foreign Representatives.

The clerk, or some other person as the court may direct, shall give the debtor, all persons or bodies authorized to administer foreign proceedings of the debtor, all entities against whom provisional relief is being sought under § 1519 of the Code, all parties to litigation pending in the United States in which the debtor is a party at the time of the filing of the petition, and such other entities as the court may direct, notice by mail of the court's intention to communicate with a foreign court or foreign representative.

(As amended Pub.L. 98–91, § 2(a), Aug. 30, 1983, 97 Stat. 607; Pub.L. 98–353, Title III, § 321, July 10, 1984, 98 Stat. 357; Mar. 30, 1987, eff. Aug. 1, 1987; Apr. 30, 1991, eff. Aug. 1, 1991; Apr. 22, 1993, eff. Aug. 1, 1993; Apr. 23, 1996, eff. Dec. 1, 1996; Apr. 11, 1997, eff. Dec. 1, 1997; Apr. 29, 1999, eff. Dec. 1, 1999; Apr. 17, 2000, eff. Dec. 1, 2000; Apr. 23, 2001, eff. Dec. 1, 2001; Mar. 27, 2003, eff. Dec. 1, 2003; Apr. 26, 2004, eff. Dec. 1, 2004; Apr. 25, 2005, eff. Dec. 1, 2005; Apr. 23, 2008, eff. Dec. 1, 2008; Mar. 26, 2009, eff. Dec. 1, 2009.)

[1] So in original. Period probably should not appear.

ADVISORY COMMITTEE NOTES

1983 Enactments

Some of the notices required by this rule may be given either by the clerk or as the court may otherwise direct. For example, the court may order the trustee or debtor in possession to transmit one or more of the notices required by this rule, such as, notice of a proposed sale of property. See § 363(b) of the Code. When publication of notices is required or desirable, reference should be made to Rule 9008.

Notice of the order for relief is required to be given by § 342 of the Code and by subdivision (f)(1) of this rule. That notice may be combined with the notice of the meeting of creditors as indicated in Official Form No. 16, the notice and order of the meeting of creditors.

Subdivision (a) sets forth the requirement that 20 days notice be given of the significant events in a case under the Bankruptcy Code. The former Act and Rules provided a ten day notice in bankruptcy and Chapter XI [former § 701 et seq. of this title] cases, and a 20 day notice in a Chapter X [former § 501 et seq. of this title] case. This rule generally makes uniform the 20 day notice provision except that subdivision (b) contains a 25 day period for certain events in a chapter 9, 11, or 13 case. Generally, Rule 9006 permits reduction of time periods. Since notice by mail is complete on mailing, the requirement of subdivision (a) is satisfied if the notices are deposited in the mail at least 20 days before the event. See Rule 9006(e). The exceptions referred to in the introductory phrase include the modifications in the notice procedure permitted by subdivision (h) as to non-filing creditors, subdivision (i) as to cases where a committee is functioning, and subdivision (k) where compliance with subdivision (a) is impracticable.

The notice of a proposed sale affords creditors an opportunity to object to the sale and raise a dispute for the court's attention. Section 363(b) of the Code permits the trustee or debtor in possession to sell property, other than in the ordinary course of business, only after notice and hearing. If no objection is raised after notice, § 102(1) provides that there need not be an actual hearing. Thus, absent objection, there would be no court involvement with respect to a trustee's sale. Once an objection is raised, only the court may pass on it.

Prior to the Code the court could shorten the notice period for a proposed sale of property or dispense with notice. This subdivision (a), permits the 20 day period to be shortened in appropriate circumstances but the rule does not contain a provision allowing the court to dispense with notice. The rule is thus consistent with the Code, §§ 363(b) and 102(1)(A) of the Code. See 28 U.S.C. § 2075. It may be necessary, in certain circumstances, however, to use a method of notice other than mail. Subdivision (a)(2) vests the court with discretion, on cause shown, to order a different method. Reference should also be made to Rule 6004 which allows a different type of notice of proposed sales when the property is of little value.

Notice of the hearing on an application for compensation or reimbursement of expenses totalling $100 or less need not be given. In chapter 13 cases relatively small amounts are sometimes allowed for post-confirmation services and it would not serve a useful purpose to require advance notice.

Subdivision (b) is similar to subdivision (a) but lengthens the notice time to 25 days with respect to those events particularly significant in chapter 9, 11 and 13 cases. The additional time may be necessary to formulate objections to a disclosure statement or confirmation of a plan and preparation for the hearing on approval of the disclosure statement or confirmation. The disclosure statement and hearing thereon is only applicable in chapter 9 cases (§ 901(a) of the Code), and chapter 11 cases (§ 1125 of the Code).

Subdivision (c) specifies certain matters that should be included in the notice of a proposed sale of property and notice of the hearing on an application for allowances. Rule 6004 fixes the time within which parties in interest may file objections to a proposed sale of property.

Subdivision (d) relates exclusively to the notices given to equity security holders in chapter 11 cases. Under chapter 11, a plan may impair the interests of the debtor's shareholders or a plan may be a relatively simple restructuring of unsecured debt. In some cases, it is necessary that equity interest holders receive various notices and in other cases there is no purpose to be served. This subdivision indicates that the court is not mandated to order notices but rather that the matter should be treated with some flexibility. The court may decide whether notice is to be given and how it is to be given. Under § 341(b) of the Code, a meeting of equity security holders is not required in each case, only when it is ordered by the court. Thus subdivision (d)(2) requires notice only when the court orders a meeting.

In addition to the notices specified in this subdivision, there may be other events or matters arising in a case as to which equity security holders should receive notice. These are situations left to determination by the court.

Subdivision (e), authorizing a notice of the apparent insufficiency of assets for the payment of any dividend, is correlated with Rule 3002(c)(5), which provides for the issuance of an additional notice to creditors if the possibility of a payment later materializes.

Subdivision (f) provides for the transmission of other notices to which no time period applies. Clause (1) requires notice of the order for relief; this complements the mandate of § 342 of the Code requiring such notice as is appropriate of the order for relief. This notice may be combined with the notice of the meeting of creditors to avoid the necessity of more than one mailing. See Official Form No. 16, notice of meeting of creditors.

Subdivision (g) recognizes that an agent authorized to receive notices for a creditor may, without a court order, designate where notices to the creditor he represents should be addressed. Agent includes an officer of a corporation, an attorney at law, or an attorney in fact if the requisite authority has been given him. It should be noted that Official Forms Nos. 17 and 18 do not include an authorization of the holder of a power of attorney to receive notices for the creditor. Neither these forms nor this rule carries any implication that such an authorization may not be given in a power of attorney or that a request for notices to be addressed to both the creditor or his duly authorized agent may not be filed.

Subdivision (h). After the time for filing claims has expired in a chapter 7 case, creditors who have not filed their claims in accordance with Rule 3002(c) are not entitled to share in the estate except as they may come within the special provisions of § 726 of the Code or Rule 3002(c)(6). The elimination of notice to creditors who have no recognized stake in the estate may permit economies in time and expense. Reduction of the list of creditors to receive notices under this subdivision is discretionary. This subdivision does not apply to the notice of the meeting of creditors.

Subdivision (i) contains a list of matters of which notice may be given a creditors' committee or to its authorized agent in lieu of notice to the creditors. Such notice may serve every practical purpose of a notice to all the creditors and save delay and expense. In re Schulte-United, Inc., 59 F.2d 553, 561 (8th Cir.1932).

Subdivision (j). The premise for the requirement that the district director of internal revenue receive copies of notices that all creditors receive in a chapter 11 case is that every debtor is potentially a tax debtor of the United States. Notice to the district director alerts him to the possibility that a tax debtor's estate is about to be liquidated or reorganized and that the debtor may be discharged. When other indebtedness to the United States is indicated, the United States attorney is notified as the person in the best position to protect the interests of the government. In addition, the provision requires notice by mail to the head of any department, agency, or instrumentality of the United States through whose action the debtor became indebted to the United States. This rule is not intended to preclude a local rule from requiring a state or local tax authority to receive some or all of the notices to creditors under these rules.

Subdivision (k) specifies two kinds of situations in which notice by publication may be appropriate: (1) when notice by mail is impracticable; and (2) when notice by mail alone is less than adequate. Notice by mail may be impracticable when, for example, the debtor has disappeared or his records have been destroyed and the names and addresses of his creditors are unavailable, or when the number of creditors with nominal claims is very large and the estate to be distributed may be insufficient to defray the costs of issuing the notices. Supplementing notice by mail is also indicated when the debtor's records are incomplete or inaccurate and it is reasonable to believe that publication may reach some of the creditors who would otherwise be missed. Rule 9008 applies when the court directs notice by publication under this rule. Neither clause (2) of subdivision (a) nor subdivision (k) of this rule is concerned with the publication of advertisement to the general public of a sale of property of the estate at public auction under Rule 6004(b). See 3 Collier, Bankruptcy 522–23 (14th ed. 1971); 4B id. 1165–67 (1967); 2 id. ¶363.03 (15th ed. 1981).

Subdivision (m). Inclusion in notices to creditors of information as to other names used by the debtor as required by Rule 1005 will assist them in the preparation of their proofs of claim and in deciding whether to file a complaint objecting to the debtor's discharge. Additional names may be listed by the debtor on his statement of affairs when he did not file the petition. The mailing of notices should not be postponed to await a delayed filing of the statement of financial affairs.

1987 Amendments

Subdivision (a) is amended to provide that notice of a hearing on an application for compensation must be given only when the amount requested is in excess of $500.

Subdivision (d). A new notice requirement is added as clause (3). When a proposed sale is of all or substantially all of the debtor's assets, it is appropriate that equity security holders be given notice of the proposed sale. The clauses of subdivision (d) are renumbered to accommodate this addition.

Subdivision (f). Clause (7) is eliminated. Mailing of a copy of the discharge order is governed by Rule 4004(g).

Subdivision (g) is amended to relieve the clerk of the duty to mail notices to the address shown in a proof of claim when a notice of no dividend has been given pursuant to Rule 2002. This amendment avoids the necessity of the clerk searching proofs of claim which are filed in no dividend cases to ascertain whether a different address is shown.

Subdivision (n) was enacted by § 321 of the 1984 amendments.

1991 Amendments

Subdivision (a)(3) is amended to exclude compromise or settlement agreements concerning adequate protection or which modify or terminate the automatic stay, provide for use of cash collateral, or create a senior or equal lien on collateral to obtain credit. Notice requirements relating to approval of such agreements are governed by Rule 4001(d).

Subdivision (a)(5) is amended to include a hearing on dismissal or conversion of a chapter 12 case. This subdivision does not apply when a hearing is not required. It is also amended to avoid the necessity of giving notice to all creditors of a hearing on the dismissal of a consumer debtor's case based on substantial abuse of chapter 7. Such hearings on dismissal under § 707(b) of the Code are governed by Rule 1017(e).

Subdivision (a)(9) is added to provide for notice of the time fixed for filing objections and the hearing to consider confirmation of a plan in a chapter 12 case. Section 1224 of the Code requires "expedited notice" of the confirmation hearing in a chapter 12 case and requires that the hearing be concluded not later than 45 days after the filing of the plan unless the time is extended for cause. This amendment establishes 20 days as the notice period. The court may shorten this time on its own motion or on motion of a party in interest. The notice includes both the date of the hearing and the date for filing objections, and must be accompanied by a copy of the plan or a summary of the plan in accordance with Rule 3015(d).

Subdivision (h) is amended to delete as unnecessary the references to subdivisions (h) and (i).

Subdivision (d) does not require notice to equity security holders in a chapter 12 case. The procedural burden of requiring such notice is outweighed by the likelihood that all equity security holders of a family farmer will be informed of the progress of the case without formal notice. Subdivision (d) is amended to recognize that the United States trustee may convene a meeting of equity security holders pursuant to § 341(b).

Subdivision (f)(2) is amended and subdivision (f)(4) is deleted to require notice of any conversion of the case, whether the conversion is by court order or is effectuated by the debtor filing a notice of conversion pursuant to §§ 1208(a) or 1307(a). Subdivision (f)(8), renumbered (f)(7), is amended to include entry of an order confirming a chapter 12 plan. Subdivision (f)(9) is amended to increase the amount to $1,500.

Subdivisions (g) and (j) are amended to delete the words "with the court" and subdivision (i) is amended to delete the words "with the clerk" because these phrases are unnecessary. See Rules 5005(a) and 9001(3).

Subdivision (i) is amended to require that the United States trustee receive notices required by subdivision (a)(2), (3) and (7) of this rule notwithstanding a court order limiting such notice to committees and to creditors and equity security holders who request such notices. Subdivision (i) is amended further to include committees elected pursuant to § 705 of the Code and to provide that committees of retired employees appointed in chapter 11 cases receive certain notices.

Subdivision (k) is derived from Rule X–1008. The administrative functions of the United States trustee pursuant to 28 U.S.C. § 586(a) and standing to be heard on issues under § 307 and other sections of the Code require that the United States trustee be informed of developments and issues in every case except chapter 9 cases. The rule omits those notices described in subdivision (a)(1) because a meeting of creditors is convened only by the United States trustee, and those notices described in subdivision (a)(4) (date fixed for filing claims against a surplus), subdivision (a)(6) (time fixed to accept or reject proposed modification of a plan), subdivision (a)(8) (time fixed for filing proofs of claims in chapter 11 cases), subdivision (f)(3) (time fixed for filing claims in chapter 7, 12, and 13 cases), and subdivision (f)(5) (time fixed for filing complaint to determine dischargeability of debt) because these notices do not relate to matters that generally involve the United States trustee. Nonetheless, the omission of these notices does not prevent the United States trustee from receiving such notices upon request. The United States trustee also receives notice of hearings on applications for compensation or reimbursement without regard to the $500 limitation contained in subdivision (a)(7) of this rule. This rule is intended to be flexible in that it permits the United States trustee in a particular judicial district to request notices in certain categories, and to request not to receive notices in other categories, when the practice in that district makes that desirable.

1993 Amendments

Subdivision (j) is amended to avoid the necessity of sending an additional notice to the Washington, D.C. address of the Securities and Exchange Commission if the Commission prefers to have notices sent only to a local office. This change also clarifies that notices required to be mailed pursuant to this rule must be sent to the Securities and Exchange Commission only if it has filed a notice of appearance or has filed a written request. Other amendments are stylistic and make no substantive change.

1996 Amendments

Paragraph (a)(4) is abrogated to conform to the abrogation of Rule 3002(c)(6). The remaining paragraphs of subdivision (a) are renumbered, and references to these paragraphs contained in other subdivisions of this rule are amended accordingly.

Paragraph (f)(8) is amended so that a summary of the trustee's final account, which is prepared after distribution of property, does not have to be mailed to the debtor, all creditors, and indenture trustees in a chapter 7 case. Parties are sufficiently protected by receiving a summary of the trustee's final report that informs parties of the proposed distribution of property.

Subdivision **(h)** is amended (1) to provide that an order under this subdivision may not be issued if a notice of no dividend is given pursuant to Rule 2002(e) and the time for filing claims has not expired as provided in Rule 3002(c)(5); (2) to clarify that notices required to be mailed by subdivision (a) to parties other than creditors must be mailed to those entities despite an order issued pursuant to subdivision (h); (3) to provide that if the court, pursuant to Rule 3002(c)(1) or 3002(c)(2), has granted an extension of time to file a proof of claim, the creditor for whom the extension has been granted must continue to receive notices despite an order issued pursuant to subdivision (h); and (4) to delete references to subdivision (a)(4) and Rule 3002(c)(6), which have been abrogated.

Other amendments to this rule are stylistic.

GAP Report on Rule 2002. No changes since publication, except for stylistic changes and the correction of a typographical error in the committee note.

1997 Amendments

Paragraph (a)(1) is amended to include notice of a meeting of creditors convened under § 1104(b) of the Code for the purpose of electing a trustee in a chapter 11 case. The court for cause shown may order the 20–day period reduced pursuant to Rule 9006(c)(1).

Subdivision (n) is amended to conform to the 1994 amendment to § 342 of the Code. As provided in § 342(c), the failure of a notice given by the debtor to a creditor to contain the information required by § 342(c) does not invalidate the legal effect of the notice.

GAP Report on Rule 2002. No changes to the published draft.

1999 Amendments

Paragraph (a)(4) is amended to conform to the amendments to Rule 1017. If the United States trustee files a motion to dismiss a case for the debtor's failure to file the list of creditors, schedules, or the statement of financial affairs within the time specified in § 707(a)(3), the amendments to this rule and to Rule 1017 eliminate the requirement that all creditors receive notice of the hearing.

Paragraph (a)(4) is amended further to conform to Rule 1017(b), which requires that notice of the hearing on dismissal of a case for failure to pay the filing fee be served on only the debtor and the trustee.

Paragraph (f)(2) is amended to provide for notice of the suspension of proceedings under § 305.

Gap Report on Rule 2002. No changes since publication.

2000 Amendments

Paragraph(a)(6) is amended to increase the dollar amount from $500 to $1,000. The amount was last amended in 1987, when it was changed from $100 to $500. The amendment also clarifies that the notice is required only if a particular entity is requesting more than $1,000 as compensation or reimbursement of expenses. If several professionals are requesting compensation or reimbursement, and only one hearing will be held on all applications, notice under paragraph (a)(6) is required only with respect to the entities that have requested more than $1,000. If each applicant requests $1,000 or less, notice under paragraph (a)(6) is not required even though the aggregate amount of all applications to be considered at the hearing is more than $1,000.

If a particular entity had filed prior applications or had received compensation or reimbursement of expenses at an earlier time in the case, the amounts previously requested or awarded are not considered when determining whether the present application exceeds $1,000 for the purpose of applying this rule.

GAP Report on Rule 2002(a). No changes since publication.

2001 Amendments

Subdivision (c)(3) is added to assure that parties given notice of a hearing to consider confirmation of a plan under subdivision (b) are given adequate notice of an injunction provided for in the plan if it would enjoin conduct that is not otherwise enjoined by operation of the Code. The validity and effect of any injunction provided for in a plan are substantive law matters that are beyond the scope of these rules.

The notice requirement of subdivision (c)(3) is not applicable to an injunction contained in a plan if it is substantially the same as an injunction provided under the Code. For example, if a plan contains an injunction against acts to collect a discharged debt from the debtor, Rule 2002(c)(3) would not apply because that conduct would be enjoined under § 524(a)(2) upon the debtor's discharge. But if a plan provides that creditors will be enjoined from asserting claims against persons who are not debtors in the case, the notice of the confirmation hearing must include the information required under Rule 2002(c)(3) because that conduct would not be enjoined by operation of the Code. See § 524(e).

The requirement that the notice identify the entities that would be subject to the injunction requires only reasonable identification under the circumstances. If the entities that would be subject to the injunction cannot be identified by name, the notice may describe them by class or category if reasonable under the circumstances. For example, it may be sufficient for the notice to identify the entities as "all creditors of the debtor" and for the notice to be published in a manner that satisfies due process requirements.

Subdivision (g) has been revised to clarify that where a creditor or indenture trustee files both a proof of claim which includes a mailing address and a separate request designating a mailing address, the last paper filed determines the proper address. The amendments also clarify that a request designating a mailing address is effective only with respect to a particular case.

Under Rule 2002(g), a duly filed proof of claim is considered a request designating a mailing address if a notice of no dividend has been given under Rule 2002(e), but has been superseded by a subsequent notice of possible dividend under Rule 3002(c)(5). A duly filed proof of interest is considered a request designating a mailing address of an equity security holder.

Rule 2002(g)(3) is added to assure that notices to an infant or incompetent person under this rule are mailed to the appropriate guardian or other legal representative. Under Rule 1007(m), if the debtor knows that a creditor is an infant or incompetent person, the debtor is required to include in the list and schedule of creditors the name and address of the person upon whom process would be served in an adversary proceeding in accordance with Rule 7004(b)(2). If the infant or incompetent person, or another person, files a request or proof of claim designating a different name and mailing

Rule 2002

BANKRUPTCY RULES

address, the notices would have to be mailed to both names and addresses until the court resolved the issue as to the proper mailing address.

The other amendments to Rule 2002(g) are stylistic.

CHANGES MADE AFTER PUBLICATION AND COMMENTS

In Rule 2002(c)(3), the word "highlighted" was replaced with "underlined" because highlighted documents are difficult to scan electronically for inclusion in the clerks' files. The Committee Note was revised to put in a more prominent position the statement that the validity and effect of any injunction provided for in a plan are substantive matters beyond the scope of the rules.

In Rule 2002(g), no changes were made.

2003 Amendments

Subdivision (a)(1) of the rule is amended to direct the clerk or other person giving notice of the § 341 or § 1104(b) meeting of creditors to include the debtor's full social security number on the notice. Official Form 9, the form of the notice of the meeting of creditors that will become a part of the court's file in the case, will include only the last four digits of the debtor's social security number. This rule, however, directs the clerk to include the full social security number on the notice that is served on the creditors and other identified parties, unless the court orders otherwise in a particular case. This will enable creditors and other parties in interest who are in possession of the debtor's social security number to verify the debtor's identity and proceed accordingly. The filed Official Form 9, however, will not include the debtor's full social security number. This will prevent the full social security number from becoming a part of the court's file in the case, and the number will not be included in the court's electronic records. Creditors who already have the debtor's social security number will be able to verify the existence of a case under the debtor's social security number, but any person searching the electronic case files without the number will not be able to acquire the debtor's social security number.

2004 Amendments

The rule is amended to reflect that the structure of the Internal Revenue Service no longer includes a District Director. Thus, rather than sending notice to the District Director, the rule now requires that the notices be sent to the location designated by the Service and set out in the register of addresses maintained by the clerk under Rule 5003(e). The other change is stylistic.

2005 Amendments

A new paragraph (g)(4) is inserted in the rule. The new paragraph authorizes an entity and a notice provider to agree that the notice provider will give notices to the entity at the address or addresses set out in their agreement. Rule 9001(9) sets out the definition of a notice provider.

The business of many entities is national in scope, and technology currently exists to direct the transmission of notice (both electronically and in paper form) to those entities in an accurate and much more efficient manner than by sending individual notices to the same creditor by separate mailings. The rule authorizes an entity and a notice provider to determine the manner of the service as well as to set the address or addresses to which the notices must be sent. For example, they could agree that all notices sent by the notice provider to

the entity must be sent to a single, nationwide electronic or postal address. They could also establish local or regional addresses to which notices would be sent in matters pending in specific districts. Since the entity and notice provider also can agree on the date of the commencement of service under the agreement, there is no need to set a date in the rule after which notices would have to be sent to the address or addresses that the entity establishes. Furthermore, since the entity supplies the address to the notice provider, use of that address is conclusively presumed to be proper. Nonetheless, if that address is not used, the notice still may be effective if the notice is otherwise effective under applicable law. This is the same treatment given under Rule 5003(e) to notices sent to governmental units at addresses other than those set out in that register of addresses.

The remaining subdivisions of Rule 2002(g) continue to govern the addressing of a notice that is not sent pursuant to an agreement described in Rule 2002(g)(4).

2008 Amendments

Subdivision (b) is amended to provide for 25 days' notice of the time for the court to make a final determination whether the plan in a small business case can serve as a disclosure statement. Conditional approval of a disclosure statement in a small business case is governed by Rule 3017.1 and does not require 25 days' notice. The court may consider this matter in a hearing combined with the confirmation hearing in a small business case.

Because of the requirements of Rule 6004(g), subdivision (c)(1) is amended to require that a trustee leasing or selling personally identifiable information under § 363(b)(1)(A) or (B) of the Code, as amended in 2005, include in the notice of the lease or sale transaction a statement as to whether the lease or sale is consistent with a policy prohibiting the transfer of the information.

Subdivisions (f)(9) and (10) are new. They reflect the 2005 amendments to §§ 342(d) and 704(b) of the Code. Section 342(d) requires the clerk to give notice to creditors shortly after the commencement of the case as to whether a presumption of abuse exists. Subdivision (f)(9) adds this notice to the list of notices that the clerk must give. Subdivision (f)(10) implements the amendment to § 704(b), which requires the court to provide a copy to all creditors of a statement by the United States trustee or bankruptcy administrator as to whether the debtor's case would be presumed to be an abuse under § 707(b) not later than five days after receiving it.

Subdivision (f)(11) is also added to provide notice to creditors of the debtor's filing of a statement in a chapter 11, 12, or 13 case that there is no reasonable cause to believe that § 522(q) applies in the case. This allows a creditor who disputes that assertion to request a delay of the entry of the discharge in the case.

Subdivision (g)(2) of the rule is amended because the 2005 amendments to § 342(f) of the Code permit creditors in chapter 7 and 13 individual debtor cases to file a notice with any bankruptcy court of the address to which the creditor wishes all notices to be sent. The amendment to Rule 2002(g)(2) therefore only limits application of the subdivision when a creditor files a notice under § 342(f).

New subdivision (g)(5) implements § 342(g)(1) which was added to the Code in 2005. Section 342(g)(1) allows a creditor to treat a notice as not having been brought to the creditor's attention, and so potentially ineffective, until it is received by a person or organizational subdivision that the creditor has designated to receive notices under the Bankruptcy Code. Under that section, the creditor must have established reasonable procedures for such notices to be delivered to the designated person or subdivision. The rule provides that, in order to challenge a notice under § 342(g)(1), a creditor must have filed the name and address of the designated notice recipient, as well as a description of the procedures for directing notices to that recipient, prior to the time that the challenged notice was issued. The filing required by the rule may be made as part of a creditor's filing under § 342(f), which allows a creditor to file a notice of the address to be used by all bankruptcy courts or by particular bankruptcy courts to provide notice to the creditor in cases under chapters 7 and 13. Filing the name and address of the designated notice recipient and the procedures for directing notices to that recipient will reduce uncertainty as to the proper party for receiving notice and limit factual disputes as to whether a notice recipient has been designated and as to the nature of procedures adopted to direct notices to the recipient.

Subdivision (k) is amended to add notices given under subdivision (q) to the list of notices which must be served on the United States trustee.

Section 1514(d) of the Code, added by the 2005 amendments, requires that such additional time as is reasonable under the circumstances be given to creditors with foreign addresses with respect to notices and the filing of a proof of claim. Thus, subdivision (p)(1) is added to this rule to give the court flexibility to direct that notice by other means shall supplement notice by mail, or to enlarge the notice period, for creditors with foreign addresses. If cause exists, such as likely delays in the delivery of mailed notices in particular locations, the court may order that notice also be given by email, facsimile, or private courier. Alternatively, the court may enlarge the notice period for a creditor with a foreign address. It is expected that in most situations involving foreign creditors, fairness will not require any additional notice or extension of the notice period. This rule recognizes that the court has discretion to establish procedures to determine, on its own initiative, whether relief under subdivision (p) is appropriate, but that the court is not required to establish such procedures and may decide to act only on request of a party in interest.

Subdivision (p)(2) is added to the rule to grant creditors with a foreign address to which notices are mailed at least 30 days' notice of the time within which to file proofs of claims if notice is mailed to the foreign address, unless the court orders otherwise. If cause exists, such as likely delays in the delivery of notices in particular locations, the court may extend the notice period for creditors with foreign addresses. The court may also shorten the additional notice time if circumstances so warrant. For example, if the court in a chapter 11 case determines that supplementing the notice to a foreign creditor with notice by electronic means, such as email or facsimile, would give the creditor reasonable notice, the court may order that the creditor be given only 20 days' notice in accordance with Rule 2002(a)(7).

Subdivision (p)(3) is added to provide that the court may, for cause, override a creditor's designation of a foreign address under Rule 2002(g). For example, if a party in interest believes that a creditor has wrongfully designated a foreign address to obtain additional time when it has a significant presence in the United States, the party can ask the court to

order that notices to that creditor be sent to an address other than the one designated by the foreign creditor.

Subdivision (q) is added to require that notice of the hearing on the petition for recognition of a foreign proceeding be given to the debtor, all administrators in foreign proceedings of the debtor, entities against whom provisional relief is sought, and entities with whom the debtor is engaged in litigation at the time of the commencement of the case. There is no need at this stage of the proceedings to provide notice to all creditors. If the foreign representative should take action to commence a case under another chapter of the Code, the rules governing those proceedings will operate to provide that notice is given to all creditors.

The rule also requires notice of the court's intention to communicate with a foreign court or foreign representative.

2009 Amendments

The rule is amended to implement changes in connection with the amendment to Rule 9006(a) and the manner by which time is computed under the rules. The deadlines in the rule are amended to substitute a deadline that is a multiple of seven days. Throughout the rules, deadlines are amended in the following manner:

- 5–day periods become 7–day periods
- 10–day periods become 14–day periods
- 15–day periods become 14–day periods
- 20–day periods become 21–day periods
- 25–day periods become 28–day periods

CROSS REFERENCES

Form and manner of publication of notices, see Fed.Rules Bankr.Proc. Rule 9008, 11 USCA.

General requirements of form for creditors' notices, see Fed.Rules Bankr.Proc. Rule 9004, 11 USCA.

Hearing on disclosure statement in municipality debt adjustment and reorganization cases, see Fed.Rules Bankr.Proc. Rule 3017, 11 USCA.

Notice by mail complete on mailing, see Fed.Rules Bankr. Proc. Rule 9006, 11 USCA.

Notice of—

> Dismissal for failure to pay filing fees, see Fed.Rules Bankr.Proc. Rule 1017, 11 USCA.

> Dividend and of time to file proof of claim in liquidation case, see Fed.Rules Bankr.Proc. Rule 3002, 11 USCA.

> Hearing on compromise or settlement to creditors, debtor, indenture trustees, and others designated by court, see Fed.Rules Bankr.Proc. Rule 9019, 11 USCA.

> Hearing on confirmation of individual debt adjustment plan to include plan or summary, see Fed.Rules Bankr. Proc. Rule 3015, 11 USCA.

> Hearing on dismissal of case, see Fed.Rules Bankr.Proc. Rule 1017, 11 USCA.

> Order of conversion to liquidation case, see Fed.Rules Bankr.Proc. Rule 1019, 11 USCA.

> Time extended to file claims against surplus in converted liquidation case, see Fed.Rules Bankr.Proc. Rule 1019, 11 USCA.

> Time fixed for filing complaint objecting to discharge in reorganization case, see Fed.Rules Bankr.Proc. Rule case, see Fed.Rules Bankr.Proc. Rule 4004, 11 USCA.

Time fixed for filing complaint to determine debt's dischargeability, see Fed.Rules Bankr.Proc. Rule 4007, 11 USCA.

Use, sale, or lease of property other than in ordinary course, see Fed.Rules Bankr.Proc. Rule 6004, 11 USCA.

Waiver, denial, or revocation of discharge, see Fed.Rules Bankr.Proc. Rule 4006, 11 USCA.

Reduction in time periods generally, see Fed.Rules Bankr.Proc. Rule 9006, 11 USCA.

Reduction in twenty-day period for notice to file claims not permitted—

Against surplus in estate in liquidation case, see Fed. Rules Bankr.Proc. Rule 9006, 11 USCA.

In municipality debt adjustment or reorganization cases, see Fed.Rules Bankr.Proc. Rule 9006, 11 USCA.

Review by court on plan's confirmation after notice and hearing pursuant to, see Fed.Rules Bankr.Proc. Rule 3020, 11 USCA.

LIBRARY REFERENCES

American Digest System

Bankruptcy ⟐2131, 3071.

Key Number System Topic No. 51.

Corpus Juris Secundum

CJS Bankruptcy § 54, Notices.

CJS Bankruptcy § 62, Appointment of Interim Trustee.

CJS Bankruptcy § 82, Meeting of Creditors and Election Procedures.

CJS Bankruptcy § 145, Compromise and Settlement.

CJS Bankruptcy § 285, Captions.

CJS Bankruptcy § 296, Notice by Mail--Proper Mailing Address.

CJS Bankruptcy § 297, Notice by Other Means.

CJS Bankruptcy § 298, Notice of Not Less Than 20 Days.

CJS Bankruptcy § 299, Notice of Not Less Than 25 Days.

CJS Bankruptcy § 301, Notice to Debtor, Creditors, and Indenture Trustees.

CJS Bankruptcy § 302, Notice to United States Trustee.

CJS Bankruptcy § 303, Notice to Committees.

CJS Bankruptcy § 304, Notice to the United States.

CJS Bankruptcy § 306, Notice to Equity Security Holders in Chapter 11 Cases.

CJS Bankruptcy § 309, Reduction.

CJS Bankruptcy § 365, Commencement and Order for Relief.

CJS Bankruptcy § 389, Cooperation and Communication With Foreign Courts and Foreign Representatives.

CJS Bankruptcy § 397, Hearing and Notice of Hearing.

CJS Bankruptcy § 416, Proceedings.

CJS Bankruptcy § 421, Proceedings.

CJS Bankruptcy § 425, Proceedings.

CJS Bankruptcy § 427, Proceedings.

CJS Bankruptcy § 431, Presumption of Abuse.

CJS Bankruptcy § 432, Presumption of Abuse--Notice.

CJS Bankruptcy § 451, Dismissal or Conversion on Request of United States Trustee.

CJS Bankruptcy § 457, Failure to Provide Copy of Debtor's Federal Income Tax Return to Trustee and Requesting Creditors.

CJS Bankruptcy § 458, Failure to File Prepetition Tax Returns in Chapter 13 Case.

CJS Bankruptcy § 459, Failure to File Postpetition Tax Return.

CJS Bankruptcy § 782, Notice and Hearing.

CJS Bankruptcy § 791, Notice.

CJS Bankruptcy § 879, Service and Content of Notices.

CJS Bankruptcy § 886, Authorization to Sell Property Free and Clear; Notice.

CJS Bankruptcy § 1016, Reorganization and Municipal Debt Cases.

CJS Bankruptcy § 1019, Extension of Time; Excuse for Delay--Lack or Insufficiency of Notice.

CJS Bankruptcy § 1047, Time for Proceedings; Extension of Time.

CJS Bankruptcy § 1082, Time for Proceedings.

CJS Bankruptcy § 1105, Closing.

CJS Bankruptcy § 1118, Filing of Plan and Disclosure Statement; Hearing on Objections.

CJS Bankruptcy § 1120, Modification of Plan Before Confirmation.

CJS Bankruptcy § 1123, Hearing and Order.

CJS Bankruptcy § 1202, Generally; Objections to Confirmation.

CJS Bankruptcy § 1203, Requirements for Confirmation; Notice and Hearing.

Rule 2003. Meeting of Creditors or Equity Security Holders

(a) Date and place

Except as otherwise provided in § 341(e) of the Code, in a chapter 7 liquidation or a chapter 11 reorganization case, the United States trustee shall call a meeting of creditors to be held no fewer than 21 and no more than 40 days after the order for relief. In a chapter 12 family farmer debt adjustment case, the United States trustee shall call a meeting of creditors to be held no fewer than 21 and no more than 35 days after the order for relief. In a chapter 13 individual's debt adjustment case, the United States trustee shall call a meeting of creditors to be held no fewer than 21 and no more than 50 days after the order for relief. If there is an appeal from or a motion to vacate the order for relief, or if there is a motion to dismiss the case, the United States trustee may set a later date for the meeting. The meeting may be held at a regular place for holding court or at any other place designated by the United States trustee within the district convenient for the parties in interest. If the United States trustee designates a place for the meeting which is not regularly staffed by the United States trustee or an assistant who may preside at the meeting, the meeting may be held not more than 60 days after the order for relief.

(b) Order of meeting

(1) Meeting of Creditors

The United States trustee shall preside at the meeting of creditors. The business of the meeting shall include the examination of the debtor under oath and, in a chapter 7 liquidation case, may include the election of a creditors' committee and, if the case is not under subchapter V of chapter 7, the election of a trustee. The presiding officer shall have the authority to administer oaths.

(2) Meeting of equity security holders

If the United States trustee convenes a meeting of equity security holders pursuant to § 341(b) of the Code, the United States trustee shall fix a date for the meeting and shall preside.

(3) Right to vote

In a chapter 7 liquidation case, a creditor is entitled to vote at a meeting if, at or before the meeting, the creditor has filed a proof of claim or a writing setting forth facts evidencing a right to vote pursuant to § 702(a) of the Code unless objection is made to the claim or the proof of claim is insufficient on its face. A creditor of a partnership may file a proof of claim or writing evidencing a right to vote for the trustee for the estate of a general partner notwithstanding that a trustee for the estate of the partnership has previously qualified. In the event of an objection to the amount or allowability of a claim for the purpose of voting, unless the court orders otherwise, the United States trustee shall tabulate the votes for each alternative presented by the dispute and, if resolution of such dispute is necessary to determine the result of the election, the tabulations for each alternative shall be reported to the court.

(c) Record of meeting

Any examination under oath at the meeting of creditors held pursuant to § 341(a) of the Code shall be recorded verbatim by the United States trustee using electronic sound recording equipment or other means of recording, and such record shall be preserved by the United States trustee and available for public access until two years after the conclusion of the meeting of creditors. Upon request of any entity, the United States trustee shall certify and provide a copy or transcript of such recording at the entity's expense.

(d) Report of election and resolution of disputes in a chapter 7 case

(1) Report of undisputed election

In a chapter 7 case, if the election of a trustee or a member of a creditors' committee is not disputed, the United States trustee shall promptly file a report of the election, including the name and address of the person or entity elected and a statement that the election is undisputed.

(2) Disputed election

If the election is disputed, the United States trustee shall promptly file a report stating that the election is disputed, informing the court of the nature of the dispute, and listing the name and address of any candidate elected under any alternative presented by the dispute. No later than the date on which the report is filed, the United States trustee shall mail a copy of the report to any party in interest that has made a request to receive a copy of the report. Pending disposition by the court of a disputed election for trustee, the interim trustee shall continue in office. Unless a motion for the resolution of the dispute is filed no later than 14 days after the United States trustee files a report of a disputed election for trustee, the interim trustee shall serve as trustee in the case.

(e) Adjournment

The meeting may be adjourned from time to time by announcement at the meeting of the adjourned date and time. The presiding official shall promptly file a statement specifying the date and time to which the meeting is adjourned.

(f) Special meetings

The United States trustee may call a special meeting of creditors on request of a party in interest or on the United States trustee's own initiative.

(g) Final meeting

If the United States trustee calls a final meeting of creditors in a case in which the net proceeds realized exceed $1,500, the clerk shall mail a summary of the trustee's final account to the creditors with a notice of the meeting, together with a statement of the amount of the claims allowed. The trustee shall attend the final meeting and shall, if requested, report on the administration of the estate.

(As amended Mar. 30, 1987, eff. Aug. 1, 1987; Apr. 30, 1991, eff. Aug. 1, 1991; Apr. 22, 1993, eff. Aug. 1, 1993; Apr. 29, 1999, eff. Dec. 1, 1999; Mar. 27, 2003, eff. Dec. 1, 2003; Apr. 23, 2008, eff. Dec. 1, 2008; Mar. 26, 2009, eff. Dec. 1, 2009; Apr. 26, 2011, eff. Dec. 1, 2011.)

ADVISORY COMMITTEE NOTES

Section 341(a) of the Code requires a meeting of creditors in a chapter 7, 11 or 13 case, and § 341(b) permits the court to order a meeting of equity security holders. A major change from prior law, however, prohibits the judge from attending or presiding over the meeting. Section 341(c).

This rule does not apply either in a case for the reorganization of a railroad or for the adjustment of debts of a municipality. Sections 1161 and 901 render §§ 341 and 343 inapplicable in these types of cases. Section 341 sets the requirement for a meeting of creditors and § 343 provides for the examination of the debtor.

Subdivision (a). The meeting is to be held between 20 and 40 days after the date of the order for relief. In a voluntary case, the date of the order for relief is the date of the filing of the petition (§ 301 of the Code); in an involuntary case, it is the date of an actual order (§ 303(i) of the Code).

Subdivision (b) provides flexibility as to who will preside at the meeting of creditors. The court may designate a person to serve as presiding officer, such as the interim trustee appointed under § 701 of the Code. If the court does not designate anyone, the clerk will preside. In either case, creditors may elect a person of their own choosing. In any event, the clerk may remain to record the proceedings and take appearances. Use of the clerk is not contrary to the legislative policy of § 341(c). The judge remains insulated from any information coming forth at the meeting and any information obtained by the clerk must not be relayed to the judge.

Although the clerk may preside at the meeting, the clerk is not performing any kind of judicial role, nor should the clerk give any semblance of performing such a role. It would be pretentious for the clerk to ascend the bench, don a robe or be addressed as "your honor". The clerk should not appear to parties or others as any type of judicial officer.

In a chapter 11 case, if a committee of unsecured creditors has been appointed pursuant to § 1102(a)(1) of the Code and a chairman has been selected, the chairman will preside or a person, such as the attorney for the committee, may be designated to preside by the chairman.

Since the judge must fix the bond of the trustee but cannot be present at the meeting, the rule allows the creditors to recommend the amount of the bond. They should be able to obtain relevant information concerning the extent of assets of the debtor at the meeting.

Paragraph (1) authorizes the presiding officer to administer oaths. This is important because the debtor's examination must be under oath.

Paragraph (3) of subdivision (b) has application only in a chapter 7 case. That is the only type of case under the Code that permits election of a trustee or committee. In all other cases, no vote is taken at the meeting of creditors. If it is necessary for the court to make a determination with respect to a claim, the meeting may be adjourned until the objection or dispute is resolved.

The second sentence recognizes that partnership creditors may vote for a trustee of a partner's estate along with the separate creditors of the partner. Although § 723(c) gives the trustee of a partnership a claim against a partner's estate for the full amount of partnership creditors' claims allowed, the purpose and function of this provision are to simplify distribution and prevent double proof, not to disfranchise partnership creditors in electing a trustee of an estate against which they hold allowable claims.

Subdivision (c) requires minutes and a record of the meeting to be maintained by the presiding officer. A verbatim record must be made of the debtor's examination but the rule is flexible as to the means used to record the examination.

Subdivision (d) recognizes that the court must be informed immediately about the election or nonelection of a trustee in a chapter 7 case. Pursuant to Rule 2008, the clerk officially informs the trustee of his election or appointment and how he is to qualify. The presiding person has no authority to resolve a disputed election.

For purposes of expediency, the results of the election should be obtained for each alternative presented by the dispute and immediately reported to the court. Thus, when an interested party presents the dispute to the court, its prompt resolution by the court will determine the dispute and a new or adjourned meeting to conduct the election may be avoided. The clerk is not an interested party.

A creditors' committee may be elected only in a chapter 7 case. In chapter 11 cases, a creditors' committee is appointed pursuant to § 1102.

While a final meeting is not required, Rule 2002(f)(10) provides for the trustee's final account to be sent to creditors.

1987 Amendments

Subdivision (a). Many courts schedule meetings of creditors at various locations in the district. Because the clerk must schedule meetings at those locations, an additional 20 days for scheduling the meetings is provided under the amended rule.

1991 Amendments

The amendment to subdivision (a) relating to the calling of the meeting of creditors in a chapter 12 case is consistent with the expedited procedures of chapter 12. Subdivision (a) is also amended to clarify that the United States trustee does not call a meeting of creditors in a chapter 9 case. Pursuant to § 901(a) of the Code, § 341 is inapplicable in chapter 9 cases. The other amendments to subdivisions (a), (b)(1), and (b)(2) and the additions of subdivisions (f) and (g) are derived from Rule X–1006 and conform to the 1986 amendments to § 341 of the Code. The second sentence of subdivision (b)(3) is amended because Rule 2009(e) is abrogated. Although the United States trustee fixes the date for the meeting, the clerk of the bankruptcy court transmits the notice of the meeting unless the court orders otherwise, as prescribed in Rule 2002(a)(1).

Pursuant to § 702 and § 705 of the Code, creditors may elect a trustee and a committee in a chapter 7 case. Subdivision (b) of this rule provides that the United States trustee shall preside over any election that is held under those sections. The deletion of the last sentence of subdivision (b)(1) does not preclude creditors from recommending to the United States trustee the amount of the trustee's bond when a trustee is elected. Trustees and committees are not elected in chapter 11, 12, and 13 cases.

If an election is disputed, the United States trustee shall not resolve the dispute. For purposes of expediency, the United States trustee shall tabulate the results of the election for each alternative presented by the dispute. However, if the court finds that such tabulation is not feasible under the circumstances, the United States trustee need not tabulate the votes. If such tabulation is feasible and if the disputed vote or votes would affect the result of the election, the tabulations of votes for each alternative presented by the dispute shall be reported to the court. If a motion is made for resolution of the dispute in accordance with subdivision (d) of this rule, the court will determine the issue and another meeting to conduct the election may not be necessary.

Subdivisions (f) and (g) are derived from Rule X–1006(d) and (e), except that the amount is increased to $1,500 to conform to the amendment to Rule 2002(f).

1993 Amendments

Subdivision (a) is amended to extend by ten days the time for holding the meeting of creditors in a chapter 13 case. This extension will provide more flexibility for scheduling the meeting of creditors. Other amendments are stylistic and make no substantive change.

1999 Amendments

Subdivision (d) is amended to require the United States trustee to mail a copy of a report of a disputed election to any party in interest that has requested a copy of it. Also, if the election is for a trustee, the rule as amended will give a party in interest ten days from the filing of the report, rather than from the date of the meeting of creditors, to file a motion to resolve the dispute.

The substitution of "United States trustee" for "presiding officer" is stylistic. Section 341(a) of the Code provides that the United States trustee shall preside at the meeting of creditors. Other amendments are designed to conform to the style of Rule 2007.1(b)(3) regarding the election of a trustee in a chapter 11 case.

Gap Report on Rule 2003. No changes since publication.

2003 Amendments

The rule is amended to reflect the enactment of subchapter V of chapter 7 of the Code governing multilateral clearing organization liquidations. Section 782 of the Code provides that the designation of a trustee or alternative trustee for the case is made by the Federal Reserve Board. Therefore, the meeting of creditors in those cases cannot include the election of a trustee.

2008 Amendments

If the debtor has solicited acceptances to a plan before commencement of the case, § 341(e), which was added to the Code by the 2005 amendments, authorizes the court, on request of a party in interest and after notice and a hearing, to order that a meeting of creditors not be convened. The rule is amended to recognize that a meeting of creditors might not be held in those cases.

2009 Amendments

The rule is amended to implement changes in connection with the amendment to Rule 9006(a) and the manner by which time is computed under the rules. The deadlines in the rule are amended to substitute a deadline that is a multiple of seven days. Throughout the rules, deadlines are amended in the following manner:

- 5–day periods become 7–day periods
- 10–day periods become 14–day periods
- 15–day periods become 14–day periods
- 20–day periods become 21–day periods
- 25–day periods become 28–day periods

2011 Amendments

Subdivision (e). Subdivision (e) is amended to require the presiding official to file a statement after the adjournment of a meeting of creditors or equity security holders designating the period of the adjournment. The presiding official is the United States trustee or the United States trustee's designee. This requirement will provide notice to parties in interest not present at the initial meeting of the date and time to which the meeting has been continued. An adjourned meeting is "held open" as permitted by § 1308(b)(1) of the Code. The filing of this statement will also discourage premature motions to dismiss or convert the case under § 1307(e).

CROSS REFERENCES

Affirmations, see Fed.Rules Bankr.Proc. Rule 9012, 11 USCA.

Election of creditors' committee in liquidation case, see 11 USCA § 705.

Eligibility to serve as and qualification of trustee, see 11 USCA §§ 321 and 322.

Enlargement of time not permitted—

    Date of meeting of creditors, see Fed.Rules Bankr.Proc. Rule 9006, 11 USCA.

    Motion for resolution of trustee election dispute, see Fed.Rules Bankr.Proc. Rule 9006, 11 USCA.

Holders of multiple proxies to file list of proxies to be voted, see Fed.Rules Bankr.Proc. Rule 2006, 11 USCA.

Inapplicability of this rule to—

    Municipality debt adjustment case, see 11 USCA § 901.

    Railroad reorganization case, see 11 USCA § 1161.

Interim trustee in liquidation case, see Fed.Rules Bankr. Proc. Rule 2001, 11 USCA, and 11 USCA § 701.

Motions; form and service, see Fed.Rules Bankr.Proc. Rule 9013, 11 USCA.

Reduction of twenty-day period for date of meeting of creditors not permitted, see Fed.Rules Bankr.Proc. Rule 9006, 11 USCA.

Selection and substitution of trustees, see Fed.Rules Bankr. Proc. Rules 2008 and 2012, 11 USCA.

Time for objections to property claimed to be exempt, see Fed.Rules Bankr.Proc. Rule 4003, 11 USCA.

LIBRARY REFERENCES

American Digest System

Bankruptcy ⟐3024.

Key Number System Topic No. 51.

Corpus Juris Secundum

CJS Bankruptcy § 50, Chapter 7 Proceedings.

CJS Bankruptcy § 78, Eligibility of Creditors to Vote.

CJS Bankruptcy § 80, Report to Court; Disputed Election.

CJS Bankruptcy § 82, Meeting of Creditors and Election Procedures.

CJS Bankruptcy § 308, Enlargement.

CJS Bankruptcy § 309, Reduction.

CJS Bankruptcy § 790, Convening of Meeting by Trustee or Other Judicial Officer.

CJS Bankruptcy § 793, Duties of Trustee or Other Judicial Officer.

CJS Bankruptcy § 794, Time of Initial Meeting.

CJS Bankruptcy § 795, Time of Initial Meeting--Rescheduling, Adjournment, and Continuance.

CJS Bankruptcy § 796, Place of Meeting.

CJS Bankruptcy § 800, United States Trustee or Other Judicial Officer; Bankruptcy Judge.

CJS Bankruptcy § 809, Voting and Elections.

Rule 2004. Examination

(a) Examination on motion

On motion of any party in interest, the court may order the examination of any entity.

(b) Scope of examination

The examination of an entity under this rule or of the debtor under § 343 of the Code may relate only to the acts, conduct, or property or to the liabilities and financial condition of the debtor, or to any matter which may affect the administration of the debtor's estate, or to the debtor's right to a discharge. In a family farmer's debt adjustment case under chapter 12, an individual's debt adjustment case under chapter 13, or a reorganization case under chapter 11 of the Code, other than for the reorganization of a railroad, the examination may also relate to the operation of any business and the desirability of its continuance, the source of any money or property acquired or to be acquired by the debtor for purposes of consummating a plan and the consideration given or offered therefor, and any other matter relevant to the case or to the formulation of a plan.

(c) Compelling attendance and production of documents

The attendance of an entity for examination and for the production of documents, whether the examination is to be conducted within or without the district in which the case is pending, may be compelled as provided in Rule 9016 for the attendance of a witness at a hearing or trial. As an officer of the court, an attorney may issue and sign a subpoena on behalf of the court for the district in which the examination is to be held if the attorney is admitted to practice in that court or in the court in which the case is pending.

(d) Time and place of examination of debtor

The court may for cause shown and on terms as it may impose order the debtor to be examined under this rule at any time or place it designates, whether within or without the district wherein the case is pending.

(e) Mileage

An entity other than a debtor shall not be required to attend as a witness unless lawful mileage and witness fee for one day's attendance shall be first tendered. If the debtor resides more than 100 miles from the place of examination when required to appear for an examination under this rule, the mileage allowed by law to a witness shall be tendered for any distance more than 100 miles from the debtor's residence at the date of the filing of the first petition commencing a case under the Code or the residence at the time the debtor is required to appear for the examination, whichever is the lesser.

(As amended Mar. 30, 1987, eff. Aug. 1, 1987; Apr. 30, 1991, eff. Aug. 1, 1991; Apr. 29, 2002, eff. Dec. 1, 2002.)

ADVISORY COMMITTEE NOTES

Subdivision (a) of this rule is derived from former Bankruptcy Rule 205(a). See generally 2 Collier, Bankruptcy ¶¶343.02, 343.08, 343.13 (15th ed. 1981). It specifies the manner of moving for an examination. The motion may be heard ex parte or it may be heard on notice.

Subdivision (b) is derived from former Bankruptcy Rules 205(d) and 11–26.

Subdivision (c) specifies the mode of compelling attendance of a witness or party for an examination and for the production of evidence under this rule. The subdivision is substantially declaratory of the practice that had developed under § 21a of the Act [former § 44(a) of this title]. See 2 Collier, supra ¶343.11.

This subdivision will be applicable for the most part to the examination of a person other than the debtor. The debtor is required to appear at the meeting of creditors for examination. The word "person" includes the debtor and this subdivision may be used if necessary to obtain the debtor's attendance for examination.

Subdivision (d) is derived from former Bankruptcy Rule 205(f) and is not a limitation on subdivision (c). Any person, including the debtor, served with a subpoena within the range of a subpoena must attend for examination pursuant to subdivision (c). Subdivision (d) applies only to the debtor and a subpoena need not be issued. There are no territorial limits on the service of an order on the debtor. See, e.g., In re Totem Lodge & Country Club, Inc., 134 F.Supp. 158 (S.D.N.Y.1955).

Subdivision (e) is derived from former Bankruptcy Rule 205(g). The lawful mileage and fee for attendance at a United States court as a witness are prescribed by 28 U.S.C. § 1821.

Definition of debtor. The word "debtor" as used in this rule includes the persons specified in the definition in Rule 9001(5).

Spousal privilege. The limitation on the spousal privilege formerly contained in § 21a of the Act [former § 44(a) of this title] is not carried over in the Code. For privileges generally, see Rule 501 of the Federal Rules of Evidence made applicable in cases under the Code by Rule 1101 thereof.

1991 Amendments

This rule is amended to allow the examination in a chapter 12 case to cover the same matters that may be covered in an examination in a chapter 11 or 13 case.

2002 Amendments

Subdivision (c) is amended to clarify that an examination ordered under Rule 2004(a) may be held outside the district in which the case is pending if the subpoena is issued by the court for the district in which the examination is to be held and is served in the manner provided in Rule 45 F.R.Civ.P., made applicable by Rule 9016.

The subdivision is amended further to clarify that, in addition to the procedures for the issuance of a subpoena set forth in Rule 45 F.R.Civ.P., an attorney may issue and sign a subpoena on behalf of the court for the district in which a Rule 2004 examination is to be held if the attorney is authorized to practice, even if admitted pro hac vice, either in the court in which the case is pending or in the court for the district in which the examination is to be held. This provision supplements the procedures for the issuance of a subpoena set forth in Rule 45(a)(3)(A) and (B) F.R.Civ.P. and is consistent with one of the purposes of the 1991 amendments to Rule 45, to ease the burdens of interdistrict law practice.

Changes Made After Publication and Comments. The typographical error was corrected, but no other changes were made.

CROSS REFERENCES

Allowances and travel expenses of witnesses, see 28 USCA § 1821.

Apprehension and removal of debtor to compel attendance for examination, see Fed.Rules Bankr.Proc. Rule 2005, 11 USCA.

Debtor as corporation or partnership for purposes of this rule, see Fed.Rules Bankr.Proc. Rule 9001, 11 USCA.

Duty of bankrupt to—

    Attend hearing on right to discharge, see 11 USCA § 524.

    Submit to examination, see Fed.Rules Bankr.Proc. Rule 4002, 11 USCA.

Duty of trustee to investigate debtor—

    Individual debt adjustment case, see 11 USCA § 1302.

    Liquidation case, see 11 USCA § 704.

Examination of debtor concerning compensation agreements with attorney, see Fed.Rules Bankr.Proc. Rule 2017, 11 USCA.

Immunity from self-incrimination, see 11 USCA § 344.

Motions; form and service, see Fed.Rules Bankr.Proc. Rule 9013, 11 USCA.

Subpoena, see Fed.Rules Civ.Proc. Rule 45, 28 USCA.

Privileges, see Fed.Rules Evid. Rule 501, 28 USCA.

LIBRARY REFERENCES

American Digest System

Bankruptcy ☞3040.1 to 3048.

Key Number System Topic No. 51.

Corpus Juris Secundum

CJS Bankruptcy § 252, Power to Examine Debtor or Any Entity.

CJS Bankruptcy § 801, Creditors.

CJS Bankruptcy § 807, Scope of Inquiry.

CJS Bankruptcy § 812, Who is Entitled to Make Examination.

CJS Bankruptcy § 813, Effect of Pending Litigation.

CJS Bankruptcy § 814, Postconfirmation Examinations.

CJS Bankruptcy § 816, Where Debtor Attempts to Avoid Examination.

CJS Bankruptcy § 818, Compelling Attendance and Production of Documentary Evidence.

CJS Bankruptcy § 820, Exclusions and Limitations.

CJS Bankruptcy § 821, Exclusions and Limitations--Privilege.

CJS Bankruptcy § 823, Who May be Required to Submit to Examination.

CJS Bankruptcy § 824, Examination of Corporations.

CJS Bankruptcy § 825, Securing Attendance.

CJS Bankruptcy § 826, Production of Documentary Evidence.

CJS Bankruptcy § 828, Exclusions.

CJS Bankruptcy § 829, Judicial Balancing of Interests.

CJS Bankruptcy § 834, Discretion of Court in Restricting Public Access.

Rule 2005. Apprehension and Removal of Debtor to Compel Attendance for Examination

(a) Order to compel attendance for examination

On motion of any party in interest supported by an affidavit alleging (1) that the examination of the debtor is necessary for the proper administration of the estate and that there is reasonable cause to believe that the debtor is about to leave or has left the debtor's residence or principal place of business to avoid examination, or (2) that the debtor has evaded service of a subpoena or of an order to attend for examination, or (3) that the debtor has willfully disobeyed a subpoena or order to attend for examination, duly served, the court may issue to the marshal, or some other officer authorized by law, an order directing the officer to bring the debtor before the court without unnecessary delay. If, after hearing, the court finds the allegations to be true, the court shall thereupon cause the debtor to be examined forthwith. If necessary, the court shall fix conditions for further examination and for the debtor's obedience to all orders made in reference thereto.

(b) Removal

Whenever any order to bring the debtor before the court is issued under this rule and the debtor is found in a district other than that of the court issuing the order, the debtor may be taken into custody under the order and removed in accordance with the following rules:

    (1) If the debtor is taken into custody under the order at a place less than 100 miles from the place of issue of the order, the debtor shall be brought forthwith before the court that issued the order.

    (2) If the debtor is taken into custody under the order at a place 100 miles or more from the place of issue of the order, the debtor shall be brought without unnecessary delay before the nearest available United States magistrate judge, bankruptcy judge, or district judge. If, after hearing, the magistrate judge, bankruptcy judge, or district judge finds that an order has issued under this rule and that the person in custody is the debtor, or if the person in custody waives a hearing, the magistrate judge, bankruptcy judge, or district judge shall order removal, and the person in custody shall be released on conditions ensuring prompt appearance before the court that issued the order to compel the attendance.

(c) Conditions of release

In determining what conditions will reasonably assure attendance or obedience under subdivision (a) of this rule or appearance under subdivision (b) of this rule, the court shall be governed by the provisions and policies of title 18, U.S.C., § 3146(a) and (b).

(As amended Mar. 30, 1987, eff. Aug. 1, 1987; Apr. 22, 1993, eff. Aug. 1, 1993.)

ADVISORY COMMITTEE NOTES

This rule is derived from former Bankruptcy Rule 206. The rule requires the debtor to be examined as soon as possible if allegations of the movant for compulsory examination under this rule are found to be true after a hearing. Subdivision (b) includes in paragraphs (1) and (2) provisions adapted from subdivisions (a) and (b) of Rule 40 of the Federal Rules of Criminal Procedure, which governs the handling of a person arrested in one district on a warrant issued in another. Subdivision (c) incorporates by reference the features of subdivisions (a) and (b) of 18 U.S.C. § 3146, which prescribe standards, procedures and factors to be considered in determining conditions of release of accused persons in noncapital cases prior to trial. The word "debtor" as used in this rule includes the persons named in Rule 9001(5).

The affidavit required to be submitted in support of the motion may be subscribed by the unsworn declaration provided for in 28 U.S.C. § 1746.

1993 Amendments

Subdivision (b)(2) is amended to conform to § 321 of the Judicial Improvements Act of 1990, Pub. L. No. 101–650, which changed the title of "United States magistrate" to "United States magistrate judge." Other amendments are stylistic and make no substantive change.

Change of Name

United States magistrate appointed under section 631 of Title 28, Judiciary and Judicial Procedure, to be known as United States magistrate judge after Dec. 1, 1990, with any reference to United States magistrate or magistrate in Title 28, in any other Federal statute, etc., deemed a reference to United States magistrate judge appointed under section 631 of Title 28, see section 321 of Pub.L. 101–650, set out as a note under section 631 of Title 28.

CROSS REFERENCES

Debtor as corporation or partnership for purposes of this rule, see Fed.Rules Bankr.Proc. Rule 9001, 11 USCA.

Motions; form and service, see Fed.Rules Bankr.Proc. Rule 9013, 11 USCA.

Commitment to another district; removal, see Fed.Rules Cr.Proc. Rule 40, 18 USCA.

LIBRARY REFERENCES

American Digest System

Bankruptcy ⚮3043.

Key Number System Topic No. 51.

Corpus Juris Secundum

CJS Bankruptcy § 252, Power to Examine Debtor or Any Entity.

CJS Bankruptcy § 816, Where Debtor Attempts to Avoid Examination.

Rule 2006. Solicitation and Voting of Proxies in Chapter 7 Liquidation Cases

(a) Applicability

This rule applies only in a liquidation case pending under chapter 7 of the Code.

(b) Definitions

(1) Proxy

A proxy is a written power of attorney authorizing any entity to vote the claim or otherwise act as the owner's attorney in fact in connection with the administration of the estate.

(2) Solicitation of proxy

The solicitation of a proxy is any communication, other than one from an attorney to a regular client who owns a claim or from an attorney to the owner of a claim who has requested the attorney to represent the owner, by which a creditor is asked, directly or indirectly, to give a proxy after or in contemplation of the filing of a petition by or against the debtor.

(c) Authorized solicitation

(1) A proxy may be solicited only by (A) a creditor owning an allowable unsecured claim against the estate on the date of the filing of the petition; (B) a committee elected pursuant to § 705 of the Code; (C) a committee of creditors selected by a majority in number and amount of claims of creditors (i) whose claims are not contingent or unliquidated, (ii) who are not disqualified from voting under § 702(a) of the Code and (iii) who were present or represented at a meeting of which all creditors having claims of over $500 or the 100 creditors having the largest claims had at least seven days' notice in writing and of which meeting written minutes were kept and are available reporting the names of the creditors present or represented and voting and the amounts of their claims; or (D) a bona fide trade or credit association, but such association may solicit only creditors who were its members or subscribers in good standing and had allowable unsecured claims on the date of the filing of the petition.

(2) A proxy may be solicited only in writing.

(d) Solicitation not authorized

This rule does not permit solicitation (1) in any interest other than that of general creditors; (2) by or on behalf of any custodian; (3) by the interim trustee or by or on behalf of any entity not qualified to vote under § 702(a) of the Code; (4) by or on behalf of an attorney at law; or (5) by or on behalf of a transferee of a claim for collection only.

(e) Data required from holders of multiple proxies

At any time before the voting commences at any meeting of creditors pursuant to § 341(a) of the Code, or at any other time as the court may direct, a holder of two or more proxies shall file and transmit to the United States trustee a verified list of the proxies to be voted and a verified statement of the pertinent facts and circumstances in connection with the execution and delivery of each proxy, including:

(1) a copy of the solicitation;

(2) identification of the solicitor, the forwarder, if the forwarder is neither the solicitor nor the owner of the claim, and the proxyholder, including their connections with the debtor and with each other. If the solicitor, forwarder, or proxyholder is an association, there shall also be included a statement that the creditors whose claims have been solicited and the creditors whose claims are to be voted were members or subscribers in good standing and had allowable unsecured claims on the date of the filing of the petition. If the solicitor, forwarder, or proxyholder is a committee of creditors, the statement shall also set forth the date and place the committee was organized, that the committee was organized in accordance with clause (B) or (C) of paragraph (c)(1) of this rule, the members of the committee, the amounts of their claims, when the claims were acquired, the amounts paid therefor, and the extent to which the claims of the committee members are secured or entitled to priority;

(3) a statement that no consideration has been paid or promised by the proxyholder for the proxy;

(4) a statement as to whether there is any agreement and, if so, the particulars thereof, between the proxyholder and any other entity for the payment of any consideration in connection with voting the proxy, or for the sharing of compensation with any entity, other than a member or regular associate of the proxyholder's law firm, which may be allowed the trustee or any entity for services rendered in the case, or for the employment of any person as attorney, accountant, appraiser, auctioneer, or other employee for the estate;

(5) if the proxy was solicited by an entity other than the proxyholder, or forwarded to the holder by an entity who is neither a solicitor of the proxy nor the owner of the claim, a statement signed and verified by the solicitor or forwarder that no consideration has been paid or promised for the proxy, and whether there is any agreement, and, if so, the particulars thereof, between the solicitor or forwarder and any other entity for the payment of any consideration in connection with voting the proxy, or for sharing compensation with any entity, other than

a member or regular associate of the solicitor's or forwarder's law firm which may be allowed the trustee or any entity for services rendered in the case, or for the employment of any person as attorney, accountant, appraiser, auctioneer, or other employee for the estate;

(6) if the solicitor, forwarder, or proxyholder is a committee, a statement signed and verified by each member as to the amount and source of any consideration paid or to be paid to such member in connection with the case other than by way of dividend on the member's claim.

(f) Enforcement of restrictions on solicitation

On motion of any party in interest or on its own initiative, the court may determine whether there has been a failure to comply with the provisions of this rule or any other impropriety in connection with the solicitation or voting of a proxy. After notice and a hearing the court may reject any proxy for cause, vacate any order entered in consequence of the voting of any proxy which should have been rejected, or take any other appropriate action.

(As amended Mar. 30, 1987, eff. Aug. 1, 1987; Apr. 30, 1991, eff. Aug. 1, 1991; Mar. 26, 2009, eff. Dec. 1, 2009.)

ADVISORY COMMITTEE NOTES

This rule is a comprehensive regulation of solicitation and voting of proxies in liquidation cases. It is derived from former Bankruptcy Rule 208. The rule applies only in chapter 7 cases because no voting occurs, other than on a plan, in a chapter 11 case. Former Bankruptcy Rule 208 did not apply to solicitations of acceptances of plans.

Creditor control was a basic feature of the Act and is continued, in part, by the Code. Creditor democracy is perverted and the congressional objective frustrated, however, if control of administration falls into the hands of persons whose principal interest is not in what the estate can be made to yield to the unsecured creditors but in what it can yield to those involved in its administration or in other ulterior objectives.

Subdivision (b). The definition of proxy in the first paragraph of subdivision (b) is derived from former Bankruptcy Rule 208.

Subdivision (c). The purpose of the rule is to protect creditors against loss of control of administration of their debtors' estates to holders of proxies having interests that differ from those of the creditors. The rule does not prohibit solicitation but restricts it to those who were creditors at the commencement of the case or their freely and fairly selected representatives. The special role occupied by credit and trade associations is recognized in the last clause of subdivision (c)(1). On the assumption that members or subscribers may have affiliated with an association in part for the purpose of obtaining its services as a representative in liquidation proceedings, an established association is authorized to solicit its own members, or its regular customers or clients, who were creditors on the date of the filing of the petition. Although the association may not solicit nonmembers or nonsubscribers for proxies, it may sponsor a meeting of creditors at which a committee entitled to solicit proxies may be selected in accordance with clause (C) of subdivision (c)(1).

Rule 2006 BANKRUPTCY RULES

Under certain circumstances, the relationship of a creditor, creditors' committee, or association to the estate or the case may be such as to warrant rejection of any proxy solicited by such a person or group. Thus a person who is forbidden by the Code to vote his own claim should be equally disabled to solicit proxies from creditors. Solicitation by or on behalf of the debtor has been uniformly condemned, e.g., In re White, 15 F.2d 371 (9th Cir. 1926), as has solicitation on behalf of a preferred creditor, Matter of Law, 13 Am.B.R. 650 (S.D.Ill. 1905). The prohibition on solicitation by a receiver or his attorney made explicit by General Order 39 has been collaterally supported by rulings rejecting proxies solicited by a receiver in equity, In re Western States Bldg.-Loan Ass'n, 54 F.2d 415 (S.D.Cal.1931), and by an assignee for the benefit of creditors, Lines v. Falstaff Brewing Co., 233 F.2d 927 (9th Cir. 1956).

Subdivision (d) prohibits solicitation by any person or group having a relationship described in the preceding paragraph. It also makes no exception for attorneys or transferees of claims for collection. The rule does not undertake to regulate communications between an attorney and his regular client or between an attorney and a creditor who has asked the attorney to represent him in a proceeding under the Code, but any other communication by an attorney or any other person or group requesting a proxy from the owner of a claim constitutes a regulated solicitation. Solicitation by an attorney of a proxy from a creditor who was not a client prior to the solicitation is objectionable not only as unethical conduct as recognized by such cases as In the Matter of Darland Company, 184 F.Supp. 760 (S.D.Iowa 1960) but also and more importantly because the practice carries a substantial risk that administration will fall into the hands of those whose interest is in obtaining fees from the estate rather than securing dividends for creditors. The same risk attaches to solicitation by the holder of a claim for collection only.

Subdivision (e). The regulation of solicitation and voting of proxies is achieved by the rule principally through the imposition of requirements of disclosure on the holders of two or more proxies. The disclosures must be made to the clerk before the meeting at which the proxies are to be voted to afford the clerk or a party in interest an opportunity to examine the circumstances accompanying the acquisition of the proxies in advance of any exercise of the proxies. In the light of the examination the clerk or a party in interest should bring to the attention of the judge any question that arises and the judge may permit the proxies that comply with the rule to be voted and reject those that do not unless the holders can effect or establish compliance in such manner as the court shall prescribe. The holders of single proxies are excused from the disclosure requirements because of the insubstantiality of the risk that such proxies have been solicited, or will be voted, in an interest other than that of general creditors.

Every holder of two or more proxies must include in the submission a verified statement that no consideration has been paid or promised for the proxy, either by the proxyholder or the solicitor or any forwarder of the proxy. Any payment or promise of consideration for a proxy would be conclusive evidence of a purpose to acquire control of the administration of an estate for an ulterior purpose. The holder of multiple proxies must also include in the submission a verified statement as to whether there is any agreement by the holder, the solicitor, or any forwarder of the proxy for the employment of any person in the administration of an estate or for the sharing of any compensation allowed in connection with the administration of the estate. The provisions requiring these statements implement the policy of the Code expressed in § 504 as well as the policy of this rule to deter the acquisition of proxies for the purpose of obtaining a share in the outlays for administration. Finally the facts as to any consideration moving or promised to any member of a committee which functions as a solicitor, forwarder, or proxyholder must be disclosed by the proxyholder. Such information would be of significance to the court in evaluating the purpose of the committee in obtaining, transmitting, or voting proxies.

Subdivision (f) has counterparts in the local rules referred to in the Advisory Committee's Note to former Bankruptcy Rule 208. Courts have been accorded a wide range of discretion in the handling of disputes involving proxies. Thus the referee was allowed to reject proxies and to proceed forthwith to hold a scheduled election at the same meeting. E.g., In re Portage Wholesale Co., 183 F.2d 959 (7th Cir. 1950); In re McGill, 106 Fed. 57 (6th Cir. 1901); In re Deena Woolen Mills, Inc., 114 F.Supp. 260, 273 (D.Me.1953); In re Finlay, 3 Am.B.R. 738 (S.D.N.Y.1900). The bankruptcy judge may postpone an election to permit a determination of issues presented by a dispute as to proxies and to afford those creditors whose proxies are rejected an opportunity to give new proxies or to attend an adjourned meeting to vote their own claims. Cf. In the Matter of Lenrick Sales, Inc., 369 F.2d 439, 442–43 (3d Cir.), cert. denied, 389 U.S. 822 (1967); In the Matter of Construction Supply Corp., 221 F.Supp. 124, 128 (E.D.Va.1963). This rule is not intended to restrict the scope of the court's discretion in the handling of disputes as to proxies.

1991 Amendments

This rule is amended to give the United States trustee information in connection with proxies so that the United States trustee may perform responsibilities as presiding officer at the § 341 meeting of creditors. See Rule 2003.

The words "with the clerk" are deleted as unnecessary. See Rules 5005(a) and 9001(3).

2009 Amendments

The rule is amended to implement changes in connection with the amendment to Rule 9006(a) and the manner by which time is computed under the rules. The deadline in the rule is amended to substitute a deadline that is a multiple of seven days. Throughout the rules, deadlines are amended in the following manner:

- 5–day periods become 7–day periods
- 10–day periods become 14–day periods
- 15–day periods become 14–day periods
- 20–day periods become 21–day periods
- 25–day periods become 28–day periods

CROSS REFERENCES

Committee of unsecured creditors selected before order for relief, solicitation pursuant to this rule, see Fed.Rules Bankr. Proc. Rule 2007, 11 USCA.

Motions; form and service, see Fed.Rules Bankr.Proc. Rule 9013, 11 USCA.

Signing and verification of papers, see Fed.Rules Bankr. Proc. Rule 9011, 11 USCA.

American Digest System

Bankruptcy ☞3024.

Key Number System Topic No. 51.

Corpus Juris Secundum

CJS Bankruptcy § 79, Solicitation and Voting of Proxies.

CJS Bankruptcy § 82, Meeting of Creditors and Election Procedures.

CJS Bankruptcy § 1100, Solicitation and Voting of Proxies in Chapter 7 Liquidations.

Rule 2007. Review of Appointment of Creditors' Committee Organized Before Commencement of the Case

(a) Motion to review appointment

If a committee appointed by the United States trustee pursuant to § 1102(a) of the Code consists of the members of a committee organized by creditors before the commencement of a chapter 9 or chapter 11 case, on motion of a party in interest and after a hearing on notice to the United States trustee and other entities as the court may direct, the court may determine whether the appointment of the committee satisfies the requirements of § 1102(b)(1) of the Code.

(b) Selection of members of committee

The court may find that a committee organized by unsecured creditors before the commencement of a chapter 9 or chapter 11 case was fairly chosen if:

(1) it was selected by a majority in number and amount of claims of unsecured creditors who may vote under § 702(a) of the Code and were present in person or represented at a meeting of which all creditors having unsecured claims of over $1,000 or the 100 unsecured creditors having the largest claims had at least seven days' notice in writing, and of which meeting written minutes reporting the names of the creditors present or represented and voting and the amounts of their claims were kept and are available for inspection;

(2) all proxies voted at the meeting for the elected committee were solicited pursuant to Rule 2006 and the lists and statements required by subdivision (e) thereof have been transmitted to the United States trustee; and

(3) the organization of the committee was in all other respects fair and proper.

(c) Failure to comply with requirements for appointment

After a hearing on notice pursuant to subdivision (a) of this rule, the court shall direct the United States trustee to vacate the appointment of the committee and may order other appropriate action if the court finds that such appointment failed to satisfy the requirements of § 1102(b)(1) of the Code.

(As amended Mar. 30, 1987, eff. Aug. 1, 1987; Apr. 30, 1991, eff. Aug. 1, 1991; Mar. 26, 2009, eff. Dec. 1, 2009.)

ADVISORY COMMITTEE NOTES

Section 1102(b)(1) of the Code permits the court to appoint as the unsecured creditors' committee, the committee that was selected by creditors before the order for relief. This provision recognizes the propriety of continuing a "prepetition" committee in an official capacity. Such a committee, however, must be found to have been fairly chosen and representative of the different kinds of claims to be represented.

Subdivision (a) does not necessarily require a hearing but does require a party in interest to bring to the court's attention the fact that a prepetition committee had been organized and should be appointed. An application would suffice for this purpose. Party in interest would include the committee, any member of the committee, or any of its agents acting for the committee. Whether or not notice of the application should be given to any other party is left to the discretion of the court.

Subdivision (b) implements § 1102(b)(1). The Code provision allows the court to appoint, as the official § 1102(a) committee, a "prepetition" committee if its members were fairly chosen and the committee is representative of the different kinds of claims. This subdivision of the rule indicates some of the factors the court may consider in determining whether the requirements of § 1102(b)(1) have been satisfied. In effect, the subdivision provides various factors which are similar to those set forth in Rule 2006 with respect to the solicitation and voting of proxies in a chapter 7 liquidation case.

1987 Amendments

The rule is amended to conform to the 1984 amendments to § 1102(b)(1) of the Code.

1991 Amendments

This rule is amended to conform to the 1986 amendments to § 1102(a). The United States trustee appoints committees pursuant to § 1102 in chapter 11 cases. Section 1102 is applicable in chapter 9 cases pursuant to § 901(a).

Although § 1102(b)(1) of the Code permits the United States trustee to appoint a prepetition committee as the statutory committee if its members were fairly chosen and it is representative of the different kinds of claims to be represented, the amendment to this rule provides a procedure for judicial review of the appointment. The factors that may be considered by the court in determining whether the committee was fairly chosen are not new. A finding that a prepetition committee has not been fairly chosen does not prohibit the appointment of some or all of its members to the creditors' committee. Although this rule deals only with judicial review of the appointment of prepetition committees, it does not preclude judicial review under Rule 2020 regarding the appointment of other committees.

2009 Amendments

The rule is amended to implement changes in connection with the amendment to Rule 9006(a) and the manner by which time is computed under the rules. The deadline in the rule is amended to substitute a deadline that is a multiple of seven days. Throughout the rules, deadlines are amended in the following manner:

- 5–day periods become 7–day periods
- 10–day periods become 14–day periods
- 15–day periods become 14–day periods
- 20–day periods become 21–day periods
- 25–day periods become 28–day periods

CROSS REFERENCES

Representation of creditors and equity security holders in municipality debt adjustment and reorganization cases, see Fed.Rules Bankr.Proc. Rule 2019, 11 USCA.

LIBRARY REFERENCES

American Digest System

Bankruptcy ☞3024.

Key Number System Topic No. 51.

Corpus Juris Secundum

CJS Bankruptcy § 1129, Appointment of Creditors" and Equity Security Holders" Committees.

Rule 2007.1. Appointment of Trustee or Examiner in a Chapter 11 Reorganization Case

(a) Order to appoint trustee or examiner

In a chapter 11 reorganization case, a motion for an order to appoint a trustee or an examiner under § 1104(a) or § 1104(c) of the Code shall be made in accordance with Rule 9014.

(b) Election of trustee

(1) Request for an election

A request to convene a meeting of creditors for the purpose of electing a trustee in a chapter 11 reorganization case shall be filed and transmitted to the United States trustee in accordance with Rule 5005 within the time prescribed by § 1104(b) of the Code. Pending court approval of the person elected, any person appointed by the United States trustee under § 1104(d) and approved in accordance with subdivision (c) of this rule shall serve as trustee.

(2) Manner of election and notice

An election of a trustee under § 1104(b) of the Code shall be conducted in the manner provided in Rules 2003(b)(3) and 2006. Notice of the meeting of creditors convened under § 1104(b) shall be given as provided in Rule 2002. The United States trustee shall preside at the meeting. A proxy for the purpose of voting in the election may be solicited only by a committee of creditors appointed under § 1102 of the Code or by any other party entitled to solicit a proxy pursuant to Rule 2006.

(3) Report of election and resolution of disputes.

(A) Report of undisputed election

If no dispute arises out of the election, the United States trustee shall promptly file a report certifying the election, including the name and address of the person elected and a statement that the election is undisputed. The report shall be accompanied by a verified statement of the person elected setting forth that person's connections with the debtor, creditors, any other party in interest, their respective attorneys and accountants, the United States trustee, or any person employed in the office of the United States trustee.

(B) Dispute arising out of an election

If a dispute arises out of an election, the United States trustee shall promptly file a report stating that the election is disputed, informing the court of the nature of the dispute, and listing the name and address of any candidate elected under any alternative presented by the dispute. The report shall be accompanied by a verified statement by each candidate elected under each alternative presented by the dispute, setting forth the person's connections with the debtor, creditors, any other party in interest, their respective attorneys and accountants, the United States trustee, or any person employed in the office of the United States trustee. Not later than the date on which the report of the disputed election is filed, the United States trustee shall mail a copy of the report and each verified statement to any party in interest that has made a request to convene a meeting under § 1104(b) or to receive a copy of the report, and to any committee appointed under § 1102 of the Code.

(c) Approval of appointment

An order approving the appointment of a trustee or an examiner under § 1104(d) of the Code shall be made on application of the United States trustee. The application shall state the name of the person appointed and, to the best of the applicant's knowledge, all the person's connections with the debtor, creditors, any other parties in interest, their respective attorneys and accountants, the United States trustee, or persons employed in the office of the United States trustee. The application shall state the names of the parties in interest with whom the United States trustee consulted regarding the appointment. The application shall be accompanied by a verified statement of the person appointed setting forth the person's connections with the debtor, creditors, any other party in interest, their respective attorneys and accountants, the United States trustee, or any person employed in the office of the United States trustee.

(Added Apr. 30, 1991, eff. Aug. 1, 1991; amended Apr. 11, 1997, eff. Dec. 1, 1997; Apr. 23, 2008, eff. Dec. 1, 2008.)

ADVISORY COMMITTEE NOTES
1991 Adoption

This rule is added to implement the 1986 amendments to § 1104 of the Code regarding the appointment of a trustee or examiner in a chapter 11 case. A motion for an order to appoint a trustee or examiner is a contested matter. Although the court decides whether the appointment is warranted under the particular facts of the case, it is the United States trustee who makes the appointment pursuant to § 1104(c) of the Code. The appointment is subject to approval of the court, however, which may be obtained by application of the United States trustee. Section 1104(c) of the Code requires that the appointment be made after consultation with parties in interest and that the person appointed be disinterested.

The requirement that connections with the United States trustee or persons employed in the United States trustee's office be revealed is not intended to enlarge the definition of "disinterested person" in § 101(13) of the Code, to supersede executive regulations or other laws relating to appointments by United States trustees, or to otherwise restrict the United States trustee's discretion in making appointments. This information is required, however, in the interest of full disclosure and confidence in the appointment process and to give the court all information that may be relevant to the exercise of judicial discretion in approving the appointment of a trustee or examiner in a chapter 11 case.

1997 Amendments

This rule is amended to implement the 1994 amendments to § 1104 of the Code regarding the election of a trustee in a chapter 11 case.

Eligibility for voting in an election for a chapter 11 trustee is determined in accordance with Rule 2003(b)(3). Creditors whose claims are deemed filed under § 1111(a) are treated for voting purposes as creditors who have filed proofs of claim.

Proxies for the purpose of voting in the election may be solicited only by a creditors' committee appointed under § 1102 or by any other party entitled to solicit proxies pursuant to Rule 2006. Therefore, a trustee or examiner who has served in the case, or a committee of equity security holders appointed under § 1102, may not solicit proxies.

The procedures for reporting disputes to the court derive from similar provisions in Rule 2003(d) applicable to chapter 7 cases. An election may be disputed by a party in interest or by the United States trustee. For example, if the United States trustee believes that the person elected is ineligible to serve as trustee because the person is not "disinterested," the United States trustee should file a report disputing the election.

The word "only" is deleted from subdivision (b), redesignated as subdivision (c), to avoid any negative inference with respect to the availability of procedures for obtaining review of the United States trustee's acts or failure to act pursuant to Rule 2020.

GAP Report on Rule 2007.1. The published draft of proposed new subdivision (b)(3) of Rule 2007.1, and the Committee Note, was substantially revised to implement Mr. Patchan's recommendations (described above), to clarify how a disputed election will be reported, and to make stylistic improvements.

2008 Amendments

Under § 1104(b)(2) of the Code, as amended in 2005, if an eligible, disinterested person is elected to serve as trustee in a chapter 11 case, the United States trustee is directed to file a report certifying the election. The person elected does not have to be appointed to the position. Rather, the filing of the report certifying the election itself constitutes the appointment. The section further provides that in the event of a dispute in the election of a trustee, the court must resolve the matter. The rule is amended to be consistent with § 1104(b)(2).

When the United States trustee files a report certifying the election of a trustee, the person elected must provide a verified statement, similar to the statement required of professional persons under Rule 2014, disclosing connections with parties in interest and certain other persons connected with the case. Although court approval of the person elected is not required, the disclosure of the person's connections will enable parties in interest to determine whether the person is disinterested.

LIBRARY REFERENCES
American Digest System
Bankruptcy ☞3623.1 to 3626.
Key Number System Topic No. 51.

Corpus Juris Secundum
CJS Bankruptcy § 67, Request for Appointment.
CJS Bankruptcy § 71, Appointment by U.S. Trustee; Judicial Approval.
CJS Bankruptcy § 82, Meeting of Creditors and Election Procedures.
CJS Bankruptcy § 86, Request for Appointment.
CJS Bankruptcy § 87, Approval of Appointment.

Rule 2007.2. Appointment of Patient Care Ombudsman in a Health Care Business Case

(a) Order to appoint patient care ombudsman

In a chapter 7, chapter 9, or chapter 11 case in which the debtor is a health care business, the court shall order the appointment of a patient care ombudsman under § 333 of the Code, unless the court, on motion of the United States trustee or a party in interest filed no later than 21 days after the commencement of the case or within another time fixed by the court, finds that the appointment of a patient care ombudsman is not necessary under the specific circumstances of the case for the protection of patients.

(b) Motion for order to appoint ombudsman

If the court has found that the appointment of an ombudsman is not necessary, or has terminated the appointment, the court, on motion of the United States trustee or a party in interest, may order the appointment at a later time if it finds that the appointment has become necessary to protect patients.

(c) Notice of appointment

If a patient care ombudsman is appointed under § 333, the United States trustee shall promptly file a notice of the appointment, including the name and address of the person appointed. Unless the person appointed is a State Long–Term Care Ombudsman, the notice shall be accompanied by a verified statement of the person appointed setting forth the person's connections with the debtor, creditors, patients, any other party in interest, their respective attorneys and accountants, the United States trustee, and any person employed in the office of the United States trustee.

(d) Termination of appointment

On motion of the United States trustee or a party in interest, the court may terminate the appointment of a patient care ombudsman if the court finds that the appointment is not necessary to protect patients.

(e) Motion

A motion under this rule shall be governed by Rule 9014. The motion shall be transmitted to the United States trustee and served on: the debtor; the trustee; any committee elected under § 705 or appointed under § 1102 of the Code or its authorized agent, or, if the case is a chapter 9 municipality case or a chapter 11 reorganization case and no committee of unsecured creditors has been appointed under § 1102, on the creditors included on the list filed under Rule 1007(d); and such other entities as the court may direct.
(Added Apr. 23, 2008, eff. Dec. 1, 2008. As amended Mar. 26, 2009, eff. Dec. 1, 2009.)

ADVISORY COMMITTEE NOTES

2008 Adoption

Section 333 of the Code, added by the 2005 amendments, requires the court to order the appointment of a health care ombudsman within the first 30 days of a health care business case, unless the court finds that the appointment is not necessary for the protection of patients. The rule recognizes this requirement and provides a procedure by which a party may obtain a court order finding that the appointment of a patient care ombudsman is unnecessary. In the absence of a timely motion under subdivision (a) of this rule, the court will enter an order directing the United States trustee to appoint the ombudsman.

Subdivision (b) recognizes that, despite a previous order finding that a patient care ombudsman is not necessary, circumstances of the case may change or newly discovered evidence may demonstrate the necessity of an ombudsman to protect the interests of patients. In that event, a party may move the court for an order directing the appointment of an ombudsman.

When the appointment of a patient care ombudsman is ordered, the United States trustee is required to appoint a disinterested person to serve in that capacity. Court approval of the appointment is not required, but subdivision (c) requires the person appointed, if not a State Long–Term Care Ombudsman, to file a verified statement similar to the statement filed by professional persons under Rule 2014 so that

parties in interest will have information relevant to disinterestedness. If a party believes that the person appointed is not disinterested, it may file a motion asking the court to find that the person is not eligible to serve.

Subdivision (d) permits parties in interest to move for the termination of the appointment of a patient care ombudsman. If the movant can show that there no longer is any need for the ombudsman, the court may order the termination of the appointment.

2009 Amendments

The rule is amended to implement changes in connection with the amendment to Rule 9006(a) and the manner by which time is computed under the rules. The deadline in the rule is amended to substitute a deadline that is a multiple of seven days. Throughout the rules, deadlines are amended in the following manner:

- 5–day periods become 7–day periods
- 10–day periods become 14–day periods
- 15–day periods become 14–day periods
- 20–day periods become 21–day periods
- 25–day periods become 28–day periods

LIBRARY REFERENCES

Corpus Juris Secundum

CJS Bankruptcy § 764, Consumer Privacy and Patient Care Ombudsmen.

Rule 2008. Notice to Trustee of Selection

The United States trustee shall immediately notify the person selected as trustee how to qualify and, if applicable, the amount of the trustee's bond. A trustee that has filed a blanket bond pursuant to Rule 2010 and has been selected as trustee in a chapter 7, chapter 12, or chapter 13 case that does not notify the court and the United States trustee in writing of rejection of the office within seven days after receipt of notice of selection shall be deemed to have accepted the office. Any other person selected as trustee shall notify the court and the United States trustee in writing of acceptance of the office within seven days after receipt of notice of selection or shall be deemed to have rejected the office.
(As amended Mar. 30, 1987, eff. Aug. 1, 1987; Apr. 30, 1991, eff. Aug. 1, 1991; Mar. 26, 2009, eff. Dec. 1, 2009.)

ADVISORY COMMITTEE NOTES

This rule is adapted from former Bankruptcy Rule 209(c). The remainder of that rule is inapplicable because its provisions are covered by §§ 701–703, 321 of the Code.

If the person selected as trustee accepts the office, he must qualify within five days after his selection, as required by § 322(a) of the Code.

In districts having a standing trustee for chapter 13 cases, a blanket acceptance of the appointment would be sufficient for compliance by the standing trustee with this rule.

1987 Amendments

The rule is amended to eliminate the need for a standing chapter 13 trustee or member of the panel of chapter 7 trustees to accept or reject an appointment.

1991 Amendments

The amendments to this rule relating to the United States trustee are derived from Rule X–1004(a) and conform to the 1986 amendments to the Code and 28 U.S.C. § 586 which provide that the United States trustee appoints and supervises trustees, and in a chapter 7 case presides over any election of a trustee. This rule applies when a trustee is either appointed or elected. This rule is also amended to provide for chapter 12 cases.

2009 Amendments

The rule is amended to implement changes in connection with the amendment to Rule 9006(a) and the manner by which time is computed under the rules. The deadline in the rule is amended to substitute a deadline that is a multiple of seven days. Throughout the rules, deadlines are amended in the following manner:

- 5–day periods become 7–day periods
- 10–day periods become 14–day periods
- 15–day periods become 14–day periods
- 20–day periods become 21–day periods
- 25–day periods become 28–day periods

CROSS REFERENCES

Appointment of trustees—

Individual debt adjustment case, see 11 USCA § 1302.

Railroad reorganization case, see 11 USCA § 1163.

Reorganization case, see 11 USCA § 1104.

Bonds of trustees, see 11 USCA § 322.

Election of trustee in liquidation case, see 11 USCA § 702.

Eligibility to serve as trustee, see 11 USCA § 321.

Limited purpose of trustee appointed in municipality debt adjustment case, see 11 USCA § 926.

Representation of creditors and equity security holders in municipality debt adjustment and reorganization cases, see Fed.Rules Bankr.Proc. Rule 2019, 11 USCA.

Right of creditors to elect single trustee when joint administration ordered, see Fed.Rules Bankr.Proc. Rule 2009, 11 USCA.

LIBRARY REFERENCES

American Digest System

Bankruptcy ⟂3006.

Key Number System Topic No. 51.

Corpus Juris Secundum

CJS Bankruptcy § 47, Notification of Bankruptcy Trustee; Trustee's Bond.

CJS Bankruptcy § 57, Qualification of Trustee.

Rule 2009. Trustees for Estates When Joint Administration Ordered

(a) Election of single trustee for estates being jointly administered

If the court orders a joint administration of two or more estates under Rule 1015(b), creditors may elect a single trustee for the estates being jointly administered, unless the case is under subchapter V of chapter 7 of the Code.

(b) Right of creditors to elect separate trustee

Notwithstanding entry of an order for joint administration under Rule 1015(b), the creditors of any debtor may elect a separate trustee for the estate of the debtor as provided in § 702 of the Code, unless the case is under subchapter V of chapter 7.

(c) Appointment of trustees for estates being jointly administered

(1) Chapter 7 liquidation cases

Except in a case governed by subchapter V of chapter 7, the United States trustee may appoint one or more interim trustees for estates being jointly administered in chapter 7 cases.

(2) Chapter 11 reorganization cases

If the appointment of a trustee is ordered, the United States trustee may appoint one or more trustees for estates being jointly administered in chapter 11 cases.

(3) Chapter 12 family farmer's debt adjustment cases

The United States trustee may appoint one or more trustees for estates being jointly administered in chapter 12 cases.

(4) Chapter 13 individual's debt adjustment cases

The United States trustee may appoint one or more trustees for estates being jointly administered in chapter 13 cases.

(d) Potential conflicts of interest

On a showing that creditors or equity security holders of the different estates will be prejudiced by conflicts of interest of a common trustee who has been elected or appointed, the court shall order the selection of separate trustees for estates being jointly administered.

(e) Separate accounts

The trustee or trustees of estates being jointly administered shall keep separate accounts of the property and distribution of each estate.

(As amended Mar. 30, 1987, eff. Aug. 1, 1987; Apr. 30, 1991, eff. Aug. 1, 1991; Mar. 27, 2003, eff. Dec. 1, 2003.)

ADVISORY COMMITTEE NOTES

This rule is applicable in chapter 7 cases and, in part, in chapter 11 and 13 cases. The provisions in subdivisions (a) and (b) concerning creditor election of a trustee apply only in a chapter 7 case because it is only pursuant to § 702 of the Code that creditors may elect a trustee. Subdivision (c) of the rule applies in chapter 11 and 13 as well as chapter 7 cases; pursuant to § 1104 of the Code, the court may order the appointment of a trustee on application of a party in interest and, pursuant to § 1163 of the Code, the court must appoint a trustee in a railroad reorganization case. Subdivision (c) should not be taken as an indication that more than one trustee may be appointed for a single debtor. Section 1104(c) permits only one trustee for each estate. In a chapter 13 case, if there is no standing trustee, the court is to appoint a person to serve as trustee pursuant to § 1302 of the Code. There is no provision for a trustee in a chapter 9 case, except for a very limited purpose; see § 926 of the Code.

This rule recognizes that economical and expeditious administration of two or more estates may be facilitated not only by the selection of a single trustee for a partnership and its partners, but by such selection whenever estates are being jointly administered pursuant to Rule 1015. See In the Matter of International Oil Co., 427 F.2d 186, 187 (2d Cir. 1970). The rule is derived from former § 5c of the Act [former § 23(c) of this title] and former Bankruptcy Rule 210. The premise of § 5c of the Act was that notwithstanding the potentiality of conflict between the interests of the creditors of the partners and those of the creditors of the partnership, the conflict is not sufficiently serious or frequent in most cases to warrant the selection of separate trustees for the firm and the several partners. Even before the proviso was added to § 5c of the Act in 1938 to permit the creditors of a general partner to elect their separate trustee for his estate, it was held that the court had discretion to permit such an election or to make a separate appointment when a conflict of interest was recognized. In re Wood, 248 Fed. 246, 249–50 (6th Cir.), cert. denied, 247 U.S. 512 (1918); 4 Collier, Bankruptcy ¶723.04 (15th ed.1980). The rule retains in subdivision (e) the features of the practice respecting the selection of a trustee that was developed under § 5 of the Act [former § 23 of this title]. Subdivisions (a) and (c) permit the court to authorize election of a single trustee or to make a single appointment when joint administration of estates of other kinds of debtors is ordered, but subdivision (d) requires the court to make a preliminary evaluation of the risks of conflict of interest. If after the election or appointment of a common trustee a conflict of interest materializes, the court must take appropriate action to deal with it.

Subdivision (f) is derived from § 5e of the Act [former § 23(e) of this title] and former Bankruptcy Rule 210(f) and requires that the common trustee keep a separate account for each estate in all cases that are jointly administered.

1991 Amendments

One or more trustees may be appointed for estates being jointly administered in chapter 12 cases.

The amendments to this rule are derived from Rule X–1005 and are necessary because the United States trustee, rather than the court, has responsibility for appointing trustees pursuant to §§ 701, 1104, 1202, and 1302 of the Code.

If separate trustees are ordered for chapter 7 estates pursuant to subdivision (d), separate and successor trustees should be chosen as prescribed in § 703 of the Code. If the occasion for another election arises, the United States trustee should call a meeting of creditors for this purpose. An order to select separate trustees does not disqualify an appointed or elected trustee from serving for one of the estates.

Subdivision (e) is abrogated because the exercise of discretion by the United States trustee, who is in the Executive Branch, is not subject to advance restriction by rule of court. United States v. Cox, 342 F.2d 167 (5th Cir.1965), cert. denied, 365 U.S. 863 (1965); United States v. Frumento, 409 F.Supp. 136, 141 (E.D.Pa.), aff'd, 563 F.2d 1083 (3d Cir.1977), cert. denied, 434 U.S. 1072 (1977); see, Smith v. United States, 375 F.2d 243 (5th Cir.1967); House Report No. 95–595, 95th Cong., 1st Sess. 110 (1977). However, a trustee appointed by the United States trustee may be removed by the court for cause. See § 324 of the Code. Subdivision (d) of this rule, as amended, is consistent with § 324. Subdivision (f) is redesignated as subdivision (e).

2003 Amendments

The rule is amended to reflect the enactment of subchapter V of chapter 7 of the Code governing multilateral clearing organization liquidations. Section 782 of the Code provides that the designation of a trustee or alternative trustee for the case is made by the Federal Reserve Board. Therefore, neither the United States trustee nor the creditors can appoint or elect a trustee in these cases.

Other amendments are stylistic.

CROSS REFERENCES

Partnerships—

    Commencement of involuntary cases, see 11 USCA § 303.

    Person defined to include partnerships, see 11 USCA § 101.

Representation of creditors and equity security holders in municipality debt adjustment and reorganization cases, see Fed.Rules Bankr.Proc. Rule 2019, 11 USCA.

LIBRARY REFERENCES

American Digest System

Bankruptcy ⟷3004.1, 3011, 3623.1 to 3626.

Key Number System Topic No. 51.

Corpus Juris Secundum

CJS Bankruptcy § 50, Chapter 7 Proceedings.

CJS Bankruptcy § 59, Election or Appointment of Trustees for Estates Ordered Jointly Administered.

CJS Bankruptcy § 1097, Trustee's Duties and Liabilities.

Rule 2010.   Qualification by Trustee; Proceeding on Bond

(a) Blanket bond

The United States trustee may authorize a blanket bond in favor of the United States conditioned on the faithful performance of official duties by the trustee or trustees to cover (1) a person who qualifies as trustee in a number of cases, and (2) a number of trustees each of whom qualifies in a different case.

(b) Proceeding on bond

A proceeding on the trustee's bond may be brought by any party in interest in the name of the United States for the use of the entity injured by the breach of the condition.

(As amended Mar. 30, 1987, eff. Aug. 1, 1987; Apr. 30, 1991, eff. Aug. 1, 1991.)

ADVISORY COMMITTEE NOTES

Subdivisions (a) and (b). Subdivision (a) gives authority for approval by the court of a single bond to cover (1) a person who qualifies as trustee in a number of cases, and (2) a number of trustees each of whom qualifies in a different case. The cases need not be related in any way. Substantial economies can be effected if a single bond covering a number of different cases can be issued and approved at one time. When a blanket bond is filed, the trustee qualifies under subdivision (b) of the rule by filing an acceptance of the office.

Subdivision (c) prescribes the evidentiary effect of a certified copy of an order approving the trustee's bond given by a trustee under this rule or, when a blanket bond has been authorized, of a certified copy of acceptance. This rule supplements the Federal Rules of Evidence, which apply in bankruptcy cases. See Rule 1101 of the Federal Rules of Evidence. The order of approval should conform to Official Form No. 25. See, however, § 549(c) of the Code which provides only for the filing of the petition in the real estate records of serve as constructive notice of the pendency of the case. See also Rule 2011 which prescribes the evidentiary effect of a certificate that the debtor is a debtor in possession.

Subdivision (d) is derived from former Bankruptcy Rule 212(f). Reference should be made to § 322(a) and (d) of the Code which requires the bond to be filed with the bankruptcy court and places a two year limitation for the commencement of a proceeding on the bond. A bond filed under this rule should conform to Official Form No. 25. A proceeding on the bond of a trustee is governed by the rules in Part VII. See the Note accompanying Rule 7001. See also Rule 9025.

1987 Amendments

Subdivision (b) is deleted because of the amendment to Rule 2008.

1991 Amendments

This rule is amended to conform to the 1986 amendment of § 322 of the Code. The United States trustee determines the amount and sufficiency of the trustee's bond. The amendment to subdivision (a) is derived from Rule X–1004(b).

Subdivision (b) is abrogated because an order approving a bond is no longer necessary in view of the 1986 amendments to § 322 of the Code. Subdivision (c) is redesignated as subdivision (b).

CROSS REFERENCES

Proceeding on trustee's bond as exception to procedural rule of prosecution in name of real party in interest, see Fed.Rules Bankr.Proc. Rule 7017, 11 USCA.

Security; proceedings against sureties, see Fed.Rules Bankr.Proc. Rule 9025, 11 USCA.

Two-year limitations period on bond proceeding, see 11 USCA § 322.

Parties plaintiff and defendant; capacity, see Fed.Rules Civ.Proc. Rule 17, 28 USCA.

Security; proceedings against sureties, see Fed.Rules Civ. Proc. Rule 65.1, 28 USCA.

LIBRARY REFERENCES

American Digest System

Bankruptcy ⊨3006.

Key Number System Topic No. 51.

Corpus Juris Secundum

CJS Bankruptcy § 47, Notification of Bankruptcy Trustee; Trustee's Bond.

CJS Bankruptcy § 57, Qualification of Trustee.

CJS Bankruptcy § 107, Suits Against Trustee--Proceeding on Trustee's Bond.

CJS Bankruptcy § 277, Real Party in Interest; Capacity.

Rule 2011. Evidence of Debtor in Possession or Qualification of Trustee

(a) Whenever evidence is required that a debtor is a debtor in possession or that a trustee has qualified, the clerk may so certify and the certificate shall constitute conclusive evidence of that fact.

(b) If a person elected or appointed as trustee does not qualify within the time prescribed by § 322(a) of the Code, the clerk shall so notify the court and the United States trustee.

(As amended Apr. 30, 1991, eff. Aug. 1, 1991.)

ADVISORY COMMITTEE NOTES

This rule prescribes the evidentiary effect of a certificate issued by the clerk that the debtor is a debtor in possession. See Official Form No. 26. Only chapter 11 of the Code provides for a debtor in possession. See § 1107(a) of the Code. If, however, a trustee is appointed in the chapter 11 case, there will not be a debtor in possession. See §§ 1101(1), 1105 of the Code.

1991 Amendments

This rule is amended to provide a procedure for proving that a trustee has qualified in accordance with § 322 of the Code. *Subdivision (b)* is added so that the court and the United States trustee will be informed if the person selected as trustee pursuant to §§ 701, 702, 1104, 1202, 1302, or 1163 fails to qualify within the time prescribed in § 322(a).

CROSS REFERENCES

Debtor in possession for purposes of reorganization case defined as debtor except when trustee is serving, see 11 USCA § 1101.

LIBRARY REFERENCES

American Digest System

Bankruptcy ⊨3006, 3622, 3623.1.

Key Number System Topic No. 51.

Corpus Juris Secundum

CJS Bankruptcy § 57, Qualification of Trustee.

CJS Bankruptcy § 131, Debtor as Debtor in Possession.

CJS Bankruptcy § 136, Rights, Powers, and Duties of Debtor in Possession.

CJS Bankruptcy § 1050, Evidence; Presumptions and Burden of Proof.

Rule 2012. Substitution of Trustee or Successor Trustee; Accounting

(a) Trustee

If a trustee is appointed in a chapter 11 case or the debtor is removed as debtor in possession in a chapter 12 case, the trustee is substituted automatically for the debtor in possession as a party in any pending action, proceeding, or matter.

(b) Successor trustee

When a trustee dies, resigns, is removed, or otherwise ceases to hold office during the pendency of a case under the Code (1) the successor is automatically substituted as a party in any pending action, proceeding, or matter; and (2) the successor trustee shall prepare, file, and transmit to the United States trustee an accounting of the prior administration of the estate. (As amended Mar. 30, 1987, eff. Aug. 1, 1987; Apr. 30, 1991, eff. Aug. 1, 1991.)

ADVISORY COMMITTEE NOTES

Paragraph (1) of this rule implements § 325 of the Code. It provides that a pending action or proceeding continues without abatement and that the trustee's successor is automatically substituted as a party whether it be another trustee or the debtor returned to possession, as such party.

Paragraph (2) places it within the responsibility of a successor trustee to file an accounting of the prior administration of the estate. If an accounting is impossible to obtain from the prior trustee because of death or lack of cooperation, prior reports submitted in the earlier administration may be updated.

1987 Amendments

Subdivision (a) is new. The subdivision provides for the substitution of a trustee appointed in a chapter 11 case for the debtor in possession in any pending litigation.

The original provisions of the rule are now in subdivision (b).

1991 Amendments

Subdivision (a) is amended to include any chapter 12 case in which the debtor is removed as debtor in possession pursuant to § 1204(a) of the Code.

Subdivision (b) is amended to require that the accounting of the prior administration which must be filed with the court is also transmitted to the United States trustee who is responsible for supervising the administration of cases and trustees. See 28 U.S.C. § 586(a)(3). Because a court order is not required for the appointment of a successor trustee, requiring the court to fix a time for filing the accounting is inefficient and unnecessary. The United States trustee has supervisory powers over trustees and may require the successor trustee to file the accounting within a certain time period. If the successor trustee fails to file the accounting within a reasonable time, the United States trustee or a party in interest may take appropriate steps including a request for an appropriate court order. See 28 U.S.C. § 586(a)(3)(G). The words "with the court" are deleted in subdivision (b)(2) as unnecessary. See Rules 5005(a) and 9001(3).

Rule 2013. Public Record of Compensation Awarded to Trustees, Examiners, and Professionals

(a) Record to be kept

The clerk shall maintain a public record listing fees awarded by the court (1) to trustees and attorneys, accountants, appraisers, auctioneers and other professionals employed by trustees, and (2) to examiners. The record shall include the name and docket number of the case, the name of the individual or firm receiving the fee and the amount of the fee awarded. The record shall be maintained chronologically and shall be kept current and open to examination by the public without charge. "Trustees," as used in this rule, does not include debtors in possession.

(b) Summary of record

At the close of each annual period, the clerk shall prepare a summary of the public record by individual or firm name, to reflect total fees awarded during the preceding year. The summary shall be open to examination by the public without charge. The clerk shall transmit a copy of the summary to the United States trustee. (As amended Mar. 30, 1987, eff. Aug. 1, 1987; Apr. 30, 1991, eff. Aug. 1, 1991.)

ADVISORY COMMITTEE NOTES

This rule is adapted from former Rule 213. The first sentence of that rule is omitted because of the provisions in 28 U.S.C. §§ 586 and 604(f) creating panels of private trustees.

The rule is not applicable to standing trustees serving in chapter 13 cases. See § 1302 of the Code.

A basic purpose of the rule is to prevent what Congress has defined as "cronyism." Appointment or employment, whether in a chapter 7 or 11 case, should not center among a small select group of individuals unless the circumstances are such that it would be warranted. The public record of appointments to be kept by the clerk will provide a means for monitoring the appointment process.

Subdivision (b) provides a convenient source for public review of fees paid from debtors' estates in the bankruptcy courts. Thus, public recognition of appointments, fairly distributed and based on professional qualifications and expertise, will be promoted and notions of improper favor dispelled. This rule is in keeping with the findings of the Congressional subcommittees as set forth in the House Report of the Committee on the Judiciary, No. 95–595, 95th Cong., 1st Sess. 89–99 (1977). These findings included the observations that there were frequent appointments of the same person, contacts developed between the bankruptcy bar and the courts, and an unusually close relationship between the bar and the judges developed over the years. A major purpose of the new statute is to dilute these practices and instill greater public confidence in the system. Rule 2013 implements that laudatory purpose.

1987 Amendments

In subdivisions (b) and (c) the word awarded is substituted for the word paid. While clerks do not know if fees are paid, they can determine what fees are awarded by the court.

1991 Amendments

Subdivision (a) is deleted. The matter contained in this subdivision is more properly left for regulation by the United States trustee. When appointing trustees and examiners and when monitoring applications for employment of auctioneers, appraisers and other professionals, the United States trustee should be sensitive to disproportionate or excessive fees received by any person.

Subdivision (b), redesignated as subdivision (a), is amended to reflect the fact that the United States trustee appoints examiners subject to court approval.

Subdivision (c), redesignated as subdivision (b), is amended to furnish the United States trustee with a copy of the annual summary which may assist that office in the performance of its responsibilities under 28 U.S.C. § 586 and the Code.

The rule is not applicable to standing trustees serving in chapter 12 cases. See § 1202 of the Code.

CROSS REFERENCES

Compensation of officers to reimburse actual and necessary services, see 11 USCA § 330.

Limitation on compensation of trustee, see 11 USCA § 326.

LIBRARY REFERENCES

American Digest System

Bankruptcy ⟨key⟩3152, 3153, 3160 to 3164, 3192.

Clerks of Courts ⟨key⟩64 to 69.

Records ⟨key⟩32.

Key Number System Topic Nos. 326, 51, 79.

Corpus Juris Secundum

CJS Bankruptcy § 112, General Rule and Limitation.

Rule 2014. Employment of Professional Persons

(a) Application for an order of employment

An order approving the employment of attorneys, accountants, appraisers, auctioneers, agents, or other professionals pursuant to § 327, § 1103, or § 1114 of the Code shall be made only on application of the trustee or committee. The application shall be filed and, unless the case is a chapter 9 municipality case, a copy of the application shall be transmitted by the applicant to the United States trustee. The application shall state the specific facts showing the necessity for the employment, the name of the person to be employed, the reasons for the selection, the professional services to be rendered, any proposed arrangement for compensation, and, to the best of the applicant's knowledge, all of the person's connections with the debtor, creditors, any other party in interest, their respective attorneys and accountants, the United States trustee, or any person employed in the office of the United States trustee. The application shall be accompanied by a verified statement of the person to be employed setting forth the person's connections with the debtor, creditors, any other party in interest, their respective attorneys and accountants, the United States trustee, or any person employed in the office of the United States trustee.

(b) Services rendered by member or associate of firm of attorneys or accountants

If, under the Code and this rule, a law partnership or corporation is employed as an attorney, or an accounting partnership or corporation is employed as an accountant, or if a named attorney or accountant is employed, any partner, member, or regular associate of the partnership, corporation or individual may act as attorney or accountant so employed, without further order of the court.

(As amended Mar. 30, 1987, eff. Aug. 1, 1987; Apr. 30, 1991, eff. Aug. 1, 1991.)

ADVISORY COMMITTEE NOTES

Subdivision (a) is adapted from the second sentence of former Bankruptcy Rule 215(a). The remainder of that rule is covered by § 327 of the Code.

Subdivision (b) is derived from former Bankruptcy Rule 215(f). The compensation provisions are set forth in § 504 of the Code.

1991 Amendments

This rule is amended to include retention of professionals by committees of retired employees pursuant to § 1114 of the Code.

The United States trustee monitors applications filed under § 327 of the Code and may file with the court comments with respect to the approval of such applications. See 28 U.S.C. § 586(a)(3)(H). The United States trustee also monitors creditors' committees in accordance with 28 U.S.C. § 586(a)(3)(E). The addition of the second sentence of subdivision (a) is designed to enable the United States trustee to perform these duties.

Subdivision (a) is also amended to require disclosure of the professional's connections with the United States trustee or persons employed in the United States trustee's office. This requirement is not intended to prohibit the employment of such persons in all cases or to enlarge the definition of "disinterested person" in § 101(13) of the Code. However, the court may consider a connection with the United States trustee's office as a factor when exercising its discretion. Also, this information should be revealed in the interest of full disclosure and confidence in the bankruptcy system, especially since the United States trustee monitors and may be heard on applications for compensation and reimbursement of professionals employed under this rule.

The United States trustee appoints committees pursuant to § 1102 of the Code which is applicable in chapter 9 cases under § 901. In the interest of full disclosure and confidence in the bankruptcy system, a connection between the United States trustee and a professional employed by the committee should be revealed in every case, including a chapter 9 case. However, since the United States trustee does not have any role in the employment of professionals in chapter 9 cases, it is not necessary in such cases to transmit to the United States trustee a copy of the application under subdivision (a) of this rule. See 28 U.S.C. § 586(a)(3)(H).

CROSS REFERENCES

Application for compensation or reimbursement, see Fed. Rules Bankr.Proc. Rule 2016, 11 USCA.

Compensation for services and reimbursement of costs, see 11 USCA § 503.

Compensation of professional persons—

Actual, necessary services, see 11 USCA § 330.

Limitation on, see 11 USCA § 328.

Sharing of, see 11 USCA § 504.

LIBRARY REFERENCES

American Digest System

Bankruptcy ⟲3029.1, 3030.

Key Number System Topic No. 51.

Corpus Juris Secundum

CJS Bankruptcy § 288, Applications.

CJS Bankruptcy § 767, Application for Order of Employment.

CJS Bankruptcy § 770, Services by Members and Associates.

CJS Bankruptcy § 774, Necessity of Court Approval.

CJS Bankruptcy § 850, Valuation and Appraisals of Property.

Rule 2015.   Duty to Keep Records, Make Reports, and Give Notice of Case or Change of Status

[Text of subdivision (a) effective until December 1, 2012, absent contrary Congressional action.]

(a) Trustee or debtor in possession

A trustee or debtor in possession shall:

(1) in a chapter 7 liquidation case and, if the court directs, in a chapter 11 reorganization case file and transmit to the United States trustee a complete inventory of the property of the debtor within 30 days after qualifying as a trustee or debtor in possession, unless such an inventory has already been filed;

(2) keep a record of receipts and the disposition of money and property received;

(3) file the reports and summaries required by § 704(8) of the Code which shall include a statement, if payments are made to employees, of the amounts of deductions for all taxes required to be withheld or paid for and in behalf of employees and the place where these amounts are deposited;

(4) as soon as possible after the commencement of the case, give notice of the case to every entity known to be holding money or property subject to withdrawal or order of the debtor, including every bank, savings or building and loan association, public utility company, and landlord with whom the debtor has a deposit, and to every insurance company which has issued a policy having a cash surrender value payable to the debtor, except that notice need not be given to any entity who has knowledge or has previously been notified of the case;

(5) in a chapter 11 reorganization case, on or before the last day of the month after each calendar quarter during which there is a duty to pay fees under 28 U.S.C. § 1930(a)(6), file and transmit to the United States trustee a statement of any disbursements made during that quarter and of any fees payable under 28 U.S.C. § 1930(a)(6) for that quarter; and

(6) in a chapter 11 small business case, unless the court, for cause, sets another reporting interval, file and transmit to the United States trustee for each calendar month after the order for relief, on the appropriate Official Form, the report required by § 308. If the order for relief is within the first 15 days of a calendar month, a report shall be filed for the portion of the month that follows the order for relief. If the order for relief is after the 15th day of a calendar month, the period for the remainder of the month shall be included in the report for the next calendar month. Each report shall be filed no later than 21 days after the last day of the calendar month following the month covered by the report. The obligation to file reports under this subparagraph terminates on the effective date of the plan, or conversion or dismissal of the case.

[Text of subdivision (a) effective December 1, 2012, absent contrary Congressional action.]

(a) Trustee or debtor in possession

A trustee or debtor in possession shall:

(1) in a chapter 7 liquidation case and, if the court directs, in a chapter 11 reorganization case file and transmit to the United States trustee a complete inventory of the property of the debtor within 30 days after qualifying as a trustee or debtor in possession, unless such an inventory has already been filed;

(2) keep a record of receipts and the disposition of money and property received;

(3) file the reports and summaries required by § 704(a)(8) of the Code, which shall include a statement, if payments are made to employees, of the amounts of deductions for all taxes required to be withheld or paid for and in behalf of employees and the place where these amounts are deposited;

(4) as soon as possible after the commencement of the case, give notice of the case to every entity known to be holding money or property subject to withdrawal or order of the debtor, including every bank, savings or building and loan association, public utility company, and landlord with whom the debtor has a deposit, and to every insurance company which has issued a policy having a cash surrender value payable to the debtor, except that notice need not be given to any entity who has knowledge or has previously been notified of the case;

(5) in a chapter 11 reorganization case, on or before the last day of the month after each calendar quarter during which there is a duty to pay fees under 28 U.S.C. § 1930(a)(6), file and transmit to the United States trustee a statement of any disbursements made during that quarter and of any fees payable under 28 U.S.C. § 1930(a)(6) for that quarter; and

(6) in a chapter 11 small business case, unless the court, for cause, sets another reporting interval, file and transmit to the United States trustee for each calendar month after the order for relief, on the appropriate Official Form, the report required by § 308. If the order for relief is within the first 15 days of a calendar month, a report shall be filed for the portion of the month that follows the order for relief. If the order for relief is after the 15th day of a calendar month, the period for the remainder of the month shall be included in the report for the next calendar month. Each report shall be filed no later than 21 days after the last day of the calendar month following the month covered by the report. The obligation to file reports under this subparagraph terminates on the effective date of the plan, or conversion or dismissal of the case.

(b) Chapter 12 trustee and debtor in possession

In a chapter 12 family farmer's debt adjustment case, the debtor in possession shall perform the duties prescribed in clauses (2)-(4) of subdivision (a) of this rule and, if the court directs, shall file and transmit to

the United States trustee a complete inventory of the property of the debtor within the time fixed by the court. If the debtor is removed as debtor in possession, the trustee shall perform the duties of the debtor in possession prescribed in this paragraph.

(c) Chapter 13 trustee and debtor

(1) Business cases

In a chapter 13 individual's debt adjustment case, when the debtor is engaged in business, the debtor shall perform the duties prescribed by clauses (2)-(4) of subdivision (a) of this rule and, if the court directs, shall file and transmit to the United States trustee a complete inventory of the property of the debtor within the time fixed by the court.

(2) Nonbusiness cases

In a chapter 13 individual's debt adjustment case, when the debtor is not engaged in business, the trustee shall perform the duties prescribed by clause (2) of subdivision (a) of this rule.

(d) Foreign representative

In a case in which the court has granted recognition of a foreign proceeding under chapter 15, the foreign representative shall file any notice required under § 1518 of the Code within 14 days after the date when the representative becomes aware of the subsequent information.

(e) Transmission of reports

In a chapter 11 case the court may direct that copies or summaries of annual reports and copies or summaries of other reports shall be mailed to the creditors, equity security holders, and indenture trustees. The court may also direct the publication of summaries of any such reports. A copy of every report or summary mailed or published pursuant to this subdivision shall be transmitted to the United States trustee.

(As amended Mar. 30, 1987, eff. Aug. 1, 1987; Apr. 30, 1991, eff. Aug. 1, 1991; Apr. 23, 1996, eff. Dec. 1, 1996; Apr. 29, 2002, eff. Dec. 1, 2002; Apr. 23, 2008, eff. Dec. 1, 2008; Mar. 26, 2009, eff. Dec. 1, 2009; Apr. 23, 2012, eff. Dec. 1, 2012, absent contrary Congressional action.)

ADVISORY COMMITTEE NOTES

This rule combines the provisions found in former Rules 218, 10–208, 11–30 and 13–208 of the Rules of Bankruptcy Procedure. It specifies various duties which are in addition to those required by §§ 704, 1106, 1302 and 1304 of the Code.

In **subdivision (a)** the times permitted to be fixed by the court in clause (3) for the filing of reports and summaries may be fixed by local rule or order.

Subdivision (b). This subdivision prescribes duties on either the debtor or trustee in chapter 13 cases, depending on whether or not the debtor is engaged in business (§ 1304 of the Code). The duty of giving notice prescribed by subdivision (a)(4) is not included in a nonbusiness case because of its impracticability.

Subdivision (c) is derived from former Chapter X Rule 10–208(c) which, in turn, was derived from § 190 of the Act [former § 590 of this title]. The equity security holders to whom the reports should be sent are those of record at the time of transmittal of such reports.

1987 Amendments

Subdivision (a) is amended to add as a duty of the trustee or debtor in possession the filing of a notice of or a copy of the petition. The filing of such notice or a copy of the petition is essential to the protection of the estate from unauthorized post-petition conveyances of real property. Section 549(c) of the Code protects the title of a good faith purchaser for fair equivalent value unless the notice or copy of the petition is filed.

1991 Amendments

This rule is amended to provide the United States trustee with information needed to perform supervisory responsibilities in accordance with 28 U.S.C. § 586(a)(3) and to exercise the right to raise, appear and be heard on issues pursuant to § 307 of the Code.

Subdivision (a)(3) is amended to conform to the 1986 amendments to § 704(8) of the Code and the United States trustee system. It may not be necessary for the court to fix a time to file reports if the United States trustee requests that they be filed within a specified time and there is no dispute regarding such time.

Subdivision (a)(5) is deleted because the filing of a notice of or copy of the petition to protect real property against unauthorized postpetition transfers in a particular case is within the discretion of the trustee.

The new subdivision (a)(5) was added to enable the United States trustee, parties in interest, and the court to determine the appropriate quarterly fee required by 28 U.S.C. § 1930(a)(6). The requirements of subdivision (a)(5) should be satisfied whenever possible by including this information in other reports filed by the trustee or debtor in possession. Nonpayment of the fee may result in dismissal or conversion of the case pursuant to § 1112(b) of the Code.

Rule X–1007(b), which provides that the trustee or debtor in possession shall cooperate with the United States trustee by furnishing information that the United States trustee reasonably requires, is deleted as unnecessary. The deletion of Rule X–1007(b) should not be construed as a limitation of the powers of the United States trustee or of the duty of the trustee or debtor in possession to cooperate with the United States trustee in the performance of the statutory responsibilities of that office.

Subdivision (a)(6) is abrogated as unnecessary. See § 1106(a)(7) of the Code.

Subdivision (a)(7) is abrogated. The closing of a chapter 11 case is governed by Rule 3022.

New subdivision (b), which prescribes the duties of the debtor in possession and trustee in a chapter 12 case, does not prohibit additional reporting requirements pursuant to local rule or court order.

1996 Amendments

Subdivision (a)(1) provides that the trustee in a chapter 7 case and, if the court directs, the trustee or debtor in possession in a chapter 11 case, is required to file and transmit to the United States trustee a complete inventory of the debtor's property within 30 days after qualifying as trustee or debtor in possession, unless such an inventory has already been filed. Subdivisions (b) and (c) are amended to clarify that a debtor in possession and trustee in a chapter 12 case, and a debtor in a chapter 13 case where the debtor is engaged in business, are not required to file and transmit to the United States trustee a complete inventory of the property of the debtor unless the court so directs. If the court so directs, the court also fixes the time limit for filing and transmitting the inventory.

GAP Report on Rule 2015. No changes since publication, except for a stylistic change in the first sentence of the committee note.

2002 Amendments

Subdivision (a)(5) is amended to provide that the duty to file quarterly disbursement reports continues only so long as there is an obligation to make quarterly payments to the United States trustee under 28 U.S.C. § 1930(a)(6).

Other amendments are stylistic.

Changes Made After Publication and Comments. No changes were made.

2008 Amendments

Subparagraph (a)(6) implements § 308 of the Code, added by the 2005 amendments. That section requires small business chapter 11 debtors to file periodic financial and operating reports, and the rule sets the time for filing those reports and requires the use of an Official Form for the report. The obligation to file reports under this rule does not relieve the trustee or debtor of any other obligations to provide information or documents to the United States trustee.

The rule also is amended to fix the time for the filing of notices under § 1518, added to the Code in 2005. Former subdivision (d) is renumbered as subdivision (e).

Other changes are stylistic.

2009 Amendments

The rule is amended to implement changes in connection with the amendment to Rule 9006(a) and the manner by which time is computed under the rules. The deadlines in the rule are amended to substitute a deadline that is a multiple of seven days. Throughout the rules, deadlines are amended in the following manner:

- 5–day periods become 7–day periods
- 10–day periods become 14–day periods
- 15–day periods become 14–day periods
- 20–day periods become 21–day periods
- 25–day periods become 28–day periods

2012 Amendments

[Effective December 1, 2012, absent contrary Congressional action.]

Subdivision (a)(3). Subdivision (a)(3) is amended to correct the reference to § 704. The 2005 amendments to the Code expanded § 704 and created subsections within it. The provision that was previously § 704(8) became § 704(a)(8). The other change to (a)(3) is stylistic.

Final approval of this technical amendment is sought without publication.

CROSS REFERENCES

Duties of trustee—

Individual debt adjustment case, see 11 USCA § 1302.

Reorganization case, see 11 USCA § 1106.

Operation of business by debtor, see 11 USCA § 1304.

Public access to papers filed in case under this title, see 11 USCA § 107.

LIBRARY REFERENCES

American Digest System

Bankruptcy ⟷3008, 3022, 3622, 3672.

Key Number System Topic No. 51.

Corpus Juris Secundum

CJS Bankruptcy § 96, Duty to File Inventory and Collect and Reduce to Money Property of Estate.

CJS Bankruptcy § 101, Chapter 11.

CJS Bankruptcy § 102, Chapter 12.

CJS Bankruptcy § 103, Chapter 13.

CJS Bankruptcy § 104, Chapter 13--Duties If Debtor is Engaged in Business.

CJS Bankruptcy § 134, Rights, Powers, and Duties of Debtor in Possession--Specific Rights, Powers, and Duties.

CJS Bankruptcy § 136, Rights, Powers, and Duties of Debtor in Possession.

CJS Bankruptcy § 836, Chapter 7 Cases.

CJS Bankruptcy § 841, Fiduciary Duties of Trustees and Debtors in Possession.

CJS Bankruptcy § 847, Operation of Family Farm in Chapter 12 Cases.

CJS Bankruptcy § 848, Operation of Business or Affairs of Chapter 13 Debtor.

Rule 2015.1. Patient Care Ombudsman

(a) Reports

A patient care ombudsman, at least 14 days before making a report under § 333(b)(2) of the Code, shall give notice that the report will be made to the court, unless the court orders otherwise. The notice shall be transmitted to the United States trustee, posted conspicuously at the health care facility that is the subject of the report, and served on: the debtor; the trustee; all patients; and any committee elected under § 705 or appointed under § 1102 of the Code or its authorized agent, or, if the case is a chapter 9 municipality case or a chapter 11 reorganization case and no committee of unsecured creditors has been appointed under § 1102, on the creditors included on the list filed under Rule 1007(d); and such other entities as the court may direct. The notice shall state the date and time when the report will be made, the manner in which the report will be made, and, if the report is in writing, the name, address, telephone number, email address, and website, if any, of the person from whom a copy of the report may be obtained at the debtor's expense.

(b) Authorization to review confidential patient records

A motion by a patient care ombudsman under § 333(c) to review confidential patient records shall be governed by Rule 9014, served on the patient and any family member or other contact person whose name and address have been given to the trustee or the debtor for the purpose of providing information regarding the patient's health care, and transmitted to the United States trustee subject to applicable non-bankruptcy law relating to patient privacy. Unless the court orders otherwise, a hearing on the motion may not be commenced earlier than 14 days after service of the motion.

(Added Apr. 23, 2008, eff. Dec. 1, 2008; amended Mar. 26, 2009, eff. Dec. 1, 2009.)

ADVISORY COMMITTEE NOTES

2008 Adoption

This rule is new and implements § 333 of the Code, added by the 2005 amendments. Subdivision (a) is designed to give parties in interest, including patients or their representatives, sufficient notice so that they will be able to review written reports or attend hearings at which reports are made. The rule permits a notice to relate to a single report or to periodic reports to be given during the case. For example, the ombudsman may give notice that reports will be made at specified intervals or dates during the case.

Subdivision (a) of the rule also requires that the notice be posted conspicuously at the health care facility in a place where it will be seen by patients and their families or others visiting the patients. This may require posting in common areas and patient rooms within the facility. Because health care facilities and the patients they serve can vary greatly, the locations of the posted notice should be tailored to the specific facility that is the subject of the report.

Subdivision (b) requires the ombudsman to notify the patient and the United States trustee that the ombudsman is seeking access to confidential patient records so that they will be able to appear and be heard on the matter. This procedure should assist the court in reaching its decision both as to access to the records and appropriate restrictions on that access to ensure continued confidentiality. Notices given under this rule are subject to the provisions of applicable federal and state law that relate to the protection of patients' privacy, such as the Health Insurance Portability and Accountability Act of 1996, Pub. L. No. 104–191 (HIPAA).

2009 Amendments

The rule is amended to implement changes in connection with the amendment to Rule 9006(a) and the manner by which time is computed under the rules. The deadlines in the rule are amended to substitute a deadline that is a multiple of seven days. Throughout the rules, deadlines are amended in the following manner:

- 5–day periods become 7–day periods
- 10–day periods become 14–day periods
- 15–day periods become 14–day periods
- 20–day periods become 21–day periods
- 25–day periods become 28–day periods

Rule 2015.2. Transfer of Patient in Health Care Business Case

Unless the court orders otherwise, if the debtor is a health care business, the trustee may not transfer a patient to another health care business under § 704(a)(12) of the Code unless the trustee gives at least 14 days' notice of the transfer to the patient care ombudsman, if any, the patient, and any family member or other contact person whose name and address has been given to the trustee or the debtor for the purpose of providing information regarding the patient's health care. The notice is subject to applicable nonbankruptcy law relating to patient privacy.

(Added Apr. 23, 2008, eff. Dec. 1, 2008; amended Mar. 26, 2009, eff. Dec. 1, 2009.)

ADVISORY COMMITTEE NOTES

2008 Adoption

This rule is new. Section 704(a)(12), added to the Code by the 2005 amendments, authorizes the trustee to relocate patients when a health care business debtor's facility is in the process of being closed. The Code permits the trustee to take this action without the need for any court order, but the notice required by this rule will enable a patient care ombudsman appointed under § 333, or a patient who contends that the trustee's actions violate § 704(a)(12), to have those issues resolved before the patient is transferred.

This rule also permits the court to enter an order dispensing with or altering the notice requirement in proper circumstances. For example, a facility could be closed immediately, or very quickly, such that 10 days' notice would not be possible in some instances. In that event, the court may shorten the time required for notice.

Notices given under this rule are subject to the provisions of applicable federal and state law that relate to the protection of patients' privacy, such as the Health Insurance Portability and Accountability Act of 1996, Pub. L. No. 104–191 (HIPAA).

2009 Amendments

The rule is amended to implement changes in connection with the amendment to Rule 9006(a) and the manner by which time is computed under the rules. The deadline in the rule is amended to substitute a deadline that is a multiple of seven days. Throughout the rules, deadlines are amended in the following manner:

- 5–day periods become 7–day periods
- 10–day periods become 14–day periods
- 15–day periods become 14–day periods
- 20–day periods become 21–day periods
- 25–day periods become 28–day periods

Rule 2015.3. Reports of Financial Information on Entities in Which a Chapter 11 Estate Holds a Controlling or Substantial Interest

(a) Reporting requirement

In a chapter 11 case, the trustee or debtor in possession shall file periodic financial reports of the value, operations, and profitability of each entity that is not a publicly traded corporation or a debtor in a case under title 11, and in which the estate holds a substantial or controlling interest. The reports shall be prepared as prescribed by the appropriate Official Form, and shall be based upon the most recent information reasonably available to the trustee or debtor in possession.

(b) Time for filing; service

The first report required by this rule shall be filed no later than seven days before the first date set for the meeting of creditors under § 341 of the Code. Subsequent reports shall be filed no less frequently than every six months thereafter, until the effective date of a plan or the case is dismissed or converted. Copies of the report shall be served on the United States trustee, any committee appointed under § 1102 of the Code, and any other party in interest that has filed a request therefor.

(c) Presumption of substantial or controlling interest; judicial determination

For purposes of this rule, an entity of which the estate controls or owns at least a 20 percent interest, shall be presumed to be an entity in which the estate has a substantial or controlling interest. An entity in which the estate controls or owns less than a 20 percent interest shall be presumed not to be an entity in which the estate has a substantial or controlling interest. Upon motion, the entity, any holder of an interest therein, the United States trustee, or any other party in interest may seek to rebut either presumption, and the court shall, after notice and a hearing, determine whether the estate's interest in the entity is substantial or controlling.

(d) Modification of reporting requirement

The court may, after notice and a hearing, vary the reporting requirement established by subdivision (a) of this rule for cause, including that the trustee or debtor in possession is not able, after a good faith effort, to comply with those reporting requirements, or that the information required by subdivision (a) is publicly available.

(e) Notice and protective orders

No later than 14 days before filing the first report required by this rule, the trustee or debtor in possession shall send notice to the entity in which the estate has a substantial or controlling interest, and to all holders—known to the trustee or debtor in possession—of an interest in that entity, that the trustee or debtor in possession expects to file and serve financial information relating to the entity in accordance with this rule. The entity in which the estate has a substantial or controlling interest, or a person holding an interest in that entity, may request protection of the information under § 107 of the Code.

(f) Effect of request

Unless the court orders otherwise, the pendency of a request under subdivisions (c), (d), or (e) of this rule shall not alter or stay the requirements of subdivision (a).

(Added Apr. 23, 2008, eff. Dec. 1, 2008; amended Mar. 26, 2009, eff. Dec. 1, 2009.)

ADVISORY COMMITTEE NOTES

2008 Adoption

This rule implements § 419 of the Bankruptcy Abuse Prevention and Consumer Protection Act of 2005 ("BAPCPA"). Reports are to be made on the appropriate Official Form. While § 419 of BAPCPA places the obligation to report upon the "debtor," this rule extends the obligation to include cases in which a trustee has been appointed. The court can order that the reports not be filed in appropriate circumstances, such as when the information that would be included in these reports is already available to interested parties.

2009 Amendments

The rule is amended to implement changes in connection with the amendment to Rule 9006(a) and the manner by which time is computed under the rules. The deadline in the rule is amended to substitute a deadline that is a multiple of seven days. Throughout the rules, deadlines are amended in the following manner:

- 5–day periods become 7–day periods
- 10–day periods become 14–day periods
- 15–day periods become 14–day periods
- 20–day periods become 21–day periods
- 25–day periods become 28–day periods

Rule 2016. Compensation for Services Rendered and Reimbursement of Expenses

(a) Application for compensation or reimbursement

An entity seeking interim or final compensation for services, or reimbursement of necessary expenses, from the estate shall file an application setting forth a detailed statement of (1) the services rendered, time expended and expenses incurred, and (2) the amounts requested. An application for compensation shall include a statement as to what payments have theretofore been made or promised to the applicant for services rendered or to be rendered in any capacity whatsoever in connection with the case, the source of the compensation so paid or promised, whether any compensation previously received has been shared and whether an agreement or understanding exists between the applicant and any other entity for the sharing of compensation received or to be received for services rendered in or in connection with the case, and the particulars of any sharing of compensation or agreement or understanding therefor, except that details of any agreement by the applicant for the sharing of compensation as a member or regular associate of a firm of lawyers or accountants shall not be required. The requirements of this subdivision shall apply to an application for compensation for services rendered by an attorney or accountant even though the application is filed by a creditor or other entity. Unless the case is a chapter 9 municipality case, the applicant shall transmit to the United States trustee a copy of the application.

(b) Disclosure of compensation paid or promised to attorney for debtor

Every attorney for a debtor, whether or not the attorney applies for compensation, shall file and transmit to the United States trustee within 14 days after the order for relief, or at another time as the court may direct, the statement required by § 329 of the Code including whether the attorney has shared or agreed to share the compensation with any other entity. The statement shall include the particulars of any such sharing or agreement to share by the attorney, but the details of any agreement for the sharing of the compensation with a member or regular associate of the attorney's law firm shall not be required. A supplemental statement shall be filed and transmitted to the United States trustee within 14 days after any payment or agreement not previously disclosed.

(c) Disclosure of compensation paid or promised to bankruptcy petition preparer

Before a petition is filed, every bankruptcy petition preparer for a debtor shall deliver to the debtor, the declaration under penalty of perjury required by § 110(h)(2). The declaration shall disclose any fee, and the source of any fee, received from or on behalf of the debtor within 12 months of the filing of the case and all unpaid fees charged to the debtor. The declaration shall also describe the services performed and documents prepared or caused to be prepared by the bankruptcy petition preparer. The declaration shall be filed with the petition. The petition preparer shall file a supplemental statement within 14 days after any payment or agreement not previously disclosed.

(As amended Mar. 30, 1987, eff. Aug. 1, 1987; Apr. 30, 1991, eff. Aug. 1, 1991; Mar. 27, 2003, eff. Dec. 1, 2003; Mar. 26, 2009, eff. Dec. 1, 2009.)

Rule 2016 BANKRUPTCY RULES

ADVISORY COMMITTEE NOTES

This rule is derived from former Rule 219. Many of the former rule's requirements are, however, set forth in the Code. Section 329 requires disclosure by an attorney of transactions with the debtor, § 330 sets forth the bases for allowing compensation, and § 504 prohibits sharing of compensation. This rule implements those various provisions.

Subdivision (a) includes within its provisions a committee, member thereof, agent, attorney or accountant for the committee when compensation or reimbursement of expenses is sought from the estate.

Regular associate of a law firm is defined in Rule 9001(9) to include any attorney regularly employed by, associated with, or counsel to that law firm. Firm is defined in Rule 9001(6) to include a partnership or professional corporation.

1987 Amendments

Subdivision (a) is amended to change "person" to "entity." There are occasions in which a governmental unit may be entitled to file an application under this rule. The requirement that the application contain a "detailed statement of services rendered, time expended and expenses incurred" gives to the court authority to ensure that the application is both comprehensive and detailed. No amendments are made to delineate further the requirements of the application because the amount of detail to be furnished is a function of the nature of the services rendered and the complexity of the case.

Subdivision (b) is amended to require that the attorney for the debtor file the § 329 statement before the meeting of creditors. This will assist the parties in conducting the examination of the debtor. In addition, the amended rule requires the attorney to supplement the § 329 statement if an undisclosed payment is made to the attorney or a new or amended agreement is entered into by the debtor and the attorney.

1991 Amendments

Subdivision (a) is amended to enable the United States trustee to perform the duty to monitor applications for compensation and reimbursement filed under § 330 of the Code. See 28 U.S.C. § 586(a)(3)(A).

Subdivision (b) is amended to give the United States trustee the information needed to determine whether to request appropriate relief based on excessive fees under § 329(b) of the Code. See Rule 2017.

The words "with the court" are deleted in subdivisions (a) and (b) as unnecessary. See Rules 5005(a) and 9001(3).

2003 Amendments

This rule is amended by adding subdivision (c) to implement § 110(h)(1) of the Code.

2009 Amendments

The rule is amended to implement changes in connection with the amendment to Rule 9006(a) and the manner by which time is computed under the rules. The deadline in the rule is amended to substitute a deadline that is a multiple of seven days. Throughout the rules, deadlines are amended in the following manner:

- 5–day periods become 7–day periods
- 10–day periods become 14–day periods
- 15–day periods become 14–day periods
- 20–day periods become 21–day periods
- 25–day periods become 28–day periods

Subdivision (c) is amended to reflect the 2005 amendment to § 110(h)(1) of the Bankruptcy Code which now requires that the declaration be filed with the petition. The statute previously required that the petition preparer file the declaration within 10 days after the filing of the petition. The amendment to the rule also corrects the cross reference to § 110(h)(1), which was redesignated as subparagraph (h)(2) of § 110 by the 2005 amendment to the Code.

Other changes are stylistic.

CROSS REFERENCES

Compensation of professional persons—
  Actual, necessary services, see 11 USCA § 330.
  Limitation on, see 11 USCA § 328.
  Sharing of, see 11 USCA § 504.
Definition of—
  Firm to include partnership or professional corporation, see Fed.Rules Bankr.Proc. Rule 9001, 11 USCA.
  Regular associate to mean attorney employed by, associated with, as counsel to firm or individual, see Fed. Rules Bankr.Proc. Rule 9001, 11 USCA.
Employment of professional persons, see Fed.Rules Bankr. Proc. Rule 2014, 11 USCA.

LIBRARY REFERENCES

American Digest System
  Bankruptcy ⚮3151 to 3205.
  Key Number System Topic No. 51.

Corpus Juris Secundum
  CJS Bankruptcy § 113, Application for Compensation or Reimbursement.
  CJS Bankruptcy § 288, Applications.
  CJS Bankruptcy § 781, Content; Detail and Documentation Required.

Rule 2017. Examination of Debtor's Transactions with Debtor's Attorney

(a) Payment or transfer to attorney before order for relief

On motion by any party in interest or on the court's own initiative, the court after notice and a hearing may determine whether any payment of money or any transfer of property by the debtor, made directly or indirectly and in contemplation of the filing of a petition under the Code by or against the debtor or before entry of the order for relief in an involuntary case, to an attorney for services rendered or to be rendered is excessive.

(b) Payment or transfer to attorney after order for relief

On motion by the debtor, the United States trustee, or on the court's own initiative, the court after notice and a hearing may determine whether any payment of money or any transfer of property, or any agreement therefor, by the debtor to an attorney after entry of an order for relief in a case under the Code is excessive, whether the payment or transfer is made or is to be made directly or indirectly, if the payment, transfer, or agreement therefor is for services in any way related to the case.

(As amended Mar. 30, 1987, eff. Aug. 1, 1987; Apr. 30, 1991, eff. Aug. 1, 1991.)

ADVISORY COMMITTEE NOTES

This rule is derived from § 60d of the Act [former § 96(d) of this title] and former Bankruptcy Rule 220 and implements § 329 of the Code. Information required to be disclosed by the attorney for a debtor by § 329 of the Code and by the debtor in his Statement of Financial Affairs (Item #15 of Form No. 7, Item #20 of Form No. 8) will assist the court in determining whether to proceed under this rule. Section 60d was enacted in recognition of "the temptation of a failing debtor to deal too liberally with his property in employing counsel to protect him in view of financial reverses and probable failure." In re Wood & Henderson, 210 U.S. 246, 253 (1908). This rule, like § 60d of the Act and § 329 of the Code, is premised on the need for and appropriateness of judicial scrutiny of arrangements between a debtor and his attorney to protect the creditors of the estate and the debtor against overreaching by an officer of the court who is in a peculiarly advantageous position to impose on both the creditors and his client. 2 Collier, Bankruptcy ¶329.02 (15th ed. 1980); MacLachlan, Bankruptcy 318 (1956). Rule 9014 applies to any contested matter arising under this rule.

This rule is not to be construed to permit post-petition payments or transfers which may be avoided under other provisions of the Code.

1991 Amendments

This rule is amended to include within subdivision (a) a payment or transfer of property by the debtor to an attorney after the filing of an involuntary petition but before the order for relief. Any party in interest should be able to make a motion for a determination of whether such payment or transfer is excessive because the funds or property transferred may be property of the estate.

The United States trustee supervises and monitors the administration of bankruptcy cases other than chapter 9 cases and pursuant to § 307 of the Code may raise, appear and be heard on issues relating to fees paid to the debtor's attorney. It is consistent with that role to expect the United States trustee to review statements filed under Rule 2016(b) and to file motions relating to excessive fees pursuant to § 329 of the Code.

CROSS REFERENCES

Court filing of compensation paid or agreed to be paid, see 11 USCA § 329.

Motions; form and service, see Fed.Rules Bankr.Proc. Rule 9013, 11 USCA.

Proceedings under this rule as nonadversarial proceedings, see Fed.Rules Bankr.Proc. Rule 7001, 11 USCA.

Process; service of summons, complaint, see Fed.Rules Bankr.Proc. Rule 7004, 11 USCA.

LIBRARY REFERENCES

American Digest System

Bankruptcy ⊶2827, 3204.

Key Number System Topic No. 51.

Corpus Juris Secundum

CJS Bankruptcy § 139, Adversary Proceedings.

CJS Bankruptcy § 261, Power to Render Declaratory Judgment.

CJS Bankruptcy § 788, Determination as to Whether Payment is Excessive.

Rule 2018.   Intervention; Right to Be Heard

(a) Permissive intervention

In a case under the Code, after hearing on such notice as the court directs and for cause shown, the court may permit any interested entity to intervene generally or with respect to any specified matter.

(b) Intervention by Attorney General of a State

In a chapter 7, 11, 12, or 13 case, the Attorney General of a State may appear and be heard on behalf of consumer creditors if the court determines the appearance is in the public interest, but the Attorney General may not appeal from any judgment, order, or decree in the case.

(c) Chapter 9 municipality case

The Secretary of the Treasury of the United States may, or if requested by the court shall, intervene in a chapter 9 case. Representatives of the state in which the debtor is located may intervene in a chapter 9 case with respect to matters specified by the court.

(d) Labor unions

In a chapter 9, 11, or 12 case, a labor union or employees' association, representative of employees of the debtor, shall have the right to be heard on the economic soundness of a plan affecting the interests of the employees. A labor union or employees' association which exercises its right to be heard under this subdivision shall not be entitled to appeal any judgment, order, or decree relating to the plan, unless otherwise permitted by law.

(e) Service on entities covered by this rule

The court may enter orders governing the service of notice and papers on entities permitted to intervene or be heard pursuant to this rule.

(As amended Mar. 30, 1987, eff. Aug. 1, 1987; Apr. 30, 1991, eff. Aug. 1, 1991.)

ADVISORY COMMITTEE NOTES

This rule is derived from former Rules 8–210, 9–15 and 10–210 and it implements §§ 1109 and 1164 of the Code.

Pursuant to § 1109 of the Code, parties in interest have a right to be heard and the Securities and Exchange Commission may raise and be heard on any issue but it may not take an appeal. That section is applicable in chapter 9 cases

(§ 901 of the Code) and in chapter 11 cases, including cases under subchapter IV thereof for the reorganization of a railroad.

In a railroad reorganization case under subchapter IV of chapter 11, § 1164 also gives the right to be heard to the Interstate Commerce Commission, the Department of Transportation and any state or local regulatory commission with jurisdiction over the debtor, but these entities may not appeal.

This rule does not apply in adversary proceedings. For intervention in adversary proceedings, see Rule 7024. The rules do not provide any right of compensation to or reimbursement of expenses for intervenors or others covered by this rule. Section 503(b)(3)(D) and (4) is not applicable to the entities covered by this rule.

Subdivision (a) is derived from former Chapter VIII Rule 8–210 and former Chapter X Rule 10–210. It permits intervention of an entity (see § 101(14), (21) of the Code) not otherwise entitled to do so under the Code or this rule. Such a party seeking to intervene must show cause therefor.

Subdivision (b) specifically grants the appropriate state's attorney General the right to appear and be heard on behalf of consumer creditors when it is in the public interest. See House Rep. No. 95–595, 95th Cong., 1st Sess. (1977) 189. While "consumer creditor" is not defined in the Code or elsewhere, it would include the type of individual entitled to priority under § 507(a)(5) of the Code, that is, an individual who has deposited money for the purchase, lease or rental of property or the purchase of services for the personal, family, or household use of the individual. It would also include individuals who purchased or leased property for such purposes in connection with which there may exist claims for breach of warranty.

This subdivision does not grant the Attorney General the status of party in interest. In other contexts, the Attorney General will, of course, be a party in interest as for example, in representing a state in connection with a tax claim.

Subdivision (c) recognizes the possible interests of the Secretary of the Treasury or of the state of the debtor's locale when a municipality is the debtor. It is derived from former Chapter IX Rule 9–15 and § 85(d) of the Act [former § 405(d) of this title].

Subdivision (d) is derived from former Chapter X Rule 10–210 which, in turn, was derived from § 206 of the Act [former § 606 of this title]. Section 206 has no counter-part in the Code.

Subdivision (e) is derived from former Chapter VIII Rule 8–210(d). It gives the court flexibility in directing the type of future notices to be given intervenors.

1987 Amendments

Subdivision (d) is amended to make it clear that the prohibition against appeals by labor unions is limited only to their participation in connection with the hearings on the plan as provided in subdivision (d). If a labor union would otherwise have the right to file an appeal or to be a party to an appeal, this rule does not preclude the labor union from exercising that right.

1991 Amendments

Subdivisions (b) and **(d)** are amended to include chapter 12.

CROSS REFERENCES

Consumer debt defined as debt primarily for personal, family, or household purpose, see 11 USCA § 101.

Definitions for purposes of this rule of—

Entity, see 11 USCA § 101.

Governmental unit, see 11 USCA § 101.

Person, see 11 USCA § 101.

Intervention of—

Department of Transportation, see 11 USCA § 1164.

Interstate Commerce Commission, see 11 USCA § 1164.

Party in interest, see 11 USCA § 1109.

Securities and Exchange Commission, see 11 USCA § 1109.

State or local regulatory commission, see 11 USCA § 1164.

Intervention in adversary proceedings, see Fed.Rules Bankr.Proc. Rule 7024, 11 USCA.

LIBRARY REFERENCES

American Digest System

Bankruptcy ⊗2160, 2204.1 to 2206, 3481.
Key Number System Topic No. 51.

Corpus Juris Secundum

CJS Bankruptcy § 279, Intervention.
CJS Bankruptcy § 1122, Objections to Confirmation.

Rule 2019. Disclosure Regarding Creditors and Equity Security Holders in Chapter 9 and Chapter 11 Cases

(a) Definitions

In this rule the following terms have the meanings indicated:

(1) "Disclosable economic interest" means any claim, interest, pledge, lien, option, participation, derivative instrument, or any other right or derivative right granting the holder an economic interest that is affected by the value, acquisition, or disposition of a claim or interest.

(2) "Represent" or "represents" means to take a position before the court or to solicit votes regarding the confirmation of a plan on behalf of another.

(b) Disclosure by Groups, Committees, and Entities

(1) In a chapter 9 or 11 case, a verified statement setting forth the information specified in subdivision (c) of this rule shall be filed by every group or committee that consists of or represents, and every entity that represents, multiple creditors or equity security holders that are (A) acting in concert to advance their common interests, and (B) not composed entirely of affiliates or insiders of one another.

(2) Unless the court orders otherwise, an entity is not required to file the verified statement described in paragraph (1) of this subdivision solely because of its status as:

(A) an indenture trustee;

(B) an agent for one or more other entities under an agreement for the extension of credit;

(C) a class action representative; or

(D) a governmental unit that is not a person.

(c) Information Required

The verified statement shall include:

(1) the pertinent facts and circumstances concerning:

(A) with respect to a group or committee, other than a committee appointed under § 1102 or § 1114 of the Code, the formation of the group or committee, including the name of each entity at whose instance the group or committee was formed or for whom the group or committee has agreed to act; or

(B) with respect to an entity, the employment of the entity, including the name of each creditor or equity security holder at whose instance the employment was arranged;

(2) if not disclosed under subdivision (c)(1), with respect to an entity, and with respect to each member of a group or committee:

(A) name and address;

(B) the nature and amount of each disclosable economic interest held in relation to the debtor as of the date the entity was employed or the group or committee was formed; and

(C) with respect to each member of a group or committee that claims to represent any entity in addition to the members of the group or committee, other than a committee appointed under § 1102 or § 1114 of the Code, the date of acquisition by quarter and year of each disclosable economic interest, unless acquired more than one year before the petition was filed;

(3) if not disclosed under subdivision (c)(1) or (c)(2), with respect to each creditor or equity security holder represented by an entity, group, or committee, other than a committee appointed under § 1102 or § 1114 of the Code:

(A) name and address; and

(B) the nature and amount of each disclosable economic interest held in relation to the debtor as of the date of the statement; and

(4) a copy of the instrument, if any, authorizing the entity, group, or committee to act on behalf of creditors or equity security holders.

(d) Supplemental Statements

If any fact disclosed in its most recently filed statement has changed materially, an entity, group, or committee shall file a verified supplemental statement whenever it takes a position before the court or solicits votes on the confirmation of a plan. The supplemental statement shall set forth the material changes in the facts required by subdivision (c) to be disclosed.

(e) Determination of Failure to Comply; Sanctions

(1) On motion of any party in interest, or on its own motion, the court may determine whether there has been a failure to comply with any provision of this rule.

(2) If the court finds such a failure to comply, it may:

(A) refuse to permit the entity, group, or committee to be heard or to intervene in the case;

(B) hold invalid any authority, acceptance, rejection, or objection given, procured, or received by the entity, group, or committee; or

(C) grant other appropriate relief.

(As amended Mar. 30, 1987, eff. Aug. 1, 1987; Apr. 30, 1991, eff. Aug. 1, 1991; Apr. 26, 2011, eff. Dec. 1, 2011.)

ADVISORY COMMITTEE NOTES

This rule is a comprehensive regulation of representation in chapter 9 municipality and in chapter 11 reorganization cases. It is derived from §§ 209 to 213 of the Act [former §§ 609 to 613 of this title] and former Chapter X Rule 10–211.

Subdivision (b) is derived from §§ 212, 213 of the Act [former §§ 612 and 613 of this title]. As used in clause (2), "other authorization" would include a power or warrant of attorney which are specifically mentioned in § 212 of the Act. This rule deals with representation provisions in mortgages, trust deeds, etc. to protect the beneficiaries from unfair practices and the like. It does not deal with the validation or invalidation of security interests generally. If immediate compliance is not possible, the court may permit a representative to be heard on a specific matter, but there is no implicit waiver of compliance on a permanent basis.

1991 Amendments

Subdivision (a) is amended to exclude from the requirements of this rule committees of retired employees appointed pursuant to § 1114 of the Code. The words "with the clerk" are deleted as unnecessary. See Rules 5005(a) and 9001(3).

2011 Amendments

The rule is substantially amended to expand the scope of its coverage and the content of its disclosure requirements. Stylistic and organizational changes are also made in order to provide greater clarity. Because the rule no longer applies only to representatives of creditors and equity security holders, the title of the rule has been changed to reflect its broadened focus on disclosure of financial information in chapter 9 and chapter 11 cases.

Subdivision (a). The content of subdivision (a) is new. It sets forth a definition of the term "disclosable economic interest," which is used in subdivisions (c)(2), (c)(3), (d), and (e). The definition of the term is intended to be sufficiently broad to cover any economic interest that could affect the legal and strategic positions a stakeholder takes in a chapter 9 or chapter 11 case. A disclosable economic interest extends beyond claims and interests owned by a stakeholder and includes, among other types of holdings, short positions, credit default swaps, and total return swaps.

The second definition is of "represent" or "represents." The definition provides that representation requires active participation in the case or in a proceeding on behalf of another entity - either by taking a position on a matter before the court or by soliciting votes on the confirmation of a plan. Thus, for example, an attorney who is retained and consulted by a creditor or equity security holder to monitor the case, but who does not advocate any position before the court or engage in solicitation activities on behalf of that client, does not represent the creditor or equity security holder for purposes of this rule.

Subdivision (b). Subdivision (b)(1) specifies who is covered by the rule's disclosure requirements. In addition to an entity, group, or committee that *represents* more than one creditor or equity security holder, the amendment extends the rule's coverage to groups or committees that *consist* of more than one creditor or equity security holder. The rule no longer excludes official committees, except as specifically indicated. The rule applies to a group of creditors or equity security holders that act in concert to advance common interests (except when the group consists exclusively of affiliates or insiders of one another), even if the group does not call itself a committee.

Subdivision (b)(2) excludes certain entities from the rule's coverage. Even though these entities may represent multiple creditors or equity security holders, they do so under formal legal arrangements of trust or contact law that preclude them from acting on the basis of conflicting economic interests. For example, an indenture trustee's responsibilities are defined by the indenture, and individual interests of bondholders would not affect the trustee's representation.

Subdivision (c). Subdivision (c) sets forth the information that must be included in a verified statement required to be filed under this rule. Subdivision (c)(1) continues to require disclosure concerning the employment of an entity or indenture trustee and the formation of a committee or group, other than an official committee, and the employment of an entity.

Subdivision (c)(2) specifies information that must be disclosed with respect to the entity and each member of the committee and group filing the statement. In the case of a committee or group, the information about the nature and amount of a disclosable economic interest must be specifically provided on a member-by-member basis, and not in the aggregate. The quarter and year in which each disclosable economic interest was acquired by each member of a committee or group (other than an official committee) that claims to represent others must also be specifically provided, except for a disclosable economic interest acquired more than a year before the filing of the petition. Although the rule no longer requires the disclosure of the precise date of acquisition or the amount paid for disclosable economic interests, nothing in this rule precludes either the discovery of that information or its disclosure when ordered by the court pursuant to authority outside this rule.

Subdivision (c)(3) specifies information that must be disclosed with respect to creditors or equity security holders that are represented by an entity, group, committee, or indenture trustee. This provision does not apply with respect to those represented by official committees. The information required to be disclosed under subdivision (c)(3) parallels that required to be disclosed under subdivision (c)(2)(A) and (B). The amendment also clarifies that under (c)(3) the nature and amount of each disclosable economic interest of represented creditors and shareholders must be stated as of the date of the verified statement.

Subdivision (c)(4) requires the attachment of any instrument authorizing the filer of the verified statement to act on behalf of creditors or equity security holders.

Subdivision (d). Subdivision (d) requires the filing of a supplemental statement at the time an entity, group, or committee takes a position before the court or solicits votes on a plan if there has been a material change in any of the information contained in its last filed statement. The supplemental verified statement must set forth the material changes that have occurred regarding the information required to be disclosed by subdivision (c) of this rule.

Subdivision (e). Subdivision (e) addresses the court's authority to determine whether there has been a violation of this rule and to impose a sanction for any violation. It no longer addresses the court's authority to determine violations of other applicable laws regulating the activities and personnel of an entity, group, or committee.

CROSS REFERENCES

Appointment of creditors' committee organized before order for relief, see Fed.Rules Bankr.Proc. Rule 2007, 11 USCA.

Motions; form and service, see Fed.Rules Bankr.Proc. Rule 9013, 11 USCA.

Trustees for estates when joint administration ordered, see Fed.Rules Bankr.Proc. Rule 2009, 11 USCA.

LIBRARY REFERENCES

American Digest System

Bankruptcy ⊙⇒3024.

Key Number System Topic No. 51.

Corpus Juris Secundum

CJS Bankruptcy § 1130, Powers and Duties of Committee.

Rule 2020.   Review of Acts by United States Trustee

A proceeding to contest any act or failure to act by the United States trustee is governed by Rule 9014. (Added Apr. 30, 1991, eff. Aug. 1, 1991.)

ADVISORY COMMITTEE NOTES

The United States trustee performs administrative functions, such as the convening of the meeting of creditors and the appointment of trustees and committees. Most of the acts of the United States trustee are not controversial and will go unchallenged. However, the United States trustee is not a judicial officer and does not resolve disputes regarding the propriety of its own actions. This rule, which is new, provides a procedure for judicial review of the United States trustee's acts or failure to act in connection with the administration of the case. For example, if the United States trustee schedules a § 341 meeting to be held 90 days after the petition is filed, and a party in interest wishes to challenge the propriety of that act in view of § 341(a) of the Code and Rule 2003 which requires that the meeting be held not more than 40 days after the order for relief, this rule permits the party to do so by motion.

This rule provides for review of acts already committed by the United States trustee, but does not provide for advisory opinions in advance of the act. This rule is not intended to limit the discretion of the United States trustee, provided that the United States trustee's act is authorized by, and in compliance with, the Code, title 28, these rules, and other applicable law.

LIBRARY REFERENCES

American Digest System

Bankruptcy ⬥3008.1.

Key Number System Topic No. 51.

Corpus Juris Secundum

CJS Bankruptcy § 42, Regulation and Review of United States Trustee's Actions.

PART III—CLAIMS AND DISTRIBUTION TO CREDITORS AND EQUITY INTEREST HOLDERS; PLANS

Rule
3001. Proof of Claim.
3002. Filing Proof of Claim or Interest.
3002.1. Notice Relating to Claims Secured by Security Interest in the Debtor's Principal Residence.
3003. Filing Proof of Claim or Equity Security Interest in Chapter 9 Municipality or Chapter 11 Reorganization Cases.
3004. Filing of Claims by Debtor or Trustee.
3005. Filing of Claim, Acceptance, or Rejection By Guarantor, Surety, Indorser, or Other Codebtor.
3006. Withdrawal of Claim; Effect on Acceptance or Rejection of Plan.
3007. Objections to Claims.
3008. Reconsideration of Claims.
3009. Declaration and Payment of Dividends in a Chapter 7 Liquidation Case.
3010. Small Dividends and Payments in Chapter 7 Liquidation, Chapter 12 Family Farmer's Debt Adjustment, and Chapter 13 Individual's Debt Adjustment Cases.
3011. Unclaimed Funds in Chapter 7 Liquidation, Chapter 12 Family Farmer's Debt Adjustment, and Chapter 13 Individual's Debt Adjustment Cases.
3012. Valuation of Security.
3013. Classification of Claims and Interests.
3014. Election Under § 1111(b) by Secured Creditor in Chapter 9 Municipality or Chapter 11 Reorganization Case.
3015. Filing, Objection to Confirmation, and Modification of a Plan in a Chapter 12 Family Farmer's Debt Adjustment or a Chapter 13 Individual's Debt Adjustment Case.
3016. Filing of Plan and Disclosure Statement in a Chapter 9 Municipality or Chapter 11 Reorganization Case.
3017. Court Consideration of Disclosure Statement in a Chapter 9 Municipality or Chapter 11 Reorganization Case.
3017.1. Court Consideration of Disclosure Statement in a Small Business Case.
3018. Acceptance or Rejection of Plan in a Chapter 9 Municipality or a Chapter 11 Reorganization Case.
3019. Modification of Accepted Plan in a Chapter 9 Municipality or a Chapter 11 Reorganization Case.
3020. Deposit; Confirmation of Plan in a Chapter 9 Municipality or Chapter 11 Reorganization Case.
3021. Distribution Under Plan.
3022. Final Decree in Chapter 11 Reorganization Case.

Rule 3001. Proof of Claim

(a) Form and content

A proof of claim is a written statement setting forth a creditor's claim. A proof of claim shall conform substantially to the appropriate Official Form.

(b) Who may execute

A proof of claim shall be executed by the creditor or the creditor's authorized agent except as provided in Rules 3004 and 3005.

[Text of subdivision (c) effective until December 1, 2012, absent contrary Congressional action.]

(c) Supporting Information

(1) Claim Based on a Writing

When a claim, or an interest in property of the debtor securing the claim, is based on a writing, the original or a duplicate shall be filed with the proof of claim. If the writing has been lost or destroyed, a statement of the circumstances of the loss or destruction shall be filed with the claim.

(2) Additional Requirements in an Individual Debtor Case: Sanctions for Failure to Comply

In a case in which the debtor is an individual:

(A) If, in addition to its principal amount, a claim includes interest, fees, expenses, or other charges incurred before the petition was filed, an itemized statement of the interest, fees, expenses, or charges shall be filed with the proof of claim.

(B) If a security interest is claimed in the debtor's property, a statement of the amount necessary to cure any default as of the date of the petition shall be filed with the proof of claim.

(C) If a security interest is claimed in property that is the debtor's principal residence, the attachment prescribed by the appropriate Official Form shall be filed with the proof of claim. If an escrow account has been established in connection with the claim, an escrow account statement prepared as of the date the petition was filed and in a form consistent with applicable nonbankruptcy law shall be filed with the attachment to the proof of claim.

(D) If the holder of a claim fails to provide any information required by this subdivision (c), the court may, after notice and hearing, take either or both of the following actions:

(i) preclude the holder from presenting the omitted information, in any form, as evidence in any contested matter or adversary proceeding in the case, unless the court determines that the failure was substantially justified or is harmless; or

(ii) award other appropriate relief, including reasonable expenses and attorney's fees caused by the failure.

[Text of subdivision (c) effective December 1, 2012, absent contrary Congressional action.]

(c) Supporting Information

(1) Claim Based on a Writing

Except for a claim governed by paragraph (3) of this subdivision, when a claim, or an interest in property of the debtor securing the claim, is based on a writing, a copy of the writing shall be filed with the proof of claim. If the writing has been lost or destroyed, a statement of the circumstances of the loss or destruction shall be filed with the claim.

(2) Additional Requirements in an Individual Debtor Case: Sanctions for Failure to Comply

In a case in which the debtor is an individual:

(A) If, in addition to its principal amount, a claim includes interest, fees, expenses, or other charges incurred before the petition was filed, an itemized statement of the interest, fees, expenses, or charges shall be filed with the proof of claim.

(B) If a security interest is claimed in the debtor's property, a statement of the amount necessary to cure any default as of the date of the petition shall be filed with the proof of claim.

(C) If a security interest is claimed in property that is the debtor's principal residence, the attachment prescribed by the appropriate Official Form shall be filed with the proof of claim. If an escrow account has been established in connection with the claim, an escrow account statement prepared as of the date the petition was filed and in a form consistent with applicable nonbankruptcy law shall be filed with the attachment to the proof of claim.

(D) If the holder of a claim fails to provide any information required by this subdivision (c), the court may, after notice and hearing, take either or both of the following actions:

(i) preclude the holder from presenting the omitted information, in any form, as evidence in any contested matter or adversary proceeding in the case, unless the court determines that the failure was substantially justified or is harmless; or

(ii) award other appropriate relief, including reasonable expenses and attorney's fees caused by the failure.

(3) Claim based on an open-end or revolving consumer credit agreement

(A) When a claim is based on an open-end or revolving consumer credit agreement—except one for which a security interest is claimed in the debtor's real property—a statement shall be filed with the proof of claim, including all of the following information that applies to the account:

(i) the name of the entity from whom the creditor purchased the account;

(ii) the name of the entity to whom the debt was owed at the time of an account holder's last transaction on the account;

(iii) the date of an account holder's last transaction;

(iv) the date of the last payment on the account; and

(v) the date on which the account was charged to profit and loss.

(B) On written request by a party in interest, the holder of a claim based on an open-end or revolving consumer credit agreement shall, within 30 days after the request is sent, provide the requesting party a copy of the writing specified in paragraph (1) of this subdivision.

(d) Evidence of perfection of security interest

If a security interest in property of the debtor is claimed, the proof of claim shall be accompanied by evidence that the security interest has been perfected.

(e) Transferred claim

(1) Transfer of claim other than for security before proof filed

If a claim has been transferred other than for security before proof of the claim has been filed, the proof of claim may be filed only by the transferee or an indenture trustee.

(2) Transfer of claim other than for security after proof filed

If a claim other than one based on a publicly traded note, bond, or debenture has been transferred other than for security after the proof of claim has been filed, evidence of the transfer shall be filed by the transferee. The clerk shall immediately notify the alleged transferor by mail of the filing of the evidence of transfer and that objection thereto, if any, must be filed within 21 days of the mailing of the notice or within any additional time allowed by the court. If the alleged transferor files a timely objection and the court finds, after notice and a hearing, that the claim has been transferred other than for security, it shall enter an order substituting the transferee for the transferor. If a timely objection is not filed by the alleged transferor, the transferee shall be substituted for the transferor.

(3) Transfer of claim for security before proof filed

If a claim other than one based on a publicly traded note, bond, or debenture has been transferred for security before proof of the claim has been filed, the transferor or transferee or both may file a proof of claim for the full amount. The proof shall be supported by a statement setting forth the terms of the transfer. If either the transferor or the transferee files a proof of claim, the clerk shall immediately notify the other by mail of the right to join in the filed claim. If both transferor and transferee file proofs of the same claim, the proofs shall be consolidated. If the transferor or transferee does not file an agreement regarding its relative rights respecting voting of the claim, payment of dividends thereon, or participation in the administration of the estate, on motion by a party in interest and after notice and a hearing, the court shall enter such orders respecting these matters as may be appropriate.

(4) Transfer of claim for security after proof filed

If a claim other than one based on a publicly traded note, bond, or debenture has been transferred for security after the proof of claim has been filed, evidence of the terms of the transfer shall be filed by the transferee. The clerk shall immediately notify the alleged transferor by mail of the filing of the evidence of transfer and that objection thereto, if any, must be filed within 21 days of the mailing of the notice or within any additional time allowed by the court. If a timely objection is filed by the alleged transferor, the court, after notice and a hearing, shall determine whether the claim has been transferred for security. If the transferor or transferee does not file an agreement regarding its relative rights respecting voting of the claim, payment of dividends thereon, or participation in the administration of the estate, on motion by a party in interest and after notice and a hearing, the court shall enter such orders respecting these matters as may be appropriate.

(5) Service of objection or motion; notice of hearing

A copy of an objection filed pursuant to paragraph (2) or (4) or a motion filed pursuant to paragraph (3) or (4) of this subdivision together with a notice of a hearing shall be mailed or otherwise delivered to the transferor or transferee, whichever is appropriate, at least 30 days prior to the hearing.

(f) Evidentiary effect

A proof of claim executed and filed in accordance with these rules shall constitute prima facie evidence of the validity and amount of the claim.

(g) [1] To the extent not inconsistent with the United States Warehouse Act or applicable State law, a warehouse receipt, scale ticket, or similar document of the type routinely issued as evidence of title by a grain storage facility, as defined in section 557 of title 11, shall constitute prima facie evidence of the validity and amount of a claim of ownership of a quantity of grain. (As amended Pub.L. 98–353, Title III, § 354, July 10, 1984, 98 Stat. 361; Apr. 30, 1991, eff. Aug. 1, 1991; Mar. 26, 2009, eff. Dec. 1, 2009; Apr. 26, 2011, eff. Dec. 1, 2011; Apr. 23, 2012, eff. Dec. 1, 2012, absent contrary Congressional action.)

[1] So in original. Subsec. (g) was enacted without a catchline.

ADVISORY COMMITTEE NOTES

This rule is adapted from former Bankruptcy Rules 301 and 302. The Federal Rules of Evidence, made applicable to cases under the Code by Rule 1101, do not prescribe the evidentiary effect to be accorded particular documents. Subdivision (f) of this rule supplements the Federal Rules of Evidence as they apply to cases under the Code.

Subdivision (c). This subdivision is similar to former Bankruptcy Rule 302(c) and continues the requirement for the filing of any written security agreement and provides that the filing of a duplicate of a writing underlying a claim authenticates the claim with the same effect as the filing of the original writing. Cf. Rules 1001(4) and 1003 of F.R. of Evid. Subdivision (d) together with the requirement in the first sentence of subdivision (c) for the filing of any written security agreement, is designed to facilitate the determination whether the claim is secured and properly perfected so as to be valid against the trustee.

Subdivision (d). "Satisfactory evidence" of perfection, which is to accompany the proof of claim, would include a duplicate of an instrument filed or recorded, a duplicate of a certificate of title when a security interest is perfected by notation on such a certificate, a statement that pledged property has been in possession of the secured party since a specified date, or a statement of the reasons why no action was necessary for perfection. The secured creditor may not be required to file a proof of claim under this rule if he is not seeking allowance of a claim for a deficiency. But see § 506(d) of the Code.

Subdivision (e). The rule recognizes the differences between an unconditional transfer of a claim and a transfer for the purpose of security and prescribes a procedure for dealing with the rights of the transferor and transferee when the transfer is for security. The rule clarifies the procedure to be followed when a transfer precedes or follows the filing of the petition. The interests of sound administration are served by requiring the post-petition transferee to file with the proof of claim a statement of the transferor acknowledging the transfer and the consideration for the transfer. Such a disclosure will assist the court in dealing with evils that may arise out of post-bankruptcy traffic in claims against an estate. Monroe v. Scofield, 135 F.2d 725 (10th Cir. 1943); In re Philadelphia & Western Ry., 64 F.Supp. 738 (E.D.Pa.1946); cf. In re Latham Lithographic Corp., 107 F.2d 749 (2d Cir. 1939). Both paragraphs (1) and (3) of this subdivision, which deal with a transfer before the filing of a proof of claim, recognize that the transferee may be unable to obtain the required statement from the transferor, but in that event a sound reason for such inability must accompany the proof of claim filed by the transferee.

Paragraphs (3) and (4) clarify the status of a claim transferred for the purpose of security. An assignee for security has been recognized as a rightful claimant in bankruptcy. Feder v. John Engelhorn & Sons, 202 F.2d 411 (2d Cir. 1953). An assignor's right to file a claim notwithstanding the assignment was sustained in In re R & L Engineering Co., 182 F.Supp. 317 (S.D.Cal.1960). Facilitation of the filing of proofs by both claimants as holders of interests in a single claim is consonant with equitable treatment of the parties and sound administration. See In re Latham Lithographic Corp., 107 F.2d 749 (2d Cir. 1939).

Paragraphs (2) and (4) of subdivision (e) deal with the transfer of a claim after proof has been filed. Evidence of the terms of the transfer required to be disclosed to the court will facilitate the court's determination of the appropriate order to be entered because of the transfer.

Paragraph (5) describes the procedure to be followed when an objection is made by the transferor to the transferee's filed evidence of transfer.

The United States Warehouse Act, referred to in subd. (g), is Part C of Act Aug. 11, 1916, c. 313, 39 Stat. 486, as amended, which is classified generally to chapter 10 (§ 241 et seq.) of Title 7, Agriculture. For complete classification of this Act to the Code, see section 241 of Title 7 and Tables.

1984 Amendments

Subdivision (g) was added by § 354 of the 1984 amendments.

Subd. (g). Pub.L. 98–353 added subd. (g).

1991 Amendments

Subdivision (a) is amended in anticipation of future revision and renumbering of the Official Forms.

Subdivision (e) is amended to limit the court's role to the adjudication of disputes regarding transfers of claims. If a claim has been transferred prior to the filing of a proof of claim, there is no need to state the consideration for the transfer or to submit other evidence of the transfer. If a claim has been transferred other than for security after a proof of claim has been filed, the transferee is substituted for the transferor in the absence of a timely objection by the alleged transferor. In that event, the clerk should note the transfer without the need for court approval. If a timely objection is filed, the court's role is to determine whether a transfer has been made that is enforceable under nonbankruptcy law. This rule is not intended either to encourage or discourage postpetition transfers of claims or to affect any remedies otherwise available under nonbankruptcy law to a transferor or transferee such as for misrepresentation in connection with the transfer of a claim. "After notice and a hearing" as used in subdivision (e) shall be construed in accordance with paragraph (5).

The words "with the clerk" in subdivision (e)(2) and (e)(4) are deleted as unnecessary. See Rules 5005(a) and 9001(3).

1984 Acts

Amendment by Pub.L. 98–353 effective with respect to cases filed 90 days after July 10, 1984, see section 553 of Pub.L. 98–353, set out as a note under section 101 of this title.

2009 Amendments

The rule is amended to implement changes in connection with the amendment to Rule 9006(a) and the manner by which time is computed under the rules. The deadlines in the rule are amended to substitute a deadline that is a multiple of seven days. Throughout the rules, deadlines are amended in the following manner:

- 5–day periods become 7–day periods
- 10–day periods become 14–day periods
- 15–day periods become 14–day periods
- 20–day periods become 21–day periods
- 25–day periods become 28–day periods

2011 Amendments

Subdivision (c). Subdivision (c) is amended to prescribe with greater specificity the supporting information required to accompany certain proofs of claim and, in cases in which the debtor is an individual, the consequences of failing to provide the required information.

Existing subdivision (c) is redesignated as (c)(l).

Subdivision (c)(2) is added to require additional information to accompany proofs of claim filed in cases in which the debtor is an individual. When the holder of a claim seeks to recover-in addition to the principal amount of a debt-interest, fees, expenses, or other charges, the proof of claim must be accompanied by a statement itemizing these additional amounts with sufficient specificity to make clear the basis for the claimed amount.

If a claim is secured by a security interest in the property of the debtor and the debtor defaulted on the claim prior to the filing of the petition, the proof of claim must be accompanied by a statement of the amount required to cure the prepetition default.

If the claim is secured by a security interest in the debtor's principal residence, the proof of claim must be accompanied by the attachment prescribed by the appropriate Official Form. In that attachment, the holder of the claim must provide the information required by subparagraphs (A) and (B) of this paragraph (2). In addition, if an escrow account has been established in connection with the claim, an escrow account statement showing the account balance, and any amount owed, as of the date the petition was filed must be submitted in accordance with subparagraph (C). The statement must be prepared in a form consistent with the requirements of nonbankruptcy law. *See, e.g.*, 12 U.S.C. § 2601 *et seq.* (Real Estate Settlement Procedure Act). Thus the holder of the claim may provide the escrow account statement using the same form it uses outside of bankruptcy for this purpose.

Subparagraph (D) of subdivision (c)(2) sets forth sanctions that the court may impose on a creditor in an individual debtor case that fails to provide information required by subdivision (c). Failure to provide the required information does not itself constitute a ground for disallowance of a claim. See § 502(b) of the Code. But when an objection to the allowance of a claim is made or other litigation arises concerning the status or treatment of a claim, if the holder of that claim has not complied with the requirements of this subdivision, the court may preclude it from presenting as evidence any of the omitted information, unless the failure to comply with this subdivision was substantially justified or harmless. The court retains discretion to allow an amendment to a proof of claim under appropriate circumstances or to impose a sanction different from or in addition to the preclusion of the introduction of evidence.

2012 Amendments

[Effective December 1, 2012,
absent contrary Congressional action.]

Subdivision (c). Subdivision (c) is amended in several respects. The former requirement in paragraph (1) to file an original or duplicate of a supporting document is amended to reflect the current practice of filing only copies. The proof of claim form instructs claimants not to file the original of a document because it may be destroyed by the clerk's office after scanning.

Subdivision (c) is further amended to add paragraph (3). Except with respect to claims secured by a security interest in the debtor's real property (such as a home equity line of credit), paragraph (3) specifies information that must be provided in support of a claim based on an open-end or revolving consumer credit agreement (such as an agreement underlying the issuance of a credit card). Because a claim of this type may have been sold one or more times prior to the debtor's bankruptcy, the debtor may not recognize the name of the person filing the proof of claim. Disclosure of the information required by paragraph (3) will assist the debtor in associating the claim with a known account. It will also provide a basis for assessing the timeliness of the claim. The date, if any, on which the account was charged to profit and loss ("charge-off" date) under subparagraph (A)(v) should be determined in accordance with applicable standards for the classification and account management of consumer credit. A proof of claim executed and filed in accordance with subparagraph (A), as well as the applicable provisions of subdivisions (a), (b), (c)(2), and (e), constitutes prima facie evidence of the validity and amount of the claim under subdivision (f).

To the extent that paragraph (3) applies to a claim, paragraph (1) of subdivision (c) is not applicable. A party in interest, however, may obtain the writing on which an open-end or revolving consumer credit claim is based by requesting in writing that documentation from the holder of the claim. The holder of the claim must provide the documentation within 30 days after the request is sent. The court, for cause, may extend or reduce that time period under Rule 9006.

Changes Made After Publication

Subdivision (c)(1). The requirement for the attachment of a writing on which a claim is based was changed to require that a copy, rather than the original or a duplicate, of the writing be provided.

Subdivision (c)(3). An exception to subparagraph (A) was added for open-end or revolving consumer credit agreements that are secured by the debtor's real property.

A time limit of 30 days for responding to a written request under subparagraph (B) was added.

Committee Note. A statement was added to clarify that if a proof of claim complies with subdivision (c)(3)(A), as well as with subdivisions (a), (b), (c)(2), and (e), it constitutes prima facie evidence of the validity and amount of the claim under subdivision (f).

Other changes. Stylistic changes were also made to the rule.

CROSS REFERENCES

Filed claims or interests deemed allowed, see 11 USCA § 502.

Filing of proofs of claims or interests, see 11 USCA § 501.

Notice to claimants in converted liquidation case, see Fed. Rules Bankr.Proc. Rule 1019, 11 USCA.

Admissibility of duplicates, see Fed.Rules Evid. Rule 1003, 28 USCA.

LIBRARY REFERENCES

American Digest System

Bankruptcy ⟷2891 to 2904.

Key Number System Topic No. 51.

Corpus Juris Secundum

CJS Bankruptcy § 1007, Generally; Who May File.

CJS Bankruptcy § 1011, Transfer or Assignment.

CJS Bankruptcy § 1025, Evidence.

CJS Bankruptcy § 1050, Evidence; Presumptions and Burden of Proof.

Rule 3002.   Filing Proof of Claim or Interest

(a) Necessity for filing

An unsecured creditor or an equity security holder must file a proof of claim or interest for the claim or interest to be allowed, except as provided in Rules 1019(3), 3003, 3004, and 3005.

(b) Place of filing

A proof of claim or interest shall be filed in accordance with Rule 5005.

(c) Time for filing

In a chapter 7 liquidation, chapter 12 family farmer's debt adjustment, or chapter 13 individual's debt adjustment case, a proof of claim is timely filed if it is filed not later than 90 days after the first date set for the meeting of creditors called under § 341(a) of the Code, except as follows:

(1) A proof of claim filed by a governmental unit, other than for a claim resulting from a tax return filed under § 1308, is timely filed if it is filed not later than 180 days after the date of the order for relief. A proof of claim filed by a governmental unit for a claim resulting from a tax return filed under § 1308 is timely filed if it is filed no later than 180 days after the date of the order for relief or 60 days after the date of the filing of the tax return. The court may, for cause, enlarge the time for a governmental unit to file a proof of claim only upon motion of the governmental unit made before expiration of the period for filing a timely proof of claim.

(2) In the interest of justice and if it will not unduly delay the administration of the case, the court may extend the time for filing a proof of claim by an infant or incompetent person or the representative of either.

(3) An unsecured claim which arises in favor of an entity or becomes allowable as a result of a judgment may be filed within 30 days after the judgment becomes final if the judgment is for the recovery of money or property from that entity or denies or avoids the entity's interest in property. If the judgment imposes a liability which is not satisfied, or a duty which is not performed within such period or such further time as the court may permit, the claim shall not be allowed.

(4) A claim arising from the rejection of an executory contract or unexpired lease of the debtor may be filed within such time as the court may direct.

(5) If notice of insufficient assets to pay a dividend was given to creditors under Rule 2002(e), and subsequently the trustee notifies the court that payment of a dividend appears possible, the clerk shall give at least 90 days' notice by mail to creditors of that fact and of the date by which proofs of claim must be filed.

(6) If notice of the time to file a proof of claim has been mailed to a creditor at a foreign address, on motion filed by the creditor before or after the expiration of the time, the court may extend the time by not more than 60 days if the court finds that the notice was insufficient under the circumstances to give the creditor a reasonable time to file a proof of claim.

(As amended Mar. 30, 1987, eff. Aug. 1, 1987; Apr. 30, 1991, eff. Aug. 1, 1991; Apr. 23, 1996, eff. Dec. 1, 1996; Apr. 23, 2008, eff. Dec. 1, 2008.)

ADVISORY COMMITTEE NOTES

Subdivision (a) of this rule is substantially a restatement of the general requirement that claims be proved and filed. The exceptions refer to Rule 3003 providing for the filing of claims in chapter 9 and 11 cases, and to Rules 3004 and 3005 authorizing claims to be filed by the debtor or trustee and the filing of a claim by a contingent creditor of the debtor.

A secured claim need not be filed or allowed under § 502 or § 506(d) unless a party in interest has requested a determination and allowance or disallowance under § 502.

Subdivision (c) is adapted from former Bankruptcy Rule 302(e) but changes the time limits on the filing of claims in chapter 7 and 13 cases from six months to 90 days after the first date set for the meeting of creditors. The special rule for early filing by a secured creditor in a chapter 13 case, in former Rule 13–302(e)(1) is not continued.

Although the claim of a secured creditor may have arisen before the petition, a judgment avoiding the security interest may not have been entered until after the time for filing claims has expired. Under Rule 3002(c)(3) the creditor who did not file a secured claim may nevertheless file an unsecured claim within the time prescribed. A judgment does not become final for the purpose of starting the 30 day period provided for by paragraph (3) until the time for appeal has expired or, if an appeal is taken, until the appeal has been disposed of. In re Tapp, 61 F.Supp. 594 (W.D.Ky.1945).

Paragraph (1) is derived from former Bankruptcy Rule 302(e). The governmental unit may move for an extension of the 90 day period. Pursuant to § 501(c) of the Code, if the government does not file its claim within the proper time period, the debtor or trustee may file on its behalf. An extension is not needed by the debtor or trustee because the right to file does not arise until the government's time has expired.

Paragraph (4) is derived from former chapter rules. See, e.g., Rule 11–33(a)(2)(B). In light of the reduced time it is necessary that a party with a claim arising from the rejection of an executory contract have sufficient time to file that claim. This clause allows the court to fix an appropriate time.

Paragraph (5) of subdivision (c) is correlated with the provision in Rule 2002(e) authorizing notification to creditors of estates from which no dividends are anticipated. The clause permits creditors who have refrained from filing claims after receiving notification to be given an opportunity to file when subsequent developments indicate the possibility of a dividend. The notice required by this clause must be given in the manner provided in Rule 2002. The information relating to the discovery of assets will usually be obtained by the clerk from the trustee's interim reports or special notification by the trustee.

Provision is made in Rule 2002(a) and (h) for notifying all creditors of the fixing of a time for filing claims against a surplus under paragraph (6). This paragraph does not deal with the distribution of the surplus. Reference must also be made to § 726(a)(2)(C) and (3) which permits distribution on late filed claims.

Paragraph (6) is only operative in a chapter 7 case. In chapter 13 cases, the plan itself provides the distribution to creditors which is not necessarily dependent on the size of the estate.

1987 Amendments

Subdivision (a) is amended by adding a reference to Rule 1019(4). Rule 1019(4) provides that claims actually filed by a creditor in a chapter 11 or 13 case shall be treated as filed in a superseding chapter 7 case. Claims deemed filed in a chapter 11 case pursuant to § 1111(a) of the Code are not considered as filed in a superseding chapter 7 case. The creditor must file a claim in the superseding chapter 7 case.

1991 Amendments

Subdivision (a) is amended to conform to the renumbering of subdivisions of Rule 1019. Subdivision (c) is amended to include chapter 12 cases. Subdivision (c)(4) is amended to clarify that it includes a claim arising from the rejection of an unexpired lease.

1996 Amendments

The amendments are designed to conform to §§ 502(b)(9) and 726(a) of the Code as amended by the Bankruptcy Reform Act of 1994.

The Reform Act amended § 726(a)(1) and added § 502(b)(9) to the Code to govern the effects of a tardily filed claim. Under § 502(b)(9), a tardily filed claim must be disallowed if an objection to the proof of claim is filed, except to the extent that a holder of a tardily filed claim is entitled to distribution under § 726(a)(1), (2), or (3).

The phrase "in accordance with this rule" is deleted from Rule 3002(a) to clarify that the effect of filing a proof of claim after the expiration of the time prescribed in Rule 3002(c) is governed by § 502(b)(9) of the Code, rather than by this rule.

Section 502(b)(9) of the Code provides that a claim of a governmental unit shall be timely filed if it is filed "before 180 days after the date of the order for relief" or such later time as the Bankruptcy Rules provide. To avoid any confusion as to whether a governmental unit's proof of claim is timely filed under § 502(b)(9) if it is filed on the 180th day after the order for relief, paragraph (1) of subdivision (c) provides that a governmental unit's claim is timely if it is filed not later than 180 days after the order for relief.

References to "the United States, a state, or subdivision thereof" in paragraph (1) of subdivision (c) are changed to "governmental unit" to avoid different treatment among foreign and domestic governments.

GAP Report on Rule 3002. After publication of the proposed amendments, the Bankruptcy Reform Act of 1994 amended sections 726 and 502(b) of the Code to clarify the rights of creditors who tardily file a proof of claim. In view of the Reform Act, proposed new subdivision (d) of Rule 3002 has been deleted from the proposed amendments because it is no longer necessary. In addition, subdivisions (a) and (c) have been changed after publication to clarify that the effect of tardily filing a proof of claim is governed by § 502(b)(9) of the Code, rather than by this rule.

The amendments to § 502(b) also provide that a governmental unit's proof of claim is timely filed if it is filed before 180 days after the order for relief. Proposed amendments to Rule 3002(c)(1) were added to the published amendments to conform to this statutory change and to avoid any confusion as to whether a claim by a governmental unit is timely if it is filed on the 180th day.

The committee note has been re-written to explain the rule changes designed to conform to the Reform Act.

2008 Amendments

Subdivision (c)(1) is amended to reflect the addition of § 1308 to the Bankruptcy Code in 2005. This provision requires that chapter 13 debtors file tax returns during the pendency of the case, and imposes bankruptcy-related consequences if debtors fail to do so. Subdivision (c)(1) provides additional time for governmental units to file a proof of claim for tax obligations with respect to tax returns filed during the pendency of a chapter 13 case. The amendment also allows the governmental unit to move for additional time to file a proof of claim prior to expiration of the applicable filing period.

Subdivision (c)(5) of the rule is amended to set a new period for providing notice to creditors that they may file a proof of claim in a case in which they were previously informed that there was no need to file a claim. Under Rule 2002(e), if it appears that there will be no distribution to creditors, the creditors are notified of this fact and are informed that if assets are later discovered and a distribution is likely that a new notice will be given to the creditors. This second notice is prescribed by Rule 3002(c)(5). The rule is amended to direct the clerk to give at least 90 days' notice of the time within which creditors may file a proof of claim. Setting the deadline in this manner allows the notices being sent to creditors to be more accurate regarding the deadline than was possible under the prior rule. The rule previously began the 90 day notice period from the time of the mailing of the notice, a date that could vary and generally would not even be known to the creditor. Under the amended rule, the notice will identify a specific bar date for filing proofs of claim thereby being more helpful to the creditors.

Subdivision (c)(6) is added to give the court discretion to extend the time for filing a proof of claim for a creditor who received notice of the time to file the claim at a foreign address, if the court finds that the notice was not sufficient, under the particular circumstances, to give the foreign creditor a reasonable time to file a proof of claim. This amendment is designed to comply with § 1514(d), added to the Code by the 2005 amendments, and requires that the rules and orders of the court provide such additional time as is reasonable under the circumstances for foreign creditors to file claims in cases under all chapters of the Code.

Other changes are stylistic.

CROSS REFERENCES

Filed claims or interests deemed allowed, see 11 USCA § 502.

Filing of—

     Claims by debtor or trustee, see Fed.Rules Bankr.Proc. Rule 3004, 11 USCA.

     Claims by guarantor, surety, indorser, or other codebtor, see Fed.Rules Bankr.Proc. Rule 3005, 11 USCA.

     Proofs of claims or interests, see 11 USCA § 501.

Filing proof of claim in liquidation or individual debt adjustment case, ninety-day period—

     Enlargement permitted as limited in this rule, see Fed. Rules Bankr.Proc. Rule 9006, 11 USCA.

     Reduction not permitted, see Fed.Rules Bankr.Proc. Rule 9006, 11 USCA.

Motions; form and service, see Fed.Rules Bankr.Proc. Rule 9013, 11 USCA.

Notice by mail of time allowed to file claims, see Fed.Rules Bankr.Proc. Rule 2002, 11 USCA.

Time extended to file claims against surplus—

     Converted liquidation case, see Fed.Rules Bankr.Proc. Rule 1019, 11 USCA.

     Notice to creditors in liquidation case, see Fed.Rules Bankr.Proc. Rule 2002, 11 USCA.

Twenty-day notice of time to file claims against surplus, see Fed.Rules Bankr.Proc. Rule 2002, 11 USCA.

LIBRARY REFERENCES

American Digest System

Bankruptcy ⚯2897.1 to 2900(2).

Key Number System Topic No. 51.

Corpus Juris Secundum

CJS Bankruptcy § 296, Notice by Mail--Proper Mailing Address.

CJS Bankruptcy § 301, Notice to Debtor, Creditors, and Indenture Trustees.

CJS Bankruptcy § 308, Enlargement.

CJS Bankruptcy § 309, Reduction.

CJS Bankruptcy § 794, Time of Initial Meeting.

CJS Bankruptcy § 1008, Necessity of Filing.

CJS Bankruptcy § 1018, Extension of Time; Excuse for Delay.

CJS Bankruptcy § 1105, Closing.

Rule 3002.1.   Notice Relating to Claims Secured by Security Interest in the Debtor's Principal Residence

(a) In General

This rule applies in a chapter 13 case to claims that are (1) secured by a security interest in the debtor's principal residence, and (2) provided for under § 1322(b)(5) of the Code in the debtor's plan.

(b) Notice of Payment Changes

The holder of the claim shall file and serve on the debtor, debtor's counsel, and the trustee a notice of any change in the payment amount, including any change that results from an interest rate or escrow account adjustment, no later than 21 days before a payment in the new amount is due.

(c) Notice of Fees, Expenses, and Charges

The holder of the claim shall file and serve on the debtor, debtor's counsel, and the trustee a notice itemizing all fees, expenses, or charges (1) that were incurred in connection with the claim after the bankruptcy case was filed, and (2) that the holder asserts are recoverable against the debtor or against the debtor's principal residence. The notice shall be served within 180 days after the date on which the fees, expenses, or charges are incurred.

(d) Form and Content

A notice filed and served under subdivision (b) or (c) of this rule shall be prepared as prescribed by the appropriate Official Form, and filed as a supplement to the holder's proof of claim. The notice is not subject to Rule 3001(f).

(e) Determination of Fees, Expenses, or Charges

On motion of the debtor or trustee filed within one year after service of a notice under subdivision (c) of this rule, the court shall, after notice and hearing, determine whether payment of any claimed fee, expense, or charge is required by the underlying agreement and applicable nonbankruptcy law to cure a default or maintain payments in accordance with § 1322(b)(5) of the Code.

(f) Notice of Final Cure Payment

Within 30 days after the debtor completes all payments under the plan, the trustee shall file and serve on the holder of the claim, the debtor, and debtor's counsel a notice stating that the debtor has paid in full the amount required to cure any default on the claim. The notice shall also inform the holder of its obligation to file and serve a response under subdivision (g). If the debtor contends that final cure payment has been made and all plan payments have been completed, and the trustee does not timely file and serve the notice required by this subdivision, the debtor may file and serve the notice.

(g) Response to Notice of Final Cure Payment

Within 21 days after service of the notice under subdivision (f) of this rule, the holder shall file and serve on the debtor, debtor's counsel, and the trustee a statement indicating (1) whether it agrees that the debtor has paid in full the amount required to cure the default on the claim, and (2) whether the debtor is otherwise current on all payments consistent with § 1322(b)(5) of the Code. The statement shall itemize the required cure or postpetition amounts, if any, that the holder contends remain unpaid as of the date of the statement. The statement shall be filed as a supplement to the holder's proof of claim and is not subject to Rule 3001(f).

(h) Determination of Final Cure and Payment

On motion of the debtor or trustee filed within 21 days after service of the statement under subdivision (g) of this rule, the court shall, after notice and hearing, determine whether the debtor has cured the default and paid all required postpetition amounts.

(i) Failure to Notify

If the holder of a claim fails to provide any information as required by subdivision (b), (c), or (g) of this rule, the court may, after notice and hearing, take either or both of the following actions:

(1) preclude the holder from presenting the omitted information, in any form, as evidence in any contested matter or adversary proceeding in the case, unless the court determines that the failure was substantially justified or is harmless; or

(2) award other appropriate relief, including reasonable expenses and attorney's fees caused by the failure.

(Adopted Apr. 26, 2011, eff. Dec. 1, 2011.)

ADVISORY COMMITTEE NOTES

2011 Adoption

This rule is new. It is added to aid in the implementation of § 1322(b)(5), which permits a chapter 13 debtor to cure a default and maintain payments of a home mortgage over the course of the debtor's plan. It applies regardless of whether the trustee or the debtor is the disbursing agent for postpetition mortgage payments.

In order to be able to fulfill the obligations of § 1322(b)(5), a debtor and the trustee must be informed of the exact amount needed to cure any prepetition arrearage, *see* Rule 3001(c)(2), and the amount of the postpetition payment obligations. If the latter amount changes over time, due to the adjustment of the interest rate, escrow account adjustments, or the assessment of fees, expenses, or other charges, notice of any change in payment amount needs to be conveyed to the debtor and trustee. Timely notice of these changes will permit the debtor or trustee to challenge the validity of any such charges, if necessary, and to adjust postpetition mortgage payments to cover any properly claimed adjustment. Compliance with the notice provision of the rule should also eliminate any concern on the part of the holder of the claim that informing a debtor of a change in postpetition payment obligations might violate the automatic stay.

Subdivision (a). Subdivision (a) specifies that this rule applies only in a chapter 13 case to claims secured by a security interest in the debtor's principal residence.

Subdivision (b). Subdivision (b) requires the holder of a claim to notify the debtor, debtor's counsel, and the trustee of any postpetition change in the mortgage payment amount at least 21 days before the new payment amount is due.

Subdivision (c). Subdivision (c) requires an itemized notice to be given, within 180 days of incurrence, of any postpetition fees, expenses, or charges that the holder of the claim asserts are recoverable in connection with a claim secured by the debtor's principal residence. This amount might include, for example, inspection fees, late charges, or attorney's fees.

Subdivision (d). Subdivision (d) provides the method of giving the notice under subdivisions (b) and (c). In both instances, the holder of the claim must give notice of the change as prescribed by the appropriate Official Form. In addition to serving the debtor, debtor's counsel, and the trustee, the holder of the claim must also file the notice on the claims register in the case as a supplement to its proof of claim. Rule 3001(f) does not apply to any notice given under subdivision (b) or (c), and therefore the notice will not constitute prima facie evidence of the validity and amount of the payment change or of the fee, expense, or charge.

Subdivision (e). Subdivision (e) permits the debtor or trustee, within a year after service of a notice under subdivision (c), to seek a determination by the court as to whether the fees, expenses, or charges set forth in the notice are required by the underlying agreement or applicable nonbankruptcy law to cure a default or maintain payments.

Subdivision (f). Subdivision (f) requires the trustee to issue a notice to the holder of the claim, the debtor, and the debtor's attorney within 30 days after completion of payments under the plan. The notice must (1) indicate that all amounts required to cure a default on a claim secured by the debtor's principal residence have been paid, and (2) direct the holder to comply with subdivision (g). If the trustee fails to file this notice within the required time, this subdivision also permits the debtor to file and serve the notice on the trustee and the holder of the claim .

Subdivision (g). Subdivision (g) governs the response of the holder of the claim to the trustee's or debtor's notice under subdivision (f). Within 21 days after service of notice of the final cure payment, the holder of the claim must file and serve a statement indicating whether the prepetition default has been fully cured and also whether the debtor is current on all payments in accordance with § 1322(b)(5) of the Code. If the holder of the claim contends that all cure payments have not been made or that the debtor is not current on other payments required by § 1322(b)(5), the response must itemize all amounts, other than regular future installment payments, that the holder contends are due.

Subdivision (h). Subdivision (h) provides a procedure for the judicial resolution of any disputes that may arise about payment of a claim secured by the debtor's principal residence. Within 21 days after the service of the statement under (g), the trustee or debtor may move for a determination by the court of whether any default has been cured and whether any other non-current obligations remain outstanding.

Subdivision (i). Subdivision (i) specifies sanctions that may be imposed if the holder of a claim fails to provide any of the information as required by subdivisions (b), (c), or (g).

If, after the chapter 13 debtor has completed payments under the plan and the case has been closed, the holder of a claim secured by the debtor's principal residence seeks to recover amounts that should have been but were not disclosed under this rule, the debtor may move to have the case reopened in order to seek sanctions against the holder of the claim under subdivision (i).

Rule 3003. Filing Proof of Claim or Equity Security Interest in Chapter 9 Municipality or Chapter 11 Reorganization Cases

(a) Applicability of rule

This rule applies in chapter 9 and 11 cases.

(b) Schedule of liabilities and list of equity security holders

(1) Schedule of liabilities

The schedule of liabilities filed pursuant to § 521(1)[1] of the Code shall constitute prima facie evidence of the validity and amount of the claims of creditors, unless they are scheduled as disputed, contingent, or unliquidated. It shall not be necessary for a creditor or equity security holder to file a proof of claim or interest except as provided in subdivision (c)(2) of this rule.

(2) List of equity security holders

The list of equity security holders filed pursuant to Rule 1007(a)(3) shall constitute prima facie evidence of the validity and amount of the equity security interests and it shall not be necessary for the holders of such interests to file a proof of interest.

(c) Filing of proof of claim

(1) Who may file

Any creditor or indenture trustee may file a proof of claim within the time prescribed by subdivision (c)(3) of this rule.

(2) Who must file

Any creditor or equity security holder whose claim or interest is not scheduled or scheduled as disputed, contingent, or unliquidated shall file a proof of claim or interest within the time prescribed by subdivision (c)(3) of this rule; any creditor who fails to do so shall not be treated as a creditor with respect to such claim for the purposes of voting and distribution.

(3) Time for filing

The court shall fix and for cause shown may extend the time within which proofs of claim or interest may be filed. Notwithstanding the expiration of such time, a proof of claim may be filed to the extent and under the conditions stated in Rule 3002(c)(2), (c)(3), (c)(4), and (c)(6).

(4) Effect of filing claim or interest

A proof of claim or interest executed and filed in accordance with this subdivision shall supersede any scheduling of that claim or interest pursuant to § 521(a)(1) of the Code.

(5) Filing by indenture trustee

An indenture trustee may file a claim on behalf of all known or unknown holders of securities issued pursuant to the trust instrument under which it is trustee.

(d) Proof of right to record status

For the purposes of Rules 3017, 3018 and 3021 and for receiving notices, an entity who is not the record holder of a security may file a statement setting forth facts which entitle that entity to be treated as the record holder. An objection to the statement may be filed by any party in interest.

(As amended Mar. 30, 1987, eff. Aug. 1, 1987; Apr. 30, 1991, eff. Aug. 1, 1991; Apr. 23, 2008, eff. Dec. 1, 2008.)

1 So in original. Probably should be "§ 521(a)(1)".

ADVISORY COMMITTEE NOTES

Subdivision (a). This rule applies only in chapter 9 and chapter 11 cases. It is adapted from former Chapter X Rule 10–401 and provides an exception to the requirement for filing proofs of claim and interest as expressed in §§ 925 and 1111(a) of the Code.

Subdivision (b). This general statement implements §§ 925 and 1111(a) of the Code.

Subdivision (c). This subdivision permits, in paragraph (1), the filing of a proof of claim but does not make it mandatory. Paragraph (2) requires, as does the Code, filing when a claim is scheduled as disputed, contingent, or unliquidated as to amount. It is the creditor's responsibility to determine if the claim is accurately listed. Notice of the provision of this rule is provided for in Official Form No. 16, the order for the meeting of creditors. In an appropriate case the court may order creditors whose claims are scheduled as disputed, contingent, or unliquidated be notified of that fact but the procedure is left to the discretion of the court.

Subdivision (d) is derived from former Chapter X Rule 10–401(f).

Except with respect to the need and time for filing claims, the other aspects concerning claims covered by Rules 3001 and 3002 are applicable in chapter 9 and 11 cases.

Holders of equity security interests need not file proofs of interest. Voting and distribution participation is dependent on ownership as disclosed by the appropriate records of a transfer agent or the corporate or other business records at the time prescribed in Rules 3017 and 3021.

1991 Amendments

Paragraph (3) of subdivision (c) is amended to permit the late filing of claims by infants or incompetent persons under the same circumstances that permit late filings in cases under chapter 7, 12, or 13. The amendment also provides sufficient time in which to file a claim that arises from a postpetition judgment against the claimant for the recovery of money or property or the avoidance of a lien. It also provides for purposes of clarification that upon rejection of an executory contract or unexpired lease, the court shall set a time for filing a claim arising therefrom despite prior expiration of the time set for filing proofs of claim.

The caption of paragraph (4) of subdivision (c) is amended to indicate that it applies to a proof of claim.

2008 Amendments

Subdivision (c)(3) is amended to implement § 1514(d) of the Code, which was added by the 2005 amendments. It makes the new Rule 3002(c)(6) applicable in chapter 9 and chapter 11 cases. This change was necessary so that creditors with

foreign addresses be provided such additional time as is reasonable under the circumstances to file proofs of claims.

CROSS REFERENCES

Acceptance or rejection of municipality debt adjustment or reorganization plan by obligor filing creditor's claim, see Fed.Rules Bankr.Proc. Rule 3005, 11 USCA.

Distribution under confirmed plan to indenture trustee filing under this rule, see Fed.Rules Bankr.Proc. Rule 3021, 11 USCA.

Exception to filing requirement for—

Municipality debt adjustment case, see 11 USCA § 925.

Reorganization case, see 11 USCA § 1111.

Filing of claims by—

Debtor or trustee, see Fed.Rules Bankr.Proc. Rule 3004, 11 USCA.

Guarantor, surety, indorser, or other codebtor, see Fed. Rules Bankr.Proc. Rule 3005, 11 USCA.

Twenty-day notice of time fixed to file proof of claim, see Fed.Rules Bankr.Proc. Rule 2002, 11 USCA.

LIBRARY REFERENCES

American Digest System

Bankruptcy ⊗2897.1 to 2900(2), 3481.

Key Number System Topic No. 51.

Corpus Juris Secundum

CJS Bankruptcy § 309, Reduction.

CJS Bankruptcy § 1014, Scheduling as Filing.

CJS Bankruptcy § 1016, Reorganization and Municipal Debt Cases.

CJS Bankruptcy § 1018, Extension of Time; Excuse for Delay.

Rule 3004.   Filing of Claims by Debtor or Trustee

If a creditor does not timely file a proof of claim under Rule 3002(c) or 3003(c), the debtor or trustee may file a proof of the claim within 30 days after the expiration of the time for filing claims prescribed by Rule 3002(c) or 3003(c), whichever is applicable. The clerk shall forthwith give notice of the filing to the creditor, the debtor and the trustee.

(As amended Mar. 30, 1987, eff. Aug. 1, 1987; Apr. 25, 2005, eff. Dec. 1, 2005.)

ADVISORY COMMITTEE NOTES

This rule is adapted from former Bankruptcy Rule 303 but conforms with the changes made by § 501(c) of the Code. Rule 303 permitted only the filing of tax and wage claims by the debtor. Section 501(c) of the Code, however, permits the filing by the debtor or trustee on behalf of any creditor.

It is the policy of the Code that debtors' estates should be administered for the benefit of creditors without regard to the dischargeability of their claims. After their estates have been closed, however, discharged debtors may find themselves saddled with liabilities, particularly for taxes, which remain unpaid because of the failure of creditors holding nondischargeable claims to file proofs of claim and receive distributions thereon. The result is that the debtor is deprived of an important benefit of the Code without any fault or omission on the debtor's part and without any objective of the Code being served thereby.

Section 501(c) of the Code authorizes a debtor or trustee to file a proof of claim for any holder of a claim. Although all claims may not be nondischargeable, it may be difficult to determine, in particular, whether tax claims survive discharge. See Plumb, Federal Tax Liens and Priorities in Bankruptcy, 43 Ref.J. 37, 43–44 (1969); 1 Collier, Bankruptcy ¶17.14 (14th ed. 1967); 3 id. ¶523.06 (15th ed. 1979). To eliminate the necessity of the resolution of this troublesome issue, the option accorded the debtor by the Code does not depend on the nondischargeability of the claim. No serious administrative problems and no unfairness to creditors seemed to develop from adoption of Rule 303, the forerunner to § 501(c). The authority to file is conditioned on the creditor's failure to file the proof of claim on or before the first date set for the meeting of creditors, which is the date a claim must ordinarily be filed in order to be voted in a chapter 7 case. Notice to the creditor is provided to enable him to file a proof of claim pursuant to Rule 3002, which proof, when filed, would supersede the proof filed by the debtor or trustee. Notice to the trustee would serve to alert the trustee to the special character of the proof and the possible need for supplementary evidence of the validity and amount of the claim. If the trustee does not qualify until after a proof of claim is filed by the debtor pursuant to this rule, he should be notified as soon as practicable thereafter.

To the extent the claim is allowed and dividends paid thereon, it will be reduced or perhaps paid in full. If the claim is also filed pursuant to Rule 3005, only one distribution thereon may be made. As expressly required by Rule 3005 and by the purpose of this rule such distribution must diminish the claim.

1987 Amendments

Under the rule as amended, the debtor or trustee in a chapter 7 or 13 case has 120 days from the first date set for the meeting of creditors to file a claim for the creditor. During the first 90 days of that period the creditor in a Chapter 7 or 13 case may file a claim as provided by Rule 3002(c). If the creditor fails to file a claim, the debtor or trustee shall have an additional 30 days thereafter to file the claim. A proof of claim filed by a creditor supersedes a claim filed by the debtor or trustee only if it is timely filed within the 90 days allowed under Rule 3002(c).

2005 Amendments

The rule is amended to conform to § 501(c) of the Code. Under that provision, the debtor or trustee may file proof of a claim if the creditor fails to do so in a timely fashion. The rule previously authorized the debtor and the trustee to file a claim as early as the day after the first date set for the meeting of creditors under § 341(a). Under the amended rule, the debtor and trustee must wait until the creditor's opportunity to file a claim has expired. Providing the debtor and the trustee with the opportunity to file a claim ensures that the claim will participate in any distribution in the case. This is particularly important for claims that are nondischargeable.

Since the debtor and trustee cannot file a proof of claim until after the creditor's time to file has expired, the rule no longer permits the creditor to file a proof of claim that will supersede the claim filed by the debtor or trustee. The rule

leaves to the courts the issue of whether to permit subsequent amendment of such proof of claim.

Other changes are stylistic.

CROSS REFERENCES

Exception to execution of proof of claim by creditor or agent, see Fed.Rules Bankr.Proc. Rule 3001, 11 USCA.

Filing of claims by debtor or trustee, see 11 USCA § 501.

LIBRARY REFERENCES

American Digest System

Bankruptcy ⊕2895.1 to 2900(2), 2929.

Key Number System Topic No. 51.

Corpus Juris Secundum

CJS Bankruptcy § 1017, Filing by Trustee, Debtor, Co-Debtor, or Surety.

Rule 3005. Filing of Claim, Acceptance, or Rejection By Guarantor, Surety, Indorser, or Other Codebtor

(a) Filing of claim

If a creditor does not timely file a proof of claim under Rule 3002(c) or 3003(c), any entity that is or may be liable with the debtor to that creditor, or who has secured that creditor, may file a proof of the claim within 30 days after the expiration of the time for filing claims prescribed by Rule 3002(c) or Rule 3003(c) whichever is applicable. No distribution shall be made on the claim except on satisfactory proof that the original debt will be diminished by the amount of distribution.

(b) Filing of acceptance or rejection; substitution of creditor

An entity which has filed a claim pursuant to the first sentence of subdivision (a) of this rule may file an acceptance or rejection of a plan in the name of the creditor, if known, or if unknown, in the entity's own name but if the creditor files a proof of claim within the time permitted by Rule 3003(c) or files a notice prior to confirmation of a plan of the creditor's intention to act in the creditor's own behalf, the creditor shall be substituted for the obligor with respect to that claim.

(As amended Mar. 30, 1987, eff. Aug. 1, 1987; Apr. 30, 1991, eff. Aug. 1, 1991; Apr. 25, 2005, eff. Dec. 1, 2005.)

ADVISORY COMMITTEE NOTES

This rule is adapted from former Rules 304 and 10–402. Together with § 501(b) of the Code, the rule makes clear that anyone who may be liable on a debt of the debtor, including a surety, guarantor, indorser, or other codebtor, is authorized to file in the name of the creditor of the debtor.

Subdivision (a). Rule 3002(c) provides the time period for filing proofs of claim in chapter 7 and 13 cases; Rule 3003(c) provides the time, when necessary, for filing claims in a chapter 9 or 11 case.

Subdivision (b). This subdivision applies in chapter 9 and 11 cases as distinguished from chapter 7 cases. It permits voting for or against a plan by an obligor who files a claim in place of the creditor.

1991 Amendments

The words "with the court" in subdivision (b) are deleted as unnecessary. See Rules 5005(a) and 9001(3).

2005 Amendments

The rule is amended to delete the last sentence of subdivision (a). The sentence is unnecessary because if a creditor has filed a timely claim under Rule 3002 or 3003(c), the codebtor cannot file a proof of such claim. The codebtor, consistent with § 501(b) of the Code, may file a proof of such claim only after the creditor's time to file has expired. Therefore, the rule no longer permits the creditor to file a superseding claim. The rule leaves to the courts the issue of whether to permit subsequent amendment of the proof of claim.

The amendment conforms the rule to § 501(b) by deleting language providing that the codebtor files proof of the claim in the name of the creditor.

Other amendments are stylistic.

CROSS REFERENCES

Exception to execution of proof of claim by creditor or agent, see Fed.Rules Bankr.Proc. Rule 3001, 11 USCA.

LIBRARY REFERENCES

American Digest System

Bankruptcy ⊗2895.1 to 2900(2).
Key Number System Topic No. 51.

Corpus Juris Secundum

CJS Bankruptcy § 1017, Filing by Trustee, Debtor, Co-Debtor, or Surety.

LIBRARY REFERENCES

Corpus Juris Secundum

CJS Bankruptcy § 1017, Filing by Trustee, Debtor, Co-Debtor, or Surety.

Rule 3006.   Withdrawal of Claim; Effect on Acceptance or Rejection of Plan

A creditor may withdraw a claim as of right by filing a notice of withdrawal, except as provided in this rule. If after a creditor has filed a proof of claim an objection is filed thereto or a complaint is filed against that creditor in an adversary proceeding, or the creditor has accepted or rejected the plan or otherwise has participated significantly in the case, the creditor may not withdraw the claim except on order of the court after a hearing on notice to the trustee or debtor in possession, and any creditors' committee elected pursuant to § 705(a) or appointed pursuant to § 1102 of the Code. The order of the court shall contain such terms and conditions as the court deems proper. Unless the court orders otherwise, an authorized withdrawal of a claim shall constitute withdrawal of any related acceptance or rejection of a plan.
(As amended Apr. 30, 1991, eff. Aug. 1, 1991.)

ADVISORY COMMITTEE NOTES

This rule is derived from former Rules 305 and 10–404.

Since 1938 is has generally been held that Rule 41 F.R.Civ.P. governs the withdrawal of a proof of claim. In re Empire Coal Sales Corp., 45 F.Supp. 974, 976 (S.C.N.Y.), aff'd sub nom. Kleid v. Ruthbell Coal Co., 131 F.2d 372, 373 (2d Cir.1942); Kelso v. MacLaren, 122 F.2d 867, 870 (8th Cir. 1941); In re Hills, 35 F.Supp. 532, 533 (W.D.Wash.1940). Accordingly the cited cases held that after an objection has been filed a proof of claim may be withdrawn only subject to approval by the court. This constitutes a restriction of the right of withdrawal as recognized by some though by no means all of the cases antedating the promulgation of the Federal Rules of Civil Procedure. See 3 Collier, Bankruptcy ¶57.12 (14th ed. 1961); Note, 20 Bost.U.L.Rev. 121 (1940).

The filing of a claim does not commence an adversary proceeding but the filing of an objection to the claim initiates a contest that must be disposed of by the court. This rule recognizes the applicability of the considerations underlying Rule 41(a) F.R.Civ.P. to the withdrawal of a claim after it has been put in issue by an objection. Rule 41(a)(2) F.R.Civ.P. requires leave of court to obtain dismissal over the objection of a defendant who has pleaded a counterclaim prior to the service of the plaintiff's motion to dismiss. Although the applicability of this provision to the withdrawal of a claim was assumed in Conway v. Union Bank of Switzerland, 204 F.2d 603, 608 (2d Cir.1953), Kleid v. Ruthbell Coal Co., supra, Kelso v. MacLaren, supra, and In re Hills, supra, this rule vests discretion in the court to grant, deny, or condition the request of a creditor to withdraw, without regard to whether the trustee has filed a merely defensive objection or a complaint seeking an affirmative recovery of money or property from the creditor.

A number of pre-1938 cases sustained denial of a creditor's request to withdraw proof of claim on the ground of estoppel or election of remedies. 2 Remington, Bankruptcy 186 (Henderson ed. 1956); cf. 3 Collier, supra ¶57.12, at 201 (1964). Voting a claim for a trustee was an important factor in the denial of a request to withdraw in Standard Varnish Works v. Haydock, 143 Fed. 318, 319–20 (6th Cir.1906), and In re Cann, 47 F.2d 661, 662 (W.D.Pa.1931). And it has frequently been recognized that a creditor should not be allowed to withdraw a claim after accepting a dividend. In re Friedmann, 1 Am.B.R. 510, 512 (Ref., S.D.N.Y.1899); 3 Collier 205 (1964); cf. In re O'Gara Coal Co., 12 F.2d 426, 429 (7th Cir.), cert. denied, 271 U.S. 683 (1926). It was held in Industrial Credit Co. v. Hazen, 222 F.2d 225 (8th Cir.1955), however, that although a claimant had participated in the first meeting of creditors and in the examination of witnesses, the creditor was entitled under Rule 41(a)(1) F.R.Civ.P. to withdraw the claim as of right by filing a notice of withdrawal before the trustee filed an objection under § 57g of the Act. While this rule incorporates the post-1938 case law referred to in the first paragraph of this note, it rejects the inference drawn in the Hazen case that Rule 41(a) F.R.Civ.P. supersedes the pre-1938 case law that vests discretion in the court to deny or restrict withdrawal of a claim by a creditor on the ground of estoppel or election of remedies. While purely formal or technical participation in a case by a creditor who has filed a claim should not deprive the creditor of the right to withdraw the claim, a creditor who has accepted a dividend or who has voted in the election of a trustee or otherwise participated actively in proceedings in a case should be permitted to withdraw only with the approval of the court on terms it deems appropriate after notice to the trustee. 3 Collier 205–06 (1964).

1991 Amendments

This amendment is stylistic. Notice of the hearing need not be given to committees of equity security holders appointed pursuant to § 1102 or committees of retired employees appointed pursuant to § 1114 of the Code.

CROSS REFERENCES

Dismissal of actions, see Fed.Rules Civ.Proc. Rule 41, 28 USCA.

LIBRARY REFERENCES

American Digest System

Bankruptcy ⟨=2903.

Key Number System Topic No. 51.

Corpus Juris Secundum

CJS Bankruptcy § 1010, Withdrawal.

CJS Bankruptcy § 1158, Number of Creditors and Amount of Claims Concurring; Withdrawal.

Rule 3007.   Objections to Claims

(a) Objections to Claims

An objection to the allowance of a claim shall be in writing and filed. A copy of the objection with notice of the hearing thereon shall be mailed or otherwise delivered to the claimant, the debtor or debtor in possession, and the trustee at least 30 days prior to the hearing.

(b) Demand for Relief Requiring an Adversary Proceeding

A party in interest shall not include a demand for relief of a kind specified in Rule 7001 in an objection to the allowance of a claim, but may include the objection in an adversary proceeding.

(c) Limitation on Joinder of Claims Objections

Unless otherwise ordered by the court or permitted by subdivision (d), objections to more than one claim shall not be joined in a single objection.

(d) Omnibus Objection

Subject to subdivision (e), objections to more than one claim may be joined in an omnibus objection if all the claims were filed by the same entity, or the objections are based solely on the grounds that the claims should be disallowed, in whole or in part, because:

(1) they duplicate other claims;

(2) they have been filed in the wrong case;

(3) they have been amended by subsequently filed proofs of claim;

(4) they were not timely filed;

(5) they have been satisfied or released during the case in accordance with the Code, applicable rules, or a court order;

(6) they were presented in a form that does not comply with applicable rules, and the objection states that the objector is unable to determine the validity of the claim because of the noncompliance;

(7) they are interests, rather than claims; or

(8) they assert priority in an amount that exceeds the maximum amount under § 507 of the Code.

(e) Requirements For Omnibus Objection

An omnibus objection shall:

(1) state in a conspicuous place that claimants receiving the objection should locate their names and claims in the objection;

(2) list claimants alphabetically, provide a cross-reference to claim numbers, and, if appropriate, list claimants by category of claims;

(3) state the grounds of the objection to each claim and provide a cross-reference to the pages in the omnibus objection pertinent to the stated grounds;

(4) state in the title the identity of the objector and the grounds for the objections;

(5) be numbered consecutively with other omnibus objections filed by the same objector; and

(6) contain objections to no more than 100 claims.

(f) Finality of Objection

The finality of any order regarding a claim objection included in an omnibus objection shall be determined as though the claim had been subject to an individual objection.

(As amended Apr. 30, 1991, eff. Aug. 1, 1991; Apr. 30, 2007, eff. Dec. 1, 2007.)

ADVISORY COMMITTEE NOTES

This rule is derived from § 47a(8) of the Act [former § 75(a)(8) of this title] and former Bankruptcy Rule 306. It prescribes the manner in which an objection to a claim shall be made and notice of the hearing thereon given to the claimant. The requirement of a writing does not apply to an objection to the allowance of a claim for the purpose of voting for a trustee or creditors' committee in a chapter 7 case. See Rule 2003.

The contested matter initiated by an objection to a claim is governed by rule 9014, unless a counterclaim by the trustee is joined with the objection to the claim. The filing of a counterclaim ordinarily commences an adversary proceeding subject to the rules in Part VII.

While the debtor's other creditors may make objections to the allowance of a claim, the demands of orderly and expeditious administration have led to a recognition that the right to object is generally exercised by the trustee. Pursuant to § 502(a) of the Code, however, any party in interest may object to a claim. But under § 704 the trustee, if any purpose would be served thereby, has the duty to examine proofs of claim and object to improper claims.

By virtue of the automatic allowance of a claim not objected to, a dividend may be paid on a claim which may thereafter be disallowed on objection made pursuant to this rule. The amount of the dividend paid before the disallowance in such event would be recoverable by the trustee in an adversary proceeding.

1991 Amendments

The words "with the court" are deleted as unnecessary. See Rules 5005(a) and 9001(3).

2007 Amendments

The rule is amended in a number of ways. First, the amendment prohibits a party in interest from including in a claim objection a request for relief that requires an adversary proceeding. A party in interest may, however, include an objection to the allowance of a claim in an adversary proceeding. Unlike a contested matter, an adversary proceeding requires the service of a summons and complaint, which puts the defendant on notice of the potential for an affirmative recovery. Permitting the plaintiff in the adversary proceeding to include an objection to a claim would not unfairly surprise the defendant as might be the case if the action were brought as a contested matter that included an action to obtain relief of a kind specified in Rule 7001.

The rule as amended does not require that a party include an objection to the allowance of a claim in an adversary proceeding. If a claim objection is filed separately from a related adversary proceeding, the court may consolidate the objection with the adversary proceeding under Rule 7042.

The rule also is amended to authorize the filing of a pleading that joins objections to more than one claim. Such filings present a significant opportunity for the efficient administration of large cases, but the rule includes restrictions on the use of these omnibus objections to ensure the protection of the due process rights of the claimants.

Unless the court orders otherwise, objections to more than one claim may be joined in a single pleading only if all of the claims were filed by the same entity, or if the objections are based solely on the grounds set out in subdivision (d) of the rule. Objections of the type listed in subdivision (d) often can be resolved without material factual or legal disputes. Objections to multiple claims permitted under the rule must comply with the procedural requirements set forth in subdivision (e). Among those requirements is the requirement in subdivision (e)(5) that these omnibus objections be consecutively numbered. Since these objections may not join more than 100 objections in any one omnibus objection, there may be a need for several omnibus objections to be filed in a particular case. Consecutive numbering of each omnibus objection and the identification of the objector in the title of the objection is essential to keep track of the objections on the court's docket. For example, the objections could be titled Debtor in Possession's First Omnibus Objection to Claims, Debtor in Possession's Second Omnibus Objection to Claims, Creditors' Committee's First Omnibus Objection to Claims, and so on. Titling the objections in this manner should avoid confusion and aid in tracking the objections on the docket.

Subdivision (f) provides that an order resolving an objection to any particular claim is treated, for purposes of finality, as if the claim had been the subject of an individual objection. A party seeking to appeal any such order is neither required, nor permitted, to await the court's resolution of all other joined objections. The rule permits the joinder of objections for convenience, and that convenience should not impede timely review of a court's decision with respect to each claim. Whether the court's action as to a particular objection is final, and the consequences of that finality, are not addressed by this amendment. Moreover, use of an omnibus objection generally does not preclude the objecting party from raising a subsequent objection to the claim on other grounds. See Restatement (Second) of Judgments § 26(1)(d) (1982) (generally applicable rule barring multiple actions based on same transaction or series of transactions is overridden when a statutory scheme permits splitting of claims).

CROSS REFERENCES

Allowance of claims or interests after objection, see 11 USCA § 502.

Contested matters, see Fed.Rules Bankr.Proc. Rule 9014, 11 USCA.

Duty of trustee to examine proofs of claims and to object to improper claims—

Individual debt adjustment case, see 11 USCA § 1302.

Liquidation case, see 11 USCA § 704.

Reorganization case, see 11 USCA § 1106.

Objection to claim for purpose of voting for trustee or creditors' committee in liquidation case, see Fed.Rules Bankr. Proc. Rule 2003, 11 USCA.

LIBRARY REFERENCES

American Digest System

Bankruptcy ⇒2922 to 2924.

Key Number System Topic No. 51.

Corpus Juris Secundum

CJS Bankruptcy § 1023, Objections.

Rule 3008.   Reconsideration of Claims

A party in interest may move for reconsideration of an order allowing or disallowing a claim against the estate. The court after a hearing on notice shall enter an appropriate order.

ADVISORY COMMITTEE NOTES

Section 502(j) of the Code deals only with the reconsideration of allowed claims as did former § 57k of the Act [former § 93(k) of this title] and General Order 21(b). It had sometimes been held that a referee had no jurisdiction to reconsider a disallowed claim, or the amount or priority of an allowed claim, at the instance of the claimant. See, e.g., In re Gouse, 7 F.Supp. 106 (M.D.Pa.1934); In re Tomlinson & Dye, Inc., 3 F.Supp. 800 (N.D.Okla.1933). This view disregarded § 2a(2) of the Act [former § 11(a)(2) of this title] and the "ancient and elementary power" of a referee as a court to reconsider orders. In re Pottasch Bros. Co., Inc., 79 F.2d 613, 616 (2d Cir.1935); Castaner v. Mora, 234 F.2d 710 (1st Cir.1956). This rule recognizes, as did former Bankruptcy Rule 307, the power of the court to reconsider an order of disallowance on appropriate motion.

Reconsideration of a claim that has been previously allowed or disallowed after objection is discretionary with the court. The right to seek reconsideration of an allowed claim, like the right to object to its allowance, is generally exercised by the trustee if one has qualified and is performing the duties of that office with reasonable diligence and fidelity. A request for reconsideration of a disallowance would, on the other hand, ordinarily come from the claimant.

A proof of claim executed and filed in accordance with the rules in this Part III is prima facie evidence of the validity and the amount of the claim notwithstanding a motion for reconsideration of an order of allowance. Failure to respond does not constitute an admission, though it may be deemed a consent to a reconsideration. In re Goble Boat Co., 190 Fed. 92 (N.D.N.Y.1911). The court may decline to reconsider an order of allowance or disallowance without notice to any adverse party and without affording any hearing to the movant. If a motion to reconsider is granted, notice and hearing must be afforded to parties in interest before the previous action in the claim taken in respect to the claim may be vacated or modified. After reconsideration, the court may allow or disallow the claim, increase or decrease the amount of a prior allowance, accord the claim a priority different from that originally assigned it, or enter any other appropriate order.

The rule expands § 502(j) which provides for reconsideration of an allowance only before the case is closed. Authorities have disagreed as to whether reconsideration may be had after a case has been reopened. Compare 3 Collier, Bankruptcy ¶57.23[4] (14th ed. 1964), see generally 3 id. ¶502.10 (15th ed. 1979), with 2 Remington, Bankruptcy 498 (Henderson ed. 1956). If a case is reopened as provided in § 350(b) of the Code, reconsideration of the allowance or disallowance of a claim may be sought and granted in accordance with this rule.

CROSS REFERENCES

Closing and reopening cases, see 11 USCA § 350.

Exception to procedural rule on new trials and amendment of judgments, see Fed.Rules Bankr.Proc. Rule 9023, 11 USCA.

Motions; form and service, see Fed.Rules Bankr.Proc. Rule 9013, 11 USCA.

Reconsideration of claim prior to closing of case, see 11 USCA § 502.

LIBRARY REFERENCES

American Digest System

Bankruptcy ⚖2933.

Key Number System Topic No. 51.

Corpus Juris Secundum

CJS Bankruptcy § 289, Motions.

CJS Bankruptcy § 1027, Reconsideration.

Rule 3009. Declaration and Payment of Dividends in a Chapter 7 Liquidation Case

In a chapter 7 case, dividends to creditors shall be paid as promptly as practicable. Dividend checks shall be made payable to and mailed to each creditor whose claim has been allowed, unless a power of attorney authorizing another entity to receive dividends has been executed and filed in accordance with Rule 9010. In that event, dividend checks shall be made payable to

the creditor and to the other entity and shall be mailed to the other entity.

(As amended Mar. 30, 1987, eff. Aug. 1, 1987; Apr. 22, 1993, eff. Aug. 1, 1993.)

ADVISORY COMMITTEE NOTES

This rule is derived from former Rules 308 and 11–35(a). The preparation of records showing dividends declared and to whom payable is subject to prescription by the Director of the Administrative Office pursuant to Rule 5003(e). The rule governs distributions to creditors having priority as well as to general unsecured creditors. Notwithstanding the detailed statutory provisions regulating the declaration of dividends, a necessarily wide discretion over this matter has been recognized to reside in the court. See 3A Collier, Bankruptcy ¶65.03 (14th ed. 1975): 1 Proceedings of Seminar for Newly Appointed Referees in Bankruptcy 173 (1964). Although the rule leaves to the discretion of the court the amount and the times of dividend payments, it recognizes the creditors' right to as prompt payment as practicable.

The second and third sentences of the rule make explicit the method of payment of dividends and afford protection of the interests of the creditor and the holder of a power of attorney authorized to receive payment.

The rule does not permit variance at local option. This represents a marked change from former Bankruptcy Rule 308.

1993 Amendments

This rule is amended to delete the requirement that the court approve the amounts and times of distributions in chapter 7 cases. This change recognizes the role of the United States trustee in supervising trustees. Other amendments are stylistic and make no substantive change.

CROSS REFERENCES

Dividend records kept by clerk, see Fed.Rules Bankr.Proc. Rule 5003, 11 USCA.

Unclaimed dividends, see 11 USCA § 347.

LIBRARY REFERENCES

American Digest System

Bankruptcy ⚖3009, 3442.1.

Key Number System Topic No. 51.

Corpus Juris Secundum

CJS Bankruptcy § 1098, Time of Payment.

Rule 3010. Small Dividends and Payments in Chapter 7 Liquidation, Chapter 12 Family Farmer's Debt Adjustment, and Chapter 13 Individual's Debt Adjustment Cases

(a) Chapter 7 cases

In a chapter 7 case no dividend in an amount less than $5 shall be distributed by the trustee to any creditor unless authorized by local rule or order of the court. Any dividend not distributed to a creditor shall be treated in the same manner as unclaimed funds as provided in § 347 of the Code.

(b) Chapter 12 and chapter 13 cases

In a chapter 12 or chapter 13 case no payment in an amount less than $15 shall be distributed by the trustee to any creditor unless authorized by local rule or order of the court. Funds not distributed because of this subdivision shall accumulate and shall be paid whenever the accumulation aggregates $15. Any funds remaining shall be distributed with the final payment.

(As amended Mar. 30, 1987, eff. Aug. 1, 1987; Apr. 30, 1991, eff. Aug. 1, 1991.)

ADVISORY COMMITTEE NOTES

This rule permits a court to eliminate the disproportionate expense and inconvenience incurred by the issuance of a dividend check of less than $5 (or $15 in a chapter 13 case). Creditors are more irritated than pleased to receive such small dividends, but the money is held subject to their specific request as are unclaimed dividends under § 347(a) of the Code. When the trustee deposits undistributed dividends pursuant to a direction in accordance with this rule the trustee should file with the clerk a list of the names and addresses, so far as known, of the persons entitled to the money so deposited and the respective amounts payable to them pursuant to Rule 3011. In a chapter 13 case, the small dividend will accumulate and will be payable at the latest, with the final dividend. Local rule or order may change the practice permitted in this rule and, in that connection, the order may be incorporated in the order confirming a chapter 13 plan.

1991 Amendments

Subdivision (b) is amended to include chapter 12 cases.

LIBRARY REFERENCES

American Digest System

Bankruptcy ☞3009, 3442.1, 3685, 3710.
Key Number System Topic No. 51.

Corpus Juris Secundum

CJS Bankruptcy § 15, Local Rules.

Rule 3011. Unclaimed Funds in Chapter 7 Liquidation, Chapter 12 Family Farmer's Debt Adjustment, and Chapter 13 Individual's Debt Adjustment Cases

The trustee shall file a list of all known names and addresses of the entities and the amounts which they are entitled to be paid from remaining property of the estate that is paid into court pursuant to § 347(a) of the Code.

(As amended Mar. 30, 1987, eff. Aug. 1, 1987; Apr. 30, 1991, eff. Aug. 1, 1991.)

ADVISORY COMMITTEE NOTES

This rule is derived from former Bankruptcy Rule 310. The operative provisions of that rule, however, are contained in § 347(a) of the Code, requiring the trustee to stop payment of checks remaining unpaid 90 days after distribution. The rule adds the requirement of filing a list of the names and addresses of the persons entitled to these dividends. This rule applies in a chapter 7 or 13 case but not in a chapter 9 or 11 case. The latter cases are governed by § 347(b) of the Code which provides for unclaimed distributions to be returned to the debtor or other entity acquiring the assets of the debtor.

1991 Amendments

The title of this rule is amended to include chapter 12 cases. The words "with the clerk" are deleted as unnecessary. See Rules 5005(a) and 9001(3).

CROSS REFERENCES

Treatment of small dividends as unclaimed funds, see Fed. Rules Bankr.Proc. Rule 3010, 11 USCA.

LIBRARY REFERENCES

American Digest System

Bankruptcy ☞3009, 3011, 3442.1, 3685, 3710.
Key Number System Topic No. 51.

Corpus Juris Secundum

CJS Bankruptcy § 1011, Transfer or Assignment.

Rule 3012. Valuation of Security

The court may determine the value of a claim secured by a lien on property in which the estate has an interest on motion of any party in interest and after a hearing on notice to the holder of the secured claim and any other entity as the court may direct.

(As amended Mar. 30, 1987, eff. Aug. 1, 1987.)

ADVISORY COMMITTEE NOTES

Pursuant to § 506(a) of the Code, secured claims are to be valued and allowed as secured to the extent of the value of the collateral and unsecured, to the extent it is enforceable, for the excess over such value. The valuation of secured claims may become important in different contexts, e.g., to determine the issue of adequate protection under § 361, impairment under § 1124, or treatment of the claim in a plan pursuant to § 1129(b) of the Code. This rule permits the issue to be raised on motion by a party in interest. The secured creditor is entitled to notice of the hearing on the motion and the court may direct that others in the case also receive such notice.

An adversary proceeding is commenced when the validity, priority, or extent of a lien is at issue as prescribed by Rule 7001. That proceeding is relevant to the basis of the lien itself while valuation under Rule 3012 would be for the purposes indicated above.

CROSS REFERENCES

Definition of—

Lien, see 11 USCA § 101.

Security, see 11 USCA § 101.

Security interest, see 11 USCA § 101.

Determination of secured status, see 11 USCA § 506.

Motions; form and service, see Fed.Rules Bankr.Proc. Rule 9013, 11 USCA.

American Digest System

Bankruptcy ☞2852.

Key Number System Topic No. 51.

Corpus Juris Secundum

CJS Bankruptcy § 1026, Secured Claims.

Rule 3013. Classification of Claims and Interests

For the purposes of the plan and its acceptance, the court may, on motion after hearing on notice as the court may direct, determine classes of creditors and equity security holders pursuant to §§ 1122, 1222(b)(1), and 1322(b)(1) of the Code.

(As amended Apr. 30, 1991, eff. Aug. 1, 1991.)

ADVISORY COMMITTEE NOTES

Sections 1122 and 1322(b)(1) set the standards for classifying claims and interests but provide that such classification is accomplished in the plan. This rule does not change the standards; rather it recognizes that it may be desirable or necessary to establish proper classification before a plan can be formulated. It provides for a court hearing on such notice as the court may direct.

1991 Amendments

This rule is amended to include chapter 12 cases.

CROSS REFERENCES

Motions; form and service, see Fed.Rules Bankr.Proc. Rule 9013, 11 USCA.

American Digest System

Bankruptcy ☞3550, 3682, 3707.

Key Number System Topic No. 51.

Corpus Juris Secundum

CJS Bankruptcy § 1173, Classification and Discrimination.

CJS Bankruptcy § 1192, Classification and Discrimination.

Rule 3014. Election Under § 1111(b) by Secured Creditor in Chapter 9 Municipality or Chapter 11 Reorganization Case

An election of application of § 1111(b)(2) of the Code by a class of secured creditors in a chapter 9 or 11 case may be made at any time prior to the conclusion of the hearing on the disclosure statement or within such later time as the court may fix. If the disclosure statement is conditionally approved pursuant to Rule 3017.1, and a final hearing on the disclosure statement is not held, the election of application of § 1111(b)(2) may be made not later than the date fixed pursuant to Rule 3017.1(a)(2) or another date the court may fix. The election shall be in writing and signed unless made at the hearing on the disclosure statement. The election, if made by the majorities required by § 1111(b)(1)(A)(i), shall be binding on all members of the class with respect to the plan.

(As amended Apr. 11, 1997, eff. Dec. 1, 1997.)

ADVISORY COMMITTEE NOTES

Pursuant to § 1111(b)(1) of the Code, a nonrecourse secured loan is converted, automatically, into a recourse loan thereby entitling the creditor to an unsecured deficiency claim if the value of the collateral is less than the debt. The class, however, may retain the loan as a nonrecourse loan by electing application of § 1111(b)(2) by the majorities stated in § 1111(b)(1)(A)(i). That section does not specify any time periods for making the election.

Rule 3014 provides that if no agreement is negotiated, the election of § 1111(b)(2) of the Code may be made at any time prior to conclusion of the hearing on the disclosure statement. Once the hearing has been concluded, it would be too late for a secured creditor class to demand different treatment unless the court has fixed a later time. This would be the case if, for example, a public class of secured creditors should have an approved disclosure statement prior to electing under § 1111(b).

Generally it is important that the proponent of a plan ascertain the position of the secured creditor class before a plan is proposed. The secured creditor class must know the prospects of its treatment under the plan before it can intelligently determine its rights under § 1111(b). The rule recognizes that there may be negotiations between the proponent of the plan and the secured creditor leading to a representation of desired treatment under § 1111(b). If that treatment is approved by the requisite majorities of the class and culminates in a written, signed statement filed with the court, that statement becomes binding and the class may not thereafter demand different treatment under § 1111(b) with respect to that plan. The proponent of the plan is thus enabled to seek approval of the disclosure statement and transmit the plan for voting in anticipation of confirmation. Only if that plan is not confirmed may the class of secured creditors thereafter change its prior election.

While this rule and the Code refer to a class of secured creditors it should be noted that ordinarily each secured creditor is in a separate and distinct class. In that event, the secured creditor has the sole power to determine application of § 1111(b) with respect to that claim.

1997 Amendments

This amendment provides a deadline for electing application of § 1111(b)(2) in a small business case in which a conditionally approved disclosure statement is finally approved without a hearing.

GAP Report on Rule 3014. No changes to the published draft.

CROSS REFERENCES

Hearing on disclosure statement, see Fed.Rules Bankr. Proc. Rule 3017, 11 USCA.

Reduction of time for election pursuant to § 1111(b) not permitted, see Fed.Rules Bankr.Proc. Rule 9006, 11 USCA.

American Digest System

Bankruptcy ☞2852.

Key Number System Topic No. 51.

Corpus Juris Secundum

CJS Bankruptcy § 309, Reduction.

Rule 3015.   Filing, Objection to Confirmation, and Modification of a Plan in a Chapter 12 Family Farmer's Debt Adjustment or a Chapter 13 Individual's Debt Adjustment Case

(a) Chapter 12 plan

The debtor may file a chapter 12 plan with the petition. If a plan is not filed with the petition, it shall be filed within the time prescribed by § 1221 of the Code.

(b) Chapter 13 plan

The debtor may file a chapter 13 plan with the petition. If a plan is not filed with the petition, it shall be filed within 14 days thereafter, and such time may not be further extended except for cause shown and on notice as the court may direct. If a case is converted to chapter 13, a plan shall be filed within 14 days thereafter, and such time may not be further extended except for cause shown and on notice as the court may direct.

(c) Dating

Every proposed plan and any modification thereof shall be dated.

(d) Notice and copies

The plan or a summary of the plan shall be included with each notice of the hearing on confirmation mailed pursuant to Rule 2002. If required by the court, the debtor shall furnish a sufficient number of copies to enable the clerk to include a copy of the plan with the notice of the hearing.

(e) Transmission to United States trustee

The clerk shall forthwith transmit to the United States trustee a copy of the plan and any modification thereof filed pursuant to subdivision (a) or (b) of this rule.

(f) Objection to confirmation; determination of good faith in the absence of an objection

An objection to confirmation of a plan shall be filed and served on the debtor, the trustee, and any other entity designated by the court, and shall be transmitted to the United States trustee, before confirmation of the plan. An objection to confirmation is governed by Rule 9014. If no objection is timely filed, the court may determine that the plan has been proposed in good faith and not by any means forbidden by law without receiving evidence on such issues.

(g) Modification of plan after confirmation

A request to modify a plan pursuant to § 1229 or § 1329 of the Code shall identify the proponent and shall be filed together with the proposed modification. The clerk, or some other person as the court may direct, shall give the debtor, the trustee, and all creditors not less than 21 days' notice by mail of the time fixed for filing objections and, if an objection is filed, the hearing to consider the proposed modification, unless the court orders otherwise with respect to creditors who are not affected by the proposed modification. A copy of the notice shall be transmitted to the United States trustee. A copy of the proposed modification, or a summary thereof, shall be included with the notice. If required by the court, the proponent shall furnish a sufficient number of copies of the proposed modification, or a summary thereof, to enable the clerk to include a copy with each notice. Any objection to the proposed modification shall be filed and served on the debtor, the trustee, and any other entity designated by the court, and shall be transmitted to the United States trustee. An objection to a proposed modification is governed by Rule 9014.

(As amended Apr. 30, 1991, eff. Aug. 1, 1991; Apr. 22, 1993, eff. Aug. 1, 1993; Mar. 26, 2009, eff. Dec. 1, 2009.)

ADVISORY COMMITTEE NOTES

Section 1321 provides only that the "debtor shall file a plan." No time periods are specified, nor is any other detail provided. The rule requires a chapter 13 plan to be filed either with the petition or within 15 days thereafter. The court may, for cause, extend the time. The rule permits a summary of the plan to be transmitted with the notice of the hearing on confirmation. The court may, however, require the plan itself to be transmitted and the debtor to supply enough copies for this purpose. In the former rules under Chapter XIII [former § 1001 et seq. of this title] the plan would accompany the notice of the first meeting of creditors. It is more important for the plan or a summary of its terms to be sent with the notice of the confirmation hearing. At that hearing objections to the plan will be heard by the court.

1991 Amendments

This rule is amended to include chapter 12 plans. Section 1221 of the Code requires the debtor to file a chapter 12 plan not later than 90 days after the order for relief, except that the court may extend the period if an extension is "substantially justified."

Subdivision (e) enables the United States trustee to monitor chapter 12 and chapter 13 plans pursuant to 28 U.S.C. § 586(a)(3)(C).

1993 Amendments

Subdivision (b) is amended to provide a time limit for filing a plan after a case has been converted to chapter 13. The substitution of "may" for "shall" is stylistic and makes no substantive change.

Subdivision (d) is amended to clarify that the plan or a summary of the plan must be included with each notice of the confirmation hearing in a chapter 12 case pursuant to Rule 2002(a).

Subdivision (f) is added to expand the scope of the rule to govern objections to confirmation in chapter 12 and chapter 13 cases. The subdivision also is amended to include a provision that permits the court, in the absence of an objection, to determine that the plan has been proposed in good faith and not by any means forbidden by law without the need to receive evidence on these issues. These matters are now governed by Rule 3020.

Subdivision (g) is added to provide a procedure for post-confirmation modification of chapter 12 and chapter 13 plans. These procedures are designed to be similar to the procedures for confirmation of plans. However, if no objection is filed with respect to a proposed modification of a plan after confirmation, the court is not required to hold a hearing. *See* § 1229(b)(2) and § 1329(b)(2) which provide that the plan as modified becomes the plan unless, after notice and a hearing, such modification is disapproved. *See* § 102(1). The notice of the time fixed for filing objections to the proposed modification should set a date for a hearing to be held in the event that an objection is filed.

Amendments to the title of this rule are stylistic and make no substantive change.

2009 Amendments

The rule is amended to implement changes in connection with the amendment to Rule 9006(a) and the manner by which time is computed under the rules. The deadlines in the rule are amended to substitute a deadline that is a multiple of seven days. Throughout the rules, deadlines are amended in the following manner:

- 5–day periods become 7–day periods
- 10–day periods become 14–day periods
- 15–day periods become 14–day periods
- 20–day periods become 21–day periods
- 25–day periods become 28–day periods

CROSS REFERENCES

Acceptance or rejection of plans, see Fed.Rules Bankr.Proc. Rule 3018, 11 USCA.

Deposit; confirmation of plan, see Fed.Rules Bankr.Proc. Rule 3020, 11 USCA.

Reduction of time for filing plan not permitted, see Fed. Rules Bankr.Proc. Rule 9006, 11 USCA.

LIBRARY REFERENCES

American Digest System

Bankruptcy ⇔3681 to 3684, 3704.1, 3713, 3715.
Key Number System Topic No. 51.

Corpus Juris Secundum

CJS Bankruptcy § 309, Reduction.

CJS Bankruptcy § 1170, Filing and Contents of Plan, Generally.

CJS Bankruptcy § 1183, Modification of Plan After Confirmation.

CJS Bankruptcy § 1188, Filing and Requisites of Plan, Generally.

CJS Bankruptcy § 1202, Generally; Objections to Confirmation.

CJS Bankruptcy § 1206, Postconfirmation Modification--Procedure and Burden of Proof.

Rule 3016. Filing of Plan and Disclosure Statement in a Chapter 9 Municipality or Chapter 11 Reorganization Case

(a) Identification of plan

Every proposed plan and any modification thereof shall be dated and, in a chapter 11 case, identified with the name of the entity or entities submitting or filing it.

(b) Disclosure statement

In a chapter 9 or 11 case, a disclosure statement under § 1125 of the Code or evidence showing compliance with § 1126(b) shall be filed with the plan or within a time fixed by the court, unless the plan is intended to provide adequate information under § 1125(f)(1). If the plan is intended to provide adequate information under § 1125(f)(1), it shall be so designated and Rule 3017.1 shall apply as if the plan is a disclosure statement.

(c) Injunction under a plan

If a plan provides for an injunction against conduct not otherwise enjoined under the Code, the plan and disclosure statement shall describe in specific and conspicuous language (bold, italic, or underlined text) all acts to be enjoined and identify the entities that would be subject to the injunction.

(d) Standard form small business disclosure statement and plan

In a small business case, the court may approve a disclosure statement and may confirm a plan that conform substantially to the appropriate Official Forms or other standard forms approved by the court.

(As amended Mar. 30, 1987, eff. Aug. 1, 1987; Apr. 30, 1991, eff. Aug. 1, 1991; Apr. 23, 1996, eff. Dec. 1, 1996; Apr. 23, 2001, eff. Dec. 1, 2001; Apr. 23, 2008, eff. Dec. 1, 2008.)

ADVISORY COMMITTEE NOTES

This rule implements the Code provisions concerning the filing of plans in chapters 9 and 11.

Chapter 9 Cases. Section 941 provides that the debtor may file a plan with the petition or thereafter but within a time fixed by the court. A rule, therefore, is unnecessary to specify the time for filing chapter 9 plans.

Chapter 11 Nonrailroad Cases. Section 1121 contains detailed provisions with respect to who may file a chapter 11 plan and, in part, the time period. Section 1121(a) permits a debtor to file a plan with the petition or at any time during the case. Section 1121(b) and (c) grants exclusive periods of 120 days and 180 days for the debtor to file and obtain acceptance of a plan. Failure to take advantage of these periods or the appointment of a trustee would permit other parties in interest to file a plan. These statutory provisions are not repeated in the rules.

Chapter 11 Railroad Cases. Pursuant to subchapter IV of chapter 11, § 1121 of the Code is applicable in railroad cases;

see §§ 1161, 103(g). A trustee, however, is to be appointed in every case; thus, pursuant to § 1121(c), any party in interest may file a plan. See discussion of subdivision (a) of this rule, infra.

Subdivision (a). Section 1121(c), while permitting parties in interest a limited right to file plans, does not provide any time limitation. This subdivision sets as the deadline, the conclusion of the hearing on the disclosure statement. The court may, however, grant additional time. It is derived from former Chapter X Rule 10–301(c)(2) which used, as the cut-off time, the conclusion of the hearing on approval of a plan. As indicated, supra, § 1121(a) permits a debtor to file a plan at any time during the chapter 11 case. Under § 1121(c), parties other than a debtor may file a plan only after a trustee is appointed or the debtor's exclusive time expires.

Subdivision (b) requires plans to be properly identified.

Subdivision (c). This provision is new. In chapter 9 and 11 cases (including railroad reorganization cases) postpetition solicitation of votes on a plan requires transmittal of a disclosure statement, the contents of which have been approved by the court. See § 1125 of the Code. A prepetition solicitation must either have been in conformity with applicable nonbankruptcy law or, if none, the disclosure must have been of adequate information as set forth in § 1125 of the Code. See § 1126(b). Subdivision (c) of this rule provides the time for filing the disclosure statement or evidence of compliance with § 1126(b) which ordinarily will be with the plan but the court may allow a later time or the court may, pursuant to the last sentence, fix a time certain. Rule 3017 deals with the hearing on the disclosure statement. The disclosure statement, pursuant to § 1125 is to contain adequate information. "Adequate information" is defined in § 1125(a) as information that would permit a reasonable creditor or equity security holder to make an informed judgment on the plan.

1991 Amendments

Subdivision (a) is amended to enlarge the time for filing competing plans. A party in interest may not file a plan without leave of court only if an order approving a disclosure statement relating to another plan has been entered and a decision on confirmation of the plan has not been entered. This subdivision does not fix a deadline beyond which a debtor may not file a plan.

1996 Amendments

Section 1121(c) gives a party in interest the right to file a chapter 11 plan after expiration of the period when only the debtor may file a plan. Under § 1121(d), the exclusive period in which only the debtor may file a plan may be extended, but only if a party in interest so requests and the court, after notice and a hearing, finds cause for an extension. Subdivision (a) is abrogated because it could have the effect of extending the debtor's exclusive period for filing a plan without satisfying the requirements of § 1121(d). The abrogation of subdivision (a) does not affect the court's discretion with respect to the scheduling of hearings on the approval of disclosure statements when more than one plan has been filed.

The amendment to subdivision (c), redesignated as subdivision (b), is stylistic.

GAP Report on Rule 3016. No changes since publication, except for a stylistic change.

2001 Amendments

Subdivision (c) is added to assure that entities whose conduct would be enjoined under a plan, rather than by operation of the Code, are given adequate notice of the proposed injunction. The validity and effect of any injunction are substantive law matters that are beyond the scope of these rules.

Specific and conspicuous language is not necessary if the injunction contained in the plan is substantially the same as an injunction provided under the Code. For example, if a plan contains an injunction against acts to collect a discharged debt from the debtor, Rule 3016(c) would not apply because that conduct would be enjoined nonetheless under § 524(a)(2). But if a plan provides that creditors will be permanently enjoined from asserting claims against persons who are not debtors in the case, the plan and disclosure statement must highlight the injunctive language and comply with the requirements of Rule 3016(c). See § 524(e).

The requirement in this rule that the plan and disclosure statement identify the entities that would be subject to the injunction requires reasonable identification under the circumstances. If the entities that would be subject to the injunction cannot be identified by name, the plan and disclosure statement may describe them by class or category. For example, it may be sufficient to identify the subjects of the injunction as "all creditors of the debtor."

CHANGES MADE AFTER PUBLICATION AND COMMENTS

The word "highlighted" in the parenthesis was replaced with "underlined" because highlighted documents are difficult to scan electronically for inclusion in the clerks' files. The Committee Note was revised to put in a more prominent position the statement that the validity and effect of any injunction provided for in a plan are substantive matters beyond the scope of the rules. Other stylistic changes were made to the Committee Note.

2008 Amendments

Subdivision (b) is amended to recognize that, in 2005, § 1125(f)(1) was added to the Code to provide that the plan proponent in a small business case need not file a disclosure statement if the plan itself includes adequate information and the court finds that a separate disclosure statement is unnecessary. If the plan is intended to provide adequate information in a small business case, it may be conditionally approved as a disclosure statement under Rule 3017.1 and is subject to all other rules applicable to disclosure statements in small business cases.

Subdivision (d) is added to the rule to implement § 433 of the Bankruptcy Abuse Prevention and Consumer Protection Act of 2005 which requires the promulgation of Official Forms for plans and disclosure statements in small business cases. Section 1125(f)(2) of the Code provides that the court may approve a disclosure statement submitted on the appropriate Official Form or on a standard form approved by the court. The rule takes no position on whether a court may require a local standard form disclosure statement or plan of reorganization in lieu of the Official Forms.

Other amendments are stylistic.

Filing of municipality debt adjustment plan, see 11 USCA § 941.

Hearing on disclosure statement, see Fed.Rules Bankr. Proc. Rule 3017, 11 USCA.

LIBRARY REFERENCES

American Digest System

Bankruptcy ⊕3481, 3533.1 to 3535, 3539.1, 3540.

Key Number System Topic No. 51.

Corpus Juris Secundum

CJS Bankruptcy § 101, Chapter 11.

CJS Bankruptcy § 1118, Filing of Plan and Disclosure Statement; Hearing on Objections.

CJS Bankruptcy § 1151, Filing and Contents of Disclosure Statement.

Rule 3017. Court Consideration of Disclosure Statement in a Chapter 9 Municipality or Chapter 11 Reorganization Case

(a) Hearing on disclosure statement and objections

Except as provided in Rule 3017.1, after a disclosure statement is filed in accordance with Rule 3016(b), the court shall hold a hearing on at least 28 days' notice to the debtor, creditors, equity security holders and other parties in interest as provided in Rule 2002 to consider the disclosure statement and any objections or modifications thereto. The plan and the disclosure statement shall be mailed with the notice of the hearing only to the debtor, any trustee or committee appointed under the Code, the Securities and Exchange Commission and any party in interest who requests in writing a copy of the statement or plan. Objections to the disclosure statement shall be filed and served on the debtor, the trustee, any committee appointed under the Code, and any other entity designated by the court, at any time before the disclosure statement is approved or by an earlier date as the court may fix. In a chapter 11 reorganization case, every notice, plan, disclosure statement, and objection required to be served or mailed pursuant to this subdivision shall be transmitted to the United States trustee within the time provided in this subdivision.

(b) Determination on disclosure statement

Following the hearing the court shall determine whether the disclosure statement should be approved.

(c) Dates fixed for voting on plan and confirmation

On or before approval of the disclosure statement, the court shall fix a time within which the holders of claims and interests may accept or reject the plan and may fix a date for the hearing on confirmation.

(d) Transmission and notice to United States trustee, creditors and equity security holders

Upon approval of a disclosure statement,— [1]except to the extent that the court orders otherwise with respect to one or more unimpaired classes of creditors or equity security holders—the debtor in possession, trustee, proponent of the plan, or clerk as the court orders shall mail to all creditors and equity security holders, and in a chapter 11 reorganization case shall transmit to the United States trustee,

(1) the plan or a court-approved summary of the plan;

(2) the disclosure statement approved by the court;

(3) notice of the time within which acceptances and rejections of the plan may be filed; and

(4) any other information as the court may direct, including any court opinion approving the disclosure statement or a court-approved summary of the opinion.

In addition, notice of the time fixed for filing objections and the hearing on confirmation shall be mailed to all creditors and equity security holders in accordance with Rule 2002(b), and a form of ballot conforming to the appropriate Official Form shall be mailed to creditors and equity security holders entitled to vote on the plan. If the court opinion is not transmitted or only a summary of the plan is transmitted, the court opinion or the plan shall be provided on request of a party in interest at the plan proponent's expense. If the court orders that the disclosure statement and the plan or a summary of the plan shall not be mailed to any unimpaired class, notice that the class is designated in the plan as unimpaired and notice of the name and address of the person from whom the plan or summary of the plan and disclosure statement may be obtained upon request and at the plan proponent's expense, shall be mailed to members of the unimpaired class together with the notice of the time fixed for filing objections to and the hearing on confirmation. For the purposes of this subdivision, creditors and equity security holders shall include holders of stock, bonds, debentures, notes, and other securities of record on the date the order approving the disclosure statement is entered or another date fixed by the court, for cause, after notice and a hearing.

(e) Transmission to beneficial holders of securities

At the hearing held pursuant to subdivision (a) of this rule, the court shall consider the procedures for transmitting the documents and information required by subdivision (d) of this rule to beneficial holders of stock, bonds, debentures, notes, and other securities, determine the adequacy of the procedures, and enter any orders the court deems appropriate.

(f) Notice and transmission of documents to entities subject to an injunction under a plan

If a plan provides for an injunction against conduct not otherwise enjoined under the Code and an entity that would be subject to the injunction is not a creditor or equity security holder, at the hearing held under Rule 3017(a), the court shall consider procedures for providing the entity with:

(1) at least 28 days' notice of the time fixed for filing objections and the hearing on confirmation of the plan containing the information described in Rule 2002(c)(3); and

(2) to the extent feasible, a copy of the plan and disclosure statement.

(As amended Mar. 30, 1987, eff. Aug. 1, 1987; Apr. 30, 1991, eff. Aug. 1, 1991; Apr. 11, 1997, eff. Dec. 1, 1997; Apr. 23, 2001, eff. Dec. 1, 2001; Mar. 26, 2009, eff. Dec. 1, 2009.)

1 So in original. The comma probably should not appear.

ADVISORY COMMITTEE NOTES

This rule is adapted from former Rule 10–303 which dealt with the approval of a Chapter X plan by the court. There is no requirement for plan approval in a chapter 9 or 11 case under the Code but there is the requirement that a disclosure statement containing adequate financial information be approved by the court after notice and a hearing before votes on a plan are solicited. Section 1125(b) of the Code is made applicable in chapter 9 cases by § 901(a). It is also applicable in railroad reorganization cases under subchapter IV of chapter 11; see § 1161 of the Code.

Subdivision (a) of this rule provides for the hearing on the disclosure statement. Thus, a hearing would be required in all cases; whether it may be ex parte would depend on the circumstances of the case, but a mere absence of objections would not eliminate the need for a hearing; see § 102(1) of the Code.

No provision similar to former Rule 10–303(f) is included. That subdivision together with former Rule 10–304 prohibited solicitation of votes until after entry of an order approving the plan. Section 1125(b) of the Code explicitly provides that votes on a plan may not be solicited until a disclosure statement approved by the court is transmitted. Pursuant to the change in rulemaking power, a comparable provision in this rule is unnecessary. 28 U.S.C. § 2075.

Copies of the disclosure statement and plan need not be mailed with the notice of the hearing or otherwise transmitted prior to the hearing except with respect to the parties explicitly set forth in the subdivision.

It should be noted that, by construction, the singular includes the plural. Therefore, the phrase "plan or plans" or "disclosure statement or statements" has not been used although the possibility of multiple plans and statements is recognized.

Subdivision (d) permits the court to require a party other than the clerk of the bankruptcy court to bear the responsibility for transmitting the notices and documents specified in the rule when votes on the plan are solicited. Ordinarily the person responsible for such mailing will be the proponent of the plan. In rare cases the clerk may be directed to mail these documents, particularly when the trustee would have the responsibility but there is insufficient money in the estate to enable the trustee to perform this task.

1987 Amendments

Subdivision (d). Section 1125(c) of the Code requires that the entire approved disclosure statement be provided in connection with voting on a plan. The court is authorized by § 1125(c) to approve different disclosure statements for different classes. Although the rule does not permit the mailing of a summary of the disclosure statement in place of the approved disclosure statement, the court may approve a summary of the disclosure statement to be mailed with the complete disclosure statement to those voting on the plan.

1991 Amendments

This rule is amended to enable the United States trustee to monitor and comment with regard to chapter 11 disclosure statements and plans. The United States trustee does not perform these functions in a chapter 9 municipal debt adjustment case. See 28 U.S.C. § 586(a)(3)(B).

Subdivision (d) is amended to give the court the discretion to direct that one or more unimpaired classes shall not receive disclosure statements, plans, or summaries of plans. Members of unimpaired classes are not entitled to vote on the plan. Although disclosure statements enable members of unimpaired classes to make informed judgments as to whether to object to confirmation because of lack of feasibility or other grounds, in an unusual case the court may direct that disclosure statements shall not be sent to such classes if to do so would not be feasible considering the size of the unimpaired classes and the expense of printing and mailing. In any event, all creditors are entitled to notice of the time fixed for filing objections and notice of the hearing to consider confirmation of the plan pursuant to Rule 2002(b) and the requirement of such notice may not be excused with respect to unimpaired classes. The amendment to subdivision (d) also ensures that the members of unimpaired classes who do not receive such documents will have sufficient information so that they may request these documents in advance of the hearing on confirmation. The amendment to subdivision (d) is not intended to give the court the discretion to dispense with the mailing of the plan and disclosure statement to governmental units holding claims entitled to priority under § 507(a)(7) because they may not be classified. See § 1123(a)(1).

The words "with the court" in subdivision (a) are deleted as unnecessary. See Rules 5005(a) and 9001(3). Reference to the Official Form number in subdivision (d) is deleted in anticipation of future revision and renumbering of the Official Forms.

Subdivision (e) is designed to ensure that appropriate measures are taken for the plan, disclosure statement, ballot and other materials which are required to be transmitted to creditors and equity security holders under this rule to reach the beneficial holders of securities held in nominee name. Such measures may include orders directing the trustee or debtor in possession to reimburse the nominees out of the funds of the estate for the expenses incurred by them in distributing materials to beneficial holders. In most cases, the plan proponent will not know the identities of the beneficial holders and therefore it will be necessary to rely on the nominal holders of the securities to distribute the plan materials to the beneficial owners.

1997 Amendments

Subdivision (a) is amended to provide that it does not apply to the extent provided in new Rule 3017.1, which applies in small business cases.

Subdivision (d) is amended to provide flexibility in fixing the record date for the purpose of determining the holders of securities who are entitled to receive documents pursuant to this subdivision. For example, if there may be a delay between the oral announcement of the judge's order approving the disclosure statement and entry of the order on the court docket, the court may fix the date on which the judge orally approves the disclosure statement as the record date so that the parties may expedite preparation of the lists necessary to facilitate the distribution of the plan, disclosure statement, ballots, and other related documents.

The court may set a record date pursuant to subdivision (d) only after notice and a hearing as provided in § 102(1) of the Code. Notice of a request for an order fixing the record date may be included in the notice of the hearing to consider approval of the disclosure statement mailed pursuant to Rule 2002(b).

If the court fixes a record date pursuant to subdivision (d) with respect to the holders of securities, and the holders are impaired by the plan, the judge also should order that the same record date applies for the purpose of determining eligibility for voting pursuant to Rule 3018(a).

Other amendments to this rule are stylistic.

GAP Report on Rule 3017. No changes to the published draft.

2001 Amendments

Subdivision (f) is added to assure that entities whose conduct would be enjoined under a plan, rather than by operation of the Code, and who will not receive the documents listed in subdivision (d) because they are neither creditors nor equity security holders, are provided with adequate notice of the proposed injunction. It does not address any substantive law issues relating to the validity or effect of any injunction provided under a plan, or any due process or other constitutional issues relating to notice. These issues are beyond the scope of these rules and are left for judicial determination.

This rule recognizes the need for adequate notice to subjects of an injunction, but that reasonable flexibility under the circumstances may be required. If a known and identifiable entity would be subject to the injunction, and the notice, plan, and disclosure statement could be mailed to that entity, the court should require that they be mailed at the same time that the plan, disclosure statement and related documents are mailed to creditors under Rule 3017(d). If mailing notices and other documents is not feasible because the entities subject to the injunction are described in the plan and disclosure statement by class or category and they cannot be identified individually by name and address, the court may require that notice under Rule 3017(f)(1) be published.

CHANGES MADE AFTER PUBLICATION AND COMMENTS

No changes were made in the text of the proposed amendments since publication. The Committee Note was revised to put in a more prominent position the statement that the rule does not address related substantive law issues which are beyond the scope of the rules.

2009 Amendments

The rule is amended to implement changes in connection with the amendment to Rule 9006(a) and the manner by which time is computed under the rules. The deadlines in the rule are amended to substitute a deadline that is a multiple of seven days. Throughout the rules, deadlines are amended in the following manner:

- 5–day periods become 7–day periods
- 10–day periods become 14–day periods
- 15–day periods become 14–day periods
- 20–day periods become 21–day periods
- 25–day periods become 28–day periods

CROSS REFERENCES

Acceptance or rejection of plan—

    Eligible persons, see Fed.Rules Bankr.Proc. Rule 3018, 11 USCA.

    Preference among more than one plan, see Fed.Rules Bankr.Proc. Rule 3018, 11 USCA.

Disclosure statement—

    Different statements as between different classes of claims, see 11 USCA § 1125.

    Right to be heard on adequacy of information, see 11 USCA § 1125.

    Solicitation of plan's acceptance, see 11 USCA § 1125.

Notice of—

    Time fixed for plan's acceptance or rejection in accord with this rule, see Fed.Rules Bankr.Proc. Rule 2002, 11 USCA.

Proof of right to record status filed by security holder, see Fed.Rules Bankr.Proc. Rule 3003, 11 USCA.

LIBRARY REFERENCES

American Digest System

Bankruptcy ⫘3481, 3539.1, 3540.

Key Number System Topic No. 51.

Corpus Juris Secundum

CJS Bankruptcy § 101, Chapter 11.

CJS Bankruptcy § 1118, Filing of Plan and Disclosure Statement; Hearing on Objections.

CJS Bankruptcy § 1119, Acceptance of Rejection of Plan by Claim Holders.

CJS Bankruptcy § 1123, Hearing and Order.

CJS Bankruptcy § 1153, In Small Business Cases.

Rule 3017.1. Court Consideration of Disclosure Statement in a Small Business Case

(a) Conditional approval of disclosure statement

In a small business case, the court may, on application of the plan proponent or on its own initiative, conditionally approve a disclosure statement filed in accordance with Rule 3016. On or before conditional approval of the disclosure statement, the court shall:

    (1) fix a time within which the holders of claims and interests may accept or reject the plan;

(2) fix a time for filing objections to the disclosure statement;

(3) fix a date for the hearing on final approval of the disclosure statement to be held if a timely objection is filed; and

(4) fix a date for the hearing on confirmation.

(b) Application of Rule 3017

Rule 3017(a), (b), (c), and (e) do not apply to a conditionally approved disclosure statement. Rule 3017(d) applies to a conditionally approved disclosure statement, except that conditional approval is considered approval of the disclosure statement for the purpose of applying Rule 3017(d).

(c) Final approval

(1) Notice

Notice of the time fixed for filing objections and the hearing to consider final approval of the disclosure statement shall be given in accordance with Rule 2002 and may be combined with notice of the hearing on confirmation of the plan.

(2) Objections

Objections to the disclosure statement shall be filed, transmitted to the United States trustee, and served on the debtor, the trustee, any committee appointed under the Code and any other entity designated by the court at any time before final approval of the disclosure statement or by an earlier date as the court may fix.

(3) Hearing

If a timely objection to the disclosure statement is filed, the court shall hold a hearing to consider final approval before or combined with the hearing on confirmation of the plan.

(Added Apr. 11, 1997, eff. Dec. 1, 1997; amended Apr. 23, 2008, eff. Dec. 1, 2008.)

ADVISORY COMMITTEE NOTES

1997 Amendment

This rule is added to implement § 1125(f), which was added to the Code by the Bankruptcy Reform Act of 1994.

The procedures for electing to be considered a small business are set forth in Rule 1020. If the debtor is a small business and has elected to be considered a small business, § 1125(f) permits the court to conditionally approve a disclosure statement subject to final approval after notice and a hearing. If a disclosure statement is conditionally approved, and no timely objection to the disclosure statement is filed, it is not necessary for the court to hold a hearing on final approval.

GAP Report on Rule 3017.1. No changes to the published draft.

2008 Amendments

Section 101 of the Code, as amended in 2005, defines a "small business case" and "small business debtor," and elimi-

nates any need to elect that status. Therefore, the reference in the rule to an election is deleted.

As provided in the amendment to Rule 3016(b), a plan intended to provide adequate information in a small business case under § 1125(f)(1) may be conditionally approved and is otherwise treated as a disclosure statement under this rule.

LIBRARY REFERENCES

American Digest System

Bankruptcy ☞3533.1 to 3535, 3539.1, 3540.

Key Number System Topic No. 51.

Corpus Juris Secundum

CJS Bankruptcy § 1118, Filing of Plan and Disclosure Statement; Hearing on Objections.

CJS Bankruptcy § 1153, In Small Business Cases.

Rule 3018. Acceptance or Rejection of Plan in a Chapter 9 Municipality or a Chapter 11 Reorganization Case

(a) Entities entitled to accept or reject plan; time for acceptance or rejection

A plan may be accepted or rejected in accordance with § 1126 of the Code within the time fixed by the court pursuant to Rule 3017. Subject to subdivision (b) of this rule, an equity security holder or creditor whose claim is based on a security of record shall not be entitled to accept or reject a plan unless the equity security holder or creditor is the holder of record of the security on the date the order approving the disclosure statement is entered or on another date fixed by the court, for cause, after notice and a hearing. For cause shown, the court after notice and hearing may permit a creditor or equity security holder to change or withdraw an acceptance or rejection. Notwithstanding objection to a claim or interest, the court after notice and hearing may temporarily allow the claim or interest in an amount which the court deems proper for the purpose of accepting or rejecting a plan.

(b) Acceptances or rejections obtained before petition

An equity security holder or creditor whose claim is based on a security of record who accepted or rejected the plan before the commencement of the case shall not be deemed to have accepted or rejected the plan pursuant to § 1126(b) of the Code unless the equity security holder or creditor was the holder of record of the security on the date specified in the solicitation of such acceptance or rejection for the purposes of such solicitation. A holder of a claim or interest who has accepted or rejected a plan before the commencement of the case under the Code shall not be deemed to have accepted or rejected the plan if the court finds after notice and hearing that the plan was not transmitted to substantially all creditors and equity security holders of the same class, that an unreasonably short time was prescribed for such creditors and equity security holders to accept or reject the plan, or that the solicitation was not in compliance with § 1126(b) of the Code.

(c) Form of acceptance or rejection

An acceptance or rejection shall be in writing, identify the plan or plans accepted or rejected, be signed by the creditor or equity security holder or an authorized agent, and conform to the appropriate Official Form. If more than one plan is transmitted pursuant to Rule 3017, an acceptance or rejection may be filed by each creditor or equity security holder for any number of plans transmitted and if acceptances are filed for more than one plan, the creditor or equity security holder may indicate a preference or preferences among the plans so accepted.

(d) Acceptance or rejection by partially secured creditor

A creditor whose claim has been allowed in part as a secured claim and in part as an unsecured claim shall be entitled to accept or reject a plan in both capacities.
(As amended Mar. 30, 1987, eff. Aug. 1, 1987; Apr. 30, 1991, eff. Aug. 1, 1991; Apr. 22, 1993, eff. Aug. 1, 1993; Apr. 11, 1997, eff. Dec. 1, 1997.)

ADVISORY COMMITTEE NOTES

This rule applies in chapter 9, 11 and 13 cases under the Code. The references in the rule to equity security holders will not, however, be relevant in chapter 9 or 13 cases. The rule will be of little utility in a chapter 13 case because only secured creditors may be requested to vote on a plan; unsecured creditors are not entitled to vote; see § 1325(a)(4), (5) of the Code.

Subdivision (a) is derived from former Rule 10–305(a). It substitutes, in a reorganization case, entry of the order approving the disclosure statement for the order approving a plan in conformity with the differences between Chapter X [former § 501 et seq. of this title] and chapter 11. In keeping with the underlying theory, it continues to recognize that the lapse of time between the filing of the petition and entry of such order will normally be significant and, during that interim, bonds and equity interests can change ownership.

Subdivision (b) recognizes the former Chapter XI [former § 701 et seq. of this title] practice permitting a plan and acceptances to be filed with the petition, as does § 1126(b) of the Code. However, because a plan under chapter 11 may affect shareholder interests, there should be reference to a record date of ownership. In this instance the appropriate record date is that used in the prepetition solicitation materials because it is those acceptances or rejections which are being submitted to the court.

While § 1126(c), (d), and (e) prohibits use of an acceptance or rejection not procured in good faith, the added provision in subdivision (b) of the rule is somewhat more detailed. It would prohibit use of prepetition acceptances or rejections when some but not all impaired creditors or equity security holders are solicited or when they are not given a reasonable opportunity to submit their acceptances or rejections. This provision together with § 1126(e) gives the court the power to nullify abusive solicitation procedures.

Subdivision (c). It is possible that multiple plans may be before the court for confirmation. Pursuant to § 1129(c) of the Code, the court may confirm only one plan but is required to consider the preferences expressed by those accepting the plans in determining which one to confirm.

Subdivisions (d) and (e) of former Rule 10–305 are not continued since comparable provisions are contained in the statute; see § 1126(c), (d), (e).

It should be noted that while the singular "plan" is used throughout, by construction the plural is included; see § 102(7).

1991 Amendments

Subdivisions (a) and (b) are amended to delete provisions that duplicate § 1126 of the Code. An entity who is not a record holder of a security, but who claims that it is entitled to be treated as a record holder, may file a statement pursuant to Rule 3003(d).

Subdivision (a) is amended further to allow the court to permit a creditor or equity security holder to change or withdraw an acceptance or rejection for cause shown whether or not the time fixed for voting has expired.

Subdivision (b) is also amended to give effect to a prepetition acceptance or rejection if solicitation requirements were satisfied with respect to substantially all members of the same class, instead of requiring proper solicitation with respect to substantially all members of all classes.

Subdivision (c) is amended to delete the Official Form number in anticipation of future revision and renumbering of the Official Forms.

1993 Amendments

The title of this rule is amended to indicate that it applies only in a chapter 9 or a chapter 11 case. The amendment of the word "Plans" to "Plan" is stylistic.

1997 Amendments

Subdivision (a) is amended to provide flexibility in fixing the record date for the purpose of determining the holders of securities who are entitled to vote on the plan. For example, if there may be a delay between the oral announcement of the judge's decision approving the disclosure statement and entry of the order on the court docket, the court may fix the date on which the judge orally approves the disclosure statement as the record date for voting purposes so that the parties may expedite preparation of the lists necessary to facilitate the distribution of the plan, disclosure statement, ballots, and other related documents in connection with the solicitation of votes.

The court may set a record date pursuant to subdivision (a) only after notice and a hearing as provided in § 102(1) of the Code. Notice of a request for an order fixing the record date may be included in the notice of the hearing to consider approval of the disclosure statement mailed pursuant to Rule 2002(b).

If the court fixes the record date for voting purposes, the judge also should order that the same record date shall apply for the purpose of distributing the documents required to be distributed pursuant to Rule 3017(d).

GAP Report on Rule 3018. No changes to the published draft.

Acceptance of altered or modified plan, see 11 USCA § 1127.

Disqualification of votes on acceptance in absence of good faith, see 11 USCA § 1126.

Filing of plan in—

Individual debt adjustment case, see Fed.Rules Bankr. Proc. Rule 3015, 11 USCA.

Municipality debt adjustment and reorganization cases, with disclosure statement, see Fed.Rules Bankr.Proc. Rule 3016, 11 USCA.

Proof of right to record status filed by security holder, see Fed.Rules Bankr.Proc. Rule 3003, 11 USCA.

LIBRARY REFERENCES

American Digest System

Bankruptcy ⊛3481, 3541.1 to 3547.

Key Number System Topic No. 51.

Corpus Juris Secundum

CJS Bankruptcy § 1119, Acceptance of Rejection of Plan by Claim Holders.

CJS Bankruptcy § 1156, Deemed Acceptance or Rejection; Unimpaired Classes.

CJS Bankruptcy § 1157, Acceptance of the Plan--Eligibility to Vote; Impairment.

CJS Bankruptcy § 1158, Number of Creditors and Amount of Claims Concurring; Withdrawal.

CJS Bankruptcy § 1202, Generally; Objections to Confirmation.

Rule 3019. Modification of Accepted Plan in a Chapter 9 Municipality or a Chapter 11 Reorganization Case

(a) Modification of plan before confirmation

In a chapter 9 or chapter 11 case, after a plan has been accepted and before its confirmation, the proponent may file a modification of the plan. If the court finds after hearing on notice to the trustee, any committee appointed under the Code, and any other entity designated by the court that the proposed modification does not adversely change the treatment of the claim of any creditor or the interest of any equity security holder who has not accepted in writing the modification, it shall be deemed accepted by all creditors and equity security holders who have previously accepted the plan.

(b) Modification of plan after confirmation in individual debtor case

If the debtor is an individual, a request to modify the plan under § 1127(e) of the Code is governed by Rule 9014. The request shall identify the proponent and shall be filed together with the proposed modification. The clerk, or some other person as the court may direct, shall give the debtor, the trustee, and all creditors not less than 21 days' notice by mail of the time fixed to file objections and, if an objection is filed, the hearing to consider the proposed modification, unless the court orders otherwise with respect to creditors who are not affected by the proposed modification. A copy of the notice shall be transmitted to the United States trustee, together with a copy of the proposed modification. Any objection to the proposed modification shall be filed and served on the debtor, the proponent of the modification, the trustee, and any other entity designated by the court, and shall be transmitted to the United States trustee.

(As amended Mar. 30, 1987, eff. Aug. 1, 1987; Apr. 22, 1993, eff. Aug. 1, 1993; Apr. 23, 2008, eff. Dec. 1, 2008; Mar. 26, 2009, eff. Dec. 1, 2009.)

ADVISORY COMMITTEE NOTES

This rule implements §§ 942, 1127 and 1323 of the Code. For example, § 1127 provides for modification before and after confirmation but does not deal with the minor modifications that do not adversely change any rights. The rule makes clear that a modification may be made, after acceptance of the plan without submission to creditors and equity security holders if their interests are not affected. To come within this rule, the modification should be one that does not change the rights of a creditor or equity security holder as fixed in the plan before modification.

1993 Amendments

This rule is amended to limit its application to chapter 9 and chapter 11 cases. Modification of plans after confirmation in chapter 12 and chapter 13 cases is governed by Rule 3015. The addition of the comma in the second sentence is stylistic and makes no substantive change.

2008 Amendments

The 2005 amendments to § 1127 of the Code provide for modification of a confirmed plan in an individual debtor chapter 11 case. Therefore, the rule is amended to establish the procedure for filing and objecting to a proposed modification of a confirmed plan.

2009 Amendments

The rule is amended to implement changes in connection with the amendment to Rule 9006(a) and the manner by which time is computed under the rules. The deadline in the rule is amended to substitute a deadline that is a multiple of seven days. Throughout the rules, deadlines are amended in the following manner:

- 5–day periods become 7–day periods
- 10–day periods become 14–day periods
- 15–day periods become 14–day periods
- 20–day periods become 21–day periods
- 25–day periods become 28–day periods

Acceptance or rejection of plans, see Fed.Rules Bankr.Proc. Rule 3018, 11 USCA.

Modification of plan in—

Individual debt adjustment case, see 11 USCA § 1323.

Municipality debt adjustment case, see 11 USCA § 942.

Reorganization case, see 11 USCA § 1127.

LIBRARY REFERENCES

American Digest System

Bankruptcy ⬥3481, 3569.
Key Number System Topic No. 51.

Corpus Juris Secundum

CJS Bankruptcy § 1120, Modification of Plan Before Confirmation.

CJS Bankruptcy § 1163, Modification of the Plan.

Rule 3020.   Deposit; Confirmation of Plan in a Chapter 9 Municipality or Chapter 11 Reorganization Case

(a) Deposit

In a chapter 11 case, prior to entry of the order confirming the plan, the court may order the deposit with the trustee or debtor in possession of the consideration required by the plan to be distributed on confirmation. Any money deposited shall be kept in a special account established for the exclusive purpose of making the distribution.

(b) Objection to and hearing on confirmation in a Chapter 9 or Chapter 11 case

(1) Objection

An objection to confirmation of the plan shall be filed and served on the debtor, the trustee, the proponent of the plan, any committee appointed under the Code, and any other entity designated by the court, within a time fixed by the court. Unless the case is a chapter 9 municipality case, a copy of every objection to confirmation shall be transmitted by the objecting party to the United States trustee within the time fixed for filing objections. An objection to confirmation is governed by Rule 9014.

(2) Hearing

The court shall rule on confirmation of the plan after notice and hearing as provided in Rule 2002. If no objection is timely filed, the court may determine that the plan has been proposed in good faith and not by any means forbidden by law without receiving evidence on such issues.

(c) Order of confirmation

(1) The order of confirmation shall conform to the appropriate Official Form. If the plan provides for an injunction against conduct not otherwise enjoined under the Code, the order of confirmation shall (1) describe in reasonable detail all acts enjoined; (2) be specific in its terms regarding the injunction; and (3) identify the entities subject to the injunction.

(2) Notice of entry of the order of confirmation shall be mailed promptly to the debtor, the trustee, creditors, equity security holders, other parties in interest, and, if known, to any identified entity subject to an injunction provided for in the plan against conduct not otherwise enjoined under the Code.

(3) Except in a chapter 9 municipality case, notice of entry of the order of confirmation shall be transmitted to the United States trustee as provided in Rule 2002(k).

(d) Retained power

Notwithstanding the entry of the order of confirmation, the court may issue any other order necessary to administer the estate.

(e) Stay of confirmation order

An order confirming a plan is stayed until the expiration of 14 days after the entry of the order, unless the court orders otherwise.

(As amended Mar. 30, 1987, eff. Aug. 1, 1987; Apr. 30, 1991, eff. Aug. 1, 1991; Apr. 22, 1993, eff. Aug. 1, 1993; Apr. 29, 1999, eff. Dec. 1, 1999; Apr. 23, 2001, eff. Dec. 1, 2001; Mar. 26, 2009, eff. Dec. 1, 2009.)

ADVISORY COMMITTEE NOTES

This rule is adapted from former Rules 10–307, 11–38, and 13–213. It applies to cases filed under chapters 9, 11 and 13. Certain subdivisions of the earlier rules have not been included, such as, a subdivision revesting title in the debtor because § 541 of the Code does not transfer title out of the debtor as did § 70a of the Bankruptcy Act [former § 110(a) of this title]; see also §§ 1141(b), 1327(b). Subdivision (b) of former Rule 13–213 is not included because its provisions are contained in the statute; see §§ 1322, 1325(b), 105.

Subdivision (a) gives discretion to the court to require in chapter 11 cases the deposit of any consideration to be distributed on confirmation. If money is to be distributed, it is to be deposited in a special account to assure that it will not be used for any other purpose. The Code is silent in chapter 11 with respect to the need to make a deposit or the person with whom any deposit is to be to made. Consequently, there is no statutory authority for any person to act in a capacity similar to the disbursing agent under former Chapter XI [former § 701 et seq. of this title] practice. This rule provides that only the debtor in possession or trustee should be appointed as the recipient of the deposit. Any consideration other than money, e.g., notes or stock may be given directly to the debtor in possession or trustee and need not be left in any kind of special account. In chapter 9 cases, § 944(b) provides for deposit with a disbursing agent appointed by the court of any consideration to be distributed under the plan.

Subdivision (d) clarifies the authority of the court to conclude matters pending before it prior to confirmation and to continue to administer the estate as necessary, e.g., resolving objections to claims.

1991 Amendments

The United States trustee monitors chapter 11, chapter 12, and chapter 13 plans and has standing to be heard regarding confirmation of a plan. See 28 U.S.C. § 586(a)(3). The amendments to subdivisions (b)(1) and (c) of this rule facilitate that role of the United States trustee. Subdivision (b)(1) is also amended to require service on the proponent of the plan of objections to confirmation. The words "with the court" in subdivision (b)(1) are deleted as unnecessary. See Rules 5005(a) and 9001(3).

In a chapter 12 case, the court is required to conduct and conclude the hearing on confirmation of the plan within the time prescribed in § 1224 of the Code.

Subdivision (c) is also amended to require that the confirmation order be mailed to the trustee. Reference to the Official Form number is deleted in anticipation of future revision and renumbering of the Official Forms.

1993 Amendments

This rule is amended to limit its application to chapter 9 and chapter 11 cases. The procedures relating to confirmation of plans in chapter 12 and chapter 13 cases are provided in rule 3015. Other amendments are stylistic and make no substantive change.

1999 Amendments

Subdivision (e) is added to provide sufficient time for a party to request a stay pending appeal of an order confirming a plan under chapter 9 or chapter 11 of the Code before the plan is implemented and an appeal becomes moot. Unless the court orders otherwise, any transfer of assets, issuance of securities, and cash distributions provided for in the plan may not be made before the expiration of the 10–day period. The stay of the confirmation order under subdivision (e) does not affect the time for filing a notice of appeal from the confirmation order in accordance with Rule 8002.

The court may, in its discretion, order that Rule 3020(e) is not applicable so that the plan may be implemented and distributions may be made immediately. Alternatively, the court may order that the stay under Rule 3020(e) is for a fixed period less than 10 days.

Gap Report on Rule 3020. No changes since publication.

2001 Amendments

Subdivision (c) is amended to provide notice to an entity subject to an injunction provided for in a plan against conduct not otherwise enjoined by operation of the Code. This requirement is not applicable to an injunction contained in a plan if it is substantially the same as an injunction provided under the Code. The validity and effect of any injunction provided for in a plan are substantive law matters that are beyond the scope of these rules.

The requirement that the order of confirmation identify the entities subject to the injunction requires only reasonable identification under the circumstances. If the entities that would be subject to the injunction cannot be identified by name, the order may describe them by class or category if reasonable under the circumstances. For example, it may be sufficient to identify the entities as "all creditors of the debtor."

CHANGES MADE AFTER PUBLICATION AND COMMENTS

No changes were made in the text of the proposed amendments. The Committee Note was revised to put in a more prominent position the statement that the validity and effect of injunctions provided for in plans is beyond the scope of the rules.

2009 Amendments

The rule is amended to implement changes in connection with the amendment to Rule 9006(a) and the manner by which time is computed under the rules. The deadline in the rule is amended to substitute a deadline that is a multiple of seven days. Throughout the rules, deadlines are amended in the following manner:

- 5–day periods become 7–day periods
- 10–day periods become 14–day periods
- 15–day periods become 14–day periods
- 20–day periods become 21–day periods
- 25–day periods become 28–day periods

CROSS REFERENCES

Modification of accepted plan before confirmation, see Fed. Rules Bankr.Proc. Rule 3019, 11 USCA.

LIBRARY REFERENCES

American Digest System

Bankruptcy ⊕3039, 3481, 3559, 3566.1 to 3570.
Key Number System Topic No. 51.

Corpus Juris Secundum

CJS Bankruptcy § 262, Postconfirmation Powers.
CJS Bankruptcy § 1122, Objections to Confirmation.
CJS Bankruptcy § 1123, Hearing and Order.
CJS Bankruptcy § 1162, Implementation of the Plan; Distribution.

Rule 3021. Distribution Under Plan

Except as provided in Rule 3020(e), after a plan is confirmed, distribution shall be made to creditors whose claims have been allowed, to interest holders whose interests have not been disallowed, and to indenture trustees who have filed claims under Rule 3003(c)(5) that have been allowed. For purposes of this rule, creditors include holders of bonds, debentures, notes, and other debt securities, and interest holders include the holders of stock and other equity securities, of record at the time of commencement of distribution, unless a different time is fixed by the plan or the order confirming the plan.

(As amended Apr. 11, 1997, eff. Dec. 1, 1997; Apr. 29, 1999, eff. Dec. 1, 1999.)

ADVISORY COMMITTEE NOTES

This rule is derived from former Chapter X Rule 10–405(a). Subdivision (b) of that rule is covered by § 1143 of the Code.

1997 Amendments

This rule is amended to provide flexibility in fixing the record date for the purpose of making distributions to holders of securities of record. In a large case, it may be impractical for the debtor to determine the holders of record with respect to publicly held securities and also to make distributions to those holders at the same time. Under this amendment, the plan or the order confirming the plan may fix a record date for distributions that is earlier than the date on which distributions commence.

This rule also is amended to treat holders of bonds, debentures, notes, and other debt securities the same as any other creditors by providing that they shall receive a distribution only if their claims have been allowed. Finally, the amendments clarify that distributions are to be made to all interest holders—not only those that are within the definition of "equity security holders" under § 101 of the Code—whose interests have not been disallowed.

GAP Report on Rule 3021. No changes to the published draft.

1999 Amendments

This amendment is to conform to the amendments to Rule 3020 regarding the ten-day stay of an order confirming a plan in a chapter 9 or chapter 11 case. The other amendments are stylistic.

Gap Report on Rule 3021. No changes since publication.

CROSS REFERENCES

Disposition of unclaimed property, see 11 USCA § 347.

Power of court to require transfers of property, see 11 USCA § 1142.

Proof of right to record status filed by security holder, see Fed.Rules Bankr.Proc. Rule 3003, 11 USCA.

Time for surrender of security or performance of required act under reorganization plan, see 11 USCA § 1143.

LIBRARY REFERENCES

American Digest System

Bankruptcy ⊕3481, 3568(2), 3570.

Key Number System Topic No. 51.

Rule 3022. Final Decree in Chapter 11 Reorganization Case

After an estate is fully administered in a chapter 11 reorganization case, the court, on its own motion or on motion of a party in interest, shall enter a final decree closing the case.

(As amended Mar. 30, 1987, eff. Aug. 1, 1987; Apr. 30, 1991, eff. Aug. 1, 1991.)

ADVISORY COMMITTEE NOTES

Section 350 of the Code requires the court to close the case after the estate is fully administered and the trustee has been discharged. Section 1143 places a five year limitation on the surrender of securities when required for participation under

a plan but this provision should not delay entry of the final decree.

1991 Amendments

Entry of a final decree closing a chapter 11 case should not be delayed solely because the payments required by the plan have not been completed. Factors that the court should consider in determining whether the estate has been fully administered include (1) whether the order confirming the plan has become final, (2) whether deposits required by the plan have been distributed, (3) whether the property proposed by the plan to be transferred has been transferred, (4) whether the debtor or the successor of the debtor under the plan has assumed the business or the management of the property dealt with by the plan, (5) whether payments under the plan have commenced, and (6) whether all motions, contested matters, and adversary proceedings have been finally resolved.

The court should not keep the case open only because of the possibility that the court's jurisdiction may be invoked in the future. A final decree closing the case after the estate is fully administered does not deprive the court of jurisdiction to enforce or interpret its own orders and does not prevent the court from reopening the case for cause pursuant to § 350(b) of the Code. For example, on motion of a party in interest, the court may reopen the case to revoke an order of confirmation procured by fraud under § 1144 of the Code. If the plan or confirmation order provides that the case shall remain open until a certain date or event because of the likelihood that the court's jurisdiction may be required for specific purposes prior thereto, the case should remain open until that date or event.

CROSS REFERENCES

Close of case after trustee's discharge, see 11 USCA § 350.

Surrender of security or performance of required act under reorganization plan, denial of distribution, see 11 USCA § 1143.

LIBRARY REFERENCES

American Digest System

Bankruptcy ⊕3441, 3444.10 to 3444.60, 3570.

Key Number System Topic No. 51.

Corpus Juris Secundum

CJS Bankruptcy § 1105, Closing.

Rule
4001. Relief from Automatic Stay; Prohibiting or Conditioning the Use, Sale, or Lease of Property; Use of Cash Collateral; Obtaining Credit; Agreements.
4002. Duties of Debtor.
4003. Exemptions.
4004. Grant or Denial of Discharge.
4005. Burden of Proof in Objecting to Discharge.
4006. Notice of No Discharge.
4007. Determination of Dischargeability of a Debt.
4008. Filing of Reaffirmation Agreement; Statement in Support of Reaffirmation Agreement.

Rule 4001. Relief from Automatic Stay; Prohibiting or Conditioning the Use, Sale, or Lease of Property; Use of Cash Collateral; Obtaining Credit; Agreements

(a) Relief from stay; prohibiting or conditioning the use, sale, or lease of property

(1) Motion

A motion for relief from an automatic stay provided by the Code or a motion to prohibit or condition the use, sale, or lease of property pursuant to § 363(e) shall be made in accordance with Rule 9014 and shall be served on any committee elected pursuant to § 705 or appointed pursuant to § 1102 of the Code or its authorized agent, or, if the case is a chapter 9 municipality case or a chapter 11 reorganization case and no committee of unsecured creditors has been appointed pursuant to § 1102, on the creditors included on the list filed pursuant to Rule 1007(d), and such other entities as the court may direct.

(2) Ex parte relief

Relief from a stay under § 362(a) or a request to prohibit or condition the use, sale, or lease of property pursuant to § 363(e) may be granted without prior notice only if (A) it clearly appears from specific facts shown by affidavit or by a verified motion that immediate and irreparable injury, loss, or damage will result to the movant before the adverse party or the attorney for the adverse party can be heard in opposition, and (B) the movant's attorney certifies to the court in writing the efforts, if any, which have been made to give notice and the reasons why notice should not be required. The party obtaining relief under this subdivision and § 362(f) or § 363(e) shall immediately give oral notice thereof to the trustee or debtor in possession and to the debtor and forthwith mail or otherwise transmit to such adverse party or parties a copy of the order granting relief. On two days notice to the party who obtained relief from the stay without notice or on shorter notice to that party as the court may prescribe, the adverse party may appear and move reinstatement of the stay or reconsideration of the order prohibiting or conditioning the use, sale, or lease of property. In that event, the court shall proceed expeditiously to hear and determine the motion.

(3) Stay of order

An order granting a motion for relief from an automatic stay made in accordance with Rule 4001(a)(1) is stayed until the expiration of 14 days after the entry of the order, unless the court orders otherwise.

(b) Use of cash collateral

(1) Motion; Service

(A) Motion

A motion for authority to use cash collateral shall be made in accordance with Rule 9014 and shall be accompanied by a proposed form of order.

(B) Contents

The motion shall consist of or (if the motion is more than five pages in length) begin with a concise statement of the relief requested, not to exceed five pages, that lists or summarizes, and sets out the location within the relevant documents of, all material provisions, including:

(i) the name of each entity with an interest in the cash collateral;

(ii) the purposes for the use of the cash collateral;

(iii) the material terms, including duration, of the use of the cash collateral; and

(iv) any liens, cash payments, or other adequate protection that will be provided to each entity with an interest in the cash collateral or, if no additional adequate protection is proposed, an explanation of why each entity's interest is adequately protected.

(C) Service

The motion shall be served on: (1) any entity with an interest in the cash collateral; (2) any committee elected under § 705 or appointed under § 1102 of the Code, or its authorized agent, or, if the case is a chapter 9 municipality case or a chapter 11 reorganization case and no committee of unsecured creditors has been appointed under § 1102, the creditors included on the list filed under Rule 1007(d); and (3) any other entity that the court directs.

(2) Hearing

The court may commence a final hearing on a motion for authorization to use cash collateral no earlier than 14 days after service of the motion. If the motion so requests, the court may conduct a preliminary hearing before such 14–day period expires, but the court may authorize the use of only that amount of cash collateral as is necessary to avoid immediate and irreparable harm to the estate pending a final hearing.

(3) Notice

Notice of hearing pursuant to this subdivision shall be given to the parties on whom service of the motion is required by paragraph (1) of this subdivision and to such other entities as the court may direct.

(c) Obtaining credit

(1) Motion; Service

(A) Motion

A motion for authority to obtain credit shall be made in accordance with Rule 9014 and shall be accompanied by a copy of the credit agreement and a proposed form of order.

(B) Contents

The motion shall consist of or (if the motion is more than five pages in length) begin with a concise statement of the relief requested, not to exceed five pages, that lists or summarizes, and sets out the location within the relevant documents of, all material provisions of the proposed credit agreement and form of order, including interest rate, maturity, events of default, liens, borrowing limits, and borrowing conditions. If the proposed credit agreement or form of order includes any of the provisions listed below, the concise statement shall also: briefly list or summarize each one; identify its specific location in the proposed agreement and form of order; and identify any such provision that is proposed to remain in effect if interim approval is granted, but final relief is denied, as provided under Rule 4001(c)(2). In addition, the motion shall describe the nature and extent of each provision listed below:

(i) a grant of priority or a lien on property of the estate under § 364(c) or (d);

(ii) the providing of adequate protection or priority for a claim that arose before the commencement of the case, including the granting of a lien on property of the estate to secure the claim, or the use of property of the estate or credit obtained under § 364 to make cash payments on account of the claim;

(iii) a determination of the validity, enforceability, priority, or amount of a claim that arose before the commencement of the case, or of any lien securing the claim;

(iv) a waiver or modification of Code provisions or applicable rules relating to the automatic stay;

(v) a waiver or modification of any entity's authority or right to file a plan, seek an extension of time in which the debtor has the exclusive right to file a plan, request the use of cash collateral under § 363(c), or request authority to obtain credit under § 364;

(vi) the establishment of deadlines for filing a plan of reorganization, for approval of a disclosure statement, for a hearing on confirmation, or for entry of a confirmation order;

(vii) a waiver or modification of the applicability of nonbankruptcy law relating to the perfection of a lien on property of the estate, or on the foreclosure or other enforcement of the lien;

(viii) a release, waiver, or limitation on any claim or other cause of action belonging to the estate or the trustee, including any modification of the statute of limitations or other deadline to commence an action;

(ix) the indemnification of any entity;

(x) a release, waiver, or limitation of any right under § 506(c); or

(xi) the granting of a lien on any claim or cause of action arising under §§[1] 544, 545, 547, 548, 549, 553(b), 723(a), or 724(a).

(C) Service

The motion shall be served on: (1) any committee elected under § 705 or appointed under § 1102 of the Code, or its authorized agent, or, if the case is a chapter 9 municipality case or a chapter 11 reorganization case and no committee of unsecured creditors has been appointed under § 1102, on the creditors included on the list filed under Rule 1007(d); and (2) on any other entity that the court directs.

(2) Hearing.

The court may commence a final hearing on a motion for authority to obtain credit no earlier than 14 days after service of the motion. If the motion so requests, the court may conduct a hearing before such 14–day period expires, but the court may authorize the obtaining of credit only to the extent necessary to avoid immediate and irreparable harm to the estate pending a final hearing.

(3) Notice

Notice of hearing pursuant to this subdivision shall be given to the parties on whom service of the motion is required by paragraph (1) of this subdivision and to such other entities as the court may direct.

(d) Agreement relating to relief from the automatic stay, prohibiting or conditioning the use, sale, or lease of property, providing adequate protection, use of cash collateral, and obtaining credit

(1) Motion; Service

(A) Motion

A motion for approval of any of the following shall be accompanied by a copy of the agreement and a proposed form of order:

(i) an agreement to provide adequate protection;

(ii) an agreement to prohibit or condition the use, sale, or lease of property;

(iii) an agreement to modify or terminate the stay provided for in § 362;

(iv) an agreement to use cash collateral; or

(v) an agreement between the debtor and an entity that has a lien or interest in property of the estate pursuant to which the entity consents to the creation of a lien senior or equal to the entity's lien or interest in such property.

(B) Contents

The motion shall consist of or (if the motion is more than five pages in length) begin with a concise statement of the relief requested, not to exceed five pages, that lists or summarizes, and sets out the location within the relevant documents of, all material provisions of the agreement. In addition, the concise statement shall briefly list or summarize, and identify the specific location of, each provision in the proposed form of order, agreement, or other document of the type listed in subdivision (c)(1)(B). The motion shall also describe the nature and extent of each such provision.

(C) Service

The motion shall be served on: (1) any committee elected under § 705 or appointed under § 1102 of the Code, or its authorized agent, or, if the case is a chapter 9 municipality case or a chapter 11 reorganization case and no committee of unsecured creditors has been appointed under § 1102, on the creditors included on the list filed under Rule 1007(d); and (2) on any other entity the court directs.

(2) Objection

Notice of the motion and the time within which objections may be filed and served on the debtor in possession or trustee shall be mailed to the parties on whom service is required by paragraph (1) of this subdivision and to such other entities as the court may direct. Unless the court fixes a different time, objections may be filed within 14 days of the mailing of the notice.

(3) Disposition; hearing

If no objection is filed, the court may enter an order approving or disapproving the agreement without conducting a hearing. If an objection is filed or if the court determines a hearing is appropriate, the court shall hold a hearing on no less than seven days' notice to the objector, the movant, the parties on whom service is required by paragraph (1) of this subdivision and such other entities as the court may direct.

(4) Agreement in settlement of motion

The court may direct that the procedures prescribed in paragraphs (1), (2), and (3) of this subdivision shall not apply and the agreement may be approved without further notice if the court determines that a motion made pursuant to subdivisions (a), (b), or (c) of this rule was sufficient to afford reasonable notice of the material provisions of the agreement and opportunity for a hearing.

(As amended Mar. 30, 1987, eff. Aug. 1, 1987; Apr. 30, 1991, eff. Aug. 1, 1991; Apr. 29, 1999, eff. Dec. 1, 1999; Apr. 30, 2007, eff. Dec. 1, 2007; Mar. 26, 2009, eff. Dec. 1, 2009; Apr. 28, 2010, eff. Dec. 1, 2010.)

1 So in original. Probably should be only one section symbol.

ADVISORY COMMITTEE NOTES

This rule implements § 362 of the Code which sets forth provisions regarding the automatic stay that arises on the filing of a petition. That section and this rule are applicable in chapter 7, 9, 11 and 13 cases. It also implements § 363(c)(2) concerning use of cash collateral.

Subdivision (a) transforms with respect to the automatic stay what was an adversary proceeding under the former rules to motion practice. The Code provides automatic stays in several sections, e.g., §§ 362(a), 1301(a), and in § 362(d) provides some grounds for relief from the stay. This rule specifies that the pleading seeking relief is by means of a motion. Thus the time period in Rule 7012 to answer a complaint would not be applicable and shorter periods may be fixed. Section 362(e) requires the preliminary hearing to be concluded within 30 days of its inception, rendering ordinary complaint and answer practice inappropriate.

This subdivision also makes clear that a motion under Rule 9014 is the proper procedure for a debtor to seek court permission to use cash collateral. See § 363(c)(2). Pursuant to Rule 5005, the motion should be filed in the court in which the case is pending. The court or local rule may specify the persons to be served with the motion for relief from the stay; see Rule 9013.

Subdivision (b) of the rule fills a procedural void left by § 362. Pursuant to § 362(e), the automatic stay is terminated 30 days after a motion for relief is made unless the court continues the stay as a result of a final hearing or, pending final hearing, after a preliminary hearing. If a preliminary hearing is held, § 362(e) requires the final hearing to be commenced within 30 days after the preliminary hearing. Although the expressed legislative intent is to require expeditious resolution of a secured party's motion for relief, § 362 is silent as to the time within which the final hearing must be concluded. Subdivision (b) imposes a 30 day deadline on the court to resolve the dispute.

At the final hearing, the stay is to be terminated, modified, annulled, or conditioned for cause, which includes, inter alia, lack of adequate protection; § 362(d). The burden of proving adequate protection is on the party opposing relief from the stay; § 362(g)(2). Adequate protection is exemplified in § 361.

Subdivision (c) implements § 362(f) which permits ex parte relief from the stay when there will be irreparable damage. This subdivision sets forth the procedure to be followed when relief is sought under § 362(f). It is derived from former Bankruptcy Rule 601(d).

1987 Amendments

The scope of this rule is expanded and the former subdivisions (a), (b) and (c) are now combined in subdivision (a). The new subdivision (a)(2) is amended to conform to the 1984 amendments to § 362(e) of the Code.

Subdivision (b) deals explicitly with the procedures which follow after a motion to use cash collateral is made and served. Filing shall be pursuant to Rule 5005. Service of the motion may be made by any method authorized by Rule 7004 and, if service is by mail, service is complete on mailing. Rule 9006(e). Under subdivision (b)(2), the court may commence a final hearing on the motion within 15 days of service. Rule 9006(f) does not extend this 15 day period when service of the motion is by mail because the party served is not required to act within the 15 day period. In addition to service of the motion, notice of the hearing must be given. Rule 9007 authorizes the court to direct the form and manner of giving notice that is appropriate to the circumstances.

Section 363(c)(3) authorizes the court to conduct a preliminary hearing and to authorize the use of cash collateral "if there is a reasonable likelihood that the trustee will prevail at a final hearing." Subdivision (b)(2) of the rule permits a preliminary hearing to be held earlier than 15 days after service. Any order authorizing the use of cash collateral shall be limited to the amount necessary to protect the estate until a final hearing is held.

The objective of subdivision (b) is to accommodate both the immediate need of the debtor and the interest of the secured creditor in the cash collateral. The time for holding the final hearing may be enlarged beyond the 15 days prescribed when required by the circumstances.

The motion for authority to use cash collateral shall include (1) the amount of cash collateral sought to be used; (2) the name and address of each entity having an interest in the cash collateral; (3) the name and address of the entity in control or having possession of the cash collateral; (4) the facts demonstrating the need to use the cash collateral; and (5) the nature of the protection to be provided those having an interest in the cash collateral. If a preliminary hearing is requested, the motion shall also include the amount of cash collateral sought to be used pending final hearing and the protection to be provided.

Notice of the preliminary and final hearings may be combined. This rule does not limit the authority of the court under § 363(c)(2)(B) and § 102(1).

Subdivision (c) is new. The service, hearing, and notice requirements are similar to those imposed by subdivision (b). The motion to obtain credit shall include the amount and type of the credit to be extended, the name and address of the

lender, the terms of the agreement, the need to obtain the credit, and the efforts made to obtain credit from other sources. If the motion is to obtain credit pursuant to § 364(c) or (d), the motion shall describe the collateral, if any, and the protection for any existing interest in the collateral which may be affected by the proposed agreement.

Subdivision (d) is new. In the event the 15 day period for filing objections to the approval of an agreement of the parties described in this subdivision is too long, the parties either may move for a reduction of the period under Rule 9006(c)(1) or proceed under subdivision (b) or (c), if applicable. Rule 9006(c)(1) requires that cause be shown for the reduction of the period in which to object. In applying this criterion the court may consider the option of proceeding under subdivision (b) or (c) and grant a preliminary hearing and relief pending final hearing.

1991 Amendments

Subdivision (a) is expanded to include a request to prohibit or condition the use, sale, or lease of property as is necessary to provide adequate protection of a property interest pursuant to § 363(e) of the Code.

Notice of the motion for relief from the automatic stay or to prohibit or condition the use, sale, or lease of property must be served on the entities entitled to receive notice of a motion to approve an agreement pursuant to subdivision (d). If the movant and the adverse party agree to settle the motion and the terms of the agreement do not materially differ from the terms set forth in the movant's motion papers, the court may approve the agreement without further notice pursuant to subdivision (d)(4).

Subdivision (a)(2) is deleted as unnecessary because of § 362(e) of the Code.

Subdivisions (b)(1), (c)(1), and (d)(1) are amended to require service on committees that are elected in chapter 7 cases. Service on committees of retired employees appointed under § 1114 of the Code is not required. These subdivisions are amended further to clarify that, in the absence of a creditors' committee, service on the creditors included on the list filed pursuant to Rule 1007(d) is required only in chapter 9 and chapter 11 cases. The other amendments to subdivision (d)(1) are for consistency of style and are not substantive.

Subdivision (d)(4) is added to avoid the necessity of further notice and delay for the approval of an agreement in settlement of a motion for relief from an automatic stay, to prohibit or condition the use, sale, or lease of property, for use of cash collateral, or for authority to obtain credit if the entities entitled to notice have already received sufficient notice of the scope of the proposed agreement in the motion papers and have had an opportunity to be heard. For example, if a trustee makes a motion to use cash collateral and proposes in the original motion papers to provide adequate protection of the interest of the secured party by granting a lien on certain equipment, and the secured creditor subsequently agrees to terms that are within the scope of those proposed in the motion, the court may enter an order approving the agreement without further notice if the entities that received the original motion papers have had a reasonable opportunity to object to the granting of the motion to use cash collateral.

If the motion papers served under subdivision (a), (b), or (c) do not afford notice sufficient to inform the recipients of the material provisions of the proposed agreement and opportunity for a hearing, approval of the settlement agreement may not be obtained unless the procedural requirements of subdivision (d)(1), (d)(2), and (d)(3) are satisfied. If the 15 day period for filing objections to the approval of the settlement agreement is too long under the particular circumstances of the case, the court may shorten the time for cause under Rule 9006(c)(1).

1999 Amendments

Paragraph (a)(3) is added to provide sufficient time for a party to request a stay pending appeal of an order granting relief from an automatic stay before the order is enforced or implemented. The stay under paragraph (a)(3) is not applicable to orders granted ex parte in accordance with Rule 4001(a)(2).

The stay of the order does not affect the time for filing a notice of appeal in accordance with Rule 8002. While the enforcement and implementation of an order granting relief from the automatic stay is temporarily stayed under paragraph (a)(3), the automatic stay continues to protect the debtor, and the moving party may not foreclose on collateral or take any other steps that would violate the automatic stay.

The court may, in its discretion, order that Rule 4001(a)(3) is not applicable so that the prevailing party may immediately enforce and implement the order granting relief from the automatic stay. Alternatively, the court may order that the stay under Rule 4001(a)(3) is for a fixed period less than 10 days.

Gap Report on Rule 4001. No changes since publication.

2007 Amendments

The rule is amended to require that parties seeking authority to use cash collateral, to obtain credit, and to obtain approval of agreements to provide adequate protection, modify or terminate the stay, or to grant a senior or equal lien on property, submit with those requests a proposed order granting the relief, and that they provide more extensive notice to interested parties of a number of specified terms. The motion must either not exceed five pages in length, or, if it is longer, begin with a concise statement of five pages or less, that summarizes or lists the material provisions and which will assist the court and interested parties in understanding the nature of the relief requested. The concise statement must also set out the location within the documents of the summarized or listed provisions. The parties to agreements and lending offers frequently have concise summaries of their transactions that contain a list of the material provisions of the agreements, even if the agreements themselves are very lengthy. A similar summary should allow the court and interested parties to understand the relief requested.

In addition to the concise statement, the rule requires that motions under subdivisions (c) and (d) state whether the movant is seeking approval of any of the provisions listed in subdivision (c)(1)(B), and where those provisions are located in the documents. The rule is intended to enhance the ability of the court and interested parties to find and evaluate those provisions.

The rule also provides that any motion for authority to obtain credit must identify any provision listed in subdivision (c)(1)(B)(i)-(xi) that is proposed to remain effective if the court grants the motion on an interim basis under Rule 4001 (c)(2), but later denies final relief.

Other amendments are stylistic.

2009 Amendments

The rule is amended to implement changes in connection with the amendment to Rule 9006(a) and the manner by which time is computed under the rules. The deadlines in the rule are amended to substitute a deadline that is a multiple of seven days. Throughout the rules, deadlines are amended in the following manner:

- 5–day periods become 7–day periods
- 10–day periods become 14–day periods
- 15–day periods become 14–day periods
- 20–day periods become 21–day periods
- 25–day periods become 28–day periods

2010 Amendments

Subdivision (d). Subdivision (d) is amended to implement changes in connection with the 2009 amendment to Rule 9006(a) and the manner by which time is computed under the rules. The deadlines in subdivision (d)(2) and (d)(3) are amended to substitute deadlines that are multiples of seven days. Throughout the rules, deadlines have been amended in the following manner:

- 5 day periods become 7 day periods
- 10 day periods become 14 day periods
- 15 day periods become 14 day periods
- 20 day periods become 21 day periods
- 25 day periods become 28 day periods

CROSS REFERENCES

Enlargement of thirty-day period after which stay will expire following commencement of final hearing not permitted, see Fed.Rules Bankr.Proc. Rule 9006, 11 USCA.

Extension of time for trustee to redeem debtor's property, see 11 USCA § 108.

Methods for providing adequate protection, see 11 USCA § 361.

Motions—

    For relief from stay filed with court in which case is pending, see Fed.Rules Bankr.Proc. Rule 5005, 11 USCA.

    Form and service, see Fed.Rules Bankr.Proc. Rule 9013, 11 USCA.

Signing and verification of papers, see Fed.Rules Bankr. Proc. Rule 9011, 11 USCA.

Stay of actions on claims against, codebtor in individual debt adjustment case, see 11 USCA § 1301.

LIBRARY REFERENCES

American Digest System

Bankruptcy ⟾2156, 2391 to 2443, 3035.1 to 3038, 3061, 3082.1 to 3084.

Key Number System Topic No. 51.

Corpus Juris Secundum

CJS Bankruptcy § 298, Notice of Not Less Than 20 Days.

CJS Bankruptcy § 309, Reduction.

CJS Bankruptcy § 522, Parties; Standing.

CJS Bankruptcy § 528, Agreement as to Relief from Stay.

CJS Bankruptcy § 529, Ex Parte Relief from Stay.

CJS Bankruptcy § 530, Determination and Relief.

CJS Bankruptcy § 856, Motion and Notice.

CJS Bankruptcy § 857, Approval of Agreement.

CJS Bankruptcy § 870, Agreement or Stipulation for Use of Cash Collateral.

CJS Bankruptcy § 871, Motion for Authorization.

CJS Bankruptcy § 872, Notice and Hearing; Ex Parte Relief.

CJS Bankruptcy § 900, Motion for Authorization to Obtain Credit; Notice and Hearing.

CJS Bankruptcy § 901, Motion for Authorization to Obtain Credit; Approval of Agreement.

Rule 4002. Duties of Debtor

(a) In general

In addition to performing other duties prescribed by the Code and rules, the debtor shall:

(1) attend and submit to an examination at the times ordered by the court;

(2) attend the hearing on a complaint objecting to discharge and testify, if called as a witness;

(3) inform the trustee immediately in writing as to the location of real property in which the debtor has an interest and the name and address of every person holding money or property subject to the debtor's withdrawal or order if a schedule of property has not yet been filed pursuant to Rule 1007;

(4) cooperate with the trustee in the preparation of an inventory, the examination of proofs of claim, and the administration of the estate; and

(5) file a statement of any change of the debtor's address.

(b) Individual debtor's duty to provide documentation

(1) Personal identification

Every individual debtor shall bring to the meeting of creditors under § 341:

(A) a picture identification issued by a governmental unit, or other personal identifying information that establishes the debtor's identity; and

(B) evidence of social-security number(s), or a written statement that such documentation does not exist.

(2) Financial information

Every individual debtor shall bring to the meeting of creditors under § 341, and make available to the trustee, the following documents or copies of them, or provide a written statement that the documentation does not exist or is not in the debtor's possession:

(A) evidence of current income such as the most recent payment advice;

(B) unless the trustee or the United States trustee instructs otherwise, statements for each of the debtor's depository and investment accounts, including checking, savings, and money market accounts, mutual funds and brokerage accounts for the time period that includes the date of the filing of the petition; and

(C) documentation of monthly expenses claimed by the debtor if required by § 707(b)(2)(A) or (B).

(3) Tax return

At least 7 days before the first date set for the meeting of creditors under § 341, the debtor shall provide to the trustee a copy of the debtor's federal income tax return for the most recent tax year ending immediately before the commencement of the case and for which a return was filed, including any attachments, or a transcript of the tax return, or provide a written statement that the documentation does not exist.

(4) Tax returns provided to creditors

If a creditor, at least 14 days before the first date set for the meeting of creditors under § 341, requests a copy of the debtor's tax return that is to be provided to the trustee under subdivision (b)(3), the debtor, at least 7 days before the first date set for the meeting of creditors under § 341, shall provide to the requesting creditor a copy of the return, including any attachments, or a transcript of the tax return, or provide a written statement that the documentation does not exist.

(5) Confidentiality of tax information

The debtor's obligation to provide tax returns under Rule 4002(b)(3) and (b)(4) is subject to procedures for safeguarding the confidentiality of tax information established by the Director of the Administrative Office of the United States Courts.

(As amended Mar. 30, 1987, eff. Aug. 1, 1987; Apr. 23, 2008, eff. Dec. 1, 2008; Mar. 26, 2009, eff. Dec. 1, 2009.)

ADVISORY COMMITTEE NOTES

This rule should be read together with §§ 343 and 521 of the Code and Rule 1007, all of which impose duties on the debtor. Clause (3) of this rule implements the provisions of Rule 2015(a).

1987 Amendments

New clause (5) of the rule imposes on the debtor the duty to advise the clerk of any change of the debtor's address.

2008 Amendments

This rule is amended to implement § 521(a)(1)(B)(iv) and (e)(2), added to the Code by the 2005 amendments. These Code amendments expressly require the debtor to file with the court, or provide to the trustee, specific documents. The amendments to the rule implement these obligations and establish a time frame for creditors to make requests for a copy of the debtor's Federal income tax return. The rule also requires the debtor to provide documentation in support of claimed expenses under § 707(b)(2)(A) and (B).

Subdivision (b) of the rule is also amended to require the debtor to cooperate with the trustee by providing materials and documents necessary to assist the trustee in the performance of the trustee's duties. Nothing in the rule, however, is intended to limit or restrict the debtor's duties under § 521, or to limit the access of the Attorney General to any information provided by the debtor in the case. Subdivision (b)(2) does not require that the debtor create documents or obtain documents from third parties; rather, the debtor's obligation is to bring to the meeting of creditors under § 341 the documents which the debtor possesses. Under subdivision (b)(2)(B), the trustee or the United States trustee can instruct debtors that they need not provide the documents described in that subdivision. Under subdivisions (b)(3) and (b)(4), the debtor must obtain and provide copies of tax returns or tax transcripts to the appropriate person, unless no such documents exist. Any written statement that the debtor provides indicating either that documents do not exist or are not in the debtor's possession must be verified or contain an unsworn declaration as required under Rule 1008.

Because the amendment implements the debtor's duty to cooperate with the trustee, the materials provided to the trustee would not be made available to any other party in interest at the § 341 meeting of creditors other than the Attorney General. Some of the documents may contain otherwise private information that should not be disseminated. For example, pay stubs and financial account statements might include the social-security numbers of the debtor and the debtor's spouse and dependents, as well as the names of the debtor's children. The debtor should redact all but the last four digits of all social-security numbers and the names of any minors when they appear in these documents. This type of information would not usually be needed by creditors and others who may be attending the meeting. If a creditor perceives a need to review specific documents or other evidence, the creditor may proceed under Rule 2004.

Tax information produced under this rule is subject to procedures for safeguarding confidentiality established by the Director of the Administrative Office of the United States Courts.

2009 Amendments

The rule is amended to implement changes in connection with the amendment to Rule 9006(a) and the manner by which time is computed under the rules. The deadline in the rule is amended to substitute a deadline that is a multiple of seven days. Throughout the rules, deadlines are amended in the following manner:

- 5–day periods become 7–day periods
- 10–day periods become 14–day periods
- 15–day periods become 14–day periods
- 20–day periods become 21–day periods
- 25–day periods become 28–day periods

CROSS REFERENCES

Debtor's duties to—
Appear at meeting of creditors, see 11 USCA § 343.
File list of creditors and assets, cooperate with trustee, and appear at discharge hearing, see 11 USCA § 521.
File lists, schedules, and statements, see Fed.Rules Bankr.Proc. Rule 1007, 11 USCA.
Keep records, make reports, and give notice, see Fed. Rules Bankr.Proc. Rule 2015, 11 USCA.

Immunity from self-incrimination, see 11 USCA § 344.

LIBRARY REFERENCES
American Digest System
Bankruptcy ⟳2261, 3022, 3273.1, 3622.
Key Number System Topic No. 51.

Corpus Juris Secundum
CJS Bankruptcy § 758, Debtor's Duties.
CJS Bankruptcy § 797, Debtor's Duty to Attend as Mandatory.
CJS Bankruptcy § 806, Documents Debtor is Required to Bring.
CJS Bankruptcy § 1054, Hearing, Determination, and Order.

Rule 4003. Exemptions

(a) Claim of exemptions

A debtor shall list the property claimed as exempt under § 522 of the Code on the schedule of assets required to be filed by Rule 1007. If the debtor fails to claim exemptions or file the schedule within the time specified in Rule 1007, a dependent of the debtor may file the list within 30 days thereafter.

(b) Objecting to a claim of exemptions

(1) Except as provided in paragraphs (2) and (3), a party in interest may file an objection to the list of property claimed as exempt within 30 days after the meeting of creditors held under § 341(a) is concluded or within 30 days after any amendment to the list or supplemental schedules is filed, whichever is later. The court may, for cause, extend the time for filing objections if, before the time to object expires, a party in interest files a request for an extension.

(2) The trustee may file an objection to a claim of exemption at any time prior to one year after the closing of the case if the debtor fraudulently asserted the claim of exemption. The trustee shall deliver or mail the objection to the debtor and the debtor's attorney, and to any person filing the list of exempt property and that person's attorney.

(3) An objection to a claim of exemption based on § 522(q) shall be filed before the closing of the case. If an exemption is first claimed after a case is reopened, an objection shall be filed before the reopened case is closed.

(4) A copy of any objection shall be delivered or mailed to the trustee, the debtor and the debtor's attorney, and the person filing the list and that person's attorney.

(c) Burden of proof

In any hearing under this rule, the objecting party has the burden of proving that the exemptions are not properly claimed. After hearing on notice, the court shall determine the issues presented by the objections.

(d) Avoidance by debtor of transfers of exempt property

A proceeding by the debtor to avoid a lien or other transfer of property exempt under § 522(f) of the Code shall be by motion in accordance with Rule 9014. Notwithstanding the provisions of subdivision (b), a creditor may object to a motion filed under § 522(f) by challenging the validity of the exemption asserted to be impaired by the lien.

(As amended Mar. 30, 1987, eff. Aug. 1, 1987; Apr. 30, 1991, eff. Aug. 1, 1991; Apr. 17, 2000, eff. Dec. 1, 2000; Apr. 23, 2008, eff. Dec. 1, 2008.)

ADVISORY COMMITTEE NOTES

This rule is derived from § 522(*l*) of the Code and, in part, former Bankruptcy Rule 403. The Code changes the thrust of that rule by making it the burden of the debtor to list his exemptions and the burden of parties in interest to raise objections in the absence of which "the property claimed as exempt on such list is exempt;" § 522(*l*).

Subdivision (a). While § 522(*l*) refers to a list of property claimed as exempt, the rule incorporates such a list as part of Official Form No. 6, the schedule of the debtor's assets, rather than requiring a separate list and filing. Rule 1007, to which subdivision (a) refers, requires that schedule to be filed within 15 days after the order for relief, unless the court extends the time.

Section 522(*l*) also provides that a dependent of the debtor may file the list if the debtor fails to do so. Subdivision (a) of the rule allows such filing from the expiration of the debtor's time until 30 days thereafter. Dependent is defined in § 522(a)(1).

Subdivision (d) provides that a proceeding by the debtor, permitted by § 522(f) of the Code, is a contested matter rather than the more formal adversary proceeding. Proceedings within the scope of this subdivision are distinguished from proceedings brought by the trustee to avoid transfers. The latter are classified as adversary proceedings by Rule 7001.

1991 Amendments

Subdivision (b) is amended to facilitate the filing of objections to exemptions claimed on a supplemental schedule filed under Rule 1007(h).

2000 Amendments

This rule is amended to permit the court to grant a timely request for an extension of time to file objections to the list of claimed exemptions, whether the court rules on the request before or after the expiration of the 30–day period. The purpose of this amendment is to avoid the harshness of the present rule which has been construed to deprive a bankruptcy court of jurisdiction to grant a timely request for an extension if it has failed to rule on the request within the 30–day period. See *In re Laurain*, 113 F.3d 595 (6th Cir. 1997); *Matter of Stoulig*, 45 F.3d 957 (5th Cir. 1995); *In re Brayshaw*, 912 F.2d 1255 (10th Cir. 1990). The amendments clarify that the extension may be granted only for cause. The amendments also conform the rule to § 522(*l*) of the Code by recognizing that any party in interest may file an objection or request for an extension of time under this rule. Other amendments are stylistic.

GAP Report on Rule 4003(b). The words "trustee or creditor" were replaced by "party in interest" to conform to § 522(*l*) of the Bankruptcy Code which permits any party in interest to object to claimed exemptions. Style revisions also were made to the published draft.

2008 Amendments

Subdivision (b) is rewritten to include four paragraphs.

Subdivision (b)(2) is added to the rule to permit the trustee to object to an exemption at any time up to one year after the closing of the case if the debtor fraudulently claimed the exemption. Extending the deadline for trustees to object to an exemption when the exemption claim has been fraudulently made will permit the court to review and, in proper circumstances, deny improperly claimed exemptions, thereby protecting the legitimate interests of creditors and the bankruptcy estate. However, similar to the deadline set in § 727(e) of the Code for revoking a discharge which was fraudulently obtained, an objection to an exemption that was fraudulently claimed must be filed within one year after the closing of the case. Subdivision (b)(2) extends the objection deadline only for trustees.

Subdivision (b)(3) is added to the rule to reflect the addition of subsection (q) to § 522 of the Code by the 2005 Act. Section 522(q) imposes a $136,875 limit on a state homestead exemption if the debtor has been convicted of a felony or owes a debt arising from certain causes of action. Other revised provisions of the Code, such as § 727(a)(12) and § 1328(h), suggest that the court may consider issues relating to § 522(q) late in the case, and the 30–day period for objections would not be appropriate for this provision.

Subdivision (d) is amended to clarify that a creditor with a lien on property that the debtor is attempting to avoid on the grounds that the lien impairs an exemption may raise in defense to the lien avoidance action any objection to the debtor's claimed exemption. The right to object is limited to an objection to the exemption of the property subject to the lien and for purposes of the lien avoidance action only. The creditor may not object to other exemption claims made by the debtor. Those objections, if any, are governed by Rule 4003(b).

Other changes are stylistic.

CROSS REFERENCES

Automatic preservation of avoided property transfers for benefit of estate, see 11 USCA § 551.

Enlargement of thirty-day period for filing objections to property claimed as exempt permitted as limited in this rule, see Fed.Rules Bankr.Proc. Rule 9006, 11 USCA.

Motions; form and service, see Fed.Rules Bankr.Proc. Rule 9013, 11 USCA.

Proceedings to avoid transfers of exempt property as non-adversarial proceedings, see Fed.Rules Bankr.Proc. Rule 7001, 11 USCA.

Reduction of time to claim property as exempt by dependent not permitted, see Fed.Rules Bankr.Proc. Rule 9006, 11 USCA.

Right of debtor's redemption of personal property from lien securing dischargeable consumer debt, see 11 USCA § 722.

LIBRARY REFERENCES

American Digest System

Bankruptcy ⬅2761 to 2802.

Key Number System Topic No. 51.

Corpus Juris Secundum

CJS Bankruptcy § 139, Adversary Proceedings.

CJS Bankruptcy § 261, Power to Render Declaratory Judgment.

CJS Bankruptcy § 308, Enlargement.

CJS Bankruptcy § 309, Reduction.

CJS Bankruptcy § 467, Filing Periods.

CJS Bankruptcy § 555, Property Subject to Liens or Mortgages--Liens Securing Unallowed or Undersecured Claims.

CJS Bankruptcy § 574, Dependents or Spouse of Debtor.

CJS Bankruptcy § 576, Filing List of Property Claimed as Exempt.

CJS Bankruptcy § 585, Extension of Time; Effect of Absence of Timely Objection.

CJS Bankruptcy § 586, Effect of Conversion on Time Allowed for Objection.

CJS Bankruptcy § 588, Burden of Proof.

CJS Bankruptcy § 794, Time of Initial Meeting.

Rule 4004. Grant or Denial of Discharge

(a) Time for objecting to discharge; notice of time fixed

In a chapter 7 case, a complaint, or a motion under § 727(a)(8) or (a)(9) of the Code, objecting to the debtor's discharge shall be filed no later than 60 days after the first date set for the meeting of creditors under § 341(a). In a chapter 11 case, the complaint shall be filed no later than the first date set for the hearing on confirmation. In a chapter 13 case, a motion objecting to the debtor's discharge under § 1328(f) shall be filed no later than 60 days after the first date set for the meeting of creditors under § 341(a). At least 28 days' notice of the time so fixed shall be given to the United States trustee and all creditors as provided in Rule 2002(f) and (k) and to the trustee and the trustee's attorney.

(b) Extension of Time

(1) On motion of any party in interest, after notice and hearing, the court may for cause extend the time to object to discharge. Except as provided in subdivision (b)(2), the motion shall be filed before the time has expired.

(2) A motion to extend the time to object to discharge may be filed after the time for objection has expired and before discharge is granted if (A) the objection is based on facts that, if learned after the discharge, would provide a basis for revocation under § 727(d) of the Code, and (B) the movant did not have knowledge of those facts in time to permit an objection. The motion shall be filed promptly after the movant discovers the facts on which the objection is based.

(c) Grant of discharge

(1) In a chapter 7 case, on expiration of the times fixed for objecting to discharge and for filing a motion to dismiss the case under Rule 1017(e), the court shall forthwith grant the discharge unless:

(A) the debtor is not an individual;

(B) a complaint, or a motion under § 727(a)(8) or (a)(9), objecting to the discharge has been filed and not decided in the debtor's favor;

(C) the debtor has filed a waiver under § 727(a)(10);

(D) a motion to dismiss the case under § 707 is pending;

(E) a motion to extend the time for filing a complaint objecting to the discharge is pending;

(F) a motion to extend the time for filing a motion to dismiss the case under Rule 1017(e)(1) is pending;

(G) the debtor has not paid in full the filing fee prescribed by 28 U.S.C. § 1930(a) and any other fee prescribed by the Judicial Conference of the United States under 28 U.S.C. § 1930(b) that is payable to the clerk upon the commencement of a case under the Code, unless the court has waived the fees under 28 U.S.C. § 1930(f);

(H) the debtor has not filed with the court a statement of completion of a course concerning personal financial management as required by Rule 1007(b)(7);

(I) a motion to delay or postpone discharge under § 727(a)(12) is pending;

(J) a motion to enlarge the time to file a reaffirmation agreement under Rule 4008(a) is pending;

(K) a presumption has arisen under § 524(m) that a reaffirmation agreement is an undue hardship; or

(L) a motion is pending to delay discharge, because the debtor has not filed with the court all tax documents required to be filed under § 521(f).

(2) Notwithstanding Rule 4004(c)(1), on motion of the debtor, the court may defer the entry of an order granting a discharge for 30 days and, on motion within that period, the court may defer entry of the order to a date certain.

(3) If the debtor is required to file a statement under Rule 1007(b)(8), the court shall not grant a discharge earlier than 30 days after the statement is filed.

(4) In a chapter 11 case in which the debtor is an individual, or a chapter 13 case, the court shall not grant a discharge if the debtor has not filed any statement required by Rule 1007(b)(7).

(d) Applicability of rules in Part VII and Rule 9014

An objection to discharge is governed by Part VII of these rules, except that an objection to discharge under

§§ 727(a)(8),[1] (a)(9), or 1328(f) is commenced by motion and governed by Rule 9014.

(e) Order of discharge

An order of discharge shall conform to the appropriate Official Form.

(f) Registration in other districts

An order of discharge that has become final may be registered in any other district by filing a certified copy of the order in the office of the clerk of that district. When so registered the order of discharge shall have the same effect as an order of the court of the district where registered.

(g) Notice of discharge

The clerk shall promptly mail a copy of the final order of discharge to those specified in subdivision (a) of this rule.

(As amended Mar. 30, 1987, eff. Aug. 1, 1987; Apr. 30, 1991, eff. Aug. 1, 1991; Apr. 23, 1996, eff. Dec. 1, 1996; Apr. 29, 1999, eff. Dec. 1, 1999; Apr. 17, 2000, eff. Dec. 1, 2000; Apr. 29, 2002, eff. Dec. 1, 2002; Apr. 23, 2008, eff. Dec. 1, 2008; Mar. 26, 2009, eff. Dec. 1, 2009; Apr. 28, 2010, eff. Dec. 1, 2010; Apr. 26, 2011, eff. Dec. 1, 2011.)

[1] So in original. Probably should be only one section symbol.

ADVISORY COMMITTEE NOTES

This rule is adapted from former Bankruptcy Rule 404.

Subdivisions (a) and (b) of this rule prescribe the procedure for determining whether a discharge will be granted pursuant to § 727 of the Code. The time fixed by subdivision (a) may be enlarged as provided in subdivision (b).

The notice referred to in subdivision (a) is required to be given by mail and addressed to creditors as provided in Rule 2002.

An extension granted on a motion pursuant to subdivision (b) of the rule would ordinarily benefit only the movant, but its scope and effect would depend on the terms of the extension.

Subdivision (c). If a complaint objecting to discharge is filed, the court's grant or denial of the discharge will be entered at the conclusion of the proceeding as a judgment in accordance with Rule 9021. The inclusion of the clause in subdivision (c) qualifying the duty of the court to grant a discharge when a waiver has been filed is in accord with the construction of the Code. 4 Collier, Bankruptcy ¶727.12 (15th ed. 1979).

The last sentence of subdivision (c) takes cognizance of § 524(c) of the Code which authorizes a debtor to enter into enforceable reaffirmation agreements only prior to entry of the order of discharge. Immediate entry of that order after expiration of the time fixed for filing complaints objecting to discharge may render it more difficult for a debtor to settle pending litigation to determine the dischargeability of a debt and execute a reaffirmation agreement as part of a settlement.

Subdivision (d). An objection to discharge is required to be made by a complaint, which initiates an adversary proceeding as provided in Rule 7003. Pursuant to Rule 5005, the complaint should be filed in the court in which the case is pending.

Subdivision (e). Official Form No. 27 to which subdivision (e) refers, includes notice of the effects of a discharge specified in § 524(a) of the Code.

Subdivision (f). Registration may facilitate the enforcement of the order of discharge in a district other than that in which it was entered. See 2 Moore's Federal Practice ¶1.04[2] (2d ed. 1967). Because of the nationwide service of process authorized by Rule 7004, however, registration of the order of discharge is not necessary under these rules to enable a discharged debtor to obtain relief against a creditor proceeding anywhere in the United States in disregard of the injunctive provisions of the order of discharge.

Subdivision (g). Notice of discharge should be mailed promptly after the order becomes final so that creditors may be informed of entry of the order and of its injunctive provisions. Rule 2002 specifies the manner of the notice and persons to whom the notice is to be given.

1991 Amendments

This rule is amended to conform to § 727(c) which gives the United States trustee the right to object to discharge. This amendment is derived from Rule X–1008(a)(1) and is consistent with Rule 2002. The amendment to subdivision (c) is to prevent a timely motion to dismiss a chapter 7 case for substantial abuse from becoming moot merely because a discharge order has been entered. Reference to the Official Form number in subdivision (e) is deleted in anticipation of future revision and renumbering of the Official Forms.

1996 Amendments

Subsection (c) is amended to delay entry of the order of discharge if a motion pursuant to Rule 4004(b) to extend the time for filing a complaint objecting to discharge is pending. Also, this subdivision is amended to delay entry of the discharge order if the debtor has not paid in full the filing fee and the administrative fee required to be paid upon the commencement of the case. If the debtor is authorized to pay the fees in installments in accordance with Rule 1006, the discharge order will not be entered until the final installment has been paid.

The other amendments to this rule are stylistic.

GAP Report on Rule 4004. No changes have been made since publication, except for stylistic changes.

1999 Amendments

Subdivision (a) is amended to clarify that, in a chapter 7 case, the deadline for filing a complaint objecting to discharge under § 727(a) is 60 days after the first date set for the meeting of creditors, whether or not the meeting is held on that date. The time for filing the complaint is not affected by any delay in the commencement or conclusion of the meeting of creditors. This amendment does not affect the right of any party in interest to file a motion for an extension of time to file a complaint objecting to discharge in accordance with Rule 4004(b).

The substitution of the word "filed" for "made" in subdivision (b) is intended to avoid confusion regarding the time when a motion is "made" for the purpose of applying these rules. See, e.g., In re Coggin, 30 F.3d 1443 (11th Cir. 1994). As amended, this rule requires that a motion for an extension of time for filing a complaint objecting to discharge be *filed* before the time has expired.

Other amendments to this rule are stylistic.

Gap Report on Rule 4004. No changes since publication.

2000 Amendments

Subdivision (c) is amended so that a discharge will not be granted while a motion requesting an extension of time to file a motion to dismiss the case under § 707(b) is pending. Other amendments are stylistic.

GAP Report on Rule 4004(c). No changes since publication except for style revisions.

2002 Amendments

Subdivision (c)(1)(D) is amended to provide that the filing of a motion to dismiss under § 707 of the Bankruptcy Code postpones the entry of the discharge. Under the present version of the rule, only motions to dismiss brought under § 707(b) cause the postponement of the discharge. This amendment would change the result in cases such as *In re Tanenbaum*, 210 B.R. 182 (Bankr. D. Colo. 1997).

Changes Made After Publication and Comments. No changes were made.

2008 Amendments

Subdivision (c)(1)(G) is amended to reflect the fee waiver provision in 28 U.S.C. § 1930, added by the 2005 amendments.

Subdivision (c)(1)(H) is new. It reflects the 2005 addition to the Code of §§ 727(a)(11) and 1328(g), which require that individual debtors complete a course in personal financial management as a condition to the entry of a discharge. Including this requirement in the rule helps prevent the inadvertent entry of a discharge when the debtor has not complied with this requirement. If a debtor fails to file the required statement regarding a personal financial management course, the clerk will close the bankruptcy case without the entry of a discharge.

Subdivision (c)(1)(I) is new. It reflects the 2005 addition to the Code of § 727(a)(12). This provision is linked to § 522(q). Section 522(q) limits the availability of the homestead exemption for individuals who have been convicted of a felony or who owe a debt arising from certain causes of action within a particular time frame. The existence of reasonable cause to believe that § 522(q) may be applicable to the debtor constitutes grounds for withholding the discharge.

Subdivision (c)(1)(J) is new. It accommodates the deadline for filing a reaffirmation agreement established by Rule 4008(a).

Subdivision (c)(1)(K) is new. It reflects the 2005 revisions to § 524 of the Code that alter the requirements for approval of reaffirmation agreements. Section 524(m) sets forth circumstances under which a reaffirmation agreement is presumed to be an undue hardship. This triggers an obligation to review the presumption and may require notice and a hearing. Subdivision (c)(1)(J) has been added to prevent the discharge from being entered until the court approves or disapproves the reaffirmation agreement in accordance with § 524(m).

Subdivision (c)(1)(L) is new. It implements § 1228(a) of Public Law Number 109–8, an uncodified provision of the Bankruptcy Abuse Prevention and Consumer Protection Act

of 2005, which prohibits entry of a discharge unless required tax documents have been provided to the court.

Subdivision (c)(3) is new. It postpones the entry of the discharge of an individual debtor in a case under chapter 11, 12, or 13 if there is a question as to the applicability of § 522(q) of the Code. The postponement provides an opportunity for a creditor to file a motion to limit the debtor's exemption under that provision.

Other changes are stylistic.

2009 Amendments

The rule is amended to implement changes in connection with the amendment to Rule 9006(a) and the manner by which time is computed under the rules. The deadline in the rule is amended to substitute a deadline that is a multiple of seven days. Throughout the rules, deadlines are amended in the following manner:

- 5–day periods become 7–day periods
- 10–day periods become 14–day periods
- 15–day periods become 14–day periods
- 20–day periods become 21–day periods
- 25–day periods become 28–day periods

2010 Amendments

Subdivision (a). Subdivision (a) is amended to include a deadline for filing a motion objecting to a debtor's discharge under §§ 727(a)(8), (a)(9), or 1328(f) of the Code. These sections establish time limits on the issuance of discharges in successive bankruptcy cases by the same debtor.

Subdivision (c). Subdivision (c)(1) is amended because a corresponding amendment to subdivision (d) directs certain objections to discharge to be brought by motion rather than by complaint. Subparagraph (c)(1)(B) directs the court not to grant a discharge if a motion or complaint objecting to discharge has been filed unless the objection has been decided in the debtor's favor.

Subdivision (c)(4) is new. It directs the court in chapter 11 and 13 cases to withhold the entry of the discharge if an individual debtor has not filed a statement of completion of a course concerning personal financial management as required by Rule 1007(b)(7).

Subdivision (d). Subdivision (d) is amended to direct that objections to discharge under §§ 727(a)(8), (a)(9), and 1328(f) be commenced by motion rather than by complaint. Objections under the specified provisions are contested matters governed by Rule 9014. The title of the subdivision is also amended to reflect this change.

2011 Amendments

Subdivision (b). Subdivision (b) is amended to allow a party, under certain specified circumstances, to seek an extension of time to object to discharge after the time for filing has expired. This amendment addresses the situation in which there is a gap between the expiration of the time for objecting to discharge and the entry of the discharge order. If, during that period, a party discovers facts that would provide grounds for revocation of discharge, it may not be able to seek revocation under § 727(d) of the Code because the facts would have been known prior to the granting of the discharge. Furthermore, during that period the debtor may commit an act that provides a basis for both denial and revocation of the discharge. In those situations, subdivision (b)(2) allows a party to file a motion for an extension of time to object to discharge based on those facts so long as they were not known to the party before expiration of the deadline for objecting. The motion must be filed promptly after discovery of those facts.

CROSS REFERENCES

Discharge—

Effect of, see 11 USCA § 524.

Exceptions to, see 11 USCA § 523.

Filing complaint to object to discharge, sixty-day period—

Enlargement permitted as limited in this rule, see Fed. Rules Bankr.Proc. Rule 9006, 11 USCA.

Reduction not permitted, see Fed.Rules Bankr.Proc. Rule 9006, 11 USCA.

Motions; form and service, see Fed.Rules Bankr.Proc. Rule 9013, 11 USCA.

Notice by mail—

Order of discharge, see Fed.Rules Bankr.Proc. Rule 2002, 11 USCA.

Time fixed to file complaint objecting to discharge, see Fed.Rules Bankr.Proc. Rule 2002, 11 USCA.

Time for filing complaint in reconverted liquidation case revived or extended as under this rule, see Fed.Rules Bankr. Proc. Rule 1019, 11 USCA.

Transfer of claim before or after proof of claim filed, see Fed.Rules Bankr.Proc. Rule 3001, 11 USCA.

LIBRARY REFERENCES

American Digest System

Bankruptcy ⟜3271 to 3322.

Key Number System Topic No. 51.

Corpus Juris Secundum

CJS Bankruptcy § 287, Complaints.

CJS Bankruptcy § 301, Notice to Debtor, Creditors, and Indenture Trustees.

CJS Bankruptcy § 308, Enlargement.

CJS Bankruptcy § 309, Reduction.

CJS Bankruptcy § 794, Time of Initial Meeting.

CJS Bankruptcy § 1047, Time for Proceedings; Extension of Time.

CJS Bankruptcy § 1054, Hearing, Determination, and Order.

Rule 4005.　Burden of Proof in Objecting to Discharge

At the trial on a complaint objecting to a discharge, the plaintiff has the burden of proving the objection. (As amended Mar. 30, 1987, eff. Aug. 1, 1987.)

ADVISORY COMMITTEE NOTES

This rule does not address the burden of going forward with the evidence. Subject to the allocation by the rule of the initial burden of producing evidence and the ultimate burden of persuasion, the rule leaves to the courts the formulation of rules governing the shift of the burden of going forward with the evidence in the light of considerations such as the difficulty of proving the nonexistence of a fact and of establishing a fact as to which the evidence is likely to be more accessible to the debtor than to the objector. <u>See, e.g., In re Haggerty</u>, 165 F.2d 977, 979–80 (2d Cir. 1948); <u>Federal Provision Co. v. Ershowsky</u>, 94 F.2d 574, 575 (2d Cir.1938); <u>In re Riceputo</u>, 41 F.Supp. 926, 927–28 (E.D.N.Y. 1941).

LIBRARY REFERENCES

American Digest System

Bankruptcy ⟜3315.

Key Number System Topic No. 51.

Corpus Juris Secundum

CJS Bankruptcy § 1050, Evidence; Presumptions and Burden of Proof.

Rule 4006.　Notice of No Discharge

If an order is entered: denying a discharge; revoking a discharge; approving a waiver of discharge; or, in the case of an individual debtor, closing the case without the entry of a discharge, the clerk shall promptly notify all parties in interest in the manner provided by Rule 2002.

(As amended Mar. 30, 1987, eff. Aug. 1, 1987; Apr. 23, 2008, eff. Dec. 1, 2008.)

ADVISORY COMMITTEE NOTES

The suspension by § 108(c) of the Code of the statute of limitations affecting any debt of a debtor terminates within 30 days after the debtor is denied a discharge or otherwise loses his right to a discharge. If, however, a debtor's failure to receive a discharge does not come to the attention of his creditors until after the statutes of limitations have run, the debtor obtains substantially the same benefits from his bankruptcy as a debtor who is discharged.

This rule requires the clerk to notify creditors if a debtor fails to obtain a discharge because a waiver of discharge was filed under § 727(a)(10) or as a result of an order denying or revoking the discharge under § 727(a) or (d).

2008 Amendments

This amendment was necessary because the 2005 amendments to the Code require that individual debtors in a chapter 7 or 13 case complete a course in personal financial management as a condition to the entry of a discharge. If the debtor fails to complete the course, the case may be closed and no discharge will be entered. Reopening the case is governed by § 350 and Rule 5010. The rule is amended to provide notice to parties in interest, including the debtor, that no discharge was entered.

CROSS REFERENCES

Notice by mail, see Fed.Rules Bankr.Proc. Rule 2002, 11 USCA.

Suspension of statute of limitations on debts of debtor, see 11 USCA § 108.

LIBRARY REFERENCES

American Digest System

Bankruptcy ⟜2131, 3318.1.

Key Number System Topic No. 51.

CJS Bankruptcy § 301, Notice to Debtor, Creditors, and Indenture Trustees.

Rule 4007. Determination of Dischargeability of a Debt

(a) Persons entitled to file complaint

A debtor or any creditor may file a complaint to obtain a determination of the dischargeability of any debt.

(b) Time for commencing proceeding other than under § 523(c) of the Code

A complaint other than under § 523(c) may be filed at any time. A case may be reopened without payment of an additional filing fee for the purpose of filing a complaint to obtain a determination under this rule.

(c) Time for filing complaint under § 523(c) in a chapter 7 liquidation, chapter 11 reorganization, chapter 12 family farmer's debt adjustment case, or chapter 13 individual's debt adjustment case; notice of time fixed

Except as otherwise provided in subdivision (d), a complaint to determine the dischargeability of a debt under § 523(c) shall be filed no later than 60 days after the first date set for the meeting of creditors under § 341(a). The court shall give all creditors no less than 30 days' notice of the time so fixed in the manner provided in Rule 2002. On motion of a party in interest, after hearing on notice, the court may for cause extend the time fixed under this subdivision. The motion shall be filed before the time has expired.

(d) Time for filing complaint under § 523(a)(6) in a chapter 13 individual's debt adjustment case; notice of time fixed

On motion by a debtor for a discharge under § 1328(b), the court shall enter an order fixing the time to file a complaint to determine the dischargeability of any debt under § 523(a)(6) and shall give no less than 30 days' notice of the time fixed to all creditors in the manner provided in Rule 2002. On motion of any party in interest, after hearing on notice, the court may for cause extend the time fixed under this subdivision. The motion shall be filed before the time has expired.

(e) Applicability of Rules in Part VII

A proceeding commenced by a complaint filed under this rule is governed by Part VII of these rules. (As amended Mar. 30, 1987, eff. Aug. 1, 1987; Apr. 30, 1991, eff. Aug. 1, 1991; Apr. 29, 1999, eff. Dec. 1, 1999; Apr. 23, 2008, eff. Dec. 1, 2008.)

ADVISORY COMMITTEE NOTES

This rule prescribes the procedure to be followed when a party requests the court to determine dischargeability of a debt pursuant to § 523 of the Code.

Although a complaint that comes within § 523(c) must ordinarily be filed before determining whether the debtor will be discharged, the court need not determine the issues presented by the complaint filed under this rule until the question of discharge has been determined under Rule 4004. A complaint filed under this rule initiates an adversary proceeding as provided in Rule 7003.

Subdivision (b) does not contain a time limit for filing a complaint to determine the dischargeability of a type of debt listed as nondischargeable under § 523(a)(1), (3), (5), (7), (8), or (9). Jurisdiction over this issue on these debts is held concurrently by the bankruptcy court and any appropriate nonbankruptcy forum.

Subdivision (c) differs from subdivision (b) by imposing a deadline for filing complaints to determine the issue of dischargeability of debts set out in § 523(a)(2), (4) or (6) of the Code. The bankruptcy court has exclusive jurisdiction to determine dischargeability of these debts. If a complaint is not timely filed, the debt is discharged. See § 523(c).

Subdivision (e). The complaint required by this subdivision should be filed in the court in which the case is pending pursuant to Rule 5005.

1991 Amendments

Subdivision (a) is amended to delete the words "with the court" as unnecessary. See Rules 5005(a) and 9001(3).

Subdivision (c) is amended to apply in chapter 12 cases the same time period that applies in chapter 7 and 11 cases for filing a complaint under § 523(c) of the Code to determine dischargeability of certain debts. Under § 1228(a) of the Code, a chapter 12 discharge does not discharge the debts specified in § 523(a) of the Code.

1999 Amendments

Subdivision (c) is amended to clarify that the deadline for filing a complaint to determine the dischargeability of a debt under § 523(c) of the Code is 60 days after the first date set for the meeting of creditors, whether or not the meeting is held on that date. The time for filing the complaint is not affected by any delay in the commencement or conclusion of the meeting of creditors. This amendment does not affect the right of any party in interest to file a motion for an extension of time to file a complaint to determine the dischargeability of a debt in accordance with this rule.

The substitution of the word "filed" for "made" in the final sentences of subdivisions (c) and (d) is intended to avoid confusion regarding the time when a motion is "made" for the purpose of applying these rules. *See, e.g., In re Coggin*, 30 F.3d 1443 (11th Cir. 1994). As amended, these subdivisions require that a motion for an extension of time be *filed* before the time has expired.

The other amendments to this rule are stylistic.

Gap Report on Rule 4007. No changes since publication, except for stylistic changes in the heading of Rule 4007(d).

2008 Amendments

Subdivision (c) is amended because of the 2005 amendments to § 1328(a) of the Code. This revision expands the exceptions to discharge upon completion of a chapter 13 plan. Subdivision (c) extends to chapter 13 the same time limits applicable to other chapters of the Code with respect to the two exceptions to discharge that have been added to § 1328(a) and that are within § 523(c).

The amendment to subdivision (d) reflects the 2005 amendments to § 1328(a) that expands the exceptions to discharge upon completion of a chapter 13 plan, including two out of three of the provisions that fall within § 523(c). However, the 2005 revisions to § 1328(a) do not include a reference to § 523(a)(6), which is the third provision to which § 523(c) refers. Thus, subdivision (d) is now limited to that provision.

CROSS REFERENCES

Costs and attorney fees to consumer debtor upon discharge of debt, see 11 USCA § 523.

Effect of dismissal on dischargeability of debt, see 11 USCA § 349.

Filing complaint to determine dischargeability of debt, sixty-day period—

Enlargement permitted as limited in this rule, see Fed. Rules Bankr.Proc. Rule 9006, 11 USCA.

Reduction not permitted, see Fed.Rules Bankr.Proc. Rule 9006, 11 USCA.

Motions; form and service, see Fed.Rules Bankr.Proc. Rule 9013, 11 USCA.

Notice by mail of time fixed to file complaint, see Fed.Rules Bankr.Proc. Rule 2002, 11 USCA.

Time for filing complaint in reconverted liquidation case revived or extended as under this rule, see Fed.Rules Bankr. Proc. Rule 1019, 11 USCA.

LIBRARY REFERENCES

American Digest System

Bankruptcy ⟺3341 to 3388, 3419.1 to 3423.
Key Number System Topic No. 51.

Corpus Juris Secundum

CJS Bankruptcy § 287, Complaints.

CJS Bankruptcy § 301, Notice to Debtor, Creditors, and Indenture Trustees.

CJS Bankruptcy § 308, Enlargement.

CJS Bankruptcy § 309, Reduction.

CJS Bankruptcy § 794, Time of Initial Meeting.

CJS Bankruptcy § 1047, Time for Proceedings; Extension of Time.

CJS Bankruptcy § 1082, Time for Proceedings.

CJS Bankruptcy § 1083, Time for Proceedings--Extension of Time.

CJS Bankruptcy § 1208, Discharge.

Rule 4008. Filing of Reaffirmation Agreement; Statement in Support of Reaffirmation Agreement

(a) Filing of reaffirmation agreement

A reaffirmation agreement shall be filed no later than 60 days after the first date set for the meeting of creditors under § 341(a) of the Code. The reaffirmation agreement shall be accompanied by a cover sheet, prepared as prescribed by the appropriate Official Form. The court may, at any time and in its discretion, enlarge the time to file a reaffirmation agreement.

(b) Statement in support of reaffirmation agreement

The debtor's statement required under § 524(k)(6)(A) of the Code shall be accompanied by a statement of the total income and expenses stated on schedules I and J. If there is a difference between the total income and expenses stated on those schedules and the statement required under § 524(k)(6)(A), the statement required by this subdivision shall include an explanation of the difference.

(As amended Apr. 30, 1991, eff. Aug. 1, 1991; Apr. 23, 2008, eff. Dec. 1, 2008; Mar. 26, 2009, eff. Dec. 1, 2009.)

ADVISORY COMMITTEE NOTES

Section 524(d) of the Code requires the court to hold a hearing to inform an individual debtor concerning the granting or denial of discharge and the law applicable to reaffirmation agreements.

The notice of the § 524(d) hearing may be combined with the notice of the meeting of creditors or entered as a separate order.

The expression "not more than" contained in the first sentence of the rule is for the explicit purpose of requiring the hearing to occur within that time period and cannot be extended.

1991 Amendments

This rule is changed to conform to § 524(d) of the Code as amended in 1986. A hearing under § 524(d) is not mandatory unless the debtor desires to enter into a reaffirmation agreement.

2008 Amendments

This rule is amended to establish a deadline for filing reaffirmation agreements. The Code sets out a number of prerequisites to the enforceability of reaffirmation agreements. Among those requirements, § 524(k)(6)(A) provides that each reaffirmation agreement must be accompanied by a statement indicating the debtor's ability to make the payments called for by the agreement. In the event that this statement reflects an insufficient income to allow payment of the reaffirmed debt, § 524(m) provides that a presumption of undue hardship arises, allowing the court to disapprove the reaffirmation agreement, but only after a hearing conducted prior to the entry of discharge. Rule 4004(c)(1)(K) accommodates this provision by delaying the entry of discharge where a presumption of undue hardship arises. However, in order for that rule to be effective, the reaffirmation agreement itself must be filed before the entry of discharge. Under Rule 4004(c)(1) discharge is to be entered promptly after the expiration of the time for filing a complaint objecting to discharge, which, under Rule 4004(a), is 60 days after the first date set for the meeting of creditors under § 341(a). Accordingly, that date is set as the deadline for filing a reaffirmation agreement.

Any party may file the agreement with the court. Thus, whichever party has a greater incentive to enforce the agreement usually will file it. In the event that the parties are unable to file a reaffirmation agreement in a timely fashion, the rule grants the court broad discretion to permit a late filing. A corresponding change to Rule 4004(c)(1)(J) accommodates such an extension by providing for a delay in the entry of discharge during the pendency of a motion to extend the time for filing a reaffirmation agreement.

Rule 4008 is also amended by deleting provisions regarding the timing of any reaffirmation and discharge hearing. As noted above, § 524(m) itself requires that hearings on undue hardship be conducted prior to the entry of discharge. In other respects, including hearings to approve reaffirmation agreements of unrepresented debtors under § 524(c)(6), the rule leaves discretion to the court to set the hearing at a time appropriate for the particular circumstances presented in the case and consistent with the scheduling needs of the parties.

2009 Amendments

Subdivision (a) of the rule is amended to require that the entity filing the reaffirmation agreement with the court also include Official Form 27, the Reaffirmation Agreement Cover Sheet. The form includes information necessary for the court to determine whether the proposed reaffirmation agreement is presumed to be an undue hardship for the debtor under § 524(m) of the Code.

CROSS REFERENCES

Confirmation of reorganization plan, see Fed.Rules Bankr. Proc. Rule 3020, 11 USCA.

Motions; form and service, see Fed.Rules Bankr.Proc. Rule 9013, 11 USCA.

LIBRARY REFERENCES

American Digest System

Bankruptcy ⟜3415.1 to 3417.

Key Number System Topic No. 51.

Corpus Juris Secundum

CJS Bankruptcy § 84, Appointment in Interests of Creditors, Equity Security Holders, or Estate.

CJS Bankruptcy § 85, Appointment Where Debts Exceed $5 Million.

CJS Bankruptcy § 1095, Hearing; Determination of Validity of Reaffirmation.

PART V—BANKRUPTCY COURTS AND CLERKS

Rule
5001. Courts and Clerks' Offices.
5002. Restrictions on Appointments.
5003. Records Kept By the Clerk.
5004. Disqualification.
5005. Filing and Transmittal of Papers.
5006. Certification of Copies of Papers.
5007. Record of Proceedings and Transcripts.
5008. Notice Regarding Presumption of Abuse in Chapter 7 Cases of Individual Debtors.
5009. Closing Chapter 7 Liquidation, Chapter 12 Family Farmer's Debt Adjustment, Chapter 13 Individual's Debt Adjustment, and Chapter 15 Ancillary and Cross–Border Cases.
5010. Reopening Cases.
5011. Withdrawal and Abstention from Hearing a Proceeding.
5012. Agreements Concerning Coordination of Proceedings in Chapter 15 Cases.

Rule 5001. Courts and Clerks' Offices

(a) Courts always open

The courts shall be deemed always open for the purpose of filing any pleading or other proper paper, issuing and returning process, and filing, making, or entering motions, orders and rules.

(b) Trials and hearings; orders in chambers

All trials and hearings shall be conducted in open court and so far as convenient in a regular court room. Except as otherwise provided in 28 U.S.C. § 152(c), all other acts or proceedings may be done or conducted by a judge in chambers and at any place either within or without the district; but no hearing, other than one ex parte, shall be conducted outside the district without the consent of all parties affected thereby.

(c) Clerk's office

The clerk's office with the clerk or a deputy in attendance shall be open during business hours on all days except Saturdays, Sundays and the legal holidays listed in Rule 9006(a).

(As amended Mar. 30, 1987, eff. Aug. 1, 1987; Apr. 30, 1991, eff. Aug. 1, 1991; Apr. 23, 2008, eff. Dec. 1, 2008.)

ADVISORY COMMITTEE NOTES

This rule is adapted from subdivisions (a), (b) and (c) of Rule 77 F.R.Civ.P.

1987 Amendments

Rule 9001, as amended, defines court to mean the bankruptcy judge or district judge before whom a case or proceeding is pending. Clerk means the bankruptcy clerk, if one has been appointed for the district; if a bankruptcy clerk has not been appointed, clerk means clerk of the district court.

1991 Amendments

Subdivision (c) is amended to refer to Rule 9006(a) for a list of legal holidays. Reference to F.R.Civ.P. is not necessary for this purpose.

2008 Amendments

The rule is amended to permit bankruptcy judges to hold hearings outside of the district in which the case is pending to the extent that the circumstances lead to the authorization of the court to take such action under the 2005 amendment to 28 U.S.C. § 152(c). Under that provision, bankruptcy judges may hold court outside of their districts in emergency situations and when the business of the court otherwise so requires. This amendment to the rule is intended to implement the legislation.

CROSS REFERENCES

Legal holiday defined, see Fed.Rules Bankr.Proc. Rule 9006, 11 USCA.

LIBRARY REFERENCES

American Digest System

Bankruptcy ⊕2121, 2127.

Key Number System Topic No. 51.

Corpus Juris Secundum

CJS Bankruptcy § 23, Sessions and Hearings; Court Always Open.

Rule 5002. Restrictions on Appointments

(a) Approval of appointment of relatives prohibited

The appointment of an individual as a trustee or examiner pursuant to § 1104 of the Code shall not be approved by the court if the individual is a relative of the bankruptcy judge approving the appointment or the United States trustee in the region in which the case is pending. The employment of an individual as attorney, accountant, appraiser, auctioneer, or other professional person pursuant to §§ 327, 1103, or 1114 shall not be approved by the court if the individual is a relative of the bankruptcy judge approving the employment. The employment of an individual as attorney, accountant, appraiser, auctioneer, or other professional person pursuant to §§ 327, 1103, or 1114 may be approved by the court if the individual is a relative of the United States trustee in the region in which the case is pending, unless the court finds that the relationship with the United States trustee renders the employment improper under the circumstances of the case. Whenever under this subdivision an individual may not be approved for appointment or employment, the individual's firm, partnership, corporation, or any other form of business association or relationship, and all members, associates and professional employees thereof also may not be approved for appointment or employment.

(b) Judicial determination that approval of appointment or employment is improper

A bankruptcy judge may not approve the appointment of a person as a trustee or examiner pursuant to § 1104 of the Code or approve the employment of a person as an attorney, accountant, appraiser, auctioneer, or other professional person pursuant to §§ 327, 1103, or 1114 of the Code if that person is or has been so connected with such judge or the United States trustee as to render the appointment or employment improper.

(As amended Apr. 29, 1985, eff. Aug. 1, 1985; Apr. 30, 1991, eff. Aug. 1, 1991.)

ADVISORY COMMITTEE NOTES

This rule is adapted from former Bankruptcy Rule 505(a). The scope of the prohibition on appointment or employment is expanded to include an examiner appointed under § 1104 of the Code and attorneys and other professional persons whose employment must be approved by the court under § 327 or § 1103.

The rule supplements two statutory provisions. Under 18 U.S.C. § 1910, it is a criminal offense for a judge to appoint a relative as a trustee and, under 28 U.S.C. § 458, a person may not be "appointed to or employed in any office or duty in any court" if he is a relative of any judge of that court. The rule prohibits the appointment or employment of a relative of a bankruptcy judge in a case pending before that bankruptcy judge or before other bankruptcy judges sitting within the district.

A relative is defined in § 101(34) of the Code to be an "individual related by affinity or consanguinity within the third degree as determined by the common law, or individual in a step or adoptive relationship within such third degree." Persons within the third degree under the common law system are as follows: first degree—parents, brothers and sisters, and children; second degree—grandparents, uncles and aunts, first cousins, nephews and nieces, and grandchildren; third degree—great grandparents, great uncles and aunts, first cousins once removed, second cousins, grand nephews and nieces, great grandchildren. Rule 9001 incorporates the definitions of § 101 of the Code.

In order for the policy of this rule to be meaningfully implemented, it is necessary to extend the prohibition against appointment or employment to the firm or other business association of the ineligible person and to those affiliated with the firm or business association. "Firm" is defined in Rule 9001 to include a professional partnership or corporation of attorneys or accountants. All other types of business and professional associations and relationships are covered by this rule.

1985 Amendments

The amended rule is divided into two subdivisions. Subdivision (a) applies to relatives of bankruptcy judges and subdivision (b) applies to persons who are or have been connected with bankruptcy judges. Subdivision (a) permits no judicial discretion; subdivision (b) allows judicial discretion. In both subdivisions of the amended rule "bankruptcy judge" has been substituted for "judge." The amended rule makes clear that it only applies to relatives of, or persons connected with, the bankruptcy judge. *See In re Hilltop Sand and Gravel, Inc.*, 35 B.R. 412 (N.D.Ohio 1983).

Subd. (a). The original rule prohibited all bankruptcy judges in a district from appointing or approving the employment of (i) a relative of any bankruptcy judge serving in the district, (ii) the firm or business association of any ineligible relative and (iii) any member or professional employee of the firm or business association of an ineligible relative. In addition, the definition of relative, the third degree relationship under the common law, is quite broad. The restriction on the employment opportunities of relatives of bankruptcy judges was magnified by the fact that many law and accounting firms have practices and offices spanning the nation.

Relatives are not eligible for appointment or employment when the bankruptcy judge to whom they are related makes the appointment or approves the employment. Canon 3(b)(4) of the Code of Judicial Conduct, which provides that the judge "shall exercise his power of appointment only on the basis of merit, avoiding nepotism and favoritism," should guide a bankruptcy judge when a relative of a judge of the same bankruptcy court is considered for appointment or employment.

Subd. (b), derived from clause (2) of the original rule, makes a person ineligible for appointment or employment if the person is so connected with a bankruptcy judge making the appointment or approving the employment as to render the appointment or approval of employment improper. The caption and text of the subdivision emphasize that application of the connection test is committed to the sound discretion of the bankruptcy judge who is to make the appointment or approve the employment. All relevant circumstances are to be taken into account by the court. The most important of those circumstances include: the nature and duration of the connection with the bankruptcy judge; whether the connection still exists, and, if not, when it was terminated; and the type of appointment or employment. These and other considerations must be carefully evaluated by the bankruptcy judge.

The policy underlying subdivision (b) is essentially the same as the policy embodied in the Code of Judicial Conduct. Canon 2 of the Code of Judicial Conduct instructs a judge to avoid impropriety and the appearance of impropriety, and Canon 3(b)(4) provides that the judge "should exercise his power of appointment only on the basis of merit, avoiding nepotism and favoritism." Subdivision (b) alerts the potential appointee or employee and party seeking approval of employment to consider the possible relevance or impact of subdivision (b) and indicates to them that appropriate disclosure must be made to the bankruptcy court before accepting appointment or employment. The information required may be made a part of the application for approval of employment. See Rule 2014(a).

Subdivision (b) departs from the former rule in an important respect: a firm or business association is not prohibited from appointment or employment merely because an individual member or employee of the firm or business association is ineligible under subdivision (b).

The emphasis given to the bankruptcy court's judicial discretion in applying subdivision (b) and the absence of a *per se* extension of ineligibility to the firm or business association or any ineligible individual complement the amendments to subdivision (a). The change is intended to moderate the prior limitation on the employment opportunities of attorneys, accountants and other professional persons who are or who have been connected in some way with the bankruptcy judge. For example, in all but the most unusual situations service as a law clerk to a bankruptcy judge is not the type of connection which alone precludes appointment or employment. Even if a bankruptcy judge determines that it is improper to appoint or approve the employment of a former law clerk in the period immediately after completion of the former law clerk's service with the judge, the firm which employs the former law clerk will, absent other circumstances, be eligible for employment. In each instance all the facts must be considered by the bankruptcy judge.

Subdivision (b) applies to persons connected with a bankruptcy judge. "Person" is defined in § 101 of the Bankruptcy Code to include an "individual, partnership and corporation." A partnership or corporation may be appointed or employed to serve in a bankruptcy case. If a bankruptcy judge is connected in some way with a partnership or corporation, it is necessary for the court to determine whether the appointment or employment of that partnership or corporation is proper.

The amended rule does not regulate professional relationships which do not require approval of a bankruptcy judge. Disqualification of the bankruptcy judge pursuant to 28 U.S.C. § 455 may, however, be appropriate. Under Rule 5004(a), a bankruptcy judge may find that disqualification from only some aspect of the case, rather than the entire case, is necessary. A situation may also arise in which the disqualifying circumstance only comes to light after services have been performed. Rule 5004(b) provides that if compensation from the estate is sought for these services, the bankruptcy judge is disqualified from awarding compensation.

1991 Amendments

The 1986 amendments to the Code provide that the United States trustee shall appoint trustees in chapter 7, chapter 12, and chapter 13 cases without the necessity of court approval. This rule is not intended to apply to the appointment of trustees in those cases because it would be inappropriate for a court rule to restrict in advance the exercise of discretion by the executive branch. See COMMITTEE NOTE to Rule 2009.

In chapter 11 cases, a trustee or examiner is appointed by the United States trustee after consultation with parties in interest and subject to court approval. Subdivision (a), as amended, prohibits the approval of the appointment of an individual as a trustee or examiner if the person is a relative of the United States trustee making the appointment or the bankruptcy judge approving the appointment.

The United States trustee neither appoints nor approves the employment of professional persons employed pursuant to §§ 327, 1103, or 1114 of the Code. Therefore, subdivision (a) is not a prohibition against judicial approval of employment of a professional person who is a relative of the United States trustee. However, the United States trustee monitors applications for compensation and reimbursement of expenses and may raise, appear and be heard on issues in the case. Employment of relatives of the United States trustee may be approved unless the court finds, after considering the relationship and the particular circumstances of the case, that the relationship would cause the employment to be improper. As used in this rule, "improper" includes the appearance of impropriety.

United States trustee is defined to include a designee or assistant United States trustee. See Rule 9001. Therefore,

subdivision (a) is applicable if the person appointed as trustee or examiner or the professional to be employed is a relative of a designee of the United States trustee or any assistant United States trustee in the region in which the case is pending.

This rule is not exclusive of other laws or rules regulating ethical conduct. See, e.g., 28 CFR § 45.735–5.

CROSS REFERENCES

Appointment of trustee or examiner, see 11 USCA § 1104.

Definition of relative, see 11 USCA § 101.

Nepotism in appointment of receiver or trustee, see 18 USCA § 1910.

Relative of justice or judge ineligible to appointment, see 28 USCA § 458.

LIBRARY REFERENCES

American Digest System

Bankruptcy ⚖3003, 3004.1, 3029.1, 3030.

Key Number System Topic No. 51.

Corpus Juris Secundum

CJS Bankruptcy § 31, Restrictions and Limitations on Activities and Practices of Judges.

CJS Bankruptcy § 56, Eligibility to Serve as Trustee or Examiner--Disinterestedness Requirement.

CJS Bankruptcy § 760, Disqualification for and Limitations Upon Employment.

CJS Bankruptcy § 786, Disqualification of Judge from Allowing Compensation.

Rule 5003. Records Kept By the Clerk

(a) Bankruptcy dockets

The clerk shall keep a docket in each case under the Code and shall enter thereon each judgment, order, and activity in that case as prescribed by the Director of the Administrative Office of the United States Courts. The entry of a judgment or order in a docket shall show the date the entry is made.

(b) Claims register

The clerk shall keep in a claims register a list of claims filed in a case when it appears that there will be a distribution to unsecured creditors.

(c) Judgments and orders

The clerk shall keep, in the form and manner as the Director of the Administrative Office of the United States Courts may prescribe, a correct copy of every final judgment or order affecting title to or lien on real property or for the recovery of money or property, and any other order which the court may direct to be kept. On request of the prevailing party, a correct copy of every judgment or order affecting title to or lien upon real or personal property or for the recovery of money or property shall be kept and indexed with the civil judgments of the district court.

(d) Index of cases; certificate of search

The clerk shall keep indices of all cases and adversary proceedings as prescribed by the Director of the Administrative Office of the United States Courts. On request, the clerk shall make a search of any index and papers in the clerk's custody and certify whether a case or proceeding has been filed in or transferred to the court or if a discharge has been entered in its records.

(e) Register of mailing addresses of federal and state governmental units and certain taxing authorities

The United States or the state or territory in which the court is located may file a statement designating its mailing address. The United States, state, territory, or local governmental unit responsible for collecting taxes within the district in which the case is pending may also file a statement designating an address for service of requests under § 505(b) of the Code, and the designation shall describe where further information concerning additional requirements for filing such requests may be found. The clerk shall keep, in the form and manner as the Director of the Administrative Office of the United States Courts may prescribe, a register that includes the mailing addresses designated under the first sentence of this subdivision, and a separate register of the addresses designated for the service of requests under § 505(b) of the Code. The clerk is not required to include in any single register more than one mailing address for each department, agency, or instrumentality of the United States or the state or territory. If more than one address for a department, agency, or instrumentality is included in the register, the clerk shall also include information that would enable a user of the register to determine the circumstances when each address is applicable, and mailing notice to only one applicable address is sufficient to provide effective notice. The clerk shall update the register annually, effective January 2 of each year. The mailing address in the register is conclusively presumed to be a proper address for the governmental unit, but the failure to use that mailing address does not invalidate any notice that is otherwise effective under applicable law.

(f) Other books and records of the clerk

The clerk shall keep any other books and records required by the Director of the Administrative Office of the United States Courts.

(As amended Mar. 30, 1987, eff. Aug. 1, 1987; Apr. 17, 2000, Dec. 1, 2000; Apr. 23, 2008, eff. Dec. 1, 2008.)

ADVISORY COMMITTEE NOTES

This rule consolidates former Bankruptcy Rules 504 and 507. The record-keeping duties of the referee under former Bankruptcy Rule 504 are transferred to the clerk. Subdivisions (a), (c), (d) and (e) are similar to subdivisions (a)–(d) of Rule 79 F.R.Civ.P.

Subdivision (b) requires that filed claims be listed on a claims register only when there may be a distribution to unsecured creditors. Compilation of the list for no asset or nominal asset cases would serve no purpose.

Rule 2013 requires the clerk to maintain a public record of fees paid from the estate and an annual summary thereof.

Former Bankruptcy Rules 507(d) and 508, which made materials in the clerk's office and files available to the public, are not necessary because § 107 of the Code guarantees public access to files and dockets of cases under the Code.

1987 Amendments

Subdivision (a) has been made more specific.

Subdivision (c) is amended to require that on the request of the prevailing party the clerk of the district court shall keep and index bankruptcy judgments and orders affecting title to or lien upon real or personal property or for the recovery of money or property with the civil judgments of the district court. This requirement is derived from former Rule 9021(b). The Director of the Administrative Office will provide guidance to the bankruptcy and district court clerks regarding appropriate paperwork and retention procedures.

2000 Amendments

Subdivision (e) is added to provide a source where debtors, their attorneys, and other parties may go to determine whether the United States or the state or territory in which the court is located has filed a statement designating a mailing address for notice purposes. By using the address in the register—which must be available to the public—the sender is assured that the mailing address is proper. But the use of an address that differs from the address included in the register does not invalidate the notice if it is otherwise effective under applicable law.

The register may include a separate mailing address for each department, agency, or instrumentality of the United States or the state or territory. This rule does not require that addresses of municipalities or other local governmental units be included in the register, but the clerk may include them.

Although it is important for the register to be kept current, debtors, their attorneys, and other parties should be able to rely on mailing addresses listed in the register without the need to continuously inquire as to new or amended addresses. Therefore, the clerk must update the register, but only once each year.

To avoid unnecessary cost and burden on the clerk and to keep the register a reasonable length, the clerk is not required to include more than one mailing address for a particular agency, department, or instrumentality of the United States or the state or territory. But if more than one address is included, the clerk is required to include information so that a person using the register could determine when each address should be used. In any event, the inclusion of more than one address for a particular department, agency, or instrumentality does not impose on a person sending a notice the duty to send it to more than one address.

GAP Report on Rule 5003. No changes since publication.

2008 Amendments

The rule is amended to implement § 505(b)(1) of the Code added by the 2005 amendments, which allows a taxing authority to designate an address to use for the service of requests under that subsection. Under the amendment, the clerk is directed to maintain a separate register for mailing addresses of governmental units solely for the service of requests under § 505(b). This register is in addition to the register of addresses of governmental units already maintained by the clerk. The clerk is required to keep only one address for a governmental unit in each register.

CROSS REFERENCES

Books and records kept by Clerk and entries therein, see Fed.Rules Civ.Proc. Rule 79, 28 USCA.

Judgment effective when entered as provided in this rule, see Fed.Rules Bankr.Proc. Rule 9021, 11 USCA.

Public access to case dockets, see 11 USCA § 107.

Public record of estate fees to be kept by clerk, see Fed.Rules Bankr.Proc. Rule 2013, 11 USCA.

LIBRARY REFERENCES

American Digest System

Bankruptcy ⊕2121.

Clerks of Courts ⊕69.

Key Number System Topic Nos. 51, 79.

Corpus Juris Secundum

CJS Bankruptcy § 12, Federal Rules of Civil Procedure.

CJS Bankruptcy § 286, Papers Filed as Public Records.

CJS Bankruptcy § 296, Notice by Mail--Proper Mailing Address.

CJS Bankruptcy § 304, Notice to the United States.

CJS Bankruptcy § 314, Judgments.

Rule 5004. Disqualification

(a) Disqualification of judge

A bankruptcy judge shall be governed by 28 U.S.C. § 455, and disqualified from presiding over the proceeding or contested matter in which the disqualifying circumstances [1] arises or, if appropriate, shall be disqualified from presiding over the case.

(b) Disqualification of judge from allowing compensation

A bankruptcy judge shall be disqualified from allowing compensation to a person who is a relative of the bankruptcy judge or with whom the judge is so connected as to render it improper for the judge to authorize such compensation.

(As amended Apr. 29, 1985, eff. Aug. 1, 1985; Mar. 30, 1987, eff. Aug. 1, 1987.)

[1] So in original. Probably should be "circumstance".

ADVISORY COMMITTEE NOTES

Subdivision (a). Disqualification of a bankruptcy judge is governed by 28 U.S.C. § 455. That section provides that the judge "shall disqualify himself in any proceeding in which his impartiality might reasonably be questioned" or under certain other circumstances. In a case under the Code it is possible that the disqualifying circumstance will be isolated to an adversary proceeding or contested matter. The rule makes it clear that when the disqualifying circumstance is limited in

that way the judge need only disqualify himself from presiding over that adversary proceeding or contested matter.

It is possible, however, that even if the disqualifying circumstance arises in connection with an adversary proceeding, the effect will be so pervasive that disqualification from presiding over the case is appropriate. This distinction is consistent with the definition of "proceeding" in 28 U.S.C. § 455(d)(1).

Subdivision (b) precludes a bankruptcy judge from allowing compensation from the estate to a relative or other person closely associated with the judge. The subdivision applies where the judge has not appointed or approved the employment of the person requesting compensation. Perhaps the most frequent application of the subdivision will be in the allowance of administrative expenses under § 503(b)(3) to (5) of the Code. For example, if an attorney or accountant is retained by an indenture trustee who thereafter makes a substantial contribution in a chapter 11 case, the attorney or accountant may seek compensation under § 503(b)(4). If the attorney or accountant is a relative of or associated with the bankruptcy judge, the judge may not allow compensation to the attorney or accountant. Section 101(34) defines relative and Rule 9001 incorporates the definitions of the Code. See the Advisory Committee's Note to Rule 5002.

1987 Amendments

The rule is amended to be gender neutral. The bankruptcy judge before whom the matter is pending determines whether disqualification is required.

1985 Amendments

Subdivision (a) was affected by the Bankruptcy Amendments and Federal Judgeship Act of 1984, P.L. 98–353, 98 Stat. 333. The 1978 Bankruptcy Reform Act, P.L. 95–598, included bankruptcy judges in the definition of United States judges in 28 U.S.C. § 451 and they were therefore subject to the provisions of 28 U.S.C. § 455. This was to become effective on April 1, 1984, P.L. 95–598, § 404(b). Section 113 of P.L. 98–353, however, appears to have rendered the amendment to 28 U.S.C. § 451 ineffective. Subdivision (a) of the rule retains the substance and intent of the earlier draft by making bankruptcy judges subject to 28 U.S.C. § 455.

The word "associated" in subdivision (b) has been changed to "connected" in order to conform with Rule 5002(b).

CROSS REFERENCES

Definition of relative, see 11 USCA § 101.

Prohibited appointments, see Fed.Rules Bankr.Proc. Rule 5002, 11 USCA.

LIBRARY REFERENCES

American Digest System

Judges ⊕39 to 56.

Key Number System Topic No. 227.

Corpus Juris Secundum

CJS Bankruptcy § 34, Bias or Knowledge.

CJS Bankruptcy § 35, Personal or Family Involvement.

CJS Bankruptcy § 36, Involvement of Former Law Associate.

CJS Bankruptcy § 37, Financial or Other Interest.

CJS Bankruptcy § 56, Eligibility to Serve as Trustee or Examiner--Disinterestedness Requirement.

CJS Bankruptcy § 786, Disqualification of Judge from Allowing Compensation.

Rule 5005.   Filing and Transmittal of Papers

(a) Filing

(1) Place of filing

The lists, schedules, statements, proofs of claim or interest, complaints, motions, applications, objections and other papers required to be filed by these rules, except as provided in 28 U.S.C. § 1409, shall be filed with the clerk in the district where the case under the Code is pending. The judge of that court may permit the papers to be filed with the judge, in which event the filing date shall be noted thereon, and they shall be forthwith transmitted to the clerk. The clerk shall not refuse to accept for filing any petition or other paper presented for the purpose of filing solely because it is not presented in proper form as required by these rules or any local rules or practices.

(2) Filing by electronic means

A court may by local rule permit or require documents to be filed, signed, or verified by electronic means that are consistent with technical standards, if any, that the Judicial Conference of the United States establishes. A local rule may require filing by electronic means only if reasonable exceptions are allowed. A document filed by electronic means in compliance with a local rule constitutes a written paper for the purpose of applying these rules, the Federal Rules of Civil Procedure made applicable by these rules, and § 107 of the Code.

(b) Transmittal to the United States trustee

(1) The complaints, motions, applications, objections and other papers required to be transmitted to the United States trustee by these rules shall be mailed or delivered to an office of the United States trustee, or to another place designated by the United States trustee, in the district where the case under the Code is pending.

(2) The entity, other than the clerk, transmitting a paper to the United States trustee shall promptly file as proof of such transmittal a verified statement identifying the paper and stating the date on which it was transmitted to the United States trustee.

(3) Nothing in these rules shall require the clerk to transmit any paper to the United States trustee if the United States trustee requests in writing that the paper not be transmitted.

(c) Error in filing or transmittal

A paper intended to be filed with the clerk but erroneously delivered to the United States trustee, the trustee, the attorney for the trustee, a bankruptcy judge, a district judge, the clerk of the bankruptcy appellate panel, or the clerk of the district court shall, after the date of its receipt has been noted thereon, be transmitted forthwith to the clerk of the bankruptcy court. A paper intended to be transmitted to the United States trustee but erroneously delivered to the clerk, the trustee, the attorney for the trustee, a bankruptcy judge, a district judge, the clerk of the bankruptcy appellate panel, or the clerk of the district court shall, after the date of its receipt has been noted thereon, be transmitted forthwith to the United States trustee. In the interest of justice, the court may order that a paper erroneously delivered shall be deemed filed with the clerk or transmitted to the United States trustee as of the date of its original delivery.

(As amended Mar. 30, 1987, eff. Aug. 1, 1987 ; Apr. 30, 1991, eff. Aug. 1, 1991; Apr. 22, 1993, eff. Aug. 1, 1993; Apr. 23, 1996, eff. Dec. 1, 1996; Apr. 12, 2006, eff. Dec. 1, 2006.)

ADVISORY COMMITTEE NOTES

Subdivision (a) is an adaptation of Rule 5(e) F.R.Civ.P. §§ 301–304 of the Code and Rules 1002 and 1003 require that cases under the Code be commenced by filing a petition "with the bankruptcy court." Other sections of the Code and other rules refer to or contemplate filing but there is no specific reference to filing with the bankruptcy court. For example, § 501 of the Code requires filing of proofs of claim and Rule 3016(c) requires the filing of a disclosure statement. This subdivision applies to all situations in which filing is required. Except when filing in another district is authorized by 28 U.S.C. § 1473, all papers, including complaints commencing adversary proceedings, must be filed in the court where the case under the Code is pending.

Subdivision (b) is the same as former Bankruptcy Rule 509(c).

1987 Amendments

Subdivision (a) is amended to conform with the 1984 amendments.

1991 Amendments

Subdivision (b)(1) is flexible in that it permits the United States trustee to designate a place or places for receiving papers within the district in which the case is pending. Transmittal of papers to the United States trustee may be accomplished by mail or delivery, including delivery by courier, and the technical requirements for service of process are not applicable. Although papers relating to a proceeding commenced in another district pursuant to 28 U.S.C. § 1409 must be filed with the clerk in that district, the papers required to be transmitted to the United States trustee must be mailed or delivered to the United States trustee in the district in which the case under the Code is pending. The United States trustee in the district in which the case is pending monitors the progress of the case and should be informed of all developments in the case wherever the developments take place.

Subdivision (b)(2) requires that proof of transmittal to the United States trustee be filed with the clerk. If papers are served on the United States trustee by mail or otherwise, the filing of proof of service would satisfy the requirements of this subdivision. This requirement enables the court to assure that papers are actually transmitted to the United States trustee in compliance with the rules. When the rules require that a paper be transmitted to the United States trustee and proof of transmittal has not been filed with the clerk, the court should not schedule a hearing or should take other appropriate action to assure that the paper is transmitted to the United States trustee. The filing of the verified statement with the clerk also enables other parties in interest to determine whether a paper has been transmitted to the United States trustee.

Subdivision (b)(3) is designed to relieve the clerk of any obligation under these rules to transmit any paper to the United States trustee if the United States trustee does not wish to receive it.

Subdivision (c) is amended to include the erroneous delivery of papers intended to be transmitted to the United States trustee.

1993 Amendments

Subdivision (a) is amended to conform to the 1991 amendment to Rule 5(e) F.R.Civ.P. It is not a suitable role for the office of the clerk to refuse to accept for filing papers not conforming to requirements of form imposed by these rules or by local rules or practices. The enforcement of these rules and local rules is a role for a judge. This amendment does not require the clerk to accept for filing papers sent to the clerk's office by facsimile transmission.

1996 Amendments

The rule is amended to permit, but not require, courts to adopt local rules that allow filing, signing, or verifying of documents by electronic means. However, such local rules must be consistent with technical standards, if any, promulgated by the Judicial Conference of the United States.

An important benefit to be derived by permitting filing by electronic means is that the extensive volume of paper received and maintained as records in the clerk's office will be reduced substantially. With the receipt of electronic data transmissions by computer, the clerk may maintain records electronically without the need to reproduce them in tangible paper form.

Judicial Conference standards governing the technological aspects of electronic filing will result in uniformity among judicial districts to accommodate an increasingly national bar. By delegating to the Judicial Conference the establishment and future amendment of national standards for electronic filing, the Supreme Court and Congress will be relieved of the burden of reviewing and promulgating detailed rules dealing with complex technological standards. Another reason for leaving to the Judicial Conference the formulation of technological standards for electronic filing is that advances in computer technology occur often, and changes in the technological standards may have to be implemented more frequently than would be feasible by rule amendment under the Rules Enabling Act process.

It is anticipated that standards established by the Judicial Conference will govern technical specifications for electronic data transmission, such as requirements relating to the formatting of data, speed of transmission, means to transmit copies of supporting documentation, and security of communication procedures. In addition, before procedures for electronic filing are implemented, standards must be established

to assure the proper maintenance and integrity of the record and to provide appropriate access and retrieval mechanisms. These matters will be governed by local rules until system-wide standards are adopted by the Judicial Conference.

Rule 9009 requires that the Official Forms shall be observed and used "with alterations as may be appropriate." Compliance with local rules and any Judicial Conference standards with respect to the formatting or presentation of electronically transmitted data, to the extent that they do not conform to the Official Forms, would be an appropriate alteration within the meaning of Rule 9009.

These rules require that certain documents be in writing. For example, Rule 3001 states that a proof of claim is a "written statement." Similarly, Rule 3007 provides that an objection to a claim "shall be in writing." Pursuant to the new subdivision (a)(2), any requirement under these rules that a paper be written may be satisfied by filing the document by electronic means, notwithstanding the fact that the clerk neither receives nor prints a paper reproduction of the electronic data.

Section 107(a) of the Code provides that a "paper" filed in a case is a public record open to examination by an entity at reasonable times without charge, except as provided in § 107(b). The amendment to subdivision (a)(2) provides that an electronically filed document is to be treated as such a public record.

Although under subdivision (a)(2) electronically filed documents may be treated as written papers or as signed or verified writings, it is important to emphasize that such treatment is only for the purpose of applying these rules. In addition, local rules and Judicial Conference standards regarding verification must satisfy the requirements of 28 U.S.C. § 1746.

GAP Report on Rule 5005. No changes since publication.

2006 Amendments

Subdivision (a). Amended Rule 5005(a)(2) acknowledges that many courts have required electronic filing by means of a standing order, procedures manual, or local rule. These local practices reflect the advantages that courts and most litigants realize from electronic filings. Courts requiring electronic filing must make reasonable exceptions for persons for whom electronic filing of documents constitutes an unreasonable denial of access to the courts. Experience with the rule will facilitate convergence on uniform exceptions in an amended Rule 5005(a)(2).

Subdivision (c). The rule is amended to include the clerk of the bankruptcy appellate panel among the list of persons required to transmit to the proper person erroneously filed or transmitted papers. The amendment is necessary because the bankruptcy appellate panels were not in existence at the time of the original promulgation of the rule. The amendment also inserts the district judge on the list of persons required to transmit papers intended for the United States trustee but erroneously sent to another person. The district judge is included in the list of persons who must transmit papers to the clerk of the bankruptcy court in the first part of the rule, and there is no reason to exclude the district judge from the list of persons who must transmit erroneously filed papers to the United States trustee.

CROSS REFERENCES

Filing of pleadings and other papers with court, see Fed. Rules Civ.Proc. Rule 5, 28 USCA.

LIBRARY REFERENCES

American Digest System

Bankruptcy ⟨=2127.1, 2163, 2321 to 2325.

Key Number System Topic No. 51.

Corpus Juris Secundum

CJS Bankruptcy § 12, Federal Rules of Civil Procedure.

CJS Bankruptcy § 54, Notices.

CJS Bankruptcy § 82, Meeting of Creditors and Election Procedures.

CJS Bankruptcy § 229, Hearing and Determining Motion for Withdrawal.

CJS Bankruptcy § 284, Signature and Verification of Basis for Filing.

CJS Bankruptcy § 310, General Procedures.

CJS Bankruptcy § 616, Prosecution and Defense of Proceedings; Expedited Procedures.

CJS Bankruptcy § 701, Form of Action as Adversary Proceeding.

Rule 5006. Certification of Copies of Papers

The clerk shall issue a certified copy of the record of any proceeding in a case under the Code or of any paper filed with the clerk on payment of any prescribed fee.

(As amended Apr. 30, 1991, eff. Aug. 1, 1991.)

ADVISORY COMMITTEE NOTES

Fees for certification and copying are fixed by the Judicial Conference under 28 U.S.C. § 1930(b).

Rule 1101 F.R.Evid. makes the Federal Rules of Evidence applicable to cases under the Code. Rule 1005 F.R.Evid. allows the contents of an official record or of a paper filed with the court to be proved by a duly certified copy. A copy certified and issued in accordance with Rule 5006 is accorded authenticity by Rule 902(4) F.R.Evid.

CROSS REFERENCES

Public records, see Fed.Rules Evid. Rule 1005, 28 USCA.

LIBRARY REFERENCES

American Digest System

Bankruptcy ⟨=2121.

Clerks of Courts ⟨=69.

Key Number System Topic Nos. 51, 79.

Rule 5007. Record of Proceedings and Transcripts

(a) Filing of record or transcript

The reporter or operator of a recording device shall certify the original notes of testimony, tape recording, or other original record of the proceeding and promptly file them with the clerk. The person preparing any transcript shall promptly file a certified copy.

(b) Transcript fees

The fees for copies of transcripts shall be charged at rates prescribed by the Judicial Conference of the United States. No fee may be charged for the certified copy filed with the clerk.

(c) Admissibility of record in evidence

A certified sound recording or a transcript of a proceeding shall be admissible as prima facie evidence to establish the record.

(As amended Mar. 30, 1987, eff. Aug. 1, 1987; Apr. 30, 1991, eff. Aug. 1, 1991.)

ADVISORY COMMITTEE NOTES

This rule supplements 28 U.S.C. § 773. A record of proceedings before the bankruptcy judge is to be made whenever practicable. By whatever means the record is made, subdivision (a) requires that the preparer of the record certify and file the original notes, tape recording, or other form of sound recording of the proceedings. Similarly, if a transcript is requested, the preparer is to file a certified copy with the clerk.

Subdivision (b) is derived from 28 U.S.C. § 753(f).

Subdivision (c) is derived from former Bankruptcy Rule 511(c). This subdivision extends to a sound recording the same evidentiary status as a transcript under 28 U.S.C. § 773(b).

1991 Amendments

The words "with the clerk" in the final sentence of subdivision (a) are deleted as unnecessary. See Rules 5005(a) and 9001(3).

CROSS REFERENCES

Reporters, see 28 USCA § 753.

Stenographer; stenographic report or transcript as evidence, see Fed.Rules Civ.Proc. Rule 80, 28 USCA.

LIBRARY REFERENCES

American Digest System

Bankruptcy ⟨=2121.

Courts ⟨=57.

Key Number System Topic Nos. 106, 51.

Rule 5008. Notice Regarding Presumption of Abuse in Chapter 7 Cases of Individual Debtors

If a presumption of abuse has arisen under § 707(b) in a chapter 7 case of an individual with primarily consumer debts, the clerk shall within 10 days after the date of the filing of the petition notify creditors of the presumption of abuse in accordance with Rule 2002. If the debtor has not filed a statement indicating whether a presumption of abuse has arisen, the clerk shall within 10 days after the date of the filing of the petition notify creditors that the debtor has not filed the statement and that further notice will be given if a later filed statement indicates that a presumption of abuse has arisen. If a debtor later files a statement indicating that a presumption of abuse has arisen, the clerk shall notify creditors of the presumption of abuse as promptly as practicable.

(Added Apr. 23, 2008, eff. Dec. 1, 2008.)

ADVISORY COMMITTEE NOTES

2008 Amendments

This rule is new. The 2005 amendments to § 342 of the Code require that clerks give written notice to all creditors not later than 10 days after the date of the filing of the petition that a presumption of abuse has arisen under § 707(b). A statement filed by the debtor will be the source of the clerk's information about the presumption of abuse. This rule enables the clerk to meet its obligation to send the notice within the statutory time period set forth in § 342. In the event that the court receives the debtor's statement after the clerk has sent the first notice, and the debtor's statement indicates a presumption of abuse, the rule requires that the clerk send a second notice.

LIBRARY REFERENCES

Corpus Juris Secundum

CJS Bankruptcy § 301, Notice to Debtor, Creditors, and Indenture Trustees.

CJS Bankruptcy § 432, Presumption of Abuse--Notice.

Rule 5009. Closing Chapter 7 Liquidation, Chapter 12 Family Farmer's Debt Adjustment, Chapter 13 Individual's Debt Adjustment, and Chapter 15 Ancillary and Cross–Border Cases

(a) Cases under chapters 7, 12, and 13

If in a chapter 7, chapter 12, or chapter 13 case the trustee has filed a final report and final account and has certified that the estate has been fully administered, and if within 30 days no objection has been filed by the United States trustee or a party in interest, there shall be a presumption that the estate has been fully administered.

(b) Notice of failure to file Rule 1007(b)(7) statement

If an individual debtor in a chapter 7 or 13 case has not filed the statement required by Rule 1007(b)(7) within 45 days after the first date set for the meeting of creditors under § 341(a) of the Code, the clerk shall promptly notify the debtor that the case will be closed without entry of a discharge unless the statement is filed within the applicable time limit under Rule 1007(c).

(c) Cases under chapter 15

A foreign representative in a proceeding recognized under § 1517 of the Code shall file a final report when the purpose of the representative's appearance in the court is completed. The report shall describe the nature and results of the representative's activities in the court. The foreign representative shall transmit the report to the United States trustee, and give notice of its filing to the debtor, all persons or bodies authorized to administer foreign proceedings of the debtor, all parties to litigation pending in the United States in which the debtor was a party at the time of the filing of the petition, and such other entities as the court may direct. The foreign representative shall file a certificate with the court that notice has been given. If no objection has been filed by the United States trustee or a party in interest within 30 days after the certificate is filed, there shall be a presumption that the case has been fully administered.

(As amended Apr. 30, 1991, eff. Aug. 1, 1991; Apr. 28, 2010, eff. Dec. 1, 2010.)

ADVISORY COMMITTEE NOTES

This rule is the same as § 350(a) of the Code. An estate may be closed even though the period allowed by Rule 3002(c) for filing claims has not expired. The closing of a case may be expedited when a notice of no dividends is given under Rule 2002(e). Dismissal of a case for want of prosecution or failure to pay filing fees is governed by Rule 1017.

1991 Amendments

The final report and account of the trustee is required to be filed with the court and the United States trustee under §§ 704(9), 1202(b)(1), and 1302(b)(1) of the Code. This amendment facilitates the United States trustee's performance of statutory duties to supervise trustees and administer cases under chapters 7, 12, and 13 pursuant to 28 U.S.C. § 586. In the absence of a timely objection by the United States trustee or a party in interest, the court may discharge the trustee and close the case pursuant to § 350(a) without the need to review the final report and account or to determine the merits of the trustee's certification that the estate has been fully administered.

Rule 3022 governs the closing of chapter 11 cases.

2010 Amendments

Subdivisions (a) and (b). The rule is amended to redesignate the former rule as subdivision (a) and to add new subdivisions (b) and (c) to the rule. Subdivision (b) requires the clerk to provide notice to an individual debtor in a chapter 7 or 13 case that the case may be closed without the entry of a discharge due to the failure of the debtor to file a timely statement of completion of a personal financial management course. The purpose of the notice is to provide the debtor with an opportunity to complete the course and file the appropriate document prior to the filing deadline. Timely filing of the document avoids the need for a motion to extend the time retroactively. It also avoids the potential for closing the case without discharge, and the possible need to pay an additional fee in connection with reopening. Timely filing also benefits the clerk's office by reducing the number of instances in which cases must be reopened.

Subdivision (c). Subdivision (c) requires a foreign representative in a chapter 15 case to file a final report setting out the foreign representative's actions and results obtained in the United States court. It also requires the foreign representative to give notice of the filing of the report, and provides interested parties with 30 days to object to the report after the foreign representative has certified that notice has been given. In the absence of a timely objection, a presumption arises that the case is fully administered, and the case may be closed.

CROSS REFERENCES

Debtor to succeed to any tax attributes of estate, see 11 USCA § 346.

Dismissal of case; suspension, see Fed.Rules Bankr.Proc. Rule 1017, 11 USCA.

Final decree, see Fed.Rules Bankr.Proc. Rule 3022, 11 USCA.

Postpetition transfers of estate property not avoidable by trustee after case closed, see 11 USCA § 549.

Scheduled property not administered before case closed deemed abandoned, see 11 USCA § 554.

LIBRARY REFERENCES

Corpus Juris Secundum

CJS Bankruptcy § 1105, Closing.

Rule 5010. Reopening Cases

A case may be reopened on motion of the debtor or other party in interest pursuant to § 350(b) of the Code. In a chapter 7, 12, or 13 case a trustee shall not be appointed by the United States trustee unless the court determines that a trustee is necessary to protect the interests of creditors and the debtor or to insure efficient administration of the case.

(As amended Mar. 30, 1987, eff. Aug. 1, 1987; Apr. 30, 1991, eff. Aug. 1, 1991.)

ADVISORY COMMITTEE NOTES

Section 350(b) of the Code provides: "A case may be reopened in the court in which such case was closed to administer assets, to accord relief to the debtor, or for other cause."

Rule 9024, which incorporates Rule 60 F.R.Civ.P., exempts motions to reopen cases under the Code from the one year limitation of Rule 60(b).

Although a case has been closed the court may sometimes act without reopening the case. Under Rule 9024, clerical errors in judgments, orders, or other parts of the record or errors therein caused by oversight or omission may be corrected. A judgment determined to be non-dischargeable pursuant to Rule 4007 may be enforced after a case is closed by a writ of execution obtained pursuant to Rule 7069.

1987 Amendments

In order to avoid unnecessary cost and delay, the rule is amended to permit reopening of a case without the appointment of a trustee when the services of a trustee are not needed.

1991 Amendments

This rule is amended to conform to the 1986 amendments to the Code that give the United States trustee the duty to appoint trustees in chapter 7, 12 and 13 cases. See §§ 701, 702(d), 1202(a), and 1302(a) of the Code. In most reopened

cases, a trustee is not needed because there are no assets to be administered. Therefore, in the interest of judicial economy, this rule is amended so that a motion will not be necessary unless the United States trustee or a party in interest seeks the appointment of a trustee in the reopened case.

CROSS REFERENCES

Motions; form and service, see Fed.Rules Bankr.Proc. Rule 9013, 11 USCA.

Relief from judgment or order, see Fed.Rules Bankr.Proc. Rule 9024, 11 USCA.

LIBRARY REFERENCES

American Digest System

Bankruptcy ⇔3444.10 to 3444.60.

Key Number System Topic No. 51.

Corpus Juris Secundum

CJS Bankruptcy § 63, Appointment of Trustee in Reopened Case.

CJS Bankruptcy § 74, Chapter 12 Cases.

CJS Bankruptcy § 75, Chapter 13 Cases.

CJS Bankruptcy § 1106, Reopening.

Rule 5011. Withdrawal and Abstention from Hearing a Proceeding

(a) Withdrawal

A motion for withdrawal of a case or proceeding shall be heard by a district judge.

(b) Abstention from hearing a proceeding

A motion for abstention pursuant to 28 U.S.C. § 1334(c) shall be governed by Rule 9014 and shall be served on the parties to the proceeding.

(c) Effect of filing of motion for withdrawal or abstention

The filing of a motion for withdrawal of a case or proceeding or for abstention pursuant to 28 U.S.C. § 1334(c) shall not stay the administration of the case or any proceeding therein before the bankruptcy judge except that the bankruptcy judge may stay, on such terms and conditions as are proper, proceedings pending disposition of the motion. A motion for a stay ordinarily shall be presented first to the bankruptcy judge. A motion for a stay or relief from a stay filed in the district court shall state why it has not been presented to or obtained from the bankruptcy judge. Relief granted by the district judge shall be on such terms and conditions as the judge deems proper.

(Added Mar. 30, 1987, eff. Aug. 1, 1987 and amended Apr. 30, 1991, eff. Aug. 1, 1991.)

ADVISORY COMMITTEE NOTES

Motions for withdrawal pursuant to 28 U.S.C. § 157(d) or abstention pursuant to 28 U.S.C. § 1334(c), like all other motions, are to be filed with the clerk as required by Rule 5005(a). If a bankruptcy clerk has been appointed for the district, all motions are filed with the bankruptcy clerk. The method for forwarding withdrawal motions to the district court will be established by administrative procedures.

Subdivision (a). Section 157(d) permits the district court to order withdrawal on its own motion or the motion of a party. Subdivision (a) of this rule makes it clear that the bankruptcy judge will not conduct hearings on a withdrawal motion. The withdrawal decision is committed exclusively to the district court.

Subdivision (b). A decision to abstain under 28 U.S.C. § 1334(c) is not appealable. The district court is vested originally with jurisdiction and the decision to relinquish that jurisdiction must ultimately be a matter for the district court. The bankruptcy judge ordinarily will be in the best position to evaluate the grounds asserted for abstention. This subdivision (b) provides that the initial hearing on the motion is before the bankruptcy judge. The procedure for review of the report and recommendation are governed by Rule 9033.

This rule does not apply to motions under § 305 of the Code for abstention from hearing a case. Judicial decisions will determine the scope of the bankruptcy judge's authority under § 305.

Subdivision (c). Unless the court so orders, proceedings are not stayed when motions are filed for withdrawal or for abstention from hearing a proceeding. Because of the district court's authority over cases and proceedings, the subdivision authorizes the district court to order a stay or modify a stay ordered by the bankruptcy judge.

1991 Amendments

Subdivision (b) is amended to delete the restriction that limits the role of the bankruptcy court to the filing of a report and recommendation for disposition of a motion for abstention under 28 U.S.C. § 1334(c)(2). This amendment is consistent with § 309(b) of the Judicial Improvements Act of 1990 which amended § 1334(c(2) so that it allows an appeal to the district court of a bankruptcy court's order determining an abstention motion. This subdivision is also amended to clarify that the motion is a contested matter governed by Rule 9014 and that it must be served on all parties to the proceeding with is the subject of the motion.

LIBRARY REFERENCES

American Digest System

Bankruptcy ☞2103.

Federal Courts ☞47.5, 65.

Key Number System Topic Nos. 170B, 51.

Corpus Juris Secundum

CJS Bankruptcy § 202, Procedure; Motion and Stay.

CJS Bankruptcy § 229, Hearing and Determining Motion for Withdrawal.

CJS Bankruptcy § 230, Stays When Withdrawal of Reference is Sought.

Rule 5012. Agreements Concerning Coordination of Proceedings in Chapter 15 Cases

Approval of an agreement under § 1527(4) of the Code shall be sought by motion. The movant shall attach to the motion a copy of the proposed agreement or protocol and, unless the court directs otherwise, give at least 30 days' notice of any hearing on the motion by transmitting the motion to the United States trustee, and serving it on the debtor, all persons or bodies authorized to administer foreign proceedings of the debtor, all entities against whom provisional relief is being sought under § 1519, all parties to litigation pending in the United States in which the debtor was a party at the time of the filing of the petition, and such other entities as the court may direct.
(Added Apr. 28, 2010, eff. Dec. 1, 2010.)

ADVISORY COMMITTEE NOTES

2010 Adoption

This rule is new. In chapter 15 cases, any party in interest may seek approval of an agreement, frequently referred to as a "protocol," that will assist with the conduct of the case. Because the needs of the courts and the parties may vary greatly from case to case, the rule does not attempt to limit the form or scope of a protocol. Rather, the rule simply requires that approval of a particular protocol be sought by motion, and designates the persons entitled to notice of the hearing on the motion. These agreements, or protocols, drafted entirely by parties in interest in the case, are intended to provide valuable assistance to the court in the management of the case. Interested parties may find guidelines published by organizations, such as the American Law Institute and the International Insolvency Institute, helpful in crafting agreements or protocols to apply in a particular case.

LIBRARY REFERENCES

Corpus Juris Secundum

CJS Bankruptcy § 389, Cooperation and Communication With Foreign Courts and Foreign Representatives.

PART VI—COLLECTION AND LIQUIDATION OF THE ESTATE

Rule
6001. Burden of Proof as to Validity of Postpetition Transfer.
6002. Accounting by Prior Custodian of Property of the Estate.
6003. Interim and Final Relief Immediately Following the Commencement of the Case—Applications for Employment; Motions for Use, Sale, or Lease of Property; and Motions for Assumption or Assignment of Executory Contracts.
6004. Use, Sale, or Lease of Property.
6005. Appraisers and Auctioneers.
6006. Assumption, Rejection or Assignment of an Executory Contract or Unexpired Lease.
6007. Abandonment or Disposition of Property.
6008. Redemption of Property from Lien or Sale.
6009. Prosecution and Defense of Proceedings by Trustee or Debtor in Possession.
6010. Proceeding to Avoid Indemnifying Lien or Transfer to Surety.
6011. Disposal of Patient Records in Health Care Business Case.

Rule 6001. Burden of Proof as to Validity of Postpetition Transfer

Any entity asserting the validity of a transfer under § 549 of the Code shall have the burden of proof.

ADVISORY COMMITTEE NOTES

This rule is derived from former Bankruptcy Rule 603. The Act contained, in § 70d [former § 110(d) of this title], a provision placing the burden of proof on the same person as did Rule 603. The Code does not contain any directive with respect to the burden of proof. This omission, in all probability, resulted from the intention to leave matters affecting evidence to these rules. See H.Rep. No. 95–595, 95th Cong. 1st Sess. (1977) 293.

LIBRARY REFERENCES

American Digest System

Bankruptcy ⬡2726.1(1).

Key Number System Topic No. 51.

Corpus Juris Secundum

CJS Bankruptcy § 703, Burden of Proof.

Rule 6002. Accounting by Prior Custodian of Property of the Estate

(a) Accounting required

Any custodian required by the Code to deliver property in the custodian's possession or control to the trustee shall promptly file and transmit to the United States trustee a report and account with respect to the property of the estate and the administration thereof.

(b) Examination of administration

On the filing and transmittal of the report and account required by subdivision (a) of this rule and after an examination has been made into the superseded administration, after notice and a hearing, the court shall determine the propriety of the administration, including the reasonableness of all disbursements.

(As amended Mar. 30, 1987, eff. Aug. 1, 1987; Apr. 30, 1991, eff. Aug. 1, 1991; Apr. 22, 1993, eff. Aug. 1, 1993.)

ADVISORY COMMITTEE NOTES

"Custodian" is defined in § 101(10) of the Code. The definition includes a trustee or receiver appointed in proceedings not under the Code, as well as an assignee for the benefit of creditors.

This rule prescribes the procedure to be followed by a custodian who under § 543 of the Code is required to deliver property to the trustee and to account for its disposition. The examination under subdivision (b) may be initiated (1) on the motion of the custodian required to account under subdivision (a) for an approval of his account and discharge thereon, (2) on the motion of, or the filing of an objection to the custodian's account by, the trustee or any other party in interest, or (3) on the court's own initiative. Rule 9014 applies to any contested matter arising under this rule.

Section 543(d) is similar to an abstention provision. It grants the bankruptcy court discretion to permit the custodian to remain in possession and control of the property. In that event, the custodian is excused from complying with § 543(a)(c) and thus would not be required to turn over the property to the trustee. When there is no duty to turn over to the trustee, Rule 6002 would not be applicable.

1991 Amendments

This rule is amended to enable the United States trustee to review, object to, or to otherwise be heard regarding the custodian's report and accounting. See §§ 307 and 543 of the Code.

1993 Amendments

Subdivision (b) is amended to conform to the language of § 102(1) of the Code.

CROSS REFERENCES

Accountability of prior custodians for estate property, see 11 USCA § 543.

Definition of custodian, see 11 USCA § 101.

Proceedings under this rule as nonadversarial proceedings, see Fed.Rules Bankr.Proc. Rule 7001, 11 USCA.

Property of estate, see 11 USCA § 541.

LIBRARY REFERENCES

American Digest System

Bankruptcy ⬡3064.

Key Number System Topic No. 51.

Corpus Juris Secundum

CJS Bankruptcy § 139, Adversary Proceedings.

CJS Bankruptcy § 261, Power to Render Declaratory Judgment.

CJS Bankruptcy § 614, Form of Action as Adversary Proceeding or Contested Matter

CJS Bankruptcy § 645, Report and Account.

Rule 6003. Interim and Final Relief Immediately Following the Commencement of the Case—Applications for Employment; Motions for Use, Sale, or Lease of Property; and Motions for Assumption or Assignment of Executory Contracts

Except to the extent that relief is necessary to avoid immediate and irreparable harm, the court shall not, within 21 days after the filing of the petition, issue an order granting the following:

(a) an application under Rule 2014;

(b) a motion to use, sell, lease, or otherwise incur an obligation regarding property of the estate, including a motion to pay all or part of a claim that arose before the filing of the petition, but not a motion under Rule 4001; or

(c) a motion to assume or assign an executory contract or unexpired lease in accordance with § 365. (Added Apr. 30, 2007, eff. Dec. 1, 2007; amended Mar. 26, 2009, eff. Dec. 1, 2009; Apr. 26, 2011, eff. Dec. 1, 2011.)

ADVISORY COMMITTEE NOTES

2007 Adoption

There can be a flurry of activity during the first days of a bankruptcy case. This activity frequently takes place prior to the formation of a creditors' committee, and it also can include substantial amounts of materials for the court and parties in interest to review and evaluate. This rule is intended to alleviate some of the time pressures present at the start of a case so that full and close consideration can be given to matters that may have a fundamental impact on the case.

The rule provides that the court cannot grant relief on applications for the employment of professional persons, motions for the use, sale, or lease of property of the estate other than such a motion under Rule 4001, and motions to assume or assign executory contracts and unexpired leases for the first 20 days of the case, unless granting relief is necessary to avoid immediate and irreparable harm. This standard is taken from Rule 4001(b)(2) and (c)(2), and decisions under those provisions should provide guidance for the application of this provision.

This rule does not govern motions and applications made more than 20 days after the filing of the petition.

2009 Amendments

The rule is amended to implement changes in connection with the amendment to Rule 9006(a) and the manner by which time is computed under the rules. The deadline in the rule is amended to substitute a deadline that is a multiple of seven days. Throughout the rules, deadlines are amended in the following manner:

- 5–day periods become 7–day periods
- 10–day periods become 14–day periods
- 15–day periods become 14–day periods
- 20–day periods become 21–day periods
- 25–day periods become 28–day periods

2011 Amendments

The rule is amended to clarify that it limits the timing of the entry of certain orders, but does not prevent the court from providing an effective date for such an order that may relate back to the time of the filing of the application or motion, or to some other date. For example, while the rule prohibits, absent immediate and irreparable harm, the court from authorizing the employment of counsel during the first 21 days of a case, it does not prevent the court from providing in an order entered after expiration of the 21–day period that the relief requested in the motion or application is effective as of a date earlier than the issuance of the order. Nor does it prohibit the filing of an application or motion for relief prior to expiration of the 21–day period. Nothing in the rule prevents a professional from representing the trustee or a debtor in possession pending the approval of an application for the approval of the employment under Rule 2014.

The amendment also clarifies that the scope of the rule is limited to granting the specifically identified relief set out in the subdivisions of the rule. Deleting "regarding" from the rule clarifies that the rule does not prohibit the court from entering orders in the first 21 days of the case that may relate to the motions and applications set out in (a), (b), and (c); it is only prohibited from granting the relief requested by those motions or applications. For example, in the first 21 days of the case, the court could grant the relief requested in a motion to establish bidding procedures for the sale of property of the estate, but it could not, absent immediate and irreparable harm, grant a motion to approve the sale of property.

LIBRARY REFERENCES

Corpus Juris Secundum

CJS Bankruptcy § 365, Commencement and Order for Relief.

CJS Bankruptcy § 767, Application for Order of Employment.

Rule 6004. Use, Sale, or Lease of Property

(a) Notice of proposed use, sale, or lease of property

Notice of a proposed use, sale, or lease of property, other than cash collateral, not in the ordinary course of business shall be given pursuant to Rule 2002(a)(2), (c)(1), (i), and (k) and, if applicable, in accordance with § 363(b)(2) of the Code.

(b) Objection to proposal

Except as provided in subdivisions (c) and (d) of this rule, an objection to a proposed use, sale, or lease of property shall be filed and served not less than seven days before the date set for the proposed action or within the time fixed by the court. An objection to the proposed use, sale, or lease of property is governed by Rule 9014.

(c) Sale free and clear of liens and other interests

A motion for authority to sell property free and clear of liens or other interests shall be made in accordance with Rule 9014 and shall be served on the parties who have liens or other interests in the property to be sold. The notice required by subdivision (a) of this rule shall include the date of the hearing on the motion and the time within which objections may be filed and served on the debtor in possession or trustee.

(d) Sale of property under $2,500

Notwithstanding subdivision (a) of this rule, when all of the nonexempt property of the estate has an aggregate gross value less than $2,500, it shall be sufficient to give a general notice of intent to sell such property other than in the ordinary course of business to all creditors, indenture trustees, committees appointed or elected pursuant to the Code, the United States trustee and other persons as the court may direct. An objection to any such sale may be filed and served by a party in interest within 14 days of the mailing of the notice, or within the time fixed by the court. An objection is governed by Rule 9014.

(e) Hearing

If a timely objection is made pursuant to subdivision (b) or (d) of this rule, the date of the hearing thereon may be set in the notice given pursuant to subdivision (a) of this rule.

(f) Conduct of sale not in the ordinary course of business

(1) Public or private sale

All sales not in the ordinary course of business may be by private sale or by public auction. Unless it is impracticable, an itemized statement of the property sold, the name of each purchaser, and the price received for each item or lot or for the property as a whole if sold in bulk shall be filed on completion of a sale. If the property is sold by an auctioneer, the auctioneer shall file the statement, transmit a copy thereof to the United States trustee, and furnish a copy to the trustee, debtor in possession, or chapter 13 debtor. If the property is not sold by an auctioneer, the trustee, debtor in possession, or chapter 13 debtor shall file the statement and transmit a copy thereof to the United States trustee.

(2) Execution of instruments

After a sale in accordance with this rule the debtor, the trustee, or debtor in possession, as the case may be, shall execute any instrument necessary or ordered by the court to effectuate the transfer to the purchaser.

(g) Sale of personally identifiable information

(1) Motion

A motion for authority to sell or lease personally identifiable information under § 363(b)(1)(B) shall include a request for an order directing the United States trustee to appoint a consumer privacy ombudsman under § 332. Rule 9014 governs the motion which shall be served on: any committee elected under § 705 or appointed under § 1102 of the Code, or if the case is a chapter 11 reorganization case and no committee of unsecured creditors has been appointed under § 1102, on the creditors included on the list of creditors filed under Rule 1007(d); and on such other entities as the court may direct. The motion shall be transmitted to the United States trustee.

(2) Appointment

If a consumer privacy ombudsman is appointed under § 332, no later than seven days before the hearing on the motion under § 363(b)(1)(B), the United States trustee shall file a notice of the appointment, including the name and address of the person appointed. The United States trustee's notice shall be accompanied by a verified statement of the person appointed setting forth the person's connections with the debtor, creditors, any other party in interest, their respective attorneys and accountants, the United States trustee, or any person employed in the office of the United States trustee.

(h) Stay of order authorizing use, sale, or lease of property

An order authorizing the use, sale, or lease of property other than cash collateral is stayed until the expiration of 14 days after entry of the order, unless the court orders otherwise.

(As amended Mar. 30, 1987, eff. Aug. 1, 1987; Apr. 30, 1991, eff. Aug. 1, 1991; Apr. 29, 1999, eff. Dec. 1, 1999; Apr. 23, 2008, eff. Dec. 1, 2008; Mar. 26, 2009, eff. Dec. 1, 2009.)

ADVISORY COMMITTEE NOTES

Subdivisions (a) and (b). Pursuant to § 363(b) of the Code, a trustee or debtor in possession may use, sell, or lease property other than in the ordinary course of business only after notice and hearing. Rule 2002(a), (c) and (i) specifies the time when notice of sale is to be given, the contents of the notice and the persons to whom notice is to be given of sales of property. Subdivision (a) makes those provisions applicable as well to notices for proposed use and lease of property.

The Code does not provide the time within which parties may file objections to a proposed sale. Subdivision (b) of the rule requires the objection to be in writing and filed not less than five days before the proposed action is to take place. The objection should also be served within that time on the person who is proposing to take the action which would be either the trustee or debtor in possession. This time period is subject to change by the court. In some instances there is a need to conduct a sale in a short period of time and the court is given discretion to tailor the requirements to the circumstances.

Subdivision (c). In some situations a notice of sale for different pieces of property to all persons specified in Rule 2002(a) may be uneconomic and inefficient. This is particularly true in some chapter 7 liquidation cases when there is property of relatively little value which must be sold by the trustee. Subdivision (c) allows a general notice of intent to sell when the aggregate value of the estate's property is less than $2,500. The gross value is the value of the property without regard to the amount of any debt secured by a lien on the property. It is not necessary to give a detailed notice specifying the time and place of a particular sale. Thus, the requirements of Rule 2002(c) need not be met. If this method of providing notice of sales is used, the subdivision specifies that parties in interest may serve and file objections to the proposed sale of any property within the class and the time for service and filing is fixed at not later than 15 days after mailing the notice. The court may fix a different time. Subdivision (c) would have little utility in chapter 11 cases. Pursuant to Rule 2002(i), the court can limit notices of sale to the creditors' committee appointed under § 1102 of the Code and the same burdens present in a small chapter 7 case would not exist.

Subdivision (d). If a timely objection is filed, a hearing is required with respect to the use, sale, or lease of property. Subdivision (d) renders the filing of an objection tantamount to requesting a hearing so as to require a hearing pursuant to §§ 363(b) and 102(1)(B)(i).

Subdivision (e) is derived in part from former Bankruptcy Rule 606(b) but does not carry forward the requirement of that rule that court approval be obtained for sales of property. Pursuant to § 363(b) court approval is not required unless timely objection is made to the proposed sale. The itemized statement or information required by the subdivision is not necessary when it would be impracticable to prepare it or set forth the information. For example, a liquidation sale of retail goods although not in the ordinary course of business may be on a daily ongoing basis and only summaries may be available.

The duty imposed by paragraph (2) does not affect the power of the bankruptcy court to order third persons to execute instruments transferring property purchased at a sale under this subdivision. See, e.g., In re Rosenberg, 138 F.2d 409 (7th Cir. 1943).

1987 Amendments

Subdivision (a) is amended to conform to the 1984 amendments to § 363(b)(2) of the Code.

Subdivision (b) is amended to provide that an objection to a proposed use, sale, or lease of property creates a contested matter governed by Rule 9014. A similar amendment is made to subdivision (d), which was formerly subdivision (c).

Subdivision (c) is new. Section 363(f) provides that sales free and clear of liens or other interests are only permitted if one of the five statutory requirements is satisfied. Rule 9013 requires that a motion state with particularity the grounds relied upon by the movant. A motion for approval of a sale free and clear of liens or other interests is subject to Rule 9014, service must be made on the parties holding liens or other interests in the property, and notice of the hearing on the motion and the time for filing objections must be included in the notice given under subdivision (a).

1991 Amendments

This rule is amended to provide notice to the United States trustee of a proposed use, sale or lease of property not in the ordinary course of business. See Rule 2002(k). Subdivision (f)(1) is amended to enable the United States trustee to monitor the progress of the case in accordance with 28 U.S.C. § 586(a)(3)(G).

The words "with the clerk" in subdivision (f)(1) are deleted as unnecessary. See Rules 5005(a) and 9001(3).

1999 Amendments

Subdivision (g) is added to provide sufficient time for a party to request a stay pending appeal of an order authorizing the use, sale, or lease of property under § 363(b) of the Code before the order is implemented. It does not affect the time for filing a notice of appeal in accordance with Rule 8002.

Rule 6004(g) does not apply to orders regarding the use of cash collateral and does not affect the trustee's right to use, sell, or lease property without a court order to the extent permitted under § 363 of the Code.

The court may, in its discretion, order that Rule 6004(g) is not applicable so that the property may be used, sold, or leased immediately in accordance with the order entered by the court. Alternatively, the court may order that the stay under Rule 6004(g) is for a fixed period less than 10 days.

Gap Report on Rule 6004. No changes since publication.

2008 Amendments

The rule is amended by inserting a new subdivision (g) to implement §§ 332 and 363(b)(1)(B) of the Code, added by the 2005 amendments. This rule governs the proposed transfer of personally identifiable information in a manner inconsistent with any policy covering the transfer of the information. Rule 2002(c)(1) requires the seller to state in the notice of the sale or lease whether the transfer is consistent with and policy governing the transfer of the information.

Under § 332 of the Code, the consumer privacy ombudsman must be appointed at least five days prior to the hearing on a sale or lease of personally identifiable information. In an appropriate case, the consumer privacy ombudsman may seek a continuance of the hearing on the proposed sale to perform the tasks required of the ombudsman by § 332 of the Code.

Former subdivision (g) is redesignated as subdivision (h).

2009 Amendments

The rule is amended to implement changes in connection with the amendment to Rule 9006(a) and the manner by which time is computed under the rules. The deadlines in the rule are amended to substitute a deadline that is a multiple of seven days. Throughout the rules, deadlines are amended in the following manner:

- 5–day periods become 7–day periods
- 10–day periods become 14–day periods
- 15–day periods become 14–day periods
- 20–day periods become 21–day periods
- 25–day periods become 28–day periods

CROSS REFERENCES

Appraisers and auctioneers, see Fed.Rules Bankr.Proc. Rule 6005, 11 USCA.

Authorization to operate debtor's business—

Individual debt adjustment case, see 11 USCA § 1304.

Liquidation case, see 11 USCA § 721.

Reorganization case, see 11 USCA § 1108.

Twenty-day notice of property disposition to include certain information, see Fed.Rules Bankr.Proc. Rule 2002, 11 USCA.

LIBRARY REFERENCES

American Digest System

Bankruptcy ⟐3061 to 3088, 3776.5.

Key Number System Topic No. 51.

Corpus Juris Secundum

CJS Bankruptcy § 856, Motion and Notice.

CJS Bankruptcy § 867, Stay of Order Authorizing Use, Sale, or Lease of Property.

CJS Bankruptcy § 877, Sale or Lease of Personally Identifiable Information.

CJS Bankruptcy § 879, Service and Content of Notices.

CJS Bankruptcy § 886, Authorization to Sell Property Free and Clear; Notice.

Rule 6005.   Appraisers and Auctioneers

The order of the court approving the employment of an appraiser or auctioneer shall fix the amount or rate of compensation. No officer or employee of the Judicial Branch of the United States or the United States Department of Justice shall be eligible to act as appraiser or auctioneer. No residence or licensing requirement shall disqualify an appraiser or auctioneer from employment.

(As amended Mar. 30, 1987, eff. Aug. 1, 1987; Apr. 30, 1991, eff. Aug. 1, 1991.)

ADVISORY COMMITTEE NOTES

This rule is derived from former Bankruptcy Rule 606(c) and implements § 327 of the Code. Pursuant to § 327, the trustee or debtor in possession may employ one or more appraisers or auctioneers, subject to court approval. This rule requires the court order approving such employment to fix the amount or rate of compensation. The second sentence of the former rule is retained to continue to safeguard against imputations of favoritism which detract from public confidence in bankruptcy administration. The final sentence is to guard against imposition of parochial requirements not warranted by any consideration having to do with sound bankruptcy administration.

Reference should also be made to Rule 2013(a) regarding the limitation on employment of appraisers and auctioneers, and Rule 2014(a) regarding the application for appointment of an appraiser or auctioneer.

CROSS REFERENCES

Employment—

Application for, see Fed.Rules Bankr.Proc. Rule 2014, 11 USCA.

Limitation on appointment, see Fed.Rules Bankr.Proc. Rule 2013, 11 USCA.

Professional persons, see 11 USCA § 327.

Sharing of compensation prohibited, see 11 USCA § 504.

LIBRARY REFERENCES

American Digest System

Bankruptcy ⟐3029.1, 3155, 3160, 3162.

Key Number System Topic No. 51.

Corpus Juris Secundum

CJS Bankruptcy § 760, Disqualification for and Limitations Upon Employment.

CJS Bankruptcy § 850, Valuation and Appraisals of Property.

Rule 6006.   Assumption, Rejection or Assignment of an Executory Contract or Unexpired Lease

(a) Proceeding to assume, reject, or assign

A proceeding to assume, reject, or assign an executory contract or unexpired lease, other than as part of a plan, is governed by Rule 9014.

(b) Proceeding to require trustee to act

A proceeding by a party to an executory contract or unexpired lease in a chapter 9 municipality case, chapter 11 reorganization case, chapter 12 family farmer's debt adjustment case, or chapter 13 individual's debt adjustment case, to require the trustee, debtor in possession, or debtor to determine whether to assume or reject the contract or lease is governed by Rule 9014.

(c) Notice

Notice of a motion made pursuant to subdivision (a) or (b) of this rule shall be given to the other party to the contract or lease, to other parties in interest as the court may direct, and, except in a chapter 9 municipality case, to the United States trustee.

(d) Stay of order authorizing assignment

An order authorizing the trustee to assign an executory contract or unexpired lease under § 365(f) is stayed until the expiration of 14 days after the entry of the order, unless the court orders otherwise.

(e) Limitations

The trustee shall not seek authority to assume or assign multiple executory contracts or unexpired leases in one motion unless: (1) all executory contracts or unexpired leases to be assumed or assigned are between the same parties or are to be assigned to the same assignee; (2) the trustee seeks to assume, but not assign to more than one assignee, unexpired leases of real property; or (3) the court otherwise authorizes the motion to be filed. Subject to subdivision (f), the trustee may join requests for authority to reject multiple executory contracts or unexpired leases in one motion.

(f) Omnibus Motions

A motion to reject or, if permitted under subdivision (e), a motion to assume or assign multiple executory contracts or unexpired leases that are not between the same parties shall:

(1) state in a conspicuous place that parties receiving the omnibus motion should locate their names and their contracts or leases listed in the motion;

(2) list parties alphabetically and identify the corresponding contract or lease;

(3) specify the terms, including the curing of defaults, for each requested assumption or assignment;

(4) specify the terms, including the identity of each assignee and the adequate assurance of future performance by each assignee, for each requested assignment;

(5) be numbered consecutively with other omnibus motions to assume, assign, or reject executory contracts or unexpired leases; and

(6) be limited to no more than 100 executory contracts or unexpired leases.

(g) Finality of Determination

The finality of any order respecting an executory contract or unexpired lease included in an omnibus motion shall be determined as though such contract or lease had been the subject of a separate motion.

(As amended Mar. 30, 1987, eff. Aug. 1, 1987; Apr. 30, 1991, eff. Aug. 1, 1991; Apr. 22, 1993, eff. Aug. 1, 1993; Apr. 29, 1999, eff. Dec. 1, 1999; Apr. 30, 2007, eff. Dec. 1, 2007; Mar. 26, 2009, eff. Dec. 1, 2009.)

ADVISORY COMMITTEE NOTES

Section 365(a) of the Code requires court approval for the assumption or rejection of an executory contract by the trustee or debtor in possession. The trustee or debtor in possession may also assign an executory contract, § 365(f)(1), but must first assume the contract, § 365(f)(2). Rule 6006 provides a procedure for obtaining court approval. It does not apply to the automatic rejection of contracts which are not assumed in chapter 7 liquidation cases within 60 days after the order for relief, or to the assumption or rejection of contracts in a plan pursuant to § 1123(b)(2) or § 1322(b)(7).

Subdivision (a) by referring to Rule 9014 requires a motion to be brought for the assumption, rejection, or assignment of an executory contract. Normally, the motion will be brought by the trustee, debtor in possession or debtor in a chapter 9 or chapter 13 case. The authorization to assume a contract and to assign it may be sought in a single motion and determined by a single order.

Subdivision (b) makes applicable the same motion procedure when the other party to the contract seeks to require the chapter officer to take some action. Section 365(d)(2) recognizes that this procedure is available to these contractual parties. This provision of the Code and subdivision of the rule apply only in chapter 9, 11 and 13 cases. A motion is not necessary in chapter 7 cases because in those cases a contract is deemed rejected if the trustee does not timely assume it.

Subdivision (c) provides for the court to set a hearing on a motion made under subdivision (a) or (b). The other party to

the contract should be given appropriate notice of the hearing and the court may order that other parties in interest, such as a creditors' committee, also be given notice.

1987 Amendments

Subdivisions (a) and (b) are amended to conform to the 1984 amendment to § 365 of the Code, which governs assumption or rejection of time share interests.

Section 1113, governing collective bargaining agreements, was added to the Code in 1984. It sets out requirements that must be met before a collective bargaining agreement may be rejected. The application to reject a collective bargaining agreement referred to in § 1113 shall be made by motion. The motion to reject creates a contested matter under Rule 9014, and service is made pursuant to Rule 7004 on the representative of the employees. The time periods set forth in § 1113(d) govern the scheduling of the hearing and disposition of a motion to reject the agreement.

1991 Amendments

References to time share interests are deleted as unnecessary. Time share interests are within the scope of this rule to the extent that they are governed by § 365 of the Code.

Subdivision (b) is amended to include chapter 12 cases.

Subdivision (c) is amended to enable the United States trustee to appear and be heard on the issues relating to the assumption or rejection of executory contracts and unexpired leases. See §§ 307, 365, and 1113 of the Code.

1993 Amendments

This rule is amended to delete the requirement for an actual hearing when no request for a hearing is made. See rule 9014.

1999 Amendments

Subdivision (d) is added to provide sufficient time for a party to request a stay pending appeal of an order authorizing the assignment of an executory contract or unexpired lease under § 365(f) of the Code before the assignment is consummated. The stay under subdivision (d) does not affect the time for filing a notice of appeal in accordance with Rule 8002.

The court may, in its discretion, order that Rule 6006(d) is not applicable so that the executory contract or unexpired lease may be assigned immediately in accordance with the order entered by the court. Alternatively, the court may order that the stay under Rule 6006(d) is for a fixed period less than 10 days.

Gap Report on Rule 6006. No changes since publication.

2007 Amendments

The rule is amended to authorize the use of omnibus motions to reject multiple executory contracts and unexpired leases. In some cases there may be numerous executory contracts and unexpired leases, and this rule permits the combining of up to one hundred of these contracts and leases in a single motion to initiate the contested matter.

The rule also is amended to authorize the use of a single motion to assume or assign executory contracts and unexpired leases (i) when such contracts and leases are with a single nondebtor party, (ii) when such contracts and leases are being assigned to the same assignee, (iii) when the trustee proposes to assume, but not assign to more than one assignee, real property leases, or (iv) the court authorizes the filing of a joint motion to assume or to assume and assign executory contracts and unexpired leases under other circumstances that are not specifically recognized in the rule.

An omnibus motion to assume, assign, or reject multiple executory contracts and unexpired leases must comply with the procedural requirements set forth in subdivision (f) of the rule, unless the court orders otherwise. These requirements are intended to ensure that the nondebtor parties to the contracts and leases receive effective notice of the motion. Among those requirements is the requirement in subdivision (f)(5) that these motions be consecutively numbered (e.g., Debtor in Possession's First Omnibus Motion for Authority to Assume Executory Contracts and Unexpired Leases, Debtor in Possession's Second Omnibus Motion for Authority to Assume Executory Contracts and Unexpired Leases, etc.). There may be a need for several of these motions in a particular case. Numbering the motions consecutively is essential to keep track of these motions on the court's docket and should avoid confusion that might otherwise result from similar or identically-titled motions.

Subdivision (g) of the rule provides that the finality of any order respecting an executory contract or unexpired lease included in an omnibus motion shall be determined as though such contract or lease had been the subject of a separate motion. A party seeking to appeal any such order is neither required, nor permitted, to await the court's resolution of all other contracts or leases included in the omnibus motion to obtain appellate review of the order. The rule permits the listing of multiple contracts or leases for convenience, and that convenience should not impede timely review of the court's decision with respect to each contract or lease.

2009 Amendments

The rule is amended to implement changes in connection with the amendment to Rule 9006(a) and the manner by which time is computed under the rules. The deadline in the rule is amended to substitute a deadline that is a multiple of seven days. Throughout the rules, deadlines are amended in the following manner:

- 5–day periods become 7–day periods
- 10–day periods become 14–day periods
- 15–day periods become 14–day periods
- 20–day periods become 21–day periods
- 25–day periods become 28–day periods

CROSS REFERENCES

Assumption or rejection of executory contracts by trustee, see 11 USCA § 365.

Commodity contracts—

Compliance by trustee with customer's instructions, see 11 USCA § 765.

Definition of, see 11 USCA § 761.

Treatment of customer property, see 11 USCA § 766.

Motions; form and service, see Fed.Rules Bankr.Proc. Rule 9013, 11 USCA.

Provisions in plan for assumption or rejection of certain executory contracts or unexpired leases, see 11 USCA §§ 1123 and 1322.

LIBRARY REFERENCES

American Digest System

Bankruptcy ⚮3101 to 3117, 3776.5.
Key Number System Topic No. 51.

Corpus Juris Secundum

CJS Bankruptcy § 922, Necessity of Court Approval; Assumption by Conduct.

CJS Bankruptcy § 923, Application for Approval.

CJS Bankruptcy § 928, Judicial Forcing of Decision Date on Request of Party to Contract.

CJS Bankruptcy § 929, Stay of Order Authorizing Assignment.

CJS Bankruptcy § 938, Rejection of Lease by Operation of Law.

CJS Bankruptcy § 945, Application for Court Approval of Rejection; Hearing and Notice.

CJS Bankruptcy § 1180, Treatment of Executory Contracts and Unexpired Leases.

Rule 6007. Abandonment or Disposition of Property

(a) Notice of proposed abandonment or disposition; objections; hearing

Unless otherwise directed by the court, the trustee or debtor in possession shall give notice of a proposed abandonment or disposition of property to the United States trustee, all creditors, indenture trustees, and committees elected pursuant to § 705 or appointed pursuant to § 1102 of the Code. A party in interest may file and serve an objection within 14 days of the mailing of the notice, or within the time fixed by the court. If a timely objection is made, the court shall set a hearing on notice to the United States trustee and to other entities as the court may direct.

(b) Motion by party in interest

A party in interest may file and serve a motion requiring the trustee or debtor in possession to abandon property of the estate.

(c) [Abrogated]

(As amended Mar. 30, 1987, eff. Aug. 1, 1987; Apr. 30, 1991, eff. Aug. 1, 1991; Apr. 22, 1993, eff. Aug. 1, 1993; Mar. 26, 2009, eff. Dec. 1, 2009.)

ADVISORY COMMITTEE NOTES

Sections 554 and 725 of the Code permit and require abandonment and disposition of property of the estate. Pursuant to § 554, the trustee may abandon property but only after notice and hearing. This section is applicable in chapter 7, 11 and 13 cases. Section 725 requires the trustee to dispose of property in which someone other than the estate has an interest, prior to final distribution. It applies only in chapter 7 cases. Notice and hearing are also required conditions. Section 102(1) provides that "notice and hearing" is construed to mean appropriate notice and an opportunity for a hearing. Neither § 554 nor § 725 specify to whom the notices are to be sent. This rule does not apply to § 554(c). Pursuant to that subsection, property is deemed abandoned if it is not administered. A hearing is not required by the statute.

Subdivision (a) requires the notices to be sent to all creditors, indenture trustees, and committees elected under § 705 or appointed under § 1102 of the Code. This may appear burdensome, expensive and inefficient but the subdivision is in keeping with the Code's requirement for notice and the Code's intent to remove the bankruptcy judge from undisputed matters. The burden, expense and inefficiency can be alleviated in large measure by incorporating the notice into or together with the notice of the meeting of creditors so that separate notices would not be required.

Subdivision (b) implements § 554(b) which specifies that a party in interest may request an order that the trustee abandon property. The rule specifies that the request be by motion and, pursuant to the Code, lists the parties who should receive notice.

Subdivision (c) requires a hearing when an objection under subdivision (a) is filed or a motion under subdivision (b) is made. Filing of an objection is sufficient to require a hearing; a separate or joined request for a hearing is unnecessary since the objection itself is tantamount to such a request.

1991 Amendments

This rule is amended to conform to the 1986 amendments to 28 U.S.C. § 586(a) and to the Code. The United States trustee monitors the progress of the case and has standing to raise, appear and be heard on the issues relating to the abandonment or other disposition of property. See §§ 307 and 554 of the Code. Committees of retired employees appointed under § 1114 are not entitled to notice under subdivision (a) of this rule.

1993 Amendments

This rule is amended to clarify that when a motion is made pursuant to subdivision (b), a hearing is not required if a hearing is not requested or if there is no opposition to the motion. *See* Rule 9014. Other amendments are stylistic and make no substantive change.

2009 Amendments

The rule is amended to implement changes in connection with the amendment to Rule 9006(a) and the manner by which time is computed under the rules. The deadline in the rule is amended to substitute a deadline that is a multiple of seven days. Throughout the rules, deadlines are amended in the following manner:

- 5–day periods become 7–day periods
- 10–day periods become 14–day periods
- 15–day periods become 14–day periods
- 20–day periods become 21–day periods
- 25–day periods become 28–day periods

CROSS REFERENCES

Abandonment of property burdensome or of little value to estate, see 11 USCA § 554.

Abandonment of railroad line—

Authorization by court, see 11 USCA § 1170.

Provision of plan, see 11 USCA § 1172.

Disposition of property with lien in liquidation case, see 11 USCA § 725.

Motions; form and service, see Fed.Rules Bankr.Proc. Rule 9013, 11 USCA.

LIBRARY REFERENCES

American Digest System

Bankruptcy ⊃3131 to 3137.

Key Number System Topic No. 51.

Corpus Juris Secundum

CJS Bankruptcy § 657, Standing; Motion.

CJS Bankruptcy § 658, Notice.

CJS Bankruptcy § 659, Objections to Abandonment.

CJS Bankruptcy § 660, Hearing.

Rule 6008. Redemption of Property from Lien or Sale

On motion by the debtor, trustee, or debtor in possession and after hearing on notice as the court may direct, the court may authorize the redemption of property from a lien or from a sale to enforce a lien in accordance with applicable law.

ADVISORY COMMITTEE NOTES

This rule is derived from former Bankruptcy Rule 609. No provision in the Code addresses the trustee's right of redemption. Ordinarily the secured creditor should be given notice of the trustee's motion so that any objection may be raised to the proposed redemption.

The rule applies also to a debtor exercising a right of redemption pursuant to § 722. A proceeding under that section is governed by Rule 9014.

CROSS REFERENCES

Motions; form and service, see Fed.Rules Bankr.Proc. Rule 9013, 11 USCA.

Tangible personal property—

Enforceability of agreement between holder of claim and debtor having consideration based on dischargeable debt, see 11 USCA § 524.

Redemption of exempt or abandoned property from lien securing dischargeable consumer debt, see 11 USCA § 722.

LIBRARY REFERENCES

American Digest System

Bankruptcy ⊃3034.

Key Number System Topic No. 51.

Corpus Juris Secundum

CJS Bankruptcy § 606, Property Subject to Liens or Mortgages.

CJS Bankruptcy § 609, Filing of Motion; Notice.

Rule 6009. Prosecution and Defense of Proceedings by Trustee or Debtor in Possession

With or without court approval, the trustee or debtor in possession may prosecute or may enter an appearance and defend any pending action or proceeding by or against the debtor, or commence and prosecute any action or proceeding in behalf of the estate before any tribunal.

ADVISORY COMMITTEE NOTES

This rule is derived from former Bankruptcy Rule 610.

CROSS REFERENCES

Suspension of statutes of limitations, see 11 USCA § 108.

Voluntary or involuntary petition filed to operate as automatic stay on other proceedings, see 11 USCA § 362.

LIBRARY REFERENCES

American Digest System

Bankruptcy ☞2159.1, 2151 to 2155, 3024, 2395.

Key Number System Topic No. 51.

Corpus Juris Secundum

CJS Bankruptcy § 105, Suits by Trustee.

CJS Bankruptcy § 106, Suits Against Trustee.

CJS Bankruptcy § 134, Rights, Powers, and Duties of Debtor in Possession--Specific Rights, Powers, and Duties.

CJS Bankruptcy § 136, Rights, Powers, and Duties of Debtor in Possession.

CJS Bankruptcy § 616, Prosecution and Defense of Proceedings; Expedited Procedures.

Rule 6010. Proceeding to Avoid Indemnifying Lien or Transfer to Surety

If a lien voidable under § 547 of the Code has been dissolved by the furnishing of a bond or other obligation and the surety thereon has been indemnified by the transfer of, or the creation of a lien upon, nonexempt property of the debtor, the surety shall be joined as a defendant in any proceeding to avoid the indemnifying transfer or lien. Such proceeding is governed by the rules in Part VII.

(As amended Apr. 30, 1991, eff. Aug. 1, 1991.)

ADVISORY COMMITTEE NOTES

This rule is derived from former Bankruptcy Rule 612.

1991 Amendments

This rule is amended to conform to § 550(a) of the Code which provides that the trustee may recover the property transferred in a voidable transfer. The value of the property may be recovered in lieu of the property itself only if the court so orders.

CROSS REFERENCES

Motions; form and service, see Fed.Rules Bankr.Proc. Rule 9013, 11 USCA.

LIBRARY REFERENCES

American Digest System

Bankruptcy ☞2723.

Key Number System Topic No. 51.

Rule 6011. Disposal of Patient Records in Health Care Business Case

(a) Notice by publication under § 351(1)(A)

A notice regarding the claiming or disposing of patient records under § 351(1)(A) shall not identify any patient by name or other identifying information, but shall:

(1) identify with particularity the health care facility whose patient records the trustee proposes to destroy;

(2) state the name, address, telephone number, email address, and website, if any, of a person from whom information about the patient records may be obtained;

(3) state how to claim the patient records; and

(4) state the date by which patient records must be claimed, and that if they are not so claimed the records will be destroyed.

(b) Notice by mail under § 351(1)(B)

Subject to applicable nonbankruptcy law relating to patient privacy, a notice regarding the claiming or disposing of patient records under § 351(1)(B) shall, in addition to including the information in subdivision (a), direct that a patient's family member or other representative who receives the notice inform the patient of the notice. Any notice under this subdivision shall be mailed to the patient and any family member or other contact person whose name and address have been given to the trustee or the debtor for the purpose of providing information regarding the patient's health care, to the Attorney General of the State where the health care facility is located, and to any insurance company known to have provided health care insurance to the patient.

(c) Proof of compliance with notice requirement

Unless the court orders the trustee to file proof of compliance with § 351(1)(B) under seal, the trustee shall not file, but shall maintain, the proof of compliance for a reasonable time.

(d) Report of destruction of records

The trustee shall file, no later than 30 days after the destruction of patient records under § 351(3), a report certifying that the unclaimed records have been destroyed and explaining the method used to effect the destruction. The report shall not identify any patient by name or other identifying information.

(Added Apr. 23, 2008, eff. Dec. 1, 2008.)

ADVISORY COMMITTEE NOTES

2008 Adoption

This rule is new. It implements § 351(1), which was added to the Code by the 2005 amendments. That provision requires the trustee to notify patients that their patient records will be destroyed if they remain unclaimed for one year after the publication of a notice in an appropriate newspaper. The

Code provision also requires that individualized notice be sent to each patient and to the patient's family member or other contact person.

The variety of health care businesses and the range of current and former patients present the need for flexibility in the creation and publication of the notices that will be given. Nevertheless, there are some matters that must be included in any notice being given to patients, their family members, and contact persons to ensure that sufficient information is provided to these persons regarding the trustee's intent to dispose of patient records. Subdivision (a) of this rule lists the minimum requirements for notices given under § 351(1)(A), and subdivision (b) governs the form of notices under § 351(1)(B). Notices given under this rule are subject to provisions under applicable federal and state law that relate to the protection of patients' privacy, such as the Health Insurance Portability and Accountability Act of 1996, Pub. L. No. 104–191 (HIPAA).

Subdivision (c) directs the trustee to maintain proof of compliance with § 351(1)(B), but because the proof of compliance may contain patient names that should or must remain confidential, it prohibits filing the proof of compliance unless the court orders the trustee to file it under seal.

Subdivision (d) requires the trustee to file a report with the court regarding the destruction of patient records. This certification is intended to ensure that the trustee properly completed the destruction process. However, because the report will be filed with the court and ordinarily will be available to the public under § 107, the names, addresses, and other identifying information of patients are not to be included in the report to protect patient privacy.

PART VII—ADVERSARY PROCEEDINGS

Rule
7001. Scope of Rules of Part VII.
7002. References to Federal Rules of Civil Procedure.
7003. Commencement of Adversary Proceeding.
7004. Process; Service of Summons, Complaint.
7005. Service and Filing of Pleadings and Other Papers.
7007. Pleadings Allowed.
7007.1. Corporate Ownership Statement.
7008. General Rules of Pleading.
7009. Pleading Special Matters.
7010. Form of Pleadings.
7012. Defenses and Objections—When and How Presented—By Pleading or Motion—Motion for Judgment on the Pleadings.
7013. Counterclaim and Cross-Claim.
7014. Third-Party Practice.
7015. Amended and Supplemental Pleadings.
7016. Pre-Trial Procedure; Formulating Issues.
7017. Parties Plaintiff and Defendant; Capacity.
7018. Joinder of Claims and Remedies.
7019. Joinder of Persons Needed for Just Determination.
7020. Permissive Joinder of Parties.
7021. Misjoinder and Non-Joinder of Parties.
7022. Interpleader.
7023. Class proceedings.
7023.1. Derivative Actions.
7023.2. Adversary Proceedings Relating to Unincorporated Associations.
7024. Intervention.
7025. Substitution of Parties.
7026. General Provisions Governing Discovery.
7027. Depositions Before Adversary Proceedings or Pending Appeal.
7028. Persons Before Whom Depositions May be Taken.
7029. Stipulations Regarding Discovery Procedure.
7030. Depositions Upon Oral Examination.
7031. Deposition Upon Written Questions.
7032. Use of Depositions in Adversary Proceedings.
7033. Interrogatories to Parties.
7034. Production of Documents and Things and Entry Upon Land for Inspection and Other Purposes.
7035. Physical and Mental Examination of Persons.
7036. Requests for Admission.
7037. Failure to Make Discovery: Sanctions.
7040. Assignment of Cases for Trial.
7041. Dismissal of Adversary Proceedings.
7042. Consolidation of Adversary Proceedings; Separate Trials.
7052. Findings by the Court.
7054. Judgments; Costs.
7055. Default.
7056. Summary Judgment.
7058. Entering Judgment in Adversary Proceeding.
7062. Stay of Proceedings to Enforce a Judgment.
7064. Seizure of Person or Property.
7065. Injunctions.
7067. Deposit in Court.
7068. Offer of Judgment.
7069. Execution.
7070. Judgment for Specific Acts; Vesting Title.

Rule
7071. Process in Behalf of and Against Persons Not Parties.
7087. Transfer of Adversary Proceeding.

Rule 7001. Scope of Rules of Part VII

An adversary proceeding is governed by the rules of this Part VII. The following are adversary proceedings:

(1) a proceeding to recover money or property, other than a proceeding to compel the debtor to deliver property to the trustee, or a proceeding under § 554(b) or § 725 of the Code, Rule 2017, or Rule 6002;

(2) a proceeding to determine the validity, priority, or extent of a lien or other interest in property, other than a proceeding under Rule 4003(d);

(3) a proceeding to obtain approval under § 363(h) for the sale of both the interest of the estate and of a co-owner in property;

(4) a proceeding to object to or revoke a discharge, other than an objection to discharge under §§ 727(a)(8), [1] (a)(9), or 1328(f);

(5) a proceeding to revoke an order of confirmation of a chapter 11, chapter 12, or chapter 13 plan;

(6) a proceeding to determine the dischargeability of a debt;

(7) a proceeding to obtain an injunction or other equitable relief, except when a chapter 9, chapter 11, chapter 12, or chapter 13 plan provides for the relief;

(8) a proceeding to subordinate any allowed claim or interest, except when a chapter 9, chapter 11, chapter 12, or chapter 13 plan provides for subordination;

(9) a proceeding to obtain a declaratory judgment relating to any of the foregoing; or

(10) a proceeding to determine a claim or cause of action removed under 28 U.S.C. § 1452.

(As amended Mar. 30, 1987, eff. Aug. 1, 1987; Apr. 30, 1991, eff. Aug. 1, 1991; Apr. 29, 1999, eff. Dec. 1, 1999; Apr. 28, 2010, eff. Dec. 1, 2010.)

1 So in original. Probably should be only one section symbol.

ADVISORY COMMITTEE NOTES

The rules in Part VII govern the procedural aspects of litigation involving the matters referred to in this Rule 7001. Under Rule 9014 some of the Part VII rules also apply to contested matters.

These Part VII rules are based on the premise that to the extent possible practice before the bankruptcy courts and the district courts should be the same. These rules either incorporate or are adaptations of most of the Federal Rules of Civil Procedure. Although the Part VII rules of the former Bankruptcy Rules also relied heavily on the F.R.Civ.P., the former Part VII rules departed from the civil practice in two significant ways: a trial or pretrial conference had to be scheduled as soon as the adversary proceeding was filed and pleadings had to be filed within periods shorter than those established by the F.R.Civ.P. These departures from the civil practice have been eliminated.

The content and numbering of these Part VII rules correlate to the content and numbering of the F.R.Civ.P. Most, but not all, of the F.R.Civ.P. have a comparable Part VII rule. When there is no Part VII rule with a number corresponding to a particular F.R.Civ.P., Parts V and IX of these rules must be consulted to determine if one of the rules in those parts deals with the subject. The list below indicates the F.R.Civ. P., or subdivision thereof, covered by a rule in either Part V or Part IX.

F.R.Civ.P.	Rule in Part V or IX
6	9006
7(b)	9013
10(a)	9004(b)
11	9011
38, 39	9015(a)–(e)
47–51	9015(f)
43, 44, 44.1	9017
45	9016
58	9021
59	9023
60	9024
61	9005
63	9028
77(a), (b), (c)	5001
77(d)	9022(d)
79(a)–(d)	5003
81(c)	9027
83	9029
92	9030

Proceedings to which the rules in Part VII apply directly include those brought to avoid transfers by the debtor under §§ 544, 545, 547, 548 and 549 of the Code; subject to important exceptions, proceedings to recover money or property; proceedings on bonds under Rules 5008(d) and 9025; proceedings under Rule 4004 to determine whether a discharge in a chapter 7 or 11 case should be denied because of an objection grounded on § 727 and proceedings in a chapter 7 or 13 case to revoke a discharge as provided in §§ 727(d) or 1328(e); and proceedings initiated pursuant to § 523(c) of the Code to determine the dischargeability of a particular debt. Those proceedings were classified as adversary proceedings under former Bankruptcy Rule 701.

Also included as adversary proceedings are proceedings to revoke an order of confirmation of a plan in a chapter 11 or 13 case as provided in §§ 1144 and 1330, to subordinate under § 510(c), other than as part of a plan, an allowed claim or interest, and to sell under § 363(h) both the interest of the estate and a co-owner in property.

Declaratory judgments with respect to the subject matter of the various adversary proceedings are also adversary proceedings.

Any claim or cause of action removed to a bankruptcy court pursuant to 28 U.S.C. § 1478 is also an adversary proceeding.

Unlike former Bankruptcy Rule 701, requests for relief from an automatic stay do not commence an adversary proceeding. Section 362(e) of the Code and Rule 4001 establish an expedited schedule for judicial disposition of requests for relief from the automatic stay. The formalities of the adversary proceeding process and the time for serving pleadings are not well suited to the expedited schedule. The motion practice prescribed in Rule 4001 is best suited to such requests because the court has the flexibility to fix hearing dates and other deadlines appropriate to the particular situation.

Clause (1) contains important exceptions. A person with an interest in property in the possession of the trustee or debtor in possession may seek to recover or reclaim that property under § 554(b) or § 725 of the Code. Since many attempts to recover or reclaim property under these two sections do not generate disputes, application of the formalities of the Part VII Rules is not appropriate. Also excluded from adversary proceedings is litigation arising from an examination under Rule 2017 of a debtor's payments of money or transfers of property to an attorney representing the debtor in a case under the Code or an examination of a superseded administration under Rule 6002.

Exemptions and objections thereto are governed by Rule 4003. Filing of proofs of claim and the allowances thereof are governed by Rules 3001–3005, and objections to claims are governed by Rule 3007. When an objection to a claim is joined with a demand for relief of the kind specified in this Rule 7001, the matter becomes an adversary proceeding. See Rule 3007.

1987 Amendment

Another exception is added to clause (1). A trustee may proceed by motion to recover property from the debtor.

1991 Amendment

Clauses (5) and (8) are amended to include chapter 12 plans.

1999 Amendments

This rule is amended to recognize that an adversary proceeding is not necessary to obtain injunctive or other equitable relief that is provided for in a plan under circumstances in which substantive law permits the relief. Other amendments are stylistic.

Gap Report on Rule 7001. No changes since publication, except for stylistic changes.

2010 Amendments

Paragraph (4) of the rule is amended to create an exception for objections to discharge under §§ 727(a)(8), (a)(9), and 1328(f) of the Code. Because objections to discharge on these grounds typically present issues more easily resolved than other objections to discharge, the more formal procedures applicable to adversary proceedings, such as commencement by a complaint, are not required. Instead, objections on these three grounds are governed by Rule 4004(d). In an appropriate case, however, Rule 9014(c) allows the court to order that additional provisions of Part VII of the rules apply to these matters.

CROSS REFERENCES

Adversarial nature of proceeding—

Avoidance of indemnifying lien or transfer to surety, see Fed.Rules Bankr.Proc. Rule 6010, 11 USCA.

Commenced by complaint objecting to discharge, see Fed.Rules Bankr.Proc. Rule 4004, 11 USCA.

Commenced by complaint to obtain determination of debt's dischargeability, see Fed.Rules Bankr.Proc. Rule 4007, 11 USCA.

Joinder of objection to claim with demand for relief, see Fed.Rules Bankr.Proc. Rule 3007, 11 USCA.

Liability of sureties on bond or stipulation or other undertaking, see Fed.Rules Bankr.Proc. Rule 9025, 11 USCA.

Applicability of rules of this part to removed claim or cause of action, see Fed.Rules Bankr.Proc. Rule 9027, 11 USCA.

Contested matters, applicability of and notice to parties of applicability of rules of this part, see Fed.Rules Bankr.Proc. Rule 9014, 11 USCA.

Effect of amendment of Federal Rules of Civil Procedure, see Fed.Rules Bankr.Proc. Rule 9032, 11 USCA.

Meanings of words in Federal Rules of Civil Procedure when applicable, see Fed.Rules Bankr.Proc. Rule 9002, 11 USCA.

LIBRARY REFERENCES

American Digest System

Bankruptcy ⊙2129, 2156.

Key Number System Topic No. 51.

Corpus Juris Secundum

CJS Bankruptcy § 11, Federal Rules of Bankruptcy Procedure.

CJS Bankruptcy § 110, Removal of Trustee or Examiner for Cause.

CJS Bankruptcy § 139, Adversary Proceedings.

CJS Bankruptcy § 140, Contested Matters.

CJS Bankruptcy § 236, Process and Pleading After Removal.

CJS Bankruptcy § 247, Procedure for Obtaining Injunction.

CJS Bankruptcy § 261, Power to Render Declaratory Judgment.

CJS Bankruptcy § 555, Property Subject to Liens or Mortgages--Liens Securing Unallowed or Undersecured Claims.

CJS Bankruptcy § 614, Form of Action as Adversary Proceeding or Contested Matter.

CJS Bankruptcy § 656, Nature of Proceeding.

CJS Bankruptcy § 701, Form of Action as Adversary Proceeding.

CJS Bankruptcy § 755, Commencement of Adversary Proceeding; Venue.

CJS Bankruptcy § 886, Authorization to Sell Property Free and Clear; Notice.

CJS Bankruptcy § 892, Setting Aside Confirmed Sale; Remedies for Collusive Bidding.

CJS Bankruptcy § 1023, Objections.

CJS Bankruptcy § 1026, Secured Claims.

CJS Bankruptcy § 1028, Procedure for Determination of Priority.

CJS Bankruptcy § 1046, Generally; Objections to Discharge.

CJS Bankruptcy § 1056, Revocation or Vacation of Discharge.

CJS Bankruptcy § 1164, Revocation of Order of Confirmation.

CJS Bankruptcy § 1184, Revocation or Vacation.

CJS Bankruptcy § 1205, Postconfirmation Modification.

CJS Bankruptcy § 1207, Revocation or Vacation.

Rule 7002. References to Federal Rules of Civil Procedure

Whenever a Federal Rule of Civil Procedure applicable to adversary proceedings makes reference to another Federal Rule of Civil Procedure, the reference shall be read as a reference to the Federal Rule of Civil Procedure as modified in this Part VII.

ADVISORY COMMITTEE NOTES

Rules 5, 12, 13, 14, 25, 27, 30, 41 and 52 F.R.Civ.P. are made applicable to adversary proceedings by Part VII. Each of those rules contains a cross reference to another Federal Rule; however, the Part VII rule which incorporates the cross-referenced Federal Rule modifies the Federal Rule in some way. Under this Rule 7002 the cross reference is to the Federal Rule as modified by Part VII. For example, Rule 5 F.R.Civ.P., which is made applicable to adversary proceedings by Rule 7005, contains a reference to Rule 4 F.R.Civ.P. Under this Rule 7002, the cross reference is to Rule 4 F.R.Civ.P. as modified by Rule 7004.

Rules 7, 10, 12, 13, 14, 19, 22, 23.2, 24–37, 41, 45, 49, 50, 52, 55, 59, 60, 62 F.R.Civ.P. are made applicable to adversary proceedings by Part VII or generally to cases under the Code by Part IX. Each of those Federal Rules contains a cross reference to another Federal Rule which is not modified by the Part VII or Part IX rule which makes the cross-referenced Federal Rule applicable. Since the cross-referenced rule is not modified by a Part VII rule this Rule 7002 does not apply.

LIBRARY REFERENCES

American Digest System

Bankruptcy ⊙2129.

Key Number System Topic No. 51.

Corpus Juris Secundum

CJS Bankruptcy § 139, Adversary Proceedings.

Rule 7003. Commencement of Adversary Proceeding

Rule 3 F.R.Civ.P. applies in adversary proceedings.

ADVISORY COMMITTEE NOTES

Rule 5005(a) requires that a complaint commencing an adversary proceeding be filed with the court in which the case under the Code is pending unless 28 U.S.C. § 1473 authorizes the filing of the complaint in another district.

CROSS REFERENCES

Complaint filed with court in which case is pending, see Fed.Rules Bankr.Proc. Rule 5005, 11 USCA.

American Digest System

Bankruptcy ☞2127.1 to 2133, 2156 to 2158.

Key Number System Topic No. 51.

Corpus Juris Secundum

CJS Bankruptcy § 139, Adversary Proceedings.

CJS Bankruptcy § 151, Original But Not Exclusive Jurisdiction of Civil Proceedings.

CJS Bankruptcy § 287, Complaints.

CJS Bankruptcy § 701, Form of Action as Adversary Proceeding.

CJS Bankruptcy § 755, Commencement of Adversary Proceeding; Venue.

CJS Bankruptcy § 886, Authorization to Sell Property Free and Clear; Notice.

CJS Bankruptcy § 892, Setting Aside Confirmed Sale; Remedies for Collusive Bidding.

Rule 7004. Process; Service of Summons, Complaint

(a) Summons; service; proof of service

(1) Except as provided in Rule 7004(a)(2), Rule 4(a), (b), (c)(1), (d)(1), (e)–(j), (*l*), and (m) F.R.Civ.P. applies in adversary proceedings. Personal service under Rule 4(e)–(j) F.R.Civ.P. may be made by any person at least 18 years of age who is not a party, and the summons may be delivered by the clerk to any such person.

(2) The clerk may sign, seal, and issue a summons electronically by putting an "s/" before the clerk's name and including the court's seal on the summons.

(b) Service by first class mail

Except as provided in subdivision (h), in addition to the methods of service authorized by Rule 4(e)–(j) F.R.Civ.P., service may be made within the United States by first class mail postage prepaid as follows:

(1) Upon an individual other than an infant or incompetent, by mailing a copy of the summons and complaint to the individual's dwelling house or usual place of abode or to the place where the individual regularly conducts a business or profession.

(2) Upon an infant or an incompetent person, by mailing a copy of the summons and complaint to the person upon whom process is prescribed to be served by the law of the state in which service is made when an action is brought against such a defendant in the courts of general jurisdiction of that state. The summons and complaint in that case shall be addressed to the person required to be served at that person's dwelling house or usual place of abode or at the place where the person regularly conducts a business or profession.

(3) Upon a domestic or foreign corporation or upon a partnership or other unincorporated association, by mailing a copy of the summons and complaint to the attention of an officer, a managing or

general agent, or to any other agent authorized by appointment or by law to receive service of process and, if the agent is one authorized by statute to receive service and the statute so requires, by also mailing a copy to the defendant.

(4) Upon the United States, by mailing a copy of the summons and complaint addressed to the civil process clerk at the office of the United States attorney for the district in which the action is brought and by mailing a copy of the summons and complaint to the Attorney General of the United States at Washington, District of Columbia, and in any action attacking the validity of an order of an officer or an agency of the United States not made a party, by also mailing a copy of the summons and complaint to that officer or agency. The court shall allow a reasonable time for service pursuant to this subdivision for the purpose of curing the failure to mail a copy of the summons and complaint to multiple officers, agencies, or corporations of the United States if the plaintiff has mailed a copy of the summons and complaint either to the civil process clerk at the office of the United States attorney or to the Attorney General of the United States.

(5) Upon any officer or agency of the United States, by mailing a copy of the summons and complaint to the United States as prescribed in paragraph (4) of this subdivision and also to the officer or agency. If the agency is a corporation, the mailing shall be as prescribed in paragraph (3) of this subdivision of this rule. The court shall allow a reasonable time for service pursuant to this subdivision for the purpose of curing the failure to mail a copy of the summons and complaint to multiple officers, agencies, or corporations of the United States if the plaintiff has mailed a copy of the summons and complaint either to the civil process clerk at the office of the United States attorney or to the Attorney General of the United States. If the United States trustee is the trustee in the case and service is made upon the United States trustee solely as trustee, service may be made as prescribed in paragraph (10) of this subdivision of this rule.

(6) Upon a state or municipal corporation or other governmental organization thereof subject to suit, by mailing a copy of the summons and complaint to the person or office upon whom process is prescribed to be served by the law of the state in which service is made when an action is brought against such a defendant in the courts of general jurisdiction of that state, or in the absence of the designation of any such person or office by state law, then to the chief executive officer thereof.

(7) Upon a defendant of any class referred to in paragraph (1) or (3) of this subdivision of this rule, it is also sufficient if a copy of the summons and complaint is mailed to the entity upon whom service

is prescribed to be served by any statute of the United States or by the law of the state in which service is made when an action is brought against such a defendant in the court of general jurisdiction of that state.

(8) Upon any defendant, it is also sufficient if a copy of the summons and complaint is mailed to an agent of such defendant authorized by appointment or by law to receive service of process, at the agent's dwelling house or usual place of abode or at the place where the agent regularly carries on a business or profession and, if the authorization so requires, by mailing also a copy of the summons and complaint to the defendant as provided in this subdivision.

(9) Upon the debtor, after a petition has been filed by or served upon the debtor and until the case is dismissed or closed, by mailing a copy of the summons and complaint to the debtor at the address shown in the petition or to such other address as the debtor may designate in a filed writing.

(10) Upon the United States trustee, when the United States trustee is the trustee in the case and service is made upon the United States trustee solely as trustee, by mailing a copy of the summons and complaint to an office of the United States trustee or another place designated by the United States trustee in the district where the case under the Code is pending.

(c) Service by publication

If a party to an adversary proceeding to determine or protect rights in property in the custody of the court cannot be served as provided in Rule 4(e)-(j) F.R.Civ.P. or subdivision (b) of this rule, the court may order the summons and complaint to be served by mailing copies thereof by first class mail, postage prepaid, to the party's last known address, and by at least one publication in such manner and form as the court may direct.

(d) Nationwide service of process

The summons and complaint and all other process except a subpoena may be served anywhere in the United States.

(e) Summons: time limit for service within the United States

Service made under Rule 4(e), (g), (h)(1), (i), or (j)(2) F. R. Civ. P. shall be by delivery of the summons and complaint within 14 days after the summons is issued. If service is by any authorized form of mail, the summons and complaint shall be deposited in the mail within 14 days after the summons is issued. If a summons is not timely delivered or mailed, another summons shall be issued and served. This subdivision does not apply to service in a foreign country.

(f) Personal jurisdiction

If the exercise of jurisdiction is consistent with the Constitution and laws of the United States, serving a summons or filing a waiver of service in accordance with this rule or the subdivisions of Rule 4 F.R.Civ.P. made applicable by these rules is effective to establish personal jurisdiction over the person of any defendant with respect to a case under the Code or a civil proceeding arising under the Code, or arising in or related to a case under the Code.

(g) Service on debtor's attorney

If the debtor is represented by an attorney, whenever service is made upon the debtor under this Rule, service shall also be made upon the debtor's attorney by any means authorized under Rule 5(b) F. R. Civ. P.

(h) Service of process on an insured depository institution

Service on an insured depository institution (as defined in section 3 of the Federal Deposit Insurance Act) in a contested matter or adversary proceeding shall be made by certified mail addressed to an officer of the institution unless—

(1) the institution has appeared by its attorney, in which case the attorney shall be served by first class mail;

(2) the court orders otherwise after service upon the institution by certified mail of notice of an application to permit service on the institution by first class mail sent to an officer of the institution designated by the institution; or

(3) the institution has waived in writing its entitlement to service by certified mail by designating an officer to receive service.

(As amended Mar. 30, 1987, eff. Aug. 1, 1987; Apr. 30, 1991, eff. Aug. 1, 1991; Oct. 22, 1994, Pub.L. 103–394, Title I, § 114, 108 Stat. 4118; Apr. 23, 1996, eff. Dec. 1, 1996; Apr. 29, 1999, eff. Dec. 1, 1999; Apr. 25, 2005, eff. Dec. 1, 2005; Apr. 12, 2006, eff. Dec. 1, 2006; Mar. 26, 2009, eff. Dec. 1, 2009.)

ADVISORY COMMITTEE NOTES

Subdivision (a) of the rule, by incorporation of Rule 4(a), (b), (d), (e) and (g)–(i) F.R.Civ.P., governs the mechanics of issuance of a summons and its form, the manner of service on parties and their representatives, and service in foreign countries.

Subdivision (b), which is the same as former Rule 704(c), authorizes service of process by first class mail postage prepaid. This rule retains the modes of service contained in former Bankruptcy Rule 704. The former practice, in effect since 1976, has proven satisfactory.

Subdivision (c) is derived from former Bankruptcy Rule 704(d)(2).

Subdivision (d). Nationwide service of process is authorized by subdivision (d).

Subdivision (e) authorizes service by delivery on individuals and corporations in foreign countries if the party to be served is the debtor or any person required to perform the duties of the debtor and certain other persons, the adversary proceeding involves property in the custody of the bankruptcy court, or if federal or state law authorizes such service in a foreign country.

Subdivision (f). The requirement of former Bankruptcy Rule 704 that the summons be served within 10 days is carried over into these rules by subdivision (f).

1987 Amendment

Subdivision (a) is amended to make Rule 4(j) F.R.Civ.P. applicable to service of the summons. If service is not completed within 120 days of the filing of the complaint, the complaint may be dismissed.

Technical amendments are made to subdivisions (a), (b), (e), and (f) to conform to recent amendments to Rule 4 F.R.Civ.P.

1991 Amendment

The United States trustee may serve as trustee in a case pursuant to 28 U.S.C. § 586(a)(2) and §§ 701(a)(2), 1202(a), and 1302(a) of the Code. This rule is amended to avoid the necessity of mailing copies of a summons and complaint or other pleadings to the Attorney General and to the United States attorney when service on the United States trustee is required only because the United States trustee is acting as a case trustee. For example, a proceeding commenced by a creditor to dismiss a case for unreasonable delay under § 707(a) is governed by Rule 9014 which requires service on the trustee pursuant to the requirements of Rule 7004 for the service of a summons and complaint. The Attorney General and the United States attorney would have no interest in receiving a copy of the motion to dismiss. Mailing to the office of the United States trustee when acting as the case trustee is sufficient in such cases.

The words "with the court" in subdivision (b)(9) are deleted as unnecessary. See Rules 5005(a) and 9001(3).

The new paragraph (10) of subdivision (b) does not affect requirements for service of process on the United States trustee when sued or otherwise a party to a litigation unrelated to its capacity as a trustee. If a proceeding is commenced against the United States trustee which is unrelated to the United States trustee's role as trustee, the requirements of paragraph (5) of subdivision (b) of this rule would apply.

Subdivision (g) is added in anticipation of substantial amendment to, and restructuring of subdivisions of, Rule 4 F.R.Civ.P. Any amendment to Rule 4 will not affect service in bankruptcy cases and proceedings until further amendment to the Bankruptcy Rules. On January 1, 1990, Rule 4 F.R.Civ.P. read as follows:

Rule 4 F.R.Civ.P.

PROCESS

(a) Summons: issuance. Upon the filing of the complaint the clerk shall forthwith issue a summons and deliver the summons of the plaintiff or the plaintiff's attorney, who shall be responsible for prompt service of the summons and a copy of the complaint. Upon request of the plaintiff separate or additional summons shall issue against any defendants.

(b) Same: form. The summons shall be signed by the clerk, be under the seal of the court, contain the name of the court and the names of the parties, be directed to the defendant, state the name and address of the plaintiff's attorney, if any, otherwise the plaintiff's address, and the time within which these rules require the defendant to appear and

defend, and shall notify the defendant that in case of the defendant's failure to do so judgment by default will be rendered against the defendant for the relief demanded in the complaint. When, under Rule 4(e), service is made pursuant to a statute or rule of court of a state, the summons, or notice, or order in lieu of summons shall correspond as nearly as may be to that required by the statute or rule.

(c) Service

(1) [Not applicable.]

(2)(A) [Not applicable.]

(B) [Not applicable.]

(C) A summons and complaint may be served upon a defendant of any class referred to in paragraph (1) or (3) of subdivision (d) of this rule—

(i) pursuant to the law of the State in which the district court held for the service of summons or other like process upon such defendant in an action brought in the courts of general jurisdiction of that State, or

(ii) [Not applicable.]

(D) [Not applicable.]

(E) [Not applicable.]

(3) [Not applicable.]

(d) Summons and complaint: person to be served. The summons and complaint shall be served together. The plaintiff shall furnish the person making service with such copies as are necessary. Service shall be made as follows:

(1) Upon an individual other than an infant or an incompetent person, by delivering a copy of the summons and of the complaint to the individual personally or by leaving copies thereof at the individual's dwelling house or usual place of abode with some person of suitable age and discretion then residing therein or by delivering a copy of the summons and of the complaint to an agent authorized by appointment or by law to receive service of process.

(2) Upon an infant or an incompetent person, by serving the summons and complaint in the manner prescribed by the law of the state in which the service is made for the service of summons or other like process upon any such defendant in an action brought in the courts of general jurisdiction of that state.

(3) Upon a domestic or foreign corporation or upon a partnership or other unincorporated association which the subject to suit under a common name, by delivering a copy of the summons and of the complaint to an officer, a managing or general agent, or to any other agent authorized by appointment or by law to receive service of process and, if the agent is one authorized by statute to receive service and the statute so requires, by also mailing a copy to the defendant.

(4) Upon the United States, by delivering a copy of the summons and of the complaint to the United States attorney for the district in which the action is brought or to an assistant United States attorney or clerical employee designated by the United States attorney in a writing filed with the clerk of the court and by sending a copy of the summons and of the complaint by registered or certified mail to the Attorney General of the United States at Washington, District of Columbia, and in any action attacking the validity of an order of an officer or agency of the United States not made a party, by also sending a copy of the summons and of the complaint by registered or certified mail to such officer or agency.

(5) Upon an officer or agency of the United States, by serving the United States and by sending a copy of the summons and of the complaint by registered or certified mail to such officer or agency. If the agency is a corporation the copy shall be delivered as provided in paragraph (3) of this subdivision of this rule.

(6) Upon a state or municipal corporation or other governmental organization thereof subject to suit, by delivering a copy of the summons and of the complaint to the chief executive officer thereof or by serving the summons and complaint in the manner prescribed by the law of that state for the service of summons or other like process upon any such defendant.

(e) Summons: service upon party not inhabitant of or found within state. Whenever a statute of the United States or an order of court thereunder provides for service of a summons, or of a notice, or of an order in lieu of summons upon a party not an inhabitant of or found within the state in which the district court is held, service may be made under the circumstances and in the manner prescribed by the statute or order, or, if there is no provision therein prescribing the manner of service, in a manner stated in this rule. Whenever a statute or rule of court of the state in which the district court is held provides (1) for service of a summons, or of a notice, or of an order in lieu of summons upon a party not an inhabitant of or found within the state, or (2) for service upon or notice to such a party to appear and respond or defend in an action by reason of the attachment or garnishment or similar seizure of the party's property located within the state, service may in either case be made under the circumstances and in the manner prescribed in the statute or rule.

(f) [Not applicable.]

(g) Return. The person serving the process shall make proof of service thereof to the court promptly and in any event within the time during which the person served must respond to the process. If service is made by a person other than a United States marshal or deputy United States marshal, such person shall make affidavit thereof. If service is made under subdivision (c)(2)(C)(ii) of this rule, return shall be made by the sender's filing with the court the acknowledgement received pursuant to such subdivision. Failure to make proof of service does not affect the validity of the service.

(h) Amendment. At any time in its discretion and upon such terms as it deems just, the court may allow any process or proof of service thereof to be amended, unless it clearly appears that material prejudice would result to the substantial rights of the party against whom the process issued.

(i) Alternative provisions for service in a foreign country.

(1) Manner. When the federal or state law referred to in subdivision (e) of this rule authorizes service upon a party not an inhabitant of or found within the state in which the district court is held, and service is to be effected upon the party in a foreign country, it is also sufficient if service of the summons and complaint is made: (A) in the manner prescribed by the law of the foreign country for service in that country in an action in any of its courts of general jurisdiction; or (B) as directed by the foreign authority in response to a letter rogatory, when service in either case is reasonably calculated to give actual notice; or (C) upon an individual, by delivery to the individual personally, and upon a corporation or partnership or association, by deliv-

ery to an officer, a managing or general agent; or (D) by any form of mail, requiring a signed receipt, to be addressed and dispatched by the clerk of the court to the party to be served; or (E) above may be made by any person who is not a party and is not less than 18 years of age or who is designated by order of the district court or by the foreign court. On request, the clerk shall deliver the summons to the plaintiff for transmission to the person or the foreign court or officer who will make the service.

(2) Return. Proof of service may be made as prescribed by subdivision (g) of this rule, or by the law of the foreign country, or by order of the court. When service is made pursuant to subparagraph (1)(D) of this subdivision, proof of service shall include a receipt signed by the addressee or other evidence of delivery to the addressee satisfactory to the court.

(j) Summons: time limit for service. If a service of the summons and complaint is not made upon a defendant within 120 days after the filing of the complaint and the party on whose behalf such service was required cannot show good cause why such service was not made within that period, the action shall be dismissed as to that defendant without prejudice upon the court's own initiative with notice to such party or upon motion. This subdivision shall not apply to service in a foreign country pursuant to subdivision (i) of this rule.

1996 Amendments

The purpose of these amendments is to conform the rule to the 1993 revisions of Rule 4 F.R.Civ.P. and to make stylistic improvements. Rule 7004, as amended, continues to provide for service by first class mail as an alternative to the methods of personal service provided in Rule 4 F.R.Civ.P., except as provided in the new subdivision (h).

Rule 4(d)(2) F.R.Civ.P. provides a procedure by which the plaintiff may request by first class mail that the defendant waive service of the summons. This procedure is not applicable in adversary proceedings because it is not necessary in view of the availability of service by mail pursuant to Rule 7004(b). However, if a written waiver of service of a summons is made in an adversary proceeding, Rule 4(d)(1) F.R.Civ.P. applies so that the defendant does not thereby waive any objection to the venue or the jurisdiction of the court over the person of the defendant.

Subdivisions (b)(4) and (b)(5) are amended to conform to the 1993 amendments to Rule 4(i)(3) F.R.Civ.P., which protect the plaintiff from the hazard of losing a substantive right because of failure to comply with the requirements of multiple service when the United States or an officer, agency, or corporation of the United States is a defendant. These subdivisions also are amended to require that the summons and complaint be addressed to the civil process clerk at the office of the United States attorney.

Subdivision (e), which has governed service in a foreign country, is abrogated and Rule 4(f) and (h)(2) F.R.Civ.P., as substantially revised in 1993, are made applicable in adversary proceedings.

The new subdivision (f) is consistent with the 1993 amendments to F.R.Civ.P. 4(k)(2). It clarifies that service or filing a waiver of service in accordance with this rule or the applicable subdivisions of F.R.Civ.P. 4 is sufficient to establish personal jurisdiction over the defendant. See the committee note to the 1993 amendments to Rule 4 F.R.Civ.P.

Subdivision (g) is abrogated. This subdivision was promulgated in 1991 so that anticipated revisions to Rule 4 F.R.Civ.P. would not affect service of process in adversary proceedings until further amendment to Rule 7004.

Subdivision (h) and the first phrase of subdivision (b) were added by § 114 of the Bankruptcy Reform Act of 1994, Pub.L. No. 103–394, 108 Stat. 4106.

GAP Report on Rule 7004. After publication of the proposed amendments, Rule 7004(b) was amended and Rule 7004(h) was added by the Bankruptcy Reform Act of 1994 to provide for service by certified mail on an insured depository institution. The above draft includes those statutory amendments (without underlining new language or striking former language). No other changes have been made since publication, except for stylistic changes.

1999 Amendments

Subdivision (e) is amended so that the ten-day time limit for service of a summons does not apply if the summons is served in a foreign country.

Gap Report on Rule 7004. No changes since publication.

2005 Amendments

This amendment specifically authorizes the clerk to issue a summons electronically. In some bankruptcy cases the trustee or debtor in possession may commence hundreds of adversary proceedings simultaneously, and permitting the electronic signing and sealing of the summonses for those proceedings increases the efficiency of the clerk's office without any negative impact on any party. The rule only authorizes electronic issuance of the summons. It does not address the service requirements for the summons. Those requirements are set out elsewhere in Rule 7004, and nothing in Rule 7004(a)(2) should be construed as authorizing electronic service of a summons.

2006 Amendments

Under current Rule 7004, an entity may serve a summons and complaint upon the debtor by personal service or by mail. If the entity chooses to serve the debtor by mail, it must also serve a copy of the summons and complaint on the debtor's attorney by mail. If the entity effects personal service on the debtor, there is no requirement that the debtor's attorney also be served.

Subdivision (b)(9). The rule is amended to delete the reference in subdivision (b)(9) to the debtor's address as set forth in the statement of financial affairs. In 1991, the Official Form of the statement of financial affairs was revised and no longer includes a question regarding the debtor's current residence. Since that time, Official Form 1, the petition, has required the debtor to list both the debtor's residence and mailing address. Therefore, the subdivision is amended to delete the statement of financial affairs as a document that might contain an address at which the debtor can be served.

Subdivision (g). The rule is amended to require service on the debtor's attorney whenever the debtor is served with a summons and complaint. The amendment makes this change by deleting that portion of Rule 7004(b)(9) that requires service on the debtor's attorney when the debtor is served by mail, and relocates the obligation to serve the debtor's attorney into new subdivision (g). Service on the debtor's attorney

is not limited to mail service, but may be accomplished by any means permitted under Rule 5(b) F. R. Civ. P.

2009 Amendments

The rule is amended to implement changes in connection with the amendment to Rule 9006(a) and the manner by which time is computed under the rules. The deadlines in the rule are amended to substitute a deadline that is a multiple of seven days. Throughout the rules, deadlines are amended in the following manner:

- 5–day periods become 7–day periods
- 10–day periods become 14–day periods
- 15–day periods become 14–day periods
- 20–day periods become 21–day periods
- 25–day periods become 28–day periods

CROSS REFERENCES

Contested matters, request for relief by motion served in manner provided in this rule, see Fed.Rules Bankr.Proc. Rule 9014, 11 USCA.

Form of pleadings, see Fed.Rules Bankr.Proc. Rule 7010, 11 USCA.

Service of—

Motion for substitution of parties, see Fed.Rules Bankr. Proc. Rule 7025, 11 USCA.

Notice of depositions before adversary proceedings or pending appeal, see Fed.Rules Bankr.Proc. Rule 7027, 11 USCA.

Pleadings and other papers, see Fed.Rules Bankr.Proc. Rule 7005, 11 USCA.

Summons and involuntary petition—

Manner of service, see Fed.Rules Bankr.Proc. Rule 1010, 11 USCA.

Time limitations, see Fed.Rules Bankr.Proc. Rule 1010, 11 USCA.

LIBRARY REFERENCES

American Digest System

Bankruptcy ☞2158.

Key Number System Topic No. 51.

Corpus Juris Secundum

CJS Bankruptcy § 140, Contested Matters.

CJS Bankruptcy § 150, Applicability of Minimum State Contacts Requirement.

CJS Bankruptcy § 257, Sanctions Resulting from Noncompliance With Requirements as to Basis for Filing--Procedure for Imposing Sanctions.

CJS Bankruptcy § 292, Service by First-Class Mail.

CJS Bankruptcy § 293, Service by Publication.

CJS Bankruptcy § 378, Service of Summons and Petition.

CJS Bankruptcy § 391, Service of Summons and Petition.

CJS Bankruptcy § 886, Authorization to Sell Property Free and Clear; Notice.

CJS Bankruptcy § 923, Application for Approval.

CJS Bankruptcy § 1048, Service of Summons and Complaint.

CJS Bankruptcy § 1084, Service of Summons and Complaint.

CJS Bankruptcy § 1122, Objections to Confirmation.

CJS Federal Courts § 28, Actions Against Nonresidents; Long-Arm Jurisdiction--Federal Long-Arm Jurisdiction.

Rule 7005. Service and Filing of Pleadings and Other Papers

Rule 5 F.R.Civ.P. applies in adversary proceedings.

ADVISORY COMMITTEE NOTES

Rule 5 F.R.Civ.P. refers to Rule 4 F.R.Civ.P. Pursuant to Rule 7002 this reference is to Rule 4 F.R.Civ.P. as incorporated and modified by Rule 7004.

CROSS REFERENCES

Applicability of this rule in proceedings on contested involuntary petition and to vacate order for relief, see Fed.Rules Bankr.Proc. Rule 1018, 11 USCA.

Form of pleadings, see Fed.Rules Bankr.Proc. Rule 7010, 11 USCA.

Service of—

  Motion for substitution, see Fed.Rules Bankr.Proc. Rule 7025, 11 USCA.

  Motion to intervene, see Fed.Rules Bankr. Proc. Rule 7024, 11 USCA.

  Notice of judgment or order, see Fed.Rules Bankr.Proc. Rule 9022, 11 USCA.

  Requests for depositions and discovery, see Fed.Rules Bankr.Proc. Rule 7027 et seq., 11 USCA.

LIBRARY REFERENCES

American Digest System

Bankruptcy ⏬2127.1, 2158.

Key Number System Topic No. 51.

Corpus Juris Secundum

CJS Bankruptcy § 397, Hearing and Notice of Hearing.

CJS Bankruptcy § 879, Service and Content of Notices.

Rule 7007. Pleadings Allowed

Rule 7 F.R.Civ.P. applies in adversary proceedings.

CROSS REFERENCES

Amended and supplemental pleadings, see Fed.Rules Bankr.Proc. Rule 7015, 11 USCA.

Counterclaim and cross-claim, see Fed.Rules Bankr.Proc. Rule 7013, 11 USCA.

Form of pleadings, see Fed.Rules Bankr.Proc. Rule 7010, 11 USCA.

Service and filing of pleadings and other papers, see Fed. Rules Bankr.Proc. Rule 7005, 11 USCA.

Third-party practice, see Fed.Rules Bankr.Proc. Rule 7014, 11 USCA.

LIBRARY REFERENCES

American Digest System

Bankruptcy ⏬2127.1, 2156, 2158, 2162, 2187.

Key Number System Topic No. 51.

Corpus Juris Secundum

CJS Bankruptcy § 289, Motions.

Rule 7007.1. Corporate Ownership Statement

(a) Required disclosure

Any corporation that is a party to an adversary proceeding, other than the debtor or a governmental unit, shall file two copies of a statement that identifies any corporation, other than a governmental unit, that directly or indirectly owns 10% or more of any class of the corporation's equity interests, or states that there are no entities to report under this subdivision.

(b) Time for Filing

A party shall file the statement required under Rule 7007.1(a) with its first appearance, pleading, motion, response, or other request addressed to the court. A party shall file a supplemental statement promptly upon any change in circumstances that this rule requires the party to identify or disclose.

(Added Mar. 27, 2003, eff. Dec. 1, 2003. As amended Apr. 30, 2007, eff. Dec. 1, 2007.)

ADVISORY COMMITTEE NOTES

2003 Adoption

This rule is derived from Rule 26.1 of the Federal Rules of Appellate Procedure. The information that parties shall supply will support properly informed disqualification decisions in situations that call for automatic disqualification under Canon 3C(1)(c) of the Code of Conduct for United States Judges. This rule does not cover all of the circumstances that may call for disqualification under the subjective financial interest standard of Canon 3C, and does not deal at all with other circumstances that may call for disqualification. Nevertheless, the required disclosures are calculated to reach the majority of circumstances that are likely to call for disqualification under Canon 3C(1)(c).

The rule directs nongovernmental corporate parties to list those corporations that hold significant ownership interests in them. This includes listing membership interests in limited liability companies and similar entities that fall under the definition of a corporation in Bankruptcy Code § 101.

Under subdivision (b), parties must file the statement with the first document that they file in any adversary proceeding. The rule also requires parties and other persons to file supplemental statements promptly whenever changed circumstances require disclosure of new or additional information.

The rule does not prohibit the adoption of local rules requiring disclosures beyond those called for in Rule 7007.1.

2007 Amendments

The rule is amended to clarify that a party must file a corporate ownership statement with its initial paper filed with the court in an adversary proceeding. The party's initial filing may be a document that is not a "pleading" as defined in Rule 7 F. R. Civ. P., which is made applicable in adversary proceedings by Rule 7007. The amendment also brings Rule 7007.1 more closely in line with Rule 7.1 F. R. Civ. P.

LIBRARY REFERENCES

American Digest System

Bankruptcy ⟲2127.1.

Key Number System Topic No. 51.

Corpus Juris Secundum

CJS Bankruptcy § 290, Corporate Ownership Statement in Adversary Proceeding.

CJS Bankruptcy § 309, Reduction.

CJS Bankruptcy § 347, List of Equity Security Holders.

CJS Bankruptcy § 348, List of Administrators and Others in Chapter 15 Case.

Rule 7008. General Rules of Pleading

(a) Applicability of Rule 8 F.R.Civ.P.

Rule 8 F.R.Civ.P. applies in adversary proceedings. The allegation of jurisdiction required by Rule 8(a) shall also contain a reference to the name, number, and chapter of the case under the Code to which the adversary proceeding relates and to the district and division where the case under the Code is pending. In an adversary proceeding before a bankruptcy judge, the complaint, counterclaim, cross-claim, or third-party complaint shall contain a statement that the proceeding is core or non-core and, if non-core, that the pleader does or does not consent to entry of final orders or judgment by the bankruptcy judge.

(b) Attorney's fees

A request for an award of attorney's fees shall be pleaded as a claim in a complaint, cross-claim, third-party complaint, answer, or reply as may be appropriate.

(As amended Mar. 30, 1987, eff. Aug. 1, 1987.)

ADVISORY COMMITTEE NOTES

1987 Amendment

Proceedings before a bankruptcy judge are either core or non-core. 28 U.S.C. § 157. A bankruptcy judge may enter a final order or judgment in a core proceeding. In a non-core proceeding, absent consent of the parties, the bankruptcy judge may not enter a final order or judgment but may only submit proposed findings of fact and conclusions of law to the district judge who will enter the final order or judgment. 28 U.S.C. § 157(c)(1). The amendment to subdivision (a) of this rule requires an allegation as to whether a proceeding is core or non-core. A party who alleges that the proceeding is non-core shall state whether the party does or does not consent to the entry of a final order or judgment by the bankruptcy judge. Failure to include the statement of consent does not constitute consent. Only express consent in the pleadings or otherwise is effective to authorize entry of a final order or judgment by the bankruptcy judge in a non-core proceeding. Amendments to Rule 7012 require that the defendant admit or deny the allegation as to whether the proceeding is core or non-core.

CROSS REFERENCES

Amended and supplemental pleadings, see Fed.Rules Bankr.Proc. Rule 7015, 11 USCA.

Applicability of this rule in proceedings on contested involuntary petition and to vacate order for relief, see Fed.Rules Bankr.Proc. Rule 1018, 11 USCA.

Defenses and objections, see Fed.Rules Bankr.Proc. Rule 7012, 11 USCA.

Joinder of claims and remedies, see Fed.Rules Bankr.Proc. Rule 7013, 11 USCA.

LIBRARY REFERENCES

American Digest System

Bankruptcy ⟲2162.

Key Number System Topic No. 51.

Corpus Juris Secundum

CJS Bankruptcy § 220, Consent to Final Determination by Bankruptcy Judge--What Constitutes Consent.

CJS Bankruptcy § 397, Hearing and Notice of Hearing.

CJS Bankruptcy § 779, Award of Attorney's Fees to Prevailing Party in Adversary Proceeding.

CJS Bankruptcy § 892, Setting Aside Confirmed Sale; Remedies for Collusive Bidding.

CJS Bankruptcy § 1049, Pleading of Grounds of Objection; Amendments.

CJS Bankruptcy § 1085, Pleading of Grounds for Exception.

Rule 7009. Pleading Special Matters

Rule 9 F.R.Civ.P. applies in adversary proceedings.

CROSS REFERENCES

Applicability of this rule in proceedings on contested involuntary petition and to vacate order for relief, see Fed.Rules Bankr.Proc. Rule 1018, 11 USCA.

Parties plaintiff and defendant; capacity, see Fed.Rules Bankr.Proc. Rule 7017, 11 USCA.

Pleading affirmative defenses, see Fed.Rules Bankr.Proc. Rule 7008, 11 USCA.

LIBRARY REFERENCES

American Digest System

Bankruptcy ⟲2162.

Key Number System Topic No. 51.

Corpus Juris Secundum

CJS Bankruptcy § 140, Contested Matters.

CJS Bankruptcy § 746, Sufficiency of Pleadings.

CJS Bankruptcy § 1049, Pleading of Grounds of Objection; Amendments.

CJS Bankruptcy § 1085, Pleading of Grounds for Exception.

Rule 7010. Form of Pleadings

Rule 10 F.R.Civ.P. applies in adversary proceedings, except that the caption of each pleading in such a proceeding shall conform substantially to the appropriate Official Form.

(As amended Apr. 30, 1991, eff. Aug. 1, 1991.)

ADVISORY COMMITTEE NOTES

1991 Amendment

Reference to the Official Form number is deleted in anticipation of future revision and renumbering of the Official Forms.

CROSS REFERENCES

Applicability of this rule in proceedings on contested involuntary petition and to vacate order for relief, see Fed.Rules Bankr.Proc. Rule 1018, 11 USCA.

General requirements of form for adversarial pleading or paper, see Fed.Rules Bankr.Proc. Rule 9004, 11 USCA.

LIBRARY REFERENCES

American Digest System

Bankruptcy ⚎2127.1, 2162.

Key Number System Topic No. 51.

Corpus Juris Secundum

CJS Bankruptcy § 285, Captions.

CJS Bankruptcy § 397, Hearing and Notice of Hearing.

Rule 7012. Defenses and Objections—When and How Presented—By Pleading or Motion—Motion for Judgment on the Pleadings

(a) When presented

If a complaint is duly served, the defendant shall serve an answer within 30 days after the issuance of the summons, except when a different time is prescribed by the court. The court shall prescribe the time for service of the answer when service of a complaint is made by publication or upon a party in a foreign country. A party served with a pleading stating a cross-claim shall serve an answer thereto within 21 days after service. The plaintiff shall serve a reply to a counterclaim in the answer within 21 days after service of the answer or, if a reply is ordered by the court, within 21 days after service of the order, unless the order otherwise directs. The United States or an officer or agency thereof shall serve an answer to a complaint within 35 days after the issuance of the summons, and shall serve an answer to a cross-claim, or a reply to a counterclaim, within 35 days after service upon the United States attorney of the pleading in which the claim is asserted. The service of a motion permitted under this rule alters these periods of time as follows, unless a different time is fixed by order of the court: (1) if the court denies the motion or postpones its disposition until the trial on the merits, the responsive pleading shall be served within 14 days after notice of the court's action; (2) if the court grants a motion for a more definite statement, the responsive pleading shall be served within 14 days after the service of a more definite statement.

(b) Applicability of Rule 12(b)–(i) F.R.Civ.P.

Rule 12(b)–(i) F.R.Civ.P. applies in adversary proceedings. A responsive pleading shall admit or deny an allegation that the proceeding is core or non-core. If the response is that the proceeding is non-core, it shall include a statement that the party does or does not consent to entry of final orders or judgment by the bankruptcy judge. In non-core proceedings final orders and judgments shall not be entered on the bankruptcy judge's order except with the express consent of the parties.

(As amended Mar. 30, 1987, eff. Aug. 1, 1987; Apr. 23, 2008, eff. Dec. 1, 2008; Mar. 26, 2009, eff. Dec. 1, 2009.)

ADVISORY COMMITTEE NOTES

Subdivision (a) continues the practice of former Bankruptcy Rule 712(a) by requiring that the answer to a complaint be filed within 30 days after the issuance of the summons. Under Rule 7004(f), the summons must be served within 10 days of issuance. The other pleading periods in adversary proceedings are the same as those in civil actions before the district courts, except that the United States is allowed 35 rather than 60 days to respond.

Rule 12(b)(7) and (h)(2) F.R.Civ.P. refers to Rule 19 F.R.Civ.P. Pursuant to Rule 7002 these references are to Rule 19 F.R.Civ.P. as incorporated and modified by Rule 7019.

1987 Amendment

The amendment to subdivision (b) requires a response to the allegation that the proceeding is core or non-core. A final order of judgment may not be entered in a non-core proceeding heard by a bankruptcy judge unless all parties expressly consent. 28 U.S.C. § 157(c).

2008 Amendments

The rule is amended to conform to the changes made to the Federal Rules of Civil Procedure through the restyling of those rules effective on December 1, 2007.

2009 Amendments

The rule is amended to implement changes in connection with the amendment to Rule 9006(a) and the manner by which time is computed under the rules. The deadlines in the rule are amended to substitute a deadline that is a multiple of seven days. Throughout the rules, deadlines are amended in the following manner:

- 5–day periods become 7–day periods
- 10–day periods become 14–day periods
- 15–day periods become 14–day periods
- 20–day periods become 21–day periods
- 25–day periods become 28–day periods

CROSS REFERENCES

Averments of defense in separate statements, see Fed. Rules Bankr.Proc. Rule 7010, 11 USCA.

Counterclaim and cross-claim, see Fed.Rules Bankr.Proc. Rule 7013, 11 USCA.

Defenses of third-party defendant, see Fed.Rules Bankr. Proc. Rule 7014, 11 USCA.

Pleadings allowed, see Fed.Rules Bankr.Proc. Rule 7007, 11 USCA.

Removed actions, see Fed.Rules Bankr.Proc. Rule 9027, 11 USCA.

Waiver of sovereign immunity, see 11 USCA § 106.

LIBRARY REFERENCES

American Digest System

Bankruptcy ⬥2127.1, 2156, 2162.

Key Number System Topic No. 51.

Corpus Juris Secundum

CJS Bankruptcy § 219, Consent to Final Determination by Bankruptcy Judge.

CJS Bankruptcy § 220, Consent to Final Determination by Bankruptcy Judge--What Constitutes Consent.

CJS Bankruptcy § 221, Consent to Final Determination by Bankruptcy Judge--Waiver of Objection.

Rule 7013. Counterclaim and Cross-Claim

Rule 13 F.R.Civ.P. applies in adversary proceedings, except that a party sued by a trustee or debtor in possession need not state as a counterclaim any claim that the party has against the debtor, the debtor's property, or the estate, unless the claim arose after the entry of an order for relief. A trustee or debtor in possession who fails to plead a counterclaim through oversight, inadvertence, or excusable neglect, or when justice so requires, may by leave of court amend the pleading, or commence a new adversary proceeding or separate action.

(As amended Mar. 30, 1987, eff. Aug. 1, 1987.)

ADVISORY COMMITTEE NOTES

Rule 13(h) F.R.Civ.P. refers to Rule 19 F.R.Civ.P. Pursuant to Rule 7002 this reference is to Rule 19 F.R.Civ.P. as incorporated and modified by Rule 7019.

CROSS REFERENCES

Amended and supplemental pleadings, see Fed.Rules Bankr.Proc. Rule 7015, 11 USCA.

Counterclaims and cross-claims of third-party defendant, see Fed.Rules Bankr.Proc. Rule 7014, 11 USCA.

Default judgment against counterclaimants and cross-claimants, see Fed.Rules Bankr.Proc. Rule 7055, 11 USCA.

Dismissal of counterclaims and cross-claims, see Fed.Rules Bankr.Proc. Rule 7041, 11 USCA.

Separate trial of counterclaims and cross-claims, see Fed. Rules Bankr.Proc. Rule 7042, 11 USCA.

LIBRARY REFERENCES

American Digest System

Bankruptcy ⬥2048.4, 2156, 2157, 2159.1 to 2161, 2162, 2671.

Key Number System Topic No. 51.

Corpus Juris Secundum

CJS Bankruptcy § 281, Counterclaims.

Rule 7014. Third-Party Practice

Rule 14 F.R.Civ.P. applies in adversary proceedings.

ADVISORY COMMITTEE NOTES

This rule does not purport to deal with questions of jurisdiction. The scope of the jurisdictional grant under 28 U.S.C. § 1471 and whether the doctrines of pendent or ancillary jurisdiction are applicable to adversary proceedings will be determined by the courts.

Rule 14 F.R.Civ.P. refers to Rules 12 and 13 F.R.Civ.P. Pursuant to Rule 7002 those references are to Rules 12 and 13 as incorporated and modified by Rules 7012 and 7013.

CROSS REFERENCES

Default judgment against third-party plaintiff, see Fed. Rules Bankr.Proc. Rule 7055, 11 USCA.

Joinder of claims, see Fed.Rules Bankr.Proc. Rule 7018, 11 USCA.

Requisites of pleading, see Fed.Rules Bankr.Proc. Rule 7008, 11 USCA.

Separate trial of third-party claim, see Fed.Rules Bankr. Proc. Rule 7042, 11 USCA.

LIBRARY REFERENCES

American Digest System

Bankruptcy ⬥2056, 2127.1, 2157, 2158, 2161.

Key Number System Topic No. 51.

Corpus Juris Secundum

CJS Bankruptcy § 275, Applicable Rules of Civil Procedure.

Rule 7015. Amended and Supplemental Pleadings

Rule 15 F.R.Civ.P. applies in adversary proceedings.

CROSS REFERENCES

Amendments to pleadings considered at pre-trial conference, see Fed.Rules Bankr.Proc. Rule 7016, 11 USCA.

Applicability of this rule in proceedings on contested involuntary petition and to vacate order for relief, see Fed.Rules Bankr.Proc. Rule 1018, 11 USCA.

Substitution of parties, see Fed.Rules Bankr.Proc. Rule 7025, 11 USCA.

LIBRARY REFERENCES

American Digest System

Bankruptcy ⬥2157, 2162.

Key Number System Topic No. 51.

Corpus Juris Secundum

CJS Bankruptcy § 397, Hearing and Notice of Hearing.

CJS Bankruptcy § 1049, Pleading of Grounds of Objection; Amendments.

CJS Bankruptcy § 1086, Pleading of Grounds for Exception--Amendment.

Rule 7016. Pre-Trial Procedure; Formulating Issues

Rule 16 F.R.Civ.P. applies in adversary proceedings.

CROSS REFERENCES

Amended and supplemental pleadings, see Fed.Rules Bankr.Proc. Rule 7015, 11 USCA.

Applicability of this rule in proceedings on contested involuntary petition and to vacate order for relief, see Fed.Rules Bankr.Proc. Rule 1018, 11 USCA.

Preliminary hearing before trial to determine merit of defenses, see Fed.Rules Bankr.Proc. Rule 7012, 11 USCA.

LIBRARY REFERENCES

American Digest System

Bankruptcy ⇔2127.1, 2187.

Key Number System Topic No. 51.

Corpus Juris Secundum

CJS Bankruptcy § 144, Pre-Trial Procedure; Status Conferences and Deadlines for Action.

CJS Bankruptcy § 397, Hearing and Notice of Hearing.

Rule 7017. Parties Plaintiff and Defendant; Capacity

Rule 17 F.R.Civ.P. applies in adversary proceedings, except as provided in Rule 2010(b).

(As amended Apr. 30, 1991, eff. Aug. 1, 1991.)

ADVISORY COMMITTEE NOTES

Rules 2010(d) and 5008(d), which implement §§ 322 and 345 of the Code, authorize a party in interest to prosecute a claim on the bond of a trustee or depository in the name of the United States.

1991 Amendment

Reference to Rule 5008(d) is deleted because of the abrogation of Rule 5008.

CROSS REFERENCES

Bond requirement for deposit or investment by trustee of estate money, see 11 USCA § 345.

Filing by trustee of bond in favor of United States as qualification to serve, see 11 USCA § 322.

Service upon infants or incompetent persons of—

Notice of application for depositions before adversary proceedings or pending appeal, see Fed.Rules Bankr. Proc. Rule 7027, 11 USCA.

Summons and complaint, see Fed.Rules Bankr.Proc. Rule 7004, 11 USCA.

LIBRARY REFERENCES

American Digest System

Bankruptcy ⇔2152.1, 2154.1, 2159.1 to 2161.

Key Number System Topic No. 51.

Corpus Juris Secundum

CJS Bankruptcy § 140, Contested Matters.

CJS Bankruptcy § 275, Applicable Rules of Civil Procedure.

CJS Bankruptcy § 277, Real Party in Interest; Capacity.

Rule 7018. Joinder of Claims and Remedies

Rule 18 F.R.Civ.P. applies in adversary proceedings.

CROSS REFERENCES

Joinder of parties—

Misjoinder and non-joinder, see Fed.Rules Bankr.Proc. Rule 7021, 11 USCA.

Permissive joinder, see Fed.Rules Bankr.Proc. Rule 7020, 11 USCA.

Persons needed for just determination, see Fed.Rules Bankr.Proc. Rule 7019, 11 USCA.

LIBRARY REFERENCES

American Digest System

Bankruptcy ⇔2127.1, 2162, 2164.1.

Key Number System Topic No. 51.

Rule 7019. Joinder of Persons Needed for Just Determination

Rule 19 F.R.Civ.P. applies in adversary proceedings, except that (1) if an entity joined as a party raises the defense that the court lacks jurisdiction over the subject matter and the defense is sustained, the court shall dismiss such entity from the adversary proceeding and (2) if an entity joined as a party properly and timely raises the defense of improper venue, the court shall determine, as provided in 28 U.S.C. § 1412, whether that part of the proceeding involving the joined party shall be transferred to another district, or whether the entire adversary proceeding shall be transferred to another district.

(As amended Mar. 30, 1987, eff. Aug. 1, 1987.)

ADVISORY COMMITTEE NOTES

This rule addresses a situation different from that encountered by the district court when its jurisdiction is based on diversity of citizenship under 28 U.S.C. § 1332. Joining of a party whose citizenship is the same as that of an adversary destroys the district court's jurisdiction over the entire civil action but under 28 U.S.C. § 1471 the attempted joinder of such a person would not affect the bankruptcy court's jurisdiction over the original adversary proceeding.

1987 Amendment

The rule is amended to delete the reference to retention of the adversary proceeding if venue is improper. See 28 U.S.C. § 1412.

CROSS REFERENCES

Additional parties for determination of counterclaim or cross-claim, see Fed.Rules Bankr.Proc. Rule 7013, 11 USCA.

Exception to procedural rule on transfer by court of adversary proceeding, see Fed.Rules Bankr.Proc. Rule 7087, 11 USCA.

Parties—

Permissive joinder, see Fed.Rules Bankr.Proc. Rule 7020, 11 USCA.

Substitution of, see Fed.Rules Bankr.Proc. Rule 7025, 11 USCA.

LIBRARY REFERENCES

American Digest System

Bankruptcy ⊕2045, 2081, 2159.1, 2162.

Key Number System Topic No. 51.

Corpus Juris Secundum

CJS Bankruptcy § 151, Original But Not Exclusive Jurisdiction of Civil Proceedings.

CJS Bankruptcy § 152, Exclusive Jurisdiction of Property of Debtor and Estate.

CJS Bankruptcy § 273, Adversary Proceedings.

CJS Bankruptcy § 275, Applicable Rules of Civil Procedure.

Rule 7020.   Permissive Joinder of Parties

Rule 20 F.R.Civ.P. applies in adversary proceedings.

CROSS REFERENCES

Additional parties for determination of counterclaim or cross-claim, see Fed.Rules Bankr.Proc. Rule 7013, 11 USCA.

Parties—

     Joinder of persons needed for just determination, see Fed.Rules Bankr.Proc. Rule 7019, 11 USCA.

     Substitution of, see Fed.Rules Bankr.Proc. Rule 7025, 11 USCA.

LIBRARY REFERENCES

American Digest System

Bankruptcy ⊕2045, 2127.1, 2159.1.

Key Number System Topic No. 51.

Corpus Juris Secundum

CJS Bankruptcy § 275, Applicable Rules of Civil Procedure.

Rule 7021.   Misjoinder and Non-Joinder of Parties

Rule 21 F.R.Civ.P. applies in adversary proceedings.

CROSS REFERENCES

Applicability of this rule in contested matters not otherwise provided for, see Fed.Rules Bankr.Proc. Rule 9014, 11 USCA.

Judgment on counterclaim or cross-claim rendered in separate trials, see Fed.Rules Bankr.Proc. Rule 7013, 11 USCA.

Separate trials—

     In furtherance of convenience or to avoid prejudice, see Fed.Rules Bankr.Proc. Rule 7042, 11 USCA.

     Of parties joined permissively, see Fed.Rules Bankr.Proc. Rule 7020, 11 USCA.

LIBRARY REFERENCES

American Digest System

Bankruptcy ⊕2127.1, 2159.1.

Key Number System Topic No. 51.

Corpus Juris Secundum

CJS Bankruptcy § 140, Contested Matters.

CJS Bankruptcy § 275, Applicable Rules of Civil Procedure.

Rule 7022.   Interpleader

Rule 22(a) F.R.Civ.P. applies in adversary proceedings. This rule supplements—and does not limit—the joinder of parties allowed by Rule 7020.

(As amended Apr. 23, 2008, eff. Dec. 1, 2008.)

ADVISORY COMMITTEE NOTES

2008 Amendments

The rule is amended to conform to the changes made to the Federal Rules of Civil Procedure through the restyling of those rules effective on December 1, 2007.

CROSS REFERENCES

Preliminary injunction in interpleader actions, see Fed. Rules Bankr.Proc. Rule 7065, 11 USCA.

LIBRARY REFERENCES

American Digest System

Bankruptcy ⊕2045, 2127.1, 2182.1.

Interpleader ⊕15 to 43.

Key Number System Topic Nos. 222, 51.

Corpus Juris Secundum

CJS Bankruptcy § 275, Applicable Rules of Civil Procedure.

Rule 7023.   Class proceedings

Rule 23 F.R.Civ.P. applies in adversary proceedings.

CROSS REFERENCES

Exception of class actions from procedural rule of necessary joinder of parties, see Fed.Rules Bankr.Proc. Rule 7019, 11 USCA.

LIBRARY REFERENCES

American Digest System

Bankruptcy ⊕2131, 2159.1, 2162, 2164.1, 2182.1, 2895.1, 3030, 3033, 3768.

Key Number System Topic No. 51.

Corpus Juris Secundum

CJS Bankruptcy § 275, Applicable Rules of Civil Procedure.

Rule 7023.1.   Derivative Actions

Rule 23.1 F.R.Civ.P. applies in adversary proceedings.

(As amended Apr. 23, 2008, eff. Dec. 1, 2008.)

ADVISORY COMMITTEE NOTES

2008 Amendments

The rule is amended to conform to the changes made to the Federal Rules of Civil Procedure through the restyling of those rules effective on December 1, 2007.

CROSS REFERENCES

Actions relating to unincorporated associations, see Fed. Rules Bankr.Proc. Rule 7023.1, 11 USCA.

LIBRARY REFERENCES

American Digest System

Bankruptcy ⬯2154.1, 2159.1, 2162.

Key Number System Topic No. 51.

Corpus Juris Secundum

CJS Bankruptcy § 275, Applicable Rules of Civil Procedure.

Rule 7023.2. Adversary Proceedings Relating to Unincorporated Associations

Rule 23.2 F.R.Civ.P. applies in adversary proceedings.

CROSS REFERENCES

Capacity of unincorporated association to sue or be sued, see Fed.Rules Bankr.Proc. Rule 7017, 11 USCA.

Derivative actions by shareholders, see Fed.Rules Bankr. Proc. Rule 7023.1, 11 USCA.

LIBRARY REFERENCES

American Digest System

Bankruptcy ⬯2159.1.

Key Number System Topic No. 51.

Corpus Juris Secundum

CJS Bankruptcy § 275, Applicable Rules of Civil Procedure.

Rule 7024. Intervention

Rule 24 F.R.Civ.P. applies in adversary proceedings.

ADVISORY COMMITTEE NOTES

A person may seek to intervene in the case under the Code or in an adversary proceeding relating to the case under the Code. Intervention in a case under the Code is governed by Rule 2018 and intervention in an adversary proceeding is governed by this rule. Intervention in a case and intervention in an adversary proceeding must be sought separately.

CROSS REFERENCES

Applicability of this rule in proceedings on contested involuntary petition and to vacate order for relief, see Fed.Rules Bankr.Proc. Rule 1018, 11 USCA.

Intervention in case under this title, see Fed.Rules Bankr. Proc. Rule 2018, 11 USCA.

LIBRARY REFERENCES

American Digest System

Bankruptcy ⬯2160.

Key Number System Topic No. 51.

Corpus Juris Secundum

CJS Bankruptcy § 275, Applicable Rules of Civil Procedure.

CJS Bankruptcy § 279, Intervention.

CJS Bankruptcy § 397, Hearing and Notice of Hearing.

Rule 7025. Substitution of Parties

Subject to the provisions of Rule 2012, Rule 25 F.R.Civ.P. applies in adversary proceedings.

ADVISORY COMMITTEE NOTES

Rule 25 F.R.Civ.P. refers to Rule 4 F.R.Civ.P. Pursuant to Rule 7002 that reference is to Rule 4 as incorporated and modified by Rule 7004.

CROSS REFERENCES

Applicability of this rule in—

Contested matters not otherwise provided for, see Fed. Rules Bankr.Proc. Rule 9014, 11 USCA.

Proceedings on contested involuntary petition and to vacate order for relief, see Fed.Rules Bankr.Proc. Rule 1018, 11 USCA.

Right to use depositions previously taken, see Fed.Rules Bankr.Proc. Rule 7026, 11 USCA.

LIBRARY REFERENCES

American Digest System

Bankruptcy ⬯2159.1.

Key Number System Topic No. 51.

Corpus Juris Secundum

CJS Bankruptcy § 140, Contested Matters.

CJS Bankruptcy § 275, Applicable Rules of Civil Procedure.

Rule 7026. General Provisions Governing Discovery

Rule 26 F.R.Civ.P. applies in adversary proceedings.

CROSS REFERENCES

Applicability of this rule in—

Contested matters not otherwise provided for, see Fed. Rules Bankr.Proc. Rule 9014, 11 USCA.

Proceedings on contested involuntary petition and to vacate order for relief, see Fed.Rules Bankr.Proc. Rule 1018, 11 USCA.

Failure to make discovery; sanctions, see Fed.Rules Bankr. Proc. Rule 7037, 11 USCA.

Subpoena for taking depositions; place of examination, see Fed.Rules Bankr.Proc. Rule 9016, 11 USCA.

LIBRARY REFERENCES

American Digest System

Bankruptcy ⬯3040.1 to 3048.

Key Number System Topic No. 51.

Corpus Juris Secundum

CJS Bankruptcy § 140, Contested Matters.

CJS Bankruptcy § 256, Sanctions Resulting from Noncompliance With Requirements as to Basis for Filing.

CJS Bankruptcy § 284, Signature and Verification of Basis for Filing.

CJS Bankruptcy § 397, Hearing and Notice of Hearing.

Rule 7027. Depositions Before Adversary Proceedings or Pending Appeal

Rule 27 F.R.Civ.P. applies to adversary proceedings.

ADVISORY COMMITTEE NOTES

Rule 27(a)(2) F.R.Civ.P. refers to Rule 4 F.R.Civ.P. Pursuant to Rule 7002 the reference is to Rule 4 F.R.Civ.P. as incorporated and modified by Rule 7004.

CROSS REFERENCES

Applicability of this rule in contested matters not otherwise provided for, see Fed.Rules Bankr.Proc. Rule 9014, 11 USCA.

LIBRARY REFERENCES

American Digest System

Bankruptcy ⟐3040.1 to 3048.
Key Number System Topic No. 51.

Corpus Juris Secundum

CJS Bankruptcy § 140, Contested Matters.

Rule 7028. Persons Before Whom Depositions May be Taken

Rule 28 F.R.Civ.P. applies in adversary proceedings.

CROSS REFERENCES

Affirmations, see Fed.Rules Bankr.Proc. Rule 9012, 11 USCA.

Applicability of this rule in—

Contested matters not otherwise provided for, see Fed. Rules Bankr.Proc. Rule 9014, 11 USCA.

Proceedings on contested involuntary petition and to vacate order for relief, see Fed.Rules Bankr.Proc. Rule 1018, 11 USCA.

LIBRARY REFERENCES

American Digest System

Bankruptcy ⟐3040.1 to 3048.
Key Number System Topic No. 51.

Corpus Juris Secundum

CJS Bankruptcy § 140, Contested Matters.
CJS Bankruptcy § 397, Hearing and Notice of Hearing.

Rule 7029. Stipulations Regarding Discovery Procedure

Rule 29 F.R.Civ.P. applies in adversary proceedings.

CROSS REFERENCES

Applicability of this rule in—

Contested matters not otherwise provided for, see Fed. Rules Bankr.Proc. Rule 9014, 11 USCA.

Proceedings on contested involuntary petition and to vacate order for relief, see Fed.Rules Bankr.Proc. Rule 1018, 11 USCA.

LIBRARY REFERENCES

American Digest System

Bankruptcy ⟐3040.1 to 3048.
Key Number System Topic No. 51.

Rule 7030. Depositions Upon Oral Examination

Rule 30 F.R.Civ.P. applies in adversary proceedings.

ADVISORY COMMITTEE NOTES

Rule 30 F.R.Civ.P. refers to Rule 4 F.R.Civ.P. Pursuant to Rule 7002 that reference is a reference to Rule 4 F.R.Civ.P. as incorporated and modified by Rule 7004.

CROSS REFERENCES

Applicability of this rule in—

Contested matters not otherwise provided for, see Fed. Rules Bankr.Proc. Rule 9014, 11 USCA.

Proceedings on contested involuntary petition and to vacate order for relief, see Fed.Rules Bankr.Proc. Rule 1018, 11 USCA.

Failure to make discovery; sanctions, see Fed.Rules Bankr. Proc. Rule 7037, 11 USCA.

Subpoena for taking depositions; place of examination, see Fed.Rules Bankr.Proc. Rule 9016, 11 USCA.

LIBRARY REFERENCES

American Digest System

Bankruptcy ⟐3040.1 to 3048.
Key Number System Topic No. 51.

Corpus Juris Secundum

CJS Bankruptcy § 824, Examination of Corporations.

Rule 7031. Deposition Upon Written Questions

Rule 31 F.R.Civ.P. applies in adversary proceedings.

CROSS REFERENCES

Applicability of this rule in—

Contested matters not otherwise provided for, see Fed. Rules Bankr.Proc. Rule 9014, 11 USCA.

Proceedings on contested involuntary petition and to vacate order for relief, see Fed.Rules Bankr.Proc. Rule 1018, 11 USCA.

Failure to make discovery; sanctions, see Fed.Rules Bankr. Proc. Rule 7037, 11 USCA.

LIBRARY REFERENCES

American Digest System

Bankruptcy ⟐3040.1 to 3048.
Key Number System Topic No. 51.

Rule 7032. Use of Depositions in Adversary Proceedings

Rule 32 F.R.Civ.P. applies in adversary proceedings.

Applicability of this rule in—

Contested matters not otherwise provided for, see Fed. Rules Bankr.Proc. Rule 9014, 11 USCA.

Proceedings on contested involuntary petition and to vacate order for relief, see Fed.Rules Bankr.Proc. Rule 1018, 11 USCA.

LIBRARY REFERENCES

American Digest System

Bankruptcy ☞3048.

Key Number System Topic No. 51.

Rule 7033.   Interrogatories to Parties

Rule 33 F.R.Civ.P. applies in adversary proceedings.

CROSS REFERENCES

Applicability of this rule in—

Contested matters not otherwise provided for, see Fed. Rules Bankr.Proc. Rule 9014, 11 USCA.

Proceedings on contested involuntary petition and to vacate order for relief, see Fed.Rules Bankr.Proc. Rule 1018, 11 USCA.

Failure to make discovery; sanctions, see Fed.Rules Bankr. Proc. Rule 7037, 11 USCA.

LIBRARY REFERENCES

American Digest System

Bankruptcy ☞3040.1 to 3048.

Key Number System Topic No. 51.

Rule 7034.   Production of Documents and Things and Entry Upon Land for Inspection and Other Purposes

Rule 34 F.R.Civ.P. applies in adversary proceedings.

CROSS REFERENCES

Applicability of this rule in—

Contested matters not otherwise provided for, see Fed. Rules Bankr.Proc. Rule 9014, 11 USCA.

Proceedings on contested involuntary petition and to vacate order for relief, see Fed.Rules Bankr.Proc. Rule 1018, 11 USCA.

Failure to make discovery; sanctions, see Fed.Rules Bankr. Proc. Rule 7037, 11 USCA.

Subpoena for production of documentary evidence, see Fed. Rules Bankr.Proc. Rule 9016, 11 USCA.

LIBRARY REFERENCES

American Digest System

Bankruptcy ☞3044.

Key Number System Topic No. 51.

Rule 7035.   Physical and Mental Examination of Persons

Rule 35 F.R.Civ.P. applies in adversary proceedings.

CROSS REFERENCES

Applicability of this rule in—

Contested matters not otherwise provided for, see Fed. Rules Bankr.Proc. Rule 9014, 11 USCA.

Proceedings on contested involuntary petition and to vacate order for relief, see Fed.Rules Bankr.Proc. Rule 1018, 11 USCA.

Failure to make discovery; sanctions, see Fed.Rules Bankr. Proc. Rule 7037, 11 USCA.

LIBRARY REFERENCES

American Digest System

Bankruptcy ☞3040.1 to 3048.

Key Number System Topic No. 51.

Rule 7036.   Requests for Admission

Rule 36 F.R.Civ.P. applies in adversary proceedings.

CROSS REFERENCES

Applicability of this rule in—

Contested matters not otherwise provided for, see Fed. Rules Bankr.Proc. Rule 9014, 11 USCA.

Proceedings on contested involuntary petition and to vacate order for relief, see Fed.Rules Bankr.Proc. Rule 1018, 11 USCA.

Pre-trial conference to obtain admissions of facts and documents, see Fed.Rules Bankr.Proc. Rule 7016, 11 USCA.

LIBRARY REFERENCES

American Digest System

Bankruptcy ☞3040.1 to 3048.

Key Number System Topic No. 51.

Rule 7037.   Failure to Make Discovery: Sanctions

Rule 37 F.R.Civ.P. applies in adversary proceedings.

CROSS REFERENCES

Applicability of this rule in—

Contested matters not otherwise provided for, see Fed. Rules Bankr.Proc. Rule 9014, 11 USCA.

Proceedings on contested involuntary petition and to vacate order for relief, see Fed.Rules Bankr.Proc. Rule 1018, 11 USCA.

LIBRARY REFERENCES

American Digest System

Bankruptcy ☞3040.1 to 3048, 3766.

Key Number System Topic No. 51.

Corpus Juris Secundum

CJS Bankruptcy § 140, Contested Matters.

CJS Bankruptcy § 256, Sanctions Resulting from Noncompliance With Requirements as to Basis for Filing.

CJS Bankruptcy § 260, Sanctions Under Fed. R. Civ. P. 37.

CJS Bankruptcy § 284, Signature and Verification of Basis for Filing.

CJS Bankruptcy § 397, Hearing and Notice of Hearing.

Rule 7040. Assignment of Cases for Trial

Rule 40 F.R.Civ.P. applies in adversary proceedings.

CROSS REFERENCES

Local bankruptcy rules on practice and procedure not inconsistent with these rules, see Fed.Rules Bankr.Proc. Rule 9029, 11 USCA.

LIBRARY REFERENCES

American Digest System

Bankruptcy ⊕2127.1.

Key Number System Topic No. 51.

Rule 7041. Dismissal of Adversary Proceedings

Rule 41 F.R.Civ.P. applies in adversary proceedings, except that a complaint objecting to the debtor's discharge shall not be dismissed at the plaintiff's instance without notice to the trustee, the United States trustee, and such other persons as the court may direct, and only on order of the court containing terms and conditions which the court deems proper.

(As amended Apr. 30, 1991, eff. Aug. 1, 1991.)

ADVISORY COMMITTEE NOTES

Dismissal of a complaint objecting to a discharge raises special concerns because the plaintiff may have been induced to dismiss by an advantage given or promised by the debtor or someone acting in his interest. Some courts by local rule or order have required the debtor and his attorney or the plaintiff to file an affidavit that nothing has been promised to the plaintiff in consideration of the withdrawal of the objection. By specifically authorizing the court to impose conditions in the order of dismissal this rule permits the continuation of this salutary practice.

Rule 41 F.R.Civ.P. refers to Rule 19 F.R.Civ.P. Pursuant to Rule 7002 that reference is to Rule 19 F.R.Civ.P. as incorporated and modified by Rule 7019.

1991 Amendment

The United States trustee has standing to object to the debtor's discharge pursuant to § 727(c) and may have refrained from commencing an adversary proceeding objecting to discharge within the time limits provided in Rule 4004 only because another party commenced such a proceeding. The United States trustee may oppose dismissal of the original proceeding.

The rule is also amended to clarify that the court may direct that other persons receive notice of a plaintiff's motion to dismiss a complaint objecting to discharge.

CROSS REFERENCES

Applicability of this rule in contested matters not otherwise provided for, see Fed.Rules Bankr.Proc. Rule 9014, 11 USCA.

Findings by court necessary when judgment rendered on merits of motion to dismiss after trial on facts, see Fed.Rules Bankr.Proc. Rule 7052, 11 USCA.

Sanction for failure to attend deposition, to answer interrogatories, or to respond to inspection request, see Fed.Rules Bankr.Proc. Rule 7037, 11 USCA.

LIBRARY REFERENCES

American Digest System

Bankruptcy ⊕2162, 2184.

Key Number System Topic No. 51.

Corpus Juris Secundum

CJS Bankruptcy § 50, Chapter 7 Proceedings.

CJS Bankruptcy § 140, Contested Matters.

CJS Bankruptcy § 1054, Hearing, Determination, and Order.

Rule 7042. Consolidation of Adversary Proceedings; Separate Trials

Rule 42 F.R.Civ.P. applies in adversary proceedings.

CROSS REFERENCES

Applicability of this rule in contested matters not otherwise provided for, see Fed.Rules Bankr.Proc. Rule 9014, 11 USCA.

Separate trials—

Joinder of party against whom no claim exists, see Fed. Rules Bankr.Proc. Rule 7020, 11 USCA.

Separate judgments rendered on counterclaim or crossclaim, see Fed.Rules Bankr.Proc. Rule 7013, 11 USCA.

LIBRARY REFERENCES

American Digest System

Bankruptcy ⊕2127.1, 2156.

Key Number System Topic No. 51.

Corpus Juris Secundum

CJS Bankruptcy § 140, Contested Matters.

Rule 7052. Findings by the Court

Rule 52 F. R. Civ. P. applies in adversary proceedings, except that any motion under subdivision (b) of that rule for amended or additional findings shall be filed no later than 14 days after entry of judgment. In these proceedings, the reference in Rule 52 F. R. Civ. P. to the entry of judgment under Rule 58 F. R. Civ. P. shall be read as a reference to the entry of a judgment or order under Rule 5003(a).

(As amended Mar. 26, 2009, eff. Dec. 1, 2009.)

ADVISORY COMMITTEE NOTES

Rule 52(a) F.R.Civ.P. refers to Rule 12 F.R.Civ.P. Pursuant to Rule 7002 this reference is to Rule 12 F.R.Civ.P. as incorporated and modified by Rule 7012.

2009 Amendments

The rule is amended to clarify that the reference in Rule 52 F. R. Civ. P. to Rule 58 F. R. Civ. P. and its provisions is construed as a reference to the entry of a judgment or order under Rule 5003(a).

The rule is amended by limiting the time for filing post judgment motions for amended or additional findings. In 2009, Rule 52 F. R. Civ. P. was amended to extend the deadline for filing those post judgment motions to no later than 28 days after entry of the judgment. That deadline corresponds to the 30–day deadline for filing a notice of appeal in a civil case under Rule 4(a)(1)(A) F. R. App. P. In a bankruptcy case, the deadline for filing a notice of appeal is 14 days. Therefore, the 28–day deadline for filing a motion for amended or additional findings would effectively override the notice of appeal deadline under Rule 8002(a) but for this amendment.

CROSS REFERENCES

Amendment of findings—

On motion for new trial, see Fed.Rules Bankr.Proc. Rule 9023, 11 USCA.

Stay of proceedings to enforce judgment pending disposition of motion to amend, see Fed.Rules Bankr.Proc. Rule 7062, 11 USCA.

Applicability of this rule in—

Contested matters not otherwise provided for, see Fed. Rules Bankr.Proc. Rule 9014, 11 USCA.

Proceedings on contested involuntary petition and to vacate order for relief, see Fed.Rules Bankr.Proc. Rule 1018, 11 USCA.

Effect of motion to amend or to add fact findings on time for appeal, see Fed.Rules Bankr.Proc. Rule 8002, 11 USCA.

Enlargement of ten-day period for motion to amend findings of court not permitted, see Fed.Rules Bankr.Proc. Rule 9006, 11 USCA.

LIBRARY REFERENCES

American Digest System

Bankruptcy ⬯2164.1.

Key Number System Topic No. 51.

Corpus Juris Secundum

CJS Bankruptcy § 140, Contested Matters.

CJS Bankruptcy § 308, Enlargement.

CJS Bankruptcy § 314, Judgments.

CJS Bankruptcy § 397, Hearing and Notice of Hearing.

Rule 7054. Judgments; Costs

(a) Judgments

Rule 54(a)–(c) F.R.Civ.P. applies in adversary proceedings.

[Text of subdivision (b) effective until December 1, 2012, absent contrary Congressional action.]

(b) Costs

The court may allow costs to the prevailing party except when a statute of the United States or these rules otherwise provides. Costs against the United States, its officers and agencies shall be imposed only to the extent permitted by law. Costs may be taxed by the clerk on one day's notice; on motion served within five days thereafter, the action of the clerk may be reviewed by the court.

[Text of subdivision (b) effective December 1, 2012, absent contrary Congressional action.]

(b) Costs

The court may allow costs to the prevailing party except when a statute of the United States or these rules otherwise provides. Costs against the United States, its officers and agencies shall be imposed only to the extent permitted by law. Costs may be taxed by the clerk on 14 days' notice; on motion served within seven days thereafter, the action of the clerk may be reviewed by the court.

(As amended Apr. 23, 2012, eff. Dec. 1, 2012, absent contrary Congressional action.)

ADVISORY COMMITTEE NOTES

2012 Amendments

[Effective December 1, 2012, absent contrary Congressional action.]

Subdivision (b). Subdivision (b) is amended to provide more time for a party to respond to the prevailing party's bill of costs. The former rule's provision of one day's notice was unrealistically short. The change to 14 days conforms to the change made to Civil Rule 54(d). Extension from five to seven days of the time for serving a motion for court review of the clerk's action implements changes in connection with the December 1, 2009, amendment to Rule 9006(a) and the manner by which time is computed under the rules. Throughout the rules, deadlines have been amended in the following manner:

- 5–day periods became 7–day periods.
- 10–day periods became 14–day periods.
- 15–day periods became 14–day periods.
- 20–day periods became 21–day periods.
- 25–day periods became 28–day periods.

Changes Made After Publication

No changes were made after publication.

CROSS REFERENCES

Amendment or alteration—

Stay of proceedings pending disposition of motion for, see Fed.Rules Bankr.Proc. Rule 7062, 11 USCA.

Time for service of motion, see Fed.Rules Bankr.Proc. Rule 9023, 11 USCA.

Applicability of this rule in—

Contested matters not otherwise provided for, see Fed. Rules Bankr.Proc. Rule 9014, 11 USCA.

Proceedings on contested involuntary petition and to vacate order for relief, see Fed.Rules Bankr.Proc. Rule 1018, 11 USCA.

Entry of judgment, district court record of judgment, see Fed.Rules Bankr.Proc. Rule 9021, 11 USCA.

Relief from judgment or order, see Fed.Rules Bankr.Proc. Rule 9024, 11 USCA.

LIBRARY REFERENCES

American Digest System

Bankruptcy ⬯2164.1, 2181 to 2191.

Key Number System Topic No. 51.

Corpus Juris Secundum

CJS Bankruptcy § 140, Contested Matters.

CJS Bankruptcy § 314, Judgments.

CJS Bankruptcy § 316, Costs and Fees.

CJS Bankruptcy § 397, Hearing and Notice of Hearing.

Rule 7055. Default

Rule 55 F.R.Civ.P. applies in adversary proceedings.

CROSS REFERENCES

Applicability of this rule in contested matters not otherwise provided for, see Fed.Rules Bankr.Proc. Rule 9014, 11 USCA.

Demand for judgment, see Fed.Rules Bankr.Proc. Rule 7054, 11 USCA.

LIBRARY REFERENCES

American Digest System

Bankruptcy ⟫2165, 2930, 3387.1.

Key Number System Topic No. 51.

Corpus Juris Secundum

CJS Bankruptcy § 314, Judgments.

Rule 7056. Summary Judgment

[Text of Rule 7056 effective until December 1, 2012, absent contrary Congressional action.]

Rule 56 F.R.Civ.P. applies in adversary proceedings.

[Text of Rule 7056 effective December 1, 2012, absent contrary Congressional action.]

Rule 56 F.R.Civ.P. applies in adversary proceedings, except that any motion for summary judgment must be made at least 30 days before the initial date set for an evidentiary hearing on any issue for which summary judgment is sought, unless a different time is set by local rule or the court orders otherwise.

(As amended Apr. 23, 2012, eff. Dec. 1, 2012, absent contrary Congressional action.)

ADVISORY COMMITTEE NOTES

2012 Amendments

[Effective December 1, 2012, absent contrary Congressional action.]

The only exception to complete adoption of Rule 56 F.R.Civ.P. involves the default deadline for filing a summary judgment motion. Rule 56(c)(1)(A) makes the default deadline 30 days after the close of all discovery. Because in bankruptcy cases hearings can occur shortly after the close of discovery, a default deadline based on the scheduled hearing date, rather than the close of discovery, is adopted. As with Rule 56(c)(1), the deadline can be altered either by local rule or court order.

Changes Made After Publication

No changes were made after publication.

CROSS REFERENCES

Applicability of this rule in—

Contested matters, not otherwise provided for, see Fed. Rules Bankr.Proc. Rule 9014, 11 USCA.

Proceedings on contested involuntary petition and to vacate order for relief, see Fed.Rules Bankr.Proc. Rule 1018, 11 USCA.

LIBRARY REFERENCES

American Digest System

Bankruptcy ⟫2164.1, 3766.1.

Key Number System Topic No. 51.

Corpus Juris Secundum

CJS Bankruptcy § 140, Contested Matters.

CJS Bankruptcy § 314, Judgments.

CJS Bankruptcy § 397, Hearing and Notice of Hearing.

Rule 7058. Entering Judgment in Adversary Proceeding

Rule 58 F.R.Civ.P. applies in adversary proceedings. In these proceedings, the reference in Rule 58 F.R.Civ.P. to the civil docket shall be read as a reference to the docket maintained by the clerk under Rule 5003(a).

(Added Mar. 26, 2009, eff. Dec. 1, 2009.)

ADVISORY COMMITTEE NOTES

2009 Adoption

This rule makes Rule 58 F.R.Civ.P. applicable in adversary proceedings and is added in connection with the amendments to Rule 9021.

LIBRARY REFERENCES

Corpus Juris Secundum

CJS Bankruptcy § 314, Judgments.

Rule 7062. Stay of Proceedings to Enforce a Judgment

Rule 62 F.R.Civ.P. applies in adversary proceedings.

(As amended Apr. 30, 1991, eff. Aug. 1, 1991; Apr. 29, 1999, eff. Dec. 1, 1999.)

ADVISORY COMMITTEE NOTES

The additional exceptions set forth in this rule make applicable to those matters the consequences contained in Rule 62(c) and (d) with respect to orders in actions for injunctions.

1991 Amendment

This rule is amended to include as additional exceptions to Rule 62(a) an order granting relief from the automatic stay of actions against codebtors provided by § 1201 of the Code, the sale or lease of property of the estate under § 363, and the assumption or assignment of an executory contract under § 365.

1999 Amendments

The additional exceptions to Rule 62(a) consist of orders that are issued in contested matters. These exceptions are deleted from this rule because of the amendment to Rule 9014 that renders this rule inapplicable in contested matters unless the court orders otherwise. See also the amendments to Rules 3020, 3021, 4001, 6004, and 6006 that delay the implementation of certain types of orders for a period of ten days unless the court otherwise directs.

Gap Report on Rule 7062. No changes since publication.

CROSS REFERENCES

Applicability of this rule in—

Contested matters not otherwise provided for, see Fed. Rules Bankr.Proc. Rule 9014, 11 USCA.

Proceedings on contested involuntary petition and to vacate order for relief, see Fed.Rules Bankr.Proc. Rule 1018, 11 USCA.

Effect of entry of judgment on availability of relief under this rule, see Fed.Rules Bankr.Proc. Rule 9021, 11 USCA.

Power of court to suspend or to order continuation of other proceedings pending appeal, see Fed.Rules Bankr.Proc. Rule 8005, 11 USCA.

Security; proceedings against sureties, see Fed.Rules Bankr.Proc. Rule 9025, 11 USCA.

Stay of new proceedings until payment of costs of previously dismissed action, see Fed.Rules Bankr.Proc. Rule 7041, 11 USCA.

LIBRARY REFERENCES

American Digest System

Bankruptcy ⟺2164.1, 3038, 3070, 3776.5(1).
Key Number System Topic No. 51.

Corpus Juris Secundum

CJS Bankruptcy § 397, Hearing and Notice of Hearing.

Rule 7064.   Seizure of Person or Property

Rule 64 F.R.Civ.P. applies in adversary proceedings.

CROSS REFERENCES

Applicability of this rule in contested matters not otherwise provided for, see Fed.Rules Bankr.Proc. Rule 9014, 11 USCA.

Writ of attachment or sequestration issued against property ordered by judgment to be conveyed, see Fed.Rules Bankr. Proc. Rule 7070, 11 USCA.

LIBRARY REFERENCES

American Digest System

Bankruptcy ⟺2164.1.
Key Number System Topic No. 51.

Corpus Juris Secundum

CJS Bankruptcy § 140, Contested Matters.

Rule 7065.   Injunctions

Rule 65 F.R.Civ.P. applies in adversary proceedings, except that a temporary restraining order or preliminary injunction may be issued on application of a debtor, trustee, or debtor in possession without compliance with Rule 65(c).

CROSS REFERENCES

Injunction pending appeal of interlocutory or final judgment concerning injunction, see Fed.Rules Bankr.Proc. Rule 7062, 11 USCA.

Security; proceedings against sureties, see Fed.Rules Bankr.Proc. Rule 9025, 11 USCA.

Signing and verification of papers, see Fed.Rules Bankr. Proc. Rule 9011, 11 USCA.

LIBRARY REFERENCES

American Digest System

Bankruptcy ⟺2367 to 2374.
Key Number System Topic No. 51.

Corpus Juris Secundum

CJS Bankruptcy § 247, Procedure for Obtaining Injunction.
CJS Bankruptcy § 288, Applications.

Rule 7067.   Deposit in Court

Rule 67 F.R.Civ.P. applies in adversary proceedings.

LIBRARY REFERENCES

American Digest System

Deposits in Court ⟺1 to 12.
Key Number System Topic No. 123.

Rule 7068.   Offer of Judgment

Rule 68 F.R.Civ.P. applies in adversary proceedings.

LIBRARY REFERENCES

American Digest System

Bankruptcy ⟺2181, 2182.1, 3032.1, 3033.
Key Number System Topic No. 51.

Corpus Juris Secundum

CJS Bankruptcy § 314, Judgments.

Rule 7069.   Execution

Rule 69 F.R.Civ.P. applies in adversary proceedings.

CROSS REFERENCES

Applicability of this rule in contested matters not otherwise provided for, see Fed.Rules Bankr.Proc. Rule 9014, 11 USCA.

Effect of entry of judgment on availability of process to enforce judgment, see Fed.Rules Bankr.Proc. Rule 9021, 11 USCA.

Writ of execution to enforce judgment to deliver possession of property, see Fed.Rules Bankr.Proc. Rule 7070, 11 USCA.

LIBRARY REFERENCES

American Digest System

Bankruptcy ⟺2164.1.
Key Number System Topic No. 51.

Corpus Juris Secundum

CJS Bankruptcy § 140, Contested Matters.
CJS Bankruptcy § 314, Judgments.

Rule 7070.   Judgment for Specific Acts; Vesting Title

Rule 70 F.R.Civ.P. applies in adversary proceedings and the court may enter a judgment divesting the title of any party and vesting title in others whenever the real or personal property involved is within the jurisdiction of the court.

(As amended Mar. 30, 1987, eff. Aug. 1, 1987.)

ADVISORY COMMITTEE NOTES
1987 Amendment

The reference to court is used in the amendment because the district court may preside over an adversary proceeding.

CROSS REFERENCES

Effect of entry of judgment on availability of relief under this rule, see Fed.Rules Bankr.Proc. Rule 9021, 11 USCA.

LIBRARY REFERENCES
American Digest System

Bankruptcy ⊚2164.1, 3776.1.
Key Number System Topic No. 51.

Corpus Juris Secundum

CJS Bankruptcy § 314, Judgments.

Rule 7071.   Process in Behalf of and Against Persons Not Parties

Rule 71 F.R.Civ.P. applies in adversary proceedings.

CROSS REFERENCES

Applicability of this rule in contested matters not otherwise provided for, see Fed.Rules Bankr.Proc. Rule 9014, 11 USCA.

LIBRARY REFERENCES
American Digest System

Bankruptcy ⊚2164.1.
Key Number System Topic No. 51.

Corpus Juris Secundum

CJS Bankruptcy § 140, Contested Matters.

Rule 7087.   Transfer of Adversary Proceeding

On motion and after a hearing, the court may transfer an adversary proceeding or any part thereof to another district pursuant to 28 U.S.C. § 1412, except as provided in Rule 7019(2).

(As amended Mar. 30, 1987, eff. Aug. 1, 1987.)

ADVISORY COMMITTEE NOTES
1987 Amendment

The reference to the venue section of title 28 is amended to conform to the 1984 amendments to title 28.

LIBRARY REFERENCES
American Digest System

Bankruptcy ⊚2083 to 2091.
Key Number System Topic No. 51.

Corpus Juris Secundum

CJS Bankruptcy § 273, Adversary Proceedings.

Rule
8001. Manner of Taking Appeal; Voluntary Dismissal; Certification to Court of Appeals.
8002. Time for Filing Notice of Appeal.
8003. Leave to Appeal.
8004. Service of the Notice of Appeal.
8005. Stay Pending Appeal.
8006. Record and Issues on Appeal.
8007. Completion and Transmission of the Record; Docketing of the Appeal.
8008. Filing and Service.
8009. Briefs and Appendix; Filing and Service.
8010. Form of Briefs; Length.
8011. Motions.
8012. Oral Argument.
8013. Disposition of Appeal; Weight Accorded Bankruptcy Judge's Findings of Fact.
8014. Costs.
8015. Motion for Rehearing.
8016. Duties of Clerk of District Court and Bankruptcy Appellate Panel.
8017. Stay of Judgment of District Court or Bankruptcy Appellate Panel.
8018. Rules by Circuit Councils and District Courts; Procedure When There is No Controlling Law.
8019. Suspension of Rules in Part VIII.
8020. Damages and Costs for Frivolous Appeal.

Rule 8001. Manner of Taking Appeal; Voluntary Dismissal; Certification to Court of Appeals

(a) Appeal as of right; how taken

An appeal from a judgment, order, or decree of a bankruptcy judge to a district court or bankruptcy appellate panel as permitted by 28 U.S.C. § 158(a)(1) or (a)(2) shall be taken by filing a notice of appeal with the clerk within the time allowed by Rule 8002. An appellant's failure to take any step other than timely filing a notice of appeal does not affect the validity of the appeal, but is ground only for such action as the district court or bankruptcy appellate panel deems appropriate, which may include dismissal of the appeal. The notice of appeal shall (1) conform substantially to the appropriate Official Form, (2) contain the names of all parties to the judgment, order, or decree appealed from and the names, addresses, and telephone numbers of their respective attorneys, and (3) be accompanied by the prescribed fee. Each appellant shall file a sufficient number of copies of the notice of appeal to enable the clerk to comply promptly with Rule 8004.

(b) Appeal by leave; how taken

An appeal from an interlocutory judgment, order, or decree of a bankruptcy judge as permitted by 28 U.S.C. § 158(a)(3) shall be taken by filing a notice of appeal, as prescribed in subdivision (a) of this rule, accompanied by a motion for leave to appeal prepared

in accordance with Rule 8003 and with proof of service in accordance with Rule 8008.

(c) Voluntary dismissal

(1) Before docketing

If an appeal has not been docketed, the appeal may be dismissed by the bankruptcy judge on the filing of a stipulation for dismissal signed by all the parties, or on motion and notice by the appellant.

(2) After docketing

If an appeal has been docketed and the parties to the appeal sign and file with the clerk of the district court or the clerk of the bankruptcy appellate panel an agreement that the appeal be dismissed and pay any court costs or fees that may be due, the clerk of the district court or the clerk of the bankruptcy appellate panel shall enter an order dismissing appeal. An appeal may also be dismissed on motion of the appellant on terms and conditions fixed by the district court or bankruptcy appellate panel.

(d) [Abrogated]

(e) Election to have appeal heard by district court instead of bankruptcy appellate panel; withdrawal of election

(1) Separate writing for election

An election to have an appeal heard by the district court under 28 U.S.C. § 158(c)(1) may be made only by a statement of election contained in a separate writing filed within the time prescribed by 28 U.S.C. § 158(c)(1).

(2) Withdrawal of election

A request to withdraw the election may be filed only by written stipulation of all the parties to the appeal or their attorneys of record. Upon such a stipulation, the district court may either transfer the appeal to the bankruptcy appellate panel or retain the appeal in the district court.

(f) Certification for direct appeal to court of appeals

(1) Timely appeal required

A certification of a judgment, order, or decree of a bankruptcy court to a court of appeals under 28 U.S.C. § 158(d)(2) shall not be effective until a timely appeal has been taken in the manner required by subdivisions (a) or (b) of this rule and the notice of appeal has become effective under Rule 8002.

(2) Court where certification made and filed

A certification that a circumstance specified in 28 U.S.C. § 158(d)(2)(A)(i)–(iii) exists shall be filed in the court in which a matter is pending for purposes of 28 U.S.C. § 158(d)(2) and this rule. A matter is pending in a bankruptcy court until the docketing, in accordance with Rule 8007(b), of an appeal taken under 28 U.S.C. § 158(a)(1) or (2), or the grant of leave to appeal under 28 U.S.C. § 158(a)(3). A matter is pending in a district court or bankruptcy appellate panel after the docketing, in accordance with Rule 8007(b), of an appeal taken under 28 U.S.C. § 158(a)(1) or (2), or the grant of leave to appeal under 28 U.S.C. § 158(a)(3).

(A) Certification by court on request or court's own initiative

(i) Before docketing or grant of leave to appeal

Only a bankruptcy court may make a certification on request or on its own initiative while the matter is pending in the bankruptcy court.

(ii) After docketing or grant of leave to appeal

Only the district court or bankruptcy appellate panel involved may make a certification on request of the parties or on its own initiative while the matter is pending in the district court or bankruptcy appellate panel.

(B) Certification by all appellants and appellees acting jointly

A certification by all the appellants and appellees, if any, acting jointly may be made by filing the appropriate Official Form with the clerk of the court in which the matter is pending. The certification may be accompanied by a short statement of the basis for the certification, which may include the information listed in subdivision (f)(3)(C) of this rule.

(3) Request for certification; filing; service; contents

(A) A request for certification shall be filed, within the time specified by 28 U.S.C. § 158(d)(2), with the clerk of the court in which the matter is pending.

(B) Notice of the filing of a request for certification shall be served in the manner required for service of a notice of appeal under Rule 8004.

(C) A request for certification shall include the following:

(i) the facts necessary to understand the question presented;

(ii) the question itself;

(iii) the relief sought;

(iv) the reasons why the appeal should be allowed and is authorized by statute or rule, including why a circumstance specified in 28 U.S.C. § 158(d)(2)(A)(i)–(iii) exists; and

(v) an attached copy of the judgment, order, or decree complained of and any related opinion or memorandum.

(D) A party may file a response to a request for certification or a cross request within 14 days after the notice of the request is served, or another time fixed by the court.

(E) Rule 9014 does not govern a request, cross request, or any response. The matter shall be submitted without oral argument unless the court otherwise directs.

(F) A certification of an appeal under 28 U.S.C. § 158(d)(2) shall be made in a separate document served on the parties.

(4) Certification on court's own initiative

(A) A certification of an appeal on the court's own initiative under 28 U.S.C. § 158(d)(2) shall be made in a separate document served on the parties in the manner required for service of a notice of appeal under Rule 8004. The certification shall be accompanied by an opinion or memorandum that contains the information required by subdivision (f)(3)(C)(i)–(iv) of this rule.

(B) A party may file a supplementary short statement of the basis for certification within 14 days after the certification.

(5) Duties of parties after certification

A petition for permission to appeal in accordance with F. R. App. P. 5 shall be filed no later than 30 days after a certification has become effective as provided in subdivision (f)(1).

(As amended Mar. 30, 1987, eff. Aug. 1, 1987; Apr. 30, 1991, eff. Aug. 1, 1991; Apr. 11, 1997, eff. Dec. 1, 1997; Apr. 23, 2008, eff. Dec. 1, 2008; Mar. 26, 2009, eff. Dec. 1, 2009.)

ADVISORY COMMITTEE NOTES

These rules in Part VIII apply only to appeals to the district courts or bankruptcy appellate panels. Subsequent appeals to the courts of appeals, or direct appeals by agreement of the parties under 28 U.S.C. § 1293(b), are governed by Federal Rules of Appellate Procedure.

Subdivisions (a) and (b) require that a notice of appeal be filed whenever a litigant seeks to secure appellate review by the district court or bankruptcy appellate panel. An appeal from an interlocutory order which will be heard only if leave is granted under 28 U.S.C. §§ 1334(b) or 1482(b) is taken by filing a notice of appeal accompanied by a motion for leave to appeal which complies with the requirements set forth in Rule 8003. Rule 8003 also governs other aspects of interlocutory appeals.

Subdivision (c) is an adaptation of Rule 42 F.R.App.P.

Subdivision (d) deals with the situation in which an appellant perfects an appeal to the district court or a bankruptcy appellate panel and also a direct appeal pursuant to 28 U.S.C. § 1293(b) to the court of appeals. This subdivision provides that once the appeal to the court of appeals is taken, a notice of appeal to the district court or bankruptcy appellate panel shall be dismissed and, if the first appeal is to the district court or bankruptcy appellate panel, the first appeal shall be dismissed. Paragraph (3) gives an appellant or cross appellant an opportunity to file an appeal to the district court or bankruptcy appellate panel if the court of appeals dismisses the direct appeal because the judgment, order, or decree appealed from is not final. Since the court of appeals has determined the judgment, order, or decree is not final, the new appeal is an appeal for which leave is necessary.

1987 Amendment

Subdivisions (a) and (b) are amended to conform to the 1984 amendments.

Subdivision (d) is abrogated because there is no direct appeal to the court of appeals under 28 U.S.C. § 158, as enacted by the 1984 amendments.

Subdivision (e) is new. Section 158(b)(1) of title 28 authorizes the circuit councils to establish bankruptcy appellate panels. Appeals may not be heard by these panels unless the district court authorizes the referral and all parties to the appeal consent. This rule requires that the parties consent to such an appeal; however, the method of consenting to an appeal may be the subject of a rule promulgated by a circuit council under Rule 8018.

1991 Amendment

Reference to the Official Form number is deleted in anticipation of future revision and renumbering of the Official Forms.

1997 Amendment

This rule is amended to conform to the Bankruptcy Reform Act of 1994 which amended 28 U.S.C. § 158. As amended, a party may—without obtaining leave of the court—appeal from an interlocutory order or decree of the bankruptcy court issued under § 1121(d) of the Code increasing or reducing the time periods referred to in § 1121.

Subdivision (e) is amended to provide the procedure for electing under 28 U.S.C. § 158(c)(1) to have an appeal heard by the district court instead of the bankruptcy appellate panel service. This subdivision is applicable only if a bankruptcy appellate panel service is authorized under 28 U.S.C. § 158(b) to hear the appeal.

GAP Report on Rule 8001. The heading of subdivision (e) is amended to clarify that it applies to the election to have an appeal heard by the district court instead of the BAP. The final paragraph of the Committee Note is revised to clarify that subdivision (e) is applicable only if a BAP is authorized to hear the appeal.

2008 Amendments

Subdivision (e) is amended by redesignating the subdivision as (e)(1) and adding new subdivision (e)(2). Subdivision (e)(2) explicitly recognizes the district court's authority to transfer an appeal to the bankruptcy appellate panel on two conditions: first, all of the parties to the appeal must have agreed to request the withdrawal of the election to have the district court hear the appeal; and, second, the district court must decide whether to grant the request for withdrawal. The district court has discretion either to keep the case or transfer it to the bankruptcy appellate panel, which will prevent strategic behavior by parties and avoid the wasting of judicial resources.

Subdivision (f) is added to the rule to implement the 2005 amendments to 28 U.S.C. § 158(d). That section authorizes appeals directly to the court of appeals, with that court's consent, upon certification that a ground for the appeal exists under § 158(d)(2)(A)(i)–(iii). Certification can be made by the court on its own initiative under subdivision (f)(4), or in response to a request of a party or a majority of the appellants and appellees (if any) under subdivision (f)(3). Certification also can be made by all of the appellants and appellees under subdivision (f)(2)(B). Under subdivision (f)(1), certification is effective only when a timely appeal is commenced under subdivision (a) or (b), and a notice of appeal has been timely filed under Rule 8002. These actions will provide sufficient notice of the appeal to the circuit clerk, so the rule dispenses with the uncodified temporary procedural requirements set out in § 1233(b)(4) of the Bankruptcy Abuse Prevention and Consumer Protection Act of 2005, Pub. L. No. 109–8.

The rule adopts a bright-line test for identifying the court in which a matter is pending. Under subdivision (f)(2), the bright-line chosen is the "docketing" under Rule 8007(b) of an appeal of an interlocutory order or decree under 28 U.S.C. § 158(a)(2) or a final judgment, order or decree under 28 U.S.C. § 158(a)(1), or the granting of leave to appeal any other interlocutory judgment, order or decree under 28 U.S.C. § 158(a)(3), whichever is earlier.

To ensure that parties are aware of a certification, the rule requires either that it be made on the Official Form (if being made by all of the parties to the appeal) or on a separate document (whether the certification is made on the court's own initiative or in response to a request by a party). This is particularly important because the rule adopts the bankruptcy practice established by Rule 8001(a) and (b) of requiring a notice of appeal in every instance, including interlocutory orders, of appeals from bankruptcy court orders, judgments, and decrees. Because this requirement is satisfied by filing the notice of appeal that takes the appeal to the district court or bankruptcy appellate panel in the first instance, the rule does not require a separate notice of appeal if a certification occurs after a district court or bankruptcy appellate panel decision.

A certification under subdivision (f)(1) does not place the appeal in the circuit court. Rather, the court of appeals must first authorize the direct appeal. Subdivision (f)(5) therefore provides that any party intending to pursue the appeal in the court of appeals must seek that permission under Rule 5 of the Federal Rules of Appellate Procedure. Subdivision (f)(5) requires that the petition for permission to appeal be filed within 30 days after an effective certification.

2009 Amendments

The rule is amended to implement changes in connection with the amendment to Rule 9006(a) and the manner by which time is computed under the rules. The deadlines in the rule are amended to substitute a deadline that is a multiple of seven days. Throughout the rules, deadlines are amended in the following manner:

- 5–day periods become 7–day periods
- 10–day periods become 14–day periods
- 15–day periods become 14–day periods
- 20–day periods become 21–day periods
- 25–day periods become 28–day periods

CROSS REFERENCES

CROSS REFERENCES

Appeals as of right, when taken, see Federal Rules of Appellate Procedure Rule 3, 28 USCA.

Effect of clerk's retention and indexing of judgment on appealability and proceedings on appeal, see Fed.Rules Bankr.Proc. Rule 9021, 11 USCA.

Suspension of this rule, see Fed.Rules Bankr.Proc. Rule 8019, 11 USCA.

Time to file and to serve items of record and statement of issues on appeal, see Fed.Rules Bankr.Proc. Rule 8006, 11 USCA.

Voluntary dismissal, see Federal Rules of Appellate Procedure Rule 42, 28 USCA.

LIBRARY REFERENCES

American Digest System

Bankruptcy ⟷3761 to 3775, 3778.
Key Number System Topic No. 51.

Corpus Juris Secundum

CJS Bankruptcy § 14, Federal Rules of Appellate Procedure.

CJS Bankruptcy § 1212, Leave for Appeal.

CJS Bankruptcy § 1220, District Court--Election.

CJS Bankruptcy § 1221, Court of Appeals.

CJS Bankruptcy § 1250, Sanctions.

Rule 8002.   Time for Filing Notice of Appeal

(a) Fourteen–day period

The notice of appeal shall be filed with the clerk within 14 days of the date of the entry of the judgment, order, or decree appealed from. If a timely notice of appeal is filed by a party, any other party may file a notice of appeal within 14 days of the date on which the first notice of appeal was filed, or within the time otherwise prescribed by this rule, whichever period last expires. A notice of appeal filed after the announcement of a decision or order but before entry of the judgment, order, or decree shall be treated as filed after such entry and on the day thereof. If a notice of appeal is mistakenly filed with the district court or the bankruptcy appellate panel, the clerk of the district court or the clerk of the bankruptcy appellate panel shall note thereon the date on which it was received and transmit it to the clerk and it shall be deemed filed with the clerk on the date so noted.

(b) Effect of motion on time for appeal

If any party makes a timely motion of a type specified immediately below, the time for appeal for all parties runs from the entry of the order disposing of the last such motion outstanding. This provision applies to a timely motion:

(1) to amend or make additional findings of fact under Rule 7052, whether or not granting the motion would alter the judgment;

(2) to alter or amend the judgment under Rule 9023;

(3) for a new trial under Rule 9023; or

(4) for relief under Rule 9024 if the motion is filed no later than 14 days after the entry of judgment. A notice of appeal filed after announcement or entry of the judgment, order, or decree but before disposition of any of the above motions is ineffective to appeal from the judgment, order, or decree, or part thereof, specified in the notice of appeal, until the entry of the order disposing of the last such motion outstanding. Appellate review of an order disposing of any of the above motions requires the party, in compliance with Rule 8001, to amend a previously filed notice of appeal. A party intending to challenge an alteration or amendment of the judgment, order, or decree shall file a notice, or an amended notice, of appeal within the time prescribed by this Rule 8002 measured from the entry of the order disposing of the last such motion outstanding. No additional fees will be required for filing an amended notice.

(c) Extension of time for appeal

(1) The bankruptcy judge may extend the time for filing the notice of appeal by any party, unless the judgment, order, or decree appealed from:

(A) grants relief from an automatic stay under § 362, § 922, § 1201, or § 1301;

(B) authorizes the sale or lease of property or the use of cash collateral under § 363;

(C) authorizes the obtaining of credit under § 364;

(D) authorizes the assumption or assignment of an executory contract or unexpired lease under § 365;

(E) approves a disclosure statement under § 1125; or

(F) confirms a plan under § 943, § 1129, § 1225, or § 1325 of the Code.

(2) A request to extend the time for filing a notice of appeal must be made by written motion filed before the time for filing a notice of appeal has expired, except that such a motion filed not later than 21 days after the expiration of the time for filing a notice of appeal may be granted upon a showing of excusable neglect. An extension of time for filing a notice of appeal may not exceed 21 days from the expiration of the time for filing a notice of appeal otherwise prescribed by this rule or 14 days from the date of entry of the order granting the motion, whichever is later.

(As amended Mar. 30, 1987, eff. Aug. 1, 1987; Apr. 30, 1991, eff. Aug. 1, 1991; Apr. 29, 1994, eff. Aug. 1, 1994; Apr. 11, 1997, eff. Dec. 1, 1997; Mar. 26, 2009, eff. Dec. 1, 2009.)

ADVISORY COMMITTEE NOTES

This rule is an adaptation of Rule 4(a) F.R.App.P. The time to appeal from a judgment, order, or decree of a bankruptcy judge is 10 days, rather than the 30 days provided for in the civil practice. The shortened time is specified in order to obtain prompt appellate review, often important to the administration of a case under the Code. If a timely notice of appeal is filed, other parties have an additional 10 days within which to file a notice of appeal. A notice of appeal filed within the additional 10 day period by an appellee is a cross appeal, but there is a separate appeal if a non-appellee files a notice of appeal within that 10 day period. The district courts and bankruptcy appellate panels have inherent authority to consolidate appeals.

Subdivision (b) is essentially the same as Rule 4(a)(4) of the F.R.App.P.

Subdivision (c) is similar to former Bankruptcy Rule 802(c). To expedite the disposition of appeals the maximum extension of time is 20 days instead of the 30 days provided by Rule 4(a)(5) of the F.R.App.P. Subject to the exceptions set forth in subdivision (c), the court may extend the time for taking an appeal when a motion for extension is filed after the expiration of the original 10 day period but no later than 20 days after the expiration of the original 10 day period. Orders of the bankruptcy court relating to the sale of property, extension of credit, confirmation of a plan, dismissal or conversion of the case, and approval of the disclosure statement are of such significance to the administration of the case, the parties in interest, and third parties that this subdivision requires that either an appeal or a motion for extension be filed within the original 10 day period.

If a timely notice of appeal is not filed, no appeal may be taken later. Former Bankruptcy Rule 803, which provided that a referee's judgment became final when the appeal period expired, has been omitted as unnecessary.

1991 Amendment

Subdivision (a) is amended to conform to F.R.App.P. 4(a)(2) which is designed to avoid the loss of the right to appeal when a notice of appeal is filed prematurely.

Subdivision (b)(1) is deleted because Rule 9015 was abrogated in 1987.

1994 Amendments

These amendments are intended to conform to the 1993 amendments to F.R.App.P. 4(a)(4) and 6(b)(2)(i).

This rule as amended provides that a notice of appeal filed before the disposition of a specified postjudgment motion will become effective upon disposition of the motion. A notice filed before the filing of one of the specified motions or after the filing of a motion but before disposition of the motion is, in effect, suspended until the motion is disposed of, whereupon, the previously filed notice effectively places jurisdiction in the district court or bankruptcy appellate panel.

Because a notice of appeal will ripen into an effective appeal upon disposition of a postjudgment motion, in some instances there will be an appeal from a judgment that has been altered substantially because the motion was granted in whole or in part. The appeal may be dismissed for want of prosecution when the appellant fails to meet the briefing schedule. But, the appellee may also move to strike the appeal. When responding to such a motion, the appellant would have an opportunity to state that, even though some relief sought in a

postjudgment motion was granted, the appellant still plans to pursue the appeal. Because the appellant's response would provide the appellee with sufficient notice of the appellant's intentions, the rule does not require an additional notice of appeal in that situation.

The amendment provides that a notice of appeal filed before the disposition of a postjudgment tolling motion is sufficient to bring the judgment, order, or decree specified in the original notice of appeal to the district court or bankruptcy appellate panel. If the judgment is altered upon disposition of a postjudgment motion, however, and if a party who has previously filed a notice of appeal wishes to appeal from the disposition of the motion, the party must amend the notice to so indicate. When a party files an amended notice, no additional fees are required because the notice is an amendment of the original and not a new notice of appeal.

Subdivision (b) is also amended to include, among motions that extend the time for filing a notice of appeal, a motion under Rule 9024 that is filed within 10 days after entry of a judgment. The addition of this motion conforms to a similar amendment to F.R.App.P. 4(a)(4) made in 1993, except that a Rule 9024 motion does not toll the time to appeal unless it is filed within the 10-day period. The reason for providing that the motion extends the time to appeal only if it is _filed_ within the 10-day period is to enable the court and the parties in interest to determine solely from the court records whether the time to appeal has been extended by a motion for relief under Rule 9024.

1997 Amendment

Subdivision (c) is amended to provide that a request for an extension of time to file a notice of appeal must be filed within the applicable time period. This amendment will avoid uncertainty as to whether the mailing of a motion or an oral request in court is sufficient to request an extension of time, and will enable the court and the parties in interest to determine solely from the court records whether a timely request for an extension has been made.

The amendments also give the court discretion to permit a party to file a notice of appeal more than 20 days after expiration of the time to appeal otherwise prescribed, but only if the motion was timely filed and the notice of appeal is filed within a period not exceeding 10 days after entry of the order extending the time. This amendment is designed to protect parties that file timely motions to extend the time to appeal from the harshness of the present rule as demonstrated in In re Mouradick, 13 F.3d 326 (9th Cir.1994), where the court held that a notice of appeal filed within the 3-day period expressly prescribed by an order granting a timely motion for an extension of time did not confer jurisdiction on the appellate court because the notice of appeal was not filed within the 20-day period specified in subdivision (c).

The subdivision is amended further to prohibit any extension of time to file a notice of appeal—even if the motion for an extension is filed before the expiration of the original time to appeal—if the order appealed from grants relief from the automatic stay, authorizes the sale or lease of property, use of cash collateral, obtaining of credit, or assumption or assignment of an executory contract or unexpired lease under § 365, or approves a disclosure statement or confirms a plan. These types of orders are often relied upon immediately after they are entered and should not be reviewable on appeal after the expiration of the original appeal period under Rule 8002(a) and (b).

GAP Report on Rule 8002. No changes to the published draft.

2009 Amendments

The rule is amended to implement changes in connection with the amendment to Rule 9006(a) and the manner by which time is computed under the rules. The deadlines in the rule are amended to substitute a deadline that is a multiple of seven days. Throughout the rules, deadlines are amended in the following manner:

- 5–day periods become 7–day periods
- 10–day periods become 14–day periods
- 15–day periods become 14–day periods
- 20–day periods become 21–day periods
- 25–day periods become 28–day periods

CROSS REFERENCES

Appeal as of right, how taken, see Fed.Rules Bankr.Proc. Rule 8001, 11 USCA.

Appeals as of right, when taken, see Federal Rules of Appellate Procedure Rule 4, 28 USCA.

Filing notice of appeal, ten-day period—

Enlargement permitted as limited in this rule, see Fed. Rules Bankr.Proc. Rule 9006, 11 USCA.

Reduction not permitted, see Fed.Rules Bankr.Proc. Rule 9006, 11 USCA.

Lack of notice of judgment has no affect on time to appeal nor relief from failure to appeal except as permitted in this rule, see Fed.Rules Bankr.Proc. Rule 9022, 11 USCA.

Suspension of this rule, see Fed.Rules Bankr.Proc. Rule 8019, 11 USCA.

LIBRARY REFERENCES

American Digest System

Bankruptcy ⇒3774.1, 3775.

Key Number System Topic No. 51.

Corpus Juris Secundum

CJS Bankruptcy § 308, Enlargement.

CJS Bankruptcy § 309, Reduction.

CJS Bankruptcy § 314, Judgments.

CJS Bankruptcy § 867, Stay of Order Authorizing Use, Sale, or Lease of Property.

CJS Bankruptcy § 929, Stay of Order Authorizing Assignment.

CJS Bankruptcy § 1242, Tolling of Time.

CJS Bankruptcy § 1243, Extension of Time.

CJS Bankruptcy § 1245, Relief from Limitation; Excusable Neglect.

Rule 8003.   Leave to Appeal

(a) Content of motion; answer

A motion for leave to appeal under 28 U.S.C. § 158(a) shall contain: (1) a statement of the facts necessary to an understanding of the questions to be presented by the appeal; (2) a statement of those questions and of the relief sought; (3) a statement of

the reasons why an appeal should be granted; and (4) a copy of the judgment, order, or decree complained of and of any opinion or memorandum relating thereto. Within 14 days after service of the motion, an adverse party may file with the clerk an answer in opposition.

(b) Transmittal; determination of motion

The clerk shall transmit the notice of appeal, the motion for leave to appeal and any answer thereto to the clerk of the district court or the clerk of the bankruptcy appellate panel as soon as all parties have filed answers or the time for filing an answer has expired. The motion and answer shall be submitted without oral argument unless otherwise ordered.

(c) Appeal improperly taken regarded as a motion for leave to appeal

If a required motion for leave to appeal is not filed, but a notice of appeal is timely filed, the district court or bankruptcy appellate panel may grant leave to appeal or direct that a motion for leave to appeal be filed. The district court or the bankruptcy appellate panel may also deny leave to appeal but in so doing shall consider the notice of appeal as a motion for leave to appeal. Unless an order directing that a motion for leave to appeal be filed provides otherwise, the motion shall be filed within 14 days of entry of the order.

(d) Requirement of leave to appeal

If leave to appeal is required by 28 U.S.C. § 158(a) and has not earlier been granted, the authorization of a direct appeal by a court of appeals under 28 U.S.C. § 158(d)(2) shall be deemed to satisfy the requirement for leave to appeal.

(As amended Mar. 30, 1987, eff. Aug. 1, 1987; Apr. 23, 2008, eff. Dec. 1, 2008; Mar. 26, 2009, eff. Dec. 1, 2009.)

ADVISORY COMMITTEE NOTES

Subdivisions (a) and (b) of this rule are derived from Rules 5 and 6 F.R.App.P. The motion for leave to appeal is addressed to the district court or the bankruptcy appellate panel, although filed with the clerk of the bankruptcy court.

Subdivision (c) provides that if a party mistakenly believes the order appealed from is final and files only a notice of appeal, the appeal is not automatically dismissed. The district court or bankruptcy appellate panel has the options to direct that a motion be filed, to decide exclusively on the papers already filed to grant leave to appeal, or to deny leave to appeal. Cf. 28 U.S.C. § 2103.

2008 Amendments

The rule is amended to add subdivision (d) to solve the jurisdictional problem that could otherwise ensue when a district court or bankruptcy appellate panel has not granted leave to appeal under 28 U.S.C. § 158(a)(3). If the court of appeals accepts the appeal, the requirement of leave to appeal is deemed satisfied. However, if the court of appeals does not authorize a direct appeal, the question of whether to grant leave to appeal remains a matter to be resolved by the district court or the bankruptcy appellate panel.

2009 Amendments

The rule is amended to implement changes in connection with the amendment to Rule 9006(a) and the manner by which time is computed under the rules. The deadlines in the rule are amended to substitute a deadline that is a multiple of seven days. Throughout the rules, deadlines are amended in the following manner:

- 5–day periods become 7–day periods
- 10–day periods become 14–day periods
- 15–day periods become 14–day periods
- 20–day periods become 21–day periods
- 25–day periods become 28–day periods

CROSS REFERENCES

Appeal—

After dismissal of direct appeal by court of appeals, when taken, see Fed.Rules Bankr.Proc. Rule 8001, 11 USCA.

By leave, how taken, see Fed.Rules Bankr.Proc. Rule 8001, 11 USCA.

Effect of clerk's retention and indexing of judgment on appealability and proceedings on appeal, see Fed.Rules Bankr.Proc. Rule 9021, 11 USCA.

LIBRARY REFERENCES

American Digest System

Bankruptcy ⟺3772.

Key Number System Topic No. 51.

Corpus Juris Secundum

CJS Bankruptcy § 1212, Leave for Appeal.

CJS Bankruptcy § 1221, Court of Appeals.

Rule 8004.   Service of the Notice of Appeal

The clerk shall serve notice of the filing of a notice of appeal by mailing a copy thereof to counsel of record of each party other than the appellant or, if a party is not represented by counsel, to the party's last known address. Failure to serve notice shall not affect the validity of the appeal. The clerk shall note on each copy served the date of the filing of the notice of appeal and shall note in the docket the names of the parties to whom copies are mailed and the date of the mailing. The clerk shall forthwith transmit to the United States trustee a copy of the notice of appeal, but failure to transmit such notice shall not affect the validity of the appeal.

(As amended Mar. 30, 1987, eff. Aug. 1, 1987; Apr. 30, 1991, eff. Aug. 1, 1991.)

ADVISORY COMMITTEE NOTES

This rule is an adaptation of Rule 3(d) F.R.App.P.

1991 Amendment

This rule is amended to keep the United States trustee informed of the progress of the case.

CROSS REFERENCES

Appeals as of right, how taken, see Federal Rules of Appellate Procedure Rule 3, 28 USCA.

Filing by appellant of sufficient number of copies of notice of appeal, see Fed.Rules Bankr.Proc. Rule 8001, 11 USCA.

Notice of appeal under 28 U.S.C. § 158(a) or (b) from a judgment, order, or decree of a Bankruptcy Judge, see Official Bankr. Form 17, 11 USCA.

LIBRARY REFERENCES

American Digest System

Bankruptcy ⟺3774.1.

Key Number System Topic No. 51.

Rule 8005.   Stay Pending Appeal

A motion for a stay of the judgment, order, or decree of a bankruptcy judge, for approval of a supersedeas bond, or for other relief pending appeal must ordinarily be presented to the bankruptcy judge in the first instance. Notwithstanding Rule 7062 but subject to the power of the district court and the bankruptcy appellate panel reserved hereinafter, the bankruptcy judge may suspend or order the continuation of other proceedings in the case under the Code or make any other appropriate order during the pendency of an appeal on such terms as will protect the rights of all parties in interest. A motion for such relief, or for modification or termination of relief granted by a bankruptcy judge, may be made to the district court or the bankruptcy appellate panel, but the motion shall show why the relief, modification, or termination was not obtained from the bankruptcy judge. The district court or the bankruptcy appellate panel may condition the relief it grants under this rule on the filing of a bond or other appropriate security with the bankruptcy court. When an appeal is taken by a trustee, a bond or other appropriate security may be required, but when an appeal is taken by the United States or an officer or agency thereof or by direction of any department of the Government of the United States a bond or other security shall not be required.

(As amended Mar. 30, 1987, eff. Aug. 1, 1987.)

ADVISORY COMMITTEE NOTES

The first, third, and fourth sentences of this rule are adaptations of Rule 8(a) and (b) F.R.App.P. The second sentence of the rule is derived from § 39(c) of the Bankruptcy Act [former § 67(c) of this title] and confers on the bankruptcy judge discretion respecting the stay or continuation of other proceedings in the case while an appeal is pending.

The last sentence of the rule, which specifically subjects a trustee to the same kind of security requirements as other litigants, is derived from former Bankruptcy Rule 805. The exemption of the United States from the bond or security requirements is the same as the exemption contained in Rule 62(e) F.R.Civ.P.

Sections 363(m) and 364(e) of the Code provide that unless an order approving a sale of property, or authorizing the obtaining of credit or the incurring of debt is stayed pending appeal, the sale of property to a good faith purchaser or a good faith extension of credit, with or without any priority or lien, shall not be affected by the reversal or modification of such order on appeal, whether or not the purchaser or creditor knows of the pendency of the appeal.

CROSS REFERENCES

Effect of clerk's retention and indexing of judgment on appealability and proceedings on appeal, see Fed.Rules Bankr.Proc. Rule 9021, 11 USCA.

Security; proceedings against sureties, see Fed.Rules Bankr.Proc. Rule 9025, 11 USCA.

Stay of proceedings to enforce judgment, see Fed.Rules Bankr.Proc. Rule 7062, 11 USCA.

LIBRARY REFERENCES

American Digest System

Bankruptcy ⟷3776.5.

Key Number System Topic No. 51.

Corpus Juris Secundum

CJS Bankruptcy § 1254, Stay.

CJS Bankruptcy § 1255, Stay--Security; Supersedeas Bond.

Rule 8006. Record and Issues on Appeal

Within 14 days after filing the notice of appeal as provided by Rule 8001(a), entry of an order granting leave to appeal, or entry of an order disposing of the last timely motion outstanding of a type specified in Rule 8002(b), whichever is later, the appellant shall file with the clerk and serve on the appellee a designation of the items to be included in the record on appeal and a statement of the issues to be presented. Within 14 days after the service of the appellant's statement the appellee may file and serve on the appellant a designation of additional items to be included in the record on appeal and, if the appellee has filed a cross appeal, the appellee as cross appellant shall file and serve a statement of the issues to be presented on the cross appeal and a designation of additional items to be included in the record. A cross appellee may, within 14 days of service of the cross appellant's statement, file and serve on the cross appellant a designation of additional items to be included in the record. The record on appeal shall include the items so designated by the parties, the notice of appeal, the judgment, order, or decree appealed from, and any opinion, findings of fact, and conclusions of law of the court. Any party filing a designation of the items to be included in the record shall provide to the clerk a copy of the items designated or, if the party fails to provide the copy, the clerk shall prepare the copy at the party's expense. If the record designated by any party includes a transcript of any proceeding or a part thereof, the party shall, immediately after filing the designation, deliver to the reporter and file with the clerk a written request for the transcript and make satisfactory arrangements for payment of its cost. All parties shall take any other action necessary to enable the clerk to assemble and transmit the record.

(As amended Mar. 30, 1987, eff. Aug. 1, 1987; Apr. 30, 1991, eff. Aug. 1, 1991; Apr. 29, 1994, eff. Aug. 1, 1994; Mar. 26, 2009, eff. Dec. 1, 2009.)

ADVISORY COMMITTEE NOTES

This rule is an adaptation of Rule 10(b) F.R.App.P. The last sentence of the rule is derived from Rule 11(a) F.R.App.P.

1991 Amendment

The seven-day time periods are changed to 10 days to conform to Rule 75(b)(2) F.R.Civ.P. and Rule 10(b)(3) F.R.App.P. The amendment requiring a party to provide a copy of the items designated for the record is to facilitate the amendments to Rule 8007 providing for retention by the bankruptcy clerk of the original record.

1994 Amendments

The amendment to the first sentence of this rule is made together with the amendment to Rule 8002(b), which provides, in essence, that certain specified postjudgment motions suspend a filed notice of appeal until the disposition of the last of such motions. The purpose of this amendment is to suspend the 10-day period for filing and serving a designation of the record and statement of the issues if a timely postjudgment motion is made and a notice of appeal is suspended under Rule 8002(b). The 10-day period set forth in the first sentence of this rule begins to run when the order disposing of the last of such postjudgment motions outstanding is entered. The other amendments to this rule are stylistic.

2009 Amendments

The rule is amended to implement changes in connection with the amendment to Rule 9006(a) and the manner by which time is computed under the rules. The deadlines in the rule are amended to substitute a deadline that is a multiple of seven days. Throughout the rules, deadlines are amended in the following manner:

- 5-day periods become 7-day periods
- 10-day periods become 14-day periods
- 15-day periods become 14-day periods
- 20-day periods become 21-day periods
- 25-day periods become 28-day periods

CROSS REFERENCES

Effect of clerk's retention and indexing of judgment on appealability and proceedings on appeal, see Fed.Rules Bankr.Proc. Rule 9021, 11 USCA.

Record on appeal for all purposes, see Fed.Rules Bankr. Proc. Rule 8007, 11 USCA.

Record on appeal, see Federal Rules of Appellate Procedure Rule 10, 28 USCA.

Transmission of record on appeal, see Federal Rules of Appellate Procedure Rule 11, 28 USCA.

LIBRARY REFERENCES

American Digest System

Bankruptcy ⟷3777.

Key Number System Topic No. 51.

Rule 8007. Completion and Transmission of the Record; Docketing of the Appeal

(a) Duty of reporter to prepare and file transcript

On receipt of a request for a transcript, the reporter shall acknowledge on the request the date it was received and the date on which the reporter expects to have the transcript completed and shall transmit the request, so endorsed, to the clerk or the clerk of the bankruptcy appellate panel. On completion of the transcript the reporter shall file it with the clerk and, if appropriate, notify the clerk of the bankruptcy appellate panel. If the transcript cannot be completed within 30 days of receipt of the request the reporter shall seek an extension of time from the clerk or the clerk of the bankruptcy appellate panel and the action of the clerk shall be entered in the docket and the parties notified. If the reporter does not file the transcript within the time allowed, the clerk or the clerk of the bankruptcy appellate panel shall notify the bankruptcy judge.

(b) Duty of clerk to transmit copy of record; docketing of appeal

When the record is complete for purposes of appeal, the clerk shall transmit a copy thereof forthwith to the clerk of the district court or the clerk of the bankruptcy appellate panel. On receipt of the transmission the clerk of the district court or the clerk of the bankruptcy appellate panel shall enter the appeal in the docket and give notice promptly to all parties to the judgment, order, or decree appealed from of the date on which the appeal was docketed. If the bankruptcy appellate panel directs that additional copies of the record be furnished, the clerk of the bankruptcy appellate panel shall notify the appellant and, if the appellant fails to provide the copies, the clerk shall prepare the copies at the expense of the appellant.

(c) Record for preliminary hearing

If prior to the time the record is transmitted a party moves in the district court or before the bankruptcy appellate panel for dismissal, for a stay pending appeal, for additional security on the bond on appeal or on a supersedeas bond, or for any intermediate order, the clerk at the request of any party to the appeal shall transmit to the clerk of the district court or the clerk of the bankruptcy appellate panel a copy of the parts of the record as any party to the appeal shall designate. (As amended Mar. 30, 1987, eff. Aug. 1, 1987; Apr. 30, 1991, eff. Aug. 1, 1991.)

ADVISORY COMMITTEE NOTES

Subdivision (a) is an adaptation of Rule 11(b) F.R.App.P.

Subdivision (b) is similar to former Bankruptcy Rule 807. The duty of the clerk of the bankruptcy court to transmit the record as soon as the record is complete is derived from the second paragraph of Rule 11(b) F.R.App.P. The last sentence of the subdivision applies to appeals to bankruptcy

appellate panels. Additional copies of the record may be needed when the appendix to the brief required under Rule 8009(b) is not adequate in the judgment of the bankruptcy appellate panel for disposition of the appeal. If additional copies are required, the appellant will arrange for the production of the copies; if the appellant fails to do so, the clerk of the bankruptcy appellate panel shall prepare the copies at the expense of the appellant.

Subdivision (c) is derived from subdivisions (c), (e) and (f) of Rule 11 F.R.App.P. and subdivision (d) is essentially the same as Rule 11(b) F.R.App.P.

1991 Amendment

This rule is amended to require that the bankruptcy clerk retain the original record and transmit a copy of the record to the clerk of the district court or bankruptcy appellate panel. Transmission of the original documents may cause disruption in the continuing administration of the case in the bankruptcy court.

CROSS REFERENCES

Docketing of appeal and filing of record, see Federal Rules of Appellate Procedure Rule 12, 28 USCA.

Effect of clerk's retention and indexing of judgment on appealability and proceedings on appeal, see Fed.Rules Bankr.Proc. Rule 9021, 11 USCA.

Time for filing and service of briefs, see Fed.Rules Bankr. Proc. Rule 8009, 11 USCA.

Transmission of record, see Federal Rules of Appellate Procedure Rule 11, 28 USCA.

LIBRARY REFERENCES

American Digest System

Bankruptcy ⊗3777.

Key Number System Topic No. 51.

Rule 8008. Filing and Service

(a) Filing

Papers required or permitted to be filed with the clerk of the district court or the clerk of the bankruptcy appellate panel may be filed by mail addressed to the clerk, but filing is not timely unless the papers are received by the clerk within the time fixed for filing, except that briefs are deemed filed on the day of mailing. An original and one copy of all papers shall be filed when an appeal is to the district court; an original and three copies shall be filed when an appeal is to a bankruptcy appellate panel. The district court or bankruptcy appellate panel may require that additional copies be furnished. Rule 5005(a)(2) applies to papers filed with the clerk of the district court or the clerk of the bankruptcy appellate panel if filing by electronic means is authorized by local rule promulgated pursuant to Rule 8018.

(b) Service of all papers required

Copies of all papers filed by any party and not required by these rules to be served by the clerk of the district court or the clerk of the bankruptcy appellate panel shall, at or before the time of filing, be served by the party or a person acting for the party on all other parties to the appeal. Service on a party represented by counsel shall be made on counsel.

(c) Manner of service

Service may be personal or by mail. Personal service includes delivery of the copy to a clerk or other responsible person at the office of counsel. Service by mail is complete on mailing.

(d) Proof of service

Papers presented for filing shall contain an acknowledgment of service by the person served or proof of service in the form of a statement of the date and manner of service and of the names of the persons served, certified by the person who made service. The clerk of the district court or the clerk of the bankruptcy appellate panel may permit papers to be filed without acknowledgment or proof of service but shall require the acknowledgment or proof of service to be filed promptly thereafter.

(As amended Mar. 30, 1987, eff. Aug. 1, 1987; Apr. 23, 1996, eff. Dec. 1, 1996.)

ADVISORY COMMITTEE NOTES

This rule is an adaptation of Rule 25 F.R.App.P. Motions, briefs, appendices when required, statements, and any other filed paper must be accompanied by the specified number of copies. Rules 8001 and 8004 govern the number of copies of the notice of appeal which must be filed.

1996 Amendment

This rule is amended to permit, but not require, district courts and, where bankruptcy appellate panels have been authorized, circuit councils to adopt local rules that allow filing of documents by electronic means, subject to the limitations contained in Rule 5005(a)(2). See the committee note to the amendments to Rule 5005. Other amendments to this rule are stylistic.

GAP Report on Rule 8008. No changes since publication, except for stylistic changes.

CROSS REFERENCES

Appeal—

    After dismissal of direct appeal by court of appeals, when taken, see Fed.Rules Bankr.Proc. Rule 8001, 11 USCA.

    By leave, how taken, see Fed.Rules Bankr.Proc. Rule 8001, 11 USCA.

Filing and service of papers, see Federal Rules of Appellate Procedure Rule 25, 28 USCA.

Manner and proof of service of emergency motions, see Fed.Rules Bankr.Proc. Rule 8011, 11 USCA.

LIBRARY REFERENCES

American Digest System

Bankruptcy ☞3773, 3774.1.

Key Number System Topic No. 51.

Rule 8009. Briefs and Appendix; Filing and Service

(a) Briefs

Unless the district court or the bankruptcy appellate panel by local rule or by order excuses the filing of briefs or specifies different time limits:

    (1) The appellant shall serve and file a brief within 14 days after entry of the appeal on the docket pursuant to Rule 8007.

    (2) The appellee shall serve and file a brief within 14 days after service of the brief of appellant. If the appellee has filed a cross appeal, the brief of the appellee shall contain the issues and argument pertinent to the cross appeal, denominated as such, and the response to the brief of the appellant.

    (3) The appellant may serve and file a reply brief within 14 days after service of the brief of the appellee, and if the appellee has cross-appealed, the appellee may file and serve a reply brief to the response of the appellant to the issues presented in the cross appeal within 14 days after service of the reply brief of the appellant. No further briefs may be filed except with leave of the district court or the bankruptcy appellate panel.

(b) Appendix to brief

If the appeal is to a bankruptcy appellate panel, the appellant shall serve and file with the appellant's brief excerpts of the record as an appendix, which shall include the following:

    (1) The complaint and answer or other equivalent pleadings;

    (2) Any pretrial order;

    (3) The judgment, order, or decree from which the appeal is taken;

    (4) Any other orders relevant to the appeal;

    (5) The opinion, findings of fact, or conclusions of law filed or delivered orally by the court and citations of the opinion if published;

    (6) Any motion and response on which the court rendered decision;

    (7) The notice of appeal;

    (8) The relevant entries in the bankruptcy docket; and

    (9) The transcript or portion thereof, if so required by a rule of the bankruptcy appellate panel.

An appellee may also serve and file an appendix which contains material required to be included by the appellant but omitted by appellant.

(As amended Mar. 30, 1987, eff. Aug. 1, 1987; Mar. 26, 2009, eff. Dec. 1, 2009.)

ADVISORY COMMITTEE NOTES

Subdivision (a) of this rule is adapted from Rules 28(a) and 31(a) F.R.App.P. The introductory clause of the rule recognizes the desirability of allowing local and individual variation in the filing of briefs. The numbered paragraphs prescribe shorter periods than the corresponding periods allowed by Rule 31(a) F.R.App.P.

Subdivision (b), which is similar to an interim rule for bankruptcy appellate panels promulgated by the Ninth Circuit, applies only when an appeal is to an appellate panel. The appellant must prepare an appendix to the brief which contains the documents relevant to the appeal. With the appendix available to each member of the appellate panel, it is unlikely that multiple copies of the record will be necessary. The last sentence of the subdivision enables the appellee to correct an omission of the appellant.

Rule 30 F.R.App.P., which governs the preparation of the appendix in appeals taken to the courts of appeals, specifies fewer documents which must be included in the appendix but permits the parties to include any other material.

1987 Amendment

The amendment to Rule 8007(c) permits a rule of the bankruptcy appellate panel to provide that the record is to be retained rather than transmitted. The new paragraph (9) of subdivision (b) of this rule complements Rule 8007(c) by authorizing a rule of the panel to require inclusion of the transcript or a portion thereof in the appendix.

2009 Amendments

The rule is amended to implement changes in connection with the amendment to Rule 9006(a) and the manner by which time is computed under the rules. The deadlines in the rule are amended to substitute a deadline that is a multiple of seven days. Throughout the rules, deadlines are amended in the following manner:

- 5–day periods become 7–day periods
- 10–day periods become 14–day periods
- 15–day periods become 14–day periods
- 20–day periods become 21–day periods
- 25–day periods become 28–day periods

LIBRARY REFERENCES

American Digest System

Bankruptcy ⬠3777.

Key Number System Topic No. 51.

Corpus Juris Secundum

CJS Bankruptcy § 1249, Briefs.

Rule 8010.   Form of Briefs; Length

(a) Form of briefs

Unless the district court or the bankruptcy appellate panel by local rule otherwise provides, the form of brief shall be as follows:

(1) Brief of the appellant. The brief of the appellant shall contain under appropriate headings and in the order here indicated:

(A) A table of contents, with page references, and a table of cases alphabetically arranged, statutes and other authorities cited, with references to the pages of the brief where they are cited.

(B) A statement of the basis of appellate jurisdiction.

(C) A statement of the issues presented and the applicable standard of appellate review.

(D) A statement of the case. The statement shall first indicate briefly the nature of the case, the course of the proceedings, and the disposition in the court below. There shall follow a statement of the facts relevant to the issues presented for review, with appropriate references to the record.

(E) An argument. The argument may be preceded by a summary. The argument shall contain the contentions of the appellant with respect to the issues presented, and the reasons therefor, with citations to the authorities, statutes and parts of the record relied on.

(F) A short conclusion stating the precise relief sought.

(2) Brief of the appellee. The brief of the appellee shall conform to the requirements of paragraph (1)(A)–(E) of this subdivision, except that a statement of the basis of appellate jurisdiction, of the issues, or of the case need not be made unless the appellee is dissatisfied with the statement of the appellant.

(b) Reproduction of statutes, rules, regulations, or similar material

If determination of the issues presented requires reference to the Code or other statutes, rules, regulations, or similar material, relevant parts thereof shall be reproduced in the brief or in an addendum or they may be supplied to the court in pamphlet form.

(c) Length of briefs

Unless the district court or the bankruptcy appellate panel by local rule or order otherwise provides, principal briefs shall not exceed 50 pages, and reply briefs shall not exceed 25 pages, exclusive of pages containing the table of contents, tables of citations and any addendum containing statutes, rules, regulations, or similar material.

ADVISORY COMMITTEE NOTES

This rule is derived from subdivisions (a), (b), (c), and (f) of Rule 28 F.R.App.P.

When an appeal is to a bankruptcy appellate panel and an appendix is filed pursuant to Rule 8009(b) and reference is made in a brief to parts of the record included in the appendix, the reference should be to the appropriate pages of the appendix at which those parts appear.

CROSS REFERENCES

Briefs, see Federal Rules of Appellate Procedure Rule 28, 28 USCA.

LIBRARY REFERENCES

American Digest System

Bankruptcy ⬠3777.

Key Number System Topic No. 51.

Rule 8011. Motions

(a) Content of motions; response; reply

A request for an order or other relief shall be made by filing with the clerk of the district court or the clerk of the bankruptcy appellate panel a motion for such order or relief with proof of service on all other parties to the appeal. The motion shall contain or be accompanied by any matter required by a specific provision of these rules governing such a motion, shall state with particularity the grounds on which it is based, and shall set forth the order or relief sought. If a motion is supported by briefs, affidavits or other papers, they shall be served and filed with the motion. Any party may file a response in opposition to a motion other than one for a procedural order within seven days after service of the motion, but the district court or the bankruptcy appellate panel may shorten or extend the time for responding to any motion.

(b) Determination of motions for procedural orders

Notwithstanding subdivision (a) of this rule, motions for procedural orders, including any motion under Rule 9006, may be acted on at any time, without awaiting a response thereto and without hearing. Any party adversely affected by such action may move for reconsideration, vacation, or modification of the action.

(c) Determination of all motions

All motions will be decided without oral argument unless the court orders otherwise. A motion for a stay, or for other emergency relief may be denied if not presented promptly.

(d) Emergency motions

Whenever a movant requests expedited action on a motion on the ground that, to avoid irreparable harm, relief is needed in less time than would normally be required for the district court or bankruptcy appellate panel to receive and consider a response, the word "Emergency" shall precede the title of the motion. The motion shall be accompanied by an affidavit setting forth the nature of the emergency. The motion shall state whether all grounds advanced in support thereof were submitted to the bankruptcy judge and, if any grounds relied on were not submitted, why the motion should not be remanded to the bankruptcy judge for reconsideration. The motion shall include the office addresses and telephone numbers of moving and opposing counsel and shall be served pursuant to Rule 8008. Prior to filing the motion, the movant shall make every practicable effort to notify opposing counsel in time for counsel to respond to the motion. The affidavit accompanying the motion shall also state when and how opposing counsel was notified or if opposing counsel was not notified why it was not practicable to do so.

(e) Power of a single judge to entertain motions

A single judge of a bankruptcy appellate panel may grant or deny any request for relief which under these rules may properly be sought by motion, except that a single judge may not dismiss or otherwise decide an appeal or a motion for leave to appeal. The action of a single judge may be reviewed by the panel.

ADVISORY COMMITTEE NOTES

Subdivisions (a), (b) and (e) of this rule conform substantially to subdivisions (a), (b) and (c) of Rule 27 F.R.App.P. Subdivisions (c) and (d) are taken from Rule 13(c) and (d) of the Rules of the First Circuit governing appeals to bankruptcy appellate panels.

CROSS REFERENCES

Motions, see Federal Rules of Appellate Procedure Rule 27, 28 USCA.

Signing and verification of papers, see Fed.Rules Bankr. Proc. Rule 9011, 11 USCA.

LIBRARY REFERENCES

American Digest System
    Bankruptcy ⊙→3773, 3778.
    Key Number System Topic No. 51.

Rule 8012. Oral Argument

Oral argument shall be allowed in all cases unless the district judge or the judges of the bankruptcy appellate panel unanimously determine after examination of the briefs and record, or appendix to the brief, that oral argument is not needed. Any party shall have an opportunity to file a statement setting forth the reason why oral argument should be allowed.

Oral argument will not be allowed if (1) the appeal is frivolous; (2) the dispositive issue or set of issues has been recently authoritatively decided; or (3) the facts and legal arguments are adequately presented in the briefs and record and the decisional process would not be significantly aided by oral argument.

ADVISORY COMMITTEE NOTES

This rule is derived from Rule 34(a) F.R.App.P. The other details of oral argument which are covered by the remaining subdivisions of Rule 34 F.R.App.P. are not in these rules and are left to local rule or order of the court.

CROSS REFERENCES

Oral argument, see Federal Rules of Appellate Procedure Rule 34, 28 USCA.

LIBRARY REFERENCES

American Digest System
    Bankruptcy ⊙→3778.
    Key Number System Topic No. 51.

Corpus Juris Secundum

CJS Bankruptcy § 1211, Oral Argument.

Rule 8013. Disposition of Appeal; Weight Accorded Bankruptcy Judge's Findings of Fact

On an appeal the district court or bankruptcy appellate panel may affirm, modify, or reverse a bankruptcy judge's judgment, order, or decree or remand with instructions for further proceedings. Findings of fact, whether based on oral or documentary evidence, shall not be set aside unless clearly erroneous, and due regard shall be given to the opportunity of the bankruptcy court to judge the credibility of the witnesses. (As amended Mar. 30, 1987, eff. Aug. 1, 1987.)

ADVISORY COMMITTEE NOTES

This rule accords to the findings of a bankruptcy judge the same weight given the findings of a district judge under Rule 52 F.R.Civ.P. See also Rules 7052(a) and 9014.

1987 Amendment

The amendment to this rule conforms the appellate review standard to Rule 52 F.R.Civ.P., as amended in August 1985.

CROSS REFERENCES

Findings by court, see Fed.Rules Bankr.Proc. Rule 7052, 11 USCA.

Findings by court, see Fed.Rules Civ.Proc. Rule 52, 28 USCA.

Suspension of this rule, see Fed.Rules Bankr.Proc. Rule 8019, 11 USCA.

LIBRARY REFERENCES

American Digest System

Bankruptcy ⊕3779 to 3790.

Key Number System Topic No. 51.

Corpus Juris Secundum

CJS Bankruptcy § 219, Consent to Final Determination by Bankruptcy Judge.

Rule 8014. Costs

Except as otherwise provided by law, agreed to by the parties, or ordered by the district court or the bankruptcy appellate panel, costs shall be taxed against the losing party on an appeal. If a judgment is affirmed or reversed in part, or is vacated, costs shall be allowed only as ordered by the court. Costs incurred in the production of copies of briefs, the appendices, and the record and in the preparation and transmission of the record, the cost of the reporter's transcript, if necessary for the determination of the appeal, the premiums paid for cost of supersedeas bonds or other bonds to preserve rights pending appeal and the fee for filing the notice of appeal shall be taxed by the clerk as costs of the appeal in favor of the party entitled to costs under this rule. (As amended Mar. 30, 1987, eff. Aug. 1, 1987.)

ADVISORY COMMITTEE NOTES

This rule is an adaptation of Rule 39(a), (c) and (e) of the F.R.App.P. Under this rule all costs are taxed by the clerk of the bankruptcy court.

CROSS REFERENCES

Costs, see Federal Rules of Appellate Procedure Rule 39, 28 USCA.

LIBRARY REFERENCES

American Digest System

Bankruptcy ⊕2189.

Key Number System Topic No. 51.

Corpus Juris Secundum

CJS Bankruptcy § 1214, Costs and Fees.

Rule 8015. Motion for Rehearing

Unless the district court or the bankruptcy appellate panel by local rule or by court order otherwise provides, a motion for rehearing may be filed within 14 days after entry of the judgment of the district court or the bankruptcy appellate panel. If a timely motion for rehearing is filed, the time for appeal to the court of appeals for all parties shall run from the entry of the order denying rehearing or the entry of subsequent judgment. (As amended Mar. 30, 1987, eff. Aug. 1, 1987; Mar. 26, 2009, eff. Dec. 1, 2009.)

ADVISORY COMMITTEE NOTES

This is an adaptation of the first sentence of Rule 40(a) F.R.App.P. The filing of a motion for rehearing does not toll the time for taking an appeal to the court of appeals from the district court or the bankruptcy appellate panel. Appeals from a district court or a bankruptcy appellate panel are to the appropriate court of appeals. Under Rule 4(a)(4) F.R.App.P. the filing of post-trial motions in the district court has the effect of vitiating any prior notice of appeal and, on the district court's disposition of those post-trial motions, a new appeal period starts. Rule 4 F.R.App.P. does not, however, contain any provision which stays or otherwise alters the time for taking an appeal to the court of appeals when a motion for rehearing is filed under Rule 8015 with the district court or bankruptcy appellate panel.

1987 Amendment

The amendment, which is derived from Rule 8002(b), Rule 4(a)(4) F.R.App.P., and Rule 11.1 Sup.Ct.R., clarifies the effect of the filing of a timely motion for rehearing. If a timely motion is filed, the appeal period to the court of appeals begins to run on the entry of an order denying the motion or the entry of a subsequent judgment.

2009 Amendments

The rule is amended to implement changes in connection with the amendment to Rule 9006(a) and the manner by which time is computed under the rules. The deadline in the rule is amended to substitute a deadline that is a multiple of seven days. Throughout the rules, deadlines are amended in the following manner:

- 5–day periods become 7–day periods
- 10 day periods become 14–day periods
- 15–day periods become 14–day periods
- 20–day periods become 21 day periods
- 25–day periods become 28–day periods

CROSS REFERENCES

Petition for rehearing, see Federal Rules of Appellate Procedure Rule 40, 28 USCA.

LIBRARY REFERENCES

American Digest System

Bankruptcy ⊗3778.

Key Number System Topic No. 51.

Corpus Juris Secundum

CJS Bankruptcy § 10, Other U.S. Code Provisions.

CJS Bankruptcy § 16, Local Rules--Appellate Practice.

CJS Bankruptcy § 1244, Appeal to Court of Appeals.

CJS Bankruptcy § 1269, Rehearing.

Rule 8016. Duties of Clerk of District Court and Bankruptcy Appellate Panel

(a) Entry of judgment

The clerk of the district court or the clerk of the bankruptcy appellate panel shall prepare, sign and enter the judgment following receipt of the opinion of the court or the appellate panel or, if there is no opinion, following the instruction of the court or the appellate panel. The notation of a judgment in the docket constitutes entry of judgment.

(b) Notice of orders or judgments; return of record

Immediately on the entry of a judgment or order the clerk of the district court or the clerk of the bankruptcy appellate panel shall transmit a notice of the entry to each party to the appeal, to the United States trustee, and to the clerk, together with a copy of any opinion respecting the judgment or order, and shall make a note of the transmission in the docket. Original papers transmitted as the record on appeal shall be returned to the clerk on disposition of the appeal. (As amended Mar. 30, 1987, eff. Aug. 1, 1987; Apr. 30, 1991, eff. Aug. 1, 1991.)

ADVISORY COMMITTEE NOTES

Subdivision (a) of this rule is adapted from Rule 36 F.R.App.P. Subdivision (b) is similar to subdivisions (c) and (d) of Rule 45 F.R.App.P.

1991 Amendment

Subdivision (b) is amended to enable the United States trustee to monitor the progress of the case. The requirements of this subdivision apply to an order of the district court or bankruptcy appellate panel staying its judgment pending appeal to the court of appeals pursuant to Rule 8017(b).

CROSS REFERENCES

Duties of clerks, see Federal Rules of Appellate Procedure Rule 45, 28 USCA.

Entry of judgment, see Federal Rules of Appellate Procedure Rule 36, 28 USCA.

LIBRARY REFERENCES

American Digest System

Clerks of Courts ⊗64.1 to 76.

Key Number System Topic No. 79.

Rule 8017. Stay of Judgment of District Court or Bankruptcy Appellate Panel

(a) Automatic stay of judgment on appeal

Judgments of the district court or the bankruptcy appellate panel are stayed until the expiration of 14 days after entry, unless otherwise ordered by the district court or the bankruptcy appellate panel.

(b) Stay pending appeal to the court of appeals

On motion and notice to the parties to the appeal, the district court or the bankruptcy appellate panel may stay its judgment pending an appeal to the court of appeals. The stay shall not extend beyond 30 days after the entry of the judgment of the district court or the bankruptcy appellate panel unless the period is extended for cause shown. If before the expiration of a stay entered pursuant to this subdivision there is an appeal to the court of appeals by the party who obtained the stay, the stay shall continue until final disposition by the court of appeals. A bond or other security may be required as a condition to the grant or continuation of a stay of the judgment. A bond or other security may be required if a trustee obtains a stay but a bond or security shall not be required if a stay is obtained by the United States or an officer or agency thereof or at the direction of any department of the Government of the United States.

(c) Power of court of appeals not limited

This rule does not limit the power of a court of appeals or any judge thereof to stay proceedings during the pendency of an appeal or to suspend, modify, restore, or grant an injunction during the pendency of an appeal or to make any order appropriate to preserve the status quo or the effectiveness of the judgment subsequently to be entered. (As amended Mar. 26, 2009, eff. Dec. 1, 2009.)

ADVISORY COMMITTEE NOTES

This rule is derived from Rule 62 F.R.Civ.P. and Rule 41 F.R.App. P.

Subdivision (a) accords to the parties to an appeal 10 days within which to decide whether to pursue an appeal to the court of appeals. In ordinary civil litigation there is a similar opportunity. Rule 62(a) F.R.Civ.P. automatically stays enforcement of a district court's judgment in a civil action and

Rule 41(a) F.R.App.P. provides that the mandate of the court of appeals shall not issue for 21 days, unless the court otherwise directs. The district court or bankruptcy appellate panel may reduce the 10 day period of this subdivision.

Subdivision (b) vests in the district courts and the bankruptcy appellate panels the same authority the courts of appeals have under Rule 41(b) F.R.App.P. to stay their judgments pending appeal. Perfection of an appeal to the court of appeals while a stay entered by the district court or bankruptcy appellate panel is in effect results in the automatic continuation of that stay during the course of the appeal in the court of appeals.

Subdivision (c) is the same as Rule 62(g) F.R.Civ.P.

2009 Amendments

The rule is amended to implement changes in connection with the amendment to Rule 9006(a) and the manner by which time is computed under the rules. The deadline in the rule is amended to substitute a deadline that is a multiple of seven days. Throughout the rules, deadlines are amended in the following manner:

- 5–day periods become 7–day periods
- 10–day periods become 14–day periods
- 15–day periods become 14–day periods
- 20–day periods become 21–day periods
- 25–day periods become 28–day periods

CROSS REFERENCES

Stay of mandate, see Federal Rules of Appellate Procedure Rule 41, 28 USCA.

LIBRARY REFERENCES

American Digest System

Bankruptcy ☞3776.5, 3789.1.
Key Number System Topic No. 51.

Rule 8018. Rules by Circuit Councils and District Courts; Procedure When There is No Controlling Law

(a) Local Rules by Circuit Councils and District Courts

(1) Circuit councils which have authorized bankruptcy appellate panels pursuant to 28 U.S.C. § 158(b) and the district courts may, acting by a majority of the judges of the council or district court, make and amend rules governing practice and procedure for appeals from orders or judgments of bankruptcy judges to the respective bankruptcy appellate panel or district court consistent with—but not duplicative of—Acts of Congress and the rules of this Part VIII. Local rules shall conform to any uniform numbering system prescribed by the Judicial Conference of the United States. Rule 83 F.R.Civ.P. governs the procedure for making and amending rules to govern appeals.

(2) A local rule imposing a requirement of form shall not be enforced in a manner that causes a party to lose rights because of a nonwillful failure to comply with the requirement.

(b) Procedure When There Is No Controlling Law. A bankruptcy appellate panel or district judge may regulate practice in any manner consistent with federal law, these rules, Official Forms, and local rules of the circuit council or district court. No sanction or other disadvantage may be imposed for noncompliance with any requirement not in federal law, federal rules, Official Forms, or the local rules of the circuit council or district court unless the alleged violator has been furnished in the particular case with actual notice of the requirement.

(As amended Mar. 30, 1987, eff. Aug. 1, 1987; Apr. 27, 1995, eff. Dec. 1, 1995.)

ADVISORY COMMITTEE NOTES

This rule is similar to Rule 47 F.R.App.P. and Rule 83 F.R.Civ.P. Local rules governing procedure before the bankruptcy courts may be promulgated under Rule 9028.

1987 Amendment

Rule 83 F.R.Civ.P. was amended in August 1985 to require greater participation by the public in the rule making process. The amendment to Rule 8018 incorporates Rule 83 F.R.Civ.P. Under 28 U.S.C. § 158(b)(2), appeals may be taken to a bankruptcy appellate panel only if the district court so authorizes. If a district court does not authorize appeals to the bankruptcy appellate panel, appeals will be to the district court. This rule is amended to authorize district courts to promulgate rules for appeals.

1995 Amendments

The amendments to this rule conform to the amendments to Rule 9029. See Committee Note to the amendments to Rule 9029.

CROSS REFERENCES

Promulgation of local rules governing bankruptcy procedure, see Fed.Rules Bankr.Proc. Rule 9029, 11 USCA.

Rules by courts of appeals, see Federal Rules of Appellate Procedure Rule 47, 28 USCA.

LIBRARY REFERENCES

American Digest System

Bankruptcy ☞2129, 3761.
Key Number System Topic No. 51.

Corpus Juris Secundum

CJS Bankruptcy § 16, Local Rules--Appellate Practice.

Rule 8019. Suspension of Rules in Part VIII

In the interest of expediting decision or for other cause, the district court or the bankruptcy appellate panel may suspend the requirements or provisions of the rules in Part VIII, except Rules 8001, 8002, and 8013, and may order proceedings in accordance with the direction.

(As amended Mar. 30, 1987, eff. Aug. 1, 1987.)

This rule is derived from Rule 2 F.R.App.P.

CROSS REFERENCES
Suspension of rules, see Federal Rules of Appellate Procedure Rule 2, 28 USCA.

LIBRARY REFERENCES
American Digest System
Bankruptcy ⟨key⟩2129, 3761.
Key Number System Topic No. 51.

Rule 8020.   Damages and Costs for Frivolous Appeal
If a district court or bankruptcy appellate panel determines that an appeal from an order, judgment, or decree of a bankruptcy judge is frivolous, it may, after a separately filed motion or notice from the district court or bankruptcy appellate panel and reasonable opportunity to respond, award just damages and single or double costs to the appellee.
(Added Apr. 11, 1997, eff. Dec. 1, 1997.)

ADVISORY COMMITTEE NOTES
1997 Amendment
This rule is added to clarify that a district court hearing an appeal, or a bankruptcy appellate panel, has the authority to award damages and costs to an appellee if it finds that the appeal is frivolous. By conforming to the language of Rule 38 F.R.App.P., this rule recognizes that the authority to award damages and costs in connection with frivolous appeals is the same for district courts sitting as appellate courts, bankruptcy appellate panels, and courts of appeals.

GAP Report on Rule 8020. No changes to the published draft.

LIBRARY REFERENCES
American Digest System
Bankruptcy ⟨key⟩2187, 2189.
Key Number System Topic No. 51.

Corpus Juris Secundum
CJS Bankruptcy § 258, Court's Inherent and Statutory Power to Sanction Abuse of Judicial Process.
CJS Bankruptcy § 1215, Costs and Fees--Frivolous Appeals.
CJS Bankruptcy § 1265, Sanctions.

PART IX—GENERAL PROVISIONS

Rule
9001. General Definitions.
9002. Meanings of Words in the Federal Rules of Civil Procedure When Applicable to Cases Under The Code.
9003. Prohibition of Ex Parte Contacts.
9004. General Requirements of Form.
9005. Harmless Error.
9005.1. Constitutional Challenge to a Statute—Notice, Certification, and Intervention.
9006. Computing and Extending Time.
9007. General Authority to Regulate Notices.
9008. Service or Notice by Publication.
9009. Forms.
9010. Representation and Appearances; Powers of Attorney.
9011. Signing of Papers; Representations to the Court; Sanctions; Verification and Copies of Papers.
9012. Oaths and Affirmations.
9013. Motions: Form and Service.
9014. Contested Matters.
9015. Jury Trials.
9016. Subpoena.
9017. Evidence.
9018. Secret, Confidential, Scandalous, or Defamatory Matter.
9019. Compromise and Arbitration.
9020. Contempt Proceedings.
9021. Entry of Judgment.
9022. Notice of Judgment or Order.
9023. New Trials; Amendment of Judgments.
9024. Relief from Judgment or Order.
9025. Security: Proceedings Against Sureties.
9026. Exceptions Unnecessary.
9027. Removal.
9028. Disability of a Judge.
9029. Local Bankruptcy Rules; Procedure When There Is No Controlling Law.
9030. Jurisdiction and Venue Unaffected.
9031. Masters Not Authorized.
9032. Effect of Amendment of Federal Rules of Civil Procedure.
9033. Review of Proposed Findings of Fact and Conclusions of Law in Non-Core Proceedings.
9034. Transmittal of Pleadings, Motion Papers, Objections, and Other Papers to the United States Trustee.
9035. Applicability of Rules in Judicial Districts in Alabama and North Carolina.
9036. Notice by Electronic Transmission.
9037. Privacy Protection For Filings Made with the Court.

Rule 9001.   General Definitions

The definitions of words and phrases in §§ 101, 902, 1101, and 1502 of the Code, and the rules of construction in § 102, govern their use in these rules. In addition, the following words and phrases used in these rules have the meanings indicated:

(1) "Bankruptcy clerk" means a clerk appointed pursuant to 28 U.S.C. § 156(b).

(2) "Bankruptcy Code" or "Code" means title 11 of the United States Code.

(3) "Clerk" means bankruptcy clerk, if one has been appointed, otherwise clerk of the district court.

(4) "Court" or "judge" means the judicial officer before whom a case or proceeding is pending.

(5) "Debtor." When any act is required by these rules to be performed by a debtor or when it is necessary to compel attendance of a debtor for examination and the debtor is not a natural person: (A) if the debtor is a corporation, "debtor" includes, if designated by the court, any or all of its officers, members of its board of directors or trustees or of a similar controlling body, a controlling stockholder or member, or any other person in control; (B) if the debtor is a partnership, "debtor" includes any or all of its general partners or, if designated by the court, any other person in control.

(6) "Firm" includes a partnership or professional corporation of attorneys or accountants.

(7) "Judgment" means any appealable order.

(8) "Mail" means first class, postage prepaid.

(9) "Notice provider" means any entity approved by the Administrative Office of the United States Courts to give notice to creditors under Rule 2002(g)(4).

(10) "Regular associate" means any attorney regularly employed by, associated with, or counsel to an individual or firm.

(11) "Trustee" includes a debtor in possession in a chapter 11 case.

(12) "United States trustee" includes an assistant United States trustee and any designee of the United States trustee.

(As amended Mar. 30, 1987, eff. Aug. 1, 1987; Apr. 30, 1991, eff. Aug. 1, 1991; Apr. 25, 2005, eff. Dec. 1, 2005; Apr. 28, 2010, eff. Dec. 1, 2010.)

ADVISORY COMMITTEE NOTES

1987 Amendment

The terms "bankruptcy clerk" and "clerk" have been defined to reflect that unless otherwise stated, for the purpose of these rules, the terms are meant to identify the court officer for the bankruptcy records. If a bankruptcy clerk is appointed, all filings are made with the bankruptcy clerk. If one has not been appointed, all filings are with the clerk of the district court. Rule 5005.

The rule is also amended to include a definition of "court or judge." Since a case or proceeding may be before a bankruptcy judge or a judge of the district court, "court or judge" is defined to mean the judicial officer before whom the case or proceeding is pending.

1991 Amendment

Section 582 of title 28 provides that the Attorney General may appoint one or more assistant United States trustees in any region when the public interest so requires. This rule is amended to clarify that an assistant United States trustee, as well as any designee of the United States trustee, is included within the meaning of "United States trustee" in the rules.

2005 Amendments

The rule is amended to add the definition of a notice provider and to renumber the final three definitions in the rule. A notice provider is an entity approved by the Administrative Office of the United States Courts to enter into agreements with entities to give notice to those entities in the form and manner agreed to by those parties. The new definition supports the amendment to Rule 2002(g)(4) that authorizes a notice provider to give notices under Rule 2002.

Many entities conduct business on a national scale and receive vast numbers of notices in bankruptcy cases throughout the country. Those entities can agree with a notice provider to receive their notices in a form and at an address or addresses that the creditor and notice provider agree upon. There are processes currently in use that provide substantial assurance that notices are not misdirected. Any notice provider would have to demonstrate to the Administrative Office of the United States Courts that it could provide the service in a manner that ensures the proper delivery of notice to creditors. Once the Administrative Office of the United States Courts approves the notice provider to enter into agreements with creditors, the notice provider and other entities can establish the relationship that will govern the delivery of notices in cases as provided in Rule 2002(g)(4).

2010 Amendments

The rule is amended to add § 1502 of the Code to the list of definitional provisions that are applicable to the Rules. That section was added to the Code by the 2005 amendments.

CROSS REFERENCES

Clerk defined, see Fed.Rules Bankr.Proc. Rule 9002, 11 USCA.

Judgment defined, see Fed.Rules Bankr.Proc. Rules 7054 and 9002, 11 USCA.

LIBRARY REFERENCES

American Digest System

Bankruptcy ⟨key⟩2129.

Key Number System Topic No. 51.

Corpus Juris Secundum

CJS Bankruptcy § 12, Federal Rules of Civil Procedure.

CJS Bankruptcy § 20, Bankruptcy Court as Unit of District Court.

CJS Bankruptcy § 41, Appointment, Oath, and Term; Vacancy in and Removal from Office.

CJS Bankruptcy § 132, Rights, Powers, and Duties of Debtor in Possession.

CJS Bankruptcy § 141, After Notice and a Hearing.

CJS Bankruptcy § 296, Notice by Mail--Proper Mailing Address.

CJS Bankruptcy § 767, Application for Order of Employment.

CJS Bankruptcy § 770, Services by Members and Associates.

CJS Bankruptcy § 781, Content; Detail and Documentation Required.

CJS Bankruptcy § 790, Convening of Meeting by Trustee or Other Judicial Officer.

CJS Bankruptcy § 793, Duties of Trustee or Other Judicial Officer.

CJS Bankruptcy § 800, United States Trustee or Other Judicial Officer; Bankruptcy Judge.

CJS Bankruptcy § 817, Where Debtor is Corporation or Partnership.

Rule 9002. Meanings of Words in the Federal Rules of Civil Procedure When Applicable to Cases Under The Code

The following words and phrases used in the Federal Rules of Civil Procedure made applicable to cases under the Code by these rules have the meanings indicated unless they are inconsistent with the context:

(1) "Action" or "civil action" means an adversary proceeding or, when appropriate, a contested petition, or proceedings to vacate an order for relief or to determine any other contested matter.

(2) "Appeal" means an appeal as provided by 28 U.S.C. § 158.

(3) "Clerk" or "clerk of the district court" means the court officer responsible for the bankruptcy records in the district.

(4) "District court," "trial court," "court," "district judge," or "judge" means bankruptcy judge if the case or proceeding is pending before a bankruptcy judge.

(5) "Judgment" includes any order appealable to an appellate court.

(As amended Mar. 30, 1987, eff. Aug. 1, 1987; Apr. 22, 1993, eff. Aug. 1, 1993.)

ADVISORY COMMITTEE NOTES

1993 Amendments

This rule is revised to include the words "district judge" in anticipation of amendments to the Federal Rules of Civil Procedure.

CROSS REFERENCES

Contested matters, see Fed.Rules Bankr.Proc. Rule 9014, 11 USCA.

Judgment defined, see Fed.Rules Civ.Proc. Rule 54, 28 USCA.

One form of action, see Fed.Rules Civ.Proc. Rule 2, 28 USCA.

Procedural rules which govern adversary proceedings, see Fed.Rules Bankr.Proc. Rule 7001 et seq., 11 USCA.

LIBRARY REFERENCES

American Digest System

Bankruptcy ☞2129.

Key Number System Topic No. 51.

Corpus Juris Secundum

CJS Bankruptcy § 314, Judgments.

Rule 9003. Prohibition of Ex Parte Contacts

(a) General prohibition

Except as otherwise permitted by applicable law, any examiner, any party in interest, and any attorney, accountant, or employee of a party in interest shall refrain from ex parte meetings and communications with the court concerning matters affecting a particular case or proceeding.

(b) United States trustee

Except as otherwise permitted by applicable law, the United States trustee and assistants to and employees or agents of the United States trustee shall refrain from ex parte meetings and communications with the court concerning matters affecting a particular case or proceeding. This rule does not preclude communications with the court to discuss general problems of administration and improvement of bankruptcy administration, including the operation of the United States trustee system.

(As amended Mar. 30, 1987, eff. Aug. 1, 1987; Apr. 30, 1991, eff. Aug. 1, 1991.)

ADVISORY COMMITTEE NOTES

This rule regulates the actions of parties in interest and their attorneys or others employed by parties in interest. This regulation of the conduct of parties in interest and their representative is designed to insure that the bankruptcy system operates fairly and that no appearance of unfairness is created. See H.Rep. No. 95–595, 95th Cong., 1st Sess. 95 et seq. (1977).

This rule is not a substitute for or limitation of any applicable canon of professional responsibility or judicial conduct. See, e.g., Canon 7, EC7–35, Disciplinary Rule 7–110(B) of the Code of Professional Responsibility: "Generally, in adversary proceedings a lawyer should not communicate with a judge relative to a matter pending before, or which is to be brought before, a tribunal over which he presides in circumstances which might have the effect or give the appearance of granting undue advantage to one party;" and Canon 3A(4) of the Code of Judicial Conduct: "A judge should . . . neither initiate nor consider ex parte or other communications concerning a pending or impending proceeding."

1987 Amendments

This rule is amended to apply to both the bankruptcy judges and the district judges of the district.

1991 Amendments

Subdivision (a) is amended to extend to examiners the prohibition on ex parte meetings and communications with the court.

Subdivision (b) is derived from Rule X–1010.

CROSS REFERENCES

Disqualification of judge, see Fed.Rules Bankr.Proc. Rule 5004, 11 USCA.

LIBRARY REFERENCES

American Digest System

Bankruptcy ☞2127.1.

Key Number System Topic No. 51.

Corpus Juris Secundum

CJS Bankruptcy § 31, Restrictions and Limitations on Activities and Practices of Judges.

CJS Bankruptcy § 34, Bias or Knowledge.

CJS Bankruptcy § 42, Regulation and Review of United States Trustee's Actions.

Rule 9004. General Requirements of Form

(a) Legibility; abbreviations

All petitions, pleadings, schedules and other papers shall be clearly legible. Abbreviations in common use in the English language may be used.

(b) Caption

Each paper filed shall contain a caption setting forth the name of the court, the title of the case, the bankruptcy docket number, and a brief designation of the character of the paper.

ADVISORY COMMITTEE NOTES

Subdivision (b). Additional requirements applicable to the caption for a petition are found in Rule 1005, to the caption for notices to creditors in Rule 2002(m), and to the caption for a pleading or other paper filed in an adversary proceeding in Rule 7010. Failure to comply with this or any other rule imposing a merely formal requirement does not ordinarily result in the loss of rights. See Rule 9005.

LIBRARY REFERENCES

American Digest System

Bankruptcy ☞2127.1, 2162.

Key Number System Topic No. 51.

Corpus Juris Secundum

CJS Bankruptcy § 285, Captions.

Rule 9005. Harmless Error

Rule 61 F.R.Civ.P. applies in cases under the Code. When appropriate, the court may order the correction of any error or defect or the cure of any omission which does not affect substantial rights.

LIBRARY REFERENCES

American Digest System

Bankruptcy ⟨⟩3788.

Key Number System Topic No. 51.

Corpus Juris Secundum

CJS Bankruptcy § 12, Federal Rules of Civil Procedure.

CJS Bankruptcy § 285, Captions.

Rule 9005.1. Constitutional Challenge to a Statute—Notice, Certification, and Intervention

Rule 5.1 F.R.Civ.P. applies in cases under the Code. (Added Apr. 30, 2007, eff. Dec. 1, 2007.)

ADVISORY COMMITTEE NOTES

2007 Adoption

The rule is added to adopt the new rule added to the Federal Rules of Civil Procedure. The new Civil Rule replaces Rule 24(c) F. R. Civ. P., so the cross reference to Civil Rule 24 contained in Rule 7024 is no longer sufficient to bring the provisions of new Civil Rule 5.1 into adversary proceedings. This rule also makes Civil Rule 5.1 applicable to all contested matters and other proceedings within the bankruptcy case.

Rule 9006. Computing and Extending Time

(a) Computing time

The following rules apply in computing any time period specified in these rules, in the Federal Rules of Civil Procedure, in any local rule or court order, or in any statute that does not specify a method of computing time.

(1) Period stated in days or a longer unit

When the period is stated in days or a longer unit of time:

(A) exclude the day of the event that triggers the period;

(B) count every day, including intermediate Saturdays, Sundays, and legal holidays; and

(C) include the last day of the period, but if the last day is a Saturday, Sunday, or legal holiday, the period continues to run until the end of the next day that is not a Saturday, Sunday, or legal holiday.

(2) Period stated in hours

When the period is stated in hours:

(A) begin counting immediately on the occurrence of the event that triggers the period;

(B) count every hour, including hours during intermediate Saturdays, Sundays, and legal holidays; and

(C) if the period would end on a Saturday, Sunday, or legal holiday, then continue the period until the same time on the next day that is not a Saturday, Sunday, or legal holiday.

(3) Inaccessibility of clerk's office

Unless the court orders otherwise, if the clerk's office is inaccessible:

(A) on the last day for filing under Rule 9006(a)(1), then the time for filing is extended to the first accessible day that is not a Saturday, Sunday, or legal holiday; or

(B) during the last hour for filing under Rule 9006(a)(2), then the time for filing is extended to the same time on the first accessible day that is not a Saturday, Sunday, or legal holiday.

(4) "Last day" defined

Unless a different time is set by a statute, local rule, or order in the case, the last day ends:

(A) for electronic filing, at midnight in the court's time zone; and

(B) for filing by other means, when the clerk's office is scheduled to close.

(5) "Next day" defined

The "next day" is determined by continuing to count forward when the period is measured after an event and backward when measured before an event.

(6) "Legal holiday" defined

"Legal holiday" means:

(A) the day set aside by statute for observing New Year's Day, Martin Luther King Jr.'s Birthday, Washington's Birthday, Memorial Day, Independence Day, Labor Day, Columbus Day, Veterans' Day, Thanksgiving Day, or Christmas Day;

(B) any day declared a holiday by the President or Congress; and

(C) for periods that are measured after an event, any other day declared a holiday by the state where the district court is located. (In this rule, "state" includes the District of Columbia and any United States commonwealth or territory.)

(b) Enlargement

(1) In general

Except as provided in paragraphs (2) and (3) of this subdivision, when an act is required or allowed to be done at or within a specified period by these rules or by a notice given thereunder or by order of court, the court for cause shown may at any time in its discretion (1) with or without motion or notice order the period enlarged if the request therefor is made before the expiration of the period originally prescribed or as extended by a previous order or (2) on motion made after the expiration of the specified period permit the act to be done where the failure to act was the result of excusable neglect.

(2) Enlargement not permitted

The court may not enlarge the time for taking action under Rules 1007(d), 2003(a) and (d), 7052, 9023, and 9024.

(3) Enlargement governed by other rules

The court may enlarge the time for taking action under Rules 1006(b)(2), 1017(e), 3002(c), 4003(b), 4004(a), 4007(c), 4008(a), 8002, and 9033, only to the extent and under the conditions stated in those rules. In addition, the court may enlarge the time to file the statement required under Rule 1007(b)(7), and to file schedules and statements in a small business case under § 1116(3) of the Code, only to the extent and under the conditions stated in Rule 1007(c).

(c) Reduction

(1) In general

Except as provided in paragraph (2) of this subdivision, when an act is required or allowed to be done at or within a specified time by these rules or by a notice given thereunder or by order of court, the court for cause shown may in its discretion with or without motion or notice order the period reduced.

(2) Reduction not permitted

The court may not reduce the time for taking action under Rules 2002(a)(7), 2003(a), 3002(c), 3014, 3015, 4001(b)(2), (c)(2), 4003(a), 4004(a), 4007(c), 4008(a), 8002, and 9033(b). In addition, the court may not reduce the time under Rule 1007(c) to file the statement required by Rule 1007(b)(7).

(d) For motions—affidavits

A written motion, other than one which may be heard ex parte, and notice of any hearing shall be served not later than seven days before the time specified for such hearing, unless a different period is fixed by these rules or by order of the court. Such an order may for cause shown be made on ex parte application. When a motion is supported by affidavit, the affidavit shall be served with the motion; and, except as otherwise provided in Rule 9023, opposing affidavits may be served not later than one day before the hearing, unless the court permits them to be served at some other time.

(e) Time of service

Service of process and service of any paper other than process or of notice by mail is complete on mailing.

(f) Additional time after service by mail or under Rule 5(b)(2)(D), (E), or (F) F. R. Civ. P.

When there is a right or requirement to act or undertake some proceedings within a prescribed period after service and that service is by mail or under Rule 5(b)(2)(D), (E), or (F) F.R.Civ.P., three days are added after the prescribed period would otherwise expire under Rule 9006(a).

(g) Grain storage facility cases

This rule shall not limit the court's authority under § 557 of the Code to enter orders governing procedures in cases in which the debtor is an owner or operator of a grain storage facility.

(As amended Mar. 30, 1987, eff. Aug. 1, 1987; Apr. 25, 1989, eff. Aug. 1, 1989; Apr. 30, 1991, eff. Aug. 1, 1991; Apr. 23, 1996, eff. Dec. 1, 1996; Apr. 29, 1999, eff. Dec. 1, 1999; Apr. 23, 2001, eff. Dec. 1, 2001; Apr. 25, 2005, eff. Dec. 1, 2005; Apr. 23, 2008, eff. Dec. 1, 2008; Mar. 26, 2009, eff. Dec. 1, 2009.)

ADVISORY COMMITTEE NOTES

Subdivision (a). This rule is an adaptation of Rule 6 F.R.Civ.P. It governs the time for acts to be done and proceedings to be had in cases under the Code and any litigation arising therein.

Subdivision (b) is patterned after Rule 6(b) F.R.Civ.P. and Rule 26(b) F.R.App.P.

Paragraph (1) of this subdivision confers on the court discretion generally to authorize extensions of time for doing acts required or allowed by these rules or orders of court. The exceptions to this general authority to extend the time are contained in paragraphs (2) and (3).

In the interest of prompt administration of bankruptcy cases certain time periods may not be extended. Paragraph (2) lists the rules which establish time periods which may not be extended: Rule 1007(d), time for filing a list of 20 largest creditors; Rule 1017(b)(3), 30 day period for sending notice of dismissal for failure to pay the filing fee; Rule 1019(2), 20 day period for notice of conversion to a chapter 7 case; Rule 2003(a), meeting of creditors not more than 40 days after order for relief; Rule 2003(d), 10 days for filing a motion for resolution of an election dispute; Rule 3014, time for the § 1111(b)(2) election; Rule 4001(b), expiration of stay 30 days following the commencement of final hearing; Rule 7052(b), 10 day period to move to amend findings of fact; Rule 9015(f), 20 day period to move for judgment notwithstanding the verdict; Rule 9023, 10 day period to move for a new trial; and Rule 9024, time to move for relief from judgment.

Many rules which establish a time for doing an act also contain a specific authorization and standard for granting an extension of time and, in some cases, limit the length of an extension. In some instances it would be inconsistent with the objective of the rule and sound administration of the case to permit extension under Rule 9006(b)(1), but with respect to the other rules it is appropriate that the power to extend time be supplemented by Rule 9006(b)(1). Unless a rule which contains a specific authorization to extend time is listed in paragraph (3) of this subdivision, an extension of the time may be granted under paragraph (1) of this subdivision. If a rule is included in paragraph (3) an extension may not be granted under paragraph (1). The following rules are listed in paragraph (3): Rule 1006(b)(2), time for paying the filing fee in installments; Rule 3002(c), 90 day period for filing a claim in a chapter 7 or 13 case; Rule 4003(b), 30 days for filing objections to a claim of exemptions; Rule 4004(a), 60 day period to object to a discharge; Rule 4007(b), 60 day period to file a dischargeability complaint; and Rule 8002, 10 days for filing a notice of appeal.

Subdivision (c). Paragraph (1) of this subdivision authorizes the reduction of the time periods established by these rules or an order of the court. Excluded from this general authority are the time periods established by the rules referred to in paragraph (2) of the subdivision: Rule 2002(a) and (b), 20 day and 25 day notices of certain hearings and actions in the case; Rule 2003(a), meeting of creditors to be not less than 20 days after the order for relief; Rule 3002(c), 90 days for filing a claim in a chapter 7 or 13 case; Rule 3014, time for § 1111(b)(2) election; Rule 3015, 10 day period after filing of petition to file a chapter 13 plan; Rule 4003(a), 15 days for a dependent to claim exemptions; Rule 4004(a), 60 day period to object to a discharge; Rule 4007(c), 60 day period to file a dischargeability complaint; and Rule 8002, 10 days for filing a notice of appeal. Reduction of the time periods fixed in the rules referred to in this subdivision would be inconsistent with the purposes of those rules and would cause harmful uncertainty.

[The Advisory Committee Note for subd. (c) above states that Rule 2002(a) and (b) are excluded from the general authority for the reduction of time periods while the text of subd. (c)(2) specifies that only Rule 2002(a)(4) and (a)(8) are excluded.]

Subdivision (d) is derived from Rule 6(d) F.R.Civ.P. The reference is to Rule 9023 instead of to Rule 59(c) F.R.Civ.P. because Rule 9023 incorporates Rule 59 F.R.Civ.P. but excepts therefrom motions to reconsider orders allowing and disallowing claims.

Subdivision (f) is new and is the same as Rule 6(e) F.R.Civ.P.

1987 Amendment

Subdivision (a) is amended to conform to the 1984 amendments to Rule 6 F.R.Civ.P.

Subdivision (b). The reference to Rule 4001(b) in paragraph (3) is deleted because of the amendments made to Rule 4001. Rule 9033, which is new, contains specific provisions governing the extension of time to file objections to proposed findings of fact and conclusions of law. Rule 9033 is added to the rules referred to in paragraph (3).

Subdivision (c). Rule 4001(b)(2) and (c)(2) provide that a final hearing on a motion to use cash collateral or a motion for authority to obtain credit may be held no earlier than 15 days after the filing of the motion. These two rules are added to paragraph (2) to make it clear that the 15 day period may not be reduced. Rule 9033 is also added to paragraph (2).

Subdivision (g) is new. Under § 557 of the Code, as enacted by the 1984 amendments, the court is directed to expedite grain storage facility cases. This subdivision makes it clear this rule does not limit the court's authority under § 557.

The original Advisory Committee Note to this rule included the 25 day notice period of Rule 2002(b) as a time period which may not be reduced under Rule 9006(C)(2). This was an error.

1989 Amendment

Prior to 1987, subdivision (a) provided that intermediate weekends and legal holidays would not be counted in the computation of a time period if the prescribed or allowed time was less than 7 days. This rule was amended in 1987 to conform to Fed. R. Civ. P. 6(a) which provides for the exclusion of intermediate weekends and legal holidays if the time prescribed or allowed is less than 11 days. An undesirable result of the 1987 amendment was that 10-day time periods prescribed in the interest of prompt administration of bankruptcy cases were extended to at least 14 calendar days.

As a result of the present amendment, 10-day time periods prescribed or allowed will no longer be extended to at least 14 calendar days because of intermediate weekends and legal holidays.

1991 Amendment

As a result of the 1989 amendment to this rule, the method of computing time under subdivision (a) is not the same as the method of computing time under Rule 6(a) F.R.Civ.P. Subdivision (a) is amended to provide that it governs the computation of time periods prescribed by the Federal Rules of Civil Procedure when the Bankruptcy Rules make a civil rule applicable to a bankruptcy case or proceeding.

Subdivision (b)(2) is amended because of the deletion of Rule 1019(2). Reference to Rule 9015(f) is deleted because of the abrogation of Rule 9015 in 1987.

Subdivision (b)(3) is amended to limit the enlargement of time regarding dismissal of a chapter 7 case for substantial abuse in accordance with Rule 1017(e).

1996 Amendment

Subdivision (c)(2) is amended to conform to the abrogation of Rule 2002(a)(4) and the renumbering of Rule 2002(a)(8) to Rule 2002(a)(7).

GAP Report on Rule 9006. No changes since publication, except for a stylistic change.

1999 Amendments

Rule 9006(b)(2) is amended to conform to the abrogation of Rule 1017(b)(3).

Gap Report on Rule 9006. The proposed amendment to Rule 9006(b)(2) has been added as a technical change to conform to the abrogation of Rule 1017(b)(3). The proposed amendment to Rule 9006(c)(2), providing that the time under Rule 1019(6) to file a request for payment of an administrative expense after a case is converted to chapter 7 could not be reduced by the court, was deleted. The proposed amendments to Rule 1019(6) have been changed so that the court will fix the time for filing the request for payment. Since the court will fix the time limit, the court should have the power to reduce it. See Gap Report to Rule 1019(6).

2001 Amendments

Rule 5(b) F. R. Civ. P., which is made applicable in adversary proceedings by Rule 7005, is being restyled and amended to authorize service by electronic means—or any other means not otherwise authorized under Rule 5(b)—if consent is obtained from the person served. The amendment to Rule 9006(f) is intended to extend the three-day "mail rule" to service under Rule 5(b)(2)(D), including service by electronic means. The three-day rule also will apply to service under Rule 5(b)(2)(C) F. R. Civ. P. when the person served has no known address and the paper is served by leaving a copy with the clerk of the court.

CHANGES MADE AFTER PUBLICATION AND COMMENTS

No changes were made.

2005 Amendments

Rule 9006(f) is amended, consistent with a corresponding amendment to Rule 6(e) of the F.R. Civ. P, to clarify the method of counting the number of days to respond after service either by mail or under Civil Rule 5(b)(2)(C) or (D).

Three days are added after the prescribed period expires. If, before the application of Rule 9006(f), the prescribed period is less than 8 days, intervening Saturdays, Sundays, and legal holidays are excluded from the calculation under Rule 9006(a). Some illustrations may be helpful.

Under existing Rule 9006(a), assuming that there are no legal holidays and that a response is due in seven days, if a paper is filed on a Monday, the seven day response period commences on Tuesday and concludes on Wednesday of the next week. Adding three days to the end of the period would extend it to Saturday, but because the response period ends on a weekend, the response day would be the following Monday, two weeks after the filing of the initial paper. If the paper is filed on a Tuesday, the seven-day response period would end on the following Thursday, and the response time would also be the following Monday. If the paper is mailed on a Wednesday, the initial seven-day period would expire nine days later on a Friday, but the response would again be due on the following Monday because of Rule 9006(f). If the paper is mailed on a Thursday, however, the seven day period ends on Monday, eleven days after the mailing of the service because of the exclusion of the two intervening Saturdays and Sundays. The response is due three days later on the following Thursday. If the paper is mailed on a Friday, the seven day period would conclude on a Tuesday, and the response is due three days later on a Friday.

No other change in the system of counting time is intended. Other changes are stylistic.

2008 Amendments

Subdivision (b)(3) is amended to implement § 1116(3) of the Code, as amended by the 2005 amendments, which places specific limits on the extension of time for filing schedules and statements of financial affairs in a small business case.

Subdivisions (b)(3) and (c)(2) are amended to provide that enlargement or reduction of the time to file the statement of completion of a personal financial management course required by Rule 1007(b)(7) are governed by Rule 1007(c). Likewise, the amendments to subdivisions (b)(3) and (c)(2) recognize that the enlargement of time to file a reaffirmation agreement is governed by Rule 4008(a), and that reduction of the time provided under that rule is not permitted.

Other amendments are stylistic.

2009 Amendments

Subdivision (a). Subdivision (a) has been amended to simplify and clarify the provisions that describe how deadlines are computed. Subdivision (a) governs the computation of any time period found in a Federal Rule of Bankruptcy Procedure, a Federal Rule of Civil Procedure, a statute, a local rule, or a court order. In accordance with Bankruptcy Rule 9029(a), a local rule may not direct that a deadline be computed in a manner inconsistent with subdivision (a).

The time-computation provisions of subdivision (a) apply only when a time period must be computed. They do not apply when a fixed time to act is set. The amendments thus carry forward the approach taken in *Violette v. P.A. Days, Inc.*, 427 F.3d 1015, 1016 (6th Cir. 2005) (holding that Civil Rule 6(a) "does not apply to situations where the court has established a specific calendar day as a deadline"), and reject the contrary holding of *In re American Healthcare Management, Inc.*, 900 F.2d 827, 832 (5th Cir. 1990) (holding that Bankruptcy Rule 9006(a) governs treatment of date-certain

deadline set by court order). If, for example, the date for filing is "no later than November 1, 2007," subdivision (a) does not govern. But if a filing is required to be made "within 10 days" or "within 72 hours," subdivision (a) describes how that deadline is computed.

Subdivision (a) does not apply when computing a time period set by a statute if the statute specifies a method of computing time. *See, e.g.*, 11 U.S.C. § 527(a)(2) (debt relief agencies must provide a written notice to an assisted person "not later than 3 business days" after providing bankruptcy assistance services).

Subdivision (a)(1). New subdivision (a)(1) addresses the computation of time periods that are stated in days. It also applies to time periods that are stated in weeks, months, or years. *See, e.g.*, Federal Rule of Civil Procedure 60(c)(1) made applicable to bankruptcy cases under Rule 9024. Subdivision (a)(1)(B)'s directive to "count every day" is relevant only if the period is stated in days (not weeks, months, or years).

Under former Rule 9006(a), a period of eight days or more was computed differently than a period of less than eight days. Intermediate Saturdays, Sundays, and legal holidays were included in computing the longer periods, but excluded in computing the shorter periods. Former Rule 9006(a) thus made computing deadlines unnecessarily complicated and led to counterintuitive results.

Under new subdivision (a)(1), all deadlines stated in days (no matter the length) are computed in the same way. The day of the event that triggers the deadline is not counted. All other days—including intermediate Saturdays, Sundays, and legal holidays—are counted, with only one exception: If the period ends on a Saturday, Sunday, or legal holiday, then the deadline falls on the next day that is not a Saturday, Sunday, or legal holiday. An illustration is provided below in the discussion of subdivision (a)(5). Subdivision (a)(3) addresses filing deadlines that expire on a day when the clerk's office is inaccessible.

Where subdivision (a) formerly referred to the "act, event, or default" that triggers the deadline, new subdivision (a) refers simply to the "event" that triggers the deadline; this change in terminology is adopted for brevity and simplicity, and is not intended to change meaning.

Periods previously expressed as less than eight days will be shortened as a practical matter by the decision to count intermediate Saturdays, Sundays, and legal holidays in computing all periods. Many of those periods have been lengthened to compensate for the change. *See, e.g.*, Rules 2008 (trustee's duty to notify court of acceptance of the appointment within five days is extended to seven days); 6004(b) (time for filing and service of objection to proposed use, sale or lease of property extended from five days prior to the hearing to seven days prior to the hearing); and 9006(d) (time for giving notice of a hearing extended from five days prior to the hearing to seven days).

Most of the 10–day periods were adjusted to meet the change in computation method by setting 14 days as the new period. *See, e.g.*, Rules 1007(h) (10–day period to file supplemental schedule for property debtor becomes entitled to acquire after the commencement of the case is extended to 14 days); 3020(e) (10–day stay of order confirming a chapter 11 plan extended to 14 days); 8002(a) (10–day period in which to file notice of appeal extended to 14 days). A 14–day period also has the advantage that the final day falls on the same day of the week as the event that triggered the period—the 14th day after a Monday, for example, is a Monday. This advantage of using week-long periods led to adopting seven-day periods to replace some of the periods set at less than 10 days, 21–day periods to replace 20–day periods, and 28–day periods to replace 25–day periods. Thirty-day and longer periods, however, were generally retained without change.

Subdivision (a)(2). New subdivision (a)(2) addresses the computation of time periods that are stated in hours. No such deadline currently appears in the Federal Rules of Bankruptcy Procedure. But some statutes contain deadlines stated in hours, as do some court orders issued in expedited proceedings.

Under subdivision (a)(2), a deadline stated in hours starts to run immediately on the occurrence of the event that triggers the deadline. The deadline generally ends when the time expires. If, however, the time period expires at a specific time (say, 2:17 p.m.) on a Saturday, Sunday, or legal holiday, then the deadline is extended to the same time (2:17 p.m.) on the next day that is not a Saturday, Sunday, or legal holiday. Periods stated in hours are not to be "rounded up" to the next whole hour. Subdivision (a)(3) addresses situations when the clerk's office is inaccessible during the last hour before a filing deadline expires.

Subdivision (a)(2)(B) directs that every hour be counted. Thus, for example, a 72–hour period that commences at 10:23 a.m. on Friday, November 2, 2007, will run until 9:23 a.m. on Monday, November 5; the discrepancy in start and end times in this example results from the intervening shift from daylight saving time to standard time.

Subdivision (a)(3). When determining the last day of a filing period stated in days or a longer unit of time, a day on which the clerk's office is not accessible because of the weather or another reason is treated like a Saturday, Sunday, or legal holiday. When determining the end of a filing period stated in hours, if the clerk's office is inaccessible during the last hour of the filing period computed under subdivision (a)(2) then the period is extended to the same time on the next day that is not a weekend, holiday, or day when the clerk's office is inaccessible.

Subdivision (a)(3)'s extensions apply "[u]nless the court orders otherwise." In some circumstances, the court might not wish a period of inaccessibility to trigger a full 24–hour extension; in those instances, the court can specify a briefer extension.

The text of the rule no longer refers to "weather or other conditions" as the reason for the inaccessibility of the clerk's office. The reference to "weather" was deleted from the text to underscore that inaccessibility can occur for reasons unrelated to weather, such as an outage of the electronic filing system. Weather can still be a reason for inaccessibility of the clerk's office. The rule does not attempt to define inaccessibility. Rather, the concept will continue to develop through caselaw. *See, e.g.,* William G. Phelps, *When Is Office of Clerk of Court Inaccessible Due to Weather or Other Conditions for Purpose of Computing Time Period for Filing Papers under Rule 6(a) of Federal Rules of Civil Procedure,* 135 A.L.R. Fed. 259 (1996) (collecting cases). In addition, many local provisions address inaccessibility for purposes of electronic filing. *See, e.g.,* D. Kan. Rule 5.4.11 ("A Filing User whose filing is made untimely as the result of a technical failure may seek appropriate relief from the court.").

Subdivision (a)(4). New subdivision (a)(4) defines the end of the last day of a period for purposes of subdivision (a)(1).

Subdivision (a)(4) does not apply in computing periods stated in hours under subdivision (a)(2), and does not apply if a different time is set by a statute, local rule, or order in the case. A local rule may provide, for example, that papers filed in a drop box after the normal hours of the clerk's office are filed as of the day that is date-stamped on the papers by a device in the drop box.

28 U.S.C. § 452 provides that "[a]ll courts of the United States shall be deemed always open for the purpose of filing proper papers, issuing and returning process, and making motions and orders." A corresponding provision exists in Rule 5001(a). Some courts have held that these provisions permit an after-hours filing by handing the papers to an appropriate official. *See, e.g., Casalduc v. Diaz,* 117 F.2d 915, 917 (1st Cir. 1941). Subdivision (a)(4) does not address the effect of the statute on the question of after-hours filing; instead, the rule is designed to deal with filings in the ordinary course without regard to Section 452.

Subdivision (a)(5). New subdivision (a)(5) defines the "next" day for purposes of subdivisions (a)(1)(C) and (a)(2)(C). The Federal Rules of Bankruptcy Procedure contain both forward-looking time periods and backward-looking time periods. A forward-looking time period requires something to be done within a period of time *after* an event. *See, e.g.,* Rules 1007(c) (the schedules, statements, and other documents shall be filed by the debtor within 14 days of the entry of the order for relief"); 1019(5)(B)(ii) ("the trustee, not later than 30 days after conversion of the case, shall file and transmit to the United States trustee a final report and account"); and 7012(a) ("If a complaint is duly served, the defendant shall serve an answer within 30 days after the issuance of the summons, except when a different time is prescribed by the court.").

A backward-looking time period requires something to be done within a period of time *before* an event. *See, e.g.,* Rules 6004(b) ("an objection to a proposed use, sale, or lease of property shall be filed and served not less than seven days before the date set for the proposed action"); 9006(d) ("A written motion, other than one which may be heard ex parte, and notice of any hearing shall be served not later than seven days before the time specified for such hearing"). In determining what is the "next" day for purposes of subdivisions (a)(1)(C) and (a)(2)(C), one should continue counting in the same direction—that is, forward when computing a forward-looking period and backward when computing a backward-looking period. If, for example, a filing is due within 10 days *after* an event, and the tenth day falls on Saturday, September 1, 2007, then the filing is due on Tuesday, September 4, 2007 (Monday, September 3, is Labor Day). But if a filing is due 10 days *before* an event, and the tenth day falls on Saturday, September 1, then the filing is due on Friday, August 31.

Subdivision (a)(6). New subdivision (a)(6) defines "legal holiday" for purposes of the Federal Rules of Bankruptcy Procedure, including the time-computation provisions of subdivision (a). Subdivision (a)(6) continues to include within the definition of "legal holiday" days that are declared a holiday by the President or Congress.

For forward-counted periods—*i.e.,* periods that are measured after an event—subdivision (a)(6)(C) includes certain state holidays within the definition of legal holidays, and defines the term "state"—for purposes of subdivision (a)(6)— to include the District of Columbia and any commonwealth or territory of the United States. Thus, for purposes of subdivision (a)(6)'s definition of "legal holiday," "state" includes the District of Columbia, Guam, American Samoa, the U.S. Virgin Islands, the Commonwealth of Puerto Rico, and the Commonwealth of the Northern Mariana Islands.

However, state legal holidays are not recognized in computing backward-counted periods. For both forward- and backward-counted periods, the rule thus protects those who may be unsure of the effect of state holidays. For forward-counted deadlines, treating state holidays the same as federal holidays extends the deadline. Thus, someone who thought that the federal courts might be closed on a state holiday would be safeguarded against an inadvertent late filing. In contrast, for backward-counted deadlines, not giving state holidays the treatment of federal holidays allows filing on the state holiday itself rather than the day before. Take, for example, Monday, April 21, 2008 (Patriot's Day, a legal holiday in the relevant state). If a filing is due 14 days after an event, and the fourteenth day is April 21, then the filing is due on Tuesday, April 22 because Monday, April 21 counts as a legal holiday. But if a filing is due 14 days before an event, and the fourteenth day is April 21, the filing is due on Monday, April 21; the fact that April 21 is a state holiday does not make April 21 a legal holiday for purposes of computing this backward-counted deadline. But note that if the clerk's office is inaccessible on Monday, April 21, then subdivision (a)(3) extends the April 21 filing deadline forward to the next accessible day that is not a Saturday, Sunday or legal holiday—no earlier than Tuesday, April 22.

The rule is amended [this Committee note relates to subdivision (d)] to implement changes in connection with the amendment to Rule 9006(a) and the manner by which time is computed under the rules. The deadline in the rule is amended to substitute a deadline that is a multiple of seven days. Throughout the rules, deadlines are amended in the following manner:

- 5–day periods become 7–day periods
- 10–day periods become 14–day periods
- 15–day periods become 14–day periods
- 20–day periods become 21–day periods
- 25–day periods become 28–day periods

Subdivision (f) is amended to conform to the changes made to Rule 5(b)(2) of the Federal Rules of Civil Procedure as a part of the Civil Rules Restyling Project. As a part of that project, subparagraphs (b)(2)(C) and (D) of that rule were rewritten as subparagraphs (b)(2)(D), (E), and (F). The cross reference to those rules contained in subdivision (f) of this rule is corrected by this amendment.

CROSS REFERENCES

Completion of service by mail upon mailing, see Fed.Rules Civ.Proc. Rule 5, 28 USCA.

Computation and extension of time, see Federal Rules of Appellate Procedure Rule 26, 28 USCA.

Motions—

Form and service, see Fed.Rules Bankr.Proc. Rule 9013, 11 USCA.

On appeal to district court or bankruptcy appellate panel acted upon without hearing at any time, see Fed.Rules Bankr.Proc. Rule 8011, 11 USCA.

Time, see Fed.Rules Civ.Proc. Rule 6, 28 USCA.

LIBRARY REFERENCES

American Digest System

Bankruptcy ⟲2127.1, 2132, 2156, 2158.

Key Number System Topic No. 51.

Corpus Juris Secundum

CJS Bankruptcy § 288, Applications.

CJS Bankruptcy § 289, Motions.

CJS Bankruptcy § 295, Notice by Mail.

CJS Bankruptcy § 307, Computation.

CJS Bankruptcy § 308, Enlargement.

CJS Bankruptcy § 309, Reduction.

CJS Bankruptcy § 315, Judgments--Relief from Judgment or Order; Collateral Attack.

CJS Bankruptcy § 345, List of Creditors and Others--Twenty Largest Unsecured Creditors.

CJS Bankruptcy § 349, Schedules and Statements Regarding Debtor's Assets, Liabilities, Income, Expenditures, and Finances.

CJS Bankruptcy § 356, Extension of Time for Filing.

CJS Bankruptcy § 358, Amendment.

CJS Bankruptcy § 616, Prosecution and Defense of Proceedings; Expedited Procedures.

CJS Bankruptcy § 678, Transfer to Occur Within Preference Period.

CJS Bankruptcy § 791, Notice.

CJS Bankruptcy § 854, Expedited Determination of Disposition of Grain Assets.

CJS Bankruptcy § 871, Motion for Authorization.

CJS Bankruptcy § 872, Notice and Hearing; Ex Parte Relief.

CJS Bankruptcy § 900, Motion for Authorization to Obtain Credit; Notice and Hearing.

CJS Bankruptcy § 1018, Extension of Time; Excuse for Delay.

CJS Bankruptcy § 1047, Time for Proceedings; Extension of Time.

CJS Bankruptcy § 1083, Time for Proceedings--Extension of Time.

Rule 9007. General Authority to Regulate Notices

When notice is to be given under these rules, the court shall designate, if not otherwise specified herein, the time within which, the entities to whom, and the form and manner in which the notice shall be given. When feasible, the court may order any notices under these rules to be combined.

(As amended Mar. 30, 1987, eff. Aug. 1, 1987.)

CROSS REFERENCES

Construction of phrase "after notice and a hearing", see 11 USCA § 102.

Notice as is appropriate of order for relief, see 11 USCA § 342.

LIBRARY REFERENCES

American Digest System

Bankruptcy ☞2131.

Key Number System Topic No. 51.

Rule 9008.   Service or Notice by Publication

Whenever these rules require or authorize service or notice by publication, the court shall, to the extent not otherwise specified in these rules, determine the form and manner thereof, including the newspaper or other medium to be used and the number of publications.

CROSS REFERENCES

Construction of phrase "after notice and a hearing", see 11 USCA § 102.

Notice as is appropriate of order for relief, see 11 USCA § 342.

LIBRARY REFERENCES

American Digest System

Bankruptcy ☞2131, 2158.

Key Number System Topic No. 51.

Corpus Juris Secundum

CJS Bankruptcy § 297, Notice by Other Means.

Rule 9009.   Forms

Except as otherwise provided in Rule 3016(d), the Official Forms prescribed by the Judicial Conference of the United States shall be observed and used with alterations as may be appropriate. Forms may be combined and their contents rearranged to permit economies in their use. The Director of the Administrative Office of the United States Courts may issue additional forms for use under the Code. The forms shall be construed to be consistent with these rules and the Code.

(As amended Apr. 30, 1991, eff. Aug. 1, 1991; Apr. 23, 2008, eff. Dec. 1, 2008.)

ADVISORY COMMITTEE NOTES

The rule continues the obligatory character of the Official Forms in the interest of facilitating the processing of the paperwork of bankruptcy administration, but provides that Official Forms will be prescribed by the Judicial Conference of the United States. The Supreme Court and the Congress will thus be relieved of the burden of considering the large number of complex forms used in bankruptcy practice. The use of the Official Forms has generally been held subject to a "rule of substantial compliance" and some of these rules, for example Rule 1002, specifically state that the filed document need only "conform substantially" to the Official Form. See also Rule 9005. The second sentence recognizes the propriety of combining and rearranging Official Forms to take advantage of technological developments and resulting economies.

The Director of the Administrative Office is authorized to issue additional forms for the guidance of the bar.

1991 Amendment

Rule 9029 is amended to clarify that local court rules may not prohibit or limit the use of the Official Forms.

2008 Amendments

The rule is amended to provide that a plan proponent in a small business chapter 11 case need not use an Official Form of a plan of reorganization and disclosure statement. The use of those forms is optional, and under Rule 3016(d) the proponent may submit a plan and disclosure statement in those cases that does not conform to the Official Forms.

CROSS REFERENCES

Correction of harmless errors or cure of harmless omissions, see Fed.Rules Bankr.Proc. Rule 9005, 11 USCA.

LIBRARY REFERENCES

American Digest System

Bankruptcy ☞2129.

Key Number System Topic No. 51.

Corpus Juris Secundum

CJS Bankruptcy § 17, Official Forms.

CJS Bankruptcy § 283, Official Forms.

CJS Bankruptcy § 336, Contents, Signature, and Verification.

Rule 9010.   Representation and Appearances; Powers of Attorney

(a) Authority to act personally or by attorney

A debtor, creditor, equity security holder, indenture trustee, committee or other party may (1) appear in a case under the Code and act either in the entity's own behalf or by an attorney authorized to practice in the court, and (2) perform any act not constituting the practice of law, by an authorized agent, attorney in fact, or proxy.

(b) Notice of appearance

An attorney appearing for a party in a case under the Code shall file a notice of appearance with the attorney's name, office address and telephone number, unless the attorney's appearance is otherwise noted in the record.

(c) Power of attorney

The authority of any agent, attorney in fact, or proxy to represent a creditor for any purpose other than the execution and filing of a proof of claim or the acceptance or rejection of a plan shall be evidenced by a power of attorney conforming substantially to the appropriate Official Form. The execution of any such power of attorney shall be acknowledged before one of the officers enumerated in 28 U.S.C. § 459, § 953, Rule 9012, or a person authorized to administer oaths under the laws of the state where the oath is administered.

(As amended Mar. 30, 1987, eff. Aug. 1, 1987; Apr. 30, 1991, eff. Aug. 1, 1991.)

ADVISORY COMMITTEE NOTES

This rule is substantially the same as former Bankruptcy Rule 910 and does not purport to change prior holdings prohibiting a corporation from appearing pro se. See In re Las Colinas Development Corp., 585 F.2d 7 (1st Cir.1978).

1987 Amendment

Subdivision (c) is amended to include a reference to Rule 9012 which is amended to authorize a bankruptcy judge or clerk to administer oaths.

1991 Amendment

References to Official Form numbers in subdivision (c) are deleted in anticipation of future revision and renumbering of the Official Forms.

CROSS REFERENCES

Ex parte relief from automatic stay, see Fed.Rules Bankr. Proc. Rule 4001, 11 USCA.

Payment of dividends to persons authorized to receive them by power of attorney executed and filed in accordance with this rule, see Fed.Rules Bankr.Proc. Rule 3009, 11 USCA.

LIBRARY REFERENCES

American Digest System

Bankruptcy ⊜2127.1.

Key Number System Topic No. 51.

Corpus Juris Secundum

CJS Bankruptcy § 142, Representation and Appearances; Powers of Attorney.

Rule 9011. Signing of Papers; Representations to the Court; Sanctions; Verification and Copies of Papers

(a) Signing of papers

Every petition, pleading, written motion, and other paper, except a list, schedule, or statement, or amendments thereto, shall be signed by at least one attorney of record in the attorney's individual name. A party who is not represented by an attorney shall sign all papers. Each paper shall state the signer's address and telephone number, if any. An unsigned paper shall be stricken unless omission of the signature is corrected promptly after being called to the attention of the attorney or party.

(b) Representations to the court

By presenting to the court (whether by signing, filing, submitting, or later advocating) a petition, pleading, written motion, or other paper, an attorney or unrepresented party is certifying that to the best of the person's knowledge, information, and belief, formed after an inquiry reasonable under the circumstances,— [1]

(1) it is not being presented for any improper purpose, such as to harass or to cause unnecessary delay or needless increase in the cost of litigation;

(2) the claims, defenses, and other legal contentions therein are warranted by existing law or by a nonfrivolous argument for the extension, modification, or reversal of existing law or the establishment of new law;

(3) the allegations and other factual contentions have evidentiary support or, if specifically so identified, are likely to have evidentiary support after a reasonable opportunity for further investigation or discovery; and

(4) the denials of factual contentions are warranted on the evidence or, if specifically so identified, are reasonably based on a lack of information or belief.

(c) Sanctions

If, after notice and a reasonable opportunity to respond, the court determines that subdivision (b) has been violated, the court may, subject to the conditions stated below, impose an appropriate sanction upon the attorneys, law firms, or parties that have violated subdivision (b) or are responsible for the violation.

(1) How initiated

(A) By motion

A motion for sanctions under this rule shall be made separately from other motions or requests and shall describe the specific conduct alleged to violate subdivision (b). It shall be served as provided in Rule 7004. The motion for sanctions may not be filed with or presented to the court unless, within 21 days after service of the motion (or such other period as the court may prescribe), the challenged paper, claim, defense, contention, allegation, or denial is not withdrawn or appropriately corrected, except that this limitation shall not apply if the conduct alleged is the filing of a petition in violation of subdivision (b). If warranted, the court may award to the party prevailing on the motion the reasonable expenses and attorney's fees incurred in presenting or opposing the motion. Absent exceptional circumstances, a law firm shall be held jointly responsible for violations committed by its partners, associates, and employees.

(B) On court's initiative

On its own initiative, the court may enter an order describing the specific conduct that appears to violate subdivision (b) and directing an attorney, law firm, or party to show cause why it has not violated subdivision (b) with respect thereto.

(2) Nature of sanction; limitations

A sanction imposed for violation of this rule shall be limited to what is sufficient to deter repetition of such conduct or comparable conduct by others similarly situated. Subject to the limitations in subparagraphs (A) and (B), the sanction may consist of, or include, directives of a nonmonetary nature, an order to pay a penalty into court, or, if imposed on motion and warranted for effective deterrence, an order directing payment to the movant of some or all of the reasonable attorneys' fees and other expenses incurred as a direct result of the violation.

(A) Monetary sanctions may not be awarded against a represented party for a violation of subdivision (b)(2).

(B) Monetary sanctions may not be awarded on the court's initiative unless the court issues its order to show cause before a voluntary dismissal or settlement of the claims made by or against the party which is, or whose attorneys are, to be sanctioned.

(3) Order

When imposing sanctions, the court shall describe the conduct determined to constitute a violation of this rule and explain the basis for the sanction imposed.

(d) Inapplicability to discovery

Subdivisions (a) through (c) of this rule do not apply to disclosures and discovery requests, responses, objections, and motions that are subject to the provisions of Rules 7026 through 7037.

(e) Verification

Except as otherwise specifically provided by these rules, papers filed in a case under the Code need not be verified. Whenever verification is required by these rules, an unsworn declaration as provided in 28 U.S.C. § 1746 satisfies the requirement of verification.

(f) Copies of signed or verified papers

When these rules require copies of a signed or verified paper, it shall suffice if the original is signed or verified and the copies are conformed to the original.
(As amended Mar. 30, 1987, eff. Aug. 1, 1987; Apr. 30, 1991, eff. Aug. 1, 1991; Apr. 11, 1997, eff. Dec. 1, 1997.)

1 So in original. The comma probably should not appear.

ADVISORY COMMITTEE NOTES

Subdivision (a). Excepted from the papers which an attorney for a debtor must sign are lists, schedules, statements of financial affairs, statements of executory contracts, Chapter 13 Statements and amendments thereto. Rule 1008 requires that these documents be verified by the debtor. Although the petition must also be verified, counsel for the debtor must sign the petition. See Official Form No. 1. An unrepresented party must sign all papers.

The last sentence of this subdivision authorizes a broad range of sanctions.

The word "document" is used in this subdivision to refer to all papers which the attorney or party is required to sign.

Subdivision (b) extends to all papers filed in cases under the Code the policy of minimizing reliance on the formalities of verification which is reflected in the third sentence of Rule 11 F.R.Civ.P. The second sentence of subdivision (b) permits the substitution of an unsworn declaration for the verification.

See 28 U.S.C. § 1746. Rules requiring verification or an affidavit are as follows: Rule 1008, petitions, schedules, statements of financial affairs, Chapter 13 Statements and amendments; Rule 2006(e), list of multiple proxies and statement of facts and circumstances regarding their acquisition; Rule 4001(c), motion for ex parte relief from stay; Rule 7065, incorporating Rule 65(b) F.R.Civ.P. governing issuance of temporary restraining order; Rule 8011(d), affidavit in support of emergency motion on appeal.

1987 Amendment

The statement of intention of the debtor under § 521(2) of the Code is added to the documents which counsel is not required to sign.

1991 Amendment

Subdivision (a) is amended to conform to Rule 11 F.R.Civ.P. where appropriate, but also to clarify that it applies to the unnecessary delay or needless increase in the cost of the administration of the case. Deletion of the references to specific statements that are excluded from the scope of this subdivision is stylistic. As used in subdivision (a) of this rule, "statement" is limited to the statement of financial affairs and the statement of intention required to be filed under Rule 1007. Deletion of the reference to the Chapter 13 Statement is consistent with the amendment to Rule 1007(b).

1997 Amendment

This rule is amended to conform to the 1993 changes to F.R.Civ.P. 11. For an explanation of these amendments, see the advisory committee note to the 1993 amendments to F.R.Civ.P. 11.

The "safe harbor" provision contained in subdivision (c)(1)(A), which prohibits the filing of a motion for sanctions unless the challenged paper is not withdrawn or corrected within a prescribed time after service of the motion, does not apply if the challenged paper is a petition. The filing of a petition has immediate serious consequences, including the imposition of the automatic stay under § 362 of the Code, which may not be avoided by the subsequent withdrawal of the petition. In addition, a petition for relief under chapter 7 or chapter 11 may not be withdrawn unless the court orders dismissal of the case for cause after notice and a hearing.

GAP Report on Rule 9011. The proposed amendments to subdivision (a) were revised to clarify that a party not represented by an attorney must sign lists, schedules, and statements, as well as other papers that are filed.

CROSS REFERENCES

Affidavit in support of—
    Complaint seeking temporary restraining order, see Fed. Rules Bankr.Proc. Rule 7065, 11 USCA.
    Emergency motion on appeal, see Fed.Rules Bankr.Proc. Rule 8011, 11 USCA.
    Motion for ex parte relief from stay, see Fed.Rules Bankr.Proc. Rule 4001, 11 USCA.
Verification of—
    Complaint seeking temporary restraining order, see Fed. Rules Bankr.Proc. Rule 7065, 11 USCA.
    List of multiple proxies and acquisition statement, see Fed.Rules Bankr.Proc. Rule 2006, 11 USCA.

Motions for ex parte relief from stay, see Fed.Rules Bankr.Proc. Rule 4001, 11 USCA.

Petitions and accompanying papers, see Fed.Rules Bankr.Proc. Rule 1008, 11 USCA.

Pleadings allowed; form of motions, see Fed.Rules Civ. Proc. Rule 7, 28 USCA.

Signing of pleadings, see Fed.Rules Civ.Proc. Rule 11, 28 USCA.

Statements in pleadings subject to obligations set forth in rule 11, see Fed.Rules Civ.Proc. Rule 8, 28 USCA.

LIBRARY REFERENCES

American Digest System

Bankruptcy ☞2187, 3782, 3784, 3786.

Key Number System Topic No. 51.

Corpus Juris Secundum

CJS Bankruptcy § 232, Notice of Removal.

CJS Bankruptcy § 236, Process and Pleading After Removal.

CJS Bankruptcy § 256, Sanctions Resulting from Noncompliance With Requirements as to Basis for Filing.

CJS Bankruptcy § 257, Sanctions Resulting from Noncompliance With Requirements as to Basis for Filing--Procedure for Imposing Sanctions.

CJS Bankruptcy § 258, Court's Inherent and Statutory Power to Sanction Abuse of Judicial Process.

CJS Bankruptcy § 284, Signature and Verification of Basis for Filing.

CJS Bankruptcy § 289, Motions.

CJS Bankruptcy § 336, Contents, Signature, and Verification.

CJS Bankruptcy § 435, Sanctions Against Debtor's Attorney.

CJS Bankruptcy § 436, Sanctions Against Party Filing Motion to Dismiss or Convert.

CJS Bankruptcy § 779, Award of Attorney's Fees to Prevailing Party in Adversary Proceeding.

CJS Bankruptcy § 816, Where Debtor Attempts to Avoid Examination.

CJS Bankruptcy § 1265, Sanctions.

Rule 9012. Oaths and Affirmations

(a) Persons authorized to administer oaths

The following persons may administer oaths and affirmations and take acknowledgments: a bankruptcy judge, clerk, deputy clerk, United States trustee, officer authorized to administer oaths in proceedings before the courts of the United States or under the laws of the state where the oath is to be taken, or a diplomatic or consular officer of the United States in any foreign country.

(b) Affirmation in lieu of oath

When in a case under the Code an oath is required to be taken, a solemn affirmation may be accepted in lieu thereof.

(As amended Mar. 30, 1987, eff. Aug. 1, 1987; Apr. 30, 1991, eff. Aug. 1, 1991.)

ADVISORY COMMITTEE NOTES

This rule is derived from Rule 43(d) F.R.Civ.P.

The provisions of former Bankruptcy Rule 912(a) relating to who may administer oaths have been deleted as unnecessary. Bankruptcy judges and the clerks and deputy clerks of bankruptcy courts are authorized by statute to administer oaths and affirmations and to take acknowledgments. 28 U.S.C. §§ 459, 953. A person designated to preside at the meeting of creditors has authority under Rule 2003(b)(1) to administer the oath. Administration of the oath at a deposition is governed by Rule 7028.

1987 Amendment

Subdivision (a) has been added to the rule to authorize bankruptcy judges and clerks to administer oaths.

1991 Amendment

This rule is amended to conform to the 1986 amendment to § 343 which provides that the United States trustee may administer the oath to the debtor at the § 341 meeting. This rule also allows the United States trustee to administer oaths and affirmations and to take acknowledgments in other situations. This amendment also affects Rule 9010(c) relating to the acknowledgment of a power of attorney. The words "United States trustee" include a designee of the United States trustee pursuant to Rule 9001 and § 102(9) of the Code.

CROSS REFERENCES

Acknowledgment of power of attorney, see Fed.Rules Bankr.Proc. Rule 9010, 11 USCA.

Administration of oaths and acknowledgments by—

Clerks of court, see 28 USCA § 953.

Justices or judges, see 28 USCA § 459.

Affirmation in lieu of oath, see Fed.Rules Civ.Proc. Rule 43, 28 USCA.

Oath defined to include affirmation, see 1 USCA § 1.

Oath or affirmation of witnesses, see Fed.Rules Evid. Rule 603, 28 USCA.

LIBRARY REFERENCES

American Digest System

Bankruptcy ☞2121, 2127.1.

Key Number System Topic No. 51.

Corpus Juris Secundum

CJS Bankruptcy § 142, Representation and Appearances; Powers of Attorney.

CJS Bankruptcy § 143, Oaths and Affirmations.

Rule 9013. Motions: Form and Service

A request for an order, except when an application is authorized by these rules, shall be by written motion, unless made during a hearing. The motion shall state with particularity the grounds therefor, and shall set forth the relief or order sought. Every written motion other than one which may be considered ex parte shall be served by the moving party on the trustee or debtor

in possession and on those entities specified by these rules or, if service is not required or the entities to be served are not specified by these rules, the moving party shall serve the entities the court directs.
(As amended Mar. 30, 1987, eff. Aug. 1, 1987.)

ADVISORY COMMITTEE NOTES

This rule is derived from Rule 5(a) and Rule 7(b)(1) F.R.Civ.P. Except when an application is specifically authorized by these rules, for example an application under Rule 2014 for approval of the employment of a professional, all requests for court action must be made by motion.

LIBRARY REFERENCES

American Digest System

Bankruptcy ⊚2127.1, 2156, 2158, 2163, 2164.1.
Key Number System Topic No. 51.

Corpus Juris Secundum

CJS Bankruptcy § 279, Intervention.
CJS Bankruptcy § 288, Applications.
CJS Bankruptcy § 289, Motions.
CJS Bankruptcy § 421, Proceedings.
CJS Bankruptcy § 425, Proceedings.
CJS Bankruptcy § 455, Chapter 12.
CJS Bankruptcy § 456, Chapter 13.
CJS Bankruptcy § 836, Chapter 7 Cases.
CJS Bankruptcy § 839, Involuntary Cases.
CJS Bankruptcy § 866, Use, Sale, or Lease of Property Other Than Cash Collateral.

Rule 9014.　Contested Matters

(a) Motion. In a contested matter not otherwise governed by these rules, relief shall be requested by motion, and reasonable notice and opportunity for hearing shall be afforded the party against whom relief is sought. No response is required under this rule unless the court directs otherwise.

(b) Service. The motion shall be served in the manner provided for service of a summons and complaint by Rule 7004. Any paper served after the motion shall be served in the manner provided by Rule 5(b) F. R. Civ. P.

(c) Application of Part VII rules. Except as otherwise provided in this rule, and unless the court directs otherwise, the following rules shall apply: 7009, 7017, 7021, 7025, 7026, 7028–7037, 7041, 7042, 7052, 7054–7056, 7064, 7069, and 7071. The following subdivisions of Fed. R. Civ. P. 26, as incorporated by Rule 7026, shall not apply in a contested matter unless the court directs otherwise: 26(a)(1) (mandatory disclosure), 26(a)(2) (disclosures regarding expert testimony) and 26(a)(3) (additional pre-trial disclosure), and 26(f) (mandatory meeting before scheduling conference/ discovery plan). An entity that desires to perpetuate testimony may proceed in the same manner as provided in Rule 7027 for the taking of a deposition before an adversary proceeding. The court may at any stage in a

particular matter direct that one or more of the other rules in Part VII shall apply. The court shall give the parties notice of any order issued under this paragraph to afford them a reasonable opportunity to comply with the procedures prescribed by the order.

(d) Testimony of witnesses. Testimony of witnesses with respect to disputed material factual issues shall be taken in the same manner as testimony in an adversary proceeding.

(e) Attendance of witnesses. The court shall provide procedures that enable parties to ascertain at a reasonable time before any scheduled hearing whether the hearing will be an evidentiary hearing at which witnesses may testify.
(As amended Mar. 30, 1987, eff. Aug. 1, 1987; Apr. 29, 1999, eff. Dec. 1, 1999; Apr. 29, 2002, eff. Dec. 1, 2002; Apr. 26, 2004, eff. Dec. 1, 2004.)

ADVISORY COMMITTEE NOTES

Rules 1017(d), 3020(b)(1), 4001(a), 4003(d), and 6006(a), which govern respectively dismissal or conversion of a case, objections to confirmation of a plan, relief from the automatic stay and the use of cash collateral, avoidance of a lien under § 522(f) of the Code, and the assumption or rejection of executory contracts or unexpired leases, specifically provide that litigation under those rules shall be as provided in Rule 9014. This rule also governs litigation in other contested matters.

Whenever there is an actual dispute, other than an adversary proceeding, before the bankruptcy court, the litigation to resolve that dispute is a contested matter. For example, the filing of an objection to a proof of claim, to a claim of exemption, or to a disclosure statement creates a dispute which is a contested matter. Even when an objection is not formally required, there may be a dispute. If a party in interest opposes the amount of compensation sought by a professional, there is a dispute which is a contested matter.

When the rules of Part VII are applicable to a contested matter, reference in the Part VII rules to adversary proceedings is to be read as a reference to a contested matter. See Rule 9002(1).

1999 Amendments

This rule is amended to delete Rule 7062 from the list of Part VII rules that automatically apply in a contested matter.

Rule 7062 provides that Rule 62 F.R.Civ.P., which governs stays of proceedings to enforce a judgment, is applicable in adversary proceedings. The provisions of Rule 62, including the ten-day automatic stay of the enforcement of a judgment provided by Rule 62(a) and the stay as a matter of right by posting a supersedeas bond provided in Rule 62(d), are not appropriate for most orders granting or denying motions governed by Rule 9014.

Although Rule 7062 will not apply automatically in contested matters, the amended rule permits the court, in its discretion, to order that Rule 7062 apply in a particular matter, and Rule 8005 gives the court discretion to issue a stay or any other appropriate order during the pendency of an appeal on such terms as will protect the rights of all parties in interest. In addition, amendments to Rules 3020, 4001, 6004, and 6006 automatically stay certain types of orders for a period of ten days, unless the court orders otherwise.

Gap Report on Rule 9014. No changes since publication.

2002 Amendments

The list of Part VII rules that are applicable in a contested matter is extended to include Rule 7009 on pleading special matters, and Rule 7017 on real parties in interest, infants and incompetent persons, and capacity. The discovery rules made applicable in adversary proceedings apply in contested matters unless the court directs otherwise.

Subdivision (b) is amended to permit parties to serve papers, other than the original motion, in the manner provided in Rule 5(b) F.R.Civ.P. When the court requires a response to the motion, this amendment will permit service of the response in the same manner as an answer is served in an adversary proceeding.

Subdivision (d) is added to clarify that if the motion cannot be decided without resolving a disputed material issue of fact, an evidentiary hearing must be held at which testimony of witnesses is taken in the same manner as testimony is taken in an adversary proceeding or at a trial in a district court civil case. Rule 43(a), rather than Rule 43(e), F.R.Civ.P. would govern the evidentiary hearing on the factual dispute. Under Rule 9017, the Federal Rules of Evidence also apply in a contested matter. Nothing in the rule prohibits a court from resolving any matter that is submitted on affidavits by agreement of the parties.

Subdivision (e). Local procedures for hearings and other court appearances in a contested matter vary from district to district. In some bankruptcy courts, an evidentiary hearing at which witnesses may testify usually is held at the first court appearance in the contested matter. In other courts, it is customary for the court to delay the evidentiary hearing on disputed factual issues until some time after the initial hearing date. In order to avoid unnecessary expense and inconvenience, it is important for attorneys to know whether they should bring witnesses to a court appearance. The purpose of the final sentence of this rule is to require that the court provide a mechanism that will enable attorneys to know at a reasonable time before a scheduled hearing whether it will be necessary for witnesses to appear in court on that particular date.

Other amendments to this rule are stylistic.

Changes Made After Publication and Comments: The Advisory Committee made two changes to subdivision (d) after considering the comments received addressing the proposed rule. First, the word "material" is inserted to make explicit that which was implied in the published version of the proposed rule. Second, the reference to F.R.Civ.P. 43(a) was removed. The purpose of proposed subdivision (d) was to recognize that testimony should be taken in the same manner in both contested matters and adversary proceedings. The revision to the published rule states this more directly.

The Committee Note was amended to reflect the changes made in the text of the rule.

2004 Amendments

The rule is amended to provide that the mandatory disclosure requirements of Fed. R. Civ. P. 26, as incorporated by Rule 7026, do not apply in contested matters. The typically short time between the commencement and resolution of most contested matters makes the mandatory disclosure provisions of Rule 26 ineffective. Nevertheless, the court may by local rule or by order in a particular case provide that these provisions of the rule apply in a contested matter.

CROSS REFERENCES

Contested matters—

Assumption, rejection, or assignment of executory contract or unexpired lease, or proceeding to require trustee to act, see Fed.Rules Bankr.Proc. Rule 6006, 11 USCA.

Avoidance by debtor of transfers of exempt property, see Fed.Rules Bankr.Proc. Rule 4003, 11 USCA.

Dismissal or conversion to another chapter, see Fed. Rules Bankr.Proc. Rule 1017, 11 USCA.

Objection to confirmation of plan, see Fed.Rules Bankr. Proc. Rule 3020, 11 USCA.

Relief from automatic stay, see Fed.Rules Bankr.Proc. Rule 4001, 11 USCA.

Request for use of cash collateral, see Fed.Rules Bankr. Proc. Rule 4001, 11 USCA.

Effect of amendment of Federal Rules of Civil Procedure, see Fed.Rules Bankr.Proc. Rule 9032, 11 USCA.

Meanings of words in Federal Rules of Civil Procedure when applicable, see Fed.Rules Bankr.Proc. Rule 9002, 11 USCA.

Motions; form and service, see Fed.Rules Bankr.Proc. Rule 9013, 11 USCA.

LIBRARY REFERENCES

American Digest System

Bankruptcy ⟨≈⟩2127.1, 2156, 2158.

Key Number System Topic No. 51.

Corpus Juris Secundum

CJS Bankruptcy § 11, Federal Rules of Bankruptcy Procedure.

CJS Bankruptcy § 42, Regulation and Review of United States Trustee's Actions.

CJS Bankruptcy § 67, Request for Appointment.

CJS Bankruptcy § 86, Request for Appointment.

CJS Bankruptcy § 140, Contested Matters.

CJS Bankruptcy § 151, Original But Not Exclusive Jurisdiction of Civil Proceedings.

CJS Bankruptcy § 202, Procedure; Motion and Stay.

CJS Bankruptcy § 253, Civil Contempt.

CJS Bankruptcy § 275, Applicable Rules of Civil Procedure.

CJS Bankruptcy § 277, Real Party in Interest; Capacity.

CJS Bankruptcy § 308, Enlargement.

CJS Bankruptcy § 314, Judgments.

CJS Bankruptcy § 316, Costs and Fees.

CJS Bankruptcy § 359, Designation of Debtor as Health Care Business.

CJS Bankruptcy § 362, Procedure on Objection or Request for Determination.

CJS Bankruptcy § 416, Proceedings.

CJS Bankruptcy § 421, Proceedings.

CJS Bankruptcy § 425, Proceedings.

CJS Bankruptcy § 427, Proceedings.

CJS Bankruptcy § 429, Proceedings.

CJS Bankruptcy § 451, Dismissal or Conversion on Request of United States Trustee.

CJS Bankruptcy § 457, Failure to Provide Copy of Debtor's Federal Income Tax Return to Trustee and Requesting Creditors.

CJS Bankruptcy § 458, Failure to File Prepetition Tax Returns in Chapter 13 Case.

CJS Bankruptcy § 459, Failure to File Postpetition Tax Return.

CJS Bankruptcy § 525, Evidence.

CJS Bankruptcy § 609, Filing of Motion; Notice.

CJS Bankruptcy § 614, Form of Action as Adversary Proceeding or Contested Matter.

CJS Bankruptcy § 701, Form of Action as Adversary Proceeding.

CJS Bankruptcy § 764, Consumer Privacy and Patient Care Ombudsmen.

CJS Bankruptcy § 856, Motion and Notice.

CJS Bankruptcy § 866, Use, Sale, or Lease of Property Other Than Cash Collateral.

CJS Bankruptcy § 871, Motion for Authorization.

CJS Bankruptcy § 877, Sale or Lease of Personally Identifiable Information.

CJS Bankruptcy § 886, Authorization to Sell Property Free and Clear; Notice.

CJS Bankruptcy § 900, Motion for Authorization to Obtain Credit; Notice and Hearing.

CJS Bankruptcy § 922, Necessity of Court Approval; Assumption by Conduct.

CJS Bankruptcy § 923, Application for Approval.

CJS Bankruptcy § 928, Judicial Forcing of Decision Date on Request of Party to Contract.

CJS Bankruptcy § 938, Rejection of Lease by Operation of Law.

CJS Bankruptcy § 945, Application for Court Approval of Rejection; Hearing and Notice.

CJS Bankruptcy § 1122, Objections to Confirmation.

CJS Bankruptcy § 1180, Treatment of Executory Contracts and Unexpired Leases.

CJS Bankruptcy § 1183, Modification of Plan After Confirmation.

CJS Bankruptcy § 1206, Postconfirmation Modification--Procedure and Burden of Proof.

Rule 9015. Jury Trials

(a) Applicability of certain Federal Rules of Civil Procedure

Rules 38, 39, 47–49, and 51, F. R. Civ. P., and Rule 81(c) F. R. Civ. P. insofar as it applies to jury trials, apply in cases and proceedings, except that a demand made under Rule 38(b) F. R. Civ. P. shall be filed in accordance with Rule 5005.

(b) Consent to have trial conducted by bankruptcy judge

If the right to a jury trial applies, a timely demand has been filed pursuant to Rule 38(b) F.R.Civ.P., and the bankruptcy judge has been specially designated to conduct the jury trial, the parties may consent to have a jury trial conducted by a bankruptcy judge under 28 U.S.C. § 157(e) by jointly or separately filing a statement of consent within any applicable time limits specified by local rule.

(c) Applicability of Rule 50 F. R. Civ. P.

Rule 50 F. R. Civ. P. applies in cases and proceedings, except that any renewed motion for judgment or request for a new trial shall be filed no later than 14 days after the entry of judgment.

(Added Apr. 11, 1997, eff. Dec. 1, 1997; amended Mar. 26, 2009, eff. Dec. 1, 2009.)

ADVISORY COMMITTEE NOTES

1987 Abrogation

Former section 1480 of title 28 preserved a right to trial by jury in any case or proceeding under title 11 in which jury trial was provided by statute. Rule 9015 provided the procedure for jury trials in bankruptcy courts. Section 1480 was repealed. Section 1411 added by the 1984 amendments affords a jury trial only for personal injury or wrongful death claims, which 28 U.S.C. § 157(b)(5) requires be tried in the district court. Nevertheless, Rule 9015 has been cited as conferring a right to jury trial in other matters before bankruptcy judges. In light of the clear mandate of 28 U.S.C. § 2075 that the "rules shall not abridge, enlarge, or modify any substantive right," Rule 9015 is abrogated. In the event the courts of appeals or the Supreme Court define a right to jury trial in any bankruptcy matters, a local rule in substantially the form of Rule 9015 can be adopted pending amendment of these rules.

1997 Amendment

This rule provides procedures relating to jury trials. This rule is not intended to expand or create any right to trial by jury where such right does not otherwise exist.

GAP Report on Rule 9015. No changes to the published draft.

2009 Amendments

The rule is amended by deleting Rule 50 F. R. Civ. P. from the list in subdivision (a) of rules made applicable in cases and proceedings. However, subdivision (c) is added to make Rule 50 applicable in cases and proceedings, but it limits the time for filing certain post judgment motions to 14 days after the entry of judgment. The amendment is necessary because Rule 50 F. R. Civ. P. was amended in 2009 to extend the deadline for the filing of these post judgment motions to 28 days. That deadline corresponds to the 30–day deadline for filing a notice of appeal in a civil case under Rule 4(a)(1)(A) F. R. App. P. In a bankruptcy case, the deadline for filing a notice of appeal is 14 days. Therefore, the 28–day deadline for filing these post judgment motions would effectively override the notice of appeal deadline under Rule 8002(a) but for this amendment.

Other amendments are stylistic.

American Digest System

Bankruptcy ☜2130.

Jury ☜19(9).

Key Number System Topic Nos. 230, 51.

Corpus Juris Secundum

CJS Bankruptcy § 12, Federal Rules of Civil Procedure.

CJS Bankruptcy § 310, General Procedures.

CJS Bankruptcy § 311, When Does Right to Trial by Jury Exist.

Rule 9016. Subpoena

Rule 45 F.R.Civ.P. applies in cases under the Code. (As amended Mar. 30, 1987, eff. Aug. 1, 1987.)

ADVISORY COMMITTEE NOTES

Although Rule 7004(d) authorizes nationwide service of process, Rule 45 F.R.Civ.P. limits the subpoena power to the judicial district and places outside the district which are within 100 miles of the place of trial or hearing.

CROSS REFERENCES

Compelling attendance of witnesses by use of subpoena—

Deposition upon oral examination, see Fed.Rules Bankr. Proc. Rule 7030, 11 USCA.

Deposition upon written questions, see Fed.Rules Bankr. Proc. Rule 7031, 11 USCA.

Examination of debtor—

Apprehension and removal of debtor to compel attendance, see Fed.Rules Bankr.Proc. Rule 2005, 11 USCA.

Compelling attendance for examination and production of documentary evidence, see Fed.Rules Bankr.Proc. Rule 2004, 11 USCA.

LIBRARY REFERENCES

American Digest System

Bankruptcy ☜2131, 2134, 2158, 3043, 3044.

Key Number System Topic No. 51.

Corpus Juris Secundum

CJS Bankruptcy § 12, Federal Rules of Civil Procedure.

CJS Bankruptcy § 818, Compelling Attendance and Production of Documentary Evidence.

CJS Bankruptcy § 825, Securing Attendance.

CJS Bankruptcy § 826, Production of Documentary Evidence.

Rule 9017. Evidence

The Federal Rules of Evidence and Rules 43, 44 and 44.1 F.R.Civ.P. apply in cases under the Code.

ADVISORY COMMITTEE NOTES

Sections 251 and 252 of Public Law 95–598, amended Rule 1101 of the Federal Rules of Evidence to provide that the Federal Rules of Evidence apply in bankruptcy courts and to any case or proceeding under the Code. Rules 43, 44 and 44.1 of the F.R.Civ.P., which supplement the Federal Rules of Evidence, are by this rule made applicable to cases under the Code.

Examples of bankruptcy rules containing matters of an evidentiary nature are: Rule 2011, evidence of debtor retained in possession; Rule 3001(f), proof of claim constitutes prima facie evidence of the amount and validity of a claim; and Rule 5007(c), sound recording of court proceedings constitutes the record of the proceedings.

CROSS REFERENCES

Applicability of rules to proceedings and cases under this title, see Fed.Rules Evid. Rule 1101, 28 USCA.

LIBRARY REFERENCES

American Digest System

Bankruptcy ☜2163, 2439(1), 2440, 2725.1, 2728, 2925.1, 2929, 3314.1, 3318.1, 3386, 3387.1.

Key Number System Topic No. 51.

Corpus Juris Secundum

CJS Bankruptcy § 12, Federal Rules of Civil Procedure.

CJS Bankruptcy § 13, Federal Rules of Evidence.

CJS Bankruptcy § 138, Rules of Practice and Procedure.

CJS Bankruptcy § 803, Interpreters.

CJS Bankruptcy § 1050, Evidence; Presumptions and Burden of Proof.

CJS Bankruptcy § 1087, Evidence; Presumptions.

Rule 9018. Secret, Confidential, Scandalous, or Defamatory Matter

On motion or on its own initiative, with or without notice, the court may make any order which justice requires (1) to protect the estate or any entity in respect of a trade secret or other confidential research, development, or commercial information, (2) to protect any entity against scandalous or defamatory matter contained in any paper filed in a case under the Code, or (3) to protect governmental matters that are made confidential by statute or regulation. If an order is entered under this rule without notice, any entity affected thereby may move to vacate or modify the order, and after a hearing on notice the court shall determine the motion.
(As amended Mar. 30, 1987, eff. Aug. 1, 1987.)

ADVISORY COMMITTEE NOTES

This rule provides the procedure for invoking the court's power under § 107 of the Code.

CROSS REFERENCES

Motion to strike scandalous matter, see Fed.Rules Civ.Proc. Rule 12, 28 USCA.

Motions; form and service, see Fed.Rules Bankr.Proc. Rule 9013, 11 USCA.

Protective orders, see Fed.Rules Civ.Proc. Rule 26, 28 USCA.

LIBRARY REFERENCES

American Digest System

Bankruptcy ☜2127.1, 3040.1.

Records ☞32.
Key Number System Topic Nos. 326, 51.

Corpus Juris Secundum

CJS Bankruptcy § 147, Protective Orders.

CJS Bankruptcy § 831, Trade Secrets, Confidential Information and Scandalous or Defamatory Matter.

Rule 9019. Compromise and Arbitration

(a) Compromise

On motion by the trustee and after notice and a hearing, the court may approve a compromise or settlement. Notice shall be given to creditors, the United States trustee, the debtor, and indenture trustees as provided in Rule 2002 and to any other entity as the court may direct.

(b) Authority to compromise or settle controversies within classes

After a hearing on such notice as the court may direct, the court may fix a class or classes of controversies and authorize the trustee to compromise or settle controversies within such class or classes without further hearing or notice.

(c) Arbitration

On stipulation of the parties to any controversy affecting the estate the court may authorize the matter to be submitted to final and binding arbitration.

(As amended Mar. 30, 1987, eff. Aug. 1, 1987; Apr. 30, 1991, eff. Aug. 1, 1991; Apr. 22, 1993, eff. Aug. 1, 1993.)

ADVISORY COMMITTEE NOTES

Subdivisions (a) and (c) of this rule are essentially the same as the provisions of former Bankruptcy Rule 919 and subdivision (b) is the same as former Rule 8–514(b), which was applicable to railroad reorganizations. Subdivision (b) permits the court to deal efficiently with a case in which there may be a large number of settlements.

1991 Amendment

This rule is amended to enable the United States trustee to object or otherwise be heard in connection with a proposed compromise or settlement and otherwise to monitor the progress of the case.

1993 Amendments

Subdivision (a) is amended to conform to the language of § 102(1) of the Code. Other amendments are stylistic and make no substantive change.

CROSS REFERENCES

Motions; form and service, see Fed.Rules Bankr.Proc. Rule 9013, 11 USCA.

LIBRARY REFERENCES

American Digest System

Bankruptcy ☞2131, 3009, 3031 to 3033, 3555.
Key Number System Topic No. 51.

Corpus Juris Secundum

CJS Bankruptcy § 145, Compromise and Settlement.

CJS Bankruptcy § 146, Submission to Arbitration.

Rule 9020. Contempt Proceedings

Rule 9014 governs a motion for an order of contempt made by the United States trustee or a party in interest.

(As amended Mar. 30, 1987, eff. Aug. 1, 1987; Apr. 30, 1991, eff. Aug. 1, 1991; Apr. 23, 2001, eff. Dec. 1, 2001.)

ADVISORY COMMITTEE NOTES

Section 1481 of Title 28 provides that a bankruptcy court "may not . . . . punish a criminal contempt not committed in the presence of the judge of the court or warranting a punishment of imprisonment." Rule 9020 does not enlarge the power of bankruptcy courts.

Subdivision (a) is adapted from former Bankruptcy Rule 920 and Rule 42 F.R.Crim.P. Paragraph (1) of the subdivision permits summary imposition of punishment for contempt if the conduct is in the presence of the court and is of such nature that the conduct "obstruct[s] the administration of justice." See 18 U.S.C. § 401(a). Cases interpreting Rule 42(a) F.R.Crim.P. have held that when criminal contempt is in question summary disposition should be the exception: summary disposition should be reserved for situations where it is necessary to protect the judicial institution. 3 Wright, Federal Practice & Procedure—Criminal § 707 (1969). Those cases are equally pertinent to the application of this rule and, therefore, contemptuous conduct in the presence of the judge may often be punished only after the notice and hearing requirements of subdivision (b) are satisfied.

If the bankruptcy court concludes it is without power to punish or to impose the proper punishment for conduct which constitutes contempt, subdivision (a)(3) authorizes the bankruptcy court to certify the matter to the district court.

Subdivision (b) makes clear that when a person has a constitutional or statutory right to a jury trial in a criminal contempt matter this rule in no way affects that right. See Frank v. United States, 395 U.S. 147 (1969).

The Federal Rules of Civil Procedure do not specifically provide the procedure for the imposition of civil contempt sanctions. The decisional law governing the procedure for imposition of civil sanctions by the district courts will be equally applicable to the bankruptcy courts.

1987 Amendment

The United States Bankruptcy Courts, as constituted under the Bankruptcy Reform Act of 1978, were courts of law, equity, and admiralty with an inherent contempt power, but former 28 U.S.C. § 1481 restricted the criminal contempt power of bankruptcy judges. Under the 1984 amendments, bankruptcy judges are judicial officers of the district court, 28 U.S.C. §§ 151, 152(a)(1). There are no decisions by the courts of appeals concerning the authority of bankruptcy judges to punish for either civil or criminal contempt under the 1984 amendments. This rule, as amended, recognizes that bankruptcy judges may not have the power to punish for contempt.

Sound judicial administration requires that the initial determination of whether contempt has been committed should be made by the bankruptcy judge. If timely objections are not filed to the bankruptcy judge's order, the order has the same force and effect as an order of the district court. If objections are filed within 10 days of service of the order, the district court conducts a de novo review pursuant to Rule 9033 and any order of contempt is entered by the district court on completion of the court's review of the bankruptcy judge's order.

1991 Amendments

The words "with the clerk" in subdivision (c) are deleted as unnecessary. See Rules 5005(a) and 9001(3).

2001 Amendments

The amendments to this rule cover a motion for an order of contempt filed by the United States trustee or a party in interest. This rule, as amended, does not address a contempt proceeding initiated by the court sua sponte.

Whether the court is acting on motion under this rule or is acting sua sponte, these amendments are not intended to extend, limit, or otherwise affect either the contempt power of a bankruptcy judge or the role of the district judge regarding contempt orders. Issues relating to the contempt power of bankruptcy judges are substantive and are left to statutory and judicial development, rather than procedural rules.

This rule, as amended in 1987, delayed for ten days from service the effectiveness of a bankruptcy judge's order of contempt and rendered the order subject to de novo review by the district court. These limitations on contempt orders were added to the rule in response to the Bankruptcy Amendments and Federal Judgeship Act of 1984, Pub. L. No. 98–353, 98 Stat. 333, which provides that bankruptcy judges are judicial officers of the district court, but does not specifically mention contempt power. See 28 U.S.C. § 151. As explained in the committee note to the 1987 amendments to this rule, no decisions of the courts of appeals existed concerning the authority of a bankruptcy judge to punish for either civil or criminal contempt under the 1984 Act and, therefore, the rule as amended in 1987 "recognizes that bankruptcy judges may not have the power to punish for contempt." Committee Note to 1987 Amendments to Rule 9020.

Since 1987, several courts of appeals have held that bankruptcy judges have the power to issue civil contempt orders. *See, e.g., Matter of Terrebonne Fuel and Lube, Inc.*, 108 F.3d 609 (5th Cir. 1997); *In re Rainbow Magazine, Inc.*, 77 F.3d 278 (9th Cir. 1996). Several courts have distinguished between a bankruptcy judge's civil contempt power and criminal contempt power. *See, e.g., Matter of Terrebonne Fuel and Lube, Inc.*, 108 F.3d at 613, n. 3 ("[a]lthough we find that bankruptcy judge's [sic] can find a party in civil contempt, we must point out that bankruptcy courts lack the power to hold persons in criminal contempt."). For other decisions regarding criminal contempt power, *see, e.g., In re Ragar*, 3 F.3d 1174 (8th Cir. 1993); *Matter of Hipp, Inc.*, 895 F.2d 1503 (5th Cir. 1990). To the extent that Rule 9020, as amended in 1987, delayed the effectiveness of civil contempt orders and required de novo review by the district court, the rule may have been unnecessarily restrictive in view of judicial decisions recognizing that bankruptcy judges have the power to hold parties in civil contempt.

Subdivision (d), which provides that the rule shall not be construed to impair the right to trial by jury, is deleted as

unnecessary and is not intended to deprive any party of the right to a jury trial when it otherwise exists.

CHANGES MADE AFTER PUBLICATION AND COMMENTS

No changes were made in the text of the proposed amendments. Stylistic changes were made to the Committee Note.

CROSS REFERENCES

Contempts, see 18 USCA §§ 401 et seq. and 3691 et seq.

Criminal contempt, see Fed.Rules Cr.Proc. Rule 42, 18 USCA.

Power of court to punish persons for contempts, see 11 USCA § 105.

LIBRARY REFERENCES

American Digest System

Bankruptcy ⬤2134, 2465.1 to 2466.

Key Number System Topic No. 51.

Corpus Juris Secundum

CJS Bankruptcy § 140, Contested Matters.

CJS Bankruptcy § 253, Civil Contempt.

Rule 9021.   Entry of Judgment

A judgment or order is effective when entered under Rule 5003.

(As amended Mar. 30, 1987, eff. Aug. 1, 1987; Mar. 26, 2009, eff. Dec. 1, 2009.)

ADVISORY COMMITTEE NOTES

Subdivision (a). This rule is derived from Rule 58 F.R.Civ.P. The requirement that a judgment entered in an adversary proceeding or contested matter be set forth on a separate document is to eliminate uncertainty as to whether an opinion or memorandum of the court is a judgment. There is no sound reason to require that every order in a case under the Code be evidenced by a separate document.

Subdivision (b) establishes a procedure for entering a judgment of a bankruptcy court for the recovery of money or property in an index of judgments kept by the clerk of the district court. It clarifies the availability of the same remedies for the enforcement of a bankruptcy court judgment as those provided for the enforcement of a district court judgment. See 28 U.S.C. §§ 1961–63. When indexed in accordance with subdivision (b) of this rule a judgment of the bankruptcy court may be found by anyone searching for liens of record in the judgment records of the district court. Certification of a copy of the judgment to the clerk of the district court provides a basis for registration of the judgment pursuant to 28 U.S.C. § 1963 in any other district. When so registered, the judgment may be enforced by issuance of execution and orders for supplementary proceedings that may be served anywhere within the state where the registering court sits. See 7 Moore, Federal Practice 2409–11 (2d ed. 1971). The procedures available in the district court are not exclusive, however, and the holder of a judgment entered by the bankruptcy court may use the remedies under Rules 7069 and 7070 even if the judgment is indexed by the clerk of the district court.

Subdivision (c) makes it clear that when a district court hears a matter reserved to it by 28 U.S.C. §§ 1471, 1481, its judgments are entered in the district court's civil docket and in the docket of the bankruptcy court. When the district court acts as an appellate court, Rule 8016(a) governs the entry of judgments on appeal.

1987 Amendment

Former subdivision (a) was derived from Rule 58 F.R.Civ.P. As amended, Rule 9021 adopts Rule 58. The reference in Rule 58 to Rule 79(a) F.R.Civ.P. is to be read as a reference to Rule 5003.

2009 Amendments

The rule is amended in connection with the amendment that adds Rule 7058. The entry of judgment in adversary proceedings is governed by Rule 7058, and the entry of a judgment or order in all other proceedings is governed by this rule.

CROSS REFERENCES

Entry of judgment, see Fed.Rules Civ.Proc. Rule 58, 28 USCA.

Entry of judgment on appeal, see Fed.Rules Bankr.Proc. Rule 8016, 11 USCA.

Findings by court, see Fed.Rules Bankr.Proc. Rule 7052, 11 USCA.

Judgments rendered by district court—

Effect as lien on local property, see 28 USCA § 1962.

Interest allowed on money judgment, see 28 USCA § 1961.

Registration of final judgments in other districts, see 28 USCA § 1963.

LIBRARY REFERENCES

American Digest System

Bankruptcy ☞2164.1, 2442, 2729, 2932, 3318.1, 3387.1, 3767, 3773, 3774.1.

Key Number System Topic No. 51.

Corpus Juris Secundum

CJS Bankruptcy § 12, Federal Rules of Civil Procedure.

CJS Bankruptcy § 314, Judgments.

CJS Bankruptcy § 315, Judgments--Relief from Judgment or Order; Collateral Attack.

Rule 9022.   Notice of Judgment or Order

(a) Judgment or order of bankruptcy judge

Immediately on the entry of a judgment or order the clerk shall serve a notice of entry in the manner provided in Rule 5(b) F.R.Civ.P. on the contesting parties and on other entities as the court directs. Unless the case is a chapter 9 municipality case, the clerk shall forthwith transmit to the United States trustee a copy of the judgment or order. Service of the notice shall be noted in the docket. Lack of notice of the entry does not affect the time to appeal or relieve or authorize the court to relieve a party for failure to appeal within the time allowed, except as permitted in Rule 8002.

(b) Judgment or order of district judge

Notice of a judgment or order entered by a district judge is governed by Rule 77(d) F.R.Civ.P. Unless the case is a chapter 9 municipality case, the clerk shall forthwith transmit to the United States trustee a copy of a judgment or order entered by a district judge. (As amended Mar. 30, 1987, eff. Aug. 1, 1987; Apr. 30, 1991, eff. Aug. 1, 1991; Apr. 23, 2001, eff. Dec. 1, 2001.)

ADVISORY COMMITTEE NOTES

Subdivision (a) of this rule is an adaptation of Rule 77(d) F.R.Civ.P.

Subdivision (b) complements Rule 9021(b). When a district court acts as an appellate court, Rule 8016(b) requires the clerk to give notice of the judgment on appeal.

1991 Amendments

This rule is amended to enable the United States trustee to be informed of all developments in the case so that administrative and supervisory functions provided in 28 U.S.C. § 586(a) may be performed.

2001 Amendments

Rule 5(b) F.R.Civ.P., which is made applicable in adversary proceedings by Rule 7005, is being restyled and amended to authorize service by electronic means—or any other means not otherwise authorized under Rule 5(b)—if consent is obtained from the person served. The amendment to Rule 9022(a) authorizes the clerk to serve notice of entry of a judgment or order by electronic means if the person served consents, or to use any other means of service authorized under Rule 5(b), including service by mail. This amendment conforms to the amendments made to Rule 77(d) F.R. Civ. P.

CHANGES MADE AFTER PUBLICATION AND COMMENTS

No changes were made.

CROSS REFERENCES

Entry of judgment; district court record of judgment, see Fed.Rules Bankr.Proc. Rule 9021, 11 USCA.

Notice of judgment on appeal, see Fed.Rules Bankr.Proc. Rule 8016, 11 USCA.

LIBRARY REFERENCES

American Digest System

Bankruptcy ☞2131, 2158, 2164.1.

Key Number System Topic No. 51.

Corpus Juris Secundum

CJS Bankruptcy § 12, Federal Rules of Civil Procedure.

CJS Bankruptcy § 314, Judgments.

Rule 9023.   New Trials; Amendment of Judgments

Except as provided in this rule and Rule 3008, Rule 59 F. R. Civ. P. applies in cases under the Code. A motion for a new trial or to alter or amend a judgment shall be filed, and a court may on its own order a new trial, no later than 14 days after entry of judgment. (As amended Mar. 26, 2009, eff. Dec. 1, 2009.)

ADVISORY COMMITTEE NOTES

Rule 59 F.R.Civ.P. regulates motions for a new trial and amendment of judgment. Those motions must be served within 10 days of the entry of judgment. No similar time limit is contained in Rule 3008 which governs reconsideration of claims.

2009 Amendments

The rule is amended to limit to 14 days the time for a party to file a post judgment motion for a new trial and for the court to order sua sponte a new trial. In 2009, Rule 59 F. R. Civ. P. was amended to extend the deadline for these actions to 28 days after the entry of judgment. That deadline corresponds to the 30–day deadline for filing a notice of appeal in a civil case under Rule 4(a)(1)(A) F. R. App. P. In a bankruptcy case, however, the deadline for filing a notice of appeal is 14 days. Therefore, the 28–day deadline for filing a motion for a new trial or a motion to alter or amend a judgment would effectively override the notice of appeal deadline under Rule 8002(a) but for this amendment.

CROSS REFERENCES

Amendment of findings by court, see Fed.Rules Bankr. Proc. Rule 7052, 11 USCA.

Effect of motion under this rule on time for appeal, see Fed.Rules Bankr.Proc. Rule 8002, 11 USCA.

Enlargement of ten-day period for motion for new trial not permitted, see Fed.Rules Bankr.Proc. Rule 9006, 11 USCA.

Time for service of opposing affidavits to motion for new trial, see Fed.Rules Bankr.Proc. Rule 9006, 11 USCA.

LIBRARY REFERENCES

American Digest System

Bankruptcy ☞2164.1, 2443, 2729, 2933, 3320.1 to 3322, 3387.1, 3773, 3774.1.

Key Number System Topic No. 51.

Corpus Juris Secundum

CJS Bankruptcy § 289, Motions.

CJS Bankruptcy § 308, Enlargement.

CJS Bankruptcy § 1207, Revocation or Vacation.

Rule 9024. Relief from Judgment or Order

Rule 60 F.R.Civ.P. applies in cases under the Code except that (1) a motion to reopen a case under the Code or for the reconsideration of an order allowing or disallowing a claim against the estate entered without a contest is not subject to the one year limitation prescribed in Rule 60(c), (2) a complaint to revoke a discharge in a chapter 7 liquidation case may be filed only within the time allowed by § 727(e) of the Code, and (3) a complaint to revoke an order confirming a plan may be filed only within the time allowed by § 1144, § 1230, or § 1330.
(As amended Apr. 30, 1991, eff. Aug. 1, 1991; Apr. 23, 2008, eff. Dec. 1, 2008.)

ADVISORY COMMITTEE NOTES

Motions to reopen cases are governed by Rule 5010. Reconsideration of orders allowing and disallowing claims is governed by Rule 3008. For the purpose of this rule all orders of the bankruptcy court are subject to Rule 60 F.R.Civ.P.

Pursuant to § 727(e) of the Code a complaint to revoke a discharge must be filed within one year of the entry of the discharge or, when certain grounds of revocation are asserted, the later of one year after the entry of the discharge or the date the case is closed. Under § 1144 and § 1330 of the Code a party must file a complaint to revoke an order confirming a chapter 11 or 13 plan within 180 days of its entry. Clauses (2) and (3) of this rule make it clear that the time periods established by §§ 727(e), 1144 and 1330 of the Code may not be circumvented by the invocation of F.R.Civ.P. 60(b).

1991 Amendment

Clause (3) is amended to include a reference to § 1230 of the Code which contains time limitations relating to revocation of confirmation of a chapter 12 plan. The time periods prescribed by § 1230 may not be circumvented by the invocation of F.R.Civ.P. 60(b).

2008 Amendments

The rule is amended to conform to the changes made to the Federal Rules of Civil Procedure through the restyling of those rules effective on December 1, 2007.

CROSS REFERENCES

Enlargement of time for motion for relief from judgment or order not permitted, see Fed.Rules Bankr.Proc. Rule 9006, 11 USCA.

Motions; form and service, see Fed.Rules Bankr.Proc. Rule 9013, 11 USCA.

Reconsideration of allowance or disallowance of claims, see Fed.Rules Bankr.Proc. Rule 3008, 11 USCA.

Reopening cases, see Fed.Rules Bankr.Proc. Rule 5010, 11 USCA.

Revocation of discharges under individual debt adjustment plan, see 11 USCA § 1328.

Setting aside judgment by default, see Fed.Rules Bankr. Proc. Rule 7055, 11 USCA.

LIBRARY REFERENCES

American Digest System

Bankruptcy ☞2164.1, 2443, 2729, 2932, 3320.1 to 3322, 3387.1, 3766.1 to 3768, 3773, 3774.1.

Key Number System Topic No. 51.

Corpus Juris Secundum

CJS Bankruptcy § 139, Adversary Proceedings.

CJS Bankruptcy § 308, Enlargement.

CJS Bankruptcy § 315, Judgments--Relief from Judgment or Order; Collateral Attack.

CJS Bankruptcy § 1056, Revocation or Vacation of Discharge.

CJS Bankruptcy § 1057, Revocation or Vacation of Discharge--Time When Revocation May be Sought.

CJS Bankruptcy § 1207, Revocation or Vacation.

Rule 9025. Security: Proceedings Against Sureties

Whenever the Code or these rules require or permit the giving of security by a party, and security is given in the form of a bond or stipulation or other undertaking with one or more sureties, each surety submits to the jurisdiction of the court, and liability may be determined in an adversary proceeding governed by the rules in Part VII.

ADVISORY COMMITTEE NOTES

This rule is an adaptation of Rule 65.1 F.R.Civ.P. and applies to any surety on a bond given pursuant to § 303(e) of the Code, Rules 2001, 2010, 5008, 7062, 7065, 8005, or any other rule authorizing the giving of such security.

CROSS REFERENCES

Bonds—

Deposit or investment by trustee of money of estates, see 11 USCA § 345.

Indemnification bond in involuntary cases, see 11 USCA § 303.

Qualification to serve as trustee, see 11 USCA § 322.

Enforcement of bond or undertaking on injunction against surety, see Fed.Rules Bankr.Proc. Rule 7065, 11 USCA.

Security; proceedings against sureties, see Fed.Rules Civ. Proc. Rule 65.1, 28 USCA.

Security defined, see 11 USCA § 101.

LIBRARY REFERENCES

American Digest System

Principal and Surety ⟨key⟩59 to 87.

Key Number System Topic No. 309.

Corpus Juris Secundum

CJS Bankruptcy § 107, Suits Against Trustee--Proceeding on Trustee's Bond.

CJS Bankruptcy § 139, Adversary Proceedings.

Rule 9026. Exceptions Unnecessary

Rule 46 F.R.Civ.P. applies in cases under the Code.

LIBRARY REFERENCES

American Digest System

Bankruptcy ⟨key⟩2127.1, 2163, 3770.

Key Number System Topic No. 51.

Corpus Juris Secundum

CJS Bankruptcy § 12, Federal Rules of Civil Procedure.

Rule 9027. Removal

(a) Notice of removal

(1) Where filed; form and content

A notice of removal shall be filed with the clerk for the district and division within which is located the state or federal court where the civil action is pending. The notice shall be signed pursuant to Rule 9011 and contain a short and plain statement of the facts which entitle the party filing the notice to remove, contain a statement that upon removal of the claim or cause of action the proceeding is core or non-core and, if non-core, that the party filing the notice does or does not consent to entry of final orders or judgment by the bankruptcy judge, and be accompanied by a copy of all process and pleadings.

(2) Time for filing; civil action initiated before commencement of the case under the code

If the claim or cause of action in a civil action is pending when a case under the Code is commenced, a notice of removal may be filed only within the longest of (A) 90 days after the order for relief in the case under the Code, (B) 30 days after entry of an order terminating a stay, if the claim or cause of action in a civil action has been stayed under § 362 of the Code, or (C) 30 days after a trustee qualifies in a chapter 11 reorganization case but not later than 180 days after the order for relief.

(3) Time for filing; civil action initiated after commencement of the case under the Code

If a claim or cause of action is asserted in another court after the commencement of a case under the Code, a notice of removal may be filed with the clerk only within the shorter of (A) 30 days after receipt, through service or otherwise, of a copy of the initial pleading setting forth the claim or cause of action sought to be removed, or (B) 30 days after receipt of the summons if the initial pleading has been filed with the court but not served with the summons.

(b) Notice

Promptly after filing the notice of removal, the party filing the notice shall serve a copy of it on all parties to the removed claim or cause of action.

(c) Filing in non-bankruptcy court

Promptly after filing the notice of removal, the party filing the notice shall file a copy of it with the clerk of the court from which the claim or cause of action is removed. Removal of the claim or cause of action is effected on such filing of a copy of the notice of removal. The parties shall proceed no further in that court unless and until the claim or cause of action is remanded.

(d) Remand

A motion for remand of the removed claim or cause of action shall be governed by Rule 9014 and served on the parties to the removed claim or cause of action.

(e) Procedure after removal

(1) After removal of a claim or cause of action to a district court the district court or, if the case under the Code has been referred to a bankruptcy judge of the district, the bankruptcy judge, may issue all necessary orders and process to bring before it all proper parties

whether served by process issued by the court from which the claim or cause of action was removed or otherwise.

(2) The district court or, if the case under the Code has been referred to a bankruptcy judge of the district, the bankruptcy judge, may require the party filing the notice of removal to file with the clerk copies of all records and proceedings relating to the claim or cause of action in the court from which the claim or cause of action was removed.

(3) Any party who has filed a pleading in connection with the removed claim or cause of action, other than the party filing the notice of removal, shall file a statement admitting or denying any allegation in the notice of removal that upon removal of the claim or cause of action the proceeding is core or non-core. If the statement alleges that the proceeding is non-core, it shall state that the party does or does not consent to entry of final orders or judgment by the bankruptcy judge. A statement required by this paragraph shall be signed pursuant to Rule 9011 and shall be filed not later than 14 days after the filing of the notice of removal. Any party who files a statement pursuant to this paragraph shall mail a copy to every other party to the removed claim or cause of action.

(f) Process after removal

If one or more of the defendants has not been served with process, the service has not been perfected prior to removal, or the process served proves to be defective, such process or service may be completed or new process issued pursuant to Part VII of these rules. This subdivision shall not deprive any defendant on whom process is served after removal of the defendant's right to move to remand the case.

(g) Applicability of Part VII

The rules of Part VII apply to a claim or cause of action removed to a district court from a federal or state court and govern procedure after removal. Repleading is not necessary unless the court so orders. In a removed action in which the defendant has not answered, the defendant shall answer or present the other defenses or objections available under the rules of Part VII within 21 days following the receipt through service or otherwise of a copy of the initial pleading setting forth the claim for relief on which the action or proceeding is based, or within 21 days following the service of summons on such initial pleading, or within seven days following the filing of the notice of removal, whichever period is longest.

(h) Record supplied

When a party is entitled to copies of the records and proceedings in any civil action or proceeding in a federal or a state court, to be used in the removed civil action or proceeding, and the clerk of the federal or state court, on demand accompanied by payment or tender of the lawful fees, fails to deliver certified copies, the court may, on affidavit reciting the facts, direct such record to be supplied by affidavit or otherwise. Thereupon the proceedings, trial and judgment may be had in the court, and all process awarded, as if certified copies had been filed.

(i) Attachment or sequestration; securities

When a claim or cause of action is removed to a district court, any attachment or sequestration of property in the court from which the claim or cause of action was removed shall hold the property to answer the final judgment or decree in the same manner as the property would have been held to answer final judgment or decree had it been rendered by the court from which the claim or cause of action was removed. All bonds, undertakings, or security given by either party to the claim or cause of action prior to its removal shall remain valid and effectual notwithstanding such removal. All injunctions issued, orders entered and other proceedings had prior to removal shall remain in full force and effect until dissolved or modified by the court.

(As amended Mar. 30, 1987, eff. Aug. 1, 1987; Apr. 30, 1991, eff. Aug. 1, 1991; Apr. 29, 2002, eff. Dec. 1, 2002; Mar. 26, 2009, eff. Dec. 1, 2009.)

ADVISORY COMMITTEE NOTES

Under 28 U.S.C. § 1478(a) "any claim or cause of action in a civil action, other than a proceeding before the United States Tax Court or a civil action by a Government unit to enforce [a] . . . regulatory or police power" may be removed "if the bankruptcy courts have jurisdiction over such claim or cause of action." This rule specifies how removal is accomplished, the procedure thereafter, and the procedure to request remand of the removed claim or cause of action. If the claim or cause of action which is removed to the bankruptcy court is subject to the automatic stay of § 362 of the Code, the litigation may not proceed in the bankruptcy court until relief from the stay is granted.

The subdivisions of this rule conform substantially to 28 U.S.C. §§ 1446–1450 and Rule 81(a) F.R.Civ.P. pertaining to removal to the district courts.

Subdivision (a)(1) is derived from 28 U.S.C. § 1446(a).

Subdivisions (a)(2) and (a)(3) are derived from paragraphs one and two of 28 U.S.C. § 1446(b). Timely exercise of the right to remove is as important in bankruptcy cases as in removals from a state court to a district court.

Subdivision (a)(2) governs the situation in which there is litigation pending and a party to the litigation becomes a debtor under the Code. Frequently, removal would be of little utility in such cases because the pending litigation will be stayed by § 362(a) on commencement of the case under the Code. As long as the stay remains in effect there is no reason to impose a time limit for removal to the bankruptcy court and, therefore, clause (B) of subdivision (a)(2) provides that a removal application may be filed within 30 days of entry of an order terminating the stay. Parties to stayed litigation will not be required to act immediately on commencement of a case under the Code to protect their right to remove. If the pending litigation is not stayed by § 362(a) of the Code, the removal application must ordinarily be filed within 90 days of the order for relief. Clause (C) contains an alternative period for a chapter 11 case. If a trustee is appointed, the removal application may be filed within 30 days of the trustee's qualification, provided that the removal application is filed not more than 180 days after the order for relief.

The removal application must be filed within the longest of the three possible periods. For example, in a chapter 11 case if the 90 day period expires but a trustee is appointed shortly thereafter, the removal application may be filed within 30 days of the trustee's qualification but not later than 180 days after the order for relief. Nevertheless, if the claim or cause of action in the civil action is stayed under § 362, the application may be filed after the 180 day period expires, provided the application is filed within 30 days of an order terminating the stay.

Subdivision (a)(3) applies to the situation in which the case under the Code is pending when the removable claim or cause of action is asserted in a civil action initiated in other than the bankruptcy court. The time for filing the application for removal begins to run on receipt of the first pleading containing the removable claim or cause of action. Only litigation not stayed by the code or by court order may properly be initiated after the case under the Code is commenced. See e.g., § 362(a).

Subdivision (b). With one exception, this subdivision is the same as 28 U.S.C. § 1446(d). The exemption from the bond requirement is enlarged to include a trustee or debtor in possession. Complete exemption from the bond requirement for removal is appropriate because of the limited resources which may be available at the beginning of a case and the small probability that an action will be improperly removed.

Recovery on the bond is permitted only when the removal was improper. If the removal is proper but the bankruptcy court orders the action remanded on equitable grounds, 28 U.S.C. § 1478(b), there is no recovery on the bond.

Subdivisions (c) and (d) are patterned on 28 U.S.C. § 1446(e).

Subdivision (e). There is no provision in the Federal Rules of Civil Procedure for seeking remand. The first sentence of this subdivision requires that a request for remand be by motion and that the moving party serve all other parties; however, no hearing is required. In recognition of the intrusion of the removal practice on the state and federal courts from which claims or causes of action are removed, the subdivision directs the bankruptcy court to decide remand motions as soon as practicable. The last sentence of this subdivision is derived from 28 U.S.C. § 1446(c).

Subdivisions (f) and (g), with appropriate changes to conform them to the bankruptcy context, are the same as 28 U.S.C. § 1447(a) and (b) and 28 U.S.C. § 1448, respectively.

Subdivisions (h) and (i) are taken from Rule 81(c) F.R.Civ.P.

Subdivisions (j) and (k) are derived from 28 U.S.C. § 1449 and § 1450, respectively.

Remand orders of bankruptcy judges are not appealable. 28 U.S.C. § 1478(b).

This rule does not deal with the question whether a single plaintiff or defendant may remove a claim or cause of action if there are two or more plaintiffs or defendants. See 28 U.S.C. § 1478.

1987 Amendment

Section 1452 of title 28, with certain exceptions, provides for removal of claims or causes of action in civil actions pending in state or federal courts when the claim or cause of action is within the jurisdiction conferred by 28 U.S.C. § 1334. An order granting or denying a motion for remand is not appealable. 28 U.S.C. § 1452(b). Under subdivision (e), as amended, the district court must enter the order on the remand motion; however, the bankruptcy judge conducts the initial hearing on the motion and files a report and recommendation. The parties may file objections. Review of the report and recommendation is pursuant to Rule 9033.

Subdivision (f) has been amended to provide that if there has been a referral pursuant to 28 U.S.C. § 157(a) the bankruptcy judge will preside over the removed civil action.

Subdivision (i) has been abrogated consistent with the abrogation of Rule 9015.

1991 Amendment

The abrogation of subdivision (b) is consistent with the repeal of 28 U.S.C. § 1446(d). The changes substituting the notice of removal for the application for removal conform to the 1988 amendments to 28 U.S.C. § 1446.

Rules 7008(a) and 7012(b) were amended in 1987 to require parties to allege in pleadings whether a proceeding is core or non-core and, if non-core, whether the parties consent to the entry of final orders or judgment by the bankruptcy judge. Subdivision (a)(1) is amended and subdivision (f)(3) is added to require parties to a removed claim or cause of action to make the same allegations. The party filing the notice of removal must include the allegation in the notice and the other parties who have filed pleadings must respond to the allegation in a separate statement filed within 10 days after removal. However, if a party to the removed claim or cause of action has not filed a pleading prior to removal, there is no need to file a separate statement under subdivision (f)(3) because the allegation must be included in the responsive pleading filed pursuant to Rule 7012(b).

Subdivision (e), redesignated as subdivision (d), is amended to delete the restriction that limits the role of the bankruptcy court to the filing of a report and recommendation for disposition of a motion for remand under 28 U.S.C. § 1452(b). This amendment is consistent with § 309(c) of the Judicial Improvements Act of 1990, which amended § 1452(b) so that it allows an appeal to the district court of a bankruptcy court's order determining a motion for remand. This subdivision is also amended to clarify that the motion is a contested matter governed by Rule 9014. The words "filed with the clerk" are deleted as unnecessary. See Rules 5005(a) and 9001(3).

2002 Amendments

Subdivision (a)(3) is amended to clarify that if a claim or cause of action is initiated after the commencement of a bankruptcy case, the time limits for filing a notice of removal of the claim or cause of action apply whether the case is still pending or has been suspended, dismissed, or closed.

Changes Made After Publication and Comments: No changes were made.

2009 Amendments

The rule is amended to implement changes in connection with the amendment to Rule 9006(a) and the manner by which time is computed under the rules. The deadlines in the rule are amended to substitute a deadline that is a multiple of seven days. Throughout the rules, deadlines are amended in the following manner:

- 5–day periods become 7–day periods
- 10–day periods become 14–day periods
- 15–day periods become 14–day periods
- 20–day periods become 21–day periods
- 25–day periods become 28–day periods

CROSS REFERENCES

Removed actions, see Fed.Rules Civ.Proc. Rule 81, 28 USCA.

Removal of actions, see 28 USCA §§ 1446 to 1450.

LIBRARY REFERENCES

American Digest System

Bankruptcy ⊜2086.1 to 2091.

Key Number System Topic No. 51.

Corpus Juris Secundum

CJS Bankruptcy § 232, Notice of Removal.

CJS Bankruptcy § 233, Notice to Parties; Filing in Nonbankruptcy Court.

CJS Bankruptcy § 234, Pending Actions.

CJS Bankruptcy § 235, Referral of Removed Claim to Bankruptcy Judge.

CJS Bankruptcy § 236, Process and Pleading After Removal.

CJS Bankruptcy § 237, Supplying of Record.

CJS Bankruptcy § 238, Attachment or Sequestration; Continued Effect of Security and Preremoval Injunctions, Orders, and Other Proceedings.

Rule 9028.   Disability of a Judge

Rule 63 F.R.Civ.P. applies in cases under the Code. (As amended Mar. 30, 1987, eff. Aug. 1, 1987.)

ADVISORY COMMITTEE NOTES

This rule is an adaptation of Rule 63 F.R.Civ.P.

1987 Amendment

Rule 9028 has been changed to adopt the procedures contained in Rule 63 of the Federal Rules of Civil Procedure for substituting a judge in the event of disability.

CROSS REFERENCES

Disability of judge, see Fed.Rules Civ.Proc. Rule 63, 28 USCA.

LIBRARY REFERENCES

American Digest System

Judges ⊜21, 32.

Key Number System Topic No. 227.

Corpus Juris Secundum

CJS Bankruptcy § 12, Federal Rules of Civil Procedure.

CJS Bankruptcy § 32, Removal of Judge; Substitution for Disabled Judge.

Rule 9029.   Local Bankruptcy Rules; Procedure When There Is No Controlling Law

(a) Local Bankruptcy Rules

(1) Each district court acting by a majority of its district judges may make and amend rules governing practice and procedure in all cases and proceedings within the district court's bankruptcy jurisdiction which are consistent with—but not duplicative of—Acts of Congress and these rules and which do not prohibit or limit the use of the Official Forms. Rule 83 F.R.Civ.P. governs the procedure for making local rules. A district court may authorize the bankruptcy judges of the district, subject to any limitation or condition it may prescribe and the requirements of 83 F.R.Civ.P., to make and amend rules of practice and procedure which are consistent with—but not duplicative of—Acts of Congress and these rules and which do not prohibit or limit the use of the Official Forms. Local rules shall conform to any uniform numbering system prescribed by the Judicial Conference of the United States.

(2) A local rule imposing a requirement of form shall not be enforced in a manner that causes a party to lose rights because of a nonwillful failure to comply with the requirement.

(b) Procedure When There Is No Controlling Law. A judge may regulate practice in any manner consistent with federal law, these rules, Official Forms, and local rules of the district. No sanction or other disadvantage may be imposed for noncompliance with any requirement not in federal law, federal rules, Official Forms, or the local rules of the district unless the alleged violator has been furnished in the particular case with actual notice of the requirement.

(As amended Mar. 30, 1987, eff. Aug. 1, 1987; Apr. 30, 1991, eff. Aug. 1, 1991; Apr. 27, 1995, eff. Dec. 1, 1995.)

ADVISORY COMMITTEE NOTES

This rule is an adaptation of Rule 83 F.R.Civ.P. and Rule 57(a) F.R.Crim.P. Under this rule bankruptcy courts may make local rules which govern practice before those courts. Circuit councils and district courts are authorized by Rule 8018 to make local rules governing appellate practice.

1987 Amendment

Rule 9029 is amended to authorize the district court to promulgate local rules governing bankruptcy practice. This rule, as amended, permits the district court to authorize the bankruptcy judges to promulgate or recommend local rules for adoption by the district court.

Effective August 1, 1985, Rule 83 F.R.Civ.P., governing adoption of local rules, was amended to achieve greater participation by the bar, scholars, and the public in the rule making process; to authorize the judicial council to abrogate local rules; and to make certain that single-judge standing orders are not inconsistent with these rules or local rules. Rule 9029 has been amended to incorporate Rule 83. The term "court" in the last sentence of the rule includes the judges of the district court and the bankruptcy judges of the district. Rule 9001(4).

1991 Amendments

This rule is amended to make it clear that the Official Forms must be accepted in every bankruptcy court.

1995 Amendments

Subdivision (a). This rule is amended to reflect the requirement that local rules be consistent not only with applicable national rules but also with Acts of Congress. The amendment also states that local rules should not repeat applicable national rules and Acts of Congress.

The amendment also requires that the numbering of local rules conform with any uniform numbering system that may be prescribed by the Judicial Conference. Lack of uniform numbering might create unnecessary traps for counsel and litigants. A uniform numbering system would make it easier for an increasingly national bar and for litigants to locate a local rule that applies to a particular procedural issue.

Paragraph (2) of subdivision (a) is new. Its aim is to protect against loss of rights in the enforcement of local rules relating to matters of form. For example, a party should not be deprived of a right to a jury trial because its attorney, unaware of—or forgetting—a local rule directing that jury demands be noted in the caption of the case, includes a jury demand only in the body of the pleading. The proscription of paragraph (2) is narrowly drawn—covering only violations that are not willful and only those involving local rules directed to matters of form. It does not limit the court's power to impose substantive penalties upon a party if it or its attorney stubbornly or repeatedly violates a local rule, even one involving merely a matter of form. Nor does it affect the court's power to enforce local rules that involve more than mere matters of form—for example, a local rule requiring that a party demand a jury trial within a specified time period to avoid waiver of the right to a trial by jury.

Subdivision (b). This rule provides flexibility to the court in regulating practice when there is no controlling law. Specifically, it permits the court to regulate practice in any manner consistent with federal law, with rules adopted under 28 U.S.C. § 2075, with Official Forms, and with the district's local rules.

This rule recognizes that courts rely on multiple directives to control practice. Some courts regulate practice through the published Federal Rules and the local rules of the court. Some courts also have used internal operating procedures, standing orders, and other internal directives. Although such directives continue to be authorized, they can lead to problems. Counsel or litigants may be unaware of various directives. In addition, the sheer volume of directives may impose an unreasonable barrier. For example, it may be difficult to obtain copies of the directives. Finally, counsel or litigants may be unfairly sanctioned for failing to comply with a directive. For these reasons, the amendment to this rule disapproves imposing any sanction or other disadvantage on a person for noncompliance with such an internal directive,

unless the alleged violator has been furnished in a particular case with actual notice of the requirement.

There should be no adverse consequence to a party or attorney for violating special requirements relating to practice before a particular judge unless the party or attorney has actual notice of those requirements. Furnishing litigants with a copy outlining the judge's practices—or attaching instructions to a notice setting a case for conference or trial—would suffice to give actual notice, as would an order in a case specifically adopting by reference a judge's standing order and indicating how copies can be obtained.

CROSS REFERENCES

Local rules to govern appellate practice, see Fed.Rules Bankr.Proc. Rule 8018, 11 USCA.

Rules by district courts, see Fed.Rules Civ.Proc. Rule 83, 28 USCA.

Rules by district courts, see Fed.Rules Cr.Proc. Rule 57, 18 USCA.

LIBRARY REFERENCES

American Digest System

Bankruptcy ⇐2129.

Key Number System Topic No. 51.

Corpus Juris Secundum

CJS Bankruptcy § 15, Local Rules.

CJS Bankruptcy § 25, Power to Regulate Practice and Make Rules.

CJS Bankruptcy § 138, Rules of Practice and Procedure.

Rule 9030.　Jurisdiction and Venue Unaffected

These rules shall not be construed to extend or limit the jurisdiction of the courts or the venue of any matters therein.

(As amended Mar. 30, 1987, eff. Aug. 1, 1987.)

ADVISORY COMMITTEE NOTES

The rule is an adaptation of Rule 82 F.R.Civ.P.

CROSS REFERENCES

Jurisdiction and venue unaffected, see Fed.Rules Civ.Proc. Rule 82, 28 USCA.

Power of Supreme Court to prescribe bankruptcy rules, see 28 USCA § 2075.

LIBRARY REFERENCES

American Digest System

Bankruptcy ⇐2041.1, 2081, 2129.

Key Number System Topic No. 51.

Corpus Juris Secundum

CJS Bankruptcy § 264, Cases Under Bankruptcy Code.

Rule 9031.　Masters Not Authorized

Rule 53 F.R.Civ.P. does not apply in cases under the Code.

This rule precludes the appointment of masters in cases and proceedings under the Code.

American Digest System

Bankruptcy ☞2127.1.

Key Number System Topic No. 51.

Corpus Juris Secundum

CJS Bankruptcy § 12, Federal Rules of Civil Procedure.

Rule 9032. Effect of Amendment of Federal Rules of Civil Procedure

The Federal Rules of Civil Procedure which are incorporated by reference and made applicable by these rules shall be the Federal Rules of Civil Procedure in effect on the effective date of these rules and as thereafter amended, unless otherwise provided by such amendment or by these rules.

(As amended Apr. 30, 1991, eff. Aug. 1, 1991.)

1991 Amendment

This rule is amended to provide flexibility so that the Bankruptcy Rules may provide that subsequent amendments to a Federal Rule of Civil Procedure made applicable by these rules are not effective with regard to Bankruptcy Code cases or proceedings. For example, in view of the anticipated amendments to, and restructuring of, Rule 4 F.R.Civ.P., Rule 7004(g) will prevent such changes from affecting Bankruptcy Code cases until the Advisory Committee on Bankruptcy Rules has an opportunity to consider such amendments and to make appropriate recommendations for incorporating such amendments into the Bankruptcy Rules.

American Digest System

Bankruptcy ☞2129.

Key Number System Topic No. 51.

Corpus Juris Secundum

CJS Bankruptcy § 12, Federal Rules of Civil Procedure.

CJS Bankruptcy § 139, Adversary Proceedings.

CJS Bankruptcy § 140, Contested Matters.

Rule 9033. Review of Proposed Findings of Fact and Conclusions of Law in Non-Core Proceedings

(a) Service

In non-core proceedings heard pursuant to 28 U.S.C. § 157(c)(1), the bankruptcy judge shall file proposed findings of fact and conclusions of law. The clerk shall serve forthwith copies on all parties by mail and note the date of mailing on the docket.

(b) Objections: time for filing

Within 14 days after being served with a copy of the proposed findings of fact and conclusions of law a party may serve and file with the clerk written objections which identify the specific proposed findings or conclusions objected to and state the grounds for such objection. A party may respond to another party's objections within 14 days after being served with a copy thereof. A party objecting to the bankruptcy judge's proposed findings or conclusions shall arrange promptly for the transcription of the record, or such portions of it as all parties may agree upon or the bankruptcy judge deems sufficient, unless the district judge otherwise directs.

(c) Extension of time

The bankruptcy judge may for cause extend the time for filing objections by any party for a period not to exceed 21 days from the expiration of the time otherwise prescribed by this rule. A request to extend the time for filing objections must be made before the time for filing objections has expired, except that a request made no more than 21 days after the expiration of the time for filing objections may be granted upon a showing of excusable neglect.

(d) Standard of review

The district judge shall make a de novo review upon the record or, after additional evidence, of any portion of the bankruptcy judge's findings of fact or conclusions of law to which specific written objection has been made in accordance with this rule. The district judge may accept, reject, or modify the proposed findings of fact or conclusions of law, receive further evidence, or recommit the matter to the bankruptcy judge with instructions.

(Added Mar. 30, 1987, eff. Aug. 1, 1987; amended Mar. 26, 2009, eff. Dec. 1, 2009.)

Section 157(c)(1) of title 28 requires a bankruptcy judge to submit proposed findings of fact and conclusions of law to the district court when the bankruptcy judge has heard a non-core proceeding. This rule, which is modeled on Rule 72 F.R.Civ.P., provides the procedure for objecting to, and for review by, the district court of specific findings and conclusions.

Subdivision (a) requires the clerk to serve a copy of the proposed findings and conclusions on the parties. The bankruptcy clerk, or the district court clerk if there is no bankruptcy clerk in the district, shall serve a copy of the proposed findings and conclusions on all parties.

Subdivision (b) is derived from Rule 72(b) F.R.Civ.P. which governs objections to a recommended disposition by a magistrate.

Subdivision (c) is similar to Rule 8002(c) of the Bankruptcy Rules and provides for granting of extensions of time to file objections to proposed findings and conclusions.

Subdivision (d) adopts the de novo review provisions of Rule 72(b) F.R.Civ.P.

2009 Amendments

The rule is amended to implement changes in connection with the amendment to Rule 9006(a) and the manner by which time is computed under the rules. The deadlines in the rule are amended to substitute a deadline that is a multiple of seven days. Throughout the rules, deadlines are amended in the following manner:

- 5–day periods become 7–day periods
- 10–day periods become 14–day periods
- 15–day periods become 14–day periods
- 20–day periods become 21–day periods
- 25–day periods become 28–day periods

LIBRARY REFERENCES

American Digest System

Bankruptcy ⚖2104, 2105.
Key Number System Topic No. 51.

Corpus Juris Secundum

CJS Bankruptcy § 218, District Court's De Novo Review.
CJS Bankruptcy § 308, Enlargement.
CJS Bankruptcy § 309, Reduction.
CJS Bankruptcy § 1216, Review of Bankruptcy Court's Proposed Findings and Conclusions.

Rule 9034.   Transmittal of Pleadings, Motion Papers, Objections, and Other Papers to the United States Trustee

Unless the United States trustee requests otherwise or the case is a chapter 9 municipality case, any entity that files a pleading, motion, objection, or similar paper relating to any of the following matters shall transmit a copy thereof to the United States trustee within the time required by these rules for service of the paper:

(a) a proposed use, sale, or lease of property of the estate other than in the ordinary course of business;

(b) the approval of a compromise or settlement of a controversy;

(c) the dismissal or conversion of a case to another chapter;

(d) the employment of professional persons;

(e) an application for compensation or reimbursement of expenses;

(f) a motion for, or approval of an agreement relating to, the use of cash collateral or authority to obtain credit;

(g) the appointment of a trustee or examiner in a chapter 11 reorganization case;

(h) the approval of a disclosure statement;

(i) the confirmation of a plan;

(j) an objection to, or waiver or revocation of, the debtor's discharge;

(k) any other matter in which the United States trustee requests copies of filed papers or the court orders copies transmitted to the United States trustee.

(Added Apr. 30, 1991, eff. Aug. 1, 1991.)

ADVISORY COMMITTEE NOTES

Section 307 of the Code gives the United States trustee the right to appear and be heard on issues in cases and proceedings under the Code. This rule is intended to keep the United States trustee informed of certain developments and disputes in which the United States may wish to be heard. This rule, which derives from Rule X–1008, also enables the United States trustee to monitor the progress of the case in accordance with 28 U.S.C. § 586(a). The requirement to transmit copies of certain pleadings, motion papers and other documents is intended to be flexible in that the United States trustee in a particular judicial district may request copies of papers in certain categories, and may request not to receive copies of documents in other categories, when the practice in that district makes that desirable. When the rules require that a paper be served on particular parties, the time period in which service is required is also applicable to transmittal to the United States trustee.

Although other rules require that certain notices be transmitted to the United States trustee, this rule goes further in that it requires the transmittal to the United States trustee of other papers filed in connection with these matters. This rule is not an exhaustive list of the matters of which the United States trustee may be entitled to receive notice.

LIBRARY REFERENCES

American Digest System

Bankruptcy ⚖2127.1, 3009.
Key Number System Topic No. 51.

Corpus Juris Secundum

CJS Bankruptcy § 768, Notice and Hearing.

Rule 9035.   Applicability of Rules in Judicial Districts in Alabama and North Carolina

In any case under the Code that is filed in or transferred to a district in the State of Alabama or the State of North Carolina and in which a United States trustee is not authorized to act, these rules apply to the extent that they are not inconsistent with any federal statute effective in the case.

(Added Apr. 30, 1991, eff. Aug. 1, 1991; amended Apr. 11, 1997, eff. Dec. 1, 1997.)

ADVISORY COMMITTEE NOTES

Section 302(d)(3) of the Bankruptcy Judges, United States Trustees, and Family Farmer Bankruptcy Act of 1986 provides that amendments to the Code relating to United States trustees and quarterly fees required under 28 U.S.C. § 1930(a)(6) do not become effective in any judicial district in the States of Alabama and North Carolina until the district elects to be included in the United States trustee system, or October 1, 1992, whichever occurs first, unless Congress extends the deadline. If the United States trustee system becomes effective in these districts, the transition provisions in the 1986 Act will govern the application of the United States trustee amendments to cases that are pending at that time. See § 302(d)(3)(F). The statute, and not the bankruptcy court, determines whether a United States trustee is authorized to act in a particular case.

Section 302(d)(3)(I) of the 1986 Act authorizes the Judicial Conference of the United States to promulgate regulations governing the appointment of bankruptcy administrators to supervise the administration of estates and trustees in cases in the districts in Alabama and North Carolina until the provisions of the Act relating to the United States trustee take effect in these districts. Pursuant to this authority, in September 1987, the Judicial Conference promulgated regulations governing the selection and appointment of bankruptcy administrators and regulations governing the establishment, duties, and functions of bankruptcy administrators. Guidelines relating to the bankruptcy administrator program have been prescribed by the Director of the Administrative Office of the United States Courts.

Many of these rules were amended to implement the United States trustee system in accordance with the 1986 Act. Since the provisions of the 1986 Act relating to the United States trustee system are not effective in cases in Alabama and North Carolina in which a bankruptcy administrator is serving, rules referring to United States trustees are at least partially inconsistent with the provisions of the Bankruptcy Code and title 28 of the United States Code effective in such cases.

In determining the applicability of these rules in cases in Alabama and North Carolina in which a United States trustee is not authorized to act, the following guidelines should be followed:

(1) The following rules do not apply because they are inconsistent with the provisions of the Code or title 28 in these cases: 1002(b), 1007(1), 1009(c), 2002(k), 2007.1(b), 2015(a)(6), 2020, 3015(b), 5005(b), 7004(b)(10), 9003(b), and 9034.

(2) The following rules are partially inconsistent with the provisions of the Code effective in these cases and, therefore, are applicable with the following modifications:

(a) **Rule 2001(a) and (c)**—The court, rather than the United States trustee, appoints the interim trustee.

(b) **Rule 2003**—The duties of the United States trustee relating to the meeting of creditors or equity security holders are performed by the officer determined in accordance with regulations of the Judicial Conference, guidelines of the Director of the Administrative Office, local rules or court orders.

(c) **Rule 2007**—The court, rather than the United States trustee, appoints committees in chapter 9 and chapter 11 cases.

(d) **Rule 2008**—The bankruptcy administrator, rather than the United States trustee, informs the trustee of how to qualify.

(e) **Rule 2009(c) and (d)**—The court, rather than the United States trustee, appoints interim trustees in chapter 7 cases and trustees in chapter 11, 12 and 13 cases.

(f) **Rule 2010**—The court, rather than the United States trustee, determines the amount and sufficiency of the trustee's bond.

(g) **Rule 5010**—The court, rather than the United States trustee, appoints the trustee when a case is reopened.

(3) All other rules are applicable because they are consistent with the provisions of the Code and title 28 effective in these cases, except that any reference to the United States trustee is not applicable and should be disregarded.

Many of the amendments to the rules are designed to give the United States trustee, a member of the Executive Branch, notice of certain developments and copies of petitions, schedules, pleadings, and other papers. In contrast, the bankruptcy administrator is an officer in the Judicial Branch and matters relating to notice of developments and access to documents filed in the clerk's office are governed by regulations of the Judicial Conference of the United States, guidelines of the Administrative Office of the United States Courts, local rules, and court orders. Also, requirements for disclosure of connections with the bankruptcy administrator in applications for employment of professional persons, restrictions on appointments of relatives of bankruptcy administrators, effects of erroneously filing papers with the bankruptcy administrator, and other matters not covered by these rules may be governed by regulations of the Judicial Conference, guidelines of the Director of the Administrative Office, local rules, and court orders.

This rule will cease to have effect if a United States trustee is authorized in every case in the districts in Alabama and North Carolina.

1997 Amendment

Certain statutes that are not codified in title 11 or title 28 of the United States Code, such as § 105 of the Bankruptcy Reform Act of 1994, Pub.L. 103–394, 108 Stat. 4106, relate to bankruptcy administrators in the judicial districts of North Carolina and Alabama. This amendment makes it clear that the Bankruptcy Rules do not apply to the extent that they are inconsistent with these federal statutes.

GAP Report on Rule 9035. No changes to the published draft.

LIBRARY REFERENCES

American Digest System

Bankruptcy ⌖2129.

Key Number System Topic No. 51.

Corpus Juris Secundum

CJS Bankruptcy § 38, Nationwide System; Not in Effect in North Carolina and Alabama.

CJS Bankruptcy § 51, Chapter 11 Proceedings.

CJS Bankruptcy § 138, Rules of Practice and Procedure.

CJS Bankruptcy § 790, Convening of Meeting by Trustee or Other Judicial Officer.

CJS Bankruptcy § 793, Duties of Trustee or Other Judicial Officer.

Rule 9036. Notice by Electronic Transmission

Whenever the clerk or some other person as directed by the court is required to send notice by mail and the entity entitled to receive the notice requests in writing that, instead of notice by mail, all or part of the information required to be contained in the notice be sent by a specified type of electronic transmission, the court may direct the clerk or other person to send the information by such electronic transmission. Notice by electronic means is complete on transmission.

(Added Apr. 22, 1993, eff. Aug. 1, 1993; amended Apr. 25, 2005, eff. Dec. 1, 2005.)

ADVISORY COMMITTEE NOTES

1993 Amendments

This rule is added to provide flexibility for banks, credit card companies, taxing authorities, and other entities that ordinarily receive notices by mail in a large volume of bankruptcy cases, to arrange to receive by electronic transmission all or part of the information required to be contained in such notices.

The use of electronic technology instead of mail to send information to creditors and interested parties will be more convenient and less costly for the sender and the receiver. For example, a bank that receives by mail, at different locations, notices of meetings of creditors pursuant to Rule 2002(a) in thousands of cases each year may prefer to receive only the vital information ordinarily contained in such notices by electronic transmission to one computer terminal.

The specific means of transmission must be compatible with technology available to the sender and the receiver. Therefore, electronic transmission of notices is permitted only upon request of the entity entitled to receive the notice, specifying the type of electronic transmission, and only if approved by the court.

Electronic transmission pursuant to the rule completes the notice requirements. The creditor or interested party is not thereafter entitled to receive the relevant notice by mail.

2005 Amendments

The rule is amended to delete the requirement that the sender of an electronic notice must obtain electronic confirmation that the notice was received. The amendment provides that notice is complete upon transmission. When the rule was first promulgated, confirmation of receipt of electronic notices was commonplace. In the current electronic environment, very few internet service providers offer the confirmation of receipt service. Consequently, compliance with the rule may be impossible, and the rule could discourage the use of electronic noticing.

Confidence in the delivery of email text messages now rivals or exceeds confidence in the delivery of printed materials. Therefore, there is no need for confirmation of receipt of electronic messages just as there is no such requirement for paper notices.

LIBRARY REFERENCES

American Digest System

Bankruptcy ⊕2131.

Key Number System Topic No. 51.

Corpus Juris Secundum

CJS Bankruptcy § 297, Notice by Other Means.

CJS Bankruptcy § 791, Notice.

CJS Bankruptcy § 1203, Requirements for Confirmation; Notice and Hearing.

Rule 9037.   Privacy Protection For Filings Made with the Court

(a) Redacted Filings

Unless the court orders otherwise, in an electronic or paper filing made with the court that contains an individual's social-security number, taxpayer-identification number, or birth date, the name of an individual, other than the debtor, known to be and identified as a minor, or a financial-account number, a party or nonparty making the filing may include only:

    (1) the last four digits of the social-security number and taxpayer-identification number;

    (2) the year of the individual's birth;

    (3) the minor's initials; and

    (4) the last four digits of the financial-account number.

(b) Exemptions from the Redaction Requirement

The redaction requirement does not apply to the following:

    (1) a financial-account number that identifies the property allegedly subject to forfeiture in a forfeiture proceeding;

    (2) the record of an administrative or agency proceeding unless filed with a proof of claim;

    (3) the official record of a state-court proceeding;

    (4) the record of a court or tribunal, if that record was not subject to the redaction requirement when originally filed;

    (5) a filing covered by subdivision (c) of this rule; and

    (6) a filing that is subject to § 110 of the Code.

(c) Filings Made Under Seal

The court may order that a filing be made under seal without redaction. The court may later unseal the filing or order the entity that made the filing to file a redacted version for the public record.

(d) Protective Orders

For cause, the court may by order in a case under the Code:

    (1) require redaction of additional information; or

    (2) limit or prohibit a nonparty's remote electronic access to a document filed with the court.

(e) Option for Additional Unredacted Filing Under Seal

An entity making a redacted filing may also file an unredacted copy under seal. The court must retain the unredacted copy as part of the record.

(f) Option for Filing a Reference List

A filing that contains redacted information may be filed together with a reference list that identifies each item of redacted information and specifies an appropriate identifier that uniquely corresponds to each item listed. The list must be filed under seal and may be amended as of right. Any reference in the case to a listed identifier will be construed to refer to the corresponding item of information.

(g) Waiver of Protection of Identifiers

An entity waives the protection of subdivision (a) as to the entity's own information by filing it without redaction and not under seal.

(Added Apr. 30, 2007, eff. Dec. 1, 2007.)

ADVISORY COMMITTEE NOTES

2007 Adoption

The rule is adopted in compliance with section 205(c)(3) of the E–Government Act of 2002, Public Law No. 107–347. Section 205(c)(3) requires the Supreme Court to prescribe rules "to protect privacy and security concerns relating to electronic filing of documents and the public availability . . . of documents filed electronically." The rule goes further than the E–Government Act in regulating paper filings even when they are not converted to electronic form, but the number of filings that remain in paper form is certain to diminish over time. Most districts scan paper filings into the electronic case file, where they become available to the public in the same way as documents initially filed in electronic form. It is electronic availability, not the form of the initial filing, that raises the privacy and security concerns addressed in the E–Government Act.

The rule is derived from and implements the policy adopted by the Judicial Conference in September 2001 to address the privacy concerns resulting from public access to electronic case files. *See* http://www.privacy.uscourts.gov/Policy.htm. The Judicial Conference policy is that documents in case files generally should be made available electronically to the same extent they are available at the courthouse, provided that certain "personal data identifiers" are not included in the public file.

While providing for the public filing of some information, such as the last four digits of an account number, the rule does not intend to establish a presumption that this information never could or should be protected. For example, it may well be necessary in individual cases to prevent remote access by nonparties to any part of an account number or social-security number. It may also be necessary to protect information not covered by the redaction requirement—such as driver's license numbers and alien registration numbers—in a particular case. In such cases, protection may be sought under subdivision (c) or (d). Moreover, the rule does not affect the protection available under other rules, such as Rules 16 and 26(c) of the Federal Rules of Civil Procedure, or under other sources of protective authority.

Any personal information not otherwise protected by sealing or redaction will be made available over the internet.

Counsel should therefore notify clients of this fact so that an informed decision may be made on what information is to be included in a document filed with the court.

An individual debtor's full social-security number or taxpayer-identification number is included on the notice of the § 341 meeting of creditors sent to creditors. Of course, that is not filed with the court, see Rule 1007(f) (the debtor "submits" this information), and the copy of the notice that is filed with the court does not include the full social-security number or taxpayer-identification number. Thus, since the full social-security number or taxpayer-identification number is not filed with the court, it is not available to a person searching that record.

The clerk is not required to review documents filed with the court for compliance with this rule. As subdivision (a) recognizes, the responsibility to redact filings rests with counsel, parties, and others who make filings with the court.

Subdivision (d) recognizes the court's inherent authority to issue a protective order to prevent remote access to private or sensitive information and to require redaction of material in addition to that which would be redacted under subdivision (a) of the rule. These orders may be issued whenever necessary either by the court on its own motion, or on motion of a party in interest.

Subdivision (e) allows an entity that makes a redacted filing to file an unredacted document under seal. This provision is derived from section 205(c)(3)(iv) of the E–Government Act. Subdivision (f) allows the option to file a reference list of redacted information. This provision is derived from section 205(c)(3)(v) of the E–Government Act, as amended in 2004.

In accordance with the E–Government Act, subdivision (f) of the rule refers to "redacted" information. The term "redacted" is intended to govern a filing that is prepared with abbreviated identifiers in the first instance, as well as a filing in which a personal identifier is edited after its preparation.

Subdivision (g) allows an entity to waive the protections of the rule as to that entity's own information by filing it in unredacted form. An entity may elect to waive the protection if, for example, it is determined that the costs of redaction outweigh the benefits to privacy. As to financial account numbers, the instructions to Schedules E and F of Official Form 6 note that the debtor may elect to include the complete account number on those schedules rather than limit the number to the final four digits. Including the complete number would operate as a waiver by the debtor under subdivision (g) as to the full information that the debtor set out on those schedules. The waiver operates only to the extent of the information that the entity filed without redaction. If an entity files an unredacted identifier by mistake, it may seek relief from the court.

Trial exhibits are subject to the redaction requirements of Rule 9037 to the extent they are filed with the court. Trial exhibits that are not initially filed with the court must be redacted in accordance with this rule if and when they are filed as part of an appeal or for other reasons.

PART X—UNITED STATES TRUSTEES [ABROGATED]

[Rules X–1001 to X–1010. Abrogated Apr. 30, 1991, eff. Aug. 1, 1991]

OFFICIAL FORMS

Form

1. Voluntary Petition.
2. Declaration Under Penalty of Perjury on Behalf of a Corporation or Partnership.
3A. Application and Order to Pay Filing Fee in Installments.
3B. Application for Waiver of the Chapter 7 Filing Fee for Individuals Who Cannot Pay the Filing Fee in Full or in Installments.
4. List of Creditors Holding 20 Largest Unsecured Claims.
5. Involuntary Petition.
6. Schedules.
7. Statement of Financial Affairs.
8. Individual Debtor's Statement of Intention.
9. Notice of Commencement of Case Under the Bankruptcy Code, Meeting of Creditors, and Deadlines.
10. Proof of Claim.
[11. Omitted. See Form 5.].
11A. General Power of Attorney.
11B. Special Power of Attorney.
12. Order and Notice for Hearing on Disclosure Statement.
13. Order Approving Disclosure Statement and Fixing Time for Filing Acceptances or Rejections of Plan, Combined with Notice Thereof.
14. Class [ ] Ballot for Accepting or Rejecting Plan of Reorganization.
15. Order Confirming Plan.
16A. Caption (Full).
16B. Caption (Short Title).
16C. Caption of Complaint in Adversary Proceeding Filed by a Debtor [Abrogated].
16D. Caption for Use in Adversary Proceeding.
17. Notice of Appeal Under 28 U.S.C. § 158(a) or (b) From a Judgment, Order, or Decree of a Bankruptcy Judge.
18. Discharge of Debtor in a Chapter 7 Case.
19. Declaration and Signature of Non–Attorney Bankruptcy Petition Preparer.
20A. Notice of Motion or Objection.
20B. Notice of Objection to Claim.
21. Statement of Social-Security Number or Individual Taxpayer-Identification Number (ITIN).
22. Statement of Current Monthly Income.
23. Debtor's Certification of Completion of Postpetition Instructional Course Concerning Personal Financial Management.
24. Certification to Court of Appeals by all Parties.
25A. Plan of Reorganization in Small Business Case Under Chapter 11.
25B. Disclosure Statement in Small Business Case Under Chapter 11.
25C. Small Business Monthly Operating Report.
26. Periodic Report Regarding Value, Operations and Profitability of Entities in Which the Debtor's Estate Holds a Substantial or Controlling Interest.
27. Reaffirmation Agreement Cover Sheet.

INTRODUCTION AND GENERAL INSTRUCTIONS

Rule 9009 of the Federal Rules of Bankruptcy Procedure states that the Official Forms prescribed by the Judicial Conference of the United States "shall be observed and used." The Official Forms, accordingly, are obligatory in character.

Rule 9009 expressly permits the user of the Official Forms to make such "alterations as may be appropriate," and the use of the Official Forms has been held to be subject to a "rule of substantial compliance." Some rules, for example Fed. R.Bankr.P. 3001(a), specifically state that the filed document need only "conform substantially" to the Official Form. A document for which an Official Form is prescribed generally will meet the standard of substantial compliance if the document contains the complete substance, that is, all of the information required by the Official Form.

Rule 9009 also expressly permits the contents of Official Forms to be rearranged, and the format of the Official Forms traditionally has been quite flexible. The forms of the voluntary petition, the schedules, and the statement of financial affairs are printed and sold by private publishers. Design features such as type face, type size, layout, and side and top margins were not prescribed by the Judicial Conference, but rather left to the professional judgment of each publisher.

A great deal of variation, accordingly, has developed. Some publishers also add forms that are not official but which have been drafted by the publisher. A form for a chapter 13 plan, for example, frequently is included with commercially printed packages of forms for filing cases under chapter 13, although there is no Official Form for this purpose. The variety of formats has accelerated since the introduction of computer software for generating the petitions, schedules, and statements of affairs. It is the policy of the Judicial Conference that such diversity is desirable and should be encouraged.

The sheer volume of bankruptcy cases, however, has compelled the Judicial Conference, for the first time, to prescribe the format of certain Official Forms. In particular, the format of Form 1, the Voluntary Petition, now is prescribed. This format is designed to assist the clerk of the bankruptcy court to enter the case in the court's computer database and ensures that all required information is available to both the clerk and the United States trustee at the inception of the case. The rule of substantial compliance continues to apply, however. Accordingly, publishers may vary the size and style of the type and may alter the size and shape of the boxes on the form, within the bounds of that rule.

The Official Forms of the petitions, schedules, and statement of financial affairs, (Forms 1, 5, 6, and 7), are to be printed on one side of the paper only. Each page is to be pre-punched with two holes at the top, and sufficient top margin allowed so that neither caption nor text is destroyed or obscured. Compliance with these standards will facilitate both the securing of the papers in the case file and review of the file by the public.

Although Rule 9009 permits alteration, for most of the Official Forms, alteration will be appropriate only in rare circumstances. The special forms for chapter 11 cases, on the other hand, seldom will be used without alterations. Forms 12 through 15, while legally sufficient in any chapter 11 case, are intended by the Judicial Conference, and most often

will be used, as a framework for drafting a document specially tailored to the particular case. These alterations generally will take the form of additions to the prescribed elements.

Rule 9009 provides for a balance of prescribed substance, to which full adherence is expected in all but the most unusual cases, and flexible formatting, under which requirements are kept to the minimum necessary for proper operation of the courts and the bankruptcy system. While Rule 9009 recognizes the overall need for flexibility, Rule 9029 makes it clear that the Official Forms must be accepted in every bankruptcy court.

Under Rule 9029, courts may not reject documents presented for filing in novel or unfamiliar formats if those documents contain the substance prescribed by the Official Form and meet the requirements for one-sided printing, pre-punched holes, and adequate top margins. Nor are courts authorized to impose local forms which vary in substance from the Official Forms or reject papers presented for filing on Official Forms on the basis that the proffered documents differ from a locally preferred version.

Special Instructions for Computer–Generated Forms

In Form 1, the Voluntary Petition, if a box contains multiple choices, a computer-generated petition that shows only the choice made is acceptable for filing. All sections of the petition must be shown and completed, however, unless instructions on the Official Form of the petition state that the box is applicable only to cases filed under a chapter other than the one selected by the debtor. If the debtor has no information to provide for a particular box, for example if the debtor has no prior bankruptcies to report, a computer-generated petition should so indicate by stating "None."

Form 6, the Schedules, on which the debtor reports all of the debtor's assets and liabilities, has been prescribed in a columnar format. Columns help to organize the information which the debtor is required to report and should be used when the printed schedules are completed on a typewriter. In a computerized law office, however, the organizational structure of the schedules can be built into the computer program, and a rigid columnar format may be a hindrance rather than a help. Schedules generated by computer which provide all of the information requested by the prescribed form are fully acceptable, regardless of the format of the printed page. The information must be appropriately labeled, however. In Schedule B, for example, all of the categories of personal property must be printed on the filed document together with the debtor's response to each. The space occupied by each category may be expanded, however, so that attachments are not needed. Instructions provided on the printed forms can simply be built into the computer program; they need not be reprinted on the filed document.

Form 7, the Statement of Financial Affairs, contains a series of questions which direct the debtor to answer by furnishing information. If the answer to a question is "None," or the question is not applicable, an affirmative statement to that effect is required. To assure that the trustee and the creditors can review the debtor's statement properly, the complete text of each question must be printed on the filed document.

Form 9, the Notice of Filing under the Bankruptcy Code, Meeting of Creditors, and Fixing of Dates, will be prepared by the clerk of the bankruptcy court in most cases. The form is designed for use with automated printing and mailing equipment. Two free lines, which do not appear on the printed blank form, have been programmed into the form. Courts may use this space to add local information, such as directions for obtaining copies of the debtor's schedules.

CONVERSION TABLE FOR OFFICIAL BANKRUPTCY FORMS

Former Official Form Number

Form No. 1. Voluntary Petition
[Revised; see new Official Form 1.]

Form No. 2. Application and Order to Pay Filing Fee in Installments
[Renumbered; see new Official Form 3.]

Form No. 3. Order for Payment of Filing Fee in Installments
[Abrogated and combined with Form No. 2; see new Official Form 3.]

Form No. 4. Unsworn Declaration under Penalty of Perjury on Behalf of a Corporation or Partnership
[Renumbered; see new Official Form 2.]

Form No. 5. Certificate of Commencement of Case
[Abrogated.]

Form No. 6. Schedules of Assets and Liabilities
[Revised; see new Official Form 6.]

Form No. 6A. Schedule of Current Income and Current Expenditures for Individual Debtor
[Revised; see new Official Form 6, Schedules I and J.]

Form No. 7. Statement of Financial Affairs for Debtor Not Engaged in Business
[Revised and combined with former Form No. 8; see new Official Form 7.]

Form No. 8. Statement of Financial Affairs for Debtor Engaged in Business
[Revised and combined with former Form No. 7; see new Official Form 7.]

Form No. 8A. Chapter 7 Individual Debtor's Statement of Intention
[Renumbered; see new Official Form 8.]

Form No. 9. List of Creditors Holding 20 Largest Unsecured Claims
[Renumbered; see new Official Form 4.]

Former Official Form Number

Form No. 10. Chapter 13 Statement
[Abrogated; see new Official Forms 6, 7, and 8.]

Form No. 11. Involuntary Case: Creditors' Petition
[Revised, combined with former Form No. 12, and renumbered; see new Official Form 5.]

Form No. 12. Involuntary Case Against Partnership; Partner's Petition
[Abrogated and combined with former Form No. 11; see new Official Form 5.]

Form No. 13. Summons to Debtor
[Abrogated.]

Form No. 14. Order for Relief
[Abrogated.]

Form No. 15. Appointment of Committee of Unsecured Creditors in Chapter 9 Municipality or Chapter 11 Reorganization Case
[Abrogated.]

Form No. 16. Order for Meeting of Creditors and Related Orders, Combined with Notice Thereof and of Automatic Stay
[Revised and renumbered; see new Official Form 9.]

Form No. 17. General Power of Attorney
[Renumbered; see new Official Form 11A.]

Form No. 18. Special Power of Attorney
[Renumbered; see new Official Form No. 11B.]

Form No. 19. Proof of Claim
[Revised and renumbered; see new Official Form 10.]

Form No. 20. Proof of Claim for Wages, Salary, or Commissions
[Abrogated and combined with former Form No. 19; see new Official Form 10.]

Form No. 21. Proof of Multiple Claims for Wages, Salary, or Commissions
[Abrogated and combined with former Form No. 19; see new Official Form No. 10.]

Form No. 22. Order Appointing Interim Trustee and Fixing Amount of Bond
[Abrogated.]

Form No. 23. Order Approving Election of Trustee and Fixing Amount of Bond
[Abrogated.]

Form No. 24. Notice to Trustee of Selection and of Time Fixed for Filing a Complaint Objecting to Discharge of Debtor

OFFICIAL FORMS

Former Official Form Number

[Abrogated.]

Form No. 25.   Bond and Order Approving Bond of Trustee
[Abrogated.]

Form No. 26.   Certificate of Retention of Debtor in Possession
[Abrogated.]

Form No. 27.   Discharge of Debtor
[Renumbered; see new Official Form 18.]

Form No. 28.   Order and Notice for Hearing on Disclosure Statement
[Renumbered; see new Official Form 12.]

Form No. 29.   Order Approving Disclosure Statement and Fixing Time for Filing Acceptances or Rejections of Plan, Combined with Notice Thereof
[Renumbered; see new Official Form 13.]

Former Official Form Number

Form No. 30.   Ballot for Accepting or Rejecting Plan
[Renumbered; see new Official Form 14.]

Form No. 31.   Order Confirming Plan
[Renumbered; see new Official Form 15.]

Form No. 32.   Notice of Filing Final Account
[Abrogated.]

Form No. 33.   Final Decree
[Abrogated.]

Form No. 34.   Caption of Adversary Proceedings
[Renumbered; see new Official Form No. 16C.]

Form No. 35.   Notice of Appeal to a District Court or Bankruptcy Appellate Panel from a Judgment of a Bankruptcy Court Entered in an Adversary Proceeding
[Revised and renumbered; see new Official Form 17.]

NOTE CONCERNING CONTINUED AVAILABILITY OF CERTAIN ABROGATED FORMS

Forms No. 5, 13, 14, 26, 32 and 33, although abrogated as Official Forms, continue to be available as procedural forms issued by the Director of the Administrative Office of the United States Courts. Members of the bar and the public may consult the Bankruptcy Forms Manual, which is available in the clerk's office at every bankruptcy court location. The contents of the Bankruptcy Forms Manual may be copied without restriction, subject to any applicable copy fee charged by the clerk.

Forms No. 15, 22, 23, 24 and 25, also abrogated as Official Forms, pertain to functions now performed by the United States trustee. Any forms deemed necessary for carrying out those functions will be issued by the Department of Justice.

Form 1. Voluntary Petition

B1 (Official Form 1) (12/11)

UNITED STATES BANKRUPTCY COURT	VOLUNTARY PETITION

Name of Debtor (if individual, enter Last, First, Middle):	Name of Joint Debtor (Spouse) (Last, First, Middle):
All Other Names used by the Debtor in the last 8 years (include married, maiden, and trade names):	All Other Names used by the Joint Debtor in the last 8 years (include married, maiden, and trade names):
Last four digits of Soc. Sec. or Individual-Taxpayer I.D. (ITIN)/Complete EIN (if more than one, state all):	Last four digits of Soc. Sec. or Individual-Taxpayer I.D. (ITIN)/Complete EIN (if more than one, state all):
Street Address of Debtor (No. and Street, City, and State): ZIP CODE	Street Address of Joint Debtor (No. and Street, City, and State): ZIP CODE
County of Residence or of the Principal Place of Business:	County of Residence or of the Principal Place of Business:
Mailing Address of Debtor (if different from street address): ZIP CODE	Mailing Address of Joint Debtor (if different from street address): ZIP CODE
Location of Principal Assets of Business Debtor (if different from street address above): ZIP CODE	

Type of Debtor
(Form of Organization)
(Check one box.)

☐ Individual (includes Joint Debtors)
 See Exhibit D on page 2 of this form.
☐ Corporation (includes LLC and LLP)
☐ Partnership
☐ Other (If debtor is not one of the above entities, check this box and state type of entity below.)

Nature of Business
(Check one box.)

☐ Health Care Business
☐ Single Asset Real Estate as defined in 11 U.S.C. § 101(51B)
☐ Railroad
☐ Stockbroker
☐ Commodity Broker
☐ Clearing Bank
☐ Other

Chapter of Bankruptcy Code Under Which the Petition is Filed (Check one box.)

☐ Chapter 7
☐ Chapter 9
☐ Chapter 11
☐ Chapter 12
☐ Chapter 13

☐ Chapter 15 Petition for Recognition of a Foreign Main Proceeding
☐ Chapter 15 Petition for Recognition of a Foreign Nonmain Proceeding

Chapter 15 Debtors

Country of debtor's center of main interests:

Each country in which a foreign proceeding by, regarding, or against debtor is pending:

Tax-Exempt Entity
(Check box, if applicable.)

☐ Debtor is a tax-exempt organization under title 26 of the United States Code (the Internal Revenue Code).

Nature of Debts
(Check one box.)

☐ Debts are primarily consumer debts, defined in 11 U.S.C. § 101(8) as "incurred by an individual primarily for a personal, family, or household purpose."
☐ Debts are primarily business debts.

Filing Fee (Check one box.)

☐ Full Filing Fee attached.

☐ Filing Fee to be paid in installments (applicable to individuals only). Must attach signed application for the court's consideration certifying that the debtor is unable to pay fee except in installments. Rule 1006(b). See Official Form 3A.

☐ Filing Fee waiver requested (applicable to chapter 7 individuals only). Must attach signed application for the court's consideration. See Official Form 3B.

Chapter 11 Debtors

Check one box:
☐ Debtor is a small business debtor as defined in 11 U.S.C. § 101(51D).
☐ Debtor is not a small business debtor as defined in 11 U.S.C. § 101(51D).

Check if:
☐ Debtor's aggregate noncontingent liquidated debts (excluding debts owed to insiders or affiliates) are less than $2,343,300 (*amount subject to adjustment on 4/01/13 and every three years thereafter*).

Check all applicable boxes:
☐ A plan is being filed with this petition.
☐ Acceptances of the plan were solicited prepetition from one or more classes of creditors, in accordance with 11 U.S.C. § 1126(b).

Statistical/Administrative Information   THIS SPACE IS FOR COURT USE ONLY

☐ Debtor estimates that funds will be available for distribution to unsecured creditors.
☐ Debtor estimates that, after any exempt property is excluded and administrative expenses paid, there will be no funds available for distribution to unsecured creditors.

Estimated Number of Creditors

☐ 1-49	☐ 50-99	☐ 100-199	☐ 200-999	☐ 1,000-5,000	☐ 5,001-10,000	☐ 10,001-25,000	☐ 25,001-50,000	☐ 50,001-100,000	☐ Over 100,000

Estimated Assets

☐ $0 to $50,000	☐ $50,001 to $100,000	☐ $100,001 to $500,000	☐ $500,001 to $1 million	☐ $1,000,001 to $10 million	☐ $10,000,001 to $50 million	☐ $50,000,001 to $100 million	☐ $100,000,001 to $500 million	☐ $500,000,001 to $1 billion	☐ More than $1 billion

Estimated Liabilities

☐ $0 to $50,000	☐ $50,001 to $100,000	☐ $100,001 to $500,000	☐ $500,001 to $1 million	☐ $1,000,001 to $10 million	☐ $10,000,001 to $50 million	☐ $50,000,001 to $100 million	☐ $100,000,001 to $500 million	☐ $500,000,001 to $1 billion	☐ More than $1 billion

B1 (Official Form 1) (12/11)   Page 2

Voluntary Petition *(This page must be completed and filed in every case.)*	**Name of Debtor(s):**	
All Prior Bankruptcy Cases Filed Within Last 8 Years (If more than two, attach additional sheet.)		
Location Where Filed:	Case Number:	Date Filed:
Location Where Filed:	Case Number:	Date Filed:
Pending Bankruptcy Case Filed by any Spouse, Partner, or Affiliate of this Debtor (If more than one, attach additional sheet.)		
Name of Debtor:	Case Number:	Date Filed:
District:	Relationship:	Judge:

Exhibit A (To be completed if debtor is required to file periodic reports (e.g., forms 10K and 10Q) with the Securities and Exchange Commission pursuant to Section 13 or 15(d) of the Securities Exchange Act of 1934 and is requesting relief under chapter 11.) ☐ Exhibit A is attached and made a part of this petition.	**Exhibit B** (To be completed if debtor is an individual whose debts are primarily consumer debts.) I, the attorney for the petitioner named in the foregoing petition, declare that I have informed the petitioner that [he or she] may proceed under chapter 7, 11, 12, or 13 of title 11, United States Code, and have explained the relief available under each such chapter. I further certify that I have delivered to the debtor the notice required by 11 U.S.C. § 342(b). X _____ Signature of Attorney for Debtor(s) (Date)

Exhibit C

Does the debtor own or have possession of any property that poses or is alleged to pose a threat of imminent and identifiable harm to public health or safety?

☐   Yes, and Exhibit C is attached and made a part of this petition.

☐   No.

Exhibit D

(To be completed by every individual debtor. If a joint petition is filed, each spouse must complete and attach a separate Exhibit D.)

☐   Exhibit D, completed and signed by the debtor, is attached and made a part of this petition.

If this is a joint petition:

☐   Exhibit D, also completed and signed by the joint debtor, is attached and made a part of this petition.

Information Regarding the Debtor - Venue
(Check any applicable box.)

☐   Debtor has been domiciled or has had a residence, principal place of business, or principal assets in this District for 180 days immediately preceding the date of this petition or for a longer part of such 180 days than in any other District.

☐   There is a bankruptcy case concerning debtor's affiliate, general partner, or partnership pending in this District.

☐   Debtor is a debtor in a foreign proceeding and has its principal place of business or principal assets in the United States in this District, or has no principal place of business or assets in the United States but is a defendant in an action or proceeding [in a federal or state court] in this District, or the interests of the parties will be served in regard to the relief sought in this District.

Certification by a Debtor Who Resides as a Tenant of Residential Property
(Check all applicable boxes.)

☐   Landlord has a judgment against the debtor for possession of debtor's residence. (If box checked, complete the following.)

_____
(Name of landlord that obtained judgment)

_____
(Address of landlord)

☐   Debtor claims that under applicable nonbankruptcy law, there are circumstances under which the debtor would be permitted to cure the entire monetary default that gave rise to the judgment for possession, after the judgment for possession was entered, and

☐   Debtor has included with this petition the deposit with the court of any rent that would become due during the 30-day period after the filing of the petition.

☐   Debtor certifies that he/she has served the Landlord with this certification. (11 U.S.C. § 362(l)).

B1 (Official Form 1) (12/11)   Page 3

Voluntary Petition	Name of Debtor(s):
(This page must be completed and filed in every case.)	

Signatures

Signature(s) of Debtor(s) (Individual/Joint)

I declare under penalty of perjury that the information provided in this petition is true and correct.

[If petitioner is an individual whose debts are primarily consumer debts and has chosen to file under chapter 7] I am aware that I may proceed under chapter 7, 11, 12 or 13 of title 11, United States Code, understand the relief available under each such chapter, and choose to proceed under chapter 7.

[If no attorney represents me and no bankruptcy petition preparer signs the petition] I have obtained and read the notice required by 11 U.S.C. § 342(b).

I request relief in accordance with the chapter of title 11, United States Code, specified in this petition.

X _____
     Signature of Debtor

X _____
     Signature of Joint Debtor

     Telephone Number (if not represented by attorney)

     Date

Signature of a Foreign Representative

I declare under penalty of perjury that the information provided in this petition is true and correct, that I am the foreign representative of a debtor in a foreign proceeding, and that I am authorized to file this petition.

(Check only **one** box.)

☐ I request relief in accordance with chapter 15 of title 11, United States Code. Certified copies of the documents required by 11 U.S.C. § 1515 are attached.

☐ Pursuant to 11 U.S.C. § 1511, I request relief in accordance with the chapter of title 11 specified in this petition. A certified copy of the order granting recognition of the foreign main proceeding is attached.

X _____
     (Signature of Foreign Representative)

     (Printed Name of Foreign Representative)

     Date

Signature of Attorney*

X _____
     Signature of Attorney for Debtor(s)

     Printed Name of Attorney for Debtor(s)

     Firm Name

     Address

     Telephone Number

     Date

*In a case in which § 707(b)(4)(D) applies, this signature also constitutes a certification that the attorney has no knowledge after an inquiry that the information in the schedules is incorrect.

Signature of Non-Attorney Bankruptcy Petition Preparer

I declare under penalty of perjury that: (1) I am a bankruptcy petition preparer as defined in 11 U.S.C. § 110; (2) I prepared this document for compensation and have provided the debtor with a copy of this document and the notices and information required under 11 U.S.C. §§ 110(b), 110(h), and 342(b); and, (3) if rules or guidelines have been promulgated pursuant to 11 U.S.C. § 110(h) setting a maximum fee for services chargeable by bankruptcy petition preparers, I have given the debtor notice of the maximum amount before preparing any document for filing for a debtor or accepting any fee from the debtor, as required in that section. Official Form 19 is attached.

     Printed Name and title, if any, of Bankruptcy Petition Preparer

     Social-Security number (If the bankruptcy petition preparer is not an individual, state the Social-Security number of the officer, principal, responsible person or partner of the bankruptcy petition preparer.) (Required by 11 U.S.C. § 110.)

     Address

X _____
     Signature

     Date

Signature of Debtor (Corporation/Partnership)

I declare under penalty of perjury that the information provided in this petition is true and correct, and that I have been authorized to file this petition on behalf of the debtor.

The debtor requests the relief in accordance with the chapter of title 11, United States Code, specified in this petition.

X _____
     Signature of Authorized Individual

     Printed Name of Authorized Individual

     Title of Authorized Individual

     Date

Signature of bankruptcy petition preparer or officer, principal, responsible person, or partner whose Social-Security number is provided above.

Names and Social-Security numbers of all other individuals who prepared or assisted in preparing this document unless the bankruptcy petition preparer is not an individual.

If more than one person prepared this document, attach additional sheets conforming to the appropriate official form for each person.

A bankruptcy petition preparer's failure to comply with the provisions of title 11 and the Federal Rules of Bankruptcy Procedure may result in fines or imprisonment or both. 11 U.S.C. § 110; 18 U.S.C. § 156.

Form 1

Exhibit "A"

B 1A (Official Form 1, Exhibit A) (9/97)

[If debtor is required to file periodic reports (e.g., forms 10K and 10Q) with the Securities and Exchange Commission pursuant to Section 13 or 15(d) of the Securities Exchange Act of 1934 and is requesting relief under chapter 11 of the Bankruptcy Code, this Exhibit "A" shall be completed and attached to the petition.]

UNITED STATES BANKRUPTCY COURT

In re _____ ,   )   Case No. _____

           Debtor   )

)

)   Chapter 11

EXHIBIT "A" TO VOLUNTARY PETITION

1. If any of the debtor's securities are registered under Section 12 of the Securities Exchange Act of 1934, the SEC file number is _____ .

2. The following financial data is the latest available information and refers to the debtor's condition on

_____ .

    a. Total assets $ _____

    b. Total debts (including debts listed in 2.c., below) $ _____

    c. Debt securities held by more than 500 holders:

                                              Approximate number of holders:

secured ☐	unsecured ☐	subordinated ☐	$ _____	_____
secured ☐	unsecured ☐	subordinated ☐	$ _____	_____
secured ☐	unsecured ☐	subordinated ☐	$ _____	_____
secured ☐	unsecured ☐	subordinated ☐	$ _____	_____
secured ☐	unsecured ☐	subordinated ☐	$ _____	_____

    d. Number of shares of preferred stock   _____   _____

    e. Number of shares common stock   _____   _____

      Comments, if any:

3. Brief description of debtor's business:

4. List the names of any person who directly or indirectly owns, controls, or holds, with power to vote, 5% or more of the voting securities of debtor:

Complete Annotation Materials, see Title 11 U.S.C.A.

Exhibit "C"

B 1C (Official Form 1, Exhibit C) (9/01)

[If, to the best of the debtor's knowledge, the debtor owns or has possession of property that poses or is alleged to pose a threat of imminent and identifiable harm to the public health or safety, attach this Exhibit "C" to the petition.]

UNITED STATES BANKRUPTCY COURT

In re _____ ,   )   Case No. _____

           Debtor   )

)

)   Chapter _____

EXHIBIT "C" TO VOLUNTARY PETITION

1. Identify and briefly describe all real or personal property owned by or in possession of the debtor that, to the best of the debtor's knowledge, poses or is alleged to pose a threat of imminent and identifiable harm to the public health or safety (attach additional sheets if necessary):

2. With respect to each parcel of real property or item of personal property identified in question 1, describe the nature and location of the dangerous condition, whether environmental or otherwise, that poses or is alleged to pose a threat of imminent and identifiable harm to the public health or safety (attach additional sheets if necessary):

Form 1

Exhibit "D"

B 1D (Official Form 1, Exhibit D) (12/09)

UNITED STATES BANKRUPTCY COURT

In re_____   Case No._____
                Debtor   (if known)

EXHIBIT D - INDIVIDUAL DEBTOR'S STATEMENT OF COMPLIANCE WITH
CREDIT COUNSELING REQUIREMENT

Warning: You must be able to check truthfully one of the five statements regarding credit counseling listed below. If you cannot do so, you are not eligible to file a bankruptcy case, and the court can dismiss any case you do file. If that happens, you will lose whatever filing fee you paid, and your creditors will be able to resume collection activities against you. If your case is dismissed and you file another bankruptcy case later, you may be required to pay a second filing fee and you may have to take extra steps to stop creditors' collection activities.

Every individual debtor must file this Exhibit D. If a joint petition is filed, each spouse must complete and file a separate Exhibit D. Check one of the five statements below and attach any documents as directed.

❏ 1. Within the 180 days **before the filing of my bankruptcy case**, I received a briefing from a credit counseling agency approved by the United States trustee or bankruptcy administrator that outlined the opportunities for available credit counseling and assisted me in performing a related budget analysis, and I have a certificate from the agency describing the services provided to me. *Attach a copy of the certificate and a copy of any debt repayment plan developed through the agency.*

❏ 2. Within the 180 days **before the filing of my bankruptcy case**, I received a briefing from a credit counseling agency approved by the United States trustee or bankruptcy administrator that outlined the opportunities for available credit counseling and assisted me in performing a related budget analysis, but I do not have a certificate from the agency describing the services provided to me. *You must file a copy of a certificate from the agency describing the services provided to you and a copy of any debt repayment plan developed through the agency no later than 14 days after your bankruptcy case is filed.*

Complete Annotation Materials, see Title 11 U.S.C.A.

B 1D (Official Form 1, Exh. D) (12/09) – Cont.

❏ 3. I certify that I requested credit counseling services from an approved agency but was unable to obtain the services during the seven days from the time I made my request, and the following exigent circumstances merit a temporary waiver of the credit counseling requirement so I can file my bankruptcy case now. *[Summarize exigent circumstances here.]*

If your certification is satisfactory to the court, you must still obtain the credit counseling briefing within the first 30 days after you file your bankruptcy petition and promptly file a certificate from the agency that provided the counseling, together with a copy of any debt management plan developed through the agency. Failure to fulfill these requirements may result in dismissal of your case. Any extension of the 30-day deadline can be granted only for cause and is limited to a maximum of 15 days. Your case may also be dismissed if the court is not satisfied with your reasons for filing your bankruptcy case without first receiving a credit counseling briefing.

❏ 4. I am not required to receive a credit counseling briefing because of: *[Check the applicable statement.]* *[Must be accompanied by a motion for determination by the court.]*

❏ Incapacity. (Defined in 11 U.S.C. § 109(h)(4) as impaired by reason of mental illness or mental deficiency so as to be incapable of realizing and making rational decisions with respect to financial responsibilities.);

❏ Disability. (Defined in 11 U.S.C. § 109(h)(4) as physically impaired to the extent of being unable, after reasonable effort, to participate in a credit counseling briefing in person, by telephone, or through the Internet.);

❏ Active military duty in a military combat zone.

❏ 5. The United States trustee or bankruptcy administrator has determined that the credit counseling requirement of 11 U.S.C. § 109(h) does not apply in this district.

I certify under penalty of perjury that the information provided above is true and correct.

Signature of Debtor: _____

Date: _____

(Added Aug. 1, 1991; amended Mar. 16, 1993; Mar. 1995; Oct. 1, 1997; Dec. 1, 2001; Dec. 1, 2002; Dec. 1, 2003; Aug. 11, 2005, eff. Oct. 17, 2005; Oct. 12, 2006; Apr. 1, 2007; revised eff. Dec. 1, 2007; Jan., 2008; Dec. 1, 2008; Dec. 2009; Apr. 1, 2010; Dec. 1, 2011.)

ADVISORY COMMITTEE NOTES

1991 Enactment

Form 1, the Voluntary Petition, is to be used to commence a voluntary case under chapter 7, 11, 12, or 13 of the Bankruptcy Code. A chapter 9 petition requires other allegations, (see § 109(c) of the Code), but this form may be adapted for such use. The form also may be adapted for use in filing a petition ancillary to a foreign proceeding under § 304 of the Code.

The form departs from the traditional format of a captioned pleading. All of the elements of the caption prescribed in Rule 1005 have been retained. Their placement on the page, however, has been changed to make the form compatible with electronic data processing by the clerk. The form of the caption of the case for use in other documents, formerly incorporated in Official Form No. 1, has been made a separate Form 16A.

All names used by the debtor, including trade names, names used in doing business, married names, and maiden names should be furnished in the spaces provided. If there is not sufficient room for all such names on the form itself, the list should be continued on an additional sheet attached to the petition. A complete list will enable creditors to identify the debtor properly when they receive notices and orders.

Redesign of this form into a box format also is intended to provide the court, the United States trustee, and other interested parties with as much information as possible during the 15–day period provided by Rule 1007(c), when schedules and statements may not have been filed. The box format sepa-

---

Complete Annotation Materials, see Title 11 U.S.C.A.

Form 1

rates into categories the data provided by the debtor, and enables the form to be used by all voluntary debtors in all chapters.

For the first time, the form requires both a street address and any separate mailing address, as well as any separate addresses used by a joint debtor. Disclosure of prior bankruptcies is new to the petition but formerly was required in the statement of financial affairs; its inclusion in the petition is intended to alert the trustee to cases in which an objection to discharge pursuant to § 727(a)(8) or (a)(9) or a motion to dismiss under § 109(g) may be appropriate. The information about pending related cases, also new to the petition, signals the clerk to assign the case to the judge to whom any related case has been assigned.

Rule 1008 requires all petitions to be verified or contain an unsworn declaration as provided in 28 U.S.C. § 1746. The unsworn declaration on page two of the petition conforms with 28 U.S.C. § 1746, which permits the declaration to be made in the manner indicated with the same force and effect as a sworn statement. The form may be adapted for use outside the United States by adding the words "under the laws of the United States" after the word "perjury."

Exhibit "A," to be attached to the petition of a corporate debtor, is for the purpose of supplying the Securities and Exchange Commission with information it needs at the beginning stages of a chapter 11 case in order to determine how actively to monitor the proceedings. Exhibit "B" was added by § 322 of Pub.L. No. 98–353, the Bankruptcy Amendments and Federal Judgeship Act of 1984. The references to chapters 11 and 12 of the Code found in Exhibit "B" and its related allegations were added by § 283(aa) of the 1986 amendments, (Pub.L. No. 99–554). This exhibit has been included in the form of the petition.

The form effects a merger of the petition and the bankruptcy cover sheet to assist the clerk in providing the statistical information required by the Director of the Administrative Office of the United States Courts pursuant to the Congressional reporting mandates of 28 U.S.C. § 604. The Director is authorized to change the particulars of the statistical portion of the form as needed in the performance of these statutory duties.

1993 Amendment

The form has been amended to require a debtor not represented by an attorney to provide a telephone number so that court personnel, the trustee, other parties in the case, and their attorneys can contact the debtor concerning matters in the case.

1995 Amendment

The form is amended to provide space for signing by a "bankruptcy petition preparer," as required under section 110 of the Code, which was added by the Bankruptcy Reform Act of 1994. In addition to signing, a bankruptcy petition preparer is required by section 110 to disclose the information requested. All signatories of Form 1 are requested to provide the clerk's office with a telephone number.

A chapter 11 debtor that qualifies as a "small business" under section 101 of the Code, as amended by the 1994 Act, may elect special, expedited treatment under amendments made to chapter 11 by the 1994 Act. The court may order that a creditors committee not be appointed in a small business case. Accordingly, the first page of the petition is

amended to require a small business filing under chapter 11 to identify itself. The petition also is amended to offer a small business chapter 11 debtor an opportunity to exercise its right to elect to be considered a small business at the commencement of the case.

Several clarifying and technical amendments also have been made to indicate that a debtor is to check only one box with respect to "Type of Debtor" and "Nature of Debt," to clarify the intent that the individual signing on behalf of a corporation or partnership is authorized to file the petition, and to require a debtor to represent that it is eligible for relief under the chapter of title 11 specified in the petition.

1997 Amendment

The form has been substantially amended to simplify its format and make the form easier to complete correctly. The Latin phrase "In re" has been deleted as unnecessary. The amount of information requested in the boxes labeled "Type of Debtor" and "Nature of Debt" has been reduced, and the reporting by a corporation of whether it is a publicly held entity has been moved to Exhibit "A" of the petition. The box labeled "Representation by Attorney" has been deleted; the information it contained is requested in the signature boxes on the second page of the form.

In the statistical information section, the labels on the ranges of estimated assets and liabilities have been rewritten to improve the accuracy of reporting. The asset/liability range of $10 million to $100 million has been divided into two categories to promote better statistical reporting of business cases. Requests for information in chapter 11 and chapter 12 cases concerning the number of the debtor's employees and equity security holders have been deleted.

The second page of the form has been simplified so that a debtor need only sign the petition once. The request for information concerning the filing of a plan has been deleted.

Exhibit "A" has been simplified. In addition, the category of chapter 11 debtors required to file Exhibit "A" is modified to include a corporation, partnership, or other entity, but only if the debtor has issued publicly-traded equity securities or debt instruments. Most small corporations will not be required to file Exhibit "A."

2001 Amendment

The form has been amended to require the debtor to disclose whether the debtor owns or has possession of any property that poses or is alleged to pose a threat of imminent and identifiable harm to public health or safety. If any such property exists, the debtor must complete and attach Exhibit "C" describing the property, its location, and the potential danger it poses. Exhibit "C" will alert the United States trustee and any person selected as trustee that immediate precautionary action may be necessary.

2002 Amendment

The form has been amended to provide a checkbox for designating a clearing bank case filed under subchapter V of chapter 7 of the Code enacted by § 112 of Pub. L. No. 106–554 (December 21, 2000).

2003 Amendment

The form is amended to require the debtor to disclose only the last four digits of the debtor's social security number to afford greater privacy to the individual debtor, whose bankruptcy case records may be available on the Internet. Pursuant to § 110(c) of the Bankruptcy Code, the certification by a non-attorney bankruptcy petition preparer requires a petition preparer to provide the full social security number of the individual who actually prepares the document.

2005 Amendments

The form is amended to implement amendments to the Bankruptcy Code contained in the Bankruptcy Abuse Prevention and Consumer Protection Act of 2005, Pub. L. No. 109–8, 119 Stat. 23 (April 20, 2005). The period for which the debtor must provide all names used and information about any prior bankruptcy cases is now eight years to match the required time between the granting of discharges to the same debtor in § 727(a)(8) of the Code as amended in 2005. The box indicating the debtor's selection of a chapter under which to file the case has been amended to delete "Sec. 304—Case ancillary to foreign proceeding" and replace it with "Chapter 15 Petition for Recognition of a Foreign Main Proceeding" and "Chapter 15 Petition for Recognition of a Foreign Nonmain Proceeding" reflecting the 2005 repeal of § 304 and enactment of chapter 15 of the Code. A statement of venue to be used in a chapter 15 case also has been added.

The section of the form labeled "Type of Debtor" has been revised and subtitled "Form of Organization." This section is revised to make it clear that a limited liability corporation ("LLC") and limited liability partnership ("LLP") should identify itself as a "corporation." A new section titled "Nature of Business" has been created that includes both existing check boxes that identify certain types of debtors for which the Bankruptcy Code provides special treatment, such as stockbrokers and railroads, and a new checkbox for a "health care business" for which the 2005 amendments to the Code include specific requirements. This section of the form also contains checkboxes for single asset real estate debtors and nonprofit organizations which will be used by trustees and creditors and by the Director of the Administrative Office of the United States Courts in preparing statistical reports and analyses. The statistical section of the form also is amended to provide more detail concerning the number of creditors in a case. A check box also has been added for a debtor to indicate that the debtor is applying for a waiver of the filing fee, to implement the 2005 enactment of 28 U.S.C. § 1930(f) authorizing the bankruptcy court to waive the filing fee in certain circumstances.

Although the 2005 Act eliminated an eligible debtor's option to elect to be treated as a "small business" in a chapter 11 case, new provisions for such debtors added to the Code in 2005 make it desirable to identify eligible debtors at the outset of the case. Accordingly, the section of the form labeled "Chapter 11 Small Business" has been revised and renamed "Chapter 11 Debtors" for this purpose. Chapter 11 debtors that meet the definition of "small business debtor" in § 101 of the Code are directed to identify themselves in this section of the form. In addition, chapter 11 debtors whose aggregate noncontingent debts owed to non-insiders or affiliates are less than $2 million are directed to identify themselves in this section.

A space is provided for individuals to certify that they have received budget and credit counseling prior to filing, as required by § 109(h) which was added to the Code in 2005, or to request a waiver of the requirement. Space also is provided for a debtor who is a tenant of residential real property to

state whether the debtor's landlord has a judgment against the debtor for possession of the premises, whether under applicable nonbankruptcy law the debtor would be permitted to cure the monetary default, and whether the debtor has made the appropriate deposit with the court. This addition to the form implements § 362(l) which was added to the Code in 2005.

The signature sections and the declaration under penalty of perjury by an individual debtor concerning the notice received about bankruptcy relief, the declaration under penalty of perjury by a bankruptcy petition preparer, and the declaration and certification by an attorney all are amended to include new material mandated by the 2005 Act. A signature section also is provided for a representative of a foreign proceeding.

2006 Amendment

Page one of the form is amended in several ways to assist the courts in evaluating their workload and fulfilling the statistical reporting requirements of 28 U.S.C. § 159. Section 159 was enacted as part of the Bankruptcy Abuse Prevention and Consumer Protection Act of 2005 (BAPCPA), Pub.L. No. 109-8 and takes effect October 17, 2006. Accordingly, in the section of the form labeled "Nature of Business," the instruction is amended to specify that only one box should be checked and only if the debtor is any of the entities listed. The "nonprofit" choice is separated into a discrete section and the language amended to the more precise "tax-exempt."

In addition, the section labeled "Type of Debtor" is amended to include, below the checkbox for "Individual or Joint," a direction to "See Exhibit D on page 2 of this form." Exhibit D replaces the certification concerning prepetition credit counseling and is described below. The section labeled "Nature of Debts" is amended to state the statutory definition of a "consumer debt" and to modify both the consumer and business categories by adding the word "primarily" to both make it clearer to individual debtors that "business" may be the more appropriate choice if personal debts have been incurred to finance a business venture.

In the section labeled "Chapter 11 Debtors," the language concerning whether the debtor owes less than $2 million is restyled for clarity. This section also is augmented to provide the court with notice when a case if [sic] filed as a "prepackaged" chapter 11 reorganization case. Two checkboxes are offered, using language adapted from § 1126(b) of the Code. Lastly, the information requested concerning estimated assets and liabilities is abbreviated, with the number of ranges reduced and the scope of each range amended. Statistical reports now will be derived from actual dollar amounts of assets and liabilities as shown on the debtor's schedules. The information on the petition, accordingly, is for case management and public information purposes only.

Exhibit D replaces the section formerly labeled "Certification Concerning Debt Counseling by Individual/Joint Debtor(s)." Early cases decided under the 2005 amendments to the Bankruptcy Code indicate that individual debtors may not be aware of the requirement to obtain prepetition credit counseling, the few and very narrow exceptions to that requirement, or the potentially dire consequences to their efforts to obtain bankruptcy relief if they fail to complete the requirement. Accordingly, page 2 of the petition instructs individual debtors to attach a completed Exhibit D and makes it clear that each spouse in a joint case must complete and attach a separate Exhibit D. Exhibit D itself includes a warning about the requirement to obtain counseling and the consequences of failing to fulfill this requirement. It further provides check-boxes and instructions concerning the additional documents that are required in particular circumstances, in order to minimize the number of cases which the court must dismiss for ineligibility.

2005–2007 Amendments

(The 2005-2007 Committee Note incorporates Committee Notes previously published in 2005 and 2006.)

The form is amended to implement amendments to the Bankruptcy Code contained in the Bankruptcy Abuse Preven-tion and Consumer Protection Act of 2005, Pub. L. No. 109–8, 119 Stat. 23 (April 20, 2005)("BAPCPA"). The period for which the debtor must provide all names used and informa-tion about any prior bankruptcy cases is now eight years to match the required time between the granting of discharges to the same debtor in § 727(a)(8) of the Code as amended in 2005. In conformity with Rule 9037, the debtor is directed to provide only the last four digits of any individual's tax-identification number.

The box indicating the debtor's selection of a chapter under which to file the case is amended to delete "Sec. 304—Case ancillary to foreign proceeding" and replace it with "Chapter 15 Petition for Recognition of a Foreign Main Proceeding" and "Chapter 15 Petition for Recognition of a Foreign Non-main Proceeding" reflecting the 2005 repeal of § 304 and enactment of chapter 15 of the Code. A statement of venue to be used in a chapter 15 case also is added on page 2 of the form.

The section labeled "Type of Debtor" is amended to include, below the checkbox for "Individual or Joint," a direction to "See Exhibit D on page 2 of this form." This addition alerts individual debtors that Exhibit D on page 2 of the form applies to them. Exhibit D, more fully described below, ad-dresses the prepetition credit counseling requirements added to the Code by BAPCPA. The subtitle, "Form of Organiza-tion," is added, and this section also is revised to make clear that a limited liability corporation ("LLC") or limited liability partnership ("LLP") should identify itself as a "corporation."

The form also is amended in several ways to assist the courts in evaluating their workload and fulfilling the statistical reporting requirements of 28 U.S.C. § 159, enacted as part of BAPCPA. Accordingly, a new section of the form labeled "Nature of Business," is added that contains both existing checkboxes that identify certain types of debtors for which the Bankruptcy Code provides special treatment, such as stockbrokers and railroads, and a new checkbox for a "health care business" for which the 2005 amendments to the Code include specific requirements. This section of the form also contains a checkbox for single asset real estate debtors, so they can be identified at the time of filing. All other busi-nesses will mark the checkbox labeled "Other." Another new section titled "Tax-Exempt Entity" contains a checkbox to be used by qualified organizations. The Judicial Conference of the United States and the Administrative Office of the United States Courts will use this information in preparing statistical reports and analyses for Congress.

A checkbox also is added for an individual debtor to indi-cate that the debtor is applying for a waiver of the filing fee, to implement the 2005 enactment of 28 U.S.C. § 1930(f) authorizing the bankruptcy court to waive the filing fee in certain circumstances. The description directs the debtor to

the Official Form for the application that must be filed for the court's consideration.

The section labeled "Nature of Debts" is amended to state the statutory definition of a "consumer debt" and to modify both the consumer and business categories by adding the word "primarily" to both choices to make it clearer to individ-ual debtors that "business" may be the appropriate choice if personal debts have been incurred to finance a business venture.

Although the 2005 Act eliminated from the Code any option to elect to be treated as a "small business" in a chapter 11 case, new provisions for "small business" debtors added by BAPCPA make it desirable to identify eligible debtors at the outset of the case. Accordingly, the section of the form labeled "Chapter 11 Small Business" is revised and renamed "Chapter 11 Debtors" for this purpose. Chapter 11 debtors that meet the definition of "small business debtor" in § 101 of the Code are directed to identify themselves in this section of the form. Chapter 11 debtors whose aggregate noncontingent debts owed to non-insiders or affiliates are less than $2,190,000 are directed to identify themselves in this section. A third part of this section attempts to identify chapter 11 cases that are filed as pre-packaged cases, using criteria taken from § 1126(b) of the Code. Identifying "pre-packs" at filing will assist judges and court staff to manage these cases appropriately.

The statistical information concerning the number of credi-tors and estimated assets and liabilities is revised to provide more detail.

BAPCPA also added a new § 109(h) to the Code. To implement this provision, a section labeled "Exhibit D" is inserted on page 2 of the form, and a separate Exhibit D is added. These additions will enable individual debtors to certi-fy that they have received budget and credit counseling prior to filing, as required by § 109(h), or request a temporary waiver of, or exemption from, the requirement, if they meet the statutory requirements for such relief. Exhibit D includes directions to attach required documentation or, if the debtor requests a temporary waiver or an exemption, a motion for a determination by the court. Exhibit D also states the require-ment that all individual debtors must obtain a briefing from an approved credit counseling agency before filing a bank-ruptcy case, unless one of the very limited exceptions applies, and further states the consequences that may be faced by any debtor who fails to comply.

Space is provided on page 2 for a debtor who is a tenant of residential real property to certify whether the debtor's land-lord has a judgment against the debtor for possession of the premises, whether under applicable nonbankruptcy law the debtor would be permitted to cure the monetary default, and whether the debtor has made the appropriate deposit with the court. This addition to the form implements § 362(l) which was added to the Code in 2005. And a box is provided that allows the debtor to certify that s/he has served the landlord with the certification as required by § 362(l)(1).

The signature sections and the declaration under penalty of perjury by an individual debtor concerning the notice received about bankruptcy relief, the declaration under penalty of perjury by a bankruptcy petition preparer, and the attorney signature box are amended to include new material mandated by the 2005 Act. The attorney signature box is also amended to remind the attorney that in a case in which § 707(b)(4)(D) applies, that the signature constitutes a certification that the attorney has no knowledge after an inquiry that the information in the schedules filed with the petition is incorrect. A signature section is also provided for a representative of a foreign proceeding.

2008 Amendments

Paragraph 3 of Exhibit D is amended to delete any reference to a requirement that a debtor file a motion with the court to obtain an order approving a request for the postponement of the debtor's obligation to obtain a credit counseling briefing prior to the commencement of the case. The paragraph immediately following numbered paragraph 3 is also amended to reflect the deletion of the need for a separate motion beyond the completion of the certification itself. That paragraph continues to warn the debtor that the case may be dismissed if the court does not find that a postponement is warranted. It also advises the debtor that, even if the court concludes that postponement of the obligation is appropriate, the debtor still must complete the briefing within the time allowed under the Code.

2011 Amendment

The form is amended to implement Rule 1004.2. Subdivision (a) of that rule requires a chapter 15 petition to state the country of the debtor's center of main interests and to identify each country in which a foreign proceeding by, regarding, or against the debtor is pending. A box is added to the first page of the form for this purpose. Minor stylistic changes are also made.

LIBRARY REFERENCES
Corpus Juris Secundum

CJS Bankruptcy § 336, Contents, Signature, and Verification.

CJS Bankruptcy § 337, Contents, Signature, and Verification--Certification of Delivery or Receipt of Prefiling Notice.

Form 2.   Declaration Under Penalty of Perjury
on Behalf of a Corporation or Partnership

Official Form 2
6/90

DECLARATION UNDER PENALTY OF PERJURY
ON BEHALF OF A CORPORATION OR PARTNERSHIP

I, [the president *or* other officer *or* an authorized agent of the corporation] [*or* a member *or* an authorized agent of the partnership] named as the debtor in this case, declare under penalty of perjury that I have read the foregoing [list *or* schedule *or* amendment *or* other document (describe)] and that it is true and correct to the best of my information and belief.

Date _____

Signature _____

_____
(Print Name and Title)

(Added Aug. 1, 1991.)

ADVISORY COMMITTEE NOTES

This form is derived from former Official Form No. 4.

Rule 1008 requires that all petitions, lists, schedules, statements, and amendments thereto be verified or contain an unsworn declaration conforming with 28 U.S.C. § 1746. This form or adaptations of the form have been incorporated into the official forms of the petitions, schedules, and statement of financial affairs. See Official Forms 1, 5, 6, and 7. The form has been amended for use in connection with other papers required by these rules to be verified or contain an unsworn declaration.

Form 3A. Application and Order to Pay Filing Fee in Installments

B 3A (Official Form 3A) (12/07)

UNITED STATES BANKRUPTCY COURT

In re _____,   Case No. _____
                  Debtor
                                                   Chapter _____

APPLICATION TO PAY FILING FEE IN INSTALLMENTS

1. In accordance with Fed. R. Bankr. P. 1006, I apply for permission to pay the filing fee amounting to $ _____ in installments.

2. I am unable to pay the filing fee except in installments.

3. Until the filing fee is paid in full, I will not make any additional payment or transfer any additional property to an attorney or any other person for services in connection with this case.

4. I propose the following terms for the payment of the Filing Fee.*

    $ _____   Check one ☐   With the filing of the petition, or
                                  ☐   On or before _____

    $ _____ on or before _____

    $ _____ on or before _____

    $ _____ on or before _____

*   The number of installments proposed shall not exceed four (4), and the final installment shall be payable not later than 120 days after filing the petition. For cause shown, the court may extend the time of any installment, provided the last installment is paid not later than 180 days after filing the petition. Fed. R. Bankr. P. 1006(b)(2).

5. I understand that if I fail to pay any installment when due, my bankruptcy case may be dismissed and I may not receive a discharge of my debts.

_____   _____   _____   _____
Signature of Attorney   Date   Signature of Debtor   Date
                                               (In a joint case, both spouses must sign.)

_____   _____   _____
Name of Attorney   Signature of Joint Debtor (if any)   Date

DECLARATION AND SIGNATURE OF NON-ATTORNEY BANKRUPTCY PETITION PREPARER (See 11 U.S.C. § 110)

I declare under penalty of perjury that: (1) I am a bankruptcy petition preparer as defined in 11 U.S.C. § 110; (2) I prepared this document for compensation and have provided the debtor with a copy of this document and the notices and information required under 11 U.S.C. §§ 110(b), 110(h), and 342(b); (3) if rules or guidelines have been promulgated pursuant to 11 U.S.C. § 110(h) setting a maximum fee for services chargeable by bankruptcy petition preparers, I have given the debtor notice of the maximum amount before preparing any document for filing for a debtor or accepting any fee from the debtor, as required under that section; and (4) I will not accept any additional money or other property from the debtor before the filing fee is paid in full.

_____   _____
Printed or Typed Name and Title, if any, of Bankruptcy Petition Preparer   Social-Security No. (Required by 11 U.S.C. § 110.)
If the bankruptcy petition preparer is not an individual, state the name, title (if any), address, and social-security number of the officer, principal, responsible person, or partner who signs the document.

_____
Address

x
_____   _____
Signature of Bankruptcy Petition Preparer   Date

Names and Social-Security numbers of all other individuals who prepared or assisted in preparing this document, unless the bankruptcy petition preparer is not an individual:

If more than one person prepared this document, attach additional signed sheets conforming to the appropriate Official Form for each person.
A bankruptcy petition preparer's failure to comply with the provisions of title 11 and the Federal Rules of Bankruptcy Procedure may result in fines or imprisonment or both. 11 U.S.C. § 110; 18 U.S.C. § 156.

Form 3A

OFFICIAL FORMS

B 3A (Official Form 3A) (12/07) - Cont.

UNITED STATES BANKRUPTCY COURT

In re _____,   Case No. _____
                    Debtor

                                            Chapter _____

ORDER APPROVING PAYMENT OF FILING FEE IN INSTALLMENTS

☐   IT IS ORDERED that the debtor(s) may pay the filing fee in installments on the terms proposed in the foregoing application.

☐   IT IS ORDERED that the debtor(s) shall pay the filing fee according to the following terms:

$ _____   Check one ☐ With the filing of the petition, or
                                 ☐ On or before _____

$ _____   on or before _____

$ _____   on or before _____

$ _____   on or before _____

☐   IT IS FURTHER ORDERED that until the filing fee is paid in full the debtor(s) shall not make any additional payment or transfer any additional property to an attorney or any other person for services in connection with this case.

BY THE COURT

Date: _____

_____
United States Bankruptcy Judge

(Added Aug. 1, 1991, and amended Mar. 1995; Oct. 1, 1997; Dec. 1, 2003; Aug. 11, 2005, eff. Oct. 17, 2005; Dec. 1, 2007.)

ADVISORY COMMITTEE NOTES

This form is derived from former Official Form No. 2.

A statement that the applicant is unable to pay the filing fee except in installments has been added as required by Rule 1006(b).

1995 Amendment

This form is a "document for filing" that may be prepared by a "bankruptcy petition preparer" as defined in 11 U.S.C. § 110, which was added to the Code by the Bankruptcy Reform Act of 1994; accordingly, a signature line is provided for such preparer. In addition to signing, a bankruptcy petition preparer is required by section 110 to disclose the information requested. A signature line for a debtor's attorney also is added, as required by Rule 9011.

1997 Amendment

The form has been reorganized and the paragraphs numbered. The debtor's certification concerning payment for services in the case has been placed ahead of the statement of proposed terms for installment payment of court fees. Acknowledgment by the debtor of the potential consequences of failure to pay any installment when due has been added. (See

11 U.S.C. § 707(a)(2).) The language of the form also has been changed to conform to Rule 1006 and to clarify that a debtor is not disqualified from paying the filing fee in installments because the debtor has paid money to a bankruptcy petition preparer.

2003 Amendment

Pursuant to § 110(c) of the Bankruptcy Code, the certification by a non-attorney bankruptcy petition preparer requires a petition preparer to provide the full Social Security number of the individual who actually prepares the document pursuant to § 110(c) of the Code.

2005 Amendment

The form is amended to direct the debtor to state that, until the filing fee is paid in full, the debtor will not make any additional payment or transfer any additional property to an attorney or any other person for services in connection with the case. The declaration and certification by a non-attorney bankruptcy petition preparer in the form are amended to include material mandated by § 110 of the Code as amended by the Bankruptcy Abuse Prevention and Consumer Protection Act of 2005, Pub. L. No. 109–8, 119 Stat. 23 (April 20, 2005). The certification by a non-attorney bankruptcy petition preparer is re-named a declaration and also is revised to include material mandated by § 110 of the Code as amended in 2005. The order is amended to provide space for the court

---

Complete Annotation Materials, see Title 11 U.S.C.A.

to set forth a payment schedule other than the one proposed by the debtor.

2005–2007 Amendments

(The 2005-2007 Committee Note incorporates the Committee Note previously published in 2005.)

The form is amended to direct the debtor to state that, until the filing fee is paid in full, the debtor will not make any additional payment or transfer any additional property to an attorney or any other person for services in connection with the case. The declaration and certification by a non-attorney bankruptcy petition preparer in the form are amended to include material mandated by § 110 of the Code as amended by the Bankruptcy Abuse Prevention and Consumer Protection Act of 2005, Pub. L. No. 109-8, 119 Stat. 23 (April 20, 2005). The certification by a non-attorney bankruptcy petition preparer is re-named a declaration and also is revised to include material mandated by § 110 of the Code as amended in 2005. The order is amended to provide space for the court to set forth a payment schedule other than the one proposed by the debtor.

LIBRARY REFERENCES

Corpus Juris Secundum

CJS Bankruptcy § 341, Fee for Filing Petition.

Form 3B. Application for Waiver of the Chapter
7 Filing Fee for Individuals Who Cannot Pay
the Filing Fee in Full or in Installments

B3B (Official Form 3B) (11/11)

**APPLICATION FOR WAIVER OF THE CHAPTER 7 FILING FEE
FOR INDIVIDUALS WHO CANNOT PAY THE FILING FEE
IN FULL OR IN INSTALLMENTS**

The court fee for filing a case under chapter 7 of the Bankruptcy Code is $306.

If you cannot afford to pay the full fee at the time of filing, you may apply to pay the fee
in installments. A form, which is available from the bankruptcy clerk's office, must be
completed to make that application. If your application to pay in installments is
approved, you will be permitted to file your petition, generally completing payment of
the fee over the course of four to six months.

If you cannot afford to pay the fee either in full at the time of filing or in installments,
you may request a waiver of the filing fee by completing this application and filing it
with the Clerk of Court. A judge will decide whether you have to pay the fee. By law,
the judge may waive the fee only if your income is less than 150 percent of the official
poverty line applicable to your family size and you are unable to pay the fee in
installments. You may obtain information about the poverty guidelines at
www.uscourts.gov or in the bankruptcy clerk's office.

Required information. Complete all items in the application, and attach requested
schedules. Then sign the application on the last page. If you and your spouse are filing a
joint bankruptcy petition, you both must provide information as requested and sign the
application.

B3B (Official Form 3B) (11/11) -- Cont.

UNITED STATES BANKRUPTCY COURT

In re: _____   Case No. _____
       Debtor(s)   (if known)

APPLICATION FOR WAIVER OF THE CHAPTER 7 FILING FEE
FOR INDIVIDUALS WHO CANNOT PAY THE FILING FEE IN FULL OR IN INSTALLMENTS

Part A. Family Size and Income

1. Including yourself, your spouse, and dependents you have listed or will list on Schedule I (Current Income of Individual Debtors(s)), how many people are in your family? (Do not include your spouse if you are separated AND are not filing a joint petition.) _____

2. Restate the following information that you provided, or will provide, on Line 16 of Schedule I. Attach a completed copy of Schedule I, if it is available.

    Total Combined Monthly Income (Line 16 of Schedule I): $_____

3. State the monthly net income, if any, of dependents included in Question 1 above. Do not include any income already reported in Item 2. If none, enter $0.

                                                                    $_____

4. Add the "Total Combined Monthly Income" reported in Question 2 to your dependents' monthly net income from Question 3.

                                                                    $_____

5. Do you expect the amount in Question 4 to increase or decrease by more than 10% during the next 6 months? Yes ___ No ___

    If yes, explain.

Part B. Monthly Expenses

6. EITHER (a) attach a completed copy of Schedule J (Schedule of Monthly Expenses), and state your total monthly expenses reported on Line 18 of that Schedule, OR (b) if you have not yet completed Schedule J, provide an estimate of your total monthly expenses.

                                                                    $_____

7. Do you expect the amount in Question 6 to increase or decrease by more than 10% during the next 6 months? Yes ___ No ___
    If yes, explain.

Part C. Real and Personal Property

EITHER (1) attach completed copies of Schedule A (Real Property) and Schedule B (Personal Property), OR (2) if you have not yet completed those schedules, answer the following questions.

8. State the amount of cash you have on hand. $_____

9. State below any money you have in savings, checking, or other accounts in a bank or other financial institution.

Bank or Other Financial Institution:	Type of Account such as savings, checking, CD:	Amount:
		$_____
_____	_____	
		$_____
_____	_____	

B3B (Official Form 3B) (11/11) -- Cont.

10. State below the assets owned by you. **Do not list ordinary household furnishings and clothing.**

Home   Address:
                _____   Value: $ _____
                _____   Amount owed on mortgages and liens: $ _____

Other real estate   Address:
                _____   Value: $ _____
                _____   Amount owed on mortgages and liens: $ _____

Motor vehicle   Model/Year: _____   Value: $ _____
                _____   Amount owed: $ _____

Motor vehicle   Model/Year: _____   Value: $ _____
                _____   Amount owed: $ _____

Other   Description_____   Value: $ _____
                _____   Amount owed: $ _____

11. State below any person, business, organization, or governmental unit that owes you money and the amount that is owed.

Name of Person, Business, or Organization that Owes You   Amount Owed
Money

                                                                 $ _____

_____ $ _____

Part D. Additional Information.

12. Have you paid an **attorney** any money for services in connection with this case, including the completion of this form, the bankruptcy petition, or schedules? Yes ___ No ___
If yes, how much have you paid? $ _____

13. Have you promised to pay or do you anticipate paying an **attorney** in connection with your bankruptcy case? Yes ___ No ___
If yes, how much have you promised to pay or do you anticipate paying? $ _____

14. Have you paid **anyone other than an attorney** (such as a bankruptcy petition preparer, paralegal, typing service, or another person) any money for services in connection with this case, including the completion of this form, the bankruptcy petition, or schedules? Yes ___ No ___
If yes, how much have you paid? $ _____

15. Have you promised to pay or do you anticipate paying **anyone other than an attorney** (such as a bankruptcy petition preparer, paralegal, typing service, or another person) any money for services in connection with this case, including the completion of this form, the bankruptcy petition, or schedules?
Yes ___ No ___
If yes, how much have you promised to pay or do you anticipate paying? $ _____

16. Has anyone paid an attorney or other person or service in connection with this case, on your behalf?
Yes ___ No ___

If yes, explain.

B3B (Official Form 3B) (11/11) -- Cont.

17. Have you previously filed for bankruptcy relief during the past eight years? Yes ___ No ___

Case Number (if known)	Year filed	Location of filing	Did you obtain a discharge? (if known)
_____	_____	_____	Yes ____ No ____ Don't know ____
_____	_____	_____	Yes ____ No ____ Don't know ____

18. Please provide any other information that helps to explain why you are unable to pay the filing fee in installments.

19. I (we) declare under penalty of perjury that I (we) cannot currently afford to pay the filing fee in full or in installments and that the foregoing information is true and correct.

Executed on: _____

_____ Date

_____ Date

_____ Signature of Debtor

_____ Signature of Codebtor

DECLARATION AND SIGNATURE OF BANKRUPTCY PETITION PREPARER (See 11 U.S.C. § 110)

I declare under penalty of perjury that: (1) I am a bankruptcy petition preparer as defined in 11 U.S.C. § 110; (2) I prepared this document for compensation and have provided the debtor with a copy of this document and the notices and information required under 11 U.S.C. §§ 110(b), 110(h), and 342(b); and (3) if rules or guidelines have been promulgated pursuant to 11 U.S.C. § 110(h) setting a maximum fee for services chargeable by bankruptcy petition preparers, I have given the debtor notice of the maximum amount before preparing any document for filing for a debtor or accepting any fee from the debtor, as required under that section.

_____
Printed or Typed Name and Title, if any, of Bankruptcy Petition Preparer   Social-Security No. (Required by 11 U.S.C. §110.)

If the bankruptcy petition preparer is not an individual, state the name, title (if any), address, and social-security number of the officer, principal, responsible person, or partner who signs the document.

_____
Address

x_____
Signature of Bankruptcy Petition Preparer   Date _____

Names and Social-Security numbers of all other individuals who prepared or assisted in preparing this document, unless the bankruptcy petition preparer is not an individual:

If more than one person prepared this document, attach additional signed sheets conforming to the appropriate Official Form for each person.
A bankruptcy petition preparer's failure to comply with the provisions of title 11 and the Federal Rules of Bankruptcy Procedure may result in fines or imprisonment or both. 11 U.S.C. § 110; 18 U.S.C. § 156.

B3B (Official Form 3B) (11/11) -- Cont.

UNITED STATES BANKRUPTCY COURT

In re: _____   Case No. _____
    Debtor(s)

ORDER ON DEBTOR'S APPLICATION FOR WAIVER OF THE CHAPTER 7 FILING FEE

Upon consideration of the debtor's "Application for Waiver of the Chapter 7 Filing Fee," the court orders that the application be:

[ ] GRANTED.

    This order is subject to being vacated at a later time if developments in the administration of the bankruptcy case demonstrate that the waiver was unwarranted.

[ ] DENIED.

    The debtor shall pay the chapter 7 filing fee according to the following terms:

    $ _____ on or before _____

    $ _____ on or before _____

    $ _____ on or before _____

    $ _____ on or before _____

    Until the filing fee is paid in full, the debtor shall not make any additional payment or transfer any additional property to an attorney or any other person for services in connection with this case.

    IF THE DEBTOR FAILS TO TIMELY PAY THE FILING FEE IN FULL OR TO TIMELY MAKE INSTALLMENT PAYMENTS, THE COURT MAY DISMISS THE DEBTOR'S CASE.

[ ] SCHEDULED FOR HEARING.

    A hearing to consider the debtor's "Application for Waiver of the Chapter 7 Filing Fee" shall be held on _____ at _____ am/pm at _____.
                       (address of courthouse)

    IF THE DEBTOR FAILS TO APPEAR AT THE SCHEDULED HEARING, THE COURT MAY DEEM SUCH FAILURE TO BE THE DEBTOR'S CONSENT TO THE ENTRY OF AN ORDER DENYING THE FEE WAIVER APPLICATION BY DEFAULT.

BY THE COURT:

DATE: _____   _____
                                United States Bankruptcy Judge

(Added Aug. 11, 2005, eff. Oct. 17, 2005. Amended Apr. 9, 2006; Dec. 1, 2007; Nov. 2011.)

ADVISORY COMMITTEE NOTES

2005 Amendment

This form is new. 28 U.S.C. § 1930(f), enacted as part of the Bankruptcy Abuse and Consumer Protection Act of 2005, Pub. L. No. 109–8, 119 Stat. 23 (April 20, 2005), provides that "under procedures prescribed by the Judicial Conference of the United States, the district court or the bankruptcy court may waive the filing fee in a case under chapter 7 of title 11 for an individual if the court determines that such individual has income less than 150 percent of the income official poverty line ... applicable to a family of the size involved and is unable to pay that fee in installments." To implement this provision, Interim Rule 1006 adds a new subdivision (c). Official Form 3B is the form referenced in that subdivision, and is to be used by individual chapter 7 debtors when applying for a waiver of the filing fee. A corresponding standard order also is included.

2005–2007 Amendments

(The 2005-2007 Committee Note incorporates the Committee Note previously published in 2005.)

This form is new. 28 U.S.C. § 1930(f), enacted as part of the Bankruptcy Abuse and Consumer Protection Act of 2005, Pub. L. No. 109-8, 119 Stat. 23 (April 20, 2005), provides that "under procedures prescribed by the Judicial Conference of the United States, the district court or the bankruptcy court may waive the filing fee in a case under chapter 7 of title 11 for an individual if the court determines that such individual has income less than 150 percent of the income official poverty line ... applicable to a family of the size involved and is unable to pay that fee in installments." To implement this provision, Fed. R. Bankr. P.1006 adds a new subdivision (c). Official Form 3B is the form referenced in that subdivision, and is to be used by individual chapter 7 debtors when applying for a waiver of the filing fee. A corresponding standard order also is included.

LIBRARY REFERENCES

Corpus Juris Secundum

CJS Bankruptcy § 342, Fee for Filing Petition--Waiver.

Form 4. List of Creditors Holding 20 Largest Unsecured Claims

B 4 (Official Form 4) (12/07)

UNITED STATES BANKRUPTCY COURT

In re _____ ,
Debtor

Case No. _____

Chapter _____

LIST OF CREDITORS HOLDING 20 LARGEST UNSECURED CLAIMS

Following is the list of the debtor's creditors holding the 20 largest unsecured claims. The list is prepared in accordance with Fed. R. Bankr. P. 1007(d) for filing in this chapter 11 [*or* chapter 9] case. The list does not include (1) persons who come within the definition of "insider" set forth in 11 U.S.C. § 101, or (2) secured creditors unless the value of the collateral is such that the unsecured deficiency places the creditor among the holders of the 20 largest unsecured claims. If a minor child is one of the creditors holding the 20 largest unsecured claims, state the child's initials and the name and address of the child's parent or guardian, such as "A.B., a minor child, by John Doe, guardian." Do not disclose the child's name. See, 11 U.S.C. §112 and Fed. R. Bankr. P. 1007(m).

(1)	(2)	(3)	(4)	(5)
Name of creditor and complete mailing address, including zip code	*Name, telephone number and complete mailing address, including zip code, of employee, agent, or department of creditor familiar with claim who may be contacted*	*Nature of claim (trade debt, bank loan, government contract, etc.)*	*Indicate if claim is contingent, unliquidated, disputed or subject to setoff*	*Amount of claim [if secured also state value of security]*

Date: _____

_____
Debtor

[Declaration as in Form 2]

(Added Aug. 1, 1991; amended Mar. 16, 1993; Aug. 11, 2005, eff. Oct. 17, 2005; Dec. 1, 2007.)

ADVISORY COMMITTEE NOTES

1991 Enactment

This form is derived from former Official Form No. 9.

In conformity with Rule 1007(d) and in recognition of the notice function served by this list under Rule 4001, governmental units must be listed if they are among the creditors holding the 20 largest claims.

Rule 1008 requires all lists to be verified or contain an unsworn declaration conforming with 28 U.S.C. § 1746.

1993 Amendment

The form has been amended to delete reference to the specific subsection of 11 U.S.C. § 101 in connection with the definition of the term "insider." Section 101 of the Bankruptcy Code contains numerous definitions, and statutory amendments from time to time have resulted in the renumbering of many of its subsections. The more general reference will avoid the necessity to amend the form further in the event of future amendments to § 101.

2005 Amendment

The form is amended to direct that the name of any minor child not be disclosed. The amendment implements § 112 of the Code, which was added by the Bankruptcy Abuse Prevention and Consumer Protection Act of 2005, Pub. L. No. 109–8, 119 Stat. 23 (April 20, 2005).

2005–2007 Amendments

(The 2005-2007 Committee Note incorporates Committee Notes previously published in 2005.)

The form is amended to direct that the name of any minor child not be disclosed. The amendment implements § 112 of the Code, which was added by the Bankruptcy Abuse Prevention and Consumer Protection Act of 2005, Pub. L. No. 109-8, 119 Stat. 23 (April 20, 2005). In addition, the form is amended to add to the reference to Rule 1007(m) a direction to include for noticing purposes the name, address, and legal relationship to the child of "a person described" in that rule. Rule 1007(m) requires the person named to be someone on whom process would be served in an adversary proceeding against the child.

LIBRARY REFERENCES

Corpus Juris Secundum

CJS Bankruptcy § 345, List of Creditors and Others-- Twenty Largest Unsecured Creditors.

Form 5

OFFICIAL FORMS

Form 5. Involuntary Petition

B 5 (Official Form 5) (12/07)

UNITED STATES BANKRUPTCY COURT	INVOLUNTARY PETITION

IN RE (Name of Debtor – If Individual: Last, First, Middle)	ALL OTHER NAMES used by debtor in the last 8 years (Include married, maiden, and trade names.)
Last four digits of Social-Security or other Individual's Tax-I.D. No./Complete EIN (If more than one, state all.):	
STREET ADDRESS OF DEBTOR (No. and street, city, state, and zip code)	MAILING ADDRESS OF DEBTOR (If different from street address)
COUNTY OF RESIDENCE OR PRINCIPAL PLACE OF BUSINESS ZIP CODE	ZIP CODE

LOCATION OF PRINCIPAL ASSETS OF BUSINESS DEBTOR (If different from previously listed addresses)

CHAPTER OF BANKRUPTCY CODE UNDER WHICH PETITION IS FILED

☐ Chapter 7   ☐ Chapter 11

INFORMATION REGARDING DEBTOR (Check applicable boxes)

Nature of Debts (Check one box.)	Type of Debtor (Form of Organization)	Nature of Business (Check one box.)
Petitioners believe: ☐ Debts are primarily consumer debts ☐ Debts are primarily business debts	☐ Individual (Includes Joint Debtor) ☐ Corporation (Includes LLC and LLP) ☐ Partnership ☐ Other (If debtor is not one of the above entities, check this box and state type of entity below.)	☐ Health Care Business ☐ Single Asset Real Estate as defined in 11 U.S.C. § 101(51)(B) ☐ Railroad ☐ Stockbroker ☐ Commodity Broker ☐ Clearing Bank ☐ Other

VENUE	FILING FEE (Check one box)
☐ Debtor has been domiciled or has had a residence, principal place of business, or principal assets in the District for 180 days immediately preceding the date of this petition or for a longer part of such 180 days than in any other District. ☐ A bankruptcy case concerning debtor's affiliate, general partner or partnership is pending in this District.	☐ Full Filing Fee attached ☐ Petitioner is a child support creditor or its representative, and the form specified in § 304(g) of the Bankruptcy Reform Act of 1994 is attached. *[If a child support creditor or its representative is a petitioner, and if the petitioner files the form specified in § 304(g) of the Bankruptcy Reform Act of 1994, no fee is required.]*

PENDING BANKRUPTCY CASE FILED BY OR AGAINST ANY PARTNER OR AFFILIATE OF THIS DEBTOR (Report information for any additional cases on attached sheets.)

Name of Debtor	Case Number	Date
Relationship	District	Judge

ALLEGATIONS
(Check applicable boxes)   COURT USE ONLY

1. ☐ Petitioner(s) are eligible to file this petition pursuant to 11 U.S.C. § 303 (b).
2. ☐ The debtor is a person against whom an order for relief may be entered under title 11 of the United States Code.
3.a. ☐ The debtor is generally not paying such debtor's debts as they become due, unless such debts are the subject of a bona fide dispute as to liability or amount;
         or
   b. ☐ Within 120 days preceding the filing of this petition, a custodian, other than a trustee receiver, or agent appointed or authorized to take charge of less than substantially all of the property of the debtor for the purpose of enforcing a lien against such property, was appointed or took possession.

Complete Annotation Materials, see Title 11 U.S.C.A.

828

B 5 (Official Form 5) (12/07)   Page 2

Name of Debtor_____

Case No._____

<table>
<tr><td colspan="2" align="center">TRANSFER OF CLAIM</td></tr>
<tr><td colspan="2">☐ Check this box if there has been a transfer of any claim against the debtor by or to any petitioner. Attach all documents that evidence the transfer and any statements that are required under Bankruptcy Rule 1003(a).</td></tr>
<tr><td colspan="2" align="center">REQUEST FOR RELIEF</td></tr>
<tr><td colspan="2">Petitioner(s) request that an order for relief be entered against the debtor under the chapter of title 11, United States Code, specified in this petition. If any petitioner is a foreign representative appointed in a foreign proceeding, a certified copy of the order of the court granting recognition is attached.</td></tr>
<tr><td colspan="2">Petitioner(s) declare under penalty of perjury that the foregoing is true and correct according to the best of their knowledge, information, and belief.</td></tr>
<tr>
<td>x_____
Signature of Petitioner or Representative (State title)</td>
<td>x_____
Signature of Attorney   Date</td>
</tr>
<tr>
<td>Name of Petitioner   Date Signed</td>
<td>Name of Attorney Firm (If any)</td>
</tr>
<tr>
<td>Name & Mailing
Address of Individual
Signing in Representative
Capacity</td>
<td>Address

Telephone No.</td>
</tr>
<tr>
<td>x_____
Signature of Petitioner or Representative (State title)</td>
<td>x_____
Signature of Attorney   Date</td>
</tr>
<tr>
<td>Name of Petitioner   Date Signed</td>
<td>Name of Attorney Firm (If any)</td>
</tr>
<tr>
<td>Name & Mailing
Address of Individual
Signing in Representative
Capacity</td>
<td>Address

Telephone No.</td>
</tr>
<tr>
<td>x_____
Signature of Petitioner or Representative (State title)</td>
<td>x_____
Signature of Attorney   Date</td>
</tr>
<tr>
<td>Name of Petitioner   Date Signed</td>
<td>Name of Attorney Firm (If any)</td>
</tr>
<tr>
<td>Name & Mailing
Address of Individual
Signing in Representative
Capacity</td>
<td>Address

Telephone No.</td>
</tr>
</table>

<table>
<tr><td colspan="3" align="center">PETITIONING CREDITORS</td></tr>
<tr><td>Name and Address of Petitioner</td><td>Nature of Claim</td><td>Amount of Claim</td></tr>
<tr><td>Name and Address of Petitioner</td><td>Nature of Claim</td><td>Amount of Claim</td></tr>
<tr><td>Name and Address of Petitioner</td><td>Nature of Claim</td><td>Amount of Claim</td></tr>
<tr><td>Note: If there are more than three petitioners, attach additional sheets with the statement under penalty of perjury, each petitioner's signature under the statement and the name of attorney and petitioning creditor information in the format above.</td><td colspan="2">Total Amount of Petitioners' Claims</td></tr>
</table>

_____continuation sheets attached

(Added Aug. 1, 1991; and amended Dec. 1, 2002; Dec. 1, 2003; Aug. 11, 2005, eff. Oct. 17, 2005; Oct. 12 2006; Dec. 1, 2007.)

ADVISORY COMMITTEE NOTES

1991 Amendment

This form has been redesigned in a box format similar to that of Form 1. See Advisory Committee Note to Form 1.

The allegations required under § 303 are grouped together, and a separate section has been provided for additional allegations based upon the prohibitions and requirements set forth in Rule 1003(a) concerning transfer of claims by petitioning creditors. Petitioners may wish to supplement the allegations set forth in the form with a further statement of facts. Additional information concerning any allegation can be requested by the debtor as part of the discovery process.

Each petitioning creditor, by signing on the line provided, signs both the petition and the unsworn declaration which 28 U.S.C. § 1746 permits instead of verification. The addresses as well as the names of individuals signing the petition in a representative capacity are required, together with disclosure of which petitioner is represented by each signatory.

This form is intended to be used in every involuntary case, including that of a partnership. The separate form for a petition by a partner has been abrogated. Pursuant to § 303(b)(3)(A) of the Code, a petition by fewer than all of the general partners seeking an order for relief with respect to the partnership is treated as an involuntary petition. Such a petition is adversarial in character because not all of the partners are joining in the petition.

Section 303(b)(3)(B) permits a petition against the partnership if relief has been ordered under the Code with respect to all of the general partners. In that event, the petition may be filed by a general partner, a trustee of a general partner's estate, or a creditor of the partnership. This form may be adapted for use in that type of case.

28 U.S.C. § 1408(1) specifies the proper venue alternatives for all persons, including partnerships, as domicile, residence, principal place of business, or location of principal assets. Venue also may be based on a pending case commenced by an affiliate, general partner, or partnership pursuant to 28 U.S.C. § 1408(2). Both options are set forth in the block labeled "Venue."

28 U.S.C. § 1746 permits the unsworn declaration instead of a verification. See Committee Note to Form 2.

1992 Amendment

The form has been amended to require the dating of signatures.

2002 Amendment

The form is amended to give notice that no filing fee is required if a child support creditor or its representative is a petitioner, and if the petitioner also files a form detailing the child support debt, its status, and other characteristics, as specified in § 304(g) of the Bankruptcy Reform Act of 1994, Pub. L. No. 103–394, 108 Stat. 4106 (Oct. 22, 1994).

2003 Amendment

The form is amended to require the petitioner to disclose the debtor's employer identification number, if any, and only the last four digits of the debtor's social security number to afford greater privacy to the individual debtor, whose bankruptcy case records may be available on the Internet. The form also is amended to delete the request for information concerning the "Type of Business," as this data no longer is collected for statistical purposes.

2005 Amendment

The form has been amended to delete statistical information no longer required and to add "as to liability or amount" to the language concerning debts that are the subject of a bona fide dispute, in conformity with § 303 of the Code as amended by the Bankruptcy Abuse Prevention and Consumer Protection Act of 2005, Pub. L. No. 109–8, 119 Stat. 23 (April 20, 2005). The petitioning creditors must now provide, to the extent known to them, all other names used by the debtor during the 8 years, rather than 6 years, before the filing of the petition. A new check box is provided for the petitioning creditors to identify the debtor that is a "health care business" as defined in § 101 of the Code, thereby alerting the court and the United States trustee of the necessity under § 333 to appoint an ombudsman to represent the interests of the patients of the health care business. These amendments also implement the 2005 amendments to the Code. A new checkbox also is provided for a "clearing bank," which may become a debtor upon the filing of a petition at the direction

of the Board of Governors of the Federal Reserve System; this addition conforms to an amendment to § 109(b)(2) of the Code which was enacted in 2000.

2006 Amendment

The section of the form labeled "Information Regarding Debtor" is amended to facilitate, to the extent available in an involuntary case, the collection of the same statistical information that is requested in a voluntary case. Accordingly, information about whether the debtor is an individual, a corporation, or some other type of entity is separated from the checklist of types of debtors, such as health care businesses and railroads, concerning which the Code provides for specialized treatment.

2005–2007 Amendments

(The 2005-2007 Committee Note incorporates Committee Notes previously published in 2005 and 2006.)

The form has been amended to delete statistical information about the debtor that no longer is required, and to substitute checkboxes similar to those on the voluntary petition form. The form also is amended to add "as to liability or amount" to the language concerning debts that are the subject of a bona fide dispute, in conformity with § 303 of the Code as amended by the Bankruptcy Abuse Prevention and Consumer Protection Act of 2005, Pub. L. No. 109–8, 119 Stat. 23 (April 20, 2005). The petitioning creditors must now provide, to the extent known to them, all other names used by the debtor during the 8 years, rather than 6 years, before the filing of the petition. In conformity with Rule 9037, the petitioning creditors are directed to provide only the last four digits of any individual's tax-identification number. A new checkbox is provided for the petitioning creditors to identify the debtor that is a "health care business" as defined in § 101 of the Code, thereby alerting the court and the United States trustee of the necessity under § 333 of the Code to appoint an ombudsman to represent the interests of the patients of the health care business. These amendments also implement the 2005 amendments to the Code. A new checkbox also is provided for a "clearing bank," which may become a debtor upon the filing of a petition at the direction of the Board of Governors of the Federal Reserve System; this addition conforms to an amendment to § 109(b)(2) of the Code, which was enacted in 2000.

Form 6. Schedules

B6 Cover (Form 6 Cover) (12/07)

FORM 6. SCHEDULES

Summary of Schedules
Statistical Summary of Certain Liabilities and Related Data (28 U.S.C. § 159)

Schedule A - Real Property
Schedule B - Personal Property
Schedule C - Property Claimed as Exempt
Schedule D - Creditors Holding Secured Claims
Schedule E - Creditors Holding Unsecured Priority Claims
Schedule F - Creditors Holding Unsecured Nonpriority Claims
Schedule G - Executory Contracts and Unexpired Leases
Schedule H - Codebtors
Schedule I - Current Income of Individual Debtor(s)
Schedule J - Current Expenditures of Individual Debtors(s)

Unsworn Declaration Under Penalty of Perjury

GENERAL INSTRUCTIONS: The first page of the debtor's schedules and the first page of any amendments thereto must contain a caption as in Form 16B. Subsequent pages should be identified with the debtor's name and case number. If the schedules are filed with the petition, the case number should be left blank.

Schedules D, E, and F have been designed for the listing of each claim only once. Even when a claim is secured only in part or entitled to priority only in part, it still should be listed only once. A claim which is secured in whole or in part should be listed on Schedule D only, and a claim which is entitled to priority in whole or in part should be listed on Schedule E only. Do not list the same claim twice. If a creditor has more than one claim, such as claims arising from separate transactions, each claim should be scheduled separately.

Review the specific instructions for each schedule before completing the schedule.

Form 6

B6 Summary (Official Form 6 - Summary) (12/07)

United States Bankruptcy Court

In re _____,   Case No. _____
                    Debtor

                                                     Chapter _____

SUMMARY OF SCHEDULES

Indicate as to each schedule whether that schedule is attached and state the number of pages in each. Report the totals from Schedules A, B, D, E, F, I, and J in the boxes provided. Add the amounts from Schedules A and B to determine the total amount of the debtor's assets. Add the amounts of all claims from Schedules D, E, and F to determine the total amount of the debtor's liabilities. Individual debtors also must complete the "Statistical Summary of Certain Liabilities and Related Data" if they file a case under chapter 7, 11, or 13.

NAME OF SCHEDULE	ATTACHED (YES/NO)	NO. OF SHEETS	ASSETS	LIABILITIES	OTHER
A - Real Property			$		
B - Personal Property			$		
C - Property Claimed as Exempt					
D - Creditors Holding Secured Claims				$	
E - Creditors Holding Unsecured Priority Claims (Total of Claims on Schedule E)				$	
F - Creditors Holding Unsecured Nonpriority Claims				$	
G - Executory Contracts and Unexpired Leases					
H - Codebtors					
I - Current Income of Individual Debtor(s)					$
J - Current Expenditures of Individual Debtors(s)					$
TOTAL			$	$	

B 6 Summary (Official Form 6 - Summary) (12/07)

United States Bankruptcy Court

In re _____,   Case No. _____
                 Debtor
                                             Chapter _____

STATISTICAL SUMMARY OF CERTAIN LIABILITIES AND RELATED DATA (28 U.S.C. § 159)

If you are an individual debtor whose debts are primarily consumer debts, as defined in § 101(8) of the Bankruptcy Code (11 U.S.C. § 101(8)), filing a case under chapter 7, 11 or 13, you must report all information requested below.

☐ Check this box if you are an individual debtor whose debts are NOT primarily consumer debts. You are not required to report any information here.

This information is for statistical purposes only under 28 U.S.C. § 159.

Summarize the following types of liabilities, as reported in the Schedules, and total them.

Type of Liability	Amount
Domestic Support Obligations (from Schedule E)	$
Taxes and Certain Other Debts Owed to Governmental Units (from Schedule E)	$
Claims for Death or Personal Injury While Debtor Was Intoxicated (from Schedule E) (whether disputed or undisputed)	$
Student Loan Obligations (from Schedule F)	$
Domestic Support, Separation Agreement, and Divorce Decree Obligations Not Reported on Schedule E.	$
Obligations to Pension or Profit-Sharing, and Other Similar Obligations (from Schedule F)	$
TOTAL	$

State the following:

Average Income (from Schedule I, Line 16)	$
Average Expenses (from Schedule J, Line 18)	$
Current Monthly Income (from Form 22A Line 12; **OR**, Form 22B Line 11; **OR**, Form 22C Line 20)	$

State the following:

1. Total from Schedule D, "UNSECURED PORTION, IF ANY" column		$
2. Total from Schedule E, "AMOUNT ENTITLED TO PRIORITY" column.	$	
3. Total from Schedule E, "AMOUNT NOT ENTITLED TO PRIORITY, IF ANY" column		$
4. Total from Schedule F		$
5. Total of non-priority unsecured debt (sum of 1, 3, and 4)		$

B6A (Official Form 6A) (12/07)

In re _____,   Case No. _____
                    Debtor   (If known)

SCHEDULE A - REAL PROPERTY

Except as directed below, list all real property in which the debtor has any legal, equitable, or future interest, including all property owned as a co-tenant, community property, or in which the debtor has a life estate. Include any property in which the debtor holds rights and powers exercisable for the debtor's own benefit. If the debtor is married, state whether the husband, wife, both, or the marital community own the property by placing an "H," "W," "J," or "C" in the column labeled "Husband, Wife, Joint, or Community." If the debtor holds no interest in real property, write "None" under "Description and Location of Property."

Do not include interests in executory contracts and unexpired leases on this schedule. List them in Schedule G - Executory Contracts and Unexpired Leases.

If an entity claims to have a lien or hold a secured interest in any property, state the amount of the secured claim. See Schedule D. If no entity claims to hold a secured interest in the property, write "None" in the column labeled "Amount of Secured Claim."

If the debtor is an individual or if a joint petition is filed, state the amount of any exemption claimed in the property only in Schedule C - Property Claimed as Exempt.

DESCRIPTION AND LOCATION OF PROPERTY	NATURE OF DEBTOR'S INTEREST IN PROPERTY	HUSBAND, WIFE, JOINT, OR COMMUNITY	CURRENT VALUE OF DEBTOR'S INTEREST IN PROPERTY, WITHOUT DEDUCTING ANY SECURED CLAIM OR EXEMPTION	AMOUNT OF SECURED CLAIM

Total▶
(Report also on Summary of Schedules.)

B 6B (Official Form 6B) (12/07)

In re _____,   Case No. _____
        Debtor   (If known)

SCHEDULE B - PERSONAL PROPERTY

Except as directed below, list all personal property of the debtor of whatever kind. If the debtor has no property in one or more of the categories, place an "x" in the appropriate position in the column labeled "None." If additional space is needed in any category, attach a separate sheet properly identified with the case name, case number, and the number of the category. If the debtor is married, state whether the husband, wife, both, or the marital community own the property by placing an "H," "W," "J," or "C" in the column labeled "Husband, Wife, Joint, or Community." If the debtor is an individual or a joint petition is filed, state the amount of any exemptions claimed only in Schedule C - Property Claimed as Exempt.

Do not list interests in executory contracts and unexpired leases on this schedule. List them in Schedule G - Executory Contracts and Unexpired Leases.

If the property is being held for the debtor by someone else, state that person's name and address under "Description and Location of Property." If the property is being held for a minor child, simply state the child's initials and the name and address of the child's parent or guardian, such as "A.B., a minor child, by John Doe, guardian." Do not disclose the child's name. See, 11 U.S.C. §112 and Fed. R. Bankr. P. 1007(m).

TYPE OF PROPERTY	N O N E	DESCRIPTION AND LOCATION OF PROPERTY	HUSBAND, WIFE, JOINT, OR COMMUNITY	CURRENT VALUE OF DEBTOR'S INTEREST IN PROPERTY, WITH-OUT DEDUCTING ANY SECURED CLAIM OR EXEMPTION
1. Cash on hand.				
2. Checking, savings or other financial accounts, certificates of deposit or shares in banks, savings and loan, thrift, building and loan, and homestead associations, or credit unions, brokerage houses, or cooperatives.				
3. Security deposits with public utilities, telephone companies, landlords, and others.				
4. Household goods and furnishings, including audio, video, and computer equipment.				
5. Books; pictures and other art objects; antiques; stamp, coin, record, tape, compact disc, and other collections or collectibles.				
6. Wearing apparel.				
7. Furs and jewelry.				
8. Firearms and sports, photographic, and other hobby equipment.				
9. Interests in insurance policies. Name insurance company of each policy and itemize surrender or refund value of each.				
10. Annuities. Itemize and name each issuer.				
11. Interests in an education IRA as defined in 26 U.S.C. § 530(b)(1) or under a qualified State tuition plan as defined in 26 U.S.C. § 529(b)(1). Give particulars. (File separately the record(s) of any such interest(s). 11 U.S.C. § 521(c).)				

B 6B (Official Form 6B) (12/07) -- Cont.

In re _____,   Case No. _____
                        Debtor   (If known)

SCHEDULE B - PERSONAL PROPERTY
(Continuation Sheet)

TYPE OF PROPERTY	N O N E	DESCRIPTION AND LOCATION OF PROPERTY	HUSBAND, WIFE, JOINT, OR COMMUNITY	CURRENT VALUE OF DEBTOR'S INTEREST IN PROPERTY, WITH-OUT DEDUCTING ANY SECURED CLAIM OR EXEMPTION
12. Interests in IRA, ERISA, Keogh, or other pension or profit sharing plans. Give particulars.				
13. Stock and interests in incorporated and unincorporated businesses. Itemize.				
14. Interests in partnerships or joint ventures. Itemize.				
15. Government and corporate bonds and other negotiable and non-negotiable instruments.				
16. Accounts receivable.				
17. Alimony, maintenance, support, and property settlements to which the debtor is or may be entitled. Give particulars.				
18. Other liquidated debts owed to debtor including tax refunds. Give particulars.				
19. Equitable or future interests, life estates, and rights or powers exercisable for the benefit of the debtor other than those listed in Schedule A – Real Property.				
20. Contingent and noncontingent interests in estate of a decedent, death benefit plan, life insurance policy, or trust.				
21. Other contingent and unliquidated claims of every nature, including tax refunds, counterclaims of the debtor, and rights to setoff claims. Give estimated value of each.				

B 6B (Official Form 6B) (12/07) -- Cont.

In re _____ ,   Case No. _____
            Debtor   **(If known)**

SCHEDULE B - PERSONAL PROPERTY
(Continuation Sheet)

TYPE OF PROPERTY	N O N E	DESCRIPTION AND LOCATION OF PROPERTY	HUSBAND, WIFE, JOINT, OR COMMUNITY	CURRENT VALUE OF DEBTOR'S INTEREST IN PROPERTY, WITH-OUT DEDUCTING ANY SECURED CLAIM OR EXEMPTION
22. Patents, copyrights, and other intellectual property. Give particulars.				
23. Licenses, franchises, and other general intangibles. Give particulars.				
24. Customer lists or other compilations containing personally identifiable information (as defined in 11 U.S.C. § 101(41A)) provided to the debtor by individuals in connection with obtaining a product or service from the debtor primarily for personal, family, or household purposes.				
25. Automobiles, trucks, trailers, and other vehicles and accessories.				
26. Boats, motors, and accessories.				
27. Aircraft and accessories.				
28. Office equipment, furnishings, and supplies.				
29. Machinery, fixtures, equipment, and supplies used in business.				
30. Inventory.				
31. Animals.				
32. Crops - growing or harvested. Give particulars.				
33. Farming equipment and implements.				
34. Farm supplies, chemicals, and feed.				
35. Other personal property of any kind not already listed. Itemize.				

_____ continuation sheets attached   Total▶ | $

(Include amounts from any continuation sheets attached. Report total also on Summary of Schedules.)

Form 6C

B 6C (Official Form 6C) (04/10)

In re _____,   Case No. _____
                    Debtor   (If known)

SCHEDULE C - PROPERTY CLAIMED AS EXEMPT

Debtor claims the exemptions to which debtor is entitled under: ☐ Check if debtor claims a homestead exemption that exceeds
(Check one box) $146,450.*
☐ 11 U.S.C. § 522(b)(2)
☐ 11 U.S.C. § 522(b)(3)

DESCRIPTION OF PROPERTY	SPECIFY LAW PROVIDING EACH EXEMPTION	VALUE OF CLAIMED EXEMPTION	CURRENT VALUE OF PROPERTY WITHOUT DEDUCTING EXEMPTION

* *Amount subject to adjustment on 4/1/13, and every three years thereafter with respect to cases commenced on or after the date of adjustment.*

Complete Annotation Materials, see Title 11 U.S.C.A.

838

Form 6D

B 6D (Official Form 6D) (12/07)

In re _____ , Case No. _____
         Debtor   (If known)

SCHEDULE D - CREDITORS HOLDING SECURED CLAIMS

State the name, mailing address, including zip code, and last four digits of any account number of all entities holding claims secured by property of the debtor as of the date of filing of the petition. The complete account number of any account the debtor has with the creditor is useful to the trustee and the creditor and may be provided if the debtor chooses to do so. List creditors holding all types of secured interests such as judgment liens, garnishments, statutory liens, mortgages, deeds of trust, and other security interests.

List creditors in alphabetical order to the extent practicable. If a minor child is the creditor, state the child's initials and the name and address of the child's parent or guardian, such as "A.B., a minor child, by John Doe, guardian." Do not disclose the child's name. See, 11 U.S.C. §112 and Fed. R. Bankr. P. 1007(m). If all secured creditors will not fit on this page, use the continuation sheet provided.

If any entity other than a spouse in a joint case may be jointly liable on a claim, place an "X" in the column labeled "Codebtor," include the entity on the appropriate schedule of creditors, and complete Schedule H – Codebtors. If a joint petition is filed, state whether the husband, wife, both of them, or the marital community may be liable on each claim by placing an "H," "W," "J," or "C" in the column labeled "Husband, Wife, Joint, or Community."

If the claim is contingent, place an "X" in the column labeled "Contingent." If the claim is unliquidated, place an "X" in the column labeled "Unliquidated." If the claim is disputed, place an "X" in the column labeled "Disputed." (You may need to place an "X" in more than one of these three columns.)

Total the columns labeled "Amount of Claim Without Deducting Value of Collateral" and "Unsecured Portion, if Any" in the boxes labeled "Total(s)" on the last sheet of the completed schedule. Report the total from the column labeled "Amount of Claim Without Deducting Value of Collateral" also on the Summary of Schedules and, if the debtor is an individual with primarily consumer debts, report the total from the column labeled "Unsecured Portion, if Any" on the Statistical Summary of Certain Liabilities and Related Data.

☐ Check this box if debtor has no creditors holding secured claims to report on this Schedule D.

CREDITOR'S NAME AND MAILING ADDRESS INCLUDING ZIP CODE AND AN ACCOUNT NUMBER (See Instructions Above.)	CODEBTOR	HUSBAND, WIFE, JOINT, OR COMMUNITY	DATE CLAIM WAS INCURRED, NATURE OF LIEN , AND DESCRIPTION AND VALUE OF PROPERTY SUBJECT TO LIEN	CONTINGENT	UNLIQUIDATED	DISPUTED	AMOUNT OF CLAIM WITHOUT DEDUCTING VALUE OF COLLATERAL	UNSECURED PORTION, IF ANY
ACCOUNT NO.								
			VALUE $					
ACCOUNT NO.								
			VALUE $					
ACCOUNT NO.								
			VALUE $					
____ continuation sheets attached			Subtotal ▶ (Total of this page)				$	$
			Total ▶ (Use only on last page)				$	$
							(Report also on Summary of Schedules.)	(If applicable, report also on Statistical Summary of Certain Liabilities and Related Data.)

Form 6D

B 6D (Official Form 6D) (12/07) – Cont.   2

In re_____,   Case No. _____
            Debtor   **(if known)**

SCHEDULE D - CREDITORS HOLDING SECURED CLAIMS
(Continuation Sheet)

CREDITOR'S NAME AND MAILING ADDRESS INCLUDING ZIP CODE AND AN ACCOUNT NUMBER (*See Instructions Above.*)	CODEBTOR	HUSBAND, WIFE, JOINT, OR COMMUNITY	DATE CLAIM WAS INCURRED, NATURE OF LIEN , AND DESCRIPTION AND VALUE OF PROPERTY SUBJECT TO LIEN	CONTINGENT	UNLIQUIDATED	DISPUTED	AMOUNT OF CLAIM WITHOUT DEDUCTING VALUE OF COLLATERAL.	UNSECURED PORTION, IF ANY
ACCOUNT NO.								
			VALUE $					
ACCOUNT NO.								
			VALUE $					
ACCOUNT NO.								
			VALUE $					
ACCOUNT NO.								
			VALUE $					
ACCOUNT NO.								
			VALUE $					
Sheet no._____of_____continuation sheets attached to Schedule of Creditors Holding Secured Claims			Subtotal (s)▶ (Total(s) of this page)				$	$
			Total(s) ▶ (Use only on last page)				$	$
							(Report also on Summary of Schedules.)	(If applicable, report also on Statistical Summary of Certain Liabilities and Related Data.)

Complete Annotation Materials, see Title 11 U.S.C.A.
840

B 6E (Official Form 6E) (04/10)

In re _____,   Case No._____
                    Debtor   (if known)

SCHEDULE E - CREDITORS HOLDING UNSECURED PRIORITY CLAIMS

A complete list of claims entitled to priority, listed separately by type of priority, is to be set forth on the sheets provided. Only holders of unsecured claims entitled to priority should be listed in this schedule. In the boxes provided on the attached sheets, state the name, mailing address, including zip code, and last four digits of the account number, if any, of all entities holding priority claims against the debtor or the property of the debtor, as of the date of the filing of the petition. Use a separate continuation sheet for each type of priority and label each with the type of priority.

The complete account number of any account the debtor has with the creditor is useful to the trustee and the creditor and may be provided if the debtor chooses to do so. If a minor child is a creditor, state the child's initials and the name and address of the child's parent or guardian, such as "A.B., a minor child, by John Doe, guardian." Do not disclose the child's name. See, 11 U.S.C. §112 and Fed. R. Bankr. P. 1007(m).

If any entity other than a spouse in a joint case may be jointly liable on a claim, place an "X" in the column labeled "Codebtor," include the entity on the appropriate schedule of creditors, and complete Schedule H-Codebtors. If a joint petition is filed, state whether the husband, wife, both of them, or the marital community may be liable on each claim by placing an "H," "W," "J," or "C" in the column labeled "Husband, Wife, Joint, or Community." If the claim is contingent, place an "X" in the column labeled "Contingent." If the claim is unliquidated, place an "X" in the column labeled "Unliquidated." If the claim is disputed, place an "X" in the column labeled "Disputed." (You may need to place an "X" in more than one of these three columns.)

Report the total of claims listed on each sheet in the box labeled "Subtotals" on each sheet. Report the total of all claims listed on this Schedule E in the box labeled "Total" on the last sheet of the completed schedule. Report this total also on the Summary of Schedules.

Report the total of amounts entitled to priority listed on each sheet in the box labeled "Subtotals" on each sheet. Report the total of all amounts entitled to priority listed on this Schedule E in the box labeled "Totals" on the last sheet of the completed schedule. Individual debtors with primarily consumer debts report this total also on the Statistical Summary of Certain Liabilities and Related Data.

Report the total of amounts <u>not</u> entitled to priority listed on each sheet in the box labeled "Subtotals" on each sheet. Report the total of all amounts not entitled to priority listed on this Schedule E in the box labeled "Totals" on the last sheet of the completed schedule. Individual debtors with primarily consumer debts report this total also on the Statistical Summary of Certain Liabilities and Related Data.

☐ Check this box if debtor has no creditors holding unsecured priority claims to report on this Schedule E.

TYPES OF PRIORITY CLAIMS (Check the appropriate box(es) below if claims in that category are listed on the attached sheets.)

☐ **Domestic Support Obligations**

Claims for domestic support that are owed to or recoverable by a spouse, former spouse, or child of the debtor, or the parent, legal guardian, or responsible relative of such a child, or a governmental unit to whom such a domestic support claim has been assigned to the extent provided in 11 U.S.C. § 507(a)(1).

☐ **Extensions of credit in an involuntary case**

Claims arising in the ordinary course of the debtor's business or financial affairs after the commencement of the case but before the earlier of the appointment of a trustee or the order for relief. 11 U.S.C. § 507(a)(3).

☐ **Wages, salaries, and commissions**

Wages, salaries, and commissions, including vacation, severance, and sick leave pay owing to employees and commissions owing to qualifying independent sales representatives up to $11,725* per person earned within 180 days immediately preceding the filing of the original petition, or the cessation of business, whichever occurred first, to the extent provided in 11 U.S.C. § 507(a)(4).

☐ **Contributions to employee benefit plans**

Money owed to employee benefit plans for services rendered within 180 days immediately preceding the filing of the original petition, or the cessation of business, whichever occurred first, to the extent provided in 11 U.S.C. § 507(a)(5).

* Amount subject to adjustment on 4/01/13, and every three years thereafter with respect to cases commenced on or after the date of adjustment.

Form 6E

B 6E (Official Form 6E) (04/10) – Cont.

In re _____ , Case No._____
                 Debtor   (if known)

☐ **Certain farmers and fishermen**

Claims of certain farmers and fishermen, up to $5,775* per farmer or fisherman, against the debtor, as provided in 11 U.S.C. § 507(a)(6).

☐ **Deposits by individuals**

Claims of individuals up to $2,600* for deposits for the purchase, lease, or rental of property or services for personal, family, or household use, that were not delivered or provided. 11 U.S.C. § 507(a)(7).

☐ **Taxes and Certain Other Debts Owed to Governmental Units**

Taxes, customs duties, and penalties owing to federal, state, and local governmental units as set forth in 11 U.S.C. § 507(a)(8).

☐ **Commitments to Maintain the Capital of an Insured Depository Institution**

Claims based on commitments to the FDIC, RTC, Director of the Office of Thrift Supervision, Comptroller of the Currency, or Board of Governors of the Federal Reserve System, or their predecessors or successors, to maintain the capital of an insured depository institution. 11 U.S.C. § 507 (a)(9).

☐ **Claims for Death or Personal Injury While Debtor Was Intoxicated**

Claims for death or personal injury resulting from the operation of a motor vehicle or vessel while the debtor was intoxicated from using alcohol, a drug, or another substance. 11 U.S.C. § 507(a)(10).

* *Amounts are subject to adjustment on 4/01/13, and every three years thereafter with respect to cases commenced on or after the date of adjustment.*

_____ continuation sheets attached

B 6E (Official Form 6E) (04/10) -- Cont.

In re _____ ,   Case No. _____
                    Debtor   **(if known)**

SCHEDULE E - CREDITORS HOLDING UNSECURED PRIORITY CLAIMS
(Continuation Sheet)

Type of **Priority for Claims Listed on This Sheet**

CREDITOR'S NAME, MAILING ADDRESS INCLUDING ZIP CODE, AND ACCOUNT NUMBER *(See instructions above.)*	CODEBTOR	HUSBAND, WIFE, JOINT, OR COMMUNITY	DATE CLAIM WAS INCURRED AND CONSIDERATION FOR CLAIM	CONTINGENT	UNLIQUIDATED	DISPUTED	AMOUNT OF CLAIM	AMOUNT ENTITLED TO PRIORITY	AMOUNT NOT ENTITLED TO PRIORITY, IF ANY
Account No.									
Account No.									
Account No.									
Account No.									

Sheet no. ____ of ____ continuation sheets attached to Schedule of Creditors Holding Priority Claims.

Subtotals▶
(Totals of this page) $ $

Total▶ $
(Use only on last page of the completed
Schedule E. Report also on the Summary
of Schedules.)

Totals▶ $ $
(Use only on last page of the completed
Schedule E. If applicable, report also on
the Statistical Summary of Certain
Liabilities and Related Data.)

Form 6F

B 6F (Official Form 6F) (12/07)

In re _____,   Case No. _____
              Debtor   **(if known)**

SCHEDULE F - CREDITORS HOLDING UNSECURED NONPRIORITY CLAIMS

State the name, mailing address, including zip code, and last four digits of any account number, of all entities holding unsecured claims without priority against the debtor or the property of the debtor, as of the date of filing of the petition. The complete account number of any account the debtor has with the creditor is useful to the trustee and the creditor and may be provided if the debtor chooses to do so. If a minor child is a creditor, state the child's initials and the name and address of the child's parent or guardian, such as "A.B., a minor child, by John Doe, guardian." Do not disclose the child's name. See, 11 U.S.C. §112 and Fed. R. Bankr. P. 1007(m). Do not include claims listed in Schedules D and E. If all creditors will not fit on this page, use the continuation sheet provided.

If any entity other than a spouse in a joint case may be jointly liable on a claim, place an "X" in the column labeled "Codebtor," include the entity on the appropriate schedule of creditors, and complete Schedule H - Codebtors. If a joint petition is filed, state whether the husband, wife, both of them, or the marital community may be liable on each claim by placing an "H," "W," "J," or "C" in the column labeled "Husband, Wife, Joint, or Community."

If the claim is contingent, place an "X" in the column labeled "Contingent." If the claim is unliquidated, place an "X" in the column labeled "Unliquidated." If the claim is disputed, place an "X" in the column labeled "Disputed." (You may need to place an "X" in more than one of these three columns.)

Report the total of all claims listed on this schedule in the box labeled "Total" on the last sheet of the completed schedule. Report this total also on the Summary of Schedules and, if the debtor is an individual with primarily consumer debts, report this total also on the Statistical Summary of Certain Liabilities and Related Data.

☐ Check this box if debtor has no creditors holding unsecured claims to report on this Schedule F.

CREDITOR'S NAME, MAILING ADDRESS INCLUDING ZIP CODE, AND ACCOUNT NUMBER (*See instructions above.*)	CODEBTOR	HUSBAND, WIFE, JOINT, OR COMMUNITY	DATE CLAIM WAS INCURRED AND CONSIDERATION FOR CLAIM. IF CLAIM IS SUBJECT TO SETOFF, SO STATE.	CONTINGENT	UNLIQUIDATED	DISPUTED	AMOUNT OF CLAIM
ACCOUNT NO.							
ACCOUNT NO.							
ACCOUNT NO.							
ACCOUNT NO.							
				Subtotal ▶			$

continuation sheets attached

Total ▶ $
(Use only on last page of the completed Schedule F.)
(Report also on Summary of Schedules and, if applicable, on the Statistical Summary of Certain Liabilities and Related Data.)

Complete Annotation Materials, see Title 11 U.S.C.A.

844

B 6F (Official Form 6F) (12/07) - Cont.

In re _____ ,   Case No. _____
        Debtor   **(if known)**

SCHEDULE F - CREDITORS HOLDING UNSECURED NONPRIORITY CLAIMS
(Continuation Sheet)

CREDITOR'S NAME, MAILING ADDRESS INCLUDING ZIP CODE, AND ACCOUNT NUMBER (See instructions above.)	CODEBTOR	HUSBAND, WIFE, JOINT, OR COMMUNITY	DATE CLAIM WAS INCURRED AND CONSIDERATION FOR CLAIM. IF CLAIM IS SUBJECT TO SETOFF, SO STATE.	CONTINGENT	UNLIQUIDATED	DISPUTED	AMOUNT OF CLAIM
ACCOUNT NO.							
ACCOUNT NO.							
ACCOUNT NO.							
ACCOUNT NO.							
ACCOUNT NO.							

Sheet no._____ of_____ continuation sheets attached to Schedule of Creditors Holding Unsecured Nonpriority Claims

Subtotal► $

Total► $
(Use only on last page of the completed Schedule F.)
(Report also on Summary of Schedules and, if applicable on the Statistical Summary of Certain Liabilities and Related Data.)

Form 6G

OFFICIAL FORMS

B 6G (Official Form 6G) (12/07)

In re _____ ,   Case No._____
            Debtor   **(if known)**

SCHEDULE G - EXECUTORY CONTRACTS AND UNEXPIRED LEASES

Describe all executory contracts of any nature and all unexpired leases of real or personal property. Include any timeshare interests. State nature of debtor's interest in contract, i.e., "Purchaser," "Agent," etc. State whether debtor is the lessor or lessee of a lease. Provide the names and complete mailing addresses of all other parties to each lease or contract described. If a minor child is a party to one of the leases or contracts, state the child's initials and the name and address of the child's parent or guardian, such as "A.B., a minor child, by John Doe, guardian." Do not disclose the child's name. See, 11 U.S.C. §112 and Fed. R. Bankr. P. 1007(m).

☐ Check this box if debtor has no executory contracts or unexpired leases.

NAME AND MAILING ADDRESS, INCLUDING ZIP CODE, OF OTHER PARTIES TO LEASE OR CONTRACT.	DESCRIPTION OF CONTRACT OR LEASE AND NATURE OF DEBTOR'S INTEREST. STATE WHETHER LEASE IS FOR NONRESIDENTIAL REAL PROPERTY. STATE CONTRACT NUMBER OF ANY GOVERNMENT CONTRACT.

B 6H (Official Form 6H) (12/07)

In re _____ ,   Case No. _____
                    Debtor   **(if known)**

SCHEDULE H - CODEBTORS

Provide the information requested concerning any person or entity, other than a spouse in a joint case, that is also liable on any debts listed by the debtor in the schedules of creditors. Include all guarantors and co-signers. If the debtor resides or resided in a community property state, commonwealth, or territory (including Alaska, Arizona, California, Idaho, Louisiana, Nevada, New Mexico, Puerto Rico, Texas, Washington, or Wisconsin) within the eight-year period immediately preceding the commencement of the case, identify the name of the debtor's spouse and of any former spouse who resides or resided with the debtor in the community property state, commonwealth, or territory. Include all names used by the nondebtor spouse during the eight years immediately preceding the commencement of this case. If a minor child is a codebtor or a creditor, state the child's initials and the name and address of the child's parent or guardian, such as "A.B., a minor child, by John Doe, guardian." Do not disclose the child's name. See, 11 U.S.C. §112 and Fed. R. Bankr. P. 1007(m).

☐ Check this box if debtor has no codebtors.

NAME AND ADDRESS OF CODEBTOR	NAME AND ADDRESS OF CREDITOR

B6I (Official Form 6I) (12/07)

In re _____ ,   Case No. _____
                    Debtor   **(if known)**

SCHEDULE I - CURRENT INCOME OF INDIVIDUAL DEBTOR(S)

The column labeled "Spouse" must be completed in all cases filed by joint debtors and by every married debtor, whether or not a joint petition is filed, unless the spouses are separated and a joint petition is not filed. Do not state the name of any minor child. The average monthly income calculated on this form may differ from the current monthly income calculated on Form 22A, 22B, or 22C.

Debtor's Marital Status:	DEPENDENTS OF DEBTOR AND SPOUSE	
	RELATIONSHIP(S):	AGE(S):
Employment: DEBTOR	SPOUSE	
Occupation		
Name of Employer		
How long employed		
Address of Employer		

INCOME: (Estimate of average or projected monthly income at time case filed)	DEBTOR	SPOUSE
1. Monthly gross wages, salary, and commissions (Prorate if not paid monthly)	$_____	$_____
2. Estimate monthly overtime	$_____	$_____
3. SUBTOTAL	$_____	$_____
4. LESS PAYROLL DEDUCTIONS		
a. Payroll taxes and social security	$_____	$_____
b. Insurance	$_____	$_____
c. Union dues	$_____	$_____
d. Other (Specify): _____	$_____	$_____
5. SUBTOTAL OF PAYROLL DEDUCTIONS	$_____	$_____
6. TOTAL NET MONTHLY TAKE HOME PAY	$_____	$_____
7. Regular income from operation of business or profession or farm (Attach detailed statement)	$_____	$_____
8. Income from real property	$_____	$_____
9. Interest and dividends	$_____	$_____
10. Alimony, maintenance or support payments payable to the debtor for the debtor's use or that of dependents listed above	$_____	$_____
11. Social security or government assistance (Specify):_____	$_____	$_____
12. Pension or retirement income	$_____	$_____
13. Other monthly income (Specify):_____	$_____	$_____
14. SUBTOTAL OF LINES 7 THROUGH 13	$_____	$_____
15. AVERAGE MONTHLY INCOME (Add amounts on lines 6 and 14)	$_____	$_____
16. COMBINED AVERAGE MONTHLY INCOME: (Combine column totals from line 15)	$_____	

(Report also on Summary of Schedules and, if applicable, on Statistical Summary of Certain Liabilities and Related Data)

17. Describe any increase or decrease in income reasonably anticipated to occur within the year following the filing of this document:

_____

B6J (Official Form 6J) (12/07)

In re _____ ,   Case No. _____
             Debtor   **(if known)**

SCHEDULE J - CURRENT EXPENDITURES OF INDIVIDUAL DEBTOR(S)

Complete this schedule by estimating the average or projected monthly expenses of the debtor and the debtor's family at time case filed. Prorate any payments made bi-weekly, quarterly, semi-annually, or annually to show monthly rate. The average monthly expenses calculated on this form may differ from the deductions from income allowed on Form22A or 22C.

☐   Check this box if a joint petition is filed and debtor's spouse maintains a separate household. Complete a separate schedule of expenditures labeled "Spouse."

1. Rent or home mortgage payment (include lot rented for mobile home)	$ _____
a. Are real estate taxes included? Yes _____ No _____	
b. Is property insurance included? Yes _____ No _____	
2. Utilities: a. Electricity and heating fuel	$ _____
b. Water and sewer	$
c. Telephone	$
d. Other _____	$ _____
3. Home maintenance (repairs and upkeep)	$
4. Food	$ _____
5. Clothing	$ _____
6. Laundry and dry cleaning	$ _____
7. Medical and dental expenses	$ _____
8. Transportation (not including car payments)	$
9. Recreation, clubs and entertainment, newspapers, magazines, etc.	$
10. Charitable contributions	$ _____
11. Insurance (not deducted from wages or included in home mortgage payments)	
a. Homeowner's or renter's	$ _____
b. Life	$ _____
c. Health	$
d. Auto	$
e. Other _____	$
12. Taxes (not deducted from wages or included in home mortgage payments) (Specify) _____	$ _____
13. Installment payments: (In chapter 11, 12, and 13 cases, do not list payments to be included in the plan)	
a. Auto	$ _____
b. Other _____	$ _____
c. Other _____	$ _____
14. Alimony, maintenance, and support paid to others	$
15. Payments for support of additional dependents not living at your home	$
16. Regular expenses from operation of business, profession, or farm (attach detailed statement)	$ _____
17. Other _____	$
18. AVERAGE MONTHLY EXPENSES (Total lines 1-17. Report also on Summary of Schedules and, if applicable, on the Statistical Summary of Certain Liabilities and Related Data.)	$

19. Describe any increase or decrease in expenditures reasonably anticipated to occur within the year following the filing of this document:

20. STATEMENT OF MONTHLY NET INCOME

a. Average monthly income from Line 15 of Schedule I	$ _____
b. Average monthly expenses from Line 18 above	$ _____
c. Monthly net income (a. minus b.)	$ _____

Form 6

B6 Declaration (Official Form 6 - Declaration) (12/07)

In re _____,   Case No. _____
                    Debtor   (if known)

DECLARATION CONCERNING DEBTOR'S SCHEDULES

DECLARATION UNDER PENALTY OF PERJURY BY INDIVIDUAL DEBTOR

I declare under penalty of perjury that I have read the foregoing summary and schedules, consisting of _____ sheets, and that they are true and correct to the best of my knowledge, information, and belief.

Date _____   Signature: _____
                                                                                        Debtor

Date _____   Signature: _____
                                                                              (Joint Debtor, if any)

                                                   [If joint case, both spouses must sign.]

DECLARATION AND SIGNATURE OF NON-ATTORNEY BANKRUPTCY PETITION PREPARER (See 11 U.S.C. § 110)

I declare under penalty of perjury that: (1) I am a bankruptcy petition preparer as defined in 11 U.S.C. § 110; (2) I prepared this document for compensation and have provided the debtor with a copy of this document and the notices and information required under 11 U.S.C. §§ 110(b), 110(h) and 342(b); and, (3) if rules or guidelines have been promulgated pursuant to 11 U.S.C. § 110(h) setting a maximum fee for services chargeable by bankruptcy petition preparers, I have given the debtor notice of the maximum amount before preparing any document for filing for a debtor or accepting any fee from the debtor, as required by that section.

_____   _____
Printed or Typed Name and Title, if any,   Social Security No.
of Bankruptcy Petition Preparer   (Required by 11 U.S.C. § 110.)

If the bankruptcy petition preparer is not an individual, state the name, title (if any), address, and social security number of the officer, principal, responsible person, or partner who signs this document.

_____
Address

X _____   _____
Signature of Bankruptcy Petition Preparer   Date

Names and Social Security numbers of all other individuals who prepared or assisted in preparing this document, unless the bankruptcy petition preparer is not an individual:

If more than one person prepared this document, attach additional signed sheets conforming to the appropriate Official Form for each person.

A bankruptcy petition preparer's failure to comply with the provisions of title 11 and the Federal Rules of Bankruptcy Procedure may result in fines or imprisonment or both. 11 U.S.C. § 110; 18 U.S.C. § 156.

DECLARATION UNDER PENALTY OF PERJURY ON BEHALF OF A CORPORATION OR PARTNERSHIP

I, the _____ [the president or other officer or an authorized agent of the corporation or a member or an authorized agent of the partnership] of the _____ [corporation or partnership] named as debtor in this case, declare under penalty of perjury that I have read the foregoing summary and schedules, consisting of _____ sheets (Total shown on summary page plus 1), and that they are true and correct to the best of my knowledge, information, and belief.

Date _____   Signature: _____

                                                   [Print or type name of individual signing on behalf of debtor.]

[An individual signing on behalf of a partnership or corporation must indicate position or relationship to debtor.]

Penalty for making a false statement or concealing property: Fine of up to $500,000 or imprisonment for up to 5 years or both. 18 U.S.C. §§ 152 and 3571.

(Added Aug. 1, 1991; amended Mar. 16, 1993; Mar. 1995; Oct. 1, 1997; Apr. 1, 1998; Dec. 1, 2003; April 1, 2004; Apr. 25, 2005, eff. Dec. 1, 2005; Aug. 11, 2005, eff. Oct. 17, 2005; Oct. 11, 2006; Apr. 1, 2007; Dec. 2007; Apr. 1, 2010.)

ADVISORY COMMITTEE NOTES

1991 Enactment

These schedules shall be used to comply with § 521(1) of the Code and Rule 1007(b). Schedules A, B, D, E, and F constitute the schedule of assets and liabilities. Schedules I and J constitute a schedule of current income and current expenditures for individual and joint debtors. Two new schedules have been created, Schedule G—Executory Contracts and Unexpired Leases, and Schedule H—Codebtors.

The order of the schedules has been arranged with the summary sheet in front and with the schedules of assets appearing first, followed by the schedules of liabilities. This structure corresponds to the customary pattern by which trustees and creditors review these documents and to the format of the accounting profession for balance sheets.

The schedules require a complete listing of assets and liabilities but leave many of the details to investigation by the trustee. Instructions in the former schedules to provide details concerning "written instruments" relating to the debtor's property or debts have been deleted. Section 521(3) of the Code requires the debtor to cooperate with the trustee, who can administer the estate more effectively by requesting any documents from the debtor rather than relying on descriptions in the schedules which may prove to be inaccurate.

Leasehold interests in both real and personal property are to be reported in Schedule G—Executory Contracts and Unexpired Leases. This information should not be repeated in the schedules of assets.

Generally in these schedules, a creditor's claim will be listed only once, even if the claim is secured only in part, or is entitled only in part to priority under § 507(a) of the Code, with the remainder of the claim to be treated as a general unsecured claim. For example, a partially secured creditor whose claim is reported in Schedule D—Creditors Holding Secured Claims will be listed together with the value of the property securing the claim and a notation of the amount of

Complete Annotation Materials, see Title 11 U.S.C.A.

850

any unsecured portion of the claim. Information concerning the unsecured portion should not be repeated in Schedule F—Creditors Holding Nonpriority Unsecured Claims. Any resulting overstatement of the amounts owed on secured and priority claims as reported on the summary sheet is offset by a corresponding understatement of the amount owed on unsecured claims.

If a debtor has no property or no creditors in a particular category, an affirmative statement to that effect is required. Married debtors should indicate whether property is jointly or separately owned and whether spouses are jointly or separately liable for debts, using the columns provided in the schedules.

Former "Schedule B–3. Property not otherwise scheduled," has been deleted and its two questions moved. Schedule B—Personal Property now includes at item 33, "Other personal property of any kind not already listed." The only other question on former Schedule B–3 concerned assignments for the benefit of creditors; it has been moved to the Statement of Financial Affairs.

Schedule A—Real Property. Instructions at the top of the form indicate the scope of the interests in property to be reported on the schedule. Leasehold interests of the debtor are not reported here but on the Schedule of Executory Contracts and Unexpired Leases. The trustee will request copies of deeds or other instruments necessary to the administration of the estate.

Schedule B—Personal Property. This schedule is to be used for reporting all of the debtor's interests in personal property except leases and executory contracts, which are to be listed on the Schedule of Executory Contracts and Unexpired Leases. Several new categories of property have been added to the schedule, i.e., aircraft, and interests in IRA, ERISA, Keogh, or other pension or profit-sharing plans. To minimize the potential for concealment of assets, the debtor must declare whether the debtor has any property in each category on the schedule. The trustee can request copies of any documents concerning the debtor's property necessary to the administration of the estate.

Schedule C—Property Claimed as Exempt. The form of the schedule has been modified to eliminate duplication of information provided elsewhere. The location of property, for example, which formerly was required here, is disclosed in the schedules of real and personal property. The requirement that the debtor state the present use of the property also has been eliminated as best left to inquiry by the trustee. Exemptions in some states are granted by constitutional provisions; accordingly, the requirement that the debtor state the "statute" creating an exemption has been changed to request a statement of the relevant "law."

This schedule adds a new requirement that the debtor state the market value of the property in addition to the amount claimed as exempt.

Schedule D—Creditors Holding Secured Claims. Schedules D, E, and F have been redesigned with address boxes sized to match the number of characters which can be accommodated on the computerized noticing systems used by the courts. The size also closely approximates that of standard mailing labels. Space is designated at the top of the box for the debtor's account number with the creditor. The design of the form is intended to reduce the volume of misdirected creditor mail.

The form requires the debtor to state affirmatively that a claim is disputed, unliquidated, or contingent. The existence

of any type of codebtor is to be disclosed, but details are to be provided in Schedule H, as they are not needed here. Duplication of information also has been kept to a minimum by deleting requests that the debtor indicate on this schedule whether a debt has been reduced to judgment and the date on which a creditor repossessed any collateral. Requests for details concerning negotiable instruments and the consideration for a claim, formerly part of the schedule, are left to the trustee's inquiries.

Schedule E—Creditors Holding Unsecured Priority Claims. The schedule lists all of the types of claims entitled to priority and requires the debtor to indicate the existence of claims in each category. Continuation sheets are provided. The type of priority claim is to be noted at the top of the continuation sheet, and each type must be reported on a separate sheet. This schedule also requires the debtor to indicate the existence of any codebtors. As in Schedule D—Creditors Holding Secured Claims, requests for information concerning judgments and negotiable instruments have been deleted.

Schedule F—Creditors Holding Unsecured Nonpriority Claims. This schedule has been revised generally in conformity with the other schedules of creditors. If a claim is subject to setoff, the debtor is required to so state.

Schedule G—Executory Contracts and Unexpired Leases. Rule 1007(b) requires the debtor to file a schedule of executory contracts and unexpired leases, unless the court orders otherwise. All unexpired leases of either real or personal property are to be reported on this schedule. The schedule also requires the debtor to disclose specific information to assist the trustee in identifying leases which must be assumed within 60 days after the order for relief or be deemed rejected under § 365(d) of the Code.

Schedule H—Schedule of Codebtors. This schedule is designed to provide the trustee and creditors with information about codebtors of all types other than spouses in joint cases. The completed schedule provides information concerning nondebtor parties, such as guarantors and non-debtor spouses having an interest in property as tenants by the entirety. In chapter 12 and chapter 13 cases, the completed schedule also indicates those persons who may be entitled to certain protections from creditor action under §§ 1201 and 1301 of the Code.

Schedule I—Schedule of Current Income of Individual Debtor(s) and Schedule J—Schedule of Current Expenditures of Individual Debtor(s). Former Official Form No. 6A has been divided into a schedule of current income and a separate schedule of current expenditures. The language is substantially the same as in former Official Form No. 6A. In light of the abrogation of Official Form No. 10, the Chapter 13 Statement, style changes have been made so that these schedules can be used by individual and joint debtors in all chapters.

1993 Amendment

Schedule E (Creditors Holding Unsecured Priority Claims) has been changed to conform to the statutory amendment that added subsection (a)(8) to § 507 of the Code. Pub.L. No. 101–647, (Crime Control Act of 1990), added the new subsection, which had the effect of creating an eighth priority for claims of certain governmental units based on commitments to maintain the capital of an insured depository institution.

Form 6

Schedule E—Creditors Holding Unsecured Priority Claims is amended to add the new seventh priority afforded to debts for alimony, maintenance, or support of a spouse, former spouse, or child of the debtor by the Bankruptcy Reform Act of 1994. Statutory references are amended to conform to the paragraph numbers of section 507(a) of the Code as renumbered by the 1994 Act. Schedule E also is amended to add commissions owed to certain independent sales representatives and to raise the maximum dollar amounts for certain priorities in accordance with amendments made by the 1994 Act to section 507(a) of the Code. The 1994 Act also amended section 104 of the Code to provide for future adjustment of the maximum dollar amounts specified in section 507(a) to be made by administrative action at three-year intervals to reflect changes in the consumer price index. Schedule E is amended to give notice that these dollar amounts are subject to change without formal amendment to the official form.

The Schedules are a "document for filing" that may be prepared by a "bankruptcy petition preparer" as defined in 11 U.S.C. § 110, which was added to the Code by the 1994 Act; accordingly, a signature line for such preparer is added. In addition to signing, a bankruptcy petition preparer is required by section 110 to disclose the information requested.

1997 Amendment

The form is amended to add to the column labels a reference to community liability for claims. The amendment is technical and corrects an editorial oversight.

2003 Amendment

The instructions to Schedule D (Creditors Holding Secured Claims), Schedule E (Creditors Holding Unsecured Priority Claims), and Schedule F (Creditors Holding Unsecured Nonpriority Claims) are amended to inform the debtor that the debtor must list the last four digits of any account number with the listed creditor, and that the debtor may, in its discretion, include the entire account number in the schedules. Schedule I (Current Income of Individual Debtor(s)) is amended to provide greater privacy to minors and other dependents of the debtor by deleting the requirement that the debtor disclose their names. Pursuant to § 110(c) of the Bankruptcy Code, the certification by a non-attorney bankruptcy petition preparer requires a petition preparer to provide the full Social Security number of the individual who actually prepares the document.

2005 Amendment

The forms of the Schedules of Assets and Liabilities are amended to implement the provisions of the Bankruptcy Abuse Prevention and Consumer Protection Act of 2005, Pub. L. No. 109–8, 119 Stat. 23, (April 20, 2005). An amendment that directs the debtor to avoid disclosing the name of any minor child occurs in several of the schedules in conformity with § 112 which was added to the Code in 2005. Section 112 provides for the debtor to provide the name of any minor child confidentially to the court, should the trustee need the information to evaluate properly the information filed by the debtor.

The "Statistical Summary of Certain Liabilities" is added to collect information needed to prepare statistical reports required under 28 U.S.C. § 159, which was enacted as part of the 2005 Act.

Schedules A, B, C, and D are amended to delete the word "market" from the columns in which the debtor reports the value of various kinds of property. Amendments to § 506 of the Code enacted in 2005 specify that "replacement value" must be used in connection with certain property. The schedules no longer specify "market" value and permit the debtor to choose the appropriate one, whether that be replacement, market, or some other value. Valuation of property, generally, is the subject of extensive provisions in the Code, and the deletion of the word "market" from the determinations of value to be made by the debtor on the schedules is intended to remove any inference about choice of valuation standard. This deletion simply indicates that the form takes no position on which Code provision or valuation standard may be applicable in any instance.

The following paragraphs describe changes that are specific to each schedule.

Schedule B—Personal Property is amended to require the debtor to list any interests in an education IRA, as § 541(b)(5), added to the Code in 2005, makes special provision for them. The schedule also is amended to require the debtor to disclose the existence of any customer lists or other compilations containing personally identifiable information provided by an individual to the debtor in connection with obtaining a product or service from the debtor for personal, family, or household purposes. This amendment implements § 332, which was added to the Code in 2005.

Schedule C—Property Claimed as Exempt is amended to delete descriptive information concerning the length of domicile required for the debtor to qualify to claim certain exemptions. Any summary of the amendments enacted in 2005 to § 522 of the Code concerning these requirements might inadvertently cause the debtor to lose important rights. Accordingly, the form now directs the debtor to indicate whether exemptions are being claimed under § 522(b)(2) or § 522(b)(3) and whether the debtor claims a homestead exemption that exceeds $125,000.

Schedule E—Creditors Holding Unsecured Priority Claims is amended to implement the changes in priority to which a claim may be entitled under 11 U.S.C. § 507 as amended by the 2005 Act and to add the new priority included in the Reform Act for claims for death or personal injury while the debtor was intoxicated. "Subtotal" and "Total" boxes have been added to the column labeled "Amount Entitled to Priority" to assist the individual debtor to complete the Means Test form.

Schedule G—Executory Contracts and Unexpired Leases is amended by deleting the note to the debtor advising that parties listed on this schedule may not receive notice of the filing of the bankruptcy case unless they also are listed on one of the schedules of liabilities. The better practice is for all parties to transactions with the debtor to receive notice of the filing of the case, and an amendment to Rule 1007 requiring the debtor to provide a mailing list that includes these parties is scheduled to take effect December 1, 2005.

Schedule H—Codebtors is amended to add specifics about community property jurisdictions in connection with the requirement to provide the name of any spouse of a debtor who resides or resided in a community property jurisdiction. This amendment also mirrors amendments made in 1997 to Official Form 7, the Statement of Financial Affairs, and will assure that these codebtors receive notice of the filing of the bankruptcy case. The form also is amended to extend from six

Complete Annotation Materials, see Title 11 U.S.C.A.

852

years to eight years the time period for which this information is reported pursuant to the 2005 amendments to § 727(a)(8) of the Code.

Schedule I—Current Income of Individual Debtor(s) is amended to require the income of a nondebtor spouse to be reported in cases filed under chapters 7 and 11. Line numbers have been added to assist the debtor in calculating and reporting totals. A new subtotal line for income from sources other than as an employee and a new "total monthly income" line provide for this form to be used in conjunction with Schedule J to satisfy the requirements of § 521(a)(1)(B)(v), which was added to the Code in 2005. The form also has been revised to provide the statement concerning any anticipated increase or decrease in income required in § 521(a)(1)(B)(vi), which also was added to the Code in 2005.

Schedule J—Current Expenditures of Individual Debtor(s). A direction has been added to require the debtor to report any increase or decrease in expenses anticipated to occur within the year following the filing of the document, as required by § 521(a)(1)(B)(vi), which was added to the Code in 2005. The form also is amended to provide, in conjunction with Schedule I, a statement of monthly net income, itemized to show how the amount is calculated, as required by § 522(a)(1)(B)(v), which was added to the Code in 2005.

Declaration Concerning Debtor's Schedules. The declaration by a non-attorney bankruptcy petition preparer is amended to include material mandated by § 110 of the Code as amended in 2005.

2006 Amendments

In order to comply fully with the statistical reporting requirements of 28 U.S.C. § 159, which was enacted as part of the 2005 Act and takes effect in October 2006, the "Statistical Summary of Certain Liabilities" is renamed "Statistical Summary of Certain Liabilities and Related Data," and additional information is required to be stated there. Collecting in one place the bulk of the information to be used in the reports required under 28 U.S.C. § 159 will assist the courts and the Director of the Administrative Office of the United States Courts to fulfill their statutory responsibilities.

Schedule D is amended to provide for creating a total of any unsecured amounts (amounts that exceed the value of the collateral) owed to creditors holding secured claims, and for stating this amount on the Statistical Summary of Certain Liabilities and Related Data.

Schedule E is amended to provide for creating totals of the amounts entitled to priority and of any amounts that exceed the statutory limits on certain priorities and to direct the debtor to report these amounts on the Statistical Summary of Certain Liabilities and Related Data. Schedule F is amended to direct the debtor to report the total of this schedule both on the Summary of Schedules and on the Statistical Summary of Certain Liabilities.

The statistical reports required under 28 U.S.C. § 159 must include "the current monthly income, average income, and average expenses" of individual debtors with primarily consumer debts as reported on the schedules filed by those debtors. Accordingly, Schedules I and J, on which debtors already are directed to report average income and average expenses are amended to label the totals arrived at by completing the schedules as " average monthly income" and "average monthly expenses." These amendments make no

substantive changes, simply conforming the terminology on these schedules to that used in § 159.

The amount of the debtor's current monthly income, which also is required by § 159, is derived from Official Forms 22A, 22B, or 22C, depending on the chapter under which the debtor files. This amount is included on the Statistical Summary of Certain Liabilities and Related Data as a convenience to make reports under § 159 easier to compile.

The declaration Concerning Debtor's Schedules is amended in the section designated for signing and verifying by an individual or joint debtor. The amendment accommodates the requirement that individual debtors must complete both the Summary of Schedules and the Statistical Summary of Certain Liabilities and Related Data by directing the debtor to state number of pages being verified as the number of sheets in the completed schedules "plus 2."

2005–2007 Amendments

(The 2005–2007 Committee Note incorporates Committee Notes previously published in 2005 and 2006.)

The forms of the Schedules of Assets and Liabilities are amended to implement the provisions of the Bankruptcy Abuse Prevention and Consumer Protection Act of 2005, Pub. L. No. 109–8, 119 Stat. 23, (April 20, 2005) ("BAPCPA"). An amendment that directs the debtor to avoid disclosing the name and address of any minor child occurs in Schedules B, D, E, F, G, and H in conformity with § 112 which was added to the Code in 2005. Section 112 provides for the debtor to furnish the name of any minor child confidentially to the court, should the trustee need the information to evaluate properly the information filed by the debtor. In addition, those schedules are amended to add to the reference to Rule 1007(m), with respect to a minor child, a direction to include for noticing purposes the name, address, and legal relationship to the child of "a person described" in that rule. Rule 1007(m) requires the person named to be someone on whom process would be served in an adversary proceeding against the child.

The "Statistical Summary of Certain Liabilities and Related Data" is added to collect from individual debtors with primarily consumer debts the information needed to prepare statistical reports required under 28 U.S.C. § 159, which was enacted as part of BAPCPA. Collecting the bulk of the information to be used in these statistical reports in the Summary of Schedules and the statistical summary will assist the courts and the Director of the Administrative Office to fulfill their statutory responsibilities. Schedules D and E are amended to provide additional totals and, together with Schedule F, to direct debtors who must complete the statistical summary to report total amounts there. Similarly, Schedules I and J are amended to conform their terminology to that used in 28 U.S.C. § 159 and direct debtors who must complete the statistical summary to report the specified amounts there.

Schedules A, B, C, and D are amended to delete the word "market" from the columns in which the debtor reports the value of various kinds of property. Amendments to § 506 of the Code enacted in 2005 specify that "replacement value" must be used in connection with certain property. The schedules no longer specify "market" value and permit the debtor to choose the appropriate one, whether that be replacement, market, or some other value. Valuation of property, generally, is the subject of extensive provisions in the Code, and the deletion of the word "market" from the determinations of value to be made by the debtor on the schedules is intended to remove any inference about choice of valuation standard. This deletion simply indicates that the form takes no position on which Code provision or valuation standard may be applicable in any particular instance.

The following paragraphs describe changes that are specific to each schedule:

Schedule B—Personal Property is amended to require the debtor to list any interests in an education IRA, because § 541(b)(5), added to the Code in 2005, makes special provision for them. The schedule is also amended to require the debtor to disclose the existence of any customer lists or other compilations containing personally identifiable information provided by an individual to the debtor in connection with obtaining a product or service from the debtor for personal, family, or household purposes. This amendment implements § 332, which was added to the Code by BAPCPA in 2005.

Schedule C—Property claimed as Exempt is amended to delete descriptive information concerning the length of domicile required for the debtor to qualify to claim certain exemptions. Any summary of the BAPCPA amendments to § 522 of the Code concerning these requirements might inadvertently cause the debtor to lose important rights. Accordingly, the form now directs the debtor to indicate whether exemptions are being claimed under § 522(b)(2) or § 522(b)(3) and whether the debtor claims a homestead exemption that exceeds $136,875.

Schedule D—Creditors Holding Secured Claims is amended to provide for creating a total of any unsecured amounts (amounts that exceed the value of the collateral) owed to creditors holding secured claims. In addition to facilitating statistical reporting, providing a breakdown of the amounts owed to creditors listed on this schedule will assist the individual debtor in completing the means test calculation under § 707(b)(2)(A)(i) of the Code.

Schedule E—Creditors Holding Unsecured Priority Claims is amended to implement the changes in priority to which a claim may be entitled under 11 U.S.C. § 507 as amended by BAPCPA and to add the new priority included in the 2005 Act for claims for death or personal injury while the debtor was intoxicated. "Subtotal" and "Total" boxes have been added to the columns labeled "Amount Entitled to Priority" and "Amount Not Entitled to Priority" for statistical reporting purposes and to assist the individual debtor in completing the means test calculation under § 707(b)(2)(A)(i) of the Code.

Schedule H—Codebtors is amended to add specifics about community property jurisdictions in connection with the requirement to provide the name of any spouse of a debtor who resides or resided in a community property jurisdiction. This amendment also mirrors amendments made in 1997 to Official Form 7, the Statement of Financial Affairs, and will assure that these codebtors receive notice of the filing of the bankruptcy case. The form also is amended to extend from six years to eight years the time period for which this information is reported pursuant to the 2005 amendments to § 727(a)(8) of the Code.

Schedule I—Current Income of Individual Debtor(s) is amended to make it clear that "every" married debtor must provide income information for both spouses, unless the spouses are separated and a joint petition is not filed. The description of the income to be reported is revised to clarify that the purpose of this schedule is to obtain information about actual income on the date the bankruptcy case is filed and which a debtor reasonably expects in the future in contrast to the debtor's "current monthly income" as defined in § 101(10A) and reported on Form 22A, 22B, or 22C. And a statement included at the top of the form also explains that the income calculated this form may be different than the current monthly income. Line numbers have been added to assist the debtor in calculating and reporting totals. A new subtotal line for income from sources other than as an employee and a new "average monthly income" line will enable this form to be used in conjunction with Schedule J to satisfy the requirements of § 521(a)(1)(B)(v), which was added to the Code by BAPCPA. New statistical reporting requirements in 28 U.S.C. § 159 also require "average monthly income." In addition, the form is revised to provide the statement concerning any anticipated increase or decrease in income required in § 521(a)(1)(B)(vi), also added to the Code in 2005.

Schedule J—Current Expenditures of Individual Debtor(s). In conjunction with amendments to Schedule I, the form is amended to provide for reporting the debtor's actual "average monthly expenses," as required by 28 U.S.C. § 159 and a statement of monthly net income, itemized to show how the amount is calculated, as required by § 522(a)(1)(B)(v), which was added to the Code by BAPCPA in 2005. In addition, line numbers have been inserted and the description of expenses revised to make it clear than the purpose of this schedule is to obtain information about a debtor's actual and reasonably foreseeable expenses on the date the bankruptcy case is filed. And a statement similar to the statement at the top of Schedule I explains that the expenses calculated on the form may differ from the expenses calculated on Forms 22A or 22C. A direction has been added to require the debtor to report any increase or decrease in expenses anticipated to occur within the year following the filing of the document, as required by § 521(a)(1)(B)(vi), which also was added to the Code in 2005.

Declaration Concerning Debtor's Schedules. The declaration by individual or joint debtors is amended to require the debtor to merely state the total number of pages being verified. The declaration and signature of any non-attorney bankruptcy petition preparer is amended to include material mandated by § 110 of the Code as amended in 2005.

LIBRARY REFERENCES

Corpus Juris Secundum

CJS Bankruptcy § 344, List of Creditors and Others.

CJS Bankruptcy § 349, Schedules and Statements Regarding Debtor's Assets, Liabilities, Income, Expenditures, and Finances.

Form 7. Statement of Financial Affairs

B 7 (Official Form 7) (04/10)

UNITED STATES BANKRUPTCY COURT

In re:_____,   Case No. _____
          Debtor   (if known)

STATEMENT OF FINANCIAL AFFAIRS

This statement is to be completed by every debtor. Spouses filing a joint petition may file a single statement on which the information for both spouses is combined. If the case is filed under chapter 12 or chapter 13, a married debtor must furnish information for both spouses whether or not a joint petition is filed, unless the spouses are separated and a joint petition is not filed. An individual debtor engaged in business as a sole proprietor, partner, family farmer, or self-employed professional, should provide the information requested on this statement concerning all such activities as well as the individual's personal affairs. To indicate payments, transfers and the like to minor children, state the child's initials and the name and address of the child's parent or guardian, such as "A.B., a minor child, by John Doe, guardian." Do not disclose the child's name. See, 11 U.S.C. §112 and Fed. R. Bankr. P. 1007(m).

Questions 1 - 18 are to be completed by all debtors. Debtors that are or have been in business, as defined below, also must complete Questions 19 - 25. **If the answer to an applicable question is "None," mark the box labeled "None."** If additional space is needed for the answer to any question, use and attach a separate sheet properly identified with the case name, case number (if known), and the number of the question.

DEFINITIONS

"In business." A debtor is "in business" for the purpose of this form if the debtor is a corporation or partnership. An individual debtor is "in business" for the purpose of this form if the debtor is or has been, within six years immediately preceding the filing of this bankruptcy case, any of the following: an officer, director, managing executive, or owner of 5 percent or more of the voting or equity securities of a corporation; a partner, other than a limited partner, of a partnership; a sole proprietor or self-employed full-time or part-time. An individual debtor also may be "in business" for the purpose of this form if the debtor engages in a trade, business, or other activity, other than as an employee, to supplement income from the debtor's primary employment.

"Insider." The term "insider" includes but is not limited to: relatives of the debtor; general partners of the debtor and their relatives; corporations of which the debtor is an officer, director, or person in control; officers, directors, and any owner of 5 percent or more of the voting or equity securities of a corporate debtor and their relatives; affiliates of the debtor and insiders of such affiliates; any managing agent of the debtor. 11 U.S.C. § 101.

---

1. **Income from employment or operation of business**

None   State the gross amount of income the debtor has received from employment, trade, or profession, or from operation of
☐   the debtor's business, including part-time activities either as an employee or in independent trade or business, from the beginning of this calendar year to the date this case was commenced. State also the gross amounts received during the **two years** immediately preceding this calendar year. (A debtor that maintains, or has maintained, financial records on the basis of a fiscal rather than a calendar year may report fiscal year income. Identify the beginning and ending dates of the debtor's fiscal year.) If a joint petition is filed, state income for each spouse separately. (Married debtors filing under chapter 12 or chapter 13 must state income of both spouses whether or not a joint petition is filed, unless the spouses are separated and a joint petition is not filed.)

AMOUNT   SOURCE

Form 7

2

2. Income other than from employment or operation of business

None ☐ State the amount of income received by the debtor other than from employment, trade, profession, operation of the debtor's business during the **two years** immediately preceding the commencement of this case. Give particulars. If a joint petition is filed, state income for each spouse separately. (Married debtors filing under chapter 12 or chapter 13 must state income for each spouse whether or not a joint petition is filed, unless the spouses are separated and a joint petition is not filed.)

AMOUNT   SOURCE

3. Payments to creditors

Complete a. or b., as appropriate, and c.

None ☐ a. *Individual or joint debtor(s) with primarily consumer debts:* List all payments on loans, installment purchases of goods or services, and other debts to any creditor made within **90 days** immediately preceding the commencement of this case unless the aggregate value of all property that constitutes or is affected by such transfer is less than $600. Indicate with an asterisk (*) any payments that were made to a creditor on account of a domestic support obligation or as part of an alternative repayment schedule under a plan by an approved nonprofit budgeting and credit counseling agency. (Married debtors filing under chapter 12 or chapter 13 must include payments by either or both spouses whether or not a joint petition is filed, unless the spouses are separated and a joint petition is not filed.)

NAME AND ADDRESS OF CREDITOR	DATES OF PAYMENTS	AMOUNT PAID	AMOUNT STILL OWING

None ☐ b. *Debtor whose debts are not primarily consumer debts: List each payment or other transfer to any creditor made* within **90 days** immediately preceding the commencement of the case unless the aggregate value of all property that constitutes or is affected by such transfer is less than $5,850*. If the debtor is an individual, indicate with an asterisk (*) any payments that were made to a creditor on account of a domestic support obligation or as part of an alternative repayment schedule under a plan by an approved nonprofit budgeting and credit counseling agency. (Married debtors filing under chapter 12 or chapter 13 must include payments and other transfers by either or both spouses whether or not a joint petition is filed, unless the spouses are separated and a joint petition is not filed.)

NAME AND ADDRESS OF CREDITOR	DATES OF PAYMENTS/ TRANSFERS	AMOUNT PAID OR VALUE OF TRANSFERS	AMOUNT STILL OWING

Amount subject to adjustment on 4/01/13, and every three years thereafter with respect to cases commenced on or after the date of adjustment.

3

None
☐   c. *All debtors:* List all payments made within **one year** immediately preceding the commencement of this case
to or for the benefit of creditors who are or were insiders. (Married debtors filing under chapter 12 or chapter 13 must
include payments by either or both spouses whether or not a joint petition is filed, unless the spouses are separated and
a joint petition is not filed.)

NAME AND ADDRESS OF CREDITOR AND RELATIONSHIP TO DEBTOR	DATE OF PAYMENT	AMOUNT PAID	AMOUNT STILL OWING

---

4. Suits and administrative proceedings, executions, garnishments and attachments

None
☐   a. List all suits and administrative proceedings to which the debtor is or was a party within **one year** immediately
preceding the filing of this bankruptcy case. (Married debtors filing under chapter 12 or chapter 13 must include
information concerning either or both spouses whether or not a joint petition is filed, unless the spouses are separated
and a joint petition is not filed.)

CAPTION OF SUIT AND CASE NUMBER	NATURE OF PROCEEDING	COURT OR AGENCY AND LOCATION	STATUS OR DISPOSITION

None
☐   b. Describe all property that has been attached, garnished or seized under any legal or equitable process within **one
year** immediately preceding the commencement of this case. (Married debtors filing under chapter 12 or chapter 13
must include information concerning property of either or both spouses whether or not a joint petition is filed, unless
the spouses are separated and a joint petition is not filed.)

NAME AND ADDRESS OF PERSON FOR WHOSE BENEFIT PROPERTY WAS SEIZED	DATE OF SEIZURE	DESCRIPTION AND VALUE OF PROPERTY

---

5.   Repossessions, foreclosures and returns

None
☐   List all property that has been repossessed by a creditor, sold at a foreclosure sale, transferred through a deed in lieu
of foreclosure or returned to the seller, within **one year** immediately preceding the commencement of this case.
(Married debtors filing under chapter 12 or chapter 13 must include information concerning property of either or both
spouses whether or not a joint petition is filed, unless the spouses are separated and a joint petition is not filed.)

NAME AND ADDRESS OF CREDITOR OR SELLER	DATE OF REPOSSESSION, FORECLOSURE SALE, TRANSFER OR RETURN	DESCRIPTION AND VALUE OF PROPERTY

---

6. Assignments and receiverships

None ☐ a. Describe any assignment of property for the benefit of creditors made within **120 days** immediately preceding the commencement of this case. (Married debtors filing under chapter 12 or chapter 13 must include any assignment by either or both spouses whether or not a joint petition is filed, unless the spouses are separated and a joint petition is not filed.)

NAME AND ADDRESS OF ASSIGNEE	DATE OF ASSIGNMENT	TERMS OF ASSIGNMENT OR SETTLEMENT

None ☐ b. List all property which has been in the hands of a custodian, receiver, or court-appointed official within **one year** immediately preceding the commencement of this case. (Married debtors filing under chapter 12 or chapter 13 must include information concerning property of either or both spouses whether or not a joint petition is filed, unless the spouses are separated and a joint petition is not filed.)

NAME AND ADDRESS OF CUSTODIAN	NAME AND LOCATION OF COURT CASE TITLE & NUMBER	DATE OF ORDER	DESCRIPTION AND VALUE OF PROPERTY

7. Gifts

None ☐ List all gifts or charitable contributions made within **one year** immediately preceding the commencement of this case except ordinary and usual gifts to family members aggregating less than $200 in value per individual family member and charitable contributions aggregating less than $100 per recipient. (Married debtors filing under chapter 12 or chapter 13 must include gifts or contributions by either or both spouses whether or not a joint petition is filed, unless the spouses are separated and a joint petition is not filed.)

NAME AND ADDRESS OF PERSON OR ORGANIZATION	RELATIONSHIP TO DEBTOR, IF ANY	DATE OF GIFT	DESCRIPTION AND VALUE OF GIFT

8. Losses

None ☐ List all losses from fire, theft, other casualty or gambling within **one year** immediately preceding the commencement of this case **or since the commencement of this case**. (Married debtors filing under chapter 12 or chapter 13 must include losses by either or both spouses whether or not a joint petition is filed, unless the spouses are separated and a joint petition is not filed.)

DESCRIPTION AND VALUE OF PROPERTY	DESCRIPTION OF CIRCUMSTANCES AND, IF LOSS WAS COVERED IN WHOLE OR IN PART BY INSURANCE, GIVE PARTICULARS	DATE OF LOSS

5

9. Payments related to debt counseling or bankruptcy

None ☐

List all payments made or property transferred by or on behalf of the debtor to any persons, including attorneys, for consultation concerning debt consolidation, relief under the bankruptcy law or preparation of a petition in bankruptcy within **one year** immediately preceding the commencement of this case.

NAME AND ADDRESS OF PAYEE	DATE OF PAYMENT, NAME OF PAYER IF OTHER THAN DEBTOR	AMOUNT OF MONEY OR DESCRIPTION AND VALUE OF PROPERTY

10. Other transfers

None ☐

a. List all other property, other than property transferred in the ordinary course of the business or financial affairs of the debtor, transferred either absolutely or as security within **two years** immediately preceding the commencement of this case. (Married debtors filing under chapter 12 or chapter 13 must include transfers by either or both spouses whether or not a joint petition is filed, unless the spouses are separated and a joint petition is not filed.)

NAME AND ADDRESS OF TRANSFEREE, RELATIONSHIP TO DEBTOR	DATE	DESCRIBE PROPERTY TRANSFERRED AND VALUE RECEIVED

None ☐

b. List all property transferred by the debtor within **ten years** immediately preceding the commencement of this case to a self-settled trust or similar device of which the debtor is a beneficiary.

NAME OF TRUST OR OTHER DEVICE	DATE(S) OF TRANSFER(S)	AMOUNT OF MONEY OR DESCRIPTION AND VALUE OF PROPERTY OR DEBTOR'S INTEREST IN PROPERTY

11. Closed financial accounts

None ☐

List all financial accounts and instruments held in the name of the debtor or for the benefit of the debtor which were closed, sold, or otherwise transferred within **one year** immediately preceding the commencement of this case. Include checking, savings, or other financial accounts, certificates of deposit, or other instruments, shares and share accounts held in banks, credit unions, pension funds, cooperatives, associations, brokerage houses and other financial institutions. (Married debtors filing under chapter 12 or chapter 13 must include information concerning accounts or instruments held by or for either or both spouses whether or not a joint petition is filed, unless the spouses are separated and a joint petition is not filed.)

NAME AND ADDRESS OF INSTITUTION	TYPE OF ACCOUNT, LAST FOUR DIGITS OF ACCOUNT NUMBER, AND AMOUNT OF FINAL BALANCE	AMOUNT AND DATE OF SALE OR CLOSING

6

12. Safe deposit boxes

None
☐

List each safe deposit or other box or depository in which the debtor has or had securities, cash, or other valuables within **one year** immediately preceding the commencement of this case. (Married debtors filing under chapter 12 or chapter 13 must include boxes or depositories of either or both spouses whether or not a joint petition is filed, unless the spouses are separated and a joint petition is not filed.)

NAME AND ADDRESS OF BANK OR OTHER DEPOSITORY	NAMES AND ADDRESSES OF THOSE WITH ACCESS TO BOX OR DEPOSITORY	DESCRIPTION OF CONTENTS	DATE OF TRANSFER OR SURRENDER, IF ANY

13. Setoffs

None
☐

List all setoffs made by any creditor, including a bank, against a debt or deposit of the debtor within **90 days** preceding the commencement of this case. (Married debtors filing under chapter 12 or chapter 13 must include information concerning either or both spouses whether or not a joint petition is filed, unless the spouses are separated and a joint petition is not filed.)

NAME AND ADDRESS OF CREDITOR	DATE OF SETOFF	AMOUNT OF SETOFF

14. Property held for another person

None
☐

List all property owned by another person that the debtor holds or controls.

NAME AND ADDRESS OF OWNER	DESCRIPTION AND VALUE OF PROPERTY	LOCATION OF PROPERTY

15. Prior address of debtor

None
☐

If debtor has moved within **three years** immediately preceding the commencement of this case, list all premises which the debtor occupied during that period and vacated prior to the commencement of this case. If a joint petition is filed, report also any separate address of either spouse.

ADDRESS	NAME USED	DATES OF OCCUPANCY

16. Spouses and Former Spouses

None
☐

If the debtor resides or resided in a community property state, commonwealth, or territory (including Alaska, Arizona, California, Idaho, Louisiana, Nevada, New Mexico, Puerto Rico, Texas, Washington, or Wisconsin) within **eight years** immediately preceding the commencement of the case, identify the name of the debtor's spouse and of any former spouse who resides or resided with the debtor in the community property state.

NAME

---

17. Environmental Information.

For the purpose of this question, the following definitions apply:

"Environmental Law" means any federal, state, or local statute or regulation regulating pollution, contamination, releases of hazardous or toxic substances, wastes or material into the air, land, soil, surface water, groundwater, or other medium, including, but not limited to, statutes or regulations regulating the cleanup of these substances, wastes, or material.

"Site" means any location, facility, or property as defined under any Environmental Law, whether or not presently or formerly owned or operated by the debtor, including, but not limited to, disposal sites.

"Hazardous Material" means anything defined as a hazardous waste, hazardous substance, toxic substance, hazardous material, pollutant, or contaminant or similar term under an Environmental Law.

None
☐

a. List the name and address of every site for which the debtor has received notice in writing by a governmental unit that it may be liable or potentially liable under or in violation of an Environmental Law. Indicate the governmental unit, the date of the notice, and, if known, the Environmental Law:

SITE NAME AND ADDRESS	NAME AND ADDRESS OF GOVERNMENTAL UNIT	DATE OF NOTICE	ENVIRONMENTAL LAW

None
☐

b. List the name and address of every site for which the debtor provided notice to a governmental unit of a release of Hazardous Material. Indicate the governmental unit to which the notice was sent and the date of the notice.

SITE NAME AND ADDRESS	NAME AND ADDRESS OF GOVERNMENTAL UNIT	DATE OF NOTICE	ENVIRONMENTAL LAW

None
☐

c. List all judicial or administrative proceedings, including settlements or orders, under any Environmental Law with respect to which the debtor is or was a party. Indicate the name and address of the governmental unit that is or was a party to the proceeding, and the docket number.

NAME AND ADDRESS OF GOVERNMENTAL UNIT	DOCKET NUMBER	STATUS OR DISPOSITION

---

18 . Nature, location and name of business

None
☐

a. *If the debtor is an individual*, list the names, addresses, taxpayer-identification numbers, nature of the businesses, and beginning and ending dates of all businesses in which the debtor was an officer, director, partner, or managing executive of a corporation, partner in a partnership, sole proprietor, or was self-employed in a trade, profession, or other activity either full- or part-time within **six years** immediately preceding the commencement of this case, or in which the debtor owned 5 percent or more of the voting or equity securities within **six years** immediately preceding the commencement of this case.

If the debtor is a partnership, list the names, addresses, taxpayer-identification numbers, nature of the businesses, and beginning and ending dates of all businesses in which the debtor was a partner or owned 5 percent or more of the voting or equity securities, within **six years** immediately preceding the commencement of this case.

If the debtor is a corporation, list the names, addresses, taxpayer-identification numbers, nature of the businesses, and beginning and ending dates of all businesses in which the debtor was a partner or owned 5 percent or more of the voting or equity securities within **six years** immediately preceding the commencement of this case.

NAME	LAST FOUR DIGITS OF SOCIAL-SECURITY OR OTHER INDIVIDUAL TAXPAYER-I.D. NO. (ITIN)/ COMPLETE EIN	ADDRESS	NATURE OF BUSINESS	BEGINNING AND ENDING DATES

None ☐
b. Identify any business listed in response to subdivision a., above, that is "single asset real estate" as defined in 11 U.S.C. § 101.

NAME   ADDRESS

The following questions are to be completed by every debtor that is a corporation or partnership and by any individual debtor who is or has been, within **six years** immediately preceding the commencement of this case, any of the following: an officer, director, managing executive, or owner of more than 5 percent of the voting or equity securities of a corporation; a partner, other than a limited partner, of a partnership, a sole proprietor, or self-employed in a trade, profession, or other activity, either full- or part-time.

*(An individual or joint debtor should complete this portion of the statement **only** if the debtor is or has been in business, as defined above, within six years immediately preceding the commencement of this case. A debtor who has not been in business within those six years should go directly to the signature page.)*

---

19. Books, records and financial statements

None ☐
a. List all bookkeepers and accountants who within **two years** immediately preceding the filing of this bankruptcy case kept or supervised the keeping of books of account and records of the debtor.

NAME AND ADDRESS   DATES SERVICES RENDERED

None ☐
b. List all firms or individuals who within **two years** immediately preceding the filing of this bankruptcy case have audited the books of account and records, or prepared a financial statement of the debtor.

NAME   ADDRESS   DATES SERVICES RENDERED

        Form 7

None ☐   c. List all firms or individuals who at the time of the commencement of this case were in possession of the books of account and records of the debtor. If any of the books of account and records are not available, explain.

     NAME   ADDRESS

None ☐   d. List all financial institutions, creditors and other parties, including mercantile and trade agencies, to whom a financial statement was issued by the debtor within **two years** immediately preceding the commencement of this case.

     NAME AND ADDRESS   DATE ISSUED

---

20. Inventories

None ☐   a. List the dates of the last two inventories taken of your property, the name of the person who supervised the taking of each inventory, and the dollar amount and basis of each inventory.

                                                  DOLLAR AMOUNT
                                                  OF INVENTORY
                                                  (Specify cost, market or other
     DATE OF INVENTORY   INVENTORY SUPERVISOR   basis)

None ☐   b. List the name and address of the person having possession of the records of each of the inventories reported in a., above.

                                                    NAME AND ADDRESSES
                                                  OF CUSTODIAN
     DATE OF INVENTORY   OF INVENTORY RECORDS

---

21. Current Partners, Officers, Directors and Shareholders

None ☐   a. If the debtor is a partnership, list the nature and percentage of partnership interest of each member of the partnership.

     NAME AND ADDRESS   NATURE OF INTEREST   PERCENTAGE OF INTEREST

None ☐   b. If the debtor is a corporation, list all officers and directors of the corporation, and each stockholder who directly or indirectly owns, controls, or holds 5 percent or more of the voting or equity securities of the corporation.

                                                    NATURE AND PERCENTAGE
     NAME AND ADDRESS   TITLE   OF STOCK OWNERSHIP

---

22 . Former partners, officers, directors and shareholders

None ☐   a.   If the debtor is a partnership, list each member who withdrew from the partnership within **one year** immediately preceding the commencement of this case.

NAME	ADDRESS	DATE OF WITHDRAWAL

None ☐   b.   If the debtor is a corporation, list all officers or directors whose relationship with the corporation terminated within **one year** immediately preceding the commencement of this case.

NAME AND ADDRESS	TITLE	DATE OF TERMINATION

---

23 . Withdrawals from a partnership or distributions by a corporation

None ☐   If the debtor is a partnership or corporation, list all withdrawals or distributions credited or given to an insider, including compensation in any form, bonuses, loans, stock redemptions, options exercised and any other perquisite during **one year** immediately preceding the commencement of this case.

NAME & ADDRESS OF RECIPIENT, RELATIONSHIP TO DEBTOR	DATE AND PURPOSE OF WITHDRAWAL	AMOUNT OF MONEY OR DESCRIPTION AND VALUE OF PROPERTY

---

24. Tax Consolidation Group.

None ☐   If the debtor is a corporation, list the name and federal taxpayer-identification number of the parent corporation of any consolidated group for tax purposes of which the debtor has been a member at any time within **six years** immediately preceding the commencement of the case.

NAME OF PARENT CORPORATION	TAXPAYER-IDENTIFICATION NUMBER (EIN)

---

25. Pension Funds.

None ☐   If the debtor is not an individual, list the name and federal taxpayer-identification number of any pension fund to which the debtor, as an employer, has been responsible for contributing at any time within **six years** immediately preceding the commencement of the case.

NAME OF PENSION FUND	TAXPAYER-IDENTIFICATION NUMBER (EIN)

* * * * * *

11

[If completed by an individual or individual and spouse]

I declare under penalty of perjury that I have read the answers contained in the foregoing statement of financial affairs and any attachments thereto and that they are true and correct.

Date _____   Signature of Debtor _____

Date _____   Signature of Joint Debtor (if any) _____

[If completed on behalf of a partnership or corporation]

I declare under penalty of perjury that I have read the answers contained in the foregoing statement of financial affairs and any attachments thereto and that they are true and correct to the best of my knowledge, information and belief.

Date _____   Signature _____

                                             Print Name and Title

[An individual signing on behalf of a partnership or corporation must indicate position or relationship to debtor.]

_____ continuation sheets attached

Penalty for making a false statement: Fine of up to $500,000 or imprisonment for up to 5 years, or both. 18 U.S.C. §§ 152 and 3571

DECLARATION AND SIGNATURE OF NON-ATTORNEY BANKRUPTCY PETITION PREPARER (See 11 U.S.C. § 110)

I declare under penalty of perjury that: (1) I am a bankruptcy petition preparer as defined in 11 U.S.C. § 110; (2) I prepared this document for compensation and have provided the debtor with a copy of this document and the notices and information required under 11 U.S.C. §§ 110(b), 110(h), and 342(b); and, (3) if rules or guidelines have been promulgated pursuant to 11 U.S.C. § 110(h) setting a maximum fee for services chargeable by bankruptcy petition preparers, I have given the debtor notice of the maximum amount before preparing any document for filing for a debtor or accepting any fee from the debtor, as required by that section.

_____   _____
Printed or Typed Name and Title, if any, of Bankruptcy Petition Preparer   Social-Security No. (Required by 11 U.S.C. § 110.)

If the bankruptcy petition preparer is not an individual, state the name, title (if any), address, and social-security number of the officer, principal, responsible person, or partner who signs this document.

_____
Address

_____   _____
Signature of Bankruptcy Petition Preparer   Date

Names and Social-Security numbers of all other individuals who prepared or assisted in preparing this document unless the bankruptcy petition preparer is not an individual:

If more than one person prepared this document, attach additional signed sheets conforming to the appropriate Official Form for each person.

A bankruptcy petition preparer's failure to comply with the provisions of title 11 and the Federal Rules of Bankruptcy Procedure may result in fines or imprisonment or both. 18 U.S.C. § 156.

(Added Aug. 1, 1991; amended Mar. 16, 1993; Mar. 1995; Sept. 2000; Dec. 1, 2003; Aug. 11, 2005, eff. Oct. 17, 2005; Apr. 1, 2007; Apr. 1, 2010.)

ADVISORY COMMITTEE NOTES

1991 Enactment

This form consolidates questions from former Official Forms No. 7, No. 8, and No. 10. This form is to be completed by all debtors. An individual debtor engaged in business as a sole proprietor, partner, family farmer, or self-employed professional should provide the information requested on this statement concerning all such activities as well as the individual's personal affairs.

The Chapter 13 Statement, former Official Form No. 10, has been abrogated. Chapter 13 debtors are to complete this statement and the schedules prescribed in Official Form 6.

All questions have been converted to affirmative directions to furnish information, and each question must be answered. If the answer is "none," or the question is not applicable, the debtor is required to so state by marking the box labeled "None" provided at each question.

See Committee Note to Form 2 for a discussion of the unsworn declaration at the end of this form.

1993 Amendment

The form has been amended in two ways. In the second paragraph of the instructions, the third sentence has been deleted to clarify that only a debtor that is or had been in business as defined in the form should answer Questions 16–21. In addition, administrative proceedings have been added to the types of legal actions to be disclosed in Question 4.a.

1995 Amendment

This form is a "document for filing" that may be prepared by a "bankruptcy petition preparer" as defined in 11 U.S.C. § 110, which was added to the Code by the Bankruptcy Reform Act of 1994; accordingly, a signature line for such preparer is added. In addition to signing, a bankruptcy petition preparer is required by section 110 to disclose the information requested.

2000 Amendment

The form has been amended to provide more information to taxing authorities, pension fund supervisors, and governmen-

Form 7

tal units charged with environmental protection and regulation. Four new questions have been added to the form, covering community property owned by a debtor and the debtor's non-filing spouse or former spouse (Question 16), environmental information (Question 17), any consolidated tax group of a corporate debtor (Question 24), and the debtor's contributions to any employee pension fund (Question 25). In addition, every debtor will be required to state on the form whether the debtor has been in business within six years before filing the petition and, if so, must answer the remaining questions on the form (Questions 19–25). This is an enlargement of the two-year period previously specified. One reason for the longer "reach back" period is that business debtors often owe taxes that have been owed for more than two years. Another is that some of the questions already addressed to business debtors request information for the six-year period before the commencement of the case. Application of a six-year period to this section of the form will assure disclosure of all relevant information.

2003 Amendment

Pursuant to § 110(c) of the Bankruptcy Code, the certification by a non-attorney bankruptcy petition preparer requires a petition preparer to provide the full Social Security number of the individual who actually prepares the document.

2005 Amendment

The form is amended in several ways to reflect changes in the Bankruptcy Code made by the Bankruptcy Abuse Prevention and Consumer Protection Act of 2005, Pub. L. No. 109–8, 119 Stat. 23 (April 20, 2005). A new sentence in the introduction advises the debtor not to disclose the name and address of any minor child.

The definition of "in business" is amended in the introductory section and in Question 1 and Question 18 to clarify that various part-time activities can result in the debtor being "in business" for purposes of the form.

Question 1 is amended to specify that, in addition to the income from the debtor's primary employment, the debtor must include income from part-time activities either as an employee or from self-employment. The debtor now also will report the source of all income from employment or operation of a business, even if there is only one source, in order to assist the trustee in reviewing the pay stubs, etc., filed by the debtor in the case.

Question 3 is amended to accommodate amendments to § 547(c) of the Code enacted in 2005 which exempt from recovery by the trustee payments by a debtor for a domestic support obligation or as part of an alternative repayment schedule negotiated by an approved nonprofit budgeting and credit counseling agency. In addition, Question 3 now requires a debtor with primarily non-consumer debts to report only those transfers that aggregate more than $5,000 to any creditor in the 90–day period prior to the filing of the petition, as a result of the addition of § 547(c)(9) to the Code in 2005.

In Question 10, the extension of the reachback period for transfers from one year to two years reflects the 2005 amendment to § 548(a)(1) of the Code to permit a trustee to avoid a fraudulent transfer made by the debtor within two years of the date of the filing of the petition. Question 10 also is amended to implement new § 548(e) added to the Code in 2005 to require the debtor to disclose all transfers to any self-

settled asset protection trust within the ten years before the filing of the petition.

Question 15 is amended to extend from two years to three years the prepetition time period for which the debtor must disclose the addresses of all premises occupied by the debtor. This information will assist the trustee, the United States trustee, and the court to ascertain whether any homestead exemption asserted by the debtor is properly claimed under § 522(v)(3)(A) as amended, and §§ 522(p) and (q) as added to the Code in 2005.

The form also is amended to extend from six years to eight years the period before the filing of the petition concerning which the debtor is required to disclose the name of the debtor's spouse or of any former spouse who resides or resided with the debtor in a community property state. In addition, the certification by a non-attorney bankruptcy petition preparer is renamed a "declaration" and is amended to include material mandated by 11 U.S.C. § 110 as amended by the 2005 Act.

2005-2007 Amendments

(The 2005-2007 Committee Note incorporates the Committee Note previously published in 2005.)

The form is amended in several ways to reflect changes in the Bankruptcy Code made by the Bankruptcy Abuse Prevention and Consumer Protection Act of 2005, Pub. L. No. 109–8, 119 Stat. 23 (April 20, 2005). A new sentence in the introduction advises the debtor not to disclose the name and address of any minor child in conformity with § 112, which was added to the Code by the 2005 Act. In addition, the form is amended to add to the reference to Rule 1007(m) with respect to a minor child a direction to include for noticing purposes the name, address, and legal relationship to the child of "a person described" in that rule. Rule 1007(m) requires the person named to be someone on whom process would be served in an adversary proceeding against the child.

The definition of "in business" is amended in the introductory section and in Question 1 and Question 18 to clarify that various part-time activities can result in the debtor being "in business" for purposes of the form.

Question 1 is amended to specify that, in addition to the income from the debtor's primary employment, the debtor must include income from part-time activities either as an employee or from self-employment. The debtor now also will report the source of all income from employment or operation of a business, even if there is only one source, in order to assist the trustee in reviewing the pay stubs, etc., filed by the debtor in the case.

Question 3 is amended to accommodate amendments to § 547(c) of the Code enacted in 2005 which exempt from recovery by the trustee payments by a debtor for a domestic support obligation or as part of an alternative repayment schedule negotiated by an approved nonprofit budgeting and credit counseling agency. In addition, Question 3 now requires a debtor with primarily non-consumer debts to report only those transfers that aggregate more than $5,475 to any creditor in the 90–day period prior to the filing of the petition, as a result of the addition of § 547(c)(9) to the Code in 2005. In addition, the language of the question is revised for clarity.

In Question 10, the extension of the reach-back period for transfers from one year to two years reflects the 2005 amendment to § 548(a)(1) of the Code to permit a trustee to avoid a fraudulent transfer made by the debtor within two years

Complete Annotation Materials, see Title 11 U.S.C.A.
866

before the date of the filing of the petition. Question 10 also is amended to implement new § 548(e) added to the Code in 2005 to require the debtor to disclose all transfers to any self-settled asset protection trust within the ten years before the filing of the petition.

Question 15 is amended to extend from two years to three years the prepetition time period for which the debtor must disclose the addresses of all premises occupied by the debtor. This information will assist the trustee, the United States trustee, and the court to ascertain whether any homestead exemption asserted by the debtor is properly claimed under § 522(b)(3)(A) as amended, and §§ 522(p) and (q) as added to the Code in 2005.

The form also is amended to extend from six years to eight years the period before the filing of the petition concerning which the debtor is required to disclose the name of the debtor's spouse or of any former spouse who resides or resided with the debtor in a community property state. In addition, the certification by a non-attorney bankruptcy petition preparer is renamed a "declaration" and is amended to include material mandated by 11 U.S.C. § 110 as amended by the 2005 Act.

Form 8.   Individual Debtor's
Statement of Intention

B 8 (Official Form 8) (12/08)

UNITED STATES BANKRUPTCY COURT

In re _____,   Case No. _____
                    Debtor   Chapter 7

CHAPTER 7 INDIVIDUAL DEBTOR'S STATEMENT OF INTENTION

PART A – Debts secured by property of the estate. *(Part A must be fully completed for **EACH** debt which is secured by property of the estate. Attach additional pages if necessary.)*

Property No. 1	
Creditor's Name:	**Describe Property Securing Debt:**

Property will be *(check one)*:
    ❐ Surrendered   ❐ Retained

If retaining the property, I intend to *(check at least one)*:
    ❐ Redeem the property
    ❐ Reaffirm the debt
    ❐ Other. Explain _____ (for example, avoid lien
using 11 U.S.C. § 522(f)).

Property is *(check one)*:
    ❐ Claimed as exempt   ❐ Not claimed as exempt

Property No. 2 *(if necessary)*	
Creditor's Name:	**Describe Property Securing Debt:**

Property will be *(check one)*:
    ❐ Surrendered   ❐ Retained

If retaining the property, I intend to *(check at least one)*:
    ❐ Redeem the property
    ❐ Reaffirm the debt
    ❐ Other. Explain _____ (for example, avoid lien
using 11 U.S.C. § 522(f)).

Property is *(check one)*:
    ❐ Claimed as exempt   ❐ Not claimed as exempt

B 8 (Official Form 8) (12/08)   Page 2

PART B – Personal property subject to unexpired leases. *(All three columns of Part B must be completed for each unexpired lease. Attach additional pages if necessary.)*

Property No. 1		
Lessor's Name:	**Describe Leased Property:**	Lease will be Assumed pursuant to 11 U.S.C. § 365(p)(2): ☐ YES ☐ NO

Property No. 2 *(if necessary)*		
Lessor's Name:	**Describe Leased Property:**	Lease will be Assumed pursuant to 11 U.S.C. § 365(p)(2): ☐ YES ☐ NO

Property No. 3 *(if necessary)*		
Lessor's Name:	**Describe Leased Property:**	Lease will be Assumed pursuant to 11 U.S.C. § 365(p)(2): ☐ YES ☐ NO

_____ continuation sheets attached *(if any)*

I declare under penalty of perjury that the above indicates my intention as to any property of my estate securing a debt and/or personal property subject to an unexpired lease.

Date: _____

_____
Signature of Debtor

_____
Signature of Joint Debtor

B 8 (Official Form 8) (12/08)   Page 3

CHAPTER 7 INDIVIDUAL DEBTOR'S STATEMENT OF INTENTION
(Continuation Sheet)

PART A - Continuation

Property No.	
Creditor's Name:	**Describe Property Securing Debt:**

Property will be *(check one)*:
☐ Surrendered   ☐ Retained

If retaining the property, I intend to *(check at least one)*:
☐ Redeem the property
☐ Reaffirm the debt
☐ Other. Explain _____ (for example, avoid lien using 11 U.S.C. § 522(f)).

Property is *(check one)*:
☐ Claimed as exempt   ☐ Not claimed as exempt

PART B - Continuation

Property No.		
Lessor's Name:	**Describe Leased Property:**	Lease will be Assumed pursuant to 11 U.S.C. § 365(p)(2): ☐ YES ☐ NO

Property No.		
Lessor's Name:	**Describe Leased Property:**	Lease will be Assumed pursuant to 11 U.S.C. § 365(p)(2): ☐ YES ☐ NO

(Added Aug. 1, 1991; and amended Mar. 1995; Oct. 1, 1997; Dec. 1, 2003; Aug. 11, 2005, eff. Oct. 17, 2005; Dec. 1, 2008.)

ADVISORY COMMITTEE NOTES

This form is derived from former Official Form No. 8A. Rule 1007(b)(2) requires the debtor to serve a copy of this statement on the trustee and all creditors named in the statement. In a joint case, if the property and debts of both debtors are the same, the form may be adapted for joint use. If joint debtors have separate debts, however, each debtor must use a separate form.

1995 Amendment

This form is a "document for filing" that may be prepared by a "bankruptcy petition preparer" as defined in 11 U.S.C. § 110, which was added to the Code by the Bankruptcy Reform Act of 1994; accordingly, a signature line for such preparer is added. In addition to signing, a bankruptcy petition preparer is required by section 110 to disclose the information requested.

1997 Amendment

The form is amended to conform more closely to the language of the Bankruptcy Code. The amendments also make clear that the form is not intended to take a position regarding whether the options stated on the form are the only choices available to the debtor. Compare *Lowry Federal Credit Union v. West*, 882 F.2d 1543 (10th Cir. 1989), with *In re Taylor*, 3 F.3d 1512 (11th Cir. 1993).

2003 Amendment

Pursuant to § 110(c) of the Bankruptcy Code, the certification by a non-attorney bankruptcy petition preparer requires a petition preparer to provide the full Social Security number of the individual who actually prepares the document.

2005 Amendment

The form is amended to conform to § 521(a)(6), which was added to the Code by the Bankruptcy Abuse Prevention and Consumer Protection Act of 2005, Pub. L. No. 109–8, 119 Stat. 23 (April 20, 2005), by adding a section covering personal property subject to an unexpired lease and an option labeled "lease will be assumed pursuant to 11 U.S.C. § 362(h)(1)(A)" to the choices a debtor may make. The certification by a non-attorney bankruptcy petition preparer in the form is renamed a "declaration" and is amended to include material mandated by the 2005 amendments to § 110 of the Code.

2008 Amendments

The form is amended to conform to § 362(h), which was added to the Code, and § 521(a)(2), which was amended, by the Bankruptcy Abuse Prevention and Consumer Protection Act of 2005, Pub. L. No. 109–8, 119 Stat. 23 (April 20, 2005), by expanding the questions directed to the debtor regarding leased personal property and property subject to security interests. The form is also amended and reformatted to require the debtor to complete a series of statements describing the property and setting out what actions the debtor intends to take for each listed asset. The amended form is intended to elicit more complete information about the debtor's intentions with regard to property subject to security interests and personal property leases than has been obtained under the current version of the form.

In addition, the form is amended to specify that the debtor's signature is a declaration under penalty of perjury, as required by Rule 1008, and to provide space for the co-debtor's signature. A continuation page has been provided for use if necessary. The Declaration of Non–Attorney Bankruptcy Petition Preparer has been deleted from the form as duplicative of Form 19, Declaration and Signature of Non–Attorney Bankruptcy Petition Preparer. Form 19 contains both the petition preparer's declaration and signature and the notice the petition preparer is required to give to the debtor under § 110 of the Code.

LIBRARY REFERENCES

Corpus Juris Secundum

CJS Bankruptcy § 350, Statement of Intention With Respect to the Retention or Surrender of Collateral.

Form 9. Notice of Commencement of Case Under the Bankruptcy Code, Meeting of Creditors, and Deadlines

Official Form 9
(9/97)

FORM 9.   NOTICE OF COMMENCEMENT OF CASE UNDER THE
BANKRUPTCY CODE, MEETING OF CREDITORS,
AND DEADLINES

9A..........Chapter	7, Individual/Joint, No-Asset Case	
9B..........Chapter	7, Corporation/Partnership, No-Asset Case	
9C..........Chapter	7, Individual/Joint, Asset Case	
9D..........Chapter	7, Corporation/Partnership, Asset Case	
9E..........Chapter	11, Individual/Joint Case	
9E(Alt.)..Chapter	11, Individual/Joint Case	
9F..........Chapter	11, Corporation/Partnership Case	
9F(Alt.)..Chapter	11, Corporation/Partnership Case	
9G..........Chapter	12, Individual/Joint Case	
9H..........Chapter	12, Corporation/Partnership Case	
9I..........Chapter	13, Individual/Joint Case	

132

B9A (Official Form 9A) (Chapter 7 Individual or Joint Debtor No Asset Case) (12/11)

UNITED STATES BANKRUPTCY COURT _____ **District of** _____

Notice of
Chapter 7 Bankruptcy Case, Meeting of Creditors, & Deadlines

[A chapter 7 bankruptcy case concerning the debtor(s) listed below was filed on _____ (date).]
or [A bankruptcy case concerning the debtor(s) listed below was originally filed under chapter _____ on
_____ (date) and was converted to a case under chapter 7 on _____ (date).]

You may be a creditor of the debtor. **This notice lists important deadlines.** You may want to consult an attorney to protect your rights. All documents filed in the case may be inspected at the bankruptcy clerk's office at the address listed below. NOTE: The staff of the bankruptcy clerk's office cannot give legal advice.

See Reverse Side for Important Explanations

Debtor(s) (name(s) and address):	Case Number:
	Last four digits of Social-Security or Individual Taxpayer-ID (ITIN) No(s)./Complete EIN:
All other names used by the Debtor(s) in the last 8 years (include married, maiden, and trade names):	Bankruptcy Trustee (name and address):
Attorney for Debtor(s) (name and address):	
Telephone number:	Telephone number:

Meeting of Creditors

Date: / /   Time: ( ) A. M.   Location:
                                          ( ) P. M.

Presumption of Abuse under 11 U.S.C. § 707(b)
See "Presumption of Abuse" on the reverse side.

Depending on the documents filed with the petition, one of the following statements will appear.

The presumption of abuse does not arise.
Or
The presumption of abuse arises.
Or
Insufficient information has been filed to date to permit the clerk to make any determination concerning the presumption of abuse. If more complete information, when filed, shows that the presumption has arisen, creditors will be notified.

Deadlines:
Papers must be *received* by the bankruptcy clerk's office by the following deadlines:
Deadline to Object to Debtor's Discharge or to Challenge Dischargeability of Certain Debts:

Deadline to Object to Exemptions:
Thirty (30) days after the *conclusion* of the meeting of creditors.

Creditors May Not Take Certain Actions:

In most instances, the filing of the bankruptcy case automatically stays certain collection and other actions against the debtor and the debtor's property. Under certain circumstances, the stay may be limited to 30 days or not exist at all, although the debtor can request the court to extend or impose a stay. If you attempt to collect a debt or take other action in violation of the Bankruptcy Code, you may be penalized. Consult a lawyer to determine your rights in this case.

Please Do Not File a Proof of Claim Unless You Receive a Notice To Do So.

Creditor with a Foreign Address:

A creditor to whom this notice is sent at a foreign address should read the information under "Do Not File a Proof of Claim at This Time" on the reverse side.

Address of the Bankruptcy Clerk's Office:	**For the Court:**
	Clerk of the Bankruptcy Court:
Telephone number:	
Hours Open:	Date:

	EXPLANATIONS	B9A (Official Form 9A) (12/11)
Filing of Chapter 7 Bankruptcy Case	A bankruptcy case under Chapter 7 of the Bankruptcy Code (title 11, United States Code) has been filed in this court by or against the debtor(s) listed on the front side, and an order for relief has been entered.	
Legal Advice	The staff of the bankruptcy clerk's office cannot give legal advice. Consult a lawyer to determine your rights in this case.	
Creditors Generally May Not Take Certain Actions	Prohibited collection actions are listed in Bankruptcy Code § 362. Common examples of prohibited actions include contacting the debtor by telephone, mail, or otherwise to demand repayment; taking actions to collect money or obtain property from the debtor; repossessing the debtor's property; starting or continuing lawsuits or foreclosures; and garnishing or deducting from the debtor's wages. Under certain circumstances, the stay may be limited to 30 days or not exist at all, although the debtor can request the court to extend or impose a stay.	
Presumption of Abuse	If the presumption of abuse arises, creditors may have the right to file a motion to dismiss the case under § 707(b) of the Bankruptcy Code. The debtor may rebut the presumption by showing special circumstances.	
Meeting of Creditors	A meeting of creditors is scheduled for the date, time, and location listed on the front side. *The debtor (both spouses in a joint case) must be present at the meeting to be questioned under oath by the trustee and by creditors.* Creditors are welcome to attend, but are not required to do so. The meeting may be continued and concluded at a later date specified in a notice filed with the court.	
Do Not File a Proof of Claim at This Time	There does not appear to be any property available to the trustee to pay creditors. *You therefore should not file a proof of claim at this time.* If it later appears that assets are available to pay creditors, you will be sent another notice telling you that you may file a proof of claim, and telling you the deadline for filing your proof of claim. If this notice is mailed to a creditor at a foreign address, the creditor may file a motion requesting the court to extend the deadline.	
Discharge of Debts	The debtor is seeking a discharge of most debts, which may include your debt. A discharge means that you may never try to collect the debt from the debtor. If you believe that the debtor is not entitled to receive a discharge under Bankruptcy Code § 727(a) *or* that a debt owed to you is not dischargeable under Bankruptcy Code § 523(a)(2), (4), or (6), you must file a complaint -- or a motion if you assert the discharge should be denied under § 727(a)(8) or (a)(9) -- in the bankruptcy clerk's office by the "Deadline to Object to Debtor's Discharge or to Challenge the Dischargeability of Certain Debts" listed on the front of this form. The bankruptcy clerk's office must receive the complaint or motion and any required filing fee by that deadline.	
Exempt Property	The debtor is permitted by law to keep certain property as exempt. Exempt property will not be sold and distributed to creditors. The debtor must file a list of all property claimed as exempt. You may inspect that list at the bankruptcy clerk's office. If you believe that an exemption claimed by the debtor is not authorized by law, you may file an objection to that exemption. The bankruptcy clerk's office must receive the objections by the "Deadline to Object to Exemptions" listed on the front side.	
Bankruptcy Clerk's Office	Any paper that you file in this bankruptcy case should be filed at the bankruptcy clerk's office at the address listed on the front side. You may inspect all papers filed, including the list of the debtor's property and debts and the list of the property claimed as exempt, at the bankruptcy clerk's office.	
Creditor with a Foreign Address	Consult a lawyer familiar with United States bankruptcy law if you have any questions regarding your rights in this case.	

Refer To Other Side For Important Deadlines and Notices

B9B (**Official Form 9B**) (Chapter 7 Corporation/Partnership No Asset Case) (12/11)

UNITED STATES BANKRUPTCY COURT_____ District of_____

Notice of
Chapter 7 Bankruptcy Case, Meeting of Creditors, & Deadlines

|A chapter 7 bankruptcy case concerning the debtor(s) listed below was filed on _____ (date).|
or |A bankruptcy case concerning the debtor(s) listed below was originally filed under chapter_____ on
_____(date) and was converted to a case under chapter 7 on_____ (date).|

You may be a creditor of the debtor. **This notice lists important deadlines.** You may want to consult an attorney to protect your
rights. All documents filed in the case may be inspected at the bankruptcy clerk's office at the address listed below. NOTE: The
staff of the bankruptcy clerk's office cannot give legal advice.

See Reverse Side for Important Explanations	
Debtor(s) (name(s) and address):	Case Number:
	Last four digits of Social-Security or Individual Taxpayer-ID (ITIN) No(s)./Complete EIN:
All other names used by the debtor(s) in the last 8 years (include trade names):	Bankruptcy Trustee (name and address):
Attorney for Debtor(s) (name and address):	
Telephone number:	Telephone number:

Meeting of Creditors
Date: / /   Time: (   ) A. M.   Location: (   ) P. M.

Creditors May Not Take Certain Actions:
In most instances, the filing of the bankruptcy case automatically stays certain collection and other actions against the debtor and the debtor's property. Under certain circumstances, the stay may be limited to 30 days or not exist at all, although the debtor can request the court to extend or impose a stay. If you attempt to collect a debt or take other action in violation of the Bankruptcy Code, you may be penalized. Consult a lawyer to determine your rights in this case.

Please Do Not File a Proof of Claim Unless You Receive a Notice To Do So.

Creditor with a Foreign Address:
A creditor to whom this notice is sent at a foreign address should read the information under "Do Not File a Proof of Claim at This Time" on the reverse side.

Address of the Bankruptcy Clerk's Office:	**For the Court:**
	Clerk of the Bankruptcy Court:
Telephone number:	
Hours Open:	Date:

	EXPLANATIONS	B9B (Official Form 9B) (12/11)
Filing of Chapter 7 Bankruptcy Case	A bankruptcy case under Chapter 7 of the Bankruptcy Code (title 11, United States Code) has been filed in this court by or against the debtor(s) listed on the front side, and an order for relief has been entered.	
Legal Advice	The staff of the bankruptcy clerk's office cannot give legal advice. Consult a lawyer to determine your rights in this case.	
Creditors Generally May Not Take Certain Actions	Prohibited collection actions are listed in Bankruptcy Code § 362. Common examples of prohibited actions include contacting the debtor by telephone, mail, or otherwise to demand repayment; taking actions to collect money or obtain property from the debtor; repossessing the debtor's property; and starting or continuing lawsuits or foreclosures. Under certain circumstances, the stay may be limited to 30 days or not exist at all, although the debtor can request the court to extend or impose a stay.	
Meeting of Creditors	A meeting of creditors is scheduled for the date, time, and location listed on the front side. *The debtor's representative must be present at the meeting to be questioned under oath by the trustee and by creditors.* Creditors are welcome to attend, but are not required to do so. The meeting may be continued and concluded at a later date specified in a notice filed with the court.	
Do Not File a Proof of Claim at This Time	There does not appear to be any property available to the trustee to pay creditors. *You therefore should not file a proof of claim at this time.* If it later appears that assets are available to pay creditors, you will be sent another notice telling you that you may file a proof of claim, and telling you the deadline for filing your proof of claim. If this notice is mailed to a creditor at a foreign address, the creditor may file a motion requesting the court to extend the deadline.	
Bankruptcy Clerk's Office	Any paper that you file in this bankruptcy case should be filed at the bankruptcy clerk's office at the address listed on the front side. You may inspect all papers filed, including the list of the debtor's property and debts and the list of the property claimed as exempt, at the bankruptcy clerk's office.	
Creditor with a Foreign Address	Consult a lawyer familiar with United States bankruptcy law if you have any questions regarding your rights in this case.	

Refer To Other Side For Important Deadlines and Notices

B9C (Official Form 9C) (Chapter 7 Individual or Joint Debtor Asset Case) (12/11)

UNITED STATES BANKRUPTCY COURT_____ District of _____

<table>
<tr><td colspan="2" align="center">Notice of
Chapter 7 Bankruptcy Case, Meeting of Creditors, & Deadlines</td></tr>
<tr><td colspan="2">[A chapter 7 bankruptcy case concerning the debtor(s) listed below was filed on _____ (date).]
or [A bankruptcy case concerning the debtor(s) listed below was originally filed under chapter_____ on _____ (date) and was converted to a case under chapter 7 on_____ (date).]</td></tr>
<tr><td colspan="2">You may be a creditor of the debtor. This notice lists important deadlines. You may want to consult an attorney to protect your rights. All documents filed in the case may be inspected at the bankruptcy clerk's office at the address listed below. NOTE: The staff of the bankruptcy clerk's office cannot give legal advice.</td></tr>
<tr><td colspan="2" align="center">See Reverse Side for Important Explanations</td></tr>
<tr><td>Debtor(s) (name(s) and address):</td><td>Case Number:</td></tr>
<tr><td rowspan="2"></td><td>Last four digits of Social-Security or Individual Taxpayer-ID (ITIN) No(s)./Complete EIN:</td></tr>
<tr><td rowspan="4">Bankruptcy Trustee (name and address):</td></tr>
<tr><td>All other names used by the Debtor(s) in the last 8 years (include married, maiden, and trade names):</td></tr>
<tr><td>Attorney for Debtor(s) (name and address):</td></tr>
<tr><td>Telephone number:</td></tr>
<tr><td></td><td>Telephone number:</td></tr>
<tr><td colspan="2" align="center">Meeting of Creditors</td></tr>
<tr><td colspan="2">Date: / /   Time: ( ) A. M.   Location:
                              ( ) P. M.</td></tr>
<tr><td colspan="2" align="center">Presumption of Abuse under 11 U.S.C. § 707(b)
See "Presumption of Abuse" on the reverse side.</td></tr>
<tr><td colspan="2">Depending on the documents filed with the petition, one of the following statements will appear.
    The presumption of abuse does not arise.
        Or
    The presumption of abuse arises.
        Or
    Insufficient information has been filed to date to permit the clerk to make any determination concerning the presumption of abuse. If more complete information, when filed, shows that the presumption has arisen, creditors will be notified.</td></tr>
<tr><td colspan="2" align="center">Deadlines:
Papers must be received by the bankruptcy clerk's office by the following deadlines:</td></tr>
<tr><td colspan="2" align="center">Deadline to File a Proof of Claim:
For all creditors (except a governmental unit):   For a governmental unit:</td></tr>
<tr><td colspan="2" align="center">Creditor with a Foreign Address:
A creditor to whom this notice is sent at a foreign address should read the information under "Claims" on the reverse side.</td></tr>
<tr><td colspan="2" align="center">Deadline to Object to Debtor's Discharge or to Challenge Dischargeability of Certain Debts:</td></tr>
<tr><td colspan="2" align="center">Deadline to Object to Exemptions:
Thirty (30) days after the conclusion of the meeting of creditors.</td></tr>
<tr><td colspan="2" align="center">Creditors May Not Take Certain Actions:
In most instances, the filing of the bankruptcy case automatically stays certain collection and other actions against the debtor and the debtor's property. Under certain circumstances, the stay may be limited to 30 days or not exist at all, although the debtor can request the court to extend or impose a stay. If you attempt to collect a debt or take other action in violation of the Bankruptcy Code, you may be penalized. Consult a lawyer to determine your rights in this case.</td></tr>
<tr><td>Address of the Bankruptcy Clerk's Office:</td><td align="center">For the Court:</td></tr>
<tr><td rowspan="2">Telephone number:</td><td>Clerk of the Bankruptcy Court:</td></tr>
<tr><td></td></tr>
<tr><td>Hours Open:</td><td>Date:</td></tr>
</table>

Form 9C

	EXPLANATIONS	B9C (Official Form 9C) (12/11)
Filing of Chapter 7 Bankruptcy Case	A bankruptcy case under Chapter 7 of the Bankruptcy Code (title 11, United States Code) has been filed in this court by or against the debtor(s) listed on the front side, and an order for relief has been entered.	
Legal Advice	The staff of the bankruptcy clerk's office cannot give legal advice. Consult a lawyer to determine your rights in this case.	
Creditors Generally May Not Take Certain Actions	Prohibited collection actions are listed in Bankruptcy Code § 362. Common examples of prohibited actions include contacting the debtor by telephone, mail, or otherwise to demand repayment; taking actions to collect money or obtain property from the debtor; repossessing the debtor's property; starting or continuing lawsuits or foreclosures; and garnishing or deducting from the debtor's wages. Under certain circumstances, the stay may be limited to 30 days or not exist at all, although the debtor can request the court to extend or impose a stay.	
Meeting of Creditors	A meeting of creditors is scheduled for the date, time, and location listed on the front side. *The debtor (both spouses in a joint case) must be present at the meeting to be questioned under oath by the trustee and by creditors.* Creditors are welcome to attend, but are not required to do so. The meeting may be continued and concluded at a later date specified in a notice filed with the court.	
Claims	A Proof of Claim is a signed statement describing a creditor's claim. If a Proof of Claim form is not included with this notice, you can obtain one at any bankruptcy clerk's office. A secured creditor retains rights in its collateral regardless of whether that creditor files a Proof of Claim. If you do not file a Proof of Claim by the "Deadline to File a Proof of Claim" listed on the front side, you might not be paid any money on your claim from other assets in the bankruptcy case. To be paid, you must file a Proof of Claim even if your claim is listed in the schedules filed by the debtor. Filing a Proof of Claim submits the creditor to the jurisdiction of the bankruptcy court, with consequences a lawyer can explain. For example, a secured creditor who files a Proof of Claim may surrender important nonmonetary rights, including the right to a jury trial. **Filing Deadline for a Creditor with a Foreign Address:** The deadlines for filing claims set forth on the front of this notice apply to all creditors. If this notice has been mailed to a creditor at a foreign address, the creditor may file a motion requesting the court to extend the deadline.	
Discharge of Debts	The debtor is seeking a discharge of most debts, which may include your debt. A discharge means that you may never try to collect the debt from the debtor. If you believe that the debtor is not entitled to receive a discharge under Bankruptcy Code § 727(a) *or* that a debt owed to you is not dischargeable under Bankruptcy Code § 523(a)(2), (4), or (6), you must file a complaint -- or a motion if you assert the discharge should be denied under § 727(a)(8) or (a)(9) -- in the bankruptcy clerk's office by the "Deadline to Object to Debtor's Discharge or to Challenge the Dischargeability of Certain Debts" listed on the front of this form. The bankruptcy clerk's office must receive the complaint or motion and any required filing fee by that deadline.	
Exempt Property	The debtor is permitted by law to keep certain property as exempt. Exempt property will not be sold and distributed to creditors. The debtor must file a list of all property claimed as exempt. You may inspect that list at the bankruptcy clerk's office. If you believe that an exemption claimed by the debtor is not authorized by law, you may file an objection to that exemption. The bankruptcy clerk's office must receive the objections by the "Deadline to Object to Exemptions" listed on the front side.	
Presumption of Abuse	If the presumption of abuse arises, creditors may have the right to file a motion to dismiss the case under § 707(b) of the Bankruptcy Code. The debtor may rebut the presumption by showing special circumstances.	
Bankruptcy Clerk's Office	Any paper that you file in this bankruptcy case should be filed at the bankruptcy clerk's office at the address listed on the front side. You may inspect all papers filed, including the list of the debtor's property and debts and the list of the property claimed as exempt, at the bankruptcy clerk's office.	
Liquidation of the Debtor's Property and Payment of Creditors' Claims	The bankruptcy trustee listed on the front of this notice will collect and sell the debtor's property that is not exempt. If the trustee can collect enough money, creditors may be paid some or all of the debts owed to them, in the order specified by the Bankruptcy Code. To make sure you receive any share of that money, you must file a Proof of Claim, as described above.	
Creditor with a Foreign Address	Consult a lawyer familiar with United States bankruptcy law if you have any questions regarding your rights in this case.	
	Refer To Other Side For Important Deadlines and Notices	

B9D (Official Form 9D) (Chapter 7 Corporation/Partnership Asset Case) (12/11)

UNITED STATES BANKRUPTCY COURT	District of

Notice of
Chapter 7 Bankruptcy Case, Meeting of Creditors, & Deadlines

[A chapter 7 bankruptcy case concerning the debtor(s) listed below was filed on _____ (date).]
or [A bankruptcy case concerning the debtor(s) listed below was originally filed under chapter _____ on
_____ (date) and was converted to a case under chapter 7 on _____ (date).]

You may be a creditor of the debtor. **This notice lists important deadlines.** You may want to consult an attorney to protect your rights. All documents filed in the case may be inspected at the bankruptcy clerk's office at the address listed below. NOTE: The staff of the bankruptcy clerk's office cannot give legal advice.

See Reverse Side for Important Explanations

Debtor(s) (name(s) and address):	Case Number:
	Last four digits of Social-Security or Individual Taxpayer-ID (ITIN) No(s)./Complete EIN:
All other names used by the Debtor(s) in the last 8 years (include trade names):	Bankruptcy Trustee (name and address):
Attorney for Debtor(s) (name and address):	
Telephone number:	Telephone number:

Meeting of Creditors

Date: / /   Time: (   ) A. M.   Location:
                              (   ) P. M.

Deadline to File a Proof of Claim

Papers must be *received* by the bankruptcy clerk's office by the following deadlines:

For all creditors (except a governmental unit):   For a governmental unit:

Creditor with a Foreign Address:
A creditor to whom this notice is sent at a foreign address should read the information under "Claims" on the reverse side.

Creditors May Not Take Certain Actions:

In most instances, the filing of the bankruptcy case automatically stays certain collection and other actions against the debtor and the debtor's property. Under certain circumstances, the stay may be limited to 30 days or not exist at all, although the debtor can request the court to extend or impose a stay. If you attempt to collect a debt or take other action in violation of the Bankruptcy Code, you may be penalized. Consult a lawyer to determine your rights in this case.

Address of the Bankruptcy Clerk's Office:	For the Court:
	Clerk of the Bankruptcy Court:
Telephone number:	
Hours Open:	Date:

	EXPLANATIONS B9D (Official Form 9D) (12/11)
Filing of Chapter 7 Bankruptcy Case	A bankruptcy case under Chapter 7 of the Bankruptcy Code (title 11, United States Code) has been filed in this court by or against the debtor(s) listed on the front side, and an order for relief has been entered.
Legal Advice	The staff of the bankruptcy clerk's office cannot give legal advice. Consult a lawyer to determine your rights in this case.
Creditors Generally May Not Take Certain Actions	Prohibited collection actions are listed in Bankruptcy Code § 362. Common examples of prohibited actions include contacting the debtor by telephone, mail, or otherwise to demand repayment; taking actions to collect money or obtain property from the debtor; repossessing the debtor's property; and starting or continuing lawsuits or foreclosures. Under certain circumstances, the stay may be limited to 30 days or not exist at all, although the debtor can request the court to extend or impose a stay.
Meeting of Creditors	A meeting of creditors is scheduled for the date, time, and location listed on the front side. *The debtor's representative must be present at the meeting to be questioned under oath by the trustee and by creditors.* Creditors are welcome to attend, but are not required to do so. The meeting may be continued and concluded at a later date specified in a notice filed with the court.
Claims	A Proof of Claim is a signed statement describing a creditor's claim. If a Proof of Claim form is not included with this notice, you can obtain one at any bankruptcy clerk's office. A secured creditor retains rights in its collateral regardless of whether that creditor files a Proof of Claim. If you do not file a Proof of Claim by the "Deadline to File a Proof of Claim" listed on the front side, you might not be paid any money on your claim from other assets in the bankruptcy case. To be paid, you must file a Proof of Claim even if your claim is listed in the schedules filed by the debtor. Filing a Proof of Claim submits the creditor to the jurisdiction of the bankruptcy court, with consequences a lawyer can explain. For example, a secured creditor who files a Proof of Claim may surrender important nonmonetary rights, including the right to a jury trial. **Filing Deadline for a Creditor with a Foreign Address:** The deadlines for filing claims set forth on the front of this notice apply to all creditors. If this notice has been mailed to a creditor at a foreign address, the creditor may file a motion requesting the court to extend the deadline.
Liquidation of the Debtor's Property and Payment of Creditors' Claims	The bankruptcy trustee listed on the front of this notice will collect and sell the debtor's property that is not exempt. If the trustee can collect enough money, creditors may be paid some or all of the debts owed to them, in the order specified by the Bankruptcy Code. To make sure you receive any share of that money, you must file a Proof of Claim, as described above.
Bankruptcy Clerk's Office	Any paper that you file in this bankruptcy case should be filed at the bankruptcy clerk's office at the address listed on the front side. You may inspect all papers filed, including the list of the debtor's property and debts and the list of the property claimed as exempt, at the bankruptcy clerk's office.
Creditor with a Foreign Address	Consult a lawyer familiar with United States bankruptcy law if you have any questions regarding your rights in this case.
	Refer To Other Side For Important Deadlines and Notices

B9E (Official Form 9E) (Chapter 11 Individual or Joint Debtor Case) (12/11)

UNITED STATES BANKRUPTCY COURT_____ District of _____

Notice of
Chapter 11 Bankruptcy Case, Meeting of Creditors, & Deadlines

[A chapter 11 bankruptcy case concerning the debtor(s) listed below was filed on _____ (date).]
or [A bankruptcy case concerning the debtor(s) listed below was originally filed under chapter_____ on
_____ (date) and was converted to a case under chapter 11 on_____ (date).]

You may be a creditor of the debtor. **This notice lists important deadlines.** You may want to consult an attorney to protect your rights. All documents filed in the case may be inspected at the bankruptcy clerk's office at the address listed below.
NOTE: The staff of the bankruptcy clerk's office cannot give legal advice.

See Reverse Side for Important Explanations

Debtor(s) (name(s) and address):	Case Number:
	Last four digits of Social-Security or Individual Taxpayer-ID (ITIN) No(s)./Complete EIN:
All other names used by the Debtor(s) in the last 8 years (include married, maiden, and trade names):	Attorney for Debtor(s) (name and address): Telephone number:

Meeting of Creditors

Date: / /   Time: (   ) A. M.   Location:
                                (   ) P. M.

Deadlines:
Papers must be *received* by the bankruptcy clerk's office by the following deadlines:

Deadline to File a Proof of Claim:
Notice of deadline will be sent at a later time.

Creditor with a Foreign Address:
A creditor to whom this notice is sent at a foreign address should read the information under "Claims" on the reverse side.

Deadline to File a Complaint to Determine Dischargeability of Certain Debts:

Deadline to File a Complaint Objecting to Discharge of the Debtor:

First date set for hearing on confirmation of plan
Notice of that date will be sent at a later time.

Deadline to Object to Exemptions:

Thirty (30) days after the *conclusion* of the meeting of creditors.

Creditors May Not Take Certain Actions:
In most instances, the filing of the bankruptcy case automatically stays certain collection and other actions against the debtor and the debtor's property. Under certain circumstances, the stay may be limited to 30 days or not exist at all, although the debtor can request the court to extend or impose a stay. If you attempt to collect a debt or take other action in violation of the Bankruptcy Code, you may be penalized. Consult a lawyer to determine your rights in this case.

Address of the Bankruptcy Clerk's Office:	For the Court:
	Clerk of the Bankruptcy Court:
Telephone number:	
Hours Open:	Date:

	EXPLANATIONS B9E (Official Form 9E) (12/11)
Filing of Chapter 11 Bankruptcy Case	A bankruptcy case under Chapter 11 of the Bankruptcy Code (title 11, United States Code) has been filed in this court by or against the debtor(s) listed on the front side, and an order for relief has been entered. Chapter 11 allows a debtor to reorganize or liquidate pursuant to a plan. A plan is not effective unless confirmed by the court. You may be sent a copy of the plan and a disclosure statement telling you about the plan, and you might have the opportunity to vote on the plan. You will be sent notice of the date of the confirmation hearing, and you may object to confirmation of the plan and attend the confirmation hearing. Unless a trustee is serving, the debtor will remain in possession of the debtor's property and may continue to operate any business.
Legal Advice	The staff of the bankruptcy clerk's office cannot give legal advice. Consult a lawyer to determine your rights in this case.
Creditors Generally May Not Take Certain Actions	Prohibited collection actions are listed in Bankruptcy Code § 362. Common examples of prohibited actions include contacting the debtor by telephone, mail, or otherwise to demand repayment; taking actions to collect money or obtain property from the debtor; repossessing the debtor's property; starting or continuing lawsuits or foreclosures; and garnishing or deducting from the debtor's wages. Under certain circumstances, the stay may be limited to 30 days or not exist at all, although the debtor can request the court to extend or impose a stay.
Meeting of Creditors	A meeting of creditors is scheduled for the date, time, and location listed on the front side. *The debtor (both spouses in a joint case) must be present at the meeting to be questioned under oath by the trustee and by creditors.* Creditors are welcome to attend, but are not required to do so. The meeting may be continued and concluded at a later date specified in a notice filed with the court. The court, after notice and a hearing, may order that the United States trustee not convene the meeting if the debtor has filed a plan for which the debtor solicited acceptances before filing the case.
Claims	A Proof of Claim is a signed statement describing a creditor's claim. If a Proof of Claim form is not included with this notice, you can obtain one at any bankruptcy clerk's office. You may look at the schedules that have been or will be filed at the bankruptcy clerk's office. If your claim is scheduled and is *not* listed as disputed, contingent, or unliquidated, it will be allowed in the amount scheduled unless you filed a Proof of Claim or you are sent further notice about the claim. Whether or not your claim is scheduled, you are permitted to file a Proof of Claim. If your claim is not listed at all *or* if your claim is listed as disputed, contingent, or unliquidated, then you must file a Proof of Claim or you might not be paid any money on your claim and may be unable to vote on a plan. The court has not yet set a deadline to file a Proof of Claim. If a deadline is set, you will be sent another notice. A secured creditor retains rights in its collateral regardless of whether that creditor files a Proof of Claim. Filing a Proof of Claim submits the creditor to the jurisdiction of the bankruptcy court, with consequences a lawyer can explain. For example, a secured creditor who files a Proof of Claim may surrender important nonmonetary rights, including the right to a jury trial. **Filing Deadline for a Creditor with a Foreign Address:** The deadline for filing claims will be set in a later court order and will apply to all creditors unless the order provides otherwise. If notice of the order setting the deadline is sent to a creditor at a foreign address, the creditor may file a motion requesting the court to extend the deadline.
Discharge of Debts	Confirmation of a chapter 11 plan may result in a discharge of debts, which may include all or part of your debt. *See* Bankruptcy Code § 1141 (d). Unless the court orders otherwise, however, the discharge will not be effective until completion of all payments under the plan. A discharge means that you may never try to collect the debt from the debtor except as provided in the plan. If you believe that a debt owed to you is not dischargeable under Bankruptcy Code § 523 (a) (2), (4), or (6), you must start a lawsuit by filing a complaint in the bankruptcy clerk's office by the "Deadline to File a Complaint to Determine Dischargeability of Certain Debts" listed on the front side. The bankruptcy clerk's office must receive the complaint and any required filing fee by that Deadline. If you believe that the debtor is not entitled to receive a discharge under Bankruptcy Code § 1141 (d)(3), you must file a complaint with the required filing fee in the bankruptcy clerk's office not later than the first date set for the hearing on confirmation of the plan. You will be sent another notice informing you of that date.
Exempt Property	The debtor is permitted by law to keep certain property as exempt. Exempt property will not be sold and distributed to creditors, even if the debtor's case is converted to chapter 7. The debtor must file a list of property claimed as exempt. You may inspect that list at the bankruptcy clerk's office. If you believe that an exemption claimed by the debtor is not authorized by law, you may file an objection to that exemption. The bankruptcy clerk's office must receive the objection by the "Deadline to Object to Exemptions" listed on the front side.
Bankruptcy Clerk's Office	Any paper that you file in this bankruptcy case should be filed at the bankruptcy clerk's office at the address listed on the front side. You may inspect all papers filed, including the list of the debtor's property and debts and the list of the property claimed as exempt, at the bankruptcy clerk's office.
Creditor with a Foreign Address	Consult a lawyer familiar with United States bankruptcy law if you have any questions regarding your rights in this case.
	Refer To Other Side For Important Deadlines and Notices

B9E ALT (Official Form 9E ALT) (Chapter 11 Individual or Joint Debtor Case) (12/11)

UNITED STATES BANKRUPTCY COURT_____ District of_____	

Notice of
Chapter 11 Bankruptcy Case, Meeting of Creditors, & Deadlines

[A chapter 11 bankruptcy case concerning the debtor(s) listed below was filed on _____ (date).]
or [A bankruptcy case concerning the debtor(s) listed below was originally filed under chapter_____ on
_____ (date) and was converted to a case under chapter 11 on_____ (date).]

You may be a creditor of the debtor. **This notice lists important deadlines.** You may want to consult an attorney to protect your rights. All documents filed in the case may be inspected at the bankruptcy clerk's office at the address listed below.
NOTE: The staff of the bankruptcy clerk's office cannot give legal advice.

See Reverse Side for Important Explanations

Debtor(s) (name(s) and address):	Case Number:
	Last four digits of Social-Security or Individual Taxpayer-ID (ITIN) No(s)./Complete EIN:
All other names used by the Debtor(s) in the last 8 years (include married, maiden, and trade names):	Attorney for Debtor(s) (name and address):
	Telephone number:

Meeting of Creditors

Date: / /   Time: (   ) A. M.   Location:
                                 (   ) P. M.

Deadlines:

Papers must be *received* by the bankruptcy clerk's office by the following deadlines:
Deadline to File a Proof of Claim:

For all creditors (except a governmental unit):   For a governmental unit:

Creditor with a Foreign Address:
A creditor to whom this notice is sent at a foreign address should read the information under "Claims" on the reverse side.

Deadline to File a Complaint to Determine Dischargeability of Certain Debts:

Deadline to File a Complaint Objecting to Discharge of the Debtor:

First date set for hearing on confirmation of plan
Notice of that date will be sent at a later time.

Deadline to Object to Exemptions:

Thirty (30) days after the *conclusion* of the meeting of creditors.

Creditors May Not Take Certain Actions:

In most instances, the filing of the bankruptcy case automatically stays certain collection and other actions against the debtor and the debtor's property. Under certain circumstances, the stay may be limited to 30 days or not exist at all, although the debtor can request the court to extend or impose a stay. If you attempt to collect a debt or take other action in violation of the Bankruptcy Code, you may be penalized. Consult a lawyer to determine your rights in this case.

Address of the Bankruptcy Clerk's Office:	For the Court:
	Clerk of the Bankruptcy Court:
Telephone number:	
Hours Open:	Date:

Complete Annotation Materials, see Title 11 U.S.C.A.
883

EXPLANATIONS   B9E ALT (Official Form 9E ALT) (12/11)

Filing of Chapter 11 Bankruptcy Case	A bankruptcy case under Chapter 11 of the Bankruptcy Code (title 11, United States Code) has been filed in this court by or against the debtor(s) listed on the front side, and an order for relief has been entered. Chapter 11 allows a debtor to reorganize or liquidate pursuant to a plan. A plan is not effective unless confirmed by the court. You may be sent a copy of the plan and a disclosure statement telling you about the plan, and you might have the opportunity to vote on the plan. You will be sent notice of the date of the confirmation hearing, and you may object to confirmation of the plan and attend the confirmation hearing. Unless a trustee is serving, the debtor will remain in possession of the debtor's property and may continue to operate any business.
Legal Advice	The staff of the bankruptcy clerk's office cannot give legal advice. Consult a lawyer to determine your rights in this case.
Creditors Generally May Not Take Certain Actions	Prohibited collection actions are listed in Bankruptcy Code § 362. Common examples of prohibited actions include contacting the debtor by telephone, mail, or otherwise to demand repayment; taking actions to collect money or obtain property from the debtor; repossessing the debtor's property; starting or continuing lawsuits or foreclosures; and garnishing or deducting from the debtor's wages. Under certain circumstances, the stay may be limited to 30 days or not exist at all, although the debtor can request the court to extend or impose a stay.
Meeting of Creditors	A meeting of creditors is scheduled for the date, time, and location listed on the front side. *The debtor (both spouses in a joint case) must be present at the meeting to be questioned under oath by the trustee and by creditors.* Creditors are welcome to attend, but are not required to do so. The meeting may be continued and concluded at a later date specified in a notice filed with the court. The court, after notice and a hearing, may order that the United States trustee not convene the meeting if the debtor has filed a plan for which the debtor solicited acceptances before filing the case.
Claims	A Proof of Claim is a signed statement describing a creditor's claim. If a Proof of Claim form is not included with this notice, you can obtain one at any bankruptcy clerk's office. You may look at the schedules that have been or will be filed at the bankruptcy clerk's office. If your claim is scheduled and is *not* listed as disputed, contingent, or unliquidated, it will be allowed in the amount scheduled unless you filed a Proof of Claim or you are sent further notice about the claim. Whether or not your claim is scheduled, you are permitted to file a Proof of Claim. If your claim is not listed at all *or* if your claim is listed as disputed, contingent, or unliquidated, then you must file a Proof of Claim by the "Deadline to File a Proof of Claim" listed on the front side or you might not be paid any money on your claim and may be unable to vote on a plan. A secured creditor retains rights in its collateral regardless of whether that creditor files a Proof of Claim. Filing a Proof of Claim submits the creditor to the jurisdiction of the bankruptcy court, with consequences a lawyer can explain. For example, a secured creditor who files a Proof of Claim may surrender important nonmonetary rights, including the right to a jury trial. **Filing Deadline for a Creditor with a Foreign Address:** The deadlines for filing claims set forth on the front of this notice apply to all creditors. If this notice has been mailed to a creditor at a foreign address, the creditor may file a motion requesting the court to extend the deadline.
Discharge of Debts	Confirmation of a chapter 11 plan may result in a discharge of debts, which may include all or part of your debt. *See* Bankruptcy Code § 1141 (d). Unless the court orders otherwise, however, the discharge will not be effective until completion of all payments under the plan. A discharge means that you may never try to collect the debt from the debtor except as provided in the plan. If you believe that a debt owed to you is not dischargeable under Bankruptcy Code § 523 (a) (2), (4), or (6), you must start a lawsuit by filing a complaint in the bankruptcy clerk's office by the "Deadline to File a Complaint to Determine Dischargeability of Certain Debts" listed on the front side. The bankruptcy clerk's office must receive the complaint and any required filing fee by that Deadline. If you believe that the debtor is not entitled to receive a discharge under Bankruptcy Code § 1141 (d) (3), you must file a complaint with the required filing fee in the bankruptcy clerk's office not later than the first date set for the hearing on confirmation of the plan. You will be sent another notice informing you of that date.
Exempt Property	The debtor is permitted by law to keep certain property as exempt. Exempt property will not be sold and distributed to creditors, even if the debtor's case is converted to chapter 7. The debtor must file a list of property claimed as exempt. You may inspect that list at the bankruptcy clerk's office. If you believe that an exemption claimed by the debtor is not authorized by law, you may file an objection to that exemption. The bankruptcy clerk's office must receive the objection by the "Deadline to Object to Exemptions" listed on the front side.
Bankruptcy Clerk's Office	Any paper that you file in this bankruptcy case should be filed at the bankruptcy clerk's office at the address listed on the front side. You may inspect all papers filed, including the list of the debtor's property and debts and the list of property claimed as exempt, at the bankruptcy clerk's office.
Creditor with a Foreign Address	Consult a lawyer familiar with United States bankruptcy law if you have any questions regarding your rights in this case.

Refer To Other Side For Important Deadlines and Notices

B9F (Official Form 9F) (Chapter 11 Corporation/Partnership Case) (12/11)

UNITED STATES BANKRUPTCY COURT_____ District of_____

Notice of
Chapter 11 Bankruptcy Case, Meeting of Creditors, & Deadlines

[A chapter 11 bankruptcy case concerning the debtor(s) listed below was filed on _____ (date).]
or [A bankruptcy case concerning the debtor(s) listed below was originally filed under chapter_____ on
_____ (date) and was converted to a case under chapter 11 on_____ (date).]

You may be a creditor of the debtor. **This notice lists important deadlines.** You may want to consult an attorney to protect your rights. All documents filed in the case may be inspected at the bankruptcy clerk's office at the address listed below. NOTE: The staff of the bankruptcy clerk's office cannot give legal advice.

See Reverse Side for Important Explanations

Debtor(s) (name(s) and address):	Case Number:
	Last four digits of Social-Security or Individual Taxpayer-ID (ITIN) No(s)./Complete EIN:
All other names used by the Debtor(s) in the last 8 years (include trade names):	Attorney for Debtor(s) (name and address):
	Telephone number:

Meeting of Creditors

Date: / /   Time: ( ) A. M.   Location:
               ( ) P. M.

Deadline to File a Proof of Claim

Proof of Claim must be *received* by the bankruptcy clerk's office by the following deadline:

Notice of deadline will be sent at a later time.

Creditor with a Foreign Address:
A creditor to whom this notice is sent at a foreign address should read the information under "Claims" on the reverse side.

Deadline to File a Complaint to Determine Dischargeability of Certain Debts:

Creditors May Not Take Certain Actions:
In most instances, the filing of the bankruptcy case automatically stays certain collection and other actions against the debtor and the debtor's property. Under certain circumstances, the stay may be limited to 30 days or not exist at all, although the debtor can request the court to extend or impose a stay. If you attempt to collect a debt or take other action in violation of the Bankruptcy Code, you may be penalized. Consult a lawyer to determine your rights in this case.

Address of the Bankruptcy Clerk's Office:	For the Court:
	Clerk of the Bankruptcy Court:
Telephone number:	
Hours Open:	Date:

	EXPLANATIONS B9F (Official Form 9F) (12/11)
Filing of Chapter 11 Bankruptcy Case	A bankruptcy case under Chapter 11 of the Bankruptcy Code (title 11, United States Code) has been filed in this court by or against the debtor(s) listed on the front side, and an order for relief has been entered. Chapter 11 allows a debtor to reorganize or liquidate pursuant to a plan. A plan is not effective unless confirmed by the court. You may be sent a copy of the plan and a disclosure statement telling you about the plan, and you might have the opportunity to vote on the plan. You will be sent notice of the date of the confirmation hearing, and you may object to confirmation of the plan and attend the confirmation hearing. Unless a trustee is serving, the debtor will remain in possession of the debtor's property and may continue to operate any business.
Legal Advice	The staff of the bankruptcy clerk's office cannot give legal advice. Consult a lawyer to determine your rights in this case.
Creditors Generally May Not Take Certain Actions	Prohibited collection actions are listed in Bankruptcy Code § 362. Common examples of prohibited actions include contacting the debtor by telephone, mail, or otherwise to demand repayment; taking actions to collect money or obtain property from the debtor; repossessing the debtor's property; and starting or continuing lawsuits or foreclosures. Under certain circumstances, the stay may be limited to 30 days or not exist at all, although the debtor can request the court to extend or impose a stay.
Meeting of Creditors	A meeting of creditors is scheduled for the date, time, and location listed on the front side. *The debtor's representative must be present at the meeting to be questioned under oath by the trustee and by creditors.* Creditors are welcome to attend, but are not required to do so. The meeting may be continued and concluded at a later date specified in a notice filed with the court. The court, after notice and a hearing, may order that the United States trustee not convene the meeting if the debtor has filed a plan for which the debtor solicited acceptances before filing the case.
Claims	A Proof of Claim is a signed statement describing a creditor's claim. If a Proof of Claim form is not included with this notice, you can obtain one at any bankruptcy clerk's office. You may look at the schedules that have been or will be filed at the bankruptcy clerk's office. If your claim is scheduled and is *not* listed as disputed, contingent, or unliquidated, it will be allowed in the amount scheduled unless you filed a Proof of Claim or you are sent further notice about the claim. Whether or not your claim is scheduled, you are permitted to file a Proof of Claim. If your claim is not listed at all *or* if your claim is listed as disputed, contingent, or unliquidated, then you must file a Proof of Claim or you might not be paid any money on your claim and may be unable to vote on a plan. The court has not yet set a deadline to file a Proof of Claim. If a deadline is set, you will be sent another notice. A secured creditor retains rights in its collateral regardless of whether that creditor files a Proof of Claim. Filing a Proof of Claim submits the creditor to the jurisdiction of the bankruptcy court, with consequences a lawyer can explain. For example, a secured creditor who files a Proof of Claim may surrender important nonmonetary rights, including the right to a jury trial. **Filing Deadline for a Creditor with a Foreign Address:** The deadline for filing claims will be set in a later court order and will apply to all creditors unless the order provides otherwise. If notice of the order setting the deadline is sent to a creditor at a foreign address, the creditor may file a motion requesting the court to extend the deadline.
Discharge of Debts	Confirmation of a chapter 11 plan may result in a discharge of debts, which may include all or part of your debt. *See* Bankruptcy Code § 1141 (d). A discharge means that you may never try to collect the debt from the debtor, except as provided in the plan. If you believe that a debt owed to you is not dischargeable under Bankruptcy Code § 1141 (d) (6) (A), you must start a lawsuit by filing a complaint in the bankruptcy clerk's office by the "Deadline to File a Complaint to Determine Dischargeability of Certain Debts" listed on the front side. The bankruptcy clerk's office must receive the complaint and any required filing fee by that deadline.
Bankruptcy Clerk's Office	Any paper that you file in this bankruptcy case should be filed at the bankruptcy clerk's office at the address listed on the front side. You may inspect all papers filed, including the list of the debtor's property and debts and the list of the property claimed as exempt, at the bankruptcy clerk's office.
Creditor with a Foreign Address	Consult a lawyer familiar with United States bankruptcy law if you have any questions regarding your rights in this case.
	Refer To Other Side For Important Deadlines and Notices

B9F ALT (Official Form 9F ALT) (Chapter 11 Corporation/Partnership Case) (12/11)

| UNITED STATES BANKRUPTCY COURT_____ District of_____ |

Notice of
Chapter 11 Bankruptcy Case, Meeting of Creditors, & Deadlines

[A chapter 11 bankruptcy case concerning the debtor(s) listed below was filed on _____(date).]
or [A bankruptcy case concerning the debtor(s) listed below was originally filed under chapter_____ on _____(date) and was converted to a case under chapter 11 on_____(date).]

You may be a creditor of the debtor. **This notice lists important deadlines.** You may want to consult an attorney to protect your rights. All documents filed in the case may be inspected at the bankruptcy clerk's office at the address listed below.
NOTE: The staff of the bankruptcy clerk's office cannot give legal advice.

See Reverse Side for Important Explanations

Debtor(s) (name(s) and address):	Case Number:
	Last four digits of Social-Security or Individual Taxpayer-ID (ITIN) No(s)./Complete EIN:
All other names used by the Debtor(s) in the last 8 years (include trade names):	Attorney for Debtor(s) (name and address):
	Telephone number:

Meeting of Creditors

Date: / /   Time: ( ) A. M.   Location:
                                ( ) P. M.

Deadline to File a Proof of Claim

Proof of Claim must be *received* by the bankruptcy clerk's office by the following deadline:

For all creditors (except a governmental unit):   For a governmental unit:

Creditor with a Foreign Address:
A creditor to whom this notice is sent at a foreign address should read the information under "Claims" on the reverse side.

Deadline to File a Complaint to Determine Dischargeability of Certain Debts:

Creditors May Not Take Certain Actions:
In most instances, the filing of the bankruptcy case automatically stays certain collection and other actions against the debtor and the debtor's property. Under certain circumstances, the stay may be limited to 30 days or not exist at all, although the debtor can request the court to extend or impose a stay. If you attempt to collect a debt or take other action in violation of the Bankruptcy Code, you may be penalized. Consult a lawyer to determine your rights in this case.

Address of the Bankruptcy Clerk's Office:	**For the Court:**
	Clerk of the Bankruptcy Court:
Telephone number:	
Hours Open:	Date:

	EXPLANATIONS **B9F ALT (Official Form 9F ALT) (12/11)**
Filing of Chapter 11 Bankruptcy Case	A bankruptcy case under Chapter 11 of the Bankruptcy Code (title 11, United States Code) has been filed in this court by or against the debtor(s) listed on the front side, and an order for relief has been entered. Chapter 11 allows a debtor to reorganize or liquidate pursuant to a plan. A plan is not effective unless confirmed by the court. You may be sent a copy of the plan and a disclosure statement telling you about the plan, and you might have the opportunity to vote on the plan. You will be sent notice of the date of the confirmation hearing, and you may object to confirmation of the plan and attend the confirmation hearing. Unless a trustee is serving, the debtor will remain in possession of the debtor's property and may continue to operate any business.
Legal Advice	The staff of the bankruptcy clerk's office cannot give legal advice. Consult a lawyer to determine your rights in this case.
Creditors Generally May Not Take Certain Actions	Prohibited collection actions are listed in Bankruptcy Code § 362. Common examples of prohibited actions include contacting the debtor by telephone, mail, or otherwise to demand repayment; taking actions to collect money or obtain property from the debtor; repossessing the debtor's property; and starting or continuing lawsuits or foreclosures. Under certain circumstances, the stay may be limited to 30 days or not exist at all, although the debtor can request the court to extend or impose a stay.
Meeting of Creditors	A meeting of creditors is scheduled for the date, time, and location listed on the front side. *The debtor's representative must be present at the meeting to be questioned under oath by the trustee and by creditors.* Creditors are welcome to attend, but are not required to do so. The meeting may be continued and concluded at a later date specified in a notice filed with the court. The court, after notice and a hearing, may order that the United States trustee not convene the meeting if the debtor has filed a plan for which the debtor solicited acceptances before filing the case.
Claims	A Proof of Claim is a signed statement describing a creditor's claim. If a Proof of Claim form is not included with this notice, you can obtain one at any bankruptcy clerk's office. You may look at the schedules that have been or will be filed at the bankruptcy clerk's office. If your claim is scheduled and is *not* listed as disputed, contingent, or unliquidated, it will be allowed in the amount scheduled unless you filed a Proof of Claim or you are sent further notice about the claim. Whether or not your claim is scheduled, you are permitted to file a Proof of Claim. If your claim is not listed at all *or* if your claim is listed as disputed, contingent, or unliquidated, then you must file a Proof of Claim by the "Deadline to File Proof of Claim" listed on the front side, or you might not be paid any money on your claim and may be unable to vote on a plan. A secured creditor retains rights in its collateral regardless of whether that creditor files a Proof of Claim. Filing a Proof of Claim submits the creditor to the jurisdiction of the bankruptcy court, with consequences a lawyer can explain. For example, a secured creditor who files a Proof of Claim may surrender important nonmonetary rights, including the right to a jury trial. **Filing Deadline for a Creditor with a Foreign Address:** The deadlines for filing claims set forth on the front of this notice apply to all creditors. If this notice has been mailed to a creditor at a foreign address, the creditor may file a motion requesting the court to extend the deadline.
Discharge of Debts	Confirmation of a chapter 11 plan may result in a discharge of debts, which may include all or part of your debt. *See* Bankruptcy Code § 1141 (d). A discharge means that you may never try to collect the debt from the debtor, except as provided in the plan. If you believe that a debt owed to you is not dischargeable under Bankruptcy Code § 1141 (d) (6) (A), you must start a lawsuit by filing a complaint in the bankruptcy clerk's office by the "Deadline to File a Complaint to Determine Dischargeability of Certain Debts" listed on the front side. The bankruptcy clerk's office must receive the complaint and any required filing fee by that deadline.
Bankruptcy Clerk's Office	Any paper that you file in this bankruptcy case should be filed at the bankruptcy clerk's office at the address listed on the front side. You may inspect all papers filed, including the list of the debtor's property and debts and the list of the property claimed as exempt, at the bankruptcy clerk's office.
Creditor with a Foreign Address	Consult a lawyer familiar with United States bankruptcy law if you have any questions regarding your rights in this case.

Refer To Other Side For Important Deadlines and Notices

B9G **(Official Form 9G)** (Chapter 12 Individual or Joint Debtor Family Farmer or Family Fisherman) (12/11)

UNITED STATES BANKRUPTCY COURT_____ District of_____

Notice of
Chapter 12 Bankruptcy Case, Meeting of Creditors, & Deadlines

[The debtor(s) listed below filed a chapter 12 bankruptcy case on _____ (date).]
or [A bankruptcy case concerning the debtor(s) listed below was originally filed under chapter_____ on_____
_____ (date) and was converted to a case under chapter 12 on_____ (date).]

You may be a creditor of the debtor. **This notice lists important deadlines.** You may want to consult an attorney to protect your rights. All documents filed in the case may be inspected at the bankruptcy clerk's office at the address listed below.
NOTE: The staff of the bankruptcy clerk's office cannot give legal advice.

See Reverse Side for Important Explanations

Debtor(s) (name(s) and address):	Case Number:
	Last four digits of Social-Security or Individual Taxpayer-ID (ITIN) No(s)./Complete EIN:
All other names used by the Debtor(s) in the last 8 years (include married, maiden, and trade names):	Bankruptcy Trustee (name and address):
Attorney for Debtor(s) (name and address):	
Telephone number:	Telephone number:

Meeting of Creditors
Date: / /   Time: (   ) A. M.   Location: (   ) P. M.

Deadlines:
Papers must be *received* by the bankruptcy clerk's office by the following deadlines:

Deadline to File a Proof of Claim:

For all creditors(except a governmental unit):   For a governmental unit:

Creditor with a Foreign Address:
A creditor to whom this notice is sent at a foreign address should read the information under "Claims" on the reverse side.

Deadline to File a Complaint to Determine Dischargeability of Certain Debts:

Deadline to Object to Exemptions:
Thirty (30) days after the *conclusion* of the meeting of creditors.

Filing of Plan, Hearing on Confirmation of Plan
[The debtor has filed a plan. The plan or a summary of the plan is enclosed. The hearing on confirmation will be held:
Date:_____ Time:_____ Location:_____]
or [The debtor has filed a plan. The plan or a summary of the plan and notice of confirmation hearing will be sent separately.]
or [The debtor has not filed a plan as of this date. You will be sent separate notice of the hearing on confirmation of the plan.]

Creditors May Not Take Certain Actions:
In most instances, the filing of the bankruptcy case automatically stays certain collection and other actions against the debtor, the debtor's property, and certain codebtors. Under certain circumstances, the stay may be limited to 30 days or not exist at all, although the debtor can request the court to extend or impose a stay. If you attempt to collect a debt or take other action in violation of the Bankruptcy Code, you may be penalized. Consult a lawyer to determine your rights in this case.

Address of the Bankruptcy Clerk's Office:	**For the Court:**
	Clerk of the Bankruptcy Court:
Telephone number:	
Hours Open:	Date:

	EXPLANATIONS	B9G (Official Form 9G) (12/11)

Filing of Chapter 12 Bankruptcy Case	A bankruptcy case under Chapter 12 of the Bankruptcy Code (title 11, United States Code) has been filed in this court by the debtor(s) listed on the front side, and an order for relief has been entered. Chapter 12 allows family farmers and family fishermen to adjust their debts pursuant to a plan. A plan is not effective unless confirmed by the court. You may object to confirmation of the plan and appear at the confirmation hearing. A copy or summary of the plan [is included with this notice] *or* [will be sent to you later], and [the confirmation hearing will be held on the date indicated on the front of this notice] *or* [you will be sent notice of the confirmation hearing]. The debtor will remain in possession of the debtor's property and may continue to operate the debtor's business unless the court orders otherwise.
Legal Advice	The staff of the bankruptcy clerk's office cannot give legal advice. Consult a lawyer to determine your rights in this case.
Creditors Generally May Not Take Certain Actions	Prohibited collection actions against the debtor and certain codebtors are listed in Bankruptcy Code § 362 and § 1201. Common examples of prohibited actions include contacting the debtor by telephone, mail, or otherwise to demand repayment; taking actions to collect money or obtain property from the debtor; repossessing the debtor's property; starting or continuing lawsuits or foreclosures; and garnishing or deducting from the debtor's wages. Under certain circumstances, the stay may be limited in duration or not exist at all, although the debtor may have the right to request the court to extend or impose a stay.
Meeting of Creditors	A meeting of creditors is scheduled for the date, time, and location listed on the front side. *The debtor (both spouses in a joint case) must be present at the meeting to be questioned under oath by the trustee and by creditors.* Creditors are welcome to attend, but are not required to do so. The meeting may be continued and concluded at a later date specified in a notice filed with the court.
Claims	A Proof of Claim is a signed statement describing a creditor's claim. If a Proof of Claim form is not included with this notice, you can obtain one at any bankruptcy clerk's office. A secured creditor retains rights in its collateral regardless of whether that creditor files a Proof of Claim. If you do not file a Proof of Claim by the "Deadline to File a Proof of Claim" listed on the front side, you might not be paid any money on your claim from other assets in the bankruptcy case. To be paid, you must file a Proof of Claim even if your claim is listed in the schedules filed by the debtor. Filing a Proof of Claim submits the creditor to the jurisdiction of the bankruptcy court, with consequences a lawyer can explain. For example, a secured creditor who files a Proof of Claim may surrender important nonmonetary rights, including the right to a jury trial. **Filing Deadline for a Creditor with a Foreign Address:** The deadlines for filing claims set forth on the front of this notice apply to all creditors. If this notice has been mailed to a creditor at a foreign address, the creditor may file a motion requesting the court to extend the deadline.
Discharge of Debts	The debtor is seeking a discharge of most debts, which may include your debt. A discharge means that you may never try to collect the debt from the debtor. If you believe that a debt owed to you is not dischargeable under Bankruptcy Code § 523 (a) (2), (4), or (6), you must start a lawsuit by filing a complaint in the bankruptcy clerk's office by the "Deadline to File a Complaint to Determine Dischargeability of Certain Debts" listed on the front side. The bankruptcy clerk's office must receive the complaint and any required filing fee by that Deadline.
Exempt Property	The debtor is permitted by law to keep certain property as exempt. Exempt property will not be sold and distributed to creditors, even if the debtor's case is converted to chapter 7. The debtor must file a list of all property claimed as exempt. You may inspect that list at the bankruptcy clerk's office. If you believe that an exemption claimed by the debtor is not authorized by law, you may file an objection to that exemption. The bankruptcy clerk's office must receive the objection by the "Deadline to Object to Exemptions" listed on the front side.
Bankruptcy Clerk's Office	Any paper that you file in this bankruptcy case should be filed at the bankruptcy clerk's office at the address listed on the front side. You may inspect all papers filed, including the list of the debtor's property and debts and the list of the property claimed as exempt, at the bankruptcy clerk's office.
Creditor with a Foreign Address	Consult a lawyer familiar with United States bankruptcy law if you have any questions regarding your rights in this case.

Refer To Other Side For Important Deadlines and Notices

B9H **(Official Form 9H)** (Chapter 12 Corporation/Partnership Family Farmer or Family Fisherman) (12/11)

UNITED STATES BANKRUPTCY COURT_____ **District of**_____

Notice of
Chapter 12 Bankruptcy Case, Meeting of Creditors, & Deadlines

[The debtor |corporation| *or* |partnership| listed below filed a chapter 12 bankruptcy case on _____ (date).|
or |A bankruptcy case concerning the debtor |corporation| *or* |partnership| listed below was originally filed under chapter_____
on _____ (date) and was converted to a case under chapter 12 on_____ (date).]

You may be a creditor of the debtor. **This notice lists important deadlines.** You may want to consult an attorney to protect your
rights. All documents filed in the case may be inspected at the bankruptcy clerk's office at the address listed below.
NOTE: The staff of the bankruptcy clerk's office cannot give legal advice.

See Reverse Side for Important Explanations

Debtor(s) (name(s) and address):	Case Number:
	Last four digits of Social-Security or Individual Taxpayer-ID (ITIN) No(s)./Complete EIN:
All other names used by the Debtor(s) in the last 8 years (include trade names):	Bankruptcy Trustee (name and address):
Attorney for Debtor(s) (name and address):	
Telephone number:	Telephone number:

Meeting of Creditors

Date: / /   Time: (   ) A. M.   Location:
                                     (   ) P. M.

Deadlines:
Papers must be *received* by the bankruptcy clerk's office by the following deadlines:

Deadline to File a Proof of Claim:

For all creditors(except a governmental unit):   For a governmental unit:

Creditor with a Foreign Address:
A creditor to whom this notice is sent at a foreign address should read the information under "Claims" on the reverse side.

Deadline to File a Complaint to Determine Dischargeability of Certain Debts:

Filing of Plan, Hearing on Confirmation of Plan

[The debtor has filed a plan. The plan or a summary of the plan is enclosed. The hearing on confirmation will be held:
Date:_____ Time:_____ Location:_____
or [The debtor has filed a plan. The plan or a summary of the plan and notice of confirmation hearing will be sent separately.]
or [The debtor has not filed a plan as of this date. You will be sent separate notice of the hearing on confirmation of the plan.]

Creditors May Not Take Certain Actions:
In most instances, the filing of the bankruptcy case automatically stays certain collection and other actions against the debtor and
the debtor's property. Under certain circumstances, the stay may be limited to 30 days or not exist at all, although the debtor can
request the court to extend or impose a stay. If you attempt to collect a debt or take other action in violation of the Bankruptcy
Code, you may be penalized. Consult a lawyer to determine your rights in this case.

Address of the Bankruptcy Clerk's Office:	**For the Court:**
	Clerk of the Bankruptcy Court:
Telephone number:	
Hours Open:	Date:

Form 9H

	EXPLANATIONS B9H (Official Form 9H) (12/11)
Filing of Chapter 12 Bankruptcy Case	A bankruptcy case under Chapter 12 of the Bankruptcy Code (title 11, United States Code) has been filed in this court by the debtor listed on the front side, and an order for relief has been entered. Chapter 12 allows family farmers and family fishermen to adjust their debts pursuant to a plan. A plan is not effective unless confirmed by the court. You may object to confirmation of the plan and appear at the confirmation hearing. A copy or summary of the plan [is included with this notice] *or* [will be sent to you later], and [the confirmation hearing will be held on the date indicated on the front of this notice] *or* [you will be sent notice of the confirmation hearing]. The debtor will remain in possession of the debtor's property and may continue to operate the debtor's business unless the court orders otherwise.
Legal Advice	The staff of the bankruptcy clerk's office cannot give legal advice. Consult a lawyer to determine your rights in this case.
Creditors Generally May Not Take Certain Actions	Prohibited collection actions against the debtor and certain codebtors are listed in Bankruptcy Code § 362 & § 1201. Common examples of prohibited actions include contacting the debtor by telephone, mail, or otherwise to demand repayment; taking actions to collect money or obtain property from the debtor; repossessing the debtor's property; and starting or continuing lawsuits or foreclosures. Under certain circumstances, the stay may be limited in duration or not exist at all, although the debtor may have the right to request the court to extend or impose a stay.
Meeting of Creditors	A meeting of creditors is scheduled for the date, time, and location listed on the front side. *The debtor's representative must be present at the meeting to be questioned under oath by the trustee and by creditors.* Creditors are welcome to attend, but are not required to do so. The meeting may be continued and concluded at a later date specified in a notice filed with the court.
Claims	A Proof of Claim is a signed statement describing a creditor's claim. If a Proof of Claim form is not included with this notice, you can obtain one at any bankruptcy clerk's office. A secured creditor retains rights in its collateral regardless of whether that creditor files a Proof of Claim. If you do not file a Proof of Claim by the "Deadline to File a Proof of Claim" listed on the front side, you might not be paid any money on your claim from other assets in the bankruptcy case. To be paid, you must file a Proof of Claim even if your claim is listed in the schedules filed by the debtor. Filing a Proof of Claim submits the creditor to the jurisdiction of the bankruptcy court, with consequences a lawyer can explain. For example, a secured creditor who files a Proof of Claim may surrender important nonmonetary rights, including the right to a jury trial. **Filing Deadline for a Creditor with a Foreign Address:** The deadlines for filing claims set forth on the front of this notice apply to all creditors. If this notice has been mailed to a creditor at a foreign address, the creditor may file a motion requesting the court to extend the deadline.
Discharge of Debts	The debtor is seeking a discharge of most debts, which may include your debt. A discharge means that you may never try to collect the debt from the debtor. If you believe that a debt owed to you is not dischargeable under Bankruptcy Code § 523 (a) (2), (4), or (6), you must start a lawsuit by filing a complaint in the bankruptcy clerk's office by the "Deadline to File a Complaint to Determine Dischargeability of Certain Debts" listed on the front side. The bankruptcy clerk's office must receive the complaint and any required filing fee by that Deadline.
Bankruptcy Clerk's Office	Any paper that you file in this bankruptcy case should be filed at the bankruptcy clerk's office at the address listed on the front side. You may inspect all papers filed, including the list of the debtor's property and debts and the list of the property claimed as exempt, at the bankruptcy clerk's office.
Creditor with a Foreign Address	Consult a lawyer familiar with United States bankruptcy law if you have any questions regarding your rights in this case.
	Refer To Other Side For Important Deadlines and Notices

B9I (Official Form 9I) (Chapter 13 Case) (12/11)

UNITED STATES BANKRUPTCY COURT_____ **District of** _____

Notice of
Chapter 13 Bankruptcy Case, Meeting of Creditors, & Deadlines

[The debtor(s) listed below filed a chapter 13 bankruptcy case on _____ (date).]
or [A bankruptcy case concerning the debtor(s) listed below was originally filed under chapter_____
on _____ (date) and was converted to a case under chapter 13 on_____ (date).]

You may be a creditor of the debtor. **This notice lists important deadlines.** You may want to consult an attorney to protect your rights. All documents filed in the case may be inspected at the bankruptcy clerk's office at the address listed below.
NOTE: The staff of the bankruptcy clerk's office cannot give legal advice.

See Reverse Side for Important Explanations

Debtor(s) (name(s) and address):	Case Number:
	Last four digits of Social-Security or Individual Taxpayer-ID (ITIN) No(s)./Complete EIN:
All other names used by the Debtor(s) in the last 8 years (include married, maiden, and trade names):	Bankruptcy Trustee (name and address):
Attorney for Debtor(s) (name and address):	
Telephone number:	Telephone number:

Meeting of Creditors

Date: /   /   Time: (   ) A. M.   Location:
                        (   ) P. M.

Deadlines:
Papers must be *received* by the bankruptcy clerk's office by the following deadlines:
Deadline to File a Proof of Claim:

For all creditors (except a governmental unit):   For a governmental unit (except as otherwise provided
                                           in Fed . R. Bankr. P. 3002(c)(1)):

Creditor with a Foreign Address:
A creditor to whom this notice is sent at a foreign address should read the information under "Claims" on the reverse side.

Deadline to Object to Debtor's Discharge or to Challenge Dischargeability of Certain Debts:

Deadline to Object to Exemptions:
Thirty (30) days after the *conclusion* of the meeting of creditors.

Filing of Plan, Hearing on Confirmation of Plan

[The debtor has filed a plan. The plan or a summary of the plan is enclosed. The hearing on confirmation will be held:
Date: Time: Location:]
or [The debtor has filed a plan. The plan or a summary of the plan and notice of confirmation hearing will be sent separately.]
or [The debtor has not filed a plan as of this date. You will be sent separate notice of the hearing on confirmation of the plan.]

Creditors May Not Take Certain Actions:

In most instances, the filing of the bankruptcy case automatically stays certain collection and other actions against the debtor, the debtor's property, and certain codebtors. Under certain circumstances, the stay may be limited to 30 days or not exist at all, although the debtor can request the court to extend or impose a stay. If you attempt to collect a debt or take other action in violation of the Bankruptcy Code, you may be penalized. Consult a lawyer to determine your rights in this case.

Address of the Bankruptcy Clerk's Office:	**For the Court:**
	Clerk of the Bankruptcy Court:
Telephone number:	
Hours Open:	Date:

	EXPLANATIONS B9I (Official Form 9I) (12/11)
Filing of Chapter 13 Bankruptcy Case	A bankruptcy case under Chapter 13 of the Bankruptcy Code (title 11, United States Code) has been filed in this court by the debtor(s) listed on the front side, and an order for relief has been entered. Chapter 13 allows an individual with regular income and debts below a specified amount to adjust debts pursuant to a plan. A plan is not effective unless confirmed by the bankruptcy court. You may object to confirmation of the plan and appear at the confirmation hearing. A copy or summary of the plan [is included with this notice] *or* [will be sent to you later], and [the confirmation hearing will be held on the date indicated on the front of this notice] *or* [you will be sent notice of the confirmation hearing]. The debtor will remain in possession of the debtor's property and may continue to operate the debtor's business, if any, unless the court orders otherwise.
Legal Advice	The staff of the bankruptcy clerk's office cannot give legal advice. Consult a lawyer to determine your rights in this case.
Creditors Generally May Not Take Certain Actions	Prohibited collection actions against the debtor and certain codebtors are listed in Bankruptcy Code § 362 and § 1301. Common examples of prohibited actions include contacting the debtor by telephone, mail, or otherwise to demand repayment; taking actions to collect money or obtain property from the debtor; repossessing the debtor's property; starting or continuing lawsuits or foreclosures; and garnishing or deducting from the debtor's wages. Under certain circumstances, the stay may be limited to 30 days or not exist at all, although the debtor can request the court to exceed or impose a stay.
Meeting of Creditors	A meeting of creditors is scheduled for the date, time, and location listed on the front side. *The debtor (both spouses in a joint case) must be present at the meeting to be questioned under oath by the trustee and by creditors.* Creditors are welcome to attend, but are not required to do so. The meeting may be continued and concluded at a later date specified in a notice filed with the court.
Claims	A Proof of Claim is a signed statement describing a creditor's claim. If a Proof of Claim form is not included with this notice, you can obtain one at any bankruptcy clerk's office. A secured creditor retains rights in its collateral regardless of whether that creditor files a Proof of Claim. If you do not file a Proof of Claim by the "Deadline to File a Proof of Claim" listed on the front side, you might not be paid any money on your claim from other assets in the bankruptcy case. To be paid, you must file a Proof of Claim even if your claim is listed in the schedules filed by the debtor. Filing a Proof of Claim submits the creditor to the jurisdiction of the bankruptcy court, with consequences a lawyer can explain. For example, a secured creditor who files a Proof of Claim may surrender important nonmonetary rights, including the right to a jury trial. **Filing Deadline for a Creditor with a Foreign Address:** The deadlines for filing claims set forth on the front of this notice apply to all creditors. If this notice has been mailed to a creditor at a foreign address, the creditor may file a motion requesting the court to extend the deadline.
Discharge of Debts	The debtor is seeking a discharge of most debts, which may include your debt. A discharge means that you may never try to collect the debt from the debtor. If you believe that the debtor is not entitled to a discharge under Bankruptcy Code § 1328(f), you must file a motion objecting to discharge in the bankruptcy clerk's office by the "Deadline to Object to Debtor's Discharge or to Challenge the Dischargeability of Certain Debts" listed on the front of this form. If you believe that a debt owed to you is not dischargeable under Bankruptcy Code § 523(a)(2) or (4), you must file a complaint in the bankruptcy clerk's office by the same deadline. The bankruptcy clerk's office must receive the motion or the complaint and any required filing fee by that deadline.
Exempt Property	The debtor is permitted by law to keep certain property as exempt. Exempt property will not be sold and distributed to creditors, even if the debtor's case is converted to chapter 7. The debtor must file a list of all property claimed as exempt. You may inspect that list at the bankruptcy clerk's office. If you believe that an exemption claimed by the debtor is not authorized by law, you may file an objection to that exemption. The bankruptcy clerk's office must receive the objection by the "Deadline to Object to Exemptions" listed on the front side.
Bankruptcy Clerk's Office	Any paper that you file in this bankruptcy case should be filed at the bankruptcy clerk's office at the address listed on the front side. You may inspect all papers filed, including the list of the debtor's property and debts and the list of the property claimed as exempt, at the bankruptcy clerk's office.
Creditor with a Foreign Address	Consult a lawyer familiar with United States bankruptcy law if you have any questions regarding your rights in this case.
	Refer To Other Side For Important Deadlines and Notices

(Added Aug. 1, 1991; amended Mar. 16, 1993; Mar. 1995; Oct. 1, 1997; Dec. 1, 2003; Aug. 11, 2005, eff. Oct. 17, 2005; Oct. 2006; Dec. 1, 2007; Dec. 1, 2008; Dec. 1, 2010; Dec. 1, 2011.)

ADVISORY COMMITTEE NOTES

1991 Enactment

The form has been redesigned to facilitate electronic generation of notice to creditors concerning the filing of the petition, the meeting of creditors, and important deadlines in the case. Adoption of a box format, with significant dates highlighted, is intended to assist creditors who may be unfamiliar with bankruptcy cases to understand the data provided. Nine variations of the form, designated 9A through 9I, have been created to meet the specialized notice requirements for chapters 7, 11, 12, and 13, asset and no-asset cases, and the various types of debtors.

1992 Amendment

Forms 9B, 9D, 9F, and 9H are amended to make a technical correction in the reference to Rule 9001(5). Form 9H also contains a technical correction deleting the reference to a complaint objecting to discharge of the debtor.

1993 Amendment

The title page of the form has been amended to conform to the headings used on Forms 9A–9I. Alternate versions of Form 9E and Form 9F have been added for the convenience of districts that routinely set a deadline for filing claims in a chapter 11 case. When a creditor receives the alternate form in a case, the box labeled "Filing Claims" will contain information about the bar date as follows: "Deadline for filing a claim: __(date)__ ." If no deadline is set in a particular case, either the court will use Form 9E or Form 9F, as appropriate, or the alternate form will be used with the following sentence appearing in the box labeled "Filing Claims": "When the court sets a deadline for filing claims, creditors will be notified."

1995 Amendment

The form is amended to provide notice of the claims filing period provided to "a governmental unit" by section 502(b)(9) of the Code as amended by the Bankruptcy Reform Act of 1994. A court that routinely sets a deadline for filing proofs of claim at the outset of chapter 11 cases and, accordingly, uses Form 9E(Alt.) or Form 9F(Alt.) retains the option in any case in which no deadlines actually are set to substitute a message stating that creditors will be notified if the court fixes a deadline.

The form also is amended to add, in the paragraph labeled "Discharge of Debts," a reference to dischargeability actions under section 523(a)(15) of the Code, which was added by the 1994 Act.

1997 Amendment

Forms 9A, 9I (and the alternate versions of Forms 9E and 9F) have been amended, redesigned, and rewritten. Minor conforming changes have been made to respond to amendments made in the Bankruptcy Reform Act of 1994: the longer claims filing period for governmental units in section 502(b)(9) of the Code (see Forms 9C, 9D, 9E(Alt.), 9F(Alt.), 9G, 9H, and 9I); and a reference to dischargeability actions under section 523(a)(15) (see Forms 9A, 9C, 9E, and 9E(Alt.), 9G, and 9H). All of the forms have been substantially revised to make them easier to read and understand. The titles have been simplified. Recipients are told why they are receiving the notice. Explanations are provided on the back of the form and are set in larger type. Plain English is used. Deadlines are highlighted on the front of the form. Recipients are told that papers must be received by the bankruptcy clerk's office by the applicable deadline. The box for the trustee has been deleted from the chapter 11 notices (Forms 9E and 9F and the alternates). Various alternatives are set out in brackets in many of the forms, permitting each bankruptcy clerk's office to tailor the forms even more precisely to fit the needs of a particular case. The court may use blank spaces on the form to include additional information applicable to the particular district.

2003 Amendment

The form is amended to add to the information provided to creditors, the trustee and the United States trustee, all the names used by the debtor during the six years prior to the filing of the petition. The form includes the debtor's full employer identification number, if any, as well as the last four digits of the debtor's social security number. Rule 2002(a)(1) also is amended to direct the clerk to include the debtor's full social security number and employer identification number on the notices served on the United States trustee, the trustee, and creditors. This will enable creditors to identify the debtor accurately. The copy of Official Form 9 included in the case file, however, will show only the last four digits of the debtor's social security number. This should afford greater privacy to the individual debtor, whose bankruptcy case records may be available on the Internet.

2005 Amendment

The form is amended in a variety of ways to implement the provisions of the Bankruptcy Abuse Prevention and Consumer Protection Act of 2005, Pub. L. No. 109–8, 119 Stat. 23 (April 20, 2005). All versions of the form are amended to advise creditors to consult an attorney concerning what rights they may have in the specific case. All versions of the form are also amended to provide information about filing claims to creditors with foreign addresses and to advise those creditors to consult a lawyer familiar with United States bankruptcy law regarding any questions they may have about their rights in a particular case. These amendments implement § 1514, which was added to the Code in 2005.

Forms 9A and 9C are amended to include a box in which the clerk can notify creditors in a chapter 7 case filed by an individual with primarily consumer debts whether the presumption of abuse has arisen under § 707(b) of the Code as amended in 2005. Under § 342(d) of the Code, the clerk has a duty to notify creditors concerning the presumption within ten days of the filing of the petition. If cases in which the debtor does not file Official Form 22A with the petition, the forms provide for the clerk to state that insufficient information has been filed, and to inform creditors that if later-filed information indicates that the presumption arises, creditors will be sent another notice.

In cases involving serial filers (debtors who have filed more than one case within a specified period), the automatic stay provided by § 362(a) of the Code as amended in 2005 may not apply or may be limited in duration, unless the stay is extended or imposed by court order. The form contains a general statement alerting debtors to this possibility.

Section 1514, added to the Code in 2005, also requires that a secured creditor with a foreign address be advised whether the creditor is required to file a proof of claim, and Forms 9B, 9D, 9E, 9E (Alt.), 9F, 9F (Alt.), 9G, 9H, and 9I are amended to include general information addressing that question. Forms 9E, 9E (Alt.), 9F, and 9F (Alt.) also are amended to inform creditors that in a case in which the debtor has filed a plan for which it has solicited acceptances before filing the case, the court may, after notice and a hearing, order that the United States trustee not convene a meeting of creditors.

Forms 9E and 9E Alt. are amended to state that, unless the court orders otherwise, an individual chapter 11 debtor's discharge is not effective until completion of all payments under the plan, as provided in § 1141(d)(5) which was added to the Code in 2005. Forms 9F and 9F (Alt.) are amended to include a deadline to file a complaint to determine the dischargeability of a debt, in conformity with § 1141(d)(6) which was added to the Code in 2005.

Form 9I is amended to include a deadline to file a complaint to determine the dischargeability of certain debts. This amendment implements 2005 amendment to § 1328(a)(1) of the Code.

2006 Amendment

Forms 9G and 9H are amended to add "family fisherman" to the title and to the description of chapter 12. The 2005 amendments to the Code added a "family fisherman," as defined in § 101(19A), to the persons eligible to file a bankruptcy case under chapter 12. Form 9I is amended to provide general notice to parties in interest of the potential for a claim to be filed late in the case.

2005–2007 Amendments

(The 2005-2007 Committee Note incorporates Committee Notes previously published in 2005 and 2006.)

The form is amended in a variety of ways to implement the provisions of the Bankruptcy Abuse Prevention and Consumer Protection Act of 2005, Pub. L. No. 109-8, 119 Stat. 23 (April 20, 2005). All versions of the form are amended to advise creditors to consult an attorney concerning what rights they may have in the specific case. All versions of the form also are amended to provide to creditors with foreign addresses information about filing claims and to advise those creditors to consult a lawyer familiar with United States bankruptcy law regarding any questions they may have about their rights in a particular case. These amendments implement § 1514, which was added to the Code in 2005.

Forms 9A and 9C are amended to include a box in which the clerk can notify creditors in a chapter 7 case filed by an individual with primarily consumer debts if the presumption of abuse has arisen under § 707(b) of the Code as amended in 2005. Under § 342(d) of the Code, the clerk has a duty to notify creditors concerning the presumption within ten days of the filing of the petition. In cases in which the debtor does not file Official Form 22A with the petition, the forms provide for the clerk to state that insufficient information has been filed, and to inform creditors that if later-filed information indicates that the presumption arises, creditors will be sent another notice. Forms 9G and 9H are amended to add "family fisher-men" to the notices used in chapter 12 cases, in conformity with the 2005 amendments to the Code extending the provisions of chapter 12 to family fishermen.

In cases involving serial filers (debtors who have filed more than one case within a specified period), the automatic stay provided by § 362(a) of the Code as amended in 2005 may not apply or may be limited in duration, unless the stay is extended or imposed by court order. The form contains a general statement alerting debtors to this possibility.

Section 1514, added to the Code in 2005, also requires that a secured creditor with a foreign address be advised whether the creditor is required to file a proof of claim, and Forms 9B, 9D, 9E, 9E (Alt.), 9F, 9F (Alt.), 9G, 9H, and 9I are amended to include general information addressing that question. Forms 9E, 9E (Alt.), 9F, and 9F (Alt.) also are amended to inform creditors that in a case in which the debtor has filed a plan for which it has solicited acceptances before filing the case, the court may, after notice and a hearing, order that the United States trustee not convene a meeting of creditors.

Forms 9E and 9E (Alt.) are amended to state that, unless the court orders otherwise, an individual chapter 11 debtor's discharge is not effective until completion of all payments under the plan, as provided in § 1141(d)(5) which was added to the Code in 2005. Forms 9F and 9F (Alt.) are amended to include a deadline to file a complaint to determine the dischargeability of a debt, in conformity with § 1141(d)(6), which also was added to the Code in 2005.

Form 9I is amended to include a deadline to file a complaint to determine the dischargeability of certain debts. This amendment implements a 2005 amendment to § 1328(a) of the Code.

In addition, all versions of the form are amended to provide to the public only the last four digits of any individual debtor's taxpayer-identification number. This amendment implements Rule 9037.

2010 Amendment

Forms 9A, 9C, and 9I are amended in the "Deadlines" section on the front and the "Discharge of Debts" section on the back. The changes conform to amendments to Bankruptcy Rules 4004 and 7001 that direct that certain objections to discharge be brought by motion rather than by complaint.

2011 Amendment

The form's explanation of the "Meeting of Creditors" is amended to take account of the amendment of Rule 2003(e). When a meeting of creditors is adjourned to another date, the rule requires the official presiding at the meeting to file a statement specifying the date and time to which the meeting is adjourned. The explanation on all versions of the form is amended to reflect that requirement. Stylistic changes to the form are also made.

Form 10. Proof of Claim

B 10 (Official Form 10) (12/11)

UNITED STATES BANKRUPTCY COURT	PROOF OF CLAIM

Name of Debtor:	Case Number:	

NOTE: *Do not use this form to make a claim for an administrative expense that arises after the bankruptcy filing. You may file a request for payment of an administrative expense according to 11 U.S.C. § 503.*

Name of Creditor (the person or other entity to whom the debtor owes money or property):

COURT USE ONLY

Name and address where notices should be sent:

☐ Check this box if this claim amends a previously filed claim.

Court Claim Number:_____
(If known)

Telephone number: email:

Filed on:_____

Name and address where payment should be sent (if different from above):

☐ Check this box if you are aware that anyone else has filed a proof of claim relating to this claim. Attach copy of statement giving particulars.

Telephone number: email:

1. Amount of Claim as of Date Case Filed: $_____

If all or part of the claim is secured, complete item 4.

If all or part of the claim is entitled to priority, complete item 5.

☐ Check this box if the claim includes interest or other charges in addition to the principal amount of the claim. Attach a statement that itemizes interest or charges.

2. Basis for Claim: _____
(See instruction #2)

3. Last four digits of any number by which creditor identifies debtor:	**3a. Debtor may have scheduled account as:**	**3b. Uniform Claim Identifier (optional):**
	(See instruction #3a)	(See instruction #3b)

4. Secured Claim (See instruction #4)
Check the appropriate box if the claim is secured by a lien on property or a right of setoff, attach required redacted documents, and provide the requested information.

Amount of arrearage and other charges, as of the time case was filed, included in secured claim, if any:

$_____

Nature of property or right of setoff: ☐ Real Estate ☐ Motor Vehicle ☐ Other
Describe:

Basis for perfection: _____

Value of Property: $_____

Amount of Secured Claim: $_____

Annual Interest Rate_____% ☐ Fixed or ☐ Variable
(when case was filed)

Amount Unsecured: $_____

5. Amount of Claim Entitled to Priority under 11 U.S.C. § 507 (a). If any part of the claim falls into one of the following categories, check the box specifying the priority and state the amount.

☐ Domestic support obligations under 11 U.S.C. § 507 (a)(1)(A) or (a)(1)(B).

☐ Wages, salaries, or commissions (up to $11,725*) earned within 180 days before the case was filed or the debtor's business ceased, whichever is earlier – 11 U.S.C. § 507 (a)(4).

☐ Contributions to an employee benefit plan – 11 U.S.C. § 507 (a)(5).

Amount entitled to priority:

☐ Up to $2,600* of deposits toward purchase, lease, or rental of property or services for personal, family, or household use – 11 U.S.C. § 507 (a)(7).

☐ Taxes or penalties owed to governmental units – 11 U.S.C. § 507 (a)(8).

☐ Other – Specify applicable paragraph of 11 U.S.C. § 507 (a)(__).

$_____

Amounts are subject to adjustment on 4/1/13 and every 3 years thereafter with respect to cases commenced on or after the date of adjustment.

6. Credits. The amount of all payments on this claim has been credited for the purpose of making this proof of claim. (See instruction #6)

Form 10

B 10 (Official Form 10) (12/11)   2

7. Documents: Attached are **redacted** copies of any documents that support the claim, such as promissory notes, purchase orders, invoices, itemized statements of running accounts, contracts, judgments, mortgages, and security agreements. If the claim is secured, box 4 has been completed, and **redacted** copies of documents providing evidence of perfection of a security interest are attached. *(See instruction #7, and the definition of "redacted".)*

DO NOT SEND ORIGINAL DOCUMENTS. ATTACHED DOCUMENTS MAY BE DESTROYED AFTER SCANNING.

If the documents are not available, please explain:

8. Signature: (See instruction #8)

Check the appropriate box.

☐ I am the creditor.   ☐ I am the creditor's authorized agent.   ☐ I am the trustee, or the debtor,   ☐ I am a guarantor, surety, indorser, or other codebtor.
          (Attach copy of power of attorney, if any.)   or their authorized agent.   (See Bankruptcy Rule 3005.)
                  (See Bankruptcy Rule 3004.)

I declare under penalty of perjury that the information provided in this claim is true and correct to the best of my knowledge, information, and reasonable belief.

Print Name:
Title:
Company:
Address and telephone number (if different from notice address above):   (Signature)   (Date)

Telephone number: email:

Penalty for presenting fraudulent claim: Fine of up to $500,000 or imprisonment for up to 5 years, or both. 18 U.S.C. §§ 152 and 3571.

INSTRUCTIONS FOR PROOF OF CLAIM FORM

The instructions and definitions below are general explanations of the law. In certain circumstances, such as bankruptcy cases not filed voluntarily by the debtor, exceptions to these general rules may apply.

Items to be completed in Proof of Claim form

Court, Name of Debtor, and Case Number:
Fill in the federal judicial district in which the bankruptcy case was filed (for example, Central District of California), the debtor's full name, and the case number. If the creditor received a notice of the case from the bankruptcy court, all of this information is at the top of the notice.

Creditor's Name and Address:
Fill in the name of the person or entity asserting a claim and the name and address of the person who should receive notices issued during the bankruptcy case. A separate space is provided for the payment address if it differs from the notice address. The creditor has a continuing obligation to keep the court informed of its current address. See Federal Rule of Bankruptcy Procedure (FRBP) 2002(g).

1. Amount of Claim as of Date Case Filed:
State the total amount owed to the creditor on the date of the bankruptcy filing. Follow the instructions concerning whether to complete items 4 and 5. Check the box if interest or other charges are included in the claim.

2. Basis for Claim:
State the type of debt or how it was incurred. Examples include goods sold, money loaned, services performed, personal injury/wrongful death, car loan, mortgage note, and credit card. If the claim is based on delivering health care goods or services, limit the disclosure of the goods or services so as to avoid embarrassment or the disclosure of confidential health care information. You may be required to provide additional disclosure if an interested party objects to the claim.

3. Last Four Digits of Any Number by Which Creditor Identifies Debtor:
State only the last four digits of the debtor's account or other number used by the creditor to identify the debtor.

3a. Debtor May Have Scheduled Account As:
Report a change in the creditor's name, a transferred claim, or any other information that clarifies a difference between this proof of claim and the claim as scheduled by the debtor.

3b. Uniform Claim Identifier:
If you use a uniform claim identifier, you may report it here. A uniform claim identifier is an optional 24-character identifier that certain large creditors use to facilitate electronic payment in chapter 13 cases.

4. Secured Claim:
Check whether the claim is fully or partially secured. Skip this section if the claim is entirely unsecured. (See Definitions.) If the claim is secured, check the box for the nature and value of property that secures the claim, attach copies of lien documentation, and state, as of the date of the bankruptcy filing, the annual interest rate (and whether it is fixed or variable), and the amount past due on the claim.

5. Amount of Claim Entitled to Priority Under 11 U.S.C. § 507 (a).
If any portion of the claim falls into any category shown, check the appropriate box(es) and state the amount entitled to priority. (See Definitions.) A claim may be partly priority and partly non-priority. For example, in some of the categories, the law limits the amount entitled to priority.

6. Credits:
An authorized signature on this proof of claim serves as an acknowledgment that when calculating the amount of the claim, the creditor gave the debtor credit for any payments received toward the debt.

7. Documents:
Attach redacted copies of any documents that show the debt exists and a lien secures the debt. You must also attach copies of documents that evidence perfection of any security interest. You may also attach a summary in addition to the documents themselves. FRBP 3001(c) and (d). If the claim is based on delivering health care goods or services, limit disclosing confidential health care information. Do not send original documents, as attachments may be destroyed after scanning.

8. Date and Signature:
The individual completing this proof of claim must sign and date it. FRBP 9011. If the claim is filed electronically, FRBP 5005(a)(2) authorizes courts to establish local rules specifying what constitutes a signature. If you sign this form, you declare under penalty of perjury that the information provided is true and correct to the best of your knowledge, information, and reasonable belief. Your signature is also a certification that the claim meets the requirements of FRBP 9011(b). Whether the claim is filed electronically or in person, if your name is on the signature line, you are responsible for the declaration. Print the name and title, if any, of the creditor or other person authorized to file this claim. State the filer's address and telephone number if it differs from the address given on the top of the form for purposes of receiving notices. If the claim is filed by an authorized agent, attach a complete copy of any power of attorney, and provide both the name of the individual filing the claim and the name of the agent. If the authorized agent is a servicer, identify the corporate servicer as the company. Criminal penalties apply for making a false statement on a proof of claim.

B 10 (Official Form 10) (12/11)

3

DEFINITIONS

INFORMATION

Debtor
A debtor is the person, corporation, or other entity that has filed a bankruptcy case.

Creditor
A creditor is a person, corporation, or other entity to whom debtor owes a debt that was incurred before the date of the bankruptcy filing. See 11 U.S.C. §101 (10).

Claim
A claim is the creditor's right to receive payment for a debt owed by the debtor on the date of the bankruptcy filing. See 11 U.S.C. §101 (5). A claim may be secured or unsecured.

Proof of Claim
A proof of claim is a form used by the creditor to indicate the amount of the debt owed by the debtor on the date of the bankruptcy filing. The creditor must file the form with the clerk of the same bankruptcy court in which the bankruptcy case was filed.

Secured Claim Under 11 U.S.C. § 506 (a)
A secured claim is one backed by a lien on property of the debtor. The claim is secured so long as the creditor has the right to be paid from the property prior to other creditors. The amount of the secured claim cannot exceed the value of the property. Any amount owed to the creditor in excess of the value of the property is an unsecured claim. Examples of liens on property include a mortgage on real estate or a security interest in a car. A lien may be voluntarily granted by a debtor or may be obtained through a court proceeding. In some states, a court judgment is a lien.

A claim also may be secured if the creditor owes the debtor money (has a right to setoff).

Unsecured Claim
An unsecured claim is one that does not meet the requirements of a secured claim. A claim may be partly unsecured if the amount of the claim exceeds the value of the property on which the creditor has a lien.

Claim Entitled to Priority Under 11 U.S.C. § 507 (a)
Priority claims are certain categories of unsecured claims that are paid from the available money or property in a bankruptcy case before other unsecured claims.

Redacted
A document has been redacted when the person filing it has masked, edited out, or otherwise deleted, certain information. A creditor must show only the last four digits of any social-security, individual's tax-identification, or financial-account number, only the initials of a minor's name, and only the year of any person's date of birth. If the claim is based on the delivery of health care goods or services, limit the disclosure of the goods or services so as to avoid embarrassment or the disclosure of confidential health care information.

Evidence of Perfection
Evidence of perfection may include a mortgage, lien, certificate of title, financing statement, or other document showing that the lien has been filed or recorded.

Acknowledgment of Filing of Claim
To receive acknowledgment of your filing, you may either enclose a stamped self-addressed envelope and a copy of this proof of claim or you may access the court's PACER system (www.pacer.psc.uscourts.gov) for a small fee to view your filed proof of claim.

Offers to Purchase a Claim
Certain entities are in the business of purchasing claims for an amount less than the face value of the claims. One or more of these entities may contact the creditor and offer to purchase the claim. Some of the written communications from these entities may easily be confused with official court documentation or communications from the debtor. These entities do not represent the bankruptcy court or the debtor. The creditor has no obligation to sell its claim. However, if the creditor decides to sell its claim, any transfer of such claim is subject to FRBP 3001(e), any applicable provisions of the Bankruptcy Code (11 U.S.C. § 101 et seq.), and any applicable orders of the bankruptcy court.

B 10A (Attachment A) (12/11)

Mortgage Proof of Claim Attachment

If you file a claim secured by a security interest in the debtor's principal residence, you must use this form as an attachment to your proof of claim. See Bankruptcy Rule 3001(c)(2).

Name of debtor: _____   Case number: _____

Name of creditor: _____   Last four digits of any number you   __ __ __ __
                                              use to identify the debtor's account:

Part 1: Statement of Principal and Interest Due as of the Petition Date

Itemize the principal and interest due on the claim as of the petition date (included in the Amount of Claim listed in Item 1 on your Proof of Claim form).

1. Principal due   (1) $ _____

2. Interest due

Interest rate	From mm/dd/yyyy	To mm/dd/yyyy	Amount
____ %	_____	_____	$ _____
____ %	_____	_____	$ _____
____ %	_____	_____	+ $ _____

Total interest due as of the petition date $ _____   Copy total here ▶ (2) + $ _____

3. Total principal and interest due   (3) $ _____

Part 2: Statement of Prepetition Fees, Expenses, and Charges

Itemize the fees, expenses, and charges due on the claim as of the petition date (included in the Amount of Claim listed in Item 1 on the Proof of Claim form).

Description	Dates incurred		Amount
1. Late charges	_____	(1)	$ _____
2. Non-sufficient funds (NSF) fees	_____	(2)	$ _____
3. Attorney's fees	_____	(3)	$ _____
4. Filing fees and court costs	_____	(4)	$ _____
5. Advertisement costs	_____	(5)	$ _____
6. Sheriff/auctioneer fees	_____	(6)	$ _____
7. Title costs	_____	(7)	$ _____
8. Recording fees	_____	(8)	$ _____
9. Appraisal/broker's price opinion fees	_____	(9)	$ _____
10. Property inspection fees	_____	(10)	$ _____
11. Tax advances (non-escrow)	_____	(11)	$ _____
12. Insurance advances (non-escrow)	_____	(12)	$ _____
13. Escrow shortage or deficiency (Do not include amounts that are part of any installment payment listed in Part 3.)	_____	(13)	$ _____
14. Property preservation expenses. Specify:_____	_____	(14)	$ _____
15. Other. Specify:_____	_____	(15)	$ _____
16. Other. Specify:_____	_____	(16)	$ _____
17. Other. Specify:_____	_____	(17) +	$ _____

18. Total prepetition fees, expenses, and charges. Add all of the amounts listed above.   (18) $ _____

B 10A (Attachment A) (12/11)

Part 3. Statement of Amount Necessary to Cure Default as of the Petition Date

Does the installment payment amount include an escrow deposit?

☐ No

☐ Yes   Attach to the Proof of Claim form an escrow account statement prepared as of the petition date in a form consistent with applicable nonbankruptcy law.

1. **Installment payments due**	Date last payment received by creditor	_____ mm/dd/yyyy	
	Number of installment payments due	(1) _____	
2. **Amount of installment payments due**	_____ installments @	$ _____	
	_____ installments @	$ _____	
	_____ installments @	+ $ _____	
	Total installment payments due as of the petition date	$ _____	Copy total here ► (2) $ _____
3. **Calculation of cure amount**	<u>Add</u> total prepetition fees, expenses, and charges		Copy total from Part 2 here ► + $ _____
	<u>Subtract</u> total of unapplied funds (funds received but not credited to account)		- $ _____
	<u>Subtract</u> amounts for which debtor is entitled to a refund		- $ _____
	Total amount necessary to cure default as of the petition date		(3) $ _____

Copy total onto Item 4 of Proof of Claim form

Form 10

B 10S1 (Supplement 1) (12/11)

UNITED STATES BANKRUPTCY COURT

In re _____.
Debtor

Case No. _____

Chapter 13

Notice of Mortgage Payment Change

If you file a claim secured by a security interest in the debtor's principal residence provided for under the debtor's plan pursuant to § 1322(b)(5), you must use this form to give notice of any changes in the installment payment amount. File this form as a supplement to your proof of claim at least 21 days before the new payment amount is due. See Bankruptcy Rule 3002.1.

Name of creditor: _____

Court claim no. (if known): _____

Last four digits of any number you use to identify the debtor's account: ___ ___ ___ ___

Date of payment change:
Must be at least 21 days after date of this notice   mm/dd/yyyy _____

New total payment: $ _____
Principal, interest, and escrow, if any

Part 1: Escrow Account Payment Adjustment

Will there be a change in the debtor's escrow account payment?

☐ No
☐ Yes   Attach a copy of the escrow account statement prepared in a form consistent with applicable nonbankruptcy law. Describe the basis for the change. If a statement is not attached, explain why: _____

Current escrow payment: $ _____   New escrow payment: $ _____

Part 2: Mortgage Payment Adjustment

Will the debtor's principal and interest payment change based on an adjustment to the interest rate in the debtor's variable-rate note?

☐ No
☐ Yes   Attach a copy of the rate change notice prepared in a form consistent with applicable nonbankruptcy law. If a notice is not attached, explain why: _____

Current interest rate: _____ %   New interest rate: _____ %

Current principal and interest payment: $ _____   New principal and interest payment: $ _____

Part 3: Other Payment Change

Will there be a change in the debtor's mortgage payment for a reason not listed above?

☐ No
☐ Yes   Attach a copy of any documents describing the basis for the change, such as a repayment plan or loan modification agreement. (Court approval may be required before the payment change can take effect.)

Reason for change: _____

Current mortgage payment: $ _____   New mortgage payment: $ _____

Part 4: Sign Here

The person completing this Notice must sign it. Sign and print your name and your title, if any, and state your address and telephone number if different from the notice address listed on the proof of claim to which this Supplement applies.

Check the appropriate box.

☐ I am the creditor.   ☐ I am the creditor's authorized agent.
(Attach copy of power of attorney, if any.)

I declare under penalty of perjury that the information provided in this Notice is true and correct to the best of my knowledge, information, and reasonable belief.

✗ _____   Date _____
Signature   mm/dd/yyyy

Print: _____   Title _____
First Name   Middle Name   Last Name

Company _____

Address _____
Number   Street

_____
City   State   ZIP Code

Contact phone _____   Email _____

B 10S2 (Supplement 2) (12/11)

UNITED STATES BANKRUPTCY COURT

In re _____,   Case No. _____
         Debtor
                                             Chapter   13

Notice of Postpetition Mortgage Fees, Expenses, and Charges

If you hold a claim secured by a security interest in the debtor's principal residence, you must use this form to give notice of any postpetition fees, expenses, and charges that you assert are recoverable against the debtor or against the debtor's principal residence. File this form as a supplement to your proof of claim. See Bankruptcy Rule 3002.1.

Name of creditor: _____   Court claim no. (if known): _____

Last four digits of any number you use to
identify the debtor's account: ___ ___ ___ ___

Does this notice supplement a prior notice of postpetition fees,
expenses, and charges?

☐   No
☐   Yes. Date of the last notice: _____
                                  mm/dd/yyyy

Part 1: Itemize Postpetition Fees, Expenses, and Charges

Itemize the fees, expenses, and charges incurred on the debtor's mortgage account after the petition was filed. Do not include any escrow account disbursements or any amounts previously itemized in a notice filed in this case or ruled on by the bankruptcy court.

Description	Dates incurred		Amount
1. Late charges	_____	(1)	$ _____
2. Non-sufficient funds (NSF) fees	_____	(2)	$ _____
3. Attorney fees	_____	(3)	$ _____
4. Filing fees and court costs	_____	(4)	$ _____
5. Bankruptcy/Proof of claim fees	_____	(5)	$ _____
6. Appraisal/Broker's price opinion fees	_____	(6)	$ _____
7. Property inspection fees	_____	(7)	$ _____
8. Tax advances (non-escrow)	_____	(8)	$ _____
9. Insurance advances (non-escrow)	_____	(9)	$ _____
10. Property preservation expenses. Specify:_____	_____	(10)	$ _____
11. Other. Specify:_____	_____	(11)	$ _____
12. Other. Specify:_____	_____	(12)	$ _____
13. Other. Specify:_____	_____	(13)	$ _____
14. Other. Specify:_____	_____	(14)	$ _____

The debtor or trustee may challenge whether the fees, expenses, and charges you listed are required to be paid. See 11 U.S.C. § 1322(b)(5) and Bankruptcy Rule 3002.1.

B 10S2 (Supplement 2) (12/11)

Page 2

Part 2: Sign Here

The person completing this Notice must sign it. Sign and print your name and your title, if any, and state your address and telephone number if different from the notice address listed on the proof of claim to which this Supplement applies.

Check the appropriate box.

☐ I am the creditor.

☐ I am the creditor's authorized agent. (Attach copy of power of attorney, if any.)

I declare under penalty of perjury that the information provided in this Notice is true and correct to the best of my knowledge, information, and reasonable belief.

✗ _____   Date _____
    Signature   mm/dd/yyyy

Print: _____   Title _____
       First Name   Middle Name   Last Name

Company _____

Address _____
        Number   Street

        _____
        City   State   ZIP Code

Contact phone _____   Email _____

(Added Aug. 1, 1991; amended Mar. 16, 1993; Mar. 1995; July, 1995; Oct. 1, 1997; Apr. 1, 1998; Dec. 1, 2003; April 1, 2004; Aug. 11, 2005, eff. Oct. 17, 2005; Apr. 1, 2007; Dec. 1, 2007; Dec. 1, 2008; Apr. 1, 2010; Dec. 1, 2011.)

ADVISORY COMMITTEE NOTES

1991 Enactment

This form replaces former Official Forms No. 19, No. 20, and No. 21. The box format and simplified language are intended to facilitate completion of the form.

The form directs the claimant to attach documents to support the claim or, if voluminous, a summary of such documents. These include any security agreement (if not included in the writing on which the claim is founded), and evidence of perfection of any security interest. See Committee Note to Rule 3001(d) concerning satisfactory evidence of perfection. If the claim includes prepetition interest or other charges such as attorney fees, a statement giving a detailed breakdown of the elements of the claim is required.

Rule 2002(g) requires the clerk to update the mailing list in the case by substituting the address provided by a creditor on a proof of claim, if that address is different from the one supplied by the debtor. The form contains checkboxes to assist the clerk in performing this duty. The form also alerts the trustee when the claim is an amendment to or replacement for an earlier claim.

1993 Amendment

The form has been amended to accommodate inclusion of the priority afforded in § 507(a)(8) of the Code, which was added by Pub.L. No. 101–647, (Crime Control Act of 1990), and to avoid the necessity of further amendment to the form if other priorities are added to § 507(a) in the future. In addition, sections 4 and 5 of the form have been amended to clarify that only prepetition arrearages and charges are to be included in the amount of the claim.

1995 Amendment

The form is amended to add the seventh priority granted by the Bankruptcy Reform Act of 1994 to debts for alimony, maintenance, or support of a spouse, former spouse, or child of the debtor. The form also amends the Code reference to the priority afforded to tax debts and the dollar maximums for the priorities granted to wages and customer deposits in conformity with amendments made by the 1994 Act to section 507(a) of the Code. The 1994 Act also amended section 104 of the Code to provide for future adjustment of the dollar amounts specified in section 507(a) to be made by administrative action at three-year intervals to reflect changes in the consumer price index. The form is amended to include notice that these dollar amounts are subject to change without formal amendment to the official form.

1997 Amendment

Numbered sections 4. and 5. of the form have been reformatted to eliminate redundant information and make it easier to complete the form correctly. A creditor will report the total amount of the claim first, and will report only that amount unless the claim is secured by collateral or entitled to a priority under § 507 of the Code.

Explanatory definitions and instructions for completing the form also have been added.

2003 Amendment

The form is amended to require a wage, salary, or other compensation creditor to disclose only the last four digits of the creditor's Social Security number to afford greater privacy to the creditor. A trustee can request the full information necessary for tax withholding and reporting at the time the trustee makes a distribution to creditors.

2005 Amendment

The form is amended to conform to changes in the priority afforded the claims of certain creditors in § 507(a) of the Code as amended by the Bankruptcy Abuse Prevention and Consumer Protection Act of 2005, Pub. L. No. 109–8, 119 Stat. 23 (April 20, 2005).

Form 10

2005-2007 Amendments

(The 2005-2007 Committee Note incorporates Committee Notes previously published in 2005.)

The form is amended to conform to changes in the priority afforded the claims of certain creditors in § 507(a) of the Code as amended by the Bankruptcy Abuse Prevention and Consumer Protection Act of 2005, Pub. L. No. 109-8, 119 Stat. 23 (April 20, 2005).

In addition, the form and its instructions are amended in several respects based on the experiences of creditors and trustees in using it and on the technological changes that have occurred in the courts' processing of claims. A definition of the word "redacted" has been added in conformity with Rule 9037.

The creditor now has a space in which to provide a separate payment address if different from the creditor's address for receiving notices in the case. The checkboxes for indicating that the creditor's address provided on the proof of claim is a new address, and that the creditor never received any notices from the court in the case have been deleted. The computer systems now used by the courts make it unnecessary for a creditor to "flag" a new address or call attention to the fact that the creditor is making its first appearance in the case. In place of the deleted items is a new checkbox to be used when a debtor or a trustee files a proof of claim for a creditor; it will alert the clerk to send the notice required by Rule 3004. The box for indicating whether the claim replaces a previously filed claim also has been deleted as no longer necessary in light of the 2005 amendments to Rules 3004 and 3005. The creditor simply will amend the claim filed by the other party.

Requests for the creditor to state the date on which the debt was incurred and the date on which any court judgment concerning the debt was obtained have been deleted, based on reports from trustees that they rely on the documents supporting the claim for this information. The checkboxes for stating the basis for the creditor's claim have been replaced with a blank in which the creditor is to provide this information. Examples of the most common categories, based on the former checkboxes, can be found in the instructions on the form. The request to state the account number by which the creditor identifies the debtor has been moved to paragraph 3 of the form and has been revised to request only the last four digits of the number, in conformity with Rule 9037. In addition, a new paragraph 3a gives the creditor a place to notify the trustee and the court of any change in the creditor's name, or that the claim has been transferred, or to provide any other information to clarify a difference between the proof of claim and the creditor's claim as scheduled by the debtor.

The adjective "total" is deleted from the sections of the form where the creditor states the amount of the claim and the creditor now simply reports the amount of the claim. If the claim is a general unsecured claim, no further details are stated on the form, although a creditor still must attach a copy of any writing on which the claim is based, as required by Rule 3001(c), and must attach a statement itemizing any interest or other charges (in addition to the principal) that are included in the claim. If the claim or any part of it is secured or entitled to priority under § 507(a) of the Code, the creditor is directed to provide details in the appropriate sections of the form. The creditor now states the amount to be afforded priority only once, in the section of the form designated for describing the specific priority being asserted. The introductory language in the section where the creditor describes any

priority to which it is entitled has been revised for clarity. The word "collateral" has been replaced with the less colloquial and more accurate phrase "lien on property" throughout the form.

Information about obtaining acknowledgment from the court of the filing of the proof of claim is revised and moved to a new section on the reverse side called "Information." This new section also alerts a creditor to the possibility that it may be approached about selling its claim, advises that the court has no role in any such solicitations, and states that a creditor is under no obligation to accept any offer to purchase its claim. A new instruction is added about signing a proof of claim. This instruction includes citations to Rules 9011 and 5005(a)(2) concerning signature requirements in an electronic filing environment.

Finally, all of the definitions and instructions on the reverse side of the form are amended generally to reflect the deletions, additions, and other changes made on page 1. These include a reminder to the creditor to keep the court informed of any changes in its address. The instructions now appear at the top of the page, and the text is revised both to reflect the substantive changes to the form and to improve the clarity and style of this explanatory material.

2008 Amendment

The form is amended at box seven on page one, and instructions two and seven on page two, to instruct the claimant that the information contained in or attached to a claim based on the delivery of health care goods or services should be limited so as to avoid embarrassment or the unnecessary disclosure of confidential information. The claimant is informed that additional disclosure may be required if the trustee or another party in interest objects to the claim.

Page two of the form is also amended to revise slightly the definitions of "creditor" and "claim" to conform more closely to the definitions of those terms in the Code.

2011 Amendment

The form is amended in several respects. A new section—3b—is added to allow the reporting of a uniform claim identifier. This identifier, consisting of 24 characters, is used by some creditors to facilitate automated receipt, distribution, and posting of payments made by means of electronic funds transfers by chapter 13 trustees. Creditors are not required to use a uniform claim identifier.

Language is added to section 4 to clarify that the annual interest rate that must be reported for a secured claim is the rate applicable at the time the bankruptcy case was filed. Checkboxes for indicating whether the interest rate is fixed or variable are also added.

Section 7 of the form is revised to clarify that, consistent with Rule 3001(c), writings supporting a claim or evidencing perfection of a security interest must be attached to the proof of claim. If the documents are not available, the filer must provide an explanation for their absence. The instructions for this section of the form explain that summaries of supporting documents may be attached only in addition to the documents themselves.

Section 8—the date and signature box—is revised to include a declaration that is intended to impress upon the filer the duty of care that must be exercised in filing a proof of claim. The individual who completes the form must sign it.

By doing so, he or she declares under penalty of perjury that the information provided "is true and correct to the best of my knowledge, information and reasonable belief." That individual must also provide identifying information—name; title; company; and, if not already provided, mailing address, telephone number, and email address—and indicate by checking the appropriate box the basis on which he or she is filing the proof of claim (for example, as creditor or authorized agent for the creditor). Because a trustee or debtor that files a proof of claim under Rule 3004 will indicate that basis for filing here, the checkbox on the first page of the form for stating the filer's status as a trustee or debtor is deleted. When a servicing agent files a proof of claim on behalf of a creditor, the individual completing the form must sign it and must provide his or her own name, as well as the name of the company that is the servicing agent.

Amendments are made to the instructions that reflect the changes made to the form, and stylistic and formatting changes are made to the form and instructions. Spaces are added for providing email addresses in addition to other contact information in order to facilitate communication with the claimant. The provision of this additional information does not affect any requirements for serving or providing official notice to the claimant.

[**Attachment A**]. This form is new. It must be completed and attached to a proof of claim secured by a security interest in a debtor's principal residence. The form, which implements Rule 3001(c)(2), requires an itemization of prepetition interest, fees, expenses, and charges included in the claim amount, as well as a statement of the amount necessary to cure any default as of the petition date. If the mortgage installment payments include an escrow deposit, an escrow account statement must also be attached to the proof of claim, as required by Rule 3001(c)(2)(C).

[**Supplement 1**]. This form is new and applies in chapter 13 cases. It implements Rule 3002.1, which requires the holder of a claim secured by a security interest in the debtor's principal residence—or the holder's agent—to provide notice at least 21 days prior to a change in the amount of the ongoing mortgage installment payments. The form requires the holder of the claim to indicate the basis for the changed payment amount and when it will take effect. The notice must be filed as a supplement to the claim holder's proof of claim, and it must be served on the debtor, debtor's counsel, and the trustee.

The individual completing the form must sign and date it. By doing so, he or she declares under penalty of perjury that the information provided is true and correct to the best of that individual's knowledge, information, and reasonable belief. The signature is also a certification that the standards of Rule 9011(b) are satisfied.

[**Supplement 2**]. This form is new and applies in chapter 13 cases. It implements Rule 3002.1, which requires the holder of a claim secured by a security interest in the debtor's principal residence—or the holder's agent—to file a notice of all postpetition fees, expenses, and charges within 180 days after they are incurred. The notice must be filed as a supplement to the claim holder's proof of claim, and it must be served on the debtor, debtor's counsel, and the trustee.

The individual completing the form must sign and date it. By doing so, he or she declares under penalty of perjury that the information provided is true and correct to the best of that individual's knowledge, information, and reasonable belief. The signature is also a certification that the standards of Rule 9011(b) are satisfied.

[Form 11. Omitted. See Form 5.]

Form 11A. General Power of Attorney

Official Form 11A
6/90

United States Bankruptcy Court

_____ District Of _____

In re

       Debtor   ,

                             Case No. _____

                             Chapter

GENERAL POWER OF ATTORNEY

To _____ of * _____ , and
_____ of * _____ .

      The undersigned claimant hereby authorizes you, or any one of you, as attorney in fact for the undersigned and with full power of substitution, to vote on any question that may be lawfully submitted to creditors of the debtor in the above-entitled case; [*if appropriate*] to vote for a trustee of the estate of the debtor and for a committee of creditors; to receive dividends; and in general to perform any act not constituting the practice of law for the undersigned in all matters arising in this case.

      Dated:

                     Signed:

                             By _____

                             as _____

                             Address: _____

                                       _____

      [*If executed by an individual*] Acknowledged before me on _____ .

      [*If executed on behalf of a partnership*] Acknowledged before me on _____ ,
by _____ , who says that he [*or* she] is a member of the partnership named above and is authorized to execute this power of attorney in its behalf.

      [*If executed on behalf of a corporation*] Acknowledged before me on _____ ,
by _____ , who says that he [*or* she] is _____ of the corporation
named above and is authorized to execute this power of attorney in its behalf.

                               _____

                               _____
                                   [*Official character.*]

* State mailing address.

(Added Aug. 1, 1991.)

ADVISORY COMMITTEE NOTES

This form previously was numbered Official Form No. 17.

Form 11B. Special Power of Attorney

Official Form 11B
6/90

United States Bankruptcy Court

_____ District Of _____

In re

Debtor

Case No. _____

Chapter _____

SPECIAL POWER OF ATTORNEY

To _____ of * _____, and

of *

The undersigned claimant hereby authorizes you, or any one of you, as attorney in fact for the undersigned [if desired: and with full power of substitution,] to attend the meeting of creditors of the debtor or any adjournment thereof, and to vote in my behalf on any question that may be lawfully submitted to creditors at such meeting or adjourned meeting, and for a trustee or trustees of the estate of the debtor.

Dated: _____

Signed:

By

as _____

Address: _____

_____

[If executed by an individual] Acknowledged before me on _____.

[If executed on behalf of a partnership] Acknowledged before me
by _____, who says that he [or she] is a member of the partnership named above and is authorized to execute this power of attorney in its behalf.

[If executed on behalf of a corporation] Acknowledged before me on _____,
by _____, who says that he [or she] is _____ of the corporation
named above and is authorized to execute this power of attorney in its behalf.

_____

[Official character.]

* State mailing address.

(Added Aug. 1, 1991.)

ADVISORY COMMITTEE NOTES

This form previously was numbered Official Form No. 18.

Form 12. Order and Notice for Hearing
on Disclosure Statement

Official Form 12
(12/03)

**Form 12. ORDER AND NOTICE FOR HEARING
ON DISCLOSURE STATEMENT**

[Caption as in Form 16A]

**ORDER AND NOTICE FOR HEARING
ON DISCLOSURE STATEMENT**

To the debtor, its creditors, and other parties in interest:

A disclosure statement and a plan under chapter 11 [*or* chapter 9] of the Bankruptcy Code having been filed by
_____ on _____ ,

IT IS ORDERED and notice is hereby given, that:

    1. The hearing to consider the approval of the disclosure statement shall be held at:
_____ , on _____ , at _____ o'clock ___.m.

    2. _____ is fixed as the last day for filing and serving in accordance with Fed. R. Bankr. P. 3017(a) written objections to the disclosure statement.

    3. Within _____ days after entry of this order, the disclosure statement and plan shall be distributed in accordance with Fed. R. Bankr. P. 3017(a).

    4. Requests for copies of the disclosure statement and plan shall be mailed to the debtor in possession [*or* trustee *or* debtor *or* _____] at * _____ .

Dated: _____

                               BY THE COURT

                                      _____
                                      United States Bankruptcy Judge

    * State mailing address

(Added Aug. 1, 1991; amended Dec. 2003.)

ADVISORY COMMITTEE NOTES

1991 Enactment

This form previously was numbered Official Form No. 28. The form is related to Rule 3017(a). Section 1125 of the Code requires court approval of a disclosure statement before votes may be solicited for or against a plan in either chapter 11 reorganization or chapter 9 municipality cases.

Objections to the disclosure statement may be filed. Rule 3017(a) specifies that the court may fix a time for the filing of objections or they can be filed at any time prior to approval of the statement.

Rule 3017(a) also specifies the persons who are to receive copies of the statement and plan prior to the hearing. These documents will not be sent to all parties in interest because at this stage of the case it could be unnecessarily expensive and confusing. However, any party in interest may request copies. The request should be made in writing (Rule 3017(a)), and sent to the person mailing the statement and plan which, as the form indicates, would usually be the proponent of the plan.

This form may be adapted for use if more than one disclosure statement is to be considered by the court.

Form 13. Order Approving Disclosure Statement and Fixing Time for Filing Acceptances or Rejections of Plan, Combined with Notice Thereof

Official Form 13
(12/03)

**Form 13. ORDER APPROVING DISCLOSURE STATEMENT AND FIXING TIME
FOR FILING ACCEPTANCES OR REJECTIONS OF PLAN,
COMBINED WITH NOTICE THEREOF**

[Caption as in Form 16A]

**ORDER APPROVING DISCLOSURE STATEMENT AND FIXING TIME
FOR FILING ACCEPTANCES OR REJECTIONS OF PLAN,
COMBINED WITH NOTICE THEREOF**

A disclosure statement under chapter 11 of the Bankruptcy Code having been filed
by _____, on _____ [*if appropriate*, and
by _____, on _____], referring to a plan under
chapter 11 of the Code filed by _____, on _____
[*if appropriate*, and by _____, on _____ respectively]
[*if appropriate*, as modified by a modification filed on _____]; and

It having been determined after hearing on notice that the disclosure statement [*or statements*]
contain[s] adequate information:

IT IS ORDERED, and notice is hereby given, that:

A. The disclosure statement filed by _____ dated _____
[*if appropriate*, and by _____, dated _____ is [are] approved.

B. _____ is fixed as the last day for filing written acceptances or rejections
of the plan [*or plans*] referred to above.

C. Within _____ days after the entry of this order, the plan [*or plans*] *or* a summary *or*
summaries thereof approved by the court, [and [*if appropriate*] a summary approved by the court of its opinion,
if any, dated _____, approving the disclosure statement [*or statements*]], the disclosure statement [*or
statements*], and a ballot conforming to Official Form 14 shall be mailed to creditors, equity security holders, and
other parties in interest, and shall be transmitted to the United States trustee, as provided in Fed. R. Bankr. P.
3017(d).

D. If acceptances are filed for more than one plan, preferences among the plans so accepted may be
indicated.

E. [*If appropriate*] _____ is fixed for the hearing on confirmation of the plan [*or plans*].

F. [*If appropriate*] _____ is fixed as the last day for filing and serving pursuant to Fed.
R. Bankr. P. 3020(b)(1) written objections to confirmation of the plan.

Dated: _____

BY THE COURT

_____
United States Bankruptcy Judge

[*If the court directs that a copy of the opinion should be transmitted in lieu of or in addition to the summary thereof, the
appropriate change should be made in paragraph C of this order.*]

(Added Aug. 1, 1991; amended Dec. 2003.)

ADVISORY COMMITTEE NOTES
1991 Enactment

This form is derived from former Official Form No. 29. The form may be adapted for use if more than one disclosure statement is approved by the court.

Form 14. Class [ ] Ballot for Accepting
or Rejecting Plan of Reorganization

Official Form 14
(12/03)

Form 14. CLASS [ ] BALLOT FOR ACCEPTING OR REJECTING
PLAN OF REORGANIZATION

[Caption as in Form 16A]

CLASS [ ] BALLOT FOR ACCEPTING OR REJECTING
PLAN OF REORGANIZATION

[Proponent] filed a plan of reorganization dated *[Date]* (the "Plan") for the Debtor in this case. The Court has *[conditionally]* approved a disclosure statement with respect to the Plan (the "Disclosure Statement"). The Disclosure Statement provides information to assist you in deciding how to vote your ballot. If you do not have a Disclosure Statement, you may obtain a copy from *[name, address, telephone number and telecopy number of proponent/proponent's attorney.]* Court approval of the disclosure statement does not indicate approval of the Plan by the Court.

You should review the Disclosure Statement and the Plan before you vote. You may wish to seek legal advice concerning the Plan and your classification and treatment under the Plan. Your *[claim] [equity interest]* has been placed in class [ ] under the Plan. If you hold claims or equity interests in more than one class, you will receive a ballot for each class in which you are entitled to vote.

If your ballot is not received by *[name and address of proponent's attorney or other appropriate address]* on or before *[date]*, and such deadline is not extended, your vote will not count as either an acceptance or rejection of the Plan.

If the Plan is confirmed by the Bankruptcy Court it will be binding on you whether or not you vote.

ACCEPTANCE OR REJECTION OF THE PLAN

[At this point the ballot should provide for voting by the particular class of creditors or equity holders receiving the ballot using one of the following alternatives:]

[If the voter is the holder of a secured, priority, or unsecured nonpriority claim:]

The undersigned, the holder of a Class [ ] claim against the Debtor in the unpaid amount of Dollars ($)

[or, if the voter is the holder of a bond, debenture, or other debt security:]

The undersigned, the holder of a Class [ ] claim against the Debtor, consisting of Dollars ($) principal amount of *[describe bond, debenture, or other debt security]* of the Debtor (For purposes of this Ballot, it is not necessary and you should not adjust the principal amount for any accrued or unmatured interest.)

[or, if the voter is the holder of an equity interest:]

The undersigned, the holder of Class [ ] equity interest in the Debtor, consisting of _____ shares or other interests of *[describe equity interest]* in the Debtor

Official Form 14 continued
(12/03)

[In each case, the following language should be included:]

(Check one box only)

| | ACCEPTS THE PLAN | | REJECTS THE PLAN

Dated: _____

Print or type name: _____

Signature: _____

Title (if corporation or partnership) _____

Address: _____

_____

RETURN THIS BALLOT TO:

[Name and address of proponent's attorney or other appropriate address]

Complete Annotation Materials, see Title 11 U.S.C.A.

(Added Aug. 1, 1991; amended Oct. 1, 1997; Dec. 2003.)

ADVISORY COMMITTEE NOTES

1991 Enactment

The form is derived from former Official Form No. 30. The form has been amended to facilitate the voting of a debtor's shares held in "street name." The form may be adapted to designate the class in which each ballot is to be tabulated. It is intended that a separate ballot will be provided for each class in which a holder may vote.

1997 Amendment

The form has been substantially amended to simplify its format and make it easier to complete correctly.

Directions or blanks for proponent to complete the text of the ballot are in italics and enclosed within brackets. A ballot should include only the applicable language from the alternatives shown on this form and should be adapted to the particular requirements of the case.

If the plan provides for creditors in a class to have the right to reduce their claims so as to qualify for treatment given to creditors whose claims do not exceed a specified amount, the ballot should make provisions for the exercise of that right. See section 1122(b) of the Code.

If debt or equity securities are held in the name of a broker/dealer or nominee, the ballot should require the furnishing of sufficient information to assure that duplicate ballots are not submitted and counted and that ballots submitted by a broker/dealer or nominee reflect the votes of the beneficial holders of such securities. See Rule 3017(e).

In the event that more than one plan of reorganization is to be voted upon, the form of ballot will need to be adapted to permit holders of claims or equity interests (a) to accept or reject each plan being proposed, and (b) to indicate preferences among the competing plans. See section 1129(c) of the Code.

Form 15. Order Confirming Plan

form b15
(Rev. 12/01)

Form 15. ORDER CONFIRMING PLAN

[Caption as in Form 16A]

ORDER CONFIRMING PLAN

The plan under chapter 11 of the Bankruptcy Code filed by _____ , on

_____ *[if applicable*, as modified by a modification filed on _____ .] or a summary

thereof, having been transmitted to creditors and equity security holders; and

It having been determined after hearing on notice that the requirements for confirmation set forth in 11 U.S.C.

§ 1129(a) *[or, if appropriate*, 11 U.S.C. § 1129(b)] have been satisfied;

IT IS ORDERED that:

The plan filed by _____ , on _____ , *[If*

appropriate, include dates and any other pertinent details of modifications to the plan] is confirmed. *[If the plan provides*

for an injunction against conduct not otherwise enjoined under the Code, include the information required by Rule 3020.]

A copy of the confirmed plan is attached.

Dated:

BY THE COURT

United States Bankruptcy Judge.

(Added Aug. 1, 1991; amended Dec. 1, 2001.)

ADVISORY COMMITTEE NOTES

This form is derived from former Official Form No. 31. The form has been simplified to avoid the necessity of repeating the statutory requirements of 11 U.S.C. § 1129(a). In the case of an individual chapter 11 debtor, Form 18 may be adapted for use together with this form.

2001 Amendment

The form is amended to conform to the December 1, 2001, amendments to Rule 3020.

Form 16A.   Caption (Full)

B16A (Official Form 16A) (12/07)

Form 16A. CAPTION (FULL)

United States Bankruptcy Court

_____ District Of _____

In re _____ ,)
[Set forth here all names including married,   )
maiden, and trade names used by debtor within   )
last 8 years.]   )
                 Debtor   ) Case No. _____
)
Address _____   )
)
          _____) Chapter _____
)
Last four digits of Social-Security or Individual Tax-
Payer-Identification (ITIN) No(s)..(if any): _____)
)
Employer Tax-Identification (EIN) No(s).(if any): _____)
)

[Designation of Character of Paper]

(Added Aug. 1, 1991; and amended Mar. 1995; Dec. 1, 2003; Aug. 11, 2005, eff. Oct. 17, 2005; Dec. 1, 2007.)

ADVISORY COMMITTEE NOTES

1991 Enactment

This form has been transferred from former Official Form No. 1, which included the form of caption for the case. Rule 9004(b) requires a caption to set forth the title of the case. Rule 1005 provides that the title of the case shall include the debtor's name, all other names used by the debtor within six years before the commencement of the case, and the debtor's social security and tax identification numbers. This form of caption is prescribed for use on the petition, the notice of the meeting of creditors, the order of discharge, and the documents relating to a chapter 11 plan, (Official Forms 1, 9, 12, 13, 14, 15, and 18). See Rule 2002(m). In the petition, (Official Form 1), and the notice of the meeting of creditors, (Official Form 9), the information required by Rule 1005 appears in a block format. A notation of the chapter of the Bankruptcy Code under which the case is proceeding has been added to the form.

1995 Amendment

The form is amended to provide for the debtor's address to appear in the caption in furtherance of the duty of the debtor to include this information on every notice given by the debtor. The Bankruptcy Reform Act of 1994 amended section 342 of the Code to add this requirement.

2003 Amendment

The form is amended to require disclosure of only the last four digits of the debtor's social security number to afford greater privacy to the individual debtor, whose bankruptcy case records may be available over the Internet.

2005 Amendment

The form is amended to require that the title of the case include all names used by the debtor within the last eight years in conformity with § 727(a)(8) as amended by the Bankruptcy Abuse Prevention and Consumer Protection Act of 2005, Pub. L. No. 109–8, 119 Stat. 23 (April 20, 2005), extending from six years to eight years the period during which a debtor is barred from receiving successive discharges.

2005–2007 Amendments

(The 2005-2007 Committee Note incorporates the Committee Note previously published in 2005.)

The form is amended to require that the title of the case include all names used by the debtor within the last eight years in conformity with § 727(a)(8) as amended by the Bankruptcy Abuse Prevention and Consumer Protection Act of 2005, Pub. L. No. 109–8, 119 Stat. 23 (April 20, 2005), extending from six years to eight years the period during which a debtor is barred from receiving successive discharges. In conformity with Rule 9037, the filer is directed to provide only the last four digits of any individual debtor's taxpayer-identification number.

Form 16B.   Caption (Short Title)

Official Form 16B
12/94

FORM 16B. CAPTION (SHORT TITLE)

(May be used if 11 U.S.C. § 342(c) is not applicable)

United States Bankruptcy Court

_____ District Of _____

In re _____ ,
_____
          Debtor

Case No. _____

Chapter _____

[Designation of Character of Paper]

(Added Aug. 1, 1991; and amended Mar. 1995.)

ADVISORY COMMITTEE NOTES

This form of caption is prescribed for general use in filing papers in a case under the Bankruptcy Code. Rule 9004(b) requires a caption to set forth the title of the case, and Rule 1005 specifies that the title must include all names used by the debtor within six years before the commencement of the case and the debtor's social security and tax identification numbers. This information is necessary in the petition, the notice of the meeting of creditors, the order of discharge, and the documents relating to the plan in a chapter 11 case. See Rule 2002(m) and Official Form 16A. In other notices, motions, applications, and papers filed in a case, however, a short title containing simply the name of the debtor or joint debtors may be used. Additional names, such as any under which the debtor has engaged in business, may be included in the short title as needed.

1995 Amendment

The title of this form is amended to specify that it can be used when section 342(c) of the Code, as added by the Bankruptcy Reform Act of 1994, is not applicable.

Form 16C.   Caption of Complaint in Adversary Proceeding Filed by a Debtor [Abrogated]

ADVISORY COMMITTEE NOTES

This form previously was numbered Official Form No. 34. A notation of the chapter of the Bankruptcy Code under which the case is proceeding has been added to the form. Rule 7010 refers to this form as providing the caption of a pleading in an adversary proceeding.

1995 Amendment

The form is amended to conform to the amendments made to section 342 of the Code by the Bankruptcy Reform Act of 1994.

2003 Amendment

The form is abrogated. An amendment to Official Form 16A directs that only the last four digits of the debtor's Social Security number should appear in a caption. Section 342(c) of the Bankruptcy Code continues to require the debtor to provide a creditor with the debtor's name, address, and taxpayer identification number on any notice the debtor is required to give to the creditor. An individual debtor can fulfill this requirement by including the debtor's Social Security account number on only the creditor's copy of any notice or summons the debtor may serve on the creditor.

Form 16D. Caption for Use in Adversary Proceeding

Official Form 16D
(12/04)

Form 16D. CAPTION FOR USE IN ADVERSARY PROCEEDING

United States Bankruptcy Court

_____ District Of _____

In re _____,	)	
Debtor	)	Case No.
	)	
	)	Chapter
_____,	)	
Plaintiff	)	
	)	
	)	
	)	
	)	
Defendant ,	)	Adv. Proc. No.

COMPLAINT [_or_ other Designation]

[If in a Notice of Appeal (see Form 17) or other notice filed and served by a debtor, this caption must be altered to include the debtor's address and Employer's Tax Identification Number(s) or last four digits of Social Security Number(s) as in Form 16A.]

(Added Mar. 1995; amended Dec. 1, 2004)

ADVISORY COMMITTEE NOTES

1995 Enactment

This form of caption may be used in an adversary proceeding when section 342(c) of the Code, as added by the Bankruptcy Reform Act of 1994, is not applicable.

2004 Amendment

The form is amended to reflect the 2003 abrogation of Form 16C. As a complaint initiating an adversary proceeding serves as a notice to the defendant of the filing of an action, a debtor filing an adversary proceeding must follow the notice requirements of § 342(c) of the Code. To protect individual privacy a debtor should use the defendant's copy of the summons to be served with the complaint to provide the information required by § 342(c) to any creditor named as a defendant.

Form 17. Notice of Appeal Under 28 U.S.C.
§ 158(a) or (b) From a Judgment, Order,
or Decree of a Bankruptcy Judge

Official Form 17
(12/04)

United States Bankruptcy Court

_____ District Of _____

In re _____,
　　　　　Debtor

Case No. _____

Chapter _____

[Caption as in Form 16A, 16B, or 16D, as appropriate]

NOTICE OF APPEAL

_____, the plaintiff [*or defendant or* other party] appeals under 28 U.S.C.
§ 158(a) or (b) from the judgment, order, or decree of the bankruptcy judge (describe) entered in this adversary
proceeding [*or other proceeding, describe type*] on the _____ day of _____, _____.
　　　　　　　　　　　　　　　　　　　　　　　　　　　　　(month)　　　　　(year)
　　　　The names of all parties to the judgment, order, or decree appealed from and the names, addresses, and
telephone numbers of their respective attorneys are as follows:

Dated: _____

Signed: _____
　　　　Attorney for Appellant (or Appellant, if not represented by an Attorney)

Attorney Name: _____

Address: _____
　　　　　_____

Telephone No: _____

　　　　If a Bankruptcy Appellate Panel Service is authorized to hear this appeal, each party has a right to have the
appeal heard by the district court. The appellant may exercise this right only by filing a separate statement of
election at the time of the filing of this notice of appeal. Any other party may elect, within the time provided in 28
U.S.C. § 158(c), to have the appeal heard by the district court.

　　　　*If a child support creditor or its representative is the appellant, and if the child support creditor or its representative
files the form specified in § 304(g) of the Bankruptcy Reform Act of 1994, no fee is required.*

(Added Aug. 1, 1991; and amended Mar. 1995; Oct. 1, 1997;
Dec. 1, 2002; Dec. 1, 2004.)

ADVISORY COMMITTEE NOTES

This form is derived from former Official Form No. 35.
The form has been amended to indicate that a final order may
be entered other than in an adversary proceeding.

1995 Amendment

The form is amended to reflect the amendments to 28
U.S.C. § 158 concerning bankruptcy appellate panels made by
the Bankruptcy Reform Act of 1994. Section 158(d) requires
an appellant who elects to appeal to a district court rather
than a bankruptcy appellate panel to do so "at the time of
filing the appeal."

The 1994 Act also amended 28 U.S.C. § 158(a) to permit
immediate appeal of interlocutory orders increasing or reducing a chapter 11 debtor's exclusive period to file a plan under
section 1121 of the Code. The form is amended to provide
appropriate flexibility.

1997 Amendment

The form has been amended to conform to Rule 8001(a),
which requires the notice to contain the names of all parties to
the judgment, order, or decree appealed from and the names,
addresses, and telephone numbers of their respective attorneys. A party filing a notice of appeal pro se should provide
equivalent information.

2002 Amendment

The form is amended to give notice that no filing fee is
required if a child support creditor or its representative is the
appellant, and if the child support creditor or its representative files a form detailing the child support debt, its status,
and other characteristics, as specified in § 304(g) of the
Bankruptcy Reform Act of 1994, Pub. L. No. 103–396, 108
Stat. 4106 (Oct. 22, 1994).

2004 Amendment   Form 16C.

The form is amended to reflect the 2003 abrogation of

**Form 18. Discharge of Debtor
in a Chapter 7 Case**
B18 (Official Form 18) (12/07)

United States Bankruptcy Court

_____ District Of _____

In re _____,
      [Set forth here all names including married,
      maiden, and trade names used by debtor within
      last 8 years.]
                     Debtor   Case No. _____

Address _____

        _____   Chapter 7

Last four digits of Social-Security or other Individual Taxpayer-
Identification No(s)(if any).: _____

Employer Tax-Identification No(s).(EIN) [if any]:_____

DISCHARGE OF DEBTOR

It appearing that the debtor is entitled to a discharge, **IT IS ORDERED:** The debtor is granted a
discharge under section 727 of title 11, United States Code, (the Bankruptcy Code).

Dated: _____

                                 BY THE COURT

                                 _____

                                 United States Bankruptcy Judge

SEE THE BACK OF THIS ORDER FOR IMPORTANT INFORMATION.

B18 (Official Form 18) (12/07) - Cont.

EXPLANATION OF BANKRUPTCY DISCHARGE
IN A CHAPTER 7 CASE

This court order grants a discharge to the person named as the debtor. It is not a dismissal of the case and it does not determine how much money, if any, the trustee will pay to creditors.

Collection of Discharged Debts Prohibited

The discharge prohibits any attempt to collect from the debtor a debt that has been discharged. For example, a creditor is not permitted to contact a debtor by mail, phone, or otherwise, to file or continue a lawsuit, to attach wages or other property, or to take any other action to collect a discharged debt from the debtor. *[In a case involving community property:* There are also special rules that protect certain community property owned by the debtor's spouse, even if that spouse did not file a bankruptcy case.] A creditor who violates this order can be required to pay damages and attorney's fees to the debtor.

However, a creditor may have the right to enforce a valid lien, such as a mortgage or security interest, against the debtor's property after the bankruptcy, if that lien was not avoided or eliminated in the bankruptcy case. Also, a debtor may voluntarily pay any debt that has been discharged.

Debts that are Discharged

The chapter 7 discharge order eliminates a debtor's legal obligation to pay a debt that is discharged. Most, but not all, types of debts are discharged if the debt existed on the date the bankruptcy case was filed. (If this case was begun under a different chapter of the Bankruptcy Code and converted to chapter 7, the discharge applies to debts owed when the bankruptcy case was converted.)

Debts that are Not Discharged.

Some of the common types of debts which are <u>not</u> discharged in a chapter 7 bankruptcy case are:

    a. Debts for most taxes;

    b. Debts incurred to pay nondischargeable taxes;

    c. Debts that are domestic support obligations;

    d. Debts for most student loans;

    e. Debts for most fines, penalties, forfeitures, or criminal restitution obligations;

    f. Debts for personal injuries or death caused by the debtor's operation of a motor vehicle, vessel, or aircraft while intoxicated;

    g. Some debts which were not properly listed by the debtor;

    h. Debts that the bankruptcy court specifically has decided or will decide in this bankruptcy case are not discharged;

    i. Debts for which the debtor has given up the discharge protections by signing a reaffirmation agreement in compliance with the Bankruptcy Code requirements for reaffirmation of debts; and

    j. Debts owed to certain pension, profit sharing, stock bonus, other retirement plans, or to the Thrift Savings Plan for federal employees for certain types of loans from these plans.

This information is only a general summary of the bankruptcy discharge. There are exceptions to these general rules. Because the law is complicated, you may want to consult an attorney to determine the exact effect of the discharge in this case.

(Added Aug. 1, 1991; and amended Mar. 1995; Oct. 1, 1997; Aug. 11, 2005, eff. Oct. 17, 2005; Dec. 1, 2007.)

ADVISORY COMMITTEE NOTES

1991 Enactment

This form previously was numbered Official Form No. 27. The form has been revised to accommodate cases commenced by the filing of either a voluntary or an involuntary petition.

1995 Amendment

The form is amended to include debts described in section 523(a)(15) of the Code, which was added by the Bankruptcy Reform Act of 1994, in the list of debts discharged unless determined by the court to be nondischargeable.

1997 Amendment

The discharge order has been simplified by deleting paragraphs which had detailed some, but not all, of the effects of the discharge. These paragraphs have been replaced with a plain English explanation of the discharge. This explanation is to be printed on the reverse of the order, to increase understanding of the bankruptcy discharge among creditors and debtors. The bracketed sentence in the second paragraph should be included when the case involves community property.

2005 Amendment

The form is amended to require that the title of the case include all names used by the debtor within the eight years prior to the filing of the petition in the case in conformity with § 727(a)(8) as amended by the Bankruptcy Abuse Prevention and Consumer Protection Act of 2005, Pub. L. No. 109–8, 119 Stat. 23 (April 20, 2005), extending from six years to eight years the period during which a debtor is barred from receiving successive discharges. The explanation part of the form is amended to include additional types of debts that are not discharged under § 523(a) as amended in 2005 and to revise certain terminology in conformity with provisions of the 2005 Act.

2005–2007 Amendments

(The 2005–2007 Committee Note incorporates the Committee Note previously published in 2005.)

The form is amended to require that the title of the case include all names used by the debtor within the eight years prior to the filing of the petition in the case in conformity with § 727(a)(8) as amended by the Bankruptcy Abuse Prevention and Consumer Protection Act of 2005, Pub. L. No. 109-8, 119 Stat. 23 (April 20, 2005), extending from six years to eight years the period during which a debtor is barred from receiving successive discharges. The explanation part of the form is amended to include additional types of debts that are not discharged under § 523(a), as amended in 2005, and to revise certain terminology in conformity with provisions of the 2005 Act. In conformity with Rule 9037 and Official Form 16A, the caption also is amended to provide only the last four digits of any individual debtor's taxpayer-identification number.

Form 19.   Declaration and Signature of Non–Attorney Bankruptcy Petition Preparer

B19 (Official Form 19) (12/07)

United States Bankruptcy Court

In re _____,   Case No. _____
                    Debtor
                                         Chapter _____

**DECLARATION AND SIGNATURE OF NON-ATTORNEY
BANKRUPTCY PETITION PREPARER** (*See* 11 U.S.C. § 110)

I declare under penalty of perjury that: (1) I am a bankruptcy petition preparer as defined in 11 U.S.C. § 110; (2) I prepared the accompanying document(s) listed below for compensation and have provided the debtor with a copy of the document(s) and the attached notice as required by 11 U.S.C. §§ 110(b), 110(h), and 342(b); and (3) if rules or guidelines have been promulgated pursuant to 11 U.S.C. § 110(h) setting a maximum fee for services chargeable by bankruptcy petition preparers, I have given the debtor notice of the maximum amount before preparing any document for filing for a debtor or accepting any fee from the debtor, as required by that section.

Accompanying documents: Printed or Typed Name and Title, if any, of
_____   Bankruptcy Petition Preparer:
_____
_____   _____
_____   Social-Security No. of Bankruptcy Petition
                                         Preparer (Required by 11 U.S.C. § 110):

                                         _____

If the bankruptcy petition preparer is not an individual, state the name, title (if any), address, and social-security number of the officer, principal, responsible person, or partner who signs this document.

_____
_____
Address

X
Signature of Bankruptcy Petition Preparer   Date

Names and social-security numbers of all other individuals who prepared or assisted in preparing this document, unless the bankruptcy petition preparer is not an individual:

If more than one person prepared this document, attach additional signed sheets conforming to the appropriate Official Form for each person.

A bankruptcy petition preparer's failure to comply with the provisions of title 11 and the Federal Rules of Bankruptcy Procedure may result in fines or imprisonment or both. 11 U.S.C. § 110; 18 U.S.C. § 156.

B19 (Official Form 19) (12/07) - Cont.

2

NOTICE TO DEBTOR BY NON-ATTORNEY BANKRUPTCY PETITION PREPARER
[Must be filed with any document(s) prepared by a bankruptcy petition preparer.]

I am a bankruptcy petition preparer. I am not an attorney and may not practice law or give legal advice. Before preparing any document for filing as defined in § 110(a)(2) of the Bankruptcy Code or accepting any fees, I am required by law to provide you with this notice concerning bankruptcy petition preparers. Under the law, § 110 of the Bankruptcy Code (11 U.S.C. § 110), I am forbidden to offer you any legal advice, including advice about any of the following:

- whether to file a petition under the Bankruptcy Code (11 U.S.C. § 101 et seq.);
- whether commencing a case under chapter 7, 11, 12, or 13 is appropriate;
- whether your debts will be eliminated or discharged in a case under the Bankruptcy Code;
- whether you will be able to retain your home, car, or other property after commencing a case under the Bankruptcy Code;
- the tax consequences of a case brought under the Bankruptcy Code;
- the dischargeability of tax claims;
- whether you may or should promise to repay debts to a creditor or enter into a reaffirmation agreement with a creditor to reaffirm a debt;
- how to characterize the nature of your interests in property or your debts; or
- bankruptcy procedures and rights.

[The notice may provide additional examples of legal advice that a bankruptcy petition preparer is not authorized to give.]

In addition, under 11 U.S.C. § 110(h), the Supreme Court or the Judicial Conference of the United States may promulgate rules or guidelines setting a maximum allowable fee chargeable by a bankruptcy petition preparer. As required by law, I have notified you of this maximum allowable fee, if any, before preparing any document for filing or accepting any fee from you.

_____   _____
Signature of Debtor   Date   Joint Debtor (if any)   Date

[In a joint case, both spouses must sign.]

(Added Mar. 1995; and amended Dec. 1, 2003; Aug. 11, 2005, eff. Oct. 17, 2005; Dec. 1, 2007.)

ADVISORY COMMITTEE NOTES

1995 Amendment

This form is new. The Bankruptcy Reform Act of 1994 requires a "bankruptcy petition preparer," as defined in 11 U.S.C. § 110, to sign any "document for filing" that the bankruptcy petition preparer prepares for compensation on behalf of a debtor, to disclose on the document certain information, and to provide the debtor with a copy of the document. This form or adaptations of this form have been incorporated into the official forms of the voluntary petition, the schedules, the statement of financial affairs, and other official forms that typically would be prepared for a debtor by a bankruptcy petition preparer. This form is to be used in connection with any other document that a bankruptcy petition preparer prepares for filing by a debtor in a bankruptcy case.

2003 Amendment

Pursuant to § 110(c) of the Bankruptcy Code, the certification by a non-attorney bankruptcy petition preparer requires a petition preparer to provide the full Social Security number of the individual who actually prepares the document.

2005 Amendment

The certification by a non-attorney bankruptcy petition preparer in this form is renamed a "declaration" and is amended to include material mandated by amendments to § 110 of the Code in the Bankruptcy Abuse Prevention and Consumer Protection Act of 2005, Pub. L. No. 109–8, 119 Stat. 23 (April 20, 2005).

2005-2007 Amendments

(The 2005–2007 Committee Note incorporates the Committee Notes to Forms 19A and 19B previously published in 2005.)

This form is new. It is derived from form 19B and replaces forms 19A and 19B (which forms are abrogated). The form contains the notice a bankruptcy petition preparer is required to give to a debtor under § 110 of the Code as amended by the Bankruptcy Abuse Prevention and Consumer Protection Act of 2005, Pub. L. No. 109-8, 119 Stat. 23 (April 20, 2005), and the bankruptcy petition preparer's signed declaration (also required by § 110 of the Code) that the notice was given to the debtor.

The notice states, in language mandated in the 2005 Act, that the bankruptcy petition preparer is not an attorney and must not give legal advice. The notice also includes examples of advice a bankruptcy petition preparer may not give that are taken from § 110(e)(2) of the Code.

Although space is provided in the declaration to list multiple documents prepared for a single filing, a new form 19 must be completed and accompany subsequent filings. For example, one form 19 listing all forms prepared by the bankruptcy petition preparer would be filed with the debtor's petition package. Another form 19 would be required if the debtor files amended schedules later in the case that were prepared by the bankruptcy petition preparer.

The form must be signed by the debtor and the bankruptcy petition preparer where indicated, and must be filed with each document for filing prepared by the bankruptcy petition preparer.

Form 20A

OFFICIAL FORMS

Form 20A. Notice of Motion or Objection

B20A (Official Form 20A) (Notice of Motion or Objection) (12/10)

United States Bankruptcy Court
_____ District of _____

In re

[Set forth here all names including married, maiden, and trade names used by debtor within last 8 years.]

Debtor

Address _____

Last four digits of Social Security or Individual Tax-payer Identification (ITIN) No(s).,(if any): _____

Employer's Tax Identification (EIN) No(s).(if any): _____

Case No. _____

Chapter _____

NOTICE OF [MOTION TO | [OBJECTION TO]

_____ has filed papers with the court to [relief sought in motion or objection].

Your rights may be affected. You should read these papers carefully and discuss them with your attorney, if you have one in this bankruptcy case. (If you do not have an attorney, you may wish to consult one.)

If you do not want the court to [relief sought in motion or objection], or if you want the court to consider your views on the [motion] [objection], then on or before (date) , you or your attorney must:

[File with the court a written request for a hearing {*or, if the court requires a written response*, an answer, explaining your position} at:

{address of the bankruptcy clerk's office}

If you mail your {request}{response} to the court for filing, you must mail it early enough so the court will **receive** it on or before the date stated above.

You must also mail a copy to:

{movant's attorney's name and address}

{names and addresses of others to be served}]

[Attend the hearing scheduled to be held on (date) , (year) , at ____ a.m./p.m. in Courtroom____, United States Bankruptcy Court, {address}.]

[Other steps required to oppose a motion or objection under local rule or court order.]

If you or your attorney do not take these steps, the court may decide that you do not oppose the relief sought in the motion or objection and may enter an order granting that relief.

Date: _____

Signature: _____
Name:
Address

(Added Oct. 1, 1997; amended Dec. 2003; Dec. 1, 2010.)

ADVISORY COMMITTEE NOTES

1997 Enactment

These forms are new. They are intended to provide uniform, plain English explanations to parties regarding what they must do to respond in certain contested matters which occur frequently in bankruptcy cases. Such explanations have been given better in some courts than in others. The forms are intended to make bankruptcy proceedings more fair, equitable, and efficient, by aiding parties, who sometimes do not have counsel, in understanding the applicable rules. It is hoped that use of these forms also will decrease the number of inquiries to bankruptcy clerks' offices.

These notices will be sent by the movant unless local rules provide for some other entity to give notice.

These forms are not intended to dictate the specific procedures to be used by different bankruptcy courts. The forms contain optional language that can be used or adapted, depending on local procedures. Similarly, the signature line will be adapted to identify the actual sender of the notice in each circumstance. All adaptations of the form should carry out the intent to give notice of applicable procedures in easily understood language.

2010 Amendment

The form is amended to require that the title of the case include all names used by the debtor within the last eight years. This change conforms to the 2005 amendment of § 727(a)(8), which extended from six years to eight years the period during which a debtor is barred from receiving successive discharges. In conformity with Rule 9037, the filer is directed to provide only the last four digits of any individual debtor's taxpayer-identification number.

Form 20B. Notice of Objection to Claim

B20B (Official Form 20B) (Notice of Objection to Claim) (12/10)

United States Bankruptcy Court

_____ District of _____

In re

[Set forth here all names including married, maiden, and trade names used by debtor within last 8 years.]

Debtor)

Address _____

_____

Last four digits of Social Security or Individual Tax-payer Identification (ITIN) No(s)..(if any): _____

Employer's Tax Identification (EIN) No(s).(if any): _____

Case No. _____

Chapter _____

NOTICE OF OBJECTION TO CLAIM

_____ has filed an objection to your claim in this bankruptcy case.

Your claim may be reduced, modified, or eliminated. You should read these papers carefully and discuss them with your attorney, if you have one.

If you do not want the court to eliminate or change your claim, then on or before _(date)_, you or your lawyer must:

{If required by local rule or court order.}

[File with the court a written response to the objection, explaining your position, at:

{address of the bankruptcy clerk's office}

If you mail your response to the court for filing, you must mail it early enough so that the court will **receive** it on or before the date stated above.

You must also mail a copy to:

{objector's attorney's name and address}

{names and addresses of others to be served}]

Attend the hearing on the objection, scheduled to be held on _(date)_, _(year)_, at ___ a.m./p.m. in Courtroom____, United States Bankruptcy Court, {address}.

If you or your attorney do not take these steps, the court may decide that you do not oppose the objection to your claim.

Date: _____

Signature: _____
Name:
Address

(Added Oct. 1, 1997; amended Dec. 2003; Dec. 1, 2010.)

ADVISORY COMMITTEE NOTES

1997 Enactment

These forms are new. They are intended to provide uniform, plain English explanations to parties regarding what they must do to respond in certain contested matters which occur frequently in bankruptcy cases. Such explanations have been given better in some courts than in others. The forms are intended to make bankruptcy proceedings more fair, equitable, and efficient, by aiding parties, who sometimes do not have counsel, in understanding the applicable rules. It is hoped that use of these forms also will decrease the number of inquiries to bankruptcy clerks' offices.

These notices will be sent by the movant unless local rules provide for some other entity to give notice.

These forms are not intended to dictate the specific procedures to be used by different bankruptcy courts. The forms contain optional language that can be used or adapted, depending on local procedures. Similarly, the signature line will be adapted to identify the actual sender of the notice in each circumstance. All adaptations of the form should carry out the intent to give notice of applicable procedures in easily understood language.

2010 Amendment

The form is amended to require that the title of the case include all names used by the debtor within the last eight years. This change conforms to the 2005 amendment of § 727(a)(8), which extended from six years to eight years the period during which a debtor is barred from receiving successive discharges. In conformity with Rule 9037, the filer is directed to provide only the last four digits of any individual debtor's taxpayer-identification number.

Form 21

Form 21. Statement of Social-Security Number or Individual Taxpayer-Identification Number (ITIN)

B 21 (Official Form 21) (12/07)

UNITED STATES BANKRUPTCY COURT

In re _____ .
  [Set forth here all names including married, maiden,)
  and trade names used by debtor within last 8 years])
)
                                Debtor   ) Case No. _____
Address _____   )
       _____   ) Chapter _____
)
Last four digits of Social-Security or Individual Taxpayer-)
Identification (ITIN) No(s).,(if any):   )
)
Employer Tax-Identification (EIN) No(s).(if any):   )
)

STATEMENT OF SOCIAL-SECURITY NUMBER(S)
(or other Individual Taxpayer-Identification Number(s) (ITIN(s)))[*]

1.Name of Debtor (Last, First, Middle):_____
(Check the appropriate box and, if applicable, provide the required information.)

  ☐ Debtor has a Social-Security Number and it is: _____
        (If more than one, state all.)
  ☐ Debtor does not have a Social-Security Number but has an Individual Taxpayer-Identification
        Number (ITIN), and it is: _____
        (If more than one, state all.)
  ☐ Debtor does not have either a Social-Security Number or an Individual Taxpayer-Identification
        Number (ITIN).

2.Name of Joint Debtor (Last, First, Middle):_____
(Check the appropriate box and, if applicable, provide the required information.)

  ☐ Joint Debtor has a Social-Security Number and it is: _____
        (If more than one, state all.)
  ☐ Joint Debtor does not have a Social-Security Number but has an Individual Taxpayer-Identification
        Number (ITIN) and it is: _____
        (If more than one, state all.)
  ☐ Joint Debtor does not have either a Social-Security Number or an Individual Taxpayer-Identification
        Number (ITIN).

I declare under penalty of perjury that the foregoing is true and correct.

  X _____
     Signature of Debtor   Date
  X _____
     Signature of Joint Debtor   Date

_____

[*] *Joint debtors must provide information for both spouses.*

Penalty for making a false statement: Fine of up to $250,000 or up to 5 years imprisonment or both. 18 U.S.C. §§ 152 and 3571.

(Added Oct. 14, 2003, eff. Dec. 1, 2003; Dec. 1, 2007.)

ADVISORY COMMITTEE NOTES

2003 Enactment

The form implements Rule 1007(f), which requires a debtor to submit a statement under penalty of perjury setting out the debtor's Social Security number. The form is necessary because Rule 1005 provides that the caption of the petition includes only the final four digits of the debtor's Social Security number. The statement provides the information necessary for the clerk to include the debtor's full Social Security number on the notice of the meeting of creditors, as required under Rule 2002(a)(1). Creditors in a case, along with the trustee and United States trustee or bankruptcy administrator, will receive the full Social Security number on their copy of the notice of the meeting of creditors. The copy of that notice which goes into the court file will show only the last four digits of the number.

2007 Amendment

The form is amended to direct an individual debtor who does not have a social-security number but has another government-issued individual taxpayer-identification number to furnish that number to the court. In light of the new Rule 9037 which limits public disclosure to all but the last four digits of any individual taxpayer-identification number, the amendment to this form will ensure that the court and creditors can properly identify a debtor who does not have a social-security number.

Form 22. Statement of Current Monthly Income

B 22A (Official Form 22A) (Chapter 7) (12-10)

In re _____	According to the information required to be entered on this statement

In re _____
            Debtor(s)

Case Number: _____
            (If known)

According to the information required to be entered on this statement (check one box as directed in Part I, III, or VI of this statement):

☐ **The presumption arises.**
☐ **The presumption does not arise.**
☐ **The presumption is temporarily inapplicable.**

CHAPTER 7 STATEMENT OF CURRENT MONTHLY INCOME
AND MEANS-TEST CALCULATION

In addition to Schedules I and J, this statement must be completed by every individual chapter 7 debtor. If none of the exclusions in Part I applies, joint debtors may complete one statement only. If any of the exclusions in Part I applies, joint debtors should complete separate statements if they believe this is required by § 707(b)(2)(C).

	Part I. MILITARY AND NON-CONSUMER DEBTORS
1A	**Disabled Veterans.** If you are a disabled veteran described in the Declaration in this Part 1A, (1) check the box at the beginning of the Declaration, (2) check the box for "The presumption does not arise" at the top of this statement, and (3) complete the verification in Part VIII. Do not complete any of the remaining parts of this statement. ☐ **Declaration of Disabled Veteran.** By checking this box, I declare under penalty of perjury that I am a disabled veteran (as defined in 38 U.S.C. § 3741(1)) whose indebtedness occurred primarily during a period in which I was on active duty (as defined in 10 U.S.C. § 101(d)(1)) or while I was performing a homeland defense activity (as defined in 32 U.S.C. §901(1)).
1B	**Non-consumer Debtors.** If your debts are not primarily consumer debts, check the box below and complete the verification in Part VIII. Do not complete any of the remaining parts of this statement. ☐ **Declaration of non-consumer debts.** By checking this box, I declare that my debts are not primarily consumer debts.

1C	**Reservists and National Guard Members; active duty or homeland defense activity.** Members of a reserve component of the Armed Forces and members of the National Guard who were called to active duty (as defined in 10 U.S.C. § 101(d)(1)) after September 11, 2001, for a period of at least 90 days, or who have performed homeland defense activity (as defined in 32 U.S.C. § 901(1)) for a period of at least 90 days, are excluded from all forms of means testing during the time of active duty or homeland defense activity and for 540 days thereafter (the "exclusion period"). If you qualify for this temporary exclusion, (1) check the appropriate boxes and complete any required information in the Declaration of Reservists and National Guard Members below, (2) check the box for "The presumption is temporarily inapplicable" at the top of this statement, and (3) complete the verification in Part VIII. **During your exclusion period you are not required to complete the balance of this form, but you must complete the form no later than 14 days after the date on which your exclusion period ends, unless the time for filing a motion raising the means test presumption expires in your case before your exclusion period ends.**
	
	☐ **Declaration of Reservists and National Guard Members.** By checking this box and making the appropriate entries below, I declare that I am eligible for a temporary exclusion from means testing because, as a member of a reserve component of the Armed Forces or the National Guard
	
	     a. ☐ I was called to active duty after September 11, 2001, for a period of at least 90 days and
	         ☐ I remain on active duty /or/
	         ☐ I was released from active duty on _____, which is less than 540 days before this bankruptcy case was filed;
	         OR
	     b. ☐ I am performing homeland defense activity for a period of at least 90 days /or/
	         ☐ I performed homeland defense activity for a period of at least 90 days, terminating on _____, which is less than 540 days before this bankruptcy case was filed.

Form B22A

B 22A (Official Form 22A) (Chapter 7) (12/10)

Part II. CALCULATION OF MONTHLY INCOME FOR § 707(b)(7) EXCLUSION		
Marital/filing status. Check the box that applies and complete the balance of this part of this statement as directed. a. ☐ **Unmarried. Complete only Column A ("Debtor's Income") for Lines 3-11.** b. ☐ Married, not filing jointly, with declaration of separate households. By checking this box, debtor declares under penalty of perjury: "My spouse and I are legally separated under applicable non-bankruptcy law or my spouse and I are living apart other than for the purpose of evading the requirements of § 707(b)(2)(A) of the Bankruptcy Code." **Complete only Column A ("Debtor's Income") for Lines 3-11.** c. ☐ Married, not filing jointly, without the declaration of separate households set out in Line 2.b above. **Complete both Column A ("Debtor's Income") and Column B ("Spouse's Income") for Lines 3-11.** d. ☐ Married, filing jointly. **Complete both Column A ("Debtor's Income") and Column B ("Spouse's Income") for Lines 3-11.** (Row 2)		
All figures must reflect average monthly income received from all sources, derived during the six calendar months prior to filing the bankruptcy case, ending on the last day of the month before the filing. If the amount of monthly income varied during the six months, you must divide the six-month total by six, and enter the result on the appropriate line.	**Column A** Debtor's Income	**Column B** Spouse's Income
3 Gross wages, salary, tips, bonuses, overtime, commissions.	$	$
4 **Income from the operation of a business, profession or farm.** Subtract Line b from Line a and enter the difference in the appropriate column(s) of Line 4. If you operate more than one business, profession or farm, enter aggregate numbers and provide details on an attachment. Do not enter a number less than zero. **Do not include any part of the business expenses entered on Line b as a deduction in Part V.** a. Gross receipts $ b. Ordinary and necessary business expenses $ c. Business income — Subtract Line b from Line a	$	$
5 **Rent and other real property income.** Subtract Line b from Line a and enter the difference in the appropriate column(s) of Line 5. Do not enter a number less than zero. **Do not include any part of the operating expenses entered on Line b as a deduction in Part V.** a. Gross receipts $ b. Ordinary and necessary operating expenses $ c. Rent and other real property income — Subtract Line b from Line a	$	$
6 Interest, dividends and royalties.	$	$
7 Pension and retirement income.	$	$
8 Any amounts paid by another person or entity, on a regular basis, for the household expenses of the debtor or the debtor's dependents, including child support paid for that purpose. Do not include alimony or separate maintenance payments or amounts paid by your spouse if Column B is completed. Each regular payment should be reported in only one column; if a payment is listed in Column A, do not report that payment in Column B.	$	$
9 Unemployment compensation. Enter the amount in the appropriate column(s) of Line 9. However, if you contend that unemployment compensation received by you or your spouse was a benefit under the Social Security Act, do not list the amount of such compensation in Column A or B, but instead state the amount in the space below: Unemployment compensation claimed to be a benefit under the Social Security Act Debtor $ _____ Spouse $ _____	$	$

B 22A (Official Form 22A) (Chapter 7) (12-10) — 3

10	**Income from all other sources.** Specify source and amount. If necessary, list additional sources on a separate page. Do not include alimony or separate maintenance payments paid by your spouse if Column B is completed, but include all other payments of alimony or separate maintenance. Do not include any benefits received under the Social Security Act or payments received as a victim of a war crime, crime against humanity, or as a victim of international or domestic terrorism.

a.		$
b.		$

Total and enter on Line 10 $ $

11	**Subtotal of Current Monthly Income for § 707(b)(7).** Add Lines 3 thru 10 in Column A, and, if Column B is completed, add Lines 3 through 10 in Column B. Enter the total(s). $ $
12	**Total Current Monthly Income for § 707(b)(7).** If Column B has been completed, add Line 11, Column A to Line 11, Column B, and enter the total. If Column B has not been completed, enter the amount from Line 11, Column A. $

Part III. APPLICATION OF § 707(b)(7) EXCLUSION

13	**Annualized Current Monthly Income for § 707(b)(7).** Multiply the amount from Line 12 by the number 12 and enter the result. $
14	**Applicable median family income.** Enter the median family income for the applicable state and household size. (This information is available by family size at www.usdoj.gov/ust/ or from the clerk of the bankruptcy court.) a. Enter debtor's state of residence: _____ b. Enter debtor's household size: _____ $
15	**Application of Section 707(b)(7).** Check the applicable box and proceed as directed. ☐ **The amount on Line 13 is less than or equal to the amount on Line 14.** Check the box for "The presumption does not arise" at the top of page 1 of this statement, and complete Part VIII; do not complete Parts IV, V, VI or VII. ☐ **The amount on Line 13 is more than the amount on Line 14.** Complete the remaining parts of this statement.

Complete Parts IV, V, VI, and VII of this statement only if required. (See Line 15.)

Part IV. CALCULATION OF CURRENT MONTHLY INCOME FOR § 707(b)(2)

16	Enter the amount from Line 12. $
17	**Marital adjustment.** If you checked the box at Line 2.c, enter on Line 17 the total of any income listed in Line 11, Column B that was NOT paid on a regular basis for the household expenses of the debtor or the debtor's dependents. Specify in the lines below the basis for excluding the Column B income (such as payment of the spouse's tax liability or the spouse's support of persons other than the debtor or the debtor's dependents) and the amount of income devoted to each purpose. If necessary, list additional adjustments on a separate page. If you did not check box at Line 2.c, enter zero.

a.		$
b.		$
c.		$

Total and enter on Line 17. $

18	**Current monthly income for § 707(b)(2).** Subtract Line 17 from Line 16 and enter the result. $

Form B22A

OFFICIAL FORMS

	Part V. CALCULATION OF DEDUCTIONS FROM INCOME	
	Subpart A: Deductions under Standards of the Internal Revenue Service (IRS)	
19A	**National Standards: food, clothing and other items.** Enter in Line 19A the "Total" amount from IRS National Standards for Food, Clothing and Other Items for the applicable number of persons. (This information is available at www.usdoj.gov/ust/ or from the clerk of the bankruptcy court.) The applicable number of persons is the number that would currently be allowed as exemptions on your federal income tax return, plus the number of any additional dependents whom you support.	$
19B	**National Standards: health care.** Enter in Line a1 below the amount from IRS National Standards for Out-of-Pocket Health Care for persons under 65 years of age, and in Line a2 the IRS National Standards for Out-of-Pocket Health Care for persons 65 years of age or older. (This information is available at www.usdoj.gov/ust/ or from the clerk of the bankruptcy court.) Enter in Line b1 the applicable number of persons who are under 65 years of age, and enter in Line b2 the applicable number of persons who are 65 years of age or older. (The applicable number of persons in each age category is the number in that category that would currently be allowed as exemptions on your federal income tax return, plus the number of any additional dependents whom you support.) Multiply Line a1 by Line b1 to obtain a total amount for persons under 65, and enter the result in Line c1. Multiply Line a2 by Line b2 to obtain a total amount for persons 65 and older, and enter the result in Line c2. Add Lines c1 and c2 to obtain a total health care amount, and enter the result in Line 19B.	

Persons under 65 years of age			Persons 65 years of age or older			
a1.	Allowance per person		a2.	Allowance per person		
b1.	Number of persons		b2.	Number of persons		
c1.	Subtotal		c2.	Subtotal		$

20A	**Local Standards: housing and utilities; non-mortgage expenses.** Enter the amount of the IRS Housing and Utilities Standards; non-mortgage expenses for the applicable county and family size. (This information is available at www.usdoj.gov/ust/ or from the clerk of the bankruptcy court). The applicable family size consists of the number that would currently be allowed as exemptions on your federal income tax return, plus the number of any additional dependents whom you support.	$
20B	**Local Standards: housing and utilities; mortgage/rent expense.** Enter, in Line a below, the amount of the IRS Housing and Utilities Standards; mortgage/rent expense for your county and family size (this information is available at www.usdoj.gov/ust/ or from the clerk of the bankruptcy court) (the applicable family size consists of the number that would currently be allowed as exemptions on your federal income tax return, plus the number of any additional dependents whom you support); enter on Line b the total of the Average Monthly Payments for any debts secured by your home, as stated in Line 42; subtract Line b from Line a and enter the result in Line 20B. **Do not enter an amount less than zero.**	

a.	IRS Housing and Utilities Standards; mortgage/rental expense	$	
b.	Average Monthly Payment for any debts secured by your home, if any, as stated in Line 42	$	
c.	Net mortgage/rental expense	Subtract Line b from Line a.	$

21	**Local Standards: housing and utilities; adjustment.** If you contend that the process set out in Lines 20A and 20B does not accurately compute the allowance to which you are entitled under the IRS Housing and Utilities Standards, enter any additional amount to which you contend you are entitled, and state the basis for your contention in the space below:	$

22A	**Local Standards: transportation; vehicle operation/public transportation expense.** You are entitled to an expense allowance in this category regardless of whether you pay the expenses of operating a vehicle and regardless of whether you use public transportation. Check the number of vehicles for which you pay the operating expenses or for which the operating expenses are included as a contribution to your household expenses in Line 8. ☐ 0 ☐ 1 ☐ 2 or more. If you checked 0, enter on Line 22A the "Public Transportation" amount from IRS Local Standards: Transportation. If you checked 1 or 2 or more, enter on Line 22A the "Operating Costs" amount from IRS Local Standards: Transportation for the applicable number of vehicles in the applicable Metropolitan Statistical Area or Census Region. (These amounts are available at www.usdoj.gov/ust/ or from the clerk of the bankruptcy court.)		$
22B	**Local Standards: transportation; additional public transportation expense.** If you pay the operating expenses for a vehicle and also use public transportation, and you contend that you are entitled to an additional deduction for your public transportation expenses, enter on Line 22B the "Public Transportation" amount from IRS Local Standards: Transportation. (This amount is available at www.usdoj.gov/ust/ or from the clerk of the bankruptcy court.)		$
23	**Local Standards: transportation ownership/lease expense; Vehicle 1.** Check the number of vehicles for which you claim an ownership/lease expense. (You may not claim an ownership/lease expense for more than two vehicles.) ☐ 1 ☐ 2 or more. Enter, in Line a below, the "Ownership Costs" for "One Car" from the IRS Local Standards: Transportation (available at www.usdoj.gov/ust/ or from the clerk of the bankruptcy court); enter in Line b the total of the Average Monthly Payments for any debts secured by Vehicle 1, as stated in Line 42; subtract Line b from Line a and enter the result in Line 23. **Do not enter an amount less than zero.**		
	a.	IRS Transportation Standards, Ownership Costs	$	
	b.	Average Monthly Payment for any debts secured by Vehicle 1, as stated in Line 42	$	
	c.	Net ownership/lease expense for Vehicle 1	Subtract Line b from Line a.	$
24	**Local Standards: transportation ownership/lease expense; Vehicle 2.** Complete this Line only if you checked the "2 or more" Box in Line 23. Enter, in Line a below, the "Ownership Costs" for "One Car" from the IRS Local Standards: Transportation (available at www.usdoj.gov/ust/ or from the clerk of the bankruptcy court); enter in Line b the total of the Average Monthly Payments for any debts secured by Vehicle 2, as stated in Line 42; subtract Line b from Line a and enter the result in Line 24. **Do not enter an amount less than zero.**		
	a.	IRS Transportation Standards, Ownership Costs	$	
	b.	Average Monthly Payment for any debts secured by Vehicle 2, as stated in Line 42	$	
	c.	Net ownership/lease expense for Vehicle 2	Subtract Line b from Line a.	$
25	**Other Necessary Expenses: taxes.** Enter the total average monthly expense that you actually incur for all federal, state and local taxes, other than real estate and sales taxes, such as income taxes, self-employment taxes, social-security taxes, and Medicare taxes. **Do not include real estate or sales taxes.**		$
26	**Other Necessary Expenses: involuntary deductions for employment.** Enter the total average monthly payroll deductions that are required for your employment, such as retirement contributions, union dues, and uniform costs. **Do not include discretionary amounts, such as voluntary 401(k) contributions.**		$
27	**Other Necessary Expenses: life insurance.** Enter total average monthly premiums that you actually pay for term life insurance for yourself. **Do not include premiums for insurance on your dependents, for whole life or for any other form of insurance.**		$
28	**Other Necessary Expenses: court-ordered payments.** Enter the total monthly amount that you are required to pay pursuant to the order of a court or administrative agency, such as spousal or child support payments. **Do not include payments on past due obligations included in Line 44.**		$

Form B22A

29	**Other Necessary Expenses: education for employment or for a physically or mentally challenged child.** Enter the total average monthly amount that you actually expend for education that is a condition of employment and for education that is required for a physically or mentally challenged dependent child for whom no public education providing similar services is available.	$
30	**Other Necessary Expenses: childcare.** Enter the total average monthly amount that you actually expend on childcare—such as baby-sitting, day care, nursery and preschool. **Do not include other educational payments.**	$
31	**Other Necessary Expenses: health care.** Enter the total average monthly amount that you actually expend on health care that is required for the health and welfare of yourself or your dependents, that is not reimbursed by insurance or paid by a health savings account, and that is in excess of the amount entered in Line 19B. **Do not include payments for health insurance or health savings accounts listed in Line 34.**	$
32	**Other Necessary Expenses: telecommunication services.** Enter the total average monthly amount that you actually pay for telecommunication services other than your basic home telephone and cell phone service—such as pagers, call waiting, caller id, special long distance, or internet service—to the extent necessary for your health and welfare or that of your dependents. **Do not include any amount previously deducted.**	$
33	**Total Expenses Allowed under IRS Standards.** Enter the total of Lines 19 through 32.	$

Subpart B: Additional Living Expense Deductions
Note: Do not include any expenses that you have listed in Lines 19-32

34	**Health Insurance, Disability Insurance, and Health Savings Account Expenses.** List the monthly expenses in the categories set out in lines a-c below that are reasonably necessary for yourself, your spouse, or your dependents.	

	a.	Health Insurance	$
	b.	Disability Insurance	$
	c.	Health Savings Account	$

Total and enter on Line 34 $

If you do not actually expend this total amount, state your actual total average monthly expenditures in the space below:
$ _____

35	**Continued contributions to the care of household or family members.** Enter the total average actual monthly expenses that you will continue to pay for the reasonable and necessary care and support of an elderly, chronically ill, or disabled member of your household or member of your immediate family who is unable to pay for such expenses.	$
36	**Protection against family violence.** Enter the total average reasonably necessary monthly expenses that you actually incurred to maintain the safety of your family under the Family Violence Prevention and Services Act or other applicable federal law. The nature of these expenses is required to be kept confidential by the court.	$
37	**Home energy costs.** Enter the total average monthly amount, in excess of the allowance specified by IRS Local Standards for Housing and Utilities, that you actually expend for home energy costs. **You must provide your case trustee with documentation of your actual expenses, and you must demonstrate that the additional amount claimed is reasonable and necessary.**	$
38	**Education expenses for dependent children less than 18.** Enter the total average monthly expenses that you actually incur, not to exceed $147.92* per child, for attendance at a private or public elementary or secondary school by your dependent children less than 18 years of age. **You must provide your case trustee with documentation of your actual expenses, and you must explain why the amount claimed is reasonable and necessary and not already accounted for in the IRS Standards.**	$

Amount subject to adjustment on 4/01/13, and every three years thereafter with respect to cases commenced on or after the date of adjustment.

39	**Additional food and clothing expense.** Enter the total average monthly amount by which your food and clothing expenses exceed the combined allowances for food and clothing (apparel and services) in the IRS National Standards, not to exceed 5% of those combined allowances. (This information is available at www.usdoj.gov/ust/ or from the clerk of the bankruptcy court.) **You must demonstrate that the additional amount claimed is reasonable and necessary.**	$
40	**Continued charitable contributions.** Enter the amount that you will continue to contribute in the form of cash or financial instruments to a charitable organization as defined in 26 U.S.C. § 170(c)(1)-(2).	$
41	**Total Additional Expense Deductions under § 707(b).** Enter the total of Lines 34 through 40	$

Subpart C: Deductions for Debt Payment

42	**Future payments on secured claims.** For each of your debts that is secured by an interest in property that you own, list the name of the creditor, identify the property securing the debt, state the Average Monthly Payment, and check whether the payment includes taxes or insurance. The Average Monthly Payment is the total of all amounts scheduled as contractually due to each Secured Creditor in the 60 months following the filing of the bankruptcy case, divided by 60. If necessary, list additional entries on a separate page. Enter the total of the Average Monthly Payments on Line 42.			

	Name of Creditor	Property Securing the Debt	Average Monthly Payment	Does payment include taxes or insurance?
a.			$	☐ yes ☐ no
b.			$	☐ yes ☐ no
c.			$	☐ yes ☐ no
			Total: Add Lines a, b and c.	$

43	**Other payments on secured claims.** If any of debts listed in Line 42 are secured by your primary residence, a motor vehicle, or other property necessary for your support or the support of your dependents, you may include in your deduction 1/60th of any amount (the "cure amount") that you must pay the creditor in addition to the payments listed in Line 42, in order to maintain possession of the property. The cure amount would include any sums in default that must be paid in order to avoid repossession or foreclosure. List and total any such amounts in the following chart. If necessary, list additional entries on a separate page.	

	Name of Creditor	Property Securing the Debt	1/60th of the Cure Amount
a.			$
b.			$
c.			$
		Total: Add Lines a, b and c	$

44	**Payments on prepetition priority claims.** Enter the total amount, divided by 60, of all priority claims, such as priority tax, child support and alimony claims, for which you were liable at the time of your bankruptcy filing. **Do not include current obligations, such as those set out in Line 28.**	$

B 22A (Official Form 22A) (Chapter 7) (12/10)   8

45	**Chapter 13 administrative expenses.** If you are eligible to file a case under chapter 13, complete the following chart, multiply the amount in line a by the amount in line b, and enter the resulting administrative expense.		
	a.	Projected average monthly chapter 13 plan payment.	$
	b.	Current multiplier for your district as determined under schedules issued by the Executive Office for United States Trustees. (This information is available at www.usdoj.gov/ust/ or from the clerk of the bankruptcy court.)	x
	c.	Average monthly administrative expense of chapter 13 case	Total: Multiply Lines a and b	$

46	**Total Deductions for Debt Payment.** Enter the total of Lines 42 through 45.	$

Subpart D: Total Deductions from Income		
47	**Total of all deductions allowed under § 707(b)(2).** Enter the total of Lines 33, 41, and 46.	$

Part VI. DETERMINATION OF § 707(b)(2) PRESUMPTION		
48	**Enter the amount from Line 18** (Current monthly income for § 707(b)(2))	$
49	**Enter the amount from Line 47** (Total of all deductions allowed under § 707(b)(2))	$
50	**Monthly disposable income under § 707(b)(2).** Subtract Line 49 from Line 48 and enter the result	$
51	**60-month disposable income under § 707(b)(2).** Multiply the amount in Line 50 by the number 60 and enter the result.	$
52	**Initial presumption determination.** Check the applicable box and proceed as directed.	
	☐ **The amount on Line 51 is less than $7,025*.** Check the box for "The presumption does not arise" at the top of page 1 of this statement, and complete the verification in Part VIII. Do not complete the remainder of Part VI.	
	☐ **The amount set forth on Line 51 is more than $11,725*.** Check the box for "The presumption arises" at the top of page 1 of this statement, and complete the verification in Part VIII. You may also complete Part VII. Do not complete the remainder of Part VI.	
	☐ **The amount on Line 51 is at least $7,025*, but not more than $11,725*.** Complete the remainder of Part VI (Lines 53 through 55).	
53	**Enter the amount of your total non-priority unsecured debt**	$
54	**Threshold debt payment amount.** Multiply the amount in Line 53 by the number 0.25 and enter the result.	$
55	**Secondary presumption determination.** Check the applicable box and proceed as directed.	
	☐ **The amount on Line 51 is less than the amount on Line 54.** Check the box for "The presumption does not arise" at the top of page 1 of this statement, and complete the verification in Part VIII.	
	☐ **The amount on Line 51 is equal to or greater than the amount on Line 54.** Check the box for "The presumption arises" at the top of page 1 of this statement, and complete the verification in Part VIII. You may also complete Part VII.	

Part VII: ADDITIONAL EXPENSE CLAIMS		
56	**Other Expenses.** List and describe any monthly expenses, not otherwise stated in this form, that are required for the health and welfare of you and your family and that you contend should be an additional deduction from your current monthly income under § 707(b)(2)(A)(ii)(I). If necessary, list additional sources on a separate page. All figures should reflect your average monthly expense for each item. Total the expenses.		

	Expense Description	Monthly Amount
a.		$
b.		$
c.		$
	Total: Add Lines a, b and c	$

*Amounts are subject to adjustment on 4/01/13, and every three years thereafter with respect to cases commenced on or after the date of adjustment.

Part VIII: VERIFICATION

| 57 | I declare under penalty of perjury that the information provided in this statement is true and correct. *(If this is a joint case, both debtors must sign.)*

 Date: _____   Signature: _____
 (Debtor)

 Date: _____   Signature: _____
 (Joint Debtor, if any) |

Form B22B   OFFICIAL FORMS

In re _____
                Debtor(s)

Case Number: _____
                (If known)

CHAPTER 11 STATEMENT OF CURRENT MONTHLY INCOME

In addition to Schedules I and J, this statement must be completed by every individual chapter 11 debtor, whether or not filing jointly. Joint debtors may complete one statement only.

Part I. CALCULATION OF CURRENT MONTHLY INCOME			
1	**Marital/filing status.** Check the box that applies and complete the balance of this part of this statement as directed. a. ☐ **Unmarried. Complete only Column A ("Debtor's Income") for Lines 2-10.** b. ☐ **Married, not filing jointly. Complete only Column A ("Debtor's Income") for Lines 2-10.** c. ☐ **Married, filing jointly. Complete both Column A ("Debtor's Income") and Column B ("Spouse's Income") for Lines 2-10.**		
	All figures must reflect average monthly income received from all sources, derived during the six calendar months prior to filing the bankruptcy case, ending on the last day of the month before the filing. If the amount of monthly income varied during the six months, you must divide the six-month total by six, and enter the result on the appropriate line.	**Column A** Debtor's Income	**Column B** Spouse's Income
2	**Gross wages, salary, tips, bonuses, overtime, commissions.**	$	$
3	**Net income from the operation of a business, profession, or farm.** Subtract Line b from Line a and enter the difference in the appropriate column(s) of Line 3. If more than one business, profession or farm, enter aggregate numbers and provide details on an attachment. Do not enter a number less than zero. a. Gross receipts — $ b. Ordinary and necessary business expenses — $ c. Business income — Subtract Line b from Line a.	$	$
4	**Net rental and other real property income.** Subtract Line b from Line a and enter the difference in the appropriate column(s) of Line 4. Do not enter a number less than zero. a. Gross receipts — $ b. Ordinary and necessary operating expenses — $ c. Rent and other real property income — Subtract Line b from Line a.	$	$
5	**Interest, dividends, and royalties.**	$	$
6	**Pension and retirement income.**	$	$
7	**Any amounts paid by another person or entity, on a regular basis, for the household expenses of the debtor or the debtor's dependents, including child support paid for that purpose.** Do not include alimony or separate maintenance payments or amounts paid by the debtor's spouse if Column B is completed. Each regular payment should be reported in only one column; if a payment is listed in Column A, do not report that payment in Column B.	$	$
8	**Unemployment compensation.** Enter the amount in the appropriate column(s) of Line 8. However, if you contend that unemployment compensation received by you or your spouse was a benefit under the Social Security Act, do not list the amount of such compensation in Column A or B, but instead state the amount in the space below: Unemployment compensation claimed to be a benefit under the Social Security Act — Debtor $ _____ Spouse $ _____	$	$

9	**Income from all other sources.** Specify source and amount. If necessary, list additional sources on a separate page. Total and enter on Line 9. **Do not include alimony or separate maintenance payments paid by your spouse if Column B is completed, but include all other payments of alimony or separate maintenance. Do not include** any benefits received under the Social Security Act or payments received as a victim of a war crime, crime against humanity, or as a victim of international or domestic terrorism. a. _____ $ b. _____ $	$	$
10	**Subtotal of current monthly income.** Add Lines 2 thru 9 in Column A, and, if Column B is completed, add Lines 2 through 9 in Column B. Enter the total(s).	$	$
11	**Total current monthly income.** If Column B has been completed, add Line 10, Column A to Line 10, Column B, and enter the total. If Column B has not been completed, enter the amount from Line 10, Column A.	$	
Part II: VERIFICATION			
12	I declare under penalty of perjury that the information provided in this statement is true and correct. *(If this a joint case, both debtors must sign.)* Date: _____ Signature: _____ *(Debtor)* Date: _____ Signature: _____ *(Joint Debtor, if any)*		

B 22C (Official Form 22C) (Chapter 13) (12/10)

In re _____
          Debtor(s)

Case Number: _____
          (If known)

<table>
<tr><td colspan="2">According to the calculations required by this statement:</td></tr>
<tr><td>☐</td><td>The applicable commitment period is 3 years.</td></tr>
<tr><td>☐</td><td>The applicable commitment period is 5 years.</td></tr>
<tr><td>☐</td><td>Disposable income is determined under § 1325(b)(3).</td></tr>
<tr><td>☐</td><td>Disposable income is not determined under § 1325(b)(3).</td></tr>
<tr><td colspan="2">(Check the boxes as directed in Lines 17 and 23 of this statement.)</td></tr>
</table>

**CHAPTER 13 STATEMENT OF CURRENT MONTHLY INCOME
AND CALCULATION OF COMMITMENT PERIOD AND DISPOSABLE INCOME**

In addition to Schedules I and J, this statement must be completed by every individual chapter 13 debtor, whether or not filing jointly. Joint debtors may complete one statement only.

	Part I. REPORT OF INCOME		
1	**Marital/filing status.** Check the box that applies and complete the balance of this part of this statement as directed. a. ☐ Unmarried. **Complete only Column A ("Debtor's Income") for Lines 2-10.** b. ☐ Married. **Complete both Column A ("Debtor's Income") and Column B ("Spouse's Income") for Lines 2-10.**		
	All figures must reflect average monthly income received from all sources, derived during the six calendar months prior to filing the bankruptcy case, ending on the last day of the month before the filing. If the amount of monthly income varied during the six months, you must divide the six-month total by six, and enter the result on the appropriate line.	**Column A** Debtor's Income	**Column B** Spouse's Income
2	**Gross wages, salary, tips, bonuses, overtime, commissions.**	$	$
3	**Income from the operation of a business, profession, or farm.** Subtract Line b from Line a and enter the difference in the appropriate column(s) of Line 3. If you operate more than one business, profession or farm, enter aggregate numbers and provide details on an attachment. Do not enter a number less than zero. **Do not include any part of the business expenses entered on Line b as a deduction in Part IV.** a. Gross receipts $ b. Ordinary and necessary business expenses $ c. Business income Subtract Line b from Line a	$	$
4	**Rent and other real property income.** Subtract Line b from Line a and enter the difference in the appropriate column(s) of Line 4. Do not enter a number less than zero. **Do not include any part of the operating expenses entered on Line b as a deduction in Part IV.** a. Gross receipts $ b. Ordinary and necessary operating expenses $ c. Rent and other real property income Subtract Line b from Line a	$	$
5	**Interest, dividends, and royalties.**	$	$
6	**Pension and retirement income.**	$	$
7	**Any amounts paid by another person or entity, on a regular basis, for the household expenses of the debtor or the debtor's dependents, including child support paid for that purpose.** Do not include alimony or separate maintenance payments or amounts paid by the debtor's spouse. Each regular payment should be reported in only one column; if a payment is listed in Column A, do not report that payment in Column B.	$	$

Form B22C

B 22C (Official Form 22C) (Chapter 13) (12/10)   2

8	**Unemployment compensation.** Enter the amount in the appropriate column(s) of Line 8. However, if you contend that unemployment compensation received by you or your spouse was a benefit under the Social Security Act, do not list the amount of such compensation in Column A or B, but instead state the amount in the space below: Unemployment compensation claimed to be a benefit under the Social Security Act Debtor $ _____ Spouse $ _____	$	$
9	**Income from all other sources.** Specify source and amount. If necessary, list additional sources on a separate page. Total and enter on Line 9. **Do not include alimony or separate maintenance payments paid by your spouse, but include all other payments of alimony or separate maintenance. Do not include any benefits received under the Social Security Act or** payments received as a victim of a war crime, crime against humanity, or as a victim of international or domestic terrorism. a. $ b. $	$	$
10	**Subtotal.** Add Lines 2 thru 9 in Column A, and, if Column B is completed, add Lines 2 through 9 in Column B. Enter the total(s).	$	$
11	**Total.** If Column B has been completed, add Line 10, Column A to Line 10, Column B, and enter the total. If Column B has not been completed, enter the amount from Line 10, Column A.	$	

	Part II. CALCULATION OF § 1325(b)(4) COMMITMENT PERIOD	
12	Enter the amount from Line 11.	$
13	**Marital adjustment.** If you are married, but are not filing jointly with your spouse, AND if you contend that calculation of the commitment period under § 1325(b)(4) does not require inclusion of the income of your spouse, enter on Line 13 the amount of the income listed in Line 10, Column B that was NOT paid on a regular basis for the household expenses of you or your dependents and specify, in the lines below, the basis for excluding this income (such as payment of the spouse's tax liability or the spouse's support of persons other than the debtor or the debtor's dependents) and the amount of income devoted to each purpose. If necessary, list additional adjustments on a separate page. If the conditions for entering this adjustment do not apply, enter zero. a. $ b. $ c. $ Total and enter on Line 13.	$
14	**Subtract Line 13 from Line 12 and enter the result.**	$
15	**Annualized current monthly income for § 1325(b)(4).** Multiply the amount from Line 14 by the number 12 and enter the result.	$
16	**Applicable median family income.** Enter the median family income for applicable state and household size. (This information is available by family size at www.usdoj.gov/ust/ or from the clerk of the bankruptcy court.) a. Enter debtor's state of residence: _____ b. Enter debtor's household size: _____	$
17	**Application of § 1325(b)(4).** Check the applicable box and proceed as directed. ☐ **The amount on Line 15 is less than the amount on Line 16.** Check the box for "The applicable commitment period is 3 years" at the top of page 1 of this statement and continue with this statement. ☐ **The amount on Line 15 is not less than the amount on Line 16.** Check the box for "The applicable commitment period is 5 years" at the top of page 1 of this statement and continue with this statement.	

	Part III. APPLICATION OF § 1325(b)(3) FOR DETERMINING DISPOSABLE INCOME	
18	Enter the amount from Line 11.	$

19	**Marital adjustment.** If you are married, but are not filing jointly with your spouse, enter on Line 19 the total of any income listed in Line 10, Column B that was NOT paid on a regular basis for the household expenses of the debtor or the debtor's dependents. Specify in the lines below the basis for excluding the Column B income (such as payment of the spouse's tax liability or the spouse's support of persons other than the debtor or the debtor's dependents) and the amount of income devoted to each purpose. If necessary, list additional adjustments on a separate page. If the conditions for entering this adjustment do not apply, enter zero.	
	a.	$	
	b.	$	
	c.	$	
	Total and enter on Line 19.	$
20	**Current monthly income for § 1325(b)(3).** Subtract Line 19 from Line 18 and enter the result.	$
21	**Annualized current monthly income for § 1325(b)(3).** Multiply the amount from Line 20 by the number 12 and enter the result.	$
22	**Applicable median family income.** Enter the amount from Line 16.	$
23	**Application of § 1325(b)(3).** Check the applicable box and proceed as directed. ☐ **The amount on Line 21 is more than the amount on Line 22.** Check the box for "Disposable income is determined under § 1325(b)(3)" at the top of page 1 of this statement and complete the remaining parts of this statement. ☐ **The amount on Line 21 is not more than the amount on Line 22.** Check the box for "Disposable income is not determined under § 1325(b)(3)" at the top of page 1 of this statement and complete Part VII of this statement. **Do not complete Parts IV, V, or VI.**	

Part IV. CALCULATION OF DEDUCTIONS FROM INCOME
Subpart A: Deductions under Standards of the Internal Revenue Service (IRS)

24A	**National Standards: food, apparel and services, housekeeping supplies, personal care, and miscellaneous.** Enter in Line 24A the "Total" amount from IRS National Standards for Allowable Living Expenses for the applicable number of persons. (This information is available at www.usdoj.gov/ust/ or from the clerk of the bankruptcy court.) The applicable number of persons is the number that would currently be allowed as exemptions on your federal income tax return, plus the number of any additional dependents whom you support.	$

24B	**National Standards: health care.** Enter in Line a1 below the amount from IRS National Standards for Out-of-Pocket Health Care for persons under 65 years of age, and in Line a2 the IRS National Standards for Out-of-Pocket Health Care for persons 65 years of age or older. (This information is available at www.usdoj.gov/ust/ or from the clerk of the bankruptcy court.) Enter in Line b1 the applicable number of persons who are under 65 years of age, and enter in Line b2 the applicable number of persons who are 65 years of age or older. (The applicable number of persons in each age category is the number in that category that would currently be allowed as exemptions on your federal income tax return, plus the number of any additional dependents whom you support.) Multiply Line a1 by Line b1 to obtain a total amount for persons under 65, and enter the result in Line c1. Multiply Line a2 by Line b2 to obtain a total amount for persons 65 and older, and enter the result in Line c2. Add Lines c1 and c2 to obtain a total health care amount, and enter the result in Line 24B.	

Persons under 65 years of age		Persons 65 years of age or older		
a1.	Allowance per person	a2.	Allowance per person	
b1.	Number of persons	b2.	Number of persons	
c1.	Subtotal	c2.	Subtotal	$

25A	**Local Standards: housing and utilities; non-mortgage expenses.** Enter the amount of the IRS Housing and Utilities Standards; non-mortgage expenses for the applicable county and family size. (This information is available at www.usdoj.gov/ust/ or from the clerk of the bankruptcy court). The applicable family size consists of the number that would currently be allowed as exemptions on your federal income tax return, plus the number of any additional dependents whom you support.	$

Form B22C   OFFICIAL FORMS

25B	**Local Standards: housing and utilities; mortgage/rent expense.** Enter, in Line a below, the amount of the IRS Housing and Utilities Standards; mortgage/rent expense for your county and family size (this information is available at www.usdoj.gov/ust/ or from the clerk of the bankruptcy court) (the applicable family size consists of the number that would currently be allowed as exemptions on your federal income tax return, plus the number of any additional dependents whom you support); enter on Line b the total of the Average Monthly Payments for any debts secured by your home, as stated in Line 47; subtract Line b from Line a and enter the result in Line 25B. **Do not enter an amount less than zero.**		
	a.	IRS Housing and Utilities Standards; mortgage/rent expense	$	
	b.	Average Monthly Payment for any debts secured by your home, if any, as stated in Line 47	$	
	c.	Net mortgage/rental expense	Subtract Line b from Line a.	$

26	**Local Standards: housing and utilities; adjustment.** If you contend that the process set out in Lines 25A and 25B does not accurately compute the allowance to which you are entitled under the IRS Housing and Utilities Standards, enter any additional amount to which you contend you are entitled, and state the basis for your contention in the space below: _____ _____ _____	$

27A	**Local Standards: transportation; vehicle operation/public transportation expense.** You are entitled to an expense allowance in this category regardless of whether you pay the expenses of operating a vehicle and regardless of whether you use public transportation. Check the number of vehicles for which you pay the operating expenses or for which the operating expenses are included as a contribution to your household expenses in Line 7. ☐ 0 ☐ 1 ☐ 2 or more. If you checked 0, enter on Line 27A the "Public Transportation" amount from IRS Local Standards: Transportation. If you checked 1 or 2 or more, enter on Line 27A the "Operating Costs" amount from IRS Local Standards: Transportation for the applicable number of vehicles in the applicable Metropolitan Statistical Area or Census Region. (These amounts are available at www.usdoj.gov/ust/ or from the clerk of the bankruptcy court.)	$

27B	**Local Standards: transportation; additional public transportation expense.** If you pay the operating expenses for a vehicle and also use public transportation, and you contend that you are entitled to an additional deduction for your public transportation expenses, enter on Line 27B the "Public Transportation" amount from IRS Local Standards: Transportation. (This amount is available at www.usdoj.gov/ust/ or from the clerk of the bankruptcy court.)	$

28	**Local Standards: transportation ownership/lease expense; Vehicle 1.** Check the number of vehicles for which you claim an ownership/lease expense. (You may not claim an ownership/lease expense for more than two vehicles.) ☐ 1 ☐ 2 or more. Enter, in Line a below, the "Ownership Costs" for "One Car" from the IRS Local Standards: Transportation (available at www.usdoj.gov/ust/ or from the clerk of the bankruptcy court); enter in Line b the total of the Average Monthly Payments for any debts secured by Vehicle 1, as stated in Line 47; subtract Line b from Line a and enter the result in Line 28. **Do not enter an amount less than zero.**		
	a.	IRS Transportation Standards, Ownership Costs	$	
	b.	Average Monthly Payment for any debts secured by Vehicle 1, as stated in Line 47	$	
	c.	Net ownership/lease expense for Vehicle 1	Subtract Line b from Line a.	$

B 22C (Official Form 22C) (Chapter 13) (12/10)   5

29	Local Standards: transportation ownership/lease expense; Vehicle 2. Complete this Line only if you checked the "2 or more" Box in Line 28. Enter, in Line a below, the "Ownership Costs" for "One Car" from the IRS Local Standards: Transportation (available at www.usdoj.gov/ust/ or from the clerk of the bankruptcy court); enter in Line b the total of the Average Monthly Payments for any debts secured by Vehicle 2, as stated in Line 47; subtract Line b from Line a and enter the result in Line 29. **Do not enter an amount less than zero.**			
	a.	IRS Transportation Standards, Ownership Costs	$	
	b.	Average Monthly Payment for any debts secured by Vehicle 2, as stated in Line 47	$	
	c.	Net ownership/lease expense for Vehicle 2	Subtract Line b from Line a.	$
30	**Other Necessary Expenses: taxes.** Enter the total average monthly expense that you actually incur for all federal, state, and local taxes, other than real estate and sales taxes, such as income taxes, self-employment taxes, social-security taxes, and Medicare taxes. **Do not include real estate or sales taxes.**			$
31	**Other Necessary Expenses: involuntary deductions for employment.** Enter the total average monthly deductions that are required for your employment, such as mandatory retirement contributions, union dues, and uniform costs. **Do not include discretionary amounts, such as voluntary 401(k) contributions.**			$
32	**Other Necessary Expenses: life insurance.** Enter total average monthly premiums that you actually pay for term life insurance for yourself. **Do not include premiums for insurance on your dependents, for whole life or for any other form of insurance.**			$
33	**Other Necessary Expenses: court-ordered payments.** Enter the total monthly amount that you are required to pay pursuant to the order of a court or administrative agency, such as spousal or child support payments. **Do not include payments on past due obligations included in Line 49.**			$
34	**Other Necessary Expenses: education for employment or for a physically or mentally challenged child.** Enter the total average monthly amount that you actually expend for education that is a condition of employment and for education that is required for a physically or mentally challenged dependent child for whom no public education providing similar services is available.			$
35	**Other Necessary Expenses: childcare.** Enter the total average monthly amount that you actually expend on childcare—such as baby-sitting, day care, nursery and preschool. **Do not include other educational payments.**			$
36	**Other Necessary Expenses: health care.** Enter the total average monthly amount that you actually expend on health care that is required for the health and welfare of yourself or your dependents, that is not reimbursed by insurance or paid by a health savings account, and that is in excess of the amount entered in Line 24B. **Do not include payments for health insurance or health savings accounts listed in Line 39.**			$
37	**Other Necessary Expenses: telecommunication services.** Enter the total average monthly amount that you actually pay for telecommunication services other than your basic home telephone and cell phone service—such as pagers, call waiting, caller id, special long distance, or internet service—to the extent necessary for your health and welfare or that of your dependents. **Do not include any amount previously deducted.**			$
38	**Total Expenses Allowed under IRS Standards.** Enter the total of Lines 24 through 37.			$
	Subpart B: Additional Living Expense Deductions **Note: Do not include any expenses that you have listed in Lines 24-37**			

Form B22C

B 22C (Official Form 22C) (Chapter 13) (12/10)
6

	Health Insurance, Disability Insurance, and Health Savings Account Expenses. List the monthly expenses in the categories set out in lines a-c below that are reasonably necessary for yourself, your spouse, or your dependents.				
39	a.	Health Insurance	$		
	b.	Disability Insurance	$		
	c.	Health Savings Account	$		
	Total and enter on Line 39				$
	If you do not actually expend this total amount, state your actual total average monthly expenditures in the space below: $ _____				
40	**Continued contributions to the care of household or family members.** Enter the total average actual monthly expenses that you will continue to pay for the reasonable and necessary care and support of an elderly, chronically ill, or disabled member of your household or member of your immediate family who is unable to pay for such expenses. **Do not include payments listed in Line 34.**				$
41	**Protection against family violence.** Enter the total average reasonably necessary monthly expenses that you actually incur to maintain the safety of your family under the Family Violence Prevention and Services Act or other applicable federal law. The nature of these expenses is required to be kept confidential by the court.				$
42	**Home energy costs.** Enter the total average monthly amount, in excess of the allowance specified by IRS Local Standards for Housing and Utilities that you actually expend for home energy costs. **You must provide your case trustee with documentation of your actual expenses, and you must demonstrate that the additional amount claimed is reasonable and necessary.**				$
43	**Education expenses for dependent children under 18.** Enter the total average monthly expenses that you actually incur, not to exceed $147.92 per child, for attendance at a private or public elementary or secondary school by your dependent children less than 18 years of age. **You must provide your case trustee with documentation of your actual expenses, and you must explain why the amount claimed is reasonable and necessary and not already accounted for in the IRS Standards.**				$
44	**Additional food and clothing expense.** Enter the total average monthly amount by which your food and clothing expenses exceed the combined allowances for food and clothing (apparel and services) in the IRS National Standards, not to exceed 5% of those combined allowances. (This information is available at www.usdoj.gov/ust/ or from the clerk of the bankruptcy court.) **You must demonstrate that the additional amount claimed is reasonable and necessary.**				$
45	**Charitable contributions.** Enter the amount reasonably necessary for you to expend each month on charitable contributions in the form of cash or financial instruments to a charitable organization as defined in 26 U.S.C. § 170(c)(1)-(2). **Do not include any amount in excess of 15% of your gross monthly income.**				$
46	**Total Additional Expense Deductions under § 707(b).** Enter the total of Lines 39 through 45.				$
	Subpart C: Deductions for Debt Payment				
47	**Future payments on secured claims.** For each of your debts that is secured by an interest in property that you own, list the name of the creditor, identify the property securing the debt, state the Average Monthly Payment, and check whether the payment includes taxes or insurance. The Average Monthly Payment is the total of all amounts scheduled as contractually due to each Secured Creditor in the 60 months following the filing of the bankruptcy case, divided by 60. If necessary, list additional entries on a separate page. Enter the total of the Average Monthly Payments on Line 47.				

47		Name of Creditor	Property Securing the Debt	Average Monthly Payment	Does payment include taxes or insurance?	
	a.			$	☐ yes ☐ no	
	b.			$	☐ yes ☐ no	
	c.			$	☐ yes ☐ no	
				Total: Add Lines a, b, and c		$

Complete Annotation Materials, see Title 11 U.S.C.A.

944

B 22C (Official Form 22C) (Chapter 13) (12/10)   7

	Other payments on secured claims. If any of debts listed in Line 47 are secured by your primary residence, a motor vehicle, or other property necessary for your support or the support of your dependents, you may include in your deduction 1/60th of any amount (the "cure amount") that you must pay the creditor in addition to the payments listed in Line 47, in order to maintain possession of the property. The cure amount would include any sums in default that must be paid in order to avoid repossession or foreclosure. List and total any such amounts in the following chart. If necessary, list additional entries on a separate page.			
48				

	Name of Creditor	Property Securing the Debt	1/60th of the Cure Amount	
a.			$	
b.			$	
c.			$	
			Total: Add Lines a, b, and c	$

49	**Payments on prepetition priority claims.** Enter the total amount, divided by 60, of all priority claims, such as priority tax, child support and alimony claims, for which you were liable at the time of your bankruptcy filing. **Do not include current obligations, such as those set out in Line 33.**	$

50	**Chapter 13 administrative expenses.** Multiply the amount in Line a by the amount in Line b, and enter the resulting administrative expense.	

a.	Projected average monthly chapter 13 plan payment.	$	
b.	Current multiplier for your district as determined under schedules issued by the Executive Office for United States Trustees. (This information is available at www.usdoj.gov/ust/ or from the clerk of the bankruptcy court.)	x	
c.	Average monthly administrative expense of chapter 13 case	Total: Multiply Lines a and b	$

51	**Total Deductions for Debt Payment.** Enter the total of Lines 47 through 50.	$

	Subpart D: Total Deductions from Income	
52	**Total of all deductions from income.** Enter the total of Lines 38, 46, and 51.	$

	Part V. DETERMINATION OF DISPOSABLE INCOME UNDER § 1325(b)(2)	
53	**Total current monthly income.** Enter the amount from Line 20.	$
54	**Support income.** Enter the monthly average of any child support payments, foster care payments, or disability payments for a dependent child, reported in Part I, that you received in accordance with applicable nonbankruptcy law, to the extent reasonably necessary to be expended for such child.	$
55	**Qualified retirement deductions.** Enter the monthly total of (a) all amounts withheld by your employer from wages as contributions for qualified retirement plans, as specified in § 541(b)(7) and (b) all required repayments of loans from retirement plans, as specified in § 362(b)(19).	$
56	**Total of all deductions allowed under § 707(b)(2).** Enter the amount from Line 52.	$
57	**Deduction for special circumstances.** If there are special circumstances that justify additional expenses for which there is no reasonable alternative, describe the special circumstances and the resulting expenses in lines a-c below. If necessary, list additional entries on a separate page. Total the expenses and enter the total in Line 57. **You must provide your case trustee with documentation of these expenses and you must provide a detailed explanation of the special circumstances that make such expenses necessary and reasonable.**	

	Nature of special circumstances	Amount of expense	
a.		$	
b.		$	
c.		$	
		Total: Add Lines a, b, and c	$

B 22C (Official Form 22C) (Chapter 13) (12/10)   8

58	**Total adjustments to determine disposable income.** Add the amounts on Lines 54, 55, 56, and 57 and enter the result.	$
59	**Monthly Disposable Income Under § 1325(b)(2).** Subtract Line 58 from Line 53 and enter the result.	$

	Part VI: ADDITIONAL EXPENSE CLAIMS	
60	**Other Expenses.** List and describe any monthly expenses, not otherwise stated in this form, that are required for the health and welfare of you and your family and that you contend should be an additional deduction from your current monthly income under § 707(b)(2)(A)(ii)(I). If necessary, list additional sources on a separate page. All figures should reflect your average monthly expense for each item. Total the expenses.	

	Expense Description	Monthly Amount	
a.		$	
b.		$	
c.		$	
	Total: Add Lines a, b, and c	$	

	Part VII: VERIFICATION	
61	I declare under penalty of perjury that the information provided in this statement is true and correct. *(If this is a joint case, both debtors must sign.)*	

Date: _____   Signature: _____
                                        (Debtor)

Date: _____   Signature: _____
                                        (Joint Debtor, if any)

Form 22

(Added Aug. 11, 2005, eff. Oct. 17, 2005 and amended Apr. 1, 2007; Jan., 2008; Nov. 18, 2008, eff. Dec. 19, 2008; Apr. 1, 2010; Dec. 1, 2010.)

ADVISORY COMMITTEE NOTES
2005 Amendment

A. Overview

Among the changes introduced by the Bankruptcy Abuse Prevention and Consumer Protection Act of 2005 are interlocking provisions defining "current monthly income" and establishing a means test to determine whether relief under Chapter 7 should be presumed abusive. Current monthly income ("CMI") is defined in § 101(10A) of the Code, and the means test is set out in § 707(b)(2). These provisions have a variety of applications. In Chapter 7, if the debtor's CMI exceeds a defined level the debtor is subject to the means test, and § 707(b)(2)(C) specifically requires debtors to file a statement of CMI and calculations to determine the applicability of the means test presumption. In Chapters 11 and 13, CMI provides the starting point for determining the disposable income that must be contributed to payment of unsecured creditors. Moreover, Chapter 13 debtors with CMI above defined levels are required by § 1325(b)(3) to complete the means test in order to determine the amount of their monthly disposable income, and pursuant to § 1325(b)(4), the level of CMI determines the "applicable commitment period" over which projected disposable income must be paid to unsecured creditors.

To provide for the reporting and calculation of CMI and for the completion of the means test where required, three separate official forms have been created—one for Chapter 7, one for Chapter 11, and one for Chapter 13. This note first describes the calculation of CMI that is common to all three of the forms, next describes the means test as set out in the Chapter 7 and 13 forms, and finally addresses particular issues that are unique to each of the separate forms.

B. Calculation of CMI

Although Chapters 7, 11, and 13 use CMI for different purposes, the basic computation is the same in each. As defined in § 101(10A), CMI is the monthly average of certain income that the debtor (and in a joint case, the debtor's spouse) received in the six calendar months before the bankruptcy filing. The definition includes in this average (1) income from all sources, whether or not taxable, and (2) any amount paid by an entity other than the debtor (or the debtor's spouse in a joint case) on a regular basis for the household expenses of the debtor, the debtor's dependents, and (in a joint case) the debtor's spouse if not otherwise a dependent. At the same time, the definition excludes from the averaged income "benefits received under the Social Security Act" and certain payments to victims of terrorism, war crimes, and crimes against humanity.

Each of the forms provides for reporting income items constituting CMI. The items are reported in a set of entry lines—Part II of the Chapter 7 form and Part I of the forms for Chapter 11 and Chapter 13—that include separate columns for reporting income of the debtor and of the debtor's spouse. The first of these entry lines includes a set of instructions and check boxes indicating when the "debtor's spouse" column must be completed. The instructions also direct the required averaging of reported income.

The subsequent entry lines specify several common types of income and are followed by a "catch-all" line for other income. The specific entry lines address (a) gross wages; (b) business

income; (c) rental income; (d) interest, dividends, and royalties; (e) pension and retirement income; (f) regular contributions to the debtor's household expenses; and (g) unemployment compensation. Gross wages (before taxes) are required to be entered. Consistent with usage in the Internal Revenue Manual and the American Community Survey of the Census Bureau, business and rental income is defined as gross receipts less ordinary and necessary expenses. Unemployment compensation is given special treatment. Because the federal government provides funding for state unemployment compensation under the Social Security Act, there may be a dispute about whether unemployment compensation is a "benefit received under the Social Security Act." The forms take no position on the merits of this argument, but give debtors the option of reporting unemployment compensation separately from the CMI calculation. This separate reporting allows parties in interest to determine the materiality of an exclusion of unemployment compensation and to challenge it. The forms provide for totaling the income lines.

C. The means test: deductions from current monthly income (CMI)

The means test operates by deducting from CMI defined allowances for living expenses and payment of secured and priority debt, leaving disposable income presumptively available to pay unsecured non-priority debt. These deductions from CMI under are set out in § 707(b)(2)(A)(ii)–(iv). The forms for Chapter 7 and Chapter 13 have identical sections (Parts V and III, respectively) for calculating these deductions. The calculations are divided into subparts reflecting three different kinds of allowed deductions.

1. Deductions under IRS standards

Subpart A deals with deductions from CMI, set out in § 707(b)(2)(A)(ii), for "the debtor's applicable monthly expense amounts specified under the National Standards and Local Standards, and the debtor's actual monthly expenses for the categories specified as Other Necessary Expenses issued by the Internal Revenue Service for the area in which the debtor resides." The forms provide entry lines for each of the specified expense deductions under the IRS standards, and instructions on the entry lines identify the website of the U.S. Trustee Program, where the relevant IRS allowances can be found. As with all of the deductions in § 707(b)(2)(A)(ii), deductions under the IRS standards are subject to the proviso that they not include "any payments for debts."

The IRS National Standards provide a single allowance for food, clothing, household supplies, personal care, and miscellany, depending on income and household size. The forms contain an entry line for the applicable allowance.

The IRS Local Standards provide one set of deductions for housing and utilities and another set for transportation expenses, with different amounts for different areas of the country, depending on the size of the debtor's family and the number of the debtor's vehicles. Each of the amounts specified in the Local Standards are treated by the IRS as a cap on actual expenses, but because § 707(b)(2)(A)(ii) provides for deductions in the "amounts specified under the ... Local Standards," the forms treat these amounts as allowed deductions. The forms again direct debtors to the website of the U.S. Trustee Program to obtain the appropriate allowances.

The Local Standards for housing and utilities, as published by the IRS for its internal purposes, present single amounts covering all housing expenses; however, for bankruptcy purposes, the IRS has separated these amounts into a non-mortgage component and a mortgage/rent component. The non-mortgage component covers a variety of expenses involved in maintaining a residence, such as utilities, repairs and maintenance. The mortgage/rent component covers the cost of acquiring the residence. For homeowners with mortgages, the mortgage/rent component involves debt payment, since the cost of a mortgage is part of the allowance. Accordingly, the forms require debtors to deduct from the mortgage/rent component their average monthly mortgage payment (including required payments for taxes and insurance), up to the full amount of the IRS mortgage/rent component, and instruct debtors that this average monthly payment is the one reported on the separate line of the forms for deductions of secured debt under § 707(b)(2)(A)(iii). The forms allow debtors to challenge the appropriateness of this method of computing the Local Standards allowance for housing and utilities and to claim any additional housing allowance to which they contend they are entitled, but the forms require specification of the basis for such a contention.

The IRS issues Local Standards for transportation in two components for its internal purposes as well as for bankruptcy: one component covers vehicle operation/public transportation expense and the other ownership/lease expense. The amount of the vehicle operation/public transportation allowance depends on the number of vehicles the debtor operates, with debtors who do not operate vehicles being given a public transportation allowance. The instruction for this line item makes it clear that every debtor is thus entitled to some transportation expense allowance. No debt payment is involved in this allowance. The ownership/lease component, on the other hand, may involve debt payment. Accordingly, the forms require debtors to reduce the allowance for ownership/lease expense by the average monthly loan payment amount (principal and interest), up to the full amount of the IRS ownership/lease expense amount. This average payment is as reported on the separate line of the forms for deductions of secured debt under § 707(b)(2)(A)(iii).

The IRS does not set out specific dollar allowances for "Other Necessary Expenses." Rather, it specifies a number of categories for such expenses, and describes the nature of the expenses that may be deducted in each of these categories. Section 707(b)(2)(A)(ii) allows a deduction for the debtor's actual expenses in these specified categories, subject to its requirement that payment of debt not be included. Several of the IRS categories deal with debt repayment and so are not included in the forms. Several other categories deal with expense items that are more expansively addressed by specific statutory allowances. Subpart A sets out the remaining categories of "Other Necessary Expenses" in individual entry lines. Instructions in these entry lines reflect limitations imposed by the IRS and the need to avoid inclusion of items deducted elsewhere on the forms.

Subpart A concludes with a subtotal of the deductions allowed under the IRS standards.

2. Additional statutory expense deductions

In addition to the expense deductions allowed under the IRS standards, the means test makes provision—in subclauses (I), (II), (IV), and (V) of § 707(b)(2)(A)(ii)—for six special expense deductions. Each of these additional expense items is set out on a separate entry line in Subpart B, introduced by an instruction that there should not be double counting of any expense already included in the IRS deductions. Contributions to tax-exempt charities provide another statutory ex-

pense deduction. Section 1325(b)(2)(A)(ii) expressly allows a deduction from CMI for such contributions (up to 15% of the debtor's gross income), and § 707(b)(1) provides that in considering whether a Chapter 7 filing is an abuse, the court may not take into consideration "whether a debtor ... continues to make [tax-exempt] charitable contributions." Accordingly, Subpart B also includes an entry line for charitable contributions. The subpart concludes with a subtotal of the additional statutory expense deductions.

3. Deductions for payment of debt

Subpart C of the forms deals with the means test's deductions from CMI for payment of secured and priority debt, as well as a deduction for administrative fees that would be incurred if the debtor paid debts through a Chapter 13 plan. In accord with § 707(b)(2)(A)(iii), the deduction for secured debt is divided into two entry lines—one for payments that are contractually due during the 60 months following the bankruptcy filing, the other for amounts needed to retain necessary collateral securing debts in default. In each situation, the instructions for the entry lines require dividing the total payment amount by 60, as the statute directs. Priority debt, deductible pursuant to § 707(b)(2)(A)(iv), is treated on a single entry line, also requiring division by 60. The defined deduction for the expenses of administering a Chapter 13 plan is allowed by § 707(b)(2)(A)(ii)(III) only for debtors eligible for Chapter 13. The forms treat this deduction in an entry line requiring the eligible debtor to state the amount of the prospective Chapter 13 plan payment and multiply that payment amount by the percentage fee established for the debtor's district by the Executive Office for United States Trustees. The forms refer debtors to the website of the U.S. Trustee Program to obtain this percentage fee. The subpart concludes with a subtotal of debt payment deductions.

4. Total deductions

Finally, the forms direct that the subtotals from Subparts A, B, and C be added together to arrive at the total of allowed deductions from CMI under the means test.

5. Additional claimed deductions

The forms do not provide for means test deductions from CMI for expenses in categories that are not specifically identified as "Other Necessary Expenses" in the Internal Revenue Manual. However, debtors may wish to claim expenses that do not fall within the categories listed as "Other Necessary Expenses" in the forms. Part VII of the Chapter 7 form and Part VI of the Chapter 13 form provide for such expenses to be identified and totaled. Although expenses listed in these sections are not deducted from CMI for purposes of the means test calculation, the listing provides a basis for debtors to assert that these expenses should be deducted from CMI under § 707(b)(2)(A)(ii)(I), and that the results of the forms' calculation, therefore, should be modified.

D. The chapter-specific forms

1. Chapter 7

The Chapter 7 form has several unique aspects. The form includes, in the upper right corner of the first page, a check box directing the debtor to state whether or not the calculations required by the form result in a presumption of abuse. The debtor is not bound by this statement and may argue, in response to a motion brought under § 707(b)(1), that there should be no presumption despite the calculations required by the form. The check box is intended to give clerks of court a conspicuous indication of the cases for which they are required to provide notice of a presumption of abuse pursuant to § 342(d).

Part I of the form implements the provision of § 707(b)(2)(D) that excludes certain disabled veterans from all means testing, making it unnecessary to compute the CMI of such veterans. Debtors who declare under penalty of perjury that they are disabled veterans within the statutory definition are directed to verify their declaration in Part VII, to check the "no presumption" box at the beginning of the form, and to disregard the remaining parts of the form.

Part II of the form is the computation of CMI. Section 707(b)(7) eliminates standing to assert the means test's presumption of abuse if the debtor's annualized CMI does not exceed a defined median state income. For this purpose, the statute directs that CMI of the debtor's spouse be combined with the debtor's CMI even if the debtor's spouse is not a joint debtor, unless the debtor declares under penalty of perjury that the spouses are legally separated or living separately other than for purposes of evading the means test. Accordingly, the calculation of CMI in Part II directs a computation of the CMI of the debtor's spouse not only in joint cases, but also in cases of married debtors who do not make the specified declaration, and the CMI of both spouses in these cases is combined for purposes of determining standing under § 707(b)(7).

Part III of the form provides for the comparison of the debtor's CMI to the applicable state median income for purposes of § 707(b)(7). It then directs debtors whose income does not exceed the applicable median to verify the form, to check the "no presumption" box at the beginning of the form, and not to complete the remaining parts of the form. Debtors whose CMI does exceed the applicable state median are required to complete the remaining parts of the form.

Part IV of the form provides for an adjustment to the CMI of a married debtor, not filing jointly, whose spouse's CMI was combined with the debtor's for purposes of determining standing to assert the means test presumption. The means test itself does not charge a married debtor in a non-joint case with the income of the non-filing spouse, but rather only with contributions made by that spouse to the household expenses of the debtor or the debtor's dependents, as provided in the definition of CMI in § 101(10A). Accordingly, Part IV calls for the combined CMI of Part II to be reduced by the amount of the non-filing spouse's income that was not contributed to the household expenses of the debtor or the debtor's dependents.

Part V of the form provides for a calculation of the means test's deductions from the debtor's CMI, as described above.

Part VI provides for a determination of whether the debtor's CMI, less the allowed deductions, gives rise to a presumption of abuse under § 707(b)(2)(A). Depending on the outcome of this determination, the debtor is directed to check the appropriate box at the beginning of the form and to sign the verification in Part VIII. Part VII allows the debtor to claim additional deductions, as discussed above.

2. Chapter 11

The Chapter 11 form is the simplest of the three, since the means-test deductions of § 707(b)(2) are not employed in determining the extent of an individual Chapter 11 debtor's disposable income. Section 1129(a)(15) requires payments of disposable income "as defined in section 1325(b)(2)," and that paragraph allows calculation of disposable income under judicially-determined standards, rather than pursuant to the

means test deductions, specified for higher income Chapter 13 debtors by § 1325(b)(3). However, § 1325(b)(2) does require that CMI be used as the starting point in the judicial determination of disposable income, and so the Chapter 11 form requires this calculation (in Part I of the form), as described above, together with a verification (in Part II).

3. Chapter 13

Like the Chapter 7 form, the form for Chapter 13 debtors contains a number of special provisions. The upper right corner of the first page includes check boxes requiring the debtor to state whether, under the calculations required by the statement, the applicable commitment period under § 1325(b)(4) is three years or five years and whether the means test deductions are required by § 1325(b)(3) to be used in determining the debtor's disposable income. The check box is intended to inform standing trustees and other interested parties about these items, but does not prevent the debtor from arguing that the calculations required by the form do not accurately reflect the debtor's disposable income.

Part I of the form is a report of income to be used for determining CMI. Section 1325(b)(4) imposes a five-year applicable commitment period—rather than a three-year period—if the debtor's annualized CMI is not less than a defined median state income. For this purpose, as under § 707(b)(4), the CMI of the debtor's spouse is required by the statute to be combined with the debtor's CMI, and there is no exception for spouses who are legally separated or living separately. Accordingly, the report of income in Part I directs a combined reporting of the income of both spouses in all cases of married debtors.

Part II of the form computes the applicable commitment period by annualizing the income calculated in Part I and comparing it to the applicable state median. The form allows debtors to contend that the income of a non-filing spouse should not be treated as CMI and permits debtors to claim a deduction for any income of a non-filing spouse to the extent that this income was not contributed to the household expenses of the debtor or the debtor's dependents. The debtor is directed to check the appropriate box at the beginning of the form, stating the applicable commitment period.

Part III of the form compares the debtor's CMI to the applicable state median, allowing a determination of whether the means-test deductions must be used, pursuant to § 1325(b)(3), in calculating disposable income. For this purpose, since § 1325(b)(3) does not provide for including the income of the debtor's spouse, the form directs a deduction of the income of a non-filing spouse that is not contributed to the household expenses of the debtor or the debtor's dependents. Again, the debtor is directed to check the appropriate box at the beginning of the form, indicating whether the means test deductions are applicable. If so, the debtor is directed to complete the remainder of the form. If not, the debtor is directed to complete the verification in Part VII but not complete the other parts of the form.

Part IV provides for calculation of the means-test deductions provided in § 707(b)(2), described above, as incorporated by § 1325(b)(3) for debtors with CMI above the applicable state median.

Part V provides for three adjustments required by special provisions affecting disposable income in Chapter 13. First, § 1325(b)(2) itself excludes from the CMI used in determining disposable income certain "child support payments, foster care payments, [and] disability payments for a dependent child." Because payments of this kind are included in the definition of CMI in § 101(10A), a line entry for deduction of these payments is provided. Second, a line entry is provided for deduction of contributions by the debtor to certain retirement plans, listed in § 541(b)(7)(B), since that provision states that such contributions "shall not constitute disposable income, as defined in section 1325(b)." Third, the same line entry also allows a deduction from disposable income for payments on loans from retirement accounts that are excepted from the automatic stay by § 362(b)(19), since § 1322(f) provides that for a "loan described in section 362(b)(19) ... any amounts required to repay such loan shall not constitute 'disposable income' under section 1325."

The Chapter 13 form does not provide a deduction from disposable income for the Chapter 13 debtor's anticipated attorney fees. There is no specific statutory allowance for such a deduction, and none appears necessary. Section 1325(b)(1)(B) requires that disposable income contributed to a Chapter 13 plan be used to pay "unsecured creditors." A debtor's attorney who has not taken a security interest in the debtor's property is an unsecured creditor who may be paid from disposable income.

Part VI of the form allows the debtor to claim additional deductions, as described above, and Part VII is the verification.

2006 Amendment

Forms 22A, Line 43, and Form 22C, Line 48, are amended to delete the phrase "in default" with respect to "Other payments on secured claims." A debtor may be required to make other payments to the creditor even when the debt is not in default, such as to retain collateral. Form 22C, Line 17, also is amended to require all chapter 13 debtors, including those whose income falls below the applicable median income, to determine their disposable income under § 1325(b)(3) of the Code by completing Part III of the form. Both forms contain stylistic amendments to conform the wording more closely to that used in the 2005 Act.

2005–2008 Amendment

(The 2005–2007 Committee Note incorporates Committee Notes previously published in 2005 and 2006.)

A. Overview

Among the changes introduced by the Bankruptcy Abuse Prevention and Consumer Protection Act of 2005 was a set of interlocking provisions defining "current monthly income" and establishing a means test to determine whether relief under Chapter 7 should be presumed abusive. Current monthly income ("CMI") is defined in § 101(10A) of the Code, and the means test is set out in § 707(b)(2). These provisions have a variety of applications. In Chapter 7, if the debtor's CMI exceeds a defined level the debtor is subject to the means test, and § 707(b)(2)(C) specifically requires debtors to file a statement of CMI and calculations to determine the applicability of the means test presumption. In Chapters 11 and 13, CMI provides the starting point for determining the disposable income that debtors may be required to pay to unsecured creditors. Moreover, Chapter 13 debtors with CMI above defined median income levels are required by § 1325(b)(3) to use the deductions from income prescribed by the means test in order to determine what part of their income is "disposable," and pursuant to § 1325(b)(4), the level of CMI determines the "applicable commitment period" over which projected disposable income must be paid to unsecured creditors.

To provide for the reporting and calculation of CMI and for the completion of the means test where required, three separate official forms have been created—one for Chapter 7, one for Chapter 11, and one for Chapter 13. This note first describes the calculation of CMI that is common to all three of the forms, next describes the means test deductions set out in the Chapter 7 and 13 forms, and finally addresses particular issues that are unique to each of the separate forms.

B. Calculation of CMI

Although Chapters 7, 11, and 13 use CMI for different purposes, the basic computation is the same in each. As defined in § 101(10A), CMI is the monthly average of certain income that the debtor (and in a joint case, the debtor's spouse) received in the six calendar months before the bankruptcy filing. The definition includes in this average (1) income from all sources, whether or not taxable, and (2) any amount paid by an entity other than the debtor (or the debtor's spouse in a joint case) on a regular basis for the household expenses of the debtor, the debtor's dependents, and (in a joint case) the debtor's spouse if not otherwise a dependent. At the same time, the definition excludes from the averaged income "benefits received under the Social Security Act" and certain payments to victims of terrorism, war crimes, and crimes against humanity.

Each of the three forms provides for reporting income items constituting CMI. The items are reported in a set of entry lines—Part II of the form for Chapter 7 and Part I of the forms for Chapter 11 and Chapter 13—that include separate columns for reporting income of the debtor and of the debtor's spouse. The first of these entry lines includes a set of instructions and check boxes indicating when the "debtor's spouse" column must be completed. The instructions also direct the required averaging of reported income.

The subsequent entry lines for income reporting specify several common types of income and are followed by a "catch-all" line for other income. The entry lines address (a) gross wages; (b) business income; (c) rental income; (d) interest, dividends, and royalties; (e) pension and retirement income; (f) regular payments of the household expenses of the debtor or the debtor's dependents; (g) unemployment compensation, and (h) all other forms of income (the "catch-all" line).

Gross wages (before taxes) are required to be entered. However, consistent with usage in the Internal Revenue Manual and the American Community Survey of the Census Bureau, business and rental income are defined as gross receipts less ordinary and necessary expenses.

Unemployment compensation is given special treatment. Because the federal government provides funding for state unemployment compensation under the Social Security Act, there may be a dispute about whether unemployment compensation is a "benefit received under the Social Security Act." The forms take no position on the merits of this argument, but give debtors the option of reporting unemployment compensation separately from the CMI calculation. This separate reporting allows parties in interest to determine the materiality of an exclusion of unemployment compensation and to challenge it.

Alimony and child support are also given special treatment. Child support is not generally considered "income" to the recipient. See 26 U.S.C. § 71(c). Thus, child support is only part of CMI if it is paid on a regular basis for the household expenses of the debtor or the debtor's dependents. On the other hand, alimony and other forms of spousal support are considered income to the recipient, and thus are within CMI regardless of the regularity and use of the payments. To address this distinction, the instruction in the entry line for regular payments of household expenses directs that the entry include regular child support payments used for household expenses of the debtor or the debtor's dependents, and the instruction for the "catch-all" line directs inclusion of all spousal support payments that are not otherwise reported as spousal income.

The forms provide for totaling the income reporting lines.

C. The means test: deductions from current monthly income

The means test operates by deducting from CMI defined allowances for living expenses and payment of secured and priority debt, leaving disposable income presumptively available to pay unsecured non-priority debt. These deductions from CMI are set out in the Code at § 707(b)(2)(A)(ii)-(iv). The forms for Chapter 7 and Chapter 13 have similar sections (Parts V and IV, respectively) for calculating these deductions. The calculations are divided into subparts reflecting three different kinds of allowed deductions.

1. Deductions under IRS standards

Subpart A deals with deductions from CMI, set out in § 707(b)(2)(A)(ii), for "the debtor's applicable monthly expense amounts specified under the National Standards and Local Standards, and the debtor's actual monthly expenses for the categories specified as Other Necessary Expenses issued by the Internal Revenue Service for the area in which the debtor resides." The forms provide entry lines for each of the specified expense deductions under the IRS standards, and instructions on the entry lines identify the website of the U.S. Trustee Program, where the relevant IRS allowances can be found. As with all of the deductions in § 707(b)(2)(A)(ii), deductions under the IRS standards are subject to the proviso that they not include "any payments for debts."

National Standards. The IRS National Standards provide a single allowance for food, clothing, household supplies, personal care, and miscellany, depending on household size, which can be entered directly from a table supplied by the IRS. There is also a National Standard for out-of-pocket health care expenses, which provides two different per-person allowances, depending on age group: the allowance for persons 65 or older is greater than the allowance for those under 65. Accordingly, the forms direct debtors to compute the National Standard allowance for health care by first multiplying each of the two age-group allowances by the number of household members within that age group and then adding subtotals for the two age groups to obtain the total allowance.

Local Standards. The IRS Local Standards provide one set of deductions for housing and utilities and another set for transportation expenses, with different amounts for different areas of the country, depending on the size of the debtor's household and the number of the debtor's vehicles. Each of the amounts specified in the Local Standards are treated by the IRS as a cap on actual expenses, but because § 707(b)(2)(A)(ii) provides for deductions in the "amounts specified under the . . . Local Standards," the forms treat these amounts as allowed deductions.

The Local Standards for housing and utilities, as published by the IRS for its internal purposes, present single amounts covering all housing expenses; however, for bankruptcy purposes, the IRS has provided the Executive Office for United States Trustees with information allowing a division of these amounts into a non-mortgage component and a mortgage/rent component. The non-mortgage component covers a variety of expenses involved in maintaining a residence, such as utilities, repairs and maintenance. The mortgage/rent component covers the cost of acquiring the residence. The forms take no position on the question of whether the debtor must actually be making payments on a home in order to claim a mortgage/rent allowance. For homeowners with mortgages, the mortgage/rent allowance involves debt payment, since the cost of a mortgage is the basis for the allowance. Accordingly, the forms require debtors to deduct from the mortgage/rent allowance their average monthly mortgage payment, up to the full amount of the IRS mortgage/rent allowance, and instruct debtors that this average monthly payment is the one reported on the separate line of the forms for deductions of secured debt under § 707(b)(2)(a)(iii). The forms allow debtors to challenge the appropriateness of this method of computing the Local Standards allowance for housing and utilities and to claim any additional housing allowance to which they contend they are entitled, but the forms require specification of the basis for such a contention.

The IRS issues Local Standards for transportation in two components for its internal purposes as well as for bankruptcy: one component covers vehicle operation/public transportation expense and the other ownership/lease expense. The amount of the vehicle operation/public transportation allowance depends on the number of vehicles the debtor operates; debtors who do not operate vehicles are given a public transportation allowance, regardless of whether they actually use public transportation. It is not clear whether the public transportation allowance may also be claimed by debtors who do make use of public transportation but also operate vehicles. The forms permit debtors to claim both a public transportation and vehicle operating allowance, but take no position as to whether it is appropriate to claim both allowances. No debt payment is involved in the vehicle operation/public transportation component of the Local Standards for transportation.

The ownership/lease component, on the other hand, may involve debt payment. Accordingly, the forms require debtors to reduce the allowance for ownership/lease expense by the average monthly loan payment amount (principal and interest), up to the full amount of the IRS ownership/lease expense amount. This average payment is as reported on the separate line of the forms for deductions of secured debt under § 707(b)(2)(a)(iii). The forms take no position on the question of whether the debtor must actually be making payments on a vehicle in order to claim the ownership/lease allowance.

Other Necessary Expenses. The IRS does not set out specific dollar allowances for "Other Necessary Expenses." Rather, it specifies a number of categories for such expenses, and describes the nature of the expenses that may be deducted in each of these categories. Section 707(b)(2)(a)(ii) allows a deduction for the debtor's actual expenses in these specified categories, subject to its requirement that payment of debt not be included. Several of the IRS categories deal with debt repayment and so are not included in the forms. Several other categories deal with expense items that are more expansively addressed by specific statutory allowances. Subpart A sets out the remaining categories of "Other Necessary Expenses" in individual entry lines. Instructions in these entry lines reflect limitations imposed by the IRS and the need to avoid inclusion of items deducted elsewhere on the forms.

Subpart A concludes with a subtotal of the deductions allowed under the IRS standards.

2. Additional statutory expense deductions

In addition to the expense deductions allowed under the IRS standards, the means test makes provision—in subclauses (I), (II), (IV), and (V) of § 707(b)(2)(A)(ii)—for six special expense deductions. Each of these additional expense items is set out on a separate entry line in Subpart B, introduced by an instruction that tracks the statutory language and provides that there should not be double counting of any expense already included in the IRS deductions.

One of these special expense deductions presents a problem of statutory construction. Section 707(b)(2)A)(ii)(I), after directing the calculation of the debtor's monthly expenses under the IRS standards, states, "Such expenses shall include reasonably necessary health insurance, disability insurance, and health saving account expenses . . . ." There is no express statutory limitation to expenses actually incurred by the debtor, and so the provision appears to allow a reasonable "monthly expense" deduction for health and disability insurance or a health savings account even if the debtor does not make such payments, similar to the way in which the National Standards give an allowance for food, clothing and personal care expenses without regard to the debtor's actual expenditures. However, the statutory language might also be read as providing that the debtor's "Other Necessary Expenses" should include reasonable insurance and health savings account payments. Since "Other Necessary Expenses" are limited to actual expenditures, such a limitation could be implied here. The forms deal with this ambiguity by allowing the debtor to claim a deduction for reasonable insurance and health savings account expenses even if not made, but also require a statement of the amount actually expended in these categories, thus allowing a challenge by any party who believes that only actual expenditures are properly deductible.

Contributions to tax-exempt charities provide another statutory expense deduction. Section 707(b)(1) provides that in considering whether a Chapter 7 filing is an abuse, the court may not take into consideration "whether a debtor . . . continues to make [tax-exempt] charitable contributions." Section 1325(b)(2)(A)(ii) expressly allows a deduction from CMI for such contributions that are "reasonably necessary" (up to 15% of the debtor's gross income), and the Religious Liberty and Charitable Donation Clarification Act of 2005 added language to § 1325(b)(3) to provide the same deduction for above-median income debtors whose disposable income is determined using means test deductions. Accordingly, Subpart B of both the Chapter 7 and Chapter 13 forms includes an entry line for charitable contributions, employing the different statutory deductions allowed in each context.

The Subpart B concludes with a subtotal of the additional statutory expense deductions.

3. Deductions for payment of debt

Subpart C deals with the means test's deductions from CMI for payment of secured and priority debt, as well as a deduction for administrative fees that would be incurred if the debtor paid debts through a Chapter 13 plan.

In accord with § 707(b)(2)(A)(iii), the deduction for secured debt is divided into two entry lines—one for payments that are contractually due during the 60 months following the bankruptcy filing, the other for amounts needed to retain necessary collateral securing debts in default. In each situation, the instructions for the entry lines require dividing the total payment amount by 60, as the statute directs. The forms recognize another ambiguity in this connection: "payments contractually due" might either be understood as limited to

payments of principal and interest (payable to secured creditor) or, in the context of a mortgage with an escrow, might be understood as including payments of property taxes and insurance (ultimately paid to taxing bodies and insurers, but initially payable to the mortgagee). The forms require the debtor to specify whether the amount deducted includes taxes and insurance, allowing a party in interest to inquire into the deduction and raise an objection.

Priority debt, deductible pursuant to § 707(b)(2)(A)(iv), is treated on a single entry line, also requiring division by 60. The instruction for this line makes clear that only past due priority debt—not anticipated debts—should be included. Thus, future support or tax obligations, and future fees that might be payable to a Chapter 13 debtor's attorney, are not included.

The defined deduction for the expenses of administering a Chapter 13 plan is allowed by § 707(b)(2)(A)(ii)(III) only for debtors eligible for Chapter 13. The forms treat this deduction in an entry line requiring the eligible debtor to state the amount of the prospective Chapter 13 plan payment and multiply that payment amount by the percentage fee established for the debtor's district by the Executive Office for United States Trustees. The forms refer debtors to the website of the U.S. Trustee Program to obtain this percentage fee.

The subpart concludes with a subtotal of debt payment deductions.

4. Total deductions

Finally, the forms direct that the subtotals from Subparts A, B, and C be added together to arrive at the total of allowed deductions from CMI under the means test.

5. Additional claimed deductions

The forms do not provide for means test deductions from CMI for expenses in categories that are not specifically identified as "Other Necessary Expenses" in the Internal Revenue Manual. However, debtors may wish to claim expenses that do not fall within the categories listed as "Other Necessary Expenses" in the forms. Part VII of the Chapter 7 form and Part VI of the Chapter 13 form provide for such expenses to be identified and totaled. Although expenses listed in these sections are not deducted from CMI for purposes of the means test calculation, the listing provides a basis for debtors to assert that these expenses should be deducted from CMI under § 707(b)(2)(A)(ii)(I), and that the results of the forms' calculation should therefore be modified.

D. The chapter-specific forms

1. Chapter 7

The Chapter 7 form has several unique aspects. The form includes, in the upper right corner of the first page, a check box directing the debtor to state whether or not the calculations required by the form result in a presumption of abuse. The debtor is not bound by this statement and may argue, in response to a motion brought under § 707(b)(1), that there should be no presumption despite the calculations required by the form. The check box is intended to give clerks of court a conspicuous indication of the cases for which they are required to provide notice of a presumption of abuse pursuant to § 342(d).

Part I implements the provision of § 707(b)(2)(D) that excludes certain disabled veterans from all means testing, making it unnecessary to compute the CMI of such veterans. Debtors who declare under penalty of perjury that they are disabled veterans within the statutory definition are directed to verify their declaration in Part VII, to check the "no presumption" box at the beginning of the form, and to disregard the remaining parts of the form.

Part I also provides an exclusion for debtors who do not have primarily consumer debts. These debtors are not subject to any of the provisions of § 707(b)—including the requirement of § 707(b)(2)(C) for filing a CMI statement—since § 707(b) applies, by its terms, only to "an individual debtor . . . whose debts are primarily consumer debts." However, a debtor may be found to have asserted non-consumer status incorrectly. Unless such a debtor has filed the CMI form within the 45 days after filing the case, the case could be subject to automatic dismissal under § 521(i). To avoid this possibility, debtors asserting principally non-consumer status may complete the appropriate portions of Part I, claim an exclusion from the balance of the form, and promptly file the form. If it is subsequently determined that the debtor does have primarily consumer debts, the form will have been filed within the deadline established by § 521(i), and can be amended to include the necessary CMI and means test information.

Part II computes CMI for purposes of the safe harbor of § 707(b)(7). Section 707(b)(7) prohibits a motion to dismiss based on the means test's presumption of abuse if the debtor's annualized CMI does not exceed a defined median state income. For this purpose, the statute directs that CMI of the debtor's spouse be combined with the debtor's CMI even if the debtor's spouse is not a joint debtor, unless the debtor declares under penalty of perjury that the spouses are legally separated or living separately other than for purposes of evading the means test. Accordingly, the calculation of CMI in Part II directs a computation of the CMI of the debtor's spouse not only in joint cases, but also in cases of married debtors who do not make the specified declaration, and the CMI of both spouses in these cases is combined for purposes of determining standing under § 707(b)(7).

Part III compares the debtor's CMI to the applicable state median income for purposes of § 707(b)(7). It then directs debtors whose income does not exceed the applicable median to verify the form, to check the "no presumption" box at the beginning of the form, and not to complete the remaining parts of the form. Debtors whose CMI does exceed the applicable state median are required to complete the remaining parts of the form.

Part IV adjusts the CMI of a married debtor, not filing jointly, whose spouse's CMI was combined with the debtor's in Part II. The means test itself does not charge a married debtor in a non-joint case with the income of the non-filing spouse, but only with payments regularly made by that spouse for the household expenses of the debtor or the debtor's dependents, as provided in the definition of CMI in § 101(10A). Accordingly, Part IV calls for the combined CMI of Part II to be reduced by the amount of the non-filing spouse's income that was not regularly paid for the household expenses of the debtor or the debtor's dependents. The form requires that the alternative uses of the spouse's income be specified.

Part V of the form provides for a calculation of the means test's deductions from the debtor's CMI, as described above in § C.

Part VI provides for a determination of whether the debtor's CMI, less the allowed deductions, gives rise to a presumption of abuse under § 707(b)(2)(A). Depending on the outcome of this determination, the debtor is directed to check

the appropriate box at the beginning of the form and to sign the verification in Part VIII. Part VII allows the debtor to claim additional deductions, as discussed above in § C.5.

2. Chapter 11

The Chapter 11 form is the simplest of the three, since the means-test deductions of § 707(b)(2) are not employed in determining the extent of an individual Chapter 11 debtor's disposable income. Section 1129(a)(15) requires payments of disposable income "as defined in section 1325(b)(2)," and that paragraph allows calculation of disposable income under judicially-determined standards, rather than pursuant to the means test deductions, specified for higher income Chapter 13 debtors by § 1325(b)(3). However, § 1325(b)(2) does require that CMI be used as the starting point in the judicial determination of disposable income, and so the Chapter 11 form requires this calculation (in Part I of the form), as described above, together with a verification (in Part II).

3. Chapter 13

Like the Chapter 7 form, the form for Chapter 13 debtors contains a number of special provisions. The upper right corner of the first page includes check boxes requiring the debtor to state whether, under the calculations required by the statement, the applicable commitment period under § 1325(b)(4) is three years or five years and whether § 1325(b)(3) requires the means-test deductions to be used in determining the debtor's disposable income. The check box is intended to inform standing trustees and other interested parties about these items, but does not prevent the debtor from arguing that the calculations required by the form do not accurately reflect the debtor's disposable income.

Part I is a report of income to be used for determining CMI. In the absence of full payment of allowed unsecured claims, § 1325(b)(4) imposes a five-year applicable commitment period—rather than a three-year period—if the debtor's annualized CMI is not less than a defined median state income. For this purpose, as under § 707(b)(7), § 1325(b)(4) requires that the CMI of the debtor's spouse be combined with the debtor's CMI, but, unlike § 707(b)(7), no exception is made for spouses who are legally separated or living separately. Accordingly, the report of income in Part I directs a combined reporting of the income of both spouses in all cases of married debtors.

Part II computes the applicable commitment period by annualizing the income calculated in Part I and comparing it to the applicable state median. The form allows debtors to contend that the income of a non-filing spouse should not be treated as CMI and permits debtors to claim a deduction for any income of a non-filing spouse to the extent that this income was not regularly paid for the household expenses of the debtor or the debtor's dependents (with the alternative uses specified). The debtor is directed to check the appropriate box at the beginning of the form, stating the applicable commitment period. The check box does not prevent a debtor from proposing an applicable commitment period of less than three or five years in conjunction with a plan that pays all allowed unsecured claims in full.

Part III compares the debtor's CMI to the applicable state median, allowing a determination of whether the means-test deductions must be used, pursuant to § 1325(b)(3), in calculating disposable income. For this purpose, since § 1325(b)(3) does not provide for including the income of the debtor's spouse, the form directs a deduction of the income of a nonfiling spouse that was not contributed to the household expenses of the debtor or the debtor's dependents. Again, the debtor is directed to check the appropriate box at the beginning of the form, indicating whether the means test deductions are applicable. If so, the debtor is directed to complete the remainder of the form. If not, the debtor is directed to complete the verification in Part VII but not complete the other parts of the form.

Part IV provides for calculation of the means-test deductions provided in § 707(b)(2), described above in § C, as incorporated by § 1325(b)(3) for debtors with CMI above the applicable state median.

Part V provides for four adjustments required by special provisions affecting disposable income in Chapter 13. First, § 1325(b)(2) itself excludes from the CMI used in determining disposable income certain "child support payments, foster care payments, [and] disability payments for a dependent child." Because payments of this kind are included in the definition of CMI in § 101(10A), a line entry for deduction of these payments is provided. Second, a line entry is provided for deduction of contributions by the debtor to certain retirement plans, listed in § 541(b)(7)(B), since that provision states that such contributions "shall not constitute disposable income, as defined in section 1325(b)." Third, the same line entry also allows a deduction from disposable income for payments on loans from retirement accounts that are excepted from the automatic stay by § 362(b)(19), since § 1322(f) provides that for a "loan described in section 362(b)(19) . . . any amounts required to repay such loan shall not constitute 'disposable income' under section 1325." Finally, § 1325(b)(3) requires that deductions from income for above-median income debtors be determined not only in accordance with the means test deductions, set out in subparagraph (A) of § 707(b)(2), but also in accordance with subparagraph (B), which sets out the grounds for rebutting a presumption of abuse based on a demonstration of additional expenses justified by special circumstances. Part V includes an entry line for such additional expenses, with a warning that the debtor will be required (as provided by § 707(b)(2)(B)) to document the expenses and provide a detailed explanation of the special circumstances that make them reasonable and necessary.

The Chapter 13 form does not provide a deduction from disposable income for the Chapter 13 debtor's anticipated attorney fees. No specific statutory allowance for such a deduction exists, and none appears necessary. Section 1325(b)(1)(B) requires that disposable income contributed to a Chapter 13 plan be used to pay "unsecured creditors." A debtor's attorney who has not taken a security interest in the debtor's property is an unsecured creditor who may be paid from disposable income.

Part VI allows the debtor to declare expenses not allowed under the form without deducting them from CMI, as described above in § C.5.

2008 Amendment

The chapter 7 form is amended to implement the temporary exclusion from means testing created by the National Guard and Reservists Debt Relief Act of 2008. That law amended § 707(b)(2)(D) for a period of three years by adding a new subsection (ii) to provide a temporary exclusion from the application of the means test for certain members of the National Guard and reserve components of the Armed Forces. The new temporary exclusion would last for the period that the qualifying debtor is on active duty or is performing a homeland defense activity, and for 540 days thereafter.

Because the exclusion for Reservists and National Guard members applies only for a defined period of time, it may expire during the course of the chapter 7 case filed by a debtor initially entitled to the exclusion. For that reason, a new check box is added to the top of the form that states that the "presumption is temporarily inapplicable." A debtor who is entitled to claim the Reservists and National Guard exclusion at the commencement of the chapter 7 case may check that box.

The new exclusion applies only to a debtor who satisfies all of the requirements of § 707(b)(2)(D)(ii), and its expiration date depends on facts specific to each debtor. Therefore, in a joint case in which the exclusion in part 1C is claimed by either or both filers, each joint filer must complete a separate statement. If only one joint debtor qualifies for the exclusion in part IC, the other joint debtor must complete the form.

Part 1C is added to the form to allow qualifying debtors to claim the temporary exclusion under § 707(b)(2)(D)(ii). Debtors who declare under penalty of perjury that they satisfy all of the requirements of that provision are directed to verify their declaration in Part VIII and to check the "temporary presumption" box at the beginning of the form. They are not required to complete the remaining parts of the form for so long as the exclusion remains applicable.

A debtor who is or has been a Reservist or a National Guard member may qualify for the exclusion described in part 1C by being called to active duty service after September 11, 2001, for a period of at least 90 days, or while performing homeland defense activity for a period of at least 90 days. After the debtor has been released from active duty or has ceased performing homeland defense activity, the exclusion applies for a period of 540 days after the release date or cessation of homeland defense activity. Under those circumstances the debtor must state the date of release from active duty or the date on which the performance of homeland defense activity terminated.

If the Reservist and National Guard exclusion terminates during the course of a chapter 7 case—because of the expiration of the 540 day period following the release from active duty or the cessation of homeland defense activity—then the debtor may be required to complete the remaining parts of the form that are applicable to the debtor. If the exclusion terminates while a timely motion to dismiss under § 707(b)(2) may still be filed, Interim Rule 1007-I(n) requires that the debtor complete the remaining parts of the form no later than 14 days after the termination. If the obligation to complete the form arises in these circumstances and the debtor has not previously completed the form, the clerk is required to give the debtor notice of the obligation.

2010 Amendment

Form 22A, lines 19A, 19B, 20A, and 20B, and Form 22C, lines 24A, 24B, 25A, and 25B, are amended to delete the terms "household" and "household size" and to replace them with "number of persons" or "family size." Under § 707(b)(2)(A)(ii)(I) means test deductions for food, clothing, and other items and for health care are permitted to be taken in the amounts specified in the IRS National Standards. The IRS National Standards are based on numbers of persons, not household size. Similarly, the IRS Local Standards are based on family, not household, size. The IRS itself generally determines the applicable number of persons or family size for these purposes according to the number of dependents that the debtor claims for federal income tax purposes.

In order for Forms 22A and 22C to reflect more accurately the manner in which the specified National and Local Standards are applied by the IRS, the references to "household" and "household size" are deleted, and the substituted terms— "number of persons" and "family size"—are defined in terms of exemptions on the debtor's federal income tax return and other dependents.

Form 22A, line 8, Form 22B, line 7, and Form 22C, line 7, are amended to add an instruction that only one joint filer should report regular payments by another person for household expenses. Reporting of the figure by both spouses results in an erroneous double-counting of this source of income.

The introductory instruction to Part I of Form 22A is amended to direct debtors in joint cases to file separate forms if only one of the debtors is entitled to an exemption under Part I and the debtors believe that the filing of separate forms is required by § 707(b)(2)(C) of the Code. The language of § 707(b) is ambiguous about how the exclusions from means testing authorized by § 707(b)(1) (for debtors whose debts are not primarily consumer debts) and (b)(2)(D) (for certain disabled veterans, National Guard members, and Armed Forces reservists) are to be applied in joint cases. The form does not impose a particular interpretation of these provisions. It leaves up to joint debtors the initial determination of whether the exclusion of one spouse from means testing relieves the other spouse from the obligation to complete the form, and allows any dispute over this matter to be resolved by the courts.

LIBRARY REFERENCES

Corpus Juris Secundum

CJS Bankruptcy § 352, Statement of Current Monthly Income.

Form 23. Debtor's Certification of Completion of Postpetition Instructional Course Concerning Personal Financial Management

B 23 (Official Form 23) (12/10)

UNITED STATES BANKRUPTCY COURT

In re _____,   Case No._____
                      Debtor

                                                   Chapter _____

**DEBTOR'S CERTIFICATION OF COMPLETION OF POSTPETITION INSTRUCTIONAL
COURSE CONCERNING PERSONAL FINANCIAL MANAGEMENT**

Every individual debtor in a chapter 7, chapter 11 in which § 1141(d)(3) applies, or chapter 13 case must file this certification. If a joint petition is filed, each spouse must complete and file a separate certification. Complete one of the following statements and file by the deadline stated below:

☐ I, _____, the debtor in the above-styled case, hereby
              (Printed Name of Debtor)
certify that on _____ *(Date)*, I completed an instructional course in personal financial management

provided by _____, an approved personal financial
                          (Name of Provider)
management provider.

Certificate No. *(if any)*:_____.

☐ I, _____, the debtor in the above-styled case, hereby
              (Printed Name of Debtor)
certify that no personal financial management course is required because of *[Check the appropriate box.]*:
    ☐ Incapacity or disability, as defined in 11 U.S.C. § 109(h);
    ☐ Active military duty in a military combat zone; or
    ☐ Residence in a district in which the United States trustee (or bankruptcy administrator) has determined that
the approved instructional courses are not adequate at this time to serve the additional individuals who would otherwise
be required to complete such courses.

Signature of Debtor: _____

Date: _____

Instructions: Use this form only to certify whether you completed a course in personal financial management. (Fed. R. Bankr. P. 1007(b)(7).) Do NOT use this form to file the certificate given to you by your prepetition credit counseling provider and do NOT include with the petition when filing your case.

Filing Deadlines: In a chapter 7 case, file within 60 days of the first date set for the meeting of creditors under § 341 of the Bankruptcy Code. In a chapter 11 or 13 case, file no later than the last payment made by the debtor as required by the plan or the filing of a motion for a discharge under § 1141(d)(5)(B) or § 1328(b) of the Code. (See Fed. R. Bankr. P. 1007(c).)

(Added Aug. 11, 2005, eff. Oct. 17, 2005; amended Oct. 11, 2006; Dec. 1, 2007; Dec. 1, 2008; Dec. 1, 2009; Dec. 1, 2010.)

ADVISORY COMMITTEE NOTES

2005 Amendment

The form is new. Sections 727(a)(11) and 1328(g)(1), which were added to the Code by the Bankruptcy Abuse Prevention and Consumer Protection Act of 2005, Pub. L. No. 109–8, 119 Stat. 23 (April 20, 2005), require the debtor to complete an instructional course concerning personal financial management as a condition for receiving a discharge. The completed form, when filed by the debtor, will signal the clerk that this condition has been satisfied.

2006 Amendment

The form is amended to direct each individual debtor, including both spouses in a joint case, to file a separate certification and to provide the certificate number of the certificate of completion issued to the debtor by the approved personal financial management counselor. The form also is amended to include the deadlines for filing the certification in cases under chapters 7 and 13 and to instruct the debtor that the form is not to be used to file the certificate provided by the debtor's prepetition credit counselor.

2005-2007 Amendments

(The 2005–2007 Committee Note incorporates Committee Notes previously published in 2005 and 2006.)

The form was issued in 2005. Sections 727(a)(11), 1141(d)(3) and 1328(g)(1), which were added to the Code by the Bankruptcy Abuse Prevention and Consumer Protection Act of 2005, Pub. L. No. 109–8, 119 Stat. 23 (April 20, 2005), require individual debtors to complete an instructional course concerning personal financial management as a condition for receiving a discharge. The completed form will signal the clerk that this condition has been satisfied. Each individual debtor, including both spouses in a joint case, must file a separate certification and provide the certificate number of the certificate of completion issued to the debtor by the approved personal financial management counselor. Instructions are included that state the deadlines for filing the certification in chapter 7, chapter 11 in which § 1141(d)(3) applies, and chapter 13 cases, and remind the debtor that the form is not to be used for filing a certification of prepetition credit counseling.

2009 Amendments

The statement of the deadline for filing the form in a chapter 7 case is amended to conform to amended Rule 1007(c).

2010 Amendment

The statement of the deadline for filing the form in a chapter 7 case is amended to conform to amended Rule 1007(c).

LIBRARY REFERENCES

Corpus Juris Secundum

CJS Bankruptcy § 353, Statement of Completion of Course in Personal Financial Management.

Form 24. Certification to Court
of Appeals by all Parties

B 24 (Official Form 24) (12/07)

[Caption as described in Fed. R. Bankr. P. 7010 or 9004(b), as applicable.]

CERTIFICATION TO COURT OF APPEALS
BY ALL PARTIES

A notice of appeal having been filed in the above-styled matter on _____ *[Date]*,
_____, _____, and _____, *[Names of all the appellants and all the appellees, if any]*, who are all the appellants [and all the appellees] hereby certify to the court under 28 U.S.C. § 158(d)(2)(A) that a circumstance specified in 28 U.S.C. § 158(d)(2) exists as stated below.

Leave to appeal in this matter ☐ is ☐ is not required under 28 U.S.C. § 158(a).

[If from a final judgment, order, or decree] This certification arises in an appeal from a final judgment, order, or decree of the United States Bankruptcy Court for the _____ District of _____ entered on _____ *[Date]*.

[If from an interlocutory order or decree] This certification arises in an appeal from an interlocutory order or decree, and the parties hereby request leave to appeal as required by 28 U.S.C. § 158(a).

[The certification shall contain one or more of the following statements, as is appropriate to the circumstances.]

The judgment, order, or decree involves a question of law as to which there is no controlling decision of the court of appeals for this circuit or of the Supreme Court of the United States, or involves a matter of public importance.

Or

The judgment, order, or decree involves a question of law requiring resolution of conflicting decisions.

Or

An immediate appeal from the judgment, order, or decree may materially advance the progress of the case or proceeding in which the appeal is taken.

B 24 (Official Form 24) (12/07) - Cont.   Page 2

[The parties may include or attach the information specified in Rule 8001(f)(3)(C).]

Signed: *[If there are more than two signatories, all must sign and provide the information requested below. Attach additional signed sheets if needed.]*

_____	_____
Attorney for Appellant (or Appellant, if not represented by an attorney)	Attorney for Appellee (or Appellee if not represented by an attorney)
_____	_____
Printed Name of Signer	Printed Name of Signer
_____	_____
Address	Address
_____	_____
Telephone No.	Telephone No.
_____	_____
Date	Date

(Added Aug. 11, 2005, eff. Oct. 17, 2005; Dec. 1, 2007.)

ADVISORY COMMITTEE NOTES
2005 Amendment

This form is new. Rule 8001, as amended in 2005, requires that any certification of an appeal, bankruptcy court judgment, order, or decree directly to the United States Court of Appeals by all the appellants and appellees (if any) acting jointly be filed on this form.

2005-2007 Amendments

(The 2005–2007 Committee Note incorporates the Committee Note previously published in 2005.)

This form was issued in 2005. Rule 8001 requires that any certification of an appeal, bankruptcy court judgment, order, or decree directly to the United States Court of Appeals by all the appellants and appellees (if any) acting jointly be filed on this form.

Form 25A. Plan of Reorganization in Small Business Case Under Chapter 11

B25A (Official Form 25A) (12/11)

United States Bankruptcy Court

_____ District of _____

In re_____,   Case No. _____
                Debtor

Small Business Case under Chapter 11

[NAME OF PROPONENT]'S PLAN OF REORGANIZATION, DATED [INSERT DATE]

ARTICLE I
SUMMARY

This Plan of Reorganization (the "Plan") under chapter 11 of the Bankruptcy Code (the "Code") proposes to pay creditors of [insert the name of the debtor] (the "Debtor") from [specify sources of payment, such as an infusion of capital, loan proceeds, sale of assets, cash flow from operations, or future income].

This Plan provides for _____ classes of secured claims; _____ classes of unsecured claims; and _____ classes of equity security holders. Unsecured creditors holding allowed claims will receive distributions, which the proponent of this Plan has valued at approximately __ cents on the dollar. This Plan also provides for the payment of administrative and priority claims [if payment is not in full on the effective date of this Plan with respect to any such claim (to the extent permitted by the Code or the claimant's agreement), identify such claim and briefly summarize the proposed treatment.]

All creditors and equity security holders should refer to Articles III through VI of this Plan for information regarding the precise treatment of their claim. A disclosure statement that provides more detailed information regarding this Plan and the rights of creditors and equity security holders has been circulated with this Plan. **Your rights may be affected. You should read these papers carefully and discuss them with your attorney, if you have one. (If you do not have an attorney, you may wish to consult one.)**

ARTICLE II
CLASSIFICATION OF CLAIMS AND INTERESTS

2.01   Class 1.   All allowed claims entitled to priority under § 507 of the Code (except administrative expense claims under § 507(a)(2), ["gap" period claims in an involuntary case under § 507(a)(3),] and priority tax claims under § 507(a)(8)).

2.02   Class 2.   The claim of _____ , to the extent allowed as a secured claim under § 506 of the Code.

[Add other classes of secured creditors, if any. Note: Section 1129(a)(9)(D) of the Code provides that a secured tax claim which would otherwise meet the description of a priority tax claim under § 507(a)(8) of the Code is to be paid in the same manner and over the same period as prescribed in § 507(a)(8).]

2.03   Class 3.   All unsecured claims allowed under § 502 of the Code.

[Add other classes of unsecured claims, if any.]

2.04   Class 4 .   Equity interests of the Debtor.   [If the Debtor is an individual, change this heading to "The interests of the individual Debtor in property of the estate."]

ARTICLE III
TREATMENT OF ADMINISTRATIVE EXPENSE CLAIMS,
U.S. TRUSTEES FEES, AND PRIORITY TAX CLAIMS

3.01   Unclassified Claims.   Under section §1123(a)(1), administrative expense claims, ["gap" period claims in an involuntary case allowed under § 502(f) of the Code,] and priority tax claims are not in classes.

3.02   Administrative Expense Claims.   Each holder of an administrative expense claim allowed under § 503 of the Code [, and a "gap" claim in an involuntary case allowed under § 502(f) of the Code,] will be paid in full on the effective date of this Plan (as defined in Article VII), in cash, or upon such other terms as may be agreed upon by the holder of the claim and the Debtor.

3.03   Priority Tax Claims.   Each holder of a priority tax claim will be paid [specify terms of treatment consistent with § 1129(a)(9)(C) of the Code].

3.04   United States Trustee Fees.   All fees required to be paid by 28 U.S.C. §1930(a)(6) (U.S. Trustee Fees) will accrue and be timely paid until the case is closed, dismissed, or converted to another chapter of the Code. Any U.S. Trustee Fees owed on or before the effective date of this Plan will be paid on the effective date.

ARTICLE IV
TREATMENT OF CLAIMS AND INTERESTS UNDER THE PLAN

4.01   Claims and interests shall be treated as follows under this Plan:

B25A (Official Form 25A) (12/11) - Cont.   3

Class	Impairment	Treatment
Class 1 - Priority Claims	[State whether impaired or unimpaired.]	[Insert treatment of priority claims in this Class, including the form, amount and timing of distribution, if any. For example: "Class 1 is unimpaired by this Plan, and each holder of a Class 1 Priority Claim will be paid in full, in cash, upon the later of the effective date of this Plan as defined in Article VII, or the date on which such claim is allowed by a final non-appealable order. Except: _____."]
Class 2 – Secured Claim of [Insert name of secured creditor.]	[State whether impaired or unimpaired.]	[Insert treatment of secured claim in this Class, including the form, amount and timing of distribution, if any.] [Add class[es] of secured claims if applicable]
Class 3 - General Unsecured Creditors	[State whether impaired or unimpaired.]	[Insert treatment of unsecured creditors in this Class, including the form, amount and timing of distribution, if any.] [Add administrative convenience class if applicable]
Class 4 - Equity Security Holders of the Debtor	[State whether impaired or unimpaired.]	[Insert treatment of equity security holders in this Class, including the form, amount and timing of distribution, if any.]

ARTICLE V
ALLOWANCE AND DISALLOWANCE OF CLAIMS

5.01   Disputed Claim. A disputed claim is a claim that has not been allowed or disallowed [by a final non-appealable order], and as to which either: (i) a proof of claim has been filed or deemed filed, and the Debtor or another party in interest has filed an objection; or (ii) no proof of claim has been filed, and the Debtor has scheduled such claim as disputed, contingent, or unliquidated.

5.02   Delay of Distribution on a Disputed Claim. No distribution will be made on account of a disputed claim unless such claim is allowed [by a final non-appealable order].

5.03   Settlement of Disputed Claims. The Debtor will have the power and authority to settle and compromise a disputed claim with court approval and compliance with Rule 9019 of the Federal Rules of Bankruptcy Procedure.

B25A (Official Form 25A) (12/11) - Cont.   4

ARTICLE VI
PROVISIONS FOR EXECUTORY CONTRACTS AND UNEXPIRED LEASES

6.01   Assumed Executory Contracts and Unexpired Leases.

(a)   The Debtor assumes the following executory contracts and/or unexpired leases effective upon the [Insert "effective date of this Plan as provided in Article VII," "the date of the entry of the order confirming this Plan," or other applicable date]:

[List assumed executory contracts and/or unexpired leases.]

(b)   The Debtor will be conclusively deemed to have rejected all executory contracts and/or unexpired leases not expressly assumed under section 6.01(a) above, or before the date of the order confirming this Plan, upon the [Insert "effective date of this Plan," "the date of the entry of the order confirming this Plan," or other applicable date]. A proof of a claim arising from the rejection of an executory contract or unexpired lease under this section must be filed no later than _____ (___) days after the date of the order confirming this Plan.

ARTICLE VII
MEANS FOR IMPLEMENTATION OF THE PLAN

[Insert here provisions regarding how the plan will be implemented as required under §1123(a)(5) of the Code. For example, provisions may include those that set out how the plan will be funded, as well as who will be serving as directors, officers or voting trustees of the reorganized debtor.]

ARTICLE VIII
GENERAL PROVISIONS

8.01   Definitions and Rules of Construction. The definitions and rules of construction set forth in §§ 101 and 102 of the Code shall apply when terms defined or construed in the Code are used in this Plan, and they are supplemented by the following definitions: [Insert additional definitions if necessary].

8.02   Effective Date of Plan. The effective date of this Plan is the first business day following the date that is fourteen days after the entry of the order of confirmation. If, however, a stay of the confirmation order is in effect on that date, the effective date will be the first business day after the date on which the stay of the confirmation order expires or is otherwise terminated.

8.03   Severability.   If any provision in this Plan is determined to be unenforceable, the determination will in no way limit or affect the enforceability and operative effect of any other provision of this Plan.

8.04   Binding Effect.   The rights and obligations of any entity named or referred to in this Plan will be binding upon, and will inure to the benefit of the successors or assigns of such entity.

8.05   Captions.   The headings contained in this Plan are for convenience of reference only and do not affect the meaning or interpretation of this Plan.

[8.06   Controlling Effect.   Unless a rule of law or procedure is supplied by federal law (including the Code or the Federal Rules of Bankruptcy Procedure), the laws of the State of _____ govern this Plan and any agreements, documents, and instruments executed in connection with this Plan, except as otherwise provided in this Plan.]

[8.07   Corporate Governance.   [If the Debtor is a corporation include provisions required by § 1123(a)(6) of the Code.]]

ARTICLE IX
DISCHARGE

[If the Debtor is not entitled to discharge under 11 U.S.C. § 1141(d)(3) change this heading to
"NO DISCHARGE OF DEBTOR."]

9.01.   **[Option 1 – If Debtor is an individual and § 1141(d)(3) is not applicable]**
Discharge. Confirmation of this Plan does not discharge any debt provided for in this Plan until the court grants a discharge on completion of all payments under this Plan, or as otherwise provided in § 1141(d)(5) of the Code. The Debtor will not be discharged from any debt excepted from discharge under § 523 of the Code, except as provided in Rule 4007(c) of the Federal Rules of Bankruptcy Procedure.

**[Option 2 -- If the Debtor is a partnership and section 1141(d)(3) of the Code
is not applicable]**
Discharge. On the confirmation date of this Plan, the debtor will be discharged from any debt that arose before confirmation of this Plan, subject to the occurrence of the effective date, to the extent specified in § 1141(d)(1)(A) of the Code. The Debtor will not be discharged from any debt imposed by this Plan.

[Option 3 -- If the Debtor is a corporation and § 1141(d)(3) is not applicable]
Discharge. On the confirmation date of this Plan, the debtor will be discharged from any debt that arose before confirmation of this Plan, subject to the occurrence of the effective date, to the extent specified in § 1141(d)(1)(A) of the Code, except that the Debtor will not be discharged of any debt: (i) imposed by this Plan; (ii) of a kind specified in § 1141(d)(6)(A) if a timely complaint was filed in accordance with Rule 4007(c) of the Federal Rules of Bankruptcy Procedure; or (iii) of a kind specified in § 1141(d)(6)(B).

[Option 4 – If § 1141(d)(3) is applicable]

No Discharge. In accordance with § 1141(d)(3) of the Code, the Debtor will not receive any discharge of debt in this bankruptcy case.

ARTICLE X
OTHER PROVISIONS

[Insert other provisions, as applicable.]

Respectfully submitted,

By: _____
The Plan Proponent

By: _____
Attorney for the Plan Proponent

(Added Dec. 1, 2008, and amended Dec. 1, 2011.)

ADVISORY COMMITTEE NOTES

2008 Enactment

This form is new. It implements § 433 of the Bankruptcy Abuse Prevention and Consumer Protection Act of 2005, Pub. L. No. 109–8, 119 Stat. 23 (April 20, 2005). This form for a small business chapter 11 plan of reorganization may be used in cases where the debtor (whether an individual or an artificial entity) is a small business debtor under § 101(51D) of the Code. The form is intended to be used in conjunction with the small business chapter 11 disclosure statement form (Official Form 25B).

Because the type of debtor and the details of the proposed plan of reorganization may vary, the form is intended to provide an illustrative format, rather than a specific prescription for the language or content of a plan in any particular case. The form includes instructions and examples of the types of information needed to complete it.

2011 Amendment

Provision 8.02 of Article VIII of the form, which specifies the plan's effective date, is amended to reflect the change in the time periods of Rules 3020(e) and 8002(a) for a stay of the confirmation order and the filing of a notice of appeal. As of December 1, 2009, both time periods were increased from ten to fourteen days. The effective date of the plan will generally be the first business day after those time periods expire. Accordingly, the effective date of the plan is extended to the first business day following the date that is fourteen days after the entry of the order of confirmation. If, however, a stay of the confirmation order remains in effect on the specified effective date, the plan will instead go into effect on the first business day after the stay expires or is terminated, so long as the order of confirmation has not been vacated.

**Form 25B.   Disclosure Statement in Small
Business Case Under Chapter 11**

B25B (Official Form 25B) (12/08)

United States Bankruptcy Court

_____ District of _____

In re_____,   Case No. _____
        Debtor

Small Business Case under Chapter 11

[NAME OF PLAN PROPONENT]'S DISCLOSURE STATEMENT, DATED [INSERT DATE]

Table of Contents

[Insert when text is finalized]

I.   **INTRODUCTION**

This is the disclosure statement (the "Disclosure Statement") in the small business chapter 11 case of _____ (the "Debtor"). This Disclosure Statement contains information about the Debtor and describes the [insert name of plan] (the "Plan") filed by [the Debtor] on [insert date]. A full copy of the Plan is attached to this Disclosure Statement as Exhibit A. *Your rights may be affected. You should read the Plan and this Disclosure Statement carefully and discuss them with your attorney. If you do not have an attorney, you may wish to consult one.*

The proposed distributions under the Plan are discussed at pages __-__ of this Disclosure Statement. [General unsecured creditors are classified in Class __, and will receive a distribution of ___% of their allowed claims, to be distributed as follows _____.]

A.   **Purpose of This Document**

This Disclosure Statement describes:

* The Debtor and significant events during the bankruptcy case,
* How the Plan proposes to treat claims or equity interests of the type you hold (*i.e.*, what you will receive on your claim or equity interest if the plan is confirmed),
* Who can vote on or object to the Plan,
* What factors the Bankruptcy Court (the "Court") will consider when deciding whether to confirm the Plan,
* Why [the Proponent] believes the Plan is feasible, and how the treatment of your claim or equity interest under the Plan compares to what you would receive on your claim or equity interest in liquidation, and
* The effect of confirmation of the Plan.

Be sure to read the Plan as well as the Disclosure Statement. This Disclosure Statement describes the Plan, but it is the Plan itself that will, if confirmed, establish your rights.

B.   **Deadlines for Voting and Objecting; Date of Plan Confirmation Hearing**

The Court has not yet confirmed the Plan described in this Disclosure Statement. This section describes the procedures pursuant to which the Plan will or will not be confirmed.

1.   *Time and Place of the Hearing to [Finally Approve This Disclosure Statement and] Confirm the Plan*

The hearing at which the Court will determine whether to [finally approve this Disclosure Statement and] confirm the Plan will take place on [insert date] , at [insert time], in Courtroom _____, at the [Insert Courthouse Name, and Full Court Address, City, State, Zip Code].

2.   *Deadline For Voting to Accept or Reject the Plan*

Form 25B

OFFICIAL FORMS

If you are entitled to vote to accept or reject the plan, vote on the enclosed ballot and return the ballot in the enclosed envelope to [insert address]. See section IV.A. below for a discussion of voting eligibility requirements.

Your ballot must be received by [insert date] or it will not be counted.

      3.   *Deadline For Objecting to the [Adequacy of Disclosure and] Confirmation of the Plan*

Objections to [this Disclosure Statement or to] the confirmation of the Plan must be filed with the Court and served upon [insert entities] by [insert date].

      4.   *Identity of Person to Contact for More Information*

If you want additional information about the Plan, you should contact [insert name and address of representative of plan proponent].

      C.   **Disclaimer**

The Court has [conditionally] approved this Disclosure Statement as containing adequate information to enable parties affected by the Plan to make an informed judgment about its terms. The Court has not yet determined whether the Plan meets the legal requirements for confirmation, and the fact that the Court has approved this Disclosure Statement does not constitute an endorsement of the Plan by the Court, or a recommendation that it be accepted. [The Court's approval of this Disclosure Statement is subject to final approval at the hearing on confirmation of the Plan. Objections to the adequacy of this Disclosure Statement may be filed until _____.]

    II.   **BACKGROUND**

      A.   **Description and History of the Debtor's Business**

The Debtor is a [corporation, partnership, etc.]. Since [insert year operations commenced], the Debtor has been in the business of _____. [Describe the Debtor's business].

      B.   **Insiders of the Debtor**

[Insert a detailed list of the names of Debtor's insiders as defined in §101(31) of the United States Bankruptcy Code (the "Code") and their relationship to the Debtor. For each insider, list all compensation paid by the Debtor or its affiliates to that person or entity during the two years prior to the commencement of the Debtor's bankruptcy case, as well as compensation paid during the pendency of this chapter 11 case.]

      C.   **Management of the Debtor Before and During the Bankruptcy**

During the two years prior to the date on which the bankruptcy petition was filed, the officers, directors, managers or other persons in control of the Debtor (collectively the "Managers") were [List the Managers of the Debtor prior to the petition date].

The Managers of the Debtor during the Debtor's chapter 11 case have been: [List Managers of the Debtor during the Debtor's chapter 11 case.]

After the effective date of the order confirming the Plan, the directors, officers, and voting trustees of the Debtor, any affiliate of the Debtor participating in a joint Plan with the Debtor, or successor of the Debtor under the Plan (collectively the "Post Confirmation Managers"), will be: [List Post Confirmation Managers of the Debtor.] The responsibilities and compensation of these Post Confirmation Managers are described in section __ of this Disclosure Statement.

D.   **Events Leading to Chapter 11 Filing**

[Describe the events that led to the commencement of the Debtor's bankruptcy case.]

E.   **Significant Events During the Bankruptcy Case**

[Describe significant events during the Debtor's bankruptcy case:

- Describe any asset sales outside the ordinary course of business, debtor in possession financing, or cash collateral orders.
- Identify the professionals approved by the court.
- Describe any adversary proceedings that have been filed or other significant litigation that has occurred (including contested claim disallowance proceedings), and any other significant legal or administrative proceedings that are pending or have been pending during the case in a forum other than the Court.
- Describe any steps taken to improve operations and profitability of the Debtor.
- Describe other events as appropriate.]

F.   **Projected Recovery of Avoidable Transfers [Choose the option that applies]**

[Option 1 – If the Debtor does not intend to pursue avoidance actions]

The Debtor does not intend to pursue preference, fraudulent conveyance, or other avoidance actions.

[Option 2 – If the Debtor intends to pursue avoidance actions]

The Debtor estimates that up to $_____ may be realized from the recovery of fraudulent, preferential or other avoidable transfers. While the results of litigation cannot be predicted with certainty and it is possible that other causes of action may be identified, the following is a summary of the preference, fraudulent conveyance and other avoidance actions filed or expected to be filed in this case:

Transaction	Defendant	Amount Claimed

[Option 3 – If the Debtor does not yet know whether it intends to pursue avoidance actions]

Form 25B

The Debtor has not yet completed its investigation with regard to prepetition transactions. If you received a payment or other transfer within 90 days of the bankruptcy, or other transfer avoidable under the Code, the Debtor may seek to avoid such transfer.

G.   Claims Objections

Except to the extent that a claim is already allowed pursuant to a final non-appealable order, the Debtor reserves the right to object to claims. Therefore, even if your claim is allowed for voting purposes, you may not be entitled to a distribution if an objection to your claim is later upheld. The procedures for resolving disputed claims are set forth in Article V of the Plan.

H.   Current and Historical Financial Conditions

The identity and fair market value of the estate's assets are listed in Exhibit B. [Identify source and basis of valuation.]

The Debtor's most recent financial statements [if any] issued before bankruptcy, each of which was filed with the Court, are set forth in Exhibit C.

[The most recent post-petition operating report filed since the commencement of the Debtor's bankruptcy case are set forth in Exhibit D.] [A summary of the Debtor's periodic operating reports filed since the commencement of the Debtor's bankruptcy case is set forth in Exhibit D.]

III.   SUMMARY OF THE PLAN OF REORGANIZATION AND TREATMENT OF CLAIMS AND EQUITY INTERESTS

A.   What is the Purpose of the Plan of Reorganization?

As required by the Code, the Plan places claims and equity interests in various classes and describes the treatment each class will receive. The Plan also states whether each class of claims or equity interests is impaired or unimpaired. If the Plan is confirmed, your recovery will be limited to the amount provided by the Plan.

B.   Unclassified Claims

Certain types of claims are automatically entitled to specific treatment under the Code. They are not considered impaired, and holders of such claims do not vote on the Plan. They may, however, object if, in their view, their treatment under the Plan does not comply with that required by the Code. As such, the Plan Proponent has *not* placed the following claims in any class:

1.   *Administrative Expenses*

Administrative expenses are costs or expenses of administering the Debtor's chapter 11 case which are allowed under § 507(a)(2) of the Code. Administrative expenses also include the value of any goods sold to the Debtor in the ordinary course of business and received within 20 days before the date of the bankruptcy petition. The Code requires that all administrative expenses be paid on the effective date of the Plan, unless a particular claimant agrees to a different treatment.

The following chart lists the Debtor's estimated administrative expenses, and their proposed treatment under the Plan:

Type	Estimated Amount Owed	Proposed Treatment
Expenses Arising in the Ordinary Course of Business After the Petition Date		Paid in full on the effective date of the Plan, or according to terms of obligation if later
The Value of Goods Received in the Ordinary Course of Business Within 20 Days Before the Petition Date		Paid in full on the effective date of the Plan, or according to terms of obligation if later
Professional Fees, as approved by the Court.		Paid in full on the effective date of the Plan, or according to separate written agreement, or according to court order if such fees have not been approved by the Court on the effective date of the Plan
Clerk's Office Fees		Paid in full on the effective date of the Plan
Other administrative expenses		Paid in full on the effective date of the Plan or according to separate written agreement
Office of the U.S. Trustee Fees		Paid in full on the effective date of the Plan
TOTAL		

    2.   *Priority Tax Claims*

Priority tax claims are unsecured income, employment, and other taxes described by § 507(a)(8) of the Code. Unless the holder of such a § 507(a)(8) priority tax claim agrees otherwise, it must receive the present value of such claim, in regular installments paid over a period not exceeding 5 years from the order of relief.

Form 25B

B25B (Official Form 25B) (12/08) – Cont.   7

The following chart lists the Debtor's estimated § 507(a)(8) priority tax claims and their proposed treatment under the Plan:

Description (name and type of tax)	Estimated Amount Owed	Date of Assessment	Treatment	
			Pmt interval	=
			[Monthly] payment	=
			Begin date	=
			End date	=
			Interest Rate %	=
			Total Payout Amount	= $
			Pmt interval	=
			[Monthly] payment	=
			Begin date	=
			End date	=
			Interest Rate %	=
			Total Payout Amount	= $

C.   **Classes of Claims and Equity Interests**

The following are the classes set forth in the Plan, and the proposed treatment that they will receive under the Plan:

1.   *Classes of Secured Claims*

Allowed Secured Claims are claims secured by property of the Debtor's bankruptcy estate (or that are subject to setoff) to the extent allowed as secured claims under § 506 of the Code. If the value of the collateral or setoffs securing the creditor's claim is less than the amount of the creditor's allowed claim, the deficiency will [be classified as a general unsecured claim].

The following chart lists all classes containing Debtor's secured prepetition claims and their proposed treatment under the Plan:

Class #	Description	Insider? (Yes or No)	Impairment	Treatment
	Secured claim of: Name = Collateral description = Allowed Secured Amount = $_____ Priority of lien = Principal owed = $_____ Pre-pet. arrearage = $_____ Total claim = $_____		[State whether impaired or unimpaired]	[Monthly] Pmt = Pmts Begin = Pmts End = [Balloon pmt] = Interest rate % = Treatment of Lien = [Additional payment required to cure defaults] =
	Secured claim of: Name = Collateral description = Allowed Secured Amount = $_____ Priority of lien = Principal owed = $_____ Pre-pet. arrearage = $_____ Total claim = $_____		[State whether impaired or unimpaired]	Monthly Pmt = Pmts Begin = Pmts End = [Balloon pmt] = Interest rate % = Treatment of Lien = [Additional payment required to cure defaults] =

    2.   *Classes of Priority Unsecured Claims*

Certain priority claims that are referred to in §§ 507(a)(1), (4), (5), (6), and (7) of the Code are required to be placed in classes. The Code requires that each holder of such a claim receive cash on the effective date of the Plan equal to the allowed amount of such claim. However, a class of holders of such claims may vote to accept different treatment.

Form 25B

B25B (Official Form 25B) (12/08) – Cont.

The following chart lists all classes containing claims under §§ 507(a)(1), (4), (5), (6), and (a)(7) of the Code and their proposed treatment under the Plan:

Class #	Description	Impairment	Treatment
	Priority unsecured claim pursuant to Section [insert] Total amt of claims = $	[State whether impaired or unimpaired]	
	Priority unsecured claim pursuant to Section [insert] Total amt of claims = $	[State whether impaired or unimpaired]	

3. *Class[es] of General Unsecured Claims*

General unsecured claims are not secured by property of the estate and are not entitled to priority under § 507(a) of the Code. [Insert description of §1122(b) convenience class if applicable.]

The following chart identifies the Plan's proposed treatment of Class[es] __ through __, which contain general unsecured claims against the Debtor:

Class #	Description	Impairment	Treatment
	[1122(b) Convenience Class]	[State whether impaired or unimpaired]	[Insert proposed treatment, such as "Paid in full in cash on effective date of the Plan or when due under contract or applicable nonbankruptcy law"]
	General Unsecured Class	[State whether impaired or unimpaired]	Monthly Pmt = Pmts Begin = Pmts End = [Balloon pmt] = Interest rate % from [date] = Estimated percent of claim paid =

4. *Class[es] of Equity Interest Holders*

Equity interest holders are parties who hold an ownership interest (*i.e.*, equity interest) in the Debtor. In a corporation, entities holding preferred or common stock are equity interest holders. In a partnership, equity interest holders include both general and limited partners. In a limited liability company ("LLC"), the equity interest holders are the members. Finally, with respect to an individual who is a debtor, the Debtor is the equity interest holder.

The following chart sets forth the Plan's proposed treatment of the class[es] of equity interest holders: [There may be more than one class of equity interests in, for example, a partnership case, or a case where the prepetition debtor had issued multiple classes of stock.]

Class #	Description	Impairment	Treatment
	Equity interest holders	[State whether impaired or unimpaired]	

D.   **Means of Implementing the Plan**

1.   *Source of Payments*

Payments and distributions under the Plan will be funded by the following:

[Describe the source of funds for payments under the Plan.]

2.   *Post-confirmation Management*

The Post-Confirmation Managers of the Debtor, and their compensation, shall be as follows:

Name	Affiliations	Insider (yes or no)?	Position	Compensation

E.   **Risk Factors**

The proposed Plan has the following risks:

[List all risk factors that might affect the Debtor's ability to make payments and other distributions required under the Plan.]

F.   **Executory Contracts and Unexpired Leases**

Form 25B

OFFICIAL FORMS

The Plan, in Exhibit 5.1, lists all executory contracts and unexpired leases that the Debtor will assume under the Plan. Assumption means that the Debtor has elected to continue to perform the obligations under such contracts and unexpired leases, and to cure defaults of the type that must be cured under the Code, if any. Exhibit 5.1 also lists how the Debtor will cure and compensate the other party to such contract or lease for any such defaults.

If you object to the assumption of your unexpired lease or executory contract, the proposed cure of any defaults, or the adequacy of assurance of performance, you must file and serve your objection to the Plan within the deadline for objecting to the confirmation of the Plan, unless the Court has set an earlier time.

All executory contracts and unexpired leases that are not listed in Exhibit 5.1 will be rejected under the Plan. Consult your adviser or attorney for more specific information about particular contracts or leases.

If you object to the rejection of your contract or lease, you must file and serve your objection to the Plan within the deadline for objecting to the confirmation of the Plan.

[The Deadline for Filing a Proof of Claim Based on a Claim Arising from the Rejection of a Lease or Contract Is _____. Any claim based on the rejection of a contract or lease will be barred if the proof of claim is not timely filed, unless the Court orders otherwise.]

G.　　**Tax Consequences of Plan**

Creditors and Equity Interest Holders Concerned with How the Plan May Affect Their Tax Liability Should Consult with Their Own Accountants, Attorneys, And/Or Advisors.

The following are the anticipated tax consequences of the Plan: [List the following general consequences as a minimum: (1)Tax consequences to the Debtor of the Plan; (2) General tax consequences on creditors of any discharge, and the general tax consequences of receipt of plan consideration after confirmation.]

IV.　　**CONFIRMATION REQUIREMENTS AND PROCEDURES**

To be confirmable, the Plan must meet the requirements listed in §§ 1129(a) or (b) of the Code. These include the requirements that: the Plan must be proposed in good faith; at least one impaired class of claims must accept the plan, without counting votes of insiders; the Plan must distribute to each creditor and equity interest holder at least as much as the creditor or equity interest holder would receive in a chapter 7 liquidation case, unless the creditor or equity interest holder votes to accept the Plan; and the Plan must be feasible. These requirements are <u>not</u> the only requirements listed in § 1129, and they are not the only requirements for confirmation.

A.   **Who May Vote or Object**

Any party in interest may object to the confirmation of the Plan if the party believes that the requirements for confirmation are not met.

Many parties in interest, however, are not entitled to vote to accept or reject the Plan. A creditor or equity interest holder has a right to vote for or against the Plan only if that creditor or equity interest holder has a claim or equity interest that is both (1) allowed or allowed for voting purposes and (2) impaired.

In this case, the Plan Proponent believes that classes _____ are impaired and that holders of claims in each of these classes are therefore entitled to vote to accept or reject the Plan. The Plan Proponent believes that classes _____ are unimpaired and that holders of claims in each of these classes, therefore, do not have the right to vote to accept or reject the Plan.

1.   *What Is an Allowed Claim or an Allowed Equity Interest?*

Only a creditor or equity interest holder with an allowed claim or an allowed equity interest has the right to vote on the Plan. Generally, a claim or equity interest is allowed if either (1) the Debtor has scheduled the claim on the Debtor's schedules, unless the claim has been scheduled as disputed, contingent, or unliquidated, or (2) the creditor has filed a proof of claim or equity interest, unless an objection has been filed to such proof of claim or equity interest. When a claim or equity interest is not allowed, the creditor or equity interest holder holding the claim or equity interest cannot vote unless the Court, after notice and hearing, either overrules the objection or allows the claim or equity interest for voting purposes pursuant to Rule 3018(a) of the Federal Rules of Bankruptcy Procedure.

The deadline for filing a proof of claim in this case was _____.
[If applicable – The deadline for filing objections to claims is_____.]

2.   *What Is an Impaired Claim or Impaired Equity Interest?*

As noted above, the holder of an allowed claim or equity interest has the right to vote only if it is in a class that is *impaired* under the Plan. As provided in § 1124 of the Code, a class is considered impaired if the Plan alters the legal, equitable, or contractual rights of the members of that class.

3.   *Who is **Not** Entitled to Vote*

The holders of the following five types of claims and equity interests are *not* entitled to vote:
- holders of claims and equity interests that have been disallowed by an order of the Court;

- holders of other claims or equity interests that are not "allowed claims" or "allowed equity interests" (as discussed above), unless they have been "allowed" for voting purposes.

- holders of claims or equity interests in unimpaired classes;

Form 25B

OFFICIAL FORMS

- holders of claims entitled to priority pursuant to §§ 507(a)(2), (a)(3), and (a)(8) of the Code; and

- holders of claims or equity interests in classes that do not receive or retain any value under the Plan;

- administrative expenses.

Even If You Are Not Entitled to Vote on the Plan, You Have a Right to Object to the Confirmation of the Plan [and to the Adequacy of the Disclosure Statement].

4. *Who Can Vote in More Than One Class*

A creditor whose claim has been allowed in part as a secured claim and in part as an unsecured claim, or who otherwise hold claims in multiple classes, is entitled to accept or reject a Plan in each capacity, and should cast one ballot for each claim.

B. **Votes Necessary to Confirm the Plan**

If impaired classes exist, the Court cannot confirm the Plan unless (1) at least one impaired class of creditors has accepted the Plan without counting the votes of any insiders within that class, and (2) all impaired classes have voted to accept the Plan, unless the Plan is eligible to be confirmed by "cram down" on non-accepting classes, as discussed later in Section [B.2.].

1. *Votes Necessary for a Class to Accept the Plan*

A class of claims accepts the Plan if both of the following occur: (1) the holders of more than one-half (1/2) of the allowed claims in the class, who vote, cast their votes to accept the Plan, and (2) the holders of at least two-thirds (2/3) in dollar amount of the allowed claims in the class, who vote, cast their votes to accept the Plan.

A class of equity interests accepts the Plan if the holders of at least two-thirds (2/3) in amount of the allowed equity interests in the class, who vote, cast their votes to accept the Plan.

2. *Treatment of Nonaccepting Classes*

Even if one or more impaired classes reject the Plan, the Court may nonetheless confirm the Plan if the nonaccepting classes are treated in the manner prescribed by § 1129(b) of the Code. A plan that binds nonaccepting classes is commonly referred to as a "cram down" plan. The Code allows the Plan to bind nonaccepting classes of claims or equity interests if it meets all the requirements for consensual confirmation except the voting requirements of § 1129(a)(8) of the Code, does not "discriminate unfairly," and is "fair and equitable" toward each impaired class that has not voted to accept the Plan.

You should consult your own attorney if a "cramdown" confirmation will affect your claim or equity interest, as the variations on this general rule are numerous and complex.

C. **Liquidation Analysis**

To confirm the Plan, the Court must find that all creditors and equity interest holders who do not accept the Plan will receive at least as much under the Plan as such claim and equity interest holders would receive in a chapter 7 liquidation. A liquidation analysis is attached to this Disclosure Statement as Exhibit E.

D. **Feasibility**

The Court must find that confirmation of the Plan is not likely to be followed by the liquidation, or the need for further financial reorganization, of the Debtor or any successor to the Debtor, unless such liquidation or reorganization is proposed in the Plan.

1. *Ability to Initially Fund Plan*

The Plan Proponent believes that the Debtor will have enough cash on hand on the effective date of the Plan to pay all the claims and expenses that are entitled to be paid on that date. Tables showing the amount of cash on hand on the effective date of the Plan, and the sources of that cash are attached to this disclosure statement as Exhibit F.

2. *Ability to Make Future Plan Payments And Operate Without Further Reorganization*

The Plan Proponent must also show that it will have enough cash over the life of the Plan to make the required Plan payments.

The Plan Proponent has provided projected financial information. Those projections are listed in Exhibit G.

The Plan Proponent's financial projections show that the Debtor will have an aggregate annual average cash flow, after paying operating expenses and post-confirmation taxes, of $\_-\_$. The final Plan payment is expected to be paid on _____.

[Summarize the numerical projections, and highlight any assumptions that are not in accord with past experience. Explain why such assumptions should now be made.]

You Should Consult with Your Accountant or other Financial Advisor If You Have Any Questions Pertaining to These Projections.

V. **EFFECT OF CONFIRMATION OF PLAN**

A. **DISCHARGE OF DEBTOR** [If the Debtor is not entitled to discharge pursuant to 11 U.S.C. § 1141(d)(3) change this heading to "**NO DISCHARGE OF DEBTOR**."]

[Option 1 – If Debtor is an individual and § 1141(d)(3) is not applicable]

Form 25B   OFFICIAL FORMS

<u>Discharge.</u> Confirmation of the Plan does not discharge any debt provided for in the Plan until the court grants a discharge on completion of all payments under the Plan, or as otherwise provided in § 1141(d)(5) of the Code. Debtor will not be discharged from any debt excepted from discharge under § 523 of the Code, except as provided in Rule 4007(c) of the Federal Rules of Bankruptcy Procedure.

[Option 2 -- If the Debtor is a partnership and § 1141(d)(3) of the Code is not applicable]

<u>Discharge.</u> On the effective date of the Plan, the Debtor shall be discharged from any debt that arose before confirmation of the Plan, subject to the occurrence of the effective date, to the extent specified in § 1141(d)(1)(A) of the Code. However, the Debtor shall not be discharged from any debt imposed by the Plan. After the effective date of the Plan your claims against the Debtor will be limited to the debts imposed by the Plan.

[Option 3 -- If the Debtor is a corporation and § 1141(d)(3) is not applicable]

<u>Discharge.</u> On the effective date of the Plan, the Debtor shall be discharged from any debt that arose before confirmation of the Plan, subject to the occurrence of the effective date, to the extent specified in § 1141(d)(1)(A) of the Code, except that the Debtor shall not be discharged of any debt (i) imposed by the Plan, (ii) of a kind specified in § 1141(d)(6)(A) if a timely complaint was filed in accordance with Rule 4007(c) of the Federal Rules of Bankruptcy Procedure, or (iii) of a kind specified in § 1141(d)(6)(B). After the effective date of the Plan your claims against the Debtor will be limited to the debts described in clauses (i) through (iii) of the preceding sentence.

[Option 4 – If § 1141(d)(3) is applicable]

<u>No Discharge.</u> In accordance with § 1141(d)(3) of the Code, the Debtor will not receive any discharge of debt in this bankruptcy case.

B.   Modification of Plan

The Plan Proponent may modify the Plan at any time before confirmation of the Plan. However, the Court may require a new disclosure statement and/or revoting on the Plan.

[If the Debtor is not an individual, add the following: "The Plan Proponent may also seek to modify the Plan at any time after confirmation only if (1) the Plan has not been substantially consummated *and* (2) the Court authorizes the proposed modifications after notice and a hearing."]

[If the Debtor is an individual, add the following: "Upon request of the Debtor, the United States trustee, or the holder of an allowed unsecured claim, the Plan may be modified at any time after confirmation of the Plan but before the completion of payments under the Plan, to (1) increase or reduce the amount of payments under the Plan on claims of a particular class, (2) extend or reduce the time period for such payments, or (3) alter the amount of distribution to a creditor whose claim is provided for by the Plan to the extent necessary to take account of any payment of the claim made other than under the Plan."]

C.   Final Decree

B25B (Official Form 25B) (12/08) – Cont.   16

     Once the estate has been fully administered, as provided in Rule 3022 of the Federal Rules of
Bankruptcy Procedure, the Plan Proponent, or such other party as the Court shall designate in the Plan
Confirmation Order, shall file a motion with the Court to obtain a final decree to close the case.
Alternatively, the Court may enter such a final decree on its own motion.

VI.   OTHER PLAN PROVISIONS

    [Insert other provisions here, as necessary and appropriate.]

_____
[Signature of the Plan Proponent]

_____
[Signature of the Attorney for the Plan Proponent]

B25B (Official Form 25B) (12/08) – Cont.   17

EXHIBITS

B25B (Official Form 25B) (12/08) – Cont.   18

Exhibit A – Copy of Proposed Plan of Reorganization

Exhibit B – Identity and Value of Material Assets of Debtor

Exhibit C – Prepetition Financial Statements
(to be taken from those filed with the court)

Exhibit D – [Most Recently Filed Postpetition Operating Report][Summary of Postpetition Operating Reports]

B25B (Official Form 25B) (12/08) – Cont.   22

Exhibit E – Liquidation Analysis

Plan Proponent's Estimated Liquidation Value of Assets

Assets

a.	Cash on hand	$
b.	Accounts receivable	$
c.	Inventory	$
d.	Office furniture & equipment	$
e.	Machinery & equipment	$
f.	Automobiles	$
g.	Building & Land	$
h.	Customer list	$
i.	Investment property (such as stocks, bonds or other financial assets)	$
j.	Lawsuits or other claims against third-parties	$
k.	Other intangibles (such as avoiding powers actions)	$

Total Assets at Liquidation Value $

Less:
Secured creditors' recoveries $
Less:
Chapter 7 trustee fees and expenses $
Less:
Chapter 11 administrative expenses $
Less:
Priority claims, excluding administrative expense claims $
[Less:
Debtor's claimed exemptions] $

(1) Balance for unsecured claims $

(2) Total dollar amount of unsecured claims $

Percentage of Claims Which Unsecured Creditors Would $
Receive Or Retain in a Chapter 7 Liquidation:

Percentage of Claims Which Unsecured Creditors Will   ____% [Divide (1) by (2)]
Receive or Retain under the Plan:

____%

Form 25B

OFFICIAL FORMS

Exhibit F – Cash on hand on the effective date of the Plan

Cash on hand on effective date of the Plan:	$

Less –

Amount of administrative expenses payable on effective date of the Plan	-
Amount of statutory costs and charges	-
Amount of cure payments for executory contracts	-
Other Plan Payments due on effective date of the Plan	-
Balance after paying these amounts...............	$

The sources of the cash Debtor will have on hand by the effective date of the Plan are estimated as follows:

$	Cash in Debtor's bank account now
+	Additional cash Debtor will accumulate from net earnings between now and effective date of the Plan [state the basis for such projections]
+	Borrowing [separately state terms of repayment]
+	Capital Contributions
+	Other
$	Total [This number should match "cash on hand" figure noted above

Exhibit G – Projections of Cash Flow and Earnings for Post-Confirmation Period

(Added Dec. 1, 2008.)

ADVISORY COMMITTEE NOTES
2008 Enactment

This form is new. It implements § 433 of the Bankruptcy Abuse Prevention and Consumer Protection Act of 2005, Pub. L. No. 109–8, 119 Stat. 23 (April 20, 2005), which provides for an official form for a disclosure statement that may be used in cases where the debtor (whether an individual or an artificial entity) is a small business debtor under § 101(51D) of the Code. The form provides a format for disseminating information to parties in interest about the plan of reorganization in a small business debtor's chapter 11 case, so that a party can make a reasonably informed judgment whether to accept, reject, or object to a proposed plan of reorganization or liquidation.

The form is intended to be used in conjunction with the form small business chapter 11 plan (Official Form 25A). As required by § 433 of the 2005 Act, the form seeks to strike a practical balance between the reasonable needs of the courts, the United States trustee, creditors, and other parties in interest for reasonably complete information, on the one hand, and economy and simplicity for debtors, on the other. The form includes instructions and examples of the types of information needed to complete it.

Because the relevant legal requirements for, and effect of, a plan's confirmation may vary depending on the nature of the debtor and the details of the proposed plan, this form is intended to provide an illustrative format for disclosure, rather than a specific prescription for the language or content of a particular disclosure statement. The form highlights the factual and legal disclosures required for adequate disclosure under § 1125 of the Code. The form is not intended to restrict a plan proponent from providing additional information where that would be useful. Plan proponents are encouraged to present material information in as clear a manner as possible, including, where feasible, by providing an accompanying executive summary, approved by the court, that highlights particular creditors' or interest holders' voting status and treatment under the plan.

Rule 3016 specifies the manner in which the disclosure statement is to be filed. Rule 3017 specifies the manner in which the court will consider it. Rule 3017.1 specifies special procedures for the court's conditional approval of a disclosure statement in a small business case.

Form 25C.   Small Business Monthly
            Operating Report

B 25C (Official Form 25C) (12/08)

UNITED STATES BANKRUPTCY COURT

In re _____,   Case No. _____
              Debtor

                                          Small Business Case under Chapter 11

SMALL BUSINESS MONTHLY OPERATING REPORT

Month: _____   Date filed: _____

Line of Business: _____   NAISC Code: _____

IN ACCORDANCE WITH TITLE 28, SECTION 1746, OF THE UNITED STATES CODE, I DECLARE UNDER PENALTY OF
PERJURY THAT I HAVE EXAMINED THE FOLLOWING SMALL BUSINESS MONTHLY OPERATING REPORT AND THE
ACCOMPANYING ATTACHMENTS AND, TO THE BEST OF MY KNOWLEDGE, THESE DOCUMENTS ARE TRUE,
CORRECT AND COMPLETE.

RESPONSIBLE PARTY:

_____
Original Signature of Responsible Party

_____
Printed Name of Responsible Party

Questionnaire: *(All questions to be answered on behalf of the debtor.)*	Yes	No
1. IS THE BUSINESS STILL OPERATING?	❐	❐
2. HAVE YOU PAID ALL YOUR BILLS ON TIME THIS MONTH?	❐	❐
3. DID YOU PAY YOUR EMPLOYEES ON TIME?	❐	❐
4. HAVE YOU DEPOSITED ALL THE RECEIPTS FOR YOUR BUSINESS INTO THE DIP ACCOUNT THIS MONTH?	❐	❐
5. HAVE YOU FILED ALL OF YOUR TAX RETURNS AND PAID ALL OF YOUR TAXES THIS MONTH	❐	❐
6. HAVE YOU TIMELY FILED ALL OTHER REQUIRED GOVERNMENT FILINGS?	❐	❐
7. HAVE YOU PAID ALL OF YOUR INSURANCE PREMIUMS THIS MONTH?	❐	❐
8. DO YOU PLAN TO CONTINUE TO OPERATE THE BUSINESS NEXT MONTH?	❐	❐
9. ARE YOU CURRENT ON YOUR QUARTERLY FEE PAYMENT TO THE U.S. TRUSTEE?	❐	❐
10. HAVE YOU PAID ANYTHING TO YOUR ATTORNEY OR OTHER PROFESSIONALS THIS MONTH?	❐	❐
11. DID YOU HAVE ANY UNUSUAL OR SIGNIFICANT UNANTICIPATED EXPENSES THIS MONTH?	❐	❐
12. HAS THE BUSINESS SOLD ANY GOODS OR PROVIDED SERVICES OR TRANSFERRED ANY ASSETS TO ANY BUSINESS RELATED TO THE DIP IN ANY WAY?	❐	❐
13. DO YOU HAVE ANY BANK ACCOUNTS OPEN OTHER THAN THE DIP ACCOUNT?	❐	❐

OFFICIAL FORMS

Form 25C

Page 2

B 25C (Official Form 25C) (12/08)

14. HAVE YOU SOLD ANY ASSETS OTHER THAN INVENTORY THIS MONTH? ☐ ☐

15. DID ANY INSURANCE COMPANY CANCEL YOUR POLICY THIS MONTH? ☐ ☐

16. HAVE YOU BORROWED MONEY FROM ANYONE THIS MONTH? ☐ ☐

17. HAS ANYONE MADE AN INVESTMENT IN YOUR BUSINESS THIS MONTH? ☐ ☐

18. HAVE YOU PAID ANY BILLS YOU OWED BEFORE YOU FILED BANKRUPTCY? ☐ ☐

TAXES

DO YOU HAVE ANY PAST DUE TAX RETURNS OR PAST DUE POST-PETITION TAX OBLIGATIONS? ☐ ☐

IF YES, PLEASE PROVIDE A WRITTEN EXPLANATION INCLUDING WHEN SUCH RETURNS WILL BE FILED, OR WHEN SUCH PAYMENTS WILL BE MADE AND THE SOURCE OF THE FUNDS FOR THE PAYMENT.

(Exhibit A)

INCOME

PLEASE SEPARATELY LIST ALL OF THE INCOME YOU RECEIVED FOR THE MONTH. THE LIST SHOULD INCLUDE ALL INCOME FROM CASH AND CREDIT TRANSACTIONS. *(THE U.S. TRUSTEE MAY WAIVE THIS REQUIREMENT.)*

TOTAL INCOME $

SUMMARY OF CASH ON HAND

Cash on Hand at Start of Month $ _____

Cash on Hand at End of Month $ _____

PLEASE PROVIDE THE TOTAL AMOUNT OF CASH CURRENTLY AVAILABLE TO YOU **TOTAL** $ _____

(Exhibit B)

EXPENSES

PLEASE SEPARATELY LIST ALL EXPENSES PAID BY CASH OR BY CHECK FROM YOUR BANK ACCOUNTS THIS MONTH. INCLUDE THE DATE PAID, WHO WAS PAID THE MONEY, THE PURPOSE AND THE AMOUNT. *(THE U.S. TRUSTEE MAY WAIVE THIS REQUIREMENT.)*

TOTAL EXPENSES $ _____

(Exhibit C)

CASH PROFIT

INCOME FOR THE MONTH *(TOTAL FROM EXHIBIT B)* $ _____

EXPENSES FOR THE MONTH *(TOTAL FROM EXHIBIT C)* $ _____

(Subtract Line C from Line B) **CASH PROFIT FOR THE MONTH** $ _____

Complete Annotation Materials, see Title 11 U.S.C.A.
989

B 25C (Official Form 25C) (12/08)

UNPAID BILLS

PLEASE ATTACH A LIST OF ALL DEBTS (INCLUDING TAXES) WHICH YOU HAVE INCURRED
SINCE THE DATE YOU FILED BANKRUPTCY BUT HAVE NOT PAID. THE LIST MUST INCLUDE
THE DATE THE DEBT WAS INCURRED, WHO IS OWED THE MONEY, THE PURPOSE OF THE
DEBT AND WHEN THE DEBT IS DUE. *(THE U.S. TRUSTEE MAY WAIVE THIS REQUIREMENT.)*

TOTAL PAYABLES $ _____

(Exhibit D)

MONEY OWED TO YOU

PLEASE ATTACH A LIST OF ALL AMOUNTS OWED TO YOU BY YOUR CUSTOMERS FOR WORK
YOU HAVE DONE OR THE MERCHANDISE YOU HAVE SOLD. YOU SHOULD INCLUDE WHO
OWES YOU MONEY, HOW MUCH IS OWED AND WHEN IS PAYMENT DUE. *(THE U.S. TRUSTEE MAY
WAIVE THIS REQUIREMENT.)*

TOTAL RECEIVABLES $ _____

(Exhibit E)

BANKING INFORMATION

PLEASE ATTACH A COPY OF YOUR LATEST BANK STATEMENT FOR EVERY ACCOUNT YOU
HAVE AS OF THE DATE OF THIS FINANCIAL REPORT OR HAD DURING THE PERIOD COVERED
BY THIS REPORT.

(Exhibit F)

EMPLOYEES

NUMBER OF EMPLOYEES WHEN THE CASE WAS FILED?

NUMBER OF EMPLOYEES AS OF THE DATE OF THIS MONTHLY REPORT? _____

PROFESSIONAL FEES

BANKRUPTCY RELATED:

PROFESSIONAL FEES RELATING TO THE BANKRUPTCY CASE PAID DURING THIS REPORTING
PERIOD? $ _____

TOTAL PROFESSIONAL FEES RELATING TO THE BANKRUPTCY CASE PAID SINCE THE FILING
OF THE CASE? $ _____

NON-BANKRUPTCY RELATED:

PROFESSIONAL FEES NOT RELATING TO THE BANKRUPTCY CASE PAID DURING THIS
REPORTING PERIOD? $ _____

TOTAL PROFESSIONAL FEES NOT RELATING TO THE BANKRUPTCY CASE PAID SINCE THE
FILING OF THE CASE? $

H 25C (Official Form 25C) (12/08)

PROJECTIONS

COMPARE YOUR ACTUAL INCOME AND EXPENSES TO THE PROJECTIONS FOR THE FIRST 180
DAYS OF YOUR CASE PROVIDED AT THE INITIAL DEBTOR INTERVIEW.

	Projected	Actual	Difference
INCOME	$	$	$
EXPENSES	$	$	$
CASH PROFIT	$	$	$

TOTAL PROJECTED INCOME FOR THE NEXT MONTH: $

TOTAL PROJECTED EXPENSES FOR THE NEXT MONTH: $

TOTAL PROJECTED CASH PROFIT FOR THE NEXT MONTH: $

ADDITIONAL INFORMATION

**PLEASE ATTACH ALL FINANCIAL REPORTS INCLUDING AN INCOME STATEMENT AND BALANCE SHEET
WHICH YOU PREPARE INTERNALLY.**

(Added Dec. 1, 2008.)

ADVISORY COMMITTEE NOTES
2008 Enactment

This form is new. It implements §§ 434 and 435 of the Bankruptcy Abuse Prevention and Consumer Protection Act of 2005, Pub. L. No. 109–8, 119 Stat. 23 (April 20, 2005), which provided for rules and an official form to assist small business debtors in chapter 11 cases to fulfill their responsibilities under § 308 of the Code, a provision added by the 2005 Act. The form directs the debtor to disclose the information required under § 308 and resembles those developed earlier by the United States trustees for use in supervising debtors in possession in chapter 11 cases.

Form 26. Periodic Report Regarding Value, Operations and Profitability of Entities in Which the Debtor's Estate Holds a Substantial or Controlling Interest

B26 (Official Form 26) (12/08)

United States Bankruptcy Court
_____ District of _____

In re_____   Case No. _____

          Debtor   Chapter 11

PERIODIC REPORT REGARDING VALUE, OPERATIONS AND PROFITABILITY OF ENTITIES IN WHICH THE ESTATE OF [NAME OF DEBTOR] HOLDS A SUBSTANTIAL OR CONTROLLING INTEREST

This is the report as of _____on the value, operations and profitability of those entities in which the estate holds a substantial or controlling interest, as required by Bankruptcy Rule 2015.3. The estate of [Name of Debtor] holds a substantial or controlling interest in the following entities:

Name of Entity	Interest of the Estate	Tab #

This periodic report (the "Periodic Report") contains separate reports ("Entity Reports") on the value, operations, and profitability of each entity listed above.

Each Entity Report shall consist of three exhibits. Exhibit A contains a valuation estimate for the entity as of a date not more than two years prior to the date of this report. It also contains a description of the valuation method used. Exhibit B contains a balance sheet, a statement of income (loss), a statement of cash flows, and a statement of changes in shareholders' or partners' equity (deficit) for the period covered by the Entity Report, along with summarized footnotes. Exhibit C contains a description of the entity's business operations.

THIS REPORT MUST BE SIGNED BY A REPRESENTATIVE OF THE TRUSTEE OR DEBTOR IN POSSESSION.

The undersigned, having reviewed the above listing of entities in which the estate of [Debtor] holds a substantial or controlling interest, and being familiar with the Debtor's financial affairs, verifies under the penalty of perjury that the listing is complete, accurate and truthful to the best of his/her knowledge.

B26 (Official Form 26) (12/08) – Cont.   2

Date: _____

_____
Signature of Authorized Individual

_____
Name of Authorized Individual

_____
Title of Authorized Individual

[If the Debtor is an individual or in a joint case]

Signature(s) of Debtor(s) (Individual/Joint)

_____
Signature of Debtor

_____
Signature of Joint Debtor

Form 26

OFFICIAL FORMS

B26 (Official Form 26) (12/08) – Cont.   3

Exhibit A
Valuation Estimate for [Name of Entity]

[Provide a statement of the entity's value and the value of the estate's interest in the entity, including a description of the basis for the valuation, the date of the valuation and the valuation method used. This valuation must be no more than two years old. Indicate the source of this information.]

Complete Annotation Materials, see Title 11 U.S.C.A.

994

B26 (Official Form 26) (12/08) – Cont.

4

Exhibit B
Financial Statements for [Insert Name of Entity]

B26 (Official Form 26) (12/08) – Cont.   5

Exhibit B-1
Balance Sheet for [Name of Entity]
As of [date]

[Provide a balance sheet dated as of the end of the most recent six-month period of the current fiscal year and as of the end of the preceding fiscal year. Indicate the source of this information.]

Exhibit B-2
Statement of Income (Loss) for [Name of Entity]
Period ending [date]

[Provide a statement of income (loss) for the following periods:

    (i) For the initial report:
        a. the period between the end of the preceding fiscal year and the end of the
           most recent six-month period of the current fiscal year; and
        b. the prior fiscal year.
    (ii) For subsequent reports, since the closing date of the last report.

Indicate the source of this information.]

OFFICIAL FORMS

Exhibit B-3
Statement of Cash Flows for [Name of Entity]
For the period ending [date]

[Provide a statement of changes in cash flows for the following periods:

    (i) For the initial report:
        a. the period between the end of the preceding fiscal year and the end of the
          most recent six-month period of the current fiscal year; and
        b. the prior fiscal year.
    (ii) For subsequent reports, since the closing date of the last report.

Indicate the source of this information.]

Exhibit B-4
Statement of Changes in Shareholders'/Partners' Equity (Deficit) for [Name of Entity]
period ending [date]

[Provide a statement of changes in shareholders'/partners equity (deficit) for the following periods:

    (i) For the initial report:
        a. the period between the end of the preceding fiscal year and the end of the most recent six-month period of the current fiscal year; and
        b. the prior fiscal year.
    (ii) For subsequent reports, since the closing date of the last report.

Indicate the source of this information.]

Form 26

B26 (Official Form 26) (12/08) – Cont.   9

Exhibit C
Description of Operations for [name of entity]

[Describe the nature and extent of the estate's interest in the entity.

Describe the business conducted and intended to be conducted by the entity, focusing on the entity's dominant business segment(s). Indicate the source of this information.]

(Added Dec. 1, 2008.)

ADVISORY COMMITTEE NOTES

2008 Enactment

This form is new. It implements § 419 of the Bankruptcy Abuse Prevention and Consumer Protection Act of 2005, Pub. L. No. 109–8, 119 Stat. 23 (April 20, 2005), which requires a chapter 11 debtor to file periodic reports on the profitability of any entities in which the estate holds a substantial or controlling interest. The form is to be used when required by Bankruptcy Rule 2015.3, with such variations as may be approved by the court pursuant to subdivisions (d) and (e) of that rule. The form includes instructions and examples of the types of information needed to complete it.

Form 27. Reaffirmation Agreement Cover Sheet

B27 (Official Form 27) (12/09)

UNITED STATES BANKRUPTCY COURT

In re _____,
          Debtor

Case No. _____
Chapter ____

REAFFIRMATION AGREEMENT COVER SHEET

This form must be completed in its entirety and filed, with the reaffirmation agreement attached, within the time set under Rule 4008. It may be filed by any party to the reaffirmation agreement.

1.   Creditor's Name: _____

2.   Amount of the debt subject to this reaffirmation agreement:
       $_____ on the date of bankruptcy $_____ to be paid under reaffirmation agreement

3.   Annual percentage rate of interest: _____% prior to bankruptcy
       _____% under reaffirmation agreement (____ Fixed Rate ____ Adjustable Rate)

4.   Repayment terms (if fixed rate): $_____ per month for _____ months

5.   Collateral, if any, securing the debt: Current market value: $_____
       Description: _____

6.   Does the creditor assert that the debt is nondischargeable? ___Yes ___ No
(If yes, attach a declaration setting forth the nature of the debt and basis for the contention that the debt is nondischargeable.)

Debtor's Schedule I and J Entries

Debtor's Income and Expenses
as Stated on Reaffirmation Agreement

7A. Total monthly income from $_____
      Schedule I, line 16

7B. Monthly income from all $_____
      sources after payroll deductions

8A. Total monthly expenses $_____
      from Schedule J, line 18

8B. Monthly expenses $_____

9A. Total monthly payments on $_____
      reaffirmed debts not listed on
      Schedule J

9B. Total monthly payments on $_____
      reaffirmed debts not included in
      monthly expenses

10B. Net monthly income $_____
      (Subtract sum of lines 8B and 9B from
      line 7B. If total is less than zero, put the
      number in brackets.)

Form 27

OFFICIAL FORMS

11. Explain with specificity any difference between the income amounts (7A and 7B):

12. Explain with specificity any difference between the expense amounts (8A and 8B):

If line 11 or 12 is completed, the undersigned debtor, and joint debtor if applicable, certifies that any explanation contained on those lines is true and correct.

_____   _____
Signature of Debtor (only required if   Signature of Joint Debtor (if applicable, and only
line 11 or 12 is completed)   required if line 11 or 12 is completed)

Other Information

☐   Check this box if the total on line 10B is less than zero. If that number is less than zero, a presumption of undue hardship arises (unless the creditor is a credit union) and you must explain with specificity the sources of funds available to the Debtor to make the monthly payments on the reaffirmed debt:

Was debtor represented by counsel during the course of negotiating this reaffirmation agreement?
_____Yes   _____No

If debtor was represented by counsel during the course of negotiating this reaffirmation agreement, has counsel executed a certification (affidavit or declaration) in support of the reaffirmation agreement?
_____Yes   _____No

FILER'S CERTIFICATION

I hereby certify that the attached agreement is a true and correct copy of the reaffirmation agreement between the parties identified on this Reaffirmation Agreement Cover Sheet.

_____
Signature

_____
Print/Type Name & Signer's Relation to Case

(Added Dec. 2009.)

ADVISORY COMMITTEE NOTES
2009 Enactment

This form is new. It gathers certain financial information, including information necessary for the court to determine whether a reaffirmation agreement creates a presumption of undue hardship under § 524(m) of the Code, and it allows the debtor to provide additional information that may rebut such a presumption.

To implement the requirements of Bankruptcy Rule 4008(b), the form also provides for a disclosure of any differences between the income and expenses reported on schedules I and J and the income and expenses reported in the debtor's statement in support of the reaffirmation agreement, together with an explanation of any such differences.

Finally, the form requires a certification that the information supplied is true and correct.

Uniform Fraudulent Transfer Act.
Uniform Commercial Code (Selected Sections).

UNIFORM FRAUDULENT TRANSFER ACT *

See, also, Uniform Fraudulent Conveyance Act, to which this act is the successor.

Sec.
1. Definitions.
2. Insolvency.
3. Value.
4. Transfers Fraudulent as to Present and Future Creditors.

Sec.
5. Transfers Fraudulent as to Present Creditors.
6. When Transfer is Made or Obligation is Incurred.
7. Remedies of Creditors.
8. Defenses, Liability, and Protection of Transferee.
9. Extinguishment of [Claim for Relief] [Cause of Action].
10. Supplementary Provisions.
11. Uniformity of Application and Construction.
12. Short Title.
13. Repeal.

§ 1. Definitions

As used in this [Act]:

(1) "Affiliate" means:

(i) a person who directly or indirectly owns, controls, or holds with power to vote, 20 percent or more of the outstanding voting securities of the debtor, other than a person who holds the securities,

(A) as a fiduciary or agent without sole discretionary power to vote the securities; or

(B) solely to secure a debt, if the person has not exercised the power to vote;

(ii) a corporation 20 percent or more of whose outstanding voting securities are directly or indirectly owned, controlled, or held with power to vote, by the debtor or a person who directly or indirectly owns, controls, or holds, with power to vote, 20 percent or more of the outstanding voting securities of the debtor, other than a person who holds the securities,

(A) as a fiduciary or agent without sole power to vote the securities; or

(B) solely to secure a debt, if the person has not in fact exercised the power to vote;

(iii) a person whose business is operated by the debtor under a lease or other agreement, or a person substantially all of whose assets are controlled by the debtor; or

(iv) a person who operates the debtor's business under a lease or other agreement or controls substantially all of the debtor's assets.

(2) "Asset" means property of a debtor, but the term does not include:

(i) property to the extent it is encumbered by a valid lien;

(ii) property to the extent it is generally exempt under nonbankruptcy law; or

(iii) an interest in property held in tenancy by the entireties to the extent it is not subject to process by a creditor holding a claim against only one tenant.

(3) "Claim" means a right to payment, whether or not the right is reduced to judgment, liquidated, unliquidated, fixed, contingent, matured, unmatured, disputed, undisputed, legal, equitable, secured, or unsecured.

(4) "Creditor" means a person who has a claim.

(5) "Debt" means liability on a claim.

(6) "Debtor" means a person who is liable on a claim.

(7) "Insider" includes:

(i) if the debtor is an individual,

* Reproduced by permission of the National Conference of Commissioners on Uniform State Laws.

(A) a relative of the debtor or of a general partner of the debtor;

(B) a partnership in which the debtor is a general partner;

(C) a general partner in a partnership described in clause (B); or

(D) a corporation of which the debtor is a director, officer, or person in control;

(ii) if the debtor is a corporation,

(A) a director of the debtor;

(B) an officer of the debtor;

(C) a person in control of the debtor;

(D) a partnership in which the debtor is a general partner;

(E) a general partner in a partnership described in clause (D); or

(F) a relative of a general partner, director, officer, or person in control of the debtor;

(iii) if the debtor is a partnership,

(A) a general partner in the debtor;

(B) a relative of a general partner in, a general partner of, or a person in control of the debtor;

(C) another partnership in which the debtor is a general partner;

(D) a general partner in a partnership described in clause (C); or

(E) a person in control of the debtor;

(iv) an affiliate, or an insider of an affiliate as if the affiliate were the debtor; and

(v) a managing agent of the debtor.

(8) "Lien" means a charge against or an interest in property to secure payment of a debt or performance of an obligation, and includes a security interest created by agreement, a judicial lien obtained by legal or equitable process or proceedings, a common-law lien, or a statutory lien.

(9) "Person" means an individual, partnership, corporation, association, organization, government or governmental subdivision or agency, business trust, estate, trust, or any other legal or commercial entity.

(10) "Property" means anything that may be the subject of ownership.

(11) "Relative" means an individual related by consanguinity within the third degree as determined by the common law, a spouse, or an individual related to a spouse within the third degree as so determined, and includes an individual in an adoptive relationship within the third degree.

(12) "Transfer" means every mode, direct or indirect, absolute or conditional, voluntary or involuntary, of disposing of or parting with an asset or an interest in an asset, and includes payment of money, release, lease, and creation of a lien or other encumbrance.

(13) "Valid lien" means a lien that is effective against the holder of a judicial lien subsequently obtained by legal or equitable process or proceedings.

§ 2. Insolvency

(a) A debtor is insolvent if the sum of the debtor's debts is greater than all of the debtor's assets at a fair valuation.

(b) A debtor who is generally not paying his [or her] debts as they become due is presumed to be insolvent.

(c) A partnership is insolvent under subsection (a) if the sum of the partnership's debts is greater than the aggregate, at a fair valuation, of all of the partnership's assets and the sum of the excess of the value of each general partner's nonpartnership assets over the partner's nonpartnership debts.

(d) Assets under this section do not include property that has been transferred, concealed, or removed with intent to hinder, delay, or defraud creditors or that has been transferred in a manner making the transfer voidable under this [Act].

(e) Debts under this section do not include an obligation to the extent it is secured by a valid lien on property of the debtor not included as an asset.

§ 3. Value

(a) Value is given for a transfer or an obligation if, in exchange for the transfer or obligation, property is transferred or an antecedent debt is secured or satisfied, but value does not include an unperformed promise made otherwise than in the ordinary course of the promisor's business to furnish support to the debtor or another person.

(b) For the purposes of Sections 4(a)(2) and 5, a person gives a reasonably equivalent value if the person acquires an interest of the debtor in an asset pursuant to a regularly conducted, noncollusive foreclosure sale or execution of a power of sale for the acquisition or disposition of the interest of the debtor upon default under a mortgage, deed of trust, or security agreement.

(c) A transfer is made for present value if the exchange between the debtor and the transferee is intended by them to be contemporaneous and is in fact substantially contemporaneous.

§ 4. Transfers Fraudulent as to Present and Future Creditors

(a) A transfer made or obligation incurred by a debtor is fraudulent as to a creditor, whether the creditor's claim arose before or after the transfer was made or the obligation was incurred, if the debtor made the transfer or incurred the obligation:

(1) with actual intent to hinder, delay, or defraud any creditor of the debtor; or

(2) without receiving a reasonably equivalent value in exchange for the transfer or obligation, and the debtor:

(i) was engaged or was about to engage in a business or a transaction for which the remaining assets of the debtor were unreasonably small in relation to the business or transaction; or

(ii) intended to incur, or believed or reasonably should have believed that he [or she] would incur, debts beyond his [or her] ability to pay as they became due.

(b) In determining actual intent under subsection (a)(1), consideration may be given, among other factors, to whether:

(1) the transfer or obligation was to an insider;

(2) the debtor retained possession or control of the property transferred after the transfer;

(3) the transfer or obligation was disclosed or concealed;

(4) before the transfer was made or obligation was incurred, the debtor had been sued or threatened with suit;

(5) the transfer was of substantially all the debtor's assets;

(6) the debtor absconded;

(7) the debtor removed or concealed assets;

(8) the value of the consideration received by the debtor was reasonably equivalent to the value of the asset transferred or the amount of the obligation incurred;

(9) the debtor was insolvent or became insolvent shortly after the transfer was made or the obligation was incurred;

(10) the transfer occurred shortly before or shortly after a substantial debt was incurred; and

(11) the debtor transferred the essential assets of the business to a lienor who transferred the assets to an insider of the debtor.

§ 5. Transfers Fraudulent as to Present Creditors

(a) A transfer made or obligation incurred by a debtor is fraudulent as to a creditor whose claim arose before the transfer was made or the obligation was incurred if the debtor made the transfer or incurred the obligation without receiving a reasonably equivalent value in exchange for the transfer or obligation and the debtor was insolvent at that time or the debtor became insolvent as a result of the transfer or obligation.

(b) A transfer made by a debtor is fraudulent as to a creditor whose claim arose before the transfer was made if the transfer was made to an insider for an antecedent debt, the debtor was insolvent at that time,

and the insider had reasonable cause to believe that the debtor was insolvent.

§ 6. When Transfer is Made or Obligation is Incurred

For the purposes of this [Act]:

(1) a transfer is made:

(i) with respect to an asset that is real property other than a fixture, but including the interest of a seller or purchaser under a contract for the sale of the asset, when the transfer is so far perfected that a good-faith purchaser of the asset from the debtor against whom applicable law permits the transfer to be perfected cannot acquire an interest in the asset that is superior to the interest of the transferee; and

(ii) with respect to an asset that is not real property or that is a fixture, when the transfer is so far perfected that a creditor on a simple contract cannot acquire a judicial lien otherwise than under this [Act] that is superior to the interest of the transferee;

(2) if applicable law permits the transfer to be perfected as provided in paragraph (1) and the transfer is not so perfected before the commencement of an action for relief under this [Act], the transfer is deemed made immediately before the commencement of the action;

(3) if applicable law does not permit the transfer to be perfected as provided in paragraph (1), the transfer is made when it becomes effective between the debtor and the transferee;

(4) a transfer is not made until the debtor has acquired rights in the asset transferred;

(5) an obligation is incurred:

(i) if oral, when it becomes effective between the parties; or

(ii) if evidenced by a writing, when the writing executed by the obligor is delivered to or for the benefit of the obligee.

§ 7. Remedies of Creditors

(a) In an action for relief against a transfer or obligation under this [Act], a creditor, subject to the limitations in Section 8, may obtain:

(1) avoidance of the transfer or obligation to the extent necessary to satisfy the creditor's claim;

[(2) an attachment or other provisional remedy against the asset transferred or other property of the transferee in accordance with the procedure prescribed by [ ];]

(3) subject to applicable principles of equity and in accordance with applicable rules of civil procedure,

(i) an injunction against further disposition by the debtor or a transferee, or both, of the asset transferred or of other property;

(ii) appointment of a receiver to take charge of the asset transferred or of other property of the transferee; or

(iii) any other relief the circumstances may require.

(b) If a creditor has obtained a judgment on a claim against the debtor, the creditor, if the court so orders, may levy execution on the asset transferred or its proceeds.

§ 8. Defenses, Liability, and Protection of Transferee

(a) A transfer or obligation is not voidable under Section 4(a)(1) against a person who took in good faith and for a reasonably equivalent value or against any subsequent transferee or obligee.

(b) Except as otherwise provided in this section, to the extent a transfer is voidable in an action by a creditor under Section 7(a)(1), the creditor may recover judgment for the value of the asset transferred, as adjusted under subsection (c), or the amount necessary to satisfy the creditor's claim, whichever is less. The judgment may be entered against:

(1) the first transferee of the asset or the person for whose benefit the transfer was made; or

(2) any subsequent transferee other than a good faith transferee who took for value or from any subsequent transferee.

(c) If the judgment under subsection (b) is based upon the value of the asset transferred, the judgment must be for an amount equal to the value of the asset at the time of the transfer, subject to adjustment as the equities may require.

(d) Notwithstanding voidability of a transfer or an obligation under this [Act], a good-faith transferee or obligee is entitled, to the extent of the value given the debtor for the transfer or obligation, to

(1) a lien on or a right to retain any interest in the asset transferred;

(2) enforcement of any obligation incurred; or

(3) a reduction in the amount of the liability on the judgment.

(e) A transfer is not voidable under Section 4(a)(2) or Section 5 if the transfer results from:

(1) termination of a lease upon default by the debtor when the termination is pursuant to the lease and applicable law; or

(2) enforcement of a security interest in compliance with Article 9 of the Uniform Commercial Code.

(f) A transfer is not voidable under Section 5(b):

(1) to the extent the insider gave new value to or for the benefit of the debtor after the transfer was made unless the new value was secured by a valid lien;

(2) if made in the ordinary course of business or financial affairs of the debtor and the insider; or

(3) if made pursuant to a good-faith effort to rehabilitate the debtor and the transfer secured present value given for that purpose as well as an antecedent debt of the debtor.

§ 9. Extinguishment of [Claim for Relief] [Cause of Action]

A [claim for relief] [cause of action] with respect to a fraudulent transfer or obligation under this [Act] is extinguished unless action is brought:

(a) under Section 4(a)(1), within 4 years after the transfer was made or the obligation was incurred or, if later, within one year after the transfer or obligation was or could reasonably have been discovered by the claimant;

(b) under Section 4(a)(2) or 5(a), within 4 years after the transfer was made or the obligation was incurred; or

(c) under Section 5(b), within one year after the transfer was made or the obligation was incurred.

§ 10. Supplementary Provisions

Unless displaced by the provisions of this [Act], the principles of law and equity, including the law merchant and the law relating to principal and agent, estoppel, laches, fraud, misrepresentation, duress, coercion, mistake, insolvency, or other validating or invalidating cause, supplement its provisions.

§ 11. Uniformity of Application and Construction

This [Act] shall be applied and construed to effectuate its general purpose to make uniform the law with respect to the subject of this [Act] among states enacting it.

§ 12. Short Title

This [Act] may be cited as the Uniform Fraudulent Transfer Act.

§ 13. Repeal

The following acts and all other acts and parts of acts inconsistent herewith are hereby repealed:

UNIFORM COMMERCIAL CODE

Selected Sections

———

Reprinted by permission of the National Conference of Commissioners on Uniform State Laws

Article 1. General Provisions

The American Law Institute and National Conference of Commissioners on Uniform State Laws

Part 2. General Definitions And Principles Of Interpretation

§ 1–201. General Definitions

* * *

(b) Subject to definitions contained in other articles of [the Uniform Commercial Code] that apply to particular articles or parts thereof:

* * *

(3) "Agreement", as distinguished from "contract", means the bargain of the parties in fact, as found in their language or inferred from other circumstances, including course of performance, course of dealing, or usage of trade as provided in Section 1–303.

* * *

(9) "Buyer in ordinary course of business" means a person that buys goods in good faith, without knowledge that the sale violates the rights of another person in the goods, and in the ordinary course from a person, other than a pawnbroker, in the business of selling goods of that kind. * * *

* * *

(11) "Consumer" means an individual who enters into a transaction primarily for personal, family, or household purposes

* * *

(13) "Creditor" includes a general creditor, a secured creditor, a lien creditor, and any representative of creditors, including an assignee for the benefit of creditors, a trustee in bankruptcy, a receiver in equity, and an executor or administrator of an insolvent debtor's or assignor's estate.

* * *

(20) "Good faith," except as otherwise provided in Article 5, means honesty in fact and the observance of reasonable commercial standards of fair dealing.

* * *

(29) "Purchase" means taking by sale, lease, discount, negotiation, mortgage, pledge, lien, security interest, issue or reissue, gift, or any other voluntary transaction creating an interest in property.

(30) "Purchaser" means a person that takes by purchase.

(31) "Record" means information that is inscribed on a tangible medium or that is stored in an electronic or other medium and is retrievable in perceivable form.

* * *

(35) "Security interest" means an interest in personal property or fixtures which secures payment or performance of an obligation. "Security interest" includes any interest of a consignor and a buyer of accounts, chattel paper, a payment intangible, or a promissory note in a transaction that is subject to Article 9. "Security interest" does not include the special property interest of a buyer of goods on identification of those goods to a contract for sale under Section 2–401, but a buyer may also acquire a "security interest" by complying with Article 9. Except as otherwise provided in Section 2–505, the right of a seller or lessor of goods under Article 2 or 2A to retain or acquire possession of the goods is not a "security interest", but a seller or lessor may also acquire a "security interest" by complying with Article 9. The retention or reservation of title by a seller of goods notwithstanding shipment or delivery to the buyer under Section 2–401 is limited in effect to a reservation of a "security interest." Whether a transaction in the form of a lease creates a "security interest" is determined pursuant to Section 1–203.

* * *

(37) "Signed" includes using any symbol executed or adopted with present intention to adopt or accept a writing.

* * *

As amended in 2003.

Uniform Commercial Code

Article 2. Sales

Official Text

The American Law Institute and National Conference of Commissioners on Uniform State Laws

Part 7. Remedies

§ 2–702. Seller's Remedies On Discovery Of Buyer's Insolvency

(1) If the seller discovers that the buyer is insolvent, the seller may refuse delivery except for cash including payment for all goods theretofore delivered under the contract, and stop delivery under Section 2–705.

(2) If the seller discovers that the buyer has received goods on credit while insolvent, the seller may reclaim the goods upon demand made within a reasonable time after the buyer's receipt of the goods. Except as provided in this subsection, the seller may not base a right to reclaim goods on the buyer's fraudulent or innocent misrepresentation of solvency or of intent to pay.

(3) The seller's right to reclaim under subsection (2) is subject to the rights of a buyer in ordinary course of business or other good-faith purchaser for value under Section 2–403. Successful reclamation of goods excludes all other remedies with respect to them.

As amended in 2003.

Uniform Commercial Code

Article 9. Secured Transactions

The American Law Institute and National Conference of Commissioners on Uniform State Laws

Part 1. General Provisions

[Subpart 1. Short Title, Definitions, And General Concepts]

§ 9–102. Definitions And Index Of Definitions

(a) [Article 9 definitions.] In this article:

* * *

(3) "Account debtor" means a person obligated on an account, chattel paper, or general intangible. The term does not include persons obligated to pay a negotiable instrument, even if the instrument constitutes part of chattel paper.

* * *

(7) "Authenticate" means:

(A) to sign; or

(B) with present intent to adopt or accept a record, to attach to or logically associate with the record an electronic sound, symbol, or process.

* * *

(9) "Cash proceeds" means proceeds that are money, checks, deposit accounts, or the like.

* * *

(12) "Collateral" means the property subject to a security interest or agricultural lien. The term includes:

(A) proceeds to which a security interest attaches;

(B) accounts, chattel paper, payment intangibles, and promissory notes that have been sold; and

(C) goods that are the subject of a consignment.

(13) "Commercial tort claim" means a claim arising in tort with respect to which:

(A) the claimant is an organization; or

(B) the claimant is an individual and the claim:

(i) arose in the course of the claimant's business or profession; and

(ii) does not include damages arising out of personal injury to or the death of an individual.

* * *

(23) "Consumer goods" means goods that are used or bought for use primarily for personal, family, or household purposes.

* * *

(28) "Debtor" means:

(A) a person having an interest, other than a security interest or other lien, in the collateral, whether or not the person is an obligor;

(B) a seller of accounts, chattel paper, payment intangibles, or promissory notes; or

(C) a consignee.

* * *

(33) "Equipment" means goods other than inventory, farm products, or consumer goods.

(34) "Farm products" means goods, other than standing timber, with respect to which the debtor is engaged in a farming operation and which are:

(A) crops grown, growing, or to be grown, including:

(i) crops produced on trees, vines, and bushes; and

(ii) aquatic goods produced in aquacultural operations;

(B) livestock, born or unborn, including aquatic goods produced in aquacultural operations;

(C) supplies used or produced in a farming operation; or

(D) products of crops or livestock in their unmanufactured states.

* * *

(44) "Goods" means all things that are movable when a security interest attaches. The term includes (i) fixtures, (ii) standing timber that is to be cut and removed under a conveyance or contract for sale, (iii) the unborn young of animals, (iv) crops grown, growing, or to be grown, even if the crops are produced on trees, vines, or bushes, and (v) manufactured homes. The term also includes a computer program embedded in goods and any supporting information provided in connection with a transaction relating to the program if (i) the program is associated with the goods in such a manner that it customarily is considered part of the goods, or (ii) by becoming the owner of the goods, a person acquires a right to use the program in connection with the goods. The term does not include a computer program embedded in goods that consist solely of the medium in which the program is embedded. The term also does not include accounts, chattel paper, commercial tort claims, deposit accounts, documents, general intangibles, instruments, investment property, letter-of-credit rights, letters of credit, money, or oil, gas, or other minerals before extraction.

* * *

(48) "Inventory" means goods, other than farm products, which:

(A) are leased by a person as lessor;

(B) are held by a person for sale or lease or to be furnished under a contract of service;

(C) are furnished by a person under a contract of service; or

(D) consist of raw materials, work in process, or materials used or consumed in a business.

(49) "Investment property" means a security, whether certificated or uncertificated, security entitlement, securities account, commodity contract, or commodity account.

* * *

(52) "Lien creditor" means:

(A) a creditor that has acquired a lien on the property involved by attachment, levy, or the like;

(B) an assignee for benefit of creditors from the time of assignment;

(C) a trustee in bankruptcy from the date of the filing of the petition; or

(D) a receiver in equity from the time of appointment.

* * *

(57) "New value" means (i) money, (ii) money's worth in property, services, or new credit, or (iii) release by a transferee of an interest in property previously transferred to the transferee. The term does not include an obligation substituted for another obligation.

* * *

(64) "Proceeds", except as used in Section 9–609(b), means the following property:

(A) whatever is acquired upon the sale, lease, license, exchange, or other disposition of collateral;

(B) whatever is collected on, or distributed on account of, collateral;

(C) rights arising out of collateral;

(D) to the extent of the value of collateral, claims arising out of the loss, nonconformity, or interference with the use of, defects or infringement of rights in, or damage to, the collateral; or

(E) to the extent of the value of collateral and to the extent payable to the debtor or the secured party, insurance payable by reason of the loss or nonconformity of, defects or infringement of rights in, or damage to, the collateral.

* * *

(70) "Record", except as used in "for record", "of record", "record or legal title", and "record owner", means information that is inscribed on a tangible medium or which is stored in an electronic or other medium and is retrievable in perceivable form.

* * *

(73) "Secured party" means:

(A) a person in whose favor a security interest is created or provided for under a security agreement, whether or not any obligation to be secured is outstanding;

(B) a person that holds an agricultural lien;

(C) a consignor;

(D) a person to which accounts, chattel paper, payment intangibles, or promissory notes have been sold;

(E) a trustee, indenture trustee, agent, collateral agent, or other representative in whose favor a security interest or agricultural lien is created or provided for; or

(F) a person that holds a security interest arising under Section 2–401, 2–505, 2–711(3), 2A–508(5), 4–210, or 5–118.

(74) "Security agreement" means an agreement that creates or provides for a security interest.

* * *

[Subpart 2. Applicability Of Article]

§ 9–109. Scope

(a) [General scope of article.] Except as otherwise provided in subsections (c) and (d), this article applies to:

(1) a transaction, regardless of its form, that creates a security interest in personal property or fixtures by contract;

(2) an agricultural lien;

(3) a sale of accounts, chattel paper, payment intangibles, or promissory notes;

(4) a consignment;

(5) a security interest arising under Section 2–401, 2–505, 2–711(3), or 2A–508(5), as provided in Section 9–110; and

(6) a security interest arising under Section 4–210 or 5–118.

* * *

Part 2. Effectiveness Of Security Agreement; Attachment Of Security Interest; Rights Of Parties To Security Agreement

[Subpart 1. Effectiveness And Attachment]

§ 9–201. General Effectiveness Of Security Agreement

(a) [General effectiveness.] Except as otherwise provided in [the Uniform Commercial Code], a security agreement is effective according to its terms between the parties, against purchasers of the collateral, and against creditors.

* * *

§ 9–203. Attachment And Enforceability Of Security Interest; Proceeds; Supporting Obligations; Formal Requisites

(a) [Attachment.] A security interest attaches to collateral when it becomes enforceable against the debtor with respect to the collateral, unless an agreement expressly postpones the time of attachment.

(b) [Enforceability.] Except as otherwise provided in subsections (c) through (i), a security interest is enforceable against the debtor and third parties with respect to the collateral only if :

(1) value has been given;

(2) the debtor has rights in the collateral or the power to transfer rights in the collateral to a secured party; and

(3) one of the following conditions is met:

(A) the debtor has authenticated a security agreement that provides a description of the collateral and, if the security interest covers timber to be cut, a description of the land concerned;

(B) the collateral is not a certificated security and is in the possession of the secured party under Section 9–313 pursuant to the debtor's security agreement;

(C) the collateral is a certificated security in registered form and the security certificate has been delivered to the secured party under Section 8–301 pursuant to the debtor's security agreement; or

(D) the collateral is deposit accounts, electronic chattel paper, investment property, letter-of-credit rights, or electronic documents, and the secured party has control under Section 7–106, 9–104, 9–105, 9–106, or 9–107 pursuant to the debtor's security agreement.

* * *

§ 9–204. After–Acquired Property; Future Advances

(a) [After-acquired collateral.] Except as otherwise provided in subsection (b), a security agreement may create or provide for a security interest in after-acquired collateral.

(b) [When after-acquired property clause not effective.] A security interest does not attach under a term constituting an after-acquired property clause to:

(1) consumer goods, other than an accession when given as additional security, unless the debtor acquires rights in them within 10 days after the secured party gives value; or

(2) a commercial tort claim.

(c) [Future advances and other value.] A security agreement may provide that collateral secures, or that accounts, chattel paper, payment intangibles, or promissory notes are sold in connection with, future ad-

UNIFORM COMMERCIAL CODE § 9–315

vances or other value, whether or not the advances or value are given pursuant to commitment.

Part 3. Perfection And Priority

[Subpart 1. Law Governing Perfection And Priority]

§ 9–301. Law Governing Perfection And Priority Of Security Interests

Except as otherwise provided in Sections 9–303 through 9–306, the following rules determine the law governing perfection, the effect of perfection or nonperfection, and the priority of a security interest in collateral:

(1) Except as otherwise provided in this section, while a debtor is located in a jurisdiction, the local law of that jurisdiction governs perfection, the effect of perfection or nonperfection, and the priority of a security interest in collateral.

(2) While collateral is located in a jurisdiction, the local law of that jurisdiction governs perfection, the effect of perfection or nonperfection, and the priority of a possessory security interest in that collateral.

* * *

§ 9–307. Location Of Debtor

(a) ["Place of business."] In this section, "place of business" means a place where a debtor conducts its affairs.

(b) [Debtor's location: general rules.] Except as otherwise provided in this section, the following rules determine a debtor's location:

(1) A debtor who is an individual is located at the individual's principal residence.

(2) A debtor that is an organization and has only one place of business is located at its place of business.

(3) A debtor that is an organization and has more than one place of business is located at its chief executive office.

* * *

[Subpart 2. Perfection]

§ 9–308. When Security Interest Or Agricultural Lien Is Perfected; Continuity Of Perfection

(a) [Perfection of security interest.] Except as otherwise provided in this section and Section 9–309, a security interest is perfected if it has attached and all of the applicable requirements for perfection in Sections 9–310 through 9–316 have been satisfied. A security interest is perfected when it attaches if the applicable requirements are satisfied before the security interest attaches.

* * *

§ 9–309. Security Interest Perfected Upon Attachment

The following security interests are perfected when they attach:

(1) a purchase-money security interest in consumer goods, except as otherwise provided in Section 9–311(b) with respect to consumer goods that are subject to a statute or treaty described in Section 9–311(a);

(2) an assignment of accounts or payment intangibles which does not by itself or in conjunction with other assignments to the same assignee transfer a significant part of the assignor's outstanding accounts or payment intangibles;

* * *

§ 9–310. When Filing Required To Perfect Security Interest Or Agricultural Lien; Security Interests And Agricultural Liens To Which Filing Provisions Do Not Apply

(a) [General rule: perfection by filing.] Except as otherwise provided in subsection (b) and Section 9–312(b), a financing statement must be filed to perfect all security interests and agricultural liens.

* * *

§ 9–313. When Possession By Or Delivery To Secured Party Perfects Security Interest Without Filing

(a) [Perfection by possession or delivery.] Except as otherwise provided in subsection (b), a secured party may perfect a security interest in tangible negotiable documents, goods, instruments, money, or tangible chattel paper by taking possession of the collateral. A secured party may perfect a security interest in certificated securities by taking delivery of the certificated securities under Section 8–301.

* * *

§ 9–315. Secured Party's Rights On Disposition Of Collateral And In Proceeds

(a) [Disposition of collateral: continuation of security interest or agricultural lien; proceeds.] Except as otherwise provided in this article and in Section 2–403(2):

(1) a security interest or agricultural lien continues in collateral notwithstanding sale, lease, license, exchange, or other disposition thereof unless the secured party authorized the disposition free of the security interest or agricultural lien; and

(2) a security interest attaches to any identifiable proceeds of collateral.

* * *

(c) [Perfection of security interest in proceeds.] A security interest in proceeds is a perfected security interest if the security interest in the original collateral was perfected.

(d) [Continuation of perfection.] A perfected security interest in proceeds becomes unperfected on the 21st day after the security interest attaches to the proceeds unless:

(1) the following conditions are satisfied:

(A) a filed financing statement covers the original collateral;

(B) the proceeds are collateral in which a security interest may be perfected by filing in the office in which the financing statement has been filed; and

(C) the proceeds are not acquired with cash proceeds;

(2) the proceeds are identifiable cash proceeds; or

(3) the security interest in the proceeds is perfected other than under subsection (c) when the security interest attaches to the proceeds or within 20 days thereafter.

(e) [When perfected security interest in proceeds becomes unperfected.] If a filed financing statement covers the original collateral, a security interest in proceeds which remains perfected under subsection (d)(1) becomes unperfected at the later of:

(1) when the effectiveness of the filed financing statement lapses under Section 9–515 or is terminated under Section 9–513; or

(2) the 21st day after the security interest attaches to the proceeds.

[Subpart 3. Priority]

§ 9–317. Interests That Take Priority Over Or Take Free Of Security Interest Or Agricultural Lien

(a) [Conflicting security interests and rights of lien creditors.] A security interest or agricultural lien is subordinate to the rights of:

(1) a person entitled to priority under Section 9–322; and

(2) except as otherwise provided in subsection (e), a person that becomes a lien creditor before the earlier of the time:

(A) the security interest or agricultural lien is perfected; or

(B) one of the conditions specified in Section 9–203(b)(3) is met and a financing statement covering the collateral is filed.

(b) [Buyers that receive delivery.] Except as otherwise provided in subsection (e), a buyer, other than a secured party, of tangible chattel paper, tangible documents, goods, instruments, or a certificated security takes free of a security interest or agricultural lien if the buyer gives value and receives delivery of the collateral without knowledge of the security interest or agricultural lien and before it is perfected.

* * *

(e) [Purchase-money security interest.] Except as otherwise provided in Sections 9–320 and 9–321, if a person files a financing statement with respect to a purchase-money security interest before or within 20 days after the debtor receives delivery of the collateral, the security interest takes priority over the rights of a buyer, lessee, or lien creditor which arise between the time the security interest attaches and the time of filing.

§ 9–320. Buyer Of Goods

(a) [Buyer in ordinary course of business.] Except as otherwise provided in subsection (e), a buyer in ordinary course of business, other than a person buying farm products from a person engaged in farming operations, takes free of a security interest created by the buyer's seller, even if the security interest is perfected and the buyer knows of its existence.

(b) [Buyer of consumer goods.] Except as otherwise provided in subsection (e), a buyer of goods from a person who used or bought the goods for use primarily for personal, family, or household purposes takes free of a security interest, even if perfected, if the buyer buys:

(1) without knowledge of the security interest;

(2) for value;

(3) primarily for the buyer's personal, family, or household purposes; and

(4) before the filing of a financing statement covering the goods.

* * *

(e) [Possessory security interest not affected.] Subsections (a) and (b) do not affect a security interest in goods in the possession of the secured party under Section 9–313.

§ 9–322. Priorities Among Conflicting Security Interests In And Agricultural Liens On Same Collateral

(a) [General priority rules.] Except as otherwise provided in this section, priority among conflicting security interests and agricultural liens in the same collateral is determined according to the following rules:

(1) Conflicting perfected security interests and agricultural liens rank according to priority in time of filing or perfection. Priority dates from the earlier of the time a filing covering the collateral is first made or the security interest or agricultural lien is first perfected, if there is no period thereafter when there is neither filing nor perfection.

(2) A perfected security interest or agricultural lien has priority over a conflicting unperfected security interest or agricultural lien.

(3) The first security interest or agricultural lien to attach or become effective has priority if conflicting security interests and agricultural liens are unperfected.

(b) [Time of perfection: proceeds and supporting obligations.] For the purposes of subsection (a)(1):

(1) the time of filing or perfection as to a security interest in collateral is also the time of filing or perfection as to a security interest in proceeds; and

(2) the time of filing or perfection as to a security interest in collateral supported by a supporting obligation is also the time of filing or perfection as to a security interest in the supporting obligation.

* * *

§ 9–323. Future Advances

* * *

(b) [Lien creditor.] Except as otherwise provided in subsection (c), a security interest is subordinate to the rights of a person that becomes a lien creditor to the extent that the security interest secures an advance made more than 45 days after the person becomes a lien creditor unless the advance is made:

(1) without knowledge of the lien; or

(2) pursuant to a commitment entered into without knowledge of the lien.

* * *

(d) [Buyer of goods.] Except as otherwise provided in subsection (e), a buyer of goods other than a buyer in ordinary course of business takes free of a security interest to the extent that it secures advances made after the earlier of:

(1) the time the secured party acquires knowledge of the buyer's purchase; or

(2) 45 days after the purchase.

(e) [Advances made pursuant to commitment: priority of buyer of goods.] Subsection (d) does not apply if the advance is made pursuant to a commitment entered into without knowledge of the buyer's purchase and before the expiration of the 45–day period.

* * *

§ 9–324. Priority Of Purchase–Money Security Interests

(a) [General rule: purchase-money priority.] Except as otherwise provided in subsection (g), a perfected purchase-money security interest in goods other than inventory or livestock has priority over a conflicting security interest in the same goods, and, except as otherwise provided in Section 9–327, a perfected security interest in its identifiable proceeds also has priority, if the purchase-money security interest is perfected when the debtor receives possession of the collateral or within 20 days thereafter.

(b) [Inventory purchase-money priority.] Subject to subsection (c) and except as otherwise provided in subsection (g), a perfected purchase-money security interest in inventory has priority over a conflicting security interest in the same inventory, has priority over a conflicting security interest in chattel paper or an instrument constituting proceeds of the inventory and in proceeds of the chattel paper, if so provided in Section 9–330, and, except as otherwise provided in Section 9–327, also has priority in identifiable cash proceeds of the inventory to the extent the identifiable cash proceeds are received on or before the delivery of the inventory to a buyer, if:

(1) the purchase-money security interest is perfected when the debtor receives possession of the inventory;

(2) the purchase-money secured party sends an authenticated notification to the holder of the conflicting security interest;

(3) the holder of the conflicting security interest receives the notification within five years before the debtor receives possession of the inventory; and

(4) the notification states that the person sending the notification has or expects to acquire a purchase-money security interest in inventory of the debtor and describes the inventory.

(c) [Holders of conflicting inventory security interests to be notified.] Subsections (b)(2) through (4) apply only if the holder of the conflicting security interest had filed a financing statement covering the same types of inventory:

(1) if the purchase-money security interest is perfected by filing, before the date of the filing; or

(2) if the purchase-money security interest is temporarily perfected without filing or possession under Section 9–312(f), before the beginning of the 20–day period thereunder.

* * *

(g) [Conflicting purchase-money security interests.] If more than one security interest qualifies for priority in the same collateral under subsection (a), (b), (d), or (f):

(1) a security interest securing an obligation incurred as all or part of the price of the collateral has priority over a security interest securing an obligation incurred for value given to enable the debtor to acquire rights in or the use of collateral; and

(2) in all other cases, Section 9–322(a) applies to the qualifying security interests.

§ 9–332. Transfer Of Money; Transfer Of Funds From Deposit Account

(a) [Transferee of money.] A transferee of money takes the money free of a security interest unless the transferee acts in collusion with the debtor in violating the rights of the secured party.

(b) [Transferee of funds from deposit account.] A transferee of funds from a deposit account takes the funds free of a security interest in the deposit account unless the transferee acts in collusion with the debtor in violating the rights of the secured party.

§ 9–333. Priority Of Certain Liens Arising By Operation Of Law

(a) ["Possessory lien."] In this section, "possessory lien" means an interest, other than a security interest or an agricultural lien:

(1) which secures payment or performance of an obligation for services or materials furnished with respect to goods by a person in the ordinary course of the person's business;

(2) which is created by statute or rule of law in favor of the person; and

(3) whose effectiveness depends on the person's possession of the goods.

(b) [Priority of possessory lien.] A possessory lien on goods has priority over a security interest in the goods unless the lien is created by a statute that expressly provides otherwise.

§ 9–339. Priority Subject To Subordination

This article does not preclude subordination by agreement by a person entitled to priority.

[Subpart 4. Rights of Bank]

§ 9–340. Effectiveness Of Right Of Recoupment Or Set–Off Against Deposit Account

(a) [Exercise of recoupment or set-off.] Except as otherwise provided in subsection (c), a bank with which a deposit account is maintained may exercise any right of recoupment or set-off against a secured party that holds a security interest in the deposit account.

(b) [Recoupment or set-off not affected by security interest.] Except as otherwise provided in subsection (c), the application of this article to a security interest in a deposit account does not affect a right of recoupment or set-off of the secured party as to a deposit account maintained with the secured party.

(c) [When set-off ineffective.] The exercise by a bank of a set-off against a deposit account is ineffective against a secured party that holds a security interest in the deposit account which is perfected by control under Section 9–104(a)(3), if the set-off is based on a claim against the debtor.

Part 4. Rights Of Third Parties

§ 9–401. Alienability Of Debtor's Rights

(a) [Other law governs alienability; exceptions.] Except as otherwise provided in subsection (b) and Sections 9–406, 9–407, 9–408, and 9–409, whether a debtor's rights in collateral may be voluntarily or involuntarily transferred is governed by law other than this article.

(b) [Agreement does not prevent transfer.] An agreement between the debtor and secured party which prohibits a transfer of the debtor's rights in collateral or makes the transfer a default does not prevent the transfer from taking effect.

§ 9–407. Restrictions On Creation Or Enforcement Of Security Interest In Leasehold Interest Or In Lessor's Residual Interest

(a) [Term restricting assignment generally ineffective.] Except as otherwise provided in subsection (b), a term in a lease agreement is ineffective to the extent that it:

(1) prohibits, restricts, or requires the consent of a party to the lease to the assignment or transfer of, or the creation, attachment, perfection, or enforcement of a security interest in an interest of a party under the lease contract or in the lessor's residual interest in the goods; or

(2) provides that the assignment or transfer or the creation, attachment, perfection, or enforcement of the

security interest may give rise to a default, breach, right of recoupment, claim, defense, termination, right of termination, or remedy under the lease.

(b) [Effectiveness of certain terms.] Except as otherwise provided in Section 2A–303(7), a term described in subsection (a)(2) is effective to the extent that there is:

(1) a transfer by the lessee of the lessee's right of possession or use of the goods in violation of the term; or

(2) a delegation of a material performance of either party to the lease contract in violation of the term.

* * *

Part 5. Filing

[Subpart 1. Filing Office; Contents And Effectiveness Of Financing Statement]

§ 9–501. Filing Office

(a) [Filing offices.] Except as otherwise provided in subsection (b), if the local law of this State governs perfection of a security interest or agricultural lien, the office in which to file a financing statement to perfect the security interest or agricultural lien is:

(1) the office designated for the filing or recording of a record of a mortgage on the related real property, if:

(A) the collateral is as-extracted collateral or timber to be cut; or

(B) the financing statement is filed as a fixture filing and the collateral is goods that are or are to become fixtures; or

(2) the office of [ ] [or any office duly authorized by [ ]], in all other cases, including a case in which the collateral is goods that are or are to become fixtures and the financing statement is not filed as a fixture filing.

* * *

§ 9–502. Contents Of Financing Statement; Record Of Mortgage As Financing Statement; Time Of Filing Financing Statement

(a) [Sufficiency of financing statement.] Subject to subsection (b), a financing statement is sufficient only if it:

(1) provides the name of the debtor;

(2) provides the name of the secured party or a representative of the secured party; and

(3) indicates the collateral covered by the financing statement.

* * *

(d) [Filing before security agreement or attachment.] A financing statement may be filed before a security agreement is made or a security interest otherwise attaches.

§ 9–515. Duration And Effectiveness Of Financing Statement; Effect Of Lapsed Financing Statement

(a) [Five-year effectiveness.] Except as otherwise provided in subsections (b), (e), (f), and (g), a filed

financing statement is effective for a period of five years after the date of filing.

* * *

(c) [Lapse and continuation of financing statement.] The effectiveness of a filed financing statement lapses on the expiration of the period of its effectiveness unless before the lapse a continuation statement is filed pursuant to subsection (d). Upon lapse, a financing statement ceases to be effective and any security interest or agricultural lien that was perfected by the financing statement becomes unperfected, unless the security interest is perfected otherwise. If the security interest or agricultural lien becomes unperfected upon lapse, it is deemed never to have been perfected as against a purchaser of the collateral for value.

(d) [When continuation statement may be filed.] A continuation statement may be filed only within six months before the expiration of the five-year period specified in subsection (a) or the 30–year period specified in subsection (b), whichever is applicable.

(e) [Effect of filing continuation statement.] Except as otherwise provided in Section 9–510, upon timely filing of a continuation statement, the effectiveness of the initial financing statement continues for a period of five years commencing on the day on which the financing statement would have become ineffective in the absence of the filing. Upon the expiration of the five-year period, the financing statement lapses in the same manner as provided in subsection (c), unless, before the lapse, another continuation statement is filed pursuant to subsection (d). Succeeding continuation statements may be filed in the same manner to continue the effectiveness of the initial financing statement.

* * *

§ 9–516. What Constitutes Filing; Effectiveness Of Filing

(a) [What constitutes filing.] Except as otherwise provided in subsection (b), communication of a record to a filing office and tender of the filing fee or acceptance of the record by the filing office constitutes filing.

* * *

Part 6. Default

[Subpart 1. Default And Enforcement Of Security Interest]

§ 9–601. Rights After Default; Judicial Enforcement; Consignor Or Buyer Of Accounts, Chattel Paper, Payment Intangibles, Or Promissory Notes

(a) [Rights of secured party after default.] After default, a secured party has the rights provided in this part and, except as otherwise provided in Section 9–602, those provided by agreement of the parties. A secured party:

(1) may reduce a claim to judgment, foreclose, or otherwise enforce the claim, security interest, or agricultural lien by any available judicial procedure; and

(2) if the collateral is documents, may proceed either as to the documents or as to the goods they cover.

* * *

§ 9–607. Collection And Enforcement By Secured Party

(a) [Collection and enforcement generally.] If so agreed, and in any event after default, a secured party:

(1) may notify an account debtor or other person obligated on collateral to make payment or otherwise render performance to or for the benefit of the secured party;

(2) may take any proceeds to which the secured party is entitled under Section 9–315;

(3) may enforce the obligations of an account debtor or other person obligated on collateral and exercise the rights of the debtor with respect to the obligation of the account debtor or other person obligated on collateral to make payment or otherwise render performance to the debtor, and with respect to any property that secures the obligations of the account debtor or other person obligated on the collateral;

(4) if it holds a security interest in a deposit account perfected by control under Section 9–104(a)(1), may apply the balance of the deposit account to the obligation secured by the deposit account; and

(5) if it holds a security interest in a deposit account perfected by control under Section 9–104(a)(2) or (3), may instruct the bank to pay the balance of the deposit account to or for the benefit of the secured party.

* * *

§ 9–609. Secured Party's Right To Take Possession After Default

(a) [Possession; rendering equipment unusable; disposition on debtor's premises.] After default, a secured party:

(1) may take possession of the collateral; and

(2) without removal, may render equipment unusable and dispose of collateral on a debtor's premises under Section 9–610.

(b) [Judicial and nonjudicial process.] A secured party may proceed under subsection (a):

(1) pursuant to judicial process; or

(2) without judicial process, if it proceeds without breach of the peace.

(c) [Assembly of collateral.] If so agreed, and in any event after default, a secured party may require the debtor to assemble the collateral and make it available to the secured party at a place to be designated by the secured party which is reasonably convenient to both parties.

§ 9–610. Disposition Of Collateral After Default

(a) [Disposition after default.] After default, a secured party may sell, lease, license, or otherwise dispose of any or all of the collateral in its present condition or following any commercially reasonable preparation or processing.

(b) [Commercially reasonable disposition.] Every aspect of a disposition of collateral, including the method, manner, time, place, and other terms, must be commercially reasonable. If commercially reasonable, a secured party may dispose of collateral by public or private proceedings, by one or more contracts, as a unit or in parcels, and at any time and place and on any terms.

* * *

§ 9–611. Notification Before Disposition Of Collateral

* * *

(b) [Notification of disposition required.] Except as otherwise provided in subsection (d), a secured party that disposes of collateral under Section 9–610 shall send to the persons specified in subsection (c) a reasonable authenticated notification of disposition.

(c) [Persons to be notified.] To comply with subsection (b), the secured party shall send an authenticated notification of disposition to:

(1) the debtor;

(2) any secondary obligor; and

(3) if the collateral is other than consumer goods:

(A) any other person from which the secured party has received, before the notification date, an authenticated notification of a claim of an interest in the collateral;

(B) any other secured party or lienholder that, 10 days before the notification date, held a security interest in or other lien on the collateral perfected by the filing of a financing statement that:

(i) identified the collateral;

(ii) was indexed under the debtor's name as of that date; and

(iii) was filed in the office in which to file a financing statement against the debtor covering the collateral as of that date; and

(C) any other secured party that, 10 days before the notification date, held a security interest in the collateral perfected by compliance with a statute, regulation, or treaty described in Section 9–311(a).

* * *

§ 9–612. Timeliness Of Notification Before Disposition Of Collateral

(a) [Reasonable time is question of fact.] Except as otherwise provided in subsection (b), whether a notification is sent within a reasonable time is a question of fact.

(b) [10–day period sufficient in non-consumer transaction.] In a transaction other than a consumer transaction, a notification of disposition sent after default and 10 days or more before the earliest time of disposition set forth in the notification is sent within a reasonable time before the disposition.

§ 9–615. Application Of Proceeds Of Disposition; Liability For Deficiency And Right To Surplus

(a) [Application of proceeds.] A secured party shall apply or pay over for application the cash proceeds of disposition under Section 9–610 in the following order to:

(1) the reasonable expenses of retaking, holding, preparing for disposition, processing, and disposing, and, to the extent provided for by agreement and not prohibited by law, reasonable attorney's fees and legal expenses incurred by the secured party;

(2) the satisfaction of obligations secured by the security interest or agricultural lien under which the disposition is made;

(3) the satisfaction of obligations secured by any subordinate security interest in or other subordinate lien on the collateral if:

(A) the secured party receives from the holder of the subordinate security interest or other lien an authenticated demand for proceeds before distribution of the proceeds is completed;

* * *

§ 9–620. Acceptance Of Collateral In Full Or Partial Satisfaction Of Obligation; Compulsory Disposition Of Collateral

(a) [Conditions to acceptance in satisfaction.] Except as otherwise provided in subsection (g), a secured party may accept collateral in full or partial satisfaction of the obligation it secures only if:

(1) the debtor consents to the acceptance under subsection (c);

(2) the secured party does not receive, within the time set forth in subsection (d), a notification of objection to the proposal authenticated by:

(A) a person to which the secured party was required to send a proposal under Section 9–621; or

(B) any other person, other than the debtor, holding an interest in the collateral subordinate to the security interest that is the subject of the proposal;

(3) if the collateral is consumer goods, the collateral is not in the possession of the debtor when the debtor consents to the acceptance; and

(4) subsection (e) does not require the secured party to dispose of the collateral or the debtor waives the requirement pursuant to Section 9–624.

* * *

(e) [Mandatory disposition of consumer goods.] A secured party that has taken possession of collateral shall dispose of the collateral pursuant to Section 9–610 within the time specified in subsection (f) if:

(1) 60 percent of the cash price has been paid in the case of a purchase-money security interest in consumer goods; or

(2) 60 percent of the principal amount of the obligation secured has been paid in the case of a non-purchase-money security interest in consumer goods.

* * *

(g) [No partial satisfaction in consumer transaction.] In a consumer transaction, a secured party may not accept collateral in partial satisfaction of the obligation it secures.

§ 9–622. Effect Of Acceptance Of Collateral

(a) [Effect of acceptance.] A secured party's acceptance of collateral in full or partial satisfaction of the obligation it secures:

(1) discharges the obligation to the extent consented to by the debtor;

(2) transfers to the secured party all of a debtor's rights in the collateral;

(3) discharges the security interest or agricultural lien that is the subject of the debtor's consent and any subordinate security interest or other subordinate lien; and

(4) terminates any other subordinate interest.

(b) [Discharge of subordinate interest notwithstanding noncompliance.] A subordinate interest is discharged or terminated under subsection (a), even if the secured party fails to comply with this article.

§ 9–623. Right To Redeem Collateral

(a) [Persons that may redeem.] A debtor, any secondary obligor, or any other secured party or lienholder may redeem collateral.

(b) [Requirements for redemption.] To redeem collateral, a person shall tender:

(1) fulfillment of all obligations secured by the collateral; and

(2) the reasonable expenses and attorney's fees described in Section 9–615(a)(1).

(c) [When redemption may occur.] A redemption may occur at any time before a secured party:

(1) has collected collateral under Section 9–607;

(2) has disposed of collateral or entered into a contract for its disposition under Section 9–610; or

(3) has accepted collateral in full or partial satisfaction of the obligation it secures under Section 9–622.

[Subpart 2. Noncompliance With Article]

§ 9–625. Remedies For Secured Party's Failure To Comply With Article

* * *

(b) [Damages for noncompliance.] Subject to subsections (c), (d), and (f), a person is liable for damages in the amount of any loss caused by a failure to comply with this article. Loss caused by a failure to comply may include loss resulting from the debtor's inability to obtain, or increased costs of, alternative financing.

* * *

FEDERAL TAX LIEN STATUTES INTERNAL REVENUE CODE—

Selected Sections

Title 26, United States Code
Subtitle F.Procedure and Administration
Chapter 64.Collection
Subchapter C.Lien for Taxes
Part II.Liens

Sec.
6321.   Lien for taxes.

Sec.
6322.   Period of lien.
6323.   Validity and priority against certain persons.

---

§ 6321.   Lien for taxes

If any person liable to pay any tax neglects or refuses to pay the same after demand, the amount (including any interest, additional amount, addition to tax, or assessable penalty, together with any costs that may accrue in addition thereto) shall be a lien in favor of the United States upon all property and rights to property, whether real or personal, belonging to such person.

(Aug. 16, 1954, c. 736, 68A Stat. 779.)

HISTORICAL AND STATUTORY NOTES

Revision Notes and Legislative Reports

1954 Acts. House Report No. 1337, Senate Report No. 1622, and Conference Report No. 2543, see 1954 U.S. Code Cong. and Adm. News, p. 4554.

Short Title

Pub.L. 89–719, § 1(a), Nov. 2, 1966, 80 Stat. 1125, provided that: "This Act [enacting sections 3505, 7425, 7426 and 7810 of this title, amending sections 545, 6322 to 6325, 6331, 6332, 6334, 6335, 6337 to 6339, 6342, 6343, 6502, 6503, 6532, 7402, 7403, 7421, 7424, 7505, 7506 and 7809 of this title, sections 1346, 1402 and 2410 of Title 28, Judiciary and Judicial Procedure, and section 270a of Title 40, Public Buildings, Property and Works, redesignating former section 7425 of this title as 7427, and enacting provisions set out as notes under this section and section 7424 of this title, and under section 1346 of Title 28] may be cited as the 'Federal Tax Lien Act of 1966'."

CROSS REFERENCES

Action to enforce lien or to subject property to payment of tax, see 26 USCA § 7403.

Liability of operators for repayments to Mine Safety and Health Fund, see 30 USCA § 934.

Lien for liability, Employee Retirement Income Security Program, see 29 USCA § 1368.

LIBRARY REFERENCES

American Digest System
Internal Revenue ⟜4765, 4771.
Key Number System Topic No. 220.

Corpus Juris Secundum
CJS Internal Revenue § 722, Creation, Accrual, and Duration.
CJS Internal Revenue § 723, Property Subject to Lien.
CJS Internal Revenue § 737, Interest.
CJS United States § 202, Retaining Out of Claims Amount Due United States.

§ 6322.   Period of lien

Unless another date is specifically fixed by law, the lien imposed by section 6321 shall arise at the time the assessment is made and shall continue until the liability for the amount so assessed (or a judgment against the taxpayer arising out of such liability) is satisfied or becomes unenforceable by reason of lapse of time.

(Aug. 16, 1954, c. 736, 68A Stat. 779; Nov. 2, 1966, Pub.L. 89–719, Title I, § 113(a), 80 Stat. 1146.)

HISTORICAL AND STATUTORY NOTES

Revision Notes and Legislative Reports

1954 Acts. House Report No. 1337, Senate Report No. 1622, and Conference Report No. 2543, see 1954 U.S.Code Cong. and Adm.News, pp. 4554, 5224.

1966 Acts. Senate Report No. 1708, see 1966 U.S.Code Cong. and Adm.News, p. 3722.

Amendments

1966 Amendments. Pub.L. 89–719 inserted phrase "(or a judgment against the taxpayer arising out of such liability)."

Effective and Applicability Provisions

1966 Acts. Amendment by Pub.L. 89–719 applicable after Nov. 2, 1966, regardless of when the title or lien of the United States arose or when the lien or interest of another person was acquired, with certain exceptions, see § 114(a)–(c) of Pub.L. 89–719, set out as a note under § 6323 of this title.

American Digest System

Internal Revenue ☞4780, 4793, 4803.
Key Number System Topic No. 220.

Corpus Juris Secundum

CJS Internal Revenue § 722, Creation, Accrual, and Duration.

§ 6323. Validity and priority against certain persons

(a) Purchasers, holders of security interests, mechanic's lienors, and judgment lien creditors.—The lien imposed by section 6321 shall not be valid as against any purchaser, holder of a security interest, mechanic's lienor, or judgment lien creditor until notice thereof which meets the requirements of subsection (f) has been filed by the Secretary.

(b) Protection for certain interests even though notice filed.—Even though notice of a lien imposed by section 6321 has been filed, such lien shall not be valid—

(1) **Securities.**—With respect to a security (as defined in subsection (h)(4))—

(A) as against a purchaser of such security who at the time of purchase did not have actual notice or knowledge of the existence of such lien; and

(B) as against a holder of a security interest in such security who, at the time such interest came into existence, did not have actual notice or knowledge of the existence of such lien.

(2) **Motor vehicles.**—With respect to a motor vehicle (as defined in subsection (h)(3)), as against a purchaser of such motor vehicle, if—

(A) at the time of the purchase such purchaser did not have actual notice or knowledge of the existence of such lien, and

(B) before the purchaser obtains such notice or knowledge, he has acquired possession of such motor vehicle and has not thereafter relinquished possession of such motor vehicle to the seller or his agent.

(3) **Personal property purchased at retail.**—With respect to tangible personal property purchased at retail, as against a purchaser in the ordinary course of the seller's trade or business, unless at the time of such purchase such purchaser intends such purchase to (or knows such purchase will) hinder, evade, or defeat the collection of any tax under this title.

(4) **Personal property purchased in casual sale.**—With respect to household goods, personal effects, or other tangible personal property described in section 6334(a) purchased (not for resale) in a casual sale for less than $1,000, as against the

purchaser, but only if such purchaser does not have actual notice or knowledge (A) of the existence of such lien, or (B) that this sale is one of a series of sales.

(5) **Personal property subject to possessory lien.**—With respect to tangible personal property subject to a lien under local law securing the reasonable price of the repair or improvement of such property, as against a holder of such a lien, if such holder is, and has been, continuously in possession of such property from the time such lien arose.

(6) **Real property tax and special assessment liens.**—With respect to real property, as against a holder of a lien upon such property, if such lien is entitled under local law to priority over security interests in such property which are prior in time, and such lien secures payment of—

(A) a tax of general application levied by any taxing authority based upon the value of such property;

(B) a special assessment imposed directly upon such property by any taxing authority, if such assessment is imposed for the purpose of defraying the cost of any public improvement; or

(C) charges for utilities or public services furnished to such property by the United States, a State or political subdivision thereof, or an instrumentality of any one or more of the foregoing.

(7) **Residential property subject to a mechanic's lien for certain repairs and improvements.**—With respect to real property subject to a lien for repair or improvement of a personal residence (containing not more than four dwelling units) occupied by the owner of such residence, as against a mechanic's lienor, but only if the contract price on the contract with the owner is not more than $5,000.

(8) **Attorneys' liens.**—With respect to a judgment or other amount in settlement of a claim or of a cause of action, as against an attorney who, under local law, holds a lien upon or a contract enforceable against such judgment or amount, to the extent of his reasonable compensation for obtaining such judgment or procuring such settlement, except that this paragraph shall not apply to any judgment or amount in settlement of a claim or of a cause of action against the United States to the extent that the United States offsets such judgment or amount against any liability of the taxpayer to the United States.

(9) **Certain insurance contracts.**—With respect to a life insurance, endowment, or annuity contract, as against the organization which is the insurer under such contract, at any time—

(A) before such organization had actual notice or knowledge of the existence of such lien;

(B) after such organization had such notice or knowledge, with respect to advances required to be made automatically to maintain such contract in force under an agreement entered into before such organization had such notice or knowledge; or

(C) after satisfaction of a levy pursuant to section 6332(b), unless and until the Secretary delivers to such organization a notice, executed after the date of such satisfaction, of the existence of such lien.

(10) **Deposit-secured loans.**—With respect to a savings deposit, share, or other account, with an institution described in section 581 or 591, to the extent of any loan made by such institution without actual notice or knowledge of the existence of such lien, as against such institution, if such loan is secured by such account.

(c) **Protection for certain commercial transactions financing agreements, etc.**—

(1) **In general.**—To the extent provided in this subsection, even though notice of a lien imposed by section 6321 has been filed, such lien shall not be valid with respect to a security interest which came into existence after tax lien filing but which—

(A) is in qualified property covered by the terms of a written agreement entered into before tax lien filing and constituting—

(i) a commercial transactions financing agreement,

(ii) a real property construction or improvement financing agreement, or

(iii) an obligatory disbursement agreement, and

(B) is protected under local law against a judgment lien arising, as of the time of tax lien filing, out of an unsecured obligation.

(2) **Commercial transactions financing agreement.**—For purposes of this subsection—

(A) **Definition.**—The term "commercial transactions financing agreement" means an agreement (entered into by a person in the course of his trade or business)—

(i) to make loans to the taxpayer to be secured by commercial financing security acquired by the taxpayer in the ordinary course of his trade or business, or

(ii) to purchase commercial financing security (other than inventory) acquired by the taxpayer in the ordinary course of his trade or business;

but such an agreement shall be treated as coming within the term only to the extent that such loan or purchase is made before the 46th day after the date of tax lien filing or (if earlier) before the lender or purchaser had actual notice or knowledge of such tax lien filing.

(B) **Limitation on qualified property.**—The term "qualified property", when used with respect to a commercial transactions financing agreement,

includes only commercial financing security acquired by the taxpayer before the 46th day after the date of tax lien filing.

(C) **Commercial financing security defined.**—The term "commercial financing security" means (i) paper of a kind ordinarily arising in commercial transactions, (ii) accounts receivable, (iii) mortgages on real property, and (iv) inventory.

(D) **Purchaser treated as acquiring security interest.**—A person who satisfies subparagraph (A) by reason of clause (ii) thereof shall be treated as having acquired a security interest in commercial financing security.

(3) **Real property construction or improvement financing agreement.**—For purposes of this subsection—

(A) **Definition.**—The term "real property construction or improvement financing agreement" means an agreement to make cash disbursements to finance—

(i) the construction or improvement of real property,

(ii) a contract to construct or improve real property, or

(iii) the raising or harvesting of a farm crop or the raising of livestock or other animals. For purposes of clause (iii), the furnishing of goods and services shall be treated as the disbursement of cash.

(B) **Limitation on qualified property.**—The term "qualified property", when used with respect to a real property construction or improvement financing agreement, includes only—

(i) in the case of subparagraph (A)(i), the real property with respect to which the construction or improvement has been or is to be made,

(ii) in the case of subparagraph (A)(ii), the proceeds of the contract described therein, and

(iii) in the case of subparagraph (A)(iii), property subject to the lien imposed by section 6321 at the time of tax lien filing and the crop or the livestock or other animals referred to in subparagraph (A)(iii).

(4) **Obligatory disbursement agreement.**—For purposes of this subsection—

(A) **Definition.**—The term "obligatory disbursement agreement" means an agreement (entered into by a person in the course of his trade or business) to make disbursements, but such an agreement shall be treated as coming within the term only to the extent of disbursements which are required to be made by reason of the intervention of the rights of a person other than the taxpayer.

(B) **Limitation on qualified property.**—The term "qualified property", when used with respect to an obligatory disbursement agreement, means property subject to the lien imposed by section

6321 at the time of tax lien filing and (to the extent that the acquisition is directly traceable to the disbursements referred to in subparagraph (A)) property acquired by the taxpayer after tax lien filing.

(C) Special rules for surety agreements.—Where the obligatory disbursement agreement is an agreement ensuring the performance of a contract between the taxpayer and another person—

(i) the term "qualified property" shall be treated as also including the proceeds of the contract the performance of which was ensured, and

(ii) if the contract the performance of which was ensured was a contract to construct or improve real property, to produce goods, or to furnish services, the term "qualified property" shall be treated as also including any tangible personal property used by the taxpayer in the performance of such ensured contract.

(d) 45-day period for making disbursements.—Even though notice of a lien imposed by section 6321 has been filed, such lien shall not be valid with respect to a security interest which came into existence after tax lien filing by reason of disbursements made before the 46th day after the date of tax lien filing, or (if earlier) before the person making such disbursements had actual notice or knowledge of tax lien filing, but only if such security interest—

(1) is in property (A) subject, at the time of tax lien filing, to the lien imposed by section 6321, and (B) covered by the terms of a written agreement entered into before tax lien filing, and

(2) is protected under local law against a judgment lien arising, as of the time of tax lien filing, out of an unsecured obligation.

(e) Priority of interest and expenses.—If the lien imposed by section 6321 is not valid as against a lien or security interest, the priority of such lien or security interest shall extend to—

(1) any interest or carrying charges upon the obligation secured,

(2) the reasonable charges and expenses of an indenture trustee or agent holding the security interest for the benefit of the holder of the security interest,

(3) the reasonable expenses, including reasonable compensation for attorneys, actually incurred in collecting or enforcing the obligation secured,

(4) the reasonable costs of insuring, preserving, or repairing the property to which the lien or security interest relates,

(5) the reasonable costs of insuring payment of the obligation secured, and

(6) amounts paid to satisfy any lien on the property to which the lien or security interest relates, but

only if the lien so satisfied is entitled to priority over the lien imposed by section 6321,

to the extent that, under local law, any such item has the same priority as the lien or security interest to which it relates.

(f) Place for filing notice; form.—

(1) Place for filing.—The notice referred to in subsection (a) shall be filed—

(A) Under State laws.—

(i) Real property.—In the case of real property, in one office within the State (or the county, or other governmental subdivision), as designated by the laws of such State, in which the property subject to the lien is situated; and

(ii) Personal property.—In the case of personal property, whether tangible or intangible, in one office within the State (or the county, or other governmental subdivision), as designated by the laws of such State, in which the property subject to the lien is situated, except that State law merely conforming to or reenacting Federal law establishing a national filing system does not constitute a second office for filing as designated by the laws of such State; or

(B) With clerk of district court.—In the office of the clerk of the United States district court for the judicial district in which the property subject to the lien is situated, whenever the State has not by law designated one office which meets the requirements of subparagraph (A); or

(C) With Recorder of Deeds of the District of Columbia.—In the office of the Recorder of Deeds of the District of Columbia, if the property subject to the lien is situated in the District of Columbia.

(2) Situs of property subject to lien.—For purposes of paragraphs (1) and (4), property shall be deemed to be situated—

(A) Real property.—In the case of real property, at its physical location; or

(B) Personal property.—In the case of personal property, whether tangible or intangible, at the residence of the taxpayer at the time the notice of lien is filed.

For purposes of paragraph (2)(B), the residence of a corporation or partnership shall be deemed to be the place at which the principal executive office of the business is located, and the residence of a taxpayer whose residence is without the United States shall be deemed to be in the District of Columbia.

(3) Form.—The form and content of the notice referred to in subsection (a) shall be prescribed by the Secretary. Such notice shall be valid notwithstanding any other provision of law regarding the form or content of a notice of lien.

(4) Indexing required with respect to certain real property.—In the case of real property, if—

(A) under the laws of the State in which the real property is located, a deed is not valid as against a purchaser of the property who (at the time of purchase) does not have actual notice or knowledge of the existence of such deed unless the fact of filing of such deed has been entered and recorded in a public index at the place of filing in such a manner that a reasonable inspection of the index will reveal the existence of the deed, and

(B) there is maintained (at the applicable office under paragraph (1)) an adequate system for the public indexing of Federal tax liens,

then the notice of lien referred to in subsection (a) shall not be treated as meeting the filing requirements under paragraph (1) unless the fact of filing is entered and recorded in the index referred to in subparagraph (B) in such a manner that a reasonable inspection of the index will reveal the existence of the lien.

(5) **National filing systems.**—The filing of a notice of lien shall be governed solely by this title and shall not be subject to any other Federal law establishing a place or places for the filing of liens or encumbrances under a national filing system.

(g) **Refiling of notice.**—For purposes of this section—

(1) **General rule.**—Unless notice of lien is refiled in the manner prescribed in paragraph (2) during the required refiling period, such notice of lien shall be treated as filed on the date on which it is filed (in accordance with subsection (f)) after the expiration of such refiling period.

(2) **Place for filing.**—A notice of lien refiled during the required refiling period shall be effective only—

(A) if—

(i) such notice of lien is refiled in the office in which the prior notice of lien was filed, and

(ii) in the case of real property, the fact of refiling is entered and recorded in an index to the extent required by subsection (f)(4); and

(B) in any case in which, 90 days or more prior to the date of a refiling of notice of lien under subparagraph (A), the Secretary received written information (in the manner prescribed in regulations issued by the Secretary) concerning a change in the taxpayer's residence, if a notice of such lien is also filed in accordance with subsection (f) in the State in which such residence is located.

(3) **Required refiling period.**—In the case of any notice of lien, the term "required refiling period" means—

(A) the one-year period ending 30 days after the expiration of 10 years after the date of the assessment of the tax, and

(B) the one-year period ending with the expiration of 10 years after the close of the preceding required refiling period for such notice of lien.

(4) **Transitional rule.**—Notwithstanding paragraph (3), if the assessment of the tax was made before January 1, 1962, the first required refiling period shall be the calendar year 1967.

(h) **Definitions.**—For purposes of this section and section 6324—

(1) **Security interest.**—The term "security interest" means any interest in property acquired by contract for the purpose of securing payment or performance of an obligation or indemnifying against loss or liability. A security interest exists at any time (A) if, at such time, the property is in existence and the interest has become protected under local law against a subsequent judgment lien arising out of an unsecured obligation, and (B) to the extent that, at such time, the holder has parted with money or money's worth.

(2) **Mechanic's lienor.**—The term "mechanic's lienor" means any person who under local law has a lien on real property (or on the proceeds of a contract relating to real property) for services, labor, or materials furnished in connection with the construction or improvement of such property. For purposes of the preceding sentence, a person has a lien on the earliest date such lien becomes valid under local law against subsequent purchasers without actual notice, but not before he begins to furnish the services, labor, or materials.

(3) **Motor vehicle.**—The term "motor vehicle" means a self-propelled vehicle which is registered for highway use under the laws of any State or foreign country.

(4) **Security.**—The term "security" means any bond, debenture, note, or certificate or other evidence of indebtedness, issued by a corporation or a government or political subdivision thereof, with interest coupons or in registered form, share of stock, voting trust certificate, or any certificate of interest or participation in, certificate of deposit or receipt for, temporary or interim certificate for, or warrant or right to subscribe to or purchase, any of the foregoing; negotiable instrument; or money.

(5) **Tax lien filing.**—The term "tax lien filing" means the filing of notice (referred to in subsection (a)) of the lien imposed by section 6321.

(6) **Purchaser.**—The term "purchaser" means a person who, for adequate and full consideration in money or money's worth, acquires an interest (other than a lien or security interest) in property which is valid under local law against subsequent purchasers without actual notice. In applying the preceding sentence for purposes of subsection (a) of this section, and for purposes of section 6324—

(A) a lease of property,

(B) a written executory contract to purchase or lease property,

(C) an option to purchase or lease property or any interest therein, or

(D) an option to renew or extend a lease of property,

which is not a lien or security interest shall be treated as an interest in property.

(i) Special rules.—

(1) Actual notice or knowledge.—For purposes of this subchapter, an organization shall be deemed for purposes of a particular transaction to have actual notice or knowledge of any fact from the time such fact is brought to the attention of the individual conducting such transaction, and in any event from the time such fact would have been brought to such individual's attention if the organization had exercised due diligence. An organization exercises due diligence if it maintains reasonable routines for communicating significant information to the person conducting the transaction and there is reasonable compliance with the routine. Due diligence does not require an individual acting for the organization to communicate information unless such communication is part of his regular duties or unless he has reason to know of the transaction and that the transaction would be materially affected by the information.

(2) Subrogation.—Where, under local law, one person is subrogated to the rights of another with respect to a lien or interest, such person shall be subrogated to such rights for purposes of any lien imposed by section 6321 or 6324.

(3) Forfeitures.—For purposes of this subchapter, a forfeiture under local law of property seized by a law enforcement agency of a State, county, or other local governmental subdivision shall relate back to the time of seizure, except that this paragraph shall not apply to the extent that under local law the holder of an intervening claim or interest would have priority over the interest of the State, county, or other local governmental subdivision in the property.

(4) Cost–of–living adjustment.—In the case of notices of liens imposed by section 6321 which are filed in any calendar year after 1998, each of the dollar amounts under paragraph (4) or (7) of subsection (b) shall be increased by an amount equal to.—

(A) such dollar amount, multiplied by

(B) the cost-of-living adjustment determined under section 1(f)(3) for the calendar year, determined by substituting "calendar year 1996" for "calendar year 1992" in subparagraph (B) thereof.

If any amount as adjusted under the preceding sentence is not a multiple of $10, such amount shall be rounded to the nearest multiple of $10.

(j) Withdrawal of notice in certain circumstances.—

(1) In general.—The Secretary may withdraw a notice of a lien filed under this section and this chapter shall be applied as if the withdrawn notice had not been filed, if the Secretary determines that—

(A) the filing of such notice was premature or otherwise not in accordance with administrative procedures of the Secretary,

(B) the taxpayer has entered into an agreement under section 6159 to satisfy the tax liability for which the lien was imposed by means of installment payments, unless such agreement provides otherwise,

(C) the withdrawal of such notice will facilitate the collection of the tax liability, or

(D) with the consent of the taxpayer or the National Taxpayer Advocate, the withdrawal of such notice would be in the best interests of the taxpayer (as determined by the National Taxpayer Advocate) and the United States.

Any such withdrawal shall be made by filing notice at the same office as the withdrawn notice. A copy of such notice of withdrawal shall be provided to the taxpayer.

(2) Notice to credit agencies, etc.—Upon written request by the taxpayer with respect to whom a notice of a lien was withdrawn under paragraph (1), the Secretary shall promptly make reasonable efforts to notify credit reporting agencies, and any financial institution or creditor whose name and address is specified in such request, of the withdrawal of such notice. Any such request shall be in such form as the Secretary may prescribe.

(Aug. 16, 1954, c. 736, 68A Stat. 779; Feb. 26, 1964, Pub.L. 88–272, Title II, § 236(a), (c)(1), 78 Stat. 127, 128; July 5, 1966, Pub.L. 89–493, § 17(a), 80 Stat. 266; Nov. 2, 1966, Pub.L. 89–719, Title I, § 101(a), 80 Stat. 1125; Oct. 4, 1976, Pub.L. 94–455, Title XII, § 1202(h)(2), Title XIX, § 1906(b)(13)(A), Title XX, § 2008(c), 90 Stat. 1688, 1834, 1892; Nov. 6, 1978, Pub.L. 95–600, Title VII, § 702(q)(1), (2), 92 Stat. 2937, 2938; Oct. 22, 1986, Pub.L. 99–514, Title XV, § 1569(a), 100 Stat. 2764; Nov. 10, 1988, Pub.L. 100–647, Title I, § 1015(s)(1), 102 Stat. 3573; Nov. 5, 1990, Pub.L. 101–508, Title XI, §§ 11317(b), 11704(a)(26), 104 Stat. 1388–458, 1388–519; July 30, 1996, Pub.L. 104–168, Title V, § 501(a), 110 Stat. 1460; July 22, 1998, Pub.L. 105–206, Title I, §§ 1102(d)(1)(A), Title III, 3435(a), (b), 112 Stat. 704, 760, 761.)

HISTORICAL AND STATUTORY NOTES

Revision Notes and Legislative Reports

1954 Acts. House Report No. 1337, Senate Report No. 1622, and House Conference Report No. 2543, see 1954 U.S.Code Cong. and Adm.News, pp. 4554, 5224, 5280, 5340, respectively.

1964 Acts. House Report No. 749, Senate Report No. 830, Senate Suppl. Report No. 830, and Conference Report No. 1149, see 1964 U.S.Code Cong. and Adm.News, p. 1313.

1966 Acts. Senate Report No. 1708, see 1966 U.S.Code Cong. and Adm.News, p. 3722.

1976 Acts. House Report Nos. 94–658, 94–1380, Senate Report No. 94–938, and House Conference Report No. 94–1515, see 1976 U.S.Code Cong. and Adm.News, p. 2897.

1978 Acts. House Report No. 95–1445, Senate Report No. 95–1263, and House Conference Report No. 95–1800, see 1978 U.S.Code Cong. and Adm.News, p. 6761.

1986 Acts. House Conference Report No. 99–841 and Statement by President, see 1986 U.S.Code Cong. and Adm. News, p. 4075.

1988 Acts. Senate Report No. 100–445 and House Conference Report No. 100–1104, see 1988 U.S.Code Cong. and Adm.News, p. 4515.

1990 Acts. House Report No. 101–881 and House Conference Report No. 101–964, see 1990 U.S.Code Cong. and Adm.News, p. 2017.

1996 Acts. House Report No. 104–506, see 1996 U.S. Code Cong. and Adm. News, p. 1143.

1998 Acts. House Conference Report No. 105–599, see 1998 U.S. Code Cong. and Adm. News, p. 297.

Amendments

1998 Amendments. Subsec. (b)(4). Pub.L. 105–206, § 3435(a)(1)(A), substituted "$1,000" for "$250".

Subsec. (b)(7). Pub.L. 105–206, § 3435(a)(1)(B), substituted "$5,000" for "$1,000".

Subsec. (b)(10). Pub.L. 105–206, § 3435(b), substituted "Deposit-secured loans" for "Passbook loans" in the par. heading, struck out ", evidenced by a passbook," following "savings deposit, share, or other account" and substituted a period for "and if such institution has been continuously in possession of such passbook from the time the loan is made." following "secured by such account".

Subsec. (i)(4). Pub.L. 105–206, § 3435(a)(2), added par. (4).

Subsec. (j)(1)(D). Pub.L. 105–206, § 1102(d)(1)(A), substituted "National Taxpayer Advocate" for "Taxpayer Advocate" each place it appeared.

1996 Amendments. Subsec. (j). Pub.L. 104–168, § 501(a) added subsec. (j).

1990 Amendments. Subsec. (a). Pub.L. 101–508, § 11704(a)(26), substituted "Purchasers" for "Purchases" in the heading.

Subsec. (g). Pub.L. 101–508, § 11317(b), substituted "10 years" for "6 years" wherever appearing.

1988 Amendments. Subsec. (f)(1)(A)(ii). Pub.L. 100–647, § 1015(s)(1)(A), added provision that State law merely conforming to or reenacting Federal law establishing a national filing system does not constitute a second office for filing as designated by the laws of such State.

Subsec. (f)(5). Pub.L. 100–647, § 1015(s)(1)(B), added par. (5).

1986 Amendments. Subsec. (i)(3). Pub.L. 99–514 added par. (3).

1978 Amendments. Subsec. (f)(4). Pub.L. 95–600, § 702(q)(1), in par. heading substituted "Indexing required with respect to certain real property" for "Index" and in text added provisions relating to the validity of a deed, under the laws of the State in which the real property is located, as against a purchaser who does not have actual notice or knowledge of the existence of such deed and provisions relating to the maintenance of an adequate system for the public indexing of Federal tax liens.

Subsec. (g)(2)(A). Pub.L. 95–600, § 702(q)(2), inserted reference to real property.

1976 Amendments. Subsecs. (a), (b). Pub.L. 94–455, § 1906(b)(13)(A), struck out "or his delegate" following "Secretary" wherever appearing.

Subsec. (f)(2). Pub.L. 94–455, § 2008(c)(1)(B), inserted introductory reference to par. (4).

Subsec. (f)(3). Pub.L. 94–455, § 1906(b)(13)(A) struck out "or his delegate" following "Secretary".

Subsec. (f)(4). Pub.L. 94–455, § 2008(c)(1)(A), added par. (4).

Subsec. (g)(2)(A). Pub.L. 94–455, § 2008(c)(2), required the fact of refiling be entered and recorded in an index in accordance with subsec. (f)(4).

Subsec. (g)(2)(B). Pub.L. 94–455, § 1906(b)(13)(A), struck out "or his delegate" following "Secretary" wherever appearing.

Subsec. (i)(3). Pub.L. 94–455, § 1202(h)(2), struck out par. (3) which provided for special rule respecting disclosure of amount of outstanding lien.

1966 Amendments. Subsec. (a). Pub.L. 89–719 redesignated as the entire subsec. (a) that part of former subsec. (a) which preceded pars. (1)–(3) thereof, and, in subsec. (a) as so redesignated, substituted holder of a security interest, mechanic's lienor, and judgment lien creditor for mortgagee, pledgee, and judgment creditor, struck out reference to an exception provided in subsecs. (c) and (d), and inserted reference to the requirements of subsec. (f).

Subsec. (a)(3). Pub.L. 89–493 substituted the Recorder of Deeds of the District of Columbia for the clerk of the United States District Court for the District of Columbia.

Subsec. (b)(1). Pub.L. 89–719 redesignated provisions of former subsec. (c)(1) as subsec. (b)(1) and, in subsec. (b)(1) as so redesignated, substituted "holder of a security interest" for "mortgagee and pledgee" and purchaser of such security interest for purchaser of such security for any adequate and full consideration of money or money's worth.

Subsec. (b)(2). Pub.L. 89–719 redesignated provisions of former subsec. (d)(1) as subsec. (b)(2) and, in subsec. (b)(2) as so redesignated, substituted purchaser of such motor vehicle for purchaser of such motor vehicle for an adequate and full consideration in money or money's worth and substituted actual notice or knowledge for notice or knowledge.

Subsec. (b)(3)–(10). Pub.L. 89–719 added pars. (3)–(10).

Subsecs. (c)–(e). Pub.L. 89–719 added subsecs. (c)–(e).

Subsec. (f)(1). Pub.L. 89–719 redesignated provisions of former subsec. (a)(1)–(3) as subsec. (f)(1).

Subsec. (f)(2). Pub.L. 89–719 added par. (2).

Subsec. (f)(3). Pub.L. 89–719 redesignated provisions of former subsec. (b) as subsec. (f)(3) and, in subsec. (f)(3) as so redesignated, substituted provisions that the form and content of the notice be prescribed by the Secretary or his delegate for provisions limiting the effectiveness of the notice to situations in which the notice is in such form as would be valid if filed with the clerk of the United States district court when state or territory law fails to designate an office for the filing of notice.

Subsec. (g). Pub.L. 89–719 added subsec. (g).

Subsec. (h)(1), (2). Pub.L. 89–719 added pars. (1), (2).

Subsec. (h)(3). Pub.L. 89–719 redesignated provisions of former subsec. (d)(2) as subsec. (h)(3).

Subsec. (h)(4). Pub.L. 89–719 redesignated provisions of former subsec. (c)(2) as subsec. (h)(4).

Subsec. (h)(5), (6). Pub.L. 89–719 added pars. (5), (6).

Subsec. (i)(1), (2). Pub.L. 89–719 added subsec. (i)(1), (2).

Subsec. (i)(3). Pub.L. 89–719 redesignated the provisions of former subsec. (e) as subsec. (i)(3) and, in subsec. (i)(3) as so redesignated, substituted "regulations" for "rules and regulations".

1964   Amendments. Subsec. (a). Pub.L. 88–272, § 236(c)(1), substituted "subsections (c) and (d)" for "subsection (c)."

Subsec. (d). Pub.L. 88–272, § 236(a), added subsec. (d) and redesignated former subsec. (d) as (e).

Subsec. (e). Pub.L. 88–272, § 236(a), redesignated former subsec. (d) as (e).

Effective and Applicability Provisions

1998 Acts. Amendment by section 1102(d)(1)(a) of Pub.L. 105–206 effective July 22, 1998, see section 1102(f) of Pub.L. 105–206, set out as a note under section 7803 of this title.

Section 3435(c) of Pub.L. 105–206 provided that: "The amendments made by this section [amending subsecs. (b) and (i) of this section] shall take effect on the date of the enactment of this Act [July 22, 1998]."

1996 Acts. Section 501(d) of Pub.L. 104–168 provided that: "The amendments made by this section [amending this section and section 6343 of this title] shall take effect on the date of the enactment of this Act [July 30, 1996]."

1990 Acts. Section 11317(c) of Pub.L. 101–508 provided that:

"The amendments made by this section [amending subsec. (g)(3) of this section and section 6502(a) of this title] shall apply to—

"**(1)** taxes assessed after the date of the enactment of this Act [Nov. 5, 1990], and

"**(2)** taxes assessed on or before such date [Nov. 5, 1990] if the period specified in section 6502 of the Internal Revenue Code of 1986 [section 6502 of this title] (determined without regard to the amendments made by subsection (a) [amending section 6502(a) of this title]) for collection of such taxes has not expired as of such date [Nov. 5, 1990]."

Amendment by section 11704 of Pub.L. 101–508 shall take effect Nov. 5, 1990, see section 11704(b) of Pub.L. 101–508, set out as a note under section 56 of this title.

1988 Acts. Section 1015(s)(2) of Pub.L. 100–647 provided that: "The amendment made by this subsection [amending subsec. (f)(1)(A)(ii) and (f)(5) of this section] shall take effect on the date of the enactment of this Act [Nov. 10, 1988]."

1986 Acts. Section 1569(b) of Pub.L. 99–514 provided that: "The amendment made by this section [enacting subsec. (i)(3) of this section] shall take effect on the date of the enactment of this Act [Oct. 22, 1986]."

1978 Acts. Section 702(q)(3) of Pub.L. 95–600 provided that:

"**(A)** The amendments made by this subsection [amending subsecs. (f)(4) and (g)(2)(A) of this section] shall apply with respect to liens, other security interests, and other interests in real property acquired after the date of the enactment of this Act [Nov. 6, 1978].

"**(B)** If, after the date of the enactment of this Act [Nov. 6, 1978], there is a change in the application (or nonapplication)

of section 6323(f)(4) of the Internal Revenue Code of 1954 [subsec. (f)(4) of this section] (as amended by paragraph (1)) with respect to any filing jurisdiction, such change shall apply only with respect to liens, other security interests, and other interests in real property acquired after the date of such change."

1976 Acts. Amendment by section 1202(h)(2) of Pub.L. 94–455 effective Jan. 1, 1977, see section 1202(i) of Pub.L. 94–455, set out as a note under section 6103 of this title.

Amendment by section 1906(b)(13)(A) of Pub.L. 94–455 effective the first day of the first month which begins more than 90 days after Oct. 4, 1976, see section 1906(d) of Pub.L. 94–455, set out as a note under section 6013 of this title.

Section 2008(d)(3) of Pub.L. 94–455 provided that:

"The amendment made by subsection (c) [amending subsecs. (f) and (g)(2)(A) of this section] shall take effect—

"**(A)** in the case of liens filed before the date of the enactment of this Act [Oct. 4, 1976], on the 270th day after such date of enactment, or

"**(B)** in the case of liens filed on or after the date of enactment of this Act [Oct. 4, 1976], on the 120th day after such date of enactment."

1966 Acts. Section 114 of Pub.L. 89–719 provided that:

"**(a) General rule.**—Except as otherwise provided, the amendments made by this title [enacting sections 3505, 7425, 7426, and 7810 of this title, amending this section and sections 545, 6311, 6322, 6324, 6325, 6332, 6334, 6335, 6337, 6338, 6339, 6342, 6343, 6502, 6503, 6532, 7402, 7403, 7421, 7424, 7505, 7506, and 7809 of this title and section 270a of former Title 40, redesignated former section 7425 of this title as 7427, and enacting material set out as notes under this section and section 7424 of this title] shall apply after the date of enactment of this Act [Nov. 2, 1966], regardless of when a lien or a title of the United States arose or when the lien or interest of any other person was acquired.

"**(b) Exceptions.**—The amendments made by this title shall not apply in any case—

"**(1)** in which a lien or a title derived from enforcement of a lien held by the United States has been enforced by a civil action or suit which has become final by judgment, sale, or agreement before the date of enactment of this Act; or

"**(2)** in which such amendments would—

"**(A)** impair a priority enjoyed by any person (other than the United States) holding a lien or interest prior to the date of enactment of this Act;

"**(B)** operate to increase the liability of any such person; or

"**(C)** shorten the time for bringing suit with respect to transactions occurring before the date of enactment of this Act.

"**(c) Liability for withheld taxes.**—

"**(1)** The amendments made by section 105(a) (relating to effect on third parties) [adding section 3505 of this title] shall apply only with respect to wages paid on or after January 1, 1967.

"**(2)** The amendments made by section 105(b) (relating to performance bonds of contractors for public buildings or works) [amending section 270a of former Title 40] shall apply to contracts entered into pursuant to invitations for bids issued after June 30, 1967."

Section 21 of Pub.L. 89–493 provided that the amendment of this section shall take effect on the first day of the first month which is at least ninety days after July 5, 1966.

1964 Acts. Section 236(d) of Pub.L. 88–272 provided that: "The amendments made by this section [to this section, and section 6324 of this title] shall apply only with respect to purchases made after the date of the enactment of this Act [Feb. 26, 1964]."

CROSS REFERENCES

Hazardous substances releases, liability, see 42 USCA § 9607.

Liability of operators for repayments to Mine Safety and Health Fund, see 30 USCA § 934.

Treatment of certain liens in liquidation, see 11 USCA § 724.

LIBRARY REFERENCES

American Digest System

Internal Revenue ☞4781, 4782.

Key Number System Topic No. 220.

Corpus Juris Secundum

CJS Bankruptcy § 669, Statutory Liens; Penalty Liens.

CJS Internal Revenue § 721, What Law Governs.

CJS Internal Revenue § 722, Creation, Accrual, and Duration.

CJS Internal Revenue § 724, Priority.

CJS Internal Revenue § 725, Enforcement and Extinguishment.

*

INDEX TO
BANKRUPTCY CODE, RULES, FORMS
AND RELATED PROVISIONS OF U.S.
CODE TITLES 18, 26 AND 28

References are to U.S. Code sections unless otherwise indicated

Bankruptcy Highlights precede Bankruptcy Code.

Related Uniform Laws and Federal Tax Lien Statutes follow the Official Bankruptcy forms.

ABANDONMENT

Bankruptcy, this index

ABATEMENT AND REVIVAL

Bankruptcy, pending actions, successor trustees, 11 § 325

ABDUCTION

Kidnapping, generally, this index

ABSTENTION

Bankruptcy, this index

ABUSE

Bankruptcy, this index

ACCEPTANCES

Bankruptcy, this index

ACCOUNTANTS

Bankruptcy, this index

ACCOUNTS AND ACCOUNTING

Bankruptcy, this index
Coverdell education savings accounts, bankruptcy, 11 §§ 521, 541

ACETIC ANHYDRIDE

Controlled Substances, generally, this index

ACETONE

Controlled Substances, generally, this index

ACETORPHINE

Controlled Substances, generally, this index

ACETYLDIHYDROCODEINE

Controlled Substances, generally, this index

ACETYLMETHADOL

Controlled Substances, generally, this index

ACIDS

Controlled Substances, generally, this index
Drugs and Medicine, generally, this index

ACTIONS AND PROCEEDINGS

Arbitration, generally, this index
Bankruptcy, this index
District Courts, generally, this index

ACTIONS AND PROCEEDINGS—Cont'd

Dockets and Docketing, generally, this index
Judges or justices, disqualification, 28 § 455
Receivers and Receivership, generally, this index
Trial, generally, this index
Trusts and trustees, 28 § 959
Witnesses, generally, this index

ADMINISTRATIVE OFFICE OF UNITED STATES COURTS

Annuities, 28 § 604
Bankruptcy, this index
Clerical court assistants, accounts and accounting, 28 § 604
Clerks of Courts, generally, this index
Contracts, Director, 28 § 604
Court of Federal Claims, this index
Director,
   Accommodations, 28 § 604
   Annuities, 28 § 604
   Audits and auditors, 28 § 604
   Contracts, 28 § 604
   Disbursements, 28 § 604
   Dockets and docketing, 28 § 604
   Expenses and expenditures, 28 § 604
   Fines, penalties and forfeitures, 28 § 604
   Judicial Conference, supervision, 28 § 604
   Librarians, compensation and salaries, 28 § 604
   Powers and duties, 28 § 604
   Recycling, 28 § 604
   Reports, 28 § 604
   Restitution, 28 § 604
   Secretaries, compensation and salaries, 28 § 604
   Statistics, 28 § 604
   Stenographers, compensation fixed by, 28 § 604
   Supervision, 28 § 604
   Supplies, 28 § 604
   Traveling expenses, 28 § 604
   United States magistrate judges, powers and duties, 28 § 604
Exchange, personal property, 28 § 604
Incentive pay or awards, 28 § 604
Librarians, compensation and salaries, 28 § 604
Officers and employees, incentive pay or awards, 28 § 604
Pretrial services. Crimes and Offenses, this index
Public utilities, contracts, 28 § 604
Reports. Director, ante
Rules and regulations, publication, 28 § 604
Secretaries, compensation and salaries, 28 § 604
Stenographers, compensation and salaries, 28 § 604

ADMINISTRATIVE OFFICE OF UNITED STATES COURTS
—Cont'd
Terminal equipment, contracts, 28 § 604
Traveling expenses, Director, 28 § 604
Volunteers, 28 § 604

ADR

Alternative Dispute Resolution, generally, this index

ADVANCES

Bankruptcy, this index

ADVERSARY PROCEEDINGS

Bankruptcy, this index

ADVERTISEMENTS

Bankruptcy, debt relief agencies, 11 § 528

AERONAUTICS AND SPACE

Aeronautics Board. Civil Aeronautics Board, generally, this index
Aircraft, generally, this index
Boards and commissions. Civil Aeronautics Board, generally, this index

AFFILIATES

Bankruptcy, this index

AGED PERSONS

Intermediate Care Facilities, generally, this index
Long term care. Nursing Homes, generally, this index
Nursing Homes, generally, this index

AGENTS AND AGENCIES

Bankruptcy, this index
Federal Agencies, generally, this index
Home Health Agencies, generally, this index

AGRICULTURAL PRODUCTS

Bankruptcy,
   Exemptions, 11 § 522
   Liens and incumbrances, exemptions, 11 § 522
Exchanges. Commodity Exchanges, generally, this index
Secretary of Agriculture, generally, this index

AGRICULTURE

Commodity Exchanges, generally, this index
Secretary of Agriculture, generally, this index

AGRICULTURE DEPARTMENT

Secretary of Agriculture, generally, this index

AGRICULTURE SECRETARY

Secretary of Agriculture, generally, this index

AIR CARRIERS

Aircraft, generally, this index

AIRCRAFT

Bankruptcy, this index
Destruction, 18 § 2516
Interception of wire, oral, or electronic communications, 18 § 2516
Propellers, destruction, 18 § 2516
Reorganization, bankruptcy, security interest, 11 § 1110
Sabotage, interception of wire, oral, or electronic communications, 18 § 2516
Security interest, bankruptcy, 11 § 1110

AIRCRAFT EQUIPMENT SETTLEMENT LEASES ACT OF 1993

Generally, 11 § 1110 nt

AIRLINES

Aircraft, generally, this index

AIRPORTS AND LANDING FIELDS

Interception of wire, oral, or electronic communications, 18 § 2516

ALABAMA

Bankruptcy, judges or justices, appointments, 28 § 152
United States trustees of judicial districts, appointment, 28 § 581

ALASKA

Bankruptcy, judges or justices, appointments, 28 § 152
United States trustees, judicial districts, appointments, 28 § 581

ALCOHOLICS AND ALCOHOLISM

Controlled Substances, generally, this index

ALIENS

Crimes and offenses, smuggling, RICO, predicate offenses, 18 § 1961
Investigations, smuggling, 18 § 2516
Smuggling,
   RICO, 18 § 1961
   Wiretapping, 18 § 2516
Wiretapping, 18 § 2516

ALIMONY

Bankruptcy, this index

ALLYLPRODINE

Controlled Substances, generally, this index

ALPHACETYLMATHADOL

Controlled Substances, generally, this index

ALPHAMEPRODINE

Controlled Substances, generally, this index

ALPHAMETHADOL

Controlled Substances, generally, this index

ALPHAPRODINE

Controlled Substances, generally, this index

ALTERNATIVE DISPUTE RESOLUTION

   Generally, 28 § 651 et seq.
Administration, 28 § 651
Confidential or privileged information, 28 § 652
Consent, arbitration referrals, 28 § 654
Damages, arbitration referrals, 28 § 654
Definitions, 28 § 651
Exemptions, 28 § 652
Jurisdiction, 28 § 652
Neutrals, 28 § 653
Referrals, arbitration referrals, 28 § 654

AMPHETAMINES

Controlled Substances, generally, this index

ANALOGUES

Controlled Substances, generally, this index

ANALOGUES—Cont'd

Drugs and Medicine, generally, this index

ANILERIDINE

Controlled Substances, generally, this index

ANIMALS

Bankruptcy, this index

ANNUITIES

Administrative Office of United States Courts, 28 § 604

Bankruptcy, exemptions, 11 § 522

Exemptions, bankruptcy, 11 § 522

ANTHRANILIC ACID

Controlled Substances, generally, this index

ANTICRAMDOWN LAW

Bankruptcy, chapter 13 proceedings, 11 § 1325

APPEAL AND REVIEW

Bankruptcy, this index

Court of Appeals for Sixth Circuit, generally, this index

Court of Federal Claims, this index

Courts of Appeals, generally, this index

International Trade Court, this index

Judges or Justices, this index

United States Magistrate Judges, this index

APPRAISAL AND APPRAISERS

Bankruptcy, this index

ARBITRATION

Arbitrators,

    Certificates and certification, 28 § 655

    Compensation and salaries, 28 § 658

    Disqualification, 28 § 655

    Privileges and immunities, 28 § 655

    Referrals, 28 § 655

Awards,

    Referrals, 28 §§ 655, 657

    Sealing, 28 § 657

Bankruptcy, this index

Certificates and certification, arbitrators, 28 § 655

Compensation and salaries, 28 § 658

Disqualification, arbitrators, 28 § 655

Dockets and docketing, new trial, 28 § 657

Hearings, referrals, 28 § 655

Judgments and decrees, 28 § 657

Neutrals, compensation and salaries, 28 § 658

New trial, 28 § 657

Oaths and affirmations, 28 § 655

Powers and duties, arbitrators, 28 § 655

Privileges and immunities, arbitrators, 28 § 655

Process, awards, 28 § 657

Production of books and papers, 28 § 656

Referrals, 28 §§ 654, 655

Sealing, awards, 28 § 657

Subpoenas, 28 § 656

Time, new trial, 28 § 657

Traveling expenses, 28 § 658

Trial de novo, 28 § 657

ARBITRATORS

Arbitration, this index

ARIZONA

Bankruptcy, judges or justices, appointments, 28 § 152

ARIZONA—Cont'd

United States trustees, appointments, 28 § 581

ARKANSAS

Bankruptcy, judges or justices, appointments, 28 § 152

United States trustees, judicial districts, appointments, 28 § 581

ARMED FORCES

Application of law, bankruptcy, reserves, chapter 7 proceedings, 11 § 707 nt

Bankruptcy,

    Chapter 7 proceedings, abuse, 11 § 707

    Counseling services, exemptions, 11 § 109

    Reserves, chapter 7 proceedings, 11 § 707

Counseling services, bankruptcy, exemptions, 11 § 109

Reserves, bankruptcy, chapter 7 proceedings, 11 § 707

ARMED SERVICES

Armed Forces, generally, this index

ASSASSINATION

Congress, this index

Interception of wire, oral, or electronic communications, 18 § 2516

Justices of Supreme Court, 18 § 2516

President of the United States, this index

Vice President of the United States, this index

ASSAULT AND BATTERY

Cabinet departments, interception of wire, oral, or electronic communications, 18 § 2516

Congress, this index

Interception of wire, oral, or electronic communications, public officers and employees, 18 § 2516

Justices of Supreme Court, interception of wire, oral, or electronic communications, 18 § 2516

President of the United States, this index

Secretary of Agriculture, this index

Secretary of Commerce, this index

Secretary of Defense, this index

Secretary of Education, this index

Secretary of Energy, this index

Secretary of Housing and Urban Development, this index

Secretary of Labor, this index

Secretary of State, this index

Secretary of the Interior, this index

Secretary of the Treasury, this index

Secretary of Transportation, this index

ASSESSMENTS

Bankruptcy, this index

ASSIGNMENTS

Bankruptcy, this index

ASSIGNMENTS FOR BENEFIT OF CREDITORS

Custodians, property, 11 § 543

ASSISTED LIVING FACILITIES

Bankruptcy,

    Definitions, 11 § 101

    Ombudsman, 11 § 333

    Records and recordation, 11 § 351

Definitions, bankruptcy, 11 § 101

Ombudsman, bankruptcy, 11 § 333

Records and recordation, bankruptcy, 11 § 351

ASSOCIATIONS AND SOCIETIES

Cooperatives, generally, this index
Racketeering, generally, this index
Religious Organizations and Societies, generally, this index

ATHLETICS

Bribery and corruption, interception of wire, oral, or electronic communications, 18 § 2516

ATOMIC ENERGY

Crimes and offenses, interception of wire, oral, or electronic communications, 18 § 2516
Interception of wire, oral, or electronic communications, 18 § 2516

ATROPINE SULFATE

Controlled Substances, generally, this index

ATTORNEY FEES

Attorneys, this index

ATTORNEY GENERAL

Assassination, interception of wire, oral, or electronic communications, 18 § 2516
Assault and battery, interception of wire, oral, or electronic communications, 18 § 2516
Bankruptcy, this index
Deputies, surveillance, 18 § 2516
Director, Administrative Office of U.S. Courts, reports, 28 § 604
Kidnapping, interception of wire, oral, or electronic communications, 18 § 2516

ATTORNEYS

Attorney General, generally, this index
Bankruptcy, this index
Fees,
 Bankruptcy, this index
 Judges or justices, discipline, 28 § 372
 Receivers and receivership, fraud, 18 § 155
 Title 11, fraud, 18 § 155
 United States magistrate judges, 28 § 372
Interception of Wire, Oral, or Electronic Communications, this index
Judges or justices, disqualification, 28 § 455
United States Tax Court, this index

AUCTIONS AND AUCTIONEERS

Bankruptcy, this index

AUDITS AND AUDITORS

Administrative Office of U.S. Courts, 28 § 604
Bankruptcy, this index
Judicial Center, 28 § 604

AUTOMATIC STAY

Bankruptcy, this index

AVIATION

Aircraft, generally, this index

AVOIDANCE

Bankruptcy, this index

AWARDS

Arbitration, this index
Incentive Pay or Awards, generally, this index

BACK PAY

Bankruptcy, 11 § 503

BAD FAITH

Bankruptcy, this index

BANKRUPTCY

 Generally, 11 § 101 et seq.; BKR 1001 et seq.
Abandonment, 11 § 347; BKR 3011, 6007
 Grain, 11 § 557
 Notice, 11 § 554
 Railroads, 11 § 1170
Abstention, 11 § 305; BKR 5011
 Comity, 28 § 1334
 Foreign representatives, appearances, 11 § 306
 Reciprocity, 28 § 1334
Abuse,
 Chapter 7 proceedings, post
 Homesteads, exemptions, 11 § 522
 Reaffirmation agreements, 18 § 158
Acceleration, contracts, 11 § 555 et seq.
Acceptances,
 Chapter 9 proceedings, BKR 3018
 Chapter 11 proceedings, post
 Plans and specifications, BKR 3005, 3006
Access, foreign countries, 11 § 1509 et seq.
Accountants, 11 § 503 et seq.; BKR 2014
 Appointments, BKR 5002
 Compensation and salaries, 11 § 504
  Administrative expenses, 11 § 503
  Priorities and preferences, 11 § 507
 Definitions, 11 § 101
Accounts and accounting,
 Coverdell education savings accounts, 11 §§ 521, 541
 Custodians, BKR 6002
 Disclosure, orders of court, 11 § 542
 Filing, 11 § 543
 Inspection and inspectors, 18 § 154
 Money, possession, 11 § 363
 Separate accounts, joint administration, BKR 2009
 Taxation, 11 § 346
 Trusts and trustees, post
 Turnovers, property, 11 § 542
Actions and proceedings, 11 § 108; BKR 6009
 Adversary proceedings, generally, post
 Alternative dispute resolution, 28 § 651 et seq.
 Automatic stay, generally, post
 Chapter 9 proceedings, post
 Community property, discharge, 11 § 524
 Compromise and settlement, generally, post
 Contracts, rejection, 11 § 365
 Core proceedings, 28 § 157
 Damages, generally, post
 Discharge, 11 § 524
 Dismissal and nonsuit, generally, post
 Ex parte proceedings, BKR 9003
 Expenses and expenditures, allowances, 11 § 503
 Foreign countries, generally, post
 Frivolous actions, generally, post
 Governmental units, 11 § 362; 28 § 1452
 Grain, 11 § 557
 Injunctions, generally, post
 Involuntary proceedings, generally, post
 Joint proceedings, generally, post
 Liens and incumbrances, generally, post
 Limitation of actions, generally, post

BANKRUPTCY—Cont'd
Actions and proceedings—Cont'd
Managers and management, 28 § 959
Noncore proceedings,
    Abstention, 28 § 157
    Findings, **BKR 9033**
Original jurisdiction, 28 § 1334
Pending actions, generally, post
Postpetition, generally, post
References, generally, post
Removal of cases or causes, generally, post
Repurchase agreements, liquidation, 11 § 559
Sales, avoidance, 11 § 363
Securities, automatic stay, 11 § 362
Stay of proceedings, generally, post
Taxation,
    Automatic stay, 11 § 362
    Contests, 11 § 505
Timeshares, rejection, 11 § 365
Trusts and trustees, post
Actual notice, transfers, 11 § 542
Addresses,
Foreign countries, 11 § 1514
Governmental units, mail and mailing, **BKR 5003**
Notice, 11 § 342; **BKR 2002**
Taxation, 11 § 505; **BKR 5003**
Adjustments,
Core proceedings, 28 § 157
Individual debtors. Chapter 13 proceedings, generally, post
Money, 11 § 104
Municipal corporations. Chapter 9 proceedings, generally, post
Administration, 11 § 301 et seq.; 28 § 604
Chapter 13 proceedings, expenses and expenditures, schedules, 11 § 707 nt
Examinations and examiners, **BKR 6002**
Exemptions, expenses and expenditures, 11 § 522
Expenses and expenditures,
    Assurance of payment, public utilities, 11 § 366
    Chapter 13 proceedings, schedules, 11 § 707 nt
    Conversion, payment, **BKR 1019**
    Exemptions, 11 § 522
    Hearings, 11 § 503
    Leases, 11 § 503
    Taxation, 11 §§ 346, 503
Foreign countries, 11 § 1519 et seq.
Hearings, expenses and expenditures, 11 § 503
Leases, expenses and expenditures, 11 § 503
Notice, expenses and expenditures, 11 § 503
Payment, expenses and expenditures, 11 § 503
Presumptions, **BKR 5009**
Reopening proceedings, 11 § 350
Taxation, expenses and expenditures, 11 §§ 346, 503
Transition, 28 § 151
Administrative Office of United States Courts,
Bankruptcy Division, compensation and salaries, 11 § 102
Judges or justices,
    Assistants, appointments, 28 § 156
    Official stations, recommendations, 28 § 152
Returns, 28 § 156
Trusts and trustees, individual debtors, money, 11 § 1302
Administrators,
Appointments, 11 § 341 nt
Employee Retirement Income Security Program, 11 §§ 521, 704

BANKRUPTCY—Cont'd
Admissions, **BKR 7036**
Advances, discharge, 11 § 523
Adversary proceedings, **BKR 7001 et seq.**
Application of rules, **BKR 7001**
Applications, **BKR 1018**
Captions, complaints, forms, **BKR Form 16D**
Claims, withdrawal, **BKR 3006**
Forms,
    Captions, complaints, **BKR Form 16D**
    Complaints, captions, **BKR Form 16D**
Adverse or pecuniary interest. Conflict of interest, generally, post
Advertisements, debt relief agencies, 11 § 528
Affidavits, time, **BKR 9006**
Affiliates,
Chapter 11 proceedings, venue, 28 § 1408
Definitions, 11 § 101
Affirmations. Oaths and affirmations, generally, post
Agents and agencies,
Committees, compensation and salaries, 11 § 504
Concealment, sentence and punishment, 18 § 152
Debt relief agencies, generally, post
Agreements. Contracts, generally, post
Agricultural Products, this index
Agriculture. Chapter 12 proceedings, generally, post
Aircraft,
Discharge, 11 § 523
Security interest, 11 § 1110
Alabama, **BKR 9035**
Alimony,
Automatic stay, 11 § 362
Avoidance, 11 § 547
Chapter 11 proceedings, 11 § 1129
Chapter 12 proceedings, 11 §§ 1208, 1222 et seq.
Chapter 13 proceedings, 11 §§ 1307, 1322 et seq.
Collection, 11 § 362
Definitions, 11 § 101
Discharge, 11 § 523
Exemptions, 11 §§ 522, 523
Priorities and preferences, 11 § 507
Allowances,
Claims, post
Compensation and salaries, generally, post
Alternative dispute resolution, 28 § 651 et seq.
Alternative repayment schedule, avoidance, 11 § 547
Amendments,
Application of law, 11 § 101 nt
Federal Rules of Civil Procedure, **BKR 9032**
Judgments and decrees, **BKR 9023**
Lists, **BKR 1009**
Pleadings, **BKR 7015**
Ancillary cases. Foreign countries, generally, post
Animals, 11 § 541
Custodians, transfers, 11 § 543
Exemptions, 11 § 522
Security interest, 11 § 363
Transfers, custodians, 11 § 543
Annuities, exemptions, 11 § 522
Answers, **BKR 7012**
Petitions, claims, **BKR 1011**
Antecedent debt, avoidance, preferences, 11 § 547
Anticramdown Law, chapter 13 proceedings, 11 § 1325
Appeal and review, **BKR 8001 et seq.**
Abstention, 11 § 305
Appendix, **BKR 8009, 8010**

BANKRUPTCY—Cont'd

Appeal and review—Cont'd
 Bankruptcy appellate panels, generally, post
 Briefs, **BKR 8009, 8010**
 Certificates and certification, **BKR 8001; BKR Form 24**
 Chapter 9 proceedings, post
 Claims, removal, 28 § 1452
 Clerks of court, **BKR 8016**
 Committees, organization, **BKR 2007**
 Contempt, **BKR 9020**
 Costs, **BKR 8014**
 Credit, extensions, 11 § 364
 Direct appeals, 28 § 158
 Disposition, **BKR 8013**
 Dockets and docketing, **BKR 8007**
 Frivolous appeals, damages, **BKR 8020**
 Grain, 11 § 557
 Issue statement, **BKR 8006**
 Jurisdiction, 28 §§ 158, 1334
 Leave of court, **BKR 8003**
 Local rules, **BKR 8018**
 Motions,
  Emergencies, **BKR 8011**
  Rehearings, **BKR 8015**
 Noncore proceedings, **BKR 9033**
 Notice,
  Filing, fees, 28 § 1930
  Forms, **BKR Form 17**
  Service, **BKR 8004**
  Time, **BKR 8002**
 Oral arguments, **BKR 8012**
 Orders of court, 28 § 157
 Records and recordation, **BKR 8006, 8007, 8016**
 Rules, revocation or suspension, **BKR 8019**
 Sales, modification, 11 § 363
 Standards, **BKR 8013**
 Statements, issues, **BKR 8006**
 Stay of proceedings, **BKR 8005, 8017**
 Transcripts, **BKR 8007**
 Trusts and trustees, indebtedness, 11 § 364
 Venue, 28 § 1408
Appearances, 11 § 521
 Chapter 11 proceedings, 11 §§ 1109, 1164
 Dismissal and nonsuit, 11 § 109
 Nonsuit, 11 § 109
 Notice, **BKR 9010**
 Parties, **BKR 9010**
 Railroads, 11 § 1164
Appellate panel. Bankruptcy appellate panels, generally, post
Appendix, appeal and review, briefs, **BKR 8009**
Appliances, exemptions, 11 § 522
Application of law, 11 § 102
 Amendments, 11 § 101 nt
 Armed Forces, reserves, chapter 7 proceedings, 11 § 707 nt
 Foreign countries, 11 § 1508
 Notice, 11 § 102
Applications, labor and employment, **BKR 6003**
Appointments,
 Consumer privacy ombudsman, **BKR 6004**
 Examinations and examiners, post
 Foreign countries, post
 Patient care ombudsman, 11 § 333; **BKR 2007.2**
 Trusts and trustees, post
 United States trustees, post
Appraisal and appraisers, 11 § 327; **BKR 2014, 6005**
 Appointments, **BKR 5002**

BANKRUPTCY—Cont'd

Appraisal and appraisers—Cont'd
 Compensation and salaries,
  Records and recordation, **BKR 2013**
  Sharing, 11 § 504
 Records and recordation, compensation and salaries, **BKR 2013**
 Sharing, compensation and salaries, 11 § 504
Apprehension, examinations and examiners, **BKR 2005**
Arbitration, **BKR 9019**
 Reference, 28 § 654
Armed Forces, this index
Assessments,
 Claims, 11 § 502
 Payment, 11 § 505
Assignments, 11 § 365
 Contracts, 11 § 365; **BKR 6003**
 Leases, 11 § 365; **BKR 6006**
Assistance,
 Definitions, 11 § 101
 Foreign countries, 11 § 1507
Assistants,
 Judges or justices, appointments, 28 § 156
 United States trustees, post
Assisted Living Facilities, this index
Assumptions,
 Contracts, 11 § 365; **BKR 6003**
 Leases, **BKR 6006**
Assurance of payment, definitions, 11 § 366
Attachment, removal of cases or causes, **BKR 9027**
Attendance, examinations and examiners, **BKR 2005, 4002**
Attorney General,
 Audits and auditors, 28 § 586 nt
 Investigations, reports, 18 § 3057
Attorneys, 11 § 327 et seq.; **BKR 2014, 9010**
 Appointments, **BKR 5002**
 Automatic stay, fees, 11 § 362
 Cancellation, fees, 11 §§ 329, 541
 Chapter 7 proceedings, fees, 11 § 707
  Consumer debt, 11 § 523
 Chapter 13 proceedings, post
 Claims, 11 § 502
  Fees, **BKR 3001**
  Services, disallowance, 11 § 502
 Committees, 11 § 504
 Consumer debts, 11 § 523
 Corporations, reorganization, fees, 11 § 503
 Counseling services, fees, 11 § 111
 Debt relief agencies, fees, 11 § 526
 Definitions, 11 § 101
 Discharge, 11 § 524
 Disclosure, fees, **BKR 2016**
 Discretion of court, fees, 11 § 503
 Examinations and examiners, **BKR 2017**
 Excessive fees, 11 § 329; **BKR 2017**
 Expenses and expenditures, allowances, 11 § 503
 Fees, 11 § 329 et seq.
  Automatic stay, 11 § 362
  Cancellation, 11 §§ 329, 541
  Chapter 7 proceedings, 11 § 707
   Consumer debt, 11 § 523
  Chapter 13 proceedings, post
  Claims, **BKR 3001**
  Consumer debts, 11 § 523
  Corporations, reorganization, 11 § 503
  Counseling services, 11 § 111

INDEX

BANKRUPTCY—Cont'd
Attorneys—Cont'd
Fees—Cont'd
Debt relief agencies, 11 § 526
Disclosure, **BKR 2016**
Discretion of court, 11 § 503
Excessive fees, 11 § 329; **BKR 2017**
Fraud, 18 § 155
Interim compensation, 11 § 331
Involuntary proceedings, 11 §§ 303, 504
Petitions, 11 § 110
Pleading, **BKR 7008**
Priorities and preferences, 11 § 507
Professional services, 11 § 503
Records and recordation, **BKR 2013**
Recovery, 11 § 541
Sales, 11 § 363
Sharing, 11 § 504
Statements, 11 § 329
Subordination, **BKR 1006**
Financial statements and reports, 11 § 542
Fraud, fees, 18 § 155
Interim compensation, fees, 11 § 331
Involuntary proceedings, fees, 11 §§ 303, 504
Judges or justices, practice of law, 28 § 153
Labor and employment, 11 § 327 et seq.
Meetings, 11 § 341
Motions, fees, examinations and examiners, **BKR 2017**
Orders of court,
Excessive compensation, 11 § 329
Interim compensation, 11 § 331
Petitions, fees, 11 § 110
Pleading, fees, **BKR 7008**
Power of attorney, generally, post
Priorities and preferences, fees, 11 § 507
Professional associations, 11 § 504
Professional services, fees, 11 § 503
Public service attorney referral program, 11 § 504
Records and recordation, fees, **BKR 2013**
Recovery, fees, 11 § 541
Sales, fees, 11 § 363
Sharing, fees, 11 § 504
Signatures, chapter 7 proceedings, 11 § 707
Statements, fees, 11 § 329
Subordination, fees, **BKR 1006**
Trusts and trustees, post
United States attorneys, generally, post
Auctions and auctioneers, **BKR 2014, 6005**
Appointments, **BKR 5002**
Compensation and salaries, 11 § 504; **BKR 2013**
Labor and employment, 11 § 327
Audits and auditors,
Attorney General, 28 § 586 nt
Automatic stay, political subdivisions, 11 § 362
Chapter 7 proceedings, discharge, 11 § 727
Judicial Conference of the United States, 28 § 586 nt
Political subdivisions, automatic stay, 11 § 362
United States trustees, 28 § 586
Automatic stay, 11 § 361; **BKR 4001**
Alimony, 11 § 362
Attorneys, fees, recovery, 11 § 362
Bad faith, 11 § 362
Chapter 9 proceedings, post
Children and minors, 11 § 362
Children born out of wedlock, 11 § 362
Commodities, 11 § 362

BANKRUPTCY—Cont'd
Automatic stay—Cont'd
Consumer debt, 11 § 362
Contracts, **BKR 6006**
Damages, 11 § 362
Divorce, 11 § 362
Domestic violence, 11 § 362
Evictions, 11 § 362
Foreign countries, 11 § 1519 et seq.
Forward contracts, 11 §§ 362, 553
Good faith, 11 § 362
Interest, 11 § 362
Joint proceedings, post
Landlord and tenant, 11 § 362
Leases, post
Liens and incumbrances, 11 § 362
Master netting agreements, 11 § 362
Medicare, 11 § 362
Negotiable instruments, 11 § 362
Notice, 11 § 362; **BKR 4001**
Objections and exceptions, 11 § 362
Pending actions, 11 § 109
Presumptions, 11 § 362
Real estate, 11 § 362
Repurchase agreements, 11 § 362
Retirement and pensions, 11 § 362
Sales, 11 § 553; **BKR 6004**
Securities, 11 §§ 362, 553
Security interest, 11 § 362
Set-off and counterclaim, 11 § 553
Repurchase agreements, 11 § 362
Support, 11 § 362
Swap agreements, 11 § 362
Taxation, post
Termination, 11 § 362
Unlawful detainer, 11 § 362
Avoidance, 11 §§ 541, 544 et seq.
Alimony, 11 § 547
Alternative repayment schedule, 11 § 547
Antecedent debt, preferences, 11 § 547
Automatic preservation, 11 §§ 541, 551
Burden of proof, preferences, 11 § 547
Chapter 9 proceedings, 11 §§ 109, 926
Commodities, 11 §§ 546, 764
Consumer debt, 11 § 547
Damages, 11 §§ 501, 550
Definitions, priorities and preferences, 11 § 547
Evidence, priorities and preferences, 11 § 547
Exemptions, 11 § 551; **BKR 4003**
Transfers, 11 § 522
Fraud, 11 § 548
Insiders, 11 § 547
Judicial liens, 11 §§ 544, 547
Liens and incumbrances, 11 §§ 349, 522, 544 et seq.
Indemnity, **BKR 6010**
Limitation of actions, 11 §§ 546, 550
Perfected security interest, 11 § 547
Postpetition transactions, 11 § 549
Preferences, 11 § 547
Priorities and preferences, 11 § 547
Real estate, good faith purchasers, 11 § 549
Reinstatement, 11 § 349
Repayment, alternative repayment schedule, 11 § 547
Security interest, 11 §§ 522, 547
Statutory liens, 11 § 545 et seq.
Support, 11 § 547

BANKRUPTCY—Cont'd
Avoidance—Cont'd
  Tax liens, **11 §§ 522, 545**
  Waiver, **11 § 522**
Awards, Crime Victims Reparation Law, exemptions, **11 § 522**
Back pay, **11 § 503**
Bad faith,
  Automatic stay, **11 § 362**
  Chapter 7 proceedings, **11 § 707**
  Chapter 13 proceedings, **11 § 348**
Ballots, reorganization, plans and specifications, forms, **BKR Form 14**
Bankruptcy Administrator, appointments, **11 § 341 nt**
Bankruptcy appellate panels, **28 § 158**
  Clerks of courts, powers and duties, **BKR 8016**
  Joint appellate panels, **28 § 158**
  Local rules, **BKR 8018**
Bankruptcy Division, Administrative Office of U.S. Courts, officers and employees, compensation and salaries, **11 § 102**
Banks and banking,
  Definitions, **11 § 101**
  Margin, transfers, **11 § 546**
  Qualifications, **11 § 109**
  Securities, liquidation, **11 § 555**
  Unsecured claims, priorities and preferences, **11 §§ 753, 767**
Barley, **11 § 557**
Beans, dry edible beans, **11 § 557**
Bias and prejudice, dismissal and nonsuit, **11 § 349**
Bifurcation of claims, chapter 13 proceedings, **11 § 1325**
Boards and commissions, National Bankruptcy Review Commission, **11 nt prec § 101**
Bodily injury, payments, exemptions, **11 § 522**
Bona fide purchasers, **11 § 544 et seq.**
  Perfection, **11 § 548**
  Preferences, real estate, **11 § 547**
  Real estate, **11 §§ 544, 547**
  Statutory liens, avoidance, **11 § 545**
Bonds (officers and fiduciaries), **BKR 9025**
  Claims, evidence, **BKR 3005**
  Deposits, money, **11 § 345**
  Involuntary proceedings, **11 § 303**
  Liens and incumbrances, **BKR 6010**
  Money, deposits, **11 § 345**
  Preferences, transfers, **11 § 547**
  Removal of cases or causes, **BKR 9027**
  Stay of proceedings, **BKR 8005**
  Transfers, preferences, **11 § 547**
  Trusts and trustees, post
  Voluntary proceedings, **11 § 303**
Bonus, retention bonuses, **11 § 503**
Books and papers, **BKR 5003**
  Certified copies, **BKR 5006**
  Concealment, crimes and offenses, **18 § 152**
  Disclosure, hearings, **11 § 542**
  Exemptions, **11 § 522**
  Filing, **BKR 5005**
  Inspection and inspectors, **11 § 107; 18 § 154**
  Liens and incumbrances, nonpossessory, **11 § 522**
  Surrender, **11 § 521**
  Trade, exemptions, **11 § 522**
Bribery and corruption, **18 § 152**
Briefs, appeal and review, **BKR 8009, 8010**
Brokers,
  Commodities, post

BANKRUPTCY—Cont'd
Brokers—Cont'd
  Shares and shareholders, post
Building and loan associations, qualifications, **11 § 109**
Buildings, **28 § 156**
  Expenses and expenditures, **28 § 156**
  National Bankruptcy Review Commission, **11 nt prec § 101**
Burden of proof. Evidence, generally, post
Burial plot, exemptions, **11 § 522**
Business and commerce,
  Claims, ordinary course of business, **11 § 507**
  Crimes and offenses, **11 § 503**
  Foreign countries, post
  Goods, wares and merchandise, returns, **11 § 546**
  Health care businesses, generally, post
  Individual debtors, operating businesses, **11 § 1304**
  Information, public access, **11 § 107**
  Involuntary proceedings, **11 § 303**
  Liens and incumbrances, **11 § 522**
  Location, **11 § 109**
  Operating businesses, **11 § 363**
    Foreign countries, **11 §§ 1520, 1522**
    Individual debtors, **11 § 1304**
    Reorganization, **11 § 1108**
    Trusts and trustees, **11 § 303**
  Ordinary course of business, claims, **11 § 507**
  Place of business, generally, post
  Public access, information, **11 § 107**
  Reorganization, operating businesses, **11 § 1108**
  Returns, goods, wares and merchandise, **11 § 546**
  Small businesses, generally, post
  Taxation, deductions, **11 § 346**
  Trusts and trustees, **11 § 303**
Cancellation,
  Attorneys, fees, **11 §§ 329, 541**
  Reaffirmation agreements, **11 § 524**
Capacity, parties, **BKR 7017**
Captions,
  Forms, post
  Notice, **BKR 2002**
  Petitions, **BKR 1005**
Carrybacks, taxation, **11 § 346**
Carryovers, taxation, **11 § 346**
Cash. Money, generally, post
Cash collateral, definitions, **11 § 363**
Cause, definitions, **11 § 1112**
Certificates and certification,
  Appeal and review, **BKR 8001; BKR Form 24**
  Copies, **BKR 5006**
  Counseling services, **11 § 521**
  Financial management training curriculum, certification of completion, forms, **BKR Form 23**
  Foreign countries, **11 § 1515 et seq.**
  Forms, nonattorney petition preparers, **BKR Form 6**
  Nonattorney petition preparers, forms, **BKR Form 6**
  Professional personnel, compensation and salaries, **11 § 330**
  Records and recordation, searches and seizures, **BKR 5003**
  Residential rental housing, possession, **11 § 362**
Certified copies, **BKR 5006**
Certiorari, fees, receipts, **28 § 1930**
Chambers, orders of court, **BKR 5001**
Changes,
  Statements, **BKR 4002**
  Venue, **28 § 1412; BKR 1014**
Chapter 7 proceedings, **11 § 701 et seq.**

INDEX

BANKRUPTCY—Cont'd
Chapter 7 proceedings—Cont'd
Abandonment,
Consumer debt, liens and incumbrances, redemption, 11 § 722
Disposition, **BKR 3011**
Abuse, 11 § 707
Notice, 11 § 342; **BKR 5008**
Trusts and trustees, 11 §§ 704, 707
Accounts and accounting, 11 § 704
Actions and proceedings, dismissal and nonsuit, 11 § 707
Addresses, notice, 11 § 342
Application of law, 11 § 103
Attorneys, fees, 11 § 707
Consumer debt, 11 § 523
Audits and auditors, discharge, 11 § 727
Bad faith, 11 § 707
Banks and banking, qualifications, 11 § 109
Building and loan associations, qualifications, 11 § 109
Business and commerce, reports, filing, 11 § 704
Chapter 11 proceedings, conversion, 11 § 707
Chapter 13 proceedings,
Automatic stay, time, 11 § 362
Consumer debts, dismissal and nonsuit, 11 § 707
Charities, contributions, dismissal and nonsuit, 11 § 707
Claims,
Amount, 11 § 702
Conversion, **BKR 1019**
Time, 11 § 348
Distributions, payment, 11 § 726
Evidence,
Examinations and examiners, 11 § 704
Filing, **BKR 3002**
Fraud, discharge, revocation or suspension, 11 § 727
General partner, 11 § 723
Liens and incumbrances, avoidance, 11 § 724
Partnership,
Allowances, objections and exceptions, 11 § 502
Deficiencies, damages, 11 § 723
Trusts and trustees, elections, 11 § 702
Unsecured claims,
Distributions, elections, 11 § 705
Payment, 11 § 726
Clearing banks, 11 § 781 et seq.
Closings, **BKR 5009**
Collection, 11 § 721 et seq.
Application of law, 11 § 103
Discharge, 11 § 727
Disposition, 11 § 725
Liens and incumbrances, 11 § 724
Money, 11 § 704
Partnership, rights, 11 § 723
Redemption, 11 § 722
Support, 11 § 704
Committees, elections, 11 §§ 703, 705
Complaints, discharge, **BKR 4004 et seq.**
Consumer debt,
Costs, discharge, 11 § 523
Discharge, costs, 11 § 523
Liens and incumbrances, redemption, 11 § 722
Redemption, liens and incumbrances, 11 § 722
Contracts, 11 § 555 et seq.
Objections and exceptions, 11 § 365
Conversion, 11 § 348; **BKR 1017, 1019**
Chapter 11 proceedings, 11 § 706; 28 § 1930
Chapter 12 proceedings, 11 § 706

BANKRUPTCY—Cont'd
Chapter 7 proceedings—Cont'd
Conversion—Cont'd
Chapter 13 proceedings, 11 §§ 706, 1301, 1307
Cooperative banks, qualifications, 11 § 109
Copies, 11 § 521
Corporations, judicial districts, offices, 11 § 321
Costs, 11 § 707
Credit unions, qualifications, 11 § 109
Crimes and offenses, dismissal and nonsuit, 11 § 707
Customs duties, discharge, objections and exceptions, 11 § 523
Damages,
Claims, distribution, payment, 11 § 726
General partners, deficiencies, damages, 11 § 723
Liens and incumbrances, avoidance, 11 § 724
Death, **BKR 1016**
Trusts and trustees, successor trustees, 11 § 703
Deficiencies, partnership, claims, damages, 11 § 723
Definitions, 11 § 707
Destruction of property, discharge, denial, 11 § 727
Discharge, 11 § 727; **BKR 4004**
Driving while intoxicated, objections and exceptions, 11 § 523
Forms, **BKR Form 18**
Good faith, 11 § 727
Opposition, 11 § 704
Dismissal and nonsuit, 11 § 707
Abuse, **BKR 1017**
Death, mental health, **BKR 1016**
Schedules, 11 § 521
Disposition, 11 § 725
Distribution, 11 § 726
Application of law, 11 § 103
Final distribution, hearings, 11 § 725
Liens and incumbrances, treatment, 11 § 724
Dividends, payment, **BKR 3009, 3010**
Divorce, discharge, objections and exceptions, 11 § 523
Drugs and medicine, trafficking, dismissal and nonsuit, 11 § 707
Education, loans, 11 § 523
Elections,
Meetings, 11 § 702
Proxies, **BKR 2006**
Termination, trusts and trustees, 11 § 701
Trusts and trustees, termination, 11 § 701
Embezzlement, discharge, objections and exceptions, 11 § 523
Evidence,
Abuse, 11 § 707
Claims, filing, **BKR 3002**
Filing, claims, **BKR 3002**
Examinations and examiners, claims, evidence, 11 § 704
Exemptions, consumer debt, liens and incumbrances, discharge, 11 § 722
Expenses and expenditures, payment, 11 § 726
Dismissal and nonsuit, 11 § 707
Fees, filing, 28 § 1930
Waiver, **BKR 1006**
Forms, **BKR Form 3B**
Filing,
Fees, 28 § 1930
Waiver, **BKR 1006**
Forms, **BKR Form 3B**
Involuntary proceedings, 11 § 303
Trusts and trustees, fees, 11 § 330

BANKRUPTCY—Cont'd
Chapter 7 proceedings—Cont'd
Filing—Cont'd
Unsecured claims, 11 § 726
Voluntary proceedings, dismissal and nonsuit, 11 § 707
Final account, 11 § 704
Financial management training curriculum, 11 § 727
Fines and penalties, 11 § 707
Claims, distributions, 11 § 726
Governmental unit, discharge, objections and exceptions, 11 § 523
Foreign banks, qualifications, 11 § 109
Forms,
Filing, fees, waiver, **BKR Form 3B**
Notice, **BKR Form 9**
Statement of intention, individual debtors, **BKR Form 8**
Fraud,
Claims, discharge, denial, 11 § 727
Discharge, objections and exceptions, 11 § 523
General partners,
Deficiencies, recovery, 11 § 723
Distributions, payment, 11 § 508
Good faith,
Claims, customers, 11 § 746
Customers, claims, 11 § 746
Discharge, 11 § 727
Schedules, filing, 11 § 521
Health care businesses, **BKR 1021**
Hearings,
Discharge, 11 § 523
Dismissal and nonsuit, 11 § 707
Distributions, 11 § 725
Party in interest, conversion, 11 § 706
Trusts and trustees, discharge, revocation or suspension, 11 § 727
Homestead associations, qualifications, 11 § 109
Indemnity, partnership, deficiencies, 11 § 723
Information, party in interest, 11 § 704
Insiders, trusts and trustees, elections, 11 § 702
Insurance, qualifications, 11 § 109
Interest, payment, time, 11 § 726
Inventories, **BKR 2015**
Investigations, 11 § 704
Involuntary proceedings, 11 § 303
Joint administration, appointments, **BKR 2009**
Judgments and decrees, consumer debts, discharge, costs, 11 § 523
Larceny, discharge, objections and exceptions, 11 § 523
Liens and incumbrances,
Avoidance, 11 § 724
Consumer debt, redemption, 11 § 722
Discharge, objections and exceptions, 11 § 523
Taxation, 11 § 724
Lists, discharge, objections and exceptions, 11 § 523
Lost property, discharge, revocation or suspension, 11 § 727
Meetings, **BKR 2003**
Corporations, forms, **BKR Form 9**
Elections, trusts and trustees, 11 § 702
Individual debtors, forms, **BKR Form 9**
Joint debtors, forms, **BKR Form 9**
Partnership, forms, **BKR Form 9**
Trusts and trustees, elections, 11 § 702
Mental health, **BKR 1016**
Money, fraud, discharge, objections and exceptions, 11 § 523

BANKRUPTCY—Cont'd
Chapter 7 proceedings—Cont'd
Motions,
Discharge, objections and exceptions, time, **BKR 4004**
Dismissal and nonsuit, abuse, **BKR 1017**
Interim trustees, appointments, **BKR 2001**
Proxies, **BKR 2006**
Reopening, **BKR 5010**
National Guard, 11 § 707
No asset notice, **BKR 2002**
Notice, **BKR 2002**
Abuse, 11 § 342; **BKR 5008**
Addresses, 11 § 342
Corporations, forms, **BKR Form 9**
Debtors in possession, **BKR 2015**
Discharge, **BKR 4004**
Forms, **BKR Form 9**
Individual debtors, forms, **BKR Form 9**
Joint debtors, forms, **BKR Form 9**
Partnership, forms, **BKR Form 9**
Proxies, **BKR 2006**
Support, 11 § 704
Oaths and affirmations, 11 § 707
Discharge, fraud, 11 § 727
Fraud, discharge, 11 § 727
Objections and exceptions, 11 § 523
Claims, allowances, 11 § 704
Closings, **BKR 5009**
Discharge, 11 § 727
Time, **BKR 4004**
Operation, businesses, 11 § 721
Pancl, trusts and trustees, 28 § 586
Appointments, 11 § 701
Parties,
Audits and auditors, discharge, 11 § 727
Conversion, hearings, 11 § 706
Information, 11 § 704
Involuntary proceedings, trusts and trustees, appointments, 11 § 303
Partnership,
Claims, objections and exceptions, 11 § 502
General partners,
Deficiencies, damages, 11 § 723
Payment, 11 § 508
Payment, dividends, **BKR 3009, 3010**
Pending actions, 11 § 727
Petitions, involuntary proceedings, 11 § 303
Political subdivisions, 11 § 523
Reports, taxation, 11 § 704
Taxation, reports, 11 § 704
Powers and duties, trusts and trustees, 11 § 704
Presumptions, 11 § 707
Abuse, **BKR 5008**
Prior bankruptcies, discharge, 11 § 727
Priorities and preferences, 11 § 726
Liens and incumbrances, 11 § 724
Partnership, deficiencies, damages, 11 § 723
Unsecured claims, 11 §§ 753, 767
Privileges and immunities, material questions, 11 § 727
Proxies, **BKR 2006**
Railroads, reorganization, 11 § 1174
Records and recordation, **BKR 2001**
Concealment, 11 § 727
Debtors in possession, **BKR 2015**
Redemption, 11 § 722
Referees, fees, **11 nt prec § 101**

BANKRUPTCY—Cont'd
Chapter 7 proceedings—Cont'd
Registration, discharge, **BKR 4004**
Reopening, **BKR 5010**
Trusts and trustees, appointments, **11 § 703**
Reorganization, railroads, **11 § 1174**
Reports, **BKR 2001**
Final, filing, **11 § 704**
Repurchase agreement, liquidation, contracts, **11 § 559**
Resignation, trusts and trustees, successor trustees, **11 § 703**
Revocation or suspension, discharge, **11 § 727**
Savings and loan association, qualifications, **11 § 109**
Savings banks, qualifications, **11 § 109**
Schedules, **11 § 523**
Dismissal and nonsuit, **11 § 521**
Securities, contracts, **11 § 555**
Self-incrimination, **11 § 727**
Senior liens, **11 § 724**
Separation agreements, discharge, objections and exceptions, **11 § 523**
Solicitation, proxies, **BKR 2006**
Spouses,
Alimony, maintenance, support, **11 § 523**
Discharge, denial, **11 § 524**
Statements,
Business and commerce, operation, filing, **11 § 704**
Intention, **BKR 1007**
Successor trustees, qualifications, **11 §§ 322, 703**
Supervision, **28 § 586**
Supplemental schedules, **BKR 1007**
Support, **11 § 704**
Tangible, consumer debt, liens and incumbrances, redemption, **11 § 722**
Taxation, **11 § 346**
Discharge, objections and exceptions, **11 § 523**
Liens and incumbrances, **11 § 724**
Tardy priority claims, **11 § 726**
Termination, **11 § 701**
Time,
Abuse, notice, **BKR 5008**
Discharge, **BKR 4007**
Objections and exceptions, **BKR 4004**
Trusts and trustees, discharge, revocation or suspension, **11 § 727**
Transfers,
Avoidance, priorities and preferences, **11 § 547**
Destruction of property, discharge, denial, **11 § 727**
Trusts and trustees,
Abuse, **11 §§ 704, 707**
Accounts and accounting, **11 § 704**
Turnovers, delivery, **11 § 542**
Application of law, **11 § 103**
Appointments, successors, **11 § 703**
Avoidance, liens and incumbrances, **11 § 724**
Candidates, elections, **11 § 702**
Committees,
Consultants, **11 § 705**
Trusts and trustees, elections, **11 § 702**
Vacancies in office, elections, **11 § 703**
Commodity brokers, contracts, objections and exceptions, **11 § 365**
Compensation and salaries, payment, **11 § 330**
Conversion, termination, **11 § 348**
Credit, **11 § 364**
Damages, general partners, deficiencies, **11 § 723**

BANKRUPTCY—Cont'd
Chapter 7 proceedings—Cont'd
Trusts and trustees—Cont'd
Death, successors, **11 § 703**
Discharge, objections and exceptions, **11 § 704**
Distribution, surplus property, **11 § 723**
Elections, **11 § 702**
Qualifications, **11 § 322**
Eligibility, domicile and residence, **11 § 321**
Filing, fees, payment, **11 § 330**
Interim trustees, **11 § 701**
Appointments, **11 § 703; BKR 2001**
Qualifications, **11 § 322**
Vacancies in office, **11 § 703**
Investigations, **11 § 704**
Objections and exceptions, discharge, **11 § 727**
Partnership, deficiencies, damages, **11 § 723**
Powers and duties, **11 § 704**
Professional persons, labor and employment, **11 § 327**
Removal from office, successors, **11 § 703**
Resignation, successors, **11 § 703**
Successor trustee, United States trustee, appointments, **11 § 703**
Support, **11 § 704**
Termination, **11 § 701**
Vacancies in office, successors, **11 § 703**
Unclaimed property, disposition, **11 § 347; BKR 3011**
Unexpired leases, objections and exceptions, **11 § 365**
United States trustees, post
Vacating or setting aside, proxies, **BKR 2006**
Veterans, disabled veterans, **11 § 707**
Voluntary proceedings, dismissal and nonsuit, filing, **11 § 707**
Waiver,
Consumer debt, liens and incumbrances, redemption, **11 § 722**
Conversion, **11 § 706**
Discharge, **11 § 524**
Fees, filing, **28 § 1930; BKR 1006**
Forms, **BKR Form 3B**
Chapter 9 proceedings, **11 § 901 et seq.**
Acceptances, plans and specifications, **BKR 3018, 3019**
Dismissal and nonsuit, **11 § 930**
Actions and proceedings, **11 § 922**
Avoidance, transfers, **11 § 926**
Confirmation of plan, **11 § 943**
Petitions, **11 § 921**
Transfers, avoidance, **11 § 926**
Administration, expenses and expenditures, **11 § 901**
Appeal and review, **11 § 901**
Stay of proceedings, **11 § 921**
Application of law, **11 §§ 103, 901**
Appointments, trusts and trustees, **11 § 926**
Automatic stay, **11 § 901**
Claims, **11 § 922**
Confirmation of plan, **BKR 3020**
Time, **11 § 362**
Avoidance, transfers, **11 §§ 109, 901, 926**
Best interest, confirmation of plan, **11 § 943**
Bonds, dealers, notice, **11 § 923**
Chief Judge, designation, **11 § 921**
Claims,
Automatic stay, petitions, enforcement, **11 § 922**
Codebtor, **11 § 901**
Confirmation of plan, **11 § 943**
Evidence, filing, **BKR 3003**

BANKRUPTCY—Cont'd
Chapter 9 proceedings—Cont'd
Claims—Cont'd
Exchanges, security, 11 § 946
Interests,
Allowances, 11 § 901
Evidence, lists, filing, 11 § 925
Lists, 11 § 925
Closings, 11 § 945
Committees, 11 § 901
Allowances, 11 § 503
Organization, **BKR 2007**
Priorities and preferences, 11 § 507
Community, 11 § 901
Compliance, confirmation of plan, 11 § 943
Confirmation of plan, 11 § 943; **BKR 3020**
Notice, 11 § 944
Contingent claim, lists, filing, 11 § 925
Contracts, qualifications, 11 § 109
Credit, 11 § 901
Damages, avoidance, 11 § 901
Debt adjustment plan, qualifications, 11 § 109
Definitions, 11 § 902
Application of law, 11 § 901
Representatives and representation, statements, **BKR 2019**
Delay,
Appeal and review, orders, 11 § 921
Unreasonable, dismissal and nonsuit, 11 § 930
Deposits, **BKR 3020**
Discharge, 11 § 524
Confirmation of plan, 11 § 944
Judgments and decrees, 11 § 901
Disclosure,
Confirmation of plan, expenses and expenditures, payment, 11 § 943
Forms, **BKR Form 12**
Statements, **BKR 3017**
Filing, **BKR 3016**
Dismissal and nonsuit, 11 § 923
Application of law, 11 § 901
Notice, 11 §§ 923, 930
Petitions, objections and exceptions, 11 § 921
Disputes, lists, filing, 11 § 925
Elections, nonrecourse loans, **BKR 3014**
Evidence,
Claims, filing, **BKR 3003**
Lists, 11 § 925
Exchanges, security, 11 § 946
Executory contracts, rejection, 11 § 365
Filing,
Claims, 11 § 901
Automatic stay, 11 § 922
Evidence, **BKR 3003**
Fees, payment, 28 § 1930
Plans and specifications, 11 § 941
Fraud, transfers, 11 §§ 901, 926
Good faith, 11 § 901
Confirmation of plan, **BKR 3020**
Negotiations, 11 § 109
Petitions, 11 § 921
Health care businesses, **BKR 1021**
Hearings, dismissal and nonsuit, 11 § 930
Injunctions,
Discharge, 11 § 901
Plans and specifications, **BKR 3017**

BANKRUPTCY—Cont'd
Chapter 9 proceedings—Cont'd
Insolvency, qualifications, 11 § 109
Intervention, **BKR 2018**
Judges or justices, designation, 11 § 921
Judgments and decrees,
Jurisdiction, 11 § 904
State laws, binding, consent, 11 § 903
Jurisdiction,
Appeal and review, 11 § 921
Confirmation of plan, 11 § 930
Plans and specifications, 11 § 945
Leases, 11 §§ 901, 929
Assumption, 11 § 365
Liens and incumbrances,
Claims, reorganization, 11 § 901
Taxation, petitions, filing, 11 § 922
Lists,
Claims, 11 § 925
Filing, 11 §§ 521, 924
Twenty largest creditors, **BKR 1007**
Material default, dismissal and nonsuit, 11 § 930
Modification, plans and specifications, 11 § 942; **BKR 3019**
Negotiations, qualifications, 11 § 109
Newspapers, notice, 11 § 923
Nonrecourse loans, elections, **BKR 3014**
Notice, 11 § 923
Disclosure, statements, **BKR 3017**
Dismissal and nonsuit, 11 § 930
Objections and exceptions,
Confirmation of plan, 11 § 943; **BKR 3020**
Disclosure, statements, **BKR 3017**
Dismissal and nonsuit, 11 § 921
Orders of court,
Appeal and review, delays, 11 § 921
Confirmation of plan, **BKR 3020**
Disclosure, statements, **BKR 3017**
Jurisdiction, 11 § 904
Notice, 11 § 923
Petitions, 11 § 921
Automatic stay, filing, 11 § 922
Time, filing, 11 § 941
Plans and specifications, 11 § 941 et seq.
Acceptances, **BKR 3018, 3019**
Closings, 11 § 945
Confirmation of plan, 11 §§ 943, 944
Dismissal and nonsuit, 11 § 930
Core proceeding, 28 § 157
Exchanges, security, 11 § 946
Executory contracts, assumption, 11 § 501
Filing, 11 § 941; **BKR 3016**
Injunctions, **BKR 3017**
Jurisdiction, 11 § 945
Leases, unexpired leases, assumption, 11 § 501
Modification, 11 § 942; **BKR 3019**
Rejection, **BKR 3018**
Political subdivisions,
Jurisdiction, 11 § 904
Powers and duties, preservation, 11 § 903
Postpetition,
Avoidance, transfers, 11 § 901
Security interest, 11 § 928
Powers and duties, transfers, avoidance, 11 § 926
Preferences, 11 § 901
Preservation, States, powers and duties, 11 § 903
Priorities and preferences, 11 § 901

BANKRUPTCY—Cont'd
Chapter 9 proceedings—Cont'd
Process, automatic stay, 11 § 922
Prosecution, dismissal and nonsuit, 11 § 930
Publication, notice, 11 § 923
Qualifications, 11 § 109
Recourse, 11 § 927
Rejection, plans and specifications, **BKR 3018**
Reopening, 11 § 901
Reorganization, 11 §§ 103, 901
Representatives and representation, statements, **BKR 2019**
Retention, dismissal and nonsuit, jurisdiction, 11 § 930
Schedules, liabilities, **BKR 3003**
Securities,
    Exchanges, 11 § 946
    Money, disposition, 11 § 347
Security interest,
    Postpetition, 11 § 928
        Set-off and counterclaim, 11 § 901
    Set-off and counterclaim, postpetition, 11 § 901
Self-incrimination, 11 § 901
Service of process, automatic stay, 11 § 922
Spouses, definitions, 11 § 902
State laws, 11 §§ 109, 903
Statute of limitations, transfers, avoidance, 11 § 901
Statutory liens, 11 § 901
Stay of proceedings, 11 § 921
    Jurisdiction, 11 § 904
    Petitions, filing, 11 § 922
Subordination, 11 § 901
Taxation,
    Confirmation of plan, objections and exceptions, 11 § 943
    Petitions, 11 § 921
    Special taxpayer, definitions, 11 § 902
Termination, 11 § 930
Time, filing of plan, 11 § 941
Transfers, avoidance, 11 §§ 109, 926
Trusts and trustees, 11 § 901
    Appointments, 11 § 926
    Compensation and salaries, priorities and preferences, 11 § 507
    Contributions, 11 § 503
    Definitions, 11 § 902
Unliquidated claims, lists, filing, 11 § 925
Unreasonable delay, dismissal and nonsuit, 11 § 930
Utilities, 11 § 901
Waiver, discharge, 11 § 524
Want of prosecution, dismissal and nonsuit, 11 § 930
Chapter 11 proceedings, 11 § 1101 et seq.
Abandonment, railroads, 11 § 1170
Acceptances, 11 § 1126
    Forms, plans and specifications, **BKR Forms 13, 14**
    Plans and specifications, **BKR 3018, 3019**
Administration, application of laws, 11 § 103
Aircraft, machinery and equipment, 11 § 1110
Alimony, 11 § 1129
Appearance, 11 § 1109
    Railroads, 11 § 1164
Application of laws,
    Administration, 11 § 103
    Railroads, 11 § 1161
Automatic stay, 11 § 362
    Confirmation of plan, **BKR 3020**
Cause, dismissal and nonsuit, 11 § 1112
Chapter 7 proceedings, conversion, 11 § 707
Claims, 11 § 1111

BANKRUPTCY—Cont'd
Chapter 11 proceedings—Cont'd
Claims—Cont'd
    Classification, 11 §§ 1122, 1123
    Evidence, filing, **BKR 3003**
    Impairment, 11 § 1124
    Railroads, priorities and preferences, 11 § 1171
Classification, claims, 11 §§ 1122, 1123
Collective bargaining agreements,
    Railroads, 11 § 1167
    Rejection, 11 § 1113
Committees, 11 §§ 1102, 1103; **BKR 2007**
Complaints, discharge, **BKR 4004**
Confirmation of plan, 11 §§ 1128, 1129; **BKR 3020**
    Dismissal and nonsuit, 11 § 1112
    Forms, objections and exceptions, **BKR Form 13**
    Orders of court, **BKR Form 15**
    Postconfirmation, 11 § 1141 et seq.
    Railroads, 11 § 1173
Consumer debts, 11 § 523
Controlling interest, financial statements and reports, **BKR 2015.3; BKR Form 26**
Conversion, 11 § 1112
    Eligibility, 11 § 706
    Individual debtors, 11 § 1301
    Liquidation, **BKR 1019**
Customs duties, discharge, objections and exceptions, 11 § 523
Debtors in possession, powers and duties, 11 § 1107
Default, 11 § 1123
    Dismissal and nonsuit, 11 § 1112
    Railroads, 11 § 1172
Definitions, 11 § 1101
    Fair and equitable, plans and specifications, 11 § 1129
    Property of the estate,
        Individual debtors, 11 § 1115
        Municipal debt adjustment, 11 § 902
    Railroads, 11 § 1162
    Representatives and representation, statements, **BKR 2019**
Delivery, plans and specifications, 11 § 1142
Deposits, **BKR 3020**
Discharge, 11 § 524; **BKR 4004**
    Confirmation of plan, 11 § 1141
Disclosure,
    Dismissal and nonsuit, 11 § 1112
    Forms, **BKR Form 12 et seq.**
    Objections and exceptions, statements, **BKR 3017, 3017.1**
    Orders of court, forms, **BKR Form 12 et seq.**
    Postpetition, 11 § 1125
    Small businesses, statements, 11 § 1125; **BKR 3017.1**
    Statements, **BKR 3016 et seq.**
    Taxation, 11 § 1125
Dismissal and nonsuit, 11 § 1112
Distribution, 11 § 1143
Divorce, discharge, objections and exceptions, 11 § 523
Elections,
    Ballots, plans and specifications, forms, **BKR Form 14**
    Nonrecourse loans, **BKR 3014**
    Plans and specifications, ballots, forms, **BKR Form 14**
Embezzlement, fiduciaries, 11 § 523
Evidence, 11 § 1111
    Claims, filing, **BKR 3003**
Examinations and examiners,
    Appointments, 11 § 1104; **BKR 2007.1**
    Powers and duties, 11 § 1106

BANKRUPTCY—Cont'd
Chapter 11 proceedings—Cont'd
Exemptions, securities, 11 § 1145
Federal, State or local laws, railroads, 11 § 1166
Fees,
Dismissal and nonsuit, 11 § 1112
Fraud, 18 § 155
Filing, 11 § 1106
Claims, evidence, **BKR 3003**
Controlling interest, financial statements and reports, **BKR 2015.3**
Dismissal and nonsuit, 11 § 1112
Plans and specifications, **BKR 3016**
Substantial or controlling interest, financial statements and reports, **BKR 2015.3**
Financial statements and reports, substantial or controlling interest, **BKR 2015.3; BKR Form 26**
Foreign countries, venue, 28 § 1408
Forms, **BKR Form 9**
Small businesses, **BKR Form 25 et seq.**
Substantial or controlling interest, financial statements and reports, **BKR Form 26**
Fraud,
Fees, 18 § 155
Taxation, discharge, 11 § 1141
Trusts and trustees, 11 § 1104
Good faith,
Collective bargaining, 11 § 1113
Confirmation of plan, 11 §§ 1129, 1144; **BKR 3020**
Plans and specifications, 11 § 1126
Postpetition, solicitation, 11 § 1125
Retirement and pensions, 11 § 1114
Health care businesses, **BKR 1021**
Hearings, confirmation of plan, 11 § 1128
Impairment, claims, 11 § 1124
Injunctions, plans and specifications, **BKR 3017**
Insurance,
Dismissal and nonsuit, 11 § 1112
Retirement and pensions, payment, 11 § 1114
Inventories, **BKR 2015**
Involuntary proceedings, 11 § 303
Joint administration, appointments, **BKR 2009**
Judgments and decrees, **BKR 3022**
Jurisdiction, 28 § 1334
Liquidation, railroads, 11 § 1174
Lists, **BKR 1007**
Filing, 11 § 1106
Losses,
Dismissal and nonsuit, 11 § 1112
Nonmonetary obligations, 11 § 1124
Managers and management, 28 § 959
Dismissal and nonsuit, 11 § 1112
Meetings, **BKR 2003; BKR Form 9**
Dismissal and nonsuit, 11 § 1112
Modification, plans and specifications, 11 § 1127; **BKR 3019**
Motions, judgments and decrees, **BKR 3022**
Nonrecourse loans, elections, **BKR 3014**
Notice, **BKR 2002**
Confirmation of plan, 11 § 1128
Controlling interest, financial statements and reports, **BKR 2015.3**
Corporations, forms, **BKR Form 9**
Discharge, **BKR 4004**
Disclosure, statements, **BKR 3017, 3017.1**
Individual debtors, forms, **BKR Form 9**

BANKRUPTCY—Cont'd
Chapter 11 proceedings—Cont'd
Notice—Cont'd
Joint debtors, forms, **BKR Form 9**
Partnership, forms, **BKR Form 9**
Substantial or controlling interest, financial statements and reports, **BKR 2015.3**
Support, 11 § 1106
Trusts and trustees, **BKR 2015**
Objections and exceptions,
Confirmation of plan, 11 §§ 1128, 1129; **BKR 3020**
Forms, **BKR Form 13**
Discharge, time, **BKR 4004**
Disclosure, statements, **BKR 3017, 3017.1**
Forms, confirmation of plan, **BKR Form 13**
Operating businesses, 11 § 1108
Orders of court,
Confirmation of plan, **BKR 3020**
Disclosure, statements, **BKR 3017; BKR Form 12 et seq.**
Dismissal and nonsuit, 11 § 1112
Parties, appearance, 11 § 1109
Payment,
Personal services, plans and specifications, 11 § 1123
Retirement and pensions, insurance, 11 § 1114
Taxation, periodic payment, 11 § 1129
Pending actions, 11 § 1141
Plans and specifications, 11 § 1121 et seq.
Acceptances, **BKR 3018, 3019**
Filing, **BKR 3016**
Forms, **BKR Form 13 et seq.**
Injunctions, **BKR 3017**
Modification, 11 § 1127; **BKR 3019**
Orders of court, 11 § 1142
Forms, **BKR Form 13 et seq.**
Revocation or suspension, 11 § 1144
Railroads, 11 § 1172
Rejection, **BKR 3018**
Revocation or suspension, 11 § 1144
Postconfirmation, 11 § 1141 et seq.
Postpetition, disclosure, 11 § 1125
Powers and duties,
Committees, 11 § 1103
Trusts and trustees, 11 § 1106
United States trustees, 28 § 586
Presumptions, substantial or controlling interest, financial statements and reports, **BKR 2015.3**
Priorities and preferences, railroads, claims, 11 § 1171
Property of the estate,
Individual debtors, definitions, 11 § 1115
Municipal debt adjustment, definitions, 11 § 902
Protective orders, substantial or controlling interest, financial statements and reports, **BKR 2015.3**
Public interest, railroads, 11 § 1165
Qualifications, trusts and trustees, 11 §§ 322, 1163
Railroads, 11 § 1161 et seq.
Abandonment, 11 § 1170
Appearance, 11 § 1164
Application of laws, 11 § 1161
Appointments, trusts and trustees, 11 § 1163
Collective bargaining, 11 § 1167
Confirmation of plan, 11 § 1173
Default, 11 § 1172
Definitions, 11 §§ 101, 1162
Federal laws, 11 § 1166
Leases, rejection, 11 § 1169

BANKRUPTCY—Cont'd
Chapter 11 proceedings—Cont'd
Railroads—Cont'd
Liquidation, 11 § 1174
Qualifications, 11 § 109
Plans and specifications, 11 § 1172
Public interest, 11 § 1165
Reorganization, default, 11 § 1172
Rolling stock, 11 § 1168
State or local laws, 11 § 1166
Trusts and trustees, appointments, 11 § 1163
Records and recordation, debtors in possession, **BKR 2015**
Registration, discharge, **BKR 4004**
Rejection,
Collective bargaining, 11 § 1113
Forms, plans and specifications, **BKR Forms 13, 14**
Plans and specifications, **BKR 3018**
Forms, **BKR Forms 13, 14**
Reports,
Confirmation of plan, 11 § 1106
Dismissal and nonsuit, 11 § 1112
Representatives and representation, statements, **BKR 2019**
Retirement and pensions, insurance, payment, 11 § 1114
Revocation or suspension, confirmation of plan, orders of court, 11 § 1144
Rolling stock, railroads, 11 § 1168
Schedules,
Filing, 11 §§ 523, 1106
Liabilities, **BKR 3003**
Secretary of the Treasury, reorganization, 11 § 1126
Securities, exemptions, 11 § 1145
Ships and shipping, 11 § 1110
Small businesses,
Disclosure, statements, 11 § 1125; **BKR 3016, 3017.1**
Forms, **BKR Form 25 et seq.**
Solicitation, postpetition, 11 § 1125
State or local laws, railroads, 11 § 1166
Substantial or controlling interest, financial statements and reports, **BKR 2015.3**; **BKR Form 26**
Supplemental schedules, **BKR 1007**
Support, 11 §§ 1106, 1129
Dismissal and nonsuit, 11 § 1112
Taxation, 11 §§ 346, 1146
Disclosure, 11 § 1125
Dismissal and nonsuit, 11 § 1112
Fraud, discharge, 11 § 1141
Periodic payment, 11 § 1129
Termination, trusts and trustees, appointments, 11 § 1105
Time,
Controlling interest, financial statements and reports, **BKR 2015.3**
Discharge, **BKR 4007**
Objections and exceptions, **BKR 4004**
Substantial or controlling interest, financial statements and reports, **BKR 2015.3**
Transportation Department, railroads, appearances, 11 § 1164
Trusts and trustees,
Appearance, 11 § 1109
Appointments, 11 §§ 1104, 1105; **BKR 2007.1**
Fraud, 11 § 1104
Powers and duties, 11 § 1106
Qualifications, 11 §§ 322, 1163
Railroads, appointments, 11 § 1163
Substitution, **BKR 2012**
Support, 11 § 1106

BANKRUPTCY—Cont'd
Chapter 11 proceedings—Cont'd
United States trustees, post
Venue, 28 §§ 1408, 1409
Chapter 12 proceedings, 11 § 1201 et seq.
Abandonment, disposition, **BKR 3011**
Actions and proceedings, stay of proceedings, 11 § 1201
Alimony, 11 §§ 1208, 1222 et seq.
Application of law, 11 §§ 103, 1205
Attorneys, fees, 11 § 329
Claims,
Allowances, 28 § 157
Evidence, filing, **BKR 3002**
Closings, **BKR 5009**
Codebtors, stay of proceedings, 11 § 1201
Compensation and salaries, trusts and trustees, 11 § 330
Confirmation of plan, 11 § 1223 et seq.
Abandoned or unclaimed property, 11 § 347
Revocation or suspension, 11 § 1230
Contracts, assumption, 11 § 365
Conversion, 11 §§ 348, 1208
Chapter 7 proceedings, 11 § 706; **BKR 1019**
Chapter 13 proceedings, 11 § 1307
Corporations, trusts and trustees, 11 § 321
Credit, 11 § 364
Debtors in possession, 11 § 1207
Powers and duties, 11 § 1203
Removal, 11 § 1204
Discharge, 11 §§ 524, 1228
Objections and exceptions, 11 § 523
Dismissal and nonsuit, 11 § 1208
Dividends, payment, **BKR 3010**
Evidence, claims, filing, **BKR 3002**
Family Farmers Protection Act of 2002, 11 §§ 101 nt, 1201 et seq.
Fees, filing, 28 § 1930
Filing,
Fees, 28 § 1930
Plans and specifications, objections and exceptions, **BKR 3015**
Pleading, demand, time, extensions, 11 § 108
Forms,
Corporations, **BKR Form 9**
Individual debtors, **BKR Form 9**
Joint debtors, **BKR Form 9**
Partnership, **BKR Form 9**
Good faith, confirmation of plan, 11 § 1225; **BKR 3015**
Interests, sales, notice, 11 § 1206
Inventories, **BKR 2015**
Involuntary proceedings, objections and exceptions, 11 § 303
Joint administration, appointments, **BKR 2009**
Leases, assumption, 11 § 365
Liquidation, conversion, 11 § 1208
Meetings, **BKR 2003**; **BKR Form 9**
Modification, plans and specifications, **BKR 3015**
Motions, reopening, **BKR 5010**
Negotiable instruments, dishonor, notice, 11 § 1201
Notice,
Corporations, forms, **BKR Form 9**
Debtors in possession, **BKR 2015**
Family farmers, forms, **BKR Form 9**
Individual debtors, forms, **BKR Form 9**
Joint debtors, forms, **BKR Form 9**
Modification, plans and specifications, **BKR 3015**
Partnership, forms, **BKR Form 9**

BANKRUPTCY—Cont'd
Chapter 12 proceedings—Cont'd
  Notice—Cont'd
    Plans and specifications, modification, **BKR 3015**
    Support, **11 § 1202**
  Objections and exceptions,
    Closings, **BKR 5009**
    Plans and specifications, **BKR 3015**
    Stay of proceedings, **11 § 1201**
  Parties, plans and specifications, objections and exceptions, **11 § 1224**
  Payment, **11 § 1226**
    Dividends, **BKR 3010**
    Time, **11 §§ 1222, 1229**
  Pending actions, **11 § 1228**
  Plans and specifications, **11 § 1221 et seq.**
    Applications, **11 § 1221 nt**
    Conversion, **11 § 348**
    Default, **11 § 1222**
    Disapproval, modification, **11 § 1229**
    Filing, **11 § 1221**
    Good faith, confirmation of plan, **11 § 1225**
    Hearings, confirmation of plan, **11 § 1224**
    Modification, confirmation of plan, **11 § 1229**
    Objections and exceptions, **BKR 3015**
      Discharge, **11 § 523**
    Parties, objections and exceptions, **11 § 1224**
    Revocation or suspension,
      Confirmation of plan, **11 § 1230**
      Discharge, **11 § 1228**
    Taxation, **11 § 1231**
    Time,
      Filing, **11 § 1221**
      Payment, **11 §§ 1222, 1229**
    Trusts and trustees, objections and exceptions, **11 § 1224**
    Unclaimed property, disposition, **11 § 347**
    Unsecured debts, discharge, objections and exceptions, **11 § 1228**
    Vested rights, confirmation of plan, **11 § 1227**
    Waiver, discharge, **11 § 524**
  Powers and duties,
    Debtors in possession, **11 § 1203**
    Trusts and trustees, **11 § 1202**
  Professional persons, labor and employment, **11 § 327**
  Qualifications, trusts and trustees, **11 § 322**
  Records and recordation, possession, **BKR 2015**
  Reinstatement, debtors in possession, notice, **11 § 1204**
  Removal, debtors in possession, **11 § 1204**
  Reopening, **BKR 5010**
  Sales, **11 § 1206**
  Stay of proceedings, codebtor, **11 § 1201**
  Supplemental schedules, **BKR 1007**
  Support, **11 §§ 1202, 1208, 1222 et seq.**
  Taxation, **11 §§ 346, 1231**
  Termination, **11 § 1201**
  Time, discharge, **BKR 4007**
  Trusts and trustees,
    Compensation and salaries, limitation, **11 §§ 326, 330**
    Eligibility, **11 § 321**
    Extension, time, filing, **11 § 108**
    Powers and duties, **11 § 1202**
      Avoidance, **11 § 546**
    Professional services, labor and employment, **11 § 327**
    Qualifications, **11 § 322**
    Residential real property, **11 § 365**
    Substitution, **BKR 2012**

BANKRUPTCY—Cont'd
Chapter 12 proceedings—Cont'd
  Trusts and trustees—Cont'd
    Support, **11 § 1202**
  Unclaimed funds, disposition, **BKR 3011**
  United States trustees, post
  Vested rights, **11 § 1227**
  Waiver, conversion, **11 §§ 706, 1208**
Chapter 13 proceedings, **11 § 1301 et seq.**
  Abandonment, disposition, **BKR 3011**
  Acceptance, confirmation of plan, **11 § 1327**
  Accounts and accounting, **11 § 1302**
  Actions and proceedings, **11 § 1301**
  Addresses, notice, **11 § 342**
  Administrative expenses, schedules, **11 § 707 nt**
  Administrative Office of United States Courts, trusts and trustees, money, **11 § 1302**
  Agriculture, **11 § 1307**
  Alimony, **11 §§ 1307, 1322 et seq.**
  Allowances, postpetition, **11 § 1305**
  Anticramdown Law, **11 § 1325**
  Appearance, trusts and trustees, valuation, **11 § 1302**
  Application of law, **11 § 103**
  Assignments, **11 § 1322**
  Assumption, contracts, **11 § 1322**
  Attorneys,
    Contracts, cancellation, **11 § 329**
    Discharge, **11 § 523**
    Fees,
      Contracts, cancellation, **11 § 329**
      Discharge, **11 § 523**
      Security interest, domicile and residence, notice, **BKR 3002.1**
    Security interest, domicile and residence, notice, **BKR 3002.1**
  Automatic stay, **11 § 362**
  Bifurcation of claims, **11 § 1325**
  Business and commerce, operating businesses, **11 § 1304**
  Chapter 7 proceedings, ante
  Claims, **11 § 348**
    Confirmation of plan, **11 § 1325**
    Disallowance, **11 § 1305**
    Evidence,
      Filing, **BKR 3002**
      Postpetition, **11 § 1305**
    Examinations and examiners, **11 § 1302**
    Postpetition, **11 § 1305**
    Priorities and preferences, payment, **11 § 1322**
    Secured claims, **11 §§ 348, 1323**
    Taxation, **11 § 1305**
  Closings, **BKR 5009**
    Stay of proceedings, objections and exceptions, **11 § 1301**
  Codebtors, stay of proceedings, **11 § 1301**
  Committees, investigations, **11 § 1302**
  Commodity brokers, qualifications, **11 § 109**
  Compensation and salaries, **11 § 1306**
    Trusts and trustees, **11 §§ 326, 330**
  Confirmation of plan, **11 § 1324 et seq.**
    Conversion, **11 § 1307**
    Hearings, **11 § 1302**
    Objections and exceptions, **11 § 1325**
    Revocation or suspension, **11 § 1330**
  Consideration, claims, **11 § 1301**
  Consumer debt, **11 § 1302**
    Claims, treatment, **11 § 1322**
    Discharge, judgments and decrees, costs, **11 § 523**

INDEX

BANKRUPTCY—Cont'd
Chapter 13 proceedings—Cont'd
Consumer debt—Cont'd
Filing, 11 § 1305
Stay of proceedings, 11 § 1301
Transfers, 11 § 547
Contracts, assumption, 11 § 1322
Conversion, 11 § 348
Good faith, 11 § 348
Liquidation, 11 §§ 706, 1301; **BKR 1019**
Notice, 11 § 1307
Reorganization, 11 §§ 1301, 1307; 28 § 1930
Waiver, 11 § 1307
Conviction of crime, restitution, objections and exceptions, 11 § 1328
Copies, 11 § 521
Corporations, eligibility, 11 § 321
Costs, security interest, domicile and residence, notice, **BKR 3002.1**
Crimes and offenses, discharge, 11 § 1328
Customs duties, objections and exceptions, 11 § 523
Damages, discharge, 11 § 1328
Debtors in possession, 11 § 1306
Declarations, **BKR Form 6**
Default, plans and specifications, 11 § 1322
Discharge, 11 § 524
Damages, 11 § 1328
Objections and exceptions, 11 §§ 523, 1302
Restitution, 11 § 1328
Waiver, 11 § 1328
Dismissal and nonsuit, 11 § 1307; **BKR 1017**
Consumer debt, stay of proceedings, objections and exceptions, 11 § 1301
Schedules, 11 § 521
Disposal, money, hearings, 11 § 1302
Distributions, confirmation of plan, 11 § 1325
Dividends, payment, **BKR 3010**
Divorce, discharge, objections and exceptions, 11 § 523
Domicile and residence, security interest, notice, **BKR 3002.1**
Driving while intoxicated, damages, discharge, 11 § 523
Education, loans, objections and exceptions, 11 § 523
Embezzlement, fiduciaries, discharge, 11 § 523
Evidence, claims,
Filing, **BKR 3002**
Postpetition, 11 § 1305
Examinations and examiners, 11 § 1302
Expenses and expenditures, 11 § 1307
Confirmation of plan, payment, 11 § 1325
Extensions, time, 11 § 108
Fees, attorneys, consumer debt, discharge, 11 § 523
Filing,
Accounts and accounting, 11 § 1302
Claims, postpetition, 11 § 1305
Fees, payment, 28 § 1930
Payment, fees, 28 § 1930
Postpetition, claims, 11 § 1305
Prepetition tax returns, 11 § 1308
Final report, 11 § 1302
Financial management training curriculum, 11 § 1328
Financial statements and reports, investigations, 11 § 1302
Fines, penalties and forfeitures, political subdivisions, objections and exceptions, 11 § 523
Forms,
Mortgages, **BKR Form 10**
Notice, **BKR Form 9**

BANKRUPTCY—Cont'd
Chapter 13 proceedings—Cont'd
Fraud, discharge, 11 § 1328
Exemptions, 11 § 523
Future earnings, 11 § 1322
Good faith,
Confirmation of plan, 11 § 1325; **BKR 3015**
Schedules, filing, 11 § 521
Hanging Law, 11 § 1325
Health insurance, 11 § 1329
Hearings,
Confirmation of plan, 11 § 1324
Conversion, 11 § 1307
Discharge,
Notice, 11 § 523
Revocation or suspension, 11 § 1328
Security interest, domicile and residence, notice, **BKR 3002.1**
Stay of proceedings, 11 § 1301
Trusts and trustees, appearance, 11 § 1302
Holders, unsecured claims, confirmation of plan, 11 § 1325
Husband and wife,
Alimony, maintenance, support, 11 § 523
Qualifications, 11 § 109
Information, 11 § 1302
Insurance, personal property, 11 § 1326
Inventories, **BKR 2015**
Investigations, financial statements and reports, 11 § 1302
Irreparable harm, consumer debt, 11 § 1301
Joint administration, appointments, **BKR 2009**
Judgments and decrees, consumer debt, discharge, fees, 11 § 523
Larceny, fiduciaries, discharge, 11 § 523
Leases, 11 § 1303
Assumption, 11 § 1322
Personal property, payment, 11 § 1326
Liens and incumbrances,
Confirmation of plan, 11 § 1325
Valuation, hearings, 11 § 1302
Limitation of actions, security interest, domicile and residence, notice, **BKR 3002.1**
Lists, filing, 11 § 523
Means test, 11 § 1325
Meetings, **BKR 2003**
Forms, **BKR Form 9**
Modification, 11 § 1307
Hearings, 11 § 1302
Plans and specifications, 11 § 1322; **BKR 3015**
Time, 11 §§ 1323, 1329
Money,
Disposal, 11 § 1302
Fraud, 11 § 523
Mortgages, forms, **BKR Form 10**
Motions,
Discharge, **BKR 4007**
Reopening, **BKR 5010**
Security interest, domicile and residence, notice, **BKR 3002.1**
Negotiable instruments, dishonor, notice, 11 § 1301
Nonpayment, fees, 11 § 1307
Notice,
Addresses, 11 § 342
Domicile and residence, security interest, **BKR 3002.1**
Forms, **BKR Form 9**
Negotiable instruments, dishonor, 11 § 1301

BANKRUPTCY—Cont'd
Chapter 13 proceedings—Cont'd
Notice—Cont'd
Plans and specifications, objections and exceptions, **BKR 3015**
Security interest, domicile and residence, **BKR 3002.1**
Support, **11 § 1302**
Trusts and trustees, **BKR 2015**
Objections and exceptions,
Claims, **11 § 1302**
Closings, **BKR 5009**
Confirmation of plan, **11 §§ 1324, 1327**
Discharge, **11 § 1302**
Plans and specifications, **BKR 3015**
Confirmation of plan, **11 §§ 1324, 1327**
Operating businesses, **11 § 1304**
Orders of court,
Consumer debt, **11 § 1305**
Conversion, **11 § 1307**
Discharge, waiver, **11 § 1328**
Stay of proceedings, **11 § 1301**
Parties,
Confirmation of plan, objections and exceptions, **11 § 1324**
Conversion, notice, **11 § 1307**
Information, **11 § 1302**
Stay of proceedings, notice, **11 § 1301**
Payment,
Claims, **11 § 1326**
Priorities and preferences, **11 § 1322**
Confirmation of plan, **11 § 1325**
Dividends, **BKR 3010**
Priorities and preferences, claims, **11 § 1322**
Time, **11 §§ 1302, 1322**
Pending actions, **11 § 1328**
Personal injuries, discharge, **11 § 1328**
Personal property, **11 § 1326**
Petitions, claims, postpetition, **11 § 1305**
Plans and specifications,
Consumer debt, unsecured claims, **11 § 1322**
Contracts, **11 § 501**
Conversion, **11 § 1307**
Core proceedings, **28 § 157**
Discharge, **11 § 1328**
Filing, **11 § 1321**
Alternate plans, **11 § 1307**
Claims, **11 § 1301**
Modification, **11 § 1323**
Objections and exceptions, **BKR 3015**
Payment, **11 § 1326**
Leases, **11 § 501**
Liquidation, **11 § 1307**
Modification, **11 §§ 1307, 1329**
Time, **11 § 1323**
Objections and exceptions, **BKR 3015**
Payment, **11 § 1326**
Time, **11 § 1302**
Time,
Conversion, **11 § 1307**
Designated plans, **11 § 1322**
Payment, **11 § 1302**
Vested rights, confirmation of plan, **11 § 1327**
Waiver, **11 § 1307**
Discharge, **11 § 1328**
Political subdivisions,
Education, loans, discharge, **11 § 523**

BANKRUPTCY—Cont'd
Chapter 13 proceedings—Cont'd
Political subdivisions—Cont'd
Taxation, **11 § 1305**
Postpetition, claims, **11 § 1305**
Prepetition tax returns, **11 § 1308**
Principal residence, liens and incumbrances, **11 § 1322**
Priorities and preferences, claims, **11 § 1322**
Proof of claim, postpetition, **11 § 1305**
Property, **11 § 1306**
Records and recordation, **BKR 2015**
Referees, fees, **11 nt prec § 101**
Rejection,
Contracts, **11 § 1322**
Plans and specification, confirmation of plan, **11 § 1327**
Secured claims, modification, **11 § 1323**
Reopening, **BKR 5010**
Reports, **11 § 1302**
Restitution,
Conviction of crime, discharge, **11 § 1328**
Objections and exceptions, **11 § 523**
Revocation or suspension,
Confirmation of plan, **11 § 1307**
Discharge, notice, **11 § 1328**
Sales, **11 § 1303**
Schedules,
Administrative expenses, **11 § 707 nt**
Dismissal and nonsuit, **11 § 521**
Filing, **11 § 523**
Security interest, **11 § 109**
Confirmation of plan, **11 § 1325**
Domicile and residence, notice, **BKR 3002.1**
Self-employment, **11 § 1304**
Separation agreement, discharge, objections and exceptions, **11 § 523**
Statements, investigations, filing, **11 § 1302**
Stay of proceedings, **11 § 1301**
Stockbrokers, qualifications, **11 § 109**
Supplemental schedules, **BKR 1007**
Support, **11 §§ 1302, 1307, 1322 et seq.**
Taxation,
Confirmation of plan, **11 § 1325**
Discharge, **11 § 523**
Dismissal and nonsuit, **11 § 1307**
Postpetition claims, **11 § 1305**
Prepetition returns, **11 § 1308**
Termination, **11 § 1307**
Tests, means test, **11 § 1325**
Time,
Confirmation of plan, hearings, **11 § 1324**
Conversion, **11 § 1307**
Designated plans, **11 § 1322**
Discharge, **BKR 4007**
Payment, **11 § 1302**
Security interest, domicile and residence, notice, **BKR 3002.1**
Timeshares, assumption, **11 § 1322**
Trusts and trustees, **11 § 1302**
Appointments, qualifications, **11 §§ 322, 1302**
Compensation and salaries, **11 § 330**
Standing trustees, payments, **11 § 1326**
Confirmation of plan, **11 § 1325**
Conversion, termination, **11 § 348**
Credit, **11 § 364**
Eligibility, **11 § 321**
Fraud, **11 § 1302**

BANKRUPTCY—Cont'd
Chapter 13 proceedings—Cont'd
Trusts and trustees—Cont'd
Investigations, 11 § 1302
Objections and exceptions, confirmation of plan, 11 § 1325
Payment, 11 § 1326
Standing trustees,
Compensation and salaries, 11 § 1326; 28 § 586
Service, 11 § 1302
Support, 11 § 1302
Time, payment, 11 § 1302
Unclaimed property, disposition, 11 § 347
Unexpired leases, assumption, 11 § 365
United States trustees, post
Unsecured claims, objections and exceptions, 11 § 1325
Unsecured debts, qualifications, 11 § 109
Valuation, hearings, 11 § 1302
Vested rights, 11 § 1327
Waiver,
Default, 11 § 1322
Discharge, 11 §§ 524, 1328
Dismissal and nonsuit, 11 § 1307
Chapter 15 proceedings. Foreign countries, generally, post
Charities,
Dismissal and nonsuit, 11 § 707
Fraud, 11 § 548
Transfers, 11 §§ 363, 541, 1129
Charters, discrimination, 11 § 525
Checks, trusts and trustees, disposition, 11 § 347
Chemical and biological warfare and weapons, claims, 11 § 362
Chief Judge. Judges or justices, post
Children and minors,
Appointments, **BKR 5002**
Automatic stay, 11 § 362
Consideration, 11 § 524
Discharge, objections and exceptions, 11 § 523
Disclosure, 11 § 112
Exemptions, 11 § 522
Petitions, **BKR 1004.1**
Priorities and preferences, 11 §§ 507, 547
Process, **BKR 1007**
Support, generally, post
Children born out of wedlock, automatic stay, 11 § 362
Citation, **BKR 1001**
Civil Aeronautics Board, 11 § 1110
Civil procedure, **BKR 7002**
Claims, 11 § 502; **BKR 3001 et seq.**
Abstention, 11 § 305
Acceptances, plans and specifications, **BKR 3005**
Adversary proceedings, withdrawal, **BKR 3006**
Allowances, 11 § 502 et seq.
Core proceeding, 28 § 157
Distributions, 11 § 508
Fines, penalties and forfeitures, damages, 11 § 522
Subordination, notice, 11 § 510
Attorneys, ante
Automatic stay, 11 §§ 362, 501
Bonds (officers and fiduciaries), evidence, **BKR 3005**
Breach of performance, 11 § 502
Chapter 7 proceedings, ante
Chapter 9 proceedings, ante
Chapter 11 proceedings, ante
Chapter 13 proceedings, ante
Chemical and biological warfare and weapons, 11 § 362

BANKRUPTCY—Cont'd
Claims—Cont'd
Classification, **BKR 3013**
Codebtors, 11 § 509; **BKR 3005**
Collection, automatic stay, petitions, 11 § 362
Commodities, 11 §§ 765, 766
Community claim,
Definitions, 11 § 101
Notice, 11 § 342
Community property,
Damages, 11 § 541
Discharge, 11 § 524
Consumer credit protection, open end or revolving consumer credit agreements, **BKR 3001**
Contingent, estimates, 11 § 502
Contracts, rejection, filing, 11 § 501
Copies, objections and exceptions, **BKR 3007**
Costs, **BKR 3001**
Credit cards and plates, **BKR 3001**
Damages, 11 §§ 501, 502
Definitions, 11 § 101
Disallowance, 11 § 502
Liens and incumbrances, 11 § 506
Elections, nonrecourse loans, **BKR 3014**
Employment contracts, termination, damages, 11 § 502
Evidence, **BKR 3001 et seq.**
Chapter 11 proceedings, 11 § 1111
Exemptions, **BKR 4003**
Foreign countries, **BKR 3002**
Forms, **BKR Form 10**
Fraud, 18 § 152
Individual debtors, postpetition, 11 § 1305
Involuntary proceedings, 11 § 501
Time, extensions, 11 § 108
Unsecured claims, reduction, 11 § 502
Exemptions, **BKR 4003**
Fees, **BKR 3001**
Filing, **BKR 5005**
Delays, 11 § 502
Evidence, 11 § 501; **BKR 3002 et seq.**
Objections and exceptions, **BKR 3007**
Foreign countries, 11 § 1513; **BKR 3002**
Forms, **BKR 3001; BKR Form 10**
Notice, **BKR Form 20B**
Secured claims, schedules, **BKR Form 6**
Unsecured claims, schedules, **BKR Form 6**
Fraud, crimes and offenses, 18 § 152
Frauds, statute of, **BKR 3001**
Nonrecourse loans, elections, **BKR 3014**
Grain, 11 § 557
Guarantors, evidence, **BKR 3005**
Indorsers, evidence, **BKR 3005**
Insider, services, disallowance, 11 § 502
Interest, **BKR 3001**
Involuntary proceedings, 11 §§ 303, 501
Ordinary course of business, filing, 11 § 501
Leases, damages, termination, 11 § 502
Liens and incumbrances,
Valuation, **BKR 3012**
Void, 11 § 506
Location, **BKR 3002**
Mortgages, forms, **BKR Form 10**
Motions, post
Nonrecourse loans, elections, **BKR 3014**
Notice, 11 § 502; **BKR 2002**
Classification, **BKR 3013**

BANKRUPTCY—Cont'd
Claims—Cont'd
  Notice—Cont'd
    Filing, **BKR 3004**
    Forms, **BKR Form 20B**
    Liens and incumbrances, valuation, **BKR 3012**
    Objections and exceptions, **BKR 3007**
    Reconsideration, **BKR 3008**
    Withdrawal, **BKR 3006**
  Objections and exceptions, **BKR 3007**
    Discharge, 11 § 502
    Exemptions, **BKR 4003**
  Omnibus objections, **BKR 3007**
  Open end credit plans, **BKR 3001**
  Open end or revolving consumer credit agreements, **BKR 3001**
  Orders of court, 11 § 348
    Reconsideration, **BKR 3008**
    Withdrawal, **BKR 3006**
  Partnership, general partner, 11 § 502
  Petitions, answer, **BKR 1011**
  Plans and specifications, **BKR 3015 et seq.**
    Acceptances, rejection, **BKR 3005**
  Predatory loans, 11 § 363
  Priorities and preferences, 11 §§ 507, 726
  Reaffirmation agreements, 11 § 524
  Reconsideration, 11 § 502; **BKR 3008**
  Recovery, allowances, 11 § 502
  Register, **BKR 5003**
  Reimbursement,
    Damages, filing, 11 § 501
    Disallowance, 11 § 502
  Rejection,
    Contracts, 11 § 501
    Plans and specifications, **BKR 3005**
  Removal, 28 § 1452
  Revolving consumer credit agreements, **BKR 3001**
  Sales, 11 § 363
  Secured claims, 11 § 501 et seq.
    Automatic stay, 11 § 362
    Chapter 13 proceedings, 11 §§ 348, 1323
    Contributions, 11 § 502
    Evidence, 11 § 501
    Fines, penalties and forfeitures, 11 § 522
    Liens and incumbrances,
      Ordinary course of business, 11 § 546
      Sales, 11 § 363
    Ordinary course of business, liens and incumbrances, 11 § 546
    Priorities and preferences, 11 § 507
    Proof of claim, 11 § 501
    Qualifications, 11 § 109
    Sales, liens and incumbrances, 11 § 363
    Schedules, forms, **BKR Form 6**
    Status, 11 § 506
    Subordination, 11 § 541
    Subrogation, 11 § 509
  Setoff and counterclaim, post
  Signatures, **BKR 3001**
    Nonrecourse loans, elections, **BKR 3014**
  Sovereign immunity, abrogation, governmental units, 11 § 106
  Subordination, 11 § 510
  Subrogation, 11 §§ 502, 507, 509
  Taxation, post
  Time, 11 § 501 et seq.; **BKR 3002 et seq.**

BANKRUPTCY—Cont'd
Claims—Cont'd
  Transfers, **BKR 3001**
  Trusts and trustees, post
  Unclaimed funds, disposition, **BKR 3011**
  Unsecured claims,
    Administration, expenses and expenditures, 11 § 364
    Avoidance, 11 § 544
    Employee benefit plans, priorities and preferences, 11 § 507
    Evidence, reduction, 11 § 502
    Exemptions, 11 § 522
    Fish and game, sales, priorities and preferences, 11 § 507
    Individual debtors, confirmation of plan, 11 §§ 1325, 1329
    Involuntary proceedings, ordinary course of business,
      Discharge, 11 § 523
      Priorities and preferences, 11 § 507
    Liquidation, priorities and preferences, 11 §§ 753, 767
    Objections and exceptions, notice, 11 § 502
    Political subdivisions, taxation, priorities and preferences, 11 § 501
    Priorities and preferences, 11 §§ 507, 753, 767
    Qualifications, 11 § 109
    Reduction, 11 § 502
    Schedules, forms, **BKR Form 6**
  Valuation, liens and incumbrances, **BKR 3012**
  Withdrawal, **BKR 3006**
Class actions, **BKR 7023**
Clearing banks, liquidation, 11 § 781 et seq.
Clearing organizations. Commodities, post
Clerks of courts, **BKR 5001**
  Appointments, 28 § 156
  Consumer debt, notice, 11 § 342
  Fees, 28 § 1930
  Fraud, notice, 28 § 586
  Statistics, 28 § 159
Closings, 11 § 350; **BKR 5009**
  Abandonment, 11 § 554
  Automatic stay, 11 § 362
  Avoidance, 11 § 546
  Foreign countries, 11 § 1517
Clothing, exemptions, 11 § 522
Codebtors,
  Claims, 11 § 509
    Evidence, **BKR 3005**
  Demand, pleading, 11 § 108
  Evidence, claims, **BKR 3005**
  Pleading, demand, 11 § 108
  Schedules, forms, **BKR Form 6**
  Stay of proceedings, family farmers, 11 § 1201
Collection, **BKR 6001 et seq.**
  Alimony, 11 § 362
  Chapter 7 proceedings, ante
  Liquidation, 11 § 103
  Maintenance, 11 § 362
  Support, post
Collective bargaining, chapter 11 proceedings,
  Railroads, 11 § 1167
  Rejection, 11 § 1113
Colleges and Universities, this index
Comity, abstention, 11 § 305; 28 § 1334
Commerce. Business and commerce, generally, ante
Commercial fishing operation, definitions, 11 § 101
Commercial fishing vessel, definitions, 11 § 101
Committees,
  Appointments, appeal and review, **BKR 2007**

BANKRUPTCY—Cont'd
Committees—Cont'd
  Chapter 9 proceedings, ante
  Equity security holders, post
  Notice, **BKR 2002**
  Priorities and preference, actual and necessary expenses, 11 § 507
  Professional persons, employment, 11 §§ 327, 328
  Reimbursement, allowances, expenses, 11 § 503
  Small businesses, 11 § 1102; **BKR 1020**
Commodities, 11 § 761 et seq.
  Acceleration, contracts, 11 § 556
  Accounts and accounting, 11 § 763
  Appearance, Commodity Futures Trading Commission, 11 § 762
  Automatic stay, 11 § 362
  Avoidance, 11 §§ 546, 764
  Board of Trade, definitions, 11 § 761
  Brokers, 11 § 761 et seq.
    Definitions, 11 § 101
    Margin, transfers, 11 § 546
    Setoff and counterclaim, margin, 11 § 362
  Cash, setoff or counterclaim, 11 § 362
  Claims, 11 §§ 765, 766
  Clearing organizations, 11 § 766
    Accounts and accounting, 11 § 763
    Definitions, 11 § 761
  Commodity Futures Trading Commission,
    Appearance, 11 § 762
    Avoidance, 11 § 764
    Rules and regulations, 11 § 766
  Compromise and settlement, fraud, 11 § 548
  Contracts, 11 § 766
    Acceleration, 11 § 556
    Damages, 11 § 562
    Liquidation, 11 § 556
      Avoidance, 11 § 764
    Margin, setoff or counterclaim, 11 § 362
    Notice, instructions, 11 § 765
    Termination, 11 § 556
  Customers,
    Accounts and accounting, 11 § 763
    Definitions, 11 § 761
    Notice, 11 § 765
    Treatment, 11 § 766
  Damages, contracts, 11 § 562
  Definitions, 11 § 761
  Distribution, 11 § 766
  Evidence, filing, notice, 11 § 765
  Forward contract merchant, setoff or counterclaim, 11 § 362
  Futures contracts,
    Automatic stay, setoff or counterclaim, 11 § 553
    Setoff or counterclaim, 11 § 362
  Instructions, customers, 11 § 765
  Margin,
    Definitions, 11 § 761
    Setoff or counterclaim, 11 § 362
  Master agreements, 11 § 761
  Net equity,
    Accounts and accounting, 11 § 763
    Definitions, 11 § 761
  Notice, 11 § 765
    Commission, 11 § 762
    Customers, instructions, 11 § 765
  Options, automatic stay, setoff or counterclaim, 11 § 553

BANKRUPTCY—Cont'd
Commodities—Cont'd
  Options dealer, definitions, 11 § 761
  Orders of court, avoidance, 11 § 764
  Securities, 11 § 766
  Setoff and counterclaim,
    Margin, 11 § 362
    Net equity, treatment, 11 § 763
  Termination, contracts, 11 § 556
  Transfers, 11 § 764 et seq.
    Avoidance, 11 §§ 546, 764
    Brokers, margin, 11 § 546
    Notice, 11 § 765
  Trusts and trustees, post
  Unsecured claims, priorities and preferences, 11 §§ 753, 767
  Voidable transfers, 11 § 764
Commodity Futures Trading Commission. Commodities, ante
Communications,
  Foreign countries, 11 § 1525 et seq.
  Interception, orders of court, 18 § 2516
Community claim,
  Definitions, 11 § 101
  Notice, 11 § 342
Community property. Husband and wife, post
Compensation and salaries, 11 § 502 et seq.
  Accountants, ante
  Allowances, 11 § 503
  Applications, **BKR 2016**
  Chapter 13 proceedings, ante
  Consumer privacy ombudsman, 11 § 330
  Custodians, post
  Denial, 11 § 328
  Disclosure, petitions, preparers, **BKR 2016**
  Employee benefit plans, contributions, priorities and preferences, 11 § 507
  Employment contract, termination, disallowance, 11 § 502
  Examinations and examiners, post
  Exclusions, 11 § 541
  Future earnings, losses, payment, exemptions, 11 § 522
  Interim compensation, 11 § 331
  Judges or justices, post
  Leases, default, 11 § 365
  Notice, **BKR 2002**
  Patient care ombudsman, 11 § 330
  Petitions, preparers, **BKR 2016**
  Priorities and preferences, 11 § 507
  Professional associations, 11 § 504
  Professional personnel, post
  Public service attorney referral program, 11 § 504
  Retired judges, recall, 28 § 155
  Sharing, 11 § 504
  Trusts and trustees, post
  Unemployment compensation, exemptions, 11 § 522
  United States trustees, post
  Vacation, allowances, priorities and preferences, 11 § 507
Complaints,
  Discharge, **BKR 4004 et seq.**
  Filing, **BKR 5005**
Compromise and settlement, 11 § 541; **BKR 9019**
  Commodity brokers,
    Avoidance, 11 § 546
    Fraud, valuation, 11 § 548
  Definitions, 11 § 101
  Discharge, objections and exceptions, 11 § 523

BANKRUPTCY—Cont'd
Compromise and settlement—Cont'd
  Exemptions, 11 § 522
  Shares and shareholders,
    Definitions, 11 § 741
    Stay of proceedings, 11 § 362
Computers, exemptions, 11 § 522
Concealment, 18 § 3284
  Books and papers, 18 § 152
  Perjury, sentence and punishment, 18 § 152
  Recovery, exemptions, 11 § 522
Concurrent proceedings, foreign countries, 11 § 1528 et seq.
Condominiums, discharge, 11 § 523
Conferences, 11 § 105
  Judicial Conference of the United States, generally, post
Confidential or privileged information,
  Income tax, returns, **BKR 4002**
  Patient care ombudsman, 11 § 333; **BKR 2015.1**
  Trade secrets, 11 § 107; **BKR 9018**
Confirmation of plan,
  Chapter 9 proceedings, ante
  Chapter 11 proceedings, ante
  Chapter 12 proceedings, ante
  Chapter 13 proceedings, ante
  Conversion, **BKR 1019**
  Core proceedings, 28 § 157
  Distribution, **BKR 3021**
  Small businesses, 11 § 1129
Conflict of interest,
  Examinations and examiners, **BKR 5002**
  Joint administration, **BKR 2009**
  Judges or justices, post
  Labor and employment, objections and exceptions, 11 § 327
  Professional personnel, 11 §§ 327, 328
  Sentence and punishment, 18 § 154
Conflict of laws, foreign countries, 11 § 1503
Consent,
  Arbitration, alternative dispute resolution, referrals, 28 § 654
  Involuntary proceedings, dismissal and nonsuit, 11 § 303
  Sales, 11 § 363
Consideration, claims, discharge, 11 § 524
Consolidations and mergers, **BKR 1015, 7042**
  Joint proceedings, 11 § 302
  Preliminary hearings, automatic stay, 11 § 362
  Sales, notice, objections and exceptions, 11 § 363
Constitution of the United States, challenges, statutes, **BKR 9005.1**
Construction, rules, 11 § 102
Consumer credit protection, open end or revolving consumer credit agreements, claims, **BKR 3001**
Consumer debt,
  Attorneys, fees, 11 § 523
  Automatic stay, 11 § 362
  Avoidance, 11 § 547
  Chapter 7 proceedings, ante
  Chapter 13 proceedings, ante
  Clerks of courts, notice, 11 § 342
  Definitions, 11 § 101
  Discharge, 11 § 523
  Extensions, open end credit plan, discharge, 11 § 523
  Fraud, notice, 11 § 342
  Good faith, discharge, 11 § 523
  Liquidation, dismissal and nonsuit, 11 § 707
  Luxury goods or services, discharge, 11 § 523
  Notice, 11 § 342; **BKR 2002**

BANKRUPTCY—Cont'd
Consumer debt—Cont'd
  Real estate,
    Discharge, exemptions, 11 § 524
      Statements, 11 §§ 521, 704
      Statements, discharge, exemptions, 11 §§ 521, 704
    Reduction, unsecured claims, 11 § 502
Consumer Price Index, adjustments, filing, 11 § 104
Consumer privacy ombudsman, 11 § 332
  Appointments, **BKR 6004**
  Compensation and salaries, 11 § 330
  Salaries, 11 § 330
Contempt, **BKR 9020**
Contests, **BKR 9014**
  Petitions, **BKR 1011, 1013**
  United States trustees, **BKR 2020**
Contracts, **BKR 6006**
  Acceleration, 11 § 555 et seq.
  Assignments, 11 § 365; **BKR 6003**
  Assumptions, 11 § 365; **BKR 6003**
  Attorneys, fees, statements, filing, 11 § 329
  Breach of performance, allowances, 11 § 502
  Chapter 7 proceedings, ante
  Claims,
    Disallowance, 11 § 502
    Fees, 11 § 506
  Commodities, ante
  Compromise and settlement, generally, ante
  Consideration, 11 § 524
  Death benefit plan, beneficiaries, 11 § 521
  Debt relief agencies, 11 §§ 526, 528
  Definitions,
    Commodities, 11 § 556
    Master agreements, 11 § 561
    Repurchase agreements, 11 § 559
    Securities, 11 § 555
    Swap agreements, 11 § 560
  Exemptions, life insurance, 11 § 522
  Forward contracts, generally, post
  Illness, payment, exemptions, 11 § 522
  Insurance, nonforfeitures, good faith, 11 § 542
  Insured depository institutions, assumptions, 11 § 365
  Intellectual property, licenses and permits, 11 § 365
  Labor and employment, damages, 11 § 502
  Leases, generally, post
  Licenses and permits, intellectual property, 11 § 365
  Life insurance, exemptions, 11 § 522
  Liquidation, 11 § 555 et seq.
  Master agreements, generally, post
  Motions, **BKR 4001**
  Reaffirmation agreements, generally, post
  Rejections, 11 §§ 365, 502
  Rent, generally, post
  Repurchase agreements, generally, post
  Sales, 11 § 363
    Avoidance, 11 §§ 363, 541
  Schedules, forms, **BKR Form 6**
  Security agreement, definitions, 11 § 101
  Security interest, generally, post
  Separation agreements, 11 §§ 522, 523
  Shares and shareholders, post
  Statutory contracts, rejection, evidence, 11 § 501
  Subordination, 11 § 510
  Swap agreements, generally, post
  Timeshares, rejection, 11 § 365

BANKRUPTCY—Cont'd

Contracts—Cont'd

Transfers,

Life insurance, premiums, payment, exemptions, 11 § 522

Real estate, priorities and preferences, 11 § 547

Trusts and trustees, post

Contributions,

Damages, filing, 11 § 501

Disallowance, 11 § 502

Employee benefit plans, 11 § 541

Priorities and preferences, 11 § 507

Rescission, subordination, 11 § 510

Controlling interest, chapter 11 proceedings, financial statements and reports, **BKR 2015.3; BKR Form 26**

Conversion, 11 § 348; **BKR 1017, 1019**

Chapter 7 proceedings, ante

Chapter 11 proceedings, ante

Chapter 12 proceedings, ante

Chapter 13 proceedings, ante

Waiver, rights, 11 § 706

Conveyances. Fraudulent conveyances, generally, post

Cooperation, foreign countries, 11 § 1525 et seq.

Cooperative banks, qualifications, 11 § 109

Cooperatives, residence, exemptions, 11 § 522

Coordination, foreign countries, 11 § 1529 et seq.

Coowners, sales, distributions, 11 § 363

Copies,

Certificates and certification, **BKR 5006**

Chapter 7 proceedings, 11 § 521

Chapter 13 proceedings, 11 § 521

Claims, objections and exceptions, **BKR 3007**

Conversion, **BKR 1019**

Debt relief agencies, 11 §§ 527, 528

Fees, 11 § 521

Income tax, returns, **BKR 4002**

Partnership, petitions, **BKR 1004**

Payment, 11 § 521

Petitions, post

Reaffirmation agreements, 11 § 524

Schedules, **BKR 1007**

Core proceedings, 28 § 157

Corn, 11 § 557

Corporations,

Bylaws, 11 § 321

Chapter 7 proceedings, ante

Chapter 11 proceedings, generally, ante

Declarations, forms, **BKR Forms 2, 6**

Definitions, 11 § 101

Disclosure, title to property, **BKR 1007, 7007.1**

Foreign countries, recognition petitions, ownership statements, **BKR 1011**

Involuntary proceedings,

Objections and exceptions, 11 § 303

Ownership statements, **BKR 1011**

Reorganization. Chapter 11 proceedings, generally, ante

Statements, title to property, **BKR 1007, 7007.1**

Taxation, 11 § 346

Title to property, statements, **BKR 1007, 7007.1**

Trusts and trustees, 11 § 321

Costs, **BKR 7054**

Appeal and review, **BKR 8014**

Chapter 7 proceedings, 11 § 707

Chapter 13 proceedings, security interest, domicile and residence, notice, **BKR 3002.1**

Claims, **BKR 3001**

Consumer debt, discharge, 11 § 523

BANKRUPTCY—Cont'd

Costs—Cont'd

Counseling services, 11 § 111

Debt relief agencies, 11 § 526

Dismissal and nonsuit, 28 § 1930

Frivolous appeals, **BKR 8020**

Political subdivisions, awards, 11 § 106

Councils. Judicial Council, generally, post

Counseling services, 11 § 109

Certificates and certification, 11 § 521

Financial management training curriculum, generally, post

Notice, 11 §§ 111, 342

Plans and specifications, 11 § 521

Statement of compliance, **BKR 1007**

Counselors. Attorneys, generally, ante

Counterclaim. Setoff and counterclaim, post

Courtesy, trusts and trustees, sales, 11 § 363

Courts,

Discretion of court, attorneys, fees, 11 § 503

Emergencies, special sessions, 28 § 152

Findings, **BKR 7052**

Judges or justices, generally, post

Jurisdiction, generally, post

Leave of court, appeal and review, **BKR 8003**

Location, 28 § 152

Orders of court, generally, post

Powers and duties, 11 § 105

Courts of appeals,

Judges or justices, appointments, 28 § 152

Jurisdiction, 28 § 158

Cover sheet, reaffirmation agreements, forms, **BKR Form 27**

Coverdell education savings accounts, 11 §§ 521, 541

Credit cards and plates, claims, **BKR 3001**

Credit (payment of indebtedness),

Core proceedings, orders of court, 28 § 157

Counseling services, generally, ante

Fraud, discharge, 11 § 523

Motions, **BKR 4001**

Taxation, 11 § 503

Trusts and trustees, 11 § 364

Credit unions, 11 § 109

Crimes and offenses, 18 § 151 et seq.

Actions and proceedings, 11 § 362

Bribery and corruption, 18 § 152

Chapter 7 proceedings, dismissal and nonsuit, 11 § 707

Concealment, 18 § 152

Conflict of interest, 18 § 154

Definitions, 18 § 151

Embezzlement, 18 § 153

Expenses and expenditures, priorities and preferences, 11 § 507

Fees, 18 § 155

Fraud, generally, post

Homesteads, exemptions, 11 § 522

Inspection and inspectors, 18 § 154

Oaths and affirmations, 18 § 152

Pending actions, statements, **BKR 1007**

Preparers, 18 § 156

Priorities and preferences, expenses and expenditures, 11 § 507

Reaffirmation agreements, 18 § 158

Reports, 18 § 3057

Victims, awards, exemptions, 11 § 522

Crockery, exemptions, 11 § 522

Crops, exemptions, 11 § 522

Cross border cases. Foreign countries, generally, post

BANKRUPTCY—Cont'd
Cross claims, **BKR 7013**
Currency. Money, generally, post
Current monthly income,
    Definitions, **11 § 707**
    Forms, current monthly income and means test calculation, **BKR Form 22**
    Statements, **BKR 1007**
Curriculum. Financial management training curriculum, generally, post
Custodians, **11 § 541**
    Accounts and accounting, **11 § 543; BKR 6002**
    Adverse or pecuniary interest, **18 § 154**
    Animals, transfers, **11 § 543**
    Assignments for benefit of creditors, **11 § 543**
    Compensation and salaries,
        Hearings, **11 § 543**
        Priorities and preferences, **11 § 507**
        Turnovers, allowances, **11 § 503**
    Conflict of interest, **18 § 154**
    Contracts, default, **11 § 365**
    Definitions, **11 § 101**
    Dismissal and nonsuit, reinstatement, **11 § 349**
    Embezzlement, **18 § 153**
    Inspection and inspectors, refusal, **18 § 154**
    Liens and incumbrances, possession, avoidance, **11 § 545**
    Motor vehicles, expenses and expenditures, objections and exceptions, **11 § 543**
    Turnovers, property, **11 §§ 503, 543**
Customers,
    Commodities, ante
    Shares and shareholders, post
Customs duties,
    Discharge, objections and exceptions, **11 § 523**
    Exemptions, **11 § 522**
Damages,
    Automatic stay, **11 § 362**
    Avoidance, transfers, **11 § 550**
    Chapter 7 proceedings, ante
    Chapter 13 proceedings, discharge, **11 § 1328**
    Claims, **11 §§ 501, 502**
    Commodities, contracts, **11 § 562**
    Contribution, **11 § 502**
    Counseling services, **11 § 111**
    Debt relief agencies, **11 § 526**
    Disallowance, **11 § 502**
    Driving while intoxicated, discharge, **11 § 523**
    Employment contracts, termination, **11 § 502**
    Exemptions, **11 § 522**
    Forward contracts, **11 § 562**
    Frivolous appeals, **BKR 8020**
    Involuntary proceedings, bad faith, petitions, **11 § 303**
    Leases, rejection, set-off and counterclaim, **11 § 365**
    Liens and incumbrances, avoidance, **11 §§ 550, 551**
    Master agreements, **11 § 562**
    Political subdivisions, awards, **11 § 106**
    Purchasers and purchasing, subordination, **11 § 510**
    Reimbursement, **11 § 502**
    Repurchase agreements, **11 § 562**
    Sales, **11 § 363**
    Securities, **11 § 562**
    Serial filers, **11 § 362**
    Swap agreements, **11 § 562**
    Taxation, post
    Time, **11 §§ 502, 562**
    Timeshares, rejection, setoff and counterclaim, **11 § 365**

BANKRUPTCY—Cont'd
Death, **BKR 1016**
    Benefit plans, **11 § 541**
    Trusts and trustees,
        Liquidation, **11 § 703**
        Successors, **BKR 2012**
    Wrongful death, generally, post
Debt relief agencies, **11 § 526 et seq.**
    Advertisements, **11 § 528**
    Attorneys, fees, **11 § 526**
    Contracts, **11 §§ 526, 528**
    Copies, **11 §§ 527, 528**
    Costs, **11 § 526**
    Damages, **11 § 526**
    Definitions, **11 § 101**
    Disclosure, **11 §§ 527, 528**
    Fees, **11 § 526**
    Fines, penalties and forfeitures, **11 § 526**
    Fraud, **11 § 526**
    Hearings, **11 § 526**
    Injunctions, **11 § 526**
    Jurisdiction, **11 § 526**
    Motions, fines and penalties, **11 § 526**
    Notice, **11 § 526 et seq.**
    Statements, **11 §§ 527, 528**
    Time,
        Contracts, **11 § 528**
        Disclosure, **11 § 527**
    Waiver, **11 § 526**
Debtors in possession,
    Actions and proceedings, **28 § 959; BKR 6009**
    Chapter 11 proceedings, **11 § 1107**
    Chapter 12 proceedings, ante
    Chapter 13 proceedings, **11 § 1306**
    Defenses, **BKR 6009**
    Evidence, **BKR 2011**
    Individual debtors, **11 § 1306**
    Notice, **BKR 2015**
    Records and recordation, **BKR 2015**
    Reorganization, **11 § 1107**
    Reports, **BKR 2015**
    Small businesses, **11 § 1116**
Debtor's monthly expenses, definitions, **11 § 707**
Debtor's principal residence, definitions, **11 § 101**
Deceit. Fraud, generally, post
Declarations,
    Corporations, forms, **BKR Forms 2, 6**
    Individual debtors, **BKR Form 6**
    Partnership, forms, **BKR Forms 2, 6**
    Petitions, preparers, **11 § 110**
        Nonattorneys, **BKR Forms 6, 19A**
    Schedules, **BKR Forms 2, 6**
Decrees. Judgments and decrees, generally, post
Deductions, taxation, **11 § 346**
Deeds and conveyances. Fraudulent conveyances, generally, post
Defamation, **11 § 107; BKR 9018**
Default, **BKR 1013**
    Chapter 11 proceedings, ante
    Chapter 12 proceedings, **11 § 1222**
    Chapter 13 proceedings, plans and specifications, **11 § 1322**
    Contracts, **11 § 365**
    Family farmers, **11 § 1222**
    Individual debtors, plans and specifications, **11 § 1322**
    Judgments and decrees, **BKR 7055**
    Railroads, reorganization, **11 § 1172**

BANKRUPTCY—Cont'd
Default—Cont'd
  Reorganization, 11 § 1123
    Railroads, 11 § 1172
  Security interest, 11 § 521
Defenses, 11 § 558; **BKR** 6009, 7012
  Petitions, **BKR** 1011
  Predatory loans, 11 § 363
  Usury, 11 § 558
Definitions, 11 § 101; **BKR** 9001, 9002
  Avoidance, priorities and preferences, 11 § 547
  Cause, 11 § 1112
  Chapter 7 proceedings, 11 § 707
  Chapter 9 proceedings, post
  Chapter 11 proceedings, ante
  Clearing banks, 11 § 781
  Contracts, ante
  Cooperation, foreign countries, 11 § 1527
  Counseling services, 11 § 109
  Foreign countries, post
  Fraud, transfers, 11 § 548
  Grain, 11 § 557
  Household goods, exemptions, 11 § 522
  Petitions, preparers, 11 § 110
  Priorities and preferences, avoidance, 11 § 547
  Profits, 11 § 308
  Property of the estate, 11 §§ 902, 1115
  Proxies, **BKR** 2006
  Reaffirmation agreements, 11 § 524
  Replacement value, 11 § 506
  Returns,
    Discharge, 11 § 523
    Prepetition returns, 11 § 1308
  Small businesses, 11 § 707
  Swap agreements, post
  Time, **BKR** 9006
  Transfers, post
  Trusts and trustees, post
Delivery, chapter 11 proceedings, plans and specifications, 11 § 1142
Demand,
  Definitions, discharge, 11 § 524
  Filing, 11 § 108
Depositions, **BKR** 7027 et seq.
Depository institutions, process, **BKR** 7004
Deposits, 11 § 345; **BKR** 7067
  Interest, 28 § 589a
  Investments, 11 § 345
  Leases, 11 § 365
  Public utilities, 11 § 366
  Unsecured claims, 11 § 507
Deputies, clerks, 28 § 156
Derivative actions, **BKR** 7023.1
Destruction,
  Health care businesses, patient records, **BKR** 6011
  Taxation, documents, 11 § 521 nt
  Trusts and trustees, health care businesses, records and recordation, 11 § 351
Devises, 11 § 541
Direct appeals, 28 § 158
Directors, Administrative Office of United States Courts, powers and duties, 28 § 604
Disability. Handicapped persons, generally, post
Disallowance, 11 § 502
Disbursements, 11 § 543
Discharge, 11 § 523 et seq.; **BKR** 4004 et seq.

BANKRUPTCY—Cont'd
Discharge—Cont'd
  Aircraft, 11 § 523
  Alimony, 11 § 523
  Chapter 7 proceedings, ante
  Chapter 9 proceedings, ante
  Chapter 11 proceedings, ante
  Chapter 12 proceedings, ante
  Chapter 13 proceedings, ante
  Claims, disallowance, 11 § 502
  Community property, 11 § 524
  Consumer debt, discharge, costs, 11 § 523
  Contracts, consideration, 11 § 524
  Core proceedings, objections and exceptions, 28 § 157
  Customs duties, 11 § 523
  Damages, 11 § 524
  Discrimination, 11 § 525
  Dismissal and nonsuit, 11 § 349
  Driving while intoxicated, damages, 11 § 523
  Elections, fines and penalties, 11 § 523
  Evidence, objections and exceptions, **BKR** 4005
  Federally insured depository institutions, exceptions, 11 § 523
  Fines, penalties and forfeitures, political subdivisions, objections and exceptions, 11 § 523
  Forma pauperis proceedings, frivolous or malicious, 11 § 523
  Forms, chapter 7 proceedings, **BKR Form** 18
  Fraud, 11 § 523
  Fraudulent conveyances, 11 § 524
  Good faith, 11 § 524
  Injunctions, 11 § 524
  Luxury goods or services, 11 § 523
  No discharge, notice, **BKR** 4006
  Nonprofit institution, education, loans, 11 § 523
  Notice, 11 § 523
    Revocation or suspension, **BKR** 4006
  Objections and exceptions, 11 § 523
    Evidence, **BKR** 4005
  Open end credit plan, money, advances, 11 § 523
  Orders of court, 11 § 523
  Personal injuries, post
  Political subdivisions, 11 § 523
  Pro se, 11 § 524
  Reaffirmation agreements, 11 § 524
  Repayment, voluntary, 11 § 524
  Restitution, 11 §§ 523, 1328
  Retirement and pensions, exemptions, 11 § 523
  Revocation or suspension, notice, **BKR** 4006
  Ships and shipping, 11 § 523
  Statements, writing, fraud, 11 § 523
  Supplemental injunction, 11 § 524
  Support, 11 § 523
  Taxation, 11 § 523
  Time, **BKR** 4007
  Trusts and trustees, bonds (officers and fiduciaries), 11 § 322
  Waiver, **BKR** 4006
Disclosure,
  Chapter 9 proceedings, ante
  Chapter 11 proceedings, ante
  Children and minors, 11 § 112
  Compensation and salaries, ante
  Consumer privacy ombudsman, 11 § 332
  Corporations, title to property, **BKR** 7007.1
  Counseling services, 11 § 111

BANKRUPTCY—Cont'd

Disclosure—Cont'd

Debt relief agencies, 11 §§ 527, 528

Definitions, chapter 9 proceedings, chapter 11 proceedings, representatives and representation, statements, **BKR 2019**

Equity security holders, representatives and representation, statements, **BKR 2019**

Forms, orders of court, **BKR Form 12 et seq.**

Lists, **BKR 1007**

Orders of court, forms, **BKR Form 12 et seq.**

Reaffirmation agreements, 11 § 524

Representatives and representation, statements, **BKR 2019**

Small businesses, post

Social security, numbers and numbering, 11 § 342

Statements, **BKR Form 12 et seq.**

Discovery, **BKR 7026 et seq.**

Discrimination, 11 § 525

Dishes, exemptions, 11 § 522

Disinterested person, definitions, 11 § 101

Dismissal and nonsuit, 11 § 349; **BKR 1017, 7041**

Abstention, 11 § 305

Automatic stay, 11 §§ 109, 362

Chapter 7 proceedings, ante

Chapter 9 proceedings, ante

Chapter 11 proceedings, 11 § 1112

Chapter 13 proceedings, ante

Costs, 28 § 1930

Death, **BKR 1016**

Exemptions, 11 § 522

Involuntary proceedings, 11 § 303

Mental health, **BKR 1016**

Orders of court, 11 § 109

Petitions, **BKR 1013, 1014**

Postpetition transfers, 11 § 549

Reinstatement, 11 § 349

Support, 11 § 1112

Taxation, post

Voluntary, 11 § 109; **BKR 8001**

Disposable income, definitions, 11 § 1325

Disposition, **BKR 6007**

Dispute resolution, 28 § 651 et seq.

Disqualification, judges or justices, 28 § 455; **BKR 5004**

Disregard, Bankruptcy Law or Rule, fines, penalties and forfeitures, 18 § 156

Distribution, 11 § 508; **BKR 3021**

Abandoned or unclaimed property, 11 § 347

Chapter 7 proceedings, ante

Chapter 11 proceedings, 11 § 1143

Claims, subordination, 11 § 510

Examinations and examiners, **BKR 6002**

Foreign countries, 11 § 1521

Retirement and pensions, exemptions, 11 § 522

Trusts and trustees, compensation and salaries, 11 § 330

District of Columbia,

Judges or justices, appointments, 28 § 152

Taxation, automatic stay, postpetition, 11 § 362

Dividends,

Chapter 7 proceedings,

No dividends, notice, **BKR 2002**

Payment, **BKR 3009**

Payment, **BKR 3010**

Divorce,

Alimony, generally, ante

Automatic stay, 11 § 362

Discharge, 11 § 523

BANKRUPTCY—Cont'd

Divorce—Cont'd

Exemptions, 11 § 522

Settlement agreements, 11 § 541

Dockets and docketing, **BKR 5003**

Access, 11 § 107

Appeal and review, **BKR 8007**

Custodians, 28 § 156

Documents. Books and papers, generally, ante

Dollar amounts, adjustments, 11 § 104

Domestic violence, automatic stay, 11 § 362

Domicile and residence, 11 § 109

Chapter 11 proceedings, 28 § 1408

Chapter 13 proceedings, security interest, notice, **BKR 3002.1**

Definitions, 11 § 101

Exemptions, 11 § 522

Foreign countries, 11 § 1516

Trusts and trustees, 11 § 321

Dower and curtesy, 11 § 363

Driving while intoxicated or under the influence. Motor vehicles, post

Drugs and medicine, trafficking, chapter 7 proceedings, dismissal and nonsuit, 11 § 707

Dry edible beans, 11 § 557

Duties. Powers and duties, generally, post

Education,

Coverdell education savings accounts, 11 §§ 521, 541

Financial management training curriculum, generally, post

Judges or justices, 11 § 101 nt

Loans, exemptions, 11 § 523

Materials, exemptions, 11 § 522

Elections,

Chapter 7 proceedings, ante

Chapter 11 proceedings, ante

Discharge, fines and penalties, 11 § 523

Exemptions, 11 § 522

Fines and penalties, discharge, 11 § 523

Meetings, **BKR 2003**

Liquidation, 11 § 702

Nonrecourse loans, **BKR 3014**

Trusts and trustees, post

Electronic filing, **BKR 5005**

Notice, **BKR 9036**

Electronic summons, **BKR 7004**

Eligibility, trusts and trustees, 11 § 321

Embezzlement, 11 § 523; 18 § 153

Emergencies,

Appeal and review, motions, **BKR 8011**

Courts, special sessions, 28 § 152

Employee Retirement Income Security Program, Administrators, 11 §§ 521, 704

Contributions, 11 § 541

Priorities and preferences, 11 § 507

Priorities and preferences, contributions, 11 § 507

Employees. Officers and employees, generally, post

Employment. Labor and employment, generally, post

Entry, judgments and decrees, **BKR 7058, 8016, 9021**

Entry upon land, **BKR 7034**

Small businesses, 11 § 1116

Equity,

Automatic stay, 11 § 362

Equity security holders, generally, post

Equity security holders, 11 § 501 et seq.

Administrators, 11 § 341 nt

Allowances, 11 § 502

BANKRUPTCY—Cont'd
Equity security holders—Cont'd
  Classification, **BKR 3013**
  Committees,
    Compensation and salaries, professional persons, 11 §§ 328, 504
    Priorities and preferences, expenses and expenditures, 11 § 507
    Professional persons, compensation and salaries, 11 §§ 328, 504
  Core proceedings, 28 § 157
  Definitions, 11 § 101
  Evidence, filing, 11 § 501; **BKR 3003**
  Expenses and expenditures, priorities and preferences, 11 § 507
  Filing, evidence, 11 § 501; **BKR 3003**
  Lists, **BKR 1007**
  Meetings, 11 § 341
  Notice, **BKR 2002**
  Priorities and preferences, expenses and expenditures, 11 § 507
  Representatives and representation, statements, **BKR 2019**
  Statements, representatives and representation, **BKR 2019**
Error,
  Filing, **BKR 5005**
  Harmless error, **BKR 9005**
Evictions, automatic stay, 11 § 362
Evidence, **BKR 9017**
  Avoidance, preferences, 11 §§ 363, 547
  Chapter 7 proceedings, ante
  Chapter 13 proceedings, claims, postpetition, 11 § 1305
  Claims, ante
  Debtors in possession, **BKR 2011**
  Discharge, objections and exceptions, **BKR 4005**
  Exemptions, claims, **BKR 4003**
  Foreign countries, 11 § 1515 et seq.; **BKR 3002**
  Loans, 11 § 364
  Postpetition transfers, validation, **BKR 6001**
  Preferences, avoidance, 11 §§ 363, 547
  Presumptions, generally, post
  Priorities and preferences, avoidance, 11 §§ 363, 547
  Privileges and immunities, 11 § 344
  Sales, 11 § 363
  Self-incrimination, 11 § 344
  Transcripts, **BKR 5007**
  Trusts and trustees, post
Ex parte proceedings, **BKR 9003**
  Identity and identification, theft, 11 § 107
Examinations and examiners, 11 § 343; **BKR 2004, 2005**
  Administration, **BKR 6002**
  Administrative expenses, 11 § 503
  Administrators, 11 § 341 nt
  Appointments,
    Foreign countries, 11 § 1522
    Judges or justices, relatives, **BKR 5002**
    United States trustees, relatives, **BKR 5002**
  Attendance, **BKR 4002**
  Attorneys, **BKR 2017**
  Books and papers, 11 § 107
  Chapter 11 proceedings, ante
  Compensation and salaries, 11 § 330
    Administrative expenses, 11 § 503
    Interim compensation, 11 § 331
    Priorities and preferences, 11 § 507
    Records and recordation, **BKR 2013**
    Sharing, 11 § 504

BANKRUPTCY—Cont'd
Examinations and examiners—Cont'd
  Conflict of interest, **BKR 5002**
  Conversion, 11 § 348
  Foreign countries, post
  Grain, 11 § 557
  Interim compensation, 11 § 331
  Labor and employment, 11 § 327
  Meetings, **BKR 2003**
  Political subdivisions, tax returns, 11 § 505
  Priorities and preferences, compensation and salaries, 11 § 507
  Privileges and immunities, 11 § 344
  Records and recordation, compensation and salaries, **BKR 2013**
  Removal, 11 § 324
  Self-incrimination, 11 § 344
  Sharing, compensation and salaries, 11 § 504
  Tax returns, governmental units, 11 § 505
  Trusts and trustees, post
  United States trustees, post
Exceptions. Objections and exceptions, generally, post
Exclusive jurisdiction, 28 § 1334
Execution, **BKR 7069**
  Avoidance, statutory liens, 11 § 545
  Railroads, reorganization, 11 § 1172
  Reorganization, railroads, 11 § 1172
  Statutory liens, avoidance, 11 § 545
  Trusts and trustees, 11 § 544
Executory contracts. Contracts, generally, ante
Exemptions, 11 § 522; **BKR 4003**
  Alimony, 11 §§ 522, 523
  Animals, 11 § 522
  Annuities, 11 § 522
  Appliances, 11 § 522
  Automatic preservation, avoided transfers, 11 § 551
  Avoidance, ante
  Books and papers, 11 § 522
  Burial plot, ante
  Chapter 11 proceedings, securities, 11 § 1145
  Clothing, 11 § 522
  Colleges and universities, financial assistance, fraud, 11 § 522
  Computers, 11 § 522
  Cooperatives, 11 § 522
  Counseling services, 11 § 109
  Crime Victims Reparation Law, 11 § 522
  Crockery, 11 § 522
  Crops, 11 § 522
  Dependents, 11 § 522
  Disability, 11 § 522
  Dishes, 11 § 522
  Domicile and residence, 11 § 522
  Elections, 11 § 522
  Filing, 11 § 522
  Fraud, 11 §§ 522, 523; **BKR 4003**
  Furniture, 11 § 522
  Future earnings, losses, 11 § 522
  Handicapped persons, benefits, 11 § 522
  Health aids, 11 § 522
  Homesteads, post
  Household goods, 11 § 522
  Hydrocarbons, 11 § 541
  Illnesses, benefits, 11 § 522
  Insured depository institutions, 11 § 522
  Jewelry, 11 § 522

BANKRUPTCY—Cont'd
Exemptions—Cont'd
  Joint proceedings, post
  Joint property, 11 § 522
  Kitchenware, 11 § 522
  Liens and incumbrances, 11 § 522; BKR 4003
  Life insurance, 11 § 522
  Linens, 11 § 522
  Lists, 11 § 522
  Livestock, 11 § 522
  Maintenance, 11 § 522
  Medical devices, 11 § 522
  Motions, avoidance, BKR 4003
  Motor vehicles, 11 § 522
  New markets venture capital companies, 11 § 109
  Objections and exceptions, 11 § 522
  Pensions, 11 § 522
  Personal effects, 11 § 522
  Personal injuries, 11 § 522
  Personal property, 11 § 522
  Privacy protection, BKR 9037
  Profit-sharing plans, 11 § 522
  Public assistance, 11 § 522
  Real estate, post
  Redemption, 11 § 541
  Retirement and pensions, 11 § 522
  Schedules, forms, BKR Form 6
  Scholarships, fraud, 11 § 522
  Securities, reorganization, 11 § 1145
  Security interest, 11 § 552
  Separate maintenance, 11 § 522
  Sickness, benefits, 11 § 522
  Social security, 11 § 522
  Stock bonus plans, 11 § 522
  Support, 11 § 522
  Television and radio, 11 § 522
  Tools of trade, 11 § 522
  Toys, 11 § 522
  Trade tools, 11 § 522
  Transfers, BKR 4003
    Avoidance, 11 §§ 522, 551
  Turnovers, property, 11 § 542
  Unemployment compensation, 11 § 522
  Veterans, benefits, 11 § 522
  Video cassette recorders, 11 § 522
  Waiver, 11 § 522
  Wrongful death, 11 § 522; 28 § 157
Expenses and expenditures, 28 § 604
  Administration, ante
  Automatic stay, 11 § 362
  Buildings, 28 § 156
  Claims, 11 § 506
  Community property, 11 § 363
  Consumer debts, discharge, 11 § 523
  Creditors, 11 § 503
  Custodians, 11 § 543
  Filing, 11 § 503
  Grain, 11 § 557
  Involuntary proceedings, post
  Mileage. Traveling expenses, generally, post
  Priorities and preferences, 11 § 507
  Professional persons, 11 § 328
  References, 11 § 102
  Reimbursement, generally, post
  Schedules, 11 § 521
    Forms, BKR Form 6

BANKRUPTCY—Cont'd
Expenses and expenditures—Cont'd
  Taxation, 11 § 503
  Traveling expenses, generally, post
  Trusts and trustees, post
  United States trustees, 28 §§ 586, 588
Extensions, 11 § 108; BKR 9006
  Appeal and review, BKR 8002
  Judicial liens, 11 § 544
  Leases, 11 § 365
  Taxation, 11 § 505
Facilities. Buildings, generally, ante
Family Farmers Protection Act of 2002, 11 §§ 101 nt, 1201 et seq.
Family fisherman, definitions, 11 § 101
Family fisherman with regular annual income, definitions, 11 § 101
Farmers. Chapter 12 proceedings, generally, ante
Federal Bureau of Investigation, powers and duties, 18 § 158
Federal depository institutions regulatory agency, definitions, 11 § 101
Federal Rules of Civil Procedure, amendments, BKR 9032
Fees, 28 § 1930
  Administrators, 28 § 1930
  Attorneys, ante
  Chapter 7 proceedings, ante
  Chapter 11 proceedings, ante
  Claims, BKR 3001
  Copies, 11 § 521
  Counseling services, 11 § 111
  Debt relief agencies, 11 § 526
  Filing, post
  Financial management training curriculum, 11 § 111
  Fraud, 18 § 155
  Judicial Conference of the United States, 28 § 1930
  Petitions,
    Filing, BKR 1006
    Preparers, 11 § 110
  Priorities and preferences, 11 § 507
  Professional persons, 11 § 330
  References, 11 nt prec § 101
  Transcripts, BKR 5007
  Treasury of United States, post
  United States trustees, post
  Witnesses, post
Fiduciaries,
  Fraud, 11 § 523
  Trusts and trustees, generally, post
Filing,
  Access, 11 § 107
  Adversary proceedings, BKR 7005
  Appeal and review, BKR 8008
    Briefs, BKR 8009
  Assets, schedules, 11 § 521
  Attorneys, fees, statements, 11 § 329
  Books and papers, BKR 5005
  Briefs, appeal and review, BKR 8009
  Chapter 7 proceedings, ante
  Chapter 9 proceedings, ante
  Chapter 11 proceedings, ante
  Chapter 12 proceedings, ante
  Chapter 13 proceedings, ante
  Claims, ante
  Consumer debts, statements, 11 § 521
  Custodians, accounts and accounting, 11 § 543
  Delays, claims, 11 § 502

BANKRUPTCY—Cont'd
Filing—Cont'd
Error, **BKR 5005**
Evidence, claims, 11 § 501
Exemptions, 11 § 522
Extension of time, 11 § 108
Fees, 28 § 1930
Dismissal and nonsuit, **BKR 1017**
Installment payments, forms, **BKR Form 3A**
Foreign countries, post
Grain, 11 § 557
Liabilities, schedules, 11 § 521
Noncore proceedings, proposed findings, **BKR 9033**
Partnership, petitions, **BKR 1004**
Petitions, post
Pleading, 11 § 108
Postpetition transactions, avoidance, 11 § 549
Privacy protection, **BKR 9037**
Public access, 11 § 107
Reaffirmation agreements, **BKR 4008**
Records and recordation, **BKR 5005, 5007**
Redacted filings, **BKR 9037**
Removal, **BKR 9027**
Schedules, 11 § 521
Serial filers, 11 § 362
Signatures, 11 § 110
Stay of proceedings, termination, proposed actions, 11 § 1301
Taxation, returns, 11 § 346
Time, extension of time, 11 § 108
Trusts and trustees, bonds (officers and fiduciaries), 11 § 322
Voluntary proceedings, 11 §§ 301, 302
Financial management training curriculum, 11 § 111
Certification of completion, forms, **BKR Form 23**
Chapter 7 proceedings, 11 § 727
Chapter 13 proceedings, 11 § 1328
Forms, certification of completion, **BKR Form 23**
Reports, 11 § 111 nt
Statement of course completion, **BKR 1007**
Discharge, **BKR 4004**
Tests, 11 § 111 nt
Financial statements and reports, **BKR 1007**
Chapter 11 proceedings, substantial or controlling interest, **BKR 2015.3; BKR Form 26**
Filing, 11 § 521
Forms, **BKR Form 7**
Small businesses, 11 §§ 308, 1116
Findings, courts, **BKR 7052**
Fines and penalties, **BKR 9011**
Administration, expenses and expenditures, 11 § 503
Bribery and corruption, 18 § 152
Chapter 7 proceedings, ante
Chapter 13 proceedings, 11 § 1328
Concealment, assets, 18 § 152
Conflict of interest, 18 § 154
Debt relief agencies, 11 § 526
Discovery, **BKR 7037**
Elections, discharge, 11 § 523
Embezzlement, 18 § 153
Equity security holders, representatives and representation, statements, **BKR 2019**
Exemptions, 11 § 522
Fraud, generally, post
Governmental units, 11 § 523
Liens and incumbrances, 11 §§ 522, 550 et seq.

BANKRUPTCY—Cont'd
Fines and penalties—Cont'd
Life insurance, 11 § 542
Petitions, preparers, 11 § 110
Priorities and preferences, 11 § 507
Representatives and representation, statements, **BKR 2019**
Taxation, post
Trusts and trustees, personal liability, 11 § 322
Fish and game,
Commercial fishing,
Chapter 12 proceedings, generally, ante
Definitions, 11 § 101
Definitions, 11 § 101
Family fishermen. Chapter 12 proceedings, generally, ante
Processing facilities,
Sales, 11 § 546
Unsecured claims, priorities and preferences, 11 § 507
Flax and flaxseed, 11 § 557
Foreign banks in the United States, 11 § 109
Foreign countries, 11 § 1501 et seq.
Abstention, 11 § 305
Access, 11 § 1509 et seq.
Addresses, 11 § 1514
Administration, 11 § 1519 et seq.
Adversary proceedings, **BKR 1018**
Appearances, 11 § 306
Application of law, 11 § 1508
Appointments, 11 § 1515
Examinations and examiners, 11 § 1522
Assistance, 11 § 1507
Automatic stay, 11 § 1519 et seq.
Business and commerce,
Operating businesses, 11 §§ 1520, 1522
Venue, 28 § 1410
Certificates and certification, 11 § 1515 et seq.
Chapter 11 proceedings, venue, 28 § 1408
Claims, 11 § 1513; **BKR 3002**
Closings, 11 § 1517
Communications, 11 § 1525 et seq.
Concurrent proceedings, 11 § 1528 et seq.
Conflict of laws, 11 § 1503
Contests, petitions, **BKR 1011**
Cooperation, 11 § 1525 et seq.
Coordination, 11 § 1529 et seq.
Core proceedings, 28 § 157
Corporations, recognition petitions, ownership statements, **BKR 1011**
Definitions, 11 §§ 101, 1502
Cooperation, 11 § 1527
Distribution, 11 § 1521
Domicile and residence, 11 § 1516
Evidence, 11 § 1515 et seq.; **BKR 3002**
Examinations and examiners,
Appointments, 11 § 1522
Powers and duties, 11 § 1505
Supervision, 11 § 1526
Fees, filing, 28 § 1930
Filing,
Fees, 28 § 1930
Petitions, 11 §§ 1504, 1509 et seq.
Information, 11 § 1521
Injunctions, 11 §§ 1519, 1521
Intervention, 11 § 1524
Involuntary proceedings, 11 § 1511
Jurisdiction,
Concurrent proceedings, 11 § 1528 et seq.

BANKRUPTCY—Cont'd
Foreign countries—Cont'd
  Jurisdiction—Cont'd
    Representatives and representation, 11 §§ 306, 1510
    Master agreements, 11 § 561
    Modification, 11 §§ 1517, 1522
      Concurrent proceedings, 11 § 1529
    Motions, **BKR 1003**
      Pending actions, petitions, **BKR 1004.2**
    Multiple proceedings, 11 § 1530
    Notice, 11 § 1514 et seq.; **BKR 2002**
      Time, **BKR 2015**
    Operating businesses, 11 §§ 1520, 1522
    Orders of court, 11 § 1509 et seq.
    Parties, 11 § 1512
    Payment, 11 § 1532
    Pending actions, 11 § 1523
      Abstention, 11 § 305
      Concurrent proceedings, 11 § 1528 et seq.
      Petitions, **BKR 1004.2**
      Venue, 28 § 1410
    Petitions, **BKR 1003, 1004.2**
      Contests, **BKR 1011**
      Filing, 11 §§ 1504, 1509 et seq.
      Recognition petitions, 11 § 1515 et seq.; **BKR 1010 et seq.**
    Pleading, **BKR 1003**
    Presumptions, 11 § 1516
      Concurrent proceedings, 11 § 1531
    Public policy, 11 §§ 1501, 1506
    Recognition petitions, 11 § 1515 et seq.; **BKR 1010 et seq.**
    Representatives and representation, 11 § 1509 et seq.
    Responsive pleadings, **BKR 1011**
    Revocation or suspension, 11 § 1520 et seq.
    Security interest, 11 § 1520
    Status, 11 § 1518
    Stay of proceedings, 11 § 1519 et seq.
    Summons, **BKR 1003**
    Supervision,
      Examinations and examiners, 11 § 1526
      Trusts and trustees, 11 § 1526
    Taxation, 11 § 1513
    Termination, 11 §§ 1517, 1522
      Concurrent proceedings, 11 § 1529
    Time, notice, **BKR 2015**
    Transfers, 11 § 1520 et seq.
    Trusts and trustees,
      Additional relief, 11 § 1521
      Powers and duties, 11 § 1505
      Supervision, 11 § 1526
    United States trustees, ante
    Venue, 28 § 1410
      Chapter 11 proceedings, 28 § 1408
    Voluntary proceedings, 11 § 1511
    Witnesses, 11 § 1521
Foreign insurance, 11 § 109
Forfeitures, 11 § 363
Forgiveness, taxation, 11 § 346
Forma pauperis, frivolous actions, 11 § 523
Forms, **BKR 9009; BKR Form 1 et seq.**
  Adversary proceedings, ante
  Ballots, reorganization, plans and specifications, **BKR Form 14**
  Captions,
    Adversary proceedings, complaints, **BKR Form 16D**
    Full captions, **BKR Form 16A**

BANKRUPTCY—Cont'd
Forms—Cont'd
  Captions—Cont'd
    Short title, **BKR Form 16B**
  Certificates and certification, ante
  Chapter 7 proceedings, ante
  Chapter 11 proceedings, ante
  Chapter 12 proceedings, ante
  Chapter 13 proceedings, ante
  Claims, ante
  Current monthly income and means test calculation, **BKR Form 22**
  Declarations, **BKR Forms 2, 6**
  Discharge, ante
  Disclosure, ante
  Evidence, claims, **BKR Form 10**
  Fees, installments, **BKR Form 3A**
  Filing, fees, installments, **BKR Form 3A**
  Financial management training curriculum, certification of completion, **BKR Form 23**
  Financial statements and reports, **BKR Form 7**
  Full captions, **BKR Form 16A**
  General power of attorney, **BKR Form 11A**
  Income, post
  Individual debtors, intentions, statements, **BKR Form 8**
  Installments, fees, **BKR Form 3A**
  Involuntary proceedings, post
  Landlord and tenant, automatic stay, 11 § 362
  Lists, unsecured claims, **BKR Form 4**
  Mortgages, **BKR Form 10**
  Motions, post
  Nonattorney petition preparers,
    Declarations, **BKR Form 6**
    Notice, **BKR Form 19B**
  Nonattorney preparers, declarations, **BKR Form 19A**
  Notice, post
  Orders of court, post
  Petitions, post
  Power of attorney,
    General power of attorney, **BKR Form 11A**
    Special power of attorney, **BKR Form 11B**
  Proof of claim, **BKR Form 10**
  Reaffirmation agreements, post
  Schedules, post
  Short titles, captions, **BKR Form 16B**
  Small businesses, **BKR Form 25 et seq.**
  Special power of attorney, **BKR Form 11B**
  Statements, post
  Statistics, 28 § 159
  Unsecured claims, lists, **BKR Form 4**
  Voluntary proceedings, petitions, **BKR Form 1**
Forward contracts,
  Acceleration, 11 § 556
  Automatic stay, 11 §§ 362, 553
  Damages, 11 § 562
  Definitions, 11 § 101
  Liquidation, 11 § 556
  Margin payments, 11 § 546
  Termination, 11 § 556
  Unsecured claims, priorities and preferences, 11 §§ 753, 767
Fraud, 18 § 152
  Attorneys, fees, 18 § 155
  Avoidance, transfers, trusts and trustees, 11 § 546 et seq.
  Chapter 9 proceedings, transfers, 11 §§ 901, 926
  Chapter 11 proceedings, ante

BANKRUPTCY—Cont'd
Fraud—Cont'd
  Chapter 13 proceedings, ante
  Charities, 11 § 548
  Clerks of courts, notice, 28 § 586
  Concealment, 18 § 157
  Consumer debt, notice, 11 § 342
  Conveyances. Fraudulent conveyances, generally, post
  Debt relief agencies, 11 § 526
  Definitions, transfers, 11 § 548
  Discharge, 11 §§ 523, 1328
  Exemptions, 11 §§ 522, 523; **BKR 4003**
  Fees, 18 § 155
  Fiduciaries, 11 § 523
  Homesteads, exemptions, 11 § 522
  Insiders, transfers, 11 § 548
  Interception of wire, oral, or electronic communications, 18 § 2516
  Liability, transfers, avoidance, 11 § 550
  Lien creditors, transfers, avoidance, 11 § 551
  Limitation of actions, transfers, 11 § 546
  Master netting agreements, 11 § 548
  Partnership, transfers, avoidance, 11 § 548
  Petitions, preparers, 11 § 110
  Racketeer influenced and corrupt organizations, 18 § 1961
  References, schedules, 18 § 158
  Religious organizations and societies, 11 § 548
  Repurchase agreements, 11 § 548
  Schedules, 18 § 158
  Securities,
    Discharge, 11 § 523
    Transfers, 11 § 548
  Security interest, 11 § 552
  Statute of frauds, 11 § 558
  Tax returns, 11 §§ 505, 523
  Transfers,
    Avoidance, trusts and trustees, 11 § 546 et seq.
    Chapter 9 proceedings, 11 §§ 901, 926
    Definitions, 11 § 548
    Exemptions, 11 § 522
    Fraudulent conveyances, generally, post
    Insiders, 11 § 548
    Liability, avoidance, 11 § 550
    Lien creditors, avoidance, 11 § 551
    Limitation of actions, 11 § 546
    Master netting agreements, 11 § 548
    Partnership, avoidance, 11 § 548
    Repurchase agreements, 11 § 548
    Security interest, 11 § 552
    Trusts and trustees, avoidance, 11 § 546 et seq.
  Trusts and trustees, avoidance, 11 § 546 et seq.
  United States trustees, reports, 28 § 586
Frauds, statute of, 11 § 558
  Claims, **BKR 3001**
  Nonrecourse loans, elections, **BKR 3014**
Fraudulent conveyances, 11 § 548
  Discharge, 11 § 524
  Judges or justices, 28 § 157
  Limitation of actions, 11 § 546
Frivolous actions,
  Appeal and review, **BKR 8020**
  Forma pauperis, 11 § 523
  Review, **BKR 8020**
Fuel, taxation, 11 § 501
Furniture, exemptions, 11 § 522
Future earnings, exemptions, 11 § 522

BANKRUPTCY—Cont'd
General power of attorney, forms, **BKR Form 11A**
Gifts, 11 § 541
  National Bankruptcy Review Commission, 11 nt prec § 101
Good faith,
  Automatic stay, 11 § 362
  Avoidance, damages, 11 § 550
  Chapter 7 proceedings, ante
  Chapter 9 proceedings, ante
  Chapter 11 proceedings, ante
  Chapter 12 proceedings, confirmation of plan, 11 § 1225; **BKR 3015**
  Chapter 13 proceedings, ante
  Consumer debt, discharge, 11 § 523
  Discharge, 11 § 524
  Leases, 11 § 363
  Liens and incumbrances, 11 § 364
  Loans, 11 § 364
  Postpetition transactions, real estate, 11 § 549
  Priorities and preferences, 11 § 364
  Real estate, postpetition transactions, 11 § 549
  Sales, 11 § 363
  Small businesses, 11 § 362
  Transfers, 11 §§ 542, 548
  Turnovers, property, 11 § 542
Goods, wares and merchandise, 11 § 546
Grain, 11 § 557
  Claims, evidence, **BKR 3001**
  Priorities and preferences, unsecured claims, 11 § 507
  Storage, 11 § 546
  Unsecured claims, priorities and preferences, 11 § 507
Grand jury, investigations, 18 § 3057
Grants, discrimination, 11 § 525
Guaranty, claims, evidence, **BKR 3005**
Handicapped persons, **BKR 9028**
  Benefits, exemptions, 11 § 522
  Exemptions, benefits, 11 § 522
  Judges or justices, 28 § 152; **BKR 9028**
Hanging Law, chapter 13 proceedings, 11 § 1325
Hardship, reaffirmation agreements, 11 § 524
Harmless error, **BKR 9005**
Health aids, exemptions, 11 § 522
Health care businesses, **BKR 1021**
  Definitions, 11 § 101
  Destruction, patient records, **BKR 6011**
  Notice, patient records, **BKR 6011**
  Patient care ombudsman, generally, post
  Records and recordation, patients, **BKR 6011**
  Reports, patient records, destruction, **BKR 6011**
  Transfers, patients, **BKR 2015.2**
Health insurance, chapter 13 proceedings, 11 § 1329
Hearings, 28 § 157; **BKR 5001**
  Abandonment, 11 § 554; **BKR 6007**
  Abstention, 11 § 305
  Administration, expenses and expenditures, 11 § 503
  Appearance, 11 § 521
  Automatic stay, 11 §§ 362, 506
  Cash, collateral, 11 § 363
  Chapter 7 proceedings, ante
  Chapter 11 proceedings, confirmation of plans, 11 § 1128
  Chapter 13 proceedings, ante
  Clearing banks, liquidation, 11 § 784
  Compensation and salaries, 11 §§ 330, 331
  Consumer privacy ombudsman, 11 § 332
  Debt relief agencies, 11 § 526
  Discharge, 11 § 523

BANKRUPTCY—Cont'd

Hearings—Cont'd
 Financial statements and reports, **11 § 542**
 Interim compensation, **11 § 331**
 Involuntary proceedings, **11 § 303**
 Judges or justices, removal, **28 § 152**
 Leases, **BKR 6004**
 Liens and incumbrances, **11 § 364**
 Loans, **11 § 364**
 Objections and exceptions, claims, **11 § 502**
 Officers and employees, removal, **11 § 324**
 Panels, bankruptcy appellate panels, **28 § 158**
 Personally identifiable information, disposition, **11 §§ 332, 363**
 Plans and specifications, **11 § 506**
 Priorities and preferences, **11 § 363**
 Public utilities, deposits, **11 § 366**
 Reaffirmation agreements, **11 § 524**
 Rules of construction, **11 § 102**
 Sales, **BKR 6004**
 Subordination, claims, **11 § 510**
 Trusts and trustees, post
 Turnovers, custodians, **11 § 543**
Holidays, **BKR 5001**
Home Health Agencies, this index
Homestead associations, **11 § 109**
Homesteads, exemptions, **11 § 522**
Hospices, this index
Hospitals, this index
Hours of labor, offices, **BKR 5001**
Household goods, exemptions, **11 § 522**
Husband and wife,
 Alimony, generally, ante
 Avoidance, preferences, **11 § 547**
 Community property, **11 § 541**
  Discharge, **11 § 524**
  Sales, **11 § 363**
 Discharge, community property, **11 § 524**
 Divorce, generally, ante
 Exemptions, **11 § 522**
 Joint proceedings, **11 § 302**
 Maintenance. Alimony, generally, ante
 Preferences, avoidance, **11 § 547**
 Qualifications, **11 § 109**
 Sales, community property, **11 § 363**
 Settlement agreements, **11 § 541**
 Support. Alimony, generally, ante
Hydrocarbons, exemptions, **11 § 541**
Identity and identification,
 Notice, **11 § 342**
 Personally identifiable information, generally, post
 Petitions, preparers, **11 § 110**
 Social security, numbers and numbering, **BKR 4002**
 Theft, **11 § 107**
Illnesses, benefits, exemptions, **11 § 522**
Immunities. Privileges and immunities, generally, post
Improvements, transfers, avoidance, liability, **11 § 550**
Incidental property, definitions, **11 § 101**
Income,
 Current monthly income, generally, ante
 Documentation, **BKR 4002**
 Forms,
  Current monthly income and means test calculation, **BKR Form 22**
  Schedules, **BKR Form 6**
 Schedules, **11 § 521**

BANKRUPTCY—Cont'd

Income—Cont'd
 Schedules—Cont'd
  Forms, **BKR Form 6**
Income tax,
 Confidential or privileged information, returns, **BKR 4002**
 Copies, returns, **BKR 4002**
 Returns, copies, **BKR 4002**
Incompetency. Mental health, generally, post
Incumbrances. Liens and incumbrances, generally, post
Indemnity,
 Involuntary proceedings, **11 § 303**
 Liens and incumbrances, **BKR 6010**
Indenture trust and trustees,
 Compensation and salaries, priorities and preferences, **11 § 507**
 Definitions, **11 § 101**
 Examinations and examiners, **11 § 343**
 Expenses and expenditures, priorities and preferences, **11 § 507**
 Involuntary proceedings, **11 § 303**
 Proof of claim, **11 § 501**
Indexes, **BKR 5003**
Individual debtors. Chapter 13 proceedings, generally, ante
Indorsers, claims, evidence, **BKR 3005**
Industrial banks, **11 § 109**
Information,
 Financial information, documentation, **BKR 4002**
 Foreign countries, **11 § 1521**
 Personally identifiable information, generally, post
Inheritances, **11 § 541**
Injunctions, **BKR 7065**
 Automatic stay, generally, ante
 Chapter 9 proceedings, plans and specifications, **BKR 3017**
 Chapter 11 proceedings, plans and specifications, **BKR 3017**
 Debt relief agencies, **11 § 526**
 Discharge, **11 § 524**
 Foreign countries, **11 §§ 1519, 1521**
 Petitions, preparers, **11 § 110**
 Plans and specifications, notice, **BKR 2002**
 Removal of cases or causes, **BKR 9027**
 Supplemental injunctions, **11 § 524**
Injuries. Personal injuries, generally, post
Insiders,
 Avoidance, **11 § 547**
 Definitions, **11 § 101**
 Fraud, transfers, **11 § 548**
 Involuntary proceedings, **11 § 303**
 Services, claims, **11 § 502**
 Subordination, claims, **11 § 747**
Inspection and inspectors,
 Lists, **BKR 1007**
 Sentence and punishment, **18 § 154**
Installments,
 Filing, fees, forms, **BKR Form 3A**
 Forms, filing, fees, **BKR Form 3A**
 Joint proceedings, **28 § 1930**
 Petitions, fees, payment, **BKR 1006**
 Voluntary proceedings, **28 § 1930**
Instructions, commodities, customers, **11 § 765**
Instruments,
 Musical instruments, **11 § 522**
 Negotiable instruments, **11 § 362**
Insurance,
 Chapter 11 proceedings, ante
 Chapter 13 proceedings, personal property, **11 § 1326**

BANKRUPTCY—Cont'd
Insurance—Cont'd
  Life insurance, generally, post
  Liquidation, 11 § 109
  Small businesses, 11 § 1116
Insured depository institutions, service of process, **BKR 7004**
Intellectual property,
  Definitions, 11 § 101
  Licenses and permits, contracts, 11 § 365
Intent, fraudulent transfers, 11 § 548
Interception of wire, oral, or electronic communications, 18 § 2516
Interest, 11 § 541
  Automatic stay, 11 § 362
  Cash, collateral, 11 § 363
  Chapter 11 proceedings, railroads, 11 § 1165
  Claims, **BKR 3001**
  Deposits, 28 § 589a
  Grain, 11 § 557
  Hydrocarbons, 11 § 541
  Railroads, reorganization, 11 § 1165
  Reaffirmation agreements, 11 § 524
  Security interest, generally, post
  Taxation, 11 § 511
  Unmatured interest, 11 § 502
Interim compensation, 11 § 331
Interim trustees. Trusts and trustees, post
Interlocutory orders, 28 § 158
Intermediate Care Facilities, this index
Interpleader, **BKR 7022**
Interpreters, 11 § 1515
Interrogatories, **BKR 7033**
Interstate commerce, 28 § 157
Intervention, **BKR 2018, 7024**
  Foreign countries, 11 § 1524
Intoxication, driving while intoxicated, damages, discharge, 11 § 523
Inventories, **BKR 2015**
  Conversion, **BKR 1019**
  Preferences, 11 § 547
  Trusts and trustees, **BKR 4002**
Investigations, 18 § 3057
  United States attorneys, 18 § 3057
Investments, deposits, 11 § 345
Involuntary proceedings, 11 § 541; **BKR 1010 et seq.**
  Adversary proceedings, **BKR 1018**
  Attorneys, 11 § 504
  Automatic stay, 11 §§ 362, 553
  Avoidance, transfers, 11 § 303
  Contests, adversary proceedings, **BKR 1018**
  Corporations,
    Objections and exceptions, 11 § 303
    Ownership statements, **BKR 1011**
  Evidence, claims, 11 § 501
  Exemptions, transfers, 11 § 522
  Expenses and expenditures,
    Allowances, 11 § 503
    Priorities and preferences, 11 § 507
  Filing,
    Claims, 11 § 501
    Petitions, 11 § 303
  Foreign countries, 11 § 1511
  Foreign representatives, 11 § 306
  Forms, petitions, **BKR Form 5**
  Joinder, 11 § 303; **BKR 1003**
  Lists, **BKR 1007**

BANKRUPTCY—Cont'd
Involuntary proceedings—Cont'd
  Orders of court,
    Claims, priorities and preferences, 11 § 507
    Petitions, 11 § 303
    Priorities and preferences, claims, 11 § 507
  Partnership, petitions, **BKR 1004**
  Petitions, **BKR 1003, 1010 et seq.**
    Contests, **BKR 1013**
    Filing, 11 § 303
    Forms, **BKR Form 5**
  Priorities and preferences, 11 § 507
  Schedules, **BKR 1007**
  Securities, automatic stay, 11 § 362
  Time, schedules, **BKR 1007**
  Transfers,
    Avoidance, 11 § 303
    Claims, **BKR 1003**
    Exemptions, 11 § 522
    Validation, 11 § 549
  Unsecured claims, discharge, 11 § 523
  Validation, transfers, 11 § 549
Irreparable injuries, automatic stay, 11 § 363
Issues, statements, appeal and review, **BKR 8006**
Jewelry,
  Exemptions, 11 § 522
  Liens and incumbrances, exemptions, 11 § 522
Joinder,
  Claims, **BKR 7018**
  Involuntary proceedings, 11 § 303; **BKR 1003**
  Liens and incumbrances, indemnity, **BKR 6010**
  Parties, **BKR 7019 et seq.**
Joint administration, **BKR 2009**
  Consolidations and mergers, **BKR 1015**
Joint appellate panels, 28 § 158
Joint proceedings, 11 §§ 302, 541
  Automatic stay, 11 § 362
    Securities, exemptions, 11 § 362
    Setoff and counterclaim, 11 § 553
  Exemptions, 11 § 522
    Automatic stay, securities, 11 § 362
    Fees, filing, 28 § 1930
    Filing, fees, 28 § 1930
    Securities, automatic stay, 11 § 362
  Fees, filing, exemptions, 28 § 1930
  Filing, fees, exemptions, 28 § 1930
  Securities, exemptions, automatic stay, 11 § 362
  Setoff and counterclaim, automatic stay, 11 § 553
Joint property, exemptions, 11 § 522
Joint tenants, 11 § 363
Judges or justices, 28 § 151 et seq.
  Adjacent districts, 28 § 152
  Annual leave, 28 § 153
  Appeal and review, 28 § 158
  Appellate panels, 28 § 158
  Appointments, 11 § 105; 28 § 152
  Chief Judge, 28 § 154
    Court of appeals, 28 § 152
  Compensation and salaries, 28 §§ 153, 604
    Relatives, disqualification, **BKR 5004**
    Retired judges, 28 § 604
      Recall, 28 § 155
  Conflict of interest, 28 § 153
    Disqualification, **BKR 5004**
  Core proceedings, 28 § 157
  Disability, **BKR 9028**

BANKRUPTCY—Cont'd
Judges or justices—Cont'd
Discipline, 28 § 372
Disqualification, 28 § 455; BKR 5004
Education, 11 § 101 nt
Expenses and expenditures, 28 § 604
Fraudulent conveyances, 28 § 157
Handicapped persons, BKR 9028
Law clerks, 28 § 156
Leave of absence, 28 § 153
Meetings, 11 § 341
Mental health, 28 § 152
Oaths and affirmations, 28 § 153
Official duty station, 28 § 152
Practice of law, 28 § 153
Puerto Rico, appointments, 28 § 152
Recall, 28 § 155
References, generally, post
Relatives, compensation and salaries, disqualification, BKR 5004
Removal from office, 28 § 372
Grounds, 28 § 152
Reports, 18 § 3057
Retirement and pensions, recall, 28 § 155
Secretaries, 28 § 156
Sick leave, 28 § 153
Staff, 28 § 156
Terms of office, 28 § 152
Territories, 28 § 152
Transfers, 28 § 155
Vacancies in office, 28 § 152
Judgments and decrees, 28 § 157; BKR 7054 et seq.
Amendments, BKR 9023
Automatic stay, 11 § 362
Chapter 11 proceedings, BKR 3022
Consumer debts, discharge, 11 § 523
Discharge, 11 § 524
Dismissal and nonsuit, 11 § 349
Entry, BKR 7058, 8016, 9021
Involuntary proceedings, dismissal and nonsuit, 11 § 303
Motions,
Amendments, time, BKR 9023
Time, BKR 9015
Notice, BKR 8016, 9022
Offers, BKR 7068
Powers and duties, 11 § 105
Records and recordation, BKR 5003
Relief, BKR 9024
Summary judgment, BKR 7056
Time, amendments, BKR 9023
Judicial Conference of the United States, 28 § 152 et seq.
Adjustments, 11 § 104
Assessments, reports, 28 § 152
Audits and auditors, 28 § 586 nt
Compensation and salaries, retired judges, 28 § 155
Fees, 28 § 1930
Filing, fees, 28 § 1930
Merger and consolidation, 28 § 156
Payment, 28 § 153
Reports, assessments, 28 § 152
Retired judges, compensation and salaries, 28 § 155
Judicial Council,
Appellate panels, 28 § 158
Appointments, 28 § 156
Joint appellate panels, 28 § 158
Recall, 28 § 155

BANKRUPTCY—Cont'd
Judicial Council—Cont'd
Removal, judges or justices, 28 §§ 152, 372
Reports, appellate panels, 28 § 158
Judicial districts,
Trusts and trustees, 11 § 321
United States trustees, appointments, 28 § 581
Judicial liens. Liens and incumbrances, post
Judicial review. Appeal and review, generally, ante
Jurisdiction, 28 § 1334; BKR 9030
Abstention, 28 § 1334
Appeal and review, 28 § 158
Chapter 9 proceedings, ante
Chapter 11 proceedings, 28 § 1334
Debt relief agencies, 11 § 526
Dismissal and nonsuit, 28 § 1930
Foreign countries, ante
Grain, 11 § 557
Jury, 28 § 157
Sureties and suretyship, BKR 9025
Jury, 28 § 157; BKR 9015
Contempt, BKR 9020
Personal injuries, 28 § 1411
Wrongful death, 28 § 1411
Justices. Judges or justices, generally, ante
Kitchenware, exemptions, 11 § 522
Labor and employment,
Applications, BKR 6003
Attorneys, 11 § 327 et seq.
Contracts, termination, damages, 11 § 502
Discrimination, 11 § 525
Priorities and preferences, taxation, 11 § 507
Professional personnel, generally, post
Taxation, priorities and preferences, 11 § 507
Unemployment compensation, exemptions, 11 § 522
Labor organizations, intervention, BKR 2018
Landlord and tenant,
Assignments, deposits, 11 § 365
Automatic stay, 11 § 362
Possession, certificates and certification, 11 § 362
Larceny,
Discharge, exemptions, 11 § 523
Fiduciaries, 11 § 523
Identity and identification, 11 § 107
Law clerks, 28 § 156
Leases, 11 § 361 et seq.; BKR 6004, 6006
Administration, expenses and expenditures, 11 § 503
Assignments, 11 § 365
Automatic stay, 11 § 362; BKR 6004, 6006
Personal property, 11 § 365
Chapter 9 proceedings, ante
Chapter 13 proceedings, ante
Consumer privacy ombudsman, 11 § 332
Damages, termination, 11 § 502
Default, 11 § 365
Definitions, 11 § 365
Good faith, 11 § 363
Motions, BKR 4001, 6003
Personally identifiable information, BKR 6004
Municipalities, 11 § 929
Nonresidential real property, 11 § 541
Automatic stay, 11 § 362
Notice, 11 § 363; BKR 2002, 4001, 6004 et seq.
Personal property, 11 § 365
Orders of court, 28 § 157
Personal property, 11 § 365

BANKRUPTCY—Cont'd
Leases—Cont'd
Personal property—Cont'd
Chapter 13 proceedings, payment, **11 § 1326**
Personally identifiable information, **11 §§ 332, 363; BKR 6004**
Proof of claim, **11 § 501**
Railroads, **11 § 1169**
Rejection, **11 §§ 365, 502**
Sales, **11 § 363**
Schedules, forms, **BKR Form 6**
Setoff and counterclaim, **11 § 553**
Termination, damages, **11 § 502**
Trusts and trustees, post
Turnovers, **11 § 542**
Leave of absence,
Judges or justices, **28 § 153**
Law clerks, **28 § 156**
Leave of court, appeal and review, **BKR 8003**
Letters of credit, **11 § 101**
Leverage transactions, stay of proceedings, **11 § 553**
Liability. Damages, generally, ante
Licenses and permits, discrimination, **11 § 525**
Liens and incumbrances, **11 § 361 et seq.**
Automatic stay, **11 § 362**
Avoidance, ante
Bona fide purchasers, **11 § 545**
Chapter 7 proceedings, ante
Chapter 13 proceedings, ante
Definitions, **11 § 101**
Exemptions, **11 § 522; BKR 4003**
Fines, penalties and forfeitures, **11 §§ 522, 550 et seq.**
Good faith, **11 § 364**
Goods, wares and merchandise, **11 § 546**
Household goods, **11 § 522**
Indemnity, **BKR 6010**
Judicial liens, **11 § 522**
Avoidance, trusts and trustees, **11 §§ 544, 547**
Definitions, **11 § 101**
Trusts and trustees, avoidance, **11 §§ 544, 547**
Notice, **11 § 364**
Taxation, **11 § 522**
Operating businesses, **11 § 364**
Priorities and preferences, **11 §§ 364, 507**
Reaffirmation agreements, **11 § 524**
Redemption, **BKR 6008**
Replacement liens, **11 § 361**
Sales, **11 § 363; BKR 6004**
Status, **11 § 506**
Statutory liens, **11 § 545 et seq.**
Automatic preservation, **11 § 551**
Avoidance, **11 § 545 et seq.**
Definitions, **11 § 101**
Exemptions, **11 § 522**
Postpetition transactions, **11 § 552**
Subordination, **11 § 510**
Taxation, post
Trusts and trustees, post
Validation, **28 § 157**
Valuation, **11 § 363; BKR 3012**
Void liens, **11 §§ 506, 541, 551**
Life insurance, **11 § 541**
Exemptions, payment, **11 § 522**
Good faith, transfers, **11 § 542**
Payment, exemptions, **11 § 522**
Transfers, good faith, **11 § 542**

BANKRUPTCY—Cont'd
Limitation of actions,
Avoidance, transfers, **11 §§ 546, 550**
Bonds (officers and fiduciaries), **11 § 322**
Chapter 13 proceedings, security interest, domicile and residence, notice, **BKR 3002.1**
Defenses, **11 § 558**
Fraudulent conveyances, **11 § 546**
Postpetition, **11 § 549**
Preferences, **11 § 546**
Priorities and preferences, **11 § 546**
Revocation or suspension, **11 § 108**
Taxation, **11 § 346**
Transfers, avoidance, **11 §§ 546, 550**
Limited appearance, foreign representatives, **11 § 306**
Linens, exemptions, **11 § 522**
Liquidations. Chapter 7 proceedings, generally, ante
Lists, **BKR 1007**
Abandonment, disposition, **BKR 3011**
Amendments, **BKR 1009**
Chapter 9 proceedings, ante
Chapter 11 proceedings, ante
Conversion, **BKR 1019**
Counseling services, **11 § 111**
Discharge, exemptions, **11 § 523**
Exemptions, discharge, **11 § 523**
Filing, **11 § 521**
Taxation, **11 § 505**
Unsecured claims, forms, **BKR Form 4**
Verification, **BKR 1008**
Livestock and livestock products. Animals, generally, ante
Loans,
Chapter 9 proceedings, nonrecourse loans, **BKR 3014**
Chapter 11 proceedings, nonrecourse loans, **BKR 3014**
Discharge, nonprofit institutions, **11 § 523**
Education, exemptions, **11 § 523**
Evidence, **11 § 364**
Good faith, **11 § 364**
Nonprofit institutions, discharge, **11 § 523**
Notice, **BKR 4001**
Predatory loans, **11 § 363**
Securities, **11 § 364**
Usury, **11 § 558**
Local rules, **BKR 8018, 9029**
Location,
Business and commerce, **11 § 109**
Claims, **BKR 3002**
Courts, **28 § 152**
Examinations and examiners, **BKR 2004**
Meetings, **BKR 2003**
Losses,
Chapter 11 proceedings, ante
Evidence, **11 § 108**
Taxation, **11 § 346**
Luxury goods or services, definitions, **11 § 523**
Mail and mailing,
Governmental units, addresses, **BKR 5003**
Notice, **BKR 2002**
Process, **BKR 7004, 9006**
Service of process, **BKR 7004, 9006**
Trusts and trustees, health care businesses, records and recordation, **11 § 351**
Maintenance. Alimony, generally, ante
Managers and management,
Actions and proceedings, **28 § 959**
Chapter 11 proceedings, ante

BANKRUPTCY—Cont'd
Managers and management—Cont'd
  Financial management training curriculum, generally, ante
Margins,
  Commodity brokers,
    Avoidance, transfers, 11 § 546
    Fraudulent transfers, 11 § 548
  Definitions, 11 § 101
  Repurchase agreements,
    Fraudulent transfers, 11 § 548
    Set-off and counterclaim, 11 §§ 362, 546
  Securities,
    Avoidance, transfers, 11 § 546
    Fraudulent transfers, 11 § 548
  Shares and shareholders, post
Mask work, definitions, 11 § 101
Master agreements,
  Acceleration, 11 § 561
  Automatic stay, 11 § 362
  Avoidance, 11 § 546
  Commodities, 11 § 761
  Damages, 11 § 562
  Definitions, 11 §§ 101, 561
  Foreign countries, 11 § 561
  Fraud, transfers, 11 § 548
  Liquidation, 11 § 561
  Offsets, 11 § 561
  Termination, 11 § 561
  Unsecured claims, priorities and preferences, 11 §§ 753, 767
Masters, **BKR 9031**
Means test, chapter 13 proceedings, 11 § 1325
Median family income, definitions, 11 § 101
Medical devices, exemptions, 11 § 522
Medicare, automatic stay, 11 § 362
Meetings, 11 § 341; **BKR 2003**
  Chapter 7 proceedings, ante
  Chapter 11 proceedings, ante
  Chapter 12 proceedings, **BKR 2003; BKR Form 9**
  Chapter 13 proceedings, ante
  Examinations and examiners, 11 § 343
  Small businesses, 11 § 1116
Mental health, **BKR 1016**
  Counseling services, 11 § 109
  Examinations and examiners, **BKR 7035**
  Judges or justices, 28 § 152
  Petitions, **BKR 1004.1**
  Process, **BKR 1007**
Mergers.   Consolidations and mergers, generally, ante
Mileage.   Traveling expenses, generally, post
Minors.   Children and minors, generally, ante
Misjoinder, parties, **BKR 7021**
Misrepresentation.   Fraud, generally, ante
Modification,
  Chapter 9 proceedings, plans and specifications, 11 § 942; **BKR 3019**
  Chapter 11 proceedings, plans and specifications, 11 § 1127; **BKR 3019**
  Chapter 12 proceedings, plans and specifications, **BKR 3015**
  Chapter 13 proceedings, ante
  Foreign countries, ante
  Grain, 11 § 557
Money, **BKR 4001**
  Adjustments, 11 § 104
  Administration, 11 § 363
  Allowances, 11 § 502

BANKRUPTCY—Cont'd
Money—Cont'd
  Definitions, 11 § 363
  Deposits, generally, ante
  Discharge, fraud, 11 § 523
  Fraud, discharge, 11 § 523
  Investments, 11 § 345
  Orders of court, 28 § 157
  Satisfaction, 11 § 363
  Set-off and counterclaim, 11 § 362
  Trusts and trustees, 11 § 363
  Unsecured claims, 11 § 507
Money orders, 11 § 541
Monopolies and combinations, notice, 11 § 363
Mortgages, 11 § 541
  Forms, **BKR Form 10**
  Secretary of HUD, 11 § 362
Motions, **BKR 9013**
  Abandonment, **BKR 6007**
  Abstention, **BKR 5011**
  Appeal and review, ante
  Attorneys, fees, examinations and examiners, **BKR 2017**
  Chapter 7 proceedings, ante
  Chapter 11 proceedings, judgments and decrees, **BKR 3022**
  Chapter 13 proceedings, ante
  Claims,
    Classification, **BKR 3013**
    Liens and incumbrances, valuation, **BKR 3012**
  Committees, appointments, appeal and review, **BKR 2007**
  Core proceedings, 28 § 157
  Debt relief agencies, fines and penalties, 11 § 526
  Dismissal and nonsuit, **BKR 1017**
  Equity security holders, representatives and representation, disclosure, statements, **BKR 2019**
  Examinations and examiners, **BKR 2005**
  Exemptions, avoidance, **BKR 4003**
  Filing, **BKR 5005**
  Foreign countries, ante
  Forms, 28 § 2075
    Notice, **BKR Form 20A**
  Grain, 11 § 557
  Health care businesses, **BKR 1021**
  Involuntary proceedings, dismissal and nonsuit, 11 § 303
  Judgments and decrees, ante
  Leases, ante
  Leave of court, appeal and review, **BKR 8003**
  Lists, impounding, **BKR 1007**
  New trial, time, **BKR 9015, 9023**
  Notice, forms, **BKR Form 20A**
  Patient care ombudsman, **BKR 2007.2**
  Petitions, preparers, fines and penalties, 11 § 110
  Reaffirmation agreements, post
  Rehearings, **BKR 8015**
  Reopening, **BKR 5010**
  Representatives and representation, disclosure, statements, **BKR 2019**
  Sales, post
  Signatures, **BKR 9011**
  State laws, claims, abstention, 28 § 1334
  Time, **BKR 9006**
    Judgments and decrees, **BKR 9015**
      Amendments, **BKR 9023**
    New trial, **BKR 9015, 9023**
  Trade secrets, 11 § 107
  Trial, new trial, time, **BKR 9015, 9023**
  United States trustees, **BKR 9034**

BANKRUPTCY—Cont'd
Motions—Cont'd
Venue, change of venue, **BKR 1014**
Withdrawal, 28 § 157; **BKR 5011**
Motor vehicles,
Claims, driving while intoxicated or under the influence, priorities and preferences, **11 § 507**
Damages, driving while intoxicated or under the influence, discharge, **11 § 523**
Driving while intoxicated or under the influence,
Claims, priorities and preferences, **11 § 507**
Damages, discharge, **11 § 523**
Discharge, damages, **11 § 523**
Priorities and preferences, claims, **11 § 507**
Exemptions, **11 § 522**
Multiple foreign proceedings, **11 § 1530**
Municipal corporations. Chapter 9 proceedings, generally, ante
Musical instruments, **11 § 522**
Names, **11 § 109 et seq.**
Petitions, **BKR 1005**
National Bankruptcy Review Commission, **11 nt prec § 101**
National Guard, chapter 7 proceedings, **11 § 707**
National securities association, **11 § 555**
Repurchase agreements, **11 § 559**
Negotiable instruments,
Automatic stay, **11 § 362**
Family farmers, dishonor, notice, **11 § 1201**
Individual debtors, dishonor, notice, **11 § 1301**
Municipalities, recourse, **11 § 927**
Net equity,
Commodity brokers, **11 § 761**
Stockbrokers, **11 § 741**
Netting agreements. Master agreements, generally, ante
New markets venture capital companies, exemptions, **11 § 109**
New trial. Trial, post
Newspapers, municipal debt adjustment, notice, **11 § 923**
No asset notice, chapter 7 proceedings, **BKR 2002**
Nonattorney preparers. Petitions, post
Noncore proceedings,
Abstention, 28 § 157
Proposed findings, **BKR 9033**
Nonjoinder, parties, **BKR 7021**
Nonparties, process, **BKR 7071**
Nonprofit corporations, involuntary proceedings, **11 § 303**
Nonprofit organizations or associations,
Counseling services, generally, ante
Discharge, loans, **11 § 523**
Loans, discharge, **11 § 523**
Nonrecourse loans, elections, **BKR 3014**
Nonresidential real property, leases,
Automatic stay, **11 § 362**
Termination, **11 § 541**
Nonsuit. Dismissal and nonsuit, generally, ante
North Carolina, **BKR 9035**
Notice, **BKR 2002, 9007**
Abandonment, 11 § 554; **BKR 6007**
Abstention, 11 § 305
Addresses, 11 § 342; **BKR 2002**
Administration, expenses and expenditures, **11 § 503**
Payment, **BKR 1019**
Appeal and review, ante
Appearances, **BKR 9010**
Application of law, **11 § 102**
Automatic stay, 11 § 362; **BKR 4001**
Avoidance, transfers, **11 § 549**

BANKRUPTCY—Cont'd
Notice—Cont'd
Chapter 7 proceedings, ante
Chapter 9 proceedings, ante
Chapter 11 proceedings, ante
Chapter 12 proceedings, ante
Chapter 13 proceedings, ante
Claims, ante
Codebtors, claims, **11 § 509**
Commodities, ante
Community claim holders, orders of court, **11 § 342**
Compensation and salaries, **11 § 330**
Compromise and settlement, **BKR 9019**
Consumer debt, ante
Consumer privacy ombudsman, **11 § 332**
Contempt, **BKR 9020**
Contracts, **BKR 6006**
Counseling services, **11 §§ 111, 342**
Courts, emergencies, special sessions, 28 § 152
Debt relief agencies, **11 § 526 et seq.**
Discharge, **11 § 523**
Revocation or suspension, **BKR 4006**
Disclosure, orders of court, **11 § 542**
Disposition, **BKR 6007**
Electronic filing, **BKR 9036**
Financial management training curriculum, **11 § 111**
Foreign countries, ante
Forms,
Appeal and review, **BKR Form 17**
Chapter 13 proceedings, **BKR Form 9**
Motions, **BKR Form 20A**
Nonattorney petition preparers, **BKR Form 19B**
Objections and exceptions, **BKR Forms 20A, 20B**
Grain, **11 § 557**
Health care businesses, patient records, **BKR 6011**
Identity and identification, numbers and numbering, **11 § 342**
Interim compensation, **11 § 331**
Interim trustees, involuntary proceedings, appointments, **11 § 303**
Intervention, **BKR 2018**
Involuntary proceedings, dismissal and nonsuit, **11 § 303**
Judgments and decrees, ante
Leases, ante
Liens and incumbrances, **11 § 364**
Taxation, **11 § 522**
Loans, **BKR 4001**
Money, collateral, **BKR 4001**
Monopolies and combinations, **11 § 363**
Negotiable instruments, dishonor, **11 § 362**
Nonattorney petition preparers, **BKR Form 19B**
Objections and exceptions, forms, **BKR Forms 20A, 20B**
Orders of court,
Community claim holders, **11 § 342**
Disclosure, **11 § 542**
Parties, post
Patient care ombudsman, **BKR 2007.2**
Reports, **BKR 2015.1**
Perfection, security interest, avoidance, **11 § 546**
Personally identifiable information, disposition, **11 §§ 332, 363**
Petitions, preparers, **11 § 110**
Public utilities, deposits, **11 § 366**
Publication, **BKR 9008**
Reaffirmation agreements, **11 § 524**

BANKRUPTCY—Cont'd
Notice—Cont'd
  Removal from office,
    Examinations and examiners, **11 § 324**
    Trusts and trustees, **11 § 324**
  Removal of cases or causes, **BKR 9027**
  Sales, **11 § 363; BKR 4001, 6004**
  Security interest, postpetition transactions, **11 § 552**
  Statements, amendments, **BKR 1009**
  Subordination, **11 § 510**
  Taxation, post
  Time, extension of time, **11 § 108**
  Transfers, avoidance, **11 § 549**
  Trusts and trustees, post
  Turnovers, **11 §§ 542, 543**
  United States trustees, post
Numbers and numbering,
  Petitions, post
  Social security, post
Nursing Homes, this index
Oaths and affirmations, **BKR 9012**
  Administrators, **11 § 341 nt**
  Chapter 7 proceedings, ante
  Examinations and examiners, **11 § 343**
  Fraud, **18 § 152**
    Liquidations, **11 § 727**
  Judges or justices, **28 § 153**
  Liquidations, fraud, **11 § 727**
  Meetings, **BKR 2003**
  Petition preparers, **11 § 110**
  United States trustees, **11 § 343**
Oats, **11 § 557**
Objections and exceptions, **11 § 541; BKR 7012, 9026**
  Abandonment, **BKR 6007**
  Automatic stay, **11 § 362**
  Chapter 7 proceedings, ante
  Chapter 9 proceedings, ante
  Chapter 11 proceedings, ante
  Chapter 12 proceedings, ante
  Chapter 13 proceedings, ante
  Claims, ante
  Closings, **BKR 5009**
  Conflict of interest, **11 § 327**
  Discharge, **11 § 523**
    Evidence, **BKR 4005**
  Executory contracts, **11 § 365**
  Exemptions, **11 § 522**
  Filing, **BKR 5005**
  Forms, notice, **BKR Forms 20A, 20B**
  Leases, **BKR 6004**
  Motions, **BKR 4001**
  Noncore proceedings, proposed findings, **BKR 9033**
  Notice, forms, **BKR Forms 20A, 20B**
  Petitions, **BKR 1011**
  Professional persons, conflict of interest, **11 § 327**
  Sales, **BKR 6004**
  Small businesses, statements, reorganization, **BKR 1020**
  Stay of proceedings, **11 § 1301**
  United States trustees, **BKR 9034**
Offenses. Crimes and offenses, generally, ante
Offers, judgments and decrees, **BKR 7068**
Officers and employees, **11 §§ 105, 321 et seq.**
  Attorneys, generally, ante
  Contracts, termination, **11 § 502**
  Custodians, generally, ante
  Discrimination, **11 § 525**

BANKRUPTCY—Cont'd
Officers and employees—Cont'd
  Examinations and examiners, generally, ante
  Paraprofessionals, **11 §§ 330, 507**
  Priorities and preferences, compensation and salaries, **11 § 507**
  Professional personnel, generally, post
  Termination, contracts, **11 § 502**
  Trusts and trustees, generally, post
  United States trustees, generally, post
Offices, **BKR 5001**
Official bankruptcy forms. Forms, generally, ante
Official stations, courts, judges or justices, **28 § 152**
Offsets, master agreements, **11 § 561**
Ombudsman,
  Consumer privacy ombudsman, generally, ante
  Patient care ombudsman, generally, post
Omnibus objections, claims, **BKR 3007**
Open end credit plans,
  Claims, **BKR 3001**
  Discharge, **11 § 523**
Open end or revolving consumer credit agreements, claims, **BKR 3001**
Operating businesses. Business and commerce, ante
Options,
  Automatic stay, **11 § 553**
  Life insurance, **11 § 542**
Oral arguments, appeal and review, **BKR 8012**
Oral examinations, depositions, **BKR 7030**
Orders of court, **28 § 157**
  Adversary proceedings, **BKR 1018**
  Appraisal and appraisers, **BKR 6005**
  Attorneys,
    Excessive compensation, **11 § 329**
    Interim compensation, **11 § 331**
  Auctions and auctioneers, **BKR 6005**
  Chambers, **BKR 5001**
  Chapter 9 proceedings, ante
  Chapter 11 proceedings, ante
  Chapter 13 proceedings, ante
  Claims, ante
  Consolidations and mergers, **BKR 1015**
  Consumer debts, discharge, **11 § 523**
  Consumer privacy ombudsman, **11 § 332**
  Conversion, **11 § 348**
  Default, **BKR 1013**
  Discharge, **11 § 523**
  Disclosure, forms, **BKR Form 12 et seq.**
  Dismissal and nonsuit, **11 § 349**
  Examinations and examiners, **BKR 2004**
    Interim compensation, **11 § 331**
  Foreign countries, **11 § 1509 et seq.**
  Forms, disclosure, **BKR Form 12 et seq.**
  Grain, **11 § 557**
  Involuntary proceedings, ante
  Issuance, **11 § 105**
  Joint administration, husband and wife, exemptions, **11 § 522**
  Joint proceedings, **11 § 302**
  Jury, **28 § 1411**
  Notice, **11 § 542; BKR 2002, 9022**
  Obedience, **11 § 109**
  Open end credit plans, **11 § 523**
  Patient care ombudsman, **11 § 333**
  Petitions, fees, payment, **BKR 1006**
  Professional personnel, labor and employment, **BKR 2014**

BANKRUPTCY—Cont'd
Orders of court—Cont'd
 Professional persons, interim compensation, 11 § 331
 Protective orders, generally, post
 Public utilities, 11 § 366
 Purchases and purchasing, 11 § 363
 Records and recordation, 11 § 542; **BKR 5003**
 Relief, **BKR 9024**
 Repurchase agreements, 11 § 559
 Sales, 11 § 363; 28 § 157
 Security interest, 11 § 552
 Sessions, 28 § 151
 Shares and shareholders, post
 Taxation, 11 § 346
 Time, extension of time, 11 § 108
 Torts, 28 § 157
 Trusts and trustees, interim compensation, 11 § 331
 Vacating or setting aside, **BKR 1018**
 Voluntary proceedings, 11 § 301
 Wiretapping, 18 § 2516
Ordinary course of business, payment, priorities and preferences, 11 § 547
Original jurisdiction, 28 § 1334
Panel trustees, 28 § 586
Panels. Bankruptcy appellate panels, generally, ante
Papers. Books and papers, generally, ante
Paraprofessionals, labor and employment, 11 §§ 330, 507
Parties,
 Abandonment, 11 § 554
 Automatic stay, 11 § 362
 Avoidance, preferences, 11 § 547
 Books and papers, 11 § 107
 Chapter 7 proceedings, post
 Chapter 11 proceedings, 11 § 1109
 Chapter 12 proceedings, 11 § 1224
 Chapter 13 proceedings, ante
 Discharge, 11 § 1328
 Exemptions, lists, 11 § 522
 Foreign countries, 11 § 1512
 Involuntary proceedings, 11 § 303
 Lists, exemptions, 11 § 522
 Notice, **BKR 2002**
  Compensation and salaries, 11 § 330
 Preferences, avoidance, 11 § 547
 Public utilities, deposits, 11 § 366
 Real party in interest, **BKR 7017**
 Substitution, **BKR 7025**
Partnership,
 Chapter 7 proceedings, ante
 Chapter 11 proceedings, venue, 28 § 1408
 Claims, general partner, 11 § 541
 Compensation and salaries, 11 § 504
 Contests, petitions, **BKR 1011**
 Copies, petitions, **BKR 1004**
 Declarations, forms, **BKR Forms 2, 6**
 Definitions, 11 § 101
 Distributions, 11 § 508
 Filing, petitions, **BKR 1004**
 Fraudulent transfers, 11 § 548
 Involuntary proceedings, 11 § 303; **BKR 1004**
 Objections and exceptions, 11 § 502
 Petitions, **BKR 1004**
  Contests, **BKR 1011**
  Involuntary proceedings, 11 § 303
 Statements, **BKR 1007**
 Summons, **BKR 1004**

BANKRUPTCY—Cont'd
Partnership—Cont'd
 Taxation, 11 § 346
 Venue, **BKR 1014**
Party in interest. Parties, generally, ante
Paternity, support, automatic stay, 11 § 362
Patient, definitions, 11 § 101
Patient care ombudsman, 11 § 333; **BKR 2007.2**
 Compensation and salaries, 11 § 330
 Confidential or privileged information, **BKR 2015.1**
 Notice, reports, **BKR 2015.1**
 Reports, notice, **BKR 2015.1**
 Salaries, 11 § 330
Patient records, definitions, 11 § 101
Payment,
 Chapter 7 proceedings, dividends, **BKR 3009, 3010**
 Chapter 11 proceedings, ante
 Chapter 12 proceedings, ante
 Chapter 13 proceedings, ante
 Claims, 11 § 502
 Codebtors, 11 § 509
 Compensation and salaries, generally, ante
 Confirmation of plan, 11 § 1326
 Copies, 11 § 521
 Distributions, 11 § 508
 Dividends, **BKR 3010**
 Foreign countries, 11 § 1532
 Margins, generally, ante
 Matured debts, 11 § 542
 Ordinary course of business, priorities and preferences, 11 § 547
 Petitions, fees, **BKR 1006**
 Reconsidered claims, 11 § 502
 Repayment, generally, post
 Taxation, post
 Trusts and trustees, post
 Unconfirmed plans, 11 § 1326
Penalties. Fines and penalties, generally, ante
Pending actions, **BKR 6009**
 Chapter 7 proceedings, 11 § 727
 Chapter 11 proceedings, 11 § 1141
 Chapter 12 proceedings, 11 § 1228
 Chapter 13 proceedings, 11 § 1328
 Crimes and offenses, statements, **BKR 1007**
 Discharge, **BKR 4004**
 Foreign countries, ante
Pensions. Retirement and pensions, generally, post
Perfection, 11 § 546 et seq.
 Automatic stay, preferences, 11 § 362
 Postpetition, 11 § 549
 Preferences, 11 § 547
  Automatic stay, 11 § 362
 Real estate, bona fide purchasers, 11 §§ 544, 547
 Security interest, evidence, **BKR 3001**
Perjury, 18 § 152
 Declarations, **BKR Forms 2, 6**
Permissive joinder, **BKR 7020**
Personal defenses, 11 § 558
Personal effects, exemptions, 11 § 522
Personal injuries,
 Chapter 13 proceedings, discharge, 11 § 1328
 Discharge, 11 § 523
  Chapter 13 proceedings, 11 § 1328
 Jury, 28 § 1411
 Liquidation, exemptions, 28 § 157
 Payments, exemptions, 11 § 522

BANKRUPTCY—Cont'd
Personal jurisdiction, **BKR 7004**
Personal property,
  Chapter 13 proceedings, 11 § 1326
  Exemptions, 11 § 522
  Forms, schedules, **BKR Form 6**
  Leases, 11 § 365
    Chapter 13 proceedings, payment, 11 § 1326
  Possession, 11 § 521
  Schedules, forms, **BKR Form 6**
Personally identifiable information, **BKR 4002**
  Consumer privacy ombudsman, 11 § 332
    Compensation and salaries, 11 § 330
  Definitions, 11 § 101
  Leases, 11 §§ 332, 363; **BKR 6004**
  Sales, 11 §§ 332, 363; **BKR 6004**
  Theft, 11 § 107
  Trusts and trustees, disposition, 11 §§ 332, 363
Petitions, 11 § 541; **BKR 1002 et seq.**
  Amendments, **BKR 1009**
  Answers, claims, **BKR 1011**
  Attorneys, fees, filing, **BKR 1006**
  Avoidance, transfers, 11 § 547 et seq.
  Captions, **BKR 1005**
  Chapter 9 proceedings, ante
  Chapter 13 proceedings, ante
  Children and minors, **BKR 1004.1**
  Claims, answer, **BKR 1011**
  Compensation and salaries, preparers, **BKR 2016**
  Contests, **BKR 1011, 1013**
  Conversion, 11 § 348
  Copies,
    Amendments, **BKR 1009**
    Numbers and numbering, **BKR 1002, 1003**
  Debt relief agencies, generally, ante
  Declarations, preparers, 11 § 110
  Defenses, **BKR 1011**
  Definitions, preparers, 11 § 110
  Dismissal and nonsuit, **BKR 1013, 1014**
  Fees,
    Filing, **BKR 1006**
    Preparers, 11 § 110
  Filing, 11 § 541; **BKR 1002, 5005**
    Automatic stay, 11 §§ 362, 553
    Avoidance, transfers, 11 § 547 et seq.
    Bad faith, dismissal and nonsuit, 11 § 303
    Bias and prejudice, 11 § 349
    Conversions, 11 § 348
    Definitions, repo participants, 11 § 101
    Fees, **BKR 1006**
    Fraudulent transfers, avoidance, 11 § 548
    Involuntary proceedings, automatic stay, 11 § 553
    Joint proceedings, automatic stay, 11 § 553
    Life insurance, 11 § 542
    Preferences, avoidance, 11 § 547
    Security interest, 11 § 552
    Setoff and counterclaim, 11 § 553
    Signatures, 11 § 110
    Single petitions, 11 § 302
    Transfers, avoidance, 11 § 547 et seq.
    Unmatured debts, disallowance, 11 § 502
    Voluntary proceedings, automatic stay, 11 § 553
  Fines, penalties and forfeitures, preparers, 11 § 110
  Foreign countries, ante
  Forms, **BKR 9004**

BANKRUPTCY—Cont'd
Petitions—Cont'd
  Forms—Cont'd
    Nonattorney preparers,
      Declarations, **BKR Forms 6, 19A**
      Notice, **BKR Form 19B**
  Fraud, preparers, 11 § 110
  Identity and identification, preparers, 11 § 110
  Injunctions, preparers, 11 § 110
  Installments, fees, payment, **BKR 1006**
  Involuntary proceedings, ante
  Mental health, **BKR 1004.1**
  Motions, preparers, fines and penalties, 11 § 110
  Names, **BKR 1005**
  Nonattorney preparers,
    Declarations, **BKR Forms 6, 19A**
    Notice, **BKR Form 19B**
  Nonresidential real property, leases, 11 § 362
  Notice, preparers, 11 § 110
    Nonattorneys, **BKR Form 19B**
  Numbers and numbering,
    Copies, **BKR 1002, 1003**
    Social security, 11 § 110; **BKR 1005**
  Objections and exceptions, **BKR 1011**
  Orders of court, fees, payment, **BKR 1006**
  Partnership, ante
  Payment, fees, **BKR 1006**
  Postpetition, generally, post
  Preferences, avoidance, 11 § 547
  Preparers, 11 § 110
    Compensation and salaries, **BKR 2016**
    Debt relief agencies, generally, ante
    Forms, nonattorney preparers,
      Declarations, **BKR Forms 6, 19A**
      Notice, **BKR Form 19B**
    Nonattorney preparers,
      Declarations, **BKR Forms 6, 19A**
      Notice, **BKR Form 19B**
  Process, **BKR 1010**
  Recognition petitions, foreign countries, 11 § 1515 et seq.;
    BKR 1010 et seq.
  Signatures, **BKR 9011**
    Nonattorney petition preparers,
      Declarations, **BKR Forms 6, 19A**
      Notice, **BKR Form 19B**
    Preparers, 11 § 110
  Social security, numbers and numbering, 11 § 110; **BKR 1005**
  Summons, **BKR 1010**
    Contests, **BKR 1011**
  TIN (taxpayer identification number), **BKR 1005**
  Transfers, avoidance, 11 § 547 et seq.
  Verification, **BKR 1008**
  Voluntary proceedings, post
Physical examinations, **BKR 7035**
Place of business, 11 § 109
  Venue, 28 §§ 1408, 1410
Plans and specifications,
  Acceptances, **BKR 3005**
    Rejection, **BKR 3006**
  Chapter 9 proceedings, ante
  Chapter 11 proceedings, ante
  Chapter 12 proceedings, ante
  Chapter 13 proceedings, ante
  Confirmation of plan, generally, ante
  Counseling services, 11 § 521

BANKRUPTCY—Cont'd
Plans and specifications—Cont'd
  Examinations and examiners, **BKR 2004**
  Exemptions, 11 § 522
  Injunctions, notice, **BKR 2002**
  Rejection, **BKR 3005**
  Small businesses, 11 § 1121
  Timeshares, generally, post
Pleading,
  Adversary proceedings, **BKR 7005 et seq.**
  Filing, 11 § 108
  Foreign proceedings, **BKR 1003**
  Forms, 28 § 2075; **BKR 7010, 9004**
  Grain, responsive pleading, 11 § 557
  Representatives and representation, **BKR 9011**
  Responsive pleading, **BKR 1011**
    Grain, 11 § 557
  Signatures, **BKR 9011**
  Special matters, **BKR 7009**
  Supplemental pleadings, **BKR 7015**
  United States trustees, **BKR 9034**
  Verification, **BKR 9011**
Political subdivisions,
  Abrogation, sovereign immunity, 11 § 106
  Actions and proceedings, 11 § 362; 28 § 1452
  Addresses, mail and mailing, **BKR 5003**
  Chapter 7 proceedings, ante
  Chapter 9 proceedings, generally, ante
  Definitions, 11 § 101
  Discrimination, 11 § 525
  Education, loans, discharge, 11 § 523
  Fines, penalties and forfeitures, discharge, 11 § 523
  Grain, 11 § 557
  Judgments and decrees, stay of proceedings, 11 § 362
  Mail and mailing, addresses, **BKR 5003**
  Money, deposits, 11 § 345
  Notice, taxation, 11 § 362
  Priorities and preferences, 11 § 507
  Process, 11 § 106
  Qualifications, 11 § 109
  Sovereign immunity, abrogation, 11 § 106
  Stay of proceedings, 11 § 362
  Taxation, generally, post
Possession,
  Automatic stay, 11 § 362
  Debtors in possession, generally, ante
  Personal property, 11 § 521
  Turnovers, property, 11 §§ 542, 543
Postpetition,
  Chapter 9 proceedings, ante
  Chapter 11 proceedings, 11 § 1125
  Chapter 13 proceedings, claims, 11 § 1305
  Conversion, **BKR 1019**
  Exemptions, 11 § 522
  Individual debtors, claims, 11 § 1305
  Limitation of actions, 11 § 549
  Reorganization, 11 § 1125
  Taxation, automatic stay, 11 § 362
  Transfers, post
Power of attorney, **BKR 9010**
  General power, forms, **BKR Form 11A**
  Special power, forms, **BKR Form 11B**
Powers and duties, 11 §§ 361 et seq., 521 et seq.; **BKR 4001 et seq.**
  Administrative Office of United States Courts, directors, 28 § 604

BANKRUPTCY—Cont'd
Powers and duties—Cont'd
  Automatic stay, 11 § 362
  Chapter 9 proceedings, transfers, avoidance, 11 § 926
  Chapter 11 proceedings, ante
  Courts, 11 § 105
  Exemptions, 11 §§ 522, 541
  Trusts and trustees, post
  United States trustees, 11 § 307
Predatory loans, 11 § 363
Preferences. Priorities and preferences, generally, post
Prejudice, dismissal and nonsuit, 11 § 349
Preliminary hearing, automatic stay, 11 § 362
Preparers. Petitions, ante
Prepetition tax returns, 11 § 1308
Prepetition taxes, automatic stay, 11 § 362
Preservation, actual, expenses and expenditures, allowances, 11 § 503
President of the United States, Judicial Conference of the United States, 11 § 104
Presumptions,
  Administration, **BKR 5009**
  Automatic stay, 11 § 362
  Chapter 7 proceedings, ante
  Chapter 11 proceedings, substantial or controlling interest, financial statements and reports, **BKR 2015.3**
  Consumer debts, 11 § 707
  Foreign countries, ante
  Open end credit plans, 11 § 523
  Preferences, 11 § 547
  Reaffirmation agreements, 11 § 524
Pretrial procedure, **BKR 7016**
Prima facie evidence. Evidence, generally, ante
Priorities and preferences,
  Alimony, 11 § 507
    Automatic stay, 11 § 362
  Antecedent debt, 11 § 547
  Automatic preservation, 11 § 551
  Automatic stay, 11 § 362
  Avoidance, 11 § 547
  Chapter 7 proceedings, ante
  Child support, automatic stay, 11 § 362
  Claims, 11 §§ 507, 726
  Compensation and salaries, 11 § 507
  Definitions, 11 § 547
  Driving while intoxicated or under the influence, claims, 11 § 507
  Evidence, 11 § 547
  Exemptions, 11 § 522
  Good faith, 11 § 364
  Goods, wares and merchandise, 11 § 546
  Inventories, 11 § 547
  Liability, transferees, 11 § 550
  Liens and incumbrances, 11 §§ 364, 507
  Limitation of actions, 11 § 546
  Loans, 11 § 364
  Motor vehicles, driving while intoxicated or under the influence, claims, 11 § 507
  Ordinary course of business, payment, 11 § 547
  Prepetition transfers, 11 § 547
  Preservation, automatic preservation, 11 § 551
  Presumptions, 11 § 547
  Railroads, 11 § 1171
  Securities, post
  Security interest, 11 § 552
  Subrogation, 11 § 507

BANKRUPTCY—Cont'd
Priorities and preferences—Cont'd
  Support, 11 § 507
  Taxation, post
  Time, 11 § 547
  Transfers, avoidance, 11 § 547
  Trusts and trustees, avoidance, 11 § 547
  Unsecured claims, 11 §§ 507, 753, 767
  Witnesses, fees, 11 § 507
Privacy, **BKR 9037**
  Consumer privacy ombudsman, generally, ante
Privileged information. Confidential or privileged information, generally, ante
Privileges and immunities, 11 §§ 344, 521
  Examinations and examiners, 11 § 344
  Support, post
  Witnesses, 18 § 6001
Procedures, 28 § 157
Proceedings. Actions and proceedings, generally, ante
Proceeds, 11 § 541
  Custodians, accounts and accounting, 11 § 543
  Grain, 11 § 557
  Security interest, 11 § 552
Process, 11 § 105
  Adversary proceedings, **BKR 7004, 7005**
  Appeal and review, **BKR 8004, 8008**
  Automatic stay, 11 § 362
  Briefs, **BKR 8009**
  Children and minors, **BKR 1007**
  Community property, 11 § 524
  Contempt, **BKR 9020**
  Governmental units, 11 § 106
  Injunctions, 11 § 524
  Intervention, **BKR 2018**
  Involuntary proceedings, petitions, **BKR 1010**
  Mail and mailing, **BKR 7004, 9006**
  Mentally ill persons, **BKR 1007**
  Motions, **BKR 9013**
  Noncore proceedings, **BKR 9033**
  Nonparties, **BKR 7071**
  Publication, **BKR 7004, 9008**
  Removal of cases or causes, **BKR 9027**
  Time, **BKR 7004**
Production of books and papers, **BKR 2004, 7034**
Professional associations, compensation and salaries, 11 § 504
Professional personnel, 11 § 326 et seq.; **BKR 2014**
  Accountants, 11 § 507
  Administration, expenses and expenditures, reimbursement, 11 § 503
  Certificates and certification, compensation and salaries, 11 § 330
  Compensation and salaries, 11 §§ 328, 504
    Certificates and certification, 11 § 330
    Interim compensation, 11 § 331
    Priorities and preferences, 11 § 507
    Records and recordation, **BKR 2013**
    Sharing, 11 § 504
  Conflict of interest, 11 §§ 327, 328
  Disclosure, records and recordation, 11 § 542
  Grain, 11 § 557
  Interim compensation, 11 § 331
  Priorities and preferences, compensation and salaries, 11 § 507
  Records and recordation,
    Compensation and salaries, **BKR 2013**
    Disclosure, 11 § 542

BANKRUPTCY—Cont'd
Professional personnel—Cont'd
  Reimbursement, administration, expenses and expenditures, 11 § 503
  Sharing, compensation and salaries, 11 § 504
Profits, 11 § 541
  Accounts and accounting, custodians, 11 § 543
  Custodians, accounts and accounting, 11 § 543
  Definitions, 11 § 308
  Exemptions, profit-sharing plans, 11 § 522
  Small businesses, 11 § 308
Proof of claim, **BKR 3001 et seq.**
Property of the estate, definitions, 11 §§ 902, 1115
Proposed findings, noncore proceedings, **BKR 9033**
Protective orders, **BKR 9018**
  Chapter 11 proceedings, substantial or controlling interest, financial statements and reports, **BKR 2015.3**
  Consolidations and mergers, **BKR 1015**
  Privacy protection, **BKR 9037**
  Securities, 11 § 742
  Shares and shareholders, 11 § 742
Proxies, chapter 7 proceedings, **BKR 2006**
Public access, books and papers, 11 § 107
Public assistance, exemptions, 11 § 522
Public policy, foreign countries, 11 §§ 1501, 1506
Public service attorney referral program, 11 § 504
Public utilities, deposits, 11 § 366
Publication,
  Municipal debt adjustment, notice, 11 § 923
  Notice, **BKR 2002**
  Process, **BKR 7004, 9008**
Puerto Rico, judges or justices, appointments, 28 § 152
Punitive damages. Damages, generally, ante
Purchasers and purchasing,
  Bona fide purchasers, generally, ante
  Damages, transfers, 11 § 550
  Definitions, 11 § 101
  Limitation of actions, 11 § 546
  Modification, 11 § 363
  Real estate, postpetition, 11 § 549
Qualifications, 11 § 109
  Trusts and trustees, 11 § 322
Racketeer influenced and corrupt organizations, fraud, 18 § 1961
Railroads. Chapter 11 proceedings, ante
Reaffirmation agreements, 11 § 524
  Abuse, 18 § 158
  Cover sheet, forms, **BKR Form 27**
  Crimes and offenses, 18 § 158
  Discharge, undue hardship, presumptions, **BKR 4004**
  Filing, **BKR 4008**
  Forms, cover sheet, **BKR Form 27**
  Motions, 11 § 524
  Statements, 11 § 524; **BKR 4008**
Real estate,
  Automatic stay, 11 § 362
  Avoidance, postpetition, 11 § 549
  Bona fide purchasers, 11 §§ 544, 547
  Consumer debt, ante
  Exemptions, 11 § 522
  Nonresidential real property, leases,
    Automatic stay, 11 § 362
    Termination, 11 § 541
  Postpetition, avoidance, 11 § 549
  Schedules, forms, **BKR Form 6**
Real party in interest, **BKR 7017**

BANKRUPTCY—Cont'd
Recall, judges or justices, 28 § 155
Receivable, definitions, 11 § 547
Receivers and receivership, 28 § 959
    Appointments, 11 § 105
    Fees, 18 § 155
    Goods, wares and merchandise, 11 § 546
    Reports, 18 § 3057
Reciprocity, abstention, 11 § 305; 28 § 1334
Reclamation,
    Goods, wares and merchandise, 11 § 546
    Shares and shareholders, 11 § 751
Recognition petitions, foreign countries, 11 § 1515 et seq.;
    BKR 1010 et seq.
Reconsideration, claims, 11 § 502; **BKR 3008**
Records and recordation, **BKR 5003**
    Access, 11 § 107
    Appeal and review, **BKR 8006, 8007, 8016**
    Assisted living facilities, 11 § 351
    Certified copies, **BKR 5006**
    Chapter 7 proceedings, ante
    Chapter 11 proceedings, ante
    Compensation and salaries, **BKR 2013**
    Custodians, 28 § 156
    Disclosure, 11 § 542
    Filing, **BKR 5005, 5007**
    Health care businesses, patients, **BKR 6011**
    Home health agencies, 11 § 351
    Hospices, 11 § 351
    Hospitals, 11 § 351
    Intermediate care facilities, 11 § 351
    Long term care, facilities, 11 § 351
    Meetings, **BKR 2003**
    Nursing homes, 11 § 351
    Patient care ombudsman, 11 § 333
    Real estate, transfers, avoidance, 11 § 549
    Removal of cases or causes, **BKR 9027**
    Skilled nursing facilities, 11 § 351
    Trusts and trustees, post
    Turnovers, **BKR 1019**
Recourse, municipalities, 11 § 927
Recovery,
    Attorneys, fees, 11 § 541
    Costs, trusts and trustees, 11 § 506
    Liens and incumbrances, trusts and trustees, good faith, 11 § 550
Redacted filings, **BKR 9037**
Redemption,
    Exemptions, 11 § 541
    Liens and incumbrances, **BKR 6008**
    Liquidation, 11 § 722
    Sales, **BKR 6008**
Reduction,
    Consumer debt, unsecured claims, 11 § 502
    Homesteads, exemptions, fraud, 11 § 522
Referees. References, generally, post
References, 28 § 157
    Alternative dispute resolution, 28 § 654
    Appellate panels, 28 § 158
    Arbitration, 28 § 654
    Assistants, 11 § 102
    Chapter 11 proceedings, 28 § 157
    Expenses and expenditures, 11 § 102
    Fees, **11 nt prec § 101**
    Fraud, schedules, 18 § 158
    Public service attorney referral program, 11 § 504

BANKRUPTCY—Cont'd
References—Cont'd
    Salary and Expense Fund, 11 § 102; **11 nt prec § 101**
    Sessions, 28 § 151
    Stay of proceedings, 11 § 362
    Stenographers, 11 § 102
    Supervision, 11 § 102
Referrals. References, generally, ante
Refunds. Taxation, post
Regional Rail Reorganization, this index
Register, claims, **BKR 5003**
Rehearings, motions, **BKR 8015**
Reimbursement, **BKR 2016**
    Custodians, liens and incumbrances, avoidance, 11 § 349
    Disallowance, 11 § 502
    Evidence, 11 § 501
    Officers and employees, 11 § 330
    Professional persons, 11 § 330
    Securities, rescission, 11 § 510
Reinstatement, transfers, avoidance, 11 § 349
Rejection,
    Chapter 11 proceedings, ante
    Chapter 13 proceedings, ante
    Collective bargaining, agreements, 11 § 1113
    Contracts, 11 § 365; **BKR 6006**
    Executory contracts, 11 § 502
    Leases, 11 §§ 365, 502; **BKR 6006**
    Plans and specifications, **BKR 3005**
    Railroads, leases, 11 § 1169
    Shares and shareholders, executory contracts, 11 § 744
    Timeshares, 11 § 365
    Trusts and trustees, **BKR 2008**
    Unexpired leases, 11 § 553
Related party, definitions, 11 § 524
Relatives,
    Definitions, 11 § 101
    Judges or justices, compensation and salaries, disqualification, **BKR 5004**
Release, examinations and examiners, **BKR 2005**
Religious organizations and societies, fraud, 11 § 548
Remand, 28 § 1452; **BKR 9027**
Removal from office,
    Judges or justices, ante
    Trusts and trustees, post
Removal of cases or causes, **BKR 2005, 9027**
    Attachment, **BKR 9027**
    Bonds (officers and fiduciaries), **BKR 9027**
    Claims, 28 § 1452
    Grounds, 28 § 152
    Injunctions, **BKR 9027**
    Process, **BKR 9027**
    Records and recordation, **BKR 9027**
Rent, 11 § 541
    Custodians, 11 § 543
    Leases, generally, ante
    Liens and incumbrances, avoidance, 11 § 545
    Security interest, 11 § 552
Reopening, **BKR 5010**
Reorganization,
    Chapter 11 proceedings, generally, ante
    Chapter 12 proceedings, generally, ante
Repayment,
    Avoidance, alternative repayment schedule, 11 § 547
    Discharge, ante
Replacement value, definitions, 11 § 506
Repo participants. Repurchase agreements, generally, post

BANKRUPTCY—Cont'd
Reports,
   Chapter 7 proceedings, **BKR 2001**
   Chapter 11 proceedings, ante
   Crimes and offenses, 18 § 3057
   Elections, **BKR 2003**
   Financial management training curriculum, 11 § 111 nt
   Financial statements and reports, generally, ante
   Health care businesses, patient records, destruction, **BKR 6011**
   Individual debtors, 11 § 1302
   National Bankruptcy Review Commission, 11 nt prec § 101
   Patient care ombudsman, notice, **BKR 2015.1**
   Reorganization, confirmation of plan, 11 § 1106
   Small businesses, monthly operating reports, **BKR Form 25**
   Statistics, 28 § 159
   Trusts and trustees, post
   United States trustees, post
Representatives and representation,
   Chapter 11 proceedings, venue, 28 § 1409
   Foreign countries, 11 § 1509 et seq.
   Parties, **BKR 9010**
   Pleading, **BKR 9011**
   Statements, **BKR 2019**
Repurchase agreements,
   Acceleration, 11 § 559
   Automatic stay, 11 § 362
   Avoidance, set-off and counterclaim, 11 § 546
   Damages, 11 § 562
   Definitions, 11 § 101
   Fraud, 11 § 548
   Liquidation, 11 § 559
   National securities association, 11 § 559
   Reverse repurchase agreements, 11 § 101
   Securities,
     Automatic stay, 11 § 362
     Liquidation, 11 § 559
   Set-off and counterclaim, 11 §§ 362, 546, 559
   Termination, 11 § 559
   Unsecured claims, priorities and preferences, 11 §§ 753, 767
Rescission, reaffirmation agreements, 11 § 524
Residence. Domicile and residence, generally, ante
Responsive pleading, **BKR 1011**
   Grain, 11 § 557
Restitution, discharge, 11 §§ 523, 1328
Retention, bonuses, 11 § 503
Retirement and pensions,
   Automatic stay, 11 § 362
   Chapter 11 proceedings, insurance, 11 § 1114
   Discharge, 11 § 523
   Education individual retirement accounts, 11 §§ 521, 541
   Employee Retirement Income Security Program, generally, ante
   Exemptions, 11 § 522
   Insurance, chapter 11 proceedings, 11 § 1114
   Judges or justices, ante
Returns,
   Attorneys, fees, cancellation, 11 §§ 329, 541
   Goods, wares and merchandise, 11 § 546
   Income tax, copies, **BKR 4002**
   Taxation, post
Reversal, orders of court, grain, 11 § 557
Reverse repurchase agreements, 11 § 101
Review. Appeal and review, generally, ante

BANKRUPTCY—Cont'd
Revocation or suspension, **BKR 1017**
   Abstention, 11 § 305
   Appeal and review, **BKR 8019**
   Foreign countries, 11 § 1520 et seq.
   Individual debtors, fraud, 11 § 1330
   Reorganization, confirmation of plan, 11 § 1144
   Taxation, 11 § 346
   Time, 11 § 108
   Trusts and trustees, 28 § 586
Revolving consumer credit agreements, claims, **BKR 3001**
Rice, 11 § 557
RICO, fraud, 18 § 1961
Rolling stock, railroads, 11 § 1168
Rye, 11 § 557
Salaries. Compensation and salaries, generally, ante
Sales, 11 § 361 et seq.; **BKR 6004**
   Administrative expenses, 11 § 503
   Automatic stay, 11 § 553; **BKR 6004**
   Chapter 13 proceedings, 11 § 1303
   Community property, 11 § 363
   Consumer privacy ombudsman, 11 § 332
   Contracts, ante
   Damages, 11 § 363
   Dower and curtesy, 11 § 363
   Good faith, 11 § 363
   Grain, 11 § 557
   Individual debtors, 11 § 1303
   Joint tenants, 11 § 363
   Liens and incumbrances, 11 § 363; **BKR 6004**
   Motions, **BKR 4001, 6003**
     Personally identifiable information, **BKR 6004**
   Notice, **BKR 2002, 6004**
   Orders of court, 11 § 363; 28 § 157
   Personally identifiable information, 11 §§ 332, 363; **BKR 6004**
   Proceeds, generally, ante
   Reclamation, 11 § 546
   Redemption, **BKR 6008**
   Taxation, 11 § 346
   Trusts and trustees, post
Satisfaction, money, 11 § 363
Savings and loan associations, 11 § 109
Savings banks, 11 § 109
Scandalous matters, 11 § 107; **BKR 9018**
Schedules, **BKR 1007**
   Abandonment, 11 § 554
   Amendments, **BKR 1009**
   Assets, filing, 11 § 521
   Chapter 7 proceedings, ante
   Chapter 9 proceedings, liabilities, **BKR 3003**
   Chapter 11 proceedings, ante
   Chapter 13 proceedings, ante
   Codebtors, forms, **BKR Form 6**
   Conversion, **BKR 1019**
   Declarations, **BKR Forms 2, 6**
   Discharge, 11 § 523
   Executory contracts, forms, **BKR Form 6**
   Exemptions, forms, **BKR Form 6**
   Expenses and expenditures, 11 § 521; **BKR Form 6**
   Filing, 11 § 521; **BKR 5005**
   Forms, **BKR 9004**
     Declarations, **BKR Forms 2, 6**
     Summaries, **BKR Form 6**
   Fraud, 18 § 158
   Income, ante

BANKRUPTCY—Cont'd

Schedules—Cont'd

Leases, forms, **BKR Form 6**

Liabilities, filing, 11 § 521

Personal property, forms, **BKR Form 6**

Real estate, forms, **BKR Form 6**

Secured claims, forms, **BKR Form 6**

Small businesses, 11 § 1116

Summaries, forms, **BKR Form 6**

Supplemental schedules, **BKR 1007**

Trusts and trustees, 11 § 704

Unsecured claims, forms, **BKR Form 6**

Verification, **BKR 1008**

Scholarships,

Discharge, 11 § 523

Fraud, exemptions, 11 § 522

Searches and seizures, **BKR 7064**

Certificates and certification, records and recordation, **BKR 5003**

Records and recordation, certificates and certification, **BKR 5003**

Secretaries, judges or justices, 28 § 156

Secretary of HUD, mortgages, foreclosure, stay of proceedings, 11 § 362

Secretary of the Treasury, reorganization, 11 § 1126

Secured claims. Claims, ante

Securities, 11 § 741 et seq.

Acceleration, contracts, 11 § 555

Automatic stay, 11 §§ 362, 553

Chapter 7 proceedings, ante

Chapter 9 proceedings, ante

Chapter 11 proceedings, ante

Compromise and settlement, 11 § 362

Damages, 11 § 562

Definitions, 11 §§ 101, 741

Discharge, fraud, 11 § 523

Dismissal and nonsuit, 11 § 349

Equity security holders, generally, ante

Exemptions, chapter 11 proceedings, 11 § 1145

Fraud,

Discharge, 11 § 523

Transfers, 11 § 548

Limitation of actions, transfers, 11 § 546

Loans, 11 § 364

Margins,

Avoidance, transfers, 11 § 546

Fraudulent transfers, 11 § 548

Names, customers, 11 § 751

Definitions, 11 § 741

National securities association, 11 § 555

Repurchase agreements, 11 § 559

Notice, orders of court, 11 § 743

Priorities and preferences, unsecured claims, 11 §§ 753, 767

Protective orders, 11 § 742

Repurchase agreements,

Automatic stay, 11 § 362

Liquidation, 11 § 559

Rescision, 11 § 510

Stay of proceedings, 11 § 555

Subordination, 11 § 510

Termination, contracts, 11 § 555

Transfers,

Fraud, 11 § 548

Limitation of actions, 11 § 546

Voidable transfers, 11 § 749

BANKRUPTCY—Cont'd

Securities—Cont'd

Unsecured claims, priorities and preferences, 11 §§ 753, 767

Voidable transfers, 11 § 749

Security interest,

Aircraft, 11 § 1110

Animals, 11 § 363

Automatic stay, 11 § 362

Avoidance, 11 §§ 522, 547

Chapter 9 proceedings, ante

Chapter 13 proceedings, ante

Default, 11 § 521

Definitions, 11 § 101

Evidence, perfection, **BKR 3001**

Foreign countries, 11 § 1520

Postpetition, 11 § 552

Reaffirmation agreements, 11 § 524

Sales, **BKR 6004**

Seizures. Searches and seizures, generally, ante

Self-employment, 11 § 1304

Self-incrimination, 11 § 344

Examinations and examiners, 11 § 344

Liquidation, 11 § 727

Sellers, goods, wares and merchandise, reclamation, 11 § 546

Sentence and punishment, 18 § 152 et seq.

Separation agreements, 11 §§ 522, 523

Sequestration, removal of cases or causes, **BKR 9027**

Serial filers, 11 § 362

Service of process. Process, generally, ante

Services,

Administration, expenses and expenditures, 11 § 503

Compensation and salaries, exemptions, 11 § 541

Setoff and counterclaim, 11 § 553; **BKR 7013**

Automatic stay, 11 § 362

Avoidance, transfers, 11 §§ 522, 550

Commodity contracts, margins, 11 § 362

Definitions, 11 § 553

Evidence, 11 § 501

Governmental units, 11 § 106

Hearings, 28 § 157

Leases, 11 § 365

Matured debts, 11 § 542

Prepetition claims, 11 § 553

Proof of claim, 11 § 501

Repurchase agreements, 11 §§ 362, 546, 559

Secured claims, 11 § 506

Swap agreements, 11 § 553

Taxation, refunds, 11 § 362

Timeshares, 11 § 365

Transfers, avoidance, 11 §§ 522, 550

Settlement. Compromise and settlement, generally, ante

Severance pay. Compensation and salaries, generally, ante

Shares and shareholders, 11 § 741 et seq.

Accounts and accounting, 11 § 745

Assumptions, executory contracts, 11 § 744

Automatic stay, 11 § 742

Banks and banking, net equity claims, 11 § 745

Bonus plans, exemptions, 11 § 522

Brokers, 11 § 741 et seq.

Contracts, liquidation, 11 § 555

Definitions, 11 § 101

Repurchase agreements, 11 § 559

Transfers, limitation of actions, 11 § 546

Compromise and settlement,

Definitions, 11 § 741

BANKRUPTCY—Cont'd
Shares and shareholders—Cont'd
  Compromise and settlement—Cont'd
    Stay of proceedings, **11 § 362**
  Contracts,
    Definitions, **11 § 741**
    Executory contracts, **11 § 744**
    Liquidation, **11 §§ 555, 752**
    Transfers, **11 § 746**
  Customers,
    Capacity, **11 § 745**
    Definitions, **11 § 741**
    Net equity claims, **11 § 745**
    Voidable transfers, **11 § 749**
  Definitions, **11 § 741**
  Derivative actions, **BKR 7023.1**
  Dismissal and nonsuit, **11 § 742**
  Distribution, **11 § 750**
  Executory contracts, **11 § 744**
  Fraudulent transfers, **11 § 548**
  Margins,
    Avoidance, transfers, **11 § 546**
    Definitions, **11 § 741**
    Fraudulent transfers, **11 § 548**
  Net equity, definitions, **11 § 741**
  Net equity claims, **11 § 745**
  Notice, orders of court, **11 § 743**
  Orders of court,
    Executory contracts, **11 § 744**
    Notice, **11 § 743**
    Voidable transfers, **11 § 749**
  Protective orders, **11 § 742**
  Qualifications, **11 § 109**
  Reclamation, **11 § 751**
  Rejection, executory contracts, **11 § 744**
  Repurchase agreements, liquidation, **11 § 559**
  Stay of proceedings, **11 §§ 362, 746, 747**
  Subordination, **11 §§ 746, 747**
  Transfers, voidable transfers, **11 § 749**
  Trusts and trustees, post
  United States trustees, **28 § 586**
  Voidable transfers, **11 § 749**
Ships and shipping,
  Automatic stay, **11 § 362**
  Discharge, **11 § 523**
  Reorganization, **11 § 1110**
Short titles, **BKR 1001**
  Captions, forms, **BKR Form 16B**
Signatures,
  Attorneys, chapter 7 proceedings, **11 § 707**
  Claims, **BKR 3001**
  Filing, **11 § 110**
  Nonrecourse loans, elections, **BKR 3014**
  Petitions, ante
  Pleading, **BKR 9011**
Single asset real estate,
  Automatic stay, **11 § 362**
  Definitions, **11 § 101**
Single petition, joint proceedings, **11 § 302**
Small business investment companies, qualifications, **11 § 109**
Small businesses,
  Chapter 11 proceedings, ante
  Committees, **11 § 1102; BKR 1020**
  Confirmation of plan, **11 § 1129**
  Debtors in possession, **11 § 1116**
  Definitions, **11 §§ 101, 707**

BANKRUPTCY—Cont'd
Small businesses—Cont'd
  Disclosure,
    Forms, statements, **BKR Form 25**
    Statements, **11 § 1125; BKR 3016, 3017.1**
      Forms, **BKR Form 25**
  Entry upon land, **11 § 1116**
  Financial statements and reports, **11 §§ 308, 1116**
  Forms, **BKR Form 25 et seq.**
  Good faith, **11 § 362**
  Insurance, **11 § 1116**
  Meetings, **11 § 1116**
  Objections and exceptions, statements, reorganization, **BKR 1020**
  Plans and specifications, **11 § 1121**
  Profits, **11 § 308**
  Reorganization, statements, **BKR 1020**
  Reports, monthly operating reports, **BKR Form 25**
  Schedules, **11 § 1116**
  Statements,
    Disclosure, **11 § 1125; BKR 3016, 3017.1**
    Reorganization, **BKR 1020**
  Taxation, returns, **11 §§ 308, 1116**
  Trusts and trustees, **11 § 1116**
  United States trustees, **28 § 586**
Social security,
  Disclosure, numbers and numbering, **11 § 342**
  Exemptions, **11 § 522**
  Forms, numbers and numbering, statements, **BKR Form 21**
  Identity and identification, numbers and numbering, **BKR 4002**
  Numbers and numbering,
    Disclosure, **11 § 342**
    Forms, statements, **BKR Form 21**
    Identity and identification, **BKR 4002**
    Petitions, **11 § 110; BKR 1005**
    Protection, **11 § 342**
    Statements, **BKR 1007, 2002**
      Forms, **BKR Form 21**
    Voluntary proceedings, amendments, **BKR 1009**
  Petitions, numbers and numbering, **11 § 110; BKR 1005**
  Protection, numbers and numbering, **11 § 342**
  Statements, numbers and numbering, **BKR 1007, 2002**
    Forms, **BKR Form 21**
  Voluntary proceedings, numbers and numbering, amendments, **BKR 1009**
Solicitation,
  Chapter 7 proceedings, proxies, **BKR 2006**
  Chapter 11 proceedings, postpetition, **11 § 1125**
Sovereign immunity, abrogation, **11 § 106**
Soybeans, **11 § 557**
Special matters, pleading, **BKR 7009**
Special power of attorney, forms, **BKR Form 11B**
Special sessions, courts, emergencies, **28 § 152**
Specific performance, **BKR 7070**
Spouses. Husband and wife, generally, ante
Standards, statutory liens, avoidance, **11 § 545**
Standing trustees. United States trustees, post
Statements,
  Amendments, **BKR 1009**
  Changes, **BKR 4002**
  Consumer debts, security interest, **11 § 521**
  Conversion, **BKR 1019**
  Corporations, title to property, **BKR 1007, 7007.1**
  Counseling services, statement of compliance, **BKR 1007**

BANKRUPTCY—Cont'd

Statements—Cont'd

Current monthly income, **BKR 1007**

Debt relief agencies, 11 §§ 527, 528

Disclosure, **BKR Form 12 et seq.**

Filing, **BKR 5005**

Financial management training curriculum, statement of course completion, **BKR 1007**

Discharge, **BKR 4004**

Financial statements and reports, generally, ante

Forms,

Disclosure, **BKR Form 12 et seq.**

Financial affairs statements, **BKR Form 7**

Individual debtors, intentions, **BKR Form 8**

Reorganization, **BKR Form 13**

Fraud, discharge, 11 § 523

Individual debtors, intentions, forms, **BKR Form 8**

Intentions, reorganization, **BKR 1007**

Issues, appeal and review, **BKR 8006**

Partnership, **BKR 1007**

Reaffirmation agreements, 11 § 524; **BKR 4008**

Representatives and representation, **BKR 2019**

Small businesses, ante

Verification, **BKR 1008**

States,

Automatic stay, income tax, 11 § 362

Chapter 9 proceedings, 11 §§ 109, 903

Chapter 11 proceedings,

Managers and management, 28 § 959

Railroads, 11 § 1166

Claims, 11 § 502

Core proceedings, 28 § 157

Exemptions, 11 § 522

Managers and management, chapter 11 proceedings, 28 § 959

Priorities and preferences, income tax, 11 § 507

Railroads, chapter 11 proceedings, 11 § 1166

Securities, sales, 11 § 364

Taxation, 11 § 346

Statistics, 28 § 159

Liabilities, summaries, **BKR Form 6**

Summaries, liabilities, **BKR Form 6**

Status,

Conferences, 11 § 105

Foreign countries, 11 § 1518

Liens and incumbrances, 11 § 506

Statute of frauds, 11 § 558

Statute of limitations. Limitation of actions, generally, ante

Statutory liens. Liens and incumbrances, ante

Stay of proceedings, 11 § 362; **BKR 7062**

Annulment, 11 § 362

Appeal and review, **BKR 8005, 8017**

Automatic stay, generally, ante

Chapter 9 proceedings, ante

Community property, discharge, 11 § 524

Core proceedings, 28 § 157

Discharge, 11 § 524

Foreign countries, 11 § 1519 et seq.

Grain, 11 § 557

Hearings, 11 § 362

Negotiable instruments, dishonor, 11 § 362

Notice, 11 § 362

Objections and exceptions, 11 § 1301

Paternity, support, 11 § 362

Petitions,

Filing, 11 § 362

BANKRUPTCY—Cont'd

Stay of proceedings—Cont'd

Petitions—Cont'd

Preparers, 11 § 110

Preliminary hearings, 11 § 362

Real estate, 11 § 362

Repurchase agreements, liquidation, 11 § 559

Securities, 11 § 555

Shares and shareholders, 11 §§ 362, 746, 747

Supplemental injunctions, 11 § 524

Swap agreements, 11 § 560

Taxation, 11 § 505

Termination, 11 § 362

Time, 11 § 362

Venue, change of venue, **BKR 1014**

Withdrawal, **BKR 5011**

Stipulations, discovery, **BKR 7029**

Stock and stockholders,

Securities, generally, ante

Shares and shareholders, generally, ante

Straight bankruptcy. Chapter 7 proceedings, generally, ante

Student loans, discrimination, 11 § 525

Subordination, 11 § 510

Subpoenas, **BKR 9016**

Subrogation, 11 § 509

Allowance of claim or interest, 11 § 502

Priorities and preferences, 11 § 507

Substantial or controlling interest, chapter 11 proceedings, financial statements and reports, **BKR 2015.3; BKR Form 26**

Substitution, parties, **BKR 7025**

Successors. Trusts and trustees, post

Summaries, schedules, forms, **BKR Form 6**

Summary judgment, **BKR 7056**

Summons,

Electronic summons, **BKR 7004**

Foreign countries, **BKR 1003**

Partnership, **BKR 1004**

Petitions, **BKR 1010**

Contests, **BKR 1011**

Service, **BKR 7004, 7005**

Supersedeas. Stay of proceedings, generally, ante

Supervision, 28 § 586

Examinations and examiners, foreign countries, 11 § 1526

Trusts and trustees, foreign countries, 11 § 1526

Supplemental injunctions, 11 § 524

Supplemental pleadings, **BKR 7015**

Supplemental schedules, **BKR 1007**

Support,

Alimony, generally, ante

Automatic stay, 11 § 362

Avoidance, 11 § 547

Chapter 7 proceedings, 11 § 704

Chapter 11 proceedings, ante

Chapter 12 proceedings, 11 §§ 1202, 1208, 1222 et seq.

Chapter 13 proceedings, 11 §§ 1302, 1307, 1322 et seq.

Collection,

Automatic stay, 11 § 362

Chapter 7 proceedings, 11 § 704

Chapter 11 proceedings, 11 § 1106

Chapter 12 proceedings, 11 § 1202

Chapter 13 proceedings, 11 § 1302

Definitions, 11 § 101

Discharge, 11 § 523

Dismissal and nonsuit, 11 § 1112

Exemptions, 11 § 522

BANKRUPTCY—Cont'd
Support—Cont'd
Priorities and preferences, 11 § 507
Privileges and immunities,
Chapter 7 proceedings, 11 § 704
Chapter 11 proceedings, 11 § 1106
Chapter 12 proceedings, 11 § 1202
Chapter 13 proceedings, 11 § 1302
Supreme Court, 28 § 2075
Surcharge, custodians, disbursements, 11 § 543
Sureties and surety bonds. Bonds (officers and fiduciaries), generally, ante
Suspension. Revocation or suspension, generally, ante
Swap agreements, 11 § 546
Acceleration, 11 § 560
Automatic stay, 11 § 362
Cleared swaps, 11 § 761
Damages, 11 § 562
Definitions, 11 §§ 101, 560
Fraud, 11 § 548
Liquidation, 11 § 560
Set-off and counterclaim, 11 § 553
Termination, 11 § 560
Unsecured claims, priorities and preferences, 11 §§ 753, 767
Taxation, 11 §§ 346, 505
Accounts and accounting, 11 § 346
Addresses, 11 § 505; BKR 5003
Administrative expenses, 11 § 503
Assessments, 11 § 502
Automatic stay, 11 § 505
Objections and exceptions, 11 § 362
Prepetition taxes, 11 § 362
Avoidance, liens and incumbrances, 11 §§ 522, 545
Business and commerce, ante
Carrybacks, 11 § 346
Carryovers, 11 § 346
Chapter 7 proceedings, ante
Chapter 9 proceedings, ante
Chapter 11 proceedings, ante
Chapter 12 proceedings, 11 §§ 346, 1231
Chapter 13 proceedings, ante
Claims, 11 § 346
Foreign countries, 11 § 1513
Priorities and preferences, 11 §§ 501, 502
Contests, 11 § 505
Copies, returns, 11 § 521
Corporations, 11 § 346
Damages, discharge, 11 § 505
Deductions, 11 § 346
Destruction, documents, 11 § 521 nt
Discharge, objections and exceptions, 11 § 523
Dismissal and nonsuit, 11 § 346
Returns, 11 § 521
Evidence, priorities and preferences, 11 § 501
Exemptions, 11 § 522
Expenses and expenditures, 11 § 503
Exports and imports, customs duties, priorities and preferences, 11 § 507
Filing, returns, 11 § 346
Fines and penalties, 11 § 505
Priorities and preferences, 11 § 503
Foreign countries, 11 § 1513
Forgiveness, 11 § 346
Fraud, returns, 11 § 523
Fuel, 11 § 501

BANKRUPTCY—Cont'd
Taxation—Cont'd
Gross receipts, priorities and preferences, 11 § 507
Individual debtors, 11 §§ 523, 1305
Interest, 11 § 511
Liens and incumbrances,
Automatic stay, 11 § 362
Avoidance, 11 §§ 522, 545
Notice, avoidance, 11 § 522
Limitation of actions, 11 § 346
Lists, 11 § 505
Losses, 11 § 346
Notice, 11 § 362
Liens and incumbrances, 11 § 522
Requests, tax determinations, 11 § 505
Stay of proceedings, 11 § 362
Orders of court, 11 § 346
Partnership, 11 § 346
Payment, 11 § 505
Secured claims, 11 § 506
Prepetition returns, 11 § 1308
Prepetition taxes, automatic stay, 11 § 362
Priorities and preferences, 11 § 507
Claims, 11 § 502
Evidence, 11 § 501
Foreign countries, 11 § 1513
Refunds, 11 § 505
Set-off and counterclaim, 11 § 362
Returns,
Copies, 11 § 521
Discharge, 11 §§ 505, 523
Dismissal and nonsuit, 11 § 521
Filing, 11 § 346
Prepetition returns, 11 § 1308
Small businesses, 11 §§ 308, 1116
Revocation or suspension, 11 § 346
Sales, 11 § 346
Set-off and counterclaim, refunds, 11 § 362
Small businesses, returns, 11 §§ 308, 1116
States, 11 § 346
Time, claims, 11 § 502
Transfers, 11 § 346
Trusts and trustees, post
Unsecured claims, 11 § 523
Withholding, 11 § 346
Telecommunications, interception, orders, 18 § 2516
Television and radio, exemptions, 11 § 522
Tenants by the entirety, sales, 11 § 363
Tenants in common, sales, 11 § 363
Tentative carryback adjustment, taxation, priorities and preferences, 11 § 507
Term overriding royalty, definitions, 11 § 101
Termination,
Air carriers, terminals, 11 § 365
Automatic stay, 11 § 362
Chapter 7 proceedings, 11 § 701
Chapter 9 proceedings, 11 § 930
Chapter 11 proceedings, ante
Chapter 12 proceedings, 11 § 1201
Chapter 13 proceedings, 11 § 1307
Commodities, contracts, 11 § 556
Foreign countries, ante
Forward contracts, 11 § 556
Master agreements, 11 § 561
Nonresidential real property, leases, 11 § 541
Patient care ombudsman, BKR 2007.2

BANKRUPTCY—Cont'd
Termination—Cont'd
  Repurchase agreements, **11 § 559**
  Securities, contracts, **11 § 555**
  Swap agreements, **11 § 560**
  Trusts and trustees, **28 § 586**
Terms of office. Judges or justices, ante
Tests,
  Chapter 13 proceedings, means test, **11 § 1325**
  Financial management training curriculum, **11 § 111 nt**
Theft. Larceny, generally, ante
Third parties, **BKR 7014**
Time, **BKR 9006**
  Appeal and review, **BKR 8002**
  Avoidance, **11 § 546**
  Chapter 7 proceedings, ante
  Chapter 11 proceedings, ante
  Chapter 12 proceedings, discharge, **BKR 4007**
  Chapter 13 proceedings, ante
  Claims, **11 § 501 et seq.; BKR 3002 et seq.**
  Consolidations and mergers, orders of court, **BKR 1015**
  Consumer debts, schedules, **11 § 521**
  Corporations, title to property, statements, **BKR 7007.1**
  Courts, findings, **BKR 7052**
  Damages, **11 §§ 502, 562**
  Debt relief agencies,
    Contracts, **11 § 528**
    Disclosure, **11 § 527**
  Definitions, **BKR 9006**
  Discharge, **BKR 4007**
  Examinations and examiners, **BKR 2004**
  Extensions, generally, ante
  Findings, courts, **BKR 7052**
  Foreign countries, notice, **BKR 2015**
  Grain, **11 § 557**
  Judgments and decrees, amendments, **BKR 9023**
  Lists, schedules, **BKR 1007**
  Meetings, **BKR 2003**
  Motions, ante
  New trial, **BKR 9015, 9023**
  Offices, **BKR 5001**
  Open end or revolving consumer credit agreements, claims, **BKR 3001**
  Preferences, **11 § 547**
  Priorities and preferences, **11 § 547**
  Process, **BKR 7004**
  Reaffirmation agreements, **11 § 524**
  Sales, notice, **11 § 363**
  Summary judgment, **BKR 7056**
  Taxation, claims, **11 § 502**
  Venue, **28 § 1408**
Timeshares,
  Definitions, **11 § 101**
  Individual debt adjustment, **11 § 1322**
  Setoff and counterclaim, **11 § 365**
TIN (taxpayer identification number), petitions, **BKR 1005**
Title of act, **11 nt prec § 101**
Title to property, **11 § 541**
  Corporations, statements, **BKR 1007, 7007.1**
  Vested rights, **BKR 7070**
Tools, exemptions, **11 § 522**
Toys, exemptions, **11 § 522**
Trade secrets, **11 § 107; BKR 9018**
Training. Financial management training curriculum, generally, ante
Transcripts, **BKR 5007**

BANKRUPTCY—Cont'd
Transcripts—Cont'd
  Appeal and review, **BKR 8007**
  Review, **BKR 8007**
Transfers,
  Actual notice, **11 § 542**
  Adversary proceedings, **BKR 7087**
  Antecedent debt, avoidance, preferences, **11 § 547**
  Avoidance, generally, ante
  Bona fide purchasers, **11 § 548**
  Chapter 7 proceedings, ante
  Chapter 9 proceedings, avoidance, **11 §§ 109, 926**
  Charities, **11 §§ 363, 541, 1129**
  Claims, **BKR 3001**
  Commodities, ante
  Consumer debt, avoidance, **11 § 547**
  Damages, avoidance, **11 § 550**
  Definitions, **11 § 101**
    Avoidance, priorities and preferences, **11 § 547**
    Fraud, **11 § 548**
  Dismissal and nonsuit, **11 § 349**
  Distributions, **11 § 508**
  Evidence, claims, **BKR 3001**
  Exemptions, **BKR 4003**
    Avoidance, **11 §§ 501, 522**
  Foreign countries, **11 § 1520 et seq.**
  Fraud, ante
  Health care businesses, patients, **BKR 2015.2**
  Improvements, avoidance, liability, **11 § 550**
  Involuntary proceedings, ante
  Judges or justices, **28 § 155**
  Judicial liens, avoidance, **11 § 547**
  Liens and incumbrances, indemnity, **BKR 6010**
  Limitation of actions, avoidance, **11 §§ 546, 550**
  Notice, claims, evidence, **BKR 3001**
  Objections and exceptions, claims, evidence, **BKR 3001**
  Ordinary course of business, payments, avoidance, **11 § 547**
  Payment, avoidance, ordinary course of business, **11 § 547**
  Perfection, preferences, **11 § 547**
    Automatic stay, **11 § 362**
  Postpetition, **BKR 6001**
    Avoidance, **11 §§ 546, 549, 551**
  Preferences, avoidance, **11 § 547**
  Priorities and preferences, avoidance, **11 § 547**
  Real estate, bona fide purchasers, preferences, **11 § 547**
  Reconsideration, claims, **11 § 502**
  Reinstatement, avoidance, **11 § 349**
  Securities, ante
  Security interest, avoidance, **11 § 547**
  Set-off and counterclaim, **11 § 553**
  Taxation, **11 § 346**
  Time, preferences, **11 § 547**
  Trusts and trustees, post
  Validation, postpetition transfers, **BKR 6001**
  Waiver, avoidance, **11 § 522**
Transportation Department, railroads, appearances, **11 § 1164**
Traveling expenses, **11 § 503**
  National Bankruptcy Review Commission, **11 nt prec § 101**
  Witnesses, **BKR 2004**
Treasury of United States,
  Fees, **28 § 156**
    Referees, **11 nt prec § 101**
    Standing trustees, **28 § 586**
  Referees, fees, **11 nt prec § 101**
  Standing trustees, fees, **28 § 586**
Treaties, **11 § 1503**

BANKRUPTCY—Cont'd
Trial, **BKR 5001**
  Assignments, **BKR 7040**
  New trial, **BKR 9023**
    Time, **BKR 9015**
Trustees. Trusts and trustees, generally, post
Trusts and trustees, 11 § 321 et seq.; **BKR 2007.1 et seq.**
  Abandonment, 11 § 554
  Accounts and accounting, 11 § 327
    Compensation and salaries, 11 § 328
    Joint administration, **BKR 2009**
    Successors, **BKR 2012**
  Actions and proceedings, 11 § 323; 28 § 959; **BKR 6009**
    Vacancies in office, 11 § 325
  Administrative expenses, credit, 11 § 364
  Appeal and review, credit, 11 § 364
  Appointments,
    Judges or justices, relatives, **BKR 5002**
    Standing trustees, 28 § 586
    United States trustees, relatives, **BKR 5002**
  Attorneys,
    Cancellation, fees, 11 § 541
    Fees, sharing, 11 § 504
    Labor and employment, 11 § 327 et seq.
  Avoidance, generally, ante
  Beneficial interest, transfers, 11 § 541
  Bonds (officers and fiduciaries), 11 § 322; **BKR 2008, 2010**
    Chapter 7 proceedings, interim trustees, **BKR 2001**
    Involuntary proceedings, 11 § 303
  Business and commerce, sales, hearings, 11 § 363
  Cash collateral, definitions, administration, 11 § 363
  Chapter 7 proceedings, ante
  Chapter 9 proceedings, ante
  Chapter 11 proceedings, ante
  Chapter 12 proceedings, ante
  Chapter 13 proceedings, ante
  Checks, disposition, 11 § 347
  Claims,
    Business and commerce, venue, 28 § 1409
    Evidence, 11 § 108; **BKR 3003, 3004**
    Grain, 11 § 557
    Time, 11 § 501
  Clearing banks, liquidation, 11 § 781 et seq.
  Commodities, 11 § 766
    Customers, instructions, 11 § 765
    Open commodity contracts, statements, 11 § 766
    Transfers, void, 11 § 764
  Community property, sales, 11 § 363
  Compensation and salaries, 11 § 326
    Administrative expenses, allowances, 11 § 503
    Contracts, 11 § 365
    Priorities and preferences, payment, 11 § 507
    Records and recordation, **BKR 2013**
    Sharing, 11 § 504
  Confirmation of plan, individual debt adjustment, objections and exceptions, 11 § 1325
  Conflict of interest, **BKR 5002**
  Consent, 11 § 363
  Consumer debt, avoidance, transfers, 11 § 547
  Contracts, **BKR 6006**
    Assumption, 11 § 364
      Sales, setoff and counterclaim, 11 § 553
    Performance, time, 11 § 365
  Conversion, termination of service, 11 § 348
  Cooperation, 11 § 521
  Corporations, 11 § 321

BANKRUPTCY—Cont'd
Trusts and trustees—Cont'd
  Credit, 11 § 364
  Custodians, appointments, 11 § 545
  Damages, avoidance, transfers, 11 § 550
  Death, successors, **BKR 2012**
  Default, curing, time, 11 § 108
  Defenses, **BKR 6009**
  Definitions,
    Chapter 9 proceedings, 11 § 902
    Powers and duties, 11 § 323
  Demand, filing, time, 11 § 108
  Deposits, 11 § 345
  Destruction, health care businesses, records and recordation, 11 § 351
  Disclosure, records and recordation, hearings, 11 § 542
  Elections, 11 § 702; **BKR 2007.1**
    Qualifications, 11 §§ 322, 702
    Reports, **BKR 2003**
  Eligibility, 11 § 321
  Embezzlement, 18 § 153
  Evidence, 11 §§ 363, 364
    Avoidance, priorities and preferences, 11 § 547
    Claims, 11 § 108; **BKR 3003, 3004**
    Qualifications, **BKR 2011**
  Examinations and examiners, 11 § 343
    Conduct, 11 § 341
    Conflict of interest, 11 § 327
  Execution, 11 § 544
    Avoidance, 11 § 545
  Exemptions, liens and incumbrances, 11 § 522
  Expenses and expenditures,
    Claims, secured claims, recovery, 11 § 506
    Loans, 11 § 364
  Extensions, actions and proceedings, 11 § 108
  Fees, contracts, fraud, 18 § 155
  Filing, claims, evidence, 11 § 108; **BKR 3003, 3004**
  Fines, penalties and forfeitures, damages, 11 § 322
  Fish and game, reclamation, 11 § 546
  Foreign countries, ante
  Fraud, avoidance, 11 §§ 548, 550
  Good faith, real estate, 11 § 549
  Grain, 11 § 557
  Hearings,
    Leases, 11 § 363
    Removal from office, 11 § 324
    Sales, 11 § 363
  Indenture trust and trustees, generally, ante
  Inspection and inspectors, records and recordation, 18 § 154
  Interim trustees, 11 § 322
    Chapter 7 proceedings, appointments, **BKR 2001**
    Compensation and salaries, 11 § 331
    Involuntary proceedings, 11 § 303
  Inventories, **BKR 4002**
  Involuntary proceedings, transfers, validation, 11 § 549
  Joint administration, **BKR 2009**
  Labor and employment, powers and duties, 11 § 327
  Leases, **BKR 6006**
    Powers and duties, 11 §§ 363, 365
    Setoff, 11 § 553
  Liens and incumbrances, 11 § 544 et seq.
    Loans, 11 § 364
  Loans, liens and incumbrances, 11 § 364
  Losses, filing, time, 11 § 108

BANKRUPTCY—Cont'd

Trusts and trustees—Cont'd

Mail and mailing, health care businesses, records and recordation, 11 § 351

Money, 11 § 363

Judgments and decrees, venue, 28 § 1409

Multiple trustees, compensation and salaries, 11 § 326

Notice, **BKR 2002, 2015**

Claims, filing, **BKR 3004**

Elections, **BKR 2007.1**

Health care businesses, records and recordation, 11 § 351

Leases, 11 § 363

Perfection, security interest, 11 § 546

Removal from office, 11 § 324

Sales, 11 § 363

Selection, **BKR 2008**

Taxation, returns, 11 § 505

Time, extensions, 11 § 108

Objections and exceptions, confirmation of plan, individual debt adjustment, 11 § 1325

Partnership,

Avoidance, fraud, 11 § 548

Claims, 11 § 541

Payment, confirmation of plan, individual debt adjustment, 11 § 1326

Perfection,

Automatic stay, 11 § 362

Avoidance, 11 § 546

Personally identifiable information, disposition, 11 §§ 332, 363

Petitions, transmission, **BKR 1002**

Plans and specifications,

Individual debt adjustment, 11 § 1326

Modifications, 11 § 1329

Pleading, filing, extensions, 11 § 108

Possession, money, 11 § 363

Postpetition,

Avoidance, 11 §§ 549, 550

Security interest, 11 § 552

Powers and duties, 11 § 323

Avoidance, 11 § 544 et seq.

Fraud, transfers, avoidance, 11 § 548

Labor and employment, 11 § 327

Leases, 11 § 363

Liens and incumbrances, avoidance, 11 § 545

Limitation of actions, avoidance, 11 § 546

Postpetition, avoidance, 11 §§ 549, 550

Priorities and preferences, avoidance, 11 § 547

Sales, 11 § 363

Priorities and preferences,

Avoidance, damages, 11 § 550

Claims, 11 § 507

Qualifications, 11 § 322

Records and recordation, **BKR 2015**

Compensation and salaries, **BKR 2013**

Health care businesses, 11 § 351

Recovery,

Costs, 11 § 506

Liens and incumbrances, good faith, 11 § 550

Rejection, **BKR 2008**

Removal from office,

Hearings, 11 § 324

Successors, **BKR 2012**

Rent, statutory liens, avoidance, 11 § 545

Reports, 18 § 3057; **BKR 2015**

BANKRUPTCY—Cont'd

Trusts and trustees—Cont'd

Reports—Cont'd

Elections, **BKR 2007.1**

Returns, taxation, 11 § 346

Revocation or suspension, 28 § 586

Sales,

Avoidance, 11 §§ 363, 541

Curtesy, 11 § 363

Dower, 11 § 363

Reclamation, 11 § 546

Turnovers, property, 11 § 542

Schedules, 11 § 704

Security interest, postpetition transactions, 11 § 552

Shares and shareholders,

Accounts and accounting, trust deeds, 11 § 745

Contracts, 11 § 744

Customers, 11 § 751

Distribution, 11 § 752

Distribution, 11 § 750

Customers, 11 § 752

Payment, net equity, subordination, 11 § 747

Reduction, 11 § 748

Small businesses, 11 § 1116

Standing trustees.   United States trustees, post

Statutory liens, avoidance, 11 §§ 545, 550

Statutory successors, 28 § 1409

Substitution, parties, **BKR 2012**

Successors, 11 § 544

Avoidance, transfers, 11 § 544 et seq.

Damages, avoidance, transfers, 11 § 550

Discharge, taxation, 11 § 505

Preservation, avoidance, transfers, 11 § 551

Qualifications, 11 §§ 322, 703

Security interests, postpetition transactions, 11 § 552

Statutory successors, 28 § 1409

Substitution, 11 § 325; **BKR 2012**

Taxation, discharge, 11 § 505

Swap agreements, 11 § 546

Taxation, 11 § 505

Returns, 11 § 346

Termination, 28 § 586

Timeshares, rejection, setoff and counterclaim, 11 § 365

Transfers,

Avoidance, 11 § 544 et seq.

Patients, 11 § 704

Unclaimed property, disposition, 11 § 347

Undivided interest, sales, 11 § 363

United States trustees, generally, post

Utilities, 11 § 366

Vacancies in office, 11 § 325

Venue, 28 § 1409

Turnovers,

Property, 11 §§ 542, 543

Records and recordation, **BKR 1019**

Unclaimed property.   Abandonment, generally, ante

Undercapitalization, avoidance, fraud, 11 § 548

Undertakings.   Bonds (officers and fiduciaries), generally, ante

Underwriters, definitions, 11 § 364

Undivided interest in property, sales, 11 § 363

Unemployment compensation, exemptions, 11 § 522

Unenforceability, conversion, waiver, 11 § 706

Unincorporated associations, adversary proceedings, **BKR 7023.2**

BANKRUPTCY—Cont'd
United States attorneys,
   Investigations, 18 § 3057
   Reaffirmation agreements, abuse, 18 § 158
   Schedules, fraud, 18 § 158
United States Marshals Service,
   Conflict of interest, 18 § 154
   Embezzlement, 18 § 153
United States Tax Court, this index
United States trustees, 28 § 581 **et seq.**
   Abuse, chapter 7 proceedings, 11 §§ 704, 707
   Applications, compensation and salaries, 28 § 586
   Appointments, 28 § 581
      Chapter 11 proceedings, committees, 11 §§ 1102, 1114
      Consumer privacy ombudsman, 11 § 332
      Standing trustees, 28 § 586
   Appropriations, System Fund, 28 § 589a
   Assistants,
      Appointments, 28 § 582
      Compensation and salaries, limitation, 28 § 587
      Official stations, 28 § 584
      Removal from office, 28 § 582
   Audits and auditors, 28 § 586
   Bonds(officers and fiduciaries), 11 § 322
   Chapter 7 proceedings, 11 § 703 **et seq.**
      Abuse, 11 §§ 704, 707
      Appointments, successor trustees, 11 § 703
      Committees, consultants, 11 § 705
      Discharge, objections and exceptions, 11 § 727
      Dismissal and nonsuit, 11 § 707
      Interim trustee, appointments, **BKR 2001**
      Motions, consumer debts, dismissal and nonsuit, 11 § 707
      Objections and exceptions,
        Conflict of interest, 11 § 327
        Discharge, 11 § 727
      Reports, filing, 11 § 704
      Revocation or suspension, discharge, 11 § 727
      Successor trustees, appointments, 11 § 703
   Chapter 11 proceedings, 28 § 586
      Appointments, committees, 11 §§ 1102, 1114
      Committees, appointments, 11 §§ 1102, 1114
   Chapter 12 proceedings,
      Appointments, 11 § 1202
      Compensation and salaries, 11 § 326; 28 § 586
      Confirmation of plan, objections and exceptions, 11 § 1224
   Chapter 13 proceedings, 11 § 1307
      Appointments, individual debtors, 11 § 1302
      Conversion, 11 § 1307
      Powers and duties, 28 § 586
   Compensation and salaries,
      Assistants, 28 § 587
      Officers and employees, notice, 11 § 330
      Standing trustees, 28 § 586
   Consumer privacy ombudsman, appointments, 11 § 332
   Contests, **BKR 2020**
   Costs, recovery, deposits, 28 § 589a
   Counseling services, 11 § 111
   Deposits, 28 § 586
   Districts, regions, appointments, 28 § 581
   Entities, 11 § 101
   Ex parte contacts, **BKR 9003**
   Examinations and examiners, 11 § 341
      Oaths and affirmations, 11 § 343
   Executive Office, Director, 28 § 156
   Expenses and expenditures, 28 §§ 586, 588

BANKRUPTCY—Cont'd
United States trustees—Cont'd
   Fees,
      Percentage fee, 28 § 586
      Quarterly fees, 28 § 1930
   Filing, records and recordation, **BKR 5005**
   Financial management training curriculum, 11 § 111
   Foreign countries, 28 § 586
      Motions, pending actions, petitions, **BKR 1004.2**
   Fraud, reports, 28 § 586
   Interest, deposits, System Fund, 28 § 589a
   Involuntary proceedings, interim trustee, 11 § 303
   Judicial districts, appointments, 28 § 581
   Meetings, 11 § 341; **BKR 2003**
   Moneys, deposits, 11 § 345
   Notice, **BKR 2002**
      Compensation and salaries, 11 § 330
   Oaths and affirmations, 11 § 343; 28 § 583
   Objections and exceptions, **BKR 9034**
      Removal from office, 11 § 324
   Officers and employees, 28 § 589
   Official stations, 28 § 584
   Panel trustees, 28 § 586
   Powers and duties, 11 § 307; 28 § 581 **et seq.**
   Private trustees, 28 § 586
   Professional persons, conflict of interest, objections and
      exceptions, 11 § 327
   Quarterly fees, payment, 28 § 1930
   Records and recordation, filing, **BKR 5005**
   Regions, judicial districts, appointments, 28 § 581
   Removal from office, 28 § 581
   Reports, 28 § 586
      System Fund, deposits, 28 § 589a
   Rules and regulations, 11 § 102
   Small businesses, 28 § 586
   Standing trustees, 11 § 307 nt
      Qualifications, 28 § 586
   Supervision, standing trustees, 28 § 586
   System Fund,
      Compensation and salaries, 11 § 330
      Investments, 28 § 589a
   Terms of office, 28 § 581
   Transmission, pleadings, **BKR 9034**
   Treasury of United States,
      Quarterly fees, deposits, 28 § 1930
      System Fund, 28 § 589a
   Vacancies in office, 28 § 585
   Voluntary proceedings, petitions, amendments, **BKR 1009**
Universities. Colleges and Universities, this index
Unlawful detainer, automatic stay, 11 § 362
Unsecured claims. Claims, ante
Usury, defenses, 11 § 558
Utilities, 11 § 366
Vacancies in office,
   Judges or justices, 28 § 152
   Trusts and trustees, 11 § 325
Vacating or setting aside,
   Chapter 7 proceedings, proxies, **BKR 2006**
   Committees, appointments, **BKR 2007**
   Orders of court, **BKR 1018**
Vacation pay. Compensation and salaries, generally, ante
Validation,
   Liens and incumbrances, 28 § 157
   Postpetition transfers, **BKR 6001**
   Taxation, 11 § 505

BANKRUPTCY—Cont'd

Valuation,
  Definitions,
    Fraud, **11 §§ 542, 548**
    Powers and duties, **11 § 522**
  Liens and incumbrances, **11 § 363; BKR 3012**
Venue, **28 § 1408 et seq.; BKR 9030**
  Change of venue, **28 § 1412; BKR 1014**
  Chapter 11 proceedings, **28 §§ 1408, 1409**
  Foreign countries, ante
  Place of business, **28 §§ 1408, 1410**
Verification,
  Lists, **BKR 1008**
  Pleadings, **BKR 9011**
Vested rights,
  Family farmers, **11 § 1227**
  Individual debtors, **11 § 1327**
  Title to property, **BKR 7070**
Veterans,
  Benefits, exemptions, **11 § 522**
  Chapter 7 proceedings, disabled veterans, **11 § 707**
  Disabled veterans, chapter 7 proceedings, **11 § 707**
  Exemptions, benefits, **11 § 522**
Video cassette recorders, exemptions, **11 § 522**
Void liens, **11 §§ 506, 541, 551**
Voluntary proceedings, **11 §§ 301, 541**
  Automatic stay, **11 § 362**
    Setoff and counterclaim, **11 § 553**
  Dismissal and nonsuit, **BKR 8001**
  Fees, filing, payment, **28 § 1930**
  Foreign countries, **11 § 1511**
  Lists, **BKR 1007**
  Petitions, **11 § 301; BKR 1002**
    Amendments, **BKR 1009**
    Forms, **BKR Form 1**
  Repayment, **11 § 524**
  Schedules, **BKR 1007**
  Securities, automatic stay, **11 § 362**
  Time, schedules, **BKR 1007**
Wage earners bankruptcy. Chapter 13 proceedings, generally, ante
Waiver,
  Chapter 7 proceedings, ante
  Chapter 13 proceedings, ante
  Community claims, property, discharge, **11 § 524**
  Contracts, claims, **11 § 524**
  Conversion, **11 § 706**
  Counseling services, **11 § 109**
  Debt relief agencies, **11 § 526**
  Defenses, **11 § 558**
  Discharge, **11 § 524; BKR 4006**
  Dismissal and nonsuit, **11 § 1307**
  Exemptions, **11 § 522**
  Powers and duties, **11 §§ 522, 524**
  Privacy protection, **BKR 9037**
  Recovery, **11 § 522**
  Sovereign immunity, abrogation, **11 § 106**
  Transfers, avoidance, **11 § 522**
Warehouses and warehousemen, liens and incumbrances, avoidance, **11 § 546**
Warrants, automatic stay, setoff and counterclaim, **11 § 553**
Wearing apparel, exemptions, **11 § 522**
Wheat, **11 § 557**
Wife. Husband and wife, generally, ante
Willful or malicious injury, exceptions, **11 § 523**
Wiretapping, orders of court, **18 § 2516**

BANKRUPTCY—Cont'd

Withdrawal, **28 § 157; BKR 5011**
  Claims, **BKR 3006**
Withholding, taxation, **11 § 346**
Witnesses,
  Fees, **11 § 503**
    Priorities and preferences, **11 § 507**
  Foreign countries, **11 § 1521**
  Priorities and preferences, fees, **11 § 507**
  Privileges and immunities, **18 § 6001**
  Traveling expenses, **BKR 2004**
Writs, **28 § 2075**
Written questions, depositions, **BKR 7031**
Wrongful death,
  Exemptions, **11 § 522; 28 § 157**
  Jury, **28 § 1411**

BANKS AND BANKING

Bankruptcy, this index
Clearing banks, liquidation, **11 § 781 et seq.**
Financial assistance. Colleges and Universities, this index
Fraud, bankruptcy, **11 §§ 522, 523**

BARBITAL

Controlled Substances, generally, this index

BARBITURIC ACID

Controlled Substances, generally, this index

BARLEY

Bankruptcy, **11 § 557**
Commodity Exchanges, generally, this index

BATTERY

Assault and Battery, generally, this index

BEANS

Bankruptcy, dry edible beans, **11 § 557**
Dry edible beans, bankruptcy, **11 § 557**

BENZETHIDINE

Controlled Substances, generally, this index

BENZILATE

Controlled Substances, generally, this index

BENZYL CHLORIDE

Controlled Substances, generally, this index

BENZYL CYANIDE

Controlled Substances, generally, this index

BENZYLMORPHINE

Controlled Substances, generally, this index

BETACETYLMETHADOL

Controlled Substances, generally, this index

BETAMEPRODINE

Controlled Substances, generally, this index

BETAMETHADOL

Controlled Substances, generally, this index

BETAPRODINE

Controlled Substances, generally, this index

BEZITRAMIDE

Controlled Substances, generally, this index

BIAS AND PREJUDICE

Bankruptcy, dismissal and nonsuit, 11 § 349
Judges or justices, 28 § 455

BIOTERRORISM

Interception of wire, oral, or electronic communications, 18 § 2516

BOARDS AND COMMISSIONS

Bankruptcy, National Bankruptcy Review Commission, 11 nt prec § 101
Civil Aeronautics Board, generally, this index
Labor Disputes, this index
National Bankruptcy Review Commission, 11 nt prec § 101

BOARDS OF TRADE

Commodity Exchanges, this index

BONA FIDE PURCHASERS

Bankruptcy, this index

BONDS (OFFICERS AND FIDUCIARIES)

Bankruptcy, this index

BONUS

Bankruptcy, retention bonuses, 11 § 503
Shares and Shareholders, this index

BOOKS AND PAPERS

Bankruptcy, this index

BRIBERY AND CORRUPTION

Athletics, this index
Bankruptcy, sentence and punishment, 18 § 152
Federal Officers and Employees, this index
Racketeering, generally, this index
Witnesses, this index

BUFOTENINE

Controlled Substances, generally, this index

BUGGING

Interception of Wire, Oral, or Electronic Communications, generally, this index

BUILDING AND LOAN CORPORATIONS OR ASSOCIATIONS

Bankruptcy, 11 § 109

BUILDINGS

Bankruptcy, this index
Intermediate Care Facilities, generally, this index

BUSINESS AND COMMERCE

Bankruptcy, this index
Boards of trade. Commodity Exchanges, this index
Commodity Exchanges, generally, this index
Interference, interception of wire, oral, or electronic communications, 18 § 2516
International Trade Court, generally, this index
Secretary of Commerce, generally, this index
Threats, interception of wire, oral, or electronic communications, 18 § 2516

BUTYL NITRITE

Controlled Substances, generally, this index

CAB

Civil Aeronautics Board, generally, this index

CABLES

Interception of Wire, Oral, or Electronic Communications, generally, this index

CABOOSES

Railroads, generally, this index

CALIFORNIA

Bankruptcy, judges or justices, appointments, 28 § 152
United States trustees, judicial districts, 28 § 581

CARRIERS

Aircraft, generally, this index
Railroads, generally, this index

CARRYING AWAY

Kidnapping, generally, this index

CARS

Railroads, generally, this index

CHAPTER 7 PROCEEDINGS

Bankruptcy, this index

CHAPTER 9 PROCEEDINGS

Bankruptcy, this index

CHAPTER 11 PROCEEDINGS

Bankruptcy, this index

CHAPTER 12 PROCEEDINGS

Bankruptcy, this index

CHAPTER 13 PROCEEDINGS

Bankruptcy, this index

CHARITIES

Bankruptcy, this index
Fraud, bankruptcy, 11 § 548
Judges or justices, disqualification, 28 § 455

CHECKS

Bankruptcy, trusts and trustees, disposition, 11 § 347

CHEMICAL AND BIOLOGICAL WARFARE AND WEAPONS

Bankruptcy, claims, 11 § 362
Claims, bankruptcy, 11 § 362

CHIEF JUDGE OR JUSTICE

Courts of Appeals, this index
International Trade Court, this index
Supreme Court, this index

CHILD

Children and Minors, generally, this index

CHILDREN AND MINORS

Bankruptcy, this index
Custody, bankruptcy, automatic stay, 11 § 362
Disqualification, judges or justices, 28 § 455

CHILDREN AND MINORS—Cont'd

Interception of wire, oral, or electronic communications, sexual exploitation, 18 § 2516

Judges or justices, disqualification, 28 § 455

Sexual exploitation, interception of wire, oral, or electronic communications, 18 § 2516

Visitation, bankruptcy, automatic stay, 11 § 362

CHILDREN BORN OUT OF WEDLOCK

Bankruptcy, automatic stay, 11 § 362

Support, bankruptcy, relief from automatic stay, 11 § 362

CHINA TRADE ACT CORPORATIONS

Federal agencies, privileges and immunities, 18 § 6001

Privileges and immunities, Federal agencies, 18 § 6001

CHLORAL BETAINE

Controlled Substances, generally, this index

CHLORAL HYDRATE

Controlled Substances, generally, this index

CHORHEXADOL

Controlled Substances, generally, this index

CHRONIC DISEASES

Nursing Homes, generally, this index

CIGARETTES AND CIGARS

Racketeering, 18 § 1961

Trafficking, racketeering, 18 § 1961

CINCINNATI, OH

Court of Appeals for Sixth Circuit, generally, this index

CITIZENS AND CITIZENSHIP

Wiretap, interception, 18 § 2516

CIVIL AERONAUTICS BOARD

Bankruptcy, 11 § 1110

Privileges and immunities, witnesses, 18 § 6001

Witnesses, privileges and immunities, 18 § 6001

CIVIL AIRCRAFT

Aircraft, generally, this index

CIVIL SERVICE

Retirement and pensions. Judges or Justices, this index

CLAIMS

Bankruptcy, this index

Court of Federal Claims, generally, this index

District Courts, generally, this index

CLAIMS COURT

Court of Federal Claims, generally, this index

CLASSROOMS

Colleges and Universities, generally, this index

CLEARING BANKS

Banks and Banking, this index

CLERKS OF COURTS

Bankruptcy, this index

Compensation and salaries,

Deputies, 28 § 604

Director of Administrative Office of U.S. Courts, 28 § 604

CLERKS OF COURTS—Cont'd

Deputies, compensation and salaries, 28 § 604

Director of Administrative Office of U.S. Courts, supervision, 28 § 604

District courts. Clerks of District Courts, generally, this index

Incentive pay or awards, 28 § 604

Supervision, Director of Administrative Office of U.S. Courts, 28 § 604

CLERKS OF DISTRICT COURTS

Compensation and salaries, Director of Administrative Office of U.S. Courts, 28 § 604

Director of Administrative Office of U.S. Courts, compensation and salaries, 28 § 604

Incentive pay or awards, 28 § 604

CLONITAZENE

Controlled Substances, generally, this index

CLOTHING

Bankruptcy, exemptions, 11 § 522

Exemptions, bankruptcy, 11 § 522

CODEBTORS

Bankruptcy, this index

CODEINE

Controlled Substances, generally, this index

COLLECTIVE BARGAINING

Bankruptcy, this index

COLLEGES AND UNIVERSITIES

Assistance,

Loans, generally, post

Scholarships, generally, this index

Bankruptcy,

Financial assistance, fraud, exemptions, 11 § 522

Robert T. Stafford Federal Student Loan Program, 11 § 525

Coverdell education savings accounts, bankruptcy, 11 §§ 521, 541

Disqualification, judges or justices, 28 § 455

Financial assistance,

Bankruptcy, fraud, exemptions, 11 § 522

Fraud, bankruptcy, exemptions, 11 § 522

Loans, generally, post

Scholarships, generally, this index

Fraud,

Financial assistance, ante

Loans, post

Income tax, tuition,

Coverdell education savings accounts, bankruptcy, 11 §§ 521, 541

Education individual retirement accounts, bankruptcy, 11 §§ 521, 541

Individual retirement account, bankruptcy, 11 §§ 521, 541

Retirement accounts, bankruptcy, 11 §§ 521, 541

Judges or justices, disqualification, 28 § 455

Loans,

Bankruptcy, fraud, exemptions, 11 § 522

Fraud, bankruptcy, exemptions, 11 § 522

Robert T. Stafford Federal Student Loan Program, bankruptcy, 11 § 525

Robert T. Stafford Federal Student Loan Program. Loans, ante

COLLEGES AND UNIVERSITIES—Cont'd
Scholarships, generally, this index
Student loans. Loans, generally, ante
Tuition. Income tax, ante

COLORADO

Bankruptcy, judges or justices, appointments, 28 § 152

COMMANDER–IN–CHIEF

President of the United States, generally, this index

COMMERCE DEPARTMENT

Secretary of Commerce, generally, this index

COMMERCE SECRETARY

Secretary of Commerce, generally, this index

COMMITTEES

Bankruptcy, this index

COMMODITIES

Bankruptcy, this index
Brokers, liquidation, 28 § 586
Exchanges. Commodity Exchanges, generally, this index

COMMODITY EXCHANGES

Boards of trade, definitions, bankruptcy, 11 § 761
Commodity Futures Trading Commission,
    Bankruptcy, this index
    Definitions, bankruptcy, 11 § 761
    Privileges and immunities, witnesses, 18 § 6001 et seq.
Witnesses, privileges and immunities, 18 § 6001 et seq.

COMMODITY FUTURES

Commodity Exchanges, generally, this index

COMMODITY FUTURES TRADING COMMISSION

Commodity Exchanges, this index

COMMONWEALTH

Northern Mariana Islands, generally, this index

COMMUNICATIONS

Bankruptcy, this index
Interception of Wire, Oral, or Electronic Communications, generally, this index

COMPENSATION AND SALARIES

Arbitration, 28 § 658
Bankruptcy, this index
Clerks of Courts, this index
Clerks of District Courts, this index
Court Criers, this index
Courts of Appeals, this index
District Judges, this index
Guam, this index
Incentive Pay or Awards, generally, this index
Judges or Justices, this index
Law Clerks, this index
Messengers, courts, 28 § 604
Northern Mariana Islands, this index
Stenographers, this index
Subsistence, generally, this index
Supreme Court, this index
United States Magistrate Judges, this index
Virgin Islands, this index

COMPLAINTS

Court of Appeals for Sixth Circuit, this index

COMPROMISE AND SETTLEMENT

Bankruptcy, this index

COMPUTERS

Bankruptcy, this index
Fraud, interception of wire, oral, or electronic communications, 18 § 2516
Interception of wire, oral, or electronic communications, 18 § 2516

CONCURRENT PROCEEDINGS

Bankruptcy, foreign countries, 11 § 1528 et seq.

CONDOMINIUMS

Bankruptcy, discharge, 11 § 523

CONFERENCES

Bankruptcy, this index
Judicial Conference of the United States, generally, this index

CONFIDENTIAL OR PRIVILEGED INFORMATION

Alternative dispute resolution, 28 § 652
Bankruptcy, this index
District courts, alternative dispute resolution, 28 § 652

CONFINEMENT

Kidnapping, generally, this index

CONFLICT OF INTEREST

Bankruptcy, this index
Judges or justices, disqualification, 28 § 455
United States Magistrate Judges, this index

CONFLICT OF LAWS

Bankruptcy, foreign countries, 11 § 1503

CONGRESS

Assassination, interception of wire, oral, or electronic communications, 18 § 2516
Assault and battery, interception of wire, oral, or electronic communications, 18 § 2516
Kidnapping, interception of wire, oral, or electronic communications, 18 § 2516

CONNECTICUT

Bankruptcy, judges or justices, appointments, 28 § 152
Judicial districts, United States trustees, appointments, 28 § 581
United States trustees, judicial districts, appointments, 28 § 581

CONSOLIDATIONS AND MERGERS

Bankruptcy, this index

CONSPIRACY

Interception of wire, oral, or electronic communications, 18 § 2516

CONSUMER CREDIT PROTECTION

Bankruptcy, this index
Fraud. Credit Cards and Plates, this index
Interception of wire, oral, or electronic communications, 18 § 2516

CONSUMER DEBT

Bankruptcy, this index

CONSUMER PRIVACY OMBUDSMAN

Bankruptcy, this index

CONTRACTS

Administrative Office of United States Courts, this index
Annuities, generally, this index
Bankruptcy, this index
Long term care. Nursing Homes, generally, this index
Nursing Homes, generally, this index

CONTRIBUTIONS

Bankruptcy, this index

CONTROLLED SUBSTANCES

Concealment, interception of wire, oral, or electronic communications, 18 § 2516
Exports and imports, interception of wire, oral, or electronic communications, 18 § 2516
Interception of wire, oral, or electronic communications, orders, 18 § 2516
Investigations, racketeering, 18 § 2516
Manufacturers and manufacturing, interception of wire, oral, or electronic communications, 18 § 2516
Marijuana, interception of wire, oral, or electronic communications, 18 § 2516
Sales, interception of wire, oral, or electronic communications, 18 § 2516

CONVERSION

Bankruptcy, this index

COOPERATIVE BANKS

Bankruptcy, 11 § 109

COOPERATIVES

Bankruptcy, exemptions, 11 §§ 522, 523
Exemptions, bankruptcy, 11 §§ 522, 523

CORN

Bankruptcy, 11 § 557
Commodity Exchanges, generally, this index

CORPORATIONS

Bankruptcy, this index
Banks and Banking, generally, this index
Railroads, generally, this index

COSTS

Bankruptcy, this index

COTTON

Commodity Exchanges, generally, this index

COUNSELING SERVICES

Armed Forces, this index
Bankruptcy, this index

COUNSELORS

Attorneys, generally, this index

COUNTERFEITING

Interception of wire, oral, or electronic communications, 18 § 2516
Mail and Mailing, this index
Racketeering, 18 § 1961

COURT CRIERS

Compensation and salaries, Director of Administrative Office of U.S. Courts, 28 § 604
Director of Administrative Office of U.S. Courts, compensation and salaries, 28 § 604

COURT OF APPEALS

Courts of Appeals, generally, this index

COURT OF APPEALS FOR FIRST CIRCUIT

Discipline, complaints, 28 § 372

COURT OF APPEALS FOR SECOND CIRCUIT

Judges or justices, complaints, 28 § 372

COURT OF APPEALS FOR THIRD CIRCUIT

Discipline, judges or justices, complaints, 28 § 372

COURT OF APPEALS FOR FOURTH CIRCUIT

Judges or justices, complaints, 28 § 372

COURT OF APPEALS FOR FIFTH CIRCUIT

Judges or justices, complaints, 28 § 372

COURT OF APPEALS FOR SIXTH CIRCUIT

Complaints, judges or justices, 28 § 372
Judges or justices,
    Complaints, 28 § 372
    Disability, complaints, 28 § 372
    Misconduct, 28 § 372

COURT OF APPEALS FOR SEVENTH CIRCUIT

Judges or justices, complaints, 28 § 372

COURT OF APPEALS FOR EIGHTH CIRCUIT

Judges or justices, discipline, 28 § 372

COURT OF APPEALS FOR NINTH CIRCUIT

Judges or justices, complaints, 28 § 372

COURT OF APPEALS FOR TENTH CIRCUIT

Judges or justices, complaints, 28 § 372

COURT OF APPEALS FOR ELEVENTH CIRCUIT

Judges or justices, complaints, 28 § 372

COURT OF APPEALS FOR THE ARMED FORCES

Privileges and immunities, witnesses, 18 § 6001 et seq.
Witnesses, privileges and immunities, 18 § 6001 et seq.

COURT OF APPEALS FOR THE DISTRICT OF COLUMBIA

Witnesses, privileges and immunities, 18 § 6001 et seq.

COURT OF CLAIMS

Court of Federal Claims, generally, this index

COURT OF FEDERAL CLAIMS

Administrative Office of United States Courts, annuities, 28 § 604
Appeal and review, judges, discipline, 28 § 372
Discipline, judges or justices, 28 § 372
Judges or justices,
    Complaints,
        Appeal and review, 28 § 372
        Discipline, 28 § 372
    Discipline, 28 § 372
    Retirement and pensions, annuities, payment, 28 § 604
Witnesses, privileges and immunities, 18 § 6001 et seq.

COURTHOUSES AND COURTROOMS

Administrative Office of United States Courts, generally, this index

COURTS

Accommodations, 28 § 604
Administrative Office of United States Courts, generally, this index
Attorneys, generally, this index
Audits and auditors, 28 § 604
Bankruptcy, this index
Calendars. Dockets and Docketing, generally, this index
Center. Judicial Center, generally, this index
Clerical assistants,
　Compensation and salaries, 28 § 604
　Salaries, 28 § 604
Clerks of Courts, generally, this index
Court of Appeals for Sixth Circuit, generally, this index
Court of Federal Claims, generally, this index
Courts of Appeals, generally, this index
District Courts, generally, this index
District Judges, generally, this index
Dockets and Docketing, generally, this index
Federal Judicial Center. Judicial Center, generally, this index
Incentive pay or awards, 28 § 604
Inspection and inspectors, overseas, dockets and docketing, 28 § 604
International Trade Court, generally, this index
Judges or Justices, generally, this index
Judicial Center, generally, this index
Judicial Conference of the United States, generally, this index
Jury, generally, this index
Law Clerks, generally, this index
Machinery and equipment, 28 § 604
Magistrates. United States Magistrate Judges, generally, this index
Marshals. United States Marshals Service, generally, this index
Messengers, compensation and salaries, 28 § 604
Office expenses, payment, 28 § 604
Officers and employees,
　Incentive pay or awards, 28 § 604
　United States Marshals Service, generally, this index
Records and recordation,
　Disqualification, judges or justices, 28 § 455
　Judges or justices, disqualification, 28 § 455
Secretaries, compensation and salaries, 28 § 604
Security, 28 § 604
Speedy trial. Trial, this index
Stenographers, compensation and salaries, 28 § 604
Supplies, 28 § 604
Supreme Court, generally, this index
Tax Court. United States Tax Court, generally, this index
United States courts of appeals. Courts of Appeals, generally, this index
United States Magistrate Judges, generally, this index
United States Marshals Service, generally, this index
United States Tax Court, generally, this index
Witnesses, generally, this index

COURTS OF APPEALS

Bankruptcy, this index
Chief Judge or Justice, disability, 28 § 372
Compensation and salaries,
　Law clerks, 28 § 604

COURTS OF APPEALS—Cont'd

Compensation and salaries—Cont'd
　Secretaries, 28 § 604
Incentive pay or awards, 28 § 604
Judges or justices,
　Additional judges, 28 § 372
　Compensation and salaries, disability, 28 § 372
　Disability, 28 § 372
　Retirement and pensions, disability, 28 § 372
　Vacancies in office, 28 § 372
Officers and employees, incentive pay or awards, 28 § 604
Privileges and immunities, 18 § 6001 et seq.
Reports, Administrative Office of U.S. Courts, 28 § 604
Sixth Circuit. Court of Appeals for Sixth Circuit, generally, this index
United States magistrate judges, 28 § 604
Witnesses, privileges and immunities, 18 § 6001 et seq.

COVERDELL EDUCATION SAVINGS ACCOUNTS

Bankruptcy, 11 §§ 521, 541

CRACK (COCAINE)

Controlled Substances, generally, this index

CREDIT CARDS AND PLATES

Fraud, Secret Service, 18 § 2516

CREDIT (PAYMENT OF INDEBTEDNESS)

Bankruptcy, this index
Usury, generally, this index

CREDIT UNIONS

Bankruptcy, 11 § 109

CRIME VICTIMS

Interception of wire, oral, or electronic communications, 18 § 2516
Restitution, generally, this index
Retaliation, interception of wire, oral, or electronic communications, 18 § 2516
Tampering, interception of wire, oral, or electronic communications, 18 § 2516

CRIMES AND OFFENSES

Aliens, this index
Assault and Battery, generally, this index
Atomic Energy, this index
Bankruptcy, this index
Battery. Assault and Battery, generally, this index
Crime Victims, generally, this index
Embezzlement, generally, this index
Explosives, this index
Immigration, this index
Interception of Wire, Oral, or Electronic Communications, generally, this index
Kidnapping, generally, this index
Misapplication of funds. Embezzlement, generally, this index
Motor Vehicles, this index
Pretrial services,
　Accommodations, 28 § 604
　Administrative Office of United States Courts, Director, 28 § 604
　Administrative personnel, 28 § 604
　Judicial Conference of the United States, 28 § 604
　Law books, 28 § 604
　Supplies, 28 § 604
　Vouchers, audits and auditing, 28 § 604

CRIMES AND OFFENSES—Cont'd
Racketeering, generally, this index
Receivers and Receivership, this index
Restitution, generally, this index
Speedy trial. Trial, this index
Trial, generally, this index
Victims. Crime Victims, generally, this index
Witnesses, generally, this index

CRIMINAL CODE

Crimes and Offenses, generally, this index

CRIMINAL JUSTICE SYSTEM

Crimes and Offenses, generally, this index

CRIMINAL PROCEDURE

Crimes and Offenses, generally, this index

CRIMINAL SYNDICALISM

Racketeering, generally, this index

CROCKERY

Bankruptcy, exemptions, 11 § 522

CURRENT MONTHLY INCOME

Bankruptcy, this index

CUSTODIANS

Bankruptcy, this index

CUSTODY

Children and minors, bankruptcy, automatic stay, 11 § 362
Kidnapping, generally, this index

CYPRENORPHINE

Controlled Substances, generally, this index

DAMAGES

Bankruptcy, this index
District Courts, this index

DANGEROUS DRUGS

Controlled Substances, generally, this index

DEATH

Bankruptcy, this index
Hospices, generally, this index
International Trade Court, this index
Justices or judges, vacancies in office, 28 § 372

DEBT RELIEF AGENCIES

Bankruptcy, this index

DEBTORS IN POSSESSION

Bankruptcy, this index

DEFAULT

Bankruptcy, this index
Railroads, this index

DEFENSE DEPARTMENT

Head of Department. Secretary of Defense, generally, this index

DEFENSE SECRETARY

Secretary of Defense, generally, this index

DEFINITIONS

Words and Phrases, generally, this index

DELAWARE

Bankruptcy, judges or justices, appointments, 28 § 152
United States trustees of judicial districts, appointment, 28 § 581

DEPENDENTS

Bankruptcy, exemptions, 11 § 522

DEPOSITS

Bankruptcy, this index
Public utilities, bankruptcy, 11 § 366

DESOMORPHINE

Controlled Substances, generally, this index

DEXTROMETHORPHAN

Controlled Substances, generally, this index

DEXTROMORAMIDE

Controlled Substances, generally, this index

DEXTRORPHAN

Controlled Substances, generally, this index

DIAMPROMIDE

Controlled Substances, generally, this index

DIETHYLTHIAMBUTENE

Controlled Substances, generally, this index

DIETHYLTRYPTAMINE

Controlled Substances, generally, this index

DIGITAL SIGNALS

Interception of Wire, Oral, or Electronic Communications, generally, this index

DIHYDROCODEINE

Controlled Substances, generally, this index

DIHYDROCODEINONE

Controlled Substances, generally, this index

DIHYDROMORPHINE

Controlled Substances, generally, this index

DIMENOXADOL

Controlled Substances, generally, this index

DIMEPHEPTANOL

Controlled Substances, generally, this index

DIMETHYLTHIAMBUTENE

Controlled Substances, generally, this index

DIMETHYLTRYPTAMINE

Controlled Substances, generally, this index

DIOXAPHETYL BUTYRATE

Controlled Substances, generally, this index

DIPHENOXYLATE

Controlled Substances, generally, this index

DIPIPANONE

Controlled Substances, generally, this index

DISBURSING OFFICIALS, CLERKS, AND AGENTS

Administrative Office of U.S. Courts, 28 § 604

DISCIPLINE

Court of Appeals for First Circuit, this index
Court of Appeals for Third Circuit, this index
Court of Federal Claims, this index
International Trade Court, this index

DISCLOSURE

Bankruptcy, this index

DISCRIMINATION

Bankruptcy, 11 § 525
Student Loan Program, bankruptcy, 11 § 525

DISEASES

Drugs and Medicine, generally, this index

DISHES

Bankruptcy, exemptions, 11 § 522

DISMISSAL AND NONSUIT

Bankruptcy, this index

DISPUTE RESOLUTION

Alternative Dispute Resolution, generally, this index
Arbitration, generally, this index

DISTRICT COURTS

Alternative Dispute Resolution, generally, this index
Appeal and review. Courts of Appeals, generally, this index
Arbitration, referrals, 28 § 654
Bankruptcy, generally, this index
Clerks of District Courts, generally, this index
Damages, alternative dispute resolution, 28 § 654
Definitions, alternative dispute resolution, 28 § 651
District Judges, generally, this index
Exemptions, alternative dispute resolution, 28 § 652
Guam, this index
Judges. District Judges, generally, this index
Jurisdiction, alternative dispute resolution, 28 § 652
Neutrals, alternative dispute resolution, 28 § 653
Northern Mariana Islands, this index
Pretrial services. Crimes and Offenses, this index
Referrals, arbitration, 28 § 654
Security, 28 § 604
United States Magistrate Judges, generally, this index
Virgin Islands, this index
Witnesses, privileges and immunities, 18 § 6001 et seq.

DISTRICT JUDGES

Appointment, disability, 28 § 372
Certificates and certification, disability, 28 § 372
Compensation and salaries,
    Disability, 28 § 372
    Secretaries, 28 § 604
Discipline, 28 § 372
Handicapped persons,
    Appointments, 28 § 372
    Retirement and pensions, 28 § 372
Law clerks, compensation and salaries, 28 § 604
Precedence, disability, 28 § 372
Resignation, disability, 28 § 372

DISTRICT JUDGES—Cont'd
United States Magistrate Judges, generally, this index
Vacancies in office, 28 § 372

DISTRICT OF COLUMBIA

Bankruptcy, this index
United States trustees, judicial districts, 28 § 581

DISTRICTS

District Courts, generally, this index

DIVORCE

Bankruptcy, this index

DOCKETS AND DOCKETING

Administrative Office of U.S. Courts, information, 28 § 604
Arbitration, this index
Bankruptcy, this index
Examinations and examiners, 28 § 604
Information, Administrative Office of U.S. Courts, 28 § 604

DOCUMENTARY EVIDENCE

Racketeer influenced and corrupt organizations, 18 § 1961

DOMESTIC VIOLENCE

Bankruptcy, automatic stay, 11 § 362

DOMICILE AND RESIDENCE

Bankruptcy, this index

DOMICILIARY CARE

Nursing Homes, generally, this index

DOWER AND CURTESY

Bankruptcy, sales, 11 § 363
Sales, bankruptcy, 11 § 363

DRUGS AND MEDICINE

Bankruptcy, trafficking, chapter 7 proceedings, dismissal and
    nonsuit, 11 § 707
Controlled Substances, generally, this index
Interception of wire, oral, or electronic communications, 18
    § 2516
Racketeering, generally, this index
Trafficking, bankruptcy, chapter 7 proceedings, dismissal and
    nonsuit, 11 § 707

EAVESDROPPING

Interception of Wire, Oral, or Electronic Communications,
    generally, this index

EDUCATION

Bankruptcy, this index
Colleges and Universities, generally, this index
Coverdell education savings accounts, bankruptcy, 11 §§ 521,
    541
Income Tax, this index
Scholarships, generally, this index
Secretary of Education, generally, this index

EDUCATION DEPARTMENT

Secretary of Education, generally, this index

EDUCATION INDIVIDUAL RETIREMENT ACCOUNTS

Bankruptcy, 11 §§ 521, 541

EDUCATION SECRETARY

Secretary of Education, generally, this index

EGGS AND EGG PRODUCTS

Commodity Exchanges, generally, this index

ELECTIONS

Bankruptcy, this index

ELECTRONIC FILING

Bankruptcy, this index

ELECTRONIC SURVEILLANCE

Interception of Wire, Oral, or Electronic Communications, generally, this index

EMBEZZLEMENT

Bankruptcy, 11 § 523; 18 § 153
Interception of wire, oral, or electronic communications, Pension and Welfare Fund, 18 § 2516

EMERGENCIES

Bankruptcy, this index

EMIGRATION

Immigration, generally, this index

EMPLOYEE RETIREMENT INCOME SECURITY PROGRAM

Bankruptcy, this index
Theft, 18 § 2516

ENERGY

Interception, wire and oral communications, 18 § 2516
Secretary of Energy, generally, this index

ENERGY DEPARTMENT

Head of Department. Secretary of Energy, generally, this index
Secretary of Energy, generally, this index

ENERGY SECRETARY

Secretary of Energy, generally, this index

ENGINE HOUSES

Railroads, generally, this index

ENTIRETIES, ESTATES BY

Bankruptcy, sales, 11 § 363

ENTRY UPON LAND

Bankruptcy, this index

EQUITY

Bankruptcy, this index
Receivers and receivership, 28 § 959
Trusts and trustees, 28 § 959

EQUITY SECURITY HOLDERS

Bankruptcy, this index

ERGONOVINE

Controlled Substances, generally, this index

ERGOTAMINE

Controlled Substances, generally, this index

ESCAPE

Interception of wire, oral, or electronic communications, 18 § 2516

ESPIONAGE

Interception of wire, oral, or electronic communications, 18 § 2516

ESTATE TAX

United States Tax Court, generally, this index

ETHCHLORVYNOL

Controlled Substances, generally, this index

ETHINAMATE

Controlled Substances, generally, this index

ETHYL ETHER

Controlled Substances, generally, this index

ETHYLMETHYLTHIAMBUTENE

Controlled Substances, generally, this index

ETHYLMORPHINE

Controlled Substances, generally, this index

ETONITAZENE

Controlled Substances, generally, this index

ETORPHINE

Controlled Substances, generally, this index

ETOXERIDINE

Controlled Substances, generally, this index

EVICTIONS

Landlord and Tenant, this index

EVIDENCE

Bankruptcy, this index
Witnesses, generally, this index

EXAMINATIONS AND EXAMINERS

Bankruptcy, this index

EXECUTION

Bankruptcy, this index

EXECUTIVE DEPARTMENTS

Justice Department, generally, this index
President of the United States, generally, this index
Secretary of Agriculture, generally, this index
Secretary of Commerce, generally, this index
Secretary of Energy, generally, this index
Secretary of Housing and Urban Development, generally, this index
Secretary of Labor, generally, this index
Secretary of State, generally, this index
Secretary of the Interior, generally, this index
Secretary of the Treasury, generally, this index
Witnesses, privileges and immunities, 18 § 6001 et seq.

EXECUTIVE MANSION

White House, generally, this index

EXECUTIVE OFFICE

President of the United States, this index

EXECUTORS AND ADMINISTRATORS

Disqualification, judges or justices, 28 § 455
Judges or justices, disqualification, 28 § 455

EXEMPTIONS

Annuities, this index
Bankruptcy, this index
Clothing, this index
Cooperatives, this index
New markets venture capital companies, bankruptcy, 11 § 109

EXPENSES AND EXPENDITURES

Administrative Office of U.S. Courts, 28 § 604
Bankruptcy, this index
Court officers and employees, payment, Administrative Office of U.S. Courts, 28 § 604
Judges or Justices, this index
Subsistence, generally, this index
Traveling Expenses, generally, this index

EXPLOSIVES

Crimes and offenses, communications, interceptions, 18 § 2516
Interception of wire, oral, or electronic communications, 18 § 2516

EXPORTS AND IMPORTS

Controlled Substances, this index
Courts. International Trade Court, generally, this index
International Trade Court, generally, this index

EXTENDED CARE SERVICES

Nursing Homes, generally, this index

EXTORTION

Credit (payment of indebtedness), 18 § 2516
Interception of wire, oral, or electronic communications, credit (payment of indebtedness), 18 § 2516

FAMILY FARMERS PROTECTION ACT OF 2002

Generally, 11 §§ 101 nt, 1201 et seq.

FATHERS

Children and Minors, generally, this index

FEDERAL AGENCIES

Arbitration, generally, this index
Interception of wire, oral, or electronic communications, 18 § 2516
Officers and employees. Federal Officers and Employees, generally, this index
Privileges and immunities, witnesses, 18 § 6001 et seq.
Witnesses, privileges and immunities, 18 § 6001 et seq.

FEDERAL BUREAU OF INVESTIGATION

Bankruptcy, powers and duties, 18 § 158
Interception of wire, oral, or electronic communications, 18 § 2516

FEDERAL CLAIMS COURT

Court of Federal Claims, generally, this index

FEDERAL DEPOSIT INSURANCE CORPORATION

Privileges and immunities, witnesses, 18 § 6001 et seq.
Witnesses, privileges and immunities, 18 § 6001 et seq.

FEDERAL JUDICIAL CENTER

Judicial Center, generally, this index

FEDERAL MARITIME COMMISSION

Privileges and immunities, 18 § 6001 et seq.
Witnesses, privileges and immunities, 18 § 6001 et seq.

FEDERAL OFFICERS AND EMPLOYEES

Bribery and corruption, interception of wire, oral, or electronic communications, 18 § 2516
Disqualification, judges or justices, 28 § 455
Influence, injuries, interception of wire, electronic or oral communications, 18 § 2516
Interception of wire, oral, or electronic communications, 18 § 2516
Judges or justices, disqualification, 28 § 455
President of the United States, generally, this index
Secretary of Agriculture, generally, this index
Secretary of Commerce, generally, this index
Secretary of Education, generally, this index
Secretary of Health and Human Services, generally, this index
Secretary of Housing and Urban Development, generally, this index
Secretary of Labor, generally, this index
Secretary of State, generally, this index
Secretary of Transportation, generally, this index
United States Marshals Service, generally, this index
Vice President of the United States, generally, this index

FEDERAL REGISTER

Administrative Office of United States Courts, rules and regulations, 28 § 604

FEDERAL TRADE COMMISSION

Witnesses, privileges and immunities, 18 § 6001 et seq.

FELONIES

Crimes and Offenses, generally, this index

FENTANYL

Controlled Substances, generally, this index

FIDUCIARIES

Bankruptcy, this index
Disqualification, judges or justices, 28 § 455
Judges or justices, disqualification, 28 § 455
Receivers and Receivership, generally, this index

FINANCIAL INSTITUTIONS

Banks and Banking, generally, this index

FINANCIAL MANAGEMENT TRAINING CURRICULUM

Bankruptcy, this index

FINANCIAL STATEMENTS AND REPORTS

Bankruptcy, this index

FINES AND PENALTIES

Bankruptcy, this index
Restitution, generally, this index

FISH AND GAME

Bankruptcy, this index
Commercial fishing. Bankruptcy, this index

FLAX AND FLAXSEED

Bankruptcy, 11 § 557
Commodity Exchanges, generally, this index

FLIGHTS

Aircraft, generally, this index

FLORIDA

Bankruptcy, judges or justices, appointments, 28 § 152
United States trustees, appointments, 28 § 581

FOREIGN AND INTERNATIONAL RELATIONS

Secretary of State, generally, this index

FOREIGN BANKS IN THE UNITED STATES

Bankruptcy, 11 § 109

FOREIGN COUNTRIES

Aliens, generally, this index
Bankruptcy, this index
Immigration, generally, this index
Secretary of State, generally, this index

FOREIGN COURTS OR TRIBUNALS

Exports and imports. International Trade Court, generally, this index

FOREIGN INSURANCE

Bankruptcy, 11 § 109

FOREIGNERS

Aliens, generally, this index

FORFEITURES

Bankruptcy, 11 § 363

FORMULARIES

Drugs and Medicine, generally, this index

FORWARD CONTRACTS

Bankruptcy, this index

FOUNDATIONS

Scholarships, generally, this index

FRATERNAL ASSOCIATIONS AND SOCIETIES

Disqualification, judges or justices, 28 § 455
Judges or justices, disqualification, 28 § 455

FRAUD

Bankruptcy, this index
Banks and Banking, this index
Charities, this index
Colleges and Universities, this index
Computers, this index
Credit Cards and Plates, this index
Passports, this index
Racketeering, generally, this index
Receivers and Receivership, this index
Religious organizations and societies, bankruptcy, 11 § 548
Scholarships, this index
Secret Service, this index

FRAUDS, STATUTE OF

Bankruptcy, this index

FRAUDULENT CONVEYANCES

Bankruptcy, this index

FREE BASE (COCAINE)

Controlled Substances, generally, this index

FRIVOLOUS ACTIONS

Bankruptcy, this index

FUEL

Bankruptcy, taxation, 11 § 501
Taxation, bankruptcy, 11 § 501

FUNDS

Retirement and Pensions, this index
Scholarships, generally, this index

FURETHIDINE

Controlled Substances, generally, this index

FURNITURE

Bankruptcy, exemptions, 11 § 522

FUTURES (COMMODITIES)

Commodity Exchanges, generally, this index

GAMBLING

Interceptions, communications, 18 § 2516
Racketeering, generally, this index
Syndicated gambling, crimes and offenses, 18 § 2516

GEORGIA

Bankruptcy, judges or justices, appointments, 28 § 152

GI

Armed Forces, generally, this index

GIFT TAX

United States Tax Court, generally, this index

GIFTS

Bankruptcy, this index
National Bankruptcy Review Commission, 11 nt prec § 101

GLUTETHIMIDE

Controlled Substances, generally, this index

GOLD

Commodity Exchanges, generally, this index

GOOD FAITH

Bankruptcy, this index

GOODS, WARES AND MERCHANDISE

Bankruptcy, liens and incumbrances, 11 § 546
Household Goods, generally, this index

GOVERNMENT EMPLOYEES

Federal Officers and Employees, generally, this index

GOVERNMENT OFFICERS AND EMPLOYEES

Federal Officers and Employees, generally, this index

GRAIN

Bankruptcy, this index
Commodity Exchanges, generally, this index
Futures. Commodity Exchanges, generally, this index

GRAND JURY

Bankruptcy, investigations, 18 § 3057

GRANTS

Bankruptcy, discrimination, 11 § 525

GUAM

Compensation and salaries,
District courts, judges or justices, 28 § 604
Judges or justices, district courts, 28 § 604
District courts,
Compensation and salaries, judges or justices, 28 § 604
Judges or justices, compensation and salaries, 28 § 604
Witnesses, 18 § 6001 et seq.
United States trustees of judicial districts, 28 § 581

GUARDIAN AND WARD

Disqualification, judges or justices, 28 § 455
Judges or justices, disqualification, 28 § 455

HABIT FORMING DRUGS

Controlled Substances, generally, this index

HANDICAPPED PERSONS

Bankruptcy, this index
District Judges, this index
Intermediate Care Facilities, generally, this index
Judges or Justices, this index
Supreme Court, this index

HANGING LAW

Bankruptcy, chapter 13 proceedings, 11 § 1325

HARDSHIP

Bankruptcy, reaffirmation agreements, 11 § 524

HAWAII

Bankruptcy, judges or justices, appointments, 28 § 152
United States, judicial district trustees, appointments, 28 § 581

HEALTH AND HUMAN SERVICES DEPARTMENT

Head of Department. Secretary of Health and Human Services, generally, this index
Secretary of Health and Human Services, generally, this index

HEALTH AND HUMAN SERVICES SECRETARY

Secretary of Health and Human Services, generally, this index

HEALTH AND SANITATION

Controlled Substances, generally, this index

HEALTH CARE BUSINESSES

Bankruptcy, this index

HEALTH CARE FACILITIES AND SERVICES

Hospitals, generally, this index

HEALTH CARE PROVIDERS

Long term care. Nursing Homes, generally, this index
Nursing Homes, generally, this index

HEALTH INSURANCE

Bankruptcy, chapter 13 proceedings, 11 § 1329
Long term care. Nursing Homes, generally, this index
Nursing Homes, generally, this index

HEARINGS

Arbitration, this index
Bankruptcy, this index

HIGH SCHOOLS OR SECONDARY SCHOOLS

Income tax, education individual retirement accounts, bankruptcy, 11 §§ 521, 541

HIGHER EDUCATION

Colleges and Universities, generally, this index

HOG (PCP)

Controlled Substances, generally, this index

HOME CARE

Agents and agencies. Home Health Agencies, generally, this index

HOME HEALTH AGENCIES

Bankruptcy,
Definitions, 11 § 101
Ombudsman, 11 § 333
Records and recordation, 11 § 351
Definitions, bankruptcy, 11 § 101
Ombudsman, bankruptcy, 11 § 333
Records and recordation, bankruptcy, 11 § 351

HOMES

Nursing Homes, generally, this index

HOMESTEAD ASSOCIATIONS

Bankruptcy, 11 § 109

HOMESTEADS

Bankruptcy, this index

HOSPICES

Bankruptcy,
Definitions, 11 § 101
Ombudsman, 11 § 333
Records and recordation, 11 § 351
Definitions, bankruptcy, 11 § 101
Ombudsman, bankruptcy, 11 § 333
Records and recordation, bankruptcy, 11 § 351

HOSPITALS

Bankruptcy,
Definitions, 11 § 101
Ombudsman, 11 § 333
Records and recordation, 11 § 351
Definitions, bankruptcy, 11 § 101
Long term care. Nursing Homes, generally, this index
Nursing Homes, generally, this index
Ombudsman, bankruptcy, 11 § 333
Records and recordation, bankruptcy, 11 § 351

HOSTAGES

Interception of wire, oral, or electronic communications, 18 § 2516

HOUSEHOLD GOODS

Bankruptcy, exemptions, 11 § 522
Definitions, bankruptcy, exemptions, 11 § 522
Exemptions, bankruptcy, 11 § 522
Liens and incumbrances, bankruptcy, 11 § 522

HOUSING

Assisted Living Facilities, generally, this index
Secretary of Housing and Urban Development, generally, this index

HOUSING AND URBAN DEVELOPMENT DEPARTMENT

Secretary of Housing and Urban Development, generally, this index

HUMAN TRAFFICKING

Trafficking, this index

HUSBAND AND WIFE

Bankruptcy, this index
Judges or justices, disqualification, 28 § 455

HYDRIODIC ACID

Controlled Substances, generally, this index

HYDROMORPHINOL

Controlled Substances, generally, this index

HYDROXYPETHIDINE

Controlled Substances, generally, this index

IBOGAINE

Controlled Substances, generally, this index

IDAHO

Bankruptcy, judges or justices, appointments, 28 § 152
United States trustees, judicial districts, 28 § 581

IDENTITY AND IDENTIFICATION

Bankruptcy, this index
Personally identifiable information. Bankruptcy, this index
Theft, bankruptcy, 11 § 107

ILLINOIS

Bankruptcy, judges or justices, appointments, 28 § 152
United States trustees, judicial districts, 28 § 581

IMMIGRATION

Crimes and offenses,
    Smuggling, 18 § 1961
    Wiretapping, 18 § 2516
Interception of wire, oral, or electronic communications, investigations, alien smuggling, 18 § 2516
Investigations, smuggling, 18 § 2516
Smuggling,
    RICO-predicate offenses, 18 § 1961
    Wiretapping, 18 §§ 1961, 2516
Wiretapping, 18 § 2516

IMMUNITIES

Privileges and Immunities, generally, this index

INCENTIVE PAY OR AWARDS

Administrative Office of United States Courts, 28 § 604
Clerks of courts, 28 § 604
Clerks of district courts, 28 § 604
Courts, 28 § 604
Courts of appeals, 28 § 604
Law clerks, 28 § 604

INCOME

Bankruptcy, this index

INCOME TAX

Bankruptcy, this index
Colleges and Universities, this index
Coverdell education savings accounts, bankruptcy, 11 §§ 521, 541

INCOME TAX—Cont'd
Education,
    Coverdell education savings accounts, bankruptcy, 11 §§ 521, 541
    Individual retirement accounts, bankruptcy, 11 §§ 521, 541
High Schools or Secondary Schools, this index
Individual retirement accounts,
    Coverdell education savings accounts, bankruptcy, 11 §§ 521, 541
    Education, bankruptcy, 11 §§ 521, 541
    Higher education, bankruptcy, 11 §§ 521, 541
Schools and School Districts, this index
Tax Court. United States Tax Court, generally, this index
Tuition. Colleges and Universities, this index
United States Tax Court, generally, this index

INDEBTEDNESS

Bankruptcy, generally, this index
Municipal corporations, chapter 9 proceedings. Bankruptcy, this index
Receivers and Receivership, generally, this index
Usury, generally, this index

INDEMNITY

Bankruptcy, this index

INDENTURE TRUST AND TRUSTEES

Bankruptcy, this index

INDEXES

Bankruptcy, this index

INDIANA

Bankruptcy, judges or justices, appointments, 28 § 152
United States trustees, judicial districts, appointments, 28 § 581

INDIVIDUAL RETIREMENT ACCOUNTS

Income Tax, this index

INFANTS

Children and Minors, generally, this index

INJUNCTIONS

Bankruptcy, this index

INSOLVENCY

Bankruptcy, generally, this index
Investigations, crimes and offenses, 18 § 3057

INSPECTION AND INSPECTORS

Bankruptcy, this index

INSTALLMENTS

Bankruptcy, this index

INSTITUTIONS OF HIGHER EDUCATION OR LEARNING

Colleges and Universities, generally, this index

INSTRUCTIONS

Bankruptcy, commodities, customers, 11 § 765

INSTRUMENTALITIES OF THE UNITED STATES

Federal Agencies, generally, this index

INSURANCE

Bankruptcy, this index
Judges or Justices, this index

INSURANCE—Cont'd

Long term care. Nursing Homes, generally, this index

Nursing Homes, generally, this index

INTELLECTUAL PROPERTY

Bankruptcy, this index

INTERCEPTION OF WIRE, ORAL, OR ELECTRONIC COMMUNICATIONS

Aircraft, 18 § 2516

Aliens, smuggling, 18 § 2516

Atomic energy, 18 § 2516

Attorneys, Federal officers and employees, felonies, 18 § 2516

Authorization, 18 § 2516

Bioterrorism, 18 § 2516

Bribery and corruption, 18 § 2516

Bureau of Investigation, 18 § 2516

Business and commerce, interference, 18 § 2516

Cabinet departments, applications, 18 § 2516

Chemical and biological warfare and weapons, 18 § 2516

Children and minors, sexual exploitation, 18 § 2516

Citizens and citizenship, naturalization, 18 § 2516

Computers, 18 § 2516

Congress, applications, 18 § 2516

Conspiracy, 18 § 2516

Controlled substances, manufacturers and manufacturing, exports and imports, 18 § 2516

Counterfeiting, 18 § 2516

Credit, extortion, 18 § 2516

Currency, exports and imports, 18 § 2516

Employee benefit plans, investigations, 18 § 2516

Energy, facilities, 18 § 2516

Escape, 18 § 2516

Espionage, 18 § 2516

Explosives, 18 § 2516

Federal agencies, 18 § 2516

Federal Officers and Employees, this index

Fraud, 18 § 2516

Fugitives from justice, 18 § 2516

Gambling, 18 § 2516

Hostages, 18 § 2516

Immigration, smuggling, 18 § 2516

Labor and employment, 18 § 2516

Labor organizations, 18 § 2516

Mail and mailing, fraud, 18 § 2516

Malicious mischief, 18 § 2516

Marihuana, 18 § 2516

Military assistance and sales, exports and imports, 18 § 2516

Money laundering, 18 § 2516

Motor vehicles, trafficking, 18 § 2516

Murder, hired killers, 18 § 2516

Narcotics, 18 § 2516

Natural gas, pipes and pipelines, 18 § 2516

Naturalization, 18 § 2516

Obscenity, 18 § 2516

Obstruction, 18 § 2516

Passports, forgery, 18 § 2516

Pension or Welfare Fund, 18 § 2516

Piracy, 18 § 2516

President of the United States, assassinations, 18 § 2516

Racketeer influenced and corrupt organizations, 18 § 2516

Railroads, 18 § 2516

Retaliation, 18 § 2516

Riots and mobs, 18 § 2516

Sabotage, 18 § 2516

Sexual exploitation, children and minors, 18 § 2516

Smallpox, 18 § 2516

INTERCEPTION OF WIRE, ORAL, OR ELECTRONIC COMMUNICATIONS—Cont'd

Smuggling, aliens, 18 § 2516

Sports, bribery and corruption, 18 § 2516

Stolen property, interstate transportation, 18 § 2516

Supreme Court, applications, 18 § 2516

Syndicated gambling, 18 § 2516

Tampering, 18 § 2516

Television and radio, fraud, 18 § 2516

Terrorists and Terrorism, this index

Treason, 18 § 2516

Vessels, destruction, 18 § 2516

Visas, 18 § 2516

Witnesses, 18 § 2516

INTEREST

Bankruptcy, this index

Usury, generally, this index

INTERIOR DEPARTMENT

Secretary of the Interior, generally, this index

INTERIOR SECRETARY

Secretary of the Interior, generally, this index

INTERLOCUTORY ORDERS

Bankruptcy, 28 § 158

INTERMEDIATE CARE FACILITIES

Bankruptcy,
  Definitions, 11 § 101
  Ombudsman, 11 § 333
  Records and recordation, 11 § 351
Definitions, bankruptcy, 11 § 101
Ombudsman, bankruptcy, 11 § 333
Records and recordation, bankruptcy, 11 § 351

INTERNAL REVENUE CODE

Income Tax, generally, this index

INTERNATIONAL TRADE COURT

Appeal and review, judges or justices, discipline, 28 § 372

Chief Judge or Justice, disability, 28 § 372

Death, judges or justices, 28 § 372

Discipline, judges or justices, 28 § 372

Judges or justices,
  Additional judges, 28 § 372
  Compensation and salaries, disability, 28 § 372
  Disability, 28 § 372
  Vacancies in office, 28 § 372
Resignation, judges or justices, 28 § 372
Retirement and pensions, judges or justices, disability, 28 § 372
Witnesses, privileges and immunities, 18 § 6001 et seq.

INTERPRETERS

Bankruptcy, 11 § 1515

INTERSTATE AND FOREIGN COMMERCE

Aircraft, destruction, 18 § 2516

Racketeering, 18 § 2516

INTERVENTION

Bankruptcy, this index

INVEIGLE AND INVEIGLING

Kidnapping, generally, this index

INVENTORIES

Bankruptcy, this index

INVESTIGATIONS

Aliens, this index
Bankruptcy, this index
Controlled Substances, this index
Immigration, this index
Interception of Wire, Oral, or Electronic Communications, generally, this index
Prostitutes and Prostitution, this index
Smuggling, aliens, interception of wire, oral, or electronic communications, 18 § 2516
United States Attorneys, this index

INVESTMENTS

Bankruptcy, this index

INVOLUNTARY BANKRUPTCY IMPROVEMENT ACT OF 2005

Generally, 11 §§ 101 nt, 303; 18 § 157

INVOLUNTARY PROCEEDINGS

Bankruptcy, this index

IOWA

Bankruptcy, judges or justices, appointments, 28 § 152
United States trustees, judicial districts, appointments, 28 § 581

ISLANDS

Northern Mariana Islands, generally, this index
Virgin Islands, generally, this index

ISOMETHADONE

Controlled Substances, generally, this index

ISONIPECAINE

Controlled Substances, generally, this index

JET AIRCRAFT

Aircraft, generally, this index

JEWELRY

Bankruptcy,
    Exemptions, 11 § 522
    Liens and incumbrances, exemptions, 11 § 522

JOINDER

Bankruptcy, this index

JOINT TENANTS

Bankruptcy, 11 § 363

JUDGES OR JUSTICES

Administrative Office of United States Courts, generally, this index
Adverse or pecuniary interest, disqualification, 28 § 455
Appeal and review, disqualification, 28 § 455
Appointments, disability, 28 § 372
Attorneys, this index
Bankruptcy, this index
Center. Judicial Center, generally, this index
Certificates and certification, disability, retirement and pensions, 28 § 372
Compensation and salaries,
    Life insurance, group premiums, 28 § 604

JUDGES OR JUSTICES—Cont'd
Compensation and salaries—Cont'd
    Resignation, 28 § 372
Conflict of interest, disqualification, 28 § 455
Court of Appeals for Second Circuit, this index
Court of Appeals for Fourth Circuit, this index
Court of Appeals for Fifth Circuit, this index
Court of Appeals for Sixth Circuit, this index
Court of Appeals for Seventh Circuit, this index
Court of Appeals for Eighth Circuit, this index
Court of Appeals for Ninth Circuit, this index
Court of Appeals for Tenth Circuit, this index
Court of Appeals for Eleventh Circuit, this index
Court of Federal Claims, this index
Courts of Appeals, this index
Definitions, disqualification, 28 § 455
Degree of relationship, definitions, 28 § 455
Discipline, complaints, 28 § 372
Disqualification, 28 § 455
Expenses and expenditures, Director of Administrative Office of U.S. Courts, 28 § 604
Federal Judicial Center. Judicial Center, generally, this index
Federal Officers and Employees, this index
Fiduciary, definitions, 28 § 455
Group insurance. Life insurance, post
Handicapped persons,
    Appointments, 28 § 372
    Retirement and pensions, 28 § 372
Insurance, group insurance, premiums, compensation and salaries, 28 § 604
International Trade Court, this index
Judicial Center, generally, this index
Life insurance,
    Group insurance, premiums, compensation and salaries, 28 § 604
    Premiums, group insurance, compensation and salaries, 28 § 604
Magistrate judges. United States Magistrate Judges, generally, this index
Office expenses, Director of Administrative Office of U.S. Courts, 28 § 604
President of the United States, disability, 28 § 372
Proceeding, definitions, 28 § 455
Recall, bankruptcy, 28 § 155
Recusal, 28 § 455
Relatives, disqualification, 28 § 455
Retirement and pensions,
    Bankruptcy, this index
    Handicapped persons, 28 § 372
    Substitutes, 28 § 372
Secretaries,
    Bankruptcy, 28 § 156
    Compensation and salaries, 28 § 604
Subsistence, 28 § 604
Substitutes, retirement and pensions, 28 § 372
Traveling expenses, 28 § 604
United States Magistrate Judges, generally, this index
Vacancies in office,
    Death, 28 § 372
    Disability, 28 § 372
Virgin Islands, this index
Waivers, disqualification, 28 § 455
Witnesses, disqualification, 28 § 455

JUDGMENTS AND DECREES

Arbitration, this index

JUDGMENTS AND DECREES—Cont'd
Bankruptcy, this index

JUDICIAL CENTER

Accommodations, 28 § 604
Audits and auditors, 28 § 604
Director, 28 § 604
Law books, 28 § 604
Machinery and equipment, 28 § 604
Subsistence, 28 § 604
Supplies, 28 § 604
Traveling expenses, 28 § 604

JUDICIAL CONFERENCE OF THE UNITED STATES

Bankruptcy, this index
Director of Administrative Office of the U.S. Courts, 28 § 604
Pretrial services, 28 § 604
Supervision, Director of Administrative Office of the U.S. Courts, 28 § 604
United States Magistrate Judges, this index

JUDICIAL COUNCIL

Bankruptcy, this index
Disability, retirement and pensions, 28 § 372
Discipline, 28 § 372

JUDICIAL DISTRICTS

Bankruptcy, this index
Connecticut, this index
New York, this index
South Dakota, this index

JURISDICTION

Bankruptcy, this index
District Courts, this index

JURY

Bankruptcy, this index
Influence, interception of wire, oral, or electronic communications, 18 § 2516
Interception of wire, oral, or electronic communications, influence, 18 § 2516
Receivers and receivership, 28 § 959
Trusts and trustees, 28 § 959

JUSTICE DEPARTMENT

Attorney General, generally, this index
Marshals. United States Marshals Service, generally, this index
Oaths and affirmations, United States trustees, 28 § 583
Trusts and trustees, United States trustees, bankruptcy, 28 § 581 et seq.
United States Marshals Service, generally, this index
United States trustees,
    Bankruptcy, 28 § 581 et seq.
    Oaths and affirmations, 28 § 583

JUSTICES

Judges or Justices, generally, this index

KANSAS

Bankruptcy, judges or justices, appointments, 28 § 152
United States trustees, appointments, 28 § 581

KENTUCKY

Bankruptcy, judges or justices, appointments, 28 § 152
United States trustees, judicial districts, 28 § 581

KETOBEMIDONE

Controlled Substances, generally, this index

KIDNAPPING

Attorney General, this index
Cabinet departments, interception of wire, oral, or electronic communications, 18 § 2516
Congress, this index
Interception of wire, oral, or electronic communications, President, Congress, 18 § 2516
Justices of Supreme Court, interception of wire, oral, or electronic communications, 18 § 2516
President of the United States, this index
Racketeering, generally, this index
Secretary of Agriculture, this index
Secretary of Housing and Urban Development, this index
Secretary of Labor, this index
Secretary of State, this index
Secretary of the Interior, this index
Secretary of the Treasury, this index
Vice President of the United States, this index

KITCHENWARE

Bankruptcy, exemptions, 11 § 522

LABOR AND EMPLOYMENT

Bankruptcy, this index
Secretary of Labor, generally, this index

LABOR DEPARTMENT

Head of Department. Secretary of Labor, generally, this index
Secretary of Labor, generally, this index

LABOR DISPUTES

Boards and commissions, witnesses, privileges and immunities, 18 § 6001 et seq.
Labor organizations, payment, loans, 18 § 2516

LABOR ORGANIZATIONS

Labor Disputes, this index

LABOR SECRETARY

Secretary of Labor, generally, this index

LANDLORD AND TENANT

Bankruptcy, automatic stay, 11 § 362
Evictions, bankruptcy, automatic stay, 11 § 362
Unlawful detainer, bankruptcy, automatic stay, 11 § 362

LARCENY

Bankruptcy, this index

LAW BOOKS

Director of Administrative Office of U.S. Courts, 28 § 604
United States magistrate judges, 28 § 604

LAW CLERKS

Bankruptcy, 28 § 156
Compensation and salaries, incentive pay or awards, 28 § 604
District Judges, this index
Incentive pay or awards, 28 § 604

LAW ENFORCEMENT

Interception of Wire, Oral, or Electronic Communications, generally, this index

LAW ENFORCEMENT OFFICERS

United States Marshals Service, generally, this index

LAW LIBRARIES

Librarians, courts, compensation and salaries, 28 § 604

LAWYERS

Attorneys, generally, this index

LEASES

Bankruptcy, this index

LEAVE OF COURT

Bankruptcy, this index
Trusts and trustees, 28 § 959

LEGAL REPRESENTATIVES

Attorneys, generally, this index

LEGAL SERVICES

Attorneys, generally, this index

LETTERS OF CREDIT

Bankruptcy, 11 § 101

LEVOMETHORPHAN

Controlled Substances, generally, this index

LEVOMORAMIDE

Controlled Substances, generally, this index

LEVOPHENACYLMORPHAN

Controlled Substances, generally, this index

LEVORPHANOL

Controlled Substances, generally, this index

LIBRARIANS

Law Libraries, this index

LICENSES AND PERMITS

Bankruptcy, discrimination, 11 § 525

LIENS AND INCUMBRANCES

Bankruptcy, this index
Household Goods, this index
Warehouses and warehousemen, bankruptcy, avoidance, 11 § 546

LIFE INSURANCE

Bankruptcy, this index
Group insurance. Judges or Justices, this index
Judges or Justices, this index

LIMITATION OF ACTIONS

Bankruptcy, this index

LINENS

Bankruptcy, exemptions, 11 § 522

LISTS

Bankruptcy, this index

LOANS

Bankruptcy, this index
Colleges and Universities, this index
Interest. Usury, generally, this index
Usury, generally, this index

LONG TERM CARE

Nursing Homes, generally, this index

LOUISIANA

Bankruptcy, judges or justices, appointments, 28 § 152
United States trustees, judicial districts, appointments, 28 § 581

LYSERGIC ACID

Controlled Substances, generally, this index

LYSERGIC ACID AMIDE

Controlled Substances, generally, this index

MAGISTRATES

United States Magistrate Judges, generally, this index

MAIL AND MAILING

Bankruptcy, this index
Counterfeiting, interception of wire, oral, or electronic communications, 18 § 2516
Interception of Wire, Oral, or Electronic Communications, this index

MAINE

United States trustees, judicial districts, appointments, 28 § 581

MALICIOUS MISCHIEF

Energy facilities, destruction, 18 § 2516
Interception of wire, oral, or electronic communications, 18 § 2516

MANAGERS AND MANAGEMENT

Bankruptcy, this index
Property, this index

MANUFACTURERS AND MANUFACTURING

Controlled Substances, this index

MARGINS

Bankruptcy, this index

MARIANA ISLANDS

Northern Mariana Islands, generally, this index

MARIJUANA

Controlled Substances, this index

MARKETS AND MARKETING

Commodity Exchanges, generally, this index

MARSHALS

United States Marshals Service, generally, this index

MARYLAND

Bankruptcy, judges or justices, appointments, 28 § 152
United States trustees, judicial districts, 28 § 581

MASSACHUSETTS

Bankruptcy, judges or justices, appointments, 28 § 152
United States trustees of judicial districts, appointment, 28 § 581

MASTER AGREEMENTS

Bankruptcy, this index

MEAL FEEDS

Commodity Exchanges, generally, this index

MEDIATION AND MEDIATORS

Alternative Dispute Resolution, generally, this index

MEDICAL CARE AND TREATMENT

Drugs and Medicine, generally, this index
Hospitals, generally, this index
Long term care. Nursing Homes, generally, this index
Nursing Homes, generally, this index

MEDICAL DEVICES

Bankruptcy, exemptions, 11 § 522

MEDICAL FACILITIES

Hospitals, generally, this index

MEDICARE

Bankruptcy, automatic stay, 11 § 362

MEDICINE

Drugs and Medicine, generally, this index

MENTAL HEALTH

Bankruptcy, this index

MEPROBAMATE

Controlled Substances, generally, this index

MESCALINE

Controlled Substances, generally, this index

MESSENGERS

Courts, compensation and salaries, 28 § 604

METAZOCINE

Controlled Substances, generally, this index

METHADONE

Controlled Substances, generally, this index

METHOHEXITAL

Controlled Substances, generally, this index

METHYLDESORPHINE

Controlled Substances, generally, this index

METHYLHYDROMORPHINE

Controlled Substances, generally, this index

METHYLPHENIDATE

Controlled Substances, generally, this index

METHYLPHENOBARBITAL

Controlled Substances, generally, this index

METHYPRYLON

Controlled Substances, generally, this index

MICHIGAN

Bankruptcy, judges or justices, appointments, 28 § 152
United States trustees, judicial districts, appointments, 28 § 581

MILEAGE

Traveling Expenses, generally, this index

MILITARY DEPARTMENTS

Privileges and immunities, witnesses, 18 § 6001 et seq.
Witnesses, privileges and immunities, 18 § 6001 et seq.

MILITARY FORCES

Armed Forces, generally, this index

MINITRIALS

Alternative Dispute Resolution, generally, this index

MINNESOTA

Bankruptcy, judges or justices, appointments, 28 § 152
United States trustees, judicial districts, appointments, 28 § 581

MINORS

Children and Minors, generally, this index

MISDEMEANORS

Crimes and Offenses, generally, this index

MISSISSIPPI

Bankruptcy, judges or justices, appointments, 28 § 152
United States trustees, judicial districts, appointments, 28 § 581

MISSOURI

Bankruptcy, judges or justices, appointments, 28 § 152
United States trustees, judicial districts, 28 § 581

MONEY

Bankruptcy, this index
Embezzlement, generally, this index
Racketeering, generally, this index
Records and recordation, interception of wire, oral or electronic communications, 18 § 2516

MONEY LAUNDERING

Definitions, organized crime, 18 § 1961
Interception of wire, oral or electronic communications, 18 § 2516

MONTANA

Bankruptcy, judges or justices, appointments, 28 § 152
United States trustees, judicial districts, appointments, 28 § 581

MORAMIDE

Controlled Substances, generally, this index

MORPHERIDINE

Controlled Substances, generally, this index

MORPHINE

Controlled Substances, generally, this index

MORTGAGES

Bankruptcy, this index

MOTHERS

Children and Minors, generally, this index

MOTIONS

Bankruptcy, this index

MOTOR VEHICLES

Bankruptcy, this index

MOTOR VEHICLES—Cont'd

Crimes and offenses, attempts, interception of wire, oral, or electronic communications, 18 § 2516

Driving while intoxicated or under the influence. Bankruptcy, this index

Stolen property, interception of wire, oral, or electronic communications, 18 § 2516

MUNICIPAL CORPORATIONS

Chapter 9 proceedings. Bankruptcy, this index

Indebtedness, chapter 9 proceedings. Bankruptcy, this index

MURDER

Interception of wire, oral, or electronic communications, 18 § 2516

Internationally protected persons, interception of wire, oral, or electronic communications, 18 § 2516

MUSIC

Bankruptcy, liens and incumbrances, exemptions, 11 § 522

MUTUAL FUNDS

Judges or justices, disqualification, 28 § 455

MUTUAL INSURANCE

Judges or justices, disqualification, 28 § 455

MYROPHINE

Controlled Substances, generally, this index

N–ACETYLANTHRANILIC ACID

Controlled Substances, generally, this index

N–PHENYL–N–[1–(2–PHENYLETHYL)–4–PIPERIDINYL] PROPANAMIDE

Controlled Substances, generally, this index

NALORPHINE

Controlled Substances, generally, this index

NAMES

Bankruptcy, 11 § 109 et seq.

United States Bankruptcy Court, 28 § 151

NARCOTICS

Controlled Substances, generally, this index

NATIONAL BANKRUPTCY REVIEW COMMISSION ACT

Generally, 11 nt prec § 101

NATIONAL DEFENSE

Armed Forces, generally, this index

Secretary of Defense, generally, this index

NATIONAL GUARD

Bankruptcy, chapter 7 proceedings, 11 § 707

NATIONAL GUARD AND RESERVISTS DEBT RELIEF ACT OF 2008

Generally, 11 §§ 101 nt, 707, 707 nt

NATIONAL GUARD AND RESERVISTS DEBT RELIEF ACT OF 2011

Generally, 11 §§ 101 nt, 707 nt

NATIONAL NARCOTICS ACT OF 1984

Controlled Substances, generally, this index

NATIONAL SECURITIES ASSOCIATION

Securities, this index

NATIONAL TRANSPORTATION SAFETY BOARD

Privileges and immunities, witnesses, 18 § 6001 et seq.

Witnesses, privileges and immunities, 18 § 6001 et seq.

NATURAL RESOURCES

Secretary of Energy, generally, this index

NEBRASKA

Bankruptcy, judges or justices, appointments, 28 § 152

United States trustees, judicial districts, appointments, 28 § 581

NEGOTIABLE INSTRUMENTS

Bankruptcy, this index

Racketeering, generally, this index

NET EQUITY

Bankruptcy, this index

NEUTRALITY

Alternative dispute resolution, 28 § 653

NEVADA

Bankruptcy, judges or justices, appointments, 28 § 152

United States trustees of judicial districts, appointment, 28 § 581

NEW HAMPSHIRE

Bankruptcy, judges or justices, appointments, 28 § 152

United States trustees, judicial districts, appointments, 28 § 581

NEW JERSEY

Bankruptcy, judges or justices, appointments, 28 § 152

United States trustees, judicial districts, appointment, 28 § 581

NEW MARKETS VENTURE CAPITAL COMPANIES

Bankruptcy, exemptions, 11 § 109

Exemptions, bankruptcy, 11 § 109

NEW MEXICO

Bankruptcy, judges or justices, appointments, 28 § 152

United States trustees, judicial districts, appointments, 28 § 581

NEW TRIAL

Arbitration, 28 § 657

NEW YORK

Bankruptcy, judges or justices, appointments, 28 § 152

Judicial districts, United States trustees, appointments, 28 § 581

United States trustees, judicial districts, appointments, 28 § 581

NEWSPAPERS

Bankruptcy, municipal debt adjustment, notice, 11 § 923

NICOCODEINE

Controlled Substances, generally, this index

NICOMORPHINE

Controlled Substances, generally, this index

NONCITIZENS

Aliens, generally, this index

NONPROFIT CORPORATIONS

Bankruptcy, involuntary proceedings, 11 § 303

NONPROFIT ORGANIZATIONS OR ASSOCIATIONS

Bankruptcy, this index

NONRESIDENTS

Aliens, generally, this index

NORACYMETHADOL

Controlled Substances, generally, this index

NORLEVORPHANOL

Controlled Substances, generally, this index

NORMETHADONE

Controlled Substances, generally, this index

NORMORPHINE

Controlled Substances, generally, this index

NORPIPANONE

Controlled Substances, generally, this index

NORPSEUDOEPHEDRINE

Controlled Substances, generally, this index

NORTH CAROLINA

Bankruptcy, judges or justices, appointments, 28 § 152
United States trustees, judicial districts, appointments, 28 § 581

NORTH DAKOTA

Bankruptcy, judges or justices, appointments, 28 § 152
United States trustees, judicial districts, appointments, 28 § 581

NORTHERN MARIANA ISLANDS

Compensation and salaries,
  District courts, judges or justices, 28 § 604
  Judges or justices, district courts, 28 § 604
District courts, judges or justices, compensation and salaries, 28 § 604
United States trustees of judicial districts, 28 § 581

NORTHERN MARIANAS, COMMONWEALTH OF

Northern Mariana Islands, generally, this index

NOTICE

Bankruptcy, this index

NURSING HOMES

Bankruptcy,
  Definitions, 11 § 101
  Ombudsman, 11 § 333
  Records and recordation, 11 § 351
Definitions, bankruptcy, 11 § 101
Ombudsman, bankruptcy, 11 § 333
Records and recordation, bankruptcy, 11 § 351

OATHS AND AFFIRMATIONS

Arbitration, 28 § 655
Bankruptcy, this index
United States trustees, 28 § 583

OATS

Bankruptcy, 11 § 557
Commodity Exchanges, generally, this index

OBJECTIONS AND EXCEPTIONS

Bankruptcy, this index

OBSCENITY

Racketeering, 18 § 1961
Wiretapping, 18 § 2516

OBSTRUCTING JUSTICE

Interception of wire, oral, or electronic communications, 18 § 2516

OFFENSES

Crimes and Offenses, generally, this index

OFFICERS AND EMPLOYEES

Administrative Office of United States Courts, this index
Bankruptcy, this index
Courts, this index
Courts of Appeals, this index
Federal Officers and Employees, generally, this index
Judges or Justices, generally, this index
White House, this index

OFFICES

White House, generally, this index

OFFICIAL STATIONS

Bankruptcy, courts, judges or justices, 28 § 152

OHIO

Bankruptcy, judges or justices, appointments, 28 § 152
United States trustees of judicial districts, appointment, 28 § 581

OIL AND GAS

Secretary of Energy, generally, this index

OKLAHOMA

Bankruptcy, judges or justices, appointments, 28 § 152
United States trustees, judicial districts, appointments, 28 § 581

OMBUDSMAN

Consumer privacy ombudsman. Bankruptcy, this index
Nursing Homes, this index
Patient care ombudsman. Bankruptcy, this index

OPTIONS

Bankruptcy, this index

ORAL COMMUNICATIONS

Interception of Wire, Oral, or Electronic Communications, generally, this index

ORDERS OF COURT

Bankruptcy, this index
Protective orders. Bankruptcy, this index

OREGON

Bankruptcy, judges or justices, appointments, 28 § 152
United States trustees, judicial districts, appointments, 28 § 581

ORGANIZED CRIME

Racketeering, generally, this index

PANELS

Bankruptcy appellate panels. Bankruptcy, this index

PARALDEHYDE

Controlled Substances, generally, this index

PARAPROFESSIONALS

Bankruptcy, labor and employment, 11 §§ 330, 507

PARENT AND CHILD

Children and Minors, generally, this index

PARTIES

Bankruptcy, this index
Disqualification, judges or justices, 28 § 455
Judges or justices, disqualification, 28 § 455

PARTNERSHIP

Bankruptcy, this index
Racketeering, generally, this index

PASSPORTS

Fraud, wiretapping, investigations and investigators, 18 § 2516
Wiretapping, investigations and investigators, 18 § 2516

PATIENT CARE OMBUDSMAN

Bankruptcy, this index

PENAL CODE

Crimes and Offenses, generally, this index

PENAL LAWS

Crimes and Offenses, generally, this index

PENNSYLVANIA

Bankruptcy, judges or justices, appointments, 28 § 152
United States trustees, appointments, 28 § 581

PERFECTION

Bankruptcy, this index

PERJURY

Bankruptcy, this index

PERSONAL EFFECTS

Bankruptcy, exemptions, 11 § 522

PERSONAL INJURIES

Bankruptcy, this index

PERSONAL PROPERTY

Bankruptcy, this index

PERSONALLY IDENTIFIABLE INFORMATION

Bankruptcy, this index

PETHIDINE

Controlled Substances, generally, this index

PETIT JURY

Jury, generally, this index

PETITIONS

Bankruptcy, this index

PETRICHLORAL

Controlled Substances, generally, this index

PHENADOXONE

Controlled Substances, generally, this index

PHENAMPROMIDE

Controlled Substances, generally, this index

PHENAZOCINE

Controlled Substances, generally, this index

PHENMETRAZINE

Controlled Substances, generally, this index

PHENOBARBITAL

Controlled Substances, generally, this index

PHENOMORPHAN

Controlled Substances, generally, this index

PHENOPERIDINE

Controlled Substances, generally, this index

PHENYLACETIC ACID

Controlled Substances, generally, this index

PHOLCODINE

Controlled Substances, generally, this index

PHRASES

Words and Phrases, generally, this index

PHYSICIANS AND SURGEONS

Drugs and Medicine, generally, this index

PIMINODINE

Controlled Substances, generally, this index

PIPRADROL

Controlled Substances, generally, this index

PIRACY

Interception of wire, oral, or electronic communications, 18 § 2516

PIRITRAMIDE

Controlled Substances, generally, this index

PLANS AND SPECIFICATIONS

Bankruptcy, this index

PLATINUM

Commodity Exchanges, generally, this index

PLEADING

Bankruptcy, this index

POISONS

Controlled Substances, generally, this index

POLITICAL SUBDIVISIONS

Bankruptcy, this index

POSTSECONDARY EDUCATION AND SCHOOLS

Colleges and Universities, generally, this index

POWER OF ATTORNEY

Bankruptcy, this index

PRESIDENT OF THE UNITED STATES

Assassination, interception of wire, oral, or electronic communications, 18 § 2516

Assault and battery, interception of wire, oral, or electronic communications, 18 § 2516

Bankruptcy, this index

Domicile and residence. White House, generally, this index

Executive mansion. White House, generally, this index

Executive Office, assassination, officers and employees, 18 § 2516

Interception of Wire, Oral, or Electronic Communications, this index

Judges or Justices, this index

Kidnapping, interception of wire, oral, or electronic communications, 18 § 2516

White House, generally, this index

PRESIDENTIAL AND EXECUTIVE OFFICE ACCOUNTABILITY

United States District Court for the District of Columbia, 28 § 1413

Venue, 28 § 1413

PRESUMPTIONS

Bankruptcy, this index

PRETRIAL SERVICES

Crimes and Offenses, this index

PRIORITIES AND PREFERENCES

Bankruptcy, this index

PRIVACY

Bankruptcy, this index

Consumer privacy ombudsman. Bankruptcy, this index

PRIVILEGES AND IMMUNITIES

Arbitrators, 28 § 655

Bankruptcy, this index

Federal Agencies, this index

Federal Deposit Insurance Corporation, this index

Federal Maritime Commission, 18 § 6001 et seq.

Military departments, witnesses, 18 § 6001 et seq.

Securities and Exchange Commission, this index

Witnesses, this index

PROCESS

Arbitration, this index

Bankruptcy, this index

PRODUCTION OF BOOKS AND PAPERS

Arbitration, 28 § 656

PROFESSIONAL PERSONNEL

Bankruptcy, this index

PROFESSIONS AND OCCUPATIONS

Attorneys, generally, this index

Receivers and Receivership, generally, this index

PROFIT–SHARING PLANS

Bankruptcy, 11 § 522

PROFITS

Bankruptcy, this index

PROHEPTAZINE

Controlled Substances, generally, this index

PROPELLERS

Aircraft, destruction, 18 § 2516

PROPERIDINE

Controlled Substances, generally, this index

PROPERTY

Bankruptcy, generally, this index

Managers and management, actions and proceedings, 28 § 959

PROSTITUTES AND PROSTITUTION

Interception of wire, oral, or electronic communications, 18 § 2516

Investigations, interception of wire, oral, or electronic communications, 18 § 2516

PROTECTION OF FAMILY FARMERS ACT OF 2002

Generally, 11 §§ 101 nt, 1201 et seq.

PSILOCYBIN

Controlled Substances, generally, this index

PSILOCYN

Controlled Substances, generally, this index

PUBLIC EDUCATION

Colleges and Universities, generally, this index

PUBLIC OFFICERS AND EMPLOYEES

Federal Officers and Employees, generally, this index

PUBLIC RECORDS

Records and Recordation, generally, this index

PUBLIC UTILITIES

Bankruptcy, deposits, 11 § 366

Deposits, bankruptcy, 11 § 366

PUBLICATION

Bankruptcy, this index

PUERTO RICO

United States trustees of judicial districts, 28 § 581

PURCHASERS AND PURCHASING

Bankruptcy, this index

RACEMETHORPHAN

Controlled Substances, generally, this index

RACEMORAMIDE

Controlled Substances, generally, this index

RACEMORPHAN

Controlled Substances, generally, this index

RACKETEERING

Generally, 18 § 1961 et seq.

Attorney General, definitions, 18 § 1961

Bankruptcy, fraud, 18 § 1961

Cigarettes and cigars, 18 § 1961

RACKETEERING—Cont'd
Counterfeiting, 18 § 1961
Definitions, 18 § 1961
Documents, definitions, 18 § 1961
Interception of wire, oral, or electronic communications, 18 § 2516
Interstate and foreign commerce, interception of wire, oral, or electronic communications, 18 § 2516
Listed chemical, definitions, 18 § 1961
Motion pictures, counterfeiting, brands, marks and labels, trafficking, 18 § 1961
Music videos, counterfeiting, brands, marks and labels, trafficking, 18 § 1961
Obscenity, 18 § 1961
Pattern of racketeering activity, definitions, 18 § 1961
Person, definitions, 18 § 1961
Sound recordings, counterfeiting, brands, marks and labels, 18 § 1961
Terrorists and terrorism, 18 § 1961
Traffickers in persons, 18 § 1961

RAIL CARRIERS
Railroads, generally, this index

RAILROAD RETIREMENT BOARD
Witnesses, privileges and immunities, 18 § 6001 et seq.

RAILROADS
Default,
  Bankruptcy, reorganization, 11 § 1172
  Reorganization, bankruptcy, 11 § 1172
Interception of wire, oral, or electronic communications, 18 § 2516

RAILWAYS
Railroads, generally, this index

REAFFIRMATION AGREEMENTS
Bankruptcy, this index

REAL ESTATE
Bankruptcy, this index
Landlord and Tenant, generally, this index
Records and Recordation, generally, this index

RECALL
Bankruptcy, judges or justices, 28 § 155
Judges or Justices, this index

RECEIVERS AND RECEIVERSHIP
Bankruptcy, this index
Crimes and offenses, investigations, 18 § 3057
Fees, fraud, 18 § 155
Fraud,
  Compensation and salaries, 18 § 155
  Fees, 18 § 155
Investigations, crimes and offenses, 18 § 3057
Managers and management, 28 § 959

RECIPROCITY
Bankruptcy, abstention, 11 § 305; 28 § 1334

RECORDS AND RECORDATION
Assisted living facilities, bankruptcy, 11 § 351
Bankruptcy, this index
Courts, this index
Home health agencies, bankruptcy, 11 § 351
Hospices, bankruptcy, 11 § 351

RECORDS AND RECORDATION—Cont'd
Hospitals, bankruptcy, 11 § 351
Intermediate care facilities, bankruptcy, 11 § 351
Long term care, bankruptcy, 11 § 351
Money, this index
Nursing homes, bankruptcy, 11 § 351
Skilled nursing facilities, bankruptcy, 11 § 351
United States Magistrate Judges, this index

RECUSAL
Judges or Justices, this index
United States magistrate judges, 28 § 455

RECYCLING AND RESOURCE RECOVERY
Courts, 28 § 604

REDEMPTION
Bankruptcy, this index

REFEREES SALARY AND EXPENSE FUND ACT OF 1984
Generally, 11 nt prec § 101

REFERENCES
Bankruptcy, this index

REGIONAL RAIL REORGANIZATION
Bankruptcy, 11 § 1166

RELATIVES
Judges or Justices, this index

RELIGION
Associations and societies. Religious Organizations and Societies, generally, this index
Corporations. Religious Organizations and Societies, generally, this index
Religious Organizations and Societies, generally, this index

RELIGIOUS LIBERTY AND CHARITABLE DONATION CLARIFICATION ACT OF 2006
Generally, 11 §§ 101 nt, 1325

RELIGIOUS ORGANIZATIONS AND SOCIETIES
Bankruptcy, fraud, 11 § 548
Disqualification, judges or justices, 28 § 455
Fraud, bankruptcy, 11 § 548
Judges or justices, disqualification, 28 § 455

REMAND
Bankruptcy, this index

REMOVAL OF CASES OR CAUSES
Bankruptcy, this index

RENT
Bankruptcy, this index

REPARATIONS
Restitution, generally, this index

REPORTS
Bankruptcy, this index
Courts of Appeals, this index

REPRESENTATIVES AND REPRESENTATION
Bankruptcy, this index
Congress, generally, this index

REPURCHASE AGREEMENTS

Bankruptcy, this index

RESERVES

Armed Forces, this index

RESIDENT ALIENS

Aliens, generally, this index

RESTITUTION

Administrative Office of U.S. Courts, Director, powers and duties, 28 § 604
Bankruptcy, discharge, 11 §§ 523, 1328

RETALIATION

Crime Victims, this index
Witnesses, this index

RETIREMENT AND PENSIONS

Annuities, generally, this index
Bankruptcy, this index
Funds,
    Embezzlement, interception of wire, oral, or electronic communications, 18 § 2516
    Interception of wire, oral, or electronic communications, embezzlement, 18 § 2516
Judges or Justices, this index

RETURNS

Bankruptcy, this index

RHODE ISLAND

Bankruptcy, judges or justices, appointments, 28 § 152
United States trustees of judicial districts, appointment, 28 § 581

RICE

Bankruptcy, 11 § 557
Commodity Exchanges, generally, this index

RICO

Racketeering, generally, this index

RICO ACT

    Generally, 18 § 1961 et seq.
Racketeering, generally, this index

RIOTS AND MOBS

Interception of wire, oral, or electronic communications, 18 § 2516

ROBBERY

Interception of wire, oral, or electronic communications, 18 § 2516
Racketeering, generally, this index

RULES OF BANKRUPTCY

Bankruptcy, generally, this index

RULES OF COURT

Court of Appeals for Sixth Circuit, generally, this index

RYE

Bankruptcy, 11 § 557
Commodity Exchanges, generally, this index

SABOTAGE

Aircraft, this index

SAINT CROIX

Virgin Islands, generally, this index

SAINT JOHN

Virgin Islands, generally, this index

SAINT THOMAS

Virgin Islands, generally, this index

SALES

Bankruptcy, this index
Commodity Exchanges, generally, this index
Controlled Substances, this index

SANATORIUMS

Hospitals, generally, this index

SAVINGS ACCOUNTS

Coverdell education savings accounts, bankruptcy, 11 §§ 521, 541

SAVINGS ASSOCIATIONS

Bankruptcy, liquidation, 11 § 109

SAVINGS BANKS AND INSTITUTIONS

Bankruptcy, 11 § 109

SCHOLARSHIPS

Bankruptcy,
    Discharge, 11 § 523
    Fraud, exemptions, 11 § 522
Fraud, bankruptcy, exemptions, 11 § 522

SCHOOLS AND SCHOOL DISTRICTS

Income tax, education individual retirement accounts, bankruptcy, 11 §§ 521, 541
Postsecondary education and schools. Colleges and Universities, generally, this index

SEARCHES AND SEIZURES

Bankruptcy, this index
Interception of Wire, Oral, or Electronic Communications, generally, this index

SECRET SERVICE

Credit cards and plates, fraud, 18 § 2516
Fraud, credit cards and plates, 18 § 2516

SECRETARIES

Bankruptcy, judges or justices, 28 § 156
Judges or Justices, this index

SECRETARY OF AGRICULTURE

Assassination, 18 § 2516
Assault and battery, interception of wire, oral, or electronic communications, 18 § 2516
Kidnapping, interception of wire, oral, or electronic communications, 18 § 2516

SECRETARY OF COMMERCE

Assassination, 18 § 2516
Assault and battery, interception of wire, oral, or electronic communications, 18 § 2516
Kidnapping, interception of wire, oral, or electronic communications, 18 § 2516

SECRETARY OF DEFENSE

Assassination, 18 § 2516

SECRETARY OF DEFENSE—Cont'd

Assault and battery, interception of wire, oral, or electronic communications, 18 § 2516

Kidnapping, interception of wire, oral, or electronic communications, 18 § 2516

SECRETARY OF EDUCATION

Assassination, 18 § 2516

Assault and battery, interception of wire, oral, or electronic communications, 18 § 2516

Kidnapping, interception of wire or oral communications, 18 § 2516

SECRETARY OF ENERGY

Assassination, 18 § 2516

Assault and battery, interception of wire, oral, or electronic communications, 18 § 2516

Kidnapping, interception of wire, oral, or electronic communications, 18 § 2516

SECRETARY OF HEALTH AND HUMAN SERVICES

Assassination, interception of wire, oral, or electronic communications, 18 § 2516

Assault and battery, interception of wire, oral, or electronic communications, 18 § 2516

Kidnapping, interception of wire, oral, or electronic communications, 18 § 2516

SECRETARY OF HOUSING AND URBAN DEVELOPMENT

Assassination, 18 § 2516

Assault and battery, interception of wire, oral, or electronic communications, 18 § 2516

Bankruptcy, mortgage or deed of trust, 11 § 362

Kidnapping, interception of wire, oral, or electronic communications, 18 § 2516

SECRETARY OF LABOR

Assassinations, 18 § 2516

Assault and battery, interception of wire, oral, or electronic communications, 18 § 2516

Kidnapping, interception of wire, oral, or electronic communications, 18 § 2516

SECRETARY OF STATE

Assassination, 18 § 2516

Assault and battery, interception of wire, oral, or electronic communications, 18 § 2516

Kidnapping, wiretapping, 18 § 2516

SECRETARY OF THE INTERIOR

Assassination, 18 § 2516

Assault and battery, interception of wire, oral, or electronic communications, 18 § 2516

Kidnapping, interception of wire, oral, or electronic communications, 18 § 2516

SECRETARY OF THE TREASURY

Assassination, 18 § 2516

Assault and battery, interception of wire, oral, or electronic communications, 18 § 2516

Bankruptcy, reorganization, 11 § 1126

Kidnapping, interception of wire, oral, or electronic communications, 18 § 2516

SECRETARY OF TRANSPORTATION

Assassination, 18 § 2516

SECRETARY OF TRANSPORTATION—Cont'd

Assault and battery, interception of wire, oral, or electronic communications, 18 § 2516

Kidnapping, interception of wire, oral, or electronic communications, 18 § 2516

SECURITIES

Bankruptcy, this index

Equity security holders. Bankruptcy, this index

National securities association, bankruptcy, 11 § 555
  Repurchase agreements, 11 § 559

SECURITIES AND EXCHANGE COMMISSION

Privileges and immunities, witnesses, 18 § 6001 et seq.

Witnesses, privileges and immunities, 18 § 6001 et seq.

SECURITY

United States Marshals Service, 28 § 604

SECURITY INTEREST

Aircraft, this index

Bankruptcy, this index

SELF–EMPLOYMENT

Bankruptcy, 11 § 1304

SELF–INCRIMINATION

Bankruptcy, this index

SENATE

Judges or justices, disability, appointments, 28 § 372

SENTENCE AND PUNISHMENT

Bankruptcy, 18 § 152 et seq.

Restitution, generally, this index

Witnesses, this index

SETOFF AND COUNTERCLAIM

Bankruptcy, this index

SEXUAL EXPLOITATION

Children and Minors, this index

SHARES AND SHAREHOLDERS

Bankruptcy, this index

Bonus, bankruptcy, payment, 11 § 522

SHIPS AND SHIPPING

Bankruptcy, this index

Interception of wire, oral, or electronic communications, theft, 18 § 2516

SIGNATURES

Bankruptcy, this index

SILVER

Commodity Exchanges, generally, this index

SKILLED NURSING FACILITIES

Nursing Homes, generally, this index

SMALL BUSINESS INVESTMENT COMPANIES

Bankruptcy, liquidation, 11 § 109

SMALL BUSINESSES

Bankruptcy, this index

SMALLPOX

Interception of wire, oral, or electronic communications, 18 § 2516

SMUGGLING

Aliens, this index
Immigration, this index

SOCIAL SECURITY

Bankruptcy, this index

SOCIAL SERVICES

Secretary of Health and Human Services, generally, this index

SOLICITATION

Bankruptcy, this index

SORGHUMS

Bankruptcy, 11 § 557
Commodity Exchanges, generally, this index

SOUTH CAROLINA

Bankruptcy, judges or justices, appointments, 28 § 152
United States trustees, judicial districts, appointment, 28 § 581

SOUTH DAKOTA

Bankruptcy, judges or justices, appointments, 28 § 152
Judicial districts, United States trustees, 28 § 581
United States trustees, judicial districts, 28 § 581

SOVEREIGN IMMUNITY

Bankruptcy, abrogation, 11 § 106

SOYBEANS

Bankruptcy, 11 § 557

SPEEDY TRIAL

Trial, this index

STATE DEPARTMENT

Secretary of State, generally, this index

STATE LAWS

Gambling, crimes and offenses, interception of wire, oral, or electronic communications, 18 § 2516
Syndicated gambling, crimes and offenses, interception of wire, oral or electronic communications, 18 § 2516
Trusts and trustees, United States courts, 28 § 959

STATES

Bankruptcy, this index
Connecticut, generally, this index
Laws. State Laws, generally, this index
New York, generally, this index
South Dakota, generally, this index
Statutes. State Laws, generally, this index

STATISTICS

Bankruptcy, this index
Savings and loan associations, 28 § 604

STATUTES

State Laws, generally, this index

STAY OF PROCEEDINGS

Automatic stay. Bankruptcy, this index

STAY OF PROCEEDINGS—Cont'd
Bankruptcy, this index

STENOGRAPHERS

Administrative Office of United States Courts, compensation and salaries, 28 § 604
Compensation and salaries, Administrative Office of United States Courts, 28 § 604

STOLEN PROPERTY

Interception of wire, oral, or electronic communications, 18 § 2516
Motor Vehicles, this index
Racketeering, generally, this index
Transportation, interception of wire, oral, or electronic communications, 18 § 2516

STUDENTS

Colleges and Universities, generally, this index

SUBPOENAS

Arbitration, 28 § 656
Bankruptcy, this index

SUBROGATION

Bankruptcy, this index

SUBSISTENCE

Administrative Office of U.S. Courts, 28 § 604
Court officers and employees, 28 § 604
Judges or Justices, this index
Judicial Center, officers and employees, 28 § 604

SUBSTANCE ABUSE

Controlled Substances, generally, this index

SULFONDIETHYLMETHANE

Controlled Substances, generally, this index

SULFONETHYLMETHANE

Controlled Substances, generally, this index

SULFONMETHANE

Controlled Substances, generally, this index

SUMMONS

Bankruptcy, this index

SUPPLIES

Courts, Administrative Office of United States Courts, 28 § 604

SUPPORT

Bankruptcy, this index
Children born out of wedlock, bankruptcy, relief from automatic stay, 11 § 362
Paternity, bankruptcy, relief from automatic stay, 11 § 362

SUPREME COURT

Bankruptcy, 28 § 2075
Chief Judge or Justice, disability, certificates and certification, 28 § 372
Compensation and salaries, Chief Judge or Justice, 28 § 372
    Disability retirement, 28 § 372
Handicapped persons, retirement and pensions, 28 § 372
Justices,
    Assassination, interception of wire, oral, or electronic communications, 18 § 2516

SUPREME COURT—Cont'd

Justices—Cont'd
   Disability, certificate of disability, 28 § 372
Witnesses, privileges and immunities, 18 § 6001 et seq.

SURCHARGE

Bankruptcy, custodians, 11 § 543

SURFACE TRANSPORTATION BOARD

Privileges and immunities, witnesses, 18 § 6001 et seq.
Witnesses, privileges and immunities, 18 § 6001 et seq.

SWAP AGREEMENTS

Bankruptcy, this index

SYNDICATED GAMBLING

Gambling, this index

TAX COURT

United States Tax Court, generally, this index

TAXATION

Bankruptcy, this index
Fuel, this index
Income Tax, generally, this index
United States Tax Court, generally, this index

TELECOMMUNICATIONS

Interception of Wire, Oral, or Electronic Communications,
   generally, this index
Wiretapping. Interception of Wire, Oral, or Electronic Communications, generally, this index

TELEVISION AND RADIO

Bankruptcy, this index
Interception of Wire, Oral, or Electronic Communications,
   this index

TENANTS

Landlord and Tenant, generally, this index

TENANTS IN COMMON

Bankruptcy, sales, 11 § 363

TENEMENTS

Landlord and Tenant, generally, this index

TENNESSEE

Bankruptcy, judges or justices, appointments, 28 § 152
United States trustees, judicial districts, appointment, 28
   § 581

TERMINALLY ILL

Hospices, generally, this index

TERRITORIES

Guam, generally, this index
Northern Mariana Islands, generally, this index
Virgin Islands, generally, this index

TERRORISTS AND TERRORISM

Interception of wire, oral, or electronic communications, 18
   § 2516
Racketeering, 18 § 1961

TESTS

Bankruptcy, this index

TETRAHYDROCANNABINOLS

Controlled Substances, generally, this index

TEXAS

Bankruptcy, judges or justices, appointments, 28 § 152
United States trustees, judicial districts, appointments, 28
   § 581

THEBACON

Controlled Substances, generally, this index

THIRD PARTIES

Bankruptcy, this index

THREATS

Business and commerce, interference, 18 § 2516

TIMESHARES

Bankruptcy, this index

TIN (TAXPAYER IDENTIFICATION NUMBER)

Bankruptcy, this index

TITLE TO PROPERTY

Bankruptcy, this index

TOLUENE

Controlled Substances, generally, this index

TOYS

Bankruptcy, exemptions, 11 § 522

TRADE SECRETS

Bankruptcy, this index

TRADEMARKS AND TRADE NAMES

Trafficking, interception of wire, oral, or electronic communications, 18 § 2516

TRAFFICKING

Cigarettes and Cigars, this index
Drugs and Medicine, this index
Human trafficking, racketeering, 18 § 1961
Racketeering, traffickers in persons, 18 § 1961
Trademarks and Trade Names, this index

TRAINS

Railroads, generally, this index

TRANSCRIPTS

Bankruptcy, this index

TRANSPORTATION

Aircraft, generally, this index
Expenses and expenditures. Traveling Expenses, generally,
   this index
Railroads, generally, this index
Secretary of Commerce, generally, this index
Secretary of Transportation, generally, this index
Stolen Property, this index

TRANSPORTATION DEPARTMENT

Bankruptcy, railroads, appearances, 11 § 1164
Secretary of Transportation, generally, this index

TRANSPORTATION SECRETARY

Secretary of Transportation, generally, this index

TRAVELING EXPENSES

Administrative Office of United States Courts, this index
Arbitration, 28 § 658
Bankruptcy, this index
Court officers and employees, 28 § 604
Judges or Justices, this index
Judicial Center, this index
National Bankruptcy Review Commission, **11 nt prec § 101**

TREASON

Interception of wire, oral, or electronic communications, 18 § 2516

TREASURY DEPARTMENT

Secretary of the Treasury, generally, this index

TREASURY OF UNITED STATES

Bankruptcy, this index

TREASURY SECRETARY

Secretary of the Treasury, generally, this index

TREATIES

Bankruptcy, 11 § 1503

TRIAL

Bankruptcy, this index
Disqualification, judges or justices, 28 § 455
Judges or justices, disqualification, 28 § 455
Jury, generally, this index
Speedy trial, 28 § 604

TRIBUNALS

Courts, generally, this index

TRIMEPERIDINE

Controlled Substances, generally, this index

TRUST TERRITORY OF PACIFIC ISLANDS

Northern Mariana Islands, generally, this index

TRUSTS AND TRUSTEES

Bankruptcy, this index
Justice Department, United States trustees, bankruptcy, 28 § 581 et seq.
United States trustees. Bankruptcy, this index

UNEMPLOYMENT COMPENSATION

Bankruptcy, exemptions, 11 § 522

UNITED STATES

Agents and agencies. Federal Agencies, generally, this index
Claims. Court of Federal Claims, generally, this index
Courts, generally, this index
Hawaii, this index
Marshals. United States Marshals Service, generally, this index
Officers and employees. Federal Officers and Employees, generally, this index
President of the United States, generally, this index

UNITED STATES ARMED FORCES

Armed Forces, generally, this index

UNITED STATES ATTORNEYS

Bankruptcy, this index
Investigations, bankruptcy, 18 § 3057

UNITED STATES COURT OF FEDERAL CLAIMS

Court of Federal Claims, generally, this index

UNITED STATES COURT OF INTERNATIONAL TRADE

International Trade Court, generally, this index

UNITED STATES COURTS OF APPEALS

Courts of Appeals, generally, this index

UNITED STATES DISTRICT COURTS

District Courts, generally, this index

UNITED STATES INSTRUMENTALITY

Federal Agencies, generally, this index

UNITED STATES JUDGES OR JUSTICES

Judges or Justices, generally, this index

UNITED STATES MAGISTRATE JUDGES

Appeal and review, disqualification, 28 § 455
Compensation and salaries, 28 § 604
Conflict of interest, 28 § 455
Courtrooms, 28 § 604
Definitions, disqualification, 28 § 455
Discipline, 28 § 372
Disqualification, 28 § 455
Judicial Conference of the United States,
    Evaluations, 28 § 604
    Rules and regulations, 28 § 604
Law books, 28 § 604
Manuals, 28 § 604
Part-time Magistrate Judges, 28 § 604
Records and recordation, preservation, 28 § 604
Reports, 28 § 604
Security, courtrooms, 28 § 604
Statistics, 28 § 604
Supervision, 28 § 604
Supplies, 28 § 604
Waiver, disqualification, 28 § 455

UNITED STATES MARSHALS SERVICE

Administrative Office of U.S. Courts, disbursements, 28 § 604
Bankruptcy, this index
Disbursements, Administrative Office of U.S. Courts, 28 § 604
Security, 28 § 604

UNITED STATES OFFICERS AND EMPLOYEES

Federal Officers and Employees, generally, this index

UNITED STATES TAX COURT

Attorneys,
    Bankruptcy, 28 § 1452
    Debtors and creditors, automatic stay, petitions, 11 § 362
Bankruptcy,
    Attorneys, 28 § 1452
    Automatic stay, 11 § 362
    Removal of cases or causes, 28 § 1452
Privileges and immunities, witnesses, 18 § 6001 et seq.
Removal of cases or causes, bankruptcy, 28 § 1452
Witnesses, privileges and immunities, 18 § 6001 et seq.

UNITED STATES TRUSTEES

Bankruptcy, this index

UNIVERSITIES

Colleges and Universities, generally, this index

UNLAWFUL DETAINER

Bankruptcy, automatic stay, 11 § 362

UNLAWFUL RESTRAINT

Kidnapping, generally, this index

USURY

Bankruptcy, defenses, 11 § 558
Defenses, bankruptcy, 11 § 558
Interception of wire, oral, or electronic communications, 18 § 2516

UTAH

Bankruptcy, judges or justices, appointments, 28 § 152
United States trustees, judicial districts, appointments, 28 § 581

VENUE

Bankruptcy, this index
Presidential and Executive Office Accountability, 28 § 1413

VERMONT

Bankruptcy, judges or justices, appointments, 28 § 152

VETERANS

Bankruptcy, this index
Benefits, bankruptcy, exemptions, 11 § 522

VICE PRESIDENT OF THE UNITED STATES

Assassination, interception of wire, oral, or electronic communications, 18 § 2516
Kidnapping, interception of wire, oral, or electronic communications, 18 § 2516
Officers and employees, assassination, kidnapping, assault, interception of wire, oral, or electronic communications, 18 § 2516

VICTIMS

Crime Victims, generally, this index

VIDEO

Bankruptcy, exemptions, video cassette recorders, 11 § 522

VIRGIN ISLANDS

Compensation and salaries, district courts, judges or justices, 28 § 604
District courts,
    Compensation and salaries, judges or justices, 28 § 604
    Judges or justices, compensation and salaries, 28 § 604
Judges or justices, compensation and salaries, district courts, 28 § 604
United States trustees of judicial districts, 28 § 581
Witnesses, privileges and immunities, 18 § 6001 et seq.

VIRGINIA

Bankruptcy, judges or justices, appointments, 28 § 152

VISAS

Wiretapping, investigations and investigators, 18 § 2516

VOLUNTARY PROCEEDINGS

Bankruptcy, this index

WAREHOUSES AND WAREHOUSEMEN

Bankruptcy, liens and incumbrances, avoidance, 11 § 546
Liens and incumbrances, bankruptcy, avoidance, 11 § 546

WARRANTS

Bankruptcy, automatic stay, setoff and counterclaim, 11 § 553

WASHINGTON (STATE)

Bankruptcy, judges or justices, appointments, 28 § 152
United States trustees, judicial districts, appointments, 28 § 581

WEST VIRGINIA

Bankruptcy, judges or justices, appointments, 28 § 152

WHEAT

Bankruptcy, 11 § 557

WHITE HOUSE

Officers and employees,
    Assassination, 18 § 2516
    Assault and battery, 18 § 2516
    Interception of wire, oral, or electronic communications, 18 § 2516
    Kidnapping, 18 § 2516

WIRETAP

Interception of Wire, Oral, or Electronic Communications, generally, this index

WISCONSIN

Bankruptcy, judges or justices, appointments, 28 § 152
United States trustees of judicial districts, appointment, 28 § 581

WITNESSES

Bankruptcy, this index
Bribery and corruption, interception of wire, oral, or electronic communications, 18 § 2516
Commodity Exchanges, this index
Court of Federal Claims, this index
District Courts, this index
Federal Agencies, this index
Federal Maritime Commission, this index
Federal Trade Commission, this index
Influencing, interception of wire, oral, or electronic communications, 18 § 2516
Injuring, interception of wire, oral, or electronic communications, 18 § 2516
Interception of wire, oral, or electronic communications, 18 § 2516
International Trade Court, this index
Judges or Justices, this index
Military Departments, this index
National Transportation Safety Board, this index
Privileges and immunities, 18 § 6001 et seq.
    Definitions, 18 § 6001
Retaliation, interception of wire, oral, or electronic communications, 18 § 2516
Securities and Exchange Commission, this index
Sentence and punishment, disclosure, relocation, 18 § 2516
Surface Transportation Board, this index
Tampering, interception of wire, oral, or electronic communications, 18 § 2516
United States Tax Court, this index
Virgin Islands, this index

WOOL

Commodity Exchanges, generally, this index

WORDS AND PHRASES

Accountant, bankruptcy, 11 § 101

Act, bankruptcy, commodity brokers, 11 § 761

Adequate information, bankruptcy, reorganization, postpetition, 11 § 1125

Affiliates, bankruptcy, 11 § 101

Agency of the United States, Federal Maritime Commission, witnesses, privileges and immunities, 18 § 6001

Alternative dispute resolution, district courts, 28 § 651

Amount reaffirmed, bankruptcy, reaffirmation agreements, 11 § 524

Annual percentage rate, bankruptcy, reaffirmation agreements, 11 § 524

Applicable commitment period, bankruptcy, individual debtors, confirmation of plan, 11 § 1325

Assisted living facility, bankruptcy, 11 § 101

Assisted person, bankruptcy, 11 § 101

Assurance of payment, public utilities, bankruptcy, 11 § 366

Attorney, bankruptcy, 11 § 101

Attorney General, racketeer influenced and corrupt organizations, 18 § 1961

Authorized representative, bankruptcy, reorganization, retirement and pensions, 11 § 1114

Avoidable preferences, bankruptcy, 11 § 547

Bankruptcy, patient, 11 § 101

Bankruptcy assistance, 11 § 101

Bankruptcy petition preparers, 11 § 110; 18 § 156

Board,
    Clearing banks, bankruptcy, liquidation, 11 § 781
    Railroads, bankruptcy, 11 § 1162

Board of Trade, bankruptcy, commodity brokers, 11 § 761

Cash collateral, bankruptcy, trusts and trustees, 11 § 363

Cause, bankruptcy, dismissal and nonsuit, 11 § 1112

Charitable contribution, bankruptcy, 11 § 548

Claim, bankruptcy, 11 § 101

Clearing bank, bankruptcy, liquidation, 11 § 781

Clearing organization, bankruptcy, commodity brokers, 11 § 761

Commercial fishing operation, bankruptcy, 11 § 101

Commercial fishing vessel, bankruptcy, 11 § 101

Commission, bankruptcy,
    Commodity brokers, 11 § 761
    Stockbrokers, 11 § 741

Commodity, bankruptcy, brokers, 11 § 751

Commodity broker, bankruptcy, 11 § 101

Commodity contracts, bankruptcy, commodity brokers, 11 § 761

Commodity option, bankruptcy, commodity brokers, 11 § 761

Commodity option dealer, bankruptcy, commodity brokers, 11 § 761

Community claim, bankruptcy, 11 § 101

Consumer debt, bankruptcy, 11 § 101

Contract market, bankruptcy, commodity brokers, 11 § 761

Contract of sale, bankruptcy, commodity brokers, 11 § 761

Contractual right, bankruptcy,
    Commodities, 11 § 556
    Master agreements, 11 § 561
    Repurchase agreements, 11 § 559
    Securities, 11 § 555
    Swap agreements, 11 § 560

Conveyances, bankruptcy, fraud, 11 § 548

Cooperation, bankruptcy, foreign countries, 11 § 1527

Core proceedings, bankruptcy, 28 § 157

Corporation, bankruptcy, 11 § 101

Court of the United States, witnesses, privileges and immunities, 18 § 6001

WORDS AND PHRASES—Cont'd

Creditor, bankruptcy, 11 § 101

Current monthly income, bankruptcy, dismissal and nonsuit, 11 § 707

Custodian, bankruptcy, 11 § 101

Customer, bankruptcy,
    Commodity brokers, 11 § 761
    Stockbrokers, 11 § 741

Customer name securities, bankruptcy, stockbrokers, 11 § 741

Customer property, bankruptcy,
    Commodity brokers, 11 § 761
    Stockbrokers, 11 § 741

Debt, bankruptcy, 11 § 101

Debt relief agency, bankruptcy, 11 § 101

Debtor, bankruptcy, 11 § 101
    Crimes and offenses, 18 § 151
    Foreign countries, 11 § 1502

Debtor in possession, bankruptcy, reorganization, 11 § 1101

Debtor's monthly expenses, bankruptcy, dismissal and nonsuit, 11 § 707

Debtor's principal residence, bankruptcy, 11 § 101

Degree of relationship, judges or justices, disqualification, 28 § 455

Demand, bankruptcy discharge, 11 § 524

Dependent, bankruptcy, exemptions, 11 § 522

Depository institution, clearing banks, bankruptcy, liquidation, 11 § 781

Disability, bankruptcy, counseling services, 11 § 109

Disinterested person, bankruptcy, 11 § 101

Disposable income, bankruptcy,
    Family farmers, confirmation of plan, 11 § 1225
    Individual debtors, confirmation of plan, 11 § 1325

Distribution, bankruptcy, retirement and pensions, exemptions, 11 § 522

Document for filing, bankruptcy, 18 § 156
    Preparers, 11 § 110

Documentary material, racketeer influenced and corrupt organizations, 18 § 1961

Domestic support obligation, bankruptcy, 11 § 101

Enterprise, racketeer influenced and corrupt organizations, 18 § 1961

Entity, bankruptcy, 11 § 101

Equity securities, bankruptcy, 11 § 101

Equity security holder, bankruptcy, 11 § 101

Establishment, bankruptcy, foreign countries, 11 § 1502

Estate, bankruptcy, 11 § 101

Fair and equitable, bankruptcy, reorganization, plans and specifications, 11 § 1129

Family farmer, bankruptcy, 11 § 101

Family farmer with regular annual income, bankruptcy, 11 § 101

Family fisherman, bankruptcy, 11 § 101

Family fisherman with regular annual income, bankruptcy, 11 § 101

Farming operation, bankruptcy, 11 § 101

Farmout agreement, bankruptcy, 11 § 101

Federal depository institutions regulatory agency, bankruptcy, 11 § 101

Fiduciary, judges or justices, disqualification, 28 § 455

Financial institution, bankruptcy, 11 § 101

Financial interest, judges or justices, disqualification, 28 § 455

Foreign court, bankruptcy, 11 § 1502

Foreign future, bankruptcy, commodity brokers, 11 § 761

WORDS AND PHRASES—Cont'd

Foreign futures commission merchant, bankruptcy, commodity brokers, 11 § 761

Foreign main proceeding, bankruptcy, 11 § 1502

Foreign nonmain proceeding, bankruptcy, 11 § 1502

Foreign proceeding, bankruptcy, 11 § 101

Foreign representative, bankruptcy, 11 § 101

Forward contract, bankruptcy, 11 § 101

Forward contract merchant, bankruptcy, 11 § 101

Fraudulent transfers, bankruptcy, 11 § 548

Futures commission merchant, bankruptcy, commodity brokers, 11 § 761

Governmental unit, bankruptcy, 11 § 101

Grain, bankruptcy, 11 § 557

Health care business, bankruptcy, 11 § 101

Household goods, bankruptcy, exemptions, 11 § 522

Improvements, bankruptcy, transfers, avoidance, liability, 11 § 550

Incapacity, bankruptcy, counseling services, 11 § 109

Incidental property, bankruptcy, 11 § 101

Indenture, bankruptcy, 11 § 101

Indenture trustee, bankruptcy, 11 § 101

Individual with regular income, bankruptcy, 11 § 101

Insider, bankruptcy, 11 § 101

Insolvent, bankruptcy, 11 § 101

Institution affiliated party, bankruptcy, 11 § 101

Insufficiency, bankruptcy, set-off and counterclaim, 11 § 553

Insured credit union, bankruptcy, 11 § 101

Intellectual property, bankruptcy, 11 § 101

Inventory, bankruptcy, 11 § 547

Investor typical of holders of claims or interest of the relative class, bankruptcy, reorganization, postpetition, 11 § 1125

Judicial lien, bankruptcy, 11 § 101

Lease,
  Aircraft, bankruptcy, 11 § 1110
  Railroads, bankruptcy, reorganization, 11 § 1168

Legal advice, bankruptcy, petitions, preparers, 11 § 110

Lessee, bankruptcy, rejection, 11 § 365

Leverage transaction, bankruptcy, commodity brokers, 11 § 761

Leverage transaction merchant, bankruptcy, commodity brokers, 11 § 761

Lien, bankruptcy, 11 § 101
  Reaffirmation agreements, 11 § 524

Listed chemicals, RICO, 18 § 1961

Luxury goods or services, bankruptcy, discharge, 11 § 523

Margin payment, bankruptcy, 11 § 101
  Commodity brokers, 11 § 761
  Stockbrokers, 11 § 741

Mask work, bankruptcy, 11 § 101

Master netting agreement, bankruptcy, 11 § 101

Master netting agreement participant, bankruptcy, 11 § 101

May, bankruptcy, reaffirmation agreements, 11 § 524

Median family income, bankruptcy, 11 § 101

Member property, bankruptcy, commodity brokers, 11 § 761

Money laundering, racketeering influenced and corrupt organizations, 18 § 1961

Municipality, bankruptcy, 11 § 101

Net equity, bankruptcy,
  Commodity brokers, 11 § 761
  Stockbrokers, 11 § 741

New value, bankruptcy, preferences, 11 § 547

Other information, witnesses, privileges and immunities, 18 § 6001

Patient, bankruptcy, 11 § 101

Patient records, bankruptcy, 11 § 101

WORDS AND PHRASES—Cont'd

Pattern of racketeering activity, 18 § 1961

Person,
  Bankruptcy, 11 § 101
  Racketeer influenced and corrupt organizations, 18 § 1961

Petition, bankruptcy, 11 § 101

Preferences, bankruptcy, avoidance, 11 § 547

Priorities and preferences, bankruptcy, avoidance, 11 § 547

Proceeding, judges or justices, disqualification, 28 § 455

Proceedings before an agency of the United States, witnesses, privileges and immunities, 18 § 6001

Producer, grain, bankruptcy, 11 § 557

Profitability, bankruptcy, 11 § 308

Property of the estate, bankruptcy,
  Individual debtors, 11 § 1115
  Municipal debt adjustment, 11 § 902

Purchaser, bankruptcy, 11 § 101

Qualified religious or charitable entity or organization, bankruptcy, 11 § 548

Racketeering activity, 18 § 1961

Racketeering investigators, 18 § 1961

Railroad, bankruptcy, 11 § 101

Receivable, bankruptcy, preferences, 11 § 547

Recognition, bankruptcy, foreign countries, 11 § 1502

Reduction payment, bankruptcy, 11 § 101

Related party, bankruptcy, discharge, 11 § 524

Relative, bankruptcy, 11 § 101

Replacement value, bankruptcy, 11 § 506

Repo participants, bankruptcy, 11 § 101

Repurchase agreement, bankruptcy, 11 § 101

Retiree benefits, bankruptcy, reorganization, 11 § 1114

Returns, bankruptcy,
  Discharge, 11 § 523
  Prepetition returns, 11 § 1308

Rolling stock equipment, railroads, bankruptcy, 11 § 1168

Secured party, railroads, bankruptcy, reorganization, 11 § 1168

Securities, bankruptcy, 11 § 101

Securities clearing agency, bankruptcy, 11 § 101

Securities contract, bankruptcy, stockbrokers, 11 § 741

Securities self regulatory organization, bankruptcy, 11 § 101

Security agreement, bankruptcy, 11 § 101

Security interest,
  Aircraft, bankruptcy, 11 § 1110
  Bankruptcy, 11 § 101

Settlement payment, bankruptcy, 11 § 101
  Stockbrokers, 11 § 741

Single asset real estate, bankruptcy, 11 § 101

SIPC, bankruptcy, stockbrokers, 11 § 741

Small business, bankruptcy, chapter 7 proceedings, dismissal and nonsuit, 11 § 707

Small business case, bankruptcy, 11 § 101

Small business debtor, bankruptcy, 11 § 101

Special taxpayer, bankruptcy, municipal debt adjustment, 11 § 902

Spouse, bankruptcy, municipal debt adjustment, 11 § 902

State,
  Bankruptcy, 11 § 101
  Racketeering, 18 § 1961

Statutory lien, bankruptcy, 11 § 101

Stockbroker, bankruptcy, 11 § 101

Student Loan Program, bankruptcy, 11 § 525

Substantial consummation, bankruptcy, reorganization, 11 § 1101

Swap agreement, bankruptcy, 11 § 101

Swap participant, bankruptcy, 11 § 101

WORDS AND PHRASES—Cont'd

Term overriding royalty, bankruptcy, **11 § 101**

Timeshare interest, bankruptcy, **11 § 101**

Timeshare plan, bankruptcy, **11 § 101**

Transfers, bankruptcy, **11 § 101**
    Fraud, **11 § 548**
    Preferences, avoidance, **11 § 547**

Trustees, bankruptcy,
    Foreign countries, **11 § 1502**
    Municipal debt adjustment, **11 § 902**
    Powers and duties, **11 § 323**

Underwriter, bankruptcy, reorganization, securities, exemptions, **11 § 1145**

Uninsured State member bank, bankruptcy, **11 § 101**

United States, bankruptcy, **11 § 101**

Unlawful debt, racketeer influenced and corrupt organizations, **18 § 1961**

WORDS AND PHRASES—Cont'd

Value, bankruptcy,
    Exemptions, **11 § 522**
    Fraud, **11 § 548**

Within the territorial jurisdiction of the United States, bankruptcy, **11 § 1502**

WRITS

Bankruptcy, this index

WRONGFUL DEATH

Bankruptcy, this index

WYOMING

Bankruptcy, judges or justices, appointments, **28 § 152**

United States trustees, judicial districts, **28 § 581**

YOUTH

Children and Minors, generally, this index

†